WEBSTER'S
NEW WRLD®
DICTIONARY

FIFTH EDITION

HOUGHTON MIFFLIN HARCOURT
BOSTON   NEW YORK

DICTIONARY STAFF

Publisher
Bruce Nichols

Executive Editor
Steven R. Kleinedler

Consulting Editor
Donald Stewart

Senior Editors
Peter Chipman
Louise E. Robbins

Associate Editor
Emily A. Neeves

Production Supervisor
Margaret Anne Miles

Database Production Supervisor
Christopher Granniss

Book Designer
David Futato

Print Production Director
Donna Baxter McCarthy

Lead Print Production Coordinator
Diane Varone

GUIDE TO THE USE OF THIS DICTIONARY

I. GUIDE WORDS

The two GUIDE WORDS at the top of each page indicate the alphabetical range of entries on that page. The first and last main entry words on a page serve as the GUIDE WORDS.

II. THE MAIN ENTRY WORD

A.   Arrangement of Entries — All main entries, including single words, hyphenated and unhyphenated compounds, proper names, prefixes, suffixes, combining forms, and abbreviations, are listed in strict alphabetical order and are set in large boldface type.

a² (ə; *stressed*, ā) *adj.* ...
a³ *abbrev.* **1** about **2** ...
a-² *prefix* ...
aard·vark (ärd′värk′) *n.* ...
Aar·on (er′ən) *n. Bible* ...
AB¹ (ā′bē′) *n.* a blood type ...
AB² *abbrev.* **1** Alberta (Canada) **2** ...
ab- [[L]] *prefix* ...
a·back (ə bak′) *adv.* [Archaic] backward; back **—taken aback** ...

In biographical entries only the last, or family, name is used in alphabetization; but when two or more persons have the same family name, they appear within the entry block in alphabetical order by first names.

John·son (jän′sən) **1** An·drew ... **2** Lyn·don Baines ... **3** Samuel ...

Biographical and geographical names that are spelled the same way are given separate entry blocks.

Idiomatic phrases after a main entry are also listed alphabetically within each group.

fly¹ (flī) *vi.* ... **—let fly (at)** ... **—on the fly** ...

B.   Alternative Spellings and Variant Forms — When different spellings of a word are some distance apart alphabetically, the definition appears with the spelling most frequently used, and the other spellings are cross-referred to this entry. If two commonly used alternative spellings are alphabetically close to each other, they appear as a joint boldface entry, but the order of entry does not necessarily indicate that the form entered first is "more correct" or is preferred.

the·a·ter or **the·a·tre** (thē′ə tər) *n.* ...

If an alternative spelling is alphabetically close to the prevailing spelling, it is given at the end of the entry block in small boldface.

cook·ie *n.* ... : also **cook′y,** *pl.* **-ies** ...

C.   Cross-references — When an entry is cross-referred to another term that has the same meaning but is more frequently used,

the entry cross-referred to is usually set in small capitals.

an·aes·the·sia ... *n.* ANESTHESIA ...

D.   Homographs — Main entries that are spelled alike but are different in meaning and origin, such as **bat** (a club), **bat** (the animal), and **bat** (to wink), have separate entry blocks and are marked by superscript numbers following the boldface spelling.

bat¹ ... *n.* ...
bat² ... *n.* ...
bat³ ... *vt.* ...

E.   Foreign Terms — Foreign words and phrases occurring with some frequency in English, but not completely naturalized, are set in boldface italic type. This is a signal to the user of the dictionary to print these terms in italics or underline them in writing.

bon·jour (bōn zhōōr′) *interj., n.* [[Fr]] ...

F.   Prefixes, Suffixes, & Combining Forms — Prefixes and initial combining forms have a hyphen at the end.

hemi- ... *prefix* half ...

Suffixes and terminal combining forms have a hyphen at the beginning.

-a·ble ... *suffix* **1** that can or will ...

The abundance of these forms, whose syllabification and pronunciation can be determined from the words containing them, makes it possible for the reader to understand and pronounce many complex terms not entered in the dictionary but formed with affixes and words that are entered.

G.   Word Division — Boldface entry words are divided into syllables that are separated by a center dot.

gen·er·a·tor
in·ter·me·di·ar·y

For information regarding stress marks, see the GUIDE TO PRONUNCIATION.

III. PRONUNCIATION

The handling of pronunciations in this dictionary is explained in the GUIDE TO PRONUNCIATION, which follows this general guide.

IV. PART-OF-SPEECH LABELS

This dictionary gives part-of-speech labels, in boldface italic type, for most main entry words that are solid or hyphenated forms. Labels are not given to prefixes, suffixes, combining forms, trademarks and service marks, abbreviations, and biographical and geographical entries.

Here are the part-of-speech labels used in this dictionary:

n.	noun
pl.n.	plural noun
sing.n.	singular noun
pron.	pronoun
v.	verb
vt.	transitive verb
vi.	intransitive verb
v.aux.	auxiliary verb
v.impersonal	impersonal verb
adj.	adjective
adv.	adverb
prep.	preposition
conj.	conjunction
interj.	interjection
definite article	
indefinite article	
possessive pronominal adj.	

When an entry word is used as more than one part of speech, long dashes introduce each separate part-of-speech label.

round ... *adj.* ... —*n.* ... —*vt.* ... —*vi.* ... —*adv.* ... —*prep.* ...

Sometimes an entry has two or more part-of-speech labels separated by commas, with a definition or cross-reference that is understood to apply to all parts of speech.

des·patch ... *vt., n.* DISPATCH

V. INFLECTED FORMS

This dictionary shows three types of inflected forms: plurals of nouns, principal parts of verbs, and comparative and superlative forms of adjectives and adverbs.

Only inflected forms regarded as irregular or offering difficulty in spelling are entered. They appear in boldface immediately after the part-of-speech label. They are shortened where possible, and syllabified and pronounced where necessary.

ci·ty ... *n., pl.* **-ies** ...
hap·py ... *adj.* **-pi·er, -pi·est** ...
an·a·lyze ... *vt.* **-lyzed′, -lyz′ing** ...

Plurals: This dictionary does not show regular plurals:

1) formed by adding *-s* to the singular (**cats**)
2) formed by adding *-es* to a singular that ends with *s, x, z,* or *sh* (**boxes or bushes**)
3) formed by adding *-es* to a singular that ends with *ch* when *ch* is pronounced [ch] (**churches**) or by adding *-s* when *ch* is pronounced [k] (**stomachs**)

Principal Parts: This dictionary does not show principal parts when:

1) the past tense and past participle are formed by simply adding *-ed* to the infinitive (**search/searched, talk/talked**)
2) the present participle is formed by simply adding *-ing* to the infinitive (**search/searching, talk/talking**)

If only two principal parts are shown, as at **love**, the first is both the past tense and the past participle (**loved**) and the second is the present participle (**loving**). If three principal parts are shown, as at **go**, the first is the past tense (**went**), the second is the past participle (**gone**), and the third is the present participle (**going**).

Comparatives & Superlatives: This dictionary does not show comparatives and superlatives formed by the simple addition of *-er* or *-est* to the base form (**tall/taller/tallest**).

VI. ETYMOLOGY

The etymology, or word history, appears inside open double brackets immediately before the definitions. The symbols and abbreviations used in the etymologies are found in the list immediately preceding page 1 of the dictionary proper.

di·shev·el ... [[< OFr *des-*, DIS- + *chevel,* hair]] ...

If the parts making up an entry word are obvious to the reader, no etymology appears at that entry.

VII. THE DEFINITIONS

A.   Order of Senses — In general, each entry lists meanings in historical order; the standard, general senses of a word appear first. Informal, slang, etc. senses come next. Technical senses preceded by field labels, such as *Astron.* or *Chem.,* follow in alphabetical order.

B.   Numbering & Grouping of Senses — Senses are numbered consecutively within a part of speech in boldface numerals. Where a primary sense of a word is subdivided into several closely related meanings, those meanings are preceded by italicized letters.

flat¹ ... *adj.* ... **1** having ... **2** lying ... **10** *Music a)* lower... *b)* below —*adv.* ... —*n.* **1** anything ... **2** ... **3** *Music a)* a note ... *b)* the symbol ... —*vt.* ... —*vi.* ...

C.   Capitalization — If a main entry word is capitalized in all its senses, the entry word itself begins with a capital letter. If a capitalized main entry word has a sense or senses that are not capitalized, these are marked with the corresponding small-boldface, lowercase letter followed by a short dash and enclosed in brackets.

Pu·ri·tan ... *n.* ... **1** ... **2** [p-] ...

If a lowercase main entry word has a meaning or meanings that are capitalized, they are marked with the corresponding small-boldface, uppercase letter followed by a short dash and enclosed in brackets.

In some of these usage notes, a self-explanatory qualifying word may be added.

left¹ ... —*n.* ... **1** ... **2** [*often* L-] ...

D.   Plural Forms — In a singular noun entry, the designation "[*pl.*]" (or "[*often pl.*]," "[*usually pl.*]," etc.) before a definition indicates that it is (or *often, usually,* etc. is) the plural form of the entry word that has the meaning given in the definition.

look ... *vi.* ... —*n.* **1** ... **2** ... **3** [Inf.] *a*) [*usually pl.*] appearance *b*) [*pl.*] personal appearance ...

If a plural is used as a singular with a singular verb, the designation [*with sing. v.*] is added.

E.   Verbs Followed by Prepositions or Objects — In many cases, one or more specific prepositions follow a particular verb in general use. This dictionary shows this either by including the preposition in the definition, italicized and usually enclosed in parentheses, or by adding a note after the definition giving the particular prepositions associated with that definition of the verb.

In definitions of transitive verbs, the specific or generalized object of the verb, where given, is enclosed in parentheses, since the object is not grammatically part of the definition of the verb.

F.   Illustrative Examples — Phrases or sentences containing the entry word and showing how it is used in context are enclosed in italic brackets. The word being illustrated is set in italics within its phrase or sentence.

a·cross ... *adv.* ... —*prep.* **1** ... **2** ... **3** into contact with by chance [*to come across an old friend*]

VIII.   USAGE LABELS

People use language in different ways depending on differences in geographic location, age, education, and employment; people's individual language varies also according to the situation they are in or their purpose in speaking or writing. The usage labels used in this dictionary are listed below, with an explanation of each.

Informal: The word or meaning is widely used in everyday talk, personal letters, etc., but not in formal speaking or writing. Abbreviated *Inf.*

Slang: The word or meaning is not generally considered standard usage but is used, even by the very best speakers and writers, in very informal situations or for creating special effects. People belonging to a certain group often use their own slang terms.

Old Informal, Old Slang: The word or meaning was informal or slang when regularly used in the recent past and is not used much today.

Obsolete: The word or meaning is no longer used but occurs in earlier writings. Abbreviated *Obs.*

Archaic: The word or meaning is not used in ordinary speech or writing today but occurs in certain special situations such as church ritual and in older books.

Old-fashioned: The word or meaning is not yet considered archaic but seems out-of-date.

Rare: The word or meaning has never been in general use.

Now Rare: The word or meaning is not used much today but was in general use in the past.

Historical: The word or meaning refers to something that no longer exists and for which there is not a modern term.

Old Poetic: The word or meaning was often used in the past, especially in poetry, but is used today only in certain kinds of traditional or somewhat old-fashioned poetry. Abbreviated *Old Poet.*

Literary: The word or meaning is regarded as having an elevated, polished, highly formal quality.

Dialect: The word or meaning is used regularly only in certain geographical areas. When a word or meaning is used mainly in some specific area of the U.S., a more specific label, such as *South* or *Northwest*, appears. Abbreviated *Dial.*

British: The word or meaning is used mainly in Great Britain and also, usually, in the other English-speaking regions of the world outside the U.S. Abbreviated *Brit.*

Canadian (or *Irish,* etc.): The word or meaning is used mainly in Canada (or Ireland, etc.). Abbreviated *Cdn.,* etc.

In addition to the above usage labels, supplementary information often appears in a short note after the definition, indicating that a word or meaning is used in an insulting, familiar, ironic, humorous, or other way.

IX.   RUN-IN DERIVED ENTRIES

It is possible in English to create an almost infinite number of derived forms simply by adding certain prefixes and suffixes to the base word. The editors have included as many of these common derived words as space permitted, as run-in entries in boldface type — but only when the meaning of such words is immediately clear from the meanings of the base words and affixes.

Thus, **greatness** and **liveliness** are run in at the end of the entries for **great** and **lively**; the suffix **-ness** is found as a separate entry meaning "state, quality, or instance of being." Many words formed with common suffixes, such as **-able, -er, -less, -like, -ly,** and **-tion,** are similarly treated as run-in entries with the base word from which they are derived. All such entries are syllabified and either accented to show stress in pronunciation or, where necessary, pronounced in full or in part.

When a derived word has a meaning or meanings different from those that can be deduced from the sum of its parts, it has been entered separately, pronounced, and fully defined (see **folder**).

GUIDE TO PRONUNCIATION

I. PRONUNCIATION STYLE

Pronunciations are provided as needed. Pronunciations are given in parentheses immediately after the boldface entry word:

mil·len·ni·um (mi len′ē əm)

Pronunciations have sometimes been shortened so as to cover only a particular part of the entry word, generally the part most likely to cause confusion or difficulty. Hyphens are used to indicate which part of the pronunciation is not shown.

home·stead (–sted′)

More than one pronunciation is sometimes given. Each variant pronunciation may be regarded as having wide currency in American English unless a qualifying note has been added to a particular variant indicating that it is less common. Variants may be also qualified with respect to particular grammatical usage.

av·o·ca·do (av′ə kä′dō, ä′və–)
ex·cuse (ek skyōōz′; *for n.,* –skyōōs′)

This dictionary does not attempt to cover all pronunciations of a given word and does not indicate differences arising out of various regional dialects.

II. PRONUNCIATION KEY

The Pronunciation Key lists the pronunciation symbols used in this dictionary along with several key words. Key words are short, familiar words that illustrate each of the various sounds represented by the symbols.

Symbol	Key Word	IPA Symbol
Vowel Sounds		
a	_a_t, c_a_p, p_a_rrot	æ
ā	_a_pe, pl_a_y, s_ai_l	eɪ
ä	c_o_t, f_a_ther, h_ea_rt	ɑ
e	t_e_n, w_ea_lth, m_e_rry	ɛ
ē	_e_ven, f_ee_t, m_o_ney	i
i	_i_s, st_i_ck, m_i_rror	ɪ
ī	_i_ce, h_i_gh, sk_y_	aɪ
ō	g_o_, _o_pen, t_o_ne	oʊ
ô	_a_ll, l_a_w, h_o_rn	ɔ
ōō	c_ou_ld, l_oo_k, p_u_ll	ʊ
yōō	c_u_re, f_u_rious, glob_u_le, _you_r	jʊ
ōō	b_oo_t, cr_e_w, t_u_ne	u
yōō	c_u_te, f_e_w, _u_se	ju
oi	b_oy_, _oi_l, r_oy_al	ɔɪ
ou	c_ow_, _ou_t, s_ou_r	aʊ
u	m_u_d, t_o_n, bl_oo_d, tr_ou_ble	ʌ
ʉr	h_er_, s_ir_, w_or_d	ɝ
ə	_a_go, _a_gent, colle_ct_, focu_s_	ə

Consonant Sounds

b	_b_ed, ta_b_le, ro_b_	b
d	_d_og, mi_dd_le, sa_d_	d
f	_f_or, _ph_one, cou_gh_	f
g	_g_et, wi_gg_le, do_g_	g
h	_h_at, _h_ope, a_h_ead	h
hw	_wh_ich, _wh_ite	hw
j	_j_oy, ba_dg_e, a_g_ent	dʒ
k	_k_ill, _c_at, quie_t_	k
l	_l_et, ye_ll_ow, ba_ll_	l
′l	catt_le_, padd_le_	l̩
m	_m_eet, nu_m_ber, ti_m_e	m
n	_n_et, ca_n_dle, to_n_	n
′n	sudde_n_, sweete_n_	n̩
p	_p_ut, sam_p_le, esca_p_e	p
r	_r_ed, w_r_ong, bo_rn_	ɹ
s	_s_it, ca_s_tle, offi_c_e	s
t	_t_op, le_tt_er, ca_t_	t
v	_v_oice, e_v_ery, lo_v_e	v
w	_w_et, al_w_ays, q_u_art	w
y	_y_es, can_y_on, on_i_on	j
z	_z_oo, mi_s_ery, ri_s_e	z
ch	_ch_ew, na_t_ure, pun_ch_	tʃ
sh	_sh_ell, ma_ch_ine, bu_sh_	ʃ
th	_th_in, no_th_ing, tru_th_	θ
th	_th_en, o_th_er, ba_th_e	ð
zh	bei_g_e, mea_s_ure, sei_z_ure	ʒ
ŋ	ri_ng_, a_ng_er, dri_nk_	ŋ

III. FOREIGN SOUNDS

A number of foreign words are entered in the dictionary. An approximation of the native pronunciation—typically French or Spanish in this dictionary—has been provided. Foreign pronunciations use sounds not generally found in English, and, therefore, some additional pronunciation symbols are required. Below is a short explanation of these symbols:

à Used in French; a sound between the [a] as in *cat* and [ä] as in *cot*.

ë Used in French; round the lips as though to say *oh* while pronouncing [e] as in *get*.

ö Used chiefly in French; round the lips as though to say *oh* while pronouncing the sound [ā] as in *ate*.

ô Used in French, German, Spanish, etc.; round the lips loosely as though to say *aw* while pronouncing [u] as in *cut*.

ü Used in French and German; round the lips to say *oh* while pronouncing [ē] as in *meet*.

kh   Used in German and Scots English; pronounce [k] while allowing the breath to escape in a stream, as in saying [h].

H   Used in German; pronounce [sh] while keeping the tip of the tongue pointed downward.

n   Used chiefly in French; this symbol indicates that the vowel sound preceding it is pronounced with air expelled through both the mouth and the nose.

r   Pronounce [r] with a vibrating of the tip of the tongue in Spanish or Italian, or with a trilling of the uvula in French or German.

ʼ   Used in French to indicate that a final consonant is short or unvoiced or that a letter *e* is silent or very lightly pronounced.

yʼ   Used in Russian; pronounce an unvoiced [y] immediately after pronouncing the preceding consonant.

IV. STRESS MARKS

A heavy mark [ʹ] after a syllable indicates that the syllable is spoken with the most force. A light mark [ʹ] after a syllable indicates that the syllable is spoken with relatively less force. Syllables with no marking are given the least force.

dic·tion·ar·y (dikʹshə nerʹē)

ABBREVIATIONS AND SYMBOLS USED IN THIS DICTIONARY

abbrev.	abbreviated, abbreviation	Gram.	Grammar
adj.	adjective	Haw	Hawaiian
adv.	adverb	Heb	Hebrew
Afr	African	Hung	Hungarian
Afrik	Afrikaans	IE	Indo-European
alt.	alternative	i.e.	that is
Am	American	in.	inch(es)
AmInd	American Indian	indic.	indicative
AmSp	American Spanish	Inf., inf.	informal
Anat.	Anatomy	infl.	influenced
Anglo-Fr	Anglo-French	intens.	intensive
Ar	Arabic	interj.	interjection
Aram.	Aramaic	Ir	Irish
Archit.	Architecture	It	Italian
Austral.	Australian	Jpn	Japanese
Biol.	Biology	km	kilometer(s)
Bot.	Botany	L	Classical Latin
Brit	British	lb.	pound(s)
C	Celsius	lit.	literally
c.	century	LL	Late Latin
c.	circa	LowG	Low German
cap.	capital city	m	meter(s)
Cdn	Canadian	masc.	masculine
Celt	Celtic	Math.	Mathematics
cf.	compare	MDu	Middle Dutch
Ch.	Church	ME	Middle English
Chem.	Chemistry	Mech.	Mechanics
Chin	Chinese	Med.	Medicine
compar.	comparative	met.	metropolitan
Comput.	Computer Science	Mex	Mexican
conj.	conjunction	MHG	Middle High German
contr.	contraction (grammar)	mi.	mile(s)
Dan	Danish	Mil.	Military
Dial., dial.	dialectal	ML	Medieval Latin
dim.	diminutive	ModGr	Modern Greek
Du	Dutch	ModL	modern scientific Latin
E	eastern, English	Myth.	Mythology
EC	east central	N	northern
Eccles.	Ecclesiastical	n.	noun
Educ.	Education	Naut.	nautical usage
e.g.	for example	NC	north central
Egypt	Egyptian	NE	northeastern
Elec.	Electricity	NormFr	Norman French
Eng	English	Norw	Norwegian
Esk	Eskimo	NW	northwestern
esp.	especially	Obs., obs.	obsolete
etc.	and the like	occas.	occasionally
Ex.	example	OE	Old English
exc.	except	OFr	Old French
F	Fahrenheit	OHG	Old High German
fem.	feminine	ON	Old Norse
Fl	Flemish	orig.	originally
fol.	following entry	OS	Old Saxon
Fr	French	OSlav	Old Church Slavonic
ft.	foot, feet	oz.	ounce(s)
Gael	Gaelic	pers.	person (grammar)
Geol.	Geology	Pers	Persian
Geom.	Geometry	Photog.	Photography
Ger	German	pl.	plural
Gmc	Germanic	pl.n.	plural noun
Gr	Classical Greek	Poet.	Poetic

Pol	Polish	sing.	singular
pop.	population	sing.n.	singular noun
Port	Portuguese	Sp	Spanish
poss.	possessive	sp.	spelling, spelled
pp.	past participle	specif.	specifically
prec.	preceding entry	sq.	square
prep.	preposition	superl.	superlative
pres.	present tense	SW	southwestern
prob.	probably	Swed	Swedish
pron.	pronoun	Theol.	Theology
Prov	Provençal	transl.	translated, translation
prp.	present participle	Turk	Turkish
pseud.	pseudonym	ult.	ultimately
Psychol.	Psychology	v.	verb
pt.	past tense	var.	variant
R.C.Ch.	Roman Catholic Church	v.aux.	auxiliary verb
Rom.	Roman	vi.	intransitive verb
Russ	Russian	VL	Vulgar Latin
S	southern	vt.	transitive verb
Sans	Sanskrit	W	western
SC	south central	WC	west central
Scand	Scandinavian	WInd	West Indian
Scot	Scottish	WWI	World War I
SE	southeastern	WWII	World War II

Symbols

<	derived from	&	and
?	uncertain or unknown	°	degree
+	plus		

A

a¹ or **A** (ā) *n.*, pl. **a's, A's** the first letter of the English alphabet

a² (ə; *stressed*, ā) *indefinite article* ⟦< AN⟧ **1** one; one sort of **2** each; any one —*prep.* per [*once a day*] Before words beginning with a consonant sound, *a* is used [*a child, a home, a uniform*] See AN

a³ *abbrev.* **1** about **2** adjective **3** alto **4** answer

A¹ (ā) *n.* **1** a blood type **2** a grade indicating excellence **3** *Music* the sixth tone in the scale of C major

A² *abbrev.* **1** answer **2** April **3** Baseball, Basketball assist(s) **4** August

a-¹ ⟦< OE⟧ *prefix* **1** in, into, on, at, to [*ashore*] **2** in the act or state of [*asleep*]

a-² *prefix* **1** ⟦< OE⟧ up, out [*arise*] **2** ⟦< OE⟧ off, of [*akin*] **3** ⟦< Gr⟧ not, without [*amoral*]

AA *abbrev.* **1** Alcoholics Anonymous **2** Associate in (or of) Arts

aard·vark (ärd′värk′) *n.* ⟦Du, earth pig⟧ a nocturnal S African mammal that eats ants and termites

Aar·on (er′ən) *n. Bible* the first high priest of the Hebrews

AB¹ (ā′bē′) *n.* a blood type

AB² *abbrev.* **1** Alberta (Canada) **2** Bachelor of Arts: also **A.B.**

ab- ⟦L⟧ *prefix* away, from, from off, down [*abdicate*]

ABA *abbrev.* American Bar Association

a·back (ə bak′) *adv.* [Archaic] backward; back —**taken aback** startled and confused; surprised

a·ba·cus (ab′ə kəs) *n.*, pl. **-cus·es** or **-ci′** (-sī′) ⟦< Gr *abax*⟧ a frame with sliding beads for doing arithmetic

a·baft (ə baft′) *adv.* ⟦< OE *on*, on + *be*, by + *œftan*, aft⟧ aft —*prep. Naut.* behind

ab·a·lo·ne (ab′ə lō′nē) *n.* ⟦< AmInd⟧ an edible sea mollusk with an oval shell lined with mother-of-pearl

a·ban·don (ə ban′dən) *vt.* ⟦< OFr *mettre a bandon*, to put under (another's) ban⟧ **1** to give up completely **2** to desert —*n.* unrestrained activity; exuberance —**a·ban′don·ment** *n.*

a·ban·doned *adj.* **1** deserted **2** shamefully wicked **3** unrestrained

a·base (ə bās′) *vt.* **a·based′, a·bas′ing** ⟦< ML *abassare*, to lower⟧ to humble —**a·base′ment** *n.*

a·bash (ə bash′) *vt.* ⟦< OFr *es-*, intens. + *baer*, gape⟧ to make ashamed and uneasy; disconcert —**a·bash′ed·ly** *adv.*

a·bate (ə bāt′) *vt., vi.* **a·bat′ed, a·bat′ing** ⟦< OFr *abattre*, beat down⟧ **1** to make or become less **2** *Law* to end —**a·bate′ment** *n.*

ab·at·toir (ab′ə twär′) *n.* ⟦Fr: see prec.⟧ a slaughterhouse

ab·bé (a′bā) *n.* ⟦Fr: see ABBOT⟧ a French priest's title

ab·bess (ab′əs) *n.* ⟦see ABBOT⟧ a woman who heads a convent of nuns

ab·bey (ab′ē) *n.* **1** a monastery or convent **2** a church belonging to an abbey

ab·bot (ab′ət) *n.* ⟦< Aram *abbā*, father⟧ a man who heads a monastery

abbr or **abbrev** *abbrev.* **1** abbreviated **2** abbreviation

ab·bre·vi·ate (ə brē′vē āt′) *vt.* **-at′ed, -at′ing** ⟦< L *ad-*, to + *brevis*, brief⟧ to make shorter; esp., to shorten (a word) by omitting letters

ab·bre·vi·a·tion (-ā′shən) *n.* **1** a shortening **2** a shortened form of a word or phrase, as *Mr.* for *Mister*

ABC (ā′bē′sē′) *n.*, pl. **ABC's** [*usually pl.*] **1** the alphabet **2** the basic elements (of a subject)

ab·di·cate (ab′di kāt′) *vt., vi.* **-cat′ed, -cat′ing** ⟦< L *ab-*, off + *dicare*, to proclaim⟧ **1** to give up formally (a throne, etc.) **2** to surrender (a right, responsibility, etc.) —**ab′di·ca′tion** *n.*

ab·do·men (ab′də mən, ab dō′-) *n.* ⟦L⟧ the part of the body between the diaphragm and the pelvis; belly —**ab·dom′i·nal** (-däm′ə nəl) *adj.*

ab·duct (ab dukt′) *vt.* ⟦< L *ab-*, away + *ducere*, to lead⟧ to kidnap —**ab·duc′tion** *n.* —**ab·duc′tor** *n.*

a·beam (ə bēm′) *adv., adj.* at right angles to a ship's length or keel

a·bed (ə bed′) *adv., adj.* in bed

A·bel (ā′bəl) *n. Bible* the second son of Adam and Eve: see CAIN

a·be·li·a (ə bēl′yə, ə bē′lē ə) *n.* an ornamental shrub with clusters of fragrant flowers

ab·er·ra·tion (ab′ər ā′shən) *n.* ⟦< L *ab-*, from + *errare*, wander⟧ **1** a deviation from what is right, true, normal, etc. **2** mental derangement or lapse **3** *Optics* the failure of light rays from one point to converge at a single focus —**ab·er′rant** (-ənt) *adj.* —**ab′er·ra′tion·al** *adj.*

a·bet (ə bet′) *vt.* **a·bet′ted, a·bet′ting** ⟦< OFr *a-*, to + *beter*, to bait⟧ to urge on or help, esp. in crime —**a·bet′tor** *n.*, **a·bet′ter**

a·bey·ance (ə bā′əns) *n.* [< OFr *a-*, to, at + *bayer*, wait expectantly] temporary suspension, as of an activity or ruling

ab·hor (ab hôr′) *vt.* **-horred′, -hor′ring** [< L *ab-*, from + *horrere*, to shudder] to regard with disgust, hatred, etc.; detest —**ab·hor′rence** *n.*

ab·hor·rent (-ənt) *adj.* causing disgust, hatred, etc.; detestable —**ab·hor′rent·ly** *adv.*

a·bide (ə bīd′) *vi.* **a·bode′** or **a·bid′ed, a·bid′ing** [< OE *ā-*, intens. + *bīdan*, bide] **1** to remain **2** [Archaic] to reside —*vt.* **1** to await **2** to put up with —**abide by 1** to live up to (a promise, etc.) **2** to submit to and carry out —**a·bid′ance** *n.*

a·bid·ing *adj.* enduring; lasting

a·bil·i·ty (ə bil′ə tē) *n.*, pl. **-ties** [< L *habilitas*] **1** a being able; power to do **2** talent or skill

-a·bil·i·ty (ə bil′ə tē) [L *-abilitas*] *suffix* a (specified) ability, capacity, or tendency

ab·ject (ab′jekt′, ab jekt′) *adj.* [< L *ab-*, from + *jacere*, to throw] **1** miserable; wretched **2** lacking self-respect; degraded —**ab′ject′ly** *adv.* —**ab·jec′tion** *n.*, **ab′ject′ness**

ab·jure (ab joor′, əb-) *vt.* **-jured′, -jur′ing** [< L *ab-*, away + *jurare*, swear] **1** to give up (rights, allegiance, etc.) on oath; renounce **2** to recant —**ab·ju·ra·tion** (ab′jə rā′shən) *n.* —**ab·jur′er** *n.*

ab·late (ab lāt′) *vt.* **-lat′ed, -lat′ing** [see fol.] **1** to remove, as by surgery **2** to wear away, burn away, or vaporize —*vi.* to be ablated, as a rocket shield in reentry —**ab·la′tion** *n.*

ab·la·tive (ab′lə tiv) *n.* [< L *ab-*, away + *ferre*, to bear] *Gram.* the case expressing removal, cause, agency, etc., as in Latin

a·blaze (ə blāz′) *adj.* **1** burning brightly **2** greatly excited

a·ble (ā′bəl) *adj.* **a′bler, a′blest** [< L *habere*, have] **1** having enough power, skill, etc. to do something **2** skilled; talented **3** *Law* competent —**a′bly** *adv.*

-a·ble (ə bəl) [< L] *suffix* **1** that can or will [*perishable*] **2** capable of being ___ed [*manageable*] **3** worthy of being ___ed [*lovable*] **4** having qualities of [*comfortable*] **5** inclined to [*peaceable*]

a·ble-bod·ied *adj.* healthy and strong

able seaman a trained or skilled seaman: also **able-bodied seaman**

a·bloom (ə bloom′) *adj.* in bloom

ab·lu·tion (ab loo′shən) *n.* [< L *ab-*, off + *luere*, to wash] [*usually pl.*] a washing of the body, esp. as a religious ceremony

-a·bly (ə blē) *suffix* in a way indicating a (specified) ability, tendency, etc.

ABM *abbrev.* anti-ballistic missile

ab·ne·gate (ab′nə gāt′) *vt.* **-gat′ed, -gat′ing** [< L *ab-*, from + *negare*, deny] to give up (rights, claims, etc.); renounce —**ab′ne·ga′tion** *n.*

ab·nor·mal (ab nôr′məl) *adj.* not normal, average, or typical; irregular —**ab·nor′mal·ly** *adv.*

ab·nor·mal·i·ty (-mal′ə tē) *n.* **1** an abnormal condition **2** *pl.* **-ties** an abnormal thing

a·board (ə bôrd′) *adv., prep.* on or in (a train, ship, etc.)

a·bode (ə bōd′) *vi., vt. alt. pt. & pp. of* ABIDE —*n.* a home; residence

a·bol·ish (ə bäl′ish) *vt.* [< L *abolere*, destroy] to do away with; void —**a·bol′ish·ment** *n.*

ab·o·li·tion (ab′ə lish′ən) *n.* **1** complete destruction; annulment **2** [*occas.* **A-**] the abolishing of slavery in the U.S. —**ab′o·li′tion·ist** *n.*

a·bom·i·na·ble (ə bäm′ə nə bəl) *adj.* [see fol.] **1** disgusting; vile **2** very bad —**a·bom′i·na·bly** *adv.*

a·bom·i·nate (-nāt′) *vt.* **-nat′ed, -nat′ing** [< L *abominari*, regard as an ill omen] **1** to hate; loathe **2** to dislike very much —**a·bom′i·na′tion** *n.*

ab·o·rig·i·nal (ab′ə rij′ə nəl) *adj.* **1** existing (in a region) from the beginning; first; indigenous **2** of aborigines —*n.* an aborigine

ab·o·rig·i·ne (-nē′) *n.*, pl. **-nes** [< L *ab-*, from + *origine*, origin] **1** any of the first known inhabitants of a region **2** [**A-**] a member of the aboriginal people of Australia

a·born·ing (ə bôr′niŋ) *adv.* while being born or created [*the plan died* aborning]

a·bort (ə bôrt′) *vi.* [< L *aboriri*, miscarry] to have a miscarriage —*vt.* **1** to cause (an embryo or fetus) to be expelled in an abortion **2** to cut short (a flight, etc.), as because of an equipment failure

a·bor·tion (ə bôr′shən) *n.* **1** induced termination of a pregnancy with destruction of the embryo or fetus **2** MISCARRIAGE (*n.* 2) —**a·bor′tion·ist** *n.*

a·bor·tive (ə bôrt′iv) *adj.* **1** unsuccessful; fruitless **2** *Biol.* arrested in development

a·bound (ə bound′) *vi.* [< L *ab-*, away + *undare*, rise in waves] **1** to be plentiful **2** to be rich (*in*) or teem (*with*)

a·bout (ə bout′) *adv.* [< OE *onbūtan*, around] **1** all around **2** near **3** in an opposite direction **4** approximately **5** [Inf.] nearly [*about* ready] —*adj.* **1** astir [he is up and *about*] **2** likely immediately [*about* to leave] —*prep.* **1** on all sides of **2** near to **3** with **4** concerning

a·bout-face *n.* a reversal of position or opinion —*vi.* **-faced′, -fac′ing** to turn or face in the opposite direction

a·bove (ə buv′) *adv.* [OE *abūfan*] **1** in a higher place; up **2** earlier (in a book, etc.) **3** higher in rank, etc. —*prep.* **1** over; on top of **2** better or more than [*above the average*] —*adj.* mentioned earlier —*n.* something that is above —**above all** most of all; mainly

a·bove-board *adv., adj.* without dishonesty or concealment

a·bove-ground *adj., adv.* **1** above or on the surface of the earth **2** not secret(ly)

a·brade (ə brād′) *vt., vi.* **a·brad′ed, a·brad′ing** [< L *ab-*, away + *radere*, to scrape] to rub off; scrape away

A·bra·ham (ā′brə ham′) *n. Bible* the first patriarch of the Hebrews

a·bra·sion (ə brā′zhən) *n.* **1** an abrading **2** an abraded spot, as on the skin

a·bra·sive (-siv) *adj.* **1** causing abrasion **2** aggressively annoying; irritating —*n.* a substance, as sandpaper, used for grinding, polishing, etc.

a·breast (ə brest′) *adv., adj.* **1** side by side **2** informed (*of*) recent happenings

a·bridge (ə brij′) *vt.* **a·bridged′, a·bridg′ing** [< LL *abbreviare*, abbreviate] **1** to shorten, lessen, or curtail **2** to shorten (a piece of writing) while keeping the substance —**a·bridg′ment** *n.,* **a·bridge′ment**

a·broad (ə brôd′) *adv.* **1** far and wide **2** in circulation; current **3** outdoors **4** to or in foreign lands —**from abroad** from a foreign land

ab·ro·gate (ab′rə gāt′) *vt.* **-gat′ed, -gat′ing** [< L *ab-*, away + *rogare*, ask] to cancel or repeal by authority —**ab′ro·ga′tion** *n.* —**ab′ro·ga′tor** *n.*

a·brupt (ə brupt′) *adj.* [< L *ab-*, off + *rumpere*, to break] **1** sudden; unexpected **2** brusque **3** very steep **4** disconnected, as some writing —**a·brupt′ly** *adv.* —**a·brupt′ness** *n.*

ABS *abbrev.* anti-lock braking system

Ab·sa·lom (ab′sə ləm) *n. Bible* David's son who rebelled against him

ab·scess (ab′ses′) *n.* [< L *ab(s)-*, from + *cedere*, go] a swollen area in body tissues, containing pus —*vi.* to form an abscess —**ab′scessed′** *adj.*

ab·scis·sa (ab sis′ə) *n., pl.* **-sas** or **-sae** (-ē) [L < *ab-*, from + *scindere*, to cut] *Math.* the horizontal distance of a point from a vertical axis

ab·scond (ab skänd′, əb-) *vi.* [< L *ab(s)-*, from + *condere*, hide] to leave hastily and secretly, esp. to escape the law —**ab·scond′er** *n.*

ab·sence (ab′səns) *n.* **1** a being absent **2** the time of this **3** a lack

ab·sent (ab′sənt; *for v.,* ab sent′) *adj.* [< L *ab-*, away + *esse*, be] **1** not present **2** not existing; lacking **3** not attentive —*vt.* to keep (oneself) away —*prep.* in the absence of [*absent* her testimony, our case is weak] —**ab′sent·ly** *adv.*

ab·sen·tee (ab′sən tē′) *n.* one who is absent, as from work —*adj.* designating, of, or from one who is absent —**ab′sen·tee′ism′** *n.*

absentee ballot a ballot to be marked and sent to a board of elections by a person (**absentee voter**) who will not be present at the polls at election time

ab·sent-mind·ed or **ab·sent-mind·ed** *adj.* **1** not attentive; preoccupied **2** habitually forgetful —**ab′sent-mind′ed·ly** *adv.* —**ab′sent-mind′ed·ness** *n.*

absent without leave *Mil.* absent from duty without official permission

ab·sinthe (ab′sinth′) *n.* [< Gr] a greenish liquor flavored with wormwood, etc.

ab·so·lute (ab′sə lōōt′) *adj.* [see ABSOLVE] **1** perfect; complete **2** not mixed; pure **3** not limited [*absolute* power] **4** positive **5** not doubted; real [*absolute* truth] **6** not relative —**ab′so·lute′ly** *adv.*

absolute value the value of a real number, disregarding its positive or negative sign [the *absolute value* of -4 or +4 is 4]

absolute zero the lower limit on physically obtainable temperatures: equal to -273.15°C or -459.67°F

ab·so·lu·tion (ab′sə lōō′shən) *n.* **1** a freeing (*from* guilt) **2** remission (*of* sin or penalty for it)

ab·so·lut·ism (ab′sə lōō tiz′əm) *n.* government by absolute rule; despotism —**ab′so·lut′ist** *n., adj.*

ab·solve (ab zälv′, əb-) *vt.* **-solved′, -solv′ing** [< L *ab-*, from + *solvere*, loosen] **1** to free from guilt, a duty, etc. **2** to give religious absolution to

ab·sorb (ab sôrb′, -zôrb′; əb-) *vt.* [< L *ab-*, from + *sorbere*, drink in] **1** to suck up into a network of pores or small spaces by capillary action **2** to interest greatly; engross **3** to assimilate **4** to pay for (costs, etc.) **5** to take in (a shock, etc.) without recoil **6** to take in and not reflect (light or sound) —**ab·sorb′ing** *adj.*

ab·sorb·ent *adj.* capable of absorbing moisture, etc. —*n.* a thing that absorbs —**ab·sorb′en·cy** *n.*

ab·sorp·tion (ab sôrp′shən, -zôrp′-; əb-) *n.* **1** an absorbing or being absorbed **2** great interest —**ab·sorp′tive** *adj.*

ab·stain (ab stān′, əb-) *vi.* [< L *ab(s)-*, from + *tenere*, to hold] to voluntarily do without; refrain (*from*) —**ab·stain′er** *n.* —**ab·sten′tion** (-sten′shən) *n.*

ab·ste·mi·ous (ab stē′mē əs, əb-) *adj.* [< L *ab(s)-*, from + *temetum*, strong drink] moderate in eating and drinking; temperate

ab·sti·nence (ab′stə nəns) *n.* **1** an abstaining from some or all food, liquor, etc. **2** an abstaining from sexual activity —**ab′sti·nent** *adj.*

ab·stract (*for adj.,* ab strakt′, ab′strakt′; *for n.* & *vt.* 2, ab′strakt′; *for vt.* 1, ab strakt′) *adj.* [< L *ab(s)-*, from + *trahere*, to draw] **1** thought of apart from material objects **2** expressing a quality so thought of **3** theoretical **4** *Art* not representing things realistically —*n.* a summary —*vt.* **1** to take away **2** to summarize —**ab·stract′ly** *adv.* —**ab·stract′ness** *n.*

ab·stract·ed *adj.* preoccupied

ab·strac·tion (ab strak′shən) *n.* **1** an abstracting; removal **2** an abstract idea, thing, etc. **3** mental withdrawal **4** an abstract painting, sculpture, etc.

ab·struse (ab strōōs′) *adj.* [< L *ab(s)-*, away + *trudere*, to thrust] hard to understand —**ab·struse′ly** *adv.* —**ab·struse′ness** *n.*

ab·surd (ab surd′, -zurd′; əb-) *adj.* [< L *ab-*, intens. + *surdus*, dull, insensible] so unreasonable as to be ridiculous —**ab·surd′i·ty** *n.* —**ab·surd′ly** *adv.*

a·bun·dance (ə bun′dəns) *n.* [see ABOUND] a great supply; more than enough —**a·bun′dant** *adj.* —**a·bun′dant·ly** *adv.*

a·buse (ə byōōz′; *for n.,* ə byōōs′) *vt.* **a·bused′, a·bus′ing** [< L *ab-*, away + *uti*, to use⟧ **1** to use wrongly **2** to mistreat, esp. by inflicting physical or sexual harm on **3** to insult; revile —*n.* **1** wrong use **2** mistreatment, esp. by the infliction of physical or sexual harm **3** a corrupt practice **4** insulting language —**a·bu·sive** (ə byōō′siv) *adj.* —**a·bu′sive·ly** *adv.*

a·but (ə but′) *vi., vt.* **a·but′ted, a·but′ting** ⟦< OFr *a*–, to + *bout*, end⟧ to border (*on* or *upon*)

a·but·ment *n.* a part supporting one end of an arch, bridge, etc.

a·bys·mal (ə biz′məl) *adj.* **1** of or like an abyss; not measurable **2** very bad; wretched —**a·bys′mal·ly** *adv.*

a·byss (ə bis′) *n.* ⟦< Gr *a*–, without + *byssos*, bottom⟧ **1** a bottomless gulf **2** anything too deep for measurement [an *abyss* of shame]

Ab·ys·sin·i·a (ab′ə sin′ē ə) *former name for* ETHIOPIA —**Ab′ys·sin′i·an** *adj., n.*

ac *abbrev.* acre(s)

Ac *Chem. symbol for* actinium

AC *abbrev.* **1** air conditioning **2** alternating current

-ac (ak, ək) ⟦< Gr⟧ *suffix* **1** characteristic of [*elegiac*] **2** relating to [*cardiac*] **3** affected by [*maniac*]

a·ca·cia (ə kā′shə) *n.* ⟦< Gr *akē*, thorn⟧ **1** a tree or shrub with yellow or white flower clusters **2** the locust tree

ac·a·dem·ic (ak′ə dem′ik) *adj.* **1** of colleges, universities, etc.; scholastic **2** having to do with the liberal arts rather than technical education **3** formal; pedantic **4** merely theoretical —**ac′a·dem′i·cal·ly** *adv.*

a·cad·e·mi·cian (ə kad′ə mish′ən, ak′ə də–) *n.* a member of an ACADEMY (*n.* 3)

a·cad·e·my (ə kad′ə mē) *n., pl.* **-mies** ⟦< Gr *akadēmeia*, place where Plato taught⟧ **1** a private secondary school **2** a school for special instruction **3** an association of scholars, writers, etc., for advancing an art or science

a·can·thus (ə kan′thəs) *n., pl.* **-thus·es** or **-thi′** (-thī′, -thē′) ⟦< Gr *akē*, a point⟧ **1** a plant with lobed, often spiny leaves **2** *Archit.* a representation of these leaves, as on the capital of a column

a cap·pel·la (ä′ kə pel′ə) ⟦It, in chapel style⟧ without instrumental accompaniment: said of vocalists or vocal groups : also sp. **a ca·pel′la**

A·ca·pul·co (ä′kə pool′kō, ak′ə–) city & seaport in S Mexico, on the Pacific: a winter resort

ac·cede (ak sēd′) *vi.* **-ced′ed, -ced′ing** ⟦< L *ad*–, to + *cedere*, go, yield⟧ **1** to enter upon the duties (of an office); attain (*to*) **2** to assent; agree (*to*)

ac·cel·er·ate (ak sel′ər āt′, ək–) *vt.* **-at′ed, -at′ing** ⟦< L *ad*–, to + *celerare*, hasten⟧ **1** to increase the speed of **2** to cause to happen sooner —*vi.* to go faster —**ac·cel′er·ant** *adj., n.* —**ac·cel′er·a′tion** *n.*

ac·cel·er·a·tor *n.* that which accelerates something; esp., the foot throttle of a motor vehicle

ac·cent (ak′sent′; *for v.,* also ak sent′) *n.* ⟦< L *ad*–, to + *canere*, sing⟧ **1** emphasis given a

spoken syllable or word **2** a mark showing such emphasis or indicating pronunciation **3** a distinguishing manner of pronunciation [an Irish *accent*] **4** special emphasis or attention **5** *Music, Prosody* rhythmic stress —*vt.* **1** to mark with an accent **2** to emphasize; stress

ac·cen·tu·ate (ak sen′choo āt′, ək–) *vt.* **-at′ed, -at′ing** to accent; emphasize —**ac·cen′tu·a′tion** *n.*

ac·cept (ak sept′, ək–) *vt.* ⟦< L *ad*–, to + *capere*, take⟧ **1** to receive, esp. willingly **2** to approve **3** to agree or consent to **4** to believe in **5** to reply "yes" to **6** to agree to pay

ac·cept·a·ble *adj.* worth accepting; satisfactory —**ac·cept′a·bil′i·ty** *n.*, **ac·cept′a·ble·ness** —**ac·cept′a·bly** *adv.*

ac·cept·ance *n.* **1** an accepting **2** approval **3** belief in; assent **4** a promise to pay

ac·cept·ed *adj.* generally regarded as true, proper, etc.; conventional; approved

ac·cess (ak′ses′) *n.* [see ACCEDE] **1** approach or means of approach **2** the right to enter, use, etc. **3** an outburst; fit [an *access* of anger] —*vt.* **1** to get data from, or add data to, a database **2** to gain access to [*accessed* the roof]

ac·ces·si·ble (ak ses′ə bəl, ək–) *adj.* **1** that can be approached or entered, esp. easily **2** obtainable **3** easily understood —**ac·ces′si·bil′i·ty** *n.* —**ac·ces′si·bly** *adv.*

ac·ces·sion (ak sesh′ən, ək–) *n.* **1** the act of attaining (a throne, power, etc.) **2** assent **3** *a)* increase by addition *b)* an addition

ac·ces·so·ry (ak ses′ər ē, ək–) *adj.* ⟦see ACCEDE⟧ **1** additional; extra **2** helping in an unlawful act —*n., pl.* **-ries** **1** something extra or complementary **2** one who, though absent, helps another to break the law

ac·ci·dent (ak′sə dənt) *n.* ⟦< L *ad*–, to + *cadere*, to fall⟧ **1** an unexpected or unintended happening, as one resulting in injury, loss, etc. **2** chance

ac·ci·den·tal (-dent′'l) *adj.* happening by chance —*n. Music* a note that is raised or lowered by one or two half steps relative to the pitch specified by the key signature —**ac′ci·den′tal·ly** *adv.*

ac·ci·dent-prone *adj.* seemingly inclined to become involved in accidents

ac·claim (ə klām′) *vt.* ⟦< L *ad*–, to + *clamare*, to cry out⟧ to greet or announce with loud approval or applause; hail —*n.* loud approval

ac·cla·ma·tion (ak′lə mā′shən) *n.* **1** loud applause or approval **2** an approving vote by voice

ac·cli·mate (ak′lə māt′, ə klī′mət) *vt., vi.* **-mat·ed, -mat·ing** ⟦< L *ad*–, to + Gr *klima*, region⟧ to accustom or become accustomed to a new climate or environment —**ac′cli·ma′tion** *n.*

ac·cli·ma·tize (ə klī′mə tīz′) *vt., vi.* **-tized′, -tiz′ing** ACCLIMATE —**ac·cli′ma·ti·za′tion** *n.*

ac·cliv·i·ty (ə kliv′ə tē) *n., pl.* **-ties** ⟦< L *ad*–, up + *clivus*, hill⟧ an upward slope

ac·co·lade (ak′ə lād′) *n.* ⟦< L *ad*, to + *collum*, neck⟧ anything done or given to show great respect, appreciation, etc.

ac·com·mo·date (ə käm′ə dāt′) *vt.* **-dat′ed, -dat′ing** ⟦< L *ad-*, to + *commodare*, to fit⟧ **1** to adapt **2** to do a favor for **3** to have space for

ac·com·mo·dat·ing *adj.* obliging

ac·com·mo·da·tion *n.* **1** adjustment **2** willingness to do favors **3** a help; convenience **4** [*pl.*] *a*) lodgings *b*) traveling space, as in a train

ac·com·pa·ni·ment (ə kum′pə nə mənt, -nē-; *often* ə kump′nə-, -nē-) *n.* **1** anything that accompanies something else, as an instrumental part supporting a solo voice, etc. **2** a food served with a main dish

ac·com·pa·ny (ə kum′pə nē; *often* ə kump′nē) *vt.* **-nied, -ny·ing** ⟦see AD- & COMPANION⟧ **1** to go with **2** to supplement **3** to play or sing an accompaniment for or to —**ac·com′pa·nist** *n.*

ac·com·plice (ə käm′plis) *n.* ⟦< ME *a* (the article) + LL *complex*, a confederate⟧ a partner in crime

ac·com·plish (ə käm′plish) *vt.* ⟦< L *ad-*, intens. + *complere*, fill up⟧ to succeed in doing; complete

ac·com·plished *adj.* **1** done; completed **2** expert; skilled

ac·com·plish·ment *n.* **1** completion **2** work completed; an achievement **3** a social art or skill: *usually used in pl.*

ac·cord (ə kôrd′) *vt.* ⟦< L *ad-*, to + *cor*, heart⟧ **1** to make agree **2** to grant —*vi.* to agree; harmonize (*with*) —*n.* mutual agreement; harmony —**of one's own accord** willingly —**with one accord** all agreeing

ac·cord·ance *n.* agreement; conformity —**ac·cord′ant** *adj.*

ac·cord·ing *adj.* in harmony —**according to 1** in agreement with **2** as stated by

ac·cord·ing·ly *adv.* **1** in a fitting and proper way **2** therefore

ac·cor·di·on (ə kôr′dē ən) *n.* ⟦prob. < It *accordare*, to be in tune⟧ a musical instrument with keys and a bellows which is squeezed to force air through reeds

ac·cost (ə kôst′) *vt.* ⟦< L *ad-*, to + *costa*, side⟧ to approach and speak to, esp. in a bold way

ac·count (ə kount′) *vt.* ⟦< OFr *a-*, to + *conter*, tell⟧ to judge to be —*vi.* **1** to give a financial reckoning (*to*) **2** to give reasons (*for*) **3** to be the reason (*for*) —*n.* **1** [*often pl.*] a record of business transactions **2** *a*) BANK ACCOUNT *b*) CHARGE ACCOUNT **3** a credit customer or client **4** worth; importance **5** an explanation **6** a report —**on account** as partial payment —**on account of** because of —**on no account** under no circumstances —**take into account** to consider

ac·count·a·ble *adj.* responsible; liable —**ac·count′a·bil′i·ty** *n.*

ac·count·ant *n.* one whose work is accounting

ac·count·ing *n.* the figuring and recording of financial accounts

ac·cou·ter (ə koōt′ər) *vt.* ⟦prob. < L *consuere*, to sew⟧ to outfit; equip

ac·cou·tre·ments or **ac·cou·ter·ments** (ə koō′trə mənts, -koōt′ər-) *pl.n.* **1** clothes **2** equipment

ac·cred·it (ə kred′it) *vt.* ⟦see CREDIT⟧ **1** to authorize; certify **2** to believe in **3** to attribute —**ac·cred′i·ta′tion** *n.*

ac·cre·tion (ə krē′shən) *n.* ⟦< L *ad-*, to + *crescere*, to grow⟧ **1** growth in size, esp. by addition **2** accumulated matter **3** a growing together of parts **4** a part added separately; addition

ac·crue (ə kroō′) *vi.* **-crued′, -cru′ing** ⟦see prec.⟧ to come as a natural growth or periodic increase, as interest on money —**ac·cru′al** *n.*

acct *abbrev.* account

ac·cul·tur·ate (ə kul′chər āt′) *vi., vt.* **-at′ed, -at′ing** to undergo, or change by, acculturation

ac·cul·tur·a·tion *n.* **1** adaptation to a culture, esp. a new or different one **2** mutual influence of different cultures

ac·cu·mu·late (ə kyoō′myə lāt′) *vt., vi.* **-lat′ed, -lat′ing** ⟦< L *ad-*, to + *cumulare*, to heap⟧ to pile up or collect —**ac·cu′mu·la′tion** *n.* —**ac·cu′mu·la′tive** (-lāt′iv, -lə tiv) *adj.*

ac·cu·ra·cy (ak′yoor ə se, -yər-) *n.* the quality or state of being accurate; precision

ac·cu·rate (-it) *adj.* ⟦< L *ad-*, to + *cura*, care⟧ **1** careful and exact **2** free from errors; precise —**ac′cu·rate·ly** *adv.* —**ac′cu·rate·ness** *n.*

ac·curs·ed (ə kur′sid, -kurst′) *adj.* **1** under a curse **2** damnable Also **ac·curst′** —**ac·curs′ed·ness** *n.*

ac·cu·sa·tion (ak′yoō zā′shən, -yə-) *n.* **1** an accusing or being accused **2** what one is accused of —**ac·cu·sa·to·ry** (ə kyoō′zə tôr′ē) *adj.*

ac·cu·sa·tive (ə kyoō′zə tiv) *n.* ⟦see fol.⟧ *Gram.* the case of the direct object of a verb; also, the objective case in English

ac·cuse (ə kyoōz′) *vt.* **-cused′, -cus′ing** ⟦< L *ad-*, to + *causa*, a cause⟧ **1** to blame **2** to bring charges against —**ac·cus′er** *n.*

ac·cus·tom (ə kus′təm) *vt.* to make familiar with something by custom, habit, or use; habituate (*to*)

ac·cus·tomed *adj.* **1** customary; usual **2** habituated (*to*)

ace (ās) *n.* ⟦< L *as*, unit⟧ **1** a playing card, etc. with one spot **2** a point, as in tennis, made by a serve one's opponent cannot return **3** an expert, esp. in combat flying —*adj.* [Inf.] first-rate —*vt.* **aced, ac′ing** [Slang] to defeat completely: often with *out* **2** [Inf.] to earn a grade of A in, on, etc.

Ace bandage ⟦< *Ace*, trademark for such a bandage⟧ an elasticized cloth bandage used to provide support, as for a sprain

ace in the hole [Slang] any advantage held in reserve

a·cer·bi·ty (ə sur′bə tē) *n., pl.* **-ties** ⟦< L *acerbus*, bitter⟧ **1** sourness **2** sharpness of temper, words, etc. —**a·cer′bic** *adj.*

a·ce·ta·min·o·phen (ə sēt′ə min′ə fən, as′ə tə-) *n.* a crystalline powder used to lessen fever and pain

ac·et·an·i·lide (as′ət an′ə lid′) *n.* [< ACETIC + ANILINE] a drug used to lessen pain and fever

ac·e·tate (as′i tāt′) *n.* **1** a salt or ester of acetic acid **2** something, esp. a fabric, made with an acetate of cellulose

a·ce·tic (ə sēt′ik) *adj.* [< L *acetum*, vinegar] of the sharp, sour liquid (**acetic acid**) found in vinegar

ac·e·tone (as′i tōn′) *n.* [see prec.] a colorless, flammable liquid used as a solvent, as for removing nail polish —**ac′e·ton′ic** (-tän′ik) *adj.*

a·ce·ty·lene (ə set′′l ēn′) *n.* a gas used for lighting and, with oxygen, in welding

a·ce·tyl·sal·i·cyl·ic acid (ə sēt′′l sal′ə sil′ik) ASPIRIN

ache (āk) *vi.* **ached, ach′ing** [< OE *acan*] **1** to have or give dull, steady pain **2** to yearn —*n.* a dull, continuous pain

a·chene (ā kēn′, ə-) *n.* [< Gr *a-*, not + *chainein*, to gape] any small, dry fruit with one seed

a·chieve (ə chēv′) *vt.* **a·chieved′, a·chiev′ing** [< OFr < *a-*, to + L *caput*, head] **1** to do; accomplish **2** to get by effort —**a·chiev′a·ble** *adj.* —**a·chiev′er** *n.*

a·chieve·ment *n.* **1** an achieving **2** a thing achieved; feat

achievement test a test for measuring a student's mastery of a given subject or skill

A·chil·les (ə kil′ēz′) *n. Gr. Myth* a hero killed in the Trojan War

Achilles' heel (one's) vulnerable spot

Achilles tendon the tendon connecting the heel to the calf muscles

a·choo (ä choo′) *interj.* used to suggest a sneeze

ach·ro·mat·ic (ak′rə mat′ik, ā′krə-) *adj.* [< Gr *a-*, without + *chrōma*, color] refracting white light without breaking it up into its component colors

ach·y (āk′ē) *adj.* **-i·er, -i·est** having an ache

ac·id (as′id) *adj.* [L *acidus*, sour] **1** sour; sharp; tart **2** of an acid —*n.* **1** a sour substance **2** [Slang] LSD **3** *Chem.* any compound that reacts with a base to form a salt —**a·cid·i·ty** (ə sid′ə tē) *n., pl.* **-ties** —**ac′id·ly** *adv.*

a·cid·i·fy (ə sid′ə fī′) *vt., vi.* **-fied′, -fy′ing 1** to make or become sour **2** to change into an acid

ac·i·do·sis (as′ə dō′sis) *n.* a condition in which there is an abnormal retention of acid or loss of alkali in the body

acid rain rain with a high concentration of acids produced by the gases from burning fossil fuels

acid reflux reflux of stomach acid, etc. into the esophagus, resulting in heartburn and other symptoms

acid test a crucial, final test

a·cid·u·lous (ə sij′oo ləs) *adj.* **1** somewhat acid or sour **2** sarcastic

-a·cious (ā′shəs) [< L] *suffix* inclined to, full of [*gracious*]

-ac·i·ty (as′ə tē) [< L] *suffix* a (specified) characteristic, quality, or tendency [*tenacity*]

ac·knowl·edge (ak näl′ij, ək-) *vt.* **-edged, -edg·ing** [see KNOWLEDGE] **1** to admit as true **2** to recognize the authority or claims of **3** to respond to **4** to express thanks for **5** to state that one has received (a letter, etc.) —**ac·knowl′edg·ment** *n.,* **ac·knowl′edge·ment**

ACL *abbrev.* anterior cruciate ligament (of the knee)

ACLU *abbrev.* American Civil Liberties Union

ac·me (ak′mē) *n.* [Gr *akmē*, a point, top] the highest point; peak

ac·ne (ak′nē) *n.* [see prec.] a skin disorder usually causing pimples on the face, etc.

ac·o·lyte (ak′ə līt′) *n.* [< Gr *akolouthos*, follower] **1** one who helps a priest at services, esp. at Mass **2** an attendant; helper

ac·o·nite (ak′ə nīt′) *n.* [< Gr] a plant with hoodlike, usually blue or violet flowers

a·corn (ā′kôrn′) *n.* [< OE *æcern*, nut] the nut of the oak tree

acorn squash a kind of winter squash, acorn-shaped with dark-green skin and yellow flesh

a·cous·tic (ə koos′tik) *adj.* [< Gr *akouein*, to hear] **1** having to do with hearing or acoustics **2** of or using a musical instrument that is not amplified Also **a·cous′ti·cal** —**a·cous′ti·cal·ly** *adv.*

a·cous·tics (-tiks) *pl.n.* the qualities of a room, etc. that determine how clearly sounds can be heard in it —*n.* the branch of physics dealing with sound

ac·quaint (ə kwānt′) *vt.* [< L *ad-*, to + *cognoscere*, know] **1** to inform **2** to make familiar (with)

ac·quaint·ance *n.* **1** knowledge gotten from personal experience **2** a person whom one knows slightly

ac·qui·esce (ak′wē es′) *vi.* **-esced′, -esc′ing** [< L *ad-*, to + *quiescere*, grow quiet] to consent without enthusiasm: often with *in* —**ac′qui·es′cence** *n.* —**ac′qui·es′cent** *adj.*

ac·quire (ə kwīr′) *vt.* **-quired′, -quir′ing** [< L *ad-*, to + *quaerere*, to seek] **1** to gain by one's own efforts **2** to get as one's own —**ac·quire′ment** *n.*

ac·qui·si·tion (ak′wə zish′ən) *n.* **1** an acquiring **2** something acquired

ac·quis·i·tive (ə kwiz′ə tiv) *adj.* eager to acquire (money, etc.); grasping —**ac·quis′i·tive·ness** *n.*

ac·quit (ə kwit′) *vt.* **-quit′ted, -quit′ting** [< L *ad-*, to + *quietare*, to quiet] **1** to release from an obligation, etc. **2** to clear (a person) of a charge **3** to conduct (oneself); behave —**ac·quit′tal** *n.*

a·cre (ā′kər) *n.* [OE *æcer*, field] a measure of land, 4,840 sq. yards

a·cre·age *n.* acres collectively

ac·rid (ak′rid) *adj.* [< L *acris*, sharp] **1** sharp or bitter to the taste or smell **2** sharp in speech, etc. —**a·crid·i·ty** (ə krid′ə tē) *n.* —**ac′rid·ly** *adv.*

ac·ri·mo·ny (ak′ri mō′nē) *n., pl.* **-nies** [< L *acer*, sharp] bitterness or harshness of manner or speech —**ac′ri·mo′ni·ous** *adj.*

ac·ro·bat (ak′rə bat′) *n.* 〖< Gr *akrobatos*, walking on tiptoe〗 one who performs gymnastic tricks, as on a trapeze or tightrope —**ac′ro·bat′ic** *adj.*

ac·ro·bat·ics *pl.n.* [*also with sing. v.*] **1** an acrobat's tricks **2** any tricks requiring great skill

ac·ro·nym (ak′rə nim′) *n.* 〖< Gr *akros*, at the end + *onyma*, name〗 a word formed from the first (or first few) letters of several words, as *radar*

ac·ro·pho·bi·a (ak′rō fō′bē ə) *n.* 〖< Gr *akros*, at the top + -PHOBIA〗 an abnormal fear of being in high places

A·crop·o·lis (ə kräp′ə lis) 〖< Gr *akros*, at the top + *polis*, city〗 the fortified hill in Athens on which the Parthenon was built

a·cross (ə krôs′) *adv.* **1** crosswise **2** from one side to the other —*prep.* **1** from one side to the other of **2** on or to the other side of **3** into contact with by chance [to come *across* an old friend]

a·cross-the-board *adj.* **1** combining win, place, and show, as a bet **2** including or affecting all classes or groups

a·cros·tic (ə krôs′tik) *n.* 〖Gr *akrostichos* < *akros*, at the end + *stichos*, line of verse〗 a poem, etc. in which certain letters in each line, as the first or last, spell out a word, motto, etc.

a·cryl·ic (ə kril′ik) *adj.* **1** designating any of a group of synthetic fibers used to make fabrics **2** designating any of a group of clear, synthetic resins used to make paints, plastics, etc.

act (akt) *n.* 〖< L *agere*, to do〗 **1** a thing done **2** an action **3** a law **4** a main division of a drama or opera **5** a short performance, as on a variety show **6** something done merely for show —*vt.* to perform in (a play or part) —*vi.* **1** to perform in a play, movie, etc. **2** to behave **3** to function **4** to have an effect (*on*) **5** to appear to be —**act up** [Inf.] to misbehave

ACTH *n.* 〖*a*(*dreno*)*c*(*ortico*)*t*(*ropic*) *h*(*ormone*)〗 a pituitary hormone that acts on the adrenal cortex

act·ing *adj.* temporarily doing the duties of another —*n.* the art of an actor

ac·ti·nide series (ak′tə nīd′) a group of radioactive chemical elements from element 89 (actinium) through element 103 (lawrencium)

ac·tin·i·um (ak tin′ē əm) *n.* 〖< Gr *aktis*, ray〗 a white, radioactive, metallic chemical element: symbol, Ac; at. no. 89

ac·tion (ak′shən) *n.* **1** the doing of something **2** a thing done **3** [*pl.*] behavior **4** the way of working, as of a machine **5** the moving parts, as of a gun **6** the sequence of events, as in a story **7** a lawsuit **8** military combat **9** [Slang] activity

action figure a plastic, doll-like toy typically resembling a superhero or movie character

ac·ti·vate (ak′tə vāt′) *vt.* **-vat′ed, -vat′ing** **1** to make active **2** to put (a military unit) on active status —**ac′ti·va′tion** *n.* —**ac′ti·va′tor** *n.*

activated charcoal a form of highly porous carbon that can adsorb gases, vapors, and colloidal particles: also **activated carbon**

ac·tive (ak′tiv) *adj.* **1** acting; working **2** causing motion or change **3** lively; agile **4** *Gram.* indicating the voice of a verb whose subject performs the action —**ac′tive·ly** *adv.*

ac·tiv·ism (-tə viz′əm) *n.* the taking of direct action to achieve a political or social end —**ac′tiv·ist** *adj., n.*

ac·tiv·i·ty (ak tiv′ə tē) *n., pl.* **-ties** **1** a being active **2** liveliness **3** a specific action or function [student *activities*]

ac·tor (ak′tər) *n.* **1** one who does a thing **2** one who acts in plays, movies, etc.

ac·tress (-tris) *n.* a woman or girl who acts in plays, movies, etc.

ac·tu·al (ak′chōō əl) *adj.* 〖< L *agere*, to do〗 **1** existing in reality **2** existing at the time —**ac′tu·al·ly** *adv.*

ac·tu·al·i·ty (-al′ə tē) *n.* **1** reality **2** *pl.* **-ties** an actual thing; fact

ac·tu·al·ize (-əl īz′) *vt.* **-ized′, -iz′ing** **1** to make actual or real **2** to make realistic

ac·tu·ar·y (ak′chōō er′ē) *n., pl.* **-ies** 〖L *actuarius*, clerk〗 one who figures insurance risks, premiums, etc. —**ac′tu·ar′i·al** *adj.*

ac·tu·ate (ak′chōō āt′) *vt.* **-at′ed, -at′ing** **1** to put into action **2** to cause to take action —**ac′tu·a′tor** *n.*

a·cu·i·ty (ə kyōō′ə tē) *n.* 〖< L *acus*, needle〗 keenness of thought or vision

a·cu·men (ə kyōō′mən, ak′yə mən) *n.* 〖< L *acuere*, sharpen〗 keenness of mind; shrewdness

ac·u·punc·ture (ak′yōō puŋk′chər) *n.* 〖< L *acus*, needle + PUNCTURE〗 in traditional Chinese medicine, the piercing of parts of the body with needles to treat disease or relieve pain —**ac′u·punc′tur·ist** *n.*

a·cute (ə kyōōt′) *adj.* 〖< L *acuere*, sharpen〗 **1** sharp-pointed **2** keen of mind **3** sensitive [*acute* hearing] **4** severe, as pain **5** severe but not chronic [an *acute* disease] **6** very serious **7** less than 90° [an *acute* angle] —**a·cute′ly** *adv.* —**a·cute′ness** *n.*

acute accent a mark (′) showing primary stress, the quality of a vowel, etc.

-a·cy (ə sē) 〖ult. < Gr〗 *suffix* quality, condition, etc. [*supremacy*]

a·cy·clo·vir (ā sī′klō vir′) *n.* a synthetic powder used in the treatment of certain viral infections, as herpes

ad (ad) *n.* [Inf.] an advertisement

AD or **A.D.** *abbrev.* 〖L *Anno Domini*, in the year of the Lord〗 of the Christian era: used with dates

ad- 〖L〗 *prefix* motion toward, addition to, nearness to: becomes *a-, ac-, af-, ag-, al-, an-*, etc. before certain consonants

ad ab·sur·dum (ad′ ab surd′əm) 〖L〗 to the point of absurdity; to a ridiculous extreme

ad·age (ad′ij) *n.* 〖< L *ad-*, to + *aio*, I say〗 an old saying; proverb

a·da·gio (ə dä′jō, -zhō) *adv.* 〖It *ad agio*, at ease〗 *Music* slowly —*adj.* slow —*n., pl.* **-gios** **1** a slow movement in music **2** a slow ballet dance Also written **a·da′gio** *pl.* **-gios**

Ad·am (ad′əm) *n.* 〖Heb < *adam*, a human〗 *Bible* the first man

ad·a·mant (ad'ə mənt) *adj.* [< Gr *a-*, not + *da-man*, subdue] inflexible; unyielding

Ad·ams (ad'əmz) **1** *John* 1735-1826; 2d president of the U.S. (1797-1801) **2** *John Quin·cy* (kwin'zē, -sē) 1767-1848; 6th president of the U.S. (1825-29): son of John

Adam's apple the projection of cartilage in the front of the throat: seen chiefly in men

a·dapt (ə dapt') *vt.* [< L *ad-*, to + *aptare*, to fit] **1** to make suitable, esp. by changing **2** to adjust (oneself) to new circumstances —*vi.* to adjust oneself —**ad·ap·ta·tion** (ad'əp tā' shən) *n.* —**a·dapt'er** *n.*, **a·dap'tor**

a·dapt·a·ble *adj.* able to adjust or be adjusted —**a·dapt'a·bil'i·ty** *n.*

add (ad) *vt.* [< L *ad-*, to + *dare*, to give] **1** to join (*to*) so as to increase **2** to state further **3** to combine (numbers) into a sum —*vi.* **1** to cause an increase (*to*) **2** to find a sum —**add up** to seem reasonable —**add up to** to mean; signify

ADD *abbrev.* attention-deficit disorder

ad·dend (ad'end') *n.* [< fol.] *Math.* a number or quantity to be added to another

ad·den·dum (ə den'dəm) *n., pl.* **-da** (-də) [L] a thing added, as an appendix

ad·der (ad'ər) *n.* [< OE *nædre*] **1** a poisonous snake of Europe **2** any of various other snakes, some harmless

ad·dict (ə dikt'; *for n.*, ad'ikt) *vt.* [< L *addicere*, give assent] **1** to give (oneself) up to a strong habit: usually in the passive voice [*addicted* to heroin] **2** to make an addict of —*n.* one addicted to a habit, as to using drugs —**ad·dic'tion** *n.* —**ad·dic'tive** *adj.*

Ad·dis A·ba·ba (ad'is ab'ə bə) capital of Ethiopia

ad·di·tion (ə dish'ən) *n.* **1** an adding of numbers to get a sum **2** a joining of one thing to another **3** a part added —**in addition (to)** besides

ad·di·tion·al *adj.* added; more; extra —**ad·di'tion·al·ly** *adv.*

ad·di·tive (ad'ə tiv) *adj.* of addition —*n.* a substance added in small quantities, as to change the properties of a food

ad·dle (ad''l) *vi., vt.* **-dled, -dling** [< OE *adela*, mud] to make or become confused

ad·dress (ə dres'; *for n.* 2, 3, & 4, *also* ad' dres') *vt.* [< L *dirigere*, to direct] **1** to direct (words) *to* **2** to speak or write *to* **3** to write the destination on (a letter, etc.) **4** to apply (oneself) *to* **5** to deal or cope with —*n.* **1** a speech **2** the place where one lives or receives mail **3** the destination indicated on an envelope, etc. **4** *Comput. a)* a code identifying the location of an item of information *b)* a string of characters serving as an email destination or Web location

ad·dress·ee (a'dres ē') *n.* the person to whom mail, etc. is addressed

ad·duce (ə dōōs') *vt.* **-duced', -duc'ing** [< L *ad-*, to + *ducere*, to lead] to give as a reason or proof

-ade (ād) [ult. < L] *suffix* **1** the act of ___ing [*blockade*] **2** participant(s) in an action [*bri-*

gade] **3** [after LEMONADE] drink made from [*limeade*]

Ad·e·laide (ad'ə lād') seaport in S Australia

A·den (äd''n, ād'n), **Gulf of** gulf of the Arabian Sea, south of Arabia

ad·e·nine (ad'ə nēn') *n.* a purine base contained in the DNA, RNA, and ADP of all tissue

ad·e·noids (ad''n oidz', ad'noidz') *pl.n.* [< Gr *adēn*, gland + -OID] lymphoid growths in the throat behind the nose: they can obstruct nasal breathing

a·dept (ə dept'; *for n.* ad'ept') *adj.* [< L *ad-*, to + *apisci*, attain] highly skilled —*n.* **ad'ept'** an expert —**a·dept'ly** *adv.* —**a·dept'ness** *n.*

ad·e·quate (ad'i kwət) *adj.* [< L *ad-*, to + *ae-quus*, equal] enough for what is required; sufficient; suitable —**ad'e·qua·cy** (-kwə sē) *n.* —**ad'e·quate·ly** *adv.*

ad·here (ad hir', əd-) *vi.* **-hered', -her'ing** [< L *ad-*, to + *haerere*, to stick] **1** to stick fast; stay attached **2** to give allegiance or support (*to*) —**ad·her'ence** *n.*

ad·her·ent *n.* a supporter or follower (*of a* person, cause, etc.)

ad·he·sion (ad hē'zhən, əd-) *n.* **1** a being stuck together **2** body tissues abnormally joined

ad·he·sive (-siv') *adj.* **1** sticking **2** sticky —*n.* a substance used to stick things together

ad hoc (ad häk') [L, to this] for a specific, usually one-time purpose [an ad hoc committee]

a·dieu (ə dyōō', -dōō'; *Fr* ä dyö') *interj., n., pl.* **a·dieus'** or **a·dieux** (ə dyōō', -dōō'; *Fr* ä dyö') [Fr] goodbye

ad in·fi·ni·tum (ad in'fə nīt'əm) [L] endlessly; without limit

a·di·os (a'dē ōs', ä'-; *Sp* ä dyôs') *interj.* [Sp] goodbye

ad·i·pose (ad'ə pōs') *adj.* [ult. < Gr *aleipha*, fat] of animal fat; fatty

Ad·i·ron·dack Mountains (ad'ə rän'dak') mountain range in NE New York: also **Ad·irondacks**

adj *abbrev.* **1** adjective **2** adjustment

ad·ja·cent (ə jā'sənt) *adj.* [< L *ad-*, to + *jacere*, to lie] near or close (*to*); adjoining —**ad·ja' cen·cy** (-sən sē) *n.* —**ad·ja'cent·ly** *adv.*

ad·jec·tive (aj'ik tiv) *n.* [< L *adjacere*, lie near] a word used to modify a noun or other substantive —**ad'jec·ti'val** (-tī'vəl) *adj.* —**ad'jec·ti'val·ly** *adv.*

ad·join (ə join') *vt.* [< L *ad-*, to + *jungere*, to join] to be next to —*vi.* to be in contact —**ad·join'ing** *adj.*

ad·journ (ə jurn') *vt.* [< OFr *a*, at + *jorn*, day] to suspend (a meeting, session, etc.) for a time —*vi.* **1** to close a meeting, etc. for a time **2** [Inf.] to retire (*to* another room, etc.) —**ad·journ'ment** *n.*

ad·judge (ə juj') *vt.* **-judged', -judg'ing** [< L *ad-*, to + *judicare*, to judge] **1** to decide by law **2** to declare, order, or award by law

ad·ju·di·cate (ə jōō'di kāt') *vt.* **-cat'ed, -cat' ing** to hear and decide (a case) —*vi.* to serve as a judge (*in* or *on*) —**ad·ju'di·ca'tion** *n.* —**ad·ju'di·ca'tor** *n.*

ad·junct (a'juŋkt') *n.* [see ADJOIN] a secondary or nonessential addition —*adj.* in a temporary or part-time position

ad·jure (ə joor') *vt.* **-jured', -jur'ing** [< L *ad-*, to + *jurare*, to swear] 1 to charge solemnly under oath 2 to ask earnestly —**ad·ju·ra·tion** (aj'oo rā'shən) *n.*

ad·just (ə just') *vt.* [< OFr *a-*, to + *joster*, to tilt] 1 to change so as to fit 2 to regulate or set (a watch, etc.) 3 to settle rightly 4 to decide the amount to be paid in settling (an insurance claim) —*vi.* to adapt oneself —**ad·just'a·ble** *adj.* —**ad·just'er** *n.,* **ad·jus'tor** —**ad·just'ment** *n.*

ad·ju·tant (aj'ə tənt) *n.* [< L *ad-*, to + *juvare*, to help] 1 an assistant 2 a military staff officer who assists the commanding officer

ad-lib (ad'lib') [Inf.] *vt., vi.* **-libbed', -lib'bing** [< L *ad libitum*, at pleasure] to improvise (words, etc. not in a prepared script, etc.) —*n.* an ad-libbed remark: also **ad lib** —*adj.* spoken or done extemporaneously —*adv.* extemporaneously: also **ad lib**

adm or **admin** *abbrev.* 1 administration 2 administrative

Adm *abbrev.* admiral

admin *abbrev.* administration

ad·min·is·ter (ad min'is tər, əd-) *vt.* [< L *ad-*, to + *ministrare*, to serve] 1 to manage; direct 2 to give out, as punishment 3 to apply (medicine, etc.) 4 to direct the taking of (an oath, etc.)

ad·min·is·trate (-trāt') *vt.* **-trat'ed, -trat'ing** to administer; manage

ad·min·is·tra·tion (-trā'shən) *n.* 1 management 2 [*often* A-] the executive officials of a government, etc. and their policies 3 their term of office 4 the administering (*of* punishment, medicine, etc.) —**ad·min'is·tra'tive** (-trāt'iv, -trə tiv) *adj.*

ad·min·is·tra·tor *n.* 1 a person who administers 2 *Law* one appointed to settle an estate

ad·mi·ra·ble (ad'mə rə bəl) *adj.* deserving admiration; excellent —**ad'mi·ra·bly** *adv.*

ad·mi·ral (ad'mə rəl) *n.* [< Ar *'amīr*, leader + *'alī,* high] 1 the commanding officer of a fleet 2 a naval officer of the highest rank

ad·mi·ral·ty *n., pl.* **-ties** [*often* A-] the governmental department in charge of naval affairs, as in England

ad·mi·ra·tion (ad'mə rā'shən) *n.* 1 an admiring 2 pleased approval

ad·mire (ad mīr', əd-) *vt.* **-mired', -mir'ing** [< L *ad-*, at + *mirari*, to wonder] 1 to regard with wonder and delight 2 to esteem highly —**ad·mir'er** *n.*

ad·mis·si·ble (ad mis'ə bəl, əd-) *adj.* that can be accepted or admitted —**ad·mis'si·bil'i·ty** *n.*

ad·mis·sion (ad mish'ən, əd-) *n.* 1 an admitting or being admitted 2 an entrance fee 3 a conceding, confessing, etc. 4 a thing conceded, confessed, etc.

ad·mit (ad mit', əd-) *vt.* **-mit'ted, -mit'ting** [< L *ad-*, to + *mittere*, to send] 1 to permit or entitle to enter or use 2 to allow; leave room

for 3 to concede or confess —*vi.* 1 to allow: with *of* 2 to concede or confess (*to*) —**ad·mit'tance** *n.*

ad·mit·ted·ly *adv.* by admission or general agreement

ad·mix·ture (ad miks'chər) *n.* [< L *ad-*, to + *miscere*, to mix] 1 a mixture 2 a thing added in mixing

ad·mon·ish (ad män'ish, əd-) *vt.* [< L *ad-*, to + *monere*, to warn] 1 to warn 2 to reprove mildly 3 to exhort —**ad·mo·ni·tion** (ad'mə nish'ən) *n.* —**ad·mon'i·to'ry** (-i tôr'ē) *adj.*

ad nau·se·am (ad nô'zē əm) [L] to the point of disgust

a·do (ə dōō') *n.* fuss; trouble

a·do·be (ə dō'bē) *n.* [Sp] 1 unburnt, sun-dried brick 2 clay for making this brick 3 a building of adobe

ad·o·les·cence (ad'ə les'əns) *n.* the time of life between puberty and maturity

ad·o·les·cent *adj.* [< L *ad-*, to + *alescere*, grow up] of or in adolescence —*n.* a person during adolescence

A·don·is (ə dän'is) *n.* 1 *Gr. Myth.* a young man loved by Aphrodite 2 a handsome young man

a·dopt (ə däpt') *vt.* [< L *ad-*, to + *optare*, to choose] 1 to take legally into one's own family and raise as one's own child 2 to take as one's own 3 to choose or accept —**a·dop'tion** *n.*

a·dop·tive (ə däp'tiv) *adj.* that has become so by adoption

a·dor·a·ble (ə dôr'ə bəl) *adj.* [Inf.] delightful; charming —**a·dor'a·bly** *adv.*

ad·o·ra·tion (ad'ə rā'shən) *n.* 1 a worshiping 2 great love or devotion

a·dore (ə dôr') *vt.* **-dored', -dor'ing** [< L *ad-*, to + *orare*, to speak] 1 to worship as divine 2 to love greatly 3 [Inf.] to like very much

a·dorn (ə dôrn') *vt.* [< L *ad-*, to + *ornare*, fit out] 1 to be an ornament to 2 to put decorations on —**a·dorn'ment** *n.*

ADP (ā'dē'pē') *n.* [a(*denosine*) d(i)p(*hosphate*)] an organic compound vital to the energy processes of all living cells

a·dre·nal (ə drē'nəl) *adj.* [AD- + RENAL] 1 near the kidneys 2 of two ductless glands (**adrenal glands**) just above the kidneys

a·dren·a·line (ə dren'ə lin) *n.* [< *Adrenalin*, a trademark] a hormone secreted by the adrenal glands, which increases endurance, strength, etc.

A·dri·at·ic (Sea) (ā'drē at'ik) sea between Italy and the Balkan Peninsula

a·drift (ə drift') *adv., adj.* floating without mooring or direction

a·droit (ə droit') *adj.* [< Fr à, to + L *dirigere*, lay straight] skillful and clever —**a·droit'ly** *adv.* —**a·droit'ness** *n.*

ad·sorb (ad sôrb', -zôrb') *vt.* [< AD- + L *sorbere*, drink in] to collect (a gas, etc.) in condensed form on a surface —**ad·sorb'ent** *adj.* —**ad·sorp'tion** (-sôrp'shən, -zôrp'-) *n.*

ad·u·late (aj'oo lāt', -jə-) *vt.* **-lat'ed, -lat'ing** [< L *adulari*, fawn upon] to admire intensely —**ad'u·la'tion** *n.* —**ad'u·la·to'ry** (-lə tôr'ē) *adj.*

a·dult (ə dult', ad'ult') *adj.* ⟦see ADOLES-CENT⟧ 1 grown up; mature 2 for adult people [*adult* education] 3 pornographic —*n.* a mature person, animal, or plant —**a·dult'-hood** *n.*

a·dul·ter·ate (ə dul'tər āt') *vt.* **-at'ed, -at'-ing** ⟦< L *ad-*, to + *alter*, other⟧ to make inferior, impure, etc. by adding an improper substance —**a·dul'ter·a'tion** *n.*

a·dul·ter·y (ə dul'tər ē) *n., pl.* **-ies** sexual intercourse between a married person and someone other than that person's spouse —**a·dul'ter·er** *n.* —**a·dul'ter·ess** *n.* —**a·dul'ter-ous** *adj.*

ad·um·brate (ad um'brāt, ad'əm brāt') *vt.* **-brat'ed, -brat'ing** ⟦< L *ad-*, to + *umbra*, shade⟧ 1 to outline vaguely 2 to foreshadow —**ad'um·bra'tion** *n.*

adv *abbrev.* 1 adverb 2 advertisement

ad·vance (ad vans', əd-) *vt.* **-vanced', -vanc'-ing** ⟦< L *ab-*, from + *ante*, before⟧ 1 to bring forward 2 to promote 3 to suggest 4 to raise the rate of 5 to lend —*vi.* 1 to go forward 2 to improve; progress 3 to rise in rank, price, etc. —*n.* 1 a moving forward 2 an improvement 3 a rise in value 4 [*pl.*] approaches to get favor 5 a payment made before it is due —*adj.* 1 in front [*advance* guard] 2 beforehand —**in advance** 1 in front 2 ahead of time —**ad·vance'ment** *n.*

ad·vanced *adj.* 1 in front 2 far on in life; old 3 ahead or higher in progress, price, etc.

advance man a person hired to travel in advance of a band, political candidate, etc. to arrange for publicity, etc.

ad·van·tage (ad vant'ij, əd-) *n.* ⟦< L *ab-* + *ante*: see ADVANCE⟧ 1 superiority 2 a favorable circumstance, event, etc. 3 gain or benefit —*vt.* **-taged, -tag·ing** to be a benefit or aid to —**take advantage of** 1 to use for one's own benefit 2 to impose upon —**ad·van·ta·geous** (ad'van tā'jəs) *adj.*

Ad·vent (ad'vent') *n.* ⟦< L *ad-*, to + *venire*, to come⟧ 1 *Christianity* the period including the four Sundays just before Christmas 2 [**a-**] a coming or arrival

ad·ven·ti·tious (ad'ven tish'əs) *adj.* ⟦see prec.⟧ not inherent; accidental

ad·ven·ture (ad ven'chər, əd-) *n.* ⟦see ADVENT⟧ 1 a daring, hazardous undertaking 2 an unusual, stirring, often romantic experience —*vi.* **-tured, -tur·ing** to engage in adventure —**ad·ven'tur·ous** *adj.*, **ad·ven'-ture·some** —**bi·ad·ven'tur·ous·ly** *adv.*

ad·ven·tur·er *n.* 1 one who has or looks for adventures 2 one who seeks to become rich, etc. by dubious schemes

ad·ven·tur·ess (-is) *n.* a woman who seeks to become rich, etc. by dubious schemes

ad·verb (ad'vurb') *n.* ⟦< L *ad-*, to + *verbum*, word⟧ a word used to modify a verb, an adjective, or another adverb, by expressing time, place, manner, degree, etc. —**ad·ver'bi·al** *adj.* —**ad·ver'bi·al·ly** *adv.*

ad·ver·sar·i·al (ad'vər ser'ē əl) *adj.* of or relating to adversaries, as in a lawsuit

ad·ver·sar·y *n., pl.* **-ies** ⟦see ADVERT⟧ an opponent; foe

ad·verse (ad vurs', ad'vurs') *adj.* ⟦see ADVERT⟧ 1 opposed 2 unfavorable —**ad·verse'ly** *adv.*

ad·ver·si·ty (ad vur'sə tē) *n.* 1 misfortune; wretched or troubled state 2 *pl.* **-ties** a calamity; disaster

ad·vert (ad vurt') *vi.* ⟦< L *ad*, to + *vertere*, to turn⟧ to call attention (*to*)

ad·ver·tise (ad'vər tīz') *vt.* **-tised', -tis'ing** ⟦see prec.⟧ to describe or praise publicly, usually so as to promote sales —*vi.* 1 to call public attention to things for sale 2 to ask (*for*) by public notice —**ad'ver·tis'er** *n.* —**ad'ver·tis'ing** *n.*

ad·ver·tise·ment (ad'vər tīz'mənt, əd vur'tis-) *n.* a public notice, usually paid for

ad·ver·to·ri·al (ad'vər tôr'ē əl) *n.* ⟦ADVER-(TISE) + (EDI)TORIAL⟧ an advertisement, as in a magazine, made to resemble an article or editorial

ad·vice (ad vīs', əd-) *n.* ⟦< L *ad-*, at + *videre*, to look⟧ opinion given as to what to do; counsel

ad·vis·a·ble (ad vīz'ə bəl, əd-) *adj.* wise; sensible —**ad·vis'a·bil'i·ty** *n.*

ad·vise (ad vīz', əd-) *vt.* **-vised', -vis'ing** ⟦< ML *advisum*, advice⟧ 1 to give advice to 2 to offer as advice 3 to notify; inform —**ad·vi'sor** *n.*, **ad·vis'er**

ad·vis·ed·ly (-id lē) *adv.* deliberately

ad·vise·ment *n.* careful consideration —**take under advisement** to consider carefully

ad·vi·so·ry (ad vī'zə rē, əd-) *adj.* advising or empowered to advise —*n., pl.* **-ries** a report, esp. about weather conditions

ad·vo·cate (ad'və kit; for *v.*, -kāt') *n.* ⟦< L *ad-*, to + *vocare*, to call⟧ one who speaks or writes in support of another or a cause —*vt.* **-cat'-ed, -cat'ing** to be an advocate of —*vi.* to act as an advocate —**ad'vo·ca·cy** (-kə sē) *n.*

advt. *abbrev.* advertisement

adz or **adze** (adz) *n.* ⟦< OE *adesa*⟧ an axlike tool for trimming and smoothing wood

Ae·ge·an (Sea) (ē jē'ən) sea between Greece and Turkey

ae·gis (ē'jis) *n.* ⟦< Gr *aigis*, shield of Zeus⟧ 1 protection 2 sponsorship

Ae·ne·as (i nē'əs) *n. Gr. & Rom. Myth.* a Trojan whose adventures are told in a poem (the **Ae·ne'id**) by Virgil

ae·on (ē'ən, ē'än') *n. alt. sp. of* EON

aer·ate (er'āt', ā'ər āt') *vt.* **-at'ed, -at'ing** ⟦AER(O)- + -ATE⟧ 1 to expose to air 2 to charge (liquid) with gas, as to make soda water —**aer·a'tion** *n.* —**aer'a'tor** *n.*

aer·i·al (er'ē əl) *adj.* ⟦< Gr *aēr*, air + -AL⟧ 1 of, in, or by air 2 unreal; imaginary 3 of aircraft or flying —*n.* a radio or TV antenna

aer·i·al·ist *n.* an acrobat on a trapeze, high wire, etc.

ae·rie (ā'ər ē, ē'rē, er'ē, ir'ē) *n.* ⟦prob. < L *ager*, field⟧ 1 the high nest of an eagle or other bird of prey 2 a house or stronghold on a high place

aero- ⟦< Gr *aēr*, air⟧ *combining form* 1 air 2

aircraft or flying **3** gas, gases Also **aer-** or **aeri-**

aer·o·bat·ics (er′ō bat′iks) *pl.n.* ⟦prec. + (ACRO)BATICS⟧ stunts done while flying an aircraft

aer·o·bic (er ō′bik) *adj.* ⟦< Gr *aēr*, air + *bios*, life⟧ **1** able to live, grow, or take place only where free oxygen is present **2** of exercise, as running, that conditions the heart and lungs by increasing efficient intake of oxygen by the body —*n.* ⟦*pl.*, *with sing. or pl. v.*⟧ aerobic exercises

aer·o·dy·nam·ics (er′ō dī nam′iks) *n.* the branch of mechanics dealing with forces exerted by air or other gases in motion —*pl.n.* the characteristics of an object that affect its efficient movement through the air —**aer′o·dy·nam′ic** *adj.* —**aer′o·dy·nam′i·cal·ly** *adv.*

aer·o·nau·tics (er′ə nôt′iks) *n.* the science of making and flying aircraft —**aer′o·nau′ti·cal** *adj.*

aer·o·sol (er′ə sôl′, -säl′) *n.* ⟦AERO- + SOL(UTION)⟧ a suspension of insoluble particles in a gas —*adj.* of or from a container in which gas under pressure dispenses liquid spray

aer·o·space (er′ō spās′) *n.* the earth's atmosphere and the space outside it —*adj.* of aerospace, or of missiles, etc. for flight in aerospace

Aes·chy·lus (es′ki ləs) 525?-456 B.C.; Gr. writer of tragedies

Ae·sop (ē′sop, -säp′) Gr. fable writer: supposedly lived 6th c. B.C.

aes·thete (es′thēt′) *n.* ⟦Gr *aisthētēs*, one who perceives⟧ a person who is or pretends to be highly sensitive to art and beauty

aes·thet·ic (es thet′ik) *adj.* **1** of aesthetics **2** of beauty **3** sensitive to art and beauty

aes·thet·ics *n.* the philosophy of art and beauty

a·far (ə fär′) *adv.* [Archaic] at or to a distance —**from afar** from a distance

af·fa·ble (af′ə bəl) *adj.* ⟦< L *ad-*, to + *fari*, to speak⟧ pleasant; friendly —**af′fa·bil′i·ty** *n.* —**af′fa·bly** *adv.*

af·fair (ə fer′) *n.* ⟦< L *ad-*, to + *facere*, to do⟧ **1** any matter, event, etc. **2** [*pl.*] matters of business **3** an event arousing public controversy **4** a social gathering **5** an adulterous sexual relationship

af·fect (ə fekt′; *for vt.* 3 & 4, *usually* a fekt′; *for n.*, af′ekt′) *vt.* ⟦< L *ad-*, to + *facere*, to do⟧ **1** to have an effect on; influence **2** to stir the emotions of **3** to like to use, wear, etc. **4** to make a pretense of being, feeling, etc. —*n.* an emotion or emotional response

af·fec·ta·tion (af′ek tā′shən) *n.* **1** a pretending to like, have, etc. **2** artificial behavior meant to impress others

af·fect·ed (ə fekt′id; *for* 4 & 5, *usually* a-) *adj.* **1** afflicted **2** influenced **3** emotionally moved **4** assumed for effect **5** full of affectation

af·fect·ing (ə fekt′iŋ) *adj.* emotionally moving

af·fec·tion (ə fek′shən) *n.* fond or tender feeling

af·fec·tion·ate *adj.* tender and loving —**af·fec′tion·ate·ly** *adv.*

af·fect·less (af′ekt′lis) *adj.* lacking emotion

af·fer·ent (af′ər ənt) *adj.* ⟦< L *ad-*, to + *ferre*, to carry⟧ leading inward to a central part, as nerves

af·fi·da·vit (af′ə dā′vit) *n.* ⟦ML, he has made oath⟧ a written statement made under oath

af·fil·i·ate (ə fil′ē āt′; *for n., usually,* -it) *vt.* -at′ed, -at′ing ⟦< ML *affiliare*, adopt as a son⟧ **1** to take in as a member **2** to associate (oneself) *with* a group, etc. —*vi.* to join —*n.* an affiliated person, club, etc. —**af·fil′i·a′tion** *n.*

af·fin·i·ty (ə fin′i tē) *n., pl.* **-ties** ⟦< L *affinis*, adjacent⟧ **1** relationship by marriage **2** close relationship **3** a likeness implying common origin **4** a natural liking or sympathy

af·firm (ə furm′) *vt.* ⟦< L *ad-*, to + *firmare*, make firm⟧ **1** to declare positively; assert **2** to confirm; ratify —*vi. Law* to make a formal statement, but not under oath —**af·fir·ma·tion** (af′ər mā′shən) *n.*

af·firm·a·tive (ə furm′ə tiv) *adj.* affirming; answering "yes" —*n.* **1** an expression of assent **2** the side upholding the proposition being debated

affirmative action a plan to offset past discrimination in employing or educating women, members of a minority, etc.

af·fix (ə fiks′; *for n.* af′iks′) *vt.* ⟦< L *ad-*, to + *figere*, fasten⟧ **1** to fasten; attach **2** to add at the end —*n.* **1** a thing affixed **2** a prefix or suffix

af·flict (ə flikt′) *vt.* ⟦< L *ad-*, to + *fligere*, to strike⟧ to cause pain or suffering to; distress greatly

af·flic·tion (ə flik′shən) *n.* **1** pain, suffering **2** any cause of suffering

af·flu·ence (af′lōō əns) *n.* ⟦< L *ad-*, to + *fluere*, to flow⟧ riches; wealth

af·flu·ent *adj.* wealthy; rich —**af′flu·ent·ly** *adv.*

af·ford (ə fôrd′) *vt.* ⟦< OE *geforthian*, to advance⟧ **1** to spare (money, time, etc.) without much inconvenience **2** to give; yield [it *affords* pleasure] —**af·ford′a·bil′i·ty** *n.* —**af·ford′a·ble** *adj.*

af·fray (ə frā′) *n.* ⟦< OFr *esfraer*, frighten⟧ a noisy brawl

af·front (ə frunt′) *vt.* ⟦< ML *ad-*, to + *frons*, forehead⟧ to insult openly —*n.* an open insult

Af·ghan (af′gan′, -gən) *n.* **1** a native of Afghanistan **2** [**a-**] a soft, crocheted or knitted blanket or shawl

Af·ghan·i·stan (af gan′i stan′) country in SC Asia, east of Iran

a·fi·cio·na·do (ə fish′ə nä′dō) *n.* ⟦Sp⟧ a devotee of some sport, art, etc.

a·field (ə fēld′) *adv.* **1** in or to the field **2** away (from home); astray

a·fire (ə fīr′) *adv., adj.* on fire

a·flame (ə flām′) *adv., adj.* **1** in flames **2** glowing

AFL-CIO *abbrev.* American Federation of Labor and Congress of Industrial Organizations

a·float (ə flōt′) *adj., adv.* 1 floating 2 at sea 3 current 4 free of debt, etc.

a·flut·ter (ə flut′ər) *adv., adj.* in a flutter

a·foot (ə foot′) *adv.* 1 on foot 2 in progress

a·fore·men·tioned (ə fôr′men′chənd) *adj.* mentioned before

a·fore·said *adj.* spoken of before

a·fore·thought *adj.* thought out beforehand; premeditated

a·foul (ə foul′) *adv., adj.* in a collision or a tangle —**run** (or **fall**) **afoul of** to get into trouble with

a·fraid (ə frād′) *adj.* [see AFFRAY] feeling frightened; followed by *of, that,* or an infinitive: often used informally to indicate regret [I'm *afraid* I must go]

Af·ri·ca (af′ri kə) second largest continent, south of Europe —**Af′ri·can** *adj., n.*

Af·ri·can-A·mer·i·can *n.* a black American of African ancestry —*adj.* of African-Americans, their culture, etc. Also written **African American**

Af·ri·can·ized bee (af′ri kən īzd′) a hybrid of African and European bees, known for its aggressiveness

African violet a tropical African plant with violet, white, or pinkish flowers and hairy leaves, often grown as a houseplant

Af·ri·kaans (af′ri käns′, -känz′) *n.* [Afrik < *Afrika,* Africa] an official language of South Africa, based on Dutch

Af·ro (af′rō′) *n., pl.* **-ros′** a full, bushy hair style, as worn by some African-Americans

Afro- [< L *Afer,* an African] *combining form* African, African and

Af·ro-A·mer·i·can *n., adj.* AFRICAN-AMERICAN

aft (aft) *adv.* [< OE *æftan*] at, near, or toward the stern of a ship or rear of an aircraft

af·ter (af′tər) *adv.* [OE *æfter*] 1 behind 2 later —*prep.* 1 behind 2 later than 3 in search of 4 as a result of 5 in spite of [*after* all I've said, he's still going] 6 lower in rank or order than 7 in imitation of 8 for [named *after* Lincoln] —*conj.* following the time when —*adj.* 1 next; later 2 nearer the rear

af·ter·birth *n.* the placenta and membranes expelled after the birth of offspring

af·ter·burn·er *n.* a device attached esp. to jet engines for burning or utilizing exhaust gases

af·ter·ef·fect *n.* an effect coming later, or as a secondary result

af·ter·life *n.* a life after death

af·ter·math (-math′) *n.* [< AFTER + OE *mæth,* cutting of grass] 1 result, esp. an unpleasant one

af·ter·noon (af′tər nōōn′; *for adj.,* also af′tər nōōn′) *n.* the time from noon to evening —*adj.* in the afternoon

af·ter·tax *adj.* occurring or remaining after the payment of taxes

af·ter·thought *n.* 1 an idea, explanation, part, etc. coming or added later 2 a thought coming too late to be apt

af·ter·ward *adv.* later; subsequently: also **af′ter·wards**

Ag [L *argentum*] *Chem. symbol for* silver

a·gain (ə gen′) *adv.* [< OE *on-,* up to + *gegn,* direct] 1 back into a former condition 2 once more 3 besides 4 on the other hand —**again and again** often; repeatedly —**as much again** twice as much

a·gainst (ə genst′) *prep.* [see prec.] 1 in opposition to 2 toward so as to strike [thrown *against* the wall] 3 in contact with 4 in preparation for 5 as a charge on

Ag·a·mem·non (ag′ə mem′nän′) *n. Gr. Myth.* commander of the Greek army in the Trojan War

a·gape (ə gāp′) *adv., adj.* [A-¹ + GAPE] wide open

a·gar (ä′gär, ā′gär) *n.* [Malay] a gelatinous product made from seaweed, used in bacterial cultures: also **a′gar-a′gar**

ag·ate (ag′it) *n.* [< L *achatēs*] a hard, semiprecious stone with striped or clouded coloring

a·ga·ve (ə gä′vē) *n.* [< proper name in Gr. myth] a desert plant with thick, fleshy leaves

agcy *abbrev.* agency

age (āj) *n.* [< L *aetas*] 1 the length of time that a person or thing has existed 2 a stage of life 3 old age 4 a historical or geological period 5 [*often pl.*] [Inf.] a long time —*vi., vt.* **aged, ag′ing** or **age′ing** to grow or make old, ripe, mature, etc. —**of age** old enough to have attained full legal rights

-age (ij) [< LL *-aticum*] *suffix* 1 act, state, or result of [*usage*] 2 amount or number of [*acreage*] 3 cost of [*postage*] 4 place of [*steerage*]

a·ged (ā′jid; *for 2* ājd) *adj.* 1 old 2 of the age of —**the aged** old people

age·ism (āj′iz′əm) *n.* [AGE + (RAC)ISM] discrimination against older people

age·less *adj.* 1 seemingly not growing older 2 eternal

a·gen·cy (ā′jən sē) *n., pl.* **-cies** [< L *agere,* to act] 1 action; power 2 means 3 a firm, etc. empowered to act for another 4 an administrative government division 5 an organization that offers assistance [a social *agency*]

a·gen·da (ə jen′də) *n., pl.* **-das** [< L *agere,* to do] a list of things to be dealt with, as at a meeting

a·gent (ā′jənt) *n.* [< L *agere,* to do] 1 an active force or substance producing an effect 2 a person, firm, etc. empowered to act for another 3 a representative of a government agency

Agent Orange [military code name, from *orange*-colored containers] a highly toxic defoliant used in the Vietnam War

age-old *adj.* ancient

ag·er·a·tum (aj′ər āt′əm) *n.* [< Gr *agēratos,* not growing old] a plant of the composite family with small, thick heads of bluish flowers

age spot a permanent, brownish spot on the skin from exposure to the sun over time

ag·glom·er·ate (ə gläm′ər āt′; *for adj. & n.*, -it) *vt., vi.* -at′ed, -at′ing [< L *ad-*, to + *glomerare*, form into a ball] to gather into a mass or ball —*adj.* gathered into a mass or ball —*n.* a jumbled heap, mass, etc.

ag·glu·ti·nate (ə glōōt′'n it; *for v.*, -āt′) *adj.* [< L *ad-*, to + *gluten*, glue] stuck together — *vt., vi.* -nat′ed, -nat′ing to stick together, as with glue —**ag·glu′ti·na′tion** *n.*

ag·gran·dize (ə gran′dīz′) *vt.* -dized′, -diz′ing [< Fr *a-*, to + *grandir*, to increase] to make greater, more powerful, richer, etc. —**ag′gran·dize·ment** (ə gran′diz mənt) *n.*

ag·gra·vate (ag′rə vāt′) *vt.* -vat′ed, -vat′ing [< L *ad-*, to + *gravis*, heavy] 1 to make worse 2 [Inf.] to annoy; vex —**ag′gra·va′tion** *n.*

ag·gra·vat·ed *adj. Law* designating a grave form of a specified offense

ag·gre·gate (ag′rə git; *for v.*, -gāt′) *adj.* [< L *ad-*, to + *grex*, a herd] total —*n.* 1 a mass of distinct things gathered into a total or whole 2 sand, pebbles, etc. used in making concrete —*vt.* -gat′ed, -gat′ing 1 to gather into a mass 2 to total —**ag′gre·ga′tion** *n.*

ag·gres·sion (ə gresh′ən) *n.* [< L *aggredi*, to attack] 1 an unprovoked attack or warlike act 2 a being aggressive —**ag·gres′sor** *n.*

ag·gres·sive (ə gres′iv) *adj.* 1 boldly hostile; quarrelsome 2 bold and active; enterprising —**ag·gres′sive·ly** *adv.* —**ag·gres′sive·ness** *n.*

ag·grieve (ə grēv′) *vt.* -grieved′, -griev′ing [see AGGRAVATE] to cause grief or injury to; offend

a·ghast (ə gast′) *adj.* [< OE *gast*, ghost] feeling great horror or dismay

ag·ile (aj′əl) *adj.* [< L *agere*, to act] quick and easy of movement —**ag′ile·ly** *adv.* —**a·gil·i·ty** (ə jil′ə tē) *n.*

ag·i·tate (aj′i tāt′) *vt.* -tat′ed, -tat′ing [< L *agere*, to act] 1 to stir up or shake up 2 to excite the feelings of —*vi.* to stir up people so as to produce changes —**ag′i·ta′tion** *n.* —**ag′i·ta′tor** *n.*

a·gleam (ə glēm′) *adv., adj.* gleaming

a·glit·ter (ə glit′ər) *adv., adj.* glittering

a·glow (ə glō′) *adv., adj.* in a glow (of color or emotion)

ag·nos·tic (ag näs′tik) *n.* [< Gr *a-*, not + base of *gignōskein*, know] one who believes it impossible to know if God exists —*adj.* of an agnostic —**ag·nos′ti·cism** (-ti siz′əm) *n.*

a·go (ə gō′) *adj.* [< OE *agan*, pass away] gone by; past [years *ago*] —*adv.* in the past [long *ago*]

a·gog (ə gäg′) *adv., adj.* [< OFr *en*, in + *gogue*, joke] with eager anticipation or excitement

ag·o·nize (ag′ə nīz′) *vi.* -nized′, -niz′ing to struggle 2 to be in agony —*vt.* to torture

ag·o·ny (ag′ə nē) *n., pl.* -nies [< Gr *agōn*, a contest] 1 great mental or physical pain 2 a strong outburst (*of* emotion)

ag·o·ra·pho·bi·a (ag′ər ə fō′bē ə, ə gôr′ ə-) *n.* [< Gr *agora*, marketplace + -PHOBIA] an abnormal fear of being in public places —**ag′o·ra·pho′bic** *adj., n.*

a·grar·i·an (ə grer′ē ən) *adj.* [< L *ager*, field] 1 of land or the ownership of land 2 of agriculture —**a·grar′i·an·ism** *n.*

a·gree (ə grē′) *vi.* -greed′, -gree′ing [< L *ad*, to + *gratus*, pleasing] 1 to consent (*to*) 2 to be in accord 3 to be of the same opinion (*with*) 4 to arrive at an understanding (*about* prices, etc.) 5 to be suitable, healthful, etc.: followed by *with* —*vt.* to grant [I *agree* that it's true]

a·gree·a·ble *adj.* 1 pleasing or pleasant 2 willing to consent 3 conformable 4 acceptable —**a·gree′a·bly** *adv.*

a·gree·ment *n.* 1 an agreeing 2 an understanding between people, countries, etc. 3 a contract 4 *Gram.* correspondence, as between subject and verb

agri- *combining form* agriculture: also, **agro-**

ag·ri·busi·ness (ag′rə biz′nis) *n.* [see fol. + BUSINESS] farming and associated businesses and industries

ag·ri·cul·ture (ag′ri kul′chər) *n.* [< L *ager*, field + *cultura*, cultivation] the growing of crops and raising of livestock; farming —**ag′ri·cul′tur·al** *adj.* —**ag′ri·cul′tur·al·ly** *adv.* —**ag′ri·cul′tur·ist** *n.*

a·gron·o·my (ə grän′ə mē) *n.* [< Gr *agros*, field + *nemein*, govern] the science and economics of crop production —**a·gron′o·mist** *n.*

a·ground (ə ground′) *adv., adj.* on or onto the shore, a reef, etc.

a·gue (ā′gyōō′) *n.* [< ML (*febris*) *acuta*, violent (fever)] a fever, usually malarial, marked by chills

ah (ä, ô) *interj.* used to express delight, surprise, pain, etc.

a·ha (ä hä′) *interj.* used to express triumph, sudden understanding, satisfaction, etc.

a·head (ə hed′) *adv., adj.* 1 in or to the front 2 forward; onward 3 in advance 4 winning or profiting —**get ahead** to advance financially, etc.

a·hem (ə hem′) *interj.* used to get someone's attention, etc.

-a·hol·ic (ə hôl′ik, -häl′-) *combining form* one preoccupied with (something specified)

a·hoy (ə hoi′) *interj.* used in hailing [ship *ahoy*!]

AI *abbrev.* artificial intelligence

aid (ād) *vt., vi.* [< L *ad-*, to + *juvare*, to help] to help; assist —*n.* 1 help or assistance 2 a helper

aide (ād) *n.* [Fr] 1 an assistant 2 an aide-de-camp

aide-de-camp or **aid-de-camp** (ād′də kamp′) *n., pl.* **aides′-** or **aids′-** [Fr] a military officer serving as an assistant to a superior

AIDS (ādz) *n.* [A(cquired) I(mmune) D(eficiency) S(yndrome)] a condition of deficiency of certain leukocytes, resulting in infections, cancer, neural degeneration, etc.: see HIV

ai·grette or **ai·gret** (ā gret′, ā′gret′) *n.* [see EGRET] a bunch of the long, white, showy plumes of the egret

ail (āl) *vt.* [OE *eglian*, to trouble] to cause pain and trouble to —*vi.* to be in poor health

ai·le·ron (ā′lə rän′) *n.* [Fr < L *ala*, wing] an adjustable airfoil at the trailing edge of an airplane wing, for controlling rolling

ail·ment (āl′mənt) *n.* a mild illness

aim (ām) *vi., vt.* [< L *ad-*, to + *aestimare*, to estimate] 1 to direct (a weapon, blow, etc.) so as to hit 2 to direct (one's efforts) 3 to intend —*n.* 1 an aiming 2 the ability to hit a target 3 intention —**take aim** to aim a weapon, etc.

aim·less *adj.* having no purpose —**aim′less·ly** *adv.* —**aim′less·ness** *n.*

ain't (ānt) [< *amn't*, contr. of *am not*] *contr.* [Inf.] am not: also a dialectal or nonstandard contraction for *is not*, *are not*, *has not*, and *have not*

ai·o·li or **ai·ö·li** (ī ō′lē) *n.* [ult. < L *allium*, garlic + *oleum*, oil] a mayonnaise containing crushed raw garlic

air (er) *n.* [< Gr *aēr*] 1 the invisible mixture of gases surrounding the earth 2 *a*) a breeze; wind *b*) fresh air 3 a song or tune 4 an outward appearance [an *air* of dignity] 5 general mood 6 [*pl.*] affected, superior manners 7 public expression 8 AIR CONDITIONING —*adj.* of or by aircraft —*vt.* 1 to let air into 2 to publicize 3 to broadcast —*vi.* to be broadcast —**in the air** current or prevalent —**on** (or **off**) **the air** that is (or is not) broadcasting —**up in the air** not settled

air·bag a bag that inflates instantly within an automobile in a collision, to protect riders

air base a base for military aircraft

air·borne *adj.* 1 carried by or through the air 2 aloft or flying

air brake a brake operated by the action of compressed air on a piston

air·brush *n.* an atomizer worked by compressed air and used for spraying on paint, etc.: also **air brush** —*vt.* to spray or modify with an airbrush

air conditioning a method of keeping air humidity and temperature at desired levels in buildings, cars, etc., esp. by means of artificial refrigeration —**air′-con·di′tion** *vt.* —**air conditioner**

air-cooled *adj.* cooled by having air passed over, into, or through it

air·craft *n., pl.* **-craft** any machine for traveling through the air

aircraft carrier a warship for carrying aircraft, having a large, flat deck for takeoffs and landings

air·date *n.* the date scheduled for a radio or TV broadcast

air·drop *n.* the dropping of supplies, troops, etc. from an aircraft in flight —**air′drop′** *vt.*

Aire·dale (er′dāl′) *n.* [after *Airedale*, valley in England] a large terrier with a wiry coat

air·fare *n.* fare for transportation on a commercial airplane

air·field *n.* a field where aircraft can take off and land

air·foil *n.* a wing, rudder, etc. of an aircraft

air force the aviation branch of a country's armed forces

air·freight *n.* cargo transported by air

air guitar the imagined guitar of someone pretending to play music

air gun a gun or gunlike device operated by compressed air

air·head *n.* [Slang] a silly, ignorant person

air lane a route for travel by air; airway

air·lift *n.* a system of transporting troops, supplies, etc. by aircraft —*vt.* to transport by airlift

air·line *n.* a system or company for moving freight and passengers by aircraft —*adj.* of or on an airline

air·lin·er *n.* a large airline-operated aircraft for carrying passengers

air lock an airtight compartment, with adjustable air pressure, between places of unequal air pressure

air·mail *n.* mail transported by air, esp. overseas: also sp. **air mail** —*adj.* of or for mail sent by air —*vt.* to send (mail) by air

air·man (-mən) *n., pl.* **-men** (-mən) 1 an aviator 2 an enlisted person in the U.S. Air Force

air mass *Meteorology* a huge, relatively uniform body of air whose temperature, humidity, etc. reflect its place of origin

air mattress a pad filled with air, used as a mattress for camping, etc.

air·plane *n.* a motor-driven or jet-propelled aircraft kept aloft by the forces of air upon its wings

air·play *n.* the playing of a recording over radio or TV

air pocket an atmospheric condition that causes an aircraft to make a sudden, short drop while in flight

air·port *n.* a place where aircraft can land and take off, usually with facilities for repair, etc.

air power the total capacity of a nation for air war

air pressure the pressure of the atmosphere or of compressed air

air raid an attack by aircraft, esp. bombers

air rifle a rifle operated by compressed air

air·ship *n.* a self-propelled, steerable aircraft that is lighter than air

air·sick *adj.* nauseated because of air travel —**air′sick′ness** *n.*

air·space *n.* the space above a nation over which it can claim jurisdiction

air·strike *n.* an attack made by aircraft

air·strip *n.* a temporary airfield

air·tight *adj.* 1 too tight for air or gas to enter or escape 2 having no weaknesses [an *airtight* alibi]

air·time *n.* *Radio & TV* the period of time during which a program, commercial, etc. may be broadcast: also **air time**

air·waves *pl.n.* the medium through which radio signals are transmitted

air·way *n.* AIR LANE

air·y (er′ē) *adj.* **-i·er**, **-i·est** 1 of air 2 open to the air; breezy 3 unsubstantial as air 4 light as air; graceful **5** lighthearted **6** affectedly nonchalant —**air′i·ly** *adv.* —**air′i·ness** *n.*

aisle (īl) *n.* [< L *ala*, wing] a passageway, as between sections of seats in rows

a·jar (ə jär′) *adv., adj.* [OE *cier*, a turn] slightly open, as a door

AK *abbrev.* Alaska

aka (ā′kä′ā′) *abbrev.* also known as: used before an alias : also **a.k.a., a k a**

a·kim·bo (ə kim′bō) *adv., adj.* [< ON *keng*, bent + *bogi*, a bow] with hands on hips and elbows bent outward [with arms *akimbo*]

a·kin (ə kin′) *adj.* **1** of one kin; related **2** similar

A·ki·ta (ə kēt′ə) *n.* [after *Akita* prefecture, Japan] a large, powerful dog breed with a thick coat, erect ears, and a bushy, curled tail

Al *Chem.* symbol for aluminum

-al (əl, 'l) [< L] *suffix* **1** of, like, or suitable for [*theatrical*] **2** the act or process of ___ing [*rehearsal*]

à la or **a la** (ä′lə, -lä) [Fr] in the manner or style of

Al·a·bam·a (al′ə ham′ə) state of the SE U.S., cap. Montgomery: abbrev. **AL** —**Al′a·bam′i·an** *adj., n.,* **Al′a·bam′an**

al·a·bas·ter (al′ə bas′tər) *n.* [< Gr *alabastros*, perfume vase] a translucent, whitish variety of gypsum, used for statues, vases, etc.

a la carte (ä′lə kärt′) [Fr] with a separate price for each item on the menu

a·lac·ri·ty (ə lak′rə tē) *n.* [< L *alacer*, lively] eager willingness, often quick, lively action

A·lad·din (ə lad′'n) *n.* a boy in *The Arabian Nights* who finds a magic lamp

à la king (ä′lə kiŋ′) in a cream sauce containing mushrooms, pimentos, etc.

Al·a·mo (al′ə mō′) Franciscan mission at San Antonio, Texas: scene of the bloody defeat of a Texan garrison by Mexican troops (1836)

a la mode (al′ə mōd′) [< Fr] **1** in fashion **2** served in a certain style, as pie with ice cream Also **à la mode**

a·lar (ā′lər) *adj.* [< L *ala*, a wing] **1** of a wing **2** having wings

a·larm (ə lärm′) *n.* [< It *all'arme*, to arms] **1** [Archaic] a sudden call to arms **2** a warning of danger **3** a mechanism that warns of danger, arouses from sleep, etc. **4** fear caused by danger —*vt.* **1** to warn of danger **2** to frighten

alarm clock a clock that can be set to buzz, flash a light, etc. at a given time, as to awaken a person

a·larm·ing *adj.* frightening

a·larm·ist *n.* one who spreads alarming rumors, exaggerated reports of danger, etc. —*adj.* of an alarmist

a·las (ə las′) *interj.* an exclamation of sorrow, pity, etc.

A·las·ka (ə las′kə) state of the U.S. in NW North America; cap. Juneau: abbrev. *AK* — **A·las′kan** *adj., n.*

alb (alb) *n.* [< L *albus*, white] a white robe worn by a priest at Mass

al·ba·core (al′bə kôr′) *n.* [< Ar *al*, the + *buko*, young camel] a tuna with unusually long pectoral fins

Al·ba·ni·a (al bā′nē ə) country in the W Balkan Peninsula —**Al·ba′ni·an** *adj., n.*

Al·ba·ny (ôl′bə nē) capital of New York, on the Hudson

al·ba·tross (al′bə trôs′) *n.* [< Sp < Ar *al qādūs*, a scoop] **1** a large, web-footed sea bird **2** a burden

al·be·it (ôl bē′it) *conj.* [ME *al be it*, al (though) it be] although

Al·ber·ta (al burt′ə) province of SW Canada: cap. Edmonton: abbrev. *AB*

al·bi·no (al bī′nō) *n., pl.* **-nos** [< L *albus*, white] a person, animal, or plant lacking normal coloration: human albinos have white skin, whitish hair, and pink eyes

al·bum (al′bəm) *n.* [< L *albus*, white] **1** a book with blank pages for mounting pictures, stamps, etc. **2** one or more compact discs, LPs, etc. packaged in a holder **3** a set of musical recordings issued together

al·bu·men (al byōō′mən) *n.* [L < *albus*, white] **1** the white of an egg **2** the nutritive protein in seeds, etc. **3** ALBUMIN

al·bu·min (al byōō′min) *n.* [see prec.] a water-soluble protein found in milk, egg, blood, vegetable tissues, etc. —**al·bu′mi·nous** *adj.*

Al·bu·quer·que (al′bə kur′kē) city in central New Mexico

al·che·my (al′kə mē) *n.* [< Ar < Gr *chēmeia*; infl. by Gr *cheein*, pour] the chemistry of the Middle Ages, the chief aim of which was to change base metals into gold —**al′che·mist** *n.*

al·co·hol (al′kə hôl′) *n.* [< Ar *alkuhl*, antimony powder] **1** a colorless, volatile, pungent liquid, used in various forms as a fuel, as an intoxicating ingredient in fermented and distilled beverages, etc. **2** any such intoxicating beverage

al·co·hol·ic *adj.* **1** of alcohol **2** suffering from alcoholism —*n.* one who has chronic alcoholism

al·co·hol·ism *n.* the habitual excessive drinking of alcoholic beverages, or a resulting diseased condition

al·cove (al′kōv′) *n.* [< Ar *al*, the + *qubba*, an arch] a recessed section of a room

al·der (ôl′dər) *n.* [OE *alor*] a small tree or shrub of the birch family

al·der·man (ôl′dər mən) *n., pl.* **-men** (-mən) [< OE *eald*, old + *man*] in some U.S. cities, a municipal officer representing a certain district or ward —**al′der·man′ic** (-man′ik) *adj.*

ale (āl) *n.* [OE *ealu*] a usually full-bodied beer

a·le·a·to·ry (ā′lē ə tôr′ē) *adj.* [< L *aleatorius*, of gambling < *alea*, chance] depending on chance or luck

a·lem·bic (ə lem′bik) *n.* [< Ar *al-anbīq* < Gr *ambix*, a cup] **1** an apparatus formerly used for distilling **2** anything that purifies

a·lert (ə lurt′) *adj.* [< L *erigere*, to erect] **1** watchful; vigilant **2** active; nimble —*n.* a warning signal; alarm —*vt.* **1** to warn to be ready, etc. **2** to make aware of [*alert* them to their duties] —**on the alert** vigilant —**a·lert′ly** *adv.* —**a·lert′ness** *n.*

A·leu·tian Islands (ə lōō′shən) chain of U.S. islands off the SW tip of Alaska —**A·leu′tian** *adj., n.*

ale·wife (āl′wīf′) *n., pl.* **-wives′** ⟦< ?⟧ a NW Atlantic fish resembling the herring, used for food and in fertilizers

Al·ex·an·der the Great (al′ig zan′dər) 356-323 B.C.; military conqueror: king of Macedonia (336-323)

Al·ex·an·dri·a (-drē ə) seaport in N Egypt

al·fal·fa (al fal′fə) *n.* ⟦Sp < Ar *al-fiṣfiṣa*, fodder⟧ a plant of the pea family, used for fodder and pasture and as a cover crop

Al′fred the Great (al′frəd) A.D. 849-899; Anglo-Saxon king (871-899)

al·fres·co (al fres′kō, äl-) *adv.* ⟦It < *al*, in the + *fresco*, cool⟧ outdoors —*adj.* outdoor Also **al fresco**

al·gae (al′jē′) *pl.n., sing.* **al′ga** (-gə) ⟦pl. of L *alga*, seaweed⟧ a group of simple organisms, one-celled or many-celled, containing chlorophyll and found in water or damp places

al·ge·bra (al′jə brə) *n.* ⟦< Ar *al*, the + *jabara*, to reunite⟧ a mathematical system using symbols, esp. letters, to generalize certain arithmetical operations and relationships —**al′ge·bra′ic** (-brā′ik) *adj.* —**al′ge·bra′i·cal·ly** *adv.*

Al·ge·ri·a (al jir′ē ə) country in N Africa —**Al·ge′ri·an** *adj., n.*

-al·gia (al′jə) ⟦< Gr *algos*⟧ *combining form* pain [*neuralgia*]

Al·giers (al jirz′) seaport & capital of Algeria

Al·gon·qui·an (al gän′kē ən, -kwē-) *adj.* designating or of a widespread family of North American Indian languages —*n.* this family of languages

al·go·rithm (al′gə rith′əm) *n.* ⟦ult. < Ar⟧ 1 any systematic method of solving a certain kind of mathematical problem 2 *Comput.* a set of instructions for solving a problem by means of a limited number of steps

a·li·as (ā′lē əs) *n., pl.* **-as·es** ⟦L < *alius*, other⟧ an assumed name —*adv.* otherwise named [Bell *alias* Jones]

A·li Ba·ba (ä′lē bä′bə, al′ə bab′ə) in *The Arabian Nights*, a poor man who finds the treasure of forty thieves

al·i·bi (al′ə bī′) *n., pl.* **-bis′** ⟦L < *alius ibi*, elsewhere⟧ 1 *Law* the plea or fact that an accused person was elsewhere than at the scene of the crime 2 [Inf.] an excuse —*vi., vt.* **-bied′, -bi′ing** [Inf.] to offer an excuse (for)

al·ien (āl′yən, āl′ē ən) *adj.* ⟦< L *alius*, other⟧ 1 foreign 2 not natural; strange 3 opposed or repugnant [beliefs *alien* to mine] 4 of aliens —*n.* 1 a foreigner 2 a foreign-born resident who is not naturalized 3 a hypothetical being from outer space

al·ien·a·ble (-ə bəl) *adj.* capable of being transferred to a new owner

al·ien·ate (-āt′) *vt.* **-at′ed, -at′ing** 1 to transfer the ownership of (property) to another 2 to make unfriendly or withdrawn 3

to cause a transference of (affection) —**al′ien·a′tion** *n.*

a·light¹ (ə līt′) *vi.* **a·light′ed** or **a·lit′, a·light′ing** ⟦ME *alihtan*⟧ 1 to get down or off; dismount 2 to come to rest after flight

a·light² (ə līt′) *adj.* lighted up; burning

a·lign (ə līn′) *vt.* ⟦< Fr *a-*, to + *ligne*, LINE¹⟧ 1 to bring into a straight line 2 to bring (components or parts) into adjustment 3 to bring into agreement, etc. —*vi.* to line up —**a·lign′ment** *n.*

a·like (ə līk′) *adj.* ⟦< OE *gelic*⟧ like one another —*adv.* 1 similarly 2 equally

al·i·ment (al′ə mənt) *n.* ⟦< L *alere*, nourish⟧ nourishment; food

al·i·men·ta·ry (-men′tə rē, -men′trē) *adj.* 1 of food or nutrition 2 nourishing

alimentary canal (*or* **tract**) the passage in the body (from the mouth to the anus) that food goes through

al·i·mo·ny (al′ə mō′nē) *n.* ⟦< L *alere*, nourish⟧ money a court orders paid to a person by that person's legally separated or divorced spouse

a·line (ə līn′) *vt., vi.* **a·lined′, a·lin′ing** ALIGN —**a·line′ment** *n.*

a·lit (ə līt′) *vi.* alt. pt. & pp. of ALIGHT¹

a·live (ə līv′) *adj.* ⟦< OE *on*, in + *life*, life⟧ 1 having life; living 2 in existence, operation, etc. 3 lively; alert —**alive to** aware of —**alive with** teeming with

a·li·yah or **a·li·ya** (ä′lē yä′) *n.* ⟦< Heb, lit., ascent⟧ immigration by Jews to Israel

al·ka·li (al′kə lī′) *n., pl.* **-lies′** or **-lis′** ⟦< Ar *al-qīlī*, the ashes of a certain plant⟧ 1 any base, as soda, that is soluble in water and gives off ions in solution 2 a mineral salt, etc. that can neutralize acids

al·ka·line (-lin, -līn′) *adj.* of or like an alkali —**al·ka·lin′i·ty** (-lin′ə tē) *n.*

al·ka·lize (-līz′) *vt.* **-lized′, -liz′ing** to make alkaline —**al·ka·li·za′tion** *n.*

al·ka·loid (-loid′) *n.* a bitter, alkaline substance, such as caffeine, morphine, etc., containing nitrogen and found esp. in plants

al·kyd (al′kid) *n.* ⟦ult. < ALKALI + (AC]I)D⟧ a synthetic resin used in paints, varnishes, etc.: also **alkyd resin**

all (ôl) *adj.* ⟦OE *eal*⟧ 1 the whole quantity of [*all* the gold] 2 every one of [*all* men] 3 the greatest possible [in *all* sincerity] 4 any [beyond *all* doubt] 5 alone; only [*all* work and no play] —*pron.* 1 [with pl. v.] everyone 2 everything 3 every part or bit —*n.* 1 one's whole property, effort, etc. [gave his *all*] 2 a totality; whole —*adv.* 1 wholly; entirely [*all* worn out] 2 apiece [a score of two *all*] —**after all** nevertheless —**all in 1** [Inf.] very tired 2 ⟦< a betting term⟧ [Slang] having a personal commitment to a cause or endeavor —**all in all 1** considering everything 2 as a whole —**all out** completely —**all the better** (or **worse**) so much the better (or worse) —**all the same** nevertheless 2 unimportant —**at all 1** in the least 2 in any way 3 under any considerations —**in all** altogether

all- *combining form* 1 wholly, entirely [*all-*

American] **2** for every [*all*-purpose] **3** of everything [*all*-inclusive]

Al·lah (alʹə, äʹlə) *n.* ⟦< Ar *al*, the + *ilāh*, god] *the Muslim name for* God

all-A·mer·i·can *adj.* representative of the U.S. as a whole, or chosen as the best in the U.S. —*n.* **1** a hypothetical football team, etc. made up of U.S. college players voted the best of the year **2** a player on such a team

all-a·round *adj.* having many abilities, talents, or uses; versatile

al·lay (a läʹ, ə-) *vt.* **-layed´, -lay´ing** ⟦< OE *a*-, down + *lecgan*, lay] **1** to calm; quiet **2** to relieve (pain, etc.)

all-clear *n.* a siren or other signal that an air raid or alert is over

al·le·ga·tion (alʹə gāʹshən) *n.* an assertion of wrongdoing, esp. one without proof or to be proved

al·lege (ə lejʹ) *vt.* **-leged´, -leg´ing** ⟦< L *ex*-, out of + *litigare*, to dispute] **1** to declare or assert, esp. without proof **2** to offer as an excuse

al·leged (ə lejd´, ə lejʹid) *adj.* **1** declared, but without proof **2** so-called [*alleged* friends] —**al·leg´ed·ly** *adv.*

Al·le·ghe·ny Mountains (alʹə gāʹnē) mountain range in Pennsylvania, Maryland, West Virginia, & Virginia: also **Al·le·ghe´nies**

al·le·giance (ə lēʹjəns) *n.* ⟦< OFr *liege*, liege] **1** the duty of being loyal to one's ruler, country, etc. **2** loyalty; devotion, as to a cause

al·le·go·ry (alʹə gôr´ē) *n., pl.* **-ries** ⟦< Gr *allos*, other + *agoreuein*, speak in assembly] a story in which people, things, and events have a symbolic meaning, often instructive —**al´le·gor´i·cal** *adj.* —**al´le·gor´i·cal·ly** *adv.* —**al´le·go´rist** *n.*

al·le·gret·to (alʹə gret´ō) *adj., adv.* ⟦It, dim. of *allegro*] *Music* moderately fast

al·le·gro (ə le´grō´, -lä´-) *adj., adv.* ⟦It] *Music* fast

al·lele (ə lēl´) *n.* ⟦< Gr *allēlōn*, of one another] a gene transferring inherited characteristics

al·le·lu·ia (alʹə lōō´yə, ä´lə-) *interj., n.* ⟦LL(Eccles.)] HALLELUJAH

al·ler·gen (alʹər jən) *n.* ⟦Ger] a substance inducing an allergic reaction —**al´ler·gen´ic** (-jen´ik) *adj.*

al·ler·gic (ə lur´jik) *adj.* **1** of, caused by, or having an allergy **2** [Inf.] averse (*to*)

al·ler·gist (alʹər jist) *n.* a doctor who specializes in treating allergies

al·ler·gy (alʹər jē) *n., pl.* **-gies** ⟦Ger < Gr *allos*, other + *ergon*, work] **1** a hypersensitivity to a specific substance (as a food, pollen, dust, etc.) or condition (as heat or cold) **2** an aversion

al·le·vi·ate (ə lē´vē āt´) *vt.* **-at´ed, -at´ing** ⟦< L *ad*-, to + *levis*, light] **1** to lessen or relieve (pain, etc.) **2** to decrease (poverty, etc.) —**al·le´vi·a´tion** *n.*

al·ley (alʹē) *n., pl.* **-leys** ⟦< OFr *aler*, go] **1** a lane bordered by trees or shrubs, as in a park **2** a narrow street between or behind buildings **3** a bowling lane

alley cat a homeless, mongrel cat

al·ley·way *n.* an alley between buildings

all-fired *adj., adv.* ⟦< *hell-fired*] [Slang] extreme(ly)

al·li·ance (ə līʹəns) *n.* [see ALLY] **1** an allying or close association, as of nations for a common objective, families by marriage, etc. **2** an agreement for this **3** the countries, groups, etc. in such association

al·lied (ə līd´, alʹīd´) *adj.* **1** united by kinship, treaty, etc. **2** closely related

al·li·ga·tor (alʹə gāt´ər) *n.* ⟦< Sp *el*, the + L *lacerta*, lizard] a large reptile of the U.S. and China, like the crocodile but with a shorter, broader snout

alligator clip a fastening device with spring-loaded jaws for making an electrical connection

alligator pear AVOCADO

all-im·por·tant *adj.* highly important; necessary; essential

all-in·clu·sive *adj.* including everything, esp. for a single price

al·lit·er·a·tion (ə lit´ər ā´shən) *n.* ⟦< L *ad*-, to + *littera*, letter] repetition of an initial sound in two or more words of a phrase —**al·lit´er·a´tive** (-āt´iv, -ə tiv) *adj.*

al·lo·cate (alʹə kāt´) *vt.* **-cat´ed, -cat´ing** ⟦< L *ad*-, to + *locus*, a place] **1** to set apart for a specific purpose **2** to distribute or allot —**al´lo·ca´tion** *n.*

al·lot (ə lät´) *vt.* **-lot´ted, -lot´ting** ⟦< OFr *a*-, to + *lot*, lot] **1** to distribute in arbitrary shares; apportion **2** to assign as one's share —**al·lot´ment** *n.*

all-out *adj.* complete or wholehearted

all-o·ver *adj.* over the whole surface

al·low (ə lou´) *vt.* [see ALLOCATE] **1** to permit; let [I'm not *allowed* to go] **2** to let have [she *allowed* herself no sweets] **3** to acknowledge as valid **4** to provide (a certain amount), as for shrinkage, waste, etc. —**allow for** to leave room, time, etc. for —**al·low´a·ble** *adj.*

al·low·ance (-əns) *n.* **1** an allowing **2** something allowed **3** an amount of money, food, etc. given regularly to a child, soldier, etc. **4** a reduction in price, as for a trade-in —**make allowance(s) for** to excuse because of mitigating factors

al·loy (alʹoi; *also, and for v. usually,* ə loi´) *n.* ⟦< L *ad*-, to + *ligare*, to bind] **1** a substance that is a mixture of two or more metals **2** something that debases another thing when mixed with it —*vt.* to make into an alloy

all-pur·pose *adj.* useful in many ways

all right 1 satisfactory; adequate **2** unhurt; safe **3** correct **4** yes; very well **5** [Inf.] certainly

all-round *adj., adv. var. of* ALL-AROUND

all·spice (ôl´spīs´) *n.* a spice made from the berry of a West Indian tree of the myrtle family

all-star *adj.* **1** made up of outstanding or star performers **2** of or characteristic of an all-star event —*n.* a member of an all-star team

all-time *adj.* unsurpassed up to the present time

al·lude (ə lōōd′) *vi.* **-lud′ed, -lud′ing** ⟦L *alludere*, to jest⟧ to refer indirectly (*to*)

al·lure (ə loor′) *vt., vi.* **-lured′, -lur′ing** ⟦< OFr *a-*, to + *loirer*, to lure⟧ to tempt with something desirable; attract; entice —*n.* fascination; charm —**al·lure′ment** *n.* —**al·lur·ing** (ə loor′iŋ, a-) *adj.*

al·lu·sion (ə lōō′zhən) *n.* an indirect or casual reference

al·lu·sive (-siv) *adj.* **1** containing an allusion **2** full of allusions —**al·lu′sive·ly** *adv.* —**al·lu′sive·ness** *n.*

al·lu·vi·um (ə lōō′vē əm) *n., pl.* **-vi·ums** or **-vi·a** (-vē ə) ⟦< L *ad-*, to + *luere*, to wash⟧ sand, clay, etc. deposited by moving water —**al·lu′vi·al** *adj.*

al·ly (ə lī′; *also, and for n. usually,* al′ī) *vt., vi.* **-lied′, -ly′ing** ⟦< L *ad-*, to + *ligare*, to bind⟧ **1** to unite or join for a specific purpose **2** to relate by similarity of structure, etc. —*n., pl.* **-lies** a country or person joined with another for a common purpose

al·ma ma·ter (al′mə mät′ər, äl′-) ⟦L, fostering mother⟧ **1** the college or school that one attended **2** its anthem

al·ma·nac (ôl′mə nak′, al′-) *n.* ⟦< *c.* 5th-c. Gr *almenichiaka*, calendar⟧ **1** a calendar with astronomical data, weather forecasts, etc. **2** a book published annually, with statistical information

al·might·y (ôl mīt′ē) *adj.* all-powerful —**the Almighty** God

al·mond (ä′mənd, al′-, ôl′-; am′ənd) *n.* ⟦< Gr *amygdalē*⟧ **1** the edible, nutlike kernel of a peachlike fruit **2** the tree it grows on **3** the light-tan color of its shell —*adj.* shaped like an almond; oval and pointed at one or both ends

al·most (ôl′mōst′, ôl mōst′) *adv.* very nearly; all but

alms (ämz, älmz) *n., pl.* **alms** ⟦< Gr *eleos*, mercy⟧ money, food, etc. given to poor people —**alms′giv′er** *n.*

alms·house *n.* **1** [Archaic] a poorhouse **2** [Brit.] a privately endowed home for the poor

al·oe (al′ō′) *n., pl.* **-oes′** ⟦< Gr *aloē*⟧ an African plant of the lily family

a·loft (ə lôft′) *adv.* ⟦ME < *o*, on+ *loft*, loft⟧ **1** high up **2** in the air; flying **3** toward or in the rigging, mastheads, etc. of a ship

a·lo·ha (ä lō′hə, -hä′; ə lō′ə) *n., interj.* ⟦Haw, love⟧ **1** hello **2** goodbye

a·lone (ə lōn′) *adj., adv.* ⟦ME < *al*, all + *one*, one⟧ **1** apart from anything or anyone else **2** without any other person **3** only **4** without equal —**let alone 1** to refrain from interfering with: also **leave alone 2** and certainly not [we hadn't a dime, *let alone* a dollar]

a·long (ə lôŋ′) *prep.* ⟦< OE *and-*, over against + *-lang*, long⟧ **1** on or beside the length of **2** in conformity with —*adv.* **1** lengthwise **2** progressively forward **3** together (with) **4** with one [take me *along*] **5** advanced [well *along* in years] —**all along** from the beginning —**be along** [Inf.] to come or arrive —**get**

along 1 to advance **2** to manage **3** to survive **4** to be compatible

a·long·shore *adv.* near or beside the shore

a·long·side *adv.* at or by the side; side by side —*prep.* beside —**alongside of** at the side of

a·loof (ə lōōf′) *adj.* ⟦< *a-*, on & Du *loef*, windward side⟧ **1** cool and reserved [an *aloof* manner] **2** uninvolved [remained *aloof* from politics] —**a·loof′ness** *n.*

a·loud (ə loud′) *adv.* **1** loudly **2** with the normal voice; not silently

alp (alp) *n.* ⟦after ALPS⟧ a high mountain

al·pac·a (al pak′ə) *n.* ⟦< AmInd⟧ **1** a South American llama **2** its silky wool, or cloth woven from it

al·pha (al′fə) *n.* **1** the first letter of the Greek alphabet (A, α) **2** the beginning of anything —*adj.* of the dominant member of a group

al·pha·bet (-bet′) *n.* ⟦< Gr *alpha* & *bēta*, first two letters of the Gr alphabet⟧ the letters used in writing a language, esp. as arranged in their conventional order —**al′pha·bet′i·cal** *adj.* —**al′pha·bet′i·cal·ly** *adv.*

al·pha·bet·ize (al′fə bə tīz′) *vt.* **-ized′, -iz′ing** to arrange in the conventional order of the alphabet —**al′pha·bet′i·za′tion** *n.*

al·pha·nu·mer·ic (-nōō mer′ik) *adj.* having both alphabetical and numerical symbols

alpha particle a positively charged particle consisting of two protons and two neutrons, given off by certain radioactive substances

alpha ray a stream of alpha particles

alpha wave an electrical brain wave indicating relaxation: also **alpha rhythm**

Al·pine (al′pīn′) *adj.* **1** of the Alps **2** [a-] of or like high mountains

Alps (alps) mountain system in SC Europe

al-Qae·da (al kä′də, äl kī′də) ⟦Ar, lit., the base, foundation⟧ a radical Islamic organization that has been responsible for many acts of terrorism: also sp. **al-Qai·da**

al·read·y (ôl red′ē) *adv.* **1** by or before the given or implied time **2** even now or even then

al·right (ôl rīt′) *adj., adv., interj.* disputed sp. of ALL RIGHT

Al·sace (al säs′, al′sas′) historical region of NE France —**Al·sa′tian** (-sā′shən) *adj., n.*

al·so (ôl′sō) *adv.* ⟦< OE *eall*, all + *swa*, so⟧ in addition; likewise; too; besides

al·so-ran *n.* [Inf.] a defeated contestant in a race, election, etc.

alt *abbrev.* **1** alternate **2** altitude **3** alto

al·tar (ôl′tər) *n.* ⟦< L *altus*, high⟧ **1** a platform where sacrifices are made to a god, etc. **2** a table, etc. for sacred purposes in a place of worship

altar boy a boy who helps a priest at religious services, esp. at Mass

altar girl a girl who helps a priest at religious services, esp. at Mass

al·ter (ôl′tər) *vt., vi.* ⟦< L *alter*, other⟧ to change; make or become different —**al′ter·a′tion** *n.*

al·ter·ca·tion (ôl′tər kā′shən) *n.* ⟦< L *altercari*, to dispute⟧ an angry or heated argument; quarrel

al·ter e·go [L, other I] **1** another aspect of oneself **2** a constant companion

al·ter·nate (ôl′tər nit; *for v.,* -nāt′) *adj.* [< L *alternus,* one after the other] **1** succeeding each other **2** every other **3** ALTERNATIVE (*adj.* 1) —*n.* a substitute —*vt.* **-nat′ed, -nat′ing** to do or use by turns —*vi.* **1** to act, happen, etc. by turns **2** to take turns regularly —**al′ter·nate·ly** *adv.* —**al′ter·na′tion** *n.*

alternating current an electric current reversing direction many times a second: abbrev. *AC*

al·ter·na·tive (ôl tur′nə tiv) *adj.* **1** providing a choice between things **2** of an institution, etc. appealing to unconventional interests [an *alternative* school] —*n.* **1** a choice between things **2** one of the things to be chosen **3** something left to choose

al·ter·na·tor (ôl′tər nāt′ər) *n.* an electric generator producing alternating current

al·though (ôl *thō′*) *conj.* [ME < *al,* even + THOUGH] in spite of the fact that; though: sometimes sp. **al·tho′**

al·tim·e·ter (al tim′ət ər) *n.* [< L *altus,* high + -METER] an instrument for measuring altitude

al·ti·tude (al′tə tōōd′) *n.* [< L *altus,* high] **1** the height of a thing, esp. above sea level **2** a high place: *usually used in pl.*

al·to (al′tō) *n., pl.* **-tos** [It < L *altus,* high] **1** the range of a voice between tenor and mezzo-soprano **2** a voice, singer, or instrument with such a range **3** a part for an alto —*adj.* of or for an alto

al·to·geth·er (ôl′tōō geth′ər) *adv.* **1** completely **2** in all **3** on the whole

al·tru·ism (al′trōō iz′əm) *n.* [< L *alter,* other] unselfish concern for the welfare of others —**al′tru·ist** *n.* —**al′tru·is′tic** *adj.* —**al′tru·is′ti·cal·ly** *adv.*

al·um¹ (al′əm) *n.* [< L *alumen*] any of a group of salts of aluminum, etc., used in manufacturing and medicine

a·lum² (ə lum′) *n.* [Inf.] an alumnus or alumna

a·lu·min·i·um (al′yōō min′ē əm) *n.* [Brit.] *var. of* ALUMINUM

a·lu·mi·num (ə lōō′mə nəm) *n.* [< L *alumen,* alum] a silvery, lightweight metallic chemical element: symbol, Al; at. no. 13

a·lum·na (ə lum′nə) *n., pl.* **-nae** (-nē) a woman or girl who has attended or is a graduate of a particular school, college, etc.

a·lum·nus (ə lum′nəs) *n., pl.* **-ni** (-nī′) [L, foster son] a man or boy who has attended or is a graduate of a particular school, college, etc.

al·ways (ôl′wāz) *adv.* [OE *ealne weg*] **1** at all times **2** all the time **3** at any time **4** in every instance

Alz·hei·mer's (disease) (älts′hī′mərz) [after A. *Alzheimer* (1864-1915), Ger doctor] a degenerative brain disease

am (am) *vi.* [OE *eom*] *1st pers. sing., pres. indic., of* BE

Am *abbrev.* **1** America **2** American

AM¹ (a′em′) *n.* amplitude-modulation broadcasting or sound transmission

AM² *abbrev.* **1** amplitude modulation **2** [L *ante meridiem*] before noon: used to designate the time from midnight to noon : also **A.M., am,** or **a.m. 3** [L *Artium Magister*] master of arts: also **A.M.**

AMA *abbrev.* American Medical Association

a·mal·gam (ə mal′gəm) *n.* [< Gr *malagma,* an emollient] **1** any alloy of mercury with another metal [a dental filling of silver *amalgam*] **2** a mixture; blend

a·mal·ga·mate (-gə māt′) *vt., vi.* **-mat′ed, -mat′ing** to unite; mix; combine —**a·mal′ga·ma′tion** *n.*

a·man·dine (ä′mən dēn′) *adj.* [Fr] prepared with almonds

a·man·u·en·sis (ə man′yōō en′sis) *n., pl.* **-ses′** (-sēz′) [L < *a-,* from + *manus,* hand + -*ensis,* relating to] a secretary: now a jocular usage

am·a·ranth (am′ə ranth′) *n.* [< Gr *amarantos,* unfading] **1** any of a large group of similar plants, some bearing showy flowers **2** [Old Poet.] an imaginary flower that never dies

am·a·ret·to (am′ə ret′ō) *n.* [It, rather bitter] [*also* A-] a liqueur with an almond flavor

am·a·ryl·lis (am′ə ril′is) *n.* [< Gr *Amaryllis,* name for a shepherdess] a lilylike plant with large white, purple, pink, or red flowers

a·mass (ə mas′) *vt.* [< Fr < L *massa,* a lump] to pile up; accumulate

am·a·teur (am′ə chər, tər) *n.* [Fr < L *amare,* to love] **1** one who does something for pleasure, not for money; nonprofessional **2** one who is somewhat unskillful —*adj.* of or done by amateurs —**am′a·teur′ish** (-′oor′-) *adj.* —**am′a·teur·ism′** *n.*

am·a·to·ry (am′ə tôr′ē) *adj.* [< L *amare,* to love] of or showing love, esp. sexual love

a·maze (ə māz′) *vt.* **a·mazed′, a·maz′ing** [OE *āmasian*] to fill with great surprise or wonder; astonish —**a·maze′ment** *n.* —**a·maz′ing** *adj.* —**a·maz′ing·ly** *adv.*

Am·a·zon¹ (am′ə zän′, -zən) *n.* **1** *Gr. Myth.* any of a race of female warriors **2** [a-] a tall, strong, aggressive woman

Am·a·zon² river in N South America flowing E from the Andes to the Atlantic Ocean

am·bas·sa·dor (am bas′ə dər) *n.* [< Prov *ambaissador*] the highest-ranking diplomatic representative of one country to another —**am·bas′sa·do′ri·al** (-dôr′ē əl) *adj.* —**am·bas·sa·dor·ship′** *n.*

am·ber (am′bər) *n.* [< Ar ′*anbar,* ambergris] **1** a brownish-yellow fossil resin used in jewelry, etc. **2** its color —*adj.* amberlike or amber-colored

Amber Alert [after *Amber* Hagerman (1986-96), U.S. child] a message about a recently missing or abducted person sent over an emergency system of radio and TV broadcasts, roadside electronic displays, etc., in order to enlist the public's help

am·ber·gris (-grēs′, -gris′) *n.* [< OFr *ambre gris,* gray amber] a grayish, waxy substance produced in the intestines of sperm whales, used in perfumes

ambi- ⟦L⟧ *combining form* both ⟦*ambidextrous*⟧

am·bi·dex·trous (am′bə deks′trəs) *adj.* ⟦< earlier *ambidexter* + -OUS⟧ using both hands with equal ease —**am′bi·dex·ter′i·ty** (-deks ter′ə tē) *n.*

am·bi·ence (am′bē əns, äm′bē äns′) *n.* ⟦Fr: see fol.⟧ an environment or its distinct atmosphere: also sp. **am′bi·ance** (-əns)

am·bi·ent (am′bē ənt) *adj.* ⟦< L *ambi*-, around + *ire*, to go⟧ surrounding; on all sides

am·bi·gu·i·ty (am′bə gyōō′ə tē) *n.* 1 a being ambiguous 2 *pl.* **-ties** an ambiguous word, statement, etc.

am·big·u·ous (am big′yōō əs) *adj.* ⟦< L *ambi*-, around + *agere*, to do⟧ 1 having two or more meanings 2 not clear; vague —**am·big′u·ous·ly** *adv.*

am·bi·tion (am bish′ən) *n.* ⟦< L *ambitio*, a going around (to solicit votes)⟧ 1 a strong desire for fame, power, etc. 2 the thing so desired

am·bi·tious (-əs) *adj.* 1 full of or showing ambition 2 demanding great effort —**am·bi′tious·ly** *adv.*

am·biv·a·lence (am biv′ə ləns) *n.* ⟦AMBI- + VALENCE⟧ simultaneous conflicting feelings —**am·biv′a·lent** *adj.* —**am·biv′a·lent·ly** *adv.*

am·ble (am′bəl) *vi.* **-bled, -bling** ⟦< L *ambulare*, to walk⟧ 1 to move at an easy gait, as a horse 2 to walk in a leisurely way —*n.* 1 a horse's ambling gait 2 a leisurely walking pace

am·bro·sia (am brō′zhə) *n.* ⟦< Gr *a*-, not + *brotos*, mortal⟧ 1 *Gr. & Rom. Myth.* the food of the gods 2 anything that tastes or smells delicious —**am·bro′sial** *adj.*

am·bu·lance (am′byə ləns) *n.* ⟦< L *ambulare*, to walk⟧ a vehicle equipped for carrying the sick or wounded

am·bu·late (am′byōō lāt′, -byə-) *vi.* **-lat′ed, -lat′ing** to move about; walk —**am′bu·la′tion** *n.*

am·bu·la·to·ry (-lə tôr′ē) *adj.* 1 of or for walking 2 able to walk

am·bus·cade (am′bəs kād′) *n., vt., vi.* **-cad′ed, -cad′ing** AMBUSH

am·bush (am′boosh) *n.* ⟦< ML *in*-, in + *boscus*, woods⟧ 1 a deployment of persons in hiding to make a surprise attack 2 their hiding place 3 a surprise attack —*vt., vi.* to attack from ambush

a·me·ba (ə mē′bə) *n., pl.* **-bas** or **-bae** (-bē) *alt. sp. of* AMOEBA —**a·me′bic** (-bik) *adj.*

a·mel·io·rate (ə mēl′yə rāt′) *vt., vi.* **-rat′ed, -rat′ing** ⟦< Fr < L *melior*, better⟧ to make or become better; improve —**a·mel′io·ra′tion** *n.*

a·men (ā′men′, ä′-) *interj.* ⟦< Heb *amen*, truly⟧ may it be so!: used after a prayer or to express approval

a·me·na·ble (ə mē′nə bəl, -men′ə-) *adj.* ⟦< OFr < L *minare*, to drive (animals)⟧ 1 responsible or answerable 2 willing 3 susceptible (to) —**a·me′na·bil′i·ty** *n.* —**a·me′na·bly** *adv.*

a·mend (ə mend′) *vt.* ⟦< L *emendare*⟧ 1 to correct; emend 2 to improve 3 to change

or revise (a law, etc.) —*vi.* to improve one's conduct —**a·mend′a·ble** *adj.*

a·mend·ment *n.* 1 a correction of errors, faults, etc. 2 improvement 3 a revision or change proposed or made in a bill, law, etc.

a·mends (ə mendz′) *pl.n.* ⟦see AMEND⟧ [*sometimes with sing. v.*] payment made or satisfaction given for injury, loss, etc.

a·men·i·ty (ə men′ə tē, -mēn′-) *n., pl.* **-ties** ⟦< L *amoenus*, pleasant⟧ 1 pleasantness 2 an attractive feature or convenience

am·ent (am′ənt, ā′mənt) *n.* ⟦< L *amentum*, thong⟧ CATKIN

Am·er·a·sian (am′ər ā′zhən) *n.* ⟦AMER(ICAN) + ASIAN⟧ a person of both American and Asian descent —*adj.* both American and Asian [*an Amerasian child*]

a·merce (ə murs′) *vt.* **a·merced′, a·merc′ing** ⟦< OFr *a merci*, at the mercy of⟧ to punish, esp. by imposing a fine —**a·merce′ment** *n.*

A·mer·i·ca (ə mer′i kə) ⟦associated with *Amerigo* VESPUCCI⟧ 1 North America, South America, and the West Indies, considered together: also **the Americas** 2 North America 3 the United States of America

A·mer·i·can (-kən) *adj.* 1 of or in America 2 of the U.S. or its people —*n.* 1 a person born or living in North or South America 2 a citizen of the U.S.

A·mer·i·can·a (ə mer′i kan′ə, -kä′nə) *pl.n.* books, papers, objects, etc. having to do with the U.S., its people, and its history

American Indian a member of any of the indigenous peoples of the Americas, esp. N America, except the Eskimos and related peoples

A·mer·i·can·ism *n.* 1 a custom or belief of or originating in the U.S. 2 a word or idiom originating in American English 3 devotion to the U.S., its customs, etc.

A·mer·i·can·ize (-īz′) *vt., vi.* **-ized′, -iz′ing** to make or become American in character, manners, etc. —**A·mer′i·can·i·za′tion** *n.*

American plan a system of hotel operation in which the price charged covers room, service, and meals

American Revolution the war (1775-83) fought by the American colonies to gain independence from Great Britain

American Samoa group of seven islands in the SW Pacific: an unincorporated territory of the U.S.

am·er·i·ci·um (am′ər ish′ē əm) *n.* ⟦after AMERICA⟧ a metallic radioactive chemical element: symbol, Am; at. no. 95

Am·er·in·di·an (am′ər in′dē ən) *n., adj.* AMERICAN INDIAN —**Am′er·ind′** *n., adj.*

am·e·thyst (am′i thist) *n.* ⟦< Gr *amethystos*, not drunken: the Greeks thought the amethyst prevented intoxication⟧ 1 a purple or violet quartz or corundum, used in jewelry 2 purple or violet

a·mi·a·ble (ā′mē ə bəl) *adj.* ⟦< L *amicus*, friend⟧ good-natured; friendly —**a′mi·a·bil′i·ty** *n.* —**a′mi·a·bly** *adv.*

am·i·ca·ble (am′i kə bəl) *adj.* ⟦see prec.⟧

friendly; peaceable —**am′i·ca·bil′i·ty** *n.*
—**am′i·ca·bly** *adv.*

a·mid (ə mid′) *prep.* in the middle of; among:
also **a·midst** (ə midst′)

am·ide (am′īd′) *n.* any of several organic compounds derived from ammonia

a·mid·ships *adv., adj.* in or toward the middle of a ship

a·mi·go (ə mē′gō) *n., pl.* **-gos′** (-gōz′) [Sp] a friend

a·mi·no acid (ə mē′nō) [< AMMONIA] any of the nitrogenous organic acids that form proteins necessary for all life

Am·ish (äm′ish, am′-) *pl.n.* [after Jacob *Ammann* (or *Amen*), the founder] the members of a Christian sect that favors plain living in an agrarian society —*adj.* of this sect

a·miss (ə mis′) *adv.* [see A-¹ & MISS¹] in a wrong way; astray —*adj.* wrong, faulty, improper, etc. [*what is amiss?*]

am·i·ty (am′i tē) *n., pl.* **-ties** [< L *amicus*, friend] peaceful relations

am·me·ter (am′mēt′ər) *n.* [AM(PERE) + -METER] an instrument for measuring an electric current in amperes

am·mo (am′ō) *n.* [Slang] ammunition

am·mo·ni·a (ə mōn′yə) *n.* [prob. from a salt found near an Egyptian shrine of Jupiter *Ammon*] 1 a colorless, pungent gas, a compound of nitrogen and hydrogen 2 a solution of this gas in water

am·mu·ni·tion (am′yōō nish′ən) *n.* [< L *munire*, fortify] 1 bullets, gunpowder, bombs, grenades, rockets, etc. 2 any means of attack or defense

am·ne·sia (am nē′zhə) *n.* [< Gr *a-*, not + *mnasthai*, to remember] partial or total loss of memory

am·nes·ty (am′nəs tē) *n., pl.* **-ties** [< Gr *amnēstia*, a forgetting] a pardon, esp. for political offenses —*vt.* **-tied, -ty·ing** to pardon

am·ni·o·cen·te·sis (am′nē ō′sen tē′sis) *n.* [< fol. + Gr *kentēsis*, a pricking] the surgical procedure of extracting amniotic fluid from a pregnant woman to determine the sex of the fetus, detect disease, etc.

am·ni·on (am′nē ən, -än′) *n., pl.* **-ni·ons** or **-ni·a** (-ə) [Gr, dim. of *amnos*, lamb] the membrane enclosing the embryo of a mammal, reptile, or bird: it is filled with a watery fluid (**amniotic fluid**) —**am′ni·ot′ic** (-ät′ik) *adj.*

a·moe·ba (ə mē′bə) *n., pl.* **-bas** or **-bae** (-bē) [< Gr *ameibein*, to change] a one-celled, microscopic organism having no fixed shape and reproducing by fission —**a·moe′bic** (-bik) *adj.*

a·mok (ə muk′) *adj., adv.* [< Malay *amuk*, attacking furiously] used chiefly in **run amok**, to lose control and behave violently

a·mong (ə muŋ′) *prep.* [< OE *on*, in + *gemang*, a crowd] 1 surrounded by [*among* friends] 2 in the group of [*best among* books] 3 to or for each or several of [*divide it among* the crowd] 4 by the joint action of Also [Chiefly Brit.] **a·mongst** (ə muŋst′)

A·mon-Re (ä′mən rā′) *n.* the ancient Egyptian sun god: also **A′mon-Ra′** (-rä′)

a·mon·til·la·do (ə män′tə lä′dō) *n.* [< Sp, after *Montilla*, town in Spain] a pale, dry sherry

a·mor·al (ā môr′əl) *adj.* 1 neither moral nor immoral 2 without moral sense —**a′mo·ral′i·ty** *n.* —**a·mor′al·ly** *adv.*

am·o·rous (am′ə rəs) *adj.* [< L *amor*, love] 1 fond of making love 2 full of love 3 of sexual love —**am′o·rous·ly** *adv.*

a·mor·phous (ə môr′fəs) *adj.* [< Gr *a-*, without + *morphē*, form] 1 without definite form 2 vague or indefinite 3 *Chem.* not crystalline

am·or·tize (am′ər tīz′, ə môr′-) *vt.* **-tized′, -tiz′ing** [< ME < L *ad*, to + *mors*, death] to put money aside at intervals for gradual payment of (a debt, etc.) —**am′or·ti·za′tion** *n.*

a·mount (ə mount′) *vi.* [< OFr *amont*, upward < L *ad*, to + *mons*, mountain] 1 to add up (*to*) 2 to be equal (*to*) in value, etc. —*n.* 1 a sum total 2 the whole value or effect 3 a quantity

a·mour (ə moor′) *n.* [< L *amor*, love] a love affair, esp. an illicit one

a·mour-pro·pre (à moōr prô′pr′) *n.* [Fr] self-esteem

amp¹ (amp) *n. short for:* 1 AMPERE 2 AMPLIFIER

amp² *abbrev.* 1 amperage 2 ampere(s)

am·per·age (am′pər ij) *n.* the strength of an electric current in amperes

am·pere (am′pir′) *n.* [< A. M. *Ampère* (1775-1836), Fr physicist] the standard unit for measuring an electric current, equal to one coulomb per second

am·per·sand (am′pər sand′) *n.* [< *and per se and*, (the sign) & by itself (is) *and*] a sign (&), meaning *and*

am·phet·a·mine (am fet′ə mēn′, -min) *n.* a drug used esp. as a stimulant and to lessen appetite

am·phib·i·an (am fib′ē ən) *n.* [see fol.] 1 any amphibious animal or plant 2 a coldblooded vertebrate that has gills when young, later usually developing lungs 3 any aircraft that can take off from or land on water or land —*adj.* AMPHIBIOUS

am·phib·i·ous *adj.* [Gr *amphibios*, living a double life < *amphi-*, around + *bios*, life] that can live or operate on land and in water

am·phi·the·a·ter or **am·phi·the·a·tre** (am′fə thē′ə tər) *n.* [< Gr *amphi-*, around + *theatron*, theater] a round or oval building with rising rows of seats around an open space

am·ple (am′pəl) *adj.* **-pler, -plest** [< L *amplus*] 1 large in size, scope, etc. 2 more than enough 3 adequate —**am′ply** *adv.*

am·pli·fi·er (am′plə fī′ər) *n.* one that amplifies; esp., a device for strengthening electrical signals

am·pli·fy (−fī′) *vt.* **-fied′, -fy′ing** [< L *amplus*, large + *facere*, to make] 1 to make stronger; esp., to strengthen (electrical signals) 2 to develop more fully —**am′pli·fi·ca′tion** *n.*

am·pli·tude (am′plə tōōd′) *n.* [see AMPLE] 1

scope, extent, breadth, etc. **2** abundance **3** range from mean to extreme of a fluctuating quantity, as of an alternating current

amplitude modulation the changing of the amplitude of the transmitting radio wave in accordance with the signal being broadcast: abbrev. *AM*

am·pule (am′pyo͞ol′, -po͞ol′) *n.* ⟦< L *ampulla*, bottle⟧ a small, sealed, glass or plastic container for a single dose of a hypodermic medicine: also **am′pul′** (-pyo͞ol′) or **am′poule′** (-po͞ol′)

am·pu·tate (am′pyo͞o tāt′) *vt., vi.* **-tat′ed, -tat′ing** ⟦< L *am-*, AMBI- + *putare*, to prune⟧ to cut off (an arm, etc.), esp. by surgery —**am′pu·ta′tion** *n.*

am·pu·tee (-tē′) *n.* one who has had a limb or limbs amputated

Am·ster·dam (am′stər dam′) constitutional capital of the Netherlands

amt *abbrev.* amount

Am·trak (am′trak′) *abbrev.* ⟦*Am(erican) tr(avel) (tr)a(c)k*⟧ a national U.S. passenger railroad system

a·muck (ə muk′) *n. alt. sp. of* AMOK

am·u·let (am′yo͞o lit) *n.* ⟦< L⟧ something worn to protect against evil

a·muse (ə myo͞oz′) *vt.* **a·mused′, a·mus′ing** ⟦< Fr < *à*, at + OFr *muser*, to gaze⟧ **1** to keep pleasantly occupied; entertain **2** to make laugh, smile, etc. —**a·mus′ed·ly** *adv.*

a·muse·ment *n.* **1** a being amused **2** something that amuses; entertainment

amusement park an outdoor place with refreshment booths and a merry-go-round, roller coaster, etc.

am·yl·ase (am′ə lās′) *n.* ⟦< Gr *amylon*, starch⟧ an enzyme that helps change starch into sugar, found in saliva, etc.

an (an; *unstressed,* ən, ′n) *indefinite article* ⟦< OE *an*, one⟧ **1** one; one sort of **2** each; any one —*prep.* per [two *an* hour] *An* is used before words beginning with a vowel sound [*an* eye, *an* honor] See also A²

-an (ən, in, ′n) ⟦< L *-anus*⟧ *suffix* **1** (one) belonging to [*diocesan*] **2** (one) born in or living in [*Mexican*] **3** (one) believing in [*Lutheran*]

a·nach·ro·nism (ə nak′rə niz′əm) *n.* ⟦< Gr *ana-*, against + *chronos*, time⟧ **1** anything out of its proper historical time **2** the representation of this —**a·nach′ro·nis′tic** *adj.*

an·a·con·da (an′ə kän′də) *n.* ⟦< Sinhalese *henacandāya,* a snake of Sri Lanka⟧ a long, heavy South American boa living mostly in and around water

an·aer·o·bic (an′ər ō′bik) *adj.* ⟦< Gr *an-*, without + *aēr,* air + *bios,* life⟧ able to live, grow, or take place without air or free oxygen [*anaerobic* bacteria]

an·aes·the·sia (an′əs thē′zhə) *n.* ANESTHESIA —**an′aes·thet′ic** (-thet′ik) *adj., n.*

an·a·gram (an′ə gram′) *n.* ⟦< Gr *anagrammatizein,* transpose letters⟧ **1** a word, etc. made by rearranging letters (Ex.: *now* — *won*) **2** [*pl., with sing. v.*] a word game based on this

a·nal (ā′nəl) *adj.* **1** of or near the anus **2** *short for* ANAL-RETENTIVE

an·al·ge·si·a (an′əl jē′zē ə) *n.* ⟦< Gr *an-,* without + *algēsia,* pain⟧ a fully conscious state in which pain is not felt

an·al·ge·sic (-zik) *adj.* of or causing analgesia —*n.* a drug that produces analgesia

an·a·log (an′ə lôg′) *adj.* **1** of electronic devices in which the signal varies continuously **2** using hands, dials, etc. to show numerical amounts, as on a clock: cf. DIGITAL (*adj.* 2) —*n.* ANALOGUE

a·nal·o·gize (ə nal′ə jīz′) *vi., vt.* **-gized′, -giz′ing** to use, or explain by, analogy

a·nal·o·gous (-gəs) *adj.* [see ANALOGY] similar in some way —**a·nal′o·gous·ly** *adv.*

an·a·logue (an′ə lôg′) *n.* something analogous

a·nal·o·gy (ə nal′ə jē) *n., pl.* **-gies** ⟦< Gr *ana-,* according to + *logos,* word, reckoning⟧ **1** similarity in some ways **2** the inference that certain resemblances imply further similarity

a·nal-re·ten·tive (ā′nəl ri ten′tiv) *adj.* excessively orderly, stingy, etc.

a·nal·y·sand (ə nal′ə sand′) *n.* a person undergoing psychoanalysis

a·nal·y·sis (-sis) *n., pl.* **-ses′** (-sēz′) ⟦< Gr *ana-,* up + *lysis,* a loosing⟧ **1** *a)* a breaking up of a whole into its parts to find out their nature, etc. *b)* any detailed examination **2** a statement of the results of this **3** PSYCHO-ANALYSIS **4** *Chem.* an analysis of compounds or mixtures —**an·a·lyt·ic** (an′ə lit′ik) *adj.,* **an′a·lyt′i·cal** —**an′a·lyt′i·cal·ly** *adv.*

an·a·lyst (an′ə list) *n.* **1** one who analyzes **2** a psychoanalyst

an·a·lyze (-līz′) *vt.* **-lyzed′, -lyz′ing 1** to make an analysis of; examine in detail **2** to psychoanalyze —**an′a·lyz′a·ble** *adj.* —**an′a·lyz′er** *n.*

an·a·pest (an′ə pest′) *n.* ⟦< Gr *ana-,* back + *paiein,* to strike⟧ a metrical foot of two unaccented syllables followed by an accented one

an·ar·chism (an′ər kiz′əm) *n.* **1** the theory that all forms of government interfere unjustly with individual liberty **2** resistance to all government —**an′ar·chist′** *n.* —**an′ar·chis′tic** *adj.*

an·ar·chy (-kē) *n., pl.* **-chies** ⟦< Gr *an-,* without + *archos,* leader⟧ **1** the absence of government **2** political disorder and violence **3** disorder; confusion —**an·ar·chic** (an är′kik) *adj.* —**an·ar′chi·cal·ly** *adv.*

a·nath·e·ma (ə nath′ə mə) *n., pl.* **-mas** ⟦Gr, thing devoted to evil⟧ **1** a thing or person accursed or damned **2** a thing or person greatly detested **3** a formal curse, as in excommunication

a·nath·e·ma·tize (-tīz′) *vt., vi.* **-tized′, -tiz′ing** to utter an anathema (against); curse

a·nat·o·mize (ə nat′ə mīz′) *vt., vi.* **-mized′, -miz′ing** [see fol.] **1** to dissect (an animal or plant) in order to examine the structure **2** to analyze —**a·nat′o·mist** *n.*

a·nat·o·my (-mē) *n., pl.* **-mies** ⟦< Gr *ana-,* up + *temnein,* to cut⟧ **1** dissection of an organism to study its structure **2** the science of the structure of animals or plants **3** the structure of an organism **4** any analysis —**a·na·tom·i·cal** (an'ə täm'i kəl) *adj.*

-ance (əns) [< L] *suffix* **1** the act or process of ___ing [*discontinuance*] **2** the quality or state of being [*forbearance*] **3** a thing that ___s [*hindrance*] **4** a thing that is ___ed [*utterance*]

an·ces·tor (an'ses'tər) *n.* [< L *ante-*, before + *cedere*, go] **1** a person, esp. one now deceased, from whom one is descended; forebear **2** a precursor or forerunner —**an·ces·tral** (an ses'trəl) *adj.*

an·ces·try (-trē) *n.*, *pl.* **-tries 1** family descent **2** ancestors collectively

an·chor (aŋ'kər) *n.* [< Gr *ankyra*, an anchor, hook] **1** a heavy object, usually an iron weight with flukes, lowered from a vessel, as by cable, to prevent drifting **2** anything that gives security by remaining fixed in place or unchanging **3** the final contestant on a relay team, etc. **4** one who reports or coordinates a newscast —*vt.* **1** to hold secure as by an anchor **2** to be the final contestant on (a relay team, etc.) **3** to report or coordinate (a newscast) —*vi.* **1** to lower an anchor overboard **2** to be or become fixed —**at anchor** kept from drifting by its anchor

an·chor·age (-ij) *n.* **1** an anchoring or being anchored **2** a place to anchor

An·chor·age (aŋ'kər ij) seaport in S Alaska

an·cho·rite (aŋ'kə rīt') *n.* [< Gr *ana-*, back + *chōrein*, retire] a religious recluse; hermit

an·chor·man *n.*, *pl.* **-men'** a man who anchors a newscast

an·chor·per·son *n.* a person who anchors a newscast

an·chor·wom·an *n.*, *pl.* **-wom'en** a woman who anchors a newscast

an·cho·vy (an'chō'vē, an chō'vē) *n.*, *pl.* **-vies** [< Port *anchova*] a herringlike fish, often salted, cured, and eaten as a relish

an·cient (ān'chənt) *adj.* [< L *ante*, before] **1** of times long past **2** very old —*n.* an aged person

an·cil·lar·y (an'sə ler'ē) *adj.* [< L *ancilla*, maidservant] **1** subordinate: often with *to* **2** auxiliary

-an·cy (ən sē) *suffix* -ANCE

and (and; *unstressed*, ənd, ən) *conj.* [OE] **1** also; in addition **2** plus **3** as a result **4** in contrast; but **5** then; following this **6** [Inf.] to [*try and* come today]

an·dan·te (än dän'tā) *adj.*, *adv.* [It < *andare*, to walk] *Music* moderate in tempo

An·der·sen (an'dər sən), **Hans Christian** (häns, hänz) 1805-75; Dan. writer of fairy tales

An·des (Mountains) (an'dēz') mountain system of W South America

and·i·ron (and'ī'ərn) *n.* [< OFr *andier*] either of a pair of metal supports for logs in a fireplace

and/or (and'ôr') *conj.* either *and* or *or* [*personal and/or* real property]

An·dor·ra (an dôr'ə) country in the E Pyrenees

an·dro·gen (an'drō jən) *n.* [< Gr *andros*, of man + -GEN] a type of steroid that acts as a male sex hormone —**an'dro·gen'ic** (-jen'ik) *adj.*

an·drog·y·nous (an drä'jə nəs) *adj.* [< Gr *andros*, of man + *gynē*, woman] **1** both male and female in one **2** blending male and female characteristics, roles, etc. **3** not differentiated as to gender [*androgynous* clothing]

an·droid (an'droid') *n.* [< Gr *andros*, of man + -OID] in science fiction, a robot made to resemble a human

an·ec·dote (an'ik dōt') *n.* [< Gr *anekdotos*, unpublished] a short, entertaining account of some event —**an'ec·dot'al** *adj.*

a·ne·mi·a (ə nē'mē ə) *n.* [< Gr *an-*, without + *haima*, blood] a condition in which the blood is low in red cells or in hemoglobin, resulting in paleness, weakness, etc. —**a·ne'mic** *adj.*

an·e·mom·e·ter (an'ə mäm'ət ər) *n.* [< Gr *anemos*, the wind + -METER] a gauge for determining the force or speed of the wind; wind gauge

a·nem·o·ne (ə nem'ə nē') *n.* [< Gr *anemos*, the wind] **1** a plant with cup-shaped flowers of white, pink, red, or purple **2** SEA ANEMONE

a·nent (ə nent') *prep.* [< OE *on efen*, on even (with)] [Now Rare] concerning; about

aneroid barometer (an'ər oid') [< Gr *a-*, without + *nēros*, liquid + -OID] a barometer working by the bending of a thin metal disk instead of by the rise or fall of mercury

an·es·the·sia (an'es thē'zhə) *n.* [< Gr *an-*, without + *aisthēsis*, feeling] a partial or total loss of the sense of pain, touch, etc., specif. when induced by an anesthetic

an·es·the·si·ol·o·gist (-thē'zē äl'ə jist) *n.* a doctor who specializes in administering anesthetics —**an'es·the'si·ol'o·gy** *n.*

an·es·thet·ic (-thet'ik) *adj.* of or producing anesthesia —*n.* a liquid, gas, etc. used as a drug to produce anesthesia, as before surgery

an·es·the·tist (ə nes'thə tist') *n.* one trained to give anesthetics

an·es·the·tize (-tīz') *vt.* **-tized'**, **-tiz'ing** to cause anesthesia in —**an·es'the·ti·za'tion** *n.*

an·eu·rysm or **an·eu·rism** (an'yōō riz'əm) *n.* [< Gr *ana-*, up + *eurys*, broad] a sac formed by an enlargement in a weakened wall of an artery, a vein, or the heart

a·new (ə nōō') *adv.* **1** once more; again **2** in a new manner or form

an·gel (ān'jəl) *n.* [< Gr *angelos*, messenger] **1** *Theol.* a supernatural being with greater than human power, etc., esp. one serving as a messenger of God **2** an image of a human figure with wings and a halo **3** a person regarded as beautiful, good, innocent, etc. **4** [Inf.] a financial backer, as for a play —**an·gel'ic** (an jel'ik) *adj.* —**an·gel'i·cal·ly** *adv.*

angel dust [Slang] a powerful psychedelic drug

An·ge·le·no (an'jə lē'nō) *n.*, *pl.* **-nos** [AmSp] a person born or living in Los Angeles

an·gel·fish (ān'jəlfish') *n.*, *pl.* **-fish'** or **-fish'es** a bright-colored tropical fish with spiny fins

angel (food) cake a light, spongy, white cake made with egg whites

an·ger (aŋ′gər) *n.* [< ON *angr*, distress] a feeling of displeasure and hostility that a person has because of being injured, mistreated, opposed, etc. —*vt., vi.* to make or become angry

an·gi·na (pec·to·ris) (an jī′nə pek′tər is) [L, lit., squeezing of the breast] a condition marked by chest pain, caused by a sudden decrease of blood to the heart

an·gi·o·gram (an′jē ō gram′) *n.* an X-ray photograph of blood vessels

an·gi·o·plas·ty (-plas′tē) *n.* any of various surgical techniques for repairing or replacing damaged blood vessels

an·gi·o·sperm (-spurm′) *n.* [< Gr *angos*, vessel + *sperma*, seed] any of a large division of plants having seeds produced within a closed pod or ovary

an·gle¹ (aŋ′gəl) *n.* [< Gr *ankylos*, bent] the shape or space made by two straight lines or plane surfaces that meet **2** the measure of this space, expressed in degrees, etc. **3** a sharp corner **4** a point of view; aspect **5** [Inf.] a tricky method for achieving a purpose —*vt., vi.* **-gled, -gling 1** to move or bend at an angle **2** [Inf.] to give a specific point of view to (a story, etc.)

an·gle² (aŋ′gəl) *vi.* **-gled, -gling** [< OE *angul*, fishhook] **1** to fish with a hook and line **2** to use tricks to get something [to *angle* for a promotion] —**an′gler** *n.*

An·gle (aŋ′gəl) *n.* a member of a Germanic people that settled in E England in the 5th c. A.D.

angle iron a piece of iron or steel bent at a right angle, for joining or reinforcing two beams, etc.

an·gle·worm *n.* [< ANGLE²] an earthworm

An·gli·can (aŋ′gli kən) *adj.* [< ML *Anglicus*, of the Angles] of or connected with the Church of England —*n.* an Anglican church member

An·gli·cize (-glə siz′) *vt., vi.* **-cized′, -ciz′ing** [*also* a-] to change to English idiom, pronunciation, customs, etc. —**An′gli·ci·za′tion** *n.*

An·glo (aŋ′glō) *n., pl.* **-glos** [AmSp] [*also* a-] a white inhabitant of the U.S. who is of non-Hispanic descent

Anglo- *combining form* **1** English **2** Anglican

An·glo-A·mer·i·can (-ə mer′i kən) *adj.* English and American —*n.* an American of English birth or ancestry

An·glo-French *adj.* English and French —*n.* the French spoken esp. by the upper classes in England from the Norman Conquest through the Middle Ages

An·glo-Sax·on *n.* **1** a member of the Germanic peoples in England at the time of the Norman Conquest **2** the language of these peoples, OLD ENGLISH **3** an Englishman —*adj.* **1** of the Anglo-Saxons **2** of the English

An·go·la (aŋ gō′lə, an-) country on the SW coast of Africa

An·go·ra (aŋ gôr′ə, an-) *n.* [former name of ANKARA] **1** a breed of cat, goat, or rabbit with

long, silky fur or hair **2** *a)* yarn of Angora rabbit hair *b)* mohair

an·gry (aŋ′grē) *adj.* **-gri·er, -gri·est 1** feeling or showing anger **2** wild and stormy —**an′gri·ly** (-grə lē) *adv.*

ang·strom (aŋ′strəm) *n.* [after A. J. *Angström* (1814-74), Swed physicist] one hundred-millionth of a centimeter: a unit used in measuring the length of light waves

an·guish (aŋ′gwish) *n.* [< L *angustia*, tightness] great mental or physical pain; agony —*vi., vt.* to feel or cause to feel anguish —**an′guished** *adj.*

an·gu·lar (aŋ′gyə lər) *adj.* **1** having or forming an angle or angles; having sharp corners **2** lean; gaunt **3** without ease or grace; stiff —**an′gu·lar′i·ty** (-lar′ə tē) *n., pl.* **-ties**

an·i·line (an′ə lin) *n.* [< Ar *an-nīl*, the indigo plant] a colorless, poisonous, oily derivative of benzene, used in making dyes, resins, etc.

an·i·mad·vert (an′i məd vurt′, -mad′-) *vi.* [L *animadvertere*, lit., to turn the mind] to comment adversely (*on* or *upon*) —**an′i·mad·ver′sion** *n.*

an·i·mal (an′i məl) *n.* [L < *anima*, breath, soul] **1** any of a group of living organisms, excluding plants, bacteria, and certain other simple organisms, typically able to move about **2** any such organism other than a human; esp., any four-footed creature **3** a brutish or inhuman person —*adj.* **1** of or like an animal **2** gross, bestial, etc.

an·i·mate (an′i māt′; *for adj.,* -mit) *vt.* **-mat′ed, -mat′ing** [see prec.] **1** to give life or motion to **2** to make energetic or spirited **3** to inspire —*adj.* living —**an′i·ma′tion** *n.* —**an′i·ma′tor** *n.*

an·i·mat·ed *adj.* **1** living or lifelike **2** lively **3** designating or of a movie or video whose frames consist of computer-generated images, photographs of drawings, etc., arranged to give the appearance of motion when viewed

an·i·ma·tron·ics (an′i mə trän′iks) *n.* [< *Audio-Animatronics*, service mark for a type of entertainment using robotics in this way] the use of electronic mechanisms to simulate lifelike motion in puppets and other figures —**an′i·ma·tron′ic** *adj.*

an·i·me (an′i mā′) *n.* [Jpn, ? ult. < Eng ANIMATION] a style of Japanese film animation, strongly influenced by MANGA and often with science-fiction or fantasy themes

an·i·mism (an′i miz′əm) *n.* [< L *anima*, soul] the belief that all life is produced by a spiritual force, or that all natural phenomena have souls —**an′i·mis′tic** *adj.*

an·i·mos·i·ty (an′ə mäs′ə tē) *n., pl.* **-ties** [see fol.] a feeling of strong dislike or hatred; hostility

an·i·mus (an′ə məs) *n.* [L, passion] animosity; hostility

an·i·on (an′i′ən) *n.* [< Gr *anion*, thing going up] a negatively charged ion: in electrolysis, anions move toward the anode

an·ise (an′is) *n.* [< Gr *anison*] **1** a dicotyledonous plant related to celery and parsley **2** its fragrant seed, used for flavoring: also **an′i·seed′** (-i sēd′)

an·i·sette (an′i zet′, -set′) *n.* ⟦Fr⟧ a sweet, anise-flavored liqueur

An·ka·ra (aŋ′kər ə, än′-) capital of Turkey

ankh (aŋk) *n.* ⟦Egypt, life, soul⟧ a cross with a loop at the top, an ancient Egyptian symbol of life

an·kle (aŋ′kəl) *n.* ⟦OE *ancleow*⟧ **1** the joint that connects the foot and the leg **2** the area of the leg between the foot and calf

an·klet (aŋk′lit) *n.* **1** an ornament worn around the ankle **2** a short sock

an·nals (an′əlz) *pl.n.* ⟦< L *annus*, year⟧ **1** a written account of events year by year **2** historical records; history **3** a journal containing reports of a society, etc. —**an′nal·ist** *n.*

An·nap·o·lis (ə nap′ə lis) capital of Maryland

an·neal (ə nēl′) *vt.* ⟦< OE *an-*, on + *æl*, fire⟧ to heat (glass, metals, etc.) and cool to prevent brittleness

an·ne·lid (an′ə lid′) *n.* ⟦< L dim. of *anulus*, a ring⟧ any of various wormlike animals, including leeches, having long, segmented bodies

an·nex (ə neks′; *for n.,* an′eks′) *vt.* ⟦< L *ad-*, to + *nectere*, to tie⟧ **1** to attach or append, esp. to something larger **2** to incorporate into a country, etc. the territory of (another country, etc.) —*n.* something annexed; esp., an addition to a building —**an·nex·a·tion** (an′ eks ā′shən) *n.*

an·ni·hi·late (ə nī′ə lāt′) *vt.* **-lat′ed, -lat′ing** ⟦< L *ad*, to + *nihil*, nothing⟧ to destroy completely —**an·ni′hi·la′tion** *n.* —**an·ni′hi·la′tor** *n.*

an·ni·ver·sa·ry (an′ə vur′sə rē) *n., pl.* **-ries** ⟦L *annus*, year + *vertere*, to turn⟧ **1** the date on which some event occurred in an earlier year **2** a celebration or commemoration of such an event

an·no·tate (an′ō tāt′) *vt., vi.* **-tat′ed, -tat′ing** ⟦< L *ad-*, to + *nota*, a sign⟧ to provide explanatory notes for (a text, etc.) —**an′no·ta′tion** *n.* —**an′no·ta′tor** *n.*

an·nounce (ə nouns′) *vt.* **-nounced′, -nounc′ing** ⟦< L *ad-*, to + *nuntius*, messenger⟧ **1** to declare publicly **2** to make known the arrival of **3** to be an announcer for —*vi.* to serve as announcer —**an·nounce′ment** *n.*

an·nounc·er *n.* one who announces; specif., one who introduces radio or TV programs

an·noy (ə noi′) *vt.* ⟦< VL *in odio*, in hate⟧ to irritate or bother, as by a repeated action —**an·noy′ance** *n.* —**an·noy′ing** *adj.* —**an·noy′ing·ly** *adv.*

an·nu·al (an′yōō əl) *adj.* ⟦< L *annus*, year⟧ **1** of or measured by a year **2** yearly **3** living only one year or season —*n.* **1** a periodical published once a year **2** a plant living only one year or season —**an′nu·al·ly** *adv.*

an·nu·i·ty (ə nōō′ə tē) *n., pl.* **-ties** ⟦see prec.⟧ **1** an investment yielding periodic payments, esp. yearly **2** such a payment —**an·nu′i·tant** *n.*

an·nul (ə nul′) *vt.* **-nulled′, -nul′ling** ⟦< L *ad-*, to + *nullum*, nothing⟧ **1** to do away with **2** to make no longer legally binding; nullify —**an·nul′ment** *n.*

an·nu·lar (an′yōō lər) *adj.* ⟦< L *anulus*, a ring⟧ like or forming a ring

an·nun·ci·a·tion (ə nun′sē ā′shən) *n.* an announcing —**the Annunciation** *Bible* the angel Gabriel's announcement to Mary that she would bear Jesus **2** the church festival commemorating this

an·ode (an′ōd′) *n.* ⟦< Gr *anodos*, a way up⟧ **1** the positive electrode in an electrolytic cell **2** the principal electrode for collecting electrons in an electron tube **3** the negative electrode in a battery

an·o·dize (an′ō dīz′) *vt.* **-dized′, -diz′ing** to put a protective film on (a metal) by an electrolytic process in which the metal is the anode

an·o·dyne (-dīn′) *adj.* ⟦< Gr *an-*, without + *odynē*, pain⟧ **1** soothing **2** bland; insipid —*n.* anything that relieves pain or soothes

a·noint (ə noint′) *vt.* ⟦< L *in-*, on + *unguere*, to smear⟧ to put oil on, as in consecrating —**a·noint′ment** *n.*

a·nom·a·lous (ə näm′ə ləs) *adj.* ⟦< Gr *an-*, not + *homos*, the same⟧ **1** abnormal **2** inconsistent or odd

a·nom·a·ly (-lē) *n., pl.* **-lies** **1** abnormality **2** anything anomalous

an·o·mie or **an·o·my** (an′ə mē) *n.* ⟦Fr < Gr *anomia*, lawlessness⟧ lack of purpose, identity, etc.

a·non (ə nän′) *adv.* ⟦< OE *on an*, into one⟧ ⟦Archaic⟧ **1** soon **2** at another time

Anon or **anon** *abbrev.* anonymous

a·non·y·mous (ə nän′ə məs) *adj.* ⟦< Gr *an-*, without + *onyma*, name⟧ **1** with no name known **2** given, written, etc. by one whose name is withheld or unknown **3** lacking individuality —**an·o·nym·i·ty** (an′ə nim′ə tē) *n.* —**a·non′y·mous·ly** *adv.*

a·noph·e·les (ə näf′ə lēz′) *n.* ⟦< Gr *anōphelēs*, harmful⟧ the mosquito that can transmit malaria

an·o·rex·i·a (an′ə reks′ē ə) *n.* ⟦< Gr *an-*, without + *orexis*, desire⟧ an eating disorder characterized by obsession with weight loss: in full **anorexia ner·vo·sa** (nər vō′sə) —**an′o·rex′ic** *adj., n.*

an·oth·er (ə nuth′ər) *adj.* **1** one more; an additional **2** a different one —*pron.* **1** one additional **2** a different one **3** one of the same kind

an·swer (an′sər) *n.* ⟦< OE *and-*, against + *swerian*, swear⟧ **1** a reply to a question, letter, etc. **2** any act in response **3** a solution to a problem —*vi.* **1** to reply **2** to be sufficient **3** to be responsible or liable (*to* a person *for* an action, etc.) **4** to conform (*to*) [he *answers* to the description] —*vt.* **1** to reply or respond to **2** to serve or fulfill [*to answer* the purpose] **3** to defend oneself against (a charge) **4** to conform to [she *answers* the description] —**answer back** [Inf.] to reply forcefully or insolently —**an′swer·a·ble** *adj.*

an·swer·ing machine a device for recording telephone messages automatically

answering service a business whose function is to answer telephone calls for its clients

ant (ant) *n.* [< OE *æmet(t)e*] any of a family of insects, generally wingless, that live in complex colonies

ant- *prefix* ANTI-

-ant (ənt) [ult. < L] *suffix* **1** that has, shows, or does [*defiant*] **2** one that [*occupant*]

ant·ac·id (ant'as'id) *adj.* counteracting acidity, specif. gastric acidity —*n.* an antacid substance

an·tag·o·nism (an tag'ə niz'əm) *n.* [see ANTAGONIZE] opposition or hostility

an·tag·o·nist *n.* an adversary; opponent —**an·tag'o·nis'tic** *adj.* —**an·tag'o·nis'ti·cal·ly** *adv.*

an·tag·o·nize (-nīz') *vt.* -**nized'**, -**niz'ing** [< Gr *anti-*, against + *agōn*, a contest] to incur the dislike of or make an enemy of

Ant·arc·tic (ant ärk'tik, -är'-) *adj.* [see ANTI- & ARCTIC] of or near the South Pole or the region around it —**the Antarctic** the region including Antarctica and the **Antarctic Ocean** surrounding it

Ant·arc·ti·ca (-ti kə) continent surrounding the South Pole, completely covered by an ice shelf

Antarctic Circle an imaginary circle parallel to the equator, *c.* 66°33' south of it

ant bear a large anteater of Central America and tropical South America

an·te (an'tē) *n.* [L, before] *Poker* the stake that each player must put into the pot before receiving cards —*vt., vi.* -**ted** or -**teed**, -**te·ing** *Poker* to put in (one's ante): also **ante up** —**up** (or **raise**) **the ante** to increase the seriousness, as of a competition

ante- [see prec.] *prefix* before in time or place

ant·eat·er *n.* a mammal with a long snout, that feeds mainly on ants

an·te·bel·lum (an'ti bel'əm) *adj.* [L] before the war; esp., before the American Civil War

an·te·ced·ent (an'tə sēd'nt) *adj.* [< L *ante-*, before + *cedere*, go] prior; previous —*n.* **1** any thing prior to another **2** [*pl.*] one's ancestry, past life, etc. **3** *Gram.* the word or phrase to which a pronoun refers

an·te·cham·ber (an'ti chām'bər) *n.* a room leading into a larger or main room

an·te·date (-dāt') *vt.* -**dat'ed**, -**dat'ing 1** to put a date on that is earlier than the actual date **2** to come before in time

an·te·di·lu·vi·an (-də lōō'vē ən) *adj.* [< ANTE- + L *diluvium*, a flood + -AN] **1** of the time before the biblical Flood **2** very old or old-fashioned

an·te·lope (an'tə lōp') *n.* [< Gr *antholops*, deer] a swift, cud-chewing, horned animal resembling the deer

an·te me·ri·di·em (an'tē mə rid'ē əm) [L] before noon

an·ten·na (an ten'ə) *n.* [L, sail yard] **1** *pl.* -**nae** (-ē) or -**nas** either of a pair of feelers on the head of an insect, crab, etc. **2** *pl.* -**nas**

Radio, TV an arrangement of wires, rods, etc. used in sending and receiving electromagnetic waves

an·te·ri·or (an tir'ē ər) *adj.* [< L *ante*, before] **1** at or toward the front **2** previous; earlier

an·te·room (an'tē rōōm') *n.* a room leading to a larger or main room

an·them (an'thəm) *n.* [< Gr *anti-*, over against + *phōnē*, voice] **1** a religious choral song **2** a song of praise or devotion, as to a nation

an·ther (an'thər) *n.* [< Gr *anthēros*, blooming] the part of a stamen that produces pollen

ant·hill *n.* the soil heaped up by ants around their nest opening

an·thol·o·gize (an thäl'ə jīz') *vi.* -**gized'**, -**giz'ing** to make anthologies —*vt.* to include in an anthology —**an·thol'o·gist** (-jist) *n.*, **an·thol'o·giz'er**

an·thol·o·gy (-jē) *n., pl.* -**gies** [< Gr *anthos*, flower + *legein*, gather] a collection of poems, stories, songs, etc., esp. by different people

An·tho·ny (an'thə nē, -tə-), **Mark** *see* ANTONY, Mark

an·thra·cite (an'thrə sīt') *n.* [< Gr *anthrax*, coal] hard coal, which gives much heat and little smoke

an·thrax (an'thraks') *n.* [< Gr, coal, carbuncle] an infectious disease of cattle, sheep, etc. that can be transmitted to humans

anthropo- [< Gr *anthrōpos*, man] *combining form* man, human

an·thro·po·cen·tric (an'thrə pō'sen'trik) *adj.* [see prec.] centering one's view of everything around humankind

an·thro·poid (an'thrə poid') *adj.* [see ANTHROPO- & -OID] resembling a human —*n.* **1** APE (*n.* 1) **2** any of a group of primates including humans, apes, and monkeys

an·thro·pol·o·gy (an'thrə päl'ə jē) *n.* [ANTHROPO- + -LOGY] the study of the characteristics, customs, etc. of humanity —**an'thro·po·log'i·cal** (-pə läj'i kəl) *adj.* —**an'thro·pol'o·gist** *n.*

an·thro·po·mor·phism (-pō'môr'fiz'əm) *n.* the attributing of human characteristics to animals, objects, etc. —**an'thro·po'mor'phic** *adj.* —**an'thro·po'mor'phi·cal·ly** *adv.* —**an'thro·po'mor'phize'** (-fīz') *vt., vi.* -**phized'**, -**phiz'ing**

an·ti (an'tī', -tē) [Inf.] *n., pl.* -**tis'** [< fol.] a person opposed to something —*prep.* opposed to

anti- [< Gr *anti*, against] *prefix* **1** against, hostile to **2** that operates against **3** that prevents, cures, or neutralizes **4** opposite, reverse **5** rivaling

an·ti·air·craft (an'tē er'kraft') *adj.* used against hostile aircraft

an·ti·bal·lis·tic missile (-bə lis'tik) a missile intended to destroy an enemy ballistic missile in flight

an·ti·bi·ot·ic (-bī ät'ik, -bē-) *n.* [< ANTI- + Gr *bios*, life] any of certain substances, as penicillin or streptomycin, produced by various microorganisms and capable of destroying or weakening bacteria, etc. —*adj.* of antibiotics

an·ti·bod·y (an′ti bäd′ē) *n., pl.* **-bod′ies** a protein produced in the body to neutralize a toxin or other antigen

an·tic (an′tik) *adj.* [< L: see ANTIQUE] odd and funny —*n.* a playful or ludicrous act, trick, etc.: *usually used in pl.*

An·ti·christ (an′ti krīst′) *n. Bible* a great opponent of Christ: 1 John 2:18

an·tic·i·pate (an tis′ə pāt′) *vt.* **-pat′ed, -pat′ing** [< L *ante-*, before + *capere*, take] 1 to look forward to 2 to forestall 3 to use or deal with in advance 4 to be ahead of in doing —**an·tic′i·pa′tion** *n.* —**an·tic′i·pa·to′ry** (-pə tôr′ē) *adj.*

an·ti·cli·max (an′ti klī′maks′) *n.* 1 a sudden drop from the important to the trivial 2 a descent which is in disappointing contrast to a preceding rise —**an′ti·cli·mac′tic** (-klī mak′ tik) *adj.*

an·ti·cline (an′ti klīn′) *n.* [< ANTI- + Gr *klinein*, to lean] *Geol.* a sharply arched fold of stratified rock

an·ti·co·ag·u·lant (an′ti kō ag′yōō lənt) *n.* a drug or substance that delays or prevents the clotting of blood

an·ti·de·pres·sant (-dē pres′ənt) *adj.* lessening emotional depression —*n.* an antidepressant drug

an·ti·dote (an′tə dōt′) *n.* [< Gr *anti-*, against + *dotos*, given] 1 a remedy to counteract a poison 2 anything that works against an evil or unwanted condition

an·ti·freeze (an′ti frēz′) *n.* a substance used, as in the radiator of an automobile, to prevent freezing

an·ti·gen (an′tə jən) *n.* [ANTI- + -GEN] any substance to which the body reacts by producing antibodies

An·ti·gua and Bar·bu·da (an tē′gwə 'n bär bōō′də) country in the E West Indies, consisting of three small islands

an·ti·he·ro (an′ti hir′ō) *n., pl.* **-roes** the protagonist of a novel, etc. who lacks the virtues of a traditional hero

an·ti·his·ta·mine (an′ti his′tə mēn′, -min) *n.* any of several drugs used to block histamine, as in allergic reactions

an·ti·in·flam·ma·to·ry (an′tē in flam′ə tôr′ ē) *adj.* reducing inflammation —*n.* an antiinflammatory medication, as aspirin

an·ti·knock (an′ti näk′) *n.* a substance added to the fuel of internal-combustion engines to reduce noise resulting from too rapid combustion

An·til·les (an til′ēz′) group of islands of the West Indies, including Cuba, Jamaica, etc. (**Greater Antilles**) & the Leeward Islands and Windward Islands (**Lesser Antilles**)

an·ti·lock (an′tē läk′) *adj.* designating an automotive braking system that prevents the wheels from locking during a sudden stop

an·ti·log·a·rithm (an′ti lôg′ə rith′əm) *n.* the number resulting when a base is raised to a power by a logarithm

an·ti·ma·cas·sar (an′ti mə kas′ər) *n.* [ANTI- + *macassar*, a hair oil] a small cover on the back or arms of a chair, sofa, etc. to prevent soiling

an·ti·mat·ter (an′ti mat′ər) *n.* a form of matter in which the electrical charge of each particle is the reverse of that in the usual matter of our universe

an·ti·mis·sile (an′tī mis′əl) *adj.* designed as a defense against ballistic missiles

an·ti·mo·ny (an′tə mō′nē) *n.* [< ML] a silvery-white, nonmetallic chemical element used in alloys to harden them: symbol, Sb; at. no. 51

an·ti·pas·to (an′ti päs′tō, -pas′-) *n.* [It < *anti-*, before + *pasto*, food] an appetizer of assorted meats, cheeses, marinated vegetables, etc.

an·tip·a·thy (an tip′ə thē) *n., pl.* **-thies** [< Gr *anti-*, against + *pathein*, to suffer] 1 strong dislike; aversion 2 the object of such dislike

an·ti·per·son·nel (an′ti pur′sə nel′) *adj.* intended to destroy people rather than objects [*antipersonnel* mines]

an·ti·per·spi·rant (-pur′spə rənt) *n.* a substance applied to the skin to reduce perspiration

an·tiph·o·nal (an tif′ə nəl) *adj.* [see ANTHEM] sung or chanted in alternation

an·tip·o·des (an tip′ə dēz′) *pl.n.* [< Gr *anti-*, opposite + *pous*, foot] any two places directly opposite each other on the earth —**an·tip′o·dal** *adj.*

an·ti·quar·i·an (an′ti kwer′ē ən) *adj.* 1 of antiques or antiquities 2 of antiquaries 3 dealing in old books —*n.* an antiquary

an·ti·quar·y (an′ti kwer′ē) *n., pl.* **-quar′ies** a collector or student of antiquities

an·ti·quate (-kwāt′) *vt.* **-quat′ed, -quat′ing** [see fol.] to make old, out-of-date, or obsolete —**an′ti·quat′ed** *adj.* —**an′ti·qua′tion** *n.*

an·tique (an tēk′) *adj.* [< L *antiquus*, ancient] 1 of ancient times 2 out-of-date 3 of, or in the style of, a former period 4 dealing in antiques —*n.* 1 any ancient relic 2 a piece of furniture, etc. from a former period —*vt.* **-tiqued′, -tiqu′ing** to make look antique —*vi.* to shop for antique furniture, etc.

an·tiq·ui·ty (an tik′wə tē) *n., pl.* **-ties** [see prec.] 1 the ancient period of history 2 great age 3 [*pl.*] relics, etc. of the distant past

an·ti·Se·mit·ic (an′tē sə mit′ik) *adj.* having or showing prejudice against Jews Also **an′ti·se·mit′ic** —**an′ti·Sem′ite′** (-sem′īt′) *n.* —**an′ti·Sem′i·tism′** (-ə tiz′əm) *n.*

an·ti·sep·sis (an′tə sep′sis) *n.* [ANTI- + SEPSIS] 1 a being antiseptic 2 the use of antiseptics

an·ti·sep·tic (-tik) *adj.* 1 preventing infection, decay, etc. by acting against bacteria, etc. 2 using antiseptics 3 sterile 4 very clean or tidy —*n.* any antiseptic substance —**an′ti·sep′ti·cal·ly** *adv.*

an·ti·se·rum (an′ti sir′əm) *n., pl.* **-rums** or **-ra** a serum containing antibodies

an·ti·slav·er·y (an′ti-) *adj.* against slavery

an·ti·so·cial *adj.* 1 not sociable; avoiding others 2 harmful to the welfare of people [vandalism and other *antisocial* behaviors]

an·ti·tank (an'tī trust') *adj.* for use against tanks in war

an·tith·e·sis (an tith'ə sis) *n., pl.* **-ses'** (-sēz') [< Gr *anti-*, against + *tithenai*, to place] 1 a contrast or opposition, as of ideas 2 the exact opposite —**an·ti·thet·i·cal** (an'tə thet'i kəl) *adj.* —**an'ti·thet'i·cal·ly** *adv.*

an·ti·tox·in (an'ti täks'in) *n.* 1 a circulating antibody formed by the body to act against a specific toxin 2 a serum containing an antitoxin, injected into a person to prevent a disease

an·ti·trust (an'tī trust') *adj.* opposed to or regulating trusts, or business monopolies

an·ti·vi·ral (an'tī vī'rəl) *adj.* capable of checking the growth of a virus

an·ti·viv·i·sec·tion·ist (-viv'ə sek'shən ist) *n.* one opposing vivisection

ant·ler (ant'lər) *n.* [< OFr *antoillier*] the branched, bony growth on the head of any animal of the deer family —**ant'lered** (-lərd) *adj.*

An·to·ny (an'tə nē), **Mark (or Marc)** 83?-30 B.C.; Rom. general

an·to·nym (an'tə nim') *n.* [< Gr *anti-*, opposite + *onyma*, name] a word meaning the opposite of another

ant·sy (ant'sē) *adj.* **-si·er, -si·est** [Slang] fidgety, nervous, impatient, etc.

Ant·werp (an'twurp') seaport in N Belgium

a·nus (ā'nəs) *n., pl.* **a'nus·es** or **a'ni'** (-nī') [L] the opening at the lower end of the alimentary canal

an·vil (an'vəl) *n.* [< OE *anfilt*] 1 an iron or steel block on which metal objects are hammered into shape 2 one of three small bones in the middle ear

anx·i·e·ty (aŋ zī'ə tē) *n., pl.* **-ties** [see fol.] 1 worry or uneasiness about what may happen 2 an eager but uneasy desire [*anxiety* to do well]

anx·ious (aŋk'shəs) *adj.* [< L *angere*, to choke] 1 worried 2 causing anxiety 3 eagerly wishing —**anx'ious·ly** *adv.*

an·y (en'ē) *adj.* [OE *ænig*] 1 one, no matter which, of more than two [*any* boy may go] 2 some [has he *any* pain?] 3 without limit [*any* number can play] 4 even one or the least amount of [I haven't *any* dimes] 5 every [*any* child can do it] —*pron.* (*sing. & pl.*) any one or ones —*adv.* to any degree or extent; at all [is he *any* better today?]

an·y·bod·y (-bäd'ē, -bud'ē) *pron.* any person

an·y·how *adv.* ANYWAY

an·y·more *adv.* now; nowadays

an·y·one *pron.* any person; anybody

an·y·place *adv.* [Inf.] in, at, or to any place

an·y·thing *pron.* any object, event, fact, etc. —*n.* a thing, no matter of what kind —*adv.* in any way —**anything but** not at all

an·y·time *adv.* at any time —*conj.* WHENEVER

an·y·way *adv.* 1 in any manner 2 nevertheless; anyhow 3 haphazardly

an·y·where *adv.* 1 in, at, or to any place 2 [Inf.] at all

A/o or **a/o** *abbrev.* account of

A-OK (ā'ō kā') *adj.* [A(LL) OK] [Inf.] excellent, fine, in working order, etc.: also **A'-O·kay'**

A one (ā' wun') [Inf.] first-class: also **A 1** or **A number 1**

a·or·ta (ā ôr'tə) *n., pl.* **-tas** or **-tae** (-tē) [< Gr *aeirein*, to raise] the main artery of the body, carrying blood from the heart —**a·or'tic** *adj.*, **a·or'tal**

AP *abbrev.* Associated Press

a·pace (ə pās') *adv.* at a fast pace

A·pach·e (ə pach'ē) *n., pl.* **-es** or **-e** [AmSp] a member of a group of North American Indians of the SW U.S.

a·part (ə pärt') *adv.* [< L *ad*, to, at + *pars*, part] 1 aside 2 away in place or time 3 in or to pieces —*adj.* separated —**apart from** other than —**tell apart** to distinguish between or among

a·part·heid (ə pär'tāt', -tīt') *n.* [Afrik., separateness] the official policy of racial segregation as practiced in South Africa, *c.* 1950-91

a·part·ment *n.* [< It *appartare*, to separate] a room or suite of rooms to live in, esp. one of a number in an **apartment building** (or **house**)

ap·a·thy (ap'ə thē) *n., pl.* **-thies** [< Gr *a-*, without + *pathos*, emotion] 1 lack of emotion 2 lack of interest; indifference; listlessness —**ap'a·thet'ic** (-thet'ik) *adj.* —**ap'a·thet'i·cal·ly** *adv.*

a·pa·tite (ap'ə tīt') *n.* [< Ger < Gr *apatē*, deceit] a mineral incorporating calcium phosphate and found in rocks, bones, and teeth

a·pat·o·saur·us (ə pat'ə sôr'əs) *n.* a huge, plant-eating dinosaur

APB (ā'pē'bē') *n.* all-points bulletin

ape (āp) *n.* [< OE *apa*] 1 any gibbon or great ape 2 loosely, any monkey 3 a mimic 4 a person who is uncouth, clumsy, etc. —*vt.* **aped, ap'ing** to mimic —**ape'like'** *adj.*

Ap·en·nines (ap'ə nīnz') mountain range of central Italy

a·pe·ri·tif (ə per'ə tēf') *n.* [Fr] an alcoholic drink taken before a meal

ap·er·ture (ap'ər chər) *n.* [< L *aperire*, to open] an opening; hole

a·pex (ā'peks') *n., pl.* **a'pex·es** or **ap·i·ces** (ap'ə sēz') [L] 1 the highest point 2 the pointed end; tip 3 the climax

a·pha·sia (ə fā'zhə) *n.* [Gr < *a-*, not + *phanai*, to say] loss of the power to use or understand words —**a·pha'sic** (-zik) *adj., n.*

a·phe·li·on (ə fē'lē ən) *n., pl.* **-li·ons** or **-li·a** (-ə) [< Gr *apo-*, from + *hēlios*, sun] the point farthest from the sun in the orbit of a planet or comet, or of a man-made satellite

a·phid (ā'fid, af'id) *n.* [< ModL *aphis*] an insect that lives on plants by sucking their juices

aph·o·rism (af'ə riz'əm) *n.* [< Gr *apo-*, from + *horizein*, to bound] a concise statement of a general truth; maxim; adage —**aph'o·ris'tic** *adj.* —**aph'o·ris'ti·cal·ly** *adv.*

aph·ro·di·si·ac (af'rə dē'zē ak') *adj.* 〖ult. after fol.〗 arousing or increasing sexual desire —*n.* an aphrodisiac drug, etc.

Aph·ro·di·te (af'rə dīt'ē) *n.* the Greek goddess of love and beauty

a·pi·ar·y (ā'pē er'ē) *n., pl.* **-ar'ies** 〖< L *apis*, bee〗 a place where bees are kept —**a'pi·a·rist** (-ə rist) *n.*

a·piece (ə pēs') *adv.* 〖ME *a pece*〗 for each one; each

a·plen·ty (ə plen'tē) *adj., adv.* [Inf.] in abundance

a·plomb (ə pläm', -plum') *n.* 〖Fr: see PLUMB〗 self-possession; poise

a·poc·a·lypse (ə päk'ə lips') *n.* 〖< Gr *apo-kalyptein*, disclose〗 **1** a revelation, esp. of a violent struggle in which evil will be destroyed **2** a disastrous event, esp. the end of the world **3** [A-] *Bible* the book of Revelation —**a·poc'a·lyp'tic** (-lip'tik) *adj.*

A·poc·ry·pha (ə päk'rə fə) *pl.n.* 〖< Gr *apo-*, away + *kryptein*, to hide〗 fourteen books of the Septuagint considered non-canonical in Judaism and Protestantism

a·poc·ry·phal (-fəl) *adj.* **1** of doubtful authenticity **2** not genuine; spurious

ap·o·gee (ap'ə jē') *n.* 〖< Gr *apo-*, from + *gē*, earth〗 the point farthest from the earth in the orbit of the moon or a satellite

a·po·lit·i·cal (ā'pə lit'i kəl) *adj.* not concerned with political matters —**a'po·lit'i·cal·ly** *adv.*

A·pol·lo (ə päl'ō) *n.* **1** the Greek and Roman god of music, poetry, prophecy, and medicine **2** *pl.* **-los** a handsome young man

a·pol·o·get·ic (ə päl'ə jet'ik) *adj.* showing regret; making an apology —**a·pol'o·get'i·cal·ly** *adv.*

a·pol·o·gist (ə päl'ə jist) *n.* one who defends or attempts to justify a doctrine, faith, action, etc.

a·pol·o·gize (-jīz') *vi.* **-gized'**, **-giz'ing** to make an apology —**a·pol'o·giz'er** *n.*

a·pol·o·gy (ə päl'ə jē) *n., pl.* **-gies** 〖< Gr *apo-*, from + *logos*, speech〗 **1** a formal defense of some idea, doctrine, etc.: also **ap·o·lo·gi·a** (ap'ə lō'jē ə) **2** an expression of regret for a fault, insult, etc.

ap·o·plec·tic (ap'ə plek'tik) *adj.* extremely angry

ap·o·plex·y (ap'ə plek'sē) *n.* 〖< Gr *apo-*, from + *plessein*, to strike〗 [Old-fashioned] STROKE (*n.* 3)

a·pos·ta·sy (ə päs'tə sē) *n., pl.* **-sies** 〖< Gr *apo-*, away + *stasis*, a standing〗 an abandoning of what one has believed in, as a faith or cause

a·pos·tate (-tāt') *n.* a person guilty of apostasy

a·pos·ta·tize (-tə tīz') *vi.* **-tized'**, **-tiz'ing** to become an apostate

a pos·te·ri·o·ri (ā' päs tir'ē ôr'ī') [L] **1** from effect to cause **2** based on observation or experience

a·pos·tle (ə päs'əl) *n.* 〖< Gr *apo-*, from + *stel-lein*, send〗 **1** [*usually* A-] any of the disciples of Jesus, esp. the original twelve **2** the leader of a new movement

ap·os·tol·ic (ap'əs täl'ik) *adj.* **1** of the Apos-

---

tles or their teachings, work, etc. **2** [*often* A-] of the pope; papal

a·pos·tro·phe (ə päs'trə fē) *n.* 〖< Gr *apo-*, from + *strephein*, to turn〗 **1** a mark (') indicating: *a)* omission of a letter or letters from a word (Ex.: *it's* for *it is*) *b)* the possessive case (Ex.: *Mary's* dress) *c)* certain plural forms (Ex.: five 6's, dot the *i*'s) **2** an exclamatory address to a person or thing

a·poth·e·car·y (ə päth'ə ker'ē) *n., pl.* **-ies** 〖< Gr *apothēkē*, storehouse〗 [Old-fashioned] a pharmacist or druggist

ap·o·thegm (ap'ə them') *n.* 〖< Gr *apo-*, from + *phthengesthai*, to utter〗 a short, pithy saying

a·poth·e·o·sis (ə päth'ē ō'sis, ap'ə thē'ə sis) *n., pl.* **-ses'** (-sēz') 〖< Gr *apo-*, from + *theos*, god〗 **1** the deifying of a person **2** the glorification of a person or thing **3** a glorified ideal

app (ap) *n.* a computer application

Ap·pa·la·chi·a (ap'ə lā'chə, -chē ə; -lach'ə) the highland region of the E U.S. extending from SW Pennsylvania through N Alabama

Ap·pa·la·chi·an Mountains mountain system extending from Newfoundland to N Alabama: also **Appalachians**

ap·pall or **ap·pal** (ə pôl') *vt.* **-palled'**, **-pall'ing** 〖ult. < L *ad*, to + *pallere*, to be pale〗 to horrify, dismay, or shock

ap·pa·loo·sa (ap'ə lōō'sə) *n.* 〖after *Palouse* Indians of NW U.S.〗 a Western saddle horse with black and white spots on the rump and loins

ap·pa·ra·tus (ap'ə rat'əs, -rāt'-) *n., pl.* **-tus** or **-tus·es** 〖< L *ad-*, to + *parare*, prepare〗 **1** the instruments, materials, tools, etc. for a specific use **2** any complex device, machine, or system

ap·par·el (ə per'əl) *n.* 〖ult. < L *ad-*, to + *parare*, prepare〗 clothing; attire —*vt.* **-eled** or **-elled**, **-el·ing** or **-el·ling** to clothe; dress

ap·par·ent (ə per'ənt) *adj.* 〖see APPEAR〗 **1** readily seen; visible **2** evident; obvious **3** appearing real or true —**ap·par'ent·ly** *adv.*

ap·pa·ri·tion (ap'ə rish'ən) *n.* 〖see APPEAR〗 **1** anything that appears unexpectedly or in a strange way **2** a ghost; phantom

ap·peal (ə pēl') *vt.* 〖< L *ad-*, to + *pellere*, to drive〗 to make an appeal of (a case) —*vi.* **1** to appeal a law case to a higher court **2** to make an urgent request (*to a person for* help, etc.) **3** to be attractive or interesting —*n.* **1** a call upon some authority for a decision **2** a request for the transference of a case to a higher court for rehearing **3** a request for help, etc. **4** a quality that arouses interest, desire, etc. —**ap·peal'ing** *adj.*

ap·pear (ə pir') *vi.* 〖< L *ad-*, to + *perere*, be visible〗 **1** to come into sight **2** to come into being **3** to become understood or obvious **4** to seem; look **5** to present oneself formally in court **6** to come before the public

ap·pear·ance *n.* **1** an appearing **2** the look or outward aspect of a person or thing **3** an outward show; pretense —**keep up appearances** to maintain an outward show of being proper, prosperous, etc.

ap·pease (ə pēz′) *vt.* **-peased′, -peas′ing**
⟦ult. < L *ad*, to + *pax*, peace⟧ to pacify, quiet,
or satisfy, esp. by giving in to the demands of
—**ap·pease′ment** *n.* —**ap·peas′er** *n.*

ap·pel·lant (ə pel′ənt) *n.* a person who appeals to a higher court

ap·pel·late (-it) *adj. Law* having to do with
appeals [an *appellate* court]

ap·pel·la·tion (ap′ə lā′shən) *n.* ⟦see AP-
PEAL⟧ **1** a naming **2** a name or title

ap·pend (ə pend′) *vt.* ⟦< L *ad-*, to + *pendere*,
hang⟧ to attach or affix; add as a supplement
or appendix

ap·pend·age *n.* **1** anything appended **2** any
external organ or part, as a tail

ap·pen·dec·to·my (ap′ən dek′tə mē) *n., pl.*
-mies ⟦see -ECTOMY⟧ the surgical removal
of the appendix

ap·pen·di·ci·tis (ə pen′də sīt′is) *n.* ⟦see -ITIS⟧
inflammation of the appendix

ap·pen·dix (ə pen′diks) *n., pl.* **-dix·es** or **-di-
ces′** (-də sēz′) ⟦L, appendage⟧ **1** additional
material at the end of a book **2** a small,
saclike appendage of the large intestine

ap·per·tain (ap′ər tān′) *vi.* ⟦< L *ad-*, to + *per-
tinere*, to reach⟧ to belong as a function, part,
etc.; pertain

ap·pe·ten·cy (ap′ə tən sē) *n., pl.* **-cies** ⟦see
fol.⟧ a craving; appetite

ap·pe·tite (ap′ə tīt′) *n.* ⟦< L *ad-*, to + *petere*,
to desire⟧ **1** a desire for food **2** any strong
desire or craving

ap·pe·tiz·er (-tī′zər) *n.* a small portion of a
tasty food served at the beginning of a meal

ap·pe·tiz·ing (-tī′ziŋ) *adj.* **1** stimulating the
appetite **2** savory; delicious

ap·plaud (ə plôd′) *vt., vi.* ⟦< L *ad-*, to + *plaudere*, clap hands⟧ **1** to show approval (of) by
clapping the hands, etc. **2** to approve —**ap·
plaud′er** *n.*

ap·plause (ə plôz′) *n.* approval, esp. as shown
by clapping hands

ap·ple (ap′əl) *n.* ⟦< OE *æppel*, fruit, apple⟧ **1** a
firm, round, edible fruit **2** the tree it grows on

apple butter a thick, sweet spread made from
apples stewed with spices

ap·ple·jack *n.* brandy distilled from fermented
cider

ap·ple-pie *adj.* [Inf.] **1** neat and tidy [*apple-
pie* order] **2** suggesting wholesomeness

ap·ple·sauce *n.* a dessert or relish of apples
cooked to a pulp in water

ap·pli·ance (ə plī′əns) *n.* a device or machine,
esp. one for household use

ap·pli·ca·ble (ap′li kə bəl) *adj.* that can be applied; appropriate —**ap′pli·ca·bil′i·ty** (-bil′
ə tē) *n.*

ap·pli·cant (-kənt) *n.* one who applies, as for
employment or help

ap·pli·ca·tion (ap′li kā′shən) *n.* **1** an applying **2** anything applied, as a remedy **3** a specific use **4** a request, or a form filled out in
making one [an employment *application*] **5**
continued effort; diligence **6** relevance or
practicality **7** a computer program for performing a specific task

ap·pli·ca·tor (ap′li kāt′ər) *n.* any device for
applying medicine, paint, polish, etc.

ap·plied (ə plīd′) *adj.* used in actual practice
[*applied* science]

ap·pli·qué (ap′li kā′) *n.* ⟦Fr⟧ a decoration
made of one material attached to another
—*vt.* **-quéd′, -qué′ing** to decorate with ap-
pliqué

ap·ply (ə plī′) *vt.* **-plied′, -ply′ing** ⟦< L *ad-*, to
+ *plicare*, to fold⟧ **1** to put or spread on [*apply* glue] **2** to put to practical or specific use
[*apply* your knowledge] **3** to devote (oneself
or one's faculties) diligently —*vi.* **1** to make
a formal request **2** to be suitable or relevant
—**ap·pli′er** *n.*

ap·point (ə point′) *vt.* ⟦< L *ad*, to + *punctum*, a
point⟧ **1** to set (a date, place, etc.) **2** to name
for an office, position, etc. **3** to furnish [*well-
appointed*] —**ap·point′ee′** *n.*

ap·point·ive *adj.* of or filled by appointment
[an *appointive* office]

ap·point·ment *n.* **1** an appointing or being appointed **2** a position filled by appointing **3** an
arrangement to meet someone or be some-
where **4** [*pl.*] furniture; equipment

Ap·po·mat·tox Court House (ap′ə mat′əks)
village in central Virginia, where Lee surren-
dered to Grant (1865)

ap·por·tion (ə pôr′shən) *vt.* ⟦see AD- &
PORTION⟧ to distribute in shares according to
a plan —**ap·por′tion·ment** *n.*

ap·pose (ə pōz′) *vt.* **-posed′, -pos′ing** ⟦< L
ad-, to + *ponere*, put⟧ to put side by side or
opposite

ap·po·site (ap′ə zit) *adj.* ⟦see prec.⟧ appropriate; apt —**ap′po·site·ly** *adv.* —**ap′po·site·
ness** *n.*

ap·po·si·tion (ap′ə zish′ən) *n.* **1** an apposing,
or the position resulting from this **2** *Gram.*
the position of a word or phrase beside another in explanation ["my niece" is in *apposi-
tion* to "Jill" in "Jill, my niece, is here"] —**ap·
pos′i·tive** (ə päz′ə tiv) *adj., n.*

ap·prais·al (ə prāz′əl) *n.* **1** an appraising **2** an
appraised value

ap·praise (ə prāz′) *vt.* **-praised′, -prais′ing**
⟦< L *ad*, to + *pretium*, price⟧ **1** to set a price
for; estimate the value of **2** to judge the quality or worth of —**ap·prais′er** *n.*

ap·pre·ci·a·ble (ə prē′shə bəl, -shē ə-) *adj.*
⟦see prec.⟧ enough to be perceived or estimated; noticeable —**ap·pre′ci·a·bly** *adv.*

ap·pre·ci·ate (ə prē′shē āt′) *vt.* **-at′ed, -at′
ing** ⟦see APPRAISE⟧ **1** to think well of; esteem **2** to recognize gratefully **3** to estimate
the quality of **4** to be fully or sensitively aware
of —*vi.* to rise in value —**ap·pre′ci·a′tor** *n.*
—**ap·pre′ci·a·to′ry** (-shə tôr′ē, -shē ə-) *adj.*

ap·pre·ci·a·tion *n.* **1** grateful recognition, as
of a favor **2** sensitive awareness, as of art **3**
a rise in value or price

ap·pre·ci·a·tive (-shə tiv, -shē ə-) *adj.* feeling or showing appreciation —**ap·pre′ci·a·
tive·ly** *adv.*

ap·pre·hend (ap′rē hend′) *vt.* ⟦< L *ad-*, to +
prehendere, take⟧ **1** to capture or arrest **2** to

perceive; understand **3** to fear; dread: now rare in legal usage

ap·pre·hen·sion (-hen′shən) *n.* **1** capture or arrest **2** perception or understanding **3** fear; anxiety

ap·pre·hen·sive (-siv) *adj.* anxious; uneasy —**ap′pre·hen′sive·ly** *adv.* —**ap′pre·hen′sive·ness** *n.*

ap·pren·tice (ə pren′tis) *n.* ⟦see APPRE-HEND⟧ **1** a person being taught a craft or trade, now usually as a member of a labor union **2** any beginner —*vt.* **-ticed, -tic·ing** to place or accept as an apprentice —**ap·pren′tice·ship′** *n.*

ap·prise or **ap·prize** (ə prīz′) *vt.* **-prised′** or **-prized′, -pris′ing** or **-priz′ing** ⟦see APPREHEND⟧ to inform or notify

ap·proach (ə prōch′) *vi.* ⟦< L *ad-*, to + *propius*, nearer⟧ to come closer —*vt.* **1** to come nearer to **2** to approximate **3** to make a proposal or request to **4** to begin dealing with —*n.* **1** a coming closer **2** an approximation **3** an overture (*to* someone): *usually used in pl.* **4** a means of reaching a person or place, access **5** a means of attaining a goal —**ap·proach′a·ble** *adj.*

ap·pro·ba·tion (ap′rə bā′shən) *n.* ⟦see APPROVE⟧ approval

ap·pro·pri·ate (ə prō′prē āt′; *for adj.,* -it) *vt.* **-at′ed, -at′ing** ⟦< L *ad-*, to + *proprius*, one's own⟧ **1** to take for one's own use, often improperly **2** to set aside (money, etc.) for a specific use —*adj.* suitable; fit; proper —**ap·pro′pri·ate·ly** *adv.* —**ap·pro′pri·ate·ness** *n.* —**ap·pro′pri·a′tor** *n.*

ap·pro·pri·a·tion *n.* **1** an appropriating or being appropriated **2** money set aside for a specific use

ap·prov·al (ə prōō′vəl) *n.* **1** the act of approving **2** favorable attitude or opinion **3** formal consent —**on approval** for the customer to examine and decide whether to buy or return

ap·prove (ə prōōv′) *vt.* **-proved′, -prov′ing** ⟦< L *ad-*, to + *probare*, test⟧ **1** to give one's consent to **2** to consider to be good, satisfactory, etc. —*vi.* to have a favorable opinion (*of*) —**ap·prov′ing·ly** *adv.*

ap·prox·i·mate (ə präk′sə mit; *for v.,* -māt′) *adj.* ⟦< L *ad-*, to + *proximus*, nearest⟧ **1** much like; resembling **2** more or less correct or exact —*vt.* **-mat′ed, -mat′ing** to come near to; be almost the same as —**ap·prox′i·mate·ly** *adv.*

ap·prox·i·ma·tion *n.* a calculation or assessment that is only meant to be approximately correct

ap·pur·te·nance (ə purt′'n əns) *n.* ⟦see APPERTAIN⟧ **1** anything added to a more important thing **2** [*pl.*] apparatus or equipment **3** *Law* an incidental right attached to some thing

APR *abbrev.* annual percentage rate

ap·ri·cot (ap′ri kät′, ā′pri–) *n.* ⟦Fr *abricot* < L *praecoquum*, early matured (fruit)⟧ **1** a small, yellowish-orange, peachlike fruit **2** the tree it grows on

A·pril (ā′prəl) *n.* ⟦< L⟧ the fourth month of the year, having 30 days: abbrev. **Apr**

a pri·o·ri (ā′ prī ôr′ī) ⟦L⟧ **1** from cause to effect; deductive or deductively **2** based on theory, logic, etc. instead of experience

a·pron (ā′prən) *n.* ⟦< L *mappa*, napkin⟧ **1** a garment worn over the front part of the body to protect one's clothes **2** any extending or protecting part **3** a paved area, as where a driveway broadens to meet the road **4** the part of a stage in front of the proscenium arch

ap·ro·pos (ap′rə pō′) *adv.* ⟦Fr *à propos*, to the purpose⟧ at the right time; opportunely —*adj.* relevant; apt —*prep.* with regard to —**apropos of** with regard to

apse (aps) *n.* ⟦L *apsis*, an arch⟧ a semicircular or polygonal projection of a church, usually domed or vaulted

apt¹ (apt) *adj.* ⟦< L *aptus*⟧ **1** appropriate; fitting [an *apt* remark] **2** tending or inclined; likely [*apt* to rain] **3** quick to learn —**apt′ly** *adv.* —**apt′ness** *n.*

apt² *abbrev.* apartment

ap·ti·tude (ap′rə tōōd′) *n.* ⟦see APT¹⟧ **1** a natural tendency **2** a natural ability or talent **3** quickness to learn

aq·ua (äk′wə, ak′–) *n., pl.* **-uas** or **-uae′** (-wē′) ⟦L⟧ water —*adj.* ⟦< AQUAMARINE⟧ bluish-green

aqua·cul·ture *n.* ⟦prec. + CULTURE⟧ the cultivation of water plants and animals for human use

aq·ua·ma·rine *n.* ⟦L *aqua marina*, sea water⟧ bluish green —*adj.* bluish-green

aq·ua·naut (-nôt′) *n.* ⟦AQUA + (ASTRO)NAUT⟧ one trained to use a watertight underwater chamber as a base for undersea experiments

aq·ua·plane *n.* ⟦AQUA + PLANE¹⟧ a board on which one rides standing up as it is pulled by a motorboat —*vi.* **-planed′, -plan′ing** to ride on such a board as a sport

a·quar·i·um (ə kwer′ē əm) *n., pl.* **-i·ums** or **-i·a** (-ə) ⟦< L *aquarius*, of water⟧ **1** a tank, etc. for keeping live water animals and plants **2** a building where such collections are exhibited

A·quar·i·us (-əs) *n.* ⟦L, water carrier⟧ the 11th sign of the zodiac

a·quat·ic (ə kwät′ik, -kwat′–) *adj.* **1** growing or living in water **2** done in or upon the water [*aquatic* sports]

aq·ua·vit (äk′wə vēt′, ak′–) *n.* ⟦< L *aqua vitae*, water of life⟧ a Scandinavian alcoholic liquor distilled from grain or potatoes and flavored with caraway

aq·ue·duct (ak′wə dukt′) *n.* ⟦< L *aqua*, water + *ductus*, a leading⟧ **1** a large pipe or conduit for bringing water from a distant source **2** an elevated structure supporting this

a·que·ous (ā′kwē əs, ak′wē–) *adj.* of, like, or formed by water

aqueous humor a watery fluid in the space between the cornea and the lens of the eye

aq·ui·fer (ak′wə fər, ak′–) *n.* ⟦< L *aqua*, water + *ferre*, carry⟧ an underground layer of porous rock, etc. containing water

aq·ui·line (ak′wə līn′, -lin) *adj.* ⟦< L *aquila*,

eagle] 1 of or like an eagle 2 curved like an eagle's beak [an *aquiline* nose]

A·qui·nas (ə kwī'nəs), Saint **Thom·as** (täm'əs) (1225?-74); It. theologian & philosopher

Ar *abbrev. Chem. symbol for* argon

AR *abbrev.* Arkansas

Ar·ab (ar'əb, er'-) *n.* 1 a person born or living in Arabia 2 a member of a Semitic people orig. living in Arabia, now throughout the Middle East and northern Africa

ar·a·besque (ar'ə besk', er'-) *n.* [< It *Arabo*, Arab] an elaborate design consisting of intertwined lines suggesting flowers, foliage, etc.

A·ra·bi·a (ə rā'bē ə) peninsula in SW Asia —**A·ra'bi·an** *adj., n.*

Arabian camel DROMEDARY

Arabian Nights, The a collection of tales from Arabia, India, Persia, etc.

Arabian Peninsula ARABIA

Ar·a·bic (ar'ə bik, er'-) *adj.* 1 of Arabia 2 of the Arabs or their language or culture —*n.* the Semitic language of the Arabs, spoken in Arabia, Syria, N Africa, etc.

Arabic numerals the figures 1, 2, 3, 4, 5, 6, 7, 8, 9, and the 0 (zero)

ar·a·ble (ar'ə bəl, er'-) *adj.* [< L *arare*, to plow] suitable for plowing and farming

a·rach·nid (ə rak'nid) *n.* [< Gr *arachnē*, spider] any of a class of arthropods with four pairs of legs, including spiders and scorpions

Ar·a·ma·ic (ar'ə mā'ik, er'-) *n.* a Semitic language spoken during the latter biblical times

ar·bi·ter (är'bət ər) *n.* [L, a witness or judge] an arbitrator; judge

ar·bi·trage (är'bə träzh') *n.* the simultaneous purchase and sale, as of stock, in two financial markets to profit from a price difference

ar·bit·ra·ment (är bit'rə mənt) *n.* 1 arbitration 2 an arbitrator's verdict or award

ar·bi·trar·y (är'bə trer'ē) *adj.* [see ARBITER] 1 left to one's judgment 2 based on one's preference or whim; capricious 3 absolute; despotic —**ar'bi·trar'i·ly** *adv.*

ar·bi·trate (-trāt') *vt., vi.* -trat'ed, -trat'ing [see ARBITER] 1 to submit (a dispute) to an arbitrator 2 to decide (a dispute) as an arbitrator —**ar'bi·tra'tion** *n.*

ar·bi·tra·tor *n.* a person selected to judge a dispute, as in collective bargaining

ar·bor (är'bər) *n.* [< L *herba*, grass, herb] a place shaded by trees or shrubs or by vines on a latticework; bower

ar·bo·re·al (är bôr'ē əl) *adj.* [< L *arbor*, tree] 1 of or like a tree 2 living in trees

ar·bo·re·tum (är'bə rēt'əm) *n., pl.* -tums or -ta (-ə) [L] a place where many kinds of trees and shrubs are grown for exhibition or study

ar·bor·vi·tae (är'bər vīt'ē) *n.* [L, tree of life] any of various cypress trees having sprays of scalelike leaves

ar·bu·tus (är byoot'əs) *n.* [L] 1 a tree or shrub with dark-green leaves and strawberry-like fruit 2 a trailing plant with white or pink flower clusters

arc (ärk) *n.* [< L *arcus*, a bow, arch] 1 a bow-like curved line or object 2 the band of incandescent light formed when a current leaps a short gap between electrodes 3 any part of a curve, esp. of a circle —*vi.* arced, arc'ing to move in a curved course or form an arc

ar·cade (är käd') *n.* [see prec.] 1 a covered passageway, esp. one lined with shops 2 a penny arcade or a similar place with coin-operated video games 3 a line of arches and their supporting columns

ar·cane (är kān') *adj.* [< L *arcanus*, hidden] secret or esoteric

arch¹ (ärch) *n.* [see ARC] 1 a curved structure used as a support over an open space, as in a doorway 2 the form of an arch 3 anything shaped like an arch —*vt.* to span with or as an arch —*vi.* to form an arch

arch² (ärch) *adj.* [< ARCH-] 1 chief; principal 2 playfully mischievous; pert [an *arch* look]

Arch or **arch** *abbrev.* 1 archaic 2 architecture

arch- [< Gr *archos*, first, ruler] *prefix* main, principal [*archenemy*]

-arch (ärk) [see prec.] *suffix* ruler [*matriarch*]

ar·chae·ol·o·gy (är'kē äl'ə jē) *n.* [< Gr *archaios*, ancient + -LOGY] the study of the life of ancient peoples, as by excavation of ancient cities or artifacts: also sp. **ar'che·ol'o·gy** —**ar'chae·o·log'i·cal** (-ə läj'i kəl) *adj.* —**ar'chae·o·log'i·cal·ly** *adv.* —**ar'chae·ol'o·gist** *n.*

ar·cha·ic (är kā'ik) *adj.* [< Gr *archaios*, ancient] 1 ancient 2 old-fashioned 3 no longer used except in poetry, church ritual, etc.: said as of the word *thou* —**ar·cha'i·cal·ly** *adv.*

ar·cha·ism (är'kā iz'əm) *n.* an archaic word, usage, style, etc. —**ar'cha·is'tic** *adj.*

arch·an·gel (ärk'ān'jəl) *n.* an angel of high rank

arch·bish·op (ärch'-) *n.* a bishop of the highest rank

arch·dea·con *n.* a church official ranking just below a bishop

arch·di·o·cese *n.* the diocese of an archbishop —**arch'di·oc'e·san** *adj.*

arch·duke *n.* a sovereign prince, esp. of the former Austrian imperial family

arch·en·e·my *n., pl.* -mies a chief enemy —**the archenemy** Satan

arch·er (är'chər) *n.* [< L *arcus*, bow] one who shoots with bow and arrow

arch·er·y *n.* the sport of shooting with bow and arrow

ar·che·type (är'kə tīp') *n.* [< Gr *archos*, first + *typos*, a mark] 1 an original pattern or model; prototype 2 a perfect example of a type or group —**ar'che·typ'al** (-tīp'əl) *adj.*, **ar'che·typ'i·cal** (-tīp'i kəl)

ar·chi·e·pis·co·pal (är'kē ē pis'kə pəl) *adj.* of or related to an archbishop

Ar·chi·me·des (är'kə mē'dēz') 287?-212 B.C.; Gr. mathematician & inventor

ar·chi·pel·a·go (är'kə pel'ə gō') *n., pl.* -goes' or -gos' [< Gr *archi-*, chief + *pelagos*, sea] 1 a portion of a body of water having many islands 2 a group of many islands

ar·chi·tect (är′kə tekt′) *n.* 〚< Gr *archi-*, chief + *tektōn*, carpenter〛 **1** one who designs buildings and supervises their construction **2** any designer or planner

ar·chi·tec·ton·ics (är′kə tek tän′iks) *pl.n.* [*usually with sing. v.*] **1** the science of architecture **2** structural design, as of a symphony —**ar′chi·tec·ton′ic** *adj.*

ar·chi·tec·ture (är′kə tek′chər) *n.* **1** the science or profession of designing and constructing buildings **2** a style of construction **3** design and construction —**ar′chi·tec′tur·al** *adj.* —**ar′chi·tec′tur·al·ly** *adv.*

ar·chi·trave (är′kə trāv′) *n.* 〚< L *archi-*, first + *trabs*, a beam〛 in a classical building, the beam resting directly on the tops of the columns

ar·chive (är′kīv′) *n.* 〚< Gr *archeion*, town hall〛 [*usually pl.*] **1** a place for keeping public records, documentary material, etc. **2** the records, material, etc. kept there —*vt.* **-chived′, -chiv′ing** to keep in or as in archives —**ar·chi·vist** (är′kə vist, -kī′-) *n.*

arch·way (ärch′wā′) *n.* a passage under an arch, or the arch itself

-ar·chy (är kē) 〚< Gr *archein*, to rule〛 *combining form* rule, government [*monarchy*]

arc·tic (ärk′tik, är′-) *adj.* 〚< Gr *arktikos*, northern〛 **1** of or near the North Pole **2** very cold —**the Arctic** the region around the North Pole

Arctic Circle [*also* **a- c-**] an imaginary circle parallel to the equator, c. 66°34′ north of it

Arctic Ocean ocean surrounding the North Pole

-ard (ərd) 〚< MHG *hart*, bold〛 *suffix* one who does something to excess [*drunkard*]

ar·dent (är′dənt) *adj.* 〚< L *ardere*, to burn〛 **1** passionate **2** zealous **3** glowing or burning —**ar′dent·ly** *adv.*

ar·dor (är′dər) *n.* 〚< L *ardor*, a flame〛 **1** emotional warmth; passion **2** zeal **3** intense heat Also, Brit. sp., **ar′dour**

ar·du·ous (är′jōō əs) *adj.* 〚L *arduus*, steep〛 **1** difficult to do; laborious **2** using much energy; strenuous —**ar′du·ous·ly** *adv.*

are (är) *vi.* 〚OE *aron*〛 *pl. & 2d pers. sing., pres. indic., of* BE

ar·e·a (er′ē ə) *n.* 〚L, vacant place〛 **1** a part of the earth's surface; region **2** the measure, in square units, of a surface **3** a location having a specific use or character [*play area*] **4** scope or extent

area code a three-digit telephone code assigned to a specific area of the U.S., Canada, etc.

a·re·na (ə rē′nə) *n.* 〚L, sandy place〛 **1** a place or building for contests, shows, etc. **2** any sphere of struggle [*political arena*]

arena theater a theater having a central stage surrounded by seats

aren't (ärnt) *contr.* are not

Ar·es (er′ēz′) *n. Gr. Myth.* the god of war

ar·gent (är′jənt) *adj.* 〚L *argentum*, silver〛 [Old Poet.] silvery

Ar·gen·ti·na (är′jən tē′nə) country in S South America —**Ar′gen·tine′** (-tēn′, -tīn′) *adj., n.,* **Ar′gen·tin′i·an** (-tin′ē ən)

ar·gon (är′gän′) *n.* 〚Gr, inert〛 a chemical element, a nonreactive gas found in the air and used in light bulbs, electron tubes, etc.: symbol, Ar; at. no. 18

Ar·go·naut (är′gə nôt′) *n. Gr. Myth.* any of those who sail with Jason to search for the Golden Fleece

ar·go·sy (är′gə sē) *n., pl.* **-sies** 〚after *Ragusa,* It name of Dubrovnik in Croatia〛 [Old Poet.] a large merchant ship or a fleet of such ships

ar·got (är′gō, -gət) *n.* 〚Fr〛 the specialized vocabulary of a particular group, as of criminals

ar·gue (är′gyōō) *vi.* **-gued, -gu·ing** 〚< L *arguere*, prove〛 **1** to give reasons (*for* or *against*) **2** to quarrel; dispute —*vt.* **1** to discuss; debate **2** to maintain; contend **3** to persuade by giving reasons —**ar′gu·a·ble** *adj.*

ar·gu·ment (är′gyōō mənt) *n.* **1** a reason or reasons offered in arguing **2** an arguing; debate **3** a summary

ar·gu·men·ta·tion (-men tā′shən) *n.* the process of arguing, debate

ar·gu·men·ta·tive (-men′tə tiv) *adj.* **1** controversial **2** apt to argue; contentious Also **ar′gu·men′tive**

ar·gyle (är′gīl′) *adj.* 〚after *Argyll,* Scotland〛 knitted or woven in a diamond-shaped pattern [*argyle* socks]

a·ri·a (ä′rē ə) *n.* 〚It < L, *aer*, air〛 a song, as in an opera, for solo voice

-ar·i·an (er′ē ən) 〚< L〛 *suffix* **1** (one) characterized by [*octogenarian*] **2** (one) believing in or associated with [*Unitarian*]

ar·id (ar′id) *adj.* 〚< L *arere*, be dry〛 **1** dry and barren **2** uninteresting; dull —**a·rid·i·ty** (ə rid′ə tē) *n.*

Ar·i·es (er′ēz′) *n.* 〚L, ram (male sheep)〛 the first sign of the zodiac

a·right (ə rīt′) *adv.* correctly

a·rise (ə rīz′) *vi.* **a·rose′** (-rōz′), **a·ris′en** (-riz′ən), **a·ris′ing** 〚< OE *a-*, out + *risan,* to rise〛 **1** to get up, as from sleeping **2** to ascend **3** to come into being **4** to result (*from*)

ar·is·toc·ra·cy (ar′i stäk′rə sē) *n., pl.* **-cies** 〚< Gr *aristos,* best + *kratos,* to rule〛 **1** government by a privileged minority, usually of inherited wealth **2** a country with such government **3** a privileged ruling class

a·ris·to·crat (ə ris′tə krat′) *n.* **1** a member of the aristocracy **2** one with the tastes, manners, etc. of the upper class —**a·ris′to·crat′ic** *adj.*

Ar·is·toph·a·nes (ar′i stäf′ə nēz′) 450?-388? B.C.; Gr. writer of comedies

Ar·is·tot·le (ar′is tät′′l) 384-322 B.C.; Gr. philosopher —**Ar·is·to·te·li·an** (ar′is tə tēl′yən) *adj., n.*

a·rith·me·tic (ə rith′mə tik) *n.* 〚< Gr *arithmos,* number〛 the science or art of computing by positive, real numbers —**ar·ith·met·ic** (ar′ith met′ik) *adj.,* **ar′ith·met′i·cal** *adj.* —**ar′ith·me·ti′cian** (-mə tish′ən) *n.*

arithmetic mean the average obtained by dividing a sum by the number of its addends

A·ri·zo·na (ar′ə zō′nə) state of the SW U.S.: cap. Phoenix: abbrev. *AZ* —**Ar′i·zo′nan** *adj.,* *n.,* **Ar′i·zo′ni·an**

ark (ärk) *n.* [< L *arcere,* enclose] **1** ARK OF THE COVENANT **2** an enclosure in a synagogue for the scrolls of the Torah **3** *Bible* the boat in which Noah, his family, and two of every kind of creature survived the Flood

Ar·kan·sas (är′kən sô′) state of the SC U.S.: cap. Little Rock: abbrev. *AR* —**Ar·kan′san** (-kan′zən) *adj.,* *n.*

ark of the covenant *Bible* the chest containing the two stone tablets inscribed with the Ten Commandments

Ar·ling·ton (är′liŋ tən) city in NE Texas

arm[1] (ärm) *n.* [OE *earm*] **1** an upper limb of the human body **2** anything like this in shape, function, position, etc. **3** anything connected to something larger [*arm* of the sea] —**with open arms** in a warm and friendly way

arm[2] (ärm) *n.* [< L *arma,* weapons] **1** a weapon: *usually used in pl.* **2** any branch of the military forces —*vt.* to provide with weapons, etc. —*vi.* to prepare for war or any struggle —**under arms** ready for war —**up in arms 1** prepared to fight **2** indignant

ARM (*often* ärm) *abbrev.* adjustable-rate mortgage

ar·ma·da (är mä′də) *n.* [Sp < L *arma,* weapons] **1** a fleet of warships **2** a fleet of military aircraft

ar·ma·dil·lo (är′mə dil′ō) *n., pl.* **-los** [Sp: see prec.] a burrowing mammal of tropical America, covered with bony plates

Ar·ma·ged·don (är′mə ged′′n) *n.* **1** *Bible* the site of the last, decisive battle between the forces of good and evil **2** any great, decisive battle

ar·ma·ment (är′mə mənt) *n.* [< L *armare,* to arm] **1** [*often pl.*] all the military forces and equipment of a nation **2** all the military equipment of a warship, tank, etc. **3** an arming or being armed for war

ar·ma·ture (är′mə chər) *n.* [< L *armare,* to arm] **1** any protective covering **2** the iron core wound with wire in which electromotive force is produced in a generator or motor

arm·chair *n.* a chair with supports at the sides for one's arms

armed forces all the military, naval, and air forces of a country

Ar·me·ni·a (är mēn′yə, -mē′nē ə) country in W Asia —**Ar·me′ni·an** *adj., n.*

arm·ful (ärm′fool) *n., pl.* **-fuls** as much as the arms or one arm can hold

arm·hole *n.* an opening for the arm in a garment

ar·mi·stice (är′mə stis) *n.* [< L *arma,* weapons + *stare,* to stand] a truce preliminary to the signing of a peace treaty

Armistice Day Nov. 11, the anniversary of the armistice of WWI in 1918

arm·let (ärm′lət) *n.* **1** an ornamental band worn around the upper arm **2** a narrow, deep inlet of the sea

arm·load *n.* an armful

ar·mor (är′mər) *n.* [< L *armare,* to arm] any defensive or protective covering — *vt., vi.* to put armor on —**ar′mored** *adj.*

armored car a vehicle covered with armor plate, as a truck for carrying money to or from a bank

ar·mo·ri·al (är môr′ē əl) *adj.* of coats of arms

armor plate a protective covering of steel plates

ar·mor·y (är′mər ē) *n., pl.* **-mor·ies** [see ARMOR] **1** an arsenal **2** a National Guard unit drill hall

arm·pit *n.* the hollow under the arm at the shoulder

arm·rest *n.* a support for the arm, as on the inside of an automobile door

ar·my (är′mē) *n., pl.* **-mies** [ult. < L *arma,* weapons] **1** a large, organized body of soldiers for waging war, esp. on land **2** a large number of persons, animals, etc. [an *army* of ants]

Ar·nold (är′nəld), **Ben·e·dict** (ben′ə dikt′) 1741-1801; Am. Revolutionary general who became a traitor

a·ro·ma (ə rō′mə) *n.* [< Gr *arōma,* spice] a pleasant odor; fragrance

a·ro·ma·ther·a·py *n.* the therapeutic use of aromatic oils from herbs, etc.

ar·o·mat·ic (ar′ə mat′ik) *adj.* of or having an aroma; fragrant or pungent —*n.* an aromatic plant, chemical, etc. —**ar′o·mat′i·cal·ly** *adv.*

a·rose (ə rōz′) *vi. pt. of* ARISE

a·round (ə round′) *adv.* [ME] **1** in a circle **2** in every direction **3** in circumference **4** to the opposite direction **5** [Inf.] nearby [stay *around*] —*prep.* **1** so as to encircle or envelop **2** on the border of **3** in various places in or on **4** about [*around* 1890]

a·rouse (ə rouz′) *vt.* **a·roused′, a·rous′ing 1** to awaken, as from sleep **2** to stir, as to action **3** to evoke [to *arouse* pity] —**a·rous′al** *n.*

ar·peg·gio (är pej′ō) *n., pl.* **-gios** [It < *arpa,* a harp] a chord whose notes are played in quick succession

ar·raign (ə rān′) *vt.* [< L *ad,* to + *ratio,* reason] **1** to bring before a law court to answer charges **2** to call to account; accuse —**ar·raign′ment** *n.*

ar·range (ə rānj′) *vt.* **-ranged′, -rang′ing** [< OFr *a-,* to + *rengier,* to range] **1** to put in the correct order **2** to classify **3** to prepare or plan **4** to arrive at an agreement about **5** *Music* to adapt (a composition) to particular instruments or voices —*vi. Music* to write arrangements, esp. as a profession —**ar·rang′er** *n.*

ar·range·ment *n.* **1** an arranging **2** a result or manner of arranging **3** [*usually pl.*] a plan **4** a settlement **5** *Music a*) an arranging of a composition *b*) the composition as thus arranged

ar·rant (ar′ənt) *adj.* [var. of ERRANT] that is plainly such; out-and-out; notorious

ar·ras (ar′əs) *n.* [after *Arras,* Fr city] a wall hanging, esp. of tapestry

ar·ray (ə rā′) *vt.* [< OFr *areer*] **1** to place in

order **2** to dress in finery —*n.* **1** an orderly grouping, esp. of troops **2** an impressive display **3** fine clothes

ar·rears (ə rirz′) *pl.n.* [< L *ad*, to + *retro*, behind] overdue debts —**in arrears** behind in paying a debt, doing one's work, etc.

ar·rest (ə rest′) *vt.* [< L *ad*-, to + *restare*, to stop] **1** to stop or check **2** to seize by authority of the law **3** to catch and keep (one's attention, etc.) —*n.* an arresting or being arrested —**under arrest** in legal custody

ar·rest·ing *adj.* attracting attention; interesting

ar·rhyth·mi·a (ə rith′mē ə) *n.* [< Gr *a*–, without + *rhythmos*, measure] an irregularity in the heart's rhythm —**ar·rhyth′mic** *adj.*, **ar·rhyth′mi·cal**

ar·riv·al (ə rī′vəl) *n.* **1** an arriving **2** a person or thing that arrives

ar·rive (ə rīv′) *vi.* –**rived′**, –**riv′ing** [< L *ad*-, to + *ripa*, shore] **1** to reach one's destination **2** to come [the time has *arrived*] **3** to attain fame, etc. —**arrive at** to reach by thinking, etc.

ar·ri·ve·der·ci (är rē′ve der′chē) *interj.* [It] goodbye

ar·ro·gant (ar′ə gənt) *adj.* [< L *arrogare*, to claim] full of or due to pride; haughty —**ar′ro·gance** *n.* —**ar′ro·gant·ly** *adv.*

ar·ro·gate (–gāt′) *vt.* –**gat′ed**, –**gat′ing** [< L *ad*-, for + *rogare*, to ask] to claim or seize without right —**ar′ro·ga′tion** *n.*

ar·row (ar′ō) *n.* [OE *arwe*] **1** a pointed shaft for shooting from a bow **2** a sign (←), used to indicate direction

ar·row·head *n.* the separable, pointed tip of an arrow

ar·row·root *n.* [from use as antidote for poisoned arrows] **1** a tropical plant with starchy roots **2** a starch made from its roots

ar·roy·o (ə roi′ō) *n.*, *pl.* –**os** [Sp < L *arrugia*, mine shaft] [Southwest] **1** a dry gully **2** a rivulet or stream

ar·se·nal (är′sə nəl) *n.* [< Ar *dār aṣṣinā′a*, workshop] **1** a place for making or storing weapons **2** a store or collection of things to be used in a conflict or struggle

ar·se·nic (är′sə nik′; *for adj.* är sen′ik) *n.* [< Gr *arsenikon*] a very poisonous chemical element, compounds of which are used in insecticides, etc.: symbol, As; at. no. 33 —*adj.* of or containing arsenic: also **ar·sen′i·cal**

ar·son (är′sən) *n.* [< L *ardere*, to burn] the crime of purposely setting fire to a building or property —**ar′son·ist** *n.*

art[1] (ärt) *n.* [< L *ars*] **1** human creativity **2** skill **3** any specific skill or its application **4** any craft or its principles **5** creative work or its principles **6** any branch of creative work, as painting or sculpture **7** products of this, as paintings or statues **8** *a)* a branch of learning *b)* [*pl.*] LIBERAL ARTS **9** cunning **10** sly trick; wile: *usually used in pl.*

art[2] (ärt) *vi. archaic* 2d *pers. sing., pres. indic., of* BE: used with *thou*

art[3] *abbrev.* **1** article **2** artificial

art dec·o (dek′ō) a decorative style of the late 1920s and the 1930s, derived from cubism

ar·te·ri·al (är tir′ē əl) *adj.* **1** of or in the arteries **2** of a main road

ar·te·ri·ole (är tir′ē ōl′) *n.* [see ARTERY] any of the small blood vessels between the arteries and capillaries

ar·te·ri·o·scle·ro·sis (är tir′ē ō′sklə rō′sis) *n.* [< Gr *artēria*, artery + SCLEROSIS] an abnormal thickening and hardening of the walls of the arteries

ar·ter·y (ärt′ər ē) *n.*, *pl.* –**ter·ies** [< Gr *aeirein*, to lift] **1** any of the blood vessels that carry blood away from the heart **2** a main route

ar·te·sian well (är tē′zhən) [Fr *artésien*, of Artois (in France)] a deep well in which water is forced up by pressure of underground water draining from higher ground

art film a film characterized by artistic sophistication, realism, etc.

art·ful (ärt′fəl) *adj.* **1** skillful or clever **2** cunning; crafty —**art′ful·ly** *adv.* —**art′ful·ness** *n.*

art house a theater that shows art films, etc.

ar·thri·tis (är thrīt′is) *n.* [Gr < *arthron*, joint + –ITIS] inflammation of a joint or joints —**ar·thrit·ic** (är thrit′ik) *adj.*

arthro- [< Gr *arthron*, joint] *combining form* joint, joints

ar·thro·pod (är′thrə päd′) *n.* [prec. + –POD] any of a phylum of invertebrates with jointed legs and a segmented body, including insects, spiders, etc.

ar·thro·scope (–skōp′) *n.* [ARTHRO- + –SCOPE] an endoscope used inside a joint —**ar′thro·scop′ic** (–skäp′ik) *adj.*

Ar·thur[1] (är′thər) *n.* legendary 6th–c. king of Britain —**Ar·thu·ri·an** (är thoor′ē ən) *adj.*

Ar·thur[2] (är′thər), **Ches·ter A(lan)** (ches′tər) 1829–86; 21st president of the U.S. (1881–85)

ar·ti·choke (ärt′ə chōk′) *n.* [ult. < Ar *al-harshaf*] **1** a thistlelike plant **2** its edible flower head

ar·ti·cle (ärt′i kəl) *n.* [< L *artus*, joint] **1** one of the sections of a document **2** a complete piece of writing, as in a newspaper, magazine, etc. **3** a separate item [an *article* of luggage] **4** *Gram.* any one of the words *a, an,* or *the,* used at the start of a noun phrase

ar·tic·u·late (är tik′yōō lit; *for v.,* –lāt′) *adj.* [see prec.] **1** jointed: usually **ar·tic′u·lat′ed 2** made up of distinct sounds, as speech **3** able to speak **4** expressing oneself clearly —*vt.* –**lat′ed**, –**lat′ing 1** to connect by joints **2** to arrange in connected sequence **3** to utter distinctly **4** to express clearly —*vi.* **1** to speak distinctly **2** to be jointed or connected —**ar·tic′u·late·ly** *adv.* —**ar·tic′u·la′tion** *n.*

ar·ti·fact (ärt′ə fakt′) *n.* **1** any object made by human work, esp. one of historical interest **2** a feature accidentally introduced into something being studied

ar·ti·fice (ärt′ə fis) *n.* [< L *ars*, art + *facere*, make] **1** skill or ingenuity **2** trickery **3** an artful trick

ar·tif·i·cer (är tif′ə sər) *n.* **1** a skilled crafts-man **2** an inventor

ar·ti·fi·cial (ärt′ə fish′əl) *adj.* 〖see ARTIFICE〗 **1** made by human work; not natu-ral **2** simulated [*artificial* teeth] **3** affected [an *artificial* smile] —**ar′ti·fi′ci·al′i·ty** (-fish′ē al′ə tē) *n.*, *pl.* **-ties** —**ar′ti·fi′cial·ly** *adv.*

artificial intelligence 1 the capability of computers to learn, solve problems, exhibit creativity, etc. **2** the science dealing with this

artificial respiration the maintenance of breathing by artificial means, as by forcing air into the mouth

ar·til·ler·y (är til′ər ē) *n.* 〖< OFr *atillier*, equip〗 **1** mounted guns, as cannon or mis-sile launchers **2** gunnery —**the artillery** the branch of an army using heavy mounted guns —**ar·til′ler·y·man** (-mən) *n.*, *pl.* **-men** (-mən)

ar·ti·san (ärt′ə zən) *n.* 〖ult. < L *ars*, art〗 a skilled craftsman

art·ist (ärt′ist) *n.* **1** one who is skilled in any of the fine arts **2** one who does anything very well **3** a professional in any of the perform-ing arts

ar·tis·tic (är tis′tik) *adj.* **1** of art or artists **2** done skillfully and tastefully **3** sensitive to beauty —**ar·tis′ti·cal·ly** *adv.*

art·ist·ry (ärt′is trē) *n.* artistic quality, ability, or work

art·less (ärt′lis) *adj.* **1** lacking skill or art **2** simple; natural **3** without guile; ingenuous; innocent —**art′less·ly** *adv.*

Arts and Crafts a movement of the late 1800s and early 1900s that promoted handwork and craftsmanship

art·y (ärt′ē) *adj.* **art′i·er**, **art′i·est** [Inf.] af-fectedly artistic —**art′i·ness** *n.*

ar·um (er′əm) *n.* 〖L〗 any of a family of plants with flowers enveloped within a hoodlike leaf

Ar·y·an (ar′ē ən) *n.* 〖< Sans *āzya-*, noble〗 **1** [Obs.] the hypothetical parent language of the Indo-European family **2** a person sup-posed to be a descendant of the prehistoric peoples that spoke this language: *Aryan* is not a valid ethnological term

as (az) *adv.* 〖< ALSO〗 **1** equally [just *as* happy at home] **2** for instance [a card game, *as* bridge] **3** when related in a speci-fied way [my view *as* contrasted with yours] —*conj.* **1** to the same amount or degree that [straight *as* an arrow] **2** in the same manner that [do *as* you are told] **3** while [she wept *as* she spoke] **4** because [*as* you object, we won't go] **5** that the consequence is [so obvious *as* to need no reply] **6** though [tall *as* he was, he couldn't reach it] —*pron.* **1** a fact that [we are tired, *as* you can see] **2** that: preceded by *such* or *the same* [such books *as* I own] —*prep.* in the role or func-tion of [he poses *as* a friend] —**as for (or to)** concerning — **as if (or though)** as it (or one) would if —**as is** [Inf.] just as it is —**as it were** as if it were so

As *Chem. symbol for* arsenic

ASAP *abbrev.* as soon as possible

as·bes·tos (as bes′təs, az-) *n.* 〖< Gr *a–*, not + *sbennynai*, extinguish〗 a nonconducting, fireproof mineral formerly used in electrical insulation, roofing, etc. but now known to cause lung cancer

as·cend (ə send′) *vi.* 〖< L *ad-*, to + *scandere*, to climb〗 to move upward; rise —*vt.* **1** to move upward along; mount **2** to succeed to (a throne)

as·cend·an·cy or **as·cend·en·cy** (ə sen′dən sē) *n.* a position of control; domination

as·cend·ant or **as·cend·ent** (-dənt) *adj.* **1** rising **2** in control; dominant —**in the ascen-dant** at or approaching the height of power, fame, etc.

as·cen·sion (-shən) *n.* **1** an ascending **2** [A-] the 40th day after Easter, celebrating the Ascension —**the Ascension** *Bible* the bodily ascent of Jesus into heaven 40 days after his resurrection

as·cent (ə sent′) *n.* **1** an ascending **2** an up-ward slope

as·cer·tain (as′ər tān′) *vt.* 〖see AD- & CERTAIN〗 to find out with certainty

as·cet·ic (ə set′ik) *adj.* 〖< Gr *askein*, to train the body〗 self-denying; austere —*n.* 〖< Gr *askētēs*, monk〗 one who leads a life of strict self-denial, esp. for religious purposes —**as·cet′i·cism′** (-ə siz′əm) *n.*

ASCII (as′kē) *n.* a code that facilitates infor-mation exchange among various computers

a·scor·bic acid (ə skôr′bik) 〖A-² + *scorbutic*, of scurvy + -IC〗 vitamin C

as·cot (as′kət, -kät′) *n.* a necktie with very broad ends hanging from the knot

as·cribe (ə skrīb′) *vt.* **-cribed′**, **-crib′ing** 〖< L *ad-*, to + *scribere*, write〗 **1** to assign (something) *to* a supposed cause **2** to regard (something) as belonging *to* or coming from someone —**as·crip·tion** (ə skrip′shən) *n.*

a·sep·tic (ā sep′tik, ə-) *adj.* free from dis-ease-producing bacteria, etc.

a·sex·u·al (ā sek′shōō əl) *adj.* **1** having no sex or sexual organs **2** without the union of male and female germ cells **3** having little or no sexual activity, desire, character, etc. —**a·sex′u·al·ly** *adv.*

ash¹ (ash) *n.* 〖< OE *æsce*〗 **1** the grayish powder left after something has burned **2** fine, volcanic lava **3** the gray color of wood ash See also ASHES

ash² (ash) *n.* 〖< OE *æsc*〗 **1** a shade tree of the olive family **2** its wood

a·shamed (ə shāmd′) *adj.* **1** feeling shame **2** reluctant because fearing shame beforehand —**a·sham·ed·ly** (ə shām′id lē) *adv.*

ash·en (ash′ən) *adj.* **1** of ashes **2** like ashes, esp. in color; pale

ash·es (ash′iz) *pl.n.* **1** the grayish powder and small particles left after a thing has burned **2** human remains left after cremation

a·shore (ə shôr′) *adv., adj.* **1** to or on the shore **2** to or on land

ash·ram (äsh′rəm) *n.* 〖< Sans *ā*, toward + *śrama*, penance〗 a usually secluded Hindu religious community

ash·tray *n.* a container for smokers' tobacco ashes, etc.: also **ash tray**

Ash Wednesday the first day of Lent: from the putting of ashes on the forehead in penitence

ash·y *adj.* **-i·er, -i·est** 1 of or covered with ashes 2 ashen; pale

A·sia (ā′zhə) largest continent, in the Eastern Hemisphere —**A′sian** *adj., n.,* less preferred **A·si·at·ic** (ā′zhē at′ik)

A·si·a·go (cheese) (ä′sē ä′gō) 《after *Asiago,* Italy》 a hard, dry, sharply flavored cheese originally of N Italy: also **asiago (cheese)**

Asia Minor large peninsula of W Asia, in Turkey between the Black Sea and the Mediterranean

a·side (ə sīd′) *adv.* 1 on or to one side 2 in reserve [put one *aside* for me] 3 apart; notwithstanding [joking *aside*] —*n.* words spoken by an actor but supposedly not heard by the other actors —**aside from** 1 with the exception of 2 apart from

as·i·nine (as′ə nīn′) *adj.* 《< L *asinus,* ass》 like an ass; stupid; silly —**as′i·nine′ly** *adv.* —**as′i·nin′i·ty** (-nin′ə tē) *n.*

ask (ask) *vt.* 《OE *āscian*》 1 to use words in seeking the answer to (a question) 2 to inquire of (a person) 3 to request or demand 4 to invite —*vi.* 1 to make a request (*for*) 2 to inquire (*about* or *after*) —**ask′er** *n.*

a·skance (ə skans′) *adv.* 《ME》 1 with a sideways glance 2 with suspicion, disapproval, etc.

a·skew (ə skyōō′) *adv.* to one side; awry —*adj.* on one side; awry

asking price the price asked by a seller, esp. as a basis for bargaining

a·slant (ə slant′) *adv.* on a slant —*prep.* on a slant across —*adj.* slanting

a·sleep (ə slēp′) *adj.* 1 sleeping 2 inactive; dull 3 numb 4 dead —*adv.* into a sleeping condition

a·so·cial (ā sō′shəl) *adj.* 1 avoiding contact with others 2 selfish

asp (asp) *n.* 《< Gr *aspis*》 a poisonous snake of Africa, Arabia, etc.

as·par·a·gus (ə spar′ə gəs, -sper′-) *n.* 《< Gr *asparagos*》 1 a plant of the lily family, with edible shoots 2 these shoots

as·par·tame (as′pər tām′) *n.* an artificial, low-calorie sweetener, used esp. in soft drinks

as·pect (as′pekt′) *n.* 《< L *ad-,* to + *specere,* to look》 1 the way one appears 2 the appearance of something from a specific position or viewpoint 3 a side facing in a given direction

as·pen (as′pən) *n.* 《OE *æspe*》 a poplar tree whose leaves flutter even in very light breezes

as·per·i·ty (ə sper′ə tē) *n., pl.* **-ties** 《< L *asper,* rough》 1 roughness or harshness 2 sharpness of temper

as·per·sion (ə spur′zhən) *n.* a damaging or disparaging remark; slander

as·phalt (as′fôlt′) *n.* 《< Gr *asphaltos*》 a brown or black tarlike substance mixed with sand or gravel and used for paving, roofing, etc. —*vt.* to pave, roof, etc. with asphalt

as·pho·del (as′fə del′) *n.* 《< Gr *asphodelos*》 a plant of the lily family, having white or yellow flowers

as·phyx·i·ate (as fik′sē āt′) *vt., vi.* **-at′ed, -at′ing** 《< Gr *a-,* not + *sphyzein,* to throb》 1 to make or become unconscious from lack of oxygen in the blood 2 to suffocate —**as·phyx′i·ant** *n.* —**as·phyx′i·a′tion** *n.*

as·pic (as′pik′) *n.* 《< OFr *aspe,* asp》 a cold jelly of meat juice, tomato juice, etc., served as a garnish or in a mold

as·pi·rant (as′pə rənt, ə spī′-) *adj.* aspiring —*n.* one who aspires

as·pi·rate (as′pə rāt′; *for n.,* -pər it) *vt.* **-rat′ed, -rat′ing** 1 to begin (a word) with the sound of English (h) 2 to follow (a consonant) with an audible puff of breath 3 to suck in or draw in 4 *Med.* to remove (fluid, etc.) by suction —*n.* an aspirated sound

as·pi·ra·tion (as′pə rā′shən) *n.* 1 a) strong desire or ambition, as for advancement b) the thing so desired 2 a drawing in by breathing or suction 3 *Med.* removal of fluid, etc. by suction

as·pi·ra·tor *n.* an apparatus using suction to remove air, fluids, etc.

as·pire (ə spīr′) *vi.* **-pired′, -pir′ing** 《< L *ad-,* to + *spirare,* breathe》 to be ambitious (*to* get or do something); seek (*after*)

as·pi·rin (as′pə rin′, -prin′) *n.* 《Ger》 1 a white, crystalline powder used for reducing fever, relieving pain, etc. 2 a tablet of this

ass (as) *n.* 《< L *asinus*》 1 a horselike animal having long ears and a short mane 2 a stupid or silly person

as·sail (ə sāl′) *vt.* 《< L *ad-,* to + *salire,* to leap》 1 to attack physically and violently 2 to attack with arguments, etc. —**as·sail′a·ble** *adj.*

as·sail·ant (-ənt) *n.* an attacker

as·sas·sin (ə sas′ən) *n.* 《< Ar *ḥashshāshīn,* hashish users》 a murderer who strikes suddenly; now, esp., the murderer of a politically important or prominent person

as·sas·si·nate (-āt′) *vt.* **-nat′ed, -nat′ing** to murder as an assassin does —**as·sas′si·na′tion** *n.*

as·sault (ə sôlt′) *n.* 《< L *ad-,* to + *salire,* to leap》 1 a violent attack 2 nonconsensual sexual contact 3 *Law* an unlawful threat or attempt to harm another physically —*vt., vi.* to make an assault (upon)

assault and battery *Law* the carrying out of threatened physical harm

as·say (as′ā, a sā′; *for v.* a sā′) *n.* 《< OFr *essai,* trial》 1 a testing 2 an analysis of the ingredients of an ore, drug, etc. —*vt.* 1 to make an assay of; test 2 to try; attempt —*vi.* to be shown by assay to have a specified proportion of something —**as·say′er** *n.*

as·sem·blage (ə sem′blij; *for 3, also* ä′sem bläzh′) *n.* 1 an assembling 2 a group of persons or things gathered together 3 *Art* objects assembled in a sculptured collage

as·sem·ble (ə sem′bəl) *vt., vi.* **-bled, -bling** 《< L *ad-,* to + *simul,* together》 1 to gather into a group; collect **2** to put together the parts of —**as·sem'bler** *n.*

as·sem·bly (-blē) *n., pl.* **-blies** **1** an assembling **2** a group of persons gathered together **3** *a*) a legislative body *b*) [A-] the lower house of some state legislatures **4** a fitting together of parts to make a whole

assembly line in many factories, a method whereby each worker performs a specific task in assembling the work as it is passed along

as·sem·bly·man (-mən) *n., pl.* **-men** a man who is a member of a legislative assembly

as·sem·bly·wom·an *n., pl.* **-wom'en** a woman who is a member of a legislative assembly

as·sent (ə sent') *vi.* [< L *ad*-, to + *sentire*, to feel] to express acceptance; agree ⟨to⟩ —*n.* consent or agreement

as·sert (ə surt') *vt.* [< L *ad*-, to + *serere*, join] **1** to declare; affirm **2** to maintain or defend (rights, etc.) —**assert oneself** to insist on one's rights, or on being recognized —**as·sert'er** *n.*, **as·ser'tor**

as·ser·tion (ə sur'shən) *n.* **1** an asserting **2** a positive statement

as·ser·tive (ə surt'iv) *adj.* persistently, forcefully, or boldly positive or confident —**as·ser'tive·ly** *adv.* —**as·ser'tive·ness** *n.*

as·sess (ə ses') *vt.* [< L *ad*-, to + *sedere*, sit] **1** to set an estimated value on (property, etc.) for taxation **2** to set the amount of (a tax, fine, etc.) **3** to impose a tax, etc. on **4** to judge the worth or importance of —**as·sess'ment** *n.* —**as·ses'sor** *n.*

as·set (as'et) *n.* [< L *ad*, to + *satis*, enough] **1** anything owned that has value **2** a desirable thing [charm is an *asset*] **3** [*pl.*] *Law* property available to pay debts

as·sev·er·ate (ə sev'ə rāt') *vt.* **-at'ed, -at'ing** [< L *ad*-, to + *severus*, earnest] to state positively; assert —**as·sev'er·a'tion** *n.*

as·sid·u·ous (ə sij'ōō əs) *adj.* [< L *assidere*, to assist] diligent; persevering; careful —**as·si·du·i·ty** (as'ə dyōō'ə tē) *n., pl.* **-ties** —**as·sid'u·ous·ly** *adv.* —**as·sid'u·ous·ness** *n.*

as·sign (ə sīn') *vt.* [< L *ad*-, to + *signare*, to sign] **1** to set apart or mark for a specific purpose; designate **2** to appoint, as to a duty **3** to give out as a task; allot **4** to ascribe; attribute **5** *Law* to transfer (a right, etc.) —**as·sign'a·ble** *adj.* —**as·sign'er** *n., Law* **as·sign·or** (ə sīn'ôr') —**as·sign·ee'** *n.*

as·sig·na·tion (as'ig nā'shən) *n.* an appointment to meet, esp. one made secretly by lovers, or the meeting itself

as·sign·ment (ə sīn'mənt) *n.* **1** an assigning or being assigned **2** anything assigned

as·sim·i·late (ə sim'ə lāt') *vt.* **-lat'ed, -lat'ing** [< L *ad*-, to + *similare*, make similar] **1** to absorb and incorporate **2** to make like or alike; with *to* —*vi.* **1** to become like or alike **2** to become absorbed and incorporated —**as·sim'i·la'tion** *n.*

as·sist (ə sist') *vt., vi.* [< L *ad*-, to + *sistere*, make stand] to help; aid —*n.* an instance or act of helping —**assist at** to be present at; attend

as·sist·ance (ə sis'təns) *n.* help; aid

as·sist·ant (-tənt) *adj.* assisting; helping —*n.* one who assists; helper; aid

assisted living a living arrangement providing assistance to elderly or disabled persons

as·siz·es (ə sīz'iz) [see ASSESS] *pl.n.* **1** court sessions held periodically in each county of England **2** the time or place of these

assn *abbrev.* association

assoc *abbrev.* **1** associate(s) **2** association

as·so·ci·ate (ə sō'shē āt', -sē-; *for n. & adj.*, -it) *vt.* **-at'ed, -at'ing** [< L *ad*-, to + *socius*, companion] **1** to connect; combine; join **2** to bring into relationship as partner, etc. **3** to connect in the mind —*vi.* to join ⟨with⟩ as a partner, friend, etc. —*n.* **1** a friend, partner, co-worker, etc. **2** a degree granted by a junior college —*adj.* **1** joined with others in work, etc. **2** having less than full status

as·so·ci·a·tion *n.* **1** an associating or being associated **2** fellowship; partnership **3** an organization, society, etc. **4** a mental connection between ideas, etc.

association football soccer

as·so·ci·a·tive (-shē āt'iv, -sē-; -shə tiv) *adj.* **1** of, by, or causing association **2** *Math.* producing the same result regardless of how the elements are grouped

as·so·nance (as'ə nəns) *n.* [< L *ad*-, to + *sonare*, to sound] **1** likeness of sound **2** a partial rhyme made by repetition of a vowel sound —**as'so·nant** *adj., n.*

as·sort (ə sôrt') *vt.* [ult. < L *ad*-, to + *sors*, lot, fate] to sort or classify

as·sort·ed *adj.* **1** various; miscellaneous **2** sorted; classified

as·sort·ment *n.* **1** an assorting **2** a miscellaneous collection; variety

asst *abbrev.* assistant

as·suage (ə swāj') *vt.* **-suaged', -suag'ing** [< L *ad*-, to + *suavis*, sweet] **1** to lessen (pain, distress, etc.) **2** to calm (anger, etc.) **3** to satisfy or slake (thirst, etc.)

as·sume (ə sōōm') *vt.* **-sumed', -sum'ing** [< L *ad*-, to + *sumere*, to take] **1** to take on (the appearance, role, etc. of) **2** to seize; usurp **3** to undertake **4** to take for granted; suppose **5** to pretend to have; feign —**as·sum'a·ble** *adj.*

as·sumed *adj.* **1** pretended; fictitious **2** taken for granted

as·sump·tion (ə sump'shən) *n.* **1** [A-] *R.C.Ch. a*) the bodily ascent of the Virgin Mary into heaven *b*) a feast on Aug. 15 celebrating this **2** an assuming **3** a supposition —**as·sump'tive** *adj.*

as·sur·ance (ə shoor'əns) *n.* **1** an assuring or being assured **2** a promise, guarantee, etc. **3** self-confidence **4** [Chiefly Brit.] insurance

as·sure (ə shoor') *vt.* **-sured', -sur'ing** [< L *ad*-, to + *securus*, secure] **1** to make (a person) sure of something **2** to give confidence to; reassure **3** to tell or promise confidently **4** to guarantee **5** [Chiefly Brit.] to insure against loss

as·sured *adj.* **1** made sure; certain **2** confident; sure of oneself —**as·sur·ed·ly** (ə shŏŏr′ id lē) *adv.*

As·syr·i·a (ə sir′ē ə) ancient empire in SW Asia —**As·syr′i·an** *adj., n.*

as·ta·tine (as′tə tēn′, -tin) *n.* ⟦< Gr *astatos,* unstable⟧ a highly unstable radioactive chemical element: symbol, At; at. no. 85

as·ter (as′tər) *n.* ⟦< Gr *astēr,* star⟧ any of several plants of the composite family with variously colored daisylike flowers

as·ter·isk (as′tər isk′) *n.* ⟦< Gr dim. of *astēr,* star⟧ a starlike sign (*) used in printing to mark footnotes, etc.

a·stern (ə sturn′) *adv.* 1 behind a ship or aircraft 2 AFT 3 backward

as·ter·oid (as′tər oid′) *n.* ⟦see ASTER & -OID⟧ any of the celestial objects that orbit the sun mainly between Mars and Jupiter

asth·ma (az′mə) *n.* ⟦Gr⟧ a chronic disorder characterized by wheezing, coughing, difficulty in breathing, etc. —**asth·mat·ic** (az mat′ik) *adj., n.*

a·stig·ma·tism (ə stig′mə tiz′əm) *n.* ⟦< Gr *a-,* without + *stigma,* a mark + -ISM⟧ an irregularity in the lens of the eye, that prevents proper focusing of light rays, causing distortion, poor eyesight, etc. —**as·tig·mat·ic** (as′ tig mat′ik) *adj., n.*

a·stil·be (ə stil′bē) *n.* a plant having spikes of white, pink, or red flowers

a·stir (ə stur′) *adv., adj.* 1 in motion 2 out of bed

as·ton·ish (ə stän′ish) *vt.* ⟦< L *ex-,* intens. + *tonare,* to thunder⟧ to fill with sudden wonder; amaze —**as·ton′ish·ing** *adj.* —**as·ton′ ish·ing·ly** *adv.* —**as·ton′ish·ment** *n.*

as·tound (ə stound′) *vt.* ⟦see prec.⟧ to astonish greatly —**as·tound′ing** *adj.* —**as·tound′ ing·ly** *adv.*

a·strad·dle (ə strad′'l) *adv.* in a straddling position

as·tra·khan (as′trə kən) *n.* ⟦after *Astrakhan,* Russ city⟧ loosely curled fur from young lamb pelts, or a wool fabric resembling this

as·tral (as′trəl) *adj.* ⟦< Gr *astron,* star⟧ of, from, or like the stars

a·stray (ə strā′) *adv., adj.* ⟦ME < pp. of OFr *estraier,* stray⟧ 1 off the right path 2 in error

a·stride (ə strīd′) *adv.* with a leg on either side —*prep.* 1 with a leg on either side of 2 extending over or across

as·trin·gent (ə strin′jənt) *adj.* ⟦< L *ad-,* to + *stringere,* to draw tight⟧ 1 that contracts body tissue and stops secretions 2 harsh; biting —*n.* an astringent substance —**as·trin′gen·cy** *n.*

astro- ⟦< Gr *astron,* star⟧ *combining form* star or stars [*astrophysics*]

as·tro·bi·ol·o·gy (as′trō bī äl′ə jē) *n.* the branch of biology that speculates about and seeks evidence of living organisms on planets other than earth

as·tro·dy·nam·ics *n.* the branch of dynamics dealing with the motion and gravitation of objects in space

as·trol·o·gy (ə sträl′ə jē) *n.* ⟦< Gr *astron,* star + *-logia,* -LOGY⟧ a method or theory based on the belief that the positions of the moon, sun, and stars affect human affairs and can be used to predict the future —**as·trol′o·ger** *n.* —**as·tro·log·i·cal** (as′trə läj′i kəl) *adj.*

as·tro·naut (as′trə nôt′) *n.* ⟦< Fr < Gr *astron,* star + *nautēs,* sailor⟧ one trained to make flights into outer space —**as′tro·nau′tics** *n.*

as·tro·nom·i·cal (as′trə näm′i kəl) *adj.* 1 of astronomy 2 extremely large: said as of numbers Also **as′tro·nom′ic** —**as·tro·nom′ i·cal·ly** *adv.*

astronomical unit a unit of length based on the mean distance of the earth from the sun, *c.* 150 million km (*c.* 93 million mi.)

as·tron·o·my (ə strän′ə mē) *n.* ⟦< Gr *astron,* star + *nomos,* law⟧ the science that studies the origin, size, motion, etc. of stars, planets, etc. —**as·tron′o·mer** *n.*

as·tro·phys·ics (as′trō fiz′iks) *n.* the branch of astronomy dealing with the physical properties of the universe —**as′tro·phys′i·cist** (-ə sist) *n.*

As·tro·Turf (-turf′) *trademark for* a grasslike synthetic carpet used in stadiums, etc.

as·tute (ə stōōt′) *adj.* ⟦< L *astus,* craft, cunning⟧ clever or shrewd; keen —**as·tute′ly** *adv.* —**as·tute′ness** *n.*

a·sun·der (ə sun′dər) *adv.* ⟦< OE *on sundran*⟧ 1 into pieces 2 apart in direction or position

a·sy·lum (ə sī′ləm) *n.* ⟦< Gr *a-,* without + *sylon,* right of seizure⟧ 1 refuge, esp. as granted by one country to a citizen of another 2 [Old-fashioned] an institution for the care of mentally ill, aged, or poor people

a·sym·me·try (ā sim′ə trē) *n.* lack of symmetry —**a·sym·met·ri·cal** (ā′sə me′tri kəl) *adj.* —**a′sym·met′ri·cal·ly** *adv.*

a·symp·to·mat·ic (ā′simp tə ma′tik) *adj.* without symptoms

at (at) *prep.* ⟦< OE *æt*⟧ 1 on; in; near; by [*at* the office] 2 to or toward [look *at* her] 3 from [visible *at* one mile] 4 attending [*at* a party] 5 busy with [*at* work] 6 in the state or manner of [*at* war, *at* a trot] 7 because of [sad *at* his death] 8 with reference to [good *at* tennis] 9 in the amount, etc. of [*at* five cents each] 10 on or near the time or age of [*at* noon, *at* twenty-one] 11 attacking, etc. [they're *at* him again]

at·a·vism (at′ə viz′əm) *n.* ⟦< L *at-,* beyond + *avus,* grandfather⟧ resemblance or reversion to a characteristic of a remote ancestor —**at′ a·vis′tic** *adj.*

a·tax·i·a (ə tak′sē ə) *n.* ⟦< Gr *a-,* not + *tassein,* arrange⟧ an inability to coordinate the body's movements, as in walking —**a·tax′ic** *adj., n.*

ate (āt; *Brit, or U.S. dial.,* et) *vt., vi. pt. of* EAT

-ate¹ (āt; *for 2,* it) *suffix* 1 to become, cause to become, form, provide with [*maturate, ulcerate*] 2 of or characteristic of, characterized by, having [*passionate*]

-ate² (āt, it) *suffix* an office, function, agent, or official [*directorate*]

at·el·ier (at′'l yā′) *n.* ⟦Fr⟧ a studio or workshop, esp. of an artist

Ath·a·bas·kan or **Ath·a·bas·can** (ath′ə bas′

kən) *n.* a family of North American Indian languages, including Navajo —*adj.* designating or of these languages or the peoples that speak them

a·the·ism (ā′thē iz′əm) *n.* ⟦< Gr *a*–, without + *theos*, god⟧ the belief that there is no God —**a′the·ist** *n.* —**a′the·is′tic** *adj.*

A·the·na (ə thē′nə) *n.* the Greek goddess of wisdom, skills, and warfare

Ath·ens (ath′ənz) capital of Greece, in the SE part —**A·the·ni·an** (ə thē′nē ən) *adj., n.*

ath·er·o·scle·ro·sis (ath′ər ō′sklə rō′sis) *n.* ⟦< Gr *athērōma*, grainy tumor + SCLEROSIS⟧ formation of fatty nodules on hardening artery walls

a·thirst (ə thurst′) *adj.* 1 [Archaic] thirsty 2 eager; longing (*for*)

ath·lete (ath′lēt′) *n.* ⟦< Gr *athlon*, a prize⟧ one who engages in exercises or games requiring strength, agility, stamina, etc.

athlete's foot ringworm of the feet

ath·let·ic (ath let′ik) *adj.* 1 of or like athletes or athletics 2 physically strong, active, fit, etc. —**ath·let′i·cal·ly** *adv.* —**ath·let′i·cism′** (-ə siz′əm) *n.*

ath·let·ics *pl.n.* [*sometimes with sing. v.*] athletic sports, games, etc.

-a·thon (ə thän′) *suffix* an event marked by length or endurance [*walk-athon*]

a·thwart (ə thwôrt′) *prep.* 1 across 2 against —*adv.* crosswise

a·tilt (ə tilt′) *adj., adv.* tilted

-a·tion (ā′shən) ⟦< Fr or L⟧ *suffix* the act, condition, or result of [*alteration*]

-a·tive (ə tiv, āt′iv) ⟦< Fr or L⟧ *suffix* of or relating to, serving to [*informative*]

At·lan·ta (at lan′tə) capital of Georgia

At·lan·tic (at lan′tik) ocean touching the Americas to the west and Europe and Africa to the east

Atlantic City city in SE New Jersey: an ocean resort

At·lan·tis (at lan′tis) *n.* ⟦< Gr⟧ legendary sunken continent in the Atlantic

At·las (at′ləs) *n.* 1 *Gr. Myth.* a giant who supports the heavens on his shoulders 2 [**a-**] a book of maps

ATM (ā′tē em′) *n.* ⟦*a(utomated) t(eller) m(achine)*⟧ a computer terminal that allows a bank customer to deposit, withdraw, or transfer funds automatically

at·mos·phere (at′məs fir′) *n.* ⟦< Gr *atmos*, vapor + *sphaira*, sphere⟧ 1 the air surrounding the earth 2 a pervading mood or spirit 3 the general tone or effect 4 a unit of pressure equal to 101,325 newtons per sq. m —**at′mos·pher′ic** (-fer′ik, -fir′-) *adj.* —**at′mos·pher′i·cal·ly** *adv.*

at. no. *abbrev.* atomic number

at·oll (a′tôl′) *n.* ⟦< Malayalam *atolu*⟧ a ring-shaped coral island surrounding a lagoon

at·om (at′əm) *n.* ⟦< Gr *a*–, not + *temnein*, to cut⟧ 1 a tiny particle; jot 2 *Chem., Physics* any of the smallest particles of an element that combine with similar particles of the same element or other elements to form molecules —**the atom** nuclear energy

atom bomb ATOMIC BOMB

a·tom·ic (ə täm′ik) *adj.* 1 of an atom or atoms 2 of or using atomic energy or atomic bombs 3 tiny —**a·tom′i·cal·ly** *adv.*

atomic bomb an extremely destructive bomb whose power results from a chain reaction of nuclear fission

atomic energy NUCLEAR ENERGY

atomic number *Chem.* a number indicating the number of protons in the nucleus of an atom of an element

atomic weight *Chem.* the weight of one atom of an element based upon the average weight of the element's isotopes

at·om·iz·er (at′əm ī zər) *n.* a device used to shoot out a fine spray, as of medicine or perfume

a·to·nal·i·ty (ā′tō nal′ə tē) *n. Music* the organization of tones without relation to a key —**a·ton·al** (ā tōn′əl) *adj.* —**a·ton′al·ly** *adv.*

a·tone (ə tōn′) *vi.* **a·toned′, a·ton′ing** ⟦< ME *at one*, in accord⟧ to make amends (*for* wrongdoing, etc.)

a·tone·ment *n.* 1 an atoning 2 amends —**the Atonement** *Theol.* the redeeming of humanity by the death of Jesus

a·top (ə täp′) *adv.* on or at the top —*prep.* on the top of

a·top·ic (ā täp′ik) *adj.* of allergic reactions, as a type of dermatitis, thought to be inherited

-a·to·ry (ə tôr′ē) ⟦< L⟧ *suffix* -ORY

ATP (ā′tē·pē′) *n.* ⟦*a(denosine) t(ri)p(hosphate)*⟧ an organic compound present in, and vital to, all living cells

a·tri·um (ā′trē əm) *n., pl.* **a′tri·a** (-ə) or **a′tri·ums** ⟦L⟧ 1 the central court or main room of an ancient Roman house 2 a court or entrance hall, usually of more than one story 3 either of the heart's upper chambers

a·tro·cious (ə trō′shəs) *adj.* ⟦< L *atrox*, fierce⟧ 1 very cruel, evil, etc. 2 very bad or unpleasant; offensive —**a·tro′cious·ly** *adv.* —**a·tro′cious·ness** *n.*

a·troc·i·ty (ə träs′ə tē) *n., pl.* **-ties** 1 atrocious behavior 2 an atrocious act 3 [Inf.] a very displeasing thing

at·ro·phy (a′trə fē) *n.* ⟦< Gr *a*–, not + *trephein*, to feed⟧ a wasting away or failure to grow, esp. of body tissue, an organ, etc. —*vi.* **-phied, -phy·ing** to undergo atrophy —*vt.* to cause atrophy in

at·ro·pine (at′rə pēn′, -pin′) *n.* ⟦< Gr *Atropos*, one of the Fates + -INE³⟧ an alkaloid obtained from belladonna, used to relieve spasms, etc.

at·tach (ə tach′) *vt.* ⟦< OFr *estache*, a post, stake⟧ 1 to fasten by sticking, tying, etc. 2 to join: often used reflexively 3 to connect by ties of affection, etc. 4 to add (a signature, etc.) 5 to ascribe 6 *Law* to take (property) by writ 7 *Comput.* to include (a file) with an email —**at·tach′a·ble** *adj.*

at·ta·ché (at′ə shā′; *chiefly Brit.* ə tash′ā) *n.* ⟦Fr: see prec.⟧ a member of an ambassador's diplomatic staff

attaché case a briefcase

at·tach·ment *n.* **1** an attaching or being attached **2** anything that attaches; fastening **3** devotion **4** anything attached **5** an accessory for an electrical appliance, etc. **6** *Law* a taking of property into custody

at·tack (ə tak′) *vt.* ⟦< It *attaccare*⟧ **1** to use force against in order to harm **2** to speak or write against **3** to undertake vigorously **4** to begin acting upon harmfully —*vi.* to make an assault —*n.* **1** an attacking **2** any hostile action, esp. with troops **3** the onset of a disease **4** a beginning of a task, undertaking, etc. —**at·tack′er** *n.*

at·tain (ə tān′) *vt.* ⟦< L *ad-*, to + *tangere*, to touch⟧ **1** to gain; accomplish; achieve **2** to reach; arrive at —**at·tain′a·bil′i·ty** *n.* —**at·tain′a·ble** *adj.*

at·tain·der (-dər) *n.* ⟦see prec.⟧ loss of civil rights and property of one sentenced to death or outlawed

at·tar (at′ər) *n.* ⟦< Ar ′*itr*, perfume⟧ a perfume made from flower petals, esp. of roses (**attar of roses**)

at·tempt (ə tempt′) *vt.* ⟦< L *ad-*, to + *temptare*, to try⟧ to try to do, get, etc. —*n.* **1** a try; endeavor **2** an attack, as on a person's life

at·tend (ə tend′) *vt.* ⟦< L *ad-*, to + *tendere*, to stretch⟧ **1** [Now Rare] to take care of **2** to go with **3** to accompany as a result **4** to be present at —*vi.* **1** to pay attention **2** to wait (*on* or *upon*) **3** to apply oneself (*to*) **4** to give the required care (*to*)

at·tend·ance *n.* **1** an attending **2** the number of persons attending

at·tend·ant *adj.* **1** attending or serving **2** being present **3** accompanying —*n.* one who attends or serves

at·ten·tion (ə ten′shən) *n.* ⟦see ATTEND⟧ **1** mental concentration or readiness **2** notice or observation **3** care or consideration **4** an act of courtesy or devotion: *usually used in pl.* **5** the erect posture of soldiers ready for a command

attention-deficit hyperactivity disorder a mental disorder marked by inability to concentrate, impulsiveness, etc.

at·ten·tive (-tiv) *adj.* **1** paying attention **2** courteous, devoted, etc. —**at·ten′tive·ly** *adv.* —**at·ten′tive·ness** *n.*

at·ten·u·ate (ə ten′yōō āt′) *vt.* **-at′ed, -at′ing** ⟦< L *ad-*, to + *tenuis*, thin⟧ **1** to make thin **2** to dilute **3** to lessen or weaken —*vi.* to become thin, weak, etc. —**at·ten′u·a′tion** *n.* —**at·ten′u·a′tor** *n.*

at·test (ə test′) *vt.* ⟦< L *ad-*, to + *testari*, to bear witness⟧ **1** to declare to be true or genuine **2** to certify, as by oath **3** to serve as proof of —*vi.* to bear witness (*to*) —**at·tes·ta·tion** (at′əs tā′shən) *n.*

at·tic (at′ik) *n.* ⟦< Gr *Attikos*, of Attica (ancient Gr state): with reference to architectural style⟧ a room or space just below a roof; garret

At·ti·la (at′′l ə, ə til′ə) A.D. 406?-453; king of the Huns: called *Attila the Hun*

at·tire (ə tīr′) *vt.* **-tired′, -tir′ing** ⟦< OFr *a*, to + *tire*, order, row⟧ to dress, esp. in fine garments; clothe —*n.* clothes, esp. fine or rich apparel

at·ti·tude (at′ə tōōd′) *n.* ⟦ult. < L *aptus*, apt⟧ **1** a bodily posture showing mood, action, etc. **2** a manner showing one's feelings or thoughts **3** one's disposition, opinion, etc. **4** [Slang] a quarrelsome or self-important manner

at·ti·tu·di·nize (at′ə tōōd′′n īz′) *vi.* **-nized′, -niz′ing** to pose for effect

Attn or **attn** *abbrev.* attention

at·tor·ney (ə tur′nē) *n., pl.* **-neys** ⟦< OFr *a-*, to + *torner*, to turn⟧ any person legally empowered to act for another; esp., a lawyer

attorney at law a lawyer

attorney general *pl.* **attorneys general** or **attorney generals** the chief law officer of a government

at·tract (ə trakt′) *vt.* ⟦< L *ad-*, to + *trahere*, to draw⟧ **1** to draw to itself or oneself **2** to get the admiration, attention, etc. of; allure —*vi.* to be attractive —**at·tract′a·ble** *adj.*

at·trac·tion (ə trak′shən) *n.* **1** an attracting or being attracted **2** power to attract; esp., charm **3** anything that attracts **4** *Physics* the mutual tendency of bodies to draw together

at·trac·tive (-tiv) *adj.* that attracts; esp., pleasing, charming, pretty, etc. —**at·trac′tive·ly** *adv.* —**at·trac′tive·ness** *n.*

at·trib·ute (ə trib′yōōt; *for n.* a′trə byōōt′) *vt.* **-ut·ed, -ut·ing** ⟦< L *ad-*, to + *tribuere*, assign⟧ to think of as belonging *to* a certain person or thing —*n.* a characteristic or quality of a person or thing —**at·trib′ut·a·ble** *adj.* —**at·tri·bu·tion** (a′trə byōō′shən) *n.*

at·trib·u·tive (ə trib′yōō tiv) *adj.* **1** attributing **2** preceding the noun it modifies: said of an adjective or of a noun used adjectively —**at·trib′u·tive·ly** *adv.*

at·tri·tion (ə trish′ən) *n.* ⟦< L *ad-*, to + *terere*, to rub⟧ **1** a wearing away by or as by friction **2** a normal loss of personnel, as by retirement

at·tune (ə tōōn′) *vt.* **-tuned′, -tun′ing 1** to tune **2** to bring into harmony

atty *abbrev.* attorney

ATV (ā′tē′vē′) *n., pl.* **ATVs** ⟦A(*ll-*) T(*errain*) V(*ehicle*)⟧ a small motor vehicle for traveling over rough ground, snow and ice, etc.

a·twit·ter (ə twit′ər) *adv., adj.* twittering

a·typ·i·cal (ā tip′i kəl) *adj.* not typical; abnormal —**a·typ′i·cal·ly** *adv.*

Au *abbrev.* ⟦L *aurum*⟧ *Chem. symbol for* gold

au·burn (ô′bərn) *adj., n.* ⟦< L *albus*, white: infl. by ME *brun*, brown⟧ reddish brown

Auck·land (ôk′lənd) seaport in N New Zealand

auc·tion (ôk′shən) *n.* ⟦< L *augere*, to increase⟧ a public sale of items, one by one, to the highest bidder for each item —*vt.* to sell at auction —**auction off** to sell at auction —**auc′tion·eer′** *n.*

au·da·cious (ô dā′shəs) *adj.* ⟦< L *audax*, bold⟧ **1** bold; daring **2** too bold; brazen; insolent —au·da′cious·ly adv. —au·da′cious·ness n.

au·dac·i·ty (ô das′ə tē) n. 1 bold courage 2 insolence; impudence 3 pl. -ties an audacious act or remark

au·di·ble (ô′də bəl) adj. [< L audire, hear] loud enough to be heard —au′di·bil′i·ty (-bil′ə tē) n. —au′di·bly adv.

au·di·ence (ô′dē əns) n. [< L audire, hear] 1 those assembled to hear and see something 2 all those reached by a TV or radio program, book, etc. 3 a hearing, esp. a formal interview

au·di·o (ô′dē ō′) adj. [< L audire, hear] 1 of frequencies corresponding to audible sound waves 2 of sound reproduction, as of the sound phase of television

au·di·o·book n. a recording of a reading of a book, as by the author

au·di·ol·o·gy (ô′dē äl′ə jē) n. evaluation and treatment of hearing defects —au′di·ol′o·gist n.

au·di·om·e·ter (—äm′ət ər) n. an instrument for measuring the sensitivity and range of hearing —au′di·o·met′ric (-ō me′trik) adj.

au·di·o·phile (ô′dē ō fīl′) n. a devotee of high-fidelity sound reproduction, as from recordings

au·di·o·vis·u·al (ô′dē ō vizh′ōō əl) adj. 1 involving both hearing and sight 2 of or using both audio and video technologies

au·dit (ôd′it) n. [< L auditus, a hearing] a formal checking of financial records — vt., vi. 1 to check (accounts, etc.) 2 to attend (a college class) as a listener receiving no credit

au·di·tion (ô dish′ən) n. [< L audire, hear] a hearing to try out an actor, singer, etc. — vt., vi. to try out in an audition

au·di·tor (ô′dit ər) n. 1 a listener 2 one who audits accounts 3 one who audits classes

au·di·to·ri·um (ô′də tôr′ē əm) n. 1 a room where an audience sits 2 a building or hall for speeches, concerts, etc.

au·di·to·ry (ô′də tôr′ē) adj. of hearing or the sense of hearing

auf Wie·der·seh·en (ouf vē′dər zā′ən) [Ger] goodbye

au·ger (ô′gər) n. [< OE nafu, hub (of a wheel) + gar, a spear] a tool for boring holes in wood

aught (ôt) n. [< OE a, ever + wiht, creature] 1 anything whatever 2 [< (N)AUGHT] a zero

aug·ment (ôg ment′) vt., vi. [< L augere, to increase] to make or become greater —aug′men·ta′tion n. —aug·ment′er n.

au gra·tin (ō grat′'n, -grät′-) [Fr] with a crust of bread crumbs and grated cheese

au·gur (ô′gər) n. [L, priest at fertility rites] a prophet; soothsayer — vt., vi. 1 to prophesy 2 to be an omen (of) —augur ill (or well) to be a bad (or good) omen

au·gu·ry (ô′gyə rē) n. 1 the practice of divination 2 pl. -ries an omen; portent

au·gust (ô gust′) adj. [L augustus] inspiring awe; imposing —au·gust′ly adv. —au·gust′ness n.

Au·gust (ô′gəst) n. [< L Augustus] the eighth month of the year, having 31 days: abbrev. Aug

Au·gus·ta (ô gus′tə) capital of Maine

Au·gus·tine (ô′gəs tēn′, ə gus′tin), Saint (A.D. 354-430); early Christian bishop and theologian

Au·gus·tus (ô gus′təs) 63 B.C.-A.D. 14; 1st Rom. emperor (27 B.C.-A.D. 14)

au jus (ō zhōō′, ō jōōs′) [Fr] served in its natural juices: said of meat

auk (ôk) n. [< ON alka] a diving bird of northern seas, with webbed feet and short wings used as paddles

auld lang syne (ôld′ laŋ′ zīn′) [Scot, lit., old long since] the good old days

aunt (ant, änt) n. [< L amita] 1 a sister of one's mother or father 2 the wife of one's mother's or father's sibling

au poi·vre (ō pwäv′rə) [Fr] with crushed black peppercorns and a sauce

au·ra (ô′rə) n., pl. -ras or -rae (-rē) [< Gr] 1 an invisible emanation 2 a particular quality surrounding a person or thing

au·ral (ô′rəl) adj. [< L auris, ear] of the ear or the sense of hearing

au·re·ole (ô′rē ōl′) n. [< L aurum, gold] 1 a halo 2 a corona around the sun

Au·re·o·my·cin (ô′rē ō mī′sin) trademark for an antibiotic used to treat infections and viruses

au re·voir (ō′rə vwär′) [Fr] goodbye

au·ri·cle (ô′ri kəl) n. [< L dim. of auris, ear] the outer part of the ear

Au·ro·ra (ô rôr′ə) n., pl. for 2 & 3 -ras or -rae (-rē) 1 the Rom. goddess of dawn 2 [a-] the dawn 3 [a-] a luminous band in the night sky, esp. at high latitudes

aurora aus·tra·lis (ô strā′lis) the aurora in the sky of the S Hemisphere

aurora bo·re·al·is (bôr′ē al′is) the aurora in the sky of the N Hemisphere

aus·cul·ta·tion (ôs′kəl tā′shən) n. [L auscultare, to listen] a listening, often with a stethoscope, to sounds in the chest, abdomen, etc. so as to determine the condition of the heart, lungs, etc. —aus′cul′tate′ vt., vi. -tat·ed, -tat′ing

aus·pice (ôs′pis) n., pl. -pi·ces (-pə siz, -sēz′) [< L auspicium, omen] 1 an omen 2 a favorable omen or sign 3 [pl.] sponsorship; patronage

aus·pi·cious (ôs pish′əs) adj. 1 favorable; propitious 2 successful —aus·pi′cious·ly adv. —aus·pi′cious·ness n.

Aus·sie (ôs′ē) adj., n. [Inf.] Australian

Aus·ten (ôs′tən), Jane 1775-1817; Eng. novelist

aus·tere (ô stir′) adj. [< Gr austēros, dry] 1 stern; severe 2 showing strict self-control; ascetic 3 very plain; lacking ornament —aus·tere′ly adv.

aus·ter·i·ty (ô ster′ə tē) n., pl. -ties 1 sternness 2 an austere practice, act, or manner 3 tightened economy

Aus·tin (ôs′tən) capital of Texas, in the central part

aus·tral (ôs′trəl) adj. [< L auster, the south] southern

Aus·tral·ia (ô strāl′yə) **1** island continent between the S Pacific and Indian oceans **2** country comprising this continent & Tasmania —**Aus·tral′i·an** *adj., n.*

Aus·tri·a (ôs′trē ə) country in central Europe —**Aus′tri·an** *adj., n.*

au·then·tic (ô then′tik) *adj.* [< Gr *authentikos*, genuine] **1** credible, reliable, etc.: said as of a news report **2** genuine; real —**au·then′ti·cal·ly** *adv.* —**au·then·tic·i·ty** (ô′thən tis′ə tē) *n.*

au·then·ti·cate (-ti kāt′) *vt.* -**cat′ed**, -**cat′ing** **1** to make authentic or valid **2** to verify **3** to prove to be genuine —**au·then′ti·ca′tion** *n.*

au·thor (ô′thər) *n.* [< L *augere*, to increase] **1** one who makes or creates something **2** a writer of books, etc. —*vt.* to be the author of

au·thor·i·tar·i·an (ə thôr′ə ter′ē ən) *adj.* believing in or characterized by absolute obedience to authority —*n.* an advocate or enforcer of such obedience —**au·thor′i·tar′i·an·ism′** *n.*

au·thor·i·ta·tive (-tāt′iv) *adj.* **1** having authority; official **2** based on competent authority; reliable —**au·thor′i·ta′tive·ly** *adv.* —**au·thor′i·ta′tive·ness** *n.*

au·thor·i·ty (-tē) *n., pl.* -**ties** [see AUTHOR] **1** the power or right to command, act, etc. **2** [*pl.*] officials with this power **3** power or influence resulting from knowledge, prestige, etc. **4** a person, writing, etc. cited to support an opinion **5** an expert

au·thor·ize (ô′thər īz′) *vt.* -**ized′**, -**iz′ing 1** to give official approval to **2** to give power or authority to **3** to justify —**au′thor·i·za′tion** *n.* —**au′thor·iz′er** *n.*

Authorized Version the revised English translation of the Bible published in England in 1611 with the authorization of King James I

au·thor·ship *n.* origin or source with regard to author or originator

au·tism (ô′tiz′əm) *n.* [AUT(O)- + -ISM] a developmental disorder marked by impaired social interaction, communication difficulties, etc. —**au·tis′tic** (-tis′tik) *adj.*

au·to (ôt′ō) *n., pl.* -**tos** an automobile

auto- [< Gr *autos*, self] *combining form* **1** self **2** by oneself or itself **3** automatic

au·to·bi·og·ra·phy (ôt′ō bī ä′grə fē) *n., pl.* -**phies** the story of one's own life written by oneself —**au′to·bi′o·graph′i·cal** (-bī′ə graf′i kəl) *adj.* —**au′to·bi′o·graph′i·cal·ly** *adv.*

au·toc·ra·cy (ô tä′krə sē) *n.* [see fol.] **1** government in which one person has absolute power **2** *pl.* -**cies** a country with such government

au·to·crat (ôt′ə krat′) *n.* [< Gr *autos*, self + *kratos*, power] **1** a ruler with absolute power **2** any domineering person —**au′to·crat′ic** *adj.* —**au′to·crat′i·cal·ly** *adv.*

au·to·di·dact (ôt′ō dī′dakt′) *n.* [see AUTO- & DIDACTIC] a person who is self-taught

au·to·graph (ôt′ə graf′) *n.* [< Gr *autos*, self + *graphein*, write] **1** a person's own signature, esp. when considered as a collector's item **2** a person's own handwriting —*vt.* to write one's signature on or in

au·to·mate (-māt′) *vt.* -**mat′ed**, -**mat′ing** [< AUTOMATION] to convert to automation or use automation in

au·to·mat·ic (ôt′ə mat′ik) *adj.* [Gr *automatos*, self-moving] **1** done unthinkingly, as by habit or reflex **2** working by itself **3** using automatic equipment **4** capable of firing continuously until the trigger is released —*n.* **1** an automatic firearm **2** a motor vehicle with a transmission that shifts gears automatically —**au′to·mat′i·cal·ly** *adv.*

automatic pilot an instrument that automatically keeps an aircraft, etc. on a predetermined course

au·to·ma·tion (-mā′shən) *n.* [AUTOMA(TIC) + -TION] a manufacturing system in which many or all of the processes are automatically performed or controlled, as by electronic devices

au·tom·a·tism (ô täm′ə tiz′əm) *n.* automatic quality, condition, or action —**au·tom′a·tize′** (-tīz′) *vt.* -**tized′**, -**tiz′ing**

au·tom·a·ton (-tän′, -tən) *n., pl.* -**tons′** or -**ta** (-tə) [see AUTOMATIC] **1** any automatic device, esp. a robot **2** a person acting like a robot

au·to·mo·bile (ôt′ə mə bēl′) *n.* [Fr: see AUTO- & MOBILE] a four-wheeled passenger car with a built-in engine

au·to·mo·tive (-mōt′iv) *adj.* [AUTO- + -MOTIVE] **1** self-moving **2** having to do with automobiles, trucks, etc.

au·to·nom·ic (-näm′ik) *adj.* of or controlled by the part of the nervous system regulating motor functions of the heart, lungs, etc.

au·ton·o·mous (ô tän′ə məs) *adj.* [< Gr *autos*, self + *nomos*, law] **1** having self-government, esp. in internal matters **2** existing or functioning independently —**au·ton′o·mous·ly** *adv.* —**au·ton′o·my** (-mē) *n.*

au·top·sy (ô′täp′sē) *n., pl.* -**sies** [< Gr *autos*, self + *opsis*, a sight] examination of a dead body to discover the cause of death

au·tumn (ôt′əm) *n.* [< L *autumnus*] the season between summer and winter; fall —**au·tum·nal** (ô tum′nəl) *adj.*

aux·il·i·a·ry (ôg zil′yə rē, -ə rē) *adj.* [< L *augere*, to increase] **1** helping **2** subsidiary **3** supplementary —*n., pl.* -**ries** an auxiliary person or thing

auxiliary verb *Gram.* a verb that helps form tenses, moods, voices, etc. of other verbs, as *have, be, do, will, must*

aux·in (ôk′sin) *n.* [< Gr *auxein*, to increase] a plant hormone that promotes and controls growth

av *abbrev.* **1** average **2** avoirdupois

Av *abbrev.* **1** Avenue **2** avoirdupois

a·vail (ə vāl′) *vi., vt.* [< L *ad*, to + *valere*, be strong] to be of use, help, or worth (to) —*n.* use or help; advantage [*to no avail*] —**avail oneself of** to take advantage of; utilize

a·vail·a·ble *adj.* **1** that can be used **2** that can be gotten or had; handy **3** not otherwise engaged or committed —**a·vail′a·bil′i·ty** *n.*

av·a·lanche (av′ə lanch′) *n.* [Fr] **1** a large mass

of loosened snow sliding down a mountain **2** a landslide **3** an overwhelming amount coming suddenly

a·vant-garde (ə vänt′gärd′, ä′-) *n.* ⟦Fr⟧ the leaders in new movements, esp. in the arts; vanguard —*adj.* of such movements

av·a·rice (av′ə ris) *n.* ⟦< L *avere*, to desire⟧ greed for money —**av·a·ri·cious** (av′ə rish′ əs) *adj.* —**av′a·ri′cious·ly** *adv.*

a·vast (ə vast′) *interj.* ⟦< Du *houd vast*, hold fast⟧ *Naut.* stop! cease!

a·va·tar (av′ə tär′) *n.* ⟦Sans *avatāra*, descent⟧ **1** *Hinduism* a god's appearance on earth in bodily form **2** an embodiment, as of a quality in a person **3** a visual representation of oneself, as on a computer network

a·vaunt (ə vônt′) *interj.* ⟦< L *ab*, from + *ante*, before⟧ ⟦Archaic⟧ go away!

avdp *abbrev.* avoirdupois

Ave *abbrev.* Avenue

A·ve Ma·ri·a (ä′vä mə rē′ə) ⟦L⟧ *R.C.Ch.* a prayer to Mary

a·venge (ə venj′) *vt.* **a·venged′, a·veng′ing** ⟦< L *ad*, to + *vindicare*, to claim⟧ **1** to get revenge for (an injury, etc.) **2** to take vengeance on behalf of —**a·veng′er** *n.*

av·e·nue (av′ə nōō′) *n.* ⟦< L *ad–*, to + *nenire*, come⟧ **1** a street, drive, etc., esp. when broad **2** a way of approach

a·ver (ə vur′) *vt.* **a·verred′, a·ver′ring** ⟦< L *ad–*, to + *verus*, true⟧ to declare to be true; affirm; assert

av·er·age (av′ər ij, av′rij) *n.* ⟦< OFr *avarie*, damage to ship or goods; hence, idea of shared losses⟧ **1** the result of dividing the sum of two or more quantities by the number of quantities **2** the usual kind, amount, etc. —*adj.* **1** constituting an average **2** ordinary; normal —*vt.* **-aged, -ag·ing 1** to figure out the average of **2** to do, take, etc. on average [to *average* six sales a day] **3** to divide proportionally —**average out** to arrive at an average eventually —**on (the) average** as an average amount, rate, etc.

a·verse (ə vurs′) *adj.* ⟦see AVERT⟧ unwilling; opposed (*to*)

a·ver·sion (ə vur′zhən) *n.* **1** an intense dislike **2** the object arousing this

a·vert (ə vurt′) *vt.* ⟦< L *a–*, from + *vertere*, to turn⟧ **1** to turn (the eyes, etc.) away **2** to ward off; prevent

avg *abbrev.* average

a·vi·an (ā′vē ən) *adj.* ⟦< L *avis*, bird + -AN⟧ of or having to do with birds

a·vi·ar·y (ā′vē er′ē) *n., pl.* **-ar′ies** ⟦< L *avis*, bird⟧ a large cage or building for keeping many birds

a·vi·a·tion (ā′vē ā′shən) *n.* ⟦see prec.⟧ **1** the art or science of flying aircraft **2** the field of aircraft design, construction, etc.

a·vi·a·tor *n.* (ā′vē āt′ər) ⟦Fr *aviateur*⟧ a pilot of an aircraft

a·vi·a·trix (ā′vē ā′triks) *n., pl.* **-trix·es** or **-tri·ces′** (-tri sēz′) a woman who is a pilot of an aircraft

av·id (av′id) *adj.* ⟦< L *avere*, to desire⟧ very

eager or greedy —**a·vid·i·ty** (ə vid′ə tē) *n.* —**av′id·ly** *adv.*

a·vi·on·ics (ā′vē än′iks) *n.* ⟦AVI(ATION) + (ELECTR)ONICS⟧ electronics as applied in aviation and astronautics

av·o·ca·do (av′ə kä′dō, ä′və-) *n., pl.* **-dos** ⟦< AmInd⟧ **1** a thick-skinned, pear-shaped tropical fruit with yellowish-green, buttery flesh **2** the tree it grows on **3** a yellowish-green color

av·o·ca·tion (av′ə kā′shən) *n.* ⟦< L *a–*, away + *vocare*, to call⟧ something done in addition to one's regular work; hobby —**av′o·ca′tion·al** *adj.*

a·void (ə void′) *vt.* ⟦ME < OFr *esvuidier*, to empty⟧ **1** to keep away from; evade; shun **2** to prevent —**a·void′a·ble** *adj.* —**a·void′a·bly** *adv.* —**a·void′ance** *n.*

av·oir·du·pois (av′ər də poiz′) *n.* ⟦< OFr *aveir de peis*, goods of weight⟧ **1** a system of weights in which 16 oz. = 1 lb.: also **avoirdupois weight 2** [Inf.] weight, esp. of a person

a·vouch (ə vouch′) *vt.* ⟦see ADVOCATE⟧ **1** to vouch for **2** to affirm **3** to avow

a·vow (ə vou′) *vt.* ⟦see ADVOCATE⟧ to declare or acknowledge openly —**a·vow′al** *n.* —**a·vowed′** *adj.* —**a·vow′ed·ly** *adv.*

a·vun·cu·lar (ə vuŋ′kyŏŏ lər) *adj.* ⟦< L *avunculus*⟧ of or like an uncle

aw (ô) *interj.* a sound of protest, sympathy, etc.

a·wait (ə wāt′) *vt., vi.* **1** to wait for or expect **2** to be in store for

a·wake (ə wāk′) *vt., vi.* **a·woke′** or **a·waked′, a·waked′** or **a·wok′en, a·wak′ing** ⟦< OE⟧ **1** to rouse from sleep **2** to rouse from inactivity —*adj.* **1** not asleep **2** active or alert

a·wak·en (ə wā′kən) *vt., vi.* to awake; wake up —**a·wak′en·ing** *n., adj.*

a·ward (ə wôrd′) *vt.* ⟦< ME < Anglo-Fr *eswarder*⟧ **1** to give, as by legal decision **2** to give (a prize, etc.); grant —*n.* **1** *Law* a decision, as by a judge **2** something awarded; prize

a·ware (ə wer′) *adj.* ⟦< OE *wær*, cautious⟧ knowing; realizing; conscious —**a·ware′ness** *n.*

a·wash (ə wôsh′) *adv., adj.* **1** at a level where the water washes over the surface **2** flooded

a·way (ə wā′) *adv.* ⟦< OE *on weg*⟧ **1** from a place [run *away*] **2** *a*) in another place or direction [*away* from here] *b*) in the proper place [put your tools *away*] **3** off; aside [turn *away*] **4** far [*away* behind] **5** from one's possession [give it *away*] **6** at once [fire *away*] **7** continuously [working *away* all night] —*adj.* **1** absent **2** at a distance [a mile *away*] —*interj.* begone! —**away with** go, come, or take away —**do away with** get rid of or kill

AWD *abbrev.* **1** all-wheel drive **2** all-wheel-drive vehicle

awe (ô) *n.* ⟦< ON *agi*⟧ a mixed feeling of reverence, fear, and wonder —*vt.* **awed, aw′ing** to fill with awe —**stand (or be) in awe of** to respect and fear

a·weigh (ə wā′) *adj.* just clear of the bottom: said of an anchor

awe·some (ô′səm) *adj.* 1 inspiring awe 2 [Slang] wonderful; impressive —**awe′some·ly** *adv.* —**awe′some·ness** *n.*

awe·struck (ô′struk′) *adj.* filled with awe: also **awe′strick·en** (-strik′ən)

aw·ful (ô′fəl) *adj.* 1 inspiring awe 2 terrifying 3 very bad —*adv.* [Inf.] very —**aw′ful·ness** *n.*

aw·ful·ly (ô′fə lē, ô′flē) *adv.* 1 in an awful way 2 [Inf.] very

a·while (ə wīl′, -hwīl′) *adv.* for a short time

awk·ward (ôk′wərd) *adj.* [< ON *ǫfugr*, turned backward] 1 clumsy; bungling 2 hard to handle; unwieldy 3 uncomfortable [an *awkward* pose] 4 embarrassed or embarrassing —**awk′ward·ly** *adv.* —**awk′ward·ness** *n.*

awl (ôl) *n.* [< OE *æl*] a small, pointed tool for making holes in wood, leather, etc.

awn (ôn) *n.* [< ON *ǫgn*] any of the bristly fibers on a head of barley, oats, etc.

awn·ing (ôn′iŋ) *n.* [< ? MFr *auvent*, a sloping roof] a structure, as of canvas, extended before a window, door, etc. as a protection from the sun or rain

a·woke (ə wōk′) *vt., vi. pt. of* AWAKE

a·wok·en *vt., vi. alt. pp. of* AWAKE

AWOL or **a·wol** (ā′wôl′) *adj., adv.* Mil. absent without leave

a·wry (ə rī′) *adv., adj.* [see A-¹ & WRY] 1 with a twist to a side; askew 2 wrong; amiss [our plans went *awry*]

ax or **axe** (aks) *n., pl.* **ax′es** [< OE *æx*] a tool with a long handle and a head with a blade, for chopping wood, etc. —*vt.* axed, ax′ing 1 to trim, split, etc. with an ax 2 to get rid of —**give (or get) the ax** [Inf.] to discharge (or be discharged) from a job —**have an ax to grind** [Inf.] to have an object of one's own to gain or promote

ax·el (ak′səl) *n.* [after Axel Paulsen (1865-1938), Norw skater] a jump in which a skater turns in the air and lands facing in the opposite direction

ax·i·al (ak′sē əl) *adj.* 1 of, like, or forming an axis 2 around, on, or along an axis —**ax′i·al·ly** *adv.*

ax·i·om (ak′sē əm) *n.* [< Gr *axios*, wor-thy] 1 *a)* a statement universally accepted as true; maxim *b)* a self-evident truth 2 an established principle, scientific law, etc. —**ax′i·o·mat′ic** (-ə mat′ik) *adj.*

ax·is (ak′sis) *n., pl.* **ax′es** (-sēz′) [L] 1 a real or imaginary straight line on which an object rotates 2 a central line around which the parts of a thing, system, etc. are symmetrically arranged —**the Axis** Germany, Italy, and Japan in WWII

ax·le (ak′səl) *n.* [< ON *ǫxull*] 1 a rod on or with which a wheel turns 2 *a)* a bar connecting two opposite wheels, as of an automobile *b)* the spindle at either end of such a bar

ax·o·lotl (ak′sə lät′'l) *n.* [< AmInd] a dark salamander of Mexico and the W U.S.

ax·on (ak′sän′) *n.* [< Gr *axōn*, axis] that part of a nerve cell through which impulses travel away from the cell body

a·ya·tol·lah (ī′yə tō′lə) *n.* [< Ar *āyat*, sign + *Allah*, Allah] a Shiite religious leader, serving as teacher, judge, etc.

aye¹ (ā) *adv.* [< ON *ei*] [Old Poet.] always; ever. also **ay**

aye² (ī) *adv.* [prob. < I, pers. pron.] yes —*n.* an affirmative vote or voter Also **ay**

AZ *abbrev.* Arizona

a·za·lea (ə zāl′yə) *n.* [< Gr *azaleos*, dry: it thrives in dry soil] 1 a shrub of the heath family, with flowers of various colors 2 the flower

Az·er·bai·jan (äz′ər bī jän′, az′-) country in W Asia

az·i·muth (az′ə məth) *n.* [< Ar *al*, the + *samt*, way] Astronomy, Surveying distance clockwise in degrees from the north point or, in the Southern Hemisphere, south point

A·zores (ā′zôrz′, ə zôrz′) group of Portuguese islands in the N Atlantic, west of Portugal

AZT (ā′zē′tē′) *n.* [*az*(*ido*)*t*(*hymidine*)] an antiviral drug used to treat AIDS

Az·tec (az′tek′) *n.* 1 a member of an Amerindian people that had an advanced civilization in Mexico before the Spanish conquest in 1519 2 the language of this people —*adj.* of the Aztecs, their language, etc.: also **Az′tec·an**

az·ure (azh′ər) *adj.* [< Pers *lāzhuward*, lapis lazuli] sky-blue —*n.* sky blue or any similar blue color

B

b¹ or **B** (bē) *n., pl.* **b's, B's** the second letter of the English alphabet

b² *abbrev.* born

B¹ (bē) *n.* 1 a blood type 2 a grade indicating above-average but not outstanding work 3 Music the seventh tone in the scale of C major

—*adj.* inferior to the best [a B movie]

B² *abbrev.* 1 bachelor 2 Baseball *a)* base *b)* baseman 3 Music bass Also **b**

B³ Chem. symbol for boron

Ba Chem. symbol for barium

BA or **B.A.** *abbrev.* Bachelor of Arts

baa (bä) *vi., n.* [echoic] bleat

Ba·al (bā′əl) *n.* [< Heb] an ancient fertility god

bab·ble (bab′əl) *vi.* **-bled, -bling** [echoic] 1 to talk like a small child; prattle 2 to talk foolishly or too much 3 to murmur, as a brook does when flowing over stones —*vt.* to say incoherently or foolishly —*n.* 1 incoherent vocal sounds 2 foolish talk 3 a murmuring sound —**bab′bler** *n.*

babe (bāb) *n.* 1 a baby 2 a naive person: also **babe in the woods** 3 [Slang] a girl or young woman, esp. an attractive one 4 [Slang] darling: used as a term of endearment

Ba·bel (bā′bəl, bab′əl) *n.* 1 *Bible* a city thwarted in its attempt to build a tower to heaven when God created a confusion of tongues 2 [*also* **b-**] a confusion of voices, sounds, etc. or the scene of this

ba·boon (ba bōōn′, bə-) *n.* [< OFr *babuin*, ape, fool] a large, fierce monkey of Africa and Arabia, having a long snout and a short tail

ba·bush·ka (bə boosh′kə) *n.* [Russ, grandmother] a woman's scarf worn on the head and tied under the chin

ba·by (bā′bē) *n., pl.* **-bies** [ME *babi*] 1 a very young child; infant 2 one who acts like an infant 3 a very young animal 4 the youngest or smallest in a group 5 [Slang] darling; honey 6 [Slang] any person or thing —*adj.* 1 of or for an infant 2 very young 3 small of its kind 4 childish —*vt.* **-bied, -by·ing** to pamper; coddle —**ba′by·hood′** *n.* —**ba′by·ish** *adj.*

baby boomer a person born during the period of elevated birthrates in the U.S., roughly 1945-1965 (the **baby boom**)

baby carriage a small vehicle, pushed by hand, for wheeling a baby about: also **baby buggy**

baby grand a small grand piano

Bab·y·lon (bab′ə län′) capital of Babylonia: often used in later literature as a symbol of luxury and wickedness

Bab·y·lo·ni·a (bab′ə lō′nē ə) ancient empire in SW Asia —**Bab′y·lo′ni·an** *adj., n.*

baby's breath a plant with small, delicate, white or pink flowers

ba·by·sit·ter *n.* a person hired to take care of a child or children, as when the parents are away for the evening —**ba′by·sit′** *vi., vt.* **-sat′, -sit′ting**

baby talk simplified, singsong talk used in speaking to or imitating a baby

bac·ca·lau·re·ate (bak′ə lôr′ē it) *n.* [< ML *baccalaris*, young nobleman seeking knighthood] 1 the degree of Bachelor of Arts, Bachelor of Science, etc. 2 a commencement address

bac·cha·nal (bak′ə nal′) *n.* a drunken or riotous celebration —**bac′cha·na′li·an** (-nä′lē ən) *adj., n.*

Bac·chus (bak′əs) *n.* the Greek and Roman god of wine and revelry

Bach (bäkh), **Jo·hann Se·bas·ti·an** (yō′hän′ zä bäs′tē än′) 1685-1750; Ger. organist & composer

bach·e·lor (bach′ə lər, bach′lər) *n.* [< ML *baccalaris*: see BACCALAUREATE] an unmarried man —**bach′e·lor·hood′** *n.*

Bachelor of Arts (or **Science**, etc.) 1 a degree given by a college or university to one who has completed a four-year course in the humanities (or in science, etc.): also **bachelor's degree** 2 one who holds this degree

bachelor's button any of several plants with white, pink, or blue flowers, as the cornflower

ba·cil·lus (bə sil′əs) *n., pl.* **-cil′li** (-ī′) [< L *bacillum*, little stick] 1 any of a genus of rod-shaped bacteria 2 loosely, any of the bacteria —**bac·il·lar·y** (bas′ə ler′ē, bə sil′ər ē) *adj.*

back (bak) *n.* [< OE *baec*] 1 the rear (or, in some animals, the top) part of the body from the nape of the neck to the end of the spine 2 the backbone 3 a part that supports or fits the back 4 the rear part or reverse of anything 5 *Sports* a player or position behind the front line —*adj.* 1 at the rear 2 remote 3 of or for the past [*back* pay] 4 backward —*adv.* 1 at, to, or toward the rear 2 to or toward a former condition, time, etc. 3 in reserve or concealment 4 in return or requital [pay him *back*] —*vt.* 1 to move backward 2 to support 3 to bet on 4 to provide or be a back for —*vi.* to go backward —**back and forth** backward and forward —**back down** to withdraw from a position or claim —**(in) back of** behind —**back off** 1 to move back 2 [Inf.] BACK DOWN —**back out (of)** 1 to withdraw from an enterprise 2 to evade keeping a promise, etc. —**back up** 1 to support 2 to move backward: also **back away** 3 to accumulate because of restricted movement [traffic *backed up*] 4 *Comput.* to make a standby copy of (data, etc.) —**go back on** [Inf.] 1 to be disloyal to; betray 2 to fail to keep (one's word, etc.) —**turn one's back on** 1 to turn away from, as in contempt 2 to abandon

back·ache *n.* an ache or pain in the back

back·bite *vt., vi.* **-bit′, -bit′ten** or **-bit′, -bit′ing** to slander (someone absent) —**back′bit′er** *n.*

back·board *n.* 1 a board at or forming the back of something 2 *Basketball* the board behind the basket

back·bone *n.* 1 the spine 2 a main support 3 willpower, courage, etc.

back·break·ing *adj.* very tiring

back·coun·try *n.* 1 a thinly populated rural area 2 a remote, uninhabited area

back·drop *n.* 1 a curtain, often scenic, at the back of a stage 2 background or setting

back·er *n.* 1 a patron; sponsor 2 one who bets on a contestant

back·field *n.* *Football* the players behind the line

back·fire *n.* 1 the intentional burning of a small area, as in a forest, to check the spread of a big fire 2 premature ignition or an explosion of gases in an internal-combustion engine 3 reverse explosion in a gun —*vi.* **-fired′, -fir′ing** 1 to explode as a backfire 2 to go awry or boomerang

back·gam·mon (-gam′ən) *n.* ⟦BACK + ME *gammen*, game⟧ a game for two, with dice governing moves of pieces on a special board

back·ground *n.* **1** the distant part of a scene **2** surroundings, sounds, etc. behind or subordinate to something **3** one's training and experience **4** events leading up to something

back·hand *n.* **1** handwriting that slants up to the left **2** a backhand catch, stroke, etc. —*adj.* **1** done with the back of the hand; specif., done with the back of the hand turned inward, as for a baseball catch, or forward, as for a tennis stroke, and with the arm across the body **2** written in backhand —*adv.* with a backhand —*vt.* to hit, catch, swing, etc. backhand

back·hand·ed *adj.* **1** BACKHAND **2** indirect or sarcastic —*adv.* with a backhand

back·hoe (-hō′) *n.* an excavating vehicle with a hinged bucket at the end of a long arm

back·ing *n.* **1** something forming a back for support **2** support given to a person or cause **3** supporters; backers

back·lash *n.* a sharp reaction or recoil

back·log *n.* an accumulation, as of uncompleted tasks — *vi., vt.* **-logged′, -log′ging** to accumulate as a backlog

back order an order not yet filled

back·pack *n.* a knapsack, esp. one attached to a frame and worn as by hikers — *vi., vt.* to hike with, or carry in, a backpack —**back′-pack′er** *n.*

back·ped·al *vi.* **-ped′aled** or **-ped′alled, -ped′al·ing** or **-ped′al·ling 1** to pedal backward, as in braking a bicycle **2** to move backward; retreat **3** to retract an earlier opinion

back·rest *n.* a support for or at the back

back·scratch·ing *n.* [Inf.] a reciprocal exchange of favors, etc.

back·side *n.* **1** the back part **2** the rump

back·slap·per (-slap′ər) *n.* [Inf.] an effusively friendly person

back·slash *n.* a short diagonal line (\): a character found esp. on computer keyboards

back·slide *vi.* **-slid′, -slid′** or **-slid′den, -slid′ing 1** to revert to bad habits, etc. **2** to reverse previous gains —**back′slid′er** *n.*

back·space *vi.* **-spaced′, -spac′ing** to move a typewriter carriage, cursor, etc. one or more spaces back along the line

back·spin *n.* a backward spin given to a ball, etc., making it reverse its normal direction upon hitting a surface

back·splash *n.* a washable surface behind a sink, etc. to protect a wall from splashes

back·stab·ber (-stab′ər) *n.* one who harms a friend, partner, etc. by treachery

back·stage *adv., adj.* behind and off the stage, as in the wings or dressing rooms

back·stairs *adj.* involving intrigue or scandal; secret: also **back′stair′**

back·stop *n.* a fence, screen, etc. to keep balls from going too far, as behind the catcher in baseball

back·stretch *n.* the part of a racetrack opposite the homestretch

back·stroke *n.* a swimming stroke made while lying face upward

back·swing *n.* that part of a player's swing in which the golf club, tennis racket, etc. is swung backward before being swung forward

back talk [Inf.] insolent replies

back-to-back *adj.* [Inf.] one right after another

back·track *vi.* **1** to return by the same path **2** to retreat or recant

back·up or **back-up** *adj.* **1** standing by as an alternate or auxiliary **2** supporting —*n.* **a** backing up; specif., *a*) an accumulation *b*) a support or help

back·ward *adv.* **1** toward the back **2** with the back foremost **3** in reverse order **4** in a way opposite to usual **5** into the past Also **back′-wards** —*adj.* **1** turned toward the rear or in the opposite way **2** shy **3** slow to develop —**back′ward·ness** *n.*

back·wash *n.* **1** water or air moved backward, as by a ship, propeller, etc. **2** a reaction caused by some event

back·wa·ter *n.* **1** water moved or held back by a dam, tide, etc. **2** an inlet, as off a river, that has little or no current **3** a place regarded as isolated, slow to change, etc.

back·woods *pl.n.* [*occas. with sing. v.*] largely wooded areas far from centers of population —*adj.* of or like the backwoods **back′woods′man** (-mən) *n., pl.* **-men** (-mən)

ba·con (bā′kən) *n.* [< OS *baco*, side of bacon] salted and smoked meat from the back or sides of a hog

Ba·con (bā′kən), **Fran·cis** (fran′sis) 1561-1626; Eng. philosopher & writer

bac·te·ri·a (bak tir′ē ə) *pl.n., sing.* **-ri·um** (-əm) or **-ri·a** [< Gr *baktērion*, small staff] microorganisms which have no chlorophyll and multiply by simple division: some bacteria cause diseases, but others are necessary for digestive health, etc. —**bac·te′ri·al** *adj.*

bac·te·ri·cide (-tir′ə sīd′) *n.* an agent that destroys bacteria —**bac·te′ri·cid′al** *adj.*

bac·te·ri·ol·o·gy (-tir′ē äl′ə jē) *n.* the science that deals with bacteria —**bac·te′ri·o·log′i·cal** (-ə läj′ə kəl) *adj.* —**bac·te′ri·ol′o·gist** *n.*

bad[1] (bad) *adj.* **worse, worst** ⟦ME⟧ **1** not good; not as it should be **2** inadequate or unfit **3** unfavorable [*bad* news] **4** rotten or spoiled **5** incorrect or faulty **6** *a*) wicked; immoral *b*) misbehaving; mischievous **7** harmful **8** severe **9** ill **10** sorry; distressed [he feels *bad* about it] **11** offensive —*adv.* [Inf.] badly —*n.* anything bad —**not bad** [Inf.] fairly good —**bad′ness** *n.*

bad[2] (bad) *vt., vi. archaic pt. of* BID

bad blood mutual ill will

bade (bad) *vt., vi. alt. pt. of* BID

bad egg [Slang] a mean or dishonest person: also **bad actor, bad apple,** or **bad lot**

bad faith insincerity; dishonesty

badge (baj) *n.* [ME *bage*] **1** an emblem worn to show rank, membership, etc. **2** any distinctive sign, etc.

badg·er (baj′ər) *n.* [< ?] **1** a carnivorous burrowing mammal with a broad back and thick, short legs **2** its fur —*vt.* to nag or torment

bad·i·nage (bad′'n äzh′) *n.* [Fr] playful talk; banter

bad·lands (bad′landz′) *pl.n.* **1** an area of barren land with dry soil and soft rocks eroded into odd shapes **2** [B-] any of several such W U.S. areas

bad·ly *adv.* **worse, worst 1** in a bad manner **2** [Inf.] very much; greatly

bad·man (-man′) *n., pl.* **-men′** (-men′) a cattle thief or desperado of the old West

bad·min·ton (bad′mint′'n) *n.* [after *Badminton,* Eng estate] a game in which players use rackets to hit a shuttlecock back and forth over a net

bad-mouth *vt.* [Slang] to find fault with, esp. to another; disparage

bad-tem·pered *adj.* irritable

Bae·de·ker (bā′də kər) *n.* **1** any of a series of guidebooks to foreign countries, first published in Germany **2** loosely, any guidebook

baf·fle (baf′əl) *vt.* **-fled, -fling** [< ?] **1** to perplex completely; bewilder **2** to impede; check —*n.* a wall or screen to deflect air, sound, etc. —**baf′fle·ment** *n.* —**baf′fler** *n.* —**baf′fling** *adj.*

bag (bag) *n.* [< ON *baggi*] **1** a nonrigid container of paper, plastic, etc., with an open top **2** a satchel; suitcase, etc. **3** a purse **4** game taken in hunting **5** a baglike shape or part **6** a bagful **7** [Slang] an unattractive woman **8** [Slang] one's special interest **9** *Baseball* a base —*vt.* **bagged, bag′ging 1** to put into a bag **2** to capture **3** to kill in hunting **4** [Slang] to obtain —*vi.* **1** to swell; bulge **2** to hang loosely —**in the bag** [Slang] having its success assured

bag·a·telle (bag′ə tel′) *n.* [Fr < L *baca,* berry] a trifle

ba·gel (bā′gəl) *n.* [Yiddish] a chewy, ring-shaped bread roll

bag·ful *n., pl.* **-fuls′** as much as a bag will hold

bag·gage (bag′ij) *n.* [< ML *bagga,* chest, bag] **1** the bags, etc. of a traveler; luggage **2** burdensome beliefs, practices, etc.

bag·gie (bag′ē) *n.* [< *Baggies,* a trademark for such bags] a small, clear plastic bag for storing food, etc.

bag·gy (bag′ē) *adj.* **-gi·er, -gi·est** puffed out or hanging loosely —**bag′gi·ly** *adv.* —**bag′gi·ness** *n.*

Bagh·dad (bag′dad) capital of Iraq: also sp. **Bag·dad**

bag lady [Slang] a homeless, poor woman who wanders city streets carrying her belongings in shopping bags

bag·pipe *n.* [*often pl.*] a wind instrument of Scotland, Ireland, etc., played by forcing air from a bag into reed pipes and fingering the stops

bah (bä, ba) *interj.* used to express contempt, scorn, or disgust

Ba·ha·mas (bə hä′məz) country on a group of islands (**Bahama Islands**) in the West Indies

Bah·rain (bä rān′) country on a group of islands in the Persian Gulf: also sp. **Bah·rein′**

bail¹ (bāl) *n.* [< L *bajulare,* bear a burden] **1** money deposited with the court to get a prisoner temporarily released **2** such a release —*vt.* **1** to have (a prisoner) set free by giving bail **2** to help out of financial or other difficulty Often with *out* —**bail′a·ble** *adj.*

bail² (bāl) *vi., vt.* [ME *baille,* bucket] to dip out (water) from (a boat): usually with *out* —**bail out 1** to parachute from an aircraft **2** [Inf.] to flee a difficult situation

bail³ (bāl) *n.* [ME *beil*] a hoop-shaped handle for a bucket, etc.

bail·iff (bā′lif) *n.* [ME *bailif*] **1** a deputy sheriff **2** a court officer who guards the jurors, keeps order in the court, etc. **3** in England, a district official **4** [Chiefly Brit.] a steward of an estate

bail·i·wick (bā′lə wik′) *n.* [ME < *baili,* bailiff + *wik,* village] **1** a bailiff's district **2** one's particular area of activity, authority, interest, etc.

bails·man (bālz′mən) *n., pl.* **-men** (-mən) a person who gives bail for another

bairn (bern) *n.* [Scot.] a child

bait (bāt) *vt.* [< ON *beita*] **1** to set dogs on for sport [to *bait* bears] **2** to torment or harass, esp. by verbal attacks **3** to goad or provoke **4** to put food on (a hook or trap) as a lure for game **5** to lure; entice; tempt —*n.* **1** food, etc. put on a hook or trap as a lure **2** anything used as a lure

bait-and-switch *adj.* of or using an unethical sales technique in which a seller lures customers by advertising an often nonexistent bargain item and then tries to switch their attention to more expensive items

baize (bāz) *n.* [< L *badius,* brown] a coarse, feltlike woolen cloth

Ba·ja Ca·li·for·nia (bä′hä kä′lē fôr′nyä) peninsula of NW Mexico, south of California

bake (bāk) *vt.* **baked, bak′ing** [< OE *bacan*] **1** to cook (food) by dry heat, esp. in an oven **2** to dry and harden (pottery, etc.) by heat; fire —*vi.* **1** to bake bread, etc. **2** to become baked —*n.* **1** a baking **2** a social affair at which baked food is served

baked beans navy beans baked with salt pork, molasses or brown sugar, etc.

bak·er (bā′kər) *n.* one whose work or business is baking bread, etc.

baker's dozen thirteen

bak·er·y *n., pl.* **-er·ies** a place where bread, etc. is baked or sold

baking powder a leavening agent containing baking soda and an acid-forming substance

baking soda sodium bicarbonate, used as a leavening agent and as an antacid

bal·a·lai·ka (bal′ə līk′ə) *n.* [Russ] a Russian stringed instrument somewhat like a guitar

bal·ance (bal′əns) *n.* [< LL *bilanx,* having two scales] **1** an instrument for weighing, esp. one with two matched hanging scales **2** a state of equilibrium in weight, value, etc. **3** bodily equilibrium **4** mental or emotional stability **5** harmonious proportion of elements in a design, etc. **6** a weight, value, etc. that counteracts another **7** equality of debits and credits, or the difference between them **8** a remainder —*vt.* **-anced, -anc·ing 1** to weigh in or as in a balance **2** to compare as to relative value, etc. **3** to counteract; offset **4** to bring into proportion, harmony, etc. **5** to make or be equal to in weight, value, etc. **6** to find the difference between, or to equalize, the debits and credits of (an account) —*vi.* **1** to be in equilibrium **2** to be equal in weight, value, etc. **3** to have the credits and debits equal —**in the balance** not yet settled

balance sheet a statement showing the financial status of a business

bal·co·ny (bal′kə nē) *n., pl.* **-nies** [< It *balcone*] **1** a platform projecting from an upper story and enclosed by a railing **2** an upper floor of seats in a theater, etc., often projecting over the main floor

bald (bôld) *adj.* [< ME] **1** lacking hair on the head **2** not covered by natural growth **3** having the tread worn off **4** plain or blunt [*bald truth*] —**bald′ly** *adv.* **bald′ness** *n.*

bald eagle a large eagle of North America, with a white-feathered head

bal·der·dash (bôl′dər dash′) *n.* nonsense

bald-faced (bôld′fāst′) *adj.* brazen; shameless [a *baldfaced* lie]

bald·ing *adj.* becoming bald

bal·dric (bôl′drik′) *n.* [ult. < L *balteus*, belt] a belt worn over one shoulder to support a sword, etc.

bale (bāl) *n.* [< OHG *balla*, ball] a large bundle, esp. a standardized quantity of hay, cotton, etc., compressed and bound —*vt.* **baled, bal′ing** to make into bales —**bal′er** *n.*

ba·leen (bə lēn′) *n.* [ult. < Gr *phallaina*, whale] the horny, elastic material hanging from the upper jaw of some whales (**baleen whales**)

bale·ful (bāl′fəl) *adj.* [< OE *bealu*, evil] deadly; harmful; ominous

Ba·li (bä′lē, bal′ē) island of Indonesia —**Ba′li·nese′** *adj., n., pl.* **-nese′**

balk (bôk) *n.* [OE *balca*, ridge] **1** an obstruction, hindrance, etc. **2** *Baseball* an illegal motion by the pitcher entitling base runners to advance one base —*vt.* to obstruct; foil —*vi.* **1** to stop and refuse to move or act **2** to hesitate (*at*)

Balkan Peninsula peninsula in SE Europe, east of Italy

Bal·kans (bôl′kənz) countries of Serbia, Montenegro, Slovenia, Croatia, Bosnia and Herzegovina, Macedonia, Romania, Bulgaria, Albania, Greece, & European Turkey, in SE Europe —**Bal′kan** *adj.*

balk·y (bôk′ē) *adj.* **-i·er, -i·est** stubbornly resisting

ball¹ (bôl) *n.* [ME *bal*] **1** any round object; sphere; globe **2** *a*) a round or egg-shaped object used in various games *b*) any of several such games, esp. baseball **3** a throw or pitch of a ball [a fast *ball*] **4** [Historical] a round projectile fired from a cannon, rifle, etc. **5** a rounded part of the body **6** *Base*-

ball a pitched ball that is not hit and is not a strike —*vi., vt.* to form into a ball —**ball up** [Slang] to muddle or confuse —**be on the ball** [Slang] to be alert; be efficient

ball² (bôl) *n.* [< Fr < Gr *ballizein*, to dance] **1** a formal social dance **2** [Slang] a good time [had a *ball*]

bal·lad (bal′əd) *n.* [< OFr *ballade*, dancing song] **1** a sentimental song with the same melody for each stanza **2** a narrative song or poem, usually anonymous, with simple words, short stanzas, and a refrain **3** a popular love song —**bal′lad·eer′** *n.* —**bal′lad·ry** *n.*

ball-and-sock·et joint a joint, as of the hip, formed by a ball in a socket

bal·last (bal′əst) *n.* [< MDu *bal*, bad] **1** anything heavy carried in a ship or vehicle to give stability **2** crushed rock or gravel, used in railroad beds, etc. **3** a device that regulates the flow of current to a fluorescent lamp —*vt.* to furnish with ballast

ball bearing 1 a bearing in which the parts turn on freely rolling metal balls **2** one of these balls

bal·le·ri·na (bal′ə rē′nə) *n.* [It] a female ballet dancer

bal·let (ba lā′, bal′ā) *n.* [Fr] **1** an artistic dance form of graceful, precise gestures and movements **2** a play, etc. performed by ballet dancers, or the music for this **3** ballet dancers

ball·game *n.* **1** a game played with a ball **2** [Inf.] a set of circumstances [a different *ballgame*]

ballistic missile a long-range guided missile designed to fall freely as it approaches its target

bal·lis·tics (bə lis′tiks) *n.* the science dealing with the motion and impact of projectiles —**bal·lis′tic** *adj.*

ball joint a ball-and-socket joint used in automotive vehicles to connect the tie rods to the turning wheels

bal·loon (bə lōōn′) *n.* [< Fr < It *palla*, ball] **1** a large, airtight bag that rises when filled with hot air or a gas lighter than air **2** an airship using such a bag to provide buoyancy **3** an inflatable rubber bag, used as a toy **4** the large final payment on certain loans —*vt.* to inflate —*vi.* to swell; expand —*adj.* like a balloon —**bal·loon′ist** *n.*

bal·lot (bal′ət) *n.* [< It *palla*, ball] **1** a ticket, card, form, etc. by which a vote is registered **2** the act or right of voting, as by ballots **3** the total number of votes cast —*vi.* to vote

ball·park *n.* a baseball stadium

ball-peen hammer a hammer with one end of the head rounded and the other end flat

ball·play·er *n.* a baseball player

ball·point (pen) a writing pen with a small ball bearing at its tip to apply the ink: also **ball′-point′** *n.*

ball·room *n.* a large hall for dancing

bal·ly·hoo (bal′ē hōō′) *n.* [< ?] noisy talk, sensational advertising, etc. — *vt., vi.* **-hooed′, -hoo′ing** [Inf.] to promote with ballyhoo

balm (bäm, bälm) *n.* [< Gr *balsamon*] 1 a fragrant, healing ointment or oil 2 anything healing or soothing

balm·y *adj.* **-i·er, -i·est** 1 soothing, mild, etc. 2 [Slang, Chiefly Brit.] crazy

ba·lo·ney (bə lō′nē) *n.* [< *bologna*] 1 bologna 2 [Slang] nonsense

bal·sa (bôl′sə) *n.* [Sp] 1 the wood, very lightweight and soft, of a tropical American tree 2 the tree

bal·sam (bôl′səm) *n.* [see BALM] 1 an aromatic resin obtained from certain trees 2 any of various aromatic, resinous oils or fluids 3 balm 4 any of various trees yielding balsam

bal·sam·ic vinegar (bôl sam′ik) aromatic, dark-brown vinegar used in salad dressings, etc.

Bal·tic Sea (bôl′tik) sea in N Europe, west of Latvia, Lithuania, & Estonia

Bal·ti·more (bôl′tə môr) seaport in N Maryland

bal·us·ter (bal′əs tər) *n.* [< Gr *balaustion*, wild pomegranate flower: from the shape] any of the small posts of a railing, as on a staircase

bal·us·trade (bal′əs trād′) *n.* a railing having an upper rail supported by balusters

Bal·zac (bál zák′; *E* bôl′zak), **Ho·no·ré de** (ô nô rä′də) 1799-1850; Fr. novelist

bam·boo (bam bōō′) *n.* [Malay *bambu*] a bush- or tree-sized tropical grass with woody, jointed, often hollow stems used for furniture, canes, etc.

bam·boo·zle (bam bōō′zəl) *vt.* **-zled, -zling** [< ?] 1 to trick; cheat; dupe 2 to confuse; puzzle

ban (ban) *vt.* **banned, ban′ning** [< OE *bannan*, summon] to prohibit or forbid, esp. officially —*n.* 1 a condemnation by church authorities 2 a curse 3 an official prohibition 4 strong public condemnation

ba·nal (bā′nəl, bə nal′) *adj.* [Fr: see prec.] trite; hackneyed —**ba·nal′i·ty** *n.*, *pl.* **-ties** —**ba′nal·ly** *adv.*

ba·nan·a (bə nan′ə) *n.* [Sp & Port] 1 a tropical plant with large clusters of edible fruit 2 the narrow, curved fruit, having soft pulp and thick, usually yellow skin

band[1] (band) *n.* [ON] 1 something that binds, ties, or encircles, as a strip or ring of wood, rubber, metal, etc. 2 a strip of color or of material 3 a range of wavelengths —*vt.* to put a band on or around

band[2] (band) *n.* [< Gothic *bandwa*, a sign] 1 a group of people united for some purpose 2 a group of musicians playing together, esp. to play lively or popular music —*vi., vt.* to unite for some purpose

band·age (ban′dij) *n.* [Fr < *bande*, a strip] a strip of cloth, etc. used to bind or cover an injury —*vt.* **-aged, -ag·ing** to put a bandage on

Band-Aid (band′ād′) [prec. + AID] *trademark for* a small bandage of gauze and adhesive tape —*n.* [*also* **band-aid**] such a bandage: also **band′aid′**

ban·dan·na or **ban·dan·a** (ban dan′ə) *n.* [Hindi *bāndhnū*, a method of dyeing] a large,

colored handkerchief often worn on the head or around the neck

band·box *n.* a light, round box to hold hats, etc.

ban·deau (ban dō′) *n.*, *pl.* **-deaux′** (-dōz′) [Fr] 1 a narrow ribbon 2 a band of material covering the breasts, as a strapless bikini top

ban·dit (ban′dit) *n.* [< It] 1 a robber; brigand 2 one who steals, defrauds, etc. —**ban′dit·ry** *n.*

ban·do·leer or **ban·do·lier** (ban′də lir′) *n.* [< Fr] a broad belt with pockets for bullets, etc., worn over one shoulder and across the chest

band saw an endless toothed steel belt on pulleys, powered for sawing

band·stand *n.* a platform for a band, esp. one for outdoor concerts

band·wag·on *n.* a wagon for a band to ride on, as in a parade —**on the bandwagon** [Inf.] on the side that is popular or appears to be winning

band·width *n.* the transmission rate of information along electronic communications lines

ban·dy[1] (ban′dē) *vt.* **-died, -dy·ing** [Fr *bander*, bandy at tennis] 1 to toss or hit back and forth 2 to pass (rumors, etc.) freely 3 to exchange (words), esp. angrily

ban·dy[2] (ban′dē) *adj.* [Fr *bandé*, bent] curved outward; bowed

ban·dy-leg·ged (-leg′id, -legd′) *adj.* bowlegged

bane (bān) *n.* [OE *bana*] 1 ruin, death, harm, or their cause 2 [Obs.] poison —**bane′ful** *adj.*

bang[1] (baŋ) *vt.* [ON *banga*, to pound] to hit, shut, etc. hard and noisily —*vi.* 1 to make a loud noise 2 to hit noisily or sharply —*n.* 1 a hard, noisy blow or impact 2 a loud, sudden noise 3 [Inf.] a burst of vigor 4 [Slang] a thrill —*adv.* 1 hard and noisily 2 abruptly —**bang up** to damage

bang[2] (baŋ) *n.* [< prec.] [*usually pl.*] hair cut to hang down on the forehead

Bang·kok (baŋ′käk′) seaport & capital of Thailand

Ban·gla·desh (bäŋ′glə desh′, baŋ′-) country in S Asia, on the Bay of Bengal

ban·gle (baŋ′gəl) *n.* [Hindi *bangrī*] a decorative bracelet or anklet

bang-up (baŋ′up′) *adj.* [Inf.] very good; excellent

ban·ish (ban′ish) *vt.* [< OFr *banir*] 1 to exile 2 to get rid of —**ban′ish·ment** *n.*

ban·is·ter (ban′is tər) *n.* [< BALUSTER] a handrail, specif. one supported by balusters

ban·jo (ban′jō′) *n.*, *pl.* **-jos′** *or* **-joes′** [of Afr orig.] a musical instrument with a long neck, circular body, and strings that are plucked —**ban′jo·ist** *n.*

bank[1] (baŋk) *n.* [ult. < OHG *bank*, bench] 1 an establishment for receiving or lending money 2 a reserve supply; pool —*vi.* to do business with a bank —*vt.* to deposit (money) in a bank —**bank on** [Inf.] to rely on —**bank′a·ble** *adj.*

bank² (baŋk) *n.* [< ON *bakki*] 1 a long mound or heap 2 a steep slope 3 a rise of land along a river, etc. 4 a shallow place, as in a sea 5 the lateral, slanting turn of an aircraft —*vt.* 1 to cover (a fire) with ashes and fuel so that it will burn slowly 2 to pile up so as to form a bank 3 to slope (a curve in a road, etc.) 4 to make (an aircraft) slant laterally on a turn 5 to make (a billiard ball) recoil from a cushion

bank³ (baŋk) *n.* [< OFr *banc*, bench] 1 a row of oars 2 a row or tier, as of keys in a keyboard —*vt.* to arrange in a row or tier

bank account money deposited in a bank and credited to the depositor

bank·book *n.* a book recording a bank depositor's deposits and withdrawals; passbook

bank card an encoded plastic card issued by a bank as for use at an ATM

bank·er *n.* a person who owns or manages a bank

bank·ing *n.* the business of a bank

bank·note *n.* a promissory note issued by a bank: a form of paper money

bank·roll *n.* a supply of money —*vt.* [Inf.] to supply with money; finance

bank·rupt (baŋk′rupt′) *n.* [< Fr < It *banca*, bench + *rotta*, broken] a person legally declared unable to pay debts —*adj.* 1 that is a bankrupt; insolvent 2 lacking in some quality [morally *bankrupt*] —*vt.* to make bankrupt —**bank′rupt′cy** *n., pl.* **-cies**

ban·ner (ban′ər) *n.* [ME *banere* < OFr *buniere*] 1 a flag 2 a headline running across a newspaper page —*adj.* foremost

banns (banz) *pl.n.* [see BAN] the proclamation made in church of an intended marriage

ban·quet (baŋ′kwət) *n.* [ult. < OHG *bank*, bench] 1 a feast 2 a formal dinner —*vt.* to honor with a banquet

ban·quette (baŋ ket′) *n.* [Fr] 1 a gunners' platform inside a trench, etc. 2 an upholstered bench

ban·shee (ban′shē) *n.* [< Ir *bean*, woman + *sith*, fairy] *Celt. Folklore* a female spirit whose wailing warns of impending death

ban·tam (ban′təm) *n.* [after *Bantam*, former province in Java] 1 any of various small domestic fowls 2 a small but aggressive person —*adj.* like a bantam

ban·tam·weight *n.* a boxer weighing 113 to 118 lb.

ban·ter (ban′tər) *vt.* [?] to tease playfully —*vi.* to exchange banter (*with* someone) —*n.* playful teasing —**ban′ter·ing·ly** *adv.*

Ban·tu (ban′tōō) *n.* [Bantu *ba–ntu*, the men] 1 a large group of languages of S Africa, including Swahili and Zulu 2 *pl.* **-tus′** or **-tu′** a member of a Bantu-speaking people

ban·yan (ban′yən) *n.* [ult. < Sans] an Indian fig tree whose branches grow shoots that take root and become new trunks over a wide area

ba·o·bab (bā′ō bab′, bä′-) *n.* [< ? Ethiopian native name] a thick-trunked tree of Africa, with edible, gourdlike fruit

bap·tism (bap′tiz′əm) *n.* [see BAPTIZE] 1 the sacrament of admitting a person into a Christian church by immersing the individual in water or by sprinkling water on the individual 2 an initiating experience —**bap·tis′mal** (-tiz′məl) *adj.*

Bap·tist (-tist) *n.* a member of a Protestant denomination practicing baptism of believers by immersion

bap·tis·ter·y (-tis tər ē, -tis trē) *n., pl.* **-ies** a place, esp. in a church, used for baptizing: also **bap′tis·try**, *pl.* **-tries**

bap·tize (bap tīz′, bap′tīz) *vt.* **-tized′**, **-tiz′ing** [< Gr *baptizein*, to immerse] 1 to administer baptism to 2 to initiate 3 to christen

bar (bär) *n.* [< ML *barra*] 1 any long, narrow piece of wood, metal, etc., often used as a barrier, lever, etc. 2 an oblong piece, as of soap 3 anything that obstructs or hinders 4 a band or strip 5 a law court, esp. that part, enclosed by a railing, where the lawyers sit 6 lawyers collectively 7 the legal profession 8 a counter, as for serving alcoholic drinks 9 a place with such a counter 10 *Music a*) a vertical line dividing a staff into measures *b*) a measure —*vt.* **barred**, **bar′ring** 1 to fasten with a bar 2 to obstruct; close 3 to oppose 4 to exclude —*prep.* excluding [the best, *bar* none] —**raise** (or **lower**) **the bar** to raise (or lower) the standard, as in a competition

barb (bärb) *n.* [< L *barba*, beard] 1 a beardlike growth 2 a sharp point projecting backward from the main point of a fishhook, harpoon, etc. 3 a cutting remark —*vt.* to provide with a barb —**barbed** *adj.*

Bar·ba·dos (bär bā′dōs, -dōz) country on an island in the West Indies

bar·bar·i·an (bär ber′ē ən) *n.* [see BARBAROUS] 1 a member of a people considered primitive, savage, etc. 2 a cruel person —*adj.* uncivilized, cruel, etc. —**bar·bar′i·an·ism′** *n.*

bar·bar·ic (-ber′ik) *adj.* 1 uncivilized; primitive 2 wild, crude, etc.

bar·ba·rism (bär′bə riz′əm) *n.* 1 a nonstandard word or expression 2 the state of being primitive or uncivilized 3 a barbarous act or custom

bar·bar·i·ty (bär ber′ə tē) *n., pl.* **-ties** 1 cruelty; brutality 2 a barbaric taste, manner, etc.

bar·ba·rize (bär′bə rīz′) *vt.,* **-rized′**, **-riz′ing** to make or become barbarous —**bar′ba·ri·za′tion** *n.*

bar·ba·rous (bär′bə rəs) *adj.* [< Gr *barbaros*, foreign] 1 uncivilized; primitive 2 crude, coarse, etc. 3 cruel; brutal —**bar′ba·rous·ly** *adv.*

bar·be·cue (bär′bə kyōō′) *n.* [AmSp *barbacoa*] 1 *a*) a hog, steer, etc. roasted whole over an open fire *b*) any meat broiled over an open fire 2 a party, picnic, etc. featuring this —*vt.,* **-cued′**, **-cu′ing** to broil over an open fire, often with a sweet, highly seasoned sauce (**barbecue sauce**)

barbed wire wire with barbs at close intervals

bar·bel (bär′bəl) *n.* [< L *barba*, beard] a threadlike growth from the lips or jaws of certain fishes

bar·bell (bär′bel′) *n.* 〚BAR + (DUMB)BELL〛 a metal bar with weights attached at each end, used for weight lifting: also **bar bell**

bar·ber (bär′bər) *n.* 〚see BARB〛 one whose work is cutting hair, shaving beards, etc.

bar·ber·ry (bär′ber′ē, -bə rē) *n., pl.* **-ries** 〚< ML *barberis*〛 1 a spiny shrub with sour, red berries 2 the berry

bar·bi·tu·rate (bär bich′ər it, -bich′ə wit) *n.* 〚< Ger〛 a salt or ester of a crystalline acid (**bar′bi·tu′ric acid**), used as a sedative

barb·wire *n.* BARBED WIRE

bar·ca·role or **bar·ca·rolle** (bär′kə rōl′) *n.* 〚< Fr < It〛 a Venetian gondolier song, or music like this

Bar·ce·lo·na (bär′sə lō′nə) seaport in NE Spain

bar code UNIVERSAL PRODUCT CODE

bard (bärd) *n.* 〚Gael & Ir〛 1 an ancient Celtic poet 2 a poet —**the Bard** SHAKESPEARE

bare (ber) *adj.* **bar′er, bar′est** 〚OE *bær*〛 1 not covered or clothed; naked 2 without furnishings; empty 3 simple; plain 4 mere [*bare* needs] —*vt.* **bared, bar′ing** to make bare; uncover —**lay bare** to uncover; expose —**bare′ness** *n.*

bare·back *adv., adj.* on a horse with no saddle

bare·bones *adj.* simple; basic

bare·faced *adj.* 1 with the face uncovered 2 open; shameless

bare·foot *adj., adv.* without shoes and stockings: also **bare′foot′ed**

bare·hand·ed *adj., adv.* 1 with hands uncovered or unprotected 2 without weapons, etc.

bare·head·ed *adj., adv.* wearing no hat or other covering on the head

bare·leg·ged (-leg′id, -legd′) *adj., adv.* with the legs bare

bare·ly (ber′lē) *adv.* 1 plainly 2 only just; scarcely 3 scantily

bar·gain (bär′gən) *n.* 〚< OFr *bargaignier*, haggle〛 1 a mutual agreement or contract 2 such an agreement with regard to worth [a bad *bargain*] 3 something sold at a price favorable to the buyer —*vi.* 1 to haggle 2 to make a bargain —**bargain for** (or **on**) to expect; count on —**into** (or **in**) **the bargain** besides —**bar′gain·er** *n.*

bargain counter a store counter for displaying goods at reduced prices

barge (bärj) *n.* 〚< ML *barga*〛 1 a large, flat-bottomed boat for freight on rivers, etc. 2 a large pleasure boat —*vi.* **barged, barg′ing** 1 to move slowly and clumsily 2 to come or go (*in* or *into*) rudely or abruptly

bar graph a graph in which the lengths of parallel bars are used to compare quantities, etc.

bar·i·tone (bar′ə tōn′) *n.* 〚< Gr *barys*, deep + *tonos*, tone〛 1 the range of a male voice between tenor and bass 2 a voice, singer, or instrument with such a range

bar·i·um (ber′ē əm) *n.* 〚< Gr *barys*, heavy〛 a metallic chemical element: symbol, Ba; at. no. 56

bark¹ (bärk) *n.* 〚< ON *borkr*〛 the outside covering of trees and woody plants —*vt.* 1 to remove bark from 2 [Inf.] to scrape; skin (the knees, etc.)

bark² (bärk) *vi.* 〚OE *beorcan*〛 1 to make the sharp, abrupt cry of a dog or a similar sound 2 to speak sharply; snap —*n.* the characteristic cry of a dog, or any noise like this —**bark up the wrong tree** to misdirect one's attack, energies, etc.

bark³ (bärk) *n.* 〚< LL *barca*〛 1 [Old Poet.] a boat 2 a sailing vessel with two square-rigged masts forward and a fore-and-aft mast aft

bar·keep·er *n.* 1 an owner of a barroom 2 a bartender Also **bar′keep′**

bark·er *n.* one who talks loud to attract customers to a sideshow, etc.

bar·ley (bär′lē) *n.* 〚OE *bærlic*〛 1 a cereal grass 2 its grain, used in making malt, in soups, etc.

bar·maid *n.* a waitress who serves alcoholic drinks in a bar

bar mitz·vah (bär mits′və) 〚< Yiddish < Aram *bar*, son of + Heb *mitsva*, commandment〛 [*also* **B- M-**] 1 a Jewish boy who has arrived at the age of religious responsibility, 13 years 2 the ceremony celebrating this event

barn (bärn) *n.* 〚OE *bern*〛 a farm building for sheltering harvested crops, livestock, machines, etc.

bar·na·cle (bär′nə kəl) *n.* 〚ME *bernacle*〛 a saltwater crustacean that attaches itself to rocks, ship bottoms, etc.

barn·burn·er *n.* [Slang] something dramatic and exciting, as a close contest

barn·storm *vi., vt.* to tour (the country, esp. rural areas) giving speeches or lectures, performing exhibitions, etc. —**barn′storm′er** *n.*

barn·yard *n.* the ground near a barn —*adj.* of, like, or fit for a barnyard; specif., earthy or crude

ba·rom·e·ter (bə räm′ət ər) *n.* 〚< Gr *baros*, weight + -METER〛 1 an instrument for measuring atmospheric pressure and thus forecasting weather 2 anything that marks change —**bar·o·met·ric** (bar′ə me′trik) *adj.*

bar·on (bar′ən) *n.* 〚ME〛 1 a member of the lowest rank of British nobility 2 a magnate —**bar′on·age** *n.* —**ba·ro·ni·al** (bə rō′nē əl) *adj.*

bar·on·ess (bar′ə nis) *n.* 1 the wife or widow of a baron 2 a noblewoman holding a baronial title

bar·on·et (-ət) *n.* a man holding the lowest hereditary British title, below a baron —**bar′on·et·cy** *n., pl.* **-cies**

ba·roque (bə rōk′) *adj.* 〚Fr < Port *barroco*, imperfect pearl〛 1 [*often* **B-**] *a)* very ornate and full of curved lines, as much art and architecture of about 1600-1750 *b)* full of highly embellished melodies, fugues, etc., as much music of that time 2 extravagantly ornate or complex

bar·racks (bar′əks) *pl.n.* 〚< Sp *barro*, clay〛 [*often with sing. v.*] a building or group of buildings for housing soldiers, etc.

bar·ra·cu·da (bar′ə kōō′də) *n., pl.* **-da** or **-das**

[[AmSp]] a fierce, pikelike fish of tropical seas

bar·rage (bə räzh′, -räj′) *n.* [[Fr < *barrer*, to stop]] **1** artillery fire that holds down the enemy while one's army attacks **2** any heavy bombardment or prolonged attack — *vi., vt.* **-raged′, -rag′ing** to subject to a barrage

barred (bärd) *adj.* **1** having bars or stripes **2** closed off with bars **3** not allowed

bar·rel (bar′əl) *n.* [[< ML *barillus*]] **1** a large, cylindrical container with slightly bulging sides and flat ends **2** a similar cylindrical container **3** the capacity of a standard barrel, used as a measure **4** the straight tube of a gun —*vt.* **-reled** or **-relled, -rel·ing** or **-rel·ling** to put in barrels —*vi.* [Slang] to go at high speed —**over a barrel** [Inf.] in a helpless position

bar·rel·ful (-fool′) *n.* **1** as much as a barrel will hold **2** [Inf.] a great amount

bar·rel·head *n.* the flat end of a barrel —**on the barrelhead** when delivered [to pay cash *on the barrelhead*]

barrel organ a mechanical musical instrument played by turning a crank

bar·ren (bar′ən) *adj.* [[< OFr]] **1** unable to bear offspring; sterile **2** without vegetation **3** unproductive **4** boring; dull **5** devoid (*of*) —**bar′ren·ness** *n.*

bar·rette (bə ret′) *n.* [[Fr]] a bar or clasp for holding a woman's hair in place

bar·ri·cade (bar′i kād′; *also, esp. for v.,* bar′ə kād′) *n.* [[Fr < It *barricare*, fortify]] a barrier, esp. one put up hastily for defense —*vt.* **-cad′ed, -cad′ing** to block with a barricade

bar·ri·er (bar′ē ər) *n.* [[< ML *barra*]] **1** an obstruction, as a fence **2** anything that blocks or hinders

bar·ring (bar′iŋ) *prep.* excepting

bar·ris·ter (bar′is tər) *n.* [[< *bar* (law court)]] in England, a lawyer authorized to plead cases in court

bar·room *n.* a room with a bar where alcoholic drinks are sold

bar·row[1] (bar′ō) *n.* [[< OE *beran*, to bear]] a handbarrow or wheelbarrow

bar·row[2] (bar′ō) *n.* [[< OE *beorg*, hill]] a heap of earth or rocks covering a grave

bar·tend·er *n.* one who serves alcoholic drinks at a bar —**bar′tend′** *vi.*

bar·ter (bürt′ər) *vi., vt.* [[< OFr *barater*]] to trade by exchanging (goods or services) without money —*n.* **1** a bartering **2** anything bartered —**bar′ter·er** *n.*

Bar·tók (bär′tôk′), **Bé·la** (bā′lä) 1881–1945; Hung. composer

bar·y·on (bar′ē än′) *n.* [[< Gr *barys,* heavy + (ELECTR)ON]] any of certain relatively massive subatomic particles including the proton and neutron

ba·sal (bā′səl) *adj.* **1** of or at the base **2** basic; fundamental

basal metabolism the minimum quantity of energy used by an organism at rest to sustain its life

ba·salt (bə sôlt′, bā′sôlt′) *n.* [[L *basaltes*]] a hard, dark volcanic rock

base[1] (bās) *n.* [[< Gr *basis*]] **1** the thing or part on which something rests **2** the most important element or principal ingredient **3** the part of a word to which affixes are attached **4** a basis **5** any of the four markers a baseball player must consecutively touch to score a run **6** a headquarters or a source of supply **7** *Chem.* a substance that forms a salt when it reacts with an acid —*adj.* forming a base —*vt.*

based, bas′ing 1 to make a base for **2** to establish

base[2] (bās) *adj.* **bas′er, bas′est** [[< VL *bassus,* low]] **1** mean; ignoble **2** menial **3** poor in quality **4** of comparatively low worth [*base metal*] —**base′ly** *adv.* —**base′ness** *n.*

base·ball *n.* **1** a game played with a ball and bat by two opposing teams on a field with four bases forming a diamond **2** the ball used in this game

base·board *n.* a board or molding at the base of a wall

base hit *Baseball* a play in which the batter hits a fair ball and gets on base without an error and without forcing out a teammate

base·less *adj.* having no basis in fact; unfounded —**base′less·ness** *n.*

base line 1 a line serving as a base **2** something serving as a basis for comparison or measurement **3** *Baseball* the lane between any two consecutive bases **4** *Basketball, Tennis* the line at either end of the court Also **base′line′** *n.*

base·man (-mən) *n., pl.* **-men** (-mən) *Baseball* an infielder stationed at first, second, or third base

base·ment *n.* the story below the main floor

base on balls *Baseball* WALK

base path *Baseball* BASE LINE (*n.* 3): also written **base′path′** *n.*

base pay the basic rate of pay not counting overtime pay, etc.

base runner *Baseball* a player who is on base or is trying to reach a base

bash (bash) *vt.* [echoic] [Inf.] to hit hard —*n.* [Slang] a party

bash·ful (-fəl) *adj.* [[(A)BASH + -FUL]] easily embarrassed; shy —**bash′ful·ly** *adv.* —**bash′ful·ness** *n.*

bas·ic (bā′sik) *adj.* **1** fundamental **2** *Chem.* alkaline —*n.* a basic principle, factor, etc. —**bas′i·cal·ly** *adv.*

BASIC (bā′sik) *n.* [B(eginner's) A(ll-purpose) S(ymbolic) I(nstruction) C(ode)] a simple computer language that uses common words and algebra

bas·il (bā′zəl, baz′əl) *n.* [[< Gr *basilikon*]] a fragrant herb of the mint family, used in cooking

ba·sil·i·ca (bə sil′i kə) *n.* [[< Gr *basilikē* (*stoa*), royal (*portico*)]] **1** a church with a broad nave, side aisles, and an apse **2** *R.C.Ch.* a church with certain ceremonial rights

ba·sin (bā′sin) *n.* [[< VL *bacca,* water vessel]] **1** a wide, shallow container for liquid **2** its contents **3** a sink **4** any shallow, rounded hollow, often containing water **5** RIVER BASIN

ba·sis (bā′sis) *n., pl.* **-ses′** (-sēz′) [[< Gr, a base]] **1** a base or foundation **2** a principal constituent 3 a fundamental principle or theory

bask (bask) vi. ⟦ME *basken*, to wallow⟧ 1 to warm oneself pleasantly 2 to enjoy a warm feeling from being in a certain situation

bas·ket (bas'kit) n. ⟦ME⟧ 1 a container made of interwoven cane, wood strips, etc. 2 its contents 3 *Basketball a)* the goal, a round, open-bottomed, hanging net *b)* a goal made by shooting the ball through this net

bas·ket·ball n. ⟦invented & named (1891) by James A. Naismith (1861-1939)⟧ 1 a team game played with a large, bouncy ball on a court having a raised basket at each end 2 this ball

basket weave a weave of fabrics resembling the weave used in making baskets

bas·ket·work n. work that is woven like a basket; wickerwork

bas mitz·vah (bäs mits'və) ⟦*also* B- M-⟧ BAT MITZVAH

Basque (bask) n. 1 a member of a people living in the W Pyrenees 2 the language of this people —adj. of the Basques

bas-re·lief (bä'ri lēf', bas'-) n. ⟦Fr < It: see fol. & RELIEF⟧ sculpture in which figures project slightly from a flat background

bass¹ (bās) n. ⟦< VL *bassus*, low⟧ 1 the range of the lowest male voice 2 a voice, singer, or instrument with such a range; specif., a double bass or a very low-pitched guitar 3 a part for a bass 4 a low, deep sound —adj. of or for a bass

bass² (bas) n., pl. **bass** or **bass'es** ⟦OE *baers*⟧ a spiny-finned food and game fish of fresh or salt water

bas·set (bas'it) n. ⟦< OFr *bas*, low⟧ a hunting hound with a long body, short forelegs, and long, drooping ears

bas·si·net (bas'ə net') n. ⟦< Fr dim. of *berceau*, a cradle⟧ a basketlike bed for an infant, often hooded and on wheels

bas·so (bas'ō, bäs'-) n., pl. **-sos** or **-si** (-sē) ⟦< VL *bassus*, low⟧ a bass voice or singer

bas·soon (ba sōōn', bə-) n. ⟦< VL *bassus*, low⟧ a low-pitched double-reed woodwind

bast (bast) n. ⟦OE *bæst*⟧ plant fiber used in ropes, mats, etc.

bas·tard (bas'tərd) n. ⟦< OFr⟧ an illegitimate child —adj. 1 of illegitimate birth 2 inferior, sham, etc. —**bas'tar·dy** (-tər dē) n.

bas·tard·ize (bas'tər dīz') vt. **-ized', -iz'ing** 1 to make, declare, or show to be a bastard 2 to make corrupt; debase —**bas'tard·i·za'tion** n.

baste¹ (bāst) vt. **bast'ed, bast'ing** ⟦< Gmc *bastjan*, make with bast⟧ to sew temporarily with long, loose stitches until properly sewed

baste² (bāst) vt. **bast'ed, bast'ing** ⟦< OFr *bassin*, basin⟧ to moisten (meat) with melted butter, drippings, etc. while roasting —**bast'er** n.

baste³ (bāst) vt. **bast'ed, bast'ing** ⟦ON *beysta*⟧ 1 to beat soundly 2 to attack with words

bas·tille (bas tēl') n. ⟦< OFr *bastir*, to build⟧

a prison —**the Bastille** a state prison in Paris destroyed (1789) in the French Revolution

bas·tion (bas'chən, -tē ən) n. ⟦see prec.⟧ 1 a projection from a fortification 2 any strong defense

bat¹ (bat) n. ⟦OE *batt*⟧ 1 a stout club 2 a club to hit the ball in baseball, etc. 3 a turn at batting 4 ⟦Inf.⟧ a blow —vt. **bat'ted, bat'ting** to hit, as with a bat —vi. to take a turn at batting —**right off the bat** ⟦Inf.⟧ at once

bat² (bat) n. ⟦< Scand⟧ a furry, nocturnal flying mammal with membranous wings

bat³ (bat) vt. **bat'ted, bat'ting** ⟦< OFr *battre*, to batter⟧ ⟦Inf.⟧ to wink —**not bat an eye** ⟦Inf.⟧ not show surprise

batch (bach) n. ⟦OE *bacan*, to bake⟧ 1 the amount (of bread, etc.) in one baking 2 one set, lot, group, etc. 3 an amount of work for processing by a computer in a single run

bate (bāt) vt. **bat'ed, bat'ing** ⟦< OFr *abattre*, beat down⟧ to abate or lessen —**with bated breath** holding the breath, as in fear

bath (bath) n., pl. **baths** (bathz, baths) ⟦OE *beth*⟧ 1 a washing, esp. of the body, in water 2 water, etc. for bathing or for soaking or treating something 3 a bathtub 4 a bathroom 5 BATHHOUSE (n. 1)

bathe (bāth) vt. **bathed, bath'ing** ⟦OE *bæth*⟧ 1 to put into a liquid 2 to give a bath to 3 to cover as with liquid —vi. 1 to take a bath 2 to swim or wade, esp. for pleasure 3 to soak oneself in something —**bath'er** (bā'thər) n.

bath·house n. 1 a public building for taking baths 2 a building used by bathers for changing clothes

bathing suit a swimsuit

bath·mat n. a mat used in or next to a bathtub

ba·thos (bā'thäs') n. ⟦< Gr *bathys*, deep⟧ 1 ANTICLIMAX (n. 1) 2 excessive sentimentality 3 triteness —**ba·thet·ic** (bə thet'ik) adj.

bath·robe n. a loose robe worn to and from the bath, etc.

bath·room n. 1 a room with a bathtub and often a toilet, etc. 2 a lavatory

bath·tub n. a tub to bathe in

bath·y·scaph (bath'ə skaf') n. ⟦< Gr *bathys*, deep + *skaphē*, boat⟧ a deep-sea diving apparatus for reaching great depths without a cable: also **bath'y·scaphe** (-skaf', -skäf')

ba·tik (bə tēk') n. ⟦Malay⟧ cloth with a design made by using wax to make certain parts of the fabric resistant to dye

ba·tiste (bə tēst', ba-) n. ⟦Fr: after supposed orig. maker, *Baptiste*⟧ a fine, thin cloth of cotton, rayon, etc.

bat mitz·vah (bät mits'və) ⟦*also* B- M-⟧ a Jewish girl who has arrived at the age of religious responsibility, 13 years 2 the ceremony celebrating this event

ba·ton (bə tän', ba-) n. ⟦Fr⟧ 1 a staff serving as a symbol of office 2 a slender stick used in directing music 3 a metal rod twirled by a drum major 4 a short, light rod used in relay races

Bat·on Rouge (bat''n rōōzh') capital of Louisiana

bat·tal·ion (bə tal'yən) n. ⟦< VL *battalia*,

battle‖ a tactical military unit forming part of a division

bat·ten¹ (bat′'n) *n.* ⟦var. of baton⟧ 1 a sawed strip of wood 2 a strip of wood put over a seam between boards as a fastening or covering —*vt.* to fasten or supply with battens

bat·ten² (bat′'n) *vi., vt.* ⟦ON batna, improve⟧ to fatten; thrive

bat·ten³ (bat′'n) *n.* ⟦< OFr battre, to batter⟧ in a loom, the movable frame that presses into place the threads of a woof

bat·ter¹ (bat′ər) *vt.* ⟦< L battuere, to beat⟧ 1 to strike with blow after blow 2 to injure by pounding, hard wear, or use —*vi.* to pound noisily and repeatedly

bat·ter² (bat′ər) *n.* Baseball, Cricket the player at bat

bat·ter³ (bat′ər) *n.* ⟦OFr bature⟧ a flowing mixture of flour, milk, etc. for making pancakes, etc.

battering ram a heavy beam or bar used for battering down gates, etc.

bat·ter·y (bat′ər ē) *n., pl.* **-ies** ⟦< OFr battre, to batter⟧ 1 a battering 2 a set of things used together 3 Baseball the pitcher and the catcher 4 Elec. a cell or group of cells storing an electrical charge and able to furnish a current 5 Law any illegal beating or touching of another person: see ASSAULT AND BATTERY 6 Mil. a set of heavy guns, rockets, etc.

bat·ting (bat′iŋ) *n.* ⟦OE batt, BAT¹⟧ cotton, wool, or synthetic fiber wadded into sheets

bat·tle (bat′'l) *n.* ⟦< L battuere, to beat⟧ 1 a large-scale fight between armed forces 2 armed fighting 3 any fight or conflict —*vt., vi.* **-tled, -tling** to fight —**give (or do) battle** to fight

bat·tle-ax or **bat·tle-axe** *n.* 1 a heavy ax formerly used as a weapon 2 [Slang] a harsh, domineering woman

bat·tle·field *n.* the site of a battle: also **bat′tle-ground′**

bat·tle·ment (-mənt) *n.* ⟦< OFr batailler, fortify⟧ a parapet with spaces for shooting, built atop a tower, wall, etc.

battle royal *pl.* **battles royal** 1 a free-for-all 2 a heated dispute

bat·tle·ship *n.* a large warship with big guns and very heavy armor

bat·ty (bat′ē) *adj.* **-ti·er, -ti·est** ⟦< BAT²⟧ [Slang] crazy or eccentric

bau·ble (bô′bəl) *n.* ⟦< L bellus, pretty⟧ a showy trifle; trinket

baud (bôd) *n.* ⟦after J. M. E. Baudot (1845-1903), Fr inventor⟧ a unit measuring rate of data transfer in digital communications

baux·ite (bôks′īt′) *n.* ⟦Fr, after (Les) Baux, town in S France⟧ a claylike sedimentary rock, the chief ore of aluminum

Ba·var·i·a (bə ver′ē ə) state of S Germany —**Ba·var′i·an** *adj., n.*

bawd (bôd) *n.* ⟦< ? OFr baud, licentious⟧ [Literary] a person, esp. a woman, who keeps a brothel

bawd·y (bô′dē) *adj.* **-i·er, -i·est** indecent; lewd —**bawd′i·ness** *n.*

bawl (bôl) *vi., vt.* ⟦< ML baulare, to bark⟧ 1 to shout 2 to weep loudly —*n.* 1 an outcry 2 a noisy weeping —**bawl out** [Slang] to scold angrily

bay¹ (bā) *n.* ⟦< ML baia⟧ a wide inlet of a sea or lake, along the shoreline

bay² (bā) *n.* ⟦< VL batare, to gape⟧ 1 an alcove or recess 2 BAY WINDOW

bay³ (bā) *vi.* ⟦< OFr baiier⟧ to bark or howl in long, deep tones —*n.* 1 the sound of baying 2 the situation of a hunted animal forced to turn and fight —**at bay** 1 cornered 2 held off —**bring to bay** to corner

bay⁴ (bā) *n.* ⟦< L baca, berry⟧ 1 LAUREL (*n.* 1) 2 [*pl.*] a laurel wreath

bay⁵ (bā) *adj.* ⟦< L badius⟧ reddish-brown —*n.* 1 a reddish-brown horse, etc. 2 reddish brown

bay·ber·ry *n., pl.* **-ries** 1 a shrub with small, wax-coated, berrylike fruit 2 the fruit

bay leaf the dried, aromatic leaf of certain laurel plants, used as a seasoning

bay·o·net (bā′ə net′, bā′ə nət) *n.* ⟦< Fr: after Bayonne, city in France⟧ a detachable blade put on a rifle muzzle, for stabbing in hand-to-hand combat —*vt., vi.* **-net′ed** or **-net′ted, -net′ing** or **-net′ting** to stab with a bayonet

bay·ou (bī′ōō) *n.* ⟦< AmInd bayuk, small stream⟧ in S U.S., a marshy or swampy backwater of a lake, river, etc.

bay window a window or set of windows jutting out from a wall

ba·zaar (bə zär′) *n.* ⟦Pers bāzār⟧ 1 a marketplace, esp. in the Middle East 2 a benefit sale for a church, etc.

ba·zoo·ka (bə zōō′kə) *n.* ⟦< name of a comic horn⟧ a portable weapon for launching armor-piercing rockets

BB (bē′bē′) *n., pl.* **BB's** ⟦designation of size⟧ a pellet of shot (diameter approximately .18 in.) fired from an air rifle (**BB gun**) or shotgun

bbl *abbrev.* barrel

BBQ (bär′bə kyōō′) *n., pl.* **BBQ's, vt. BBQed, BBQing** *inf. sp. of* BARBECUE

BC *abbrev.* 1 before Christ: also **B.C.** 2 British Columbia

B cell any of the lymphatic leukocytes not derived from the thymus, that build antibodies: cf. T CELL

be (bē) *vi.* **was** or **were, been, being** ⟦OE beon⟧ 1 to exist; live 2 to happen; occur 3 to remain or continue Note: be is used to link its subject to a predicate complement [she is nice] or as an auxiliary: (1) with a past participle: a) to form the passive voice [he will be sued] b) [Archaic] to form the perfect tense [Christ is risen] (2) with a present participle to express continuation [he is running] (3) with a present participle or infinitive to express futurity, possibility, obligation, intention, etc. [she is going soon, he is to cut it] Be is conjugated in the present indicative: (1) am, (he, she, it) is, (we, you, they) are; in the past indicative: (I, he, she, it) was, (we, you, they) were

Be *Chem. symbol for* beryllium

be- [< OE *bi-*, *be-*, at] *prefix* **1** around [*beset*] **2** completely [*bedeck*] **3** away [*betake*] **4** about [*bemoan*] **5** to make [*besot*] **6** to furnish with, affect by [*becloud*]

beach (bēch) *n.* [E dial., pebbles] a sandy shore — *vt., vi.* to ground (a boat, whale, etc.) on a beach

beach·comb·er (-kōm'ər) *n.* **1** COMBER (*n.* 2) **2** one who lives on items found on beaches **3** one who roams beaches looking for interesting things —**beach'comb'ing** *n.*

beach·head *n.* a position gained, specif. by invading an enemy shore

beach·wear *n.* garments worn at the beach, as swimsuits

bea·con (bē'kən) *n.* [< OE *beacen*, a signal] **1** a light for warning or guiding **2** a radio transmitter sending guiding signals for aircraft

bead (bēd) *n.* [< OE *bed*, prayer bead] **1** a small ball of glass, etc., pierced for stringing **2** [*pl.*] a rosary **3** [*pl.*] a string of beads **4** any small, round object, as the front sight of a rifle **5** a drop or bubble **6** the rim edge of a rubber tire — *vt.* to decorate with beads —**draw a bead on** to take careful aim at —**say one's beads** to pray with a rosary —**bead'y** *adj.* **-i·er, -i·est**

bea·dle (bēd'l) *n.* [ME *bidel*] [Historical] a minor officer in the Church of England, who kept order in church

bea·gle (bē'gəl) *n.* [< ? Fr *bee gueule*, wide throat] a small hound with short legs and drooping ears

beak (bēk) *n.* [< L *beccus*] **1** a bird's bill **2** a beaklike part, as the snout of various insects

beak·er (bēk'ər) *n.* [< ? Gr *bíkos*, vessel with handles] **1** a goblet **2** *Chem.* a glass or metal container with a beaklike lip for pouring

beam (bēm) *n.* [ME] **1** a long, thick piece of wood, metal, etc. **2** the crossbar of a balance **3** a ship's breadth at its widest point **4** a shaft of light, etc. **5** a radiant look, smile, etc. **6** a steady radio or radar signal for guiding aircraft or ships — *vt.* **1** to give out (shafts of light) **2** to direct (a radio signal, etc.) — *vi.* **1** to shine brightly **2** to smile warmly —**on the beam** [Inf.] working well

bean (bēn) *n.* [OE *bean*] **1** a plant of the pea family, bearing kidney-shaped seeds in pods **2** the edible, smooth seed of this plant **3** a pod with such seeds **4** any beanlike seed or pod [*coffee bean*, vanilla *bean*] **5** [Slang] the head or brain — *vt.* [Slang] to hit on the head —**full of beans** [Slang] lively —**spill the beans** [Inf.] to tell a secret

bear¹ (ber) *vt.* **bore, borne** or **born, bear'ing** [OE *beran*] **1** to carry **2** to have or show **3** to give birth to **4** to produce or yield **5** to support or sustain **6** to withstand or endure **7** to need [this *bears* watching] **8** to carry or conduct (oneself) **9** to give [to *bear* witness] — *vi.* **1** to be productive **2** to lie, point, or move in a given direction **3** to have bearing (*on*) **4** to tolerate —**bear down (on) 1** to exert pressure or effort (*on*) **2** to approach —**bear out** to confirm —**bear up** to endure —**bear'a·ble** *adj.* —**bear'er** *n.*

bear² (ber) *n., pl.* **bears** or **bear** [OE *bera*] **1** a large, heavy mammal with shaggy fur and a short tail **2** one who is clumsy, rude, etc. **3** one who sells stocks, etc. hoping to buy them back later at a lower price **4** [Slang] a difficult task — *adj.* falling in price —**bear'like'** *adj.*

beard (bird) *n.* [OE] **1** the hair on the chin and cheeks of a man **2** any beardlike part **3** an awn — *vt.* **1** to defy **2** to provide with a beard —**beard'ed** *adj.* —**beard'less** *adj.*

bear·ing (ber'iŋ) *n.* **1** way of carrying and conducting oneself **2** a supporting part **3** a producing or ability to produce **4** endurance **5** [*often pl.*] relative direction or position **6** [*pl.*] awareness of one's situation **7** relevance; relation **8** a part of a machine on which another part revolves, slides, etc.

bear·ish *adj.* **1** bearlike; rude, rough, etc. **2** falling, or causing, expecting, etc. a fall, in prices on the stock exchange —**bear'ish·ly** *adv.*

bé·ar·naise sauce [Fr.] (bā'är nāz') a creamy sauce, esp. for meat or fish

bear·skin *n.* **1** the fur or hide of a bear **2** a rug, coat, etc. made from this

beast (bēst) *n.* [< L *bestia*] **1** a nonhuman animal, esp. a large, four-footed mammal **2** one who is gross, brutal, etc.

beast·ly *adj.* **-li·er, -li·est 1** of or like a beast; brutal, etc. **2** [Inf.] disagreeable; unpleasant —**beast'li·ness** *n.*

beast of burden any animal used for carrying things

beast of prey any animal that hunts and kills other animals for food

beat (bēt) *vt.* **beat, beat'en, beat'ing** [OE *beatan*] **1** to hit repeatedly; pound **2** to punish by so hitting; whip, spank, etc. **3** to dash repeatedly against **4** *a*) to form (a path, etc.) by repeated treading or riding *b*) to keep walking on **5** to mix (eggs, etc.) by hard stirring **6** to move (esp. wings) up and down **7** to search through (a forest, etc.) **8** to defeat or outdo **9** to mark (time or rhythm) by tapping, etc. **10** [Inf.] to baffle **11** [Slang] to escape the penalties of (an indictment, rap, etc.) — *vi.* **1** to hit or dash repeatedly **2** to throb, vibrate, etc. — *n.* **1** a beating, as of the heart **2** any of a series of movements, blows, etc. **3** a throb **4** a habitual route **5** the unit of musical rhythm **6** BEATNIK — *adj.* **1** [Inf.] tired out **2** of a group of young persons, esp. of the 1950s, expressing social disillusionment by unconventional dress, actions, etc. —**beat down** to put or force down —**beat it!** [Slang] go away! —**beat off** to drive back —**beat up (on)** [Slang] to give a beating to —**beat'er** *n.*

beat·en *adj.* **1** shaped by hammering **2** much traveled [a *beaten* path] **3** crushed in spirit; defeated **4** tired out

be·a·tif·ic (bē'ə tif'ik) *adj.* **1** making blessed **2** showing happiness or delight

be·at·i·fy (bē at'ə fī') *vt.* **-fied'**, **-fy'ing** [< L *beatus*, happy + *facere*, to make] **1** to make blissfully happy **2** R.C.Ch. to declare (a deceased person) to be in heaven **—be·at'i·fi·ca'tion** *n.*

beat·ing *n.* **1** the act of one that beats **2** a whipping **3** a throbbing **4** a defeat

be·at·i·tude (bē at'ə tōōd') *n.* [< L *beatus*, happy] perfect blessedness or happiness **—the Beatitudes** the pronouncements in the Sermon on the Mount

beat·nik (bēt'nik) *n.* a member of the beat group

beat-up *adj.* [Slang] worn-out, dilapidated, etc.

beau (bō) *n.*, *pl.* **beaus** or **beaux** (bōz) [Fr < L *bellus*, pretty] [Old-fashioned] a woman's sweetheart

beau·te·ous (byōōt'ē əs) *adj.* [ME] beautiful **—beau'te·ous·ly** *adv.*

beau·ti·cian (byōō tish'ən) *n.* one who works in a beauty shop

beau·ti·ful (byōōt'ə fəl) *adj.* having beauty **—beau'ti·ful·ly** *adv.*

beau·ti·fy (-fī') *vt.*, *vi.* **-fied'**, **-fy'ing** to make or become beautiful **—beau'ti·fi·ca'tion** *n.* **—beau'ti·fi'er** *n.*

beau·ty (byōōt'ē) *n.*, *pl.* **-ties** [< L *bellus*, pretty] **1** the quality of being very pleasing, as in form, color, etc. **2** a thing with this quality **3** good looks **4** a very attractive person, feature, etc.

beauty salon (or **shop, parlor,** etc.) a place where people, esp. women, go for hair styling, manicuring, etc.

bea·ver (bē'vər) *n.* [< OE *beofor*] **1** a large amphibious rodent with soft, brown fur, webbed hind feet, and a flat, broad tail **2** its fur

be·calm (bē käm', bi-) *vt.* **1** to make calm **2** to make (a ship) motionless from lack of wind

be·cause (bē kôz', -kuz'; bi-) *conj.* [ME *bi*, by + *cause*] for the reason or cause that **—because of** by reason of

beck (bek) *n.* a beckoning gesture **—at the beck and call of** at the service of

beck·on (bek'n) *vi.*, *vt.* [OE *beacnian*] **1** to summon by a gesture **2** to lure; entice

be·cloud (bē kloud', bi-) *vt.* **1** to cloud over **2** to confuse; muddle

be·come (bē kum', bi kum') *vi.* **-came'**, **-come'**, **-com'ing** [OE *becuman*] to come or grow to be **—vt.** to befit; suit [modesty *becomes* her] **—become of** to happen to

be·com·ing *adj.* **1** appropriate; fit **2** suitable to or attractive on the wearer

bed (bed) *n.* [OE] **1** a piece of furniture for lying on while sleeping or resting **2** a plot of soil where plants are raised **3** the bottom of a river, lake, etc. **4** any flat surface used as a foundation **5** a geologic layer; stratum **6** the flat surface of a truck **—vt.** **bed'ded, bed'ding 1** to put to bed **2** to provide with a sleeping place **3** to embed **4** to plant in a bed of earth **5** to arrange in layers

bed and breakfast a hotel or private home that provides breakfast as part of the price

be·daz·zle (bē daz'əl, bi-) *vt.* **-zled, -zling** to dazzle thoroughly; bewilder

bed·bug *n.* a small, wingless, biting insect that infests beds, etc.

bed·clothes *pl.n.* sheets, blankets, etc. for a bed

bed·cov·er *n.* a cover for a bed; bedspread

bed·ding *n.* **1** mattresses and bedclothes **2** a bottom layer; base **3** straw, etc. for animals to sleep on

be·deck (bē dek', bi-) *vt.* to adorn

be·dev·il (bē dev'əl, bi-) *vt.* **-iled** or **-illed, -il·ing** or **-il·ling** to plague or bewilder **—be·dev'il·ment** *n.*

bed·fel·low *n.* **1** a person who shares one's bed **2** an associate, ally, etc.

be·dim (bē dim', bi-) *vt.* **-dimmed', -dim'ming** to make (the eyes or the vision) dim

bed·lam (bed'ləm) *n.* [after (the old London mental hospital of St. Mary of) *Bethlehem*] any place or condition of noise and confusion

bed of roses [Inf.] a situation or position of ease and luxury

Bed·ou·in (bed'ōō in') *n.*, *pl.* **-ins'** or **-in'** [< Ar *badāwīn*, desert dwellers] [*also* **b-**] an Arab of the desert tribes of Arabia, Syria, or N Africa

bed·pan *n.* a shallow pan for use as a toilet by one confined to bed

be·drag·gle (bē drag'əl, bi-) *vt.* **-gled, -gling** to make wet, limp, and dirty, as by dragging through mire

bed·rid·den (-rid'n) *adj.* confined to bed by illness, infirmity, etc.

bed·rock *n.* **1** solid rock beneath the soil, etc. **2** a foundation or bottom

bed·roll *n.* a portable roll of bedding, as for sleeping outdoors

bed·room *n.* a room for sleeping

bed·side *n.* the space beside a bed **—adj.** near a bed

bed·sore *n.* a sore on the body of a bedridden person, caused by chafing

bed·spread *n.* an ornamental spread covering the blanket on a bed

bed·stead (-sted') *n.* a framework for supporting the mattress, etc. of a bed

bed·time *n.* one's usual time for going to bed

bee¹ (bē) *n.* [OE *beo*] a broad-bodied, four-winged, hairy insect that gathers pollen and nectar and that can sting

bee² (bē) *n.* [OE *ben*, compulsory service] **1** a meeting of people to work together [a quilting *bee*] **2** a competition [a spelling *bee*]

beech (bēch) *n.* [OE *bece*] **1** a tree with smooth, gray bark, hard wood, and edible nuts **2** its wood

beech·nut *n.* the small, three-cornered, edible nut of the beech tree

beef (bēf) *n.*, *pl.* for **1 & 5, beefs**; for **1**, also **beeves** [< L *bos*, ox] **1** a full-grown ox, cow, bull, or steer, esp. one bred for meat **2** such animals collectively **3** their meat **4** [Inf.] *a)* human flesh *b)* strength **5** [Slang] a complaint —*vi.* [Slang] to complain —**beef up** [Inf.] to reinforce

beef·cake *n.* (prec.) + (CHEESE)CAKE) [Inf.] display of the figure of a nude or partly nude, muscular man, as in a photograph

beef·steak *n.* a thick slice of beef for broiling or frying

beef·y *adj.* **-i·er, -i·est** brawny —**beef′i·ness** *n.*

bee·hive *n.* 1 a shelter for a colony of bees 2 a place of great activity

bee·keep·er *n.* one who keeps bees for producing honey —**bee′keep′ing** *n.*

bee·line *n.* a straight line or direct route

Be·el·ze·bub (bē el′zə bub′) *n.* Bible the chief devil; Satan

been (bin; *often* ben) *vi. pp. of* BE

beep (bēp) *n.* [echoic] the brief, high-pitched sound of a horn or electronic signal — *vi., vt.* to make or cause to make this sound

beer (bir) *n.* [OE *beor*] 1 an alcoholic, fermented drink made from malt and hops 2 a soft drink made from extracts of roots, etc. [root *beer*]

bees·wax *n.* wax secreted by honeybees, used to make their honeycombs: it is used in candles, etc.

beet (bēt) *n.* [< L *beta*] 1 a plant with edible leaves and a thick, fleshy, usually purplish-red root 2 the edible root, also a source of sugar

Bee·tho·ven (bā′tō′vən), **Lud·wig van** (lŏŏt′ viH vän) 1770-1827; Ger. composer

bee·tle[1] (bēt′'l) *n.* [OE *bitan*, to bite] an insect with hard front wings that act as covers for the membranous hind wings when these are folded

bee·tle[2] (bēt′'l) *vi.* **-tled, -tling** [prob. < fol.] to overhang —*adj.* overhanging: also **bee′tling**

bee·tle-browed (-broud′) *adj.* [< ME < ? *bitel*, sharp + *brouwe*, brow] 1 having overhanging or bushy eyebrows 2 frowning

be·fall (bē fôl′, bi-) *vi., vt.* **-fell′, -fall′en, -fall′ing** [< OE *be-*, BE- + *feallan*, to fall] to happen or occur (to)

be·fit (bē fit′, bi-) *vt.* **-fit′ted, -fit′ting** to be suitable or proper for; be suited to —**be·fit′ting** *adj.*

be·fog (bē fôg′, -fäg′; bi-) *vt.* **-fogged′, -fog′ging** 1 to envelop in fog; make foggy 2 to obscure; confuse

be·fore (bē fôr′, bi-) *adv.* [OE *be-*, by + *fo-ran*, fore] 1 ahead; in front 2 previously 3 earlier; sooner —*prep.* 1 ahead of in time, space, order, etc. 2 located in front of 3 in or into the sight, presence, etc. of 4 earlier than; prior to 5 in preference to 6 being considered, judged, or decided by [a case *before* the court] —*conj.* 1 earlier than the time that [call *before* you go] 2 rather than [I'd die *before* I'd tell]

be·fore·hand *adv., adj.* ahead of time; in anticipation

be·foul (bē foul′, bi-) *vt.* 1 to make filthy 2 to slander

be·friend (bē frend′, bi-) *vt.* to act as a friend to

be·fud·dle (bē fud′'l, bi-) *vt.* **-dled, -dling** to confuse or stupefy

beg (beg) *vt., vi.* **begged, beg′ging** [< Du *beggaert*, religious mendicant] 1 to ask for (alms) 2 to ask earnestly; entreat —**beg off** to ask to be released or excused from —**go begging** to be available but unwanted

be·gan (bē gan′, bi-) *vi., vt. pt. of* BEGIN

be·get (bē get′, bi-) *vt.* **-got′** or [Archaic] **-gat′** (-gat′), **-got′ten** or **-got′, -get′ting** [< OE *begietan*, acquire] 1 to be the father of 2 to produce; cause

beg·gar (beg′ər) *n.* 1 one who begs 2 a pauper —*vt.* 1 to make poor 2 to make (a description, etc.) seem inadequate —**beg′gar·y** *n., pl.* **-ies**

beg·gar·ly *adj.* very poor, worthless, inadequate, etc.

be·gin (bē gin′, bi-) *vi., vt.* **-gan′, -gun′, -gin′ning** [< OE *beginnan*] 1 to start doing, acting, etc. 2 to originate 3 to have a first part or be the first part of

be·gin·ner *n.* one just beginning to do or learn something; novice

be·gin·ning *n.* 1 a starting 2 the time or place of starting; origin 3 the first part 4 [*usually pl.*] an early stage or example

be·gone (bē gôn′, bi-) *interj., vi.* (to) be gone; go away; get out

be·gon·ia (bi gōn′yə) *n.* [after M. *Bégon* (1638-1710), Fr patron of science] a tropical plant with showy flowers and ornamental leaves

be·got (bē gät′, bi-) *vt. pt. & alt. pp. of* BEGET

be·got·ten *vt. alt. pp. of* BEGET

be·grime (bē grīm′, bi-) *vt.* **-grimed′, -grim′ing** to cover with grime; soil

be·grudge (bē gruj′, bi gruj′) *vt.* **-grudged′, -grudg′ing** 1 to resent another's possession of (something) 2 to give with reluctance —**be·grudg′ing·ly** *adv.*

be·guile (bē gīl′, bi-) *vt.* **-guiled′, -guil′ing** 1 to mislead by tricking, etc.; deceive 2 to deprive of or cheat *out of* by deceit 3 to pass (time) pleasantly 4 to charm or delight —**be·guile′ment** *n.* —**be·guil′er** *n.*

be·gun (bē gun′, bi-) *vi., vt. pp. of* BEGIN

be·half (bē haf′, bi-) *n.* [OE *be*, by + *healf*, side] support —**in (or on) behalf of** in the interest of; for

be·have (bē hāv′, bi-) *vt., vi.* **-haved′, -hav′ing** [see BE- & HAVE] 1 to conduct (oneself) in a specified way; act 2 to conduct (oneself) properly

be·hav·ior (-yər) *n.* way of behaving; conduct or action —**be·hav′ior·al** *adj.*

behavioral science any of the sciences, as sociology and psychology, that study human behavior

be·head (bē hed′, bi-) *vt.* to cut off the head of

be·held (bē held′, bi-) *vt. pt. & pp. of* BEHOLD

be·he·moth (bə hē′məth) *n.* [< Heb *behema*, beast] 1 Bible some huge animal 2 any huge or powerful animal or thing

be·hest (bē hest′, bi-) *n.* [< OE *behæs*, a vow] an order, command, or request

be·hind (bē hīnd′, bi-) *adv.* [< OE *behindan*] 1 in or to the rear 2 in a former time, place, etc. 3 in or into arrears 4 slow; late —*prep.* 1 remaining after 2 in or to the rear of 3 inferior to in position, achievement, etc. 4 later than [*behind* schedule] 5 beyond 6 gone by or ended for [school was *behind* him now] 7 supporting [*behind* their team] 8 prompting or instigating [*behind* the plot] 9 hidden by [what's *behind* this news] —*n.* [Inf.] the buttocks

be·hind·hand *adv., adj.* behind in payment, time, or progress

be·hold (bē hōld′, bi-) *vt.* **-held′, -hold′ing** [< OE *bihealdan*] to look at; see —*interj.* look! see! —**be·hold′er** *n.*

be·hold·en *adj.* obliged to feel grateful; indebted

be·hoove (bē hōōv′, bi-) *vt.* **-hooved′, -hoov′ing** [< OE *behofian*, to need] to be incumbent upon or proper for [it *behooves* you to drive carefully]

beige (bāzh) *n., adj.* [Fr] grayish tan

Bei·jing (bā′jiŋ′, -zhiŋ′) capital of China, in the NE part

be·ing (bē′iŋ) *n.* [see BE] 1 existence; life 2 fundamental nature 3 one that lives or exists 4 personality —**being as** (or **that**) [Inf. or Dial.] since; because —**for the time being** for now

Bei·rut (bā rōōt′) seaport & capital of Lebanon

be·jew·el (bē jōō′əl, bi-) *vt.* **-eled** or **-elled, -el·ing** or **-el·ling** to decorate with or as with jewels

be·la·bor (bē lā′bər, bi-) *vt.* 1 to beat severely 2 to scold 3 to spend too much time on

Bel·a·rus (bel′ə rōōs′) country in eastern Europe

be·lat·ed (bē lāt′id, bi-) *adj.* late or too late —**be·lat′ed·ly** *adv.*

be·lay (bi lā′) *vt., vi.* **-layed′, -lay′ing** [< OE *belecgan*, make fast] 1 to make (a rope) secure by winding around a cleat, etc. 2 [Inf.] *Naut.* to hold; stop 3 to secure (a climber) by a rope so as to arrest a fall if needed

bel can·to (bel′kän′tō) [It] a style of singing with brilliant vocal display

belch (belch) *vi., vt.* [OE *bealcian*] 1 to expel (gas) through the mouth from the stomach 2 to throw forth (its contents) violently —*n.* a belching

be·lea·guer (bē lē′gər, bi-) *vt.* [< Du < *be-*, around + *leger*, a camp] 1 to besiege by encircling 2 to beset or harass

Bel·fast (bel′fast) seaport & capital of Northern Ireland

bel·fry (bel′frē) *n., pl.* **-fries** [ult. < OHG] 1 a bell tower 2 the part of a tower that holds the bells

Belg *abbrev.* Belgium

Bel·gium (bel′jəm) kingdom in W Europe —**Bel′gian** *adj., n.*

Bel·grade (bel′grād′, -grād′) capital of Serbia

be·lie (bē lī′, bi-) *vt.* **-lied′, -ly′ing** 1 to disguise or misrepresent 2 to leave unfulfilled; disappoint 3 to prove false

be·lief (bə lēf′, bē-) *n.* [< OE *geleafa*] 1 conviction that certain things are true 2 religious faith 3 trust or confidence 4 creed or doctrine 5 an opinion; expectation; judgment

be·lieve (bə lēv′, bē-) *vt.* **-lieved′, -liev′ing** [< OE *geliefan*] 1 to take as true, real, etc. 2 to trust a statement or promise of (a person) 3 to suppose or think —*vi.* to have trust, faith, or confidence (*in*) —**be·liev′a·bil′i·ty** *n.* —**be·liev′a·ble** *adj.* —**be·liev′a·bly** *adv.* —**be·liev′er** *n.*

be·lit·tle (bē lit′'l, bi-) *vt.* **-tled, -tling** to make seem little, less important, etc. —**be·lit′tle·ment** *n.*

Be·lize (bə lēz′) country in Central America, on the Caribbean

bell (bel) *n.* [OE *belle*] 1 a hollow, cuplike object, as of metal, which rings when struck 2 the sound of a bell 3 anything shaped like a bell 4 *Naut.* a bell rung to mark the periods of the watch —*vt.* to attach a bell to —*vi.* to flare out like a bell

Bell (bel), **Al·ex·an·der Gra·ham** (al′ig zan′dər grā′əm) 1847-1922; U.S. inventor of the telephone, born in Scotland

bel·la·don·na (bel′ə dän′ə) *n.* [< It, beautiful lady] 1 a poisonous plant with purplish flowers and black berries 2 ATROPINE

bell-bot·tom *adj.* of or having pant legs that flare toward the ankles: also **bell′-bot′tomed** —*n.* [*pl.*] bell-bottom pants

bell·boy *n.* BELLHOP

belle (bel) *n.* [Fr, fem. of *beau*] a pretty woman or girl

belles-let·tres (bel le′tr′, -trə) *pl.n.* [Fr] essays written in a literary style

bell·hop *n.* one employed by a hotel, club, etc. to carry luggage and do errands

bel·li·cose (bel′i kōs′) *adj.* [< L *bellicus*, of war] quarrelsome; warlike —**bel′li·cos′i·ty** (-käs′ə tē) *n.*

bel·lig·er·ent (bə lij′ər ənt) *adj.* [< L *bellum*, war + *gerere*, carry on] 1 at war 2 of war 3 warlike 4 ready to fight or quarrel —*n.* a belligerent person, group, or nation —**bel·lig′er·ence** *n.* —**bel·lig′er·en·cy** *n.* —**bel·lig′er·ent·ly** *adv.*

bell jar a bell-shaped container made of glass, used to keep air, moisture, etc. in or out: also **bell glass**

bel·low (bel′ō) *vi.* [< OE *bylgan*] 1 to roar with a reverberating sound, as a bull 2 to cry out loudly, as in anger —*vt.* to utter loudly or powerfully —*n.* a bellowing sound

bel·lows (bel′ōz′) *n.* [< ME *beli*, belly] [*with sing.* or *pl. v.*] 1 a device that forces air out when its sides are pressed together: used in pipe organs, for lighting fires, etc. 2 anything like a bellows

bell pepper a large, sweet red pepper

Bell's palsy [after C. *Bell* (1774-1842), Scot anatomist] a sudden, usually temporary paralysis of the muscles on one side of the face

bell·weth·er (bel′weth′ər) *n.* ⟦ME⟧ **1** a male sheep, usually wearing a bell, that leads the flock **2** a leader

bel·ly (bel′ē) *n.*, *pl.* **-lies** [< OE *belg*, leather bag] **1** the part of the body between the chest and thighs; abdomen **2** the underside of an animal's body **3** the stomach **4** the deep interior, as of a ship —*vt.*, *vi.* **-lied**, **-ly·ing** to swell out: used esp. of a sail in the wind

bel·ly·ache *n.* pain in the abdomen —*vi.* **-ached′**, **-ach′ing** [Slang] to complain

bel·ly·but·ton *n.* [Inf.] the navel

bel·ly·ful (-fool′) *n.* **1** enough or more than enough to eat **2** [Slang] all that one can bear

belly laugh [Inf.] a hearty laugh

be·long (bē lôŋ′, bi-) *vi.* [< ME] **1** to have a proper place [it *belongs* here] **2** to be related (*to*) **3** to be a member: with *to* **4** to be owned: with *to*

be·long·ings *pl.n.* possessions

be·lov·ed (bi luv′id, -luvd′) *adj.* ⟦ME *biloven*⟧ dearly loved person

be·low (bi lō′) *adv.*, *adj.* [see BE- & LOW[1]] **1** in or to a lower place; beneath **2** later (in a book, etc.) **3** in or to hell **4** on earth **5** under in rank, amount, etc. —*prep.* **1** lower than **2** unworthy of

Bel·shaz·zar (bel shaz′ər) *n.* *Bible* the last king of Babylon, warned of defeat by mysterious writing on a wall

belt (belt) *n.* [ult. < L *balteus*] **1** a band of leather, etc. worn around the waist **2** any encircling thing like this **3** an endless band for transferring motion, as with pulleys, or conveying things **4** a distinctive geographic area [the Corn *Belt*] **5** [Inf.] a hard blow; punch **6** [Slang] *a*) a gulp, esp. of liquor *b*) a thrill —*vt.* **1** to encircle or fasten with a belt **2** [Inf.] to hit hard **3** [Inf.] to sing loudly: usually with *out* **4** [Slang] to gulp (liquor): often with *down* —**below the belt** unfair(ly) —**tighten one's belt** to live more thriftily —**under one's belt** [Inf.] as part of one's experience

belt·way *n.* an expressway passing around an urban area

be·moan (bē mōn′, bi-) *vt.*, *vi.* to lament

be·muse (bē myooz′, bi-) *vt.* **-mused′**, **-mus′ing** [BE- + MUSE] **1** to confuse or stupefy **2** to preoccupy: usually used in the passive —**be·muse′ment** *n.*

bench (bench) *n.* ⟦OE *benc*⟧ **1** a long, hard seat **2** the place where judges sit in a court **3** [*sometimes* B-] *a*) the status of a judge *b*) judges collectively *c*) a law court **4** WORK-BENCH **5** a seat on which members of a sports team sit when they are not playing —*vt.* *Sports* to take (a player) out of a game

bench mark a standard in measuring, judging quality, etc.: also **bench′mark′** *n.*

bench press a weight-lifting exercise, done while one is lying on a bench, in which a barbell is pushed upward from the chest —**bench′-press′** *vt.*

bench·warm·er *n.* [Inf.] an athlete who is

present at but seldom participates in games and hence spends much time on the bench

bench warrant an order issued by a judge or court for the arrest of a person

bend[1] (bend) *vt.* **bent**, **bend′ing** [< OE *bendan*, confine with a string] **1** to make curved or crooked **2** to turn, esp. from a straight line **3** to make submit —*vi.* **1** to turn, esp. from a straight line **2** to yield by curving, as from pressure **3** to curve the body; stoop (*over* or *down*) **4** to give in; yield —*n.* **1** a bending or being bent **2** a bent part —**bend′a·ble** *adj.*

bend[2] (bend) *n.* ⟦ME < prec.⟧ any of various knots esp. for tying one rope to another

be·neath (bē nēth′, bi-) *adv.*, *adj.* ⟦OE *beneothan*⟧ in a lower place; underneath —*prep.* **1** below **2** under; underneath **3** unworthy of [it is *beneath* him to cheat]

ben·e·dic·tion (ben′ə dik′shən) *n.* [< L *bene*, well + *dicere*, speak] **1** a blessing **2** an invocation of blessing, esp. at the end of a religious service

ben·e·fac·tion (ben′ə fak′shen) *n.* [< L *bene*, well + *facere*, do] **1** the act of helping, esp. by charitable gifts **2** the money or help given

ben·e·fac·tor (ben′ə fak′tər) *n.* one who has given help, esp. financially; patron

ben·e·fac·tress (ben′ə fak′tris) *n.* a woman who has given help, esp. financially

ben·e·fice (ben′ə fis) *n.* [< L *beneficium*, a kindness] an endowed church office providing a living for a vicar, rector, etc.

be·nef·i·cence (bə nef′ə səns) *n.* [see BENEFACTION] **1** the quality of doing good **2** a charitable act or gift

be·nef·i·cent (-sənt) *adj.* showing beneficence; doing or resulting in good —**be·nef′i·cent·ly** *adv.*

ben·e·fi·cial (ben′ə fish′əl) *adj.* producing benefits; advantageous; favorable —**ben′e·fi′cial·ly** *adv.*

ben·e·fi·ci·ar·y (-fish′ē er′ē, -fish′ər ē) *n.*, *pl.* **-ar′ies** anyone receiving or designated to receive benefits, as funds from a will or insurance policy

ben·e·fit (ben′ə fit) *n.* [see BENEFACTION] **1** anything contributing to improvement; advantage **2** [*often pl.*] payments made by an insurance company, public agency, etc. as during sickness or retirement **3** a public performance, bazaar, etc. the proceeds of which are to help some person or cause —*vt.* **-fit·ed**, **-fit·ing** to help; aid —*vi.* to receive advantage; profit

be·nev·o·lence (bə nev′ə ləns) *n.* [< L *bene*, well + *volens*, wishing] **1** an inclination to do good; kindliness **2** a kindly, charitable act —**be·nev′o·lent** *adj.* —**be·nev′o·lent·ly** *adv.*

Ben·gal (ben gôl′), **Bay of** part of the Indian Ocean, east of India

be·night·ed (bē nīt′id, bi-) *adj.* **1** surrounded by darkness **2** not enlightened; ignorant

be·nign (bi nīn′) *adj.* [< L *benignus*, good, lit., well-born] **1** good-natured; kindly **2** favorable; beneficial **3** *Med.* not malignant; specif., not cancerous —**be·nign′ly** *adv.*

be·nig·nant (bi nig′nənt) *adj.* [< prec.] 1 kindly or gracious 2 BENIGN (*adj.* 2 & 3)

be·nig·ni·ty (-nə tē) *n.* 1 kindliness 2 *pl.* **-ties** a kind act

Be·nin (be nēn′) country in WC Africa

ben·i·son (ben′ə zən, -sən) *n.* [OFr < L: see BENEDICTION] [Archaic] a blessing

bent[1] (bent) *vt., vi. pt. & pp.* of BEND[1] —*adj.* 1 curved or crooked 2 strongly determined: with *on* 3 [Slang] *a)* dishonest *b)* eccentric; odd —*n.* a natural leaning; propensity

bent[2] (bent) *n.* [OE *beonot*] a dense, low-growing grass that spreads by runners, used for lawns: also **bent′grass′**

bent·wood *adj.* of furniture made of wood bent into various forms

be·numb (bē num′, bi-) *vt.* 1 to make numb 2 to deaden the mind, will, etc. of

ben·zene (ben′zēn, ben zēn′) *n.* [ult. < Ar *lubān jāwī*, incense of Java] a clear, flammable, poisonous, aromatic liquid used as a solvent, in plastics, etc.

ben·zo·caine (ben′zō kān′, -zə-) *n.* [< prec. & COCAINE] a white, odorless powder used in ointments as a local anesthetic

be·queath (bē kwēth′, -kwēth′; bi-) *vt.* [< OE *be-*, BE- + *cwethan*, say] 1 to leave (property) to another by one's will 2 to hand down; pass on

be·quest (-kwest′) *n.* 1 a bequeathing 2 anything bequeathed

be·rate (bē rāt′, bi-) *vt.* **-rat′ed, -rat′ing** [BE- + RATE[2]] to scold severely

Ber·ber (bur′bər) *n.* 1 a member of a Muslim people of N Africa 2 the language of this people —*adj.* of the Berbers

be·reave (bē rēv′, bi-) *vt.* **-reaved′** or **-reft′** (-reft′), **-reav′ing** [< OE *be-*, BE- + *reafian*, rob] 1 to deprive: now usually in the pp *be-reft* [*bereft* of hope] 2 to leave forlorn, as by death —**be·reave′ment** *n.*

be·ret (bə rā′) *n.* [< Fr < L *birrus*, a hood] a flat, round cap of felt, wool, etc.

berg (burg) *n.* ICEBERG

ber·i·ber·i (ber′ē ber′ē) *n.* [Sinhalese, intens. of *beri*, weakness] a disease caused by lack of vitamin B₁ and characterized by nerve disorders, etc.

Ber·ing Sea (ber′iŋ) part of the N Pacific, between Siberia & Alaska

Bering Strait strait joining the Bering Sea with the Arctic Ocean

berke·li·um (burk′lē əm) *n.* [after *Berkeley*, Calif.] a radioactive, metallic chemical element: symbol, Bk; at. no. 97

Ber·lin (bər lin′) capital of Germany, in the NE part

berm (burm) *n.* [< MDu *baerm*] 1 a ledge 2 an artificial bank of earth 3 [Dial.] a shoulder, as along the edge of a paved road

Ber·mu·da (bər myoo′də) group of British islands in the W Atlantic

Bermuda shorts knee-length pants: also **ber·mu′das** *pl.n.*

Bern or **Berne** (burn) capital of Switzerland

ber·ry (ber′ē) *n., pl.* **-ries** [OE *berie*] 1 any

small, juicy, fleshy fruit, as a strawberry 2 the dry seed of various plants, as a coffee bean —*vi.* **-ried, -ry·ing** 1 to produce berries 2 to pick berries —**ber′ry·like′** *adj.*

ber·serk (bər surk′, -zurk′; bə-) *adj., adv.* [ON *berserkr*, warrior] in or into a violent rage or frenzy

berth (burth) *n.* [< BEAR[1] + -TH[1]] 1 a place where a ship anchors or moors 2 a position, job, etc. 3 a built-in bed, as on a ship or train —*vt.* to put into or furnish with a berth —*vi.* to occupy a berth —**give (a) wide berth to** to keep well clear of

ber·yl (ber′əl) *n.* [< Gr *bēryllos*] a very hard mineral of which emerald and aquamarine are two varieties

be·ryl·li·um (bə ril′ē əm) *n.* [< L *beryllus*, beryl] a hard, silver-white, metallic chemical element used in forming alloys: symbol, Be; at. no. 4

be·seech (bē sēch′, bi-) *vt.* **-sought′** or **-seeched′, -seech′ing** [< OE *be-* + *secan*, seek] 1 to ask (someone) earnestly; entreat 2 to beg for —**be·seech′ing·ly** *adv.*

be·seem (bē sēm′, bi-) *vi.* [Archaic] to be suitable or appropriate (to)

be·set (bē set′, bi-) *vt.* **-set′, -set′ting** [< OE *be-* + *settan*, set] 1 to attack from all sides; harass 2 to surround or hem in

be·set·ting *adj.* constantly harassing

be·side (bē sīd′, bi-) *prep.* [OE *bi sidan*] 1 at the side of; near 2 in comparison with [*beside* yours my share seems small] 3 in addition to 4 other than 5 not relevant to [that's *beside* the point] —**beside oneself** wild or upset, as with fear or rage

be·sides (-sīdz′) *adv.* 1 in addition 2 except for that mentioned 3 moreover —*prep.* 1 in addition to 2 other than

be·siege (bē sēj′, bi-) *vt.* **-sieged′, -sieg′ing** 1 to surround (an enemy's castle, city, etc., or its occupants) with armed forces 2 to crowd around 3 to overwhelm, harass, etc. [she was *besieged* with queries]

be·smear (bē smir′, bi-) *vt.* [OE *bismerian*] to smear over; soil

be·smirch (bē smurch′, bi-) *vt.* to soil

be·som (bē′zəm) *n.* [OE *besma*] a broom, esp. one made of twigs tied to a handle

be·sot (bē sät′, bi-) *vt.* **-sot′ted, -sot′ting** to stupefy, as with liquor

be·sought (bē sôt′, bi-) *vt.* alt. *pt. & alt. pp.* of BESEECH

be·span·gle (bē spaŋ′gəl, bi-) *vt.* **-gled, -gling** to cover with or as with spangles

be·spat·ter (bē spat′ər, bi-) *vt.* to spatter, as with mud or slander

be·speak (bē spēk′, bi-) *vt.* **-spoke′** (-spōk′), **-spo′ken** or **-spoke′, -speak′ing** 1 to speak for in advance; reserve 2 to be indicative of; show

best (best) *adj.* [OE *betst*] 1 superl. of GOOD 2 most excellent 3 most suitable, desirable, etc. 4 largest [the *best* part of a day] —*adv.* 1 superl. of WELL[2] 2 in the most excellent manner 3 in the highest degree —*n.* 1

the most excellent person, thing, etc. **2** the utmost [she did her *best*] **—vt.** to defeat or outdo **—all for the best** beneficial after all **—at best** under the most favorable conditions **—get the best of 1** to defeat **2** to outwit **—make the best of** to do as well as one can with

bes·tial (bes′chəl, -tyəl; *often* bēs′-) *adj.* [< L *bestia*, beast] like a beast; savage, brutal, etc. **—bes·ti·al·i·ty** (bes′′ē al′ə tē, -tē-; *often* bēs′-) *n.*, *pl.* **-ties**

bes·tial·ize (bes′chəl īz′, -tyəl-; *often* bēs′-) *vt.* **-ized′, -iz′ing** to make bestial

bes·ti·ar·y (bes′tē er′ē) *n.*, *pl.* **-ies** [< L *bestia*, beast] a medieval book with fanciful descriptions of real or mythical animals

be·stir (bē stur′, bi-) *vt.* **-stirred′, -stir′ring** to stir to action; busy (oneself)

best man the principal attendant of the bridegroom at a wedding

be·stow (bē stō′, bi-) *vt.* [see BE- & STOW] to present as a gift: often with *on* or *upon* **—bestow′al** *n.*

be·strew (bē strōō′, bi-) *vt.* **-strewed′, -strewed′** or **-strewn′, -strew′ing 1** to cover (a surface) *with* something **2** to strew or scatter about a surface

be·stride (bē strīd′, bi-) *vt.* **-strode′** (-strōd′) **-strid′den** (-strid′'n), **-strid′ing** to sit on, mount, or stand over with a leg on each side

bet (bet) *n.* [prob. < ABET] **1** an agreement in which the person proved wrong about something will do or pay what is stipulated **2** the thing or sum thus staked **3** a person or thing with regard to its likelihood of bringing about some result [a good *bet* to win the election] **—vt.**, **vi. bet** or **bet′ted, bet′ting 1** to declare as in a bet **2** to stake (money, etc.) in a bet with (someone)

be·ta (bāt′ə) *n.* the second letter of the Greek alphabet (B, β)

beta blocker a drug used to control heartbeat, treat hypertension, etc.

beta car·o·tene (kar′ə tēn′) a hydrocarbon found in butter, carrots, etc. and converted by the liver into vitamin A

be·take (bē tāk′, bi-) *vt.* **-took′** (-tōōk′), **-tak′en, -tak′ing** [ME *bitaken*] to go (used reflexively) [he *betook* himself to his castle]

beta particle an electron or positron ejected from the nucleus of an atom during radioactive disintegration

beta ray a stream of beta particles

be·tel nut (bēt′'l) [Port < Malayalam *veṭṭilai*] the fruit of a palm (**betel palm**), chewed together with slaked lime and the leaves of a pepper plant (**betel pepper**) by some Asians as a mild stimulant

be·think (bē thiŋk′, bi-) [Archaic] *vt.* **-thought′** (-thôt′), **-think′ing** [OE *bethencan*] to remind (oneself)

Beth·le·hem (beth′lə hem′) ancient town in Judea, now in the West Bank: traditionally regarded as Jesus' birthplace

be·tide (bē tīd′, bi-) *vi.*, *vt.* **-tid′ed, -tid′ing**

[< ME *be-*, BE- + *tiden*, happen] to happen (to); befall

be·times (bē tīmz′, bi-) *adv.* [Archaic] **1** early or early enough **2** promptly

be·to·ken (bē tō′kən, bi-) *vt.* [ME *betocnen*] **1** to be a token or sign of **2** to show beforehand; presage

be·tray (bē trā′, bi-) *vt.* [< L *tradere*, hand over] **1** to help the enemy of (one's country, etc.) **2** to expose treacherously **3** to fail to uphold [to *betray* a trust] **4** to deceive; specif., to seduce and then desert **5** to reveal unknowingly **6** to disclose (secrets, etc.) **—be·tray′al** *n.* **—be·tray′er** *n.*

be·troth (bē trōth′; -trôth′, bi-) *vt.* [< ME: see BE- & TRUTH] to promise in marriage **—be·troth′al** *n.*

be·trothed (-trōthd′, -trôtht′) *adj.* engaged to be married **—n.** the person to whom one is engaged

bet·ta (bet′ə) *n.* [ModL] a brightly colored gourami of SE Asia: often an aquarium fish

bet·ter (bet′ər) *adj.* [OE *betera*] **1** *compar. of* GOOD **2** more excellent **3** more suitable, desirable, etc. **4** larger [the *better* part of a day] **5** improved in health **—adv. 1** *compar. of* WELL² **2** in a more excellent manner **3** in a higher degree **4** more **—n. 1** a person superior in authority, social class, etc. **2** a more excellent thing, condition, etc. **—vt. 1** to outdo; surpass **2** to improve **—better off** in a better situation **—for the better** to a better condition **—get** (or **have**) **the better of 1** to outdo **2** to outwit **—had better** ought to

bet·ter·ment (-mənt) *n.* a bettering; improvement

bet·tor (bet′ər) *n.* one who bets: also **bet′ter**

be·tween (bē twēn′, bi-) *prep.* [OE *betweonum*] **1** in the space, time, etc. that separates (two things) **2** connecting [a bond *between* friends] **3** by the joint action of **4** possessed jointly by **5** from one or the other of [choose *between* us] **6** involving [disagreements *between* siblings] **—adv.** in an intermediate space, time, etc. **—between ourselves** as a secret: also **between you and me**

be·twixt (bē twikst′, bi-) *prep.*, *adv.* [< OE *be*, by + *twegen*, twain] between: archaic except in **betwixt and between**, in an intermediate position

BeV or **bev** (bev) *abbrev.* one billion (10⁹) electron-volts

bev·el (bev′əl) *n.* [< ?] **1** a tool for measuring or marking angles, etc. **2** an angle other than a right angle **3** a sloping part or surface **—adj.** beveled **—vt. -eled** or **-elled, -el·ing** or **-el·ling** to cut so as to form an angle other than a right angle **—vi.** to slope at an angle; slant

bevel gear a gearwheel meshed with another at an angle

bev·er·age (bev′ər ij′, bev′rij) *n.* [< L *bibere*, to drink] any liquid for drinking, esp. one other than water

bev·y (bev′ē) *n.*, *pl.* **-ies** [ME *bevey*] **1** a group, esp. of girls or women **2** a flock: now used chiefly of quail

be·wail (bē wāl′, bi-) *vt.* to wail over; lament; mourn

be·ware (bē wer′, bi-) *vi., vt.* **-wared′, -war′ ing** [prob. < OE *bewarian*, keep watch] to be wary or careful (of)

be·wigged (bē wigd′, bi-) *adj.* wearing a wig

be·wil·der (bē wil′dər, bi-) *vt.* [ult. < OE *wilde*, wild] to confuse hopelessly; puzzle —**be·wil′der·ing·ly** *adv.* —**be·wil′der·ment** *n.*

be·witch (bē wich′, bi-) *vt.* [< OE *wicca*, sorcerer] **1** to cast a spell over **2** to attract and delight greatly —**be·witch′ing** *adj.*

bey (bā) *n.* [Turk] a Turkish title of respect and former title of rank

be·yond (bē änd′) *prep.* [< OE *be*, by + *geond*, yonder] **1** farther on than; past **2** later than **3** outside the reach of [*beyond* help] **4** more than —*adv.* farther away —**the (great) beyond** whatever follows death

bez·el (bez′əl) *n.* [< ?] **1** a sloping surface, as the cutting edge of a chisel **2** the slanting faces of the upper part of a cut gem **3** the groove and flange holding a gem, watch crystal, etc. in place

Bhu·tan (bōō tän′) kingdom in the Himalayas, SC Asia

Bi *Chem. symbol for* bismuth

bi- [L] *prefix* **1** having two **2** doubly **3** happening every two (specified periods) **4** happening twice during every (specified period) **5** using two or both **6** joining or involving two

bi·an·nu·al (bī an′yōō əl) *adj.* coming twice a year; semiannual —**bi·an′nu·al·ly** *adv.*

bi·as (bī′əs) *n., pl.* **-as·es** [MFr *biais*, a slant] **1** a slanting or diagonal line, cut or sewn in cloth **2** partiality; prejudice —*adj.* slanting; diagonal —*vt.* **-ased** or **-assed, -as·ing** or **-as·sing** to prejudice —**on the bias** diagonally

bi·ath·lon (bī ath′län′) *n.* [BI- + Gr *athlon*, contest] a winter sports event combining cross-country skiing and rifle marksmanship

bib (bib) *n.* [< L *bibere*, to drink] **1** a cloth or plastic cover tied under a child's chin at meals **2** the upper front part of an apron or pair of overalls

Bib *abbrev.* **1** Bible **2** Biblical

bibb lettuce (bib) [after J. *Bibb* (1789-1884), who developed it] a type of lettuce with loose heads of crisp, dark-green leaves

Bi·ble (bī′bəl) *n.* [< Gr *biblos*, papyrus < *Byblos*, Phoenician city that exported papyrus] **1** the sacred book of Christianity, consisting of the Old Testament and New Testament **2** the Holy Scriptures of Judaism, also constituting the Christian Old Testament **3** [b-] any book regarded as authoritative or official —**bib·li·cal** *adj.*, **Bib·li·cal** (bib′li kəl)

biblio- [< Gr *biblion*, book] *combining form* book, books [*bibliophile*]

bib·li·og·ra·phy (bib′lē äg′rə fē) *n., pl.* **-phies** a list of writings on a given subject or by a given author, or of those used by the author of a given work —**bib′li·og′ra·pher** *n.* —**bib′li·o·graph′ic** (-ə graf′ik) *adj.*

bib·li·o·phile (-ə fīl′) *n.* a person who loves or collects books

bib·u·lous (bib′yōō ləs) *adj.* [< L *bibere*, to drink] addicted to or fond of alcoholic beverages

bi·cam·er·al (bī kam′ər əl) *adj.* [< BI- + L *camera*, chamber] having two legislative chambers

bi·car·bon·ate of soda (bī kär′bən it) SODIUM BICARBONATE

bi·cen·ten·ni·al (bī′sen ten′ē əl) *adj.* happening once in every 200 years —*n.* a 200th anniversary

bi·ceps (bī′seps′) *n., pl.* **-ceps** [< L < *bis*, two + *caput*, head] a muscle with two points of origin; esp., the large muscle in the front of the upper arm

bick·er (bik′ər) *vi.* [ME *bikeren*] to squabble; quarrel —**bick′er·er** *n.*

bi·con·cave (bī kän′kāv′) *adj.* concave on both surfaces [a *biconcave* lens]

bi·con·vex (-veks′) *adj.* convex on both surfaces [a *biconvex* lens]

bi·cus·pid (bī kus′pid) *adj.* [< BI- + L *cuspis*, pointed end] having two points —*n.* any of eight adult teeth with two-pointed crowns

bi·cy·cle (bī′sik′əl, -si kəl) *n.* [Fr: see BI- & CYCLE] a vehicle with two wheels, the rear wheel usually being powered by pedals via a sprocket and chain —*vi.* **-cled, -cling** to ride or travel on a bicycle —*vt.* to travel over by bicycle **bi′cy′clist** *n.*

bid (bid) *vt.* **bade** or **bid, bid′den** or **bid, bid′ding** [< OE *biddan*, to urge & *beodan*, to command] **1** to command, ask, or tell **2** to state (an amount) as the price one will pay or accept **3** to express [to *bid* farewell] **4** *Card Games* to state (a number of tricks) or declare (trump) —*vi.* to make a bid —*n.* **1** a bidding **2** an amount bid **3** a chance to bid **4** an attempt or try (*for*) **5** [Inf.] an invitation —**bid fair** to seem likely —**bid′der** *n.*

bid·dy (bid′ē) *n., pl.* **-dies** [< ?] **1** a hen **2** [Inf.] an elderly woman regarded as annoying, gossipy, etc.

bide (bīd) *vi.* **bode** or **bid′ed, bid′ed, bid′ing** [OE *bidan*] [Now Chiefly Dial.] **1** to stay; continue **2** to dwell **3** to wait —*vt.* [Now Chiefly Dial.] to endure or tolerate —**bide one's time** to wait patiently for an opportunity

bi·det (bē dā′) *n.* [Fr] a low, bowl-shaped bathroom fixture, with running water, for bathing the crotch

bi·en·ni·al (bī en′ē əl) *adj.* [< L *bi-*, BI- + *annus*, year] **1** happening every two years **2** lasting for two years —*n.* **1** a biennial event **2** *Bot.* a plant that lasts two years —**bi·en′ni·al·ly** *adv.*

bier (bir) *n.* [OE *bær*] a portable framework on which a coffin is placed

bi·fo·cals (bī′fō′kəlz) *pl.n.* eyeglasses with lenses having one part ground for close focus and the other for distant focus

bi·fur·cate (bī′fər kāt′) *vt., vi.* **-cat′ed, -cat′ ing** [< L *bi-*, BI- + *furca*, a fork] to divide into two parts or branches —**bi′fur·ca′tion** *n.*

big (big) *adj.* **big′ger, big′gest** 〚ME〛 **1** of great size; large **2** great in amount or force **3** full-grown **4** elder 〚his *big* sister〛 **5** noticeably pregnant (*with*) **6** loud **7** important 〚*big* plans〛 **8** famous **9** extravagant 〚*big* talk〛 **10** noble 〚a *big* heart〛 —*adv.* [Inf.] **1** boastfully **2** impressively —**big′ness** *n.*

big·a·my (big′ə mē) *n.* 〚< L *bi*-, BI- + Gr *gamos*, marriage〛 the crime of marrying a second time when one is already legally married —**big′a·mist** *n.* —**big′a·mous** *adj.* —**big′a·mous·ly** *adv.*

Big Bang theory a theory that the universe began with a sudden expansion (**Big Bang**) from a single point between 12 and 14 billion years ago

Big Dipper, the a dipper-shaped group of bright stars in the northern sky

big game 1 large wild animals hunted for sport, as lions, tigers, moose, etc. **2** the object of any important or dangerous undertaking

big·heart·ed (-här′tid) *adj.* quick to give or forgive; generous —**big′heart′ed·ly** *adv.*

big·horn *n., pl.* **-horns** or **-horn′** a wild sheep of W North America having large horns

bight (bīt) *n.* 〚OE *byht*, a bend〛 **1** a slack part in a rope **2** a curve in a coastline **3** a bay formed by such a curve

big·mouth *n.* [Slang] one who talks too much, esp. in an opinionated way

big·ot (big′ət) *n.* 〚Fr < ?〛 **1** one who holds blindly and intolerantly to a creed, opinion, etc. **2** a prejudiced person —**big′ot·ed** *adj.* —**big′ot·ry** *n.*

big shot [Slang] an important or influential person: also **big wheel**

big-time *adj., adv.* [Slang] at, of, or to a very great degree, extent, etc.

bike (bīk) *n.* [Inf.] **1** a bicycle **2** a motorcycle —**bik′er** *n.*

bi·ki·ni (bi kē′nē) *n.* 〚Fr, after *Bikini*, Pacific atoll〛 **1** a very brief two-piece swimsuit for women **2** very brief, legless underpants or swimming trunks

bi·lat·er·al (bī lat′ər əl) *adj.* **1** of, having, or involving two sides, factions, etc. **2** affecting both sides equally; reciprocal 〚a *bilateral* pact〛 —**bi·lat′er·al·ly** *adv.*

bile (bīl) *n.* 〚Fr < L *bilis*〛 **1** the bitter, greenish fluid secreted by the liver: it aids digestion **2** bad temper; anger

bilge (bilj) *n.* 〚var. of BULGE〛 **1** the rounded lower part of a ship's hold **2** stagnant water that collects there: also **bilge water 3** [Slang] nonsense

bi·lin·gual (bī liŋ′gwəl) *adj.* 〚< L *bi*-, BI- + *lingua*, tongue〛 of, in, or able to use two languages —**bi·lin′gual·ism′** *n.*

bil·ious (bil′yəs) *adj.* 〚< L *bilis*, bile〛 **1** having or appearing to have an ailment of the bile or liver **2** bad-tempered

bilk (bilk) *vt.* 〚? < BALK〛 to cheat or swindle; defraud —**bilk′er** *n.*

bill¹ (bil) *n.* 〚< ML *bulla*, sealed document〛 **1** a statement of charges for goods or services; invoice **2** a list, as a menu or theater program **3** a poster or handbill **4** a draft of a proposed law **5** a bill of exchange **6** a piece of paper money **7** *Law* a written declaration of charges or complaints filed —*vt.* **1** to make out a bill of (items) **2** to present a statement of charges to **3** *a)* to advertise by bills *b)* to book (a performer) —**fit (or fill) the bill** [Inf.] to meet the requirements —**bill′a·ble** *adj.*

bill² (bil) *n.* 〚OE *bile*〛 **1** the projecting jaws of a bird, usually pointed; beak **2** a beaklike part of the mouth, as that of a turtle —*vi.* to touch bills together —**bill and coo** to kiss, talk softly, etc. in a loving way

bill·board *n.* a signboard, usually outdoors, for displaying advertisements

bil·let (bil′it) *n.* [see BILL¹] **1** *a)* a written order to provide lodging for military personnel *b)* the lodging **2** a position, job, or situation —*vt.* to assign to lodging by billet

bil·let-doux (be′yā dōō′) *n., pl.* **bil·lets-doux** (be′yā dōō′) 〚Fr, sweet letter〛 a love letter

bill·fold (bil′fōld′) *n.* a wallet

bil·liard (bil′yərd) *adj.* of or for billiards

bil·liards (-yərdz) *n.* 〚< Fr *billard*, orig., a cue〛 **1** a game played with a cue and three hard balls on a table with raised, cushioned edges **2** any of several similar games, such as pool

bill·ing (bil′iŋ) *n.* **1** the listing of actors' names on a theater marquee, etc. **2** the order in which the names are listed

bil·lings·gate (bil′iŋz gāt′) *n.* 〚after a London fish market〛 foul, vulgar, abusive talk

bil·lion (bil′yən) *n.* 〚Fr < *bi*-, two + (*mi*)*llion*〛 **1** a thousand millions (1,000,000,000) **2** *former Brit.* term for TRILLION (a million millions) —**bil′lionth** *adj., n.*

bil·lion·aire (-yə ner′) *n.* a person whose wealth comes to at least a billion dollars, pounds, francs, etc.

bill of exchange a written order to pay a certain sum of money to the person named

bill of fare a menu

bill of lading a receipt issued to a shipper by a carrier, describing the goods to be shipped

Bill of Rights the first ten amendments to the U.S. Constitution, which guarantee civil liberties

bill of sale a written statement transferring ownership of something by sale

bil·low (bil′ō) *n.* 〚ON *bylgja*〛 **1** a large wave **2** any large swelling mass, as of smoke —*vi.* to surge or swell in a billow —**bil′low·y** *adj.* **-i·er, -i·est**

bil·ly club (bil′ē) *n.* 〚ult. < OFr *bille*, tree trunk〛 a policeman's heavy stick

billy goat a male goat

Bi·lox·i (bə luk′sē, -läks′ē) city in SE Mississippi, on the Gulf of Mexico

bi·me·tal·lic (bī′mə tal′ik) *adj.* 〚< Fr *bi*-, BI- + *métallique*, metallic〛 **1** of, containing, or using two metals **2** of or based on bimetallism

bi·met·al·lism (bī met′'l iz′əm) *n.* the use of two metals, esp. gold and silver, as the monetary standard, with fixed values in relation to each other

bi·month·ly (bī munth′lē) *adj., adv.* **1** once every two months **2** [Now Rare] twice a month

bin (bin) *n.* [OE, crib] a box or enclosed space used for storage

bi·na·ry (bī′nə rē) *adj.* [< L *bis*, double] **1** made up of two parts; double **2** designating or of a number system in which the base used is two, each number being expressed by using the digits 0 and 1 —*n., pl.* **-ries** something with two parts

bi·na·tion·al (bī nash′ə nəl) *adj.* involving two nations or two nationalities

bin·au·ral (bī nôr′əl) *adj.* **1** of or involving both ears **2** of or using two sources of sound

bind (bīnd) *vt.* **bound**, **bind′ing** [< OE *bindan*] **1** to tie together, as with rope **2** to hold or restrain **3** to encircle with a band, etc. **4** to bandage: often with *up* **5** to constipate **6** to reinforce or ornament the edges of by a band, as of tape **7** to fasten together the pages of (a book) and enclose in a cover **8** to obligate by duty, love, etc. **9** to compel, as by oath, legal restraint, or contract —*vi.* **1** to do the act of binding **2** to be or become tight or stiff **3** to stick together —*n.* **1** anything that binds **2** [Inf.] a difficult or restrictive situation

bind·er *n.* **1** one that binds **2** a substance that binds, as tar **3** a cover for holding sheets of paper together

bind·er·y *n., pl.* **-er·ies** a place where books are bound

bind·ing *n.* a thing that binds, esp. the covers and backing of a book —*adj.* that binds, obligates, etc.

binge (binj) [Inf.] *n.* unrestrained activity; spree —*vi.* **binged**, **binge′ing** to indulge without restraint

bin·go (biŋ′gō) *n.* a game played with cards having rows of numbered squares: the first player with an entire row drawn by lot wins —*interj.* used to signify sudden success, etc.

bin·na·cle (bin′ə kəl) *n.* [ult. < L *habitaculum*, dwelling place] the case holding a ship's compass

bin·oc·u·lar (bī näk′yə lər; *for n.*, bi-) *adj.* [< L *bini*, double + *oculus*, eye] using, or for, both eyes —*n.* [*pl.*] a small, portable binocular telescope

bi·no·mi·al (bī nō′mē əl) *n.* [< L *bi-*, BI- + Gr *nomos*, law] **1** *Math.* an expression consisting of two terms connected by a plus or minus sign **2** a two-word scientific name of a plant or animal, indicating the genus and species

bi·o (bī′ō) *n., pl.* **bi′os** [Inf.] a biography

bio- [Gr < *bios*, life] *combining form* life, of living things

bi·o·chem·is·try (bī′ō kem′is trē) *n.* the study of the chemistry of life processes —**bi′o·chem′ist** *n.*

bi·o·cide (bī′ō sīd′) *n.* [BIO- + -CIDE] a substance that kills microorganisms

bi·o·de·grad·a·ble (bī′ō di grā′də bəl) *adj.* [BIO- + *degrad(e)*, decompose + -ABLE] capable of being readily decomposed by the action of microbes, as some detergents

bi·o·di·ver·si·ty *n.* variety in the living things of a particular area

bi·o·eth·ics *n.* the study of the ethical problems arising from scientific advances —**bi′o·eth′i·cist** *n.*

bi·o·feed·back *n.* a technique of seeking to train oneself, using electronic devices, to modify autonomic body functions, such as heartbeat

bi·o·fu·el *n.* any fuel derived from renewable biological sources, as plants (esp. corn or soybean oil) or animal waste

biog *abbrev.* **1** biographical **2** biography

bi·og·ra·phy (bī äg′rə fē) *n., pl.* **-phies** [< Gr: see BIO- & -GRAPHY] a person's life story written by another —**bi·og′ra·pher** *n.* —**bi·o·graph·i·cal** (bī′ə graf′i kəl) *adj.*

biol *abbrev.* **1** biological **2** biology

biological warfare the use of toxic microorganisms, etc. in war

biological weapon a weapon that consists of or that disperses toxic microorganisms

bi·ol·o·gy (bī äl′ə jē) *n.* [see BIO- & -LOGY] the science that deals with the origin, history, characteristics, etc. of living things —**bi·o·log·i·cal** (bī′ə läj′i kəl) *adj.* —**bi′o·log′i·cal·ly** *adv.* —**bi·ol′o·gist** *n.*

bi·on·ic (bī än′ik) *adj.* [see fol.] **1** of bionics **2** having an artificial body part or parts, as in science fiction, so as to enhance strength, etc.

bi·on·ics *n.* [BI(O)- + (ELECTRON)ICS] the science of designing instruments or systems modeled after living organisms

bi·o·phys·ics (bī′ō fiz′iks) *n.* the study of biological phenomena in relation to physics —**bi′o·phys′i·cal** *adj.* —**bi′o·phys′i·cist** *n.*

bi·o·pic (bī′ō pik′) *n.* [Inf.] a film dramatizing the life of a famous person

bi·op·sy (bī′äp′sē) *n., pl.* **-sies** [< BI(O)- + Gr *opsis*, a sight] *Med.* the removal of bits of living tissue for diagnosis

bi·o·rhythm (bī′ō rith′əm) *n.* any biological cycle that involves periodic changes in blood pressure, body temperature, etc.

bi·o·tin (bī′ə tin) *n.* [< Gr *bios*, life] a factor of the vitamin B group

bi·par·ti·san (bī pär′tə zən) *adj.* of, representing, or supported by two parties —**bi·par′ti·san·ship′** *n.*

bi·par·tite (bī pär′tīt′) *adj.* [< L *bi-*, BI- + *partire*, to divide] **1** having two parts **2** involving two

bi·ped (bī′ped′) *n.* [< L *bi-*, BI- + *pes*, foot] any two-footed animal —**bi·ped′al** *adj.*

bi·plane (bī′plān′) *n.* an airplane with two sets of wings, one above the other

bi·po·lar (bī pō′lər) *adj.* **1** of or involving poles or polarity **2** having alternating periods of mania and mental depression

bi·ra·cial (bī rā′shəl) *adj.* consisting of or involving two races

birch (burch) *n.* [OE *beorc*] **1** a tree having smooth, often whitish bark in thin layers, and hard, close-grained wood **2** its wood **3** a bunch of birch twigs used for whipping —*vt.* to flog

bird (burd) *n.* [< OE *bridd*, young bird] a warmblooded vertebrate with feathers and wings —*vi.* to observe wild birds in their habitat —**birds of a feather** people with the same traits or tastes —**for the birds** [Slang] ridiculous, foolish, etc.

bird·er *n.* a bird-watcher

bird·ie *n. Golf* a score of one stroke under par for a hole

bird·ing *n.* bird-watching

bird's-eye *adj.* having marks resembling birds' eyes [*bird's-eye* maple]

bird's-eye view **1** a view from high above **2** an overall, but cursory, view

bird-watch·ing *n.* a hobby involving observation of wild birds in their habitat —**bird'-watch'er** *n.*

bi·ret·ta (bə ret′ə) *n.* [< LL *birrettum*, small cloak] a square ceremonial hat with three or four vertical projections, worn by Roman Catholic clergy

Bir·ming·ham (bur′miŋ əm; *for 2*, -ham′) **1** city in central England **2** city in N Alabama

birth (burth) *n.* [< ON *byrth*] **1** the act of bringing forth offspring **2** a being born **3** origin or descent **4** the beginning of anything —*vi., vt.* to give birth (to) —**give birth (to) 1** to bring forth (offspring) **2** to create

birth·day *n.* the anniversary of the day of a person's birth

birth·ing *adj., n.* (of or for) giving birth

birth·mark *n.* a skin blemish or mark present at birth

birth·place *n.* the place of one's birth or of a thing's origin

birth·rate *n.* the number of births per year per thousand people in a given area, group, etc.: also **birth rate**

birth·right *n.* any right that a person has by birth

birth·stone *n.* a gem symbolizing the month of a person's birth

bis·cot·ti (bi skät′ē) *pl.n., sing.* **-to** (-ō-) or **-ti** [It, cognate with fol.] a hard, bar-shaped cookie made with almonds, etc.

bis·cuit (bis′kit) *n., pl.* **–cuits** or **–cuit** [< L *bis*, twice + *coquere*, to cook] **1** [Chiefly Brit.] a cracker or cookie **2** a quick bread made from a small lump of dough

bi·sect (bī sekt′) *vt.* [< L *bi–*, BI– + *secare*, to cut] **1** to cut in two **2** *Geom.* to divide into two equal parts —*vi.* to divide; fork —**bi·sec′tor** (-sekt′ər) *n.*

bi·sex·u·al (bī sek′shōō əl) *adj.* having a sexual orientation to persons of either sex —*n.* one who is bisexual —**bi′sex·u·al′i·ty** (-al′i tē) *adj.*

bish·op (bish′əp) *n.* [< Gr *episkopos*, overseer] **1** a high-ranking member of the Christian clergy, governing a diocese or church district **2** a chess piece that can move in a diagonal direction only

bish·op·ric (bish′əp rik) *n.* the district, office, or rank of a bishop

Bis·marck¹ (biz′märk′), Prince **Ot·to von** (ät′ō vän) 1815–98; Prussian chancellor (1871–90) who unified Germany

Bis·marck² (biz′märk′) capital of North Dakota

bis·muth (biz′məth) *n.* [< Ger *wismut*] a brittle, grayish-white metallic chemical element used in alloys of low melting point: symbol, Bi; at. no. 83

bi·son (bī′sən) *n., pl.* **bi′son** [< L, wild ox] a bovine ruminant having a shaggy mane and a humped back, as the American buffalo

bisque (bisk) *n.* [Fr] a thick, creamy soup made as from shellfish or vegetables

bis·tro (bē′strō′) *n.* [Fr] a small cafe

bit¹ (bit) *n.* [< OE *bite*, a bite] **1** the part of a bridle in the horse's mouth, used as a control **2** anything that curbs or controls **3** a drilling or boring tool for use in a brace, drill press, etc.

bit² (bit) *n.* [< OE *bita*, a piece] **1** *a)* a small piece or quantity *b)* small extent [a *bit* bored] *c)* a short time **2** [Inf.] 12½ cents: now usually in *two bits* —*adj.* very small [a *bit* role] —**bit by bit** gradually —**do one's bit** to do one's share

bit³ (bit) *n.* [*b(inary)* (*dig*)*it*] **1** a single digit in a binary number system **2** a unit of information

bitch (bich) *n.* [OE *bicce*] **1** a female dog, fox, etc. **2** [Slang] a woman regarded as bad-tempered, malicious, etc.: often considered an offensive term **3** [Slang] anything especially difficult —*vi.* [Slang] to complain

bitch·y *adj.* **-i·er, -i·est** [Slang] bad-tempered or malicious: used esp. of a woman

bite (bīt) *vt.* **bit** (bit), **bit·ten** (bit′'n) or **bit, bit′ing** [OE *bitan*] **1** to seize or pierce with or as with the teeth **2** to cut into, as with a sharp weapon **3** to sting, as an insect **4** to cause to smart **5** to eat into; corrode —*vi.* **1** to press or snap the teeth (*into, at*, etc.) **2** to cause a biting sensation **3** to grip **4** to seize a bait **5** to be caught, as by a trick —*n.* **1** a biting **2** biting quality; sting **3** a wound or sting from biting **4** *a)* a mouthful *b)* a snack **5** [Inf.] a sum deducted, as by a tax —**bite the bullet** to confront a painful situation bravely: from the patient's biting a bullet during battlefield surgery without an anesthetic

bit·ing (bīt′iŋ) *adj.* **1** cutting; sharp **2** sarcastic —**bit′ing·ly** *adv.*

bit·ter (bit′ər) *adj.* [OE *biter*, akin to *bitan*, to bite] **1** having a sharp, often unpleasant taste **2** causing or showing sorrow, pain, etc. **3** sharp and disagreeable; harsh [a *bitter* wind] **4** resentful or cynical —**bit′ter·ly** *adv.* —**bit′ter·ness** *n.*

bit·tern (bit′ərn) *n.* [< OFr *butor*] a wading bird with a thumping cry

bit·ters *pl.n.* a liquor containing bitter herbs, etc., used esp. as a flavoring in cocktails

bit·ter·sweet *n.* **1** a woody vine bearing small orange fruits with bright-red fleshy seeds **2** a poisonous vine with purple flowers and red berries —*adj.* **1** both bitter and sweet **2** pleasant and sad

bi·tu·men (bi tōō′mən) *n.* 〖L < Celt〗 any of various black mixtures of hydrocarbons obtained in the distillation of coal or petroleum, used for paints, roofing, etc. —**bi·tu′mi·nous** (-mə nəs) *adj.*

bituminous coal coal that contains bitumen; soft coal

bi·va·lent (bī vā′lənt) *adj. Chem.* DIVALENT

bi·valve (bī′valv′) *n.* any mollusk having a shell made of two parts hinged together, as a clam

biv·ou·ac (biv′wak′) *n.* 〖Fr < OHG *bi*-, by + *wahta*, watchman〗 a temporary encampment in the open, as by soldiers or mountaineers —*vi.* **-acked′**, **-ack′ing** to encamp in the open

bi·week·ly (bī wēk′lē) *adj., adv.* **1** once every two weeks **2** [Now Rare] semiweekly

bi·zarre (bi zär′) *adj.* 〖Fr < Basque *bizar*, beard〗 **1** odd; grotesque **2** unexpected; fantastic

bk *abbrev.* **1** bank **2** book

bl *abbrev.* **1** bale(s) **2** barrel(s)

B/L or **b/l** *abbrev.* bill of lading

blab (blab) *vt., vi.* **blabbed**, **blab′bing** 〖ME *blabben*〗 **1** to reveal (a secret) **2** to chatter; prattle Also **blab′ber** —*n.* gossip

blab·ber·mouth *n.* [Inf.] one who blabs

black (blak) *adj.* 〖OE *blæc*〗 **1** opposite to white; of the color of coal **2** [*sometimes* B-] of or relating to the dark-skinned peoples of Africa, etc. or their descendants elsewhere, specif. African-Americans in the U.S. [*black studies*] **3** without light; dark **4** dirty **5** evil; wicked **6** sad; dismal **7** sullen —*n.* **1** black color or pigment **2** black clothes, esp. when worn in mourning **3** [*sometimes* B-] a member of a black people **4** darkness —*vt., vi.* to blacken —**black out** to lose consciousness —**in the black** operating at a profit —**black′ish** *adj.* —**black′ly** *adv.* —**black′ness** *n.*

black-and-blue *adj.* discolored, as by a bruise

black·ball *n.* a vote against —*vt.* **1** to vote against **2** to ostracize

black belt a black belt or sash awarded to an expert in judo or karate

black·ber·ry (-ber′ē, -bər ē) *n., pl.* **-ries 1** the fleshy, purple or black, edible fruit of various brambles of the rose family **2** a bush or vine bearing this fruit

black·bird *n.* any of various birds the male of which is almost entirely black

black·board *n.* a smooth, usually dark surface on which to write with chalk

Black Death 〖so called from the dark spots it makes on the skin〗 a pandemic of bubonic plague and related diseases that devastated Europe and Asia in the 1300s

black·en (-ən) *vi.* to become black or dark —*vt.* **1** to make black; darken **2** to slander; defame

black eye 1 a discoloration of the skin around an eye, resulting from a blow or contusion **2** [Inf.] dishonor, or its cause

black-eyed Su·san (-sōō′zən) a yellow, daisylike wildflower with a dark center

Black Friday the Friday after Thanksgiving, traditionally the beginning of U.S. Christmas shopping and a day of brisk retail sales

black·guard (blag′ərd) *n.* a scoundrel; villain

black·head *n.* a dark plug of dried fatty matter in a pore of the skin

black·heart·ed *adj.* wicked; evil

black hole 1 an exceptionally dense object in space with intense gravitation from which light, etc. cannot escape **2** *a)* an emptiness or void *b)* anything endlessly devouring resources, etc.

black ice a thin, nearly invisible layer of ice on pavement

black·jack *n.* **1** a small, leather-covered bludgeon with a flexible handle **2** a gambling card game in which a player getting closer to 21 points than the dealer, without exceeding it, wins —*vt.* to hit with a blackjack

black light ultraviolet or infrared radiation used for fluorescent effects

black·list *n.* a list of those who are censured, refused employment, etc. —*vt.* to put on a blacklist

black lung (disease) a disease of the lungs caused by the inhalation of coal dust

black magic sorcery

black·mail *n.* 〖lit., black rent < ME *male*, *rent*〗 **1** payment extorted to prevent disclosure of information that could bring disgrace **2** extortion of such payment —*vt.* to get or try to get blackmail from —**black′mail′er** *n.*

black mark an unfavorable item in one's record

black market a system for selling goods illegally —**black marketeer (or marketer)**

black·out *n.* **1** an extinguishing of stage lights to end a scene **2** a concealing of lights that might be visible to enemy aircraft at night **3** a temporary loss of electric power **4** temporary unconsciousness **5** suppression, as of news by censorship

Black Sea sea between Asia & SE Europe, north of Turkey

black sheep a family or group member regarded as less respectable than the others

black·smith *n.* a smith who works in iron

black·thorn *n.* a thorny shrub with purple or black, plumlike fruit; sloe

black tie a tuxedo and related accessories

black-tie *adj.* being or of a social function characterized by formalwear

black·top *n.* a bituminous mixture, usually asphalt, used as a surface for roads, etc. —*vt.* **-topped′**, **-top′ping** to cover with blacktop

black widow a black spider with a red mark underneath: the female has a poisonous bite and sometimes eats its mate

blad·der (blad′ər) *n.* 〖OE *blæddre*〗 **1** a sac that fills with fluid or gas, esp. one that holds urine flowing from the kidneys **2** a thing like this

blade (blād) *n.* 〖OE *blæd*, leaf〗 **1** *a)* the leaf

of a plant, esp. of grass *b*) the flat part of a leaf **2** a broad, flat surface or part, as of an oar or snowplow **3** the cutting part of a tool, knife, etc. **4** a sword or swordsman

blam·a·ble or **blame·a·ble** (blām′ə bəl) *adj.* that deserves blame —**blam′a·bly** *adv.*

blame (blām) *vt.* **blamed, blam′ing** [see BLASPHEME] **1** to accuse of being at fault; condemn (*for*) **2** to put the responsibility of (an error, etc.) *on* —*n.* **1** a blaming **2** responsibility for a fault —**be to blame** to be at fault —**blame′less** *adj.* —**blame′less·ly** *adv.* —**blame′less·ness** *n.*

blame·wor·thy *adj.* deserving to be blamed

blanch (blanch) *vt.* [< OFr *blanc*, white] **1** to whiten or bleach **2** to make pale **3** to scald (vegetables, almonds, etc.) —*vi.* to turn pale

bland (bland) *adj.* [L *blandus*, mild] **1** gently agreeable **2** mild; not harsh **3** insipid —**bland′ly** *adv.* —**bland′ness** *n.*

blan·dish (blan′dish) *vt., vi.* [< L *blandiri*, to flatter] to flatter; coax; cajole —**blan′dish·ment** *n.*

blank (blaŋk) *adj.* [< OFr *blanc*, white] **1** not written on **2** empty; plain **3** dazed or vacant [a *blank* look] —*n.* **1** an empty space, esp. one to be filled out in a printed form **2** such a printed form **3** an empty place or time **4** a powder-filled cartridge without a bullet —*vt.* to hold (an opponent) scoreless —**blank out** to conceal by covering over —**draw a blank** [Inf.] **1** to be unsuccessful **2** to be unable to remember a particular thing —**blank′ly** *adv.* —**blank′ness** *n.*

blank check 1 a bank check not yet filled in **2** a signed check with no amount filled in **3** permission to use unlimited money, authority, etc.

blan·ket (blaŋ′kit) *n.* [< OFr dim. of *blanc*, white] **1** a large piece of cloth used for warmth, esp. as a bed cover **2** any covering like this [a *blanket* of leaves] —*adj.* including many or all items [*blanket* insurance] —*vt.* **1** to cover; overlie **2** to obscure

blank verse unrhymed verse having five usually iambic feet per line

blan·quette (blän ket′) *n.* [Fr] a stew, as of chicken or veal, in cream sauce

blare (bler) *vt., vi.* **blared, blar′ing** [ME *bleren*, to wail] to sound or exclaim loudly —*n.* a loud, harsh sound

blar·ney (blär′nē) *n.* [< the *Blarney* stone in Ireland, traditionally kissed to gain skill in flattery] smooth or flattering talk

bla·sé (blä zā′) *adj.* [Fr] unexcited or jaded

blas·pheme (blas fēm′) *vt.* **-phemed′, -phem′ing** [< Gr *blasphēmein*, to speak evil of] **1** to speak profanely of or to (God or sacred things) **2** to curse —*vi.* to utter blasphemy —**blas·phem′er** *n.*

blas·phe·my (-fə mē) *n., pl.* **-mies** profane speech, writing, or action concerning God or sacred things —**blas′phe·mous** *adj.*

blast (blast) *n.* [OE *blǣst*, puff of wind] **1** a strong rush of air or gas **2** the sound of a sudden rush of air, as through a horn **3** a blight **4** an explosion, as of dynamite **5** an outburst, as of criticism **6** [Slang] an exciting, enjoyable experience —*vi.* **1** to make a loud, harsh sound **2** to set off explosives, etc. —*vt.* **1** to wither; ruin **2** to blow up; explode **3** to criticize sharply —**blast off** to take off: said of a rocket, etc. —**(at) full blast** at full speed or capacity

blast furnace a smelting furnace in which a blast of air forced in from below produces the intense heat

blast·off or **blast-off** *n.* the launching of a rocket, spacecraft, etc.

bla·tant (blāt′nt) *adj.* [prob. < L *blaterare*, to babble] **1** disagreeably loud; noisy **2** boldly conspicuous or obtrusive —**bla′tan·cy** *n.*

blaze[1] (blāz) *n.* [OE *blæse*] **1** a bright burst of flame; fire **2** a very bright light **3** a spectacular outburst or display —*vi.* **blazed, blaz′ing 1** to burn rapidly or shine brightly **2** to be excited, as with anger

blaze[2] (blāz) *n.* [< ON *blesi*] **1** a light-colored spot on an animal's face **2** a mark made on a tree by cutting off bark or applying paint, etc. —*vt.* **blazed, blaz′ing** to mark (a tree or trail) with blazes

blaze[3] (blāz) *vt.* **blazed, blaz′ing** [ME *blasen*, to blow < OE or ON] to proclaim

blaz·er (blā′zər) *n.* a light sport coat usually in a solid color and with metal buttons

bla·zon (blā′zən) *n.* [OFr *blason*, a shield] a coat of arms —*vt.* **1** to proclaim **2** to adorn

bldg *abbrev.* building

bleach (blēch) *vt., vi.* [OE *blǣcan*] to make or become white or colorless —*n.* a substance for bleaching

bleach·ers *pl.n.* benches in tiers, for spectators as at sporting events

bleak (blēk) *adj.* [ON *bleikr*, pale] **1** exposed to wind and cold; bare **2** cold; harsh **3** gloomy **4** not hopeful —**bleak′ly** *adv.* —**bleak′ness** *n.*

blear·y (blir′ē) *adj.* **-i·er, ⁼i·est** [< ME *blere*] dim or blurred, as the eyes by tears, fatigue, etc.: also **blear**

bleat (blēt) *vi.* [OE *blǣtan*] to make the cry of a sheep, goat, or calf —*n.* a bleating cry or sound

bleed (blēd) *vi.* **bled** (bled), **bleed′ing** [< OE *blod*, blood] **1** to emit or lose blood **2** to feel pain, grief, or sympathy **3** to ooze sap, juice, etc. **4** to show through or run together: said of dyes, stains, etc. —*vt.* **1** to draw blood from **2** to ooze (sap, juice, etc.) **3** to draw off (liquid, etc.) slowly —**bleed′er** *n.*

bleep (blēp) *n., vi.* [echoic] beep —*vt.* to censor (something said) in a telecast, etc., as with a beep

blem·ish (blem′ish) *vt.* [< OFr *blesmir*, injure] to mar; spoil —*n.* a flaw, defect, etc., as a spot or scar

blench (blench) *vt., vi.* to blanch

blend (blend) *vt.* **blend′ed** or **blent, blend′ing** [OE *blendan*] **1** to mix or mingle (varieties of tea, etc.) **2** to mix thoroughly **3** to purée in a blender —*vi.* **1** to mix or merge **2**

to pass gradually into each other, as colors **3** to harmonize —*n.* **1** a blending **2** a mixture of varieties

blend·er *n.* an electrical appliance that can chop, whip, mix, or liquefy foods

bless (bles) *vt.* **blessed** or **blest, bless′ing** ⟦< OE *bletsian,* consecrate with blood⟧ **1** to make holy **2** to ask divine favor for **3** to endow (*with*) **4** to make happy **5** to glorify **6** to make the sign of the cross over

bless·ed (bles′id, blest) *adj.* **1** holy; sacred **2** blissful **3** beatified **4** bringing comfort or joy —**bless′ed·ly** *adv.* —**bless′ed·ness** *n.*

bless·ing *n.* **1** an invocation or benediction **2** a grace said before or after eating **3** good wishes or approval **4** anything that gives happiness

blew (bloo) *vi., vt. pt. of* BLOW¹ & BLOW³

blight (blīt) *n.* ⟦? < ON *blikja,* turn pale⟧ **1** any insect, disease, etc. that destroys plants **2** anything that destroys, frustrates, etc. —*vt.* **1** to wither **2** to destroy

blimp (blimp) *n.* [Inf.] a nonrigid or semirigid airship

blind (blīnd) *adj.* ⟦OE⟧ **1** without the power of sight **2** of or for sightless persons **3** lacking insight **4** hard to see; hidden **5** closed at one end [a *blind* alley] **6** not controlled by intelligence [*blind* destiny] **7** guided only by instruments, as under foggy conditions [a *blind* landing] —*vt.* **1** to make sightless **2** to dazzle **3** to deprive of insight —*n.* **1** anything that obscures sight or keeps out light, as a window shade **2** a place of concealment **3** a decoy —*adv.* **1** blindly **2** guided only by instruments [to fly *blind*] —**blind′ly** *adv.* —**blind′ness** *n.*

blind date [Inf.] **1** a date with a stranger, usually arranged by a third person **2** either person involved

blind·ers *pl.n.* bridle flaps for preventing a horse from seeing to the side

blind·fold *vt.* ⟦< ME *blindfeld,* struck blind⟧ to cover the eyes of, as with a cloth —*n.* a cloth used to cover the eyes — *adj., adv.* with the eyes covered

blind·side *vt.* **-sid′ed, -sid′ing 1** to attack or strike (someone) from an unexpected direction **2** to surprise, as with bad news

blink (bliŋk) *vi.* ⟦ME *blenken*⟧ **1** to wink one or more times **2** to flash on and off **3** to ignore (with *at*) —*vt.* **1** to cause (eyes, light, etc.) to blink **2** to evade or avoid —*n.* **1** a blinking **2** a glimmer —**on the blink** [Slang] not working right

blink·er *n.* a flashing warning light

blintz (blints) *n.* ⟦Yiddish *blintze* < Russ *blin,* pancake⟧ a thin, rolled pancake filled with cottage cheese, fruit, etc.

blip (blip) *n.* ⟦echoic of a brief sound⟧ **1** a luminous image on an oscilloscope **2** a brief interruption of a pattern

bliss (blis) *n.* ⟦< OE *blithe,* blithe⟧ **1** great happiness **2** spiritual joy —**bliss′ful** *adj.* —**bliss′ful·ly** *adv.* —**bliss′ful·ness** *n.*

blis·ter (blis′tər) *n.* ⟦< ?⟧ **1** a raised patch of skin, filled with watery matter and caused as by a burn **2** anything like a blister —*vt.* **1** to raise blisters on **2** to lash with words —*vi.* to form blisters

blis·ter·ing *adj.* very hot, intense, etc.

blithe (blīth, blith) *adj.* ⟦OE⟧ cheerful; carefree —**blithe′ly** *adv.* —**blithe′ness** *n.*

blitz (blits) *n.* ⟦< Ger *blitz,* lightning⟧ a sudden overwhelming attack or campaign —*vt.* to subject to a blitz

bliz·zard (bliz′ərd) *n.* ⟦? < dial. *bliz,* violent blow⟧ a violent snowstorm

bloat (blōt) *vt., vi.* ⟦< ON *blautr,* soft⟧ **1** to swell, as with water or air **2** to puff up, as with pride

blob (bläb) *n.* ⟦echoic⟧ **1** a drop or a small lump or spot **2** something of indefinite shape —*vt.* **blobbed, blob′bing** to splash, as with blobs

bloc (bläk) *n.* ⟦Fr < MDu *block,* log⟧ an alliance of persons, nations, etc.

block (bläk) *n.* ⟦< OFr *bloc* & MDu *block*⟧ **1** a large, solid piece of wood, stone, metal, etc. **2** a heavy stand on which chopping, etc. is done **3** an auctioneer's platform **4** an obstruction or hindrance **5** a pulley in a frame **6** [Now Brit.] a group or row of buildings **7** an area with streets or buildings on four sides **8** a number of things regarded as a unit **9** a toy brick **10** *Printing* a piece of wood, etc. engraved with a design —*vt.* **1** to obstruct, hinder **2** to mount or mold on a block **3** to sketch roughly: often with *out* —**block′er** *n.*

block·ade (blä käd′) *n.* [prec. + -ADE] **1** a shutting off of a place by troops or ships to prevent passage **2** any strategic barrier —*vt.* **-ad′ed, -ad′ing** to subject to a blockade

block and tackle an arrangement of pulley blocks and ropes, used for lifting heavy objects

block·bust·er *n.* a particularly effective person or thing; specif., an expensive film, etc. generating widespread appeal

block·bust·ing *n.* [Inf.] the inducing of owners to sell their homes out of fear that a minority group may move into the neighborhood

block grant a grant of federal funds to a state or local government to fund a block of programs

block·head *n.* a stupid person

block·house *n.* **1** [Historical] a wooden, two-story fortified building **2** a reinforced structure for observers

blog (bläg) *n.* ⟦(*We*)*blog* < WEB (*n.* 6) + LOG¹ (*n.* 3)⟧ a journal or diary written for viewing on a website —*vi.* **blogged, blog′ging** to keep a blog —**blog′ger** *n.*

blog·o·sphere (bläg′ə sfir′) *n.* ⟦BLOG + -*osphere,* as in *stratosphere,* etc.⟧ internet blogs collectively, regarded as an informal social or journalistic community

blond *adj.* ⟦OFr < ? Gmc⟧ **1** having light-colored hair **2** light in color —*n.* a blond person Also, esp. with reference to a woman or girl, **blonde** (bländ) —**blond′ness** *n.*

blood (blud) *n.* ⟦OE *blod*⟧ **1** the usually red fluid circulating in the arteries and veins of animals **2** bloodshed **3** the essence of life; life **4** the sap of a plant **5** passion, temperament, etc. **6** parental heritage; lineage **7** kinship **8** people, esp. youthful people [new *blood* in a group] —**bad blood** anger; hatred —**in cold blood** deliberately and without compassion

blood bank a supply of blood stored for future use in transfusion

blood count the number of red or white cells in a given volume of blood

blood·cur·dling (-kʉrd'liŋ) *adj.* frightening; terrifying

blood·ed *adj.* **1** having (a specified kind of) blood [hot-*blooded*] **2** of fine breed

blood·hound *n.* any of a breed of large tracking dogs with a keen sense of smell

blood·less *adj.* **1** without bloodshed **2** anemic or pale **3** lacking in vigor —**blood′less·ly** *adv.* —**blood′less·ness** *n.*

blood·line *n.* line of descent

blood·mo·bile (-mō bēl′) *n.* a traveling unit for collecting blood from donors for blood banks

blood poisoning *nontechnical term for* SEPTICEMIA

blood pressure the pressure of the blood against the blood-vessel walls

blood relation (*or* **relative**) a person related by birth

blood·shed *n.* the shedding of blood; killing

blood·shot *adj.* tinged with red because small blood vessels are swollen: said of eyes

blood·suck·er *n.* an animal that sucks blood, esp. a leech

blood·thirst·y *adj.* murderous; very cruel —**blood′thirst′i·ness** *n.*

blood vessel an artery, vein, or capillary

blood·y *adj.* **-i·er, -i·est 1** of, like, containing, or covered with blood **2** involving bloodshed **3** bloodthirsty **4** [Brit. Slang] cursed; damned —*adv.* [Brit. Slang] very —*vt.* **-ied, -y·ing** to stain with blood —**blood′i·ly** *adv.* —**blood′i·ness** *n.*

bloody mar·y (mer′ē) *pl.* **bloody mar′ys** a drink made of vodka and tomato juice

bloom (blo͞om) *n.* ⟦< ON *blomi*, flowers⟧ **1** a flower; blossom **2** the state or time of flowering **3** a period of greatest health, vigor, etc. **4** a youthful, healthy glow **5** the powdery coating on some fruits and leaves —*vi.* **1** to blossom **2** to be in one's prime **3** to glow with health, etc.

bloom·ers *pl.n.* ⟦after Amelia *Bloomer* (1818-94), U.S. feminist⟧ baggy trousers gathered at the knee, once worn by women for athletics

bloom·ing *adj.* **1** blossoming **2** flourishing **3** [Chiefly Brit.] complete [a *blooming* idiot]

bloop·er (blo͞op′ər) *n.* ⟦*bloop*, echoic + -ER⟧ **1** a stupid mistake **2** *Baseball* a fly that falls just beyond the infield

blos·som (bläs′əm) *n.* ⟦OE *blostma*⟧ **1** a flower, esp. of a fruit-bearing plant **2** a state or time of flowering —*vi.* **1** to have or open into blossoms **2** to begin to flourish —**blos′som·y** *adj.*

blot (blät) *n.* ⟦ME < ?⟧ **1** a spot or stain, esp. of ink **2** anything that spoils or mars **3** disgrace —*vt.* **blot′ted, blot′ting 1** to spot; stain **2** to disgrace **3** to erase, obscure, or get rid of: often with *out* **4** to dry, as with blotting paper —*vi.* **1** to make blots **2** to become blotted **3** to be absorbent

blotch (bläch) *n.* ⟦? < prec.⟧ **1** a discoloration on the skin **2** any large blot or stain —*vt.* to mark with blotches —**blotch′y** *adj.* **-i·er, -i·est**

blot·ter (blät′ər) *n.* **1** a piece of blotting paper **2** a book for recording events as they occur [a police *blotter*]

blotting paper a thick, soft, absorbent paper used to dry a surface freshly written on in ink

blouse (blous) *n.* ⟦Fr, workman's smock⟧ **1** a garment like a shirt, worn by women and girls **2** a uniform coat worn by soldiers, etc. —*vi., vt.* **bloused, blous′ing** to gather in and drape over loosely

blow¹ (blō) *vi.* **blew, blown, blow′ing** ⟦OE *blawan*⟧ **1** to move with some force, as the wind **2** to send forth air, as with the mouth **3** to pant **4** to give sound by blowing or being blown **5** to spout water and air, as whales do **6** to be carried by the wind **7** to be stormy **8** to burst suddenly: often with *out* **9** [Slang] to leave —*vt.* **1** to force air from, into, onto, or through **2** to drive or expel by blowing **3** to sound by blowing **4** to form by blown air or gas **5** to burst by an explosion: often with *up* **6** to melt (a fuse, etc.) **7** [Inf.] to spend (money) freely **8** [Slang] to leave **9** [Slang] to bungle **10** [Slang] to reveal [to *blow* one's cover] —*n.* **1** a blowing **2** a blast of air or a gale —**blow over** to pass over or by —**blow up 1** to enlarge or exaggerate **2** [Inf.] to lose one's temper —**blow′er** *n.*

blow² (blō) *n.* ⟦ME *blowe*⟧ **1** a hard hit, as with the fist **2** a sudden attack **3** a sudden calamity; shock —**come to blows** to begin fighting one another

blow³ (blō) *vi.* **blew, blown, blow′ing** ⟦OE *blowan*⟧ [Archaic] to bloom

blow-by-blow *adj.* told in great detail

blow-dry *vt.* **-dried′, -dry′ing** to dry (wet hair) with hot air blown from an electric device (**blow′-dry′er**)

blow·fly *n., pl.* **-flies′** a fly that lays its eggs on meat, in wounds, etc.

blow·gun *n.* a long tube through which darts, etc. are blown

blow·hard *n.* [Slang] a loudly boastful person

blow·out *n.* **1** the bursting of a tire **2** [Slang] a party, banquet, etc.

blow·torch *n.* a small torch that shoots out a hot flame

blow·up *n.* **1** an explosion **2** an enlarged photograph **3** [Inf.] an angry outburst

blow·y *adj.* **-i·er, -i·est** windy

blowz·y (blou′zē) *adj.* **-i·er, -i·est** ⟦< obs. *blouze*, wench⟧ slovenly: also **blows′y**

BLT (bē′el′tē′) *n.* a bacon, lettuce, and tomato sandwich

blub·ber¹ (blub′ər) n. 〖ME blober, a bubble〗 the insulating fat of a whale, seal, etc. —**blub′ber·y** adj.

blub·ber² (blub′ər) vi. 〖ME bloberen, to bubble〗 to weep loudly, like a child

bludg·eon (bluj′ən) n. 〖? < earlier Fr bouge, club〗 a short club with a heavy end — vt., vi. 1 to strike with a bludgeon 2 to bully or coerce

blue (blōō) adj. 〖< ?〗 1 of the color of the clear sky 2 sad and gloomy 3 puritanical 4 [Inf.] indecent; risqué —n. 1 the color of the clear sky 2 any blue pigment —**out of the blue** unexpectedly —**the blue** 1 the sky 2 the sea

blue·bell n. any of various plants with blue, bell-shaped flowers

blue·ber·ry (-ber′ē, -bər ē) n., pl. -ries 1 a shrub bearing small, edible, blue-black berries 2 any of the berries

blue·bird n. a small North American songbird with a bluish back

blue blood an aristocrat: also **blue′blood′** n. —**blue′-blood′ed** adj.

blue cheese a strong cheese containing bluish mold

blue-chip adj. 〖< high-value blue chips of poker〗 1 of or relating to high-priced stocks having good earnings and a stable price 2 [Inf.] valuable

blue-col·lar adj. 〖< color of work shirts〗 designating or of industrial workers

blue·gill n. a freshwater sunfish of a bluish color

blue·grass n. 1 a type of grass with bluish-green horizontal stems 2 fast, bluesy country music

blue·jack·et n. an enlisted person in the navy

blue jay a common crested bird with a blue upper body and head

blue jeans jeans made of blue denim: also **blue′jeans′** (-jēnz′) pl.n.

blue law a puritanical law, esp. one prohibiting certain activities on Sunday

blue·nose n. [Inf.] a puritanical person

blue-pen·cil vt. -ciled or -cilled, -cil·ing or -cil·ling to edit or correct with or as with a blue pencil

blue-plate special an inexpensive restaurant meal served at a fixed price

blue·print n. 1 a reproduction in white on a blue background, as of architectural plans 2 any detailed plan or outline —vt. to make a blueprint of

blues (blōōz) pl.n. [with sing. or pl. v.] 1 [Inf.] a depressed feeling: with the 2 black folk music having, usually, slow tempo, melancholy words, etc.: often with the —**blues′y** adj. -i·er, -i·est

blue state 〖< the media's use of blue on maps to designate "Democratic"〗 a U.S. state whose voters chose predominantly the Democratic candidate in the most recent presidential election

blue·stock·ing n. a learned or bookish woman

blu·et (blōō′it) n. 〖< Fr dim. of bleu, blue〗 a small plant having little, pale-blue flowers

blue whale a baleen whale with a blue-gray back: the largest animal

bluff¹ (bluf) vt., vi. 〖prob. < Du bluffen, to brag, or verbluffen, to baffle〗 to mislead (a person) by a false, bold front —n. an act of bluffing

bluff² (bluf) adj. 〖? < Du blaf, flat〗 1 having a flat, steep front 2 having a rough, frank manner —n. a high, steep bank or cliff

blu·ing (blōō′iŋ) n. a blue rinse used on white fabrics to counteract yellowing

blu·ish (-ish) adj. somewhat blue: also **blue′ish**

blun·der (blun′dər) vi. 〖< ON blunda, shut the eyes〗 1 to move clumsily 2 to make a foolish mistake —n. a foolish mistake —**blun′der·er** n.

blun·der·buss (-bus′) n. 〖< Du donderbus, thunder box〗 [Historical] a short gun with a broad muzzle

blunt (blunt) adj. 〖< ?〗 1 having a dull edge, etc. 2 plain-spoken — vt., vi. to make or become dull —**blunt′ly** adv. —**blunt′ness** n.

blur (blur) vt., vi. blurred, blur′ring 〖< ?〗 1 to smudge 2 to make or become indistinct in shape, etc. 3 to dim —n. anything indistinct or hazy —**blur′ry** adj. -ri·er, -ri·est —**blur′ri·ness** n.

blurb (blurb) n. 〖a coinage〗 a brief testimonial or excerpt of a review, as on a book jacket

blurt (blurt) vt. 〖prob. echoic〗 to say impulsively: often with out

blush (blush) vi. 〖< OE blyscan, to shine〗 1 to become red in the face, as from shame 2 to be ashamed: usually with at or for 3 to become rosy —n. 1 a reddening of the face, as from shame 2 a rosy color 3 BLUSHER (n. 2) —adj. rosy —**at first blush** at first sight

blush·er n. 1 one who blushes readily 2 a reddish cosmetic for the cheeks; rouge

blush wine a dry, pale-pink wine

blus·ter (blus′tər) vi. 〖? < LowG blüstern〗 1 to blow stormily: said of wind 2 to speak in a noisy, swaggering manner —n. 1 stormy blowing or noisy commotion 2 noisy or swaggering talk —**blus′ter·er** n. —**blus′ter·y** adj.

Blvd abbrev. Boulevard

BM abbrev. [Inf.] bowel movement

BMI abbrev. BODY MASS INDEX

BO abbrev. [Inf.] 1 body odor 2 box office

bo·a (bō′ə) n. 〖L〗 1 a tropical snake that suffocates its prey in its coils, as the anaconda 2 a woman's long scarf, as of fur or feathers

boar (bôr) n., pl. boars or boar 〖OE bar〗 1 a mature, uncastrated male pig 2 a wild hog

board (bôrd) n. 〖OE bord, plank〗 1 a long, flat piece of sawed wood 2 a flat piece of wood, etc. for some special use [bulletin board] 3 pasteboard 4 meals, esp. as provided regularly for pay 5 a group of administrators; council 6 [also B-] [pl.] Educ. a qualifying examination for admission to an academic program —vt. 1 to cover (up) with boards 2 to provide with meals, or room and meals, regularly for pay 3 to get on (a ship, train, etc.) —vi. to receive meals, or room and meals, regularly for pay —**on board** 1 on a ship, aircraft, etc. **2** in a group as a member, etc. —**the boards** the stage (of a theater) —**board′er** n.

board·ing·house n. a house where room and meals can be had for pay: also **boarding house**

board·walk n. a walk made of thick boards, esp. one along a beach

boast (bōst) vi. [< Anglo-Fr] to talk, esp. about oneself, with too much pride; brag —vt. **1** to brag about **2** glory in having or doing (something) —n. **1** a boasting **2** anything boasted of —**boast′er** n. —**boast′ful** adj. —**boast′ful·ly** adv.

boat (bōt) n. [OE bat] **1** a small vehicle for traveling on water **2** loosely, a ship **3** an elongated dish —**in the same boat** in the same unfavorable situation —**rock the boat** [Inf.] to disturb the status quo —**boat′man** (-mən) n., pl. **-men** (-mən)

boat·er n. a stiff straw hat with a flat crown and brim

boat·ing n. rowing, sailing, etc.

boat·swain (bō′sən) n. a ship's petty officer in charge of the deck crew, the rigging, anchors, boats, etc.

bob (bäb) n. [ME bobbe, hanging cluster; 3 < the v.] **1** any knoblike hanging weight **2** a woman's or child's short haircut **3** a quick, jerky motion —vt. **bobbed, bob′bing** [ME bobben, knock against] **1** to make move with a jerky motion **2** to cut (hair, etc.) short —vi. to move with a jerky motion —**bob up** to appear suddenly

bob·bin (bäb′in) n. [Fr bobine < ?] a spool for thread or yarn, used in spinning, machine sewing, etc.

bob·ble (bäb′əl) [Inf.] Sports n. an awkward fumbling of the ball —vt. **-bled, -bling** to make a bobble with (a ball)

bob·ble·head n. a figurine, typically resembling a cartoon character, famous athlete, etc., with a spring-mounted head that bobbles

bob·by (bäb′ē) n., pl. **-bies** [after Sir Robert (Bobby) Peel (1788-1850), who reorganized the London police force] [Inf.] a British policeman

bobby pin [from use with bobbed hair] a small metal hairpin with the sides pressing close together

bobby socks (or **sox**) [< BOB (vt. 2)] [Inf.] esp. in the 1940s and 1950s, girls' ankle-length socks

bob·by·sox·er (-säks′ər) n. [Inf.] esp. in the 1940s, a teenage girl

bob·cat n. a small North American lynx

bob·sled n. a long racing sled with a protective shell —vi. **-sled′ded, -sled′ding** to ride or race on a bobsled

Boc·cac·ci·o (bō käch′ē ō), **Gio·van·ni** (jô vän′nē) 1313-75; It. writer

boc·cie or **boc·ce** or **boc·ci** (bäch′ē) [It bocce, (wooden) balls] an Italian game similar to lawn bowling

bode¹ (bōd) vt. **bod′ed, bod′ing** [< OE boda, messenger] to be an omen of —**bode ill** (or **well**) to be a bad (or good) omen

bode² (bōd) vi. alt. pt. of BIDE

bod·ice (bäd′is) n. [altered < bodies, pl. of body] the upper part of a dress

bod·i·ly (bäd′′l ē) adj. **1** physical **2** of, in, by, or to the body —adv. **1** in person **2** as a single group

bod·kin (bäd′kin) n. [ME bodekin < ?] [Obs.] a dagger

bod·y (bäd′ē) n., pl. **-ies** [OE bodig, cask] **1** the whole physical substance of a human, animal, or plant **2** the trunk of a human or other animal **3** a corpse **4** [Inf.] a person **5** a distinct group of people or things **6** the main part **7** a distinct mass [a body of water] **8** density or consistency, as of paint or fabric **9** richness of flavor

bod·y·guard n. a person or persons assigned to guard someone

body language gestures, unconscious bodily movements, etc. that serve as nonverbal communication

body mass index a measurement for estimating body fat, calculated by dividing one's weight (in kg) by the square of one's height (in m)

body politic the people who collectively constitute a political unit under a government

body stocking a tightfitting garment, usually of one piece, that covers the torso and, sometimes, the legs

bod·y·suit n. a one-piece, tightfitting garment that covers the torso, usually worn with slacks, a skirt, etc.

Boer (bôr, boor, bō′ər) n. [Du boer, peasant] a South African of Dutch descent

bog (bäg, bôg) n. [< Gael & Ir bog, soft, moist] wet, spongy ground, esp. where peat moss is found —vt., vi. **bogged, bog′ging** to sink in or as in a bog: often with down —**bog′gy** adj.

bo·gey (bō′gē; for 1, usually boog′ē) n. **1** BOGY **2** [after an imaginary Col. Bogey] one stroke more than par on a hole: also **bo′gie**

bog·gle (bäg′əl) vi. **-gled, -gling** [< Scot bogle, specter] **1** to be startled (at) **2** to hesitate (at) —vt. to confuse (the mind, imagination, etc.)

BOGO (bō′gō′) abbrev. buy one, get one

Bo·go·tá (bō′gə tä′) capital of Colombia

bo·gus (bō′gəs) adj. [< ?] not genuine; false

bo·gy (boog′ē, bō′gē) n., pl. **-gies** [< Scot bogle, specter] an imaginary evil spirit; goblin: also **bo′gie**

bo·gy·man or **bo·gey·man** (boog′ē man′, bō′ gē-) n., pl. **-men** (-′men′) BOOGEYMAN

Bo·he·mi·a (bō hē′mē ə) region of Czech Republic: a former kingdom

Bo·he·mi·an (-ən) n. **1** CZECH (n. 2) **2** a person born or living in Bohemia **3** [usually b-] one who lives unconventionally —adj. **1** of Bohemia or its people, etc. **2** [usually b-] like a bohemian —**Bo·he′mi·an·ism′** n.

bo·ho (bō′hō′) [Slang] n. BOHEMIAN (n. 3) —adj. BOHEMIAN (adj. 2)

bohr·i·um (bôr′ē əm) n. [after Niels Bohr (1885-1962), Dan physicist] an artificially produced radioactive chemical element: symbol Bh; at. no. 107

boil¹ (boil) *vi.* [< L *bulla*, a bubble] **1** to bubble up and vaporize over direct heat **2** to seethe like a boiling liquid **3** to be agitated, as with rage **4** to cook in boiling liquid —*vt.* **1** to heat to the boiling point **2** to cook in boiling liquid —*n.* the act or state of boiling —**boil down 1** to lessen in quantity by boiling **2** to condense **3** to be ultimately equivalent (to)

boil² (boil) *n.* [OE *byle*] an inflamed, painful, pus-filled swelling on the skin

boil·er *n.* **1** a container in which things are boiled or heated **2** a tank in which water is turned to steam **3** a tank for heating water and storing it

boiling point 1 the temperature at which a specified liquid boils **2** the point at which one loses one's temper

Boi·se (boi′zē, -sē) capital of Idaho

bois·ter·ous (bois′tər əs) *adj.* [ME *boistreous*, crude] **1** rough and stormy; turbulent **2** loud and exuberant; rowdy —**bois′ter·ous·ly** *adv.*

bok choy (bäk′ choi′) [Chin] a variety of Chinese cabbage

bo·la (bō′lə) *n.* [< Sp, a ball] a set of cords with heavy balls at the ends, thrown to immobilize cattle by entangling their legs

bold (bōld) *adj.* [OE *beald*] **1** daring; fearless **2** too free in manner; impudent **3** steep **4** prominent and clear —**bold′ly** *adv.* **bold′ness** *n.*

bold·face *n.* a heavy, dark printing type

bold·faced *adj.* impudent

bole (bōl) *n.* [ON *bolr*] a tree trunk

bo·le·ro (bō ler′ō) *n.*, *pl.* **-ros** [Sp < L *bulla*, a bubble] **1** a lively Spanish dance, or the music for it **2** a short, open vest

Bol·í·var (bäl′ə vər), **Si·món** (sī′mən) 1783-1830; South American revolutionary leader

Bo·liv·i·a (bə liv′ē ə) landlocked country in WC South America —**Bo·liv′i·an** *adj.*, *n.*

boll (bōl) *n.* [ME *bolle*, BOWL¹] the roundish seed pod of a plant, esp. of cotton or flax

boll weevil a small weevil whose larvae destroy cotton bolls

bo·lo·gna (bə lō′nē) *n.* [after *Bologna*, It city] a large smoked sausage of beef, pork, or veal

Bol·she·vik (bōl′shə vik′) *n.*, *pl.* **-viks′** or **-vi′ki** (-vē′kē) [Russ < *ból′she*, larger] [*also* **b-**] **1** a member of a faction that seized power in Russia in 1917 **2** a Communist, esp. of the Soviet Union —**Bol′she·vism′** *n.* —**Bol′she·vist** *n.*, *adj.*

bol·ster (bōl′stər) *n.* [OE] **1** a long, narrow pillow **2** any bolsterlike object or support —*vt.* to prop up as with a bolster: often with *up*

bolt¹ (bōlt) *n.* [OE] **1** a short, blunt arrow shot from a crossbow **2** a flash of lightning **3** a sudden dash **4** a sliding bar for locking a door, etc. **5** a threaded metal rod used with a nut for joining parts **6** a roll (*of* cloth, paper, etc.) —*vt.* **1** to swallow (food) hurriedly **2** to fasten as with a bolt —*vi.* **1** to start suddenly; spring away **2** to withdraw support

from one's party, etc. —**bolt upright** erect or erectly

bolt² (bōlt) *vt.* [< OFr *buleter*] to sift (flour, grain, etc.)

bo·lus (bō′ləs) *n.* [< Gr *bōlos*] **1** a small, round lump **2** a mass injected into a blood vessel, as a radioactive tracer **3** a large pill

bomb (bäm) *n.* [prob. < Gr *bombos*, hollow sound] **1** a container filled as with an explosive or incendiary chemical, for dropping, hurling, etc. **2** a small container with compressed gas in it [an aerosol *bomb*] **3** [Inf.] a complete failure —*vt.* to attack with bombs —*vi.* [Inf.] to be a complete failure

bom·bard (bäm bärd′) *vt.* [< Fr *bombarde*, mortar] **1** to attack with artillery or bombs **2** to attack with questions, etc. **3** to direct a stream of particles at (atomic nuclei) —**bom·bard′ment** *n.*

bom·bar·dier (-bər dir′) *n.* one who releases the bombs in a bomber

bom·bast (bäm′bast′) *n.* [< Pers *pambak*, cotton] grand, pompous language with little real meaning —**bom·bas′tic** *adj.* —**bom·bas′ti·cal·ly** *adv.*

Bom·bay (bäm′bā′) *former name for* MUMBAI

bomb·er (bäm′ər) *n.* **1** an airplane for dropping bombs **2** one who bombs

bomb·shell *n.* **1** a bomb **2** any sudden, shocking surprise

bo·na fi·de (hō′nə fīd′, bō′nə fī′dē) [L] **1** in good faith; without fraud [a *bona fide* offer] **2** genuine; real [a *bona fide* movie star]

bo·nan·za (bə nan′zə) *n.* [Sp, prosperity] **1** a rich vein of ore **2** any source of wealth

Bo·na·parte (bō′nə pärt′), **Na·po·le·on** (nə pō′lē ən) 1769-1821; Fr. military leader & emperor (1804-15)

bon·bon (bän′bän′; *Fr* bôn bôn′) *n.* [< Fr *bon*, good] a small piece of candy

bond (bänd) *n.* [ult. < Gothic *bindan*, bind] **1** anything that binds, fastens, or unites **2** [*pl.*] shackles **3** a binding agreement **4** an obligation imposed by a contract, etc. **5** the status of goods kept in a warehouse until taxes or duties are paid **6** an interest-bearing certificate issued by a government or business, redeemable on a specified date **7** surety provided against theft, etc. **8** an amount paid for bail, etc. **9** *Chem.* a connection between atoms, as in a molecule —*vt.* **1** to join; bind **2** to furnish surety for (someone) **3** to place or hold (goods) in bond

bond·age (bän′dij) *n.* [ult. < ON *bua*, inhabit] **1** serfdom or slavery **2** subjection to some force, influence, etc.

bond·ing *n.* the development of a close relationship, esp. between family members

bond·man (-mən) *n.*, *pl.* **-men** (-mən) a man who is a bondservant

bond paper [orig. used for bonds, etc.] high-quality writing paper

bond·serv·ant *n.* **1** one obliged to serve without wages **2** a slave or serf

bonds·man (bändz′mən) *n.*, *pl.* **-men** (-mən) **1** BONDMAN **2** one who furnishes bail, etc.

bond·wom·an *n., pl.* **-wom′en** a woman who is a bondservant

bone (bōn) *n.* [< OE *ban*] **1** any of the parts forming the skeleton of most vertebrates **2** the hard tissue these parts are made of —*vt.* **boned, bon′ing** to remove the bones from —*vi.* [Slang] to study hard: usually with *up* —**have a bone to pick** [Inf.] to have cause to quarrel —**make no bones about** [Inf.] to admit freely —**boneless** *adj.*

bone china translucent china made of white clay to which the ash of burned bones has been added

bone-dry *adj.* [Inf.] very dry

bone meal crushed or ground bones, used as feed, fertilizer, etc.

bon·er (bōn′ər) *n.* [Slang] a blunder

bon·fire (bän′fīr′) *n.* [ME *banefyre*, bone fire, pyre] a large outdoor fire

bong (bôŋ, bäŋ) *n.* [echoic] a deep ringing sound, as of a large bell —*vi.* to make this sound

bon·go (bäŋ′gō) *n., pl.* **-gos** [AmSp < ?] either of a pair of small drums of different pitch struck with the fingers: in full **bongo drum**

bo·ni·to (bō nēt′ō, bə-) *n., pl.* **-tos, -toes** [Sp] a saltwater food fish similar to a tuna

bon·jour (bôn zhōōr′) *interj., n.* [Fr] good day; hello

bonk·ers (bäŋ′kərz) *adj.* [Slang] crazy

bon mot (bôn′ mō′; Fr bôn mō′) *pl.* **bons mots** (bôn′ mōz′; Fr, -mō′) [Fr, lit., good word] a clever or witty remark

Bonn (bän) city in W Germany: capital of West Germany (1949-90)

bon·net (bän′it) *n.* [< OFr *bonet*] [Inf.] any hat worn by a woman or girl

bon·ny or **bon·nie** (bän′ē) *adj.* **-ni·er, -ni·est** [< L *bonus*, good] [Now Chiefly Scot.] **1** handsome or pretty, with a healthy glow **2** pleasant

bo·no·bo (bə nō′bō) *n., pl.* **-bos** a kind of chimpanzee, small with long limbs

bon·sai (bän′sī′) *n., pl.* **-sai′** [Jpn] a tree or shrub grown in a pot and dwarfed by regular pruning, etc.

bo·nus (bō′nəs) *n., pl.* **-nus·es** [L, good] anything given in addition to the customary or required amount

bon voy·age (bän′ voi äzh′) [Fr] pleasant journey

bon·y (bō′nē) *adj.* **-i·er, -i·est** **1** of, like, or having bones **2** thin; emaciated

bony fish any fish with an air bladder, covered gills, and a bony skeleton

boo (bōō) *interj., n., pl.* **boos** a sound made to express disapproval, etc., or to startle someone — *vi., vt.* **booed, boo′ing** to shout "boo" (at)

boo-boo or **boo·boo** (bōō′bōō′) *n., pl.* **-boos′** [Slang] **1** a stupid mistake **2** a minor injury

boob tube [Slang] TV or a TV set

boo·by (bōō′bē) *n., pl.* **-bies** [prob. < Sp *bobo*] a fool; nitwit: also **boob** (bōōb)

booby trap any scheme or device for tricking a person unexpectedly

boo·dle (bōōd′'l) *n.* [< Du *boedel*, property] [Old Slang] **1** something given as a bribe; graft **2** the loot taken in a robbery

boo·gey·man (bōōg′ē man′, bō′gē-) *n., pl.* **-men′** (-men′) a frightening imaginary being

book (book) *n.* [OE *boc*] **1** a printed work on sheets of paper bound together, usually between protective covers **2** a main division of a literary work **3** [*usually pl.*] the records or accounts as of a business **4** [*pl.*] studies; lessons **5** *a*) a libretto *b*) the script of a play **6** a booklike package, as of matches —*vt.* **1** to record in a book; list **2** to engage (rooms, etc.) ahead of time **3** to record charges against on a police record —**by the book** according to the rules —**the (Good) Book** the Bible

book·bind·ing *n.* the art, trade, or business of binding books —**book′bind′er** *n.*

book·case *n.* a set of shelves or a cabinet for holding books

book·end *n.* a support, usually one of a pair, used to keep a row of books upright

book·ie (-ē) *n.* [Slang] a bookmaker

book·ing *n.* an engagement, as for a concert

book·ish (-ish) *adj.* **1** inclined to read and study **2** pedantic

book·keep·ing *n.* the work of keeping a record of business transactions —**book′keep′er** *n.*

book·let (-lit) *n.* a small book

book·mak·er *n.* a person in the business of taking bets, as on horses

book·mark *n.* **1** a thing put between the pages of a book to mark a place **2** *Comput.* a shortcut as to a Web page —*vt.* to create a computer bookmark

book matches safety matches made of paper and fastened into a cardboard cover

book·mo·bile (-mō bēl′) *n.* a lending library in a van that visits rural schools, etc.

book·plate *n.* a label pasted in a book to identify its owner

book·shelf *n., pl.* **-shelves′** a shelf on which books are kept

book·store *n.* a store where books are sold: also **book′shop′**

book·worm *n.* **1** an insect larva that feeds on the bindings, etc. of books **2** one who reads or studies frequently

boom¹ (bōōm) *vi., vt.* [echoic] to make, or say with, a deep, hollow, resonant sound —*n.* this sound

boom² (bōōm) *n.* [Du, a beam] **1** a spar extending from a mast to hold the bottom of a sail outstretched **2** a long beam extending as from an upright for supporting and guiding anything lifted (the *boom* of a derrick) **3** a barrier, as of logs, to prevent floating logs, etc. from dispersing —*vi.* to go rapidly along

boom³ (bōōm) *vi.* [< ? prec. *vi.*] to increase or grow rapidly —*n.* a period of prosperity

boom·box *n.* [Slang] a large portable radio and tape player

boom·er *n. short for* BABY BOOMER

boom·er·ang (bōōm′ər aŋ′) *n.* [< Australian native name] **1** a flat, curved stick that can be thrown so that it returns to the thrower **2** a scheme gone awry, to the schemer's harm —*vi.* to act as a boomerang

boom·town *n.* a town that has grown very rapidly: also **boom town**

boon[1] (bōōn) *n.* ⟦ON *bon*, a petition⟧ a welcome benefit; blessing

boon[2] (bōōn) *adj.* ⟦< L *bonus*, good⟧ merry; convivial: now only in **boon companion**, a close friend

boon·docks (bōōn′däks′) *pl.n.* ⟦< native Philippine name⟧ [Inf.] **1** a jungle or wilderness **2** any remote rural region Used with *the*

boon·dog·gle (bōōn′dôg′əl, -däg′-) *n.* a trifling, pointless project —*vi.* -**gled, -gling** to engage in a boondoggle —**boon′dog′gler** *n.*

boor (boor) *n.* ⟦Du *boer*, a peasant⟧ a rude, awkward, or ill-mannered person —**boor′ish** *adj.* —**boor′ish·ly** *adv.*

boost (bōōst) *vt.* ⟦< ?⟧ **1** to raise as by a push from below **2** to urge others to support **3** to increase —*n.* **1** a push upward or forward **2** an increase —**boost′er** *n.*

booster shot a later injection of a vaccine, for maintaining immunity

boot[1] (bōōt) *n.* ⟦OFr *bote*⟧ **1** a covering of leather, rubber, etc. for the foot and part of the leg **2** a kick —*vt.* **1** to put boots on **2** to kick **3** [Inf.] to dismiss (a person) **4** to start (a computer): often with *up* —*vi.* to start a computer: usually with *up* —**the boot** [Slang] dismissal

boot[2] (bōōt) *n., vt., vi.* ⟦OE *bot*, advantage⟧ [Archaic] profit —**to boot** besides; in addition

boot·black *n.* one whose work is shining shoes or boots

booth (bōōth) *n., pl.* **booths** (bōōths, bōōthz) ⟦< ON *bua*, dwell⟧ **1** a stall for selling goods, providing information, etc. **2** a small enclosure for voting **3** a small structure to house a public telephone, etc. **4** an eating area in a restaurant having a table and benchlike seats

boot·ie (bōōt′ē) *n.* **1** a short boot for women or children **2** a baby's knitted or cloth shoe

boot·leg *vt., vi.* -**legged′, -leg′ging** ⟦< hiding liquor in a boot⟧ to make or sell (liquor, etc.) illegally —*adj.* bootlegged; illegal —*n.* bootlegged liquor, etc. —**boot′leg′ger** *n.*

boot·less *adj.* ⟦BOOT[2] + -LESS⟧ useless

boo·ty (bōōt′ē) *n., pl.* -**ties** ⟦LowG *bute*⟧ **1** spoils of war **2** plunder

booze (bōōz) *vi.* **boozed, booz′ing** ⟦< MDu *busen*⟧ [Inf.] to drink too much liquor —*n.* [Inf.] liquor —[Slang] **booz′er** *n.*

bop[1] (bäp) *vt.* **bopped, bop′ping** [Inf.] to hit; punch

bop[2] (bäp) *n.* a style of jazz (c. 1945-55) marked by complex rhythms, harmonic experimentation, etc. —*vi.* **bopped, bop′ping** [Slang] to walk, esp. in an easy, strutting way

bo·rax (bôr′aks′) *n.* ⟦< Pers *būrah*⟧ a white crystalline salt used in the manufacture of glass, soaps, etc.

Bor·deaux (bôr dō′) *n.* ⟦after *Bordeaux*, city and region in SW France⟧ [*also* **b-**] a red or white wine from the Bordeaux region

bor·der (bôr′dər) *n.* ⟦< OFr *border*, to border⟧ **1** an edge or part near an edge; margin **2** a dividing line between two countries, etc. **3** a narrow strip along an edge —*vt.* **1** to provide with a border **2** to extend along the edge of —*adj.* of or near a border —**border on** (or **upon**) **1** to be next to **2** to be like; almost be

bor·der·land *n.* land near a border

bor·der·line *n.* a boundary —*adj.* **1** on a boundary **2** indefinite

bore[1] (bôr) *vt.* **bored, bor′ing** ⟦< OE *bor*, auger⟧ **1** to make a hole in with a drill, etc. **2** to make (a well, etc.) as by drilling **3** to weary by being dull —*vi.* to bore a hole or passage —*n.* **1** a hole made as by boring **2** *a)* the hollow part of a tube or gun barrel *b)* its inside diameter **3** a dull person or thing

bore[2] (bôr) *vt., vi. pt. of* BEAR[1]

bore·dom (bôr′dəm) *n.* the condition of being bored or uninterested

bo·ric acid (bôr′ik) a white crystalline compound, used as an antiseptic, in making glass, etc.

born (bôrn) *vt., vi. alt. pp. of* BEAR[1] —*adj.* **1** brought into life **2** natural, as if from birth [a *born* athlete]

born-a·gain (bôrn′ə gen′) *adj.* having a new, strong faith or belief

borne (bôrn) *vt., vi. alt. pp. of* BEAR[1]

Bor·ne·o (bôr′nē ō′) large island in the Malay Archipelago

bo·ron (bôr′än′) *n.* ⟦< BORAX⟧ a nonmetallic chemical element: symbol, B; at. no. 5

bor·ough (bur′ō) *n.* ⟦OE *burg*, town⟧ **1** a self-governing, incorporated town **2** any of the five administrative units of New York City

bor·row (bär′ō, bôr′-) *vt., vi.* ⟦OE *borgian*⟧ **1** to take or receive (something) with the intention of returning it **2** to adopt (an idea, etc.) as one's own —**bor′row·er** *n.*

borscht or **borsch** (bôrsh) *n.* ⟦Russ *borshch*⟧ a beet soup, served usually with sour cream

bor·zoi (bôr′zoi′) *n.* ⟦Russ *borzój*, swift⟧ a large dog with a narrow head, long legs, and silky coat

bosh (bäsh) *n., interj.* ⟦Turk, empty⟧ [Inf.] nonsense

Bos·ni·a and Her·ze·go·vi·na (bäz′nē ə and hert′sə gō vē′nə) country in SE Europe —**Bos′ni·an** *adj., n.*

bos·om (booz′əm; *also* bōō′zəm) *n.* ⟦OE *bosm*⟧ **1** the human breast **2** the breast regarded as the source of feelings **3** the inside; midst [in the *bosom* of one's family] —*adj.* close; intimate [a *bosom* friend]

bos·om·y *adj.* having large breasts

bos·on (bō′sän) *n.* ⟦after S. N. *Bose* (1894-1974), Indian physicist + -ON⟧ any of certain subatomic particles, including photons and mesons

boss[1] (bôs, bäs) *n.* ⟦Du *baas*, a master⟧ **1** an employer or manager **2** one who controls a political organization —*vt.* **1** to act as boss of **2** [Inf.] to order (a person) about —*adj.* [Slang] excellent

boss² (bôs, bäs) *n.* [OFr *boce*, a swelling] a protruding ornament or knob

boss·y *adj.* **-i·er, -i·est** [Inf.] domineering —**boss'i·ness** *n.*

Bos·ton (bôs'tən, bäs'-) seaport & capital of Massachusetts —**Bos·to'ni·an** (-tō'nē ən) *adj., n.*

bo·sun (bō'sən) *n.* phonetic sp. of BOATSWAIN

bot·a·ny (bät''n ē) *n.* [< Gr *botanē*, a plant] the scientific study of plants —**bo·tan·i·cal** (bə tan'i kəl) *adj.,* **bo·tan'ic** —**bot'a·nist** *n.*

botch (bäch) *vt.* [ME *bocchen*, to repair < ?] to bungle —*n.* a bungled piece of work —**botch'er** *n.*

bot·fly (bät'flī') *n., pl.* **-flies'** a fly whose larvae are parasitic on mammals

both (bōth) *adj., pron.* [OE *ba tha*, both these] the two [*both* birds sang loudly] —*conj., adv.* together; equally [*both* tired and hungry]

both·er (bäth'ər) *vt., vi.* [prob. < *pother*] 1 to worry; harass 2 to concern (oneself) —*n.* 1 worry; trouble 2 one who gives trouble —**both'er·some** (-səm) *adj.*

Bot·swa·na (bät swä'nə) country in S Africa

Bot·ti·cel·li (bät'ə chel'ē; *It* bôt'tē chel'ē), **San·dro** (sän'drō) 1445?-1510; It. painter

bot·tle (bät''l) *n.* [< LL *buttis*, a cask] 1 a narrow-necked container for liquids, usually of glass 2 its contents —*vt.* **-tled, -tling** to put into a bottle —**bottle up** to restrain —**hit the bottle** [Slang] to drink much alcoholic liquor —**bot'tler** *n.*

bot·tle·neck *n.* 1 a narrow passage or road where traffic is slowed or stopped 2 any similar hindrance to movement or progress

bot·tom (bät'əm) *n.* [OE *botm*, ground] 1 the lowest part or place 2 the part on which something rests 3 the side underneath 4 the seat of a chair 5 the ground beneath a body of water 6 basis; cause; source 7 [Inf.] the buttocks —*adj.* lowest; last; basic —**at bottom** fundamentally —**bot'tom·less** *adj.*

bottom line 1 [Inf.] profits or losses, as of a business 2 [Slang] *a)* the basic factor, etc. *b)* the final statement, decision, etc.

bot·u·lism (bäch'ə liz'əm) *n.* [< L *botulus,* sausage] poisoning, often fatal, by the toxin produced by a bacterium sometimes found in foods improperly canned or preserved

bou·doir (bōō dwär', bōō'dwär') *n.* [< Fr, lit., pouting room] a woman's bedroom

bouf·fant (bōō fänt') *adj.* [< Fr *bouffer*, puff out] puffed out; full —*n.* a puffy hairstyle

bou·gain·vil·le·a or **bou·gain·vil·lae·a** (bōō'gən vil'ē ə, -vil'yə, -vē'yə) *n.* [ModL] a woody tropical vine having large, showy purple or red bracts

bough (bou) *n.* [OE *bog*, shoulder or arm] a main branch of a tree

bought (bôt) *vt. pt. & pp.* of BUY

bouil·lon (bōō'yän', -yən) *n.* [< Fr *bouillir,* to boil] a clear broth

boul·der (bōl'dər) *n.* [< ME *bulderston,* noisy stone] a large rock worn by weather and water

bou·le·vard (bōōl'ə värd') *n.* [Fr < MDu *bolwerc,* bulwark] a broad street lined with trees, etc.

bounce (bouns) *vi.* **bounced, bounc'ing** [ME *bounsen,* to thump] 1 to spring back, as upon impact; rebound 2 to spring; leap 3 [Slang] to be returned: said of a worthless check —*vt.* 1 to cause (a ball, etc.) to bounce 2 [Slang] to expel, dismiss, etc. —*n.* 1 *a)* a bouncing; rebound *b)* a leap or jump 2 capacity for bouncing 3 [Inf.] energy, zest, etc. —**the bounce** [Slang] dismissal —**bounc'y** *adj.*

bounc·er *n.* [Slang] a person hired to remove disorderly people from a nightclub, restaurant, etc.

bounc·ing *adj.* big, healthy, etc.

bound¹ (bound) *vi.* [< OFr *bondir,* to leap] 1 to move with a leap or leaps 2 to bounce; rebound —*vt.* to cause to bound or bounce —*n.* 1 a jump; leap 2 a bounce; rebound

bound² (bound) *vt., vi. pt. & pp.* of BIND —*adj.* 1 tied 2 closely connected 3 certain; sure [*bound* to lose] 4 obliged 5 having a binding: said as of a book 6 [Inf.] determined; resolved

bound³ (bound) *adj.* [< ON *bua,* prepare] going; headed [*bound* for home]

bound⁴ (bound) *n.* [< ML *butina,* boundary] 1 a boundary 2 [*pl.*] an area near a boundary —*vt.* 1 to limit 2 to be a limit or boundary to 3 to name the boundaries of —**out of bounds** 1 beyond the boundaries 2 forbidden

bound·a·ry (boun'drē, -də rē) *n., pl.* **-ries** anything marking a limit; bound

bound·en *adj.* [old pp. of BIND] 1 [Archaic] obligated; indebted 2 obligatory [one's *bounden* duty]

bound·er *n.* [< BOUND¹] [Inf., Chiefly Brit.] a cad

bound·less *adj.* unlimited; vast

boun·te·ous (boun'tē əs) *adj.* [see BOUNTY] 1 generous 2 plentiful —**boun'te·ous·ly** *adv.*

boun·ti·ful (-tə fəl) *adj.* BOUNTEOUS

boun·ty (-tē) *n., pl.* **-ties** [< L *bonus,* good] 1 generosity 2 a generous gift 3 a reward or premium

bou·quet (bōō kā', bō-) *n.* [Fr] 1 a bunch of flowers 2 aroma, as of wine

bour·bon (bur'bən) *n.* [after *Bourbon* County, KY] [*sometimes* B-] a whiskey distilled from corn mash

bour·geois (boor zhwä', boo-) *n., pl.* **-geois'** [Fr < OFr *borc,* town] a member of the bourgeoisie —*adj.* of the bourgeoisie: used variously to mean conventional, smug, materialistic, etc.

bour·geoi·sie (boor'zhwä zē', boo'-) *n.* [*with sing. or pl. v.*] the social class between the very wealthy and the working class; middle class

bout (bout) *n.* [ME *bught*] 1 a struggle or contest, esp. a boxing or wrestling match 2 a period of some activity, as a spell of illness

bou·tique (bōō tēk'; *occas.,* bō-) *n.* [Fr < L *apotheca,* storehouse] a small shop where fashionable articles are sold

bou·ton·niere or **bou·ton·niè·re** (bōo'tə nir', -tən yer') *n.* 〖Fr, buttonhole〗 a flower worn in a buttonhole

bo·vine (bō'vīn', -vēn') *adj.* 〖< L *bos*, ox〗 1 of an ox, cow, etc. 2 dull, stupid, etc.

bow¹ (bou) *vi.* 〖< OE *bugan*, to bend〗 1 to bend down the head or body in respect, agreement, etc. 2 to give in —*vt.* 1 to bend (the head or body) down in respect, etc. 2 to weigh (*down*) —*n.* a bending down of the head or body, as in respect or greeting —**take a bow** to acknowledge applause, etc.

bow² (bō) *n.* 〖OE *boga*〗 1 anything curved [a *rainbow*] 2 a curve; bend 3 a flexible, curved strip or bar with a cord connecting the two ends, for shooting arrows 4 a slender stick strung with horsehairs, as for playing a violin 5 a decorative knot as in a ribbon, usually having two loops and two loose ends —*adj.* curved —*vt., vi.* 1 to bend; curve 2 to play (a violin, etc.) with a bow

bow³ (bou) *n.* 〖< LowG *bug*〗 the front part of a ship, etc.

bowd·ler·ize (boud'lər īz') *vt.* **-ized', iz'ing** 〖after T. *Bowdler* (1754–1825), Eng editor〗 to expurgate —**bowd'ler·ism'** *n.* —**bowd'ler·i·za'tion** *n.*

bow·el (bou'əl) *n.* 〖< L *botulus*, sausage〗 1 an intestine, esp. of a human 2 [*pl.*] the inner part —**move one's bowels** to defecate

bow·er (bou'ər) *n.* 〖< OE *bur*, dwelling〗 a place enclosed by boughs or vines; arbor

bow·ie knife (bōō'ē, bō'-) 〖after Col. J. *Bowie* (1796?–1836)〗 a long single-edged hunting knife

bowl¹ (bōl) *n.* 〖OE *bolla*〗 1 a deep, rounded dish 2 the contents of a bowl 3 a bowllike thing or part 4 an amphitheater or stadium —**bowl'like'** *adj.*

bowl² (bōl) *n.* 〖< L *bulla*, bubble〗 1 the wooden ball used in the game of lawn bowling 2 a roll of the ball in bowling —*vi.* 1 to roll a ball or participate in bowling 2 to move swiftly and smoothly —**bowl over** 1 to knock over 2 [Inf.] to astonish —**bowl'er** *n.*

bowl·der (bōl'dər) *n. alt. sp. of* BOULDER

bow·leg (bō'leg') *n.* a leg that curves outward —**bow'leg'ged** (-leg'id, -legd') *adj.*

bowl·ing *n.* 1 a game in which a heavy ball is rolled along a wooden lane (**bowling alley**) at ten wooden pins 2 LAWN BOWLING

bowling green a lawn for lawn bowling

bowls (bōlz) *n.* LAWN BOWLING

bow·man (bō'mən) *n., pl.* **-men** (-mən) an archer

bow·sprit (bou'sprit', bō'-) *n.* 〖prob. < Du〗 a tapered spar extending forward from the bow of a sailing ship

bow tie (bō) a necktie tied in a bow

box¹ (bäks) *n.* 〖< L *pyxos*, BOX³〗 1 a container, usually rectangular and lidded; case 2 the contents of a box 3 a boxlike thing or space [a jury *box*] 4 a small, enclosed group of seats, as in a theater 5 a booth [a sentry *box*] 6 *Baseball* an area designated for the batter, catcher, etc. —*vt.* to put into a box

—**box in** (or **up**) to shut in or keep in; surround or confine —**box'like'** *adj.* —**box'y** *adj.* **-i·er, -i·est**

box² (bäks) *n.* 〖< ?〗 a blow struck with the hand —*vt.* 1 to strike with such a blow 2 to engage in boxing with —*vi.* to fight with the fists

box³ (bäks) *n.* 〖< Gr *pyxos*〗 an evergreen shrub with small leathery leaves: also **box'wood'**

box·car *n.* a fully enclosed railroad freight car

box·er *n.* 1 one who boxes; prizefighter 2 a medium-sized dog with a sturdy body and a smooth coat 3 [*pl.*] men's undershorts resembling loose trunks: in full **boxer shorts**

box·ing *n.* the skill or sport of fighting with the fists, esp. in padded leather mittens (**boxing gloves**)

box office 1 a place where admission tickets are sold, as in a theater 2 [Inf.] *a*) the power of a show or performer to attract a paying audience *b*) all money paid by such an audience

box seat a seat in a box at a theater, stadium, etc.

box spring a support for a mattress consisting of a cloth-enclosed frame containing rows of coil springs fastened together and to the frame

box wrench a wrench with an enclosed head

boy (boi) *n.* 〖ME *boie*〗 1 a male child 2 any man: familiar term 3 any male servant: a patronizing term —*interj.* [Slang] used to express pleasure, surprise, etc.: often **oh, boy!** —**boy'hood'** *n.* —**boy'ish** *adj.*

boy·cott (boi'kät') *vt.* 〖after Capt. *Boycott*, Irish land agent so treated in 1880〗 to join together in refusing to deal with, buy, etc. so as to punish or coerce —*n.* a boycotting

boy·friend *n.* [Inf.] a sweetheart who is a boy or man

Boy Scout a member of the **Boy Scouts**, a boys' organization that stresses outdoor life and service to others

boy·sen·ber·ry (boi'zən ber'ē) *n., pl.* **-ries** 〖after R. *Boysen*, U.S. horticulturist, developer (*c.* 1935)〗 a berry that is a cross of the raspberry, loganberry, and blackberry

BPD *abbrev.* barrels per day

Br¹ *abbrev.* 1 Branch 2 British 3 Brother

Br² *Chem. symbol for* bromine

bra (brä) *n.* 〖< BRASSIERE〗 a woman's undergarment for supporting the breasts

brace (brās) *vt.* **braced, brac'ing** 〖< Gr *brachiōn*, arm〗 1 to bind 2 to strengthen by supporting the weight of, on 3 to make ready for an impact, shock, etc. 4 to stimulate; invigorate —*n.* 1 a couple; pair 2 a thing that clasps or connects 3 [*pl.*] [Brit.] suspenders 4 either of the signs { }, used to connect words, lines, etc. 5 any propping device 6 *a*) a device for supporting a weak part of the body *b*) [often *pl.*] a device worn for straightening teeth 7 a tool for holding a drilling bit —**brace up** to call forth one's courage, etc.

brace and bit a tool for boring, consisting of

a removable drill (*bit*) in a rotating handle (*brace*)

brace·let (brās′lit) *n.* [< Gr *brachiōn*, arm] an ornamental band or chain worn around the wrist or arm —**brace′let·ed** *adj.*

brack·en (brak′ən) *n.* [ME *braken*] a large, weedy fern found in meadows, woods, etc.

brack·et (brak′it) *n.* [< Fr *brague*, knee pants] **1** a support projecting from a wall, etc. **2** any angle-shaped support **3** either of the signs [ ], used to enclose a word, etc. **4** the part of a classified grouping within certain limits [high income *bracket*] **5** *Sports* a diagram of the matchups in a tournament —*vt.* ͺ1 to support with brackets **2** to enclose within brackets **3** to classify together

brack·ish (brak′ish) *adj.* [< MDu *brak*] somewhat salty: used of water —**brack′ish·ness** *n.*

bract (brakt) *n.* [L *bractea*, thin metal plate] a modified leaf growing at the base of a flower or on its stalk

brad (brad) *n.* [ON *broddr*, arrow] a thin wire nail with a small head

brae (brā, brē) *n.* [ON *bra*, brow] [Scot.] a sloping bank; hillside

brag (brag) *vt., vi.* **bragged, brag′ging** [ME *braggen* < ?] to boast —*n.* boastful talk —**brag′ger** *n.*

brag·gart (-ərt) *n.* a boastful person

Brah·ma (brä′mə) *n.* Hindu god regarded as the creator of the universe

Brah·man (brä′mən) *n., pl.* **-mans** [Hindi < Sans, worship] **1** a member of the Hindu priestly caste: also **Brah′min 2** a breed of domestic cattle developed from the zebu of India and having a large hump

Brahms (brämz), **Jo·han·nes** (yō hän′əs) 1833-97; Ger. composer

braid (brād) *vt.* [< OE *bregdan*, to move quickly] **1** to interweave three or more strands of (hair, straw, etc.) **2** to make by such interweaving —*n.* **1** a length of hair, etc. formed by braiding **2** a woven band of cloth, etc., used to bind or decorate clothing

Braille (brāl) *n.* [after L. *Braille* (1809-52), its Fr inventor] [*also* **b-**] a system of printing for the blind, using raised dots felt with the fingers

brain (brān) *n.* [OE *brægen*] **1** the mass of nerve tissue in the cranium of vertebrates **2** [*often pl.*] intelligence **3** [Inf.] an intelligent person —*vt.* [Slang] to hit hard on the head

brain·child *n.* [Inf.] a product of a person's own creative mental labor

brain drain [Inf.] an exhausting of the intellectual or professional resources of a country, region, etc., esp. through emigration

brain·less *adj.* foolish or stupid

brain·storm [Inf.] *n.* a sudden inspiration, idea, or plan —*vi.* to engage in brainstorming

brain·storm·ing *n.* the unrestrained offering of ideas by all members of a group to seek solutions to problems

brain·wash *vt.* [Inf.] to indoctrinate so thoroughly as to effect a radical change of beliefs and attitudes

brain wave a series of rhythmic electric impulses in the nerves of the brain

brain·y *adj.* **-i·er, -i·est** [Inf.] having a good mind; intelligent

braise (brāz) *vt.* **braised, brais′ing** [< Fr *braise*, live coals] to brown (meat, etc.) and then simmer slowly

brake (brāk) *n.* [< ODu *breken*, to break] any device for slowing or stopping a vehicle or machine, as by causing a block, band, etc. (**brake shoe**) to press against a moving part —*vt., vi.* **braked, brak′ing** to slow down or stop with or as with a brake —**brake′less** *adj.*

brake·man (-mən) *n., pl.* **-men** (-mən) a railroad worker who operated the brakes on a train, but is now chiefly an assistant to the conductor

bram·ble (bram′bəl) *n.* [< OE *brom*, broom (the plant)] a prickly shrub of the rose family, as the raspberry or blackberry —**bram′bly** *adj.*

bran (bran) *n.* [OFr *bren*] the husk of grains of wheat, rye, etc. separated from the flour

branch (branch) *n.* [< LL *branca*, a claw] **1** any woody extension from a tree or shrub; limb **2** a tributary stream **3** any part or extension of a main body or system, as a division of a family or a separately located unit of a business, library, etc. —*vi.* **1** to put forth branches **2** to come out (*from* the main part) as a branch —**branch off 1** to separate into branches **2** to diverge —**branch out** to extend one's interests, activities, etc. —**branched** (bran′t) *adj.* —**branch′like′** *adj.*

brand (brand) *n.* [OE < *biernan*, to burn] **1** a burning or partially burned stick **2** a mark burned on the skin, formerly used to punish criminals, now used on cattle to show ownership **3** the iron used in branding **4** a stigma **5** *a*) an identifying mark or label on a company's products *b*) the make of a commodity [a *brand* of coffee] *c*) a special kind —*vt.* **1** to mark with a brand **2** to put a stigma on —**brand′er** *n.*

brand·ing *n.* the marketing of products by connecting them with a popular brand name

bran·dish (bran′dish) *vt.* [< OFr *brandir*] to wave menacingly or as a challenge; flourish

brand name the name by which a certain brand or make of commodity is known —**brand′-name′** *adj.*

brand-new *adj.* [orig., fresh from the fire: see BRAND] entirely new

bran·dy (bran′dē) *n., pl.* **-dies** [< Du *brandewijn*, distilled wine] an alcoholic liquor distilled from wine or from other fermented fruit juice —*vt.* **-died, -dy·ing** to flavor or preserve with brandy

brash (brash) *adj.* [orig. Brit dial.; < ?] **1** hasty and reckless **2** insolent; impudent

Bra·sí·lia (brä zē′lyä; E brə zil′yə) capital of Brazil, in the central part

brass (bras) *n., pl.* **brass′es** [OE *bræs*] **1** a yellowish metal, an alloy of copper and zinc **2** [*often with pl. v.*] musical instruments often made of brass and blown like a trumpet **3**

[Inf.] bold impudence 4 [*often with pl. v.*] [Slang] officers or officials of high rank —*adj.* of brass —**brass′y** *adj.* **-i·er, -i·est**

bras·siere or **bras·sière** (brə zir′) *n.* [Fr < *bras*, an arm] a bra

brass tacks [Inf.] practical details: used chiefly in **get down to brass tacks**

brat[1] (brat) *n.* [< Gael *bratt*, cloth, rag, ? child's bib] a child, esp. an impudent, unruly child: scornful or playful term

brat[2] (brät, brat) *n.* [Inf.] a link of bratwurst

Bra·ti·sla·va (brä′ti slä′və) capital of Slovakia, on the Danube

brat·wurst (brät′wurst′) *n.* [Ger < OHG, *brato*, lean meat + *wurst*, sausage] highly seasoned, fresh sausage of veal and pork

braun·schwei·ger (broun′shwī′gər) *n.* [after *Braunschweig*, Germany, where orig. made] smoked liver sausage

bra·va·do (brə vä′dō) *n.* [< Sp < *bravo*, brave] feigned courage

brave (brāv) *adj.* **brav′er, brav′est** [Fr < It *bravo*] 1 not afraid; having courage 2 having a fine appearance —*n.* 1 any brave man 2 a North American Indian warrior —*vt.* **braved, brav′ing** 1 to face with courage 2 to defy; dare —**brave′ly** *adv.* —**brave′ness** *n.*

brav·er·y (brā′vər ē) *n.* courage; valor

bra·vo (brä′vō) *interj.* [It] well done! —*n., pl.* **-vos** a shout of "bravo!"

bra·vu·ra (brə vyoor′ə) *n.* [It < *bravo*, brave] 1 bold daring; dash 2 brilliant musical technique

brawl (brôl) *vi.* [ME *braulen*, to cry out] to quarrel or fight noisily —*n.* a noisy quarrel or fight

brawn (brôn) *n.* [< OFr *braon*, muscle] 1 strong, well-developed muscles 2 muscular strength —**brawn′y** *adj.* **-i·er, -i·est** —**brawn′i·ness** *n.*

bray (brā) *vi.* [< OFr *braire*] to make the loud, harsh cry of a donkey —*n.* such a cry, or a sound resembling this

braze (brāz) *vt.* **brazed, braz′ing** [Fr *braser*] to solder with a metal having a high melting point

bra·zen (brā′zən) *adj.* [< OE *bræsen*, brass] 1 of brass 2 like brass in color, etc. 3 shameless; bold; impudent 4 harsh and piercing —**brazen it out** to act in a bold, unashamed way —**bra′zen·ly** *adv.* —**bra′zen·ness** *n.*

bra·zier[1] (brā′zhər) *n.* [see BRAISE] a metal container to hold burning coals

bra·zier[2] (brā′zhər) *n.* [see BRASS] a person who works in brass

Bra·zil (brə zil′) country in South America, on the Atlantic —**Bra·zil′ian** *adj., n.*

Brazil nut the edible, three-sided seed of a tree of South America

breach (brēch) *n.* [< OE *brecan*, to break] 1 a failure to observe a law, promise, etc. 2 an opening made by a breakthrough 3 a break in friendly relations —*vt.* 1 to make a breach in 2 to violate (a contract, etc.) —**breach of promise** a breaking of a promise, esp. to marry

bread (bred) *n.* [OE, crumb] 1 a baked food made of flour or meal mixed with water, etc. 2 livelihood [to earn one's *bread*] —*vt.* to coat with bread crumbs before cooking —**break bread** to eat

breadth (bredth) *n.* [< OE *brad*, broad] 1 width 2 scope; extent

bread·win·ner (bred′win′ər) *n.* one who supports dependents by his or her earnings

break (brāk) *vt.* **broke, bro′ken, break′ing** [OE *brecan*] 1 to split or crack into pieces; smash [*broke* the vase] 2 to cut open the surface of (soil, the skin, etc.) 3 to make unusable by cracking, disrupting, etc. 4 to tame as with force 5 to get rid of (a habit) 6 to demote 7 to make poor, ill, bankrupt, etc. 8 to surpass (a record) 9 to violate (a law, promise, etc.) 10 to disrupt the order of [*break* ranks] 11 to interrupt (a journey, electric circuit, etc.) 12 to reduce the force of by interrupting (a fall, etc.) 13 to bring to an end suddenly or by force 14 to penetrate (silence, darkness, etc.) 15 to disclose 16 to decipher or solve [*break* a code] —*vi.* 1 to split into pieces; come apart 2 to force one's way (*through* obstacles, etc.) 3 to stop associating (*with*) 4 to become unusable 5 to change suddenly [his voice *broke*] 6 to begin suddenly [to *break* into song] 7 to come suddenly into being, notice, etc. [the story *broke*] 8 to stop activity temporarily [we *broke* for lunch] 9 to suffer a collapse as of spirit —*n.* 1 a breaking 2 a broken place 3 a beginning or appearance [the *break* of day] 4 an interruption of regularity 5 a gap, interval, or rest 6 a sudden change 7 an escape 8 a chance piece of luck —**break down** 1 to go out of working order 2 to have a physical or nervous collapse 3 to analyze —**break in** 1 to enter forcibly 2 to interrupt 3 to train (a beginner) 4 to prepare (something new) by use or wear —**break off** to stop abruptly —**break out** 1 to become covered with pimples, etc. 2 to escape suddenly —**break up** 1 to separate; disperse 2 to stop 3 [Inf.] to laugh or make laugh —**give someone a break** [Inf.] to stop treating someone harshly —**break′a·ble** *adj., n.*

break·age *n.* 1 a breaking 2 things broken 3 loss due to breaking or the sum allowed for it

break·down *n.* 1 a breaking down 2 a failure of health 3 an analysis

break·er *n.* 1 a person or thing that breaks 2 a wave that breaks into foam

break·fast (brek′fəst) *n.* the first meal of the day —*vi.* to eat breakfast

break·front (brāk′frunt′) *n.* a cabinet having a projecting center section in front

break-in *n.* the act of forcibly entering a building, esp. in order to rob

break·neck *adj.* very fast, reckless, or dangerous [*breakneck* speed]

break·through *n.* 1 the act of forcing a way through, as in warfare 2 a very important advance or discovery

break·up *n.* 1 a dispersion 2 a disintegration 3 a collapse

break·wa·ter *n.* a barrier to break the impact of waves, as before a harbor

breast (brest) *n.* ⟦OE *breost*⟧ **1** either of two milk-secreting glands on a woman's chest **2** the upper front part of the body **3** the part of a garment, etc. over the breast **4** the breast regarded as the center of emotions —*vt.* to face firmly; oppose

breast·bone *n.* STERNUM

breast-feed *vt.* **-fed´**, **-feed´ing** to feed (a baby) milk from the breast

breast·plate *n.* a piece of armor for the breast

breast stroke a swimming stroke in which both arms are brought out sideways from the chest

breast·work *n.* a low wall put up quickly as a defense in battle

breath (breth) *n.* ⟦< OE *bræth*, odor⟧ **1** air taken into the lungs and then let out **2** respiration **3** the power to breathe easily **4** life; spirit **5** a fragrant odor **6** a slight breeze **7** a whisper; murmur —**catch one's breath 1** to gasp **2** [Inf.] to rest or pause —**in the same breath** almost simultaneously —**save one's breath** [Inf.] to refrain from useless talk —**out of breath** breathless, as from exertion —**take someone's breath away** to thrill someone —**under (or below) one's breath** in a whisper

breathe (brēth) *vi., vt.* breathed, breath´ing **1** to take (air) into the lungs and let it out again; inhale and exhale **2** to live **3** to rest —breath´a·ble *adj.*

breath·er (brē´thər) *n.* **1** one who breathes **2** [Inf.] a pause for rest

breath·less (breth´lis) *adj.* **1** without breath **2** panting; gasping **3** unable to breathe easily because of emotion —**breath´less·ly** *adv.*

breath·tak·ing *adj.* very exciting

breath·y *adj.* -i·er, -i·est marked by an audible emission of breath

bred (bred) *vt., vi. pt. & pp. of* BREED

breech (brēch) *n.* ⟦OE *brec*⟧ **1** the buttocks **2** the part of a gun behind the barrel

breech-cloth *n.* LOINCLOTH

breech·es (brich´iz) *pl.n.* ⟦see BREECH⟧ **1** pants reaching to the knees **2** [Inf.] any pants

breed (brēd) *vt.* bred, breed´ing ⟦< OE *brod*, fetus⟧ **1** to bring forth (offspring) **2** to be the source of; produce **3** to raise (animals) **4** to rear; train —*vi.* **1** to be produced; originate **2** to reproduce —*n.* **1** a stock; strain **2** a sort; type —breed´er *n.*

breed·ing *n.* **1** the producing of young **2** good upbringing **3** the producing of plants and animals, esp. for improving the stock

breeze (brēz) *n.* ⟦perhaps < OSp *briza*, northeast wind⟧ **1** a gentle wind **2** [Inf.] a thing easy to do —*vi.* breezed, breez´ing [Inf.] to move or go quickly

breeze·way *n.* a covered passageway, as between a house and garage

breez·y *adj.* -i·er, -i·est **1** slightly windy **2** light and lively —breez´i·ly *adv.* —breez´i·ness *n.*

Bre·men (brem´ən) seaport in NW Germany

breth·ren (breth´rən) *pl.n.* ⟦ME *bretheren*⟧ brothers: now chiefly religious

bre·vet (brə vet´) *n.* ⟦< L *brevis*, brief⟧ [Historical] *Mil.* a temporary or honorary commission of higher rank without extra pay —*vt.* -vet´ted or -vet´ed, -vet´ting or -vet´ing to give a brevet to

bre·vi·ar·y (brē´vē er´ē) *n., pl.* -ar´ies ⟦< L *brevis*, brief⟧ a book of Psalms, prayers, etc. to be recited daily by priests, nuns, etc.

brev·i·ty (brev´ə tē) *n.* ⟦< L *brevis*, brief⟧ **1** briefness **2** conciseness

brew (broō) *vt.* ⟦OE *breowan*⟧ **1** to make (beer, etc.) from malt and hops by boiling and fermenting **2** to steep (tea, etc.) **3** to plot —*vi.* to begin to form —*n.* a brewed beverage —brew´er *n.*

brew·er·y (broō´ər ē) *n., pl.* -er·ies a place where beer is brewed

bri·ar¹ (brī´ər) *n.* BRIER¹

bri·ar² (brī´ər) *n.* a tobacco pipe made from the root of the BRIER²

bribe (brīb) *n.* ⟦< OFr *briber*, to beg⟧ anything given or promised as an inducement, esp. to do something illegal or wrong —*vt.* bribed, brib´ing to offer or give a bribe to —brib´er·y *n.*

bric-a-brac (brik´ə brak´) *n.* ⟦< Fr *de bric et de brac*, by hook or by crook⟧ **1** small artistic objects used to ornament a room **2** knickknacks

brick (brik) *n.* ⟦MDu < *breken*, piece of baked clay⟧ **1** an oblong block of baked clay, used in building, etc. **2** anything shaped like a brick **3** bricks collectively —*adj.* built or paved with brick —*vt.* to build or cover with brick

brick·bat *n.* **1** a piece of brick used as a missile **2** an unfavorable remark

brick·lay·er *n.* one whose work is building with bricks —brick´lay´ing *n.*

brid·al (brīd´'l) *adj.* ⟦< OE *bryd ealu*, marriage feast⟧ **1** of a bride **2** of a wedding

bride (brīd) *n.* ⟦OE *bryd*⟧ a woman just married or about to be married

bride·groom *n.* ⟦< OE *bryd*, bride + *guma*, man⟧ a man just married or about to be married

brides·maid (brīdz´mād´) *n.* a woman who attends the bride at a wedding

bridge¹ (brij) *n.* ⟦OE *brycge*⟧ **1** a structure built over a river, etc. to provide a way across **2** a thing that provides connection, contact, etc. **3** the bony upper part of the nose **4** a raised platform on a ship, from which it is commanded **5** a mounting for false teeth **6** *Music* a connecting passage —*vt.* bridged, bridg´ing to build or be a bridge over —**burn one's bridges (behind one)** to follow a course from which there is no retreat —bridge´a·ble *adj.*

bridge² (brij) *n.* ⟦< ? Russ⟧ a card game, for two pairs of players, in which they bid for the right to name the trump suit or declare no-trump

bridge·head *n.* a fortified position established by an attacking force on the enemy's side of a bridge, river, etc.

bridge·work *n.* a dental bridge or bridges

bri·dle (brīd′'l) *n.* [< OE *bregdan,* move quickly] 1 a head harness for guiding a horse: it has a bit for the mouth to which the reins are fastened 2 anything that controls or restrains —*vt.* **bri′dled, bri′dling** 1 to put a bridle on 2 to curb or control —*vi.* 1 to pull one's head back quickly as an expression of anger, scorn, etc. 2 to take offense (*at*)

bridle path a path for horseback riding

brief (brēf) *adj.* [< L *brevis*] 1 short 2 concise —*n.* 1 a summary, esp. of the main points of a law case 2 [*pl.*] legless undershorts —*vt.* 1 to summarize 2 to supply with all pertinent information —**brief′ly** *adv.* —**brief′ness** *n.*

brief·case *n.* a flat, flexible case for carrying papers, books, etc.

brief·ing *n.* a supplying of pertinent information

bri·er¹ (brī′ər) *n.* [OE *brer*] any thorny bush, as a bramble

bri·er² (brī′ər) *n.* [Fr *bruyère*] a variety of heath, whose root is used for making tobacco pipes

brig¹ (brig) *n.* [< BRIGANTINE] a two masted ship with square sails

brig² *n.* [< ?] a prison, as on a warship

bri·gade (bri gād′) *n.* [< OIt *briga,* strife] 1 a military unit composed of two or more battalions with service and administrative units 2 a group of people organized to function as a unit in some work [a fire *brigade*]

brig·a·dier general (brig′ə dir′) *U.S. Mil.* a military officer ranking just above a colonel

brig·and (brig′ənd) *n.* [see BRIGADE] a bandit, esp. one of a roving band

brig·and·age *n.* plundering by brigands

brig·an·tine (brig′ən tēn′) *n.* [< OIt *brigantino,* pirate vessel] a ship with a square-rigged foremast and a usually fore-and-aft-rigged mainmast

bright (brīt) *adj.* [OE *bryht*] 1 shining with light 2 brilliant in color or sound; vivid 3 lively; cheerful 4 mentally quick; smart 5 favorable or hopeful —**bright′ly** *adv.* —**bright′ness** *n.*

bright·en *vt., vi.* to make or become bright or brighter

bril·liant (bril′yənt) *adj.* [< Fr < It *brillare,* to sparkle] 1 shining brightly 2 vivid; intense 3 very splendid 4 very intelligent, talented, etc. —**bril′liance** *n.,* **bril′lian·cy** —**bril′liant·ly** *adv.*

bril·lian·tine (bril′yən tēn′) *n.* [< Fr] an oily substance for grooming the hair

brim (brim) *n.* [ME *brimme*] 1 the topmost edge of a cup, glass, etc. 2 a projecting rim, as of a hat — *vt., vi.* **brimmed, brim′ming** to fill or be full to the brim —**brim′less** *adj.*

brim·ful (-fool′) *adj.* full to the brim

brim·stone *n.* [< OE *bærnan,* to kindle + *stan,* stone] sulfur

brin·dle (brin′dəl) *adj.* BRINDLED —*n.* 1 a brindled color 2 a brindled animal

brin·dled (-dəld) *adj.* [prob. < ME *brennen,* to burn] having a gray or tawny coat streaked or spotted with a darker color

brine (brīn) *n.* [OE] salty water —**brin′y** *adj.* **-i·er, -i·est**

bring (briŋ) *vt.* **brought, bring′ing** [OE *bringan*] 1 to carry or lead "here" or "along" 2 to cause to be at a place where the speaker will be 2 to cause to be, happen, appear, etc. 3 to lead to an action or belief 4 to sell for —**bring about** to cause —**bring forth** to give birth to; produce —**bring off** to accomplish —**bring out** to reveal —**bring up** 1 to rear (children) 2 to introduce, as into discussion

brink (briŋk) *n.* [< MLowG or Dan, shore] the edge, esp. at the top of a steep place; verge

brink·man·ship (-mən ship′) *n.* the policy of pursuing a risky course of action to the brink of disaster: also **brinks′man·ship′**

bri·oche (brē ōsh′) *n.* [Fr] a light, rich roll made with flour, butter, eggs, and yeast

bri·quette or **bri·quet** (bri ket′) *n.* [Fr < *brique,* brick] a small block of charcoal, etc., used for fuel or kindling

Bris·bane (briz′bān′, -bən) seaport in E Australia

brisk (brisk) *adj.* [< ? Fr *brusque,* brusque] 1 quick in manner; energetic 2 keen, bracing, etc. —**brisk′ly** *adv.* —**brisk′ness** *n.*

bris·ket (bris′kit) *n.* [ME *brusket*] meat cut from the breast of an animal

bris·tle (bris′əl) *n.* [< OE *byrst*] 1 any short, stiff hair 2 such a hair, or a piece like it, in a brush —*vi.* **-tled, -tling** 1 to be stiff and erect 2 to have the bristles become erect 3 to stiffen with anger 4 to be thickly covered (*with*) —**bris′tly** (-lē) *adj.* **-tli·er, -tli·est**

bris·tle·cone pine a Rocky Mountain pine tree of the W U.S.

Brit *abbrev.* British

Brit·ain (brit′'n) GREAT BRITAIN

britch·es (brich′iz) *pl.n.* [Inf.] BREECHES (*pl.n.* 2)

Brit·i·cism (brit′ə siz′əm) *n.* a word or idiom peculiar to British English

Brit·ish (brit′ish) *adj.* of Great Britain or its people, language, etc. —**the British** the people of Great Britain

British Columbia province of SW Canada; cap. Victoria: abbrev. *BC*

British Commonwealth (of Nations) *former name for* THE COMMONWEALTH

British Isles group of islands including Great Britain, Ireland, etc.

British thermal unit a unit of heat equal to about 252 calories

Brit·on (brit′'n) *n.* 1 a member of an early Celtic people of S Britain 2 a person born or living in Great Britain, esp. in England

brit·tle (brit′'l) *adj.* [< OE *breotan,* to break] easily broken or shattered —*n.* a brittle, crunchy candy with nuts in it —**brit′tle·ness** *n.*

broach (brōch) *n.* [< ML *brocca,* a spike] a tapering bit for boring holes —*vt.* 1 to make a hole in so as to let out liquid 2 to ream with a broach 3 to start a discussion of

broad (brôd) *adj.* [OE *brad*] 1 of large extent from side to side; wide 2 extending about; full [*broad* daylight] 3 obvious [a *broad* hint] **4** tolerant; liberal [a *broad* view] **5** wide in range [a *broad* variety] **6** not detailed; general [in *broad* outline] —**broad′ly** *adv.* —**broad′ness** *n.*

broad·band *adj.* designating communication networks, etc. allowing the transmission of much data at high speeds

broad-based *adj.* comprehensive or extensive

broad·cast (-kast′) *vt., vi.* **-cast′** or **-cast′ed, -cast′ing** **1** to scatter or spread widely **2** to transmit by radio, TV, or the internet —*adj.* of or for broadcasting by radio, TV, or the internet —*n.* a program on radio, TV, or the internet —*adv.* far and wide —**broad′ cast′er** *n.*

broad·cloth *n.* a fine, smooth woolen, cotton, or silk cloth

broad·en *vt., vi.* to widen

broad jump *former name for* LONG JUMP

broad·loom *adj.* woven on a wide loom

broad-mind·ed *adj.* tolerant of unconventional opinions and behavior; liberal —**broad′- mind′ed·ly** *adv.* —**broad′-mind′ed·ness** *n.*

broad·side *n.* **1** the firing of all guns on one side of a warship **2** a vigorous attack in words —*adv.* **1** with the side facing **2** in the side [hit *broadside*] **3** indiscriminately

broad-spec·trum *adj.* effective against a wide range of germs

broad·sword *n.* a broad-bladed sword for slashing

Broad·way (brôd′wā′) street in New York City, with many theaters, etc.

bro·cade (brō kād′) *n.* [< Sp < It *broccare*, embroider] a rich cloth with a raised design woven into it —*vt.* **-cad′ed, -cad′ing** to weave a raised design into (cloth)

broc·co·li (bräk′ə lē) *n.* [It < ML *brocca*, a spike] a plant related to the cauliflower but bearing tender shoots with green flower buds

bro·chette (brō shet′) *n.* [Fr] a skewer for broiling chunks of meat, etc.

bro·chure (brō shoor′) *n.* [Fr < *brocher*, to stitch] a pamphlet

brogue[1] (brōg) *n.* [< ?] a dialectal pronunciation, esp. that of English by the Irish or Scots

brogue[2] (brōg) *n.* [< Ir *brōg*, a shoe] a man's heavy oxford shoe

broil (broil) *vt., vi.* [< OFr *bruillir*] to cook by exposure to direct heat

broil·er *n.* **1** a pan, grill, etc. for broiling **2** a chicken suitable for broiling

broke (brōk) *vt., vi. pt. of* BREAK —*adj.* [Inf.] without money; bankrupt

bro·ken (brō′kən) *vt., vi. pp. of* BREAK —*adj.* **1** splintered, fractured, etc. **2** not in working order **3** violated [a *broken* promise] **4** ruined **5** interrupted; discontinuous **6** imperfectly spoken **7** tamed —**bro′ken·ly** *adv.*

bro·ken-down *adj.* **1** sick or worn out **2** out of order; useless

bro·ken·heart·ed *adj.* crushed by sorrow, grief, etc.

bro·ker (brō′kər) *n.* [< OFr *brokier*, to tap; orig. sense "wine dealer"] **1** a person hired as an agent in negotiating contracts, buying and selling, etc. **2** STOCKBROKER —*vt., vi.* **1** to act as a broker (for) **2** to negotiate

bro·ker·age *n.* **1** the business or office of a broker **2** a broker's fee

bro·mide (brō′mīd′) *n.* **1** a compound of bromine with another element or a radical **2** potassium bromide, formerly used as a sedative **3** a trite saying

bro·mid·ic (-mid′ik) *adj.* trite or dull

bro·mine (brō′mēn′) *n.* [< Gr *brōmos*, stench] a chemical element, a reddish-brown, corrosive liquid

bron·chi (brän′kī) *pl.n., sing.* **-chus** (-kəs) [< Gr *bronchos*, windpipe] the two main branches of the windpipe —**bron′chi·al** (-kē əl) *adj.*

bron·chi·tis (-kīt′is) *n.* an inflammation of the bronchial tubes

bron·co (brän′kō) *n., pl.* **-cos** [Sp, rough] a wild or only partly tamed horse or pony of the W U.S.

bron·co·bust·er *n.* [Inf.] a tamer of broncos —**bron′co·bust′ing** *n.*

Bron·të (brän′të) **1 Char·lotte** (shär′lət) 1816-55; Eng. novelist **2 Em·i·ly** (em′ə lē) 1818-48; Eng. novelist: sister of Charlotte

bron·to·saur (brän′tō sôr′, -tə-) *n.* [< Gr *brontē*, thunder + *sauros*, lizard] APATOSAURUS: also **bron′to·saur′us**

Bronx (bräŋks) borough of New York City: used with *the*

bronze (bränz) *n.* [Fr, prob. ult. < Pers *biring*, copper] **1** an alloy of copper and tin **2** a reddish-brown color —*adj.* of or like bronze —*vt.* **bronzed, bronz′ing** [Fr *bronzer* < the *n.*] to make bronze in color

Bronze Age the period in human culture when bronze tools were used

brooch (brōch, broō′) *n.* [see BROACH] a large ornamental pin with a clasp

brood (brood) *n.* [OE *brod*] **1** a group of birds hatched at one time **2** the children in a family —*vi.* **1** to sit on and hatch eggs **2** to worry: often with *on, over,* or *about*

brood·mare *n.* a mare kept for breeding

brook[1] (brook) *n.* [< OE *broc*] a small stream

brook[2] (brook) *vt.* [OE *brucan*, to use] to put up with; endure

Brook·lyn (brook′lən) borough of New York City

broom (broom, broom) *n.* [OE *brom*, brushwood] **1** a flowering shrub of the pea family **2** a bundle of fibers or straws fastened to a long handle (**broom′stick′**), used for sweeping

Bros or **bros** *abbrev.* brothers

broth (brôth) *n.* [OE] a thin soup made by boiling meat, etc. in water

broth·el (bräth′əl) *n.* [< OE *broethan*, go to ruin] a house of prostitution

broth·er (bruth′ər) *n., pl.* **-ers** [OE *brothor*] **1** a male related to one by having the same parents **2** a friend who is like a brother **3** a fellow member of the same race, church, profession, etc. **4** [*often* B-] a lay member of a men's religious order

broth·er·hood *n.* **1** the state of being brothers **2** an association of men united in some interest, work, etc. **3** a feeling of unity among all people

broth·er-in-law *n., pl.* **broth′ers-in-law′ 1** the brother of one's spouse **2** the husband of one's sibling **3** the husband of the sibling of one's spouse

broth·er·ly *adj.* **1** of or like a brother **2** friendly, kind, loyal, etc.

brought (brôt) *vt. pt. & pp. of* BRING

brou·ha·ha (broō′hä hä′) *n.* ⟦Fr⟧ an uproar or commotion

brow (brou) *n.* ⟦OE *bru*⟧ **1** the eyebrow **2** the forehead **3** the edge of a cliff

brow·beat *vt.* **-beat′, -beat′en, -beat′ing** to intimidate with harsh, stern looks and talk; bully

brown (broun) *adj.* ⟦OE *brun*⟧ **1** having the color of chocolate, a mixture of red, black, and yellow **2** having dark skin —*n.* brown color —*vt., vi.* to make or become brown —**brown′ish** *adj.*

brown-bag *vt., vi.* **-bagged′, -bag′ging** to carry (one's lunch) to work or school, as in a brown paper bag

brown·ie (broun′ē) *n.* **1** *Eng. Folklore* a small, helpful elf **2** a small square cut from a flat chocolate cake

Brown·ing (broun′iŋ), **Rob·ert** (räb′ərt) 1812–89; Eng. poet

brown·out *n.* a dimming of lights in a city, as during an electric power shortage

brown rice rice that has not had its bran and germ removed

brown·stone *n.* **1** a reddish-brown sandstone, used for building **2** a house built with such stone

brown study deep thought; reverie

brown sugar sugar containing some molasses

browse (brouz) *n.* ⟦< OS *brustian*, to sprout⟧ leaves, shoots, etc. which animals feed on —*vt., vi.* **browsed, brows′ing 1** to nibble at (leaves, shoots, etc.) **2** to examine (a book, articles for sale, etc.) in a casual way

brows·er *n.* **1** one that browses **2** software for gaining access to the World Wide Web

bru·in (broō′in) *n.* ⟦Du, brown⟧ a bear

bruise (broōz) *vt.* **bruised, bruis′ing** ⟦< OE *brysan*, crush⟧ **1** to injure and discolor (body tissue) without breaking the skin **2** to injure the surface of, causing spoilage, denting, etc. **3** to hurt (the feelings, spirit, etc.) —*vi.* to be or become bruised —*n.* a bruised area, as of tissue

bruis·er *n.* [Inf.] a strong, pugnacious man

bruit (broōt) *vt.* ⟦< OFr, noise, rumor⟧ to spread (*about*) by rumor

brunch (brunch) *n.* a combined breakfast and lunch —*vi.* to eat brunch

Bru·nei (broō nī′) country on the N coast of Borneo

bru·net (broō net′) *adj.* ⟦< OFr, dim. of *brun*, brown⟧ having black or dark-brown hair —*n.* a brunet person

bru·nette (-net′) *adj.* BRUNET —*n.* a brunette woman or girl

brunt (brunt) *n.* ⟦ME *bront*⟧ **1** the shock (of an attack) or impact (of a blow) **2** the hardest part

brush¹ (brush) *n.* ⟦< OFr *broce*, bush⟧ **1** BRUSHWOOD **2** sparsely settled country **3** a device for cleaning, painting, etc., having bristles, wires, etc. fastened into a back **4** a brushing **5** a light, grazing stroke **6** a bushy tail, as of a fox —*vt.* **1** to clean, paint, etc. with a brush **2** to apply, remove, etc. as with a brush **3** to touch or graze in passing —*vi.* to graze past something —**brush up** to refresh one's memory

brush² (brush) *n.* ⟦< ME *bruschen*, to rush⟧ a short, quick fight

brush-off *n.* [Slang] a curt dismissal, esp. in the phrase **give** (or **get**) **the brushoff**

brush·wood *n.* **1** chopped-off tree branches **2** underbrush

brusque (brusk) *adj.* ⟦Fr < ML *bruscus*, brushwood⟧ rough and abrupt in manner or speech; curt   **brusque′ly** *adv.* —**brusque′ ness** *n.*

Brus·sels (brus′əlz) capital of Belgium

Brussels sprout 1 *often* **Brussels sprouts** a plant that bears small cabbagelike heads on an erect stem **2** one of its edible heads

bru·tal (broōt′l) *adj.* **1** like a brute; very savage, cruel, etc. **2** very harsh —**bru′tal·ly** *adv.*

bru·tal·i·ty (broō tal′ə tē) *n.* **1** a being brutal **2** *pl.* **-ties** a brutal act

bru·tal·ize (broōt′'l īz′) *vt.* **-ized′, -iz′ing 1** to make brutal **2** to treat in a brutal way —**bru′tal·i·za′tion** *n.*

brute (broōt) *adj.* ⟦< L *brutus*, irrational⟧ of or like an animal; specif., savage, stupid, etc. —*n.* **1** an animal **2** a brutal person —**brut′ ish** *adj.* —**brut′ish·ly** *adv.*

bs *abbrev.* bill of sale

BS *abbrev.* Bachelor of Science: also **B.S.**

Btu *abbrev.* British thermal unit(s): also **BTU** or **btu**

BTW *abbrev.* by the way

bu *abbrev.* bushel(s)

bub·ble (bub′əl) *n.* ⟦echoic⟧ **1** a film of liquid forming a ball around air or gas **2** a tiny ball of air or gas in a liquid or solid **3** a transparent dome **4** a plausible scheme that proves worthless **5** a period of extreme overvaluation, as in a stock market —*vi.* **-bled, -bling 1** to rise in bubbles; boil **2** to make a gurgling sound —**on the bubble** with the outcome uncertain —**bub′bly** *adj.* **-bli·er, -bli·est**

bubble gum a kind of chewing gum that can be blown into large bubbles

bub·ble·head *n.* a person who is silly, ignorant, etc.

Bubble Wrap *trademark for* plastic packaging material with air bubbles —**[b- w-]** such packaging material

bu·bo (byoō′bō′) *n., pl.* **-boes′** ⟦< Gr *boubōn*, groin⟧ an inflamed swelling of a lymph node, esp. in the armpit or groin

bu·bon·ic plague (-bän'ik) a contagious disease characterized by buboes, fever, and delirium

buc·ca·neer (buk'ə nir') *n.* [< Fr *boucanier*] a pirate

Bu·chan·an (byōō kan'ən), **James** (jāmz) 1791-1868; 15th president of the U.S. (1857-61)

Bu·cha·rest (bōō'kə rest') capital of Romania

buck¹ (buk) *n.* [OE *bucca*, male goat] 1 a male deer, rabbit, etc.: see DOE 2 the act of bucking 3 BUCKSKIN 4 [Inf.] a bold, vigorous young man —*vi.* 1 to leap upward quickly, as to throw off a rider: said of a horse, bull, etc. 2 [Inf.] to resist something as if plunging against it —*vt.* 1 to dislodge or throw by bucking 2 [Inf.] to resist stubbornly —**buck for** [Slang] to work eagerly for (a promotion, etc.) —**buck up** [Inf.] to cheer up

buck² (buk) *n.* [< ?] [Slang] a dollar —**pass the buck** [Inf.] to try to shift blame or responsibility onto another person

buck·board *n.* [BUCK¹, *vi.* + BOARD] an open carriage whose floorboards rest directly on the axles

buck·et (buk'it) *n.* [< OE *buc*, pitcher] 1 a cylindrical container with a curved handle, for carrying water, etc.; pail 2 the amount held by a bucket: also **buck'et·ful'**, *pl.* **-fuls'** 3 a thing like a bucket, as a scoop on a steam shovel —**kick the bucket** [Slang] to die

bucket seat a single contoured seat with a movable back, as in sports cars

buck·eye (buk'ī') *n.* [BUCK¹ + EYE < the appearance of the seed] 1 any of several American horse chestnut trees 2 the seed of such a tree

buck·le¹ (buk'əl) *n.* [< L *buccula*, cheek strap of a helmet] a clasp for fastening a strap, belt, etc. —*vt., vi.* **-led, -ling** to fasten with a buckle —**buckle down** to apply oneself energetically

buck·le² (buk'əl) *vt., vi.* **-led, -ling** [prob. infl. by OFr *bocler*, to bulge: see prec.] to bend or crumple —*n.* a bend, bulge, etc.

buck·ler (buk'lər) *n.* [< OFr *bocler*] a small, round shield

buck-pass·er *n.* [Inf.] one who regularly tries to shift blame or responsibility to someone else —**buck'-pass'ing** *n.*

buck·ram (buk'rəm) *n.* [? < *Bukhara*, city in central Asia] a coarse, stiff cloth used in bookbinding, etc.

buck·saw *n.* a wood-cutting saw set in a frame

buck·shot *n.* large lead shot for shooting deer and other large game

buck·skin *n.* 1 a soft leather made from the skins of deer or sheep 2 [*pl.*] clothes made of buckskin

buck·tooth *n.*, *pl.* **-teeth'** a projecting front tooth —**buck'toothed'** *adj.*

buck·wheat *n.* [< OE *boc-*, beech + WHEAT] 1 a plant with grainlike seeds 2 a dark flour made from the seeds

bu·col·ic (byōō käl'ik) *adj.* [< Gr *boukolos*, herdsman] 1 of shepherds; pastoral 2 of country life; rustic —**bu·col'i·cal·ly** *adv.*

bud (bud) *n.* [ME *budde*] 1 a small swelling on a plant, from which a shoot, leaf, or flower develops 2 an early stage of development —*vi.* **bud'ded, bud'ding** 1 to put forth buds 2 to begin to develop —**in (the) bud** 1 in a budding condition 2 in an early stage —**bud'like'** *adj.*

Bu·da·pest (bōō'də pest') capital of Hungary

Bud·dha (bōō'də) religious leader who lived in India 563?-483? B.C.; founder of Buddhism

Bud·dhism (bōō'diz'əm) *n.* a religion of Asia teaching that by right thinking and self-denial one achieves nirvana, a state of enlightenment —**Bud'dhist** *n., adj.*

bud·dy (bud'ē) *n., pl.* **-dies** [< ?] [Inf.] a close friend; comrade

budge (buj) *vt., vi.* **budged, budg'ing** [< OFr *bouger*, to move] to move even a little

budg·er·i·gar (buj'ər i gär') *n.* [native name] a blue, green, or yellow Australian parakeet: also [Inf.] **budg'ie**

budg·et (buj'it) *n.* [< L *bulga*, bag] 1 a plan adjusting expenses to income 2 estimated cost of living, operating, etc. 3 amount allotted for a specific use —*vt.* 1 to put on a budget 2 to plan [*budget* your time] —**budg'et·ar'y** *adj.*

Bue·nos Ai·res (bwä'nəs er'ēz) seaport & capital of Argentina

buff (buf) *n.* [< Fr < It *bufalo*, buffalo] 1 a soft, brownish-yellow leather 2 a dull brownish yellow 3 [Inf.] a devotee; fan —*adj.* of the color buff —*vt.* to polish or shine, as with soft leather —**in the buff** naked

buf·fa·lo (buf'ə lō') *n., pl.* **-loes', -lo', -los'** [It *bufalo* < Gr *bous*, ox] 1 any of various wild oxen, as the water buffalo of India 2 the American bison —*vt.* **-loed', -lo'ing** [Slang] to baffle, bluff, etc.

Buf·fa·lo (buf'ə lō') city in W New York, on Lake Erie

Buffalo wings [after prec.] [*also* **b-w-**] spicy fried segments of chicken wings

buff·er¹ (buf'ər) *n.* [BUFF, *v.* + -ER] 1 one who buffs 2 something used for buffing

buff·er² (buf'ər) *n.* [< OFr *buffe*, a blow] 1 anything that lessens shock, as of collision 2 a temporary storage area in a computer, for data being transferred to another device

buf·fet¹ (buf'it) *n.* [OFr < *buffe*, a blow] a blow or shock —*vt.* 1 to punch; hit 2 to thrust about

buf·fet² (bə fā', boo-) *n.* [Fr] 1 a sideboard 2 a counter or table at which guests, etc. serve themselves food 3 a meal served on such a table, etc.

buf·foon (bə fōōn') *n.* [< Fr < It *buffare*, to jest] one who is always clowning and trying to be funny; clown —**buf·foon'er·y** *n.* —**buf·foon'ish** *adj.*

bug (bug) *n.* [prob. < ME *bugge*: see fol.] 1 an insect with sucking mouthparts 2 any arthropod, as a cockroach or spider 3 a defect, as in a machine 4 [Inf.] a germ or virus 5 [Inf.] a hidden microphone —*vt.* **bugged, bug'ging** 1 [Inf.] to hide a microphone in (a room, etc.) **2** [Slang] to annoy, anger, etc.

bug·bear *n.* [ME *bugge*, a hobgoblin + BEAR²] **1** an imaginary evil being **2** a cause of needless fear Also **bug'a·boo'** (-ə boo') *n., pl.* **-boos'**

bug-eyed *adj.* [Slang] with bulging eyes

bug·gy¹ (bug'ē) *n., pl.* **-gies** [< ?] **1** a light one-horse carriage with one seat **2** BABY CARRIAGE

bug·gy² (bug'ē) *adj.* **-gi·er, -gi·est** infested with bugs

bu·gle (byoo'gəl) *n.* [< L *buculus*, young ox] a brass instrument like a small trumpet, usually without valves — *vi., vt.* **-gled, -gling** to signal by blowing a bugle —**bu'gler** *n.*

build (bild) *vt.* **built, build'ing** [< OE *bold*, house] **1** to make by putting together materials, parts, etc.; construct **2** to establish; base [*build* a theory on facts] **3** to create or develop: often with *up* —*vi.* **1** to put up buildings **2** to grow or intensify: often with *up* —*n.* the way a thing is built or shaped [a stocky *build*] —**build up** to make more attractive, healthy, etc. —**build'er** *n.*

build·ing *n.* **1** anything that is built, esp. a roofed structure for human use **2** the work or business of making houses, etc.

build-up or **build-up** *n.* [Inf.] **1** praise or favorable publicity **2** a gradual increase or expansion

built (bilt) *vt., vi. pt. & pp. of* BUILD

built-in *adj.* **1** made as part of the structure **2** inherent

built-up *adj.* **1** made higher, stronger, etc. with added parts **2** having many buildings on it

bulb (bulb) *n.* [< Gr *bolbos*] **1** an underground bud with roots and a short, scaly stem, as in a lily or onion **2** an underground plant structure resembling a bulb, as in a crocus **3** anything shaped like a bulb [an electric light *bulb*] —**bul'bous** *adj.*

Bul·gar·i·a (bəl gerʹē ə, bool-) country in SE Europe —**Bul·garʹi·an** *adj., n.*

bulge (bulj) *n.* [< L *bulga*, leather bag] an outward swelling; protuberance — *vi., vt.* **bulged, bulg'ing** to swell or bend outward —**bulg'y** *adj.* **-i·er, -i·est**

bu·lim·i·a (byoo lēʹmē ə) *n.* [< Gr *bous*, ox + *limos*, hunger] **1** *Med.* a continuous, abnormal hunger **2** a disorder characterized by overeating followed by self-induced vomiting, etc.: in full **bulimia ner·vo·sa** (nər vōʹsə) —**bu·limʹic** *adj.*

bulk (bulk) *n.* [< ON *bulki*, a heap] **1** size, mass, or volume, esp. if great **2** the main mass; largest part —*vi.* to have, or to increase in, size or importance —*adj.* **1** total; aggregate **2** not put up in individual packages —**bulk'y** *adj.* **-i·er, -i·est**

bulk·head (bulk'hed') *n.* [< ON *balkr*, partition + HEAD] **1** an upright partition, as in a ship, that is watertight, fireproof, etc. **2** a boxlike structure over an opening

bull¹ (bool) *n.* [< OE *bula*, a steer] **1** the adult male of any bovine animal, as the ox, or of

certain other large animals, as the elephant or whale **2** a speculator who buys stocks expecting their prices to rise **3** [Slang] insincere talk; nonsense —*adj.* **1** male **2** rising in price

bull² (bool) *n.* [< LL *bulla*, a seal] an official document from the pope

bull·dog *n.* a short-haired, heavily built dog with a strong grip

bull·doze (-dōz') *vt.* **-dozed', -doz'ing** [< *bull*, a flogging + DOSE] **1** [Inf.] to force or frighten by threatening; bully **2** to move, make level, etc. with a bulldozer

bull·doz·er *n.* a tractor with a large blade for pushing earth, debris, etc.

bul·let (boolʹit) *n.* [< L *bulla*, a knob] a small, shaped piece of lead, steel, etc., to be shot from a firearm

bul·le·tin (boolʹə tin) *n.* [< LL *bulla*, a seal] **1** a brief statement of the latest news **2** a regular publication, as of an organization

bulletin board a board or wall area on which bulletins, notices, etc. are put up

bul·let·proof *adj.* that bullets cannot pierce —*vt.* to make bulletproof

bull·fight *n.* a spectacle in which a bull is usually provoked in various ways and then killed with the thrust of a sword by a matador —**bull'fight'er** *n.* —**bull'fight'ing** *n.*

bull·frog *n.* a large North American frog with a deep, loud croak

bull·head·ed *adj.* blindly stubborn; headstrong —**bull'head'ed·ness** *n.*

bull·horn *n.* a portable electronic voice amplifier

bul·lion (boolʹyən) *n.* [< OFr *billon*, small coin] ingots, bars, etc. of gold or silver

bull·ish (boolʹish) *adj.* **1** of or like a bull **2** rising, or causing a rise, in prices on the stock exchange **3** optimistic

bull·ock (-ək) *n.* [< OE dim. of *bula*, steer] a castrated bull; steer

bull·pen *n.* **1** [Inf.] a temporary detention room in a jail **2** *Baseball a)* a warm-up area for relief pitchers *b)* the relief pitchers of one team

bull's-eye *n.* **1** the central mark of a target **2** a direct hit

bul·ly (boolʹē) *n., pl.* **-lies** [< MHG *buole*, lover; later infl. by BULL¹] a person who hurts or browbeats those who are weaker —*vt.* **-lied, -ly·ing** to behave as a bully toward — *adj., interj.* [Inf.] fine; good

bul·rush (boolʹrush') *n.* [< ME *bol*, stem + *rusche*, a rush] a tall plant of the sedge family, found in wet places

bul·wark (boolʹwərk) *n.* [MDu *bolwerc*] **1** a defensive wall; rampart **2** a defense; protection **3** [*usually pl.*] a ship's side above the deck

bum¹ (bum) *n.* [prob. < Ger *bummeln*, go slowly] [Inf.] **1** a vagrant **2** a loafer **3** a devotee, as of golf or skiing —*vi.* **bummed, bum'ming** [Inf.] to live as a bum or by begging —*vt.* [Slang] to get by begging [to *bum* a cigarette] —*adj.* **bum'mer, bum'mest** [Slang] **1** poor in quality **2** false **3** lame

—bum someone out [Slang] to depress or sadden someone **—on the bum** [Inf.] **1** living as a vagrant **2** out of repair

bum² (bum) [Brit. Slang] the buttocks

bum·ble (bum′bəl) *vi.* **-bled, -bling** to blunder **—***vt.* to bungle or botch **—bum′bler** *n.*

bum·ble·bee *n.* [< ME *bomben*, to buzz] a large, hairy, yellow-and-black bee, living in underground colonies

bummed *adj.* [< BUM¹] [Slang] depressed, sad, etc.: usually with *out*

bum·mer (bum′ər) *n.* [Slang] an unpleasant experience

bump (bump) *vt., vi.* [echoic] to collide (with) or hit (against) with a jolt **—***n.* **1** a knock; light jolt **2** a swelling, esp. one caused by a blow **—bump into** [Inf.] to meet unexpectedly **—bump off** [Slang] to murder **—bump′y** *adj.* **-i·er, -i·est**

bump·er¹ *n.* a device to absorb the shock of a collision; esp., either of the bars at the front and rear of a motor vehicle

bump·er² *adj.* [prob. < obs. *bombard*, liquor jug] unusually abundant [a *bumper* crop]

bumper sticker a gummed paper with a printed slogan, witticism, etc., for sticking on a vehicle's bumper

bump·kin (bump′kin) *n.* [prob. < MDu *bommekijn*, small cask] an awkward or simple person from the country

bump·tious (-shəs) *adj.* [prob. < BUMP] disagreeably conceited or forward **—bump′tious·ly** *adv.* **—bump′tious·ness** *n.*

bun (bun) *n.* [prob. < OFr *buigne*, a swelling] **1** a small roll made of bread dough, sometimes sweetened **2** hair worn in a roll or knot

bunch (bunch) *n.* [< Fl *boudje*, little bundle] **1** a cluster of similar things growing or grouped together **2** [Inf.] a group of people **—***vt., vi.* to collect into a bunch **—bunch′y** *adj.* **-i·er, -i·est**

bun·combe (bun′kəm) *n.* [after *Buncombe* county, NC] BUNKUM

bun·dle (bun′dəl) *n.* [MDu *bondel*] **1** a number of things bound together **2** a package **3** a bunch; collection **—***vt.* **-dled, -dling 1** to make into a bundle **2** to hustle (*away, off, out,* or *into*) **—bundle up** to dress warmly

bundt cake (bunt) a cake baked in a deep pan with a tube in the center and grooved sides

bung (bung) *n.* [< MDu *bonge*] a stopper for a bunghole

bun·ga·low (bun′gə lō′) *n.* [< Hindi *bānglā*, thatched house] a small house or cottage, usually of one story and having a veranda

bun·gee cord (bun′jē) elasticized cord used as to secure luggage or to hold persons leaping for sport from great heights

bung·hole (bun′hōl′) *n.* a hole in a barrel or keg for pouring in or drawing out liquid

bun·gle (bun′gəl) *vt., vi.* **-gled, -gling** [< ?] to do or make (something) badly or clumsily **—***n.* **1** a bungling **2** a bungled piece of work **—bun′gler** *n.* **—bung′ling·ly** *adv.*

bun·ion (bun′yən) *n.* [< OFr: see BUN] an inflamed swelling at the base of the big toe

bunk¹ (bunk) *n.* [prob. < Scand cognate of BENCH] **1** a shelflike bed built against a wall, as in a ship **2** [Inf.] any sleeping place **—***vi.* to sleep in a bunk **—***vt.* to provide a sleeping place for

bunk² (bunk) *n.* [Slang] *short for* BUNKUM

bunk·er (bunk′ər) *n.* [Scot < ?] **1** a large bin, as for a ship's fuel **2** an underground fortification **3** a sand trap or other area serving as a hazard on a golf course

bunk·house *n.* a barracks for ranch hands

bun·kum (bun′kəm) *n.* [respelling of BUNCOMBE] [Inf.] empty, insincere talk

bun·ny (bun′ē) *n., pl.* **-nies** [dim. of dial. *bun*] a rabbit: a child's term

buns (bunz) *pl.n.* [Slang] the human buttocks

Bun·sen burner (bun′sən) [after R. W. *Bunsen* (1811-99), Ger chemist] a small tubular gas burner that produces a hot, blue flame

bunt (bunt) *vt., vi.* [< ? ME *bounten*, to return] *Baseball* to bat (a pitch) lightly without swinging so that it rolls a short distance **—***n.* a bunted ball

bun·ting¹ (bun′tin) *n.* [< ? ME *bonten*, sift] **1** a thin cloth for making flags, etc. **2** decorative flags

bun·ting² (bun′tin) *n.* [ME] a small, brightly colored, short-billed bird

Bun·yan (bun′yən), **Paul** *American Folklore* a giant lumberjack who performs superhuman feats

buoy (bōō′ē, boi) *n.* [< L *boia*, fetter] **1** a floating object anchored in water as to warn of a hazard, etc. **2** a ring-shaped life preserver **—***vt.* [< Sp *boyar*, to float] **1** to mark with a buoy **2** to keep afloat **3** to lift up in spirits

buoy·ant (boiy′ənt; *also* bōō′yənt) *adj.* [< ? Sp *boyar*, to float] **1** having the ability or tendency to float **2** cheerful **—buoy′an·cy** *n.*

bur (bur) *n.* [< Scand] **1** a rough, prickly seed capsule of certain plants **2** a plant with burs **3** BURR¹ & BURR²

Bur *abbrev.* Bureau

bur·den¹ (burd′'n) *n.* [< OE *byrthen*] **1** anything that is carried; load **2** heavy load, as of work, care, or duty **3** the carrying capacity of a ship **—***vt.* to put a burden on; oppress **—bur′den·some** *adj.*

bur·den² (burd′'n) *n.* [< OFr *bourdon*, a humming] **1** a chorus or refrain of a song **2** a repeated, central idea; theme

bur·dock (bur′däk′) *n.* [BUR + DOCK³] a plant with large leaves and purple flower heads with prickly hooks

bu·reau (byoor′ō) *n., pl.* **-reaus** or **-reaux** (-ōz) [Fr, desk] **1** a chest of drawers, as for clothing **2** an agency **3** a government department

bu·reauc·ra·cy (byoo rä′krə sē) *n., pl.* **-cies 1** government by departmental officials following an inflexible routine **2** the officials collectively **3** inflexible governmental routine **4** the concentration of authority in administrative bureaus **—bu·reau·crat** (byoor′ə krat′) *n.* **—bu′reau·crat′ic** *adj.*

bu·reauc·ra·tize (-tīz′) *vt., vi.* **-tized′, -tiz′ing** to develop into a bureaucracy —**bu·reauc′ra·ti·za′tion** *n.*

burg (burg) *n.* [Inf.] a quiet or dull town

bur·geon (bur′jən) *vi.* [< OFr *burjon*, a bud] **1** to put forth buds, etc. **2** to grow or develop rapidly

bur·ger (bur′gər) *n.* [Inf.] a hamburger, cheeseburger, etc.

-bur·ger (bur′gər) *combining form* sandwich of ground meat, etc. [*hamburger*]

burgh (burg; *Scot* bu′rə) *n.* [Scot var. of BOROUGH] **1** [Brit.] a borough **2** in Scotland, a chartered town

burgh·er (bur′gər) *n.* a citizen of a town

bur·glar (bur′glər) *n.* [< OFr *burgeor*] one who commits burglary

bur·glar·ize *vt.* **-ized′, -iz′ing** to commit burglary in

bur·gla·ry (-glə rē) *n., pl.* **-ries** the act of breaking into a building to commit a felony, as theft, or a misdemeanor

bur·gle (bur′gəl) *vt., vi.* **-gled, -gling** [Inf.] to burglarize or commit burglary

bur·go·mas·ter (bur′gō mas′tər, -gə-) *n.* [< MDu *burg*, town + *meester*, master] the mayor of a town in the Netherlands, Flanders, Austria, or Germany

Bur·gun·dy (bur′gən dē) *n., pl.* **-dies** [*often* **b-**] a red or white wine, typically dry, orig. made in Burgundy, a region in E France —**Bur·gun·di·an** (bər gun′dē ən) *adj., n.*

bur·i·al (ber′ē əl) *n.* the burying of a dead body in a grave, tomb, etc.

bur·ka (bur′kə) *n.* alt. sp. of BURQA

Bur·ki·na Fa·so (boor kē′nə fä′sō) country in W Africa

burl (burl) *n.* [< OFr *bourle*, ends of threads] **1** a knot in thread or yarn that makes cloth look nubby **2** a knot on some tree trunks **3** veneer from wood with burls —**burled** *adj.*

bur·lap (bur′lap′) *n.* [< ? ME *borel*] a coarse cloth of jute or hemp

bur·lesque (bər lesk′) *n.* [Fr < It *burla*, a jest] **1** a broadly comic or satirical imitation **2** a sort of vaudeville with low comedy, striptease acts, etc. — *vt., vi.* **-lesqued′, -lesqu′ing** to imitate comically

bur·ly (bur′lē) *adj.* **-li·er, -li·est** [ME *borlich*, excellent] **1** big and strong **2** hearty in manner

Bur·ma (bur′mə) *former name for* MYANMAR —**Bur·mese** (bər mēz′) *adj., n., pl.* **-mese′**

burn (burn) *vt.* **burned** or **burnt, burn′ing** [< OE *beornan*, to be on fire] **1** to set on fire, as in order to produce heat, light, or power **2** to destroy by fire **3** to injure or damage by fire, acid, etc. **4** to consume as fuel **5** to sunburn **6** to cause (a hole, etc.) as by fire **7** to cause a sensation of heat in **8** to transform (body fat, etc.) into energy **9** [Slang] to cheat or trick [I got *burned* in that deal] —*vi.* **1** to be on fire **2** to give out light or heat **3** to be destroyed or injured by fire or heat **4** to feel hot **5** to be excited —*n.* **1** an injury or damage caused by fire, heat, etc. **2** the process or result of burning —**burn down** to burn to the ground —**burn out** to exhaust or become exhausted from overwork, etc. —**burn up** [Slang] to make or become angry —**burn′a·ble** *adj., n.*

burn·er *n.* **1** the part of a stove, furnace, etc. from which the flame comes **2** a similar part producing heat as with an electric coil

bur·nish (bur′nish) *vt., vi.* [< OFr *brunir*, make brown] to make or become shiny by rubbing —*n.* a gloss or polish —**bur′nish·er** *n.*

bur·noose (bər nōōs′) *n.* [< Ar *burnus*] a hooded cloak worn by Arabs

burn·out (burn′out′) *n.* **1** the point at which a rocket's fuel is burned up **2** a state of emotional exhaustion from mental stress

Burns (burnz), **Rob·ert** (rä′bərt) 1759-96; Scot. poet

burnt (burnt) *vt., vi.* alt. pt. & pp. of BURN

burp (burp) *n., vi.* [echoic] belch —*vt.* to cause (a baby) to belch

bur·qa (bur′kə) *n.* [< Ar *burqu*′] a long, loose outer garment that covers the entire body with only a small opening for the eyes, worn outside the home by some Muslim women

burr[1] (bur) *n.* [var. of BUR] **1** a bur **2** a rough edge left on metal, etc. by cutting or drilling —*vt.* to form a rough edge on

burr[2] (bur) *n.* [prob. echoic] **1** the trilling of *r*, as in Scottish speech **2** a whir

bur·ri·to (bə rē′tō) *n., pl.* **-tos** [MexSp < Sp, little burro] a Mexican dish consisting of a flour tortilla wrapped around a filling of meat, cheese, fried beans, etc.

bur·ro (bur′ō) *n., pl.* **-ros** [Sp < LL *burricus*, small horse] a donkey

bur·row (bur′ō) *n.* [see BOROUGH] **1** a hole dug in the ground by an animal **2** any similar hole —*vi.* **1** to make a burrow **2** to live or hide in a burrow **3** to search, as if by digging

bur·sa (bur′sə) *n., pl.* **-sae** (-sē) or **-sas** [< Gr *byrsa*, a hide] *Anat.* a sac or cavity with a lubricating fluid, as between a tendon and bone

bur·sar (bur′sər) *n.* [< ML *bursa*, a purse] a treasurer, as of a college

bur·si·tis (bər sīt′is) *n.* [< BURSA + -ITIS] inflammation of a bursa

burst (burst) *vi.* **burst, burst′ing** [OE *berstan*] **1** to come apart suddenly and violently; explode **2** to give sudden vent; break (*into* tears, etc.) **3** to appear, start, etc. suddenly **4** *a*) to be as full or crowded as possible *b*) to be filled (*with* pride, etc.) —*vt.* to cause to burst —*n.* **1** a bursting **2** a break or rupture **3** a sudden action or effort; spurt **4** a volley of shots

Bu·run·di (boo roon′dē, -run′-) country in EC Africa

bur·y (ber′ē) *vt.* **-ied, -y·ing** [OE *byrgan*] **1** to put (a dead body) into the earth, tomb, etc. **2** to hide or cover **3** to put away **4** to immerse [to *bury* oneself in work]

bus (bus) *n., pl.* **bus′es** or **bus′ses** [< (OMNI)BUS] a large motor coach for many passengers, usually following a regular route —*vt.* **bused** or **bussed, bus'ing** or **bus'sing** 1 to transport by bus 2 to clear dirty dishes from —*vi.* 1 to go by bus 2 to do the work of a busboy

bus·boy *n.* a restaurant worker who clears tables, brings water, etc.

bus·by (buz'bē) *n., pl.* **-bies** ⟦prob. < name *Busby*⟧ a tall fur hat worn with a full-dress uniform

bush (boosh) *n.* ⟦OE *busc*⟧ 1 a low woody plant with spreading branches; shrub 2 anything like a bush 3 uncleared land —*vi.* to grow thickly —**beat around the bush** to talk around a subject without getting to the point

Bush (boosh) 1 **George (Herbert Walker)** 1924- ; 41st president of the U.S. (1989-93) 2 **George W(alker)** 1946- ; 43d president of the U.S. (2001-09): son of George

bushed (boosht) *adj.* [Inf.] very tired; exhausted

bush·el (boosh'əl) *n.* ⟦< OFr *boisse*, grain measure⟧ a dry measure equal to 4 pecks or 32 quarts

bush·ing (boosh'iŋ) *n.* ⟦< MDu *busse*, box⟧ a removable metal lining for reducing friction on moving parts

bush league [Slang] a small or second-rate minor league, etc. —**bush'-league'** *adj.* —**bush leaguer**

bush·man (-mən) *n., pl.* **-men** (-mən) 1 one who lives in the Australian bush 2 [B-] a member of a nomadic people of S Africa: now somewhat offensive

bush·mas·ter *n.* a large poisonous snake of Central and South America

bush·whack *vt., vi.* to ambush —**bush'whack'er** *n.*

bush·y *adj.* **-i·er, -i·est** thick and spreading out like a bush [a *bushy* beard]

bush·y-tailed *adj.* used mainly in **bright-eyed and bushy-tailed**, alert, eager, etc.

bus·i·ly (biz'ə lē) *adv.* in a busy manner

busi·ness (biz'nis) *n.* ⟦OE *bisignes*: see BUSY⟧ 1 one's work; occupation 2 a special task, duty, etc. 3 rightful concern [no one's *business* but his own] 4 a matter or activity 5 commerce; trade 6 a commercial or industrial establishment —*adj.* of or for business —**mean business** [Inf.] to be in earnest

business administration college studies covering finance, management, etc. to prepare for a business career

business card a small card identifying one's business connection, given to clients, etc.

business college a school of typing, bookkeeping, etc.

busi·ness·like *adj.* efficient, methodical, systematic, etc.

busi·ness·man *n., pl.* **-men'** (-men') a man in business, esp. as an owner

busi·ness·per·son *n.* a person in business, esp. as an owner

busi·ness·wom·an *n., pl.* **-wom'en** a woman in business, esp. as an owner

bus·ing or **bus·sing** (bus'iŋ) *n.* the transport-

ing of children by bus to a school outside of their neighborhood, esp. so as to desegregate the school

bus·kin (bus'kin) *n.* ⟦? < MDu *brosekin*, small boot⟧ 1 a high, laced boot worn in ancient tragedy 2 tragic drama

buss (bus) *n., vt., vi.* ⟦prob. of echoic orig.⟧ [Now Chiefly Dial.] kiss

bust¹ (bust) *n.* ⟦< It *busto*⟧ 1 a sculpture of a person's head and shoulders 2 a woman's bosom

bust² (bust) [Inf.] *vt., vi.* ⟦< BURST⟧ 1 to burst or break 2 to make or become bankrupt or demoted 3 to hit 4 to arrest —*n.* 1 a failure 2 financial collapse 3 an arrest —**bust'ed** *adj.*

bus·tle¹ (bus'əl) *vi., vt.* **-tled, -tling** ⟦< ME *busken*, prepare⟧ to hurry busily —*n.* busy and noisy activity

bus·tle² (bus'əl) *n.* ⟦< ?⟧ a padding formerly worn to fill out the upper back of a woman's skirt

bus·y (biz'ē) *adj.* **-i·er, -i·est** ⟦OE *bisig*⟧ 1 active; at work 2 full of activity 3 in use, as a telephone 4 too detailed —*vt.* **bus'ied, bus'y·ing** to make or keep busy —**bus'y·ness** *n.*

bus·y·bod·y *n., pl.* **-ies** a meddler in the affairs of others

but (but) *prep.* ⟦OE *butan*, without⟧ except; save [nobody went *but* me] —*conj.* 1 yet; still [it's good, *but* not great] 2 on the contrary [I am old, *but* you are young] 3 unless [it never rains *but* it pours] 4 that [I don't doubt *but* you're right] 5 without the result that [I never gamble *but* I lose] —*adv.* 1 only [if I had *but* known] 2 merely [he is *but* a child] —*pron.* who . . . not; which . . . not [not a man *but* felt it] —**but for** if it were not for

bu·tane (byoo'tān') *n.* ⟦ult. < L *butyrum*, butter⟧ a hydrocarbon used as a fuel, etc.

butch (booch) *adj.* ⟦< ? fol.⟧ [Slang] masculine: sometimes said of a lesbian —*n.* [Inf.] BUZZ CUT

butch·er (booch'ər) *n.* ⟦< OFr *bouc*, he-goat⟧ 1 one whose work is killing and dressing animals for meat 2 one who cuts meat for sale 3 a brutal killer —*vt.* 1 to kill or dress (animals) for meat 2 to kill brutally or senselessly 3 to botch —**butch'er·y** *n., pl.* **-ies**

but·ler (but'lər) *n.* ⟦< OFr *bouteille*, bottle⟧ a manservant, usually the head servant of a household

butt¹ (but) *n.* ⟦< ?⟧ 1 the thick end of anything 2 a stub or stump, as of a cigar 3 a target 4 an object of ridicule 5 [Slang] a cigarette 6 [Inf.] the buttocks — *vt., vi.* to join end to end

butt² (but) *vt., vi.* ⟦< OFr *buter*, thrust against⟧ 1 to ram with the head 2 to project —*n.* a butting —**butt in (or into)** [Inf.] to intrude into (another's business, conversation, etc.)

butt³ (but) *n.* ⟦< LL *buttis*, cask⟧ a large cask for wine or beer

butte (byoot) *n.* ⟦Fr, mound⟧ a steep hill with a flat top, surrounded by a plain

but·ter (but′ər) *n.* [< Gr *bous,* cow + *tyros,* cheese] 1 the solid, yellowish, edible fat produced by churning cream 2 any substance resembling butter —*vt.* 1 to spread with butter 2 [Inf.] to flatter: often with *up* —**but′ter·y** *adj.*

butter bean a light-colored bean, as a lima bean or wax bean

but·ter·cup *n.* a plant with yellow, cup-shaped flowers

but·ter·fat *n.* the fatty part of milk, from which butter is made

but·ter·fin·gers *n.* [Inf.] one who often fumbles and drops things

but·ter·fly *n., pl.* **-flies′** [OE *buttorfleoge*] an insect with a slender body and four broad, often colorful wings

but·ter·milk *n.* the liquid left after churning butter from cream

but·ter·nut *n.* 1 a walnut tree of E North America 2 its edible, oily nut

but·ter·scotch *n.* 1 a hard, sticky candy made with brown sugar, butter, etc. 2 the flavor of this candy 3 a syrup with this flavor

but·tock (but′ək) *n.* [< OE *buttuc,* end] 1 either of the fleshy, rounded parts behind the hips 2 [*pl.*] the rump

but·ton (but′'n) *n.* [< OFr *boton*] 1 any small disk or knob used as a fastening, ornament, etc., as on a garment 2 anything small and shaped like a button 3 a small knob, as on a keyboard, that can be pressed in controlling a device —*vi., vt.* to fasten with a button or buttons

but·ton-down *adj.* 1 designating a collar, as on a shirt, fastened down by small buttons 2 conservative, unimaginative, etc.

but·ton·hole *n.* a slit or loop through which a button is inserted —*vt.* **-holed′, -hol′ing** 1 to make buttonholes in 2 to accost and hold in conversation

but·tress (bu′tris) *n.* [see BUTT²] 1 a structure built against a wall to support or reinforce it 2 a support or prop —*vt.* to prop up; bolster

bux·om (buk′səm) *adj.* [ME, humble] having a shapely, full-bosomed figure: said of a woman

buy (bī) *vt.* **bought, buy′ing** [OE *bycgan*] 1 to get by paying money; purchase 2 to get by an exchange [*buy* victory with human lives] 3 to bribe 4 [Slang] to accept as true [I can't *buy* this excuse] —*n.* 1 anything bought 2 [Inf.] something worth its price —**buy in** [Slang] to pay money so as to participate —**buy into** [Slang] BUY (*vt.* 4) —**buy off** to bribe —**buy out** to buy all the stock, rights, etc. of —**buy up** to buy all that is available of

buy·back *n. Finance* the buying by a corporation of its own stock to reduce the overall number of shares

buy·er *n.* 1 one who buys; consumer 2 one whose work is to buy merchandise for a retail store

buy·out *n.* the outright purchase of a business, as by the employees or management

buzz (buz) *vi.* [echoic] 1 to hum like a bee 2 to gossip 3 to be filled with noisy activity or talk —*vt.* 1 to fly an airplane low over (a building, etc.) 2 to signal with a buzzer —*n.* 1 a sound like a bee's hum 2 [Inf.] BUZZ CUT

buz·zard (buz′ərd) *n.* [< L *buteo,* kind of hawk] 1 a kind of hawk that is slow and heavy in flight 2 TURKEY VULTURE

buzz cut [Inf.] a man's very short haircut

buzz·er *n.* an electrical device that makes a buzzing sound as a signal

buzz saw a circular saw

bx *abbrev.* box

by (bī) *prep.* [OE *be, bi*] 1 near; at [sit *by* the fire] 2 *a*) in or during [to travel *by* day] *b*) not later than [be back *by* noon] 3 *a*) through; via [to Boston *by* Route 6] *b*) past; beyond [he walked right *by* me] 4 toward [east *by* northeast] 5 within a distance of [missed *by* a foot] 6 in behalf of [she did well *by* me] 7 through the agency of [gained *by* fraud] 8 according to [to go *by* the book] 9 at the rate of [getting dark *by* degrees] 10 following in series [marching two *by* two] 11 *a*) in or to the amount of [apples *by* the peck] *b*) and in another dimension [two *by* four] *c*) using (the given number) as multiplier or divisor —*adv.* 1 close at hand [stand *by*] 2 away; aside [to put money *by*] 3 past [she sped *by*] 4 at the place specified [stop *by* on your way] —**by and by** soon or eventually —**by and large** considering everything —**by the by** incidentally

by- *prefix* 1 near 2 secondary; incidental [*by-product*]

by-and-by (bī′ən bī′) *n.* a future time

bye¹ (bī) *n.* [var. of BY] the privilege, granted a contestant in a tournament with an uneven number of participants, of not having to compete in the first round

bye² (bī) *interj.* [Inf.] short for GOODBYE

bye-bye (bī′bī′) *n., interj.* [Inf.] goodbye

by·gone (bī′gôn′) *adj.* past; former —*n.* anything gone or past

by·law *n.* [< ME *bi,* village + *laue,* law] any of a set of rules adopted by an organization or assembly for its own meetings or affairs

by·line *n.* a line identifying the writer of a newspaper or magazine article

by·pass *n.* 1 a way, pipe, channel, etc. between two points that avoids or is auxiliary to the main way 2 a surgical operation to allow fluid to pass around a diseased or blocked part or organ —*vt.* 1 to detour 2 to furnish with a bypass 3 to ignore

by·path or **by-path** *n.* a byway

by·play *n.* action, gestures, etc. going on aside from the main action or conversation

by·prod·uct or **by-prod·uct** *n.* anything produced in the course of making another thing

By·ron (bī′rən), **George Gor·don** (jôrj gôrd′'n) 1788-1824; Eng. poet

by·stand·er *n.* a person who stands near but does not participate

byte (bīt) *n.* ⟦arbitrary formation⟧ a string of binary digits (*bits*), usually eight, operated on as a basic unit by a digital computer

by·way *n.* a secondary road or path, esp. one not much used

by·word *n.* **1** a proverb **2** one well-known for some quality **3** an object of scorn or ridicule **4** a favorite word or phrase

Byz·an·tine Empire (biz′ən tēn′, -tīn′; bi zan′ tin) empire (A.D. 395-1453) in SE Europe & SW Asia; originally the E portion of the Roman Empire

C

c or **C** (sē) *n.*, *pl.* **c's**, **C's** the third letter of the English alphabet

C¹ (sē) *n.* **1** a Roman numeral for 100 **2** *Educ.* a grade for average work **3** *Music* the first tone in the scale of C major

C² *abbrev.* **1** carat(s) **2** *Baseball* catcher **3** Catholic **4** Celsius (or centigrade) **5** cent(s) **6** *Sports* center **7** Central **8** century **9** chapter **10** circa: also **ca 11** copyright **12** cup(s) Also, except 3, 4, & 7, **c**

C³ *Chem. symbol for* carbon

Ca *Chem. symbol for* calcium

CA *abbrev.* California

cab (kab) *n.* ⟦< Fr *cabriole*, a leap⟧ **1** [Historical] a carriage for public hire **2** TAXICAB **3** the place in a truck, crane, etc. where the operator sits —*vi.* **cabbed**, **cab′bing** [Inf.] to take or drive a taxicab

ca·bal (kə bäl′) *n.* ⟦Fr, intrigue⟧ **1** a small group joined in a secret intrigue **2** an intrigue; plot

ca·bal·le·ro (kab′ə ler′ō, -əl yer′ō) *n.*, *pl.* **-ros** [Sp] **1** a Spanish gentleman **2** [Southwest] *a*) a horseman *b*) a lady's escort

ca·ban·a (kə ban′ə, -bä′nə) *n.* ⟦Sp < LL *capanna*⟧ **1** a cabin or hut **2** a small private pavilion, as at a beach

cab·a·ret (kab′ə rā′) *n.* ⟦Fr, tavern⟧ a cafe with musical entertainment

cab·bage (kab′ij) *n.* ⟦OFr *caboche* < ?⟧ a vegetable with thick leaves formed into a round head

cab·by or **cab·bie** (kab′ē) *n.*, *pl.* **-bies** [Inf.] one who drives a cab

ca·ber·net (kab′ər nā′) *n.* [also C-] a dry red wine; esp., CABERNET SAUVIGNON

cabernet sau·vi·gnon (sō vē nyên′) [also C-S-] a fragrant, dry red wine

cab·in (kab′in) *n.* ⟦< LL *capanna*, hut⟧ **1** a small, crudely or simply built house; hut **2** a room on a ship or boat **3** the space for passengers, crew, or cargo in an aircraft

cab·i·net (kab′ə nit) *n.* ⟦Fr, prob. ult. < L *cavea*, cage⟧ **1** a case with drawers or shelves **2** a case holding a TV, radio, etc. **3** [often C-] a body of official advisors to a chief executive

cab·i·net·mak·er *n.* a maker of fine furniture

cab·i·net·work *n.* articles made by a cabinetmaker: also **cab′i·netry**

cabin fever a condition of anxiety or restlessness caused by being confined or isolated, as by inclement weather

ca·ble (kā′bəl) *n.* ⟦< L *capere*, to take hold⟧ **1** a thick, heavy rope, often of wire strands **2** a bundle of insulated wires to carry an electric current **3** a cablegram **4** CABLE TV —*vt.* **-bled**, **-bling 1** to fasten with a cable **2** to send a cablegram to —*vi.* to send a cablegram

cable car a car drawn by a moving cable, as up a steep incline

ca·ble·gram *n.* a message sent by undersea cable

cable TV a TV system in which program content is transmitted by cable to subscribers' receivers

cab·o·chon (kab′ə shän′) *n.* ⟦Fr < *caboche*, head⟧ any precious stone cut in convex shape

ca·bood·le (kə bōōd′'l) *n.* ⟦< BOODLE⟧ [Inf.] lot; group [the whole *caboodle*]

ca·boose (kə bōōs′) *n.* ⟦MDu *kambuis*, cabin house⟧ the car at the rear of a freight train, used by the crew when eating, sleeping, etc.

ca·ca·o (kə kā′ō, -kä′-) *n.*, *pl.* **-os** ⟦Sp < AmInd (Mexico)⟧ **1** the seed of a tropical American tree from which cocoa and chocolate are made: also **cacao bean 2** this tree

cac·cia·to·re (kä′chə tôr′ē) *adj.* ⟦It, in the manner of hunters⟧ cooked in a casserole with olive oil and tomatoes, onions, spices, wine, etc. [chicken *cacciatore*]

cache (kash) *n.* ⟦Fr < L *cogere*, to collect⟧ **1** a place where stores of food, supplies, etc. are hidden **2** anything so hidden —*vt.* **cached**, **cach′ing** to place in a cache

cache·pot (kash′pät, -pō′) *n.* ⟦Fr < *cacher*, to hide⟧ a decorative jar for holding potted plants: also **cache pot**

ca·chet (ka shā′) *n.* ⟦Fr⟧ **1** a stamp or official seal, as on a document **2** any sign of official approval, authenticity, superior quality, etc. **3** distinction; prestige

cack·le (kak′əl) *vi.* **-led**, **-ling** ⟦echoic⟧ **1** to make the shrill, broken vocal sounds of a hen **2** to laugh or chatter with similar sounds —*n.* a cackling

ca·coph·o·ny (kə käf′ə nē) *n.*, *pl.* **-nies** ⟦< Gr *kakos*, bad + *phōnē*, voice⟧ harsh, jarring sound; discord —**ca·coph′o·nous** *adj.*

cac·tus (kak′təs) *n.*, *pl.* **-tus·es** or **-ti′** (-tī′) 〖< Gr *kaktos*, kind of thistle〗 any of various desert plants with fleshy stems and spinelike leaves

cad (kad) *n.* 〖< CADET〗 a man whose behavior is ungentlemanly —**cad′dish** *adj.* —**cad′dish·ly** *adv.* —**cad′dish·ness** *n.*

CAD (kad) *n.* 〖C(omputer-) A(ided) D(e-sign)〗 design by means of a computer system, as for complex wiring diagrams

ca·dav·er (kə dav′ər) *n.* 〖L, prob. < *cadere*, to fall〗 a corpse, as for dissection

ca·dav·er·ous *adj.* 〖< L〗 of or like a cadaver; esp., pale, ghastly, etc.

cad·die (kad′ē) *n.* 〖Scot form of Fr *cadet:* see CADET〗 one who attends a golfer, carrying the clubs, etc. —*vi.* **-died**, **-dy·ing** to act as a caddie

cad·dy¹ (kad′ē) *n.*, *pl.* **-dies** 〖< Malay *kātī*, unit of weight〗 a small container for holding or storing

cad·dy² (kad′ē) *n.*, *vi.* CADDIE

-cade (kād) 〖< (CAVAL)CADE〗 *suffix* procession, parade [*motorcade*]

ca·dence (kād′ⁿs) *n.* 〖< L *cadere*, to fall〗 1 fall of the voice in speaking 2 any rhythmic flow of sound 3 measured movement, as in marching

ca·den·za (kə den′zə) *n.* 〖It: see prec.〗 an elaborate passage for the solo instrument in a concerto

ca·det (kə det′) *n.* 〖Fr < L dim. of *caput*, head〗 1 a student in training at an armed forces academy 2 any trainee, as a practice teacher

cadge (kaj) *vt.*, *vi.* **cadged**, **cadg′ing** 〖< ?〗 to beg or get by begging; sponge —**cadg′er** *n.*

cad·mi·um (kad′mē əm) *n.* 〖< L *cadmia*, zinc ore (with which it occurs)〗 a silver-white, metallic chemical element used in alloys, pigments, etc.: symbol, Cd; at. no. 48

ca·dre (ka′drē, -drä; kä′-) *n.* 〖< Fr < L *quadrum*, a square〗 1 a small, unified group around which an expanded organization, as a military unit, can be built 2 a member of such a group

ca·du·ce·us (kə dōō′sē əs) *n.*, *pl.* **-ce·i** (-sē ī′) 〖L〗 the winged staff of Mercury: now a symbol of the medical profession

Cae·sar¹ (sē′zər) *n.* 〖after fol.〗 1 the title of the Roman emperors 2 [*often* **c-**] any emperor or dictator

Cae·sar² (sē′zər), **Jul·ius** (jōōl′yəs) 100?-44 B.C.; Rom. general & dictator (49-44)

Cae·sar·e·an section (sə zer′ē ən) CESAREAN (SECTION)

cae·su·ra (si zyoor′ə, -zhoor′ə) *n.*, *pl.* **-ras** or **-rae** (-ē) 〖L < *caedere*, to cut down〗 a break or pause in a line of verse, usually in the middle

ca·fe or **ca·fé** (ka fā′, ka-) *n.* 〖Fr, coffeehouse〗 a small restaurant, barroom, nightclub, etc.

caf·e·te·ri·a (kaf′ə tir′ē ə) *n.* 〖AmSp, coffee store〗 a self-service restaurant

caf·feine or **caf·fein** (ka fēn′, kaf′ēn′) *n.* 〖Ger *kaffein*〗 the stimulant alkaloid present in coffee, tea, cola, etc.

caf·tan (kaf′tən, -tan′) *n.* 〖Turk *qaftān*〗 1 a long-sleeved robe worn in eastern Mediterranean countries 2 a long, loose dress with wide sleeves

cage (kāj) *n.* 〖< L *cavea*, hollow place〗 1 a structure of wires, bars, etc., for confining animals 2 any openwork structure or frame —*vt.* **caged**, **cag′ing** to put or confine, as in a cage

cag·er (kāj′ər) *n.* 〖Slang〗 a basketball player

ca·gey or **ca·gy** (kā′jē) *adj.* **-gi·er**, **-gi·est** 〖< ?〗 [Inf.] 1 sly; tricky; cunning 2 cautious —**ca′gi·ly** *adv.* —**ca′gi·ness** *n.*

ca·hoots (kə hōōts′) *pl.n.* 〖< ?〗 [Slang] used chiefly in **in cahoots (with)**, in league (with): usually applied to questionable dealing, etc.

Cain (kān) *n. Bible* oldest son of Adam and Eve: he killed his brother Abel —**raise Cain** [Slang] to create a great commotion, cause trouble, etc.

cairn (kern) *n.* 〖Scot〗 a conical heap of stones built as a monument

Cai·ro (kī′rō) capital of Egypt

cais·son (kā′sən) *n.* 〖Fr < L *capsa*, box〗 1 a two-wheeled wagon with a chest for ammunition 2 a watertight box for underwater construction work

cai·tiff (kāt′if) *n.* 〖< L *captivus*, CAPTIVE〗 a mean or cowardly person —*adj.* mean or cowardly

ca·jole (kə jōl′) *vt.*, *vi.* **-joled′**, **-jol′ing** 〖< Fr〗 to coax with flattery and insincere talk —**ca·jol′er** *n.* —**ca·jol′er·y** *n.*

Ca·jun or **Ca·jan** (kā′jən) *n.* 1 a native of Louisiana of Canadian French ancestry 2 the dialect of Cajuns —*adj.* of the Cajuns, their culture, cuisine, etc.

cake (kāk) *n.* 〖< ON〗 1 a small, flat mass of baked or fried dough, batter, hashed food, etc. 2 a mixture of flour, eggs, sugar, etc. baked as in a loaf and often covered with icing 3 a shaped, solid mass, as of soap —*vt.*, *vi.* **caked**, **cak′ing** to form into a hard mass or crust —**take the cake** [Inf.] to be the prime example of something: usually used ironically —**cak′y** *adj.*, **cak′ey -i·er**, **-i·est**

cal *abbrev.* 1 caliber 2 calorie(s)

cal·a·bash (kal′ə bash′) *n.* 〖< Sp *calabaza*〗 1 the gourdlike fruit of a tropical American tree 2 *a)* the bottle-shaped, gourdlike fruit of a tropical vine *b)* a large smoking pipe made from it 3 a gourd

cal·a·boose (kal′ə bōōs′) *n.* 〖Sp *calabozo*〗 [Old Slang] a prison; jail

ca·la·ma·ri (kä′lə mä′rē) *n.* squid cooked as food, esp. as an Italian dish

cal·a·mine (kal′ə mīn′) *n.* 〖Fr < L *cadmia*, zinc ore〗 a zinc oxide powder used in skin lotions

ca·lam·i·ty (kə lam′ə tē) *n.*, *pl.* **-ties** 〖< L *calamitas*〗 a great misfortune; disaster —**ca·lam′i·tous** *adj.*

cal·car·e·ous (kal ker′ē əs) *adj.* 〖< L *calx*, lime〗 of or like limestone, calcium, or lime

cal·ci·fy (kal′sə fī′) *vt.*, *vi.* **-fied′**, **-fy′ing** 〖<

L *calx*, lime + -FY] to change into a stony substance by the deposit of lime or calcium salts —cal'ci·fi·ca'tion *n.*

cal·ci·mine (-mīn') *n.* [< L *calx*, lime] a white liquid, used as a wash for plastered surfaces —*vt.* -mined', -min'ing to coat with calcimine

cal·cine (kal'sīn) *vt., vi.* -cined', -cin'ing [< L *calx*, lime] to change to an ashy powder by heat

cal·cite (kal'sīt') *n.* CALCIUM CARBONATE

cal·ci·um (kal'sē əm) *n.* [< L *calx*, lime] a soft, silver-white, metallic chemical element found combined in limestone, chalk, etc.: symbol, Ca; at. no. 20

calcium carbonate a white powder or crystalline compound found in limestone, chalk, marble, bones, shells, etc.

cal·cu·late (kal'kyə lāt') *vt.* -lat'ed, -lat'ing [< L *calculare*, reckon] 1 to determine by using mathematics; compute 2 to determine by reasoning; estimate 3 to plan or intend for a purpose —*vi.* 1 to compute 2 to rely (*on*) —cal'cu·la·ble (-lə bəl) *adj.*

cal·cu·lat·ed *adj.* deliberately planned or carefully considered —cal'cu·lat'ed·ly *adv.*

cal·cu·lat·ing *adj.* shrewd or scheming

cal·cu·la·tion *n.* 1 a calculating 2 something deduced by calculating 3 careful planning or forethought —cal'cu·la'tive *adj.*

cal·cu·la·tor *n.* 1 one who calculates 2 a device or software application for performing mathematical operations

cal·cu·lus (-ləs) *n., pl.* -li' (-lī') or -lus·es [L, pebble used in counting] 1 an abnormal stony mass in the body 2 *Math.* a system of calculation or analysis using special symbolic notation

Cal·cut·ta (kal kut'ə) former name for KOL-KATA

cal·de·ra (kal der'ə) *n.* [Sp < L *caldarium*, room for hot baths] a broad, craterlike basin of a volcano

cal·dron (kôl'drən) *n. alt. sp. of* CAULDRON

cal·en·dar (kal'ən dər) *n.* [< L *kalendarium*, account book] 1 a system of determining the length and divisions of a year 2 a table that shows the days, weeks, and months of a given year 3 a schedule, as of programs

cal·en·der (kal'ən dər) *n.* [< Gr *kylindros*, cylinder] a machine with rollers for giving paper, cloth, etc. a smooth or glossy finish

calf[1] (kaf) *n., pl.* calves [< OE *cealf*] 1 a young cow or bull 2 the young of some other large animals, as the elephant or seal 3 CALFSKIN

calf[2] (kaf) *n., pl.* calves [ON *kalfi*] the fleshy back part of the leg below the knee

calf·skin *n.* soft leather made from the skin of a calf

Cal·ga·ry (kal'gə rē) city in S Alberta, Canada

cal·i·ber (kal'ə bər) *n.* [Fr & Sp, ult. < Gr *kalopodion*, shoemaker's last] 1 the diameter of a cylindrical body, esp. of a bullet or shell 2 the diameter of the bore of a gun 3 quality or ability Also, esp. Brit., cal'i·bre

cal·i·brate (kal'ə brāt') *vt.* -brat'ed, -brat'-ing 1 to determine the caliber of 2 to fix or correct the graduations of (a measuring instrument) —cal'i·bra'tion *n.* —cal'i·bra'tor *n.*

cal·i·co (kal'i kō') *n., pl.* -coes' or -cos' [after *Calicut*, city in India] a printed cotton fabric —*adj.* spotted like calico [a *calico* cat]

Cal·i·for·nia (kal'ə fôr'nyə) state of the SW U.S., on the Pacific; cap. Sacramento: abbrev. CA —Cal'i·for'nian *adj., n.*

cal·i·for·ni·um (kal'ə fôr'nē əm) *n.* [see prec.] an artificially produced radioactive, metallic chemical element: symbol, Cf; at. no. 98

cal·i·per (kal'ə pər) *n.* [var. of CALIBER] 1 [*usually pl.*] an instrument consisting of a pair of hinged legs, for measuring thickness or diameter 2 a part of a braking system as on a bicycle

ca·liph (kā'lif; *also,* kal'if) *n.* [Ar *khalifa*] supreme ruler: the title taken by Muhammad's successors as heads of Islam —ca'liph·ate (-ət, -āt') *n.*

cal·is·then·ics (kal'is then'iks) *pl.n.* [< Gr *kallos*, beauty + *sthenos*, strength] athletic exercises —cal'is·then'ic *adj.*

calk (kôk) *vt.* CAULK —calk'er *n.*

call (kôl) *vt.* [< ON *kalla*] 1 to say in a loud tone; shout 2 to summon 3 to give or apply a name to 4 to describe as specified 5 to telephone 6 to give orders for (a strike, etc.) 7 to stop (a game, etc.) 8 to demand payment of (a loan, etc.) 9 to expose (someone's bluff) by challenging it 10 *Poker* to equal (the preceding bet) or to equal the bet of (the last previous bettor) —*vi.* 1 to shout 2 to visit for a short while: often with *on* 3 to telephone —*n.* 1 a calling 2 a loud utterance 3 the distinctive cry of an animal or bird 4 a summons; invitation 5 an act of telephoning 6 CALLING (*n.* 3) 7 an economic demand, as for a product 8 need [no *call* for tears] 9 a demand for payment 10 a brief visit 11 an option to buy a stock, commodity, etc. at a specified price and time 12 a decision, as by a referee —call down [Inf.] to scold —call for 1 to demand 2 to come and get —call off to cancel (a scheduled event) —call up 1 to recall 2 to summon for duty 3 to telephone —on call available when summoned —call'er *n.*

cal·la (kal'ə) *n.* [< L, a plant (of uncert. kind)] a plant with a large, white leaf around a yellow flower spike: also calla lily

call forwarding a telephone service that allows incoming calls to be transferred automatically to another number

call girl a prostitute who is called by telephone to assignations

cal·lig·ra·phy (kə lig'rə fē) *n.* [< Gr *kallos*, beauty + *graphein*, write] artistic handwriting —cal·lig'ra·pher *n.* —cal·li·graph·ic (kal'ə graf'ik) *adj.*

call-in *adj.* of a radio or TV program whose audience members telephone to comment, ask questions, etc.

call·ing *n.* 1 the act of one that calls 2 one's

work or profession **3** an inner urging toward some vocation

calling card 1 a small card with one's name and address on it **2** PHONE CARD

cal·li·o·pe (kə lī′ə pē′, kal′ē ōp′) *n.* ⟦< Gr *kallos*, beauty + *ops*, voice⟧ a keyboard instrument like an organ, having a series of steam whistles

call letters the letters, and sometimes numbers, that identify a radio or TV station

cal·lous (kal′əs) *adj.* ⟦< L *callum*, hard skin⟧ **1** hardened: usually **calloused 2** unfeeling —**cal′los·i·ty** (kə läs′ə tē) *n.* —**cal′lous·ly** *adv.* —**cal′lous·ness** *n.*

cal·low (kal′ō) *adj.* ⟦OE *calu*, bare⟧ immature; inexperienced —**cal′low·ness** *n.*

cal·lus (kal′əs) *n.*, *pl.* **-lus·es** ⟦L, var. of *callum*, hard skin⟧ a hardened, thickened place on the skin

call waiting a telephone service that allows the user to put a call on hold in order to answer another incoming call.

calm (käm, kälm) *n.* **1** lack of motion; stillness **2** lack of excitement; tranquillity —*adj.* **1** still; quiet **2** not excited, tranquil —*vt., vi.* to make or become calm: often with *down* —**calm′ly** *adv.* —**calm′ness** *n.*

ca·lor·ic (kə lôr′ik) *adj.* of calories —**ca·lor′i·cal·ly** *adv.*

cal·o·rie (kal′ə rē) *n.* ⟦Fr < L *calor*, heat⟧ a unit for measuring heat, esp. for measuring the energy produced by food when oxidized in the body

cal·o·rif·ic (kal′ə rif′ik) *adj.* ⟦< L *calor*, heat + *facere*, make⟧ producing heat

cal·u·met (kal′yə met′) *n.* ⟦CdnFr < L *calamus*, reed⟧ a long-stemmed ceremonial pipe, smoked by North American Indians as a token of peace

ca·lum·ni·ate (kə lum′nē āt′) *vt., vi.* **-at′ed, -at′ing** ⟦see fol.⟧ to slander

cal·um·ny (kal′əm nē) *n.*, *pl.* **-nies** ⟦< L *calumnia*, slander⟧ a false and malicious statement; slander

Cal·va·ry (kal′və rē) *n. Bible* the hilltop outside ancient Jerusalem where Jesus was crucified

calve (kav) *vi., vt.* **calved, calv′ing** to give birth to (a calf)

calves (kavz) *n. pl. of* CALF¹ & CALF²

Cal·vin (kal′vin), **John** 1509-64; Fr. Protestant reformer

Cal·vin·ism *n.* the Christian doctrines of John Calvin and his followers —**Cal′vin·ist** *n., adj.* —**Cal′vin·is′tic** *adj.*

ca·lyp·so (kə lip′sō) *n.* ⟦< ?⟧ a kind of lively, topical folk song that originated in Trinidad

ca·lyx (kā′liks′; *also* kal′iks′) *n., pl.* **-lyx′es** *or* **-ly·ces′** ⟦L, pod⟧ the outer whorl of protective leaves, or sepals, of a flower

cal·zo·ne (kal zōn′, -zō′nē) *n.* ⟦It, pant leg: so named from its shape⟧ an Italian turnover filled with cheese, meat, or vegetables

cam¹ (kam) *n.* ⟦Du *cam*, orig., a comb⟧ a wheel, projection on a wheel, etc. that gives irregular motion, as to a wheel or shaft, or receives such motion from it

cam² (kam) *n. short for* CAMERA: often used in compounds [*weather cam*]

ca·ma·ra·de·rie (käm′ə räd′ə rē) *n.* ⟦Fr⟧ loyalty and warm, friendly feeling among comrades

cam·ber (kam′bər) *n.* ⟦OFr < L *camur*, arched⟧ a slight convex curve of a surface, as of a road —*vt., vi.* to arch slightly

cam·bi·um (kam′bē əm) *n.* ⟦< LL *cambiare*, to change⟧ a layer of cells between the wood and bark in woody plants, which will eventually become more wood and bark —**cam′bi·al** *adj.*

Cam·bo·di·a (kam bō′dē ə) country in S Indochina; cap. Phnom Penh —**Cam·bo′di·an** *adj., n.*

cam·bric (kām′brik) *n.* ⟦after *Cambrai*, Fr city⟧ a fine linen or cotton cloth

Cam·bridge (kām′brij′) **1** city in EC England **2** city in E Massachusetts

cam·cord·er (kam′kôrd′ər) *n.* a small, portable video camera and recorder

came (kām) *vi. pt. of* COME

cam·el (kam′əl) *n.* ⟦ult. < Heb *gāmāl*⟧ a large, domesticated mammal with a humped back and long neck: it is used as a steed and beast of burden in Asian and African deserts

ca·mel·lia (kə mēl′yə, -mē′lē ə) *n.* ⟦after G. J. *Kamel* (1661-1706), missionary to the Far East⟧ **1** an Asiatic evergreen tree or shrub with glossy leaves and roselike flowers **2** the flower

Cam·e·lot (kam′ə lät′) *n.* the English town where King Arthur has his court and Round Table

Cam·em·bert (cheese) (kam′əm ber′, -bərt) *n.* ⟦after *Camembert*, Fr village⟧ a soft, rich, creamy cheese

cam·e·o (kam′ē ō′) *n., pl.* **-os′** ⟦< It < ML *camaeus*⟧ **1** a gem carved with a figure raised in relief **2** a choice minor role, esp. one played by a notable actor

cam·er·a (kam′ər ə, kam′rə) *n.* ⟦L, vault⟧ any of various devices for recording or transmitting images or sequences of images, consisting essentially of a closed case with a lens that focuses incoming light on a sensitive material, as film, or on an electronic receptor —**in camera** in privacy or secrecy

cam·er·a·man (-man′) *n., pl.* **-men** (-men′) a man who operates a film or TV camera

cam·er·a·per·son *n.* an operator of a film or TV camera

cam·er·a·wom·an *n., pl.* **-wom′en** a woman who operates a film or TV camera

Cam·e·roon (kam′ə rōōn′) country in WC Africa, on the Atlantic —**Cam′e·roon′i·an** *adj., n.*

cam·i·sole (kam′i sōl′) *n.* ⟦Fr < LL *camisia*, shirt⟧ a woman's sleeveless undergarment for the upper body

cam·o·mile (kam′ə mīl′, -mēl′) *n.* ⟦< Gr *chamaimēlon*, earth apple⟧ a plant whose dried, daisylike flower heads are used in a medicinal tea

cam·ou·flage (kam′ə fläzh′, -fläj′) *n.* ⟦Fr < *camoufler*, to disguise⟧ **1** a disguising, as of ships or guns, to conceal them from the enemy 2 a disguise; deception —vt., vi. **-flaged**, **-flag'ing** to disguise (a thing or person) for concealment —**cam'ou·flag' er** n.

camp (kamp) n. ⟦< L *campus*, field⟧ 1 a) a place where temporary tents, huts, etc. are put up, as for soldiers b) a group of such tents, etc. 2 the supporters of a particular cause 3 a recreational place in the country for vacationers, esp. children 4 the people living in a camp 5 [Slang] banality, artifice, etc. so extreme as to amuse or have a perversely sophisticated appeal —vi. 1 to set up a camp 2 to live or stay in a camp: often with *out* —**break camp** to dismantle a camp and depart

cam·paign (kam pān') n. ⟦Fr < L *campus*, field⟧ 1 a series of military operations with a particular objective 2 a series of planned actions, as to elect a candidate —vi. to participate in a campaign —**cam·paign'er** n.

cam·pa·ni·le (kam'pə nē'lē) n., pl. **-les** or **-li** (-lē) ⟦It < LL *campana*, a bell⟧ a bell tower

camp·er (kam'pər) n. 1 a vacationer at a camp 2 a motor vehicle or trailer equipped for camping out

camp·fire n. 1 an outdoor fire at a camp 2 a social gathering around such a fire

cam·phor (kam'fər) n. ⟦< Sans *karpuraḥ*, camphor tree⟧ an aromatic crystalline substance derived from the wood of an E Asian evergreen tree (**camphor tree**): used to repel moths, in liniments, etc. —**cam'phor·at'ed** adj.

camp meeting a religious meeting held outdoors or in a tent, etc.

camp·site n. 1 any site for a camp 2 an area in a park set aside for camping

cam·pus (kam'pəs) n., pl. **-pus·es** ⟦L, a field⟧ the grounds, and sometimes buildings, of a school or college —adj. of a school or college [*campus* politics]

camp·y adj. **-i·er**, **-i·est** [Slang] characterized by CAMP (n. 5)

cam·shaft n. a shaft having a cam, or to which a cam is fastened

can¹ (kan; *unstressed* kən) vi., v.aux. pt. **could** ⟦< OE *cunnan*, to know⟧ 1 know(s) how (to) 2 am, are, or is able (to) 3 am, are, or is likely (to) [*can* that be true?] 4 have or has the right (to) 5 [Inf.] am, are, or is permitted (to); may —**can but** can only

can² (kan) n. ⟦OE *canne*, a cup⟧ 1 a container, usually metal, with a separate cover [a garbage *can*] 2 a tinned metal container in which foods, etc. are sealed for preservation 3 the amount a can holds —vt. **canned**, **can'ning** 1 to put up in cans or jars for preservation 2 [Slang] to dismiss from employment; fire

Ca·naan (kā'nən) ancient region at the SE end of the Mediterranean: the Biblical Promised Land

Can·a·da (kan'ə də) country in N North America; cap. Ottawa —**Ca·na·di·an** (kə nā' dē ən) adj., n.

Canadian bacon cured, smoked pork taken from the loin

Ca·na·di·an·ism n. 1 a custom or belief originating in Canada 2 a word or phrase originating in Canadian English

ca·nal (kə nal') n. ⟦< L *canalis*, channel⟧ 1 an artificial waterway for transportation or irrigation 2 *Anat.* a tubular passage or duct

Canal Zone *former name* for a strip of land on either side of the Panama Canal: leased by the U.S. (1904-79)

ca·na·pé (kan'ə pā', kan'ə pē) n. ⟦Fr⟧ a small piece of bread or a cracker, spread with spiced meat, cheese, etc., served as an appetizer

ca·nard (kə närd') n. ⟦Fr, a duck⟧ a false, esp. malicious, report

ca·nar·y (kə ner'ē) n., pl. **-ies** [after *Canary* Islands] 1 a small, yellow finch 2 a light yellow

Canary Islands group of Spanish islands off NW Africa

ca·nas·ta (kə nas'tə) n. ⟦Sp, basket⟧ a card game using a double deck

Can·ber·ra (kan'ber'ə, -bə rə) capital of Australia

can·can (kan'kan') n. ⟦Fr⟧ a lively dance with much high kicking

can·cel (kan'səl) vt. **-celed** or **-celled**, **-cel·ing** or **-cel·ling** ⟦< L *cancellus*, lattice⟧ 1 to mark over with lines, etc., as in deleting written matter or marking a postage stamp, check, etc. as used 2 to make invalid 3 to do away with; abolish 4 to neutralize or balance: often with *out* 5 *Math.* to remove (a common factor, equivalents, etc.) —**can' cel·la'tion** n.

can·cer (kan'sər) n. ⟦L, crab⟧ 1 [C-] the fourth sign of the zodiac 2 a malignant tumor that can spread 3 anything bad or harmful that spreads —**can'cer·ous** adj.

can·de·la·brum (kan'də lä'brəm, -lä'-) n., pl. **-bra** (-brə) or **-brums** ⟦L: see CHANDELIER⟧ a large branched candlestick: also **can'de·la' bra** pl. **-bras**

can·did (kan'did) adj. ⟦L *candidus*, white, pure, sincere⟧ 1 very honest or frank 2 unposed and informal [a *candid* photo] —**can' did·ly** adv.

can·di·date (kan'də dāt', -dət) n. ⟦L *candidatus*, white-robed, as were Roman office seekers⟧ one seeking an office, award, etc.

can·died (kan'dēd') adj. cooked in sugar or syrup until glazed or encrusted

can·dle (kan'dəl) n. ⟦< L *candela*⟧ a cylinder of tallow or wax with a wick through it, which gives light when burned

can·dle·stick n. a cupped or spiked holder for a candle or candles

can-do adj. [Inf.] confident of one's ability to accomplish something

can·dor (kan'dər) n. ⟦L, openness⟧ unreserved honesty or frankness in expressing oneself: Brit. sp. **can'dour**

can·dy (kan'dē) n., pl. **-dies** ⟦< Pers *qand*, cane sugar⟧ a solid confection of sugar or syrup with flavoring, fruit, nuts, etc. —vt.

–died, –dy·ing 1 to cook in sugar, esp. so as to preserve **2** to crystallize into sugar

cane (kān) *n.* ⟦< Gr *kanna*⟧ **1** the slender, jointed stem of certain plants, as bamboo **2** a plant with such a stem, as sugar cane **3** WALKING STICK **4** split rattan —*vt.* **caned, can′ing 1** to flog with a cane **2** to make (chair seats, etc.) with cane —**can′er** *n.*

cane·brake (kān′brāk′) *n.* a dense growth of cane plants

ca·nine (kā′nīn′) *adj.* ⟦< L *canis*, dog⟧ **1** of or like a dog **2** of the family of carnivores that includes dogs, wolves, and foxes —*n.* **1** a dog or other canine animal **2** any of the sharp-pointed teeth next to the incisors: in full **canine tooth**

can·is·ter (kan′is tər) *n.* ⟦< Gr *kanastron*, wicker basket⟧ a small box or can for coffee, tea, etc.

can·ker (kaŋ′kər) *n.* ⟦< L *cancer*, a crab⟧ an ulcerlike sore, esp. in the mouth —**can′ker·ous** *adj.*

can·na·bis (kan′ə bis) *n.* ⟦L, hemp⟧ **1** HEMP **2** marijuana or any other substance made from the flowering tops of the hemp

canned (kand) *adj.* **1** preserved, as in cans **2** [Slang] recorded for reproduction, as on radio or TV

can·nel (coal) (kan′əl) a dense bituminous coal that burns with a steady, bright flame

can·ner·y (kan′ər ē) *n., pl.* **-ies** a factory where foods are canned

can·ni·bal (kan′ə bəl) *n.* ⟦Sp *canibal*⟧ **1** a person who eats human flesh **2** an animal that eats its own kind —*adj.* of or like cannibals —**can′ni·bal·ism′** *n.* —**can′ni·bal·is′tic** *adj.*

can·ni·bal·ize (-īz′) *vt., vi.* **-ized′, -iz′ing 1** to strip (old or worn equipment) of parts for use in other units **2** to eat (one of one's own species)

can·non (kan′ən) *n., pl.* **-nons** or **-non** ⟦< L *canna*, cane⟧ **1** a large, mounted piece of artillery **2** an automatic gun on an aircraft

can·non·ade (-ād′) *n.* a continuous firing of artillery —*vt., vi.* **-ad′ed, -ad′ing** to fire artillery (at)

can·not (kan′ät′, kə nät′) can not —**cannot but** have or has no choice but to

can·ny (kan′ē) *adj.* **-ni·er, -ni·est** ⟦< CAN[1]⟧ cautious and shrewd —**can′ni·ly** *adv.* —**can′ni·ness** *n.*

ca·noe (kə nōō′) *n.* ⟦< Sp *canoa* < WInd⟧ a light, narrow boat moved by paddles —*vi.* **-noed′, -noe′ing** to paddle, or go in, a canoe —**ca·noe′ist** *n.*

ca·no·la (oil) (kə nō′lə) an oil from the seed of the rape plant, used in cooking

can·on (kan′ən) *n.* ⟦OE, a rule < L⟧ **1** a law or body of laws of a church **2** *a)* a basic rule or principle *b)* a criterion **3** an official list, as of books of the Bible **4** the complete works, as of an author **5** *Music* a round **6** a clergyman serving in a cathedral

ca·ñon (kan′yən) *n. alt. sp. of* CANYON

ca·non·i·cal (kə nän′i kəl) *adj.* **1** of or according to church law **2** of or belonging to a canon

can·on·ize (kan′ən īz′) *vt.* **-ized′, -iz′ing 1** to declare (a deceased person) a saint **2** to glorify —**can′on·i·za′tion** *n.*

can·o·py (kan′ə pē) *n., pl.* **-pies** ⟦< Gr *kōnōpeion*, couch with mosquito nets⟧ **1** a drapery, etc. fastened above a bed, throne, etc., or held over a person **2** a rooflike projection —*vt.* **-pied, -py·ing** to place or form a canopy over; cover

cant[1] (kant) *n.* ⟦< L *cantus*, song⟧ **1** the secret slang of beggars, thieves, etc.; argot **2** the special vocabulary of a certain occupation; jargon **3** insincere talk, esp. when pious —*vi.* to use cant

cant[2] (kant) *n.* ⟦L *cantus*, tire of a wheel⟧ **1** an outside angle **2** a beveled edge **3** a tilt, turn, slant, etc. —*vt., vi.* to slant; tilt

can't (kant, känt) *contr.* cannot

can·ta·loupe or **can·ta·loup** (kant′ə lōp′) *n.* ⟦Fr < It *Cantalupo*, estate near Rome, where first grown in Europe⟧ a muskmelon with a rough rind and juicy, orange flesh

can·tan·ker·ous (kan taŋ′kər əs) *adj.* ⟦prob. < ME *cōntakour*, troublemaker⟧ bad-tempered; quarrelsome —**can·tan′ker·ous·ly** *adv.* —**can·tan′ker·ous·ness** *n.*

can·ta·ta (kän tät′ə, kən-) *n.* ⟦It < *cantare*, to sing⟧ a choral composition in several movements with orchestral accompaniment

can·teen (kan tēn′) *n.* ⟦< Fr < It *cantina*, wine cellar⟧ **1** a recreation center for military personnel, teenagers, etc. **2** a place where food is dispensed, as in a disaster area **3** a small flask for carrying water

can·ter (kant′ər) *n.* ⟦< *Canterbury gallop*, a riding pace⟧ a moderate gallop — *vi., vt.* to ride at a canter

can·ti·cle (kan′ti kəl) *n.* ⟦< L *cantus*, song⟧ a hymn with words taken from the Bible

can·ti·le·ver (kant′'l ē′vər, -ev′ər) *n.* ⟦< ?⟧ a bracket or block projecting as a support; esp., a projecting structure anchored at one end to a pier or wall —*vt.* to support by means of cantilevers —**can′ti·le′vered** *adj.*

can·to (kan′tō) *n., pl.* **-tos** ⟦It < L *cantus*, song⟧ any of the main divisions of certain long poems

can·ton (kan′tən, -tän′) *n.* ⟦Fr < LL *cantus*, corner⟧ any of the states of Switzerland

Can·ton (kan tän′) *a former transliteration of* GUANGZHOU

Can·ton·ese (kan′tə nēz′) *n.* **1** *pl.* **-ese′** a person born or living in Canton, China **2** the variety of Chinese spoken in Canton —*adj.* of Canton

can·ton·ment (kan tän′mənt, -tōn′–) *n.* ⟦Fr: see CANTON⟧ temporary quarters for troops

can·tor (kan′tər) *n.* ⟦L, singer⟧ a singer of liturgical solos in a synagogue

can·vas (kan′vəs) *n.* ⟦< L *cannabis*, hemp⟧ **1** a coarse cloth of hemp, cotton, etc., used for tents, sails, etc. **2** a painting on canvas

can·vas·back *n.* a North American wild duck with a grayish back

can·vass (kan′vəs) *vt., vi.* ⟦< *canvas* < ? use of canvas for sifting⟧ to go through (places) or among (people) asking for (votes, opinions, orders, etc.) —*n.* a canvassing —**can′vass·er** *n.*

can·yon (kan′yən) *n.* ⟦Sp *cañon*, tube < L *canna*, a reed⟧ a long, narrow valley between high cliffs

cap¹ (kap) *n.* ⟦< LL *cappa*, hooded cloak⟧ **1** any closefitting head covering, with or without a visor or brim **2** a caplike part or thing; cover or top —*vt.* **capped, cap′ping 1** to put a cap on **2** to cover the top or end of **3** to equal or excel

cap² *abbrev.* **1** capacity **2** capital

ca·pa·ble (kā′pə bəl) *adj.* ⟦< L *capere*, to take⟧ having ability; competent —**capable of 1** having the qualities necessary for **2** able or ready to —**ca′pa·bil′i·ty** *n., pl.* **-ties** —**ca′pa·bly** *adv.*

ca·pa·cious (kə pā′shəs) *adj.* ⟦< L *capere*, to take⟧ roomy; spacious —**ca·pa′cious·ly** *adv.* —**ca·pa′cious·ness** *n.*

ca·pac·i·tor (kə pas′ə tər) *n.* a device for storing an electric charge

ca·pac·i·ty (-tē) *n., pl.* **-ties** ⟦< L *capere*, take⟧ **1** the ability to contain, absorb, or receive **2** all that can be contained; volume **3** ability **4** maximum output **5** position; function

ca·par·i·son (kə par′i sən, -zən) *n.* ⟦< LL *cappa*, cloak⟧ trappings for a horse —*vt.* to cover (a horse) with trappings

cape¹ (kāp) *n.* ⟦see prec.⟧ a sleeveless garment fastened at the neck and hanging over the back and shoulders

cape² (kāp) *n.* ⟦< L *caput*, head⟧ a piece of land projecting into a body of water

ca·per¹ (kā′pər) *vi.* ⟦? < Fr *capriole*, a leap⟧ to skip about in a playful manner —*n.* **1** a playful leap **2** a prank **3** [Slang] a criminal act, esp. a robbery —**cut a caper (or cut capers)** to caper

ca·per² (kā′pər) *n.* ⟦< Gr *kapparis*⟧ the green flower bud of a Mediterranean bush, pickled and used as a seasoning

Cape Town seaport in South Africa: seat of the legislature

Cape Verde (vurd) country on a group of islands in the Atlantic, west of Senegal

cap·il·lar·y (kap′ə ler′ē) *adj.* ⟦< L *capillus*, hair⟧ very slender —*n., pl.* **-ies 1** a tube with a very small bore: also **capillary tube 2** any of the tiny blood vessels connecting the arteries with the veins

capillary attraction the action by which liquids in contact with solids, as in a capillary tube, rise or fall: also **capillary action**

cap·i·tal (kap′ət ′l) *adj.* ⟦< L *caput*, head⟧ **1** punishable by death **2** principal; chief **3** of, or being, the seat of government **4** of capital, or wealth **5** excellent —*n.* **1** CAPITAL LETTER **2** a city that is the seat of government of a state or nation **3** money or property owned or used in business **4** [*often* **C-**] capitalists collectively **5** the top part of a column

capital gain profit resulting from the sale of capital investments such as stocks

cap·i·tal·ism *n.* an economic system in which the means of production and distribution are privately owned and operated for profit

cap·i·tal·ist *n.* **1** an owner of wealth used in business **2** an upholder of capitalism —**cap′i·tal·is′tic** *adj.*

cap·i·tal·ize (-īz′) *vt.* **-ized′, -iz′ing 1** to use as or convert into capital **2** to supply capital to or for **3** to begin (a word) with a capital letter —**capitalize on** to use to one's advantage —**cap′i·tal·i·za′tion** *n.*

capital letter the form of an alphabetical letter used to begin a sentence or proper name, as *A, B,* or *C*

cap·i·tal·ly *adv.* very well

capital punishment the penalty of death for a crime

Cap·i·tol (kap′ət ′l) *n.* ⟦< L *Capitolium*, temple of Jupiter in Rome⟧ **1** the building in which the U.S. Congress meets in Washington, DC **2** [*usually* **c-**] the building in which a state legislature meets

ca·pit·u·late (kə pich′yoo lāt′, -pich′ə lāt′) *vi.* **-lat′ed, -lat′ing** ⟦< LL *capitulare*, arrange conditions⟧ **1** to give up (*to* an enemy) on prearranged conditions **2** to stop resisting —**ca·pit′u·la′tion** *n.*

cap·let (kap′lit) *n.* a medicine tablet coated for easy swallowing

ca·pon (kā′pän′, -pən) *n.* ⟦< L *capo*⟧ a castrated rooster fattened for eating

cap·puc·ci·no (kä′pə chē′nō, kap′ə-) *n.* ⟦It⟧ espresso coffee mixed with steamed milk and topped with cinnamon, etc.

ca·price (kə prēs′) *n.* ⟦Fr < It⟧ **1** a sudden, impulsive change in thinking or acting **2** a capricious quality

ca·pri·cious (kə prish′əs) *adj.* subject to caprices; erratic —**ca·pri′cious·ly** *adv.* —**ca·pri′cious·ness** *n.*

Cap·ri·corn (kap′ri kôrn′) *n.* ⟦< L *caper*, goat + *cornu*, horn⟧ the tenth sign of the zodiac

cap·size (kap′sīz′, kap sīz′) *vt., vi.* **-sized′, -siz′ing** ⟦< ?⟧ to overturn or upset: said esp. of a boat

cap·stan (kap′stən) *n.* ⟦? < L *capere*, take⟧ an upright cylinder, as on ships, around which cables are wound for hoisting anchors, etc.

cap·sule (kap′səl, -syōōl′) *n.* ⟦Fr < L *capsa*, box⟧ **1** a soluble gelatin container enclosing a dose of medicine **2** a detachable portion of a spacecraft, designed to hold people, instruments, etc.: in full **space capsule 3** *Bot.* a seed vessel —*adj.* in a concise form —**cap′su·lar** *adj.*

cap·sul·ize (-īz′) *vt.* **-ized′, -iz′ing 1** to enclose in a capsule **2** to condense

Capt *abbrev.* Captain

cap·tain (kap′tən) *n.* ⟦< L *caput*, head⟧ **1** a chief; leader **2** *U.S. Mil.* an officer ranking just above first lieutenant **3** *U.S. Navy* an officer ranking just above commander **4** *a)* the person in command of a ship *b)* the pilot of an airplane **5** the leader of a team, as in sports —*vt.* to be captain of —**cap′tain·cy** *n., pl.* **-cies**

cap·tion (kap'shən) *n.* ⟦< L *capere*, to take⟧ 1 a heading or title, as of a newspaper article or illustration 2 *Film, TV* a subtitle —*vt.* to supply a caption for

cap·tious (-shəs) *adj.* ⟦see prec.⟧ 1 made only for the sake of argument or faultfinding [a *captious* remark] 2 quick to find fault —**cap'tious·ly** *adv.* —**cap'tious·ness** *n.*

cap·ti·vate (kap'tə vāt') *vt.* **-vat'ed, -vat'ing** to capture the attention or affection of —**cap'ti·vat'ing·ly** *adv.* —**cap'ti·va'tion** *n.* —**cap'ti·va'tor** *n.*

cap·tive (kap'tiv) *n.* ⟦< L *capere*, to take⟧ a prisoner —*adj.* 1 taken or held prisoner 2 obliged to listen [a *captive* audience] —**cap·tiv'i·ty** *n., pl.* **-ties**

cap·tor (-tər) *n.* one who captures

cap·ture (-chər) *vt.* **-tured, -tur·ing** ⟦< L *capere*, to take⟧ 1 to take or seize by force, surprise, etc. 2 to represent in a more permanent form [to *capture* her charm on canvas] —*n.* a capturing or being captured

car (kär) *n.* ⟦< L *carrus*, chariot⟧ 1 any vehicle on wheels 2 a vehicle that moves on rails, as a streetcar 3 an automobile 4 an elevator cage

Ca·ra·cas (kə räk'əs, -rak'-) capital of Venezuela

car·a·cul (kar'ə kul', -kəl) *n. alt. sp. of* KARA-KUL (esp. *n.* 2)

ca·rafe (kə raf', -räf') *n.* ⟦Fr⟧ a glass bottle for serving wine, water, or coffee

car·a·mel (kär'məl, kar'ə məl) *n.* ⟦Fr⟧ 1 burnt sugar used to color or flavor food 2 a chewy candy made from sugar, milk, etc.

car·a·mel·ize (-īz') *vt., vi.* **-ized', -iz'ing** 1 to turn into CARAMEL (*n.* 1) 2 to brown and sweeten with heat

car·a·pace (kar'ə pās') *n.* ⟦Fr < Sp⟧ the upper shell of a turtle, crab, etc.

car·at (kar'ət) *n.* ⟦Fr < Gr *keration*, little horn⟧ a unit of weight for precious stones, equal to 200 milligrams

car·a·van (kar'ə van') *n.* ⟦< Pers *kārwān*⟧ 1 a company of people traveling together for safety, as through a desert 2 VAN²

car·a·van·sa·ry (kar'ə van'sə rē) *n., pl.* **-ries** ⟦< Pers *kārwān*, caravan + *sarāī*, palace⟧ in the Middle East, an inn for caravans

car·a·way (kar'ə wā') *n.* ⟦< Ar *al-karawiyā'*⟧ the spicy seeds of an herb, used to flavor bread, etc.

car·bide (kär'bīd') *n.* a solid compound of a metal with carbon

car·bine (kär'bīn', -bēn') *n.* ⟦Fr *scarabée*, beetle⟧ 1 a short-barreled rifle 2 a light, semiautomatic or automatic rifle of relatively limited range

carbo- *combining form* carbon: also **carb-**

car·bo·hy·drate (kär'bō hī'drāt, -bə-) *n.* ⟦prec. + HYDRATE⟧ an organic compound composed of carbon, hydrogen, and oxygen, as a sugar or starch

car·bol·ic acid (kär bäl'ik) *see* PHENOL

car·bon (kär'bən) *n.* ⟦< L *carbo*, coal⟧ 1 a nonmetallic chemical element found esp. in all organic compounds: diamond and graph-

ite are pure carbon: a radioactive isotope of carbon (**carbon-14**) is used in dating fossils, etc. 2 CARBON PAPER 3 a copy made with carbon paper —*adj.* of or like carbon

car·bon·ate (-bə nit; *also, and for v. always,* -nāt') *n.* a salt or ester of carbonic acid —*vt.* **-at'ed, -at'ing** to charge with carbon dioxide —**car'bon·a'tion** *n.*

carbon black carbon produced by the incomplete burning of oil or gas

carbon copy 1 a copy made with carbon paper 2 anything very much like another

carbon dating a method of establishing the approximate age of bones, artifacts, etc. by measuring the amount of carbon-14 in them —**car'bon-date'** *vt.* **-dat'ed, -dat'ing**

carbon di·ox·ide (dī äks'īd') a heavy, colorless, odorless gas: it passes out of the lungs in respiration

car·bon·ic acid (kär bän'ik) a weak acid formed by carbon dioxide in water

car·bon·if·er·ous (kär'bə nif'ər əs) *adj.* containing carbon or coal

carbon mon·ox·ide (mə näks'īd') a colorless, odorless, highly poisonous gas

carbon paper thin paper coated on one side, as with a carbon preparation, used to make copies of letters, etc.

carbon tet·ra·chlo·ride (te'trə klôr'īd') a nonflammable liquid, used as a solvent for fats and oils, etc

Car·bo·run·dum (kär'bə run'dəm) ⟦CARB(ON) + (c)orundum⟧ *trademark for* a hard silicon carbide abrasive

car·boy (kär'boi') *n.* ⟦< Pers *qarābah*⟧ a large bottle often enclosed in a protective container, used as for storing chemicals or in brewing

car·bun·cle (kär'buŋ'kəl) *n.* ⟦< L dim. of *carbo*, coal⟧ a painful bacterial infection deep beneath the skin —**car·bun'cu·lar** (-kyōō lər) *adj.*

car·bu·ret·or (kär'bə rāt'ər) *n.* a device for mixing air with gasoline spray to make an explosive mixture in an internal-combustion engine

car·cass (kär'kəs) *n.* ⟦< Fr *carcasse*⟧ 1 the dead body of an animal 2 a framework or shell

car·cin·o·gen (kär sin'ə jən) *n.* ⟦< fol. + -GEN⟧ a substance that causes cancer —**car·ci·no·gen·ic** (kär'sə nō jen'ik) *adj.*

car·ci·no·ma (kär'sə nō'mə) *n., pl.* **-mas** or **-ma·ta** (-mə tə) ⟦L < Gr *karkinos*, crab⟧ any of several kinds of epithelial cancer

car coat a short overcoat

card¹ (kärd) *n.* ⟦< Gr *chartēs*, layer of papyrus⟧ 1 a flat, stiff piece of paper or pasteboard; specif., *a)* any of a pack of playing cards *b)* a card identifying a person, esp. as a member, agent, etc. *c)* POSTCARD *d)* GREETING CARD *e)* any of a series of cards on which information is recorded 2 a small, plug-in circuit board 3 [Inf.] a witty or clowning person —**put (or lay) one's cards on the table** to reveal something frankly

card² (kärd) *n.* [< L *carrere*, to card] a metal comb or a machine with wire teeth for combing fibers of wool, cotton, etc. —*vt.* to use a card on

card·board *n.* stiff, thick paper or pasteboard, used for cards, boxes, etc.

car·di·ac (kär′dē ak′) *adj.* [< Gr *kardia*, heart] of or relating to the heart

cardiac arrest the complete failure of the heart to pump blood

car·di·gan (kär′di gən) *n.* [after 7th Earl of *Cardigan*] a sweater or jacket, usually knitted and collarless, that opens down the front

car·di·nal (kärd′n əl) *adj.* [< L *cardo*, pivot] 1 principal; chief 2 bright-red —*n.* 1 an official appointed by the pope to his council 2 a bright-red American songbird 3 CARDINAL NUMBER

cardinal number any number used in counting or in showing how many (e.g., two, 40)

cardio- [< Gr *kardia*, heart] *combining form of* the heart

car·di·o·gram (kär′dē ō gram′, -dē ə-) *n.* ELECTROCARDIOGRAM

car·di·o·graph *n.* ELECTROCARDIOGRAPH

car·di·ol·o·gy (-äl′ə jē) *n.* the branch of medicine dealing with the heart —**car′di·ol′o·gist** *n.*

car·di·o·pul·mo·nar·y (kär′dē ō pool′mə ner′ē) *adj.* of or involving the heart and lungs

car·di·o·vas·cu·lar (-vas′kyə lər) *adj.* of the heart and the blood vessels as a unified body system

card·play·er *n.* one who plays cards

cards *pl.n.* any game played with a deck of playing cards, as poker

card·sharp *n.* [Inf.] a professional cheater at cards: also **card shark**

care (ker) *n.* [< OE *caru*, sorrow] 1 *a*) a troubled state of mind; worry *b*) a cause of such a mental state 2 close attention; heed 3 a liking or regard (*for*) 4 custody; protection 5 a responsibility —*vi.* **cared, car′ing** 1 to feel concern 2 to feel love or a liking (*for*) 3 to look after; provide (*for*) 4 to wish (*for*); want —*vt.* 1 to feel concern about or interest in 2 to wish —**(in) care of** at the address of —**take care of** 1 to attend to 2 to provide for

ca·reen (kə rēn′) *vt., vi.* [< L *carina*, keel] to lean or cause to lean sideways; tip; tilt; lurch

ca·reer (kə rir′) *n.* [< L *carrus*, car] 1 [Archaic] a swift course 2 one's progress through life 3 a profession or occupation —*vi.* to rush wildly

care·free *adj.* free from worry

care·ful *adj.* 1 cautious; wary 2 accurate; thorough; painstaking —**care′ful·ly** *adv.* —**care′ful·ness** *n.*

care·giv·er *n.* one who takes care of a child, invalid, etc.

care·less *adj.* 1 carefree; untroubled 2 not paying enough heed; neglectful 3 done or made without enough attention, precision, etc. —**care′less·ly** *adv.* —**care′less·ness** *n.*

ca·ress (kə res′) *vt.* [ult. < L *carus*, dear] to touch lovingly or gently —*n.* an affectionate touch

car·et (kar′it, ker′-) *n.* [L, there is lacking] a mark (‸) used to show where something is to be inserted in a written or printed line

care·tak·er *n.* 1 a person hired to take care of something or someone 2 one acting as temporary replacement

care·worn *adj.* worn out by, or showing the effects of, troubles and worry

car·fare (kär′fer′) *n.* the price of a ride on a subway, bus, etc.

car·go (kär′gō) *n., pl.* **-goes** or **-gos** [< Sp *cargar*, to load] the load carried by a ship, truck, etc.; freight

Car·ib·be·an (Sea) (kar′ə bē′ən, kə rib′ē ən) part of the Atlantic, bounded by the West Indies, Central America, and N South America

car·i·bou (kar′ə boo′) *n.* [CdnFr] a large North American reindeer

car·i·ca·ture (kar′i kə chər) *n.* [Fr < It *caricare*, exaggerate] 1 the exaggerated imitation of a person, literary style, etc. for satirical effect 2 a picture, etc. in which this is done —*vt.* **-tured, -tur·ing** to depict as in a caricature —**car′i·ca·tur·ist** *n.*

car·ies (ker′ēz′) *n.* [L, decay] decay of bones or, esp., of teeth

car·il·lon (kar′ə län′) *n.* [Fr, chime of four bells < L *quattuor*, four] a set of bells tuned to a chromatic scale

ca·ri·tas (kär′ē täs′) *n.* love for all people

car·jack·ing (kär′jak′in) *n.* the taking of a car and its passengers by force —**car′jack′** *vt.* —**car′jack′er** *n.*

car·mine (kär′min, -mīn′) *n.* [ult. < Ar *qirmiz*, crimson] a red or purplish-red color —*adj.* red or purplish-red

car·nage (kär′nij) *n.* [Fr < L *caro*, flesh] extensive slaughter, as in battle

car·nal (-nəl) *adj.* [< L *caro*, flesh] 1 of the flesh; material; worldly 2 sensual or sexual —**car·nal′i·ty** (-nal′i tē) *n., pl.* **-ties** —**car′nal·ly** *adv.*

car·na·tion (kär nā′shən) *n.* [< L *caro*, flesh] 1 a plant of the pink family, widely cultivated for its white, pink, or red flowers 2 its flower

car·nel·ian (kär nēl′yən) *n.* [< L *carnis*, of flesh (color)] a red variety of chalcedony, used in jewelry

car·ni·val (kär′nə vəl) *n.* [< Fr *carnaval* (or It *carnevale*)] 1 the period of feasting and revelry just before Lent 2 a reveling; festivity 3 an entertainment with sideshows, rides, etc.

car·ni·vore (kär′nə vôr′) *n.* 1 a carnivorous animal or plant 2 any of a group of usually meat-eating mammals, including dogs, cats, bears, etc.

car·niv·o·rous (kär niv′ə rəs) *adj.* [< L *caro*, flesh + *vorare*, to devour] 1 flesh-eating 2 of the carnivores —**car·niv′o·rous·ness** *n.*

car·ob (kar′əb) *n.* a tree of the E Mediterranean region with sweet pods used in making candy, etc.

car·ol (kar′əl) *n.* [< OFr *carole*, kind of dance] a song of joy or praise; esp., a Christmas song

— *vi.*, *vt.* **-oled** or **-olled, -ol·ing** or **-ol·ling** to sing; esp., to sing Christmas carols —**car′ol·er** *n.*, **car′ol·ler**

car·om (kar′əm) *n.* [< Sp *carambola*] **1** *Billiards* a shot in which the cue ball hits two balls in succession **2** a hitting and rebounding —*vi.* **1** to make a carom **2** to hit and rebound

ca·rot·id (kə rät′id) *adj.* [Gr *karōtis*] designating or of either of the two main arteries, one on each side of the neck, which convey blood to the head —*n.* a carotid artery

ca·rouse (kə rouz′) *vi.* **-roused′, -rous′ing** [< Ger *gar austrinken*, to drink] to engage in a noisy drinking party —*n.* a noisy drinking party

car·ou·sel (kar′ə sel′) *n.* [Fr < It dial. (Naples) *carusiello*, kind of tournament] **1** a merry-go-round **2** a circular baggage conveyor in an airport

carp[1] (kärp) *n.*, *pl.* **carp** or **carps** [< VL *carpa*] an edible freshwater fish widely cultivated for food

carp[2] (kärp) *vi.* [< ON *karpa*, to brag] to find fault in a petty or nagging way —**carp′er** *n.*

car·pal (kär′pəl) *adj.* of the carpus —*n.* a bone of the carpus

carpal tunnel syndrome a condition of a pinched nerve in the wrist, often caused by repetitive movement

car·pel (kär′pəl) *n.* [< Gr *karpos*, fruit] a simple pistil, regarded as a modified leaflike structure

car·pen·ter (kär′pən tər) *n.* [< L *carpentum*, a cart] one who builds and repairs wooden things, esp. buildings, ships, etc. —**car′pen·try** (-trē) *n.*

carpenter ant a large ant that gnaws holes in trees, wooden buildings, etc. for its nest

car·pet (kär′pət) *n.* [< L *carpere*, to card] **1** a heavy fabric for covering a floor **2** anything that covers like a carpet —*vt.* to cover as with a carpet —**on the carpet** being reprimanded

car·pet·bag *n.* an old-fashioned traveling bag, made of carpeting

car·pet·bag·ger *n.* a politician, promoter, etc. from the outside who is seen as opportunistic

car·pet·ing *n.* carpets or carpet fabric

car pool a plan by a group to rotate the use of their cars, as for going to work —**car′pool′** *vi.*, *vt.*

car·port (kär′pôrt′) *n.* an automobile shelter built as a roof extending from the side of a building

car·pus (kär′pəs) *n.*, *pl.* **-pi′** (-pī′) [< Gr *karpos*, wrist] *Anat.* the wrist, or the wrist bones

car·rel or **car·rell** (kar′əl) *n.* [< ML *carula*] a small enclosure in a library, for privacy in studying or reading

car·riage (kar′ij) *n.* [ult. < L *carrus*, chariot] **1** a carrying; transportation **2** the manner of carrying oneself; bearing **3** *a*) a horse-drawn passenger vehicle, esp. one with four wheels *b*) a baby carriage **4** a moving part, as on a typewriter, that supports something

car·ri·er (kar′ē ər) *n.* **1** one that carries **2** one

in the business of transporting **3** one that transmits disease germs **4** AIRCRAFT CARRIER **5** *a*) a telephone-service company *b*) an insurance company

carrier pigeon former name for HOMING PIGEON

car·ri·on (kar′ē ən) *n.* [< L *caro*, flesh] the decaying flesh of a dead body

Car·roll (kar′əl), **Lew·is** (loō′is), (pseud. of C. L. Dodgson) 1832–98; Eng. writer

car·rot (kar′ət) *n.* [< Gr *karōton*] **1** a plant with an edible, fleshy, orange-red root **2** the root

car·rou·sel (kar′ə sel′) *n.* alt. sp. of CAROUSEL

car·ry (kar′ē) *vt.* **-ried, -ry·ing** [< L *carrus*, chariot] **1** to hold or support **2** to take from one place to another **3** to keep with one [to carry an ID] **4** to transmit [air carries sounds] **5** to transfer or extend **6** to have as a quality, consequence, etc. [to carry a guarantee] **7** to bear (oneself) in a specified way **8** to win (an election, argument, etc.) **9** *a*) to keep in stock *h*) to keep on one's account books, etc. **10** to publish or broadcast [to carry a syndicated column, a TV show, etc.] —*vi.* to cover a range or distance: said of a voice, missile, etc. —*n.*, *pl.* **-ries** the distance covered by a gun, ball, etc. —**be (or get) carried away** to become very emotional or enthusiastic —**carry on 1** to engage in **2** to go on (*with*) **3** [Inf.] to behave wildly or childishly —**carry out (or through) 1** to put (plans, etc.) into practice **2** to accomplish —**carry over** to postpone

carrying charge interest paid on the balance owed in installment buying

car·ry-on *adj.* small enough to fit under an airplane seat or in an overhead compartment —*n.* a piece of carry-on luggage

car·ry-out *adj.* designating or of prepared food sold as by a restaurant to be consumed elsewhere

car·ry-o·ver *n.* something carried over or left over

car seat a seat in an automobile, specif., a portable seat for securing a small child

car·sick *adj.* nauseated from riding in an automobile, bus, etc.

Car·son City (kär′sən) capital of Nevada, in the W part

cart (kärt) *n.* [< ON *kartr*] **1** a small wagon, carriage, etc. **2** a handcart —*vt.*, *vi.* to carry as in a cart, truck, etc.; transport

cart·age (kärt′ij) *n.* **1** the work of carting **2** the charge for this

carte blanche (kärt′ blänsh′) [Fr, lit., white card] full authority or freedom

car·tel (kär tel′) *n.* [< Ger < Fr] an association of businesses in an international monopoly; trust

Car·ter (kärt′ər), **Jim·my** (jim′ē) (legal name *James Earl Carter, Jr.*) 1924– ; 39th president of the U.S. (1977–81)

car·ti·lage (kärt′'l ij) *n.* [< L *cartilago*] tough, elastic tissue forming parts of the skeleton; gristle —**car′ti·lag′i·nous** (-aj′ə nəs) *adj.*

car·tog·ra·phy (kär täg′rə fē) *n.* ⟦see CARD¹ & -GRAPHY⟧ the art of making maps or charts —**car·tog′ra·pher** *n.*

car·ton (kärt′'n) *n.* ⟦Fr < It *carta*, card⟧ a cardboard box or container

car·toon (kär tōōn′) *n.* ⟦< Fr: see prec.⟧ 1 a drawing caricaturing a person or event 2 *a*) COMIC STRIP *b*) an animated cartoon —*vi.* to draw a cartoon —**car·toon′ist** *n.*

car·tridge (kär′trij) *n.* ⟦< Fr < It *carta*, card⟧ 1 a cylindrical case containing the charge and primer, and usually the projectile, for a firearm 2 a small container, as for ink for a printer

cart·wheel *n.* a handspring performed sideways

carve (kärv) *vt.* **carved, carv′ing** ⟦OE *ceorfan*⟧ 1 to make or shape by or as by cutting 2 to decorate with cut designs 3 to divide by cutting; slice —*vi.* 1 to carve statues or designs 2 to carve meat —**carv′er** *n.* —**carv′ing** *n.*

car·wash *n.* an establishment at which automobiles are washed

car·y·at·id (kar′ē at′id) *n., pl.* **-ids** or **-i·des′** (-ə dēz′) ⟦< Gr *karyatides*, priestesses at Karyai, in ancient Greece⟧ a supporting column having the form of a draped female figure

ca·sa·ba (kə sä′bə) *n.* ⟦after *Kasaba*, town in Asia Minor⟧ a kind of cultivated melon with a hard, yellow rind

Ca·sa·blan·ca (kas′ə blaŋ′kə, kä′sə bläŋ′kə) seaport in NW Morocco

Ca·sa·no·va (kaz′ə nō′və, kas′ə-) *n.* ⟦after G. *Casanova* (1725-98), It adventurer⟧ a man who has many love affairs

cas·cade (kas kād′) *n.* ⟦Fr < L *cadere*, to fall⟧ 1 a small waterfall or series of waterfalls 2 anything resembling this, as a shower of sparks — *vt., vi.* **-cad′ed, -cad′ing** to fall or drop in a cascade

cas·car·a (kas ker′ə) *n.* ⟦Sp *cáscara*, bark⟧ a small tree growing on the Pacific coast of the U.S.

case¹ (kās) *n.* ⟦< L *casus*, a chance < *cadere*, to fall⟧ 1 an example or instance [a case of flu] 2 a person being helped, as by a doctor 3 any matter requiring study or investigation 4 *a*) the argument of one side, as in a law court *b*) convincing arguments [he has no *case*] 5 a lawsuit 6 *Gram.* the syntactic function of a noun or pronoun [nominative, objective, or possessive *case*] —*vt.* **cased, cas′ing** [Slang] to look over carefully, esp. before committing a crime —**in any case** anyhow —**in case** 1 in the event that; if 2 to be prepared for the possibility that —**in case of** in the event of —**in no case** never

case² (kās) *n.* ⟦< L *capsa*, box⟧ 1 a container, as a box 2 a protective cover [a watch *case*] 3 a full box or its contents [a *case* of beer] 4 a frame, as for a window —*vt.* **cased, cas′ing** 1 to put in a container 2 to enclose; encase

case·hard·en (-härd′'n) *vt. Metallurgy* to form a hard surface on (an iron alloy)

ca·se·in (kā′sē in, -sēn′) *n.* ⟦< L *caseus*, cheese⟧ a protein that is one of the chief constituents of milk

case·load *n.* the number of cases handled by a court, social agency, etc.

case·ment (-mənt) *n.* ⟦ult. < OFr *enchassement*⟧ a window frame that opens on hinges along the side

case·work *n.* social work in which the worker gives guidance to an individual or family —**case′work′er** *n.*

cash (kash) *n.* ⟦< L *capsa*, box⟧ 1 money that a person actually has; esp., ready money 2 bills and coins 3 money, a check, etc. paid at the time of purchase —*adj.* of or for cash —**cash in** to exchange for cash

cash·ew (kash′ōō; *also,* kə shōō′) *n.* ⟦< AmInd (Brazil) *acajú*⟧ 1 a tropical tree bearing kidney-shaped nuts 2 the nut

cash·ier¹ (ka shir′) *n.* ⟦Fr⟧ a person handling the cash transactions of a bank or store

cash·ier² (ka shir′) *vt.* ⟦< LL *cassare*, destroy⟧ to dismiss in dishonor

cash·mere (kash′mir′, kazh′-) *n.* ⟦after *Kashmir*, region in S Asia⟧ 1 a fine carded wool from goats originally of N India and Tibet 2 a soft, twilled cloth as of this wool

cash register a device, usually with a money drawer, used for registering visibly the amount of a sale

cas·ing (kās′iŋ) *n.* 1 the skin of a sausage 2 the outer covering of a pneumatic tire 3 a frame, as for a door

ca·si·no (kə sē′nō) *n., pl.* **-nos** ⟦It < *casa*, house⟧ 1 a room or building used for gambling 2 a card game for two to four players

cask (kask) *n.* ⟦ult. < L *quassare*, shatter⟧ 1 a barrel of any size, esp. one for liquids 2 its contents

cas·ket (kas′kit) *n.* ⟦< NormFr *casse*, box⟧ 1 a small box or chest, as for valuables 2 a coffin

Cas·pi·an (Sea) (kas′pē ən) inland salt sea between Asia and extreme SE Europe

Cas·san·dra (kə san′drə) *n. Gr. Myth.* a Trojan prophetess whose prophecies of doom are never believed

cas·sa·va (kə sä′və) *n.* ⟦< Fr < WInd *casáví*⟧ 1 a tropical American plant with starchy roots 2 a starch made from these roots, used in tapioca

cas·se·role (kas′ə rōl′) *n.* ⟦Fr < Gr *kyathos*, a bowl⟧ 1 a baking dish in which food can be cooked and served 2 the food baked in such a dish

cas·sette (kə set′, ka-) *n.* ⟦< NormFr *casse*, box⟧ a case with magnetic tape or film in it, for loading a tape recorder, VCR, camera, etc. quickly

cas·sia (kash′ə, kas′ē ə) *n.* ⟦ult. < Heb *qeṣî'āh*, lit., something scraped off⟧ 1 *a*) the bark of a tree of SE Asia: a source of cinnamon *b*) the tree 2 any of various tropical plants whose leaves yield senna

cas·si·no (kə sē′nō) *n. alt. sp. of* CASINO (*n.* 2)

cas·sock (kas′ək) *n.* ⟦prob. < Turk *qazaq*,

nomad] a long, closefitting vestment worn by clergymen, etc.

cast (kast) *vt.* **cast, cast′ing** [< ON *kasta*] **1** to throw with force; hurl **2** to deposit (a ballot or vote) **3** to direct [to *cast* one's eyes] **4** to project [to *cast* light] **5** to throw off or shed (a skin) **6** to shape (molten metal, etc.) by pouring into a mold **7** to select (an actor) for (a role or play) **8** to calculate —*vi.* to throw —*n.* **1** a casting; throw **2** *a)* something formed in a mold *b)* a mold or impression **3** a plaster form for immobilizing a broken limb **4** the set of actors in a play, movie, etc. **5** an appearance, as of features **6** a kind; quality **7** a tinge; shade —**cast about** to look (*for*) —**cast aside** (or **away** or **off**) to discard

cas·ta·nets (kas′tə nets′) *pl.n.* [< Sp < L *castanea*, chestnut: from the shape] a pair of small, hollowed pieces of hard wood, ivory, etc., clicked together in the hand in time to music

cast·a·way *n.* a shipwrecked person —*adj.* **1** discarded **2** shipwrecked

caste (kast) *n.* [Fr < L *castus*, pure] **1** any of the hereditary Hindu social classes of a formerly segregated system of India **2** any exclusive group **3** rigid class distinction based on birth, wealth, etc. —**lose caste** to lose social status

cast·er *n.* **1** a container for vinegar, oil, etc. at the table **2** any of a set of small wheels for supporting and moving a piece of furniture

cas·ti·gate (kas′tə gāt′) *vt.* **-gat′ed, -gat′ing** [< L *castigare*] to rebuke severely, esp. by public criticism —**cas′ti·ga′tion** *n.* —**cas′ti·ga′tor** *n.*

cast·ing *n.* a thing, esp. of metal, cast in a mold

cast iron a hard, brittle alloy of iron used for casting —**cast′-i′ron** *adj.*

cas·tle (kas′əl) *n.* [< L *castrum*, fort] **1** a large, fortified building or group of buildings used as a dwelling **2** any massive dwelling like this **3** *Chess* ROOK²

cast·off *adj.* discarded; abandoned —*n.* a person or thing cast off

cas·tor-oil plant (kas′tər oil′) a tropical plant with large seeds that yield an oil (**castor oil**) used as a cathartic

cas·trate (kas′trāt′) *vt.* **-trat′ed, -trat′ing** [< L *castrare*] to remove the testicles of; emasculate —**cas·tra′tion** *n.*

cas·u·al (kazh′oo əl) *adj.* [< L *casus*, chance] **1** happening by chance; not planned; incidental **2** occasional **3** careless or cursory **4** nonchalant **5** *a)* informal *b)* for informal use —**cas′u·al·ly** *adv.* —**cas′u·al·ness** *n.*

cas·u·al·ty (kazh′oo əl tē) *n., pl.* **-ties** **1** an accident, esp. a fatal one **2** a member of the armed forces killed, wounded, captured, etc. **3** anyone hurt or killed in an accident **4** anything lost, destroyed, etc.

cas·u·ist·ry (kazh′oo is trē) *n., pl.* **-ries** [< L *casus*, CASE¹] subtle but false reasoning, esp. about moral issues; sophistry —**cas′u·ist** *n.*

cat (kat) *n.* [OE] **1** a small, soft-furred animal, often kept as a pet or for killing mice **2**

any flesh-eating mammal related to this, as the lion, tiger, leopard, etc. **3** [Slang] a person, esp. a man —**let the cat out of the bag** to let a secret be found out

cat·a·clysm (kat′ə kliz′əm) *n.* [< Gr *kata-*, down + *klyzein*, to wash] any sudden, violent change, as in war —**cat′a·clys′mic** (-kliz′ mik) *adj.*

cat·a·comb (kat′ə kōm′) *n.* [< ? L *cata*, by + *tumba*, tomb] a gallery in an underground burial place: *usually used in pl.*

cat·a·falque (-falk′, -fôlk′) *n.* [Fr < It *catafalco*, funeral canopy] a wooden framework on which a body in a coffin lies in state

cat·a·lep·sy (-lep′sē) *n.* [< Gr *katalēpsis*, a seizing] a condition of muscle rigidity and sudden, temporary loss of consciousness —**cat′a·lep′tic** *adj., n.*

cat·a·log or **cat·a·logue** (kat′ə lôg′) *n.* [< Gr *kata-*, down + *legein*, to count] a complete list, as a card file of the books in a library, a list of articles for sale, etc. —*vt., vi.* **-loged′** or **-logued′, -log′ing** or **-logu′ing** to arrange (an item or items) in a catalog —**cat′a·log′er** *n.*, **cat′a·logu′er**

ca·tal·pa (kə tal′pə) *n.* [< AmInd] a tree with large, heart-shaped leaves and slender, bean-like pods

ca·tal·y·sis (kə tal′ə sis) *n., pl.* **-ses** (-sēz′) [< Gr *katalysis*, dissolution] the speeding up or, sometimes, slowing down of a chemical reaction by adding a substance which itself is not changed thereby

cat·a·lyst (kat′ə list) *n.* **1** a substance serving as the agent in catalysis **2** anything bringing about or hastening a result —**cat′a·lyt′ic** (-lit′ik) *adj.*

catalytic converter a device connected to the exhaust system of an automotive vehicle, to reduce air pollution by using a catalyst to break down exhaust gases

cat·a·ma·ran (kat′ə mə ran′) *n.* [Tamil *kattumaram*] **1** a narrow log raft propelled by sails or paddles **2** a boat like this having two parallel hulls

cat·a·mount (kat′ə mount′) *n.* a wildcat, esp. a cougar

cat·a·pult (kat′ə pult′) *n.* [< Gr *kata-*, down + *pallein*, to hurl] **1** an ancient military contrivance for throwing large stones, etc. **2** a device for launching an airplane, missile, etc. as from a deck or ramp —*vt.* to shoot or launch as from a catapult —*vi.* to leap

cat·a·ract (kat′ə rakt′) *n.* [< Gr *kata-*, down + *rhassein*, to strike or ? *arassein*, to smite] **1** a large waterfall **2** *a)* an eye disease in which the lens becomes opaque, causing partial or total blindness *b)* the opaque area

ca·tas·tro·phe (kə tas′trə fē) *n.* [< Gr *kata-*, down + *strephein*, to turn] any great and sudden disaster —**cat·a·stroph·ic** (kat′ə strāf′ik) *adj.*

cat·a·ton·ic (kat′ə tän′ik) *adj.* [< Gr *kata-*, down + *tonos*, tension] of or having a psychiatric condition involving catalepsy —*n.* a catatonic person

cat·bird *n.* a slate-gray North American song-bird with a call like a cat's

cat·boat *n.* a sailboat with a single sail on a mast set well forward

cat·call *n.* a shrill shout or whistle expressing derision, etc. —*vi.* to make catcalls

catch (kach, kech) *vt.* **caught, catch′ing** [< L *capere*, to take hold] **1** to seize and hold; capture **2** to take by a trap **3** to deceive **4** to surprise in some act **5** *a)* to get to in time [to *catch* a train] *b)* to overtake **6** to lay hold of; grab [to *catch* a ball] **7** to become infected with [he *caught* a cold] **8** to understand **9** to cause to be entangled or snagged **10** [Inf.] to see, hear, etc. —*vi.* **1** to become held, fastened, etc. **2** to take hold, as fire **3** to keep hold, as a lock —*n.* **1** a catching **2** a thing that catches **3** something caught **4** one worth catching, esp. a desirable marriage partner **5** a break in the voice **6** [Inf.] a tricky qualification or condition —**catch at** to seize desperately —**catch on 1** to understand **2** to become popular —**catch up 1** to seize; snatch **2** to overtake

catch·all *n.* a container or place for holding all sorts of things

catch·er *n. Baseball* the player behind home plate, who catches pitched balls

catch·ing *adj.* **1** contagious; infectious **2** attractive

catch·phrase *n.* a phrase that has become popular

Catch-22 *n.* [from the title of a novel (1961) by J. Heller (1923-99), U.S. writer] [*often* **catch-22**] a paradox in a law, regulation, or practice that makes one a victim of its provisions no matter what one does

catch·y *adj.* **-i·er, -i·est 1** attracting attention and easily remembered [a *catchy* tune] **2** tricky

cat·e·chism (kat′ə kiz′əm) *n.* [< Gr *kata-*, thoroughly + *ēchein*, to sound] **1** a handbook of questions and answers for teaching the principles of a religion **2** a close questioning

cat·e·gor·i·cal (kat′ə gôr′i kəl) *adj.* **1** positive; explicit: said of a statement, etc. **2** of, as, or in a category —**cat′e·gor′i·cal·ly** *adv.*

cat·e·go·rize (kat′ə gə rīz′) *vt.* **-rized′, -riz′ing** to place in a category; classify

cat·e·go·ry (-gôr′ē) *n., pl.* **-ries** [< Gr *katēgorein*, to assert] a division in a scheme of classification

ca·ter (kāt′ər) *vi.* [< L *ad-*, to + *capere*, take hold] **1** to provide food and service, as for parties **2** to seek to gratify another's needs or desires: with *to* —*vt.* to serve as caterer for (a banquet, etc.) —**ca′ter·er** *n.*

cat·er-cor·nered (kat′ə kôr′nərd, kat′ē-) *adj.* [< OFr *catre*, four + CORNERED] diagonal —*adv.* diagonally Also **cat′er-cor′ner**

cat·er·pil·lar (kat′ər pil′ər, kat′ə-) *n.* [< L *catta pilosus*, hairy cat] the wormlike larva of a butterfly, moth, etc. —[C-] *trademark for* a kind of tractor for rough or muddy ground

cat·er·waul (kat′ər wôl′) *vi.* [prob. echoic] to make a shrill sound like that of a cat; wail —*n.* such a sound

cat·fight *n.* [Inf.] a fight between two women

cat·fish *n., pl.* **-fish′** or **-fish′es** a fish with long, whiskerlike feelers about the mouth

cat·gut *n.* a tough thread made from dried intestines, as of sheep, and used for surgical sutures, etc.

ca·thar·sis (kə thär′sis) *n.* [< Gr *katharos*, pure] a relieving of emotional tensions, as through the arts or psychotherapy

ca·thar·tic (-tik) *adj.* purging —*n.* a medicine for purging the bowels; purgative

ca·the·dral (kə thē′drəl) *n.* [< Gr *kata-*, down + *hedra*, a seat] **1** the main church of a bishop's see **2** any large, imposing church

cath·e·ter (kath′ət ər) *n.* [< Gr *kata-*, down + *hienai*, to send] a slender tube inserted into a body passage, as into the bladder for drawing off urine —**cath′e·ter·ize′** (-īz′) *vt.* **-ized′, -iz′ing** —**cath′e·ter·i·za′tion** *n.*

cath·ode (kath′ōd′) *n.* [< Gr < *kata-*, down + -ODE] **1** the negative electrode in an electrolytic cell **2** the electron emitter in an electron tube **3** the positive terminal of a battery

cathode rays streams of electrons projected from a cathode: they produce X-rays when they strike solids

cath·ode-ray tube a vacuum tube in which a stream of electrons can be focused on a fluorescent screen: formerly widely used as picture tubes, etc.

cath·o·lic (kath′ə lik, kath′lik) *adj.* [< Gr *kata-*, completely + *holos*, whole] **1** all-inclusive; universal **2** broad in sympathies, tastes, etc. **3** [C-] ROMAN CATHOLIC —*n.* [C-] ROMAN CATHOLIC —**Ca·thol′i·cism** (kə thäl′ə siz′əm) *n.* —**cath·o·lic·i·ty** (kath′ə lis′i tē) *n.*

cat·i·on (kat′ī′ən) *n.* [< Gr *kata*, down + *ienai*, to go] a positively charged ion: in electrolysis, cations move toward the cathode

cat·kin (kat′kin) *n.* [< Du *katte*, cat] an often drooping spike of small flowers without petals, as on poplars, walnuts, etc.

cat·nap *n.* a short nap; doze —*vi.* **-napped′, -nap′ping** to doze briefly

cat·nip *n.* [CAT + dial. *nep*, catnip] an herb of the mint family: cats are strongly attracted to a compound in its leaves

cat-o'-nine-tails (kat′ə nīn′tālz′) *n., pl.* **-tails′** a whip made of nine knotted cords attached to a handle

CAT scan (kat) [c(*omputerized*) a(*xial*) t(*omography*)] CT SCAN —**CAT scanner** —**CAT scanning**

cat's cradle a game in which a string looped over the fingers is transferred back and forth on the hands of the players so as to form designs

Cats·kill Mountains (kats′kil′) mountain range in SE New York: also **Cats′kills′**

cat's-paw (kats′pô′) *n.* a person used to do distasteful or unlawful work

cat·sup (kat′səp) *n.* KETCHUP

cat·tail *n.* a tall marsh plant with long, brown, fuzzy spikes

cat·tle (kat′l) *pl.n.* [ult. < L *caput*, head] **1** [Archaic] farm animals **2** cows, bulls, steers, or oxen —**cat'tle·man** (-mən) n., pl. **-men** (-mən)

cat·ty (kat'ē) adj. **-ti·er, -ti·est** 1 of or like a cat 2 spiteful, mean, malicious, etc. —**cat'ti·ness** n.

cat·ty-cor·nered adj., adv. CATER-COR-NERED: also **cat'ty-cor'ner**

cat·walk n. a narrow, elevated walk

Cau·ca·sian (kô kā'zhən) adj. 1 of the Caucasus or its people, etc. 2 CAUCASOID —n. 1 a person born or living in the Caucasus 2 CAUCASOID

Cau·ca·soid (kô'kə soid') adj. designating or of a human racial group including most of the peoples native to Europe, N Africa, and W Asia: no longer in scientific use —n. a member of the Caucasoid population

Cau·ca·sus (kô'kə səs) 1 border region between SE Europe & W Asia, between the Black and Caspian seas: often called **the Caucasus** 2 mountain range in this region

cau·cus (kô'kəs) n. [< ?] 1 a meeting of a party or faction to decide on policy, pick candidates, etc. 2 the group attending such a meeting 3 a faction of politicians —vi. **-cused** or **-cussed, -cus·ing** or **-cus·sing** to hold a caucus

cau·dal (kôd'l) adj. [< L cauda, tail + -AL] of, like, at, or near the tail

caught (kôt) vt., vi. pt. & pp. of CATCH

caul (kôl) n. the membrane enveloping the head of a child at birth

caul·dron (kôl'drən) n. [< L calidus, warm, hot] 1 a large kettle or boiler 2 a state of violent agitation

cau·li·flow·er (kô'lə flou'ər) n. [< It cavolo, cabbage + fiore, flower] 1 a variety of cabbage with a dense white head of fleshy flower stalks 2 the head, eaten as a vegetable

caulk (kôk) vt. [< L calx, a heel] to stop up (cracks, etc.) of (a boat, etc.) as with putty, oakum, etc. —n. a soft, puttylike compound used in caulking: also **caulking compound** —**caulk'er** n.

caus·al (kôz'əl) adj. 1 of, being, or expressing a cause 2 relating to cause and effect —**cau·sal·i·ty** (kô zal'i tē) n., pl. **-ties** —**caus'al·ly** adv.

cau·sa·tion (kô zā'shən) n. 1 a causing 2 a causal agency; anything producing an effect

cause (kôz) n. [< L causa] 1 anything producing an effect or result 2 a reason or motive for producing an effect 3 any objective or movement that people are interested in and support 4 Law a case to be resolved by a court —vt. **caused, caus'ing** to be the cause of; bring about —**caus'a·tive** adj. —**cause'less** adj. —**caus'er** n.

cau·se·rie (kō'zə rē') n. [Fr] 1 a chat 2 a short, informal piece of writing

cause·way (kôz'wā') n. [ult. < L calx, lime + WAY] a raised path or road, as across wet ground or shallow water

caus·tic (kôs'tik) adj. [< Gr kaiein, to burn] 1 that can burn tissue by chemical action; corrosive 2 sarcastic; biting —n. a caustic substance —**caus'ti·cal·ly** adv. —**caus·tic'i·ty** (-tis'i tē) n.

cau·ter·ize (kôt'ər īz') vt. **-ized', -iz'ing** [see prec.] to burn with a hot needle, a laser, etc. so as to destroy dead tissue, etc. —**cau'ter·i·za'tion** n.

cau·tion (kô'shən) n. [< L cautio] 1 a warning 2 wariness; prudence —vt. to warn —**cau'tion·ar'y** adj.

cau·tious (kô'shəs) adj. full of caution; careful to avoid danger —**cau'tious·ly** adv. —**cau'tious·ness** n.

cav·al·cade (kav'əl kād', kav'əl kād') n. [Fr < L caballus, horse] a procession, as of horsemen, carriages, etc.

cav·a·lier (kav'ə lir') n. [Fr: see prec.] 1 an armed horseman; knight 2 a gallant gentleman, esp. a lady's escort —adj. 1 casual or indifferent toward important matters 2 arrogant —**cav'a·lier'ly** adv.

cav·al·ry (kav'əl rē) n., pl. **-ries** [< Fr: see CAVALCADE] combat troops mounted originally on horses but now often riding in tanks, etc. —**cav'al·ry·man** (-mən) n., pl. **-men** (-mən)

cave (kāv) n. [< L cavus, hollow] a hollow place inside the earth; cavern —vi. **caved, cav'ing** to give in; yield —**cave in** 1 to collapse 2 [Inf.] to give in; yield

ca·ve·at (kā'vē at', kav'ē-; -ät') [L] a warning, stipulation, qualification, etc.

ca·ve·at emp·tor (emp'tôr') [L] let the buyer beware

cave-in n. 1 a caving in 2 a place where the ground, etc. has caved in

cave man a prehistoric human of the Stone Age who lived in caves

cav·ern (kav'ərn) n. a cave, esp. a large cave —**cav'ern·ous** adj.

cav·i·ar or **cav·i·are** (kav'ē är') n. [Fr < Pers khāya, egg + -dār, bearing] the salted eggs of sturgeon, etc. eaten as a delicacy

cav·il (kav'əl) vi. **-iled** or **-illed, -il·ing** or **-il·ling** [< L cavilla, jeering] to object unnecessarily —n. a trivial objection; quibble —**cav'il·er** n., **cav'il·ler**

cav·i·ty (kav'i tē) n., pl. **-ties** [see CAVE] 1 a natural hollow place within the body 2 a hollow place, as one caused by decay in a tooth

ca·vort (kə vôrt') vi. [< ?] 1 to prance or caper 2 to romp; frolic

caw (kô) n. [echoic] the harsh cry of a crow —vi. to make this sound

cay·enne (pepper) (kī en', kā-) [< AmInd (Brazil) kynnha] very hot red pepper made from the dried fruit of a pepper plant

cay·use (kī'yōōs', kī yōōs') n., pl. **-us'es** or **-use'** [< AmInd tribal name] a small Western horse used by cowboys

CB (sē'bē') adj. [c(itizens') b(and)] designating or of shortwave radio frequencies set aside by the FCC for local use by private persons or businesses

CBO abbrev. Congressional Budget Office

cc abbrev. 1 carbon copy 2 cubic centimeter(s)

CC *abbrev.* **1** carbon copy (or copies) **2** closed-captioned

Cd *Chem. symbol for* cadmium

CD¹ (sē'dē') *n.* a compact disc

CD² (sē'dē') *n.* a certificate of deposit

CDC *abbrev.* Centers for Disease Control and Prevention

Cdn *abbrev.* Canadian

CD-ROM (sē'dē'räm') *n.* a compact disc on which stored data can be accessed

cease (sēs) *vt., vi.* **ceased, ceas′ing** ⟦see CEDE⟧ to end; stop

cease-fire *n.* a temporary cessation of warfare; truce

cease·less *adj.* unceasing; continual

ce·cum (sē'kəm) *n., pl.* **-ca** (-kə) ⟦< L *caecus*, blind⟧ the pouch at the beginning of the large intestine

ce·dar (sē'dər) *n.* ⟦< Gr *kedros*⟧ **1** a tree in the pine family having fragrant, durable wood **2** its wood —*adj.* of cedar

cede (sēd) *vt.* **ced′ed, ced′ing** ⟦< L *cedere*, to yield⟧ **1** to surrender formally **2** to transfer the title of

ce·dil·la (sə dil′ə) *n.* ⟦Sp dim. of *zeda*, a zeta or z⟧ a hooklike mark put under *c*, as in some French words (Ex.: *façade*) to show that it has an *s* sound

ceil·ing (sēl′iŋ) *n.* ⟦< L *caelum*, heaven⟧ **1** the inside top part of a room, opposite the floor **2** an upper limit [a price *ceiling*] **3** *Aeronautics* cloud cover affecting visibility, or the height of this —**hit the ceiling** [Slang] to lose one's temper

cel·an·dine (sel′ən dīn′, -dēn′) *n.* **1** a plant related to the poppy, with yellow flowers **2** a plant of the buttercup family, with yellow flowers

cel·e·brate (sel′ə brāt′) *vt.* **-brat′ed, -brat′ing** ⟦< L *celebrare*, to honor⟧ **1** to perform (a ritual, etc.) **2** to commemorate (an anniversary, holiday, etc.) with festivity **3** to honor publicly —*vi.* to mark a happy occasion with festive activities —**cel′e·brant** (-brənt) *n.* —**cel·e·bra′tion** *n.* —**cel′e·bra′tor** *n.*

cel·e·brat·ed *adj.* famous; renowned

ce·leb·ri·ty (sə leb′rə tē) *n.* **1** fame **2** *pl.* **-ties** a famous person

ce·ler·i·ty (sə ler′i tē) *n.* ⟦< L *celer*, swift⟧ swiftness; speed

cel·er·y (sel′ər ē, sel′rē) *n.* ⟦< Gr *selinon*, parsley⟧ a plant whose crisp leafstalks are eaten as a vegetable

ce·les·tial (sə les′chəl) *adj.* ⟦< L *caelum*, heaven⟧ **1** of or in the sky or universe **2** of heaven; divine **3** of the finest kind

cel·i·ba·cy (sel′ə bə sē) *n.* **1** the state of being unmarried **2** sexual abstinence

cel·i·bate (sel′ə bət) *n.* ⟦< L *caelebs*⟧ **1** an unmarried person **2** one who abstains from sexual intercourse —*adj.* of or in a state of celibacy

cell (sel) *n.* ⟦< L *cella*⟧ **1** a small room, as in a prison **2** a small hollow, as in a honeycomb **3** a small unit of protoplasm: all plants and animals are made up of one or more cells **4** a container holding an electrolyte, used to generate electricity **5** a small, often secret unit of an organization —**celled** *adj.*

cel·lar (sel′ər) *n.* ⟦see prec.⟧ a room or rooms below ground and usually under a building

cel·lo (chel′ō) *n., pl.* **-los** or **-li** (-ē) ⟦< VIOLONCELLO⟧ an instrument of the violin family, between the viola and double bass in size and pitch —**cel′list** *n.*

cel·lo·phane (sel′ə fān′) *n.* ⟦< CELLULOSE⟧ a thin, clear material made from cellulose, used as a wrapping

cell phone *n. short for* CELLULAR PHONE

cel·lu·lar (sel′yoo lər) *adj.* of, like, or containing a cell or cells

cellular phone a mobile radio phone used in a communications system of geographically distributed transmitters: also **cellular telephone**

cel·lu·lite (sel′yoo līt′) *n.* ⟦Fr⟧ fatty deposits on the hips and thighs: a nonmedical term

cel·lu·loid (sel′yoo loid′) *n.* ⟦fol. + -OID⟧ a tough, flammable plastic formerly used for making photographic film, etc.

cel·lu·lose (sel′yoo lōs′) *n.* ⟦Fr < L *cella*, cell + -OSE¹⟧ the chief substance in the cell walls of plants, used in making paper, textiles, etc.

cellulose acetate any of several nonflammable thermoplastics, used in making lacquers, etc.

ce·lo·sia (sə lō′shə, -sē ə) *n.* an annual garden plant with large clusters of tiny, brilliant red or yellow flowers

Cel·si·us (sel′sē əs) *adj.* ⟦after A. *Celsius* (1701-44), Swed astronomer, the inventor⟧ designating or of a thermometer on which 0° is the freezing point and 100° is the boiling point of water

Celt (kelt; *also* selt) *n.* ⟦< L⟧ a Celtic-speaking person

Celt·ic *adj.* of the Celts, their languages, etc. —*n.* a subfamily of languages including Gaelic and Welsh

ce·ment (sə ment′) *n.* ⟦< L *caementum*, rough stone⟧ **1** a powdered substance of lime and clay, mixed with water and sand to make mortar or with water, sand, and gravel to make concrete: it hardens upon drying **2** CONCRETE **3** anything that bonds —*vt.* **1** to unite as with cement **2** to cover with cement

cem·e·ter·y (sem′ə ter′ē) *n., pl.* **-ies** ⟦< Gr < *koiman*, to put to sleep⟧ a place for the burial of the dead

cen·o·bite (sen′ə bīt′) *n.* ⟦< Gr < *koinos*, common + *bios*, life⟧ a member of a religious order living in a monastery or convent

cen·o·taph (sen′ə taf′) *n.* ⟦< Gr *kenos*, empty + *taphos*, tomb⟧ a monument honoring a dead person whose remains are elsewhere

Ce·no·zo·ic (sē′nə zō′ik, sen′ə-) *adj.* ⟦ceno- (< Gr *kainos*, recent) + ZO(O)- + -IC⟧ designating the geologic era that includes the present, during which mammals have developed

cen·ser (sen′sər) *n.* a container in which incense is burned

cen·sor (sen′sər) *n.* ⟦L < *censere*, to judge⟧

an official with the power to examine literature, mail, etc. and remove or prohibit anything considered obscene, objectionable, etc. —*vt.* **1** to subject (a book, etc.) to a censor's examination **2** to restrict, ban, or delete (potentially objectionable content) —**cen′sor·ship′** *n.*

cen·so·ri·ous (sen sôr′ē əs) *adj.* inclined to find fault; harshly critical

cen·sure (sen′shər) *n.* 〖< L *censor*, censor〗 strong disapproval; condemnation —*vt.* **-sured, -sur·ing** to condemn as wrong —**cen′sur·a·ble** *adj.*

cen·sus (sen′səs) *n.* 〖L < *censere*, enroll〗 an official count of population and gathering of demographic data

cent[1] (sent) *n.* 〖< L *centum*, hundred〗 a 100th part of a dollar, or a coin of this value; penny

cent[2] *abbrev.* century; centuries

cen·taur (sen′tôr′) *n.* 〖< Gr *Kentauros*〗 *Gr. Myth.* a creature with a man's head, trunk, and arms, and a horse's body and legs

cen·ta·vo (sen tä′vō) *n., pl.* **-vos** 〖Sp, a hundredth < L *centum*, hundred〗 a 100th part of the monetary unit of various countries

cen·te·nar·i·an (sen′tə ner′ē ən) *n.* 〖< fol.〗 a person at least 100 years old

cen·te·nar·y (sen′tə ner′ē, sen ten′ər ē) *adj.* 〖< L < *centum*, hundred〗 **1** of a century **2** of a centennial —*n., pl.* **-ies** CENTENNIAL

cen·ten·ni·al (sen ten′ē əl) *adj.* 〖< L *centum*, hundred + *annus*, year + -AL〗 of or lasting 100 years —*n.* a 100th anniversary or its commemoration

cen·ter (sent′ər) *n.* 〖< Gr *kentron*, sharp point〗 **1** a point equally distant from all points on the circumference of a circle or surface of a sphere **2** a pivot **3** the approximate middle point or part of anything **4** a focal point of activity **5** [*often* C-] a group or position between the left (liberals) and right (conservatives) **6** *Sports* a player whose position is at the center of the line or playing area —*vt.* **1** to place in or near the center **2** to gather to one place —*vi.* to be focused

cen·ter·board *n.* a board or plate lowered through a slot in the floor of a sailboat to function as a movable keel

cen·ter·fold *n.* the center facing pages of a magazine, often with an extra fold, showing a photograph, as of a nude woman or man

center of gravity that point in a body or system around which its weight is evenly balanced

cen·ter·piece *n.* an ornament for the center of a table

centi- 〖L〗 *combining form* **1** one hundred **2** a 100th part of

cen·ti·grade (sen′tə grād′) *adj.* 〖Fr: see prec. & GRADE〗 CELSIUS

cen·time (sän′tēm′; *Fr* sän tēm′) *n.* 〖Fr〗 a 100th part of a franc

cen·ti·me·ter (sen′tə mēt′ər) *n.* 〖Fr: see CENTI- & METER[1]〗 a unit of measure, ¹⁄₁₀₀ meter

cen·ti·pede (sen′tə pēd′) *n.* 〖Fr < L *centi-*,

CENTI- + *pes*, FOOT〗 an elongated arthropod with a pair of legs for each body segment

cen·tral (sen′trəl) *adj.* 〖L *centralis*〗 **1** in, near, or of the center **2** equally accessible from various points **3** main; basic **4** of a controlling source in a system —**cen·tral′i·ty** (-tral′i tē) *n.* —**cen′tral·ly** *adv.*

Central African Republic country in central Africa

Central America part of North America between Mexico and South America —**Central American**

cen·tral·ize (-īz′) *vt.* **-ized′, -iz′ing 1** to make central; bring to a center **2** to organize under one control —*vi.* to become centralized —**cen′tral·i·za′tion** *n.* —**cen′tral·iz′er** *n.*

cen·tre (sent′ər) *n., vt., vi.* **-tred, -tring** *Brit. sp. of* CENTER

centri- *combining form* CENTRO-

cen·trif·u·gal (sen trif′ə gəl) *adj.* 〖< prec. + L *fugere*, to flee + -AL〗 of or relating to an apparent force (**centrifugal force**) that tends to make rotating bodies move away from the center of rotation

cen·tri·fuge (sen′trə fyōōj′) *n.* a machine using centrifugal force to separate particles of varying density

cen·trip·e·tal (sen trip′ət'l) *adj.* 〖< CENTRI- + L *petere*, rush at〗 of or relating to a force (**centripetal force**) that tends to make rotating bodies move toward the center of rotation

cen·trist (sen′trist) *n.* a person with moderate political opinions —**cen′trism′** *n.*

centro- 〖< L *centrum*, center〗 *combining form* center

cen·tu·ri·on (sen toor′ē ən) *n.* 〖see fol.〗 the commanding officer of an ancient Roman military unit, originally of 100 men

cen·tu·ry (sen′chə rē) *n., pl.* **-ries** 〖L < *centum*, hundred〗 a period of 100 years, esp. as reckoned from A.D.1

CEO *abbrev.* chief executive officer

ce·phal·ic (sə fal′ik) *adj.* 〖< Gr < *kephalē*, head〗 **1** of the head or skull **2** in, on, near, or toward the head

cephalo- 〖see prec.〗 *combining form* the head, skull, or brain

ce·ram·ic (sə ram′ik) *adj.* 〖Gr < *keramos*, potter's clay〗 of pottery, porcelain, etc. **2** of ceramics —*n.* **1** [*pl., with sing v.*] the art or work of making pottery, etc. of baked clay **2** an object made of baked clay: *often used in pl.* **3** any of various materials formed by baking clay, etc. at a high temperature

ce·ram·ist (ser′ə mist, sə ram′ist) *n.* one who works in ceramics; ceramic artist: also **ce·ram·i·cist** (sə ram′ə sist)

ce·re·al (sir′ē əl) *adj.* 〖< L *Cerealis*, of Ceres, Rom goddess of agriculture〗 of grain —*n.* **1** any grain used for food, as wheat, rice, etc. **2** any grass producing such grain **3** food made from grain, as oatmeal

cer·e·bel·lum (ser′ə bel′əm) *n., pl.* **-lums** or **-la** (-ə) 〖L, dim. of *cerebrum*〗 the section of the brain behind and below the cerebrum

cer·e·bral (ser'ə brəl, sə rē'-) *adj.* 1 of the brain or cerebrum 2 of, by, or for the intellect

cerebral palsy a muscular disorder resulting from damage to the nervous system, esp. at birth

cer·e·brate (ser'ə brāt') *vi.* **-brat'ed, -brat'ing** [< L *cerebrum*, the brain + -ATE[1]] to think —**cer'e·bra'tion** *n.*

cer·e·brum (ser'ə brəm, sə rē'brəm) *n., pl.* **-brums** or **-bra** (-brə) [L] the upper, main part of the brain of vertebrates

cer·e·ment (ser'ə mənt, sir'mənt) *n.* [< Gr *kēros*, wax] [*usually pl.*] a shroud for a dead person

cer·e·mo·ni·al (ser'ə mō'nē əl) *adj.* of or consisting of ceremony; formal —*n.* 1 a system of rites 2 a rite or ceremony —**cer'e·mo'ni·al·ly** *adv.*

cer·e·mo·ni·ous (-nē əs) *adj.* 1 full of ceremony 2 very polite or formal —**cer'e·mo'ni·ous·ly** *adv.*

cer·e·mo·ny (ser'ə mō'nē) *n., pl.* **-nies** [< L *caerimonia*] 1 a set of formal acts proper to a special occasion, as a religious rite 2 behavior that follows rigid etiquette 3 empty or meaningless formality —**stand on ceremony** to insist on formality

ce·rise (sə rēz', -rēs') *n., adj.* [< OFr *cerise*, cherry] cherry red

ce·ri·um (sir'ē əm) *n.* [after the dwarf planet *Ceres*] a lustrous, malleable chemical element used in metallurgy and in manufacturing glass: symbol, Ce; at. no. 58

cert *abbrev.* 1 certificate 2 certified

cer·tain (surt'ʼn) *adj.* [< L *certus*, determined] 1 fixed; settled 2 inevitable 3 reliable; dependable 4 sure; positive 5 definite, but unnamed [a *certain* person] 6 some [to a *certain* extent] —**for certain** without doubt

cer·tain·ly *adv.* undoubtedly; surely

cer·tain·ty *n.* 1 the state or fact of being certain 2 *pl.* **-ties** anything certain

cer·tif·i·cate (sər tif'i kit; *for v.,* -kāt') *n.* [see CERTIFY] a document attesting to a fact, qualification, etc. —*vt.* **-cat'ed, -cat'ing** to issue a certificate to

certificate of deposit a bank certificate issued for a specified deposit of money that draws interest, usually at a fixed rate and for a specified term

certified public accountant a public accountant certified as having passed a state examination

cer·ti·fy (surt'ə fī') *vt.* **-fied', -fy'ing** [< L *certus*, certain + -FY] 1 to declare (a thing) true, accurate, etc. by formal statement 2 to declare officially insane 3 to guarantee (a check, document, etc.) 4 to issue a certificate or license to —**cer'ti·fi'a·ble** *adj.* —**cer'ti·fi·ca'tion** *n.*

cer·ti·tude (surt'ə tōōd') *n.* sureness; inevitability

ce·ru·le·an (sə rōō'lē ən) *adj.* [< L < *caelum*, heaven] sky-blue; azure

Cer·van·tes (sər van'tēz', -vän'tes;), **Mi·guel de** (mē gel' de) 1547-1616; Sp. writer

cer·vix (sur'viks) *n., pl.* **cer·vi·ces** (sər vī'sēz', sur'və-) or **-vix·es** [L, neck] a necklike part, esp. of the uterus —**cer'vi·cal** (-vi kəl) *adj.*

ce·sar·e·an (section) (sə zer'ē ən) [from the ancient story that Julius CAESAR[2] was born this way] surgery to deliver a baby by cutting through the mother's abdominal and uterine walls

ce·si·um (sē'zē əm) *n.* [ult. < L *caesius*, bluish-gray] a metallic chemical element, used in photoelectric cells, radiation therapy, etc.: symbol, Cs; at. no. 55

ces·sa·tion (se sā'shən) *n.* [< L *cessare*, cease] a ceasing or stopping

ces·sion (sesh'ən) *n.* [< L *cedere*, to yield] a ceding (of rights, property, etc.) to another

cess·pool (ses'pōōl') *n.* [< ? L *cesso*, privy] a deep hole in the ground to receive drainage or sewage from the sinks, toilets, etc. of a house

ce·ta·cean (se tā'shən) *n.* [< L *cetus*, whale] any of certain fishlike marine mammals, including whales, porpoises, etc. —*adj.* of the cetaceans

Cey·lon (sə län', sā-, sē-) *former name for* SRI LANKA —**Cey·lo·nese** (sel'ə nēz', sā'lə-) *adj., n., pl.* **-nese'**

Cé·zanne (sā zän'), **Paul** 1839-1906; Fr. painter

cf *abbrev.* [L *confer*] compare

CFO *abbrev.* chief financial officer

cg or **cgm** *abbrev.* centigram(s)

CGI *abbrev.* computer-generated image (or imaging)

Ch or **ch** *abbrev.* 1 chapter 2 church

Cha·blis (sha blē') *n.* [*occas.* **c-**] a dry white Burgundy wine, orig. from Chablis, France

chad (chad) *n.* [< ?] any of the bits of paper separated from a PUNCH CARD when holes are punched in it

Chad (chad) country in NC Africa

chafe (chāf) *vt.* **chafed, chaf'ing** [< L *calefacere*, make warm] 1 to rub so as to make warm 2 to wear away or make sore by rubbing 3 to annoy; irritate —*vi.* 1 to rub (on or against) 2 to be annoyed or impatient

chaff (chaf) *n.* [OE *ceaf*] 1 threshed or winnowed husks of grain 2 anything worthless 3 teasing; banter — *vt., vi.* to tease in a good-natured way

chaf·ing dish (chāf'iŋ) a pan with a heating apparatus beneath it, as to cook food at the table

cha·grin (shə grin') *n.* [Fr] embarrassment and annoyance due to failure, disappointment, etc. —*vt.* **-grined', -grin'ing** to cause to feel chagrin

chai (chī) *n.* [via an Indian language; ult. < Mandarin *ch'a*, tea] a hot drink of black tea with spices and milk

chain (chān) *n.* [< L *catena*] 1 a flexible series of joined links 2 [*pl.*] *a)* bonds; shackles *b)* captivity 3 a chainlike measuring instrument, as for surveying 4 a series of things connected causally, logically, physically, etc. 5 a number of stores, etc. owned by one company —*vt.* **1** to fasten with chains **2** to restrain

chain gang a gang of prisoners chained together, as when working

chain-link fence (chān′liŋk′) a heavy-duty fence of interwoven steel links

chain reaction 1 a self-sustaining series of chemical or nuclear reactions in which the reaction products keep the process going **2** a series of events, each of which results in the following one

chain-saw *n.* a portable power saw with an endless loop of chain that carries the cutting teeth

chair (cher) *n.* [< L *cathedra*: see CATHE-DRAL] **1** a piece of furniture with a back, for one person to sit on **2** an important or official position **3** a chairperson —*vt.* to preside over as chairperson

chair-lift *n.* a series of seats suspended from a loop of power-driven cable, used to carry skiers up a slope

chair-man (-mən) *n., pl.* **-men** (-mən) a person in charge of a meeting, etc. —**chair′man·ship′** *n.*

chair-per-son *n.* a person in charge of a meeting, etc.

chair-wom-an *n., pl.* **-wom′en** a woman in charge of a meeting, etc.

chaise (shāz) *n.* [Fr] a lightweight carriage, having two or four wheels

chaise longue (lôŋ; *also* lounj) [Fr, lit., long chair] a couchlike chair with a long seat: also **chaise lounge** (lounj)

chal-ced-o-ny (kal sed′n ē) *n.* quartz having a waxy luster and, often, colored bands

cha-let (shal ā′, shal′ā) *n.* [Swiss-Fr] **1** a Swiss house with overhanging eaves **2** any similar building

chal-ice (chal′is) *n.* [< L *calix*, cup] **1** a cup; goblet **2** the cup for Communion wine

chalk (chôk) *n.* [< L *calx*, limestone] **1** a soft, whitish limestone **2** a piece of chalk or chalklike substance used for writing on a blackboard —*adj.* made with chalk —*vt.* to mark or rub with chalk —**chalk up 1** to score, get, or achieve **2** to ascribe —**chalk′i·ness** *n.* —**chalk′y** *adj.* **-i·er, -i·est**

chalk-board *n.* BLACKBOARD

chal-lenge (chal′ənj) *n.* [< L *calumnia*, calumny] **1** a demand for identification **2** a calling into question **3** a call to a duel, contest, etc. **4** anything that calls for special effort —*vt.* **-lenged, -leng·ing** to subject to a challenge —*vi.* to make a challenge —**chal′leng·er** *n.*

chal-lenged *adj.* disabled or handicapped

cham-ber (chām′bər) *n.* [< LL *camera*, a chamber, room] **1** a room, esp. a bedroom **2** [*pl.*] a judge's office near the courtroom **3** an assembly hall **4** a legislative or judicial body **5** a council [*chamber* of commerce] **6** an enclosed compartment; specif. the part of a gun holding a cartridge —**cham′bered** *adj.*

cham-ber-lain (-lin) *n.* [< OHG *chamarlinc*] **1** an officer in charge of the household of a ruler or lord; steward **2** [Brit.] a treasurer

cham-ber-maid *n.* a woman whose work is taking care of bedrooms, as in a hotel

chamber music music for performance by a small group, as a string quartet

chamber of commerce an association established to further the business interests of its community

cham-bray (sham′brā′) *n.* [var. of *cambric*] a smooth fabric of cotton, etc. with white threads woven across a colored warp

cha-me-le-on (kə mēl′ē ən, -mēl′yən) *n.* [< Gr *chamai*, on the ground + *leōn*, LION] any of various lizards that can change the color of their skin

cham-ois (sham′ē) *n., pl.* **-ois** [Fr] **1** a small, goatlike antelope of the mountains of Europe and the Caucasus **2** a soft leather made from the skin of chamois, sheep, deer, etc.: also **cham-my** (sham′ē), *pl.* **-mies**

cham-o-mile (kam′ə mīl′, -mēl′) *n.* alt. sp. of CAMOMILE

champ¹ (champ) *vt.* [prob. echoic] to chew hard and noisily; munch —**champ at the bit** to be impatient when held back

champ² (champ) *n.* [Inf.] CHAMPION (*n.* 2)

cham-pagne (sham pān′) *n.* **1** a sparkling white wine made in the region of Champagne in NE France **2** any of various similar sparkling wines

cham-paign (sham pān′) *n.* [< L *campus*, field] flat, open country

cham-pi-on (cham′pē ən) *n.* [< LL *campio*, gladiator] **1** one who fights for another or for a cause; defender **2** a winner of first place in a competition —*adj.* excelling all others —*vt.* to fight for; defend —**cham′pi·on·ship′** *n.*

chance (chans) *n.* [< L *cadere*, to fall] **1** the happening of events without apparent cause; luck **2** an unpredictable event **3** a risk or gamble **4** a ticket in a lottery **5** an opportunity **6** [*often pl.*] a possibility or probability —*adj.* accidental —*vi.* **chanced, chanc′ing** to have the fortune, good or bad —*vt.* to risk —**by chance** accidentally —**chance on (or upon)** to find or meet by chance —**(the) chances are** the likelihood is —**on the (off) chance** relying on the (remote) possibility

chan-cel (chan′səl) *n.* [< L *cancelli*, lattices] the part of a church around the altar, for the clergy and the choir

chan-cel-ler-y (-sə lər ē) *n., pl.* **-ies** [< ML *cancellaria*] the rank or position of a chancellor

chan-cel-lor (-sə lər) *n.* [< LL *cancellarius*, secretary] **1** a high government official, as, in certain countries, a prime minister **2** in some universities, the president or other executive officer

chan-cer-y (chan′sər ē) *n., pl.* **-ies** [< ML *cancellaria*] **1** a court of equity **2** an office of public archives **3** *R.C.Ch.* the office managing the records and documents of a diocese

chan-cre (shaŋ′kər) *n.* [Fr: see CANCER] a sore or ulcer of syphilis

chanc-y (chan′sē) *adj.* **-i·er, -i·est** risky; uncertain —**chanc′i·ness** *n.*

chan·de·lier (shan′də lir′) *n.* 〚Fr < L *candela*, candle〛 a lighting fixture that is hung from a ceiling, with branches for candles, light bulbs, etc.

chan·dler (chand′lər) *n.* 〚< L *candela*, candle〛 1 a maker of candles 2 a retailer of supplies, as for ships

Chang (chäŋ) river in central China, flowing into the East China Sea: former transliteration YANGTZE

change (chānj) *vt.* **changed**, **chang′ing** 〚< L *cambire*, to barter〛 1 to put or take (a thing) in place of something else [to *change* jobs] 2 to exchange [to *change* seats] 3 to make different; alter —*vi.* 1 to alter; vary 2 to leave one train, plane, etc. and board another 3 to put on other clothes —*n.* 1 a substitution, alteration, or variation 2 variety 3 another set of clothes 4 *a)* money returned as the difference between the price and the greater sum presented *b)* coins or bills that together equal a single larger coin or bill *c)* small coins —**change off** to take turns —**ring the changes** to ring a set of bells with all possible variations —**change′a·ble** *adj.* —**change′less** *adj.*

change·ling (-liŋ) *n.* a child secretly put in the place of another, as, in folk tales, by fairies

change of life MENOPAUSE

change·o·ver *n.* a complete change, as in goods produced

chan·nel (chan′əl) *n.* 〚see CANAL〛 1 the bed or deeper part of a river, harbor, etc. 2 a body of water joining two larger ones 3 any means of passage 4 [*pl.*] the official course of transmission of communications 5 a groove or furrow 6 a frequency band assigned to a radio or television station 7 an ongoing program of audio or video content, esp. on television —*vt.* **-neled** or **-nelled**, **-nel·ing** or **-nel·ling** 1 to make a channel in 2 to send through a channel

Channel Islands group of British islands in the English Channel

chan·nel·ize (-īz′) *vt.* **-ized′**, **-iz′ing** to provide a channel for

chan·son (shän sôn′) *n.*, *pl.* **-sons′** (-sôn′) 〚Fr〛 a song

chant (chant) *n.* 〚< L *cantare*, to sing〛 1 a song; esp., a liturgical song with a free rhythm, sung in unison without accompaniment 2 a singsong way of speaking 3 a phrase, slogan, etc. called out rhythmically and repeatedly — *vi.*, *vt.* to sing or say in a chant —**chant′er** *n.*

chan·teuse (shän tööz′) *n.* 〚Fr〛 a woman singer, esp. of popular ballads

chan·tey (shan′tē, chan′-) *n.*, *pl.* **-teys** a song formerly sung by sailors while working

chan·ti·cleer (chan′ti klir′) *n.* 〚< OFr *chantecler*, lit., sing loud〛 a rooster

Cha·nu·ka or **Cha·nu·kah** (khä′noo kä′, -kə; hä′-) *n.* HANUKKAH

cha·os (kā′äs′) *n.* 〚< Gr, space〛 extreme confusion or disorder —**cha·ot·ic** (kā ät′ik) *adj.*

chap¹ (chap) *n.* 〚< Brit *chapman*, peddler〛 [Inf.] a man; fellow

chap² (chap) *vt.*, *vi.* **chapped**, **chap′ping** 〚ME *chappen*, cut〛 to crack open; split; roughen, as skin —*n.* a chapped place in the skin

chap³ *abbrev.* 1 chaplain 2 chapter

chap·ar·ral (shap′ə ral′, chap′-) *n.* 〚Sp < *chaparro*, evergreen oak〛 [Southwest] a thicket of shrubs, etc.

cha·peau (sha pō′) *n.*, *pl.* **-peaus′** or **-peaux′** (-pōz′) 〚Fr〛 a hat

chap·el (chap′əl) *n.* 〚< ML *cappella*, dim. of *cappa*, cape〛 1 a small church 2 a private place of worship, as in a hospital 3 a religious service

chap·er·one or **chap·er·on** (shap′ər ōn′, shap′ər ōn′) *n.* 〚< OFr, hood〛 one who accompanies young, unmarried people to supervise their behavior, as at dances — *vt.*, *vi.* **-oned′**, **-on′ing** to act as chaperone (to)

chap·lain (chap′lən) *n.* 〚see CHAPEL〛 1 a clergyman attached to a chapel 2 a clergyman serving in a religious capacity with the armed forces, or in a prison, hospital, etc.

chap·let (chap′lit) *n.* 〚< LL *cappa*, cape〛 1 a garland for the head 2 a string of beads, esp. prayer beads

chaps (chaps, shaps) *pl.n.* 〚< MexSp *chaparreras*〛 leather trousers without a seat, worn over ordinary trousers, as by cowboys to protect their legs

chap·ter (chap′tər) *n.* 〚< L *caput*, head〛 1 a main division, as of a book 2 a local branch of an organization

chapter book a book divided into chapters, intended for very young readers

chapter house *n.* a fraternity or sorority house

char (chär) *vt.*, *vi.* **charred**, **char′ring** 〚< CHARCOAL〛 1 to reduce to charcoal by burning 2 to burn slightly; scorch

char·ac·ter (kar′ik tər) *n.* 〚< Gr *charassein*, engrave〛 1 any letter, figure, or symbol used in writing and printing 2 a distinctive trait, quality, etc.; characteristic 3 kind or sort 4 behavior typical of a person or group 5 moral strength 6 reputation 7 status; position 8 a person in a play, novel, etc. 9 [Inf.] an eccentric person

char·ac·ter·is·tic (-is′tik) *adj.* typical; distinctive —*n.* a distinguishing trait or quality —**char′ac·ter·is′ti·cal·ly** *adv.*

char·ac·ter·ize (-īz′) *vt.* **-ized′**, **-iz′ing** 1 to describe the particular traits of 2 to be a characteristic of —**char′ac·ter·i·za′tion** *n.*

cha·rade (shə räd′) *n.* 〚Fr < Prov *charrar*, to gossip〛 1 [*pl.*] a game in which words to be guessed are pantomimed, often syllable by syllable 2 an obvious pretense or fiction

char·broil or **char-broil** (chär′broil′) *vt.* to broil over a charcoal fire

char·coal (chär′kōl′) *n.* 〚ME *char cole*〛 1 a dark, porous form of carbon made by partially burning wood in a kiln, etc. with very little oxygen: used for fuel, etc. 2 a very dark gray or brown

chard (chärd) *n.* 〚< L *carduus*, thistle〛 a kind of beet with edible leaves and stalks

char·don·nay (shär′də nā′) *n.* [*also* C–] a dry white wine

charge (chärj) *vt.* **charged, charg′ing** [ult. < L *carrus*, wagon] **1** to load or fill (*with* something) **2** to add an electrical charge to (a battery, etc.) **3** to give as a duty, command, etc. to **4** to accuse **5** to make liable for (an error, etc.) **6** to ask as a price **7** to record as a debt **8** to pay for by using a credit card **9** to attack vigorously —*vi.* **1** to ask payment (*for*) **2** to attack vigorously —*n.* **1** a load or burden **2** the necessary quantity, as of fuel, for a container or device **3** the amount of chemical energy stored in a battery **4** a cartridge or shell, or the amount of gunpowder needed to discharge a gun, etc. **5** responsibility or care (*of*) **6** a person or thing entrusted to someone's care **7** instruction; command **8** accusation; indictment **9** cost **10** a debt, debit, or expense **11** an onslaught **12** the signal for an attack —**in charge (of)** having the responsibility, control, or supervision (of) —**charge′a·ble** *adj.*

charge account an arrangement by which a customer may pay for purchases within a specified future period

charge card a thin, flat, plastic card embossed with the owner's name, account number, etc., used when charging purchases

charg·er *n.* **1** a person or thing that charges **2** a horse ridden in battle **3** a device used to charge storage batteries

char·grill (chär′gril′) *vt.* to grill (meat) over a charcoal fire, etc.

char·i·ly (cher′ə lē, char′-) *adv.* cautiously —**char′i·ness** *n.*

char·i·ot (char′ē ət) *n.* [see CAR] a horse-drawn, two-wheeled cart used in ancient times for war, racing, etc. —**char′i·ot·eer′** (-ə tir′) *n.*

cha·ris·ma (kə riz′mə) *n.* [< Gr, favor, grace] a special quality in one that inspires devotion or fascination

char·is·mat·ic (kar′iz mat′ik) *adj.* **1** of or having charisma **2** designating or of a religious group that stresses direct divine inspiration, manifested as in glossolalia, etc. —*n.* a member of a charismatic group

char·i·ta·ble (char′i tə bəl) *adj.* **1** generous to the needy **2** of or for charity **3** kind and forgiving; lenient —**char′i·ta·bly** *adv.*

char·i·ty (char′i tē) *n., pl.* **-ties** [< L *caritas*, affection] **1** *Christian Theol.* love for one's fellow humans **2** leniency in judging others **3** *a*) generosity toward the needy *b*) help so given **4** a welfare institution, fund, etc.

char·la·tan (shär′lə tən) *n.* [ult. < VL *cerretanus*, seller of papal indulgences] a fraud; quack

Char·le·magne (shär′lə mān′) A.D. 742-814; king of the Franks (768-814): emperor of the Holy Roman Empire (800-814)

Charles·ton[1] (chärls′tən) *n.* [< fol.] a lively dance of the 1920s

Charles·ton[2] (chärls′tən) capital of West Virginia, in the W part

char·ley horse (chär′lē) [Inf.] a cramp in a muscle, esp. a thigh muscle

Char·lotte (shär′lət) city in S North Carolina

Char·lotte·town (shär′lət toun′) capital of Prince Edward Island, Canada

charm (chärm) *n.* [< L *carmen*] **1** an action, object, or words assumed to have magic power **2** a trinket worn on a bracelet, etc. **3** a quality that attracts or delights **4** *Particle Physics* a property of certain quarks — *vt., vi.* **1** to act on as if by magic **2** to fascinate; delight —**charm′er** *n.* —**charm′ing** *adj.* —**charm′ing·ly** *adv.*

char·meuse (shär mōōz′, -mōōs′) *n.* [Fr < *charmer*, to bewitch] a smooth fabric of silk or polyester

char·nel (house) (chär′nəl) *n.* [< LL *carnale*, graveyard] a building or place where corpses or bones are deposited

Cha·ron (ker′ən) *n. Gr. Myth.* the ferryman on the river Styx

chart (chärt) *n.* [< Gr *chartēs*, layer of papyrus] **1** a map, esp. for use in navigation **2** a table, graph, etc. —*vt.* **1** to make a chart of **2** to plan (a course of action)

char·ter (chärt′ər) *n.* [see prec.] **1** a franchise granted by a government **2** a written statement of basic laws or principles; constitution **3** written permission to form a local chapter or lodge of a society **4** the hire or lease of an airplane, bus, etc. —*vt.* **1** to grant a charter to **2** to hire for exclusive use

charter member a founder or original member

charter school a publicly-funded alternative school founded on a charter with the government

char·treuse (shär trōōz′, -trōōs′) *n.* [Fr] pale, yellowish green

char·wom·an (chär′woom′ən) *n., pl.* **-wom′en** [see CHORE] a cleaning woman

char·y (cher′ē, char′ē) *adj.* **-i·er, -i·est** [< OE *cearig*, sorrowful] **1** careful; cautious **2** sparing

chase[1] (chās) *vt.* **chased, chas′ing** [ult. < L *capere*, to take] **1** to follow so as to catch **2** to run after; pursue **3** to drive away **4** to hunt —*vi.* **1** to go in pursuit **2** [Inf.] to rush —*n.* **1** a chasing; pursuit **2** the hunting of game —**give chase** to pursue

chase[2] (chās) *vt.* **chased, chas′ing** [< OFr *enchasser*] to ornament (metal) as by engraving

chas·er *n.* **1** one that chases or hunts; pursuer **2** a mild drink, as water, taken after whiskey, etc.

chasm (kaz′əm) *n.* [< Gr *chasma*] **1** a deep crack in the earth's surface; abyss **2** any break or gap

chas·sis (chas′ē, shas′ē) *n., pl.* **-sis′** (-ēz′) [Fr] **1** the frame, wheels, engine, etc. of a motor vehicle, but not the body **2** *a*) a frame, as for the parts of a TV set *b*) the assembled frame and parts

chaste (chāst) *adj.* [< L *castus*, pure] **1** not indulging in unlawful sexual activity; virtuous **2**

decent; modest **3** simple in style; not ornate —**chaste′ly** *adv.*

chas·ten (chās′ən) *vt.* ⟦< L *castigare*, punish⟧ **1** to punish so as to correct **2** to restrain or subdue

chas·tise (chas tīz′, chas′tīz′) *vt.* **-tised′, -tis′ing** ⟦see prec.⟧ **1** to punish, esp. by beating **2** to scold sharply —**chas·tise′ment** *n.* —**chas·tis′er** *n.*

chas·ti·ty (chas′tə tē) *n.* a being chaste; specif., *a)* adherence to rules of sexual morality *b)* sexual abstinence *c)* simplicity of style

chas·u·ble (chaz′ə bəl, chas′-) *n.* ⟦< ML *casula*⟧ a sleeveless outer vestment worn by priests at Mass

chat (chat) *vi.* **chat′ted, chat′ting** ⟦< CHATTER⟧ **1** to talk in a light, informal manner **2** *Comput.* to hold a real-time electronic conversation by exchanging typed messages —*n.* **1** light, informal talk **2** *Comput.* the act or an instance of chatting by means of typed messages

châ·teau (sha tō′) *n.,* *pl.* **-teaux′** (-tōz′, -tō′) or **-teaus′** ⟦Fr < L *castellum*, castle⟧ **1** a French feudal castle **2** a large country house and estate, esp. in France Also **cha·teau′**

chat·e·laine (shat′′l ān′) *n.* ⟦Fr⟧ **1** the mistress of a château **2** a woman's ornamental chain or clasp

chat·tel (chat′′l) *n.* ⟦see CATTLE⟧ **1** a movable item of personal property, as furniture **2** a person considered another's property

chat·ter (chat′ər) *vi.* ⟦echoic⟧ **1** to make short, rapid, indistinct sounds, as squirrels do **2** to talk much and foolishly **3** to click together rapidly, as teeth do from cold —*n.* **1** a chattering **2** foolish talk —**chat′ter·er** *n.*

chat·ter·box *n.* an incessant talker

chat·ty (chat′ē) *adj.* **-ti·er, -ti·est** fond of chatting —**chat′ti·ness** *n.*

Chau·cer (chô′sər), **Geof·frey** (jef′rē) 1340?-1400; Eng. poet

chauf·feur (shō′fər, shō fur′) *n.* ⟦Fr, lit., stoker⟧ one hired to drive a private automobile for someone else —*vt.* to act as chauffeur to

chau·vin·ism (shō′vin iz′əm) *n.* ⟦after N. *Chauvin*, fanatical Fr patriot⟧ **1** militant and boastful patriotism; jingoism **2** unreasoning and boastful devotion to one's race, sex, etc. —**chau′vin·ist** *n., adj.* —**chau′vin·is′tic** *adj.* —**chau′vin·is′ti·cal·ly** *adv.*

cheap (chēp) *adj.* ⟦ult. < L *caupo*, tradesman⟧ **1** low in price **2** worth more than the price **3** easily gotten [a *cheap* victory] **4** of little value **5** contemptible **6** [Inf.] stingy —*adv.* at a low cost —**cheap′ly** *adv.* —**cheap′ness** *n.*

cheap·en *vt., vi.* to make or become cheap or cheaper

cheap shot [Slang] an unnecessarily hurtful action or remark

cheap·skate *n.* [Slang] a stingy person

cheat (chēt) *n.* ⟦< L *ex-*, out + *cadere*, to fall⟧ **1** a fraud; swindle **2** a swindler —*vt.* **1** to defraud; swindle **2** to foil, deprive, or elude [to *cheat* death] —*vi.* **1** to be dishonest or deceitful **2** [Slang] to be sexually unfaithful: often with *on* —**cheat′er** *n.*

check (chek) *n.* ⟦< OFr *eschec*, a check in chess⟧ **1** a sudden stop **2** any restraint **3** one that restrains **4** a supervision or test of accuracy, etc. **5** a mark (✓) to show verification **6** an identification ticket, token, etc. [a hat *check*] **7** one's bill at a restaurant or bar **8** a written order to a bank to pay a sum of money **9** a pattern of squares **10** *Chess* the state of a king that is in danger **11** *Hockey* a bumping of an opponent —*interj.* [Inf.] agreed! right! —*vt.* **1** to stop suddenly **2** to restrain; curb; block **3** to test, verify, etc. by examination or comparison: often with *out* **4** to mark with a check (✓): often with *off* **5** to mark with a pattern of squares **6** to deposit temporarily, as in a checkroom **7** to clear (esp. luggage) for shipment **8** *Chess* to place (the opponent's king) in check **9** *Hockey* to bump (an opponent) —*vi.* **1** to agree with one another, item for item: often with *out* **2** to investigate or verify: often with *on, up on* —**check in 1** to register at a hotel, etc. **2** [Inf.] to present oneself, as at work —**check out 1** to pay and leave a hotel, etc. **2** to add up the prices of (items selected) for payment **3** to prove to be accurate, in good condition, etc. —**in check** under control —**check′er** *n.*

check·book *n.* a book of detachable forms for writing bank checks

checked (chekt) *adj.* having a pattern of squares

check·er·board *n.* a square board with 64 squares of two alternating colors, used in checkers and chess

check·ered (chek′ərd) *adj.* **1** having a pattern of squares **2** marked by varied features, often specif. dishonorable acts [a *checkered* career]

check·ers (-ərz) *n.* **1** a game for two played with flat disks on a checkerboard **2** the disks

checking account a bank account against which the depositor can draw checks

check·list *n.* a list of things, names, etc. to be referred to: also **check list**

check·mate *n.* ⟦ult. < Pers *shāh māt*, the king is dead⟧ **1** *Chess a)* the move that wins the game by checking the opponent's king so that it cannot be protected *b)* the condition of the king after this move **2** total defeat, frustration, etc. —*vt.* **-mat′ed, -mat′ing 1** *Chess* to place in checkmate **2** to defeat; thwart

check·out *n.* **1** the act or place of checking out purchases **2** the act of checking out of a hotel, etc.

check·point *n.* a place on a road, etc. where traffic is inspected

check·room *n.* a room in which hats, coats, etc. may be left until called for

check·up *n.* an examination, esp. a medical one

ched·dar (cheese) (ched′ər) *n.* ⟦after *Cheddar*, England⟧ [often C-] a firm, smooth cheese

cheek (chēk) *n.* ⟦OE *ceoke*, jaw⟧ **1** either side

of the face below the eye **2** either of the buttocks **3** [Inf.] sauciness; impudence

cheek·bone *n.* the bone across the upper cheek, just below the eye

cheek·y *adj.* **-i·er, -i·est** [Inf.] saucy; impudent —**cheek′i·ness** *n.*

cheep (chēp) *n.* ⟦echoic⟧ the short, shrill sound made by a young bird — *vt., vi.* to make, or utter with, this sound —**cheep′er** *n.*

cheer (chir) *n.* ⟦< Gr *kara*, the head⟧ **1** state of mind or of feeling; spirit [be of good *cheer*] **2** gladness; joy **3** festive entertainment **4** encouragement **5** *a*) a glad, excited shout to urge on, greet, etc. *b*) a rallying cry, etc. —*vt.* **1** to gladden; comfort: often with *up* **2** to urge on, greet, or applaud with cheers —*vi.* **1** to become cheerful: usually with *up* **2** to shout cheers

cheer·ful *adj.* **1** full of cheer; joyful **2** bright and attractive **3** willing; ready [a *cheerful* helper] —**cheer′ful·ly** *adv.* —**cheer′ful·ness** *n.*

cheer·i·o (-ē ō′) *interj.* [Brit. Inf.] **1** goodbye **2** good health: used as a toast

cheer·lead (-lēd′) *vi., vi.* to act as a cheerleader (for) —**cheer′lead′ing** *n.*

cheer·lead·er *n.* a leader of cheers, as at football games

cheer·less *adj.* not cheerful; dismal; dreary —**cheer′less·ly** *adv.* —**cheer′less·ness** *n.*

cheers (chirz) *interj.* good health: used as a toast

cheer·y *adj.* **-i·er, -i·est** cheerful; bright —**cheer′i·ly** *adv.* —**cheer′i·ness** *n.*

cheese (chēz) *n.* ⟦OE *cyse*⟧ a solid food made from milk curds

cheese·burg·er *n.* a hamburger topped with melted cheese

cheese·cake *n.* **1** a cake made with cottage cheese or cream cheese **2** [Inf.] photographic display of the figure, esp. the legs, of a pretty woman

cheese·cloth *n.* ⟦from its use for straining curds to make cheese⟧ a thin cotton cloth with a very loose weave

cheese·steak *n.* a sandwich of sautéed beef slices, onion, green pepper, and melted cheese, on a long roll

chees·y *adj.* **-i·er, -i·est 1** like cheese **2** [Slang] inferior; poor

chee·tah (chēt′ə) *n.* ⟦Hindi < Sans *chitraka*, spotted⟧ a swift cat of Africa and SW Asia, with long legs and a spotted coat

chef (shef) *n.* ⟦Fr, head, chief⟧ **1** a head cook **2** any cook

Che·khov (chek′ôf), **An·ton** (än tôn′) 1860-1904; Russ. writer

chem *abbrev.* **1** chemical(s) **2** chemistry

chem·i·cal (kem′i kəl) *adj.* **1** of, made by, or used in chemistry **2** made with or operated by chemicals **3** of or involving a drug, alcohol, etc. [*chemical* dependency] —*n.* **1** any substance used in or obtained by a chemical process **2** [Slang] a drug, alcoholic beverage, etc. —**chem′i·cal·ly** *adv.*

chemical engineering the science or profession of applying chemistry to industrial uses —**chemical engineer**

chemical warfare warfare by means of poisonous gases, etc.

che·mise (shə mēz′) *n.* ⟦< LL *camisia*, tunic⟧ **1** a woman's loose, short slip **2** a straight, loose dress

chem·ist (kem′ist) *n.* ⟦ult. < Ar < ? Gr *cheein*, to pour⟧ **1** a specialist in chemistry **2** [Brit.] a pharmacist

chem·is·try (kem′is trē) *n.* [< prec.] **1** the science dealing with the composition and properties of substances, and with the reactions by which substances are produced from or converted into other substances **2** [Inf.] rapport

che·mo (kē′mō) *n.* [Inf.] *short for* CHEMOTHERAPY

chemo- *combining form* of, with, or by chemicals: also, before a vowel, **chem-**

che·mo·ther·a·py (kē′mō-) *n.* the use of drugs to prevent or treat a disease

chem·ur·gy (kem′ər jē) *n.* chemistry dealing with the use of organic, esp. farm, products in industrial manufacture

che·nille (shə nēl′) *n.* ⟦Fr, lit., caterpillar⟧ **1** a tufted, velvety yarn **2** a fabric filled or woven with this

cheque (chek) *n.* Brit. *sp. of* CHECK (*n.* 8)

cher·ish (cher′ish) *vt.* [< L *carus*, dear] **1** to feel or show love for **2** to protect; foster **3** to cling to the idea or feeling of

Cher·o·kee (cher′ə kē′) *n., pl.* **-kees′** or **-kee′** a member of a North American Indian people now chiefly of Oklahoma and North Carolina

che·root (shə rōōt′) *n.* [< Tamil] a cigar with both ends cut square

cher·ry (cher′ē) *n., pl.* **-ries** [< Gr *kerasion*] **1** a small, fleshy fruit with a smooth, hard pit **2** the tree that bears this fruit **3** the wood of this tree **4** a bright red color —*adj.* bright-red

chert (churt) *n.* a very dense type of quartz, including jasper and flint

cher·ub (cher′əb) *n., pl.* **-ubs**; for 1 usually **-u·bim′** (-yōō bim′, -ə bim′) or **-u·bims′** ⟦< Heb *kerūbh*⟧ **1** an angel depicted as a chubby, rosy-faced child with wings **2** a child having a sweet, innocent face —**che·ru·bic** (chə rōō′bik) *adj.*

cher·vil (chur′vəl) *n.* [< Gr *chairephyllon*] an herb like parsley, with leaves used to flavor salads, soups, etc.

Ches·a·peake Bay (ches′ə pēk′) arm of the Atlantic, extending into Virginia and Maryland

chess (ches) *n.* [< OFr *eschec*, a check in chess] a game played on a chessboard by two players, using a variety of pieces (**chess′men**)

chess·board *n.* a checkerboard used for chess

chest (chest) *n.* [< Gr *kistē*, a box] **1** a box with a lid **2** a cabinet with drawers, as for clothes **3** a cabinet with shelves, as for medicines **4** the part of the body enclosed by the ribs, breastbone, and diaphragm

ches·ter·field (ches′tər fēld′) *n.* ⟦after a 19th-c. Earl of *Chesterfield*⟧ **1** a single-breasted topcoat, usually with a velvet collar **2** [Chiefly Cdn.] a sofa

chest·nut (ches'nut') *n.* [< Gr *kastaneia*] 1 the edible nut of various trees of the beech family 2 such a tree, or its wood 3 reddish brown 4 a reddish-brown horse 5 [Inf.] an old, stale joke, story, etc. —*adj.* reddish-brown

chev·i·ot (shev'ē ət; *also* chev'ē ət) *n.* [after *Cheviot* Hills, on the Scottish-English border] [*sometimes* C-] a rough, twilled wool fabric

chèvre or **che·vre** (shev'ē) (shev'rə) *n.* a soft cheese made from goat's milk

chev·ron (shev'rən) *n.* [< OFr, rafter] a V-shaped bar on the sleeve of a uniform, showing rank

chew (chōō) *vt., vi.* [OE *ceowan*] to bite and crush with the teeth —*n.* 1 a chewing 2 something chewed or for chewing —**chew'er** *n.* —**chew'y** *adj.* -i·er, -i·est

chewing gum a gummy substance, as chicle, flavored for chewing

Chey·enne¹ (shi an', -en') *n., pl.* -**ennes'** or -**enne'** a member of a North American Indian people now chiefly of Oklahoma

Chey·enne² (shi an', -en') capital of Wyoming, in the SE part

chg(d) *abbrev.* charge(d)

chi (kī, kē) *n.* the 22d letter of the Greek alphabet (X, χ)

Chi·an·ti (kē än'tē, -an'-) *n.* [It] [*also* c-] a dry red wine

chi·a·ro·scu·ro (kē är'ə skoor'ō) *n., pl.* -**ros** [It < L *clarus*, clear + *obscurus*, dark] 1 light and shade in a painting, etc. treated to suggest depth or for effect 2 a style of painting, etc. emphasizing this 3 an artwork in which this is used

chic (shēk) *n.* [Fr < medieval LowG *schick*, skill] smart elegance of style —*adj.* pleasingly stylish —**chic'ness** *n.*

Chi·ca·go (shə kä'gō, -kô'-) city and port in NE Illinois

Chi·ca·na (chi kä'nə) *n.* a woman or girl who is a U.S. citizen or inhabitant of Mexican descent

chi·can·er·y (shi kän'ər ē) *n., pl.* -**ies** [< Fr] 1 trickery 2 a trick

Chi·ca·no (chi kä'nō) *n., pl.* -**nos** [< AmSp] a U.S. citizen or inhabitant of Mexican descent

chi·chi or **chi·chi** (shē'shē) *adj.* [Fr] extremely chic, specif. in a showy way

chick (chik) *n.* [ME *chike*] 1 a young chicken or bird 2 [Slang] a young woman: now often dismissive

chick·a·dee (chik'ə dē') *n.* [echoic] any of various titmice

chick·en (chik'ən) *n.* [< OE *cycen*] 1 a common farm bird raised for its edible eggs or flesh; hen or rooster, esp. a young one 2 its flesh 3 [Slang] a cowardly person —*adj.* [Slang] cowardly —*vi.* [Slang] to quit from fear: usually *with out*

chicken feed [Slang] a small sum of money

chick·en-fried *adj.* coated with seasoned flour or batter and fried

chick·en-heart·ed *adj.* cowardly; timid: also **chick'en-liv'ered**

chick·en·pox *n.* an acute, contagious viral disease, esp. of children, characterized by skin eruptions

chicken wire light, pliable wire fencing

chick·weed *n.* a low-growing plant often found as a weed in lawns, etc.

chic·le (chik'əl) *n.* [AmSp] a gumlike substance from a tropical American tree, used in chewing gum

chic·ly (shek'lē) *adv.* in a chic way

chic·o·ry (chik'ə rē) *n., pl.* -**ries** [< Gr *kichora*] 1 a plant usually with blue flowers: the leaves are used for salad 2 its root, ground for mixing with coffee or for use as a coffee substitute

chide (chīd) *vt., vi.* **chid'ed** or **chid** (chid), **chid'ed** or **chid** or **chid·den** (chid'n), **chid'ing** [OE *cidan*] to reprove mildly —**chid'ing·ly** *adv.*

chief (chēf) *n.* [< L *caput*, head] a leader; head —*adj.* main; principal

chief·ly *adv.* 1 most of all 2 mainly —*adj.* of or like a chief

chief·tain (-tən) *n.* [< L *caput*, head] a chief, esp. of a clan or tribe

chif·fon (shi fän') *n.* [Fr] a sheer, silky fabric —*adj.* 1 of chiffon 2 made fluffy as with beaten egg whites [lemon *chiffon* pie]

chif·fo·nier (shif'ə nir') *n.* [Fr] a high chest of drawers, often with a mirror

chig·ger (chig'ər) *n.* [of Afr orig.] the tiny, red larva of certain mites, whose bite causes severe itching

chi·gnon (shēn'yän') *n.* [Fr < L *catena*, chain] a coil of hair worn at the back of the neck

Chi·hua·hua¹ (chi wä'wä) *n.* [after fol.] a Mexican breed of very small dog with large, pointed ears

Chi·hua·hua² (chi wä'wä) state of N Mexico, on the U.S. border

chil·blain (chil'blān') *n.* [CHIL(L) + *blain* < OE *blegen*, a sore] a painful swelling, esp. on the fingers or toes, caused by exposure to cold

child (chīld) *n., pl.* **chil'dren** [OE *cild*] 1 an infant 2 a boy or girl before puberty 3 a son or daughter; offspring —**with child** pregnant —**child'hood'** *n.* —**child'less** *adj.*

child·birth *n.* the act of giving birth to a child

child·ish *adj.* of or like a child; specif., immature, silly, etc. —**child'ish·ly** *adv.* —**child'ish·ness** *n.*

child·like *adj.* of or like a child; specif., innocent, trusting, etc.

chil·dren (chil'drən) *n. pl. of* CHILD

child's play any very simple task

Chi·le (chil'ē) country on the SW coast of South America —**Chil·e·an** ('i lā'ən, 'il'ē ən) *adj., n.*

chi·le re·lle·no (chē'le re yä'nō) *pl.* **chi·les re·lle·nos** (chē'les re yä'nōs) [MexSp] a hot, green pepper stuffed with cheese, meat, etc. and fried

chil·i (chil'ē) *n., pl.* -**ies** or -**is** [MexSp] 1 the very hot, dried pod of red pepper, often ground with other ingredients for use as a seasoning (**chili powder**) 2 any of certain other peppers used in Mexican cooking **3** a highly spiced dish of beef, chilies or chili powder, and often beans and tomatoes: in full **chil′i con car′ne** (-kän kär′nē) Also **chil′e**

chili dog a hot dog served with chili con carne

chili sauce a spiced sauce of chopped tomatoes, sweet peppers, onions, etc.

chill (chil) *n.* ⟦< OE *ciele*⟧ **1** coldness or coolness causing shivers **2** a moderate coldness **3** a sudden fear, etc. **4** unfriendliness —*adj.* CHILLY —*vi.* **1** to become cold **2** to shake or shiver **3** [Slang] to relax or calm down: usually with *out* —*vt.* **1** to make cool or cold **2** to cause a chill in **3** to check (enthusiasm, etc.)

chill factor WINDCHILL FACTOR

chill·y *adj.* **-i·er, -i·est 1** moderately cold **2** unfriendly —**chill′i·ness** *n.*

chime (chīm) *n.* ⟦< Gr *kymbalon*, cymbal⟧ **1** [*usually pl.*] *a*) a set of tuned bells or metal tubes *b*) the musical sounds made by these **2** a single bell, as in a clock —*vi.* **chimed, chim′ ing 1** to sound as a chime or bells **2** to agree —*vt.* to give (the time) by chiming —**chime in 1** to join in **2** to agree —**chim′er** *n.*

Chi·me·ra (kī mir′ə, ki-) *n.* ⟦< Gr *chimaira*, orig., she-goat⟧ **1** *Gr. Myth.* a monster having a lion's head, goat's body, and serpent's tail **2** [**c-**] an impossible fancy

chi·mer·i·cal (-mer′i kəl) *adj.* **1** imaginary; unreal **2** fanciful

chim·ney (chim′nē) *n., pl.* **-neys** ⟦ult. < Gr *kaminos*, oven⟧ **1** the passage or structure through which smoke escapes from a fireplace, furnace, etc., usually extending above the roof **2** a glass tube around the flame of a lamp **3** a crevice extending up a cliff face

chim·pan·zee (chim′pan zē′, chim pan′zē) *n.* ⟦< Bantu⟧ a medium-sized great ape of Africa: also [Inf.] **chimp** (chimp)

chin (chin) *n.* ⟦OE *cin*⟧ the part of the face below the lower lip —*vt.* **chinned, chin′ning** to pull (oneself) up, while hanging by the hands from a bar, until the chin is just above the bar

Chin *abbrev.* Chinese

chi·na (chī′nə) *n.* ⟦orig. made in China⟧ **1** porcelain or any ceramic ware like porcelain **2** dishes, etc. made of china **3** any earthenware Also **chi′na·ware′**

Chi·na (chī′nə) country in E Asia

chin·chil·la (chin chil′ə) *n.* ⟦prob. dim. of Sp *chinche*, a small bug⟧ **1** a small rodent of South America **2** its soft, gray fur

chine (chīn) *n.* ⟦< OFr *eschine*, spine⟧ a cut of meat from the backbone

Chi·nese (chī nēz′, -nēs′) *n.* **1** *pl.* **-nese′** a person born or living in China **2** the standard language of China, any related language of China, or the group consisting of these languages —*adj.* of China or its people, language, etc.

Chinese checkers a game in which marbles are moved as checkers, on a board with holes arranged in the shape of a six-pointed star

Chinese lantern a paper lantern that can be folded up

chink¹ (chiŋk) *n.* ⟦OE *chine*⟧ a crack —*vt.* to close up the chinks in

chink² (chiŋk) *n.* ⟦echoic⟧ a sharp, clinking sound —*vi., vt.* to make or cause to make this sound

chi·no (chē′nō, shē′-) *n., pl.* **-nos** ⟦< ?⟧ **1** a strong, twilled cotton, khaki cloth **2** [*pl.*] pants of chino for casual wear

Chi·nook (shə nook′, -nook′; chə-) *n., pl.* **-nooks′** or **-nook′** ⟦< AmInd name⟧ a member of a North American Indian people of Washington and Oregon

chinook salmon a large salmon of the N Pacific and nearby waters

chintz (chints) *n.* ⟦< Hindi *chhint*⟧ a cotton cloth printed in colored designs and usually glazed

chintz·y (-ē) *adj.* **-i·er, -i·est** ⟦prec. + -Y³⟧ **1** like chintz **2** [Inf.] cheap, stingy, etc.

chin-up *n.* PULL-UP

chip (chip) *vt.* **chipped, chip′ping** ⟦< OE⟧ to break or cut off small pieces from —*vi.* **1** to break off in small pieces **2** *Golf* to make a short, lofted shot (**chip shot**) —*n.* **1** a small piece of wood, etc. cut or broken off **2** a place where a small piece has been chipped off **3** a small disk used in gambling games as a counter **4** a thin slice of food (a potato *chip*) **5** INTEGRATED CIRCUIT —**chip in** [Inf.] to contribute (money, etc.) —**chip on one's shoulder** [Inf.] an inclination to fight or quarrel

chip·munk (-muŋk′) *n.* ⟦< AmInd⟧ a small, striped North American squirrel

chipped beef dried or smoked beef sliced into shavings

chip·per¹ (chip′ər) *adj.* ⟦< N Brit Dial.⟧ [Inf.] sprightly; in good spirits

chip·per² *n.* a person or thing that chips, esp. a tool or machine for chipping

chiro- ⟦< Gr *cheir*, hand⟧ *combining form* hand

chi·rog·ra·phy (kī räg′rə fē) *n.* ⟦prec. + -GRAPHY⟧ handwriting

chi·rop·o·dy (kī räp′ə dē) *n.* ⟦CHIRO- + -POD + -Y⁴⟧ PODIATRY —**chi·rop′o·dist** *n.*

chi·ro·prac·tic (kī′rō prak′tik) *n.* ⟦< CHIRO- + Gr *praktikos*, practical⟧ a method of treating disease by manipulation of the body joints, esp. of the spine —**chi′ro·prac′tor** *n.*

chirp (churp) *vi., vt.* ⟦echoic⟧ to make, or utter in, short, shrill tones, as some birds do —*n.* this sound

chir·rup (chir′əp) *vi.* ⟦< prec.⟧ to chirp repeatedly —*n.* a chirruping sound

chis·el (chiz′əl) *n.* ⟦< L *caedere*, to cut⟧ a sharp-edged hand tool for cutting or shaping wood, stone, etc. —*vi., vt.* **-eled** or **-elled, -el·ing** or **-el·ling 1** to cut or shape with a chisel **2** [Inf.] to swindle or get by swindling —**chis′el·er** *n.*, **chis′el·ler**

chit (chit) *n.* ⟦< Hindi⟧ **1** a voucher of a small sum owed for drink, food, etc. **2** a token, etc. that may be exchanged as for food and drink

chit·chat (chit′chat′) *n.* ⟦< CHAT⟧ **1** light, informal talk **2** gossip

chi·tin (kī′tin) *n.* ⟦< Gr *chitōn*, tunic⟧ the tough, horny outer covering of insects, crustaceans, etc.

chi·ton (kī′tən) *n.* ⟦Gr *chitōn*, tunic⟧ a small

marine mollusk with a dorsal shell of eight plates

chit·ter·lings, chit·lins, or **chit·lings** (chit′linz) *pl.n.* [< Gmc base] small intestines of pigs, used for food

chiv·al·rous (shiv′əl rəs) *adj.* 1 gallant, courteous, etc. like an ideal knight 2 of chivalry Also **chiv·al·ric′** (-rik′, shi val′rik) —**chiv′al·rous·ly** *adv.*

chiv·al·ry (-rē) *n.* [< OFr *chevaler,* knight < *cheval,* horse] 1 medieval knighthood 2 the qualities of an ideal knight, as courage, honor, etc.

chives (chīvz) *pl.n.* [< L *cepa,* onion] [*sometimes with sing. v.*] an herb with slender, hollow leaves and a mild onion odor, used for flavoring

chla·myd·i·a (klə mid′ē ə) *n.* a widespread venereal disease

chlo·ral (hydrate) (klôr′əl) a colorless, crystalline compound used as a sedative

chlo·ride (-īd′) *n.* a compound of chlorine with another element or radical

chlo·ri·nate (-ə nāt′) *vt.* **-nat′ed, -nat′ing** to combine (a substance) with chlorine; esp., to treat (water or sewage) with chlorine to kill bacteria, etc. —**chlo′ri·na′tion** *n.*

chlo·rine (-ēn′) *n.* [< Gr *chlōros,* pale green] a greenish-yellow, poisonous, gaseous chemical element with a disagreeable odor, used in bleaching, water treatment, etc.: symbol, Cl; at. no. 17

chloro- [< Gr *chlōros,* pale green] *combining form* 1 green 2 having chlorine in the molecule

chlo·ro·fluo·ro·car·bon (klôr′ō flôr′ə kär′bən, -floor′-) *n.* any compound containing only carbon, fluorine, chlorine, and hydrogen, formerly used as a refrigerant, etc.: these compounds are thought to damage the atmosphere

chlo·ro·form (klôr′ə fôrm′) *n.* [< Fr: see prec. & FORMIC] a colorless, volatile liquid used as a solvent and, formerly, as an anesthetic —*vt.* to anesthetize or kill with chloroform

chlo·ro·phyll (-fil′) *n.* [< Gr *chlōros,* green + *phyllon,* leaf] the green pigment found in plant cells, essential to photosynthesis

chock (chäk) *n.* [NormFr *choque,* a block] a block or wedge placed under a wheel, etc. to prevent motion —*vt.* to wedge fast as with a chock —*adv.* as close or tight as can be

chock-full *adj.* as full as possible

choc·o·late (chôk′lət, chäk′-; chôk′ə lət, chäk′ə-) *n.* [ult. < AmInd (Mexico)] 1 a substance made from roasted and ground cacao seeds 2 a drink or candy made with chocolate 3 reddish brown —*adj.* 1 made of or flavored with chocolate 2 reddish-brown —**choc′o·lat·y** *adj.,* **choc′o·lat·ey**

choice (chois) *n.* [< OFr < Gothic *kausjan,* to test] 1 a choosing; selection 2 the right or power to choose 3 a person or thing chosen 4 the best part 5 a variety from which to choose 6 an alternative —*adj.* **choic′er, choic′est** 1 of special excellence 2 carefully chosen —**of choice** that is preferred

choir (kwīr) *n.* [< L < Gr *choros*] 1 a group of singers, esp. in a church 2 the part of a church they occupy

choke (chōk) *vt.* **choked, chok′ing** [< OE *āceocian*] 1 to prevent from breathing by blocking the windpipe; strangle; suffocate 2 to obstruct by clogging 3 to hinder the growth or action of 4 to cut off some air from the carburetor of (a gasoline engine) so as to make a richer gasoline mixture —*vi.* 1 to be suffocated 2 [Inf.] to be unable to perform because of fear, tension, etc. —*n.* 1 a choking 2 a sound of choking 3 the valve that chokes a carburetor —**choke back** to hold back (feelings, sobs, etc.) —**choke down** to swallow with difficulty —**choke off** to bring to an end

choke collar a training collar for a dog, that tightens when the dog strains at the leash: also **choke chain**

choke·hold *n.* 1 a locking one's arms around another's neck 2 absolute control

chok·er *n.* a closefitting necklace

chol·er (käl′ər) *n.* [< L *cholera:* see fol.] [Now Rare] anger or ill humor

chol·er·a (käl′ər ə) *n.* [< Gr *cholē,* bile] any of several severe, highly contagious intestinal diseases

chol·er·ic *adj.* easily angered

cho·les·ter·ol (kə les′tər ôl′, -ōl′) *n.* [< Gr *cholē,* bile + *stereos,* solid] a crystalline alcohol found esp. in animal fats, blood, nerve tissue, and bile

chomp (chämp) *vt., vi.* [var. of CHAMP¹] 1 to chew hard and noisily 2 to bite down (*on*) repeatedly —**chomp at the bit** to be impatient when held back

Chong·qing (choong′chin′) city in SC China

choose (chōōz) *vt., vi.* **chose, cho′sen, choos′ing** [OE *ceosan*] 1 to take as a choice; select 2 to decide or prefer [*to choose* to go] —**cannot choose but** cannot do otherwise than —**choos′er** *n.*

choos·y or **choos·ey** *adj.* **-i·er, -i·est** [Inf.] careful or fussy in choosing

chop (chäp) *vt.* **chopped, chop′ping** [ME *choppen*] 1 to cut by blows with a sharp tool 2 to cut into small bits; mince —*vi.* to make quick, cutting strokes —*n.* 1 a short, sharp stroke 2 a cut of meat and bone from the rib, loin, or shoulder 3 a short, broken movement of waves

Cho·pin (shō′pan; Fr shô pan′), **Fré·dé·ric** (fred′rik; Fr frā dā rēk′) 1810-49; Pol. composer, in France after 1831

chop·per (chäp′ər) *n.* 1 one that chops 2 [*pl.*] [Slang] teeth 3 [Inf.] a helicopter

chop·py *adj.* **-pi′er, -pi·est** 1 rough with short, broken waves, as the sea 2 making abrupt starts and stops —**chop′pi·ness** *n.*

chops (chäps) *pl.n.* 1 the jaws 2 the mouth and lower cheeks

chop·sticks *pl.n.* [Pidgin English] two small sticks held together in one hand and used, mainly in parts of Asia, as an eating utensil

chop su·ey (chäp′ sōō′ē) [< Chin *tsa-sui,* various pieces] a dish of meat, bean sprouts, etc., served with rice

cho·ral (kôr′əl) *adj.* of, for, or sung by a choir or chorus —**cho′ral·ly** *adv.*

cho·rale (kə ral′, -räl′) *n.* 1 a hymn tune 2 a choir or chorus

chord[1] (kôrd) *n.* 【altered (infl. by L *chorda*) < CORD】 1 [Archaic] the string of a musical instrument 2 *Geom.* a straight line joining any two points on an arc

chord[2] (kôrd) *n.* 【< ME *accord*, accord】 *Music* a combination of three or more tones sounded together in harmony

chor·date (kôr′dāt′) *n.* 【L *chorda*, CORD + -ATE[1]】 any of a phylum of animals having a dorsal nerve cord, including the vertebrates

chore (chôr) *n.* 【< OE *cierr*, job】 1 a routine task 2 a hard task

chor·e·o·graph (kôr′ē ə graf′) *vt., vi.* 【< fol.】 1 to design or plan the movements of (a dance) 2 to plan (something) in careful detail —**chor′e·og′ra·pher** (-äg′rə fər) *n.*

chor·e·og·ra·phy (kôr′ē äg′rə fē) *n.* 【Gr *choreia*, dance + -GRAPHY】 1 dancing, esp. ballet dancing 2 the devising of dances, esp. ballets —**chor′e·o·graph′ic** (-ə graf′ik) *adj.*

chor·is·ter (kôr′is tər) *n.* 【see CHORUS】 a member of a choir

cho·roid (kôr′oid′) *n.* 【Gr < *chorion*, fetal membrane + -*eidēs*, -OID】 the dark, middle membrane of the eye

chor·tle (chôrt′'l) *vi.* —**tled**, **-tling** 【prob. < CHUCKLE + SNORT】 to make a gleeful chuckling or snorting sound —*n.* such a sound —**chor′tler** *n.*

cho·rus (kôr′əs) *n.* 【< Gr *choros*】 1 a group of dancers and singers performing together 2 the part of a drama, song, etc. performed by a chorus 3 a group singing or speaking something together 4 music written for group singing 5 the refrain of a song —*vt., vi.* to sing, speak, or say in unison —**in chorus** in unison

chose (chōz) *vt., vi. pt. & obs. pp.* of CHOOSE

cho·sen (chō′zən) *vt., vi. pp.* of CHOOSE —*adj.* selected

chow (chou) *n.* 【< Chin】 1 any of a breed of medium-sized dog, originally from China: also **chow chow** 2 [Slang] food

chow·der (chou′dər) *n.* 【Fr *chaudière*, a pot】 a thick soup usually of onions and potatoes and, often, clams and milk

chow·hound *n.* [Slang] a glutton

chow mein (chou′ mān′) 【Chin *ch'ao*, fry + *mien*, flour】 a dish of meat, bean sprouts, etc., served with fried noodles

chrism (kriz′əm) *n.* 【< Gr *chrisma*, oil】 holy oil used as in baptism

Christ (krīst) *n.* 【< Gr *christos*, the anointed】 Jesus of Nazareth, regarded by Christians as the prophesied Messiah and the Son of God —**Christ′like′** *adj.*

chris·ten (kris′ən) *vt.* 1 to baptize 2 to give a name to, as at baptism 3 [Inf.] to use for the first time —**chris′ten·ing** *n.*

Chris·ten·dom (-dəm) *n.* 1 Christians collec-

tively 2 those parts of the world where most of the inhabitants profess Christianity

Chris·tian (kris′chən) *n.* a believer in Jesus as the prophesied Messiah and the Son of God, or in the religion based on the teachings of Jesus —*adj.* 1 of Jesus Christ 2 of or professing the religion based on his teachings 3 having the qualities taught by Jesus Christ, as love, kindness, humility, etc. 4 of Christians or Christianity

Chris·ti·an·i·ty (kris′chē an′ə tē) *n.* 1 Christians collectively 2 the Christian religion 3 the state of being a Christian

Chris·tian·ize (kris′chən īz′) *vt.* -**ized**′, -**iz**′ **ing** to make Christian

Christian name the baptismal name or given name, as distinguished from the surname or family name

Christian Science a religion and system of healing: official name **Church of Christ, Scientist**

Chris·tie (kris′tē) *n., pl.* -**ties** 【after *Christiania*, former name of Oslo, Norway】 *Skiing* a high-speed turn with the skis parallel

Christ·mas (kris′məs) *n.* 【see CHRIST & MASS】 a holiday on Dec. 25 celebrating the birth of Jesus Christ and also widely celebrated as a secular festivity —**Christ′mas·sy** *adj.*

chro·mat·ic (krō mat′ik) *adj.* 【< Gr *chrōma*, color】 1 of or having color or colors 2 *Music* progressing by semitones —**chro·mat′i·cal·ly** *adv.*

chro·ma·tin (krō′mə tin) *n.* 【< Gr *chrōma*, color】 a substance in cell nuclei containing the genes: it readily absorbs a coloring agent, as for observation under a microscope

chrome (krōm) *n.* 【Fr: see CHROMIUM】 chromium or chromium alloy —*adj.* designating any of various pigments (**chrome red**, **chrome yellow**) made from chromium compounds —*vt.* **chromed**, **chrom′ing** to plate with chromium

-chrome (krōm) 【< Gr *chrōma*, color】 *combining form* 1 color or coloring agent 2 chromium

chro·mi·um (krō′mē əm) *n.* 【< Gr *chrōma*, color】 a hard, metallic chemical element resistant to corrosion: symbol, Cr; at. no. 24

chromo- 【< Gr *chrōma*, color】 *combining form* color or pigment [*chromosome*]: also **chrom-**

chro·mo·some (krō′mə sōm′) *n.* 【< prec.】 any of the microscopic rod-shaped bodies made up of DNA and carrying the genes

chron·ic (krän′ik) *adj.* 【< Gr *chronos*, time】 1 lasting a long time or recurring: said of a disease 2 having had an ailment for a long time 3 habitual —**chron′i·cal·ly** *adv.*

chron·i·cle (krän′i kəl) *n.* 【< Gr *chronika*, annals】 a historical record of events in the order in which they happened —*vt.* **-cled**, **-cling** to tell the history of; recount; record —**chron′i·cler** *n.*

chrono- 【< Gr *chronos*, time】 *combining form* time: also **chron-**

chro·nol·o·gy (krə näl′ə jē) *n., pl.* **-gies** ⟦prec. + -LOGY⟧ **1** the science of measuring time and of dating events **2** the arrangement of events in the order of occurrence —**chron·o·log·i·cal** (krän′ə läj′i kəl) *adj.* —**chron′o·log′i·cal·ly** *adv.*

chro·nom·e·ter (-näm′ət ər) *n.* ⟦CHRONO- + -METER⟧ a highly accurate kind of clock or watch

chrys·a·lis (kris′ə lis) *n., pl.* **chry·sal·i·des** (kri sal′ə dēz′) or **chrys′a·lis·es** ⟦< Gr *chrysallis*⟧ **1** the pupa of a butterfly, encased in a cocoon **2** the cocoon

chrys·an·the·mum (kri san′thə məm) *n.* ⟦< Gr *chrysos*, gold + *anthemon*, flower⟧ **1** a late-blooming plant of the composite family, with showy flowers **2** the flower

chub (chub) *n., pl.* **chub** or **chubs** a small freshwater fish often used as bait

chub·by (chub′ē) *adj.* **-bi·er**, **-bi·est** round and plump —**chub′bi·ness** *n.*

chuck¹ (chuk) *vt.* ⟦< ? Fr *choquer*, strike against⟧ **1** to tap playfully, esp. under the chin **2** to throw; toss **3** [Slang] to get rid of —*n.* a chucking

chuck² (chuk) *n.* ⟦prob. var. of CHOCK⟧ **1** a cut of beef from around the neck and shoulder blade **2** a clamplike holding device, as on a lathe

chuck-full *adj. var. of* CHOCK-FULL

chuck·hole *n.* ⟦see CHOCK & HOLE⟧ POTHOLE

chuck·le (chuk′əl) *vi.* **-led**, **-ling** ⟦? < var. of CLUCK⟧ to laugh softly in a low tone —*n.* a soft, low-toned laugh

chuck wagon a wagon equipped as a kitchen for feeding cowboys, etc.

chuck·wal·la (chuk′wäl′ə) *n.* ⟦< AmInd (Mexico)⟧ a large lizard of the iguana family, native to deserts of Mexico and SW U.S.

chug (chug) *n.* ⟦echoic⟧ any of a series of puffing or explosive sounds, as of a locomotive —*vi.* **chugged**, **chug′ging** to make, or move with, such sounds —*vt.* [Slang] to drink in gulps

chuk·ka (boot) (chuk′ə) *n.* an ankle-high bootlike shoe

chum (chum) [Inf.] *n.* ⟦prob. < *chamber (mate)*⟧ a close friend —*vi.* **chummed**, **chum′ming** to be close friends —**chum′my** *adj.* **-mi·er**, **-mi·est** —**chum′mi·ness** *n.*

chump (chump) *n.* ⟦akin to MHG *kumpf*, dull⟧ [Inf.] a fool or dupe

Chung·king (chooŋ′kiŋ′) *a former transliteration of* CHONGQING

chunk (chuŋk) *n.* ⟦< ? CHUCK²⟧ a short, thick piece

chunk·y *adj.* **-i·er**, **-i·est 1** short and thick **2** stocky **3** containing chunks —**chunk′i·ness** *n.*

church (chʉrch′) *n.* ⟦< Gr *kyriakē (oikia)*, Lord's (house)⟧ **1** a building for public worship, esp. Christian worship **2** religious service **3** [*usually* C-] *a*) all Christians *b*) a particular Christian denomination **4** a religious congregation **5** ecclesiastical, as opposed to secular, government

church-go·er (-gō′ər) *n.* a person who attends church, esp. regularly

Church·ill (chʉr′il), Sir **Win·ston** (win′stən) 1874-1965; Brit. prime minister (1940-45; 1951-55)

church·man (-mən) *n., pl.* **-men** (-mən) **1** a man who is a cleric **2** a man who is a member of a church

Church of England the episcopal church of England; Anglican Church: it is an established church headed by the sovereign

church·war·den *n.* a lay officer handling certain secular matters in a church

church·wom·an *n., pl.* **-wom′en 1** a woman who is a cleric **2** a woman who is a member of a church

church·yard *n.* the ground adjoining a church, esp. when used as a cemetery

churl (chʉrl) *n.* ⟦OE *ceorl*, peasant⟧ **1** a peasant **2** a surly person; boor —**churl′ish** *adj.* —**churl′ish·ness** *n.*

churn (chʉrn) *n.* ⟦OE *cyrne*⟧ a container in which milk or cream is stirred or shaken to form butter —*vt., vi.* **1** to stir or shake (milk or cream) in a churn **2** to make (butter) thus **3** to stir up or move vigorously —**churn out** to produce in abundance, esp. mechanically or formulaically

chute¹ (shoot) *n.* ⟦Fr, a fall⟧ an inclined or vertical trough or passage down which things slide or drop

chute² (shoot) *n.* [Inf.] *short for* PARACHUTE

chut·ney (chut′nē) *n., pl.* **-neys** ⟦Hindi *chatnī*⟧ a relish of fruits, spices, herbs, and vinegar

chutz·pah or **chutz·pa** (hoots′pə, khoots′-) *n.* ⟦Yiddish < Heb⟧ [Inf.] impudence; brass

chyme (kīm) *n.* ⟦< Gr *chymos*, juice⟧ the semifluid mass formed as the stomach digests food: it passes into the small intestine

CIA *abbrev.* Central Intelligence Agency

cia·bat·ta (chə bät′ə) *n.* ⟦It, slipper: so named from its shape⟧ an Italian yeast bread made with white flour and olive oil in a long, somewhat flat loaf

ci·ca·da (si kā′də) *n., pl.* **-das** or **-dae** (-dē) ⟦L⟧ a large, flylike insect with transparent wings: the male makes a loud, shrill sound

cic·a·trix (sik′ə triks′) *n., pl.* **cic·a·tri·ces** (sik′ə trī′sēz′) or **cic′a·trix′es** ⟦L⟧ a scar

Cic·e·ro (sis′ə rō′) 106-43 B.C.; Rom. statesman & orator

-cide (sīd) ⟦< L *caedere*, to kill⟧ *suffix* **1** a killer **2** a killing

ci·der (sī′dər) *n.* ⟦< Gr *sikera*, an intoxicant⟧ juice pressed from apples, used as a drink or for making vinegar: **hard cider** is fermented, **sweet cider** is not

ci·gar (si gär′) *n.* ⟦Sp *cigarro*⟧ a roll of cut tobacco wrapped in a tobacco leaf for smoking

cig·a·rette or **cig·a·ret** (sig′ə ret′, sig′ə ret′) *n.* ⟦Fr⟧ a small roll of finely cut tobacco wrapped in thin paper for smoking

cig·a·ril·lo (sig′ə ril′ō) *n., pl.* **-los** ⟦Sp, dim. of *cigarro*, cigar⟧ a small, thin cigar

ci·lan·tro (si lan′trō, -län′-) *n.* coriander leaves used as an herb

cil·i·a (sil′ē ə) *pl.n.*, *sing.* **-i·um** (-ē əm) ‖< L‖ small hairlike projections, as those extending from certain plant cells or from around protozoa

ci·met·i·dine (sə met′ə dēn′) *n.* a drug that reduces gastric secretion: used to treat peptic ulcers

cinch (sinch) *n.* ‖< Sp < L *cingulum,* girdle‖ 1 a saddle or pack girth 2 [Slang] a thing easy to do —*vt.* 1 to fasten (a saddle) on (a horse, etc.) with a cinch 2 [Slang] to make sure of

cin·cho·na (sin kō′nə) *n.* ‖reputedly after Peruvian Countess del *Chinchón* (1576-1639)‖ 1 a tropical tree with a bitter bark from which quinine is made 2 this bark

Cin·cin·nat·i (sin′sə nat′ē, -ə) city in SW Ohio

Cin·co de Ma·yo (siŋ′kō də mī′ō) ‖Sp, fifth (lit., five) of May‖ May 5, Mexican anniversary of an 1862 victory over French forces

cinc·ture (siŋk′chər) *n.* ‖L *cinctura*‖ a belt or girdle

cin·der (sin′dər) *n.* ‖OE *sinder,* slag‖ 1 a tiny piece of partly burned coal, wood, etc. 2 [*pl.*] ashes from coal or wood

Cin·der·el·la (sin′dər el′ə) *n.* in a fairy tale, a household drudge who eventually marries a prince

cin·e·ma (sin′ə mə) *n.* ‖< Gr *kinēma,* motion‖ a film theater —**the cinema** the making of films 2 films collectively —**cin′e·mat′ic** *adj.*

cin·e·ma·tog·ra·phy (sin′ə mə täg′rə fē) *n.* the art, science, and work of photography in making films —**cin′e·ma·tog′ra·pher** *n.* —**cin′e·mat′o·graph′ic** (-mat′ə graf′ik) *adj.*

cin·na·bar (sin′ə bär′) *n.* ‖< Gr *kinnabari*‖ mercuric sulfide, a heavy, bright-red mineral

cin·na·mon (sin′ə mən) *n.* ‖< Heb *qinnāmōn*‖ 1 a reddish-brown spice made from the dried inner bark of a laurel tree of the East Indies 2 this tree

ci·phor (sī′fər) *n.* ‖< Ar *ṣifr*‖ 1 the symbol 0; zero 2 a nonentity 3 secret writing based on a key; code 4 the key to such a code

cir·ca (sur′kə) *prep.* [L] about: used before an approximate date or figure: also written **cir′ca**

cir·ca·di·an (sər kā′dē ən) *adj.* ‖coined < L *circa,* about + *dies,* day‖ of the behavioral or physiological rhythms associated with the 24-hour cycle of the earth's rotation

Cir·ce (sur′sē) *n.* in the *Odyssey,* an enchantress who turns men into swine

cir·cle (sur′kəl) *n.* ‖< Gr *kirkos*‖ 1 a plane figure bounded by a single curved line every point of which is equally distant from the center 2 this curved line 3 anything like a circle, as a ring 4 a complete or recurring series; cycle 5 a group of people with common interests 6 extent, as of influence; scope —*vt.* **-cled, -cling** 1 to form a circle around 2 to move around, as in a circle —*vi.* to go around in a circle —**cir′cler** *n.*

cir·clet (-klit) *n.* 1 a small circle 2 a circular ornament, as for the head

cir·cuit (sur′kit) *n.* ‖< L *circum,* around + *ire,* go‖ 1 a boundary line or its length 2 a going around something 3 the regular journey through a district of a person at work, as a preacher 4 the district of a U.S. Court of Appeals 5 a series of venues at which performers are booked in turn 6 the path or line of an electric current —*vi.* to go in a circuit —*vt.* to make a circuit about —**cir′cuit·al** *adj.*

circuit breaker a device that automatically interrupts the flow of an electric current, as in the event of a short circuit

circuit court a court that holds sessions in various places within its district

cir·cu·i·tous (sər kyōō′ət əs) *adj.* roundabout; indirect —**cir·cu′i·tous·ly** *adv.* —**cir·cu′i·tous·ness** *n.*

cir·cuit·ry (sur′kə trē) *n.* the system or the elements of an electric circuit

cir·cu·lar (sur′kyə lər) *adj.* 1 in the shape of a circle; round 2 moving in a circle 3 circuitous —*n.* an advertisement, etc., intended for many readers —**cir′cu·lar′i·ty** (-ler′ə tē) *n.*

circular saw a power saw having a rotating, toothed disk as its blade

cir·cu·late (sur′kyə lāt′) *vi.* **-lat′ed, -lat′ing** ‖< L *circulari,* form a circle‖ 1 to move in a circle or circuit and return, as the blood 2 to go from person to person or from place to place —*vt.* to make circulate —**cir′cu·lat′or** *n.* —**cir′cu·la·to′ry** (-lə tôr′ē) *adj.*

cir·cu·la·tion (sur′kyə lā′shən) *n.* 1 a circulating 2 the movement of blood through the arteries and veins 3 the distribution of newspapers, magazines, etc. 4 the average number of copies of a periodical sold in a given period

circum- ‖< L *circum*‖ *prefix* around, about, surrounding

cir·cum·cise (sur′kəm sīz′) *vt.* **-cised′, -cis′ing** ‖< L *circum,* around + *caedere,* to cut‖ to cut off all or part of the foreskin of —**cir′cum·ci·sion** (-sizh′ən) *n.*

cir·cum·fer·ence (sər kum′fər əns, -frəns) *n.* ‖< L *circum,* around + *ferre,* to carry‖ 1 the line bounding a circle, ball, etc. 2 the length of this line

cir·cum·flex (sur′kəm fleks′) *n.* ‖< L *circum,* around + *flectere,* to bend‖ a mark (^ or ~) used over a vowel to indicate pronunciation

cir·cum·lo·cu·tion (-lō kyōō′shən) *n.* ‖< L: see CIRCUM- & LOCUTION‖ a roundabout way of saying something

cir·cum·nav·i·gate (-nav′ə-) *vt.* **-gat′ed, -gat′ing** ‖< L: see CIRCUM- & NAVIGATE‖ 1 to sail or fly around (the earth, etc.) 2 to travel all the way around —**cir′cum·nav′i·ga′tion** *n.*

cir·cum·scribe (-skrīb′) *vt.* **-scribed′, -scrib′ing** ‖< L: see CIRCUM- & SCRIBE‖ 1 to trace a line around; encircle 2 to limit; confine —**cir′cum·scrip′tion** (-skrip′shən) *n.*

cir·cum·spect (-spekt′) *adj.* ‖< L *circumspicere,* look about‖ cautious; discreet —**cir′cum·spec′tion** *n.* —**cir′cum·spect′ly** *adv.*

cir·cum·stance (-stans′) *n.* ‖< L *circum,* around + *stare,* to stand‖ 1 a fact or event, specif. one accompanying another 2 [*pl.*] conditions affecting a person, esp. financial conditions **3** chance; luck **4** ceremony; show —*vt.* **-stanced′, -stanc′ing** to place in certain circumstances —**under no circumstances** never —**cir′cum·stanced′** *adj.*

cir·cum·stan·tial (-stan′shəl) *adj.* **1** having to do with, or depending on, circumstances **2** incidental **3** complete in detail —**cir′cum·stan′tial·ly** *adv.*

circumstantial evidence *Law* indirect evidence of a fact at issue, based on attendant circumstances

cir·cum·vent (-vent′) *vt.* ⟦< L *circum,* around + *venire,* come⟧ to bypass or avoid by craft or ingenuity —**cir′cum·ven′tion** *n.*

cir·cus (sur′kəs) *n.* ⟦L, a circle⟧ **1** in ancient Rome, an amphitheater **2** a traveling show of acrobats, trained animals, clowns, etc. **3** [Inf.] a place or event regarded as being frenzied, wildly entertaining, etc.

ci·ré (sē rā′) *adj.* ⟦< Fr *cire,* wax⟧ having a smooth, glossy finish

cir·rho·sis (sə rō′sis) *n.* ⟦< Gr *kirrhos,* tawny + -OSIS⟧ a degenerative disease, esp. of the liver, marked by excess formation of connective tissue —**cir·rhot′ic** (-rät′ik) *adj.*

cir·rus (sir′əs) *n., pl.* **cir′rus** ⟦L, a curl⟧ a high, wispy cloud

CIS *abbrev.* Commonwealth of Independent States

cis- ⟦< L *cis,* on this side⟧ *prefix* on this side of

cis·tern (sis′tərn) *n.* ⟦< L *cista,* chest⟧ a large tank for storing water, esp. rainwater

cit·a·del (sit′ə del′) *n.* ⟦< L *civitas,* city⟧ a fortress

cite (sīt) *vt.* **cit′ed, cit′ing** ⟦< L *citare,* summon⟧ **1** to summon before a court of law **2** to quote **3** to mention by way of example, proof, etc. **4** to mention in an official report as meritorious —**ci·ta′tion** *n.*

cit·i·fied (sit′i fīd′) *adj.* having the manners, dress, etc. of city people

cit·i·zen (sit′ə zən) *n.* ⟦< L *civis,* townsman⟧ a member of a state or nation who owes allegiance to it by birth or naturalization and is entitled to full civil rights —**cit′i·zen·ship′** *n.*

cit·i·zen·ry *n.* citizens as a group

cit·ric (si′trik) *adj.* designating or of an acid obtained from citrus fruits

cit·ron (-trən) *n.* ⟦< Fr, lemon⟧ **1** a yellow, thick-skinned, lemonlike fruit **2** its candied rind

cit·ron·el·la (si′trə nel′ə) *n.* ⟦see prec.⟧ a sharp-smelling oil used in soap, insect repellents, etc.

cit·rus (-trəs) *n.* ⟦L⟧ **1** any of the trees that bear oranges, lemons, limes, etc. **2** any such fruit —*adj.* of these trees

cit·y (sit′ē) *n., pl.* **-ies** ⟦< L *civis,* townsman⟧ **1** a population center larger or more important than a town **2** in the U.S., an incorporated municipality with boundaries and powers defined by state charter **3** the people of a city —*adj.* of, in, or for a city —**cit′y·wide′** *adj.*

city hall (a building that houses) a municipal government

civ·et (siv′it) *n.* ⟦< Ar *zabād*⟧ **1** the musky secretion of a catlike carnivore (**civet cat**) of Africa and S Asia: used in some perfumes **2** the animal, or its fur

civ·ic (siv′ik) *adj.* ⟦< L *civis,* townsman⟧ of a city, citizens, or citizenship

civ·ic-mind·ed *adj.* having or showing concern for the welfare of one's community

civ·ics (-iks) *n.* the study of civic affairs and the duties and rights of citizenship

civ·il (siv′əl) *adj.* ⟦see CIVIC⟧ **1** of a citizen or citizens **2** polite **3** of citizens in matters not military or religious **4** having to do with the private rights of individuals —**civ′il·ly** *adv.*

civil disobedience nonviolent opposition to a law through refusal to comply with it, on grounds of conscience

civil engineering engineering dealing with the construction of highways, bridges, harbors, etc. —**civil engineer**

ci·vil·ian (sə vil′yən) *n.* ⟦see CIVIC⟧ a person not in the armed services, the police, etc. —*adj.* of or for civilians

ci·vil·i·ty (-ə tē) *n.* **1** politeness **2** *pl.* **-ties** a civil, or polite, act

civ·i·li·za·tion (siv′ə lə zā′shən) *n.* **1** a civilizing or being civilized **2** the total culture of a people, period, etc. **3** the peoples considered to have attained a high social development

civ·i·lize (-līz′) *vt.* **-lized′, -liz′ing** ⟦see CIVIC⟧ **1** to bring out of a primitive condition to a higher level of social organization and of cultural and technological development **2** to make refined, sophisticated, etc. —**civ′i·lized′** *adj.*

civil law the body of law having to do with private rights

civil liberties liberties guaranteed to all individuals by law, custom, court decisions, etc.; rights, as of speaking or acting as one likes

civil rights those rights guaranteed to all individuals by the 13th, 14th, 15th, and 19th Amendments to the U.S. Constitution, as the right to vote and the right to equal treatment under the law

civil servant a civil service employee

civil service all those employed in government administration, esp. through competitive public examination

civil war war between different factions of the same nation —**the Civil War** the war between the North (the Union) and the South (the Confederacy) in the U.S. (1861-65)

civ·vies (siv′ēz) *pl.n.* [Inf.] civilian clothes: also **civ′ies**

ck *abbrev.* check

cl *abbrev.* centiliter(s)

Cl *Chem. symbol for* chlorine

clack (klak) *vi., vt.* ⟦prob. echoic < ON⟧ to make or cause to make a sudden, sharp sound —*n.* this sound

clad (klad) *vt. alt. pt. & pp. of* CLOTHE —*adj.* **1** clothed; dressed **2** having a bonded outer layer of another metal or an alloy [*clad* steel]

clad·ding *n.* a layer of some metal or alloy bonded to another metal

claim (klām) *vt.* ⟦< L *clamare,* cry out⟧ **1** to

demand as rightfully belonging to one **2** to require; deserve [to *claim* attention] **3** to assert —*n.* **1** a claiming **2** a right to something **3** something claimed **4** an assertion —**claim′a·ble** *adj.* —**claim′ant** *n.*, **claim′er**

clair·voy·ance (kler voi′əns) *n.* [Fr < *clair,* clear + *voyant,* seeing] the supposed ability to perceive things that are not in sight —**clair·voy′ant** *n., adj.*

clam (klam) *n.* [< obs. *clam,* a clamp] any of various hard-shelled, usually edible, bivalve mollusks —*vi.* **clammed, clam′ming** to dig for clams —**clam up** [Inf.] to keep silent —**clam′mer** *n.*

clam·bake *n.* a picnic at which steamed or baked clams are served

clam·ber (klam′bər) *vi.* [ME *clambren*] to climb clumsily, esp. by using both the hands and the feet

clam·my (klam′ē) *adj.* **-mi·er, -mi·est** [ME, prob. < OE *clam,* mud] unpleasantly moist, cold, and sticky —**clam′mi·ly** *adv.* —**clam′mi·ness** *n.*

clam·or (klam′ər) *n.* [< L *clamare,* cry out] **1** a loud outcry **2** a loud demand or complaint, as by the public —*vi.* to make a clamor —**clam′or·ous** *adj.*

clamp (klamp) *n.* [< MDu *klampe*] a device for clasping or fastening things together —*vt.* to fasten or brace, as with a clamp —**clamp down (on)** to become more strict (with)

clan (klan) *n.* [< Gael < L *planta,* offshoot] **1** a group of families claiming descent from a common ancestor **2** a group of people with interests in common —**clans·man** (klanz′mən) *n., pl.* **-men** (-mən)

clan·des·tine (klan des′tin) *adj.* [< L *clam,* secret] secret or hidden; furtive —**clan·des′tine·ly** *adv.*

clang (klaŋ) *vi., vt.* [echoic] to make or cause to make a loud, ringing sound, as by striking metal —*n.* this sound

clang·or (-ər) *n.* [L < *clangere,* to sound] a continuous clanging sound

clank (klaŋk) *n.* [echoic] a sharp, metallic sound —*vi., vt.* to make or cause to make this sound

clan·nish (klan′ish) *adj.* **1** of a clan **2** tending to associate closely with one's own group only —**clan′nish·ly** *adv.* —**clan′nish·ness** *n.*

clap (klap) *vi.* **clapped, clap′ping** [OE *clæppan,* to beat] **1** to make a sudden, loud sound, as of two flat surfaces struck together **2** to strike the hands together, as in applauding —*vt.* **1** to strike together briskly **2** to strike with an open hand **3** to put, move, etc. swiftly [*clapped* him into jail] —*n.* **1** the sound or act of clapping **2** a sharp slap

clap·board (klab′ərd) *n.* [transl. of MDu *klapholt* < *klappen,* to fit + *holt,* wood] a thin board with one thicker edge, used as siding —*vt.* to cover with clapboards

clap·per *n.* **1** a person who claps **2** the moving part of a bell, that strikes the side of the bell

clap·trap *n.* [CLAP + TRAP] insincere, empty talk intended to get applause

claque (klak) *n.* [Fr < *claquer,* to clap] **1** a group of people paid to applaud at a play, etc. **2** a group of fawning admirers

clar·et (klar′it) *n.* [< OFr (*vin*) *claret,* clear (wine)] a dry red wine

clar·i·fy (klar′ə fī′) *vt., vi.* **-fied′, -fy′ing** [< L *clarus,* clear + *facere,* to make] to make or become clear —**clar′i·fi·ca′tion** *n.*

clar·i·net (klar′ə net′) *n.* [< Fr < L *clarus,* clear] a single-reed woodwind instrument played by means of holes and keys —**clar′i·net′ist** *n.*, **clar′i·net′tist**

clar·i·on (klar′ē ən) *adj.* [< L *clarus,* clear] clear, sharp, and ringing [a *clarion* call]

clar·i·ty (klar′ə tē) *n.* [< L *clarus,* clear] the quality of being clear; clearness

clash (klash) *vi.* [echoic] **1** to collide with a loud, harsh, metallic noise **2** to conflict; disagree —*vt.* to strike with a clashing noise —*n.* **1** the sound of clashing **2** conflict

clasp (klasp) *n.* [ME *claspe*] **1** a fastening, as a hook, to hold things together **2** a holding or grasping; embrace **3** a grip of the hand —*vt.* **1** to fasten with a clasp **2** to hold or embrace tightly **3** to grip with the hand

class (klas) *n.* [< L *classis*] **1** a number of people or things grouped together because of certain likenesses; sort **2** a social or economic rank [the working *class*] **3** *a)* a group of students taught together *b)* a meeting of such a group *c)* a group graduating together **4** grade or quality **5** [Inf.] excellence, as of style or appearance —*vt.* to classify —**class′less** *adj.*

class action (suit) a legal action that is brought by one or more persons on behalf of themselves and a much larger group

clas·sic (klas′ik) *adj.* [< L *classis,* class] **1** being an excellent model of its kind **2** CLASSICAL (*adj.* 2 & 3) **3** balanced, formal, regular, simple, etc. **4** famous as traditional or typical —*n.* **1** a literary or artistic work of the highest excellence **2** [*pl.*] the works of outstanding ancient Greek and Roman authors: usually with *the* **3** a famous traditional or typical event

clas·si·cal (klas′i kəl) *adj.* **1** CLASSIC (*adj.* 1 & 3) **2** of or relating to the art, literature, etc. of the ancient Greeks and Romans **3** typical of or derived from the artistic standards of the ancient Greeks and Romans **4** standard and traditional [*classical* economics] **5** of or relating to music, esp. of the period 1750–1830 in Europe, that conforms to certain standards of form, complexity, etc. —**clas′si·cal·ly** *adv.* —**class′i·cal′i·ty** (-kal′ə tē) *n.*

clas·si·cism (-ə siz′əm) *n.* **1** the aesthetic principles of ancient Greece and Rome **2** adherence to these principles **3** knowledge of classical literature and art —**clas′si·cist** *n.*

clas·si·fied (klas′ə fīd′) *adj.* **1** confidential and available only to authorized persons **2** of classified advertising —*n.* [*pl.*] a listing of classified advertisements

classified advertising advertising arranged

according to subject, under such listings as *help wanted* —**classified advertisement**

clas·si·fy (klas′ə fī′) *vt.* **-fied′, -fy′ing 1** to arrange in categories **2** to designate (government documents) as secret or for use by authorized persons only —**clas′si·fi′a·ble** *adj.* —**clas′si·fi·ca′tion** *n.* —**clas′si·fi′er** *n.*

class·mate *n.* a member of the same class at a school or college

class·room *n.* a room in a school or college in which classes are taught

class·y *adj.* **-i·er, -i·est** [Inf.] first-class, esp. in style; elegant —**class′i·ness** *n.*

clat·ter (klat′ər) *vi., vt.* [ME *clateren*] to make or cause to make a clatter —*n.* **1** a rapid succession of loud, sharp noises **2** a tumult; hubbub

clause (klôz) *n.* [< L *claudere*, to close] **1** a group of words containing a subject and a finite verb: see DEPENDENT CLAUSE, INDEPENDENT CLAUSE **2** a provision in a document —**claus′al** *adj.*

claus·tro·pho·bi·a (klôs′trə fō′bē ə) *n.* [< L *claustrum*, enclosed place + -PHOBIA] an abnormal fear of being in an enclosed or confined place —**claus′tro·pho′bic** *adj.*

clav·i·chord (klav′i kôrd′) *n.* [< L *clavis*, key + *chorda*, string] a stringed musical instrument with a keyboard, predecessor of the piano

clav·i·cle (klav′i kəl) *n.* [< L *clavis*, key] a bone connecting the breastbone with the shoulder blade

cla·vier (klə vir′) *n.* [Fr < L *clavis*, key] any stringed keyboard instrument

claw (klô) *n.* [OE *clawu*] **1** a sharp, hooked nail on an animal's or bird's foot **2** the pincers of a lobster, etc. — *vt., vi.* to scratch, clutch, tear, etc. with or as with claws

clay (klā) *n.* [OE *clæg*] **1** a firm, plastic earth, used in making bricks, etc. **2** *a)* earth *b)* the human body —**clay′ey** *adj.* **clay′i·er, clay′i·est**

clean (klēn) *adj.* [OE *clæne*] **1** *a)* free from dirt and impurities; unsoiled *b)* free from disease, radioactivity, pollutants, etc. **2** morally pure **3** fair; sportsmanlike **4** neat and tidy **5** well-formed **6** clear **7** thorough —*adv.* [Inf.] completely — *vt., vi.* to make or be made clean —**clean up 1** to make neat **2** [Inf.] to finish **3** [Slang] to make much profit —**come clean** [Slang] to confess —**clean′ly** *adv.* —**clean′ness** *n.*

clean-cut *adj.* **1** with a sharp edge or outline **2** well-formed **3** trim, neat, etc.

clean·er *n.* a person or thing that cleans; specif., one who dry-cleans clothing

clean·ly (klen′lē) *adj.* **-li·er, -li·est 1** keeping oneself or one's surroundings clean **2** always kept clean —**clean′li·ness** *n.*

clean room a room designed to be nearly 100% free of dust, pollen, etc.

cleanse (klenz) *vt.* **cleansed, cleans′ing** [OE *clænsian*] to make clean, pure, etc. —**cleans′er** *n.*

clean-up *n.* **1** a cleaning up **2** elimination of crime

clear (klir) *adj.* [< L *clarus*] **1** free from clouds; bright **2** transparent **3** easily seen or heard; distinct **4** keen or logical [a *clear* mind] **5** not obscure; obvious **6** certain; positive **7** free from guilt **8** free from deductions; net **9** free from debt **10** free from obstruction; open —*adv.* **1** in a clear way **2** completely —*vt.* **1** to make clear **2** to free from impurities, blemishes, etc. **3** to make lucid; clarify **4** to open [to *clear* a path] **5** to get rid of **6** to prove the innocence of **7** to pass or leap over, by, etc., esp. without touching **8** to be passed or approved by **9** to give approval to; authorize **10** to make as profit **11** *Banking* to pass (a check, etc.) through a clearinghouse —*vi.* **1** to become clear **2** *Banking* to pass through a clearinghouse: said of a check —**clear away** (or **off**) to remove so as to leave a cleared space —**clear out** [Inf.] to depart —**clear up** to make or become clear —**in the clear 1** free from obstructions **2** [Inf.] guiltless —**clear′ly** *adv.* —**clear′ness** *n.*

clear·ance (-əns) *n.* **1** the clear space between a moving object and that which it is passing **2** official approval or authorization

clear-cut *adj.* **1** clearly outlined **2** distinct; definite **3** with all its trees cut down

clear·ing *n.* an area of land cleared of trees

clear·ing·house *n.* **1** an office maintained by several banks for exchanging checks, balancing accounts, etc. **2** a central office, as for exchanging information

cleat (klēt) *n.* [ME *clete*] a piece of wood or metal fastened to something to strengthen it or give secure footing

cleav·age (klēv′ij) *n.* **1** a cleaving; dividing **2** a cleft; fissure; division **3** the hollow between a woman's breasts

cleave[1] (klēv) *vt., vi.* **cleaved** or **cleft** or **clove, cleaved** or **cleft** or **clo′ven, cleav′ing** [OE *cleofan*] to divide by a blow; split; sever —**cleav′a·ble** *adj.*

cleave[2] (klēv) *vi.* **cleaved, cleav′ing** [OE *cleofian*] **1** to adhere; cling (*to*) **2** to be faithful (*to*)

cleav·er (klēv′ər) *n.* a heavy cutting tool with a broad blade, used by butchers

clef (klef) *n.* [Fr < L *clavis*, key] a symbol used at the beginning of a musical staff to indicate the pitch of the notes

cleft[1] (kleft) *n.* [< OE *cleofan*: see CLEAVE[1]] an opening or hollow made by or as if by cleaving; crevice

cleft[2] (kleft) *vt., vi. alt. pt. & pp. of* CLEAVE[1] —*adj.* split; divided

cleft lip a vertical cleft in the upper lip, often accompanying a CLEFT PALATE

cleft palate a cleft from front to back along the middle of the roof of the mouth, due to incomplete prenatal development

clem·a·tis (klem′ə tis) *n.* [< Gr *klēma*, vine] a vine of the buttercup family, with bright-colored flowers

clem·en·cy (klem′ən sē) *n.* mercy; forbearance

Clem·ens (klem′ənz), **Sam·u·el Lang·horne** (sam′yōō əl laŋ′hôrn) (pseud. *Mark Twain*) 1835-1910; U.S. writer & humorist

clem·ent (-ənt) *adj.* 〖L *clemens*〗 **1** lenient **2** mild: said as of weather

clench (klench) *vt.* 〖< OE *(be)clencan*, to make *cling*〗 **1** to close (the teeth or fist) firmly **2** to grip tightly —*n.* a firm grip

Cle·o·pa·tra (klē′ō pa′trə, klē′ə-) 69?-30 B.C.; queen of Egypt (51-49; 48-30)

clere·sto·ry (klir′stôr′ē) *n., pl.* **-ries** 〖< ME *cler*, clear + *storie*, story (of a building)〗 the upper part of a wall, as of a church, having windows for lighting the central space

cler·gy (klur′jē) *n., pl.* **-gies** 〖see CLERK〗 the body of people ordained or recognized by a religious community as spiritual or ritual leaders

cler·gy·man (-mən) *n., pl.* **-men** (-mən) a man who is a member of the clergy

cler·gy·wom·an *n., pl.* **-wom′en** a woman who is a member of the clergy

cler·ic (kler′ik) *n.* a member of the clergy

cler·i·cal (kler′i kəl) *adj.* **1** of the clergy or one of its members **2** of office clerks or their work

cler·i·cal·ism (-iz′əm) *n.* a policy or system giving political power to the clergy —**cler′i·cal·ist** *n.*

clerk (klurk) *n.* 〖< Gr *klērikos*, a cleric〗 **1** a lay member of a church with minor duties **2** an office worker who types, files, etc. **3** an official who keeps the records of a court, town, etc. **4** a salesclerk —*vi.* to work as a salesclerk

Cleve·land¹ (klēv′lənd), **(Stephen) Gro·ver** (grō′vər) 1837-1908; 22d and 24th president of the U.S. (1885-89; 1893-97)

Cleve·land² (klēv′lənd) city and port in NE Ohio

clev·er (klev′ər) *adj.* 〖? < Norw *klōver*〗 **1** skillful; adroit **2** intelligent; ingenious; smart —**clev′er·ly** *adv.* —**clev′er·ness** *n.*

clev·is (klev′is) *n.* 〖see CLEAVE²〗 a U-shaped piece of iron with holes for a pin, for attaching one thing to another

clew (klōō) *n.* 〖OE *cliwen*〗 **1** a ball of thread or yarn **2** *archaic sp. of* CLUE

cli·ché (klē shā′) *n.* 〖Fr < pp. of *clicher*, to stereotype〗 a trite expression or idea

cli·chéd (klē shād′) *adj.* trite; stereotyped

click (klik) *n.* 〖echoic〗 a slight, sharp sound like that of a door latch snapping into place — *vi., vt.* to make or cause to make a click

cli·ent (klī′ənt) *n.* 〖< L *cliens*, follower〗 **1** one for whom a lawyer, accountant, etc. is acting **2** a customer

cli·en·tele (klī′ən tel′) *n.* 〖< Fr < L *clientela*, patronage〗 all one's clients or customers, collectively

cliff (klif) *n.* 〖OE *clif*〗 a high, steep face of rock

cliff·hang·er or **cliff-hang·er** *n.* a suspenseful film, story, situation, etc.

cli·mac·ter·ic (klī mak′tər ik, klī′mak ter′ik) *n.* 〖< Gr *klimax*, ladder〗 a crucial period in life; esp., menopause —*adj.* crucial

cli·mate (klī′mət) *n.* 〖< Gr *klima*, region〗 **1** the prevailing weather conditions of a place **2** the prevailing conditions, as of society, at a particular place and time —**cli·mat′ic** (-mat′ik) *adj.*

cli·max (klī′maks′) *n.* 〖L < Gr *klimax*, ladder〗 **1** the final, culminating element in a series; highest point of interest, excitement, etc. **2** the turning point of action in a drama, etc. **3** an orgasm —*vi., vt.* to reach, or bring to, a climax —**cli·mac′tic** (-mak′tik) *adj.*

climb (klīm) *vi., vt.* **climbed, climb′ing** 〖OE *climban*〗 **1** to move up by using the feet and, often, the hands **2** to ascend gradually **3** to move (*down, over, along*, etc.) using the hands and feet **4** to grow upward on (a wall, etc.) —*n.* **1** a climbing **2** a thing or place to be climbed —**climb′a·ble** *adj.* —**climb′er** *n.*

clime (klīm) *n.* 〖see CLIMATE〗 [Old Poet.] a region, esp. with regard to climate

clinch (klinch) *vt.* 〖var. of CLENCH〗 **1** to fasten (a driven nail, etc.) by bending the projecting end **2** to settle (an argument, bargain, etc.) definitely —*vi.* **1** *Boxing* to grip the opponent with the arms so as to hinder punching effectiveness **2** [Slang] to embrace —*n.* a clinching

clinch·er *n.* **1** one that clinches **2** a decisive point, argument, act, etc.

cling (kliŋ) *vi.* **clung, cling′ing** 〖OE *clingan*〗 **1** to adhere; hold fast, as by embracing **2** to be or stay near **3** to be emotionally attached —**cling′er** *n.* —**cling′y** *adj.* **-i·er, -i·est**

clin·ic (klin′ik) *n.* 〖< Gr *klinē*, bed〗 **1** the teaching of medicine by treatment of patients in the presence of students **2** a place where medical specialists practice as a group **3** an outpatient department, as in a hospital **4** an intensive session of group instruction, as in a certain skill

clin·i·cal (-i kəl) *adj.* **1** of or connected with a clinic or sickbed **2** having to do with the treatment and observation of patients, as distinguished from theoretical study **3** purely scientific; detached —**clin′i·cal·ly** *adv.*

cli·ni·cian (kli nish′ən) *n.* one who practices clinical medicine, psychology, etc.

clink (kliŋk) *vi., vt.* 〖echoic〗 to make or cause to make a slight, sharp sound, as of glasses striking together —*n.* **1** such a sound **2** [Inf.] a jail

clink·er (kliŋ′kər) *n.* 〖Du *klinker*〗 **1** a hard mass of fused stony matter, formed as from burned coal **2** [Slang] a mistake

Clin·ton (klint′'n), **Bill** (bil) (legal name *William Jefferson Clinton*; born *William Jefferson Blythe IV*) 1946- ; 42d president of the U.S. (1993-2001)

clip¹ (klip) *vt.* **clipped, clip′ping** 〖< ON *klippa*〗 **1** to cut, as with shears **2** to cut short **3** to cut the hair of **4** [Inf.] to hit sharply **5** [Slang] to swindle —*vi.* to move rapidly —*n.* **1** a clipping **2** an excerpt from a film, videotape, etc. **3** a rapid pace **4** [Inf.] a quick, sharp blow

clip² (klip) *vi., vt.* **clipped, clip′ping** 〖OE *clyppan*, to embrace〗 to grip tightly; fasten —*n.*

any of various devices that clip, fasten, hold, etc.

clip·board *n.* a writing board with a hinged clip at the top to hold papers

clip joint [Slang] a nightclub, store, etc. that charges excessive prices

clipped form a shortened form of a word, as *pike* (for *turnpike*) or *fan* (for *fanatic*)

clip·per (klip′ər) *n.* 1 [*usually pl.*] a tool for cutting or trimming 2 a sailing ship built for great speed

clip·ping *n.* a piece cut out or off, as an item clipped from a newspaper

clique (klik, klēk) *n.* [Fr < OFr *cliquer*, make a noise] a small, exclusive circle of people; coterie —**cliqu′ish** *adj.* —**cliqu′ish·ly** *adv.*

clit·o·ris (klit′ər is) *n., pl.* **clit′o·ris·es** (–is iz) or **cli·tor·i·des** (kli tôr′i dēz′) [< Gr] a small, sensitive, erectile organ at the upper end of the vulva

clo·a·ca (klō ā′kə) *n., pl.* **-cae** (-sē′, -kē′) or **-cas** [L < *cluere*, to cleanse] a cavity, as in reptiles and birds, into which both the intestinal and the genitourinary tracts empty

cloak (klōk) *n.* [< ML *clocca*, bell: from its shape] 1 a loose outer garment, worn over the shoulders and often having a hood 2 something that covers or conceals; disguise —*vt.* 1 to cover with a cloak 2 to conceal

clob·ber (kläb′ər) *vt.* [< ?] [Slang] 1 to beat or hit repeatedly 2 to defeat decisively

cloche (klōsh) *n.* [Fr, a bell] a woman's close-fitting, bell-shaped hat

clock¹ (kläk) *n.* [ME *clokke*, orig., clock with bells < ML *clocca*, bell] a device for measuring and indicating time, usually by means of pointers moving over a dial: clocks are not meant to be worn or carried about —*vt.* 1 to record the time of (a race, etc.) with a stopwatch 2 [Inf.] to hit (someone), esp. in the head

clock² (kläk) *n.* [< ? prec., because of original bell shape] a woven or embroidered ornament on a sock, going up from the ankle

clock radio a radio with a built-in clock that can turn it on or off

clock·wise *adv., adj.* in the direction in which the hands of a clock rotate

clock·work *n.* 1 the mechanism of a clock 2 any similar mechanism, with springs and gears —**like clockwork** very regularly

clod (kläd) *n.* [OE] 1 a lump, esp. of earth or clay 2 a dull, stupid person —**clod′dish** *adj.*

clod·hop·per *n.* [prec. + HOPPER] 1 a plowman 2 a clumsy, stupid person 3 a coarse, heavy shoe

clog (kläg) *n.* [ME *clogge*, lump of wood] 1 anything that hinders or obstructs; hindrance 2 a shoe with a thick, usually wooden, sole —*vt.* **clogged, clog′ging** 1 to hinder 2 to obstruct (a passage); jam —*vi.* to become clogged

cloi·son·né (kloi′zə nā′) *adj.* [Fr, lit., partitioned] designating enamel work in which the surface decoration is set in hollows formed by thin strips of wire

clois·ter (klois′tər) *n.* [< L *claudere*, to close] 1 a monastery or convent 2 monastic life 3 a covered walk along a courtyard wall in a monastery, etc., with an open colonnade —*vt.* to confine as in a cloister —**clois′tered** *adj.*

clomp (klämp) *vi.* to walk heavily or noisily

clone (klōn) *n.* [< Gr *klōn*, a twig] 1 all the descendants derived asexually from a single organism 2 a genetically identical duplicate of an organism 3 [Inf.] a person or thing very much like another —*vt.* **cloned, clon′ing** to produce a clone of —**clon′al** *adj.*

clop (kläp) *n.* [echoic] a clattering sound, like hoofbeats —*vi.* **clopped, clop′ping** to make, or move with, such a sound

close¹ (klōs) *adj.* **clos′er, clos′est** [see fol.] 1 confined or confining [*close* quarters] 2 secretive; reserved 3 miserly; stingy 4 warm and stuffy 5 with little space between; near together 6 compact; dense [*close* weave] 7 near to the surface [a *close* shave] 8 intimate; familiar [a *close* friend] 9 strict; careful [*close* attention] 10 nearly alike [a *close* resemblance] 11 nearly equal or even [a *close* contest] 12 nearly in a given condition [*close* to despair] —*adv.* in a close manner —**close′ly** *adv.* —**close′ness** *n.*

close² (klōz) *vt.* **closed, clos′ing** [< L *claudere*, to close] 1 to shut 2 to fill up or stop (an opening) 3 to finish —*vi.* 1 to undergo shutting 2 to come to an end 3 to come close or together —*n.* an end or conclusion —**close down** (or **up**) to shut or stop entirely —**close in** to draw near from all directions —**close out** to dispose of (goods) by sale

close call (klōs) [Inf.] a narrow escape from danger: also **close shave**

close-cropped (klōs′kräpt′) *adj.* clipped very short [*close-cropped* hair]

closed-cap·tioned (klōzd′kap′shən) *adj.* broadcast with captions that are visible only when the viewer opts to enable them

closed circuit a system for telecasting by cable, etc. only to receivers connected in the circuit —**closed′-cir′cuit** *adj.*

close-fist·ed (klōs′fis′tid) *adj.* stingy

close-fit·ting (-fit′in) *adj.* fitting tightly

close-knit (-nit′) *adj.* closely united or joined

close-mouthed (-mouthd′, -mouthd′) *adj.* not talking much; taciturn

close-out *n.* a discounted sale of goods no longer carried, or of those of a business being liquidated

clos·er (klō′zər) *n.* a person adept at completing a deal, an assignment, etc. successfully

clos·et (kläz′it) *n.* [< L *claudere*, to close] 1 a small room or cupboard for clothes, supplies, etc. 2 a small, private room 3 a state of secrecy —*vt.* to shut up in a private room for confidential talk —*adj.* being such only in secret [a *closet* drinker]

clos·et·ed (kläz′it id) *adj.* concealing one's identity, esp. one's sexual orientation

close-up (klōs′up′) *n.* a photograph, etc. taken at very close range

clo·sure (klō′zhər) *n.* ⟦< L *claudere*, to close⟧ **1** a closing or being closed **2** a finish; end **3** anything that closes **4** CLOTURE **5** a sense of resolution, as after an unhappy experience

clot (klät) *n.* ⟦OE⟧ a soft lump or thickened mass [a blood *clot*] — *vt., vi.* **clot′ted, clot′ting** to form into a clot or clots; coagulate

cloth (klôth) *n., pl.* **cloths** (klôthz, klôths) ⟦OE *clath*⟧ **1** a woven, knitted, or pressed fabric of fibrous material, as cotton, wool, silk, or synthetic fibers **2** a tablecloth, washcloth, etc. —*adj.* made of cloth —**the cloth** the clergy collectively

clothe (klōth) *vt.* **clothed** or **clad, cloth′ing** ⟦see prec.⟧ **1** to provide with or dress in clothes **2** to cover

clothes (klōthz, klōz) *pl.n.* ⟦OE *clathas*⟧ articles, usually of cloth, for covering, protecting, or adorning the body

clothes·pin *n.* a small clip for fastening clothes on a line, as for drying

cloth·ier (klōth′yər) *n.* a dealer in clothes or cloth

cloth·ing (klō′thiŋ) *n.* **1** clothes; garments **2** a covering

clo·ture (klō′chər) *n.* ⟦see CLOSURE⟧ the ending of legislative debate by having the bill put to an immediate vote

cloud (kloud) *n.* ⟦OE *clud*, mass of rock⟧ **1** a visible mass of condensed water droplets or ice crystals in the sky **2** a mass of smoke, dust, etc. **3** a crowd; swarm [a *cloud* of locusts] **4** anything that darkens, obscures, etc. **5** *Comput.* the data storage and computation services accessed via the internet —*vt.* **1** to darken or obscure as with clouds **2** to make gloomy **3** to sully (a reputation, etc.) —*vi.* to become cloudy, gloomy, etc. —**under a cloud** under suspicion —**cloud′less** *adj.* —**cloud′y** *adj.* **-i·er, -i·est** —**cloud′i·ness** *n.*

cloud·burst *n.* a sudden, heavy rain

clout (klout) *n.* ⟦< OE *clut*, a patch⟧ **1** a blow, as with the hand **2** [Inf.] power, esp. political power —*vt.* **1** [Inf.] to strike, as with the hand **2** to hit (a ball) hard

clove¹ (klōv) *n.* ⟦< L *clavus*, nail: from its shape⟧ **1** the dried flower bud of a tropical evergreen tree, used as a spice **2** the tree

clove² (klōv) *n.* ⟦OE *clufu*⟧ a segment of a bulb, as of garlic

clove³ (klōv) *vt., vi.* alt. pt. of CLEAVE¹

clo·ven (klō′vən) *vt., vi.* alt. pp. of CLEAVE¹ —*adj.* divided; split [a *cloven* foot]

clo·ver (klō′vər) *n.* ⟦OE *clafre*⟧ any of various low-growing plants of the pea family, with leaves of three leaflets and small flowers in dense heads

clo·ver·leaf *n., pl.* **-leafs′** a highway interchange with an overpass and curving ramps, allowing traffic to move unhindered in any of four directions

clown (kloun) *n.* ⟦< ? Scand⟧ **1** a clumsy or boorish person **2** one who entertains, as in a circus, by antics, jokes, etc. **3** a buffoon —*vi.* to act as a clown does —**clown′ish** *adj.*

cloy (kloi) *vt.* ⟦< OFr *encloyer*, nail up < L *clavus*, nail⟧ to surfeit with too much of something that is sweet, rich, etc.

cloy·ing *adj.* **1** displeasing because of excess [*cloying* sweetness] **2** overly sweet or sentimental

club (klub) *n.* ⟦< ON *klubba*, cudgel⟧ **1** a heavy stick used as a weapon **2** an implement used to hit the ball in golf **3** *a)* a group of people based on a common interest *b)* its meeting place **4** *a)* any of a suit of playing cards marked with black figures shaped like leaves of clover (♣) *b)* [*pl.*] this suit —*vt.* **clubbed, club′bing** to strike as with a club —*vi.* to unite for a common purpose

club·foot *n., pl.* **-feet′** a congenitally misshapen, often clublike, foot

club·house *n.* **1** a building used by a club **2** a locker room used by an athletic team

club soda SODA WATER

cluck (kluk) *vi.* ⟦echoic⟧ to make a low, sharp, clicking sound, as of a hen calling her chicks —*n.* this sound

clue (kloō) *n.* **1** a fact, object, etc. that helps to solve a problem or mystery **2** [Inf.] a vague or rudimentary notion —*vt.* **clued, clu′ing** [Inf.] to provide with clues or needed facts: often with *in*

clue·less *adj.* [Inf.] **1** stupid **2** uninformed, esp. about a given situation

clump (klump) *n.* ⟦< LowG *klump*⟧ **1** a lump; mass **2** a cluster, as of trees **3** the sound of heavy footsteps —*vi.* **1** to walk heavily **2** to form clumps —**clump′y** *adj.* **-i·er, -i·est**

clum·sy (klum′zē) *adj.* **-si·er, -si·est** ⟦ME *clumsid*, numb with cold⟧ **1** lacking grace or skill; awkward **2** awkwardly shaped or made —**clum′si·ly** *adv.* —**clum′si·ness** *n.*

clung (kluŋ) *vi. pt. & pp. of* CLING

clunk (kluŋk) *n.* ⟦echoic⟧ a dull, heavy, hollow sound —*vi.* to move with a clunk or clunks

clunk·er [Slang] *n.* **1** an old machine or automobile in poor repair **2** something ill-conceived or badly done

clus·ter (klus′tər) *n.* ⟦OE *clyster*⟧ a number of persons or things grouped together — *vi., vt.* to gather or grow in a cluster

cluster bomb a bomb that explodes in midair, scattering smaller bombs widely

clutch¹ (kluch) *vt.* ⟦OE *clyccan*, to clench⟧ to grasp or hold eagerly or tightly —*vi.* to snatch or seize (*at*) —*n.* **1** [*usually pl.*] power; control **2** a grasp; grip **3** a device for engaging and disengaging a motor or engine **4** a woman's small purse

clutch² (kluch) *n.* ⟦< ON *klekja*, to hatch⟧ **1** a nest of eggs **2** a brood of chicks **3** a cluster

clut·ter (klut′ər) *n.* ⟦< CLOT⟧ a number of things scattered in disorder; jumble —*vt.* to put into disorder; jumble: often with *up*

cm *abbrev.* centimeter(s)

Cmdr *abbrev.* Commander

cni·dar·i·an (ni der′ē ən) *n.* any of a phylum of invertebrates, as jellyfishes, having stinging cells and a saclike body with only one opening

Co¹ or **co** *abbrev.* **1** company **2** county

Co² *Chem. symbol for* cobalt

CO *abbrev.* **1** Colorado **2** Commanding Officer **3** conscientious objector

co- ⟦var. of COM-⟧ *prefix* **1** together **2** equally [*coextensive*] **3** joint or jointly [*copilot*]

C/O or **c/o** *abbrev.* care of

coach (kōch) *n.* ⟦after *Kócs*, village in Hungary⟧ **1** a large, covered, four-wheeled carriage **2** a railroad passenger car **3** the lowest-priced class of airline accommodations **4** a bus **5** an instructor or trainer, as of athletes, actors, or singers — *vt., vi.* to instruct and train (athletes, actors, etc.) —**coach′a-ble** *adj.*

coach·man (-mən) *n., pl.* **-men** (-mən) the driver of a coach, or carriage

co·ad·ju·tor (kō aj′ə tər) *n.* ⟦< L *co-*, together + *adjuvare*, to help⟧ an assistant, esp. to a bishop

co·ag·u·late (kō ag′yōō lāt′) *vt.* **-lat′ed, -lat′ing** ⟦< L *co-*, together + *agere*, to drive⟧ to cause (a liquid) to become somewhat firm; clot — *vi.* to become coagulated —**co·ag′u·lant** (-lənt) *n.* —**co·ag′u·la′tion** *n.*

coal (kōl) *n.* ⟦OE *col*⟧ **1** a black rock consisting chiefly of carbon from decomposed plant matter, used as fuel **2** a piece (or pieces) of this **3** an ember — *vt., vi.* to supply or be supplied with coal —**haul** (or **rake, drag,** or **call**) **over the coals** to criticize sharply

co·a·lesce (kō′ə les′) *vi.* **-lesced′, -lesc′ing** ⟦< L *co-*, together + *alescere*, grow up⟧ to unite into a single body or group —**co′a·les′cence** (-əns) *n.*

co·a·li·tion (-lish′ən) *n.* ⟦see prec.⟧ a combination or alliance, as of factions, esp. a temporary one

coal oil **1** kerosene **2** oil produced from coal, used as a lamp fuel

coal tar a thick, black liquid obtained from the distillation of bituminous coal: used in making dyes, medicines, etc.

co·an·chor (kō′aŋ′kər) *n.* one of the usually two anchors of a TV or radio newscast

coarse (kôrs) *adj.* **coars′er, coars′est** ⟦< COURSE in the sense "ordinary or usual order"⟧ **1** of poor quality; common **2** consisting of rather large particles [*coarse* sand*/* **3** rough; harsh **4** unrefined; vulgar; crude —**coarse′ly** *adv.* —**coarse′ness** *n.*

coars·en (kôr′sən) *vt., vi.* to make or become coarse

coast (kōst) *n.* ⟦< L *costa*, rib, side⟧ **1** land alongside the sea; seashore **2** a slide down an incline, as on a sled — *vi.* **1** to sail near or along a coast **2** to go down an incline, as on a sled **3** to continue in motion on momentum —**coast·al** (kōs′təl) *adj.*

coast·er *n.* **1** a person or thing that coasts **2** a small mat, disk, etc. placed under a glass to protect a table or other surface **3** short for ROLLER COASTER

coaster brake a brake on a bicycle, operated by reverse pressure on the pedals

coast guard **1** a governmental force employed to defend a nation's coasts, aid vessels in distress, etc. **2** [C- G-] such a branch of the U.S. armed forces

coast·line *n.* the outline of a coast

coat (kōt) *n.* ⟦OFr *cote*, a coat⟧ **1** a sleeved outer garment opening down the front **2** the natural covering of an animal or plant **3** a layer of some substance, as paint, over a surface — *vt.* to cover with a coat or layer

coat·ing *n.* a surface coat or layer

coat of arms *pl.* **coats of arms** a group of heraldic emblems, as on a shield, used as the insignia of a family or group

coat·tail *n.* either half of the divided lower back part of a coat

co·au·thor (kō′ô′thər) *n.* a joint author; collaborator

coax (kōks) *vt., vi.* ⟦< obs. slang *cokes*, a fool⟧ to urge with or use soft words, flattery, etc. —**coax′er** *n.* —**coax′ing·ly** *adv.*

co·ax·i·al (kō ak′sē əl) *adj.* **1** having a common axis **2** designating a high-frequency cable, as for television transmission, having two conductors, one inside the other

cob (käb) *n.* ⟦prob. < LowG⟧ **1** a corncob **2** a short-legged, thickset horse

co·balt (kō′bôlt′) *n.* ⟦< Ger *kobold*, lit., goblin⟧ a hard, steel-gray, metallic chemical element: symbol, Co; at. no. 27

cob·ble (käb′əl) *vt.* **-bled, -bling** ⟦ME < *cobelere*, cobbler⟧ **1** to mend (shoes, etc.) **2** to put together clumsily: often with *up*

cob·bler¹ (käb′lər) *n.* ⟦< ?⟧ a kind of deep-dish fruit pie

cob·bler² (käb′lər) *n.* ⟦ME *cobelere* < ?⟧ one who makes or mends shoes

cob·ble·stone *n.* a rounded stone formerly much used for paving streets

co·bra (kō′brə) *n.* ⟦< Port⟧ a very poisonous snake of Asia and Africa

cob·web (käb′web′) *n.* ⟦ME *coppe*, spider + WEB⟧ **1** a web spun by a spider **2** anything flimsy, gauzy, or ensnaring like this —**cob′web′by** *adj.*

co·caine (kō kān′) *n.* ⟦< *coca*, tropical shrub from whose leaves it is extracted⟧ a crystalline alkaloid that is a highly addictive stimulant

coc·cus (käk′əs) *n., pl.* **coc′ci** (-sī′) ⟦< Gr *kokkos*, kernel⟧ a spherical bacterium

coc·cyx (käk′siks′) *n., pl.* **coc·cy·ges** (käk sī′jēz′) ⟦< Gr *kokkyx*, cuckoo: it is shaped like a cuckoo's beak⟧ a small bone at the base of the spine

co-chair (kō chār′, kō′chər′) *n.* one who presides over a meeting, etc. jointly with another — *vt.* to preside over as co-chair

coch·le·a (käk′lē ə) *n., pl.* **-ae′** (-ē′) or **-as** ⟦< Gr *kochlias*, snail⟧ the spiral-shaped part of the inner ear —**coch′le·ar** *adj.*

cock¹ (käk) *n.* ⟦OE *coc*⟧ **1** a rooster or other male bird **2** a faucet or valve **3** *a)* the hammer of a gun *b)* its firing position **4** a jaunty tilt, as of a hat — *vt.* **1** to tilt jauntily **2** to raise erectly **3** to turn toward **4** to set (a gun) to fire

cock² (käk) *n.* ⟦ME *cokke*⟧ a small, cone-shaped pile, as of hay

cock·ade (käk äd′) *n.* ⟦< OFr *coq*, COCK[1] (*n.* 1)⟧ a rosette, knot of ribbon, etc. worn on the hat as a badge

cock·a·ma·mie (käk′ə mä′mē) *adj.* ⟦< *decalcomania*: see DECAL⟧ [Slang] 1 inferior 2 ridiculous

cock-and-bull story an absurd, improbable story

cock·a·too (käk′ə tōō′) *n.*, *pl.* **-toos′** ⟦< Malay *kakatua*⟧ a crested parrot of Australia and the East Indies

cock·a·trice (-tris′) *n.* ⟦< L *calcare*, to tread⟧ a mythical serpent supposedly able to kill by a look

cocked hat a three-cornered hat with a turned-up brim

cock·er·el (-əl) *n.* a young rooster, less than a year old

cocker spaniel ⟦< use in hunting woodcock⟧ a small spaniel with long, silky hair and drooping ears

cock-eyed *adj.* ⟦< COCK[1], *v.* + EYE⟧ 1 cross-eyed 2 [Slang] *a*) awry *b*) silly; foolish *c*) drunk

cock·fight *n.* a fight between gamecocks, usually wearing metal spurs —**cock′fight′ing** *n.*

cock·le (käk′əl) *n.* ⟦< Gr *konchē*, mussel⟧ an edible mollusk having two heart-shaped shells —**warm the cockles of someone's heart** to make someone pleased or cheerful

cock·ney (käk′nē) *n.*, *pl.* **-neys** ⟦ME *cokenei*, spoiled child, milksop⟧ [*often* C-] 1 one born in the East End of London, England, speaking a characteristic dialect 2 this dialect

cock·pit *n.* 1 an enclosed area for cockfights 2 a sunken space in the deck of a boat, usually near the stern and for use by the helmsman 3 the space in a small airplane for the crew and passengers, or in a large one for the crew

cock·roach *n.* ⟦Sp *cucaracha*⟧ an insect with long feelers and a flat, soft body: a household pest

cocks·comb (käks′kōm′) *n.* the red, fleshy growth on a rooster's head

cock·sure *adj.* ⟦COCK[1] + SURE⟧ absolutely sure or self-confident, esp. stubbornly or overbearingly

cock·tail *n.* ⟦< ?⟧ 1 a mixed alcoholic drink, usually iced 2 an appetizer, as of shrimp or juice

cock·y *adj.* **-i·er**, **-i·est** ⟦COCK[1] + -Y[2]⟧ [Inf.] jauntily conceited or self-confident —**cock′i·ly** *adv.* —**cock′i·ness** *n.*

co·co (kō′kō′) *n.*, *pl.* **-cos′** ⟦Sp < Gr *kokkos*, berry⟧ 1 the coconut palm tree 2 its fruit; coconut

co·coa (kō′kō′) *n.* ⟦var. of CACAO⟧ 1 powder made from roasted cacao seeds 2 a drink made of this and sugar, hot milk, etc. 3 a reddish-yellow brown

cocoa butter a yellowish-white fat prepared from cacao seeds

co·co·nut or **co·coa·nut** (kō′kənut′) *n.* the oval fruit of a tropical tree (**coconut palm**), with a hard, brown husk, edible white meat, and a sweet, milky fluid (**coconut water**) inside

coconut milk 1 coconut water 2 a milky, fatty liquid obtained by pressing coconut flesh

co·coon (kə kōōn′) *n.* ⟦< Fr < ML *coco*, shell⟧ the silky or fibrous case which the larva of certain insects spins about itself for shelter during the pupa stage

cod (käd) *n.*, *pl.* **cod** or **cods** ⟦ME⟧ a food fish of northern seas

Cod (käd), **Cape** hook-shaped peninsula in E Massachusetts

COD or **cod** *abbrev.* cash, or collect, on delivery

co·da (kō′də) *n.* ⟦It < L *cauda*, tail⟧ an added concluding passage, as in music

cod·dle (käd′l) *vt.* **-dled**, **-dling** ⟦< ?⟧ 1 to cook (esp. eggs in shells) in water not quite boiling 2 to pamper

code (kōd) *n.* ⟦< L *codex*, wooden tablet⟧ 1 a systematized body of laws 2 a set of principles, as of ethics 3 a set of signals for sending messages 4 a system of symbols for secret writing, etc. 5 instructions in a computer programming language —*vt.* **cod′ed**, **cod′ing** to put into code —*vi.* to write or modify a computer program —**cod′er** *n.*

co·deine (kō′dēn′) *n.* ⟦< Gr *kōdeia*, poppy head⟧ an alkaloid derived from opium: used for pain relief and in cough medicines: also **co′dein′**

co·de·pend·ent or **co-de·pend·ent** (kō′dē pen′dənt) *adj.* psychologically influenced by or needing another who is addicted to alcohol, etc. —*n.* one who is codependent —**co′de·pend′ence** *n.*, **co′-de·pend′ence** —**co′de·pend′en·cy** *n.*, **co′-de·pend′en·cy** *n.*, *pl.* **-cies**

co·dex (kō′deks′) *n.*, *pl.* **co·di·ces** (kō′də sēz′, käd′ə-) ⟦L: see CODE⟧ a manuscript volume, esp. of the Scriptures or of a classic text

cod·fish *n.*, *pl.* **-fish′** or **-fish′es** a cod

codg·er (käj′ər) *n.* ⟦prob. var. of CADGER⟧ [Inf.] an elderly person, sometimes one who is eccentric

cod·i·cil (käd′i səl) *n.* ⟦see CODE⟧ an addition to a will

cod·i·fy (käd′ə fī′) *vt.* **-fied′**, **-fy′ing** to arrange (laws, rules, etc.) systematically —**cod′i·fi·ca′tion** *n.* —**cod′i·fi′er** *n.*

cod-liv·er oil oil from the liver of the cod: it is rich in vitamins A & D

co·ed or **co-ed** (kō′ed′) [Inf.] *n.* a young woman attending a coeducational college: now somewhat old-fashioned or patronizing —*adj.* 1 coeducational 2 of a coed

co·ed·u·ca·tion (kō′ej′ə kā′shən) *n.* an educational system in which students of both sexes attend classes together —**co′ed′u·ca′tion·al** *adj.*

co·ef·fi·cient (kō′ə fish′ənt) *n.* ⟦CO- + EFFICIENT⟧ 1 a factor that contributes to a result 2 a multiplier of a variable or unknown quantity (Ex.: 6 in 6*ab*) 3 a number used as a multiplier in measuring some property

coe·len·ter·ate (si len′tər it′) *n.* ⟦< Gr *koilos*, hollow + *enteron*, intestine⟧ CNIDARIAN

co·e·qual (kō ē′kwəl) *adj.*, *n.* equal —**co′e·qual′i·ty** (-ē kwäl′ə tē) *n.* —**co·e′qual·ly** *adv.*

co·erce (kō urs′) *vt.* **-erced′, -erc′ing** [< L *co-*, together + *arcere*, confine] 1 to restrain by force 2 to compel by threats, etc. 3 to bring about by force, threats, etc. —**co·er′cion** (-ur′shən) *n.* —**co·er′cive** (-siv) *adj.*

co·e·val (kō ē′vəl) *adj., n.* [< L *co-*, together + *aevum*, age] contemporary

co·ex·ist (-ig zist′) *vi.* 1 to exist together at the same time or in the same place 2 to live together peacefully, despite differences —**co′ex·ist′ence** *n.* —**co′ex·ist′ent** *adj.*

co·ex·ten·sive (-ik sten′siv) *adj.* extending equally in time or space

C of E *abbrev.* Church of England

cof·fee (kôf′ē) *n.* [< Ar *qahwa*] 1 a drink made from the roasted, ground, beanlike seeds of a tall tropical shrub of the madder family 2 the seeds, whole or ground, or the shrub 3 light brown

coffee break a brief respite from work when coffee, etc. is taken

cof·fee·cake *n.* a kind of cake or roll to be eaten as with coffee

cof·fee·house *n.* a place where coffee is served and people gather for talk, entertainment, etc.

cof·fee·pot *n.* a container with a spout, for making or serving coffee

coffee shop a small, informal restaurant serving coffee and light refreshments or meals

coffee table a low table, usually in front of a sofa

cof·fer (kôf′ər) *n.* [see fol.] 1 a chest for holding money or valuables 2 [*pl.*] a treasury; funds

cof·fin (kôf′in) *n.* [< Gr *kophinos*, basket] the case or box in which a dead body is buried

cog (käg) *n.* [ME] 1 one of the teeth on the rim of a cogwheel 2 a cogwheel

co·gent (kō′jənt) *adj.* [< L *co-*, together + *agere*, to drive] convincingly to the point —**co′gen·cy** *n.*

cog·i·tate (käj′ə tāt′) *vi., vt.* **-tat′ed, -tat′ing** [< L] to think deeply (about); ponder —**cog′i·ta′tion** *n.* —**cog′i·ta′tive** *adj.* —**cog′i·ta′tor** *n.*

co·gnac (kōn′yak′, kôn′-) *n.* [Fr] 1 a brandy from Cognac, France 2 loosely, any brandy

cog·nate (käg′nāt′) *adj.* [< L *co-*, together + *gnasci*, to be born] 1 related by family 2 derived from a common original form, as two words 3 related or similar —*n.* a cognate person or thing

cog·ni·tion (käg nish′ən) *n.* [< L *co-*, together + *gnoscere*, know] 1 the process of knowing, perceiving, etc. 2 an idea, perception, etc. —**cog′ni·tive** (-nə tiv) *adj.*

cognitive science the study of cognition

cog·ni·za·ble (käg′ni zə bəl) *adj.* 1 that can be known or perceived 2 *Law* within the jurisdiction of a court

cog·ni·zance (-zəns) *n.* 1 perception or knowledge 2 notice; heed —**cog′ni·zant** *adj.*

cog·no·men (käg nō′mən) *n.* [< L *co-*, with + *nomen*, name] 1 surname 2 any name; esp., a nickname

cog·wheel *n.* a wheel rimmed with teeth that mesh with those of another wheel, etc., to transmit or receive motion

co·hab·it (kō hab′it) *vi.* [< L *co-*, together + *habitare*, dwell] to live together, esp. as if legally married —**co·hab′i·ta′tion** *n.*

co·heir (kō′er′, kō er′) *n.* one who inherits jointly with another or others

co·here (kō hir′) *vi.* **-hered′, -her′ing** [< L *co-*, together + *haerere*, to stick] 1 to stick together 2 to be connected naturally or logically

co·her·ent (-hir′ənt, -her′-) *adj.* 1 sticking together; cohering 2 logically connected and intelligible 3 capable of logical, intelligible speech, thought, etc. —**co·her′ence** *n.* —**co·her′ent·ly** *adv.*

co·he·sion (-hē′zhən) *n.* a cohering; tendency to stick together —**co·he′sive** (-hēs′iv) *adj.*

co·hort (kō′hôrt′) *n.* [< L *cohors*, enclosure] 1 a band of soldiers 2 any group or band 3 an associate

co·ho salmon (kō′hō′) a small salmon of the N Pacific and nearby waters

coif (koif; *for 2 usually* kwäf) *n.* 1 [< LL *cofea*, a cap] a closefitting cap 2 [< fol.] a hairstyle

coif·fure (kwä fyoor′) *n.* [Fr] 1 a headdress 2 a hairstyle

coil (koil) *vt., vi.* [< L *com-*, together + *legere*, gather] to wind into circular or spiral form —*n.* 1 a series of rings or a spiral, or anything in this form 2 a single turn of a coil 3 *Elec.* a spiral of wire

coin (koin) *n.* [< L *cuneus*, a wedge] 1 a piece of stamped metal, issued by a government as money 2 such pieces collectively —*vt.* 1 to make (coins) by stamping metal 2 to invent (a new word, phrase, etc.) —**coin′age** *n.*

co·in·cide (kō′in sīd′) *vi.* **-cid′ed, -cid′ing** [< L *co-*, together + *incidere*, fall upon] 1 to take up the same place in space 2 to occur at the same time 3 to agree exactly

co·in·ci·dence (kō in′sə dəns) *n.* 1 a coinciding 2 an accidental, but seemingly planned, occurrence of events, ideas, etc. at the same time —**co·in′ci·dent** *adj.,* **co·in′ci·den′tal** —**co·in′ci·den′tal·ly** *adv.*

co·i·tus (kō′it əs, koi′təs) *n.* [< L < *co-*, together + *ire*, go] sexual intercourse: also **co·i·tion** (kō ish′ən)

coke¹ (kōk) *n.* [< ME *colke*, core] coal from which most of the volatile components have been removed by heating: used as an industrial fuel

coke² (kōk) *n.* [Slang] COCAINE

col *abbrev.* column

COL *abbrev.* 1 Colonel 2 cost of living

col- *prefix* COM-: used before *l*

co·la (kō′lə) *n.* [< Afr name] 1 an African tree with nuts that yield an extract used in soft drinks and medicine 2 a carbonated soft drink flavored with this extract

col·an·der (kul′ən dər, käl′-) *n.* [prob. ult. < L *colum*, strainer] a perforated pan for draining off liquids

cold (kōld) *adj.* [OE *cald*] 1 of a temperature

much lower than normal, expected, or comfortable **2** not warmed or warmed up **3** unfriendly, indifferent, or depressing **4** devoid of feeling; emotionless **5** *a)* not fresh (said of a hunting scent) *b)* off the track **6** [Inf.] unconscious [knocked *cold*] **7** [Inf.] unlucky or ineffective [a *cold* streak in shooting a basketball] —*adv.* [Inf.] **1** completely [she was stopped *cold*] **2** without preparation —*n.* **1** lack of heat or warmth **2** cold weather **3** a viral infection of the respiratory tract, causing sneezing, coughing, etc. —**catch (or take) cold** to become ill with a cold —**have (or get) cold feet** [Inf.] to be (or become) timid —**in the cold** neglected —**cold′ly** *adv.* —**cold′ness** *n.*

cold-blood·ed *adj.* **1** having a body temperature that varies with the surrounding air, water, etc., as fish and reptiles **2** cruel or callous

cold cream a creamy preparation for softening and cleansing the skin

cold cuts sliced cold meats and, usually, cheeses

cold front the forward edge of a cold air mass advancing under a warmer mass

cold shoulder [Inf.] a slight; rebuff; snub —**cold′-shoul′der** *vt.*

cold sore a sore, caused by a viral infection, consisting of little blisters in or around the mouth during a cold or fever

cold turkey [Slang] **1** totally and abruptly: said of withdrawal from drugs or tobacco by an addict or user **2** without preparation

cold war an extended period of conflict between nations that does not include direct warfare

cole (kōl) *n.* [< L *caulis*, cabbage] any of various plants related to the cabbage; esp., rape or kale

cole·slaw (-slô′) *n.* [< Du: see prec. & SLAW] a salad of shredded raw cabbage: also **cole slaw**

co·le·us (kō′lē əs) *n.* [< Gr *koleos*, a sheath] any of various plants of the mint family with bright-colored leaves

col·ic (käl′ik) *n.* [< Gr *kōlon*, colon] **1** acute abdominal pain **2** a condition of infants with frequent crying from discomfort —**col′ick·y** *adj.*

col·i·se·um (käl′ə sē′əm) *n.* [< L *colosseum*] a large stadium

co·li·tis (kō līt′is) *n.* [< COLON² + -ITIS] inflammation of the large intestine

coll *abbrev.* **1** collect **2** college

col·lab·o·rate (kə lab′ə rāt′) *vi.* -rat′ed, -rat′ing [< L *com-*, with + *laborare*, to work] **1** to work together, esp. in some creative or scientific undertaking **2** to cooperate with the enemy —**col·lab′o·ra′tion** *n.* —**col·lab′o·ra′tor** *n.*

col·lage (kə läzh′) *n.* [Fr, a pasting] an art form in which bits of objects are pasted together on a surface

col·la·gen (käl′ə jən) *n.* a fibrous protein in bone and cartilage

col·lapse (kə laps′) *vi.* -lapsed′, -laps′ing [< L *com-*, together + *labi*, to fall] **1** to fall down or cave in **2** to break down suddenly **3** to fail suddenly in health **4** to fold together compactly —*vt.* to make collapse —*n.* a collapsing —**col·laps′i·ble** *adj.*

col·lar (käl′ər) *n.* [< L *collum*, neck] **1** the part of a garment that encircles the neck **2** a band of leather, etc. for an animal's neck **3** anything like a collar —*vt.* **1** to put a collar on **2** [Inf.] to seize, as by the collar

col·lar·bone *n.* CLAVICLE

col·lard (käl′ərd) *n.* [< ME] a kind of kale with coarse leaves

col·late (kō′lāt′, käl′-) *vt.* -lat′ed, -lat′ing [< L *com-*, together + *latus*, brought] **1** to compare (texts, etc.) carefully **2** to put (pages) in proper order —**col·la′tor** *n.*

col·lat·er·al (kə lat′ər əl) *adj.* [< L *com-*, together + *lateralis*, lateral] **1** parallel or corresponding **2** accompanying or supporting [collateral evidence] **3** having the same ancestors but in a different line **4** designating or of security given as a pledge for the repayment of a loan, etc. —*n.* **1** a collateral relative **2** collateral security

col·la·tion (kə lā′shən) *n.* **1** the act or result of collating **2** a light meal

col·league (käl′ēg′) *n.* [< Fr < L *com-*, with + *legare*, appoint as deputy] a fellow worker in the same profession

col·lect (kə lekt′) *vt.* [< L *com-*, together + *legere*, gather] **1** to gather together **2** to gather (stamps, etc.) as a hobby **3** to call for and receive (money) for (bills, etc.) **4** to regain control of (oneself) —*vi.* to assemble or accumulate —*adj., adv.* with payment to be made by the receiver [to telephone someone *collect*] —**col·lect′i·ble** *adj., n.,* **col·lect′a·ble** —**col·lec′tor** *n.*

col·lect·ed *adj.* **1** gathered together **2** in control of oneself; calm

col·lec·tion *n.* **1** a collecting **2** things collected **3** a mass or pile; accumulation **4** money collected

col·lec·tive *adj.* **1** formed by collecting **2** of, as, or by a group [collective effort] **3** designating a singular noun, as *tribe*, denoting a collection of individuals —*n.* **1** any collective enterprise; specif., a collective farm **2** the people who work together in it **3** a collective noun —**col·lec′tive·ly** *adv.*

collective bargaining negotiation between organized workers and their employer concerning wages, hours, etc.

col·lec·tiv·ism *n.* collective ownership and control —**col·lec′tiv·ist** *n., adj.* —**col·lec′tiv·ize′** *vt.* -ized′, -iz′ing —**col·lec′ti·vi·za′tion** *n.*

col·leen (kä lēn′) *n.* [< Ir *caile*, girl] [Irish] a girl

col·lege (käl′ij) *n.* [see COLLEAGUE] **1** a group of individuals with certain powers and duties [the electoral *college*] **2** an institution of higher education that grants degrees **3** any of the schools of a university **4** a school offering specialized instruction [a business *col-*

lege] **5** the building or buildings of a college

col·le·gial (kə lē′jəl) *adj.* **1** collegiate **2** characterized by consideration and respect among colleagues —**col·le′gi·al′i·ty** (-jē al′ə tē) *n.*

col·le·gian (kə lē′jən) *n.* a college student

col·le·giate (-jit) *adj.* of or relating to a college or college students

col·lide (kə līd′) *vi.* **-lid′ed, -lid′ing** [< L *com-*, together + *laedere*, to strike] **1** to come into violent contact; crash **2** to conflict; clash

col·lid·er *n.* a research device for directing beams of subatomic particles at each other to observe the results of their collisions

col·lie (käl′ē) *n.* [< ?] a large, long-haired dog, orig. bred as a sheepdog

col·lier (käl′yər) *n.* [< ME: see COAL & -IER] [Chiefly Brit.] **1** a coal miner **2** a coal freighter

col·lier·y *n., pl.* **-ies** [Chiefly Brit.] a coal mine and its buildings, etc.

col·li·sion (kə lizh′ən) *n.* **1** a colliding **2** a clash or conflict

col·lo·cate (käl′ə kāt′) *vt.* **-cat′ed, -cat′ing** [< L *com-*, together + *locare*, to place] to arrange; esp., to set side by side —**col·lo·ca′tion** *n.*

col·lo·di·on (kə lō′dē ən) *n.* a nitrocellulose solution that dries into a tough, elastic film

col·loid (käl′oid′) *n.* [< Gr *kolla*, glue + -OID] a substance made up of tiny particles suspended in a medium of different matter —**col·loi′dal** *adj.*

col·lo·qui·al (kə lō′kwē əl) *adj.* [see COLLOQUY] **1** conversational **2** INFORMAL (sense *d*) —**col·lo′qui·al·ism′** *n.* —**col·lo′qui·al·ly** *adv.*

col·lo·qui·um (-əm) *n., pl.* **-qui·a** (-ə) or **-qui·ums** [L: see fol.] an organized conference or seminar on some subject

col·lo·quy (käl′ə kwē) *n., pl.* **-quies** [< L *com-*, together + *loqui*, speak] a conversation or conference

col·lude (kə lood′) *vi.* **-lud′ed, -lud′ing** to act in collusion; conspire

col·lu·sion (kə loo′zhən) *n.* [< L *com-*, with + *ludere*, to play] a secret agreement for fraudulent or illegal purpose; conspiracy —**col·lu′sive** (-siv) *adj.* —**col·lu′sive·ly** *adv.*

co·logne (kə lōn′) *n.* [< Fr *eau de cologne*, lit., water of COLOGNE] a perfumed toilet water made of alcohol and aromatic oils

Co·logne (kə lōn′) city in W Germany, on the Rhine

Co·lom·bi·a (kə lum′bē ə) country in NW South America —**Co·lom′bi·an** *adj., n.*

co·lon[1] (kō′lən) *n.* [< Gr *kōlon*, verse part] a mark of punctuation (:) used before a long quotation, explanation, example, series, etc. and after the salutation of a formal letter

co·lon[2] (kō′lən) *n., pl.* **-lons** or **-la** (-lə) [< Gr *kolon*] that part of the large intestine extending from the cecum to the rectum

colo·nel (kur′nəl) *n.* [< It *colonna*, (military) column] a military officer ranking just above a lieutenant colonel

co·lo·ni·al (kə lō′nē əl) *adj.* of, in, or having

a colony **2** [*often* C-] of the thirteen British colonies that became the U.S. —*n.* an inhabitant of a colony

co·lo·ni·al·ism *n.* the system by which a country maintains foreign colonies, esp. for economic exploitation —**co·lo′ni·al·ist** *n., adj.*

co·lon·ic (kə län′ ik) *n.* an enema

col·o·nist (käl′ə nist) *n.* a settler or inhabitant of a colony

col·o·nize (-nīz′) *vt., vi.* **-nized′, -niz′ing 1** to found a colony (in) **2** to settle in a colony —**col′o·ni·za′tion** *n.* —**col′o·niz′er** *n.*

col·on·nade (käl′ə nād′) *n.* [< L *columna*, column] *Archit.* a row of columns, as along the side of a building

co·lon·os·co·py (kō′lən äs′kə pē) *n.* an examination of the inside of the colon using a fiber-optic device

col·o·ny (käl′ə nē) *n., pl.* **-nies** [< L *colere*, cultivate] **1** *a)* a group of settlers in a distant land, under the jurisdiction of their native land *b)* the region settled **2** any territory ruled over by a distant state **3** a community of the same nationality or pursuits, as within a city **4** *Biol.* a group living or growing together

co·lo·phon (käl′ə fən, -fän′) *n.* [LL < Gr *kolophōn*, top] a publisher's emblem

col·or (kul′ər) *n.* [L] **1** the property of reflecting light of a particular visible wavelength or combination of wavelengths: the *colors* of the spectrum are red, orange, yellow, green, blue, indigo, and violet **2** any coloring matter; dye; pigment **3** color of the face or skin **4** [*pl.*] a colored badge, etc. to identify the wearer **5** [*pl.*] a flag **6** outward appearance **7** vivid quality —*vt.* **1** to give color to; paint, dye, etc. **2** to change the color of **3** to alter, as by distorting [to *color* a story] —*vi.* **1** to become colored **2** to change color **3** to blush or flush **4** to draw or color pictures with wax crayons —**of color** of or designating a person who has a racial identity other than white —**show one's (true) colors** to reveal one's true self

Col·o·ra·do (käl′ə rad′ō, -rä′dō) Mountain State of the W U.S.; cap. Denver: abbrev. CO —**Col′o·rad′an** *adj., n.*

col·or·ant (kul′ər ənt) *n.* a coloring agent

col·or·a·tion (-ə′shən) *n.* a coloring

col·o·ra·tu·ra (kul′ə rə toor′ə) *n.* [It] **1** brilliant runs, trills, etc., used to display a singer's skill **2** a soprano capable of singing such music

col·or·blind *adj.* **1** unable to distinguish certain colors or any colors **2** not influenced by considerations of race —**col′or·blind′ness** *n.*

co·lo·rec·tal (kō′lə rek′təl) *adj.* of the colon and rectum

col·ored (kul′ərd) *adj.* **1** having color **2** BLACK (*adj.* 2): an old-fashioned usage when referring to African-Americans

col·or·fast *adj.* with color not subject to fading or running

col·or·ful *adj.* **1** full of color **2** picturesque, vivid, etc. —**col′or·ful·ly** *adv.* —**col′or·ful·ness** *n.*

col·or·ing *n.* **1** anything applied to impart color; pigment; etc. **2** the way a thing is colored **3** false appearance

coloring book a book of drawings intended to be colored as by children with crayons

col·or·less *adj.* **1** without color **2** lacking interest; dull —**col′or·less·ness** *n.*

color line a set of restrictions limiting interactions between people of different races

co·los·sal (kə läs′əl) *adj.* enormous in size, degree, etc.; astonishingly great —**co·los′sal·ly** *adv.*

co·los·sus (kə läs′əs) *n., pl.* **-si′** (-ī′) or **-sus·es** [< Gr] **1** a gigantic statue **2** anything huge or important

co·los·to·my (kə läs′tə mē) *n., pl.* **-mies** a surgical construction of an artificial anal opening from the colon

co·los·trum (kə läs′trəm) *n.* [L] fluid secreted by a mother's mammary glands just after giving birth

col·our (kul′ər) *n., vt., vi.* Brit. *sp.* of COLOR

colt (kōlt) *n.* [OE] a young male horse, etc.

colt·ish *adj.* of or like a colt; esp., frisky, frolicsome, etc. —**colt′ish·ly** *adv.*

Co·lum·bi·a (kə lum′bē ə, -byə) **1** capital of South Carolina **2** river flowing from Canada through Washington, & along the Washington–Oregon border into the Pacific

col·um·bine (käl′əm bin′) *n.* [< L *columbinus*, dovelike] a plant of the buttercup family, having dainty, spurred flowers of various colors

Co·lum·bus¹ (kə lum′bəs), **Chris·to·pher** (kris′tə fər) 1451?–1506; It. explorer: discovered America (1492)

Columbus² **1** capital of Ohio, in the central part **2** city in W Georgia

col·umn (käl′əm) *n.* [< L *columna*] **1** a slender upright structure, usually a supporting member in a building **2** anything like a column [the spinal *column*] **3** a file formation of troops, etc. **4** any of the vertical sections of printed matter on a page **5** a feature article appearing regularly in a newspaper, etc. —**co·lum·nar** (kə lum′nər) *adj.*

col·um·nist (käl′əm nist′) *n.* a writer of a COLUMN (*n.* 5)

Com *abbrev.* **1** Commissioner **2** Committee

com- [< L *com-*, with] *prefix* with, together: also used as an intensive

co·ma (kō′mə) *n.* [< Gr *kōma*, deep sleep] a period of deep, prolonged unconsciousness caused by injury or disease

co·ma·tose (kō′mə tōs′, käm′ə-) *adj.* **1** of, like, or in a coma **2** lethargic

comb (kōm) *n.* [< OE *camb*] **1** a thin strip of hard rubber, plastic, etc., with teeth, used to arrange or clean the hair **2** any similar tool, as for cleaning and straightening wool, flax, etc. **3** a red, fleshy outgrowth on the head, as of a rooster **4** a honeycomb —*vt.* **1** to arrange, etc. with a comb **2** to search thoroughly

com·bat (kəm bat′; *for n.* & *adj.*, käm′bat′) *vi.* **-bat′ed** or **-bat′ted, -bat′ing** or **-bat′ting** [< Fr < L *com-*, with + *battuere*, to fight] to

fight, contend, or struggle —*vt.* to fight or actively oppose —*n.* **1** armed fighting; battle **2** any struggle or conflict —*adj.* of or for military combat —**com·bat′ant** *adj., n.*

combat fatigue a psychiatric condition involving anxiety, depression, etc., as after prolonged combat in warfare

com·bat·ive *adj.* ready or eager to fight

comb·er *n.* **1** one that combs **2** a large wave that breaks on a beach, etc.

com·bi·na·tion (käm′bə nā′shən) *n.* **1** a combining or being combined **2** a thing formed by combining **3** an association of persons, firms, etc. for a common purpose **4** the series of numbers to which a dial is turned on a lock (**combination lock**) to open it

com·bine (kəm bīn′; *for n.* käm′bīn′) *vt., vi.* **-bined′, -bin′ing** [< L *com-*, together + *bini*, two by two] to join into one, as by blending; unite —*n.* **1** a machine for harvesting and threshing grain **2** an association of persons, corporations, etc. for commercial or political purposes —**com·bin′er** *n.*

comb·ings *pl.n.* loose hair, wool, etc. removed in combing

combining form a word form occurring only in compounds and derivatives (Ex.: *tele-* in *telegraph*)

com·bo (käm′bō) *n., pl.* **-bos** **1** [Inf.] a combination **2** a small jazz ensemble

com·bust (kəm bust′) *vi.* to burn

com·bus·ti·ble (kəm bus′tə bəl) *adj.* that can burn; flammable —**com·bus′ti·bil′i·ty** *n.* —**com·bus′ti·bly** *adv.*

com·bus·tion (-chən) *n.* [< L *com-*, intens. + *urere*, to burn] the act or process of burning

come (kum) *vi.* **came, come, com′ing** [< OE *cuman*] **1** to approach the speaker or some other specified place **2** to arrive or appear [help will *come*] **3** to extend; reach [the train line *comes* near the hotel] **4** to happen [success *came* to her early in life] **5** to occur mentally [the answer *came* to me] **6** to occur in a certain order [after 8 *comes* 9] **7** to be derived or descended **8** to be a native or resident: with *from* [to come from Ohio] **9** to be caused; result [illness may *come* from a poor diet] **10** to proceed or progress (*along*) **11** to become [to *come* loose] **12** to be available [it *comes* in four sizes] **13** to amount (*to*) —*interj.* used to express irritation, impatience, etc. —**come about 1** to happen **2** to turn about —**come across** (or **upon**) to meet or find by chance —**come along 1** to appear or arrive **2** to proceed or succeed —**come around** (or **round**) **1** to recover **2** to yield —**come by** to get; gain —**come down with** to contract (a flu, etc.) —**come into 1** to enter into **2** to inherit —**come off 1** to become detached **2** to end up **3** [Inf.] to prove effective, etc. —**come on!** [Inf.] used to indicate *a*) invitation *b*) encouragement *c*) objection —**come out 1** to be disclosed **2** to make a debut **3** to end up **4** to reveal oneself to be gay, lesbian, or bisexual —**come out for** to announce endorsement of —**come**

through 1 to complete something successfully **2** [Inf.] to do or give what is wanted —**come to** to recover consciousness —**come up** to arise, as a point in a discussion —**how come?** [Inf.] why?

come·back n. **1** a return to a previous state or position, as of power **2** a witty answer; retort

co·me·di·an (kə mē′dē ən) n. an entertainer who tells jokes or plays comic parts

co·me·dic (-dik) adj. having to do with comedy

co·me·di·enne (kə mē′dē en′) n. a female entertainer who tells jokes or plays comic parts

come·down n. a loss of status

com·e·dy (käm′ə dē) n., pl. **-dies** [< Gr kōmos, revel + aeidein, sing] **1** a humorous play, etc. with a nontragic ending **2** an amusing event

come·ly (kum′lē) adj. **-li·er, -li·est** [< OE cymlic] attractive; fair —**come′li·ness** n.

come-on n. [Slang] an inducement

co·mes·ti·ble (kə mes′tə bəl) n. [< L com-, intens. + edere, to eat] [usually pl.] food

com·et (käm′it) n. [< Gr komē, hair] a small mass of dust, ice, frozen carbon dioxide, etc. orbiting the sun: as it nears the sun it vaporizes, usually forming a long, luminous tail

come·up·pance (kum′up′əns) n. [Inf.] deserved punishment

com·fit (kum′fit, käm′-) n. [< L com-, with + facere, do] a candied fruit, nut, etc.

com·fort (kum′fərt) vt. [< L com-, intens. + fortis, strong] to soothe in distress or sorrow; console —n. **1** relief from distress, etc. **2** one that comforts **3** a state of, or thing that provides, ease and quiet enjoyment —**com′fort·ing** adj. —**com′fort·less** adj.

com·fort·a·ble (kumf′tər bəl, kum′fərt ə bəl) adj. **1** providing comfort **2** at ease in body or mind **3** [Inf.] sufficient to satisfy [a comfortable salary] —**com′fort·a·bly** adv.

com·fort·er n. **1** one that comforts **2** a quilted bed covering

comfort station a public toilet or restroom

com·fy (kum′fē) adj. **-fi·er, -fi·est** [Inf.] comfortable

com·ic (käm′ik) adj. **1** of comedy **2** amusing; funny —n. **1** a comedian **2** the humorous element in art or life **3** a) COMIC STRIP b) [pl.] a section of comic strips c) a comic book

com·i·cal (-i kəl) adj. causing amusement; humorous; funny —**com′i·cal′i·ty** (-kal′ə tē) n. —**com′i·cal·ly** adv.

comic strip a series of cartoons telling a humorous or adventurous story, as in a newspaper or in a booklet (**comic book**)

com·ing (kum′iŋ) adj. **1** approaching; next **2** showing promise of being successful, etc. —n. arrival or approach

com·i·ty (käm′ə tē) n. [< L comis, polite] civility

comm abbrev. **1** commission **2** committee

com·ma (käm′ə) n. [< Gr komma, clause] a mark of punctuation (,) used to indicate a slight separation of sentence elements

com·mand (kə mand′) vt. [< L com-, intens. + mandare, entrust] **1** to give an order to; direct **2** to have authority over; control **3** to have for use [to command a fortune] **4** to deserve and get [to command respect] **5** to control (a position); overlook —vi. to have authority —n. **1** an order; direction **2** controlling power or position **3** mastery **4** military or naval force, or district, under a specified authority

com·man·dant (käm′ən dant′, -dänt′) n. a commanding officer, as of a fort

com·man·deer (-dir′) vt. [see COMMAND] **1** to seize (property) for military or government use **2** [Inf.] to take forcibly

com·mand·er n. **1** one who commands **2** U.S. Navy an officer ranking just above a lieutenant commander

commander in chief pl. **commanders in chief** the supreme commander of the armed forces of a nation

com·mand·ing adj. **1** having authority **2** impressive **3** very large: [a commanding lead]

com·mand·ment n. a command; specif., any of the TEN COMMANDMENTS

com·man·do (kə man′dō) n., pl. **-dos** or **-does** [Afrik < Port] a member of a small military force trained to operate within enemy territory

command post the field headquarters of a military unit, from which operations are directed

com·mem·o·rate (kə mem′ə rāt′) vt. **-rat′ed, -rat′ing** [< L com-, intens. + memorare, remind] **1** to honor the memory of, as by a ceremony **2** to serve as a memorial to —**com·mem′o·ra′tion** n. —**com·mem′o·ra′tor** n.

com·mem·o·ra·tive (-rə tiv, -rā′tiv) adj. commemorating —n. a stamp or coin marking an event, honoring a person, etc.

com·mence (kə mens′) vi., vt. **-menced′, -menc′ing** [< L com-, together + initiare, begin] to begin; start

com·mence·ment n. **1** a beginning; start **2** the ceremony of conferring degrees or diplomas at a school

com·mend (kə mend′) vt. [see COMMAND] **1** to entrust to the care of another **2** to praise —**com·mend′a·ble** adj. —**com·mend′a·bly** adv. —**com·men·da·tion** (käm′ən dā′shən) n.

com·mend·a·to·ry (kə men′də tôr′ē) adj. praising or recommending

com·men·su·ra·ble (kə men′shoor ə bəl, -sər-) adj. [< L com-, together + mensura, measurement] measurable by the same standard or measure

com·men·su·rate (-shoor it, -sər-) adj. [see prec.] **1** equal in measure or size; coextensive **2** proportionate **3** commensurable

com·ment (käm′ent′) n. [< L com-, intens. + meminisse, remember] **1** an explanatory or critical note **2** a remark or observation **3** talk; gossip —vi. to make a comment or comments

com·men·tar·y (käm′ən ter′ē) n., pl. **-ies** a series of explanatory notes or remarks

com·men·tate (-tāt′) vi. **-tat′ed, -tat′ing** to perform as a commentator

com·men·ta·tor (-tāt′ər) *n.* one who reports and analyzes events, trends, etc., as on television

com·merce (käm′ərs) *n.* [< L *com-*, together + *merx*, merchandise] trade on a large scale, as between countries

com·mer·cial (kə mur′shəl) *adj.* 1 of commerce or business 2 made or done for profit —*n.* Radio, TV a paid advertisement —**com·mer′cial·ism′** *n.* —**com·mer′cial·ly** *adv.*

com·mer·cial·ize (-īz′) *vt.* -ized′, -iz′ing to make use of mainly for profit —**com·mer′cial·i·za′tion** *n.*

com·min·gle (kə miŋ′gəl) *vt., vi.* -gled, -gling to mingle together

com·mis·er·ate (kə miz′ər āt′) *vi.* -at′ed, -at′ing [< L *com-*, intens. + *miserari*, to pity] to sympathize (*with*) —**com·mis′er·a′tion** *n.*

com·mis·sar (käm′ə sär′) *n.* [Russ *komissar*] the head of any former U.S.S.R. commissariat

com·mis·sar·i·at (-ser′ē ət) *n.* [Fr < L: see COMMIT] 1 an army branch providing food and supplies 2 a former government department in the U.S.S.R.

com·mis·sar·y (-ser′ē) *n., pl.* -ies [see COMMIT] 1 a store, as in an army camp, where food and supplies are sold 2 a restaurant in a movie or TV studio

com·mis·sion (kə mish′ən) *n.* [see COMMIT] 1 *a)* an authorization to perform certain duties or tasks *b)* a document giving such authorization *c)* the authority so granted 2 that which one is authorized to do 3 a group of people appointed to perform specified duties 4 a committing; doing 5 a percentage of money from sales, allotted to an agent, etc. 6 a request or order, as for the creation of a work of art 7 *Mil. a)* an official certificate conferring rank *b)* the rank conferred —*vt.* 1 to give a commission to 2 to authorize 3 to put (a ship or boat) into service 4 to request the creation of —**in** (or **out of**) **commission** in (or not in) working order

commissioned officer an officer in the armed forces holding a commission

com·mis·sion·er *n.* 1 a person authorized to do certain things by a commission or warrant 2 a member of a COMMISSION (*n.* 3) 3 an official in charge of a government bureau, etc. 4 a person selected to regulate and control a professional sport, an amateur league, etc.

com·mit (kə mit′) *vt.* -mit′ted, -mit′ting [L *com-*, together + *mittere*, send] 1 to deliver for safekeeping; entrust; consign 2 to put in custody or confinement [*committed* to prison] 3 to do or perpetrate (a crime) 4 to bind, as by a promise; pledge — *vi.* [Inf.] to make a pledge: often with *to* —**com·mit′ment** *n.* —**com·mit′tal** *n.*

com·mit·tee (kə mit′ē) *n.* [see prec.] a group of people chosen to report or act upon a certain matter —**com·mit′tee·man** (-mən) *n., pl.* -men (-men) —**com·mit′tee·wom′an** *n., pl.* -wom′en

com·mode (kə mōd′) *n.* [Fr < L: see COM- & MODE] 1 a chest of drawers 2 a toilet

com·mod·i·fy (kə mäd′ə fī′) *vt.* -fied′, -fy′ing to treat like or make into a mere commodity —**com·mod′i·fi·ca′tion** *n.*

com·mo·di·ous (kə mō′dē əs) *adj.* [see COMMODE] spacious; roomy

com·mod·i·ty (kə mäd′ə tē) *n., pl.* -ties [see COMMODE] 1 any useful thing 2 anything bought and sold 3 [*pl.*] basic products, as of agriculture

com·mo·dore (käm′ə dôr′) *n.* [see COMMAND] U.S. Navy [Historical] an officer ranking just above a captain

com·mon (käm′ən) *adj.* [< L *communis*] 1 belonging to or shared by each or all 2 general; widespread 3 familiar; usual 4 not of the upper classes [the *common* people] 5 vulgar; coarse 6 designating a noun (as *book*) that refers to any of a group —*n.* [*sometimes pl.*] land owned or used by all the inhabitants of a place —**in common** shared by each or all —**com′mon·al′i·ty** (-al′ə tē) *n.* —**com′mon·ly** *adv.*

com·mon·al·ty (-al tē) *n.* the common people

common carrier a person or company that transports people or goods for a fee

common denominator 1 a common multiple of the denominators of two or more fractions 2 a characteristic, etc. held in common

com·mon·er *n.* a person not of the nobility; one of the common people

common law the law based on custom, usage, and judicial decisions

com·mon-law marriage Law a marriage not solemnized by religious or civil ceremony

common market an association of countries for closer economic union

common multiple Math. a multiple of each of two or more quantities

com·mon·place *n.* 1 a platitude 2 anything common or ordinary —*adj.* trite or ordinary

common pleas Law in some U.S. states, a court having jurisdiction over civil and criminal trials

com·mons *pl.n.* 1 the common people 2 [C-] HOUSE OF COMMONS 3 [*often with sing. v.*] a room, building, etc. for dining, as at a college

common sense good sense or practical judgment —**com′mon-sense′** *adj.*, **com′mon·sen′si·cal**

common stock stock in a company without the privileges of preferred stock, but usually giving its owner a vote

com·mon·weal (-wēl′) *n.* the public good; general welfare

com·mon·wealth (-welth′) *n.* 1 the people of a nation or state 2 a democracy or republic 3 a federation of states —**the Commonwealth** association of independent nations united under the British crown for purposes of consultation and mutual assistance: in full **the Commonwealth of Nations**

Commonwealth of Independent States a loose confederation of countries that were part of the U.S.S.R.

com·mo·tion (kə mō′shən) *n.* [< L *com-*, together + *movere*, to move] 1 violent motion 2 confusion; bustle

com·mu·nal (kə myoon′əl, käm′yə nəl) *adj.* 1 of a commune 2 of the community; public 3 marked by common ownership of property —**com·mu′nal·ize′** *vt.* -ized′, -iz′ing —**com·mu′nal·ly** *adv.*

com·mune¹ (kə myoon′) *vi.* -muned′, -mun′ing [< OFr *comuner*, to share] 1 to talk together intimately 2 to be in close rapport

com·mune² (käm′yoon′) *n.* [< L *communis*, common] 1 the smallest administrative district of local government in some European countries 2 a small group of people living communally

com·mu·ni·ca·ble (kə myoo′ni kə bəl) *adj.* that can be communicated, as an idea, or transmitted, as a disease —**com·mu′ni·ca·bil′i·ty** *n.*

com·mu·ni·cant (-kənt) *n.* one who receives Holy Communion

com·mu·ni·cate (kə myoo′ni kāt′) *vt.* -cat′ed, -cat′ing [< L *communicare*] 1 to impart; transmit 2 to give (information, etc.) —*vi.* 1 to give or exchange information 2 to have a meaningful relationship 3 to be connected, as rooms —**com·mu′ni·ca′tor** *n.*

com·mu·ni·ca·tion *n.* 1 a transmitting 2 *a)* a giving or exchanging of information, etc. *b)* a message, letter, etc. 3 a means of communicating —**com·mu′ni·ca′tive** (-kāt′iv, -kə tiv) *adj.*

com·mun·ion (kə myoon′yən) *n.* [[see COMMON]] 1 possession in common 2 a communing 3 a Christian denomination 4 [C-] HOLY COMMUNION

com·mu·ni·qué (kə myoo′ni kā′, kə myoo′ni kā′) *n.* [[Fr]] an official communication

com·mu·nism (käm′yoo niz′əm, -yə-) *n.* [[see COMMON]] 1 any theory or system of common ownership of property 2 [*often* C-] *a)* socialism as formulated by Marx, Lenin, etc. *b)* any government or political movement supporting this

com·mu·nist (-nist) *n.* 1 an advocate or supporter of communism 2 [C-] a member of a Communist Party —*adj.* of, like, or supporting communism or communists —**com′mu·nis′tic** *adj.*

com·mu·ni·ty (kə myoo′nə tē) *n.*, *pl.* -ties [[see COMMON]] 1 *a)* any group living in the same area or having interests, work, etc. in common *b)* such an area 2 the general public 3 a sharing in common 4 the state of living with others 5 friendly association; fellowship

community college a junior college serving a certain community

community service unpaid work for the community

com·mu·ta·tive (kə myoot′ə tiv, käm′yə tāt′iv) *adj.* 1 involving exchange or replacement 2 *Math.* of an operation in which the order of the elements does not affect the result, as, in addition, 3 + 2 = 2 + 3

com·mute (kə myoot′) *vt.* -mut′ed, -mut′ing

[< L *com-*, intens. + *mutare*, to change] 1 to exchange; substitute 2 to change (an obligation, punishment, etc.) to a less severe one —*vi.* to travel as a commuter —*n.* [Inf.] the trip of a commuter —**com·mu·ta·tion** (käm′yə tā′shən) *n.*

com·mut·er *n.* a person who travels regularly by train, bus, etc., esp. between home and work

Com·o·ros (käm′ə rōz′) country on a group of islands in the W Indian Ocean

comp *abbrev.* 1 comparative 2 compound

com·pact¹ (kəm pakt′, käm′pakt; *for n.* käm′pakt) *adj.* [< L *com-*, with, together + *pangere*, to fix] 1 closely and firmly packed 2 taking little space 3 terse; concise —*vt.* 1 to pack or join firmly together 2 to make by putting together —*n.* 1 a small cosmetic case, usually containing face powder and a mirror 2 a relatively small car —**com·pact′ly** *adv.* —**com·pact′ness** *n.*

com·pact² (käm′pakt) *n.* an agreement; covenant

compact disc (*or* **disk**) a digital disc on which music, data, etc. may be encoded for playing on a device using a laser beam to read the encoded matter

com·pac·tor (kəm pak′tər, käm′pak′tər) *n.* a device that compresses trash into small bundles

com·pan·ion (kəm pan′yən) *n.* [< L *com-*, with + *panis*, bread] 1 an associate; comrade 2 a person paid to live or travel with another 3 one of a pair or set —**com·pan′ion·a·ble** *adj.* —**com·pan′ion·ship′** *n.*

com·pan·ion·way *n.* a stairway leading from one deck of a ship to another

com·pa·ny (kum′pə nē) *n.*, *pl.* -nies [[see COMPANION]] 1 companionship; society 2 a group of people associated for some purpose, esp. as a business venture 3 a guest or guests 4 a body of troops 5 a ship's crew —**keep company** to associate (*with*) —**keep (someone) company** to stay with (someone) so as to provide companionship —**part company** to stop associating (*with*)

com·pa·ra·ble (käm′pə rə bəl, kəm par′ə bəl) *adj.* 1 that can be compared 2 worthy of comparison 3 approximately equal —**com′pa·ra·bly** *adv.*

com·par·a·tive (kəm par′ə tiv) *adj.* 1 involving comparison 2 not absolute; relative 3 *Gram.* designating the second degree of comparison of adjectives and adverbs —*n. Gram.* the comparative degree ["finer" is the *comparative* of "fine"] —**com·par′a·tive·ly** *adv.*

com·pare (kəm per′) *vt.* -pared′, -par′ing [< L *com-*, with + *parare*, make equal] 1 to liken (*to*) 2 to examine for similarities or differences 3 *Gram.* to form the degrees of comparison of —*vi.* 1 to be worth comparing (*with*) 2 to make comparisons —**beyond** (*or* **past** *or* **without**) **compare** incomparably good, bad, great, etc.

com·par·i·son (kəm par′ə sən) *n.* 1 a comparing or being compared 2 likeness; simi-

larity 3 *Gram.* change in an adjective or adverb to show the positive, comparative, and superlative degrees —**in comparison with** compared with

com·part·ment (kəm pärt'mənt) *n.* ⟦< L *com-*, intens. + *partire*, divide⟧ **1** any of the divisions into which a space is partitioned off **2** a separate section or category —**com·part·men·tal·ize** (käm'pärt ment''l īz') *vt.* **-ized', -iz'ing**

com·pass (kum'pəs; *also* käm'-) *vt.* ⟦< L *com-*, together + *passus*, a step⟧ **1** [Archaic] to go around **2** to surround **3** to understand **4** to achieve or contrive —*n.* **1** [*often pl.*] an instrument with two adjustable legs, for drawing circles, for measuring, etc. **2** a boundary **3** an enclosed area **4** range; scope **5** an instrument for showing direction, esp. one with a swinging magnetic needle pointing north

com·pas·sion (kəm pash'ən) *n.* ⟦< L *com-*, together + *pati*, suffer⟧ deep sympathy; pity —**com·pas'sion·ate** *adj.* —**com·pas'sion·ate·ly** *adv.*

com·pat·i·ble (kəm pat'ə bəl) *adj.* ⟦see prec.⟧ **1** getting along or going well together **2** that can be mixed, used, etc. together effectively —**com·pat'i·bil'i·ty** *n.* —**com·pat'i·bly** *adv.*

com·pa·tri·ot (kəm pā'trē ət) *n.* ⟦see COM- & PATRIOT⟧ **1** a person of one's own country **2** a colleague

com·peer (käm'pir', käm pir') *n.* ⟦see COM- & PAR⟧ **1** an equal; peer **2** a comrade

com·pel (kəm pel') *vt.* **-pelled', -pel'ling** ⟦< L *com-*, together + *pellere*, to drive⟧ to force or get by force —**com·pel'ling·ly** *adv.*

com·pen·di·um (kəm pen'dē əm) *n., pl.* **-ums** or **-a** (-ə) ⟦< L *com-*, together + *pendere*, weigh⟧ a concise but comprehensive summary

com·pen·sate (käm'pən sāt') *vt.* **-sat'ed, -sat'ing** ⟦< L *com-*, with + *pendere*, weigh⟧ **1** [Now Rare] to make up for; counterbalance **2** to make suitable payment to —*vi.* to make or serve as amends (*for*) —**com'pen·sa'tion** *n.* —**com·pen·sa·to·ry** (kəm pen'sə tôr'ē) *adj.*

com·pete (kəm pēt') *vi.* **-pet'ed, -pet'ing** ⟦< L *com-*, together + *petere*, to desire⟧ to be in rivalry; contend; vie (*in* a contest, etc.)

com·pe·tence (käm'pə təns) *n.* **1** sufficient means for one's needs **2** ability; fitness **3** legal power, jurisdiction, etc. Also **com'pe·ten·cy** (-tən sē)

com·pe·tent (-tənt) *adj.* ⟦see COMPETE⟧ **1** capable; fit **2** sufficient; adequate **3** having legal competence —**com'pe·tent·ly** *adv.*

com·pe·ti·tion (käm'pə tish'ən) *n.* ⟦L *competitio*⟧ **1** a competing; rivalry **2** a contest; match **3** rivalry in business **4** those against whom one competes —**com·pet·i·tive** (kəm pet'ə tiv) *adj.*

com·pet·i·tor (kəm pet'ət ər) *n.* ⟦L⟧ one who competes, as a business rival

com·pile (kəm pīl') *vt.* **-piled', -pil'ing** ⟦<

L *com-*, together + *pilare*, to compress⟧ **1** to collect and assemble (statistics, facts, etc.) **2** to compose (a book, etc.) of materials from various sources —**com·pi·la·tion** (käm'pə lā'shən) *n.*

com·pla·cen·cy (kəm plā'sən sē) *n.* ⟦< L *com-*, intens. + *placere*, to please⟧ contentment; often, specif., self-satisfaction, or smugness: also **com·pla'cence** —**com·pla'cent** *adj.*

com·plain (kəm plān') *vi.* ⟦< L *com-*, intens. + *plangere*, to strike⟧ **1** to express pain, displeasure, etc. **2** to find fault **3** to make an accusation —**com·plain'er** *n.*

com·plain·ant (-ənt) *n. Law* a plaintiff

com·plaint (-plānt') *n.* **1** a complaining **2** a cause for complaining **3** an ailment **4** *Law* a formal charge or accusation

com·plai·sant (kəm plā'zənt, -sənt) *adj.* ⟦see COMPLACENCY⟧ willing to please; obliging —**com·plai'sant·ly** *adv.* —**com·plai'sance** *n.*

com·plect·ed (-plek'tid) *adj.* COMPLEXIONED

com·ple·ment (käm'plə mənt; *for v.,* -ment') *n.* ⟦see fol.⟧ **1** that which completes or perfects **2** the amount needed to fill or complete **3** *Math.* the number of degrees that must be added to a given angle to make it equal 90 degrees —*vt.* to make complete —**com'ple·men'ta·ry** (-men'tə rē) *adj.*

com·plete (kəm plēt') *adj.* ⟦< L *com-*, intens. + *plere*, fill⟧ **1** entire **2** finished **3** thorough; absolute —*vt.* **-plet'ed, -plet'ing 1** to finish **2** to make whole or perfect **3** to successfully execute —**com·plete'ly** *adv.* —**com·plete'ness** *n.* —**com·ple'tion** (plē'shən) *n.*

com·plex (käm pleks', käm'pleks'; *for n.* käm'pleks') *adj.* ⟦< L *com-*, with + *plectere*, to weave⟧ **1** consisting of two or more related parts **2** complicated —*n.* **1** a complex whole **2** an assemblage of units, as buildings **3** *Psychoanalysis a*) a group of mainly unconscious impulses, etc. strongly influencing behavior *b*) popularly, an exaggerated dislike or fear —**com·plex'i·ty** *n.*

complex fraction a fraction with a fraction in its numerator or denominator, or in both

com·plex·ion (kəm plek'shən) *n.* ⟦see COMPLEX⟧ **1** the color, texture, etc. of the skin, esp. of the face **2** nature; character; aspect

com·plex·ioned *adj.* having a (specified) complexion [light-*complexioned*]

complex sentence a sentence consisting of an independent clause and one or more dependent clauses

com·pli·ance (kəm plī'əns) *n.* **1** a complying; acquiescence **2** a tendency to give in readily to others Also **com·pli'an·cy** —**com·pli'ant** *adj.*

com·pli·cate (käm'pli kāt') *vt., vi.* **-cat'ed, -cat'ing** ⟦< L *com-*, together + *plicare*, to fold⟧ to make or become intricate, difficult, or involved —**com'pli·ca'tion** *n.*

com·pli·cat·ed *adj.* intricately involved; hard to solve, analyze, etc.

com·plic·it (kəm plis'it) *adj.* having complicity; implicated: also **com·plic'i·tous** (-ə təs)

com·plic·i·ty (-tē) *n.*, *pl.* **-ties** [see COMPLICATE] partnership in wrongdoing

com·pli·ment (käm′plə mənt; *for v.*, -ment′) *n.* [Fr < L: see COMPLETE] 1 a formal act of courtesy 2 something said in praise 3 [*pl.*] respects —*vt.* to pay a compliment

com·pli·men·ta·ry (-men′tə rē) *adj.* 1 paying or containing a compliment 2 given free as a courtesy

com·ply (kəm plī′) *vi.* **-plied′, -ply′ing** [see COMPLETE] to act in accordance (*with* a request, order, etc.)

com·po·nent (kəm pō′nənt) *adj.* [see COMPOSITE] serving as one of the parts of a whole —*n.* a part, element, or ingredient

com·port (kəm pôrt′) *vt.* [< L *com-*, together + *portare*, carry] to behave (oneself) in a specified manner —*vi.* to accord (*with*) —**com·port′ment** *n.*

com·pose (kəm pōz′) *vt.* **-posed′, -pos′ing** [< OFr *com-*, with + *poser*, to place] 1 to make up; constitute 2 to put in proper form 3 to create (a musical or literary work) 4 to make calm 5 *a*) to set (type) *b*) to produce (printed matter) as by computer, etc. —*vi.* to create musical works, etc. —**com·pos′er** *n.*

com·posed *adj.* calm; self-possessed

com·pos·ite (kəm päz′it) *adj.* [< L *com-*, together + *ponere*, to place] 1 made from two or more ingredients or parts 2 *Bot.* designating a large family of plants with flower heads composed of dense clusters of small flowers, including the daisy and the chrysanthemum —*n.* a thing of distinct parts —**com·pos′ite·ly** *adv.*

com·po·si·tion (käm′pə zish′ən) *n.* 1 a composing, esp. of literary or musical works 2 the makeup of a person or thing 3 something composed

com·pos·i·tor (kəm päz′ət ər) *n.* one who sets matter for printing, esp. a typesetter

com·post (käm′pōst) *n.* [see COMPOSITE] a mixture of decomposing organic matter for fertilizing soil —*vt.* to convert (organic matter) into compost

com·po·sure (kəm pō′zhər) *n.* [see COMPOSE] calmness; self-possession

com·pote (käm′pōt) *n.* [Fr: see COMPOSITE] 1 a dish of stewed fruits 2 a long-stemmed dish, as for candy

com·pound¹ (käm pound′, käm′pound′; *for adj. usually & for n. always,* käm′pound′) *vt.* [see COMPOSITE] 1 to mix or combine 2 to make by combining parts 3 to compute (compound interest) 4 to increase or intensify by adding something new —*adj.* made up of two or more parts —*n.* 1 a thing formed by combining parts 2 a substance containing two or more elements chemically combined —**compound a felony** (or **crime**) to agree, for payment, not to inform about or prosecute a felony (or crime)

com·pound² (käm′pound′) *n.* [Malay *kampong*] an enclosed area with a building or buildings in it

compound eye an eye made up of numerous simple eyes functioning collectively, as in insects

compound fracture a fracture in which the broken bone pierces the skin

compound interest interest paid on both the principal and the accumulated unpaid interest

compound sentence a sentence consisting of two or more independent, coordinate clauses

com·pre·hend (käm′prē hend′, -pri-) *vt.* [< L *com-*, with + *prehendere*, seize] 1 to grasp mentally; understand 2 to include; take in; comprise —**com′pre·hen′si·ble** (-hen′sə bəl) *adj.* —**com′pre·hen′sion** *n.*

com·pre·hen·sive (-hen′siv) *adj.* wide in scope; inclusive —**com′pre·hen′sive·ly** *adv.* —**com′pre·hen′sive·ness** *n.*

com·press (kəm pres′; *for n.* käm′pres′) *vt.* [< L *com-*, together + *premere*, to press] to press together and make more compact —*n.* a pad of folded cloth, often wet or medicated, applied to the skin —**com·pressed′** *adj.* —**com·pres′sion** *n.*

com·pres·sor (-pres′ər) *n.* a machine for compressing air, gas, etc.

com·prise (-prīz′) *vt.* **-prised′, -pris′ing** [see COMPREHEND] 1 to consist of 2 to make up; form

com·pro·mise (käm′prə mīz′) *n.* [< L *com-*, together + *promittere*, to promise] 1 a settlement in which each side makes concessions 2 something midway — *vt.*, *vi.* **-mised′, -mis′ing** 1 to adjust by compromise 2 to lay open to suspicion, disrepute, etc. 3 to weaken

comp·trol·ler (kən trō′lər) *n.* [altered (infl. by Fr *compte*, an account) < CONTROLLER] CONTROLLER (*n.* 1, esp. in government usage)

com·pul·sion (kəm pul′shən) *n.* 1 a compelling or being compelled 2 a driving force 3 an irresistible impulse to perform some act —**com·pul′sive** (-siv) *adj.* —**com·pul′sive·ly** *adv.*

com·pul·so·ry (-sə rē) *adj.* 1 obligatory; required 2 compelling

com·punc·tion (kəm puŋk′shən) *n.* [< L *com-*, intens. + *pungere*, to prick] an uneasy feeling prompted by guilt; remorse

com·pute (kəm pyōot′) *vt.* **-put′ed, -put′ing** [< L *com-*, with + *putare*, reckon] to calculate (an amount, etc.) —*vi.* 1 to calculate an amount, etc. 2 [Inf.] to make sense —**com·pu·ta·tion** (käm′pyōo tā′shən) *n.*

com·put·er *n.* an electronic machine that performs rapid, complex calculations or compiles and manipulates data —**com·put′er·ize′** *vt.* **-ized′, -iz′ing** —**com·put′er·i·za′tion** *n.*

com·rade (käm′rad′, -rəd) *n.* [< Sp *camarada*, chamber mate < L *camera*, room] 1 a friend; close companion 2 an associate —**com′rade·ship′** *n.*

con¹ (kän) *adv.* [< L *contra*] against —*n.* an opposing reason, vote, etc.

con² (kän) *vt.* **conned, con′ning** [< OE *cunnan*, know] to study carefully

con³ (kän) [Inf.] *adj.* CONFIDENCE [a *con* man] —*vt.* **conned, con′ning** to swindle or trick —*n.* a swindle

con⁴ (kän) *n.* [Slang] *short for* CONVICT

con⁵ (kän) *n.* [Inf.] *short for* CONVENTION

con- *prefix* COM-: used before *c, d, g, j, n, q, s, t, v,* and sometimes *f*

con·cat·e·na·tion (kan kat''n ā'shən, kän-) *n.* ⟦< L *com-*, together + *catena*, a chain⟧ a connected series, as of events

con·cave (kän kāv', kän'kāv') *adj.* ⟦< L *com-*, intens. + *cavus*, hollow⟧ hollow and curved like the inside of a bowl —**con·cav'i·ty** (-kav' ə tē) *n., pl.* **-ties**

con·ceal (kən sēl') *vt.* ⟦< L *com-*, together + *celare*, to hide⟧ 1 to hide 2 to keep secret —**con·ceal'ment** *n.*

con·cede (kən sēd') *vt.* **-ced'ed, -ced'ing** ⟦< L *com-*, with + *cedere*, cede⟧ 1 to admit as true, valid, certain, etc. 2 to grant as a right

con·ceit (kən sēt') *n.* ⟦see CONCEIVE⟧ 1 an exaggerated opinion of oneself, one's merits, etc.; vanity 2 a fanciful expression or notion, esp. a metaphor

con·ceit·ed *adj.* vain

con·ceiv·a·ble (kən sēv'ə bəl) *adj.* that can be understood, imagined, or believed —**con·ceiv'a·bil'i·ty** *n.* —**con·ceiv'a·bly** *adv.*

con·ceive (kən sēv') *vt.* **-ceived', -ceiv'ing** ⟦< L *com-*, together + *capere*, take⟧ 1 to become pregnant with 2 to form in the mind; imagine 3 to understand —*vi.* 1 to become pregnant 2 to form an idea (*of*)

con·cen·trate (kän'sən trāt') *vt.* **-trat'ed, -trat'ing** ⟦< L *com-*, together + *centrum*, center + -ATE¹⟧ 1 to focus (one's thoughts, efforts, etc.) 2 to increase the strength, density, etc. of —*vi.* to fix one's attention (*on* or *upon*) —*n.* a concentrated substance —**con'cen·tra'tion** *n.*

concentration camp a prison camp for political dissidents, ethnic minorities, etc.

con·cen·tric (kən sen'trik) *adj.* ⟦< L *com-*, together + *centrum*, center⟧ having a common center: said of circles —**con·cen'tri·cal·ly** *adv.*

con·cept (kän'sept') *n.* ⟦see CONCEIVE⟧ an idea or thought; abstract notion

con·cep·tion (kən sep'shən) *n.* 1 a conceiving or being conceived in the womb 2 the beginning, as of a process 3 the formulation of ideas 4 a concept 5 an original idea or design

con·cep·tu·al (-chōō əl) *adj.* of conception or concepts —**con·cep'tu·al·ly** *adv.*

con·cep·tu·al·ize (-īz') *vt.* **-ized', -iz'ing** to form a concept of —**con·cep'tu·al·i·za'tion** *n.*

con·cern (kən surn') *vt.* ⟦< L *com-*, with + *cernere*, sift⟧ 1 to have a relation to 2 to engage or involve 3 to cause to feel uneasy —*n.* 1 a matter of interest to one 2 interest in or regard for a person or thing 3 worry; anxiety 4 a business firm —**as concerns** in regard to —**concern oneself** 1 to busy oneself 2 to be worried

con·cerned *adj.* 1 involved or interested (*in*) 2 uneasy or anxious

con·cern·ing *prep.* relating to; about

con·cert (kän'sərt) *n.* ⟦< L *com-*, with + *certare*, strive⟧ 1 mutual agreement; concord 2 a performance of music —**in concert** in unison

con·cert·ed (kən surt'id) *adj.* 1 mutually arranged or agreed upon; combined 2 deliberate and determined —**con·cert'ed·ly** *adv.*

con·cer·ti·na (kän'sər tē'nə) *n.* ⟦< CONCERT⟧ a small accordion

con·cert·mas·ter *n.* the leader of the first violin section of a symphony orchestra, and often the assistant to the conductor

con·cer·to (kən cher'tō) *n., pl.* **-tos** or **-ti** (-tē) ⟦It⟧ a musical composition for one or more solo instruments and an orchestra, usually in three movements

con·ces·sion (kən sesh'ən) *n.* 1 a conceding 2 a thing conceded; acknowledgment 3 a privilege granted by a government, company, etc., as the right to sell food at a park

con·ces·sion·aire (-ə ner') *n.* ⟦< Fr⟧ the holder of a CONCESSION (*n.* 3)

conch (käŋk, känch) *n., pl.* **conchs** (käŋks) or **conch·es** (kän'′iz) ⟦< Gr *konchē*⟧ the spiral, one-piece shell of various sea mollusks

con·ci·erge (kän'sē erzh'; Fr kôn syerzh') *n.* ⟦Fr < L *conservus*, fellow slave⟧ 1 a custodian, as of an apartment house 2 a hotel employee who assists guests by booking theater reservations, etc.

con·cil·i·ar (kən sil'ē ər) *adj.* of, from, or by means of a council

con·cil·i·ate (-āt') *vt.* **-at'ed, -at'ing** ⟦see COUNCIL⟧ to win over; make friendly; placate —**con·cil'i·a'tion** *n.* —**con·cil'i·a'tor** *n.* —**con·cil'i·a·to'ry** (-ə tôr'ē) *adj.*

con·cise (kən sīs') *adj.* ⟦< L *com-*, intens. + *caedere*, to cut⟧ brief and to the point; short and clear —**con·cise'ly** *adv.* —**con·cise'ness** *n.* —**con·ci'sion** (-sizh'ən) *n.*

con·clave (kän'klāv') *n.* ⟦< L *com-*, with + *clavis*, a key⟧ 1 a private meeting; specif., one held by cardinals to elect a pope 2 any large convention

con·clude (kən klōōd') *vt., vi.* **-clud'ed, -clud'ing** ⟦< L *com-*, together + *claudere*, to shut⟧ 1 to end; finish 2 to deduce 3 to decide; determine 4 to arrange (a treaty, etc.)

con·clu·sion (-klōō'zhən) *n.* 1 the end 2 a judgment or opinion formed after thought 3 an outcome 4 a concluding (*of* a treaty, etc.) —**in conclusion** lastly; in closing

con·clu·sive (-siv) *adj.* final; decisive —**con·clu'sive·ly** *adv.* —**con·clu'sive·ness** *n.*

con·coct (kən käkt') *vt.* ⟦< L *com-*, together + *coquere*, to cook⟧ 1 to make by combining ingredients 2 to devise; plan —**con·coc'tion** *n.*

con·com·i·tant (-käm'ə tənt) *adj.* ⟦< L *com-*, together + *comes*, companion⟧ accompanying; attendant —*n.* a concomitant thing —**con·com'i·tant·ly** *adv.*

con·cord (kän'kôrd', kän'-) *n.* ⟦< L *com-*, together + *cor*, heart⟧ 1 agreement; harmony 2 peaceful relations, as between nations

Con·cord (käŋ'kərd) capital of New Hampshire

con·cord·ance (kən kôrd''ns) *n.* 1 agreement 2 an alphabetical list of the words used in a book, with references to the passages in which they occur

con·cord·ant *adj.* agreeing

con·cor·dat (kən kôr′dat′) *n.* ⟦Fr < L: see CONCORD⟧ a formal agreement

Con·cord (grape) (käŋ′kərd) a large, dark-blue grape used esp. for juice and jelly

con·course (kän′kôrs′) *n.* ⟦see CONCUR⟧ 1 a crowd; throng 2 an open space for crowds, as in a park 3 a broad thoroughfare

con·crete (kän′krēt′, kän krēt′) *adj.* ⟦< L *com-*, together + *crescere*, grow⟧ 1 having a material existence; real; actual 2 specific, not general 3 made of concrete —*n.* 1 anything concrete 2 a hard building material made of sand and gravel, bonded together with cement — *vt., vi.* **-cret′ed, -cret′ing** 1 to solidify 2 to cover with concrete —**con·crete′ly** *adv.* —**con·crete′ness** *n.*

con·cre·tion (kən krē′shən) *n.* 1 a solidifying 2 a solidified mass

con·cu·bine (käŋ′kyŏŏ bīn′, käŋ′-) *n.* ⟦< L *com-*, with + *cubare*, lie down⟧ in some societies, a secondary wife, of inferior social and legal status

con·cu·pis·cence (kən kyōōp′ə səns) *n.* ⟦< L *com-*, intens. + *cupiscere*, to desire⟧ strong desire, esp. sexual desire; lust —**con·cu′pis·cent** *adj.*

con·cur (kən kur′) *vi.* **-curred′, -cur′ring** ⟦< L *com-*, together + *currere*, to run⟧ 1 to occur at the same time 2 to act together 3 to agree (*with*) —**con·cur′rence** *n.*

con·cur·rent *adj.* 1 occurring at the same time 2 acting together 3 *Law* having equal authority —**con·cur′rent·ly** *adv.*

con·cus·sion (kən kush′ən) *n.* ⟦< L *com-*, together + *quatere*, to shake⟧ 1 a violent shaking; shock, as from impact 2 a condition of impaired functioning, esp. of the brain, caused by a violent blow —**con·cus′sive** (-kus′iv) *adj.*

con·demn (kən dem′) *vt.* ⟦< L *com-*, intens. + *damnare*, to harm⟧ 1 to disapprove of strongly 2 to declare guilty 3 to inflict a penalty upon 4 to doom 5 to appropriate (property) for public use 6 to declare unfit for use —**con·dem·na·tion** (kän′dem nā′shən) *n.* —**con·dem·na·to·ry** (kən dem′nə tôr′ē) *adj.* —**con·demn′er** *n.*

con·dense (kən dens′) *vt.* **-densed′, -dens′ing** ⟦< L *com-*, intens. + *densus*, dense⟧ 1 to make more dense or compact 2 to express in fewer words 3 to change to a denser form, esp. from gas to liquid —*vi.* to become condensed —**con·den·sa·tion** (kän′dən sā′shən) *n.*

condensed milk milk made very thick by evaporation, sweetened then with sugar

con·dens·er *n.* one that condenses; specif., *a)* an apparatus for liquefying gases *b)* a lens for concentrating light rays *c)* *Elec.* CAPACITOR

con·de·scend (kän′di send′) *vi.* ⟦< L *com-*, together + *descendere*, descend⟧ 1 to be gracious about doing a thing regarded as beneath one's dignity 2 to deal with others in a proud

or haughty way —**con′de·scend′ing·ly** *adv.* —**con′de·scen′sion** (-sen′shən) *n.*

con·dign (kən dīn′, kän′dīn′) *adj.* ⟦< L *com-*, intens. + *dignus*, worthy⟧ deserved; suitable: said esp. of punishment

con·di·ment (kän′də mənt) *n.* ⟦< L *condire*, to pickle⟧ a seasoning or relish, as pepper, mustard, or a sauce

con·di·tion (kən dish′ən) *n.* ⟦< L *com-*, together + *dicere*, to speak⟧ 1 anything required for the performance, completion, or existence of something else; provision or prerequisite 2 *a)* state of being *b)* an illness *c)* a healthy state 3 social position; rank —*vt.* 1 to stipulate 2 to impose a condition on 3 to bring into fit condition 4 *Psychol.* *a)* to cause to develop a habitual response *b)* to make accustomed (*to*) —**on condition that** provided that; if —**con·di′tion·er** *n.*

con·di·tion·al *adj.* containing, expressing, or dependent on a condition; qualified —*n.* *Gram.* a word, clause, tense, etc. expressing a condition —**con·di′tion·al·ly** *adv.*

con·di·tioned *adj.* 1 subject to conditions 2 in a desired condition 3 affected by conditioning 4 accustomed (*to*)

con·do (kän′dō) *n., pl.* **-dos** or **-does** *short for* CONDOMINIUM (*n.* 3)

con·dole (kən dōl′) *vi.* **-doled′, -dol′ing** ⟦< L *com-*, with + *dolere*, grieve⟧ to express sympathy; commiserate —**con·do′lence** *n.*

con·dom (kän′dəm, kun′-) *n.* ⟦< It *guanto*, a glove⟧ a thin, latex sheath for the penis, used as a prophylactic or contraceptive

con·do·min·i·um (kän′də min′ē əm) *n.* ⟦ult. < L *com-*, with + *dominium*, ownership⟧ 1 joint rule by two or more states 2 the territory ruled 3 one of the units in a multiunit dwelling, each separately owned; also, the dwelling as a whole

con·done (kən dōn′) *vt.* **-doned′, -don′ing** ⟦< L *com-*, intens. + *donare*, give⟧ to forgive or overlook (an offense) —**con·don′a·ble** *adj.*

con·dor (kän′dər, -dôr) *n.* ⟦< Sp < AmInd (Peru)⟧ 1 a large vulture of the South American Andes, with a bare head and neck 2 a similar vulture of S California

con·duce (kən dōōs′) *vi.* **-duced′, -duc′ing** ⟦< L *com-*, together + *ducere*, to lead⟧ to tend or lead (*to* an effect) —**con·du′cive** *adj.*

con·duct (kän′dukt′; *for v.* kən dukt′) *n.* ⟦< L *com-*, together + *ducere*, to lead⟧ 1 management 2 behavior —*vt.* 1 to lead 2 to manage 3 to direct (an orchestra, etc.) 4 to behave (oneself) 5 to transmit or convey —**con·duc′tion** (-duk′shən) *n.* —**con·duc′tive** *adj.* —**con·duc·tiv·i·ty** (kän duk′tiv′ə tē) *n.*

con·duct·ance (kən duk′təns) *n.* the ability to conduct electricity

con·duc·tor *n.* 1 the leader of an orchestra, etc. 2 one in charge of the passengers on a train 3 a thing that conducts electricity, heat, etc.

con·du·it (kän′dōō it) *n.* ⟦see CONDUCE⟧ 1 a channel for conveying fluids 2 a tube for electric wires

cone (kōn) *n.* [< Gr *kōnos*] **1** a solid with a circle for its base and a curved surface tapering to a point **2** any cone-shaped object **3** the scaly fruit of certain mostly evergreen trees **4** a light-sensitive cell in the retina

Co·ney Island (kō′nē) beach & amusement park in Brooklyn, New York

con·fab (kän′fab′) *n.* [ult. < L *com-*, together + *fabulari*, to converse] [Inf.] a chat

con·fec·tion (kən fek′shən) *n.* [< L *com-*, with + *facere*, make] a candy or other sweet, as ice cream

con·fec·tion·er *n.* one who makes or sells candy and other confections

con·fec·tion·er·y (-er′ē) *n.*, *pl.* **-ies** a confectioner's shop; candy store

con·fed·er·a·cy (kən fed′ər ə sē) *n.*, *pl.* **-cies** a league or alliance —**the Confederacy** the 11 Southern states that seceded from the U.S. in 1860 & 1861: official name, **Confederate States of America**

con·fed·er·ate (-it; *for v.*, -āt′) *adj.* [< L *com-*, together + *foedus*, a league] **1** united in an alliance **2** [C-] of the Confederacy —*n.* **1** an ally; associate **2** an accomplice **3** [C-] a Southern supporter of the Confederacy — *vt.*, *vi.* **-at′ed**, **-at′ing** to unite in a confederacy; ally

con·fed·er·a·tion *n.* a league or federation

con·fer (kən fur′) *vt.* **-ferred′**, **-fer′ring** [< L *com-*, together + *ferre*, to bear] to give or bestow —*vi.* to have a conference —**con·fer·ee** (kän′fər ē′) *n.* —**con·fer′rer** *n.*

con·fer·ence (kän′fər əns) *n.* **1** a formal meeting for discussion **2** an association of schools, churches, etc.

con·fer·ral (kən fur′əl) *n.* the bestowing of an honor, degree, or favor: also **con·fer′ment** *n.*

con·fess (kən fes′) *vt.*, *vi.* [< L *com-*, together + *fateri*, acknowledge] **1** to admit or acknowledge (a fault, crime, belief, etc.) **2** *a*) to tell (one's sins) to God or a priest *b*) to hear the confession of (a person) (said of a priest) —**confess to** to acknowledge

con·fess·ed·ly (-id lē) *adv.* admittedly

con·fes·sion (kən fesh′ən) *n.* **1** a confessing **2** something confessed **3** *a*) a creed *b*) a church having a creed

con·fes·sion·al *n.* an enclosure in a church, where a priest hears confessions

con·fes·sor *n.* **1** one who confesses **2** a priest who hears confessions

con·fet·ti (kən fet′ē) *n.* [< It, sweetmeats] colored paper in small pieces or streamers, scattered about at celebrations

con·fi·dant (kän′fə dant′, -dänt′) *n.* a close, trusted friend

con·fide (kən fīd′) *vi.* **-fid′ed**, **-fid′ing** [< L *com-*, intens. + *fidere*, to trust] to trust (*in* someone), esp. by sharing secrets —*vt.* **1** to tell about as a secret **2** to entrust

con·fi·dence (kän′fə dəns) *n.* **1** trust; reliance **2** assurance **3** belief in one's own abilities **4** the belief that another will keep a secret **5** something told as a secret —*adj.* swindling or used so as to swindle

confidence game a swindle effected by one (**confidence man**) who first gains the confidence of the victim

con·fi·dent (-dənt) *adj.* full of confidence; specif., *a*) certain *b*) sure of oneself —**con′fi·dent·ly** *adv.*

con·fi·den·tial (-den′shəl) *adj.* **1** secret **2** of or showing trust **3** entrusted with private matters —**con′fi·den′ti·al·i·ty** (-shē al′ə tē) *n.* —**con′fi·den′tial·ly** *adv.*

con·fig·u·ra·tion (kən fig′yə rā′shən) *n.* [< L *com-*, together + *figurare*, to form] arrangement of parts

con·fig·ure (-yər) *vt.* **-ured**, **-ur·ing** to arrange in a certain way

con·fine (kän′fīn′; *for v.* kən fīn′) *n.* [< L *com-*, with + *finis*, an end] [*usually pl.*] a boundary or bounded region —*vt.* **-fined′**, **-fin′ing 1** to keep within limits; restrict **2** to keep shut up, as in prison or a sickbed —**con·fine′ment** *n.*

con·firm (kən furm′) *vt.* [< L *com-*, intens. + *firmare*, strengthen] **1** to make firm **2** to give formal approval to **3** to prove the truth of **4** to cause to undergo religious confirmation

con·fir·ma·tion (kän′fər mā′shən) *n.* **1** a confirming **2** something that confirms **3** a Christian ceremony admitting a person to full church membership, etc. **4** a Jewish ceremony reaffirming basic beliefs

con·firmed *adj.* **1** firmly established; habitual **2** corroborated

con·fis·cate (kän′fis kāt′) *vt.* **-cat′ed**, **-cat′ing** [< L *com-*, together + *fiscus*, treasury] **1** to seize (private property) for the public treasury as a penalty **2** to seize by or as by authority —**con′fis·ca′tion** *n.* —**con′fis·ca′tor** *n.*

con·fis·ca·to·ry (kən fis′kə tôr′ē) *adj.* of or effecting confiscation

con·fla·gra·tion (kän′flə grā′shən) *n.* [< L *com-*, intens. + *flagrare*, to burn] a big, destructive fire

con·flate (kən flāt′) *vt.* **-flat′ed**, **-flat′ing** [< L *conflare*] to combine or mix (two variant readings into a single text, etc.)

con·flict (kən flikt′; *for n.* kän′flikt′) *vi.* [< L *com-*, together + *fligere*, to strike] to be antagonistic, incompatible, etc. —*n.* **1** a fight or war **2** sharp disagreement, as of interests or ideas **3** emotional disturbance due to conflicting impulses, ideas, etc.

con·flict·ed *adj.* in emotional conflict

conflict of interest a conflict between one's obligation to the public, as that of a public officeholder, and one's self-interest

con·flic·tu·al (kän′flik′chōō əl) *adj.* of or relating to conflict

con·flu·ence (kän′flōō əns) *n.* [< L *com-*, together + *fluere*, to flow] **1** a flowing together, esp. of streams **2** the place of this **3** a crowd —**con′flu·ent** *adj.*

con·form (kən fôrm′) *vt.* [< L *com-*, together + *formare*, to form] **1** to make similar **2** to bring into agreement —*vi.* **1** to be or become similar **2** to be in agreement **3** to act in accordance with accepted rules, customs, etc. —con·form'ism' n. —con·form'ist n.

con·for·ma·tion (kän'fôr mā'shən) n. 1 a symmetrical arrangement of the parts of a thing 2 the shape or outline, as of an animal

con·form·i·ty (kən fôr'mə tē) n., pl. -ties 1 agreement; correspondence; similarity 2 conventional behavior

con·found (kən found'; for 2 kän'-) vt. [< L com-, together + fundere, pour] 1 to confuse or bewilder 2 to damn: a mild oath —con·found'ed adj.

con·fra·ter·ni·ty (kän'frə tur'nə tē) n., pl. -ties [see CON- & FRATERNAL] 1 brotherhood 2 a religious society, usually of laymen

con·frere (kän'frer', kän frer') n. [OFr] a colleague or associate

con·front (kən frunt') vt. [< L com-, together + frons, forehead] 1 to face, esp. boldly or defiantly 2 to bring face to face (with) —con·fron·ta·tion (kän'frən tā'shən) n. —con'fron·ta'tion·al adj.

Con·fu·cius (kən fyoo'shəs) 551?-479? B.C.; Chin. philosopher —Con·fu'cian (-shən) adj., n.

con·fuse (kən fyooz') vt. -fused', -fus'ing [see CONFOUND] 1 to put into disorder 2 to bewilder or embarrass 3 to mistake the identity of —con·fus'ed·ly adv.

con·fu·sion (-fyoo'zhən) n. a confusing or being confused; specif., disorder, bewilderment, etc.

con·fute (kən fyoot') vt. -fut'ed, -fut'ing [L confutare] to prove to be in error or false —con·fu·ta·tion (kän'fyoo tā'shən) n.

Cong abbrev. 1 Congregational 2 Congress

con·geal (kən jēl') vt., vi. [< L com-, together + gelare, freeze] 1 to freeze 2 to coagulate; jell —con·geal'ment n.

con·ge·nial (kən jēn'yəl) adj. [see CON- & GENIAL] 1 kindred; compatible 2 likeminded; friendly 3 suited to one's liking; agreeable —con·ge'ni·al'i·ty (-jē'nē al'ə tē) n. —con·ge'nial·ly adv.

con·gen·i·tal (kən jen'ə təl) adj. [< L congenitus, born together with] existing as such at birth —con·gen'i·tal·ly adv.

con·ger (eel) (käŋ'gər) [< Gr gongros] a large, edible saltwater eel

con·ge·ries (käŋ'jə rēz') n., pl. -ries' [L: see fol.] a heap or pile of things

con·gest (kən jest') vt. [< L com-, together + gerere, carry] 1 to cause too much blood, mucus, etc. to accumulate in (a part of the body) 2 to fill to excess; overcrowd —con·ges'tion n. —con·ges'tive adj.

con·glom·er·ate (kən gläm'ər ät'; for adj. & n., -it) vt., vi. -at'ed, -at'ing [< L com-, together + glomus, ball] to form into a rounded mass —adj. 1 formed into a rounded mass 2 formed of substances collected into a single mass, esp. of rock fragments or pebbles cemented together by clay, silica, etc. —n. 1 a conglomerate mass 2 a large corporation formed by merging many diverse compa-

nies 3 a conglomerate rock —con·glom'er·a'tion n.

Con·go (käŋ'gō) 1 river in central Africa, flowing into the Atlantic 2 Democratic Republic of the Congo country in central Africa: formerly Belgian Congo (1908-60), Zaire (1971-97) 3 Republic of the Congo country in WC Africa, west of Democratic Republic of the Congo: formerly People's Republic of the Congo —Con·go·lese (käŋ'gə lēz') adj., n.

con·grat·u·late (kən grach'ə lāt') vt. -lat'ed, -lat'ing [< L com-, together + gratulari, to wish joy] to express to (another) one's pleasure at that person's good fortune, etc.; felicitate [congratulate the winner] —con·grat'u·la·to'ry (-lə tôr'ē) adj.

con·grat·u·la·tion (-lā'shən) n. 1 a congratulating 2 [pl.] expressions of pleasure in another's good fortune, etc.

con·gre·gate (käŋ'grə gāt') vt., vi. -gat'ed, -gat'ing [< L com-, together + grex, a flock] to gather into a crowd; assemble

con·gre·ga·tion (-gā'shən) n. 1 a gathering; assemblage 2 an assembly of people for religious worship 3 its members

con·gre·ga·tion·al adj. 1 of or like a congregation 2 [C-] of a Protestant denomination in which each member church is self-governing

con·gress (käŋ'grəs) n. [< L com-, together + gradi, to walk] 1 an association or society 2 an assembly or conference 3 a legislature, esp. of a republic 4 [C-] the legislature of the U.S.; the Senate and the House of Representatives —con·gres·sion·al (kən gresh'ə nəl) adj. —con·gres'sion·al·ly adv. —con'gress·man n., pl. -men (mən) —con'gress·per'son n. —con'gress·wom'an n., pl. -wom'en

con·gru·ent (käŋ'grōō ənt, kən grōō'ənt) adj. [< L congruere, agree] 1 corresponding; harmonious 2 of geometric figures of the same shape and size —con'gru·ence n.

con·gru·ous (käŋ'grōō əs) adj. 1 congruent 2 fitting; appropriate —con·gru·i·ty (kän grōō'ə tē) n., pl. -ties —con'gru·ous·ly adv. —con'gru·ous·ness n.

con·i·cal (kän'i kəl) adj. 1 of a cone 2 shaped like a cone Also con'ic —con'i·cal·ly adv.

con·i·fer (kän'ə fər, kō'nə-) n. [L < conus, cone + ferre, to bear] any of a class of conebearing trees and shrubs, mostly evergreens —co·nif·er·ous (kō nif'ər əs, kə-) adj.

conj abbrev. 1 conjugation 2 conjunction

con·jec·ture (kən jek'chər) n. [< L com-, together + jacere, to throw] 1 the act of inferring, theorizing, or predicting from incomplete evidence 2 a guess —vt., vi. -tured, -tur·ing to guess —con·jec'tur·al adj. —con·jec'tur·al·ly adv.

con·join (kən join') vt., vi. [< L com-, together + jungere, join] to join together —con·joint' adj.

con·ju·gal (kän'jə gəl) adj. [< L conjunx, spouse] of marriage or the relation between spouses —con'ju·gal·ly adv.

con·ju·gate (kän'jə gət; also, and for v. always, -gāt') adj. [< L com-, together + jugare, join] joined together; coupled —vt. **-gat′ed, -gat′ing** Gram. to give in order the inflectional forms of (a verb) —**con′ju·ga′tion** n.

con·junc·tion (kən junk′shən) n. [see CONJOIN] 1 a joining together; union 2 coincidence 3 a word used to connect words, phrases, or clauses (Ex.: *and, but, or, if*) —**con·junc′tive** adj.

con·junc·ti·va (kän′jəŋk tī′və) n., pl. **-vas** or **-vae** (-vē) [see CONJOIN] the mucous membrane covering the inner eyelids and the front of the eyeball

con·junc·ti·vi·tis (kən junk′tə vīt′is) n. inflammation of the conjunctiva

con·junc·ture (kən junk′chər) n. [see CONJOIN] a combination of events creating a crisis

con·jure (kun′jər, kän′-; for vi. kən joor′) vi. **-jured, -jur·ing** [< L com-, together + jurare, swear] 1 to summon a demon or spirit by magic 2 to practice magic —vt. to entreat solemnly —**conjure up** to cause to appear as by magic —**con′ju·ra′tion** (-jə rā′shən) n. —**con′jur·er** n., **con′ju·ror**

conk (käŋk, kôŋk) n., vt. [< CONCH] [Slang] hit on the head —**conk out** [Slang] 1 to fail suddenly: said as of a motor 2 to fall asleep from fatigue

con man [Slang] a confidence man; swindler

con·nect (kə nekt′) vt. [< L com-, together + nectere, fasten] 1 to join (two things together, or one thing with or to another) 2 to show or think of as related —vi. to join —**con·nec′tor** n., **con·nect′er**

Con·nect·i·cut (kə net′ə kət) New England state of the U.S.; cap. Hartford: abbrev. CT

con·nec·tion (kə nek′shən) n. 1 a connecting or being connected 2 a thing that connects 3 a relationship; association 4 a) a relative, as by marriage b) an influential associate, etc.: *usually used in pl.* 5 [often pl.] a transferring from one bus, plane, etc. to another

con·nec·tive (-tiv) adj. connecting —n. that which connects, esp. a connecting word, as a conjunction

connective tissue body tissue, as cartilage, serving to connect and support other tissues

con·nip·tion (kə nip′shən) n. [pseudo-L] [often pl.] [Inf.] a fit of anger, hysteria, etc.; tantrum: also **conniption fit**

con·nive (kə nīv′) vi. **-nived′, -niv′ing** [< L conivere, to wink, connive] 1 to pretend not to look (at crime, etc.), thus giving tacit consent 2 to cooperate secretly (with someone), esp. in wrongdoing; scheme —**con·niv′ance** n. —**con·niv′er** n.

con·nois·seur (kän′ə sur′) n. [< Fr < L cognoscere, know] one who has expertise and keen discrimination, esp. in the arts —**con′nois·seur′ship** n.

con·note (kə nōt′) vt. **-not′ed, -not′ing** [< L com-, together + notare, to mark] to suggest or convey (associations, etc.) in addition to the explicit, or denoted, meaning —**con·no·ta·tion** (kän′ə tā′shən) n. —**con′no·ta′tive** adj., **con′no·ta′tion·al**

con·nu·bi·al (kə nōō′bē əl) adj. [< L com-, together + nubere, marry] of marriage; conjugal —**con·nu′bi·al·ly** adv.

con·quer (käŋ′kər) vt. [< L com-, intens. + quaerere, seek] 1 to get control of as by winning a war 2 to overcome; defeat —vi. to win —**con′quer·a·ble** adj. —**con′quer·or** n.

con·quest (kän′kwest′) n. 1 a conquering 2 something conquered 3 a winning of someone's affection

con·quis·ta·dor (kän kwis′tə dôr′, -kēs′-) n., pl. **-dors′** or **con·quis′ta·do′res′** (-dôr′ez′) [Sp, conqueror] any of the Spanish conquerors of the 1500s of Mexico, Peru, etc.

con·san·guin·e·ous (kän′saŋ gwin′ē əs) adj. [see CON- & SANGUINE] having the same ancestor —**con′san·guin′i·ty** n.

con·science (kän′shəns) n. [< L com-, with + scire, know] a sense of right and wrong, with an urge to do right —**con′science·less** adj.

con·sci·en·tious (kän′shē en′shəs) adj. [see prec. & -OUS] 1 governed by one's conscience; scrupulous 2 painstaking —**con′sci·en′tious·ly** adv. —**con′sci·en′tious·ness** n.

conscientious objector one who for religious or moral reasons refuses to take part in warfare

con·scious (kän′shəs) adj. [< L: see SCIENCE] 1 having an awareness (of or that) 2 able to feel and think; awake 3 aware of oneself as a thinking being 4 intentional [conscious humor] 5 known to oneself —**con′scious·ly** adv.

con·scious·ness n. 1 the state of being conscious; awareness 2 the totality of one's thoughts and feelings

con·script (kən skript′; for n. kän′skript′) vt. [ult. < L com-, with + scribere, write] to enroll for compulsory service in the armed forces; draft —n. a draftee —**con·scrip′tion** n.

con·se·crate (kän′si krāt′) vt. **-crat′ed, -crat′ing** [< L com-, together + sacrare, make holy] 1 to set apart as holy 2 to devote to sacred or serious use —**con′se·cra′tion** n.

con·sec·u·tive (kən sek′yōō tiv) adj. [see CONSEQUENCE] following in order, without interruption —**con·sec′u·tive·ly** adv. —**con·sec′u·tive·ness** n.

con·sen·sus (kən sen′səs) n. [see fol.] 1 an opinion held by all or most 2 general agreement, esp. in opinion

con·sent (kən sent′) vi. [< L com-, with + sentire, feel] to agree, permit, or assent —n. 1 permission; approval 2 agreement [by common consent] —**con·sen′su·al** (-sen′shōō əl) adj.

con·se·quence (kän′si kwens′, -kwəns) n. [< L com-, with + sequi, follow] 1 a result; effect 2 importance —**take the consequences** to accept the results of one's actions

con·se·quent (-kwent′, -kwənt) adj. following as a result; resulting —**con′se·quent′ly** adv.

con·se·quen·tial (-kwen′shəl) adj. 1 consequent 2 important

con·ser·va·tion (kän′sər vā′shən) n. 1 a conserving; preservation 2 the official care or management of natural resources —**con'ser·va'tion·ist** *n.*

con·serv·a·tive (kən sur'və tiv) *adj.* **1** tending to conserve **2** tending to preserve established institutions, etc.; opposed to change **3** moderate; cautious —*n.* a conservative person —**con·serv'a·tism'** *n.* —**con·serv'a·tive·ly** *adv.*

con·serv·a·to·ry (-tôr'ē) *n.*, *pl.* **-ries** **1** a greenhouse, esp. one where plants are grown for display **2** a music school

con·serve (kən surv'; *for n., usually* kän'surv') *vt.* **-served'**, **-serv'ing** [< L *com-*, with + *servare*, keep] to keep from being damaged, lost, or wasted; save —*n.* [*often pl.*] a jam, esp. one made of two or more kinds of fruit

con·sid·er (kən sid'ər) *vt.* [< L *considerare*, observe] **1** to think about in order to understand or decide **2** to keep in mind **3** to be thoughtful of (others) **4** to regard as

con·sid·er·a·ble *adj.* **1** worth considering; important **2** much or large —**con·sid'er·a·bly** *adv.*

con·sid·er·ate (-it) *adj.* having regard for others and their feelings —**con·sid'er·ate·ly** *adv.* —**con·sid'er·ate·ness** *n.*

con·sid·er·a·tion (-ā'shən) *n.* **1** the act of considering; deliberation **2** thoughtful regard for others **3** something considered in making a decision **4** a recompense; fee **5** something given, as to make a binding contract —**take into consideration** to keep in mind —**under consideration** being thought over or discussed

con·sid·ered *adj.* arrived at after careful thought

con·sid·er·ing *prep.* in view of; taking into account

con·sign (kən sīn') *vt.* [< L *consignare*, to seal] **1** to hand over; deliver **2** to entrust **3** to assign to an inferior place **4** to send (goods to be sold)

con·sign·ment *n.* **1** a consigning or being consigned **2** a shipment of goods sent to a dealer for sale —**on consignment** with payment due after sale of the consignment

con·sist (kən sist') *vi.* [< L *com-*, together + *sistere*, to stand] **1** to be formed or composed (*of*) **2** to be contained or inherent (*in*)

con·sis·ten·cy (-sis'tən sē) *n.*, *pl.* **-cies** **1** firmness or thickness, as of a liquid or paste **2** agreement; harmony **3** conformity with previous practice

con·sis·tent (-tənt) *adj.* **1** in agreement or harmony; compatible **2** holding to the same principles or practice —**con·sis'tent·ly** *adv.*

con·sis·to·ry (-tə rē) *n.*, *pl.* **-ries** [see CONSIST] **1** a church council or court **2** its session

con·so·la·tion (kän'sə lā'shən) *n.* **1** comfort; solace **2** one that consoles

con·sole¹ (kən sōl') *vt.* **-soled'**, **-sol'ing** [< L *com-*, with + *solari*, to comfort, solace] to cause to feel less sad or disappointed; comfort —**con·sol'a·ble** *adj.* —**con·sol'ing·ly** *adv.*

con·sole² (kän'sōl') *n.* [Fr] **1** the desklike frame containing the keys, stops, etc. of an organ **2** a radio, television, or phonograph cabinet designed to stand on the floor **3** a unit containing displays or controls, as for operating aircraft, computers, electronic systems, etc. **4** a raised portion between automobile bucket seats

con·sol·i·date (kən säl'ə dāt') *vt.*, *vi.* **-dat'ed**, **-dat'ing** [< L *com-*, together + *solidus*, solid] **1** to combine into a single whole; unite **2** to make or become strong or stable [*to consolidate* one's *power*] —**con·sol'i·da'tion** *n.* —**con·sol'i·da'tor** *n.*

con·som·mé (kän'sə mā') *n.* [Fr] a clear, strained meat soup

con·so·nance (kän'sə nəns) *n.* [< L *com-*, with + *sonus*, sound] **1** harmony of parts or elements **2** musical harmony **3** repetition of consonants

con·so·nant (-nənt) *adj.* in harmony or accord —*n.* **1** a speech sound made by obstructing the air stream **2** a letter representing such a sound, as *p*, *t*, *l*, or *f*

con·sort (kän'sôrt'; *for v.* kən sôrt') *n.* [< L *com-*, with + *sors*, a share] **1** a wife or husband, esp. of a reigning king or queen **2** a chamber music ensemble, esp. of the Renaissance —*vt.*, *vi.* to associate

con·sor·ti·um (kən sôrt'ē əm, -sôr'shē əm) *n.*, *pl.* **-ti·a** (-ə) [see prec.] an international alliance, as of business firms

con·spec·tus (kən spek'təs) *n.* [L: see fol.] **1** a general view **2** a summary; digest

con·spic·u·ous (kən spik'yōō əs) *adj.* [< L *com-*, intens. + *specere*, see] **1** easy to see **2** outstanding; striking —**con·spic'u·ous·ly** *adv.* —**con·spic'u·ous·ness** *n.*

con·spir·a·cy (kən spir'ə sē) *n.*, *pl.* **-cies** **1** a conspiring **2** an unlawful plot **3** a conspiring group

con·spire (kən spīr') *vi.* **-spired'**, **-spir'ing** [< L *com-*, together + *spirare*, breathe] **1** to plan together secretly, esp. to commit a crime **2** to work together for any purpose or effect —**con·spir'a·tor** (-spir'ət ər) *n.* —**con·spir'a·to'ri·al** (-spir'ə tôr'ē əl) *adj.*

con·sta·ble (kän'stə bəl) *n.* [< LL *comes stabuli*, lit., count of the stable] **1** a peace officer in a small town **2** [*Chiefly Brit.*] a police officer

con·stab·u·lar·y (kən stab'yə ler'ē) *n.*, *pl.* **-ies** **1** constables, collectively **2** militarized police

con·stant (kän'stənt) *adj.* [< L *com-*, together + *stare*, to stand] **1** not changing; faithful, regular, stable, etc. **2** continual; persistent —*n.* anything that does not change or vary —**con'stan·cy** *n.* —**con'stant·ly** *adv.*

Con·stan·tine I (kän'stən tēn', -tīn') A.D. 280?-337; first Christian emperor of Rome (306-337)

Con·stan·ti·no·ple (kän'stan tə nō'pəl) *former name* (A.D. 330-1930) *for* ISTANBUL

con·stel·la·tion (kän'stə lā'shən) *n.* [< L *com-*, with + *stella*, star] **1** a visible grouping of stars in the sky, usually named for some object, animal, etc. suggested by its outline **2** any brilliant group or gathering

con·ster·na·tion (kän′stər nā′shən) *n.* ⟦< L *consternare*, terrify⟧ great fear or shock

con·sti·pate (kän′stə pāt′) *vt.* **-pat′ed, -pat′ing** ⟦< L *com-*, together + *stipare*, cram⟧ to cause constipation in

con·sti·pa·tion (-pā′shən) *n.* infrequent and difficult movement of the bowels

con·stit·u·en·cy (kən stich′ōō ən sē) *n., pl.* **-cies 1** the voters in a district **2** a group of clients, supporters, etc.

con·stit·u·ent (-ənt) *adj.* ⟦see fol.⟧ **1** necessary to the whole; component [a *constituent* part] **2** that elects —*n.* **1** a voter in a district **2** a client, supporter, etc. **3** a component

con·sti·tute (kän′stə tōōt′) *vt.* **-tut′ed, -tut′ing** ⟦< L *com-*, together + *statuere*, to set⟧ **1** to establish (a law, government, etc.) **2** to set up (an assembly, etc.) in a legal form **3** to appoint **4** to make up; form —**con′sti·tu′tive** *adj.*

con·sti·tu·tion (-tōō′shən) *n.* **1** a constituting **2** structure; organization **3** *a)* the system of basic laws and principles of a government, society, etc. *b)* a document stating these laws and principles *c)* [**C-**] such a document of the U.S.

con·sti·tu·tion·al (-shə nəl) *adj.* **1** of or in one's constitution or structure; basic **2** of or in accordance with the constitution of a government, society, etc. —*n.* a walk taken for one's health —**con′sti·tu′tion·al′i·ty** (-shə nal′ə tē) *n.* —**con′sti·tu′tion·al·ly** *adv.*

con·strain (kən strān′) *vt.* ⟦< L *com-*, together + *stringere*, draw tight⟧ **1** to confine **2** to restrain **3** to compel

con·straint (-strānt′) *n.* **1** confinement or restriction **2** force; compulsion **3** forced, unnatural manner **4** something that constrains

con·strict (kən strikt′) *vt.* ⟦see CONSTRAIN⟧ to make smaller or narrower by squeezing, etc. —**con·stric′tion** *n.*

con·stric·tor (-strik′tər) *n.* a snake that kills its prey by squeezing

con·struct (kən strukt′; *for n.* kän′strukt′) *vt.* ⟦< L *com-*, together + *struere*, pile up⟧ to build, devise, etc. —*n.* **1** something put together systematically **2** a concept or theory —**con·struc′tor** *n.*

con·struc·tion (-struk′shən) *n.* **1** a constructing or manner of being constructed **2** a structure **3** an interpretation, as of a statement **4** the arrangement of words in a sentence

construction paper sturdy, colored paper for children's art projects, etc.

con·struc·tive *adj.* leading to improvement; positive

con·strue (kən strōō′) *vt., vi.* **-strued′, -stru′ing** ⟦see CONSTRUCT⟧ **1** to analyze the construction of (a sentence) **2** to explain; interpret

con·sul (kän′səl) *n.* ⟦< L *consulere*, to deliberate⟧ **1** a chief magistrate of ancient

Rome **2** a government official appointed to live in a foreign city and look after his or her country's citizens and business there —**con′su·lar** (-ər) *adj.*

con·su·late (-it) *n.* **1** the position, powers, etc. of a consul **2** the office or residence of a consul

con·sult (kən sult′) *vi.* ⟦< L *consulere*, consider⟧ to talk things over; confer —*vt.* **1** to seek advice or information from **2** to consider —**con·sul·ta·tion** (kän′səl tā′shən) *n.*

con·sult·ant *n.* an expert who gives professional or technical advice —**con·sult′an·cy** *n., pl.* **-cies**

con·sume (-sōōm′) *vt.* **-sumed′, -sum′ing** ⟦< L *com-*, together + *sumere*, to take⟧ **1** to destroy, as by fire **2** to use up or waste (time, money, etc.) **3** to eat or drink up; devour **4** to engross

con·sum·er *n.* one that consumes; specif., one who buys goods or services for personal needs only rather than for resale or to produce other goods

con·sum·mate (kän′sə mit, kən sum′it; *for v.* kän′sə māt′) *adj.* ⟦< L *com-*, together + *summa*, a sum⟧ perfect; supreme —*vt.* **-mat′ed, -mat′ing 1** to complete **2** to complete (a marriage) by sexual intercourse —**con′sum·mate·ly** *adv.* —**con·sum·ma·tion** (kän′sə mā′shən) *n.*

con·sump·tion (kən sump′shən) *n.* **1** a consuming or being consumed **2** the using up of goods or services **3** the amount consumed **4** [Old-fashioned] tuberculosis of the lungs

cont *abbrev.* continued

con·tact (kän′takt′) *n.* ⟦< L *com-*, together + *tangere*, to touch⟧ **1** a touching or meeting **2** the state of being in association (*with*) **3** a connection **4** an influential acquaintance **5** *short for* CONTACT LENS —*vt.* **1** to come into contact with **2** to get in touch with —*vi.* to come into contact

contact lens a tiny, thin correctional lens worn on the cornea of the eye

con·ta·gion (kən tā′jən) *n.* ⟦see CONTACT⟧ **1** the spreading of disease by contact **2** a contagious disease **3** the spreading of an emotion, idea, etc.

con·ta·gious (-jəs) *adj.* **1** spread by contact: said of diseases **2** carrying the causative agent of a contagious disease **3** spreading from person to person —**con·ta′gious·ness** *n.*

con·tain (kən tān′) *vt.* ⟦< L *com-*, together + *tenere*, to hold⟧ **1** to have in it; hold **2** to have the capacity for holding **3** to hold back or restrain within fixed limits —**con·tain′ment** *n.*

con·tain·er *n.* a thing for containing something; box, can, etc.

con·tain·er·ize (-ized′, -iz′ing) to pack (cargo) into huge, standardized containers for shipment

con·tam·i·nant (kən tam′ə nənt) *n.* a contaminating substance

con·tam·i·nate (-nāt′) *vt.* **-nat′ed, -nat′ing** ⟦< L *com-*, together + *tangere*, to touch⟧ to make impure, corrupt, etc. by contact —**con·tam′i·na′tion** *n.*

contd *abbrev.* continued

con·tem·plate (kän′təm plāt′) *vt.* **-plat′ed, -plat′ing** [< L *contemplari*, observe] 1 to look at or think about intently 2 to expect or intend —*vi.* to muse —**con′tem·pla′tion** (-plā′shən) *n.* —**con·tem·pla·tive** (kən tem′plə tiv, kän′təm plāt′iv) *adj.*

con·tem·po·ra·ne·ous (kən tem′pə rā′nē əs) *adj.* [see fol.] happening in the same period —**con·tem′po·ra·ne′i·ty** (-rə nē′ə tē, -nā′-) *n.* —**con·tem′po·ra′ne·ous·ly** *adv.*

con·tem·po·rar·y (-rer′ē) *adj.* [< L *com-,* with + *tempus,* time] 1 living or happening in the same period 2 of about the same age 3 of the present time; modern —*n., pl.* **-ies** one living in the same period as another or others

con·tempt (kən tempt′) *n.* [< L *com-,* intens. + *temnere,* to scorn] 1 the feeling one has toward somebody or something one considers low, worthless, etc. 2 the condition of being despised 3 a showing disrespect for the dignity of a court (or legislature)

con·tempt·i·ble *adj.* deserving of contempt or scorn; despicable —**con·tempt′i·bly** *adv.*

con·temp·tu·ous (kən temp′chōō əs) *adj.* full of contempt; scornful —**con·temp′tu·ous·ly** *adv.* —**con·temp′tu·ous·ness** *n.*

con·tend (kən tend′) *vi.* [< L *com-,* together + *tendere,* to stretch] 1 to fight or argue 2 to compete —*vt.* to assert —**con·tend′er** *n.*

con·tent[1] (kən tent′) *adj.* [see CONTAIN] happy with one's lot; satisfied —*vt.* to satisfy —*n.* contentment

con·tent[2] (kän′tent′) *n.* [see CONTAIN] 1 [*usually pl.*] *a)* what is in a container *b)* what is dealt with in a book, speech, etc. 2 substance or meaning 3 amount contained

con·tent·ed *adj.* satisfied —**con·tent′ed·ly** *adv.* —**con·tent′ed·ness** *n.*

con·ten·tion (kən ten′shən) *n.* [see CONTEND] 1 strife, dispute, etc. 2 a point asserted —**in (or out of) contention** having a (or no) chance to win —**con·ten′tious** *adj.* —**con·ten′tious·ly** *adv.* —**con·ten′tious·ness** *n.*

con·tent·ment *n.* the state or fact of being contented

con·ter·mi·nous (kən tʉr′mə nəs) *adj.* [< L *com-,* together + *terminus,* an end] 1 having a common boundary 2 contained within the same boundaries —**con·ter′mi·nous·ly** *adv.*

con·test (kən test′; *for n.* kän′test′) *vt.* [< L *com-,* together + *testis,* a witness] 1 to dispute (a point, etc.) 2 to fight for (a position, etc.) —*vi.* to struggle (*with* or *against*) —*n.* 1 a fight; struggle 2 a competitive game, race, etc. —**con·test′a·ble** *adj.*

con·test·ant *n.* [Fr] a competitor in a game, etc.

con·text (kän′tekst′) *n.* [< L *com-,* together + *texere,* to weave] 1 the parts just before and after a passage, that determine its meaning 2 the background or environment, as of an event —**con·tex·tu·al** (kən teks′chōō əl) *adj.*

con·tex·tu·al·ize (kən teks′chōō əl īz′) *vt.* **-ized′, -iz′ing** to put in a context, as for analysis

con·tig·u·ous (kən tig′yōō əs) *adj.* [see CONTACT] 1 in contact; touching 2 near or next —**con·ti·gu·i·ty** (kän′tə gyōō′ə tē) *n.*

con·ti·nence (känt′'n əns) *n.* [see CONTAIN] 1 self-restraint; specif., a refraining from all sexual activity 2 ability to control one's bodily functions, esp. urination and defecation

con·ti·nent (-ənt) *adj.* [see CONTAIN] characterized by continence —*n.* any of the main large land areas of the earth

con·ti·nen·tal (-ent′'l) *adj.* 1 of a continent 2 [*sometimes* C-] European 3 [C-] of the American colonies at the time of the American Revolution

continental breakfast a light breakfast, as of rolls and coffee

continental drift the slow change in the relative positions of the continents

continental shelf submerged land sloping out gradually from the edge of a continent

con·tin·gen·cy (kən tin′jən sē) *n., pl.* **-cies** 1 dependence on chance 2 a possible or chance event

con·tin·gent *adj.* [see CONTACT] 1 possible 2 accidental 3 dependent (*on* or *upon* an uncertainty) —*n.* 1 a quota, as of troops 2 a part of a larger group

con·tin·u·al (kən tin′yōō əl) *adj.* 1 repeated often 2 continuous —**con·tin′u·al·ly** *adv.*

con·tin·u·ance *n.* 1 a continuing 2 duration 3 *Law* postponement or adjournment

con·tin·u·a·tion (-ā′shən) *n.* 1 a continuing 2 a beginning again; resumption 3 a part added; sequel

con·tin·ue (kən tin′yōō) *vi.* **-ued, -u·ing** [< L *continuare,* join] 1 to last; endure 2 to go on in a specified course of action or condition 3 to extend 4 to stay 5 to go on again after an interruption —*vt.* 1 to go on with 2 to extend 3 to cause to remain, as in office 4 *Law* to postpone

con·ti·nu·i·ty (kän′tə nōō′ə tē, -nyōō′-) *n., pl.* **-ties** [OFr < L *continuitas*] 1 the state or quality of being continuous 2 an unbroken, coherent whole

con·tin·u·ous (kən tin′yōō əs) *adj.* going on without interruption; unbroken —**con·tin′u·ous·ly** *adv.*

con·tin·u·um (-yōō əm) *n., pl.* **-u·a** (-yōō ə) or **-u·ums** [L] a continuous whole, quantity, or series

con·tort (kən tôrt′) *vt., vi.* [< L *com-,* together + *torquere,* to twist] to twist or wrench out of shape; distort —**con·tor′tion** *n.*

con·tor·tion·ist *n.* one who can contort his or her body into unnatural positions

con·tour (kän′toor′) *n.* [Fr < L *com-,* intens. + *tornare,* to turn] the outline of a figure, land, etc. —*vt.* to shape to the contour of something —*adj.* conforming to the shape or contour of something

con·tra (kän′trə) *prep.* against

contra- [< L *contra*] *prefix* against, opposite, opposed to

con·tra·band (kän'trə band') *n.* [< Sp < It] smuggled goods —*adj.* illegal to import or export

con·tra·cep·tion (kän'trə sep'shən) *n.* [CONTRA- + (CON)CEPTION] prevention of pregnancy, as by special devices or drugs —**con'tra·cep'tive** *adj., n.*

con·tract (kän'trakt' *for n. & usually for vt. 1 & vi. 1;* kən trakt' *for v. generally*) *n.* [< L *com-*, together + *trahere*, draw] an agreement between two or more people, esp. a written one enforceable by law —*vt.* 1 to undertake by contract 2 to get or incur (a disease, debt, etc.) 3 to reduce in size; shrink —*vi.* 1 to make a contract 2 to become smaller

con·trac·tile (kən trak'til) *adj.* having the power of contracting

con·trac·tion (kən trak'shən) *n.* 1 a contracting or being contracted 2 the shortening of a muscle of the uterus during labor 3 the shortened form of a word or phrase (Ex.: *aren't* for *are not*)

con·trac·tor (kän'trak'tər) *n.* a builder, etc. who contracts to do work or supply materials

con·trac·tu·al (kən trak'chōō əl) *adj.* of, or having the nature of, a contract —**con·trac'tu·al·ly** *adv.*

con·tra·dict (kän'trə dikt') *vt.* [< L *contra-*, against + *dicere*, speak] 1 to assert the opposite of (something said) 2 to deny the statement of (someone) 3 to be contrary to —**con'tra·dic'tion** *n.* —**con'tra·dic'to·ry** *adj.*

con·tra·dis·tinc·tion (-dis tiŋk'shən) *n.* distinction by contrast

con·trail (kän'trāl') *n.* [CON(DENSATION) + TRAIL] a white trail of condensed water vapor in an aircraft's wake

con·tra·in·di·cate (kän'trə in'di kāt') *vt.* -**cat'ed**, -**cat'ing** to make (as an indicated medical treatment) inadvisable

con·tral·to (kən tral'tō) *n., pl.* -**tos** [It: see CONTRA- & ALTO] 1 the range of the lowest female voice; alto 2 a voice or singer with such a range

con·trap·tion (kən trap'shən) *n.* [< ?] a contrivance or gadget

con·tra·pun·tal (kän'trə punt''l) *adj.* [< It *contrappunto*, counterpoint] of or characterized by counterpoint

con·trar·i·an (kän trer'ē ən) *n., adj.* (one) characterized by thought or action that is contrary to accepted opinion

con·trar·i·wise (kän'trer'ē wīz') *adv.* 1 on the contrary 2 in the opposite way, order, etc.

con·trar·y (kän'trer'ē; *for adj. 4, often* kən trer'ē) *adj.* [< L *contra*, against] 1 opposed 2 opposite in nature, order, etc.; altogether different 3 unfavorable 4 always resisting or disagreeing —*n., pl.* -**ies** the opposite —**on the contrary** as opposed to what has been said —**to the contrary** to the opposite effect —**con'tra·ri'e·ty** (-trə rī'ə tē) *n.* —**con'trar'i·ly** *adv.* —**con'trar'i·ness** *n.*

con·trast (kən trast'; *for n.* kän'trast') *vt.* [< L *contra*, against + *stare*, to stand] to compare so as to point out the differences —*vi.* to show differences when compared —*n.* 1 a contrasting or being contrasted 2 a striking difference between things being compared 3 a person or thing showing differences when compared with another

con·tra·vene (kän'trə vēn') *vt.* -**vened'**, -**ven'ing** [< L *contra*, against + *venire*, come] 1 to go against; violate 2 to contradict —**con'tra·ven'tion** (-ven'shən) *n.*

con·tre·temps (kän'trə tän') *n., pl.* -**temps'** (-tän') [Fr] a confusing, embarrassing, or awkward occurrence

con·trib·ute (kən trib'yōōt) *vt., vi.* -**ut·ed**, -**ut·ing** [< L: see CON- & TRIBUTE] 1 to give jointly with others 2 to write (an article, etc.) as for a magazine 3 to furnish (ideas, etc.) —**contribute to** be partly responsible for (a result) —**con·trib'u·tor** *n.* —**con·trib'u·to'ry** *adj.*

con·tri·bu·tion (kän'trə byōō'shən) *n.* 1 a contributing 2 something contributed, as money

con·trite (kən trīt') *adj.* [< L *com-*, together + *terere*, to rub] having or showing deep sorrow for having done wrong —**con·trite'ly** *adv.* —**con·trite'ness** *n.* —**con·tri'tion** (-trish'ən) *n.*

con·triv·ance (kən trī'vəns) *n.* 1 the act, way, or power of contriving 2 something contrived; device, invention, etc.

con·trive (kən trīv') *vt.* -**trived'**, -**triv'ing** [ult. < VL *contropare*, compare] 1 to think up; devise 2 to make inventively 3 to bring about —**con·triv'er** *n.*

con·trol (kən trōl') *vt.* -**trolled'**, -**trol'ling** [< ML *contrarotulus*, a register] 1 to regulate 2 to verify (an experiment) by comparison 3 to exercise authority over; direct 4 to restrain —*n.* 1 power to direct or regulate 2 a means of controlling; check 3 an apparatus to regulate a mechanism: *usually used in pl.* —**con·trol'la·ble** *adj.*

control group the group, in an experiment, that is not given the drug, etc. being tested

controlled substance a drug whose sale is regulated by law

con·trol·ler *n.* 1 the person in charge of auditing accounts, as in a business 2 a person or device that controls

control tower an airport tower from which air traffic is directed

con·tro·ver·sial (kän'trə vur'shəl) *adj.* subject to or stirring up controversy

con·tro·ver·sy (-sē) *n., pl.* -**sies** [< L *contra*, against + *vertere*, to turn] a conflict of opinion; dispute

con·tro·vert (kän'trə vurt', kän'trə vurt') *vt.* to argue against; dispute —**con'tro·vert'i·ble** *adj.*

con·tu·ma·cy (kän'tyōō mə sē) *n., pl.* -**cies** [< L *com-*, intens. + *tumere*, swell up] stubborn resistance to authority —**con'tu·ma'cious** (-mā'shəs) *adj.*

con·tu·me·ly (kän′tōō mə lē, -tōōm lē; kən tōō′mə lē) *n.*, *pl.* **-lies** [< L *contumelia*, abuse] 1 humiliating treatment 2 a scornful insult —**con′tu·me′li·ous** (-mē′lē əs) *adj.*

con·tu·sion (kən tyōō′zhən, -tōō′-) *n.* [< L *com-*, intens. + *tundere*, to beat] a bruise

co·nun·drum (kə nun′drəm) *n.* [pseudo-L] 1 a riddle whose answer contains a pun 2 any puzzling problem

con·ur·ba·tion (kän′ər bā′shən) *n.* [< CON- + L *urbs*, city + -ATION] an urban area centered on a large city

con·va·lesce (kän′və les′) *vi.* **-lesced′**, **-lesc′ing** [< L *com-*, intens. + *valere*, be strong] to regain strength and health —**con′va·les′cence** *n.* —**con′va·les′cent** *adj.*, *n.*

con·vec·tion (kən vek′shən) *n.* [< L *com-*, together + *vehere*, carry] 1 a transmitting 2 *a)* movement of parts of a fluid within the fluid because of differences in density due to heat, etc. *b)* heat transference by such movement —**con·vec′tion·al** *adj.* —**con·vec′tive** *adj.*

con·vene (kən vēn′) *vi.*, *vt.* **-vened′**, **-ven′ing** [< L *com-*, together + *venire*, come] to assemble for a meeting —**con·ven′er** *n.*

con·ven·ience (kən vēn′yəns) *n.* [see prec.] 1 the quality of being convenient 2 comfort 3 anything that adds to one's comfort or saves work —**at someone's convenience** at a time or place suitable to someone

con·ven·ient (-yənt) *adj.* easy to do, use, or get to; handy —**con·ven′ient·ly** *adv.*

con·vent (kän′vənt, -vent′) *n.* [see CONVENE] 1 the residence of a religious community, esp. of women 2 the community itself

con·ven·ti·cle (kən ven′ti kəl) *n.* [see CONVENE] a religious assembly held illegally and secretly

con·ven·tion (kən ven′shən) *n.* [see CONVENE] 1 *a)* an assembly, often periodical, of members or delegates *b)* such members or delegates 2 a large public exhibition centered around a particular activity [a comic book *convention*] 3 an agreement, as between nations 4 a customary practice 5 customary practices collectively —**con·ven′tion·eer′** *n.*

con·ven·tion·al *adj.* 1 having to do with a convention 2 sanctioned by or following custom or usage; customary 3 formal 4 nonnuclear [*conventional* weapons] —**con·ven′tion·al′i·ty** (-nal′ə tē) *n.* —**con·ven′tion·al·ly** *adv.*

con·ven·tion·al·ize *vt.* **-ized′**, **-iz′ing** to make conventional

con·verge (kən vʉrj′) *vi.* **-verged′**, **-verg′ing** [< L *com-*, together + *vergere*, to bend] to come together at a point —**con·ver′gence** *n.* —**con·ver′gent** *adj.*

con·ver·sant (kən vʉr′sənt, kän′vər-) *adj.* familiar or acquainted (*with*)

con·ver·sa·tion (kän′vər sā′shən) *n.* a conversing; informal talk —**con′ver·sa′tion·al** *adj.* —**con′ver·sa′tion·al·ist** *n.* —**con′ver·sa′tion·al·ly** *adv.*

conversation piece something, as an unusual article of furniture, that invites comment

con·verse¹ (kən vʉrs′; *for n.* kän′vʉrs′) *vi.* **-versed′**, **-vers′ing** [< L *conversari*, live with] to hold a conversation; talk —*n.* conversation

con·verse² (kän′vʉrs′; *also, for adj.*, kən vʉrs′) *adj.* [see CONVERT] reversed in position, order, etc.; opposite; contrary —*n.* a thing related in a converse way; the opposite —**con·verse′ly** *adv.*

con·ver·sion (kən vʉr′zhən) *n.* a converting or being converted

con·vert (kən vʉrt′; *for n.* kän′vʉrt′) *vt.* [< L *com-*, together + *vertere*, to turn] 1 to change; transform 2 to change from one religion, doctrine, etc. to another 3 to exchange for something equal in value —*vi.* to be converted —*n.* a person converted, as to a religion —**con·vert′er** *n.*

con·vert·i·ble (kən vʉrt′ə bəl) *adj.* that can be converted —*n.* an automobile with a folding or removable top

con·vex (kän veks′, kän′veks′) *adj.* [< L *com-*, together + *vehere*, bring] curving outward like the surface of a sphere —**con·vex′i·ty** *n.*

con·vey (kən vā′) *vt.* [< L *com-*, together + *via*, way] 1 to take from one place to another; transport; carry 2 to transmit 3 *Law* to transfer (property, etc.) —**con·vey′a·ble** *adj.*

con·vey·ance *n.* 1 a conveying 2 a means of conveying; esp., a vehicle

con·vey·or (belt) a device, consisting of a continuous moving belt, for conveying things

con·vict (kən vikt′; *for n.* kän′vikt′) *vt.* [see CONVINCE] to prove or find (a person) guilty —*n.* a convicted person serving a prison sentence

con·vic·tion (kən vik′shən) *n.* 1 a convicting or being convicted 2 a being convinced; strong belief

con·vince (kən vins′) *vt.* **-vinced′**, **-vinc′ing** [< L *com-*, intens. + *vincere*, conquer] to persuade by argument or evidence; make feel sure —**con·vinc′ing** *adj.* —**con·vinc′ing·ly** *adv.*

con·viv·i·al (kən viv′ē əl) *adj.* [< L *com-*, together + *vivere*, to live] 1 festive 2 fond of eating, drinking, and good company —**con·viv′i·al′i·ty** (-al′ə tē) *n.*

con·vo·ca·tion (kän′vō kā′shən) *n.* 1 a convoking 2 an ecclesiastical or academic assembly

con·voke (kən vōk′) *vt.* **-voked′**, **-vok′ing** [< L *com-*, together + *vocare*, to call] to call together; convene

con·vo·lut·ed (kän′və lōōt′id) *adj.* 1 having convolutions; coiled 2 involved; complicated

con·vo·lu·tion (-lōō′shən) *n.* [< L *com-*, together + *volvere*, to roll] 1 a twisting, coiling, or winding together 2 a fold, twist, or coil

con·voy (kän′voi′) *vt.* [see CONVEY] to escort in order to protect —*n.* 1 a convoying 2 a protecting escort 3 a group of ships, vehicles, etc. traveling together

con·vulse (kən vuls′) *vt.* **-vulsed′**, **-vuls′ing** [< L *com-*, together + *vellere*, to pluck] 1 to shake violently **2** to cause to shake with laughter, rage, etc. **—con·vul′sive** *adj.* **—con·vul′sive·ly** *adv.*

con·vul·sion (-vul′shən) *n.* **1** a violent, involuntary spasm of the muscles: *often used in pl.* **2** a fit of laughter **3** a violent disturbance

coo (ko̅o̅) *vi.* ⟦echoic⟧ to make the soft, murmuring sound of pigeons or doves **—n.** this sound

COO *abbrev.* chief operating officer

cook (kook) *n.* ⟦< L *coquere*, to cook⟧ one who prepares food **—vt.** to prepare (food) by boiling, baking, frying, etc. **—vi.** **1** to be a cook **2** to undergo cooking **—cook up** [Inf.] to devise; invent **—cook′er** *n.*

cook·book *n.* a book containing recipes and other food-preparation information

cook·er·y *n.* [Chiefly Brit.] the art or practice of cooking

cook·ie *n.* ⟦prob. < Du *koek,* cake⟧ a small, sweet cake, usually flat and either crisp or chewy

cook·out *n.* a meal cooked and eaten outdoors

cook·top *n.* a stove top, with burners, or such a unit installed as a on a kitchen counter

cool (ko̅o̅l) *adj.* ⟦OE *col*⟧ **1** moderately cold **2** tending to reduce the effects of heat [*cool* clothes] **3** not excited; composed **4** showing dislike or indifference **5** calmly bold **6** [Inf.] without exaggeration [a *cool* $1,000] **7** [Slang] *a*) very good *b*) popular, fashionable, etc. **—n.** a cool place, time, etc. [the *cool* of the evening] **2** [Slang] cool, dispassionate manner **—vt., vi.** to make or become cool or colder **—cool′ly** *adv.* **—cool′ness** *n.*

cool·ant *n.* a fluid or other substance for cooling engines, etc.

cool·er *n.* **1** a container or room for keeping things cool **2** a cold, refreshing drink **3** [Slang] jail: with *the*

Coo·lidge (ko̅o̅l′lij), **(John) Calvin** 1872-1933; 30th president of the U.S. (1923-29)

coo·lie (ko̅o̅l′lē) *n.* ⟦Hindi *qulī,* servant⟧ an unskilled native laborer, esp. formerly, in India, China, etc.

coon (ko̅o̅n) *n. short for* RACCOON

coon·skin *n.* the skin of a raccoon, used as a fur

coop (ko̅o̅p) *n.* ⟦< L *cupa,* cask⟧ a small pen as for poultry **—vt.** to confine as in a coop: usually with *up*

co-op (ko̅′äp′) *n.* [Inf.] a cooperative

coop·er (ko̅o̅p′ər) *n.* ⟦see COOP⟧ one whose work is making or repairing barrels and casks

co·op·er·ate (ko̅ äp′ər āt′) *vi.* **-at′ed, -at′ing** ⟦< L *co-,* with + *opus,* work⟧ to act or work together with another or others **—co·op′er·a′tion** *n.,* **co·op′er·a′tion**

co·op·er·a·tive (-ər ə tiv, -ər āt′iv) *adj.* **1** co-operating **2** owned collectively by members who share in its benefits **—n.** a cooperative store, etc.

co-opt (ko̅ äpt′, ko̅′äpt′) *vt.* ⟦< L < *co-,* with + *optare,* choose⟧ **1** to get (an opponent) to join one's side **2** to take over for one's own purposes

co·or·di·nate or **co·or·di·nate** (ko̅ ôrd′'n it;

for *v.,* -āt′) *adj.* ⟦< L *co-,* with + *ordo,* order⟧ **1** of the same order, importance, etc. [*coordinate* clauses in a sentence] **2** of coordination or coordinates **—n.** **1** a coordinate person or thing **2** [*pl.*] items of clothing, etc. that form a pleasing ensemble **—vt.** **-nat′ed, -nat′ing 1** to make coordinate **2** to bring into proper order or relation **—co·or′di·na′tor** *n.,* **co·or′di·na′tor**

coordinating conjunction a conjunction connecting coordinate words, clauses, etc. (Ex.: *and, but, nor*)

co·or·di·na·tion *n.* **1** a coordinating or being coordinated **2** harmonious action, as of muscles

coot (ko̅o̅t) *n.* ⟦ME *cote*⟧ **1** a ducklike water bird **2** [Inf.] an eccentric old man

coot·ie (ko̅o̅t′ē) *n.* [Slang] a louse

cop (käp) *vt.* **copped, cop′ping** ⟦prob. < L *capere,* take⟧ [Slang] to seize, steal, etc. **—n.** [Slang] a policeman **—cop out** [Slang] **1** to renege **2** to give up; quit

co·part·ner (ko̅ pärt′nər, ko̅′pärt′-) *n.* an associate

co·pay·ment (ko̅′pā′mənt) *n.* the part of a medical bill, often a fixed fee, not covered by insurance: also **co′-pay′**

COPD *abbrev.* chronic obstructive pulmonary disease

cope¹ (ko̅p) *vi.* **coped, cop′ing** ⟦< OFr *coper,* to strike⟧ **1** to fight or contend (*with*) successfully **2** to deal with problems, etc.

cope² (ko̅p) *n.* ⟦< LL *cappa*⟧ **1** a large, capelike vestment worn by priests **2** any cover like this

Co·pen·hag·en (ko̅′pən hā′gən, -hä′-) capital of Denmark

co·per·ni·ci·um (ko̅′pər nē′sē əm, -nish′ē əm) *n.* ⟦after fol.⟧ an artificially produced radioactive chemical element with a very short half-life: symbol, Cn; at. no. 112

Co·per·ni·cus (ko̅ pur′ni kəs), **Nic·o·la·us** (nik′ə lā′əs) 1473-1543; Pol. astronomer **—Co·per′ni·can** *adj.*

cop·i·er (käp′ē ər) *n.* **1** one who copies **2** a duplicating machine

co·pi·lot (ko̅′pī′lət) *n.* the assistant pilot of an airplane

cop·ing (ko̅′piŋ) *n.* ⟦< COPE²⟧ the top layer of a masonry wall

co·pi·ous (ko̅′pē əs) *adj.* ⟦< L *copia,* abundance⟧ plentiful; abundant **—co′pi·ous·ly** *adv.* **—co′pi·ous·ness** *n.*

cop-out [Slang] *n.* **1** a copping out, as by reneging or quitting **2** an excuse for inaction or failure

cop·per (käp′ər) *n.* ⟦< LL *cuprum*⟧ **1** a reddish-brown, ductile, metallic chemical element: symbol, Cu; at. no. 29 **2** a reddish brown **—adj.** **1** of copper **2** reddish-brown **—cop′per·y** *adj.*

cop·per·head *n.* a poisonous North American snake

co·pra (kä′prə, ko̅′-) *n.* ⟦Port < Hindi *khoprā*⟧ dried coconut meat, the source of coconut oil

copse (käps) *n.* ⟦< OFr *coper,* to strike⟧ a

thicket of small trees or shrubs: also **cop·pice** (käp′is)

cop·ter (käp′tər) *n.* short for HELICOPTER

cop·u·la (käp′yŏŏ lə) *n., pl.* **-las** ⟦L, a link⟧ LINKING VERB —**cop′u·la′tive** (-lāt′iv) *adj.*

cop·u·late (käp′yŏŏ lāt′) *vi.* **-lat′ed, -lat′ing** ⟦< L *co-*, together + *apere*, to join⟧ to have sexual intercourse —**cop′u·la′tion** *n.*

cop·y (käp′ē) *n., pl.* **-ies** ⟦< L *copia*, plenty⟧ 1 a thing made just like another; imitation or reproduction 2 one of a number of books, magazines, etc. having the same contents 3 matter to be typeset 4 the words of an advertisement —*vt., vi.* **cop′ied, cop′y·ing** 1 to make a copy of 2 to imitate 3 [Inf.] to provide (with) a copy —**cop′y·ist** *n.*

cop·y·cat *n.* an imitator: chiefly a child's term —*adj.* done in imitation *[a copycat crime]*

cop·y·right *n.* the exclusive right to the publication, sale, etc. of a literary or artistic work —*vt.* to protect (a book, etc.) by copyright

cop·y·writ·er *n.* a writer of copy, esp. for advertisements

co·quette (kō ket′) *n.* ⟦Fr⟧ a girl or woman who flirts —**co·quet′tish** *adj.*

cor- *prefix* COM-: used before *r*

cor·al (kôr′əl) *n.* ⟦< Gr *korallion*⟧ 1 the hard skeleton secreted by certain marine polyps: reefs and atolls of coral occur in tropical seas 2 a piece of coral 3 a yellowish red —*adj.* of coral

coral snake a small, poisonous snake marked with red, yellow, and black bands

cor·bel (kôr′bəl) *n.* ⟦< L *corvus*, raven⟧ a piece of stone, wood, etc. projecting from a wall and supporting a cornice, arch, etc.

cord (kôrd) *n.* ⟦< Gr *chordē*⟧ 1 a thick string 2 a measure of wood cut for fuel (128 cubic feet) 3 a rib on the surface of a fabric 4 ribbed cloth 5 [*pl.*] corduroy trousers 6 *Anat.* any part like a cord 7 *Elec.* a slender cable

cord·age *n.* cords and ropes

cor·dial (kôr′jəl) *adj.* ⟦< L *cor*, heart⟧ warm; hearty; sincere —*n.* a liqueur —**cor′di·al′i·ty** (-jē al′ə tē) *n.* —**cor′dial·ly** *adv.*

cor·dil·le·ra (kôr′dil yer′ə, -də ler′ə) *n.* ⟦Sp < L *chorda*, a cord⟧ a system or chain of mountains

cord·ite (kôr′dīt′) *n.* ⟦< CORD: it is stringy⟧ a smokeless explosive made of nitroglycerin, etc.

cord·less (kôrd′lis) *adj.* operated by batteries, as an electric shaver

cor·don (kôr′dən) *n.* ⟦see CORD⟧ a line or circle of police, troops, etc. guarding an area —*vt.* to encircle with a cordon

cor·do·van (kôr′də vən) *n.* ⟦after *Córdoba*, Spain⟧ a soft, colored leather

cor·du·roy (kôr′də roi′) *n.* ⟦prob. < CORD + obs. *duroy*, a coarse fabric⟧ a heavy, ribbed cotton fabric

core (kôr) *n.* ⟦prob. < L *cor*, heart⟧ 1 the central part of an apple, pear, etc. 2 the central part of anything 3 the most important part —*vt.* **cored, cor′ing** to remove the core of

co·re·spond·ent (kō′ri spän′dənt) *n.* ⟦CO- + RESPONDENT⟧ *Law* a person charged with having committed adultery with the wife or husband from whom a divorce is being sought

co·ri·an·der (kôr′ē an′dər) *n.* ⟦< Gr *koriandron*⟧ an annual herb with aromatic seedlike fruit used as a flavoring

cork (kôrk) *n.* ⟦ult. < L *quercus*, oak⟧ 1 the light, thick, elastic outer bark of an oak tree (**cork oak**) 2 a stopper made of cork, for a bottle, etc. 3 any stopper —*adj.* of cork —*vt.* to stop with a cork

cork·board *n.* a bulletin board made of granulated cork

cork·screw *n.* a spiral-shaped device for pulling corks out of bottles —*adj.* spiral — *vi., vt.* to move in a spiral; twist

corm (kôrm) *n.* ⟦< Gr *kormos*, a log⟧ a fleshy, underground stem, as that of the gladiolus or crocus

cor·mo·rant (kôr′mə rənt) *n.* ⟦< L *corvus*, raven + *marinus*, marine⟧ a large, voracious sea bird

corn¹ (kôrn) *n.* ⟦OE⟧ 1 a small, hard seed, esp. of a cereal grass; kernel 2 *a)* an American cereal plant with kernels growing in rows along a woody husk-enclosed core (**corncob**) *b)* the kernels 3 [Brit.] grain, esp. wheat 4 the leading cereal crop in a place 5 [Inf.] ideas, humor, etc. regarded as dated, trite, etc. —*vt.* to pickle (meat, etc.) in brine

corn² (kôrn) *n.* ⟦< L *cornu*, horn⟧ a hard, thick, painful growth of skin, esp. on a toe

corn·ball *adj.* ⟦CORN¹ (*n.* 5) + (SCREW)BALL⟧ [Slang] corny

corn bread bread made with cornmeal

cor·ne·a (kôr′nē ə) *n.* ⟦< L *cornu*, horn⟧ the transparent outer coat of the eyeball —**cor′ne·al** *adj.*

cor·ner (kôr′nər) *n.* ⟦< L *cornu*, horn⟧ 1 the point or place where two lines or surfaces join and form an angle 2 the angle formed 3 any of the angles at a street intersection 4 a remote, secluded place 5 a region; quarter 6 a position hard to escape from 7 a monopoly acquired on a stock or commodity to raise the price —*vt.* 1 to force into a CORNER (*n.* 6) 2 to get a monopoly on (a stock, etc.) —*vi.* to turn corners: said of a vehicle —*adj.* at, on, or for a corner —**cut corners** to cut down expenses, time, etc. —**cor′nered** *adj.*

cor·ner·back *n.* *Football* either of two defensive backs positioned outside the linebackers

cor·ner·stone *n.* 1 a stone laid at a corner of a building, esp. at a ceremony for the beginning of construction 2 the basic part; foundation

cor·net (kôr net′) *n.* ⟦< L *cornu*, horn⟧ a brass instrument similar to the trumpet but more compact

corn·flow·er *n.* an annual plant with tiny, white, pink, or blue flowers that form a round head

cor·nice (kôr′nis) *n.* ⟦< Gr *korōnis*, wreath⟧ 1 a horizontal molding projecting along the top of a wall, etc. 2 a decorative cover for a curtain rod

corn·meal *n.* meal made from corn

corn·starch *n.* a powdery starch made from corn, used in cooking

corn syrup a syrup made from cornstarch

cor·nu·co·pi·a (kôr′nə kō′pē ə) *n.* ⟦L *cornu copiae,* horn of plenty⟧ **1** a horn-shaped container overflowing with fruits, flowers, etc. **2** an abundance

corn·y (kôr′nē) *adj.* **-i·er, -i·est** [Inf.] trite, sentimental, etc.

co·rol·la (kə rōl′ə, -räl′ə) *n.* ⟦< L, dim. of *corona,* crown⟧ the petals of a flower

cor·ol·lar·y (kôr′ə ler′ē) *n., pl.* **-ies** [see prec.] **1** a proposition that follows from one already proved **2** a normal result

co·ro·na (kə rō′nə) *n., pl.* **-nas** or **-nae** (-nē) ⟦L⟧ **1** the layer of ionized gas surrounding the sun **2** a ring of colored light seen around a luminous body, as the sun or moon

cor·o·nar·y (kôr′ə ner′ē) *adj.* **1** of or like a crown **2** of the arteries supplying blood to the heart muscle —*n., pl.* **-ies** a thrombosis in a coronary artery: in full **coronary thrombosis**

cor·o·na·tion (kôr′ə nā′shən) *n.* the crowning of a sovereign

cor·o·ner (kôr′ə nər) *n.* ⟦ME, officer of the crown⟧ a public officer who must determine the cause of any death not obviously due to natural causes

cor·o·net (kôr′ə net′, kôr′ə net′) *n.* ⟦< OFr *corone,* crown⟧ **1** a small crown worn by nobility **2** a band of jewels, flowers, etc. for the head

Corp *abbrev.* **1** Corporal **2** Corporation: also **corp**

cor·po·ral[1] (kôr′pə rəl, -prəl) *n.* ⟦< L *caput,* head⟧ the lowest-ranking noncommissioned officer, just below a sergeant

cor·po·ral[2] (kôr′pə rəl, -prəl) *adj.* ⟦< L *corpus,* body⟧ of the body; bodily

corporal punishment bodily punishment, as flogging

cor·po·rate (kôr′pə rit, -prit) *adj.* ⟦< L *corpus,* body⟧ **1** of, like, or being a corporation **2** shared; joint

cor·po·ra·tion (-pə rā′shən) *n.* a legal entity, usually a group of people, that has a charter granting it certain legal powers generally given to individuals, as to buy and sell property or to enter into contracts

cor·po·re·al (kôr pôr′ē əl) *adj.* ⟦< L *corpus,* body⟧ **1** of or for the body; physical **2** of a material nature; tangible

corps (kôr) *n., pl.* **corps** (kôrz) ⟦< L *corpus,* body⟧ **1** a body of people associated under common direction **2** *Mil. a)* a specialized branch of the armed forces *b)* a tactical subdivision of an army

corpse (kôrps) *n.* ⟦var. of prec.⟧ a dead body, esp. of a person

cor·pu·lence (kôr′pyōō ləns, -pyə-) *n.* ⟦< L *corpus,* body⟧ fatness; obesity —**cor′pu·lent** *adj.*

cor·pus (kôr′pəs) *n., pl.* **cor′po·ra** (-pə rə) ⟦L⟧ **1** a body, esp. a dead one **2** a complete collection, as of laws

cor·pus·cle (kôr′pus′əl) *n.* ⟦< L dim. of *corpus,* body⟧ an unattached body cell, esp. a red or white blood cell —**cor·pus′cu·lar** (-kyōō lər) *adj.*

corpus de·lic·ti (də lik′tī′) ⟦ModL, lit., body of the crime⟧ **1** the facts constituting a crime **2** loosely, the body of a murder victim

cor·ral (kə ral′) *n.* ⟦Sp < L *currere,* to run⟧ an enclosure for horses, cattle, etc.; pen —*vt.* **-ralled′, -ral′ling 1** to drive into or confine in a corral **2** to surround or capture

cor·rect (kə rekt′) *vt.* ⟦< L *com-,* together + *regere,* to rule⟧ **1** to make right **2** to point out or mark the errors of **3** to scold or punish **4** to cure or remove (a fault, etc.) —*adj.* **1** conforming to an established standard **2** true; accurate; right —**cor·rect′a·ble** *adj.* —**cor·rec′tive** *adj., n.* —**cor·rect′ly** *adv.* —**cor·rect′ness** *n.*

cor·rec·tion (-rek′shən) *n.* **1** a correcting or being corrected **2** a change that corrects a mistake **3** punishment to correct faults **4** *Finance* a temporary reversal in rising stock prices, etc. —**cor·rec′tion·al** *adj.*

cor·re·late (kôr′ə lāt′) *vi., vt.* **-lat′ed, -lat′ing** [see COM– & RELATE] to be in or bring into mutual relation —**cor′re·la′tion** *n.*

cor·rel·a·tive (kə rel′ə tiv) *adj.* **1** having a mutual relationship **2** *Gram.* expressing mutual relation and used in pairs, as the conjunctions *neither* and *nor* —*n.* a correlative word, etc.

cor·re·spond (kôr′ə spänd′) *vi.* ⟦< L *com-,* together + *respondere,* respond⟧ **1** to be in agreement (*with* something) **2** to be similar or equal (*to* something) **3** to communicate by letters —**cor·re·spond′ing·ly** *adv.*

cor·re·spond·ence *n.* **1** agreement; conformity **2** similarity **3** *a)* communication by letters *b)* the letters

cor·re·spond·ent *adj.* corresponding; agreeing; analogous —*n.* **1** a thing that corresponds **2** one who exchanges letters with another **3** one hired by a newspaper, radio network, etc. to furnish news, etc. from a distant place

cor·ri·dor (kôr′ə dər, -dôr′) *n.* ⟦Fr < L *currere,* to run⟧ **1** a long hall or passageway **2** a heavily traveled route [birds' migration *corridors*]

cor·rob·o·rate (kə räb′ə rāt′) *vt.* **-rat′ed, -rat′ing** ⟦< L *com-,* intens. + *robur,* strength⟧ to confirm; support —**cor·rob′o·ra′tion** *n.* —**cor·rob′o·ra′tive** (-ə rāt′iv, -ər ə tiv) *adj.* —**cor·rob′o·ra′tor** *n.*

cor·rode (kə rōd′) *vt., vi.* **-rod′ed, -rod′ing** ⟦< L *com-,* intens. + *rodere,* gnaw⟧ to eat into or wear away gradually, as by rusting or the action of chemicals —**cor·ro′sion** (-rō′zhən) *n.* —**cor·ro′sive** (-rō′siv) *adj., n.*

cor·ru·gate (kôr′ə gāt′) *vt., vi.* **-gat′ed, -gat′ing** ⟦< L *com-,* intens. + *rugare,* to wrinkle⟧ to shape into parallel grooves and ridges —**cor′ru·ga′tion** *n.*

cor·rupt (kə rupt′) *adj.* ⟦< L *com-,* together + *rumpere,* to break⟧ **1** evil; depraved **2** taking bribes **3** containing alterations, errors, etc.

— *vt., vi.* to make or become corrupt —**cor·rupt′i·ble** *adj.* —**cor·rup′tion** *n.* —**cor·rupt′ly** *adv.*

cor·sage (kôr säzh′) *n.* [see CORPS & -AGE] a small bouquet for a woman to wear, as at the waist or shoulder

cor·sair (kôr′ser′) *n.* [< Fr < L *cursus*, course] 1 a pirate 2 a pirate ship

cor·set (kôr′sit) *n.* [see CORPS] a closefitting undergarment worn, chiefly by women, to support or shape the body

cor·tege or **cor·tège** (kôr tezh′, -täzh′) *n.* [Fr < L *cohors*] 1 a retinue 2 a ceremonial procession

cor·tex (kôr′teks) *n., pl.* **-ti·ces′** (-tə sēz′) [L, bark of a tree] 1 the outer part of an internal organ; esp., the outer layer of gray matter over most of the brain 2 an outer layer of plant tissue —**cor′ti·cal** (-ti kəl) *adj.*

cor·ti·sone (kôrt′ə sōn′, -zōn′) [so named by E. C. Kendall (1886-1972), U.S. physician] a hormone used to treat adrenal insufficiency, inflammatory diseases, etc.

co·run·dum (kə run′dəm) *n.* [< Sans *kuruvinda*, ruby] a very hard mineral used for grinding and polishing

cor·us·cate (kôr′ə skāt′) *vi.* **-cat′ed, -cat′ing** [< L *coruscus*, vibrating] to glitter; sparkle —**cor′us·ca′tion** *n.*

cor·vette (kôr vet′) *n.* [Fr] a fast warship smaller than a destroyer and used chiefly for convoy duty

Co·sa Nos·tra (kō′sə nō′strə) [It, our thing] *name for* MAFIA, esp. in U.S.

co·sign (kō′sīn′) *vt., vi.* 1 to sign (a promissory note) in addition to the maker, thus becoming responsible if the maker defaults 2 to sign jointly —**co′sign′er** *n.*

co·sig·na·to·ry (-sig′nə tôr′ē) *n., pl.* **-ries** one of two or more joint signers, as of a treaty

cos·met·ic (käz met′ik) *adj.* [< Gr *kosmos*, order] 1 beautifying the face, hair, etc. 2 improving the appearance without making fundamental changes [*cosmetic* repairs to a house] —*n.* a cosmetic preparation, as lipstick —**cos·met′i·cal·ly** *adv.*

cos·me·tol·o·gy (-mə täl′ə jē) *n.* the work of a beautician —**cos′me·tol′o·gist** *n.*

cos·mic (käz′mik) *adj.* [< Gr *kosmos*, universe] 1 of the cosmos 2 vast

cosmic rays streams of high-energy charged particles from outer space

cos·mog·o·ny (käz mäg′ə nē) *n.* [< Gr *kosmos*, universe + *-gonos*, generation] 1 the study of the origin of the universe 2 *pl.* **-nies** a theory of this

cos·mol·o·gy (-mäl′ə jē) *n.* [< ML] 1 the scientific study of the form, evolution, etc. of the universe 2 the branch of metaphysics dealing with the origin and structure of the universe —**cos′mo·log′i·cal** (-mə läj′ə kəl) *adj.*

cos·mo·naut (käz′mə nôt′) *n.* [Russ *kosmonavt*] a Soviet or Russian astronaut

cos·mo·pol·i·tan (käz′mə päl′ə tən) *adj.* [< Gr *kosmos*, universe + *polis*, city-state] 1 common to or representative of all or many parts of the world 2 not bound by local or national habits or prejudices; at home in all places —*n.* a cosmopolitan person or thing: also **cos·mop′o·lite′** (-mäp′ə lit′)

cos·mos (käz′məs, -mōs) *n.* [< Gr *kosmos*, universe] 1 the universe considered as an orderly system 2 any complete and orderly system

cos·play (käs′plā′) *n.* [COS(TUME) + PLAY] a social activity in which fans dress up like characters from manga, anime, science fiction, etc. —**cos′play′er** *n.*

co·spon·sor (kō′spän′sər) *n.* a joint sponsor, as of a proposed piece of legislation —*vt.* to be a cosponsor of —**co′spon′sor·ship′** *n.*

Cos·sack (käs′ak, -ak) *n.* a people living in autonomous communal settlements, esp. in the Ukraine, until the late 1800s: renowned as cavalrymen under the czars

cost (kôst) *vt.* **cost, cost′ing** [< L *com-*, together + *stare*, to stand] 1 to be obtained for (a certain price) 2 to require the expenditure, loss, etc. of —*n.* 1 the amount of money, etc. asked or paid for a thing; price 2 the time, effort, etc. needed to do something 3 loss; sacrifice —**at all costs** by any means required

co·star (kō′stär′; *for v., usually* kō′stär′) *n.* any featured actor or actress given equal billing with another in a movie, play, etc. — *vt., vi.* **-starred′, -star′ring** to present as or be a costar

Cos·ta Ri·ca (käs′tə rē′kə, kôs′-, kōs′-) country in Central America —**Cos′ta Ri′can**

cost-ef·fec·tive (kôst′ə fek′tiv) *adj.* producing good results for the amount of money spent; efficient or economical —**cost′-ef·fec′tive·ness** *n.*

cos·tive (käs′tiv, kôs′-) *adj.* [< L *constipare*, to press together] constipated or constipating

cost·ly *adj.* **-li·er, -li·est** [ME] 1 costing much; expensive 2 magnificent —**cost′li·ness** *n.*

cost of living the average cost of the necessities of life, as food, shelter, etc.

cos·tume (käs′tōōm′, -tyōōm′) *n.* [< L *consuetudo*, custom] 1 *a)* the style of dress typical of a certain country, period, etc. *b)* a set of such clothes, as worn in a play 2 a set of outer clothes —*vt.* **-tumed′, -tum′ing** to provide with a costume

co·sy (kō′zē) *adj., n., -si·er, -si·est, n., pl. -sies* chiefly Brit. sp. of COZY —**co′si·ly** *adv.* —**co′si·ness** *n.*

cot¹ (kät) *n.* [< Sans *khátvā*] a narrow, collapsible bed, as one made of canvas on a folding frame

cot² (kät) *n.* [OE] a small shelter

cote (kōt) *n.* [ME] a small shelter for doves, sheep, etc.

Côte d′I·voire (kōt dē vwàr′) *official name for* IVORY COAST

co·te·rie (kōt′ər ē) *n.* [Fr] a close circle of friends; clique

co·ter·mi·nous (kō tur′mə nəs) *adj.* CONTERMINOUS

co·til·lion (kō til′yən) *n.* ⟦< OFr *cote*, coat⟧ **1** an intricate, formal group dance **2** a formal ball Also sp. **co·til′lon**

cot·tage (kät′ij) *n.* ⟦ME⟧ **1** a small house **2** a house used for vacations —**cot′tag·er** *n.*

cottage cheese a soft, white cheese made from the curds of sour milk

cottage industry 1 any relatively small-scale business operation carried on as from the home **2** a small, loosely organized, yet flourishing activity or industry

cot·ter pin (kät′ər) a pin with two stems that can be spread apart to fasten the pin in place

cot·ton (kät′'n) *n.* ⟦< Ar *qutun*⟧ **1** the soft, white hairs around the seeds of certain plants of the mallow family **2** such a plant or plants **3** thread or cloth made of cotton —**cotton to** [Inf.] to take a liking to —**cot′ton·y** *adj.*

cotton gin ⟦see GIN²⟧ a machine for separating cotton from the seeds

cot·ton·mouth *n.* WATER MOCCASIN

cot·ton·seed *n.* the seed of the cotton plant, yielding an oil (**cottonseed oil**) used in cooking oil, soap, etc.

cot·ton·tail *n.* a common American rabbit with a short, fluffy tail

cot·ton·wood *n.* a poplar that has seeds thickly covered with cottony or silky hairs

cot·y·le·don (kät′ə lēd′'n) *n.* ⟦< Gr *kotylē*, cavity⟧ the first leaf or one of the first pair of leaves produced by the embryo of a flowering plant

couch (kouch) *n.* ⟦< OFr *coucher*, lie down⟧ an article of furniture on which one may sit or lie down; sofa —*vt.* **1** to place as on a couch **2** to word in a certain way; phrase; express

cou·gar (kōō′gər) *n.* ⟦< AmInd (Brazil)⟧ **1** a large, powerful, tawny cat; mountain lion; puma **2** [Slang] a woman who sexually pursues much younger men

cough (kôf) *vi.* ⟦ME *coughen*⟧ to expel air suddenly and noisily from the lungs —*vt.* to expel by coughing —*n.* **1** the act of coughing **2** a condition causing frequent coughing —**cough up** [Slang] to hand over (money, etc.)

cough drop a small medicated tablet for the relief of coughs, etc.

could (kood) *v.aux.* **1** *pt. of* CAN¹ **2** an auxiliary verb generally equivalent to CAN¹, expressing esp. a shade of doubt [it *could* be so]

cou·lomb (kōō′läm′, -lōm′) *n.* ⟦after C. A. de *Coulomb* (1736–1806), Fr physicist⟧ a unit of electric charge equal to the charge of 6.281 × 10¹⁸ electrons

coun·cil (koun′səl) *n.* ⟦< L *com-*, together + *calere*, to call⟧ **1** a group of people called together for discussion, advice, etc. **2** an administrative, advisory, or legislative body —**coun′cil·man** (-mən) *n., pl.* **-men** (-mən) —**coun′cil·per′son** *n.* —**coun′cil·wom′an** *n., pl.* **-wom′en**

coun·ci·lor (-sə lər) *n.* a member of a council

coun·sel (koun′səl) *n.* ⟦< L *consilium*⟧ **1** advice **2** a lawyer or group of lawyers **3** a consultant —*vt.* **-seled** or **-selled**, **-sel·ing** or **-sel·ling 1** to give advice to **2** to recommend (an action, etc.)

coun·se·lor or **coun·sel·lor** (-sə lər) *n.* **1** an advisor **2** a lawyer **3** one in charge of children at a camp

count¹ (kount) *vt.* ⟦< L *computare*, compute⟧ **1** to name or add up, unit by unit, to get a total **2** to take account of; include **3** to believe to be; consider —*vi.* **1** to name numbers or add up items in order **2** to be taken into account; have importance **3** to have a specified value: often with *for* **4** to rely or depend (on or *upon*) —*n.* **1** a counting **2** the total number **3** a reckoning **4** *Law* any of the charges in an indictment

count² (kount) *n.* ⟦< L *comes*, companion⟧ a European nobleman with a rank equal to that of an English earl

count·down *n.* **1** the schedule of operations just before the firing of a rocket, etc. **2** the counting off, in reverse order, of time units in this schedule

coun·te·nance (koun′tə nəns, kount′'n əns) *n.* ⟦< L *continentia*, bearing⟧ **1** facial expression **2** the face **3** approval; support —*vt.* **-nanced**, **-nanc·ing** to approve or tolerate

count·er¹ (kount′ər) *n.* **1** a person, device, etc. that counts something **2** a small disk for keeping count in games **3** an imitation coin or token **4** a long table, cabinet top, etc. for the displaying of goods, serving of food, etc. —**under the counter** in a secret manner: said of sales, etc. made illegally

coun·ter² (kount′ər) *adv.* ⟦< L *contra*, against⟧ in opposition; opposite —*adj.* contrary; opposed —*n.* the opposite; contrary —*vt., vi.* to act, do, etc. counter to; oppose

counter- ⟦< L *contra-*, against⟧ *combining form* **1** contrary to [*counterclockwise*] **2** in retaliation [*counterattack*] **3** complementary [*counterpart*]

coun·ter·act *vt.* to act against; neutralize —**coun′ter·ac′tion** *n.*

coun·ter·at·tack *n.* an attack made in opposition to another attack — *vt., vi.* to attack so as to offset the enemy's attack

coun·ter·bal·ance *n.* a weight, force, etc. that balances another —*vt.* **-anced**, **-anc·ing** to be a counterbalance to

coun·ter·claim *n.* an opposing claim — *vt., vi.* to present as, or make, a counterclaim

coun·ter·clock·wise *adj., adv.* in a direction opposite to that in which the hands of a clock move

coun·ter·cul·ture *n.* a culture with a lifestyle that is opposed to the prevailing culture within which it exists

coun·ter·es·pi·o·nage *n.* actions to prevent or thwart enemy espionage

coun·ter·feit (-fit′) *adj.* ⟦< OFr *contre-*, counter- + *faire*, to make⟧ **1** made in imitation of something genuine so as to deceive; forged **2** sham; pretended —*n.* an imitation made to deceive; forgery —*vt., vi.* **1** to make an imitation of (money, etc.), usually to deceive **2** to pretend —**coun′ter·feit′er** *n.*

count·er·man (-man′) *n., pl.* **-men′** (-men′) a man who serves customers at a counter, as of a lunchroom or deli

coun·ter·mand (-mand′) *vt.* ⟦< L *contra*, against + *mandare*, to command⟧ to cancel or revoke by a contrary order

coun·ter·mel·o·dy *n.* a melody distinct from the principal melody

coun·ter·pane (-pān′) *n.* ⟦ult. < L *culcita puncta*, embroidered quilt⟧ a bedspread

coun·ter·part *n.* 1 one that closely resembles another 2 a copy or duplicate

coun·ter·point *n.* ⟦< It: see COUNTER- & POINT⟧ 1 the technique of combining two or more distinct lines of music that sound simultaneously 2 any melody played or sung against a basic melody 3 a thing set up in contrast with another

coun·ter·poise *n.* ⟦see COUNTER² & POISE⟧ 1 a counterbalance 2 equilibrium —*vt.* **-poised′, -pois′ing** to counterbalance

coun·ter·pro·duc·tive *adj.* having results contrary to those intended

coun·ter·rev·o·lu·tion *n.* a political movement against a government set up by a previous revolution —**coun′ter·rev′o·lu′tion·ar′y** *adj., n., pl.* **-ies**

coun·ter·sign *n.* 1 a signature added to a previously signed document, as for confirmation 2 a secret signal to another, as a password —*vt.* to confirm with one's own signature

coun·ter·sink *vt.* **-sunk′, -sink′ing** 1 to enlarge the top part of (a hole) so that the head of a bolt, etc. will fit flush with the surface 2 to sink (a bolt, etc.) into such a hole

coun·ter·ten·or *n.* 1 the range of the highest male voice, above tenor 2 a voice or singer with such a range

coun·ter·ter·ror·ism *n.* actions to prevent or thwart terrorism

count·er·top *n.* the upper surface of a COUNTER¹ (*n.* 4)

coun·ter·weight *n.* a counterbalance

count·ess (kount′is) *n.* 1 the wife or widow of a count or earl 2 a woman of nobility with a rank equal to that of a count or earl

count·less (kount′lis) *adj.* too many to count; innumerable; myriad

coun·try (kun′trē) *n., pl.* **-tries** ⟦< L *contra*, against⟧ 1 an area of land; region 2 the whole land, or the people, of a nation 3 the land of one's birth or citizenship 4 land with farms and small towns 5 *short for* COUNTRY MUSIC

country club a social club with a clubhouse, golf course, etc.

coun·try·man (-mən) *n., pl.* **-men** (-mən) a person from one's own country

country music popular music that derives from the rural folk music of the S U.S.

coun·try·side *n.* a rural region

coun·try·wide *adj., adv.* throughout the entire nation

coun·try·wom·an *n., pl.* **-wom′en** a woman from one's own country

coun·ty (kount′ē) *n., pl.* **-ties** ⟦< ML *comitatus*, jurisdiction of a count⟧ a small adminis-

trative district of a country, U.S. state, etc.

coup (kōō) *n., pl.* **coups** (kōōz) ⟦Fr < L *colaphus*, a blow⟧ 1 a sudden, successful action 2 COUP D'ÉTAT

coup de grâce (kōō′ də gräs′) ⟦Fr, stroke of mercy⟧ 1 the blow, shot, etc. that brings death to a sufferer 2 a finishing stroke

coup d'é·tat (kōō′ dā tä′) ⟦Fr, stroke of state⟧ the sudden, forcible overthrow as of a ruler or government

coupe (kōōp) *n.* ⟦< Fr *couper*, to cut⟧ a closed, two-door automobile

cou·ple (kup′əl) *n.* ⟦< L *copula*⟧ 1 a link 2 a pair of things or persons, as two people who are engaged, married, etc. 3 [Inf.] a few — *vt., vi.* **-pled, -pling** to link or unite

cou·plet (kup′lit) *n.* two successive lines of poetry, esp. two that rhyme

cou·pling (kup′liŋ) *n.* 1 a joining together 2 a mechanical device for joining parts together

cou·pon (kōō′pän′, kyōō′-) *n.* ⟦Fr < *couper*, to cut⟧ 1 a detachable printed statement on a bond, specifying the interest due at a given time 2 a certificate entitling one to a specified right, as a discount or gift

cour·age (kur′ij) *n.* ⟦< L *cor*, heart⟧ the quality of being brave; valor

cou·ra·geous (kə rā′jəs) *adj.* having or showing courage; brave —**cou·ra′geous·ly** *adv.*

cou·ri·er (koor′ē ər, kur′-) *n.* ⟦< L *currere*, to run⟧ a messenger

course (kôrs) *n.* ⟦< L *currere*, to run⟧ 1 an onward movement; progress 2 a way, path, or channel 3 the direction taken 4 a regular manner of procedure or conduct [our wisest *course*] 5 a series of like things in order 6 a part of a meal served at one time 7 *Educ. a)* a complete series of studies, as for a degree *b)* any of the separate units of such a series —*vi.* **coursed, cours′ing** to run or race —**in due course** in the usual sequence (of events) —**in the course of** during —**of course** 1 naturally 2 certainly

cours·er (kôr′sər) *n.* a graceful, spirited, or swift horse

court (kôrt) *n.* ⟦< L *cohors*, enclosure⟧ 1 a courtyard 2 a short street 3 a space for playing a game, as basketball 4 *a)* the palace, or the family, etc., of a sovereign *b)* a sovereign and councilors, etc. as a governing body *c)* a formal gathering held by a sovereign 5 attention paid to someone in order to get something 6 *Law a)* a judge or judges *b)* a place where trials are held —*vt.* 1 to pay attention to (a person) so as to get something 2 to seek as a mate; woo 3 to try to get [to *court* favor] —*vi.* to carry on a courtship

cour·te·ous (kurt′ē əs) *adj.* ⟦see prec. & -EOUS⟧ polite and gracious —**cour′te·ous·ly** *adv.*

cour·te·san (kôrt′ə zən) *n.* ⟦see COURT⟧ a prostitute, esp. one catering to men of wealth or nobility

cour·te·sy (kurt′ə sē) *n., pl.* **-sies** 1 courteous behavior 2 a polite or considerate act or remark —*adj.* provided free; complimentary

court·house *n.* **1** a building housing law courts **2** a building housing offices of a county government

cour·ti·er (kôrt′ē ər, -yər) *n.* an attendant at a royal court

court·ly *adj.* **-li·er, -li·est** suitable for a king's court; dignified; elegant —**court′li·ness** *n.*

court-mar·tial *n., pl.* **courts′-mar′tials** for 2, now often **court′-mar′tials 1** a court in the armed forces for the trial of persons accused of breaking military law **2** a trial by a court-martial **3** a conviction by a court-martial —*vt.* **-tialed** or **-tialled, -tial·ing** or **-tial·ling** to try or convict by a court-martial

court reporter one who records exactly what is said in a courtroom during a trial

court·room *n. Law* a room in which trials are held

court·ship *n.* the act, process, or period of wooing

court·side *n. Sports* the area immediately around a basketball court, tennis court, etc.

court·yard *n.* a space enclosed by walls, adjoining or within a large building

cous·cous (kŏŏs′kŏŏs′) *n.* 〖Fr < Ar kaskasa, to grind〗 a N African dish made with crushed grain, usually steamed

cous·in (kuz′ən) *n.* 〖ult. < L com-, with + soror, sister〗 **1** the son or daughter of one's uncle or aunt **2** loosely, any relative by blood or marriage

cous·in·age (-ij) *n.* **1** the relationship between cousins **2** a group of cousins or relatives

cou·tu·ri·er (kŏŏ′tŏŏr ē ā′) *n.* 〖Fr〗 a designer of women's fashions

cove (kōv) *n.* 〖OE cofa, cave〗 a small bay or inlet

cov·en (kuv′ən) *n.* 〖see CONVENE〗 a gathering or meeting of witches

cov·e·nant (kuv′ə nənt) *n.* 〖see CONVENE〗 an agreement; compact —*vt.* to promise by a covenant —*vi.* to make a covenant

cov·er (kuv′ər) *vt.* 〖< L co-, intens. + operire, to hide〗 **1** to place something on or over **2** to extend over **3** to clothe **4** to conceal; hide **5** to shield, protect, or watch (someone or something) **6** to include; deal with [to cover a subject] **7** to protect financially [to cover a loss] **8** to accept (a bet) **9** to travel over **10** to point a firearm at **11** to remake or perform (a song popularized by another) **12** Journalism to gather the details of (a news story) —*vi.* **1** to spread over a surface, as a liquid does **2** to provide an alibi (for) —*n.* **1** anything that covers, as a lid, top, etc. **2** a shelter for protection **3** a tablecloth and setting **4** COVER CHARGE **5** something used to hide one's real actions, etc. **6** a remake or performance of a song popularized by another —**cover up** to keep blunders, crimes, etc. from being known —**take cover** to seek shelter —**under cover** in secrecy or concealment

cov·er·age (-ij) *n.* **1** the amount, extent, etc. covered by something **2** Insurance the risks covered by a policy

cov·er·all *n.* [usually pl.] a one-piece outer garment, often worn over regular clothing while working, etc.

cover charge a fixed charge in addition to the cost of food and drink, as at a nightclub or restaurant

cover crop a crop, as clover, grown to prevent erosion, restore soil fertility, etc.

covered wagon a large wagon with an arched cover of canvas

cover girl *n.* a woman model whose picture appears on magazine covers

cov·er·ing *n.* anything that covers

cov·er·let (-lit) *n.* 〖< OFr covrir, to cover + lit, bed〗 a bedspread

cover letter an explanatory letter sent with an enclosure or package

cover story the article in a magazine that deals with the subject depicted on the cover

cov·ert (kō′vərt, kuv′ərt) *adj.* 〖see COVER〗 hidden or disguised —*n.* a protected place, as for game —**cov′ert·ly** *adv.*

cov·er·up *n.* an attempt to hide blunders, crimes, etc.

cov·et (kuv′it) *vt., vi.* 〖< L cupiditas, cupidity〗 to want intensely (esp., something that another person has)

cov·et·ous *adj.* tending to covet; greedy —**cov′et·ous·ly** *adv.* —**cov′et·ous·ness** *n.*

cov·ey (kuv′ē) *n., pl.* **-eys** 〖< OFr cover, to hatch〗 a small flock of birds, esp. partridges or quail

cow[1] (kou) *n.* 〖OE cu〗 **1** the mature female of domestic cattle, valued for its milk **2** the mature female of certain other mammals, as the whale

cow[2] (kou) *vt.* 〖< ON kūga, subdue〗 to make timid; intimidate

cow·ard (kou′ərd) *n.* 〖ult. < L cauda, tail〗 a person who lacks courage, esp. one who is shamefully afraid

cow·ard·ice (-ər dis′) *n.* lack of courage

cow·ard·ly *adj.* of or like a coward —*adv.* in the manner of a coward —**cow′ard·li·ness** *n.*

cow·boy *n.* a man who is a ranch worker who herds cattle

cow·er (kou′ər) *vi.* 〖ME couren〗 to crouch or huddle up, as from fear or cold; shrink; cringe

cow·girl *n.* a woman who is a ranch worker who herds cattle

cow·hand *n.* a cowboy or cowgirl

cow·hide *n.* **1** the hide of a cow **2** leather from it

cowl (koul) *n.* 〖< L cucullus, hood〗 **1** a monk's hood or a monk's cloak with a hood **2** a hood-shaped part or structure

cow·lick (kou′lik′) *n.* 〖< its looking as if licked by a cow〗 a tuft of hair that resists being combed flat

cowl·ing (koul′iŋ) *n.* 〖see COWL〗 a metal covering for an airplane engine, etc.

co-work·er (kō′wur′kər) *n.* a fellow worker; colleague: also **co′work′er**

cow·poke *n.* [Inf.] COWBOY

cow pony a horse for herding cattle

cow·pox *n.* a disease of cows: a vaccine with its virus gives temporary immunity to smallpox

cox·comb (käks′kōm′) *n.* [for *cock's comb*] a silly, vain fellow; dandy

cox·swain (käk′sən, -swān′) *n.* [< *cock*, small boat + SWAIN] one who steers a boat or racing shell

coy (koi) *adj.* [ME, quiet] 1 bashful; shy 2 pretending to be shy —**coy′ly** *adv.* —**coy′ness** *n.*

coy·o·te (ki ōt′ē, ki′ōt′) *n.* [< AmInd (Mex)] a small, wolflike mammal of North America

coz·en (kuz′ən) *vt., vi.* [< ME *cosin*, fraud] to cheat; deceive —**coz′en·age** *n.*

co·zy (kō′zē) *adj.* **-zi·er, -zi·est** [Scot] warm and comfortable; snug —*n., pl.* **-zies** a padded cover for a teapot, to keep the tea hot —**cozy up to** [Inf.] to try to ingratiate oneself with —**co′zi·ly** *adv.* —**co′zi·ness** *n.*

CPA *abbrev.* Certified Public Accountant

CPI *abbrev.* consumer price index

CPO *abbrev.* Chief Petty Officer

CPR *abbrev.* cardiopulmonary resuscitation

CPU (sē′pē′yōō′) *n.* central processing unit: also **cpu**

Cr *Chem. symbol for* chromium

crab (krab) *n.* [OE *crabba*] 1 a crustacean with four pairs of legs and a pair of pincers 2 a peevish person —*vi.* **crabbed, crab′bing** [Inf.] to complain

crab·ap·ple *n.* 1 a small, very sour apple 2 a tree bearing crabapples: also **crab tree**

crab·bed (krab′id) *adj.* [< CRAB(APPLE)] 1 peevish 2 hard to read or understand, as handwriting —**crab′bed·ness** *n.*

crab·by *adj.* **-bi·er, -bi·est** [see prec.] cross and complaining —**crab′bi·ly** *adv.* —**crab′bi·ness** *n.*

crab grass a weedy grass, with freely rooting stems, that spreads rapidly

crack¹ (krak) *vi.* [< OE *cracian*, resound] 1 to make a sudden, sharp noise, as in breaking 2 to break or split, usually without separation of parts 3 to rasp or shift erratically in register: said of the voice 4 [Inf.] to break down as from strain —*vt.* 1 to cause to make a sharp, sudden noise 2 to cause to break or split 3 to break down (petroleum) into the lighter hydrocarbons of gasoline, etc. 4 to hit hard 5 to solve 6 [Inf.] to break into or force open 7 [Slang] to make (a joke) —*n.* 1 a sudden, sharp noise 2 a partial break; fracture 3 a chink; crevice 4 a cracking of the voice 5 a sudden, sharp blow 6 [Inf.] an attempt or try 7 [Slang] a joke or gibe —*adj.* [Inf.] excellent; first-rate —**crack down (on)** to become strict (with) —**cracked up to be** [Inf.] believed to be —**crack up** 1 to crash 2 [Inf.] *a)* to break down physically or mentally *b)* to laugh or cry

crack² (krak) *n.* [Slang] a very potent, purified form of cocaine for smoking

crack·down *n.* a resorting to strict or stricter discipline or punishment

cracked *adj.* 1 having a crack or cracks 2 sounding harsh or strident 3 [Inf.] crazy

crack·er *n.* 1 a firecracker 2 a thin, crisp wafer

crack·er·jack *adj.* [Slang] outstanding; excellent —*n.* [Slang] an excellent person or thing

crack·head *n.* [Slang] a habitual user of CRACK²

crack·le (krak′əl) *vi.* **-led, -ling** [ME *crakelen*, to crack] to make a series of slight, sharp, popping sounds —*n.* 1 a series of such sounds 2 the fine, irregular surface cracks on some pottery, etc.

crack·pot [Inf.] *n.* a crazy or eccentric person —*adj.* crazy or eccentric

crack·up *n.* 1 a crash 2 [Inf.] a physical or mental breakdown

-cra·cy (krə sē) [< Gr *kratos*, rule] *combining form* a (specified) type of government; rule by [*autocracy*]

cra·dle (krād′'l) *n.* [OE *cradol*] 1 a baby's small bed, usually on rockers 2 infancy 3 the place of a thing's beginning 4 anything like a cradle —*vt.* **-dled, -dling** 1 to place, rock, or hold in or as in a cradle 2 to take care of in infancy

cra·dle·song *n.* a lullaby

craft (kraft) *n.* [OE *cræft*, power] 1 a special skill or art 2 an occupation requiring special skill 3 the members of a skilled trade 4 guile; slyness 5 *pl.* **craft** a boat, ship, or aircraft —**crafts′man** (-mən) *n., pl.* **-men** (-mən) —**crafts′man·ship′** *n.* —**crafts′per′son** *n.* —**crafts′wom′an** *n., pl.* **-wom′en**

craft·y *adj.* **-i·er, -i·est** [ME *crafti*, sly] subtly deceitful; sly —**craft′i·ly** *adv.* —**craft′i·ness** *n.*

crag (krag) *n.* [< Celt] a steep, rugged rock rising from a rock mass —**crag′gy** *adj.* **-gi·er, -gi·est**

cram (kram) *vt.* **crammed, cram′ming** [OE *crammian*] 1 to pack full or too full 2 to stuff; force 3 to feed to excess —*vi.* 1 to eat too much or too quickly 2 to study a subject in a hurried, intensive way, as for an examination

cramp (kramp) *n.* [< OFr *crampe*, bent] 1 a sudden, painful, involuntary contraction of a muscle from chill, strain, etc. 2 [*usually pl.*] abdominal or uterine spasms and pain —*vt.* 1 to cause a cramp or cramps in 2 [< MDu *krampe*, bent in] to hamper; restrain

cramped *adj.* 1 confined or restricted 2 irregular and crowded, as some handwriting

cran·ber·ry (kran′ber′ē, -bər ē) *n., pl.* **-ries** [< Du *kranebere*] 1 a firm, sour, edible, red berry, the fruit of a low evergreen shrub 2 the shrub

crane (krān) *n.* [OE *cran*] 1 a large wading bird with very long legs and neck 2 a machine for lifting or moving heavy weights, using a movable arm or a horizontal traveling beam —*vt., vi.* **craned, cran′ing** to stretch (the neck)

cra·ni·um (krā′nē əm) *n., pl.* **-ni·ums** or **-ni·a** (-ə) [< Gr *kranion*] the skull, esp. the part containing the brain —**cra′ni·al** *adj.*

crank (kraŋk) *n.* [OE *cranc-*, something twisted] 1 a handle or arm bent at right angles and connected to a machine shaft to transmit motion 2 [Inf.] an eccentric or irritable person —*vt.* to start or operate by a

crank —**crank out** [Inf.] to produce steadily and prolifically

crank·case *n.* the metal casing that encloses the crankshaft of an internal-combustion engine

crank·shaft *n.* a shaft with one or more cranks for transmitting motion

crank·y *adj.* **-i·er, -i·est** 1 apt to operate poorly 2 irritable 3 eccentric —**crank′i·ly** *adv.* —**crank′i·ness** *n.*

cran·ny (kran′ē) *n., pl.* **-nies** [< VL *crena*, a notch] a crevice; crack

crap (krap) *n.* [< ML *crappa*, chaff] [Slang] 1 nonsense 2 junk; trash 3 excrement: somewhat vulgar —**crap′py** *adj.* **-pi·er, -pi·est**

crape (krāp) *n.* 1 CREPE (*n.* 1) 2 a piece of black crepe worn or hung as a sign of mourning

crap·pie (krap′ē) *n.* a small North American sunfish

craps (kraps) *n.* [Fr *crabs*] a gambling game played with two dice

crap·shoot *n.* [Inf.] a very risky undertaking

crap·shoot·er (krap′shoot′ər) *n.* a gambler at craps

crash (krash) *vi.* [ME] 1 to fall, collide, or break with a loud noise 2 to collapse; fail 3 [Slang] to sleep or get a temporary place to sleep —*vt.* 1 to cause (a car, airplane, etc.) to crash 2 to force with or as with a crashing noise: with *in, out, through,* etc. 3 [Inf.] to get into (a party, etc.) without an invitation, etc. —*n.* 1 a loud, sudden noise 2 a crashing 3 a sudden collapse, as of business —*adj.* [Inf.] using all possible resources, effort, and speed [*a crash program to build roads*]

crash-land *vt., vi.* to bring (an airplane) down in a forced landing, esp. without use of the landing gear —**crash landing**

crash pad [Slang] a place to live or sleep temporarily

crass (kras) *adj.* [L *crassus*, thick] 1 tasteless, insensitive, etc. 2 materialistic —**crass′ly** *adv.* —**crass′ness** *n.*

-crat (krat) [< Gr *kratos*, rule] *combining form* member or supporter of (a specified kind of) government

crate (krāt) *n.* [L *cratis*, wickerwork] a packing case made of slats of wood —*vt.* **crat′ed, crat′ing** to pack in a crate

cra·ter (krāt′ər) *n.* [< Gr *kratēr*, mixing bowl] 1 a bowl-shaped cavity, as at the mouth of a volcano 2 a pit made by an exploding bomb, meteor impact, etc. —*vt.* to make craters in —*vi.* to form craters

cra·vat (krə vat′) *n.* [< Fr] a necktie

crave (krāv) *vt.* **craved, crav′ing** [OE *crafian*] 1 to ask for earnestly; beg 2 to desire strongly

cra·ven (krā′vən) *adj.* [< L *crepare*, to rattle] cowardly —*n.* a coward —**cra′ven·ly** *adv.* —**cra′ven·ness** *n.*

crav·ing *n.* an intense and prolonged desire, as for affection or for a food or drug

craw (krô) *n.* [ME *craue*] 1 the crop of a bird 2 the stomach

craw·fish (krô′fish′) *n., pl.* **-fish′** or **-fish′es** crayfish

crawl (krôl) *vi.* [< ON *krafla*] 1 to move slowly by dragging the body along the ground 2 to go on hands and knees; creep 3 to move slowly 4 to behave in a servile manner 5 to swarm (*with* crawling things) —*n.* 1 a slow movement 2 an overarm swimming stroke

crawl space an unfinished space, as under a floor, allowing access to wiring, plumbing, etc.

crawl·y *adj.* **-i·er, -i·est** CREEPY

cray·fish (krā′fish′) *n., pl.* **-fish′** or **-fish′es** [< OHG *krebiz*] a freshwater crustacean resembling a little lobster

cray·on (krā′ən, -än′) *n.* [Fr, pencil < L *creta*, chalk] 1 a small stick of chalk, charcoal, or colored wax, used for drawing, coloring, or writing 2 a drawing made with crayons —*vt.* to draw or color with crayons

craze (krāz) *vt., vi.* **crazed, craz′ing** [ME *crasen*, to crack] 1 to make or become insane 2 to cover or become covered with many fine cracks —*n.* a fad

cra·zy (krā′zē) *adj.* **-zi·er, -zi·est** [< prec.] 1 unsound of mind; insane 2 [Inf.] foolish; not sensible 3 [Inf.] very enthusiastic or eager —*n., pl.* **-zies** [Slang] a crazy person —**like crazy** [Inf.] with great energy, intensity, etc. —**cra′zi·ly** *adv.* —**cra′zi·ness** *n.*

crazy bone FUNNY BONE

crazy quilt 1 a patchwork quilt with no regular design 2 a hodgepodge

creak (krēk) *vi., vt.* [echoic] to make, cause to make, or move with a harsh, squeaking sound —*n.* such a sound —**creak′y** *adj.* **-i·er, -i·est** —**creak′i·ly** *adv.* —**creak′i·ness** *n.*

cream (krēm) *n.* [< OFr] 1 the thick liquid that rises to the top of raw milk and contains the butterfat 2 a cosmetic, emulsion, or food with a creamy consistency 3 the best part 4 yellowish white —*adj.* made of or with cream —*vt.* 1 to add cream to 2 to beat into a creamy consistency 3 [Slang] *a*) to beat or defeat soundly *b*) to hurt, damage, etc., as by striking with great force —**cream of** creamed purée of —**cream′y** *adj.* **-i·er, -i·est** —**cream′i·ness** *n.*

cream cheese a soft, white cheese made of cream or of milk and cream

cream·er *n.* 1 a pitcher for cream 2 a nondairy substance used in place of cream

cream·er·y *n., pl.* **-ies** a place where dairy products are processed or sold

cream of tartar a white substance used in baking powder, etc.

crease (krēs) *n.* [< ME *creste*, crest] 1 a line made by folding and pressing 2 a fold or wrinkle —*vt.* **creased, creas′ing** to make a crease in 2 to wrinkle —*vi.* to become creased

cre·ate (krē āt′) *vt.* **-at′ed, -at′ing** [< L *creare*] 1 to cause to come into existence; make; originate 2 to bring about; give rise to; cause

cre·a·tion (-ā′shən) *n.* 1 a creating or being

created **2** the universe **3** anything created —**the Creation** God's creating of the world

cre·a·tion·ism (-iz′əm) *n. Theol.* a doctrine holding that matter, species, etc. were supernaturally created by God; often, specif., such a doctrine based on the description of Creation in the Book of Genesis —**cre·a′tion· ist** *n.*

cre·a·tive (-āt′iv) *adj.* **1** creating or able to create **2** showing inventiveness [a *creative* solution] **3** stimulating the imagination [*creative* toys] —**cre·a′tive·ly** *adv.* —**cre·a′ tive·ness** *n.* —**cre′a·tiv′i·ty** (-â tiv′ə tē) *n.*

cre·a·tor (-āt′ər) *n.* [L] one who creates —**the Creator** God

crea·ture (krē′chər) *n.* [< L *creatura*] a living being, animal or human

crèche (kresh, krāsh) *n.* [Fr] a display of the stable scene of Jesus' birth

cred (kred) *n.* [shortened < CREDIBILITY] [Slang] credibility and acceptance, as in a particular field

cre·dence (krēd′ns) *n.* [< L *credere*, believe] belief, esp. in the reports or testimony of another

cre·den·tial (kri den′shəl) *n.* [see prec.] [*usually pl.*] a letter or certificate showing one's right to a certain position or authority

cre·den·za (kri den′zə) *n.* [It] **1** a type of buffet or sideboard **2** a low office cabinet

credibility gap 1 a disparity between what is said and the facts **2** the inability to have one's truthfulness or honesty accepted

cred·i·ble (kred′ə bəl) *adj.* [< L *credere*, believe] that can be believed; reliable —**cred′ i·bil′i·ty** *n.* —**cred′i·bly** *adv.*

cred·it (kred′it) *n.* [< L *credere*, believe] **1** belief; confidence **2** favorable reputation **3** praise or approval **4** a person or thing bringing approval or honor **5** *a)* acknowledgment of work done *b)* [*pl.*] a list of such acknowledgments in a film, book, etc. **6** a sum available to one, as in a bank account **7** the entry, in an account, of payment on a debt **8** trust in one's ability to meet payments when due **9** a completed unit of study in a school —*vt.* **1** to believe; trust **2** to give credit to or commendation for **3** to give credit in a bank account, etc. —**do credit to** to bring honor to —**on credit** with an agreement to pay later

cred·it·a·ble *adj.* deserving some credit or praise —**cred′it·a·bly** *adv.*

credit card a card entitling one to charge purchases, etc. at certain businesses

cred·i·tor (-it ər) *n.* one to whom money is owed

credit union a cooperative association for pooling savings of members and making low-interest loans to them

cred·it·wor·thy *adj.* sufficiently sound financially to be granted credit —**cred′it·wor′thi· ness** *n.*

cre·do (krē′dō′, krā′-) *n., pl.* -**dos′** [L, I believe] a creed

cred·u·lous (krej′oo ləs, -ə ləs) *adj.* [< L *credere*, believe] tending to believe too readily —**cre·du·li·ty** (krə doo′lə tē, -dyoo-) *n.* —**cred′u·lous·ly** *adv.*

creed (krēd) *n.* [< L *credo*, I believe] **1** a brief statement of religious belief, esp. one accepted as authoritative by a church **2** any statement of belief, principles, etc. **3** religious affiliation

creek (krēk, krik) *n.* [< ON *kriki*, a bend, winding] a small stream —**up the creek** [Slang] in trouble

creel (krēl) *n.* [< L *cratis*, wickerwork] a wicker basket for holding fish

creep (krēp) *vi.* **crept, creep′ing** [OE *creopan*] **1** to move with the body close to the ground, as on hands and knees **2** to move slowly or stealthily **3** to grow along the ground or a wall, as ivy —*n.* **1** the act of creeping **2** [Slang] an annoying or disgusting person —**make one's flesh creep** to give one a feeling of fear, disgust, etc. —**the creeps** [Inf.] a feeling of fear, disgust, etc. —**creep′ er** *n.*

creep·y *adj.* -**i·er,** -**i·est** having or causing a feeling of fear or disgust —**creep′i·ly** *adv.* —**creep′i·ness** *n.*

cre·mains (krē mānz′) *pl.n.* the ashes remaining after cremation

cre·mate (krē′māt′, kri māt′) *vt.* -**mat′ed, -mat′ing** [< L *cremare*] to burn (a dead body) to ashes —**cre·ma′tion** *n.*

cre·ma·to·ry (krē′mə tôr′ē, krem′ə-) *n., pl.* -**ries** a furnace for cremating: also **cre·ma· to′ri·um** (-ē əm), *pl.* -**ri·ums, -ri·a** (-ē ə), or -**ries** —*adj.* of or for cremation

crème de menthe (krem′ də mänt′, menth′, mint′) [Fr, cream of mint] a sweet, mint-flavored liqueur

crème fraîche (krem′ fresh′) [Fr, fresh cream] slightly fermented high-fat cream, used in sauces, desserts, etc.

cren·el·ate or **cren·el·late** (kren′əl āt′) *vt.* -**el·at′ed** or -**el·lat′ed,** -**el·at′ing** or -**el· lat′ing** [< VL *crena*, a notch] to furnish with battlements or with squared notches —**cren′ el·a′tion** *n.*, **cren′el·la′tion**

Cre·ole (krē′ōl′) *n.* [< Fr < Port *crioulo*, native] **1** a person of European parentage born in the West Indies, Latin America, etc. **2** a person descended from the original French settlers of Louisiana **3** a person of mixed Creole and black descent **4** [c-] a language that develops when different languages remain in contact with each other —*adj.* [*usually* c-] prepared with sautéed tomatoes, green peppers, onions, spices, etc.

cre·o·sote (krē′ə sōt′) *n.* [< Gr *kreas*, flesh + *sōzein*, to save] **1** an oily liquid distilled from tar and used as a wood preservative, etc. **2** a flammable buildup of condensed flue gases, as inside a chimney

crepe or **crêpe** (krāp; *for 5, also* krep) *n.* [< Fr < L *crispus*, curly] **1** a thin, crinkled cloth of silk, rayon, wool, etc. **2** CRAPE (*n.* 2) **3** wrinkled soft rubber used for shoe soles: also **crepe rubber 4** thin, crinkled paper: also **crepe pa· per 5** a thin pancake, rolled and filled

crêpes su·zette (krāp′ sōō zet′) [Fr] crêpes rolled in a hot, orange-flavored sauce and served in flaming brandy

crept (krept) *vi. pt. & pp. of* CREEP

cre·scen·do (kri shen′dō′) *adj., adv.* [It < L *crescere,* grow] *Music* with a gradual increase in loudness: also written **cre·scen′do′** —*n., pl.* **-dos′** 1 a gradual increase in loudness, force, etc. 2 loosely, a state of great loudness, intensity, etc.

cres·cent (kres′ənt) *n.* [< L *crescere,* grow] 1 a phase of a planet or a moon, when it appears to have one concave edge and one convex edge 2 anything shaped like this —*adj.* shaped like a crescent

crescent wrench [< *Crescent,* a trademark] a wrench with a crescent-shaped head and an adjustable jaw

cress (kres) *n.* [OE *cressa*] a plant with pungent leaves, as watercress, used in salads, etc.

crest (krest) *n.* [< L *crista*] 1 any growth on the head of an animal, as a comb or tuft 2 a heraldic device placed on seals, silverware, etc. 3 the top line or surface; summit 4 the highest point, level, degree, etc. —*vi.* to form or reach a crest —**crest′ed** *adj.*

crest·fall·en *adj.* dejected, disheartened, etc.

Cre·ta·ceous (kri tā′shəs, krē-) *adj.* [< L *creta,* chalk] of the latest period of the Mesozoic Era, marked by the extinction of dinosaurs, the rise of mammals and flowering plants, and the formation of oil deposits

Crete (krēt) Greek island in the E Mediterranean —**Cre′tan** (krēt′n) *adj., n.*

cre·tonne (krē tän′, krē′tän′) *n.* [Fr, after *Creton,* village in Normandy] a heavy, printed cotton or linen cloth, used for curtains, slipcovers, etc.

cre·vasse (krə vas′) *n.* [Fr] a deep crack, esp. in the ice of a glacier

crev·ice (krev′is) *n.* [< L *crepare,* to rattle] a narrow opening caused by a crack or split; fissure

crew¹ (krōō) *n.* [< L *crescere,* grow] 1 a group of people working together [a road *crew*] 2 a ship's personnel, excluding the officers 3 the sport of rowing racing shells —**crew′man** (-mən) *n., pl.* **-men** (-mən)

crew² (krōō) *vi. alt. pt. of* [Chiefly Brit.] CROW² (*vi.* 1)

crew cut a man's haircut in which the hair is cropped close to the head

crew·el (krōō′əl) *n.* [ME *crule*] a loosely twisted, worsted yarn —**crew′el·work′** *n.*

crib (krib) *n.* [OE, ox stall] 1 a rack or box for fodder 2 a small bed with high sides, for a baby 3 an enclosure for storing grain 4 an underwater structure serving as a pier, water intake, etc. 5 [Inf.] a translation or other aid used dishonestly in doing schoolwork —*vt.* **cribbed, crib′bing** 1 to confine 2 to furnish with a crib 3 [Inf.] to plagiarize —*vi.* [Inf.] to do schoolwork dishonestly

crib·bage (krib′ij) *n.* a card game in which the object is to form combinations for points

crib death SUDDEN INFANT DEATH SYNDROME

crick¹ (krik) *n.* [< ON *kriki,* bend] a painful cramp in the neck, back, etc.

crick² (krik) *n.* [Dial.] CREEK

crick·et¹ (krik′it) *n.* [< OFr *criquer,* to creak] a leaping insect similar to a grasshopper

crick·et² (krik′it) *n.* [OFr *criquet,* a bat] an outdoor game played by two teams of eleven players each, using a ball, bats, and wickets

cried (krīd) *vi., vt. pt. & pp. of* CRY

cri·er (krī′ər) *n.* 1 one who cries 2 one who shouts out announcements, news, etc.

crime (krīm) *n.* [< L *crimen,* offense] 1 an act in violation of a law; specif., a serious violation, as a felony 2 a sin

Cri·me·a (krī mē′ə) peninsula in SE Europe, extending into the Black Sea —**Cri·me′an** *adj.*

crim·i·nal (krim′ə nəl) *adj.* 1 having the nature of crime 2 relating to or guilty of crime —*n.* a person guilty of a crime —**crim′i·nal′i·ty** (-nal′ə tə) *n.* —**crim′i·nal·ly** *adv.*

crim·i·nal·ist (-nəl ist) *n.* an expert in the scientific analysis of criminal evidence

crim·i·nol·o·gy (-näl′ə jē) *n.* the scientific study of crime and criminals —**crim′i·nol′o·gist** *n.*

crimp (krimp) *vt.* [< MDu *crimpen,* to wrinkle] 1 to press into narrow folds; pleat 2 to curl (hair) 3 to pinch together —*n.* 1 a crimping 2 anything crimped —**put a crimp in** [Inf.] to hinder

crim·son (krim′zən, -sən) *n.* [< Ar *qirmiz*] deep red —*adj.* deep-red —*vt., vi.* to redden or become crimson

cringe (krinj) *vi.* **cringed, cring′ing** [< OE *cringan,* to fall (in battle)] 1 to draw back, cower, etc., as from fear, embarrassment, etc. 2 to act timidly servile

crin·kle (kriŋ′kəl) *vi., vt.* **-kled, -kling** [see prec.] 1 to wrinkle 2 to rustle or crackle, as crushed paper —**crin′kly** *adj.* **-kli·er, -kli·est**

crin·o·line (krin′ə lin) *n.* [Fr < It < *crino,* horsehair + *lino,* linen] 1 a coarse, stiff cloth used as a lining in garments 2 HOOP SKIRT

crip·ple (krip′əl) *n.* [< OE *creopan,* to creep] a disabled person: now somewhat offensive —*vt.* **-pled, -pling** 1 to lame 2 to disable; impair

cri·sis (krī′sis) *n., pl.* **-ses′** (-sēz′) [L < Gr *krinein,* to separate] 1 the turning point of a disease for better or worse 2 a decisive or crucial time, etc. 3 a time of great danger, etc.

crisp (krisp) *adj.* [< L *crispus,* curly] 1 easily crumbled 2 fresh and firm 3 sharp and clear 4 fresh and invigorating 5 curled and wiry Also **crisp′y, -i·er, -i·est** —**crisp′ly** *adv.* —**crisp′ness** *n.*

criss·cross (kris′krôs′) *n.* [ME *Christcros,* Christ's cross] a mark or pattern made of crossed lines —*adj.* marked by crossing lines —*vt.* 1 to mark with crossing lines 2 to move to and fro across —*vi.* to move to and fro —*adv.* 1 crosswise 2 awry

cri·te·ri·on (krī tir′ē ən) *n., pl.* **-ri·a** (-ē ə) or **-ri·ons** [< Gr *kritēs,* judge] a standard, test, etc. by which a thing can be judged

crit·ic (krit′ik) *n.* [< Gr *krinein,* discern] 1

one who publicly evaluates books, music, etc. **2** one who finds fault

crit·i·cal (-i kəl) *adj.* **1** tending to find fault **2** of critics or criticism **3** of or forming a crisis; decisive or dangerous —**crit′i·cal·ly** *adv.*

crit·i·cism (-ə siz′əm) *n.* **1** the act of making judgments, esp. of literary or artistic work **2** a review, article, etc. expressing such judgment **3** censure **4** the principles or methods of critics

crit·i·cize (-ə siz′) *vi., vt.* **-cized′, -ciz′ing 1** to analyze and judge as a critic **2** to find fault (with) —**crit′i·ciz′a·ble** *adj.* —**crit′i·ciz′er** *n.*

cri·tique (kri tēk′) *n.* [Fr] a critical analysis or review —*vt., vi.* **-tiqued′, -tiqu′ing** to criticize (a subject, art work, etc.)

crit·ter (krit′ər) *n. dial. var. of* CREATURE

croak (krōk) *vi.* [echoic] **1** to make a deep, hoarse sound, as a frog does **2** [Slang] to die —*vt.* to utter in deep, hoarse tones —*n.* a croaking sound

Cro·at (krō′at′, -ət) *n.* a person born or living in Croatia

Cro·a·tia (krō ā′shə) country in SE Europe

cro·chet (krō shā′) *n.* [Fr, small hook] needlework done with one hooked needle — *vi., vt.* **-cheted′** (-shād′), **-chet′ing** to do, or make by, crochet —**cro·chet′er** *n.*

crock (kräk) *n.* [OE *crocca*] an earthenware pot or jar —**crock′er·y** *n.*

crocked (kräkt) *adj.* [< *crock*, to disable] [Slang] drunk

croc·o·dile (kräk′ə dil′) *n.* [< Gr *krokodilos*, lizard] a large, lizardlike reptile of tropical streams, having a long, narrow head with massive jaws

cro·cus (krō′kəs) *n., pl.* **-cus·es** or **-ci′** (krō′sī′) [< Gr *krokos*, saffron] a spring-blooming plant of the iris family, with a yellow, purple, or white flower

Croe·sus (krē′səs) flourished 6th c. B.C.; king noted for his great wealth

crois·sant (krə sänt′; Fr krwä sän′) *n.* [Fr, crescent] a crescent-shaped, flaky bread roll

Cro-Mag·non (krō mag′nən) *adj.* [after *Cro-Magnon* cave in France] of a Stone Age type of tall human living in Europe

Crom·well (kräm′wel), **Ol·i·ver** (äl′ə vər) 1599-1658; Eng. revolutionary leader & ruler (Lord Protector) of England (1653-58)

crone (krōn) *n.* [< MDu *kronje*, old ewe] an ugly, withered old woman

cro·ny (krō′nē) *n., pl.* **-nies** [< Gr *chronos*, time] a close companion

crook (krook) *n.* [< ON *krōkr*, hook] **1** a hooked or curved staff, etc.; hook **2** a bend or curve **3** [Inf.] a swindler or thief —*vt., vi.* **crooked** (krookt), **crook′ing** to bend or curve

crook·ed (krookt; *for 2 & 3* krook′id) *adj.* **1** having a crook **2** not straight; bent **3** dishonest —**crook′ed·ly** *adv.* —**crook′ed·ness** *n.*

crook·neck *n.* a squash with a long, curved neck

croon (krōōn) *vi., vt.* [ME *cronen*] **1** to

sing or hum in a low, gentle tone **2** to sing (popular songs) softly and sentimentally —*n.* a low, gentle singing or humming —**croon′er** *n.*

crop (kräp) *n.* [OE *croppa*, a cluster] **1** a saclike part of a bird's gullet, in which food is stored before digestion **2** any agricultural product, growing or harvested **3** the yield of any product in one season or place **4** a group appearing together **5** the handle of a whip **6** a riding whip **7** hair cut close to the head —*vt.* **cropped, crop′ping 1** to cut or bite off the tops or ends of **2** to cut (the hair, etc.) short —**crop out** (or **up**) to appear unexpectedly

crop-dust·ing *n.* the spraying of crops with pesticides from an airplane —**crop′-dust′** *vi., vt.*

crop·per *n.* **1** one that crops **2** a sharecropper —**come a cropper** [Inf.] to come to ruin; fail

cro·quet (krō kā′) *n.* [Fr, dial. form of *crochet*, small hook] an outdoor game in which the players use mallets to drive a ball through hoops in the ground

cro·quette (krō ket′) *n.* [Fr < *croquer*, to crunch] a small mass of meat, fish, etc. fried in deep fat

cro·sier (krō′zhər) *n.* [< OFr *croce*] the staff carried by a bishop or abbot, usually having a coiled ornament at the top

cross (krôs) *n.* [< L *crux*] **1** an upright post with a bar across it, on which the ancient Romans executed people **2** a representation of this as a symbol of the crucifixion of Jesus, hence of Christianity **3** any trouble or affliction **4** any design or mark made by two intersecting lines, bars, etc. **5** a crossing of varieties or breeds —*vt., vi.* **1** to make the sign of the cross (upon) **2** to place or lie across or crosswise **3** to intersect **4** to draw a line or lines across **5** to go or extend across **6** to meet and pass (each other) **7** to oppose **8** to interbreed (animals or plants) —*adj.* **1** lying or passing across **2** contrary; opposed **3** cranky; irritable **4** of mixed variety or breed —**cross off** (or **out**) to cancel as by drawing lines across —**cross someone's mind** to come suddenly to someone's mind —**cross someone's path** to meet someone —**cross′ly** *adv.*

cross·bar *n.* a bar, line, or stripe placed crosswise

cross·beam *n.* any transverse beam in a structure

cross·bones *n.* a representation of two crossed bones, usually under a skull: a symbol of death or danger

cross·bow (-bō′) *n.* a weapon consisting of a bow set transversely on a grooved wooden stock —**cross′bow′man** (-mən) *n., pl.* **-men** (-mən)

cross·breed *vt., vi.* **-bred′, -breed′ing** HYBRIDIZE —*n.* HYBRID (n. 1)

cross-coun·try *adj., adv.* across open country or fields [a *cross-country* race]

cross·court *adv., adj. Sports* into, toward, or

in the other side of the court [to hit the ball *crosscourt*, a *crosscourt* pass]

cross·cut saw a saw designed to cut across the grain of wood

cross-dress·ing *n.* the wearing of clothing usually worn by the opposite sex

cross-ex·am·ine *vt., vi.* **-ined, -in·ing** *Law* to question (a witness called by the opposing side) in order to challenge the witness's previous testimony —**cross′-ex·am′i·na′tion** *n.*

cross-eye *n.* an abnormal condition in which the eyes are turned toward each other —**cross′-eyed′** *adj.*

cross·fire *n.* **1** lines of fire from two or more positions that cross **2** an energetic exchange, as by opposing forces or of opposing opinions

cross·hatch *vt., vi.* to shade (a drawing) with two sets of parallel lines that cross each other

cross·ing *n.* **1** the act of passing across, interbreeding, etc. **2** an intersection, as of streets **3** a place where a street, etc. may be crossed

cross·piece *n.* a piece lying across another

cross-pol·li·nate *vt., vi.* **-nat′ed, -nat′ing** to transfer pollen from the anther of (a flower) to the stigma of (a genetically different flower) —**cross′-pol′li·na′tion** *n.*

cross-pur·pose *n.* a contrary purpose —**at cross-purposes** having a misunderstanding as to each other's purposes

cross-ref·er·ence *n.* a reference from one part of a book, etc. to another —*vt.* **-enced, -enc·ing** to provide (an index, etc.) with cross-references

cross·road *n.* **1** a road that crosses another **2** [*usually pl., often with sing. v.*] *a)* the place where roads intersect *b)* any center of activity, etc. *c)* a time of important changes or major decisions

cross section 1 *a)* a cutting through something *b)* a piece so cut off *c)* a representation of this **2** a representative part of a whole —**cross′-sec′tion** *vt.*

cross·town *adj.* **1** going across a city [a *cross-town* bus] **2** on the other side of a city [a *crosstown* rival]

cross·walk *n.* a lane marked off for pedestrians to use in crossing a street

cross·wise *adv.* so as to cross: also **cross′ways′**

cross·word puzzle a grid of squares to be filled in with the letters of words, arranged vertically and horizontally, based on a list of clues

crotch (kräch) *n.* [ME *crucche*, crutch] **1** a forked place, as on a tree **2** the place where the legs fork from the human body or from the upper part of a pair of trousers

crotch·et (kräch′it) *n.* [ult. < OFr *croc*, a hook] a peculiar whim or stubborn notion —**crotch′et·y** *adj.*

crouch (krouch) *vi.* [< OFr *croc*, a hook] to stoop low with legs bent —*n.* a crouching position

croup (kroop) *n.* [< obs. or dial. *croup*, speak hoarsely] an inflammation of the respira-

tory passages, with labored breathing, hoarse coughing, etc.

crou·pi·er (kroo′pē ā′, -ər) *n.* [Fr] one in charge of a gambling table

crou·ton (kroo′tän′, kroo tän′) *n.* [Fr < *croûte*, a crust] a small, crisp piece of toasted bread served in soup or salads

crow¹ (krō) *n.* [OE *crawa*] a large, glossy-black bird with a harsh call —**as the crow flies** in a straight, direct line —**eat crow** [Inf.] to admit an error

crow² (krō) *vi.* **crowed, crowed, crow′ing** [OE *crawan*] **1** to make the shrill cry of a rooster **2** to boast in triumph **3** to make a sound of pleasure —*n.* a crowing sound

crow·bar *n.* a long metal bar used as a lever for prying, etc.

crowd (kroud) *vi.* [< OE *crudan*] **1** to push one's way (*into*) **2** to throng —*vt.* **1** to press or push **2** to fill too full; cram —*n.* **1** a large number of people or things grouped closely **2** the common people; the masses **3** [Inf.] a set; clique —**crowd′ed** *adj.*

crow·foot *n., pl.* **-foots′** or **-feet′** a plant of the buttercup family, with leaves resembling a crow's foot

crown (kroun) *n.* [< Gr *korōnē*, wreath] **1** a wreath worn on the head in victory **2** a reward; honor **3** a monarch's headdress **4** [*often* **C-**] *a)* the power of a monarch *b)* the monarch **5** a British coin equal to 5 shillings: no longer minted **6** the top part, as of the head **7** the highest quality, state, etc. of anything **8** *a)* the part of a tooth outside the gum *b)* an artificial substitute for this —*vt.* **1** to put a crown on **2** to make (a person) a monarch **3** to honor **4** to be the highest part of **5** to complete successfully

crown prince the male heir apparent to a throne

crown princess 1 the female heir apparent to a throne **2** the wife of a crown prince

crow's-foot (krōz′foot′) *n., pl.* **-feet′** any of the wrinkles that often develop at the outer corners of the eyes of adults

crow's-nest (-nest′) *n.* a lookout's platform high on a ship's mast

cro·zier (krō′zhər) *n.* CROSIER

CRT (sē′är′tē′) *n.* a cathode-ray tube

cru·cial (kroo′shəl) *adj.* [< L *crux*, a cross] decisive; critical —**cru′cial·ly** *adv.*

cru·ci·ate (kroo′shē it, -āt′) *adj.* [< ModL *cruciatus* < L *crux*, CROSS] cross-shaped

cru·ci·ble (kroo′sə bəl) *n.* [ML *crucibulum*, lamp] **1** a heat-resistant container for melting ores, metals, etc. **2** a severe trial

cru·ci·fix (kroo′sə fiks′) *n.* [see CRUCIFY] a cross with the figure of the crucified Jesus Christ on it

cru·ci·fix·ion (-fik′shən) *n.* **1** a crucifying **2** [**C-**] the crucifying of Jesus, or a representation of this

cru·ci·form (-fôrm′) *adj.* cross-shaped

cru·ci·fy (-fī′) *vt.* **-fied′, -fy′ing** [< L *crux*, a cross + *figere*, fasten] **1** to execute by nailing or binding to a cross and leaving to die **2** to be very cruel to; torment

crude (krōōd) *adj.* **crud′er, crud′est** [< L *crudus*, raw] **1** in a raw or natural condition **2** lacking grace, tact, taste, etc. **3** roughly made —**crude′ly** *adv.* —**crude′ness** *n.* —**cru·di·ty** (krōō′də tē) *n.*

cru·di·tés (krōō′də tā′) *pl.n.* [Fr, raw things] raw vegetables cut up and served as hors d'oeuvres, usually with a dip or sauce

cru·el (krōō′əl) *adj.* [see CRUDE] causing pain and suffering; pitiless —**cru′el·ly** *adv.* —**cru′el·ness** *n.* —**cru′el·ty** *n., pl.* **-ties**

cru·et (krōō′it) *n.* [< OFr *crue*, earthen pot] a small glass bottle, as for holding vinegar or oil for the table

cruise (krōōz) *vi.* **cruised, cruis′ing** [< Du *kruisen*, to cross] **1** to sail or ride about from place to place, as for pleasure or in search of something **2** to move at the most efficient speed for sustained travel **3** to operate at a predetermined speed by use of a regulating mechanism (**cruise control**) —*vt.* to sail or journey over or about —*n.* a cruising voyage

cruise missile a long-range, jet-propelled winged missile that can be launched from an airplane, submarine, ship, etc. and guided to its target by remote control

cruis·er *n.* **1** anything that cruises, as a police car **2** a fast warship smaller than a battleship

crul·ler (krul′ər) *n.* [Du < *krullen*, to curl] a kind of twisted doughnut

crumb (krum) *n.* [< OE *cruma*, a bit scraped from bread crust] **1** a small piece broken off, as of bread **2** any bit or scrap [*crumbs of knowledge*] —**crumb·y** (krum′ē) *adj.* **-i·er, -i·est**

crum·ble (krum′bəl) *vt.* **-bled, -bling** [< prec.] to break into crumbs —*vi.* to fall to pieces; disintegrate —**crum′bly** (-blē) *adj.* **-bli·er, -bli·est**

crum·my (krum′ē) *adj.* **-mi·er, -mi·est** [Slang] **1** dirty, cheap, etc. **2** inferior, worthless, etc.

crum·pet (krum′pit) *n.* [< OE *crump*, twisted] an unsweetened batter cake baked on a griddle

crum·ple (krum′pəl) *vt.* **-pled, -pling** [ult. < MDu *crimpen*, to wrinkle] to crush together into wrinkles

crunch (krunch) *vi., vt.* [echoic] **1** to chew, press, grind, etc. with a noisy, crackling sound **2** [Inf.] to process (a large quantity of data) rapidly [*crunching* numbers on a computer] —*n.* **1** the act or sound of crunching **2** [Slang] a showdown or tight situation **3** a partial sit-up —**crunch′y** *adj.* **-i·er, -i·est**

crunch-time *n.* [Slang] the tense, crucial phase of some activity

crup·per (krup′ər, krōōp′-) *n.* [< OFr *crope*, rump] a leather strap attached to a saddle or harness and passed under a horse's tail

cru·sade (krōō sād′) *n.* [ult. < L *crux*, a cross] **1** [*sometimes* C-] any of the Christian military expeditions (1000s to 1200s) to recover the Holy Land from the Muslims **2** a

vigorous, concerted action for some cause, or against some abuse —*vi.* **-sad′ed, -sad′ing** to engage in a crusade —**cru·sad′er** *n.*

cruse (krōōs, krōōz) *n.* [OE] a small container for water, oil, etc.

crush (krush) *vt.* [< OFr *croisir*, to crash, break] **1** to press with force so as to break or put out of shape **2** to grind or pound into small bits **3** to subdue; overwhelm —*vi.* to become crushed —*n.* **1** a crushing; severe pressure **2** a crowded mass of people **3** [Inf.] *a)* an infatuation *b)* the object of such infatuation —**crush′er** *n.*

crush·ing *adj.* **1** overwhelming **2** hurtful

Cru·soe (krōō′sō′), **Ro′bin·son** (rä′bən sən) the title hero of Defoe's novel (1719) about a shipwrecked sailor

crust (krust) *n.* [< L *crusta*] **1** the hard, outer part of bread **2** any dry, hard piece of bread **3** the pastry shell of a pie **4** any hard surface layer **5** *Geol.* the solid outer layer of the earth —*vt., vi.* to cover or become covered with a crust —**crust′y** *adj.* **-i·er, -i·est**

crus·ta·cean (krus tā′shən) *n.* [see prec.] any of a class of arthropods, including shrimps, crabs, and lobsters, that have a hard outer shell

crutch (kruch) *n.* [< OE *crycce*, staff] **1** a device used by lame people as an aid in walking, typically a staff with a crosspiece on top that fits under the armpit **2** any prop or support

crux (kruks) *n., pl.* **crux′es** or **cru·ces** (krōō′sēz′) [L, a cross] **1** a difficult problem **2** the essential or deciding point

cry (krī) *vi.* **cried, cry′ing** [< L *quiritare*, to wail] **1** to utter a loud sound, as in pain or fright **2** to sob and shed tears; weep **3** to plead or clamor (*for*) **4** to show a great need (*for*) **5** to utter its characteristic call: said of an animal —*vt.* to utter loudly; shout —*n., pl.* **cries 1** a shout **2** a plea **3** a fit of weeping **4** the characteristic call of an animal —**a far cry** a great distance or difference

cry·ba·by *n., pl.* **-bies 1** [Inf.] a person, esp. a child, who cries often or with little cause **2** one who complains when failing to get his or her own way

cry·o·gen·ics (krī′ō jen′iks, -ə-) *n.* [< Gr *kryos*, cold + -GEN + -ICS] the science that deals with very low temperatures and their effect on the properties of matter —**cry′o·gen′ic** *adj.*

cry·o·sur·ger·y *n.* [< Gr *kryos*, cold + SUR-GERY] surgery that destroys selected tissues by freezing them

crypt (kript) *n.* [< Gr *kryptein*, to hide] an underground vault, esp. one under a church, used for burial

cryp·tic (krip′tik) *adj.* **1** hidden or mysterious; baffling **2** obscure and curt in expression —**cryp′ti·cal·ly** *adv.*

crypto- [see CRYPT] *combining form* **1** secret or hidden [*cryptogram*] **2** being such secretly and not publicly [*a crypto*-Fascist]

cryp·to·gram (krip′tō gram′, -tə-) *n.* [prec. + -GRAM] a message in code or cipher

cryp·tog·ra·phy (krip tä′grə fē) *n.* 〖CRYPTO- + -GRAPHY〗 the art of writing or deciphering messages in code —**cryp·tog′ra·pher** *n.*

crys·tal (kris′təl) *n.* 〖< Gr *krystallos*, crystal, ice < *kryos*, frost〗 **1** pure quartz **2** *a)* a very clear, brilliant glass *b)* articles of such glass, as goblets **3** anything clear like crystal, as the cover on a watch face **4** a solidified form of a substance having plane faces arranged in a symmetrical, three-dimensional pattern —*adj.* **1** of or made of crystal **2** like crystal; clear

crys·tal·line (-tə lin) *adj.* **1** made of crystal **2** like crystal; clear and transparent

crys·tal·lize (-tə līz′) *vi., vt.* **-lized′, -liz′ing 1** to become or cause to become crystalline **2** to take on or cause to take on a definite form —**crys′tal·li·za′tion** *n.*

cs *abbrev.* case(s)

Cs *Chem. symbol for* cesium

C-sec·tion (sē′sek′shən) *n.* [Inf.] CESAREAN (SECTION)

CST *abbrev.* Central Standard Time

ct *abbrev.* **1** cent **2** court

CT *abbrev.* **1** Central Time **2** Connecticut

CT scan 〖*c*(*omputerized*) *t*(*omography*)〗 **1** a diagnostic X-raying of soft tissues, using many single-plane X-rays (*tomograms*) to form the image **2** such an image —**CT scanner** —**CT scanning**

cu *abbrev.* cubic

Cu [L *cuprum*] *Chem. symbol for* copper

cub (kub) *n.* 〖< ? Old Ir *cuib*, a whelp〗 **1** a young fox, bear, lion, whale, etc. **2** an inexperienced or immature person

Cu·ba (kyōō′bə) country on an island in the West Indies south of Florida —**Cu′ban** *adj., n.*

cub·by·hole (kub′ē hōl′) *n.* 〖< Brit dial. *cub*, little shed + HOLE〗 a small, enclosed space: also **cub′by**

cube (kyōōb) *n.* 〖< Gr *kybos*〗 **1** a solid with six equal, square sides **2** the product obtained by multiplying a given number by its square [the *cube* of 3 is 27] —*vt.* **cubed, cub′ing 1** to obtain the cube of (a number) **2** to cut or shape into cubes —**cub′er** *n.*

cube root the number of which a given number is the cube [the *cube root* of 8 is 2]

cu·bic (kyōō′bik) *adj.* **1** having the shape of a cube: also **cu′bi·cal** (-bi kəl) **2** having the volume of a cube whose length, width, and depth each measure the given unit [a *cubic* foot]

cu·bi·cle (kyōō′bi kəl) *n.* 〖< L *cubare*, lie down〗 a small compartment

cub·ism (kyōōb′iz′əm) *n.* a school of modern art characterized by the use of geometric forms in abstract arrangements —**cub′ist** *n., adj.* —**cu·bis′tic** *adj.*

cu·bit (kyōō′bit) *n.* 〖< L *cubitum*, elbow〗 an ancient measure of length, about 18 to 22 inches

cuck·old (kuk′əld) *n.* 〖see fol.〗 a man whose wife has committed adultery —*vt.* to make a cuckold of —**cuck′old·ry** (-rē) *n.*

cuck·oo (kōō′kōō′) *n.* 〖< OFr *cucu*, echoic〗 **1** a gray-brown bird with a long, slender body: many species lay eggs in the nests of other birds **2** its call —*adj.* [Slang] crazy; foolish

cu·cum·ber (kyōō′kum′bər) *n.* 〖< L *cucumis*〗 a long, green-skinned fruit with firm, white flesh, used in salads or preserved as pickles

cud (kud) *n.* 〖OE *cudu*〗 a mouthful of swallowed food regurgitated from the first two parts of the stomach of cattle and other ruminants and chewed again

cud·dle (kud′′l) *vt.* **-dled, -dling** 〖early Modern Eng, make comfortable〗 to hold lovingly in one's arms —*vi.* to lie close and snug; nestle —*n.* an embrace; hug

cud·dly (-lē) *adj.* **-dli·er, -dli·est** that invites cuddling: also **cud′dle·some**

cudg·el (kuj′əl) *n.* 〖< OE *cycgel*〗 a short, thick stick or club —*vt.* **-eled** or **-elled, -el·ing** or **-el·ling** to beat with a cudgel

cue¹ (kyōō) *n.* 〖< *q*, *Q* (? for L *quando*, when) found in plays of the 1500s〗 **1** a signal in dialogue, etc. for an actor's entrance or speech **2** any signal to do something **3** a hint —*vt.* **cued, cu′ing** or **cue′ing** to give a cue to

cue² (kyōō) *n.* 〖var. of QUEUE〗 a long, tapering rod used in billiards and pool to strike the white ball (**cue ball**)

cuff (kuf) *n.* 〖< ME *cuffe*, glove〗 **1** a band or fold at the end of a sleeve **2** a turned-up fold at the bottom of a trouser leg **3** a slap —*vt.* to slap —**off the cuff** [Slang] extemporaneously —**on the cuff** [Slang] on credit

cuff link a pair of linked buttons or any similar small device for fastening a shirt cuff

cui·sine (kwi zēn′, kwē-) *n.* 〖Fr < L *coquere*, to cook〗 **1** a style of cooking or preparing food **2** the food prepared, as at a restaurant

cuke (kyōōk) *n.* [Inf.] *short for* CUCUMBER

cul-de-sac (kul′də sak′) *n., pl.* **-sacs′** 〖Fr, bottom of a sack〗 a dead-end street, esp. one with a turnaround at its end

cu·li·nar·y (kyōō′lə ner′ē, kul′ə-) *adj.* 〖< L *culina*, kitchen〗 of cooking

cull (kul) *vt.* 〖< L *colligere*, collect〗 **1** to pick out and discard **2** to select and gather —*n.* something rejected as not being up to standard

cul·mi·nate (kul′mə nāt′) *vi.* **-nat′ed, -nat′ing** 〖< L *culmen*, peak〗 to reach a peak or climax —**cul′mi·na′tion** *n.*

cu·lotte (kōō′lät′) *n.* 〖Fr < L *culus*, posterior〗 [*often pl.*] a woman's garment consisting of trousers made full in the legs to resemble a skirt

cul·pa·ble (kul′pə bəl) *adj.* 〖< L *culpa*, fault〗 deserving blame —**cul′pa·bil′i·ty** *n.* —**cul′pa·bly** *adv.*

cul·prit (kul′prit) *n.* 〖< Anglo-Fr *culpable*, guilty + *prit*, ready (to prove)〗 **1** a person guilty of a crime or offense **2** the cause of a particular problem

cult (kult) *n.* 〖< L *cultus*, care, cultivation〗 **1** a system of religious worship or ritual **2** devoted attachment to a person, principle, etc. **3** a sect —**cult′ism′** *n.* —**cult′ist** *n.*

cul·ti·vate (kul′tə vāt′) *vt.* **-vat′ed, -vat′ing** [< L *colere*, to till] **1** to prepare (land) for growing crops; till **2** to loosen the soil and kill weeds around (plants) **3** to grow (plants) **4** to develop or improve [*cultivate* your mind] **5** to seek to become familiar with —**cul′ti·va·ble** (-və bəl) *adj.*, **cul′ti·vat′a·ble** *adj.* —**cul′ti·va′tor** *n.*

cul·ti·va·tion *n.* **1** the act of cultivating **2** refinement, or culture

cul·ture (kul′chər) *n.* [see CULT] **1** cultivation of the soil **2** a growth of bacteria, etc. in a prepared substance **3** improvement of the mind, manners, etc. **4** development by special training or care **5** the skills, arts, etc. of a given people in a given period; civilization —*vt.* **-tured, -tur·ing** to cultivate —**cul′tur·al** *adj.* —**cul′tur·al·ly** *adv.*

culture shock the alienation, confusion, etc. experienced by someone encountering an unfamiliar culture

cul·vert (kul′vərt) *n.* [< ?] a drain or conduit under a road or embankment

cum (kum, koom) *prep.* [L] with

cum·ber (kum′bər) *vt.* [< OFr *combre*, a barrier] to hinder; hamper

cum·ber·some *adj.* burdensome; unwieldy: also **cum′brous** (-brəs)

cu·min (kyōō′min, kōō′-, kum′in) *n.* [< Gr *kyminon*] **1** an herb related to parsley and celery **2** its aromatic fruits, used as a seasoning

cum·mer·bund (kum′ər bund′) *n.* [< Ar-Pers *kamar*, loins + Pers *band*, band] a wide sash worn as a waistband, esp. with men's formal dress

cu·mu·la·tive (kyōō′myə lə tiv′, -lāt′iv) *adj.* [< L *cumulus*, a heap] increasing in effect, size, etc. by successive additions

cu·mu·lus (kyōō′myə ləs) *n., pl.* **-li′** (-lī′) [L, a heap] a bright, billowy type of cloud with a dark, flat base

cu·ne·i·form (kyōō nē′ə fôrm′) *adj.* [< L *cuneus*, a wedge + -FORM] **1** wedge-shaped **2** designating the characters in ancient Assyrian and Babylonian inscriptions —*n.* cuneiform writing

cun·ning (kun′iŋ) *adj.* [< ME *cunnen*, know] **1** sly; crafty **2** made with skill **3** pretty and delicate; cute —*n.* slyness; craftiness —**cun′ning·ly** *adv.*

cup (kup) *n.* [< L *cupa*, tub] **1** a small, open container for beverages, usually bowl-shaped and often having a handle **2** a cup and its contents **3** a cupful **4** anything shaped like a cup —*vt.* **cupped, cup′ping** to shape like a cup

cup·board (kub′ərd) *n.* a closet or cabinet with shelves for cups, plates, food, etc.

cup·cake *n.* a very small, round cake, often iced

cup·ful *n., pl.* **-fuls′** as much as a cup will hold; specif., eight fluid ounces

Cu·pid (kyōō′pid) *n.* **1** *Rom. Myth.* the god of love **2** [**c-**] a representation of Cupid as a naked cherub with bow and arrow

cu·pid·i·ty (kyōō pid′ə tē) *n.* [< L *cupere*, to desire] strong desire for wealth; avarice

cu·po·la (kyōō′pə lə) *n.* [It < L *cupa*, a tub] a small dome, etc. on a roof

cu·pro·nick·el (kyōō′prō nik′əl) *n.* an alloy of copper and nickel, used as in coins

cur (kur) *n.* [prob. < ON *kurra*, to growl] **1** a dog of mixed breed; mongrel **2** a contemptible person

cu·rate (kyoor′it) *n.* [< L *cura*, care] a member of the clergy who assists a vicar or rector —*vt.* **-rat′ed, -rat′ing** to act as curator for —**cu′ra·cy** (-ə sē) *n., pl.* **-cies**

cu·ra·tive (kyoor′ət iv) *adj.* having the power to cure —*n.* a remedy

cu·ra·tor (kyōō rāt′ər, kyoor′āt′ər) *n.* [< L *curare*, take care of] a person in charge of a collection or exhibition, as at a museum —**cu·ra·to·ri·al** (kyoor′ə tôr′ē əl) *adj.* —**cu·ra′tor·ship** *n.*

curb (kurb) *n.* [< L *curvus*, bent] **1** a chain or strap attached to a horse's bit, used to check the horse **2** anything that checks or restrains **3** a stone or concrete edging along a street —*vt.* to restrain; control

curb service service offered to customers in parked cars, as at some restaurants

curb·side *adj.* at the curb or on the sidewalk adjacent to the street

curb·stone *n.* any of a row of stones making up a curb

curd (kurd) *n.* [< ME *crud*, coagulated substance] [*often pl.*] the coagulated part of soured milk, from which cheese is made

cur·dle (kurd′l) *vt., vi.* **-dled, -dling** to form into curd; coagulate

cure (kyoor) *n.* [< L *cura*, care] **1** a healing or being healed **2** a remedy **3** a method of medical treatment —*vt.* **cured, cur′ing 1** to restore to health **2** to get rid of (an ailment, evil, etc.) **3** *a*) to preserve (meat), as by salting or smoking *b*) to process (tobacco, leather, etc.), as by drying or aging —**cur′a·ble** *adj.* —**cur′er** *n.*

cu·ré (kyōō rā′) *n.* [Fr < L *cura*, care] in France, a parish priest

cure-all *n.* something supposed to cure all ailments or evils

cu·ret·tage (kyōō ret′ij, kyōō′rə täzh′) *n.* [Fr] the process of cleaning or scraping the walls of a body cavity with a spoonlike surgical instrument

cur·few (kur′fyōō′) *n.* [< OFr *covrefeu*, lit., cover fire: orig. a nightly signal to cover fires and go to bed] a time in the evening beyond which children, etc. may not appear on the streets or in public places

Cu·ri·a (kyoor′ē ə) *n., pl.* **-ri·ae′** (-ē′) [L] the official body governing the Roman Catholic Church under the authority of the pope

Cu·rie (kyoo rē′, kyoor′ē), **Ma·rie** (mə rē′) 1867-1934; Pol. chemist in France

cu·ri·o (kyoor′ē ō′) *n., pl.* **-os′** [contr. of fol.] an unusual or rare article

cu·ri·os·i·ty (kyoor′ē äs′ə tē) *n., pl.* **-ties 1** a desire to learn or know **2** inquisitiveness **3** anything curious, rare, etc.

cu·ri·ous (kyoor′ē əs) *adj.* [< L *curiosus*,

careful 1 eager to learn or know 2 prying or inquisitive 3 unusual; strange —**cu'ri·ous·ly** *adv.*

cu·ri·um (kyŏŏ′rē əm) *n.* ⟦after Pierre & Marie CURIE⟧ an artificially produced, very radioactive, metallic chemical element: symbol, Cm; at. no. 96

curl (kurl) *vt.* ⟦< ME *crul*, curly⟧ 1 to twist (esp. hair) into ringlets 2 to cause to bend around —*vi.* 1 to form curls 2 to form a spiral or curve —*n.* 1 a ringlet of hair 2 anything with a curled shape —**curl′er** *n.* —**curl′y** *adj.* **-i·er, -i·est** —**curl′i·ness** *n.*

cur·lew (kur′lōō′, kurl′yōō′) *n.* ⟦echoic⟧ a large, brownish wading bird with long legs

curl·i·cue (kur′li kyōō′) *n.* ⟦< CURLY + CUE²⟧ a fancy curve, flourish, etc.

curl·ing (kur′liŋ) *n.* a game played on ice by two teams, in which a heavy disk of stone or iron is slid toward a target

cur·rant (kur′ənt) *n.* ⟦ult. < *Corinth*, ancient Gr city⟧ 1 a small, seedless raisin from the Mediterranean region 2 *a)* the sour berry of several species of hardy shrubs, made into jelly or jam *b)* any such shrub

cur·ren·cy (kur′ən sē) *n., pl.* **-cies** ⟦see fol.⟧ 1 circulation 2 the money in circulation in any country 3 general use or acceptance

cur·rent (kur′ənt) *adj.* ⟦< L *currere*, to run⟧ 1 now going on; of the present time 2 circulating 3 commonly accepted; prevalent —*n.* 1 a flow of water or air in a definite direction 2 a general tendency or drift, as of opinion 3 the flow or rate of flow of electricity in a conductor —**cur′rent·ly** *adv.*

cur·ric·u·lum (kə rik′yōō ləm, -yə-) *n., pl.* **-la** (-lə) or **-lums** ⟦L, course for racing⟧ a course of study in a school —**cur·ric′u·lar** *adj.*

cur·ry¹ (kur′ē) *vt.* **-ried, -ry·ing** ⟦< OFr *correier*, to put in order⟧ 1 to use a currycomb on 2 to prepare (tanned leather) —**curry favor** to try to win favor as by flattery

cur·ry² (kur′ē) *n., pl.* **-ries** ⟦Tamil *kari*, sauce⟧ 1 a powder prepared from various spices, or a sauce made with this 2 a stew made with curry —*vt.* **-ried, -ry·ing** to prepare with curry

cur·ry·comb *n.* a circular comb with teeth or ridges, for rubbing down and cleaning a horse's coat —*vt.* to use a currycomb on

curse (kurs) *n.* ⟦OE *curs*⟧ 1 a calling on God or the gods to bring evil on some person or thing 2 a profane or obscene oath 3 evil or injury that seems to come in answer to a curse —*vt.* **cursed, curs′ing** 1 to call evil down on 2 to swear at 3 to afflict —*vi.* to swear; blaspheme —**be cursed with** to suffer from

curs·ed (kur′sid, kurst) *adj.* 1 under a curse 2 deserving to be cursed; evil; hateful

cur·sive (kur′siv) *adj.* ⟦ult. < L *currere*, to run⟧ designating writing in which the letters are joined

cur·sor (kur′sər) *n.* ⟦L, runner⟧ a movable indicator light on a computer video screen, marking the current position at which a character may be entered, changed, etc.

cur·so·ry (kur′sə rē) *adj.* ⟦ult. < L *currere*, to run⟧ hastily or superficially done —**cur′so·ri·ly** *adv.* —**cur′so·ri·ness** *n.*

curt (kurt) *adj.* ⟦L *curtus*, short⟧ brief, esp. to the point of rudeness —**curt′ly** *adv.* —**curt′ness** *n.*

cur·tail (kər tāl′) *vt.* ⟦< L *curtus*, short⟧ to cut short; reduce —**cur·tail′ment** *n.*

cur·tain (kurt′'n) *n.* ⟦< LL *cortina*⟧ 1 a piece of cloth, etc. hung at a window, in front of a stage, etc. to decorate or conceal 2 the opening or closing of such a piece of cloth at the start or end of a play, etc. 3 [*pl.*] [Slang] the end; death —*vt.* to provide with or shut off as with a curtain

curtain call 1 a call, usually by applause, for performers to return to the stage 2 such a return

curt·sy (kurt′sē) *n., pl.* **-sies** ⟦var. of COURTESY⟧ a woman's gesture of respect, etc. made by bending the knees and bowing slightly —*vi.* **-sied, -sy·ing** to make a curtsy Also sp. **curt′sey**

cur·va·ceous (kər vā′shəs) *adj.* ⟦< CURVE⟧ having a full, shapely figure: said of a woman

cur·va·ture (kur′və chər) *n.* 1 a curving or being curved 2 a curve

curve (kurv) *n.* ⟦< L *curvus*, bent⟧ 1 a line having no straight part; bend with no angles 2 something shaped like, or moving in, a curve 3 a statistical distribution, as of test scores —*vt., vi.* **curved, curv′ing** 1 to form a curve by bending 2 to move in a curve —**curv′y** *adj.* **-i·er, -i·est**

cush·ion (koosh′ən) *n.* ⟦< ML *coxinum*⟧ 1 a pillow or pad 2 a thing like this in shape or use 3 anything that absorbs shock —*vt.* to provide with a cushion

cush·y (koosh′ē) *adj.* **-i·er, -i·est** ⟦< Pers *khūsh*, pleasant⟧ [Slang] easy; comfortable

cusp (kusp) *n.* ⟦L *cuspis*⟧ a point or pointed end, as on the chewing surface of a tooth —**on the cusp** at a time of transition

cus·pid (kus′pid) *n.* ⟦see prec.⟧ a tooth with one cusp; canine tooth

cus·pi·dor (kus′pə dôr′) *n.* ⟦< Port *cuspir*, to spit⟧ a spittoon

cuss (kus) *n., vt., vi.* [Inf.] CURSE

cus·tard (kus′tərd) *n.* ⟦< L *crusta*, crust⟧ a mixture of eggs, milk, sugar, etc., boiled or baked

cus·to·di·an (kəs tō′dē ən) *n.* ⟦< fol.⟧ 1 one who is responsible for the custody or care of something; caretaker 2 a person responsible for the maintenance of a building

cus·to·dy (kus′tə dē) *n., pl.* **-dies** ⟦< L *custos*, a guard⟧ a guarding or keeping safe; guardianship —**in custody** under arrest —**cus·to′di·al** (-tō′dē əl) *adj.*

cus·tom (kus′təm) *n.* ⟦< L *com-*, intens. + *suere*, be accustomed⟧ 1 a usual practice; habit 2 *a)* a social practice carried on by tradition *b)* such practices collectively 3 [*pl.*] duties or taxes imposed on imported goods 4 the regular patronage of a business —*adj.* 1

made or done to order **2** making things to order

cus·tom·ar·y *adj.* in keeping with custom; usual; habitual —**cus′tom·ar′i·ly** *adv.*

cus·tom-built *adj.* built to order, to the customer's specifications

cus·tom·er *n.* a person who buys, esp. one who buys regularly

cus·tom·house *n.* an office where customs or duties are paid

cus·tom·ize *vt.* **-ized′, -iz′ing** to make or modify according to individual specifications

cus·tom-made *adj.* made to order, to the customer's specifications

cut (kut) *vt.* **cut, cut′ting** [ME *cutten*] **1** to make an opening in with a sharp-edged instrument; gash **2** to pierce sharply so as to hurt **3** to have (a new tooth) grow through the gum **4** to divide into parts with a sharp-edged instrument; sever **5** to intersect; divide [the path *cuts* the meadow diagonally] **6** to hew **7** to mow or reap **8** to reduce; curtail [*cut* salaries] **9** to trim; pare **10** to divide (a pack of cards) **11** to make or do as by cutting **12** [Inf.] to pretend not to recognize (a person) **13** [Inf.] to stay away from (a school class, etc.) without being excused **14** [Slang] to stop —*vi.* **1** to pierce, sever, gash, etc. **2** to take cutting [pine *cuts* easily] **3** to go (*across* or *through*) **4** to change direction suddenly **5** to make a sudden shift, as from one scene to another in a film —*adj.* **1** that has been cut **2** made or formed by cutting —*n.* **1** a cutting or being cut **2** a stroke or opening made by a sharp-edged instrument **3** a piece cut off, as of meat **4** a reduction **5** a passage or channel cut out **6** the style in which a thing is cut **7** an act, remark, etc. that hurts one's feelings **8** a block or plate engraved for printing, or the impression from this **9** [Inf.] an unauthorized absence from school, etc. **10** [Inf.] a share, as of profits —**cut and dried 1** arranged beforehand **2** lifeless; dull —**cut down** to reduce; lessen —**cut it out** [Inf.] to stop doing what one is doing —**cut off 1** to sever **2** to stop abruptly; shut off —**cut out** [Inf.] fit or suited —**cut up 1** to cut into pieces **2** [Slang] to clown, joke, etc.

cu·ta·ne·ous (kyōō tā′nē əs) *adj.* [< L *cutis,* skin] of or on the skin

cut·back *n.* a reduction or discontinuance, as of production

cute (kyōōt) *adj.* **cut′er, cut′est** [< ACUTE] [Inf.] **1** clever; shrewd **2** pretty or attractive, esp. in a dainty way —**cute′ly** *adv.* —**cute′ness** *n.*

cute·sy or **cute·sie** (kyōōt′sē) *adj.* **-si·er, -si·est** [Inf.] cute in an affected way

cut·i·cle (kyōōt′i kəl) *n.* [< L *cutis,* skin] **1** the outer layer of the skin **2** hardened skin, as at the base and sides of a fingernail

cut·lass (kut′ləs) *n.* [< L *culter,* plowshare] a short, thick, curved sword

cut·ler·y (kut′lər ē) *n.* [< L *culter,* plow-

share] **1** cutting implements, as knives and scissors **2** implements used in preparing and eating food

cut·let (kut′lit) *n.* [< L *costa,* rib] **1** a small slice of meat from the ribs or leg **2** a small, flat croquette of chopped meat or fish

cut·off *n.* a road, etc. that is a shortcut

cut-rate *adj.* selling at a lower price

cut·ter (kut′ər) *n.* **1** a person or thing that cuts **2** a small, swift boat or ship

cut·throat *n.* a murderer —*adj.* **1** murderous **2** merciless; ruthless

cut·ting (kut′iŋ) *n.* a shoot cut away from a plant for rooting or grafting —*adj.* **1** that cuts; sharp **2** chilling or piercing **3** sarcastic; wounding —**cut′ting·ly** *adv.*

cutting edge the leading or most advanced position; vanguard —**cut′ting-edge′** *adj.*

cut·tle·fish (kut′'l fish′) *n., pl.* **-fish′** or **-fish′es** [OE *cudele*] a sea mollusk with eight arms and two tentacles and a hard internal shell (**cuttlebone**)

cwt *abbrev.* hundredweight

-cy (sē) [< Gr *-kia*] *suffix* **1** quality, condition, or fact of being [*idiocy*] **2** position, rank, or office of [*captaincy*]

cy·a·nide (sī′ə nīd′) *n.* a white, extremely poisonous crystalline compound

cyber- [< CYBERNETIC or CYBERNETICS] *combining form* computer, computer network [*cybercrime*]

cy·ber·net·ics (sī′bər net′iks) *n.* [< Gr *kybernan,* to steer + -ICS] the comparative study of human control systems, as the brain, and complex electronic systems —**cy′ber·net′ic** *adj.*

cy·ber·punk (sī′bər puŋk′) *n.* [CYBER- + PUNK²] science fiction describing a future filled with violence, computers, and drugs

cy·ber·space (-spās′) *n.* the electronic system of computer networks, etc., thought of as an unlimited environment for accessing information, etc.

cy·borg (sī′bôrg′) *n.* in science fiction, a human that has been modified by the substitution of artificial organs or other body parts

cy·cla·men (sī′klə mən) *n.* [< Gr] a plant of the primrose family with heart-shaped leaves

cy·cle (sī′kəl) *n.* [< Gr *kyklos,* a circle] **1** *a)* a period within which a round of regularly recurring events is completed *b)* a complete set of such events **2** a series of poems or songs on one theme **3** a bicycle, motorcycle, etc. **4** *Elec.* one complete period of the reversal of an alternating current from positive to negative and back again —*vi.* **-cled, -cling 1** to ride a bicycle, etc. **2** to pass through a cycle

cy·cli·cal (sik′li kəl) *adj.* of, or having the nature of, a cycle; occurring in cycles

cy·clist (sīk′list, sī′klə list) *n.* one who rides a bicycle, motorcycle, etc.

cyclo- [< Gr *kyklos,* a circle] *combining form* of a circle or wheel; circular

cy·clom·e·ter (sī kläm′ət ər) *n.* [prec. + -METER] an instrument that records the revolutions of a wheel for measuring distance traveled

cy·clone (sī′klōn′) *n.* [< Gr *kyklōma*, wheel] a storm with strong winds rotating about a center of low pressure

Cy·clops (sī′kläps′) *n., pl.* **Cy·clo·pes** (sī klō′pēz′) *Gr. Myth.* any of a race of one-eyed giants

cy·clo·tron (sī′klō trän′, -klə-) *n.* a circular device for accelerating charged particles, used in physical research

cyg·net (sig′net, -nit) *n.* [< Gr *kyknos*, swan] a young swan

cyl·in·der (sil′ən dər) *n.* [< Gr *kylindein*, to roll] **1** a solid, tubular figure consisting of two equal, parallel, circular bases joined by a smooth, continuous surface **2** anything with this shape; specif., *a)* the turning part of a revolver *b)* the piston chamber of an engine —**cy·lin·dri·cal** (sə lin′dri kəl) *adj.*

cym·bal (sim′bəl) *n.* [< Gr *kymbē*, hollow of a vessel] *Music* a circular brass plate that makes a sharp, ringing sound when hit —**cym′bal·ist** *n.*

cyn·ic (sin′ik) *n.* [< Gr *kynikos*, doglike] a cynical person

cyn·i·cal (-i kəl) *adj.* **1** denying the sincerity of people's motives **2** sarcastic, sneering, etc. —**cyn′i·cal·ly** *adv.*

cyn·i·cism (-ə siz′əm) *n.* **1** the attitude or beliefs of a cynic **2** a cynical remark, idea, etc.

cy·no·sure (sī′nə shoor′, sin′ə-) *n.* [< Gr *kynosoura*, dog's tail] a center of attention or interest

cy·pher (sī′fər) *n., vi. Brit. sp. of* CIPHER

cy·press (sī′prəs) *n.* [< Gr *kyparissos*] **1** an evergreen tree with cones and dark foliage **2** its wood

Cy·prus (sī′prəs) country on an island at the E end of the Mediterranean —**Cyp·ri·ot** (sip′rē ət) *adj., n.*

cyst (sist) *n.* [< Gr *kystis*, sac] a saclike structure in plants or animals, esp. one filled with diseased matter —**cyst′ic** *adj.*

cystic fibrosis a children's disease marked by fibrosis of the pancreas and by frequent respiratory infections

cy·tol·o·gy (sī täl′ə jē) *n.* [< Gr *kytos*, a hollow + -LOGY] the branch of biology dealing with cells —**cy·tol′o·gist** *n.*

cy·to·plasm (sīt′ō plaz′əm) *n.* [< Gr *kytos*, a hollow + *plasma*, something molded] the protoplasm of a cell, outside the nucleus

cy·to·sine (sīt′ō sēn′) *n.* [< Ger *zytosin*] one of the four bases that combine to form DNA

czar (zär) *n.* [Russ < L *Caesar*] **1** a king or emperor, esp. one of the former emperors of Russia **2** a person, esp. a political appointee, with wide-ranging power

cza·ri·na (zä rē′nə) *n.* the wife of a Russian czar

Czech (chek) *n.* **1** a member of a Slavic people of central Europe **2** the West Slavic language of the Czechs **3** loosely, a person born or living in Czechoslovakia **4** a person born or living in the Czech Republic —*adj.* of the Czech Republic, its people, or their language

Czech·o·slo·va·ki·a (chek′ə slō vä′kē ə) former country in central Europe: divided (1993) into Czech Republic and Slovakia —**Czech′o·slo′vak** *adj., n.,* **Czech′o·slo·vak′i·an**

Czech Republic country in central Europe: formerly the W republic of Czechoslovakia

D

d¹ or **D** (dē) *n., pl.* **d's, D's** the fourth letter of the English alphabet

d² *abbrev.* **1** day(s) **2** degree **3** diameter **4** died **5** [L *denarii*] penny; pence

D¹ (dē) *n.* **1** a Roman numeral for 500 **2** a grade for below-average work **3** *Music* the second tone in the scale of C major

D² *abbrev.* **1** December **2** Democrat

-'d *contr.* **1** had or would: a shortened form used in contractions [*I'd* seen; *they'd* see] **2** *old sp. of* -ED [*foster'd*]

DA or **D.A.** *abbrev.* District Attorney

dab (dab) *vt., vi.* **dabbed, dab′bing** [ME *dabben*, to strike] **1** to touch lightly and quickly; pat **2** to put on (paint, etc.) with light, quick strokes —*n.* **1** a tap; pat **2** a small amount, esp. of something semisolid

dab·ble (dab′əl) *vi.* **-bled, -bling** [Du *dab-*

belen, freq. of MDu *dabben,* to strike, dab] **1** to play, dip, or paddle in water **2** to do something superficially: with *in* or *at*

Dac·ca (dä′kä) *former sp. of* DHAKA

dace (dās) *n., pl.* **dace** or **daces** a small freshwater fish related to the carp

dachs·hund (däks′hoont′) *n.* [Ger < *dachs,* badger + *hund,* dog] a small dog with a long body, short legs, and drooping ears

Da·cron (dä′krän′, dak′rän′) *trademark for* a synthetic wrinkle-resistant fabric —*n.* [*also* **d-**] this fabric

dac·tyl (dak′təl) *n.* [< Gr *daktylos,* finger] a metrical foot consisting of one accented syllable followed by two unaccented ones —**dac·tyl′ic** (-til′ik) *adj.*

dad (dad) *n.* [< child's cry *dada*] [Inf.] father: *also* **dad·dy** (dad′ē), *pl.* **-dies**

daddy long·legs an arachnid with long legs

da·do (dā′dō) *n., pl.* **-does** [< L *datum*, a die] 1 the part of a pedestal between the cap and the base 2 the lower part of a wall if decorated differently from the upper part 3 a rectangular groove cut in a board, used in forming a joint

daf·fo·dil (daf′ə dil′) *n.* [< Gr *asphodelos*] a narcissus with long leaves and usually yellow flowers

daf·fy (daf′ē) *adj.* **-fi·er, -fi·est** [< ME *dafte*, daft] [Inf.] crazy; silly **—daf′fi·ness** *n.*

daft (daft) *adj.* [< OE *(ge)dæfte*, mild] 1 silly 2 insane

dag·ger (dag′ər) *n.* [< Prov *daga*] 1 a weapon with a short, pointed blade, used for stabbing 2 *Printing* a reference mark (†)

da·guerre·o·type (də ger′ō tīp′) *n.* [after L. J. M. *Daguerre* (1789–1851), Fr inventor] an early kind of photograph made on a chemically treated metal plate **—vt. -typed′, -typ′ing** to photograph by this method

dahl·ia (dal′yə, däl′) *n.* [after A. *Dahl* (1751–87), Swed botanist] a perennial plant with large, showy flowers

dai·li·ness (dā′lē nəs) *n.* the ordinary, routine aspects of a way of life

dai·ly (dā′lē) *adj.* done, happening, or published every (week)day **—n., pl.** **-lies** a daily newspaper **—adv.** every day

daily double a bet or betting procedure in which winning depends on choosing both winners in two specified races

dain·ty (dān′tē) *n., pl.* **-ties** [< OFr *deinté*] a delicacy **—adj. -ti·er, -ti·est** 1 delicious and choice 2 delicately pretty 3 *a)* of refined taste; fastidious *b)* squeamish **—dain′ti·ly** *adv.* **—dain′ti·ness** *n.*

dai·qui·ri (dak′ər ē) *n.* [after *Daiquirí*, Cuban village] a cocktail made of rum, sugar, and lime or lemon juice

dair·y (der′ē) *n., pl.* **-ies** [ME *daie*, dairymaid] 1 a building or room where milk and cream are made into butter and cheese, etc. 2 a farm that produces, or a store that sells, milk and milk products **—adj.** of milk and milk products **—dair′y·man** (-mən) *n., pl.* **-men** (-mən)

dair·y·ing *n.* the business of producing or selling dairy products

da·is (dā′is) *n., pl.* **da′is·es** [< ML *discus*, table] a raised platform, as for a speaker

dai·sy (dā′zē) *n., pl.* **-sies** [< OE *dæges eage*, day's eye] a plant of the composite family, bearing flowers with white rays around a yellow disk

Da·lai La·ma (dä′lī lä′mə) the leader of the chief branch of Tibetan Buddhism

dale (dāl) *n.* [OE *dæl*] a valley

Da·lit (dul′it, däl′-) *n.* in India, a member of the lowest castes

Dal·las (dal′əs) city in NE Texas

dal·ly (dal′ē) *vi.* **-lied, -ly·ing** [< OFr *dalier*, to trifle] 1 to flirt 2 to deal carelessly (*with*); toy 3 to waste time; loiter **—dal·li·ance** (dal′yəns, -ē əns) *n.*

Dal·ma·tian (dal mā′shən) *n.* a large, short-haired dog with dark spots on a white coat

dam¹ (dam) *n.* [ME] a barrier built to hold back flowing water **—vt.** **dammed, dam′ming** 1 to build a dam in 2 to keep back or confine

dam² (dam) *n.* [see DAME] the female parent of any four-legged mammal

dam·age (dam′ij) *n.* [< L *damnum*] 1 injury or harm resulting in a loss 2 [*pl.*] *Law* money compensating for injury, loss, etc. **—vt. -aged, -ag·ing** to do damage to **—dam′age·a·ble** *adj.*

Da·mas·cus (də mas′kəs) capital of Syria

dam·ask (dam′əsk) *n.* [after prec.] 1 a reversible fabric in figured weave, used for table linen, etc. 2 deep pink **—adj.** 1 of or like damask 2 deep-pink

dame (dām) *n.* [< L *domina*, lady] 1 [D-] in Great Britain, a woman's title of honor 2 [Slang] any woman

damn (dam) *vt.* **damned, damn′ing** [< L *damnare*, condemn] 1 to condemn to an unhappy fate 2 *Theol.* to condemn to hell 3 to condemn as bad, inferior, etc. 4 to swear at by saying "damn" **—n.** the saying of "damn" as a curse **—adj., adv.** short for [Inf.] DAMNED **—interj.** used to express anger, etc.

dam·na·ble (dam′nə bəl) *adj.* 1 deserving damnation 2 deserving to be sworn at **—dam′na·bly** *adv.*

dam·na·tion (-nā′shən) *n.* a damning or being damned **—interj.** used to express anger, etc.

damned (damd) *adj.* 1 condemned, as to hell 2 [Inf.] deserving cursing; outrageous **—adv.** [Inf.] very

Dam·o·cles (dam′ə klēz′) *n. Classical Legend* a man whose king seated him under a sword hanging by a hair to show him the perils of a ruler's life

damp (damp) *n.* [MDu, vapor] 1 a slight wetness 2 a noxious vapor **—adj.** somewhat moist or wet; humid **—vt.** 1 to bank (a fire): usually with *down* 2 to check or reduce **—damp′ness** *n.*

damp-dry *vt.* **-dried′, -dry′ing** to dry (laundry) so that some moisture is retained **—adj.** designating or of laundry so treated

damp·en (dam′pən) *vt.* 1 to make damp; moisten 2 to deaden, depress, or reduce **—damp′en·er** *n.*

damp·er (dam′pər) *n.* [see DAMP] 1 anything that deadens or depresses 2 a valve in a flue to control the draft 3 a device to check vibration in piano strings

dam·sel (dam′zəl) *n.* [see DAME] [Old-fashioned] a girl; maiden

dam·sel·fly *n., pl.* **-flies′** a slow-flying, brightly colored dragonfly

dam·son (dam′zən) *n.* [ult. < *Damascenus*, of DAMASCUS] a small, purple plum

Dan *abbrev.* Danish

dance (dans) *vi.* **danced, danc′ing** [< OFr *danser*] 1 to move the body and feet in rhythm, ordinarily to music 2 to move lightly, rapidly, gaily, etc. **—vt.** 1 to perform (a dance) **2** to cause to dance —*n.* **1** rhythmic movement, ordinarily to music **2** a particular kind of dance **3** the art of dancing **4** a party for dancing **5** a piece of music for dancing **6** rapid movement —**danc′er** *n.*

D and C dilation (of the cervix) and curettage (of the uterus)

dan·de·li·on (dan′də lī′ən) *n.* [< OFr *dent*, tooth + *de*, of + *lion*, lion] a common weed with yellow flowers

dan·der (dan′dər) *n.* [< ?] **1** tiny, allergenic particles from fur, etc. **2** [Inf.] anger or temper

dan·dle (dan′dəl) *vt.* **-dled, -dling** [< ?] to move (a child) up and down on the knee or in the arms

dan·druff (dan′drəf) *n.* [< earlier *dandro* + dial. *hurf*, scab] little scales of dead skin on the scalp

dan·dy (dan′dē) *n., pl.* **-dies** [< ?] **1** a man overly attentive to his clothes and appearance **2** [Inf.] something very good —*adj.* **-di·er, -di·est** [Inf.] very good; fine

Dane (dān) *n.* a person born or living in Denmark

dan·ger (dān′jər) *n.* [ult. < L *dominus*, a master] **1** liability to injury, damage, loss, etc.; peril **2** a thing that may cause injury, pain, etc.

dan·ger·ous *adj.* full of danger; unsafe; perilous —**dan′ger·ous·ly** *adv.*

dan·gle (dan′gəl) *vi.* **-gled, -gling** [< Scand] to hang loosely so as to swing back and forth —*vt.* to cause to dangle —**dan′gler** *n.*

Dan·iel (dan′yəl) *n. Bible* a Hebrew prophet whose faith saved him in the lions' den to which he was condemned

Dan·ish (dān′ish) *adj.* of Denmark or its people, language, etc. —*n.* **1** the Germanic language of the Danes **2** [also **d-**] (a) rich, flaky pastry filled with fruit, cheese, etc.: in full **Danish pastry**

dank (daŋk) *adj.* [ME] disagreeably damp —**dank′ly** *adv.* —**dank′ness** *n.*

dan·seur (dän sur′) *n.* [Fr] a man or boy who is a ballet dancer

dan·seuse (dän sooz′) *n.* [Fr] a woman or girl who is a ballet dancer

Dan·te (Alighieri) (dän′tā, dan′tē) 1265-1321; It. poet

Dan·ube (dan′yoōb) river in S Europe, flowing from S Germany into the Black Sea

Dao·ism (dou′iz′əm) *n. var. of* TAOISM —**Dao′ist** *n., adj.*

dap·per (dap′ər) *adj.* [MDu, nimble] **1** small and active **2** trim, neat, or dressed stylishly

dap·ple (dap′əl) *adj.* [< ON *depill*, a spot] marked with spots; mottled: also **dap′pled** —*vt.* **-pled, -pling** to cover with spots

Dar·da·nelles (där′də nelz′) strait separating the Balkan Peninsula from Asia Minor

dare (der) *vt., vi.* **dared, dar′ing** [OE *durran*] **1** to have enough courage for (some act) **2** to challenge (someone) to do something —*n.* a challenge —**dare say** to think probable —**dar′er** *n.*

dare·dev·il (-dev′əl) *adj.* bold and reckless —*n.* **1** a bold, reckless person **2** one who performs dangerous stunts

dar·ing *adj.* fearless; bold —*n.* bold courage —**dar′ing·ly** *adv.*

dark (därk) *adj.* [< OE *deorc*] **1** entirely or partly without light **2** *a)* almost black *b)* not light in color **3** hidden; secret **4** gloomy **5** evil; sinister **6** ignorant —*n.* **1** the state of being dark **2** night or nightfall —**in the dark** uninformed; ignorant —**dark′ly** *adv.* —**dark′ness** *n.*

Dark Ages the Middle Ages, esp. the earlier part, from about 500 to 1000 AD

dark·en (där′kən) *vt., vi.* to make or become dark or darker —**dark′en·er** *n.*

dark horse a little-known contestant thought unlikely to win

dark·room *n.* a darkened room for developing photographs

dar·ling (där′liŋ) *n.* [OE *deorling*] a person much loved by another —*adj.* **1** very dear; beloved **2** [Inf.] cute or attractive

darm·stadt·i·um (därm stat′ē əm) *n.* [after *Darmstadt*, Germany] an artificially produced radioactive chemical element: symbol, Ds; at. no. 110

darn[1] (därn) *vt., vi.* [< Fr dial. *darner*] to mend (cloth) by sewing a network of stitches across the gap —*n.* a darned place in fabric

darn[2] (därn) *vt., n., adj., adv., interj.* [Inf.] damn: a euphemism —**darned** *adj., adv.*

dart (därt) *n.* [< OFr] **1** *a)* a small, pointed missile for throwing or shooting *b)* [*pl., with sing. v.*] a game in which such missiles are thrown at a target **2** a sudden movement **3** a short, tapered tuck sewed into a garment —*vt., vi.* to send out or move suddenly and fast

Dar·win (där′win), **Charles (Robert)** (chärlz) 1809-82; Eng. naturalist: originated theory of evolution —**Dar·win′i·an** *adj., n.* —**Dar′win·ism′** *n.*

dash (dash) *vt.* [< Scand] **1** to throw so as to break; smash **2** to throw or thrust (*away, down,* etc.) **3** to splash **4** to destroy, frustrate —*vi.* **1** to strike violently (*against*) **2** to rush —*n.* **1** a splash **2** a bit of something added [*a dash of salt*] **3** a rush **4** a short, fast race **5** spirit; vigor **6** the mark of punctuation (— or -) used to indicate a break, omission, etc. —**dash off** to do, write, etc. hastily —**dash′er** *n.*

dash·board *n.* a panel with controls and gauges, as in an automobile

da·shi·ki (dä shē′kē) *n.* a loosefitting, brightly colored robe or tunic, modeled after an African tribal garment

dash·ing *adj.* **1** full of dash or spirit; lively **2** showy; striking; stylish —**dash′ing·ly** *adv.*

das·tard·ly (das′tərd lē) *adj.* [< ME *dastard*, a craven] mean, cowardly, etc.

dat *abbrev.* dative

da·ta (dāt′ə, dat′ə) *pl.n.* [*now usually with sing. v.*] **1** facts or figures **2** information in a form suitable for computer storage, etc.

da·ta·base *n.* a mass of data, as in a computer,

arranged for easy modification and retrieval: also **data base**

data processing the handling of large amounts of information, esp. by a computer —**data processor**

date¹ (dāt) *n.* [< L *dare*, give] 1 the time at which a thing happens, was made, etc. 2 the day of the month 3 [*pl.*] a person's birth and death dates 4 *a*) an appointment *b*) a romantic social engagement with a person *c*) this person —*vt.* **dat′ed, dat′ing** 1 to mark (a letter, etc.) with a date 2 to find out or give the date of 3 to make seem old-fashioned 4 to have romantic social engagements with —*vi.* 1 to belong to a definite period in the past: usually with *from* 2 to have romantic social engagements —**to date** up to now —**dat′er** *n.*

date² (dāt) *n.* [< Gr *daktylos*, a date] the sweet, fleshy fruit of a desert palm tree (**date palm**)

date-book *n.* a notebook for entering appointments, etc.

date-line *n.* the date and place of writing or issue, as given in a line in a newspaper story, etc.

da-tive (dāt′iv) *n.* [< L *dativus*, relating to giving] *Gram.* the case of the indirect object of a verb

da-tum (dāt′əm, dat′-) *n.* [L, what is given] *sing. of* DATA

daub (dôb) *vt., vi.* [< L *de-*, intens. + *albus*, white] 1 to cover or smear with sticky, soft matter 2 to paint badly —*n.* 1 anything daubed on 2 a daubing stroke —**daub′er** *n.*

daugh-ter (dôt′ər) *n.* [< OE *dohtor*] 1 a girl or woman as she is related to either or both parents 2 a female descendant —**daugh′ter-ly** *adj.*

daugh-ter-in-law *n., pl.* **daugh′ters-in-law′** the wife of one's child

daunt (dônt) *vt.* [< L *domare*, to tame] to intimidate or dishearten

daunt-less *adj.* that cannot be daunted; fearless —**daunt′less-ly** *adv.* —**daunt′less-ness** *n.*

dau-phin (dô′fin) *n.* [Fr, dolphin] the eldest son of the king of France: a title used from 1349 to 1830

dav-en-port (dav′ən pôrt′) *n.* [< ?] a large couch or sofa

Da-vid (dā′vid) *n. Bible* the second king of Israel and Judah

da Vin-ci (də vin′chē), **Leonardo** (lē′ə när′dō) 1452-1519; It. painter, sculptor, architect, & scientist

Da-vis (dā′vis), **Jefferson** 1808-89; president of the Confederacy (1861-65)

da-vit (dā′vit, dav′it) *n.* [OFr dim. of *David*] either of a pair of small cranes on the side of a ship for lowering or raising a small boat

daw-dle (dôd′'l) *vi., vt.* -**dled, -dling** [< ?] to waste (time) in trifling or by being slow —**daw′dler** *n.*

dawn (dôn) *vi.* [< OE *dagian*] 1 to begin to be day 2 to begin to appear, develop, etc. 3

to begin to be understood or felt —*n.* 1 daybreak 2 the beginning (*of* something)

day (dā) *n.* [OE *dæg*] 1 the period of light between sunrise and sunset 2 the time (24 hours) that it takes the earth to rotate once on its axis 3 [*also pl.*] a period; era 4 a time of power, glory, etc. 5 daily work period [an 8-hour *day*] —**day after day** every day: also **day in, day out**

day-bed *n.* a couch that can also be used as a bed

day-break *n.* the time in the morning when light first appears

day care daytime care given to children, as at a day-care center, or to the elderly, as at a social agency: also **day′care′**

day-dream *n.* 1 a pleasant, dreamy series of thoughts 2 a visionary scheme —*vi.* to have daydreams

day-light *n.* 1 the light of day 2 dawn 3 understanding

daylight saving time [*often* D- S- T-] time that is one hour later than standard time: also **daylight savings time**

Day of Atonement Yom Kippur

day-time *n.* the time between dawn and sunset

day-to-day *adj.* daily; routine

day trading rapid buying and selling of stocks, esp. on the internet —**day trader**

daze (dāz) *vt.* **dazed, daz′ing** [< ON *dasi*, tired] to stun or bewilder —*n.* a dazed condition —**daz′ed-ly** *adv.*

daz-zle (daz′əl) *vt., vi.* -**zled, -zling** [< prec.] 1 to overpower or be overpowered by bright light 2 to surprise or arouse admiration with brilliant qualities, display, etc. —*n.* a dazzling —**daz′zler** *n.*

db or **dB** *abbrev.* decibel(s)

DC *abbrev.* 1 direct current: also **dc** 2 District of Columbia

DD or **D.D.** *abbrev.* Doctor of Divinity

DDS or **D.D.S.** *abbrev.* Doctor of Dental Surgery

DDT (dē′dē′tē′) *n.* [< its chemical name] a powerful insecticide

DE *abbrev.* Delaware

de- [< Fr *dé-* or L *de*] *prefix* 1 away from, off [*derail*] 2 down [*degrade*] 3 entirely [*defunct*] 4 reverse the action of [*decode*]

DEA *abbrev.* Drug Enforcement Administration

dea-con (dē′kən) *n.* [< Gr *diakonos*, servant] 1 a cleric ranking just below a priest 2 a member of the laity who helps the minister

dea-con-ess (dē′kə nis) *n.* 1 2 a laywoman who serves as an assistant to a minister

de-ac-ti-vate (dē ak′tə vāt′) *vt.* -**vat′ed, -vat′ing** 1 to make (an explosive, chemical, etc.) inactive 2 *Mil.* to demobilize

dead (ded) *adj.* [OE] 1 no longer living 2 without life 3 deathlike 4 lacking warmth, interest, brightness, etc. 5 without feeling, motion, or power 6 extinguished or extinct 7 no longer used; obsolete 8 unerring [a *dead* shot] 9 complete [a *dead* stop] 10 precise [*dead* center] 11 [Inf.] very tired —*n.* the time of most darkness, most cold, etc. [the *dead* of night] —*adv.* 1 completely 2 directly [*dead* ahead] —**the dead** those who have died

dead-beat *n.* [Slang] one who tries to evade paying debts

dead-bolt *n.* a lock for a door, with a bolt that can be moved only by turning the key or a small knob on one side of the door

dead-en (ded′'n) *vt.* 1 to lessen the vigor or intensity of; dull 2 to numb

dead end 1 a street, alley, etc. closed at one end 2 an impasse —**dead′-end′** *adj.*

dead heat a race in which two or more contestants finish even; tie

dead letter 1 a rule, law, etc. no longer enforced 2 an unclaimed postal letter

dead-line *n.* the latest time by which something must be done

dead-lock *n.* a standstill resulting from the action of equal and opposed forces —*vt., vi.* to bring or come to a deadlock

dead-ly *adj.* -li-er, -li-est 1 causing or likely to cause death 2 implacable [*deadly* enemies] 3 typical of death [*deadly* pallor] 4 extreme 5 very boring 6 very accurate [*deadly* aim] —*adv.* extremely —**dead′li-ness** *n.*

dead-on *adj.* [Inf.] completely accurate

dead-pan *adj., adv.* without expression; blank(ly)

Dead Sea inland body of salt water abutting Israel, Jordan, and the West Bank

dead-wood *n.* anything useless or burdensome

deaf (def) *adj.* [OE] 1 unable to hear 2 unwilling to respond, as to a plea —**deaf′ness** *n.*

deaf-en (-ən) *vt.* 1 to make deaf 2 to overwhelm with noise —**deaf′en-ing** *adj.*

deaf-mute *n.* a person who is deaf and has not learned to speak: now somewhat offensive

deal¹ (dēl) *vt.* **dealt** (delt), **deal′ing** [< OE *dǣlan*] 1 to portion out or distribute 2 to give; administer (a blow, etc.) 3 [Slang] to sell (illegal drugs) —*vi.* 1 to have to do (*with*) [*science deals* with facts] 2 to conduct oneself [*deal* fairly with others] 3 to do business (*with* or *in*) 4 to distribute playing cards to the players —*n.* 1 the distributing of playing cards 2 a business transaction 3 a bargain or agreement, esp. when secret 4 [Inf.] *a)* the situation [what's the *deal?*] *b)* treatment [a fair *deal*] —**deal′er** *n.*

deal² (dēl) *n.* [OE *dǣl*, a part] an indefinite amount —**a good** (or **great**) **deal** 1 a large amount 2 very much

deal-er-ship *n.* a franchise to sell a product in a specified area

deal-ing *n.* 1 way of acting 2 [*usually pl.*] transactions or relations

dean (dēn) *n.* [< LL *decanus*, chief of ten (monks, etc.)] 1 the presiding official of a cathedral 2 a college official in charge of students or faculty 3 the senior or preeminent member of a group

dean's list a list of students at a college who have earned high grades

dear (dir) *adj.* [OE *deore*] 1 much loved 2 esteemed: a polite form of address [*Dear Sir*] 3 high-priced; costly 4 earnest [our *dearest* wish] —*n.* darling —**dear′ly** *adv.* —**dear′ness** *n.*

Dear John (letter) [Inf.] a letter, as to a fiancé, breaking off a close relationship

dearth (durth) *n.* [ME *derth*] scarcity or lack

death (deth) *n.* [OE] 1 the act or fact of dying 2 the state of being dead 3 end or destruction 4 the cause of death —**death′like′** *adj.*

death-bed *n.* used chiefly in the phrase **on one's deathbed**, during the last hours of one's life

death-blow *n.* 1 a blow that kills 2 a thing fatal (*to* something)

death-less *adj.* that cannot die; immortal —**death′less-ly** *adv.*

death-ly *adj.* like or characteristic of death —*adv.* extremely [*deathly* ill]

death-trap *n.* an unsafe building, vehicle, etc.

Death Valley dry, hot desert basin in E California & S Nevada. lowest point in N America

deb (deb) *n.* [Inf.] short for DEBUTANTE

de-ba-cle (di bä′kəl) *n.* [Fr *débâcler*, break up] 1 a crushing defeat 2 a ruinous collapse

de-bar (dē bär′) *vt.* **-barred′, -bar′ring** [< Anglo-Fr: see DE- & BAR] to keep (a person) *from* some right, etc. —**de-bar′ment** *n.*

de-bark (dē bärk′) *vt., vi.* [< Fr: see DE- & BARK³] to unload from or leave a ship or aircraft —**de-bar-ka-tion** (dē′bär kā′shən) *n.*

de-base (dē bās′) *vt.* **-based′, -bas′ing** [DE- + BASE²] to make lower in value, dignity, etc. —**de-base′ment** *n.*

de-bate (dē bāt′) *vi., vt.* **-bat′ed, -bat′ing** [< OFr: see DE- & BATTER¹] 1 to discuss reasons for and against (something) 2 to take part in a debate with (a person) or about (a question) —*n.* 1 a discussion of opposing reasons 2 a formal contest of skill in reasoned argument —**de-bat′a-ble** *adj.* —**de-bat′er** *n.*

de-bauch (dē bôch′) *vt.* [< OFr *desbaucher*, seduce] to lead astray morally; corrupt —*n.* an orgy —**de-bauch′er-y** *n., pl.* **-ies**

deb-au-chee (deb′ô shē′, di bôch′ē′) *n.* a dissipated person

de-ben-ture (di ben′chər) *n.* [< L: see DEBT] 1 a voucher acknowledging a debt 2 an interest-bearing bond issued without specified security

de-bil-i-tate (dē bil′ə tāt′) *vt.* **-tat′ed, -tat′ing** [< L *debilis*, weak] to weaken

de-bil-i-ty (də bil′ə tē) *n., pl.* **-ties** [see prec.] weakness; feebleness

deb-it (deb′it) *n.* [< L *debere*, owe] 1 an entry in an account of money owed 2 the total of such entries —*vt.* to enter as a debit

debit card a bank card that allows the cost of purchases to be deducted from a bank account

deb-o-nair (deb′ə ner′) *adj.* [< OFr *de bon aire*, lit., of good breed] 1 carefree; jaunty 2 urbane Also sp. **deb′o-naire′** —**deb′o-nair′ly** *adv.*

de·brief (dē brēf′) *vt.* 〖DE- + BRIEF〗 to receive information from (a pilot, emissary, etc.) about a recent mission

de·bris or **dé·bris** (də brē′) *n.* 〖Fr < OFr *desbrisier*, break apart〗 bits and pieces of stone, rubbish, etc.

debt (det) *n.* 〖< L *debere*, owe〗 **1** something owed to another **2** the condition of owing [to be in *debt*]

debt·or (-ər) *n.* one who owes a debt

de·bug (dē bug′) *vt.* **-bugged′**, **-bug′ging** 〖DE- + BUG〗 **1** to correct defects in **2** [Inf.] to find and remove hidden electronic listening devices from

de·bunk (dē buŋk′) *vt.* 〖DE- + BUNK²〗 to show to be false, exaggerated, etc.

De·bus·sy (də bü sē′; *E* deb′yoo sē′), **Claude** (klōd; *E* klôd) 1862-1918; Fr. composer

de·but or **dé·but** (dā byoo′, dā′byoo′) *n.* 〖Fr < *débuter*, to lead off〗 **1** a first public appearance **2** the formal introduction of a young woman into society —*vi.* to make a debut

deb·u·tante (deb′yoo tänt′) *n.* 〖Fr〗 a young woman making a debut into society

dec *abbrev.* deceased

Dec *abbrev.* December

deca- 〖< Gr *deka*, ten〗 *combining form* ten: also **dek-**

dec·ade (dek′ād) *n.* 〖< Gr *deka*, ten〗 a period of ten years

dec·a·dence (dek′ə dəns, di kād′ns) *n.* 〖< L *de-*, from + *cadere*, to fall〗 a decline, as in morals, art, etc.; deterioration —**dec′a·dent** *adj., n.*

de·caf (dē′kaf′) *n.* [Inf.] decaffeinated coffee

de·caf·fein·at·ed (dē kaf′ə nāt′id) *adj.* with caffeine removed

de·cal (dē′kal, di kal′) *n.* 〖< *decalcomania* < Fr < L *calcare*, to tread + Gr *mania*, madness〗 a picture or design transferred from prepared paper to glass, wood, etc.

Dec·a·logue or **Dec·a·log** (dek′ə lôg′) *n.* 〖see DECA- & -LOGUE〗 [*sometimes* d-] TEN COMMANDMENTS

de·camp (dē kamp′) *vi.* 〖< Fr〗 **1** to break camp **2** to go away suddenly and secretly

de·cant (dē kant′) *vt.* 〖< Fr < L *de-*, from + *canthus*, tire of a wheel〗 to pour gently from one container into another

de·cant·er *n.* a decorative glass bottle for serving wine, etc.

de·cap·i·tate (dē kap′ə tāt′) *vt.* **-tat′ed**, **-tat′ing** 〖< L *de-*, off + *caput*, head〗 to behead —**de·cap′i·ta′tion** *n.*

de·cath·lon (di kath′län′) *n.* 〖DEC(A)- + Gr *athlon*, a prize〗 an athletic contest in which each contestant takes part in ten TRACK (6b) events

de·cay (dē kā′) *vi.* 〖see DECADENCE〗 **1** to lose strength, prosperity, etc. gradually; deteriorate **2** to rot **3** to undergo radioactive disintegration —*vt.* to cause to decay —*n.* **1** deterioration **2** a rotting or rottenness

de·cease (dē sēs′) *n.* 〖< L *de-*, from + *cedere*, go〗 death

de·ceased (dē sēst′) *adj.* dead —**the deceased** the dead person or persons

de·ce·dent (dē sēd′′nt) *n.* 〖see DECEASE〗 *Law* a deceased person

de·ceit (dē sēt′) *n.* **1** a deceiving or lying **2** a dishonest action **3** deceitful quality

de·ceit·ful *adj.* **1** apt to lie or cheat **2** deceptive; false —**de·ceit′ful·ly** *adv.*

de·ceive (dē sēv′) *vt., vi.* **-ceived′**, **-ceiv′ing** 〖< L *de-*, from + *capere*, take〗 to make (a person) believe what is not true; mislead —**de·ceiv′er** *n.* —**de·ceiv′ing·ly** *adv.*

de·cel·er·ate (dē sel′ər āt′) *vt., vi.* **-at′ed**, **-at′ing** 〖DE- + (AC)CELERATE〗 to reduce the speed (of); slow down —**de·cel′er·a′tion** *n.*

De·cem·ber (dē sem′bər) *n.* 〖< L *decem*, ten: tenth month in Roman calendar〗 the twelfth and last month of the year, having 31 days

de·cen·cy (dē′sən sē) *n., pl.* **-cies** a being decent; propriety, courtesy, etc.

de·cen·ni·al (dē sen′ē əl) *adj.* 〖< L *decem*, ten + *annus*, year〗 **1** happening every ten years **2** lasting ten years

de·cent (dē′sənt) *adj.* 〖< L *decere*, befit〗 **1** proper and fitting **2** *a)* not obscene *b)* clothed **3** respectable **4** adequate [*decent* wages] **5** fair and kind —**de′cent·ly** *adv.*

de·cen·tral·ize (dē sen′trə līz′) *vt.* **-ized′**, **-iz′ing** to break up a concentration of (governmental authority, industry, etc.) and distribute more widely —**de·cen′tral·i·za′tion** *n.*

de·cep·tion (dē sep′shən) *n.* **1** a deceiving or being deceived **2** an illusion or fraud —**de·cep′tive** *adj.*

deci- 〖< L *decem*, ten〗 *combining form* one tenth part of

dec·i·bel (des′ə bəl) *n.* 〖prec. + *bel*, after Alexander Graham BELL〗 a unit for measuring relative loudness of a sound

de·cide (dē sīd′) *vt.* **-cid′ed**, **-cid′ing** 〖< L *de-*, off + *caedere*, to cut〗 **1** to end (a contest, dispute, etc.) by giving one side the victory **2** to reach a decision about; resolve —*vi.* to reach a decision —**de·cid′a·ble** *adj.*

de·cid·ed *adj.* **1** definite; clear-cut **2** determined —**de·cid′ed·ly** *adv.*

de·cid·u·ous (dē sij′oō əs) *adj.* 〖< L *de-*, off, down + *cadere*, to fall〗 **1** falling off or out at a certain season or stage of growth, as some teeth or antlers do **2** shedding leaves annually

dec·i·mal (des′ə məl) *adj.* 〖< L *decem*, ten〗 of or based on the number 10 —*n.* a fraction with a denominator of 10 or some power of 10, shown by a point (**decimal point**) before the numerator (Ex.: .5 = $^5/_{10}$)

dec·i·mate (des′ə māt′) *vt.* **-mat′ed**, **-mat′ing** 〖< L *decem*, ten〗 to destroy or kill a large part of (lit., a tenth part of) —**dec′i·ma′tion** *n.*

de·ci·pher (dē sī′fər) *vt.* 〖DE- + CIPHER〗 **1** DECODE **2** to make out the meaning of (illegible writing, etc.)

de·ci·sion (dē sizh′ən) *n.* **1** the act of deciding or settling a dispute or question **2** the act of making up one's mind **3** a judgment or conclusion **4** determination; firmness of mind

de·ci·sive (dē sī′siv) *adj.* **1** that settles a dispute, question, etc.; conclusive **2** critically important; crucial **3** showing firmness —**de·ci′sive·ly** *adv.*

deck¹ (dek) *n.* ⟦prob. < earlier LowG *verdeck*⟧ **1** a floor of a ship **2** any platform, floor, etc., like a ship's deck **3** a pack of playing cards —*vt.* ⟦Slang⟧ to knock (someone) down

deck² (dek) *vt.* ⟦MDu *decken*, to cover⟧ to array or adorn: often with *out*

de·claim (dē klām′) *vi., vt.* ⟦< L *de-*, intens. + *clamare*, to cry⟧ to recite or speak in a studied or dramatic way —**dec·la·ma·tion** (dek′lə mā′shən) *n.* —**de·clam·a·to·ry** (dē klam′ə tôr′ē) *adj.*

dec·la·ra·tion (dek′lə rā′shən) *n.* **1** a declaring; announcement **2** a formal statement

de·clar·a·tive (dē kler′ə tiv) *adj.* making a statement or assertion

de·clare (dē kler′) *vt.* -**clared′**, -**clar′ing** ⟦< L *de-*, intens. + *clarus*, clear⟧ **1** to announce openly or formally **2** to show or reveal **3** to say emphatically —**de·clar′er** *n.*

de·clas·si·fy (dē klas′ə fī′) *vt.* -**fied′**, -**fy′ing** to make (secret documents, etc.) available to the public —**de·clas′si·fi·ca′tion** *n.*

de·clen·sion (dē klen′shən) *n.* ⟦see fol.⟧ **1** a descent **2** a decline **3** *Gram.* the inflection of nouns, pronouns, or adjectives

dec·li·na·tion (dek′lə nā′shən) *n.* **1** variation from a given direction, esp. of magnetic north from true north **2** *Astron.* position in degrees north or south of the celestial equator

de·cline (dē klīn′) *vi.* -**clined′**, -**clin′ing** ⟦< L *de-*, from + *clinare*, to bend⟧ **1** to bend or slope downward **2** to deteriorate; decay **3** to refuse something —*vt.* **1** to cause to bend or slope downward **2** to refuse politely **3** *Gram.* to give the inflected forms of (a noun, pronoun, or adjective) —*n.* **1** a declining, dropping, failing, decay, etc. **2** a period of decline **3** a downward slope —**de·clin′er** *n.*

de·cliv·i·ty (dē kliv′ə tē) *n., pl.* -**ties** ⟦< L *de-*, down + *clivus*, a slope⟧ a downward slope

de·code (dē kōd′) *vt.* -**cod′ed**, -**cod′ing** to decipher (a coded message)

dé·col·le·tage (dā käl′ə tàzh′, dā kôl tàzh′) *n.* ⟦Fr < *décolleter*, lower a neckline⟧ a low neckline, esp. on a dress

de·col·o·ni·za·tion (dē käl′ə nə zā′shən) *n.* a freeing or being freed from colonial status —**de·col′o·nize′** (-ə nīz′) *vt., vi.* -**nized′**, -**niz′ing**

de·com·mis·sion (dē′kə mish′ən) *vt.* **1** to end or revoke the commission of **2** to take (a ship, nuclear power plant, etc.) out of service

de·com·pose (dē′kəm pōz′) *vt., vi.* -**posed′**, -**pos′ing** ⟦< Fr: see DE- & COMPOSE⟧ **1** to break up into basic parts **2** to rot —**de·com·po·si·tion** (dē käm pə zish′ən) *n.*

de·com·press (dē′kəm pres′) *vt.* to free from pressure, esp. from air pressure —**de′com·pres′sion** *n.*

de·con·gest·ant (dē′kən jes′tənt) *n.* a medication that relieves congestion, as in the nasal passages

de·con·struct (dē′kən strukt′) *vt.* ⟦Fr⟧ **1** to analyze rigorously **2** to take apart; disassemble —**de′con·struc′tion** *n.*

de·con·tam·i·nate (dē′kən tam′ə nāt′) *vt.* -**nat′ed**, -**nat′ing** to rid of a harmful substance, as radioactive material

de·cor or **dé·cor** (dā kôr′) *n.* ⟦Fr⟧ a decorative scheme, as of a room

dec·o·rate (dek′ə rāt′) *vt.* -**rat′ed**, -**rat′ing** ⟦< L *decus*, an ornament⟧ **1** to adorn; ornament **2** to paint or wallpaper **3** to give a medal or similar honor to —**dec·o·ra·tive** (dek′ə rə tiv, -ə rāt′iv) *adj.* —**dec′o·ra′tor** *n.*

dec·o·ra·tion *n.* **1** a decorating **2** an ornament **3** a medal, etc.

Decoration Day MEMORIAL DAY

dec·o·rous (dek′ə rəs, di kôr′əs) *adj.* having or showing decorum, good taste, etc. —**dec′o·rous·ly** *adv.*

de·co·rum (di kôr′əm) *n.* ⟦< L *decorus*, proper⟧ propriety in behavior, speech, etc.

de·cou·page or **dé·cou·page** (dā′kōō päzh′) *n.* ⟦< Fr *dé-*, DE- + *couper*, to cut⟧ the art of decorating a surface with varnished paper cutouts

de·coy (dē′koi′; *for v.*, dē koi′) *n.* ⟦< Du *de kooi*, the cage⟧ **1** an artificial or trained bird, etc. used to lure game within gun range **2** a thing or person used to lure into danger —*vt.* to lure into danger

de·crease (dē krēs′; *for n.*, usually dē′krēs′) *vi., vt.* -**creased′**, -**creas′ing** ⟦< L *de-*, from + *crescere*, grow⟧ to become or make less, smaller, etc.; diminish —*n.* **1** a decreasing **2** amount of decreasing

de·cree (dē krē′) *n.* ⟦< L *de-*, from + *cernere*, to judge⟧ an official order or decision —*vt.* -**creed′**, -**cree′ing** to order or decide by decree

de·crep·it (dē krep′it) *adj.* ⟦< L *de-*, intens. + *crepare*, to creak⟧ broken down or worn out by old age or long use —**de·crep′i·tude′** (-ə tōōd′) *n.*

de·cre·scen·do (dā′krə shen′dō, dē′-) ⟦*also in italics*⟧ *Music adj., adv.* ⟦It < L, DECREASE⟧ gradually decreasing in loudness —*n., pl.* -**dos** a gradual decrease in loudness

de·crim·i·nal·ize (dē krim′ə nəl īz′) *vt.* -**ized′**, -**iz′ing** to eliminate or reduce the penalties for (a crime)

de·cry (dē krī′) *vt.* -**cried′**, -**cry′ing** ⟦< Fr: see DE- & CRY⟧ to speak out against openly; denounce

ded·i·cate (ded′i kāt′) *vt.* -**cat′ed**, -**cat′ing** ⟦< L *de-*, intens. + *dicare*, proclaim⟧ **1** to set apart for, or devote to, a special purpose **2** to address (a book, etc.) to someone as a sign of honor —**ded′i·ca′tion** *n.*

ded·i·cat·ed *adj.* **1** devoted; faithful **2** designating a device, etc. to be used only for a particular purpose

de·duce (dē dōōs′) *vt.* -**duced′**, -**duc′ing** ⟦< L *de-*, down + *ducere*, to lead⟧ to infer by reasoning —**de·duc′i·ble** *adj.*

de·duct (dē dukt′) *vt.* ⟦see prec.⟧ to take away or subtract (a quantity)

de·duct·i·ble (-duk′tə bəl) *adj.* that can be deducted —*n.* an amount stipulated in an insurance policy to be paid by the insured in the event of a loss, etc., with the insurer paying the rest

de·duc·tion (-duk′shən) *n.* 1 a deducting; subtraction 2 an amount deducted 3 *a)* reasoning from the general to the specific *b)* a conclusion reached by such reasoning —**de·duc′tive** *adj.*

deed (dēd) *n.* [< OE *dēd*] 1 a thing done; act 2 a feat of courage, skill, etc. 3 a legal document which transfers a property —*vt.* to transfer (property) by deed

deem (dēm) *vt., vi.* [< OE *dēman*, to judge] to think, believe, or judge

de·em·pha·size (dē em′fə sīz′) *vt.* -**sized′**, -**siz′ing** to lessen the importance of —**de·em′pha·sis** (-sis) *n.*

deep (dēp) *adj.* [OE *dēop*] 1 extending far downward, inward, backward, etc. 2 hard to understand; abstruse 3 serious; profound 4 dark and rich [a *deep* red] 5 absorbed by: with *in* [*deep* in thought] 6 great in degree; intense 7 of low pitch [a *deep* voice] 8 large; big —*n.* a deep place —*adv.* far down, far back, etc. —**the deep** [Old Poet.] the ocean —**deep′ly** *adv.* —**deep′ness** *n.*

deep·en *vt., vi.* to make or become deep or deeper

deep·freeze *n.* a condition of suspended activity, etc. —*vt.* -**froze′**, -**fro′zen**, -**freez′ing** to subject (foods) to sudden freezing so as to preserve and store

deep-fry *vt.* -**fried′**, -**fry′ing** to fry in a deep pan of boiling fat or oil

deep-root·ed *adj.* 1 having deep roots 2 firmly fixed

deep-seat·ed *adj.* 1 buried deep 2 firmly fixed

deep-six *vt.* [< six fathoms] [Slang] to get rid of, as by throwing overboard

deep space OUTER SPACE

deer (dir) *n., pl.* **deer** or **deers** [OE *dēor*, wild animal] any of various ruminants, including the elk, moose, and reindeer, the male of which grows and sheds antlers annually

de·es·ca·late (dē es′kə lāt′) *vi., vt.* -**lat′ed**, -**lat′ing** to reduce in scope, magnitude, etc.: used esp. of a conflict —**de·es·ca·la′tion** *n.*

de·face (dē fās′) *vt.* -**faced′**, -**fac′ing** [see DE- & FACE] to spoil the look of; mar —**de·face′ment** *n.*

de fac·to (dē fak′tō) [L] actually existing but not officially approved

de·fal·cate (dē fal′kāt′) *vi.* -**cat′ed**, -**cat′ing** [< L *de-*, from + *falx*, a sickle] to steal or misuse funds entrusted to one's care; embezzle —**de·fal·ca′tion** *n.*

de·fame (dē fām′) *vt.* -**famed′**, -**fam′ing** [< L *dis-*, from + *fama*, fame] to attack the reputation of; slander or libel —**def·a·ma·tion** (def′ə mā′shən) *n.* —**de·fam·a·to·ry** (dē fam′ə tôr′ē) *adj.* —**de·fam′er** *n.*

de·fang (dē faŋ′) *vt.* 1 to remove the fangs of 2 to make harmless —**de·fanged′** *adj.*

de·fault (dē fôlt′) *n.* [< L *de-*, away + *fallere*, fail] failure to do or appear as required; specif., failure to pay money due —*vi., vt.* 1 to fail to do or pay when required 2 to lose (a contest) by default —**de·fault′er** *n.*

de·feat (dē fēt′) *vt.* [< L *dis-*, from + *facere*, do] 1 to win victory over 2 to bring to nothing; frustrate —*n.* a defeating or being defeated

de·feat·ist *n.* one who too readily accepts or expects defeat —**de·feat′ism′** *n.*

def·e·cate (def′i kāt′) *vi.* -**cat′ed**, -**cat′ing** [< L *de-*, from + *faex*, dregs] to excrete waste matter from the bowels —**def′e·ca′tion** *n.*

de·fect (dē′fekt′; *for v.* dē fekt′) *n.* [< L *de-*, from + *facere*, do] 1 lack of something necessary for completeness 2 an imperfection —*vi.* to forsake a party, cause, etc., esp. so as to join the opposition —**de·fec′tion** *n.* —**de·fec′tor** *n.*

de·fec·tive (dē fek′tiv) *adj.* having defects; imperfect; faulty

de·fend (dē fend′) *vt.* [< L *de-*, away + *fendere*, to strike] 1 to guard from attack; protect 2 to support or justify 3 *Law a)* to oppose (an action) *b)* to act as lawyer for (an accused) —**de·fend′er** *n.*

de·fend·ant (dē fen′dənt, -dant′) *n.* *Law* the person sued or accused

de·fense (dē fens′, dē′fens′) *n.* 1 a defending against attack 2 something that defends 3 justification by speech or writing 4 *a)* the arguments of a defendant *b)* the defendant and his or her counsel Brit. sp. **de·fence** —**de·fense′less** *adj.* —**de·fen′si·ble** *adj.*

defense mechanism any thought process used unconsciously to protect oneself against painful feelings

de·fen·sive *adj.* 1 defending 2 of or for defense —*n.* a position of defense —**de·fen′sive·ly** *adv.*

de·fer[1] (dē fur′) *vt., vi.* -**ferred′**, -**fer′ring** [see DIFFER] 1 to postpone; delay 2 to postpone the induction of (a person) into compulsory military service —**de·fer′ment** *n.*, **de·fer′ral** *n.*

de·fer[2] (dē fur′) *vi.* -**ferred′**, -**fer′ring** [< L *de-*, down + *ferre*, to BEAR[1]] to yield with courtesy (*to*)

def·er·ence (def′ər əns) *n.* 1 a yielding in opinion, judgment, etc. 2 courteous respect

def·er·en·tial (-en′shəl) *adj.* showing deference; very respectful

de·fi·ance (dē fī′əns) *n.* a defying; open, bold resistance to authority —**de·fi′ant** *adj.* —**de·fi′ant·ly** *adv.*

de·fi·cien·cy (dē fish′ən sē) *n.* [< L *de-*, from + *facere*, do] 1 a being deficient 2 *pl.* -**cies** a shortage

deficiency disease a disease caused by a lack of vitamins, minerals, etc. in the diet

de·fi·cient (dē fish′ənt) *adj.* [see DEFICIEN-CY] 1 lacking in some essential; incomplete 2 inadequate in amount

def·i·cit (def′ə sit) *n.* [L < *deficere*, to lack] the amount by which a sum of money is less than the required amount, as when there are more expenditures than income

de·file¹ (dē fīl′) *vt.* **-filed′, -fil′ing** [< OFr *defouler*, tread underfoot] **1** to make filthy **2** to profane; sully —**de·file′ment** *n.* —**de·fil′er** *n.*

de·file² (dē fīl′, dē′fīl′) *vi.* **-filed′, -fil′ing** [< Fr *dé-*, from + *fil*, thread] to go in single file —*n.* a narrow pass, valley, etc.

de·fine (dē fīn′) *vt.* **-fined′, -fin′ing** [< L *de-*, from + *finis*, boundary] **1** to determine the limits or nature of; describe exactly **2** to state the meaning of (a word, etc.) —**de·fin′er** *n.*

def·i·nite (def′ə nit) *adj.* [see prec.] **1** having exact limits **2** precise in meaning; explicit **3** certain; positive **4** *Gram.* limiting or specifying ["the" is the *definite* article] —**def′i·nite·ly** *adv.* —**def′i·nite·ness** *n.*

def·i·ni·tion (-nish′ən) *n.* **1** a defining or being defined **2** a statement of the meaning of a word **3** clarity of outline, sound, etc.

de·fin·i·tive (dē fin′ə tiv) *adj.* **1** conclusive; final **2** most nearly complete **3** serving to define

de·flate (dē flāt′) *vt., vi.* **-flat′ed, -flat′ing** [DE- + (IN)FLATE] **1** to collapse by letting out air or gas **2** to lessen in size, importance, etc. **3** to cause deflation of (currency, etc.)

de·fla·tion *n.* **1** a deflating **2** a reduction in prices resulting from severe economic decline

de·flect (dē flekt′) *vt., vi.* [< L *de-*, from + *flectere*, to bend] to turn or make go to one side —**de·flec′tion** *n.* —**de·flec′tive** *adj.* —**de·flec′tor** *n.*

De·foe (di fō′), **Daniel** 1660-1731; Eng. writer

de·fog·ger (dē fôg′ər) *n.* an apparatus for clearing condensed moisture, as from a car window

de·fo·li·ant (dē fō′lē ənt) *n.* a chemical substance that causes leaves to fall from growing plants

de·fo·li·ate (-āt′) *vt.* **-at′ed, -at′ing** [< L *de-*, from + *folium*, leaf] to strip (trees, etc.) of leaves —**de·fo′li·a′tion** *n.*

de·form (dē fôrm′) *vt.* [< L *de-*, from + *forma*, form] **1** to impair the form of **2** to make ugly —**de·for·ma·tion** (dē′fôr mā′shən, def′ ər-) *n.*

de·formed *adj.* misshapen

de·form·i·ty *n., pl.* **-ties 1** a deformed part, as of the body **2** ugliness or depravity

de·fraud (dē frôd′) *vt.* to take property, etc. from by fraud —**de·fraud′er** *n.*

de·fray (dē frā′) *vt.* [Fr *défrayer*] to pay (the cost or expenses) —**de·fray′a·ble** *adj.* —**de·fray′al** *n.*

de·frost (dē frôst′) *vt., vi.* to rid or get rid of frost or ice —**de·frost′er** *n.*

deft (deft) *adj.* [see DAFT] skillful; dexterous —**deft′ly** *adv.*

de·funct (dē funkt′) *adj.* [< L *defungi*, to finish] no longer existing; dead or extinct

de·fuse (dē fyo͞oz′) *vt.* **-fused′, -fus′ing 1** to remove the fuse from (a bomb, etc.) **2** to make harmless, less tense, etc.

de·fy (dē fī′) *vt.* **-fied′, -fy′ing** [< LL *dis-*, from + *fidus*, faithful] **1** to resist or oppose boldly or openly **2** to dare to do or prove something

de·gen·er·ate (dē jen′ər it; *for v.,* -āt′) *adj.* [< L *de-*, from + *genus*, race] **1** having sunk below a former or normal condition, etc.; deteriorated **2** depraved —*n.* a degenerate person —*vi.* **-at′ed, -at′ing** to lose former normal or higher qualities —**de·gen′er·a·cy** (-ə sē) *n.* —**de·gen′er·a′tion** *n.* —**de·gen′er·a·tive** (-ə tiv, -āt′iv) *adj.*

de·grad·a·ble (dē grād′ə bəl) *adj.* capable of being broken down chemically, as some plastics

de·grade (dē grād′) *vt.* **-grad′ed, -grad′ing** [< L *de-*, down + *gradus*, a step] **1** to demote **2** to lower in quality, moral character, dignity, etc.; debase, dishonor, etc. —**deg·ra·da·tion** (deg′rə dā′shən) *n.*

de·gree (di grē′) *n.* [see prec.] **1** any of the steps in a process **2** social or official rank **3** extent, amount, or intensity **4** a rank given by a college or university to one who has completed a course of study, or to a distinguished person as an honor **5** a grade of comparison of adjectives and adverbs [the superlative *degree*] **6** *Law* the seriousness of a crime [murder in the first *degree*] **7** *Math.* a unit of measure for angles or arcs, one 360th of a full circle **8** *Physics* a unit of measure for temperature —**to a degree** somewhat

de·greed (-grēd′) *adj.* having a college or university degree

de·hu·man·ize (dē hyo͞o′mə nīz′) *vt.* **-ized′, -iz′ing** to deprive of human qualities; make machinelike —**de·hu′man·i·za′tion** *n.*

de·hu·mid·i·fy (dē′hyo͞o mid′ə fī′) *vt.* **-fied′, -fy′ing** to remove moisture from (air, etc.) —**de′hu·mid′i·fi′er** *n.*

de·hy·drate (dē hī′drāt′) *vt.* **-drat′ed, -drat′ing** to remove water from (a substance, etc.); dry —*vi.* to lose water —**de′hy·dra′tion** *n.* —**de·hy′dra′tor** *n.*

de·ice (dē īs′) *vt.* **-iced′, -ic′ing** to melt ice from —**de·ic′er** *n.*

de·i·fy (dē′ə fī′) *vt.* **-fied′, -fy′ing** [< L *deus*, god + *facere*, make] **1** to make a god of **2** to look upon as a god —**de′i·fi·ca′tion** (-fi kā′shən) *n.*

deign (dān) *vi., vt.* [< L *dignus*, worthy] to condescend (to do or give)

de·ism (dē′iz′əm) *n.* [< L *deus*, god] the belief that God exists and created the world but takes no part in its functioning —**de′ist** *n.*

de·i·ty (dē′ə tē) *n.* [< L *deus*, god] **1** the state of being a god **2** *pl.* **-ties** a god or goddess —**the Deity** God

dé·jà vu (dā′zhə vo͞o′) [Fr, already seen] a feeling of having been in the same place or experienced the same thing before

de·ject (dē jekt′) *vt.* [< L *de-*, down + *jacere*, throw] to dishearten; depress —**de·ject′ed** *adj.* —**de·jec′tion** *n.*

Del·a·ware (del′ə wer′, -wär′) state of the E U.S.; cap. Dover: abbrev. *DE* —**Del′a·war′e·an** *adj., n.*

de·lay (dē lā′) *vt.* [< OFr *de-*, intens. + *laier*, to

leave 1 to put off; postpone 2 to make late; detain —*vi.* to linger —*n.* 1 a delaying or being delayed 2 the time one is delayed

de·lec·ta·ble (dē lek′tə bəl) *adj.* ⟦see DE-LIGHT⟧ delightful or delicious

de·lec·ta·tion (dē′lek tā′shən) *n.* ⟦see DELIGHT⟧ delight; enjoyment

del·e·gate (del′ə git; *for v.,* -gāt′) *n.* ⟦< L *de-,* from + *legare,* send⟧ a person authorized to act for others; representative —*vt.* **-gat′ed, -gat′ing** 1 to appoint as a delegate 2 to entrust (authority, etc.) to another

del·e·ga·tion (-gā′shən) *n.* 1 a delegating or being delegated 2 a body of delegates

de·lete (dē lēt′) *vt.* **-let′ed, -let′ing** ⟦< L *delere,* destroy⟧ to take out (a word, etc.); cross out —**de·le′tion** *n.*

del·e·te·ri·ous (del′ə tir′ē əs) *adj.* ⟦< Gr *dēleisthai,* injure⟧ harmful to health or well-being

delft·ware (delft′wer′) *n.* ⟦after *Delft,* city in the Netherlands⟧ glazed earthenware, usually blue and white: also **delft**

Del·hi (del′ē) city in N India: see also NEW DELHI

del·i (del′ē) *n. short for* DELICATESSEN

de·lib·er·ate (di lib′ər it; *for v.,* -āt′) *adj.* ⟦< L *de-,* intens. + *librare,* weigh⟧ 1 carefully thought out; premeditated 2 not rash or hasty 3 unhurried —*vi., vt.* **-at′ed, -at′ing** to consider carefully —**de·lib′er·ate·ly** *adv.* —**de·lib′er·a′tive** (-āt′iv, -ə tiv) *adj.*

de·lib·er·a·tion (-ā′shən) *n.* 1 a deliberating 2 [*often pl.*] consideration of alternatives 3 carefulness; slowness

del·i·ca·cy (del′i kə sē) *n., pl.* **-cies** 1 the quality of being delicate 2 a choice food

del·i·cate (-kit) *adj.* ⟦< L *delicatus,* delightful⟧ 1 pleasing in its lightness, mildness, etc. 2 beautifully fine in texture, workmanship, etc. 3 slight and subtle 4 easily damaged 5 frail in health 6 *a)* needing careful handling *b)* showing tact, consideration, etc. 7 finely sensitive —**del′i·cate·ly** *adv.* —**del′i·cate·ness** *n.*

del·i·ca·tes·sen (del′i kə tes′ən) *n.* ⟦< Ger pl. < Fr *délicatesse,* delicacy⟧ 1 prepared cooked meats, fish, cheeses, salads, etc., collectively 2 a shop where such foods are sold

de·li·cious (di lish′əs) *adj.* ⟦see fol.⟧ 1 delightful 2 very pleasing to taste or smell —**de·li′cious·ly** *adv.* —**de·li′cious·ness** *n.*

de·light (di līt′) *vt.* ⟦< L *de-,* from + *lacere,* entice⟧ to give great pleasure to —*vi.* 1 to give great pleasure 2 to be highly pleased; rejoice —*n.* 1 great pleasure 2 something giving great pleasure —**de·light′ed** *adj.*

de·light·ful *adj.* giving delight; very pleasing —**de·light′ful·ly** *adv.*

De·li·lah (di lī′lə) *n. Bible* the mistress and betrayer of Samson

de·lim·it (dē lim′it) *vt.* to fix the limits of —**de·lim′i·ta′tion** *n.*

de·lin·e·ate (di lin′ē āt′) *vt.* **-at′ed, -at′ing** ⟦< L *de-,* from + *linea,* a line⟧ 1 to draw; sketch 2 to depict in words —**de·lin′e·a′tion** *n.*

de·lin·quent (di liŋ′kwənt) *adj.* ⟦< L *de-,* from + *linquere,* leave⟧ 1 failing to do what duty or law requires 2 overdue, as taxes —*n.* a delinquent person; esp., a juvenile delinquent —**de·lin′quen·cy** *n., pl.* **-cies** —**de·lin′quent·ly** *adv.*

de·li·quesce (del′i kwes′) *vi.* **-quesced′, -quesc′ing** ⟦< L < *de-,* from + *liquere,* be liquid⟧ 1 to become liquid 2 *Biol.* to melt away in the course of growth or decay 3 *Chem.* to become liquid by absorbing moisture from the air —**del′i·ques′cent** *adj.*

de·lir·i·ous (di lir′ē əs) *adj.* 1 in a state of delirium 2 of or caused by delirium 3 wildly excited —**de·lir′i·ous·ly** *adv.*

de·lir·i·um (-əm) *n.* ⟦< L *de-,* from + *lira,* a line⟧ 1 a temporary mental disturbance, as during a fever, marked by confused speech and hallucinations 2 uncontrollably wild excitement

de·liv·er (di liv′ər) *vt.* ⟦< L *de-,* intens. + *liber,* free⟧ 1 to set free or rescue 2 to assist in the birth of 3 to make (a speech, etc.) 4 to hand over 5 to distribute (mail, etc.) 6 to strike (a blow) 7 to throw (a ball, etc.) —*vi.* 1 to make deliveries 2 to produce, etc. something promised

de·liv·er·ance *n.* a freeing or being freed; rescue

de·liv·er·y *n., pl.* **-er·ies** 1 a handing over 2 a distributing, as of mail 3 a giving birth 4 any giving forth 5 the act or manner of delivering a speech, ball, etc. 6 something delivered

dell (del) *n.* ⟦OE *dell*⟧ a small, secluded valley or glen, usually wooded

del·phin·i·um (del fin′ē əm) *n.* ⟦< Gr *delphin,* dolphin⟧ a tall plant bearing spikes of flowers, usually blue

del·ta (del′tə) *n.* 1 the fourth letter of the Greek alphabet (Δ, δ) 2 a deposit of soil, often roughly triangular, formed at the mouth of a large river

de·lude (di lōōd′) *vt.* **-lud′ed, -lud′ing** ⟦< L *de-,* from + *ludere,* to play⟧ to mislead; deceive

del·uge (del′yōōj′) *n.* ⟦< L *dis,* off + *luere,* to wash⟧ 1 a great flood 2 a heavy rainfall 3 an overwhelming rush of anything —*vt.* **-uged′, -ug′ing** 1 to flood 2 to overwhelm

de·lu·sion (di lōō′zhən) *n.* 1 a deluding or being deluded 2 a false belief, specif. one that persists psychotically —**de·lu′sive** *adj.,* **de·lu′sion·al, de·lu′so·ry** (-lōō′sə rē) *adj.*

de·luxe (di luks′, -looks′) *adj.* ⟦Fr, of luxury⟧ of extra fine quality —*adv.* in a deluxe manner

delve (delv) *vi.* **delved, delv′ing** ⟦OE *delfan*⟧ 1 [Now Dial., Chiefly Brit.] to dig 2 to search (*into*) —**delv′er** *n.*

Dem *abbrev.* 1 Democrat 2 Democratic

de·mag·net·ize (dē mag′nə tīz′) *vt.* **-ized′, -iz′ing** to remove magnetism or magnetic properties from —**de·mag′net·i·za′tion** *n.*

dem·a·gogue or **dem·a·gog** (dem′ə gäg′) *n.* ⟦< Gr *dēmos,* the people + *agōgos,* leader⟧ one who stirs up people's emotions to win them over and so gain power —**dem′a·gog′y** (-gä′jē, -gäg′ē) *n.,* **dem′a·gogu′er·y** (-gäg′ər ē)

de·mand (di mand′) *vt.* ⟦< L *de*-, from + *mandare*, entrust⟧ **1** to ask for boldly or urgently **2** to ask for as a right **3** to require; need —*vi.* to make a demand —*n.* **1** a demanding **2** a thing demanded **3** a strong request **4** an urgent requirement **5** *Economics* the desire for a commodity together with ability to pay for it; also, the amount people are ready to buy at a certain price —**in demand** wanted or sought —**on demand 1** when presented for payment **2** when needed or requested

de·mand·ing *adj.* making difficult demands on one's patience, energy, etc.

de·mar·ca·tion (dē′mär kā′shən) *n.* ⟦< Sp *de*-, from + *marcar*, to mark⟧ **1** the act of setting and marking limits or boundaries **2** a limit or boundary

de·mean[1] (dē mēn′) *vt.* ⟦DE- + MEAN[2]⟧ to degrade; humble

de·mean[2] (dē mēn′) *vt.* ⟦see fol.⟧ to behave or conduct (oneself)

de·mean·or (di mēn′ər) *n.* ⟦< OFr *demener*, to lead⟧ outward behavior; conduct; deportment: Brit. sp. **de·mean′our**

de·ment·ed (dē ment′id) *adj.* ⟦see fol.⟧ mentally deranged; insane

de·men·tia (di men′shə) *n.* ⟦< L *de* -, out from + *mens*, the mind⟧ a disorder of the mind impairing perception, memory, etc.

de·mer·it (dē mer′it) *n.* ⟦< L *de*-, intens. + *merere*, to deserve, with *de*- taken as negative⟧ **1** a fault; defect **2** a mark recorded against a student, etc. for poor conduct or work

de·mesne (di mān′, -mēn′) *n.* ⟦see DOMAIN⟧ a region or domain

De·me·ter (di mēt′ər) *n.* *Gr. Myth.* the goddess of agriculture

demi- ⟦< L *dimidius*, half⟧ *prefix* **1** half **2** less than usual in size, power, etc. [*demigod*]

dem·i·god (dem′i gäd′) *n.* **1** a minor deity **2** a godlike person

dem·i·john (-jän′) *n.* ⟦Fr *dame-jeanne*⟧ a large bottle of glass or earthenware in a wicker casing

de·mil·i·ta·rize (dē mil′ə tə rīz′) *vt.* **-rized′, -riz′ing** to free from organized military control

dem·i·monde (dem′i mänd′) *n.* ⟦Fr < *demi*- + *monde*, world⟧ **1** the class of women who have lost social standing because of sexual promiscuity **2** any group considered lacking in respectability

de·mise (dē mīz′) *n.* ⟦< L *de*-, down + *mittere*, send⟧ **1** *Law* a transfer of an estate by lease **2** death —*vt.* **-mised′, -mis′ing** to transfer (an estate) by lease

dem·i·tasse (dem′i täs′, -tas′) *n.* ⟦Fr < *demi*- + *tasse*, cup⟧ a small cup of or for after-dinner coffee

dem·o[1] (dem′ō) *n., pl.* **-os 1** a recording made to demonstrate a song, the talent of a performer, etc. **2** a product used in demonstrations

demo[2] *n., pl.* **-os** [Inf.] demolition

de·mo·bi·lize (dē mō′bə līz′) *vt.* **-lized′, -liz′ing** to disband (troops) —**de·mo′bi·li·za′tion** *n.*

de·moc·ra·cy (di mäk′rə sē) *n., pl.* **-cies** ⟦< Gr *dēmos*, the people + *kratein*, to rule⟧ **1** government by the people, directly or through representatives **2** a country, etc. with such government **3** equality of rights and opportunity

dem·o·crat (dem′ə krat′) *n.* **1** one who supports or practices democracy **2** [D-] a Democratic Party member

dem·o·crat·ic *adj.* **1** of or for democracy **2** or for all the people **3** not snobbish **4** [D-] of the Democratic Party —**dem′o·crat′i·cal·ly** *adv.*

Democratic Party one of the two major political parties in the U.S.

de·mod·u·la·tion (dē mä′jə lā′shən) *n.* *Radio* the recovery, at the receiver, of a signal that has been modulated on a carrier wave

dem·o·graph·ic (dem′ə graf′ik) *adj.* of or relating to the age, sex, income, etc. of the members of a population —*n.* a subgroup of a population sharing a particular characteristic, such as age range —**dem′o·graph′i·cal·ly** *adv.*

dem·o·graph·ics (dem′ə graf′iks) *pl.n.* demographic characteristics of a population, as age, sex, or income, used for research, etc.

de·mog·ra·phy (di mä′grə fē) *n.* ⟦< Gr *dēmos*, the people + -GRAPHY⟧ the statistical study of human populations —**de·mog′ra·pher** *n.*

de·mol·ish (di mäl′ish) *vt.* ⟦< L *de*-, down + *moliri*, build⟧ **1** to pull down or smash **2** to destroy, ruin —**dem·o·li·tion** (dem′ə lish′ən) *n.*

de·mon (dē′mən) *n.* ⟦< L *daemon*⟧ **1** a devil; evil spirit **2** one regarded as evil, cruel, etc. **3** one with great energy, skill, etc. —**de·mon·ic** (di män′ik) *adj.* —**de·mon′i·cal·ly** *adv.*

de·mon·e·tize (dē män′ə tīz′) *vt.* **-tized′, -tiz′ing** to deprive (esp. currency) of its standard value

de·mon·ize (dē′mən īz′) *vt.* **-ized′, -iz′ing 1** to make into a demon **2** to characterize as evil, cruel, etc. —**de′mon·i·za′tion** *n.*

de·mon·stra·ble (di män′strə bəl) *adj.* that can be demonstrated, or proved —**de·mon′stra·bly** *adv.*

dem·on·strate (dem′ən strāt′) *vt.* **-strat·ed, -strat′ing** ⟦< L *de*-, from + *monstrare*, to show⟧ **1** to show by reasoning; prove **2** to explain by using examples, etc. **3** to show how something works —*vi.* to express views publicly by meetings, etc. —**dem′on·stra′tion** *n.* —**dem′on·stra′tor** *n.*

de·mon·stra·tive (di män′strə tiv) *adj.* **1** illustrative **2** giving proof (*of*) **3** showing feelings openly **4** *Gram.* pointing out [*"this"* is a *demonstrative* pronoun] —*n. Gram.* a demonstrative pronoun or adjective —**de·mon′stra·tive·ly** *adv.*

de·mor·al·ize (dē môr′ə līz′) *vt.* **-ized′, -iz′ing 1** to lower the morale of **2** to throw into confusion —**de·mor′al·i·za′tion** *n.*

De·mos·the·nes (di mäs′thə nēz′) 384-322 B.C.; Athenian orator

de·mote (dē mōt′) *vt.* **-mot′ed, -mot′ing** ⟦DE- + (PRO)MOTE⟧ to reduce to a lower rank —**de·mo′tion** *n.*

de·mul·cent (dē mul′sənt) *adj.* ⟦< L *de*-,

down + *mulcere*, to stroke] soothing —*n.* a soothing ointment

de·mur (di mur′, di-) *vi.* **-murred′, -mur′ring** [< L *de-*, from + *mora*, a delay] to object or decline —*n.* a demurring: also **de·mur′ral**

de·mure (di myoor′) *adj.* [< ME *de-* (prob. intens.) + OFr *mëur*, mature] 1 modest or reserved 2 affectedly modest; coy —**de·mure′ly** *adv.*

de·mur·rage (di mur′ij) *n.* 1 the compensation payable for delaying a vehicle or vessel carrying freight, as by failure to load or unload 2 the delay itself

de·mur·rer (di mur′ər) *n.* [see DEMUR] 1 a plea for dismissal of a lawsuit because statements supporting a claim are defective 2 an objection

den (den) *n.* [OE *denn*] 1 the lair of a wild animal 2 a haunt, as of thieves 3 a small, cozy room where a person can be alone to read, work, etc.

De·na·li (di nä′ lē) mountain in Alaska: highest peak in North America: 20,310 ft.

de·na·ture (dē nä′chər) *vt.* **-tured, -tur·ing** 1 to change the nature of 2 to make (alcohol) unfit to drink

den·drite (den′drīt′) *n.* [< Gr *dendron*, tree] the part of a nerve cell that carries impulses toward the cell body

Deng Xiao·ping (duŋ′ shou′piŋ′) 1904-97; Chin. Communist leader

de·ni·al (dē nī′əl) *n.* 1 a denying; saying "no" (to a request, etc.) 2 a contradiction 3 a refusal to believe or accept (a doctrine, etc.) 4 SELF-DENIAL

de·nier′ (den′yər) *n.* [< L *deni*, by tens] a unit of weight for measuring the fineness of threads of silk, nylon, etc.

de·ni·er² (dē nī′ər) *n.* one who denies

den·i·grate (den′ə grāt′) *vt.* **-grat′ed, -grat′ing** [< L < *de-*, entirely + *nigrare*, blacken] to belittle the character of; defame —**den′i·gra′tion** *n.* —**den′i·gra′tor** *n.*

den·im (den′im) *n.* [< Fr (*serge*) *de Nîmes*, (serge) of Nîmes, town in France] a coarse, twilled cotton cloth

den·i·zen (den′ə zən) *n.* [< L *de intus*, from within] an inhabitant or frequenter of a particular place

Den·mark (den′märk′) country in Europe, on a peninsula & several islands in the North & Baltic seas

de·nom·i·nate (dē näm′ə nāt′) *vt.* **-nat′ed, -nat′ing** [< L *de-*, intens. + *nominare*, to name] to name; call

de·nom·i·na·tion (-nā′shən) *n.* 1 the act of naming 2 a name 3 a class or kind, as of coins, having a specific name or value 4 a particular religious body

de·nom·i·na·tion·al *adj.* of, or under the control of, a religious denomination

de·nom·i·na·tor (-nāt′ər) *n.* 1 a shared characteristic 2 *Math.* the term below the line in a fraction

de·note (dē nōt′) *vt.* **-not′ed, -not′ing** [< L

de-, down + *notare*, to mark] 1 to indicate 2 to signify; mean —**de·no·ta·tion** (dē′nō tā′shən) *n.*

de·noue·ment or **dé·noue·ment** (dā′noo män′) *n.* [Fr] the outcome or unraveling of a plot in a drama, story, etc.

de·nounce (dē nouns′) *vt.* **-nounced′, -nounc′ing** [see DENUNCIATION] 1 to accuse publicly; inform against 2 to condemn strongly and usually publicly —**de·nounce′ment** *n.*

dense (dens) *adj.* **dens′er, dens′est** [< L *densus*, compact] 1 packed tightly together 2 difficult to get through, penetrate, etc. 3 stupid —**dense′ly** *adv.* —**dense′ness** *n.*

den·si·ty (den′sə tē) *n., pl.* **-ties** 1 a dense condition 2 stupidity 3 number per unit, as of area [population *density*] 4 ratio of the mass of an object to its volume

dent (dent) *n.* [ME, var. of DINT] 1 a slight hollow made in a surface by a blow 2 [Inf.] a noticeable effect, esp. in lessening —*vt., vi.* to make or receive a dent (in)

den·tal (dent′'l) *adj.* [< L *dens*, tooth] of or for the teeth or dentistry

dental floss thread for removing food particles from between the teeth

den·ti·frice (den′tə fris) *n.* [< L *dens*, tooth + *fricare*, rub] any preparation for cleaning teeth

den·tin (den′tin) *n.* [see DENTAL] the hard tissue under the enamel of a tooth: also **den′tine** (-tēn′, -tin)

den·tist (den′tist) *n.* one whose profession is the care and repair of teeth —**den′tist·ry** *n.*

den·ti·tion (den tish′ən) *n.* the arrangement of teeth in the mouth

den·ture (den′chər) *n.* [see DENTAL] [often *pl.*] a set of artificial teeth

de·nu·cle·ar·ize (dē noo′klē ər īz′) *vt.* **-ized′, -iz′ing** 1 to prohibit nuclear weapons in 2 to remove nuclear weapons from

de·nude (dē nood′) *vt.* **-nud′ed, -nud′ing** [< L *de-*, off + *nudare*, to strip] to make bare or naked; strip

de·nun·ci·a·tion (dē nun′sē ā′shən) *n.* [< L *de-*, intens. + *nuntiare*, announce] the act of denouncing

Den·ver (den′vər) capital of Colorado

de·ny (dē nī′) *vt.* **-nied′, -ny′ing** [< L *de-*, intens. + *negare*, to deny] 1 to declare (a statement) untrue 2 to refuse to accept as true or right 3 to repudiate 4 to refuse to grant or give 5 to refuse the request of

de·o·dor·ant (dē ō′dər ənt) *adj.* that can counteract undesired odors —*n.* any deodorant preparation, esp. one for use on the body

de·o·dor·ize (-dər īz′) *vt.* **-ized′, -iz′ing** to counteract the odor of —**de·o′dor·iz′er** *n.*

de·part (dē pärt′) *vi.* [< L *dis-*, apart + *partire*, divide] 1 to go away 2 to die 3 to deviate (*from*) —*vt.* to leave

de·part·ed *adj.* 1 gone away 2 dead —**the de·parted** the dead

de·part·ment (dē pärt′mənt) *n.* 1 a separate part or division, as of a business 2 a field of activity —**de·part·men′tal** (-ment′'l) *adj.*

de·part·men·tal·ize (-men′t'l īz′) *vt.* **-ized′, -iz′ing** to organize into departments —**de′part·men′tal·i·za′tion** *n.*

department store a large retail store for the sale of many kinds of goods arranged in departments

de·par·ture (dē pär′chər) *n.* **1** a departing **2** a starting out, as on a trip **3** a deviation (*from*)

de·pend (dē pend′) *vi.* [< L *de-*, down + *pendere*, to hang] **1** to be determined by something else; be contingent (*on*) **2** to have trust; rely (*on*) **3** to rely (*on*) for support or aid

de·pend·a·ble *adj.* trustworthy; reliable —**de·pend′a·bil′i·ty** *n.* —**de·pend′a·bly** *adv.*

de·pend·ence *n.* **1** a being dependent **2** reliance (*on*) for support or aid **3** reliance; trust **4** DEPENDENCY (*n.* 4)

de·pend·en·cy *n., pl.* **-cies 1** dependence **2** something dependent **3** a territory, as a possession, subordinate to its governing country **4** addiction to alcohol or drugs

de·pend·ent *adj.* **1** hanging down **2** determined by something else **3** relying (*on*) for support, etc. **4** subordinate **5** addicted —*n.* one relying on another for support, etc. Also **de·pend′ant** —**de·pend′ent·ly** *adv.*

dependent clause *Gram.* a clause that cannot function as a complete sentence by itself

de·pict (dē pikt′) *vt.* [< L *de-*, intens. + *pingere*, to paint] **1** to represent by drawing, painting, etc. **2** to describe —**de·pic′tion** *n.*

de·pil·a·to·ry (di pil′ə tôr′ē) *adj.* [< L *de-*, from *pilus*, hair] serving to remove unwanted hair —*n., pl.* **-ries** a depilatory substance or device

de·plane (dē plān′) *vi.* **-planed′, -plan′ing** to get out of an airplane after it lands

de·plete (dē plēt′) *vt.* **-plet′ed, -plet′ing** [< L *de-*, from + *plere*, fill] **1** to use up (funds, etc.) **2** to use up the resources, etc. of —**de·ple′tion** *n.*

de·plor·a·ble (dē plôr′ə bəl) *adj.* regrettable, very bad, wretched, etc.

de·plore (dē plôr′) *vt.* **-plored′, -plor′ing** [< L *de-*, intens. + *plorare*, weep] **1** to be sorry about **2** to disapprove of

de·ploy (dē ploi′) *vt.* [< L *dis-*, apart + *plicare*, to fold] **1** to spread out or position (troops, etc.) according to a plan **2** to bring forth for use, action, etc. —*vi.* to be deployed —**de·ploy′ment** *n.*

de·po·lar·ize (dē pō′lər īz′) *vt.* **-ized′, -iz′ing** to destroy or counteract the polarization of —**de·po′lar·i·za′tion** *n.*

de·po·lit·i·cize (dē pə lit′ə sīz′) *vt.* **-cized′, -ciz′ing** to remove from the influence of politics

de·pon·ent (dē pōn′ənt) *n.* [< L *de-*, down + *ponere*, put] *Law* one who makes a deposition

de·pop·u·late (dē päp′yə lāt′) *vt.* **-lat′ed, -lat′ing** to reduce the population of —**de·pop′u·la′tion** *n.*

de·port (dē pôrt′) *vt.* [< L *de-*, from + *portare*, carry] **1** to conduct (oneself) in a specified way **2** to expel (a citizen of another country) —**de′por·ta′tion** *n.*

de·port·ment *n.* conduct; behavior

de·pose (dē pōz′) *vt.* **-posed′, -pos′ing** [< OFr *de-*, from + *poser*, cease] **1** to remove from office **2** *Law* to take the deposition of

de·pos·it (dē päz′it) *vt.* [< L *de-*, down + *ponere*, put] **1** to place (money, etc.) for safekeeping, as in a bank **2** to give as a collateral or partial payment **3** to put or set down **4** to cause (sediment, etc.) to settle —*n.* **1** something placed for safekeeping, as money in a bank **2** a collateral or partial payment **3** a natural accumulation, as of minerals —**de·pos′i·tor** *n.*

dep·o·si·tion (dep′ə zish′ən) *n.* **1** a deposing or being deposed, as from office **2** something deposited **3** *Law* testimony made under oath that is written down for later use

de·pos·i·to·ry (dē päz′ə tôr′ē) *n., pl.* **-ries** a place where things are put for safekeeping

de·pot (dē′pō; *military & Brit* dep′ō) *n.* [< Fr: see DEPOSIT] **1** a warehouse **2** a railroad or bus station **3** a storage place for military supplies

de·prave (dē prāv′) *vt.* **-praved′, -prav′ing** [< L *de-*, intens. + *pravus*, crooked] to make morally bad; corrupt —**de·praved′** *adj.* —**de·prav′i·ty** (-prav′ə tē) *n., pl.* **-ties**

dep·re·cate (dep′rə kāt′) *vt.* **-cat′ed, -cat′ing** [< L *de-*, off + *precari*, pray] **1** to express disapproval of **2** to belittle —**dep′re·ca′tion** *n.* —**dep′re·ca·to′ry** (-kə tôr′ē) *adj.*

de·pre·ci·ate (dē prē′shē āt′) *vt., vi.* **-at′ed, -at′ing** [< L *de-*, from + *pretium*, price] **1** to lessen in value or price **2** to belittle —**de·pre′ci·a′tion** *n.*

dep·re·da·tion (dep′rə dā′shən) *n.* [< L *de-*, intens. + *praedari*, to plunder] a robbing or plundering

de·press (dē pres′) *vt.* [< L *de-*, down + *premere*, to press] **1** to press down **2** to sadden or discourage **3** to weaken or make less active **4** to lower in value, price, etc. —**de·pressed′** *adj.*

de·pres·sant *n.* a medicine, drug, etc. that lessens nervous activity

de·pres·sion (dē presh′ən) *n.* **1** a depressing or being depressed **2** a hollow or low place **3** low spirits; dejection **4** a condition marked by hopelessness, self-doubt, lethargy, etc. **5** a decrease in force, activity, etc. **6** an extended period of reduced business, much unemployment, etc.

de·pres·sive (dē pres′iv) *adj.* **1** tending to depress **2** characterized by psychological depression —*n.* one suffering from psychological depression

de·pres·sur·ize (dē presh′ər īz′) *vt.* **-ized′, -iz′ing** to reduce pressure in

de·prive (dē prīv′) *vt.* **-prived′, -priv′ing** [< L *de-*, intens. + *privare*, to separate] **1** to take away from forcibly **2** to keep from having, etc. —**dep·ri·va·tion** (dep′rə vā′shən) *n.*

de·pro·gram (dē prō′gram′, -grəm) *vt.* **-grammed′** or **-gramed′, -gram′ming** or **-gram′ing** to cause to abandon rigidly held beliefs, etc. by undoing the effects of indoctrination

dept *abbrev.* **1** department **2** deputy

depth (depth) *n.* 〖< ME *dep*, deep + -TH¹〗 **1** the distance from the top downward, or from front to back **2** deepness **3** intensity **4** profundity of thought **5** [*usually pl.*] the deepest or inmost part —**in depth** comprehensively

dep·u·ta·tion (dep′yŏŏ tā′shən) *n.* **1** a deputing **2** a delegation

de·pute (dē pyŏŏt′) *vt.* -put′ed, -put′ing 〖< L *de*-, from + *putare*, cleanse〗 **1** to give (authority, etc.) to a deputy **2** to appoint as one's substitute, etc.

dep·u·tize (dep′yŏŏ tiz′) *vt.* -tized′, -tiz′ing to appoint as deputy

dep·u·ty (dep′yŏŏ tē) *n., pl.* -ties a person appointed to act as a substitute or assistant, as for law enforcement

de·rail (dē rāl′) *vt., vi.* to run off the rails, as a train —**de·rail′ment** *n.*

de·rail·leur (də rāl′ər) *n.* 〖Fr〗 a mechanism on a bicycle for shifting the chain from one sprocket wheel to another

de·range (dē rānj′) *vt.* -ranged′, -rang′ing 〖< OFr *des*-, apart + *rengier*, to range〗 **1** to upset or disturb **2** to make insane —**de·range′ment** *n.*

Der·by (dur′bē; *Brit* där′-) *n., pl.* -bies **1** [after an Earl of *Derby*, who founded the race held in England] any of various horse races, as ones held annually in England, Kentucky, etc. **2** [d-] any of various contests or races, open to anyone **3** [d-] a stiff felt hat with a round crown

de·reg·u·late (dē reg′yə lāt′) *vt.* -lat′ed, -lat′ing to remove regulations governing —**de·reg′u·la′tion** *n.*

der·e·lict (der′ə likt′) *adj.* 〖< L *de*-, intens. + *relinquere*: see RELINQUISH〗 **1** deserted by the owner; abandoned **2** negligent —*n.* **1** an abandoned ship on the open sea **2** a destitute and rejected person

der·e·lic·tion (-lik′shən) *n.* **1** a forsaking or being forsaken **2** a neglect of, or failure in, duty

de·ride (di rīd′) *vt.* -rid′ed, -rid′ing 〖< L *de*-, down + *ridere*, to laugh〗 to ridicule —**de·ri′sion** (-rizh′ən) *n.* —**de·ri′sive** (-rī′siv) *adj.* —**de·ri′sive·ly** *adv.*

der·i·va·tion (der′ə vā′shən) *n.* **1** a deriving or being derived **2** the source or origin of something, specif. of a word

de·riv·a·tive (də riv′ə tiv) *adj.* derived; specif., not original or novel —*n.* something derived

de·rive (di rīv′) *vt.* -rived′, -riv′ing 〖< L *de*-, from + *rivus*, a stream〗 **1** to get or receive (something) *from* a source **2** to deduce or infer **3** to trace from or to a source —*vi.* to come (*from*)

der·ma·bra·sion (dur′mə brā′zhən) *n.* 〖DERM(IS) + ABRASION〗 the surgical procedure of scraping off upper layers of the skin to remove acne scars, etc.

der·ma·ti·tis (dur′mə tīt′is) *n.* 〖< Gr *derma*, skin + -ITIS〗 inflammation of the skin

der·ma·tol·o·gy (dur′mə täl′ə jē) *n.* 〖< Gr *derma*, skin + -LOGY〗 the branch of medicine dealing with the skin —**der′ma·tol′o·gist** *n.*

der·mis (dur′mis) *n.* 〖see EPIDERMIS〗 the layer of skin just below the epidermis

der·o·gate (der′ə gāt′) *vi., vt.* -gat′ed, -gat′ing 〖< L *de*-, from + *rogare*, ask〗 to detract (*from*) or disparage —**der′o·ga′tion** *n.*

de·rog·a·to·ry (di räg′ə tôr′ē) *adj.* 〖see prec.〗 disparaging; belittling —**de·rog′a·to′ri·ly** *adv.*

der·rick (der′ik) *n.* 〖after Thos. *Derrick*, London hangman of the early 1600s: orig. applied to a gallows〗 **1** a pivoted beam for lifting and moving heavy objects **2** a tall framework, as over an oil well, to support drilling machinery, etc.

der·ri·ère (der′ē er′) *n.* 〖Fr, back part〗 the buttocks

der·rin·ger (der′in jər) *n.* 〖after H. *Deringer* (1786–1868), U.S. gunsmith〗 a small, short-barreled pistol

der·vish (dur′vish) *n.* 〖< Pers *darvēsh*, beggar〗 a member of any of various Muslim ascetic religious groups

de·sal·i·na·tion (dē′sal′ə nā′shən) *n.* 〖DE- + SALIN(E) + -ATION〗 the removal of salt, esp. from sea water to make it drinkable —**de′sal′i·nate′** *vt.* -nat′ed, -nat′ing

Des·cartes (dā kärt′), **Re·né** (rə nā′) 1596–1650; Fr. philosopher

de·scend (dē send′) *vi.* 〖< L *de*-, down + *scandere*, climb〗 **1** to move down to a lower place **2** to pass from an earlier to a later time, from greater to less, etc. **3** to slope downward **4** to come down (*from* a source) **5** to lower oneself or stoop (*to*) **6** to make a sudden raid (*on* or *upon*) —*vt.* to move down along

de·scend·ant (-sen′dənt) *n.* an offspring of a certain ancestor, family, group, etc.

de·scent (-sent′) *n.* **1** a coming down or going down **2** ancestry **3** a downward slope **4** a way down **5** a sudden attack (*on* or *upon*) **6** a decline

de·scribe (di skrīb′) *vt.* -scribed′, -scrib′ing 〖< L *de*-, from + *scribere*, write〗 **1** to tell or write about **2** to trace the outline of —**de·scrib′er** *n.*

de·scrip·tion (di skrip′shən) *n.* **1** the act or technique of describing **2** a statement or passage that describes **3** sort; kind [books of every *description*] —**de·scrip′tive** *adj.*

de·scry (di skrī′) *vt.* -scried′, -scry′ing 〖< OFr *descrier*, proclaim〗 **1** to catch sight of; discern **2** to detect

des·e·crate (des′i krāt′) *vt.* -crat′ed, -crat′ing 〖DE-(CON)SECRATE〗 to violate the sacredness of; profane —**des′e·cra′tion** *n.*

de·seg·re·gate (dē seg′rə gāt′) *vt., vi.* -gat′ed, -gat′ing to abolish segregation, esp. racial segregation, in (public schools, etc.) —**de·seg′re·ga′tion** *n.*

de·sen·si·tize (dē sen′sə tiz′) *vt.* -tized′, -tiz′ing to make less sensitive, as to an allergen

de·sert¹ (di zurt′) *vt., vi.* 〖< L *de*-, from + *serere*, join〗 **1** to abandon; forsake **2** to leave (one's military post, etc.) without permission and with no intent to return —**de·sert′er** *n.* —**de·ser′tion** (-zur′shən) *n.*

des·ert² (dez′ərt) *n.* [see prec.] 1 an uninhabited region; wilderness 2 a dry, barren region, often one that is hot —*adj.* uninhabited [a *desert* island]

de·sert³ (di zurt′) *n.* [see fol.] [*often pl.*] deserved reward or punishment [one's just *deserts*]

de·serve (di zurv′) *vt., vi.* -served′, -serv′ing [< L *de-*, intens. + *servire*, serve] to be worthy (of); merit —**de·serv′ed·ly** (-zur′vid lē) *adv.*

des·ic·cate (des′i kāt′) *vt., vi.* -cat′ed, -cat′ing [< L *de-*, intens. + *siccus*, dry] to dry out completely —**des·ic·ca′tion** *n.*

de·sid·er·a·tum (di sid′ə rāt′əm) *n., pl.* -ta (-ə) [see DESIRE] something needed and wanted

de·sign (di zīn′) *vt.* [< L *de-*, out + *signum*, a mark] 1 to sketch an outline for; plan 2 to contrive 3 to intend —*vi.* to make original plans, etc. —*n.* 1 a plan; scheme 2 purpose; aim 3 a working plan; pattern 4 arrangement of parts, form, color, etc. —**by design** purposely —**de·sign′er** *n.*

des·ig·nate (dez′ig nāt′) *vt.* -nat′ed, -nat′ing [see prec.] 1 to point out; specify 2 to name 3 to appoint —**des′ig·na′tion** *n.*

designated driver the one in a group who refrains from drinking alcoholic beverages so as to be able to safely transport the others in a motor vehicle

de·sign·ing *adj.* scheming; crafty —*n.* the art of creating designs, etc.

de·sir·a·ble (di zīr′ə bəl) *adj.* 1 worth having 2 arousing desire —**de·sir′a·bil′i·ty** *n.* —**de·sir′a·bly** *adv.*

de·sire (di zīr′) *vt.* -sired′, -sir′ing [< L *desiderare*] 1 to long for 2 to ask for —*vi.* to have a desire —*n.* 1 a wish; craving 2 sexual appetite 3 a request 4 a thing desired —**de·sir′ous** *adj.*

de·sist (di zist′, -sist′) *vi.* [< L *de-*, from + *stare*, to stand] to cease; stop

desk (desk) *n.* [< ML *desca*, table] a piece of furniture with a flat surface for writing, etc. —*adj.* of, for, or at a desk [a *desk* job]

desk·top *n., adj.* (equipment, as a microcomputer) for use on a desk or table

desktop publishing the production of printed matter by means of a computer and special software for laying out text and illustrations

Des Moines (də moin′) capital of Iowa

des·o·late (des′ə lit; *for v.*, -lāt′) *adj.* [< L *de-*, intens. + *solus*, alone] 1 lonely; solitary 2 uninhabited 3 laid waste 4 forlorn —*vt.* -lat′ed, -lat′ing 1 to rid of inhabitants 2 to lay waste 3 to make forlorn

des·o·la·tion *n.* 1 a making desolate 2 a desolate condition or place 3 misery 4 loneliness

de·spair (di sper′) *vi.* [< L *de-*, without + *sperare*, to hope] to lose hope —*n.* 1 loss of hope 2 a person or thing causing despair

des·patch (di spach′) *n.* DISPATCH

des·per·a·do (des′pər ä′dō, -ā′-) *n., pl.* -does or -dos [< Sp < L *desperare:* see DESPAIR] a dangerous criminal; bold outlaw

des·per·ate (des′pər it) *adj.* 1 rash or violent because of despair 2 having a very great need 3 very serious, dangerous, etc. 4 drastic —**des′per·ate·ly** *adv.*

des·per·a·tion (des′pər ā′shən) *n.* 1 the state of being desperate 2 recklessness resulting from despair

des·pi·ca·ble (di spik′ə bəl) *adj.* deserving scorn; contemptible

de·spise (di spīz′) *vt.* -spised′, -spis′ing [< L *de*, down + *specere*, look at] 1 to scorn 2 to loathe

de·spite (di spīt′) *prep.* [see prec.] in spite of; notwithstanding

de·spoil (dē spoil′) *vt.* [< L *de-*, intens. + *spoliare*, to strip] to rob; plunder —**de·spo·li·a·tion** (di spō′lē ā′shən) *n.*

de·spond·en·cy (di spän′dən sē) *n.* [< L *de-*, from + *spondere*, to promise] loss of hope; dejection: also **de·spond′ence** —**de·spond′ent** *adj.*

des·pot (des′pət) *n.* [< Gr *despotēs*, a master] 1 an absolute ruler 2 anyone like a tyrant —**des·pot′ic** (-pät′ik) *adj.* —**des′pot·ism′** (-pə tiz′əm) *n.*

des·sert (di zurt′) *n.* [< L *de*, from + *servire*, serve] the final course of a meal, typically cake, pie, or some other sweet food

des·ti·na·tion (des′tə nā′shən) *n.* the place toward which one is going or sent

des·tine (des′tin) *vt.* -tined, -tin·ing [< L *de-*, intens. + *stare*, to stand] 1 to predetermine, as by fate 2 to intend —**destined for** 1 headed for 2 intended for

des·ti·ny (des′tə nē) *n., pl.* -nies 1 the seemingly inevitable succession of events 2 (one's) fate

des·ti·tute (des′tə tōōt′) *adj.* [< L *de-*, down + *statuere*, to set] 1 lacking: with *of* 2 totally impoverished —**des′ti·tu′tion** *n.*

de·stroy (di stroi′) *vt.* [< L *de-*, down + *struere*, to build] 1 to tear down; demolish 2 to ruin 3 to do away with 4 to kill

de·stroy·er *n.* 1 one that destroys 2 a small, fast warship

de·struct (di strukt′, dē′strukt′) *vi.* [< fol.] to be automatically destroyed

de·struc·tion (di struk′shən) *n.* 1 a destroying or being destroyed 2 the cause or means of destroying —**de·struc′tive** *adj.* —**de·struc′tive·ly** *adv.* —**de·struc′tive·ness** *n.*

des·ue·tude (des′wi tōōd′) *n.* [< L *de-*, from + *suescere*, be accustomed] a state of disuse

des·ul·to·ry (des′əl tôr′ē) *adj.* [< L *de-*, from + *salire*, to leap] 1 aimless; disconnected 2 random

de·tach (dē tach′) *vt.* [< Fr: see DE- & ATTACH] 1 to unfasten and remove; disconnect; disengage 2 to send (troops, etc.) on a special mission —**de·tach′a·ble** *adj.*

de·tached *adj.* 1 not connected 2 aloof; disinterested; impartial

de·tach·ment *n.* 1 a detaching 2 a unit of troops, etc. on a special mission 3 impartiality or aloofness

de·tail (di tāl′, dē′tāl′) *n.* [< Fr < *dé-*, from

+ *tailler*, to cut] **1** a dealing with things item by item **2** a minute account [to go into *detail*] **3** a small part; item **4** *a)* one or more soldiers, etc. on special duty *b)* the duty —*vt.* **1** to tell, item by item **2** to assign to special duty **3** to clean (a car, etc.) with special attention to details —**in detail** with particulars

de·tain (dē tān′) *vt.* [< L *de-*, off + *tenere*, to hold] **1** to keep in custody; confine **2** to keep from going on —**de·tain·ee′** (-ē′) *n.* —**de·tain′ment** *n.*

de·tect (dē tekt′) *vt.* [< L *de-*, from + *tegere*, to cover] to discover (something hidden, not clear, etc.) —**de·tect′a·ble** *adj.*, **de·tect′i·ble** —**de·tec′tion** *n.* —**de·tec′tor** *n.*

de·tec·tive (-tek′tiv) *n.* one whose work is to investigate crimes, uncover evidence, etc.

dé·tente or **de·tente** (dā tänt′) *n.* [Fr] a lessening of tension, esp. between nations

de·ten·tion (dē ten′shən) *n.* **1** a detaining or being detained **2** the punishment of having to stay after school

de·ter (dē tur′) *vt.* **-terred′**, **-ter′ring** [< L *de-*, from + *terrere*, frighten] to keep or discourage (a person or group) from doing something through fear, doubt, etc. —**de·ter′ment** *n.* —**de·ter′rence** *n.*

de·ter·gent (dē tur′jənt) *adj.* [< L *de-*, off + *tergere*, wipe] cleansing —*n.* a cleansing substance that emulsifies dirt and oil

de·te·ri·o·rate (dē tir′ē ə rāt′) *vt.*, *vi.* **-rat′ed**, **-rat′ing** [< L *deterior*, worse] to make or become worse —**de·te′ri·o·ra′tion** *n.*

de·ter·mi·nant (dē tur′mi nənt) *n.* a thing or factor that determines

de·ter·mi·nate (-nit) *adj.* clearly determined; fixed; settled

de·ter·mi·na·tion (-nā′shən) *n.* **1** a determining or being determined **2** a firm intention **3** firmness of purpose

de·ter·mine (-mən) *vt.* **-mined**, **-min·ing** [< L *de-*, from + *terminus*, a limit] **1** to set limits to **2** to settle conclusively **3** to decide or decide upon **4** to affect the nature or quality of **5** to find out exactly —*vi.* to decide —**de·ter′mi·na·ble** *adj.*

de·ter·mined (-mənd) *adj.* **1** having one's mind made up **2** resolute; firm

de·ter·rent *adj.* deterring —*n.* something that deters

de·test (dē test′) *vt.* [< L *detestari*, to curse by the gods] to dislike intensely; hate —**de·test′a·ble** *adj.* —**de·tes·ta·tion** (-tes tā′shən) *n.* —**de·test′er** *n.*

de·thatch (dē thach′) *vt.* to remove the dead blades of grass from (a lawn)

de·throne (dē thrōn′) *vt.* **-throned′**, **-thron′ing** to depose (a monarch)

det·o·nate (det′′n āt′) *vi.*, *vt.* **-nat′ed**, **-nat′ing** [< L *de-*, intens. + *tonare*, to thunder] to explode violently —**det′o·na′tion** *n.* —**det′o·na′tor** *n.*

de·tour (dē′toor′) *n.* [< Fr: see DE- & TURN] **1** a roundabout way **2** a substitute route —*vi.*, *vt.* to go or route on a detour

de·tox (dē täks′; *for n.* dē′täks′) [Inf.] *vt.* short for DETOXIFY —*n.* short for DETOXIFICATION

de·tox·i·fy (dē täk′si fī′) *vt.* **-fied′**, **-fy′ing** [DE- + TOXI(N) + -FY] **1** to remove a poison or poisonous effect from **2** to treat for drug or alcohol addiction —**de·tox′i·fi·ca′tion** *n.*

de·tract (dē trakt′) *vt.* [< L *de-*, from + *trahere*, to draw] to take away —*vi.* to take something desirable (*from*) —**de·trac′tion** *n.*

de·trac·tor (-trak′tər) *n.* one who disparages

det·ri·ment (de′trə mənt) *n.* [< L *de-*, off + *terere*, to rub] **1** damage; injury **2** anything that causes this —**det′ri·men′tal** (-ment′'l) *adj.*

de·tri·tus (dē trīt′əs) *n.* [L, a rubbing away: see prec.] debris, specif. rock fragments

De·troit (di troit′) city & port in SE Michigan

deuce (dōōs) *n.* [< L *duo*, two] **1** a playing card or side of a die with two spots **2** *Tennis, Badminton, etc.* a tie score after which one side must score twice in a row to win

deu·te·ri·um (dōō tir′ē əm) *n.* [< Gr *deuteros*, second] a hydrogen isotope whose nucleus has one proton and one neutron

Deu·ter·on·o·my (dōōt′ər än′ə mē) *n.* [< Gr *deuteros*, second + *nomos*, law] the fifth book of the Pentateuch

deutsche mark (doich′ märk′) the former monetary unit of Germany: also written **deutsche′mark′**

de·val·ue (dē val′yōō) *vt.* **-ued**, **-u·ing** **1** to lessen the value of **2** to lower the exchange value of (a currency) —**de·val′u·a′tion** *n.*

dev·as·tate (dev′ə stāt′) *vt.* **-tat′ed**, **-tat′ing** [< L *de-*, intens. + *vastus*, empty] **1** to lay waste; ravage; destroy **2** to make helpless; overwhelm —**dev′as·ta′tion** *n.* —**dev′as·ta′tor** *n.*

de·vel·op (di vel′əp) *vt.* [< OFr *des-*, apart + *voloper*, to wrap] **1** to make fuller, bigger, better, etc. **2** to show or work out by degrees **3** to enlarge upon **4** *Photog.* to put (film, etc.) into chemicals to make the picture visible —*vi.* **1** to come into being or activity; occur **2** to become developed —**de·vel′op·er** *n.* —**de·vel′op·ment** *n.* —**de·vel′op·men′tal** (-ment′'l) *adj.*

de·vi·ant (dē′vē ənt) *adj.* deviating, esp. from what is considered normal —*n.* one whose behavior is deviant —**de′vi·ance** *n.*, **de′vi·an·cy** *n.*

de·vi·ate (dē′vē āt′; *for adj. & n.*, -it) *vi.* **-at′ed**, **-at′ing** [< L *de-*, from + *via*, road] to turn aside (*from* a course, standard, etc.); diverge —*adj.* DEVIANT —*n.* a deviant, esp. in sexual behavior —**de′vi·a′tion** *n.* —**de′vi·a′tor** *n.*

de·vice (di vīs′) *n.* [see DEVISE] **1** a plan, scheme, or trick **2** a mechanical contrivance **3** an ornamental figure or design **4** an emblem, as on a coat of arms —**leave to one's own devices** to allow to do as one wishes

dev·il (dev′əl) *n.* [ult. < Gr *diabolos*, slanderous] **1** *Theol. a)* [often D-] the chief evil spirit; Satan (with *the*) *b)* any evil spirit; demon **2** a very wicked person **3** a person who is mischievous, reckless, unlucky, etc. **4**

anything hard to operate, control, etc. —*vt.* **-iled** or **-illed**, **-il·ing** or **-il·ling 1** to prepare (food) with hot seasoning **2** to annoy; tease —**dev′il·ish** *adj.*

dev·il·fish *n., pl.* **-fish′** or **fish′es** MANTA

dev·il-may-care *adj.* careless or reckless

dev·il·ment *n.* mischievous action

devil's-advocate a person upholding a contrary viewpoint for argument's sake

devil's-food cake a rich chocolate cake

dev·il·try (-trē) *n., pl.* **-tries** reckless mischief

de·vi·ous (dē′vē əs) *adj.* [< L *de-*, off + *via*, road] **1** not direct; roundabout or deviating **2** not straightforward; dishonest —**de′vi·ous·ness** *n.*

de·vise (di vīz′) *vt., vi.* **-vised′**, **-vis′ing** [< L *dividere*, to divide] **1** to work out or create (a plan, device, etc.) **2** *Law* to bequeath (real property) by a will —*n. Law* a bequest of property

de·vi·tal·ize (dē vīt′'l īz′) *vt.* **-ized′**, **-iz′ing** to deprive of vitality

de·void (di void′) *adj.* [see DE- & VOID] completely without; empty (*of*)

de·volve (di välv′, vôlv′) *vt., vi.* **-volved′**, **-volv′ing** [< L *de-*, down + *volvere*, to roll] **1** to pass (*on*) to another: said of duties, responsibilities, etc. **2** to degenerate —**dev·o·lu·tion** (dev′ə loo̅′shən) *n.*

de·vote (di vōt′) *vt.* **-vot′ed**, **-vot′ing** [< L *de-*, from + *vovere*, to vow] to set apart for or give up to some purpose, activity, or person; dedicate

de·vot·ed (-id) *adj.* very loving, loyal, or faithful —**de·vot′ed·ly** *adv.*

dev·o·tee (dev′ə tē′, -tā′) *n.* one who is strongly devoted to something

de·vo·tion (di vō′shən) *n.* **1** a devoting or being devoted to **2** piety **3** religious worship **4** [*often pl.*] one or more prayers, etc. **5** loyalty or deep affection —**de·vo′tion·al** *adj.*

de·vour (di vour′) *vt.* [< L *de-*, intens. + *vorare*, swallow whole] **1** to eat hungrily **2** to swallow up **3** to take in greedily, as with the eyes

de·vout (di vout′) *adj.* [see DEVOTE] **1** very religious; pious **2** earnest; sincere —**de·vout′ly** *adv.*

dew (doo) *n.* [OE *deaw*] **1** atmospheric moisture condensed in drops on cool surfaces at night **2** anything refreshing, pure, etc., like dew —**dew′y** *adj.* **-i·er**, **-i·est**

dew·ber·ry *n., pl.* **-ries 1** a trailing blackberry plant **2** its fruit

dew·drop *n.* a drop of dew

dew·lap *n.* [see DEW & LAP[1]] a loose flap of skin under the throat of certain cattle, etc.

dew point the temperature at which water vapor in the air starts to condense into liquid

dex·ter·i·ty (deks ter′ə tē) *n.* [see fol.] skill in using one's hands, body, or mind

dex·ter·ous (deks′tər əs, -trəs) *adj.* [< L *dexter*, right] having or showing dexterity: also **dex′trous**

dex·trose (deks′trōs′) *n.* a glucose found in plants and animals

Dhak·a (däk′ə, dak′ə) capital of Bangladesh

dho·ti (dō′tē) *n.* [Hindi *dhotī*] a loincloth worn by Hindu men

dhur·rie (dʉr′ē, du̇r′ē) *n.* a coarse rug woven in India

di-[1] [Gr *di-* < *dis-*, twice] *prefix* twice, double, twofold

di-[2] *prefix* DIS-

di·a·be·tes (dī′ə bēt′ēz′, -is) *n.* [< Gr *diabainein*, to pass through] a disease caused by an insulin deficiency and characterized by excess sugar in the blood and urine: also **sugar diabetes** —**di′a·bet′ic** (-bet′ik) *adj., n.*

di·a·bol·ic (dī′ə bäl′ik) *adj.* [see DEVIL] very wicked or cruel; fiendish: also **di′a·bol′i·cal**

di·a·crit·i·cal mark (dī′ə krit′i kəl) [< Gr *dia-*, across + *krinein*, discern] a mark, as a macron, put on a letter or symbol to show pronunciation, etc.: also **di′a·crit′ic** *n.*

di·a·dem (dī′ə dem′) *n.* [< Gr *diadēma*, a band, fillet] **1** a crown **2** an ornamental headband

di·ag·nose (dī′əg nōs′) *vt., vi.* **-nosed′**, **-nos′ing** to make a diagnosis (of)

di·ag·no·sis (-nō′sis) *n., pl.* **-ses′** (-sēz′) [< Gr *dia-*, through + *gignoskein*, to know] **1** the act of deciding the nature of a disease, situation, problem, etc. by examination and analysis **2** the resulting decision —**di′ag·nos′tic** (-näs′tik) *adj.* —**di′ag·nos·ti′cian** (-tish′ən) *n.*

di·ag·o·nal (dī ag′ə nəl, -ag′nəl) *adj.* [< Gr *dia-*, through + *gōnia*, an angle] **1** extending slantingly between opposite corners **2** slanting; oblique —*n.* a diagonal line, plane, course, part, etc. —**di·ag′o·nal·ly** *adv.*

di·a·gram (dī′ə gram′) *n.* [< Gr *dia-*, across + *graphein*, write] a sketch, plan, graph, etc. that explains something, as by outlining its parts —*vt.* **-gramed′** or **-grammed′**, **-gram′ing** or **-gram′ming** to make a diagram of

di·al (dī′əl) *n.* [< L *dies*, day] **1** the face of a clock, etc. **2** the face of a meter, etc., for indicating, as by a pointer, an amount, direction, etc. **3** a graduated knob, etc., as on a radio for tuning in stations, etc. **4** a rotating disk on a telephone, formerly used to make automatic connections — *vt., vi.* **-aled** or **-alled**, **-al·ing** or **-al·ling 1** to tune in (a radio station, etc.) **2** to call using a telephone

dial[2] *abbrev.* **1** dialect(al) **2** dialectic(al)

di·a·lect (dī′ə lekt′) *n.* [< Gr *dia*, between + *legein*, to talk] the form of a spoken language peculiar to a region, social group, etc. —**di′a·lec′tal** *adj.*

di·a·lec·tic (dī′ə lek′tik) *n.* **1** [*often pl.*] the practice of examining ideas logically **2** logical argumentation —*adj.* DIALECTICAL

di·a·lec·ti·cal (-ti kəl) *adj.* **1** of or using dialectic **2** of a dialect

di·a·logue (dī′ə lôg′, -läg′) *n.* [see DIALECT] **1** interchange of ideas by open discussion **2** the passages of talk in a play, story, etc. Also sp. **di′a·log′**

di·al·y·sis (dī al′ə sis) *n., pl.* **-ses′** (-sēz′) [< Gr *dia-*, apart + *lyein*, dissolve] the separation of smaller dissolved molecules from the larger molecules in a solution by diffusion through a membrane: used in purifying the blood of those with impaired kidney function

di·am·e·ter (dī am′ət ər) *n.* [< Gr *dia-*, through + *metron*, a measure] 1 a line segment passing through the center of a circle, sphere, etc. from one side to the other 2 its length

di·a·met·ri·cal (dī′ə me′tri kəl) *adj.* designating an opposite, a difference, etc. that is wholly so; complete

di·a·mond (dī′mənd, dī′ə mənd) *n.* [< Gr *adamas*] 1 nearly pure, colorless, crystalline carbon, the hardest mineral known, used for gems or cutting tools 2 a gem or other piece cut from this 3 *a)* a conventionalized figure of a diamond (◇) *b)* any of a suit of playing cards marked with such figures in red 4 *Baseball* the infield or the whole field —*adj.* 1 of a diamond 2 marking the 60th, or sometimes 75th, year

di·a·mond·back *n.* a large, poisonous rattlesnake of the S U.S.

Di·an·a (dī an′ə) *n. Rom. Myth.* the goddess of the moon and of hunting

di·a·pa·son (dī′ə pā′zən) *n.* [< Gr *dia*, through + *pas*, all] an organ stop covering the instrument's entire range

di·a·per (dī′pər, dī′ə pər) *n.* [< ML *diasprum*, flowered cloth] a soft, absorbent pad of cloth or other material arranged between the legs and around the waist, as of a baby —*vt.* to put a diaper on (a baby)

di·aph·a·nous (dī af′ə nəs) *adj.* [< Gr *dia-*, through + *phainein*, to show] transparent or translucent

di·a·phragm (dī′ə fram′) *n.* [< Gr *dia-*, through + *phragma*, fence] 1 the muscular partition between the chest cavity and abdominal cavity 2 a vibrating disk producing sound waves, as in a telephone receiver 3 a vaginal contraceptive device

di·ar·rhe·a (dī′ə rē′ə) *n.* [< Gr *dia-*, through + *rhein*, to flow] too frequent and loose bowel movements: chiefly Brit. sp. **di′ar·rhoe′a**

di·a·ry (dī′ə rē) *n., pl.* **-ries** [< L *dies*, day] a daily written record of the writer's experiences, etc. —**di′a·rist** *n.*

di·a·stase (dī′ə stās′) *n.* [< Gr *dia*, apart + *histanai*, stand] an enzyme in the seed of grains and malt capable of changing starches into dextrose

di·as·to·le (dī as′tə lē′) *n.* [< Gr *dia-*, apart + *stellein*, put] the usual rhythmic expansion of the heart —**di·a·stol·ic** (dī′ə stäl′ik) *adj.*

di·a·ther·my (dī′ə thur′mē) *n.* [< Gr *dia-*, through + *thermē*, heat] medical treatment by means of heat produced under the skin, as by high-frequency electric current

di·a·tom (dī′ə täm′) *n.* [< Gr *diatomos*, cut in two] any of various microscopic algae that are an important source of food for marine life

di·a·tom·ic (dī′ə täm′ik) *adj.* [DI-¹ + ATOMIC] having two atoms or radicals in the molecule

di·a·ton·ic (dī′ə tän′ik) *adj.* [< Gr *dia-*, through + *teinein*, to stretch] *Music* designating or of a scale of eight tones, esp. a MAJOR SCALE or a MINOR SCALE

di·a·tribe (dī′ə trīb′) *n.* [< Gr *dia-*, through + *tribein*, to rub] a bitter, abusive denunciation

dib·ble (dib′əl) *n.* [ME *dibbel*] a pointed tool used for making holes in the soil

dice (dīs) *pl.n., sing.* **die** or **dice** [see DIE²] small cubes marked on each side with a different number of spots (from one to six), used in games of chance —*vi.* **diced, dic′ing** to play or gamble with dice —*vt.* to cut (vegetables, etc.) into small cubes —**no dice** [Inf.] 1 no: used in refusing a request 2 no luck

di·chot·o·my (dī kät′ə mē) *n., pl.* **-mies** [< Gr *dicha*, in two + *temnein*, to cut] division into two parts or groups

dick (dik) *n.* [Slang] a detective

Dick·ens (dik′ənz), **Charles** (chärlz) (pseud. *Boz*) 1812-70; Eng. novelist —**Dick·en′si·an** *adj.*

dick·er (dik′ər) *vi.* [ult. < L *decem*, ten] to bargain or haggle

dick·ey (dik′ē) *n., pl.* **-eys** [< nickname *Dick*] 1 a detachable shirt front 2 a small bird: also **dickey bird** Also **dick′y,** *pl.* **-ies**

Dick·in·son (dik′in sən), **Em·i·ly** (em′ə lē) 1830-86; U.S. poet

di·cot·y·le·don (dī′kät′ə lēd′'n) *n.* a plant with two seed leaves (*cotyledons*): also **di′cot′** —**di′cot′y·le′don·ous** *adj.*

Dic·ta·phone (dik′tə fōn′) *trademark for* a machine that records and plays back speech for typed transcripts, etc. —*n.* [*sometimes* **d-**] any such machine

dic·tate (dik′tāt′) *vt., vi.* **-tat′ed, -tat′ing** [< L *dicere*, speak] 1 to speak (something) aloud for someone else to write down 2 to command forcefully 3 to give (orders) with authority —*n.* 1 an authoritative order 2 an imposed constraint or requirement —**dic·ta′tion** *n.*

dic·ta·tor *n.* one who dictates; esp., a ruler or tyrant with absolute power —**dic′ta·to′ri·al** (-tə tôr′ē əl) *adj.* —**dic·ta′tor·ship′** *n.*

dic·tion (dik′shən) *n.* [< L *dicere*, say] 1 manner of expression in words; wording 2 enunciation

dic·tion·ar·y (dik′shə ner′ē) *n., pl.* **-ar′ies** [see prec.] a book of alphabetically listed words in a language, with definitions, pronunciations, etymologies, etc.

dic·tum (dik′təm) *n., pl.* **-tums** or **-ta** (-tə) [< L *dicere*, say] a formal statement of opinion; pronouncement

did (did) *vt., vi. pt. of* DO¹

di·dac·tic (dī dak′tik) *adj.* [< Gr *didaskein*, teach] 1 intended for instruction 2 morally instructive

did·dle (did′'l) *vt., vi.* **-dled, -dling** [< ?] [Inf.] 1 to cheat 2 to waste (time) in trifling —**did′dler** *n.*

di·do (dī′dō) *n., pl.* **-does** or **-dos** [< ?] [Inf.] a mischievous or foolish action

die¹ (dī) *vi.* **died, dy′ing** [< ON *deyja*] 1 to stop living 2 to stop functioning; end 3 to lose force or activity 4 [Inf.] to wish very much [I'm *dying* to go] —**die away (or down)**

to cease gradually —**die off** to die one by one until all are gone —**die out** to stop existing

die² (dī) *n., pl.* for 2, **dies** (dīz) ⟦< L *dare*, give⟧ **1** *sing.* of DICE **2** a tool for shaping, punching, etc. metal or other material

die-hard or **die·hard** *n.* a person stubbornly resistant to new ideas, reform, etc.

di·e·lec·tric (dī′i lek′trik) *n.* ⟦< *dia*-, across + ELECTRIC⟧ a material that does not conduct electricity

di·er·e·sis (dī er′ə sis) *n., pl.* **-ses′** (-sēz′) ⟦< Gr *dia*-, apart + *hairein*, to take⟧ a mark (¨) placed over the second of two consecutive vowels to show that it is pronounced separately

die·sel (dē′zəl, -səl) *n.* ⟦after R. *Diesel* (1858-1913), Ger inventor⟧ ⟦*often* D-⟧ **1** an internal-combustion engine that burns oil ignited by heat from air compression: also **diesel engine (or motor) 2** fuel for such an engine —*vi.* to continue to run after the ignition is turned off: said of an internal-combustion engine

di·et¹ (dī′ət) *n.* ⟦< Gr *diaita*, way of life⟧ **1** what a person or animal usually eats or drinks **2** a special or limited selection of food and drink, chosen or prescribed as to bring about weight loss —*vi., vt.* to adhere to or place on a diet —**di′et·er** *n.* —**di′e·tar′y** (-ə ter′ē) *adj.*

di·et² (dī′ət) *n.* ⟦< ML *dieta*⟧ **1** a formal assembly **2** in some countries, a legislative assembly

di·e·tet·ic (-ə tet′ik) *adj.* of or for a particular diet of food and drink

di·e·tet·ics (iks) *n.* the study of the kinds and quantities of food needed for health

di·e·ti·tian (dī′ə tish′ən) *n.* an expert in dietetics

dif- *prefix* DIS-: used before *f*

dif·fer (dif′ər) *vi.* ⟦< L *dis*-, apart + *ferre*, to bring⟧ **1** to be unlike or not the same **2** to be of opposite or unlike opinions; *disagree*

dif·fer·ence (dif′ər əns, dif′rəns) *n.* **1** a being different **2** the way in which people or things are different **3** a differing in opinion; disagreement **4** a dispute **5** *Math.* the amount by which one quantity is less than another

dif·fer·ent *adj.* **1** not alike **2** not the same **3** various **4** unusual —**dif′fer·ent·ly** *adv.*

dif·fer·en·tial (dif′ər en′shəl) *adj.* of, showing, or constituting a difference —*n.* **1** a differentiating amount, degree, etc. **2** a differential gear

differential gear (or gearing) a gear arrangement allowing one wheel of an automobile to turn faster than the corresponding wheel on the other side

dif·fer·en·ti·ate (-shē āt′) *vt.* **-at′ed, -at′ing 1** to constitute a difference in or between **2** to make unlike **3** to distinguish between —*vi.* **1** to become different or differentiated **2** to note a difference —**dif′fer·en′ti·a′tion** *n.*

dif·fi·cult (dif′i kult′, -kəlt) *adj.* **1** hard to do, understand, etc. **2** hard to satisfy, deal with, etc.

dif·fi·cul·ty *n., pl.* **-ties** ⟦< L *dis*-, not + *facilis*, easy⟧ **1** a being difficult **2** something difficult, as a problem, obstacle, or objection **3** trouble

dif·fi·dent (-dənt) *adj.* ⟦< L *dis*-, not + *fidere*, to trust⟧ lacking self-confidence; shy —**dif′fi·dence** *n.*

dif·frac·tion (di frak′shən) *n.* ⟦< L *dis*-, apart + *frangere*, to break⟧ **1** the breaking up of light waves as into the colors of the spectrum **2** a similar breaking up as of sound waves

dif·fuse (di fyoos′; *for v.*, -fyooz′) *adj.* ⟦< L *dis*-, apart + *fundere*, to pour⟧ **1** spread out; not concentrated **2** using more words than are needed —*vt., vi.* **-fused′, -fus′ing** to pour in every direction; spread widely —**dif·fuse′ly** *adv.* —**dif·fuse′ness** *n.* —**dif·fu′sion** *n.* —**dif·fu′sive** *adj.*

dig (dig) *vt.* **dug, dig′ging** ⟦< OFr < Du *dijk*, dike⟧ **1** to turn up or remove (ground, etc.) with a spade, the hands, etc. **2** to make (a hole, etc.) by digging **3** to get out by digging **4** to find out, as by careful study **5** to jab **6** [Slang] *a)* to understand *b)* to like —*vi.* **1** to dig the ground **2** to make a way by digging —*n.* **1** [Inf.] *a)* a poke, nudge, etc. *b)* a taunt **2** an archaeological excavation —**dig′ger** *n.*

di·gest (dī′jest′; *for v.* di jest′, dī-) *n.* ⟦< L *dis*-, apart + *gerere*, to carry⟧ an organized collection of condensed information; summary —*vt.* **1** to summarize **2** to change (food taken into the body) into an absorbable form **3** to absorb mentally —*vi.* to undergo digestion —**di·gest′i·ble** *adj.*

di·ges·tion *n.* **1** a digesting or being digested **2** the ability to digest —**di·ges′tive** *adj.*

dig·it (dij′it) *n.* ⟦< L *digitus*, a finger⟧ **1** a finger or toe **2** any number from 0 to 9

dig·i·tal (dij′i təl, -it′l) *adj.* **1** of or like a digit **2** using a row of digits, rather than numbers on a dial [a *digital* watch] **3** designating, of, or used by a computer that processes data represented by groups of electronic bits **4** designating a recording technique in which sounds or images are converted into electronic bits

dig·i·tal·is (dij′i tal′is) *n.* ⟦ModL, foxglove: see DIGIT⟧ **1** a plant with long spikes of thimblelike flowers; foxglove **2** a medicine made from the leaves of the purple foxglove, used as a heart stimulant

dig·i·tize (dij′i tīz′) *vt.* **-tized′, -tiz′ing** to translate (analog data) into digital data

dig·ni·fied (dig′nə fīd′) *adj.* having or showing dignity

dig·ni·fy (dig′nə fī′) *vt.* **-fied′, -fy′ing** ⟦< L *dignus*, worthy + *facere*, make⟧ to give dignity to; exalt

dig·ni·tar·y (-ter′ē) *n., pl.* **-tar′ies** ⟦< L *dignitas*, dignity⟧ a person holding a high position or office

dig·ni·ty (-tē) *n., pl.* **-ties** ⟦< L *dignus*, worthy⟧ **1** honorable quality; worthiness **2** high repute or honor, or the degree of this **3** a high position, rank, or title **4** stately appearance or manner **5** self-respect

di·graph (dī′graf′) *n.* a combination of two

letters to represent one sound (Ex.: read, graphic)

di·gress (di gres′, dī-) *vi.* ⟦< L *dis-*, apart + *gradi*, to go⟧ to wander temporarily from the subject, in talking or writing —**di·gres′sion** (-gresh′ən) *n.* —**di·gres′sive** *adj.*

Di·jon mustard (dē zhän′, dē′zhän′) ⟦after *Dijon*, city in France⟧ a mustard paste blended with white wine

dike (dīk) *n.* ⟦OE *dic*, ditch⟧ an embankment or dam made to prevent flooding as by the sea

di·lap·i·dat·ed (də lap′ə dāt′id) *adj.* ⟦< L *dis-*, apart + *lapidare*, throw stones at⟧ falling to pieces; broken down —**di·lap′i·da′tion** *n.*

di·late (dī′lāt′, dī lāt′) *vt.* **-lat′ed, -lat′ing** ⟦< L *dis-*, apart + *latus*, wide⟧ to make wider or larger —*vi.* **1** to become wider or larger **2** to speak or write in detail (*on* or *upon* a subject) —**di·la′tion** *n.,* **dil·a·ta·tion** (dil′ə tā′shən) *n.*

dil·a·to·ry (dil′ə tôr′ē) *adj.* ⟦see prec.⟧ **1** causing delay **2** inclined to delay; slow; tardy —**dil′a·to′ri·ness** *n.*

di·lem·ma (di lem′ə) *n.* ⟦< LGr *di-*, two + *lēmma*, proposition⟧ **1** any situation requiring a choice between unpleasant alternatives **2** any serious problem

dil·et·tante (dil′ə tänt′, dil′ə tänt′) *n., pl.* **-tantes′** or **-tan′ti** (-tän′tē) ⟦It < L *delectare*, to delight⟧ one who dabbles in an art, science, etc. in a superficial way —**dil′et·tant′ish** *adj.* —**dil′et·tant′ism** *n.*

dil·i·gent (dil′ə jənt) *adj.* ⟦< L *di-*, apart + *legere*, choose⟧ **1** persevering and careful in work; hard-working **2** done carefully —**dil′i·gence** *n.* —**dil′i·gent·ly** *adv.*

dill (dil) *n.* ⟦OE *dile*⟧ an herb related to parsley, with bitter seeds and aromatic leaves, used to flavor pickles, soups, etc.

dil·ly (dil′ē) *n., pl.* **-lies** ⟦? < DEL(IGHTFUL) + -Y²⟧ [Slang] a remarkable person or thing

dil·ly·dal·ly (dil′ē dal′ē) *vi.* **-lied, -ly·ing** ⟦< DALLY⟧ to waste time by hesitating; loiter or dawdle

di·lute (di lo͞ot′, dī-) *vt.* **-lut′ed, -lut′ing** ⟦< L *dis-*, off + *lavare*, to wash⟧ to thin down or weaken as by mixing with water —*adj.* diluted —**di·lu′tion** *n.*

dim¹ (dim) *adj.* **dim′mer, dim′mest** ⟦OE⟧ **1** not bright, clear, or distinct; dull, obscure, etc. **2** not seeing, hearing, or understanding clearly **3** [Inf.] stupid —*vt., vi.* **dimmed, dim′ming** to make or grow dim —**dim′ly** *adv.* —**dim′ness** *n.*

dim² *abbrev.* diminutive

dime (dīm) *n.* ⟦< L *decem*, ten⟧ a U.S. or Canadian 10-cent coin

di·men·sion (də men′shən) *n.* ⟦< L *dis-*, off, from + *metiri*, to measure⟧ **1** any measurable extent, as length, width, or depth **2** [*pl.*] measurements in length, width, and often depth **3** [*often pl.*] extent; scope —**di·men′sion·al** *adj.*

dime store FIVE-AND-TEN-CENT STORE

di·min·ish (də min′ish) *vt., vi.* ⟦< L *diminuere*, reduce⟧ to make or become smaller in size,

degree, importance, etc.; lessen —**dim·i·nu·tion** (dim′ə no͞o′shən, -nyo͞o′-) *n.*

di·min·u·en·do (də min′yo͞o en′dō) *adj., adv.* ⟦It: see prec.⟧ *Music* with gradually diminishing volume

di·min·u·tive (də min′yo͞o tiv) *adj.* ⟦see DIMINISH⟧ very small; tiny —*n.* a word having a suffix that expresses smallness, endearment, etc. (Ex.: *piglet*)

dim·i·ty (dim′ə tē) *n., pl.* **-ties** ⟦< Gr *dis-*, two + *mitos*, a thread⟧ a thin, corded or patterned cotton cloth

dim·mer *n.* a device, as a rheostat, for dimming electric lights

dim·ple (dim′pəl) *n.* ⟦ME *dimpel*⟧ a small, natural hollow, as on the cheek or chin —*vt.* **-pled, -pling** to form dimples (in) —**dim′ply** (-plē) *adj.*

dim sum (dim′ sum′, -so͞om′) ⟦Chin⟧ small dumplings filled with meat, vegetables, etc.; also, a light meal of these together with other foods

dim·wit *n.* [Slang] a stupid person; simpleton —**dim′wit′ted** *adj.*

din (din) *n.* ⟦OE *dyne*⟧ a loud, continuous noise; confused uproar —*vt.* **dinned, din′ning** to repeat insistently or noisily —*vi.* to make a din

din-din (din′din′) *n.* [Inf.] dinner

dine (dīn) *vi.* **dined, din′ing** ⟦ult. < L *dis-*, away + *jejunus*, hungry⟧ to eat dinner —*vt.* to provide a dinner for

din·er (dīn′ər) *n.* **1** a person eating dinner **2** a railroad car equipped to serve meals **3** a small restaurant serving quick meals, esp. one built to look like such a car

di·nette (dī net′) *n.* an alcove or small space used as a dining room

ding (diŋ) *n.* ⟦< Scand⟧ the sound of a bell: also **ding′-dong′** (-dôŋ′)

din·ghy (diŋ′gē) *n., pl.* **-ghies** ⟦Hindi *ḍiṅgī*⟧ any of various small boats, as one carried on a ship

din·gle (diŋ′gəl) *n.* ⟦ME *dingel*, abyss⟧ a small, deep, wooded valley

din·go (diŋ′gō) *n., pl.* **-goes** ⟦native name⟧ the Australian wild dog, usually tawny in color

ding·us (diŋ′əs) *n.* ⟦< Du *ding*, thing⟧ [Inf.] any device; gadget

din·gy (din′jē) *adj.* **-gi·er, -gi·est** ⟦orig. dial. var. < DUNG⟧ **1** not bright or clean; grimy **2** dismal; shabby —**din′gi·ness** *n.*

dining room a room where meals are eaten

dink·y (diŋ′kē) *adj.* **-i·er, -i·est** ⟦< Scot *dink*, trim⟧ [Inf.] small and unimportant

din·ner (din′ər) *n.* ⟦see DINE⟧ **1** the main meal of the day **2** a banquet in honor of a person or event

dinner jacket a tuxedo jacket

din·ner·ware *n.* plates, cups, saucers, etc., collectively

di·no·saur (dī′nə sôr′) *n.* ⟦< Gr *deinos*, terrible + *sauros*, lizard⟧ an extinct prehistoric reptile, often huge

dint (dint) *n.* ⟦OE *dynt*⟧ force; exertion: now chiefly in **by dint of**

di·o·cese (dī′ə sis, -sēz′) *n.* [< Gr *dioikein*, to keep house] the district under a bishop's jurisdiction —**di·oc′e·san** (-äs′ə sən) *adj.*

di·ode (dī′ōd′) *n.* [DI-¹ + -ODE] an electron tube used esp. to convert alternating current into direct current

Di·og·e·nes (dī äj′ə nēz′) 412?-323? B.C.; Gr. philosopher

Di·o·ny·sus or **Di·o·ny·sos** (dī′ə nī′səs) *n. Gr. Myth.* the god of wine and revelry

di·o·ram·a (dī′ə ram′ə) *n.* [< Gr *dia-*, through + *horama*, a view] a scenic display, as of three-dimensional figures against a painted background

di·ox·in (dī äk′sin) *n.* a highly toxic chemical contaminant found in some herbicides and industrial wastes

dip (dip) *vt.* **dipped**, **dip′ping** [OE *dyppan*] 1 to immerse briefly 2 to scoop (liquid) up or out 3 to lower (a flag, etc.) and immediately raise again —*vi.* 1 to plunge into a liquid and quickly come out 2 to sink suddenly 3 to decline slightly 4 to slope down 5 to lower a container, the hand, etc. as into water 6 to read or inquire superficially: with *into* —*n.* 1 a dipping or being dipped 2 a brief plunge into water, etc. 3 a liquid, sauce, etc. into which something is dipped 4 a portion removed by dipping 5 a downward slope or plunge

diph·the·ri·a (dif thir′ē ə, dip-) *n.* [< Gr *diphthera*, leather] an acute infectious disease marked by high fever and difficult breathing

diph·thong (dif′thôŋ; *often* dip′-) *n.* [< Gr *di-*, two + *phthongos*, a sound] a sound made by gliding from one vowel to another within one syllable, as the sound (oi) in *oil*

di·plo·ma (də plō′mə) *n.* [< Gr *diplōma*, folded letter] a certificate issued by a school, college, etc. indicating graduation or the conferring of a degree

di·plo·ma·cy (-sē) *n.* 1 the conducting of relations between nations 2 tact

dip·lo·mat (dip′lə mat′) *n.* 1 a representative of a government who conducts relations with another government 2 a tactful person

dip·lo·mat·ic *adj.* 1 of diplomacy 2 tactful —**dip′lo·mat′i·cal·ly** *adv.*

di·pole (dī′pōl′) *n.* a kind of radio or TV antenna with a single line separated at the center for connection to the receiver

dip·per (dip′ər) *n.* a long-handled cup, etc. for dipping

dip·so·ma·ni·a (dip′sə mā′nē ə) *n.* [< Gr *dipsa*, thirst + *mania*, madness] an abnormal craving for alcoholic drink —**dip′so·ma′ni·ac′** (-ak′) *n.*

dip·stick *n.* a graduated rod for measuring quantity or depth

dir *abbrev.* director

dire (dīr) *adj.* **dir′er**, **dir′est** [L *dirus*] 1 dreadful; terrible: also **dire′ful** 2 urgent [a *dire* need]

di·rect (də rekt′; *also* dī-) *adj.* [< L *di-*, apart + *regere*, to rule] 1 not roundabout or interrupted; straight 2 honest; frank [a *direct* answer] 3 with nothing between; immedi-

ate 4 in an unbroken line of descent; lineal 5 exact; complete [the *direct* opposite] 6 in the exact words [a *direct* quote] —*vt.* 1 to manage; guide 2 to order; command 3 to turn or point; aim; head 4 to tell (a person) the way to a place 5 to address (a letter, etc.) 6 *a)* to plan and supervise the action and effects of (a play, film, etc.) *b)* to conduct the performance of (a choir, band, etc.) —*adv.* directly —**di·rect′ness** *n.*

direct current an electric current flowing continuously in one direction

di·rec·tion (də rek′shən; *also* dī-) *n.* 1 a directing 2 [*usually pl.*] instructions for doing, using, etc. 3 a command 4 the point toward which something faces or the line along which it moves or lies —**di·rec′tion·al** *adj.*

di·rec·tive (-rek′tiv) *adj.* directing —*n.* a general order issued authoritatively

di·rect·ly *adv.* 1 in a direct way or line; straight 2 with nothing or no one between [*directly* responsible] 3 exactly [*directly* opposite] 4 instantly; right away

direct object *Gram.* the word or words denoting the receiver of the action of a transitive verb (Ex.: *me* in "he saw me")

di·rec·tor (-rek′tər) *n.* one who directs a school, corporation, etc. or a play, choir, etc. —**di·rec′tor·ship′** *n.*

di·rec·tor·ate (-it) *n.* 1 the position of director 2 a board of directors

di·rec·to·ry (-tə rē) *n., pl.* -**ries** a book listing the names, addresses, etc. of a specific group of persons

dirge (dərj) *n.* [< L *dirige* (direct), first word of a prayer] a song, poem, etc. of grief or mourning

dir·i·gi·ble (dir′ə jə bəl, də rij′ə-) *n.* [see DIRECT & -IBLE] AIRSHIP

dirk (dərk) *n.* [< ?] a long dagger

dirn·dl (dərn′dəl) *n.* [< Ger *dirne*, girl] a full-skirted dress with a tight bodice

dirt (dərt) *n.* [< ON *drita*, excrement] 1 any unclean matter, as soil or mud; filth 2 dirtiness, corruption, etc. 3 obscenity 4 malicious gossip

dirt bike a small motorcycle for off-road riding

dirt-cheap *adj., adv.* [Inf.] very inexpensive(ly)

dirt-poor *adj.* extremely poor

dirt·y *adj.* -**i·er**, -**i·est** 1 not clean 2 obscene 3 contemptible or nasty 4 unfair; dishonest 5 showing anger [a *dirty* look] 6 rough [*dirty* weather] —*vt., vi.* **dirt′ied**, **dirt′y·ing** to make or become dirty —**dirt′i·ly** *adv.* —**dirt′i·ness** *n.*

dis (dis) *vt.* **dissed**, **dis′sing** [Slang] to insult

dis- [< L] *prefix* separation, negation, reversal [*disbar, disable, disintegrate*]

dis·a·bil·i·ty (dis′ə bil′ə tē) *n., pl.* -**ties** 1 a disabled condition 2 that which disables, as an illness or physical limitation

dis·a·ble (dis ā′bəl) *vt.* -**bled**, -**bling** to make unable or unfit; cripple; incapacitate

dis·a·bled *adj.* having a physical or mental disability

dis·a·buse (dis'ə byo͞oz') *vt.* **-bused', -bus'ing** to rid of false ideas

dis·ad·van·tage (dis'əd vant'ij) *n.* **1** an unfavorable situation or circumstance **2** detriment —**dis'ad·van·ta'geous** (-ad'vən tā'jəs) *adj.*

dis·ad·van·taged *adj.* underprivileged

dis·af·fect (dis'ə fekt') *vt.* to make unfriendly, discontented, or disloyal —**dis'af·fect'ed** *adj.* —**dis'af·fec'tion** *n.*

dis·af·fil·i·ate (-ə fil'ē āt') *vt., vi.* **-at'ed, -at'ing** to end an affiliation (with) —**dis'af·fil'i·a'tion** *n.*

dis·a·gree (-ə grē') *vi.* **-greed', -gree'ing 1** to fail to agree; differ **2** to differ in opinion **3** to cause distress or discomfort, esp. physical discomfort: with [damp weather *disagrees* with me] —**dis'a·gree'ment** *n.*

dis·a·gree·a·ble *adj.* **1** unpleasant; offensive **2** quarrelsome —**dis'a·gree'a·bly** *adv.*

dis·al·low (dis'ə lou') *vt.* to refuse to allow (a claim, etc.); reject

dis·ap·pear (-ə pir') *vi.* **1** to cease to be seen; vanish **2** to cease existing —**dis'ap·pear'ance** *n.*

dis·ap·point (-ə point') *vt.* to fail to satisfy the hopes or expectations of —**dis'ap·point'ment** *n.*

dis·ap·pro·ba·tion (dis'ap'rə bā'shən) *n.* disapproval

dis·ap·prove (dis'ə pro͞ov') *vt., vi.* **-proved', -prov'ing 1** to have or express an unfavorable opinion (of) **2** to refuse to approve —**dis'ap·prov'al** *n.* —**dis'ap·prov'ing·ly** *adv.*

dis·arm (dis ärm') *vt.* **1** to take away weapons from **2** to make harmless **3** to make friendly —*vi.* to reduce armed forces and armaments —**dis·ar'ma·ment** (-är'mə mənt) *n.*

dis·ar·range (dis'ə rānj') *vt.* **-ranged', -rang'ing** to undo the order of; make less neat

dis·ar·ray (-ə rā') *n.* disorder

dis·as·sem·ble (-ə sem'bəl) *vt.* **-bled, -bling** to take apart

dis·as·so·ci·ate (-ə sō'shē āt', -sē-) *vt.* **-at'ed, -at'ing** to disconnect or separate; dissociate

dis·as·ter (di zas'tər) *n.* [< L *dis-*, away + *astrum*, a star] any happening that causes great harm or damage; calamity —**dis·as'trous** (-trəs) *adj.*

dis·a·vow (dis'ə vou') *vt.* to deny any knowledge of or responsibility for; disclaim —**dis'a·vow'al** *n.*

dis·band (dis band') *vt., vi.* to break up: said as of an organization

dis·bar (-bär') *vt.* **-barred', -bar'ring** to deprive (a lawyer) of the right to practice law —**dis·bar'ment** *n.*

dis·be·lieve (dis'bə lēv') *vt., vi.* **-lieved', -liev'ing** to refuse to believe —**dis'be·lief'** (-lēf') *n.*

dis·burse (dis burs') *vt.* **-bursed', -burs'ing** [< OFr *desbourser*] to pay out; expend —**dis·burse'ment** *n.* —**dis·burs'er** *n.*

disc (disk) *n.* **1** DISK **2** a phonograph record

dis·card (dis kärd'; *for n.* dis'kärd) *vt.* [< OFr: see DIS- & CARD¹] **1** *Card Games* to remove (a card or cards) from one's hand **2** to get rid of as no longer useful —*n.* **1** a discarding or being discarded **2** something discarded

disc brake a brake, as on a car, with two friction pads that press on a disc rotating with the wheel

dis·cern (di surn', -zurn') *vt.* [< L *dis-*, apart + *cernere*, to separate] to perceive or recognize clearly —**dis·cern'i·ble** *adj.* —**dis·cern'i·bly** *adv.* —**dis·cern'ment** *n.*

dis·cern·ing *adj.* having good judgment; astute

dis·charge (dis chärj'; *also, and for n. usually,* dis'chärj') *vt.* **-charged', -charg'ing** [< L *dis-*, from + *carrus*, wagon] **1** to release or dismiss **2** to unload (a cargo) **3** to shoot (a gun or projectile) **4** to emit [to *discharge* pus] **5** to pay (a debt) or perform (a duty) **6** *Elec.* to remove stored energy from (a battery, etc.) —*vi.* **1** to get rid of a load, etc. **2** to go off, as a gun —*n.* **1** a discharging or being discharged **2** that which discharges or is discharged

dis·ci·ple (di sī'pəl) *n.* [< L *dis-*, apart + *capere*, to hold] **1** a pupil or follower of any teacher or school **2** an early follower of Jesus, esp. one of the Apostles —**dis·ci'ple·ship'** *n.*

dis·ci·pli·nar·i·an (dis'ə pli ner'ē ən) *n.* a person who believes in or enforces strict discipline

dis·ci·pline (dis'ə plin') *n.* [see DISCIPLE] **1** a branch of learning **2** training that develops self-control, efficiency, etc. **3** strict control to enforce obedience **4** self-control **5** a system of rules, as for a church **6** treatment that corrects or punishes —*vt.* **-plined', -plin'ing 1** to train; control **2** to punish —**dis'ci·pli·nar'y** (-pli ner'ē) *adj.*

disc jockey DJ

dis·claim (dis klām') *vt.* **1** to give up any claim to **2** to repudiate; deny

dis·claim·er *n.* a denial or renunciation, as of responsibility

dis·close (dis klōz') *vt.* **-closed', -clos'ing** to reveal —**dis·clo'sure** (-klō'zhər) *n.*

dis·co (dis'kō) *n.,* **1** *pl.* **-cos 1** a place for dancing to recorded music **2** a kind of popular dance music with a strong beat

dis·col·or (dis kul'ər) *vt., vi.* to change in color as by fading, streaking, or staining: Brit. sp. **dis·col'our** —**dis'col·or·a'tion** *n.*

dis·com·fit (dis kum'fit) *vt.* [< L *dis-*, away + *conficere*, prepare] to frustrate or disconcert —**dis·com'fi·ture** (-fi chər) *n.*

dis·com·fort (dis kum'fərt) *n.* **1** lack of comfort; uneasiness **2** anything causing this —*vt.* to cause discomfort to

dis·com·mode (dis'kə mōd') *vt.* **-mod'ed, -mod'ing** [< DIS- + L *commodare*, to make suitable] to cause bother to; inconvenience

dis·com·pose (-kəm pōz') *vt.* **-posed', -pos'ing** to disturb; fluster —**dis'com·po'sure** (-pō'zhər) *n.*

dis·con·cert (-kən surt') *vt.* to cause to lose one's composure —**dis'con·cert'ing** *adj.* —**dis'con·cert'ing·ly** *adv.*

dis·con·nect (-kə nekt′) *vt.* to break the connection of; separate —**dis′con·nec′tion** *n.*

dis·con·nect·ed *adj.* 1 separated 2 incoherent

dis·con·so·late (dis kän′sə lit) *adj.* 〚see DIS- & CONSOLE[1]〛 inconsolable; dejected —**dis′con′so·late·ly** *adv.*

dis·con·tent (dis′kən tent′) *adj.* 〚ME〛 DISCONTENTED —*n.* dissatisfaction with one's situation: also **dis′con·tent′ment** —*vt.* to make discontented

dis·con·tent·ed *adj.* not contented; wanting something more or different

dis·con·tin·ue (dis′kən tin′yo̅o̅) *vt., vi.* -**ued,** -**u·ing** to stop; cease —**dis′con·tin′u·ance** *n.,* **dis′con·tin′u·a′tion** *n.*

dis·con·tin·u·ous (-yo̅o̅ əs) *adj.* not continuous; having interruptions or gaps

dis·cord (dis′kôrd) *n.* 〚< L *dis-,* apart + *cor,* heart〛 1 disagreement 2 harsh noise 3 a lack of musical harmony —**dis·cord′ant** *adj.*

dis·co·thèque (dis′kə tek′) *n.* 〚Fr〛 DISCO (*n.* 1)

dis·count (dis′kount′; *for v., also* dis kount′) *n.* 〚see DIS- & COMPUTE〛 1 a reduction from a usual price 2 the rate of interest charged on a discounted bill, note, etc.: also called **discount rate** —*vt.* 1 to pay or receive the value of (a bill, promissory note, etc.), minus a deduction for interest 2 to deduct an amount from (a bill, price, etc.) 3 to sell at less than the regular price 4 *a)* to allow for exaggeration, etc. in (a story, etc.) *b)* to disregard 5 to lessen the effect of by anticipating

dis·coun·te·nance (dis kount′′n əns) *vt.* -**nanced,** -**nanc·ing** 1 to make ashamed or embarrassed 2 to refuse approval or support

discount store a retail store that sells goods for less than regular prices

dis·cour·age (di skur′ij) *vt.* -**aged,** -**ag·ing** 1 to deprive of courage or confidence 2 to persuade (a person) to refrain 3 to try to prevent by disapproving —**dis·cour′age·ment** *n.*

dis·course (dis′kôrs′; *also, and for v. usually,* dis kôrs′) *n.* 〚< L *dis-,* from + *currere,* to run〛 1 talk; conversation 2 a formal treatment of a subject, in speech or writing —*vi.* -**coursed′,** -**cours′ing** to talk; confer

dis·cour·te·ous (dis kur′tē əs) *adj.* impolite; rude; ill-mannered

dis·cour·te·sy (-kurt′ə sē) *n.* 1 lack of courtesy 2 *pl.* -**sies** a rude or impolite act or remark

dis·cov·er (di skuv′ər) *vt.* 〚see DIS- & COVER〛 1 to be the first to find out, see, etc. 2 to learn of the existence of —**dis·cov′er·er** *n.*

dis·cov·er·y (di skuv′ər ē) *n., pl.* -**er·ies** 1 a discovering 2 anything discovered

dis·cred·it (dis kred′it) *vt.* 1 to disbelieve 2 to cast doubt on 3 to disgrace —*n.* 1 loss of belief; doubt 2 disgrace —**dis·cred′it·a·ble** *adj.*

dis·creet (di skrēt′) *adj.* 〚see DISCERN〛 1 careful about what one says or does 2 keeping silent or preserving confidences when necessary —**dis·creet′ly** *adv.*

dis·crep·an·cy (di skrep′ən sē) *n., pl.* -**cies** 〚< L *dis-,* from + *crepare,* to rattle〛 (a) lack of agreement; inconsistency

dis·crete (di skrēt′) *adj.* 〚see DISCERN〛 separate and distinct; unrelated

dis·cre·tion (di skresh′ən) *n.* 1 the freedom to make decisions 2 the quality of being discreet —**dis·cre′tion·ar′y** *adj.*

dis·crim·i·nate (di skrim′i nāt′) *vi.* -**nat′ed,** -**nat′ing** 〚see DISCERN〛 1 to distinguish 2 to make distinctions in treatment; show partiality or prejudice —**dis·crim′i·nat′ing** *adj.* —**dis·crim′i·na′tion** *n.*

dis·crim·i·na·to·ry (-nə tôr′ē) *adj.* showing discrimination or bias

dis·cur·sive (di skur′siv) *adj.* 〚see DISCOURSE〛 wandering from one topic to another; rambling

dis·cus (dis′kəs) *n.* 〚< Gr *diskos*〛 a heavy disk thrown for distance at a track meet

dis·cuss (di skus′) *vt.* 〚< L *dis-,* apart + *quatere,* to shake〛 to talk or write about; consider the pros and cons of —**dis·cus′sion** (-skush′ən) *n.*

dis·cus·sant (-ənt) *n.* a participant in an organized discussion

dis·dain (dis dān′) *vt.* 〚< L *dis-,* DIS- + *dignari,* deign〛 to regard as beneath one's dignity; scorn —*n.* aloof contempt —**dis·dain′ful** *adj.*

dis·ease (di zēz′) *n.* 〚< OFr *des-,* DIS- + *aise,* ease〛 1 illness in general 2 a particular destructive process in an organism; specif., an illness 3 any harmful condition, as of society —**dis·eased′** *adj.*

dis·em·bark (dis′im bärk′) *vi., vt.* to leave, or unload from, a ship, aircraft, etc. —**dis′em·bar·ka′tion** *n.*

dis·em·bod·y (-im bäd′ē) *vt.* -**bod′ied,** -**bod′y·ing** to free from bodily existence —**dis′em·bod′i·ment** *n.*

dis·em·bow·el (-im bou′əl) *vt.* -**eled** or -**elled,** -**el·ing** or -**el·ling** to take out the entrails of

dis·en·chant (-in chant′) *vt.* 1 to free from an enchantment 2 DISILLUSION (*vt.* 2) —**dis′en·chant′ment** *n.*

dis·en·cum·ber (-in kum′bər) *vt.* to relieve of a burden

dis·en·fran·chise (dis′in fran′chīz′) *vt.* -**chised′,** -**chis′ing** to deprive of a right, privilege, etc., esp. the right to vote

dis·en·gage (-in gāj′) *vt., vi.* -**gaged′,** -**gag′ing** to release or get loose from something that engages, holds, entangles, etc. —**dis′en·gage′ment** *n.*

dis·en·tan·gle (-in taŋ′gəl) *vt.* -**gled,** -**gling** to free from something that entangles, confuses, etc.; extricate

dis·es·teem (-i stēm′) *n.* lack of esteem; disfavor

dis·fa·vor (dis fā′vər) *n.* 1 an unfavorable opinion; dislike; disapproval 2 the state of being disliked, etc.

dis·fig·ure (-fig′yər) *vt.* -**ured,** -**ur·ing** to hurt the appearance of; deface —**dis·fig′ure·ment** *n.*

dis·gorge (-gôrj′) *vt., vi.* -**gorged′,** -**gorg′ing** 〚< OFr: see DIS- & GORGE〛 1 to vomit 2 to pour forth (its contents); empty (itself)

dis·grace (-grās′) *n.* 〚< It *dis-,* not + *grazia,*

favor] 1 loss of favor or respect; shame; disrepute 2 a person or thing bringing shame —*vt.* **-graced′, -grac′ing** to bring shame or dishonor upon —**dis·grace′ful** *adj.*

dis·grun·tle (-grunt′'l) *vt.* **-tled, -tling** [ult. < DIS- + GRUNT] to make peevishly discontented; make sullen

dis·guise (-gīz′) *vt.* **-guised′, -guis′ing** [< OFr: see DIS- & GUISE] 1 to make appear, sound, etc. so different as to be unrecognizable 2 to hide the real nature of —*n.* 1 anything that disguises 2 a being disguised

dis·gust (-gust′) *n.* [< DIS- + L *gustus*, a taste] a sickening dislike —*vt.* to cause to feel disgust —**dis·gust′ed** *adj.* —**dis·gust′ing** *adj.*

dish (dish) *n.* [see DISCUS] 1 a container, generally shallow and concave, for holding food 2 as much as a dish holds 3 a particular kind of food 4 any dishlike object —*vt.* to serve in a dish: with *up* or *out* —**dish it out** [Slang] to subject others to criticism, etc.

dis·ha·bille (dis′ə bēl′) *n.* [< Fr *dés-*, DIS- + *habiller*, to dress] the state of being dressed only partially or in night clothes

dish antenna a radio or TV antenna with a dish-shaped reflector

dis·har·mo·ny (dis här′mə nē) *n.* absence of harmony; discord —**dis′har·mo′ni·ous** (-mō′nē əs) *adj.*

dish·cloth *n.* a cloth for washing or drying dishes, etc.

dis·heart·en (dis härt′'n) *vt.* to discourage; depress —**dis·heart′en·ing** *adj.*

di·shev·el (di shev′əl) *vt.* **-eled** or **-elled, -el·ing** or **-el·ling** [< OFr *des-*, DIS- + *chevel*, hair] to cause (hair, clothing, etc.) to become disarranged; rumple —**di·shev′el·ment** *n.*

dis·hon·est (dis än′ist) *adj.* not honest; lying, cheating, etc. —**dis·hon′est·ly** *adv.*

dis·hon·es·ty *n.* 1 a being dishonest 2 *pl.* **-ties** a dishonest act

dis·hon·or (dis än′ər) *n.* 1 loss of honor or respect 2 a cause of dishonor —*vt.* 1 to insult or disgrace 2 to refuse to pay (a check, etc.) —**dis·hon′or·a·ble** *adj.*

dish·pan *n.* a pan in which dishes, cups, etc. are washed

dish·rag *n.* DISHCLOTH

dish·wash·er *n.* a person or machine that washes dishes, cups, etc.

dis·il·lu·sion (dis′i lōō′zhən) *vt.* 1 to free from illusion 2 to take away the idealism of and make bitter, etc. —**dis′il·lu′sion·ment** *n.*

dis·in·clined (dis′in klīnd′) *adj.* unwilling; reluctant

dis·in·fect (dis′in fekt′) *vt.* to destroy the harmful bacteria, viruses, etc. in —**dis′in·fect′ant** *n.*

dis·in·for·ma·tion (-in′fər mā′shən) *n.* deliberately false information leaked so as to confuse another nation's intelligence operations

dis·in·gen·u·ous (dis′in jen′yōō əs) *adj.* not candid or frank; insincere

dis·in·her·it (dis′in her′it) *vt.* to deprive of an inheritance, as by modifying one's will

dis·in·te·grate (dis in′tə grāt′) *vt., vi.* **-grat′ed, -grat′ing** 1 to separate into parts or fragments; break up 2 to undergo nuclear transformation —**dis·in′te·gra′tion** *n.*

dis·in·ter (dis′in tur′) *vt.* **-terred′, -ter′ring** to remove from a grave, etc.; exhume

dis·in·ter·est·ed (dis in′trəs tid, -int′ər əs tid) *adj.* 1 impartial; unbiased 2 uninterested; indifferent

dis·in·ter·me·di·a·tion (-in′tər mē′dē ā′shən) *n.* the withdrawal of funds from banks to invest them at higher rates of interest, as in government securities

dis·joint (-joint′) *vt.* 1 to put out of joint 2 to dismember 3 to destroy the unity, etc. of —**dis·joint′ed** *adj.*

disk (disk) *n.* [L *discus*: see DISCUS] 1 any thin, flat, circular thing 2 DISC 3 a layer of fibrous cartilage between adjacent vertebrae 4 a thin, flat, circular plate coated with magnetic particles, for storing computer data 5 an optical disc, such as a DVD

dis·like (dis līk′) *vt.* **-liked′, -lik′ing** to have a feeling of not liking —*n.* a feeling of not liking

dis·lo·cate (dis′lō kāt′) *vt.* **-cat′ed, -cat′ing** 1 to displace (a bone) from its proper position 2 to disarrange; disrupt —**dis′lo·ca′tion** *n.*

dis·lodge (dis läj′) *vt.* **-lodged′, -lodg′ing** to force from a place

dis·loy·al (-loi′əl) *adj.* not loyal or faithful —**dis·loy′al·ty** *n.*

dis·mal (diz′məl) *adj.* [< ML *dies mali*, evil days] 1 causing gloom or misery 2 dark and gloomy

dis·man·tle (dis mant′'l) *vt.* **-tled, -tling** [see DIS- & MANTLE] 1 to strip (a ship, etc.), as of equipment 2 to take apart —**dis·man′tle·ment** *n.*

dis·may (-mā′) *vt.* [< Anglo-Fr] to make startled and discouraged by some problem, etc. difficult to resolve —*n.* upset and discouragement caused by a problem, etc. difficult to resolve

dis·mem·ber (-mem′bər) *vt.* [see DIS- & MEMBER] 1 to cut or tear the limbs from 2 to pull or cut to pieces —**dis·mem′ber·ment** *n.*

dis·miss (-mis′) *vt.* [< L *dis-*, from + *mittere*, send] 1 to cause or allow to leave 2 to discharge from employment, etc. 3 to put aside mentally 4 *Law* to reject (a claim, etc.) —**dis·miss′al** *n.*

dis·mis·sive (-mis′iv) *adj.* showing lack of concern or regard

dis·mount (-mount′) *vi.* to get off, as from a horse —*vt.* 1 to remove (a thing) from its mounting 2 to take apart; dismantle

dis·o·be·di·ence (dis′ō bē′dē əns) *n.* refusal to obey; insubordination —**dis′o·be′di·ent** *adj.*

dis·o·bey (-ō bā′) *vt., vi.* to refuse to obey

dis·o·blige (-ə blīj′) *vt.* **-bliged′, -blig′ing** 1 to refuse to oblige 2 to offend

dis·or·der (-ôr′dər) *n.* 1 a lack of order; confusion 2 a breach of public peace; riot 3 an ailment —*vt.* 1 to throw into disorder 2 to upset the normal functions of

dis·or·der·ly *adj.* 1 untidy 2 violating public peace, safety, etc. —**dis·or′der·li·ness** *n.*

dis·or·gan·ize (dis ôr′gə nīz′) *vt.* **-ized′, -iz′ing** to break up the order or system of; throw into confusion —**dis·or′gan·i·za′tion** *n.*

dis·o·ri·ent (-ôr′ē ent′) *vt.* [see DIS- & ORI-ENT, *v.*] 1 to cause to lose one's bearings 2 to confuse mentally —**dis·o′ri·en·ta′tion** *n.*

dis·own (-ōn′) *vt.* to refuse to acknowledge as one's own; repudiate

dis·par·age (di spar′ij) *vt.* **-aged, -ag·ing** [< OFr *des-* (see DIS-) + *parage*, rank] 1 to discredit 2 to belittle —**dis·par′age·ment** *n.*

dis·pa·rate (dis′pə rət) *adj.* [< L *dis-*, not + *par*, equal] distinct or different in kind; unequal —**dis·par·i·ty** (di spar′ə tē) *n., pl.* **-ties**

dis·pas·sion·ate (dis pash′ə nət) *adj.* free from passion or bias; impartial —**dis·pas′sion·ate·ly** *adv.*

dis·patch (di spach′; *for n., also* dis′pach′) *vt.* [< L *dis-*, away + *pes*, foot] 1 to send promptly, as on an errand 2 to kill 3 to finish quickly —*n.* 1 a sending off 2 a killing 3 speed; promptness 4 a message 5 a news story sent by a reporter —**dis·patch′er** *n.*

dis·pel (di spel′) *vt.* **-pelled′, -pel′ling** [< L *dis-*, apart + *pellere*, to drive] to scatter and drive away

dis·pen·sa·ble (di spen′sə bəl) *adj.* 1 that can be dealt out 2 that can be dispensed with; not important

dis·pen·sa·ry (-sə rē) *n., pl.* **-ries** a room or place where medicines and first-aid treatment are available

dis·pen·sa·tion (dis′pən sā′shən) *n.* 1 a dispensing 2 something dispensed 3 an administrative system 4 a release from an obligation 5 *Theol.* the ordering of events under divine authority

dis·pense (di spens′) *vt.* **-pensed′, -pens′ing** [< L *dis-*, out + *pendere*, weigh] 1 to give out; distribute 2 to prepare and give out (medicines) 3 to administer (the law or justice) —**dispense with** 1 to get rid of 2 to do without —**dis·pens′er** *n.*

dis·perse (di spurs′) *vt.* **-persed′, -pers′ing** [< L *dis-*, out + *spargere*, scatter] 1 to break up and scatter 2 to dispel (mist, etc.) —*vi.* to scatter —**dis·per′sal** *n.* —**dis·per′sion** *n.*

dis·pir·it (di spir′it) *vt.* to depress; discourage —**dis·pir′it·ed** *adj.*

dis·place (dis plās′) *vt.* **-placed′, -plac′ing** 1 to move from its usual place 2 to remove from office; discharge 3 to supplant

displaced person one forced from one's country, esp. as a result of war

dis·place·ment *n.* 1 a displacing or being displaced 2 the weight or volume of air, water, or other fluid displaced by a floating object

dis·play (di splā′) *vt.* [< L *dis-*, apart + *plicare*, to fold] 1 [Obs.] to spread out; unfold 2 to exhibit —*n.* 1 an exhibition 2 anything displayed

dis·please (dis plēz′) *vt., vi.* **-pleased′, -pleas′ing** to fail to please; offend

dis·pleas·ure (-plezh′ər) *n.* a being displeased

dis·port (di spôrt′) *vi.* [< OFr *des-* (see DIS-) + *porter*, carry] to play; frolic —*vt.* to amuse (oneself)

dis·pos·al (di spō′zəl) *n.* 1 a disposing 2 a device in the drain of a kitchen sink to grind up garbage

dis·pose (-spōz′) *vt.* **-posed′, -pos′ing** [see DIS- & POSITION] 1 to arrange 2 to settle (affairs) 3 to make willing; incline —**dispose of** 1 to settle 2 to give away or sell 3 to get rid of —**dis·pos′a·ble** *adj.*

dis·po·si·tion (dis′pə zish′ən) *n.* 1 arrangement 2 management of affairs 3 a selling or giving away 4 the authority to settle, etc.; control 5 a tendency 6 one's temperament

dis·pos·sess (-pə zes′) *vt.* to deprive of the possession of land, a house, etc.

dis·praise (-prāz′) *vt.* **-praised′, -prais′ing** [< OFr *despreisier*] to blame; censure —*n.* blame

dis·pro·por·tion (-prə pôr′shən) *n.* a lack of proportion —**dis′pro·por′tion·al** *adj.*, **dis′pro·por′tion·ate** *adj.*

dis·prove (-proōv′) *vt.* **-proved′, -proved′** or **-prov′en, -prov′ing** to prove to be false

dis·pu·ta·tion (dis′pyoō tā′shən) *n.* 1 a disputing 2 debate

dis·pu·ta·tious (-pyoō tā′shəs) *adj.* inclined to dispute; contentious —**dis·pu·ta′tious·ly** *adv.*

dis·pute (di spyoōt′) *vi.* **-put′ed, -put′ing** [< L *dis-*, apart + *putare*, to think] 1 to argue; debate 2 to quarrel —*vt.* 1 to argue (a question) 2 to doubt 3 to oppose —*n.* 1 a disputing; debate 2 a quarrel —**in dispute** not settled —**dis·put′a·ble** *adj.* —**dis·pu′tant** *adj., n.*

dis·qual·i·fy (dis kwôl′ə fī′) *vt.* **-fied′, -fy′ing** to make or declare unfit or ineligible —**dis·qual′i·fi·ca′tion** *n.*

dis·qui·et (dis kwī′ət) *vt.* to make uneasy; disturb —*n.* restlessness: also **dis·qui′e·tude′** (-ə toōd′)

dis·qui·si·tion (dis′kwi zish′ən) *n.* [< L *dis-*, apart + *quaerere*, to seek] a formal discussion; treatise

dis·re·gard (dis′ri gärd′) *vt.* 1 to pay little or no attention to 2 to treat without due respect —*n.* 1 lack of attention 2 lack of due regard or respect

dis·re·pair (-ri per′) *n.* the condition of needing repairs; state of neglect

dis·rep·u·ta·ble (-rep′yoō tə bəl) *adj.* 1 not reputable 2 not fit to be seen

dis·re·pute (-ri pyoōt′) *n.* lack or loss of repute; bad reputation; disgrace

dis·re·spect (-ri spekt′) *n.* lack of respect; discourtesy —*vt.* to show a lack of respect for —**dis′re·spect′ful** *adj.*

dis·robe (dis rōb′) *vt., vi.* **-robed′, -rob′ing** to undress

dis·rupt (dis rupt′) *vt., vi.* [< L *dis-*, apart + *rumpere*, to break] 1 to break apart 2 to disturb or interrupt —**dis·rup′tion** *n.* —**dis·rup′tive** *adj.*

dis·sat·is·fy (-sat′is fī′) *vt.* **-fied′, -fy′ing**

to fail to satisfy; displease —**dis·sat'is·fac'tion** *n.*

dis·sect (di sekt') *vt.* ⟦< L *dis-*, apart + *secare*, to cut⟧ 1 to cut apart piece by piece, as a body for purposes of study 2 to examine or analyze closely —**dis·sec'tion** *n.* —**dis·sec'tor** *n.*

dis·sem·ble (di sem'bəl) *vt., vi.* **-bled, -bling** ⟦< OFr *dessembler*⟧ to conceal (the truth, one's feelings, motives, etc.) under a false appearance —**dis·sem'blance** *n.* —**dis·sem'bler** *n.*

dis·sem·i·nate (di sem'ə nāt') *vt.* **-nat'ed, -nat'ing** ⟦< L *dis-*, apart + *seminare*, to sow⟧ to scatter about; spread widely —**dis·sem'i·na'tion** *n.*

dis·sen·sion (di sen'shən) *n.* a dissenting; disagreement or quarreling

dis·sent (di sent') *vi.* ⟦< L *dis-*, apart + *sentire*, feel⟧ 1 to disagree 2 to reject doctrines of an established church —*n.* a dissenting —**dis·sent'er** *n.*

dis·ser·ta·tion (dis'ər tā'shən) *n.* ⟦< L *dis-*, apart + *serere*, join⟧ a formal discourse or treatise, esp. one written to fulfill the requirements for a doctorate from a university

dis·serv·ice (dis sur'vis) *n.* harm

dis·sev·er (di sev'ər) *vt.* 1 to sever; separate 2 to divide into parts —*vi.* to separate; disunite

dis·si·dence (dis'ə dəns) *n.* ⟦< L *dis-*, apart + *sidere*, sit⟧ disagreement; dissent —**dis'si·dent** (-dənt) *adj., n.*

dis·sim·i·lar (dis sim'ə lər) *adj.* not similar; different —**dis·sim'i·lar'i·ty** (-lar'ə tē) *n., pl.* **-ties**

dis·si·mil·i·tude (dis'si mil'ə tōōd') *n.* difference

dis·sim·u·late (di sim'yōō lāt') *vt., vi.* **-lat'ed, -lat'ing** ⟦see DIS- & SIMULATE⟧ to dissemble —**dis·sim'u·la'tion** *n.* —**dis·sim'u·la'tor** *n.*

dis·si·pate (dis'ə pāt') *vt.* **-pat'ed, -pat'ing** ⟦< L *dis-*, apart + *supare*, to throw⟧ 1 to scatter; disperse 2 to make disappear 3 to waste or squander —*vi.* 1 to vanish 2 to indulge in pleasure to the point of harming oneself —**dis'si·pa'tion** *n.*

dis·so·ci·ate (di sō'shē āt') *vt.* **-at'ed, -at'ing** ⟦< L *dis-*, apart + *sociare*, join⟧ to break the connection between; disunite —**dis·so'ci·a'tion** *n.*

dis·so·lute (dis'ə lōōt') *adj.* ⟦see DISSOLVE⟧ dissipated and immoral; profligate —**dis'so·lute'ly** *adv.* —**dis'so·lute'ness** *n.*

dis·so·lu·tion (dis'ə lōō'shən) *n.* a dissolving or being dissolved; specif., *a)* a breaking up or into parts *b)* a termination *c)* death

dis·solve (di zälv', -zôlv') *vt., vi.* **-solved', -solv'ing** ⟦< L *dis-*, apart + *solvere*, loosen⟧ 1 to make or become liquid; melt 2 to pass or make pass into solution 3 to break up 4 to end as by breaking up; terminate 5 to disappear or make disappear

dis·so·nance (dis'ə nəns) *n.* ⟦< L *dis-*, apart + *sonus*, a sound⟧ 1 an inharmonious combination of sounds 2 lack of harmony or agreement —**dis'so·nant** *adj.*

dis·suade (di swād') *vt.* **-suad'ed, -suad'-**

ing ⟦< L *dis-*, away + *suadere*, to persuade⟧ to turn (a person) aside (*from* a course, etc.) by persuasion or advice —**dis·sua'sion** (-swā'zhən) *n.*

dist *abbrev.* 1 distance 2 district

dis·taff (dis'taf') *n.* ⟦< OE *dis-*, flax + *stæf*, staff⟧ a staff on which flax, wool, etc. is wound for use in spinning —*adj.* female; specif., of the maternal side of a family

dis·tal (dis'təl) *adj.* [DIST(ANT) + -AL] *Anat.* farthest from the point of attachment or origin; terminal —**dis'tal·ly** *adv.*

dis·tance (dis'təns) *n.* ⟦< L *dis-*, apart + *stare*, to stand⟧ 1 separation in space or time; remoteness 2 an interval between two points in space or time 3 remoteness in behavior; reserve 4 a faraway place —*vt.* **-tanced, -tanc·ing** to place at an emotional distance (*from*)

dis·tant (-tənt) *adj.* 1 far away in space or time 2 away [100 miles *distant*] 3 far apart in relationship 4 aloof; reserved 5 from or at a distance —**dis'tant·ly** *adv.*

dis·taste (dis tāst') *n.* dislike —**dis·taste'ful** *adj.*

dis·tem·per (dis tem'pər) *n.* ⟦< ML *distemperare*, to disorder⟧ an infectious viral disease of young dogs, horses, etc.

dis·tend (di stend') *vt., vi.* ⟦< L *dis-*, apart + *tendere*, to stretch⟧ 1 to stretch out 2 to expand, as by pressure from within; swell —**dis·ten'tion** *n.*

dis·till or **dis·til** (di stil') *vi., vt.* **-tilled', -till'ing** ⟦< L *de-*, down + *stillare*, to drop⟧ 1 to fall or let fall in drops 2 to undergo, subject to, or produce by distillation 3 to reduce to what is essential —**dis·till'er** *n.*

dis·til·late (dis'tə lāt', -lit) *n.* a liquid obtained by distilling

dis·til·la·tion (dis'tə lā'shən) *n.* 1 the process of heating a mixture and condensing the resulting vapor to produce a more nearly pure substance 2 anything distilled

dis·till·er·y (di stil'ər ē) *n., pl.* **-ies** a place where liquor is distilled

dis·tinct (di stiŋkt') *adj.* [see DISTINGUISH] 1 not alike 2 separate 3 clearly perceived or marked off 4 unmistakable; definite —**dis·tinct'ly** *adv.*

dis·tinc·tion (-stiŋk'shən) *n.* 1 the act of making or keeping distinct 2 difference 3 a quality or feature that differentiates 4 fame; eminence 5 the quality that makes one seem superior 6 a mark of special recognition or honor

dis·tinc·tive *adj.* making distinct; characteristic —**dis·tinc'tive·ly** *adv.* —**dis·tinc'tive·ness** *n.*

dis·tin·guish (di stiŋ'gwish) *vt.* ⟦< L *dis-*, apart + *-stinguere*, to prick⟧ 1 to perceive or show the difference in 2 to characterize 3 to perceive clearly 4 to classify 5 to make famous —*vi.* to make a distinction (*between* or *among*) —**dis·tin'guish·a·ble** *adj.*

dis·tin·guished *adj.* celebrated; famous

dis·tort (di stôrt') *vt.* ⟦< L *dis-*, intens. + *torquere*, to twist⟧ 1 to twist out of shape 2 to misrepresent (facts, etc.) **3** to modify so as to reproduce unfaithfully —**dis·tor′tion** *n.*

dis·tract (di strakt′) *vt.* [< L *dis-*, apart + *trahere*, draw] **1** to draw (the mind, etc.) away in another direction **2** to confuse; bewilder —**dis·tract′ed** *adj.* —**dis·tract′ing** *adj.*

dis·trac·tion *n.* **1** a distracting or being distracted **2** anything that distracts **3** great mental distress

dis·trait (di strā′) *adj.* [see DISTRACT] absent-minded; inattentive

dis·traught (−strôt′) *adj.* [var. of prec.] **1** mentally confused; distracted **2** driven mad; crazed

dis·tress (di stres′) *vt.* [ult. < L *dis-*, apart + *stringere*, to stretch] to cause misery or suffering to —*n.* **1** pain, suffering, etc. **2** an affliction **3** a state of danger or trouble —**dis·tressed′** *adj.*

dis·trib·ute (di strib′yōōt) *vt.* **-ut·ed, -ut·ing** [< L *dis-*, apart + *tribuere*, allot] **1** to give out in shares **2** to spread out **3** to classify **4** to put (things) in various distinct places —**dis′tri·bu′tion** *n.*

dis·trib·u·tor *n.* one that distributes; specif., *a*) a dealer who distributes goods to retailers or consumers *b*) a device for distributing electric current to the spark plugs of a gasoline engine

dis·trict (dis′trikt) *n.* [< L *dis-*, apart + *stringere*, to stretch] **1** a division of a state, city, etc. made for a specific purpose **2** any region

district attorney the prosecuting attorney for the state or the federal government in a specified district

District of Columbia federal district of the U.S., on the Potomac; coextensive with the city of Washington: abbrev. *DC*

dis·trust (dis trust′) *n.* a lack of trust; doubt —*vt.* to have no trust in; doubt —**dis·trust′ful** *adj.*

dis·turb (di sturb′) *vt.* [< L *dis-*, intens. + *turbare*, to disorder] **1** to break up the quiet or settled order of **2** to make uneasy; upset **3** to interrupt —**dis·turb′er** *n.*

dis·turb·ance *n.* **1** a disturbing or being disturbed **2** anything that disturbs **3** commotion; disorder

dis·u·nite (dis′yōō nīt′) *vt., vi.* **-nit′ed, -nit′ing** to divide or separate into parts, factions, etc. —**dis·u′ni·ty** *n.*

dis·use (−yōōs′) *n.* lack of use

ditch (dich) *n.* [OE *dic*] a long, narrow channel dug into the earth, as for drainage —*vt.* **1** to make a ditch in **2** [Slang] to get rid of

dith·er (dith′ər) *vi.* [ME *dideren*] **1** to be nervously excited or confused **2** to be indecisive —*n.* a nervously excited or confused state

dit·sy (dit′sē) *adj.* **-si·er, -si·est** [? < DIZZY] [Slang] silly, flighty, eccentric, etc.: also sp. **dit′zy**

dit·to (dit′ō) *n., pl.* **-tos** [It < L *dicere*, to say] **1** the same (as above or before) **2** DITTO MARK

ditto mark a mark (″) used in lists or tables to show that the item above is to be repeated

dit·ty (dit′ē) *n., pl.* **-ties** [< L *dicere*, to say] a short, simple song

di·u·ret·ic (dī′yōō ret′ik) *adj.* [< Gr *dia-*, through + *ourein*, urinate] increasing the flow of urine —*n.* a diuretic drug or substance

di·ur·nal (dī ur′nəl) *adj.* [< L *dies*, day] **1** daily **2** of the daytime —**di·ur′nal·ly** *adv.*

div *abbrev.* **1** dividend **2** division

di·va (dē′və) *n., pl.* **-vas** or **-ve** (−ve) [It < L, goddess] **1** a leading woman singer **2** [Inf.] one who demands special treatment, overreacts, etc.

di·va·lent (dī′vā′lənt, dī vā′-) *adj. Chem.* having two valences or a valence of two

di·van (di van′, dī′van′) *n.* [< Pers *dīwān*] a large, low couch or sofa

dive (dīv) *vi.* **dived** or **dove, dived, div′ing** [OE *dyfan*] **1** to plunge headfirst into water **2** to submerge **3** to plunge suddenly into something **4** to make a steep descent, as an airplane —*n.* **1** a diving **2** any sudden plunge **3** a sharp descent **4** [Inf.] a cheap, disreputable saloon, etc. —**div′er** *n.*

di·verge (di vurj′, dī-) *vi.* **-verged′, -verg′ing** [< L *dis-*, apart + *vergere*, to turn] **1** to go or move in different directions; branch off **2** to differ, as in opinion —**di·ver′gence** *n.* —**di·ver′gent** *adj.*

di·vers (dī′vərz) *adj.* [see fol.] various

di·verse (də vurs′, dī-) *adj.* [< L *dis-*, apart + *vertere*, to turn] **1** different **2** varied —**di·verse′ly** *adv.*

di·ver·si·fy (də vur′sə fī′) *vt.* **-fied′, -fy′ing 1** to make diverse; vary **2** to divide up (investments, etc.) among various stocks, etc. —*vi.* to expand product lines, etc. —**di·ver′si·fi·ca′tion** *n.*

di·ver·sion (də vur′zhən, dī-) *n.* **1** a diverting or turning aside **2** distraction of attention **3** a pastime

di·ver·sion·ar·y *adj.* serving to divert or distract [*diversionary* tactics]

di·ver·si·ty (də vur′sə tē, dī-) *n., pl.* **-ties 1** difference **2** variety, as of ethnic background

di·vert (də vurt′, dī-) *vt.* [see DIVERSE] **1** to turn (a person or thing) aside from a course, etc. **2** to distract **3** to amuse

di·ver·tic·u·li·tis (dī′vər tik′yōō līt′is) *n.* [< L *de-*, from + *vertere*, to turn + *-ITIS*] inflammation of a sac (**di·ver·tic′u·lum**) opening out from a tubular organ or main cavity

di·vest (də vest′, dī-) *vt.* [< L *dis-*, from + *vestire*, to dress] **1** to strip of clothing, etc. **2** to deprive *of* rank, rights, etc. **3** to rid of something unwanted —*vi.* to sell off an investment or other asset

di·vide (də vīd′) *vt.* **-vid′ed, -vid′ing** [< L *dividere*] **1** to separate into parts; sever **2** to classify **3** to make or keep separate **4** to apportion **5** to cause to disagree **6** *Math.* to separate into equal parts by a divisor —*vi.* **1** to be or become separate **2** to disagree **3** to share **4** *Math.* to do division —*n.* a boundary; specif., a ridge that divides two drainage areas —**di·vid′er** *n.*

div·i·dend (div′ə dend′) *n.* **1** the number or

quantity to be divided **2** *a)* a sum to be divided among stockholders, etc. *b)* a single share of this **3** a bonus

div·i·na·tion (div′ə nā′shən) *n.* ⟦see fol.⟧ **1** the practice of trying to foretell the future **2** a prophecy

di·vine (də vīn′) *adj.* ⟦< L *divus*, god⟧ **1** of, like, or from God or a god; holy **2** devoted to God; religious **3** [Inf.] very pleasing, etc. —*n.* a member of the clergy —*vt.* **-vined′**, **-vin′ing 1** to prophesy **2** to guess **3** to find out by intuition —**di·vine′ly** *adv.*

divining rod a forked stick believed to dip downward when held over an underground supply of water, etc.

di·vin·i·ty (də vin′ə tē) *n.* **1** a being divine **2** *pl.* **-ties** a god **3** theology —**the Divinity** God

di·vis·i·ble (də viz′ə bəl) *adj.* that can be divided, esp. without leaving a remainder —**di·vis·i·bil′i·ty** *n.*

di·vi·sion (də vizh′ən) *n.* **1** a dividing or being divided **2** an apportioning **3** a difference of opinion **4** anything that divides **5** a segment, section, department, class, etc. **6** the process of finding how many times a number (the *divisor*) is contained in another (the *dividend*) **7** a major military unit

di·vi·sive (də vī′siv) *adj.* causing disagreement or dissension —**di·vi′sive·ly** *adv.* —**di·vi′sive·ness** *n.*

di·vi·sor (də vī′zər) *n.* the number by which the dividend is divided

di·vorce (də vôrs′) *n.* ⟦< L *dis-*, apart + *vertere*, to turn⟧ **1** legal dissolution of a marriage **2** any complete separation —*vt.* **-vorced′**, **-vorc′ing 1** to dissolve legally a marriage between **2** to dissolve the marriage with (one's spouse) **3** to separate —**di·vorce′ment** *n.*

di·vor·cé (di vôr′sā′, -sē′) *n.* ⟦Fr⟧ a divorced man

di·vor·cée (di vôr′sā′, -sē′) *n.* ⟦Fr⟧ a divorced woman

div·ot (div′ət) *n.* ⟦Scot⟧ *Golf* a lump of turf dislodged in making a stroke

di·vulge (də vulj′) *vt.* **-vulged′**, **-vulg′ing** ⟦< L *dis-*, apart + *vulgare*, make public⟧ to make known; reveal

div·vy (div′ē) *vt., vi.* **-vied**, **-vy·ing** [Slang] to share; divide (*up*)

Dix·ie (dik′sē) ⟦< *Dixie*, the minstrel song⟧ the Southern states of the U.S.

Dix·ie·land *adj.* in, of, or like a style of jazz with a ragtime tempo

DIY (dē′ī′wī′) *n.* DO-IT-YOURSELF

diz·zy (diz′ē) *adj.* **-zi·er**, **-zi·est** ⟦OE *dysig*, foolish⟧ **1** feeling giddy or unsteady **2** causing giddiness **3** confused **4** [Inf.] silly; harebrained —**diz′zi·ly** *adv.* —**diz′zi·ness** *n.*

DJ (dē′jā′) *n.* ⟦(DISC) J(OCKEY)⟧ **1** a person who conducts a radio program of recorded music **2** a person who plays recorded music for dancing, as at a party or disco

Dji·bou·ti (ji bōōt′ē) country in E Africa

DMV *abbrev.* Department (or Division) of Motor Vehicles

DMZ *abbrev.* demilitarized zone

DNA (dē′en′ā′) *n.* ⟦< d(*eoxyribo*)n(*ucleic*) a(*cid*)⟧ the basic chromosome material, containing and transmitting the hereditary pattern

Dne·pr (nē′pər) river in W Russia, Belarus, & Ukraine, flowing into the Black Sea: also **Dnie′per**

DNR *abbrev.* **1** Department of Natural Resources **2** do not resuscitate

do¹ (dōō) *vt.* **did**, **done**, **do′ing** ⟦OE *don*⟧ **1** to perform (an action, etc.) **2** to complete; finish **3** to cause [it *does* no harm] **4** to exert [*do* your best] **5** to deal with as is required [*do* the ironing] **6** to have as one's occupation; work at **7** to move at a speed of [to *do* 65 mph] **8** [Inf.] to serve (a jail term) **9** [Slang] to ingest [to *do* drugs] —*vi.* **1** to behave or perform [*do* as you please] **2** to be active [up and *doing*] **3** to get along; fare [he is *doing* well after surgery] **4** to be adequate [casual dress will *do*] **5** to take place [anything *doing* tonight?] —*v.aux.* **1** used to give emphasis [*do* stay a while] **2** used to ask a question [*did* you go?] **3** used as a substitute verb [act as I *do* (act)] **4** used in a negative construction [*do* not go] —**do in 1** [Slang] to kill **2** [Inf.] to tire out —**do over** [Inf.] to redecorate —**do up** to wrap up —**do with** to make use of —**do without** to get along without —**have to do with** to be related to

do² (dō) *n.* ⟦It⟧ *Music* the first or last tone of the diatonic scale

DOA *abbrev.* dead on arrival

do·a·ble (dōō′ə bəl) *adj.* that can be done

Do·ber·man (pin·scher) (dō′bər mən pin′chər) *n.* ⟦< Ger after K. F. L. *Dobermann* (1834–94), breeder + *pinscher*, terrier⟧ a large dog with a short, dark coat

doc (däk) *n.* [Slang] doctor

do·cent (dō′sənt) *n.* ⟦< L *docere*, to teach⟧ a lecturer or tour guide, as at a museum

doc·ile (däs′əl) *adj.* [see prec.] easily led or directed; submissive —**do·cil·i·ty** (dō sil′ə tē, dä-) *n.*

dock¹ (däk) *n.* ⟦< It *doccia*, canal⟧ **1** an excavated basin for receiving ships **2** a wharf; pier **3** the water between two piers **4** a platform for loading and unloading trucks, etc. —*vt., vi.* to bring or come to or into a dock: said of a ship

dock² (däk) *n.* ⟦< Fl *dok*, a cage⟧ the place where the accused stands or sits in court

dock³ (däk) *n.* ⟦OE *docce*⟧ a tall, coarse weed of the buckwheat family

dock⁴ (däk) *vt.* ⟦ME *dok*, tail⟧ **1** to cut off the end of (a tail, etc.); bob **2** to deduct from (wages, etc.)

dock·et (däk′it) *n.* ⟦< ?⟧ **1** a list of cases to be tried by a law court **2** an agenda —*vt.* to enter in a docket

dock·yard *n.* SHIPYARD

doc·tor (däk′tər) *n.* ⟦< L, teacher⟧ **1** one who holds a doctorate **2** a physician or surgeon **3** one licensed to practice any of the healing arts —*vt.* [Inf.] **1** to try to heal **2** to tamper with

doc·tor·ate (-it) *n.* the highest degree awarded by universities —**doc′tor·al** *adj.*

Doctor of Philosophy the highest doctorate awarded for original research

doc·tri·naire (däk′tri ner′) *adj.* 〖Fr〗 adhering to a doctrine dogmatically

doc·trine (däk′trin) *n.* 〖see DOCTOR〗 something taught, esp. as the principles of a religion, political party, etc. —**doc′tri·nal** (-tri nəl) *adj.*

doc·u·dra·ma (däk′yōō drä′mə) *n.* a TV dramatization of real events

doc·u·ment (däk′yōō mənt, -yə-; *for v.,* -ment′) *n.* 〖< L *documentum,* proof〗 anything printed, written, etc. that contains information or is relied upon to record or prove something —*vt.* to provide with or support by documents

doc·u·men·ta·ry (-ment′ə rē) *adj.* 1 of or supported by documents 2 depicting news events, social conditions, etc. in nonfictional but dramatic form —*n., pl.* **-ries** a documentary film, etc.

doc·u·men·ta·tion (-mən tā′shən, -men-) *n.* 1 the supplying of documents 2 the documents thus supplied 3 instructions for using computer hardware or software

dod·der (däd′ər) *vi.* 〖ME *daderen*〗 1 to shake or tremble, as from old age 2 to totter —**dod′der·ing** *adj.*

dodge (däj) *vi., vt.* **dodged, dodg′ing** 〖< ?〗 1 to move quickly aside, or avoid by so moving 2 to use tricks or evasions, or evade by so doing —*n.* 1 a dodging 2 a trick used in evading or cheating —**dodg′er** *n.*

do·do (dō′dō) *n., pl.* **-dos** or **-does** 〖Port *doudo,* lit., stupid〗 1 a large, flightless bird, now extinct 2 〖Slang〗 a stupid person

doe (dō) *n.* 〖OE *da*〗 a female deer, antelope, rabbit, goat, etc.

do·er (dōō′ər) *n.* 1 one who does something 2 one who gets things done

does (duz) *vt., vi. 3d pers. sing., pres. indic., of* DO[1]

doe·skin *n.* 1 leather from the skin of a female deer 2 a soft woolen cloth

doff (däf, dôf) *vt.* 〖see DO[1] & OFF〗 to take off (one's hat, clothes, etc.)

dog (dôg) *n.* 〖OE *docga*〗 1 any of various canines, esp. one of a domesticated breed kept as a pet, for hunting, etc. 2 a mean, contemptible fellow 3 〖*pl.*〗 〖Slang〗 feet 4 〖Slang〗 an unattractive person or unsatisfactory thing 5 *Mech.* a device for holding or grappling —*vt.* **dogged, dog′ging** to follow or hunt doggedly —**go to the dogs** 〖Inf.〗 to deteriorate

dog days the hot, uncomfortable days in July and August

dog-ear *n.* a turned-down corner of a page —**dog′-eared′** *adj.*

dog·fight *n.* a violent fight; specif., combat between fighter planes

dog·fish *n., pl.* **-fish′** or **-fish′es** any of various small sharks

dog·ged (dôg′id) *adj.* persistent; stubborn —**dog′ged·ly** *adv.*

dog·ger·el (dôg′ər əl) *n.* 〖ME *dogerel*〗 trivial poetry with a clumsy or monotonous rhythm

dog·gie bag (dôg′ē) a bag supplied by a restaurant for carrying leftovers, as for one's dog

dog·gone *interj.* damn! darn! —*adj.* 〖Inf.〗 damned

dog·house *n.* a structure for sheltering a dog —**in the doghouse** 〖Slang〗 in disfavor

do·gie (dō′gē) *n.* 〖< ?〗 〖West〗 a stray calf

dog·ma (dôg′mə) *n.* 〖< Gr, opinion〗 a doctrine; tenet, esp. a theological doctrine strictly adhered to

dog·mat·ic (-mat′ik) *adj.* 1 of or like dogma 2 asserted without proof 3 stating opinion positively or arrogantly —**dog·mat′i·cal·ly** *adv.*

dog·ma·tism (-mə tiz′əm) *n.* dogmatic assertion of opinion —**dog′ma·tist** *n.*

do-good·er *n.* 〖Inf.〗 an idealistic but impractical person who seeks to correct social ills

dog-tired *adj.* very tired; exhausted

dog·trot *n.* a slow, easy trot

dog·wood *n.* a small, flowering tree of the E U.S.

doi·ly (doi′lē) *n., pl.* **-lies** a small mat, as of lace, put under a vase, etc. as a decoration or to protect a surface

do·ings (dōō′inz) *pl.n.* actions or events

do-it-your·self *n.* the practice of making or fixing things oneself, instead of hiring another —**do′-it-your·self′er** *n.*

Dol·by (dōl′bē) 〖after R. *Dolby,* U.S. recording engineer〗 *trademark for* an audio recording and playback system used to reduce unwanted noise

dol·drums (dōl′drəmz, däl′-) *pl.n.* 〖< ? DULL〗 1 *a)* low spirits *b)* sluggishness 2 equatorial ocean regions having little wind

dole (dōl) *n.* 〖OE *dal,* a share〗 1 money or food given in charity 2 money paid by a government to the unemployed —*vt.* doled, dol′ing to give (*out*) sparingly or as a dole

dole·ful (-fəl) *adj.* 〖< L *dolere,* suffer〗 sad; mournful —**dole′ful·ly** *adv.*

doll (däl) *n.* 〖< nickname for *Dorothy*〗 1 a child's toy made to resemble a human 2 〖Slang〗 any attractive or lovable person —*vt., vi.* 〖Inf.〗 to dress stylishly or showily: with *up*

dol·lar (däl′ər) *n.* 〖< Ger *thaler,* a coin〗 1 the monetary unit of the U.S., equal to 100 cents 2 the monetary unit of various other countries, as of Canada 3 a piece of money worth one dollar

dol·lop (däl′əp) *n.* 〖< ?〗 1 a soft mass 2 a quantity, often a small one

dol·ly (däl′ē) *n., pl.* **-lies** 1 a doll: child's word 2 a low, flat, wheeled frame for moving heavy objects

dol·men (dōl′mən, däl′-) *n.* 〖Fr〗 a prehistoric monument consisting of a large, flat stone laid across upright stones

do·lo·mite (dō′lə mīt′, däl′ə-) *n.* 〖after D. *Dolomieu* (1750-1801), Fr geologist〗 1 a mineral used in making cement, etc. 2 a sedimentary rock used as a building stone

do·lor·ous (dō′lər əs, däl′ər-) *adj.* 〖< L *dolere,* suffer〗 sorrowful; sad —**do′lor·ous·ly** *adv.*

dol·phin (däl′fin, dôl′-) *n.* ⟦< Gr *delphis*⟧ a small, highly intelligent toothed whale with a beaklike snout

dolt (dōlt) *n.* ⟦prob. < ME *dolte*⟧ a stupid person —**dolt′ish** *adj.*

-dom (dəm) ⟦OE *dom*, state⟧ *suffix* 1 rank or domain of [*kingdom*] 2 fact or state of being [*martyrdom*] 3 all who are [*officialdom*]

do·main (dō mān′) *n.* ⟦< L *dominus*, a lord⟧ 1 territory under one government or ruler 2 field of activity or influence

dome (dōm) *n.* ⟦< Gr *dōma*, housetop⟧ 1 a rounded roof or ceiling 2 any dome-shaped structure or object; specif., a sports stadium covered with a dome

do·mes·tic (dō mes′tik, də-) *adj.* ⟦< L *domus*, house⟧ 1 of the home or family 2 of or made in one's country 3 tame: said of animals 4 enjoying family life —*n.* a maid, cook, etc. in the home —**do·mes′ti·cal·ly** *adv.*

do·mes·ti·cate (-ti kāt′) *vt.* **-cat′ed, -cat′ing** 1 to accustom to home life 2 to tame or cultivate for human use —**do·mes′ti·ca′tion** *n.*

do·mes·tic·i·ty (dō′mes tis′ə tē) *n.* home life or devotion to it

dom·i·cile (däm′ə sīl′, -sil′; *also* dō′mə-) *n.* ⟦< L *domus*, home⟧ a home; residence —*vt.* **-ciled′, -cil′ing** to establish in a domicile

dom·i·nant (däm′ə nənt) *adj.* dominating; ruling; prevailing —**dom′i·nance** *n.* —**dom′i·nant·ly** *adv.*

dom·i·nate (-nāt′) *vt., vi.* **-nat′ed, -nat′ing** ⟦< L *dominus*, a master⟧ 1 to rule or control by superior power 2 to rise above (the surroundings) —**dom′i·na′tion** *n.*

dom·i·neer (däm′ə nir′) *vi., vt.* ⟦< Du: see prec.⟧ to rule (*over*) in a harsh or arrogant way; tyrannize

dom·i·neer·ing *adj.* overbearing

Do·min·i·can Republic (dō min′i kən, də-) country in the E part of Hispaniola, in the West Indies —**Do·min′i·can** *adj., n.*

do·min·ion (də min′yən) *n.* ⟦see DOMINATE⟧ 1 rule or power to rule 2 a governed territory or country 3 [D-] [Historical] a self-governing nation of the Commonwealth

dom·i·no (däm′ə nō′) *n., pl.* **-noes′** or **-nos′** ⟦Fr & It⟧ 1 a hooded cloak and a mask, worn at masquerades 2 a small mask that covers the area around the eyes 3 *a)* a small, oblong tile marked with dots *b)* [*pl., with sing. v.*] a game played with such tiles

don¹ (dän) *n.* ⟦Sp < L *dominus*, master⟧ 1 [D-] Sir; Mr.: a Spanish title of respect 2 a Spanish gentleman 3 [Chiefly Brit.] a teacher at a British university 4 a Mafia leader

don² (dän) *vt.* **donned, don′ning** ⟦contr. of *do on*⟧ to put on (clothes)

Don (dän) river in SC European Russia, flowing into the Black Sea

Do·ña (dō′nyä) *n.* ⟦Sp⟧ Lady; Madam: a Spanish title of respect

do·nate (dō′nāt′) *vt., vi.* **-nat′ed, -nat′ing** ⟦< L *donum*, gift⟧ to give or contribute —**do·na′tion** *n.* —**do′nat·or** (-ər) *n.*

done (dun) *vt., vi. pp. of* DO¹ —*adj.* 1 completed 2 cooked —**done (for)** [Inf.] dead, ruined, etc.

Don Juan (dän′ wän′) *Sp. Legend* a dissolute nobleman and seducer of women

don·key (dän′kē, dôn′-, dun′-) *n., pl.* **-keys** ⟦< ?⟧ 1 a domesticated ass 2 a stupid or foolish person

don·ny·brook (dän′ē brook′) *n.* ⟦after a fair formerly held near Dublin⟧ [Inf.] a rowdy fight or free-for-all

do·nor (dō′nər, -nôr′) *n.* one who donates

Don Qui·xo·te (dän′ kē hōt′ē) 1 a satirical novel by Cervantes 2 its chivalrous but unrealistic hero

don't (dōnt) *contr.* do not

do·nut (dō′nut′) *n. inf. sp. of* DOUGHNUT

doo·dle (dōōd′'l) *vi.* **-dled, -dling** ⟦Ger *dudeln*, to trifle⟧ to scribble aimlessly —*n.* a mark made in doodling —**doo′dler** *n.*

doo-doo (dōō′dōō′) *n.* 1 [Inf.] excrement 2 [Slang] trouble

doom (dōōm) *n.* ⟦OE *dom*⟧ 1 a judgment; sentence 2 fate 3 ruin or death —*vt.* 1 to pass judgment on; condemn 2 to destine to a tragic fate

dooms·day *n.* Judgment Day

doom·y *adj.* filled with a sense of doom or disaster

door (dôr) *n.* ⟦OE *duru*⟧ 1 a movable structure for opening or closing an entrance 2 a doorway 3 a means of access —**out of doors** outdoors

door·bell *n.* a bell, etc. at the entrance of a building or room, rung by visitors to signal their presence

door·man (-man′, -mən) *n., pl.* **-men′** (-men′, -mən) one whose work is opening the door of a building, hailing taxicabs, etc.

door·mat *n.* a mat to wipe the shoes on before entering a house, etc.

door·step *n.* a step that leads from an outer door to a path, lawn, etc.

door-to-door *adj., adv.* from one home to the next, calling on each in turn

door·way *n.* 1 an opening in a wall that can be closed by a door 2 any means of access

door·yard *n.* a yard onto which a door of a house opens

do·pa (dō′pə) *n.* ⟦< chemical name⟧ an amino acid that is converted by an enzyme in the blood into certain biological chemicals: one isomer (*L-dopa*) is used in treating Parkinson's disease

dope (dōp) *n.* ⟦Du *doop*, sauce⟧ 1 any thick liquid used as a lubricant, filler, etc. 2 [Inf.] a drug or narcotic 3 [Inf.] a stupid person 4 [Slang] information —*vt.* **doped, dop′ing** to drug

dop·er *n.* [Slang] a drug addict

dop·ey or **dop·y** (dō′pē) *adj.* **-i·er, -i·est** [Inf.] 1 lethargic 2 stupid

Dor·ic (dôr′ik) *adj.* designating or of a classical style of architecture marked by fluted columns with plain capitals

dorm (dôrm) *n.* [Inf.] DORMITORY

dor·mant (dôr′mənt) *adj.* ⟦< L *dormire*, to sleep⟧ 1 inactive 2 *Biol.* in a resting or torpid state —**dor′man·cy** *n.*

dor·mer (dôr′mər) *n.* ⟦see prec.⟧ 1 a window set upright in a structure projecting from a sloping roof: also **dormer window** 2 such a structure

dor·mi·to·ry (dôr′mə tôr′ē) *n., pl.* **-ries** ⟦see DORMANT⟧ 1 a room with beds for a number of people 2 a building with rooms for many people to sleep and live in, as at a college

dor·mouse (dôr′mous′) *n., pl.* **-mice′** (-mīs′) ⟦ME *dormous*⟧ a small, furry-tailed Old World rodent

dor·sal (dôr′səl) *adj.* ⟦< L *dorsum*, the back⟧ of, on, or near the back

do·ry (dôr′ē) *n., pl.* **-ries** ⟦< ? AmInd (Central America) *dori*, dugout⟧ a flat-bottomed fishing boat with high sides, a sharp bow, and a narrow stern

dose (dōs) *n.* ⟦< Gr *dosis*, a giving⟧ an amount of a medicine to be taken at one time —*vt.* **dosed, dos′ing** to give doses to —**dos′age** *n.*

do·sim·e·ter (dō sim′ət ər) *n.* a device for measuring exposure to ionizing radiation

dos·si·er (däs′ē ā′) *n.* ⟦Fr⟧ a collection of documents about some person, etc.

dost (dust) *vt., vi. archaic* 2d pers. sing., pres. indic., of DO¹: used with *thou*

Dos·to·ev·ski or **Dos·to·yev·sky** (dôs′tô yef′skē), **Feo·dor** (fyô′dôr) 1821–81; Russ. novelist

dot (dät) *n.* ⟦OE *dott*, head of boil⟧ 1 a tiny speck or mark 2 a small, round spot —*vt.* **dot′ted, dot′ting** to mark with or as with a dot or dots —**on the dot** [Inf.] at the exact time

dot·age (dōt′ij) *n.* ⟦ME < *doten*, DOTE⟧ childish state due to old age

dot·ard (-ərd) *n.* one in his or her dotage

dot.com (dät′käm′) *adj.* [Inf.] designating or of a company doing business mostly on the Web: also **dot-com**

dote (dōt) *vi.* **dot′ed, dot′ing** ⟦ME *doten*⟧ to be excessively fond: with *on* or *upon*

doth (duth) *vt., vi. archaic* 3d pers. sing., pres. indic., of DO¹

dot·ing (dōt′iŋ) *adj.* foolishly or excessively fond —**dot′ing·ly** *adv.*

dot-ma·trix *adj.* of or by printing in which characters are formed of closely spaced dots

Dou·ay Bible (dōō ā′) an English version of the Bible for Roman Catholics, published 1582–1610

dou·ble (dub′əl) *adj.* ⟦< L *duplus*⟧ 1 twofold 2 having two layers 3 paired or repeated [a *double* consonant] 4 being of two kinds [a *double* standard] 5 twice as much, as many, etc. 6 made for two —*adv.* 1 twofold or twice 2 two together —*n.* 1 anything twice as much, as many, etc. as normal 2 a duplicate; counterpart 3 a fold 4 [*pl.*] a game of tennis, etc. with two players on each side 5 *Baseball* a hit on which the batter reaches second base 6 *Bridge* the doubling of an opponent's bid —*vt.* **-bled, -bling** 1 to make twice as

much or as many 2 to fold 3 to repeat or duplicate 4 *Bridge* to multiply by two the value or penalty of (an opponent's bid) —*vi.* 1 to become double 2 to turn sharply backward 3 to serve as a double 4 to serve an additional purpose 5 *Baseball* to hit a double —**double back** to turn back in the direction from which one came —**double up 1** to clench (one's fist) 2 to bend over, as in pain 3 to share a room, etc. with someone —**on the double** [Inf.] quickly

double agent a spy employed by two rival espionage organizations

dou·ble-bar·reled *adj.* 1 having two barrels, as a kind of shotgun 2 having a double purpose or meaning

double bass (bās) the largest, deepest-toned instrument of the violin family

dou·ble-blind *adj.* designating or of a test of the effects of a drug, treatment, etc. in which neither the subjects nor the researchers know who is receiving the drug, treatment, etc.

double boiler a cooking utensil in which one pan, for food, fits in or on another, for boiling water

dou·ble-breast·ed *adj.* overlapping across the breast, as a coat

dou·ble-cross *vt.* [Inf.] to betray —**dou′ble-cross′er** *n.*

double date [Inf.] a romantic social engagement shared by two couples —**dou′ble-date′** *vi., vt.* **-dat′ed, -dat′ing**

dou·ble-deal·ing *n.* duplicity

dou·ble-deck·er *n.* 1 any structure or vehicle with an upper deck 2 [Inf.] a sandwich with two layers of filling and three slices of bread

dou·ble-dig·it *adj.* amounting to ten percent or more [*double-digit* inflation]

double dipping an unethical receiving of pay from two or more sources

dou·ble-en·ten·dre (dub′'l än tän′drə, dōō′blôn tôn′drə) *n.* ⟦< Fr⟧ a term with two meanings, esp. when one is risqué

dou·ble-head·er *n.* two games, esp. of baseball, played in succession on the same day

dou·ble-joint·ed *adj.* having joints that permit limbs, fingers, etc. to bend at other than the usual angles

dou·ble-knit *adj.* knit with a double stitch that makes the fabric extra thick

double play *Baseball* a play in which two players are put out

dou·ble-reed *adj.* designating or of a woodwind instrument, as the oboe, having two reeds separated by a narrow opening

double standard a system, code, etc. applied unequally, as a moral code stricter for women than for men

dou·blet (dub′lit) *n.* ⟦< OFr *double*, orig., something folded⟧ 1 a man's closefitting jacket of the 1300s to the 1500s 2 a pair, or one of a pair

double take a delayed reaction, as a second glance, following unthinking acceptance

double talk 1 ambiguous and deceptive talk 2 meaningless syllables made to sound like talk

dou·bloon (də blōōn′) *n.* [< Fr < Sp < L *duplus*, double] an obsolete Spanish gold coin

dou·bly (dub′lē) *adv.* 1 twice as much 2 two at a time

doubt (dout) *vi.* [< L *dubius*, uncertain] to be uncertain or undecided —*vt.* 1 to be uncertain about 2 to tend to disbelieve —*n.* 1 *a)* a wavering of opinion or belief *b)* lack of trust 2 a condition of uncertainty —**beyond (or without) doubt** certainly —**no doubt** 1 certainly 2 probably —**doubt′er** *n.* —**doubt′ing·ly** *adv.*

doubt·ful *adj.* 1 uncertain 2 causing doubt or suspicion 3 feeling doubt —**doubt′ful·ly** *adv.*

doubt·less *adv.* 1 without doubt; certainly 2 probably —**doubt′less·ly** *adv.*

douche (dōōsh) *n.* [Fr < It *doccia*] 1 a jet of liquid applied externally or internally to the body 2 a device for douching — *vt., vi.* **douched, douch′ing** to apply a douche (to)

dough (dō) *n.* [OE *dag*] 1 a mixture of flour, liquid, etc. worked into a soft mass for baking 2 [Slang] money

dough·nut *n.* a small, usually ring-shaped cake, fried in deep fat

dough·ty (dout′ē) *adj.* **-ti·er, -ti·est** [OE *dohtig*] [Now Rare] valiant; brave

dough·y (dō′ē) *adj.* **-i·er, -i·est** of or like dough; soft, pasty, etc.

Doug·las fir (dug′ləs) [after D. *Douglas* (1798-1834), Scot botanist] a large North American evergreen tree valued for its wood

dour (door, dour) *adj.* [< L *durus*, hard] 1 [Scot.] stern; severe 2 sullen; gloomy

douse (dous) *vt.* **doused, dous′ing** [< ?] 1 to thrust suddenly into liquid 2 to drench 3 [Inf.] to put out (a light or fire) quickly

dove[1] (duv) *n.* [ME *douve*] 1 any of the smaller species of pigeon: often used as a symbol of peace 2 an advocate of measures which avoid or end wars —**dov′ish** *adj.*

dove[2] (dōv) *vi. alt. pt. of* DIVE

dove·cote *n.* a structure with compartments for nesting pigeons

Do·ver (dō′vər) capital of Delaware

dove·tail (duv′tāl′) *n.* a projecting part that fits into a corresponding cut-out space to form a joint —*vt.* to join, piece together, or fasten, as with dovetails —*vi.* to fit together logically or closely

dow·a·ger (dou′ə jər) *n.* [< L *dotare*, to endow] 1 a widow with a title or property derived from her dead husband 2 an elderly, wealthy woman

dow·dy (dou′dē) *adj.* **-di·er, -di·est** [< ME *doude*, plain woman] not neat or smart in dress —**dow′di·ness** *n.*

dow·el (dou′əl) *n.* [ME *doule*] a peg of wood, etc., usually fitted into corresponding holes in two pieces to fasten them together —*vt.* **-eled** or **-elled, -el·ing** or **-el·ling** to fasten with dowels

dow·er (dou′ər) *n.* [< L *dare*, give] that part of a man's property which his widow inherits for life

down[1] (doun) *adv.* [OE *adune*, from the hill] 1 to, in, or on a lower place or level 2 in or to a low or lower condition, amount, etc. 3 southward [*down* to Mexico] 4 from an earlier to a later period 5 out of one's hands [*put it down*] 6 in a serious manner [*get down* to work] 7 completely [*loaded down*] 8 when purchased [$5 *down* and $5 a week] 9 in writing [take *down* notes] —*adj.* 1 descending 2 in a lower place 3 gone, brought, etc. down 4 dejected; discouraged 5 ill 6 finished [four *down*, six to go] 7 inoperative [the computer is *down*] —*prep.* down toward, along, through, into, or upon —*vt.* 1 to put or throw down 2 to swallow quickly —*n.* 1 a misfortune [ups and *downs*] 2 *Football* one of a series of plays in which a team tries to advance the ball ten yards or more —**down and out** penniless, ill, etc. —**down on** [Inf.] angry or annoyed with —**down with!** do away with!

down[2] (doun) *n.* [< ON *dūnn*] 1 soft, fine feathers 2 soft, fine hair

down[3] (doun) *n.* [OE *dun*, hill] an expanse of open, high, grassy land: *usually used in pl.*

down-and-dirt·y *adj.* [Slang] 1 vulgar; coarse 2 unscrupulous 3 fiercely competitive

down·beat *n. Music* an accented beat, esp. the first beat of a measure

down·cast *adj.* 1 directed downward 2 unhappy; dejected

Down East [*also* d- e-] [Inf.] in or into New England, esp. eastern coastal Maine

down·er *n.* [Slang] any depressant or sedative

down·fall *n.* 1 a sudden fall, as from power 2 the cause of this

down·grade *n.* a downward slope —*vt.* **-grad′ed, -grad′ing** 1 to demote 2 to belittle

down·heart·ed *adj.* discouraged

down·hill *adv.* toward the bottom of a hill —*adj.* 1 going downward 2 without difficulty

Down·ing Street (doun′iŋ) street in London, site of the usual residence of the prime minister

down·load *vt., vi.* to transfer (information) as from a network or main computer to another computer —**down′load′a·ble** *adj.*

down payment a partial payment at the time of purchase

down·play *vt.* to play down; minimize

down·pour *n.* a heavy rain

down·right *adv.* utterly —*adj.* 1 absolute; utter 2 plain; frank

down·scale *adj.* of or for people who are unstylish, not affluent, etc. — *vt., vi.* **-scaled′, -scal′ing** to make smaller, less, cheaper, etc.

down·size *vt., vi.* **-sized′, -siz′ing** to make or become smaller, as by eliminating employees

down·stage *adj., adv.* of or toward the front of the stage

down·stairs *adv.* 1 down the stairs 2 on or to a lower floor —*adj.* on a lower floor —*n.* a lower floor

down·state *adj., adv.* in, to, or from the southerly part of a U.S. state

down·stream *adv., adj.* in the direction of the current of a stream

down·swing *n.* 1 a downward swing, as of a golf club 2 a downward trend: also **down′turn′**

Down (*or* **Down's**) **syndrome** ⟦after J. *Down* (1828-96), Brit physician⟧ a congenital condition characterized by mental deficiency, a broad face, etc.

down·time *n.* 1 the time a machine, factory, etc. is not working or functioning 2 time for rest or relaxation

down-to-earth *adj.* 1 realistic or practical 2 without affectation

down·town *adj., adv.* in or toward the main business section of a city —*n.* the downtown section of a city

down·trod·den *adj.* oppressed

Down Under [*also* **d- u-**] *informal name for* Australia and New Zealand

down·ward (-wərd) *adv., adj.* toward a lower place, position, state, etc.: also **down′wards** *adv.*

down·y *adj.* -i·er, -i·est 1 covered with soft, fine feathers or hair 2 soft and fluffy

dow·ry (dou′rē) *n., pl.* -ries ⟦see DOWER⟧ property a woman brings to her husband at marriage

dowse (douz) *vi.* dowsed, dows′ing ⟦< ?⟧ to use a divining rod —dows′er *n.*

dox·ol·o·gy (däks äl′ə jē) *n., pl.* -gies ⟦< Gr *doxa*, praise + -*logia*, -LOGY⟧ a hymn of praise to God

doz *abbrev.* dozen(s)

doze (dōz) *vi.* dozed, doz′ing ⟦prob. < Scand⟧ to sleep lightly; nap —*n.* a light sleep —doz′er *n.*

doz·en (duz′ən) *n., pl.* -ens *or* -en ⟦< L *duo*, two + *decem*, ten⟧ a set of twelve —doz′enth *adj.*

dpt *abbrev.* 1 department 2 deponent

Dr *or* **Dr.** *abbrev.* 1 Doctor 2 Drive

drab (drab) *n.* ⟦< VL *drappus*, cloth⟧ a dull yellowish brown —*adj.* **drab′ber, drab′best** 1 dull yellowish-brown 2 dull; dreary —drab′ness *n.*

drach·ma (drak′mə) *n.* ⟦< Gr *drachmē*⟧ 1 an ancient Greek coin 2 the former monetary unit of modern Greece, superseded in 2002 by the EURO

Drac·u·la (drak′yə lə) *n.* the title character in a novel (1897): a Romanian vampire and count

draft (draft) *n.* ⟦OE *dragan*, to draw⟧ 1 a drawing or pulling, as of a vehicle or load 2 *a*) a drawing in of a fish net *b*) the amount of fish caught in one draw 3 *a*) a drinking or the amount taken at one drink *b*) [Inf.] a portion of beer, etc. drawn from a cask 4 an inhalation 5 a preliminary or tentative piece of writing 6 a plan or drawing of a work to be done 7 a current of air, esp. indoors 8 a device for regulating the current of air in a heating system 9 a written order for payment of money; check 10 *a*) the choosing or taking of persons, esp. for compulsory military service *b*) those so taken 11 the depth of water that a ship needs in order to float —*vt.* 1 to take, as for military service, by drawing from a group 2 to make a sketch of

or plans for —*adj.* 1 used for pulling loads 2 drawn from a cask [*draft* beer] —**on draft** ready to be drawn from a keg —**draft′er** *n.*

draft·ee (draf tē′) *n.* a person drafted, esp. for military service

drafts·man (drafts′mən) *n., pl.* -men (-mən) 1 one who draws plans, as of machinery 2 an artist skillful in drawing —**drafts′man·ship′** *n.*

draft·y *adj.* -i·er, -i·est open to drafts of air

drag (drag) *vt., vi.* dragged, drag′ging ⟦see DRAW⟧ 1 to pull or be pulled with effort, esp. along the ground 2 to search (a lake bottom, etc.) with a dragnet or the like 3 to draw (something) out over a period of time; move or pass too slowly: often with *on* or *out* —*n.* 1 a dragging 2 a dragnet, grapnel, etc. 3 anything that hinders 4 [Slang] clothing characteristic of one sex when worn by the opposite sex 5 [Slang] a puff of a cigarette, etc. 6 [Slang] street [the main *drag*] 7 [Slang] a dull person, situation, etc.

drag·gy (-ē) *adj.* -gi·er, -gi·est dragging; slow-moving, dull, etc.

drag·net *n.* 1 a net dragged along a lake bottom, etc., as for catching fish 2 an organized system or network for catching criminals, etc.

drag·on (drag′ən) *n.* ⟦< Gr *drakōn*⟧ a mythical monster, usually shown as a large, winged reptile breathing out fire

drag·on·fly *n., pl.* -flies′ a large, long-bodied insect with transparent, net-veined wings

dra·goon (drə gōōn′) *n.* ⟦< Fr *dragon*, DRAGON⟧ a heavily armed cavalryman —*vt.* to force *into* doing something; coerce

drag race a race between cars accelerating from a standstill on a short, straight course (**drag strip**) —**drag′-race′** *vi.* -raced′, -rac′ing

drain (drān) *vt.* ⟦OE *dryge*, dry⟧ 1 to draw off (liquid) gradually 2 to draw liquid from gradually 3 to drink all the liquid from (a cup, etc.) 4 to exhaust (strength) gradually —*vi.* 1 to flow off gradually 2 to become dry by draining 3 to disappear gradually; fade —*n.* 1 a channel or pipe for draining 2 a draining 3 that which gradually exhausts strength, etc. —**drain′er** *n.*

drain·age *n.* 1 a draining 2 a system of drains 3 that which is drained off 4 an area drained

drain·pipe *n.* a pipe used to carry off water, sewage, etc.

drake (drāk) *n.* ⟦ME⟧ a male duck

dram (dram) *n.* ⟦< Gr *drachmē*, handful⟧ 1 a unit of apothecaries' weight equal to 3.89 grams 2 a unit of avoirdupois weight equal to 1.77 grams 3 a small drink of alcoholic liquor

dra·ma (drä′mə, dram′ə) *n.* ⟦< Gr⟧ 1 a literary composition to be performed by actors; play, esp. one that is not a comedy 2 the art of writing, acting, or producing plays 3 a series of events suggestive of those of a play 4 dramatic quality

Dram·a·mine (dram′ə mēn′) *trademark for* a drug to relieve motion sickness

dra·mat·ic (drə mat′ik) *adj.* 1 of drama 2 like a play 3 vivid, striking, etc. —**dra·mat′i·cal·ly** *adv.*

dra·mat·ics *pl.n.* 1 [*usually with sing. v.*] the performing or producing of plays 2 exaggerated emotionalism

dram·a·tist (dram′ə tist, drä′mə-) *n.* a playwright

dram·a·tize (-tīz′) *vt.* **-tized′, -tiz′ing** 1 to make into a drama 2 to regard or show in a dramatic manner —**dram′a·ti·za′tion** *n.*

drank (draŋk) *vt., vi. pt. of* DRINK

drape (drāp) *vt.* **draped, drap′ing** [< VL *drappus*, cloth] 1 to cover or hang as with cloth in loose folds 2 to arrange (a garment, etc.) in folds or hangings —*n.* 1 cloth hanging in loose folds 2 a heavy curtain hanging in loose folds

drap·er (drā′pər) *n.* [Brit.] a dealer in cloth and dry goods

drap·er·y *n., pl.* **-er·ies** 1 [Brit.] DRY GOODS 2 hangings or clothing arranged in loose folds 3 [*pl.*] curtains of heavy material

dras·tic (dras′tik) *adj.* [Gr *drastikos*, active] having a strong effect; extreme —**dras′ti·cal·ly** *adv.*

draught (draft) *n., vt., adj. now chiefly Brit. sp. of* DRAFT

draughts (drafts) *n.* [Brit.] the game of checkers

draw (drô) *vt.* **drew, drawn, draw′ing** [OE *dragan*] 1 to make move toward one; pull 2 to pull up, down, back, in, or out 3 to need (a specified depth of water) to float in: said of a ship 4 to attract 5 to breathe in 6 to elicit (a reply, etc.) 7 to bring on; provoke 8 to receive [to *draw* a salary] 9 to withdraw (money) held in an account 10 to write (a check or draft) 11 to reach (a conclusion, etc.); deduce 12 to take or get (a playing card, etc.) 13 to stretch 14 to make (lines, pictures, etc.), as with a pencil 15 to make (comparisons, etc.) 16 to cause to flow —*vi.* 1 to draw something 2 to be drawn 3 to come; move 4 to shrink 5 to allow a draft of air, smoke, etc. to move through 6 to make a demand (*on*) —*n.* 1 a drawing or being drawn 2 the result of drawing 3 a thing drawn 4 a tie; stalemate 5 a thing that attracts 6 a shallow ravine —**draw out** 1 to extend 2 to take out; extract 3 to get (a person) to talk —**draw up** 1 to arrange in order 2 to draft (a document) 3 to stop

draw·back *n.* anything that prevents or lessens satisfaction; shortcoming

draw·bridge *n.* a bridge that can be raised or drawn aside, as to permit passage of ships

draw·er (drô′ər; *for* 2 drôr) *n.* 1 one that draws 2 a sliding box in a table, chest, etc.

drawers (drôrz) *pl.n.* UNDERPANTS

draw·ing *n.* 1 the act of one that draws; specif., the art of making pictures, etc., as with a pencil 2 a picture, etc. thus made 3 a lottery

drawing board a flat board to hold paper, etc. for making drawings —**back to the drawing board** [Inf.] back to the beginning, as to correct previous errors

drawing card an entertainer, show, etc. that draws a large audience

drawing room [< *withdrawing room*: guests withdrew there after dinner] a room where guests are received or entertained; living room

drawl (drôl) *vt., vi.* [prob. < DRAW, *v.*] to speak slowly, prolonging the vowels —*n.* such a way of speaking

drawn (drôn) *vt., vi. pp. of* DRAW —*adj.* 1 pulled out 2 disemboweled 3 tense; haggard

drawn butter melted butter

draw·string *n.* a string drawn through a hem, as to tighten a garment

dray (drā) *n.* [OE *dragan*, to draw] a low cart for carrying heavy loads

dread (dred) *vt.* [OE *ondrædan*] to anticipate with fear or distaste —*n.* 1 intense fear 2 fear mixed with awe 3 reluctance and uneasiness —*adj.* inspiring dread

dread·ful (-fəl) *adj.* 1 inspiring fear or awe 2 [Inf.] very bad, offensive, etc. —**dread′ful·ly** *adv.*

dread·locks *pl.n.* hair worn in long, thin braids or uncombed, twisted locks

dread·nought *or* **dread·naught** (-nôt′) *n.* a large, heavily armored battleship

dream (drēm) *n.* [OE, joy, music] 1 a sequence of images, etc. passing through a sleeping person's mind 2 a daydream; reverie 3 a fond hope 4 anything dreamlike —*vi., vt.* **dreamed** *or* **dreamt** (dremt), **dream′ing** to have a dream or remote idea (*of*) —**dream up** [Inf.] to devise (a fanciful plan, etc.) —**dream′er** *n.* —**dream′less** *adj.* —**dream′like′** *adj.*

dream·land *n.* 1 any lovely but imaginary place 2 sleep

dream world 1 DREAMLAND 2 the realm of fantasy

dream·y *adj.* **-i·er, -i·est** 1 filled with dreams 2 fond of daydreaming 3 like something in a dream 4 soothing 5 [Slang] wonderful —**dream′i·ly** *adv.*

drear·y (drir′ē) *adj.* **-i·er, -i·est** [OE *dreorig*, sad] dismal: also [Old Poet.] **drear** —**drear′i·ly** *adv.* —**drear′i·ness** *n.*

dredge¹ (drej) *n.* [prob. < MDu] an apparatus for scooping up mud, etc., as in deepening channels — *vt., vi.* **dredged, dredg′ing** 1 to search for or gather (*up*) as with a dredge 2 to enlarge or clean out with a dredge

dredge² (drej) *vt.* **dredged, dredg′ing** [ME *dragge*, sweetmeat] to coat (food) with flour, powdered sugar, etc.

dregs (dregz) *pl.n.* [< ON *dregg*] 1 particles settling at the bottom in a liquid 2 the most worthless part

Drei·ser (drī′sər, -zər), **The·o·dore (Herman Albert)** (thē′ə dôr′) 1871-1945; U.S. novelist

drench (drench) *vt.* [OE *drincan*, to drink] to make wet all over; soak

Dres·den (drez′dən) city in E Germany

dress (dres) *vt.* [< L *dirigere*, lay straight] 1 to put clothes on; clothe 2 to trim; adorn 3 to arrange (the hair) in a certain way 4 to align (troops) **5** to apply medicines and bandages to (a wound, etc.) **6** to prepare for use, esp. for cooking [to *dress* a fowl] **7** to smooth or finish (stone, wood, etc.) —*vi.* **1** to put on clothes **2** to dress formally **3** to line up in rank —*n.* **1** clothing **2** the usual outer garment of women, generally of one piece with a skirt —*adj.* **1** of or for dresses **2** for formal wear —**dress down 1** to scold **2** to wear casual clothes to work, etc. —**dress up** to dress formally, elegantly, etc.

dres·sage (dre säzh′) *n.* [Fr, training] horsemanship using slight movements to control the horse

dress circle a semicircle of seats in a theater, etc., usually behind and above the orchestra seats

dress code a set of rules governing clothing to be worn, as in a given school or business

dress·er *n.* **1** one who dresses (in various senses) **2** a chest of drawers for clothes, usually with a mirror

dress·ing *n.* **1** the act of one that dresses **2** bandages, etc. applied to wounds **3** a sauce for salads, etc. **4** a stuffing for roast fowl, etc.

dress·ing–down *n.* a sound scolding

dressing gown a loose robe for one not fully clothed, as when lounging

dress·mak·er *n.* one who makes dresses, etc. —**dress′mak′ing** *n.*

dress rehearsal a final rehearsal, as of a play, with costumes, etc.

dress·y *adj.* **-i·er, -i·est 1** showy or elaborate in dress or appearance **2** stylish, elegant, etc. —**dress′i·ness** *n.*

drew (drōō) *vt., vi. pt. of* DRAW

drib·ble (drib′əl) *vi., vt.* **-bled, -bling** [< DRIP] **1** to flow, or let flow, in drops **2** to drool **3** *Sports* to move (a ball or puck) along by repeated bouncing, kicking, or tapping —*n.* **1** a dribbling **2** a tiny amount: also **drib′let** (-lit) —**drib′bler** *n.*

dried (drīd) *vt., vi. pt. & pp. of* DRY

dri·er (drī′ər) *n.* **1** a substance added to paint, etc. to make it dry fast **2** DRYER —*adj. compar. of* DRY

dri·est (-ist) *adj. superl. of* DRY

drift (drift) *n.* [OE *drifan*, to drive] **1** *a)* a being carried along, as by a current *b)* the course of this **2** a trend; tendency **3** general meaning; intent **4** a heap of snow, etc. piled up by wind —*vi.* **1** to be carried along, as by a current **2** to go aimlessly **3** to pile up in drifts —*vt.* to cause to drift —**drift apart** to gradually lose affection for each other —**drift off** to fall asleep

drift·er *n.* a person who drifts from place to place

drift·wood *n.* wood drifting in the water or washed ashore

drill¹ (dril) *n.* [< Du *drillen*, to bore] **1** a tool for boring holes **2** *a)* systematic military or physical training *b)* the method or practice of teaching by repeated exercises — *vt., vi.* **1** to bore with a drill (the tool) **2** to train in, or teach by means of a drill —**drill′er** *n.*

drill² (dril) *n.* [< ?] a planting machine for

making holes or furrows and dropping seeds into them

drill³ (dril) *n.* [< L *trilix*, three-threaded] a coarse, twilled cotton cloth

drill·mas·ter *n.* **1** an instructor in military drill **2** one who teaches by drilling

drill press a power-driven machine for drilling holes in metal, etc.

dri·ly (drī′lē) *adv.* DRYLY

drink (driŋk) *vt.* **drank, drunk, drink′ing** [OE *drincan*] **1** to swallow (liquid) **2** to absorb (liquid) **3** to swallow the contents of —*vi.* **1** to swallow liquid **2** to drink alcoholic liquor, esp. to excess —*n.* **1** any liquid for drinking **2** a serving of such a liquid **3** alcoholic liquor —**drink in** to take in eagerly with the senses or mind —**drink to** to drink a toast to —**drink′a·ble** *adj.* —**drink′er** *n.*

drip (drip) *vi., vt.* **dripped** or **dript, drip′ping** [OE *dryppan*] to fall, or let fall, in drops —*n.* **1** a dripping **2** the sound of falling drops of a liquid **3** [Slang] a dull person —**drip′per** *n.*

drip-dry *adj.* designating garments that dry quickly when hung wet and require little or no ironing

drive (drīv) *vt.* **drove, driv·en** (driv′ən), **driv′ing** [OE *drifan*] **1** to force to go; push forward **2** to force into or from a state or act **3** to force to work, esp. to excess **4** to hit (a ball, etc.) hard **5** to make penetrate **6** *a)* to control the movement of; operate (a car, bus, etc.) *b)* to transport in a car, etc. **7** to push (a bargain, etc.) through **8** to motivate, influence, etc. —*vi.* **1** to advance violently **2** to try hard, as to reach a goal **3** to drive a blow, ball, etc. **4** to be driven: said of a car, bus, etc. **5** to operate, or go in, a car, etc. —*n.* **1** a driving **2** a trip in a car, etc. **3** *a)* a road for cars, etc. *b)* a driveway **4** a rounding up of animals **5** an organized effort to gain an objective **6** energy and initiative **7** a strong impulse or urge **8** the propelling mechanism of a machine, etc. **9** a computer device that reads and writes data —**drive at** to mean; intend —**drive in** in *Baseball* to cause (a runner) to score or (a run) to be scored

drive-by *n., pl.* **-bys′** a shooting in which the shots are fired from a passing car, etc. —*adj.* performed from a passing car, etc.

drive-in *n.* a restaurant, movie theater, bank, etc. designed to serve people seated in their cars

driv·el (driv′əl) *vi., vt.* **-eled** or **-elled, -el·ing** or **-el·ling** [OE *dreflian*] **1** to let (saliva) drool **2** to speak or say in a silly, stupid way —*n.* silly, stupid talk

driv·en (-ən) *adj.* acting because of urgency or compulsion

driv·er (drī′vər) *n.* a person or thing that drives, as *a)* one who drives a car, etc. *b)* one who herds cattle *c)* a golf club for hitting from the tee

drive shaft a shaft that transmits motion, as to the rear axle of a car

drive-through *n.* **1** a restaurant, bank, etc.

that provides service through a window, etc. to a person in a car **2** the window through which this service is provided Also sp. [Inf.] **drive′-thru′**

drive·train *n.* the system that transmits an engine's power to wheels, a propeller, etc.

drive·way *n.* a path for cars, from a street to a garage, house, etc.

driz·zle (driz′əl) *vi.*, *vt.* **-zled**, **-zling** ⟦prob. < ME⟧ to rain in fine, misty drops —*n.* a fine, misty rain —**driz′zly** *adj.*

drogue (drōg) *n.* ⟦prob. < Scot *drug*, drag⟧ a funnel-shaped device towed behind an aircraft, etc., as for its drag effect or as a target

droll (drōl) *adj.* ⟦< Fr < MDu *drol*, stout fellow⟧ amusing in an odd or wry way — **droll′er·y** (-ər ē) *n.*, *pl.* **-ies** —**droll′ness** *n.* —**drol′ly** *adv.*

drom·e·dar·y (dräm′ə der′ē) *n.*, *pl.* **-ies** ⟦< LL *dromedarius* (*camelus*), running (camel)⟧ a one-humped camel ranging from N Africa to India

drone[1] (drōn) *n.* ⟦OE *dran*⟧ **1** a male bee or ant that does no work **2** an idler; loafer **3** a drudge **4** a pilotless aircraft

drone[2] (drōn) *vi.* **droned**, **dron′ing** ⟦< prec.⟧ **1** to make a continuous humming sound **2** to talk in a monotonous way —*vt.* to utter in a monotonous tone —*n.* a droning sound

drool (drōōl) *vi.* ⟦< DRIVEL⟧ **1** to let saliva flow from one's mouth **2** to flow from the mouth, as saliva —*n.* saliva running from the mouth

droop (drōōp) *vi.* ⟦< ON *drūpa*⟧ **1** to sink, hang, or bend down **2** to lose strength or vitality **3** to become dejected —*vt.* to let hang down —*n.* a drooping —**droop′y** *adj.* **-i·er**, **-i·est** —**droop′i·ness** *n.*

drop (dräp) *n.* ⟦OE *dropa*⟧ **1** a bit of liquid rounded in shape by surface tension **2** anything like this in shape, etc. **3** a very small quantity **4** a sudden fall, descent, slump, etc. **5** something that drops, as a curtain or trapdoor **6** the distance between a higher and lower level —*vi.* **dropped**, **drop′ping 1** to fall in drops **2** to fall; come down **3** to fall exhausted, wounded, or dead **4** to pass into a specified state [*to drop* off to sleep] **5** to come to an end [let the matter *drop*] **6** to become lower —*vt.* **1** to let or make fall **2** to utter (a hint, etc.) casually **3** to send (a letter) **4** to stop, end, or dismiss **5** to lower or lessen **6** [Inf.] to leave at a specified place: often with *off* **7** to omit or remove **8** [Slang] to lose (money, etc.) —**drop in** (or **over** or **by**) to pay a casual visit —**drop off** [Inf.] to fall asleep —**drop out** to stop participating — **drop′let** (-lit) *n.*

drop-dead *adv.* [Slang] extremely

drop kick Rugby, etc. a kick of a dropped ball just as it hits the ground —**drop′-kick′** *vt.*, *vi.* —**drop′-kick′er** *n.*

drop-off *n.* **1** a very steep drop **2** a decline, as in sales or prices **3** a place where a person or thing can be left

drop·out *n.* one who withdraws from school before graduating

drop·per *n.* a small tube with a hollow rubber bulb at one end, used to measure out a liquid in drops

drop·sy (dräp′sē) *n.* ⟦< Gr *hydrōps* < *hydōr*, water⟧ *former term for* EDEMA

dross (drôs) *n.* ⟦OE *dros*⟧ **1** scum on molten metal **2** refuse; rubbish

drought (drout) *n.* ⟦OE *drugoth*, dryness⟧ **1** prolonged dry weather **2** a prolonged shortage

drove[1] (drōv) *n.* ⟦OE *draf*⟧ **1** a number of cattle, sheep, etc. driven or moving along as a group; flock; herd **2** a moving crowd of people: *usually used in pl.*

drove[2] (drōv) *vt.*, *vi.* *pt. of* DRIVE

dro·ver (drō′vər) *n.* one who herds droves of animals, esp. to market

drown (droun) *vi.* ⟦ME *drounen*⟧ to die by suffocation in water —*vt.* **1** to kill by such suffocation **2** to flood **3** to be so loud as to overcome (another sound): usually with *out*

drowse (drouz) *vi.* **drowsed**, **drows′ing** ⟦< OE *drusian*, become sluggish⟧ to be half asleep; doze —*n.* a doze

drows·y (drou′zē) *adj.* **-i·er**, **-i·est** being or making sleepy or half asleep —**drows′i·ly** *adv.* —**drows′i·ness** *n.*

drub (drub) *vt.* **drubbed**, **drub′bing** ⟦< Ar *daraba*, to cudgel⟧ **1** to beat as with a stick **2** to defeat soundly —**drub′ber** *n.* — **drub′bing** *n.*

drudge (druj) *n.* ⟦ME *druggen*⟧ one who does hard or tedious work —*vi.* **drudged**, **drudg′ing** to do such work —**drudg′er·y** *n.*, *pl.* **-ies**

drug (drug) *n.* ⟦< OFr *drogue*⟧ **1** any substance used as or in a medicine **2** a narcotic, hallucinogen, etc. —*vt.* **drugged**, **drug′ging 1** to put a harmful drug in (a drink, etc.) **2** to stupefy as with a drug —**drug on the market** a thing in plentiful supply for which there is little or no demand

drug·gie (-ē) *n.* [Slang] a habitual user of drugs

drug·gist (-ist) *n.* **1** a dealer in drugs, medical supplies, etc. **2** a pharmacist **3** a drugstore owner or manager

drug·store *n.* a store where drugs, medical supplies, and various items are sold and prescriptions are filled

dru·id (drōō′id) *n.* ⟦< Celt⟧ [*often* D-] a member of a Celtic religious order in ancient Britain, Ireland, and France —**dru′id·ism′** *n.*

drum (drum) *n.* ⟦< Du *trom*⟧ **1** a percussion instrument consisting of a hollow cylinder with a membrane stretched over the end or ends **2** the sound produced by beating a drum **3** any drumlike cylindrical object [an oil *drum*] **4** the eardrum —*vi.* **drummed**, **drum′ming 1** to beat a drum **2** to tap continually —*vt.* **1** to play (a rhythm, etc.) as on a drum **2** to instill (ideas, facts, etc.) *into* by continued repetition —**drum out of** to expel from in disgrace —**drum up** to get (business, etc.) by soliciting

drum·lin (drum′lin) *n.* ⟦< Ir⟧ a low, flattened, oval mound or hill formed by a glacier

drum major one who leads a marching band, keeping time with a baton

drum ma·jor·ette (-et′) a woman or girl who leads a marching band, keeping time with a baton

drum·mer *n.* 1 a drum player

drum·stick *n.* 1 a stick for beating a drum 2 the lower half of the leg of a cooked fowl

drunk (druŋk) *vt., vi. pp.* of DRINK —*adj.* 1 overcome by alcoholic liquor; intoxicated 2 overcome by any powerful emotion 3 [Inf.] DRUNKEN (*adj.* 2) Usually used in the predicate —*n.* 1 [Inf.] a drunken person 2 [Slang] a drinking spree

drunk·ard *n.* a person who often gets drunk

drunk·en *adj.* 1 intoxicated 2 caused by or occurring during intoxication Used before a noun —**drunk′en·ly** *adv.* —**drunk′en·ness** *n.*

drupe (drōōp) *n.* [< Gr *druppa* (*elaa*), olive] any fleshy fruit with an inner stone, as a peach, olive, cherry, etc.

druth·ers (druth′ərz) *n.* [Inf. or Dial.] a preference [if I had my *druthers*]

dry (drī) *adj.* **dri′er, dri′est** [OE *dryge*] 1 not under water [*dry* land] 2 not wet or damp 3 lacking rain or water; arid 4 thirsty 5 not yielding milk 6 solid; not liquid 7 not sweet [*dry* wine] 8 prohibiting alcoholic beverages [a *dry* town] 9 funny in a quiet but sharp way [*dry* wit] 10 unproductive 11 boring; dull —*n., pl.* **drys** [Inf.] a prohibitionist — *vt., vi.* **dried, dry′ing** to make or become dry —**dry up** 1 to make or become thoroughly dry 2 to make or become unproductive 3 [Slang] to stop talking —**dry′ly** *adv.* —**dry′ness** *n.*

dry·ad (drī′ad′) *n.* [< Gr *drys*, tree] [*also* D-] *Gr. & Rom. Myth.* a tree nymph

dry cell a voltaic cell containing a moist, paste-like electrolyte which cannot spill

dry-clean *vt.* to clean (garments, etc.) with a solvent other than water, as naphtha —**dry cleaner**

dry dock a berth from which the water can be emptied, used for building and repairing ships

dry·er *n.* 1 one that dries; specif., an appliance for drying clothes with heat 2 DRIER

dry-eyed *adj.* not crying

dry farming farming without irrigation, by conserving moisture, etc.

dry goods cloth, cloth products, etc.

dry ice solidified carbon dioxide: used as a refrigerant

dry run [Inf.] a simulated or practice performance; rehearsal

dry·wall *n.* PLASTERBOARD — *vt., vi.* to cover (a wall, etc.) with plasterboard

DSL *abbrev.* digital subscriber line

DST *abbrev.* daylight saving time

Du *abbrev.* Dutch

du·al (dōō′əl) *adj.* [< L *duo*, two] 1 of two 2 double; twofold —**du′al·ism′** *n.* —**du·al′i·ty** (-al′ə tē) *n.*

dub¹ (dub) *vt.* **dubbed, dub′bing** [< OE *dubbian*, to strike] 1 *a*) to confer a title or rank upon *b*) to name or nickname 2 to smooth by hammering, scraping, etc. —**dub′ber** *n.*

dub² (dub) *vt.* **dubbed, dub′bing** [< DOUBLE] to provide with a soundtrack, esp. one with dialogue in another language —**dub in** to insert (dialogue, music, etc.) in the soundtrack —**dub′ber** *n.*

du·bi·e·ty (dōō bī′ə tē) *n.* 1 a being dubious 2 *pl.* **-ties** a doubtful thing

du·bi·ous (dōō′bē əs) *adj.* [< L *dubius*, uncertain] 1 causing doubt 2 skeptical 3 questionable —**du′bi·ous·ly** *adv.*

Dub·lin (dub′lən) capital of Ireland

dub·ni·um (dōōb′nē əm) *n.* [after *Dubna*, Russia] an artificially produced radioactive chemical element: symbol, Db; at. no. 105

du·cal (dōō′kəl) *adj.* [< LL *ducalis*, of a leader] of a duke or dukedom

duc·at (duk′ət) *n.* [see DUCHY] any of several former European coins

duch·ess (duch′is) *n.* 1 a duke's wife or widow 2 a woman ruling a duchy

duch·y (-ē) *n., pl.* **-ies** [< L *dux*, leader] the territory ruled by a duke or duchess

duck¹ (duk) *n.* [< OE *duce*, diver] 1 a small waterfowl with a flat bill, a short neck, and webbed feet 2 the flesh of a duck as food

duck² (duk) *vt., vi.* [ME *douken*] 1 to plunge or dip under water for a moment 2 to lower or bend (the head, body, etc.) suddenly, as to avoid a blow 3 [Inf.] to avoid (an issue, etc.) —*n.* a ducking

duck³ (duk) *n.* [Du *doek*] a cotton or linen cloth like canvas

duck·bill *n.* PLATYPUS

duck·ling *n.* a young duck

duck·pins *n.* a game like bowling, played with smaller pins and balls

duct (dukt) *n.* [< L *ducere*, to lead] a tube, channel, or pipe, as for passage of a liquid —**duct′less** *adj.*

duc·tile (duk′til) *adj.* [see prec.] 1 that can be drawn or hammered thin without breaking: said of metals 2 easily led; tractable —**duc·til′i·ty** (-til′ə tē) *n.*

ductless gland an endocrine gland

duct tape a very strong, waterproof tape, used to seal ducts, hoses, etc.

duct·work *n.* a system of ducts used to circulate air for heating, cooling, etc.

dud (dud) *n.* [prob. < Du *dood*, dead] [Inf.] 1 a bomb, etc. that fails to explode 2 a failure

dude (dōōd) *n.* [< ?] 1 a dandy; fop 2 a tourist at a ranch 3 [Slang] any man or boy — *vt., vi.* **dud′ed, dud′ing** [Slang] to dress up, esp. in showy clothes: usually with *up*

dude ranch a vacation resort on a ranch, with horseback riding, etc.

dud·geon (duj′ən) *n.* now chiefly in **in high dudgeon**, very angry, offended, etc.

duds (dudz) *pl.n.* [ME *dudde*, cloth, cloak < ?] [Inf.] 1 clothes 2 belongings

due (dōō, dyōō) *adj.* [< L *debere*, owe] 1 owed or owing as a debt; payable 2 suitable; proper 3 enough [*due* care] 4 expected or scheduled to arrive —*adv.* exactly; directly [*due* west] —*n.* 1 deserved recognition 2 [*pl.*] fees or other charges [union *dues*] —

due to 1 caused by **2** [Inf.] because of —**pay one's dues** [Slang] to earn a right, etc., as by having suffered in struggle

due bill a receipt for money paid, exchangeable for goods or services only

du·el (dōō′əl) *n.* [< medieval L *duellum*] **1** a prearranged, formalized fight between two persons armed with deadly weapons **2** any contest for supremacy between two persons — *vi., vt.* **-eled** or **-elled, -el·ing** or **-el·ling** to fight a duel with —**du′el·ist** or **du′el·list, du′el·er** or **du′el·ler** *n.*

due process (of law) legal proceedings established to protect individual rights and liberties

du·et (dōō et′) *n.* [< L *duo*, two] **1** a composition for two voices or instruments **2** the two performers of this

duf·fel (or **duf·fle**) **bag** (duf′əl) [after *Duffel*, town in Belgium] a large cloth bag for carrying clothing, etc.

duff·er (duf′ər) *n.* [< thieves' slang *duff*, to fake] [Inf.] **1** a slow-witted or dawdling elderly person **2** a relatively unskilled golfer

dug (dug) *vt., vi. pt. & pp.* of DIG

dug·out *n.* **1** a boat hollowed out of a log **2** a shelter, as in warfare, dug in the ground **3** *Baseball* a covered shelter, one for each team

DUI (dē′yōō′ī′) *n.* a citation for driving while under the influence of alcohol, drugs, etc.

du jour (dōō zhoor′) offered on this day [soup *du jour*]

duke¹ (dōōk) *n.* [< L *dux*, leader] **1** a prince ruling an independent duchy **2** a nobleman next in rank to a prince —**duke′dom** *n.*

duke² (dōōk) *n.* [pl.] [Slang] the fists or hands —**duke it out** to fight, esp. with the fists

dul·cet (dul′sit) *adj.* [< L *dulcis*, sweet] soothing or pleasant to hear

dul·ci·mer (dul′sə mər) *n.* [< L *dulce*, sweet + *melos*, song] a musical instrument with metal strings, which are struck with two small hammers or plucked with a plectrum or quill

dull (dul) *adj.* [OE *dol*] **1** mentally slow; stupid **2** physically slow; sluggish **3** boring; tedious **4** not sharp; blunt **5** not feeling or felt keenly **6** not vivid or bright [a *dull* color] **7** not distinct; muffled [a *dull* thud] — *vt., vi.* to make or become dull —**dull′ness** *n.* —**dul′ly** *adv.*

dull·ard (-ərd) *n.* a stupid person

du·ly (dōō′lē) *adv.* in due manner; in the proper way, at the right time, etc.

Du·mas (dōō mä′), **Alexandre** (al′ig zan′dər) 1802–70; Fr. novelist & playwright

dumb (dum) *adj.* [OE] **1** lacking the power of speech; mute **2** silent **3** [Ger *dumm*] [Inf.] stupid —**dumb down** [Inf.] to make less intellectually demanding —**dumb′ly** *adv.* —**dumb′ness** *n.*

dumb·bell *n.* **1** a device consisting of round weights joined by a short bar, lifted for muscular exercise **2** [Slang] a stupid person

dumb·found or **dum·found** *vt.* [DUMB + (CON)-FOUND] to make speechless by shocking; amaze

dumb·wait·er *n.* a small elevator for sending food, etc. between floors

dum-dum (bullet) (dum′dum′) [after *Dum-dum*, arsenal in India] a soft-nosed bullet that expands when it hits, causing a large wound

dum·my (dum′ē) *n., pl.* **-mies 1** a figure made in human form, as for displaying clothing **2** an imitation; sham **3** [Slang] a stupid person **4** *Bridge* the declarer's partner, whose hand is exposed on the table and played by the declarer —*adj.* sham

dump (dump) *vt.* [prob. < ON] **1** to unload in a heap or mass **2** to throw away (rubbish, etc.) **3** to sell (a commodity) in a large quantity at a low price **4** *Comput. a)* to transfer (data) to another section of storage *b)* to make a printout of (data) —*n.* **1** a place for dumping rubbish, etc. **2** *Mil.* a temporary storage center in the field **3** an ugly, rundown place —**(down) in the dumps** [Inf.] in low spirits —**dump on** [Slang] to treat with contempt

dump·ling (dump′liŋ) *n.* [< ?] **1** a small piece of steamed or boiled dough served with meat or soup **2** a crust of baked dough filled with fruit

dump·ster (dump′stər) *n.* a large metal trash bin, often one emptied by a special truck

dump·y *adj.* **-i·er, -i·est 1** short and thick; squat **2** [Inf.] ugly, run-down, etc.

dun¹ (dun) *adj., n.* [OE] dull grayish-brown

dun² (dun) *vt., vi.* **dunned, dun′ning** [? dial. var. of DIN] to ask (a debtor) repeatedly for payment —*n.* an insistent demand for payment

dunce (duns) *n.* [after John *Duns* Scotus (1265?–1308), Scot theologian] a dull, ignorant person

dune (dōōn) *n.* [Fr < MDu] a rounded hill or ridge of drifted sand

dung (duŋ) *n.* [OE] animal excrement; manure

dun·ga·ree (duŋ′gə rē′) *n.* [Hindi *dungri*] **1** a sturdy, usually blue denim **2** [pl.] work trousers or overalls made of this

dun·geon (dun′jən) *n.* [< OFr *donjon*] a dark underground cell or prison

dung·hill *n.* a heap of dung

dunk (duŋk) *vt.* [Ger *tunken*] **1** to dip (bread, etc.) into coffee, etc. before eating it **2** to immerse briefly

Dun·kirk (dun′kurk′) seaport in N France: scene of the evacuation of Allied troops under fire (1940)

du·o (dōō′ō) *n., pl.* **du′os** [It] **1** DUET (esp. *n.* 2) **2** a pair; couple

du·o·de·num (dōō′ō dē′nəm, dōō äd′n əm) *n., pl.* **-na** (-nə) or **-nums** [< L *duodeni*, twelve each: its length is about twelve fingers' breadth] the first section of the small intestine, below the stomach —**du′o·de′nal** *adj.*

dup *abbrev.* duplicate

dupe (dōōp) *n.* [< L *upupa*, stupid bird] a person easily tricked —*vt.* duped, dup′ing to deceive; fool —**dup′er** *n.*

du·plex (dōō′pleks′) *adj.* [L < *duo*, TWO +

-*plex*, -*fold*] double —*n.* 1 an apartment with rooms on two floors 2 a house consisting of two separate family units

du·pli·cate (dōō′pli kit; *for v.*, -kāt′) *adj.* [< L *duplicare*, to double] 1 double 2 corresponding exactly —*n.* an exact copy —*vt.* -cat′ed, -cat′ing 1 to make an exact copy of 2 to make or do again —du′pli·ca′tion *n.*

duplicating machine a machine for making copies of a letter, drawing, etc.

du·plic·i·ty (dōō plis′ə tē) *n., pl.* -ties [< LL *duplicitas*] hypocritical cunning or deception

du·ra·ble (door′ə bəl) *adj.* [< L *durare*, to last] 1 lasting in spite of hard wear or frequent use 2 stable —du′ra·bil′i·ty *n.* —du′ra·bly *adv.*

du·ra ma·ter (door′ə māt′ər) [< ML, lit., hard mother, transl. of Ar term] the tough, outermost membrane covering the brain and spinal cord

dur·ance (door′əns) *n.* [see DURABLE] long imprisonment: mainly in **in durance vile** (vīl)

du·ra·tion (dōō rā′shən) *n.* [see DURABLE] the time that a thing continues or lasts

du·ress (dōō res′) *n.* [< L *durus*, hard] coercion

dur·ing (door′iŋ) *prep.* [see DURABLE] 1 throughout the entire time of 2 in the course of

durst (durst) *vt., vi. now chiefly dial. pt. of* DARE

du·rum (door′əm) *n.* [< L *durus*, hard] a hard wheat that yields flour for macaroni, spaghetti, etc.

dusk (dusk) *n.* [< OE *dox*, dark-colored] 1 the dim part of twilight 2 dusky quality —dusk′y *adj.* -i·er, -i·est

dust (dust) *n.* [OE] 1 powdery earth or any finely powdered matter 2 earth 3 disintegrated mortal remains 4 anything worthless —*vt.* 1 to sprinkle with dust, powder, etc. 2 to rid of dust, as by wiping: often with *off* —*vi.* to remove dust, as from furniture —**bite the dust** [Inf.] to die, esp. in battle —dust′less *adj.*

dust bowl an arid region with eroded topsoil easily blown off by winds

dust·er *n.* 1 a person or thing that dusts 2 a long, lightweight overcoat 3 a lightweight housecoat

dust·pan *n.* a shovel-like pan into which floor dust is swept

dust·y *adj.* -i·er, -i·est 1 covered with or full of dust 2 powdery 3 muted with gray: said of a color —dust′i·ness *n.*

Dutch (duch) *n.* the language of the Netherlands —*adj.* of the Netherlands or its people, language, or culture —**go Dutch** [Inf.] to have each pay his or her own expenses —**in Dutch** [Inf.] in trouble or disfavor —**the Dutch** Dutch people

Dutch door a door with upper and lower halves that open separately

Dutch oven a heavy pot with an arched lid, for pot roasts, etc.

Dutch treat [Inf.] any date, etc. on which each pays his or her own expenses

Dutch uncle [Inf.] one who bluntly and sternly lectures another, often with benevolent intent

du·te·ous (dōōt′ē əs) *adj.* dutiful; obedient —du′te·ous·ly *adv.*

du·ti·a·ble (dōōt′ē ə bəl) *adj.* necessitating payment of a duty or tax

du·ti·ful (dōōt′i fəl) *adj.* showing, or resulting from, a sense of duty; obedient —du′ti·ful·ly *adv.*

du·ty (dōōt′ē) *n., pl.* -ties [see DUE & -TY] 1 obedience or respect to be shown to one's parents, elders, etc. 2 any action required by one's position or by moral or legal considerations, etc. 3 service, esp. military service [*overseas duty*] 4 a tax, as on imports —**on (or off) duty** at (or temporarily relieved from) one's work

du·vet (dōō vā′, dyōō-) *n.* a comforter, often down-filled, within a slipcover

DVD *n.* [< *d*(*igital*) *v*(*ideo*) *d*(*isc*)] a digital optical disc used esp. for recording video content

DVR (dē′vē′är′) *n.* DIGITAL VIDEO RECORDER

dwarf (dwôrf) *n., pl.* dwarfs or dwarves (dwôrvz) [< OE *dweorg*] 1 any abnormally small person, animal, or plant 2 *Folklore* a little being in human form, with magic powers —*vt.* 1 to stunt the growth of 2 to make seem small in comparison —*vi.* to become dwarfed —*adj.* undersized —dwarf′ish *adj.* —dwarf′ism′ *n.*

dwarf planet a solid body like a very small planet, that orbits a star

dweeb (dwēb) *n.* [Slang] a person regarded as dull, awkward, unsophisticated, etc.

dwell (dwel) *vi.* dwelt or dwelled, dwell′ing [< OE *dwellan*, to hinder] to make one's home; reside —**dwell on** (or **upon**) to think or talk about at length —dwell′er *n.*

dwell·ing (place) [ME: see prec.] a residence; abode

DWI (dē′dub′əl yōō′i′) *n.* a citation for driving while intoxicated — driving while intoxicated

dwin·dle (dwin′dəl) *vi.* -dled, -dling [< OE *dwinan*, waste away] to keep on becoming smaller or less; diminish; shrink

dyb·buk (dib′ək) *n.* [Heb *dibbûq*] *Jewish Folklore* the spirit of a dead person that enters the body of a living person

dye (dī) *n.* [< OE *deag*] a substance or solution for coloring fabric, hair, etc.; also, the color produced —*vt.* dyed, dye′ing to color with dye —dy′er *n.*

dyed-in-the-wool *adj.* not changing, as in beliefs

dy·ing (dī′iŋ) *vi. prp. of* DIE[1] —*adj.* 1 about to die or end 2 at death —*n.* death

dy·nam·ic (dī nam′ik) *adj.* [< Gr *dynasthai*, be able] 1 relating to bodies in motion 2 energetic; vigorous —dy·nam′i·cal·ly *adv.*

dy·nam·ics *n.* 1 the science dealing with motions produced by given forces 2 variation in loudness and softness in music —*pl.n.* the forces operating in any field

dy·na·mite (dī′nə mīt′) *n.* [see DYNAMIC] a

powerful explosive made with nitroglycerin
—*vt.* **-mit′ed, -mit′ing** to blow up with dynamite

dy·na·mo (dī′nə mō′) *n., pl.* **-mos′** [see DYNAMIC] **1** *former term for* GENERATOR **2** a dynamic person

dy·nas·ty (dī′nəs tē) *n., pl.* **-ties** [< Gr *dynasteia*, rule] a succession of rulers who are members of the same family —**dy·nas′tic** (-nas′tik) *adj.*

dys- [Gr] *prefix* bad, ill, difficult, etc.

dys·en·ter·y (dis′ən ter′ē) *n.* [< Gr *dys-*, bad + *entera*, bowels] an intestinal inflammation characterized by abdominal pain and bloody diarrhea

dys·func·tion (dis funk′shən) *n.* abnormal or impaired functioning —**dys·func′tion·al** *adj.*

dys·lex·i·a (dis lek′sē ə) *n.* [< DYS- + L *lexis*, speech] impairment of the ability to read —**dys·lex′ic** *adj., n.,* **dys·lec′tic**

dys·pep·si·a (dis pep′sē ə, -shə) *n.* [< Gr *dys-*, bad + *pepsis*, digestion] indigestion —**dys·pep′tic** *adj., n.*

dys·pro·si·um (dis prō′zē əm) *n.* [ModL < Gr *dysprositos*, difficult to approach] a chemical element with strong magnetic properties esp. at very low temperatures: symbol, Dy; at. no. 66

dys·to·pi·a (dis tō′pē ə) *n.* [DYS- + (U)TOPIA] **1** a hypothetical society or place with dreadful conditions and quality of life **2** a novel or other work depicting a dystopian society or place —**dys·to′pi·an** *adj.,* **dys·to′pic** *adj.*

dz *abbrev.* dozen(s)

E

e or **E** (ē) *n., pl.* **e′s, E′s** the fifth letter of the English alphabet

E¹ (ē) *n. Music* the third tone in the scale of C major

E² *abbrev.* **1** east(ern) **2** *Baseball* error(s) **3** *Physics* energy

e-¹ *prefix* EX-

e-² *prefix* done, etc. electronically on the internet [*e-commerce*]

each (ēch) *adj., pron.* [OE *ǣlc*] every one of two or more considered separately —*adv.* apiece Abbrev. **ea.** —**each other** each one the other or others; one another

ea·ger (ē′gər) *adj.* [< L *acer*] keenly desiring; impatient or anxious —**ea′ger·ly** *adv.* —**ea′ger·ness** *n.*

ea·gle (ē′gəl) *n.* [< L *aquila*] **1** a large bird of prey, with sharp vision and powerful wings **2** a representation of the eagle, as the U.S. emblem **3** *Golf* a score of two under par on a hole

ea·gle-eyed *adj.* having keen vision

ea·glet (ē′glit) *n.* a young eagle

ear¹ (ir) *n.* [OE *ēare*] **1** the part of the body that perceives sound **2** the visible, external part of the ear **3** one's sense of hearing or hearing ability **4** anything like an ear —**be all ears** to listen attentively —**give** (or **lend**) **an ear** to give attention; heed —**play by ear** to play (music) without using notation —**play it by ear** [Inf.] to improvise

ear² (ir) *n.* [< OE *ēar*] the grain-bearing spike of a cereal plant, esp. of corn —*vi.* to sprout ears

ear·ache *n.* an ache in the ear

ear·bud *n.* an earphone inserted into or placed just outside of the outer ear canal

ear·drum *n.* TYMPANIC MEMBRANE

earl (url) *n.* [< OE *eorl*, warrior] a British

nobleman ranking above a viscount —**earl′dom** *n.*

ear·lobe *n.* the fleshy lower part of the external ear

ear·ly (ur′lē) *adv., adj.* **-li·er, -li·est** [< OE *ær*, before + *-lice*, -ly] **1** near the beginning **2** before the expected or usual time **3** in the distant past **4** in the near future —**early on** at an early stage —**ear′li·ness** *n.*

ear·mark *n.* **1** a mark put on the ear of livestock **2** an identifying mark or feature **3** a special government spending appropriation —*vt.* **1** to put such a mark on **2** to reserve for a special purpose

ear·muffs (-mufs′) *pl.n.* coverings worn over the ears in cold weather

earn (urn) *vt.* [OE *earnian*] **1** to receive (wages, etc.) for one's work **2** to get as deserved **3** to receive (interest, etc.) as from a bank account —**earn′er** *n.*

ear·nest¹ (ur′nist) *adj.* [OE *eornoste*] serious and intense; not joking —**in earnest 1** serious **2** in a determined way —**ear′nest·ly** *adv.* —**ear′nest·ness** *n.*

ear·nest² (ur′nist) *n.* [ult. < Heb *eravon*] money, etc. given as a pledge in binding a bargain

earn·ings *pl.n.* **1** wages or other recompense **2** profits, interest, etc.

ear·phone *n.* a receiver for radio, etc., held to, or put into, the ear

ear·ring *n.* a ring or other small ornament for the lobe of the ear

ear·shot *n.* the distance within which a sound can be heard

ear·split·ting *adj.* so loud as to hurt the ears; deafening

earth (urth) *n.* [OE *eorthe*] **1** [*often* E-]

the planet we live on, the third planet from the sun: see PLANET **2** this world, as distinguished from heaven and hell **3** land, as distinguished from sea or sky **4** soil; ground —**down to earth 1** practical; realistic **2** without affectation

Earth Day April 22, a day on which events are held to raise awareness about environmental concerns

earth·en *adj.* made of earth or clay

earth·en·ware *n.* clay pottery

earth·ling *n.* a human: now mainly in science fiction

earth·ly *adj.* **1** *a)* terrestrial *b)* worldly **2** conceivable [no *earthly* reason]

earth·quake *n.* a trembling of the earth's crust, caused by underground volcanic forces or shifting of rock along faults, etc.

earth·ward *adv., adj.* toward the earth: also **earth′wards** *adv.*

earth·work *n.* an embankment made by piling up earth, esp. as a fortification

earth·worm *n.* a round, segmented worm that burrows in the soil

earth·y *adj.* **-i·er, -i·est 1** of or like earth **2** *a)* coarse; unrefined *b)* simple and natural — **earth′i·ness** *n.*

ease (ēz) *n.* ⟦< L *adjacens*, lying nearby⟧ **1** freedom from pain or trouble; comfort **2** natural manner; poise **3** freedom from difficulty; facility **4** affluence —*vt.* **eased, eas′ing 1** to free from pain or trouble; comfort **2** to lessen (pain, anxiety, etc.) **3** to facilitate **4** to reduce the strain or pressure of **5** to move by careful shifting, etc. —*vi.* to become less tense, severe, etc.

ea·sel (ē′zəl) *n.* ⟦ult. < L *asinus*, ass⟧ an upright frame or tripod to hold an artist's canvas, etc.

ease·ment (ēz′mənt) *n. Law* a right that one may have in another's land, as the right to pass through

eas·i·ly (ē′zə lē) *adv.* **1** with ease **2** certainly **3** very likely

east (ēst) *n.* ⟦OE⟧ **1** the direction in which sunrise occurs at the equinoxes (90° on the compass) **2** a region in or toward this direction —*adj.* **1** in, of, toward, or facing the east **2** from the east [an *east* wind] —*adv.* in or toward the east —**the East 1** the eastern part of the U.S. **2** Asia and the nearby islands

East Asia countries of E Asia, including China, Japan, North & South Korea, and Mongolia —**East Asian**

East China Sea part of the Pacific Ocean, between China & Japan

Eas·ter (ēs′tər) *n.* ⟦< OE *Eastre*, dawn goddess⟧ an annual Christian festival in the spring, celebrating the Resurrection of Jesus

east·er·ly *adj., adv.* **1** in or toward the east **2** from the east

east·ern *adj.* **1** in, of, or toward the east **2** from the east **3** [E-] of the East

east·ern·er *n.* a person born or living in the east

Eastern Hemisphere that half of the earth which includes Europe, Africa, Asia, and Australia

Eastern Orthodox Church the Christian church dominant in E Europe and W Asia

East In·dies (in′dēz′) Malay Archipelago; esp., the islands of Indonesia —**East Indian**

East Ti·mor (tē′môr′, tē môr′) country on the E half of an island (*Timor*) in SE Asia, in the Malay Archipelago, & nearby islands

east·ward *adv., adj.* toward the east: also **east′wards** *adv.*

eas·y (ē′zē) *adj.* **-i·er, -i·est** ⟦see EASE⟧ **1** not difficult **2** free from anxiety, pain, etc. **3** comfortable; restful **4** free from constraint; not stiff **5** not strict or severe **6** *a)* unhurried *b)* gradual —*adv.* [Inf.] easily —**take it easy** [Inf.] **1** to refrain from anger, haste, etc. **2** to relax; rest —**eas′i·ness** *n.*

easy chair a stuffed armchair

eas·y·go·ing *adj.* **1** acting in a relaxed manner **2** not strict; lenient

eat (ēt) *vt.* **ate, eat′en, eat′ing** ⟦OE *etan*⟧ **1** to chew and swallow (food) **2** to consume or ravage: with *away* or *up* **3** to destroy, as acid does; corrode **4** to make by or as by eating [acid *eats* holes in cloth] **5** [Slang] to worry or bother —*vi.* to eat food; have a meal —**eat′a·ble** *adj.* —**eat′er** *n.*

eat·er·y (ēt′ər ē) *n., pl.* **-ies** [Inf.] a restaurant

eaves (ēvz) *pl.n., sing.* **eave** ⟦< OE *efes*, edge⟧ the projecting lower edge or edges of a roof

eaves·drop *vi.* **-dropped′, -drop′ping** ⟦prob. < *eavesdropper*, one who stands under the eaves to listen⟧ to listen secretly to a private conversation

ebb (eb) *n.* ⟦OE *ebba*⟧ **1** the flow of the tide back toward the sea **2** a lessening —*vi.* **1** to recede, as the tide **2** to lessen; decline

Ebitda or **EBITDA** *abbrev.* earnings before interest, taxes, depreciation, and amortization

eb·on·y (eb′ə nē) *n., pl.* **-ies** ⟦< Gr *ebenos*⟧ the hard, heavy, dark wood of certain tropical trees —*adj.* **1** of ebony **2** like ebony; specif., dark or black

e·bul·lient (i bool′yənt, -bul′-) *adj.* ⟦< L *e-*, out + *bullīre*, to boil⟧ **1** bubbling; boiling **2** enthusiastic; exuberant —**e·bul′lience** *n.*

EC *abbrev.* European Community

ec·cen·tric (ək sen′trik) *adj.* ⟦< Gr *ek-*, out of + *kentron*, center⟧ **1** not concentric: said of two circles, one inside the other **2** with its axis off center [an *eccentric* wheel] **3** not exactly circular **4** odd, as in conduct; unconventional —*n.* **1** a disk set off center on a shaft, for converting circular motion into back-and-forth motion **2** an eccentric person —**ec·cen′tri·cal·ly** *adv.* —**ec·cen·tric·i·ty** (ek′sen tris′ə tē) *n., pl.* **-ties**

Ec·cle·si·as·tes (e klē′zē as′tēz′) *n.* ⟦< Gr *ek-*, out + *kalein*, to call⟧ a book of the Old Testament

ec·cle·si·as·tic (-tik) *adj.* [see prec.] ECCLESIASTICAL —*n.* a member of the clergy

ec·cle·si·as·ti·cal (-ti kəl) *adj.* of the church or the clergy

ech·e·lon (esh′ə län′) *n.* 〖Fr < L *scala*, ladder〗 **1** a steplike formation of ships, troops, or aircraft **2** a subdivision of a military force **3** any of the levels of responsibility in an organization

e·chi·no·derm (ē kī′nō dụrm′) *n.* 〖< ModL〗 a marine animal with a hard, spiny exoskeleton and radial body, as the starfish

ech·o (ek′ō) *n., pl.* **-oes** 〖< Gr *ēchō*〗 **1** the repetition of a sound by reflection of sound waves from a surface **2** a sound so produced **3** any repetition or imitation of the words, ideas, etc. of another —*vi.* **-oed, -o·ing 1** to reverberate **2** to make an echo —*vt.* to repeat (another's words, ideas, etc.)

e·cho·ic (e kō′ik) *adj.* imitative in sound, as the word *tinkle*

é·clair (ā kler′, i-, ē-) *n.* 〖Fr, lit., lightning〗 an oblong pastry shell filled with custard, etc.

é·clat (ā klä′, i-, ē-) *n.* 〖Fr < *éclater*, burst (out)〗 **1** brilliant success **2** striking effect **3** acclaim; fame

ec·lec·tic (ek lek′tik) *adj.* 〖< Gr *ek-*, out + *legein*, choose〗 selecting or selected from various sources —*n.* one who uses eclectic methods —**ec·lec′ti·cal·ly** *adv.* —**ec·lec′ti·cism′** (-tə siz′əm) *n.*

e·clipse (i klips′, ē-) *n.* 〖< Gr *ek-*, out + *leipein*, leave〗 **1** the obscuring of the sun when the moon comes between it and the earth (**solar eclipse**), or of the moon when the earth's shadow is cast upon it (**lunar eclipse**) **2** any obscuring of light, or of fame, glory, etc. —*vt.* **e·clipsed′, e·clips′ing 1** to cause an eclipse of **2** to surpass

e·clip·tic (i klip′tik) *n.* the sun's apparent annual path relative to the stars, as seen from the orbiting earth

ec·logue (ek′lôg′) *n.* 〖see ECLECTIC〗 a short pastoral poem

eco- 〖< Gr *oikos*, house〗 *combining form* **1** environment or habitat **2** ecology

ec·o·cide (ē′kō sīd′) *n.* 〖prec. + -CIDE〗 the destruction of the environment

e·col·o·gy (ē käl′ə jē) *n.* 〖< Gr *oikos*, house + *-logia*, -LOGY〗 the branch of biology that deals with the relations between living organisms and their environment —**ec′o·log′i·cal** *adj.* —**ec′o·log′i·cal·ly** *adv.* —**e·col′o·gist** *n.*

econ *abbrev.* economic(s)

ec·o·nom·ic (ek′ə näm′ik, ē′kə-) *adj.* **1** of the management of income, expenditures, etc. **2** of economics **3** of the satisfaction of the material needs of people

ec·o·nom·i·cal *adj.* **1** not wasting money, time, etc.; thrifty **2** that uses no more of something than is necessary —**ec′o·nom′i·cal·ly** *adv.*

ec·o·nom·ics *n.* the science that deals with the production, distribution, and consumption of wealth —*pl.n.* economic factors

e·con·o·mist (i kän′ə mist, ē-) *n.* a specialist in economics

e·con·o·mize (-mīz′) *vi.* **-mized′, -miz′ing** to reduce waste or expenses —**e·con′o·miz′er** *n.*

e·con·o·my (-mē) *n., pl.* **-mies** 〖< Gr *oikos*, house + *nomos*, law〗 **1** the management of the income, expenditures, etc. of a household, government, etc. **2** careful management of wealth, etc.; thrift **3** efficient use of one's materials **4** an instance of thrift **5** a system of producing and distributing wealth —*adj.* costing less or less per unit than the standard kind

ec·o·sys·tem (ē′kō sis′təm) *n.* 〖< Gr *oikos*, house + SYSTEM〗 a community of animals and plants, together with its environment

ec·sta·sy (ek′stə sē) *n., pl.* **-sies** 〖< Gr *ek-*, out + *histanai*, to set〗 a state or feeling of overpowering joy; rapture —**ec·stat·ic** (ek stat′ik) *adj.* —**ec·stat′i·cal·ly** *adv.*

-ec·to·my (ek′tə mē) *combining form* 〖< Gr *ek-*, out + *temnein*, to cut〗 surgical excision of

Ec·ua·dor (ek′wə dôr′) country on the NW coast of South America —**Ec′ua·do′re·an** *adj., n.,* **Ec′ua·do′ri·an, Ec′ua·dor′an**

ec·u·men·i·cal (e′kyə men′i kəl, -yōō-) *adj.* 〖< Gr *oikoumenē* (*gē*), the inhabited (world)〗 **1** general, or universal; esp., of the Christian church as a whole **2** furthering religious unity, esp. among Christian churches —**ec′u·men′i·cal·ly** *adv.*

ec·u·men·ism (e kyoō′mə niz′əm, ek′yə-) *n.* the ecumenical movement, esp. among Christian churches —**ec·u′men·ist** *n.*

ec·ze·ma (ek′zə mə, eg′zə-) *n.* 〖< Gr *ek-*, out + *zein*, to boil〗 a skin disorder characterized by inflammation, itching, and scaliness

ed *abbrev.* **1** edited (by) **2** *a)* edition *b)* editor *c)* education

-ed 〖OE〗 *suffix* **1** forming the past tense or past participle of certain verbs **2** forming adjectives from nouns or verbs [*cultured, bearded*]

E·dam (cheese) (ē′dəm, -dam′) 〖after *Edam*, Netherlands〗 a mild, yellow cheese

ed·dy (ed′ē) *n., pl.* **-dies** 〖prob. < ON *itha*〗 a little whirlpool or whirlwind —*vi.* **-died, -dy·ing** to move in an eddy

e·del·weiss (ā′dəl vīs′) *n.* 〖Ger < *edel*, noble + *weiss*, white〗 a small, flowering plant, esp. of the Alps, with whitish, woolly leaves

e·de·ma (ē dē′mə) *n., pl.* **-mas** or **-ma·ta** (-mə tə) 〖< Gr *oidēma*, swelling〗 an abnormal accumulation of fluid in body tissues or cavities

E·den (ēd′'n) *n.* **1** *Bible* the garden where Adam and Eve first lived; Paradise **2** any delightful place —**E·den′ic** *adj.,* **e·den·ic** (ē den′ik)

edge (ej) *n.* 〖OE *ecg*〗 **1** the sharp, cutting part of a blade **2** sharpness; keenness **3** the projecting ledge of a cliff, etc.; brink **4** the part farthest from the middle; border; margin **5** [Inf.] advantage [he has the *edge* on me] —*vt., vi.* **edged, edg′ing 1** to form an edge (on) **2** to make (one's way) sideways **3** to move gradually —**on edge 1** very tense; irritable **2** impatient —**edg′er** *n.*

edge·ways (-wāz′) *adv.* with the edge foremost: also **edge′wise′** (-wīz′)

edg·ing *n.* a fringe, trimming, etc. for a border

edg·y (ej′ē) *adj.* **-i·er, -i·est** 1 irritable; on edge 2 [Inf.] innovative, daring, etc. —**edg′i·ness** *n.*

ed·i·ble (ed′ə bəl) *adj.* [< L *edere*, eat] fit to be eaten —*n.* anything fit to be eaten: *usually used in pl.* —**ed′i·bil′i·ty** (-bil′ə tē) *n.*

e·dict (ē′dikt′) *n.* [< L *e-*, out + *dicere*, speak] a public order; decree

ed·i·fice (ed′i fis) *n.* [see fol.] a building, esp. a large, imposing one

ed·i·fy (ed′i fī′) *vt.* **-fied′, -fy′ing** [< L *aedificare*, build] to instruct so as to improve or uplift morally —**ed′i·fi·ca′tion** *n.* —**ed′i·fi′er** *n.*

Ed·in·burgh (ed′n bur′ə, -ō) capital of Scotland

Ed·i·son (ed′i sən), **Thom·as Al·va** (täm′əs al′və) 1847-1931; U.S. inventor

ed·it¹ (ed′it) *vt.* [< EDITOR] 1 to prepare (a manuscript) for publication by arranging, revising, etc. 2 to control the policy and publication of (a newspaper, etc.) 3 to prepare (a film, tape, etc.) for presentation by cutting, dubbing, etc. 4 to make changes in (a computer file) —**ed′it·a·ble** *adj.*

edit² *abbrev.* 1 edited (by) 2 edition 3 editor

e·di·tion (i dish′ən) *n.* [see fol.] 1 the size or form in which a book is published 2 the total number of copies of a book, etc. published at one time 3 any particular issue of a newspaper

ed·i·tor (ed′it ər) *n.* [L < *e-*, out + *dare*, give] 1 one that edits 2 a department head of a newspaper, etc.

ed·i·to·ri·al (ed′i tôr′ē əl) *adj.* of or by an editor —*n.* a statement of opinion in a newspaper, etc., as by an editor, publisher, or owner —**ed′i·to′ri·al·ly** *adv.*

ed·i·to·ri·al·ize (-īz′) *vi.* **-ized′, -iz′ing** to express editorial opinions

editor in chief *pl.* **editors in chief** the head of the editorial staff of a publication

Ed·mon·ton (ed′mən tən) capital of Alberta, Canada

educ *abbrev.* 1 education 2 educational

ed·u·ca·ble (ej′ōō kə bəl, ej′ə-) *adj.* that can be educated or trained —**ed′u·ca·bil′i·ty** *n.*

ed·u·cate (-kāt′) *vt.* **-cat′ed, -cat′ing** [< L *e-*, out + *ducere*, to lead] 1 to develop the knowledge, skill, or character of, esp. by formal schooling; teach 2 to pay for the schooling of —**ed′u·ca′tor** *n.*

ed·u·cat·ed *adj.* 1 having much education 2 based on experience

ed·u·ca·tion (-kā′shən) *n.* 1 the process of educating; teaching 2 knowledge, etc. thus developed 3 formal schooling —**ed′u·ca′tion·al** *adj.*

e·duce (ē dōōs′) *vt.* **e·duced′, e·duc′ing** [see EDUCATE] 1 to draw out; elicit 2 to deduce

-ee (ē) [< Anglo-Fr pp. ending] *suffix* 1 the recipient of a (specified) action [*appointee*] 2 one in a (specified) condition [*absentee*]

EEG *abbrev.* electroencephalogram

eel (ēl) *n.* [OE *æl*] a long, slippery, snakelike fish

EEOC *abbrev.* Equal Employment Opportunity Commission

e′er (er, ar) *adv.* [Old Poet.] EVER

-eer (ir) [< L *-arius*] *suffix* 1 *a)* one having to do with [*auctioneer*] *b)* one who writes, makes, etc. [*profiteer*] 2 to have to do with [*electioneer*]

ee·rie or **ee·ry** (ir′ē) *adj.* **-ri·er, -ri·est** [< OE *earg*, timid] mysterious, uncanny, or weird —**ee′ri·ly** *adv.* —**ee′ri·ness** *n.*

ef- *prefix* EX-: used before *f* [*efface*]

ef·face (ə fās′, i-) *vt.* **-faced′, -fac′ing** [< L *ex-*, out + *facies*, face] 1 to rub out; erase 2 to make (oneself) inconspicuous —**ef·face′ment** *n.*

ef·fect (e fekt′, i-) *n.* [< L *ex-*, out + *facere*, do] 1 anything brought about by a cause; result 2 the power to cause results 3 influence 4 meaning [spoke to this *effect*] 5 an impression made on the mind, etc.; its cause 6 a being operative or in force 7 [*pl.*] belongings; property —*vt.* to bring about; accomplish —**in effect** 1 actually 2 virtually 3 in operation　**take effect** to become operative

ef·fec·tive *adj.* 1 producing a desired effect; efficient 2 in effect; operative 3 impressive —**ef·fec′tive·ly** *adv.* —**ef·fec′tive·ness** *n.*

ef·fec·tu·al (e fek′chōō əl, i-) *adj.* 1 producing, or able to produce, the desired effect 2 having legal force; valid —**ef·fec′tu·al·ly** *adv.*

ef·fec·tu·ate (-āt′) *vt.* **-at′ed, -at′ing** to bring about; effect

ef·fem·i·nate (e fem′ə nit, i-) *adj.* [< L *ex-*, out + *femina*, woman] having or showing qualities or characteristics more often associated with females than males: used of a man or boy —**ef·fem′i·na·cy** *n.*

ef·fer·ent (ef′ər ənt) *adj.* [< L *ex-*, out + *ferre*, to bear] carrying away from a central part, as nerves

ef·fer·vesce (ef′ər ves′) *vi.* **-vesced′, -vesc′ing** [< L *ex-*, out + *fervere*, to boil] 1 to give off gas bubbles; bubble 2 to be lively —**ef′fer·ves′cence** *n.* —**ef′fer·ves′cent** *adj.*

ef·fete (e fēt′, i-) *adj.* [< L *ex-*, out + *fetus*, productive] 1 no longer able to produce; sterile 2 decadent, soft, too refined, etc. —**ef·fete′ly** *adv.* —**ef·fete′ness** *n.*

ef·fi·ca·cious (ef′i kā′shəs) *adj.* [see EFFECT] that produces the desired effect —**ef·fi·ca′ci·ous·ly** *adv.* —**ef′fi·ca·cy** (-kə sē) *n.*

ef·fi·cien·cy *n.* 1 the quality of being efficient 2 a small, usually one-room, apartment: in full **efficiency apartment**

ef·fi·cient (e fish′ənt, i-) *adj.* [see EFFECT] producing the desired result with a minimum of effort, expense, or waste —**ef·fi′cient·ly** *adv.*

ef·fi·gy (ef′i jē) *n., pl.* **-gies** [< L *ex-*, out + *fingere*, to form] a statue or other image; often, a crude representation of a despised person

ef·flu·ent (ef′lōō ənt) *adj.* [< L *effluere*, flow out] flowing out —*n.* the outflow of a sewer, etc. —**ef′flu·ence** *n.*

ef·flu·vi·um (e flōō′vē əm) *n., pl.* **-vi·a** (-ə) or **-vi·ums** [see prec.] a disagreeable vapor or odor

ef·fort (ef′ərt) *n.* [< L *ex-*, intens. + *fortis*, strong] 1 the use of energy to do something 2 a try; attempt 3 a result of working or trying —**ef′fort·less** *adj.* —**ef′fort·less·ly** *adv.*

ef·fron·ter·y (e frunt′ər ē, i-) *n.* [< L *ex-*, from + *frons*, forehead] impudence; audacity

ef·ful·gence (e ful′jəns, i-) *n.* [< L *ex-*, forth + *fulgere*, shine] radiance; brilliance —**ef·ful′gent** *adj.*

ef·fuse (e fyōōz′, i-) *vt., vi.* **-fused′, -fus′ing** [< L *ex-*, out + *fundere*, pour] 1 to pour out or forth 2 to spread out; diffuse

ef·fu·sion (-fyōō′zhən) *n.* 1 a pouring forth 2 unrestrained expression in speaking or writing —**ef·fu′sive** *adj.* —**ef·fu′sive·ly** *adv.* —**ef·fu′sive·ness** *n.*

e.g. *abbrev.* [L *exempli gratia*] for example

e·gad (ē gad′) *interj.* [prob. < *oh God*] [Archaic] used as a softened oath

e·gal·i·tar·i·an (ē gal′ə ter′ē ən) *adj.* [< Fr *égalité*, equality] advocating political, social, and economic equality for all people —*n.* one advocating this

egg¹ (eg) *n.* [ON] 1 the oval or round body laid by a female bird, fish, etc., containing the germ of a new individual 2 a reproductive cell produced by a female; ovum 3 a hen's egg, raw or cooked

egg² (eg) *vt.* [< ON *eggja*, give edge to] to urge or incite: with *on*

egg·beat·er *n.* a kitchen utensil for beating eggs, whipping cream, etc.

egg foo yong (*or* **young** *or* **yung**) (eg′fōō yuŋ′) a dish of beaten eggs cooked with bean sprouts, onions, minced pork or shrimp, etc.

egg·head *n.* [Slang] an intellectual

egg·nog (-näg′) *n.* [EGG¹ + *nog*, strong ale] a drink made of eggs, milk, sugar, nutmeg, and, often, whiskey or rum

egg·plant *n.* 1 a plant with a large, ovoid, purple-skinned fruit eaten as a vegetable 2 the fruit

egg roll a Chinese-American dish, a thin egg pancake wrapped around minced vegetables, meat, etc. and deep-fried

eg·lan·tine (eg′lən tīn′, -tēn′) *n.* [< L *aculeus*, a sting] a European rose with sweet-scented leaves and pink flowers

e·go (ē′gō) *n., pl.* **-gos** [L, I²] 1 the self; the individual as self-aware 2 egotism 3 *Psychoanalysis* the part of the psyche that organizes thoughts rationally and governs action

e·go·cen·tric (-sen′trik) *adj.* viewing everything in relation to oneself —**e′go·cen′tri·cal·ly** *adv.* —**e′go·cen′trism′** *n.*

e·go·ism *n.* 1 selfishness; self-interest 2 egotism; conceit —**e′go·ist** *n.* —**e′go·is′tic** *adj.*, **e′go·is′ti·cal**

e·go·tism *n.* 1 excessive reference to oneself in speaking or writing 2 conceit; vanity —**e′go·tist** *n.* —**e′go·tis′ti·cal** *adj.* —**e′go·tis′ti·cal·ly** *adv.*

ego trip [Slang] an experience that gratifies or indulges the ego

e·gre·gious (ē grē′jəs, i-) *adj.* [< L *e-*, out + *grex*, a herd] remarkably bad; flagrant [an *egregious* error] —**e·gre′gious·ly** *adv.* —**e·gre′gious·ness** *n.*

e·gress (ē′gres′) *n.* [< L *e-*, out + *gradi*, go] a way out; exit

e·gret (ē′gret′, -grit) *n.* [< OFr *aigrette*] 1 a kind of heron with long, white plumes 2 AI-GRETTE

E·gypt (ē′jipt) country in NE Africa, on the Mediterranean

E·gyp·tian (ē jip′shən, i-) *n.* 1 the language of the ancient Egyptians 2 a person born or living in Egypt —*adj.* of Egypt or its people, language, etc.

eh (ā, e) *interj.* 1 used to express doubt or surprise 2 used to make an inquiry

ei·der (i′dər) *n.* [ult. < ON *æthr*] 1 a large sea duck of northern regions EIDERDOWN

ei·der·down *n.* the fine, soft down of the eider, used as a stuffing for quilts, pillows, etc.

eight (āt, āth) *adj., n.* [< OE *eahta*] one more than seven; 8; VIII —**eighth** (ātth, āth) *adj., n.*

eight ball a black ball with the number eight on it, used in playing pool —**behind the eight ball** [Slang] in a very unfavorable position

eight·een (ā′tēn′) *adj., n.* eight more than ten; 18; XVIII —**eight′eenth′** *adj., n.*

eight·y *adj., n., pl.* **-ies** eight times ten; 80; LXXX —**the eighties** the numbers or years, as of a century, from 80 through 89 —**eight′i·eth** *adj., n.*

Ein·stein (īn′stīn′), **Al·bert** (al′bərt) 1879-1955; U.S. physicist, born in Germany: formulated theory of relativity

ein·stein·i·um (īn stīn′ē əm) *n.* [after prec.] a radioactive, metallic chemical element: symbol, Es; at. no. 99

Eir·e (er′ə) *Ir. name for* IRELAND

Ei·sen·how·er (ī′zen hou′ər), **Dwight David** (dwīt) 1890-1969; U.S. general & 34th president of the U.S. (1953-61)

ei·ther (ē′thər, ī′-) *adj.* [OE *æghwæther*] 1 one or the other (of two) 2 each (of two) —*pron.* one or the other (of two) —*conj.* a correlative used with *or* to imply a choice of alternatives [*either* go or stay] —*adv.* any more than the other; also [if you don't go, I won't *either*]

e·jac·u·late (ē jak′yōō lāt′, i-) *vt., vi.* **-lat′ed, -lat′ing** [see fol.] 1 to eject (esp. semen) 2 to utter suddenly; exclaim —**e·jac′u·la′tion** *n.*

e·ject (ē jekt′, i-) *vt.* [< L *e-*, out + *jacere*, to throw] to throw or force out; expel —**e·jec′tion** *n.* —**e·jec′tor** *n.*

eke (ēk) *vt.* **eked, ek′ing** [< OE *eacan*, to increase] 1 to supplement 2 to manage to make (a living) with difficulty: with *out*

EKG *abbrev.* electrocardiogram

e·lab·o·rate (ē lab′ə rit, i-; *for v.,* -rāt′) *adj.* [< L *e-*, out + *labor*, work] developed in detail; complicated —*vt.* **-rat′ed, -rat′ing** to work out in detail —*vi.* to add more details: usually with *on* or *upon* —**e·lab′o·**

rate·ly *adv.* —**e·lab′o·rate·ness** *n.* —**e·lab′o·ra′tion** *n.*

é·lan (ā län′, +län′) *n.* 〖Fr < *élancer*, to dart〗 spirited self-assurance; dash

e·lapse (ē laps′, i-) *vi.* **e·lapsed′, e·laps′ing** 〖< L *e-*, out + *labi*, to glide〗 to slip by; pass: said of time

e·las·tic (ē las′tik, i-) *adj.* 〖< Gr *elaunein*, set in motion〗 **1** able to spring back to its original size, shape, etc. after being stretched, squeezed, etc.; flexible **2** able to recover easily, as from dejection; buoyant **3** adaptable **4** made of or containing rubber —*n.* an elastic band or fabric —**e·las·tic′i·ty** (-tis′ə tē) *n.*

e·las·ti·cize (-tə sīz′) *vt.* **-cized′, -ciz′ing** to make (fabric) elastic by incorporating strands of rubber

e·late (ē lāt′, i-) *vt.* **-lat′ed, -lat′ing** 〖< L *ex-*, out + *ferre*, to bear〗 to raise the spirits of; make very proud, happy, etc. —**e·la′tion** *n.*

el·bow (el′bō′) *n.* 〖see ELL² & BOW²〗 **1** the joint between the upper and lower arm; esp., the outer angle made by a bent arm **2** anything bent like an elbow — *vt.*, *vi.* to shove as with the elbows

elbow grease [Inf.] vigorous physical effort

el·bow·room *n.* ample space or room

eld·er¹ (el′dər) *adj.* 〖< OE *eald*, old〗 older —*n.* **1** an older or aged person **2** an older person with some authority, as in a tribe **3** any of certain church officers

el·der² (el′dər) *n.* 〖OE *ellern*〗 a shrub or tree of the honeysuckle family, with red or purple berries

el·der·ber·ry (-ber′ē) *n.*, *pl.* **-ries 1** ELDER² **2** its berry, used for making wine, jelly, etc.

eld·er·ly *adj.* **1** somewhat old **2** in old age; aged

eld·est (el′dist) *adj.* oldest; esp., firstborn

El Do·ra·do or **El·do·ra·do** (el′də rä′dō) *n.*, *pl.* **-dos** 〖Sp, the gilded one〗 any place supposed to be rich in gold, opportunity, etc.

e·lect (ē lekt′, i-) *adj.* 〖< L *e-*, out + *legere*, choose〗 **1** chosen **2** elected but not yet installed in office: usually used in combination [mayor-*elect*] — *vt.*, *vi.* **1** to select for an office by voting **2** to choose; select —**e·lect′a·ble** *adj.* —**e·lect′a·bil′i·ty** *n.*

e·lec·tion (ē lek′shən, i-) *n.* **1** a choosing or choice **2** a choosing or being chosen by vote

e·lec·tion·eer *vi.* to canvass votes in an election

e·lec·tive (-tiv) *adj.* **1** *a*) filled by election [an *elective* office] *b*) chosen by election **2** having the power to choose **3** optional —*n.* an optional course or subject in a school curriculum

e·lec·tor (-tər) *n.* **1** one who elects; specif., a qualified voter **2** a member of the electoral college —**e·lec′tor·al** *adj.*

electoral college an assembly elected by the voters to perform the formal duty of electing the president and vice president of the U.S.

e·lec·tor·ate (-it) *n.* all those qualified to vote in an election

E·lec·tra (ē lek′trə, i-) *n. Gr. Myth.* a daugh-ter of Agamemnon: she plots the death of her mother to avenge her father

e·lec·tric (ē lek′trik, i-) *adj.* 〖< Gr *ēlektron*, amber: from the effect of friction upon amber〗 **1** of, charged with, or conducting electricity **2** producing, or produced by, electricity **3** operated by electricity **4** using electronic amplification [an *electric* guitar] **5** very tense or exciting Also **e·lec′tri·cal** —**e·lec′tri·cal·ly** *adv.*

electric chair a chair equipped for use in electrocuting persons sentenced to death

e·lec·tri·cian (ē′lek trish′ən, ē lek′-) *n.* one whose work is the construction and repair of electric apparatus

e·lec·tric·i·ty (-tris′i tē) *n.* **1** a property of certain fundamental particles of all matter, as electrons (negative charges) and protons or positrons (positive charges): electrical charges can be produced by friction, induction, or chemical change **2** an electric current **3** electric current as a public utility for lighting, heating, etc.

e·lec·tri·fy (ē lek′trə fī′, i-) *vt.* **-fied′, -fy′ing 1** to charge with electricity **2** to excite; thrill **3** to equip for the use of electricity —**e·lec′tri·fi·ca′tion** *n.* —**e·lec′tri·fi′er** *n.*

electro- *combining form* electric, electricity

e·lec·tro·car·di·o·gram (ē lek′trō kär′dē ə gram′, i-) *n.* a tracing showing the variations in electric force which trigger heart contractions

e·lec·tro·car·di·o·graph (-graf′) *n.* an instrument for making electrocardiograms

e·lec·tro·cute (-trə kyoōt′) *vt.* **-cut′ed, -cut′ing** 〖ELECTRO- + (EXE)CUTE〗 to kill or execute with electricity —**e·lec′tro·cu′tion** *n.*

e·lec·trode (-trōd′) *n.* 〖ELECTR(O)- + -ODE〗 any terminal by which electricity enters or leaves a battery, etc.

e·lec·tro·en·ceph·a·lo·gram (-trō en sef′ə lō gram′) *n.* 〖see ENCEPHALITIS & -GRAM〗 a tracing of the variations in electric force in the brain

e·lec·tro·en·ceph·a·lo·graph (-graf′) *n.* an instrument for making electroencephalograms

e·lec·trol·y·sis (ē lek′trǎl′ə sis, i-) *n.* 〖ELECTRO- + -LYSIS〗 **1** the decomposition of an electrolyte by the action of an electric current passing through it **2** the eradication of unwanted hair with an electrified needle

e·lec·tro·lyte (ē lek′trō lit′, i-) *n.* 〖ELECTRO- + -LYTE〗 any chemical compound that ionizes when molten or in solution and becomes capable of conducting electricity —**e·lec′tro·lyt′ic** (-lit′ik) *adj.*

e·lec·tro·mag·net (-mag′nit) *n.* a soft iron core that temporarily becomes a magnet when an electric current flows through a surrounding coil —**e·lec′tro·mag·net′ic** (-net′ik) *adj.*

electromagnetic wave a wave generated by an oscillating electric charge

e·lec·tro·mo·tive (-mōt′iv) *adj.* producing an electric current through differences in potential

e·lec·tron (ē lek′trän′, i-) *n.* ⟦see ELECTRIC⟧ a negatively charged elementary particle that forms a part of all·atoms, orbiting the positively charged nucleus

e·lec·tron·ic (ē′lek trän′ik) *adj.* **1** of electrons **2** operating, produced, or done by the action of electrons —**e·lec′tron′i·cal·ly** *adv.*

electronic mail EMAIL

electronic music music in which the sounds are originated or altered by electronic devices

e·lec·tron·ics *n.* the science dealing with the action of electrons, and with the use of electron tubes, transistors, etc.

electron microscope a device that focuses a beam of electrons on a fluorescent screen, etc. to form a greatly enlarged image of an object

electron tube a sealed glass tube with gas or a vacuum inside, used to control the flow of electrons

e·lec·tro·plate (ē lek′trō plāt′, i-) *vt.* **-plat′ ed, -plat′ing** to deposit a coating of metal on by electrolysis

e·lec·tro·scope (-skōp′) *n.* a device for detecting very small charges of electricity or radiation —**e·lec′tro·scop′ic** (-skäp′ik) *adj.*

e·lec·tro·shock therapy a form of SHOCK THERAPY using electricity

e·lec·tro·type *n. Printing* a plate made by electroplating a wax or plastic impression of the surface to be reproduced

el·ee·mos·y·nar·y (el′i mäs′ə ner′ē, el′ē ə-) *adj.* ⟦< Gr *eleēmosynē*, pity⟧ of, for, or supported by charity

el·e·gant (el′ə gənt) *adj.* ⟦< L *e-*, out + *legere*, choose⟧ **1** having dignified richness and grace, as of manner, design, or dress; tastefully luxurious **2** cleverly apt and simple *[an elegant solution]* —**el′e·gance** *n.* —**el′e·gant·ly** *adv.*

el·e·gi·ac (el ē′jē ak′, el′ə ji′ak′) *adj.* **1** of, like, or fit for an elegy **2** sad; mournful

el·e·gy (el′ə jē) *n., pl.* **-gies** ⟦< Gr *elegos*, a lament⟧ a mournful poem, esp. of lament and praise for the dead

el·e·ment (el′ə mənt) *n.* ⟦< L *elementum*⟧ **1** the natural or suitable environment for a person or thing **2** a component part or quality, often one that is basic or essential **3** *Chem.* any substance that cannot be separated into different substances by ordinary chemical methods, but only by radioactive decay or by nuclear reactions: all matter is composed of such substances —**the elements 1** the first principles; rudiments **2** wind, rain, etc.; forces of the atmosphere

el·e·men·tal (el′ə ment′'l) *adj.* **1** of or like basic, natural forces; primal **2** ELEMENTARY (*adj.* 2a) **3** being an essential part or parts

el·e·men·ta·ry (-ə rē) *adj.* **1** ELEMENTAL **2** *a)* of first principles or fundamentals; basic; simple *b)* of the formal instruction of children in basic subjects

elementary particle a subatomic particle that cannot be divided

elementary school a school for younger children, where basic subjects are taught

el·e·phant (el′ə fənt) *n.* ⟦< Gr *elephas*⟧ a huge, thick-skinned mammal with a long, flexible snout and, usually, two ivory tusks

el·e·phan·ti·a·sis (el′ə fən tī′ə sis) *n.* a chronic disease causing the enlargement of certain body parts and hardening of the surrounding skin

el·e·phan·tine (el′ə fan′tēn′) *adj.* like an elephant; huge, clumsy, etc.

el·e·vate (el′ə vāt′) *vt.* **-vat′ed, -vat′ing** ⟦< L *e-*, out + *levare*, to lift⟧ **1** to lift up; raise **2** to raise in rank **3** to raise to a higher intellectual or moral level **4** to elate; exhilarate

el·e·va·tion (-vā′shən) *n.* **1** an elevating or being elevated **2** a high place or position **3** height above the surface of the earth or above sea level

el·e·va·tor (-vāt′ər) *n.* **1** one that elevates, or lifts up **2** a suspended cage for hoisting or lowering people or things **3** a tall warehouse for storing and discharging grain: in full **grain elevator**

el·ev·en (ē lev′ən, i-) *adj., n.* ⟦OE *endleofan*⟧ one more than ten; 11; XI —**el·ev′enth** (-ənth) *adj., n.*

elf (elf) *n., pl.* **elves** (elvz) ⟦OE *ælf*⟧ *Folklore* a tiny, often mischievous fairy —**elf′in** *adj.*, **elf′ish**

El Gre·co (el grek′ō) 1541?-1614?; painter in Italy & Spain, born in Crete

e·lic·it (ē lis′it, i-) *vt.* ⟦< L *e-*, out + *lacere*, entice⟧ to draw forth; evoke (a response, etc.) —**e·lic′i·ta′tion** *n.*

e·lide (ē līd′, i-) *vt.* **e·lid′ed, e·lid′ing** ⟦< L *e-*, out + *laedere*, to hurt⟧ to leave out; esp., to slur over (a vowel, etc.) in pronunciation —**e·li′sion** (-lizh′ən) *n.*

el·i·gi·ble (el′i jə bəl) *adj.* ⟦see ELECT⟧ fit to be chosen; qualified —**el′i·gi·bil′i·ty** *n.* —**el′i·gi·bly** *adv.*

E·li·jah (ē lī′jə, i-) *n. Bible* a prophet of Israel in the 9th c. B.C.

e·lim·i·nate (ē lim′ə nāt′, i-) *vt.* **-nat′ed, -nat′ing** ⟦< L *e-*, out + *limen*, threshold⟧ **1** to remove; get rid of **2** to leave out of consideration; omit **3** to excrete —**e·lim′i·na′tion** *n.* —**e·lim′i·na′tor** *n.*

El·i·ot (el′ē ət) **1 George** (pseud. of *Mary Ann Evans*) 1819-80; Eng. novelist **2 T(homas) S(tearns)** 1885-1965; Brit. poet, born in the U.S.

e·lite (i lēt′, ā-) *n.* ⟦Fr < L: see ELECT⟧ *[also with pl. v.]* a group regarded as the best, most powerful, etc.

e·lit·ism *n.* government or control by an elite —**e·lit′ist** *adj., n.*

e·lix·ir (i liks′ir) *n.* ⟦< Ar *al-iksīr*⟧ **1** a hypothetical substance sought by medieval alchemists to change base metals into gold or (in full **elixir of life**) to prolong life indefinitely **2** *Pharmacy* a sweetened solution used for medicines, etc.

E·liz·a·beth (ē liz′ə bəth, i-) **Elizabeth I** 1533-1603; queen of England (1558-1603)

E·liz·a·be·than (ē liz′ə bē′thən) *adj.* of or characteristic of the time of Elizabeth I's reign —*n.* an English person, esp. a writer, of that time

elk (elk) *n.* ‖< OE *eolh*‖ **1** MOOSE: the common term in Europe **2** WAPITI

ell¹ (el) *n.* **1** an extension or wing of a building, esp. one at right angles to the main structure **2** an L-shaped pipe, etc.

ell² (el) *n.* ‖< OE *eln*‖ a former English unit of measure, equal to 45 inches

el·lipse (e lips′, i-) *n.*, *pl.* **-lip′ses′** (-sēz′) ‖< Gr *elleipein*, fall short‖ *Geom.* a closed curve in the form of a symmetrical oval

el·lip·sis (-lip′sis) *n.*, *pl.* **-ses′** (-sēz′) ‖see prec.‖ **1** *Gram.* the omission of a word or words understood in the context (Ex.: "if possible" for "if it is possible") **2** a mark (. . .) indicating an omission of words: in full **ellipsis points**

el·lip·ti·cal (-ti kəl) *adj.* **1** of, or having the form of, an ellipse **2** of or characterized by the omission of words Also **el·lip′tic** —**el·lip′ti·cal·ly** *adv.*

elm (elm) *n.* ‖OE‖ **1** a tall, deciduous shade tree **2** its hard, heavy wood

El Ni·ño (el nēn′yō) **1** a warm inshore current annually flowing south along the coast of Ecuador **2** the period of anomalous climate conditions caused every several years by changes in this current

el·o·cu·tion (el′ə kyōō′shən) *n.* ‖see ELOQUENT‖ the art of public speaking —**el′o·cu′tion·ar′y** *adj.* **el′o·cu′tion·ist** *n.*

e·lo·de·a (ē lō′dē ə, el′ə dē′ə) *n.* ‖< Gr *helōdēs*, swampy‖ a submerged water plant with whorls of short leaves

e·lon·gate (ē lôŋ′gāt′, i-) *vt.*, *vi.* **-gat′ed, -gat′ing** ‖< L *e-*, out + *longus*, long‖ to make or become longer; stretch —**e·lon·ga′tion** *n.*

e·lope (ē lōp′, i-) *vi.* **e·loped′, e·lop′ing** ‖prob. < OE *a-*, away + *hleapan*, to run‖ to run away secretly, esp. in order to get married —**e·lope′ment** *n.*

el·o·quent (el′ə kwənt) *adj.* ‖< L *e-*, out + *loqui*, speak‖ vivid, forceful, fluent, etc. in speech or writing —**el′o·quence** *n.* —**el′o·quent·ly** *adv.*

El Pas·o (el pas′ō) city in westernmost Texas

El Sal·va·dor (el sal′və dôr′) country in Central America, on the Pacific

else (els) *adj.* ‖OE *elles*‖ **1** different; other [somebody *else*] **2** in addition [is there anything *else*?] —*adv.* **1** differently; otherwise [where *else* can I go?] **2** if not [study, (or) *else* you will fail]

else·where *adv.* in or to some other place; somewhere else

e·lu·ci·date (ə lōō′sə dāt′) *vt.*, *vi.* **-dat′ed, -dat′ing** ‖< L *e-*, out + *lucidus*, clear‖ to make (something) clear; explain —**e·lu′ci·da′tion** *n.*

e·lude (ē lōōd′, i-) *vt.* **e·lud′ed, e·lud′ing** ‖< L *e-*, out + *ludere*, to play‖ **1** to avoid or escape from by quickness, cunning, etc. **2** to escape the mental grasp of [his name *eludes* me]

e·lu·sive (-lōō′siv) *adj.* tending to elude; evasive —**e·lu′sive·ly** *adv.* —**e·lu′sive·ness** *n.*

elves (elvz) *n.* *pl.* *of* ELF

elv·ish *adj.* of or like the elves

E·ly·si·um (ē lizh′əm, -liz′ē əm; i-) *n.* **1** *Gr. Myth.* the dwelling place of virtuous people after death **2** any state of ideal bliss; paradise —**E·ly′si·an** (-lizh′ən, -liz′ē ən) *adj.*

'em (əm) *pron.* [Inf.] them

em (em) *n.* ‖< the letter M‖ *Printing* a unit of measure, as of column width

em- *prefix* EN-: used before *b, m,* or *p*

e·ma·ci·ate (ē mā′shē āt′, -sē-; i-) *vt.* **-at′ed, -at′ing** ‖< L *e-*, out + *macies*, leanness‖ to cause to become abnormally lean —**e·ma′ci·a′tion** *n.*

e·mail or **e-mail** (ē′māl′) *n.* **1** a system for transmitting messages electronically over a computer network **2** a message or messages transmitted by such a system — *vt.*, *vi.* to send (such a message) to (someone)

em·a·nate (em′ə nāt′) *vi.* **-nat′ed, -nat′ing** ‖< L *e-*, out + *manare*, to flow‖ to come forth; issue, as from a source —**em′a·na′tion** *n.*

e·man·ci·pate (ē man′sə pāt′, i-) *vt.* **-pat′ed, -pat′ing** ‖< L *e-*, out + *manus*, the hand + *capere*, to take‖ **1** to set free (a slave, etc.) **2** to free from restraint —**e·man′ci·pa′tion** *n.* —**e·man′ci·pa′tor** *n.*

e·mas·cu·late (ē mas′kyōō lāt′) *vt.* **-lat′ed, -lat′ing** ‖< L *e-*, out + *masculus*, male‖ **1** to castrate **2** to weaken —**e·mas′cu·la′tion** *n.*

em·balm (em bäm′, im-) *vt.* ‖see EN- & BALM‖ to preserve (a dead body) with various chemicals —**em·balm′er** *n.*

em·bank (em baŋk′, im-) *vt.* to protect, support, or enclose with a bank of earth, etc. —**em·bank′ment** *n.*

em·bar·go (em bär′gō, im-) *n.*, *pl.* **-goes** ‖Sp < L *in-*, in + ML *barra*, a bar‖ **1** a government order prohibiting the entry or departure of commercial ships at its ports **2** any legal restriction of commerce —*vt.* **-goed, -go·ing** to put an embargo upon

em·bark (em bärk′, im-) *vt.* ‖ult. < L *in-*, in + *barca*, small boat‖ to put or take (passengers or goods) aboard a ship, aircraft, etc. —*vi.* **1** to go aboard a ship, aircraft, etc. **2** to begin; start —**em′bar·ka′tion** (-bär kā′shən) *n.*

em·bar·rass (em bar′əs, im-) *vt.* ‖< It *in-*, in + ML *barra*, a bar‖ **1** to cause to feel self-conscious **2** to hinder **3** to cause to be in debt —**em·bar′rass·ing** *adj.* —**em·bar′rass·ment** *n.*

em·bas·sy (em′bə sē) *n.*, *pl.* **-sies** ‖see AMBASSADOR‖ **1** the residence or offices of an ambassador **2** an ambassador and his or her staff **3** a group sent on an official mission

em·bat·tled (em bat′′ld) *adj.* ‖< OFr‖ engaged in battle or conflict

em·bed (em bed′, im-) *vt.* **-bed′ded, -bed′ding 1** to set or fix firmly in earth, in the mind or memory, etc. **2** to assign (an observer), as to a combat unit —**em·bed′ment** *n.*

em·bel·lish (em bel′ish, im-) *vt.* ‖< OFr *em-*, in + *bel*, beautiful‖ **1** to adorn **2** to improve (a story, etc.) by adding details, often fictitious —**em·bel′lish·ment** *n.*

em·ber (em′bər) *n.* ‖OE *æmerge*‖ **1** a glowing

piece of coal, wood, etc. **2** [*pl.*] the smoldering remains of a fire

em·bez·zle (em bez′əl, im-) *vt.* **-zled, -zling** 〚< OFr *en-*, in + *besillier*, destroy〛 to steal (money, etc. entrusted to one) —**em·bez′zle·ment** *n.* —**em·bez′zler** *n.*

em·bit·ter (-bit′ər) *vt.* to make bitter —**em·bit′ter·ment** *n.*

em·bla·zon (-blā′zən) *vt.* 〚EM- (see EN-) + BLAZON〛 **1** to decorate (*with* coats of arms, etc.) **2** to display brilliantly **3** to extol —**em·bla′zon·ment** *n.*

em·blem (em′bləm) *n.* 〚< Gr *en-*, in + *ballein*, throw〛 a visible symbol of a thing, idea, etc.; sign; badge —**em′blem·at·ic** (-blə mat′ik) *adj.*

em·bod·y (em bäd′ē, im-) *vt.* **-ied, -y·ing 1** to give bodily form to **2** to give definite form to **3** to bring together into an organized whole —**em·bod′i·ment** *n.*

em·bold·en (-bōl′dən) *vt.* to give courage to

em·bo·lism (em′bə liz′əm) *n.* 〚< Gr *en-*, in + *ballein*, to throw〛 the obstruction of a blood vessel as by a blood clot or air bubble

em·boss (em bôs′, -bäs′; im-) *vt.* 〚see EN- & BOSS[2]〛 **1** to decorate with raised designs, patterns, etc. **2** to raise (a design, etc.) in relief —**em·boss′er** *n.*

em·bou·chure (äm′boo shoor′) *n.* 〚Fr < L *in*, in + *bucca*, cheek〛 the method of applying the lips and tongue to the mouthpiece of a wind instrument

em·brace (em brās′, im-) *vt.* **-braced′, -brac′ing** 〚< L *im-*, in + *brachium*, an arm〛 **1** to clasp in the arms lovingly; hug **2** to accept readily **3** to take up or adopt **4** to encircle **5** to include —*vi.* to clasp each other in the arms —*n.* an embracing; hug —**em·brace′a·ble** *adj.*

em·bra·sure (em brā′zhər, im-) *n.* 〚Fr < obs. *embraser*, widen an opening〛 **1** an opening (for a door, window, etc.) wider on the inside than on the outside **2** an opening in a wall or parapet for a gun, with the sides slanting outward

em·broi·der (em broi′dər, im-) *vt., vi.* 〚< OFr *en-*, on + *brosder*, embroider〛 **1** to make (a design, etc.) on (fabric) with needlework **2** to embellish (a story); exaggerate

em·broi·der·y *n., pl.* **-ies 1** the art of embroidering **2** embroidered work or fabric **3** embellishment

em·broil (em broil′, im-) *vt.* 〚< OFr *en-*, in + *brouillier*, to dirty〛 **1** to confuse; muddle **2** to involve in conflict or trouble —**em·broil′ment** *n.*

em·bry·o (em′brē ō′) *n., pl.* **-os′** 〚< Gr *en-*, in + *bryein*, to swell〛 **1** an animal in the earliest stages of its development in the uterus or egg **2** the rudimentary plant contained in a seed **3** an early stage of something —**em′bry·on′ic** (-än′ik) *adj.*

em·bry·ol·o·gy (-äl′ə jē) *n.* 〚prec. + -LOGY〛 the branch of biology dealing with the formation and development of embryos —**em′bry·ol′o·gist** *n.*

em·cee (em′sē′) *vi., vt.* **-ceed′, -cee′ing** 〚< MC〛 [Inf.] to act as master of ceremonies (for) —*n.* [Inf.] a master of ceremonies

e·mend (ē mend′, i-) *vt.* 〚< L *emendare*, to correct〛 to make scholarly corrections in (a text) —**e·men·da·tion** (ē′men dā′shən, em′ən-) *n.*

em·er·ald (em′ər əld) *n.* 〚< Gr *smaragdos*〛 **1** a transparent, bright-green precious stone, a form of beryl **2** bright green

e·merge (ē murj′, i-) *vi.* **e·merged′, e·merg′ing** 〚< L *e-*, out + *mergere*, to dip〛 **1** to rise as from a fluid **2** to become visible or apparent **3** to evolve —**e·mer′gence** *n.* —**e·mer′gent** *adj.*

e·mer·gen·cy (ē mur′jən sē, i-) *n., pl.* **-cies** 〚orig. sense, emergence〛 a sudden, generally unexpected occurrence demanding immediate action —*adj.* for use in an emergency

emergency room a hospital unit for accident victims and others needing immediate treatment

e·mer·i·ta (ē mer′i tə, i-) *adj.* EMERITUS: used of a woman

e·mer·i·tus (-təs) *adj.* 〚< L *e-*, out + *mereri*, to serve〛 retired from active service, usually for age, but retaining one's title [*professor emeritus*]

Em·er·son (em′ər sən), **Ralph Wal·do** (ralf wôl′dō) 1803-82; U.S. writer & philosopher

em·er·y (em′ər ē) *n.* 〚< Gr *smyris*〛 a dark, coarse variety of corundum used for grinding, polishing, etc.

emery board a small, flat stick coated with powdered emery, used to shape fingernails

e·met·ic (ē met′ik, i-) *adj.* 〚< Gr *emein*, to vomit〛 causing vomiting —*n.* an emetic substance

-e·mi·a (ē′mē ə) 〚< Gr *haima*, blood〛 *combining form* a (specified) condition of the blood [*leukemia*]

em·i·grate (em′i grāt′) *vi.* **-grat′ed, -grat′ing** 〚< L *e-*, out + *migrare*, to move〛 to leave one country or region to settle in another —**em′i·grant** (-grənt) *adj., n.* —**em′i·gra′tion** *n.*

é·mi·gré or **e·mi·gré** (em′i grā′) *n.* 〚Fr〛 **1** one who emigrates **2** one forced to flee his or her country for political reasons

em·i·nence (em′i nəns) *n.* 〚< L *eminere*, stand out〛 **1** a high place, thing, etc. **2** superiority in rank, position, etc. **3** [E-] a title of a cardinal: preceded by *Your* or *His*

em·i·nent (-nənt) *adj.* 〚< L *eminens*〛 **1** high; lofty **2** projecting; prominent **3** renowned; distinguished **4** outstanding —**em′i·nent·ly** *adv.*

eminent domain the right of a government to purchase private property for public use

e·mir (e mir′, ə-) *n.* 〚< Ar *amara*, to command〛 in Muslim countries, a ruler or prince

em·is·sar·y (em′i ser′ē) *n., pl.* **-ies** 〚see EMIT〛 a person or agent sent on a specific mission

e·mis·sion (ē mish′ən, i-) *n.* **1** an emitting **2** something emitted; discharge

e·mit (ē mit′, i-) *vt.* **e·mit′ted, e·mit′ting** 〚< L *e-*, out + *mittere*, send〛 **1** to send out; give forth;

discharge 2 to utter (words, etc.) —e·mit′· ter *n.*

e·mo (ē′mō) *n.* 〚< emo(*tional hardcore*)〛 an offshoot of punk rock with sentimental lyrics conveying desperation, etc.

e·mol·li·ent (ē mäl′yənt, i-) *adj.* 〚< L *e-*, out + *mollire*, soften〛 softening; soothing —*n.* something that softens or soothes, as a preparation applied to the skin

e·mol·u·ment (-yōō mənt) *n.* 〚< L *e-*, out + *molere*, to grind〛 payment received for work; salary, fees, etc.

e·mote (ē mōt′, i-) *vi.* e·mot′ed, e·mot′ing [Inf.] to act in an emotional or theatrical manner

e·mo·ti·con (ē mōt′i kän′) *n.* 〚fol. + ICON〛 a combination of typed keyboard characters that represent a stylized face to convey a writer's tone, as in email or text messages; e.g., :) suggests happiness

e·mo·tion (ē mō′shən, i-) *n.* 〚< L *e-*, out + *movere*, to move〛 1 strong feeling 2 any specific feeling, as love, hate, fear, or anger

e·mo·tion·al *adj.* 1 of or showing emotion 2 easily aroused to emotion 3 appealing to the emotions; moving —e·mo′tion·al·ism′ *n.* —e·mo′tion·al·ly *adv.*

e·mo·tion·al·ize *vt.* -ized′, -iz′ing to treat in an emotional way

em·pa·thet·ic (em′pə thet′ik) *adj.* of or showing empathy: also em·path′ic (-path′ik)

em·pa·thize (em′pə thīz′) *vt.* -thized′, -thiz′ing to feel empathy (*with*)

em·pa·thy (-thē) *n.* 〚< Gr *en-*, in + *pathos*, feeling〛 the ability to share in another's emotions, thoughts, or feelings

em·per·or (em′pər ər) *n.* 〚< L *in-*, in + *parare*, to set in order〛 the supreme ruler of an empire

em·pha·sis (em′fə sis) *n., pl.* -ses′ (-sēz′) 〚< Gr *en-*, in + *phainein*, to show〛 1 force of expression, action, etc. 2 special stress given to a word or phrase in speaking 3 importance; stress

em·pha·size (-sīz′) *vt.* -sized′, -siz′ing to give emphasis to; stress

em·phat·ic (em fat′ik, im-) *adj.* 1 felt or done with emphasis 2 using emphasis in speaking, etc. 3 forcible; striking —em·phat′i·cal·ly *adv.*

em·phy·se·ma (em′fə sē′mə, -zē′-) *n.* 〚< Gr *en-*, in + *physaein*, to blow〛 a condition of the lungs in which the air sacs become distended and lose elasticity

em·pire (em′pīr′) *n.* 〚see EMPEROR〛 1 supreme rule 2 government by an emperor or empress 3 a group of states or territories under one ruler 4 an extensive organization under the control of a single person, corporation, etc.

em·pir·i·cal (em pir′i kəl) *adj.* 〚< Gr *en-*, in + *peira*, trial〛 relying or based on experiment or experience —em·pir′i·cal·ly *adv.* —em·pir′i·cism′ (-siz′əm) *n.*

em·place·ment (em pläs′mənt, im-) *n.* the prepared position from which a heavy gun or guns are fired

em·ploy (em ploi′, im-) *vt.* 〚< L *in-*, in + *plicare*, to fold〛 1 to use 2 to keep busy or occupied 3 to engage the services of; hire —*n.* employment

em·ploy·a·ble *adj.* that can be employed; specif., physically or mentally fit to be hired for work

em·ploy·ee (im-) *n.* one hired by another for wages or salary

em·ploy·er *n.* one who employs others for wages or salary

em·ploy·ment *n.* 1 an employing or being employed 2 work; occupation 3 the number or percentage of persons gainfully employed

em·po·ri·um (em pôr′ē əm) *n., pl.* -ri·ums or -ri·a (-ə) 〚< Gr *en-*, in + *poros*, way〛 a large store with a wide variety of things for sale

em·pow·er (em pou′ər, im-) *vt.* 1 to give power to; authorize 2 to enable —em·pow′er·ment *n.*

em·press (em′pris) *n.* 1 an emperor's wife 2 a woman ruler of an empire

emp·ty (emp′tē) *adj.* -ti·er, -ti·est 〚OE *æmettig*〛 1 having nothing or no one in it; unoccupied 2 worthless [*empty pleasure*] 3 insincere [*empty promises*] —*vt.* -tied, -ty·ing 1 to make empty 2 to remove (the contents) of something —*vi.* 1 to become empty 2 to pour out —*n., pl.* -ties an empty truck, bottle, etc. —emp′ti·ly *adv.* —emp′ti·ness *n.*

emp·ty-hand·ed *adj.* bringing or carrying away nothing

em·py·re·an (em pir′ē ən, em′pī rē′ən) *n.* 〚< Gr *en-*, in + *pyr*, fire〛 1 the highest heaven 2 the sky; firmament

EMT *abbrev.* emergency medical technician

e·mu (ē′myōō) *n.* 〚< Port *ema*, a crane〛 a large, flightless Australian bird, somewhat like the ostrich but smaller

em·u·late (em′yōō lāt′, -yə-) *vt.* -lat′ed, -lat′ing 〚< L *aemulus*, trying to equal or excel〛 1 to try to equal or surpass 2 to imitate (a person or thing admired) 3 to rival successfully 4 *Comput.* to duplicate the functions and interface of —em′u·la′tion *n.* —em′u·la′tive *adj.* —em′u·la′tor *n.*

e·mul·si·fy (ē mul′sə fī′, i-) *vt., vi.* -fied′, -fy′ing to form into an emulsion —e·mul′si·fi·ca′· tion *n.*

e·mul·sion (-shən) *n.* 〚< L *e-*, out + *mulgere*, to milk〛 a colloidal suspension of one liquid in another, as photographic film coatings, some medications, etc.

en- 〚< L *in-*, in〛 *prefix* 1 to put or get into or on [*enthrone*] 2 to make, cause to be [*endanger*] 3 in or into [*encase*]

-en (ən, ′n) 〚OE〛 *suffix* 1 *a*) to become or cause to be [*darken*] *b*) to cause to have [*heighten*] 2 made of [*wooden*] 3 forming plurals [*children*]

en·a·ble (en ā′bəl, in-) *vt.* -bled, -bling 1 to make able; provide with means, power, etc. (*to do something*) 2 to support the dysfunctional behavior of, as by compensating for it —en·a′bler *n.*

en·act (en akt′, in-) *vt.* **1** to pass (a bill, law, etc.) **2** to represent as in a play —**en·act′ment** *n.*

en·am·el (e nam′əl, i-) *n.* [< OFr *esmail*] **1** a glassy, opaque substance fused to metal, pottery, etc. as an ornamental or protective coating **2** the hard, white coating of teeth **3** paint that dries to a smooth, glossy surface — *vt.* **-eled** or **-elled, -el·ing** or **-el·ling** to coat with enamel —**en·am′el·er** *n.*, **en·am′el·ler**

en·am·or (en am′ər, in-) *vt.* [ult. < L *in-*, in + *amor*, love] to fill with love; charm: now mainly in the passive voice, with *of [enamored of her]*

en bloc (en bläk′) [Fr, lit., in a block] in a mass; all together

en bro·chette (än brô shet′) [Fr] broiled on small skewers

en·camp (en kamp′, in-) *vi., vt.* to set up, or put in, a camp —**en·camp′ment** *n.*

en·cap·su·late (en kap′sə lāt′) *vt.* **-lat′ed, -lat′ing 1** to enclose in a capsule **2** to make concise; condense Also **en·cap′sule** (-səl, -syool′) **-suled, -sul·ing** —**en·cap′su·la′tion** *n.*

en·case (en kās′, in-) *vt.* **-cased′, -cas′ing** to enclose, as in a case

en cas·se·role (än käs rêl′, en käs′ə rōl′) [Fr] (baked and served) in a casserole

-ence (əns, ′ns) [< L] *suffix* act, state, or result *[conference]*

en·ceph·a·li·tis (en sef′ə līt′is) *n.* [< Gr *en-*, in + *kephalē*, the head + *-ITIS*] inflammation of the brain

en·chain (en chān′) *vt.* to bind with chains; fetter

en·chant (en chant′, in-) *vt.* [< L *in-*, intens. + *cantare*, sing] **1** to cast a spell over **2** to charm greatly; delight —**en·chant′er** *n.* —**en·chant′ing** *adj.* —**en·chant′ment** *n.*

en·chi·la·da (en′chi lä′də) *n.* [AmSp] a tortilla rolled with meat inside, served with a chili-flavored sauce

en·cir·cle (en sur′kəl, in-) *vt.* **-cled, -cling 1** to surround **2** to move in a circle around — **en·cir′cle·ment** *n.*

encl *abbrev.* enclosure

en·clave (en′klāv′, än′-) *n.* [< L *in*, in + *clavis*, a key] **1** a territory surrounded by another country's territory **2** a minority group living within an area where another group predominates

en·close (en klōz′, in-) *vt.* **-closed′, -clos′ing 1** to shut in all around; surround **2** to insert in an envelope, etc., often along with something else

en·clo·sure (-klō′zhər) *n.* **1** an enclosing or being enclosed **2** something that encloses, as a fence **3** something enclosed, as in an envelope or by a wall

en·code (en kōd′, in-) *vt.* **-cod′ed, -cod′ing** to put (a message, etc.) into code

en·co·mi·um (en kō′mē əm) *n.*, *pl.* **-ums** or **-a** (-ə) [< Gr *en-*, in + *kōmos*, a revel] high praise; eulogy

en·com·pass (en kum′pəs, in-) *vt.* **1** to surround **2** to contain; include

en·core (än′kôr′) *interj.* [Fr] again; once more —*n.* a further performance, etc. in answer to an audience's applause

en·coun·ter (en koun′tər, in-) *vt.* [< L *in*, in + *contra*, against] **1** to meet unexpectedly **2** to meet in conflict **3** to meet with (difficulties, etc.) —*n.* **1** a direct meeting, as in battle **2** a meeting, esp. when unexpected

en·cour·age (en kur′ij, in-) *vt.* **-aged, -ag·ing 1** to give courage, hope, or confidence to **2** to give support to; help —**en·cour′age·ment** *n.*

en·croach (en krōch′, in-) *vi.* [< OFr *en-*, in + *croc*, a hook] to trespass or intrude (*on* or *upon*) —**en·croach′ment** *n.*

en croûte (än krōōt′) [Fr] wrapped in pastry and baked: said esp. of meats

en·crust (en krust′) *vt.* to cover as with a crust —*vi.* to form a crust —**en′crus·ta′tion** (-krus tā′shən) *n.*

en·cum·ber (en kum′bər, in-) *vt.* [see EN- & CUMBER] **1** to hold back the motion or action of; hinder **2** to burden —**en·cum′brance** *n.*

-en·cy (ən sē) [L *-entia*] *suffix* -ENCE *[dependency]*

en·cyc·li·cal (en sik′li kəl, in-) *n.* [< Gr *en-*, in + *kyklos*, a circle] a papal document addressed to the bishops

en·cy·clo·pe·di·a or **en·cy·clo·pae·di·a** (en sī′klə pē′dē ə) *n.* [< Gr *enkyklios*, general + *paideia*, education] a book or set of books with alphabetically arranged articles on all branches, or on one field, of knowledge —**en·cy′clo·pe′dic** *adj.*, **en·cy′clo·pae′dic**

en·cyst (en sist′) *vt., vi.* to enclose or become enclosed in a cyst, sac, etc. —**en·cyst′ment** *n.*

end (end) *n.* [OE *ende*] **1 a** limit; boundary **b** the last part of anything; finish; conclusion **c** a ceasing to exist; death or destruction **4** the part at or near an extremity; tip **5** an object; purpose **6** an outcome; result **7** *Football* a player at either end of the line — *vt., vi.* to bring or come to an end; finish; stop —*adj.* at the end; final —**make (both) ends meet** to manage to keep one's expenses within one's income —**put an end to 1** to stop **2** to do away with

en·dan·ger (en dän′jər, in-) *vt.* to expose to danger, harm, etc.; imperil —**en·dan′ger·ment** *n.*

endangered species a species of animal, plant, etc. in danger of becoming extinct

en·dear (en dir′, in-) *vt.* to make dear or beloved —**en·dear′ing** *adj.*

en·dear·ment *n.* **1** an endearing **2** a word or act expressing affection

en·deav·or (en dev′ər, in-) *vi.* [< EN- + OFr *deveir*, duty] to make an earnest attempt; try: usually with an infinitive —*n.* an earnest attempt or effort Brit. sp. **en·deav′our**

en·dem·ic (en dem′ik) *adj.* [< Gr *en-*, in + *dēmos*, people] native to, or constantly present in, a particular place, as a plant or disease —**en·dem′i·cal·ly** *adv.*

end·ing *n.* **1** the last part; finish **2** death

en·dive (en′dīv′, än′dēv′) *n.* [< Gr *entybon*] **1**

a cultivated plant with curled, narrow leaves used in salads **2** young leaves of chicory, used in salads

end·less *adj.* **1** having no end; eternal; infinite **2** lasting too long [an *endless* speech] **3** continual [*endless* problems] **4** with the ends joined to form a closed unit [an *endless* chain] **—end′less·ly** *adv.* **—end′less·ness** *n.*

end·most *adj.* at the end; farthest

endo- [< Gr *endon*] *combining form* within, inner

en·do·crine (en′dō krin′, -krīn′; -də-) *adj.* [prec. + Gr *krinein*, to separate] designating or of any gland producing a hormone

en·dorse (en dôrs′, in-) *vt.* **-dorsed′, -dors′ing** [< L *in*, on + *dorsum*, the back] **1** to write on the back of (a title, check, etc.) to transfer ownership, make a deposit, etc. **2** to sanction, approve, or support **3** to recommend (an advertised product) for a fee **—en·dorse′ment** *n.* **en·dors′er** *n.*

en·do·scope (en′dō skōp′, -də-) *n.* an instrument for examining visually the inside of a hollow organ or body cavity

en·dow (en dou′, in-) *vt.* [< OFr *en-*, in + *dot-are*, to endow] **1** to provide with some talent, quality, etc. [*endowed* with courage] **2** to give money or property to (a college, etc.) **—en·dow′ment** *n.*

end point *n.* a point of completion or furthest progress

end product the final result of a series of changes, processes, etc.

end table a small table placed at the end of a sofa, etc.

en·due (en dōō′, in-) *vt.* **-dued′, -du′ing** [< L *in-*, in + *ducere*, to lead] to provide (*with* qualities)

en·dur·ance (en door′əns, in-) *n.* the ability to last, stand pain, etc.

en·dure (en door′, in-) *vt.* **-dured′, -dur′ing** [< L *durus*, hard] **1** to hold up under (pain, etc.) **2** to tolerate **—vi.** **1** to continue; last **2** to bear pain, etc. without flinching **—en·dur′a·ble** *adj.*

end·ways (-wāz′) *adv.* **1** upright **2** with the end foremost **3** lengthwise Also **end′wise′** (-wīz′)

-ene (ēn) [after Gr *-enos*, adj. suffix] *Chem. suffix* a certain type of hydrocarbon [*benzene*]

en·e·ma (en′ə mə) *n.* [< Gr *en-*, in + *hienai*, send] the forcing of a liquid, as a purgative, medicine, etc., into the colon through the anus

en·e·my (en′ə mē) *n.*, *pl.* **-mies** [< L *in-*, not + *amicus*, friend] **1** one who hates and wishes to injure another **2** *a)* a nation or force hostile to another *b)* troops, ship, etc. of a hostile nation **3** one hostile to an idea, cause, etc. **4** anything injurious or harmful

en·er·get·ic (en′ər jet′ik) *adj.* having or showing energy; vigorous **—en′er·get′i·cal·ly** *adv.*

en·er·gize (en′ər jīz′) *vt.* **-gized′, -giz′ing** to give energy to **—en′er·giz′er** *n.*

en·er·gy (en′ər jē) *n.*, *pl.* **-gies** [< Gr *en-*, in + *ergon*, work] **1** force of expression **2** *a)*

inherent power; capacity for action *b)* [often *pl.*] such power, esp. in action **3** a resource, as oil or gas, from which usable energy can be produced **4** *Physics* the capacity for doing work

en·er·vate (en′ər vāt′) *vt.* **-vat′ed, -vat′ing** [< L *e-*, out + *nervus*, nerve] to deprive of strength, force, vigor, etc.; devitalize **—en′er·va′tion** *n.*

en·fee·ble (en fē′bəl, in-) *vt.* **-bled, -bling** to make feeble

en·fi·lade (en′fə lād′, en′fə lād′) *n.* [Fr] gunfire directed along a line of troops

en·fold (en fōld′, in-) *vt.* **1** to wrap in folds; wrap up **2** to embrace

en·force (en fôrs′, in-) *vt.* **-forced′, -forc′ing 1** to impose by force [to *enforce* one's will] **2** to compel observance of (a law, etc.) **—en·force′a·ble** *adj.* **—en·force′ment** *n.* **—en·forc′er** *n.*

en·fran·chise (en fran′chīz′, in-) *vt.* **-chised′, -chis′ing 1** to free from slavery **2** to give the right to vote **—en·fran′chise·ment** (-chiz mənt) *n.*

Eng *abbrev.* **1** England **2** English

en·gage (en gāj′, in-) *vt.* **-gaged′, -gag′ing** [see EN- & GAGE[1]] **1** to pledge (oneself) **2** to bind by a promise of marriage **3** to hire **4** to involve or occupy **5** to attract and hold (the attention, etc.) **6** to enter into conflict with (the enemy) **7** to mesh (gears, etc.) **—vi.** **1** to pledge oneself **2** to occupy or involve oneself [to *engage* in dramatics] **3** to enter into conflict **4** to mesh

en·gaged *adj.* **1** betrothed **2** occupied; employed **3** involved in combat, as troops **4** in gear; meshed

en·gage·ment *n.* an engaging or being engaged; specif., *a)* a betrothal *b)* an appointment *c)* a conflict; battle

en·gag·ing *adj.* attractive; pleasant; charming **—en·gag′ing·ly** *adv.*

en·gen·der (en jen′dər, in-) *vt.* [< L *in-*, in + *generare*, beget] to bring into being; cause; produce

en·gine (en′jən) *n.* [< L *in-*, in + base of *gignere*, beget] **1** any machine that uses energy to provide mechanical power **2** a railroad locomotive **3** any machine

en·gi·neer (en′jə nir′) *n.* **1** one skilled in some branch of engineering **2** one who operates or supervises the operation of engines or technical equipment [a locomotive *engineer*] **—vt.** **1** to plan, construct, etc. as an engineer **2** to manage skillfully

en·gi·neer·ing *n.* **1** the science concerned with putting scientific knowledge to practical uses **2** the planning, designing, construction, or management of machinery, roads, bridges, etc.

Eng·land (iŋ′glənd) division of the United Kingdom in S Great Britain

Eng·lish (iŋ′glish) *adj.* **1** of England, its people, etc. **2** of the language of England, the U.S., etc. **—n.** **1** the Germanic language of England and the U.S., also spoken in the

Commonwealth, etc. 2 [*sometimes* e-] a spinning motion given to a ball —**the English** the people of England —**Eng′lish·man** (-mən) *n., pl.* -**men** (-mən) —**Eng′lish·wom′an** *n., pl.* -**wom′en**

English Channel arm of the Atlantic, between England & France

English horn a double-reed woodwind instrument, slightly larger than the oboe

en·gorge (en gôrj′, in-) *vt.* -**gorged′**, -**gorg′ing** [< OFr *en-*, in + *gorge*, gorge] 1 to devour greedily 2 *Med.* to congest (tissue, etc.) with fluid, as blood

en·grave (en grāv′, in-) *vt.* -**graved′**, -**grav′ing** [< Fr *en-*, in + *graver*, to incise] 1 to cut or etch letters, designs, etc. in or on (a metal plate, etc.) 2 to print with such a plate 3 to impress deeply —**en·grav′er** *n.*

en·grav·ing *n.* 1 the act or art of one who engraves 2 an engraved plate, drawing, etc. 3 a print made from an engraved surface

en·gross (en grōs′, in-) *vt.* [< OFr *engroissier*, become thick] to take the entire attention of; occupy wholly —**en·gross′ing** *adj.*

en·gulf (en gulf′, in-) *vt.* to swallow up

en·hance (en hans′, in-) *vt.* -**hanced′**, -**hanc′ing** [< L *in-*, in + *altus*, high] to make greater, better, etc.; heighten —**en·hance′ment** *n.*

e·nig·ma (i nig′mə, e-) *n.* [< Gr *ainos*, story] 1 a riddle 2 one that is perplexing or baffling —**en·ig·mat·ic** (en′ig mat′ik) *adj.*

en·jamb·ment or **en·jambe·ment** (en jam′mənt) *n.* [< Fr *enjamber*, to encroach] in poetry, movement from one line to the next without a pause

en·join (en join′, in-) *vt.* [< L *in-*, in + *jungere*, join] 1 to command; order; impose 2 to prohibit, esp. by legal injunction

en·joy (en joi′, in-) *vt.* [< OFr *en-*, in + *joir*, rejoice] 1 to get pleasure from; relish 2 to have the use or benefit of —**enjoy oneself** to have a good time —**en·joy′a·ble** *adj.* —**en·joy′ment** *n.*

en·large (en lärj′, in-) *vt.* -**larged′**, -**larg′ing** to make larger; expand —*vi.* 1 to become larger; expand 2 to speak or write at greater length: with *on* or *upon* —**en·large′ment** *n.*

en·light·en (en līt′'n, in-) *vt.* 1 to free from ignorance, prejudice, etc. 2 to inform —**en·light′en·ment** *n.*

en·list (en list′, in-) *vt., vi.* 1 to enroll in some branch of the armed forces 2 to engage in support of a cause or movement —**en·list′ment** *n.*

en·list·ed *adj.* of a person in the armed forces who is not a commissioned officer or warrant officer

en·liv·en (en lī′vən, in-) *vt.* to make active, cheerful, etc.; liven up

en masse (en mas′) [Fr, lit., in mass] in a group; as a whole

en·mesh (en mesh′, in-) *vt.* to catch as in the meshes of a net; entangle

en·mi·ty (en′mə tē) *n., pl.* -**ties** [see ENEMY] the bitter attitude or feelings of an enemy or enemies; hostility

en·no·ble (e nō′bəl, i-) *vt.* -**bled**, -**bling** 1 to raise to aristocratic rank 2 to give a noble quality to; dignify —**en·no′ble·ment** *n.*

en·nui (än′wē′) *n.* [Fr] weariness and dissatisfaction from lack of interest; boredom

e·nor·mi·ty (ē nôr′mə tē, i-) *n., pl.* -**ties** [< L *enormis*, immense] 1 great wickedness 2 an outrageous act 3 enormous size or extent

e·nor·mous (ē nôr′məs, i-) *adj.* [see prec.] of great size, number, etc.; huge; vast; immense —**e·nor′mous·ly** *adv.*

e·nough (ē nuf′, i-) *adj.* [OE *genoh*] as much or as many as necessary; sufficient —*n.* the amount needed —*adv.* 1 sufficiently 2 fully; quite [*oddly enough*] 3 tolerably

e·now (ē nou′, i-) *adj., n., adv.* [Archaic] enough

en·plane (en plān′, in-) *vi.* -**planed′**, -**plan′ing** to board an airplane

en·quire (en kwīr′, in-) *vt., vi.* -**quired′**, -**quir′ing** INQUIRE —**en·quir′y** (-ē) *n., pl.* -**ies**

en·rage (en rāj′, in-) *vt.* -**raged′**, -**rag′ing** to put into a rage; infuriate

en·rap·ture (en rap′chər, in-) *vt.* -**tured**, -**tur·ing** to fill with delight

en·rich (en rich′, in-) *vt.* 1 to make wealthier 2 to give greater value, better quality, etc. to —**en·rich′ment** *n.*

en·roll or **en·rol** (en rōl′, in-) *vt., vi.* -**rolled′**, -**roll′ing** 1 to record or be recorded in a roll or list 2 to enlist 3 to make or become a member —**en·roll′ment** *n.*, **en·rol′ment** *n.*

en route (än rōōt′, en-) [Fr] on the way

en·sconce (en skäns′, in-) *vt.* -**sconced′**, -**sconc′ing** [< Du *schans*, small fort] to place or settle snugly or securely

en·sem·ble (än säm′bəl) *n.* [Fr < L *in-*, in + *simul*, at the same time] 1 total effect 2 a whole costume of matching parts 3 *a)* a small group of musicians, actors, etc. *b)* the performance of such a group

en·shrine (en shrīn′, in-) *vt.* -**shrined′**, -**shrin′ing** 1 to enclose in a shrine 2 to hold as sacred; cherish —**en·shrine′ment** *n.*

en·shroud (en shroud′, in-) *vt.* to cover as if with a shroud; hide; obscure

en·sign (en′sīn′; *also, & for 2 always*, -sən) *n.* [see INSIGNIA] 1 a flag or banner 2 *U.S. Navy* a commissioned officer of the lowest rank

en·si·lage (en′sə lij) *n.* [ult. < L *in-*, in + Gr *siros*, silo] the preserving of green fodder in a silo

en·slave (en slāv′, in-) *vt.* -**slaved′**, -**slav′ing** 1 to make a slave of 2 to subjugate —**en·slave′ment** *n.*

en·snare (en sner′, in-) *vt.* -**snared′**, -**snar′ing** to catch in or as in a snare

en·sue (en sōō′, in-) *vi.* -**sued′**, -**su′ing** [< L *in-*, in + *sequi*, follow] 1 to come afterward 2 to result

en·sure (en shoor′, in-) *vt.* -**sured′**, -**sur′ing** 1 to make sure 2 to protect

—**ent** (ənt) [< OFr -*ent*, L -*ens*, prp. ending] *suffix* 1 that has, shows, or does [*insistent*] 2 a person or thing that [*superintendent, solvent*]

en·tail (en tāl′, in-) *vt.* 〚< OFr *taillier*, to cut〛 1 *Law* to limit the inheritance of (real property) to a specific line of heirs 2 to make necessary; require

en·tan·gle (en taŋ′gəl, in-) *vt.* **-gled, -gling** 1 to involve in a tangle 2 to involve in difficulty 3 to confuse 4 to complicate —**en·tan′gle·ment** *n.*

en·tente (än tänt′) *n.* 〚Fr < OFr *entendre*, understand〛 1 an understanding or agreement, as between nations 2 the parties to this

en·ter (ent′ər) *vt.* 〚< L *intra*, within〛 1 to come or go into 2 to penetrate 3 to insert 4 to write down in a list, etc. 5 to become a member of or participant in 6 to get (a person, etc.) admitted 7 to begin 8 to put on record, formally or before a law court 9 to input (data, etc.) into a computer —*vi.* 1 to come or go into some place 2 to penetrate —**enter into** 1 to take part in 2 to form a part of —**enter on** (or **upon**) to begin; start

en·ter·i·tis (ent′ər īt′is) *n.* 〚< Gr *enteron*, intestine + -ITIS〛 inflammation of the intestine

en·ter·prise (ent′ər prīz′) *n.* 〚ult. < L *inter*, in + *prehendere*, take〛 1 an undertaking, esp. a big, bold, or difficult one 2 energy and initiative

en·ter·pris·ing *adj.* showing enterprise; full of energy and initiative

en·ter·tain (ent′ər tān′) *vt.* 〚ult. < L *inter*, between + *tenere*, to hold〛 1 [Archaic] to provide with sustenance, lodging, etc. 2 to amuse; divert 3 to have as a guest 4 to have in mind; consider —*vi.* to give hospitality to guests

en·ter·tain·er *n.* one who entertains; esp., a popular singer, comedian, etc.

en·ter·tain·ing *adj.* interesting and pleasurable; amusing

en·ter·tain·ment *n.* 1 an entertaining or being entertained 2 something that entertains; esp., a show or performance

en·thrall or **en·thral** (en thrôl′, in-) *vt.* **-thralled′, -thrall′ing** 〚see EN- & THRALL〛 to captivate; fascinate —**en·thrall′ment** *n.*, **en·thral′ment**

en·throne (en thrōn′, in-) *vt.* **-throned′, -thron′ing** 1 to place on a throne 2 to exalt

en·thuse (en thōōz′, in-) [Inf.] *vi.* **-thused′, -thus′ing** to express enthusiasm —*vt.* to make enthusiastic

en·thu·si·asm (en thōō′zē az′əm, in-) *n.* 〚< Gr *en-*, in + *theos*, god〛 intense or eager interest; zeal —**en·thu′si·ast′** (-ast′, -əst) *n.* —**en·thu′si·as′tic** *adj.* —**en·thu′si·as′ti·cal·ly** *adv.*

en·tice (en tīs′, in-) *vt.* **-ticed′, -tic′ing** 〚< L *in*, in + *titio*, a burning brand〛 to tempt with hope of reward or pleasure —**en·tice′ment** *n.*

en·tire (en tīr′, in-) *adj.* 〚< L *integer*, whole〛 not lacking any parts; whole; complete; intact —**en·tire′ly** *adv.*

en·tire·ty (-tē) *n.*, *pl.* **-ties** 1 the state or fact of being entire; wholeness 2 an entire thing; whole

en·ti·tle (en tīt′'l, in-) *vt.* **-tled, -tling** 1 to give a title or name to 2 to give a right or claim to

en·ti·tle·ment *n.* something to which one is entitled, esp. a benefit, as Medicare, provided by certain government programs

en·ti·ty (en′tə tē) *n.*, *pl.* **-ties** 〚ult. < L *esse*, to be〛 1 existence 2 a thing that has definite existence

en·tomb (en tōōm′, in-) *vt.* to place in a tomb; bury —**en·tomb′ment** *n.*

en·to·mol·o·gy (en′tə mäl′ə jē) *n.* 〚< Gr *entomon*, insect + -LOGY〛 the branch of zoology that deals with insects —**en′to·mo·log′i·cal** (-mə läj′i kəl) *adj.* —**en′to·mol′o·gist** *n.*

en·tou·rage (än′tōō räzh′) *n.* 〚Fr < *entourer*, surround〛 a group of accompanying attendants, etc.; retinue

en·trails (en′trālz, -trəlz) *pl.n.* 〚< L *interaneus*, internal〛 the inner organs; specif., the intestines

en·trance[1] (en′trəns) *n.* 1 the act of entering 2 a place for entering; door, etc. 3 permission or right to enter; admission

en·trance[2] (en trans′, in-) *vt.* **-tranced′, -tranc′ing** 〚see EN- & TRANCE〛 to fill with delight; enchant

en·trant (en′trənt) *n.* one who enters

en·trap (en trap′, in-) *vt.* **-trapped′, -trap′ping** to catch in or as in a trap —**en·trap′ment** *n.*

en·treat (en trēt′, in-) *vt., vi.* 〚< OFr *en-*, in + *traiter*, to treat〛 to ask earnestly; beg; implore

en·treat·y *n.*, *pl.* **-ies** an earnest request; prayer

en·tree or **en·trée** (än′trā′) *n.* 〚Fr < OFr *entrer*, enter〛 1 right to enter, use, etc.; access 2 the main course of a meal

en·trench (en trench′, in-) *vt.* 1 to surround or fortify with trenches 2 to establish securely

en·tre·pre·neur (än′trə prə nur′) *n.* 〚Fr: see ENTERPRISE〛 one who organizes a business undertaking, assuming the risk for the sake of the profit —**en′tre·pre·neur′i·al** *adj.*

en·tro·py (en′trə pē) *n.* 〚< Gr *entropē*, a turning toward〛 1 a thermodynamic measure of the energy unavailable for useful work in a system 2 a process of degeneration with increasing uncertainty, chaos, etc., as in a social system

en·trust (en trust′, in-) *vt.* 1 to charge with a trust or duty 2 to turn over for safekeeping

en·try (en′trē) *n.*, *pl.* **-tries** 〚< OFr: see ENTER〛 1 an entering; entrance 2 a way by which to enter 3 an item or note in a list, journal, etc. 4 one entered in a race, etc.

en·try-lev·el *adj.* 1 designating a job with low pay but possible advancement 2 basic; introductory

en·twine (en twīn′, in-) *vt., vi.* **-twined′, -twin′ing** to twine together or around

e·nu·mer·ate (ē nōō′mər āt′, i-) *vt.* **-at′ed, -at′ing** 〚< L *e-*, out + *numerare*, to count〛 1 to count 2 to name one by one —**e·nu′mer·a′tion** *n.*

e·nun·ci·ate (ē nun′sē āt′, i-) *vt., vi.* **-at′ed,**

-at′ing ⟦< L *e-*, out + *nuntiare*, announce⟧ 1 to state definitely 2 to announce 3 to pronounce (words), esp. clearly —**e·nun′ci·a′tion** *n.*

en·u·re·sis (en′yōō rē′sis) *n.* ⟦ult. < L *in*, in + Gr *ouron*, urine⟧ inability to control urination

en·vel·op (en vel′əp, in-) *vt.* ⟦< OFr: see EN- & DEVELOP⟧ 1 to wrap up; cover completely 2 to surround 3 to conceal; hide —**en·vel′op·ment** *n.*

en·ve·lope (än′və lōp′, en′-) *n.* 1 a thing that envelops; covering 2 a folded paper container for a letter, etc., usually with a gummed flap

en·ven·om (en ven′əm, in-) *vt.* 1 to put venom into 2 to fill with hate

en·vi·a·ble (en′vē ə bəl) *adj.* good enough to be envied or desired —**en′vi·a·bly** *adv.*

en·vi·ous (en′vē əs) *adj.* feeling or showing envy —**en′vi·ous·ly** *adv.*

en·vi·ron·ment (en vī′rən mənt, in-) *n.* ⟦see ENVIRONS⟧ 1 surroundings 2 all the conditions, etc. surrounding and affecting the development of an organism, food chain, etc. —**en·vi′ron·men′tal** *adj.*

en·vi·ron·men·tal·ist *n.* one working to solve environmental problems, as air and water pollution —**en·vi′ron·men′tal·ism** *n.*

en·vi·rons (en vī′rənz, in-) *pl.n.* ⟦< OFr *en-*, in + *viron*, a circuit⟧ 1 the districts surrounding a city; suburbs 2 surrounding area; vicinity

en·vis·age (en viz′ij, in-) *vt.* -**aged**, -**ag·ing** ⟦see EN- & VISAGE⟧ to form an image of in the mind; visualize

en·vi·sion (en vizh′ən, in-) *vt.* ⟦EN- + VISION⟧ to imagine (something not yet in existence)

en·voy (än′voi′, en′-) *n.* ⟦< Fr < L *in*, in + *via*, way⟧ 1 a messenger 2 a diplomatic agent just below an ambassador

en·vy (en′vē) *n., pl.* -**vies** ⟦< L *in-*, in + *videre*, to look⟧ 1 discontent and ill will over another's advantages, possessions, etc. 2 desire for something that another has 3 an object of such feeling —*vt.* -**vied**, -**vy·ing** to feel envy toward or because of —**en′vy·ing·ly** *adv.*

en·zyme (en′zīm′) *n.* ⟦< Gr *en-*, in + *zymē*, leaven⟧ any of various proteins, formed in living cells or made synthetically, that act as catalysts in chemical reactions

e·on (ē′ən, ē′än′) *n.* ⟦< Gr *aiōn*, an age⟧ an extremely long, indefinite period of time

-e·ous (ē əs) ⟦< L *-eus* + -OUS⟧ *suffix* var. of -OUS [*gaseous*]

EPA *abbrev.* Environmental Protection Agency

ep·au·let or **ep·au·lette** (ep′ə let′, ep′ə let′) *n.* ⟦< Fr dim. of *épaule*, shoulder⟧ a shoulder ornament, esp. on military uniforms

e·pee or **é·pée** (ā pā′) *n.* ⟦Fr⟧ a fencing sword like a foil, but heavier and more rigid

e·phed·rine (e fe′drin) *n.* ⟦< L *ephedra*, the plant horsetail⟧ an alkaloid used to relieve nasal congestion and asthma

e·phem·er·al (e fem′ər əl, i-) *adj.* ⟦< Gr *epi-*, upon + *hēmera*, day⟧ 1 lasting one day 2 short-lived; transitory

epi- ⟦< Gr *epi*, at, on⟧ *prefix* on, upon, over, among [*epiglottis*]

ep·ic (ep′ik) *n.* ⟦< Gr *epos*, a word, song, epic⟧ 1 a long narrative poem in a dignified style about the deeds of a hero or heroes 2 a novel, film, etc. resembling such a poem, as in length, subject matter, etc. —*adj.* of or like an epic; heroic; grand

ep·i·cen·ter (ep′i sent′ər) *n.* 1 the area of the earth's surface directly above the place of origin of an earthquake 2 a focal or central point

ep·i·cure (ep′i kyoor′) *n.* ⟦after *Epicurus*, ancient Gr philosopher⟧ one who enjoys and has a discriminating taste for fine foods and drinks

ep·i·cu·re·an (ep′i kyōō rē′ən, ep′i kyoor′ē ən) *adj.* fond of sensuous pleasure, esp. that of eating and drinking —*n.* an epicure

ep·i·dem·ic (ep′ə dem′ik) *adj.* ⟦< Fr < Gr *epi-*, among + *dēmos*, people⟧ spreading rapidly among many people in a community, as a disease —*n.* 1 an epidemic disease 2 the spreading of such a disease 3 a rapid, widespread growth —**ep′i·dem′i·cal·ly** *adv.*

ep·i·de·mi·ol·o·gy (ep′ə dē′mē äl′ə jē) *n.* ⟦prec. + -LOGY⟧ the branch of medicine that studies epidemics

ep·i·der·mis (ep′ə dur′mis) *n.* ⟦< Gr *epi-*, upon + *derma*, the skin⟧ the outermost layer of the skin —**ep′i·der′mal** *adj.*, **ep′i·der′mic** *adj.*

ep·i·du·ral (ep′ə door′əl) *adj.* on or outside the dura mater —*n.* local anesthesia of the lower body by epidural injection

ep·i·glot·tis (ep′ə glät′is) *n.* ⟦see EPI- & GLOTTIS⟧ the thin, lidlike piece of cartilage that covers the windpipe during swallowing

ep·i·gram (ep′ə gram′) *n.* ⟦< Gr *epi-*, upon + *graphein*, write⟧ a terse, witty, pointed statement —**ep′i·gram·mat′ic** (-grə mat′ik) *adj.*

e·pig·ra·phy (ē pig′rə fē, i-) *n.* the study of inscriptions, esp. ancient ones

ep·i·lep·sy (ep′ə lep′sē) *n.* ⟦< Gr *epi-*, upon + *lambanein*, seize⟧ a recurrent disorder of the nervous system, characterized by seizures that cause convulsions, unconsciousness, etc.

ep·i·lep·tic (-tik) *adj.* of or having epilepsy —*n.* one who has epilepsy

ep·i·logue or **ep·i·log** (ep′ə lôg′) *n.* ⟦< Gr *epi-*, upon + *legein*, speak⟧ a closing section added to a novel, play, etc., providing further comment, as a speech by an actor to the audience

E·piph·a·ny (ē pif′ə nē, i-) *n., pl.* -**nies** ⟦< Gr *epiphainein*, show forth⟧ 1 a Christian feast day (Jan. 6) commemorating the revealing of Jesus as the Christ to the Gentiles 2 [**e-**] *a*) a flash of insight *b*) an experience that brings this about

e·pis·co·pa·cy (ē pis′kə pə sē, i-) *n., pl.* -**cies** ⟦< Gr *epi-*, upon + *skopein*, to look⟧ 1 church government by bishops 2 EPISCOPATE

e·pis·co·pal (-pəl) *adj.* 1 of or governed by bishops 2 [**E-**] designating of or of any of various churches governed by bishops

E·pis·co·pa·lian (-pāl′yən) *adj.* Episcopal —*n.* a member of the Protestant Episcopal Church

e·pis·co·pate (-pit, -pāt′) *n.* 1 the position,

rank, etc. of a bishop **2** bishops collectively

ep·i·sode (ep′ə sōd′) *n.* [< Gr *epi-*, upon + *ei-sodos*, entrance] **1** any part of a novel, poem, etc. that is complete in itself **2** an event or series of events complete in itself **3** an installment, as of a weekly TV show —**ep′i·sod′ic** (-säd′ik) *adj.* —**ep′i·sod′i·cal·ly** *adv.*

e·pis·tle (ē pis′əl) *n.* [< Gr *epi-*, to + *stellein*, send] **1** a letter **2** [**E—**] any of the letters in the New Testament —**e·pis′to·lar′y** (-tə ler′ē) *adj.*

ep·i·taph (ep′ə taf′) *n.* [< Gr *epi-*, upon + *taphos*, tomb] an inscription on a tomb, etc. in memory of a dead person

ep·i·the·li·um (ep′i thē′lē əm) *n., pl.* **-li·ums** or **-li·a** (-ə) [< Gr *epi-*, upon + *thēlē*, nipple] cellular tissue covering external body surfaces or lining internal surfaces —**ep′i·the′li·al** (-əl) *adj.*

ep·i·thet (ep′ə thet′) *n.* [< Gr *epi-*, on + *tithenai*, put] a word or phrase characterizing some person or thing

e·pit·o·me (ē pit′ə mē′, i-) *n., pl.* **-mes** (-mēz′) [< Gr *epi-*, upon + *temnein*, to cut] **1** an abstract; summary **2** a person or thing that shows the typical qualities of something

e·pit·o·mize (-mīz′) *vt.* **-mized′, -miz′ing** to make or be an epitome of

e plu·ri·bus u·num (ē′ ploor′ē bo͞os′ o͞o′nŏŏm) [L] out of many, one: a motto of the U.S.

ep·och (ep′ək) *n.* [< Gr *epi-*, upon + *echein*, to hold] **1** the start of a new period in the history of anything **2** a period of time in terms of noteworthy events, persons, etc. —**ep′och·al** *adj.*

ep·ox·y (ē päk′sē, i-) *adj.* [EP(I)- + OXY(GEN)] designating a resin used in strong, resistant glues, enamels, etc. —*n., pl.* **-ies** an epoxy resin

ep·si·lon (ep′sə län′) *n.* [Gr *e psilon*, plain *e*] the fifth letter of the Greek alphabet (E, ε)

Ep·som salts (*or* **salt**) (ep′səm) [after Epsom, town in England] a white, crystalline salt, magnesium sulfate, used as a cathartic, in bath salts, etc.

Ep·stein-Barr virus (ep′stīn bär′) a herpeslike virus that causes infectious mononucleosis and may cause various forms of cancer

eq·ua·ble (ek′wə bəl) *adj.* [see foll.] steady; uniform; even; tranquil —**eq′ua·bil′i·ty** *n.* —**eq′ua·bly** *adv.*

e·qual (ē′kwəl) *adj.* [< L *aequus*, even] **1** of the same quantity, size, value, etc. **2** having the same rights, ability, rank, etc. **3** evenly proportioned **4** having the necessary ability, strength, etc.: with *to* —*n.* any person or thing that is equal —*vt.* **e′qualed** *or* **e′qualled, e′qual·ing** *or* **e′qual·ling 1** to be equal to **2** to do or make something equal to —**e·qual′i·ty** (ē kwôl′ə tē, -kwäl′-) *n., pl.* **-ties** —**e′qual·ly** *adv.*

e·qual·ize (ē′kwəl īz′) *vt.* **-ized′, -iz′ing** to make equal or uniform —**e′qual·i·za′tion** *n.* —**e′qual·iz′er** *n.*

e·qual-op·por·tu·ni·ty *adj.* treating all employees and job applicants equally, without regard to race, sex, etc.

equal sign the sign (=), indicating that the terms on either side of it are equal or equivalent

e·qua·nim·i·ty (ek′wə nim′ə tē, ē′kwə-) *n.* [< L *aequus*, even + *animus*, mind] evenness of temper; composure

e·quate (ē kwāt′, i-) *vt.* **e·quat′ed, e·quat′ing 1** to make equal **2** to treat, regard, or express as equal —**e·quat′a·ble** *adj.*

e·qua·tion (ē kwā′zhən, i-) *n.* **1** an equating or being equated **2** a statement of equality between two quantities, as shown by the equal sign (=)

e·qua·tor (ē kwāt′ər, i-) *n.* **1** an imaginary circle around the earth, equally distant from the North Pole and the South Pole **2** a similar circle dividing the sky as seen from Earth into northern and southern halves: in full **celestial equator** —**e·qua·to·ri·al** (ē′kwə tôr′ē əl, ek′wə-) *adj.*

Equatorial Guinea country in WC Africa

eq·uer·ry (ek′wər ē, ē kwer′ē) *n., pl.* **-ries** [< Fr] **1** [Historical] an officer in charge of royal horses **2** an officer who attends a person of royalty

e·ques·tri·an (ē kwes′trē ən, i-) *adj.* [< L *equus*, horse] **1** of horses or horsemanship **2** on horseback —*n.* a rider or circus performer on horseback

equi- *combining form* equal, equally [*equidistant*]

e·qui·dis·tant (ē′kwi dis′tənt) *adj.* equally distant

e·qui·lat·er·al (-lat′ər əl) *adj.* [< L *aequus*, even + *latus*, side] having all sides equal

e·qui·lib·ri·um (-lib′rē əm) *n., pl.* **-ri·ums** or **-ri·a** (-ə) [< L *aequus*, even + *libra*, a balance] a state of balance between opposing forces

e·quine (ē′kwīn′) *adj.* [< L *equus*, horse] of or like a horse

e·qui·nox (ē′kwi näks′, ek′wə-) *n.* [< L *aequus*, even + *nox*, night] either of the times (in late March and late September) when the sun crosses the equator, making night and day of equal length in all parts of the earth —**e′qui·noc′tial** (-näk′shəl) *adj.*

e·quip (ē kwip′, i-) *vt.* **e·quipped′, e·quip′ping** [< OFr *esquiper*, embark] to provide with what is needed

eq·ui·page (ek′wi pij) *n.* a carriage with horses and liveried servants

e·quip·ment (ē kwip′mənt, i-) *n.* **1** an equipping or being equipped **2** supplies, tools, etc. for a particular activity

eq·ui·poise (ek′wi poiz′, ē′kwi-) *n.* [EQUI- + POISE] **1** state of equilibrium **2** a counterbalance

eq·ui·ta·ble (ek′wit ə bəl) *adj.* [see EQUITY] fair; just —**eq′ui·ta·bly** *adv.*

eq·ui·ta·tion (ek′wi tā′shən) *n.* [< L *equitare*, to ride] the art of riding on horseback

eq·ui·ty (ek′wit ē) *n., pl.* **-ties** [< L *aequus*, even] **1** fairness; impartiality; justice **2** the value of property beyond the amount owed on it **3** *Finance a)* assets minus liabilities; net worth *b)* [*pl.*] shares of stock **4** *Law* a system of doctrines supplementing common and statute law

e·quiv·a·lent (ē kwiv′ə lənt, i-) *adj.* [< L *aequus*, equal + *valere*, be worth] equal in quantity, value, force, meaning, etc. —*n.* an equivalent thing —**e·quiv′a·lence** *n.*

e·quiv·o·cal (ē kwiv′ə kəl, i-) *adj.* [< L *ae-quus*, even + *vox*, voice] **1** having two or more meanings; purposely ambiguous **2** uncertain; doubtful **3** suspicious [*equivocal* conduct] —**e·quiv′o·cal·ly** *adv.* —**e·quiv′o·cal·ness** *n.*

e·quiv·o·cate (-kāt′) *vi.* **-cat′ed, -cat′ing** to use equivocal terms in order to deceive, hedge, etc. —**e·quiv′o·ca′tion** *n.* —**e·quiv′o·ca′tor** *n.*

ER *abbrev.* emergency room

-er (ər) [ME] *suffix* **1** *a)* a person or thing having to do with [*hatter*] *b)* a person living in [*New Yorker*] *c)* one that ___s [*roller*] **2** forming the comparative degree [*later*] **3** repeatedly: added to verbs [*flicker*]

e·ra (ir′ə, er′ə) *n.* [LL *aera*] **1** a period of time measured from some important event **2** a period of time having some special characteristic

ERA *abbrev.* **1** *Baseball* earned run average: also **era 2** Equal Rights Amendment

e·rad·i·cate (ē rad′i kāt′, i-) *vt.* **-cat′ed, -cat′ing** [< L e-, out + *radix*, root] to uproot; wipe out; destroy —**e·rad′i·ca′tion** *n.* —**e·rad′i·ca′tor** *n.*

e·rase (ē rās′, i-) *vt.* **e·rased′, e·ras′ing** [< L e-, out + *radere*, scrape] **1** to rub, scrape, or wipe out (esp. writing) **2** to remove (recorded data) from (a hard drive, etc.) **3** to obliterate, as from the mind —**e·ras′a·ble** *adj.*

e·ras·er *n.* a thing that erases; specif., a rubber device for erasing ink or pencil marks, or a pad for removing chalk marks from a blackboard

E·ras·mus (i raz′məs), **Des·i·der·i·us** (des′ə dir′ē əs) 1466?-1536; Du. humanist & theologian

e·ra·sure (ē rā′shər, i-) *n.* **1** an erasing **2** an erased word, mark, etc.

er·bi·um (ur′bē əm) *n.* [after *Ytterby*, Sweden] a soft, malleable chemical element, used in metallurgy and to color glass and porcelain: symbol, Er; at. no. 68

ere (er) [Old Poet.] *prep.* [OE *ær*] before (in time) —*conj.* **1** before **2** rather than

e·rect (ē rekt′, i-) *adj.* [< L e-, up + *regere*, make straight] upright —*vt.* **1** to construct (a building, etc.) **2** to set in an upright position; raise **3** to set up; assemble —**e·rec′tion** *n.* —**e·rect′ly** *adv.* —**e·rect′ness** *n.* —**e·rec′tor** *n.*

e·rec·tile (ē rek′til, i-; -tīl′) *adj.* that can become erect: used esp. of tissue that becomes rigid when filled with blood

erg (urg) *n.* [< Gr *ergon*, work] *Physics* a unit of work or energy

er·go (er′gō, ur′-) *adv.* [L] therefore

er·go·nom·ics (ur′gō näm′iks) *n.* [ult. < Gr *ergon*, work + (EC)ONOMICS] the science of adapting working conditions to the needs of the worker

Er·ie (ir′ē), **Lake** one of the Great Lakes, between Lake Huron & Lake Ontario

Er·in (er′in) *old poet. name for* IRELAND

Er·i·tre·a (er′ə trē′ə) country in E Africa —**Er′i·tre′an** *adj.*, *n.*

er·mine (ur′min) *n.* [prob. < OHG *harmo*, weasel] **1** a weasel whose fur is white in winter **2** its white fur

e·rode (ē rōd′, i-) *vt.* **e·rod′ed, e·rod′ing** [< L e-, out + *rodere*, gnaw] **1** to wear away **2** to form by wearing away gradually —*vi.* to become eroded

e·rog·e·nous (ē räj′ə nəs, i-) *adj.* [< Gr *erōs*, love + -GEN + -OUS] sensitive to sexual stimulation: also **e·ro·to·gen·ic** (er′ə tō′jen′ik)

E·ros (er′äs′, ir′-) *n.* **1** *Gr. Myth.* the god of love **2** [e-] sexual love or desire

e·ro·sion (ē rō′zhən, i-) *n.* an eroding or being eroded —**e·ro′sive** (-siv) *adj.*

e·rot·ic (ē rät′ik, i-) *adj.* [< Gr *erōs*, love] of or arousing sexual feelings or desires; amatory —**e·rot′i·cal·ly** *adv.*

e·rot·i·ca (-i kə) *pl.n.* [often with sing. v.] erotic books, pictures, etc.

err (ur, er) *vi.* [< L *errare*, wander] **1** to be wrong or mistaken **2** to deviate from the established moral code

er·rand (er′ənd) *n.* [OE *ærende*, mission] **1** a trip to do a thing, often esp. for someone else **2** the thing to be done

er·rant (er′ənt) *adj.* [see ERR] **1** roving or wandering, esp. in search of adventure [a knight-*errant*] **2** erring **3** shifting about [an *errant* wind]

er·rat·ic (i rat′ik) *adj.* [< L *errare*, wander] **1** irregular; random **2** eccentric; queer —**er·rat′i·cal·ly** *adv.*

er·ra·tum (e rät′əm, -rät′-) *n., pl.* **-ta** (-ə) [see ERR] an error in a work already printed

er·ro·ne·ous (ə rō′nē əs) *adj.* containing error; mistaken; wrong —**er·ro′ne·ous·ly** *adv.*

er·ror (er′ər) *n.* [see ERR] **1** the state of believing what is untrue **2** a wrong belief **3** something incorrectly done; mistake **4** a transgression **5** *Baseball* any misplay in fielding

er·satz (er′zäts′, er zäts′) *n., adj.* [Ger] substitute or synthetic, usually inferior

Erse (urs) *adj., n.* [ME *Erish*, var. of *Irisc*, Irish] (of) GAELIC and, sometimes, IRISH (*n.* 1)

erst·while (urst′hwil′) *adv.* [Archaic] formerly —*adj.* former

e·ruct (ē rukt′) *vt., vi.* [< L e-, out + *ructare*, to belch] to belch —**e·ruc·ta′tion** *n.*

er·u·dite (er′yōō dit′, -ōō-) *adj.* [< L e-, out + *rudis*, rude] learned; scholarly —**er·u′dite·ly** *adv.*

er·u·di·tion (er′yōō dish′ən) *n.* learning acquired by reading and study

e·rupt (ē rupt′, i-) *vi.* [< L e-, out + *rumpere*, to break] **1** to burst forth or out [lava *erupt-*

ing] **2** to throw forth lava, water, etc. **3** to break out in a rash —*vt.* to cause to burst forth

e·rup·tion (ē rup/shən, i-) *n.* **1** a bursting forth or out **2** *a)* a breaking out in a rash *b)* a rash

-er·y (ər ē, er/ē) [< LL -*aria*] *suffix* **1** a place to [*tannery*] **2** a place for [*nunnery*] **3** the practice or act of [*midwifery*] **4** the product of [*pottery*] **5** a collection of [*greenery*] **6** the condition of [*drudgery*]

er·y·sip·e·las (er/i sip/ə ləs) *n.* [ult. < Gr *erythros*, red + *-pelas*, skin] a bacterial infection of the skin or mucous membranes

e·ryth·ro·cyte (e rith/rō sit/) *n.* [< Gr *erythros*, red + *kytos*, a hollow] a mature red blood cell that contains hemoglobin, which carries oxygen to the body tissues

-es (iz, əz, z) [< OE] *suffix* **1** forming plurals [*glasses*] **2** forming the 3d person sing., pres. indic., of verbs [*he kisses*]

E·sau (ē/sô) *n. Bible* Isaac's son who sold his birthright to his brother, Jacob

es·ca·late (es/kə lāt/) *vi.* -**lat**'ed, -**lat**'ing **1** to rise as on an escalator **2** to expand step by step **3** to increase rapidly —**es'ca·la'tion** *n.*

es·ca·la·tor (-ər) *n.* [ult. < L *scala*, ladder] a moving stairway on an endless belt

es·ca·pade (es/kə pād/) *n.* [Fr: see fol.] a reckless adventure or prank

es·cape (e skāp/, i-) *vi.* -**caped**', -**cap**'ing [< L *ex-*, out of + LL *cappa*, cloak] **1** to get free **2** to avoid an illness, accident, etc. **3** to leak away —*vt.* **1** to get away from **2** to avoid [to *escape* death] **3** to come from involuntarily [a scream *escaped* her lips] **4** to be missed or forgotten by [his name *escapes* me] —*n.* **1** an escaping **2** a means of escape **3** a leakage **4** a temporary mental release from reality —*adj.* providing an escape

es·cap·ee (e skāp/ē', es/kā pē') *n.* one who has escaped, as from prison

es·cape·ment *n.* a notched wheel with a detaining catch that controls the action of a mechanical clock or watch

escape velocity the minimum speed required for a particle, space vehicle, etc. to escape permanently from the gravitational attraction of a planet, star, etc. without further propulsion

es·cap·ism *n.* a tendency to escape from reality, responsibilities, etc. through the imagination —**es·cap'ist** *adj., n.*

es·car·got (es/kär gō/) *n.* [Fr] an edible snail

es·ca·role (es/kə rōl/) *n.* [Fr] ENDIVE

es·carp·ment (e skärp/mənt) *n.* [< Fr] a steep slope or cliff

-es·cence (es/əns) [see fol.] *suffix* the process of becoming [*obsolescence*]

-es·cent (es/ənt) [L -*escens*] *suffix* **1** starting to be, being, or becoming [*obsolescent*] **2** giving off light (as specified) [*phosphorescent*]

es·chew (es chōō/) *vt.* [< OHG *sciuhan*, to fear] to shun; avoid —**es·chew'al** *n.*

es·cort (es/kôrt'; *for v.* i skôrt/) *n.* [< L *ex-*, out + *corrigere*, set right] **1** one or more persons, cars, etc. accompanying another or others to give protection or show honor **2** a man accompanying a woman **3** a person who is paid to act as a date for another —*vt.* to go with as an escort

es·cri·toire (es/kri twär/) *n.* [OFr < L *scribere*, write] a writing desk

es·crow (es/krō/) *n.* [see SCROLL] used chiefly in **in escrow,** put in the care of a third party until certain conditions are fulfilled

es·cutch·eon (e skuch/ən, i-) *n.* [< L *scutum*, shield] a shield on which a coat of arms is displayed

-ese (ēz, ēs) [< L -*ensis*] *suffix* **1** of a country or place [*Javanese*] **2** (in) the language of [*Cantonese*] **3** a person born or living in [*Portuguese*]

Es·ki·mo (es/kə mō/) *n.* [prob. < Fr < AmInd] **1** *pl.* -**mos**' or -**mo**' a member of a group of peoples native to Greenland, N Canada, and Alaska: often considered derogatory, esp. in Canada, *Inuit* being preferred for native peoples of the Canadian Arctic and Greenland **2** any of the languages of the Eskimos —**Es/ki·mo**' *adj.,* **Es/ki·mo'an**

ESL *abbrev.* English as a second language

e·soph·a·gus (i säf/ə gəs) *n., pl.* -**gi**' (-jī') [< Gr *oisophagos*] the tube through which food passes from the pharynx to the stomach

es·o·ter·ic (es/ə ter/ik) *adj.* [< Gr *esōteros*, inner] intended for or understood by only a chosen few

ESP (ē'es'pē') *n.* extrasensory perception

esp. *abbrev.* especially

es·pa·drille (es/pə dril/) *n.* [Fr < Sp *esparto*, coarse grass] a casual shoe with a canvas upper and a sole of twisted rope

es·pal·ier (es pal/yər) *n.* [Fr < It *spalla*, shoulder] **1** a lattice on which trees or shrubs are trained to grow flat **2** a plant trained in this way —*vt.* to provide with an espalier

es·pe·cial (e spesh/əl, i-) *adj.* special; particular —**es·pe'cial·ly** *adv.*

Es·pe·ran·to (es/pə rän/tō, -ran/-) *n.* an invented international language based on European word roots and having a highly regular grammar

es·pi·o·nage (es/pē ə näzh/) *n.* [< Fr < It *spia*, spy] the act or practice of spying

es·pla·nade (es/plə näd/, -näd/) *n.* [< Fr < It < L *explanare*, to level] a level, open stretch of ground, esp. one serving as a public walk

es·pous·al (e spou/zəl, i-) *n.* an espousing (of some cause, idea, etc.); advocacy

es·pouse (e spouz/, i-) *vt.* -**poused**', -**pous**'ing [see SPOUSE] **1** to marry **2** to advocate (some cause, idea, etc.)

es·pres·so (e spres/ō) *n., pl.* -**sos** [It] coffee made by forcing steam through finely ground coffee beans

es·prit de corps (e sprē' də kôr') [Fr] group spirit; pride, etc. shared by those in the same group

es·py (e spī/, i-) *vt.* -**pied**', -**py**'ing [see SPY] to catch sight of; spy

-esque (esk) [Fr < It -*esco*] *suffix* **1** in the

manner or style of [*Romanesque*] 2 like [*statuesque*]

es·quire (es′kwīr′) *n.* [< L *scutum*, a shield] 1 [Historical] a candidate for knighthood; squire 2 in England, a member of the gentry ranking just below a knight 3 [E-] a title of courtesy: in the U.S., now specif. used for lawyers: usually abbrev. **Esq** or **Esqr**

-ess (es, is, əs) [< LL *-issa*] *suffix* female [*lioness*]

es·say (for *n.* e sā′; *for n.* 1 usually, & *for n.* 2 always, es′ā) *vt.* [< LL *ex-*, out of + *agere*, to do] to try; attempt —*n.* 1 a trying or testing 2 a short literary composition in which the author analyzes or interprets something in a personal way —**es·say′er** *n.* —**es′say·ist** *n.*

es·sence (es′əns) *n.* [< L *esse*, to be] 1 the basic nature (of something) 2 *a)* a concentrated substance that keeps the flavor, etc. of that from which it is extracted *b)* perfume —**of the essence** critically important

Es·sene (es′ēn′, e sēn′) *n.* a member of an ancient Jewish ascetic sect that existed to the middle of the 1st c. A.D.

es·sen·tial (ə sen′shəl, i-) *adj.* 1 of or constituting the essence of something; basic 2 absolutely necessary; indispensable —*n.* something necessary or fundamental —**es·sen′tial·ly** *adv.*

est 1 established: also **estab** 2 estimate 3 estimated

EST *abbrev.* Eastern Standard Time

-est (est, ist, əst) [OE] *suffix* forming the superlative degree [*greatest*]

es·tab·lish (ə stab′lish, i-) *vt.* [< L *stabilis*, stable] 1 to order, ordain, or enact (a law, etc.) permanently 2 to set up (a nation, business, etc.) 3 to cause to be; bring about 4 to set up in a business, etc. 5 to cause to be accepted 6 to prove; demonstrate

es·tab·lish·ment *n.* 1 an establishing or being established 2 a thing established, as a business —**the Establishment** an inner circle thought of as holding decisive power in a nation, etc.

es·tate (ə stāt′, i-) *n.* [< OFr *estat*] 1 a condition or stage of life 2 property; possessions 3 a large, individually owned piece of land containing a residence

es·teem (ə stēm′, i-) *vt.* [< L *aestimare*, to value] 1 to value highly; respect 2 to consider —*n.* favorable opinion

es·ter (es′tər) *n.* [Ger < *essig*, vinegar + *äther*, ether] an organic compound formed by the reaction of an acid and an alcohol

Es·ther (es′tər) *n. Bible* the Jewish wife of a Persian king: she saved her people from slaughter

es·thete (es′thēt′) *n.* AESTHETE —**es·thet′ic** (-thet′ik) *adj.* —**es·thet′ics** (-thet′iks) *n.*

es·ti·ma·ble (es′tə mə bəl) *adj.* worthy of esteem

es·ti·mate (es′tə māt′; *for n.*, -mit) *vt.* **-mat′ed, -mat′ing** [see ESTEEM] 1 to form an opinion about 2 to calculate approximately

(size, cost, etc.) —*n.* 1 a general calculation; esp., an approximate computation of probable cost 2 an opinion or judgment —**es′ti·ma′tor** *n.*

es·ti·ma·tion *n.* 1 an estimate or judgment 2 esteem; regard

Es·to·ni·a (e stō′nē ə, -stōn′yə) country in N Europe —**Es·to′ni·an** *adj., n.*

es·trange (e strānj′, i-) *vt.* **-tranged′, -trang′ing** [< L *extraneus*, strange] to turn (a person) from an affectionate attitude to an indifferent or unfriendly one —**es·trange′ment** *n.*

es·tro·gen (es′trə jən) *n.* [< Gr *oistros*, frenzy + -GEN] any of several female sex hormones or synthetic compounds

es·trus (es′trəs) period in the reproductive cycle in which the female becomes sexually receptive

es·tu·ar·y (es′tyōō er′ē, -chōō-) *n., pl.* **-ies** [< L *aestus*, the tide] the wide mouth of a river into which the tide flows from the sea

ET *abbrev.* Eastern Time

-et (et, it, ət) [< LL *-itus*] *suffix* little [*islet*]

e·ta (āt′ə, ēt′ə) *n.* the seventh letter of the Greek alphabet (H, η)

ETA *abbrev.* estimated time of arrival

é·ta·gère (ā′tä zher′) *n.* [Fr] a stand with open shelves, for displaying art objects, ornaments, etc.

et al. *abbrev.* [L *et alii*] and others

et cet·er·a (et set′ər ə, se′trə) [L] and others; and the like: abbrev. **etc.**

etch (ech) *vt.* [< MHG *ezzen*, eat] to make (a drawing, design, etc.) on metal, glass, etc., esp. by the action of an acid —**etch′er** *n.*

etch·ing *n.* 1 the art of an etcher 2 a print made from an etched plate

e·ter·nal (ē tur′nəl, i-) *adj.* [< L *aeturnus*] 1 without beginning or end; everlasting 2 always the same; unchanging 3 seeming never to stop —**e·ter′nal·ly** *adv.* —**e·ter′nal·ness** *n.*

e·ter·ni·ty (ē tur′nə tē, i-) *n., pl.* **-ties** 1 the state or fact of being eternal 2 infinite or endless time 3 a long period of time that seems endless 4 the endless time after death

eth·ane (eth′ān′) *n.* [< fol.] an odorless, colorless, gaseous hydrocarbon, found in natural gas and used as a fuel

e·ther (ē′thər) *n.* [< Gr *aithein*, to burn] 1 an imaginary substance once thought to pervade space 2 the upper regions of space 3 a volatile, colorless, highly flammable liquid used as an anesthetic and a solvent

e·the·re·al (ē thir′ē əl, i-) *adj.* 1 very light; airy; delicate 2 not earthly; heavenly; celestial —**e·the′re·al·ly** *adv.*

eth·ic (eth′ik) *n.* [see fol.] a system of moral standards

eth·i·cal (eth′i kəl) *adj.* [< Gr *ēthos*, character] 1 having to do with ethics; of or conforming to moral standards 2 conforming to professional standards of conduct —**eth′i·cal·ly** *adv.*

eth·ics (eth′iks) *n.* 1 the study of standards of conduct and moral judgment 2 [*with sing. or* *pl. verb*] the system of morals of a particular person, religion, group, etc.

E·thi·o·pi·a (ē'thē ō'pē ə) *n.* country in E Africa —**E'thi·o'pi·an** *adj., n.*

eth·nic (eth'nik) *adj.* [< Gr *ethnos*, nation] designating or of a group of people having common customs, characteristics, language, etc. —*n.* a member of an ethnic group, esp. a minority or nationality group —**eth'ni·cal·ly** *adv.*

eth·nic·i·ty (eth nis'ə tē) *n.* ethnic classification or affiliation

eth·nog·ra·phy (eth nä̆g'rə fē) *n.* [ult. < Gk- *ethnos*, nation & -GRAPHY] the branch of anthropology that deals descriptively with specific cultures —**eth'nog'ra·pher** *n.*

eth·nol·o·gy (eth näl'ə jē) *n.* [< Gr *ethnos*, nation + -LOGY] the branch of anthropology that studies contemporary or recent cultures comparatively —**eth'no·log'i·cal** (-nə lä̆j'i kəl) *adj.* —**eth·nol'o·gist** *n.*

e·thos (ē'thäs') *n.* [Gr *ēthos*, character] the characteristic attitudes, habits, etc. of an individual or group

eth·yl (eth'əl) *n.* [< ETHER] the hydrocarbon radical that forms the base of ethyl alcohol, ether, etc.

ethyl alcohol ALCOHOL (*n.* 1)

eth·yl·ene (eth'əl ēn') *n.* [ETHYL + -ENE] a colorless, flammable, gaseous hydrocarbon used to synthesize organic chemicals, esp. polyethylene

ethylene gly·col (glī'kôl') a colorless, viscous liquid used as an antifreeze, solvent, etc.

e·ti·ol·o·gy (ēt'ē äl'ə jē) *n., pl.* -**gies** [< Gr *aitia*, cause + *logia*, description] 1 the cause assigned, as for a disease 2 the science of causes or origins —**e'ti·o·log'ic** (-ə läj'ik) *adj.*

et·i·quette (et'i kit) *n.* [Fr *étiquette*, lit., ticket] the forms, manners, etc. conventionally acceptable or required in society, a profession, etc.

Et·na (et'nə), **Mount** volcanic mountain in E Sicily

E·trus·can (i trus'kən) *adj.* of an ancient country (*Etruria*) in what is now central Italy

et seq. *abbrev.* [L *et sequens*] and the following

-ette (et) [Fr: see -ET] *suffix* 1 little [*statu-ette*] 2 female [*majorette*]

é·tude (ā'tood') *n.* [Fr, a study] a musical composition for a solo instrument, intended as or resembling an exercise

et·y·mol·o·gy (et'ə mäl'ə jē) *n., pl.* -**gies** [< Gr *etymos*, true + *logos*, word] 1 the origin and development of a word 2 the linguistic study of word origins —**et'y·mo·log'i·cal** (-mə läj'i kəl) *adj.* —**et'y·mol'o·gist** *n.*

EU *abbrev.* European Union

eu- [Fr < Gr] *prefix* good, well [*eulogy, euphony*]

eu·ca·lyp·tus (yoo'kə lip'təs) *n., pl.* -**tus·es** or **-ti'** (-ti') [< Gr *eu-*, well + *kalyptos*, covered] a tall, aromatic, chiefly Australian evergreen tree of the myrtle family

Eu·cha·rist (yoo'kə rist) *n.* [< Gr *eucharistia*, gratitude] 1 HOLY COMMUNION 2 the conse-

crated bread and wine used in this —**Eu'cha·ris'tic** *adj.*

eu·chre (yoo'kər) *n.* [< ?] a card game played with twenty-four cards

Eu·clid (yoo'klid) flourished 4th c. B.C.; Gr. mathematician: author of a basic work in geometry —**Eu·clid'e·an** (-ē ən) *adj.*, **Eu·clid'i·an**

eu·gen·ics (yoo jen'iks) *n.* [see EU- & GENESIS] the movement seeking to improve the genetic fitness of humanity —**eu·gen'ic** *adj.* —**eu·gen'i·cal·ly** *adv.* —**eu·gen'i·cist** (-ə sist) *n.*

eu·lo·gize (yoo'lə jīz') *vt.* -**gized'**, -**giz'ing** [see fol.] to praise highly —**eu'lo·gist** *n.*, **eu'lo·giz'er**

eu·lo·gy (-jē) *n., pl.* -**gies** [< Gr *eulegein*, speak well of] 1 speech or writing praising a person or thing; esp., a funeral oration 2 high praise —**eu'lo·gis'tic** (-jis'tik) *adj.*

eu·nuch (yoo'nək) *n.* [< Gr *eunouchos*, guardian of the bed] a castrated man

eu·phe·mism (yoo'fə miz'əm) *n.* [< Gr *eu-*, good + *phēmē*, speech] 1 the use of a less direct word or phrase for one considered offensive 2 a word or phrase so substituted —**eu'phe·mis'tic** *adj.* —**eu'phe·mis'ti·cal·ly** *adv.*

eu·pho·ni·ous (yoo fō'nē əs) *adj.* having a pleasant sound; harmonious —**eu·pho'ni·ous·ly** *adv.*

eu·pho·ny (yoo'fə nē) *n., pl.* -**nies** [< Gr *eu-*, good + *phōnē*, voice] a pleasant combination of agreeable sounds, as in speech

eu·pho·ri·a (yoo fôr'ē ə) *n.* [< Gr *eu-*, well + *pherein*, to bear] a feeling of well-being —**eu·phor'ic** *adj.*

Eu·phra·tes (yoo frāt'ēz) river flowing from EC Turkey through Syria & Iraq into the Persian Gulf: cf. TIGRIS

Eur·a·sia (yoor a'zhə) land mass made up of Europe & Asia

Eur·a·sian (-zhən) *adj.* 1 of Eurasia 2 of mixed European and Asian descent —*n.* a person of Eurasian descent

eu·re·ka (yoo rē'kə) *interj.* [< Gr *heurēka*, I have found] used to express triumphant achievement

Eu·rip·i·des (yoo rip'ə dēz') 480-406 B.C.; Gr. writer of tragedies

eu·ro (yoor'ō) *n.* the basic monetary unit of the European Monetary Union

Eu·rope (yoor'əp) continent between Asia & the Atlantic —**Eu·ro·pe·an** (yoor'ə pē'ən) *adj., n.*

European Community an organization of European countries established in 1967 to bring about the political and economic unification of W Europe

European Monetary Union a union of those members of the European Union that use the euro as their only legal currency

European plan a system of hotel operation in which guests are charged for rooms and pay for meals separately

European Union a union of European nations created in 1993 to bring about the gradual unification of Europe

eu·ro·pi·um (yŏŏ rō′pē əm) *n.* 〖after EUROPE〗 a soft ductile chemical element, used to dope glass and plastics for lasers and to absorb neutrons in research: symbol, Eu; at. no. 63

eu·ro·zone (yŏŏr′ō zōn′) 〖*also* E-〗 loosely, those nations of the European Union that have adopted the euro as their legal currency

eu·ryth·mics (yŏŏ rith′miks) *n.* 〖< Gr *eu-*, good + *rhythmos*, rhythm〗 the art of performing bodily movements in rhythm, usually to music

eu·sta·chian tube (yŏŏ stā′shən) 〖after B. *Eustachio* (1510-74), It anatomist〗 〖*also* E-t-〗 a slender tube between the middle ear and the pharynx

eu·tha·na·si·a (yŏŏ′thə nā′zhə) *n.* 〖< Gr *eu-*, good + *thanatos*, death〗 the act of causing death painlessly, so as to end suffering

eu·tha·nize (yŏŏ′thə nīz′) *vt.* **-nized′, -niz′ing** to put to death by euthanasia

EV (ē′vē′) *n., pl.* **EVs** 〖*e*(*lectric*) *v*(*ehicle*)〗 an automotive vehicle with an engine powered by an electric battery that can be recharged

e·vac·u·ate (ē vak′yŏŏ āt′) *vt.* **-at′ed, -at′ing** 〖< L *e-*, out + *vacuus*, empty〗 1 to make empty 2 to discharge (bodily waste, esp. feces) 3 to withdraw from, esp. because of imminent danger —*vi.* to withdraw —**e·vac′u·a′tion** *n.* —**e·vac′u·ee′** (-ē′) *n.*

e·vade (ē vād′, i-) *vt., vi.* **e·vad′ed, e·vad′ing** 〖< L *e-*, out, from + *vadere*, go〗 1 to avoid or escape (from) by deceit or cleverness 2 to avoid doing or answering directly —**e·vad′er** *n.*

e·val·u·ate (ē val′yŏŏ āt′, i-) *vt.* **-at′ed, -at′ing** 〖ult. < L *valere*, be worth〗 1 to find the value or amount of 2 to judge the worth of —**e·val′u·a′tion** *n.*

ev·a·nes·cent (ev′ə nes′ənt) *adj.* 〖< L *e-*, out + *vanescere*, vanish〗 tending to fade from sight; fleeting; ephemeral —**ev′a·nes′cence** *n.*

e·van·gel·i·cal (ē′van jel′i kəl, ev′ən-) *adj.* 〖< Gr *euangelos*, bringing good news〗 1 of or according to the Gospels or the New Testament 2 of those Protestant churches that emphasize salvation by faith in Jesus

e·van·ge·list (ē van′jə list) *n.* 1 〖E-〗 any of the four writers of the Gospels: Matthew, Mark, Luke, or John 2 a revivalist or a preacher who holds large public services in various cities, now often televised —**e·van′ge·lism′** *n.*

e·van·ge·lize (-līz′) *vt.* **-lized′, -liz′ing** to convert to Christianity —*vi.* to preach the gospel

e·vap·o·rate (ē vap′ə rāt′) *vt.* **-rat′ed, -rat′ing** 〖< L *e-*, out, from + *vaporare*, emit vapor〗 1 to change (a liquid or solid) into vapor 2 to remove moisture from (milk, etc.), as by heating, so as to get a concentrated product —*vi.* 1 to become vapor 2 to give off vapor 3 to disappear like vapor; vanish —**e·vap′o·ra′tion** *n.* —**e·vap′o·ra′tor** *n.*

e·va·sion (ē vā′zhən, i-) *n.* 1 an evading; specif., an avoiding of a duty, question, etc. 2 a way of doing this; subterfuge

e·va·sive (-siv) *adj.* 1 tending or seeking to evade 2 elusive —**e·va′sive·ly** *adv.* —**e·va′sive·ness** *n.*

eve (ēv) *n.* 〖< OE *æfen*, evening〗 1 〖Old Poet.〗 evening 2 〖*often* E-〗 the evening or day before a holiday 3 the period just prior to some event

Eve (ēv) *n. Bible* the first woman, Adam's wife

e·ven (ē′vən) *adj.* 〖OE *efne*〗 1 flat; level; smooth 2 not varying; constant 〖an *even* tempo〗 3 calm; tranquil 〖an *even* temper〗 4 in the same plane or line 〖*even* with the rim〗 5 owing and being owed nothing 6 equal in number, quantity, etc. 7 exactly divisible by two 8 exact 〖an *even* mile〗 9 revenged for a wrong, etc. —*adv.* 1 however improbable; indeed 2 exactly; just 〖it happened *even* as I expected〗 3 still; yet 〖he's *even* better〗 —*vt., vi.* to make or become even —**even if** though —**e′ven·ly** *adv.* —**e′ven·ness** *n.*

e·ven-hand·ed *adj.* impartial; fair

eve·ning (ēv′niŋ) *n.* 〖< OE *æfnung*〗 1 the last part of the day and early part of night 2 〖Dial.〗 afternoon

even money equal stakes in betting, with no odds

e·vent (ē vent′) *n.* 〖< L *e-*, out + *venire*, come〗 1 an occurrence, esp. when important 2 a particular contest in a program of sports 3 any organized activity, celebration, etc. —**in any event** no matter what happens; anyway —**in the event of** in case of —**in the event that** if it should happen that

e·ven-tem·pered *adj.* not quickly angered; calm

e·vent·ful *adj.* 1 full of outstanding events 2 having an important outcome —**e·vent′ful·ly** *adv.*

e·ven·tide (ē′vən tīd′) *n.* 〖Archaic〗 evening

e·ven·tu·al (ē ven′chŏŏ əl) *adj.* ultimate; final —**e·ven′tu·al·ly** *adv.*

e·ven·tu·al·i·ty (-al′ə tē) *n., pl.* **-ties** a possible event or outcome

e·ven·tu·ate (-āt′) *vi.* **-at′ed, -at′ing** to happen in the end; result

ev·er (ev′ər) *adv.* 〖< OE *æfre*〗 1 always 〖*ever* the same〗 2 at any time 〖do you *ever* see her?〗 3 at all; by any chance 〖how can I *ever* repay you?〗 —**ever so** 〖Inf.〗 very

Ev·er·est (ev′ər ist, ev′rist), **Mount** peak of the Himalayas: highest mountain in the world: 29,035 ft.

ev·er·glade *n.* marshy land

ev·er·green *adj.* having green leaves all year long, as most conifers —*n.* an evergreen plant or tree

ev·er·last·ing *adj.* lasting forever; eternal —*n.* eternity

ev·er·more *adv.* 〖Archaic〗 forever; constantly

ev·er·y (ev′rē) *adj.* 〖OE *æfre ælc*, lit., ever each〗 1 each, individually and separately 2 the greatest possible 〖to make *every* effort〗 3 each interval 〖take a pill *every* three hours〗 —**every now and then** occasionally: also 〖Inf.〗 **every so often** —**every other** each alternate, as the first, third, fifth, etc. —**every which way** 〖Inf.〗 in complete disorder

ev·er·y·bod·y (-bäd′ē, -bud′ē) *pron.* every person; everyone

ev·er·y·day *adj.* 1 daily 2 suitable for ordinary days [*everyday* shoes] 3 usual; common

ev·er·y·one *pron.* every person

every one every person or thing of those named [*every one* of the boys]

ev·er·y·thing *pron.* every thing; all

ev·er·y·where *adv.* in or to every place

e·vict (ē vikt′) *vt.* ‖< L *e-*, intens. + *vincere*, conquer‖ to remove (a tenant) by legal procedure —**e·vic′tion** *n.*

ev·i·dence (ev′ə dəns) *n.* 1 something that makes another thing evident; sign 2 a statement of a witness, an object, etc. bearing on or establishing the point in question in a court of law —*vt.* –**denced**, –**denc·ing** to make evident —**in evidence** plainly seen, heard, etc.

ev·i·dent (ev′ə dənt) *adj.* ‖< L *e-*, from + *videre*, see‖ easy to see or perceive; clear —**ev′i·dent·ly** *adv.*

e·vil (ē′vəl) *adj.* ‖OE *yfel*‖ 1 morally bad or wrong; wicked 2 harmful; injurious 3 unlucky; disastrous —*n.* 1 wickedness; sin 2 anything that causes harm, pain, etc. —**e′vil·ly** *adv.*

e·vil·do·er *n.* one who does evil —**e′vil·do′ing** *n.*

e·vince (ē vins′) *vt.* **e·vinced′**, **e·vinc′ing** ‖< L *e-*, intens. + *vincere*, conquer‖ to show plainly; make clear

e·vis·cer·ate (ē vis′ər āt′) *vt.* –**at′ed**, –**at′ing** ‖< L *e-*, out + *viscera*, viscera‖ 1 to remove the entrails from 2 to deprive of an essential part —**e·vis′cer·a′tion** *n.*

e·voc·a·tive (ē väk′ə tiv, i-) *adj.* ‖L *evocativus*‖ tending to evoke a reaction or response, esp. an emotional one —**e·voc′a·tive·ly** *adv.*

e·voke (ē vōk′) *vt.* **e·voked′**, **e·vok′ing** ‖< L *e-*, out, from + *vox*, voice‖ 1 to call forth 2 to elicit (a reaction, etc.) —**ev·o·ca·tion** (ev′ə kā′shən, ē′vō-) *n.*

ev·o·lu·tion (ev′ə lōō′shən) *n.* [see fol.] 1 an unfolding; process of development or change 2 a thing evolved 3 a movement that is part of a series 4 *Biol.* a) the development of a species, organism, etc. from its original to its present form b) the theory that all species developed from earlier forms, esp. by natural selection —**ev′o·lu′tion·ar′y** *adj.*

e·volve (ē välv′, -vôlv′) *vt., vi.* **e·volved′**, **e·volv′ing** ‖< L *e-*, out + *volvere*, to roll‖ 1 to develop gradually 2 to develop by evolution

ewe (yōō) *n.* ‖OE *eowu*‖ a female sheep

ew·er (yōō′ər) *n.* ‖< L *aqua*, water‖ a large, wide-mouthed water pitcher

ex *abbrev.* 1 example 2 exchange

ex- ‖< OFr or L‖ *prefix* 1 a) from, out [*expel*] b) beyond c) thoroughly d) upward 2 former, previous [*ex-*president]

ex·ac·er·bate (eg zas′ər bāt′) *vt.* –**bat′ed**, –**bat′ing** ‖< L *ex-*, intens. + *acerbus*, bitter‖ 1 to aggravate (pain, annoyance, etc.) 2 to exasperate; annoy; irritate —**ex·ac′er·ba′tion** *n.*

ex·act (eg zakt′) *adj.* ‖< L *ex-*, out + *agere*, to do‖ 1 characterized by or requiring accuracy; methodical; correct 2 without variation; precise —*vt.* 1 to extort 2 to demand; require —**ex·act′ly** *adv.* —**ex·act′ness** *n.*

ex·act·ing *adj.* 1 making severe demands; strict 2 demanding care, effort, etc.; arduous —**ex·act′ing·ly** *adv.*

ex·ac·tion (eg zak′shən) *n.* 1 an exacting 2 an extortion 3 an exacted fee, tax, etc.

ex·ac·ti·tude (-tə tōōd′) *n.* ‖Fr‖ the quality of being exact; accuracy

ex·ag·ger·ate (eg zaj′ər āt′) *vt., vi.* –**at′ed**, –**at′ing** ‖< L *ex-*, out + *agger*, a heap‖ to think or tell of (something) as greater than it is; overstate —**ex·ag′ger·a′tion** *n.* —**ex·ag′ger·a′tive** *adj.* —**ex·ag′ger·a′tor** *n.*

ex·alt (eg zôlt′) *vt.* ‖< L *ex-*, up + *altus*, high‖ 1 to raise in status, dignity, etc. 2 to praise; glorify 3 to fill with joy, pride, etc.; elate —**ex·al·ta·tion** (eg′zôl tā′shən) *n.*

ex·am·i·na·tion (eg zam′ə nā′shən) *n.* 1 an examining or being examined 2 a set of questions asked in testing: also **ex·am′**

ex·am·ine (eg zam′ən) *vt.* –**ined**, –**in·ing** ‖< L *examinare*, weigh‖ 1 to look at critically or methodically; investigate; inspect 2 to test by questioning —**ex·am′in·er** *n.*

ex·am·ple (eg zam′pəl) *n.* ‖< L *eximere*, take out‖ 1 something selected to show the character of the rest; sample 2 a case that serves as a warning 3 a model; pattern 4 an instance that illustrates a principle

ex·as·per·ate (eg zas′pər āt′) *vt.* –**at′ed**, –**at′ing** ‖< L *ex-*, out + *asper*, rough‖ to irritate; anger; vex —**ex·as′per·a′tion** *n.*

ex·ca·vate (eks′kə vāt′) *vt.* –**vat′ed**, –**vat′ing** ‖< L *ex-*, out + *cavus*, hollow‖ 1 to make a hole or cavity in 2 to form (a tunnel, etc.) by hollowing out 3 to unearth 4 to dig out (earth, soil, etc.) —**ex′ca·va′tion** *n.* —**ex′ca·va′tor** *n.*

ex·ceed (ek sēd′) *vt.* ‖< L *ex-*, out + *cedere*, to go‖ 1 to go to or be beyond (a limit, etc.) 2 to surpass

ex·ceed·ing *adj.* surpassing; extreme —**ex·ceed′ing·ly** *adv.*

ex·cel (ek sel′) *vi., vt.* –**celled′**, –**cel′ling** ‖< L *ex-*, out of + -*cellere*, to rise‖ to be better or greater than

ex·cel·lence (ek′sə ləns) *n.* 1 the fact or state of excelling; superiority 2 a particular virtue

ex·cel·len·cy (-lən sē) *n., pl.* –**cies** ‖E-‖ a title of honor for certain dignitaries 2 EXCELLENCE

ex·cel·lent (ek′sə lənt) *adj.* [see EXCEL] outstandingly good of its kind; of exceptional merit —**ex′cel·lent·ly** *adv.*

ex·cel·si·or (eks sel′sē ôr′; *for n.* eks sel′sē ər) *interj.* [see EXCEL] always upward! —*n.* long, thin wood shavings used for packing

ex·cept (ek sept′) *vt.* ‖< L *ex-*, out + *capere*, to take‖ to leave out or take out; exclude —*prep.* leaving out; but for —*conj.* 1 [Archaic] unless 2 [Inf.] were it not that; only —**except for** if it were not for

ex·cept·ing *prep., conj.* EXCEPT

ex·cep·tion *n.* **1** an excepting **2** *a)* a case to which a rule does not apply *b)* a person or thing different from others of the same class **3** an objection —**take exception 1** to object **2** feel offended

ex·cep·tion·a·ble *adj.* open to objection

ex·cep·tion·al *adj.* **1** unusual; esp., unusually good **2** needing special education, as because intellectually gifted or disabled —**ex·cep′·tion·al·ly** *adv.*

ex·cerpt (ek surpt′; *for n.* ek′surpt′) *vt.* [< L *ex-*, out + *carpere*, to pick] to select or quote (passages from a book, etc.); extract —*n.* a passage selected or quoted; extract

ex·cess (ek ses′; *also, esp. for adj.*, ek′ses′) *n.* [see EXCEED] **1** action that goes beyond a reasonable limit **2** an amount greater than is necessary **3** the amount by which one thing exceeds another —*adj.* extra; surplus —**in excess of** more than

ex·ces·sive *adj.* being too much; immoderate —**ex·ces′sive·ly** *adv.*

ex·change (eks chānj′) *vt., vi.* **-changed′, -chang′ing** [see EX- & CHANGE] **1** to give or receive (something) *for* another thing; barter; trade **2** to interchange (similar things) —*n.* **1** an exchanging; interchange **2** a thing exchanged **3** a place for exchanging [a stock *exchange*] **4** a central office providing telephone service **5** the value of one currency in terms of another —**ex·change′a·ble** *adj.*

exchange rate the rate at which one currency can be exchanged for another

ex·cheq·uer (eks chek′ər) *n.* [ME *escheker*, lit., chessboard < OFr *eschekier*: accounts of revenue were kept on a squared board] **1** a national treasury **2** funds; finances

ex·cise¹ (ek′sīz′) *n.* [ult. < L *assidere*, assist (in office)] a tax on various commodities, as liquor or tobacco, within a country: also **excise tax**

ex·cise² (ek sīz′) *vt.* **-cised′, -cis′ing** [< L *ex-*, out + *caedere*, to cut] to remove by cutting out —**ex·ci′sion** (-sizh′ən) *n.*

ex·cit·a·ble (ek sīt′ə bəl) *adj.* easily excited —**ex·cit′a·bil′i·ty** *n.*

ex·cite (ek sīt′) *vt.* **-cit′ed, -cit′ing** [< L *ex-*, out + *ciere*, to call] **1** to make active; stir up **2** to arouse; provoke **3** to arouse the feelings of —**ex·ci·ta·tion** (ek′sī tā′shən) *n.* —**ex·cit′ed·ly** *adv.* —**ex·cit′er** *n.*

ex·cite·ment *n.* **1** an exciting or being excited; agitation **2** that which excites

ex·cit·ing *adj.* causing excitement; stirring, thrilling, etc.

ex·claim (eks klām′) *vi., vt.* [< L *ex-*, out + *clamare*, to shout] to cry out; say suddenly and vehemently

ex·cla·ma·tion (ek′sklə mā′shən) *n.* **1** an exclaiming **2** something exclaimed; interjection —**ex·clam·a·to·ry** (ek sklam′ə tôr′ē) *adj.*

exclamation point (*or* **mark**) a mark (!) used in punctuating to show surprise, strong emotion, etc.

ex·clude (eks klōōd′) *vt.* **-clud′ed, -clud′ing** [< L *ex-*, out + *claudere*, to close] **1** to refuse to admit, consider, etc.; reject **2** to put or force out —**ex·clu′sion** (-klōō′zhən) *n.*

ex·clu·sive (-klōō′siv) *adj.* **1** excluding all others **2** not shared; sole [an *exclusive* right] **3** excluding certain people, as for social or economic reasons —*n.* something exclusive; specif., a news item distributed by only one news organization —**ex·clu′sive·ly** *adv.* —**ex·clu′sive·ness** *n.* —**exclusive of** not including

ex·com·mu·ni·cate (eks′kə myōō′ni kāt′) *vt.* **-cat′ed, -cat′ing** to exclude from the rights, privileges, etc. of a church, esp. from the right to receive Holy Communion —**ex′com·mu′ni·ca′tion** *n.*

ex·co·ri·ate (eks kôr′ē āt′) *vt.* **-at′ed, -at′ing** [< L *ex-*, off + *corium*, the skin] to denounce harshly —**ex·co′ri·a′tion** *n.*

ex·cre·ment (eks′krə mənt) *n.* waste matter excreted from the bowels

ex·cres·cence (eks kres′əns) *n.* [< L *ex-*, out + *crescere*, grow] an abnormal outgrowth or addition

ex·cre·ta (eks krēt′ə) *pl.n.* waste matter excreted from the body

ex·crete (eks krēt′) *vt., vi.* **-cret′ed, -cret′ing** [< L *ex-*, out of + *cernere*, sift] to eliminate (waste matter) from the body —**ex·cre′tion** *n.* —**ex·cre·to·ry** (eks′krə tôr′ē) *adj.*

ex·cru·ci·at·ing (eks krōō′shē āt′iŋ) *adj.* **1** intensely painful; agonizing **2** intense or extreme

ex·cul·pate (eks′kəl pāt′) *vt.* **-pat′ed, -pat′ing** [< L *ex*, out + *culpa*, fault] to free from blame; prove guiltless —**ex′cul·pa′tion** *n.* —**ex·cul′pa·to·ry** *adj.*

ex·cur·sion (eks kur′zhən) *n.* [< L *ex-*, out + *currere*, to run] **1** a short trip; jaunt **2** a round trip at reduced rates —*adj.* for an excursion

ex·cur·sive (eks kur′siv) *adj.* rambling; digressive —**ex·cur′sive·ly** *adv.* —**ex·cur′sive·ness** *n.*

ex·cuse (ek skyōōz′; *for n.*, -skyōōs′) *vt.* **-cused′, -cus′ing** [< L *ex-*, from + *causa*, a charge] **1** to apologize or give reasons for **2** to overlook (an offense or fault) **3** to release from an obligation, etc. **4** to permit to leave **5** to justify —*n.* **1** a defense of some action; apology **2** something that excuses **3** a pretext —**excuse oneself** to apologize **2** to ask for permission to leave —**ex·cus′a·ble** *adj.*

exec *abbrev.* **1** executive **2** executor

ex·e·cra·ble (ek′si krə bəl) *adj.* [see fol.] **1** detestable **2** very inferior

ex·e·crate (-krāt′) *vt.* **-crat′ed, -crat′ing** [< L *execrare*, to curse] **1** to denounce scathingly **2** to loathe; abhor —**ex′e·cra′tion** *n.*

ex·e·cute (ek′si kyōōt′) *vt.* **-cut′ed, -cut′ing** [see EXECUTOR] **1** to carry out; do **2** to administer (laws, etc.) **3** to put to death by a legal sentence **4** to create in accordance with a plan, etc. **5** to make valid (a deed, will, etc.) **6** *Comput.* to run (a program, etc.)

ex·e·cu·tion (-kyōō′shən) *n.* **1** an executing; carrying out, performing, etc. *a)* a putting to death by a legal sentence **2** the manner of performing

ex·e·cu·tion·er *n.* one who carries out a court-imposed death penalty

ex·ec·u·tive (eg zek'yōō tiv) *adj.* ⟦see fol.⟧ **1** of or capable of carrying out duties, functions, etc. **2** empowered to administer (laws, government affairs, etc.) —*n.* **1** the branch of government administering the laws and business affairs of a nation **2** one who administers business affairs of a corporation, etc.

ex·ec·u·tor (eg zek'yōō tər) *n.* ⟦< L *ex-*, intens. + *sequi*, to follow⟧ a person appointed to carry out the provisions of a will

ex·e·ge·sis (ek'sə jē'sis) *n.*, *pl.* **-ses'** (-sēz') ⟦< Gr *ex-*, out + *hēgeisthai*, to lead⟧ interpretation of a word, passage, etc., esp. in the Bible

ex·em·plar (eg zem'plər, -plär') *n.* ⟦< L *exemplum*, a pattern⟧ **1** a model; pattern **2** a typical specimen

ex·em·pla·ry (eg zem'plə rē) *adj.* ⟦< L *exemplum*, a pattern⟧ serving as a model or example ⟦an *exemplary* life⟧

ex·em·pli·fy (eg zem'plə fī') *vt.* **-fied'**, **-fy'ing** ⟦< L *exemplum*, example + *facere*, to make⟧ to show by example —**ex·em'pli·fi·ca'tion** *n.*

ex·empt (eg zempt') *vt.* ⟦< L *ex-*, out + *emere*, to buy⟧ to free from a rule or obligation which applies to others —*adj.* freed from a usual rule, duty, etc. —**ex·emp'tion** *n.*

ex·er·cise (ek'sər sīz') *n.* ⟦< L *exercere*, put to work⟧ **1** active use or operation **2** performance (of duties, etc.) **3** activity for developing the body or mind **4** a task to be practiced for developing some skill **5** ⟦*pl.*⟧ a program of speeches, etc. —*vt.* **-cised'**, **-cis'ing 1** to put into action; use **2** to carry out (duties, etc.); perform **3** to put into use so as to develop or train **4** to exert (influence, etc.) **5** to engage so as to worry, harass, etc. —*vi.* to do exercises

ex·ert (eg zurt') *vt.* ⟦< L *exserere*, stretch out⟧ **1** to put into action **2** to apply (oneself) with great effort

ex·er·tion *n.* **1** active use of strength, power, etc. **2** effort

ex·fo·li·ant (eks fō'lē ənt) *n.* a soap, moisturizer, cosmetic preparation, etc. that removes dead cells from the surface of the skin

ex·fo·li·ate (eks fō'lē āt') *vt., vi.* **-at'ed, -at'ing** ⟦< LL *exfoliatus*, stripped of leaves < L *ex-*, out + *folium*, a leaf⟧ to cast or come off in flakes, scales, or layers: said of skin, bark, rock, etc. —**ex·fo'li·a'tion** *n.*

ex·hale (eks hāl') *vt., vi.* **-haled', -hal'ing** ⟦< L *ex-*, out + *halare*, breathe⟧ **1** to breathe out (air) **2** to give off (vapor, etc.) —**ex·ha·la·tion** (eks'hə lā'shən) *n.*

ex·haust (eg zôst') *vt.* ⟦< L *ex-*, out + *haurire*, to draw⟧ **1** to use up **2** to empty completely; drain **3** to tire out **4** to deal with thoroughly —*n.* **1** the discharge of used steam, gas, etc. from an engine **2** the pipes through which it is released **3** fumes, etc. given off —**ex·haust'i·ble** *adj.*

ex·haus·tion (eg zôs'chən) *n.* **1** an exhausting **2** great fatigue

ex·haus·tive *adj.* leaving nothing out —**ex·haus'tive·ly** *adv.*

ex·hib·it (eg zib'it) *vt.* ⟦< L *ex-*, out + *habere*, to hold⟧ **1** to show; display **2** to present to public view —*vi.* to put art objects, etc. on public display —*n.* **1** a display **2** a thing exhibited **3** *Law* an object produced as evidence in a court —**ex·hib'i·tor** *n.*

ex·hi·bi·tion (ek'sə bish'ən) *n.* **1** an exhibiting **2** that which is exhibited **3** a public showing, as of art

ex·hi·bi·tion·ism *n.* **1** a tendency to call attention to oneself or show off **2** a tendency to expose oneself sexually —**ex'hi·bi'tion·ist** *n.*

ex·hil·a·rate (eg zil'ə rāt') *vt.* **-rat'ed, -rat'ing** ⟦< L *ex-*, intens. + *hilaris*, glad⟧ **1** to make cheerful or lively **2** to stimulate —**ex·hil'a·ra'tion** *n.* —**ex·hil'a·ra'tive** *adj.*

ex·hort (eg zôrt') *vt., vi.* ⟦< L *ex-*, out + *hortari*, to urge⟧ to urge earnestly; advise strongly —**ex'hor·ta'tion** *n.*

ex·hume (eks hyōōm', eg zyōōm') *vt.* **-humed', -hum'ing** ⟦< L *ex-*, out + *humus*, the ground⟧ **1** to dig out of the earth; disinter **2** to bring to light; reveal —**ex'hu·ma'tion** *n.*

ex·i·gen·cy (eks'ə jən sē) *n.*, *pl.* **-cies** ⟦< L *exigere*, drive out⟧ **1** urgency **2** a situation calling for immediate attention **3** ⟦*pl.*⟧ pressing needs —**ex'i·gent** *adj.*

ex·ig·u·ous (eg zig'yōō əs) *adj.* ⟦see prec.⟧ scanty; meager

ex·ile (ek'sīl', eg'zīl') *n.* ⟦< L *exul*, an exile⟧ **1** a prolonged living away from one's country, usually enforced **2** a person in exile —*vt.* **-iled', -il'ing** to force (a person) into exile; banish

ex·ist (eg zist') *vi.* ⟦< L *ex-*, out + *sistere*, to set, place⟧ **1** to have reality or being; be **2** to occur or be present **3** to continue being; live

ex·ist·ence *n.* **1** the act or fact of being **2** life; living **3** occurrence —**ex·ist'ent** *adj.*

ex·is·ten·tial (eg'zis ten'shəl) *adj.* **1** of existence **2** of existentialism

ex·is·ten·tial·ism *n.* a philosophical movement stressing individual existence and holding that humans are totally free and responsible for their acts —**ex'is·ten'tial·ist** *adj., n.*

ex·it (ek'sit, eg'zit) *n.* ⟦< L *ex-*, out + *ire*, to go⟧ **1** an actor's departure from the stage **2** a going out; departure **3** a way out **4** a road leading from an expressway —*vi.* to leave a place —*vt.* to leave (a building, expressway, etc.)

exo- ⟦< Gr *exō*⟧ *prefix* outside, outer, outer part

ex·o·bi·ol·o·gy (eks'ō bī äl'ə jē) *n.* the branch of biology investigating the possibility of extraterrestrial life

ex·o·dus (eks'ə dəs) *n.* ⟦< Gr *ex-*, out + *hodos*, way⟧ **1** [E—] the departure of the Israelites from Egypt: with *the* **2** [E—] the second book of the Bible, describing this **3** a going out or forth

ex of·fi·ci·o (eks' ə fish'ē ō') ⟦L, lit., from office⟧ by virtue of one's position

ex·on·er·ate (eg zän'ər āt') *vt.* **-at'ed, -at'ing** ⟦< L *ex-*, out + *onerare*, to load⟧ to declare or prove blameless —**ex·on'er·a'tion** *n.*

ex·or·bi·tant (eg zôr'bi tənt) *adj.* [< L *ex-*, out + *orbita*, a track] going beyond what is reasonable, just, etc.; excessive —**ex·or'bi·tance** *n.*

ex·or·cise or **ex·or·cize** (eks'ôr sīz') *vt.* **-cised'** or **-cized'**, **-cis'ing** or **-ciz'ing** [< Gr *ex-*, out + *horkos*, an oath] 1 to drive out (an evil spirit) by ritual prayers, etc. 2 to free from such a spirit —**ex'or·cism'** (-siz'əm) *n.* —**ex'or·cist** *n.*

ex·o·skel·e·ton (eks'ō skel'ə tən) *n.* any hard, external supporting structure, as the shell of an oyster

ex·o·ther·mic (-thur'mik) *adj.* designating or of a chemical change in which heat is liberated

ex·ot·ic (eg zät'ik) *adj.* [< Gr *exō*, outside] 1 foreign 2 strangely beautiful, enticing, etc. — **ex·ot'i·cal·ly** *adv.*

exp *abbrev.* experience(d)

ex·pand (ek spand') *vt., vi.* [< L *ex-*, out + *pandere*, to spread] 1 to spread out; unfold 2 to increase in size, scope, etc.

ex·panse (ek spans') *n.* a large area or unbroken surface; wide extent

ex·pan·si·ble *adj.* that can be expanded: also **ex·pand'a·ble**

ex·pan·sion *n.* 1 an expanding or being expanded; enlargement 2 an expanded thing or part 3 the degree or extent of expansion

expansion bolt a bolt with an attachment that expands as the bolt is turned

ex·pan·sive *adj.* 1 that can expand 2 broad; extensive 3 effusive; demonstrative —**ex·pan'sive·ly** *adv.*

ex·pa·ti·ate (ek pā'shē āt') *vi.* **-at'ed**, **-at'ing** [< L *ex(s)patiari*, wander] to speak or write at length (*on* or *upon*) —**ex·pa'ti·a'tion** *n.*

ex·pa·tri·ate (eks pā'trē āt'; *for n.* -it) *vt., vi.* **-at'ed**, **-at'ing** [< L *ex*, out of + *patria*, fatherland] to exile (a person or oneself) —*n.* one who lives in a foreign country temporarily or permanently —**ex·pa'tri·a'tion** *n.*

ex·pect (ek spekt') *vt.* [< L *ex-*, out + *spectare*, to look] 1 to look for as likely to occur or appear 2 to look for as proper or necessary 3 [Inf.] to suppose; guess —**be expecting** [Inf.] to be pregnant

ex·pect·an·cy *n., pl.* **-cies** 1 EXPECTATION 2 that which is expected, esp. on a statistical basis

ex·pect·ant *adj.* that expects; expecting —**ex·pect'ant·ly** *adv.*

ex·pec·ta·tion (ek'spek tā'shən) *n.* 1 an expecting; anticipation 2 a thing looked forward to 3 [*also pl.*] a reason for expecting something

ex·pec·to·rant (ek spek'tə rənt) *n.* [see fol.] a medicine that helps to bring up phlegm

ex·pec·to·rate (-tə rāt') *vt., vi.* **-rat'ed**, **-rat'ing** [< L *ex-*, out + *pectus*, breast] to spit —**ex·pec'to·ra'tion** *n.*

ex·pe·di·en·cy (ek spē'dē ən sē) *n., pl.* **-cies** 1 a being suitable for a given purpose 2 the doing of what will benefit oneself rather than

what is right or just 3 an expedient Also **ex·pe'di·ence**

ex·pe·di·ent *adj.* [see fol.] 1 useful for effecting a desired result 2 based on or guided by self-interest —*n.* an expedient thing; means to an end

ex·pe·dite (eks'pə dīt') *vt.* **-dit'ed**, **-dit'ing** [< L *expedire*, lit., to free the foot] 1 to speed up the progress of; facilitate 2 to do quickly

ex·pe·dit·er *n.* one employed to expedite urgent or involved projects: also sp. **ex'pe·di'tor**

ex·pe·di·tion (eks'pə dish'ən) *n.* [see EXPEDITE] 1 *a*) a voyage, march, etc., as for exploration or battle *b*) those on such a journey 2 efficient speed —**ex'pe·di'tion·ar'y** *adj.*

ex·pe·di·tious (-dish'əs) *adj.* efficient and speedy; prompt —**ex'pe·di'tious·ly** *adv.*

ex·pel (ek spel') *vt.* **-pelled'**, **-pel'ling** [< L *ex-*, out + *pellere*, to thrust] 1 to drive out by force 2 to dismiss by authority [*expelled* from college] —**ex·pel'la·ble** *adj.* —**ex·pel'ler** *n.*

ex·pend (ek spend') *vt.* [< L *ex-*, out + *pendere*, to weigh] 1 to spend 2 to use up

ex·pend·a·ble *adj.* 1 that can be expended 2 *Mil.* designating equipment (or personnel) expected to be used up (or sacrificed) in service

ex·pend·i·ture (ek spen'di chər) *n.* 1 an expending of money, time, etc. 2 the amount of money, time, etc. expended

ex·pense (ek spens') *n.* [see EXPEND] 1 financial cost; charge 2 any cost or sacrifice 3 [*pl.*] charges met with in doing one's work, etc.

ex·pen·sive *adj.* costly; high-priced

ex·pe·ri·ence (ek spir'ē əns) *n.* [< L *experiri*, to try] 1 the act of living through an event 2 anything or everything observed or lived through 3 *a*) training and personal participation *b*) knowledge, skill, etc. resulting from this —*vt.* **-enced**, **-enc·ing** to have experience of; undergo

ex·pe·ri·enced *adj.* having had or having learned from experience

ex·per·i·ment (ek sper'ə mənt; *also, and for v. usually*, -ment') *n.* [< L *experimentum*, a trial] a test, trial, action, etc. undertaken to discover or demonstrate something —*vi.* to make, perform, conduct, etc. experiments —**ex·per'i·men·ta'tion** (-mən tā'shən) *n.* —**ex·per'i·ment'er** *n.*

ex·per·i·men·tal *adj.* 1 based on or used for experiments 2 designed to test 3 tentative —**ex·per'i·men'tal·ly** *adv.*

ex·pert (eks'pərt) *adj.* [see EXPERIENCE] very skillful —*n.* one who is very skillful or well-informed in some special field —**ex'pert·ly** *adv.* —**ex'pert·ness** *n.*

ex·per·tise (ek'spər tēz') *n.* [Fr] the skill or knowledge of an expert

ex·pi·ate (eks'pē āt') *vt.* **-at'ed**, **-at'ing** [< L *ex-*, out + *piare*, to appease] to make amends for (wrongdoing or guilt); atone for —**ex'pi·a'tion** *n.* —**ex'pi·a·to'ry** (-ə tôr'ē) *adj.*

ex·pire (ek spīr') *vi.* **-pired'**, **-pir'ing** [< L *ex-*, out + *spirare*, breathe] 1 to exhale 2 to die 3 to come to an end —**ex·pi·ra·tion** (ek′ spə rā′shən) *n.*

ex·plain (ek splān′) *vt.* [< L *ex*-, out + *planus*, level] 1 to make plain or clear 2 to give the meaning of; expound 3 to account for —*vi.* to give an explanation —**ex·plain′a·ble** *adj.*

ex·pla·na·tion (eks′plə nā′shən) *n.* 1 an explaining 2 something that explains; interpretation, meaning, etc.

ex·plan·a·to·ry (ek splan′ə tôr′ē) *adj.* explaining or intended to explain

ex·ple·tive (eks′plə tiv) *n.* [< L *ex*-, out, up + *plere*, to fill] an oath or exclamation

ex·pli·ca·ble (eks′pli kə bəl, ik splik′ə bəl) *adj.* [see fol.] that can be explained

ex·pli·cate (eks′pli kāt′) *vt.* -cat′ed, -cat′ing [< L *ex*-, out + *plicare*, to fold] to make clear; explain fully

ex·plic·it (eks plis′it) *adj.* [see prec.] 1 clearly stated or shown; definite 2 outspoken —**ex·plic′it·ly** *adv.*

ex·plode (ek splōd′) *vt.* -plod′ed, -plod′ing [orig., to drive off the stage < L *ex*-, off + *plaudere*, applaud] 1 to expose as false 2 to make burst with a loud noise 3 to cause to change suddenly and violently, as from a solid to an expanding gas —*vi.* to burst forth noisily — **ex·plod′a·ble** *adj.*

ex·ploit (eks′ploit′; *also, and for v. usually*, ek sploit′) *n.* [see EXPLICATE] a daring act; bold deed —*vt.* 1 to make use of 2 to make unethical use of for one's own profit —**ex′ploi·ta′tion** *n.* —**ex·ploit′a·tive** *adj.* —**ex·ploit′er** *n.*

ex·plore (ck splôr′) *vt., vi.* -plored′, -plor′ing [< L *ex*-, out + *plorare*, cry out] 1 to examine (something) carefully; investigate 2 to travel in (a little-known region) to learn about it —**ex·plo·ra·tion** (eks′plə rā′shən) *n.* —**ex·plor′a·to′ry** *adj.* —**ex·plor′er** *n.*

ex·plo·sion (ek splō′zhən) *n.* 1 an exploding 2 the noise made by exploding 3 a noisy outburst 4 a sudden, widespread increase

ex·plo·sive (-siv) *adj.* 1 of, causing, or like an explosion 2 tending to explode —*n.* a substance that can explode, as gunpowder —**ex·plo′sive·ly** *adv.* —**ex·plo′sive·ness** *n.*

ex·po·nent (ek spōn′ənt; *also, esp. for 3*, eks′ pōn′-) *n.* 1 one who expounds or promotes (principles, etc.) 2 a person or thing that is an example or symbol (*of* something) 3 *Algebra* a symbol placed at the upper right of another to show how many times the latter is to be multiplied by itself (Ex.: $b^2 = b \times b$)

ex·po·nen·tial (eks′pō nen′shəl) *adj.* 1 *Math.* of an exponent 2 of or increasing by very large amounts, etc.

ex·port (ek spôrt′; *also, and for n. always*, eks′ pôrt′) *vt.* [< L *ex*-, out + *portare*, to carry] 1 to send (goods) to another country, esp. for sale 2 to send (ideas, culture, etc.) from one place to another —*n.* 1 something exported 2 an exporting —**ex′por·ta′tion** *n.* —**ex·port′er** *n.*

ex·pose (ek spōz′) *vt.* -posed′, -pos′ing [see EXPOUND] 1 to lay open (*to* danger, etc.) 2 to reveal; exhibit 3 to make (a crime, etc.) known 4 *Photog.* to subject (a sensitized film or plate) to light, etc.

ex·po·sé (eks′pō zā′) *n.* [Fr] a public disclosure of a scandal, crime, etc.

ex·po·si·tion (eks′pə zish′ən) *n.* 1 a detailed explanation 2 writing or speaking that explains 3 a large public exhibition or show

ex·pos·i·tor (ek späz′ət ər) *n.* one who expounds or explains

ex·pos·i·to·ry (-ə tôr′ē) *adj.* of or containing exposition; explanatory

ex post fac·to (eks′ pōst fak′tō) [L, from (the thing) done afterward] done afterward, but retroactive

ex·pos·tu·late (ek späs′chə lāt′) *vi.* -lat′ed, -lat′ing [< L *ex*-, intens. + *postulare*, to demand] to reason with a person earnestly, objecting to that person's actions —**ex·pos′tu·la′tion** *n.*

ex·po·sure (ek spō′zhər) *n.* 1 an exposing or being exposed 2 a location, as of a house, in relation to the sun, etc. [an eastern *exposure*] 3 frequent appearance before the public 4 *Photog. a*) the subjection of a sensitized film or plate to light, X-rays, etc. *b*) a section of a film for one picture *c*) the time during which a camera's shutter is open

ex·pound (ek spound′) *vt.* [< L *ex*-, out + *ponere*, to put] 1 to state in detail 2 to explain

ex·press (ek spres′) *vt.* [< L *ex*-, out + *premere*, to press] 1 to squeeze out (juice, etc.) 2 to put into words; state 3 to reveal; show 4 to symbolize; signify 5 to send by express —*adj.* 1 stated; expressed; explicit 2 specific 3 fast, direct, and making few stops [an *express* bus] 4 marked by speed [an *express* highway] 5 having to do with an express train, bus, service, etc. —*adv.* by express —*n.* 1 an express train, bus, etc. 2 *a*) a service for transporting things rapidly *b*) the things sent by express

ex·pres·sion (ek spresh′ən) *n.* 1 a putting into words; stating 2 a manner of expressing, esp. with eloquence 3 a particular word or phrase 4 a showing of feeling, character, etc. 5 a look, intonation, etc. that conveys meaning 6 a mathematical symbol or set of symbols —**ex·pres′sion·less** *adj.*

ex·pres·sion·ism *n.* [*often* E–] a movement in art, literature, etc. during the early 1900s seeking to give symbolic, objective expression to inner experience —**ex·pres′sion·ist** *adj., n.* —**ex·pres′sion·is′tic** *adj.*

ex·pres·sive *adj.* 1 that expresses 2 full of meaning or feeling —**ex·pres′sive·ly** *adv.*

ex·press·ly *adv.* 1 plainly; definitely 2 especially; particularly

ex·press·way *n.* a divided highway for high-speed, through traffic, with overpasses and exit ramps at intersections

ex·pro·pri·ate (eks prō′prē āt′) *vt.* -at′ed, -at′ing [< L *ex*-, out + *proprius*, one's own] to take (land, etc.) from its owner, esp. for public use —**ex·pro′pri·a′tion** *n.*

ex·pul·sion (ek spul′shən) *n.* an expelling or being expelled

ex·punge (ek spunj′) *vt.* **-punged′, -pung′ ing** ⟦< L *ex-*, out + *pungere*, to prick⟧ to blot or strike out; erase

ex·pur·gate (eks′pər gāt′) *vt.* **-gat′ed, -gat′ ing** ⟦< L *ex-*, out + *purgare*, cleanse⟧ to remove (passages considered obscene, etc.) from (a book, etc.) **—ex′pur·ga′tion** *n.*

ex·qui·site (eks′kwi zit, ek skwiz′it) *adj.* ⟦< L *ex-*, out + *quaerere*, to ask⟧ **1** carefully or elaborately done **2** very beautiful, delicate, etc. **3** of highest quality **4** very intense; keen

ext *abbrev.* extension

ex·tant (eks′tənt, ek stant′) *adj.* ⟦< L *ex-*, out + *stare*, to stand⟧ still existing; not extinct

ex·tem·po·ra·ne·ous (eks′tem′pə rā′nē əs) *adj.* ⟦see fol.⟧ done or spoken with little preparation **—ex′tem′po·ra′ne·ous·ly** *adv.*

ex·tem·po·re (ek stem′pə rē) *adv., adj.* ⟦< L *ex-*, out of + *tempus*, time⟧ with little preparation; offhand

ex·tem·po·rize (-rīz′) *vi., vt.* **-rized′, -riz′ing** to speak, perform, etc. extempore; improvise

ex·tend (ek stend′) *vt.* ⟦< L *ex-*, out + *tendere*, to stretch⟧ **1** to make longer; stretch out; prolong **2** to enlarge in area, scope, etc.; expand **3** to stretch forth **4** to offer; grant **5** to make (oneself) work hard **—vi.** to be extended **—ex·tend′ed** *adj.* **—ex·tend′er** *n.* **—ex·ten′si·ble** (-sten′sə bəl) *adj.*, **ex·tend′i·ble**

extended care nursing care for a limited time after hospitalization

extended family a nuclear family together with other relatives living with or near them

ex·ten·sion (-sten′shən) *n.* **1** an extending or being extended **2** range; extent **3** a part forming a continuation or addition **4** an extra telephone connected to the main line

ex·ten·sive (-siv) *adj.* having great extent; vast; far-reaching **—ex·ten′sive·ly** *adv.* **—ex·ten′sive·ness** *n.*

ex·tent (ek stent′) *n.* **1** the space, amount, or degree to which a thing extends; size **2** scope; limits **3** an extended space; vast area

ex·ten·u·ate (ek sten′yōō āt′) *vt.* **-at′ed, -at′ ing** ⟦< L *ex-*, out + *tenuis*, thin⟧ to make (an offense, etc.) seem less serious **—ex·ten′u·a′tion** *n.*

ex·te·ri·or (ek stir′ē ər) *adj.* **1** *a)* on the outside; outer *b)* to be used on the outside [*exterior* paint] **2** coming from without **—n.** an outside or outside surface

ex·ter·mi·nate (ek stur′mə nāt′) *vt.* **-nat′ed, -nat′ing** ⟦< L *ex-*, out + *terminus*, boundary⟧ to destroy entirely; wipe out **—ex·ter′mi·na′ tion** *n.*

ex·ter·mi·na·tor (-nāt′ər) *n.* one that exterminates; specif., one whose work is exterminating vermin

ex·ter·nal (ek stur′nəl) *adj.* ⟦< L *externus*⟧ **1** on or of the outside **2** existing apart from the mind; material **3** coming from without **4** superficial **5** foreign **—n.** an outside surface or part **—ex·ter′nal·ly** *adv.*

ex·tinct (ek stinkt′) *adj.* ⟦see EXTINGUISH⟧ **1** having died down; extinguished **2** no longer in existence

ex·tinc·tion *n.* **1** an extinguishing **2** a destroying or being destroyed **3** a dying out: said of a species

ex·tin·guish (ek stin′gwish) *vt.* ⟦< L *ex-*, out + *stinguere*, extinguish⟧ **1** to put out (a fire, etc.) **2** to destroy **—ex·tin′guish·er** *n.*

ex·tir·pate (eks′tər pāt′) *vt.* **-pat′ed, -pat′ ing** ⟦< L *ex-*, out + *stirps*, root⟧ to destroy completely **—ex′tir·pa′tion** *n.*

ex·tol or **ex·toll** (ek stōl′) *vt.* **-tolled′, -tol′ ling** ⟦< L *ex-*, up + *tollere*, to raise⟧ to praise highly; laud

ex·tort (ek stôrt′) *vt.* ⟦< L *ex-*, out + *torquere*, to twist⟧ to get (money, etc.) from someone by force or threats

ex·tor·tion *n.* **1** an extorting **2** something extorted **—ex·tor′tion·ate** *adj.* **—ex·tor′tion·ist** *n.*, **ex·tor′tion·er** *n.*

ex·tra (eks′trə) *adj.* ⟦< L *extra*, more than⟧ more or better than normal, expected, etc. **—n.** an extra person or thing; specif., *a)* a special edition of a newspaper *b)* an extra benefit *c)* an actor hired by the day to play a minor part **—adv.** more so than usual

extra- ⟦see EXTERNAL⟧ *prefix* outside, beyond, besides

ex·tract (ek strakt′; *for n.* eks′trakt′) *vt.* ⟦< L *ex-*, out + *trahere*, to draw⟧ **1** to draw out by effort **2** to obtain by pressing, distilling, etc. **3** to deduce, derive, or elicit **4** to select or quote (a passage, etc.) **—n.** something extracted; specif., *a)* a concentrate [*beef extract*] *b)* an excerpt

ex·trac·tion *n.* **1** the act or process of extracting **2** origin; descent

ex·tra·cur·ric·u·lar (eks′trə kə rik′yōō lər) *adj.* not part of the required curriculum

ex·tra·dite (eks′trə dīt′) *vt.* **-dit′ed, -dit′ing** ⟦< L *ex*, out + *traditio*, a surrender⟧ to turn over (an alleged criminal, etc.) to the jurisdiction of another country, U.S. state, etc. **—ex′tra·di′tion** (-dish′ən) *n.*

ex·tra·le·gal (eks′trə lē′gəl) *adj.* outside of legal control

ex·tra·mar·i·tal (-mar′ət′l) *adj.* having to do with sexual intercourse with someone other than one's spouse

ex·tra·ne·ous (ek strā′nē əs) *adj.* ⟦L *extraneus*, foreign⟧ **1** coming from outside; foreign **2** not pertinent; irrelevant **—ex·tra′ne·ous·ly** *adv.*

ex·tra·or·di·nar·y (ek strôrd′'n ər′ē) *adj.* ⟦< L *extra ordinem*, out of order⟧ **1** not ordinary **2** going far beyond the ordinary; remarkable

ex·trap·o·late (ek strap′ə lāt′) *vt., vi.* **-lat′ed, -lat′ing** ⟦see EXTRA- & INTERPOLATE⟧ to estimate (something unknown) on the basis of known facts **—ex·trap′o·la′tion** *n.*

ex·tra·sen·so·ry (eks′trə sen′sə rē) *adj.* apart from, or in addition to, normal sense perception

ex·tra·ter·res·tri·al (-tə res′trē əl) *adj.* being, of, or from outside the earth's limits **—n.** an extraterrestrial being, as in science fiction

ex·trav·a·gant (ek strav′ə gənt) *adj.* ⟦< L *extra*, beyond + *vagari*, to wander⟧ **1** going beyond reasonable limits; excessive **2** costing or spending too much **—ex·trav′a·gance** *n.*

ex·trav·a·gan·za (ek strav′ə gan′zə) *n.* a spectacular theatrical production

ex·treme (ek strēm′) *adj.* ⟦< L *exterus*, outer⟧ **1** farthest away; utmost **2** *a)* very great *b)* excessive **3** unconventional or radical, as in politics **4** harsh; drastic **5** involving great risk, difficulty, etc. [*extreme sports*] **—***n.* **1** either of two things that are as different or far as possible from each other **2** an extreme act, state, etc. **3** *Math.* the first or last term of a proportion **—ex·treme′ly** *adv.*

ex·trem·ism *n.* a going to extremes, esp. in politics **—ex·trem′ist** *adj., n.*

ex·trem·i·ty (ek strem′ə tē) *n., pl.* **-ties 1** the outermost part; end **2** the greatest degree **3** great need, danger, etc. **4** an extreme measure: *usually used in pl.* **5** [*pl.*] the hands and feet

ex·tri·cate (eks′tri kāt′) *vt.* **-cat′ed, -cat′ing** ⟦< L *ex-*, out + *tricae*, vexations⟧ to set free (*from* a net, difficulty, etc.) **—ex·tri·ca′tion** *n.*

ex·trin·sic (eks trin′sik, -zik) *adj.* ⟦< L *exter*, without + *secus*, otherwise⟧ not inherent **—ex·trin′si·cal·ly** *adv.*

ex·tro·vert (eks′trə vurt′) *n.* ⟦< L *extra-*, outside + *vertere*, to turn⟧ one who is active and expressive rather than introspective **—ex′tro·ver′sion** (-vur′zhən) *n.* **—ex′tro·vert′ed** *adj.*

ex·trude (ek strōōd′) *vt.* **-trud′ed, -trud′ing** ⟦< L *ex-*, out + *trudere*, to thrust⟧ to force out, as through a small opening **—***vi.* to be extruded **—ex·tru′sion** *n.*

ex·u·ber·ant (eg zōō′bər ənt) *adj.* ⟦< L *ex-*, intens. + *uberare*, bear abundantly⟧ **1** growing profusely; luxuriant **2** characterized by high spirits **—ex·u′ber·ance** *n.* **—ex·u′ber·ant·ly** *adv.*

ex·ude (eg zōōd′) *vt., vi.* **-ud′ed, -ud′ing** ⟦< L *ex-*, out + *sudare*, to sweat⟧ **1** to ooze **2** to seem to radiate [*to exude* joy] **—ex·u·da·tion** (eks′yōō dā′shən, egz′-) *n.*

ex·ult (eg zult′) *vi.* ⟦< L *ex-*, intens. + *saltare*, to leap⟧ to rejoice greatly; glory **—ex·ult′ant** *adj.* **—ex·ul·ta·tion** (eg′zəl tā′shən, eks′əl-) *n.*

ex·ur·bi·a (eks ur′bē ə) *n.* ⟦EX- + (SUB)URBIA⟧ the semirural communities beyond the suburbs, typically lived in by upper-income families **—ex·ur′ban** *adj.* **—ex·ur′ban·ite′** *adj., n.*

eye (ī) *n.* ⟦OE *ēage*⟧ **1** the organ of sight in humans and animals **2** *a)* the eyeball *b)* the iris [*brown eyes*] **3** the area around the eye [a black *eye*] **4** [*often pl.*] sight; vision **5** a look; glance **6** attention; observation **7** the power of judging, etc. by eyesight [a good *eye* for detail] **8** [*often pl.*] judgment; opinion [in the *eyes* of the law] **9** a thing like an eye in appearance or function **—***vt.* eyed, eye′ing or ey′ing to look at; observe **—have an eye for** to have a keen appreciation of **—keep an eye on** to look after **—lay (or set or clap) eyes on** to look at **—make eyes at** to look at amorously **—see eye to eye** to agree completely **—with an eye to** paying attention to; considering

eye·ball *n.* the ball-shaped part of the eye **—***vt.* [Inf.] to examine or measure visually

eye·brow *n.* the bony arch over each eye, or the hair growing on this

eye·catch·er *n.* something that especially attracts one's attention **—eye′-catch′ing** *adj.*

eye·drops *pl.n.* liquid medicine for the eyes, applied as with a dropper

eye·ful (-fool′) *n.* [Slang] a person or thing that looks striking or unusual

eye·glass *n.* **1** a lens to help faulty vision **2** [*pl.*] a pair of such lenses in a frame; glasses

eye·lash *n.* any of the hairs on the edge of the eyelid

eye·let (-lit) *n.* **1** a small hole for receiving a cord, hook, etc. **2** a metal ring for reinforcing such a hole **3** a small hole edged by stitching in embroidery

eye·lid *n.* either of the two folds of flesh that cover and uncover the eyeball

eye-o·pen·er (-ō′pə nər) *n.* a surprising piece of news, sudden realization, etc. **—eye′-o′pen·ing** *adj.*

eye·piece *n.* in a telescope, microscope, etc., the lens or lenses nearest the viewer's eye

eye·sight *n.* **1** the power of seeing; sight **2** the range of vision

eye·sore *n.* an unpleasant sight

eye·strain *n.* a tired or strained condition of the eye muscles

eye·tooth *n., pl.* **-teeth′** a canine tooth of the upper jaw

eye·wear *n.* eyeglasses, sunglasses, etc.

eye·wit·ness *n.* one who sees or has seen something happen, as a crime, etc.

ey·rie or **ey·ry** (er′ē, ir′ē) *n., pl.* **-ries** AERIE

F

f¹ or **F** (ef) *n., pl.* **f's, F's** the sixth letter of the English alphabet

f² *abbrev.* ⟦It⟧ *Music* FORTE²

F¹ (ef) *n.* **1** *Educ.* a grade for failing work or, sometimes, fair or average work **2** *Music* the fourth tone in the scale of C major

F² *abbrev.* **1** Fahrenheit **2** female or feminine **3** folio(s) **4** following **5** franc(s) **6** Friday

F³ *Chem. symbol for* fluorine

fa (fä) *n.* ⟦< ML⟧ *Music* the fourth tone of the diatonic scale

FAA *abbrev.* Federal Aviation Administration

fa·ble (fā′bəl) *n.* ⟦< L *fabula*, a story⟧ **1** a fictitious story, usually about animals, meant to teach a moral lesson **2** a myth or legend **3** a falsehood

fa·bled *adj.* **1** mythical; legendary **2** unreal; fictitious

fab·ric (fab′rik) *n.* ⟦< L *fabrica*, workshop⟧ **1** a framework; structure **2** a material, as cloth, that is made from fibers, etc. by weaving, felting, etc.

fab·ri·cate (fab′ri kāt′) *vt.* **-cat′ed, -cat′ing** ⟦see prec.⟧ **1** to make, build, construct, etc. **2** to make up (a lie, etc.); invent —**fab′ri·ca′tion** *n.* —**fab′ri·ca′tor** *n.*

fab·u·lous (fab′yōō ləs) *adj.* ⟦see FABLE⟧ **1** of or like a fable; fictitious **2** incredible; astounding **3** [Inf.] wonderful —**fab′u·lous·ly** *adv.*

fa·cade *or* **fa·çade** (fə säd′) *n.* ⟦Fr: see fol.⟧ **1** the front or main face of a building **2** an imposing appearance concealing something inferior

face (fās) *n.* ⟦< L *facies*⟧ **1** the front of the head **2** the expression of the countenance **3** the main or front surface **4** the surface that is marked, as of a clock, etc., or that is finished, as of fabric, etc. **5** the appearance; outward aspect **6** dignity; self-respect: usually in **lose** (or **save**) **face** —*vt.* **faced, fac′ing 1** to turn, or have the face turned, toward **2** to confront with boldness, etc. **3** to cover with a new surface —*vi.* to turn, or have the face turned, in a specified direction —**face to face 1** confronting each other **2** very near to: with *with* —**face up to** to face with courage —**in the face of 1** in the presence of **2** in spite of —**make a face** to grimace —**on the face of it** apparently

-faced (fāst) *combining form* having a (specified kind of) face [round-*faced*]

face·less *adj.* without individuality; anonymous

face-lift *n.* **1** plastic surgery to remove wrinkles, etc. from the face **2** an altering, cleaning, etc., as of a building's exterior Also **face lift** —*vt.* to perform a face-lift on

face-off *n.* **1** *Hockey* the start or resumption of play when the referee drops the puck between two opposing players **2** [Inf.] a confrontation

face-sav·ing *adj.* preserving one's dignity or self-respect

fac·et (fas′it) *n.* ⟦see FACE⟧ **1** any of the polished plane surfaces of a cut gem **2** any of a number of sides or aspects, as of a personality —*vt.* **-et·ed** *or* **-et·ted, -et·ing** *or* **-et·ting** to cut or make facets on

fa·ce·tious (fə sē′shəs) *adj.* ⟦< L *facetus*, witty⟧ joking, esp. about something serious —**fa·ce′tious·ly** *adv.*

face value 1 the value printed on a bill, bond, etc. **2** the seeming value

fa·cial (fā′shəl) *adj.* of or for the face —*n.* a cosmetic treatment, massage, etc. for the skin of the face

facial tissue a sheet of soft tissue paper used as a handkerchief, etc.

fac·ile (fas′il) *adj.* ⟦Fr < L *facere*, do⟧ **1** not hard to do **2** working or done easily **3** superficial

fa·cil·i·tate (fə sil′ə tāt′) *vt.* **-tat′ed, -tat′ing** ⟦see prec.⟧ to make easier —**fa·cil′i·ta′tion** *n.* —**fa·cil′i·ta′tor** *n.*

fa·cil·i·ty (-tē) *n., pl.* **-ties 1** ease of doing **2** skill; dexterity **3** [*usually pl.*] the means by which something can be done **4** a building, room, etc. for some activity

fac·ing (fās′iŋ) *n.* **1** a lining on the edge of a garment **2** a covering of contrasting material on a building

fac·sim·i·le (fak sim′ə lē) *n.* ⟦< L *facere*, make + *simile*, similar⟧ an exact reproduction or copy

fact (fakt) *n.* ⟦< L *facere*, do⟧ **1** a deed, esp. a criminal deed [an accessory before (or after) the *fact*] **2** a thing that has actually happened or is really true **3** reality; truth **4** something stated to be true —**as a matter of fact** in reality: also **in fact**

fac·tion (fak′shən) *n.* ⟦see prec.⟧ **1** a group of people in an organization working together in a common cause against the main body **2** dissension —**fac′tion·al** *adj.* —**fac′tion·al·ism′** *n.*

fac·tious (-shəs) *adj.* causing dissension or faction

fac·ti·tious (fak tish′əs) *adj.* ⟦see FACT⟧ forced or artificial

fac·toid (fak′toid) *n.* ⟦FACT + -OID⟧ **1** a spurious fact **2** a trivial or useless fact or statistic

fac·tor (fak′tər) *n.* ⟦< L *facere*, do⟧ **1** one who transacts business for another **2** any of the conditions, etc. that bring about a result **3** *Math.* any of the quantities which form a product when multiplied together —*vt. Math.* to resolve into factors —**factor in** (or **into**) to include as a factor

fac·to·ry (fak′tə rē; *often* fak′trē) *n., pl.* **-ries** ⟦see prec.⟧ a building or buildings in which things are manufactured

fac·to·tum (fak tōt′əm) *n.* ⟦< L *facere*, do + *totum*, all⟧ a handyman

fac·tu·al (fak′chōō əl) *adj.* **1** of or containing facts **2** real; actual

fac·ul·ty (fak′əl tē) *n., pl.* **-ties** ⟦see FACILE⟧ **1** any natural or specialized power of a living organism **2** special aptitude or skill **3** all the teachers of a school or of one of its departments

fad (fad) *n.* ⟦< Brit dial.⟧ a style, etc. that interests many people for a short time; passing fashion —**fad′dish** *adj.*

fade (fād) *vi.* **fad′ed, fad′ing** ⟦< OFr *fade*, pale⟧ **1** to lose color, brilliance, etc. **2** to lose freshness or strength **3** to disappear slowly; die out —*vt.* to cause to fade —**fade in** (or **out**) *Film, Radio, TV* to appear (or disappear) gradually

fa·er·ie or **fa·er·y** (fā′ər ē, fer′ē) *n.* [Archaic] 1 fairyland 2 *pl.* **-ies** a fairy

fag (fag) *vi., vt.* **fagged, fag′ging** [< ?] to make or become very tired by hard work

fag·ot or **fag·got** (fag′ət) *n.* [ult. < Gr *phakelos*, a bundle] a bundle of sticks or twigs, esp. for use as fuel

fag·ot·ing or **fag·got·ing** *n.* 1 a hemstitch with wide spaces 2 openwork with crisscross or barlike stitches across the open seam

Fahr·en·heit (fer′ən hīt′) *adj.* [after G. D. *Fahrenheit* (1686-1736), Ger physicist] designating or of a temperature scale in which 32° is the freezing point and 212° is the boiling point of water

fail (fāl) *vi.* [< L *fallere*, deceive] 1 to be insufficient; fall short 2 to weaken; die away 3 to stop operating 4 to be negligent in a duty, expectation, etc. 5 to be unsuccessful 6 to become bankrupt 7 *Educ.* to get a grade of failure —*vt.* 1 to be of no help to; disappoint 2 to leave; abandon 3 to neglect: used with an infinitive 4 *Educ.* to give a grade of failure to or get such a grade in —**without fail** 1 without failing (to occur, do, etc.) 2 consistently every time

fail·ing *n.* 1 a failure 2 a fault —*prep.* without; lacking

fail-safe *adj.* of an intricate procedure or mechanism for preventing a malfunction or accidental operation, as of nuclear weapons —*n.* such a procedure or mechanism

fail·ure (fāl′yər) *n.* 1 *a)* a falling short *b)* a weakening *c)* a breakdown in operation *d)* neglect *e)* a not succeeding *f)* a becoming bankrupt 2 one that does not succeed 3 *Educ.* a failing to pass, or a grade showing this

fain (fān) *adj., adv.* [< OE *fægen*, glad] [Archaic] glad(ly); willing(ly)

faint (fānt) *adj.* [see FEIGN] 1 weak; feeble 2 timid 3 feeling weak and dizzy 4 indistinct —*n.* a state of temporary unconsciousness —*vi.* to fall into a faint —**faint′ly** *adv.*

fair¹ (fer) *adj.* [< OE *fæger*] 1 attractive; beautiful 2 unblemished; clean 3 blond [*fair* hair] 4 clear and sunny 5 easy to read [a *fair* hand] 6 just and honest 7 according to the rules 8 moderately large 9 average [in *fair* condition] 10 *Baseball* that is not foul —*adv.* in a fair manner —**fair′ness** *n.*

fair² (fer) *n.* [< L *feriae*, festivals] 1 [Historical] a regular gathering for barter and sale of goods 2 a carnival or bazaar, often for charity 3 a competitive exhibition of farm, household, and manufactured products, with various amusements and educational displays 4 a show or convention with exhibits, vendors, etc. [a science *fair*]

fair game a legitimate object of attack or pursuit

fair-haired *adj.* 1 having blond hair 2 [Inf.] favorite

fair·ly *adv.* 1 justly; honestly 2 somewhat; moderately

fair shake [Inf.] fair or just treatment

fair·way *n.* the mowed part of a golf course between a tee and a green

fair·y (fer′ē) *n., pl.* **-ies** [< OFr *fée*] an imaginary being in human form, with magic powers —*adj.* 1 of fairies 2 graceful; delicate

fair·y·land *n.* 1 the imaginary land where the fairies live 2 a lovely, enchanting place

fairy tale 1 a story about fairies, magic deeds, etc. 2 an unbelievable or untrue story

fait ac·com·pli (fe tà kōn plē′; E fāt′ə käm′ plē′) [Fr] something already done, making opposition useless

faith (fāth) *n.* [< L *fidere*, to trust] 1 unquestioning belief, specif. in God, a religion, etc. 2 a particular religion 3 complete trust or confidence 4 loyalty

faith·ful (-fəl) *adj.* 1 loyal 2 conscientious 3 accurate; reliable —**faith′ful·ly** *adv.* —**faith′ ful·ness** *n.*

faith·less (-lis) *adj.* 1 dishonest or disloyal 2 unreliable —**faith′less·ly** *adv.* —**faith′less· ness** *n.*

fa·ji·ta (fä hē′tä) *n.* [AmSp] a dish of grilled strips of beef, chicken, etc., often wrapped in a soft tortilla

fake (fāk) *vt., vi.* **faked, fak′ing** [< ?] to make (something) seem real, etc. by deception —*n.* a fraud; counterfeit —*adj.* 1 sham; false 2 artificial —**fak′er** *n.* —**fak′er·y** *n.*

fa·kir (fə kir′) *n.* [Ar *faqīr*, lit., poor] a Muslim or Hindu itinerant beggar, often one reputed to perform marvels

fa·la·fel (fə läf′əl) *n.* [< Ar] a deep-fried patty of ground chickpeas

fal·con (fal′kən, fôl′-, fäl′-) *n.* [ult. < L *falx*, sickle] any bird of prey trained to hunt small game —**fal′con·er** *n.* —**fal′con·ry** *n.*

fall (fôl) *vi.* **fell, fall′en, fall′ing** [OE *feallan*] 1 to come down by gravity; drop; descend 2 to come down suddenly from an upright position; tumble or collapse 3 to be wounded or killed in battle 4 to take a downward direction 5 to become lower, less, weaker, etc. 6 to lose power, status, etc. 7 to do wrong; sin 8 to be captured 9 to take on a sad look [my face *fell*] 10 to take place; occur 11 to come by lot, inheritance, etc. 12 to pass into a specified condition [to *fall* ill] 13 to be directed by chance 14 to be divided (*into*) —*n.* 1 a dropping; descending 2 a coming down suddenly from an upright position 3 a downward direction or slope 4 a becoming lower or less 5 an overthrow; ruin 6 a loss of status, reputation, etc. 7 a yielding to temptation 8 autumn 9 the amount of what has fallen [a six-inch *fall* of snow] 10 the distance that something falls 11 [*usually pl.*, *often with sing. v.*] water falling over a cliff, etc. 12 a long tress of hair, added to a woman's hairdo —*adj.* of, in, for, or like autumn —**fall back** to withdraw; retreat —**fall for** [Inf.] 1 to fall in love with 2 to be tricked by —**fall in** to line up in formation —**fall off** to become smaller, worse, etc. —**fall on** (or **upon**) to attack —**fall out** 1 to quarrel 2 to leave one's place in a formation —**fall short** to fail to reach, suffice, etc. —**fall through** to fail —**fall to** 1 to begin 2 to start eating

fal·la·cious (fə lā′shəs) *adj.* ⟦see fol.⟧ 1 erroneous 2 misleading or deceptive —**fal·la′cious·ly** *adv.*

fal·la·cy (fal′ə sē) *n., pl.* **-cies** ⟦< L *fallere*, deceive⟧ 1 a mistaken idea; error 2 a flaw in reasoning

fall·en (fôl′ən) *adj.* that fell; dropped, prostrate, ruined, dead, etc.

fall guy [Slang] one put in a position to take the blame, etc. for a scheme that has miscarried

fal·li·ble (fal′ə bəl) *adj.* ⟦< L *fallere*, deceive⟧ liable to be mistaken, deceived, or erroneous —**fal′li·bil′i·ty** *n.*, **fal′li·ble·ness** —**fal′li·bly** *adv.*

fall·ing-out *n.* a quarrel

falling star METEOR (*n.* 1)

fall·off *n.* a decline

fal·lo·pi·an tube (fə lō′pē ən) ⟦after G. *Fallopius* (1523–62), It anatomist⟧ [*also* **F- t-**] either of two tubes that carry ova from the ovaries to the uterus

fall·out *n.* 1 the descent to earth of radioactive particles, as after a nuclear explosion 2 these particles 3 an incidental consequence, esp. when harmful

fal·low (fal′ō) *adj.* ⟦< OE *fealh*⟧ 1 left unplanted 2 inactive

false (fôls) *adj.* **fals′er, fals′est** ⟦< L *fallere*, deceive⟧ 1 not true; incorrect; wrong 2 untruthful; lying 3 unfaithful 4 misleading 5 not real; artificial —*adv.* in a false manner —**false′ly** *adv.* —**false′ness** *n.*

false·hood *n.* 1 falsity 2 a lie

false start in a race, the act of starting before the official signal has been given —**false′-start′** *adj., vi.*

fal·set·to (fôl set′ō) *n., pl.* **-tos** ⟦It, dim. of *falso*, false⟧ an artificial way of speaking or singing in which the voice is much higher pitched than normal

fal·si·fy (fôl′sə fī′) *vt.* **-fied′, -fy′ing** 1 to misrepresent 2 to alter (a record, etc.) fraudulently —**fal′si·fi·ca′tion** *n.* —**fal′si·fi′er** *n.*

fal·si·ty (-tē) *n.* 1 the quality of being false 2 *pl.* **-ties** a lie

Fal·staff (fôl′staf′), Sir **John** in Shakespeare's plays, a fat, witty, boastful but cowardly knight

fal·ter (fôl′tər) *vi.* ⟦prob. < ON⟧ 1 to move unsteadily; stumble 2 to stammer 3 to act hesitantly; waver —**fal′ter·ing·ly** *adv.*

fame (fām) *n.* ⟦< L *fama*⟧ 1 reputation, esp. for good 2 the state of being well known —**famed** *adj.*

fa·mil·ial (fə mil′yəl) *adj.* of or common to a family

fa·mil·iar (fə mil′yər) *adj.* ⟦see FAMILY⟧ 1 friendly or intimate 2 too friendly; unduly intimate 3 closely acquainted (*with*) 4 common; ordinary —**fa·mil′iar·ly** *adv.*

fa·mil·iar·i·ty (-ē er′ə tē) *n., pl.* **-ties** 1 intimacy 2 informal behavior 3 undue intimacy 4 close acquaintance (*with* something)

fa·mil·iar·ize (-yər īz′) *vt.* **-ized′, -iz′ing** 1 to make commonly known 2 to make (another

or oneself) fully acquainted —**fa·mil′iar·i·za′tion** *n.*

fam·i·ly (fam′ə lē, fam′lē) *n., pl.* **-lies** ⟦< L *familia*⟧ 1 parents and their children 2 relatives 3 all those descended from a common ancestor; lineage 4 a group of similar or related things —*adj.* suitable for a family; specif., wholesome

family planning the regulation, as by birth control methods, of the size, etc. of a family

family practitioner a doctor specializing in the general medical needs of the family

family room a room in a home set apart for relaxation and recreation

family tree a genealogical chart for a given family

fam·ine (fam′in) *n.* ⟦< L *fames*, hunger⟧ 1 an acute and general shortage of food 2 any acute shortage

fam·ish (-ish) *vt., vi.* ⟦see prec.⟧ to make or be very hungry

fa·mous (fā′məs) *adj.* 1 having fame; renowned 2 [Inf.] excellent; very good

fa·mous·ly *adv.* 1 in a way, statement, etc. that has become famous 2 very well [*getting along famously*]

fan¹ (fan) *n.* ⟦< L *vannus*, basket for winnowing grain⟧ any device used to set up a current of air for ventilating or cooling —*vt.* **fanned**, **fan′ning** 1 to move (air) as with a fan 2 to direct air toward as with a fan 3 to stir up; excite 4 to strike (a batter) out —*vi. Baseball* to strike out —**fan out** to spread out

fan² (fan) *n.* ⟦< fol.⟧ a person enthusiastic about a specified sport, performer, etc.

fa·nat·ic (fə nat′ik) *n.* ⟦< L *fanum*, temple⟧ a fanatic person —*adj.* fanatical —**fa·nat′i·cism′** *n.*

fa·nat·i·cal *adj.* unreasonably enthusiastic; overly zealous —**fa·nat′i·cal·ly** *adv.*

fan·ci·er (fan′sē ər) *n.* a person with a special interest in something, specif. in plant or animal breeding

fan·ci·ful (fan′sə fəl) *adj.* 1 full of fancy; imaginative 2 imaginary; not real —**fan′ci·ful·ly** *adv.*

fan·cy (fan′sē) *n., pl.* **-cies** ⟦contr. < ME *fantasie*, fantasy⟧ 1 imagination when light, playful, etc. 2 a mental image 3 a notion; caprice; whim 4 a liking or fondness —*adj.* **-ci·er, -ci·est** 1 ornamental; elaborate [*a fancy necktie*] 2 of superior skill or quality —*vt.* **-cied, -cy·ing** 1 to imagine 2 to be fond of 3 to suppose —**fan′ci·ly** *adv.* —**fan′ci·ness** *n.*

fan·cy-free *adj.* carefree

fan·cy·work *n.* embroidery, crocheting, and other ornamental needlework

fan·dom (fan′dəm) *n.* fans collectively, as of a sport or entertainer

fan·fare (fan′fer′) ⟦Fr, prob. < *fanfaron*, braggart⟧ *n.* 1 a loud flourish of trumpets 2 noisy or showy display

fang (faŋ) *n.* ⟦OE < *fon*, seize⟧ 1 one of the long, pointed teeth of carnivorous animals 2 one of the long, hollow teeth through which poisonous snakes inject venom

fan·ta·sia (fan tā′zhə) *n.* a musical composition having no fixed form

fan·ta·size (fant′ə sīz′) *vt., vi.* **-sized′, -siz′ing** to indulge in fantasies or have daydreams (about)

fan·tas·tic (fan tas′tik) *adj.* [see fol.] **1** imaginary; unreal **2** grotesque; odd **3** extravagant **4** incredible **—fan·tas′ti·cal·ly** *adv.*

fan·ta·sy (fant′ə sē) *n., pl.* **-sies** [< Gr *phainein,* to show] **1** imagination or fancy **2** an illusion or reverie **3** fiction portraying highly fanciful settings or events

fan·ta·sy·land *n.* any imaginary or unreal place

far (fär) *adj.* **far′ther, far′thest** [OE *feorr*] **1** distant in space or time **2** more distant *[the far side]* **3** very different in quality or nature *[far from poor]* —*adv.* **1** very distant in space, time, or degree **2** to or from a distance in time or position **3** very much *[far better]* **—as far as** to the distance or degree that — **by far** very much; considerably: also **far and away —(in) so far as** to the extent that **—so far** up to this place, time, or degree

far·a·way *adj.* **1** distant in time, place, etc. **2** dreamy

farce (färs) *n.* [Fr < L *farcire,* to stuff] **1** (an) exaggerated comedy based on broadly humorous situations **2** an absurd or ridiculous action, pretense, etc. **—far·ci·cal** (fär′si kəl) *adj.*

fare (fer) *vi.* **fared, far′ing** [< OE *faran,* go] **1** to happen; result **2** to be in a specified condition *[to fare well]* —*n.* **1** money paid for transportation **2** a passenger who pays a fare **3** food

Far East EAST ASIA

fare·well (fer wel′; *for adj.* fer′wel′) *interj.* goodbye —*n.* good wishes at parting —*adj.* parting; final *[a farewell gesture]*

far-fetched (fär′fecht′) *adj.* barely believable; strained; unlikely

far-flung (-fluŋ′) *adj.* extending over a wide area

fa·ri·na (fə rē′nə) *n.* [< L, meal] flour or meal made from cereal grains, potatoes, etc. and eaten as a cooked cereal

far·i·na·ceous (far′ə nā′shəs) *adj.* [see prec.] **1** consisting of or made from flour or meal **2** like meal

farm (färm) *n.* [< ML *firma,* fixed payment] **1** a piece of land (with house, barns, etc.) on which crops or animals are raised: orig., such land let out to tenants **2** any place where certain things are raised *[a fish farm]* —*vt.* to cultivate (land) —*vi.* to work on or operate a farm **—farm out** to send (work) to be completed elsewhere

farm·er *n.* a person who manages or operates a farm

farm·hand *n.* a hired farm worker

farm·house *n.* a house on a farm

farm·ing *n.* the business of operating a farm; agriculture

farm·yard *n.* the yard surrounding or enclosed by farm buildings

far·o (fer′ō) *n.* [Fr *pharaon,* Pharaoh: from the picture of a Pharaoh on early French faro cards] a gambling game played with cards

far-off *adj.* distant; remote

far-out *adj.* [Inf.] nonconformist; esp., avant-garde

far·ra·go (fə rä′gō, -rä′-) *n., pl.* **-goes** [< L *far,* kind of grain] a jumble

far-reach·ing *adj.* having a wide range, extent, influence, or effect

far·ri·er (far′ē ər) *n.* [< L *ferrum,* iron] [Chiefly Brit.] a blacksmith

far·row (far′ō) *n.* [< OE *fearh,* young pig] a litter of pigs —*vt., vi.* to give birth to (a litter of pigs)

far·sight·ed (fär′sīt′id; *for 2,* -sīt′əd) *adj.* **1** planning ahead; provident: also **far′see′ing 2** seeing distant objects more clearly than near ones **—far′sight′ed·ness** *n.*

far·ther (fär′thər) *adj.* **1** *compar. of* FAR **2** more distant **3** additional; further —*adv.* **1** *compar. of* FAR **2** at or to a greater distance **3** to a greater degree; further Cf. FURTHER

far·thest (fär′thist) *adj.* **1** *superl. of* FAR **2** most distant —*adv.* **1** *superl. of* FAR **2** at or to the greatest distance or degree

far·thing (fär′thiŋ) *n.* [OE *feorthing*] a former British coin worth ¼ penny

fas·ci·nate (fas′ə nāt′) *vt.* **-nat′ed, -nat′ing** [< L *fascinum,* a charm] to hold the attention of, as by being very interesting or delightful; charm; captivate **—fas′ci·na′tion** *n.*

fas·cism (fash′iz′əm) *n.* [< It < L *fasces,* rods bound about an ax, ancient Roman symbol of authority] *[sometimes* F-] a system of government characterized by dictatorship, militaristic nationalism, racism, etc. **—fas′cist** *n., adj.*

fash·ion (fash′ən) *n.* [< L *factio,* a making] **1** the form or shape of a thing **2** way; manner **3** the current style of dress, conduct, etc. —*vt.* **1** to make; form **2** to fit; accommodate *(to)* **—after (or in) a fashion** to some extent **—fash′ion·er** *n.*

fash·ion·a·ble *adj.* **1** stylish **2** of or used by people who follow fashion **—fash′ion·a·bly** *adv.*

fast¹ (fast) *adj.* [OE *fæst*] **1** firm; firmly fastened **2** loyal; devoted **3** nonfading *[fast colors]* **4** swift; quick **5** ahead of time *[a fast watch]* **6** wild, promiscuous, or reckless **7** [Inf.] glib —*adv.* **1** firmly; fixedly **2** thoroughly *[fast asleep]* **3** rapidly

fast² (fast) *vi.* [OE *fæstan*] to abstain from all or certain foods —*n.* **1** a fasting **2** a period of fasting

fas·ten (fas′ən) *vt.* [see FAST¹] **1** to attach; connect **2** to make secure, as by locking, buttoning, etc. **3** to fix (the attention, etc.) *on* something —*vi.* to become fastened **—fas′ten·er** *n.*

fas·ten·ing *n.* anything used to fasten; bolt, clasp, hook, etc.

fast-food *adj.* designating a business that offers food, as hamburgers, prepared and served quickly (**fast food**)

fast forward 1 the setting on a DVD player, etc. that allows the user to advance quickly to a later point in the recording **2** the act or condition of speeding up and advancing —**fast'-for'ward** *vi., vt.*

fas·tid·i·ous (fa stid′ē əs) *adj.* [< L *fastus*, disdain] **1** not easy to please **2** daintily refined; oversensitive —**fas·tid′i·ous·ly** *adv.* —**fas·tid′i·ous·ness** *n.*

fast·ness *n.* **1** a being fast **2** a stronghold

fast-talk *vt.* [Inf.] to persuade with smooth, but often deceitful talk

fast-track *adj.* speedy or accelerated; expeditious [*fast-track* approval of a new drug] —*vt.* to speed up the progress of

fat (fat) *adj.* **fat′ter, fat′test** [< OE *fætt*] **1** containing fat; oily **2** *a)* fleshy; plump *b)* too plump **3** thick; broad **4** fertile [*fat* land] **5** profitable [a *fat* job] **6** plentiful —*n.* **1** an oily or greasy material found in animal tissue and plant seeds **2** the richest part of anything **3** superfluous part —**chew the fat** [Slang] to chat —**fat′ly** *adv.* —**fat′ness** *n.*

fa·tal (fāt′'l) *adj.* **1** fateful; decisive **2** resulting in death **3** destructive; disastrous —**fa′tal·ly** *adv.*

fa·tal·ism *n.* the belief that all events are determined by fate and are hence inevitable —**fa′tal·ist** *n.* —**fa′tal·is′tic** *adj.* —**fa′tal·is′ti·cal·ly** *adv.*

fa·tal·i·ty (fā tal′ə tē, fə-) *n., pl.* **-ties** **1** a deadly effect; deadliness **2** a death caused by a disaster or accident

fat·back *n.* fat from a hog's back, usually dried and salted in strips

fat cat [Slang] a wealthy, influential donor, esp. to a political campaign

fate (fāt) *n.* [< L *fatum*, oracle] **1** the power supposed to determine the outcome of events; destiny **2** one's lot or fortune **3** final outcome **4** death; destruction

fat·ed (fāt′id) *adj.* **1** destined **2** doomed

fate·ful (-fəl) *adj.* **1** prophetic **2** significant; decisive **3** controlled as if by fate —**fate′ful·ly** *adv.*

Fates (fāts) *pl.n. Gr. & Rom. Myth.* the three goddesses who control human destiny and life

fa·ther (fä′thər) *n.* [OE *feeder*] **1** a male parent **2** an ancestor **3** an originator, founder, or inventor **4** [*often* F-] a Christian priest: used esp. as a title **5** [F-] God —*vt.* to be the father of —**fa′ther·hood′** *n.* —**fa′ther·less** *adj.*

fa·ther-in-law *n., pl.* **fa′thers-in-law′** the father of one's spouse

fa·ther·land *n.* one's native land

fa·ther·ly *adj.* of or like a father; kind, protective, etc. —**fa′ther·li·ness** *n.*

fath·om (fath′əm) *n.* [< OE *fæthm*, the two arms outstretched] a length of 6 feet, used as a nautical unit of depth or length —*vt.* **1** to measure the depth of **2** to understand thoroughly —**fath′om·a·ble** *adj.* —**fath′om·less** *adj.*

fa·tigue (fə tēg′) *n.* [Fr < L *fatigare*, to weary] **1** exhaustion; weariness **2** [*pl.*] soldiers' work clothing **3** weakness developed in metal, etc. after continued stress —*vt., vi.* **-tigued′, -tigu′ing** to tire out

fat·so (fat′sō) *n., pl.* **-sos** or **-soes** [Slang] a fat person: somewhat derisive or contemptuous

fat·ten (fat′'n) *vt., vi.* to make or become fat (in various senses)

fat·ty *adj.* **-ti·er, -ti·est** **1** of or containing fat **2** like fat; greasy

fatty acid any of a group of organic acids in animal or vegetable fats and oils

fat·u·ous (fach′ōō əs) *adj.* [L *fatuus*] complacently stupid; foolish —**fa·tu·i·ty** (fə tōō′ə tē) *n.* —**fat′u·ous·ly** *adv.* —**fat′u·ous·ness** *n.*

fat·wa (fät′wä, fat′wə) *n.* [Ar] *Islam* a religious and legal decree issued by a council of religious leaders: also **fat′wa**

fau·cet (fô′sit) *n.* [prob. < OFr *fausser*, to breach] a device with a valve for regulating the flow of a liquid from a pipe, etc.; tap

Faulk·ner (fôk′nər), **Wil·liam** (wil′yəm) 1897-1962; U.S. novelist

fault (fôlt) *n.* [< L *fallere*, deceive] **1** something that mars; defect or failing **2** a misdeed or mistake **3** blame for something wrong **4** a fracture in bedrock produced by forces within the earth's crust, etc. **5** *Tennis, etc.* an improper serve —**at fault** deserving blame —**find fault (with)** to criticize

fault·find·ing *n., adj.* criticizing

fault·less *adj.* perfect

fault·y *adj.* **fault′i·er, fault′i·est** having a fault or faults; defective —**fault′i·ly** *adv.* —**fault′i·ness** *n.*

faun (fôn) *n.* [< L *faunus*] any of a class of minor Roman deities, half man and half goat

fau·na (fô′nə) *n.* [< LL *Fauna*, Roman goddess] the animals of a specified region or time

Faust (foust) *n.* a man in legend and literature who sells his soul to the devil for knowledge and power —**Faus′ti·an** *adj.*

faux pas (fō pä′) *pl.* **faux pas** (fō päz′) [Fr, lit., false step] a social blunder

fa·vor (fā′vər) *n.* [< L *favere*, to favor] **1** friendly regard; approval **2** partiality **3** a kind or obliging act **4** a small gift or token —*vt.* **1** to approve or like **2** to be partial to **3** to support; advocate **4** to make easier; help **5** to do a kindness for **6** to resemble [to *favor* one's mother] **7** to use gently [to *favor* a sore leg] Brit. sp. **fa′vour** —**in favor of** approving **2** to the advantage of —**fa′vor·er** *n.*

fa·vor·a·ble *adj.* **1** approving **2** helpful **3** pleasing —**fa′vor·a·bly** *adv.*

fa·vor·ite (fā′vər it) *n.* **1** a person or thing regarded with special liking **2** a contestant regarded as most likely to win —*adj.* most highly regarded; preferred

fa·vor·it·ism *n.* partiality; bias

fawn¹ (fôn) *vi.* [< OE *fægen*, glad] **1** to show friendliness by licking hands, etc.: said of a dog **2** to try to gain favor by acting humble, flattering, etc. —**fawn′er** *n.* —**fawn′ing·ly** *adv.*

fawn² (fôn) *n.* [< L *fetus*, progeny] **1** a deer less than one year old **2** a pale, yellowish brown —*adj.* of this color

fax (faks) *n.* [< FACSIMILE] **1** the electronic

sending (as over a telephone line) and reproduction of pictures, print, etc. **2** a reproduction made in this way —*vt.* to send by fax

fay (fā) *n.* [see FATE] a fairy

faze (fāz) *vt.* **fazed, faz′ing** [< OE *fesian*, to drive] to disturb; disconcert

FBI *abbrev.* Federal Bureau of Investigation

FCC *abbrev.* Federal Communications Commission

FDA *abbrev.* Food and Drug Administration

FDIC *abbrev.* Federal Deposit Insurance Corporation

Fe [L *ferrum*] *Chem. symbol for* iron

fe·al·ty (fē′əl tē) *n., pl.* **-ties** [< L *fidelitas*, fidelity] loyalty, esp. as owed to a feudal lord

fear (fir) *n.* [< OE *fær*, sudden attack] **1** anxiety caused by real or possible danger, pain, etc.; fright **2** awe; reverence **3** apprehension; concern **4** a cause for fear — *vt., vi.* **1** to be afraid (of) **2** to be in awe (of) **3** to expect with misgiving [I *fear* it will rain] —**fear′less** *adj.* —**fear′less·ly** *adv.*

fear·ful (-fəl) *adj.* **1** causing, feeling, or showing fear **2** [Inf.] very bad, great, etc. —**fear′ful·ly** *adv.* —**fear′ful·ness** *n.*

fear·some *adj.* causing fear; frightful

fea·si·ble (fē′zə bəl) *adj.* [< OFr *faire*, to do] **1** capable of being done; possible **2** likely; probable **3** suitable —**fea′si·bil′i·ty** *n.* —**fea′si·bly** *adv.*

feast (fēst) *n.* [< L *festus*, festal] **1** a religious festival **2** a rich and elaborate meal; banquet —*vi.* to have a feast —*vt.* **1** to entertain at a feast **2** to delight [to *feast* one's eyes on a sight] lō′) *n.* [< *mother-* (or *father-*, etc.) *in-law*] [Inf.] a relative by marriage

feat (fēt) *n.* [L *factum*, a deed] a deed of unusual daring or skill; exploit

feath·er (feth′ər) *n.* [OE *fether*] any of the soft, light growths covering the body of a bird —*vt.* **1** to provide or adorn with feathers **2** to turn (an oar or propeller blade) so that the edge is foremost —**feather in one's cap** a distinctive achievement —**feath′er·y** *adj.*

feath·er·bed·ding *n.* the practice of limiting output or requiring superfluous workers, as by union contract

feath·er·weight *n.* **1** a boxer with a maximum weight of 126 pounds **2** any person or thing of light weight or small size

fea·ture (fē′chər) *n.* [< L *facere*, to make] **1** *a*) [*pl.*] facial form or appearance *b*) any of the parts of the face **2** a distinct or outstanding part or quality of something **3** a special attraction, sale item, newspaper article, etc. **4** a film running more than 40 minutes —*vt.* **-tured, -tur·ing** to make a feature of —*vi.* to have a prominent part —**fea′ture·less** *adj.*

fea·tur·ette (fē′chər et′) *n.* a short film

fe·brile (fē′brəl, feb′rəl) *adj.* [< L *febris*, FEVER] feverish

Feb·ru·ar·y (feb′rōō er′ē, feb′yōō-) *n., pl.* **-ies** or **-ys** [< L *Februarius* (*mensis*), orig. month of expiation] the second month of the year, having 28 days (or 29 days in leap years): abbrev. **Feb.**

fe·ces (fē′sēz′) *pl.n.* [< L *faeces*, dregs] excrement —**fe′cal** (-kəl) *adj.*

feck·less (fek′lis) *adj.* [Scot < *feck*, effect + -LESS] **1** weak; ineffective **2** irresponsible —**feck′less·ly** *adv.*

fe·cund (fē′kənd, fek′ənd) *adj.* [< L *fecundus*] fertile; productive —**fe·cun·di·ty** (fē kun′də tē) *n.*

fe·cun·date (fē′kən dāt′, fek′ən-) *vt.* **-dat′ed, -dat′ing 1** to make fecund **2** to fertilize

fed¹ (fed) *vt., vi. pt. & pp. of* FEED —**fed up** [Inf.] having had enough to become disgusted, bored, etc.

fed² *n.* [Slang] a U.S. federal agent or officer

Fed *abbrev.* **1** Federal **2** Federation

fed·a·yeen (fed′ä yēn′) *pl.n.* [Ar *fidā'iyīn*, sacrificers] Arab guerrillas

fed·er·al (fed′ər əl) *adj.* [< L *foedus*, a league] **1** designating or of a union of states, etc. in which each member subordinates its power to a central authority **2** *a*) designating or of a central government in such a union *b*) [*often* F-] designating or of the central government of the U.S. **3** [F-] of or supporting a former U.S. political party (**Federalist Party**) which favored a strong centralized government **4** [F-] of or supporting the Union in the Civil War —*n.* [F-] a supporter or soldier of the Union in the Civil War —**fed′er·al·ism′** *n.* —**fed′er·al·ist** *adj., n.* —**fed′er·al·ly** *adv.*

fed·er·al·ize (-īz′) *vt.* **-ized′, -iz′ing 1** to unite (states, etc.) in a federal union **2** to put under federal authority —**fed′er·al·i·za′tion** *n.*

fed·er·ate (fed′ər āt′) *vt., vi.* **-at′ed, -at′ing** to unite in a federation

fed·er·a·tion (fed′ər ā′shən) *n.* [see FEDERAL] **1** a union of states, groups, etc. in which each subordinates its power to that of the central authority **2** a federated organization

fe·do·ra (fə dôr′ə) *n.* [Fr] a soft felt hat worn by men

fee (fē) *n.* [ult < Gmc] a charge for professional services, licenses, etc.

fee·ble (fē′bəl) *adj.* **-bler, -blest** [< L *flere*, weep] **1** weak; infirm [a *feeble* old man] **2** without force or effectiveness [a *feeble* attempt] —**fee′ble·ness** *n.* —**fee′bly** *adv.*

feed (fēd) *vt.* **fed, feed′ing** [< OE *foda*, food] **1** to give food to **2** to provide something necessary for the growth, operation, etc. of **3** to gratify [to *feed* one's vanity] —*vi.* to eat: said esp. of animals —*n.* **1** food for animals; fodder **2** *a*) the material fed into a machine *b*) the part of the machine supplying this material **3** *Radio, TV* a transmission sent by a network, etc. to individual stations for broadcast **4** *Comput.* a service which alerts subscribers about updated information, as on selected websites —**feed′er** *n.*

feed·back *n.* **1** the transfer of part of the output back to the input, as of electricity or information **2** a response

feed·stock *n.* raw material for industrial processing

feel (fēl) *vt.* **felt, feel′ing** ⟦OE *felan*⟧ 1 to touch; examine by handling 2 to be aware of through physical sensation 3 to experience (an emotion or condition); be affected by 4 to be aware of 5 to think or believe —*vi.* 1 to have physical sensation 2 to appear to be to the senses [it *feels* warm] 3 to grope 4 to be aware of being [I *feel* sad] 5 to be moved to sympathy, pity, etc. (*for*) —*n.* 1 the act of feeling 2 the sense of touch 3 the nature of a thing as perceived through touch 4 an instinctive ability or appreciation [a *feel* for politics] —**feel like** [Inf.] to have a desire for —**feel one's way** to advance cautiously —**feel out** to try cautiously to find out the opinions of (someone) —**feel up to** [Inf.] to feel capable of

feel·er *n.* 1 a specialized organ of touch in an animal or insect, as an antenna 2 a cautious remark, offer, etc. made to learn more about something

feel·ing *n.* 1 the sense of touch 2 the ability to experience physical sensation 3 an awareness; sensation 4 an emotion 5 [*pl.*] sensibilities [hurt *feelings*] 6 sympathy; pity 7 an opinion or sentiment

fee simple absolute and unrestricted ownership of real property

feet (fēt) *n. pl. of* FOOT

feign (fān) *vt., vi.* ⟦< L *fingere*, to shape⟧ 1 to make up (an excuse, etc.) 2 to pretend; dissemble

feint (fānt) *n.* [see prec.] a pretended attack intended to take the opponent off guard, as in boxing —*vi., vt.* to deliver (such an attack)

feist·y (fīs′tē) *adj.* **-i·er, -i·est** ⟦< Norw *fisa*, to puff + -y²⟧ [Inf. or Dial.] full of spirit; specif., quarrelsome, spunky, etc. —**feist′i·ly** *adv.* —**feist′i·ness** *n.*

feld·spar (feld′spär′) *n.* ⟦< Ger *feld*, field + *spath*, a mineral⟧ any of several hard, glassy minerals

fe·lic·i·tate (fə lis′i tāt′) *vt.* **-tat′ed, -tat′ing** ⟦< L *felix*, happy⟧ to wish happiness to; congratulate —**fe·lic′i·ta′tion** *n.* —**fe·lic′i·ta′tor** *n.*

fe·lic·i·tous (-təs) *adj.* ⟦< fol.⟧ used or expressed in a way suitable to the occasion; appropriate

fe·lic·i·ty (-tē) *n., pl.* **-ties** ⟦< L *felix*, happy⟧ 1 happiness; bliss 2 anything producing happiness 3 apt and pleasing expression in writing, etc.

fe·line (fē′līn) *adj.* ⟦< L *feles*, cat⟧ 1 of a cat or the cat family 2 catlike; sly —*n.* any animal of the cat family

fell¹ (fel) *vi., vt. pt. of* FALL

fell² (fel) *vt.* ⟦OE *fellan*⟧ 1 to knock down 2 to cut down (a tree)

fell³ (fel) *adj.* ⟦< ML *fello*⟧ fierce; cruel

fel·low (fel′ō, -ə) *n.* ⟦Late OE *feolaga*, partner⟧ 1 an associate 2 one of the same rank; equal 3 one of a pair; mate 4 one holding a fellowship in a college, etc. 5 a member of a learned society 6 [Inf.] a man or boy —*adj.* 1 having the same position, work, etc. 2 associated [*fellow* workers]

fel·low·ship *n.* 1 companionship 2 a mutual sharing 3 a group of people with the same interests 4 an endowment for the support of a student or scholar doing advanced work

fellow traveler a nonmember who supports the cause of a party

fel·on (fel′ən) *n.* ⟦< ML *felo*, villain⟧ a person guilty of a felony; criminal

fel·o·ny (fel′ə nē) *n., pl.* **-nies** ⟦< ML *felonia*, treachery⟧ a major crime, as murder, arson, etc. —**fe·lo·ni·ous** (fə lō′nē əs) *adj.*

felt¹ (felt) *n.* ⟦< OE⟧ a fabric made of fibers of wool, etc., worked together by pressure, etc. —*adj.* made of felt —*vt.* to make into felt

felt² (felt) *vt., vi. pt. and pp. of* FEEL

fem *abbrev.* 1 female 2 feminine

fe·male (fē′māl′) *adj.* ⟦< L *femina*, woman⟧ 1 designating or of the sex that bears offspring 2 of, like, or suitable to women or girls; feminine 3 consisting of women or girls 4 having a hollow part for receiving an inserted part (called *male*): said of pipe fittings, electric sockets, etc. —*n.* a female person, animal, or plant

fem·i·nine (fem′ə nin) *adj.* ⟦< L *femina*, woman⟧ 1 of women or girls 2 having qualities considered characteristic of or suitable to women; gentle, delicate, etc. 3 *Gram.* designating or of the gender of words referring to females or other words with no distinction of sex —**fem′i·nin′i·ty** *n.*

fem·i·nism (-niz′əm) *n.* the movement to win political, economic, and social equality for women —**fem′i·nist** *n., adj.* —**fem′i·nis′tic** *adj.*

fe·mur (fē′mər) *n., pl.* **fe′murs** or **fem·o·ra** (fem′ə rə) ⟦< L, thigh⟧ the bone extending from the hip to the knee —**fem′o·ral** *adj.*

fen (fen) *n.* ⟦OE⟧ an area of low, flat, marshy land; swamp; bog

fence (fens) *n.* ⟦< ME *defens*, defense⟧ 1 a protective or confining barrier of posts, wire mesh, etc. 2 one who deals in stolen goods —*vt.* **fenced, fenc′ing** 1 to enclose, as with a fence: with *in*, *off*, etc. 2 to keep (*out*) as by a fence 3 to sell (stolen property) to a fence —*vi.* 1 to practice the art of fencing 2 to avoid giving a direct reply —**on the fence** uncommitted or undecided —**fenc′er** *n.*

fenc·ing *n.* 1 the art of fighting with a foil or other sword 2 material for making fences 3 a system of fences

fend (fend) *vt.* ⟦ME *fenden*, defend⟧ to turn aside; ward (*off*) —*vi.* to resist; parry —**fend for oneself** to manage by oneself

fend·er *n.* anything that fends off or protects something else, as the part of an automobile body over the wheel

fen·nel (fen′əl) *n.* ⟦< L *fenum*, hay⟧ a tall herb with aromatic seeds used to flavor foods and medicines

fe·ral (fir′əl, fer′-) *adj.* ⟦< L *ferus*, wild⟧ 1 untamed; wild 2 savage; fierce

fer·ment (fur′ment′; *for v.* fər ment′) *n.* ⟦< L *fervere*, to boil⟧ 1 a substance causing fermentation, as yeast 2 excitement or agitation

—vt. 1 to cause fermentation in **2** to excite; agitate **—vi. 1** to be in the process of fermentation **2** to be excited or agitated; seethe

fer·men·ta·tion (fur'mən tā'shən) *n.* **1** the breakdown of complex molecules in organic compounds, caused by microorganisms; esp., the conversion of sugars to alcohol by yeasts **2** excitement; agitation

fer·mi·on (fer'mē än', fur'–) *n.* ⟦after E. *Fermi*, (1901-54), U.S. physicist⟧ any of a major subdivision of subatomic particles, including leptons and baryons

fer·mi·um (fer'mē əm, furʼ–) *n.* ⟦see prec.⟧ an artificially produced radioactive, metallic chemical element: symbol, Fm; at. no. 100

fern (furn) *n.* ⟦< OE *fearn*⟧ any of a large group of nonflowering plants having roots, stems, and fronds, and reproducing by spores

fe·ro·cious (fə rō'shəs) *adj.* ⟦< L *ferus*, wild⟧ **1** fierce; savage; violently cruel **2** [Inf.] very great [a *ferocious* appetite] **—fe·ro'cious·ly** *adv.* **—fe·roc'i·ty** (fə räs'ə tē) *n.*

-fer·ous (fər əs) ⟦< L *ferre*, to bear⟧ *suffix* bearing, yielding

fer·ret (ferʼət) *n.* ⟦< L *fur*, thief⟧ a small European polecat, easily tamed for hunting rats, etc. **—vt. 1** to force out of hiding with or as if with a ferret **2** to find out by investigation: with *out*

fer·ric (ferʼik) *adj.* ⟦< L *ferrum*, iron⟧ of, containing, or derived from iron

Fer·ris wheel (ferʼis) ⟦after G. *Ferris* (1859-96), U.S. engineer⟧ a large, upright wheel revolving on a fixed axle and having suspended seats: used as an amusement ride

ferro- ⟦< L *ferrum*, iron⟧ *combining form* **1** iron **2** iron and

fer·rous (ferʼəs) *adj.* ⟦< L *ferrum*, iron⟧ of, containing, or derived from iron

fer·rule (ferʼəl, –ōol′) *n.* ⟦< L *viriae*, bracelets⟧ a metal ring or cap put around the end of a cane, tool handle, etc. to give added strength

fer·ry (ferʼē) *vt.* **-ried, -ry·ing** ⟦OE *ferian*⟧ **1** to take (people, cars, etc.) across a river, etc. **2** to deliver (airplanes) by flying them **3** to transport by airplane **—n., pl. -ries 1** a system for carrying people, goods, etc. across a river, etc. by boat **2** a boat used for this: also **fer'ry·boat' 3** the place where such a crossing begins or ends

fer·tile (furt'l) *adj.* ⟦< L *ferre*, to bear⟧ **1** producing abundantly; fruitful **2** able to produce young, seeds, fruit, pollen, spores, etc. **3** fertilized [a *fertile* egg] **—fer·til·i·ty** (fər til'ə tē) *n.*

fer·til·ize (–īz′) *vt.* **-ized', -iz'ing 1** to make fertile **2** to spread fertilizer on **3** to make (the female cell or female) fruitful by pollinating, or impregnating, with the male gamete **—fer'til·i·za·ble** *adj.* **—fer'til·i·za'tion** *n.*

fer·til·iz·er *n.* manure, chemicals, etc., used to enrich the soil

fer·ule (ferʼəl, –ōol′) *n.* ⟦< L *ferula*, a whip, rod⟧ a flat stick or ruler used for punishing children

fer·vent (furʼvənt) *adj.* ⟦< L *fervere*, to glow⟧

showing great warmth of feeling; intensely devoted or earnest **—fer'ven·cy** *n.* **—fer'vent·ly** *adv.*

fer·vid (furʼvid) *adj.* ⟦see prec.⟧ impassioned; fervent **—fer'vid·ly** *adv.*

fer·vor (furʼvər) *n.* ⟦see FERVENT⟧ great warmth of emotion; ardor; zeal

fess (or **'fess**) **up** (fes) [Inf.] to admit; confess

-fest (fest) ⟦< Ger *fest*, a feast⟧ *combining form* an occasion of much or many [*songfest*]

fes·tal (fes'təl) *adj.* ⟦< L *festum*, feast⟧ of or like a joyous celebration; festive

fes·ter (fes'tər) *n.* ⟦< L *fistula*, ulcer⟧ a small sore filled with pus **—vi. 1** to form pus **2** to grow more bitter, virulent, etc.

fes·ti·val (fes'tə vəl) *n.* ⟦see fol.⟧ **1** a time or day of feasting or celebration **2** a celebration or series of performances

fes·tive (fes'tiv) *adj.* ⟦< L *festum*, feast⟧ **1** of or for a feast or festival **2** merry; joyous [a *festive* mood] **—fes'tive·ly** *adv.* **—fes'tive·ness** *n.*

fes·tiv·i·ty (fes tiv'ə tē) *n., pl.* **-ties 1** merrymaking; gaiety **2** a festival **3** [*pl.*] things done in celebration

fes·toon (fes tōon') *n.* ⟦< It *festa*, feast⟧ a wreath or garland of flowers, etc. hanging in a loop or curve **—vt.** to adorn with festoons

fet·a (cheese) (fet'ə) ⟦< ModGr < It *fetta*, a slice⟧ a soft, white, salty cheese, first made in Greece

fe·tal (fēt'l) *adj.* of a fetus

fetch (fech) *vt.* ⟦OE *feccan*⟧ **1** to go after and bring back; get **2** to cause to come **3** to sell for

fetch·ing *adj.* attractive; charming

fete or **fête** (fāt, fet) *n.* ⟦Fr *fête*: see FEAST⟧ a festival; entertainment, esp. outdoors **—vt.** **fet'ed** or **fêt'ed, fet'ing** or **fêt'ing** to honor with a fete

fet·id (fet'id) *adj.* ⟦< L *foetere*, to stink⟧ having a bad smell; stinking; putrid **—fet'id·ness** *n.*

fet·ish (fet'ish) *n.* ⟦< Port *feitiço*⟧ **1** any object believed to have magic power **2** anything to which one is irrationally devoted **3** any nonsexual object that abnormally excites erotic feelings **—fet'ish·ism'** *n.* **—fet'ish·ist** *n.*

fet·lock (fet'läk′) *n.* ⟦< ME *fet*, feet⟧ **1** a tuft of hair on the back of a horse's leg above the hoof **2** the joint bearing this tuft

fe·to·scope (fē'tə skōp') *n.* **1** an endoscope used to examine a fetus in the womb **2** a special stethoscope used to listen to the fetal heartbeat

fet·ter (fet'ər) *n.* ⟦< OE *fot*, foot⟧ **1** a shackle or chain for the feet **2** any check or restraint **—vt. 1** to bind with fetters **2** to restrain

fet·tle (fet'l) *n.* ⟦ME *fetlen*, make ready⟧ condition; state [in fine *fettle*]

fe·tus (fēt'əs) *n., pl.* **-tus·es** ⟦L, a bringing forth⟧ the unborn young of an animal, esp. in its later stages and specif., in humans, from about the eighth week after conception until birth

feud (fyōod) *n.* ⟦< OFr *faide*⟧ a deadly quarrel, esp. between clans or families **—vi.** to carry on a feud; quarrel

feu·dal (fyōōd′'l) *adj.* ⟦ML *feudalis*⟧ of or like feudalism

feu·dal·ism *n.* the economic, political, and social system in medieval Europe, in which land, worked by serfs, was held by vassals in exchange for military and other services rendered to overlords —**feu′dal·is′tic** *adj.*

fe·ver (fē′vər) *n.* ⟦< L *febris*⟧ 1 an abnormally increased body temperature 2 any disease that is marked by a high fever 3 a restless excitement —**fe′ver·ish** *adj.* —**fe′ver·ish·ly** *adv.*

fever blister (*or* **sore**) COLD SORE

few (fyōō) *adj.* ⟦OE *feawe*⟧ not many; a small number of —*pron.* not many; a small number of —**few and far between** scarce; rare —**the few** the minority

fey (fā) *adj.* ⟦OE *fǣge*, fated⟧ strange or unusual; specif., eccentric, whimsical, etc. —**fey′ness** *n.*

fez (fez) *n.*, *pl.* **fez′zes** ⟦after *Fez*, city in Morocco⟧ a red, brimless felt hat, shaped like a truncated cone, worn formerly by Turkish men

ff *abbrev.* 1 folios 2 following (pages, etc.)

fi·an·cé (fē′än sā′) *n.* ⟦Fr < OFr *fiance*, a promise⟧ a man to whom one is engaged to be married

fi·an·cée (fē′än sā′) *n.* ⟦Fr: see prec.⟧ a woman to whom one is engaged to be married

fi·as·co (fē as′kō) *n.*, *pl.* **-coes** or **-cos** ⟦Fr < It⟧ a complete, ridiculous failure

fi·at (fē′ät, fī′at′) *n.* ⟦L, let it be done⟧ 1 a decree; order 2 a sanction; authorization 3 any arbitrary order

fib (fib) *n.* ⟦< ? FABLE⟧ a small or trivial lie —*vi.* fibbed, **fib′bing** to tell such a lie —**fib′ber** *n.*

fi·ber (fī′bər) *n.* ⟦< L *fibra*⟧ 1 a threadlike structure that combines with others to form animal or vegetable tissue 2 any substance that can be separated into threadlike parts for weaving, etc. 3 texture 4 character or nature 5 ROUGHAGE —**fi′brous** (-brəs) *adj.*

fi·ber·board *n.* a building material consisting of fibers of wood, etc. pressed into stiff sheets

fi·ber·glass (-glas′) *n.* finespun filaments of glass made into textiles, insulating material, or molded plastic

fiber optics 1 the science of transmitting light and images, as around curves, through transparent fibers 2 such fibers —**fi′ber·op′tic** *adj.*, **fiber optic**

fi·bril·la·tion (fib′ri lā′shən) *n.* ⟦< L *fibra*, fiber + -ATION⟧ very rapid contractions of part of the heart muscle, causing irregular heartbeats

fi·brin (fī′brin) *n.* a fibrous, insoluble blood protein formed in blood clots

fi·brin·o·gen (fī brin′ə jən) *n.* ⟦prec. + -GEN⟧ a protein in the blood from which fibrin is formed

fi·broid (fī′broid′) *adj.* like or composed of fibrous tissue: said as of a tumor

fi·bro·my·al·gia (fī′brō mī al′jə) *n.* a chronic condition characterized by widespread body pain and tenderness along with fatigue and other symptoms

fi·bro·sis (fī brō′sis) *n.* an excessive growth of fibrous connective tissue in an organ, part, etc.

fib·u·la (fib′yōō lə) *n.*, *pl.* **-lae′** (-lē′) or **-las** ⟦L, a clasp⟧ the long, thin outer bone of the lower leg —**fib′u·lar** *adj.*

-fic (fik) ⟦< L *facere*, make⟧ *suffix* making [*terrific*]

FICA (fī′kə) *abbrev.* Federal Insurance Contributions Act

-fi·ca·tion (fi kā′shən) ⟦see -FIC⟧ *suffix* a making [*glorification*]

fich·u (fish′ōō) *n.* ⟦Fr⟧ a triangular lace or muslin cape for women, worn tied in front

fick·le (fik′əl) *adj.* ⟦< OE *ficol*, tricky⟧ changeable or unstable; capricious

fic·tion (fik′shən) *n.* ⟦< L *fingere*, to form⟧ 1 an imaginary statement, story, etc. 2 *a*) literary narratives, collectively, with imaginary characters or events *b*) a narrative of this kind —**fic′tion·al** *adj.*

fic·tion·al·ize (-shə nəl īz′) *vt.* **-ized′**, **-iz′ing** to deal with (historical events) in fictional form —**fic′tion·al·i·za′tion** *n.*

fic·ti·tious (fik tish′əs) *adj.* 1 of or like fiction; imaginary 2 false 3 assumed for disguise [*a fictitious name*]

fic·tive (fik′tiv) *adj.* 1 of fiction 2 imaginary —**fic′tive·ly** *adv.*

fi·cus (fī′kəs) *n.*, *pl.* **fi′cus** ⟦< L, fig tree⟧ any of a genus of tropical shrubs, trees, etc. with glossy, leathery leaves

fid·dle (fid′'l) ⟦Inf.⟧ *n.* ⟦OE *fithele*⟧ a violin —*vi.* **-dled**, **-dling** 1 to play a fiddle 2 to tinker (*with*) nervously —**fid′dler** *n.*

fid·dle·sticks *interj.* nonsense!

fi·del·i·ty (fə del′ə tē) *n.*, *pl.* **-ties** ⟦< L *fides*, faith⟧ 1 faithful devotion to duty; loyalty 2 accuracy of description, sound reproduction, etc.

fidg·et (fij′it) *n.* ⟦< ME < ?⟧ a restless or nervous state: esp. in phrase **the fidgets** —*vi.* to move about restlessly or nervously —**fidg′et·y** *adj.*

Fi·do (fī′dō) *n.* ⟦< L *fidus*, faithful < *fides*, FAITH⟧ a traditional name for a pet dog

fi·du·ci·ar·y (fi dōō′shē er′ē) *adj.* ⟦< L *fiducia*, trust⟧ holding or held in trust —*n.*, *pl.* **-ies** TRUSTEE (*n.* 1)

fie (fī) *interj.* [Archaic] for shame!

fief (fēf) *n.* ⟦Fr: see FEE⟧ in feudalism, heritable land held by a vassal

fief·dom (-dəm) *n.* 1 FIEF 2 anything under a person's complete control

field (fēld) *n.* ⟦OE *feld*⟧ 1 a stretch of open land 2 a piece of cleared land for crops or pasture 3 a piece of land used for a particular purpose [*a landing field*] 4 any wide, unbroken expanse [*a field of ice*] 5 *a*) a battlefield *b*) a battle 6 a realm of knowledge or work 7 the background, as on a flag 8 *a*) an area for athletics or games *b*) all the entrants in a contest 9 *Physics* a physical force, etc. having a specific value at each point throughout a region of space —*vt.* 1 to stop or catch and throw (a baseball, etc.) 2 to put (a player or team) into active play **3** [Inf.] to answer (a question) extemporaneously — **play the field** to not confine one's activities to one object —**field′er** *n.*

field day 1 a day set aside, as at a school, for outdoor activities, etc. **2** an occasion of extraordinary opportunity or highly successful activity

field glasses binoculars

field goal 1 *Basketball* a shot, made from play, scoring two points or, if from a certain distance, three points **2** *Football* a goal kicked from the field, scoring three points

field guide a handbook for identifying plants, etc., as while hiking

field hand a hired farm laborer

field hockey HOCKEY (*n.* 2)

field marshal in some armies, an officer of the highest rank

field-test *vt.* to test (a device, method, etc.) under operating conditions

fiend (fēnd) *n.* ⟦OE *feond*, the one hating⟧ **1** an evil spirit; devil **2** an inhumanly wicked person **3** [Inf.] an addict [a dope *fiend*] —**fiend′ish** *adj.*

fierce (firs) *adj.* **fierc′er, fierc′est** ⟦< L *ferus*, wild⟧ **1** savage **2** violent **3** intense [a *fierce* embrace] —**fierce′ly** *adv.* —**fierce′ness** *n.*

fi·er·y (fī′ər ē) *adj.* **-er·i·er, -er·i·est 1** like fire; glaring, hot, etc. **2** ardent; spirited **3** excitable **4** inflamed

fi·es·ta (fē es′tə) *n.* ⟦Sp < L *festus*, festal⟧ **1** a religious festival **2** any gala celebration; holiday

fife (fīf) *n.* ⟦Ger *pfeife*⟧ a small, shrill-toned flute used mainly with drums in playing marches

fif·teen (fif′tēn′) *adj., n.* ⟦OE *fiftene*⟧ five more than ten; 15; XV —**fif′teenth′** (-tēnth′) *adj., n., adv.*

fifth (fifth) *adj.* ⟦< OE *fif*, five⟧ preceded by four others in a series; 5th —*n.* **1** the one following the fourth **2** any of the five equal parts of something; ⅕ **3** a fifth of a gallon [4 F-] [Inf.] FIFTH AMENDMENT —*adv.* in the fifth place, rank, etc. —**plead (or take) the Fifth** to invoke the Fifth Amendment

Fifth Amendment an amendment to the U.S. Constitution mainly guaranteeing certain protections in criminal cases, including protection from being compelled to testify against oneself

fifth column a group of people aiding an enemy from within their own country

fifth wheel a superfluous person or thing

fif·ty (fif′tē) *adj., n., pl.* **-ties** ⟦OE *fiftig*⟧ five times ten; 50; L —**the fifties** the numbers or years, as of a century, from 50 through 59 —**fif′ti·eth** (-ith) *adj., n.*

fif·ty-fif·ty [Inf.] *adj.* equal; even —*adv.* equally

fig¹ (fig) *n.* ⟦< L *ficus*⟧ **1** *a)* a small, sweet, pear-shaped fruit that grows on a tree related to the mulberry *b)* the tree **2** a trifle [not worth a *fig*]

fig² *abbrev.* **1** figurative(ly) **2** figure(s)

fight (fīt) *vi.* **fought, fight′ing** ⟦OE *feohtan*⟧ to take part in a struggle, contest, etc., esp. against a foe or for a cause —*vt.* **1** to oppose physically or in battle **2** to struggle against **3** to engage in (a war, etc.) **4** to gain (one's way) by struggle —*n.* **1** any struggle, contest, or quarrel **2** power or readiness to fight

fight·er *n.* **1** one that fights **2** a prizefighter **3** a fast, highly maneuverable combat airplane

fig·ment (fig′mənt) *n.* ⟦< L *fingere*, to form⟧ something merely imagined

fig·ur·a·tive (fig′yoor ə tiv′) *adj.* **1** representing by means of a figure or symbol **2** not in its literal sense; metaphorical **3** using figures of speech —**fig′ur·a·tive′ly** *adv.*

fig·ure (fig′yər) *n.* ⟦< L *fingere*, to form⟧ **1** an outline or shape; form **2** the human form **3** a person thought of in a specified way [a historical *figure*] **4** a likeness of a person or thing **5** an illustration; diagram **6** a design; pattern **7** the symbol for a number **8** [*pl.*] arithmetic **9** a sum of money **10** *Geom.* a surface or space bounded by lines or planes —*vt.* **-ured, -ur·ing 1** to represent in definite form **2** to imagine **3** to ornament with a design **4** to compute with figures **5** [Inf.] to believe; consider —*vi.* **1** to appear prominently **2** to do arithmetic —**figure in** to include —**figure on** to rely on —**figure out 1** to solve **2** to understand

fig·ure·head *n.* **1** a carved figure on the bow of a ship **2** one put in a position of leadership, but having no real power or authority

figure of speech an expression, as a metaphor or simile, using words in a nonliteral sense or unusual way

figure skating ice skating with emphasis on intricate footwork, leaps and spins, etc. —**figure skater**

fig·u·rine (fig′yōō rēn′) *n.* ⟦Fr⟧ a small sculptured or molded figure

Fi·ji (fē′jē) country on a group of islands (**Fiji Islands**) in the SW Pacific

fil·a·ment (fil′ə mənt) *n.* ⟦< L *filum*, thread⟧ a very slender thread or threadlike part; specif., the fine wire in an incandescent light bulb

fil·bert (fil′bərt) *n.* ⟦ME *filberde*⟧ the edible nut of a hazel tree

filch (filch) *vt.* ⟦ME *filchen*⟧ to steal (usually something small or petty)

file¹ (fīl) *vt.* **filed, fil′ing** ⟦< L *filum*, thread⟧ **1** to put (papers, etc.) in order for future reference **2** to dispatch or register (a news story, application, etc.) **3** to put on public record —*vi.* **1** to move in a line **2** to make application (*for* divorce, etc.) —*n.* **1** a container for keeping papers in order **2** an orderly arrangement of papers, etc. **3** a line of persons or things **4** *Comput.* a collection of data stored as a single unit —**file′a·ble** *adj.* —**fil′er** *n.*

file² (fīl) *n.* ⟦OE *feol*⟧ a steel tool with a rough, ridged surface for smoothing or grinding —*vt.* **filed, fil′ing** to smooth or grind, as with a file

fi·let (fi lā′, fil′ā′) *n.* ⟦< OFr: see FILLET⟧ FILLET (*n.* 2) —*vt.* FILLET

fi·let mi·gnon (fi lā′min yōn′, -yän′) ⟦Fr, lit.,

tiny fillet] a thick, round cut of lean beef tenderloin

fil·i·al (fil′ē əl, fil′yəl) *adj.* [< L *filius*, son] of, suitable to, or due from a son or daughter

fil·i·bus·ter (fil′i bus′tər) *n.* [< Sp < MDu *vrijbuiter*, freebooter] 1 the making of long speeches, etc. to obstruct a bill's passage in the Senate 2 a Senator who does this — *vt.*, *vi.* to obstruct (a bill) by a filibuster

fil·i·gree (fil′i grē′) *n.* [< L *filum*, thread + *granum*, grain] lacelike ornamental work of gold, silver, etc. — *vt.* **-greed′**, **-gree′ing** to ornament with filigree

fil·ing (fil′iŋ) *n.* a small piece scraped off with a file: *usually used in pl.*

Fil·i·pi·na (fil′i pē′nə) *n.* [Sp] a Filipino woman or girl

Fil·i·pi·no (fil′i pē′nō) *n., pl.* **-nos** [Sp] a person born or living in the Philippines —*adj.* of the Philippines or its people, etc.

fill (fil) *vt.* [OE *fyllan*] 1 to put as much as possible into 2 to occupy wholly 3 to put a person into or to occupy (a position, etc.) 4 to supply the things called for in (an order, etc.) 5 to close or plug (holes, etc.) —*vi.* to become full —*n.* enough to make full or to satisfy 2 anything that fills —**fill in** 1 to complete by supplying something 2 to supply for completion 3 to be a substitute —**fill out** 1 to make or become larger, etc. 2 to make (a document, etc.) complete by supplying information —**fill up** to make or become completely full —**fill′er** *n.*

fil·let (fil′it; *for n. 2 & vt., usually* fi lā′, fil′ā′) *n.* [OFr *filet* < L *filum*, thread] 1 a thin strip or band 2 a lean, boneless piece of meat or fish —*vt.* to bone and slice (meat or fish)

fill-in *n.* one that fills a vacancy or gap, often temporarily

fill·ing *n.* a substance used to fill something, as gold in a tooth cavity

filling station SERVICE STATION

fil·lip (fil′ip) *n.* [< FLIP¹] 1 an outward snap of a finger from the thumb 2 something that stimulates —*vt.* to strike or toss with a fillip

Fill·more (fil′môr), **Mill·ard** (mil′ərd) 1800-74; 13th president of the U.S. (1850-53)

fil·ly (fil′ē) *n., pl.* **-lies** [< ON *fylja*] a young female horse

film (film) *n.* [OE *filmen*] 1 a fine, thin skin, coating, etc. 2 a flexible cellulose material coated with an emulsion sensitive to light and used in photography 3 a haze or blur 4 a series of still pictures projected on a screen in such rapid succession as to create the illusion of moving persons and objects 5 a play, story, etc. in this form — *vt., vi.* 1 to cover or be covered as with a film 2 to photograph or make a film (of)

film noir (film′ nwär′) [Fr, lit., black film] a movie, esp. of the 1940s and 1950s, marked by low-key lighting, a bleak urban setting, and corrupt, cynical characters

film·strip *n.* a length of film with transparencies, often of illustrations, charts, etc., for projection separately

film·y *adj.* **-i·er**, **-i·est** 1 gauzy; sheer; thin 2 blurred; hazy —**film′i·ness** *n.*

fil·ter (fil′tər) *n.* [< ML *filtrum*, FELT¹] 1 a device for straining out solid particles, impurities, etc. from a liquid or gas 2 a device or substance for screening out electric oscillations, light waves, etc. of certain frequencies — *vt., vi.* 1 to pass through or as through a filter 2 to remove with a filter —**fil′ter·a·ble** *adj.*, **fil′tra·ble** (-trə bəl)

filth (filth) *n.* [OE *fylthe*] 1 foul dirt 2 obscenity —**filth′y** *adj.* **-i·er**, **-i·est** —**filth′i·ness** *n.*

fil·trate (fil′trāt′) *vt.* **-trat·ed**, **-trat·ing** to filter —*n.* a filtered liquid —**fil·tra′tion** *n.*

fin (fin) *n.* [OE *finn*] 1 any of several winglike organs on the body of a fish, dolphin, etc., used in swimming 2 anything like a fin in shape or use

fi·na·gle (fə nā′gəl) *vt., vi.* **-gled**, **-gling** [< ?] [Inf.] to get by, or use, craftiness, trickery, etc. —**fi·na′gler** *n.*

fi·nal (fī′nəl) *adj.* [< L *finis*, end] 1 of or coming at the end; last 2 deciding; conclusive —*n.* 1 anything final 2 [*pl.*] the last of a series of contests 3 a final examination —**fi·nal′i·ty** (-nal′ə tē) *n.* —**fi′nal·ly** *adv.*

fi·na·le (fə nal′ē) *n.* [It] the concluding part of a musical work, etc.

fi·nal·ist *n.* a contestant in the final, deciding contest of a series

fi·nal·ize *vt.* **-ized′**, **-iz′ing** [FINAL + -IZE] to make final; complete —**fi′nal·i·za′tion** *n.*

fi·nance (fī′nans′, fə nans′) *n.* [< L *finis*, end] 1 [*pl.*] money resources, income, etc. 2 the science of managing money —*vt.* **-nanced′**, **-nanc′ing** to supply or get money for —**fi·nan′cial** (-nan′shəl) *adj.* —**fi·nan′cial·ly** *adv.*

fin·an·cier (fin′ən sir′, fī′nən-) *n.* [Fr] one skilled in finance

finch (finch) *n.* [OE *finc*] any of various small, seed-eating birds, including canaries, goldfinches, etc.

find (fīnd) *vt.* **found**, **find′ing** [OE *findan*] 1 to discover by chance; come upon 2 to get by searching 3 to perceive; learn 4 to recover (something lost) 5 to reach; attain 6 to decide and declare to be —*vi.* to reach a decision [the jury *found* for the accused] —*n.* 1 a finding 2 something found —**find out** to discover; learn —**find′er** *n.*

find·ing *n.* 1 discovery 2 something found 3 [*often pl.*] the verdict of a judge, scholar, etc.

fine¹ (fīn) *adj.* **fin′er**, **fin′est** [< L *finis*, end] 1 very good; excellent 2 with no impurities; refined 3 in good health 4 clear and bright [*fine* weather] 5 composed of small parts or particles [*fine* sand] 6 very thin or small [*fine* print] 7 sharp [a *fine* edge] 8 subtle; delicate [a *fine* distinction] 9 elegant —*adv.* in a fine manner —**fine′ly** *adv.* —**fine′ness** *n.*

fine² (fīn) *n.* [see prec.] a sum of money paid as a penalty —*vt.* **fined**, **fin′ing** to order to pay a fine

fine art any of the art forms that include drawing, painting, sculpture, etc.: *usually used in pl.*

fin·er·y (fīn′ər ē) *n., pl.* **-ies** elaborate clothes, jewelry, etc.

fines herbes (fēn zerb′) [Fr] a seasoning of chopped herbs, traditionally parsley, chives, tarragon, and chervil

fi·nesse (fə nes′) *n.* [see FINE¹] 1 adroitness; skill 2 the ability to handle difficult situations diplomatically 3 cunning; artfulness —*vt.* **-nessed′, -ness′ing** 1 to manage or bring about by finesse 2 to evade (a problem, etc.)

fine-tune *vt.* **-tuned′, -tun′ing** to adjust for greater efficiency

fin·ger (fiŋ′gər) *n.* [OE] 1 any of the five jointed parts extending from the palm of the hand, esp. one other than the thumb 2 anything like a finger in shape or use —*vt.* 1 to touch with the fingers 2 *Music* to play by using the fingers in a certain way —**have (or keep) one's fingers crossed** to hope for or against something —**put one's finger on** to ascertain exactly

fin·ger·board *n.* the part of a stringed instrument against which the strings are pressed to change the pitches they produce

finger bowl a small water bowl for rinsing the fingers at a meal

fin·ger·ling (-liŋ) *n.* a small fish

fin·ger·nail *n.* the horny substance at the upper end of a finger

finger painting a painting done by using the fingers, hand, or arm to spread, on wet paper, paints (**finger paints**) made of starch, glycerin, and pigments —**fin′ger-paint′** *vi., vt.*

fin·ger-point·ing *n.* the act of assigning blame to others, often so as to deflect blame from oneself

fin·ger·print *n.* an impression of the lines and whorls on a finger tip, used to identify a person —*vt.* to take the fingerprints of

fin·ger·tip *n.* the tip of a finger —**have at one's fingertips** to have available for instant use

fin·i·al (fin′ē əl) *n.* [ult. < L *finis*, end] a decorative terminal part at the tip of a lamp, etc.

fin·ick·y (fin′ik ē) *adj.* [< FINE¹] too particular; fussy: also **fin′i·cal** (-i kəl) or **fin′ick·ing**

fin·is (fin′is; *also, as if Fr,* fē nē′) *n., pl.* **-nis·es** the end; finish

fin·ish (fin′ish) *vt.* [< L *finis*, an end] 1 *a)* to bring to an end *b)* to come to the end of 2 to consume all of 3 to give final touches to; perfect 4 to give (wood, etc.) a desired surface effect —*vi.* to come to an end —*n.* 1 the last part; end 2 *a)* anything used to finish a surface *b)* the finished effect 3 means or manner of completing or perfecting 4 polished manners, speech, etc. —**finish off** 1 to end 2 to kill or ruin —**finish with** to bring to an end —**fin′ished** *adj.* —**fin′ish·er** *n.*

fi·nite (fī′nīt′) *adj.* [< L *finis*, end] having definable limits; not infinite

fink (fiŋk) *n.* [Ger., lit., finch] [Slang] 1 an informer 2 a strikebreaker —*vi.* [Slang] to inform (*on*)

Fin·land (fin′lənd) country in N Europe

Finn (fin) *n.* a person born or living in Finland

Finn·ish (fin′ish) *n.* the language spoken in Finland —*adj.* of Finland or its people, language, etc.

fin·ny (fin′ē) *adj.* 1 having fins 2 like a fin 3 of or being fish

fir (fur) *n.* [OE] 1 a cone-bearing evergreen tree of the pine family 2 its wood

fire (fīr) *n.* [OE *fyr*] 1 the flame, heat, and light of combustion 2 something burning 3 a destructive burning [a forest *fire*] 4 strong feeling 5 a discharge of firearms — *vt., vi.* **fired, fir′ing** 1 to start burning; ignite 2 to supply with fuel 3 to bake (bricks, etc.) in a kiln 4 to excite or become excited 5 to shoot (a gun, bullet, etc.) 6 to hurl or direct with force 7 to dismiss from a position; discharge —**catch (on) fire** to ignite —**on fire** 1 burning 2 greatly excited —**under fire** under attack —**fir′er** *n.*

fire·arm *n.* any hand weapon from which a shot is fired by explosive force, as a rifle or pistol

fire·base *n.* a military base in a combat zone, from which artillery, rockets, etc. are fired

fire·bomb *n.* an incendiary bomb —*vt.* to attack or damage with a firebomb

fire·brand *n.* 1 a piece of burning wood 2 one who stirs up others, as to rebellion

fire·break *n.* a strip of forest or prairie land cleared or plowed to stop the spread of fire

fire·brick *n.* a highly heat-resistant brick for lining fireplaces, furnaces, etc.

fire·bug *n.* [Inf.] one who deliberately starts destructive fires; pyromaniac

fire·crack·er *n.* a roll of paper containing an explosive, set off as a noisemaker at celebrations, etc.

fire·damp *n.* an explosive gas, largely methane, encountered in coal mines

fire engine a motor truck with equipment for fighting fires

fire escape an outside stairway for escaping from a burning building

fire·fight *n.* a short, intense exchange of gunfire between small groups of combatants

fire·fight·er *n.* a person whose work is putting out fires —**fire′fight′ing** *n.*

fire·fly *n., pl.* **-flies′** a winged beetle whose abdomen glows with a luminescent light

fire·man (-mən) *n., pl.* **-men** (-mən) 1 FIREFIGHTER 2 a person who tends a fire in a furnace, etc.

fire·place *n.* a place for a fire, esp. an open place built in a wall under a chimney

fire·plug *n.* a street hydrant supplying water for fighting fires

fire·proof *adj.* not easily destroyed by fire —*vt.* to make fireproof

fire·side *n.* 1 the space around a fireplace 2 home or home life

fire·storm *n.* 1 an intense fire over a large area, as one caused by an atomic explosion with its high winds 2 a strong, often violent, outburst

fire tower a tower used as a lookout for forest fires

fire·trap *n.* a building easily set on fire or hard to get out of if on fire

fire-truck *n.* FIRE ENGINE

fire wall 1 a fireproof wall to prevent the spread of fire **2** a program or system designed to protect a computer network from unauthorized access also **fire′wall′** *n.*

fire-wa-ter *n.* alcoholic beverage: now humorous

fire-wood *n.* wood used as fuel

fire-works *pl.n.* **1** firecrackers, rockets, etc., for noisy effects or brilliant displays: *sometimes used in sing.* **2** a noisy quarrel or display of anger

firing line 1 the line from which gunfire is directed at the enemy **2** the forefront in any kind of activity

firm¹ (furm) *adj.* [< L *firmus*] **1** solid; hard **2** not moved easily; fixed **3** unchanging; steady **4** resolute; constant **5** showing determination; strong **6** definite [a *firm* contract] — *vt., vi.* to make or become firm —**firm′ly** *adv.* —**firm′ness** *n.*

firm² (furm) *n.* [< It < L *firmus*: see prec.] a business company

fir-ma-ment (fur′mə mənt) *n.* [< L *firmare*, strengthen] the sky, considered or described poetically as a solid arch or vault

first (furst) *adj.* [OE *fyrst*] **1** before all others in a series; 1st **2** earliest **3** foremost, as in rank or quality —*adv.* **1** before any other person or thing **2** for the first time **3** sooner; preferably —*n.* **1** any person or thing that is first **2** the beginning **3** a first happening or thing of its kind **4** the winning place, as in a race **5** the slowest forward gear ratio of a motor vehicle transmission

first aid emergency treatment for injury or sudden illness, before regular medical care is available —**first′-aid′** *adj.*

first-born *adj.* born first in a family; oldest —*n.* the firstborn child

first-class *adj.* **1** of the highest class, quality, etc. **2** designating the most expensive accommodations **3** designating or of the most expensive class of ordinary mail —*adv.* **1** with first-class accommodations **2** as or by first-class mail

first family [*often* F- F-] the family of the U.S. president

first-hand *adj., adv.* from the original producer or source; direct

first lady [*often* F- L-] the wife of the U.S. president

first lieutenant a military officer ranking just above a second lieutenant

first-ly *adv.* in the first place; first

first person the form of a pronoun or verb that refers to the speaker or writer

first-rate *adj.* highest in rank, quality, etc. —*adv.* [Inf.] very well

first responder any of those charged with responding first to the scene of an emergency, as police officers, firefighters, and ambulance medics

first-string *adj.* [Inf.] *Sports* that is the first choice for regular play at a specified position

firth (furth) *n.* [< ON *fjörthr*] a narrow inlet or arm of the sea, esp. in Scotland

FISA (fi′zə) *abbrev.* Foreign Intelligence Surveillance Act

fis-cal (fis′kəl) *adj.* [< L *fiscus*, public chest] **1** relating to the public treasury or revenues **2** financial **3** designating or of government policies of spending and taxation —**fis′cal·ly** *adv.*

fish (fish) *n., pl.* **fish** or (for different species) **fish′es** [OE *fisc*] **1** any of a large group of coldblooded vertebrate animals living in water and having fins, gills for breathing, and, usually, scales **2** the flesh of a fish used as food —*vi.* **1** to catch or try to catch fish **2** to try to get something indirectly: often with *for* —*vt.* to grope for, find, and bring to view: often with *out*

fish-er *n.* **1** one who fishes; fisherman **2** the largest marten, having very dark fur **3** this fur

fish-er-man (-mən) *n., pl.* **-men** (-mən) **1** a person who fishes for sport or for a living **2** a commercial fishing vessel

fish-er-y *n., pl.* **-ies** **1** the business of catching, selling, etc. fish **2** a place where fish, etc. are caught or bred

fish-hook *n.* a hook, usually barbed, for catching fish

fish-ing *n.* the catching of fish for sport or for a living

fish meal ground, dried fish, used as fertilizer or fodder

fish-wife *n., pl.* **-wives′ 1** a woman who sells fish **2** a coarse, scolding woman

fish-y *adj.* **-i-er, -i-est 1** like a fish in odor, taste, etc. **2** dull or expressionless [*fishy* eyes] **3** [Inf.] questionable; odd —**fish′i-ly** *adv.* —**fish′i-ness** *n.*

fis-sion (fish′ən, fizh′-) *n.* [< L *findere*, to split] **1** a splitting apart; cleavage **2** NUCLEAR FISSION —**fis′sion-a-ble** *adj.*

fis-sure (fish′ər) *n.* [see prec.] a cleft or crack

fist (fist) *n.* [OE *fyst*] a hand with the fingers closed tightly into the palm

fist-i-cuffs (fis′ti kufs′) *pl.n.* [Old-fashioned] a fight with the fists

fis-tu-la (fis′tyoo lə, -chə lə) *n., pl.* **-las** or **-lae′** (-lē′) [L, a pipe, ulcer] an abnormal passage, as from an abscess to the skin

fit¹ (fit) *vt.* **fit′ted** or **fit, fit′ting** [ME *fitten*] **1** to be suitable to **2** to be the proper size, shape, etc. for **3** to adjust so as to fit **4** to equip; outfit —*vi.* **1** [Archaic] to be suitable or proper **2** to have the proper size or shape —*adj.* **fit′ter, fit′test 1** suited to some purpose **2** proper; right **3** healthy, esp. from regular exercise or other physical activity **4** [Inf.] inclined [she was *fit* to scream] —*n.* the manner of fitting [a tight *fit*] —**fit′ly** *adv.* —**fit′ness** *n.* —**fit′ter** *n.*

fit² (fit) *n.* [OE *fitt*, conflict] **1** any sudden, uncontrollable attack, as of coughing **2** an outburst, as of anger **3** a seizure involving convulsions, loss of consciousness, etc. —**by fits (and starts)** in an irregular way —**have**

(or throw) a fit [Inf.] to become very angry or upset

fit·ful (-fəl) *adj.* characterized by intermittent activity; spasmodic —**fit'ful·ly** *adv.* —**fit'ful·ness** *n.*

fit·ting *adj.* suitable; proper —*n.* **1** an adjustment or trying on of clothes, etc. **2** a small part used to join or adapt other parts **3** [*pl.*] fixtures

five (fīv) *adj., n.* [OE *fīf*] one more than four; 5; V

five-and-ten-cent store a store that sells a wide variety of inexpensive merchandise: also **five'-and-ten'** *n.*

five-star *adj.* having the highest rating, based on a given set of criteria for excellence

fix (fiks) *vt.* **fixed, fix'ing** [< L *figere*, fasten] **1** to fasten firmly **2** to set firmly in the mind **3** to direct (one's eyes) steadily at something **4** to make rigid **5** to make permanent **6** to establish (a date, etc.) definitely **7** to set in order; adjust **8** to repair **9** to prepare (food or meals) **10** [Inf.] to influence the result or action of (a race, jury, etc.), as by bribery **11** [Inf.] to punish —*vi.* **1** to become fixed **2** [Inf. or Dial.] to prepare or intend —*n.* **1** the position of a ship, etc. determined from the bearings of two known positions **2** [Inf.] a predicament **3** [Slang] a contest, etc. that has been fixed **4** [Slang] something craved, esp. a dose of a drug craved by an addict —**fix up** [Inf.] **1** to repair **2** to arrange; set in order —**fix'a·ble** *adj.* —**fix'er** *n.*

fixa·tion (fik sā'shən) *n.* **1** a fixing or being fixed **2** an obsession **3** a remaining at an early stage of psychosexual development

fix·a·tive (fik'sə tiv) *adj.* that is able or tends to make permanent, prevent fading, etc. —*n.* a fixative substance

fixed (fikst) *adj.* **1** firmly in place **2** established, settled **3** resolute; unchanging **4** persistent [a *fixed* idea] —**fix·ed·ly** (fiks'id lē) *adv.*

fix·ings (fik'sinz') *pl.n.* [Inf.] accessories or trimmings [turkey and all the *fixings*]

fix·i·ty (fik'si tē) *n.* the quality or state of being fixed or steady

fix·ture (fiks'chər) *n.* [see FIX] **1** anything firmly in place **2** any attached piece of equipment in a house, etc. **3** a person long established in a job, etc.

fizz (fiz) *n.* [? akin to fol.] **1** a hissing, sputtering sound **2** an effervescent drink —*vi.* **1** to make a hissing sound **2** to effervesce

fiz·zle (fiz'əl) *vi.* **-zled, -zling** [< ME] **1** FIZZ (*vi.* 1) **2** [Inf.] to fail, esp. after a good start —*n.* **1** a hissing sound **2** [Inf.] a failure

fjord (fyôrd) *n.* [Norw < ON *fjörthr*] a narrow inlet of the sea bordered by steep cliffs

fl *abbrev.* **1** floor **2** [L *floruit*] (he or she) flourished **3** fluid

FL *abbrev.* Florida

flab (flab) *n.* [< FLABBY] [Inf.] sagging, fatty flesh

flab·ber·gast (flab'ər gast') *vt.* [?] to dumbfound

flab·by (flab'ē) *adj.* **-bi·er, -bi·est** [< FLAP] **1** limp and soft **2** weak —**flab'bi·ly** *adv.* —**flab'bi·ness** *n.*

flac·cid (flas'id, flak'sid) *adj.* [< L *flaccus*] soft and limp; flabby

flack (flak) *n.* [< ?] [Slang] PRESS AGENT —**flack'er·y** *n.*

fla·con (flak'ən; *Fr* flå kōn') *n., pl.* **-cons** (-enz; *Fr,* -kōn') [Fr] a small flask with a stopper, as for perfume

flag[1] (flag) *n.* [< FLAG[4], in obs. sense "to flutter"] a cloth with colors, patterns, etc., used as a symbol of a nation, state, etc., or as a signal —*vt.* **flagged, flag'ging 1** to signal with or as with a flag; esp., to signal to stop: often with *down* **2** to mark with a symbol, as to draw attention to a particular item

flag[2] (flag) *n.* [< ON *flaga*, slab of stone] FLAGSTONE

flag[3] (flag) *n.* [ME *flagge*] any of various irises, or a flower or leaf of one

flag[4] (flag) *vi.* **flagged, flag'ging** [prob. < ON *flogra*, to flutter] **1** to become limp; droop **2** to grow weak or tired

flag·el·late (flaj'ə lāt') *vt.* **-lat'ed, -lat'ing** [< L *flagellum*, a whip] to whip; flog —**flag'el·la'tion** *n.*

fla·gel·lum (flə jel'əm) *n., pl.* **-la** (-ə) or **-lums** [L, a whip] a whiplike part of some cells, as of bacteria or protozoans, used as for moving about

flag·on (flag'ən) *n.* [< LL *flasco*] a container for liquids, with a handle, a narrow neck, a spout, and, often, a lid

flag·pole *n.* a pole on which a flag is raised and flown: also **flag'staff'**

fla·grant (flā'grənt) *adj.* [< L *flagrare*, to blaze] glaringly bad; outrageous —**fla'gran·cy** (-grən sē) *n.,* **fla'grance** —**fla'grant·ly** *adv.*

flag·ship *n.* **1** the ship that carries the commander of a fleet or other large naval unit **2** the largest or most important member or part, as of a group

flag·stone *n.* a flat paving stone

flail (flāl) *n.* [< L *flagellum*, a whip] a farm tool for threshing grain by hand —*vt., vi.* **1** to thresh with a flail **2** to beat **3** to move (one's arms) like flails

flair (fler) *n.* [< L *fragrare*, to smell] **1** a natural talent; aptitude **2** a sense of style; dash

flak (flak) *n.* [Ger acronym] **1** the fire of antiaircraft guns **2** [Inf.] strong criticism Also sp. **flack**

flake (flāk) *n.* [< Scand] **1** a small, thin mass **2** a piece split off; chip —*vt., vi.* **flaked, flak'ing 1** to form into flakes **2** to peel off in flakes

flak·y *adj.* **-i·er, -i·est 1** of or producing flakes **2** [Slang] eccentric, erratic, etc.

flam·bé (fläm bā') *adj.* [Fr] served with a sauce of flaming brandy, rum, etc. —*n.* a dessert so served

flam·boy·ant (flam boi'ənt) *adj.* [Fr < L *flamma*, a flame] **1** flamelike or brilliant **2** too showy or ornate —**flam·boy′ance** *n.*, **flam·boy′an·cy** —**flam·boy′ant·ly** *adv.*

flame (flām) *n.* [< L *flamma*] 1 the burning gas of a fire, appearing as a tongue of light 2 the state of burning with a blaze 3 a thing like a flame 4 an intense emotion 5 a sweetheart —*vi.* **flamed, flam′ing** 1 to burst into flame 2 to grow red or hot 3 to become excited —*vt.* [Inf.] to attack, as in a post or comment on an electronic forum

fla·men·co (flə men′kō) *n.* [Sp] a Spanish gypsy style of dance or music

flame·out *n.* 1 a failure of combustion in a jet's engine during flight 2 a sudden and complete failure

flame·throw·er *n.* a weapon that shoots flaming oil, napalm, etc.

fla·min·go (flə miŋ′gō′) *n.*, *pl.* **-gos′** or **-goes′** [Port] a tropical wading bird with long legs and pink or red feathers

flam·ma·ble (flam′ə bəl) *adj.* easily set on fire; that will burn readily or quickly —**flam′ma·bil′i·ty** *n.*

Flan·ders (flan′dərz) region in NW Europe, in France & Belgium

flange (flanj) *n.* [< ? ME] a projecting rim on a wheel, etc., that serves to hold it in place, give it strength, etc.

flank (flaŋk) *n.* [< OFr *flanc*] 1 the side of an animal between the ribs and the hip 2 the side of anything 3 Mil. the right or left side of a formation or force —*vt.* 1 to be at the side of 2 Mil. to attack, or pass around, the side of (enemy troops)

flan·nel (flan′əl) *n.* [prob. < Welsh *gwlan*, wool] 1 a soft, loosely woven cloth of wool or cotton 2 [pl.] trousers, etc. made of this

flan·nel·ette or **flan·nel·et** (flan′əl et′) *n.* a soft, napped cotton cloth

flap (flap) *n.* [ME *flappe*] 1 anything flat and broad hanging loose at one end 2 the motion or sound of a swinging flap 3 [Inf.] a commotion; stir —*vt.* **flapped, flap′ping** 1 to slap 2 to move back and forth or up and down

flap·jack *n.* a pancake

flap·per *n.* [Inf.] in the 1920s, a bold, unconventional young woman

flare (fler) *vi.* **flared, flar′ing** [ME *fleare* < ?] 1 *a)* to blaze brightly *b)* to burn unsteadily 2 to burst out suddenly, as in anger: often with *up* or *out* 3 to curve outward, as a bell's rim —*n.* 1 a bright, unsteady blaze 2 a brightly flaming light for signaling, etc. 3 an outburst, as of emotion 4 a curving outward

flare-up *n.* a sudden outburst of flame or of anger, trouble, etc.

flash (flash) *vi.* [ME *flashen*, to splash] 1 to send out a sudden, brief light 2 to sparkle 3 to come or pass suddenly —*vt.* 1 to cause to flash 2 to send (news, etc.) swiftly 3 [Inf.] to display or expose briefly —*n.* 1 a sudden, brief light 2 a brief moment 3 a sudden, brief display 4 a brief item of late news 5 a gaudy display —*adj.* 1 happening swiftly or suddenly 2 Comput. of an erasable computer

memory device that retains stored data when power is turned off —**flash′er** *n.*

flash·back *n.* 1 a break in the continuity of a story, etc. by the telling or showing of an earlier episode 2 a sudden, vivid recollection of a past event

flash·bulb *n.* a bulb giving a brief, bright light, for taking photographs

flash·cube *n.* a rotating cube with flashbulbs in four sides

flash drive Comput. a very small, portable memory device that plugs into a USB port

flash·for·ward *n.* a break in the continuity of a story, etc. by the telling or showing of a future episode

flash·ing *n.* sheets of metal used to weatherproof roof joints or edges

flash·light *n.* a portable, usually hand-held electric light

flash mob a sudden, unannounced public gathering of people, organized by means of social media

flash point the lowest temperature at which vapor, as of an oil, will ignite with a flash

flash·y *adj.* **-i·er, -i·est** 1 dazzling 2 gaudy; showy —**flash′i·ness** *n.*

flask (flask) *n.* [< L *flasca*, bottle] 1 any bottle-shaped container used in laboratories, etc. 2 a small, flat container for liquor, etc., to be carried in the pocket

flat¹ (flat) *adj.* **flat′ter, flat′test** [< ON *flatr*] 1 having a smooth, level surface 2 lying spread out 3 broad, even, and thin 4 absolute [a *flat* denial] 5 not fluctuating [a *flat* rate] 6 tasteless; insipid 7 not interesting 8 emptied of air [a *flat* tire] 9 without gloss [*flat* paint] 10 Music *a)* lower in pitch by a half step *b)* below true pitch —*adv.* 1 in a flat manner or position 2 exactly 3 Music below true pitch —*n.* 1 anything flat, esp. a surface, part, or expanse 2 a deflated tire 3 Music *a)* a note one half step below another *b)* the symbol (♭) for this —*vt.* **flat′ted, flat′ting** Music to make flat —*vi.* to sing or play below true pitch —**fall flat** to fail in the desired effect —**flat′ly** *adv.* —**flat′ness** *n.* —**flat′tish** *adj.*

flat² (flat) *n.* [< Scot dial. *flet*, floor] [Chiefly Brit.] an apartment or suite of rooms

flat·bed *n.* a truck, trailer, etc. having a bed or platform without sides or stakes

flat·boat *n.* a flat-bottomed boat for carrying freight in shallow bodies of water or on rivers

flat·bread *n.* bread made in thin, circular pieces or sheets

flat·car *n.* a railroad freight car without sides or a roof

flat·fish *n.*, *pl.* **-fish′** or **-fish′es** a fish, such as a flounder or sole, having both eyes and mouth on the upper side of a very flat body

flat·foot *n.* 1 a condition of the foot in which the instep arch is flattened 2 *pl.* **-foots′** or **-feet′** [Slang] a policeman —**flat′-foot′ed** *adj.*

flat·i·ron *n.* an iron for clothes

flat·line *n.* the unfluctuating readout line on a medical monitor, indicating the stopping of the heartbeat —*vi.* **-lined′**, **-lin′ing** [Inf.] to cease to live, flourish, or succeed; die literally or figuratively

flat-out *adj.* [Inf.] **1** at full speed, with maximum effort, etc. **2** absolute; thorough

flat–panel *adj.* being a thin, flat electronic display screen: also **flat-screen**

flat·ten (flat′'n) *vt., vi.* to make or become flat or flatter

flat·ter (flat′ər) *vt.* [< OFr *flater,* to smooth] **1** to praise insincerely **2** to try to please, as by praise **3** to make seem more attractive than is so **4** to gratify the vanity of —**flat′ter·er** *n.* —**flat′ter·ing·ly** *adv.* —**flat′ter·y** *n.*

flat·top *n.* [Slang] **1** an aircraft carrier **2** a haircut in which the hair on top of the head is cut so as to form a flat surface

flat·u·lent (flach′ə lənt) *adj.* [see fol.] **1** having or producing gas in the intestines **2** pompous —**flat′u·lence** *n.*

fla·tus (flāt′əs) *n.* [L < *flare,* to blow] intestinal gas

flat·ware *n.* knives, forks, and spoons

flat·worm *n.* any of various worms with flat bodies, as the tapeworm

Flau·bert (flō ber′), **Gus·tave** (güs tàv′) 1821–80; Fr. novelist

flaunt (flônt) *vi.* [? < dial. *flant,* to strut] to make a gaudy or defiant display —*vt.* **1** to show off proudly or defiantly **2** FLOUT: usage objected to by many —**flaunt′ing·ly** *adv.*

flau·tist (flôt′ist, flout′-) *n.* [< It] *var. of* FLUTIST

fla·vor (flā′vər) *n.* [ult. < L *flare,* to blow] **1** that quality of a substance that is a mixing of its characteristic taste and smell **2** flavoring **3** characteristic quality —*vt.* to give flavor to Brit. sp. **fla′vour** —**fla′vor·ful** *adj.* —**fla′vor·less** *adj.*

fla·vor·ing *n.* an essence, extract, etc. that adds flavor to food or drink

flaw (flô) *n.* [ME, a flake, splinter] **1** a crack, etc. as in a gem **2** a fault, as in reasoning —**flaw′less** *adj.* —**flaw′less·ly** *adv.* —**flaw′less·ness** *n.*

flax (flaks) *n.* [< OE *fleax*] **1** a slender, erect plant with delicate blue flowers: its seed (**flax′seed′**) is used to make linseed oil **2** the fibers of this plant, which are spun into linen thread

flax·en (flak′sən) *adj.* **1** of or made of flax **2** pale-yellow

flay (flā) *vt.* [OE *flean*] **1** to strip off the skin of, as by whipping **2** to criticize harshly

flea (flē) *n.* [OE *fleah*] a small, wingless jumping insect that is a bloodsucking parasite as an adult

flea market an outdoor bazaar dealing mainly in cheap, secondhand goods

fleck (flek) *n.* [ON *flekkr*] a spot, speck, or flake —*vt.* to spot; speckle

fled (fled) *vi., vt. pt. & pp. of* FLEE

fledg·ling (flej′lin) *n.* [< ME *flegge,* ready to fly] **1** a young bird just able to fly **2** a young, inexperienced person Also [Chiefly Brit.] **fledge′ling**

flee (flē) *vi.* **fled, flee′ing** [OE *fleon*] **1** to go swiftly or escape, as from danger **2** to pass away swiftly —*vt.* to run away or try to escape from

fleece (flēs) *n.* [OE *fleos*] **1** the wool covering a sheep or similar animal **2** a soft, warm, napped fabric —*vt.* **fleeced, fleec′ing 1** to shear the fleece from **2** to swindle —**fleec′er** *n.*

fleec·y (flēs′ē) *adj.* **-i·er, -i·est** of or like fleece; soft and light —**fleec′i·ness** *n.*

fleet¹ (flēt) *n.* [OE *fleot*] **1** a number of warships under one command **2** any group of ships, trucks, etc. under one control or engaged in a common activity

fleet² (flēt) *adj.* [< OE *fleotan,* to float] swift; rapid —**fleet′ness** *n.*

fleet·ing *adj.* passing swiftly —**fleet′ing·ly** *adv.* —**fleet′ing·ness** *n.*

Flem·ish (flem′ish) *adj.* of Flanders or its people, language, etc. —*n.* any of the dialects of Dutch spoken in Flanders

fler·o·vi·um (fle rō′vē əm) *n.* [after the *Flerov* Laboratory of Nuclear Reactions in Russia] an artificially produced, radioactive chemical element: symbol, Fl; at. no. 114

flesh (flesh) *n.* [OE *flæsc*] **1** the soft substance of the body; esp., the muscular tissue **2** meat **3** the pulpy or edible part of fruits and vegetables **4** the body as distinct from the soul **5** all humankind **6** yellowish pink —**in the flesh 1** alive **2** in person —**one's (own) flesh and blood** one's close relatives —**flesh′y** *adj.* **-i·er, -i·est**

flesh-and-blood *adj.* **1** alive **2** actual **3** present; in person

flesh·ly *adj.* **-li·er, -li·est 1** of the body; corporeal **2** sensual

fleur-de-lis (flur′də lē′) *n., pl.* **fleurs-de-lis** (flur′ də lē′, -lēz′) [< OFr *flor de lis,* lit., flower of the lily] a lilylike emblem: the coat of arms of the former French royal family

flew (flōō) *vi., vt. pt. of* FLY¹

flex (fleks) *vt., vi.* [< L *flectere,* to bend] **1** to bend (an arm, knee, etc.) **2** to shorten and thicken (a muscle) in action

flex·i·ble (flek′sə bəl) *adj.* **1** able to bend without breaking; pliant **2** easily influenced **3** adjustable to change —**flex′i·bil′i·ty** *n.*

flex·time *n.* a system allowing individual employees some flexibility in choosing when they work

flib·ber·ti·gib·bet (flib′ər tē jib′it) *n.* [< ?] a frivolous, flighty person

flick¹ (flik) *n.* [echoic] a light, quick stroke —*vt.* to strike, remove, etc. with a light, quick stroke

flick² (flik) *n.* [< fol.] [Slang] a film —**the flicks** [Slang] a showing of a film

flick·er¹ (flik′ər) *vi.* [OE *flicorian*] **1** to move with a quick, light, wavering motion **2** to burn or shine unsteadily —*n.* **1** a flickering **2** a dart of flame or light

flick·er² [echoic of its cry] *n.* any of several N American woodpeckers

fli·er (flī′ər) *n.* **1** *alt sp. of* FLYER **2** [Inf] a reckless gamble

flight¹ (flīt) *n.* 〖OE *flyht*〗 **1** the act or power of flying **2** the distance flown **3** a group of things flying together **4** an airplane flying a scheduled trip **5** a trip by airplane **6** a soaring above the ordinary [a *flight* of fancy] **7** a set of stairs, as between landings

flight² (flīt) *n.* 〖< OE *fleon*, flee〗 a fleeing from or as from danger

flight attendant an airplane attendant who sees to passengers' comfort and safety

flight·less *adj.* not able to fly

flight·y *adj.* **-i·er, -i·est** **1** given to sudden whims; frivolous **2** easily excited, upset, etc. —**flight′i·ness** *n.*

flim·sy (flim′zē) *adj.* **-si·er, -si·est** 〖< ?〗 **1** easily broken or damaged; frail **2** ineffectual [a *flimsy* excuse] —**flim′si·ly** *adv.* —**flim′si·ness** *n.*

flinch (flinch) *vi.* 〖< OFr *flenchir*〗 to draw back from a blow or anything difficult or painful —*n.* a flinching

fling (fliŋ) *vt.* **flung, fling′ing** 〖< ON *flengia*, to whip〗 **1** to throw, esp. with force; hurl **2** to put abruptly or violently **3** to move (one's limbs, head, etc.) suddenly —*n.* **1** a flinging **2** a brief time of wild pleasures **3** a spirited dance **4** [Inf.] a try **5** [Inf.] a brief love affair

flint (flint) *n.* 〖OE〗 a very hard, siliceous rock, usually gray, that produces sparks when struck against steel —**flint′y** *adj.* **-i·er, -i·est**

flip¹ (flip) *vt.* **flipped, flip′ping** 〖echoic〗 **1** to toss with a quick jerk; flick **2** to snap (a coin) into the air with the thumb **3** to turn or turn over —*vi.* **1** to move jerkily **2** [Slang] to lose self-control —*n.* a flipping —**flip one's lid (or wig)** [Slang] to go berserk

flip² (flip) *adj.* **flip′per, flip′pest** [Inf.] flippant

flip chart a series of large paper sheets containing information, charts, etc., fastened loosely for sequential display

flip·pant (-ənt) *adj.* 〖prob. < FLIP¹〗 frivolous and disrespectful —**flip′pan·cy** *n., pl.* **-cies** —**flip′pant·ly** *adv.*

flip·per (-ər) *n.* 〖< FLIP¹〗 **1** a broad, flat limb adapted for swimming, as in seals **2** a paddlelike rubber device worn on each foot by skin divers, etc.

flirt (flurt) *vt.* 〖< ?〗 to move jerkily [the bird *flirted* its tail] —*vi.* **1** to pay amorous attention to someone, without serious intentions **2** to trifle or toy [to *flirt* with an idea] —*n.* **1** a quick, jerky movement **2** one who flirts with others

flir·ta·tion (flər tā′shən) *n.* **1** the act or an instance of flirting **2** a frivolous love affair —**flir·ta′tious** *adj.*

flit (flit) *vi.* **flit′ted, flit′ting** 〖< ON *flytja*〗 to pass or fly lightly and rapidly

float (flōt) *n.* 〖< OE *flota*, a ship〗 **1** anything that stays on the surface of a liquid, as a raftlike platform for swimmers, a cork on a fishing line, etc. **2** a floating ball, etc. that regulates a valve, as in a water tank **3** a low, flat vehicle decorated for exhibit in a parade **4** a beverage with ice cream floating in it —*vi.* **1**

to stay on the surface of a liquid **2** to drift easily on water, in air, etc. **3** to move about aimlessly **4** to fluctuate freely: said of exchange rates —*vt.* **1** to cause to float **2** to put into circulation [to *float* a bond issue] **3** to arrange for (a loan) —**float′er** *n.*

flock (fläk) *n.* 〖OE *flocc*〗 **1** a group of certain animals, as sheep, birds, etc., living or feeding together **2** any group, esp. a large one —*vi.* to assemble or travel in a flock or crowd

flock·ing (fläk′iŋ) *n.* 〖< L *floccus*, tuft of wool〗 **1** tiny fibers of wool, rayon, etc. applied to a fabric, wallpaper, etc. as a velvetlike surface: also **flock 2** such a fabric, etc.

floe (flō) *n.* 〖? < Norw *flo*, layer〗 ICE FLOE

flog (fläg, flôg) *vt.* **flogged, flog′ging** 〖? < L *flagellare*, to whip〗 to beat with a stick, whip, etc. —**flog′ger** *n.*

flood (flud) *n.* 〖OE *flod*〗 **1** an overflowing of water on an area normally dry **2** the rising of the tide **3** a great outpouring, as of words —*vt.* **1** to cover or fill, as with a flood **2** to put too much water, fuel, etc. on or in —*vi.* **1** to gush out **2** to become flooded —**the Flood** *Bible* the great flood in Noah's time

flood·light *n.* **1** a lamp that casts a broad beam of bright light **2** such a beam of light —*vt.* **-light′ed** *or* **-lit′, -light′ing** to illuminate by a floodlight

flood tide the rising tide

floor (flôr) *n.* 〖OE *flor*〗 **1** the inside bottom surface of a room **2** the bottom surface of anything [the ocean *floor*] **3** a story in a building **4** the right to speak in an assembly —*vt.* **1** to furnish with a floor **2** to knock down **3** [Inf.] *a)* to defeat *b)* to flabbergast; astound

floor·board *n.* **1** a board in a floor **2** the floor of an automobile, etc.

floor exercise any gymnastic exercise done without apparatus

floor·ing *n.* **1** a floor or floors **2** material for making a floor

floor model (*or* **sample**) a sample sale item, as a piece of furniture, on display in a store and often offered for sale at a reduced price

floor show a show presenting singers, dancers, etc., as in a nightclub

flop (fläp) *vt.* **flopped, flop′ping** 〖var. of FLAP〗 to flap or throw noisily and clumsily —*vi.* **1** to move, drop, or flap around loosely or clumsily **2** [Inf.] to fail —*n.* **1** the act or sound of flopping **2** [Inf.] a failure —**flop′py** *adj.* **-pi·er, -pi·est**

flop·house *n.* [Inf.] a cheap hotel for indigents

floppy disk a small, flexible computer disk for storing data

flo·ra (flôr′ə) *n.* 〖L < *flos*, a flower〗 the plants of a specified region or time

flo·ral (-əl) *adj.* of or like flowers

Flor·ence (flôr′əns) city in central Italy —**Flor′en·tine** (-ən tēn′) *adj., n.*

flo·res·cence (flō res′əns) *n.* 〖< L *flos*, a flower〗 a blooming or flowering —**flo·res′cent** *adj.*

flor·id (flôr′id) *adj.* 〖< L *flos*, a flower〗 **1**

ruddy: said of the complexion 2 gaudy; showy; ornate

Flor·i·da (flôr′ə də, flär′-) state of the SE U.S.; cap. Tallahassee: abbrev. *FL* —**Flo·rid·i·an** (flô rid′ē ən) *adj., n.,* **Flor′i·dan**

flor·in (flôr′in) *n.* ⟦< L *flos*, a flower⟧ any of various European coins, esp. a gold coin of medieval Florence

flo·rist (flôr′ist) *n.* ⟦< L *flos*, a flower⟧ one who grows or sells flowers

floss (flôs, fläs) *n.* ⟦ult. < L *floccus*, tuft of wool⟧ 1 the short, downy waste fibers of silk 2 a soft, loosely twisted thread or yarn, as of silk, for embroidery 3 a substance like this 4 DENTAL FLOSS — *vt., vi.* to clean (the teeth) with dental floss —**floss′y** *adj.* **-i·er, -i·est**

flo·ta·tion (flō tā′shən) *n.* the act or condition of floating

flo·til·la (flō til′ə) *n.* ⟦Sp, dim. of *flota*, a fleet⟧ 1 a small fleet 2 a fleet of boats or small ships

flot·sam (flät′səm) *n.* ⟦< MDu *vloten*, to float⟧ the wreckage of a ship or its cargo floating at sea: used in the phrase **flotsam and jetsam**

flounce[1] (flouns) *vi.* **flounced, flounc′ing** ⟦< ? Scand⟧ to move with quick, flinging motions of the body, as in anger —*n.* a flouncing

flounce[2] (flouns) *n.* ⟦< OFr *froncir*, to wrinkle⟧ a wide ruffle sewn to a skirt, sleeve, etc. —**flounc′y** *adj.* **-i·er, -i·est**

floun·der[1] (floun′dər) *vi.* ⟦< ? FOUNDER⟧ 1 to struggle awkwardly, as in deep mud 2 to speak or act in an awkward, confused manner

floun·der[2] (floun′dər) *n.* ⟦< Scand⟧ any of various flatfishes caught for food, as the halibut

flour (flour) *n.* ⟦orig., flower (i.e., best) of meal⟧ 1 a fine, powdery substance produced by grinding and sifting grain, esp. wheat 2 any finely powdered substance —**flour′y** *adj.*

flour·ish (flur′ish) *vi.* ⟦< L *flos*, a flower⟧ 1 to grow vigorously; thrive 2 to be at the peak of development, etc. —*vt.* to brandish (a sword, etc.) —*n.* 1 anything done in a showy way 2 a brandishing 3 decorative lines in handwriting 4 a musical fanfare

flout (flout) *vt., vi.* ⟦< ? ME *flouten*, play the flute⟧ to mock or scoff —*n.* a scornful act or remark —**flout′er** *n.*

flow (flō) *vi.* ⟦OE *flowan*⟧ 1 to move as a liquid does 2 to move gently and smoothly 3 to pour out 4 to issue; proceed 5 to hang loose [*flowing* hair] 6 to be plentiful —*n.* 1 a flowing 2 the rate of flow 3 anything that flows 4 the rising of the tide

flow·chart *n.* a diagram showing steps in a sequence of operations

flow·er (flou′ər) *n.* ⟦< L *flos*⟧ 1 the seed-producing structure of a flowering plant; blossom 2 a plant cultivated for its blossoms 3 the best or finest part —*vi.* 1 to produce blossoms 2 to reach the best stage —**in flower** flowering

flow·er·pot *n.* a container in which to grow plants

flow·er·y *adj.* **-i·er, -i·est** 1 covered or decorated with flowers 2 full of ornate expressions and fine words —**flow′er·i·ness** *n.*

flown (flōn) *vi., vt. pp. of* FLY[1]

flu (flo͞o) *n.* 1 *short for* INFLUENZA 2 a respiratory or intestinal infection caused by a virus

flub (flub) [Inf.] *vt., vi.* **flubbed, flub′bing** ⟦< ? FL(OP) + (D)UB⟧ to bungle (a job, stroke, etc.) —*n.* a blunder

fluc·tu·ate (fluk′cho͞o āt′) *vi.* **-at′ed, -at′ing** ⟦< L *fluctus*, a wave⟧ to be continually varying in an irregular way —**fluc′tu·a′tion** *n.*

flue (flo͞o) *n.* ⟦< ? OFr *fluie*, a flowing⟧ a tube or shaft for the passage of smoke, hot air, etc., esp. in a chimney

flu·ent (flo͞o′ənt) *adj.* ⟦< L *fluere*, to flow⟧ 1 flowing or moving smoothly 2 able to write or speak easily, expressively, etc. —**flu′en·cy** *n.* —**flu′ent·ly** *adv.*

fluff (fluf) *n.* ⟦? blend of *flue*, soft mass + PUFF⟧ 1 soft, light down 2 a loose, soft mass, as of hair 3 something trivial —*vt.* 1 to shake or pat until loose or fluffy 2 to bungle (one's lines), as in acting

fluff·y *adj.* **-i·er, -i·est** soft and light like fluff; feathery

flu·id (flo͞o′id) *adj.* ⟦< L *fluere*, to flow⟧ 1 that can flow as a liquid or gas does 2 that can change rapidly or easily 3 available for investment or as cash —*n.* a liquid or gas —**flu·id′i·ty** *n.* —**flu′id·ly** *adv.*

fluke[1] (flo͞ok) *n.* ⟦OE *floc*, a flatfish⟧ TREMATODE

fluke[2] (flo͞ok) *n.* ⟦< ?⟧ 1 a pointed end of an anchor, which catches in the ground 2 a barb of a harpoon, etc. 3 a lobe of a whale's tail 4 [Inf.] a stroke of luck

flung (flun) *vt. pt. & pp. of* FLING

flunk (flunk) *vt., vi.* ⟦< ?⟧ [Inf.] to fail, as in a school assignment

flunk·y (flun′kē) *n., pl.* **-ies** ⟦orig. Scot⟧ 1 a toady 2 a person with menial tasks Also **flunk′ey**

fluo·resce (flô res′) *vi.* **-resced′, -resc′ing** to produce, show, or undergo fluorescence

fluo·res·cence (-res′əns) *n.* ⟦ult. < L *fluor*, flux⟧ 1 the property of producing light when acted upon by radiant energy 2 the production of such light 3 light so produced

fluo·res·cent (flo͞o res′ənt) *adj.* 1 of or having to do with fluorescence 2 glowing and vivid [*fluorescent* colors]

fluorescent lamp (*or* **tube**) a glass tube coated on the inside with a fluorescent substance that gives off light (**fluorescent light**) when mercury vapor in the tube is acted upon by a stream of electrons

fluo·ri·date (flôr′ə dāt′, floor′-) *vt.* **-dat′ed, -dat′ing** to add fluorides to (a supply of drinking water) in order to reduce tooth decay —**fluo′ri·da′tion** *n.*

fluo·ride (flôr′īd′, floor′īd′) *n.* any of various compounds of fluorine, esp. one put in toothpaste, drinking water, etc. to prevent tooth decay

fluo·rine (-ēn′) *n.* ⟦< L *fluor*, flux⟧ a greenish-yellow, gaseous chemical element: symbol, F; at. no. 9

fluo·ro·car·bon (-kär′bən) *n.* any of certain compounds containing carbon, fluorine, and, sometimes, hydrogen

fluo·ro·scope (-skōp′) *n.* a machine for examining internal structures by viewing the shadowy images produced on a fluorescent screen by objects through which X-rays are directed

flur·ry (flur′ē) *n., pl.* **-ries** [< ?] 1 a sudden gust of wind, rain, or snow 2 a sudden commotion —*vt.* **-ried, -ry·ing** to confuse; agitate

flush[1] (flush) *vi.* 1 to flow rapidly 2 to blush or glow 3 to be washed out with a sudden flow of water 4 to start up from cover: said of birds, etc. —*vt.* 1 to wash out with a sudden flow of water 2 to make blush or glow 3 to excite [*flushed* with victory] 4 to drive (birds, etc.) from cover —*n.* 1 a rapid flow, as of water 2 a sudden, vigorous growth 3 sudden excitement 4 a blush; glow 5 a sudden feeling of heat, as in a fever —*adj.* 1 well supplied, esp. with money 2 abundant 3 level or even (*with*) 4 direct; full —*adv.* 1 so as to be level 2 directly

flush[2] (flush) *n.* [< L *fluere*, to flow] a hand of cards all in the same suit

flus·ter (flus′tər) *vt., vi.* [prob. < Scand] to make or become confused

flute (flōōt) *n.* [< Prov *fläut*] 1 a high-pitched wind instrument consisting of a long, slender tube with keys or open finger holes 2 a groove in the shaft of a column, etc. —**flut′ed** *adj.* —**flut′ing** *n.* —**flut′ist** *n.*

flut·ter (flut′ər) *vi.* [< OE *fleotan*, to float] 1 to flap the wings rapidly, without flying 2 to wave, move, or beat rapidly —*vt.* to cause to flutter —*n.* 1 a fluttering movement 2 an excited or confused state —**flut′ter·y** *adj.*

flux (fluks) *n.* [< L *fluere*, to flow] 1 a flowing 2 a continual change 3 a substance used to help metals fuse together, as in soldering

fly[1] (flī) *vi.* **flew, flown, fly′ing** [OE *fleogan*] 1 to move through the air in an aircraft or by using wings, as a bird does 2 to wave or float in the air 3 to move or pass swiftly 4 to flee 5 **flied, fly′ing** *Baseball* to hit a fly —*vt.* 1 to cause to float in the air 2 to operate (an aircraft) 3 to flee from —*n., pl.* **flies** 1 a flap that conceals the zipper, etc. on a pair of pants 2 *a*) a flap serving as the door of a tent *b*) an outer covering for a tent, usually waterproof 3 *Baseball* a ball batted high in the air 4 [*pl.*] *Theater* the space above a stage

fly[2] (flī) *n., pl.* **flies** [OE *fleoge*] 1 any of a large group of insects with two or four wings 2 an artificial fly used as a lure in fishing

fly·a·ble *adj.* suitable for flying

fly·by or **fly-by** *n., pl.* **-bys′** a flight past a designated point or place, as by an aircraft

fly-by-night *adj.* financially irresponsible

fly·catch·er *n.* a small bird that catches insects in flight

fly·er *n.* 1 one that flies 2 a bus, train, etc. with a fast schedule 3 a handbill 4 *alt. sp. of* FLIER

fly-fish·ing *n.* the act of fishing by casting artificial flies

flying buttress a buttress connected with a wall by an arch, for resisting outward pressure

flying colors used in **with flying colors**, with notable success

flying fish a fish with winglike fins used in gliding through the air

flying saucer a UFO

fly·leaf *n., pl.* **-leaves′** a blank leaf at the beginning or end of a book

fly·pa·per *n.* a sticky or poisonous paper set out to catch flies

fly·speck *n.* 1 a speck of fly excrement 2 any tiny spot or petty flaw

fly·way *n.* a route taken regularly by birds migrating to and from breeding grounds

fly·weight *n.* a boxer who weighs 112 pounds or less

fly·wheel *n.* a heavy wheel on a machine, for regulating its speed

FM[1] (ef′em′) *n.* frequency-modulation broadcasting or sound transmission

FM[2] *abbrev.* frequency modulation

f-num·ber (ef′num′bər) *n. Photog.* a number indicating the relative aperture of a lens: a higher number means a smaller opening

foal (fōl) *n.* [OE *fola*] a young horse, mule, etc. —*vt., vi.* to give birth to (a foal)

foam (fōm) *n.* [OE *fam*] 1 the whitish mass of bubbles formed on or in liquids by agitation, fermentation, etc. 2 something like foam, as frothy saliva 3 a rigid or spongy cellular mass, made from liquid rubber, plastic, etc. —*vi.* to produce foam —**foam′y** *adj.* **-i·er, -i·est**

fob (fäb) *n.* [prob. < dial. Ger *fuppe*, a pocket] 1 a short ribbon or chain attached to a pocket watch 2 any ornament worn on such a chain, etc. 3 an object or device, such as a remote control, that attaches to a key ring, etc.

fo·cal (fō′kəl) *adj.* of or at a focus

focal length the distance from the center of a lens or concave mirror to the point where the light rays converge

fo′c'sle or **fo·c's·le** (fōk′səl) *n.* phonetic sp. of FORECASTLE

fo·cus (fō′cəs) *n., pl.* **-cus·es** or **-ci′** (-sī′) [L, hearth] 1 the point where rays of light, heat, etc. come together; specif., the point where rays of reflected or refracted light meet 2 FO-CAL LENGTH 3 an adjustment of this to make a clear image [bring a lens into *focus*] 4 any center of activity, attention, etc. —*vt.* **-cused** or **-cussed, -cusing** or **-cussing** 1 to bring into focus 2 to adjust the focal length of (the eye, a lens, etc.) so as to produce a clear image 3 to concentrate —**in focus** clear and sharp —**out of focus** blurred

focus group a small group of people recruited to provide opinions, as about a particular product or service, a politcal candidate, etc.

fod·der (fäd′ər) *n.* [OE *fodor*] coarse food for cattle, horses, etc., as hay

foe (fō) *n.* [OE *fah*, hostile] an enemy

foe·tus (fēt′əs) *n. alt. sp. of* FETUS

fog (fôg, fäg) *n.* [prob. < Scand] 1 a large mass of water vapor condensed to fine particles, at or just above the earth's surface 2 a state of mental confusion —*vt.*, *vi.* **fogged**, **fog′ging** to make or become foggy

fog·gy *adj.* **-gi·er**, **-gi·est** 1 full of fog 2 dim; blurry 3 confused —**fog′gi·ness** *n.*

fog·horn *n.* a horn blown to warn ships in a fog

fo·gy (fō′gē) *n.*, *pl.* **-gies** [< ?] one who is old-fashioned: usually with *old* : also **fo′gey**, *pl.* **-geys**

foi·ble (foi′bəl) *n.* [< Fr *faible*, feeble] a small weakness in character

foil¹ (foil) *vt.* [< OFr *fuler*, trample] to keep from being successful; thwart

foil² (foil) *n.* [< L *folium*, leaf] 1 a very thin sheet of metal 2 a person or thing that sets off another by contrast 3 [< ?] a long, thin, blunted fencing sword

foist (foist) *vt.* [prob. < dial. Du *vuisten*, to hide in the hand] to get (a thing) accepted, sold, etc. by fraud, deception, etc.; palm off: with *on* or *upon*

fol *abbrev.* 1 folio(s) 2 following

fold¹ (fōld) *vt.* [OE *faldan*] 1 to double (material) up on itself 2 to draw together and intertwine [to *fold* the arms] 3 to embrace 4 to wrap up; envelop —*vi.* 1 to be or become folded 2 [Inf.] *a)* to fail, as a business, play, etc. *b)* to fail suddenly; collapse —*n.* a folded part

fold² (fōld) *n.* [OE *fald*] 1 a pen for sheep 2 a flock of sheep 3 a group sharing a common faith, goal, etc.

-fold (fōld) [< OE *feald*] *suffix* 1 having (a specified number of) parts 2 (a specified number of) times as many or as much [to profit *tenfold*]

fold·a·way *adj.* that can be folded together for easy storage

fold·er *n.* a sheet of heavy paper folded for holding loose papers

fo·li·age (fō′lē ij) *n.* [< L *folia*] leaves, as of a plant or tree

fo·lic acid (fō′lik) [< L *folium*, leaf] a substance belonging to the vitamin B complex, used in treating anemia

fo·li·o (fō′lē ō′) *n.*, *pl.* **-os′** [< L *folium*, leaf] 1 a large sheet of paper folded once 2 a large size of book, about 12 by 15 inches, made of sheets so folded 3 the number of a page in a book

folk (fōk) *n.*, *pl.* **folks** or **folk** [OE *folc*] 1 a people or nation 2 [*pl.*] people; persons —*adj.* of or originating among the common people —**one's (or the) folks** [Inf.] one's family, esp. one's parents

folk·lore *n.* [prec. + LORE] the traditional beliefs, legends, etc. of a culture

folk song 1 a song made and handed down among the common people 2 a song composed in imitation of this —**folk singer**

folk·sy (-sē) *adj.* **-si·er**, **-si·est** [Inf.] friendly or sociable

fol·li·cle (fäl′i kəl) *n.* [< L *follis*, bellows] any small sac, cavity, or gland for excretion or secretion [a hair *follicle*]

fol·low (fäl′ō) *vt.* [< OE *folgian*] 1 to come or go after 2 to pursue 3 to go along [*follow* the road] 4 to take up (a trade, etc.) 5 to result from 6 to take as a model; imitate 7 to obey 8 to watch or listen to closely 9 to be interested in developments in [to *follow* local politics] 10 to understand —*vi.* 1 to come or go after something else in place, time, etc. 2 to result —**follow out (or up)** to carry out fully —**follow through** to complete a stroke or action

fol·low·er *n.* one that follows; specif., *a)* one who follows another's teachings; disciple *b)* an attendant

fol·low·ing *adj.* that follows; next after —*n.* a group of followers —*prep.* after [*following* dinner they left]

fol·low-up *n.* a letter, visit, etc. that follows as a review, addition, etc.

fol·ly (fäl′ē) *n.*, *pl.* **-lies** [see FOOL] 1 a lack of sense; foolishness 2 a foolish action or belief 3 a foolish and useless but expensive undertaking

fo·ment (fō ment′) *vt.* [< L *fovere*, keep warm] to stir up (trouble); incite —**fo′men·ta′tion** *n.*

fond (fänd) *adj.* [< ME *fonnen*, be foolish] 1 tender and affectionate; loving or doting 2 cherished [a *fond* hope] —**fond of** having a liking for —**fond′ly** *adv.* —**fond′ness** *n.*

fon·dle (fän′dəl) *vt.* **-dled**, **-dling** [< prec.] to caress or handle lovingly

fon·due or **fon·du** (fän do̅o̅′, fän′do̅o̅′) *n.* [Fr < *fondre*, melt] melted cheese, etc. used as a dip for cubes of bread

font¹ (fänt) *n.* [< L *fons*, spring] 1 a basin to hold baptismal water 2 a container for holy water 3 a source

font² (fänt) *n.* [see FOUND²] *Printing* a complete assortment of type in one size and style

fon·ta·nel or **fon·ta·nelle** (fänt′'n el′) *n.* [ME *fontinel*, a hollow] a natural gap in the skull of a baby or young animal, that gradually closes up as bone is formed

food (fo̅o̅d) *n.* [OE *foda*] 1 any substance, esp. a solid, taken in by a plant or animal to enable it to live and grow 2 anything that nourishes

food chain *Ecology* a sequence (as grass, rabbit, fox) of organisms in a community in which each member feeds on the one below it

food poisoning sickness caused by contaminants, as bacteria, in food, or by naturally poisonous foods

food processor an electrical appliance that can purée, chop, etc. foods rapidly

food stamp any of the federal coupons given to qualifying low-income persons for use in buying food

food·stuff *n.* any substance used as food

fool (fo̅o̅l) *n.* [< L *follis*, windbag] 1 a silly or stupid person 2 a jester 3 a victim of a trick, etc.; dupe —*vi.* 1 to act like a fool 2 to joke 3 [Inf.] to meddle (*with*) —*vt.* to trick; deceive —**fool around** [Inf.] to trifle —**fool′er·y** *n.*

fool·har·dy *adj.* **-di·er**, **-di·est** foolishly daring; reckless —**fool′har′di·ly** *adv.* —**fool′har′di·ness** *n.*

fool·ish *adj.* 1 silly; unwise 2 ridiculous 3

embarrassed —**fool′ish·ly** adv. —**fool′ish·ness** n.

fool·proof adj. so simple, well-designed, etc. as not to be mishandled, damaged, etc. even by a fool

fools·cap (foolz′kap′) n. ⟦from a watermark of a jester's cap⟧ a size of writing paper, 13 by 16 in. in the U.S.

foot (foot) n., pl. **feet** ⟦OE fot⟧ 1 the end part of the leg, on which one stands 2 the base or bottom [the foot of a page] 3 the muscular part of a mollusk used in burrowing, moving, etc. 4 a measure of length equal to 12 inches: symbol ′ 5 [with pl. v.] [Brit.] infantry 6 a group of syllables serving as a unit of meter in verse —vt. 1 to add (a column of figures): often with up 2 [Inf.] to pay (costs, etc.) —**on foot** walking —**put one's foot down** [Inf.] to act firmly —**under foot** in the way

foot·age (-ij) n. 1 measurement in feet, as of film 2 a length of film that has been shot 3 recorded video, esp. of a given subject

foot-and-mouth disease a contagious disease of cloven-footed animals, causing blisters in the mouth and around the hoofs

foot·ball n. 1 a game played on a rectangular field with an inflated, oval leather ball by two teams that try to score touchdowns 2 [Brit.] a) soccer b) rugby 3 the ball used in any of these games

foot·bridge n. a bridge for pedestrians

foot-can·dle n. a unit for measuring illumination

foot·ed adj. having feet of a specified number or kind [four-footed]

foot·fall n. the sound of a footstep

foot·hill n. a low hill at or near the foot of a mountain or mountain range

foot·hold n. 1 a secure place for a foot, as in climbing 2 a secure position

foot·ie (foot′ē) n. a very short sock, extending to or below the ankle

foot·ing n. 1 a secure placing of the feet 2 the condition of a surface, as for walking 3 a foothold 4 a secure position 5 a basis for relationship

foot·less (-lis) adj. 1 without a foot or feet 2 without basis 3 [Inf.] clumsy; inept

foot·lights pl.n. a row of lights along the front of a stage floor —**the footlights** the theater or the profession of acting

foot·lock·er n. a small trunk, usually kept at the foot of a bed as by a soldier

foot·loose adj. free to go wherever, or do whatever, one likes

foot·man (-mən) n., pl. -**men** (-mən) a male servant who assists the butler

foot·note n. 1 a note of comment or reference at the bottom of a page 2 such a note at the end of a chapter or a book 3 an additional comment, etc. —vt. -**not′ed**, -**not′ing** to add a footnote or footnotes to

foot·path n. a narrow path for use by pedestrians only

foot-pound n. a unit of energy or work, the amount required to raise one pound a distance of one foot

foot·print n. 1 a mark made by a foot 2 an area, or its shape, which something affects, occupies, etc.

foot·sore adj. having sore or tender feet, as from much walking

foot·step n. 1 the distance covered in a step 2 the sound of a step 3 FOOTPRINT (n. 1) —**follow in someone's footsteps** to follow someone's example, etc.

foot·stool n. a low stool for supporting the feet of a seated person

foot·wear n. shoes, boots, etc.

foot·work n. the act or manner of using the feet, as in boxing or dancing

fop (fäp) n. ⟦ME foppe, a fool⟧ DANDY (n. 1) —**fop′per·y** n., pl. -**ies** —**fop′pish** adj. —**fop′pish·ly** adv.

for (fôr, fur) prep. ⟦OE⟧ 1 in place of [use a rope for a belt] 2 in the interest of [to act for another] 3 in favor of [vote for the levy] 4 in honor of [a party for her] 5 in order to be, get, have, keep, find, etc. [walk for exercise, start for home] 6 meant to be received by [flowers for a friend] 7 suitable to [a room for sleeping] 8 with regard to; concerning [an ear for music] 9 as being [to know for a fact] 10 considering the nature of [cool for July] 11 because of [a cry for pain] 12 at the price of [sold for $20,000] 13 to the length, amount, or duration of —conj. because; since —**for all** in spite of

for- ⟦OE⟧ prefix away, apart, off [forbid, forgo]

for·age (fôr′ij, fär′-) n. ⟦< OFr forre, fodder⟧ 1 food for domestic animals 2 a search for food —vi. -**aged**, -**ag·ing** 1 to search for food 2 to search for something one wants —vt. to take food from; raid —**for′ag·er** n.

for·ay (fôr′ā) vt., vi. ⟦< OFr forrer, to forage⟧ to plunder —n. a raid in order to seize things

for·bear¹ (fôr ber′) vt. -**bore′**, -**borne′**, -**bear′ing** ⟦see FOR- & BEAR¹⟧ to refrain from (doing, saying, etc.) —vi. 1 to refrain 2 to remain calm when provoked

for·bear² (fôr′ber′) n. alt. sp. of FOREBEAR

for·bear·ance n. 1 the act of forbearing 2 self-restraint

for·bid (fər bid′, fôr-) vt. -**bade′** (-bad′) or -**bad′**, -**bid′den**, -**bid′ding** ⟦see FOR- & BID⟧ 1 to order (a person) not to do (something); prohibit 2 to prevent

for·bid·ding adj. looking dangerous or intimidating —**for·bid′ding·ly** adv.

force (fôrs) n. ⟦< L fortis, strong⟧ 1 strength; power 2 physical coercion against a person or thing 3 the power to control, persuade, etc.; effectiveness 4 military power 5 any group of people organized for some activity [a sales force] 6 energy that causes or alters motion 7 Law binding power; validity —vt. **forced**, **forc′ing** 1 to make do something by force; compel 2 to break open, into, or through by force 3 to take by force; extort 4 to impose by force: with on or upon 5 to produce as by force [to force a smile] 6 to cause (plants, etc.) to develop faster by artificial means —**in force 1** in full strength **2** in effect; valid —**force′less** *adj.*

forced (fôrst) *adj.* **1** compulsory [*forced* labor] **2** not natural; strained [a *forced* smile] **3** due to necessity [a *forced* landing] **4** at a faster pace [a *forced* march] —**forc·ed·ly** (fôrs′id lē) *adv.*

force-feed *vt.* **-fed′, -feed′ing** to feed as by a tube through the throat to the stomach

force·ful (-fəl) *adj.* full of force; powerful, vigorous, effective, etc. —**force′ful·ly** *adv.* —**force′ful·ness** *n.*

for·ceps (fôr′seps) *n., pl.* **-ceps** [L < *for-mus*, warm + *capere*, to take] small tongs or pincers for grasping, pulling, etc.

for·ci·ble (fôr′sə bəl) *adj.* **1** done by force **2** having force —**for′ci·bly** *adv.*

ford (fôrd) *n.* [OE] a shallow place in a stream, etc. where one can cross by wading, on horseback, in a car, etc. —*vt.* to cross at a ford —**ford′a·ble** *adj.*

Ford (fôrd) **1** Ger·ald R(udolph), Jr. (jer′əld) 1913-2006; 38th president of the U.S. (1974-77) **2** Henry 1863-1947; U.S. automobile manufacturer

fore (fôr) *adv., adj.* [OE] at, in, or toward the front part, as of a ship —*n.* the front —*interj.* *Golf* a shout warning that one is about to hit the ball

fore- [OE] *prefix* **1** before in time, place, etc. [*forenoon*] **2** the front part of [*forehead*]

fore-and-aft (fôr′ən aft′) *adj. Naut.* from the bow to the stern; set lengthwise, as sails

fore·arm[1] (fôr′ärm′) *n.* the part of the arm between the elbow and the wrist

fore·arm[2] (fôr ärm′) *vt.* to arm in advance

fore·bear (fôr′ber′) *n.* [< FORE + BE + -ER] an ancestor

fore·bode (-bōd′) *vt., vi.* **-bod′ed, -bod′ing** [< OE] **1** to foretell; predict **2** to have a presentiment of (something bad) —**fore·bod′ing** *n.*

fore·cast *vt.* **-cast′** or **-cast′ed, -cast′ing 1** to predict **2** to serve as a prediction of —*n.* a prediction —**fore′cast′er** *n.*

fore·cas·tle (fōk′səl, fôr′kas′əl) *n.* **1** the upper deck of a ship in front of the foremast **2** the front part of a merchant ship, where the crew's quarters are

fore·close (fôr klōz′) *vt., vi.* **-closed′, -clos′ing** [< OFr *fors*, outside + *clore*, CLOSE[2]] to take away the right to redeem (a mortgage) —**fore·clo′sure** (-klō′zhər) *n.*

fore·doom *vt.* to doom in advance

fore·fa·ther *n.* an ancestor

fore·fin·ger *n.* the finger nearest the thumb

fore·foot *n., pl.* **-feet′** either of the front feet of an animal

fore·front *n.* **1** the extreme front **2** the position of most importance, activity, etc.

fore·go[1] *vt., vi.* **-went′, -gone′, -go′ing** to go before in place, time, etc.; precede

fore·go[2] *vt. alt. sp. of* FORGO

fore·go·ing *adj.* previously said, written, etc.; preceding

fore·gone *adj.* **1** previous **2** previously determined; inevitable

fore·ground *n.* **1** the part of a scene, etc. nearest to the viewer **2** the most noticeable position —*vt.* to place in the foreground; emphasize

fore·hand *n.* a stroke, as in tennis, made with the palm of the hand turned forward —*adj.* done as with a forehand

fore·head (fôr′ed′, -hed′; fär′-) *n.* the part of the face between the eyebrows and the line where the hair normally begins

for·eign (fôr′in, fär′-) *adj.* [< L *foras*, out-of-doors] **1** situated outside one's own country, locality, etc. **2** of, from, or having to do with other countries **3** not belonging; not characteristic

for·eign-born *adj.* born in some other country; not native

for·eign·er *n.* a person from another country; alien

foreign minister a member of a governmental cabinet in charge of foreign affairs for the country

fore·know (fôr nō′) *vt.* **-knew′, -known′, -know′ing** to have knowledge of beforehand —**fore′knowl′edge** (-näl′ij) *n.*

fore·leg *n.* either of the front legs of an animal

fore·lock *n.* a lock of hair growing just above the forehead

fore·man (-mən) *n., pl.* **-men** (-mən) **1** a man who chairs and speaks for a jury **2** a man in charge of a group of workers

fore·mast *n.* the mast nearest the bow of a ship

fore·most *adj.* first in place, time, etc. —*adv.* first

fore·noon *n.* the time from sunrise to noon; morning

fo·ren·sic (fə ren′sik, -zik) *adj.* [< L *forum*, marketplace] **1** of or suitable for public debate **2** involving the application of scientific knowledge to legal matters, as in investigating crimes —*n.* **1** [*pl.*] debate or formal argumentation **2** techniques used in investigating crimes —**fo·ren′si·cal·ly** *adv.*

forensic medicine MEDICAL JURISPRUDENCE

fore·or·dain *vt.* to ordain beforehand; predestine —**fore′or′di·na′tion** *n.*

fore·run·ner *n.* **1** a herald **2** a sign that tells or warns of something to follow **3** a predecessor; ancestor

fore·sail (-sāl′, -səl) *n.* the lowest sail on the foremast of a square-rigged ship or a schooner

fore·see *vt.* **-saw′, -seen′, -see′ing** to see or know beforehand —**fore·see′a·ble** *adj.* —**fore·se′er** *n.*

fore·shad·ow *vt.* to indicate or suggest beforehand; prefigure

fore·short·en *vt.* in drawing, etc., to shorten some lines of (an object) to give the illusion of proper relative size

fore·sight *n.* **1** *a*) the act of foreseeing *b*) the power to foresee **2** prudent regard or provision for the future

fore·skin *n.* the fold of skin that covers the end of the penis, often removed for medical or religious reasons

for·est (fôr′ist) *n.* [< L *foris*, out-of-doors] a thick growth of trees, etc. covering a large tract of land —*vt.* to plant with trees

fore·stall *vt.* [< OE *foresteall*, ambush] 1 to prevent by doing something ahead of time 2 to act in advance of

for·est·a·tion (fôr′is tā′shən) *n.* the planting or care of forests

for·est·ed *adj.* covered with trees and underbrush

for·est·er *n.* one trained in forestry

for·est·ry *n.* the science of planting and taking care of forests

fore·taste (fôr′tāst′) *n.* a taste or sample of what can be expected

fore·tell *vt.* -told′, -tell′ing to tell or indicate beforehand; predict

fore·thought *n.* 1 a thinking or planning beforehand 2 foresight

for·ev·er (fôr ev′ər, fər-) *adv.* 1 for always; endlessly 2 at all times; always Also **for·ev′er·more′**

fore·warn (fôr wôrn′) *vt.* to warn beforehand

fore·wom·an *n.,* pl. -wom′en 1 a woman who chairs and speaks for a jury 2 a woman in charge of a group of workers

fore·word *n.* an introductory statement in a book

for·feit (fôr′fit) *n.* [< OFr *forfaire*, transgress] 1 a fine or penalty for some crime, fault, or neglect 2 the act of forfeiting —*adj.* lost or taken away as a forfeit —*vt.* to lose or be deprived of as a forfeit

for·fei·ture (-fə chər) *n.* 1 the act of forfeiting 2 anything forfeited

for·gath·er (fôr gath′ər) *vi.* to come together; meet; assemble

for·gave (fôr gāv′, fər-) *vt., vi. pt. of* FORGIVE

forge¹ (fôrj) *n.* [< L *faber*, workman] 1 a furnace for heating metal to be wrought 2 a place where metal is heated and wrought; smithy —*vt.* **forged, forg′ing** 1 to form or shape (metal) by heating and hammering 2 to form; shape 3 to imitate (a signature) fraudulently, counterfeit (a check), etc. —*vi.* 1 to work at a forge 2 to commit forgery —forg′er *n.*

forge² (fôrj) *vi.* **forged, forg′ing** [prob. < FORCE] to move forward steadily: often with *ahead*

for·ger·y *n.,* pl. -ies 1 the act or crime of imitating or counterfeiting documents, signatures, etc. to deceive 2 anything forged

for·get (fər get′, fôr-) *vt., vi.* -got′, -got′ten or -got′, -get′ting [OE *forgietan*] 1 to be unable to remember 2 to overlook or neglect (something) —forget oneself to act in an improper manner —for·get′ta·ble *adj.*

for·get·ful *adj.* 1 apt to forget 2 heedless or negligent —for·get′ful·ly *adv.* —for·get′ful·ness *n.*

for·get-me-not *n.* a marsh plant with small blue, white, or pink flowers

for·give (fər giv′, fôr-) *vt., vi.* -gave′, -giv′en, -giv′ing [OE *forgiefan*] 1 to give up resentment against or the desire to punish; pardon (an offense or offender) 2 to cancel (a debt) —for·giv′a·ble *adj.* —for·give′ness *n.* —for·giv′er *n.*

for·giv·ing *adj.* inclined to forgive —for·giv′ing·ly *adv.*

for·go (fôr gō′) *vt.* -went′, -gone′, -go′ing [OE *forgan*] to do without; abstain from; give up —for·go′er *n.*

for·got (fər gät′) *vt., vi. pt. & alt. pp. of* FORGET

for·got·ten *vt., vi. alt. pp. of* FORGET

fork (fôrk) *n.* [< L *furca*] 1 a utensil or tool with prongs at one end, as for eating food, pitching hay, etc. 2 something like a fork in shape, etc. 3 the place where a road, etc. divides into branches 4 any of these branches —*vi.* to divide into branches —*vt.* to pick up or pitch with a fork —fork over (or out) [Inf.] to pay out; hand over —fork′ful′ *n.,* pl. -fuls′

fork·lift *n.* 1 a device for lifting heavy objects by means of projecting prongs that are slid under the load 2 a small truck with such a device

for·lorn (fôr lôrn′) *adj.* [< OE *forleosan*, lose utterly] 1 abandoned 2 wretched; miserable 3 without hope —for·lorn′ly *adv.*

form (fôrm) *n.* [< L *forma*] 1 shape; general structure 2 the figure of a person or animal 3 a mold 4 a particular mode, kind, type, etc. [ice is a *form* of water, the *forms* of poetry] 5 arrangement; style 6 a way of doing something requiring skill 7 a customary or conventional way of acting; ceremony 8 a printed or electronic document with blanks to be filled in 9 condition of mind or body 10 RACING FORM 11 a changed appearance of a word to show inflection, etc. 12 what is expected, based on past performances [according to *form*] —*vt.* 1 to shape; fashion 2 to train; instruct 3 to develop (habits) 4 to make up; constitute 5 to organize into [to *form* a club] —*vi.* to be formed

-form (fôrm) [< L *forma*] *combining form* having the form of [*cuneiform*]

for·mal (fôr′məl) *adj.* [< L *formalis*] 1 according to fixed customs, rules, etc. 2 stiff in manner 3 *a)* designed for wear at ceremonies, etc. *b)* requiring clothes of this kind 4 done or made in an explicit form [a *formal* contract] 5 designating language usage characterized by long words, complex syntax, etc. 6 designating education in schools, etc. —*n.* 1 a formal dance 2 a woman's evening dress —for′mal·ly *adv.*

form·al·de·hyde (fôr mal′də hīd′) *n.* [FORM(IC) + *aldehyde*] a pungent gas used in solution as a disinfectant and preservative

for·mal·ism *n.* strict attention to outward forms and traditions

for·mal·i·ty (fôr mal′ə tē) *n.,* pl. -ties 1 *a)* an observing of customs, rules, etc.; propriety *b)* excessive attention to convention 2 a formal act, esp. one having no practical effect

for·mal·ize (fôr′mə līz′) *vt.* **-ized′, -iz′ing** 1 to shape 2 to make formal —**for′mal·i·za′tion** *n.*

for·mal·wear *n.* formal clothes, as tuxedos

for·mat (fôr′mat′) *n.* [< L *formatus*, formed] 1 the shape, size, and arrangement of a book, etc. 2 the arrangement or plan, as of a TV program 3 a specific way in which computer data is stored, etc. 4 a particular type of audio or video recording and playback system —*vt.* **-mat′ted, -mat′ting** to arrange according to a format

for·ma·tion (fôr mā′shən) *n.* 1 a forming or being formed 2 a thing formed 3 the way in which something is formed; structure 4 an arrangement or positioning, as of troops

form·a·tive (fôr′mə tiv) *adj.* helping or involving formation or development

for·mer (fôr′mər) *adj.* [ME *formere*] 1 earlier; past [*in former times*] 2 being the first mentioned of two

for·mer·ly *adv.* in the past

form-fit·ting *adj.* fitting the body closely: also **form′fit′ting**

For·mi·ca (fôr mī′kə) *trademark* for a laminated, heat-resistant plastic used for counter tops, etc.

for·mic acid (fôr′mik) [< L *formica*, ant] a colorless acid found in the venom of many ants

for·mi·da·ble (fôr′mə də bəl, fôr mid′ə bəl) *adj.* [< L *formidare*, to dread] 1 causing fear, dread, or awe 2 hard to handle

form·less *adj.* shapeless; amorphous

form letter a standardized letter with the date, address, etc. filled in separately

for·mu·la (fôr′myōō lə, -myə-) *n., pl.* **-las** or **-lae** (-lē′, -lī′) [L < *forma*, form] 1 a fixed form of words, esp. a conventional expression 2 a conventional rule for doing something 3 a prescription or recipe 4 fortified milk for a baby 5 a set of symbols expressing a mathematical rule, fact, etc. 6 *Chem.* an expression of the composition, as of a compound, using symbols and figures

for·mu·late (-lāt′) *vt.* **-lat′ed, -lat′ing** 1 to express in a formula 2 to express in a definite way 3 to work out in one's mind; devise —**for′mu·la′tion** *n.* —**for′mu·la′tor** *n.*

for·ni·cate (fôr′ni kāt′) *vi.* **-cat′ed, -cat′ing** [< L *fornix*, a brothel] to commit fornication —**for′ni·ca′tor** *n.*

for·ni·ca·tion *n.* sexual intercourse between unmarried persons

for·sake (fôr sāk′) *vt.* **-sook′** (-sook′), **-sak′en, -sak′ing** [< OE *for-*, FOR- + *sacan*, to strive] 1 to give up (a habit, etc.) 2 to leave; abandon

for·sooth (fôr sōōth′) *adv.* [ME *forsooth*] [Archaic] indeed

for·swear (fôr swer′) *vt.* **-swore′, -sworn′, -swear′ing** to deny or renounce on oath —*vi.* to commit perjury

for·syth·i·a (fôr sith′ē ə, fər-) *n.* [after W. *Forsyth* (1737-1804), Eng botanist] a shrub with yellow, bell-shaped flowers that bloom in early spring

fort (fôrt) *n.* [< L *fortis*, strong] 1 a fortified place for military defense 2 a permanent army post

forte[1] (fôrt; *often* fôr′tā′) *n.* [< OFr: see prec.] that which one does particularly well

for·te[2] (fôr′tā′) *adj., adv.* [It < L *fortis*, strong] [*also in italics*] *Music* loud

forth (fôrth) *adv.* [OE] 1 forward; onward 2 out into view

Forth (fôrth), **Firth of** long estuary of the Forth River in SE Scotland

forth·com·ing *adj.* 1 about to appear; approaching 2 ready when needed 3 friendly, outgoing, etc. 4 open; frank

forth·right *adj.* direct and frank

forth·with (-with′, -with′) *adv.* at once

for·ti·fy (fôrt′ə fī′) *vt.* **-fied′, -fy′ing** [< L *fortis*, strong + *facere*, to make] 1 to strengthen physically, emotionally, etc. 2 to strengthen against attack, as with forts 3 to support 4 to add alcohol to (wine, etc.) 5 to add vitamins, etc. to (milk, etc.) —**for′ti·fi·ca′tion** *n.* —**for′ti·fi′er** *n.*

for·tis·si·mo (fôr tis′ə mō′) *adj., adv.* [It, superl. of *forte*, strong] [*also in italics*] *Music* very loud

for·ti·tude (fôrt′ə tōōd′) *n.* [< L *fortis*, strong] patient endurance of trouble, pain, etc.; courage

Fort Knox (näks) military reservation in N Kentucky: site of U.S. gold bullion depository

fort·night (fôrt′nīt′) *n.* [< OE *feowertyn niht*, lit., fourteen nights] [Chiefly Brit.] a period of two weeks —**fort′night′ly** *adj., adv.*

for·tress (fôr′tris) *n.* [< L *fortis*, strong] a fortified place; fort

for·tu·i·tous (fôr tōō′ə təs) *adj.* [< L *fors*, luck] 1 happening by chance 2 lucky —**for·tu′i·tous·ly** *adv.*

for·tu·nate (tôr′chə nət) *adj.* 1 having good luck 2 coming by good luck; favorable —**for′tu·nate·ly** *adv.*

for·tune (fôr′chən) *n.* [< L *fors*, luck] 1 luck; chance; fate 2 [*also pl.*] one's future lot, good or bad 3 good luck; success 4 wealth; riches

for·tune·tell·er *n.* one who professes to foretell the future of others —**for′tune·tell′ing** *n., adj.*

Fort Worth (wurth) city in N Texas

for·ty (fôrt′ē) *adj., n., pl.* **-ties** [OE *feowertig*] four times ten; 40; XL —**the forties** the numbers or years, as of a century, from 40 through 49 —**for′ti·eth** (-ith) *adj.*

fo·rum (fôr′əm) *n.* [L] 1 the public square of an ancient Roman city 2 a meeting, website, etc. devoted to public discussion

for·ward (fôr′wərd) *adj.* [OE *foreweard*] 1 at, toward, or of the front 2 advanced 3 onward; advancing 4 prompt; ready 5 bold; presumptuous 6 of or for the future —*adv.* toward the front; ahead —*n. Basketball, Hockey, etc.* a player positioned ahead of the rest of the team, esp. when on the offense —*vt.* 1 to promote 2 to send on

for·wards *adv.* FORWARD

fos·sil (fäs′əl) *n.* [< L *fossilis*, dug up] 1 any

hardened remains or imprints of a plant or animal of a previous geologic period, preserved in the earth's crust **2** a person with outmoded ideas or ways —*adj.* **1** of or like a fossil **2** dug from the earth [coal is a *fossil* fuel] **3** antiquated

fos·sil·ize (-īz′) *vt., vi.* **-ized′, -iz′ing 1** to change into a fossil **2** to make or become out of date, rigid, etc. —**fos′sil·i·za′tion** *n.*

fos·ter (fôs′tər) *vt.* [OE *fostrian*, to nourish] **1** to bring up; rear **2** to help to develop; promote —*adj.* having a specified standing in a family but not by birth or adoption [a *foster* brother]

fought (fôt) *vi., vt.* *pt. & pp. of* FIGHT

foul (foul) *adj.* [OE *ful*] **1** stinking; loathsome **2** extremely dirty **3** indecent; profane **4** wicked; abominable **5** stormy [*foul* weather] **6** tangled [a *foul* rope] **7** not within the limits or rules set **8** designating lines setting limits on a playing area **9** dishonest **10** [Inf.] unpleasant, disagreeable, etc. —*adv.* in a foul manner —*n.* Sports a hit, blow, move, etc. that is FOUL (*adj.* 7) —*vt.* **1** to make filthy **2** to dishonor **3** to obstruct [grease *fouls* drains] **4** to entangle (a rope, etc.) **5** to make a foul against, as in a game **6** Baseball to bat (the ball) foul —*vi.* to be or become fouled —**foul up** [Inf.] to bungle —**foul′ly** *adv.* —**foul′ness** *n.*

fou·lard (foo lärd′) *n.* [Fr] a lightweight printed fabric of silk, etc.

foul play 1 unfair play **2** murder

foul-up *n.* [Inf.] a mix-up; botch

found[1] (found) [OE *funden*] *vt., vi. pp. & pt. of* FIND

found[2] (found) *vt.* [< L *fundus*, bottom] **1** to set for support; base **2** to bring into being; establish —**found′er** *n.*

found[3] (found) *vt.* [< L *fundere*, pour] **1** to melt and pour (metal) into a mold **2** to make by founding metal

foun·da·tion (foun dā′shən) *n.* **1** a founding or being founded; establishment **2** *a)* an endowment for an institution *b)* such an institution **3** basis **4** the base of a wall, house, etc. **5** cosmetic over which other makeup is applied

foun·der (foun′dər) *vi.* [< L *fundus*, bottom] **1** to stumble, fall, or go lame **2** to fill with water and sink: said of a ship **3** to break down

found·ling (found′liŋ′) *n.* an infant of unknown parents, found abandoned

found·ry (foun′drē) *n., pl.* **-ries** a place where metal is cast

fount (fount) *n.* [< L *fons*] **1** [Old Poet.] a fountain or spring **2** a source

foun·tain (fount′'n) *n.* [< L *fons*] **1** a natural spring of water **2** a source **3** *a)* an artificial jet or flow of water [a drinking *fountain*] *b)* the basin where this flows **4** a reservoir, as for ink

foun·tain·head *n.* the source, as of a stream

fountain pen a pen which is fed ink from a built-in reservoir or cartridge

four (fôr) *adj., n.* [OE *feower*] one more than

three; 4; IV —**on all fours 1** on all four feet **2** on hands and knees

four-in-hand *n.* a necktie tied in a slipknot with the ends left hanging

four·score *adj., n.* [Archaic] four times twenty; eighty

four·some (-səm) *n.* four people

four·square (fôr′skwer′) *adj.* **1** square **2** unyielding; firm **3** frank; forthright —*adv.* in a square form or manner

four·teen (fôr′tēn′) *adj., n.* [OE *feowertyne*] four more than ten; 14; XIV —**four′teenth′** *adj., n.*

fourth (fôrth) *adj.* [OE *feortha*] preceded by three others in a series; 4th —*n.* **1** the one following the third **2** any of the four equal parts of something; ¼ **3** the fourth forward gear

fourth dimension in the theory of relativity, time added as a dimension to those of length, width, and depth

fourth estate [often F- E-] journalism or journalists

Fourth of July *see* INDEPENDENCE DAY

4WD *abbrev.* four-wheel-drive (vehicle)

four-wheel *adj.* **1** having four wheels **2** affecting four wheels [a *four-wheel* drive]

fowl (foul) *n.* [OE *fugol*] **1** any bird **2** any of the domestic birds used as food, as the chicken, duck, etc. **3** the flesh of these birds used for food

fowl·ing *n.* hunting or snaring wild birds —**fowl′er** *n.*

fox (fäks) *n.* [OE] **1** a small, wild animal of the dog family **2** its fur **3** a sly, crafty person —*vt.* to trick by slyness

fox·glove *n.* DIGITALIS

fox·hole *n.* a hole dug in the ground as a protection against enemy gunfire

fox·hound *n.* a sturdy breed of hound originally bred for hunting foxes

fox terrier a small terrier with a smooth or wiry coat, formerly trained to drive foxes from hiding

fox trot a dance for couples in 4/4 time, or music for it —**fox′-trot′** *vi.* **-trot′ted, -trot′ting**

fox·y *adj.* **-i·er, -i·est 1** foxlike; crafty; sly **2** [Slang] attractive or sexy

foy·er (foi′ər; *also* foi′ā′, -yā′) *n.* [Fr < L *focus*, hearth] an entrance hall or lobby, as in a theater or hotel

Fr *abbrev.* **1** Father **2** French

fra·cas (frā′kəs) *n.* [Fr < It *fracassare*, to smash] a noisy fight; brawl

frack·ing (frak′iŋ) *n.* [< *hydraulic fracturing*] the injection of water at high pressure into a well hole to open underground fissures for the extraction of natural gas or oil

frac·tion (frak′shən) *n.* [< L *frangere*, to break] **1** a small part, amount, etc. **2** *Math. a)* a quotient of two whole numbers, as ¹³⁄₄, ⅖ *b)* any quantity expressed in terms of a numerator and denominator —**frac′tion·al** *adj.* —**frac′tion·al·ly** *adv.*

frac·tious (frak′shəs) *adj.* [< ?] **1** hard to manage; unruly **2** peevish; cross —**frac′tious·ly** *adv.* —**frac′tious·ness** *n.*

frac·ture (frak′chər) *n.* ⟦< L *frangere*, to break⟧ a breaking or break, esp. in a bone —*vt., vi.* **-tured, -tur·ing** to break, crack, or split

frag·ile (fraj′əl) *adj.* ⟦< L *frangere*, to break⟧ easily broken or damaged; delicate —**fra·gil·i·ty** (frə jil′ə tē) *n.*

frag·ment (frag′mənt; *for v., also,* -ment′) *n.* ⟦< L *frangere*, to break⟧ **1** a part broken away **2** an incomplete part, as of a novel —*vt., vi.* to break up —**frag′men·ta′tion** (-mən tā′shən) *n.*

frag·men·tar·y (-mən ter′ē) *adj.* consisting of fragments; not complete

fra·grant (frā′grənt) *adj.* ⟦< L *fragrare*, to emit a (sweet) smell⟧ having a pleasant odor; sweet-smelling —**fra′grance** *n.* —**fra′grant·ly** *adv.*

frail (frāl) *adj.* ⟦see FRAGILE⟧ **1** easily broken; delicate **2** not robust; weak **3** easily tempted; morally weak —**frail′ly** *adv.*

frail·ty (-tē) *n.* **1** a being frail; esp., moral weakness **2** *pl.* **-ties** a fault arising from such weakness

frame (frām) *vt.* **framed, fram′ing** ⟦prob. < ON *frami*, profit or benefit⟧ **1** to form according to a pattern; design [*to frame laws*] **2** to construct **3** to put into words [*to frame an excuse*] **4** to enclose (a picture, etc.) in a border **5** [Inf.] to falsify evidence in order to make (an innocent person) appear guilty —*n.* **1** body structure **2** the framework, as of a house **3** the structural case enclosing a window, door, etc. **4** an ornamental border, as around a picture **5** the way anything is put together; form **6** condition; state [*a good frame of mind*] **7** one exposure in a strip of film **8** *Bowling, etc.* a division of a game —*adj.* having a wooden framework [*a frame house*] —**fram′er** *n.*

frame-up *n.* [Inf.] a secret, deceitful scheme, as a falsifying of evidence to make a person seem guilty

frame·work *n.* **1** a structure to hold together or support something **2** the basic structure, system, etc.

franc (fraŋk) *n.* ⟦Fr < L *Francorum rex*, king of the French, phrase on the coin in 1360⟧ **1** the former monetary unit of France, Belgium, and Luxembourg **2** the monetary unit of Switzerland, Chad, Mali, etc.

France (frans, fräns) country in W Europe

fran·chise (fran′chīz′) *n.* ⟦< OFr *franc*, free⟧ **1** any special right or privilege granted by a government **2** the right to vote; suffrage **3** the right to sell a product or service, esp. under a given brand name **4** a business granted this right —*vt.* **-chised′, -chis′ing** to grant a franchise to —**fran′chi·see′** *n.*

fran·ci·um (fran′sē əm) *n.* ⟦after FRANCE⟧ a very unstable radioactive chemical element of the alkali metals: symbol, Fr; at. no. 87

Franco- *combining form* French, French and

fran·gi·ble (fran′jə bəl) *adj.* ⟦< L *frangere*, to break⟧ breakable; fragile

frank (fraŋk) *adj.* ⟦< OFr *franc*, free⟧ free in expressing oneself; candid —*vt.* to send (mail) free of postage —*n.* **1** the right to send mail free **2** a mark indicating this right —**frank′ly** *adv.* —**frank′ness** *n.*

Frank (fraŋk) *n.* a member of the Germanic peoples whose 9th-c. empire extended over what is now France, Germany, and Italy

Frank·en·stein (fran′kən stīn′) *n.* **1** the title character in a novel (1818), creator of a monster that destroys him **2** popularly, the monster

Frank·fort (fraŋk′fərt) capital of Kentucky

Frank·furt (fraŋk′fərt; *Ger* fränk′foort) city in W Germany

frank·furt·er (fraŋk′fər tər) *n.* ⟦Ger: after prec.⟧ a smoked sausage of beef, beef and pork, etc.; wiener: also [Inf.] **frank**

frank·in·cense (fran′kin sens′) *n.* ⟦see FRANK & INCENSE[1]⟧ a gum resin burned as incense

Frank·ish (fran′kish) *n.* the West Germanic language of the Franks —*adj.* of the Franks or their language, etc.

Frank·lin (fraŋk′lin), **Ben·ja·min** (ben′jə mən) 1706–90; Am. statesman, scientist, inventor, & writer

fran·tic (fran′tik) *adj.* ⟦< Gr *phrenitis*, delirium⟧ wild with anger, pain, worry, etc. —**fran′ti·cal·ly** *adv.*

frap·pé (fra pā′) *n.* ⟦Fr < *frapper*, to strike⟧ **1** a dessert made of partly frozen fruit juices, etc. **2** a beverage poured over shaved ice **3** [New England] a milkshake Also, esp. for 3, **frappe** (frap)

frat (frat) *n.* [Inf.] a college fraternity

fra·ter·nal (frə tur′nəl) *adj.* ⟦< L *frater*, brother⟧ **1** of brothers; brotherly **2** designating or of a society organized for fellowship **3** designating twins developed from separate ova and thus not identical —**fra·ter′nal·ly** *adv.*

fra·ter·ni·ty (frə tur′nə tē) *n., pl.* **-ties 1** brotherliness **2** a group of men joined together for fellowship, etc., as in college **3** a group of people with the same beliefs, work, etc.

frat·er·nize (frat′ər nīz′) *vi.* **-nized′, -niz′ing** to associate in a friendly way —**frat′er·ni·za′tion** *n.*

frat·ri·cide (fra′trə sīd′) *n.* ⟦< L *frater*, brother + *caedere*, to kill⟧ **1** the killing of one's own sibling **2** one who commits fratricide —**frat′ri·ci′dal** *adj.*

Frau (frou) *n., pl.* **Frau′en** (-ən) ⟦Ger⟧ **1** Mrs.; Madam: a German title of respect, used to address a married woman and now also a single woman **2** a wife

fraud (frôd) *n.* ⟦< L *fraus*⟧ **1** deceit; trickery **2** *Law* intentional deception **3** a trick **4** an impostor or cheat —**fraud′ster** *n.*

fraud·u·lent (frô′jə lənt) *adj.* **1** based on or using fraud **2** done or obtained by fraud —**fraud′u·lence** *n.* —**fraud′u·lent·ly** *adv.*

fraught (frôt) *adj.* ⟦< MDu *vracht*, a load⟧ **1** filled or loaded (*with*) [*a life fraught with hardship*] **2** tense, anxious, etc.

Fräu·lein (froi′līn′; E froi′-) *n., pl.* **-lein′,**

-leins' [[Ger]] **1** Miss: a German title of respect **2** an unmarried woman: in both senses somewhat dated; see note at Frau

fray¹ (frā) *n.* [[< AFFRAY]] a noisy quarrel or fight; brawl

fray² (frā) *vt., vi.* [[< L *fricare*, to rub]] **1** to make or become worn or ragged **2** to make or become weakened or strained

fraz·zle (fraz'əl) [Inf.] *vt., vi.* **-zled, -zling** [[< dial. *fazle*]] **1** to wear to tatters; fray **2** to make or become exhausted —*n.* the state of being frazzled

freak (frēk) *n.* [[< ?]] **1** an odd notion; whim **2** an unusual happening **3** any abnormal animal, person, or plant **4** [Slang] *a)* a user of a specified drug *b)* a devotee; buff [a chess *freak*] —*adj.* oddly different; abnormal [a *freak* blizzard] —**freak out** [Slang] **1** to have hallucinations, etc., as from a psychedelic drug **2** to make or become very excited, distressed, etc. —**freak'ish** *adj.*, **freak'y -i·er, -i·est** —**freak'ish·ly** *adv.*

freak·out *n.* [Slang] the act or an instance of freaking out

freck·le (frek'əl) *n.* [[< Scand]] a small, brownish spot on the skin — *vt., vi.* **-led, -ling** to make or become spotted with freckles — **freck'led** *adj.*

Fred·er·ick the Great (fred'rik, -ər ik) 1712-86; king of Prussia (1740-86)

Fred·er·ic·ton (fred'ə rik tən) capital of New Brunswick, Canada

free (frē) *adj.* **fre'er, fre'est** [[< OE *freo*]] **1** not under the control or power of another; having liberty; independent **2** having civil and political liberty **3** able to move in any direction; loose **4** not burdened by obligations, debts, discomforts, etc. **5** not confined to the usual rules [*free* verse] **6** not exact [a *free* translation] **7** generous; profuse [a *free* spender] **8** frank **9** with no charge or cost **10** exempt from taxes, duties, etc. **11** clear of obstructions [a *free* road ahead] **12** not fastened [a rope's *free* end] —*adv.* **1** without cost **2** in a free manner —*vt.* **freed, free'ing** to make free; specif., *a)* to release from bondage, obligation, etc. *b)* to clear of obstruction, etc. —**free from** (or **of**) without —**free up** to make available for use [he *freed up* funds] —**make free with** to use freely — **free'ly** *adv.* —**free'ness** *n.*

-free (frē) *combining form* free of or from, exempt from, without

free·base *n.* a concentrated form of cocaine for smoking — *vt., vi.* **-based', -bas'ing** to prepare or use such a form of (cocaine)

free·bie or **free·bee** (frē'bē) *n.* [Slang] something given or gotten free of charge, as a theater ticket

free·boot·er (-boot'ər) *n.* [[< Du *vrij*, free + *buit*, plunder]] a pirate

freed·man (frēd'mən) *n., pl.* **-men** (-mən) a man legally freed from slavery

free·dom (frē'dəm) *n.* **1** a being free; esp., *a)* independence *b)* civil or political liberty *c)* exemption from an obligation, discomfort, etc. *d)* a being able to act, use, etc. freely *e)* ease of movement *f)* frankness **2** a right or privilege

free fall any unchecked fall, as of a parachutist before the parachute opens

free flight any flight or part of a flight, as of a rocket, occurring without propulsion —**free'-flight'** *adj.*

free-for-all *n.* a disorganized, general fight; brawl —*adj.* open to anyone

free-form *adj.* **1** irregular in shape **2** spontaneous, unrestrained, etc.

free·hand *adj.* drawn by hand without the use of instruments, etc.

free·hold *n.* an estate in land held for life or with the right to pass it on to heirs —**free'hold'er** *n.*

free·lance or **free-lance** *adj.* of or relating to a writer, artist, etc. who sells his or her services to individual buyers —*vi.* **-lanced', -lanc'ing** to work in such a way —**free'lanc'er** *n.*

free·load·er (-lōd'ər) *n.* [Inf.] a person who habitually imposes on others for free food, etc. —**free'load'** *vi.*

free·man (frē'mən) *n., pl.* **-men** (-mən) **1** a person not in slavery **2** a citizen

Free·ma·son (frē'mā'sən) *n.* a member of an international secret society based on brotherliness and mutual aid —**Free'ma'son·ry** *n.*

free on board delivered (by the seller) aboard the train, ship, etc. at no extra charge to the buyer

free·stone *n.* **1** any stone, such as limestone, that cuts easily **2** a peach, etc. in which the pit does not cling to the pulp

free·think·er *n.* one who forms opinions about religion, morals, etc. independently

free throw *Basketball* an unhindered shot at the basket allowed to a fouled player: each successful shot scores one point

Free·town seaport & capital of Sierra Leone

free trade trade carried on without protective tariffs, quotas, etc.

free verse poetry without regular meter, esp. when unrhymed

free·ware *n.* copyrighted computer software that is available free of charge but whose distribution, resale, etc. typically are restricted

free·way *n.* a multiple-lane divided highway with fully controlled access

free·will *adj.* voluntary

freeze (frēz) *vi.* **froze, fro'zen, freez'ing** [[OE *freosan*]] **1** to be formed into, or become covered with, ice; be solidified by cold **2** to become very cold **3** to be damaged or killed by cold **4** to become motionless **5** to be made speechless by strong emotion **6** to become formal or unfriendly —*vt.* **1** to form into, or cover with, ice; solidify by cold **2** to make very cold **3** to preserve (food) by refrigeration below the point at which water becomes ice **4** to kill or damage by cold **5** to make motionless **6** to make formal or unfriendly **7** *a)* to fix (prices, etc.) at a given level *b)* to make (funds, etc.) unavailable to the owners —*n.* **1**

a freezing or being frozen **2** a period of freezing weather —**freeze out 1** to die out through freezing, as plants do **2** [Inf.] to keep out by a cold manner, competition, etc. —**freeze over** to become covered with ice —**freez′a·ble** adj.

freeze-dry vt. **-dried′, -dry′ing** to quick-freeze and then dry (food, etc.) under high vacuum

freez·er n. **1** a refrigerator, compartment, etc. for freezing and storing perishable foods **2** a machine for making ice cream

freezing point the temperature at which a liquid freezes: the freezing point of water is 32°F or 0°C

freight (frāt) n. [< MDu vracht, a load] **1** the transporting of goods **2** the cost for this **3** the goods transported **4** a railroad train for transporting goods: in full **freight train** —vt. **1** to load; burden **2** to send by freight

freight·er n. a ship for freight

French (french) adj. of France or its people, language, etc. —n. the language of France, also spoken in Belgium, Canada, etc. —**the French** the people of France —**French′man** (-mən) n., pl. **-men** (-mən)

French bread bread with a crisp crust made with white flour in a long, slender loaf

French cuff a shirt-sleeve cuff turned back on itself and fastened with a cuff link

French doors a pair of doors hinged at the sides to open in the middle

French dressing 1 VINAIGRETTE **2** a creamy, orange-colored salad dressing

French fries [often f- f-] strips of potato that have been French fried

French fry [often f- f-] to fry in hot deep fat

French Gui·a·na (gē an′ə, -ä′nə) French administrative division in NE South America

French horn a mellow-toned brass instrument with a long, spiral tube and a flaring bell: in classical music, now usually **horn**

French leave an unauthorized departure

French toast sliced bread dipped in a batter of egg and milk and then fried

fre·net·ic (frə net′ik) adj. [see PHRENETIC] frantic; frenzied —**fre·net′i·cal·ly** adv.

fren·zy (fren′zē) n., pl. **-zies** [< Gr phrenitis, madness] wild excitement; delirium

Fre·on (frē′än′) trademark for any of a series of gaseous compounds of fluorine, carbon, etc.: used as refrigerants, aerosol propellants, etc.

fre·quen·cy (frē′kwən sē) n., pl. **-cies** **1** frequent occurrence **2** the number of times any event recurs in a given period **3** Physics the number of oscillations or cycles per unit of time

frequency modulation the transmission of a signal by varying the frequency of a carrier wave: abbrev. FM

fre·quent (frē′kwənt; for v. frē kwent′) adj. [< L frequens, crowded] **1** occurring often **2** constant; habitual —vt. to go to or be at often —**fre′quent·ly** adv.

fres·co (fres′kō) n., pl. **-coes** or **-cos** [It, fresh] a painting made with watercolors applied to wet plaster

fresh¹ (fresh) adj. [OE fersc] **1** recently made, grown, etc. [fresh coffee] **2** not salted, pickled, etc. **3** not spoiled **4** not tired; lively **5** not worn, soiled, etc. **6** new; recent **7** inexperienced **8** cool and refreshing [a fresh spring day] **9** brisk: said of wind **10** not salt: said of water —**fresh′ly** adv. —**fresh′ness** n.

fresh² (fresh) adj. [< Ger frech, bold] [Slang] bold; saucy; impertinent

fresh·en vt., vi. to make or become fresh —**freshen up** to bathe, change into fresh clothes, etc. —**fresh′en·er** n.

fresh·man (-mən) n., pl. **-men** (-mən) [FRESH¹ + MAN] **1** a beginner **2** a person in his or her first year in college, Congress, etc.

fresh·wa·ter adj. **1** of or living in water that is not salty **2** sailing only on inland waters

Fres·no (frez′nō) city in central California

fret¹ (fret) vt., vi. **fret′ted, fret′ting** [OE fretan, to devour] **1** to gnaw, wear away, rub, etc. **2** to make or become rough or disturbed [wind fretting the water] **3** to irritate or be irritated; worry —n. irritation; worry —**fret′ter** n.

fret² (fret) n. [ME frette] a running design of interlacing small bars

fret³ (fret) n. [OFr frette, a band] any of the ridges on the fingerboard of a banjo, guitar, etc.

fret·ful (-fəl) adj. irritable; peevish —**fret′ful·ly** adv. —**fret′ful·ness** n.

fret·work n. decorative carving or openwork, as of interlacing lines

Freud (froid), **Sig·mund** (sig′mənd) 1856-1939; Austrian physician: founder of psychoanalysis —**Freud′i·an** adj., n.

Freudian slip a mistake made in speaking that, it is thought, reveals unconscious motives, desires, etc.

Fri abbrev. Friday

fri·a·ble (frī′ə bəl) adj. [Fr < L friare, to rub] easily crumbled

fri·ar (frī′ər) n. [< L frater, brother] R.C.Ch. a member of certain religious orders

fric·as·see (frik′ə sē′, frik′ə sē′) n. [< Fr fricasser, cut up and fry] a dish consisting of meat cut into pieces, stewed or fried, and served in a sauce of its own gravy —vt. **-seed′, -see′ing** to prepare in this way

fric·tion (frik′shən) n. [< L fricare, to rub] **1** a rubbing of one object against another **2** conflict, as because of differing opinions **3** Mech. the resistance to motion of moving surfaces that touch —**fric′tion·al** adj. —**fric′tion·less** adj.

Fri·day (frī′dā) n. [after Frigg, Germanic goddess] the sixth day of the week

fridge (frij) n. [Inf.] a refrigerator

fried (frīd) vt., vi. pt. & pp. of FRY¹

friend (frend) n. [OE freond] **1** a person whom one knows well and is fond of **2** an ally or sympathizer **3** [F—] a member of the Society of Friends; Quaker —**make** (or **be**) **friends with** to become (or be) a friend of —**friend′less** adj.

friend·ly adj. **-li·er, -li·est 1** of or like a friend;

kindly 2 not hostile; amicable 3 supporting; helping —friend′li·ly adv. —friend′li·ness n.

friend·ship n. 1 the state of being friends 2 friendly feeling

fries (frīz) pl.n. [Inf.] short for FRENCH FRIES

frieze (frēz) n. [< ML frisium] an ornamental band with designs or carvings, positioned along a wall, etc.

frig·ate (frig′it) n. [< It fregata] 1 a fast, medium-sized sailing warship of the 1700s and early 1800s 2 a small-to-medium-sized modern warship

fright (frīt) n. [OE fyrhto] 1 sudden fear; alarm 2 an ugly, startling, etc. person or thing

fright·en vt. 1 to make suddenly afraid; scare 2 to force (away, out, or off) by scaring —fright′en·ing·ly adv.

fright·ful (-fəl) adj. 1 causing fright; alarming 2 shocking; terrible 3 [Inf.] a) unpleasant; annoying b) great [in a frightful hurry] —fright′ful·ly adv. —fright′ful·ness n.

frig·id (frij′id) adj. [< L frigus, coldness] 1 extremely cold 2 not warm or friendly 3 sexually unresponsive: said of a woman: often offensive —fri·gid·i·ty (fri jid′ə tē) n. —frig′id·ly adv

Frigid Zone either of two zones (North Frigid Zone or South Frigid Zone) between the polar circles and the poles

frill (fril) n. [< ?] 1 any unnecessary ornament 2 a ruffle 3 a minor luxury —frill′y adj. -i·er, -i·est

fringe (frinj) n. [< LL fimbria] 1 a border of threads, etc. hanging loose or tied in bunches 2 an outer edge; border 3 a marginal or minor part —vt. fringed, fring′ing to be or make a fringe for —adj. 1 at the outer edge 2 additional 3 minor

fringe benefit any form of employee compensation other than wages, as insurance or a pension

frip·per·y (frip′ər ē) n., pl. -ies [< OFr frepe, a rag] 1 cheap, gaudy clothes 2 showy display in dress, manners, etc.

Fris·bee (friz′bē) n. [< "Mother Frisbie's" pie tins] trademark for a saucer-shaped plastic disk tossed back and forth in a simple game —n. [also f–] 1 such a disk 2 the game

fri·sé (frē zā′, fri-) n. [Fr < friser, to curl] an upholstery fabric with a thick pile in loops

Fri·sian (frizh′ən) n. the West Germanic language of an island chain (the Frisian Islands) along the coast of N Netherlands, Germany, & Denmark

frisk (frisk) vi. [< OHG frisc, lively] to move about in a lively way; frolic —vt. to search (a person) for weapons, etc. by passing the hands quickly over the person's clothing

frisk·y (fris′kē) adj. -i·er, -i·est lively; playful —frisk′i·ly adv. —frisk′i·ness n.

frit·ter¹ (frit′ər) vt. [< L frangere, to break] to waste (money, time, etc.) bit by bit: usually with away

frit·ter² (frit′ər) n. [< L frigere, to fry] a small cake of fried batter, usually containing corn, fruit, etc.

friv·o·lous (friv′ə ləs) adj. [< L frivolus, silly] 1 of little importance 2 silly and light-minded; giddy —fri·vol·i·ty (fri väl′ə tē) n., pl. -ties —friv′o·lous·ly adv.

frizz or friz (friz) vt., vi. frizzed, friz′zing [Fr friser] to form into small, tight curls —n. hair, etc. that is frizzed —friz′zy adj. -zi·er, -zi·est

friz·zle¹ (friz′əl) vi., vt. -zled, -zling [< FRY¹] to sizzle, as in frying

friz·zle² (friz′əl) n., vt., vi. -zled, -zling FRIZZ —friz′zly adj.

fro (frō) adv. [< ON frā] backward; back: now only in TO AND FRO (at TO)

frock (fräk) n. [< OFr froc] 1 a robe worn by friars, monks, etc. 2 a dress

frog (frôg, fräg) n. [OE frogga] 1 a tailless, leaping amphibian with long hind legs and webbed feet 2 a fancy loop, as of braid, used to fasten clothing —frog in one's throat temporary hoarseness

frog·man (-man′) n., pl. -men′ (-men′) a person trained and equipped for underwater demolition, exploration, etc.

frol·ic (fräl′ik) n. [< MDu vrō, merry] 1 a lively party or game 2 merriment; fun —vi. -icked, -ick·ing 1 to make merry; have fun 2 to romp about; gambol —frol′ick·er n.

frol·ic·some (-səm) adj. playful; merry

from (frum) prep. [OE] 1 beginning at; starting with [from noon to midnight] 2 out of [from her purse] 3 originating with [a letter from me] 4 out of the possibility of or use of [kept from going] 5 as unlike [to know good from evil] 6 because of [to tremble from fear]

frond (fränd) n. [< L frons, leafy branch] the leaf of a fern or palm

front (frunt) n. [< L frons, forehead] 1 a) outward behavior [a bold front] b) [Inf.] an appearance of social standing, wealth, etc. 2 the part facing forward 3 the first part; beginning 4 a forward or leading position 5 the land bordering a lake, street, etc. 6 the advanced battle area in warfare 7 an area of activity [the home front] 8 a person or group used to hide another's activity 9 Meteorol. the boundary between two differing air masses —adj. at, to, in, on, or of the front —vt., vi. 1 to face 2 to serve as a front (for) —in front of before —front′al adj.

front·age (frunt′ij) n. 1 the front part of a building 2 the front boundary line of a lot or the length of this line 3 land bordering a street, lake, etc.

fron·tier (frun tir′) n. [see FRONT] 1 the border between two countries 2 the part of a country which borders an unexplored or undeveloped region 3 any new field of learning, etc. or any part of a field that is not fully investigated —adj. of, on, or near a frontier —fron·tiers′man (-tirz′mən) n., pl. -men (-mən)

fron·tis·piece (frunt′is pēs′) n. [ult. < L frons, front + specere, to look] an illustration facing the title page of a book

front office the management or administration, as of a company

front-run·ner *n.* a leading contestant

front-wheel drive an automotive design in which only the front wheels receive driving power

frost (frôst, fräst) *n.* ⟦OE < *freosan*, to freeze⟧ **1** a temperature low enough to cause freezing **2** frozen dew or vapor —*vt.* **1** to cover with frost **2** to cover with frosting **3** to give a frostlike, opaque surface to (glass) — **frost′y** *adj.* **-i·er, -i·est**

Frost (frôst, fräst), **Rob·ert (Lee)** (rä′bərt) 1874-1963; U.S. poet

frost·bite *n.* injury caused by exposure of body tissues to intense cold —**frost′bit′ten** *adj.*

frost·ing *n.* **1** a mixture of sugar, butter, flavoring, etc. for covering a cake; icing **2** a dull finish on glass, etc.

frost line the limit of penetration of soil by frost

froth (frôth, fräth) *n.* ⟦< ON *frotha*⟧ **1** foam **2** foaming saliva **3** light, trifling talk, ideas, etc. —*vi.* to foam —**froth′y** *adj.* **-i·er, -i·est**

frou-frou (froo′froo′) *adj.* ⟦Fr⟧ [Inf.] excessively ornate

fro·ward (frô′wərd, -ərd) *adj.* [see FRO & -WARD] not easily controlled; willful; contrary —**fro′ward·ness** *n.*

frown (froun) *vi.* ⟦< OFr *froigne*, sullen face⟧ **1** to contract the brows and lower the corners of the mouth, as in displeasure **2** to show disapproval: with *on* or *upon* —*n.* a frowning

frow·zy (frou′zē) *adj.* **-zi·er, -zi·est** ⟦< ?⟧ dirty and untidy; slovenly —**frow′zi·ly** *adv.* —**frow′zi·ness** *n.*

froze (frōz) *vi., vt. pt. of* FREEZE

fro·zen (frō′zən) *vi., vt. pp. of* FREEZE —*adj.* **1** turned into or covered with ice; solidified by cold **2** damaged or killed by freezing **3** preserved by freezing: said as of food **4** made motionless **5** kept at a fixed level **6** not readily convertible into cash [*frozen* assets]

frozen custard a food resembling soft ice cream, but with less butterfat

fruc·ti·fy (fruk′tə fī′) *vi., vt.* **-fied′, -fy′ing** ⟦< L *fructificare*⟧ to bear or cause to bear fruit

fruc·tose (fruk′tōs′, frook′-) *n.* ⟦< L *fructus*, fruit + -OSE¹⟧ a sugar found in sweet fruits and in honey

fru·gal (froo′gəl) *adj.* ⟦< L *frugi*, fit for food⟧ **1** not wasteful; thrifty **2** inexpensive or meager —**fru·gal′i·ty** (-gal′ə tē) *n., pl.* **-ties** —**fru′gal·ly** *adv.*

fruit (froot) *n.* ⟦< L *fructus*⟧ **1** any plant product, as grain or vegetables: *usually used in pl.* **2** *a)* an edible plant structure containing the seeds inside an often sweet and juicy pulp: many true fruits that are not sweet, as cucumbers, are popularly called *vegetables b) Bot.* the mature seed-bearing part of a flowering plant **3** the result or product of any action

fruit·cake *n.* a rich cake containing nuts, preserved fruit, citron, spices, etc.

fruit fly any of various small flies whose larvae feed on fruits and vegetables

fruit·ful (-fəl) *adj.* **1** bearing much fruit **2** productive; prolific **3** profitable

fru·i·tion (froo ish′ən) *n.* **1** the bearing of fruit **2** a coming to fulfillment

fruit·less (-lis) *adj.* **1** without results; unsuccessful **2** bearing no fruit; sterile; barren — **fruit′less·ly** *adv.* —**fruit′less·ness** *n.*

frump (frump) *n.* ⟦prob. < Du *rompelen*, rumple⟧ a dowdy woman —**frump′ish** *adj.* —**frump′y** *adj.* **-i·er, -i·est**

frus·trate (frus′trāt′) *vt.* **-trat′ed, -trat′ing** ⟦< L *frustra*, in vain⟧ **1** to cause to have no effect **2** to prevent from achieving a goal or gratifying a desire **3** to cause to feel impatience or annoyance due to an unsatisfied desire —**frus·tra′tion** *n.*

fry¹ (frī) *vt., vi.* **fried, fry′ing** ⟦< L *frigere*, to fry⟧ to cook in a pan over direct heat, usually in hot fat —*n., pl.* **fries 1** [*pl.*] fried potatoes **2** a social gathering at which food is fried and eaten [a fish *fry*]

fry² (frī) *pl.n., sing.* **fry** ⟦< OFr *freier*, to rub, spawn⟧ young fish

fry·er *n.* **1** a utensil for deep-frying **2** a chicken for frying

FSLIC *abbrev.* Federal Savings and Loan Insurance Corporation

ft *abbrev.* foot; feet

Ft *abbrev.* Fort

FTC *abbrev.* Federal Trade Commission

fuch·sia (fyoo′shə) *n.* ⟦after L. *Fuchs* (1501-66), Ger botanist⟧ **1** a shrubby plant with pink, red, or purple flowers **2** purple-red

fud·dle (fud′'l) *vt.* **-dled, -dling** ⟦< ?⟧ to confuse or stupefy as with alcoholic liquor —*n.* a fuddled state

fud·dy-dud·dy (fud′ē dud′ē) *n., pl.* **-dies** [Inf.] a fussy or old-fashioned person

fudge (fuj) *n.* ⟦< ?⟧ a soft candy made of butter, milk, sugar, chocolate or other flavoring, etc. —*vi.* **fudged, fudg′ing 1** to refuse to commit oneself; hedge **2** to be dishonest, cheat —**fudg′y** *adj.* **-i·er, -i·est**

fu·el (fyoo′əl, fyool) *n.* ⟦ult. < L *focus*, fireplace⟧ **1** coal, oil, gas, wood, etc., burned to supply heat or power **2** material from which nuclear energy can be obtained **3** anything that intensifies strong feeling — *vt., vi.* **fu′eled** or **fu′elled, fu′el·ing** or **fu′el·ling** to supply with or get fuel

fuel injection a system for injecting a fine spray of fuel into the combustion chambers of an engine

fu·gi·tive (fyoo′ji tiv) *adj.* ⟦< L *fugere*, to flee⟧ **1** fleeing, as from danger or justice **2** fleeting —*n.* one who is fleeing from justice, etc. —**fu′gi·tive·ly** *adv.*

fugue (fyoog) *n.* ⟦< L *fugere*, to flee⟧ a musical work in which a theme is taken up successively and developed by the various parts or voices in counterpoint

-ful (fəl; *for 2, usually* fool) *suf.* ⟦< FULL¹⟧ suffix **1** *a)* full of, having [*joyful*] *b)* having the qualities of or tendency to [*helpful*] **2** the quantity that will fill [*handful*]

ful·crum (fool′krəm, ful′-) *n., pl.* **-crums** or **-cra** (-krə) ⟦L, a support⟧ the support on which a lever turns in raising something

ful·fill (fool fil′) *vt.* **-filled′, -fill′ing** [OE *fullfyllan*] **1** to carry out (a promise, etc.) **2** to do (a duty, etc.); obey **3** to satisfy (a condition) Brit. sp. **ful·fil′ -filled′, -fill′ing** — **ful·fill′ment** *n.,* **ful·fil′ment**

full¹ (fool) *adj.* [OE] **1** having in it all there is space for; filled **2** having eaten all that one wants **3** having a great deal or number (*of*) **4** complete [a *full* dozen] **5** having reached the greatest size, extent, etc. [a *full* moon] **6** plump; round [a *full* face] **7** with wide folds; flowing [a *full* skirt] —*n.* the greatest amount, extent, etc. —*adv.* **1** to the greatest degree; completely **2** directly; exactly —**full′ness** *n.,* **ful′ness**

full² (fool) *vt., vi.* [< L *fullo*, cloth fuller] to shrink and thicken (wool cloth) —**full′er** *n.*

full·back *n. Football* one of the running backs, used typically for blocking an opponent

full-blood·ed *adj.* **1** of unmixed breed or race **2** vigorous

full-blown *adj.* **1** in full bloom **2** fully developed; matured

full-bore *adv.* to the greatest degree or extent —*adj.* all-out

full-fledged *adj.* completely developed or trained; of full status

full moon the moon when it reflects light as a full disk

full-scale *adj.* **1** according to the original or standard scale **2** to the point of being so completely [a *full-scale* riot]

full-size *adj.* **1** of the usual or standard size **2** of a large size Also **full′-sized′**

full-throat·ed *adj.* **1** having or producing deep, rich sound **2** complete and unmitigated

full-time *adj.* of or engaged in work, study, etc. that takes all of one's regular working hours

full·y *adv.* **1** completely; thoroughly **2** at least

ful·mi·nate (ful′mə nāt′) *vi.* **-nat′ed, -nat′ing** [< L *fulmen*, lightning] to express strong disapproval —**ful′mi·na′tion** *n.*

ful·some (fool′səm) *adj.* [see FULL¹ & -SOME¹, but infl. by ME *ful*, foul] disgusting, esp. because excessive

fum·ble (fum′bəl) *vi., vt.* **-bled, -bling** [prob. < ON *famla*] **1** to grope (*for*) or handle (a thing) clumsily **2** to lose one's grasp on (a football, etc.) —*n.* a fumbling —**fum′bler** *n.*

fume (fyoom) *n.* [< L *fumus*] [*often pl.*] a gas, smoke, or vapor, esp. if offensive or suffocating —*vi.* **fumed, fum′ing 1** to give off fumes **2** to show anger

fu·mi·gate (fyoo′mə gāt′) *vt.* **-gat′ed, -gat′ing** [< L *fumus*, smoke + *agere*, do] to expose to fumes, esp. so as to disinfect or kill the vermin in —**fu′mi·ga′tion** *n.* —**fu′mi·ga′tor** *n.*

fum·y (fyoom′ē) *adj.* **-i·er, -i·est** full of or producing fumes; vaporous

fun (fun) *n.* [< ME *fonne*, foolish] **1** *a)* lively, joyous play or playfulness *b)* pleasure **2** a source of amusement —*adj.* [Inf.] giving pleasure or amusement —**make fun of** to ridicule

func·tion (funk′shən) *n.* [< L *fungi*, to perform] **1** the normal or characteristic action of anything **2** a special duty required in work **3** a formal ceremony or social occasion **4** a thing that depends on and varies with something else —*vi.* to act in a required manner; work; be used —**func′tion·less** *adj.*

func·tion·al *adj.* **1** of a function **2** performing a function **3** *Med.* affecting a function of some organ without apparent organic changes —**func′tion·al′i·ty** *n. pl.,* **-ties**

functional illiterate a person who cannot read well enough to carry out everyday activities

func·tion·ar·y (-shə ner′ē) *n., pl.* **-ies** an official performing some function

function word a word, as an article or conjunction, serving mainly to show grammatical relationship

fund (fund) *n.* [L *fundus*, bottom] **1** a supply that can be drawn upon; stock **2** *a)* a sum of money set aside for a purpose *b)* [*pl.*] ready money —*vt.* **1** to put or convert into a long-term debt that bears interest **2** to provide funds for (a project, retirement of a debt, etc.)

fun·da·men·tal (fun′də ment′'l) *adj.* [see prec.] of or forming a foundation or basis; basic; essential —*n.* a principle, theory, law, etc. serving as a basis —**fun′da·men′tal·ly** *adv.*

fun·da·men·tal·ism *n.* [*sometimes* F-] religious beliefs based on a literal interpretation of the Bible or other scriptures —**fun′da·men′tal·ist** *n., adj.*

fund·rais·er (-rā′zər) *n.* **1** one soliciting money for a charity, political party, etc. **2** an event held to obtain such money —**fund′·rais′ing** *n.*

fu·ner·al (fyoo′nər əl) *n.* [< L *funus*] the ceremonies connected with burial or cremation of a dead person

funeral director one who manages a funeral home

funeral home (*or* **parlor**) an establishment where the bodies of the dead are prepared for burial or cremation and where funeral services can be held

fu·ne·re·al (fyoo nir′ē əl) *adj.* suitable for a funeral; sad and solemn; dismal —**fu·ne′re·al·ly** *adv.*

fun·gi·cide (fun′jə sīd′) *n.* [see -CIDE] any substance that kills fungi

fun·gus (fun′gəs) *n., pl.* **fun·gi** (fun′jī′) *or* **fun′gus·es** [< L] any of various plantlike organisms, as molds, mildews, mushrooms, etc., that lack chlorophyll, stems, and leaves and reproduce by spores —**fun′gal** *adj.,* **fun′gous** *adj.*

fu·nic·u·lar (fyoo nik′yoo lər) *n.* [< L *funiculus*, little rope] a mountain railway with a pair of counterbalanced cable cars that ascend and descend in turns: also **funicular railway**

funk¹ (funk) *n.* [< ? Fl *fonck*, dismay] **1** [Inf.] a state of great fear; panic **2** [Inf.] a depressed mood

funk² (funk) *n.* [fol.] [Inf.] popular music derived from rhythm and blues

funk·y (fun′kē) *adj.* **-i·er, -i·est** [orig., earthy] **1** *Jazz* having an earthy style derived from early blues **2** [Slang] unconventional, eccentric, offbeat, etc.

fun·nel (fun'əl) *n.* [ult. < L *fundere*, to pour] **1** a tapering tube with a cone-shaped mouth, for pouring things into small-mouthed containers **2** the smokestack of a steamship — *vi., vt.* **-neled** or **-nelled, -nel·ing** or **-nel·ling** to move or pour as through a funnel

fun·nies (fun'ēz) *pl.n.* [Inf.] comic strips

fun·ny (fun'ē) *adj.* **-ni·er, -ni·est 1** causing laughter; humorous **2** *a)* puzzling or suspicious *b)* [Inf.] eccentric —**fun'ni·ly** *adv.* —**fun'ni·ness** *n.*

funny bone a place on the elbow where a sharp impact on a nerve causes a tingling sensation

funny farm [Slang] an institution for the mentally ill: somewhat offensive

fur (fur) *n.* [< OFr *fuerre*, sheath] **1** the soft, thick hair covering certain animals **2** a processed skin bearing such hair —*adj.* of fur —**furred** *adj.*

fur·be·low (fur'bə lō') *n.* [ult. < Fr *falbala*] **1** a flounce or ruffle **2** a showy, useless decorative addition

fur·bish (fur'bish) *vt.* [< OFr *forbir*] **1** to polish; burnish **2** to renovate

Fu·ries (fyoor'ēz) *pl.n. Gr. & Rom. Myth.* the three terrible female spirits who punish the perpetrators of unavenged crimes

fu·ri·ous (fyoor'ē əs) *adj.* **1** full of fury; very angry **2** very great, intense, wild, etc. —**fu'ri·ous·ly** *adv.*

furl (furl) *vt.* [< L *firmus,* FIRM[1] + *ligare,* to tie] to roll up (a sail, flag, etc.) tightly and make secure

fur·long (fur'lôŋ') *n.* [< OE *furh,* a furrow + *lang,* LONG[1]] a measure of distance equal to ⅛ of a mile

fur·lough (fur'lō) *n.* [< Du *verlof*] a leave of absence, esp. for military personnel —*vt.* to grant a furlough to

fur·nace (fur'nəs) *n.* [< L *fornax*] an enclosed structure in which heat is produced, as by burning fuel

fur·nish (fur'nish) *vt.* [< OFr *furnir*] **1** to supply with furniture, etc.; equip **2** to supply; provide

fur·nish·ings *pl.n.* **1** the furniture, carpets, etc. as for a house **2** things to wear [*men's furnishings*]

fur·ni·ture (fur'ni chər) *n.* [Fr *fourniture*] **1** the things in a room, etc. which equip it for living, as chairs, beds, etc. **2** necessary equipment

fu·ror (fyoor'ôr') *n.* [< L] **1** fury; frenzy **2** *a)* a widespread enthusiasm; craze *b)* a commotion or uproar Also [Chiefly Brit.] **fu'rore'**

fur·ri·er (fur'ē ər) *n.* one who processes furs or deals in fur garments

fur·ring (fur'iŋ) *n.* thin strips of wood fixed on a wall, floor, etc. before adding boards or plaster

fur·row (fur'ō) *n.* [< OE *furh*] **1** a narrow groove made in the ground by a plow **2** anything like this, as a deep wrinkle —*vt.* to make furrows in —*vi.* to become wrinkled

fur·ry (fur'ē) *adj.* **-ri·er, -ri·est 1** of or like fur **2** covered with fur —**fur'ri·ness** *n.*

fur·ther (fur'thər) *adj.* [OE *furthor*] **1** *alt. compar. of* FAR **2** additional **3** more distant; farther —*adv.* **1** *alt. compar. of* FAR **2** to a greater degree or extent **3** in addition **4** at or to a greater distance; farther —*vt.* to give aid to; promote In sense 3 of the *adj.* and sense 4 of the *adv.,* FARTHER is more commonly used

fur·ther·ance *n.* advancement or promotion

fur·ther·more *adv.* in addition; besides; moreover

fur·thest (fur'thist) *adj.* **1** *alt. superl. of* FAR **2** most distant; farthest: also **fur'ther·most'** —*adv.* **1** *alt. superl. of* FAR **2** at or to the greatest distance or degree

fur·tive (fur'tiv) *adj.* [< L *fur,* a thief] done or acting in a stealthy manner —**fur'tive·ly** *adv.* —**fur'tive·ness** *n.*

fu·ry (fyoor'ē) *n., pl.* **-ries** [< L *furere,* to rage] **1** violent anger; wild rage **2** violence; vehemence **3** [F-] any of the FURIES

furze (furz) *n.* [OE *fyrs*] a prickly evergreen shrub native to Europe

fuse[1] (fyo͞oz) *vt., vi.* **fused, fus'ing** [< L *fundere,* to pour out] **1** to melt **2** to unite as if by melting together

fuse[2] (fyo͞oz) *n.* [< L *fusus,* spindle] **1** a tube or wick filled with combustible material, for setting off an explosive charge **2** *Elec.* a strip of easily melted metal placed in a circuit: it melts and breaks the circuit if the current becomes too strong

fu·see (fyo͞o zē') *n.* [Fr *fusée,* a rocket] a colored flare used as a signal by railroad workers, truck drivers, etc.

fu·se·lage (fyo͞o'sə läzh', -läj') *n.* [Fr] the body of an airplane, exclusive of the wings, tail assembly, and engines

fu·si·ble (fyo͞o'zə bəl) *adj.* that can be fused or easily melted

fu·si·lier or **fu·sil·eer** (fyo͞o'zə lir') *n.* [Fr] [Historical] a soldier armed with a flintlock musket

fu·sil·lade (fyo͞o'sə läd', -läd') *n.* [Fr < *fusiller,* to shoot] a simultaneous or continuous discharge of many firearms

fu·sion (fyo͞o'zhən) *n.* [L *fusio*] **1** a fusing or melting together **2** a blending; coalition **3** NUCLEAR FUSION **4** a style of popular music blending elements of jazz, rock, etc.

fuss (fus) *n.* [prob. echoic] **1** nervous, excited activity; bustle **2** a nervous state **3** a quarrel **4** a showy display of approval, etc. —*vi.* **1** to bustle about or worry over trifles **2** to whine, as a baby

fuss·budg·et (-buj'it) *n.* [prec. + BUDGET] [Inf.] a fussy person: also [Inf., Chiefly Brit.] **fuss'pot'** (-pät')

fuss·y *adj.* **-i·er, -i·est 1** *a)* worrying over trifles *b)* hard to please *c)* whining, as a baby **2** full of unnecessary details —**fuss'i·ly** *adv.* —**fuss'i·ness** *n.*

fus·tian (fus'chən) *n.* [< L *fustis,* wooden stick] pompous, pretentious talk or writing; bombast

fus·ty (fus'tē) *adj.* **-ti·er, -ti·est** ⟦< OFr *fust*, a cask⟧ **1** musty; moldy **2** old-fashioned —**fus'ti·ly** *adv.* —**fus'ti·ness** *n.*

fut *abbrev.* future

fu·tile (fyōōt'l) *adj.* ⟦< L *futilis*, lit., that easily pours out⟧ useless; vain —**fu'tile·ly** *adv.* —**fu·til·i·ty** (fyōō til'ə tē) *n., pl.* **-ties**

fu·ton (fōō'tän') *n.* ⟦Sino-Jpn⟧ a thin mattress placed on the floor or a platform frame for use as a bed

fu·ture (fyōō'chər) *adj.* ⟦< L *futurus*, about to be⟧ **1** that is to be or come **2** indicating time to come [the *future* tense] —*n.* **1** the time that is to come **2** what is going to be **3** the chance to succeed, etc. **4** [*usually pl.*] a contract for a commodity bought or sold for delivery at a later date —**fu'tur·is'tic** *adj.*

fu·tur·ism (fyōō'chər iz'əm) *n.* [*often* F-] a modernist artistic movement esp. of the early 1900s, emphasizing the speed, flux, and violence of the machine age

fu·tur·ist (fyōō'chər ist) *n.* **1** an adherent of futurism **2** a futurologist

fu·tu·ri·ty (fyōō toor'ə tē, -tyoor'-) *n., pl.* **-ties 1** the future **2** a future condition or event **3** a race for two-year-old horses in which the entries are selected before birth: in full **futurity race**

fu·tur·ol·o·gy (fyōō'chər äl'ə jē) *n.* ⟦FUTUR(E) + -OLOGY⟧ the prediction of future conditions, esp. social or technological developments, as extrapolated from known facts —**fu'tur·ol'o·gist** *n.*

futz (futs) *vi.* ⟦? < Yiddish⟧ [Slang] to trifle or fool (*around*)

fuzz (fuz) *n.* ⟦< ?⟧ loose, light particles of down, wool, etc.; fine hairs or fibers —**the fuzz** [Slang] a policeman or the police —**fuzz'y** *adj.* **-i·er, -i·est**

fuzzy logic ⟦< *fuzzy* (set), coined (1965) by L. A. Zadeh, U.S. scientist⟧ a type of logic used in computers for processing imprecise or variable data

-fy (fī) ⟦< L *facere*, do⟧ *suffix* **1** to make [*liquefy*] **2** to cause to have [*glorify*] **3** to become [*putrefy*]

FYI *abbrev.* for your information

G

g or **G** (jē) *n., pl.* **g's, G's** the seventh letter of the English alphabet

G¹ (jē) *n. Music* the fifth tone in the scale of C major

G² *trademark for* a film rating indicating content suitable for persons of all ages

G³ *abbrev.* **1** game(s) **2** German **3** goal(s) **4** gram(s) **5** guard **6** gulf Also, except for 2 & 6, **g**

Ga *Chem. symbol for* gallium

GA *abbrev.* Georgia

gab (gab) *n., vt.* **gabbed, gab'bing** ⟦ON *gabba*, to mock⟧ [Inf.] chatter

gab·ar·dine (gab'ər dēn') *n.* ⟦< OFr *gaverdine*, kind of cloak⟧ a twilled cloth of wool, cotton, etc., with a fine, diagonal weave: Brit. sp. **gab'er·dine'**

gab·ble (gab'əl) *vi., vt.* **-bled, -bling** ⟦< GAB⟧ to talk or utter rapidly or incoherently —*n.* such talk

gab·by (gab'ē) *adj.* **-bi·er, -bi·est** [Inf.] talkative —**gab'bi·ness** *n.*

gab·fest (-fest') *n.* [Inf.] an informal gathering of people to talk with one another

ga·ble (gā'bəl) *n.* ⟦< Gmc⟧ a triangular part of a wall enclosed by the sloping sides of a peaked roof —**ga'bled** *adj.*

Ga·bon (ga bōn') country on the W coast of Africa

Ga·bri·el (gā'brē əl) *n. Bible* one of the archangels, the herald of good news

gad (gad) *vi.* **gad'ded, gad'ding** ⟦ME *gadden*, to hurry⟧ to wander about in an idle or restless way —**gad'der** *n.*

gad·a·bout *n.* one who gads about, looking for fun, etc.

gad·fly *n., pl.* **-flies'** ⟦see GOAD & FLY²⟧ **1** a large fly that bites livestock **2** one who annoys others, esp. by rousing them from complacency

gadg·et (gaj'it) *n.* ⟦< ?⟧ any small mechanical contrivance or device —**gadg'et·ry** *n.*

gad·o·lin·i·um (gad'ō lin'ē əm) *n.* ⟦after Johan *Gadolin* (1760-1852), Finnish chemist⟧ a malleable, metallic chemical element that is highly magnetic at low temperatures and a superconductor: symbol, Gd; at. no. 64

Gael·ic (gā'lik) *adj.* of the Celtic people of Ireland, Scotland, or the Isle of Man —*n.* **1** the Celtic language of Scotland **2** the language group that includes GAELIC (*n.* 1), IRISH (*n.* 1), etc.

gaff (gaf) *n.* ⟦< OProv *gaf* or Sp *gafa*⟧ **1** a large hook on a pole for landing fish **2** a spar supporting a fore-and-aft sail

gaffe (gaf) *n.* ⟦Fr⟧ a blunder

gaf·fer (gaf'ər) *n.* a person in charge of lighting on the set of a film

gag (gag) *vt.* **gagged, gag'ging** ⟦echoic⟧ **1** to cause to retch **2** to keep from speaking, as by stopping up the mouth of —*vi.* to retch —*n.* **1** something put into or over the mouth to prevent talking, etc. **2** any restraint of free speech **3** a joke

gage¹ (gāj) *n.* ⟦< OFr, a pledge⟧ a glove, etc. thrown down as by a knight as a challenge to fight

gage² (gāj) *n., vt.* **gaged**, **gag'ing** *alt. sp. of* GAUGE

gag·gle (gag'əl) *n.* ⟦echoic⟧ **1** a flock of geese **2** any group or cluster

gai·e·ty (gā'ə tē) *n., pl.* **-ties 1** the quality of being cheerful and merry **2** merrymaking

gai·ly (gā'lē) *adv.* in a gay manner; specif., *a)* merrily *b)* brightly

gain (gān) *n.* ⟦< OFr *gaaigne*⟧ **1** an increase; specif., *a)* [*often pl.*] profit *b)* an increase in advantage **2** acquisition —*vt.* **1** to earn **2** to win **3** to attract **4** to get as an addition, profit, or advantage **5** to make an increase in **6** to get to; reach —*vi.* **1** to make progress **2** to increase in weight —**gain on** to draw nearer to (an opponent in a race, etc.)

gain·er *n.* **1** a person or thing that gains **2** a fancy dive forward, but with a backward somersault

gain·ful *adj.* producing gain; profitable —**gain'ful·ly** *adv.*

gain·say (gān'sā') *vt.* **-said'** (-sed'), **-say'ing** ⟦< OE *gegn*, against + *secgan*, to say⟧ **1** to deny **2** to contradict —**gain'say'er** *n.*

gait (gāt) *n.* ⟦< ON *gata*, path⟧ **1** manner of walking or running **2** any of the various foot movements of a horse, as a trot, pace, canter, etc.

gai·ter (gāt'ər) *n.* ⟦< Fr *guêtre*⟧ a cloth or leather covering for the instep, ankle, and lower leg

gal¹ (gal) *n.* [Slang] a girl or woman

gal² *abbrev.* gallon(s)

ga·la (gā'lə, gal'ə) *n.* ⟦ult. < It *gala*⟧ a celebration —*adj.* festive

Gal·a·had (gal'ə had') *n. Arthurian Legend* the knight who, because of his purity, succeeds in finding the Holy Grail

gal·ax·y (gal'ək sē) *n., pl.* **-ies** ⟦< Gr *gala*, milk⟧ **1** [*often* G-] MILKY WAY **2** a large, independent system of stars **3** a group of illustrious people —**ga·lac·tic** (gə lak'tik) *adj.*

gale (gāl) *n.* ⟦< ?⟧ **1** a strong wind **2** an outburst [*a gale of laughter*]

ga·le·na (gə lē'nə) *n.* ⟦L, lead ore⟧ native lead sulfide, a soft, lead-gray mineral with a metallic luster

Gal·i·lee (gal'ə lē') region of N Israel on the W shore of a large lake (the **Sea of Galilee**) on the Syrian border

Gal·i·le·o (gal'ə lē'ō, -lā'-) 1564-1642; It. astronomer & physicist

gall¹ (gôl) *n.* ⟦OE *galla*⟧ **1** BILE (*n.* 1) **2** something bitter or distasteful **3** bitter feeling **4** impudence

gall² (gôl) *n.* [see fol.] a sore on the skin caused by chafing —*vt.* **1** to make sore by rubbing **2** to annoy; vex

gall³ (gôl) *n.* ⟦< L *galla*⟧ a tumor on plant tissue caused by fungi, insects, etc.

gal·lant (gal'ənt; *for adj.* **3** *& n., usually* gə lant'),

-länt') *adj.* ⟦< OFr *galer*, to make merry⟧ **1** stately; imposing **2** brave and noble **3** polite and attentive to women —*n.* **1** [Now Rare] a high-spirited, stylish man **2** a man attentive and polite to women

gal·lant·ry (gal'ən trē) *n., pl.* **-ries 1** heroic courage **2** the behavior of a gallant **3** a courteous act or remark

gall·blad·der (gôl'blad'ər) *n.* a membranous sac closely attached to the liver, in which excess gall, or bile, is stored

gal·le·on (gal'ē ən) *n.* ⟦ult. < Gr *galeos*, shark⟧ a large sailing ship of the 1400s and 1500s

gal·le·ri·a (gal'ə rē'ə) *n.* a large arcade or court, sometimes with a glass roof

gal·ler·y (gal'ər ē) *n., pl.* **-ies** ⟦< ML *galeria*⟧ **1** a covered walk or porch open at one side or having the roof supported by pillars **2** a long, narrow, outside balcony **3** *a)* a balcony in a theater, etc.; esp., the highest balcony with the cheapest seats *b)* the people in these seats **4** the spectators at a sports event, etc. **5** a place for exhibiting or selling works of art; specif., a display room in a museum

gal·ley (gal'ē) *n., pl.* **-leys** ⟦< Gr *galeos*, shark⟧ **1** a long, low ship of ancient times, propelled by oars and sails **2** a ship's kitchen **3** *Printing a)* a shallow tray for holding composed type *b)* proof printed from such type (in full **galley proof**)

Gal·lic (gal'ik) *adj.* **1** of ancient Gaul or its people **2** French

Gal·li·cism (gal'i siz'əm) *n.* ⟦< prec.⟧ [*also* g-] a French idiom, custom, etc.

gal·li·um (gal'ē əm) *n.* ⟦named after L *Gallia*, France⟧ a bluish-white, metallic chemical element used in semiconductors, lasers, etc.: symbol, Ga; at. no. 31

gal·li·vant (gal'ə vant') *vi.* ⟦arbitrary elaboration of GALLANT⟧ to go about in search of amusement

gal·lon (gal'ən) *n.* ⟦< OFr *jalon*⟧ a liquid measure equal to four quarts

gal·lop (gal'əp) *vi., vt.* ⟦< OFr *galoper*⟧ to go, or cause to go, at a gallop —*n.* the fastest gait of a horse, etc., a succession of leaping strides

gal·lows (gal'ōz) *n., pl.* **-lows** or **-lows·es** ⟦OE *galga*⟧ an upright frame with a crossbeam and a rope, for hanging condemned persons

gall·stone (gôl'stōn') *n.* a small, solid mass sometimes formed in the gallbladder or bile duct

ga·lore (gə lôr') *adj.* ⟦Ir *go leór*, enough⟧ in abundance; plentifully [*to attract crowds galore*]

ga·losh (gə läsh') *n.* ⟦< OFr *galoche*⟧ a high, warmly lined overshoe of rubber and fabric

gal·van·ic (gal van'ik) *adj.* ⟦after L. *Galvani* (1737-98), It physicist⟧ **1** of or producing direct current from a chemical reaction, as in a battery **2** startling

gal·va·nize (gal'və nīz') *vt.* **-nized'**, **-niz'ing 1** to stimulate as if by electric shock; rouse; stir **2** to plate (metal) with zinc

gal·va·nom·e·ter (-näm′ət ər) *n.* an instrument for detecting and measuring a small electric current

Gam·bi·a (gam′bē ə) country on the W coast of Africa

gam·bit (gam′bit) *n.* [< Sp *gambito*, a tripping] 1 *Chess* an opening in which a pawn, etc. is sacrificed to get an advantage in position 2 an action intended to gain an advantage

gam·ble (gam′bəl) *vi.* **-bled, -bling** [ME *gamen*, to play] 1 to play games of chance for money, etc. 2 to take a risk for some advantage —*vt.* to risk in gambling; bet —*n.* an undertaking involving risk —**gam′bler** *n.*

gam·bol (gam′bəl) *n.* [< It *gamba*, leg] a gamboling; frolic —*vi.* **-boled** or **-bolled, -boling** or **-bol·ling** to jump and skip about in play; frolic

gam·brel (roof) (gam′brəl) a roof with two slopes on each of its two sides

game¹ (gām) *n.* [OE *gamen*] 1 any form of play; amusement 2 *a)* any specific amusement or sport involving competition under rules *b)* a single contest in such a competition 3 the number of points required for winning 4 a scheme; plan 5 wild birds or animals hunted for sport or food 6 [Inf.] a business or job, esp. one involving risk —*vi.* **gamed, gam′ing** to play cards, etc. for stakes; gamble —*vt.* to manipulate the rules of to one's advantage —*adj.* 1 designating or of wild birds or animals hunted for sport or food 2 *a)* plucky; courageous *b)* enthusiastic; ready (*for* something) —**ahead of the game** [Inf.] in a successful position —**the game is up** failure is certain —**game′ly** *adv.* —**game′ness** *n.*

game² (gām) *adj.* [< ?] lame or injured [a *game leg*]

game·cock *n.* a specially bred rooster trained for cockfighting

game·keep·er *n.* a person who takes care of game birds and animals, as on an estate

game plan 1 the strategy planned before a game 2 any long-range strategy

game point 1 the situation when the next point scored could win a game 2 the winning point

game show a television show in which contestants compete for prizes by playing games that involve knowledge, skill, or chance

games·man·ship (gāmz′mən ship′) *n.* skill in using ploys to gain an advantage

game·ster (gām′stər) *n.* a gambler

gam·ete (gam′ēt, gə mēt′) *n.* [< Gr *gamos*, marriage] a reproductive cell that unites with another to form the cell that develops into a new individual

gam·in (gam′in) *n.* [Fr] 1 a neglected child who roams the streets 2 a girl with saucy charm: also **ga·mine** (ga mēn′)

gam·ma (gam′ə) *n.* the third letter of the Greek alphabet (Γ, γ)

gamma glob·u·lin (gläb′yoo lin) that fraction of blood serum which contains most antibodies

gamma ray a stream of electromagnetic radiation with a very short wavelength, produced as by nuclear reactions

gam·ut (gam′ət) *n.* [< Gr letter *gamma*, for the lowest note of the medieval scale] 1 any complete musical scale 2 the entire range or extent, as of emotions

gam·y (gām′ē) *adj.* **-i·er, -i·est** 1 having the strong flavor of cooked game 2 slightly tainted 3 risqué 4 coarse or crude —**gam′i·ness** *n.*

gan·der (gan′dər) *n.* [OE *gan(d)ra*] 1 a male goose 2 [Slang] a look: chiefly in **take a gander**

Gan·dhi (gän′dē), **Mo·han·das** (mō hän′dəs) 1869-1948; Hindu nationalist leader: called *Mahatma Gandhi*

gang (gaŋ) *n.* [< OE *gangan*, to go] a group of people working or acting together; specif., a group of criminals or juvenile delinquents —**gang up on** [Inf.] to attack as a group

Gan·ges (gan′jēz) river in N India & Bangladesh

gan·gling (gaŋ′gliŋ) *adj.* [< ?] thin, tall, and awkward: also **gan′gly**

gan·gli·on (gaŋ′glē ən) *n., pl.* **-gli·a** (-ə) or **-gli·ons** [ult. < Gr, tumor] a mass of nerve cells from which nerve impulses are transmitted

gang·plank *n.* a movable ramp by which to board or leave a ship

gan·grene (gaŋ′grēn′, gaŋ grēn′) *n.* [< Gr *gran*, gnaw] decay of body tissue when the blood supply is obstructed —**gan′gre·nous** (-grə nəs) *adj.*

gang·ster (gaŋ′stər) *n.* a member of a gang of criminals —**gang′ster·ism′** *n.*

gang·way *n.* [OE *gangweg*] 1 a passageway 2 *a)* an opening in a ship's bulwarks for loading, etc. *b)* GANGPLANK —*interj.* clear the way!

gant·let (gônt′lit, gänt′-, gant′-) *n.* [< Swed *gata*, lane + *lopp*, a run] 1 a former punishment in which the offender ran between two rows of men who struck him 2 a series of troubles Now sp. equally *gauntlet*

gan·try (gan′trē) *n., pl.* **-tries** [< L *canterius*, beast of burden] 1 a framework, often on wheels, for a traveling crane 2 a wheeled framework with a crane, platforms, etc., for readying a rocket to be launched

GAO *abbrev.* Government Accountability Office

gaol (jāl) *n.* Brit. sp. of JAIL

gap (gap) *n.* [< ON *gapa*, to gape] 1 an opening made by breaking or parting 2 a mountain pass or ravine 3 a blank space; lacuna 4 a lag or disparity

gape (gāp) *vi.* **gaped, gap′ing** [< ON *gapa*] 1 to open the mouth wide, as in yawning 2 to stare with the mouth open 3 to open wide —*n.* 1 a gaping 2 a wide opening —**gap′ing·ly** *adv.*

gar (gär) *n., pl.* **gar** or **gars** [< OE *gar*, a spear] a freshwater fish with a long, beaklike snout: also **gar′fish′**, *pl.* **-fish′** or **-fish′es**

ga·rage (gə räzh′, -räj′) *n.* [Fr < *garer*, to

protect] 1 a shelter for motor vehicles 2 a business place where motor vehicles are stored, repaired, etc.

garage sale a sale of used or unwanted household articles, etc.

garb (gärb) *n.* [< It *garbo*, elegance] clothing; style of dress [clerical *garb*] —*vt.* to clothe

gar·bage (gär′bij) *n.* [ME, entrails of fowls] 1 spoiled or waste food 2 any worthless, offensive, etc. matter

gar·ble (gär′bəl) *vt.* **-bled, -bling** [< Ar *gharbāl*, a sieve] to distort or confuse (a story, etc.)

gar·çon (gàr sōn′) *n., pl.* **-çons′** (-sōn′) [Fr] a waiter

gar·den (gärd′'n) *n.* [< Frankish] 1 a piece of ground for growing vegetables, flowers, etc. 2 an area of fertile land: also **garden spot** 3 [*often pl.*] a public, parklike place, sometimes having displays of animals or plants —*vi.* to take care of a garden —*adj.* of, for, or grown in a garden —**gar′den·er** *n.*

gar·de·ni·a (gär dēn′yə) *n.* [after A. *Garden* (1730-91), Am botanist] a plant with fragrant, waxy flowers

gar·den-va·ri·e·ty *adj.* ordinary; commonplace

Gar·field (gär′fēld), **James A(bram)** (jāmz) 1831-81; 20th president of the U.S. (1881): assassinated

gar·gan·tu·an (gär gan′chōō ən) [after *Gargantua*, a giant king in a satire by Rabelais] *adj.* of extraordinary size; gigantic

gar·gle (gär′gəl) *vt., vi.* **-gled, -gling** [< Fr *gargouille*, throat] to rinse (the throat) with a liquid kept in motion by the expulsion of air from the lungs —*n.* a liquid for gargling

gar·goyle (gär′goil′) *n.* [see prec.] 1 a waterspout often formed like a grotesque creature, projecting from a building 2 a projecting ornament in the form of a grotesque creature, carved in the form of a grotesque creature

Gar·i·bal·di (gar′ə bôl′dē), **Giu·sep·pe** (jōō zep′pe) 1807-82; It. patriot & general

gar·ish (gar′ish, ger′-) *adj.* [prob. < ME *gauren*, to stare] too bright or gaudy —**gar′ish·ly** *adv.* —**gar′ish·ness** *n.*

gar·land (gär′lənd) *n.* [< OFr *garlande*] a wreath of flowers, leaves, etc. —*vt.* to decorate with garlands

gar·lic (gär′lik) *n.* [< OE *gar*, a spear + *leac*, leek] 1 an herb of the lily family 2 its strong-smelling bulb, used as seasoning —**gar′lick·y** *adj.*

gar·ment (gär′mənt) *n.* [see GARNISH] any article of clothing

gar·ner (gär′nər) *vt.* [< L *granum*, grain] 1 to gather and store 2 to get or earn

gar·net (gär′nit) *n.* [< ML *granatum*] a hard, glasslike mineral: red varieties are often gems

gar·nish (gär′nish) *vt.* [< OFr *garnir*, furnish] 1 to decorate 2 to decorate (food) with something that adds color or flavor 3 *Law* to attach (a debtor's property, wages, etc.) so that it can be used to pay the debt —*n.* 1 a decoration 2 something used to garnish food, as parsley

gar·nish·ee (gär′ni shē′) *vt.* **-eed′, -ee′ing** [< prec.] GARNISH (*vt.* 3): now rare in legal usage

gar·nish·ment *n.* *Law* a proceeding by which a creditor seeks to attach a debtor's wages, etc.

gar·ret (gar′it) *n.* [< OFr *garite*, watchtower] an attic

gar·ri·son (gar′ə sən) *n.* [< OFr *garir*, to watch] 1 troops stationed in a fort or fortified place 2 a military post or station —*vt.* to station (troops) in (a fortified place) for its defense

gar·rote (gə rät′, -rōt′) *n.* [Sp] 1 a cord, thong, etc. used in strangling a person in a surprise attack 2 a strangling in this way —*vt.* **-rot′ed** or **-rot′ted, -rot′ing** or **-rot′ting** to execute or attack by such strangling Also **ga·rotte′** or **gar·rotte′** —**gar·rot′er** *n.*

gar·ru·lous (gar′ə ləs) *adj.* [< L *garrire*, to chatter] talking much, esp. about unimportant things —**gar·ru·li·ty** (gə rōō′lə tē) *n.*, **gar′ru·lous·ness** —**gar′ru·lous·ly** *adv.*

gar·ter (gärt′ər) *n.* [< OFr *garet*, the back of the knee] an elastic band or strap for holding a stocking in place

garter belt a belt of elastic fabric with hanging garters, worn by women

garter snake a small, harmless snake common in North America

gas (gas) *n., pl.* **gas′es** or **gas′ses** [coined < Gr *chaos*, space] 1 the fluid form of a substance in which it can expand indefinitely; vapor 2 any mixture of flammable gases used for lighting or heating 3 any gas used as an anesthetic 4 any poisonous substance dispersed in the air, as in war 5 a gaseous substance formed in the bowels 6 [Inf.] GASOLINE —*vt.* **gassed, gas′sing** to injure or kill by gas —**gas up** [Inf.] to supply (a vehicle) with gasoline —**gas′e·ous** (-ē əs) *adj.*

gas chamber a room in which people are put to be killed with poison gas

gash (gash) *vt.* [< Gr *charassein*, to cut] to make a long, deep cut in; slash —*n.* a long, deep cut

gas·ket (gas′kit) *n.* [prob. < OFr *garcete*, small cord] a piece or ring of rubber, metal, etc. used to seal a joint

gas mask a filtering mask worn to prevent the breathing in of poisonous gases

gas·o·hol (gas′ə hôl′) *n.* a motor fuel mixture of gasoline and alcohol

gas·o·line (gas′ə lēn′, gas′ə lēn′) *n.* [< *gas* + L *oleum*, oil] a volatile, flammable liquid distilled from petroleum, used chiefly as a fuel in internal-combustion engines

gasp (gasp) *vi.* [< ON *geispa*, to yawn] to inhale suddenly, as in surprise, or breathe with effort —*vt.* to say with gasps —*n.* a gasping

gas station SERVICE STATION

gas·sy *adj.* **-si·er, -si·est** 1 full of gas; esp., flatulent 2 like gas

gas·tric (gas′trik) *adj.* [GASTR(O)- + -IC] of, in, or near the stomach

gastric juice the clear, acidic digestive fluid produced by glands in the stomach lining

gas·tri·tis (gas trīt′is) *n.* ⟦fol. + -ITIS⟧ inflammation of the stomach

gastro- ⟦< Gr *gastēr*⟧ *combining form* stomach (and)

gas·tron·o·my (gas trän′ə mē) *n.* ⟦< Gr *gastēr*, stomach + *nomos*, a rule⟧ the art or science of good eating —**gas′tro·nom′ic** (-trə näm′ik) *adj.*, **gas′tro·nom′i·cal**

gas·tro·pod (gas′trō päd′) *n.* ⟦GASTRO- + -POD⟧ a mollusk of the class including snails, slugs, etc.

gate (gāt) *n.* ⟦OE⟧ **1** a movable structure controlling passage through an opening in a fence or wall **2** a gateway **3** a movable barrier **4** a structure controlling the flow of water, as in a canal **5** the total amount or number of paid admissions to a performance —**give (or get) the gate** [Slang] to subject (or be subjected) to dismissal

-gate (gāt) ⟦< (*Water*)*gate*, political scandal, after the *Watergate*, building in Washington, D.C., site of 1972 burglary⟧ *combining form* a scandal marked by charges of corruption on the part of public officials, etc.

gate-crash·er *n.* [Inf.] one who attends a social affair without an invitation or attends a performance without paying

gate·fold *n.* an oversize page, as in a magazine, bound so it can be unfolded and opened out

gate·way *n.* **1** an entrance as in a wall, fitted with a gate **2** a means of access

gath·er (gath′ər) *vt.* ⟦OE *gad(e)rian*⟧ **1** to bring together **2** to get gradually; accumulate **3** to collect by picking; harvest **4** to infer; conclude **5** to draw (cloth) into folds or puckers —*vi.* **1** to assemble **2** to increase —*n.* a pucker or fold —**gath′er·er** *n.*

gath·er·ing *n.* **1** a meeting; crowd **2** a gather in cloth

ga·tor or *contr.* **'ga·tor** (gā′tər) *n.* short for ALLIGATOR

gauche (gōsh) *adj.* ⟦Fr < MFr *gauchir*, become warped⟧ lacking social grace; awkward; tactless

gau·che·rie (gō′shə rē) *n.* gauche behavior or a gauche act

gau·cho (gou′chō) *n., pl.* **-chos** ⟦AmSp⟧ a South American cowboy

gaud·y (gô′dē) *adj.* **-i·er, -i·est** ⟦< ME *gaude*, trinket⟧ bright and showy, but lacking in good taste —**gaud′i·ly** *adv.* —**gaud′i·ness** *n.*

gauge (gāj) *n.* ⟦NormFr⟧ **1** a standard measure or criterion **2** any device for measuring **3** the distance between the rails of a railroad **4** the size of the bore of a shotgun **5** the thickness of sheet metal, wire, etc. —*vt.* **gauged, gaug′ing 1** to measure the size, amount, etc. of **2** to judge

Gaul¹ (gôl) *n.* a member of the people of ancient Gaul

Gaul² (gôl) ancient division of the Roman Empire, in W Europe

Gaul·ish *n.* the Celtic language of ancient Gaul

gaunt (gônt) *adj.* ⟦ME *gawnte*⟧ **1** thin and bony; haggard, as from great hunger **2** looking grim or forbidding —**gaunt′ness** *n.*

gaunt·let¹ (gônt′lit, gänt′-) *n.* ⟦< OFr *gant*, glove⟧ **1** a knight's armored glove **2** a long glove with a flaring cuff —**throw down the gauntlet** to challenge, as to combat

gaunt·let² (gônt′lit, gänt′-) *n. see* GANTLET

gauze (gôz) *n.* ⟦< Fr *gaze* < Ar *kazz*, silk⟧ any very thin, transparent, loosely woven material, as of cotton or silk —**gauz′y** *adj.* **-i·er, -i·est**

gave (gāv) *vt., vi. pt. of* GIVE

gav·el (gav′əl) *n.* ⟦? < Scot *gable*, fork⟧ a small mallet rapped on the table, as by a judge, to call for attention, etc.

ga·votte (gə vät′) *n.* ⟦Fr⟧ a dance of the 1600s like the minuet, but livelier

gawk (gôk) *vi.* ⟦prob. < *gowk*, stupid person⟧ to stare stupidly

gawk·y (gô′kē) *adj.* **-i·er, -i·est** ⟦see prec.⟧ clumsy; ungainly —**gawk′i·ly** *adv.* —**gawk′i·ness** *n.*

gay (gā) *adj.* ⟦OFr *gai*⟧ **1** joyous and lively; merry **2** bright; brilliant [*gay* colors] **3** of or having a sexual orientation to people of the same sex: can apply either to men only or to men and women —*n.* one whose sexual orientation is to people of the same sex: often offensive in the singular, but generally acceptable in the plural

gay·e·ty (gā′ə tē) *n., pl.* **-ties** *alt. sp. of* GAIETY

gay·ly (gā′lē) *adv. alt. sp. of* GAILY

gaze (gāz) *vi.* **gazed, gaz′ing** ⟦< Scand⟧ to look steadily; stare —*n.* a steady look

ga·ze·bo (gə zē′bō, -zā′-) *n., pl.* **-bos** or **-boes** ⟦< prec.⟧ a summerhouse, windowed balcony, etc. from which one can gaze at the scenery around it

ga·zelle (gə zel′) *n.* ⟦< Ar *ghazāl*⟧ a small antelope of Africa and Asia

ga·zette (gə zet′) *n.* ⟦Fr < It dial. *gazeta*, a small coin, price of the newspaper⟧ **1** a newspaper: now mainly in newspaper titles **2** in England, an official publication —*vt.* **-zet′ted, -zet′ting** [Brit.] to publish or announce in a gazette

gaz·et·teer (gaz′ə tir′) *n.* a dictionary or index of geographical names

ga·zil·lion (gə zil′yən) *n.* [Slang] a very large, indefinite number

gaz·pa·cho (gäs pä′chō, gäz-) *n.* ⟦Sp⟧ a cold Spanish soup of chopped raw tomatoes, cucumbers, onions, and peppers, mixed with oil, vinegar, etc.

GB *abbrev.* **1** gigabyte(s) **2** Great Britain

GDP *abbrev.* gross domestic product

Ge *Chem. symbol for* germanium

gear (gir) *n.* ⟦prob. < ON *gervi*, preparation⟧ **1** clothing **2** equipment, esp. for some task **3** *a*) a toothed wheel designed to mesh with another *b*) [*often pl.*] a system of such gears meshed together to pass motion along *c*) a specific adjustment of such a system *d*) a part of a mechanism with a specific function [the steering *gear*] —*vt.* **1** to connect by or furnish with gears **2** to adapt (one thing) to conform with another [to *gear* supply to demand] —**in (or out of) gear 1** (not) connected to the motor **2** (not) in proper working order

gear·shift *n.* the lever for engaging or disengaging any of several sets of transmission gears to a motor, etc.

gear·wheel *n.* a toothed wheel in a system of gears; cogwheel

geck·o (gek′ō) *n., pl.* **-os** or **-oes** [prob. < Malay] a tropical lizard with suction pads on its feet

GED¹ *trademark for* General Educational Development

GED² *abbrev.* general equivalency diploma

gee (jē) *interj.* [< JE(SUS)] [Slang] used to express surprise, wonder, etc.

geek (gēk) *n.* [Slang] **1** a person considered to be different from others in a negative way, as in being socially awkward **2** a person regarded as knowledgeable and enthusiastic about technical matters —**geek′y** *adj.* **-i·er, -i·est**

geese (gēs) *n. pl. of* GOOSE

gee whiz an exclamation used to express surprise, enthusiasm, etc.

gee·zer (gē′zər) *n.* [< GUISE] [Slang] an old man

ge·fil·te fish (gə fil′tə) [E Yiddish] chopped, seasoned fish, boiled and served in balls or cakes

Gei·ger counter (gī′gər) [after H. *Geiger* (1882-1945), Ger physicist] an instrument for detecting and counting ionizing particles, as from radioactive ores

gei·sha (gā′shə, gē′-) *n., pl.* **-sha** or **-shas** [Sino-Jpn *gei*, art + *sha*, person] a Japanese woman trained in singing, conversation, etc. to serve as a hired companion to men

gel (jel) *n.* [< fol.] **1** a jellylike substance formed from a colloidal solution **2** any of various jellylike preparations for setting hair, brushing teeth, etc. —*vi.* **gelled, gel′ling 1** to form a gel **2** to assume definite form

gel·a·tin (jel′ə tin) *n.* [< L *gelare*, freeze] a tasteless, odorless substance extracted by boiling bones, horns, etc., or a similar vegetable substance: dissolved and cooled, it forms a jellylike substance used in foods, photographic film, etc.: also **gel′a·tine** (-tēn, -tin) —**ge·lat·i·nous** (jə lat′′n əs) *adj.*

geld (geld) *vt.* **geld′ed** or **gelt, geld′ing** [< ON *geldr*, barren] to castrate (esp. a horse)
geld·ing *n.* a castrated horse

gel·id (jel′id) *adj.* [< L *gelu*, frost] extremely cold; frozen

gem (jem) *n.* [< L *gemma*, a bud] **1** a cut and polished gemstone or a pearl **2** someone or something very precious or valuable

Gem·i·ni (jem′ə nī′, -nē′) *n.* [L, twins] the third sign of the zodiac

gem·stone *n.* any mineral that can be used in a piece of jewelry when cut and polished

ge·müt·lich (gə müt′liH) *adj.* [Ger] agreeable, cheerful, cozy, etc.

gen *abbrev.* general

Gen *abbrev.* **1** General **2** *Bible* Genesis

-gen (jən, jen) [< Gr *-genēs*, born] *suffix* **1** something that produces [*hydrogen*] **2** something produced (in a specified way)

gen·darme (zhän därm′) *n.* [Fr < *gens d'armes*, men-at-arms] a French police officer

gen·der (jen′dər) *n.* [< L *genus*, origin] **1** *Gram.* the classification by which words are grouped as masculine, feminine, or neuter **2** the fact of being a male or female human, esp. as it affects a person's self-image, social relationships, etc.

gen·dered *adj.* having or making gender-based distinctions

gene (jēn) *n.* [see -GEN] any of the units in the chromosomes by which hereditary characteristics are transmitted

ge·ne·al·o·gy (jē′nē äl′ə jē) *n., pl.* **-gies** [< Gr *genea*, race + *-logia*, -LOGY] **1** a recorded history of a person's ancestry **2** the study of family descent **3** lineage —**ge′ne·a·log′i·cal** (-ə läj′i kəl) *adj.* —**ge′ne·al′o·gist** *n.*

gen·er·a (jen′ər ə) *n. pl. of* GENUS

gen·er·al (jen′ər əl) *adj.* [< L *genus*, class] **1** of, for, or from all; not local, special, or specialized **2** of or for a whole genus, kind, etc. **3** widespread [*general unrest*] **4** most common; usual **5** not specific or precise [in *general* terms] **6** highest in rank [*attorney general*] —*n.* a military officer ranking above a colonel, specif. one ranking above a lieutenant general —**in general 1** usually **2** without specific details —**gen′er·al·ship′** *n.*

general assembly [*often* G- A-] **1** the legislative assembly in some U.S. states **2** the deliberative assembly of the United Nations

general delivery delivery of mail at the post office, to be picked up by the addressee

gen·er·al·is·si·mo (jen′ər ə lis′i mō′) *n., pl.* **-mos′** [It] in some countries, the commander in chief of the armed forces

gen·er·al·i·ty (jen′ər al′ə tē) *n., pl.* **-ties 1** the quality of being general **2** a general or vague statement, idea, etc. **3** the main body

gen·er·al·ize (jen′ər əl īz′) *vt.* **-ized′, -iz′ing 1** to state in terms of a general law **2** to infer or derive (a general law) from (particular instances) —*vi.* **1** to formulate general principles **2** to talk in generalities

gen·er·al·ly *adv.* **1** widely; popularly **2** usually **3** not specifically

general practitioner a practicing physician who does not specialize in a particular field of medicine

gen·er·ate (jen′ər āt′) *vt.* **-at′ed, -at′ing** [< L *genus*, race] **1** to produce (offspring); beget **2** to bring into being —**gen′er·a′tive** (-āt′iv, -ə tiv) *adj.*

gen·er·a·tion (jen′ər ā′shən) *n.* **1** the producing of offspring **2** production **3** a single stage in the succession of descent **4** the average period (*c.* 30 years) between human generations **5** all the people born and living at about the same time —**gen′er·a′tion·al** *adj.*

generation gap the differences in attitudes, experiences, etc. between contemporary older and younger generations

Generation X (eks) the generation of persons born in the 1960s and 1970s

gen·er·a·tor *n.* a machine for changing mechanical energy into electrical energy; dynamo

ge·ner·ic (jə ner′ik) *adj.* ‖< L *genus*, race, kind‖ **1** of a whole kind, class, or group; inclusive **2** without a brand name **3** lacking distinctive qualities —*n.* a product, as a drug, without a brand name: *often used in pl.* —**ge·ner′i·cal·ly** *adv.*

gen·er·ous (jen′ər əs) *adj.* ‖< L *generosus*, noble‖ **1** noble-minded; magnanimous **2** willing to give or share; unselfish **3** large; ample —**gen·er·os·i·ty** (jen′ər äs′ə tē) *n.* —**gen′er·ous·ly** *adv.*

gen·e·sis (jen′ə sis) *n.* ‖Gr‖ **1** the beginning; origin **2** [G-] the first book of the Bible

gene therapy the experimental treatment of diseases with new chemicals or organisms created by the recombining of units of DNA

genetic code the arrangement of chemical substances in DNA or RNA that determines the characteristics of an organism

ge·net·ics (jə net′iks) *n.* ‖ult. < GENESIS‖ the branch of biology dealing with heredity and variation in animal and plant species —**ge·net′ic** *adj.* —**ge·net′i·cal·ly** *adv.* —**ge·net′i·cist** (-ə sist) *n.*

Ge·ne·va (jə nē′və) city in SW Switzerland

Gen·ghis Khan (geŋ′gis kän′, jeŋ′-) 1162?-1227; Mongol conqueror

gen·ial (jēn′yəl) *adj.* [see GENIUS] **1** good for life and growth [a *genial* climate] **2** cheerful and friendly; amiable —**ge·ni·al·i·ty** (jē′nē al′ə tē) *n.* —**gen′ial·ly** *adv.*

ge·nie (jē′nē) *n.* ‖< Fr < Ar *jinnī*‖ JINN

gen·i·tal (jen′i təl) *adj.* ‖< L *genere*, beget‖ of reproduction or the sexual organs

gen·i·tals *pl.n.* [see prec.] the reproductive organs; esp., the external sex organs: also **gen′i·ta′li·a** (-tä′lē ə, -täl′yə)

gen·i·tive (jen′i tiv) *n.* ‖< Gr *genos*, genus‖ *Gram.* a case expressing possession, source, etc., or referring to a part of a whole

gen·i·to·u·ri·nar·y (jen′i tō yoor′ə ner′ē) *adj.* of the genital and urinary organs

gen·ius (jēn′yəs) *n.* ‖L, guardian spirit‖ **1** the particular spirit or nature of a nation, place, age, etc. **2** natural ability; strong inclination (*for*) **3** great mental capacity and inventive ability **4** one having such capacity or ability

Gen·o·a (jen′ə wə) seaport in NW Italy

gen·o·cide (jen′ə sīd′) *n.* ‖< L *genos*, race + -CIDE‖ the systematic killing of a people or nation —**gen′o·ci′dal** *adj.*

ge·nome (jē′nōm′) *n.* ‖Ger *genom* < *gen*, GENE + (*chromos*)*om*, CHROMOSOME‖ **1** one complete haploid set of chromosomes of an organism **2** an organism's genetic material —**ge·nom′ic** (-nō′mik) *adj.*

gen·o·type (jen′ə tīp′, jē′nə-) *n.* the genetic constitution of an organism —**gen′o·typ′ic** *adj.* **gen′o·typ′i·cal**

gen·re (zhän′rə) *n.* ‖Fr < L *genus*, a kind‖ **1** a kind, or type, of works of literature, art, or

popular fiction **2** painting in which everyday subjects are treated realistically

gent (jent) *n.* [Inf.] a gentleman

gen·teel (jen tēl′) *adj.* ‖< Fr *gentil*‖ polite or well-bred; now, esp., affectedly refined, polite, etc. —**gen·teel′ly** *adv.*

gen·tian (jen′shən) *n.* ‖< L *gentiana*‖ a plant typically having fringed, blue flowers

gen·tile (jen′tīl′) *n.* [*also* G-] ‖< L *gentilis*, of the same clan‖ any person not a Jew —*adj.* not Jewish

gen·til·i·ty (jen til′ə tē) *n.* [see fol.] the quality of being genteel

gen·tle (jent′'l) *adj.* **-tler, -tlest** ‖< L *gentilis*, of the same clan‖ **1** of the upper classes **2** generous; kind **3** tame [a *gentle* dog] **4** kindly; patient **5** not harsh or rough [a *gentle* tap] **6** gradual [a *gentle* slope] —**gen′tle·ness** *n.* —**gen′tly** *adv.*

gen·tle·man (-mən) *n., pl.* **-men** (-mən) **1** [Obs.] a man of good family and high social standing **2** a courteous, gracious, and honorable man **3** any man: a polite term, esp. as (in pl.) a form of address —**gen′tle·man·ly** *adj.*

gen·tle·wom·an *n., pl.* **-wom′en** **1** [Obs.] a woman of good family and high social standing **2** a courteous, gracious woman —**gen′tle·wom′an·ly** *adj.*

gen·tri·fy (jen′tri fī′) *vt.* **-fied′, -fy′ing** ‖< fol. + -FY‖ **1** to convert (a run-down neighborhood) into a more affluent one, as by remodeling homes **2** to raise to a higher status —**gen′tri·fi·ca′tion** *n.*

gen·try (jen′trē) *n.* [see GENTLE] people of high social standing

gen·u·flect (jen′yə flekt′) *vi.* ‖< L *genu*, knee + *flectere*, to bend‖ to bend the knee, as in worship —**gen′u·flec′tion** *n.*

gen·u·ine (jen′yoō in) *adj.* ‖L *genuinus*, inborn‖ **1** not counterfeit or artificial; real; true **2** sincere —**gen′u·ine·ly** *adv.* —**gen′u·ine·ness** *n.*

ge·nus (jē′nəs) *n., pl.* **gen·er·a** (jen′ər ə) or **ge′nus·es** ‖L, race, kind‖ **1** a class; kind; sort **2** a category used in classifying plants or animals that are related in structure

geo- ‖< Gr *gē*‖ *combining form* earth, of the earth

ge·o·cen·tric (jē′ō sen′trik) *adj.* **1** viewed as from the center of the earth **2** having the earth as a center —**ge′o·cen′tri·cal·ly** *adv.*

ge·ode (jē′ōd′) *n.* ‖< Gr *geōdēs*, earthlike‖ a globular stone with a cavity lined with crystals or silica

ge·o·des·ic (jē′ə des′ik) *adj.* **1** GEODETIC (*adj.* 1) **2** *a)* designating the shortest line between two points on a curved surface *b)* of the geometry of such lines **3** having a surface formed of straight bars in a grid of polygons [*geodesic* dome]

ge·o·det·ic (jē′ə det′ik) *adj.* **1** of or concerned with the measurement of the earth and its surface **2** GEODESIC (*adj.* 2)

ge·og·ra·phy (jē äg′rə fē) *n.* ‖< Gr *gē*, earth + *graphein*, write‖ **1** the science dealing with the earth's surface, continents, climates, plants, animals, resources, etc. **2** the physical features of a region —**ge·og'ra·pher** *n.* —**ge'o·graph'i·cal** (-ə graf'i kəl) *adj.*, **ge'o·graph'ic** —**ge'o·graph'i·cal·ly** *adv.*

ge·ol·o·gy (jē äl'ə jē) *n.* ⟦see GEO- & -LOGY⟧ the science dealing with the development of the earth's crust, its rocks and fossils, etc. —**ge'o·log'ic** (-ə läj'ik) *adj.*, **ge'o·log'i·cal** —**ge'o·log'i·cal·ly** *adv.* —**ge·ol'o·gist** *n.*

ge·o·mag·net·ic (jē'ō mag net'ik) *adj.* of the magnetic properties of the earth —**ge'o·mag'ne·tism'** *n.*

ge·om·e·try (jē äm'ə trē) *n.* ⟦< Gr *gē*, earth + *metrein*, to measure⟧ the branch of mathematics dealing with the properties, measurement, and relationships of points, lines, planes, and solids —**ge'o·met'ric** (-ə me'trik) *adj.*, **ge'o·met'ri·cal** —**ge'o·met'ri·cal·ly** *adv.*

ge·o·phys·ics (jē'ō fiz'iks) *n.* the science dealing with the effects of winds, tides, earthquakes, etc. on the earth —**ge'o·phys'i·cal** *adj.* —**ge'o·phys'i·cist** *n.*

George III (jôrj) 1738-1820; king of Great Britain & Ireland (1760-1820)

George·town section of Washington, DC

Geor·gia (jôr'jə) **1** state of the SE U.S.; cap. Atlanta: abbrev *GA* **2** country in W Asia in the Caucasus —**Geor'gian** (jôr'jən) *adj.*, *n.*

ge·o·sta·tion·ar·y (jē'ō stā'shə ner'ē) *adj.* designating or of a satellite orbiting the earth at a speed which keeps it always above the same point on the earth's surface

ge·o·syn·chro·nous (-sin'krə nəs) *adj.* designating or of a satellite orbiting the earth precisely once a day

ge·o·syn·cline (-sin'klīn') *n.* a very large depression in the earth's surface

ge·o·ther·mal (-thur'məl) *adj.* ⟦GEO- + Gr *thermē*, heat⟧ of the heat inside the earth

Ger *abbrev.* **1** German **2** Germany

ge·ra·ni·um (jə rā'nē əm) *n.* ⟦< Gr *geranos*, a crane⟧ **1** a common garden plant with showy red, white, etc. flowers **2** a related wildflower

ger·bil (jur'bəl) *n.* ⟦ult. < Ar⟧ a small rodent with long hind legs, often kept as a pet

ger·i·at·rics (jer'ē a'triks) *n.* ⟦< Gr *gēras*, old age + -IATRICS⟧ the branch of medicine dealing with the diseases of old age —**ger'i·at'ric** *adj.*

germ (jurm) *n.* ⟦< L *germen*⟧ **1** the rudimentary form, esp. a part of a seed, from which a new organism is developed **2** any microscopic disease-bearing organism; esp., one of the bacteria **3** an origin [the *germ* of an idea]

Ger·man (jur'mən) *n.* **1** a person born or living in Germany **2** the language of Germany, Austria, etc. —*adj.* of Germany or its people, language, etc.

ger·mane (jər mān') *adj.* ⟦see GERMAN⟧ truly relevant; pertinent

Ger·man·ic (jər man'ik) *adj.* designating or of GERMANIC (*n.* 2) —*n.* **1** [Obs.] the original language of the German people **2** the group of languages descended from it, including English

ger·ma·ni·um (jər mā'nē əm) *n.* ⟦< L *Ger-*

mania, Germany⟧ a nonmetallic chemical element used in making transistors, etc.: symbol, Ge; at. no. 32

German measles RUBELLA

German shepherd a large dog with a bushy tail and erect ears, originally used to herd sheep, now often used as a guard dog

Ger·ma·ny (jur'mə nē) country in NC Europe: formerly partitioned (1949-90) into the **Federal Republic of Germany**, also called *West Germany*, and the **German Democratic Republic**, also called *East Germany*

germ cell an ovum or sperm cell

ger·mi·cide (jur'mə sīd') *n.* ⟦< GERM + -CIDE⟧ any antiseptic, etc. used to destroy germs —**ger'mi·ci'dal** *adj.*

ger·mi·nal (jur'mə nəl) *adj.* **1** of or like germ cells **2** in the first stage of growth

ger·mi·nate (-nāt') *vi.*, *vt.* -**nat'ed**, -**nat'ing** ⟦< L *germen*, a sprout⟧ **1** to sprout or cause to sprout, as from a seed **2** to start developing —**ger'mi·na'tion** *n.*

germ·y *adj.* -**i·er**, -**i·est** full of germs

ger·on·tol·o·gy (jer'ən täl'ə jē) *n.* ⟦< Gr *gerōn*, old man + -LOGY⟧ the study of aging and the problems of the aged —**ger'on·to·log'i·cal** (-tə läj'i kəl) *adj.* —**ger'on·tol'o·gist** *n.*

ger·ry·man·der (jer'ē man'dər) *vt.*, *vi.* ⟦after Elbridge *Gerry*, governor of MA (1812) + (SALA)MANDER (from the shape of an election district in eastern MA)⟧ to divide (a voting area) unfairly, so as to give one political party an advantage

ger·und (jer'ənd) *n.* ⟦< L *gerere*, carry out⟧ *Gram.* an English verbal noun ending in *-ing*

Ge·sta·po (gə stä'pō) *n.* ⟦< Ger *Ge*(*heime*) *Sta*(*ats*)*po*(*lizei*), secret state police⟧ the terrorist secret police force of Nazi Germany

ges·ta·tion (jes tā'shən) *n.* ⟦< L *gerere*, to bear⟧ the act or period of carrying young in the uterus; pregnancy —**ges'tate'** *vt.* -**tat'ed**, -**tat'ing**

ges·tic·u·late (jes tik'yōō lāt') *vi.* -**lat'ed**, -**lat'ing** ⟦see fol.⟧ to make gestures, esp. with the hands —**ges·tic'u·la'tion** *n.*

ges·ture (jes'chər) *n.* ⟦< L *gerere*, to bear⟧ **1** a movement of part of the body to express or emphasize ideas, emotions, etc. **2** any act or remark conveying a state of mind, intention, etc., often made merely for effect —*vi.* -**tured**, -**tur·ing** to make gestures

get (get) *vt.* **got**, **got'ten** or **got**, **get'ting** ⟦< ON *geta*⟧ **1** to come into the state of having; receive, obtain, acquire, etc. **2** to arrive at [*get* home early] **3** to go and bring [*get* your books] **4** to catch **5** to persuade [*get* him to leave] **6** to cause to be [*get* the jar open] **7** to prepare [to *get* lunch] **8** to manage or contrive [to *get* to do something] **9** [Inf.] *a*) to be obliged (with *have* or *has*) [he's *got* to pass] *b*) to possess (with *have* or *has*) [he's *got* red hair] *c*) to strike, kill, baffle, defeat, etc. *d*) to understand **10** [Slang] to cause an emotional response in [her singing *gets* me] —*vi.* **1** to come, go, or arrive [when I *get* to work] **2** to come to be [to *get* caught] *Get* is used as an auxiliary for emphasis in passive constructions [to *get* praised] —*n.* the young of an animal —**get anywhere** to have any success —**get around 1** to move from place to place; circulate: also **get about 2** to circumvent **3** to influence as by flattery —**get away 1** to go away **2** to escape —**get away with** [Inf.] to do without being discovered or punished —**get by** [Inf.] to survive; manage —**get it** [Inf.] **1** to understand **2** to be punished —**get off 1** to come off, down, or out of **2** to leave or start **3** to escape or help to escape —**get on 1** to go on or into **2** to put on **3** to proceed **4** to grow older **5** to succeed —**get out 1** to go out or away **2** to take out **3** to be disclosed **4** to publish —**get over 1** to recover from **2** to forget —**get through 1** to finish **2** to manage to survive —**get together 1** to assemble **2** [Inf.] to reach an agreement —**get up 1** to rise (from sleep, etc.) **2** to organize

get·a·way *n.* **1** the act of starting, as in a race **2** the act of escaping **3** a place, as a cottage, used for vacationing

get-go *n.* [Inf.] beginning: used chiefly in **from the get-go**

get-to·geth·er *n.* an informal social gathering or meeting

Get·tys·burg (get′iz burg′) town in S Pennsylvania: site of a crucial Civil War battle (July, 1863)

get-up *n.* [Inf.] costume; dress

GeV *abbrev.* one billion electron-volts

gew·gaw (gyōō′gô′) *n.* [ME] a trinket

gey·ser (gī′zər) *n.* [< ON *gjosa*, to gush] a spring from which columns of boiling water and steam gush into the air at intervals

Gha·na (gä′nə) country on the W coast of Africa

ghast·ly (gast′lē) *adj.* -**li·er**, -**li·est** [< OE *gast*, spirit] **1** horrible; frightful **2** ghostlike; pale **3** [Inf.] very bad —**ghast′li·ness** *n.*

gher·kin (gur′kin) *n.* [< Pers *angārah*, watermelon] an immature, pickled cucumber

ghet·to (get′ō) *n., pl.* -**tos** *or* -**toes** [It] **1** a section of some European cities to which Jews were once restricted **2** any section of a city in which many members of a minority group live, or to which they are restricted as by social discrimination

ghet·to·ize (-īz′) *vt.* -**ized′**, -**iz′ing 1** to restrict to a ghetto **2** to make into a ghetto

ghost (gōst) *n.* [< OE *gast*] **1** *Folklore* the disembodied spirit of a dead person, appearing as a pale, shadowy apparition **2** a slight trace; shadow [not a *ghost* of a chance] —**give up the ghost** to die —**ghost′ly** *adj.*

ghost·writ·er *n.* one who writes books, articles, etc. for another who professes to be the author —**ghost′write′** *vt., vi.* -**wrote′**, -**writ′ten**, -**writ′ing**

ghoul (gōōl) *n.* [< Ar *ghāla*, to seize] *Muslim Folklore* an evil spirit that robs graves and feeds on the dead —**ghoul′ish** *adj.* —**ghoul′ish·ness** *n.* —**ghoul′ish·ly** *adv.*

GHQ *abbrev.* General Headquarters

GI (jē′ī′) *adj.* **1** government issue: designating clothing, etc. issued to military personnel **2** [Inf.] of or characteristic of the U.S. armed forces [a *GI* haircut] —*n., pl.* **GI's** *or* **GIs** [Inf.] a U.S. enlisted soldier

gi·ant (jī′ənt) *n.* [< Gr *gigas*] **1** any imaginary being of superhuman size **2** a person or thing of great size, strength, intellect, etc. —*adj.* of great size, strength, etc.

gi·ant·ess (jī′ən tis) *n.* [< Gr *gigas*] a female giant

gib·ber (jib′ər) *vi., vt.* [echoic] to speak rapidly and incoherently

gib·ber·ish *n.* unintelligible or incoherent chatter

gib·bet (jib′it) *n.* [< OFr *gibet*] **1** a gallows **2** a structure from which bodies of executed criminals were hung and exposed to public scorn —*vt.* to hang on a gibbet

gib·bon (gib′ən) *n.* [Fr] a small, slender, long-armed ape of SE Asia and the East Indies

Gib·bon (gib′ən), **Ed·ward** (ed′wərd) 1737-94; Eng. historian

gibe (jīb) *vi., vt.* gibed, gib′ing [< ?] to jeer or taunt —*n.* a jeer or taunt

gib·let (jib′lit) *n.* [< OFr *gibelet*, stew made of game] any of the edible internal organs of a fowl, as the gizzard or heart

Gi·bral·tar (ji brôl′tər) British colony occupying a peninsula consisting mostly of a rocky hill (**Rock of Gibraltar**) at the S tip of Spain

gid·dy (gid′ē) *adj.* -**di·er**, -**di·est** [< OE *gydig*, insane] **1** having or causing a whirling, unsteady sensation; dizzy **2** frivolous —**gid′di·ly** *adv.* —**gid′di·ness** *n.*

Gid·e·on (gid′ē ən) *n. Bible* a judge of Israel and a victorious leader in battle

gift (gift) *n.* [< OE *giefan*, give] **1** something given; present **2** the act of giving **3** a natural ability —*vt.* **1** to present a gift to **2** to present as a gift

gift·ed *adj.* **1** having a natural ability; talented **2** of superior intelligence

gig¹ (gig) *n.* [ME *gigge*, whirligig] **1** a light, two-wheeled open carriage **2** a long, light ship's boat

gig² (gig) *n.* [< ?] [Slang] a job, esp. one performing music

gig³ (gig) *n.* [Inf.] short for GIGABYTE

gi·ga·byte (gig′ə bit′) *n.* 2^{30} bytes, or, loosely, one billion bytes

gi·gan·tic (jī gan′tik) *adj.* [see GIANT] huge; enormous; immense

gig·gle (gig′əl) *vi.* -**gled**, -**gling** [< Du *giggelen*] to laugh with high, quick sounds in a silly or nervous way —*n.* such a sound —**gig′gly** *adj.* -**gli·er**, -**gli·est**

gig·o·lo (jig′ə lō′) *n., pl.* -**los′** [Fr] a man paid to be a woman's escort

Gi·la monster (hē′lə) [after the *Gila* River, AZ] a stout, poisonous lizard of SW U.S. deserts

gild (gild) *vt.* **gild′ed** *or* **gilt**, **gild′ing** [< OE *gyldan*] **1** to coat with gold leaf or a gold color **2** to make seem more attractive or valuable than it is —**gild′er** *n.* —**gild′ing** *n.*

gill¹ (gil) *n.* [ME *gile*] the breathing organ of most water animals, as fish

gill² (jil) *n.* [< LL *gillo*, cooling vessel] a unit of liquid measure equal to ¼ pint

gilt (gilt) *vt. alt. pt. & pp. of* GILT —*n.* gold leaf or color —*adj.* coated with gilt

gilt-edged *adj.* of the highest quality [*gilt-edged* securities]: also **gilt'-edge'**

gim·bal (gim'bəl, jim'-) *n.* [< L *gemellus*, twin] [*often pl.*] a device consisting of a pivoted ring or rings mounted on a fixed frame, used as to keep a ship's compass level

gim·crack (jim'krak') *adj.* [< ME *gibbecrak*, an ornament] showy but cheap and useless —*n.* a gimcrack thing —**gim'crack'er·y** *n.*

gim·let (gim'lit) *n.* [< MDu *wimmel*] a small tool for making holes

gim·mick (gim'ik) *n.* [< ?] [Inf.] 1 a tricky device 2 an attention-getting device or feature —**gim'mick·y** *adj.*

gimp·y (gim'pē) *adj.* [prob. < Norw dial. *gimpa*, to rock] [Inf.] lame; limping

gin¹ (jin) *n.* [ult. < L *juniperus*, juniper] a distilled alcoholic liquor typically flavored with juniper berries

gin² (jin) *n.* [< OFr *engin*, engine] 1 a snare, as for game 2 COTTON GIN —*vt.* **ginned, gin'ning** to remove seeds from (cotton) with a gin

gin³ (jin) *n.* GIN RUMMY

gin·ger (jin'jər) *n.* [< Gr *zingiberi*] 1 a tropical herb with rhizomes used esp. as a spice 2 this spice 3 [Inf.] a redhead 4 [Inf.] vigor; spirit —**gin'ger·y** *adj.*

ginger ale a carbonated soft drink flavored with ginger

gin·ger·bread *n.* 1 a cake flavored with ginger and molasses 2 showy ornamentation, esp. on a building

gin·ger·ly *adv.* very carefully —*adj.* very careful; cautious

gin·ger·snap *n.* a crisp cookie flavored with ginger and molasses

ging·ham (giŋ'əm) *n.* [< Malay *ginggang*] a cotton cloth, usually woven in stripes, checks, or plaids

gin·gi·vi·tis (jin'jə vīt'is) *n.* [< L *gingiva*, the gum + -ITIS] inflammation of the gums

gink·go (giŋ'kō) *n., pl.* **-goes** [Jpn *ginkyo*] an Asian tree with fan-shaped leaves: also **ging'ko**

gin rummy (jin) a variety of the card game rummy

gip (jip) *n., vt., vi. alt. sp. of* GYP

Gip·sy (jip'sē) *n.* GYPSY

gi·raffe (jə raf') *n.* [< Ar *zarāfa*] a large African ruminant with a very long neck and long legs

gird (gurd) *vt.* **gird'ed** or **girt, gird'ing** [OE *gyrdan*] 1 to encircle or fasten with a belt 2 to surround 3 to prepare (oneself) for action

gird·er (gur'dər) *n.* a large wooden or steel beam for supporting joists, the framework of a building, etc.

gir·dle (gurd''l) *n.* [OE *gyrdel*] 1 [Archaic] a belt for the waist 2 anything that encircles 3 a woman's elasticized undergarment for supporting the waist and hips —*vt.* **-dled, -dling** to encircle or bind, as with a girdle

girl (gurl) *n.* [ME *girle*, youngster] 1 a female child 2 a young, unmarried woman 3 a female servant 4 [Inf.] a woman of any age 5 [Inf.] a female sweetheart —**girl'hood'** *n.* —**girl'ish** *adj.*

girl'friend *n.* [Inf.] 1 a female sweetheart 2 a girl who is someone's friend 3 a woman friend of a woman

Girl Scout a member of the **Girl Scouts of the United States of America**, a girls' organization providing healthful, character-building activities

girt¹ (gurt) *vt. alt. pt. & pp. of* GIRD

girt² (gurt) *vt.* to fasten with a girth

girth (gurth) *n.* [< ON *gyrtha*, encircle] 1 a band put around the belly of a horse, etc. to hold a saddle or pack 2 the circumference, as of a tree trunk

gist (jist) *n.* [< OFr *giste*, point at issue] the essence or main point, as of an article or argument

give (giv) *vt.* **gave, giv'en, giv'ing** [OE *giefan*] 1 to make a gift of 2 to hand over [to *give* the porter a bag] 3 to hand over in or for payment 4 to pass (regards, etc.) along 5 to cause to have [to *give* pleasure] 6 to act as host or sponsor of 7 to produce; supply [cows *give* milk] 8 to devote or sacrifice 9 to concede; yield 10 to offer [to *give* advice] 11 to perform [to *give* a concert] 12 to utter [to *give* a reply] 13 to inflict (punishment, etc.) —*vi.* 1 to bend, yield, etc. under force or pressure 2 to make gifts, etc. —*n.* a bending, moving, etc. under pressure —**give away** 1 to make a gift of 2 to present (the bride) to the bridegroom 3 [Inf.] to reveal or betray —**give forth** (or **off**) to emit —**give in** to yield —**give it to** [Inf.] to beat or scold —**give or take** plus or minus —**give out** 1 to emit 2 to make public 3 to distribute 4 to become worn out, etc. —**give up** 1 to hand over 2 to cease 3 to stop trying 4 to despair of 5 to sacrifice —**giv'er** *n.*

give-and-take *n.* 1 mutual concession 2 repartee or banter

give·a·way *n.* 1 an unintentional revelation 2 something given free or sold cheap 3 an instance of giving something away free 4 a radio or television program giving prizes

give·back *n.* a previously negotiated workers' benefit relinquished to management, as for some concession

giv·en (giv'ən) *vt., vi. pp. of* GIVE —*adj.* 1 accustomed (*to*) by habit, etc.; prone (*to*) 2 specified; stated 3 assumed; granted —*n.* something assumed or accepted as fact

given name a person's first name

giz·mo (giz'mō) *n., pl.* **-mos** [< ?] [Slang] a gadget: also sp. **gis'mo**

giz·zard (giz'ərd) *n.* [< L *gigeria*, cooked entrails of poultry] the muscular second stomach of a bird

Gk *abbrev.* Greek

gla·cé (gla sā') *adj.* [< L *glacies*, ice] 1 glossy, as silk 2 candied, as fruits —*vt.* **-céed', -cé'ing** to glaze (fruits, etc.)

gla·cial (glā'shəl) *adj.* **1** of or relating to a glacier or glaciers **2** very cold **3** very slow —**gla'cial·ly** *adv.*

gla·cier (glā'shər) *n.* [< L *glacies*, ice] a large mass of ice and snow moving slowly down a mountain or valley

glad (glad) *adj.* **glad'der, glad'dest** [OE *glæd*] **1** happy **2** causing joy **3** very willing **4** bright —**glad'ly** *adv.* —**glad'ness** *n.*

glad·den (glad''n) *vt.* to make glad

glade (glād) *n.* [ME] an open space in a forest

glad hand [Inf.] a cordial or effusive welcome —**glad'-hand'er** *n.*

glad·i·a·tor (glad'ē āt'ər) *n.* [L < *gladius*, sword] **1** in ancient Rome, a man, often a slave, who fought in an arena as a public show **2** any person taking part in a fight —**glad'i·a·to'ri·al** (-ə tôr'ē əl) *adj.*

glad·i·o·lus (glad'ē ō'ləs) *n., pl.* **-lus·es** or **-li'** (-lī') [L, small sword] a plant of the iris family with swordlike leaves and tall spikes of funnel-shaped flowers: also **glad'i·o'la** (-lə), *pl.* **-las**

glad·some (glad'səm) *adj.* joyful or cheerful —**glad'some·ly** *adv.*

glam·or·ize (glam'ər īz') *vt.* **-ized', -iz'ing** to make glamorous: also sp. **glam'our·ize** —**glam'or·i·za'tion** *n.*

glam·our (glam'ər) *n.* [Scot var. of *grammar*, magic] **1** seemingly mysterious allure; bewitching charm **2** elegance, luxury, etc. Also sp. **glam'or** —**glam'or·ous** *adj.*, **glam'our·ous**

glance (glans) *vi.* **glanced, glanc'ing** [ME *glansen*] **1** to strike a surface obliquely and go off at an angle: with *off* **2** to flash **3** to take a quick look —*n.* **1** a glancing off **2** a flash **3** a quick look

gland (gland) *n.* [< L *glans*, acorn] any organ or group of cells that produces secretions, as insulin, or excretions, as urine —**glan·du·lar** (glan'jə lər) *adj.*

glans (glanz) *n.* [L, lit., acorn] **1** the head of the penis **2** the tip of the clitoris

glare (gler) *vi.* **glared, glar'ing** [ME *glaren*] **1** to shine with a steady, dazzling light **2** to stare fiercely —*n.* **1** a steady, dazzling light **2** a fierce stare

glar·ing *adj.* **1** dazzlingly bright **2** too showy **3** staring fiercely **4** flagrant [a *glaring* error] —**glar'ing·ly** *adv.*

Glas·gow (glas'kō, glaz'gō) seaport in SC Scotland

glas·nost (gläs'nôst) *n.* [Russ, lit., openness] Soviet policy after 1985 of publicly acknowledging internal problems

glass (glas) *n.* [OE *glæs*] **1** a hard, brittle substance, usually transparent, made by fusing silicates with soda, lime, etc. **2** GLASS-WARE **3** *a*) a glass article, esp. a drinking container, mirror, or lens *b*) [*pl.*] eyeglasses or binoculars **4** the amount held by a drinking glass —*vt.* to equip with glass panes; glaze —*adj.* of or made of glass —**glass'ful'** *n.*

glass ceiling an unofficial policy that prevents women or minorities from advancing within an organization

glass·ware *n.* articles made of glass

glass·y *adj.* **-i·er, -i·est** **1** like glass, as in smoothness **2** expressionless [a *glassy* stare] —**glass'i·ly** *adv.* —**glass'i·ness** *n.*

glau·co·ma (glô kō'mə) *n.* [< Gr *glaukos*, gleaming] any of various eye disorders marked by increased pressure within the eye causing impaired vision, etc.

glaze (glāz) *vt.* **glazed, glaz'ing** [ME *glasen*] **1** to fit (windows, etc.) with glass **2** to give a hard, glossy finish to (pottery, etc.) **3** to cover (foods) with a coating of sugar syrup, etc. —*vi.* to become glassy or glossy —*n.* **1** a glassy finish or coating **2** a thin coating of ice

gla·zier (glā'zhər) *n.* one whose work is fitting glass in windows, etc.

gleam (glēm) *n.* [OE *glæm*] **1** a flash or beam of light **2** a faint light **3** a reflected brightness, as from a polished surface **4** a faint manifestation, as of hope, understanding, etc. —*vi.* **1** to shine with a gleam **2** to appear suddenly —**gleam'y** *adj.*

glean (glēn) *vt., vi.* [< Celt] **1** to collect (grain left by reapers) **2** to collect (facts, etc.) gradually —**glean'ings** *pl.n.*

glee (glē) *n.* [OE *gleo*] lively joy; merriment —**glee'ful** *adj.*

glee club a group that sings part songs, etc.

glen (glen) *n.* [medieval Scot] a narrow, secluded valley

glen plaid [*also* G- p-] a plaid pattern with thin crossbarred stripes

glib (glib) *adj.* **glib'ber, glib'best** [< or akin to Du *glibberig*, slippery] speaking or spoken smoothly, often too smoothly to be convincing —**glib'ly** *adv.* —**glib'ness** *n.*

glide (glīd) *vi.* **glid'ed, glid'ing** [OE *glidan*] **1** to move smoothly and easily **2** *Aeronautics* to descend with little or no engine power —*vt.* to cause to glide —*n.* **1** a gliding **2** a disk or ball, as of nylon, under a furniture leg to allow easy sliding

glid·er (glīd'ər) *n.* **1** an engineless aircraft carried along by air currents **2** a seat suspended in a frame so as to swing back and forth

glim·mer (glim'ər) *vi.* [< OE *glæm*, gleam] **1** to give a faint, flickering light **2** to appear faintly —*n.* **1** a faint, flickering light **2** a faint manifestation —**glim'mer·ing** *n.*

glimpse (glimps) *vt.* **glimpsed, glimps'ing** [< OE *glæm*, gleam] to catch a brief, quick view of —*vi.* to look quickly (*at*) —*n.* a brief, quick view

glint (glint) *vi.* [ME *glenten*] to gleam or glitter —*n.* a gleam, flash, etc.

glis·san·do (gli sän'dō) *n., pl.* **-di** (-dē) or **-dos** [as if It < Fr *glisser*, to slide] *Music* a sliding effect achieved by a rapid sounding of tones

glis·ten (glis'ən) *vi.* [OE *glisnian*] to shine with reflected light, as a wet surface

glitch (glich) *n.* [< Ger *glitsche*, a slip] [Slang] a mishap, error, etc.

glit·ter (glit'ər) *vi.* [prob. < ON *glitra*] **1** to shine brightly; sparkle **2** to be brilliant or showy —*n.* **1** a bright, sparkling light **2** striking or showy brilliance **3** bits of glittering material —**glit′ter·y** *adj.*

glitz (glits) *n.* [< ?] [Inf.] gaudy or glittery showiness —**glitz′y** *adj.* **-i·er, -i·est**

gloam·ing (glōm′iŋ) *n.* [< OE *glom*] evening dusk; twilight

gloat (glōt) *vi.* [prob. < ON *glotta,* grin scornfully] to gaze or think with malicious pleasure: often with *over*

glob (gläb) *n.* [prob. < GLOBULE] a rounded mass or lump, as of jelly

glob·al (glō′bəl) *adj.* **1** worldwide **2** complete or comprehensive —**glob′al·ly** *adv.*

glob·al·ism (-iz′əm) *n.* a policy, outlook, etc. that is worldwide in scope

global warming a slight, continuing rise in atmospheric temperature, usually attributed to an intensifying of the greenhouse effect by the burning of fossil fuels

globe (glōb) *n.* [< L *globus,* a ball] **1** anything spherical or somewhat spherical **2** the earth, or a model of the earth

globe-trot·ter *n.* one who travels widely about the world —**globe′-trot′ting** *n., adj.*

glob·u·lar (gläb′yə lər) *adj.* **1** spherical **2** made up of globules

glob·ule (-yool′) *n.* [< L *globulus*] **1** a tiny ball or globe **2** a drop of liquid

glock·en·spiel (gläk′ən spēl′) *n.* [Ger *glocke,* bell + *spiel,* to play] a percussion instrument with tuned metal bars in a frame, played with small hammers

gloom (glōom) *n.* [prob. < Scand] **1** darkness; dimness **2** deep sadness; dejection —**gloom′y** *adj.* **-i·er, -i·est**

glop (gläp) *n.* [< ? GL(UE) + (SL)OP] [Inf.] any soft, gluey substance —**glop′py** *adj.*

glo·ri·fy (glôr′ə fī′) *vt.* **-fied′, -fy′ing** [< L *gloria,* glory + *facere,* to make] **1** to give glory to **2** to exalt (God), as in worship **3** to honor; extol **4** to make seem better, greater, etc. than is so —**glo′ri·fi·ca′tion** *n.*

glo·ri·ous (-ē əs) *adj.* **1** having, giving, or deserving glory **2** splendid **3** [Inf.] very delightful or enjoyable —**glo′ri·ous·ly** *adv.*

glo·ry (glôr′ē) *n., pl.* **-ries** [< L *gloria*] **1** great honor or fame, or its source **2** adoration **3** great splendor, prosperity, etc. **4** heavenly bliss —*vi.* **-ried, -ry·ing** to exult (*in*)

gloss[1] (glôs, gläs) *n.* [< ? Scand] **1** the shine of a polished surface **2** a deceptive outward show —*vt.* **1** to give a shiny surface to **2** to hide (an error, etc.) or make seem right or trivial: often with *over* —**gloss′y** *adj.* **-i·er, -i·est**

gloss[2] (glôs, gläs) *n.* [< Gr *glōssa,* tongue] a note of comment or explanation, as in a footnote —*vt.* to provide glosses for

glos·sa·ry (glôs′ə rē, gläs′-) *n., pl.* **-ries** [see prec.] a list of difficult terms with explanations, as at the end of a book

glos·so·la·li·a (gläs′ō lā′lē ə, glôs′-) *n.* [< Gr *glōssa,* tongue + *lalein,* to speak] an uttering of unintelligible sounds, as in a religious ecstasy

glot·tis (glät′is) *n.* [ModL < Gr *glōssa,* tongue] the opening between the vocal cords in the larynx —**glot′tal** *adj.*

glove (gluv) *n.* [OE *glof*] **1** a covering for the hand, with separate sheaths for the fingers and thumb **2** a baseball player's mitt **3** a padded mitten worn by boxers —*vt.* **gloved, glov′ing** to cover with a glove

glow (glō) *vi.* [OE *glowan*] **1** to give off a bright light as a result of great heat **2** to give out a steady light **3** to give out heat **4** to be elated **5** to be bright with color **6** to be ruddy, flushed, etc., as from enthusiasm —*n.* **1** a light given off, as a result of great heat **2** steady, even light **3** warmth, ardor, etc. —**glow′ing** *adj.* —**glow′ing·ly** *adv.*

glow·er (glou′ər) *vi.* [prob. < ON] to stare with sullen anger; scowl —**glow′er·ing** *adj.*

glow·worm (glō′-) *n.* a wingless, luminescent female or larva of the firefly

glu·cose (glōō′kōs′) *n.* [Fr < Gr *gleúkos,* sweetness] **1** a crystalline sugar occurring naturally in fruits, honey, etc. **2** a sweet syrup prepared by the hydrolysis of starch

glue (glōo) *n.* [< LL *glus*] **1** a sticky, viscous liquid made from animal gelatin, used as an adhesive **2** any similar substance —*vt.* **glued, glu′ing** to make stick as with glue —**glu′ey** *adj.* **-i·er, -i·est**

glum (glum) *adj.* **glum′mer, glum′mest** [prob. < ME *glomen,* gloom] gloomy; sullen —**glum′ly** *adv.* —**glum′ness** *n.*

glut (glut) *vi.* **glut′ted, glut′ting** [< L *gluttire,* to swallow] to eat to excess —*vt.* **1** to feed, fill, etc. to excess **2** to supply (the market) beyond demand —*n.* **1** a glutting or being glutted **2** a supply greater than the demand

glu·ten (glōot′'n) *n.* [L, glue] a gray, sticky, nutritious mixture of proteins found in wheat, etc. —**glu′ten·ous** *adj.*

glu·ti·nous (glōot′'n əs) *adj.* [see prec.] gluey; sticky —**glu′ti·nous·ly** *adv.*

glut·ton (glut′'n) *n.* [see GLUT] **1** one who eats to excess **2** one with a great capacity for something —**glut′ton·ous** *adj.* —**glut′ton·ous·ly** *adv.*

glut·ton·y *n., pl.* **-ies** the habit or act of eating too much

glyc·er·in (glis′ər in) *n.* [< Gr *glykeros,* sweet] *nontechnical term for* GLYCEROL: also **glyc′er·ine** (-in, -ēn′)

glyc·er·ol (glis′ər ôl′, -ōl′) *n.* [< prec.] a colorless, syrupy liquid made from fats and oils: used in skin lotions, in making explosives, etc.

gly·co·gen (glī′kə jən) *n.* [< Gr *glykys,* sweet + -GEN] a substance in animal tissues that is changed into glucose as the body needs it

GM *abbrev.* General Manager

Gmc *abbrev.* Germanic

gnarl (närl) *n.* [< ME *knorre*] a knot on a tree trunk or branch —*vt.* to make knotted; twist

gnarled *adj.* **1** knotty and twisted **2** roughened, hardened, etc.: said as of hands Also **gnarl′y -i·er, -i·est**

gnash (nash) *vt., vi.* [prob. < ON] to grind (the teeth) together, as in anger —*n.* a gnashing

gnat (nat) *n.* [OE *gnæt*] any of various small flying insects, which often bite

gnaw (nô) *vt.* ⟦OE *gnagen*⟧ **1** to bite away bit by bit; consume **2** to harass or vex —*vi.* **1** to bite repeatedly: with *on*, *away*, etc. **2** to produce a corroding, tormenting, etc. effect: with *on*, *at*, etc. —**gnaw′ing** *n.*

gneiss (nīs) *n.* ⟦< OHG *gneisto*, a spark⟧ a granitelike rock formed of layers of quartz, mica, etc.

gnoc·chi (nä′kē, nô′-, nyô′-) *n.* ⟦It, pl. of *gnocco*, dumpling⟧ **1** pasta in the form of small dumplings of flour, and often potato, served with a sauce **2** *pl.* **-chi** or **-chis** one of these dumplings

gnome (nōm) *n.* ⟦< Gr *gnōmē*, thought⟧ *Folklore* a dwarf who dwells in the earth and guards its treasures —**gnom′ish** *adj.*

GNP *abbrev.* gross national product

gnu (nōō) *n.* ⟦< the native name⟧ a large African antelope with an oxlike head and a horse-like tail

go (gō) *vi.* **went**, **gone**, **go′ing** ⟦< OE *gan*⟧ **1** to move along; travel; proceed **2** to work properly; operate [the clock is *going*] **3** to act, sound, etc. as specified [the balloon *went* "pop"] **4** to turn out; result [the war went badly] **5** to pass: said of time **6** to pass from person to person **7** to become [to go mad] **8** to be expressed, sung, etc. [as the saying *goes*] **9** to harmonize; agree [blue *goes* with gold] **10** to be accepted, valid, etc. **11** to leave; depart **12** to come to an end; fail [his eyesight is *going*] **13** to be allotted (*to*) or sold (*for*) **14** to extend, reach, etc. **15** to be able to pass (*through*), fit (*into*), etc. **16** to belong [socks *go* in that drawer] —*vt.* **1** to travel along [to go the wrong way] **2** [Inf.] to furnish (bail) for an arrested person **3** [Inf.] to say [he goes "Wow!"] —*n., pl.* **goes 1** a success [to make a go of marriage] **2** [Inf.] animation; energy **3** [Inf.] a try; attempt —**go back on** [Inf.] **1** to betray **2** to break (a promise, etc.) —**go for 1** to try to get **2** [Inf.] to attack **3** [Inf.] to be attracted by —**go in for** [Inf.] to engage or indulge in —**go into** to be contained in [5 goes into 10 twice] —**go off 1** to depart **2** to explode **3** to happen, esp. after preparation —**go on 1** to proceed; continue **2** to happen, esp. over some time **3** [Inf.] to chatter —**go out 1** to be extinguished, become outdated, etc. **2** to attend social affairs, etc. —**go over 1** to examine thoroughly **2** to do again **3** [Inf.] to be successful —**go through 1** to endure; experience **2** to look through —**go through with** to pursue to the end —**go together 1** to match; harmonize **2** [Inf.] to date only each other —**go under** to fail, as in business —**let go 1** to let escape **2** to release one's hold **3** to dismiss from a job; fire —**let oneself go** to be unrestrained —**on the go** [Inf.] in constant motion or action —**to go** [Inf.] **1** to be taken out: said of food in a restaurant **2** still to be done, etc.

goad (gōd) *n.* ⟦OE *gad*⟧ **1** a sharp-pointed stick used in driving oxen **2** any driving impulse; spur —*vt.* to drive as with a goad; urge on

go-a·head *n.* permission or a signal to proceed: usually with *the*

goal (gōl) *n.* ⟦ME *gol*, boundary⟧ **1** the place at which a race, trip, etc. is ended **2** an end that one strives to attain **3** in some games, *a*) the line or net over or into which the ball or puck must go to score *b*) the score made

goal·keep·er *n.* in some games, a player stationed at a goal to prevent the ball or puck from entering it: also **goal′ie** or **goal′tend′er**

goat (gōt) *n.* ⟦OE *gat*⟧ **1** a cud-chewing mammal with hollow horns, closely related to sheep **2** a lecherous man **3** [Inf.] a scapegoat —**get someone's goat** [Inf.] to annoy someone

goat·ee (gō tē′) *n.* a small, pointed beard on a man's chin

goat·herd *n.* one who herds goats

goat·skin *n.* the skin of a goat, or leather made from this skin

gob¹ (gäb) *n.* ⟦< OFr *gobe*, mouthful⟧ **1** a soft lump or mass **2** [*pl.*] [Inf.] a large quantity

gob² (gäb) *n.* ⟦< ?⟧ [Slang] a sailor in the U.S. Navy

gob·ble¹ (gäb′əl) *n.* ⟦echoic⟧ the throaty sound made by a male turkey —*vi.* **-bled**, **-bling** to make this sound

gob·ble² (gäb′əl) *vt., vi.* **-bled**, **-bling** ⟦< OFr *gobet*, mouthful⟧ **1** to eat quickly and greedily **2** to seize eagerly; snatch (*up*)

gob·ble·dy·gook (-dē gook′, -gōōk′) *n.* ⟦? echoic of turkey cries⟧ [Slang] wordy, meaningless, or unclear talk or writing

gob·bler (gäb′lər) *n.* a male turkey

go-be·tween *n.* one who makes arrangements between each of two sides; intermediary

Go·bi (gō′bē) large desert plateau in E Asia, chiefly in Mongolia

gob·let (gäb′lit) *n.* ⟦< OFr *gobel*⟧ a drinking glass with a base and stem

gob·lin (gäb′lin) *n.* ⟦< ML *gobelinus*⟧ *Folklore* an evil or mischievous spirit

go-by *n.* [Inf.] an intentional disregard or slight

god (gäd, gôd) *n.* ⟦OE⟧ **1** any of various beings conceived of as supernatural and immortal; esp., a male deity **2** an idol **3** a person or thing deified **4** [G-] in monotheistic religions, the creator and ruler of the universe —**god′like′** *adj.*

god·child *n., pl.* **-chil′dren** the person a godparent sponsors

god·daugh·ter *n.* a female godchild

god·dess (gäd′is) *n.* **1** a female god **2** a woman of great beauty, charm, etc.

god·fa·ther *n.* **1** a male godparent **2** [often G-] *a*) [Inf.] the head of a Mafia crime syndicate *b*) [Slang] a very influential or authoritative person

god·head *n.* **1** godhood **2** [G-] God: usually with *the*

god·hood *n.* the state of being a god; divinity

Go·di·va (gə dī′və) *n. Eng. Legend* an 11th-c. noblewoman who rode naked through the streets so that her husband would abolish a heavy tax

god·less *adj.* 1 irreligious; atheistic 2 wicked —**god′less·ness** *n.*

god·ly *adj.* **-li·er, -li·est** devoted to God; devout —**god′li·ness** *n.*

god·moth·er *n.* a female godparent

god·par·ent *n.* a person who sponsors a child, as at baptism, taking responsibility for its faith

god·send *n.* anything unexpected and needed or desired that comes at the opportune moment, as if sent by God

god·son *n.* a male godchild

God·win Aus·ten (gäd′win ôs′tən) mountain in the Himalayas: 2d highest mountain in the world: 28,250 ft.: commonly called *K2*

Goe·the (gû′tə; *E* gur′tə), **Jo·hann Wolf·gang von** (yō′hän vôlf′gäŋk fôn) 1749–1832; Ger. poet & dramatist

go·fer or **go·pher** (gō′fər) *n.* [from being asked to *go for* something] [Slang] an employee who performs menial tasks, as running errands

go·get·ter (gō′get′ər) *n.* [Inf.] an enterprising and aggressive person who usually achieves ambitions, goals, etc.

gog·gle (gäg′əl) *vi.* **-gled, -gling** [ME *gogelen*] to stare with bulging eyes —*n.* [*pl.*] large spectacles to protect the eyes against dust, wind, sparks, etc. —*adj.* bulging or rolling: said of the eyes

go-go *adj.* [short for *à gogo* < Fr, in plenty] 1 of dancing to rock music, as in discothèques 2 of a dancer performing erotic movements to rock music, as in a bar

go·ing (gō′iŋ) *n.* 1 a departure 2 the condition of the ground or land as it affects traveling, walking, etc. 3 [Slang] current situation [tough *going* in the trial] —*adj.* 1 moving; working 2 conducting its business successfully [a *going* concern] 3 available 4 commonly accepted; current [the *going* rate] — **be going to** will or shall

go·ing-over *n.* [Inf.] 1 a thorough inspection 2 a severe scolding or beating

go·ings-on *pl.n.* [Inf.] actions or events, esp. when disapproved of

goi·ter (goit′ər) *n.* [< L *guttur*, throat] an enlargement of the thyroid gland, as from iodine deficiency, often visible as a swelling in the front of the neck: also [Chiefly Brit.] **goi′tre**

gold (gōld) *n.* [OE] 1 a heavy, yellow, metallic, highly malleable chemical element: it is a precious metal: symbol, Au; at. no. 79 2 money; wealth 3 bright yellow

gold-brick *n.* [Mil. Slang] one who avoids work: also **gold′brick′er** —*vi.* [Mil. Slang] to shirk a duty or avoid work

gol·den (gōl′dən) *adj.* 1 made of or containing gold 2 bright-yellow 3 very valuable; excellent 4 flourishing 5 marking the 50th year [*golden* anniversary] 6 favorable [a *golden* opportunity]

Golden Fleece *Gr. Myth.* the fleece of gold captured by Jason

Golden Gate strait between San Francisco Bay & the Pacific

gold·en·rod *n.* a North American plant with long, branching stalks bearing clusters of small, yellow flowers

golden rule the precept that one should act toward others as one would want them to act toward oneself

gold-filled *adj.* made of a base metal overlaid with gold

gold·finch *n.* [OE *goldfinc*] any of various yellow-and-black finches

gold·fish *n., pl.* **-fish′** a small, golden-yellow or orange fish, often kept in ponds or aquariums

gold leaf gold beaten into very thin sheets, used for gilding

gold·smith *n.* an artisan who makes and repairs articles of gold

gold standard a monetary standard in which the basic currency unit equals a specified quantity of gold

golf (gôlf, gälf) *n.* [? < Du *kolf*, a club] an outdoor game played with a small, hard ball and a set of clubs, the object being to hit the ball into each of a series of 9 or 18 holes with the fewest possible strokes —*vi.* to play golf —**golf′er** *n.*

golf course (*or* **links**) a tract of land for playing golf

Go·li·ath (gə lī′əth) *n. Bible* the Philistine giant killed by David

gol·ly (gäl′ē) *interj.* used to express surprise, wonder, etc.: orig. a euphemism for *God*

Go·mor·rah *n. see* SODOM AND GOMORRAH

-gon (gän, gən) [< Gr *gōnia*, an angle] *combining form* a figure having (a specified number of) angles

go·nad (gō′nad′) *n.* [< Gr *gonē*, a seed] an animal organ that produces reproductive cells; esp., an ovary or testis

gon·do·la (gän′də lə, gän dō′lə) *n.* [It] 1 a narrow boat used on the canals of Venice 2 a railroad freight car with no top and, often, with low sides 3 a cabin suspended under an airship or balloon

gon·do·lier (-lir′) *n.* a man who propels a gondola

gone (gôn, gän) *vi., vt. pp. of* GO —*adj.* [ME *gon* < OE *gan*] 1 departed 2 ruined 3 lost 4 dead 5 used up; consumed 6 ago; past

gon·er (gôn′ər) [Inf.] *n.* a person or thing certain to die, be ruined, etc.

gong (gôŋ, gän) *n.* [Malay *guñ*] a slightly convex metallic disk that gives a loud, resonant tone when struck

gon·or·rhe·a or **gon·or·rhoe·a** (gän′ə rē′ə) *n.* [< Gr *gonos*, semen + *rhein*, to flow] a venereal disease marked by inflammation of the genital organs, discharge of pus, etc.

goo (gōō) *n.* [Inf.] 1 anything sticky, or sticky and sweet 2 excessive sentimentality —**goo′ey** *adj.* **-i·er, -i·est**

goo·ber (gōō′bər) *n.* [< Afr *nguba*] [Chiefly South] a peanut

good (good) *adj.* **bet′ter, best** [OE *gōd*] 1 effective; efficient 2 beneficial 3 valid; real [*good* money] 4 healthy or sound [*good* eyesight, *good* investments] **5** honorable [one's *good* name] **6** enjoyable, pleasant, etc. **7** reliable **8** thorough **9** excellent **10** virtuous, devout, kind, dutiful, etc. **11** proper; correct **12** skilled **13** considerable [a *good* many] **14** at least [waiting a *good* six hours] —*n.* something good; worth, benefit, etc. —*adv.* [Inf. or Dial.] well; fully —**as good as** virtually; nearly —**for good (and all)** permanently —**good and** [Inf.] very or altogether —**good for** able to endure or be used for (a period of time) **2** worth **3** able to pay or give —**no good** useless; worthless

good·bye or **good-bye** (-bī′) *interj., n., pl.* **-byes′** [contr. of *God be with ye*] farewell: also sp. **good′by′, good′-by′**

good faith good intentions; sincerity

Good Friday the Friday before Easter, commemorating the Crucifixion

good-heart·ed *adj.* kind and generous —**good′-heart′ed·ly** *adv.* —**good′-heart′ed·ness** *n.*

Good Hope, Cape of cape at the SW tip of Africa

good humor a cheerful, agreeable mood —**good′-hu′mored** *adj.* —**good′-hu′mored·ly** *adv.*

good-look·ing *adj.* handsome or beautiful

good·ly *adj.* **-li·er, -li·est 1** of good appearance or quality **2** ample

good-na·tured *adj.* agreeable; affable —**good′-na′tured·ly** *adv.*

good·ness *n.* the state or quality of being good; virtue, kindness, etc. —*interj.* used to express surprise or wonder: orig. a euphemism for *God*

goods (goodz) *pl.n.* **1** movable personal property **2** merchandise; wares **3** fabric; cloth —**get (or have) the goods on** [Slang] to discover (or know) something incriminating about

good Sa·mar·i·tan (sə mer′ə tən) one who helps another or others unselfishly: see Luke 10:30–37

good-sized *adj.* ample; fairly big

good-tem·pered *adj.* amiable

good turn a friendly, helpful act; favor

good·will *n.* **1** benevolence **2** willingness **3** the value of a business as a result of patronage, reputation, etc. Also **good will**

good·y *n., pl.* **-ies** [Inf.] something good to eat, as a piece of candy —*interj.* used to express approval or delight: mainly a child's term

good·y-good·y [Inf.] *adj.* affectedly moral or pious —*n.* a goody-goody person

goof (goof) [Inf.] *n.* **1** a stupid or silly person **2** a mistake; blunder —*vi.* **1** to err or blunder **2** to waste time, shirk duties, etc.: with *off* or *around* —**goof′y** *adj.* **-i·er, -i·est**

gook (gook, gook) *n.* [GOO + (GUN)K] [Slang] any sticky or slimy substance

goon (goon) *n.* [Slang] **1** a ruffian or thug **2** a grotesque or stupid person

goop (goop) *n.* [GOO + (SOU)P] [Slang] any sticky, semiliquid substance

goose (goos) *n., pl.* **geese** [< OE *gos*] **1** a long-necked, web-footed waterfowl like a duck but larger **2** its flesh as food **3** a silly person —**cook someone's goose** [Inf.] to spoil someone's chances

goose·ber·ry *n., pl.* **-ries 1** a small, sour berry **2** the shrub it grows on

goose bumps a momentary roughened condition of the skin, induced by cold, fear, etc.: also **goose flesh (or pimples)**

GOP (je′o′pe′) *n.* [G(rand) O(ld) P(arty)] *name for* REPUBLICAN PARTY

go·pher (go′fər) *n.* [< ? Fr *gaufre*, honeycomb: from its burrowing] **1** a burrowing rodent with wide cheek pouches **2** a ground squirrel of the prairies of North America

gore¹ (gor) *n.* [OE *gor*, filth] blood from a wound, esp. when clotted

gore² (gor) *vt.* **gored, gor′ing** [< OE *gar*, a spear] **1** to pierce with or as with a horn or tusk **2** to insert gores in —*n.* **1** a narrow, triangular piece of land **2** a tapering piece of cloth inserted in a skirt, sail, etc. to give it fullness

gorge (gôrj) *n.* [< L *gurges*, whirlpool] **1** the throat or gullet **2** the contents of the stomach **3** resentment, disgust, etc. **4** a deep, narrow pass between steep heights —*vi., vt.* **gorged, gorg′ing** to eat greedily or swallow gluttonously

gor·geous (gôr′jəs) *adj.* [< OFr *gorgias*] **1** brilliantly showy; magnificent **2** [Inf.] beautiful, delightful, etc. —**gor′geous·ly** *adv.*

go·ril·la (gə ril′ə) *n.* [ult. < name in an ancient W Afr language] the largest of the great apes, native to Africa

Gor·ki or **Gor·ky** (gôr′ke) *name* (1932–90) *for* NIZHNY NOVGOROD

gor·mand·ize (gôr′mən diz′) *vi., vt.* **-ized′, -iz′ing** [< Fr *gourmandise*, gluttony] to eat like a glutton

go-round *n.* one of a series of actions, encounters, etc., often involving conflict

gorp (gôrp) *n.* TRAIL MIX

gorse (gôrs) *n.* [OE *gorst*] FURZE

gor·y (gôr′e) *adj.* **-i·er, -i·est 1** covered with gore; bloody **2** with much bloodshed —**gor′i·ness** *n.*

gosh (gäsh, gôsh) *interj.* used to express surprise, wonder, etc.: a euphemism for *God*

gos·ling (gäz′liŋ) *n.* a young goose

gos·pel (gäs′pəl) *n.* [< OE *godspel*, good news] **1** [*often* G-] the teachings of Jesus and the Apostles **2** [G-] any of the first four books of the New Testament **3** anything proclaimed or accepted as the absolute truth: also **gospel truth**

gos·sa·mer (gäs′ə mər) *n.* [ME *gosesomer*, lit., goose summer] **1** a filmy cobweb **2** a very thin, filmy cloth —*adj.* light, thin, and filmy

gos·sip (gäs′əp) *n.* [< Late OE *godsibbe*, godparent] **1** one who chatters idly about others **2** such talk —*vi.* to be a gossip —**gos′sip·y** *adj.*

got (gät) *vt., vi. pt. & alt. pp. of* GET

Goth (gäth, gôth) *n.* **1** a member of a Germanic people that conquered most of the Roman Empire in the 3d, 4th, and 5th c. A.D. **2** [*usually* **g-**] *a*) a kind of rock music with morbid lyrics *b*) a style of black clothing and makeup *c*) a devotee of this music or clothing

Goth·ic (gäth′ik) *adj.* **1** of the Goths or their language **2** designating or of a style of architecture developed in W Europe between the 1100s and the 1500s, with pointed arches, steep roofs, etc. **3** [*sometimes* **g-**] of a type of fiction that uses remote, gloomy settings and a sinister atmosphere to suggest mystery —*n.* **1** the East Germanic language of the Goths **2** Gothic style, esp. in architecture

got·ten (gät′n) *vt., vi.* alt. *pp.* of GET

Gou·da (cheese) (gōō′də, gou′-) [after *Gouda*, Netherlands] a mild cheese sometimes coated with red wax

gouge (gouj) *n.* [< L *gulbia*] **1** a chisel for cutting grooves or holes in wood **2** such a groove or hole —*vt.* **gouged, goug′ing 1** to make a groove, etc. in (something) as with a gouge **2** to scoop out **3** [Inf.] to cheat out of money —**goug′er** *n.*

gou·lash (gōō′läsh′) *n.* [< Hung *gulyás*] a beef or veal stew seasoned with paprika

gou·ra·mi (gōō rä′mē, goor′ə mē) *n., pl.* **-mies** or **-mi** [Malay *gurami*] any of various freshwater fishes, esp. a food fish of SE Asia

gourd (gôrd, goord) *n.* [< L *cucurbita*] **1** any trailing or climbing plant of a family that includes the squash, melon, etc. **2** the fruit of one inedible species or its dried, hollowed-out shell, used as a cup, dipper, etc.

gour·mand (goor mänd′) *n.* [OFr] one who indulges in good food and drink excessively

gour·met (goor′mā, gôr-) *n.* [Fr < OFr, *gormet*, wine taster] one who likes and is an excellent judge of fine food and drink

gout (gout) *n.* [< L *gutta*, a drop] a form of arthritis characterized by painful swelling of the joints, esp. in the big toe —**gout′y** *adj.* **-i·er, -i·est**

gov or **Gov** *abbrev.* **1** government **2** governor

gov·ern (guv′ərn) *vt., vi.* [< Gr *kybernan*, to steer] **1** to exercise authority over; rule, control, etc. **2** to influence the action of; guide **3** to determine —**gov′ern·a·ble** *adj.*

gov·ern·ance (-ər nəns) *n.* the action, function, or power of government

gov·ern·ess (-ər nis) *n.* a woman employed in a private home to train and teach the children

gov·ern·ment (guv′ərn mənt, -ər mənt) *n.* **1** the exercise of authority over a state, organization, etc. **2** a system of ruling, political administration, etc. **3** those administering the affairs of a state, etc. —**gov′ern·men′tal** *adj.*

gov·er·nor (guv′ə nər, -ər nər) *n.* **1** one who governs; esp., *a*) one appointed to govern a province, etc. *b*) the elected head of any state of the U.S. **2** a mechanical device for automatically controlling the speed of an engine —**gov′er·nor·ship′** *n.*

governor general *pl.* **governors general** or **governor generals** a governor who has subordinate or deputy governors

govt or **Govt** *abbrev.* government

gown (goun) *n.* [< LL *gunna*] **1** a long, loose outer garment; specif., *a*) a nightgown *b*) a long robe worn by judges, scholars, etc. **2** a woman's formal dress

GP or **gp** *abbrev.* general practitioner

gr *abbrev.* **1** grain(s) **2** gross

Gr *abbrev.* **1** Greece **2** Greek

grab (grab) *vt.* **grabbed, grab′bing** [prob. < MDu *grabben*] **1** to snatch suddenly **2** to get by unscrupulous methods **3** [Slang] to impress greatly —*n.* a grabbing —**grab′ber** *n.*

grab·by *adj.* **-bi·er, -bi·est** [Inf.] greedy; avaricious

grace (grās) *n.* [< L *gratus*, pleasing] **1** beauty or charm of form, movement, or expression **2** goodwill; favor **3** a delay granted for payment of an obligation **4** a short prayer of thanks for a meal **5** [G-] a title of an archbishop, duke, or duchess **6** the love and favor of God toward humans —*vt.* **graced, grac′ing 1** to decorate **2** to dignify —**in the good** (or **bad**) **graces of** in favor (or disfavor) with

grace·ful *adj.* having beauty of form, movement, etc. —**grace′ful·ly** *adv.* —**grace′ful·ness** *n.*

grace·less *adj.* **1** lacking any sense of what is proper **2** clumsy or inelegant —**grace′less·ly** *adv.* —**grace′less·ness** *n.*

gra·cious (grā′shəs) *adj.* [see GRACE] **1** having or showing kindness, courtesy, charm, etc. **2** compassionate **3** polite to supposed inferiors **4** marked by luxury, ease, etc. [*gracious living*] —**gra′cious·ly** *adv.* —**gra′cious·ness** *n.*

grack·le (grak′əl) *n.* [L *graculus*, jackdaw] any of several blackbirds somewhat smaller than a crow

grad[1] (grad) *n.* [Inf.] a graduate

grad[2] *abbrev.* **1** graduate **2** graduated

gra·da·tion (grā dā′shən) *n.* **1** an arranging in grades, or stages **2** a gradual change by stages **3** a step or degree in a graded series

grade (grād) *n.* [< L *gradus*] **1** a stage or step in a progression **2** *a*) a degree in a scale of quality, rank, merit, etc. *b*) a group of people of the same rank, merit, etc. **3** *a*) the rise or descent of a sloping surface *b*) such a surface **4** the ground level around a building, road, etc. **5** any of the divisions of a school curriculum, usually by years **6** a mark or rating on an examination, etc. —*vt.* **grad′ed, grad′ing 1** to classify by grades; sort **2** to give a GRADE (*n.* 6) to **3** to make (ground) level or evenly sloped, as for a road —**make the grade** to succeed

grade crossing the place where a railroad intersects another railroad or a roadway on the same level

grade school ELEMENTARY SCHOOL —**grade school′er** *n.*

grade separation a crossing with an overpass or underpass

gra·di·ent (grā′dē ənt) *n.* [< L *gradi*, to step] **1** a slope, as of a road **2** the degree of such slope

grad·u·al (graʹjōō əl) *adj.* [< L *gradus*, a step] taking place by degrees; developing little by little —**gradʹu·al·ly** *adv.* —**gradʹu·al·ness** *n.*

grad·u·al·ism *n.* the principle of promoting gradual rather than rapid change

grad·u·ate (graʹjōō it; *for v.,* -āt′) *n.* [< L *gradus*, a step] one who has completed a course of study at a school or college —*vt.* **-atʹed,** **-atʹing** 1 to give a degree or diploma to upon completion of a course of study 2 [Inf.] to become a graduate of [to *graduate* college] 3 to mark with degrees for measuring 4 to classify into grades according to amount, size, etc. —*vi.* to become a graduate of a school, etc. —*adj.* 1 having been graduated from a school, etc. 2 of or for degrees above the bachelor's

grad·u·a·tion *n.* 1 a graduating from a school or college 2 the ceremony connected with this

graf·fi·ti (grə fēʹtē) *pl.n., sing.* **-to** (-tō) [It < L: see fol.] [*now usually with sing. v.*] inscriptions or drawings on a wall or other public surface

graft (graft) *n.* [ult. < Gr *grapheion,* stylus] 1 *a)* a shoot or bud of one plant or tree inserted into another, where it grows permanently *b)* the inserting of such a shoot 2 the transplanting of skin, bone, etc. 3 *a)* the dishonest use of one's position to gain money, etc., as in politics *b)* anything so gained —*vt., vi.* to insert (a graft) —**graftʹer** *n.*

gra·ham (grāʹəm, gram) *adj.* [after S. Graham (1794-1851), U.S. dietary reformer] designating or made of whole-wheat flour [*graham* crackers]

Grail (grāl) *n.* [< ML *gradalis,* cup] *Medieval Legend* the cup used by Jesus at the Last Supper: also **Holy Grail**

grain (grān) *n.* [< L *granum*] 1 the small, hard seed of any cereal plant, as wheat or corn 2 cereal plants 3 a tiny, solid particle, as of salt or sand 4 a tiny bit 5 the smallest unit in the system of weights used in the U.S. 6 *a)* the arrangement or direction of fibers, layers, etc. of wood, leather, etc. *b)* the markings or texture due to this 7 disposition; nature [goes against my *grain*]

grain·y (grānʹē) *adj.* **-i·er, -i·est** 1 having a clearly defined grain: said as of wood 2 coarsely textured; granular —**grainʹi·ness** *n.*

gram[1] (gram) *n.* [< L *gramma,* small weight] the basic unit of mass in the metric system, equal to 0.03527 ounce

gram[2] *abbrev.* grammar

-gram (gram) [< Gr *gramma,* writing] combining form something written [*telegram*]

gram·mar (gramʹər) *n.* [< Gr *gramma,* writing] 1 language study dealing with the forms of words and with their arrangement in sentences 2 a system of rules for speaking and writing a given language 3 one's manner of speaking or writing as judged by such rules —**gram·mar·i·an** (grə merʹē ən) *n.* —**gram·mat·i·cal** (-matʹi kəl) *adj.* —**gram·mat·i·cal·ly** *adv.*

grammar school ELEMENTARY SCHOOL

gran·a·ry (granʹə rē, grānʹ-) *n., pl.* **-ries** [< L *granum,* grain] a building for storing threshed grain

grand (grand) *adj.* [< L *grandis,* large] 1 higher in rank than others [a *grand* duke] 2 most important; main [the *grand* ballroom] 3 imposing in size, beauty, and extent 4 distinguished; illustrious 5 complete; overall [the *grand* total] 6 [Inf.] excellent; delightful —*n., pl.* **grand** [Slang] a thousand dollars —**grandʹly** *adv.*

grand- combining form of the generation older (or younger) than [grandmother, grandson]

grand·child *n., pl.* **-chilʹdren** a child of one's son or daughter

grand·daugh·ter *n.* a daughter of one's son or daughter

grande dame (gränd däm′) [Fr] a woman, esp. an older one, of great dignity

gran·dee (gran dē′) *n.* [Sp & Port *grande*: see GRAND] a man of high rank

gran·deur (granʹjər, -joor′; -dyoor′) *n.* [see GRAND] splendor; magnificence

grand·fa·ther *n.* 1 the father of one's father or mother 2 a forefather —*vt.* [Inf.] to exempt (a practice, person, etc.) from a new law or regulation

grandfather (or **grandfather's**) **clock** a large clock with a pendulum, in a tall, narrow case

gran·dil·o·quent (gran dilʹə kwənt) *adj.* [< L *grandis,* grand + *loqui,* speak] using pompous, bombastic words —**gran·dilʹo·quence** *n.* —**gran·dilʹo·quent·ly** *adv.*

gran·di·ose (granʹdē ōs′) *adj.* [< L *grandis,* great] 1 having grandeur; imposing 2 pompous and showy —**gran·di·os·i·ty** (-äsʹə tē) *n.*

grand jury a jury that investigates accusations and indicts persons for trial if there is sufficient evidence

grand·ma (granʹmə, -mä′) *n.* [Inf.] GRANDMOTHER

grand·mas·ter *n.* a chess player of the highest rating

grand·moth·er *n.* 1 the mother of one's father or mother 2 a female ancestor

grand opera opera in which the whole text is set to music

grand·pa (granʹpə, -pä′) *n.* [Inf.] GRANDFATHER

grand·par·ent *n.* a grandfather or grandmother

grand piano a large piano with strings horizontally in a wing-shaped case

grand prix (grän prē′, gran-) *pl.* **grand prix** (-prēz′) or **grands prix** (grän prē′, gran-) [Fr, great prize] [*often* G- P-] any of a series of auto races leading to an overall championship: often used attributively [the *grand prix* circuit]

grand slam 1 *Baseball* a home run hit when there is a runner on each base 2 *Bridge* the winning of all the tricks in a deal 3 the winning of all of the most elite competitions in a single year, as in tennis

grand·son *n.* a son of one's son or daughter

grand·stand *n.* the main seating structure for spectators at a sporting event —*vi.* [Inf.] to try to gain admiration by performing in a showy manner

grange (grānj) *n.* [< L *granum*, grain] a farm —**the Grange** a fraternal organization, originally of farmers, in the U.S.

gran·ite (gran′it) *n.* [< L *granum*, grain] a hard, grainy igneous rock consisting mainly of feldspar and quartz —**gra·nit·ic** (grə nit′ik) *adj.*

gran·ny or **gran·nie** (gran′ē) *n.*, *pl.* **-nies** [Inf.] 1 a grandmother 2 an old woman —*adj.* of a style like that formerly worn by elderly women [*granny* glasses]

gran·o·la (grə nō′lə) *n.* [< ? L *granum*, grain] a breakfast cereal of rolled oats, wheat germ, sesame seeds, brown sugar or honey, dried fruit or nuts, etc.

grant (grant) *vt.* [ult. < L *credere*, believe] 1 to give (what is requested, as permission) 2 to give or transfer by legal procedure 3 to admit as true; concede —*n.* 1 a granting 2 something granted, as property or a right —**take for granted** to consider as true, already settled, etc. —**grant′er** *n.*

Grant (grant), **Ulysses S(impson)** 1822-85; 18th president of the U.S. (1869-77): Union commander in the Civil War

grant-in-aid *n.*, *pl.* **grants′-in-aid′** a grant of funds, as by the federal government to a state or by a foundation to a scientist, artist, etc., to support a specific project

grants·man·ship *n.* skill in acquiring grants-in-aid

gran·u·lar (gran′yə lər) *adj.* 1 containing or consisting of grains 2 like grains 3 highly detailed [*granular* sales data] —**gran′u·lar′i·ty** (-ler′ə tē) *n.*

gran·u·late (-lāt′) *vt.*, *vi.* **-lat′ed**, **-lat′ing** to form into grains or granules —**gran′u·la′tion** *n.*

gran·ule (gran′yool) *n.* [< L *granum*, grain] a small grain or particle

grape (grāp) *n.* [< OFr *graper*, to gather with a hook] 1 a small, round, juicy berry, growing in clusters on a woody vine 2 a grapevine 3 a dark purplish red

grape·fruit *n.* a large, round, sour citrus fruit with a yellow rind

grape hyacinth a small plant of the lily family, with spikes of small, bell-shaped flowers of blue or white

grape·shot *n.* a cluster of small iron balls, formerly fired from a cannon

grape·vine *n.* 1 a woody vine bearing grapes 2 a secret means of spreading information 3 a rumor

graph (graf) *n.* [< *graph(ic formula)*] a diagram representing quantitative information and relationships, such as successive changes in a variable quantity —*vt.* to represent by a graph

-graph (graf) [< Gr *graphein*, to write] *combining form* 1 something that writes or records [*telegraph*] 2 something written, etc. [*monograph*]

graph·ic (graf′ik) *adj.* [< Gr *graphein*, to write] 1 described in realistic detail; vivid 2 of those arts (**graphic arts**) that use visual artistic representation, esp. painting, drawing, etching, etc. Also **graph′i·cal** —**graph′i·cal·ly** *adv.*

graphic novel a book containing a lengthy story in comic-strip format

graph·ics *n.* 1 design as employed in the graphic arts 2 the graphic arts

graph·ite (graf′īt′) *n.* [< Gr *graphein*, to write] a soft, black form of carbon used in pencils, electrodes, etc.

graph·ol·o·gy (graf äl′ə jē) *n.* [< Fr: see GRAPHIC & -LOGY] the study of handwriting, esp. as a clue to character —**graph·ol′o·gist** *n.*

-gra·phy (grə fē) [< Gr *graphein*, to write] *combining form* 1 a process or method of writing or graphically representing [*calligraphy*] 2 a descriptive science [*geography*]

grap·nel (grap′nəl) *n.* [< Prov *grapa*, a hook] a small anchor with several curved, pointed arms

grap·ple (grap′əl) *n.* [OFr *grapil*] 1 GRAPNEL 2 a hand to hand fight —*vt.* **-pled**, **-pling** to grip and hold —*vi.* 1 to use a GRAPNEL 2 to wrestle 3 to try to cope (*with*)

grappling iron (*or* hook) GRAPNEL

grasp (grasp) *vt.* [ME *graspen*] 1 to grip, as with the hand 2 to take hold of eagerly; seize 3 to comprehend —*vi.* 1 to try to seize: with *at* 2 to accept eagerly: with *at* —*n.* 1 a grasping; grip 2 control; possession 3 the power to hold or seize 4 comprehension —**grasp′a·ble** *adj.*

grasp·ing *adj.* avaricious; greedy

grass (gras, gräs) *n.* [OE *græs*] 1 a plant with long, narrow leaves, jointed stems, and seedlike fruit, as wheat or rye 2 any of various green plants with narrow leaves, growing densely in meadows, lawns, etc. 3 pasture or lawn 4 [Slang] marijuana —**grass′y** *adj.* **-i·er**, **-i·est**

grass·hop·per *n.* any of various winged, plant-eating insects with powerful hind legs for jumping

grass roots [Inf.] 1 the common people 2 the basic source or support, as of a movement —**grass′-roots′** *adj.*

grate¹ (grat) *vt.* **grat′ed**, **grat′ing** [< OFr *grater*] 1 to grind into particles by scraping 2 to rub against (an object) or grind (the teeth) together with a harsh sound 3 to irritate; annoy; fret —*vi.* 1 to rub with or make a rasping sound 2 to be irritating —**grat′er** *n.*

grate² (grāt) *n.* [< L *cratis*, a hurdle] 1 GRATING¹ 2 a frame of metal bars for holding fuel in a fireplace, etc.

grate·ful (grāt′fəl) *adj.* [obs. *grate*, pleasing (< L *gratus*)] 1 thankful 2 welcome —**grate′ful·ly** *adv.* —**grate′ful·ness** *n.*

grat·i·fy (grat′i fī′) *vt.* **-fied′**, **-fy′ing** [< L *gratus*, pleasing + -*ficare*, -FY] 1 to please or satisfy 2 to indulge; humor —**grat′i·fi·ca′tion** *n.* —**grat′i·fy′ing** *adj.*

grat·ing[1] (grāt′iŋ) *n.* a framework of bars set in a window, door, etc.

grat·ing[2] *adj.* 1 rasping 2 irritating

gra·tis (grat′is, grāt′-) *adv., adj.* [L < *gratia*, a favor] free of charge

grat·i·tude (grat′i tōōd′) *n.* [< L *gratus*, pleasing] thankful appreciation for favors or benefits received

gra·tu·i·tous (grə tōō′i təs, -tyōō′-) *adj.* [< L *gratus*, pleasing] 1 given free of charge 2 uncalled-for —**gra·tu′i·tous·ly** *adv.*

gra·tu·i·ty (-tē) *n., pl.* **-ties** a gift of money for a service; tip

gra·va·men (grə vā′mən) *n., pl.* **-mens** or **gra·vam′i·na** (-vam′i nə) [LL, a burden] *Law* the essential part of a complaint or accusation

grave[1] (grāv) *adj.* **grav′er**, **grav′est** [< L *gravis*, heavy] 1 important 2 serious [a *grave* illness] 3 solemn or sedate 4 somber; dull — **grave′ly** *adv.* —**grave′ness** *n.*

grave[2] (grāv) *n.* [< OE *grafan*, to dig] 1 *a)* a hole in the ground in which to bury a dead body *b)* any burial place; tomb 2 death —*vt.* **graved**, **grav′en** or **graved**, **grav′ing** 1 [Archaic] to sculpture or engrave 2 to impress sharply

grave accent (grāv, grāv) a mark (`) showing stress, vowel quality, etc.

grav·el (grav′əl) *n.* [< OFr *grave*, coarse sand] a loose mixture of pebbles and rock fragments coarser than sand

grav·el·ly (-ē) *adj.* 1 full of or like gravel 2 harsh or rasping [a *gravelly* voice]

grav·en (grāv′ən) *vt. alt. pp. of* GRAVE[2]

grave·stone *n.* a tombstone

grave·yard *n.* a cemetery

graveyard shift [Inf.] a work shift at night, esp. one starting at midnight

grav·id (grav′id) *adj.* [< L *gravis*, heavy] pregnant

gra·vim·e·ter (grə vim′ət ər) *n.* [< L *gravis*, heavy + Fr *-mètre*, -METER] 1 a device for determining specific gravity 2 an instrument for measuring the earth's gravitational pull

grav·i·tate (grav′i tāt′) *vi.* **-tat′ed**, **-tat′ing** 1 to move or tend to move in accordance with the force of gravity 2 to be attracted (*toward*)

grav·i·ta·tion *n.* 1 a gravitating 2 *Physics* the force by which every mass attracts and is attracted by every other mass —**grav′i·ta′tion·al** *adj.*

grav·i·ty (grav′i tē) *n., pl.* **-ties** [< L *gravis*, heavy] 1 graveness; seriousness 2 weight [*specific gravity*] 3 *Physics* gravitation; esp., the pull on all bodies on or near the earth toward the earth's center

gra·vy (grā′vē) *n., pl.* **-vies** [< ?] 1 the juice given off by meat in cooking 2 a sauce made from this juice 3 [Slang] any benefit beyond what is expected

gray (grā) *n.* [< OE *grǣg*] a color that is a blend of black and white —*adj.* 1 of this color 2 having hair this color 3 *a)* darkish; dull *b)* dreary; dismal 4 designating a vague, inter-mediate area —*vt., vi.* to make or become gray —**gray′ish** *adj.* —**gray′ness** *n.*

gray·beard *n.* an old man

gray matter 1 grayish nerve tissue of the brain and spinal cord 2 [Inf.] intellectual capacity; brains

graze[1] (grāz) *vt.* **grazed**, **graz′ing** [< OE *grœs*, grass] 1 to put livestock to feed on (growing grass, etc.) 2 to tend (feeding livestock) — *vi.* to feed on growing grass, etc.

graze[2] (grāz) *vt., vi.* **grazed**, **graz′ing** [prob. < prec.] to scrape or rub lightly in passing —*n.* a grazing

Gr Brit or **Gr Br** Great Britain

grease (grēs; *for v., also* grēz) *n.* [< L *crassus*, fat] 1 melted animal fat 2 any thick, oily substance or lubricant —*vt.* **greased**, **greas′ing** to smear or lubricate with grease

grease·paint *n.* greasy coloring matter used in making up for the stage

greas·y (grē′sē, -zē) *adj.* **-i·er**, **-i·est** 1 soiled with grease 2 containing much grease 3 oily —**greas′i·ness** *n.*

great (grāt) *adj.* [OE] 1 of much more than ordinary size, extent, etc. [the *Great* Lakes] 2 much above the average; esp., *a)* intense [*great* pain] *b)* eminent [a *great* writer] 3 most important; main 4 [Inf.] skillful: often with *at* 5 [Inf.] excellent; fine —*n.* a distinguished person or thing —**great′ly** *adv.* —**great′ness** *n.*

great- *combining form* older (or younger) by one generation [*great*-aunt, *great*-great-grandson]

great ape any of various large primates including the gorilla, chimpanzee, and orangutan

Great Britain principal island of the United Kingdom, including England, Scotland, & Wales

Great Dane a very large, muscular dog with a short, smooth coat

great-grand·child *n., pl.* **-chil′dren** a child of any of one's grandchildren

great-grand·par·ent *n.* a parent of any of one's grandparents

great·heart·ed *adj.* 1 brave; fearless 2 generous; unselfish

Great Lakes chain of five freshwater lakes in EC North America

Great Salt Lake shallow saltwater lake in NW Utah

grebe (grēb) *n.* [Fr *grèbe*] a diving and swimming bird with broadly lobed webbed feet

Gre·cian (grē′shən) *adj., n.* GREEK

Greco- [< L *Graecus*] *combining form* Greek, Greek and [*Greco*-Roman]

Greece (grēs) country in the S Balkan Peninsula, on the Mediterranean

greed (grēd) *n.* [< fol.] excessive desire, esp. for wealth; avarice

greed·y (grēd′ē) *adj.* **-i·er**, **-i·est** [OE *grǣdig*] 1 desiring more than one needs or deserves 2 having too strong a desire for food and drink; gluttonous —**greed′i·ly** *adv.* —**greed′i·ness** *n.*

Greek (grēk) *n.* 1 a person born or living in

Greece 2 the language, ancient or modern, of the Greeks —*adj.* of Greece or its people, language, etc.

green (grēn) *adj.* [OE *grene*] 1 of the color of growing grass 2 overspread with green plants or foliage 3 sickly or bilious 4 unripe 5 inexperienced or naive 6 not dried or seasoned 7 environmentally responsible 8 [Inf.] jealous —*n.* 1 the color of growing grass 2 [*pl.*] green leafy vegetables, as spinach 3 an area of smooth turf [a putting *green*] —**green'ish** *adj.* —**green'ly** *adv.* —**green'ness** *n.*

green·back *n.* any piece of U.S. paper money printed in green ink on the back

Green Bay city & port in Wisconsin

green bean the edible, immature green pod of the kidney bean

green·belt *n.* a beltlike area around a city, reserved for park land or farms

green·er·y *n.* green vegetation; verdure

green-eyed *adj.* very jealous

green·gro·cer *n.* [Brit.] a retail dealer in fresh vegetables and fruit

green·horn *n.* 1 an inexperienced person 2 a person easily deceived

green·house *n.* a heated building, mainly of glass, for growing plants

greenhouse effect the warming of the earth and its lower atmosphere, caused by trapped solar radiation

greenhouse gas an atmospheric gas that contributes to the greenhouse effect

Green·land (grēn'lənd) self-governing Danish island northeast of North America

green light [Inf.] permission to proceed with some undertaking —**green'light'** *vt.* **-light'ed** or **-lit'**, **-light'ing**

green manure a crop, as of clover, plowed under to fertilize the soil

green onion an immature onion with green leaves, often eaten raw; scallion

green pepper the green immature fruit of a red bell pepper

green power money as the source of economic power

green·sward *n.* green, grassy turf

green thumb a talent for growing plants

Green·wich (gren'ich; *chiefly Brit,* grin'ij) borough of London, on the prime meridian

Green·wich Village (gren'ich) section of New York City: once noted as a center for artists, writers, etc.

green·wood *n.* a forest in leaf

greet (grēt) *vt.* [OE *gretan*] 1 to address with friendliness 2 to meet or receive (a person, event, etc.) in a specified way 3 to come or appear to; meet —**greet'er** *n.*

greet·ing *n.* 1 the act or words of one who greets 2 [*often pl.*] a message of regards

greeting card an illustrated, usually folded card bearing a greeting

gre·gar·i·ous (grə ger'ē əs) *adj.* [< L *grex,* herd] 1 living in herds 2 fond of the company of others; sociable —**gre·gar'i·ous·ly** *adv.* —**gre·gar'i·ous·ness** *n.*

Gre·go·ri·an calendar (grə gôr'ē ən) the cal-

endar now widely used, introduced by Pope Gregory XIII in 1582

Gregorian chant [after Pope Gregory I] a kind of plainsong formerly widely used in the Roman Catholic Church

grem·lin (grem'lin) *n.* [prob. < Dan *gram,* a devil] a small imaginary creature humorously blamed for malfunctions or disruptions

Gre·na·da (grə nā'də) country on an island group in the West Indies

gre·nade (grə nād') *n.* [Fr < OFr, pomegranate] a small bomb detonated by a fuse and usually thrown by hand

gren·a·dier (gren'ə dir') *n.* 1 [Archaic] a soldier who threw grenades 2 a member of a special regiment or corps

gren·a·dine (gren'ə dēn') *n.* [Fr] a red syrup made from pomegranate juice

grew (grōō) *vi., vt.* pt. of GROW

grey (grā) *n., adj., vt., vi.* chiefly Brit. sp. of GRAY

grey·hound *n.* a tall, slender, swift dog with a narrow head

grid (grid) *n.* [short for GRIDIRON] 1 a framework of parallel bars; grating 2 a network of evenly spread lines at right angles 3 a system for distributing electrical power in a region 4 a metallic plate in a storage battery 5 an electrode, in spiral or gridlike shape, for controlling the flow of electrons in an electron tube

grid·dle (grid''l) *n.* [< L *craticula,* gridiron] a flat, heavy metal pan for cooking pancakes, etc.

grid·dle·cake *n.* a pancake

grid·i·ron (grid'ī'ərn) *n.* [see GRIDDLE] 1 GRILL (*n.* 1) 2 a football field

grid·lock *n.* a traffic jam in which no vehicle can move in any direction

grief (grēf) *n.* [see GRIEVE] 1 intense emotional suffering caused as by a loss 2 a cause of such suffering —**come to grief** to fail or be ruined

griev·ance (grēv'əns) *n.* 1 a circumstance thought to be unjust and ground for complaint 2 complaint against a real or imagined wrong

grieve (grēv) *vi., vt.* grieved, griev'ing [< L *gravis,* heavy] to feel or cause to feel grief

griev·ous (grēv'əs) *adj.* 1 causing grief 2 showing or full of grief 3 severe 4 deplorable; atrocious —**griev'ous·ly** *adv.*

grif·fin (grif'in) *n.* [< Gr *gryps*] a mythical monster, part lion and part eagle

grill (gril) *n.* [see GRIDDLE] 1 a unit for broiling meat, etc., consisting of a framework of metal bars or wires 2 a large griddle 3 grilled food 4 a restaurant that specializes in grilled foods —*vt.* 1 to broil 2 to question relentlessly

grille (gril) *n.* [see GRIDDLE] an open grating forming a screen

grim (grim) *adj.* grim'mer, grim'mest [OE *grimm*] 1 hard and unyielding; stern 2 appearing forbidding, harsh, etc. 3 repellent; ghastly —**grim'ly** *adv.* —**grim'ness** *n.*

gri·mace (gri mās', grim'is) *n.* [Fr] a distortion of the face, as in expressing pain, disgust, etc. —*vi.* **-maced′**, **-mac′ing** to make grimaces

grime (grīm) *n.* ⟦prob. < F *grijm*⟧ dirt rubbed into or covering a surface, as of the skin — **grim′y** *adj.* **-i·er**, **-i·est** —**grim′i·ness** *n.*

Grimm (grim) 1 **Ja·kob (Ludwig Karl)** (yä′ kôp) 1785-1863; Ger. philologist 2 **Wil·helm (Karl)** (vil′helm) 1786-1859; Ger. philologist: brother of Jakob, with whom he collected fairy tales

grin (grin) *vi.* **grinned**, **grin′ning** ⟦< OE *grennian*, bare the teeth⟧ 1 to smile broadly as in amusement 2 to show the teeth in pain, scorn, etc. —*n.* the act or look of grinning

grind (grīnd) *vt.* **ground**, **grind′ing** ⟦OE *grindan*⟧ 1 to crush or chop into fine particles 2 to oppress 3 to sharpen or smooth by friction 4 to rub (the teeth, etc.) together gratingly 5 to operate by turning the crank of —*vi.* [Inf.] to work hard and steadily —*n.* 1 a grinding 2 long, difficult work or study 3 [Inf.] a student who studies hard —**grind out** to produce by steady or laborious effort

grind·er (grīn′dər) *n.* 1 a person or thing that grinds 2 [*pl.*] [Inf.] the teeth 3 *chiefly New England var. of* HERO SANDWICH

grind·stone *n.* a revolving stone disk for sharpening tools or polishing things —**keep one's nose to the grindstone** to work hard and steadily

grin·go (griŋ′gō) *n., pl.* **-gos** ⟦MexSp⟧ in Latin America, a foreigner, esp. an American or Englishman: often somewhat contemptuous

grip (grip) *n.* ⟦< OE *gripan*, seize⟧ 1 a secure grasp; firm hold 2 the manner of holding a club, bat, etc. 3 the power of grasping firmly 4 mental grasp 5 firm control 6 a handle 7 a small traveling bag —*vt.* **gripped** or **gript**, **grip′ping** 1 to take firmly and hold fast 2 to get and hold the attention of —*vi.* to get a grip —**come to grips** to struggle (*with*) —**grip′per** *n.*

gripe (grīp) *vt.* **griped**, **grip′ing** ⟦OE *grīpan*, seize⟧ 1 to cause sharp pain in the bowels of 2 [Slang] to annoy —*vi.* [Slang] to complain —*n.* 1 a sharp pain in the bowels: *usually used in pl.* 2 [Slang] a complaint —**grip′er** *n.*

grippe (grip) *n.* ⟦Fr⟧ *former term for* INFLUENZA

gris-gris (grē′grē′) *n., pl.* **gris′-gris′** ⟦of Afr orig.⟧ an amulet, charm, or spell of African origin

gris·ly (griz′lē) *adj.* **-li·er**, **-li·est** ⟦OE *grislic*⟧ terrifying; ghastly —**gris′li·ness** *n.*

grist (grist) *n.* ⟦OE⟧ grain that is to be or has been ground

gris·tle (gris′əl) *n.* ⟦OE⟧ cartilage, esp. as found in meat —**gris′tly** (-lē) *adj.*

grist-mill *n.* a mill for grinding grain

grit (grit) *n.* ⟦< OE *greot*⟧ 1 rough particles, as of sand 2 coarse sandstone 3 stubborn courage —*vt.* **grit′ted**, **grit′ting** to clench or grind (the teeth) as in determination —*vi.* to make a grating sound —**grit′ty** *adj.* **-ti·er**, **-ti·est**

grits (grits) *pl.n.* ⟦OE *grytte*⟧ [*often with sing. v.*] coarsely ground grain; esp., hominy

griz·zled (griz′əld) *adj.* ⟦< OFr *gris*, gray⟧ 1 gray or streaked with gray 2 having gray hair

griz·zly (-lē) *adj.* **-zli·er**, **-zli·est** grayish; grizzled

grizzly (bear) a large, brown bear of W North America

groan (grōn) *vi., vt.* ⟦< OE *granian*⟧ to utter (with) a deep sound expressing pain, distress, etc. —*n.* such a sound

gro·cer (grō′sər) *n.* ⟦< OFr *grossier*⟧ a dealer in food and household supplies

gro·cer·y *n., pl.* **-ies** 1 a grocer's store 2 [*pl.*] the food and supplies sold by a grocer

grog (gräg) *n.* ⟦after Old *Grog*, nickname of E. Vernon (1684-1757), Brit admiral⟧ 1 rum diluted with water 2 any alcoholic liquor

grog·gy *adj.* **-gi·er**, **-gi·est** ⟦< prec. + -Y²⟧ 1 [Archaic] intoxicated 2 dizzy 3 sluggish or dull —**grog′gi·ly** *adv.* —**grog′gi·ness** *n.*

groin (groin) *n.* ⟦prob. < OE *grynde*, abyss⟧ 1 the fold where the abdomen joins either thigh 2 *Archit.* the sharp, curved edge at the junction of two vaults

grom·met (gräm′it) *n.* ⟦< obs. Fr *gromette*, a curb⟧ 1 a ring of rope 2 a metal eyelet in cloth, etc.

groom (grōōm) *n.* ⟦ME *grom*, boy⟧ 1 one whose work is tending horses 2 a bridegroom —*vt.* 1 to clean and curry (a horse, etc.) 2 to make neat and tidy 3 to train for a particular purpose

groove (grōōv) *n.* ⟦< ON *grof*, a pit⟧ 1 a long, narrow furrow cut with a tool 2 any channel or rut 3 a settled routine, esp. one in which one is productive, effective, etc. —*vt.* **grooved**, **groov′ing** to make a groove in

groov·y *adj.* **-i·er**, **-i·est** [Slang] very pleasing or attractive

grope (grōp) *vi.* **groped**, **grop′ing** ⟦< OE *grapian*, to touch⟧ to feel or search about blindly or uncertainly —*vt.* 1 to seek or find (one's way) by groping 2 [Slang] to fondle sexually —**grop′er** *n.* —**grop′ing·ly** *adv.*

gros·beak (grōs′bēk′) *n.* ⟦Fr: see GROSS & BEAK⟧ a songbird with a thick, strong, conical bill

gros·grain (grō′grān′) *n.* ⟦Fr, lit., coarse grain⟧ a ribbed silk or rayon fabric for ribbons, etc.

gross (grōs) *adj.* ⟦< LL *grossus*, thick⟧ 1 fat and coarse-looking 2 flagrant; very bad 3 lacking in refinement 4 vulgar; coarse 5 with no deductions; total 6 [Slang] disgusting —*n.* 1 *pl.* **gross′es** overall total 2 *pl.* **gross** twelve dozen —*vt., vi.* to earn (a specified total amount) before expenses are deducted —**gross out** [Slang] to disgust —**gross′ly** *adv.*

gross national product the total value of a nation's annual output of goods and services

gro·tesque (grō tesk′) *adj.* ⟦< It *grotta*, grotto: from designs found in caves⟧ 1 distorted or fantastic in appearance, shape, etc. 2 ridiculous; absurd —**gro·tesque′ly** *adv.*

grot·to (grät′ō) *n., pl.* **-toes** or **-tos** ⟦< It L *crypta*, crypt] 1 a cave 2 a cavelike structure used as a summerhouse, shrine, etc.

grouch (grouch) *vi.* [< ME *grucchen*] to grumble or complain sulkily —*n.* 1 one who grouches 2 a sulky mood —**grouch′y** *adj.* **-i·er, -i·est** —**grouch′i·ly** *adv.* —**grouch′i·ness** *n.*

ground¹ (ground) *n.* [OE *grund*, bottom] 1 the solid surface of the earth 2 soil; earth 3 [*often pl.*] a tract of land [*grounds* of an estate] 4 area, as of discussion 5 [*often pl.*] basis; foundation 6 valid reason or motive: *often used in pl.* 7 the background, as in a design 8 [*pl.*] sediment [coffee *grounds*] 9 the connection of an electrical conductor with a ground —*adj.* of, on, or near the ground —*vt.* 1 to set on the ground 2 to cause to run aground 3 to base; found; establish 4 to instruct in the first principles of 5 *a*) to keep (an aircraft or pilot) from flying *b*) [Inf.] to punish (a young person, esp. a teenager) by not permitting him or her to leave home for dates, etc. 6 *Elec.* to connect (a conductor) to a ground —*vi.* 1 to run ashore 2 *Baseball* to be put out on a grounder: usually with *out* — **break ground** 1 to dig; excavate 2 to plow 3 to start building —**break new ground** to innovate —**gain** (or **lose**) **ground** to gain (or lose) in achievement, popularity, etc. —**give ground** to retreat; yield —**hold** (or **stand**) **one's ground** to remain firm, not yielding — **on the ground** in reality rather than theory

ground² (ground) *vt., vi. pt. & pp. of* GRIND

ground control personnel and equipment on the ground, for guiding airplanes and spacecraft in takeoff, landing, etc.

ground cover low, dense-growing plants used for covering bare ground

ground crew a group of workers who maintain and repair aircraft

ground·er *n. Baseball* a batted ball that travels along the ground: also **ground ball**

ground floor that floor of a building approximately level with the ground; first floor —**in on the ground floor** [Inf.] in at the start (of a business, etc.)

ground glass glass with a surface that has been ground to render it translucent rather than transparent

ground·hog *n.* WOODCHUCK: also **ground hog**

ground·less *adj.* without reason or cause

ground rule 1 *Baseball* a rule adapted to playing conditions in a specific ballpark 2 any basic rule: *usually used in pl.*

ground·swell *n.* 1 a violent rolling of the ocean 2 a wave of popular feeling

ground·wa·ter *n.* water found underground

ground·work *n.* a foundation; basis

group (grōōp) *n.* [< It *gruppo*] a number of persons or things gathered or classified together —*vt., vi.* to form into a group or groups

grou·per (grōō′pər) *n.* [Port *garupa*] a large sea bass found in warm seas

group·ie (grōō′pē) *n.* [Inf.] 1 a usually female fan of a rock group, etc., who follows them about 2 a fan; devotee

group therapy (*or* **psychotherapy**) a form of treatment for a group of patients with similar emotional problems, as by group discussions

grouse¹ (grous) *n., pl.* **grouse** [< ?] a game bird with a plump body and mottled feathers

grouse² (grous) *vi.* **groused, grous′ing** [< ?] [Inf.] to complain

grout (grout) *n.* [ME] a thin mortar used as between tiles

grove (grōv) *n.* [< OE *graf*] a group of trees, without undergrowth

grov·el (gräv′əl, gruv′-) *vi.* **-eled** or **-elled, -el·ing** or **-el·ling** [< ME *grufelinge*, down on one's face] 1 to lie or crawl in a prostrate position, esp. abjectly 2 to behave abjectly — **grov′el·er** *n.,* **grov′el·ler**

grow (grō) *vi.* **grew, grown, grow′ing** [< OE *growan*] 1 to come into being or be produced naturally 2 to develop or thrive, as a living thing 3 to increase in size, quantity, etc. 4 to become [to *grow* weary] —*vt.* to cause to or let grow; raise; cultivate —**grow on** [Inf.] to come gradually to seem more likable, attractive, etc. to —**grow up** to mature —**grow′er** *n.*

growl (groul) *n.* [ME *groulen*] a rumbling, menacing sound such as an angry dog makes — *vi., vt.* to make, or express by, such a sound

grown (grōn) *vi., vt. pp. of* GROW —*adj.* having completed its growth; mature

grown-up *adj., n.* adult: also, for *n.,* **grown′up′**

growth (grōth) *n.* 1 a growing or developing 2 *a*) increase in size, etc. *b*) the full extent of this 3 something that grows or has grown 4 a tumor or other abnormal mass of tissue

grub (grub) *vi.* **grubbed, grub′bing** [ME *grubben*] 1 to dig in the ground 2 to work hard —*vt.* 1 to clear (ground) of roots 2 to uproot —*n.* 1 a wormlike larva, esp. of a beetle 2 [Slang] food

grub·by *adj.* **-bi·er, -bi·est** dirty; untidy — **grub′bi·ness** *n.*

grub·stake *n.* [GRUB (*n.* 2) + STAKE] [Inf.] 1 money or supplies advanced, as to a prospector 2 money advanced for any enterprise

grudge (gruj) *vt.* **grudged, grudg′ing** [< OFr *grouchier*] 1 BEGRUDGE 2 to give with reluctance —*n.* a feeling of resentment or ill will over some grievance —**grudg′ing·ly** *adv.*

gru·el (grōō′əl) *n.* [< ML *grutum*, meal] thin porridge made by cooking meal in water or milk

gru·el·ing or **gru·el·ling** *adj.* [prp. of obs. v. *gruel*, punish] very trying; exhausting

grue·some (grōō′səm) *adj.* [< dial. *grue*, to shudder + -SOME¹] causing horror or disgust; grisly

gruff (gruf) *adj.* [< Du *grof*] 1 rough or surly 2 harsh and throaty; hoarse —**gruff′ly** *adv.* —**gruff′ness** *n.*

grum·ble (grum′bəl) *vi.* **-bled, -bling** [prob. < Du *grommelen*] 1 to growl 2 to mutter in discontent 3 to rumble —*vt.* to express by grumbling —*n.* a grumbling —**grum′bler** *n.*

grump·y (grum'pē) *adj.* **-i·er, -i·est** [prob. echoic] grouchy; peevish

grunge (grunj) *n.* [Slang] garbage or dirt

grun·gy (grun'jē) *adj.* **-gi·er, -gi·est** [Slang] dirty, messy, etc.

grun·ion (grun'yən) *n.* [prob. < Sp *gruñón*, grumbler] a fish of the California coast: it spawns on sandy beaches

grunt (grunt) *vi., vt.* [< OE *grunian*] to utter (with) the deep, hoarse sound of a hog —*n.* **1** this sound **2** [Slang] one whose job involves routine tasks, strenuous labor, etc.; specif., a U.S. infantryman

Gru·yère (cheese) (grōō yer', grē-) [after *Gruyère*, Switzerland] [*often* **g- c-**] a light-yellow Swiss cheese, rich in butterfat

Gua·da·la·ja·ra (gwäd'′l ə här'ə) city in W Mexico: capital of Jalisco

Guam (gwäm) island in the W Pacific: an unincorporated territory of the U.S.

Guang·zhou (gwäŋ'jō) seaport in SE China

gua·nine (gwä'nēn') *n.* [< nucl. + -INE³] a crystalline base contained in the nucleic acids of all tissue

gua·no (gwä'nō) *n., pl.* **-nos** [Sp < AmInd (Peru)] manure of seabirds or bats, used as fertilizer

guar *abbrev.* guaranteed

guar·an·tee (gar'ən tē') *n.* **1** GUARANTY (*n.* 1) **2** *a)* a pledge to replace something if it is not as represented *b)* an assurance that something will be done as specified **3** a guarantor —*vt.* **-teed', -tee'ing 1** to give a guarantee for **2** to promise

guar·an·tor (gar'ən tôr') *n.* one who gives a guaranty or guarantee

guar·an·ty (-tē) *n., pl.* **-ties** [< OFr *garant*, a warrant] **1** a pledge or security for another's debt or obligation **2** an agreement that secures the existence or maintenance of something —*vt.* **-tied, -ty·ing** GUARANTEE

guard (gärd) *vt.* [< OFr *garder*] **1** to watch over and protect; defend **2** to keep from escaping or from trouble **3** to control or restrain —*vi.* **1** to keep watch (*against*) **2** to act as a guard —*n.* **1** defense; protection **2** a posture of readiness for defense **3** any device to protect against injury or loss **4** a person or group that guards **5** *Basketball* either of two players who are the main ball handlers **6** *Football* either of two players next to the center —**on (one's) guard** vigilant

guard·ed *adj.* **1** kept safe **2** cautious [a *guarded* reply] —**guard'ed·ly** *adv.*

guard·house *n. Mil.* **1** a building used by a guard when not walking a post **2** a jail for temporary confinement

guard·i·an (-ē ən) *n.* **1** one who guards or protects; custodian **2** a person legally in charge of the affairs of a minor or of a person of unsound mind —*adj.* protecting —**guard'i·an·ship'** *n.*

guard·rail *n.* a protective railing

Gua·te·ma·la (gwät'ə mä'lə) country in Central America

gua·va (gwä'və) *n.* [< native name] a yellow, pear-shaped tropical American fruit

gua·ya·be·ra (gwä'yä ber'ə) *n.* [AmSp] a kind of loosefitting shirt worn with the shirttail outside the trousers

gu·ber·na·to·ri·al (gōō'bər nə tôr'ē əl) *adj.* [L *gubernator*, governor] of a governor or the office of governor

Guern·sey (gurn'zē) *n., pl.* **-seys** [after *Guernsey*, one of the Channel Islands] a breed of dairy cattle, usually fawn-colored with white markings

guer·ril·la (gə ril'ə) *n.* [Sp, dim. of *guerra*, war] a member of a small force of irregular soldiers, making surprise raids —*adj.* **1** of or by guerrillas **2** clandestine, subversive, etc. Also sp. **gue·ril'la**

guess (ges) *vt., vi.* [ME *gessen*] **1** to form a judgment or estimate of (something) without actual knowledge; surmise **2** to judge correctly by doing this **3** to think or suppose —*n.* **1** a guessing **2** something guessed; conjecture —**guess'er** *n.*

guess·ti·mate (ges'tə mit; *for v.,* -māt') [Inf.] *n.* an estimate based on a guess —*vt.* **-mat'ed, -mat'ing** to form a guesstimate of

guess·work *n.* **1** a guessing **2** a judgment, result, etc. arrived at by guessing

guest (gest) *n.* [< ON *gestr*] **1** a person entertained at the home, club, etc. of another **2** any paying customer of a hotel, restaurant, etc. —*adj.* **1** for guests **2** performing by special invitation [a *guest* artist]

guff (guf) *n.* [echoic] [Slang] insolent talk

guf·faw (gə fô') *n.* [echoic] a loud, coarse burst of laughter —*vi.* to laugh in this way

guid·ance (gīd'ns) *n.* **1** a guiding; leadership **2** advice or assistance

guide (gīd) *vt.* **guid'ed, guid'ing** [< OFr *guider*] **1** to point out the way for; lead **2** to direct the course of; control —*n.* **1** one whose work is conducting tours, etc. **2** a controlling device **3** a book of basic instruction

guide·book *n.* a book containing directions and information for tourists

guided missile a military missile whose course is controlled by electronic signals

guide·line *n.* a principle by which to determine a course of action

guild (gild) *n.* [< OE *gieldan*, to pay] an association for mutual aid and the promotion of common interests, esp. among craftsmen

guil·der (gil'dər) *n.* [< MDu *gulden*, golden] the former monetary unit of the Netherlands

guile (gīl) *n.* [< OFr] slyness and cunning in dealing with others —**guile'ful** *adj.* —**guile'less** *adj.*

guil·lo·tine (gil'ə tēn', gē'ə-; *for v., usually* gil'ə tēn', gē'ə-) *n.* [Fr: after J. *Guillotin* (1738-1814), Fr physician who advocated its use] an instrument for beheading, having a heavy blade dropped between two grooved uprights —*vt.* **-tined', -tin'ing** to behead with a guillotine

guilt (gilt) *n.* [OE *gylt*, a sin] **1** the state of having done a wrong or committed an offense **2**

a feeling of self-reproach from believing that one has done a wrong —**guilt'less** *adj.*

guilt·y *adj.* **-i·er, -i·est 1** having guilt **2** legally judged an offender **3** of or showing guilt [a *guilty* look] —**guilt'i·ly** *adv.* —**guilt'i·ness** *n.*

guin·ea (gin'ē) *n.* [first coined of gold from *Guinea*] a former English gold coin equal to 21 shillings

Guin·ea (gin'ē) country on the W coast of Africa

Guin·ea-Bis·sau (-bi sou') country on the W coast of Africa

guinea fowl (*or* **hen**) [orig. imported from *Guinea*] a domestic fowl with a rounded body and speckled feathers

guinea pig [prob. orig. brought to England by ships plying between England, *Guinea*, and South America] **1** a small, plump rodent, often used in biological experiments **2** any subject used in an experiment

Guin·e·vere (gwin'ə vir') the wife of King Arthur

guise (gīz) *n.* [< OHG *wisa*, manner] **1** manner of dress; garb **2** outward appearance **3** a false appearance; pretense

gui·tar (gi tär') *n.* [ult. < Gr *kithara*, lyre] a musical instrument with usually six strings plucked with the fingers or a plectrum —**gui·tar'ist** *n.*

gulch (gulch) *n.* [prob. < dial., to swallow greedily] a deep, narrow ravine

gulf (gulf) *n.* [ult. < Gr *kolpos*, bosom] **1** a large area of ocean reaching into land **2** a wide, deep chasm **3** a wide gap or separation

Gulf Stream a warm ocean current flowing from the Gulf of Mexico northward and then eastward toward Europe

gull¹ (gul) *n.* [< Celt] a white and gray water bird with webbed feet

gull² (gul) *n.* [ME, lit., unfledged bird] a person easily tricked; dupe —*vt.* to cheat or trick

gul·let (gul'ət) *n.* [< L *gula*, throat] **1** the esophagus **2** the throat

gul·li·ble (gul'ə bəl) *adj.* easily gulled; credulous —**gul'li·bil'i·ty** *n.*

gul·ly (gul'ē) *n., pl.* **-lies** [see GULLET] a small, narrow ravine

gulp (gulp) *vt.* [prob. < Du *gulpen*] to swallow hastily or greedily —*vi.* to catch the breath as in swallowing —*n.* a gulping or swallowing — to catch the breath as in swallowing

gum¹ (gum) *n.* [< LL *gumma*] **1** a sticky substance found in certain trees and plants **2** an adhesive **3** CHEWING GUM —*vt.* **gummed, gum'ming** to coat or unite with gum —**gum up** [Slang] to cause to go awry —**gum'my** *adj.* **-mi·er, -mi·est**

gum² (gum) *n.* [OE *goma*] [*often pl.*] the firm flesh surrounding the base of the teeth —*vt.* **gummed, gum'ming** to chew with toothless gums

gum arabic a gum from certain acacias, used in medicine, candy, etc.

gum·bo (gum'bō) *n.* [< Bantu name for okra] a soup thickened with okra

gum·drop *n.* a small, firm candy made of sweetened gelatin, etc.

gump·tion (gump'shən) *n.* [< Scot] [Inf.] courage and initiative

gun (gun) *n.* [< ME *gonnilde*, cannon < ON] **1** any weapon with a metal tube from which a projectile is discharged by the force of an explosive **2** any similar device not discharged by an explosive [an air *gun*] **3** anything like a gun in shape or use —*vi.* **gunned, gun'ning** to shoot or hunt with a gun —*vt.* **1** [Inf.] to shoot (a person) **2** [Slang] to advance the throttle of (an engine) —**gun for** [Slang] to try to get —**jump the gun** [Inf.] to begin before the proper time —**stick to one's guns** [Inf.] to be resolute —**under the gun** [Inf.] in a tense situation, often one involving a deadline

gun·boat *n.* a small armed ship

gun·fight *n.* a fight between combatants using firearms —**gun'fight'er** *n.*

gun·fire *n.* the firing of guns

gung-ho (guŋ'hō') *adj.* [Chin *kung-ho*, lit., work together] [Inf.] enthusiastic

gunk (guŋk) *n.* [< ?] [Slang] any viscous or thick, messy substance

gun·man (-mən) *n., pl.* **-men** (-mən) an armed gangster or hired killer

gun·met·al *n.* **1** a bronze with a dark tarnish **2** its dark-gray color

gun·ner *n.* **1** a soldier, etc. who helps fire artillery **2** a naval warrant officer in charge of guns, missiles, etc.

gun·ner·y *n.* the science of making and using heavy guns and projectiles

gun·ny (gun'ē) *n., pl.* **-nies** [< Sans *gōnī*, a sack] a coarse fabric of jute or hemp

gun·ny·sack *n.* a sack made of gunny

gun·play *n.* an exchange of gunshots, as between gunmen and police

gun·point *n.* used chiefly in **at gunpoint**, under threat of being shot with a gun at close range

gun·pow·der *n.* an explosive powder used in guns, for blasting, etc.

gun·ship *n.* a heavily armed helicopter used to assault enemy ground forces

gun·shot *n.* the shooting of a gun

gun-shy *adj.* **1** easily frightened at the firing of a gun [a *gun-shy* dog] **2** wary, mistrustful, etc., esp. because of a previous experience

gun·smith *n.* one who makes or repairs small guns

gun·wale (gun'əl) *n.* [< bulwarks supporting a ship's guns] the upper edge of the side of a ship or boat

gup·py (gup'ē) *n., pl.* **-pies** [after R. J. L. *Guppy*, of Trinidad] a very small freshwater fish of the West Indies, etc.

gur·gle (gur'gəl) *vi.* **-gled, -gling** [< L *gurgulio*, gullet] to make a bubbling sound —*n.* such a sound

gur·ney (gur'nē) *n., pl.* **-neys** [< ?] a hospital stretcher on wheels

gu·ru (gōō'rōō'; *also* goo rōō') *n.* [< Sans *guruh*, venerable] **1** in Hinduism, one's personal spiritual advisor or teacher **2** an influential or charismatic leader, mentor, etc.

gush (gush) *vi.* [ME *guschen*] **1** to flow out

plentifully **2** to have a sudden flow **3** to talk or write effusively —*vt.* to cause to gush —*n.* a gushing —**gush′y** *adj.* **-i·er, -i·est**

gush·er *n.* **1** one who gushes **2** an oil well from which oil spouts forth

gus·set (gus′it) *n.* [< OFr *gousset*] a triangular piece inserted in a garment, etc. to make it stronger or roomier

gus·sy or **gus·sie** (gus′ē) *vt., vi.* **-sied, -sy·ing** [< ?] [Slang] to dress (*up*) in a fine or showy way

gust (gust) *n.* [< ON *gjosa*, to gush] **1** a sudden, strong rush of air **2** a sudden outburst of rain, laughter, etc. —**gust′y** *adj.* **-i·er, -i·est**

gus·ta·to·ry (gus′tə tôr′ē) *adj.* [< L *gustus*, taste] of the sense of taste

gus·to (gus′tō) *n.* [see prec.] **1** zest; relish **2** great vigor or liveliness

gut (gut) *n.* [< OE *geotan*, to pour] **1** [*pl.*] the entrails **2** the stomach or belly **3** the intestine **4** tough cord made from animal intestines **5** [*pl.*] [Inf.] daring; courage —*vt.* **gut′ted, gut′ting 1** to remove the intestines from **2** to destroy the interior of —*adj.* **1** [Inf.] based on intuition [a *gut* feeling] **2** [Slang] easy [a *gut* college course]

gut·less *adj.* [Inf.] lacking courage

guts·y (gut′sē) *adj.* **-i·er, -i·est** [Inf.] courageous, forceful, etc.

gut·ter (gut′ər) *n.* [< L *gutta*, a drop] **1** a channel to carry off water, as along the eaves of a roof or the side of a street **2** a place or condition characterized by squalor —*vi.* to flow in a stream

gut·tur·al (gut′ər əl) *adj.* [L *guttur*, throat] harsh; rasping: said of vocal sounds

guv (guv) *n.* slang var. of GOVERNOR

guy¹ (gī) *n.* [< OFr *guier*, to guide] a rope, chain, etc. used to steady or guide something —*vt.* to guide or steady with a guy

guy² (gī) [Inf.] *n.* [after *Guy* Fawkes, Eng conspirator] **1** a man or boy **2** any person —*vt.* to make fun of; ridicule

Guy·a·na (gī an′ə) country in NE South America

guz·zle (guz′əl) *vi., vt.* **-zled, -zling** [< ? OFr *gosier*, throat] to drink greedily or immoderately

gym (jim) *n.* [Inf.] **1** short for GYMNASIUM **2** PHYSICAL EDUCATION

gym·na·si·um (jim nā′zē əm) *n., pl.* **-si·ums** or **-si·a** (-ə) [< Gr *gymnos*, naked] a room or building equipped for physical training and sports

gym·nas·tics (jim nas′tiks) *n.* a sport combining tumbling and acrobatic feats —**gym′nast′** *n.* —**gym·nas′tic** *adj.* —**gym·nas′ti·cal·ly** *adv.*

gym·no·sperm (jim′nō spurm′, -nə-) *n.* [< Gr *gymnos*, naked + *sperma*, seed] any of a large division of seed plants, as seed ferns, conifers, etc., having the ovules not enclosed within an ovary

GYN *abbrev.* **1** gynecologic(al) **2** gynecologist **3** gynecology

gy·ne·col·o·gy (gī′nə käl′ə jē) *n.* [< Gr *gynē*, woman + -LOGY] the branch of medicine dealing with women's diseases, etc. —**gy′ne·co·log′ic** (-kə läj′ik) *adj.*, **gy′ne·co·log′i·cal** —**gy′ne·col′o·gist** *n.*

gyp (jip) [Inf.] *n.* [prob. < GYPSY] **1** a swindle **2** a swindler —*vt., vi.* **gypped, gyp′ping** to swindle; cheat: In all senses now often considered offensive

gyp·sum (jip′səm) *n.* [< Gr *gypsos*] a sulfate of calcium used to make plaster of Paris and cement

Gyp·sy (jip′sē) *n., pl.* **-sies** [< *Egipcien,* Egyptian: orig. thought to be from Egypt] **1** [*also* **g-**] a member of the Roma people: in technical use, ROMANI is now preferred **2** [**g-**] one whose lifestyle is itinerant, unconventional, etc. **3** [**g-**] [Inf.] unlicensed or nonunion

gypsy moth a moth in the E U.S.: its larvae feed on leaves, damaging trees

gy·rate (jī′rāt′) *vi.* **-rat′ed, -rat′ing** [< Gr *gyros*, a circle] to move in a circular or spiral path; whirl —**gy·ra′tion** *n.* —**gy′ra′tor** *n.*

gy·ro (yir′ō, jī′rō′) *n., pl.* **-ros** [see prec.] **1** layers of lamb and beef roasted and sliced **2** a pita sandwich of this

gyro- [see GYRATE] *combining form* gyrating [*gyroscope*]

gy·ro·scope (jī′rō skōp′, -rə-) *n.* [prec. + -SCOPE] a wheel mounted in a set of rings so that its axis is free to turn in any direction: when the wheel is spun rapidly, it will keep its original plane of rotation

H

h or **H** (āch) *n., pl.* **h's, H's** the eighth letter of the English alphabet

H¹ or **h** *abbrev.* **1** height **2** high **3** *Baseball* hit(s) **4** hour(s) **5** hundred(s)

H² *Chem. symbol for* hydrogen

ha (hä) *interj.* [echoic] used to express surprise, wonder, anger, triumph, etc.

ha·be·as cor·pus (hā′bē əs kôr′pəs) [L, (that) you have the body] *Law* a writ requiring that a detained person be brought before a court to decide the legality of the detention

hab·er·dash·er (hab′ər dash′ər) *n.* [< ME] a dealer in men's hats, shirts, neckties, etc. —**hab′er·dash′er·y** *n.*

ha·bil·i·ment (hə bil′ə mənt) *n.* [< MFr *habiller*, to clothe] 1 [*usually pl.*] clothing; attire 2 [*pl.*] equipment; trappings

hab·it (hab′it) *n.* [< L *habere*, to have] 1 a distinctive costume, as of a nun 2 a thing done often and, hence, easily 3 a usual way of doing 4 an addiction, esp. to narcotics

hab·it·a·ble *adj.* fit to be lived in

hab·i·tat (hab′i tat′) *n.* [L, it inhabits] 1 the region where a plant or animal naturally lives 2 the place where a person is ordinarily found

hab·i·ta·tion (hab′i tā′shən) *n.* 1 the act of inhabiting 2 a dwelling; home

hab·it-form·ing *adj.* resulting in the formation of a habit or in addiction

ha·bit·u·al (hə bich′ōō əl) *adj.* 1 done or acquired by habit 2 steady; inveterate [a *habitual* smoker] 3 much seen, done, or used; usual —**ha·bit′u·al·ly** *adv.* —**ha·bit′u·al·ness** *n.*

ha·bit·u·ate (-āt′) *vt.* **-at′ed, -at′ing** to accustom (*to*) —**ha·bit′u·a′tion** *n.*

ha·bit·u·é (-ā′) *n.* [Fr] one who frequents a certain place

ha·ci·en·da (hä′sē en′də) *n.* [Sp < L *facere*, do] in Spanish America, a large estate or ranch, or its main house

hack¹ (hak) *vt.* [OE *haccian*] to chop or cut roughly —*vi.* 1 to make rough cuts 2 to give harsh, dry coughs —*n.* 1 a gash 2 a harsh, dry cough

hack² (hak) *n.* [< HACKNEY] 1 a horse for hire 2 an old, worn-out horse 3 one hired to do routine or dull writing 4 a horse-drawn coach for hire 5 [Inf.] a taxicab —*vt., vi.* to gain unauthorized access to (a computer network, etc.) —*adj.* 1 employed as, or done by, a hack [*hack* writer] 2 trite; hackneyed

hack·er *n.* 1 an unskilled golfer, etc. 2 a highly skilled user of computers 3 one who seeks to gain unauthorized access to computer networks, etc.

hack·le (hak′əl) *n.* [ME *hechele*] 1 the neck feathers of a rooster, pigeon, etc. 2 [*pl.*] the hairs on a dog's neck and back that bristle

hack·ney (hak′nē) *n., pl.* **-neys** [after *Hackney*, England] 1 a horse for driving or riding 2 a carriage for hire

hack·neyed (-nēd′) *adj.* made trite by overuse

hack·saw *n.* a fine-toothed saw for cutting metal: also **hack saw**

had (had) *vt.* **pt. & pp. of** HAVE

had·dock (had′ək) *n., pl.* **-dock** or **-docks** [ME *hadok*] an Atlantic food fish, related to the cod

Ha·des (hā′dēz) *n.* [Gr *Haidēs*] 1 Gr. Myth. the home of the dead 2 [*often* **h-**] hell

haf·ni·um (haf′nē əm) *n.* [after *Hafnia*, L name of Copenhagen, Denmark] a metallic chemical element used in tungsten filament alloys and in nuclear reactor control rods: symbol, Hf; at. no. 72

haft (haft, häft) *n.* [OE *hæft*] the handle or hilt of a knife, ax, etc.

hag (hag) *n.* [< OE *hægtes*] 1 a witch 2 an ugly, often vicious, old woman —**hag′gish** *adj.*

hag·gard (hag′ərd) *adj.* [MFr *hagard*, untamed (hawk)] having a wild, wasted, worn look; gaunt

hag·gle (hag′əl) *vi.* **-gled, -gling** [< Scot *hag*, to hack] to argue about terms, price, etc. —*n.* a haggling —**hag′gler** *n.*

Hague (hāg), **The** political capital of the Netherlands (cf. AMSTERDAM)

hah (hä) *interj., n.* HA

hai·ku (hi′kōō′) *n.* [Jpn] 1 a Japanese verse form of three unrhymed lines of 5, 7, and 5 syllables, respectively 2 *pl.* **-ku′** a poem in this form

hail¹ (hāl) *vt.* [< ON *heill*, whole, sound] 1 to greet with cheers; acclaim 2 to call out to [to *hail* a cab] —*n.* a greeting —*interj.* used to signify tribute, greeting, etc. —**hail from** to be from

hail² (hāl) *n.* [OE *hægel*] 1 frozen pellets of ice falling during thunderstorms 2 a shower of or like hail —*vt., vi.* to pour down like hail

hail·stone *n.* a pellet of hail

hail·storm *n.* a storm with hail

hair (her, har) *n.* [OE *hær*] 1 any of the threadlike outgrowths from the skin of an animal or human 2 a growth of these, as on the human head 3 material woven from hair 4 a very small space, degree, etc. 5 a threadlike growth on a plant —**get in someone's hair** [Slang] to annoy someone —**split hairs** to quibble —**hair′less** *adj.* —**hair′like′** *adj.*

hair·ball *n.* a ball of hair that may form in the stomach of a cow, cat, or other animal that licks its coat

hair·breadth (-bredth′) *n.* a very small space or amount —*adj.* very narrow; close Also **hairs′breadth′** or **hair's′-breadth′**

hair·cut *n.* the act of, or a style of, cutting the hair

hair·do (-dōō′) *n., pl.* **-dos′** the style in which hair is arranged; coiffure

hair·dress·er *n.* one whose work is dressing, or arranging, hair

-haired (herd) having (a specified kind of) hair [short-*haired*]

hair·line *n.* 1 a very thin line 2 the outline of the hair on the head

hair·piece *n.* a toupee or wig

hair·pin *n.* a small, bent piece of wire, etc., for keeping the hair in place —*adj.* U-shaped [a *hairpin* turn in the road]

hair-rais·ing *adj.* terrifying or shocking

hair·split·ting *adj., n.* making petty distinctions

hair·spring *n.* a slender, hairlike coil spring, as in a watch

hair·y *adj.* **-i·er, -i·est** covered with hair —**hair′i·ness** *n.*

Hai·ti (hāt′ē) country occupying the W portion of the island of Hispaniola, West Indies —**Hai·tian** (hā′shən) *adj., n.*

hake (hāk) *n.* ⟦prob. < ON⟧ a marine food fish related to the cod

ha·lal (hä läl′) *adj.* ⟦Ar⟧ characterized by adherence to the requirements of Islamic dietary law, esp. in slaughtering animals for meat

hal·berd (hal′bərd) *n.* ⟦ult. < MHG *helmbarte*⟧ a combined spear and battle-ax of the 1400s and 1500s

hal·cy·on (hal′sē ən) *adj.* ⟦< Gr *alkyōn*, king-fisher (fabled calmer of the sea)⟧ tranquil, idyllic, etc. ⟦*halcyon* days⟧

hale¹ (hāl) *adj.* **hal′er, hal′est** ⟦OE *hal*⟧ vigorous and healthy

hale² (hāl) *vt.* **haled, hal′ing** ⟦< ΘFr *haler*⟧ to force (a person) to go ⟦*haled* him into court⟧

half (haf, häf) *n., pl.* **halves** ⟦OE *healf*⟧ 1 either of the two equal parts of something 2 either of the two equal parts of some games —*adj.* 1 being a half 2 incomplete; partial —*adv.* 1 to the extent of a half 2 partly ⟦*half* done⟧ 3 at all: used with *not* ⟦not *half* bad⟧

half- *combining form* 1 one half ⟦*half*-life⟧ 2 partly ⟦*half*-baked⟧

half-and-half *n.* something that is half of one thing and half of another, as a mixture of milk and cream —*adj.* combining two things equally —*adv.* in two equal parts

half·back *n. Football* one of the running backs, typically smaller and faster than a fullback

half-breed *n.* one whose parents are of different ethnic types: an offensive term

half brother a brother through one parent only

half dollar a coin of the U.S., Canada, etc., worth 50 cents

half-heart·ed *adj.* with little enthusiasm, determination, interest, etc. —**half′heart′ed·ly** *adv.*

half-life *n.* 1 the constant time period required for the disintegration of half of the atoms in a sample of a radioactive substance 2 the time during which something has a lingering effect

half-mast *n.* the position of a flag halfway down its staff, esp. as a sign of mourning

half note *Music* a note having one half the duration of a whole note

half·pen·ny (hāp′nē, hā′pən ē) *n., pl.* **-pence** (hā′pəns) or **-pen·nies** a former British coin equal to half a penny

half sister a sister through one parent only

half sole a sole (of a shoe or boot) from the arch to the toe

half-track *n.* an army truck, armored vehicle, etc. with tractor treads instead of rear wheels

half·way *adj.* 1 midway between two points, etc. 2 partial ⟦*halfway* measures⟧ —*adv.* 1 to the midway point 2 partially —**meet halfway** to be willing to compromise (with)

halfway house a place for helping people adjust to society after being imprisoned, hospitalized, etc.

half-wit *n.* a stupid or silly person; fool —**half′-wit′ted** *adj.*

hal·i·but (hal′ə bət) *n., pl.* **-but** or **-buts** ⟦ME *hali*, holy + *butt*, a flounder (so called because eaten on holidays)⟧ a large, edible flounder of northern seas

Hal·i·fax (hal′ə faks′) capital of Nova Scotia, Canada

hal·ite (hal′īt′, hā′līt′) *n.* rock salt

hal·i·to·sis (hal′i tō′sis) *n.* ⟦< L *halitus*, breath⟧ bad-smelling breath

hall (hôl) *n.* ⟦OE *heall*⟧ 1 the main dwelling on an estate 2 a public building with offices, etc. 3 a large room for gatherings, exhibits, etc. 4 a college building 5 a vestibule at the entrance of a building 6 an area onto which rooms open

hal·le·lu·jah or **hal·le·lu·iah** (hal′ə lōō′yə) *interj.* ⟦< Heb < *hallelū*, praise (imper.) + *yāh*, Jehovah⟧ used to express praise, thanks, etc., esp. to God —*n.* a hymn of praise to God

hall·mark (hôl′märk′) *n.* ⟦< the mark stamped on gold and silver articles at Goldsmith's Hall⟧ a mark or symbol of genuineness or high quality

hal·loo (hə lōō′) *n., interj.* (a shout or call) used esp. to attract attention —*vi., vt.* **-looed′, -loo′ing** to call out (to)

hal·low (hal′ō) *vt.* ⟦OE *halgian*⟧ to make or regard as holy

hal·lowed (-ōd) *adj.* holy or sacred

Hal·low·een or **Hal·low·e'en** (hal′ə wēn′, häl′-) *n.* ⟦contr. < *all hallow even*⟧ the evening of Oct. 31, followed by All Saints' Day: now celebrated with masquerading, etc.

hal·lu·ci·nate (hə lōō′si nāt′) *vi., vt.* **-nat′ed, -nat′ing** ⟦see fol.⟧ to have or cause to have hallucinations

hal·lu·ci·na·tion (hə lōō′si nā′shən) *n.* ⟦< L *hallucinari*, to wander mentally⟧ 1 the apparent perception of sights, sounds, etc. that are not actually present 2 the thing perceived —**hal·lu′ci·na·to′ry** (-nə tôr′ē) *adj.*

hal·lu·ci·no·gen (hə lōō′si nə jən) *n.* a drug or other substance that produces hallucinations —**hal·lu′ci·no·gen′ic** *adj.*

hall·way *n.* a passageway; corridor

ha·lo (hā′lō) *n., pl.* **-los** or **-loes** ⟦< Gr *halōs*, circular threshing floor⟧ 1 a ring of light, as around the sun 2 a symbolic ring of light around the head of a saint, etc., as in pictures

hal·o·gen (hal′ə jən) *n.* ⟦< Gr *hals*, salt⟧ any of the five nonmetallic chemical elements fluorine, chlorine, bromine, astatine, and iodine

halt¹ (hôlt) *n., vi., vt.* ⟦< Ger *halt machen*⟧ stop

halt² (hôlt) ⟦Archaic⟧ *vi.* ⟦< OE *healt*⟧ 1 to limp 2 to hesitate —*adj.* lame —**the halt** those who are lame

hal·ter (hôl′tər) *n.* ⟦OE *hælftre*⟧ 1 a rope or strap for tying or leading an animal 2 a hangman's noose 3 a woman's upper garment, held up by a loop around the neck

halve (hav, häv) *vt.* **halved, halv′ing** 1 to divide into two equal parts 2 to reduce to half

halves (havz, hävz) *n. pl. of* HALF —**by halves** halfway; imperfectly —**go halves** to share expenses equally

hal·yard (hal′yərd) *n.* ⟦< ME *halier*: see

HALE²] a rope or tackle for raising or lowering a flag, sail, etc.

ham (ham) *n.* ⟦OE *hamm*⟧ **1** the back of the thigh **2** the upper part of a hog's hind leg, salted, smoked, etc. **3** [Inf.] an amateur radio operator **4** [Slang] an actor who overacts —**ham′my** *adj.* **-mi·er, -mi·est**

Ham·burg (ham′bərg) seaport in N Germany

ham·burg·er (ham′bur′gər) *n.* ⟦after *Hamburg*, Germany⟧ **1** ground beef **2** a cooked patty of such meat, often in a sandwich Also **ham′burg** (-bərg)

Ham·il·ton (ham′əl tən), **Alexander** 1755?-1804; Am. statesman

ham·let (ham′lit) *n.* ⟦< OFr *hamelete* < LowG *hamm*, enclosed area⟧ a very small village

Ham·let (ham′lit) *n.* a Danish prince, the title hero of a tragedy by Shakespeare

ham·mer (ham′ər) *n.* ⟦OE *hamor*⟧ **1** a tool for pounding, having a metal head and a handle **2** a thing like this in shape or use, as the part of a gun that strikes the firing pin **3** one of the three small bones in the middle ear — *vt., vi.* **1** to strike repeatedly, as with a hammer **2** to drive, force, or shape, as with hammer blows —**hammer (away) at** to keep emphasizing —**ham′mer·er** *n.*

hammer and sickle the emblem of Communist parties in some countries

ham·mer·head *n.* **1** the head of a hammer **2** a shark with a mallet-shaped head having an eye at each end

ham·mer·toe *n.* a toe that is deformed, with its first joint bent downward

ham·mock (ham′ək) *n.* ⟦Sp *hamaca*, of WInd orig.⟧ a kind of bed of canvas, etc. swung from ropes at both ends

ham·per¹ (ham′pər) *vt.* ⟦ME *hampren*⟧ to hinder; impede; encumber

ham·per² (ham′pər) *n.* ⟦< OFr *hanap*, a cup⟧ a large basket, usually with a lid

ham·ster (ham′stər) *n.* ⟦< OHG *hamustro*⟧ a rodent of Europe and Asia, used in scientific experiments or kept as a pet

ham·string (ham′striŋ′) *n.* a tendon at the back of the knee —*vt.* **-strung′, -string′ing 1** to disable by cutting a hamstring **2** to lessen the power of

hand (hand) *n.* ⟦OE⟧ **1** the body part attached to the wrist, used for grasping **2** a side or direction [at my right *hand*] **3** [*pl.*] possession or care [the land is in my *hands*] **4** control [to strengthen one's *hand*] **5** an active part [take a *hand* in the work] **6** a promise to marry **7** skill **8** one having a special skill **9** manner of doing something **10** handwriting **11** applause **12** help [to lend a *hand*] **13** a hired worker [a farm *hand*] **14** a source [to get news at first *hand*] **15** anything like a hand, as a pointer on a clock **16** the breadth of a hand: used as in measuring the height of a horse **17** *Card Games a)* the cards held by a player at one time *b)* a round of play —*adj.* of, for, or controlled by the hand —*vt.* **1** to give as with the hand **2** to help or conduct with the hand —**at hand** near —**hand in hand** together —

hand it to [Slang] to give credit to —**hand over fist** [Inf.] easily and in large amounts —**hands down** easily —**on hand 1** near **2** available **3** present —**on the one** (or **other**) **hand** from one (or the opposed) point of view

hand·bag *n.* a woman's purse

hand·ball *n.* a game in which players bat a small rubber ball against a wall with their hands

hand·bar·row *n.* a frame carried by two people holding handles at the ends

hand·bill *n.* a small printed notice to be passed out by hand

hand·book *n.* a compact reference book; manual

hand·breadth *n.* the breadth of the human palm, about 4 inches

hand·car *n.* a small, open car, originally hand-powered, used on railroads

hand·cart *n.* a small cart moved by hand

hand·clasp *n.* HANDSHAKE

hand·craft *n.* HANDICRAFT —*vt.* to make skillfully by hand —**hand′craft′ed** *adj.*

hand·cuff *n.* either of a pair of connected rings for shackling the wrists of a prisoner: *usually used in pl.* —*vt.* to put handcuffs on; manacle

-hand·ed (han′did) *combining form* having or involving (a specified kind or number of) hands [right-*handed*, two-*handed*]

Han·del (han′dəl), **George Fri·der·ic** (frē′dər ik, -drik) 1685-1759; Eng. composer, born in Germany

hand·ful *n.,* *pl.* **-fuls′ 1** as much or as many as the hand will hold **2** a few; not many **3** [Inf.] someone or something that is hard to manage

hand·gun *n.* any firearm that is held and fired with one hand, as a pistol

hand-held *adj.* small enough to be held in the hand while being used

hand·i·cap (hand′dē kap′) *n.* ⟦< *hand in cup*, former kind of lottery⟧ **1** a competition in which difficulties are imposed on, or advantages given to, the various contestants to equalize their chances **2** such a difficulty or advantage **3** *a)* any hindrance *b)* a physical or mental disability —*vt.* **-capped′, -cap′ping 1** to give a handicap to **2** to hinder —**the handicapped** those who are physically or intellectually disabled

hand·i·capped *adj.* physically or intellectually disabled

hand·i·cap·per *n.* a person, as a sportswriter, who tries to predict the winners in horse races

hand·i·craft (han′dē kraft′) *n.* skill with the hands, or work calling for it

hand·i·work *n.* **1** HANDWORK **2** anything made or done by a particular person

hand·ker·chief (haŋ′kər chif′) *n.* ⟦HAND + KERCHIEF⟧ a small cloth used for wiping the nose, face, etc., or worn for ornament

han·dle (han′dəl) *n.* ⟦OE < *hand*⟧ that part of a tool, etc. by which it is held, lifted, etc. —*vt.* **-dled, -dling 1** to touch, lift, operate, etc. with the hand **2** to manage; control **3** to deal with; treat **4** to sell or deal in —*vi.* to respond to control [the car *handles* well] —**han'dler** *n.*

han·dle·bar *n.* [*often pl.*] a curved metal bar with handles on the ends, for steering a bicycle, etc.

hand·made *adj.* made by hand, not by machine

hand·maid·en *n.* [Archaic] a female servant: also **hand'maid'**

hand-me-down *n.* [Inf.] a used garment, etc. passed on to another person

hand·out *n.* 1 a gift of food, clothing, etc., as to a beggar 2 a leaflet handed out 3 a news release

hand·pick *vt.* 1 to pick by hand 2 to choose with care or for a purpose

hand·rail *n.* a rail serving as a guard or support, as along a staircase

hand·set *n.* a telephone mouthpiece and receiver in a single unit

hand·shake *n.* a gripping of each other's hand in greeting, agreement, etc.

hands-off *adj.* designating or of a policy, etc. of not interfering or intervening

hand·some (han'səm, hand'-) *adj.* [orig., easily handled] 1 large; considerable 2 generous; gracious 3 good-looking, esp. in a manly or impressive way —**hand'some·ly** *adv.* —**hand'some·ness** *n.*

hand·spring *n.* an acrobatic feat in which one turns over in midair with one or both hands touching the ground

hand-to-hand *adj.* at close quarters: said of fighting

hand-to-mouth *adj.* needing to consume all that is obtained

hand·work *n.* work done or made by hand

hand-wring·ing or **hand·wring·ing** *n.* expression of distress or anxiety

hand·writ·ing *n.* 1 writing done by hand, with a pen, pencil, etc. 2 a style of such writing —**hand'writ'ten** *adj.*

hand·y *adj.* **-i·er, -i·est** 1 close at hand; easily reached 2 easily used; convenient 3 clever with the hands; deft —**hand'i·ly** *adv.* —**hand'i·ness** *n.*

hand·y·man (-man') *n.*, *pl.* **-men'** (-men') a man who does odd jobs

hand·y·wom·an *n.*, *pl.* **-wom'en** a woman who does odd jobs

hang (haŋ) *vt.* **hung, hang'ing, hanged** [OE *hangian*] 1 to attach from above with no support from below; suspend 2 to attach (a door, etc.) so as to permit free motion at the point of attachment 3 to kill by suspending from a rope about the neck 4 to attach (wallpaper, etc.) to walls 5 to let (one's head) droop downward 6 to deadlock (a jury) —*vi.* 1 to be attached above with no support from below 2 to hover in the air 3 to swing freely 4 to fall or drape: said as of cloth 5 to die by hanging 6 to droop; bend —*n.* the way that a thing hangs —**get (or have) the hang of** 1 to learn (or have) the knack of 2 to understand the meaning or idea of —**hang around** [Inf.] to loiter around —**hang around with** [Inf.] to socialize with —**hang**

back to be reluctant, as from shyness —**hang in (there)** [Inf.] to persevere —**hang loose** [Slang] to be relaxed, easygoing, etc. —**hang on 1** to go on; persevere **2** to depend on **3** to listen attentively to **4** to wait for a while —**hang out** [Slang] to spend much time —**hang up 1** to put on a hanger, hook, etc. **2** to end a telephone call **3** to delay —**hang with** [Slang] to socialize with

hang·ar (haŋ'ər) *n.* [Fr] a repair shed or shelter for aircraft

hang·dog *adj.* abject or ashamed

hang·er *n.* 1 one who hangs things 2 a thing on which something is hung

hang gliding the sport of gliding through the air while hanging suspended by a harness from a kitelike glider (**hang glider**)

hang·ing *adj.* that hangs —*n.* 1 a killing by hanging 2 something hung on a wall, etc.

hang·man (-mən) *n.*, *pl.* **-men** (-mən) one who hangs convicted criminals

hang·nail *n.* [OE *angnægl*, a corn (on the toe)] a bit of torn skin hanging next to a fingernail

hang·o·ver *n.* headache, nausea, etc. as an aftereffect of drinking much alcoholic liquor

hang-up *n.* [Slang] an emotional or psychological problem, difficulty, etc.

hank (haŋk) *n.* [prob. < Scand] a skein of yarn or thread

han·ker (haŋ'kər) *vi.* [prob. < Du] to long or yearn: used with *for* —**han'ker·ing** *n.*

han·ky-pan·ky (haŋ'kē paŋ'kē) *n.* [Inf.] trickery or deception, as with illicit sex

Ha·noi (ha noi') capital of Vietnam, in the N part

han·som (cab) (han'səm) [after J. A. *Hansom* (1803–82), Eng inventor] a two-wheeled covered carriage pulled by one horse, with the driver's seat above and behind

Ha·nuk·kah (khä'noo kä', -kə; hä'-) *n.* [< Heb *chanuka*, lit., dedication] an 8-day Jewish festival commemorating the rededication of the Temple: also **Ha'nu·ka'**

hap (hap) *n.* [< ON *happ*] [Archaic] luck

hap·haz·ard (hap'haz'ərd) *adj.* not planned; random —*adv.* by chance

hap·less (hap'lis) *adj.* unlucky

hap·loid (hap'loid') *adj. Biol.* having the full number of chromosomes normally occurring in the mature germ cell, or half the number of the usual somatic cell —*n.* a haploid cell or gamete

hap·ly *adv.* [Archaic] by chance; perhaps

hap·pen (hap'ən) *vi.* [ME *happenen*] 1 to take place; occur 2 to be, occur, or come by chance 3 to have the luck or occasion [I *happened* to see it] —**happen on (or upon)** to meet or find by chance

hap·pen·ing *n.* occurrence; event

hap·pen·stance (-stans') *n.* [Inf.] a chance or accidental happening

hap·py (hap'ē) *adj.* **-pi·er, -pi·est** [< HAP] 1 lucky; fortunate 2 having, showing, or causing great pleasure or joy 3 suitable and clever; apt —**hap'pi·ly** *adv.* —**hap'pi·ness** *n.*

hap·py-go-luck·y *adj.* easygoing

happy hour a time, as in the late afternoon or

early evening, when a bar features drinks, appetizers, etc. at reduced prices

har·a·kir·i (här′ə kir′ē; *also* her′ē ker′ē) *n.* [Jpn < *hara*, belly + *kiri*, a cutting] ritual suicide by cutting the abdomen

ha·rangue (hə raŋ′) *n.* [< OIt *aringo*, site for public assemblies] a long, blustering speech; tirade — *vi., vt.* **-rangued′, -rangu′ing** to speak or address in a harangue

har·ass (har′əs, hə ras′) *vt.* [< OFr *harer*, to set a dog on] 1 to worry or torment 2 to trouble by repeated raids or attacks —**har′ass·ment** *n.*

Har·bin (här′bin) city in NE China

har·bin·ger (här′bin jər) *n.* [< OFr *herberge*, a shelter] a forerunner; herald

har·bor (här′bər) *n.* [< OE *here*, army + *beorg*, shelter] 1 a shelter 2 a protected inlet for anchoring ships; port —*vt.* 1 to shelter or house 2 to hold in the mind [to *harbor* envy] —*vi.* to take shelter Brit. sp. **har′bour**

hard (härd) *adj.* [OE *heard*] 1 firm and unyielding to the touch; solid and compact 2 powerful [a *hard* blow] 3 difficult to do, understand, or deal with 4 a) unfeeling [a *hard* heart] b) unfriendly [*hard* feelings] 5 harsh; severe 6 having mineral salts that interfere with lathering 7 energetic [a *hard* worker] 8 a) fermented; alcoholic [*hard* cider] b) containing much alcohol [*hard* liquor] 9 addictive and harmful [heroin is a *hard* drug] 10 a) of currency, not credit (said of money) b) readily accepted as foreign exchange [a *hard* currency] —*adv.* 1 energetically [*work hard*] 2 with strength [hit *hard*] 3 with difficulty [*hard*-earned] 4 close; near [we live *hard* by] 5 so as to be solid [frozen *hard*] 6 fully [turn *hard* right] —**hard and fast** invariable; strict —**hard of hearing** partially deaf —**hard up** [Inf.] in great need of money —**hard′ness** *n.*

hard·back *n.* a hardcover book

hard·ball *n.* BASEBALL

hard·bit·ten *adj.* tough; dogged

hard-boiled *adj.* 1 boiled until solid: said of an egg 2 [Inf.] unfeeling; tough; callous

hard copy a computer printout, often supplied along with or instead of a video screen display

hard·core *adj.* 1 absolute; unqualified 2 extremely explicit [*hardcore* pornography]

hard·cov·er *adj.,* *n.* (designating) any book bound in a stiff cover

hard disk a rigid magnetic disk fixed permanently within a drive unit and used for storing computer data

hard drive a computer drive for hard disks

hard·en (härd′′n) *vt., vi.* to make or become hard —**hard′en·er** *n.*

hard hat 1 a protective helmet worn by construction workers, miners, etc. **2** [Slang] such a worker

hard·head·ed *adj.* 1 shrewd and unsentimental; practical 2 stubborn; dogged

hard·heart·ed *adj.* unfeeling; cruel

har·di·hood (här′dē hood′) *n.* boldness

Har·ding (här′diŋ), **War·ren G(amaliel)** (wôr′ən, wär′-) 1865-1923; 29th president of the U.S. (1921-23)

hard-line *adj.* aggressive; unyielding, as in politics, etc.

hard-lin·er (-ər) *n.* one who takes a hard-line position

hard·ly (härd′lē) *adv.* **1** only just; scarcely **2** probably not; not likely

hard-nosed *adj.* [Inf.] tough and stubborn or shrewd

hard-pressed *adj.* confronted with a difficulty

hard science NATURAL SCIENCE

hard·scrab·ble (härd′skrab′əl) *adj.* producing or earning only a very small amount; barren [a *hardscrabble* farm, life, etc.]

hard sell high-pressure salesmanship

hard·ship *n.* a thing hard to bear, as poverty

hard·tack *n.* unleavened bread made in large, hard wafers

hard·top *n.* a motor vehicle having a rigid top

hard·ware *n.* **1** articles made of metal, as tools, nails, or fittings **2** the mechanical, magnetic, and electronic devices of a computer

hard·wood *n.* **1** any tough, heavy timber with a compact texture **2** the wood of any tree with broad, flat leaves, as the oak or maple

har·dy (här′dē) *adj.* **-di·er, -di·est** [< OFr *hardir*, to make bold] **1** bold and resolute **2** robust; vigorous —**har′di·ly** *adv.* —**har′di·ness** *n.*

hare (her, har) *n.* [OE *hara*] a mammal related to and resembling the rabbit

hare-brained *adj.* having or showing little sense; flighty, etc.

hare·lip *n.* CLEFT LIP

ha·rem (her′əm, har′-) *n.* [Ar *harīm,* lit., prohibited (place)] **1** the part of a Muslim household in which the women live **2** the women in a harem **3** a group of female animals that breed with a single male

hark (härk) *vi.* [ME *herkien*] to listen carefully: usually in the imperative —**hark back** to go back in thought or speech

hark·en (här′kən) *vi. alt. sp. of* HEARKEN

Har·lem (här′ləm) section of New York City, in N Manhattan

Har·le·quin (här′li kwin, -kin) *n.* **1** a comic character in pantomime, who wears a mask and diamond-patterned tights of many colors **2** [h-] a clown

har·lot (här′lət) *n.* [< OFr, rogue] [Old-fashioned] PROSTITUTE —**har′lot·ry** (-lə trē) *n.*

harm (härm) *n.* [OE *hearm*] hurt; injury; damage —*vt.* to do harm to

harm·ful *adj.* causing harm; hurtful —**harm′ful·ly** *adv.* —**harm′ful·ness** *n.*

harm·less *adj.* causing no harm —**harm′less·ly** *adv.* —**harm′less·ness** *n.*

har·mon·ic (här män′ik) *adj.* of or in harmony —*n. Music* a pure tone making up a composite tone —**har·mon′i·cal·ly** *adv.*

har·mon·i·ca (-i kə) *n.* a small wind instrument with metal reeds that vibrate and produce tones when air is blown or sucked across them

har·mo·ni·ous (här mō′nē əs) *adj.* **1** having

parts arranged in an orderly or pleasing way **2** having similar ideas, interests, etc. **3** having musical tones combined to give a pleasing effect —**har·mo·ni·ous·ly** *adv.*

har·mo·nize (här′mə nīz′) *vi.* **-nized′, -niz′ing 1** to be in harmony **2** to sing in harmony —*vt.* to make harmonious —**har′mo·ni·za′tion** *n.* —**har′mo·niz′er** *n.*

har·mo·ny (här′mə nē) *n., pl.* **-nies** [< Gr *harmos,* a fitting] **1** pleasing arrangement of parts in color, size, etc. **2** agreement in action, ideas, etc.; friendly relations **3** the sounding of two or more tones together in a chord, esp. when satisfying

har·ness (här′nis) *n.* [< OFr *harneis,* armor] **1** [Archaic] armor, etc. for a man or horse **2** the combination of leather straps and metal pieces by which a horse, etc. is fastened to a vehicle, etc. **3** anything like this —*vt.* **1** to put a harness on **2** to make use of the power of

harp (härp) *n.* [OE *hearpe*] a musical instrument having strings stretched vertically in an open, triangular frame and played by plucking —*vi.* **1** to play a harp **2** to persist in talking or writing tediously (*on* or *upon* something) —**harp′ist** *n.*

Har·pers Ferry (här′pərz) town in West Virginia: site of an antislavery raid (1859)

har·poon (här pōōn′) *n.* [< ON *harpa,* to squeeze] a barbed spear with a line attached to it, used for spearing whales, etc. —*vt.* to strike or catch with a harpoon

harp·si·chord (härp′si kôrd′) *n.* [< It *arpa,* harp + *corda,* CORD] a pianolike keyboard instrument whose strings are plucked rather than struck —**harp′si·chord′ist** *n.*

Har·py (här′pē) *n., pl.* **-pies** [< Gr *harpazein,* to snatch] **1** *Gr. Myth.* any of several monsters, part woman and part bird **2** [**h-**] *a)* a greedy person *b)* a shrewish woman

har·ri·dan (har′i dən) *n.* [prob. < Fr *haridelle,* worn-out horse] a nasty, bad-tempered old woman

har·ri·er (har′ē ər) *n.* [< HARE + -IER] **1** a small hound used for hunting hares **2** a cross-country runner

Har·ris·burg (har′is burg′) capital of Pennsylvania, in the S part

Har·ri·son (har′ə sən) **1** *Ben·ja·min* (ben′jə mən) 1833-1901; 23d president of the U.S. (1889-93): grandson of William Henry **2** *William Henry* 1773-1841; 9th president of the U.S. (1841)

har·row (har′ō) *n.* [prob. < ON] a heavy frame with spikes or disks, used for breaking up and leveling plowed ground, etc. —*vt.* **1** to draw a harrow over (land) **2** to cause mental distress to —**har′row·ing** *adj.*

har·ry (har′ē) *vt.* **-ried, -ry·ing** [< OE *here,* army] **1** to raid and ravage or rob **2** to torment or worry

harsh (härsh) *adj.* [ME *harsk*] **1** unpleasantly rough or sharp to the eye, ear, taste, or touch **2** offensive to the mind or feelings **3** cruel or severe —**harsh′ly** *adv.* —**harsh′ness** *n.*

hart (härt) *n.* [OE *heorot*] a full-grown, male European red deer

har·te·beest (här′tə bēst′, härt′bēst′) *n.* [obs. Afrik < *harte,* hart + *beest,* beast] a large African antelope with long horns curved backward

Hart·ford (härt′fərd) capital of Connecticut, in the central part

har·um-scar·um (her′əm sker′əm) *adj.* [< ?] reckless or irresponsible —*adv.* in a harum-scarum way

har·vest (här′vist) *n.* [OE *hærfest*] **1** the time of the year when grain, fruit, etc. are gathered in **2** a season's crop **3** the gathering in of a crop **4** the outcome of any effort — *vt., vi.* to gather in (a crop, etc.) —**har′vest·er** *n.*

has (haz; *before* "to", has) *vt. 3d pers. sing., pres. indic., of* HAVE

has-been *n.* [Inf.] a person or thing whose popularity is past

hash[1] (hash) *vt.* [< Fr *hacher,* to chop] to chop up (meat or vegetables) for cooking —*n.* **1** a chopped mixture of cooked meat and vegetables **2** a mixture **3** a muddle **4** [Slang] hashish —**hash out** [Inf.] to settle by long discussion —**hash over** [Inf.] to discuss at length

hash[2] (hash) *n.* [Slang] *short for* HASHISH

hash[3] (hash) *n.* [Chiefly Brit.] the symbol (#); pound sign: also **hash sign**

hash·ish (hash′ēsh′, ha shēsh′) *n.* [Ar *ḥashīsh,* dried hemp] a narcotic and intoxicant made from hemp

hash·tag (hash′tag′) *n.* [< HASH[3] + TAG] a word or phrase after the (#) symbol, used in social networking to facilitate searches for a particular subject

hasp (hasp, häsp) *n.* [OE *hæsp*] a hinged fastening for a door, etc.; esp., a metal piece fitted over a staple and held in place by a pin or padlock

has·si·um (has′ē əm) *n.* [after the L name for *Hesse,* a region of Germany] an artificially produced radioactive chemical element: symbol, Hs: at. no. 108

has·sle (has′əl) *n.* [< ?] [Inf.] **1** a heated argument; squabble **2** an annoyance, impediment, etc. —*vi.* **-sled, -sling** [Inf.] to have a hassle —*vt.* [Slang] to annoy, harass, etc.

has·sock (has′ək) *n.* [OE *hassuc,* (clump of) coarse grass] a firm cushion used as a footstool or seat

hast (hast) *vt. archaic 2d pers. sing., pres. indic., of* HAVE: used with *thou*

haste (hāst) *n.* [OFr] **1** quickness of motion; rapidity **2** careless or reckless hurrying — **make haste** to hurry

has·ten (hās′ən) *vt.* to cause to be or come faster; speed up —*vi.* to move or act swiftly; hurry

hast·y (hās′tē) *adj.* **-i·er, -i·est 1** done with haste; hurried **2** done, made, or acting rashly or too quickly —**hast′i·ly** *adv.* —**hast′i·ness** *n.*

hat (hat) *n.* [OE *hætt*] a head covering, usually with a brim and a crown —**pass the hat** to take up a collection —**talk through one's hat** [Inf.] to talk nonsense —**throw one's**

hat into the ring to enter a contest, esp. one for political office —**under one's hat** [Inf.] strictly confidential

hatch¹ (hach) *vt.* [ME *hacchen*] 1 to bring forth (young) from (an egg or eggs) 2 to contrive (a plan, plot, etc.) —*vi.* 1 to bring forth young: said of eggs 2 to emerge from the egg

hatch² (hach) *n.* [OE *hæcc*, grating] 1 HATCH-WAY 2 a lid for a hatchway

hatch·back *n.* [prec. + BACK] an automobile with a rear section that swings up, giving wide entry to a storage area

hat·check *adj.* of or working in a checkroom for hats, coats, etc.

hatch·er·y *n.*, *pl.* -**ies** a place for hatching eggs, esp. of fish or poultry

hatch·et (hach′it) *n.* [< OFr *hache*, an ax] a small ax with a short handle —**bury the hatchet** to make peace

hatchet job [Inf.] a biased, malicious attack on another's character

hatch·way *n.* an opening in a ship's deck, or in a floor or roof

hate (hāt) *vt.* **hat′ed**, **hat′ing** [OE *hatian*] 1 to have strong dislike or ill will for 2 to wish to avoid [to *hate* fights] —*vi.* to feel hatred —*n.* 1 a strong feeling of dislike or ill will; hatred 2 a person or thing hated —**hat′er** *n.*

hate·ful *adj.* 1 causing or deserving hate; loathsome 2 full of or expressing hate —**hate′ful·ly** *adv.* —**hate′ful·ness** *n.*

hath (hath) *vt.* archaic 3d pers. sing., pres. in dic., of HAVE

ha·tred (hā′trid) *n.* strong dislike or ill will; hate

hat·ter (hat′ər) *n.* one who makes, sells, or cleans hats, esp. men's hats

hau·berk (hô′bərk) *n.* [< Frankish *hals*, neck + *bergan*, to protect] a medieval coat of armor, usually of chain mail

haugh·ty (hôt′ē) *adj.* -**ti·er**, -**ti·est** [< OFr *haut*, high] having or showing great pride in oneself and contempt for others; arrogant —**haugh′ti·ly** *adv.* —**haugh′ti·ness** *n.*

haul (hôl) *vt.* [< OFr *haler*] 1 to move by pulling; drag 2 to transport by wagon, truck, etc. —*n.* 1 the act of hauling; pull 2 [Inf.] the amount gained, earned, etc. at one time 3 the distance over which something is transported —**haul off** [Inf.] to draw the arm back before hitting —**in** (or **over**) **the long haul** over a long period of time

haunch (hônch, hänch) *n.* [< OFr *hanche* < Gmc] 1 the hip, buttock, and upper thigh together 2 an animal's loin and leg together

haunt (hônt) *vt.* [< OFr *hanter*, to frequent] 1 to visit often or continually: often used of ghosts and spirits 2 to recur repeatedly to [*haunted* by memories] —*n.* a place often visited

haunt·ed *adj.* frequented by ghosts

haunt·ing *adj.* not easily forgotten

haute cou·ture (ōt′ kōō tōōr′) [Fr, high sewing] high fashion

haute cui·sine (ōt′ kwē zēn′) [Fr, high kitch-en] 1 the preparation of fine food by skilled chefs 2 food prepared in this way

hau·teur (hō tur′) *n.* [Fr < *haut*, high] disdainful pride; haughtiness

Ha·van·a¹ (hə van′ə) *n.* a cigar made of Cuban tobacco

Havana² capital of Cuba

have (hav; *before* "to" haf) *vt.* **had**, **hav′ing** [OE *habban*] 1 to hold; own; possess [to *have* money, a week *has* 7 days] 2 to experience [*have* a good time] 3 to hold mentally [to *have* an idea] 4 to state [so rumor *has* it] 5 to get, take, consume, etc. [*have* a drink] 6 to bear or beget (offspring) 7 to engage in [to have a fight] 8 to cause to or cause to be [*have* her sing] 9 to permit; tolerate [I won't *have* this noise!] 10 [Inf.] *a*) to hold at a disadvantage *b*) to deceive; cheat *Have* is used as an auxiliary to express completed action (Ex.: I *had* left) and with infinitives to express obligation or necessity (Ex.: we *have* to go). *Have got* often replaces *have*. *Have* is conjugated in the present indicative: (I) *have*, (he, she, it) *has*, (we, you, they) *have* —*n.* a wealthy person or nation —**have it out** to settle an issue by fighting or discussion —**have on** to be wearing

ha·ven (hā′vən) *n.* [OE *hæfen*] 1 a port 2 any sheltered place; refuge

have-not (hav′nät′) *n.* a person, nation, etc. with little or no wealth

hav·er·sack (hav′ər sak′) *n.* [< Ger *habersack*, lit., sack of oats] a bag for rations, etc., worn over one shoulder, as by a soldier

hav·oc (hav′ək, -äk′) *n.* [< OFr *havot*] great destruction and devastation —**play havoc with** to devastate; ruin

haw¹ (hô) *n.* [OE *haga*] 1 the berry of the hawthorn 2 HAWTHORN

haw² (hô) *vi.* [echoic] see HEM AND HAW *under* HEM²

Ha·wai·i (hə wä′ē, -wī′ē) 1 state of the U.S., consisting of a group of islands (**Hawaiian Islands**) in the N Pacific; cap. Honolulu: abbrev. HI 2 the largest of these islands —**Ha·wai′ian** (-yən) *adj.*, *n.*

hawk¹ (hôk) *n.* [OE *hafoc*] 1 a bird of prey with broad wings and a hooked beak and claws 2 an advocate of war

hawk² (hôk) *vt.* [< HAWKER] to advertise or peddle (goods) in the streets by shouting

hawk³ (hôk) *vi.*, *vt.* [echoic] to clear the throat (of) audibly

hawk·er *n.* [< Old LowG *hoker*] a peddler or huckster

hawk-eyed (-īd′) *adj.* keen-sighted

haw·ser (hô′zər) *n.* [< OFr *haucier* < L *altus*, high] a large rope used as for mooring a ship

haw·thorn (hô′thôrn′) *n.* [< OE *haga*, hedge + THORN] a thorny shrub or small tree of the rose family, with flowers and small, red fruits

Haw·thorne (hô′thôrn′), **Na·than·iel** (nə than′yəl) 1804–64; U.S. writer

hay (hā) *n.* [< OE *hieg*] grass, clover, etc. cut and dried for fodder —*vi.* to mow and dry grass, etc. for hay —**hit the hay** [Slang] to go to bed to sleep

hay·cock *n.* a small, conical heap of hay drying in a field

Hay·dn (hīd′'n), **(Franz) Jo·seph** (yō′zef) 1732-1809; Austrian composer

Hayes (hāz), **Ruth·er·ford B(irchard)** (ruth′ ər fərd) 1822-93; 19th president of the U.S. (1877-81)

hay fever an allergy to pollen, causing inflammation of the eyes and respiratory tract

hay·loft *n.* a loft, or upper story, in a barn or stable, for storing hay

hay·mow (-mou′) *n.* **1** a pile of hay in a barn **2** HAYLOFT

hay·stack *n.* a large heap of hay piled up outdoors

hay·wire *adj.* [Inf.] **1** out of order; disorganized **2** crazy —**go haywire** [Inf.] **1** to behave erratically or crazily **2** to become crazy

haz·ard (haz′ərd) *n.* [< OFr *hasard*, game of dice] **1** risk; danger **2** an obstacle on a golf course —*vt.* to risk —**haz′ard·ous** *adj.*

haze[1] (hāz) *n.* [prob. < HAZY] **1** a thin cloud of fog, smoke, etc. in the air **2** a slight vagueness of mind —*vi., vt.* **hazed, haz′ing** to make or become hazy: often with *over*

haze[2] (hāz) *vt.* **hazed, haz′ing** [< ?] to initiate or discipline by forcing to do ridiculous or painful things

ha·zel (hā′zəl) *n.* [OE *hæsel*] **1** a shrub or tree of the birch family, with edible nuts **2** a reddish brown —*adj.* **1** light reddish-brown **2** greenish-gray or greenish-brown: said of eyes

ha·zel·nut *n.* FILBERT

ha·zy (hā′zē) *adj.* **-zi·er, -zi·est** [prob. < OE *hasu*, dusky] **1** somewhat foggy or smoky **2** somewhat vague —**ha′zi·ly** *adv.* —**ha′zi·ness** *n.*

H-bomb (āch′bäm′) *n.* HYDROGEN BOMB

HD *abbrev.* high-definition

hdqrs *abbrev.* headquarters

HDTV *abbrev.* high-definition television

he (hē) *pron., pl. see* THEY [OE] **1** the man, boy, or male animal previously mentioned **2** anyone [*he* who laughs last laughs best] —*n., pl.* **hes** a male

He *Chem. symbol for* helium

head (hed) *n.* [OE *heafod*] **1** the part of the body containing the brain, jaws, eyes, ears, nose, mouth, etc. **2** the mind; intelligence **3** *pl.* **head** a unit of counting [ten *head* of cattle] **4** the main side of a coin: often **heads 5** the uppermost part or thing; top **6** the topic or title of a section, chapter, etc. **7** the foremost or projecting part; front **8** the part designed for holding, striking, etc. [the *head* of a nail] **9** the part of a tape recorder that records or reads the magnetic signals on the tape **10** the membrane across the end of a drum, etc. **11** the source of a river, etc. **12** froth, as on beer **13** a position of leadership or honor **14** a leader, ruler, etc. **15** *Bot.* a dense cluster of small flowers **16** [Slang] a person dedicated to, addicted to, etc. some interest, activity, etc. —*adj.* **1** most important; principal **2** at the top or front **3** striking against the front [*head* winds] —*vt.* **1** to be

the chief of; command **2** to lead; precede **3** to cause to go in a specified direction —*vi.* to set out; travel —**come to a head 1** to be about to suppurate, as a boil **2** to culminate, or reach a crisis —**go to someone's head 1** to confuse or intoxicate someone **2** to make someone vain —**head off** to get ahead of and intercept —**heads up!** [Inf.] look out! completely —**heads up!** [Inf.] look out! — **keep** (or **lose**) **one's head** to keep (or lose) one's poise, self-control, etc. —**on** (or **upon**) **someone's head** as someone's responsibility or misfortune —**over someone's head 1** too difficult for someone to understand **2** to a higher authority —**turn someone's head** to make one vain —**head′less** *adj.*

head·ache *n.* **1** a continuous pain in the head **2** [Inf.] a cause of worry, annoyance, or trouble

head·board *n.* a board that forms the head of a bed, etc.

head cold a common cold with congestion of the nasal passages

head·dress *n.* a ceremonial head covering

-head·ed (hed′id) *combining form* having a (specified kind or number of) head or heads [lightheaded, two-headed]

head·er *n.* **1** a pipe, etc. that brings other pipes together, as in an exhaust system **2** in word processing, text repeated at the top of each page **3** [Inf.] a headlong fall or dive

head·first *adv.* **1** with the head in front; headlong **2** recklessly —*adj.* with the head first

head·gear *n.* a hat, cap, etc.

head·ing *n.* **1** something forming the head, top, or front **2** the title, topic, etc., as of a chapter **3** the direction in which a ship, plane, etc. is moving

head·land (-lənd) *n.* a cape or point of land reaching out into the water; promontory

head·light *n.* a light with a reflector and lens, at the front of a vehicle

head·line *n.* words in large type at the top of an article, as in a newspaper, giving the topic —*vt.* **-lined′, -lin′ing 1** to give (a performer, etc.) featured billing or publicity **2** to be the featured performer, etc. in

head·long (-lôŋ′) *adv., adj.* [ME *hedelinge(s)*] **1** with the head first **2** with uncontrolled speed or force **3** reckless(ly); rash(ly)

head·mas·ter *n.* a man who is the principal of a private school

head·mis·tress *n.* a woman who is the principal of a private school

head-on *adj., adv.* **1** with the head or front foremost [a *head-on* collision] **2** directly [to meet a problem *head-on*]

head·phone *n.* [*usually pl.*] a listening device for a radio, stereo, etc. worn over the head to position its speakers over the ears

head·quar·ters *n.* [*with sing. or pl. v.*] **1** the main office, or center of operations, of one in command, as in an army **2** the main office in any organization

head·rest *n.* a support for the head

head·room *n.* space overhead, as in a doorway, tunnel, etc.

head start an early start or other competitive advantage

head·stone *n.* a stone marker placed at the head of a grave

head·strong *adj.* determined to do as one pleases

heads-up (hedz′up′) [Inf.] *adj.* [< phrase HEADS UP!: see HEAD] —*n.* the act or an instance of warning or alerting someone in advance

head·wa·ters *pl.n.* the small streams that are the sources of a river

head·way *n.* 1 forward motion 2 progress or success

head·y *adj.* -i·er, -i·est 1 intoxicating 2 having, using, etc. good judgment or intelligence

heal (hēl) *vt., vi.* [OE *hælan*] 1 to make or become well or healthy again 2 to cure (a disease) or mend, as a wound —**heal′er** *n.*

health (helth) *n.* [OE *hælth*] 1 physical and mental well-being; freedom from disease, etc. 2 condition of body or mind [poor *health*] 3 a wish for one's health and happiness, as in a toast 4 soundness, as of a society or culture

health·care *n.* the prevention and treatment of illness or injury on an ongoing basis

health food food thought to be especially healthful; specif., food grown with natural fertilizers, free of chemical additives, etc.

health·ful *adj.* helping to produce or maintain health; wholesome

health·y *adj.* -i·er, -i·est 1 having good health 2 showing or resulting from good health [a *healthy* color] 3 HEALTHFUL —**health′i·ness** *n.*

heap (hēp) *n.* [< OE *heap*, a troop] 1 a pile or mass of jumbled things 2 [*often pl.*] [Inf.] a large amount —*vt.* 1 to make a heap of 2 to give in large amounts 3 to fill (a plate, etc.) full or to overflowing —*vi.* to rise in a heap

hear (hir) *vt.* **heard** (hurd), **hear′ing** [OE *hieran*] 1 to be aware of (sounds) by the ear 2 to listen to 3 to conduct a hearing of (a law case, etc.) 4 to be informed of; learn 5 to understand —*vi.* 1 to be able to hear sounds 2 to be told (*of* or *about*) —**hear from** to get a call, etc. from —**hear! hear!** well said! —**will** (or **would**) **not hear of** to refuse to consider —**hear′er** *n.*

hear·ing *n.* 1 the act or process of perceiving sounds 2 the ability to hear 3 an opportunity to be heard 4 an appearance before a judge, investigative committee, etc. 5 the distance a sound will carry [within *hearing*]

heark·en (härk′ən) *vi.* [OE *heorcnian*] [Now Literary] to listen carefully; pay heed: with *to*

hear·say (hir′sā′) *n.* 1 rumor; gossip 2 *Law* inadmissible testimony consisting of a report given by another

hearse (hurs) *n.* [< L *hirpex*, a harrow] a vehicle used in a funeral for carrying the corpse

heart (härt) *n.* [OE *heorte*] 1 the hollow, muscular organ that circulates the blood by alternate dilation and contraction 2 the central, vital, or main part; core 3 the human heart considered as the center of emotions, etc.; specif., *a*) inmost thought and feeling *b*) love, sympathy, etc. *c*) spirit or courage 4 a conventionalized design of a heart (♡) 5 any of a suit of playing cards marked with such symbols in red —**after someone's own heart** that one finds congenial —**by heart** by or from memorization —**set one's heart on** to have a fixed desire for —**take to heart** 1 to consider seriously 2 to be troubled by

heart·ache *n.* sorrow or grief

heart attack any sudden instance of heart failure; esp., a coronary

heart·beat *n.* 1 one full contraction and dilation of the heart 2 a moment; instant

heart·break *n.* overwhelming sorrow, grief, etc. —**heart′break′ing** *adj.* —**heart′bro′ken** *adj.*

heart·break·er *n.* one that causes heartbreak

heart·burn *n.* a burning, acid sensation beneath the breastbone

-heart·ed (härt′id) [ME] *combining form* having a (specified kind of) heart [stouthearted]

heart·en (härt′'n) *vt.* to encourage

heart failure the inability of the heart to pump enough blood to supply the body tissues adequately

heart·felt *adj.* sincere; genuine

hearth (härth) *n.* [OE *heorth*] 1 the stone or brick floor of a fireplace 2 *a*) the fireside *b*) family life; home

heart·land *n.* a geographically central area having crucial importance

heart·less *adj.* unkind; unfeeling —**heart′less·ly** *adv.* —**heart′less·ness** *n.*

heart-rend·ing *adj.* causing much grief or mental anguish

heart·sick *adj.* sick at heart; extremely unhappy or despondent

heart·strings *pl.n.* deepest feelings

heart-to-heart *adj.* intimate and candid —*n.* an intimate and candid conversation

heart·warm·ing *adj.* causing genial feelings

heart·y *adj.* -i·er, -i·est 1 warm and friendly; cordial 2 strongly felt; unrestrained [hearty laughter] 3 strong and healthy 4 nourishing and plentiful [a *hearty* meal] —**heart′i·ly** *adv.* —**heart′i·ness** *n.*

heat (hēt) *n.* [OE *hætu*] 1 the quality of being hot; hotness, or the perception of this 2 much hotness 3 hot weather or climate 4 the warming of a house, etc. 5 *a*) strong feeling; ardor, anger, etc. *b*) the period of this 6 a single bout, round, or trial 7 the period of sexual excitement in a female animal 8 [Slang] coercion —*vt., vi.* 1 to make or become warm or hot 2 to make or become excited

heat·ed *adj.* 1 hot 2 vehement or angry —**heat′ed·ly** *adv.*

heat·er *n.* an apparatus for giving heat; stove, furnace, radiator, etc.

heath (hēth) *n.* [OE *hæth*] 1 a tract of open wasteland, esp. in the British Isles 2 any of various shrubs that grow on heaths, as heather

hea·then (hē′thən) *n., pl.* -**thens** or -**then** [OE *hæthen*] 1 anyone not a Jew, Christian, or Muslim; esp., a polytheist: often a disparaging term **2** a person regarded as irreligious, uncivilized, etc. —*adj.* **1** pagan **2** irreligious, uncivilized, etc. —**hea'then·ish** *adj.*

heath·er (heth'ər) *n.* ⟦ME *haddyr*⟧ a low-growing plant of the heath family with very small leaves and small, bell-shaped, purplish-pink flowers

heat index a number calculated from temperature and relative humidity, used to indicate perceived temperature

heating pad a pad consisting of an electric heating element covered with fabric, for applying heat to the body

heat lightning lightning without thunder, seen on hot evenings

heat rash a rash caused by inflammation of the sweat glands

heat·stroke *n.* a condition of high fever, collapse, etc. resulting from exposure to intense heat: also **heat stroke**

heat wave 1 unusually hot weather **2** a period of such weather

heave (hēv) *vt.* **heaved** or (esp. *Naut.*) **hove,** **heav'ing** ⟦OE *hebban*⟧ **1** to lift, esp. with effort **2** to lift in this way and throw **3** to utter (a sigh, etc.) with effort —*vi.* **1** to swell up **2** to rise and fall rhythmically **3** *a)* to vomit *b)* to pant; gasp —*n.* the act or effort of heaving —**heave to** *Naut.* to stop

heave-ho (-hō') *n.* [Inf.] dismissal, as from a job: chiefly in **give** (or **get**) **the** (**old**) **heave-ho**

heav·en (hev'ən) *n.* ⟦OE *heofon*⟧ **1** [*usually pl.*] the visible sky; firmament **2** [*often* H-] *Theol. a)* a state or place of complete happiness, etc. attained by the good after death *b)* the abode of God, his angels, and the blessed *c)* God **3** any place of great beauty or state of great happiness —**heav'en·ly** *adj.*

heav·en·ward *adv., adj.* toward heaven: also **heav'en·wards** *adv.*

heav·y (hev'ē) *adj.* **-i·er, -i·est** ⟦OE *hefig*⟧ **1** hard to lift because of great weight **2** of more than the usual, expected, or defined weight **3** larger, greater, or more intense than usual [*a heavy blow, a heavy vote*] **4** to an unusual extent [*a heavy drinker*] **5** hard to do [*heavy work*] **6** sorrowful [*a heavy heart*] **7** burdened with sleep [*heavy eyelids*] **8** hard to digest [*a heavy meal*] **9** clinging; penetrating [*a heavy odor*] **10** cloudy; gloomy [*a heavy sky*] **11** designating any large, basic industry that uses massive machinery **12** [Slang] serious and, often, depressing —*adv.* in a heavy manner —*n., pl.* **-ies 1** *Film, Theater, etc.* a villain **2** [Slang] an important person —**heav'i·ly** *adv.* —**heav'i·ness** *n.*

heav·y-du·ty *adj.* made to withstand great strain, bad weather, etc.

heav·y-hand·ed *adj.* **1** clumsy or tactless **2** oppressive or tyrannical

heav·y-heart·ed *adj.* sad; depressed

heav·y-set *adj.* having a stocky build

heav·y·weight *n.* **1** one weighing more than average; esp., a boxer in the heaviest weight

class **2** [Inf.] a very influential or important person

He·bra·ic (hē brā'ik, hi-) *adj.* of or characteristic of the Hebrews, their language, or culture; Hebrew

He·brew (hē'brōō') *n.* **1** *a)* a member of an ancient Semitic people; Israelite *b)* a Jew **2** *a)* the ancient Semitic language of the Israelites *b)* its modern form, the language of Israel —*adj.* **1** of Hebrew or the Hebrews **2** JEWISH

Heb·ri·des (heb'rə dēz') group of islands off the W coast of Scotland

heck (hek) *interj., n.* [Inf.] *euphemism for* HELL

heck·le (hek'əl) *vt.* **-led, -ling** ⟦ME *hechele*⟧ to harass (a speaker) by interrupting with questions or taunts —**heck'ler** *n.*

hec·tare (hek'ter') *n.* ⟦Fr⟧ a metric unit of area, 10,000 square meters

hec·tic (hek'tik) *adj.* ⟦< Gr *hektikos,* habitual⟧ **1** feverish; flushed **2** confused, rushed, etc. —**hec'ti·cal·ly** *adv.*

Hec·tor (hek'tər) *n.* in Homer's *Iliad,* a Trojan hero, killed by Achilles —*vt., vi.* [h-] to browbeat; bully

hedge (hej) *n.* ⟦OE *hecg*⟧ **1** a dense row of shrubs, etc. forming a boundary **2** any fence or barrier **3** a hedging —*vt.* **hedged, hedg'ing 1** to put a hedge around **2** to hinder or guard as with a barrier: often with *in* **3** to try to avoid loss in (a bet, etc.) by making counterbalancing bets, etc. —*vi.* to avoid giving a direct answer

hedge fund a partnership of investors who pool large sums for speculating in securities

hedge·hog *n.* **1** a small, insect-eating mammal of the Old World, with sharp spines on the back **2** the American porcupine

he·don·ism (hēd''n iz'əm) *n.* ⟦< Gr *hēdonē,* pleasure + -ISM⟧ the self-indulgent pursuit of pleasure as a way of life —**he'don·ist** *n.* —**he'do·nis'tic** *adj.*

-he·dron (hē'drən) ⟦< Gr⟧ *combining form* a geometric figure or crystal having (a specified number of) surfaces

heed (hēd) *vt., vi.* ⟦OE *hedan*⟧ to pay close attention (to) —*n.* close attention —**heed'ful** *adj.* —**heed'less** *adj.* —**heed'less·ly** *adv.* —**heed'less·ness** *n.*

hee-haw (hē'hô') *n., vi.* [echoic] bray

heel[1] (hēl) *n.* ⟦OE *hela*⟧ **1** the back part of the foot, under the ankle **2** that part of a stocking, shoe, etc. at the heel **3** anything like a heel in location, shape, crushing power, etc. **4** [Inf.] a despicable person —*vt.* **1** to furnish with a heel **2** to follow closely **3** [Inf.] to provide (a person) with money, etc. —*vi.* to follow along at the heels of someone —**down at** (**the**) **heel** (or **heels**) shabby; seedy —**kick up one's heels** have fun —**on** (or **upon**) **the heels of** close behind

heel[2] (hēl) *vi.* ⟦OE *hieldan*⟧ to lean to one side: said esp. of a ship —*vt.* to cause (a ship) to heel

heft (heft) [Inf.] *n.* ⟦< base of HEAVE⟧ **1**

weight; heaviness **2** importance; influence —*vt.* to try to judge the weight of by lifting

heft·y *adj.* **-i·er, -i·est** [Inf.] **1** heavy **2** large and powerful **3** big —**heft′i·ness** *n.*

he·gem·o·ny (hi jem′ə nē) *n., pl.* **-nies** [< Gr *hēgeisthai*, to lead] leadership or dominance, esp. that of one state or nation over others

he·gi·ra (hi jī′rə) *n.* [< Ar *hijrah*, flight] **1** [*often* H-] Muhammad's flight from Mecca in A.D. 622 **2** a journey, esp. one made to escape

Hei·del·berg (hīd′′l burg′) city in SW Germany: site of a famous university

heif·er (hef′ər) *n.* [OE *heahfore*] a young cow that has not borne a calf

height (hīt) *n.* [< OE *heah*, high] **1** the topmost point **2** the highest limit; extreme **3** the distance from the bottom to the top **4** elevation above a given level; altitude **5** a relatively great distance above a given level **6** [*often pl.*] an elevation; hill

height·en (-'n) *vt., vi.* **1** to bring or come to a higher position **2** to make or become larger, greater, etc.

Heim·lich maneuver (hīm′lik) [after H. J. *Heimlich*, 20th-c. U.S. surgeon] an emergency technique for dislodging an object stuck in the windpipe, using air forced up the windpipe by applying sharp pressure to the abdomen

hei·nous (hā′nəs) *adj.* [< OFr *hair*, to hate] outrageously evil —**hei′nous·ly** *adv.* —**hei′nous·ness** *n.*

heir (er) *n.* [< L *heres*] one who inherits or is entitled to inherit another's property, title, etc.

heir apparent *pl.* **heirs apparent** the heir whose right to inherit cannot be denied if the heir outlives the ancestor and the ancestor dies intestate

heir·ess (-is) *n.* a female heir, esp. to great wealth

heir·loom *n.* [see HEIR & LOOM[1]] any treasured possession handed down from generation to generation

heist (hīst) [Slang] *n.* [< HOIST] a robbery —*vt.* to rob or steal

held (held) *vt., vi. pt. & pp.* of HOLD[1]

Hel·e·na (hel′ə nə) capital of Montana

Helen of Troy *Gr. Legend* the beautiful wife of the king of Sparta: the Trojan War is started because of her abduction by Paris to Troy

hel·i·cal (hel′i kəl) *adj.* [< Gr *helix*, spiral] shaped like a helix; spiral

hel·i·cop·ter (hel′i käp′tər) *n.* [< Gr *helix*, spiral + *pteron*, wing] a vertical-lift aircraft, capable of hovering or moving in any direction, having a motor-driven, horizontal rotor —*vi., vt.* to travel or convey by helicopter

he·li·o·cen·tric (hē′lē ō sen′trik) *adj.* [< Gr *hēlios*, the sun + *kentron*, a point] having or regarding the sun as the center

he·li·o·trope (hē′lē ə trōp′) *n.* [< Gr *hēlios*, the sun + *trepein*, to turn] **1** a plant with fragrant clusters of small, white or reddish-purple flowers **2** reddish purple —*adj.* reddish-purple

hel·i·pad (hel′i pad′) *n.* a landing pad for helicopters

hel·i·port *n.* an airport for helicopters

he·li·um (hē′lē əm) *n.* [< Gr *hēlios*, the sun] a chemical element, a colorless, odorless, very light, nonreactive gas having the lowest known boiling and melting points: symbol, He; at. no. 2

he·lix (hē′liks) *n., pl.* **-lix·es** or **hel·i·ces** (hel′i sēz′) [L & Gr] a spiral

hell (hel) *n.* [< OE *helan*, to hide] **1** [*often* H-] *Theol.* the state or place of total and final separation from God and so of eternal misery and suffering, arrived at by those who die unrepentant in grave sin **2** any place or condition of evil, pain, etc. —**catch** (or **get**) **hell** [Slang] to receive a severe scolding, punishment, etc.

hell-bent or **hell·bent** *adj.* [Slang] **1** recklessly determined **2** moving fast or recklessly

hell·cat *n.* an evil, spiteful woman

hel·le·bore (hel′ə bôr′) *n.* [< Gr *helleboros*] a plant with buttercuplike flowers, whose rhizomes were once used in medicine

Hel·len·ic (hə len′ik) *adj.* **1** Greek **2** of the history, language, or culture of the ancient Greeks —**Hel·len·ism** (hel′ən iz′əm) *n.* —**Hel′len·is′tic** *adj.*

hell·gram·mite or **hell·gra·mite** (hel′grəm īt′) *n.* [< ?] a dark-brown, aquatic fly larva, often used as fish bait

hell·ion (hel′yən) *n.* [< Scot dial. *hallion*, a low fellow] [Inf.] one who is recklessly mischievous; troublemaker

hell·ish *adj.* **1** devilish; fiendish **2** [Inf.] very unpleasant —**hell′ish·ly** *adv.* —**hell′ish·ness** *n.*

hel·lo (he lō′, hel′ō′) *interj.* used to express greeting

helm (helm) *n.* [OE *helma*] **1** the wheel or tiller by which a ship is steered **2** the control or leadership of an organization, government, etc.

hel·met (hel′mət) *n.* [< OFr *helme*] a protective, rigid head covering for use in combat, certain sports, etc.

helms·man (helmz′mən) *n., pl.* **-men** (-mən) a man who steers a ship

hel·ot (hel′ət) *n.* [after *Helos*, ancient Greek town] a serf or slave

help (help) *vt.* [OE *helpan*] **1** to make things easier or better for; aid; assist **2** to relieve [to *help* a cough] **3** to keep from; avoid [can't *help* crying] **4** to serve or wait on (a customer, etc.) —*vi.* to give aid; be useful —*n.* **1** a helping; aid; assistance **2** relief **3** one that helps; esp., a hired person or persons; servant(s), farmhand(s), etc. —*interj.* used to summon assistance, esp. urgently —**cannot help but** cannot fail to —**help oneself** to take without asking —**help out** to help in getting or doing something —**help′er** *n.*

help·ful *adj.* giving help; useful —**help′ful·ly** *adv.* —**help′ful·ness** *n.*

help·ing *n.* a portion of food served to one person

help·less *adj.* **1** not able to help oneself;

weak 2 lacking help or protection 3 incompetent or ineffective —**help′less·ly** *adv.* —**help′less·ness** *n.*

help·mate *n.* [< fol.] a helpful companion; specif., a wife or husband

help·meet *n.* [misreading of "an *help meet* for him" (Genesis 2:18)] HELPMATE

Hel·sin·ki (hel′siŋ kē) capital of Finland

hel·ter-skel·ter (hel′tər skel′tər) *adv.* in haste and confusion —*adj.* disorderly

helve (helv) *n.* [OE *helfe*] the handle of a tool, esp. of an ax

Hel·ve·tian (hel vē′shən) *adj., n.* Swiss

hem[1] (hem) *n.* [OE] the border on a garment, etc. made by folding the edge and sewing it down —*vt.* **hemmed, hem′ming** to fold back the edge of and sew down —**hem in 1** to encircle **2** to confine

hem[2] (hem) *interj., n.* the sound made in clearing the throat —*vi.* **hemmed, hem′ming 1** to make this sound, as in trying to get attention **2** to grope about in speech for the right words: usually used in the phrase **hem and haw**

he·ma- *combining form* HEMO-

he-man *n.* [Inf.] a strong, virile man

hem·a·tite (hem′ə tīt′, hē′mə-) *n.* [< Gr *haimatitēs*, bloodlike] native ferric oxide, an important iron ore

he·ma·tol·o·gy (hē′mə täl′ə jē) *n.* [< Gr *haima*, blood + -LOGY] the study of blood and blood diseases —**he′ma·tol′o·gist** *n.*

he·ma·to·ma (-tō′mə) *n., pl.* **-mas** or **-ma·ta** (-mə tə) [< Gr *haima*, blood + -ōma, a mass] a swelling in a bodily tissue, filled with blood

heme (hēm) *n.* [ult. < Gr *haima*, blood] the iron-containing pigment in hemoglobin

hemi- [Gr *hēmi-*] *prefix* half [*hemisphere*]

Hem·ing·way (hem′iŋ wā′), **Er·nest** (ur′nist) 1899-1961; U.S. writer

hem·i·sphere (hem′i sfir′) *n.* [< Gr *hēmisphairion*] **1** half of a sphere, globe, celestial body, etc. **2** any of the halves (northern, southern, eastern, or western) of the earth —**hem′i·spher′i·cal** (-sfer′i kəl) *adj.,* **hem′i·spher′ic**

hem·line *n.* the bottom edge of a dress, skirt, coat, etc.

hem·lock (hem′läk′) *n.* [OE *hemlic*] **1** *a)* a poisonous European plant related to parsley *b)* a poison made from this plant **2** *a)* an evergreen tree of the pine family *b)* the wood of this tree

hemo- [< Gr *haima*] *combining form* blood

he·mo·glo·bin (hē′mə glō′bin) *n.* [< prec. + GLOBULE] the red coloring matter of the red blood corpuscles

he·mo·phil·i·a (hē′mə fil′ē ə) *n.* [< HEMO- + -PHILE] a hereditary disorder in which the blood fails to clot normally, causing prolonged bleeding from even minor cuts —**he′mo·phil′i·ac′** (-ak′) *n.*

hem·or·rhage (hem′ər ij′, hem′rij′) *n.* [< Gr *haima*, blood + *rhēgnynai*, to break] the escape of large quantities of blood from a blood vessel; heavy bleeding —*vi.* **-rhaged′,**

-rhag′ing to have a hemorrhage —*vt.* to lose (something) quickly and continuously —**hem′or·rhag′ic** (-aj′ik) *adj.*

hem·or·rhoid (hem′ər oid′, hem′roid′) *n.* [< Gr *haima*, blood + *rhein*, to flow] a painful swelling of a vein in the region of the anus, often with bleeding: *usually used in pl.* —**hem′or·rhoi′dal** *adj.*

he·mo·stat (hē′mō stat′) *n.* [see HEMO- & STATIC] anything used to stop bleeding, as a surgical clamp

hemp (hemp) *n.* [OE *hænep*] **1** a tall Asiatic plant having tough fiber **2** the fiber, used to make rope, sailcloth, etc. **3** a substance, as marijuana, made from its leaves and flowers

hem·stitch *n.* an ornamental stitch, used esp. at a hem, made by pulling out several parallel threads and tying the cross threads into small bunches —*vt.* to put hemstitches on

hen (hen) *n.* [OE *henn*] **1** the female of the domesticated chicken **2** the female of various other birds **3** the female of certain invertebrates, such as the lobster or octopus

hence (hens) *adv.* [< OE *heonan*, from here] **1** from this place; away [*go hence*] **2** from this time [a year *hence*] **3** as a result; therefore

hence·forth *adv.* from this time on; after this: also **hence′for′ward**

hench·man (hench′mən) *n., pl.* **-men** (-mən) [< OE *hengest*, stallion + -*man*] a trusted helper or follower

hen·na (hen′ə) *n.* [Ar *ḥinnā′*] **1** an Old World plant with tiny, white or red flowers **2** a dye extracted from its leaves, used to tint the hair auburn and to decorate the skin **3** reddish brown —*adj.* reddish-brown —*vt.* **-naed, -na·ing** to tint with henna

hen·peck (hen′pek′) *vt.* to nag and domineer over (one's husband) —**hen′pecked′** *adj.*

Hen·ry VIII (hen′rē) 1491-1547; king of England (1509-47)

hep (hep) *adj.* [Slang] *var. of* HIP[2]

hep·a·rin (hep′ə rin) *n.* [< Gr *hēpar*, liver] a substance found in the liver, that slows the clotting of blood

he·pat·ic (hi pat′ik) *adj.* [< Gr *hēpar*, liver] of or like the liver

hep·a·ti·tis (hep′ə tīt′is) *n.* [< Gr *hēpar*, liver + -ITIS] inflammation of the liver

her (hur) *pron.* [OE *hire*] *objective form of* SHE —*poss. pronominal adj.* of, belonging to, or done by her

He·ra (hir′ə, her′ə) *n.* Gr. Myth. the wife of Zeus and queen of the gods

her·ald (her′əld) *n.* [< OFr *herault*] **1** [Historical] an official who made proclamations, carried state messages, etc. **2** one who announces significant news, etc. **3** a forerunner; harbinger —*vt.* to announce, foretell, etc.

he·ral·dic (hə ral′dik) *adj.* of heraldry or heralds

her·ald·ry *n.* **1** the study of coats of arms, genealogies, etc. **2** ceremony or pomp

herb (urb, hurb) *n.* [< L *herba*] **1** any seed plant whose stem dies back annually **2** any plant used as a medicine, seasoning, or flavor-

ing —**her·ba·ceous** (hər bā′shəs, ər-) *adj.*
—**herb′al** *adj.*

herb·al·ist (hur′bəl ist, ur′-) *n.* one who
grows or deals in herbs

her·bi·cide (hur′bə sīd′, ur′-) *n.* any chemical
substance used to destroy plants, esp. weeds
—**her′bi·ci′dal** *adj.*

her·bi·vore (hur′bə vôr′) *n.* [Fr] a herbivorous animal

her·biv·o·rous (hər biv′ər əs) *adj.* [< L *herba*,
herb + *vorare*, devour] feeding chiefly on
plants

her·cu·le·an (hər kyoo′lē ən, hur′kyoo lē′ən)
adj. [*sometimes* H-] 1 having the great size
or strength of Hercules 2 calling for great
strength, size, or courage [a *herculean* en-
deavor]

Her·cu·les (hur′kyoo lēz′) *n.* 1 *Gr. & Rom.
Myth.* a hero famous for feats of strength 2
[h-] a very large, strong man

herd (hurd) *n.* [OE *heord*] 1 a number of
cattle or other animals feeding or living together 2 *a)* a crowd *b)* the common people;
masses (a contemptuous term) — *vt., vi.* to
gather or move as a herd

herds·man (hurdz′mən) *n., pl.* -**men** (-mən)
one who keeps or tends a herd

here (hir) *adv.* [OE *her*] 1 at or in this place:
often used as an intensive [John *here* is an ac-
tor] 2 to or into this place [come *here*] 3 at
this point; now 4 in earthly life —*n.* this place
—**neither here nor there** irrelevant

here·a·bout *adv.* in this general vicinity: also
here′a·bouts′

here·af·ter *adv.* 1 from now on; in the future 2 following this —*n.* 1 the future 2 the
state after death

here·by *adv.* by this means

he·red·i·tar·y (hə red′i ter′ē) *adj.* 1 *a)* of, or
passed down by, inheritance from an ances-
tor *b)* having title, etc. by inheritance 2 of,
or passed down by, heredity

he·red·i·ty (hə red′i tē) *n., pl.* -**ties** [< L *heres*,
heir] the transmission of characteristics from
parent to offspring by means of genes

here·in *adv.* 1 in here 2 in this writing

here·of *adv.* of or concerning this

here's (hirz) *contr.* here is

her·e·sy (her′ə sē) *n., pl.* -**sies** [< Gr *hairesis*,
selection, sect] 1 a religious belief opposed to
the orthodox doctrines of a church 2 any opinion opposed to official or established views

her·e·tic (-tik) *n.* one who professes a heresy;
esp., a church member who holds beliefs opposed to church dogma —**he·ret·i·cal** (hə ret′
i kəl) *adj.* —**he·ret′i·cal·ly** *adv.*

here·to·fore *adv.* up until now

here·up·on *adv.* 1 immediately following this;
at once 2 concerning this subject, etc.

here·with *adv.* 1 along with this 2 by this
method or means

her·it·a·ble (her′it ə bəl) *adj.* that can be inherited

her·it·age (her′i tij) *n.* 1 property that is or
can be inherited 2 tradition, etc. handed
down from one's ancestors or the past

her·maph·ro·dite (hər maf′rə dīt′) *n.* [after
Hermaphroditos, son of Hermes and Aphrodite, who became united in a single body with
a nymph] a person, animal, or plant with the
sexual organs of both the male and the female
—**her·maph′ro·dit′ic** (-dit′ik) *adj.*

Her·mes (hur′mēz′) *n. Gr. Myth.* the god who
is the messenger of the other gods

her·met·ic (hər met′ik) *adj.* [after prec. (reputed founder of alchemy)] airtight: also **her·**
met′i·cal —**her·met′i·cal·ly** *adv.*

her·mit (hur′mit) *n.* [< Gr *erēmos*, desolate]
one who lives alone in a secluded spot

her·mit·age (-mə tij) *n.* a secluded retreat, as
the place where a hermit lives

hermit crab a soft-bodied crab that lives in an
empty mollusk shell

her·ni·a (hur′nē ə) *n., pl.* -**as** or -**ae′** (-ē′,
-ī′) [L] the protrusion of all or part of an
organ, esp. the intestine, through a tear in the
wall of the surrounding structure; rupture —
her′ni·al *adj.*

her·ni·ate (-āt′) *vi.* -**at′ed**, -**at′ing** to protrude so as to form a hernia —**her′ni·a′tion** *n.*

he·ro (hir′ō, hē′rō) *n., pl.* -**roes** [< Gr
hērōs] 1 in mythology and legend, a man celebrated for bold exploits 2 a person admired
for courage, nobility, etc. 3 the principal
character in a novel, play, etc.

He·rod·o·tus (hə räd′ə təs) 484?-425? B.C.;
Gr. historian

he·ro·ic (hi rō′ik) *adj.* 1 of or like a hero 2 of
or about a hero and his deeds 3 daring and
risky —*n.* [*pl.*] heroic behavior, talk, or deeds
— **he·ro′i·cal·ly** *adv.*

her·o·in (her′ō in) *n.* [Ger, orig. a trademark]
a habit-forming narcotic derived from morphine

her·o·ine (her′ō in) *n.* a female hero in life or
literature

her·o·ism *n.* the qualities and actions of a hero

her·on (her′ən) *n.* [< OFr *hairon*] a wading
bird with a long neck, long legs, and a long,
tapered bill

hero sandwich a long roll sliced and filled with
meats, cheeses, vegetables, etc.

her·pes (hur′pēz′) *n.* [L < Gr *herpein*, to
creep] any of several viral diseases causing
small blisters on the skin and mucous membranes

herpes sim·plex (sim′pleks′) a recurrent,
incurable form of herpes usually affecting the
mouth, lips, face, or genitals

herpes zos·ter (zäs′tər) [< HERPES + Gr
zōstēr, a girdle] a viral infection of certain
sensory nerves, causing pain and an eruption
of blisters; shingles

her·pe·tol·o·gy (hur′pə täl′ə jē) *n.* [< Gr *her-
peton*, reptile] the branch of zoology dealing
with the study of reptiles and amphibians —
her′pe·tol′o·gist *n.*

Herr (her) *n., pl.* **Herr′en** (-ən) [Ger] 1 Mr.;
Sir: a German title of respect 2 a man; gentleman

her·ring (her′iŋ) *n.* [OE *hæring*] a small, silvery food fish of the North Atlantic

her·ring·bone *n.* **1** the spine of a herring, having numerous thin, parallel bony extensions on each side **2** a pattern with such a pattern, or anything having such a pattern, as a twill weave

hers (hurz) *pron.* that or those belonging to her: poss. form of SHE [*hers* are better]

her·self (hər) *pron.* a form of SHE, used as an intensive [she went *herself*], as a reflexive [she hurt *herself*], or with the meaning "her true self" [she is not *herself* today]

hertz (hurts) *n.*, *pl.* **hertz** [after H. R. *Hertz* (1857-94), Ger physicist] the international unit of frequency, equal to one cycle per second

Hertz·i·an waves (hert′sē ən, hurt′-) [see prec.] radio waves or other electromagnetic radiation resulting from the oscillations of electricity in a conductor

he's (hēz) *contr.* **1** he is **2** he has

hes·i·tant (hez′i tənt) *adj.* hesitating or undecided; doubtful **—hes′i·tan·cy** *n.* **—hes′i·tant·ly** *adv.*

hes·i·tate (-tāt′) *vi.* **-tat′ed**, **-tat′ing** [< L *haerere*, to stick] **1** to stop because of indecision **2** to pause **3** to be reluctant [I *hesitate* to ask] **4** to pause continually in speaking **—hes′i·tat′ing·ly** *adv.* **—hes′i·ta′tion** *n.*

hetero- [Gr *hetero-*] *combining form* other, another, different: also **heter-**

het·er·o·dox (het′ər ə däks′) *adj.* [< prec. + Gr *doxa*, opinion] opposed to the usual beliefs, esp. in religion; unorthodox **—het′er·o·dox′y** *n.*, *pl.* **-ies**

het·er·o·ge·ne·ous (het′ər ə jē′nē əs) *adj.* [< HETERO- + Gr *genos*, a kind] **1** differing in structure, quality, etc.; dissimilar **2** composed of unlike parts

het·er·o·sex·u·al (-sek′shōō əl) *adj.* **1** of or characterized by sexual desire for those of the opposite sex **2** *Biol.* of different sexes **—n.** a heterosexual individual **—het′er·o·sex·u·al′i·ty** *n.*

heu·ris·tic (hyōō ris′tik) *adj.* [< Gr *heuriskein*, invent] helping to learn, as by a method of education based on following rules to find answers

hew (hyōō) *vt.* **hewed**, **hewed** or **hewn**, **hew′ing** [OE *heawan*] **1** to chop or cut as with an ax **2** to make or shape in this way **—vi.** to conform (*to* a line, rule, etc.)

hex (heks) *n.* [Pennsylvania Ger *hexe*, witch] a sign, spell, etc. believed to bring bad luck **—vt.** to cause to have bad luck

hexa- [< Gr *hex*, six] *combining form* six: also, **hex-**

hex·a·gon (heks′ə gän′) *n.* [< Gr *hex*, six + *gōnia*, an angle] a plane figure with six angles and six sides **—hex·ag·o·nal** (hek sag′ə nəl) *adj.*

hex·am·e·ter (hek sam′ə tər) *n.* [see HEXA- & METER[1]] a line of verse containing six metrical feet

hey (hā) *interj.* used to attract attention, express surprise, etc.

hey·day (hā′dā′) *n.* the time of greatest health, vigor, etc.; prime

HFC *abbrev.* hydrofluorocarbon

Hg [L *hydrargyrum*] *Chem. symbol for* mercury

hgt *abbrev.* height

HHS *abbrev.* (Department of) Health and Human Services

hi (hī) *interj.* [Inf.] hello

HI *abbrev.* Hawaii

hi·a·tus (hī āt′əs) *n.*, *pl.* **-tus·es** or **-tus** [L < *hiare*, to gape] **1** a gap or break, as where a part is missing **2** any gap or interruption, as in time

hi·ba·chi (hi bä′chē) *n.*, *pl.* **-chis** [Jpn < *hi*, fire + *bachi*, bowl] a small charcoal-burning grill

hi·ber·nate (hī′bər nāt′) *vi.* **-nat′ed**, **-nat′ing** [< L *hibernus*, wintry] to spend the winter in a dormant state **—hi′ber·na′tion** *n.*

hi·bis·cus (hī bis′kəs, hi-) *n.* [< L] a plant of the mallow family, with large, colorful flowers

hic·cup (hik′up′, -əp) *n.* [echoic] **1** a sudden contraction of the diaphragm that causes the glottis to close, producing an abrupt sound **2** an anomalous event, esp. an unexpected minor setback **—vi. -cuped′** or **-cupped′**, **-cup′ing** or **-cup′ping** to make a hiccup with the diaphragm Also sp. **hic′cough′**

hick (hik) *n.* [altered < *Richard*] [Inf.] an awkward, unsophisticated person regarded as typical of rural areas: a contemptuous term

hick·ey (hik′ē) *n.*, *pl.* **-eys** or **-ies** [Inf.] a bruise made on the skin by sucking

hick·o·ry (hik′ə rē, hik′rē) *n.*, *pl.* **-ries** [< AmInd *pawchiccora*] **1** a North American tree of the walnut family **2** its hard, tough wood **3** its hard, edible nut: usually **hickory nut**

hid·den (hid′'n) *vt.*, *vi.* [OE *gehydd*] *alt. pp. of* HIDE[1] **—adj.** concealed; secret

hide[1] (hīd) *vt.* **hid** (hid), **hid′den** or **hid**, **hid′ing** [OE *hydan*] **1** to put or keep out of sight; conceal **2** to keep secret **3** to keep from sight by obscuring, etc. **—vi.** to conceal oneself

hide[2] (hīd) *n.* [OE *hid*] an animal skin or pelt, either raw or tanned

hide·a·way *n.* [Inf.] a place where one can hide, be secluded, etc.

hide·bound *adj.* obstinately conservative and narrow-minded

hid·e·ous (hid′ē əs) *adj.* [< OFr *hide*, fright] horrible; very ugly; dreadful **—hid′e·ous·ly** *adv.* **—hid′e·ous·ness** *n.*

hide·out *n.* [Inf.] a hiding place

hie (hī) *vi.*, *vt.* **hied**, **hie′ing** or **hy′ing** [OE *higian*] to hasten: usually used reflexively

hi·er·ar·chy (hī′ər är′kē) *n.*, *pl.* **-chies** [< Gr *hieros*, sacred + *archos*, ruler] **1** church government by clergy in graded ranks **2** the highest officials in such a system **3** a group of persons or things arranged in order of rank, grade, etc. **—hi′er·ar′chi·cal** (-ki kəl) *adj.*

hi·er·o·glyph·ic (hī′ər ō glif′ik, hī′rō-) *n.* [< Gr *hieros*, sacred + *glyphein*, to carve] **1** a picture or symbol representing a word, syllable, or sound, used by the ancient Egyptians and others **2** [usually *pl.*] picture writing **3** a symbol, etc. that is hard to understand —*adj.* of or like hieroglyphics

hi-fi (hī′fī′) [Inf.] *n.* a radio, phonograph, etc. having high fidelity —*adj.* of or having high fidelity of sound reproduction

high (hī) *adj.* ⟦OE *heah*⟧ **1** lofty; tall **2** extending upward a (specified) distance **3** reaching to, situated at, or done from a height **4** above others in rank, position, etc.; superior **5** grave [*high* treason] **6** greater in size, amount, degree, etc. than usual [*high* prices] **7** luxurious [*high* living] **8** raised in pitch [a high note] **9** slightly tainted: said of meat, esp. game **10** excited [*high* spirits] **11** [Slang] *a*) drunk *b*) under the influence of a drug —*adv.* in or to a high level, place, degree, etc. —*n.* **1** a high level, place, etc. **2** an area of high barometric pressure **3** the gear of a motor vehicle, etc. producing the greatest speed **4** [Slang] a condition of euphoria induced as by drugs —**high and dry 1** out of the reach of the water **2** alone and helpless —**high and low** everywhere —**high on** [Inf.] enthusiastic about —**on high** in heaven

high·ball *n.* whiskey or brandy mixed with water, soda water, ginger ale, etc.

high·born *adj.* of noble birth

high·boy *n.* a high chest of drawers mounted on legs

high·brow *n.* one having or affecting highly cultivated tastes; intellectual —*adj.* of or for a highbrow

high·chair *n.* a baby's chair with long legs and, usually, a tray for food

high-def·i·ni·tion *adj.* designating video recording, transmission, or playback systems that offer greater clarity of image than that of earlier systems: also [Inf.] **high′-def′**

high-end *adj.* [Inf.] expensive and of very high quality

higher education college or university education

high·er-up *n.* [Inf.] a person of higher rank or position

high·fa·lu·tin (-fə lōōt′'n) *adj.* [Inf.] pretentious or pompous: also sp. **high′fa·lu′ting**

high fidelity in radio, sound recording, etc., nearly exact reproduction of sound

high-five *n.* [Inf.] a slapping of the upraised open hand of another person, as in celebration

high-flown *adj.* **1** extravagantly ambitious **2** bombastic

high frequency any radio frequency between 3 and 30 megahertz

High German the group of West Germanic dialects spoken in central and S Germany and in Austria, Switzerland, etc.

high ground a morally superior position

high·hand·ed *adj.* overbearing —**high′hand′ed·ly** *adv.* —**high′hand′ed·ness** *n.*

high-hat (-hat′; *for v., usually,* -hat′) *adj.* [Slang] snobbish

high·land (-lənd) *n.* a region with many hills or mountains —**the Highlands** mountainous region occupying most of N Scotland —**High′land·er** *n.*

high-lev·el *adj.* **1** of or by persons of high office or rank **2** in a high office

high·light *n.* **1** a part on which light is brightest: also **high light 2** the most important or interesting part, scene, etc. —*vt.* **1** to give highlights to **2** to give prominence to; emphasize

high·light·er *n.* a pen with a broad felt tip for marking passages as in a textbook

high·ly *adv.* **1** very much **2** favorably **3** at a high level, wage, etc.

high-mind·ed *adj.* having high ideals, principles, etc. —**high′-mind′ed·ly** *adv.*

high·ness *n.* **1** height **2** [H—] a title used in speaking to or of a member of a royal family

high-pres·sure *adj.* **1** having or withstanding high pressure **2** using forcefully persuasive or insistent methods —*vt.* **-sured**, **-sur·ing** [Inf.] to urge with such methods

high-pro·file *adj.* well-known, highly publicized, etc.

high-rise *adj.* tall and having many stories —*n.* a high-rise building

high road 1 [Chiefly Brit.] a highway **2** an easy or direct way **3** a selfless position or course

high roller 1 a person who gambles for high stakes **2** a person who spends money freely

high school a secondary school that includes grades 10, 11, 12, and often 9

high seas open ocean waters outside the territorial limits of any nation

high sign a secret signal, given as in warning

high-spir·it·ed (-spir′it tid) *adj.* **1** courageous **2** spirited; fiery **3** lively or merry

high-strung *adj.* highly sensitive or nervous and tense

high tech (tek) **1** of specialized, complex technology: in full **high technology 2** furnishings, fashions, etc. whose design or look suggests industrial use **high′-tech′** *adj.*

high-ten·sion *adj.* having or carrying a high voltage

high tide 1 the highest level to which the tide rises **2** the time at which this occurs

high time time beyond the proper time but before it is too late

high·way *n.* **1** a public road **2** a main road; thoroughfare

high·way·man (-mən) *n., pl.* **-men** (-mən) a man who formerly robbed travelers on a highway

high wire a cable stretched high above the ground, on which aerialists perform

hi·jack (hī′jak′) *vt.* **1** to steal (goods in transit, etc.) by force **2** to seize control forcibly of (an aircraft, etc.), esp. in order to go to a nonscheduled destination —**hi′jack′er** *n.*

hike (hīk) *vi.* **hiked**, **hik′ing** [< dial. *heik*] to take a long walk —*vt.* [Inf.] **1** to pull up; hoist **2** to raise (prices, etc.) —*n.* **1** a long walk **2** [Inf.] an increase —**hik′er** *n.*

hi·lar·i·ous (hi ler′ē əs) *adj.* [< Gr *hilaros*, cheerful] **1** noisily merry **2** very funny —**hi·lar′i·ous·ly** *adv.* —**hi·lar′i·ty** (-i tē) *n.*

hill (hil) *n.* ⟦OE *hyll*⟧ **1** a natural raised part of the earth's surface, smaller and usually less rugged than a mountain **2** a small pile, heap, or mound

hill·bil·ly *n., pl.* **-lies** ⟦prec. + *Billy*⟧ [Inf.] one who lives in or comes from the mountains or backwoods of the South, specif. Appalachia: often a contemptuous term

hill·side *n.* the side of a hill

hill·top *n.* the top of a hill

hill·y *adj.* **-i·er, -i·est** full of hills —**hill′i·ness** *n.*

hilt (hilt) *n.* ⟦OE⟧ the handle of a sword, dagger, tool, etc.

him (him) *pron.* ⟦OE⟧ *objective form of* HE

Hi·ma·la·yas (him′ə lā′əz) mountain system of SC Asia, mostly in India & China —**Hi′ma·la′yan** *adj.*

him·self *pron.* a form of HE, used as an intensive [he went *himself*], as a reflexive [he hurt *himself*], or with the meaning "his true self" [he is not *himself* today]

hind¹ (hīnd) *adj.* back; rear

hind² (hīnd) *n.* ⟦OE⟧ the female of the red deer

Hind *abbrev.* **1** Hindi **2** Hindu

hin·der (hin′dər) *vt.* ⟦OE *hindrian*⟧ **1** to keep back; stop **2** to impede; thwart

Hin·di (hin′dē) *n.* the main (and official) language of India

hind·most *adj.* farthest back; last

hind·quar·ter *n.* either of the two hind legs and the adjoining part of a carcass of veal, beef, etc.

hin·drance (hin′drəns) *n.* **1** the act of hindering **2** an obstacle

hind·sight *n.* ability to see, after the event, what should have been done

Hin·du (hin′dōō′) *n.* a follower of Hinduism —*adj.* designating or of the Hindus or Hinduism

Hin·du·ism *n.* the principal religion of India, characterized by a belief in reincarnation and in many gods

Hin·du·stan (hin′dōō stan′) **1** [Historical] region in N India **2** the entire Indian subcontinent **3** the republic of India

hinge (hinj) *n.* ⟦< ME *hengen*, to hang⟧ **1** a joint on which a door, lid, etc. swings **2** a natural joint, as of the shell of a clam —*vt.* **hinged, hing′ing** to attach by a hinge —*vi.* to hang as on a hinge; depend

hint (hint) *n.* ⟦prob. < OE *hentan*, to grasp⟧ a slight indication; indirect suggestion — *vt., vi.* to give a hint (of)

hin·ter·land (hin′tər land′) *n.* ⟦Ger⟧ a remote area

hip¹ (hip) *n.* ⟦OE *hype*⟧ the part of the body around the joint formed by each thighbone and the pelvis

hip² (hip) *adj.* **hip′per, hip′pest** ⟦< ? HEP⟧ [Inf.] **1** aware of the latest cultural developments; sophisticated **2** fashionable; trendy

hip-hop *n.* a style of music and dance usually based on rap and often including other styles such as funk or rhythm and blues

hip·pie (hip′ē) *n.* **1** a young person of the 1960s and 1970s who, in a state of alienation

from conventional society, turned variously to mysticism, psychedelic drugs, etc. **2** any person having a similar lifestyle

hip·po (hip′ō) *n., pl.* **-pos** [Inf.] HIPPOPOTAMUS

Hip·poc·ra·tes (hi päk′rə tēz′) 460?–377? B.C.; Gr. physician

Hip·po·crat·ic oath (hip′ə krat′ik) the oath, attributed to Hippocrates, generally taken by medical school graduates: it sets forth their ethical code

hip·po·drome (hip′ə drōm′) *n.* ⟦< Gr *hippos*, horse + *dromos*, course⟧ an arena for circuses, games, etc.

hip·po·pot·a·mus (hip′ə pät′ə məs) *n., pl.* **-a·mus·es, -a·mi′** (-mī′), **-a·mus** ⟦< Gr *hippos*, a horse + *potamos*, river⟧ a large, plant-eating mammal with a heavy, thick-skinned body and short legs: it lives chiefly in or near African rivers

hip·py (hip′ē) *n., pl.* **-pies** *alt. sp. of* HIPPIE

hire (hīr) *n.* ⟦< OE *hyr*, wages⟧ **1** the amount paid in hiring **2** a hiring —*vt.* **hired, hir′ing** to pay for the services of (a person) or the use of (a thing) —**hire out** to work for pay

hire·ling (-liŋ) *n.* one who will follow anyone's orders for pay; mercenary

Hi·ro·shi·ma (hir′ə shē′mə, hi rō′shi mə) seaport in SW Honshu, Japan: largely destroyed (Aug. 6, 1945) by a U.S. atomic bomb, the first ever used in warfare

hir·sute (hur′sōōt′, hər sōōt′) *adj.* ⟦L *hirsutus*⟧ hairy; shaggy

his (hiz) *pron.* ⟦OE⟧ that or those belonging to him: poss. form of HE [*his* are better] — *poss. pronominal adj.* of, belonging to, or done by him

His·pan·ic (hi span′ik) *adj.* **1** Spanish **2** of or relating to Hispanics —*n.* a person of Spanish-speaking Latin American origin who lives in the U.S. For *adj.* **2** and the *n.*, *Latino* and *Latina* are now often preferred

His·pan·io·la (his′pən yō′lə) island in the West Indies, between Cuba & Puerto Rico

hiss (his) *vi.* ⟦echoic⟧ **1** to make a sound like that of a prolonged *s* **2** to show disapproval by hissing —*vt.* to say or indicate by hissing —*n.* the act or sound of hissing

his·sy fit (his′ē) [Dial.] a fit of anger: usually in **have** (or **throw**) **a hissy fit**: also **his′sy** *n., pl.* **-sies**

hist¹ (st) *interj.* [Inf.] used to attract attention

hist² *abbrev.* history

his·ta·mine (his′tə mēn′, -min′) *n.* ⟦< Gr *histos*, web + AMMONIA⟧ an ammonia derivative in all organic matter: it is released in allergic reactions, lowers the blood pressure, etc.

his·tol·o·gy (his täl′ə jē) *n.* ⟦< Gr *histos*, web + -LOGY⟧ *Biol.* the microscopic study of tissue structure —**his·tol′o·gist** *n.*

his·to·ri·an (his tôr′ē ən) *n.* a writer of, or authority on, history

his·tor·ic (-ik) *adj.* having, or likely to have, lasting importance

his·tor·i·cal (-i kəl) *adj.* **1** of or concerned

with history **2** based on people or events of the past **3** established by history; factual —**his·tor′i·cal·ly** *adv.*

historical present the present tense used for the narration of past events

his·to·ric·i·ty (his′tə ris′ə tē) *n.* historical authenticity

his·to·ri·og·ra·phy (his tôr′ē äg′rə fē) *n.* the study of the techniques of historical research

his·to·ry (his′tə rē, -trē) *n., pl.* **-ries** [< Gr *histōr*, knowing] **1** an account of what has happened, esp. in the life of a people, country, etc. **2** all recorded past events **3** the branch of knowledge that deals systematically with the past **4** a known or recorded past [the odd *history* of his coat]

his·tri·on·ic (his′trē än′ik) *adj.* [< L *histrio*, actor] **1** of acting or actors **2** overacted or overacting; affected

his·tri·on·ics *pl.n.* [*sometimes with sing. v.*] **1** dramatics **2** an artificial manner, display of emotion, etc.

hit (hit) *vt., vi.* **hit, hit′ting** [< ON *hitta*, meet with] **1** to come against (something) with force; knock **2** to give a blow (to); strike **3** to strike with a missile **4** to affect strongly [a town hard *hit* by floods] **5** to come (upon) by accident or after search **6** to arrive at [stocks *hit* a new high] **7** *Baseball* to get (a hit) —*n.* **1** a blow that strikes its mark **2** a collision **3** a successful and popular song, book, etc. **4** an instance of finding particular data in a computer search **5** [Slang] a murder **6** [Slang] a dose of a drug, a drink of liquor, etc. **7** *Baseball* BASE HIT —**hit it off** to get along well together —**hit′ter** *n.*

hit-and-run (hit′′n run′) *adj.* hitting a person, car, etc. with a moving vehicle and fleeing the scene immediately

hitch (hich) *vi.* [ME *hicchen*] **1** to move jerkily **2** to become fastened or caught **3** [Slang] to hitchhike —*vt.* **1** to move, pull, etc. with jerks **2** to fasten with a hook, knot, etc. —*n.* **1** a tug; jerk **2** a limp **3** a hindrance; obstacle **4** a fastening or catch **5** [Slang] a period of time served **6** a kind of knot

hitch·hike *vi.* **-hiked′, -hik′ing** to travel by asking or signaling for rides from passing drivers —**hitch′hik′er** *n.*

hith·er (hith′ər) *adv.* [< OE *hider*] to this place; here

hith·er·to *adv.* until this time

Hit·ler (hit′lər), **Ad·olf** (ad′ôlf′, ä′dôlf′) 1889–1945; Nazi dictator of Germany (1933–45), born in Austria —**Hit·ler′i·an** (-lir′ē ən) *adj.*

hit man [Inf.] a hired murderer

hit-or-miss *adj.* haphazard; random

HIV *n.* a retrovirus that infects human T cells and causes AIDS

hive (hīv) *n.* [< OE *hyfe*] **1** a shelter for a colony of bees; beehive **2** a colony of bees; swarm **3** a crowd of busy people **4** a place of great activity —*vt.* **hived, hiv′ing** to gather (bees) into a hive —*vi.* to enter a hive —**hive off 1** to depart from a group **2** to separate and establish newly

hives (hīvz) *pl.n.* [orig. Scot dial.] [*with sing. or pl. v.*] an allergic skin condition characterized by itching, burning, and the formation of smooth patches

HMO *n., pl.* **HMO's** [*h*(ealth) *m*(aintenance) *o*(rganization)] a healthcare system in which an organization hires medical professionals to provide services for its subscribers

HMS *abbrev.* **1** Her (or His) Majesty's Service **2** Her (or His) Majesty's Ship

hoa·gie or **hoa·gy** (hō′gē) *n., pl.* **-gies** HERO SANDWICH

hoard (hôrd) *n.* [OE *hord*] a supply stored up and hidden —*vi., vt.* to accumulate and store away (money, goods, etc.) —**hoard′er** *n.* —**hoard′ing** *n.*

hoar·frost (hôr′frôst′) *n.* FROST (*n.* 2)

hoarse (hôrs) *adj.* **hoars′er, hoars′est** [OE *has*] **1** harsh and grating in sound **2** having a rough, husky voice —**hoarse′ly** *adv.* —**hoarse′ness** *n.*

hoar·y (hôr′ē) *adj.* **-i·er, -i·est** [< OE *har*] **1** white or gray **2** having white or gray hair from old age **3** very old Also **hoar** —**hoar′i·ness** *n.*

hoax (hōks) *n.* [< ? HOCUS-POCUS] a trick or fraud; esp., a practical joke —*vt.* to deceive with a hoax

hob·ble (häb′əl) *vi.* **-bled, -bling** [ME *hobelen*] to go unsteadily; limp —*vt.* **1** to cause to limp **2** to hamper (a horse, etc.) by tying two feet together **3** to hinder —*n.* **1** a limp **2** a rope, etc. used to hobble a horse

hob·by (häb′ē) *n., pl.* **-bies** [ME *hobi*] **1** HOBBYHORSE **2** something that one likes to do in one's spare time —**hob′by·ist** *n.*

hob·by·horse *n.* **1** a child's toy consisting of a stick with a horse's head **2** ROCKING HORSE **3** an idea with which one is preoccupied

hob·gob·lin (häb′gäb′lin) *n.* [*hob*, elf or goblin + GOBLIN] **1** an elf **2** a bugbear

hob·nail *n.* [*hob*, a peg + NAIL] a short nail with a broad head, put on the soles of heavy shoes to prevent wear or slipping —*vt.* to put hobnails on

hob·nob (-näb′) *vi.* **-nobbed′, -nob′bing** [< ME *habben*, have + *nabben*, not to have] to be on close terms (*with*)

ho·bo (hō′hō) *n., pl.* **-bos** or **-boes 1** a migratory worker **2** a tramp

Ho Chi Minh City (hō′chē′min′) seaport in S Vietnam: formerly (as *Saigon*) capital of South Vietnam (1954–76)

hock[1] (häk) *n.* [< OE *hoh*, heel] the joint bending backward in the hind leg of a horse, ox, etc.

hock[2] (häk) *vt., n.* [< Du *hok*, prison] [Slang] PAWN[1] —**in (or out of) hock** [Slang] **1** pledged to (or redeemed from) a pawnbroker **2** in (or out of) debt

hock·ey (häk′ē) *n.* [prob. < OFr *hoquet*, bent stick] **1** a team game played on ice skates, with curved sticks and a hard rubber disk (*puck*); ice hockey **2** a similar game played on foot on a field, with a small ball; field hockey

hock·shop *n.* [Slang] PAWNSHOP

ho·cus-po·cus (hō′kəs pō′kəs) *n.* ⟦imitation L⟧ **1** meaningless words used as a formula by conjurers **2** a magician's trick or tricks **3** trickery

hod (häd) *n.* ⟦prob. < MDu *hodde*⟧ **1** a V-shaped device with a long handle, used for carrying bricks, mortar, etc. on the shoulder **2** a coal scuttle

hodge·podge (häj′päj′) *n.* ⟦< OFr *hochepot*, a stew⟧ a jumbled mixture

Hodg·kin's disease (häj′kinz) ⟦after T. *Hodgkin* (1798-1866), Brit physician⟧ a type of lymphoma: also **Hodgkin lymphoma**

hoe (hō) *n.* ⟦< OHG *houwan*, to cut⟧ a tool with a thin, flat blade set across the end of a long handle, used for weeding, loosening soil, etc. — *vt., vi.* **hoed, hoe′ing** to cultivate, dig, weed, etc. with a hoe

hoe·cake *n.* a thin bread made of cornmeal

hoe·down *n.* **1** a lively, rollicking dance **2** a party with such dances

hog (hôg, häg) *n.* ⟦OE *hogg*⟧ **1** any swine, esp. a domesticated adult ready for market **2** [Inf.] a greedy, gluttonous, or filthy person —*vt.* **hogged, hog′ging** [Slang] to take all of or an unfair share of —**go (the) whole hog** [Slang] to go all the way —**high on (or off) the hog** [Inf.] in a luxurious or costly way —**hog′gish** *adj.* —**hog′gish·ly** *adv.*

ho·gan (hō′gôn′, -gən) *n.* ⟦< AmInd⟧ a Navajo Indian dwelling, built of earth walls supported by timbers

hog·back *n.* a ridge with a sharp crest and abruptly sloping sides

hogs·head (hôgz′hed′) *n.* **1** a large barrel or cask holding from 63 to 140 gallons **2** a liquid measure, esp. one equal to 63 gallons

hog·tie *vt.* **-tied′, -ty′ing** or **-tie′ing 1** to tie the four feet of (an animal) **2** to tie the feet and hands of (a person) **3** [Inf.] to make incapable of effective action

hog·wash *n.* **1** refuse fed to hogs; swill **2** insincere talk, writing, etc.

ho-hum (hō′hum′) *interj.* used to show boredom: an utterance suggesting a yawn —*adj.* [Inf.] boring or tiresome

hoi pol·loi (hoi′pə loi′) ⟦Gr, the many⟧ the common people; the masses

hoist (hoist) *vt.* ⟦< Du *hijschen*⟧ to raise aloft; lift, esp. with a pulley, crane, etc. —*n.* **1** a hoisting **2** an apparatus for lifting; elevator; tackle

ho·key (hō′kē) *adj.* sentimental, corny, or contrived

ho·kum (hō′kəm) *n.* ⟦< HOCUS(-POCUS)⟧ [Slang] **1** trite sentiment, crude humor, etc. **2** nonsense or humbug

hold¹ (hōld) *vt.* **held, hold′ing** ⟦OE *haldan*⟧ **1** to keep in the hands, arms, etc.; grasp **2** to keep in a certain position or condition **3** to restrain or control; keep back **4** to possess; occupy [to *hold* an office] **5** to guard; defend [*hold* the fort] **6** to carry on (a meeting, etc.) **7** to contain [the jar *holds* a pint] **8** to regard; consider [I *hold* the story to be true] **9** *Law* to decide; decree —*vi.* **1**

to go on being firm, loyal, etc. **2** to remain unbroken or unyielding [the rope *held*] **3** to be true or valid [this rule *holds* for any case] **4** to continue [the wind *held* steady] —*n.* **1** a grasping or seizing; grip **2** a thing to hold on by **3** a dominating force [she has a *hold* over him] —**catch (or get, lay, or take) hold of** to take, seize, acquire, etc. —**hold forth** to preach; lecture —**hold on** [Inf.] stop! wait! —**hold out 1** to last; endure **2** to stand firm **3** to offer **4** [Inf.] to refuse to give (what is to be given) —**hold over 1** to postpone **2** to keep for an additional period —**hold up 1** to prop up **2** to show **3** to last; endure **4** to stop; delay **5** to stop forcibly and rob —**hold′er** *n.*

hold² (hōld) *n.* ⟦< HOLE or < MDu *hol*⟧ **1** the interior of a ship below decks, where the cargo is carried **2** the compartment for cargo in an aircraft

hold·ing *n.* **1** land, esp. a farm, rented from another **2** [*pl.*] property owned, as stocks and bonds

hold·o·ver *n.* [Inf.] one staying on from a previous period

hold·up *n.* **1** a delay **2** the act of stopping forcibly and robbing

hole (hōl) *n.* ⟦OE *hol*⟧ **1** a hollow place; cavity **2** an animal's burrow; den **3** a small, dingy, squalid place **4** an opening in anything; break; gap; tear **5** *Golf a)* a small cup sunk into a green, into which the ball is to be hit *b)* a section of a course including the tee, fairway, and green —**hole up** [Inf.] **1** to hibernate **2** to shut oneself in **3** to hide out —**in the hole** [Inf.] financially embarrassed or behind

-hol·ic (häl′ik) *combining form* -AHOLIC

hol·i·day (häl′ə dā′) *n.* **1** a religious festival; holy day **2** a day of freedom from labor, often one set aside by law **3** [*often pl.*] [Chiefly Brit.] a vacation —*adj.* of or for a holiday; joyous; gay

ho·li·er-than-thou (hō′lē ər thən thou′) *adj.* annoyingly self-righteous

ho·li·ness (hō′lē nis) *n.* **1** a being holy **2** [H-] a title of the pope

ho·lis·tic (hō lis′tik) *adj.* of or dealing with wholes or integrated systems rather than with their parts —**ho·lis′ti·cal·ly** *adv.*

Hol·land (häl′ənd) NETHERLANDS —**Hol′land·er** *n.*

hol·lan·daise sauce (häl′ən dāz′) ⟦Fr, of Holland⟧ a creamy sauce made of butter, egg yolks, lemon juice, etc.

hol·ler (häl′ər) *vi., vt., n.* [Inf.] shout or yell

hol·low (häl′ō) *adj.* ⟦OE *holh*⟧ **1** having a cavity inside; not solid **2** shaped like a bowl; concave **3** sunken [*hollow* cheeks] **4** empty or worthless [*hollow* praise] **5** hungry **6** deep-toned and muffled —*n.* **1** a hollow place; cavity **2** a valley — *vt., vi.* to make or become hollow —**hol′low·ness** *n.*

hol·ly (häl′ē) *n., pl.* **-lies** ⟦OE *holegn*⟧ an evergreen shrub or tree with stiff, glossy, sharp-pointed leaves and bright-red berries

hol·ly·hock (-häk′) *n.* ⟦< OE *halig*, holy + *hoc*,

mallow] a tall plant of the mallow family, with large, showy flowers

Hol·ly·wood (häl′ē wood′) section of Los Angeles, once the site of many film studios

Holmes (hōmz, hōlmz) **1 Ol·i·ver Wen·dell** (äl′ə vər wen′dəl) 1841-1935; associate justice, U.S. Supreme Court (1902-32) **2 SHER·LOCK HOLMES**

hol·mi·um (hōl′mē əm) n. [after Holmia, L name of Stockholm, Sweden] a soft, malleable chemical element: symbol, Ho; at. no. 67

hol·o·caust (häl′ə kôst′, hō′lə-) n. [< Gr holos, whole + kaustos, burnt] a great destruction of life, esp. by fire —**the Holocaust** [also **the h-**] the systematic killing of millions of European Jews by the Nazis before and during WWII

Hol·o·cene (häl′ō sēn′, hō′lə-) adj. [< Gr holos, whole + kainos, recent] designating the present epoch of geologic time

hol·o·gram (häl′ə gram′, hō′lə-) n. a photographic image produced by holography

hol·o·graph (-graf′) n. [< Gr holos, whole + graphein, to write] a document, letter, etc. in the handwriting of the person under whose name it appears

hol·o·graph·ic (-graf′ik) adj. 1 of or in the form of a holograph 2 of holography

ho·log·ra·phy (hō läg′rə fē) n. [< Gr holos, whole + -GRAPHY] a method of making three-dimensional photographs using a laser beam

Hol·stein (hōl′stēn′, -stīn′) n. [after the region of Schleswig-Holstein, Germany] a breed of large, black-and-white dairy cattle

hol·ster (hōl′stər) n. [Du] a pistol case attached to a belt, saddle, etc.

ho·ly (hō′lē) adj. **-li·er** or **-li·est** [OE halig] [often H-] 1 dedicated to religious use; sacred 2 spiritually pure; sinless 3 deserving deep respect, awe, etc.

Holy Communion a Christian rite in which bread and wine are consecrated and received as the body and blood of Jesus or as symbols of them

Holy Land PALESTINE

Holy Roman Empire empire of WC Europe, from A.D. 962 until 1806

Holy Spirit (or **Ghost**) the third person of the Trinity; spirit of God

hom·age (häm′ij, äm′-) n. [< L homo, man] anything given or done to show reverence, honor, etc.

hom·burg (häm′bərg) n. [after Homburg, Prussia] a man's felt hat with a stiff, curved brim

home (hōm) n. [OE hām] 1 the place where one lives 2 the place where one was born or reared 3 a place thought of as home 4 a household and its affairs 5 an institution for orphans, the aged, etc. 6 the natural environment of an animal, plant, etc. 7 HOME PLATE —adj. 1 of one's home or country; domestic 2 central [home office] —adv. 1 at, to, or in the direction of home 2 to the point aimed at [to drive a nail home] —at home 1 in one's home 2 at ease —bring

home to to impress upon —**home′less** adj. —**home′like′** adj.

home·boy n. [Slang] 1 a boy or man from one's neighborhood, town, etc. 2 a close male friend

home-care adj. of medical care, etc. provided in a person's home

home economics the science and art of homemaking, nutrition, etc.

home fries raw or boiled potatoes, sliced and fried in a frying pan

home·girl n. [Slang] 1 a girl or woman from one's neighborhood, town, etc. 2 a close female friend

home·land n. the country in which one was born or makes one's home

home·ly adj. **-li·er, -li·est** 1 suitable for home life; everyday 2 crude 3 plain or unattractive —**home′li·ness** n.

home·made adj. made, or as if made, at home

home·mak·er n. one who manages a household

ho·me·op·a·thy (hō′mē äp′ə thē) n. the treatment of a disease using, in small doses, drugs that produce symptoms like those of the disease —**ho′me·o·path′ic** (-ə path′ik) adj.

home page 1 the main page of a website 2 the Web page first displayed when a browser is opened

home plate Baseball the base that the batter stands beside

Ho·mer (hō′mər) semilegendary Gr. epic poet of c. 8th c. B.C. —**Ho·mer·ic** (hō mer′ik) adj.

home run n. Baseball a hit that allows the batter to touch all bases and score a run: also [Inf.] **hom′er** n.

home·sick adj. unhappy at being away from home —**home′sick′ness** n.

home·spun n. coarse loosely-woven cloth —adj. 1 spun at home 2 plain; homely

home·stead (-sted′) n. 1 a place where a family makes its home 2 a tract of land granted by the U.S. government to a settler —**home′stead′er** n.

home·stretch n. 1 the part of a racetrack between the last turn and the finish line 2 the final part of any long undertaking

home·ward adv., adj. toward home [homeward bound] : also **home′wards** adv.

home·work n. 1 work, esp. piecework, done at home 2 lessons to be done outside the classroom 3 preparation for some project: usually in **do one's homework**

home·y adj. **hom′i·er, hom′i·est** familiar, cozy, etc. —**home′y·ness** n.

hom·i·cide (häm′ə sīd′) n. [< L homo, a man + caedere, to kill] 1 the killing of one person by another 2 a person who kills another —**hom′i·ci′dal** adj.

hom·i·let·ics (häm′ə let′iks) pl.n. [see fol.] the art of preparing and delivering sermons

hom·i·ly (häm′ə lē) n., pl. **-lies** [< Gr homilos, assembly] a sermon

homing pigeon a pigeon trained to find its way home from distant places

hom·i·nid (häm′ə nid) n. [< L homo, a man] a primate belonging to the family that includes humans, their extinct relatives, and the great apes

hom·i·ny (häm′ə nē) *n.* ⟦< AmInd⟧ dry corn hulled and coarsely ground (**hominy grits**): it is boiled for food

homo- ⟦< Gr *homos*⟧ *combining form* same, equal, like

ho·mo·ge·ne·ous (hō′mō jē′nē əs, häm′ō-) *adj.* ⟦see prec. & GENUS⟧ **1** the same in structure, quality, etc.; similar **2** composed of similar parts —**ho′mo·ge·ne′i·ty** (-jə nē′rə tē, -nā′-) *n.*

ho·mog·e·nize (hə mäj′ə nīz′) *vt.* **-nized′, -niz′ing** to make homogeneous, or more uniform throughout; specif., to process (milk) so that fat particles are so finely emulsified that the cream does not separate

hom·o·graph (häm′ə graf′, hō′mə-) *n.* ⟦HOMO- + -GRAPH⟧ a word with the same spelling as another but with a different meaning and origin

ho·mol·o·gous (hō mäl′ə gəs) *adj.* ⟦Gr *homologos*, agreeing⟧ matching in structure, position, etc.

hom·o·nym (häm′ə nim′) *n.* ⟦< Gr *homos*, same + *onyma*, name⟧ a word with the same pronunciation as another but with a different meaning, origin, and, usually, spelling

ho·mo·pho·bi·a (hō′mə fō′bē ə) *n.* ⟦HOMO-(SEXUAL) + -PHOBIA⟧ hatred or fear of homosexuals or homosexuality —**ho′mo·pho′bic** (-fō′bik) *adj.*

Ho·mo sa·pi·ens (hō′mō sā′pē enz′) ⟦ModL *homo*, man + *sapiens*, prp. of *sapere*, to know⟧ **1** humankind **2** a human being

ho·mo·sex·u·al (hō′mō sek′shōō əl, -mə-) *adj.* of or having sexual orientation to persons of the same sex —*n.* a homosexual person —**ho′mo·sex′u·al′i·ty** (-al′ə tē) *n.*

Hon *abbrev.* honorable

hon·cho (hän′chō) *n., pl.* **-chos** ⟦< Jpn⟧ [Slang] a leader

Hon·du·ras (hän door′əs) country in Central America

hone (hōn) *n.* ⟦OE *han*, a stone⟧ a hard stone used to sharpen cutting tools —*vt.* **honed, hon′ing** to sharpen, as with a hone

hon·est (än′ist) *adj.* ⟦< L *honor*, honor⟧ **1** truthful; trustworthy **2** *a)* sincere or fair [*honest* effort] *b)* gained by fair means [an *honest* living] **3** being what it seems **4** frank and open [an *honest* face] —**hon′est·ly** *adv.* —**hon′es·ty** *n.*

hon·ey (hun′ē) *n., pl.* **-eys** ⟦OE *hunig*⟧ **1** a sweet, syrupy substance that bees make as food from the nectar of flowers **2** sweetness **3** darling

hon·ey·comb *n.* the structure of six-sided wax cells made by bees to hold their honey or eggs —*vt.* to cause to have holes like a honeycomb —*adj.* of or like a honeycomb: also **hon′ey·combed′**

hon·ey·dew melon a variety of melon with a smooth, whitish rind and sweet, greenish flesh

hon·ey·lo·cust *n.* a North American tree having featherlike foliage and large, twisted pods Also **honey locust**

hon·ey·moon *n.* the vacation spent together by a newly married couple —*vi.* to have or spend a honeymoon —**hon′ey·moon′er** *n.*

hon·ey·suck·le *n.* a plant with small, fragrant flowers of red, yellow, or white

Hong Kong (häŋ′käŋ′, hôŋ′kôŋ′) administrative region of China, on the South China Sea: formerly a British colony

honk (hôŋk, häŋk) *n.* ⟦echoic⟧ **1** the call of a wild goose **2** a similar sound, as of an automobile horn —*vi., vt.* to make or cause to make such a sound

hon·ky-tonk (hôŋ′kē tôŋk′) *n.* **1** [Old Slang] a cheap, noisy nightclub **2** [Slang] a bar, esp. one where country music is played —*adj.* designating music played on a piano with a tinkling sound

Ho·no·lu·lu (hän′ə lōō′lōō) capital of Hawaii: seaport on Oahu

hon·or (än′ər) *n.* ⟦L⟧ **1** high regard or respect; esp., *a)* glory; fame *b)* good reputation **2** adherence to principles considered right; integrity **3** chastity **4** high rank; distinction **5** [**H-**] a title of certain officials, as judges **6** something done or given as a token of respect **7** a source of respect and fame —*vt.* **1** to respect greatly **2** to show high regard for **3** to do or give something in honor of **4** to accept and pay [to *honor* a check] Brit. sp. **hon′our** —**do the honors** to act as host

hon·or·a·ble *adj.* **1** worthy of being honored **2** honest; upright **3** bringing honor —**hon′or·a·bly** *adv.*

hon·o·ra·ri·um (än′ə rer′ē əm) *n., pl.* **-ri·ums** or **-ri·a** (-ə) ⟦L⟧ a payment, as to a professional person, for services on which no fee is set

hon·or·ar·y (än′ə rer ′ē) *adj.* **1** given as an honor **2** designating or in an office held as an honor, without service or pay —**hon′or·ar′i·ly** *adv.*

honor guard a ceremonial guard, as one assigned to escort a distinguished person or to accompany a casket at a funeral

hon·or·if·ic (-ə rif′ik) *adj.* ⟦< L *honor* + *facere*, to make⟧ conferring honor; showing respect

honor roll a list of people achieving a distinction, as students earning high grades

Hon·shu (hän′shōō′) largest of the islands forming Japan

hood (hood) *n.* ⟦OE *hod*⟧ **1** a covering for the head and neck, often part of a coat, etc. **2** anything resembling a hood, as the metal cover over an automobile engine —*vt.* to cover as with a hood —**hood′ed** *adj.*

-hood (hood) ⟦OE *had*⟧ *suffix* **1** state or quality [*childhood*] **2** the whole group of [*priesthood*]

hood·ie (hood′ē) *n.* a hooded garment, esp. a sweatshirt or sweater

hood·lum (hood′ləm, hōōd′-) *n.* ⟦prob. < Ger dial. *hudilump*, wretch⟧ a lawless person, as a member of a gang of criminals

hoo·doo (hōō′dōō′) *n., pl.* **-doos′** ⟦var. of VOODOO⟧ **1** VOODOO **2** [Inf.] bad luck or its cause

hood·wink *vt.* 〚HOOD + WINK〛 to mislead by trickery; dupe

hoo·ey (hōō′ē) *interj., n.* [Slang] nonsense

hoof (hōōf, hoof) *n., pl.* **hoofs** or **hooves** (hōōvz, hoovz) 〚OE *hof*〛 the horny covering on the feet of cattle, horses, etc., or the entire foot —*vt., vi.* [Inf.] to walk: often with *it* —**hoofed** *adj.*

hook (hook) *n.* 〚OE *hoc*〛 1 a bent piece of metal, etc. used to catch, hold, or pull something 2 a fishhook 3 something shaped like a hook 4 something moving in a hooklike path, as a punch delivered with the elbow bent —*vt.* to catch, fasten, throw, etc. with a hook —*vi.* 1 to curve as a hook does 2 to be fastened or caught by a hook —**by hook or by crook** by any means, honest or dishonest —**hook up** 1 to connect or set up (a computer, etc.) 2 [Inf.] to meet up 3 [Slang] to engage in casual sexual activity, as with a friend or acquaintance —**off the hook** [Inf.] out of trouble

hook·ah or **hook·a** (hook′ə, hōō′kə) *n.* 〚Ar *ḥuqqa*〛 a tobacco pipe with a tube for drawing the smoke through a vessel of water to cool it

hooked (hookt) *adj.* 1 like a hook 2 made with a hook [*hooked* rug] 3 [Slang] *a)* obsessed with or addicted to (often with *on*) *b)* married

hook·er *n.* [Slang] a prostitute

hook·up *n.* 1 the arrangement and connection of parts, circuits, etc., as in a radio 2 [Slang] a casual sexual encounter

hook·worm *n.* a small, parasitic, intestinal roundworm with hooks around the mouth

hook·y *n.* [Inf.] used only in **play hooky**, be a truant

hoo·li·gan (hōō′li gən) *n.* 〚< ? *Hooligan*, a family name〛 [Slang] a hoodlum

hoop (hōōp) *n.* 〚OE *hop*〛 1 a circular band for holding together the staves of a barrel, etc. 2 anything like this, as a metal basketball rim —*vt.* to bind or fasten as with a hoop —**jump through hoops** [Inf.] to do many things in achieving something

hoop·la (hōōp′lä′) *n.* 〚< ?〛 [Inf.] 1 great excitement 2 showy publicity

hoop skirt a skirt worn over a framework of hoops

hoo·ray (hoo rā′, hə–; hōō–) *interj., n., vi., vt.* *var. of* HURRAY

hoose·gow (hōōs′gou′) *n.* 〚< Sp *juzgado*, court of justice〛 [Old Slang] a jail

Hoo·sier (hōō′zhər) *n.* [Inf.] a person born or living in Indiana

hoot (hōōt) *n.* 〚echoic〛 1 the sound that an owl makes 2 any sound like this, as a shout of scorn 3 [Inf.] an amusing person, thing, etc. —*vi.* to utter a hoot —*vt.* to express (scorn) of (someone) by hooting —**hoot′er** *n.*

hoot·en·an·ny (hōōt′'n an′ē) *n., pl.* **-nies** a meeting of folk singers, as for public entertainment

Hoo·ver (hōō′vər), **Her·bert (Clark)** (hur′bərt) 1874-1964; 31st president of the U.S. (1929-33)

hop¹ (häp) *vi.* **hopped, hop′ping** 〚OE *hoppian*〛 1 to make a short leap or leaps on one foot 2 to leap with both, or all, feet at once, as a frog 3 [Inf.] *a)* to go briskly *b)* to take a short trip —*vt.* 1 to jump over 2 to get aboard —*n.* 1. a hopping 2 [Inf.] *a)* a dance *b)* a short flight in an airplane

hop² (häp) *n.* 〚< MDu *hoppe*〛 a twining vine with flowers borne in small cones 2 [*pl.*] the dried ripe cones, used for flavoring beer —**hop up** [Slang] to stimulate, as by a drug

hope (hōp) *n.* 〚OE *hopa*〛 1 a feeling that what is wanted may possibly happen 2 the object of this 3 a person or thing on which one may base some hope —*vt.* **hoped, hop′ing** to want and expect —*vi.* to have hope (*for*) —**hope′ful** *adj.* —**hope′ful·ly** *adv.* —**hope′less** *adj.* —**hope′less·ly** *adv.*

hop·head *n.* [Slang] a drug addict

hop·per (häp′ər) *n.* 1 one that hops 2 any hopping insect 3 a box, tank, etc. from which the contents can be emptied slowly and evenly

hop·scotch (häp′skäch′) *n.* a children's game in which a player hops from section to section of a figure drawn on the ground

Hor·ace (hôr′is, här′–) 65-8 B.C.; Rom. poet

horde (hôrd) *n.* 〚ult. < Tatar *urdu*, a camp〛 a crowd or throng; swarm —*vi.* **hord′ed, hord′ing** to form or gather in a horde

hore·hound (hôr′hound′) *n.* 〚OE *harhune*〛 1 a bitter plant of the mint family 2 medicine or candy made from its juice

ho·ri·zon (hə rī′zən) *n.* 〚< Gr *horos*, boundary〛 1 the line where the sky seems to meet the earth 2 [*usually pl.*] the limit of one's experience, interest, etc.

hor·i·zon·tal (hôr′i zänt′'l) *adj.* 1 parallel to the plane of the horizon; not vertical 2 flat and even; level —**hor′i·zon′tal·ly** *adv.*

hor·mone (hôr′mōn′) *n.* 〚< Gr *hormē*, impulse〛 a substance formed in some organ of the body and carried to another part, where it takes effect —**hor·mo′nal** *adj.*

horn (hôrn) *n.* 〚OE〛 1 a hard, bonelike projection growing on the head of a cow, goat, etc. 2 the substance horns are made of 3 anything like a horn in position, shape, etc. 4 any brass instrument; specif., FRENCH HORN 5 a device sounded to give a warning —*adj.* made of horn —**horn in (on)** [Inf.] to intrude or meddle (in) —**horned** *adj.* —**horn′less** *adj.* —**horn′like′** *adj.*

Horn, Cape southernmost point of South America, on an island of Chile

horn·blende (hôrn′blend′) *n.* 〚Ger〛 a hard, heavy, dark-colored mineral

horned toad a small, scaly, insect-eating lizard with hornlike spines: also **horned lizard**

hor·net (hôr′nit) *n.* 〚OE *hyrnet*〛 a large, yellow and black wasp

horn of plenty CORNUCOPIA

horn·pipe *n.* 〚ME〛 a lively dance formerly popular with sailors

horn·y (hôr′nē) *adj.* **-i·er, -i·est** 1 made of horn 2 toughened and calloused [*horny* hands] 3 [Slang] yearning for sex

ho·rol·o·gy (hō räl′ə jē) *n.* 〖< Gr *hōra*, hour + -LOGY〗 the science of measuring time or making timepieces

hor·o·scope (hôr′ə skōp′) *n.* 〖< Gr *hōra*, hour + *skopos*, watcher〗 1 an astrological chart of the zodiacal signs and positions of planets, etc., esp. at the time of a person's birth 2 an astrological forecast

hor·ren·dous (hô ren′dəs) *adj.* [see HORRID] horrible; frightful

hor·ri·ble (hôr′ə bəl) *adj.* 〖see fol.〗 1 causing horror; terrible; dreadful 2 [Inf.] very bad, ugly, unpleasant, etc. —**hor′ri·bly** *adv.*

hor·rid (hôr′id) *adj.* 〖< L *horrere*, to bristle, shake, be afraid〗 1 causing horror; terrible 2 very bad, ugly, unpleasant, etc. —**hor′rid·ly** *adv.*

hor·rif·ic (hô rif′ik, hə-) *adj.* horrifying

hor·ri·fy (hôr′ə fī′) *vt.* -**fied′**, -**fy′ing** 1 to cause to feel horror 2 [Inf.] to shock or disgust

hor·ror (hôr′ər) *n.* [see HORRID] 1 the strong feeling caused by something frightful or shocking 2 strong dislike 3 something that causes horror

hors de com·bat (ôr də kōn bä′) 〖Fr, out of combat〗 disabled

hors d'oeuvre (ôr′durv′) *pl.* **hors′ d'oeuvres′** 〖Fr, lit., outside of work〗 a canapé or other appetizer

horse (hôrs) *n.* 〖OE *hors*〗 1 a large, four-legged, solid-hoofed animal with flowing mane and tail, domesticated for drawing loads, carrying riders, etc. 2 a frame with legs to support something —*adj.* of or on horses —**hold one's horses** [Slang] to curb one's impatience —**horse around** [Slang] to engage in horseplay

horse·back *n.* the back of a horse —*adv.* on horseback

horse chestnut 1 a flowering tree with large leaves and glossy brown seeds 2 its seed

horse·feath·ers *n., interj.* [Slang] nonsense

horse·fly *n., pl.* -**flies′** a large fly that sucks the blood of horses, etc.

horse·hair *n.* 1 hair from the mane or tail of a horse 2 a stiff fabric made from this hair

horse·hide *n.* 1 the hide of a horse 2 leather made from this

horse·laugh *n.* a loud, boisterous, usually derisive laugh; guffaw

horse·man (-mən) *n., pl.* -**men** (-mən) a man skilled in the riding, managing, or care of horses —**horse′man·ship′** *n.*

horse opera [Slang] WESTERN (*n.*)

horse·play *n.* rough, boisterous fun

horse·pow·er *n., pl.* -**pow′er** a unit for measuring the power of engines, etc., equal to 746 watts or 33,000 foot-pounds per minute

horse·rad·ish *n.* 1 a plant with a pungent, white, fleshy root 2 a relish made of the grated root

horse sense [Inf.] common sense

horse·shoe *n.* 1 a flat, U-shaped metal plate nailed to a horse's hoof to protect it 2 anything shaped like this 3 [*pl.*, *with sing. v.*] a game in which players toss horseshoes at two stakes

horseshoe crab a marine arthropod with a large, rounded shell and a long, spinelike tail

horse·tail *n.* a common rushlike plant found in moist areas

horse·whip *n.* a whip for driving horses —*vt.* -**whipped′**, -**whip′ping** to lash with a horse-whip

horse·wom·an *n., pl.* -**wom′en** a woman skilled in the riding, managing, or care of horses

hors·y (hôr′sē) *adj.* -**i·er**, -**i·est** 1 of, like, or suggesting a horse 2 of or like people who are fond of horses, fox-hunting, horse racing, etc. Also **hors′ey**

hor·ta·to·ry (hôr′tə tôr′ē) *adj.* 〖< L *hortari*, incite〗 exhorting; advising

hor·ti·cul·ture (hôr′tə kul′chər) *n.* 〖< L *hortus*, garden + *cultura*, cultivation〗 the art or science of growing flowers, fruits, and vegetables —**hor′ti·cul′tur·al** *adj.*

ho·san·na (hō zan′ə, -zä′nə) *n., interj.* 〖< Heb *hōshī′āh nnā*, lit., save, we pray〗 an exclamation of praise to God

hose (hōz) *n., pl.* **hose** or, for 2, usually **hos′es** 〖OE *hosa*〗 1 [*pl.*] stockings or socks 2 a flexible tube used to convey fluids —*vt.* **hosed**, **hos′ing** to water with a hose: often with *down*

ho·sier·y (hō′zhər ē) *n.* stockings

hos·pice (häs′pis) *n.* 〖< L *hospes*, host, guest〗 1 a shelter for travelers 2 a homelike facility for the care of terminally ill patients

hos·pi·ta·ble (häs′pit ə bəl, häs pit′-) *adj.* [see prec.] welcoming toward guests, new arrivals, etc. —**hos′pi·ta·bly** *adv.*

hos·pi·tal (häs′pit′'l) *n.* 〖< L *hospes*, host, guest〗 an institution providing medical treatment for people who are ill, injured, pregnant, etc.

hos·pi·tal·i·ty (häs′pi tal′ə tē) *n., pl.* -**ties** the act, practice, or quality of being hospitable

hos·pi·tal·ize (häs′pit′'l īz′) *vt.* -**ized′**, -**iz′ing** to put in, or admit to, a hospital —**hos′pi·tal·i·za′tion** *n.*

host¹ (hōst) *n.* 〖< ML *hostia*〗 a wafer of the bread used in the Eucharist

host² (hōst) *n.* 〖< L *hospes*, host, guest〗 1 one who entertains guests, esp. at home 2 a person who keeps an inn or hotel 3 any organism on or in which a parasitic organism lives —*vi., vt.* to act as host (to)

host³ (hōst) *n.* 〖< ML *hostis*, army〗 1 an army 2 a great number

hos·tage (häs′tij) *n.* 〖< OFr〗 a person kept or given as a pledge until certain conditions are met

hos·tel (häs′təl) *n.* 〖< L *hospes*, host, guest〗 an inn: also **hos′tel·ry** (-rē), *pl.* -**ries**

hos·tel·er *n.* a traveler who stops at hostels

host·ess (hōs′tis) *n.* 1 a woman who entertains guests, esp. at home; sometimes, the host's wife 2 a woman employed in a restaurant to supervise serving, seating, etc.

hos·tile (häs′təl) *adj.* 〖< L *hostis*, enemy〗 1 of or characteristic of an enemy 2 unfriendly; antagonistic —**hos′tile·ly** *adv.*

hos·til·i·ty (häs til′ə tē) *n., pl.* **-ties 1** a feeling of enmity, ill will, etc. **2** *a)* an expression of enmity, ill will, etc. *b)* [*pl.*] warfare

hos·tler (häs′lər, äs′-) *n.* ⟦contr. of HOSTELER⟧ one who takes care of horses at an inn, stable, etc.

hot (hät) *adj.* **hot′ter, hot′test** ⟦OE *hat*⟧ **1** *a)* having a temperature higher than that of the human body *b)* having a relatively high temperature **2** producing a burning sensation [*hot* pepper] **3** characterized by strong feeling or intense activity, etc.; specif., *a)* impetuous [a *hot* temper] *b)* violent [a *hot* battle] *c)* lustful *d)* very controversial **4** following closely [in *hot* pursuit] **5** electrically charged [a *hot* wire] **6** [Inf.] recent; fresh [*hot* news] **7** [Slang] *a)* recently stolen or smuggled *b)* excellent; good *c)* sexually attractive —**make it hot for** [Inf.] to make things uncomfortable for —**hot′ly** *adv.* —**hot′ness** *n.*

hot air [Slang] empty talk

hot·bed *n.* **1** a bed of earth covered with glass and heated, as by manure, for forcing plants **2** a place of rapid growth or extensive activity

hot·blood·ed *adj.* easily excited; excitable

hot·box *n.* an overheated bearing on an axle or shaft

hot cake a pancake —**sell like hot cakes** [Inf.] to be sold rapidly and in large quantities

hot dog a wiener, esp. one served hot in a long, soft roll

ho·tel (hō tel′) *n.* ⟦< OFr *hostel*, hostel⟧ an establishment providing lodging and, usually, meals for travelers, etc.

ho·tel·ier (hō tel′yər) *n.* ⟦Fr *hôtelier*⟧ an owner or manager of a hotel

hot flash the sensation of a wave of heat passing over the body, often experienced by women during menopause

hot·foot *vi.* [Inf.] to hurry; hasten: with *it*

hot·head·ed *adj.* **1** quick-tempered **2** impetuous —**hot′head′** *n.*

hot·house *n.* GREENHOUSE

hot·line *n.* an emergency telephone line, as between government leaders or to a social agency

hot plate a small portable electric heating element for cooking food

hot potato [Inf.] a troubling problem that no one wants to handle

hot rod [Slang] an automobile, often an old one, rebuilt for great speed —**hot rod′der**

hot seat [Slang] **1** ELECTRIC CHAIR **2** a difficult situation

hot·shot *n.* [Slang] one seen as an expert or as very aggressive: often used ironically

hot-tem·pered *adj.* having a fiery temper

hot tub a large tub in which several people can soak in hot water together

hound (hound) *n.* ⟦OE *hund*, dog⟧ **1** any of several breeds of hunting dog **2** any dog —*vt.* **1** to hunt or chase with or as with hounds **2** to urge on

hounds·tooth (check) (houndz′tōōth′) a pattern of irregular broken checks, used in woven material

hour (our) *n.* ⟦< Gr *hōra*⟧ **1** one of the twenty-four parts of a day; sixty minutes **2** the time for a particular activity [lunch *hour*] **3** [*pl.*] a period fixed for work, etc. [office *hours*] **4** the time of day [the *hour* is 2:30] **5** *Educ.* a credit, equal to one hour spent in class per week —**after hours** after the regular hours for business, school, etc.

hour·glass *n.* an instrument for measuring time by the trickling of sand, etc. from one glass bulb to another

hour hand the short hand of a clock or watch, which indicates the hours

hou·ri (hoo′rē, hou′-) *n., pl.* **-ris** ⟦< Ar *ḥūrīyah*, black-eyed woman⟧ a beautiful nymph of the Muslim Paradise

hour·ly *adj.* **1** happening every hour **2** done during an hour **3** frequent —*adv.* **1** once an hour **2** often

house (hous; *for v.* houz) *n., pl.* **hous·es** (hou′ziz) ⟦OE *hus*⟧ **1** a building to live in; specif., a building occupied by one family or person **2** the people who live in a house; household **3** [*often* H-] a family as including kin, ancestors, and descendants, esp. a royal family **4** shelter, living or storage space, etc. **5** *a)* a theater *b)* the audience in a theater **6** a business firm **7** [*often* H-] a legislative assembly —*adj.* of a salad dressing, wine, etc. at a particular restaurant —*vt.* **housed, hous′ing 1** to provide a house or lodgings for **2** to cover, shelter, etc. — **keep house** to take care of a home —**on the house** at the expense of the establishment

house·boat *n.* a large, flat-bottomed boat used as a residence

house·bound *adj.* confined to one's home, as by illness

house·break·ing *n.* the act of breaking into and entering another's house to commit theft or another felony

house·bro·ken *adj.* trained to live in a house (i.e., to urinate, etc. in a special place or outside): said of a dog, cat, etc.

house·fly *n., pl.* **-flies′** a two-winged fly found in and around houses

house·guest *n.* a person who stays overnight in another's home

house·hold *n.* **1** all those living in one house **2** the home and its affairs —**house′hold′er** *n.*

household word a common saying or thing, familiar to nearly everyone

house·hus·band *n.* a married man whose job is keeping house and taking care of domestic affairs

house·keep·er *n.* **1** one who runs a home, esp. a woman hired to do this **2** a chambermaid, as at a hotel —**house′keep′ing** *n.*

house·maid *n.* a maid who does housework

House of Commons the lower house of the legislature of Great Britain or Canada

House of Lords the upper house of the legislature of Great Britain

House of Representatives the lower house of the legislature of the U.S. and most of the states of the U.S.

house·plant *n.* a plant grown indoors, esp. for decoration

house·wares (-werz′) *pl.n.* articles for household use, esp. in the kitchen

house·warm·ing *n.* a party to celebrate moving into a new home

house·wife *n., pl.* **-wives′** a married woman whose job is keeping house and taking care of domestic affairs

house·work *n.* the work involved in keeping house; cleaning, cooking, etc.

hous·ing (hou′zin) *n.* **1** the providing of shelter or lodging **2** shelter or lodging **3** houses collectively **4** *Mech.* a frame, box, etc. for containing some part, mechanism, etc.

Hous·ton (hyōōs′tən) city & port in SE Texas

hove (hōv) *vt., vi. alt. pt. & pp. of* HEAVE

hov·el (huv′əl, häv′-) *n.* 〖ME〗 any small, miserable dwelling; hut

hov·er (huv′ər, häv′-) *vi.* 〖< ME *hoven*, to stay (suspended)〗 **1** to flutter in the air near one place **2** to linger close by **3** to waver (*between*)

how (hou) *adv.* 〖OE *hu*〗 **1** in what manner or way **2** in what state or condition **3** for what reason **4** to what extent, degree, etc. *How* is also used as an intensive —**how about** [Inf.] what is your opinion, etc. concerning?

how·be·it (hou bē′it) *adv.* [Archaic] however it may be; nevertheless

how·dah (hou′də) *n.* 〖< Hindi *hauda*〗 a seat for riding on the back of an elephant or camel

how·ev·er *adv.* **1** in whatever manner **2** to whatever degree **3** nevertheless

how·itz·er (hou′it sər) *n.* 〖< Czech *houfnice*, orig., a sling〗 a short cannon, firing shells in a high trajectory

howl (houl) *vi.* 〖ME *hulen*〗 **1** to utter the long, wailing cry of wolves, dogs, etc. **2** to utter a similar cry of pain, anger, etc. **3** to shout or laugh in scorn, mirth, etc. —*vt.* **1** to utter with a howl **2** to drive by howling —*n.* **1** the wailing cry of a wolf, dog, etc. **2** any similar sound **3** [Inf.] a joke

howl·er *n.* **1** one that howls **2** [Inf., Chiefly Brit.] a ludicrous blunder

how·so·ev·er (hou′sō ev′ər) *adv.* **1** to whatever degree or extent **2** by whatever means

hoy·den (hoid′'n) *n.* 〖< ? Du〗 a bold, boisterous girl; tomboy

Hoyle (hoil) *n.* a book of rules for card games, orig. compiled by E. Hoyle (1672-1769) — **according to Hoyle** according to the rules

HP *abbrev.* horsepower: usually written *abbrev.* **hp**

HQ or **hq** *abbrev.* headquarters

hr *abbrev.* hour

HR *abbrev.* **1** *Baseball* home run(s) **2** House of Representatives **3** human resources

HRH *abbrev.* Her (or His) Royal Highness

HS *abbrev.* high school

ht *abbrev.* height

HTML *abbrev.* Hypertext Markup Language

Huang (hwän) river in N China, flowing into the Yellow Sea

hua·ra·ches (wə rä′chēz, hə-) *pl.n.* 〖MexSp〗 flat sandals with uppers made of straps or woven leather strips

hub (hub) *n.* 〖< ?〗 **1** the center part of a wheel **2** a center of activity

hub·bub (hub′bub′) *n.* 〖prob. < Gael exclamation〗 an uproar; tumult

hub·cap *n.* a tight cap over the hub of a wheel, esp. on an automobile

hu·bris (hyōō′bris) *n.* 〖Gr *hybris*〗 arrogance caused by excessive pride

huck·le·ber·ry (huk′əl ber′ē) *n., pl.* **-ries** 〖prob. ult. < ME *hurtilberye*〗 **1** a shrub with blue berries **2** this berry

huck·ster (huk′stər) *n.* 〖< MDu *hoeken*, peddle〗 **1** a peddler **2** [Inf.] one engaged in advertising —*vt.* to peddle

HUD *abbrev.* (Department of) Housing and Urban Development

hud·dle (hud′'l) *vi., vt.* **-dled, -dling** 〖< ?〗 **1** to crowd close together **2** to draw (oneself) up —*n.* **1** a confused crowd or heap **2** [Inf.] a private conference **3** *Football* a grouping of a team to get signals before a play

Hud·son (hud′sən) river in E New York

Hudson Bay inland sea in NE Canada; arm of the Atlantic

hue¹ (hyōō) *n.* 〖< OE *heow*〗 **1** color **2** a particular shade or tint of a color

hue² (hyōō) *n.* 〖< OFr *hu*, outcry〗 a shouting: now only in **hue and cry**

huff (huf) *vi.* to blow; puff —*n.* a state of smoldering anger or resentment —**huff′y** *adj.* **-i·er, -i·est**

hug (hug) *vt.* **hugged, hug′ging** 〖prob. < ON *hugga*, to comfort〗 **1** to clasp closely and fondly in the arms; embrace **2** to cling to (a belief, etc.) **3** to keep close to (*small boats hugged the shore*) —*vi.* to embrace each other —*n.* a close embrace

huge (hyōōj) *adj.* **hug′er, hug′est** 〖< OFr *ahuge*〗 very large; gigantic; immense —**huge′ly** *adv.*

Hu·go (hyōō′gō), **Vic·tor (Marie)** (vik′tər) 1802-85; Fr. poet, novelist, & playwright

Hu·gue·not (hyōō′gə nät′) *n.* a French Protestant of the 1500s or 1600s

huh (hu, hun) *interj.* [Inf.] used to express contempt, surprise, etc., or to ask a question

hu·la (hōō′lə) *n.* 〖Haw〗 a native Hawaiian dance: also **hu′la·hu′la**

hulk (hulk) *n.* 〖< Gr *holkas*, towed ship〗 **1** the hull of an old, dismantled ship **2** a big, clumsy person or thing

hulk·ing *adj.* bulky and clumsy

hull (hul) *n.* 〖OE *hulu*〗 **1** the outer covering of a seed or fruit, as the husk of grain or shell of a nut **2** the frame or main body of a ship, airship, etc. **3** any outer covering —*vt.* to take the hulls off (nuts, etc.) —**hull′er** *n.*

hul·la·ba·loo (hul′ə bə lōō′) *n.* 〖echoic〗 noise and confusion; hubbub

hum (hum) *vi.* **hummed, hum′ming** 〖echoic〗 **1** to make a low, continuous, murmuring sound **2** to sing with closed lips **3** [Inf.] to be full of activity —*vt.* to sing (a tune) with closed lips —*n.* a continuous murmur

hu·man (hyōō'mən) *adj.* ⟦< L *humanus*⟧ of, characteristic of, or having the qualities typical of people, or human beings —*n.* a person: also **human being** —**hu'man·ness** *n.*

hu·mane (hyōō mān') *adj.* ⟦var. of prec.⟧ 1 kind, tender, merciful, etc. 2 civilizing; refining —**hu·mane'ly** *adv.* —**hu·mane'ness** *n.*

hu·man·ism (hyōō'mə niz'əm) *n.* 1 any system of thought based on the interests and ideals of humanity 2 [H–] the intellectual movement that stemmed from the study of the Greek and Latin classics during the Middle Ages —**hu'man·ist** *n., adj.* —**hu'man·is'tic** *adj.* —**hu'man·is'ti·cal·ly** *adv.*

hu·man·i·tar·i·an (hyōō man'ə ter'ē ən) *n.* a person devoted to promoting the welfare of humanity —*adj.* helping humanity —**hu·man'i·tar'i·an·ism'** *n.*

hu·man·i·ty (hyōō man'ə tē) *n., pl.* **-ties** 1 the fact or quality of being human or humane 2 people —**the humanities** literature, philosophy, history, etc., as distinguished from the sciences

hu·man·ize (hyōō'mə nīz') *vt.* **-ized', -iz'ing** to make or become human or humane —**hu'man·i·za'tion** *n.* —**hu'man·iz'er** *n.*

hu·man·kind *n.* the human race; people

hu·man·ly *adv.* 1 in a human manner 2 within human ability or knowledge

hu·man·oid (-mə noid') *adj.* nearly human —*n.* a nearly human creature

human resources a department responsible for personnel records, company benefits, hiring and training employees, etc.

hum·ble (hum'bəl) *adj.* **-bler, -blest** ⟦< L *humilis*, low⟧ 1 having or showing a consciousness of one's shortcomings; modest 2 lowly; unpretentious —*vt.* **-bled, -bling** 1 to lower in condition or rank; abase 2 to lower in pride; make modest —**hum'ble·ness** *n.* —**hum'bly** *adv.*

hum·bug (hum'bug') *n.* ⟦< ?⟧ 1 fraud; sham; hoax 2 an impostor —*vt.* **-bugged', -bug'ging** to dupe; deceive —*interj.* nonsense!

hum·drum (hum'drum') *adj.* ⟦echoic⟧ dull

hu·mer·us (hyōō'mər əs) *n., pl.* **-mer·i'** (-ī') ⟦L⟧ the bone of the upper arm or forelimb —**hu'mer·al** *adj.*

hu·mid (hyōō'mid) *adj.* ⟦< L *umere*, be moist⟧ damp; moist

hu·mid·i·fy (hyōō mid'ə fī') *vt.* **-fied', -fy'ing** to make humid; dampen —**hu·mid'i·fi'er** *n.*

hu·mid·i·ty (-ə tē) *n.* 1 moistness; dampness 2 the amount of moisture in the air

hu·mi·dor (hyōō'mə dôr') *n.* a case or jar for keeping tobacco moist

hu·mil·i·ate (hyōō mil'ē āt') *vt.* **-at'ed, -at'ing** ⟦< L *humilis*, humble⟧ to hurt the pride or dignity of; mortify —**hu·mil'i·a'tion** *n.*

hu·mil·i·ty (-ə tē) *n.* the state or quality of being humble

hum·ming·bird (hum'iŋ burd') *n.* a very small, brightly colored bird with narrow wings that vibrate rapidly, allowing it to hover while drinking nectar from flowers

hum·mock (hum'ək) *n.* ⟦< ?⟧ a low, rounded hill; knoll —**hum'mock·y** *adj.*

hum·mus (hum'əs) *n.* ⟦Turk *humus*⟧ a Middle Eastern puree of chickpeas, garlic, sesame paste, etc.

hu·mon·gous (hyōō mäŋ'gəs, -muŋ'-) *adj.* ⟦? a blend of HUGE + MONSTROUS⟧ [Slang] enormous

hu·mor (hyōō'mər) *n.* ⟦< L *humor*, fluid: after former belief in four body fluids (*humors*) held responsible for one's disposition⟧ 1 mood; state of mind 2 whim; caprice 3 a comical quality 4 *a)* the ability to appreciate or express what is funny, amusing, etc. *b)* the expression of this —*vt.* to comply with the mood or whim of; indulge Brit. sp. **hu'mour** —**out of humor** not in a good mood —**hu'mor·ist** *n.* —**hu'mor·less** *adj.*

hu·mor·ous *adj.* funny; amusing; comical —**hu'mor·ous·ly** *adv.*

hump (hump) *n.* ⟦prob. < LowG⟧ a rounded, protruding lump, as on a camel's back —*vt.* to hunch; arch —**over the hump** [Inf.] past the worst or most difficult part

hump·back *n.* 1 a humped, deformed back 2 HUNCHBACK (*n.* 2) 3 a large whale with long flippers and a raised back —**hump'backed'** *adj.*

hu·mus (hyōō'məs) *n.* ⟦L, earth⟧ the dark part of the soil, from partially decayed leaves, etc.

Hun (hun) *n.* a member of a warlike Asiatic people that invaded Europe in the 4th and 5th c. A.D.

hunch (hunch) *vt.* ⟦< ?⟧ to arch into a hump —*vi.* to move forward jerkily —*n.* 1 a hump 2 a feeling not based on known facts; premonition

hunch·back (hunch'bak') *n.* 1 HUMPBACK (*n.* 1) 2 a person having a back with a hump —**hunch'backed'** *adj.*

hun·dred (hun'drəd) *n., adj.* ⟦OE⟧ ten times ten; 100; C —**hun'dredth** (-drədth) *adj., n.*

hun·dred·fold *adj., adv.* (having) a hundred times as much or as many

hun·dred·weight *n.* a unit of weight equal to 100 pounds in the U.S. and 112 pounds in Great Britain

hung (huŋ) *vt., vi. pt. & pp. of* HANG —**hung over** [Slang] having a hangover —**hung up (on)** [Slang] disturbed, frustrated, or obsessed (by)

Hung *abbrev.* 1 Hungarian 2 Hungary

Hun·gar·i·an (huŋ ger'ē ən) *n.* 1 the language of Hungary 2 a person born or living in Hungary —*adj.* of Hungary or its people, language, etc.

Hun·ga·ry (huŋ'gə rē) country in SC Europe

hun·ger (huŋ'gər) *n.* ⟦OE *hungor*⟧ 1 discomfort caused by a need for food 2 starvation 3 a desire for food 4 any strong desire —*vi.* 1 to be hungry 2 to desire —**hun'gry** *adj.* **-gri·er, -gri·est** —**hun'gri·ly** *adv.*

hunger strike the refusal of a prisoner, demonstrator, etc. to eat until certain demands are met

hung jury a jury unable to reach a verdict

hunk (huŋk) *n.* [Fl *hunke*] [Inf.] **1** a large piece **2** a muscular, sexually attractive man

hun·ker (huŋ′kər) *vi.* [< dial.] to squat or crouch: often with *down* —*n.* [*pl.*] haunches or buttocks

hunt (hunt) *vt., vi.* [OE *huntian*] **1** to kill or catch (game) for food or sport **2** to try to find; search (for) **3** to chase —*n.* **1** a hunting **2** a group of people who hunt together **3** a search —**hunt′er** *n.*, **hunts′man** (-mən) *n.*, *pl.* **-men** (-mən) —**hunt′ress** *n.*

hur·dle (hurd′'l) *n.* [OE *hyrdel*] **1** a frame-like barrier over which horses or runners must leap in a race **2** an obstacle —*vt.* **-dled, -dling 1** to jump over **2** to overcome (an obstacle) —**hur′dler** *n.*

hur·dy-gur·dy (hur′dē gur′dē) *n., pl.* **-dies** [? echoic] a barrel organ

hurl (hurl) *vt.* [prob. < ON] **1** to throw with force or violence **2** to cast down **3** to utter vehemently —*vi.* [Inf.] *Baseball* to pitch —**hurl′er** *n.*

hurl·y-burl·y (hur′lē bur′lē) *n., pl.* **-burl′ies** a turmoil; uproar

Hu·ron (hyōōr′än) *,* **Lake** second largest of the Great Lakes, between Michigan & Canada

hur·rah (hə rä′, -rô′) *n., interj.* HURRAY

hur·ray (hə rā′) *n., interj.* [echoic] (exclamation) used to express joy, approval, etc.

hur·ri·cane (hur′i kān′) *n.* [< WInd *huracan*] a violent tropical cyclone with winds moving at least 74 mph

hurricane lamp 1 an oil lamp or candlestick with a glass chimney to protect the flame **2** an electric lamp like this

hur·ry (hur′ē) *vt.* **-ried, -ry·ing** [prob. akin to HURL] **1** to move or send with haste **2** to cause to occur or be done more rapidly or too rapidly **3** to urge to act soon or too soon —*vi.* to move or act with haste —*n.* **1** rush; urgency **2** eagerness to do, go, etc. quickly —**hur′ried·ly** *adv.*

hurt (hurt) *vt.* hurt, **hurt′ing** [< OFr *hurter*, to hit] **1** to cause pain or injury to **2** to harm **3** to offend —*vi.* **1** to cause injury, pain, etc. **2** to have pain; be sore —*n.* **1** a pain or injury **2** harm; damage —*adj.* injured; damaged

hurt·ful *adj.* causing hurt; harmful

hur·tle (hurt′'l) *vi., vt.* **-tled, -tling** [ME *hurtlen*] to move or throw with great speed or much force

hus·band (huz′bənd) *n.* [< ON *hūs,* house + *bondi,* freeholder] a married man —*vt.* to manage economically; conserve

hus·band·ry *n.* **1** thrift **2** farming

hush (hush) *vt.* [< ME *huscht,* quiet (adj.)] **1** to make quiet or silent **2** to soothe; lull —*vi.* to become quiet or silent —*n.* quiet; silence —*interj.* used to call for silence

hush-hush *adj.* [Inf.] very secret

hush puppy a small ball of fried cornmeal dough

husk (husk) *n.* [prob. < MDu *huus,* house] **1** the dry outer covering of various fruits or seeds, as of an ear of corn **2** any dry, rough, or useless covering —*vt.* to remove the husk from

hus·ky¹ (hus′kē) *n., pl.* **-kies** [< a var. of Eskimo] [*also* H-] a dog of any of several breeds for pulling sleds in the Arctic

husk·y² (hus′kē) *adj.* **-i·er, -i·est 1** hoarse; rough **2** [< toughness of a *husk*] big and strong **3** wide in girth

hus·sar (hoo zär′) *n.* [< Serb *husar*] a European light-armed cavalryman, usually with a brilliant dress uniform

hus·sy (huz′ē, hus′-) *n., pl.* **-sies** [< ME *huswife,* housewife] **1** a woman of low morals **2** a bold, saucy girl

hus·tings (hus′tiŋz) *pl.n.* [< ON *hūsthing,* house council] [*usually with sing. v.*] **1** the process of, or a place for, political campaigning

hus·tle (hus′əl) *vt.* **-tled, -tling** [Du *husselen,* shake up] **1** to push about; jostle **2** to force in a rough, hurried manner **3** to entice with deceptive or high-pressure tactics —*vi.* **1** to move hurriedly **2** [Inf.] to work energetically **3** [Slang] to obtain money aggressively or dishonestly —*n.* **1** a hustling **2** [Inf.] energetic action; drive —**hus′tler** *n.*

hut (hut) *n.* [< OHG *hutta*] a very plain or crude little house or cabin

hutch (huch) *n.* [< ML *hutica,* chest] **1** a chest or cupboard **2** a pen or coop for small animals **3** a hut

hutz·pah (hoots′pə) *n.* CHUTZPAH

huz·zah or **huz·za** (hə zä′) *n., interj., vi., vt. archaic var. of* HURRAH (see HURRAY)

HVAC *abbrev.* heating, ventilating, and air conditioning

hwy *abbrev.* highway

hy·a·cinth (hī′ə sinth′) *n.* [< Gr *hyakinthos*] a plant of the lily family, with spikes of bell-shaped flowers

hy·brid (hī′brid) *n.* [L *hybrida*] **1** the offspring of two animals or plants of different varieties, species, etc. **2** anything of mixed origin —*adj.* of or like a hybrid —**hy′brid·ism′** *n.*

hy·brid·ize (hī′bri dīz′) *vi., vt.* **-ized′, -iz′ing** to produce or cause to produce hybrids; crossbreed

Hy·der·a·bad (hī′dər ə bad′, -bäd′) city in SC India

hy·dra (hī′drə) *n., pl.* **-dras** or **-drae′** (-drē′) [< Gr, water serpent] **1** a small, freshwater polyp with a soft, tubelike body **2** [H-] *Gr. Myth.* a monster with many heads

hy·dran·ge·a (hī drān′jə, -dran′-; -jē ə) *n.* [< HYDR(O)- + Gr *angeion,* vessel] a shrub with showy clusters of white, blue, or pink flowers

hy·drant (hī′drənt) *n.* [< Gr *hydōr,* water] a large pipe with a valve for drawing water from a water main; fireplug

hy·drate (hī′drāt′) *n.* [HYDR(O)- + -ATE¹] a chemical compound of water and some other substance

hy·drau·lic (hī drô′lik) *adj.* [ult. < Gr *hydōr,* water + *aulos,* tube] **1** of hydraulics **2** operated by the movement and force of liquid [*hydraulic* brakes] —**hy·drau′li·cal·ly** *adv.*

hy·drau·lics *n.* the science dealing with the mechanical properties of liquids, as water, in motion and their application in engineering

hydro- [< Gr *hydōr*, WATER] *combining form* **1** water [*hydrometer*] **2** hydrogen

hy·dro·car·bon (hī′drə kär′bən) *n.* any compound containing only hydrogen and carbon

hy·dro·chlo·ric acid (hī′drə klôr′ik) a strong, highly corrosive acid that is a solution of the gas hydrogen chloride in water

hy·dro·e·lec·tric (hī′drō ē lek′trik) *adj.* producing, or relating to the production of, electricity by water power —**hy′dro·e′lec′tric′i·ty** *n.*

hy·dro·fluo·ro·car·bon (-flôr′ə kär′bən, -floor′-) *n.* any of various compounds containing only carbon, fluorine, and hydrogen, used as a refrigerant, etc.: these compounds are not thought to damage the atmosphere but are greenhouse gases

hy·dro·foil (hī′drə foil′) *n.* [HYDRO- + (AIR)FOIL] **1** a winglike structure that lifts and carries a watercraft just above the water at high speed **2** such a watercraft

hy·dro·gen (hī′drə jən) *n.* [see HYDRO- & -GEN] a flammable, colorless, odorless, gaseous chemical element: the lightest known substance: symbol, H; at. no. 1

hy·drog·e·nate (hī dräj′ə nāt′) *vt.* **-nat′ed, -nat′ing** to combine with or treat with hydrogen: vegetable oil is hydrogenated to make a solid fat

hydrogen bomb an extremely destructive nuclear bomb in which an atomic bomb explosion starts a chain reaction of nuclear fusion of heavy hydrogen atoms

hydrogen peroxide a colorless liquid used as a bleach or disinfectant

hy·drol·o·gy (hī dräl′ə jē) *n.* [see HYDRO- & -LOGY] the study of the earth's waters, their distribution, and the cycle involving evaporation, precipitation, flow, etc.

hy·drol·y·sis (-ə sis) *n., pl.* **-ses′** (-sēz′) [HYDRO- + -LYSIS] a chemical reaction in which a substance reacts with water so as to be changed into one or more other substances

hy·drom·e·ter (hī dräm′ət ər) *n.* [HYDRO- + -METER] an instrument for measuring the specific gravity of liquids —**hy·drom′e·try** *n.*

hy·dro·pho·bi·a (hī′drə fō′bē ə) *n.* [see HYDRO- & -PHOBIA] **1** an abnormal fear of water **2** [from symptomatic inability to swallow liquids] RABIES

hy·dro·phone (hī′drə fōn′) *n.* [HYDRO- + -PHONE] an instrument for registering the distance and direction of sound transmitted through water

hy·dro·plane (-plān′) *n.* **1** a small, high-speed motorboat with hydrofoils or a flat bottom **2** SEAPLANE —*vi.* **-planed′, -plan′ing 1** to ride in or drive a hydroplane **2** to skim along on water or on a wet surface

hy·dro·pon·ics (-pän′iks) *n.* [< HYDRO- & Gr *ponos*, labor] the science of growing plants in nutrient-rich solutions —**hy′dro·pon′ic** *adj.*

hy·dro·sphere (-sfir′) *n.* [HYDRO- + -*sphere*] a layer of the earth's atmosphere] all the water on the surface of the earth, including oceans, etc.

hy·dro·ther·a·py *n.* the treatment of disease, etc. by the use of water

hy·drous (hī′drəs) *adj.* [HYDR(O)- + -OUS] containing water, esp. in chemical combination

hy·drox·ide (hī dräk′sīd′) *n.* [HYDR(O)- + OXIDE] a compound consisting of an element or radical combined with the radical OH

hy·e·na (hī ē′nə) *n.* [< Gr *hyaina*] a wolflike, flesh-eating animal of Africa and Asia, with a shrill cry

hy·giene (hī′jēn′) *n.* [< Gr *hygiēs*, healthy] **1** the science of maintaining health **2** cleanliness

hy·gi·en·ic (hī jen′ik) *adj.* **1** of hygiene or health **2** sanitary —**hy′gi·en′i·cal·ly** *adv.*

hy·grom·e·ter (hī gräm′ət ər) *n.* [< Gr *hygros*, wet + *metron*, a measure] an instrument for measuring humidity

hy·men (hī′mən) *n.* [Gr *hymēn*, membrane] the thin mucous membrane that closes part or sometimes all of the opening of the vagina

hy·me·ne·al (hī′mə nē′əl) *adj.* [< Gr *Hymēn*, god of marriage] of marriage

hymn (him) *n.* [< Gr *hymnos*] a song of praise, esp. in honor of God

hym·nal (him′nəl) *n.* a collection of hymns: also **hymn′book′**

hype[1] (hīp) *vt.* **hyped, hyp′ing** [Slang] to stimulate, excite, etc.: usually with *up*

hype[2] (hīp) [Inf.] *n.* [? < HYPERBOLE] **1** deception **2** excessive promotion —*vt.* **hyped, hyp′ing** to promote in a sensational way

hy·per (hī′pər) *adj.* [Inf.] high-strung; keyed up

hyper- [< Gr *hyper*] *prefix* over, above, excessive

hy·per·ac·tive (hī′pər ak′tiv) *adj.* abnormally active —**hy′per·ac·tiv′i·ty** *n.*

hy·per·bo·la (hī pur′bə lə) *n., pl.* **-las** or **-lae′** (-lē′) [< Gr *hyperbolē*, a throwing beyond, excess] *Geom.* a curve formed by the intersection of a cone with a plane more steeply inclined than its side

hy·per·bo·le (hī pur′bə lē) *n.* [see prec.] exaggeration for effect, not meant to be taken literally —**hy·per·bol·ic** (hī′pər bäl′ik) *adj.*

hy·per·crit·i·cal (hī′pər krit′i kəl) *adj.* too critical

hy·per·ex·tend (-ek stend′) *vt.* to injure (a knee, etc.) by bending it beyond its normal straightened position

hy·per·gly·ce·mi·a (-glī sē′mē ə) *n.* [< HYPER- + Gr *glykys*, sweet + -EMIA] an abnormally high amount of sugar in the blood

hy·per·link *n.* a text segment or graphical item that serves as a cross-reference, as between hypertext documents

hy·per·sen·si·tive *adj.* excessively sensitive —**hy′per·sen′si·tiv′i·ty** *n.*

hy·per·ten·sion *n.* abnormally high blood pressure

hy·per·text *n.* digital text that can be navigated by means of hyperlinks

hy·per·thy·roid·ism (-thī′roid iz′əm) *n.* excessive activity of the thyroid gland, causing nervousness, rapid pulse, etc. —hy'per·thy'roid' *adj.*, *n.*

hy·per·ven·ti·la·tion (-vent′′l ā′shən) *n.* extremely rapid or deep breathing that may cause dizziness, fainting, etc. —hy'per·ven'ti·late' *vi.*, *vt.* -lat'ed, -lat'ing

hy·phen (hī′fən) *n.* 〚< Gr *hypo*-, under + *hen*, one〛 a mark (-) used between the parts of a compound word or the syllables of a divided word

hy·phen·ate (hī′fə nāt′) *vt.* -at'ed, -at'ing to connect or write with a hyphen —hy'phen·a'tion *n.*

hyp·no·sis (hip nō′sis) *n.*, *pl.* -ses' (-sēz′) 〚< Gr *hypnos*, sleep + -OSIS〛 a trancelike condition usually induced by another person, in which the subject responds to suggestions made by that person

hyp·not·ic (-nät′ik) *adj.* 1 causing sleep; soporific 2 of, like, or inducing hypnosis —*n.* any agent causing sleep —hyp·not'i·cal·ly *adv.*

hyp·no·tism (-nə tiz′əm) *n.* the act or practice of inducing hypnosis —hyp'no·tist *n.*

hyp·no·tize (-tīz′) *vt.* -tized', -tiz'ing to induce hypnosis in

hy·po (hī′pō) *n.*, *pl.* -pos *short for* HYPODERMIC

hypo- 〚Gr < *hypo*, under〛 *prefix* 1 under, beneath [*hypodermic*] 2 less than

hy·po·chon·dri·a (hī′pə kän′drē ə) *n.* 〚LL, *pl.*, abdomen (supposed seat of the condition)〛 abnormal anxiety over one's health, often with imaginary symptoms —hy'po·chon'dri·ac' (-ak′) *adj.*, *n.*

hy·poc·ri·sy (hi päk′rə sē) *n.*, *pl.* -sies 〚< Gr *hypokrisis*, acting a part〛 a pretending to be what one is not, or to feel what one does not feel; esp., a pretense of virtue, piety, etc.

hyp·o·crite (hip′ə krit′) *n.* 〚see prec.〛 one who pretends to be pious, virtuous, etc. without really being so —hyp'o·crit'i·cal *adj.*

hy·po·der·mic (hī′pə dur′mik) *adj.* 〚< HYPO- + Gr *derma*, skin〛 injected under the skin —*n.* a hypodermic syringe or injection

hypodermic syringe a syringe attached to a hollow needle (**hypodermic needle**) and used for the injection of a medicine or drug under the skin

hy·po·gly·ce·mi·a (hī′pō glī sē′mē ə) *n.* 〚< HYPO- + Gr *glykys*, sweet + -EMIA〛 an abnormally low amount of sugar in the blood

hy·pot·e·nuse (hī pät′′n ōōs′) *n.* 〚< Gr *hypo*-, under + *teinein*, to stretch〛 the side of a right-angled triangle located opposite the right angle

hy·po·thal·a·mus (hī′pō thal′ə məs) *n.*, *pl.* -mi' (-mī′) 〚see HYPO- & THALAMUS〛 the part of the brain that regulates many basic body functions, as temperature

hy·po·ther·mi·a (-thur′mē ə) *n.* 〚< HYPO- + Gr *thermē*, heat〛 a subnormal body temperature —hy'po·ther'mic *adj.*

hy·poth·e·sis (hī päth′ə sis) *n.*, *pl.* -ses' (-sēz′) 〚< Gr *hypo*-, under + *tithenai*, to place〛 an unproved theory, etc. tentatively proposed as an explanation for certain facts —hy'poth'e·size' (-sīz′) *vi.*, *vt.* -sized', -siz'ing

hy·po·thet·i·cal (hī′pə thet′i kəl) *adj.* based on a hypothesis; assumed; supposed —hy'po·thet'i·cal·ly *adv.*

hy·po·thy·roid·ism (hī′pō thī′roid iz′əm) *n.* deficient activity of the thyroid gland, causing sluggishness, puffiness, etc. —hy'po·thy'roid' *adj.*, *n.*

hys·sop (his′əp) *n.* 〚< Heb *ēzōbh*〛 a fragrant, blue-flowered herb of the mint family

hys·ter·ec·to·my (his′tər ek′tə mē) *n.*, *pl.* -mies 〚< Gr *hystera*, uterus + -ECTOMY〛 surgical removal of all or part of the uterus

hys·te·ri·a (hi ster′ē ə, -stir′-) *n.* 〚< Gr *hystera*, uterus: orig. thought to occur more often in women than in men〛 1 a psychiatric condition characterized by excitability, anxiety, etc. 2 any outbreak of wild, uncontrolled feeling: also **hys·ter'ics** —hys·ter'i·cal *adj.*, **hys·ter'ic** —hys·ter'i·cal·ly *adv.*

Hz *abbrev.* hertz

I

i or **I** (ī) *n.*, *pl.* **i's, I's** the ninth letter of the English alphabet

I¹ (ī) *n.* a Roman numeral for 1

I² (ī) *pron.* 〚OE *ic*〛 the person speaking or writing

I³ *abbrev.* 1 island(s) 2 isle(s)

I⁴ *symbol for Chem.* iodine

IA *abbrev.* Iowa

-i·al (ē əl, yəl) 〚L *-ialis*〛 *suffix* -AL

i·amb (ī′amb′, -am′) *n.* 〚< Gr *iambos*〛 a metrical foot of one unaccented syllable followed by one accented one

i·am·bic (ī am′bik) *adj.* 〚< Gr *iambikos*〛 of or made up of iambs —*n.* an iamb

-i·at·rics (ē a′triks′) 〚< Gr *iatros*, physician〛 *combining form* treatment of disease [*pediatrics*]

-i·a·try (ī′ə trē) 〚< Gr *iatreia*, healing〛 *combining form* medical treatment [*psychiatry*]

I·be·ri·a (ī bir′ē ə) peninsula in SW Europe, comprising Spain & Portugal: also **Iberian Peninsula** —**I·be'ri·an** *adj.*, *n.*

i·bex (ī′beks′) *n.*, *pl.* **i'bex'es** or **i·bi·ces** (ī′bə sēz′) 〚L〛 a wild goat of the Old World, with large, backward-curved horns

ibid. *abbrev.* ⟦L *ibidem*⟧ in the same place, i.e., the book, page, etc. just cited: also **ib.**

-i·bil·i·ty (ə bil′ə tē) ⟦L *-ibilitas*⟧ *suffix* -ABIL-ITY

i·bis (ī′bis) *n.* ⟦Egypt *hb*⟧ a large wading bird with a long, curved bill, found chiefly in tropical regions

-i·ble (i bəl, ə bəl) ⟦L *-ibilis*⟧ *suffix* -ABLE

Ib·sen (ib′sən), **Hen·rik** (hen′rik) 1828-1906; Norw. playwright

i·bu·pro·fen (ī′byōō prō′fən) *n.* a drug used to reduce fever and relieve pain, esp. arthritic pain

IC (ī′sē′) *n.* INTEGRATED CIRCUIT

-ic (ik) ⟦< Gr *-ikos*⟧ *suffix* **1** *a)* of, having to do with [*volcanic*] *b)* like [*angelic*] *c)* produced by [*anaerobic*] *d)* consisting of, containing [*dactylic*] *e)* having, showing [*lethargic*] **2** a person or thing: *a)* having [*paraplegic*] *b)* supporting [*heretic*] *c)* producing [*hypnotic*] Also **-i·cal** (i kəl, ə kəl)

ICBM *n.* an intercontinental ballistic missile

ICC *abbrev.* Interstate Commerce Commission

ice (īs) *n.* ⟦OE *īs*⟧ **1** water frozen solid by cold **2** a frozen dessert of fruit juice, sugar, etc. **3** [Slang] diamonds —*vt.* **iced, ic′ing 1** to change into ice; freeze **2** to cool with ice **3** to cover with icing —*vi.* to freeze: often with *up* or *over* —**break the ice** to make a start, as in getting acquainted —**on ice** [Slang] in readiness; in reserve —**on thin ice** [Inf.] in danger

Ice *abbrev.* **1** Iceland **2** Icelandic

ice·berg (-bʉrg′) *n.* ⟦prob. < Du *ijsberg*, ice mountain⟧ a great mass of ice broken off from a glacier and floating in the sea or in a lake

ice·bound *adj.* held fast or shut in by ice

ice·box *n.* a refrigerator, esp. one using ice

ice·break·er *n.* a sturdy boat for cutting channels through ice

ice·cap *n.* a mass of glacial ice that spreads slowly from the center of a mountain or polar region

ice cream ⟦orig., *iced cream*⟧ a sweet, frozen food of flavored cream or milk —**ice′-cream′** *adj.*

ice floe a piece of floating sea ice

ice hockey HOCKEY (*n.* 1)

Ice·land (īs′lənd) country on an island in the North Atlantic, southeast of Greenland — **Ice′land·er** *n.*

Ice·lan·dic (īs lan′dik) *n.* the Germanic language of Iceland —*adj.* of Iceland or its people, language, etc.

ice·man (īs′man′, -mən) *n., pl.* **-men′** (-men′, -mən) one who sells or delivers ice

ice milk a frozen dessert like ice cream, but with less butterfat

ice skate SKATE (*n.* 1) —**ice′-skate′** *vi.* **-skat′ed, -skat′ing**

ich·thy·ol·o·gy (ik′thē äl′ə jē) *n.* ⟦< Gr *ichthys*, a fish + -LOGY⟧ the branch of zoology dealing with fish —**ich′thy·ol′o·gist** *n.*

i·ci·cle (ī′sik′əl, -sə kəl) *n.* ⟦< OE *īs*, ice + *gicel*, piece of ice⟧ a hanging piece of ice, formed by the freezing of dripping water

ic·ing (īs′iŋ) *n.* a mixture variously of sugar, butter, flavoring, egg whites, etc. for covering a cake; frosting

ick·y (ik′ē) *adj.* **-i·er, -i·est** ⟦< STICKY⟧ [Slang] **1** unpleasantly sticky or sweet **2** disgusting

i·con (ī′kän′) *n.* ⟦< Gr *eikōn*, image⟧ **1** *a)* an image; figure *b)* a stylized figure on a computer screen, representing a function, file, etc. **2** *Eastern Orthodox Ch.* a sacred image or picture of Jesus, Mary, etc. **3** one that is revered or that represents an era, etc. —**i·con′ic** *adj.*

i·con·o·clast (ī kän′ə klast′) *n.* ⟦< *c.* 6th-c. Gr *eikōn*, image + *klaein*, to break⟧ one who attacks widely accepted ideas, beliefs, etc. —**i·con′o·clasm′** *n.* —**i·con′o·clas′tic** *adj.*

-ics (iks) ⟦-IC + -S (pl.)⟧ *suffix* [usually with *sing. v.*] art, science, study [*mathematics*]

ICU *abbrev.* intensive care unit

i·cy (ī′sē) *adj.* **i′ci·er, i′ci·est 1** full of or covered with ice **2** of or like ice; specif., *a)* slippery *b)* very cold **3** cold in manner; unfriendly —**i′ci·ly** *adv.* —**i′ci·ness** *n.*

id (id) *n.* ⟦L, it⟧ *Psychoanalysis* that part of the psyche which is the source of psychic energy, unconscious impulses, etc.

ID′ (ī′dē′) *n., pl.* **ID's** or **IDs** [Inf.] a document, as a license to drive a car, serving as identification

ID² *abbrev.* identification

Id. *abbrev.* ⟦L *idem*⟧ the same

I·da·ho (ī′də hō′) Mountain State of the NW U.S.; cap. Boise: abbrev. **ID** —**I′da·ho′an** *adj., n.*

i·de·a (ī dē′ə) *n.* ⟦L < Gr, appearance of a thing⟧ **1** a thought; mental conception or image **2** an opinion or belief **3** a plan; scheme **4** meaning or significance

i·de·al (ī dē′əl, -dēl′) *adj.* ⟦see prec.⟧ **1** existing as an idea, model, etc. **2** thought of as perfect **3** imaginary —*n.* **1** a conception of something in its most excellent form **2** a perfect model **3** a noble goal or principle

i·de·al·ism *n.* **1** behavior or thought based on a conception of things as one thinks they should be **2** a striving to achieve one's ideals —**i·de′al·ist** *n.* —**i′de·al·is′tic** *adj.*

i·de·al·ize (ī dē′əl īz′) *vt.* **-ized′, -iz′ing** to regard or portray as perfect or more nearly perfect than is actually the case —**i·de′al·i·za′tion** *n.* —**i·de′al·iz′er** *n.*

i·de·al·ly *adv.* **1** in an ideal manner; perfectly **2** in theory

i·den·ti·cal (ī den′ti kəl) *adj.* ⟦< L *idem*, the same⟧ **1** the very same **2** exactly alike —**i·den′ti·cal·ly** *adv.*

i·den·ti·fi·ca·tion (ī den′tə fi kā′shən) *n.* **1** an identifying or being identified **2** anything by which one can be identified

i·den·ti·fy (ī den′tə fī′) *vt.* **-fied′, -fy′ing 1** to treat as the same **2** to fix the identity of [to *identify* a biological specimen] **3** to connect or associate closely —*vi.* **1** to perceive oneself as connected (with) **2** to publicly present oneself (as)

i·den·ti·ty (ī den′tə tē) *n., pl.* **-ties** 1 the state or fact of being the same 2 *a)* the state or fact of being a specific person or thing; individuality *b)* the state of being as described 3 information used to establish or prove a person's individuality, as in providing access to a credit account

identity crisis the state of being uncertain about oneself regarding character, goals, etc., esp. in adolescence

identity theft the unauthorized use of a person's private information, as a Social Security or PIN number, to engage fraudulently in activities under that person's name

id·e·o·gram (id′ē ō gram′, ī′dē–) *n.* ⟦see IDEA & -GRAM⟧ a symbol representing an object or idea without expressing the word for it: also **id′e·o·graph′** (-graf′)

i·de·ol·o·gy (ī′dē äl′ə jē, id′ē–) *n., pl.* **-gies** ⟦see IDEA & -LOGY⟧ the doctrines, etc. on which a particular political or social system is based —**i′de·o·log′i·cal** *adj.* —**i′de·ol′o·gist** *n.*

ides (īdz) *pl.n.* ⟦< L *idus*⟧ *[often with sing. v.]* in the ancient Roman calendar, the 15th day of March, May, July, or October, or the 13th of the other months

id·i·o·cy (id′ē ə sē) *n.* 1 great foolishness or stupidity 2 *pl.* **-cies** an idiotic act or remark

id·i·om (id′ē əm) *n.* ⟦< Gr *idios*, one's own⟧ 1 the language or dialect of a people, region, class, etc. 2 the usual way that the words of a language are joined to express thought 3 a phrase or expression with an unusual syntactic pattern or with a meaning differing from the literal meaning of its parts 4 a characteristic style, as in art or music —**id′i·o·mat′ic** (-ə mat′ik) *adj.*

id·i·o·path·ic (id′ē ə′path′ik) *adj.* ⟦< Gr *idiopatheia*, feeling for oneself alone⟧ of a disease whose cause is unknown

id·i·o·syn·cra·sy (id′ē ō siŋ′krə sē) *n., pl.* **-sies** ⟦< Gr *idio-*, one's own + *synkrasis*, a mixing⟧ any personal peculiarity, mannerism, etc. — **id′i·o·syn·crat′ic** (-sin krat′ik) *adj.*

id·i·ot (id′ē ət) *n.* ⟦< Gr *idiōtēs*, ignorant person⟧ a foolish or stupid person —**id′i·ot′ic** (-ät′ik) *adj.* —**id′i·ot′i·cal·ly** *adv.*

i·dle (īd′'l) *adj.* **i′dler, i′dlest** ⟦OE *idel*, empty⟧ 1 useless; futile *[an idle wish]* 2 unfounded *[idle rumors]* 3 *a)* unemployed; not busy *b)* inactive; not in use 4 lazy —*vi.* **i′dled, i′dling** 1 to move slowly or aimlessly 2 to be unemployed or inactive 3 to operate without transmitting power *[the motor idled]* —*vt.* 1 to waste: usually with *away* 2 to cause (a motor, etc.) to idle —**i′dle·ness** *n.* —**i′dler** *n.* —**i′dly** *adv.*

i·dol (īd′'l) *n.* ⟦< Gr *eidōlon*, image⟧ 1 an image of a god, used as an object of worship 2 any object of ardent or excessive devotion

i·dol·a·try (ī däl′ə trē) *n., pl.* **-tries** 1 worship of idols 2 excessive reverence for or devotion to a person or thing —**i·dol′a·ter** *n.* —**i·dol′a·trous** *adj.*

i·dol·ize (īd′'l īz′) *vt.* **-ized′, -iz′ing** 1 to make an idol of 2 to love or admire excessively

i·dyll or **i·dyl** (īd′'l; *Brit* id′'l) *n.* ⟦< Gr *eidos*, a form⟧ 1 a short poem, etc. describing a simple, peaceful scene of rural life 2 a scene or incident suitable for this —**i·dyl·lic** (ī dil′ik) *adj.*

IE *abbrev.* Indo-European

-ie (ē) ⟦earlier form of -Y¹⟧ *suffix* 1 small or little (one, as specified) *[lassie]* 2 *a)* one that is as specified *[softie]* *b)* one connected with *[groupie]*

i.e. *abbrev.* ⟦L *id est*⟧ that is (to say)

IED *abbrev.* improvised explosive device

IEEE (ī′trip′əl ē′) *abbrev.* Institute of Electrical and Electronics Engineers

-ier (ē′ər, yər, ir, ər) ⟦< L *-arius*⟧ *suffix* a person concerned with (a specified action or thing) *[bombardier]*

if (if) *conj.* ⟦OE *gif*⟧ 1 on condition that; in case that *[if I were you, I would quit]* 2 allowing that *[if she was there, I didn't see her]* 3 whether *[ask him if he knows her]*

if·fy (if′ē) *adj.* **-fi·er, -fi·est** *[Inf.]* not definite; containing doubtful elements

ig·loo (ig′lōō′) *n., pl.* **-loos′** ⟦Inuit *iglu*, snow house⟧ a house made of blocks of snow, such as those built by the Inuit

ig·ne·ous (ig′nē əs) *adj.* ⟦< L *ignis*, a fire⟧ 1 of fire 2 produced by volcanic action or intense heat *[igneous rock]*

ig·nite (ig nīt′) *vt.* **-nit′ed, -nit′ing** ⟦see prec.⟧ to set fire to —*vi.* to catch on fire; start burning —**ig·nit′a·ble** *adj.*, **ig·nit′i·ble**

ig·ni·tion (ig nish′ən) *n.* 1 an igniting or being ignited 2 the switch or system for igniting the mixture of fuel and air in the cylinder of an internal-combustion engine

ig·no·ble (ig nō′bəl) *adj.* ⟦< L *in-*, not + *nobilis* (< earlier *gnobilis*, known)⟧ not noble; base; mean —**ig·no′bly** *adv.*

ig·no·min·y (ig′nə min′ē) *n.* ⟦< L *in-*, no, not + *nomen*, name⟧ loss of reputation; shame; disgrace —**ig′no·min′i·ous** *adj.* —**ig′no·min′i·ous·ly** *adv.*

ig·no·ra·mus (ig′nə rā′məs, -ram′əs) *n., pl.* **-mus·es** an ignorant person

ig·no·rant (ig′nə rənt) *adj.* ⟦see fol.⟧ 1 lacking knowledge or experience 2 caused by or showing lack of knowledge 3 unaware (*of*) —**ig′no·rance** *n.* —**ig′no·rant·ly** *adv.*

ig·nore (ig nôr′) *vt.* **-nored′, -nor′ing** ⟦< L *in-*, not + *gnarus*, knowing⟧ to disregard; pay no attention to

i·gua·na (i gwä′nə) *n.* ⟦Sp < WInd⟧ a large tropical American lizard

IL *abbrev.* Illinois

il- *prefix* 1 IN-¹ 2 IN-² Used before *l*

-ile (il, əl, ′l, īl) *suffix* of or like

Il·i·ad (il′ē əd) *n.* ⟦< Gr *Ilios*, Troy⟧ a Greek epic poem, ascribed to Homer, set during the Trojan War

ilk (ilk) *n.* ⟦< OE *ilca*, same⟧ kind; sort; class: only in *of that* (or *his, her,* etc.) *ilk*

ill (il) *adj.* **worse, worst** ⟦< ON *illr*⟧ 1 bad *[ill* repute, *ill* will, *ill* omen*]* 2 not well; sick —*n.* an evil or a disease —*adv.* **worse, worst** 1 badly 2 scarcely [I can *ill* afford it] —**ill at ease** uneasy; uncomfortable

ill-ad·vised (il′əd vīzd′) *adj.* showing or resulting from poor advice; unwise

ill-bred *adj.* rude; impolite

il·le·gal (i lē′gəl) *adj.* prohibited by law; against the law —**il·le·gal·i·ty** (il′ē gal′i tē) *n., pl.* **-ties** —**il·le′gal·ly** *adv.*

il·leg·i·ble (i lej′ə bəl) *adj.* hard or impossible to read because badly written or printed —**il·leg′i·bly** *adv.*

il·le·git·i·mate (il′ə jit′ə mət) *adj.* 1 born of parents not married to each other 2 not legal or logical —**il′le·git′i·ma·cy** (-mə sē) *n., pl.* **-cies**

ill-fat·ed (il′fāt′id) *adj.* 1 certain to have an evil fate or unlucky end 2 unlucky

ill-fa·vored *adj.* ugly or unpleasant

ill-got·ten *adj.* obtained unlawfully or dishonestly

il·lib·er·al (i lib′ər əl) *adj.* 1 narrow-minded 2 not generous

il·lic·it (i lis′it) *adj.* [< L *illicitus*, not allowed] unlawful; improper —**il·lic′it·ly** *adv.* —**il·lic′it·ness** *n.*

il·lim·it·a·ble (i lim′i tə bəl) *adj.* without limit; immeasurable

Il·li·nois (il′ə noi′) Midwestern state of the U.S.; cap. Springfield: abbrev. **IL** —**Il′li·nois′an** *adj., n.*

il·liq·uid (i lik′wid) *adj.* not readily convertible into cash

il·lit·er·a·cy (i lit′ər ə sē) *n.* 1 a being illiterate 2 *pl.* **-cies** a mistake in grammar suggesting this

il·lit·er·ate (i lit′ər it) *adj.* uneducated; esp., not knowing how to read or write —*n.* an illiterate person

ill-man·nered (il′man′ərd) *adj.* having bad manners; rude; impolite

ill nature a disagreeable or mean disposition —**ill′-na′tured** *adj.*

ill·ness *n.* 1 the condition of being ill 2 a sickness; disease

il·log·i·cal (i läj′i kəl) *adj.* not logical or reasonable —**il·log′i·cal·ly** *adv.*

ill-starred (il′stärd′) *adj.* unlucky

ill-suit·ed *adj.* not suited or appropriate

ill-tem·pered *adj.* sullen; irritable

ill-timed *adj.* inopportune

ill-treat *vt.* to treat unkindly, unfairly, etc. —**ill′-treat′ment** *n.*

il·lu·mi·nate (i lōō′mə nāt′) *vt.* **-nat′ed, -nat′ing** [< L *in-*, in + *luminare*, to light] 1 to give light to; light up 2 *a)* to make clear; explain *b)* to inform 3 to decorate with lights 4 to decorate (a page border, etc.) by hand —**il·lu′mi·na·ble** (-nə bəl) *adj.*

il·lu·mi·na·tion *n.* 1 an illuminating 2 the intensity of light per unit of area

il·lu·mine (-mən) *vt.* **-mined, -min·ing** to light up

illus *abbrev.* 1 illustrated 2 illustration 3 illustrator

ill-us·age (il′yōō′sij) *n.* unkind or cruel treatment; abuse: also **ill usage**

ill-use (-yōōz′; *for n.,* -yōōs′) *vt.* **-used′, -us′ing** to treat unkindly; abuse —*n.* ILL-USAGE

il·lu·sion (i lōō′zhən) *n.* [< L *illudere,* to mock] 1 a false idea or conception 2 an unreal or misleading appearance or image —**il·lu′so·ry** (-sə rē) *adj.,* **il·lu′sive** (-siv)

il·lus·trate (il′ə strāt′) *vt.* **-trat′ed, -trat′ing** [< L *in-,* in + *lustrare,* illuminate] 1 to explain; make clear, as by examples 2 to furnish (books, etc.) with explanatory or decorative pictures, etc. —**il·lus′tra·tor** *n.*

il·lus·tra·tion (-strā′shən) *n.* 1 an illustrating 2 an example, etc. used to help explain 3 a picture, diagram, etc. used to decorate or explain

il·lus·tra·tive (i lus′trə tiv, il′ə strāt′iv) *adj.* serving as an illustration or example

il·lus·tri·ous (i lus′trē əs) *adj.* [< L *illustris,* clear] distinguished; famous; outstanding —**il·lus′tri·ous·ly** *adv.* —**il·lus′tri·ous·ness** *n.*

ill will hostility; hate; dislike

IM *abbrev.* 1 instant message 2 instant messaging

im- *prefix* 1 IN-[1] 2 IN-[2] Used before *b, m,* or *p*

I'm (īm) *contr.* I am

im·age (im′ij) *n.* [< L *imago*] 1 a representation of a person or thing; esp., a statue 2 the visual impression of something in a mirror, through a lens, etc. 3 a copy 4 *a)* a mental picture; idea *b)* the concept of a person, product, etc. held by the general public 5 a vivid description, esp. one employing metaphor or simile —*vt.* **-aged, -ag·ing** 1 to make a representation of 2 to reflect 3 to imagine

im·age·ry (im′ij rē) *n.* 1 mental images 2 vividly descriptive or figurative language

i·mag·i·na·ble (i maj′i nə bəl) *adj.* that can be imagined

i·mag·i·nar·y (-ner′ē) *adj.* existing only in the imagination; unreal

i·mag·i·na·tion (-nā′shən) *n.* 1 *a)* the act or power of forming mental images of what is not present *b)* the act or power of creating new ideas by combining previous experiences 2 the ability to understand the imaginative creations of others 3 resourcefulness

i·mag·i·na·tive (-nə tiv) *adj.* 1 having, using, or showing imagination 2 of or resulting from imagination —**i·mag′i·na·tive·ly** *adv.*

i·mag·ine (i maj′in) *vt., vi.* **-ined, -in·ing** [< L *imago,* image] 1 to make a mental image (of); conceive in the mind 2 to suppose; think

im·ag·ing *n.* the production of images, esp. by electronic means as in a CAT scan, ultrasound, etc.

i·mam (i mäm′) *n.* [*often* I-] a Muslim leader, as of prayer, or ruler: often used as a title

im·bal·ance (im bal′əns) *n.* lack of balance, as in proportion or force

im·be·cile (im′bə sil, -səl) *n.* [< L *imbecilis,* feeble] a foolish or stupid person —*adj.* foolish or stupid: also **im′be·cil′ic** (-sil′ik) —**im′be·cil′i·ty** *n.*

im·bed (im bed′) *vt. var. of* EMBED

im·bibe (im bīb′) *vt.* **-bibed′, -bib′ing** [< L

in-, in + *bibere*, to drink] **1** to drink (esp. alcoholic liquor) **2** to take in with the senses or mind —*vi.* to drink, esp. alcoholic liquor

im·bro·glio (im brōl′yō) *n.*, *pl.* **-glios** [It < *imbrogliare*, embroil] **1** an involved and confusing situation **2** a confused misunderstanding

im·bue (im byōō′) *vt.* **-bued′, -bu′ing** [< L *imbuere*, to wet] **1** to dye **2** to permeate (*with* ideas, emotions, etc.)

im·i·tate (im′i tāt′) *vt.* **-tat′ed, -tat′ing** [< L *imitari*] **1** to seek to follow the example of **2** to mimic **3** to reproduce in form, color, etc. **4** to resemble —**im′i·ta′tor** *n.*

im·i·ta·tion (-tā′shən) *n.* **1** an imitating **2** the result of imitating; copy —*adj.* not real; sham [*imitation* leather] —**im′i·ta′tive** *adj.*

im·mac·u·late (im mak′yə lit) *adj.* [< L *in-*, not + *macula*, a spot] **1** perfectly clean **2** without a flaw or error **3** pure; innocent; sinless —**im·mac′u·late·ly** *adv.* —**im·mac′u·late·ness** *n.*

im·ma·nent (im′ə nənt) *adj.* [< L *in-*, in + *manere*, remain] **1** operating within; inherent **2** present throughout the universe: said of God —**im′ma·nence** *n.* —**im′ma·nent·ly** *adv.*

im·ma·te·ri·al (im′ə tir′ē əl) *adj.* **1** not consisting of matter **2** not pertinent; unimportant

im·ma·ture (im′ə toor′, -choor′) *adj.* **1** not mature; not completely developed **2** characteristic of one who is not fully developed [*immature* behavior] **3** not finished or perfected —**im′ma·tu′ri·ty** *n.*

im·meas·ur·a·ble (i mezh′ər ə bəl) *adj.* that cannot be measured; boundless; vast —**im·meas′ur·a·bly** *adv.*

im·me·di·a·cy (i mē′dē ə sē) *n.* a being immediate; esp., direct relevance to the present time, purpose, etc.

im·me·di·ate (i mē′dē it) *adj.* [see IN-² & MEDIATE] **1** not separated in space; closest **2** without delay; instant **3** next in order or relation **4** direct; firsthand —**im·me′di·ate·ly** *adv.*

im·me·mo·ri·al (im′e môr′ē əl) *adj.* extending back beyond memory or record; ancient

im·mense (i mens′) *adj.* [< L *in-*, not + *metiri*, to measure] very large; vast —**im·mense′ly** *adv.* —**im·men′si·ty** *n.*

im·merse (i murs′) *vt.* **-mersed′, -mers′ing** [< L *immergere*] **1** to plunge into or as if into a liquid **2** to baptize by submerging in water **3** to absorb deeply; engross [*immersed* in study] —**im·mer′sion** (-mur′zhən, -shən) *n.*

immersion heater an electric coil or rod immersed in water to heat it

im·mi·grant (im′ə grənt) *n.* one who immigrates —*adj.* immigrating

im·mi·grate (-grāt′) *vi.* **-grat′ed, -grat′ing** [see IN-¹ & MIGRATE] to come into a new country, etc., esp. to settle there —**im′mi·gra′tion** *n.*

im·mi·nent (im′ə nənt) *adj.* [< L *in-*, on + *minere*, to project] likely to happen without delay; impending

im·mo·bile (i mō′bəl) *adj.* **1** firmly placed; stable **2** motionless —**im′mo·bil′i·ty** *n.* —**im·mo′bi·lize′** (-bə liz′) *vt.* **-lized′, -liz′ing**

im·mod·er·ate (i mäd′ər it) *adj.* without due restraint; unreasonable; excessive

im·mod·est (i mäd′ist) *adj.* **1** indecent **2** not shy; forward —**im·mod′est·ly** *adv.* —**im·mod′es·ty** *n.*

im·mo·late (im′ə lāt′) *vt.* **-lat′ed, -lat′ing** [< L *immolare*, sprinkle with sacrificial meal] **1** to kill as a sacrifice **2** to kill or destroy by fire —**im′mo·la′tion** *n.*

im·mor·al (i môr′əl) *adj.* **1** not moral **2** lewd —**im·mor′al·ly** *adv.*

im·mo·ral·i·ty (im′ôr al′i tē) *n.* **1** a being immoral **2** *pl.* **-ties** an immoral act or practice; vice

im·mor·tal (i môrt′'l) *adj.* **1** not mortal; living forever **2** enduring **3** having lasting fame —*n.* an immortal being —**im·mor·tal′i·ty** (im′ môr tal′i tē) *n.*

im·mor·tal·ize (-īz′) *vt.* **-ized′, -iz′ing** to make immortal, esp. in fame

im·mov·a·ble (i mōōv′ə bəl) *adj.* **1** firmly fixed **2** unyielding; steadfast

im·mune (i myōōn′) *adj.* [< L *in-*, without + *munia*, duties] **1** exempt from or protected against something disagreeable or harmful **2** not susceptible to some specified disease

im·mu·ni·ty (i myōōn′ə tē) *n.*, *pl.* **-ties 1** exemption from something burdensome, as a legal obligation [*immunity* from prosecution] **2** resistance to infection or a specified disease

im·mu·nize (im′yōō nīz′) *vt.* **-nized′, -niz′ing** to make immune, as by inoculation —**im′mu·ni·za′tion** *n.*

im·mu·nol·o·gy (im′yōō näl′ə jē) *n.* the branch of science dealing with immunity, as to infection or disease, and with the body mechanisms producing it —**im′mu·nol′o·gist** *n.*

im·mure (i myoor′) *vt.* **-mured′, -mur′ing** [< L *in-*, in + *murus*, wall] to shut up within walls; confine

im·mu·ta·ble (i myōōt′ə bəl) *adj.* unchangeable —**im·mu′ta·bly** *adv.*

imp (imp) *n.* [< Gr *em-*, in + *phyton*, growth] **1** a young demon **2** a mischievous child —**imp′ish** *adj.*

im·pact (im pakt′; *for n.* im′pakt′) *vt.* [< L *impingere*, press firmly together] **1** to force tightly together **2** to affect —*vi.* **1** to hit with force **2** to have an effect (*on*) —*n.* **1** a violent contact **2** the power to move feelings, influence thinking, etc.

im·pact·ed *adj.* lodged inside the jaw: said of a tooth

im·pair (im per′) *vt.* [< L *in-*, intens. + *pejor*, worse] to make worse, less, etc. —**im·pair′ment** *n.*

im·paired (im perd′) *adj.* disabled; handicapped: often used in combination [visually *impaired*]

im·pa·la (im pä′lə) *n.*, *pl.* **-la** or **-las** a reddish antelope of central and S Africa

im·pale (im pāl′) *vt.* **-paled′, -pal′ing** [< L *in-*, on + *palus*, a pole] to pierce through with, or fix on, something pointed —**im·pale′ment** *n.*

im·pal·pa·ble (im pal′pə bəl) *adj.* **1** not perceptible to the touch **2** too subtle to be easily understood

im·pan·el (im pan′əl) *vt.* **-eled** or **-elled**, **-el·ing** or **-el·ling** to choose (a jury) in a law case —**im·pan′el·ment** *n.*

im·part (im pärt′) *vt.* ⟦see IN-¹ & PART⟧ **1** to give a share or amount of **2** to make known; reveal

im·par·tial (im pär′shəl) *adj.* without bias; fair —**im·par′ti·al′i·ty** (-shē al′i tē) *n.* —**im·par′tial·ly** *adv.*

im·pass·a·ble (im pas′ə bəl) *adj.* that cannot be passed or traveled over

im·passe (im′pas′, im pas′) *n.* ⟦Fr⟧ a situation offering no escape or resolution, as a deadlocked argument

im·pas·sioned (im pash′ənd) *adj.* passionate; fiery; ardent

im·pas·sive (im pas′iv) *adj.* not feeling or showing emotion; calm —**im·pas·siv·i·ty** (im′pa siv′i tē) *n.*

im·pas·to (im päs′tō) *n.* ⟦It⟧ painting in which the paint is laid on thickly

im·pa·tient (im pā′shənt) *adj.* lacking patience; *specif., a)* annoyed because of delay, opposition, etc. *b)* restlessly eager to do something, etc. —**im·pa′tience** *n.*

im·peach (im pēch′) *vt.* ⟦< L *in-*, in + *pedica*, a fetter⟧ **1** to discredit (a person's honor, etc.) **2** to charge (a public official) with wrongdoing —**im·peach′a·ble** *adj.* —**im·peach′ment** *n.*

im·pec·ca·ble (im pek′ə bəl) *adj.* ⟦< L *in-*, not + *peccare*, to sin⟧ without defect or error; flawless —**im·pec′ca·bil′i·ty** *n.* —**im·pec′ca·bly** *adv.*

im·pe·cu·ni·ous (im′pi kyōō′nē əs) *adj.* ⟦< L *in-*, not + *pecunia*, money⟧ having no money; poor

im·ped·ance (im pēd′ns) *n.* ⟦< fol. + -ANCE⟧ the resistance in an electric circuit to a flow of alternating current

im·pede (im pēd′) *vt.* **-ped′ed**, **-ped′ing** ⟦< L *in-*, in + *pes*, foot⟧ to hinder the progress of; obstruct

im·ped·i·ment (im ped′ə mənt) *n.* **1** one that impedes **2** a speech defect

im·ped·i·men·ta (-men′tə) *pl.n.* encumbrances, as baggage or supplies

im·pel (im pel′) *vt.* **-pelled′**, **-pel′ling** ⟦< L *in-*, in + *pellere*, to drive⟧ **1** to drive or move forward **2** to force, compel, or urge —**im·pel′ler** *n.*

im·pend (im pend′) *vi.* ⟦< L *in-*, in + *pendere*, hang⟧ to be about to happen; be imminent [*impending* disaster] —**im·pend′ing** *adj.*

im·pen·e·tra·ble (im pen′i trə bəl) *adj.* **1** that cannot be penetrated **2** that cannot be solved or understood

im·pen·i·tent (im pen′ə tənt) *adj.* without regret, shame, or remorse

im·per·a·tive (im per′ə tiv) *adj.* ⟦< L *imperare*, to command⟧ **1** indicating authority or command **2** necessary; urgent **3** designating or of the mood of a verb that expresses a command, etc. —*n.* a command

im·per·cep·ti·ble (im′pər sep′tə bəl) *adj.* not easily perceived by the senses or the mind; very slight, subtle, etc. —**im′per·cep′ti·bly** *adv.*

im·per·cep·tive (-tiv) *adj.* not perceiving —**im′per·cep′tive·ness** *n.*

im·per·fect (im pur′fikt) *adj.* **1** not complete **2** not perfect **3** designating a verb tense that indicates a past action or state as uncompleted or continuous —**im·per′fect·ly** *adv.*

im·per·fec·tion (im′pər fek′shən) *n.* **1** a being imperfect **2** a defect; fault

im·pe·ri·al (im pir′ē əl) *adj.* ⟦< L *imperium*, empire⟧ **1** of an empire, emperor, or empress **2** having supreme authority **3** majestic; august **4** of great size or superior quality —*n.* a small, pointed chin beard

imperial gallon the standard British gallon, equal to 4.546 liters (about 1⅕ U.S. gallons)

im·pe·ri·al·ism *n.* **1** imperial state or authority **2** the policy of forming and maintaining an empire, as by establishing colonies, protectorates, etc. **3** the policy of seeking to dominate the affairs of weaker countries —**im·pe′ri·al·ist** *n., adj.* —**im·pe′ri·al·is′tic** *adj.*

im·per·il (im per′əl) *vt.* **-iled** or **-illed**, **-il·ing** or **-il·ling** to put in peril; endanger

im·pe·ri·ous (im pir′ē əs) *adj.* ⟦< L *imperium*, empire⟧ **1** overbearing, arrogant, etc. **2** urgent; imperative —**im·pe′ri·ous·ly** *adv.*

im·per·ish·a·ble (im per′ish ə bəl) *adj.* not perishable; indestructible

im·per·ma·nent (im pur′mə nənt) *adj.* not permanent; temporary —**im·per′ma·nent·ly** *adv.*

im·per·son·al (im pur′sə nəl) *adj.* **1** without reference to any particular person **2** not existing as a person [an *impersonal* force] **3** designating or of a verb occurring only in the third person singular, usually with *it* as subject —**im·per′son·al·ly** *adv.*

im·per·son·ate (im pur′sə nāt′) *vt.* **-at′ed**, **-at′ing** to assume the role of or pretend to be, for purposes of entertainment or fraud —**im·per′son·a′tion** *n.* —**im·per′son·a′tor** *n.*

im·per·ti·nent (im purt′'n ənt) *adj.* **1** not pertinent **2** insolent; impudent —**im·per′ti·nence** *n.*

im·per·turb·a·ble (im′pər tur′bə bəl) *adj.* that cannot be disconcerted, disturbed, or excited

im·per·vi·ous (im pur′vē əs) *adj.* **1** incapable of being penetrated, as by moisture **2** not affected by: with *to*

im·pe·ti·go (im′pə tī′gō) *n.* ⟦see IMPETUS⟧ a contagious skin disease characterized by pustules

im·pet·u·ous (im pech′ōō əs) *adj.* ⟦see fol.⟧ acting or done suddenly with little thought; rash —**im·pet′u·os′i·ty** (-äs′i tē) *n.* —**im·pet′u·ous·ly** *adv.*

im·pe·tus (im′pə təs) *n., pl.* **-tus·es** ⟦< L *in-*, in + *petere*, rush at⟧ **1** the force with which a body moves against resistance **2** motivation; incentive

im·pi·e·ty (im pī′ə tē) *n.* **1** lack of reverence for God **2** *pl.* **-ties** an impious act or remark

im·pinge (im pinj′) *vi.* **-pinged′, -ping′ing** [< L *in-*, in + *pangere*, to strike] **1** to strike, hit, etc. (*on* or *upon*) **2** to encroach (*on* or *upon*) —**im·pinge′ment** *n.*

im·pi·ous (im′pē əs) *adj.* not pious; specif., lacking reverence for God

im·plac·a·ble (im plak′ə bəl, -plā′kə-) *adj.* not to be placated or appeased; relentless —**im·plac′a·bly** *adv.*

im·plant (im plant′; *for n.* im′plant′) *vt.* **1** to plant firmly **2** to fix firmly in the mind **3** to insert surgically —*n.* an implanted organ, device, etc.

im·plau·si·ble (im plô′zə bəl) *adj.* not plausible —**im·plau′si·bly** *adv.*

im·ple·ment (im′plə mənt; *for v.*, -ment′) *n.* [< L *in-*, in + *plere*, to fill] something used in a given activity; tool, instrument, etc. —*vt.* to carry into effect; accomplish —**im′ple·men·ta′tion** (-mən tā′shən) *n.*

im·pli·cate (im′pli kāt′) *vt.* **-cat′ed, -cat′ing** [see IMPLY] to show to be party to a crime, etc. —**im′pli·ca′tive** *adj.*

im·pli·ca·tion (-kā′shən) *n.* **1** an implicating or being implicated **2** an implying or being implied **3** something implied

im·plic·it (im plis′it) *adj.* [see IMPLY] **1** suggested though not plainly expressed; implied **2** necessarily involved though not apparent; inherent **3** without reservation or doubt —**im·plic′it·ly** *adv.*

im·plode (im plōd′) *vt., vi.* **-plod′ed, -plod′ing** [< IN-[1] + (EX)PLODE] to burst or cause to burst inward —**im·plo′sion** (-plō′zhən) *n.* —**im·plo′sive** (-plō′siv) *adj.*

im·plore (im plôr′) *vt.* **-plored′, -plor′ing** [< L *in-*, intens. + *plorare*, cry out] **1** to ask earnestly for **2** to beg (a person) to do something —**im·plor′ing·ly** *adv.*

im·ply (im plī′) *vt.* **-plied′, -ply′ing** [< L *in-*, in + *plicare*, to fold] **1** to have as a necessary part, condition, etc. **2** to indicate indirectly; hint; suggest

im·po·lite (im′pə līt′) *adj.* not polite; discourteous —**im′po·lite′ly** *adv.*

im·pol·i·tic (im päl′ə tik′) *adj.* not politic; unwise

im·pon·der·a·ble (im pän′dər ə bəl) *adj.* that cannot be weighed, evaluated, etc. —*n.* anything imponderable

im·port (im pôrt′, *also, and for n. always*, im′pôrt′) *vt.* [< L *in-*, in + *portare*, carry] **1** to bring in (goods) from another country, especially for sale **2** to mean; signify —*n.* **1** something imported **2** meaning; signification **3** importance —**im′por·ta′tion** *n.* —**im·port′er** *n.*

im·por·tant (im pôrt′'nt) *adj.* [see prec.] meaning a great deal; having much significance or value **2** having, or acting as if having, power, authority, etc. —**im·por′tance** *n.* —**im·por′tant·ly** *adv.*

im·por·tu·nate (im pôr′chə nət) *adj.* persistent in asking or demanding

im·por·tune (im′pôr tōōn′) *vt., vi.* **-tuned′, -tun′ing** [< L *importunus*, troublesome] to urge or entreat persistently or repeatedly —**im′por·tu′ni·ty** *n., pl.* **-ties**

im·pose (im pōz′) *vt.* **-posed′, -pos′ing** [< L *in-*, on + *ponere*, to place] **1** to place (a burden, tax, etc. *on* or *upon*) **2** to force (oneself) on others —**impose on** (or **upon**) **1** to take advantage of **2** to cheat or defraud —**im·po·si′tion** (-pə zish′ən) *n.*

im·pos·ing *adj.* impressive because of great size, strength, dignity, etc. —**im·pos′ing·ly** *adv.*

im·pos·si·ble (im päs′ə bəl) *adj.* **1** not capable of being, being done, or happening **2** not capable of being endured, used, etc. because disagreeable or unsuitable —**im·pos′si·bil′i·ty** *n., pl.* **-ties** —**im·pos′si·bly** *adv.*

im·post (im′pōst′) *n.* [see IMPOSE] a tax; esp., a duty on imported goods

im·pos·tor or **im·post·er** (im päs′tər) *n.* [see IMPOSE] one who deceives or cheats others by pretending to be what he or she is not

im·pos·ture (-chər) *n.* the act or practice of an impostor; fraud

im·po·tent (im′pə tənt) *adj.* **1** lacking physical strength **2** ineffective; powerless **3** unable to engage in sexual intercourse: said of males —**im′po·tence** *n.*, **im′po·ten·cy** *n.* —**im′po·tent·ly** *adv.*

im·pound (im pound′) *vt.* **1** to shut up (an animal) in a pound **2** to take and hold in legal custody **3** to gather and enclose (water), as for irrigation

im·pov·er·ish (im päv′ər ish) *vt.* [< L *in-*, in + *pauper*, poor] **1** to make poor **2** to deprive of strength, resources, etc. —**im·pov′er·ish·ment** *n.*

im·prac·ti·ca·ble (im prak′ti kə bəl) *adj.* not capable of being done in practice

im·prac·ti·cal (im prak′ti kəl) *adj.* not practical

im·pre·ca·tion (im′pri kā′shən) *n.* [< L *in-*, on + *precari*, pray] a curse

im·pre·cise (im′pri sīs′) *adj.* not precise; vague —**im′pre·cise′ly** *adv.* —**im′pre·ci′sion** (-sizh′ən) *n.*

im·preg·na·ble (im preg′nə bəl) *adj.* **1** that cannot be captured or entered by force **2** unyielding —**im·preg′na·bil′i·ty** *n.* —**im·preg′na·bly** *adv.*

im·preg·nate (im preg′nāt) *vt.* **-nat′ed, -nat′ing 1** to make pregnant; fertilize **2** to saturate **3** to imbue (*with* ideas, etc.) —**im′preg·na′tion** *n.*

im·pre·sa·ri·o (im′prə sä′rē ō) *n., pl.* **-os** [It] one who manages an opera, organizes concert series, etc.

im·press[1] (im pres′) *vt.* [< IN-[1] + PRESS[2]] **1** to force (a person) into military service **2** to seize for public use

im·press[2] (im pres′; *for n.* im′pres′) *vt.* [see IMPRINT] **1** to stamp; imprint **2** to affect strongly the mind or emotions of **3** to fix in the memory: with *on* or *upon* —*n.* **1** an impressing **2** an imprint

im·press·i·ble (-ə bəl) *adj.* that can be impressed —**im·press′i·bil′i·ty** *n.*

im·pres·sion (im presh′ən) *n.* **1** an impressing 2 a) a mark, imprint, etc. b) an effect produced on the mind 3 a vague notion 4 an amusing impersonation; mimicking

im·pres·sion·a·ble adj. easily impressed or influenced; sensitive

im·pres·sion·ism n. a theory of art, music, etc. whose aim is to capture a brief, immediate impression —**im·pres′sion·ist** n. —**im·pres′sion·is′tic** adj.

im·pres·sive (im pres′iv) adj. tending to impress the mind or emotions; eliciting awe, admiration, etc. —**im·pres′sive·ly** adv.

im·pri·ma·tur (im′pri mät′ər) n. ⟦ModL, lit., let it be printed⟧ 1 permission to publish a book, etc., as granted by a Catholic bishop 2 any sanction or approval

im·print (im print′; for n. im′print′) vt. ⟦< L in-, on + premere, to press⟧ to mark or fix as by pressing or stamping —n. 1 a mark made by imprinting 2 a lasting effect 3 a note in a book giving facts of its publication

im·pris·on (im priz′ən) vt. to put in or as in prison —**im·pris′on·ment** n.

im·prob·a·ble (im präb′ə bəl) adj. not probable; unlikely —**im·prob·a·bil′i·ty** n., pl. -**ties** —**im·prob′a·bly** adv.

im·promp·tu (im prämp′tōō′) adj., adv. ⟦< L in promptu, in readiness⟧ without preparation; offhand

im·prop·er (im präp′ər) adj. 1 not suitable; unfit 2 incorrect 3 not in good taste —**im·prop′er·ly** adv.

im·pro·pri·e·ty (im′prō prī′ə tē) n., pl. -**ties** 1 a being improper 2 an improper act, word usage, etc.

im·prove (im prōōv′) vt. -**proved′**, -**prov′ing** ⟦< Anglo-Fr en-, in + prou, gain⟧ 1 to make better 2 to make (real estate) more valuable by cultivation, construction, etc. —vi. to become better —**improve on** (or **upon**) to do or make better than —**im·prov′a·ble** adj.

im·prove·ment n. 1 an improving or being improved 2 an addition or change that improves something

im·prov·i·dent (im präv′ə dənt) adj. lacking foresight or thrift —**im·prov′i·dence** n. —**im·prov′i·dent·ly** adv.

im·pro·vise (im′prə vīz′) vt., vi. -**vised′**, -**vis′ing** ⟦< L in-, not + providere, foresee⟧ 1 to compose and perform without preparation 2 to make or do with whatever is at hand —**im·prov′i·sa′tion** (-präv′i zā′shən) n. —**im·prov′i·sa′tion·al** adj.

im·pru·dent (im prōōd′'nt) adj. not prudent; rash —**im·pru′dence** n.

im·pu·dent (im′pyōō dənt) adj. ⟦< L in-, not + pudere, feel shame⟧ shamelessly bold; insolent —**im′pu·dence** n. —**im′pu·dent·ly** adv.

im·pugn (im pyōōn′) vt. ⟦< L in-, against + pugnare, to fight⟧ to challenge as false or questionable

im·pulse (im′puls′) n. [see IMPEL] 1 a) an impelling force; impetus b) the motion or effect caused by such a force 2 a) incitement to action by a stimulus b) a sudden inclina-

tion to act 3 a brief surge in an electric current

im·pul·sion (im pul′shən) n. 1 an impelling or being impelled 2 IMPULSE (n. 1a) 3 IMPULSE (n. 2)

im·pul·sive (im pul′siv) adj. 1 driving forward 2 tending to act on impulse —**im·pul′sive·ly** adv.

im·pu·ni·ty (im pyōō′ni tē) n. ⟦< L in-, without + poena, punishment⟧ exemption from punishment, harm, etc.

im·pure (im pyoor′) adj. 1 unclean; dirty 2 immoral; obscene; 3 mixed with foreign matter; adulterated —**im·pure′ly** adv. —**im·pure′ness** n.

im·pu·ri·ty (-pyoor′ə tē) n. 1 a being impure 2 pl. -**ties** an impure thing or part

im·pute (im pyōōt′) vt. -**put′ed**, -**put′ing** ⟦< L in-, in, to + putare, to think⟧ to attribute (a fault, etc.) to another —**im′pu·ta′tion** (-pyōō tā′shən) n.

in¹ (in) prep. ⟦OE⟧ 1 contained in [in the room] 2 wearing [dressed in furs] 3 during [done in a day] 4 at the end of [due in an hour] 5 not beyond [in sight] 6 employed, enrolled, etc. at [in college] 7 out of a group of [one in ten] 8 amidst [in a storm] 9 affected by [in trouble] 10 with regard to [to vary in size] 11 using [speak in English] 12 because of; for [to cry in pain] 13 into [come in the house] 14 living or located at [in Rome] —adv. 1 to the inside [he went in] 2 to or at a certain place 3 so as to be contained by a certain space, condition, etc. 4 inside one's home, etc. (to stay in) —adj. 1 that is in power [the in group] 2 inner; inside 3 gathered, counted, etc. 4 [Inf.] currently smart, popular, etc. —n. 1 one that is in power: usually used in pl. 2 [Inf.] special influence; pull —**have it in for** [Inf.] to hold a grudge against —**ins and outs** details and intricacies —**in that** because; since —**in with** associated with

in² abbrev. inch(es)

IN abbrev. Indiana

-in (in) combining form a mass action or gathering of a (specified) type [pray-in, be-in]

in-¹ ⟦< the prep. IN¹ or L in, in⟧ prefix in, into, within, on, toward [inbreed]

in-² ⟦L⟧ prefix no, not, without, NON- The following list includes some common compounds formed with in-, with no special meanings; they will be understood if "not" or "lack of" is used with the meaning of the base word:

inability	inapplicable
inaccessible	inappropriate
inaccuracy	inapt
inaccurate	inaudible
inaction	inauspicious
inactive	incapable
inadequacy	incautious
inadequate	incivility
inadmissible	incombustible
inadvisable	incommensurate
inanimate	incommunicable

incomprehensible
inconceivable
inconclusive
inconsistency
inconsistent
incorrect
incurable
indecorous
indefinable
indiscernible
indisputable
indistinct
indivisible
inedible
ineffective
ineffectual
inefficacious
inelastic
ineligible

inequality
inequitable
inequity
inexact
inexcusable
inexpensive
infertile
inhospitable
inhumane
injudicious
inseparable
insignificance
insignificant
insolvable
insufficient
insurmountable
insusceptible
invariable

in·ab·sen·ti·a (in ab sen′shə, -shē ə) [L] although not present [to receive an award *in absentia*]

in·ac·ti·vate (in ak′tə vāt′) *vt.* **-vat′ed, -vat′ ing** to make inactive —**in·ac′ti·va′tion** *n.*

in·ad·vert·ent (in′ad vurt′′nt, -əd-) *adj.* not on purpose; accidental —**in′ad·vert′ence** *n.* —**in′ad·vert′ent·ly** *adv.*

in·al·ien·a·ble (in āl′yən ə bəl) *adj.* [see ALIEN] that may not be taken away or transferred —**in·al′ien·a·bly** *adv.*

in·am·o·ra·ta (in am′ə rät′ə) *n.* [It] a sweetheart or lover: said of a woman

in·ane (in ān′) *adj.* [L *inanis,* empty] lacking sense; silly —**in·an′i·ty** (-an′i tē) *n.*

in·ar·tic·u·late (in′är tik′yōō lit, -yə-) *adj.* **1** without the articulation of normal speech [an *inarticulate* cry] **2** not able to speak; mute **3** unable to speak clearly or coherently **4** unexpressed or unexpressible

in·as·much as (in′əz much′ az′) **1** since; because **2** to the extent that

in·at·ten·tion (in′ə ten′shən) *n.* failure to pay attention; negligence —**in′at·ten′tive** *adj.*

in·au·gu·ral (in ô′gyə rəl) *adj.* [Fr] **1** of an inauguration **2** first in a series —*n.* **1** a speech made at an inauguration **2** an inauguration

in·au·gu·rate (-rāt′) *vt.* **-rat′ed, -rat′ing** [< L *inaugurare,* to practice augury] **1** to induct into office with a formal ceremony **2** to make a formal beginning of **3** to dedicate formally —**in·au′gu·ra′tion** *n.*

in·au·then·tic (in′ô then′tik) *adj.* not authentic

in·board (in′bôrd′) *adv., adj.* **1** inside the hull of a ship or boat **2** close to the fuselage of an aircraft —*n.* a boat with an inboard motor

in·born (in′bôrn′) *adj.* present in the organism at birth; innate

in·bound (in′bound′) *adj.* traveling or going inward —*vt., vi. Basketball* to put (the ball) in play from out of bounds

in·bred (in′bred′) *adj.* **1** innate; inborn **2** resulting from inbreeding

in·breed (in′brēd′) *vt.* **-bred′, -breed′ing** to breed by continual mating of individuals of closely related stocks —*vi.* **1** to engage in

such breeding **2** to become too refined, effete, etc. —**in′breed′ing** *n.*

inc *abbrev.* **1** incorporated: also **Inc. 2** increase

In·ca (iŋ′kə) *n.* **1** a member of an American Indian people of ancient Peru, having a highly developed civilization **2** a ruler of this people —**In′can** *adj.*

in·cal·cu·la·ble (in kal′kyōō lə bəl) *adj.* **1** that cannot be calculated; too great or too many to be counted **2** unpredictable

in·can·des·cent (in′kən des′ənt) *adj.* [< L *in-,* in + *candere,* to shine] **1** glowing with intense heat **2** very bright —**in′can·des′cence** *n.*

incandescent lamp (*or* **bulb**) a lamp with a filament in a vacuum heated to incandescence by an electric current

in·can·ta·tion (in′kan tā′shən) *n.* [< L *in-,* intens. + *cantare,* to sing] words chanted in magic spells or rites

in·ca·pac·i·tate (in′kə pas′ə tāt′) *vt.* **-tat′ed, -tat′ing** to make unable or unfit

in·ca·pac·i·ty *n.* lack of capacity, power, or fitness

in·car·cer·ate (in kär′sər āt′) *vt.* **-at′ed, -at′ ing** [< L *in-,* in + *carcer,* prison] to imprison —**in·car′cer·a′tion** *n.*

in·car·na·dine (in kär′nə dīn′) *vt.* **-dined′, -din′ing** to make red

in·car·nate (in kär′nit; *also, and for v. always,* -nāt′) *adj.* [< L *in-,* in + *caro,* flesh] endowed with a human body; personified —*vt.* **-nat′ed, -nat′ing** **1** to give bodily form to **2** to be the type or embodiment of —**in′car·na′tion** *n.*

in·cen·di·ar·y (in sen′dē er′ē) *adj.* [< L *incendium,* a fire] **1** having to do with the willful destruction of property by fire **2** designed to cause fires, as certain bombs **3** willfully stirring up strife, riot, etc. —*n., pl.* **-ar′ies 1** one who willfully stirs up strife, riot, etc. **2** an incendiary bomb, etc.

in·cense¹ (in′sens′) *n.* [< L *in-,* in + *candere,* to burn] **1** any substance burned to produce a pleasant odor **2** the odor from this

in·cense² (in sens′) *vt.* **-censed′, -cens′ing** [see prec.] to make very angry

in·cen·tiv·ize *vt.* **-ized′, -iz′ing** to provide an incentive for —**in·cen′tiv·i·za′tion** *n.*

in·cen·tive (in sent′iv) *n.* [< L *in-,* in, on + *canere,* sing] a stimulus; motive

in·cep·tion (in sep′shən) *n.* [see INCIPIENT] the beginning of something; start

in·cer·ti·tude (in surt′ə tōōd′) *n.* **1** doubt **2** insecurity

in·ces·sant (in ses′ənt) *adj.* [< L *in-,* not + *cessare,* cease] never ceasing; constant —**in·ces′sant·ly** *adv.*

in·cest (in′sest′) *n.* [< L *in-,* not + *castus,* chaste] sexual intercourse between persons too closely related to marry legally —**in·ces·tu·ous** (in ses′tyōō əs, -chōō-) *adj.* —**in·ces′tu·ous·ly** *adv.* —**in·ces′tu·ous·ness** *n.*

inch (inch) *n.* [< L *uncia,* twelfth part] a measure of length equal to ¹⁄₁₂ foot: symbol, " —*vt., vi.* to move slowly, or by degrees —**every inch** in all respects —**inch by inch** gradually: also **by inches** —**within an inch of** very close to

in·cho·ate (in kō′it) *adj.* [< L *inchoare*, begin] **1** just begun; rudimentary **2** not yet clearly formed

in·ci·dence (in′sə dəns) *n.* **1** the degree or range of occurrence or effect **2** [Inf.] an instance

in·ci·dent (-dənt) *adj.* [< L *in-*, on + *cadere*, to fall] **1** likely to happen as a result **2** falling upon or affecting [*incident* rays] —*n.* **1** an event, esp. a minor one **2** a minor conflict

in·ci·den·tal (-dent′′l) *adj.* **1** happening in connection with something more important; casual **2** secondary or minor —*n.* **1** something incidental **2** [*pl.*] miscellaneous items

in·ci·den·tal·ly *adv.* **1** in an incidental manner **2** by the way

in·cin·er·ate (in sin′ər āt′) *vt., vi.* -at′ed, -at′ing [< L *in*, in + *cinis*, ashes] to burn to ashes; burn up —**in·cin′er·a′tion** *n.*

in·cin·er·a·tor *n.* a furnace for burning trash

in·cip·i·ent (in sip′ē ənt) *adj.* [< L *in-*, in + *capere*, to take] just beginning to exist or appear —**in·cip′i·ence** *n.*

in·cise (in sīz′) *vt.* -cised′, -cis′ing [< L *in-*, into + *caedere*, to cut] to cut into with a sharp tool; to engrave or carve

in·ci·sion (in sizh′ən) *n.* **1** an incising **2** a cut; specif., one made surgically

in·ci·sive (in sī′siv) *adj.* **1** cutting into **2** sharp; penetrating —**in·ci′sive·ly** *adv.* —**in·ci′sive·ness** *n.*

in·ci·sor (in sī′zər) *n.* any of the front cutting teeth between the canines

in·cite (in sīt′) *vt.* -cit′ed, -cit′ing [< L *in-*, on + *citare*, to urge] to urge to action; rouse —**in·cite′ment** *n.*

incl *abbrev.* **1** including **2** inclusive

in·clem·ent (in klem′ənt) *adj.* [< L *in-*, on + *clemens*, lenient] **1** rough; stormy **2** lacking mercy; harsh —**in·clem′en·cy** *n., pl.* -cies

in·cli·na·tion (in′klə nā′shən) *n.* **1** a bending, leaning, or sloping **2** an inclined surface; slope **3** *a*) a bias; tendency *b*) a preference

in·cline (in klīn′; *for n., usually* in′klīn′) *vi.* -clined′, -clin′ing [< L *in-*, on + *clinare*, to lean] **1** to lean; slope **2** to have a tendency **3** to have a preference or liking —*vt.* **1** to cause to lean, slope, etc. **2** to make willing; influence —*n.* a slope; grade

inclined plane a sloping plane surface, esp. one sloping slightly

in·close (in klōz′) *vt.* -closed′, -clos′ing EN-CLOSE —**in·clo′sure** (-klō′zhər) *n.*

in·clude (in klōōd′) *vt.* -clud′ed, -clud′ing [< L *in-*, in + *claudere*, to close] **1** to have as part of a whole; contain **2** to make part of a whole **3** to take into account —**in·clu′sion** (-klōō′zhən) *n.*

in·clu·sive (-klōō′siv) *adj.* **1** taking everything into account **2** including the terms or limits mentioned [the third to the fifth *inclusive*] —**inclusive of** including —**in·clu′sive·ly** *adv.*

in·cog·ni·to (in′käg nē′tō′, in käg′ni tō′) *adj., adv.* [It < L *in-*, not + *cognitus*, known] with true identity unrevealed or disguised

in·co·her·ent (in′kō hir′ənt, -her′-) *adj.* **1** not logically connected; disjointed **2** characterized by speech, etc. like this —**in′co·her′ence** *n.* —**in′co·her′ent·ly** *adv.*

in·come (in′kum′) *n.* money, etc. received in a given period, as wages, rent, interest, etc.

in·com·ing *adj.* coming in [an *incoming* tide; *incoming* email]

in·com·mu·ni·ca·do (in′kə myōō′ni kä′dō) *adj., adv.* [Sp] not allowed or willing to communicate with others

in·com·pa·ra·ble (in käm′pə rə bəl) *adj.* **1** having no basis of comparison **2** beyond comparison; matchless

in·com·pat·i·ble (in′kəm pat′ə bəl) *adj.* not compatible; specif., unable to live together harmoniously —**in′com·pat′i·bil′i·ty** *n., pl.* -ties

in·com·pe·tent (in käm′pə tənt) *adj.* without adequate ability, mental fitness, etc. —*n.* an incompetent person —**in·com′pe·tence** *n.* —**in·com′pe·tent·ly** *adv.*

in·com·plete (in′kəm plēt′) *adj.* **1** lacking a part or parts **2** unfinished —*n. Educ.* a grade, etc. indicating assigned work is not complete

in·con·gru·ous (in kän′grōō əs) *adj.* **1** lacking harmony or agreement of parts, etc. **2** inappropriate —**in′con·gru′i·ty** (-kän grōō′i tē) *n.*

in·con·se·quen·tial (in kän′si kwen′shəl) *adj.* unimportant; trivial

in·con·sid·er·a·ble (in′kən sid′ər ə bəl) *adj.* trivial; small

in·con·sid·er·ate (-it) *adj.* without thought or consideration for others; thoughtless —**in′con·sid′er·ate·ly** *adv.* —**in′con·sid′er·ate·ness** *n.,* **in′con·sid′er·a′tion** (-ər ā′shən)

in·con·sol·a·ble (in′kən sōl′ə bəl) *adj.* that cannot be consoled

in·con·spic·u·ous (in′kən spik′yōō əs) *adj.* attracting little attention

in·con·stant (in kän′stənt) *adj.* changeable; irregular —**in·con′stan·cy** *n.*

in·con·test·a·ble (in′kən tes′tə bəl) *adj.* unquestionable; indisputable —**in′con·test′a·bil′i·ty** *n.* —**in′con·test′a·bly** *adv.*

in·con·ti·nent (in känt′′n ənt) *adj.* **1** without self-restraint, esp. in sexual activity **2** unable to restrain excretion, as of urine —**in·con′ti·nence** *n.*

in·con·ven·ience (in′kən vēn′yəns) *n.* **1** lack of comfort, ease, etc. **2** anything inconvenient —*vt.* -ienced, -ienc·ing to cause inconvenience to

in·con·ven·ient (-yənt) *adj.* not favorable to one's comfort; causing bother, etc.

in·cor·po·rate (in kôr′pə rāt′) *vt.* -rat′ed, -rat′ing [see IN-[1] & CORPORATE] **1** to combine; include; embody **2** to bring together into a single whole; merge **3** to form into a corporation —*vi.* **1** to combine into a single whole **2** to form a corporation —**in·cor′po·ra′tion** *n.*

in·cor·ri·gi·ble (in kôr′ə jə bəl) *adj.* [< LL *incorrigibilis*] that cannot be corrected or reformed, esp. because set in bad habits —**in·cor′ri·gi·bil′i·ty** *n.* —**in·cor′ri·gi·bly** *adv.*

in·cor·rupt·i·ble (in′kə rup′tə bəl) *adj.* **1** not

susceptible to decay **2** that cannot be corrupted, esp. morally

in·crease (in krēs′, in′krēs′) *vi.* **-creased′, -creas′ing** ⟦< L *in-*, in + *crescere*, grow⟧ to become greater in size, amount, degree, etc. —*vt.* to make greater in size, etc. —*n.* **1** an increasing or becoming increased **2** the result or amount of an increasing —**on the increase** increasing

in·creas·ing·ly *adv.* more and more

in·cred·i·ble (in kred′ə bəl) *adj.* **1** not credible **2** seeming too unusual to be possible **3** [Inf.] extraordinarily good —**in·cred′i·bly** *adv.*

in·cred·u·lous (in krej′oo ləs) *adj.* **1** unwilling to believe **2** showing doubt or disbelief — **in·cre·du·li·ty** (in′krə dōō′lə tē) *n.*

in·cre·ment (in′krə mənt, iŋ′-) *n.* ⟦< L *incrementum*⟧ **1** an increase **2** amount of increase —**in′cre·men′tal** *adj.*

in·crim·i·nate (in krim′i nāt′) *vt.* **-nat′ed, -nat′ing** ⟦< L *in-*, in + *crimen*, offense⟧ **1** to accuse of a crime **2** to involve in, or make appear guilty of, a crime or fault —**in·crim′i·na′tion** *n.*

in·crust (in krust′) *vt., vi.* ENCRUST —**in·crus·ta·tion** (in′krus tā′shən) *n.*

in·cu·bate (in′kyoo bāt′, iŋ′-) *vt.* **-bat′ed, -bat′ing** ⟦< L *in-*, on + *cubare*, to lie⟧ **1** to sit on and hatch (eggs) **2** to heat, etc. so as to hatch or grow, as in an incubator **3** to develop, as by planning —*vi.* to undergo incubation —**in′cu·ba′tion** *n.*

in·cu·ba·tor *n.* **1** a heated container for hatching eggs **2** any similar device, as for protecting premature babies, growing cell cultures, etc.

in·cu·bus (in′kyə bəs, iŋ′-) *n., pl.* **-bus·es, -bi** (-bī′) ⟦LL⟧ a demon who haunts sleeping women

in·cul·cate (in kul′kāt′, in′kul-) *vt.* **-cat′ed, -cat′ing** ⟦< L *in-*, in + *calcare*, trample underfoot⟧ to impress upon the mind, as by training —**in′cul·ca′tion** *n.*

in·cul·pate (in kul′pāt′, in′kul-) *vt.* **-pat′ed, -pat′ing** ⟦< L *in*, on + *culpa*, blame⟧ IN-CRIMINATE

in·cum·ben·cy (in kum′bən sē) *n., pl.* **-cies** tenure of office

in·cum·bent (-bənt) *adj.* ⟦< L *in-*, on + *cubare*, lie down⟧ currently in office —*n.* one currently in office —**incumbent on** (or **upon**) resting upon as a duty or obligation

in·cum·ber (-bər) *vt.* ENCUMBER —**in·cum′brance** (-brəns) *n.*

in·cu·nab·u·la (in′kyoo nab′yoo lə) *pl.n., sing.* **-u·lum** (-ləm) ⟦< L *in-*, in + *cunabula*, pl., a cradle⟧ books printed before 1500

in·cur (in kur′) *vt.* **-curred′, -cur′ring** ⟦< L *in-*, in + *currere*, to run⟧ **1** to acquire (something undesirable) **2** to bring upon oneself

in·cu·ri·ous (in kyoor′ē əs) *adj.* not curious; uninterested

in·cur·sion (in kur′zhən) *n.* ⟦see INCUR⟧ an invasion or raid

ind *abbrev.* **1** independent **2** index

Ind *abbrev.* **1** India **2** Indian

in·debt·ed (in det′id) *adj.* **1** in debt **2** owing gratitude, as for a favor

in·debt·ed·ness *n.* **1** a being indebted **2** the amount owed

in·de·cent (in dē′sənt) *adj.* not decent; specif., *a)* improper *b)* morally offensive; obscene —**in·de′cen·cy** *n.* —**in·de′cent·ly** *adv.*

in·de·ci·pher·a·ble (in′dē sī′fər ə bəl) *adj.* that cannot be deciphered

in·de·ci·sion (in′dē sizh′ən) *n.* inability to decide; vacillation

in·de·ci·sive (-sī′siv) *adj.* **1** not conclusive or final **2** showing indecision —**in′de·ci′sive·ly** *adv.* —**in′de·ci′sive·ness** *n.*

in·deed (in dēd′) *adv.* certainly; truly —*interj.* used to express surprise, doubt, sarcasm, etc.

in·de·fat·i·ga·ble (in′di fat′i gə bəl) *adj.* ⟦< L *in-*, not + *defatigare*, tire out⟧ that cannot be tired out

in·de·fen·si·ble (in′dē fen′sə bəl) *adj.* **1** that cannot be defended **2** that cannot be justified

in·def·i·nite (in def′ə nit) *adj.* not definite; specif., *a)* having no exact limits *b)* not precise in meaning; vague *c)* blurred; indistinct *d)* uncertain *e)* *Gram.* not limiting or specifying ["a" and "an" are *indefinite* articles] —**in·def′i·nite·ly** *adv.*

in·del·i·ble (in del′ə bəl) *adj.* ⟦< L *in-*, not + *delere*, destroy⟧ **1** that cannot be erased, blotted out, etc. **2** leaving an indelible mark — **in·del′i·bly** *adv.*

in·del·i·cate (in del′i kit) *adj.* lacking propriety or modesty; coarse —**in·del′i·ca·cy** *n., pl.* **-cies**

in·dem·ni·fy (in dem′ni fī′) *vt.* **-fied′, -fy′ing** ⟦< L *indemnis*, unhurt + -FY⟧ **1** to insure against loss, damage, etc. **2** to repay for (loss or damage) —**in·dem′ni·fi·ca′tion** *n.*

in·dem·ni·ty (-tē) *n., pl.* **-ties 1** insurance against loss, damage, etc. **2** repayment for loss, damage, etc.

in·dent¹ (in dent′) *vt.* ⟦< L *in*, in + *dens*, tooth⟧ **1** to notch **2** to place (a line, paragraph, etc.) some number of spaces away from the regular margin

in·dent² (in dent′) *vt.* ⟦IN-¹ + DENT⟧ to make a dent in

in·den·ta·tion (in′den tā′shən) *n.* **1** a being indented **2** a notch, cut, inlet, etc. **3** a dent **4** a spacing in from a margin, or a blank space so made

in·den·ture (in den′chər) *n.* **1** a written contract **2** [*often pl.*] a contract binding a person to work for another —*vt.* **-tured, -tur·ing** to bind by indenture

in·de·pend·ence (in′dē pen′dəns) *n.* a being independent; freedom from the influence or control of others

Independence Day the anniversary of the adoption of the Declaration of Independence on July 4, 1776

in·de·pend·ent (-dənt) *adj.* **1** free from the influence or control of others; specif., *a)* self-governing *b)* self-reliant *c)* not adhering to any political party *d)* not connected with others [an *independent* grocer] 2 not depending on another for financial support —*n.* one who is independent in thinking, action, etc. —**in′de·pend′ent·ly** *adv.*

independent clause a clause that can function as a complete sentence

in-depth *adj.* detailed; thorough

in·de·scrib·a·ble (in′di skrīb′ə bəl) *adj.* beyond the power of description —**in′de·scrib′a·bly** *adv.*

in·de·struct·i·ble (in′di struk′tə bəl) *adj.* that cannot be destroyed —**in′de·struct′i·bil′i·ty** *n.*

in·de·ter·mi·nate (in′dē tur′mi nit, -di-) *adj.* 1 indefinite; vague 2 doubtful or inconclusive —**in′de·ter′mi·na·cy** (-nə sē) *n.*

in·dex (in′deks′) *n., pl.* **-dex′es** or **-di·ces′** (-di sēz′) [L, indicator] 1 forefinger: in full **index finger** 2 a pointer or indicator 3 an indication [an *index* of ability] 4 an alphabetical list of names, subjects, etc. indicating pages where found, as in a book 5 a number used to measure change in prices, wages, etc. —*vt.* to make or be an index of or for

index fund a mutual fund tied to a particular stock-market index

In·di·a (in′dē ə) 1 region in S Asia, south of the Himalayas 2 republic in the central & S part of this region

India ink a black liquid ink

In·di·an *n.* 1 a person born or living in India or the East Indies 2 AMERICAN INDIAN —*adj.* 1 of India, or the East Indies, their people, etc. 2 of the American Indians, their culture, etc.

In·di·an·a (in′dē an′ə) Midwestern state of the U.S.; cap. Indianapolis: abbrev. IN —**In′di·an′an** *adj., n.,* **In′di·an′i·an** (-an′ē ən)

In·di·an·ap·o·lis (in′dē ə nap′ə lis) capital of Indiana, in the central part

Indian corn CORN¹ (*n.* 2), esp. when colorful and grown for its decorative qualities

Indian file SINGLE FILE

Indian Ocean ocean south of Asia, between Africa & Australia

Indian summer mild, warm weather following the first frosts of late autumn

in·di·cate (in′di kāt′) *vt.* **-cat′ed, -cat′ing** [< L *in-*, in + *dicare*, declare] 1 to direct attention to; point out 2 to be a sign of; signify 3 to show the need for 4 to express briefly or generally —**in′di·ca′tion** *n.*

in·dic·a·tive (in dik′ə tiv) *adj.* 1 giving an indication 2 designating or of the mood of a verb used to express an act, state, etc. as actual, or to ask a question of fact —*n.* the indicative mood

in·di·ca·tor (in′di kāt′ər) *n.* one that indicates; specif., a gauge, dial, etc.

in·dict (in dīt′) *vt.* [ult. < L *in,* against + *dicere,* speak] to charge with a crime —**in·dict′ment** *n.*

in·dif·fer·ent (in dif′ər ənt, -dif′rənt) *adj.* 1 neutral 2 unconcerned; apathetic 3 of no importance 4 average —**in·dif′fer·ence** *n.* —**in·dif′fer·ent·ly** *adv.*

in·dig·e·nous (in dij′ə nəs) *adj.* [< L *indigena,* a native] 1 relating to the original inhabitants

of a region or country 2 existing or growing naturally in a region or country; native

in·di·gent (in′di jənt) *adj.* [< L *indegere,* to be in need] poor; needy —*n.* an indigent person —**in′di·gence** *n.* —**in′di·gent·ly** *adv.*

in·di·gest·i·ble (in′di jes′tə bəl) *adj.* not easily digested

in·di·ges·tion (-jes′chən) *n.* 1 difficulty in digesting food 2 discomfort caused by this

in·dig·nant (in dig′nənt) *adj.* [< L *in-,* not + *dignus,* worthy] feeling or expressing anger, esp. at unjust or mean action —**in·dig′nant·ly** *adv.*

in·dig·na·tion (in′dig nā′shən) *n.* righteous anger

in·dig·ni·ty (in dig′nə tē) *n., pl.* **-ties** an insult or affront to one's dignity or self-respect

in·di·go (in′di gō′) *n., pl.* **-gos** or **-goes** [Sp < Gr *Indikos,* Indian] 1 a blue dye obtained from certain plants or made synthetically 2 a deep violet blue —*adj.* of this color

in·di·rect (in′də rekt′) *adj.* 1 not straight 2 not straight to the point 3 dishonest [*indirect* dealing] 4 not immediate; secondary [an *indirect* result] —**in′di·rect′ly** *adv.* —**in′di·rect′ness** *n.*

indirect object *Gram.* the word or words denoting the person or thing indirectly affected by the action of the verb (Ex.: *him* in "give *him* the ball")

in·dis·creet (in′di skrēt′) *adj.* not prudent, as in speech or action; unwise

in·dis·cre·tion (-skresh′ən) *n.* 1 lack of discretion; imprudence 2 an indiscreet act or remark

in·dis·crim·i·nate (in′di skrim′i nit) *adj.* 1 mixed or random 2 not making careful distinctions —**in′dis·crim′i·nate·ly** *adv.*

in·dis·pen·sa·ble (in′di spen′sə bəl) *adj.* absolutely necessary

in·dis·posed (in′di spōzd′) *adj.* 1 slightly ill 2 unwilling; disinclined —**in·dis·po·si·tion** (in′dis pə zish′ən) *n.*

in·dis·sol·u·ble (in′di säl′yōō bəl) *adj.* that cannot be dissolved or destroyed; lasting

in·dite (in dīt′) *vt.* **-dit′ed, -dit′ing** [see INDICT] to compose and write

in·di·um (in′dē əm) *n.* [ult. < INDIGO (< its two indigo spectral lines) + -IUM] a soft, malleable metallic chemical element, used in plating aircraft bearings and mirrors: symbol, In; at. no. 49

in·di·vid·u·al (in′də vij′oo əl) *adj.* [< L < *in-,* not + *dividere,* to divide] 1 existing as a separate thing or being 2 of or relating to a single person or thing —*n.* 1 a single being or being 2 a person

in·di·vid·u·al·ism *n.* 1 individuality 2 the doctrine that the state exists for the individual 3 the leading of one's life in one's own way —**in′di·vid′u·al·ist** *n., adj.* —**in′di·vid′u·al·is′tic** *adj.*

in·di·vid·u·al·i·ty (-al′ə tē) *n., pl.* **-ties** 1 the sum of the characteristics that set one person or thing apart 2 the condition of being different from others

in·di·vid·u·al·ize (-īz′) *vt.* **-ized′, -iz′ing** 1 to make individual 2 to treat as an individual —**in′di·vid′u·al·i·za′tion** *n.*

in·di·vid·u·al·ly *adv.* 1 as individuals; separately 2 distinctively

In·do·chi·na (in′dō chī′nə) 1 large peninsula south of China, including Myanmar, Thailand, etc. 2 E part of this peninsula, consisting of Laos, Cambodia, & Vietnam

in·doc·tri·nate (in däk′trə nāt′) *vt.* **-nat′ed, -nat′ing** to instruct in, or imbue with, doctrines, theories, etc. —**in·doc′tri·na′tion** *n.*

In·do-Eu·ro·pe·an (in′dō yoor′ə pē′ən) *adj.* designating a family of languages including most of those of Europe and many of those of Asia

in·do·lent (in′də lənt) *adj.* [< L *in-*, not + *dolere*, feel pain] idle; lazy —**in′do·lence** *n.* —**in′do·lent·ly** *adv.*

in·dom·i·ta·ble (in däm′i tə bəl) *adj.* [< L *in-*, not + *domitare*, to tame] not easily discouraged or defeated

In·do·ne·sia (in′də nē′zhə) republic in the Malay Archipelago, consisting of Java, Sumatra, numerous small islands, half of New Guinea, & most of Borneo

In·do·ne·sian *n.* 1 a person born or living in Indonesia 2 the official Malay language of Indonesia —*adj.* of Indonesia, its people, language, etc.

in·door *adj.* living, belonging, etc. in a building

in·doors *adv.* in or into a building

in·dorse (in dôrs′) *vt.* **-dorsed′, -dors′ing** ENDORSE

in·du·bi·ta·ble (in dōō′bi tə bəl) *adj.* that cannot be doubted; certain —**in·du′bi·ta·bly** *adv.*

in·duce (in dōōs′) *vt.* **-duced′, -duc′ing** [< L *in-*, in + *ducere*, to lead] 1 to persuade 2 to bring on or about; cause 3 to draw (a conclusion) from particular facts 4 to bring about (an electric or magnetic effect) in a body by placing it within a field of force —**in·duc′er** *n.*

in·duce·ment *n.* 1 an inducing or being induced 2 a motive; incentive

in·duct (in dukt′) *vt.* [see INDUCE] 1 to place formally in an office, a society, etc. 2 to enroll (esp. a draftee) in the armed forces

in·duct·ance *n.* the property of an electric circuit by which a varying current in it produces a magnetic field that induces voltages in the same or a nearby circuit

in·duct·ee (in′duk tē′) *n.* a person inducted, esp. into the armed forces

in·duc·tion (in duk′shən) *n.* 1 an inducting or being inducted 2 reasoning from particular facts to a general conclusion 3 the inducing of an electric or magnetic effect by a field of force —**in·duc′tive** *adj.*

in·dulge (in dulj′) *vt.* **-dulged′, -dulg′ing** [L *indulgere*, be kind to] 1 to satisfy (a desire) 2 to gratify the wishes of; humor —*vi.* to give way to one's own desires —**in·dulg′er** *n.*

in·dul·gence (in dul′jəns) *n.* 1 an indulging or being indulgent 2 a thing indulged in 3 a favor or privilege 4 *R.C.Ch.* remission of punishment still due in Purgatory for a sin committed but forgiven

in·dul·gent (-jənt) *adj.* indulging or inclined to indulge; kind or lenient, often to excess —**in·dul′gent·ly** *adv.*

in·dus·tri·al (in dus′trē əl) *adj.* 1 having to do with industry, its workers, etc. 2 made as for industrial use —**in·dus′tri·al·ly** *adv.*

industrial arts the mechanical and technical skills used in industry

in·dus·tri·al·ism *n.* social and economic structure characterized by large industries, machine production, etc.

in·dus·tri·al·ist *n.* one who owns or controls an industrial enterprise

in·dus·tri·al·ize (-īz′) *vt., vi.* **-ized′, -iz′ing** 1 to establish or develop industrialism (in) 2 to organize as an industry —**in·dus′tri·al·i·za′tion** *n.*

industrial park a planned area for industrial use, usually on the outskirts of a city

Industrial Revolution [*often* i- r-] the societal change resulting from the introduction of machinery and large-scale production; esp., this change in England from *c.* 1760

in·dus·tri·ous (in dus′trē əs) *adj.* diligent; hardworking —**in·dus′tri·ous·ly** *adv.* —**in·dus′tri·ous·ness** *n.*

in·dus·try (in′dəs trē) *n., pl.* **-tries** [< L *industrius*, active] 1 earnest, steady effort 2 *a*) any particular branch of productive enterprise, esp. manufacturing *b*) manufacturing enterprises collectively 3 any large-scale business activity [the tourist *industry*] 4 the owners and managers of industry

-ine¹ (′in, in, ēn, ən) [< L *-inus*] *suffix* of, having the nature of, like [*aquiline, crystalline*]

-ine² (in, ən) [< L *-ina*] *suffix* forming abstract nouns [*discipline, doctrine*]

-ine³ (ēn, in, īn, ən) [< L *-inus*] *suffix* forming chemical names, as of *a*) halogens [*iodine*] *b*) alkaloids or nitrogenous bases [*morphine*]

in·e·bri·ate (in ē′brē āt′; *for n.,* -it′) *vt.* **-at′ed, -at′ing** [< L *in-*, intens. + *ebrius*, drunk] to make drunk —*n.* a drunkard —**in·e′bri·a′tion** *n.*

in·ed·u·ca·ble (in ej′ōō kə bəl, -ej′ə-) *adj.* incapable of being educated

in·ef·fa·ble (in ef′ə bəl) *adj.* [< L *in-*, not + *effabilis*, utterable] 1 inexpressible 2 too sacred to be spoken

in·ef·fi·cient (in′ə fish′ənt) *adj.* not producing the desired effect with minimum energy, time, etc. —**in′ef·fi′cien·cy** *n.* —**in′ef·fi′cient·ly** *adv.*

in·el·e·gant (in el′ə gənt) *adj.* not elegant; crude —**in·el′e·gant·ly** *adv.*

in·e·luc·ta·ble (in′i luk′tə bəl) *adj.* [< L *in-*, not + *eluctari*, to struggle] not to be avoided or escaped; inevitable [an *ineluctable* conclusion] —**in′e·luc′ta·bly** *adv.*

in·ept (in ept′) *adj.* [< L *in-*, not + *aptus*, apt] 1 unsuitable; unfit 2 foolish 3 awkward; clumsy —**in·ep′ti·tude′** (-ep′tə tōōd′) *n.* —**in·ept′ness** *n.*

in·ert (in urt′) *adj.* [< L *in-*, not + *ars*, skill] 1 without power to move or to resist 2 inactive; dull; slow 3 exhibiting little or no chemical activity [an *inert* gas]

in·er·tia (in ur′shə) *n.* [see prec.] 1 *Physics* the tendency of matter to remain at rest or to continue in a fixed direction unless affected by some outside force 2 a disinclination to move or act —**in·er′tial** *adj.*

in·es·cap·a·ble (in′e skāp′ə bəl) *adj.* that cannot be escaped or avoided

in·es·ti·ma·ble (in es′tə mə bəl) *adj.* too great to be properly measured

in·ev·i·ta·ble (in ev′i tə bəl) *adj.* [< L *in-*, not + *evitabilis*, avoidable] certain to happen; unavoidable —**in·ev′i·ta·bil′i·ty** *n.* —**in·ev′i·ta·bly** *adv.*

in·ex·haust·i·ble (in′eg zôs′tə bəl) *adj.* 1 that cannot be used up or emptied 2 tireless

in·ex·o·ra·ble (in eks′ə rə bəl) *adj.* [< L *in-*, not + *exorare*, move by entreaty] 1 that cannot be influenced by persuasion or entreaty; unrelenting 2 that cannot be altered, stopped, etc. —**in·ex′o·ra·bly** *adv.*

in·ex·pe·ri·ence (in′ek spir′ē əns) *n.* lack of experience or of the knowledge or skill resulting from experience —**in′ex·pe′ri·enced** *adj.*

in·ex·pert (in ek′spərt, in′ek spurt′) *adj.* not expert; unskillful

in·ex·pli·ca·ble (in eks′pli kə bəl) *adj.* that cannot be explained or understood

in·ex·press·i·ble (in′eks pres′ə bəl) *adj.* that cannot be expressed; indescribable

in·ex·tin·guish·a·ble (in′ek stin′gwish ə bəl) *adj.* that cannot be put out or stopped

in ex·tre·mis (in′ eks trē′mis) [L, in extremity] at the point of death

in·ex·tri·ca·ble (in eks′tri kə bəl) *adj.* 1 that one cannot extricate oneself from 2 that cannot be untied 3 so complicated as to be unsolvable

in·fal·li·ble (in fal′ə bəl) *adj.* [see IN-² & FALLABLE] 1 incapable of error 2 dependable; reliable —**in·fal′li·bil′i·ty** *n.* —**in·fal′li·bly** *adv.*

in·fa·mous (in′fə məs) *adj.* 1 having a very bad reputation; notorious 2 causing a bad reputation; scandalous

in·fa·my (-mē) *n., pl.* **-mies** 1 very bad reputation; disgrace 2 great wickedness 3 an infamous act

in·fan·cy (in′fən sē) *n., pl.* **-cies** 1 the state or period of being an infant 2 the earliest stage of anything

in·fant (in′fənt) *n.* [< L *in-*, not + *fari*, speak] a very young child; baby —*adj.* 1 of or for infants 2 in a very early stage

in·fan·ti·cide (in fan′tə sīd′) *n.* 1 the murder of a baby 2 a person guilty of this

in·fan·tile (in′fən til′) *adj.* 1 of infants 2 like an infant; babyish

in·fan·try (in′fən trē) *n., pl.* **-tries** [< L *infans*, child] 1 that branch of an army consisting of soldiers trained to fight on foot 2 such soldiers collectively —**in′fan·try·man** (-mən) *n., pl.* **-men** (-mən)

in·farct (in färkt′) *n.* [< L *in-*, in + *farcire*, to stuff] an area of dying or dead tissue resulting from inadequate blood flow to that area: also **in·farc′tion** (-färk′shən)

in·fat·u·at·ed (in fach′ōō āt′id) *adj.* [< L *in-*, intens. + *fatuus*, foolish] completely carried away by foolish love or affection

in·fat·u·a·tion *n.* a being infatuated

in·fect (in fekt′) *vt.* [< L *inficere*, to stain] 1 to contaminate or cause to become diseased by contact with a disease-producing organism or matter 2 to imbue with one's feelings, beliefs, etc.

in·fec·tion (in fek′shən) *n.* 1 an infecting or being infected 2 an infectious disease

in·fec·tious (-shəs) *adj.* 1 likely to cause infection 2 designating a disease that can be communicated by certain bacteria, viruses, etc. 3 tending to affect others to respond similarly, as a laugh —**in·fec′tious·ly** *adv.* —**in·fec′tious·ness** *n.*

in·fe·lic·i·tous (in′fə lis′ə təs) *adj.* not felicitous; unfortunate or unsuitable —**in′fe·lic′i·ty** *n., pl.* **-ties**

in·fer (in fur′) *vt.* **-ferred′, -fer′ring** [< L *in-*, in + *ferre*, to carry] 1 to conclude by reasoning from something known or assumed 2 to imply: often regarded as a loose usage —**in·fer′ence** (in′fər əns) *n.*

in·fer·en·tial (in′fər en′shəl) *adj.* based on or having to do with inference

in·fe·ri·or (in fir′ē ər) *adj.* [< L *inferus*, low] 1 located below or lower down 2 lower in order, status, etc. 3 lower in quality than: with *to* 4 poor in quality —*n.* an inferior person or thing —**in·fe′ri·or′i·ty** (-ôr′ə tē) *n.*

in·fer·nal (in fur′nəl) *adj.* [< L *inferus*, below] 1 of hell or Hades 2 hellish; fiendish

in·fer·no (in fur′nō) *n., pl.* **-nos** [see prec.] 1 HELL 2 any place characterized by flames or great heat

in·fest (in fest′) *vt.* [< L *infestus*, hostile] 1 to overrun in large numbers, usually so as to be harmful 2 to be parasitic in or on —**in′fes·ta′tion** *n.* —**in·fest′er** *n.*

in·fi·del (in′fə del′) *n.* [< L *in-*, not + *fidelis*, faithful] 1 one who does not believe in a particular religion 2 one who has no religion

in·fi·del·i·ty (in′fə del′ə tē) *n.* 1 unfaithfulness, esp. in marriage 2 *pl.* **-ties** an unfaithful act

in·field (in′fēld′) *n.* 1 the diamond-shaped area enclosed by the four base lines on a baseball field 2 the players (**in′field′ers**) whose field positions are there

in·fight·ing (in′fīt′iŋ) *n.* 1 fighting, esp. boxing, at close range 2 personal conflict within a group —**in′fight′er** *n.*

in·fil·trate (in fil′trāt′, in′fil trāt′) *vi., vt.* **-trat′ed, -trat′ing** 1 to filter or pass gradually through or into 2 to penetrate (enemy lines, a region, etc.) gradually or stealthily, so as to attack or to seize control from within —**in′fil·tra′tion** *n.* —**in′fil·tra′tor** *n.*

in·fi·nite (in′fə nit) *adj.* [see IN-² & FINITE] 1 lacking limits or bounds; endless 2 very great; vast —*n.* something infinite —**in′fi·nite·ly** *adv.*

in·fin·i·tes·i·mal (in′fin i tes′i məl) *adj.* [< L *infinitus*, infinite] too small to be measured —**in′fin·i·tes′i·mal·ly** *adv.*

in·fin·i·tive (in fin′i tiv) *n.* [see INFINITE] the form of a verb without reference to person, number, or tense: typically with *to*, as in "I want *to go*" —**in·fin′i·ti′val** (-tī′vəl) *adj.*

in·fin·i·tude (-tōōd′, -tyōōd′) *n.* [< L *infinitus*, INFINITE, prob. infl. by MAGNITUDE] 1 a being infinite 2 an infinite quantity

in·fin·i·ty (-tē) *n., pl.* **-ties** [< L *infinitas*] 1 the quality of being infinite 2 unlimited space, time, etc. 3 an indefinitely large quantity

in·firm (in furm′) *adj.* 1 weak; feeble, as from old age 2 not firm; unstable; frail; shaky —**in·firm′ly** *adv.* —**in·firm′ness** *n.*

in·fir·ma·ry (in fur′mə rē) *n., pl.* **-ries** a place for the care of sick or injured people, esp. at a school, college, or other institution

in·fir·mi·ty (-mə tē) *n., pl.* **-ties** (a) physical weakness or defect

in·flame (in flame′) *vt., vi.* **-flamed′, -flam′ing** [see IN-¹ & FLAME] 1 to arouse, excite, etc. or become aroused, excited, etc. 2 to undergo or cause to undergo inflammation

in·flam·ma·ble (in flam′ə bəl) *adj.* 1 FLAMMABLE 2 easily excited —**in·flam′ma·bil′i·ty** *n.*

in·flam·ma·tion (in′flə mā′shən) *n.* 1 an inflaming or being inflamed 2 redness, pain, heat, and swelling in the body, due to injury, disease, etc.

in·flam·ma·to·ry (in flam′ə tôr′ē) *adj.* 1 rousing excitement, anger, etc. 2 *Med.* of or caused by inflammation

in·flate (in flāt′) *vt.* **-flat′ed, -flat′ing** [< L *in-*, in + *flare*, to blow] 1 to blow full as with air or gas 2 to puff up with pride 3 to increase beyond what is normal; specif., to cause inflation of (money, credit, etc.) —*vi.* to become inflated —**in·flat′a·ble** *adj.*

in·fla·tion *n.* 1 an inflating or being inflated 2 *a)* an increase in the amount of money and credit relative to the supply of goods and services *b)* an excessive or persistent increase in prices as a result of this, causing a decline in purchasing power —**in·fla′tion·ar′y** *adj.*

in·flect (in flekt′) *vt.* [< L *in-*, in + *flectere*, to bend] 1 to vary the tone of (the voice) 2 *Gram.* to change the form of (a word) by inflection

in·flec·tion (in flek′shən) *n.* 1 a change in the tone of the voice 2 the change of form in a word to indicate number, case, tense, etc. Brit. sp. **in·flex′ion** —**in·flec′tion·al** *adj.*

in·flex·i·ble (in flek′sə bəl) *adj.* not flexible; stiff, rigid, fixed, unyielding, etc. —**in·flex′i·bil′i·ty** *n.*

in·flict (in flikt′) *vt.* [< L *in-*, on + *fligere*, to strike] 1 to cause (pain, wounds, etc.) as by striking 2 to impose (a punishment, etc.) *on* or *upon* —**in·flic′tion** *n.* —**in·flic′tive** *adj.*

in·flight (in′flīt′) *adj.* done, shown, etc. while an aircraft is in flight *[in-flight movies]*

in·flo·res·cence (in′flô res′əns, -flō-) *n.* *Bot.* 1 the producing of blossoms 2 the arrangement of flowers on a stem 3 a flower cluster 4 flowers collectively

in·flu·ence (in′flōō əns) *n.* [< L *in-*, in + *fluere*, to flow] 1 power to affect others 2 power to produce effects because of wealth, high position, etc. 3 one that has influence —*vt.* **-enced, -enc·ing** to have influence or an effect on

in·flu·en·tial (-en′shəl) *adj.* exerting influence, esp. great influence

in·flu·en·za (in′flōō en′zə) *n.* [It, an (astrological) influence] an acute, contagious viral disease, characterized by inflammation of the respiratory tract, fever, and muscular pain

in·flux (in′fluks′) *n.* [see INFLUENCE] a flowing in or streaming in

in·fo (in′fō) *n.* [Slang] *short for* INFORMATION (*n.* 2)

in·fold (in fōld′) *vt. var. of* ENFOLD

in·fo·mer·cial (in′fō mur′shəl) *n.* [INFO(RMATION) + (COM)MERCIAL] a long TV commercial made to resemble a talk show, interview, etc.

in·form (in fôrm′) *vt.* [see IN-¹ & FORM] to give knowledge of something to —*vi.* to give information, esp. in accusing another: usually with *on*

in·for·mal (in fôr′məl) *adj.* not formal; specif., *a)* not according to fixed customs, rules, etc. *b)* casual, relaxed, etc. *c)* not requiring formal dress *d)* designating or of the words, phrases, etc. characteristic of casual speech or writing —**in′for·mal′i·ty** (-mal′ə tē) *n., pl.* **-ties** —**in·for′mal·ly** *adv.*

in·form·ant (in fôr′mənt) *n.* a person who gives information; specif., an informer

in·for·ma·tion (in′fər mā′shən) *n.* 1 a being informed 2 something told or facts learned; news or knowledge 3 data stored in or retrieved from a computer

information science the science dealing with the collection, storage, and retrieval of information

in·form·a·tive (in fôr′mə tiv) *adj.* giving information; instructive

in·formed *adj.* having or based on knowledge or education

in·form·er *n.* one who secretly gives evidence against another

in·fo·tain·ment (in′fō tān′mənt) *n.* [INFO(RMATION) + (ENTER)TAINMENT] TV programming of information, as about celebrities, in a dramatic or sensational style

infra- [< L] *prefix* below, beneath

in·frac·tion (in frak′shən) *n.* [see INFRINGE] a violation of a law, pact, etc.

in·fra·red (in′frə red′) *adj.* designating or of those invisible rays just beyond the red of the visible spectrum, given off by hot objects and tending to heat objects that absorb them

in·fra·son·ic (-sän′ik) *adj.* of a frequency of sound below the range audible to the human ear

in·fra·struc·ture (-struk′chər) *n.* basic installations and facilities, as roads, power plants, transportation and communication systems, etc.

in·fre·quent (in frē′kwənt) *adj.* not frequent; uncommon —**in·fre′quen·cy** *n.*, **in·fre′quence** —**in·fre′quent·ly** *adv.*

in·fringe (in frinj′) *vt.* **-fringed′, -fring′ing** [< L *in-*, in + *frangere*, to break] to break (a law or pact) —**infringe on** (or **upon**) to encroach on (the rights, etc. of others) —**in·fringe′ment** *n.*

in·fu·ri·ate (in fyoor′ē āt′) *vt.* **-at′ed, -at′ing** [< L *in-*, in + *furia*, rage] to make very angry; enrage

in·fuse (in fyo͞oz′) *vt.* **-fused′, -fus′ing** [< L *in-*, in + *fundere*, pour] **1** to instill or impart (qualities, etc.) **2** to fill; inspire **3** to steep (tea leaves, etc.) to extract the essence —**in·fus′er** *n.* —**in·fu′sion** *n.*

-ing (iŋ) [< OE] *suffix* used to form the present participle or verbal nouns [*talking, painting*]

in·gath·er·ing (in′gath′ər iŋ) *n.* a gathering together

in·gen·ious (in jēn′yəs) *adj.* [< L *in-*, in + *gignere*, to produce] **1** clever, resourceful, etc. **2** made or done in a clever or original way —**in·gen′ious·ly** *adv.*

in·gé·nue (an′zhə no͞o′, än′-) *n.* [Fr, ingenuous] *Theater* the role of an inexperienced young woman, or an actress in this role

in·ge·nu·i·ty (in′jə no͞o′ə tē, -nyo͞o′-) *n.* the quality of being ingenious; cleverness

in·gen·u·ous (in jen′yo͞o əs) *adj.* [< L *in-*, in + *gignere*, to produce] **1** frank; open **2** simple; naïve —**in·gen′u·ous·ly** *adv.* —**in·gen′u·ous·ness** *n.*

in·gest (in jest′) *vt.* [< L *in-*, into + *gerere*, carry] to take (food, etc.) into the body, as by swallowing, inhaling, or absorbing —**in·ges′tion** *n.*

in·glo·ri·ous (in glôr′ē əs) *adj.* shameful; disgraceful

in·got (iŋ′gət) *n.* [prob. < OFr *lingo*, tongue] a mass of metal cast into a bar or other convenient shape

in·grained (in′grānd′) *adj.* **1** firmly established, as habits **2** inveterate [*an ingrained liar*]

in·grate (in′grāt′) *n.* [< L *in-*, not + *gratus*, grateful] an ungrateful person

in·gra·ti·ate (in grā′shē āt′) *vt.* **-at′ed, -at′ing** [< L *in-*, in + *gratia*, favor] to bring (oneself) into another's favor —**in·gra′ti·a′tion** *n.*

in·grat·i·tude (in grat′i to͞od′) *n.* lack of gratitude; ungratefulness

in·gre·di·ent (in grē′dē ənt) *n.* [see fol.] **1** any of the things that a mixture is made of **2** a component

in·gress (in′gres′) *n.* [< L *in-*, into + *gradi*, to go] entrance

in·grown (in′grōn′) *adj.* grown inward, esp. into the flesh, as a toenail

in·gui·nal (iŋ′gwi nəl) *adj.* [< L *inguen*, groin] of or near the groin

in·hab·it (in hab′it) *vt.* [< L *in-*, in + *habitare*, dwell] to live in —**in·hab′it·a·ble** *adj.*

in·hab·it·ant (-i tənt) *n.* a person or animal inhabiting a specified place

in·hal·ant (in hāl′ənt) *n.* a medicine, etc. to be inhaled

in·hale (in hāl′) *vt., vi.* **-haled′, -hal′ing** [< L *in-*, in + *halare*, breathe] to breathe in (air, vapor, etc.) —**in·ha·la·tion** (in′hə lā′shən) *n.*

in·hal·er (in hāl′ər) *n.* **1** one who inhales **2** RESPIRATOR (*n.* 1) **3** a device used in inhaling medicinal vapors, as for treating asthma

in·here (in hir′) *vi.* **-hered′, -her′ing** [< L *in-*, in + *haerere*, to stick] to be inherent

in·her·ent (in her′ənt, -hir′-) *adj.* existing in someone or something as a natural and inseparable quality —**in·her′ent·ly** *adv.*

in·her·it (in her′it) *vt., vi.* [< L *in*, in + *heres*, heir] **1** to receive (property, etc.) as an heir **2** to have (certain characteristics) as by heredity —**in·her′i·tor** *n.*

in·her·it·ance (in her′i təns) *n.* **1** the action of inheriting **2** something inherited

in·hib·it (in hib′it) *vt.* [< L *in-*, in, on + *habere*, to hold] to check or repress

in·hi·bi·tion (in′hi bish′ən, in′i-) *n.* **1** an inhibiting or being inhibited **2** a mental process that restrains an action, emotion, or thought

in-house *adj., adv.* (done) within an organization, company, etc. rather than outside it

in·hu·man (in hyo͞o′mən) *adj.* lacking pity, compassion, decency, etc. —**in′hu·man′i·ty** (-man′ə tē) *n.*

in·im·i·cal (i nim′i kəl) *adj.* [< L *in-*, not + *amicus*, friend] **1** hostile; unfriendly **2** in opposition; adverse

in·im·i·ta·ble (i nim′i tə bəl) *adj.* that cannot be imitated or matched

in·iq·ui·ty (i nik′wi tē) *n.* [< L *in-*, not + *aequus*, equal] **1** wickedness **2** *pl.* **-ties** a wicked or unjust act —**in·iq′ui·tous** *adj.*

in·i·tial (i nish′əl) *adj.* [< L *in-*, into, in + *tre*, go] of or at the beginning; first —*n.* the first letter of a name —*vt.* **-tialed** or **-tialled, -tial·ing** or **-tial·ling** to mark with initials —**in·i′tial·ly** *adv.*

in·i·ti·ate (i nish′ē āt′) *vt.* **-at′ed, -at′ing** [see prec.] **1** to bring into practice or use **2** to teach the fundamentals of a subject to **3** to admit as a member into a fraternity, club, etc., esp. with a special or secret ceremony —**in·i′ti·a′tion** *n.* —**in·i′ti·a·to′ry** (-ə tôr′ē) *adj.*

in·i·ti·a·tive (i nish′ə tiv, -ē ə tiv) *n.* **1** the action of taking the first step or move **2** ability in originating and implementing new ideas or methods **3** the introduction of proposed legislation, as by voters' petitions

in·ject (in jekt′) *vt.* [< L *in-*, in + *jacere*, to throw] **1** to force (a fluid) into a cavity or chamber; esp., to introduce (a liquid) into a vein, tissue, etc. with a syringe **2** to introduce (a remark, quality, etc.) —**in·jec′tion** *n.* —**in·jec′tor** *n.*

in·junc·tion (in juŋk′shən) *n.* [< L *in-*, in + *jungere*, join] **1** a command; order **2** a court order prohibiting or ordering a given action

in·jure (in′jər) *vt.* **-jured, -jur·ing** [see

INJURY] 1 to do harm or damage to; hurt 2 to wrong or offend

in·ju·ri·ous (in joor′ē əs) *adj.* injuring or likely to injure; harmful

in·ju·ry (in′jə rē) *n., pl.* **-ries** ⟦< L *in-*, not + *jus*, right⟧ 1 harm or damage 2 an injurious act

in·jus·tice (in jus′tis) *n.* 1 a being unjust 2 an unjust act; wrong

ink (iŋk) *n.* ⟦< Gr *en-*, in + *kaiein*, to burn⟧ 1 a colored liquid used for writing, printing, etc. 2 a dark, liquid secretion ejected by cuttlefish, squid, etc. —*vt.* 1 to cover, mark, or color with ink 2 [Inf.] to sign (a contract, etc.)

ink·blot *n.* any of the patterns made by blots of ink that are used in the RORSCHACH TEST

ink·ling (iŋk′liŋ) *n.* ⟦ME *ingkiling*⟧ 1 a hint 2 a vague notion

ink·well *n.* a container for ink, into which the point of a pen can be dipped

ink·y *adj.* **-i·er, -i·est** like ink in color; dark; black 2 covered with ink —**ink′i·ness** *n.*

in·laid (in′lād′, in lād′) *adj.* set into a surface or formed, decorated, etc. by inlaying

in·land (in′lənd; *for n. & adv.,* -land′, -lənd) *adj.* of or in the interior of a region —*n.* an inland region —*adv.* into or toward this region

in·law (in′lô′) *n.* ⟦< *mother-* (or *father-,* etc.) *in-law*⟧ [Inf.] a relative by marriage

in·lay (in′lā′, in lā′; *for n.* in′lā′) *vt.* **-laid′, -lay′ing** 1 to set (pieces of wood, etc.) into a surface, specif. for decoration 2 to decorate thus —*n.* 1 inlaid decoration or material 2 a shaped filling, as of gold, cemented into the cavity of a tooth

in·let (in′let′) *n.* a narrow strip of water extending into a body of land

in-line skate a kind of roller skate with its wheels in a line from toe to heel

in·mate (in′māt′) *n.* 1 [Archaic] a person living with others in the same building 2 a person confined with others in a prison or mental institution

in me·mo·ri·am (in′ mə môr′ē əm) ⟦L⟧ in memory (of): used on tombstones, in obituaries, etc.

in·most (in′mōst′) *adj.* INNERMOST

inn (in) *n.* ⟦OE⟧ 1 a hotel or motel 2 a restaurant or tavern: now usually only in the names of such places

in·nards (in′ərdz) *pl.n.* ⟦< INWARDS⟧ [Inf. or Dial.] the inner organs or parts

in·nate (i nāt′, in′āt′) *adj.* ⟦< L *in-*, in + *nasci,* be born⟧ inborn; natural

in·ner (in′ər) *adj.* 1 farther within 2 of the mind or spirit [*inner* peace] 3 more secret

inner circle the small, exclusive, most influential part of a group

inner city the central sections of a large city, esp. when crowded or run-down

inner ear the part of the ear consisting of the semicircular canals, vestibule, and cochlea

in·ner·most *adj.* 1 farthest within 2 most secret

in·ner·sole *n.* INSOLE

in·ner·spring mattress a mattress with built-in coil springs

in·ning (in′iŋ) *n.* ⟦< OE *innung,* getting in⟧ [*pl.* for *Cricket*] Baseball, Cricket 1 a team's turn at bat 2 a round of play in which both teams have a turn at bat

inn·keep·er *n.* the owner of an inn

in·no·cent (in′ə sənt) *adj.* ⟦< L *in-*, not + *nocere,* to harm⟧ 1 free from sin, evil, etc.; specif., not guilty of a specific crime 2 harmless 3 knowing no evil 4 without guile —*n.* an innocent person, as a child —**in′no·cence** *n.* —**in′no·cent·ly** *adv.*

in·noc·u·ous (i näk′yoo əs) *adj.* ⟦see prec.⟧ 1 harmless 2 not controversial or offensive —**in·noc′u·ous·ly** *adv.* —**in·noc′u·ous·ness** *n.*

in·no·va·tion (in′ə vā′shən) *n.* ⟦< L *in-*, in + *novus,* new⟧ 1 the process of introducing new methods, devices, etc. 2 a new method, custom, device, etc. —**in′no·vate′** *vi., vt.* **-vat′ed, -vat′ing** —**in′no·va′tive** *adj.* —**in′no·va′tor** *n.*

in·nu·en·do (in′yōō en′dō) *n., pl.* **-does** or **-dos** ⟦< L *in-*, in + *-nuere,* to nod⟧ a hint or sly remark, usually derogatory; insinuation

in·nu·mer·a·ble (i nōō′mer ə bəl) *adj.* too numerous to be counted

in·oc·u·late (i näk′yə lāt′) *vt.* **-lat′ed, -lat′ing** ⟦< L *in-*, in + *oculus,* eye⟧ to inject a serum, vaccine, etc. into, esp. in order to create immunity —**in·oc′u·la′tion** *n.*

in·of·fen·sive (in′ə fen′siv) *adj.* causing no harm or annoyance; not objectionable —**in′of·fen′sive·ly** *adv.*

in·op·er·a·ble (in äp′ər ə bəl) *adj.* not operable; specif., incapable of being treated by surgery

in·op·er·a·tive (in äp′ər ə tiv, -ər āt′iv) *adj.* not working or functioning

in·or·di·nate (in ôrd′n it) *adj.* ⟦ult. < L *in-*, not + *ordo,* order⟧ excessive; immoderate —**in·or′di·nate·ly** *adv.*

in·or·gan·ic (in′ôr gan′ik) *adj.* not organic; specif., designating or of matter not derived from living things

in·pa·tient (in′pā′shənt) *n.* a patient who stays in a hospital, etc. while receiving treatment

in·put (in′poot′) *n.* 1 what is put in; specif., *a)* power put into a machine, etc. *b)* data or programs entered into a computer 2 opinion; advice —*vt.* **-put′, -put′ting** to enter (data) into a computer —**in′put′ter** *n.*

in·quest (in′kwest′) *n.* ⟦see INQUIRE⟧ a judicial inquiry, esp. before a jury, as a coroner's investigation of a death

in·qui·e·tude (in kwī′ə tood′) *n.* restlessness; uneasiness

in·quire (in kwīr′) *vi.* **-quired′, -quir′ing** ⟦< L *in-*, into + *quaerere,* seek⟧ 1 to ask a question or questions 2 to investigate: usually with *into* —*vt.* to seek information about —**in·quir′er** *n.*

in·quir·y (in′kwər ē, in kwīr′ē) *n., pl.* **-ies** 1 an inquiring; investigation 2 a question

in·qui·si·tion (in′kwə zish′ən) *n.* 1 an investigation or inquest 2 [I-] the Roman Catholic tribunal established in the 1200s for suppressing heresy 3 any relentless questioning or harsh suppression —**in·quis·i·tor** (in kwiz′ə tər) *n.*

in·quis·i·tive (in kwiz′ə tiv) *adj.* 1 inclined to ask many questions 2 unnecessarily curious; prying —**in·quis′i·tive·ness** *n.*

in re (in rē′, -rā′) [L] in the matter (of)

-in·res·i·dence *combining form* appointed to work at, and usually residing at, an institution, as a college, for a certain period

in·road (in′rōd′) *n.* an encroachment: *usually used in pl.*

ins *abbrev.* insurance

in·sane (in sān′) *adj.* 1 not sane; mentally ill or deranged 2 of or for insane people [an *insane* asylum] 3 very foolish, extravagant, etc. —**in·sane′ly** *adv.* —**in·san′i·ty** (-san′ə tē) *n.*

in·sa·ti·a·ble (in sā′shə bəl, -shē ə bəl) *adj.* [see IN-² & SATIATE] that cannot be satisfied —**in·sa′ti·a·bil′i·ty** *n.* —**in·sa′ti·a·bly** *adv.*

in·scribe (in skrīb′) *vt.* **-scribed′, -scrib′ing** [< L *in-*, in + *scribere*, write] 1 to mark or engrave (words, etc.) on (a surface) 2 *a)* to dedicate (a book, etc.) to someone *b)* to autograph 3 to fix in the mind —**in·scrip′tion** (-skrip′shən) *n.*

in·scru·ta·ble (in skrōōt′ə bəl) *adj.* [< L *in-*, not + *scrutari*, examine] not easily understood; enigmatic —**in·scru′ta·bly** *adv.*

in·seam (in′sēm′) *n.* an inner seam; specif., the seam from the crotch to the bottom of a trouser leg

in·sect (in′sekt′) *n.* [< L *insectum*, lit., notched] any of a large class of small, usually winged, invertebrates, as beetles, flies, or wasps, having six legs

in·sec·ti·cide (in sek′tə sīd′) *n.* any substance used to kill insects —**in·sec′ti·ci′dal** *adj.*

in·sec·ti·vore (in sek′tə vôr′) *n.* [see fol.] any of various small mammals, as moles and shrews, that are active mainly at night and that feed principally on insects

in·sec·tiv·o·rous (in′sek tiv′ə rəs) *adj.* [< IN-SECT + L *vorare*, devour] feeding chiefly on insects

in·se·cure (in′si kyoor′) *adj.* 1 not safe from danger 2 feeling anxiety 3 not firm or dependable —**in′se·cure′ly** *adv.* —**in′se·cu′ri·ty** *n., pl.* **-ties**

in·sem·i·nate (in sem′ə nāt′) *vt.* **-nat′ed, -nat′ing** [< L *in-*, in + *semen*, seed] 1 to impregnate 2 to imbue (with ideas, etc.) —**in·sem′i·na′tion** *n.*

in·sen·sate (in sen′sāt′, -sit) *adj.* 1 not feeling sensation 2 foolish 3 cold; insensitive

in·sen·si·ble (in sen′sə bəl) *adj.* 1 unable to perceive with the senses 2 unconscious 3 unaware; indifferent 4 so small as to be virtually imperceptible —**in·sen′si·bil′i·ty** *n.*

in·sen·si·tive (-sə tiv) *adj.* 1 not sensitive; not responsive 2 tactless —**in·sen′si·tive·ly** *adv.* —**in·sen′si·tiv′i·ty** *n.*

in·sen·tient (in sen′shənt, -shē ənt) *adj.* not

sentient; not having life, consciousness, or feeling —**in·sen′tience** *n.*

in·sert (in surt′; *for n.* in′surt′) *vt.* [< L *in-*, in + *serere*, join] to put or fit (something) into something else —*n.* anything inserted or for insertion —**in·ser′tion** *n.*

in·set (in set′; *for n.* in′set′) *vt.* **-set′, -set′ting** to set in; insert —*n.* something inserted

in·shore (in′shôr′, in shôr′) *adv., adj.* in, near, or toward the shore

in·side (in′sīd′, in′sīd′, in sīd′) *n.* 1 the inner side, surface, or part 2 [pl.] [Inf.] the internal organs of the body —*adj.* 1 internal 2 known only to insiders; secret —*adv.* 1 on or to the inside; within 2 indoors —*prep.* in or within —**inside of** within the space or time of —**inside out** 1 reversed 2 [Inf.] thoroughly

in·sid·er (in′sīd′ər, in sīd′ər) *n.* 1 one inside a given place or group 2 one having confidential information

in·sid·i·ous (in sid′ē əs) *adj.* [< L *insidiae*, an ambush] 1 characterized by treachery or slyness 2 more dangerous than seems evident

in·sight (in′sīt′) *n.* 1 the ability to see and understand clearly the inner nature of things, esp. by intuition 2 an instance of such understanding

in·sig·ni·a (in sig′nē ə) *pl.n., sing.* **in·sig′ni·ne** (-nē) [ult. < L *in-*, in + *signum*, a mark] badges, emblems, or distinguishing marks, as of rank or membership —*n., pl.* **in·sig′ni·as** such a badge, etc.

in·sin·cere (in′sin sir′) *adj.* not sincere; deceptive or hypocritical —**in′sin·cere′ly** *adv.* —**in′sin·cer′i·ty** (-ser′ə tē) *n., pl.* **-ties**

in·sin·u·ate (in sin′yōō āt′) *vt.* **-at′ed, -at′ing** [< L *in-*, in + *sinus*, a curve] 1 to introduce or work into gradually, indirectly, etc. 2 to hint or suggest indirectly; imply —**in·sin′u·a′tion** *n.* —**in·sin′u·a′tive** *adj.* —**in·sin′u·a′tor** *n.*

in·sip·id (in sip′id) *adj.* [< L *in-*, not + *sapidus*, savory] 1 without flavor; tasteless 2 not exciting or interesting; dull

in·sist (in sist′) *vi.* [< L *in-*, in, on + *sistere*, to stand] to take and maintain a stand: often with *on* or *upon* —*vt.* 1 to demand strongly 2 to declare firmly —**in·sist′ing·ly** *adv.*

in·sist·ent *adj.* insisting; persistent —**in·sist′ence** *n.* —**in·sist′ent·ly** *adv.*

in si·tu (in sī′tōō′) [L] in position; in its original place

in·so·far (in′sō fär′) *adv.* to such a degree or extent: usually with *as*

in·sole (in′sōl′) *n.* 1 the inside sole of a shoe 2 a removable inside sole put in for comfort

in·so·lent (in′sə lənt) *adj.* [< L *in-*, not + *solere*, be accustomed] boldly disrespectful; impudent —**in′so·lence** *n.*

in·sol·u·ble (in säl′yə bəl) *adj.* 1 that cannot be solved 2 that cannot be dissolved —**in·sol′u·bil′i·ty** *n.*

in·sol·vent (in säl′vənt) *adj.* not solvent; unable to pay debts; bankrupt —**in·sol′ven·cy** *n.*

in·som·ni·a (in säm′nē ə) *n.* [< L *in-*, without

+ *somnus*, sleep⟧ abnormal inability to sleep —in·som′ni·ac′ (-ak′) *n., adj.*

in·so·much (in′sō much′) *adv.* 1 to such a degree or extent; so: with *that* 2 inasmuch (*as*)

in·sou·ci·ant (in sōō′sē ənt) *adj.* ⟦Fr < *in-*, not + *soucier*, to care⟧ carefree

in·spect (in spekt′) *vt.* ⟦< L *in-*, at + *specere*, look at⟧ 1 to look at carefully 2 to examine or review officially —in·spec′tion *n.*

in·spec·tor *n.* 1 one who inspects 2 an officer on a police force, ranking next below a superintendent or police chief

in·spi·ra·tion (in′spə rā′shən) *n.* 1 an inspiring or being inspired mentally or emotionally 2 *a)* any stimulus to creative thought or action *b)* an inspired idea, action, etc. —in′spi·ra′tion·al *adj.*

in·spire (in spīr′) *vt.* -spired′, -spir′ing ⟦< L *in-*, in, on + *spirare*, breathe⟧ 1 to inhale 2 to stimulate or impel, as to some creative effort 3 to motivate as by divine influence 4 to arouse (a thought or feeling) in (someone) 5 to occasion or cause —*vi.* 1 to inhale 2 to give inspiration

in·spir·it (in spir′it) *vt.* to put spirit into; cheer; hearten

inst *abbrev.* 1 institute 2 institution

in·sta·bil·i·ty (in′stə bil′ə tē) *n.* lack of firmness, determination, etc.

in·stall or in·stal (in stôl′) *vt.* -stalled′, -stall′ing ⟦< ML *in-*, in + *stallum*, a place⟧ 1 to place in an office, rank, etc., with ceremony 2 to establish in a place 3 to fix in position for use [to *install* new fixtures] —in·stal·la·tion (in′stə lā′shən) *n.* —in·stall′er *n.*

in·stall·ment or in·stal·ment *n.* 1 an installing or being installed 2 any of the parts of a sum of money to be paid at regular specified times 3 any of several parts, as of a serial

installment plan a credit system by which debts, as for purchased articles, are paid in installments

in·stance (in′stəns) *n.* [see fol.] 1 an example; case 2 a step in proceeding; occasion [in the first *instance*] —*vt.* -stanced, -stanc·ing to give as an example; cite —at the instance of at the suggestion or instigation of

in·stant (in′stənt) *adj.* ⟦< L *in-*, in, upon + *stare*, to stand⟧ 1 immediate 2 dehydrated, concentrated, or precooked for quick preparation: said of a food or beverage —*n.* 1 a moment 2 a particular moment —the instant as soon as

in·stan·ta·ne·ous (in′stən tā′nē əs) *adj.* done or happening in an instant —in′stan·ta′ne·ous·ly *adv.*

in·stan·ter (in stan′tər) *adv.* ⟦L⟧ *Law* immediately

in·stant·ly *adv.* immediately

instant messaging an online service enabling subscribers to CHAT (*vi.* 2) with one another —instant message

in·state (in stāt′) *vt.* -stat′ed, -stat′ing ⟦IN-¹ + STATE⟧ to put in a particular position, rank, etc.; install

in·stead (in sted′) *adv.* ⟦IN¹ + STEAD⟧ in place of the one mentioned —instead of in place of

in·step (in′step′) *n.* the top surface of the foot, between the ankle and the toes

in·sti·gate (in′stə gāt′) *vt.* -gat′ed, -gat′ing ⟦< L *in-*, on + *-stigare*, to prick⟧ 1 to urge on to some action 2 to foment (rebellion, etc.) —in′sti·ga′tion *n.* —in′sti·ga′tor *n.*

in·still or in·stil (in stil′) *vt.* -stilled′, -still′ing ⟦< L *in-*, in + *stilla*, a drop⟧ 1 to put in drop by drop 2 to put (an idea, etc.) in or *into* gradually

in·stinct (in′stiŋkt′) *n.* ⟦< L *instinguere*, to impel⟧ 1 (an) inborn tendency to behave in a way characteristic of a species 2 a natural or acquired tendency; knack —in·stinc′tive *adj.* —in·stinc′tu·al *adj.*

in·sti·tute (in′stə tōōt′) *vt.* -tut′ed, -tut′ing ⟦< L *in-*, in, on + *statuere*, to cause to set up⟧ 1 to set up; establish 2 to start; initiate —*n.* something instituted; specif., *a)* an organization for the promotion of art, science, etc. *b)* a school or college specializing in some field —in′sti·tut′er *n.*, in′sti·tu′tor

in·sti·tu·tion (in′stə tōō′shən) *n.* 1 an instituting or being instituted 2 an established law, custom, etc. 3 *a)* an organization having a public character, as a school, church, bank, or hospital *b)* the building housing it 4 a person or thing long established in a place —in′sti·tu′tion·al *adj.*

in·sti·tu·tion·al·ize (-īz′) *vt.* -ized′, -iz′ing 1 to make into an institution 2 to place in an institution, as for treatment —in′sti·tu′tion·al·i·za′tion *n.*

in·struct (in strukt′) *vt.* ⟦< L *in-*, in + *struere*, pile up⟧ 1 to teach; educate 2 to inform 3 to order or direct

in·struc·tion (-struk′shən) *n.* 1 an instructing; education 2 something taught 3 any of the steps to be followed, as in operating something: *usually used in pl.* 4 a sequence of bits specifying an operation to be performed by a computer —in·struc′tion·al *adj.*

in·struc·tive *adj.* giving knowledge

in·struc·tor *n.* a teacher 2 a college teacher of the lowest rank

in·stru·ment (in′strə mənt) *n.* [see IN-STRUCT] 1 a thing by means of which something is done 2 a tool or implement 3 any of various devices for indicating, measuring, controlling, etc. 4 any of various devices producing musical sound when played by a musician 5 *Law* a formal document

in·stru·men·tal (-mənt′'l) *adj.* 1 serving as a means; helpful 2 of, performed on, or written for a musical instrument or instruments, esp. without vocals

in·stru·men·tal·ist *n.* a person who performs on a musical instrument

in·stru·men·tal·i·ty (-men′tal′ə tē) *n., pl.* -ties a means; agency

in·stru·men·ta·tion (-tā′shən) *n.* 1 the writing or scoring of music for instruments 2 the use of or an equipping with instruments

instrument flying the flying of an aircraft by the use of instruments only

in·sub·or·di·nate (in′sə bôrd′'n it) *adj.* not submitting to authority; disobedient —**in′sub·or′di·na′tion** *n.*

in·sub·stan·tial (in′səb stan′shəl) *adj.* not substantial; specif., *a)* not real; imaginary *b)* weak or flimsy

in·suf·fer·a·ble (in suf′ər ə bəl) *adj.* intolerable; unbearable

in·su·lar (in′sə lər) *adj.* ⟦< L *insula*, island⟧ 1 of or like an island or islanders 2 narrow-minded; illiberal

in·su·late (-lāt′) *vt.* -lat′ed, -lat′ing ⟦< L *insula*, island⟧ 1 to set apart; isolate 2 to cover with a nonconducting material in order to prevent the escape of electricity, heat, sound, etc.

in·su·la·tion *n.* 1 an insulating or being insulated 2 material for this

in·su·lin (in′sə lin) *n.* ⟦< L *insula*, island⟧ 1 a hormone vital to carbohydrate metabolism, secreted by the islets of Langerhans 2 a synthesized form of this hormone, used in the treatment of diabetes

insulin shock the abnormal condition caused by an excess of insulin: it is characterized by tremors, cold sweat, convulsions, and coma

in·sult (in sult′; *for n.* in′sult′) *vt.* ⟦< L *in-*, on + *salire*, to leap⟧ to subject to an act, remark, etc. meant to hurt the feelings or pride —*n.* an insulting act, remark, etc.

in·su·per·a·ble (in soo′pər ə bəl) *adj.* ⟦< L *insuperabilis*⟧ that cannot be overcome [an *insuperable* obstacle]

in·sup·port·a·ble (in′sə pôrt′ə bəl) *adj.* intolerable; unbearable 2 incapable of being upheld, proved, etc.

in·sur·ance (in shoor′əns) *n.* 1 an insuring or being insured against loss 2 a contract (**insurance policy**) purchased to guarantee compensation for a specified loss by fire, death, etc. 3 the amount for which something is insured 4 the business of insuring against loss

in·sure (in shoor′) *vt.* -sured′, -sur′ing ⟦ME *ensuren*: see ENSURE⟧ 1 to take out or issue insurance on 2 ENSURE —**in·sur′a·ble** *adj.*

in·sured *n.* a person whose life, property, etc. is insured against loss

in·sur·er *n.* a person or company that insures others against loss

in·sur·gence (-jəns) *n.* a rising in revolt; uprising: also **in·sur′gen·cy**, *pl.* -**cies**

in·sur·gent (in sur′jənt) *adj.* ⟦< L *in-*, upon + *surgere*, rise⟧ rising up against established authority —*n.* an insurgent person

in·sur·rec·tion (in′sə rek′shən) *n.* ⟦see prec.⟧ a rising up against established authority —**in′sur·rec′tion·ist** *n.*

int *abbrev.* 1 interest 2 interjection 3 international

in·tact (in takt′) *adj.* ⟦< L *in-*, not + *tactus*, touched⟧ unimpaired or uninjured; kept or left whole

in·ta·glio (in tal′yō′) *n.*, *pl.* -**glios′** ⟦It < *in-*, in + *tagliare*, to cut⟧ a design carved or engraved below the surface

in·take (in′tāk′) *n.* 1 a taking in 2 the amount taken in 3 the place in a pipe, etc. where a fluid is taken in

in·tan·gi·ble (in tan′jə bəl) *adj.* 1 that cannot be touched; incorporeal 2 of certain business assets, esp. goodwill, having monetary value but no material being 3 that cannot be easily defined; vague —*n.* something intangible

in·te·ger (in′tə jər) *n.* ⟦L, whole⟧ a whole number (e.g., 5, -10) or zero

in·te·gral (in′tə grəl; *often* in teg′rəl) *adj.* ⟦see prec.⟧ 1 necessary for completeness; essential 2 made up of parts forming a whole

in·te·grate (-grāt′) *vt., vi.* -grat′ed, -grat′ing ⟦< L *integer*, whole⟧ 1 to make or become whole or complete 2 to bring (parts) together into a whole 3 *a)* to remove barriers imposing segregation upon (racial groups) *b)* to abolish segregation in —**in′te·gra′tion** *n.* —**in′te·gra′tive** *adj.*

integrated circuit an electronic circuit with many interconnected circuit elements formed on a single body, or chip, of semiconductor material

in·teg·ri·ty (in teg′rə tē) *n.* ⟦see INTEGER⟧ 1 completeness 2 unimpaired condition; soundness 3 adherence to ethical principles

in·teg·u·ment (in teg′yoo mənt) *n.* ⟦< L *in-*, upon + *tegere*, to cover⟧ an outer covering; skin, shell, rind, etc.

in·tel·lect (in′tə lekt′) *n.* ⟦< L *inter-*, between + *legere*, choose⟧ 1 the ability to reason or understand 2 high intelligence 3 a very intelligent person

in·tel·lec·tu·al (in′tə lek′choo əl) *adj.* 1 of, involving, or appealing to the intellect 2 requiring intelligence 3 having intellectual interests or tastes 4 showing high intelligence —*n.* one with intellectual interests or tastes —**in′tel·lec′tu·al·ly** *adv.* —**in′tel·lec′tu·al′i·ty** *n.*

in·tel·lec·tu·al·ize (-īz′) *vt.* -ized′, -iz′ing to examine or interpret rationally, often without regard for emotional considerations

intellectual property something produced by the mind, the rights to which may be protected by a copyright, patent, etc.

in·tel·li·gence (in tel′ə jəns) *n.* ⟦see INTELLECT⟧ 1 *a)* the ability to learn or understand *b)* the ability to cope with a new situation 2 news or information 3 those engaged in gathering secret, esp. military, information 4 an intelligent spirit or being

intelligence quotient *see* IQ

in·tel·li·gent (-jənt) *adj.* having or showing intelligence; clever, wise, etc. —**in·tel′li·gent·ly** *adv.*

intelligent design the concept that the order and complexity seen in nature must be the result of a rational design, as by God

in·tel·li·gent·si·a (-jent′sē ə) *pl.n.* ⟦< Russ⟧ [*also with sing. v.*] intellectuals collectively

in·tel·li·gi·ble (in tel′i jə bəl) *adj.* that can be understood; clear —**in·tel′li·gi·bil′i·ty** *n.* —**in·tel′li·gi·bly** *adv.*

in·tem·per·ate (in tem′pər it, -prit) *adj.* **1** not temperate or moderate; excessive **2** drinking too much alcoholic liquor —**in·tem′per·ance** *n.*

in·tend (in tend′) *vt.* ⟦< L *in-*, at + *tendere*, to stretch⟧ **1** to plan; have in mind as a purpose **2** to mean (something) to be or be used (*for*) **3** to mean; signify

in·tend·ed *n.* [Inf.] one's prospective spouse

in·tense (in tens′) *adj.* ⟦see INTEND⟧ **1** very strong [an *intense* light] **2** strenuous; earnest [*intense* thought] **3** characterized by much action, strong emotion, etc. —**in·tense′ly** *adv.*

in·ten·si·fy (in ten′sə fī′) *vt., vi.* **-fied′, -fy′ ing** to make or become intense or more intense —**in·ten′si·fi·ca′tion** *n.*

in·ten·si·ty *n., pl.* **-ties 1** a being intense **2** great energy or vehemence, as of emotion **3** the amount of force or energy of heat, light, sound, etc.

in·ten·sive *adj.* **1** of or characterized by intensity; thorough **2** designating very attentive care given to critically ill patients **3** *Gram.* giving force or emphasis ["very" is an *intensive* adverb] —*n. Gram.* an intensive word, prefix, etc. —**in·ten′sive·ly** *adv.* —**in·ten′sive·ness** *n.*

-in·ten·sive *combining form* intensively using or requiring large amounts of (a specified thing) [energy-*intensive*]

in·tent (in tent′) *adj.* ⟦see INTEND⟧ **1** firmly directed; earnest **2** having one's attention or purpose firmly fixed [*intent* on going] —*n.* **1** an intending **2** something intended; purpose or meaning —**to all intents and purposes** in almost every respect; practically; virtually —**in·tent′ly** *adv.* —**in·tent′ness** *n.*

in·ten·tion (in ten′shən) *n.* **1** determination to act in a specified way **2** anything intended; purpose

in·ten·tion·al *adj.* done purposely —**in·ten′tion·al·ly** *adv.*

in·ter (in tur′) *vt.* **-terred′, -ter′ring** ⟦< L *in*, in + *terra*, earth⟧ to put (a dead body) into a grave or tomb; bury

inter- ⟦L⟧ *prefix* **1** between or among: the second element of the compound is singular in form [*interstate*] **2** with or on each other (or one another) [*interact*]

in·ter·act (in′tər akt′) *vi.* to act on one another —**in′ter·ac′tion** *n.*

in·ter·ac·tive (-ak′tiv) *adj.* **1** acting on one another **2** designating of audio or video programming or electronic equipment that allows users to participate, as by making a response **3** of or involving the continual exchange of information between the computer and the user

in·ter·breed (in′tər brēd′, in′tər brēd′) *vt., vi.* **-bred′, -breed′ing** HYBRIDIZE

in·ter·cede (-sēd′) *vi.* **-ced′ed, -ced′ing** ⟦< L *inter-*, between + *cedere*, go⟧ **1** to plead or make a request in behalf of another **2** to mediate; intervene

in·ter·cept (-sept′) *vt.* ⟦< L *inter-*, between + *capere*, take⟧ **1** to seize or stop in its course [to *intercept* a message] **2** *Math.* to cut off or

mark off between two points, lines, etc. —*n. Math.* a point where a curve, etc. intersects an axis —**in′ter·cep′tion** *n.*

in·ter·ces·sion (-sesh′ən) *n.* an interceding; mediation or prayer in behalf of another —**in′ter·ces′sor** (-ses′ər) *n.* —**in′ter·ces′so·ry** *adj.*

in·ter·change (in′tər chānj′; *for n.* in′tər chānj′) *vt.* **-changed′, -chang′ing 1** to give and take mutually; exchange **2** to put (each of two things) in the other's place **3** to alternate —*n.* **1** an interchanging **2** a junction which allows movement of traffic between highways on different levels, as a cloverleaf —**in′ter·change′a·ble** *adj.*

in·ter·col·le·gi·ate (-kə lē′jit) *adj.* between or among colleges and universities

in·ter·com (in′tər käm′) *n.* a radio or telephone intercommunication system, as between rooms

in·ter·com·mu·ni·cate (-kə myōō′ni kāt′) *vt., vi.* **-cat′ed, -cat′ing** to communicate with or to one another —**in′ter·com·mu′ni·ca′tion** *n.*

in·ter·con·nect (-kə nekt′) *vt., vi.* to connect or be connected with one another —**in′ter·con·nec′tion** *n.*

in·ter·con·ti·nen·tal (-känt′'n ent′'l) *adj.* **1** between or among continents **2** able to travel from one continent to another: said of a missile

in·ter·cos·tal (-käs′təl, -kôs′-) *adj.* between the ribs —*n.* an intercostal muscle, etc.

in·ter·course (in′tər kôrs′) *n.* ⟦see INTER- & COURSE⟧ **1** communication or dealings between or among people, countries, etc. **2** *short for* SEXUAL INTERCOURSE

in·ter·de·nom·i·na·tion·al (-dē näm′ə nā′shən əl) *adj.* between or among religious denominations

in·ter·de·part·men·tal (-dē′pärt ment′'l) *adj.* between or among departments

in·ter·de·pend·ence (-dē pen′dəns) *n.* mutual dependence: also **in′ter·de·pend′en·cy**, *pl.* **-cies** —**in′ter·de·pend′ent** *adj.*

in·ter·dict (in′tər dikt′; *for n.* in′tər dikt′) *vt.* ⟦< L *inter-*, between + *dicere*, speak⟧ **1** to prohibit (an action) **2** to restrain from doing or using something —*n.* an official prohibition —**in′ter·dic′tion** *n.*

in·ter·dis·ci·pli·nar·y (-dis′ə pli nar′ē) *adj.* involving two or more disciplines, or branches of learning

in·ter·est (in′trist; *for v., also,* -tə rest′) *n.* ⟦< L *inter-*, between + *esse*, be⟧ **1** a right to, or a share in, something **2** anything in which one has a share **3** [*often pl.*] advantage; benefit **4** [*usually pl.*] those having a common concern or power in some industry, cause, etc. [the steel *interests*] **5** *a*) a feeling of concern, curiosity, etc. about something *b*) the power of causing this feeling *c*) something causing this feeling **6** *a*) money paid for the use of money *b*) the rate of such payment —*vt.* **1** to involve or excite the interest or attention of **2** to cause to have an interest or take part in —**in the interest(s) of** for the sake of

in·ter·est·ed adj. **1** having an interest or share **2** influenced by personal interest; biased **3** feeling or showing interest

in·ter·est·ing adj. exciting curiosity or attention; of interest

in·ter·face (in′tər fās′) n. **1** a plane forming the common boundary between two parts of matter or space **2** a point or means of interaction between two systems, groups, etc. — vt., vi. **-faced′, -fac′ing** to interact with (another system, group, etc.)

in·ter·faith (-fāth′) adj. between or involving persons adhering to different religions

in·ter·fere (in′tər fir′) vi. **-fered′, -fer′ing** [ult. < L inter-, between + ferire, to strike] **1** to clash; collide **2** a) to come in or between; intervene b) to meddle **3** to hinder an opposing player in any of various illegal ways —**interfere with** to hinder

in·ter·fer·ence (in′tər fir′əns) n. **1** an act or instance of interfering **2** something that interferes **3** Sports the hindering of an opposing player, esp. one who is trying to catch a pass **4** Physics the phenomenon by which two waves, esp. of the same frequency, reinforce or neutralize each other depending on their relative phases **5** Radio, TV, etc. a) static, unwanted signals, etc., preventing good reception b) such distorted reception

in·ter·fer·on (in′tər fir′än′) n. [prec. + -on, arbitrary suffix] a cellular protein produced in response to infection by a virus and acting to inhibit viral growth

In·ter·gen·er·a·tion·al (-jen′ə rā′shə nəl) adj. of or involving persons of different generations

in·ter·im (in′tər im) n. [< L inter, between] the period of time between; meantime —adj. temporary

in·te·ri·or (in tir′ē ər) adj. [< L inter, between] **1** situated within; inner **2** inland **3** private —n. **1** the interior part, as of a building or country **2** the internal, or domestic, affairs of a country

interior decoration the art or business of decorating and furnishing the interiors of houses, offices, etc. —**interior decorator**

in·te·ri·or·ize (-īz′) vt. **-ized′, -iz′ing** to make (a concept, value, etc.) part of one's inner nature

interj abbrev. interjection

in·ter·ject (in′tər jekt′) vt. [< L inter-, between + jacere, to throw] to interrupt with; insert

in·ter·jec·tion (-jek′shən) n. **1** an interjecting **2** something interjected **3** Gram. an exclamation or other word(s) inserted into an utterance without grammatical connection to it

in·ter·lace (-lās′) vt., vi. **-laced′, -lac′ing** to lace or weave together

in·ter·lard (-lärd′) vt. [see INTER- & LARD] to intersperse; diversify [to interlard a talk with quotations]

in·ter·leu·kin (in′tər lōō′kin) n. any of several proteins derived from many cell types and affecting the activity of other cells, as in stimulating the growth of T cells

in·ter·line (-līn′) vt. **-lined′, -lin′ing** to put an inner lining under the ordinary lining of (a garment)

in·ter·lock (-läk′) vt., vi. to lock together; join with one another

in·ter·loc·u·tor (in′tər läk′yōō tər, -yə-) n. a person taking part in a dialogue

in·ter·loc·u·to·ry (in′tər läk′yōō tôr′ē, -yə-) adj. Law not final [an interlocutory divorce decree]

in·ter·lop·er (in′tər lō′pər) n. [INTER- + -loper < Du lopen, to run] one who meddles

in·ter·lude (in′tər lōōd′) n. [< L inter, between + ludus, a play] **1** anything that fills time between two events, as music between acts of a play **2** intervening time

in·ter·mar·ry (-mar′ē) vi. **-ried, -ry·ing 1** to become connected by marriage: said of different clans, races, etc. **2** to marry each other: said of closely related persons —**in′ter·mar′riage** n.

in·ter·me·di·ar·y (-mē′dē er′ē) adj. **1** acting as a go-between or mediator **2** intermediate —n., pl. **-ar′ies** a go-between; mediator

in·ter·me·di·ate (-mē′dē it) adj. [< L inter-, between + medius, middle] **1** in the middle; in between **2** of an automobile larger than a compact but smaller than the standard size —n. an intermediate automobile

in·ter·ment (in tur′mənt) n. the act of interring; burial

in·ter·mez·zo (in′tər met′sō′) n., pl. **-zos′** or **-zi′** (-sē′) [It < L: see INTERMEDIATE] a short piece of music, as between parts of a composition

in·ter·mi·na·ble (in tur′mi nə bəl) adj. lasting, or seeming to last, forever; endless —**in·ter′mi·na·bly** adv.

in·ter·min·gle (in′tər miŋ′gəl) vt., vi. **-gled, -gling** to mix together; mingle

in·ter·mis·sion (in′tər mish′ən) n. [< L inter-, between + mittere, send] an interval of time between periods of activity, as between acts of a play

in·ter·mit·tent (-mit′'nt) adj. [see prec.] stopping and starting at intervals; periodic —**in′ter·mit′tent·ly** adv.

in·tern (in′turn′; for vt. in turn′, in′turn′) n. [< L internus, inward] **1** a doctor serving as assistant resident in a hospital generally just after graduation from medical school **2** a student, etc. doing supervised temporary work in a field to gain experience —vi. to serve as an intern —vt. to detain or confine (foreign persons, etc.), as during a war —**in·tern′ment** n. —**in′tern′ship′** n.

in·ter·nal (in tur′nəl) adj. [< L internus] **1** of or on the inside; inner **2** to be taken inside the body [internal remedies] **3** intrinsic [internal evidence] **4** domestic [internal revenue] —**in·ter′nal·ly** adv.

in·ter·nal-com·bus·tion engine an engine, as in an automobile, powered by the explosion of a fuel-and-air mixture within the cylinders

in·ter·nal·ize (-īz′) vt. **-ized′, -iz′ing** to make

(others' ideas, etc.) a part of one's thinking —**in·ter'nal·i·za'tion** n.

internal medicine the branch of medicine that deals with the diagnosis and nonsurgical treatment of diseases

internal revenue governmental income from taxes on income, profits, etc.

in·ter·na·tion·al (in'tər nash'ə nəl) *adj.* **1** between or among nations **2** concerned with the relations between nations **3** for the use of all nations **4** of or for people in various nations —**in'ter·na'tion·al·ize'** *vt.* **-ized', -iz'ing** —**in'ter·na'tion·al·ly** *adv.*

International Phonetic Alphabet a set of phonetic symbols for international use: each symbol represents a single human speech sound

in·ter·ne·cine (in'tər nē'sin) *adj.* [< L *inter-*, between + *necare*, kill] **1** deadly or harmful to both sides of a group in a conflict **2** of or involving conflict within a group

in·ter·net or **In·ter·net** (in'tər net') *n.* the accessible system of networks that connects computers worldwide: usually with *the*

in·tern·ist (in'turn'ist, in turn'ist) *n.* a doctor who specializes in INTERNAL MEDICINE

in·ter·of·fice (in'tər ôf'is) *adj.* between or among the offices of an organization [an *interoffice* memo]

in·ter·per·son·al (-pur'sə nəl) *adj.* between persons [*interpersonal* relationships]

in·ter·plan·e·tar·y (-plan'ə ter'ē) *adj.* between planets

in·ter·play (-plā') *n.* action, effect, or influence on each other or one another

in·ter·po·late (in tur'pə lāt') *vt.* **-lat'ed, -lat'ing** [< L *inter-*, between + *polire*, to polish] **1** to change (a text, etc.) by inserting new material **2** to insert between or among others **3** *Math.* to estimate (a value) based on known higher and lower values —**in·ter'po·la'tion** n.

in·ter·pose (in'tər pōz') *vt., vi.* **-posed', -pos'ing 1** to place or come between **2** to intervene (with) **3** to interrupt (with) —*in'ter·po·si'tion* (-pə zish'ən) n.

in·ter·pret (in tur'prət) *vt.* [< L *interpres*, agent, broker] **1** to explain or translate **2** to construe [to *interpret* a silence as contempt] **3** to give one's own conception of (a work of art), as in performance or criticism —*vi.* to explain or translate —**in·ter'pre·ta'tion** n. —**in·ter'pret·er** n.

in·ter·pre·tive (in tur'prə tiv) *adj.* that interprets; explanatory: also **in·ter'pre·ta'tive** (-tāt'iv)

in·ter·ra·cial (in'tər rā'shəl) *adj.* between, among, or for members of different races: also **in'ter·race'**

in·ter·re·late (-rē lāt') *vt., vi.* **-lat'ed, -lat'ing** to make or be mutually related —**in'ter·re·lat'ed** *adj.*

in·ter·ro·gate (in ter'ə gāt') *vi., vt.* **-gat'ed, -gat'ing** [< L *inter-*, between + *rogare*, ask] to ask questions (of), esp. formally —**in·ter'ro·ga'tion** n. —**in·ter'ro·ga'tor** n.

in·ter·rog·a·tive (in'tə räg'ə tiv) *adj.* asking a question: also **in'ter·rog'a·to'ry** (-ə tôr' ē)

in·ter·rupt (in'tə rupt') *vt.* [< L *inter-*, between + *rumpere*, to break] **1** to break into (a discussion, etc.) or to break in upon (a speaker, worker, etc.) **2** to make a break in the continuity of —*vi.* to interrupt an action, talk, etc. —**in'ter·rup'tion** n.

in·ter·scho·las·tic (in'tər skə las'tik) *adj.* between or among schools

in·ter·sect (in'tər sekt') *vt.* [< L *inter-*, between + *secare*, to cut] to divide into two parts by passing through or across —*vi.* to cross each other

in·ter·sec·tion (-sek'shən) n. **1** an intersecting **2** the place where two lines, roads, etc. meet

in·ter·serv·ice (-sur'vis) *adj.* between or among branches of the armed forces

in·ter·ses·sion (-sesh'ən) n. a short session between regular sessions of a college year, devoted to special projects

in·ter·sex (in'tər seks') n. the condition of being intersexual

in·ter·sex·u·al (-seks'yōō əl) n. **1** existing or occurring between the sexes [*intersexual* competition] **2** having anatomical characteristics that are neither typically male nor typically female

in·ter·sperse (in'tər spurs') *vt.* **-spersed', -spers'ing** [< L *inter-*, among + *spargere*, scatter] **1** to put here and there; scatter **2** to vary with things scattered here and there

in·ter·state (-stāt') *adj.* between or among states, esp. of the U.S. —n. one of a network of U.S. highways

in·ter·stel·lar (-stel'ər) *adj.* between or among the stars

in·ter·stice (in tur'stis) n., pl. **-sti·ces'** (-stə siz', -sēz') [< L *inter-*, between + *sistere*, to set] a crack; crevice

in·ter·twine (-twin') *vt., vi.* **-twined', -twin'ing** to twine together

in·ter·ur·ban (-ur'bən) *adj.* between cities or towns —n. an interurban railway, etc.

in·ter·val (in'tər vəl) n. [< L *inter-*, between + *vallum*, wall] **1** a space between things; gap **2** the time between events **3** the difference in pitch between two tones —**at intervals 1** once in a while **2** here and there

in·ter·vene (in'tər vēn') *vi.* **-vened', -ven'ing** [< L *inter-*, between + *venire*, come] **1** to come or be between **2** to occur between two events, etc. **3** to come between to modify, settle, or hinder some action, etc.

in·ter·ven·tion (-ven'shən) n. **1** an intervening **2** interference, esp. of one country in the affairs of another

in·ter·view (-vyōō') n. **1** a meeting of people face to face to confer **2** *a)* a meeting in which a person is asked about personal views, etc., as by a reporter *b)* a published, taped, or filmed account of this —*vt.* to conduct an interview with [*interviewed* an applicant] —**in'ter·view·ee'** n. —**in'ter·view'er** n.

in·ter·weave (-wēv′) *vt.*, *vi.* **-wove′, -wo′ ven, -weav′ing** **1** to weave together **2** to connect closely

in·tes·ta·cy (in tes′tə sē) *n.* the fact or state of dying intestate

in·tes·tate (in tes′tāt′, -tit) *adj.* [< L *in-*, not + *testari*, make a will] having made no will

in·tes·tine (in tes′tən) *n.* [< L *intus*, within] [*usually pl.*] the lower part of the alimentary canal, extending from the stomach to the anus and consisting of the SMALL INTESTINE and the LARGE INTESTINE; bowels —**in·tes′ tin·al** *adj.*

in·ti·mate (in′tə mət; *for vt.*, -māt′) *adj.* [< L *intus*, within] **1** most private or personal **2** very close or familiar **3** deep and thorough —*n.* an intimate friend —*vt.* **-mat′ed, -mat′ ing** to hint or imply —**in′ti·ma·cy** (-mə sē) *n.*, *pl.* **-cies** —**in′ti·mate·ly** *adv.* —**in′ti·ma′tion** *n.*

in·tim·i·date (in tim′ə dāt′) *vt.* **-dat′ed, -dat′ ing** [< L *in-*, in + *timidus*, afraid] to make afraid, as with threats —**in·tim′i·da′tion** *n.*

intl *abbrev.* international: also **intnl**

in·to (in′tōō) *prep.* [OE] **1** from the outside to the inside of [*into* a room] **2** continuing to the midst of [to talk *into* the night] **3** to the form, substance, or condition of [divided *into* parts] **4** so as to strike [to run *into* a wall] **5** [Inf.] involved or interested in [she's *into* jazz now]

in·tol·er·a·ble (in tä′lər ə bəl) *adj.* unbearable; too severe, painful, etc. to be endured —**in· tol′er·a·bly** *adv.*

in·tol·er·ant (-ənt) *adj.* unwilling to tolerate others' beliefs, etc. —**intolerant of** not able or willing to tolerate —**in·tol′er·ance** *n.*

in·to·na·tion (in′tō nā′shən, -tə-) *n.* **1** an intoning **2** the production of tones in or out of tune relative to a given standard of pitch **3** variations in pitch in speaking

in·tone (in tōn′) *vt.*, *vi.* **-toned′, -ton′ing** to speak or recite in a singing tone; chant —**in· ton′er** *n.*

in to·to (in tō′tō) [L] as a whole

in·tox·i·cate (in täk′si kāt′) *vt.* **-cat′ed, -cat′ ing** [< L *in-*, in + *toxicum*, poison] **1** to make drunk **2** to excite greatly —**in·tox′i·cant** *n.* — **in·tox′i·ca′tion** *n.*

intra- [L, within] *prefix* within, inside

in·tra·cit·y (in′trə sit′ē) *adj.* of or within a large municipality, often, specif. the inner city

in·trac·ta·ble (in trak′tə bəl) *adj.* hard to manage; unruly or stubborn

in·tra·der·mal (in′trə dur′məl) *adj.* within the skin or between the layers of the skin

in·tra·mu·ral (-myoor′əl) *adj.* [INTRA- + MURAL] between or among members of the same school, college, etc. [*intramural* athletics]

in·tra·net (in′trə net′) *n.* a private computer network for an organization, company, etc., accessible only by authorized users

in·tran·si·gent (in tran′sə jənt, -zə-) *adj.* [< L *in-*, not + *transigere*, to settle] refusing to compromise —**in·tran′si·gence** *n.*

in·tran·si·tive (in tran′sə tiv, -zə-) *adj.* not

transitive; designating a verb that does not require a direct object —**in·tran′si·tive·ly** *adv.*

in·tra·u·ter·ine device (in′trə yōōt′ər in) any of various devices inserted in the uterus as a contraceptive

in·tra·vas·cu·lar (-vas′kyōō lər) *adj.* directly into a blood vessel

in·tra·ve·nous (-vē′nəs) *adj.* [INTRA- + VENOUS] directly into a vein —**in′tra·ve′ nous·ly** *adv.*

in·trep·id (in trep′id) *adj.* [< L *in-*, not + *trepidus*, alarmed] bold; fearless; brave —**in·trep′ id·ly** *adv.*

in·tri·cate (in′tri kit) *adj.* [< L *in-*, in + *tricae*, vexations] **1** hard to follow or understand because full of puzzling parts, details, etc. **2** full of elaborate detail —**in′tri·ca·cy** (-kə sē) *n.*, *pl.* **-cies** —**in′tri·cate·ly** *adv.*

in·trigue (in trēg′; *for n., also* in′trēg′) *vi.* **-trigued′, -trigu′ing** [see prec.] to plot secretly or underhandedly —*vt.* to excite the interest or curiosity of —*n.* **1** a secret or underhanded plotting **2** a secret or underhanded plot or scheme **3** a secret love affair —**in·trigu′er** *n.* —**in·trigu′ing** *adj.* —**in·trigu′ ing·ly** *adv.*

in·trin·sic (in trin′sik, -zik) *adj.* [< L *intra-*, within + *secus*, following] belonging to the real nature of a thing; inherent —**in·trin′si· cal·ly** *adv.*

intro- [L] *prefix* into, within, inward

in·tro·duce (in′trə dōōs′) *vt.* **-duced′, -duc′ ing** [< L *intro-*, in + *ducere*, to lead] **1** to put in; insert **2** to bring in as a new feature **3** to bring into use or fashion **4** *a)* to make acquainted; present [*introduce* me to her] *b)* to give experience of [they *introduced* him to music] **5** to bring forward **6** to start; begin [to *introduce* a talk with a joke]

in·tro·duc·tion (-duk′shən) *n.* **1** an introducing or being introduced **2** the preliminary section of a book, speech, etc.; preface

in·tro·duc·to·ry (-duk′tə rē) *adj.* serving to introduce; preliminary

in·tro·it (in trō′it, in′troit′) *n.* [< L *intro-*, in + *ire*, to go] **1** a psalm or hymn at the opening of a Christian worship service **2** [I-] *R.C.Ch.* the first variable part of the Mass

in·tro·spec·tion (in′trə spek′shən) *n.* [< L *in tro-*, within + *specere*, to look] examination of one's own mind, feelings, etc. —**in′tro·spec′ tive** *adj.*

in·tro·vert (in′trə vurt′) *n.* [< L *intro-*, within + *vertere*, to turn] one who tends to be introspective and socially retiring —**in′tro·ver′ sion** (-vur′zhən) *n.* —**in′tro·vert′ed** *adj.*

in·trude (in trōōd′) *vt.*, *vi.* **-trud′ed, -trud′ ing** [< L *in-*, in + *trudere*, to push] to force (oneself) upon others unasked —**in·trud′ er** *n.*

in·tru·sion (in trōō′zhən) *n.* an intruding —**in· tru′sive** (-siv) *adj.* —**in·tru′sive·ly** *adv.* —**in· tru′sive·ness** *n.*

in·trust (in trust′) *vt.* ENTRUST

in·tu·bate (in′tōō bāt′) *vt.* **-bat′ed, -bat′ing**

to insert a tube into (an orifice or hollow organ) to admit air, etc.

in·tu·i·tion (in'tōō ish'ən) *n.* 〖< L *in-*, in + *tueri* to view〗 the direct knowing of something without the conscious use of reasoning —**in·tu·i·tive** (in tōō'i tiv) *adj.*

In·u·it (in'ōō it) *n.* 〖Esk〗 **1** the members of the Eskimo peoples of the Arctic from NW Alaska eastward to E Greenland, esp. those of Canada **2** any or all the languages of the Inuit

in·un·date (in'ən dāt') *vt.* **-dat'ed, -dat'ing** 〖< L *in-*, in + *unda*, a wave〗 to cover with or as with a flood; deluge —**in'un·da'tion** *n.*

in·ure (in yoor') *vt.* **-ured', -ur'ing** 〖ME *in ure*, in practice〗 to accustom to pain, trouble, etc.

in u·ter·o (in yōōt'ər ō) 〖L〗 in the uterus

in·vade (in vād') *vt.* **-vad'ed, -vad'ing** 〖< L *in-*, in + *vadere*, to come, go〗 **1** to enter forcibly or hostilely **2** to intrude upon; violate —**in·vad'er** *n.*

in·va·lid¹ (in'və lid) *adj.* 〖< L *in-*, not + *validus*, strong〗 **1** weak and sickly **2** of or for invalids —*n.* one who is ill or disabled

in·val·id² (in val'id) *adj.* not valid

in·val·i·date (-ə dāt') *vt.* **-dat'ed, -dat'ing** to make invalid; deprive of legal force —**in·val'i·da'tion** *n.*

in·val·u·a·ble (in val'yōō ə bəl) *adj.* too valuable to be measured; priceless —**in·val'u·a·bly** *adv.*

in·va·sion (in vā'zhən) *n.* an invading or being invaded, as by an army

in·va·sive (-siv) *adj.* **1** having to do with (an) invasion **2** penetrating into the body **3** spreading beyond the native range [*invasive* plants]

in·vec·tive (in vek'tiv) *n.* 〖see fol.〗 a violent verbal attack; vituperation

in·veigh (in vā') *vi.* 〖< L *in-*, in + *vehere*, carry〗 to make a violent verbal attack; rail (*against*)

in·vei·gle (in vā'gəl) *vt.* **-gled, -gling** 〖< MFr *aveugler*, to blind〗 to entice or trick into doing or giving something —**in·vei'gler** *n.*

in·vent (in vent') *vt.* 〖< L *in-*, in + *venire*, come〗 **1** to think up [to *invent* excuses] **2** to think out or produce (a new device, process, etc.); originate —**in·ven'tor** *n.*

in·ven·tion (-ven'shən) *n.* **1** an inventing **2** the power of inventing **3** something invented

in·ven·tive (-tiv) *adj.* **1** of invention **2** skilled in inventing —**in·ven'tive·ly** *adv.* —**in·ven'tive·ness** *n.*

in·ven·to·ry (in'vən tôr'ē) *n.,* pl. **-ries** 〖see INVENT〗 **1** an itemized list of goods, property, etc., as of a business **2** the store of goods, etc. for such listing; stock —*vt.* **-ried, -ry·ing** to make an inventory of

in·verse (in vurs', in'vurs') *adj.* inverted; directly opposite —*n.* any inverse thing —**in·verse'ly** *adv.*

in·ver·sion (in vur'zhən) *n.* **1** an inverting or being inverted **2** something inverted; reversal **3** *Meteorol.* a temperature reversal in which a layer of warm air traps cooler air near the surface of the earth

in·vert (in vurt') *vt.* 〖< L *in-*, to + *vertere*, to turn〗 **1** to turn upside down **2** to reverse the order, position, etc. of

in·ver·te·brate (in vur'tə brit, -brāt') *adj.* not vertebrate; having no backbone —*n.* any invertebrate animal

in·vest (in vest') *vt.* 〖< L *in-*, in + *vestis*, clothing〗 **1** to clothe **2** to install in office with ceremony **3** to furnish with power, authority, etc. **4** to put (money) into business, stocks, etc. in order to get a profit —*vi.* to invest money —**in·ves'tor** *n.*

in·ves·ti·gate (in ves'tə gāt') *vi., vt.* **-gat'ed, -gat'ing** 〖< L *in-*, in + *vestigare*, to track〗 to search (into); inquire —**in·ves'ti·ga'tor** *n.*

in·ves·ti·ga·tion (-gā'shən) *n.* **1** a careful search **2** a systematic inquiry

in·ves·ti·ture (-chər) *n.* a formal investing, as with an office

in·vest·ment (in vest'mənt) *n.* **1** an investing or being invested **2** *a)* money invested *b)* anything in which money is or may be invested

in·vet·er·ate (in vet'ər it) *adj.* 〖< pp. of L *inveterare*, to age〗 **1** firmly established **2** habitual —**in·vet'er·a·cy** *n.*

in·vid·i·ous (in vid'ē əs) *adj.* 〖< L *invidia*, envy〗 such as to excite ill will; giving offense, as by discriminating unfairly —**in·vid'i·ous·ly** *adv.* —**in·vid'i·ous·ness** *n.*

in·vig·or·ate (in vig'ər āt') *vt.* **-at'ed, -at'ing** to give vigor to; fill with energy —**in·vig'or·a'tion** *n.*

in·vin·ci·ble (in vin'sə bəl) *adj.* 〖< L *invincibilis*, not easily overcome〗 that cannot be overcome; unconquerable —**in·vin'ci·bil'i·ty** *n.*

in·vi·o·la·ble (in vī'ə lə bəl) *adj.* **1** not to be violated; not to be profaned or injured; sacred **2** indestructible —**in·vi'o·la·bil'i·ty** *n.*

in·vi·o·late (-lit) *adj.* not violated; kept sacred or unbroken

in·vis·i·ble (in viz'ə bəl) *adj.* **1** not visible; that cannot be seen **2** out of sight **3** imperceptible —**in·vis'i·bil'i·ty** *n.* —**in·vis'i·bly** *adv.*

in·vi·ta·tion (in'və tā'shən) *n.* **1** an inviting **2** a message used in inviting

in·vi·ta·tion·al *adj.* only for those invited to take part: said as of an art show, athletic tournament, etc.

in·vite (in vīt'; *for n.* in'vīt') *vt.* **-vit'ed, -vit'ing** 〖< L *invitare*〗 **1** to ask to come somewhere or do something **2** to ask for **3** to give occasion for [action that *invites* scandal] **4** to tempt; entice —*n.* [Inf.] an invitation —**in'vit·ee'** *n.*

in·vit·ing *adj.* tempting; enticing

in vi·tro (in vē'trō) 〖L, in glass〗 isolated from the living organism and artificially maintained, as in a test tube

in·vo·ca·tion (in'və kā'shən) *n.* an invoking of God, the Muses, etc.

in·voice (in'vois') *n.* 〖prob. < ME *envoie*, message〗 a list of goods shipped or services rendered, stating prices, etc.; bill —*vt.* **-voiced', -voic'ing** to present an invoice for or to

in·voke (in vōk′) *vt.* **-voked′, -vok′ing** [< L *in-*, in, on + *vocare*, to call] **1** to call on (God, the Muses, etc.) for blessing, help, etc. **2** to resort to (a law, ruling, etc.) as pertinent **3** to conjure **4** to beg for; implore

in·vol·un·tar·y (in väl′ən ter′ē) *adj.* **1** not done by choice **2** not consciously controlled —**in·vol′un·tar′i·ly** *adv.* —**in·vol′un·tar′i·ness** *n.*

in·vo·lu·tion (in′və lōō′shən) *n.* **1** an involving or being involved **2** a complication; intricacy

in·volve (in välv′, -vôlv′) *vt.* **-volved′, -volv′ing** [< L *in-*, in, in + *volvere*, to roll] **1** to make intricate or complicated **2** to entangle in difficulty, danger, etc.; implicate **3** to affect or include [the riot *involved* thousands] **4** to require [saving *involves* thrift] **5** to make busy; occupy [*involved* the class in research] —**in·volved′** *adj.* —**in·volve′ment** *n.*

in·vul·ner·a·ble (in vul′nər ə bəl) *adj.* **1** that cannot be wounded or injured **2** proof against attack —**in·vul′ner·a·bil′i·ty** *n.*

in·ward (in′wərd) *adj.* **1** situated within; internal **2** mental or spiritual **3** directed toward the inside **4** sensitive, subtle, reticent, etc. —*adv.* **1** toward the inside **2** into the mind or soul Also **in′wards** *adv.*

in·ward·ly *adv.* **1** in or on the inside **2** in the mind or spirit **3** toward the inside

in-your-face *adj.* [Slang] direct, aggressive, assertive, etc.

I/O *abbrev.* input/output

IOC *abbrev.* International Olympic Committee

i·o·dine (ī′ə dīn′, -din) *n.* [< Gr *iōdēs*, violetlike] **1** a nonmetallic chemical element, used in medicine, etc.: symbol, I; at. no. 53 **2** a tincture of iodine, used as an antiseptic

i·o·dize (-dīz′) *vt.* **-dized′, -diz′ing** to treat with iodine

i·on (ī′ən, -än′) *n.* [ult. < Gr *ienai*, to go] an electrically charged atom or group of atoms

-ion (ən) [< L *-io*] *suffix* **1** the act or condition of **2** the result of

I·on·ic (ī än′ik) *adj.* designating or of a Greek or Roman style of architecture, distinguished by ornamental scrolls on the capitals

i·on·ize (ī′ən īz′) *vt., vi.* **-ized′, -iz′ing** to dissociate into ions, as a salt dissolved in water, or become electrically charged, as a gas under radiation —**i′on·i·za′tion** *n.* —**i′on·iz′er** *n.*

i·on·o·sphere (ī än′ə sfir′) *n.* the outer layers of the earth's atmosphere, with some of its gases ionized by solar radiation

i·o·ta (ī ōt′ə) *n.* **1** the ninth letter of the Greek alphabet (I, ι) **2** a very small quantity; jot

IOU (ī′ō′yōō′) *n., pl.* **IOU's** [for I *owe you*] a signed paper, often bearing the letters *IOU*, acknowledging a specified debt

-i·ous (ē əs, yəs, əs) [see -OUS] *suffix* characterized by [*furious*]

I·o·wa (ī′ə wə) Midwestern state of the U.S.; cap. Des Moines: abbrev. IA —**I′o·wan** *adj., n.*

ip·e·cac (ip′i kak′) *n.* [< AmInd (Brazil) name] an emetic made as from the dried roots of a South American plant

IPO *abbrev.* initial public offering

ip·so fac·to (ip′sō fak′tō) [L] by that very fact

IQ *n., pl.* **IQ's** [I(NTELLIGENCE) Q(UOTIENT)] a number intended as a measure of a person's intelligence, calculated based on a test

I·qa·lu·it (ē kä′lōō ēt′) capital of Nunavut, Canada

Ir¹ *abbrev.* **1** Ireland **2** Irish

Ir² *Chem.* symbol for iridium

ir- *prefix* **1** IN-¹ **2** IN-² Used before *r*

IRA (ī′är′ā′; ī′rə) *n., pl.* **IRA's** [I(*individual*) R(*etirement*) A(*ccount*)] a personal retirement plan with taxes on the earnings deferred until funds are withdrawn

I·ran (i ran′, -rän′) country in SW Asia; : former name PERSIA —**I·ra·ni·an** (i rä′nē ən, ī-; -rä′-) *adj., n.*

I·raq (i räk′, -rak′) country in SW Asia, at the head of the Persian Gulf —**I·ra·qi** (i rä′kē, -rak′ē) *adj., n., pl.* **-qis**

i·ras·ci·ble (i ras′ə bəl) *adj.* [see fol.] easily angered; hot-tempered

i·rate (i rāt′, ī′rāt′) *adj.* [< L *ira*, anger] angry; wrathful; incensed —**i·rate′ly** *adv.* —**i·rate′ness** *n.*

ire (īr) *n.* [< L *ira*] anger; wrath

Ire·land (īr′lənd) **1** one of the British Isles, west of Great Britain **2** republic comprising most of this island

i·ren·ic (ī ren′ik) *adj.* [< Gr *eirēnē*, peace] promoting peace

ir·i·des·cent (ir′i des′ənt) *adj.* [< Gr *iris*, rainbow] having or showing an interplay of rainbowlike colors —**ir′i·des′cence** *n.*

i·rid·i·um (i rid′ē əm) *n.* [see fol.] a white metallic chemical element: symbol, Ir; at. no. 77

i·ris (ī′ris) *n., pl.* **i′ris·es** [Gr, rainbow] **1** the round, pigmented membrane surrounding the pupil of the eye **2** a plant with sword-shaped leaves and a showy flower

I·rish (ī′rish) *adj.* of Ireland or its people, language, etc. —*n.* **1** the Celtic language of Ireland **2** the English dialect of Ireland — **the Irish** the people of Ireland —**I′rish·man** (-mən) *n., pl.* **-men** (-mən) —**I′rish·wom′an** *n., pl.* **-wom′en**

Irish coffee brewed coffee with Irish whiskey, topped with whipped cream

Irish Sea arm of the Atlantic between Ireland & Great Britain

irk (ʉrk) *vt.* [ME *irken*, be weary of] to annoy, irritate, tire out, etc.

irk·some (-səm) *adj.* tending to irk; tiresome or annoying

i·ron (ī′ərn) *n.* [OE *iren*] **1** a metallic chemical element, the most common of all metals: symbol, Fe; at. no. 26 **2** any device of iron; esp., such a device with a flat undersurface, heated for pressing cloth **3** [*pl.*] iron shackles **4** firm strength; power **5** any of certain golf clubs with angled metal heads —*adj.* **1** of iron **2** like iron; strong; firm — *vt., vi.* to press with a hot iron —**iron out** to smooth out; eliminate

Iron Age the period in human culture when iron tools were first widely used

i·ron·clad *adj.* **1** covered or protected with iron **2** difficult to change or break [*an ironclad lease*] —*n.* an ironclad warship

iron curtain 1 [*often* I- C-] a barrier of secrecy and censorship seen as isolating the U.S.S.R., etc.: often with *the* **2** any similar barrier

i·ron-fist·ed (-fis′tid) *adj.* despotic and brutal

i·ron·ic (ī rän′ik) *adj.* **1** meaning the contrary of what is expressed **2** using irony **3** opposite to what is or might be expected Also **i·ron′i·cal** —**i·ron′i·cal·ly** *adv.*

i·ron·man (ī′ərn man′) *n., pl.* **-men'** (-men′) [*often* I-] a man of great physical strength

i·ron·ware *n.* things made of iron

i·ro·ny (ī′rə nē, ī′ər nē) *n., pl.* **-nies** [< Gr *eirōn*, dissembler in speech] **1** expression in which the intended meaning of the words is the direct opposite of their usual sense **2** an event or result that is the opposite of what is expected

Ir·o·quois (ir′ə kwoi′) *n., pl.* **-quois** (-kwoi′, -kwoiz′) a member of a confederation of North American Indian peoples that lived in upstate New York —*adj.* of the Iroquois —**Ir′o·quoi′an** *n., adj.*

ir·ra·di·ate (i rā′dē āt′) *vt.* **-at'ed, -at'ing 1** to shine upon; light up **2** to enlighten **3** to radiate **4** to expose to X-rays or other radiant energy —*vi.* to emit rays; shine —**ir·ra′di·a′tion** *n.*

ir·ra·tion·al (i rash′ə nəl) *adj.* **1** lacking the power to reason **2** senseless; unreasonable —**ir·ra′tion·al′i·ty** (-ə nal′ə tē) *n., pl.* **-ties** —**ir·ra′tion·al·ly** *adv.*

ir·re·claim·a·ble (ir′i klām′ə bəl) *adj.* that cannot be reclaimed

ir·re·con·cil·a·ble (i rek′ən sīl′ə bəl) *adj.* that cannot be brought into agreement; incompatible

ir·re·cov·er·a·ble (ir′i kuv′ər ə bəl) *adj.* that cannot be recovered, rectified, or remedied

ir·re·deem·a·ble (ir′i dēm′ə bəl) *adj.* **1** that cannot be bought back **2** that cannot be converted into coin: said of certain paper money **3** that cannot be changed or reformed

ir·re·fut·a·ble (i ref′yoo tə bəl, ir′i fyoot′ə bəl) *adj.* indisputable —**ir·ref′u·ta·bly** *adv.*

ir·re·gard·less (ir′i gärd′lis) *adj., adv.* REGARDLESS: a nonstandard usage

ir·reg·u·lar (i reg′yə lər) *adj.* **1** not conforming to an established rule, standard, etc. **2** not straight, even, or uniform **3** *Gram.* not inflected in the usual way —**ir·reg′u·lar′i·ty** *n., pl.* **-ties**

ir·rel·e·vant (i rel′ə vənt) *adj.* not pertinent; not to the point —**ir·rel′e·vance** *n.* —**ir·rel′e·vant·ly** *adv.*

ir·re·li·gious (ir′i lij′əs) *adj.* **1** not religious or indifferent or hostile to religion **3** profane; impious —**ir·re·li′gious·ly** *adv.*

ir·re·me·di·a·ble (ir′i mē′dē ə bəl) *adj.* that cannot be remedied or corrected —**ir′re·me′di·a·bly** *adv.*

ir·rep·a·ra·ble (i rep′ə rə bəl) *adj.* that cannot be repaired, mended, etc.

ir·re·place·a·ble (ir′i plās′ə bəl) *adj.* that cannot be replaced

ir·re·press·i·ble (-pres′ə bəl) *adj.* that cannot be repressed

ir·re·proach·a·ble (-prō′chə bəl) *adj.* blameless; faultless

ir·re·sist·i·ble (-zis′tə bəl) *adj.* that cannot be resisted; too strong, fascinating, etc. to be withstood —**ir′re·sist′i·bly** *adv.*

ir·res·o·lute (i rez′ə loot′) *adj.* not resolute; wavering; indecisive —**ir·res′o·lu′tion** (-loo′ shən) *n.*

ir·re·spec·tive (ir′i spek′tiv) *adj.* regardless (*of*)

ir·re·spon·si·ble (-spän′sə bəl) *adj.* **1** not responsible for actions **2** lacking a sense of responsibility **3** showing poor judgment, disregard for consequences, etc. —**ir′re·spon′si·bil′i·ty** *n.* —**ir′re·spon′si·bly** *adv.*

ir·re·triev·a·ble (-trēv′ə bəl) *adj.* that cannot be retrieved —**ir′re·triev′a·bly** *adv.*

ir·rev·er·ence (i rev′ər əns) *n.* lack of reverence; disrespect —**ir·rev′er·ent** *adj.*

ir·re·vers·i·ble (ir′i vur′sə bəl) *adj.* that cannot be reversed; esp., that cannot be annulled or turned back

ir·rev·o·ca·ble (i rev′ə kə bəl) *adj.* that cannot be revoked or undone —**ir·rev′o·ca·bly** *adv.*

ir·ri·ga·ble (ir′i gə bəl) *adj.* that can be irrigated

ir·ri·gate (ir′ə gāt′) *vt.* **-gat'ed, -gat'ing** [< L *in-*, in + *rigare*, to water] **1** to supply (land) with water, as by means of artificial ditches **2** *Med.* to wash out (a cavity, wound, etc.) —**ir′ri·ga′tion** *n.*

ir·ri·ta·ble (ir′i tə bəl) *adj.* **1** easily annoyed or provoked **2** *Med.* excessively sensitive to a stimulus —**ir′ri·ta·bil′i·ty** *n.* —**ir′ri·ta·bly** *adv.*

ir·ri·tant (-tənt) *adj.* causing irritation —*n.* a thing that irritates

ir·ri·tate (-tāt′) *vt.* **-tat'ed, -tat'ing** [< L *irritare*, excite] **1** to provoke to anger; annoy **2** to make inflamed or sore —**ir′ri·ta′tion** *n.*

ir·rupt (i rupt′) *vi.* [< L *in-*, in + *rumpere*, to break] to burst suddenly or violently (*into*) —**ir·rup′tion** *n.* —**ir·rup′tive** *adj.*

IRS *abbrev.* Internal Revenue Service

is¹ (iz) *vi.* [OE] *3d pers. sing., pres. indic.,* of BE

is² *abbrev.* **1** island(s) **2** islet(s)

I·saac (ī′zək) *n. Bible* one of the patriarchs, son of Abraham, and father of Jacob and Esau

I·sa·iah (ī zā′ə) *n. Bible* **1** a Hebrew prophet of the 8th c. B.C. **2** the book containing his teachings

ISBN *abbrev.* International Standard Book Number

-ise (īz) *suffix chiefly Brit. sp.* of -IZE

-ish (ish) [< OE *-isc*] *suffix* **1** of (a specified people) [*Irish*] **2** somewhat [*tallish*] **3** [Inf.] approximately [*thirtyish*] **4** like or characteristic of

Ish·tar (ish′tär′) *n.* the Babylonian and Assyrian goddess of fertility

i·sin·glass (ī′zin glas′, -ziŋ-) *n.* [prob. < MDu *huizen*, sturgeon + *blas*, bladder] **1** gelatin made from fish bladders, used in brewing, etc. **2** mica, esp. in thin sheets

I·sis (ī′sis) *n.* the Egyptian goddess of fertility

isl *abbrev.* **1** island **2** isle

Is·lam (is′läm′, iz′–) *n.* ⟦Ar *islām*, lit., submission (to God's will)⟧ **1** the Muslim religion, a monotheistic religion founded by Muhammad **2** Muslims collectively or the lands in which they predominate —**Is·lam′ic** (–läm′ik) *adj.*

Is·lam·a·bad (is läm′ə bäd′) capital of Pakistan, in the NE part

Is·lam·ism (iz′ləm ism′) *n.* a movement advocating social and political establishment of Islamic fundamentalism —**Is·lam′ist** *adj., n.*

is·land (ī′lənd) *n.* ⟦< OE *igland*, lit., island land: sp. after *isle*⟧ **1** a land mass smaller than a continent and surrounded by water **2** anything like this in position or isolation

is·land·er *n.* a person born or living on an island

isle (īl) *n.* ⟦< L *insula*⟧ an island, esp. a small island

is·let (ī′lit) *n.* a very small island

islets (*or* **islands**) **of Lang′er·hans′** (läŋ′ər häns′) ⟦after P. *Langerhans* (1847–88), Ger histologist⟧ endocrine cells in the pancreas that produce the hormone insulin

ism (iz′əm) *n.* a doctrine, theory, system, etc. whose name ends in *-ism*

-ism (iz′əm) ⟦< Gr *-ismos*⟧ *suffix* **1** act or result of [*terrorism*] **2** condition, conduct, or qualities of [*patriotism*] **3** theory of [*socialism*] **4** devotion to [*nationalism*] **5** an instance of [*witticism*]

is·n't (iz′ənt) *contr.* is not

ISO *abbrev.* International Standards Organization

iso- ⟦< Gr *isos*⟧ *combining form* equal, similar, identical [*isomorph*]

i·so·bar (ī′sō bär′) *n.* ⟦< prec. + Gr *baros*, weight⟧ a line on a map connecting points of equal barometric pressure

i·so·late (ī′sə lāt′; *for n., usually,* -lit) *vt.* **-lat′ed, -lat′ing** ⟦< It *isola* (< L *insula*), island⟧ to set apart from others; place alone —*n.* a person or thing that is isolated —**i′so·lat′ed** *adj.* —**i′so·la′tion** *n.* —**i′so·la′tor** *n.*

i·so·la·tion·ist *n.* one who opposes the involvement of a country in international alliances, etc. —*adj.* of isolationists —**i′so·la′tion·ism′** *n.*

i·so·mer (ī′sə mər) *n.* ⟦< Gr *isos*, equal + *meros*, a part⟧ any of two or more compounds that have the same chemical formula but different molecular structures —**i′so·mer′ic** (-mer′ik) *adj.*

i·so·met·ric (-met′rik) *adj.* ⟦< Gr *isos*, equal + *metron*, measure⟧ **1** equal in measure **2** of isometrics —*n.* [*pl.*] exercise in which muscles are briefly tensed in opposition to other muscles or to an immovable object —**i′so·met′ri·cal·ly** *adv.*

i·sos·ce·les (ī säs′ə lēz′) *adj.* ⟦< Gr *isos*, equal + *skelos*, leg⟧ designating a triangle with two equal sides

i·so·tope (ī′sə tōp′) *n.* ⟦< ISO- + Gr *topos*, place⟧ any of two or more forms of an element having the same atomic number but different atomic weights

ISP *n., pl.* **ISPs** ⟦*i(nternet) s(ervice) p(rovider)*⟧ a company that provides access to the internet

Is·ra·el¹ (iz′rē əl) *n. Bible* Jacob

Is·ra·el² (iz′rē əl) **1** ancient land of the Hebrews at the SE end of the Mediterranean **2** kingdom in the N part of this land **3** country between the Mediterranean Sea & Jordan

Is·rae·li (iz rā′lē) *n.* a person born or living in modern Israel —*adj.* of modern Israel or its people

Is·ra·el·ite (iz′rē ə līt′) *n.* any of the people of ancient Israel; Hebrew

ISSN *abbrev.* International Standard Serial Number

is·su·ance (ish′ōō əns) *n.* an issuing; issue

is·sue (ish′ōō) *n.* ⟦< L *ex-*, out + *ire*, go⟧ **1** an outgoing; outflow **2** a result; consequence **3** offspring **4** a point under dispute **5** a sending or giving out **6** all that is put forth at one time [an *issue* of bonds, a periodical, etc.] —*vi.* **-sued, -su·ing 1** to go or flow out; emerge **2** to result (*from*) or end (*in*) —*vt.* **1** to give or deal out [to *issue* supplies] **2** to publish —**at issue** in dispute —**take issue** to disagree —**is′su·er** *n.*

-ist (ist, əst) ⟦< Gr *-istēs*⟧ *suffix* **1** one who does, makes, or practices [*satirist*] **2** one skilled in or occupied with [*druggist, violinist*] **3** an adherent of [*anarchist*]

Is·tan·bul (is′tan bool′, -tän-) seaport in NW Turkey: former name CONSTANTINOPLE

isth·mus (is′məs) *n., pl.* **-mus·es** *or* **-mi′** (-mī′) ⟦< Gr *isthmos*, a neck⟧ a narrow strip of land having water at each side and connecting two larger land masses

it (it) *pron., pl. see* THEY ⟦< OE *hit*⟧ **1** the animal or thing previously mentioned **2** *it* is also used as: *a)* the subject of an impersonal verb [*it* is snowing] *b)* a subject or object of indefinite sense in various idiomatic constructions [*it's* all right, he lords *it* over us] —*n.* the player, as in tag, who must try to catch another —**with it** [Slang] **1** alert **2** aware of recent trends; hip

It *or* **Ital** *abbrev.* **1** Italian **2** Italy

IT *abbrev.* information technology

I·tal·ian (i tal′yən) *adj.* of Italy or its people, language, etc. —*n.* **1** a person born or living in Italy **2** the Romance language of Italy

i·tal·ic (i tal′ik, ī-) *adj.* ⟦< its early use in *Italy*⟧ designating a type in which the characters slant upward to the right (Ex.: *this is italic type*) —*n.* [*usually pl., sometimes with sing. v.*] italic type or print: abbrev. **ital**

i·tal·i·cize (i tal′ə sīz′, ī-) *vt.* **-cized′, -ciz′ing** to print in italics

It·a·ly (it′'l ē) country in S Europe

itch (ich) *vi.* ⟦OE *giccan*⟧ **1** to feel a tingling of the skin, with the desire to scratch **2** to have a restless desire —*vt.* [Inf.] SCRATCH —*n.* **1** an itching **2** a restless desire —**itch′y** *adj.* **-i·er, -i·est**

-ite (īt) ⟦< Gr *-itēs*⟧ *suffix* **1** an inhabitant of

[*Akronite*] **2** an adherent of [*laborite*] **3** a manufactured product [*dynamite*] **4** a mineral, rock, etc.

i·tem (it′əm) *n.* [< L *ita*, so, thus] **1** an article; unit; separate thing **2** a bit of news or information

i·tem·ize (-īz′) *vt.* **-ized′, -iz′ing** to specify individually —**i′tem·i·za′tion** *n.*

it·er·ate (it′ər āt′) *vt.* **-at′ed, -at′ing** [< L *iterum*, again] to utter or do again —**it′er·a′tion** *n.*

i·tin·er·ant (ī tin′ər ənt) *adj.* [< L *iter*, a walk] traveling from place to place —*n.* a traveler

i·tin·er·ar·y (-er′ē) *n., pl.* **-ar′ies** **1** a route **2** a record of a journey **3** a detailed plan for a journey

-i·tis (īt′is) [< Gr *-itis*] *suffix* inflammation of (a specified part or organ) [*neuritis*]

its (its) *pron.* that or those belonging to it —*poss. pronominal adj.* of, belonging to, or done by it

it's (its) *contr.* **1** it is **2** it has

it·self (it self′) *pron.* a form of IT, used as an intensive [the work *itself* is easy], as a reflexive [the dog bit *itself*], or with the meaning "its true self" [the bird is not *itself* today]

it·ty-bit·ty (it′ē bit′ē) *adj.* [baby talk < *little bit*] [Inf.] very small; tiny: also **it·sy-bit·sy** (it′sē bit′sē)

-i·ty (ə tē, i-) [< L *-itas*] *suffix* state, quality, or instance [*chastity*]

IUD *abbrev.* intrauterine device

IV¹ (ī′vē′) *n., pl.* **IVs** [< I(NTRA)V(ENOUS)] *Med.* **1** a procedure in which a hypodermic needle is inserted into a vein to supply blood, nutrients, etc. **2** the apparatus used for this, including the bag of fluid, tubing, and needle

IV² *abbrev.* intravenous(ly)

-ive (iv) [< L *-ivus*] *suffix* **1** of or having the nature of [*sportive*] **2** tending to [*retrospective*]

i·vied (ī′vēd) *adj.* covered or overgrown with ivy

i·vo·ry (ī′vər ē, īv′rē) *n., pl.* **-ries** [ult. < Egypt *3bw*] **1** the hard, white substance forming the tusks of elephants, walruses, etc. **2** any substance like ivory **3** creamy white —*adj.* **1** of or like ivory **2** creamy-white

Ivory Coast country on the W coast of Africa: offical name CÔTE D'IVOIRE

ivory tower a retreat away from reality or action

i·vy (ī′vē) *n., pl.* **i′vies** [OE *ifig*] **1** a climbing vine with a woody stem and evergreen leaves **2** any of various similar climbing plants

-ize (īz) [< Gr *-izein*] *suffix* **1** to cause to be [*sterilize*] **2** to become (like) [*crystallize*] **3** to combine with [*oxidize*] **4** to engage in [*soliloquize*]

J

j or **J** (jā) *n., pl.* **j's, J's** the tenth letter of the English alphabet

jab (jab) *vt., vi.* **jabbed, jab′bing** [< ME *jobben*, to peck] **1** to poke, as with a sharp instrument **2** to punch with short, straight blows —*n.* a quick thrust or blow

jab·ber (jab′ər) *vi., vt.* [prob. echoic] to speak or say quickly, incoherently, or foolishly; chatter —*n.* chatter —**jab′ber·er** *n.*

ja·bot (zha bō′) *n.* [Fr, bird's crop] a ruffle or frill down the front of a blouse, etc.

jack (jak) *n.* [< the name *Jack*] **1** [*often* J-] a man or boy **2** any of various machines used to lift something heavy a short distance [an automobile *jack*] **3** a playing card with a picture of a royal male servant or soldier **4** a small flag flown on a ship's bow to show nationality **5** any of the small, 6-pronged metal pieces tossed and picked up in a game (**jacks**) **6** *Elec.* a plug-in receptacle used to make electrical contact —*vt.* to raise by means of a jack: usually with *up* —**jack up** [Inf.] to raise (prices, wages, etc.)

jack- [see prec.] *combining form* **1** male [*jack-*

ass] **2** large or sturdy [*jackboot*] **3** boy; fellow [*jack-in-the-box*]

jack·al (jak′əl) *n.* [< Sans] a wild dog of Asia and N Africa

jack·ass (jak′as′) *n.* [JACK- + ASS] **1** a male donkey **2** a fool

jack·boot (-bōōt′) *n.* [JACK- + BOOT¹] a long, heavy military boot that covers the knee

jack·daw (-dô′) *n.* [JACK- + ME *dawe*, jackdaw] a small European crow

jack·et (jak′it) *n.* [< Ar *shakk*] **1** a short coat **2** an outer covering, as the removable paper cover on a book, the metal casing of a bullet, etc.

Jack Frost frost or cold weather personified

jack·ham·mer *n.* a portable type of pneumatic hammer, used for breaking up concrete, rock, etc.

jack-in-the-box *n., pl.* **-box′es** a toy consisting of a box from which a figure on a spring jumps up when the lid is lifted: also **jack′-in-a-box′**

jack-in-the-pul·pit (-pōōl′pit) *n., pl.* **-pits** a plant with a flower spike partly arched over by a hoodlike covering

jack·knife *n.*, *pl.* **-knives′ 1** a large pocket-knife **2** a dive in which the diver keeps knees unbent, touches the feet, and then straightens out —*vi.*, *vt.* **-knifed′**, **-knif′ing** to bend or fold at the middle or at a connection

jack-of-all-trades *n.*, *pl.* **jacks′-** [*often* J-] one who is competent at many kinds of work

jack-o'-lan·tern (jak′ə lant′ərn) *n.*, *pl.* **-terns** a hollow pumpkin cut to look like a face and used esp. as a decoration at Halloween

jack·pot *n.* [*jack*, playing card + *pot*] **1** cumulative stakes, as in poker **2** any large prize, etc.

jack rabbit a large hare of W North America, with long ears and strong hind legs

Jack·son¹ (jak′sən), **An·drew** (an′drōō′) 1767–1845; 7th president of the U.S. (1829–37)

Jack·son² (jak′sən) capital of Mississippi, in the SW part

Jack·son·ville (jak′sən vil′) port in NE Florida

Ja·cob (jā′kəb) *n. Bible* a son of Isaac

jac·quard (jak′ärd, jə kärd′) *n.* [after J. M. *Jacquard* (1752–1834), Fr inventor] [*sometimes* J-] a fabric with a figured weave, woven on an automated loom

Ja·cuz·zi (jə kōō′zē) [< *Jacuzzi*, U.S. developers] *trademark for* a kind of whirlpool bath

jade (jād) *n.* [< Sp (*piedra de*) *ijada*, (stone of) the side: supposed to cure pains in the side] **1** a hard, greenish, ornamental gemstone **2** a medium green color

jad·ed (jād′id) *adj.* **1** tired; worn-out **2** dulled or satiated —**jad′ed·ly** *adv.* —**jad′ed·ness** *n.*

jade plant a thick-leaved plant native to S Africa and Asia

jag¹ (jag) *n.* [ME *jagge*] a sharp, toothlike projection

jag² (jag) *n.* [< ?] [Slang] a drunken spree

jag·ged (jag′id) *adj.* having sharp projecting points; notched or ragged —**jag′ged·ly** *adv.* —**jag′ged·ness** *n.*

jag·uar (jag′wär′) *n.* [Port < AmInd (Brazil)] a large, leopardlike cat found from SW U.S. to Argentina

jai a·lai (hī′lī′, hī′ə lī′) [< Basque *jai*, celebration + *alai*, merry] a game like handball, played with a basketlike racket

jail (jāl) *n.* [ult. < L *cavea*, cage] a prison, esp. for persons awaiting trial or those convicted of minor offenses —*vt.* to put or keep in jail

jail·break *n.* a breaking out of jail

jail·er or **jail·or** *n.* a person in charge of a jail or of prisoners

Ja·kar·ta (jə kär′tə) capital of Indonesia, on Java island

ja·la·pe·ño (hä′lə pān′yō) *n.* [Mex] a kind of hot pepper, orig. from Mexico

Ja·lis·co (hä lēs′kō) state of W Mexico, on the Pacific

ja·lop·y (jə läp′ē) *n.*, *pl.* **-lop′ies** [< ?] [Slang] an old, ramshackle car

jal·ou·sie (jal′ə sē′) *n.* [Fr < It *gelosia*, jealousy] a window, shade, or door formed of adjustable horizontal slats of wood, metal, or glass

jam¹ (jam) *vt.* **jammed**, **jam′ming** [< ?] **1** to squeeze into a confined space **2** to crush **3** to crowd **4** to crowd into or block (a passageway, etc.) **5** to make stick so that it cannot move or work **6** to make (radio broadcasts, etc.) unintelligible, as by sending out other signals on the same wavelength —*vi.* **1** *a*) to become stuck fast *b*) to become unworkable because of jammed parts **2** to become squeezed into a confined space **3** [Inf.] *Jazz* to improvise, as in a gathering of musicians (**jam session**) —*n.* **1** a jamming or being jammed [a traffic *jam*] **2** [Inf.] a difficult situation

jam² (jam) *n.* [< ? prec.] fruit boiled with sugar to a thick mixture

Ja·mai·ca (jə mā′kə) country on an island in the West Indies, south of Cuba —**Ja·mai′can** *adj.*, *n.*

jamb (jam) *n.* [< LL *gamba*, hoof] a side post of a doorway, window, etc.

jam·bo·ree (jam′bə rē′) *n.* [< ?] **1** a noisy party, gathering, etc. **2** a large assembly of Boy Scouts from many places

James (jāmz), **Henry** 1843–1916; U.S. novelist, in England

James·town (jāmz′toun′) former village in Virginia: the 1st permanent English colonial settlement in America (1607)

jam-packed (jam′pakt′) *adj.* [Inf.] tightly packed

jan·gle (jaŋ′gəl) *vi.* **-gled**, **-gling** [< OFr *jangler*] to make a harsh, usually metallic sound —*vt.* **1** to cause to jangle **2** to irritate [to *jangle* someone's nerves] —*n.* a jangling —**jan′gler** *n.*

jan·i·tor (jan′i tər) *n.* [L, doorkeeper] one who takes care of a building, doing routine repairs, cleaning, etc. —**jan′i·to′ri·al** (-i tôr′ē əl) *adj.*

Jan·u·ar·y (jan′yōō er′ē) *n.*, *pl.* **-ar′ies** [< L < *Janus*, Roman god who was a patron of beginnings and endings] the first month of the year, having 31 days: abbrev. **Jan.**

ja·pan (jə pan′) *n.* [orig. made in Japan] a lacquer giving a hard, glossy finish

Ja·pan (jə pan′) **1** island country in the Pacific, off the E coast of Asia **2 Sea of** arm of the Pacific, between Japan & E Asia

Jap·a·nese (jap′ə nēz′) *adj.* of Japan or its people, language, etc. —*n.* **1** *pl.* **-nese′** a person born or living in Japan **2** the language of Japan

Japanese beetle a shiny, iridescent green-and-brown beetle, orig. from Japan, damaging to crops

jape (jāp) *vi.* **japed**, **jap′ing** [< OFr *japer*, to howl] **1** to joke **2** to play tricks —*n.* **1** a joke **2** a trick

jar¹ (jär) *vi.* **jarred**, **jar′ring** [ult. echoic] **1** to make a harsh sound; grate **2** to have an irritating effect (*on* one) **3** to vibrate from an impact **4** to clash; conflict —*vt.* to jolt —*n.* **1** a grating sound **2** a vibration due to impact **3** a jolt

jar² (jär) *n.* [< Ar *jarrah*, earthen container] **1** a container made of glass, earthenware, etc., with a large opening **2** as much as a jar will hold: also **jar′ful′**

jar·di·niere (jär′də nir′) *n.* [< Fr < *jardin*, a garden] an ornamental pot or stand for flowers or plants

jar·gon (jär′gən) *n.* [< MFr, a chattering] 1 unintelligible talk 2 the specialized vocabulary of those practicing the same occupation, hobby, etc.

jas·mine (jaz′min, jas′-) *n.* [< Pers *yāsamīn*] any of certain plants of warm regions, with fragrant flowers of yellow, red, or white

Ja·son (jā′sən) *n. Gr. Myth.* the leader of the Argonauts: cf. ARGONAUT

jas·per (jas′pər) *n.* [< Gr *iaspis*] an opaque variety of colored quartz, usually reddish

jaun·dice (jôn′dis) *n.* [< L *galbus*, yellow] a diseased condition in which the eyeballs, skin, and urine become abnormally yellowish as a result of increased bile in the blood —*vt.* **-diced**, **-dic·ing** 1 to cause to have jaundice 2 to make bitter through envy, etc.

jaunt (jônt) *vi.* [< ?] to take a short pleasure trip —*n.* such a trip

jaun·ty (jôn′tē) *adj.* **-ti·er**, **-ti·est** [< Fr *gentil*, genteel] showing an easy confidence; sprightly or perky —**jaun′ti·ly** *adv.* —**jaun′ti·ness** *n.*

Ja·va¹ (jä′və, jav′ə) *n.* 1 a coffee grown on Java 2 [*often* j-] [Slang] any coffee

Ja·va² (jä′və, jav′ə) large island of Indonesia —**Ja·va·nese** (jä′və nēz′) *adj., n., pl.* **-nese′**

jav·e·lin (jav′lin, jav′ə lin) *n.* [MFr *javeline*] a light spear, esp. one thrown for distance in an athletic contest

jaw (jô) *n.* [< OFr *joue*, cheek] 1 either of the two bony parts that hold the teeth and frame the mouth 2 either of two movable parts that grasp or crush something, as in a vise —*vi.* [Slang] to talk

jaw·bone *n.* a bone of a jaw, esp. of the lower jaw —*vt., vi.* **-boned′**, **-bon′ing** to try to persuade by using the influence of one's office or position

jaw·break·er *n.* 1 a hard, usually round candy 2 [Slang] a word hard to pronounce

jaw·less fish a fish with an eel-like body and a circular sucking mouth, as the lamprey

jay (jā) *n.* [< LL *gaius*, jay] any of several birds, usually strikingly colored, as the blue jay

jay·walk *vi.* to cross a street without obeying traffic rules and signals —**jay′walk′er** *n.*

jazz (jaz) *n.* [< ?] 1 a kind of syncopated, highly rhythmic music originated by Southern blacks in the early 1900s 2 [Slang] talk, acts, etc. regarded disparagingly —*vt.* [Slang] to enliven or embellish: usually with *up*

jazz·y *adj.* **-i·er**, **-i·est** 1 of or like jazz 2 [Slang] lively, flashy, etc.

JD *abbrev.* 1 [L *Jurum Doctor*] Doctor of Laws: also **J.D.** 2 juvenile delinquent: also **jd**

jeal·ous (jel′əs) *adj.* [see ZEAL] 1 watchful in guarding [*jealous* of one's rights] 2 *a*) resentfully suspicious of rivalry [a *jealous* lover] *b*) resentfully envious *c*) resulting from such feelings [a *jealous* rage] —**jeal′ous·ly** *adv.*

jeal·ous·y *n.* 1 the quality or condition of being jealous 2 *pl.* **-ous·ies** a jealous feeling

jean (jēn) *n.* [< L *Genua*, Genoa, city in Italy] 1 a durable, twilled cotton cloth 2 [*pl.*] trousers of this or of denim

jeep (jēp) *n.* [< creature in comic strip by E. C. Segar (1894-1938)] a small, rugged military vehicle of WWII —[**J-**] *trademark for* a similar vehicle for civilian use

jeer (jir) *vt., vi.* [< ? CHEER] to make fun of (a person or thing) in a rude, sarcastic manner; scoff (at) —*n.* a jeering remark

Jef·fer·son (jef′ər sən), **Thom·as** (täm′əs) 1743-1826; 3d president of the U.S. (1801-09)

Jefferson City capital of Missouri

jeg·gings (jeg′iŋz, -inz) *pl.n.* [blend of JEAN & *leggings*] stretch pants that fit like long leggings, made with a denimlike fabric

Je·ho·vah (ji hō′və) *n.* [< Heb] God

je·june (ji jōōn′) *adj.* [L *jejunus*, empty] 1 not interesting or satisfying 2 not mature; childish

je·ju·num (jē jōō′nəm) *n., pl.* **-na** (-nə) [< L *jejunus*, empty] the middle part of the small intestine

jell (jel) *vi., vt.* [< L *gelare*, freeze] 1 to become, or make into, jelly 2 [Inf.] to crystallize [plans haven't *jelled* yet]

Jell·o (jel′ō) *n.* [< *Jell*-O, a trademark] a flavored gelatin used as a dessert, etc.

jel·ly (jel′ē) *n., pl.* **-lies** [< L *gelare*, freeze] 1 a soft, gelatinous food made from cooked fruit syrup or meat juice 2 any substance like this —*vi., vt.* **-lied**, **-ly·ing** JELL (*v.* 1)

jelly bean a small, bean-shaped, gelatinous candy, usually fruit-flavored and brightly colored: also **jel′ly·bean′** *n.*

jel·ly·fish *n., pl.* **-fish′** *or* **-fish′es** 1 a sea animal with an umbrella-shaped, jellylike body and long tentacles 2 [Inf.] a weak-willed person

jel·ly·roll *n.* a thin sheet of sponge cake spread with jelly and rolled up

jeop·ard·ize (jep′ər dīz′) *vt.* **-ized′**, **-iz′ing** to put in jeopardy

jeop·ard·y (-dē) *n.* [< OFr *jeu parti*, lit., a game with even chances] great danger or risk

jer·e·mi·ad (jer′ə mī′ad′, -əd) *n.* a long lamentation or complaint: in allusion to the biblical book of Lamentations, attributed to Jeremiah

Jer·e·mi·ah (-ə) *n. Bible* a Hebrew prophet of the 7th and 6th c. B.C.

Jer·i·cho (jer′i kō′) city in the West Bank: site of an ancient city in Canaan

jerk (jurk) *n.* [< ?] 1 a sharp, abrupt pull, twist, etc. 2 a sudden muscular contraction 3 [Slang] a person regarded as disagreeable, contemptible, etc. — *vi., vt.* 1 to move with a jerk; pull sharply 2 to twitch

jer·kin (jur′kin) *n.* [< ?] a short, closefitting jacket, often sleeveless

jerk·wa·ter *adj.* [Inf.] small, unimportant, etc. [a *jerkwater* town]

jerk·y¹ (jur′kē) *adj.* **jerk′i·er**, **jerk′i·est** 1 moving by jerks; spasmodic 2 [Slang] foolish, mean, etc. —**jerk′i·ly** *adv.*

jer·ky² (jur′kē) *n.* [< Sp *charqui*] meat preserved by being sliced into strips and dried in the sun

jer·ry-built (jer′ē bilt′) *adj.* built poorly, of cheap materials

jer·sey (jur′zē) *n.*, *pl.* **-seys** [after *Jersey*, one of the Channel Islands] 1 [J-] any of a breed of reddish-brown dairy cattle, orig. from Jersey 2 a soft, knitted cloth 3 a closefitting, knitted upper garment

Je·ru·sa·lem (jə rōōz′ə ləm) capital of Israel (the country), partly in the West Bank

jest (jest) *n.* [< L *gerere*, perform] 1 a mocking remark; taunt 2 a joke 3 fun; joking 4 something to be laughed at —*vi.* 1 to jeer 2 to joke

jest·er *n.* one who jests; esp., a man employed to amuse a medieval ruler

Jes·u·it (jezh′ōō it, jez′-) *n.* a member of the Society of Jesus, a Roman Catholic religious order for men, founded in 1534

Je·sus (jē′zəz, -zəs) *c.* 8-4 B.C.–A.D. 29?; founder of the Christian religion: also **Jesus Christ** or **Jesus of Nazareth**

jet¹ (jet) *vt.*, *vi.* **jet′ted**, **jet′ting** [< L *jacere*, to throw] 1 to gush out in a stream 2 to travel or convey by jet airplane —*n.* 1 a stream of liquid or gas suddenly emitted 2 a spout or nozzle for emitting a jet 3 a jet-propelled airplane: in full **jet (air)plane** —*adj.* driven by jet propulsion

jet² (jet) *n.* [after *Gagas*, town in Asia Minor] 1 a hard, black mineral like coal, polished and used in jewelry 2 a lustrous black —*adj.* black like jet

jet lag a disruption of the daily body rhythms, caused by high-speed travel to distant time zones —**jet′-lagged′** *adj.*

jet·port *n.* a large airport with long runways, for use by jetliners

jet propulsion propulsion of airplanes, boats, etc. by the forcing of compressed outside air and hot exhaust gases through a jet nozzle —**jet′-pro·pelled′** (-prə peld′) *adj.*

jet·sam (jet′səm) *n.* [var. of JETTISON] cargo thrown overboard to lighten a ship in danger

jet set fashionable, wealthy people who frequently travel, often by jet, as for pleasure —**jet′-set′ter** *n.*

Jet Ski *trademark for* a motorcyclelike watercraft propelled by a jet of water

jet stream high-velocity winds moving from west to east, high above the earth

jet·ti·son (jet′ə sən) *vt.* [< L *jactare*, to throw] 1 to throw (goods) overboard so as to lighten a ship in danger 2 to discard

jet·ty (jet′ē) *n.*, *pl.* **-ties** [see JET¹] 1 a wall built out into the water to protect a harbor, etc. 2 a landing pier

Jew (jōō) *n.* [< Heb *yehūdī*, citizen of Judah] 1 a person descended, or regarded as descended, from the ancient Hebrews 2 a person whose religion is Judaism

jew·el (jōō′əl) *n.* [ult. < L *jocus*, a joke] 1 a valuable ring, necklace, etc., esp. one set with gems 2 a precious stone; gem 3 any person or thing that is very precious or valuable 4 a small gem used as a bearing in a watch —*vt.* **-eled** or **-elled**, **-el·ing** or **-el·ling** to decorate or set with jewels

jew·el·er or **jew·el·ler** (-ər) *n.* [ME *jueler* < OFr *joieleor* < *joel*: see JEWEL] one who makes, repairs, or deals in jewelry, watches, etc.

jew·el·ry *n.* ornaments such as rings, bracelets, etc., collectively

Jew·ish (jōō′ish) *adj.* of or having to do with Jews or Judaism —**Jew′ish·ness** *n.*

Jew·ry (jōō′rē) *n.* the Jewish people

jew's-harp or **jews'-harp** (jōōz′härp′) *n.* [< Du *jeugdtromp*, child's trumpet] a small, metal musical instrument held between the teeth and plucked to produce twanging tones

Jez·e·bel (jez′ə bel′) *n.* *Bible* a wicked queen of Israel

jib (jib) *n.* [Dan *gib*] a triangular sail secured forward of the mast or foremast

jibe¹ (jīb) *vi.* **jibed**, **jib′ing** [< Du *gijpen*] 1 to shift from one side of a ship to the other: used of a fore-and-aft sail 2 to change the course of a ship so that the sails jibe 3 [Inf.] to be in agreement or accord: often with *with*

jibe² (jīb) *vi.*, *vt.* **jibed**, **jib′ing** GIBE

jif·fy (jif′ē) *n.*, *pl.* **-fies** [< ?] [Inf.] a very short time: also **jiff**

jig (jig) *n.* [prob. < MFr *giguer*, to dance] 1 a fast, springy dance in triple time, or music for this 2 a device used to guide a tool — *vi.*, *vt.* **jigged**, **jig′ging** to dance (a jig) —**in jig time** [Inf.] very quickly —**the jig is up** [Slang] no chance is left

jig·ger (jig′ər) *n.* 1 a small glass, usually of 1½ ounces, used to measure liquor 2 the contents of a jigger

jig·gle (jig′əl) *vt.*, *vi.* **-gled**, **-gling** [< JIG] to move in quick, slight jerks —*n.* a jiggling

jig·saw (jig′sô′) *n.* a saw with a narrow blade set in a frame, for cutting curves, etc.

jigsaw puzzle a puzzle consisting of a picture cut up into irregularly shaped pieces, which must be put together again

ji·had (ji häd′) *n.* [Ar] *Islam* the religious duty to struggle for righteousness, often but not always interpreted as entailing warfare against unbelievers

jilt (jilt) *vt.* [< *Jill*, sweetheart] to reject or cast off (a previously accepted lover, etc.)

Jim Crow [name of an early black minstrel song] [also **j- c-**] discrimination against or segregation of blacks —**Jim′-Crow′** *adj.*

jim·my (jim′ē) *n.*, *pl.* **-mies** [< *James*] a short crowbar, used as by burglars to pry open windows, etc. —*vt.* **-mied**, **-my·ing** to pry open with or as with a jimmy

jim·son weed (jim′sən) [< *Jamestown weed*] a poisonous weed with white or purplish, trumpet-shaped flowers

jin·gle (jiŋ′gəl) *vi.* **-gled**, **-gling** [echoic] to make light, ringing sounds, as small bells —*vt.* to cause to jingle —*n.* 1 a jingling sound 2 a catchy verse or song with easy rhythm, simple rhymes, etc.

jin·go·ism (jiŋ′gō iz′əm) *n.* ⟦< phrase *by jingo* in patriotic Brit song⟧ chauvinistic advocacy of an aggressive, warlike foreign policy —**jin′go·ist** *n.* —**jin′go·is′tic** *adj.*

jin·n (jin) *n.*, *pl.* **jinns** or **jinn** ⟦Ar⟧ *Muslim Folklore* a supernatural being that can influence human affairs: also **jin·ni** (ji nē′, jin′ē), *pl.* **jinn**

jin·rik·i·sha (jin rik′shô′) *n.* ⟦Jpn < *jin*, a man + *riki*, power + *sha*, carriage⟧ a small, two-wheeled carriage, pulled by a person, esp. formerly in East Asia: also sp. **jin·rick′sha′** or **jin·rik′sha′**

jinx (jiŋks) [Inf.] *n.* ⟦< Gr *iynx*, the wryneck (bird used in black magic)⟧ 1 a person or thing supposed to bring bad luck 2 a streak of bad luck —*vt.* to bring bad luck to

jit·ney (jit′nē) *n.*, *pl.* **-neys** ⟦< ? Fr *jeton*, a token⟧ a small bus or a car carrying passengers for a low fare

jit·ter·bug (jit′ər bug′) *n.* a fast, acrobatic dance for couples, esp. in the 1940s —*vi.* **-bugged′, -bug′ging** to do this dance

jit·ters (jit′ərz) *pl.n.* [Inf.] an uneasy, nervous feeling; fidgets with the —**jit′ter·y** *adj.*

jive¹ (jīv) [Slang] *vt.*, *vi.* **jived, jiv′ing** ⟦< JIBE²⟧ to speak (to someone) in an insincere or flippant way —*n.* foolish, exaggerated, or insincere talk —*adj.* insincere, fraudulent, etc.

jive² (jīv) *vi.*, *vt.* **jived, jiv′ing** GIBE

Joan of Arc (jōn əv ärk), Saint (1412-31); Fr. military heroine: burned at the stake for witchcraft

job (jäb) *n.* ⟦< ?⟧ 1 a piece of work done for pay 2 a task; duty 3 the thing or material being worked on 4 employment; work —*adj.* hired or done by the job —*vt.*, *vi.* **jobbed, job′bing** 1 to deal in (goods) as a jobber 2 to let or sublet (work, contracts, etc.) —**job′hold′er** *n.* —**job′less** *adj.*

Job (jōb) *n. Bible* a man who suffered much but kept his faith in God

job action a refusal by a group of employees (esp. a group forbidden by law to strike) to perform their duties in an effort to win certain demands

job·ber (jäb′ər) *n.* 1 a wholesaler 2 one who works by the job or does piecework

job lot an assortment of goods for sale as one quantity

jock (jäk) *n.* 1 *short for: a)* JOCKEY *b)* JOCK-STRAP 2 [Slang] an athlete

jock·ey (jäk′ē) *n.*, *pl.* **-eys** ⟦< Scot dim. of JACK⟧ one whose work is riding horses in races —*vt.*, *vi.* **-eyed, -ey·ing** 1 to cheat; swindle 2 to maneuver for position or advantage

jock·strap (jäk′strap′) *n.* ⟦slang *jock*, penis + STRAP⟧ an elastic belt with a pouch for supporting the genitals, worn by male athletes

jo·cose (jō kōs′) *adj.* ⟦< L *jocus*, a joke⟧ joking or playful —**jo·cose′ly** *adv.* —**jo·cos′i·ty** (-käs′ə tē) *n.*, *pl.* **-ties**, **jo·cose′ness** *n.*

joc·u·lar (jäk′yə lər) *adj.* ⟦< L *jocus*, a joke⟧ joking; full of fun —**joc′u·lar′i·ty** (-lar′ə tē) *n.*, *pl.* **-ties**

joc·und (jäk′ənd) *adj.* ⟦< L *jucundus*, pleasant⟧ cheerful; genial —**joc′und·ly** *adv.*

jodh·purs (jäd′pərz) *pl.n.* ⟦after *Jodhpur*, former state in India⟧ riding breeches made loose and full above the knees and closefitting below

jog¹ (jäg) *vt.* **jogged, jog′ging** ⟦ME *joggen*, to spur (a horse)⟧ 1 to give a little shake to; nudge 2 to rouse (the memory) —*vi.* to move along at a slow, steady, jolting pace or trot; specif., to engage in jogging as a form of exercise —*n.* 1 a little shake or nudge 2 a slow, steady, jolting motion or trot 3 a jogging —**jog′ger** *n.*

jog² (jäg) *n.* [var. of JAG¹] 1 a projecting or notched part in a surface or line 2 a sharp change of direction

jog·ging *n.* trotting slowly and steadily as a form of exercise

jog·gle (jäg′əl) *vt.*, *vi.* **-gled, -gling** ⟦< JOG¹⟧ to shake or jolt slightly —*n.* a slight jolt

Jo·han·nes·burg (jō han′is burg′) city in NE South Africa

john (jän) *n.* [Slang] 1 a toilet 2 [*also* J-] a prostitute's customer

John (jän) *n. Bible* 1 a Christian apostle, the reputed author of the fourth Gospel 2 this book

John Bull *personification of* England or an Englishman

John Doe (dō) a fictitious name used in legal papers for one whose identity is unknown or secret

John·son (jän′sən) 1 **An·drew** (an′drōō′) 1808-75; 17th president of the U.S. (1865-69) 2 **Lyn·don Baines** (lin′dən bānz′) 1908-73; 36th president of the U.S. (1963-69) 3 **Samuel** 1709-84; Eng. lexicographer & writer

John the Baptist *Bible* the forerunner and baptizer of Jesus

join (join) *vt.*, *vi.* ⟦< L *jungere*⟧ 1 to bring or come together (with); connect; unite 2 to become a part or member of (a club, etc.) 3 to participate (*in* a conversation, etc.)

join·er *n.* a carpenter who finishes interior woodwork

joint (joint) *n.* ⟦< L *jungere*⟧ 1 a place where, or way in which, two things are joined 2 any of the parts of a jointed whole 3 a large cut of meat with the bone still in it 4 [Slang] a cheap bar, restaurant, etc., or any house, building, etc. 5 [Slang] a marijuana cigarette —*adj.* 1 common to two or more [*joint* property] 2 sharing with another [a *joint* owner] —*vt.* 1 to connect by or provide with a joint or joints 2 to cut (meat) into joints —**out of joint** 1 dislocated 2 disordered

joint·ly *adv.* in common

joist (joist) *n.* ⟦< OFr *giste*, a bed⟧ any of the parallel beams that hold up the planks of a floor or the laths of a ceiling

joke (jōk) *n.* [L *jocus*] 1 anything said or done to arouse laughter, as a funny anecdote 2 a thing done or said merely in fun 3 a person or thing to be laughed at —*vi.* **joked, jok′ing** to make jokes —**jok′ing·ly** *adv.*

jok·er n. 1 one who jokes: also **joke′ster** 2 a deceptively worded provision, as in a legal document 3 a playing card with the image of a jester on it 4 [Slang] a contemptibly foolish or inept person

jok·ey adj. comical; lighthearted: also **jok′y** —**jok′i·ness** n.

jol·li·ty (jäl′ə tē) n. a being jolly

jol·ly (jäl′ē) adj. **-li·er, -li·est** [OFr joli] 1 full of high spirits and good humor; merry 2 [Inf.] enjoyable —vt., vi. **-lied, -ly·ing** [Inf.] to try to make (a person) feel good, as by coaxing: often with along —**jol′li·ly** adv. —**jol′li·ness** n.

jolt (jōlt) vt. [< earlier jot] 1 to shake up, as with a bumpy ride 2 to shock or surprise —vi. to move along in a bumpy manner —n. 1 a sudden jerk, bump, etc. 2 a shock or surprise

Jo·nah (jō′nə) n. 1 Bible a Hebrew prophet: cast overboard and swallowed by a big fish, he was later cast up unharmed 2 one who brings bad luck

Jones (jōnz), **John Paul** 1747-92; Am. naval officer in the Revolutionary War, born in Scotland

jon·quil (jän′kwil, jän′-) n. [< L juncus, a rush] a species of narcissus with small, yellow flowers

Jon·son (jän′sən), **Ben** (ben) 1572?-1637; Eng. dramatist & poet

Jor·dan (jôrd′'n) 1 river in the Near East, flowing into the Dead Sea 2 country east of Israel —Jor·da·ni·an (jôr dā′nē ən) adj., n.

Jo·seph (jō′zəf, -səf) n. Bible 1 one of Jacob's sons, who became a high official in Egypt 2 the husband of Mary, mother of Jesus

josh (jäsh) vt., vi. [< ?] [Inf.] to tease; banter

Josh·u·a (jäsh′yōō ə, -ōō-) n. Bible Moses' successor, who led the Israelites into the Promised Land

jos·tle (jäs′əl) vt., vi. **-tled, -tling** [see JOUST] to push, as in a crowd; shove roughly —n. a jostling

jot (jät) n. [< Gr iōta, the smallest letter] a very small amount —vt. **jot′ted, jot′ting** to make a brief note of: usually with down —**jot′ter** n.

joule (jōōl) n. [after J. P. Joule (1818-89), Eng physicist] Physics a unit of work or energy

jounce (jouns) vt., vi. **jounced, jounc′ing** [< ?] to jolt or bounce —n. a jolt —**jounc′y** adj.

jour·nal (jur′nəl) n. [< L diurnalis, daily] 1 a daily record of happenings, as a diary 2 a newspaper or periodical 3 Bookkeeping a book for recording transactions in the order in which they occur 4 [orig. Scot] the part of an axle or shaft that turns in a bearing

jour·nal·ese (-ēz′) n. a facile style of writing found in many newspapers, magazines, etc.

jour·nal·ism n. the work of gathering news for, or producing, a newspaper, etc. —**jour′nal·ist** n. —**jour′nal·is′tic** adj.

jour·ney (jur′nē) n., pl. **-neys** [< OFr journee; ult. < L dies, day] a trip from one place to another, esp. when long or arduous —vi. **-neyed, -ney·ing** to travel —**jour′ney·er** n.

jour·ney·man (-mən) n., pl. **-men** (-mən) [ME < journee, day's work + man] 1 a worker qualified to work at a specified trade 2 any sound, experienced, but not brilliant performer

joust (joust) n. [ult. < L juxta, close to] a combat with lances between two knights on horseback —vi. to engage in a joust

jo·vi·al (jō′vē əl) adj. [< LL Jovialis, of Jupiter: from astrological notion of planet's influence] full of playful good humor —**jo′vi·al′i·ty** (-al′ə tē) n. —**jo′vi·al·ly** adv.

jowl[1] (joul) n. [OE ceafl, jaw] 1 the lower jaw 2 the cheek, esp. of a hog

jowl[2] (joul) n. [OE ceole, throat] [usually pl.] the fleshy hanging part under the jaw —**jowl′y** adj.

joy (joi) n. [ult. < L gaudium, joy] 1 a very glad feeling; happiness; delight 2 anything causing this

Joyce (jois), **James** 1882-1941; Ir. novelist

joy·ful adj. feeling, expressing, or causing joy; glad —**joy′ful·ly** adv.

joy·ous adj. joyful; happy —**joy′ous·ly** adv.

joy ride [Inf.] an automobile ride, often at a reckless speed, taken for pleasure, esp. in a car belonging to another —**joy rider** —**joy riding**

joy·stick n. 1 [Slang] the control stick of an airplane 2 a device resembling this, used as a controller for a video game

JP abbrev. Justice of the Peace

Jpn abbrev. 1 Japan 2 Japanese

Jr abbrev. junior: also **jr**

Ju·ba (jōō′bə) capital of South Sudan

ju·bi·lant (jōō′bə lənt) adj. [< L jubilum, wild shout] joyful and triumphant; elated; rejoicing

ju·bi·la·tion (jōō′bə lā′shən) n. 1 a rejoicing 2 a happy celebration

ju·bi·lee (jōō′bə lē′) n. [< Heb yōbēl, a ram's horn (trumpet)] 1 a 50th or 25th anniversary 2 a time of rejoicing 3 jubilation

Ju·dah[1] (jōō′də) n. Bible one of Jacob's sons

Ju·dah[2] (jōō′də) ancient kingdom in the S part of Palestine

Ju·da·ism (jōō′dā iz′əm, -dē-, -də-) n. the Jewish religion —**Ju·da′ic** (-dā′ik) adj.

Ju·das (jōō′dəs) n. 1 Bible the disciple who betrayed Jesus for money: in full **Judas Is·car·i·ot** (is ker′ē ət) 2 a traitor or betrayer

Ju·de·a (jōō dē′ə) ancient region of S Palestine

Judeo- combining form Jewish, Jewish and

judge (juj) n. [< L jus, law + dicere, say] 1 a public official with authority to hear and decide cases in a court of law 2 a person designated to determine the winner, settle a controversy, etc. 3 a person qualified to decide on the relative worth of anything 4 a governing leader of the Israelites before the time of the kings —vt., vi. **judged, judg′ing** 1 to hear and pass judgment on in a court of law 2 to determine the winner of (a contest) or settle (a controversy) 3 to form an opinion about 4 to criticize or censure 5 to think or suppose —**judge′ship′** n.

judg·ment (juj′mənt) *n.* 1 a judging; deciding 2 a legal decision; order given by a judge, etc. 3 an opinion 4 the ability to come to decide wisely, as in choosing a course of action 5 [J-] *short for* LAST JUDGMENT Also [Chiefly Brit.] **judge′ment**

judg·men·tal (-ment′′l) *adj.* making judgments as to value, etc., often, specif., judgments considered to be lacking in tolerance, objectivity, etc.

Judgment Day *Theol.* the time of God's final judgment of all people

ju·di·ca·to·ry (jōō′di kə tôr′ē) *adj.* [see JUDGE] having to do with administering justice —*n., pl.* **-ries** a law court, or law courts collectively

ju·di·ca·ture (-chər) *n.* 1 the administering of justice 2 jurisdiction 3 judges or courts collectively

ju·di·cial (jōō dish′əl) *adj.* 1 of judges, courts, or their functions 2 allowed, enforced, etc. by a court 3 befitting a judge 4 fair; impartial

ju·di·ci·ar·y (jōō dish′ē er′ē) *adj.* of judges or courts —*n., pl.* **-ar′ies** 1 the branch of government that administers justice 2 judges collectively

ju·di·cious (-dish′əs) *adj.* having or showing sound judgment —**ju·di′cious·ly** *adv.*

ju·do (jōō′dō) *n.* [Jpn < *jū*, soft + *dō*, way] a form of jujitsu

jug (jug) *n.* [pet form of *Judith* or *Joan*] a large container for liquids, with a small opening and a handle

jug·ger·naut (jug′ər nôt′) *n.* [< Sans *Jagannātha*, lord of the world] a relentless, irresistible force

jug·gle (jug′əl) *vt.* **-gled, -gling** [< L *jocus*, a joke] 1 to perform skillful tricks of sleight of hand with (balls, etc.), esp. by continually tossing and catching them 2 to catch or hold awkwardly 3 to manipulate so as to deceive —*vi.* to toss up balls, etc. and keep them in the air —**jug′gler** *n.*

jug·u·lar (jug′yōō lər) *adj.* [< L *jugum*, a yoke] of the neck or throat —*n.* JUGULAR VEIN

jugular vein either of two large veins in the neck carrying blood from the head

juice (jōōs) *n.* [< L *jus*, broth, juice] 1 the liquid part of a plant, fruit, etc. 2 a liquid in or from animal tissue 3 [Inf.] vitality 4 [Slang] *a*) electricity *b*) alcoholic liquor *c*) power or influence —*vt.* **juiced, juic′ing** to extract juice from —*vi.* [Slang] to drink alcoholic beverages to excess

juiced (jōōst) *adj.* [Slang] drunk; intoxicated

juic·er (jōō′sər) *n.* 1 a device for extracting juice from fruit 2 [Slang] a drunkard

juic·y (jōō′sē) *adj.* **-i·er, -i·est** 1 full of juice 2 [Inf.] *a*) full of interest [*juicy* gossip] *b*) highly profitable —**juic′i·ness** *n.*

ju·jit·su (jōō jit′sōō′) *n.* [< Jpn *jū*, soft, pliant + *jutsu*, art] a Japanese system of wrestling in which an opponent's strength and weight are used against him or her

ju·ju·be (jōō′jōō bē′) *n.* [< Gr *zizyphon*, name of a fruit] a fruit-flavored, jellylike lozenge

ju·jut·su (jōō jit′sōō′, -jut′-) *n.* JUJITSU

juke·box (jōōk′bäks′) *n.* [< Am black *juke*, wicked] a coin-operated player for records, CD's, etc. as in a bar

ju·lep (jōō′ləp) *n.* [< Pers *gul*, rose + *āb*, water] MINT JULEP

ju·li·enne (jōō′lē en′) *adj.* [Fr] cut into strips: said of vegetables, cheese, etc.: also **ju′li·enned′** (-end′)

Ju·li·et (jōō′lē et′, jōō′lē et′) *n.* the heroine of Shakespeare's tragedy *Romeo and Juliet*

Ju·ly (jōō lī′) *n.* [< L < *Julius* Caesar] the seventh month of the year, having 31 days: abbrev. Jul

jum·ble (jum′bəl) *vt., vi.* **-bled, -bling** [? blend of JUMP + TUMBLE] to mix or be mixed in a confused heap —*n.* a confused mixture or heap

jum·bo (jum′bō) *n., pl.* **-bos** [< Am black *jamba*, elephant] a large person, animal, or thing —*adj.* very large

jump (jump) *vi.* [< ?] 1 to spring or leap from the ground, a height, etc. 2 to jerk; bob 3 to move or act eagerly: often with *at* 4 to pass suddenly, as to a new topic 5 to rise suddenly, as prices 6 [Slang] to be lively —*vt.* 1 *a*) to leap over *b*) to pass over 2 to cause to leap 3 to leap upon 4 to cause (prices, etc.) to rise 5 [Inf.] *a*) to attack suddenly *b*) to react to prematurely 6 [Slang] to leave suddenly [to *jump* town] —*n.* 1 a jumping 2 a distance jumped 3 a sudden transition 4 a sudden rise, as in prices 5 a sudden, nervous start —**get (or have) the jump on** [Slang] to get (or have) an advantage over —**jump bail** to forfeit bail by fleeing

jump·er[1] (jum′pər) *n.* 1 one that jumps 2 a short wire to make a temporary electrical connection

jump·er[2] (jum′pər) *n.* [< dial. *jump*, short coat] 1 a loose jacket 2 a sleeveless dress for wearing over a blouse, etc.

jumper cables a pair of thick, insulated electrical wires with clamplike terminals, used to jump-start a motor vehicle that has a dead battery

jump-start *vt.* 1 to start (a motor-vehicle engine) with jumper cables 2 [Inf.] to energize, revive, etc. —*n.* a starting in such a way

jump·suit *n.* 1 a coverall worn by paratroops, etc. 2 a lounging outfit like this

jump·y (jum′pē) *adj.* **-i·er, -i·est** 1 moving in jumps or jerks 2 easily startled 3 nervous —**jump′i·ly** *adv.* —**jump′i·ness** *n.*

jun·co (juŋ′kō′) *n., pl.* **-cos′** [< Sp] a small bird with a gray or black head

junc·tion (juŋk′shən) *n.* [< L *jungere*, join] 1 a joining or being joined 2 a place of joining, as of roads —**junc′tion·al** *adj.*

junc·ture (juŋk′chər) *n.* 1 a junction 2 a point in time 3 a crisis

June (jōōn) *n.* [< L *Junius*, of *Juno*] the sixth month of the year, having 30 days: abbrev. Jun

Ju·neau (jōō′nō′) capital of Alaska: seaport on the SE coast

jun·gle (juŋ′gəl) *n.* [< Sans *jaṅgala*, waste-land] **1** land densely covered with trees, vines, etc., as in the tropics **2** [Slang] a situation in which people struggle fiercely for survival

jun·ior (jōōn′yər) *adj.* [L < *juvenis*, young] **1** the younger: written *Jr.* after a son's name if it is the same as his father's **2** of more recent position or lower status [a *junior* partner] **3** of juniors —*n.* **1** one who is younger, of lower rank, etc. **2** a student in the next-to-last year, as of college

junior college a school offering courses two years beyond high school

junior high school a school usually including grades 7, 8, and 9

ju·ni·per (jōō′ni pər) *n.* [L *juniperus*] an evergreen shrub or tree with fragrant berrylike cones used in flavoring gin, etc.

junk[1] (juŋk) *n.* [< ?] **1** old metal, paper, rags, etc. that might be reusable in some way **2** [Inf.] worthless stuff; trash **3** [Slang] heroin —*vt.* [Inf.] to scrap; discard —**junk′y** *adj.* **-i·er, -i·est**

junk[2] (juŋk) *n.* [< Malay *adjong*] a Chinese or Japanese flat-bottomed ship

junk bond [Inf.] a speculative BOND (*n.* 6), often issued to finance the takeover of a corporation

junk·er (juŋ′kər) *n.* [Slang] an old, dilapidated car or truck

Jun·ker (yoŏŋ′kər) *n.* [Ger] [Historical] a Prussian of the militaristic landowning class

jun·ket (juŋ′kit) *n.* [ME *joncate*, cream cheese] **1** milk sweetened, flavored, and thickened into curd **2** a picnic **3** an excursion, esp. one by an official at public expense —*vi.* to go on a junket —**jun′ket·eer′** (-ki tir′) *n.*, **jun′ket·er**

junk food snack food with chemical additives and little food value

junk·ie or **junk·y** (juŋ′kē) *n.*, *pl.* **-ies** [< JUNK[1], n. 3] [Slang] **1** a narcotics addict **2** one who is addicted to a specified activity, food, etc.

junk mail advertisements, solicitations, etc. mailed in large quantities

Ju·no (jōō′nō) *n.* Gr. Myth. the wife of Jupiter and queen of the gods

jun·ta (hoon′tə, jun′) *n.* [Sp < L *jungere*, join] a group of political intriguers, esp. military men, in power after a coup d'état

Ju·pi·ter (jōō′pit ər) *n.* **1** the chief Roman god **2** the largest planet of the solar system: see PLANET

Ju·ras·sic (jōō ras′ik) *adj.* [< Fr, after *Jura* Mountains, between France and Switzerland] of the geologic period characterized by the dominance of dinosaurs

ju·rid·i·cal (jōō rid′i kəl, joo-) *adj.* [< L *jus*, law + *dicere*, declare] of judicial proceedings or law

ju·ried (joor′ēd) *adj.* of a competition in which the winners are selected by a jury

ju·ris·dic·tion (joor′is dik′shən) *n.* [see JURIDICAL] **1** legal authority **2** the range of authority

ju·ris·pru·dence (joor′is prood′′ns) *n.* [< L *jus*, law + *prudentia*, a foreseeing] **1** the science or philosophy of law **2** a division of law [medical *jurisprudence*]

ju·rist (joor′ist) *n.* [< L *jus*, law] **1** an expert in law **2** JUDGE (*n.* 1)

ju·ror (joor′ər, -ôr′) *n.* a member of a jury

ju·ry (joor′ē) *n.*, *pl.* **-ries** [L *jurare*, to swear] **1** a group of people sworn to hear evidence in a law case and to give a decision **2** a committee that decides winners in a contest

just (just) *adj.* [< L *jus*, law] **1** right or fair [a *just* decision] **2** righteous [a *just* man] **3** deserved [*just* praise] **4** lawful **5** proper **6** correct or true **7** accurate; exact —*adv.* **1** exactly [*just* one o'clock] **2** nearly **3** only [*just* a taste] **4** barely [*just* missed him] **5** a very short time ago [she's *just* left] **6** immediately [*just* east of here] **7** [Inf.] really [*just* beautiful] —**just the same** nevertheless —**just′ly** *adv.* —**just′ness** *n.*

jus·tice (jus′tis) *n.* **1** a being righteous **2** fairness **3** rightfulness **4** reward or penalty as deserved **5** the use of authority to uphold what is just **6** the administration of law **7** *a*) JUDGE (*n.* 1) *b*) JUSTICE OF THE PEACE —**do justice to** to treat fairly

justice of the peace a local magistrate who decides minor cases, performs marriages, etc.

jus·ti·fy (jus′tə fī′) *vt.* **-fied′, -fy′ing** [< L *justus*, just + *facere*, to do] **1** to show to be just, right, etc. **2** Theol. to free from blame or guilt **3** to supply grounds for —**jus′ti·fi′a·ble** *adj.* **jus′ti·fi·ca′tion** (fi kā′shən) *n.*

Jus·tin·i·an I (jus tin′ē ən) A.D. 483-565; ruler of Byzantine Empire (527-565): codified Roman law

jut (jut) *vi.*, *vt.* **jut′ted, jut′ting** [prob. var. of JET[1]] to stick out; project —*n.* a part that juts

jute (jōōt) *n.* [< Sans *jūta*, matted hair] **1** a strong fiber used for making burlap, rope, etc. **2** a S Asian plant yielding this fiber

ju·ve·nile (jōō′və nil′, nəl) *adj.* [< L *juvenis*, young] **1** young; immature **2** of or for young persons —*n.* **1** a young person **2** an actor who plays youthful roles **3** a book for children —**ju′ve·nil′i·ty** (-nil′i tē) *n.*, *pl.* **-ties**

juvenile delinquency antisocial or illegal behavior by minors —**juvenile delinquent**

jux·ta·pose (juks′tə pōz′) *vt.* **-posed′, -pos′ing** [< Fr < L *juxta*, beside + POSE] to put side by side —**jux′ta·po·si′tion** *n.*

JV *abbrev.* junior varsity

K

k or **K** (kā) *n., pl.* **k's, K's** the eleventh letter of the English alphabet

K¹ *n.* **1** *Comput.* KILOBYTE **2** [Inf.] a thousand dollars

K² *abbrev.* **1** karat (carat) **2** kilometer **3** kindergarten **4** *Baseball* strikeout **5** *Comput.* the number 1,024, or 2¹⁰ Also, for 1 & 2, **k**

K³ ⟦ModL *kalium*⟧ *Chem. symbol for* potassium

kab·ba·lah (kab′ə lə, kə bä′lə) *n.* ⟦< Heb *kabala*, tradition⟧ **1** a Jewish mystical movement **2** any esoteric or secret doctrine

Ka·bu·ki (kä boo′kē) *n.* [*also* **k–**] a form of Japanese drama, chiefly in formalized pantomime

Kad·dish (käd′ish) *n.* ⟦Aram *kadish*, lit., holy⟧ *Judaism* a hymn in praise of God, recited at the daily service or as a mourner's prayer

kaf·fee·klatsch (kä′fä kläch′, kô′fē klach′) *n.* ⟦Ger < *kaffee*, coffee + *klatsch*, gossip⟧ [*also* **K–**] an informal gathering to drink coffee and chat

Kaf·ka (käf′kə), **Franz** (fränts) 1883–1924; Austrian–Czech writer

Kai·ser (kī′zər) *n.* ⟦ME *caiser*, emperor < L *Caesar*⟧ the title of the former rulers of Austria and Germany

kaiser roll ⟦Ger *kaisersemmel*, kaiser bun⟧ a large, round roll with a hard crust

kale (kāl) *n.* [var. of COLE] a hardy cabbage with spreading leaves

ka·lei·do·scope (kə lī′də skōp′) *n.* ⟦< Gr *kalos*, beautiful + *eidos*, form + -SCOPE⟧ **1** a small tube containing bits of colored glass reflected by mirrors to produce symmetrical patterns that constantly change when the tube is rotated **2** anything that constantly changes — **ka·lei′do·scop′ic** (-skäp′ik) *adj.*

ka·mi·ka·ze (kä′mə kä′zē) *adj.* ⟦Jpn, divine wind⟧ of a suicidal attack by a WWII Japanese airplane pilot

kan·ga·roo (kaŋ′gə roo′) *n.* ⟦< ?⟧ a leaping marsupial of Australia and nearby islands, with short forelegs and strong, large hind legs

kangaroo court [Inf.] an irregular court, usually disregarding normal legal procedure

Kan·sas (kan′zəs) Midwestern state of the U.S.; cap. Topeka: abbrev. *KS* **—Kan′san** *adj., n.*

Kansas City 1 city in W Missouri, on the Missouri River **2** city opposite this, in NE Kansas

Kant (känt), **Im·man·u·el** (i man′yoo el′) 1724–1804; Ger. philosopher

ka·o·lin (kā′ə lin) *n.* ⟦Fr < Chin name of hill where found⟧ a white clay used in porcelain, etc.

ka·pok (kā′päk′) *n.* ⟦Malay⟧ the silky fibers around the seeds of certain tropical trees, used for stuffing mattresses, life preservers, etc.

kap·pa (kap′ə) *n.* the tenth letter of the Greek alphabet (Κ, κ)

ka·put (kə poot′, -poot′) *adj.* ⟦Ger *kaputt*⟧ [Slang] ruined, destroyed, etc.

Ka·ra·chi (kə rä′chē) seaport in S Pakistan: former capital

kar·a·kul (kar′ə kul′, -kəl) *n.* ⟦ult. < Turkic *qara köl*, dark lake⟧ **1** a sheep native to central Asia **2** the curly black fur from the fleece of its lambs: usually sp. *caracul*

ka·ra·o·ke (kar′ē ō′kē) *n.* a form of entertainment in which bar patrons, etc. take turns singing while a special device plays prerecorded accompaniment

kar·at (kar′ət) *n.* ⟦var. of CARAT⟧ one 24th part (of pure gold)

ka·ra·te (kə rät′ē) *n.* ⟦Jpn⟧ a Japanese system of self-defense by sharp, quick blows with the hands and feet

kar·ma (kär′mə) *n.* ⟦Sans, act⟧ **1** *Buddhism, Hinduism* the totality of one's acts in each state of one's existence **2** loosely, fate

kart (kärt) *n.* ⟦< CART⟧ a small, flat, motorized vehicle, used in racing (**kart′ing**)

ka·ty·did (kāt′ē did′) *n.* ⟦echoic of the male's shrill sound⟧ a large, green tree insect

kay·ak (kī′ak′) *n.* ⟦Inuit *qajaq*⟧ a canoe with only a small opening in its shell for the paddler —*vi.* to go in a kayak **—kay′ak′er** *n.*

kay·o (kā′ō′) [Slang] *vt.* **-oed′, -o′ing** ⟦< KO⟧ *Boxing* to knock out —*n. Boxing* a knockout

Ka·zakh·stan (kä′zäk stän′) country in W Asia

ka·zoo (kə zoo′) *n.* ⟦echoic⟧ a toy musical instrument that makes buzzing tones when hummed into

KB *abbrev.* kilobyte(s)

kc *abbrev.* kilocycle(s)

Keats (kēts), **John** 1795–1821; Eng. poet

ke·bab or **ke·bob** (kə bäb′) *n.* ⟦Ar *kabāb*⟧ **1** any of the small pieces of marinated meat used in making shish kebab **2** [*often pl.*] SHISH KEBAB

keel (kēl) *n.* ⟦< ON *kjǫlr*⟧ **1** the chief timber or piece extending along the length of the bottom of a boat or ship **2** a projecting fin on the bottom of a boat or ship, for stability and directional control **—keel over 1** to capsize **2** to fall over suddenly **—on an even keel** upright or steady

keen¹ (kēn) *adj.* ⟦OE *cene*, wise⟧ **1** having a sharp edge or point [a keen knife] **2** cutting [a keen wind] **3** very perceptive [keen eyes] **4** shrewd **5** eager **6** intense **—keen′ly** *adv.* **—keen′ness** *n.*

keen² (kēn) *vt., vi.* ⟦< Ir *caoinim*, I wail⟧ to make a mournful, wailing sound

keep (kēp) *vt.* **kept, keep′ing** ⟦OE *cœpan*,

behold】 1 to celebrate; observe [to *keep* the Sabbath] 2 to fulfill (a promise, etc.) 3 to protect; guard; take care of; tend 4 to preserve 5 to provide for; support 6 to make regular entries in [to *keep* a diary] 7 to maintain in a specified state, position, etc. [to *keep* prices down] 8 to hold for the future; retain 9 to hold and not let go; detain, withhold, restrain, etc. 10 to stay in or on (a course, place, etc.) —*vi.* 1 to stay in a specified state, position, etc. 2 to continue; go on 3 to refrain [to *keep* from eating] 4 to stay fresh; not spoil —*n.* 1 food and shelter; support 2 the inner stronghold of a castle —**for keeps** [Inf.] 1 with the winner keeping what he wins 2 permanently —**keep to oneself** 1 to avoid others 2 to refrain from telling — **keep up** 1 to maintain in good condition 2 to continue 3 to maintain the pace 4 to remain informed about: with *on* or *with*

keep·er *n.* 1 one that keeps; specif., *a*) a guard *b*) a guardian *c*) a custodian 2 [Inf.] something worth keeping

keep·ing *n.* 1 observance (of a rule, holiday, etc.) 2 care; charge —**in keeping with** in conformity or accord with

keep·sake *n.* something kept, or to be kept as a reminder of an absent person, a past event, etc.

keg (keg) *n.* 〖< ON *kaggi*, keg〗 1 a small barrel 2 a unit of weight for nails, equal to 100 lb.

keg party a boisterous party where beer in kegs is served: also 〖Slang〗 **keg·ger** (keg'ər) *n.*

kelp (kelp) *n.* 〖ME *culp*〗 a large, coarse, brown seaweed, rich in iodine

Kel·vin (kel'vin) *adj.* 〖after 1st Baron *Kelvin* (1824-1907), Brit physicist〗 designating of a scale of temperature measured from absolute zero (-273.16°C)

ken (ken) *vt.* **kenned, ken'ning** 〖OE *cennan*, cause to know〗 [Scot.] to know —*n.* range of knowledge

Ken·ne·dy (ken'ə dē), **John Fitz·ger·ald** (fits jer'əld) 1917-63; 35th president of the U.S. (1961-63): assassinated

ken·nel (ken'əl) *n.* 〖< L *canis*, dog〗 1 a doghouse 2 [*often pl.*] a place where dogs are bred or kept —*vt.* **-neled** or **-nelled, -nel·ing** or **-nel·ling** to keep in a kennel

Ken·tuck·y (kən tuk'ē) state of the EC U.S.; cap. Frankfort: abbrev. KY —**Ken·tuck'i·an** *adj., n.*

Ken·ya (ken'yə, kēn'-) country on the E coast of Africa

kept (kept) *vt., vi. pt. & pp. of* KEEP —*adj.* maintained so as to be a sexual partner [a *kept* woman]

ker·a·tin (ker'ə tin) *n.* 〖< Gr *keras*, horn〗 a tough, fibrous protein, the basic substance of hair, nails, etc.

kerb (kurb) *n.* Brit. sp. *of* CURB (*n.* 3)

ker·chief (kur'chif) *n.* 〖< OFr *covrir*, to cover + *chef*, head〗 1 a piece of cloth worn over the head or around the neck 2 a handkerchief

ker·nel (kur'nəl) *n.* 〖< OE *cyrnel*〗 1 a grain or seed, as of corn 2 the inner, softer part of a

nut, etc. 3 the central, most important part; essence

ker·o·sene (ker'ə sēn') *n.* 〖Gr *kēros*, wax〗 a thin oil distilled from petroleum, used as a fuel, solvent, etc.: also sp. **ker'o·sine'**

kes·trel (kes'trəl) *n.* 〖echoic of its cry〗 a small European falcon

ketch (kech) *n.* 〖ME *cache*〗 a small sailing vessel with two masts rigged fore-and-aft, the larger mast being toward the bow

ketch·up (kech'əp) *n.* 〖? Malay *kēchap*, sauce〗 a sauce for meat, fish, etc.; esp., a thick sauce (**tomato ketchup**) of tomatoes, onions, spices, etc.

ket·tle (ket'l) *n.* 〖< L *catinus*, container for food〗 1 a metal container for boiling or cooking things 2 a teakettle

ket·tle·drum *n.* a hemispheric percussion instrument of copper with a parchment top that can be tightened or loosened to change the pitch

Kev·lar (kev'lär') *trademark for* a tough, light, synthetic fiber used in bulletproof vests, boat hulls, etc.

key[1] (kē) *n., pl.* **keys** 〖OE *cæge*〗 1 a device for moving the bolt of a lock and thus locking or unlocking something 2 any of the buttons, levers, etc. pressed in operating a piano, computer, etc. 3 a thing that explains or solves something else, as a code, the legend of a map, etc. 4 an essential person or thing 5 tone or style of expression 6 *Music* a system of related tones based on a keynote and forming a given scale —*adj.* essential; important —*vt.* **keyed, key'ing** 1 to furnish with a key 2 to regulate the tone or pitch of 3 to bring into harmony —**key in** to input (data) by means of a keyboard —**key up** to make tense or excited

key[2] (kē) *n., pl.* **keys** 〖Sp *cayo*〗 a reef or low island

key·board *n.* 1 the row or rows of keys of a piano, computer, etc. 2 a musical instrument with a keyboard —*vt., vi.* to write (text) or input (data) by means of a keyboard —**key'board'er** *n.*

key·hole *n.* an opening (in a lock) into which a key is inserted

key·note *n.* 1 the lowest, basic note of a musical scale 2 the basic idea or ruling principle —*vt.* **-not'ed, -not'ing** 1 to give the keynote of 2 to give the keynote speech at —**key'not'er** *n.*

keynote speech (*or* **address**) a speech, as at a convention, setting forth the main line of policy

key·pad *n.* the keys or push buttons on a computer keyboard, telephone, etc.

key·stone *n.* 1 the central, topmost stone of an arch 2 the most important part or principle

key·stroke *n.* any of the strokes made in operating a computer keyboard

Key West island off S Florida, in the Gulf of Mexico

key·word *n.* a word or phrase submitted to a

SEARCH ENGINE in an effort to locate relevant documents or websites

kg *abbrev.* kilogram(s)

KGB *abbrev.* [Russ abbrev.] the security police and intelligence agency (1954-91) of the Soviet Union

kha·ki (kak′ē, kä′kē) *adj.* [< Pers *khāk*, dust] 1 dull yellowish-brown 2 made of khaki (cloth) —*n.*, *pl.* **-kis** 1 a dull yellowish brown 2 strong, twilled cloth of this color 3 [*often pl.*] a khaki uniform or pants

khan (kän, kan) *n.* [< Mongolian *qan*, lord] 1 a title of Tatar or Mongol rulers in the Middle Ages 2 a title of various dignitaries in Iran, Afghanistan, etc.

Khar·kov (kär′kôf′) city in NE Ukraine

Khar·toum (kär tōōm′) capital of Sudan, on the Nile

kHz *abbrev.* kilohertz

kib·butz (ki bōōts′, -bōōts′) *n.*, *pl.* **kib·but·zim** (kē′bōō tsēm′) [ModHeb] an Israeli collective settlement, esp. a collective farm

kib·itz·er (kib′it sər) *n.* [Yiddish < Ger *kiebitz*] [Inf.] 1 an onlooker at a card game, etc., esp. one who volunteers advice 2 a giver of unwanted advice or meddler in others' affairs —**kib′itz** *vi.*

ki·bosh (kī′bäsh′, ki bäsh′) *n.* [< ?] used chiefly in **put the kibosh on**, to check, squelch, etc.

kick (kik) *vi.* [ME *kiken*] 1 to strike out with the foot 2 to recoil, as a gun 3 [Inf.] to complain 4 *Football* to kick the ball —*vt.* 1 to strike with the foot 2 to drive, force, etc., as by kicking 3 to score (a goal, etc.) by kicking 4 [Slang] to get rid of (a habit) —*n.* 1 an act or method of kicking 2 a sudden recoil 3 a complaint 4 [Inf.] an intoxicating effect 5 [*often pl.*] [Inf.] pleasure —**kick in** [Slang] to pay (one's share) —**kick over** to start up, as an automobile engine —**kick′er** *n.*

kick·back *n.* [Slang] 1 a giving back of part of money received as payment, often because of coercion or a previous agreement 2 the money so returned

kick·off *n.* 1 *Football* a kick that puts the ball into play 2 a beginning, as of a campaign

kick·stand *n.* a pivoting metal bar that can be kicked down to support a bicycle, etc. in an upright position

kick-start *vt.* 1 to start (a motorcycle, etc.) with a lever attached to a pedal that one kicks downward 2 [Inf.] to start, energize, revive, etc.

kick·y *adj.* **-i·er**, **-i·est** [Slang] 1 fashionable 2 exciting

kid (kid) *n.* [ME *kide*] 1 a young goat 2 leather from the skin of young goats 3 [Inf.] a child —*adj.* [Inf.] younger [my *kid* sister] —*vt.*, *vi.* **kid′ded**, **kid′ding** [Inf.] to tease or fool playfully —**with kid gloves** [Inf.] with great tact, gentleness, etc.

kid·die or **kid·dy** (-ē) *n.*, *pl.* **-dies** [dim. of prec.] [Inf.] a child

kid·nap (kid′nap′) *vt.* **-napped′** or **-naped′**, **-nap′ping** or **-nap′ing** [KID (*n.* 3) + dial.

nap, to snatch] to seize and hold (a person) by force or fraud, as in order to get a ransom —**kid′nap′per** *n.*, **kid′nap′er** *n.*

kid·ney (kid′nē) *n.*, *pl.* **-neys** [< ?] 1 either of a pair of glandular organs that separate water and waste products from the blood and excrete them as urine 2 an animal's kidney, used as food 3 *a)* disposition *b)* class; kind

kidney bean the kidney-shaped seed of the common garden bean

kidney stone a hard mineral deposit sometimes formed in the kidney

kid·skin *n.* leather from the skin of young goats

kiel·ba·sa (kēl bä′sə, kil-) *n.*, *pl.* **-si** (-sē) or **-sas** [Pol] a Polish smoked sausage

Ki·ev (kē′ef′, -ev′) capital of Ukraine, on the Dnepr

kill (kil) *vt.* [< ? OE *cwellan*] 1 to cause the death of; slay 2 to destroy; put an end to 3 to defeat or veto (legislation) 4 to spend (time) on trivial matters 5 to turn off (an engine, etc.) 6 to stop publication of —*n.* 1 the act of killing 2 an animal or animals killed —**kill′er** *n.*

killer bee AFRICANIZED BEE

killer whale a large black and white dolphin that hunts in packs and preys on large fish, seals, etc.; orca

kill·ing *adj.* 1 causing death; deadly 2 exhausting; fatiguing —*n.* 1 slaughter; murder 2 [Inf.] a sudden great profit

kill·joy *n.* one who lessens or lessens other people's enjoyment: also **kill′-joy′**

kiln (kil, kiln) *n.* [< L *culina*, cookstove] a furnace or oven for seasoning lumber, making charcoal, hardening pottery, etc.

ki·lo (kē′lō, kil′ō) *n.*, *pl.* **-los** [Fr] 1 KILOGRAM 2 KILOMETER

kilo- [< Gr *chilioi*] *combining form* one thousand

kil·o·byte (kil′ə bīt′) *n.* 1,024 bytes, or, loosely, 1,000 bytes

kilocycle (-sī′kəl) *n.* former term for KILOHERTZ

kil·o·gram (-gram′) *n.* 1,000 grams

kil·o·hertz (-herts′, -hurts′) *n.*, *pl.* **-hertz′** 1,000 hertz

kil·o·li·ter (-lēt′ər) *n.* 1,000 liters, or one cubic meter

kil·o·me·ter (kə läm′ət ər, kil′ə mēt′ər) *n.* 1,000 meters

kil·o·ton (kil′ə tun′) *n.* the explosive force of 1,000 tons of TNT

kil·o·watt (-wät′) *n.* 1,000 watts

kilt (kilt) *n.* [prob. < ON] a knee-length, pleated tartan skirt traditionally worn by men of the Scottish Highlands

kil·ter (kil′tər) *n.* [< ?] [Inf.] good condition; proper order: now chiefly in **out of kilter**

ki·mo·no (kə mō′nə, -nō′) *n.*, *pl.* **-nos** [Jpn] 1 a robe with wide sleeves and a sash, part of the traditional Japanese costume 2 a woman's dressing gown

kin (kin) *n.* [OE *cynn*] relatives; family -**kin** (kin) [< MDu *-ken*] *suffix* little [*lambkin*]

kind (kīnd) *n.* [OE *cynd*] 1 a natural group or

division 2 essential character 3 sort; variety; class —*adj.* sympathetic, gentle, benevolent, etc. —**in kind** in the same way —**kind of** [Inf.] somewhat; rather —**of a kind** alike

kin·der·gar·ten (kin′dər gärt′'n) *n.* [Ger < *kinder*, child + *garten*, garden] a school or class for young children, usually four to six years old, that develops basic skills and social behavior by games, music, handicrafts, etc. —**kin′der·gart′ner** *n.*, **kin′der·gar′ten·er** (-gärt′nər)

kind·heart·ed *adj.* kind

kin·dle (kin′dəl) *vt.* **-dled, -dling** [< ON *kynda*] 1 to set on fire; ignite 2 to excite (interest, feelings, etc.) —*vi.* 1 to catch fire 2 to become excited

kin·dling (kind′liŋ) *n.* material, esp. bits of dry wood, for starting a fire

kind·ly (kind′lē) *adj.* **-li·er, -li·est** 1 kind; gracious 2 agreeable; pleasant —*adv.* 1 in a kind, gracious manner 2 agreeably; favorably 3 please [*kindly* shut the door] —**kind′li·ness** *n.*

kind·ness *n.* 1 the state, quality, or habit of being kind 2 a kind act

kin·dred (kin′drid) *n.* [< OE *cynn*, kin + *rǣden*, condition] relatives —*adj.* of like nature; similar [*kindred* spirits]

kine (kīn) *pl.n.* [< OE *cy*, cows] [Archaic] cows; cattle

ki·net·ic (ki net′ik) *adj.* [< Gr *kinein*, to move] of or resulting from motion

kin·folk (kin′fōk′) *pl.n.* family; relatives; kin: also **kin′folks′**

king (kiŋ) *n.* [< OE *cyning*] 1 a male ruler of a nation 2 a man who is supreme in some field 3 something supreme in its class 4 a playing card with a picture of a king on it 5 *Chess* the chief piece —*adj.* chief (in size, importance, etc.) —**king′ly** *adj.*

King (kiŋ), **Mar·tin Luther, Jr.** (märt′'n) 1929–68; U.S. clergyman & leader in the civil rights movement: assassinated

king·dom (-dəm) *n.* 1 a country headed by a king or queen; monarchy 2 a realm; domain [the *kingdom* of poetry] 3 *Biol.* any of several divisions into which living things have been classified, such as the animals, plants, or fungi

king·fish·er *n.* a short-tailed diving bird that feeds chiefly on fish

King James Version AUTHORIZED VERSION

King Lear (lir) the title character of a tragedy by Shakespeare

king·pin *n.* 1 the pin at the front of a triangle of bowling pins 2 [Inf.] the essential person or thing

king-size *adj.* larger than the regular kind: also **king′-sized′**

kink (kiŋk) *n.* [< Scand] 1 a short twist, curl, or bend in a rope, wire, hair, etc. 2 a painful cramp in the neck, back, etc. 3 a mental twist; eccentricity — *vi., vt.* to form or cause to form a kink or kinks

kink·y *adj.* **-i·er, -i·est** 1 tightly curled 2 [Slang] weird, eccentric, etc.; specif., in sexual preferences or practices

kin·ship (kin′ship′) *n.* 1 family relationship 2 close connection

kins·man (kinz′mən) *n., pl.* **-men** (-mən) a relative; esp., a male relative

kins·wom·an *n., pl.* **-wom′en** a female relative

ki·osk (kē′äsk′) *n.* [< Pers *kūshk*, palace] 1 a small structure used as a newsstand, information booth, etc. 2 a small structure housing an interactive terminal, etc.

kip·per (kip′ər) *vt.* [< ?] to cure (herring, salmon, etc.) by salting and drying or smoking —*n.* a kippered herring, etc.

Kir·i·ba·ti (kir′ə bas′) country on a group of islands in the WC Pacific

kirk (kurk) *n.* [Scot. or North Eng.] a church

kis·met (kiz′met) *n.* [< Ar *qasama*, to divide] fate; destiny

kiss (kis) *vt., vi.* [OE *cyssan*] 1 to touch or caress with the lips as an act of affection, greeting, etc. 2 to touch lightly or gently —*n.* 1 an act of kissing 2 a light, gentle touch 3 any of various small candies —**kiss′a·ble** *adj.*

kiss·er *n.* 1 one who kisses 2 [Slang] *a)* the mouth *b)* the face

kit (kit) *n.* [ME *kyt*, tub] 1 *a)* personal equipment, esp. as packed for travel *b)* a set of tools *c)* equipment for some particular activity, etc. *d)* a set of parts to be assembled 2 a box, bag, etc. for carrying such parts, equipment, or tools —**the whole kit and caboodle** [Inf.] the whole lot

kitch·en (kich′ən) *n.* [ult. < L *coquere*, to cook] a room or place for the preparation and cooking of food

kitch·en·ette (-et′) *n.* a small kitchen

kitch·en·ware (-wer′) *n.* kitchen utensils

kite (kīt) *n.* [< OE *cyta*] 1 any of several hawk-like birds of prey with long wings 2 a light wooden frame covered with paper or cloth, to be flown in the wind at the end of a string

kith (kith) *n.* [< OE *cyth*] friends: now only in **kith and kin,** *a)* friends and relatives *b)* relatives

kitsch (kich) *n.* [Ger, gaudy trash] pretentious but shallow art or writing —**kitsch′y** *adj.*

kit·ten (kit′'n) *n.* [< OFr dim. of *chat*, cat] a young cat —**kit′ten·ish** *adj.*

kit·ty¹ (kit′ē) *n., pl.* **-ties** 1 a kitten 2 *a pet name for* a cat

kit·ty² (kit′ē) *n., pl.* **-ties** [prob. < KIT] 1 the stakes in a poker game 2 money pooled for some purpose

kit·ty-cor·nered (kit′ē kôr′nərd) *adj., adv.* CATER-CORNERED: also **kit′ty-cor′ner**

ki·wi (kē′wē) *n., pl.* **-wis** [echoic of its cry] 1 a flightless bird of New Zealand 2 [*also* K–] a hairy, egg-sized fruit with sweet, green flesh

KKK *abbrev.* Ku Klux Klan

Klee·nex (klē′neks′) *trademark for* soft tissue paper used as a handkerchief, etc. —*n.* [*occas.* k–] a piece of such paper

klep·to·ma·ni·a (klep′tō mā′nē ə) *n.* [< Gr *kleptēs*, thief + -MANIA] a persistent, abnormal impulse to steal —**klep′to·ma′ni·ac′** *n., adj.*

klieg light (klēg) [after A. & J. *Kliegl*, who developed it in 1911] a very bright arc light used on motion picture sets

Klon·dike (klän'dīk') gold-mining region in W Yukon Territory, Canada

klutz (kluts) *n.* [< Yiddish *klots*, lit., wooden block] [Slang] a clumsy or stupid person

km *abbrev.* kilometer(s)

knack (nak) *n.* [ME *knak*, sharp blow] 1 a clever expedient 2 ability to do something easily

knack·wurst (näk'wurst') *n.* [Ger < *knacken*, to burst + *wurst*, sausage] a thick, highly seasoned sausage

knap·sack (nap'sak') *n.* [< Du *knappen*, eat + *zak*, a sack] a bag of leather, canvas, or nylon for carrying equipment or supplies on the back

knave (nāv) *n.* [< OE *cnafa*, boy] 1 a dishonest, deceitful person; rogue 2 JACK (*n.* 3) —**knav'ish** *adj.*

knav·er·y (nāv'ər ē) *n., pl.* -ies rascality; dishonesty

knead (nēd) *vt.* [< OE *cnedan*] 1 to work (dough, clay, etc.) into a pliable mass by folding, pressing, and squeezing 2 to massage —**knead'er** *n.*

knee (nē) *n.* [< OE *cneow*] 1 the joint between the thigh and the lower leg 2 anything shaped like a bent knee —*vt.* kneed, knee'ing to hit or touch with the knee

knee·cap *n.* PATELLA

knee-deep *adj.* 1 up to the knees [*knee-deep* mud] 2 very much involved

knee-jerk *adj.* [< the reflex when the knee is tapped] [Inf.] of or reacting with an automatic, predictable response

kneel (nēl) *vi.* knelt or kneeled, kneel'ing [< OE *cneow*, knee] to bend or rest on a knee or the knees

kneel·er *n.* a cushion, stool, etc. to kneel on, as in a church pew

knell (nel) *vi.* [< OE *cnyllan*] 1 to ring slowly; toll 2 to sound ominously —*vt.* to call or announce by or as by a knell —*n.* 1 the sound of a bell rung slowly, as at a funeral 2 an omen of death, failure, etc.

knelt (nelt) *vi. alt. pt. and pp. of* KNEEL

knew (nōō) *vt., vi. pt. of* KNOW

knick·ers (nik'ərz) *pl.n.* [after D. *Knickerbocker*, fictitious Du author of W. Irving's *History of New York*] loose breeches gathered just below the knees: also **knick'er·bock'ers** (-ər bäk'ərz)

knick·knack (nik'nak') *n.* [< KNACK] a small ornamental article

knife (nīf) *n., pl.* knives [< OE *cnif*] 1 a cutting instrument with a sharp-edged blade set in a handle 2 a cutting blade, as in a machine —*vt.* knifed, knif'ing 1 to cut or stab with a knife 2 [Inf.] to injure or defeat by treachery —**under the knife** [Inf.] undergoing surgery

knight (nīt) *n.* [< OE *cniht*, boy] 1 in medieval times, a man formally raised to special military rank and pledged to chivalrous conduct 2 in Great Britain, a man who for some achievement is given honorary rank entitling him to use *Sir* before his given name 3 a chess piece shaped like a horse's head —*vt.* to make (a man) a knight

knight-er·rant (nīt'er'ənt) *n., pl.* knights'-er'rant 1 a medieval knight wandering in search of adventure 2 a chivalrous or quixotic person

knight·hood *n.* 1 the rank, status, or vocation of a knight 2 knights collectively

knight·ly *adj.* of, like, or befitting a knight; chivalrous, brave, etc.

K-9 or **K9** (kā'nīn') *abbrev.* [phonetic pun on *canine*] canine: informal except in law-enforcement or military use [a police *K-9* unit]

knit (nit) *vt., vi.* knit'ted or knit, knit'ting [< OE *cnotta*, a knot] 1 to make (a fabric) by looping yarn or thread together with special needles 2 to join or grow together closely and firmly: said as of a broken bone 3 to draw or become drawn together in wrinkles: said of the brows —**knit'ter** *n.*

knit·wear *n.* knitted clothing

knob (näb) *n.* [ME *knobbe*] 1 a rounded lump or protuberance 2 *a*) a handle, usually round, of a door, drawer, etc. *b*) a similar device that can be turned to control a radio, TV, etc.

knob·by *adj.* -bi·er, -bi·est 1 covered with knobs 2 like a knob

knock (näk) *vi.* [< OE *cnocian*] 1 to strike a blow 2 to rap on a door 3 to bump; collide 4 to make a thumping noise: said of an engine, etc. —*vt.* 1 to hit; strike 2 to make by hitting [to *knock* a hole in a wall] 3 [Inf.] to find fault with —*n.* 1 a knocking 2 a hit; rap 3 a thumping noise in an engine, etc., as because of faulty combustion 4 [Inf.] an adverse criticism —**knock about** (or **around**) [Inf.] to wander about —**knock down** 1 to hit so as to cause to fall 2 to take apart 3 to indicate the sale of (an article) at an auction —**knock off** 1 [Inf.] to stop working 2 [Inf.] to deduct 3 [Slang] to kill, overcome, etc. —**knock out** to make unconscious or exhausted —**knock together** to make or compose hastily —**knock up** [Slang] to make pregnant

knock·er *n.* one that knocks; esp., a small ring, knob, etc. on a door for use in knocking

knock-kneed (-nēd') *adj.* having legs that bend inward at the knees

knock·out *n.* 1 a knocking out or being knocked out 2 [Slang] a very attractive person or thing 3 *Boxing* a victory won when the opponent is unable to continue to fight, as because of having been knocked unconscious

knock·wurst (näk'wurst') *n. alt. sp. of* KNACK-WURST

knoll (nōl) *n.* [OE *cnoll*] a small hill; mound

knot (nät) *n.* [< OE *cnotta*] 1 a lump in a thread, etc., formed by a tightened loop or a tangle 2 a fastening made by tying together pieces of string, rope, etc. 3 an ornamental bow of ribbon, etc. 4 a small group or cluster 5 something that ties closely; esp., the bond of marriage 6 a problem; difficulty 7 a hard lump on a tree where a branch grows out, or a cross section of such a lump in a board **8** *Naut.* a unit of speed of one nautical mile (6,076.12 feet) an hour — *vt., vi.* **knot'ted, knot'ting 1** to make or form a knot (in) **2** to entangle or become entangled —**tie the knot** [Inf.] to get married

knot·hole *n.* a hole in a board, etc. where a knot has fallen out

knot·ty *adj.* **-ti·er, -ti·est** [ME] **1** full of knots [*knotty* pine] **2** hard to solve; puzzling [a *knotty* problem]

know (nō) *vt.* **knew, known, know'ing** [< OE *cnawan*] **1** to be well informed about **2** to be aware of [to *know* that one is loved] **3** to be acquainted with **4** to recognize or distinguish [to *know* right from wrong] **5** [Archaic] to have sexual relations with —*vi.* **1** to have knowledge **2** to be sure or aware —**in the know** [Inf.] having confidential information

know-how *n.* [Inf.] technical skill

know·ing *adj.* **1** having knowledge **2** shrewd; clever **3** implying shrewd or secret understanding [a *knowing* look] —**know'ing·ly** *adv.*

know-it-all *n.* [Inf.] one claiming to know much about almost everything

knowl·edge (näl'ij) *n.* **1** the fact or state of knowing **2** range of information or understanding **3** what is known; learning

knowl·edge·a·ble *adj.* having knowledge or intelligence —**knowl'edge·a·bly** *adv.*

known (nōn) *vt., vi. pp. of* KNOW —*adj.* **1** familiar **2** recognized, proven, etc. [a *known* expert]

knuck·le (nuk'əl) *n.* [< or akin to MDu & LowG *knokel*, dim. of *knoke*, bone] **1** a joint of the finger; esp., the joint connecting a finger to the rest of the hand **2** the knee or hock joint of an animal, used as food —**knuckle down** [Inf.] to work hard —**knuckle under** [Inf.] to yield; give in

knuck·le·head *n.* [Inf.] a stupid person

knurl (nurl) *n.* [prob. < *knur*, a knot + GNARL] **1** a knot, knob, etc. **2** any of a series of small ridges, as along the edge of a coin — *vt.* to make knurls on

KO (kā'ō') [Slang] *vt.* **KO'd, KO'ing** *Boxing* to knock out —*n., pl.* **KO's** *Boxing* a knockout Also **K.O.** or **k.o.**

ko·a·la (kō ä'lə) *n.* [< native name] a tree-dwelling Australian marsupial with thick, gray fur

Ko·di·ak (kō'dē ak') island off the SW coast of Alaska

kohl·ra·bi (kōl rä'bē) *n., pl.* **-bies** [< It *cavolo rapa*] a vegetable related to the cabbage, with an enlarged, edible stem

ko·la (kō'lə) *n.* COLA (*n.* 1)

Kol·ka·ta (kōl kut'ə) seaport in NE India

kook (kook) *n.* [prob. < CUCKOO] [Slang] a person regarded as silly, eccentric, etc. — **kook'y** *adj.* **-i·er, -i·est**

kook·a·bur·ra (kook'ə bur'ə) *n.* [< native name] an Australian kingfisher with a harsh cry like loud laughter

ko·peck or **ko·pek** (kō'pek') *n.* [Russ < *kopye*, a lance] a 100th part of a ruble

Ko·ran (kə ran', kôr'an') *n.* [< Ar *qur'ān*, book] the sacred book of Islam

Ko·re·a (kə rē'ə) peninsula & country northeast of China: divided (1948) into **Korean People's Democratic Republic** (**North Korea**) and **Republic of Korea** (**South Korea**) —**Ko·re'an** *adj., n.*

ko·sher (kō'shər) *adj.* [< Heb *kāshēr*, proper] *Judaism* clean or fit to eat according to the dietary laws

kow·tow (kou'tou') *vi.* [Chin *k'o-t'ou*, lit., bump head] to show great deference, respect, etc. (*to*)

KP *abbrev.* kitchen police: a detail to assist the cooks in an army kitchen

kraal (kräl) *n.* [Afrik] **1** a village of South African native people **2** in South Africa, an enclosure for cattle or sheep

Krem·lin (krem'lin) *n.* [< Russ *kryeml'*] **1** the citadel of Moscow, housing many Russian, or, formerly, Soviet, government offices **2** the Russian, or, formerly, Soviet, government

Krish·na (krish'nə) *n.* a Hindu god, an incarnation of Vishnu

kro·na (krō'nə) *n., pl.* **-nor** (-nôr') [ult. < L *corona*, crown] the monetary unit of Sweden

kró·na (krō'nə) *n., pl.* **-nur** (-nər) [see prec.] the monetary unit of Iceland

kro·ne (krō'nə) *n., pl.* **-ner** (-nər) [see KRONA] the monetary unit of Denmark and Norway

kryp·ton (krip'tän') *n.* [< Gr *kryptos*, hidden] a mostly inert chemical element and one of the noble gases, used chiefly in fluorescent lamps: symbol, Kr; at. no. 36

KS *abbrev.* Kansas

K2 GODWIN AUSTEN

ku·chen (kōō'kən) *n.* [Ger, cake] a coffeecake made of yeast dough, often with raisins, nuts, etc.

ku·dos (kyōō'däs', kōō'-) *n.* [Gr *kydos*] credit for an achievement; glory; fame: often wrongly taken to be the plural (*pron.* -dōz') of an assumed word "*kudo*"

kud·zu (kood'zōō') *n.* [Jpn] a fast-growing perennial vine with large, three-part leaves, invasive in SE U.S.

Kui·per belt (ki'pər) [after G. P. *Kuiper* (1905-73), U.S. astronomer] a belt of icy debris orbiting in the outer solar system in the same plane as the planets, thought to be the source of many comets

Ku Klux Klan (kōō' kluks' klan') [< Gr *kyklos*, circle] a U.S. secret society that is anti-black, anti-Semitic, anti-Catholic, etc., and uses terrorist methods

kum·quat (kum'kwät') *n.* [< Mandarin *chin-chü*, lit., golden orange] a small, orange-colored, oval fruit with a sour pulp and a sweet rind

kung fu (koon' foo', goon'-) [< Chin] a Chinese system of self-defense, like karate but with circular movements

Ku·wait (kōō wāt′) independent Arab state in E Arabia —**Ku·wai′ti** (-wāt′ē) *adj., n.*

kvetch (kə vech′) *vi.* [< Yiddish] [Slang] to complain in a nagging way

kW or **kw** *abbrev.* kilowatt(s)

Kwang·chow (kwäŋ′chō′) *a former transliteration of* GUANGZHOU

Kwan·zaa (kwän′zä) *n.* [ult. < Swahili] an African-American cultural festival, Dec. 26 through Jan. 1

KY *abbrev.* Kentucky

Kyo·to (kē ōt′ō) city in S Honshu, Japan

Kyr·gyz·stan (kir′gi stan′) country in south-central Asia

L

l¹ or **L** (el) *n., pl.* **l's, L's** the 12th letter of the English alphabet

l² *abbrev.* **1** latitude **2** left **3** length **4** line **5** liter(s) **6** long **7** loss(es)

L¹ (el) *n., pl.* **L's 1** an extension forming an L with the main structure **2** a Roman numeral for 50

L² *abbrev.* **1** Lake **2** large **3** Latin **4** left **5** length **6** liter(s) **7** longitude **8** [L *libra, pl. librae*] pound(s): now usually £

la (lä) *n.* [< L] *Music* the sixth tone of the diatonic scale

LA *abbrev.* **1** Los Angeles **2** Louisiana

lab (lab) *n.* [Inf.] a laboratory

Lab (lab) *n. short for* LABRADOR RETRIEVER

la·bel (lā′bəl) *n.* [OFr, a rag] **1** a card, paper, etc. marked and attached to an object to indicate its contents, owner, destination, etc. **2** a term of generalized classification **3** a brand name, as of a record company —*vt.* **-beled** or **-belled, -bel·ing** or **-bel·ling 1** to attach a label to **2** to classify as

la·bi·al (lā′bē əl) *adj.* **1** of the lips **2** *Phonetics* articulated with one or both lips: said as of (f), (b), and (ü)

la·bi·um (lā′bē əm) *n., pl.* **-bi·a** (-ə) [L, lip] any of the four folds of tissue of the female external genitals

la·bor (lā′bər) *n.* [< L] **1** physical or mental exertion; work **2** a specific task **3** all wage-earning workers **4** labor unions collectively **5** the process of childbirth —*vi.* **1** to work **2** to work hard **3** to move slowly and with difficulty **4** to be burdened with a liability or limitation (with *under*) **5** to be in childbirth —*vt.* to develop in too great detail; belabor

lab·o·ra·to·ry (lab′rə tôr′ē) *n., pl.* **-ries** [see prec.] a room, building, etc. for scientific experimentation or research

Labor Day the first Monday in September, a legal holiday honoring working people

la·bored (lā′bərd) *adj.* made or done with great effort; strained

la·bor·er *n.* one who labors; esp., a wage-earning worker whose work is largely hard physical labor

la·bo·ri·ous (lə bôr′ē əs) *adj.* **1** involving much hard work; difficult **2** LABORED —**la·bo′ri·ous·ly** *adv.*

labor union an association of workers to promote and protect the welfare, rights, etc. of its members

la·bour (lā′bər) *n., vi., vt. Brit. sp. of* LABOR

lab·ra·doo·dle (lab′rə dōōd′'l) *n.* [< fol. + POODLE] a dog crossbred from a Labrador retriever and a poodle

Lab·ra·dor (lab′rə dôr′) **1** region along the Atlantic in NE Canada: the mainland part of Newfoundland and Labrador **2** large peninsula between the Atlantic & Hudson Bay, containing this region & much of Quebec

Labrador retriever a retriever with a short, dense, black, yellow, or brown coat

la·bur·num (lə bur′nəm) *n.* [< L] a small tree or shrub of the pea family, with drooping yellow flowers

lab·y·rinth (lab′ə rinth′) *n.* [< Gr *labyrinthos*] a structure containing winding passages hard to follow without losing one's way; maze

lac (lak) *n.* [< Sans *lākṣā*] a resinous substance secreted by a species of insect on certain trees in Asia: source of shellac

lace (lās) *n.* [< L *laqueus,* noose] **1** a string, etc. used to draw together and fasten the parts of a shoe, corset, etc. **2** a fine netting of cotton, silk, etc., woven in ornamental designs —*vt.* **laced, lac′ing 1** to fasten with a lace **2** to weave together; intertwine **3** to hit hard **4** *a)* to add a dash of alcoholic liquor to (a drink) *b)* to add a drug, poison, etc. to

lac·er·ate (las′ər āt′) *vt.* **-at′ed, -at′ing** [< L *lacer,* lacerated] to tear jaggedly; mangle (flesh, etc.) —**lac′er·a′tion** *n.*

lace·work *n.* lace, or any openwork decoration like lace

lach·ry·mal (lak′ri məl) *adj.* [< L *lacrima,* TEAR²] **1** of or producing tears **2** LACRIMAL (*adj.* 1)

lach·ry·mose (-mōs′) *adj.* [see prec.] shedding, or causing to shed, tears; tearful or sad

lack (lak) *n.* [< or akin to medieval LowG *lak*] **1** the fact or state of not having enough or not having any **2** the thing that is needed —*vt., vi.* to be deficient in or entirely without (something)

lack·a·dai·si·cal (lak′ə dā′zi kəl) *adj.* 〚< archaic *lackaday*, an exclamation of regret, etc.〛 showing lack of interest or spirit; listless

lack·ey (lak′ē) *n., pl.* **-eys** 〚< Sp *lacayo*〛 1 a male servant of low rank 2 a servile follower; toady

lack·lus·ter (lak′lus′tər) *adj.* 1 lacking brightness; dull 2 lacking vitality; boring

la·con·ic (lə kän′ik) *adj.* 〚< Gr *Lakōn*, a Spartan〛 terse in expression; concise —**la·con′i·cal·ly** *adv.*

lac·quer (lak′ər) *n.* 〚< Fr < Port *laca*, lac〛 1 a coating substance made of shellac, gum resins, etc. dissolved in ethyl alcohol or another volatile solvent 2 a resinous varnish obtained from certain E Asian trees —*vt.* to coat with lacquer

lac·ri·mal (lak′ri məl) *adj.* 1 of or near the glands that secrete tears 2 LACHRYMAL (*adj.* 1)

la·crosse (lə krôs′) *n.* 〚CdnFr, lit., the crutch〛 a ballgame played by two teams using long-handled, pouched rackets

lac·tate (lak′tāt′) *vi.* **-tat′ed, -tat′ing** to secrete milk

lac·ta·tion (lak tā′shən) *n.* 〚< L *lac*, milk〛 1 the secretion of milk by a mammary gland 2 the period during which milk is secreted

lac·te·al (lak′tē əl) *adj.* 〚< L *lac*, milk〛 of or like milk; milky

lac·tic (lak′tik) *adj.* 〚< L *lac*, milk〛 of or obtained from milk

lactic acid a clear, syrupy acid formed when milk sours

lac·tose (lak′tōs′) *n.* 〚< L *lac*, milk〛 a sugar found in milk: used in foods

la·cu·na (lə kyōō′nə) *n., pl.* **-nas** or **-nae** (-nē) 〚L, a ditch〛 a blank space; esp., a missing portion in a text, etc.

lac·y (lās′ē) *adj.* **-i·er, -i·est** of or like lace —**lac′i·ness** *n.*

lad (lad) *n.* 〚ME *ladde*〛 a boy; youth

lad·der (lad′ər) *n.* 〚OE *hlæder*〛 1 a framework consisting of two sidepieces connected by a series of rungs, for use in climbing up or down 2 any means of climbing

lad·die (lad′ē) *n.* [Chiefly Scot.] a young lad

lad·en (lād′'n) *adj.* 〚< OE〛 1 loaded 2 burdened

la-di-da (lä′dē dä′) *adj.* 〚imitative〛 [Inf.] affectedly refined: also **la′-de-da′**

lad·ing (lād′iŋ) *n.* a load; cargo; freight

la·dle (lād′'l) *n.* 〚OE *hlædel*〛 a long-handled, cuplike spoon, used for serving soup, etc. —*vt.* **-dled, -dling** to dip out with a ladle

la·dy (lād′ē) *n., pl.* **-dies** 〚< OE *hlāf*, loaf + *dæge*, kneader〛 1 a) a woman of high social position b) a woman who is polite, refined, etc. 2 any woman: used (in pl.) to address a group 3 [**L-**] a British title given to women of certain ranks

la·dy·bug *n.* a small, roundish beetle with a spotted back: also **la′dy·bird′**

la·dy·fin·ger *n.* a small spongecake shaped somewhat like a finger

la·dy-in-wait·ing *n., pl.* **la′dies-in-wait′ing** a woman acting as an attendant to a queen or princess

la·dy·like *adj.* like or suitable for a lady; refined; well-bred

la·dy·love *n.* [Old-fashioned] a female sweetheart

la·dy·ship *n.* 1 the rank or position of a lady 2 [*usually* L-] a title used in speaking to or of a woman holding the rank of lady

la·dy's-slip·per *n.* an orchid with flowers shaped like slippers: also **la′dy-slip′per**

la·e·trile (lā′ə tril′) *n.* any of several compounds obtained chiefly from apricot kernels, claimed by some to be effective in treating cancer

La·fa·yette (lä′fē et′, -fä-), Marquis **de** 1757-1834; Fr. general: served (1777-81) in the American Revolutionary army

lag (lag) *vi.* **lagged, lag′ging** 〚< ?〛 1 to fall behind or move slowly; loiter 2 to become less intense —*n.* 1 a falling behind 2 the amount of this

la·ger (beer) (lä′gər) 〚Ger *lagerbier*, storehouse beer〛 a beer aged at a low temperature

lag·gard (lag′ərd) *n.* 〚< LAG + -ARD〛 a slow person, esp. one who falls behind —*adj.* slow; falling behind

la·gniappe or **la·gnappe** (lan yap′, lan′yap′) *n.* 〚Creole < Fr & Sp〛 1 [Chiefly South] a small present given to a customer 2 a gratuity

la·goon (lə gōōn′) *n.* 〚< L *lacuna*, pool〛 1 a shallow lake or pond, esp. one connected with a larger body of water 2 the water enclosed by a circular coral reef 3 an area of shallow salt water separated from the sea by sand dunes

La·hore (lə hôr′) city in NE Pakistan

laid (lād) *vt., vi. pt. & pp. of* LAY[1]

laid-back *adj.* [Slang] relaxed, easygoing, etc.; not frenetic or hurried

lain (lān) *vi. pp. of* LIE[1]

lair (ler) *n.* 〚OE *leger*〛 a resting place of a wild animal; den

lais·sez faire (les′ā fer′) 〚Fr, allow to do〛 noninterference; specif., absence of government control over industry and business

la·i·ty (lā′i tē) *n., pl.* **-ties** 〚< LAY[3]〛 laymen collectively

lake (lāk) *n.* 〚< L *lacus*〛 1 a large inland body of usually fresh water 2 a pool of oil or other liquid

lake·front *n.* the land along the shore of a lake —*adj.* near, at, or of the lakefront

lal·ly·gag (lä′lē gag′) *vi.* **-gagged′, -gag′ging** [Inf.] LOLLYGAG

lam (lam) [Slang] *n.* 〚< ?〛 headlong flight —*vi.* **lammed, lam′ming** to flee; escape —**on the lam** in flight, as from the police

la·ma (lä′mə) *n.* 〚Tibetan *blama*〛 a priest or monk in Lamaism

La·ma·ism (lä′mə iz′əm) *n.* a form of Buddhism in Tibet and Mongolia

la·ma·ser·y (lä′mə ser′ē) *n., pl.* **-ies** a monastery of lamas

La·maze (lə mäz′) *n.* 〚after F. *Lamaze* (1890-1957), Fr physician〛 a training program in natural childbirth, involving the help of the father

lamb (lam) *n.* ⟦OE⟧ **1** a young sheep **2** its flesh, used as food **3** a gentle, innocent, or gullible person

lam·baste (lam bāst′, -bast′) *vt.* **-bast′ed, -bast′ing** [< *lam*, to beat + *baste*, to flog] [Inf.] **1** to beat soundly **2** to scold or denounce severely

lamb·da (lam′də) *n.* the 11th letter of the Greek alphabet (Λ, λ)

lam·bent (lam′bənt) *adj.* [< L *lambere*, to lick] **1** playing lightly over a surface: said of a flame, etc. **2** glowing softly **3** light and graceful *[lambent* wit] —**lam′ben·cy** *n.*

lam·bic (lam′bik) *n.* [Fr < Du] a Belgian beer of malted barley and unmalted wheat fermented by naturally occurring airborne yeast, often flavored with fruit

lame (lām) *adj.* ⟦OE *lama*⟧ **1** crippled; esp., having an injury that makes one limp **2** stiff and painful **3** poor; ineffectual *[a lame* excuse] —*vt.* **lamed, lam′ing** to make lame —**lame′ly** *adv.* —**lame′ness** *n.*

la·mé (la mā′, lä-) *n.* [< Fr *lame*, metal plate] a cloth interwoven with metal threads, as of gold

lame duck an elected official regarded as ineffective because his or her term is about to end

la·mel·la (lə mel′ə) *n., pl.* **-lae** (-ē) or **-las** [L] a thin plate, scale, or layer

la·ment (lə ment′) *vi., vt.* [< L *lamentum,* a wailing] to feel or express deep sorrow (for); mourn —*n.* **1** a lamenting **2** an elegy, dirge, etc. mourning some loss or death —**lam·en·ta·ble** (lam′ən tə bəl, lə men′-) *adj.* —**lam·en·ta·tion** (lam′ən tā′shən) *n.*

lam·i·na (lam′i nə) *n., pl.* **-nae** (-nē′) or **-nas** [L] a thin scale or layer, as of metal, tissue, etc.

lam·i·nate (lam′i nāt′; *for adj. usually,* -nit) *vt.* **-nat′ed, -nat′ing** [see prec.] **1** to cover with one or more thin layers **2** to make by building up in layers —*adj.* **LAMINATED** —**lam′i·na′tion** *n.*

lam·i·nat·ed *adj.* **1** built in thin sheets or layers **2** covered with a thin protective layer, as of clear plastic

lamp (lamp) *n.* [< Gr *lampein,* to shine] **1** a container with a wick for burning oil, etc. to produce light or heat **2** any device for producing light or heat, as an electric light bulb **3** a holder or base for such a device

lamp·black *n.* fine soot used as a black pigment

lam·poon (lam pōōn′) *n.* [< Fr *lampons,* let us drink: used as a refrain] a satirical writing attacking someone —*vt.* to attack in a lampoon

lamp·post (lamp′pōst′) *n.* a post supporting a street lamp

lam·prey (lam′prē) *n., pl.* **-preys** [< ML *lampreda*] an eel-like fish with a jawless, sucking mouth, often parasitic on other fish

la·na·i (lə nä′ē, -nī′) *n.* [Haw] a veranda or open-sided living room

lance (lans) *n.* [< L *lancea*] **1** a long, wooden

spear with a sharp metal head **2** *a)* LANCER *b)* LANCET **3** any instrument like a lance —*vt.* **lanced, lanc′ing 1** to pierce with a lance **2** to cut open (a boil, etc.) with a lancet

Lan·ce·lot (lan′sə lät′, -lət) *n.* the most celebrated of the Knights of the Round Table

lanc·er (lans′ər) *n.* a cavalry soldier armed with a lance

lan·cet (lan′sit) *n.* [< OFr dim. of *lance,* lance] a small, pointed surgical knife, usually two-edged

land (land) *n.* ⟦OE⟧ **1** the solid part of the earth's surface **2** a country or nation **3** ground or soil **4** real estate —*vt.* **1** to put on shore from a ship **2** to bring to a particular place or condition *[it landed* him in jail] **3** to set (an aircraft) down on land or water **4** to catch *[to land* a fish] **5** [Inf.] to get or secure *[to land* a job] **6** [Inf.] to deliver (a blow) —*vi.* **1** to leave a ship and go on shore **2** to come to a port, etc.: said of a ship **3** to arrive at a specified place **4** to come to rest

land contract a real estate contract in which a buyer pays in installments, receiving title to the property once the full price is paid

land·ed *adj.* owning land *[landed* gentry]

land·fall *n.* **1** a sighting of land from a ship at sea **2** the land sighted

land·fill *n.* **1** a place used to dispose of garbage by burying it in the ground **2** garbage, etc. so disposed of

land grant a grant of land by the government for a railroad, state college, etc.

land·hold·er *n.* an owner of land —**land′hold′ ing** *adj., n.*

land·ing *n.* **1** the act of coming to shore **2** a place where a ship or boat is loaded or unloaded **3** a platform at the end of a flight of stairs **4** the act of alighting, as after a flight or jump

landing gear the system of parts on an aircraft or spacecraft used for support or mobility on land or water

land·line *n.* **1** a telephone line that is part of a network of lines connected by wires and cables underground or on poles **2** a telephone connected to such a line

land·locked *adj.* **1** surrounded by land, as a country **2** cut off from the open sea and confined to fresh water *[landlocked* salmon]

land·lord *n.* **1** a person who leases land, houses, etc. to others **2** a man who keeps a rooming house, inn, etc.

land·la·dy *n.* **1** a woman who leases land, houses, etc. to others **2** a woman who keeps a rooming house, inn, etc.

land·lub·ber (-lub′ər) *n.* one who has had little experience on boats or ships

land·mark *n.* **1** an object that marks the boundary of a piece of land **2** any prominent feature of the landscape, distinguishing a locality **3** an important event or turning point

land·mass *n.* a very large area of land; esp., a continent

land office a government office that handles the sales of public lands

land·scape (-skāp′) *n.* ⟦< Du *land*, land + *-schap*, -ship⟧ **1** a picture of natural, inland scenery **2** an expanse of natural scenery **3** the conditions of a particular time and place [the *political* landscape] —*vt.* **-scaped′, -scap′ing** to make (a plot of ground) more attractive, as by adding a lawn, trees, bushes, etc. —**land′scap′er** *n.*

land·slide *n.* **1** the sliding of a mass of earth or rocks down a slope **2** the mass sliding down **3** an overwhelming victory, esp. in an election

land·ward (-wərd) *adv., adj.* toward the land: also **land′wards** *adv.*

lane (lān) *n.* ⟦OE *lanu*⟧ **1** a narrow way, path, road, etc. **2** a path or route designated, for reasons of safety, for ships, aircraft, automobiles, etc. **3** *Bowling* a long, narrow strip of polished wood, along which the balls are rolled

lan·guage (laŋ′gwij) *n.* ⟦< L *lingua*, tongue⟧ **1** human speech or the written symbols for speech **2** *a)* any means of communicating, as by gestures, signs, etc. *b)* a system of rules and instructions used in programming a computer, etc. **3** the speech of a particular nation, etc. [the French *language*] **4** the particular style of verbal expression characteristic of a person, group, profession, etc.

lan·guid (laŋ′gwid) *adj.* ⟦< L *languere*, be weary⟧ **1** without vigor or vitality; weak **2** listless; indifferent **3** slow; dull —**lan′guid·ly** *adv.*

lan·guish (-gwish) *vi.* [see prec.] **1** to become weak; droop **2** to live under distressing conditions [to *languish* in poverty] **3** to long; pine **4** to put on an air of sentimental tenderness

lan·guor (laŋ′gər) *n.* [see LANGUID] lack of vigor or vitality; weakness; listlessness —**lan′guor·ous** *adj.*

lank (laŋk) *adj.* ⟦OE *hlanc*⟧ **1** long and slender **2** straight and limp: said of hair

lank·y (laŋ′kē) *adj.* **-i·er, -i·est** awkwardly tall and lean

lan·o·lin (lan′ə lin′) *n.* ⟦< L *lana*, wool + *oleum*, oil⟧ a fatty substance obtained from wool and used in ointments, cosmetics, etc.

Lan·sing (lan′siŋ) capital of Michigan, in the SC part

lan·tern (lan′tərn) *n.* ⟦ult. < Gr *lampein*, to shine⟧ a transparent case for holding and shielding a light

lan·tern-jawed *adj.* having long, thin jaws and sunken cheeks

lan·tha·num (lan′thə nəm) *n.* ⟦< Gr *lanthanein*, to escape notice⟧ a soft, malleable, silvery-white chemical element: symbol, La; at. no. 57

lan·yard (lan′yərd) *n.* ⟦< OFr *lasne*, noose⟧ a short rope used on board ship for holding or fastening something

La·os (lä′ōs′) country in the NW part of Indochina —**La·o·tian** (lā ō′shən) *adj., n.*

lap¹ (lap) *n.* ⟦OE *læppa*⟧ **1** the front part, from the waist to the knees, of a sitting person **2** the part of the clothing covering this **3** that in which a person or thing is cared for **4** *a)* an overlapping *b)* a part that overlaps **5** one complete circuit of a racetrack —*vt.* **lapped, lap′ping 1** to fold (*over* or *on*) **2** to wrap; enfold **3** to overlap **4** to get a lap ahead of (an opponent) in a race —*vi.* **1** to overlap **2** to extend beyond something in space or time: with *over*

lap² (lap) *vi., vt.* **lapped, lap′ping** ⟦OE *lapian*⟧ **1** to drink (a liquid) by dipping it up with the tongue as a dog does **2** to strike gently with a light splash: said of waves —*n.* **1** a lapping **2** the sound of lapping

La Paz (lə päz′) city & seat of government of Bolivia

lap·board *n.* a board placed on the lap for use as a table or desk

lap dog 1 any pet dog small enough to be held in the lap **2** a fawning or submissive person Also written **lap′dog′** *n.*

la·pel (lə pel′) *n.* ⟦dim. of LAP¹⟧ the front part of a coat folded back and forming a continuation of the collar

lap·i·dar·y (lap′ə der′ē) *n., pl.* **-dar′ies** ⟦< L *lapis*, a stone⟧ one who cuts and polishes precious stones —*adj.* **1** of the art of a lapidary **2** precise and elegant [*lapidary* prose]

lap·in (lap′in) *n.* ⟦Fr, rabbit⟧ rabbit fur, often dyed to resemble other skins

lap·is laz·u·li (lap′is laz′yōō li′, -lazh′-; -lē′) ⟦< L *lapis*, a stone + ML *lazulus*, azure⟧ an azure, opaque, semiprecious stone

Lap·land (lap′land′) region of N Europe, including the N parts of Norway, Sweden, & Finland

Lapp (lap) *n.* ⟦Swed⟧ the indigenous people of Lapland: now somewhat dated, the preferred term being SAMI

lap·pet (lap′it) *n.* ⟦dim. of LAP¹⟧ a loose flap or fold of a garment or head covering

lapse (laps) *n.* ⟦< L *labi*, to slip⟧ **1** a small error **2** *a)* a moral slip *b)* a falling into a lower condition **3** a passing, as of time **4** the termination as of a privilege through failure to meet requirements —*vi.* **lapsed, laps′ing 1** to fall into a specified state [he *lapsed* into silence] **2** to backslide **3** to elapse **4** to come to an end; stop **5** to become void because of failure to meet requirements

lap·top *n.* a small, light, portable computer having, in a single unit, a CPU, keyboard, screen, etc.

lar·board (lär′bərd) *adj., n.* ⟦< OE *hladan*, lade + *bord*, side⟧ (of) the port side of a ship

lar·ce·ny (lär′sə nē) *n., pl.* **-nies** ⟦ult. < L *latro*, robber⟧ the unlawful taking of another's property; theft —**lar′ce·nist** *n.* —**lar′ce·nous** *adj.*

larch (lärch) *n.* ⟦< L *larix*⟧ **1** a tree of the pine family that sheds its needles annually **2** its tough wood

lard (lärd) *n.* ⟦< L *lardum*⟧ a white, soft solid made by melting the fat of hogs —*vt.* **1** to put strips of fat pork, bacon, etc. on (meat, etc.) before cooking **2** to embellish [a talk *larded* with jokes]

lard·er *n.* **1** a place where food supplies are kept; pantry **2** a stock of food supplies

large (lärj) *adj.* **larg′er**, **larg′est** ⟦< L *largus*⟧ **1** of great extent or amount; big, bulky, spacious, etc. **2** bigger than others of its kind **3** operating on a big scale [a large producer] —*adv.* in a large way [write *large*] —**at large 1** free; not confined **2** taken altogether **3** representing no particular district [a congressman *at large*] —**large′ness** *n.* —**larg′ish** *adj.*

large·heart·ed *adj.* generous; kindly

large intestine the relatively large section of the intestines of vertebrates, including the cecum, colon, and rectum

large·ly *adv.* for the most part; mainly

large-scale *adj.* **1** drawn to a large scale **2** of wide scope; extensive

lar·gess or **lar·gesse** (lär jes′, lär′jis) *n.* ⟦see LARGE⟧ **1** generous giving **2** a gift or gifts generously given

lar·go (lär′gō) *adj., adv.* ⟦It, slow⟧ *Music* slow and stately

lar·i·at (lar′ē ət) *n.* ⟦Sp *la reata*, the rope⟧ **1** a rope used for tethering grazing horses, etc. **2** LASSO

lark[1] (lärk) *n.* ⟦< OE *lœwerce*⟧ any of a large family of chiefly Old World birds, esp. the skylark

lark[2] (lärk) *vi.* ⟦? < ON *leika*⟧ to play or frolic —*n.* a frolic or spree

lark·spur (lärk′spur′) *n.* DELPHINIUM

lar·va (lär′və) *n., pl.* **-vae′** (-vē′) or **-vas** ⟦L, ghost⟧ the early form of any animal that changes structurally when it becomes an adult [the tadpole is the *larva* of the frog] —**lar′val** *adj.*

lar·yn·gi·tis (lar′in jīt′is) *n.* an inflammation of the larynx, often with a temporary loss of voice

lar·ynx (lar′iŋks) *n., pl.* **lar′ynx·es** or **la·ryn·ges** (lə rin′jēz′) ⟦< Gr⟧ the structure at the upper end of the trachea, containing the vocal cords

la·sa·gna (lə zän′yə) *n.* ⟦It⟧ a dish of wide noodles baked in layers usually with tomato sauce, ground meat, and cheese

las·civ·i·ous (lə siv′ē əs) *adj.* ⟦< L *lascivus*, wanton⟧ **1** characterized by or expressing lust **2** exciting lust

la·ser (lā′zər) *n.* ⟦*l(ight) a(mplification by) s(timulated) e(mission of) r(adiation)*⟧ a device containing a substance whose atoms or molecules can be raised to a higher energy state, so that it emits light in an intense, narrow beam

la·ser·disc *n.* an optical disk for recording audio and video data: also **la′ser·disk′**, **laser disc**, or **laser disk**

lash[1] (lash) *n.* ⟦< ?⟧ **1** the flexible striking part of a whip **2** a stroke as with a whip **3** an eyelash —*vt.* **1** to strike or drive as with a lash **2** to jerk or swing sharply [the cat *lashed* her tail] **3** to censure or rebuke —*vi.* to make strokes as with a whip —**lash out 1** to strike out violently **2** to speak angrily

lash[2] (lash) *vt.* ⟦see LACE⟧ to fasten or tie with a rope, etc.

LASIK (lā′sik, -zik) *n.* ⟦*las(er-assisted) i(n situ) k(eratomileusis)* < ModL *keratomileusis*, a cutting of the cornea⟧ a type of eye surgery to correct vision, involving the use of a laser to reshape the cornea

lass (las) *n.* ⟦prob. < ON *lskr*, weak⟧ a young woman

las·sie (las′ē) *n.* [Scot.] a young woman

las·si·tude (las′i tōōd′) *n.* ⟦< L *lassus*, faint⟧ weariness; languor

las·so (las′ō) *n., pl.* **-sos** or **-soes** ⟦< Sp < L *laqueus*, noose⟧ a rope with a sliding noose used to catch cattle, etc. —*vt.* **-soed**, **-so·ing** to catch with a lasso

last[1] (last) *adj.* **1** *alt. superl.* of LATE **2** being or coming after all others in place or time; final **3** only remaining **4** most recent [last month] **5** least likely [the *last* person to suspect] **6** conclusive [the *last* word] —*adv.* **1** after all others **2** most recently **3** finally; in conclusion —*n.* the one coming last —**at (long) last** after a long time; finally

last[2] (last) *vi.* ⟦OE *lœstan*⟧ to remain in existence, use, etc.; endure —*vt.* **1** to continue during **2** to be enough for

last[3] (last) *n.* ⟦< OE *lāst*, footstep⟧ a form shaped like the foot, used in making or repairing shoes

last hurrah a final attempt or appearance

last·ing *adj.* that lasts a long time —**last′ing·ly** *adv.*

Last Judgment *Theol.* the final judgment at the end of the world

last·ly *adv.* in conclusion; finally

last straw ⟦< the straw that broke the camel's back⟧ a final trouble that results in a defeat, loss of patience, etc.: with *the*

Las Ve·gas (läs vā′gəs) city in SE Nevada

lat *abbrev.* latitude

Lat *abbrev.* Latin

latch (lach) *n.* ⟦< OE *lœccan*⟧ a fastening for a door, gate, or window; esp., a bar that fits into a notch —*vt., vi.* to fasten with a latch —**latch onto** [Inf.] to get or obtain

late (lāt) *adj.* **lat′er** or **lat′ter**, **lat′est** or **last** ⟦OE *lœt*⟧ **1** happening, coming, etc. after the usual or expected time, or at a time far advanced in a period [late to class, *late* Victorian] **2** recent **3** having recently died —*adv.* **lat′er**, **lat′est** or **last 1** after the expected time **2** at or until an advanced time of the day, year, etc. **3** toward the end of a period **4** recently —**of late** recently —**late′ness** *n.*

late·ly *adv.* recently; not long ago

la·tent (lāt′'nt) *adj.* ⟦< L *latere*, lurk⟧ lying hidden and undeveloped in a person or thing —**la′ten·cy** *n.*

lat·er·al (lat′ər əl) *adj.* ⟦< L *latus*, a side⟧ of, at, from, or toward the side; sideways —**lat′er·al·ly** *adv.*

la·tex (lā′teks′) *n.* ⟦L, a fluid⟧ **1** a milky liquid in certain plants and trees: used esp. as the basis of rubber **2** a suspension in water of particles of rubber or plastic: used in adhesives, paints, etc.

lath (lath) *n., pl.* **laths** (la*th*z, laths) ⟦< ME⟧ **1** any of the thin, narrow strips of wood used as a foundation for plaster, etc. **2** any foundation for plaster

lathe (lā*th*) *n.* ⟦prob. < MDu *lade*⟧ a machine for shaping wood, metal, etc. by spinning it rapidly on an axis while applying a chisel or other cutting tool —*vt.* **lathed**, **lath′ing** to shape on a lathe

lath·er (la*th*′ər) *n.* ⟦OE *leathor*, soap⟧ **1** a foam of soap and water **2** foamy sweat, as on a racehorse **3** [Slang] an excited state —*vt., vi.* to cover with or form lather

Lat·in (lat′'n) *adj.* ⟦< *Latium*, ancient country in central Italy⟧ **1** of ancient Rome or its people, language, etc. **2** designating one of the languages derived from Latin, the peoples that speak them, their countries, etc. —*n.* **1** a person born or living in ancient Rome **2** the language of ancient Rome **3** a person whose language is derived from Latin, as a Spaniard, Italian, or Latin American

Latin America that part of the Western Hemisphere south of the U.S. where Spanish, Portuguese, & French are the official languages —**Latin American**

La·ti·no (la tē′nō) *n., pl.* **-nos** ⟦< L *Latīnus*, LATIN⟧ a Latin American, esp. one from a Spanish-speaking culture who lives in the U.S. —*adj.* of or relating to Latinos Now often preferred to *Hispanic*—

La·ti·na (-nə) *n.* ⟦see prec.⟧ a Latin American girl or woman, esp. one from a Spanish-speaking culture who lives in the U.S. —*adj.* of or relating to Latinas

lat·ish (lāt′ish) *adj., adv.* somewhat late

lat·i·tude (lat′ə tōōd′) *n.* ⟦< L *latus*, wide⟧ **1** freedom from narrow restrictions **2** *a*) distance, measured in degrees, north or south from the equator *b*) a region with reference to this distance

la·trine (lə trēn′) *n.* ⟦< L *lavare*, to wash⟧ a toilet for the use of a large number of people, as in an army camp

lat·te (lä′tä) *n.* ⟦It⟧ espresso coffee mixed with steamed milk

lat·ter (lat′ər) *adj.* ⟦orig. compar. of LATE⟧ **1** *alt. compar. of* LATE **2** *a*) later; more recent *b*) nearer the end or close **3** being the last mentioned of two

lat·tice (lat′is) *n.* ⟦< OHG *latta*, lath⟧ an openwork structure of crossed strips of wood, metal, etc. used as a screen, support, etc.

lat·tice·work *n.* **1** a lattice **2** lattices collectively

Lat·vi·a (lat′vē ə) country in N Europe —**Lat′vi·an** *adj., n.*

laud (lôd) *vt.* ⟦< L *laus*, glory⟧ to praise; extol

laud·a·ble *adj.* praiseworthy; commendable

lau·da·num (lôd′'n əm) *n.* ⟦< L *ladanum*, a dark resin⟧ a solution of opium in alcohol

laud·a·to·ry (lôd′ə tôr′ē) *adj.* expressing praise; commendary

laugh (laf) *vi.* ⟦< OE *hleahhan*⟧ to make the

sounds and facial movements that express mirth, ridicule, etc. —*n.* **1** the act or sound of laughing **2** a cause of laughter **3** [*pl.*] [Inf.] mere diversion or pleasure —**laugh at 1** to be amused by **2** to make fun of

laugh·a·ble *adj.* amusing or ridiculous —**laugh′a·bly** *adv.*

laugh·ing·stock *n.* an object of ridicule

laugh·ter *n.* the action or sound of laughing

launch¹ (lônch) *vt.* ⟦< L *lancea*, a lance⟧ **1** to hurl or send forth with some force [to launch a rocket] **2** to slide (a new vessel) into the water **3** to set in operation or on some course; start [to launch an attack] —*vi.* **1** to start something new: often with *out* or *forth* **2** to plunge (*into*) —*n.* a launching —**launch′er** *n.*

launch² (lônch) *n.* ⟦Sp or Port *lancha*⟧ an open, or partly enclosed, motorboat

launch·pad *n.* the platform from which a rocket, etc. is launched: also **launching pad**

laun·der (lôn′dər) *vt.* ⟦< L *lavare*, to wash⟧ **1** to wash, or wash and iron (clothes, etc.) **2** to exchange or invest (illegally gotten money) so as to conceal its source —**laun′der·er** *n.* —**laun′dress** (-dris) *n.*

laun·dro·mat (lôn′drə mat′) *n.* ⟦< *Laundromat*, a former service mark⟧ a self-service laundry

laun·dry (lôn′drē) *n., pl.* **-dries 1** a place for laundering **2** clothes, etc. laundered or to be laundered

lau·re·ate (lôr′ē it) *adj.* ⟦< L *laurus*, laurel⟧ honored, as with a crown of laurel —*n.* POET LAUREATE

lau·rel (lôr′əl) *n.* ⟦< L *laurus*⟧ **1** an evergreen tree or shrub of S Europe, with large, glossy leaves **2** its foliage, esp. as woven into wreaths once used to crown the victors in contests **3** [*pl.*] fame; honor **4** any of various trees and shrubs resembling the true laurel

la·va (lä′və, lav′ə) *n.* ⟦It < L *labi*, to slide⟧ **1** melted rock issuing from a volcano **2** such rock when solidified by cooling

lav·a·liere or **lav·a·lier** (lav′ə lir′, lä′və-) *n.* ⟦< Fr⟧ an ornament on a chain, worn around the neck

lav·a·to·ry (lav′ə tôr′ē) *n., pl.* **-ries** ⟦< L *lavare*, to wash⟧ a room with a washbowl and a toilet

lave (lāv) *vt., vi.* **laved**, **lav′ing** ⟦< L *lavare*⟧ [Old Poet.] to wash or bathe

lav·en·der (lav′ən dər) *n.* ⟦< ML *lavandria*⟧ **1** a fragrant European plant of the mint family with spikes of pale-purplish flowers **2** its dried flowers and leaves, used to perfume clothes, etc. **3** a pale purple —*adj.* pale-purple

lav·ish (lav′ish) *adj.* ⟦< OFr *lavasse*, downpour⟧ **1** very generous; prodigal **2** very abundant —*vt.* to give or spend generously —**lav′ish·ly** *adv.*

law (lô) *n.* ⟦OE *lagu*⟧ **1** *a*) all the rules of conduct established by the authority or custom of a nation, etc. *b*) any one of such rules **2** obedience to such rules **3** the study of such rules; jurisprudence **4** the seeking of justice in courts under such rules **5** the profession of lawyers, judges, etc. **6** *a)* a sequence of natural events occurring with unvarying uniformity under the same conditions *b)* the stating of such a sequence 7 any rule expected to be observed *[the laws of health]* —**the Law 1** the Mosaic law, or the part of the Jewish Scriptures containing it **2** [**the l–**] [Inf.] a policeman or the police

law·a·bid·ing *adj.* obeying the law

law·break·er *n.* a person who violates the law —**law′break′ing** *adj., n.*

law·ful *adj.* **1** in conformity with the law **2** recognized by law *[lawful debts]* —**law′ful·ly** *adv.*

law·giv·er *n.* a lawmaker; legislator

law·less *adj.* **1** not regulated by the authority of law **2** not in conformity with law; illegal **3** not obeying the law; unruly —**law′less·ness** *n.*

law·mak·er *n.* one who makes or helps to make laws; esp., a legislator

lawn¹ (lôn) *n.* [< OFr *launde*, heath] land covered with grass kept closely mowed, esp. around a house

lawn² (lôn) *n.* [after *Laon*, city in France] a fine, sheer cloth of linen or cotton

lawn bowling a bowling game played on a smooth lawn with wooden balls

lawn mower a machine for cutting the grass of a lawn

Law·rence (lôr′əns), **D(avid) H(erbert)** 1885–1930; Eng. novelist & poet

law·ren·ci·um (lô ren′sē əm) *n.* [after Ernest *Lawrence* (1901-58), U.S. physicist] a radioactive, metallic chemical element; symbol, Lr; at. no. 103

law·suit *n.* a suit between private parties in a law court

law·yer (lô′yər) *n.* one whose profession is advising others in matters of law or representing them in lawsuits

lax (laks) *adj.* [< L *laxus*] **1** loose; slack **2** not strict or exact —**lax′ly** *adv.*

lax·a·tive (lak′sə tiv) *adj.* [see prec.] making the bowels loose and relieving constipation —*n.* any laxative medicine

lax·i·ty (lak′si tē) *n.* lax quality or condition

lay¹ (lā) *vt.* **laid**, **lay′ing** [< OE *lecgan*] **1** to cause to fall with force; knock down **2** to place or put in a resting position: often with *on* or *in* **3** to put down (bricks, carpeting, etc.) in the correct position or way **4** to place; put; set *[to lay emphasis on accuracy]* **5** to produce (an egg) **6** to allay, suppress, etc. **7** to bet (a specified sum, etc.) **8** to devise *[to lay plans]* **9** to present or assert *[to lay claim to property]* —*n.* the way or position in which something is situated *[the lay of the land]* —**lay aside** to put away for future use; save: also **lay away** or **lay by** —**lay in** to get and store away —**lay into** [Slang] to attack with blows or words —**lay off 1** to discharge (an employee), esp. to cut costs or because of reorganization **2** [Slang] to cease —**lay open 1** to cut open **2** to expose —**lay out 1** to

spend **2** to arrange according to a plan **3** to spread out (clothes, etc.) ready for wear, etc. —**lay over** to stop a while in a place before going on —**lay to rest** to inter —**lay up 1** to store for future use **2** to confine to a sickbed

lay² (lā) *vi. pt. of* LIE¹

lay³ (lā) *adj.* [< Gr *laos*, the people] **1** of a layman **2** not belonging to a given profession

lay⁴ (lā) *n.* [ME & OFr *lai*] **1** a short poem, esp. a narrative poem, orig. for singing **2** [Obs.] a song

lay·a·way *n.* a method of buying by making a deposit on something which is delivered only after full payment

lay·er *n.* **1** a person or thing that lays **2** a single thickness, fold, etc.

lay·ette (lā et′) *n.* [< MDu *lade*, chest] a complete outfit of clothes, bedding, etc. for a newborn baby

lay·man (lā′mən) *n., pl.* **-men** (-mən) **1** a man who is not a cleric **2** a man who is not a professional in a given field

lay·off *n.* the dismissal of one or more employees, esp. to cut costs or because of reorganization

lay·out *n.* **1** the manner in which anything is laid out; specif., the makeup of a newspaper, advertisement, etc. **2** the thing laid out

lay·o·ver *n.* a stop during a journey

lay·per·son *n.* **1** one who is not a cleric **2** one who is not a professional in a given field

lay·wom·an *n., pl.* **-wom′en 1** a woman who is not a cleric **2** a woman who is not a professional in a given field

Laz·a·rus (laz′ə rəs) *n. Bible* a man raised from the dead by Jesus

laze (lāz) *vi., vt.* **lazed**, **laz′ing** to idle or loaf

la·zy (lā′zē) *adj.* **-zi·er**, **-zi·est** [prob. < medieval LowG or MDu] **1** not eager or willing to work or exert oneself **2** sluggish — *vi., vt.* **-zied**, **-zy·ing** LAZE —**la′zi·ly** *adv.* —**la′zi·ness** *n.*

la·zy·bones *n.* [Inf.] a lazy person

Lazy Su·san (sōō′zən) a rotating tray for food

lb *symbol* [abbrev. for *libra*: see LIRA] pound; pounds: also, for the plural, **lbs**

l.c. *abbrev.* [L *loco citato*] in the place cited

LCD *n.* [l(iquid-)c(rystal) d(isplay)] a device for electronic displays using a crystalline liquid

LD *abbrev.* **1** learning disability **2** learning-disabled

lea (lē) *n.* [OE *leah*] [Old Poet.] a meadow

leach (lēch) *vt.* [prob. < OE *leccan*, to water] **1** to wash (some material) with a filtering liquid **2** to extract (a soluble substance) from some material —*vi.* to dissolve and be washed away

lead¹ (lēd) *vt.* **led**, **lead′ing** [OE *lædan*] **1** to direct, as by going before or along with, by physical contact, pulling a rope, etc.; guide **2** to guide by influence **3** to be the head of (an expedition, orchestra, etc.) **4** to be at the head of *[to lead one's class]* **5** to be ahead of in a contest **6** to live; spend *[to lead a hard life]* —*vi.* **1** to show the way, as by going before **2** to tend in a certain direction: with *to,* *from,* etc. **3** to bring as a result: with *to* [hate *led* to war] **4** to be or go first —*n.* **1** the role or example of a leader **2** first or front place **3** the amount or distance ahead [to hold a safe *lead*] **4** anything that leads, as a clue **5** the leading role in a play, etc. **6** the right of playing first in cards or the card played **7** the most important news story, as in a newspaper or telecast —**lead off** to begin —**lead on** to lure

lead² (led) *n.* [OE.] **1** a heavy, soft, toxic metallic chemical element: symbol, Pb; at. no. 82 **2** a weight for measuring depth at sea **3** bullets **4** a stick of graphite, used in pencils —*adj.* of or containing lead —*vt.* to cover, line, or weight with lead

lead·ed (led′əd) *adj.* containing a lead compound: said of gasoline

lead·en (led′'n) *adj.* **1** of lead **2** heavy **3** sluggish **4** gloomy **5** gray

lead·er (lēd′ər) *n.* one that leads; guiding head —**lead′er·ship′** *n.*

lead·ing (lēd′iŋ) *adj.* **1** that leads; guiding **2** principal; chief

leading question a question put in such a way as to suggest the answer sought

lead time (lēd) the period of time available for preparation before an event, action, etc.

leaf (lēf) *n., pl.* **leaves** [OE.] **1** any of the flat, thin parts, usually green, growing from the stem of a plant **2** a sheet of paper **3** a very thin sheet of metal **4** a hinged or removable section of a table top —*vi.* **1** to bear leaves **2** to turn the pages of a book: with *through* —**leaf′less** *adj.*

leaf·let (-lit) *n.* **1** a small or young leaf **2** a separate sheet of printed matter, often folded

leaf·stalk *n.* the part of a leaf supporting the blade and attached to the stem

leaf·y *adj.* **-i·er, -i·est** having many or broad leaves [a *leafy* vegetable]

league¹ (lēg) *n.* [< L *ligare,* bind] **1** an association of nations, groups, etc. for promoting common interests **2** *Sports* a group of teams organized to play one another — *vt.,* *vi.* **leagued, leagu′ing** to form into a league

league² (lēg) *n.* [ult. < OE *leowe,* mile] a measure of distance, usually three miles

leak (lēk) *vi.* [< ON *leka,* to drip] **1** to let a fluid out or in accidentally **2** to pass in or out of a container thus **3** to become known gradually, by accident, etc. —*vt.* to allow to leak —*n.* **1** an accidental crack, etc. that lets something out or in **2** any accidental means of escape **3** leakage **4** a disclosure of confidential information —**leak′y** *adj.* **-i·er, -i·est**

leak·age *n.* **1** a leaking **2** that which leaks or the amount that leaks

lean¹ (lēn) *vi.* **leaned** or [Chiefly Brit.] **leant** (lent), **lean′ing** [OE *hlinian*] **1** to bend or slant from an upright position **2** to bend the body so as to rest part of one's weight on something **3** to rely (*on* or *upon*) **4** to tend (*toward* or *to*) —*vt.* to cause to lean —**lean on** [Inf.] to pressure as by intimidation —**lean′er** *n.*

lean² (lēn) *adj.* [OE *hlæne*] **1** having little flesh or fat; thin; spare **2** meager —**lean′ness** *n.*

lean·ing *n.* a tendency; inclination

lean-to *n., pl.* **-tos′** **1** a structure whose sloping roof abuts another building, a wall, etc. **2** an open-fronted shelter with a roof sloping to or close to the ground behind

leap (lēp) *vi.* **leaped** or **leapt** (lept, lēpt), **leap′ing** [OE *hleapan*] **1** to jump; spring; bound **2** to accept eagerly something offered: with *at* —*vt.* **1** to pass over by a jump **2** to cause to leap —*n.* **1** a jump; spring **2** the distance covered in a jump **3** a sudden transition —**leap′er** *n.*

leap·frog *n.* a game in which each player in turn leaps over the bent backs of the other players — *vt., vi.* **-frogged′, -frog′ging** to leap or jump in or as in this way; skip (*over*)

leap year every fourth year, containing an extra day in February

learn (lurn) *vt., vi.* **learned** (lurnd) or [Chiefly Brit.] **learnt** (lurnt), **learn′ing** [OE *leornian*] **1** to get knowledge of (a subject) or skill in (an art, trade, etc.) by study, experience, etc. **2** to come to know; hear (*of* or *about*) **3** to memorize —**learn′er** *n.*

learn·ed (lurn′id; *for 2* lurnd) *adj.* **1** having or showing much learning **2** acquired by study, experience, etc.

learn·ing *n.* **1** the acquiring of knowledge or skill **2** acquired knowledge or skill

learning disability any of several conditions, believed to involve the nervous system, that interfere with mastering a skill such as reading or writing —**learn′ing-dis·a′bled** *adj.*

lease (lēs) *n.* [< L *laxus,* loose] a contract by which a landlord rents lands, buildings, etc. to a tenant for a specified time —*vt.* **leased, leas′ing** to give or get by a lease —**leas′er** *n.*

lease·hold *n.* **1** the act of holding by lease **2** land, buildings, etc. held by lease

leash (lēsh) *n.* [< L *laxus,* loose] **1** a cord, strap, etc. by which a dog or the like is held in check **2** a cord, strap, etc. used to keep an object from getting lost, etc. —*vt.* to check or control as by a leash

least (lēst) *adj.* [OE *læst*] **1** *alt. superl. of* LITTLE **2** smallest or slightest in size, degree, etc. —*adv.* **1** *superl. of* LITTLE **2** in the smallest degree —*n.* the smallest in amount, importance, etc. —**at (the) least 1** at the lowest **2** at any rate —**not in the least** not at all

least·wise *adv.* [Inf.] at least; anyway: also [Chiefly Dial.] **least′ways′**

leath·er (leth′ər) *n.* [< OE *lether-*] animal skin prepared for use by removing the hair and tanning —*adj.* of leather

leath·er·neck *n.* [< former leather-lined uniform collar] [Slang] a U.S. Marine

leath·er·y *adj.* like leather; tough and flexible —**leath′er·i·ness** *n.*

leave¹ (lēv) *vt.* **left, leav′ing** [OE *læfan,* let remain] **1** to allow to remain [*leave* it open] **2** to have remaining behind or after one **3** to bequeath **4** to go away from **5** to abandon **6** [Chiefly Dial.] to let [*leave* us go]

—*vi.* to go away or set out —**leave off** to stop —**leave out** to omit —**leav′er** *n.*

leave² (lēv) *n.* 〖OE *leaf*〗 **1** permission **2** *a)* permission to be absent from duty *b)* the period for which this is granted —**take leave of** to say goodbye to —**take one's leave** to depart

leave³ (lēv) *vi.* leaved, leav′ing to bear leaves; leaf

leav·en (lev′ən) *n.* 〖< L *levare*, raise〗 **1** LEAVENING (*n.* 1) **2** LEAVENING (*n.* 2) —*vt.* **1** to make (dough) rise **2** to spread through, causing gradual change

leav·en·ing *n.* **1** a substance, as baking powder or yeast, used to make dough rise **2** a tempering or modifying quality or thing **3** a causing to be leavened

Leav·en·worth (lev′ən wurth′) city in NE Kansas: site of a federal prison

leave of absence permission to be absent from work or duty, esp. for a long time; also, the period for which this is granted

leaves (lēvz) *n.* pl. of LEAF

leave-tak·ing *n.* a parting; farewell

leav·ings (lēv′iŋz) *pl.n.* leftovers, remnants, refuse, etc.

Leb·a·non (leb′ə nän′) country in SW Asia, on the Mediterranean —**Leb′a·nese′** (-nēz′) *adj., n., pl.* **-nese′**

lech·er (lech′ər) *n.* 〖OFr *lechier*, live debauchedly〗 a lewd, grossly sensual man —**lech′er·ous** *adj.* —**lech′er·y** *n.*

lec·i·thin (les′i thin) *n.* 〖< Gr *lekithos*, egg yolk〗 a nitrogenous, fatty compound found in animal and plant cells: used in medicine, foods, etc.

lec·tern (lek′tərn) *n.* 〖< L *legere*, to read〗 a reading stand

lec·ture (-chər) *n.* 〖< L *legere*, read〗 **1** an informative talk to a class, etc. **2** a lengthy scolding — *vt., vi.* -tured, -tur·ing **1** to give a lecture (to) **2** to scold —**lec′tur·er** *n.*

led (led) *vt., vi. pt. & pp.* of LEAD¹

LED (el′ē′dē′) *n.* 〖*l(ight-)e(mitting) d(iode)*〗 a semiconductor diode that emits light when voltage is applied: used in lamps and traffic signals

ledge (lej) *n.* 〖ME *legge*〗 **1** a shelf or shelflike projection **2** a projecting ridge of rocks

ledg·er (lej′ər) *n.* 〖ME *legger*〗 a book in which a record of debits and credits is kept

lee (lē) *n.* 〖OE *hleo*, shelter〗 **1** shelter **2** *Naut.* the side or direction away from the wind —*adj.* of or on the side away from the wind

Lee (lē), **Rob·ert E(dward)** (räb′ərt) 1807-70; commander in chief of the Confederate army

leech (lēch) *n.* 〖OE *lœce*〗 **1** a bloodsucking worm living in water and used, esp. formerly, to bleed patients **2** one who clings to another for personal advantage —*vi.* to cling (onto) thus

leek (lēk) *n.* 〖OE *leac*〗 a vegetable that resembles a thick green onion

leer (lir) *n.* 〖OE *hleor*〗 a sly, sidelong look showing lust, malicious triumph, etc. —*vi.* to look with a leer —**leer′ing·ly** *adv.*

leer·y *adj.* -i·er, -i·est wary; suspicious

lees (lēz) *pl.n.* 〖< ML *lia*〗 dregs or sediment, as of wine

lee·ward (lē′wərd′; naut. lōō′ərd) *adj.* away from the wind —*n.* the side or direction away from the wind —*adv.* toward the lee

Lee·ward Islands (lē′wərd′) N group of islands in the Lesser Antilles of the West Indies

lee·way (lē′wā′) *n.* **1** the leeward drift of a ship or aircraft from its course **2** [Inf.] *a)* margin of time, money, etc. *b)* room for freedom of action

left¹ (left) *adj.* 〖< OE *lyft*, weak〗 **1** of or on the side that is toward the west when one faces north **2** closer to the left side of one who is facing the thing mentioned —*n.* **1** the left side **2** [*often* L-] *Politics* a liberal or radical position, party, etc.: often with *the* —*adv.* on or toward the left hand or side

left² (left) *vt., vi. pt. & pp.* of LEAVE¹

left-hand *adj.* **1** on or toward the left **2** of, for, or with the left hand

left-hand·ed *adj.* **1** using the left hand more skillfully than the right **2** done with or made for use with the left hand **3** ambiguous or backhanded [*a left-handed compliment*] —*adv.* **1** with the left hand [*to write left-handed*] **2** in such a way that the bat, club, etc. swings rightward

left·ist *n., adj.* liberal or radical

left·o·ver *n.* **1** something remaining unused, etc. **2** [*usually pl.*] food left from a previous meal —*adj.* remaining unused, uneaten, etc.

left wing the more liberal or radical section of a political party, group, etc. —**left′-wing′** *adj.* —**left′-wing′er** *n.*

left·y *n., pl.* **-ies** [Slang] a left-handed person

leg (leg) *n.* 〖ON *leggr*〗 **1** one of the parts of the body by means of which humans and animals stand and walk **2** the part of a garment covering the leg **3** anything like a leg in shape or use **4** a stage, as of a trip —*vi.* **legged, leg′ging** [Inf.] to walk or run: chiefly in the phrase **leg it**

leg·a·cy (leg′ə sē) *n., pl.* **-cies** 〖ult. < L *lex*, law〗 **1** money or property left to someone by a will **2** anything handed down as from an ancestor **3** a student applying or admitted to a college, etc., who is a relative of an alumnus or alumna

le·gal (lē′gəl) *adj.* 〖< L *lex*, law〗 **1** of or based upon law **2** permitted by law **3** of or for lawyers —**le′gal·ly** *adv.*

le·gal·ese (-ēz′) *n.* the special language of legal forms, etc., often considered incomprehensible

legal holiday a holiday set by law

le·gal·ism *n.* strict or too strict adherence to the law —**le′gal·is′tic** *adj.*

le·gal·i·ty (li gal′i tē) *n., pl.* **-ties** quality, condition, or instance of being legal or lawful

le·gal·ize (lē′gəl iz′) *vt.* **-ized′, -iz′ing** to make legal or lawful —**le′gal·i·za′tion** *n.*

legal pad a pad of lined writing paper, 8 ½ by 13 or 14 inches

legal tender money acceptable by law in payment of an obligation

leg·ate (leg′it) *n.* [< L *lex*, law] an envoy or ambassador

leg·a·tee (leg′ə tē′) *n.* one to whom a legacy is bequeathed

le·ga·tion (li gā′shən) *n.* **1** a diplomatic minister and staff collectively **2** the headquarters of such a group

le·ga·to (li gät′ō) *adj., adv.* [< L *ligare*, to tie] *Music* in a smooth, even style, with no breaks between notes

leg·end (lej′ənd) *n.* [< L *legere*, read] **1** a story or body of stories handed down for generations and popularly believed to have a historical basis **2** a notable person or the stories told about his or her exploits **3** an inscription on a coin, etc. **4** a title, key, etc. accompanying an illustration or map

leg·end·ar·y (lej′ən der′ē) *adj.* **1** of, based on, or presented in legends **2** famous or remarkable

leg·er·de·main (lej′ər di mān′) *n.* [< Fr *leger de main*, light of hand] **1** sleight of hand **2** trickery

-leg·ged (leg′id, legd) *combining form* having (a specified number or kind of) legs [*short-legged*]

leg·ging (leg′iŋ, -in) *n.* **1** a covering for the lower leg **2** [*pl.*] a child's outer garment with legs **3** [*pl.*] a garment like tights but without feet

leg·gy (leg′ē) *adj.* **-gi·er, -gi·est 1** having long legs **2** [Inf.] having long, spindly stems

leg·horn (leg′hôrn′, -ərn) *n.* [after *Leghorn*, It seaport] [*sometimes* **L-**] any of a breed of small chicken

leg·i·ble (lej′ə bəl) *adj.* [< L *legere*, read] that can be read —**leg′i·bil′i·ty** *n.* —**leg′i·bly** *adv.*

le·gion (lē′jən) *n.* [< L *legere*, choose] **1** a large group of soldiers; army **2** a large number; multitude —*adj.* very numerous: used in the predicate [*their difficulties were legion*] —**le′gion·naire′** (-jə ner′) *n.*

leg·is·late (lej′is lāt′) *vi.* **-lat′ed, -lat′ing** [see fol.] to make or pass a law or laws —*vt.* to cause to be, go, etc. by making laws —**leg′is·la′tor** *n.*

leg·is·la·tion *n.* [< L *lex*, law + *latio*, a bringing] **1** the making of laws **2** the law or laws made

leg·is·la·tive *adj.* **1** of legislation or a legislature **2** having the power to make laws

leg·is·la·ture (-chər) *n.* a body of persons given the power to make laws

le·git·i·mate (lə jit′ə mət; *for v.,* -māt′) *adj.* [< L *lex*, law] **1** born of parents married to each other **2** lawful **3** *a)* reasonable *b)* justifiable **4** conforming to accepted rules, standards, etc. **5** of stage plays, as distinguished from films, vaudeville, etc. —*vt.* **-mat′ed, -mat′ing** LEGITIMIZE —**le·git′i·ma·cy** (-mə sē) *n.* —**le·git′i·mate·ly** *adv.*

le·git·i·ma·tize (-mə tīz′) *vt.* **-tized′, -tiz′ing** LEGITIMIZE

le·git·i·mize (-mīz′) *vt.* **-mized′, -miz′ing** to make or declare legitimate —**le·git′i·mi·za′tion** *n.*

leg·room *n.* adequate space for the legs while seated, as in a car

leg·ume (leg′yōōm′, li gyōōm′) *n.* [< L *legere*, gather] **1** any of an order of plants having seeds growing in pods, including peas, beans, etc. **2** the pod or seed of such a plant —**le·gu·mi·nous** (lə gyōō′mə nəs) *adj.*

leg·work *n.* [Inf.] necessary, routine work, typically involving walking or traveling about as part of a job

lei (lā, lā′ē) *n., pl.* **leis** [Haw] in Hawaii, a garland of flowers, generally worn about the neck

Leip·zig (līp′sig) city in E Germany

lei·sure (lē′zhər, lezh′ər) *n.* [< L *licere*, be permitted] free time during which one may indulge in rest, recreation, etc. —*adj.* **1** free and unoccupied **2** done or used during one's leisure

lei·sure·ly *adj.* without haste; slow —*adv.* in an unhurried manner

leit·mo·tif or **leit·mo·tiv** (līt′mō tēf′) *n.* [Ger *leitmotiv* < *leiten*, to guide + *motiv*, motive] a dominant theme, as in a musical composition

lem·ming (lem′iŋ) *n.* [< ON *læmingi*] a small arctic rodent with a short tail

lem·on (lem′ən) *n.* [< Pers *līmūn*] **1** a small, sour, yellow citrus fruit **2** the spiny, semitropical tree that it grows on **3** [Slang] something that is defective —*adj.* yellow

lem·on·ade (-ād′) *n.* a drink made of lemon juice, sugar, and water

le·mur (lē′mər) *n.* [< L *lemures*, ghosts] a small, tree-dwelling primate with large eyes

lend (lend) *vt.* **lent, lend′ing** [< OE *læn*, a loan] **1** to let another use or have (a thing) temporarily **2** to let out (money) at interest **3** to impart —*vi.* to make loans —**lend itself (**or **oneself) to** to be useful for or adapted to —**lend′er** *n.*

length (leŋkth) *n.* [< OE *lang*, long] **1** the distance from end to end of a thing **2** extent in space or time **3** a long stretch or extent **4** a piece of a certain length —**at length 1** finally **2** for a long time or in great detail

length·en *vt., vi.* to make or become longer

length·wise *adv., adj.* in the direction of the length: also **length′ways′** *adv.*

length·y *adj.* **-i·er, -i·est** long; esp., too long —**length′i·ly** *adv.*

le·ni·ent (lēn′yənt, lē′nē ənt) *adj.* [< L *lenis*, soft] not harsh or severe; merciful —**le′ni·en·cy** *n.,* **le′ni·ence** —**le′ni·ent·ly** *adv.*

Len·in (len′in), **V(ladimir) I(lyich)** 1870-1924; Russ. leader of the Communist revolution of 1917

Len·in·grad (-grad′) *name* (1924-91) *for* St. Petersburg (Russia)

len·i·tive (len′ə tiv) *adj.* [< L *lenire*, to soften] lessening pain or distress

lens (lenz) *n.* [L, lentil: < its shape] **1** a curved piece of glass, plastic, etc. for bringing together or spreading rays of light passing through it: used in optical instruments to form an image **2** a similar transparent part of the eye: it focuses light rays upon the retina **3** any device used to focus microwaves, sound waves, etc.

lent (lent) *vt., vi. pt. & pp. of* LEND

Lent (lent) *n.* 〚OE *lengten*, the spring〛 *Christianity* the forty weekdays of fasting and penitence from Ash Wednesday to Easter —**Lent'en** *adj.*, **lent'en**

len·til (lent'ʼl) *n.* 〚< L *lens*〛 **1** a kind of legume, with small, edible seeds **2** this seed

Le·o (lē'ō) *n.* 〚L, lion〛 the fifth sign of the zodiac

Leonardo da Vinci *see* DA VINCI

le·o·nine (lē'ə nīn') *adj.* 〚< L *leo*, lion〛 of or like a lion

leop·ard (lep'ərd) *n.* 〚< Gr *leōn*, lion + *pardos*, panther〛 any of various large, wild cats, esp. one with a black-spotted, tawny coat, found in Africa and Asia

le·o·tard (lē'ə tärd') *n.* 〚after J. *Léotard* (1830-70), Fr aerial performer〛 a tightfitting garment for acrobats, dancers, etc.

lep·er (lep'ər) *n.* 〚< Gr *lepros*, scaly〛 a person having leprosy

lep·re·chaun (lep'rə kôn', -kän') *n.* 〚< Old Ir *lu*, little + *corp*, body〛 *Ir. Folklore* a fairy who can reveal hidden treasure

lep·ro·sy (lep'rə sē) *n.* 〚see LEPER〛 a progressive, mildly infectious disease of the skin, flesh, nerves, etc., characterized by ulcers, white scaly scabs, deformities, etc. —**lep'rous** *adj.*

lept (lept) *vi., vt. alt. pt. of* LEAP

lep·ton (lep'tän') *n.* 〚< Gr *leptos*, thin〛 any of certain atomic particles, as the electron or neutrino

les·bi·an (lez'bē ən) *n.* 〚after *Lesbos*, Gr. island home of the poet Sappho〛 a woman whose sexual orientation is to women —**les'bi·an·ism'** *n.*

lèse-ma·jest·é (lez'ma'zhes tā', -maj'is tē) *n.* 〚Fr < L *laesa majestas*, injured majesty〛 **1** a crime or offense against the sovereign **2** any lack of proper respect toward a person in authority

le·sion (lē'zhən) *n.* 〚< L *laedere*, to harm〛 an injury of an organ or tissue resulting in impairment of function

Le·sot·ho (lə sōō'tōō) country in SE Africa, surrounded by South Africa

less (les) *adj.* 〚OE *læs(sa)*〛 **1** *alt. compar. of* LITTLE **2** not so much **3** fewer —*adv.* **1** *compar. of* LITTLE **2** to a smaller extent —*n.* a smaller amount —*prep.* minus —**less and less** decreasingly

-less (lis, ləs) 〚OE *leas*, free〛 *suffix* **1** without **2** not able to **3** not able to be ___ed

les·see (les ē') *n.* 〚see LEASE〛 one to whom a lease is given; tenant

less·en *vt., vi.* to make or become less; decrease

less·er *adj.* **1** *alt. compar. of* LITTLE **2** smaller, less, or less important

les·son (les'ən) *n.* 〚< L *legere*, to read〛 **1** an exercise for a student to learn **2** something learned for one's safety, etc. **3** [*pl.*] course of

instruction **4** a selection from the Bible read as part of a religious service

les·sor (les'ôr') *n.* 〚see LEASE〛 one who gives a lease; landlord

lest (lest) *conj.* 〚< OE *thy læs the*, lit., by the less that〛 for fear that

let¹ (let) *vt.* **let**, **let'ting** 〚OE *lætan*, leave behind〛 **1** to leave: now only in the phrases **let alone** and **let be 2** *a*) to rent *b*) to assign (a contract) **3** to cause to escape [to *let* blood] **4** to allow; permit Also used as an auxiliary in commands or suggestions [*let* us go] —*vi.* to be rented [a house to *let*] —**let down 1** to lower **2** to slow up **3** to disappoint —**let off 1** to give forth **2** to deal leniently with —**let on 1** to indicate one's awareness **2** to pretend —**let out 1** to release **2** to rent out **3** to make a garment larger —**let up 1** to relax **2** to cease

let² (let) *n.* 〚< OE *lettan*, make late〛 *Law* an obstacle: in **without let or hindrance**

-let (lit, lət) 〚Fr -*el* + -*et*, dim. suffixes〛 *suffix* small [*piglet*]

let·down *n.* **1** a slowing up **2** a disappointment

le·thal (lē'thəl) *adj.* 〚< L *letum*, death〛 causing death; fatal

leth·ar·gy (leth'ər jē) *n., pl.* -**gies** 〚< Gr *lēthē*, oblivion + *argos*, idle〛 **1** an abnormal drowsiness **2** sluggishness, apathy, etc. —**le·thar·gic** (li thär'jik) *adj.* —**le·thar'gi·cal·ly** *adv.*

let's (lets) *contr.* let us

let·ter (let'ər) *n.* 〚< L *littera*〛 **1** any character in an alphabet **2** a written or printed message, usually sent by mail **3** [*pl.*] *a*) literature *b*) learning; knowledge **4** the literal meaning —*vt.* to mark with letters —**let'ter·er** *n.*

letter carrier a postal employee who delivers mail

let·ter·head *n.* **1** the name, address, etc. as a heading on stationery **2** stationery printed with such a name, address, etc.

let·ter·ing *n.* the act of making or inscribing letters, or such letters

let·ter·per·fect *adj.* entirely correct

let·tuce (let'əs) *n.* 〚< L *lac*, milk〛 **1** a plant with crisp, green leaves **2** the leaves, much used for salads

let·up (let'up') *n.* [*Inf.*] **1** a slackening **2** a stop or pause

leu·ke·mi·a (lōō kē'mē ə) *n.* [see fol. & -EMIA] a disease that is characterized by an abnormal increase in the number of leukocytes

leu·ko·cyte (lōō'kō sīt', -kə-) *n.* 〚< Gr *leukos*, white + *kytos*, hollow〛 a colorless cell in the blood, etc. that destroys pathogens; white blood cell

lev·ee (lev'ē) *n.* 〚ult. < L *levare*, to raise〛 an embankment to prevent a river from flooding bordering land

lev·el (lev'əl) *n.* 〚< L *libra*, a balance〛 **1** an instrument for determining an even horizontal plane **2** a horizontal plane or line [*sea level*] **3** a horizontal area **4** normal position with reference to height [water seeks its *level*] **5** position in a scale of values [*income level*] —*adj.* **1** perfectly flat and even **2**

not sloping **3** even in height (*with*) **4** equal in importance, advancement, quality, etc. **5** calm or steady —*vt., vi.* **-eled** or **-elled, -el·ing** or **-el·ling** **1** to make or become level **2** to demolish **3** to aim (a gun, etc.) —**level with** [Slang] to be honest with —**lev′el·er** *n.,* **lev′el·ler**

lev·el·head·ed *adj.* having an even temper and sound judgment

lev·er (lev′ər, lē′vər) *n.* [< L *levare,* to raise] **1** a bar used as a pry **2** a means to an end **3** a device consisting of a bar turning about a fixed point, using force at a second point to lift a weight at a third

lev·er·age (-ij) *n.* **1** the action or mechanical power of a lever **2** means of accomplishing something —*vt.* **-aged, -ag·ing** *Finance* to speculate in (a business venture) with borrowed funds

le·vi·a·than (lə vī′ə thən) *n.* [< Heb *liwyā-thān*] **1** *Bible* a sea monster **2** anything huge

Le·vi's (lē′vīz′) [after *Levi* Strauss, U.S. manufacturer] *trademark for* trousers of heavy denim —*pl.n.* such trousers: also written **Le′vis** or **le′vis**

lev·i·ta·tion (lev′ə tā′shən) *n.* [< L *levis,* light] the raising a body in the air with no apparent support —**lev′i·tate′** *vt., vi.* **-tat′ed, -tat′ing**

Le·vit·i·cus (lə vit′i kəs) *n.* the third book of the Pentateuch

Lev·it·town (lev′it toun′) city in SE New York: post–WWII planned community of mass-produced houses

lev·i·ty (lev′i tē) *n., pl.* **-ties** [< L *levis,* light] gaiety, esp. improper gaiety; frivolity

lev·y (lev′ē) *n., pl.* **lev′ies** [< L *levare,* to raise] **1** an imposing and collecting of a tax, fine, etc. **2** the amount imposed **3** compulsory enlistment for military service **4** a group so enlisted —*vt.* **-ied, -y·ing** **1** to impose (a tax, fine, etc.) **2** to enlist (troops) **3** to wage (war)

lewd (lōōd) *adj.* [OE *lewede,* unlearned] indecent; lustful; obscene —**lewd′ly** *adv.* —**lewd′ness** *n.*

lex·i·cog·ra·phy (lek′sə käg′rə fē) *n.* [see fol. & -GRAPHY] the act, art, or work of writing a dictionary —**lex′i·cog′ra·pher** *n.*

lex·i·con (lek′si kän′) *n.* [< Gr *lexis,* word] **1** a dictionary **2** a special vocabulary —**lex′i·cal** *adj.*

lg *abbrev.* large

LGBT *abbrev.* lesbian, gay, bisexual, and transgender

Li *Chem. symbol for* lithium

li·a·bil·i·ty (lī′ə bil′ə tē) *n., pl.* **-ties** **1** the state of being liable **2** anything for which a person is liable **3** a debt of a person or business **4** something that works to one's disadvantage

li·a·ble (lī′ə bəl) *adj.* [< L *ligare,* bind] **1** legally bound or responsible **2** subject to [*liable* to heart attacks] **3** likely to [*liable* to get hurt]

li·ai·son (lē ā′zän′, -zən) *n.* [< L *ligare,*

bind] **1** a linking up, as of units of a military force **2** an illicit love affair

li·ar (lī′ər) *n.* one who tells lies

lib (lib) *n.* [Inf.] *short for* LIBERATION

li·ba·tion (lī bā′shən) *n.* [< L *libare,* pour out] **1** the ritual of pouring out wine or oil in honor of a god **2** this liquid **3** an alcoholic drink

li·bel (lī′bəl) *n.* [< L *liber,* book] **1** any written or printed matter tending to injure a person's reputation unjustly **2** the act or crime of publishing such a thing **3** loosely, any description, etc. that is unfair to the subject it is dealing with —*vt.* **-beled** or **-belled, -bel·ing** or **-bel·ling** to make a libel against —**li′bel·er** *n.,* **li′bel·ler** —**li′bel·ous** *adj.,* **li′bel·lous**

lib·er·al (lib′ər əl) *adj.* [< L *liber,* free] **1** generous **2** ample; abundant **3** not literal or strict **4** tolerant; broad-minded **5** favoring reform or progress —*n.* one who favors reform or progress —**lib′er·al·ism′** *n.* —**lib′er·al·ly** *adv.* —**lib′er·al·ness** *n.*

liberal arts literature, languages, history, etc. as courses or a course of study

lib·er·al·i·ty (-al′i tē) *n., pl.* **-ties** **1** generosity **2** broad-mindedness

lib·er·al·ize (-əl īz′) *vt., vi.* **-ized′, -iz′ing** to make or become liberal —**lib′er·al·i·za′tion** *n.*

lib·er·ate (lib′ər āt′) *vt.* **-at′ed, -at′ing** [< L *liber,* free] to release from slavery, oppression, enemy occupation, etc. —**lib′er·a′tion** *n.* —**lib′er·a′tor** *n.*

Li·be·ri·a (lī bir′ē ə) country on the W coast of Africa: founded (1821) as settlement for freed U.S. slaves —**Li·be′ri·an** *adj., n.*

lib·er·tar·i·an (lib′ər ter′ē ən) *n.* an advocate of full individual freedom of thought and action

lib·er·tine (lib′ər tēn′) *n.* [< L *liber,* free] one who is sexually promiscuous —*adj.* licentious

lib·er·ty (lib′ər tē) *n., pl.* **-ties** [< L *liber,* free] **1** freedom from slavery, captivity, etc. **2** a particular right, freedom, etc. **3** a too free or impertinent action or attitude **4** permission given to a sailor to go ashore See also CIVIL LIBERTIES —**at liberty 1** not confined **2** permitted (to do or say something) **3** not busy or in use —**take liberties 1** to be too familiar or impertinent **2** to deal inaccurately (*with* facts, data, etc.)

li·bid·i·nous (li bid′'n əs) *adj.* [see fol.] lustful; lascivious

li·bi·do (li bē′dō) *n.* [< L, pleasure] **1** the sexual urge **2** *Psychoanalysis* psychic energy; specif., that comprising the positive, loving instincts

Li·bra (lē′brə) *n.* [L, balance, scales] the seventh sign of the zodiac

li·brar·i·an (lī brer′ē ən) *n.* one in charge of a library or trained in library science

li·brar·y (lī′brer′ē) *n., pl.* **-ies** [< L *liber,* book] **1** a collection of books, etc. **2** a room or building for, or an institution in charge of, such a collection

li·bret·to (li bret′ō) *n., pl.* **-tos** or **-ti** (-ē) [It < L *liber,* book] the words, or text, of an opera, oratorio, etc. —**li·bret′tist** *n.*

Lib·y·a (lib′ē ə) country in N Africa, on the Mediterranean —**Lib′y·an** *adj.*, *n.*

lice (līs) *n. pl. of* LOUSE

li·cense (lī′səns) *n.* ⟦< L *licere*, be permitted⟧ **1** formal or legal permission to do something specified **2** a document, etc. indicating such permission **3** freedom to deviate from rule, practice, etc. [*poetic license*] **4** excessive freedom, constituting an abuse of liberty Brit. sp. **li′cence** —*vt.* **-censed, -cens·ing** to permit formally

li·cen·see (lī′səns ē′) *n.* a person to whom a license is granted

li·cen·ti·ate (lī sen′shē it, -āt′) *n.* a person having a professional license

li·cen·tious (lī sen′shəs) *adj.* ⟦see LICENSE⟧ sexually unrestrained; lascivious —**li·cen′-tious·ness** *n.*

li·chen (lī′kən) *n.* ⟦< Gr *leichein*, to lick⟧ an organism resembling moss but actually a combination of fungus and algae, growing in patches on rock, wood, soil, etc.

lic·it (lis′it) *adj.* ⟦< L *licitus*, permitted⟧ lawful —**lic′it·ly** *adv.*

lick (lik) *vt.* ⟦OE *liccian*⟧ **1** to pass the tongue over **2** to pass lightly over like a tongue **3** [Inf.] *a)* to thrash *b)* to vanquish —*vi.* to move lightly, as a flame —*n.* **1** a licking with the tongue **2** a small quantity **3** *short for* SALT LICK **4** [Inf.] a sharp blow —**lick up** to consume as by licking

lic·o·rice (lik′ə rish) *n.* ⟦< Gr *glykys*, sweet + *rhiza*, root⟧ **1** a black flavoring extract made from the root of a European plant **2** candy flavored with this extract or in imitation of it

lid (lid) *n.* ⟦OE *hlid*⟧ **1** a movable cover, as for a box, pot, etc. **2** *short for* EYELID **3** [Inf.] a restraint

lid·ded (lid′id) *adj.* **1** having a lid **2** having (a specified kind of) eyelids [*heavy-lidded*]

lie¹ (lī) *vi.* **lay, lain, ly′ing** ⟦OE *licgan*⟧ **1** to be or put oneself in a reclining or horizontal position **2** to rest on a support in a horizontal position **3** to be in a specified condition **4** to be situated [Canada *lies* to the north] **5** to extend **6** to be or be found —*n.* the way in which something is situated; lay

lie² (lī) *vi.* **lied, ly′ing** ⟦OE *leogan*⟧ to make a statement that one knows is false —*vt.* to accomplish, etc. by lying [to *lie* his way into office] —*n.* a false statement made with intent to deceive

Lieb·frau·milch (lēb′frou milk′) *n.* ⟦Ger⟧ a white wine

Liech·ten·stein (lik′tən stīn′) country between Switzerland & Austria

lie detector a polygraph used on persons suspected of lying

lief (lēf) *adv.* ⟦< OE *leof*, dear⟧ willingly; gladly: only in **would** (*or* **had**) **as lief**

liege (lēj) *adj.* ⟦OFr⟧ loyal; faithful —*n.* Feudal Law **1** a lord or sovereign **2** a subject or vassal

lien (lēn, lē′ən) *n.* ⟦Fr < L *ligare*, to bind⟧ a legal claim on another's property until a debt is paid

lieu (lōō) *n.* ⟦< L *locus*⟧ place: chiefly in **in lieu of**, instead of

Lieut *abbrev.* Lieutenant

lieu·ten·ant (lōō ten′ənt) *n.* ⟦< Fr *lieu*, place + *tenant*, holding⟧ **1** one who acts for a superior **2** U.S. Mil. an officer ranking below a captain: see FIRST LIEUTENANT, SECOND LIEUTENANT **3** U.S. Navy an officer ranking just above a lieutenant junior grade —**lieu·ten′an·cy** *n.*

lieutenant colonel U.S. Mil. an officer ranking just above a major

lieutenant commander U.S. Navy an officer ranking just above a lieutenant

lieutenant general U.S. Mil. an officer ranking just above a major general

lieutenant governor an elected official of a U.S. state who ranks below and substitutes for the governor

lieutenant junior grade U.S. Navy an officer ranking just above an ensign

life (līf) *n., pl.* **lives** ⟦OE *lif*⟧ **1** that property of plants, animals, etc. (ending at death) which makes it possible for them to take in food, get energy from it, grow, reproduce, etc. **2** the state of having this property **3** a human [100 *lives* were lost] **4** living things collectively [plant *life*] **5** the time a person or thing is alive or exists **6** one's manner of living [a *life* of ease] **7** the people and activities of a given time, place, etc. [military *life*] **8** *a)* one's animate existence *b)* a biography **9** the source of liveliness [the *life* of the party] **10** vigor; liveliness

life belt a life preserver in belt form

life·blood *n.* **1** the blood necessary to life **2** a vital element

life·boat *n.* one of the small boats carried by a ship for use in an emergency

life-form *n.* a particular type of organism, often one that is unusual or newly found

life·guard *n.* an expert swimmer employed as at a beach to prevent drownings

life insurance insurance for a stipulated sum paid at the death of the insured

life jacket (*or* **vest**) a life preserver that is like a sleeveless jacket

life·less *adj.* **1** without life; specif., *a)* inanimate *b)* dead **2** dull

life·like *adj.* resembling real life or a real person or thing

life·line *n.* **1** a rope or line for saving life, as one thrown to a person in the water **2** a very important commercial route

life·long *adj.* lasting or not changing during one's whole life

life net a strong net used as by firefighters to catch people jumping from a burning building

life-or-death *adj.* **1** having death as a possible result [a *life-or-death* struggle] **2** crucial [a *life-or-death* business decision]

life preserver a buoyant device for saving a person from drowning by keeping the body afloat

lif·er *n.* [Slang] **1** a person sentenced to prison for life **2** a person whose whole working life is spent with one organization

life raft a small, inflatable raft for emergency use at sea

life·sav·er *n.* **1** a lifeguard **2** [Inf.] a help in time of need

life science a science, as botany or zoology, dealing with organisms and their life processes

life-size *adj.* as big as the person or thing represented [a *life-size* portrait]: also **life'-sized'**

life style *n.* an individual's way of living

life-sup·port *adj. Med.* for providing support needed to maintain life [a *life-support* system]

life·time *n.* **1** the period of time that someone lives or that a thing lasts **2** a very long time

life·work *n.* the work to which a person's life is devoted

lift (lift) *vt.* [< ON *lopt*, air] **1** to bring up to a higher position; raise **2** to raise in rank, condition, etc.; exalt **3** to pay off (a mortgage, debt, etc.) **4** to end (a blockade, etc.) **5** [Slang] to steal —*vi.* **1** to exert strength in raising something **2** to rise; go up —*n.* **1** a lifting or rising **2** the distance something is lifted **3** lifting power or influence **4** elevation of mood **5** a ride in the direction one is going **6** help of any kind **7** *a*) [Brit.] ELEVA-TOR *b*) SKI LIFT

lift·off *n.* **1** the initial vertical takeoff as of a rocket **2** the time this occurs

lig·a·ment (lig'ə mənt) *n.* [< L *ligare*, bind] a band of tissue connecting bones or holding organs in place

lig·a·ture (lig'ə chər) *n.* [< L *ligare*, bind] **1** a tying or binding together **2** a tie, bond, etc. **3** two or more letters united, as æ, th **4** *Surgery* a thread used to tie up an artery, etc.

light¹ (līt) *n.* [OE *leoht*] **1** *a*) the form of electromagnetic energy acting on the retina of the eye to make sight possible *b*) ultraviolet or infrared radiation **2** brightness; illumination **3** a source of light, as the sun, a lamp, etc. **4** daylight **5** a thing used to ignite something **6** a window or windowpane **7** knowledge; enlightenment **8** public view [to bring new facts to *light*] **9** aspect [viewed in another *light*] —*adj.* **1** having light; bright **2** pale in color; fair —*adv.* palely [a *light* blue color] —*vt.* **light'ed** or **lit, light'ing 1** to ignite [to *light* a bonfire] **2** to cause to give off light **3** to furnish with light **4** to brighten; animate —*vi.* **1** to catch fire **2** to be lighted: usually with *up* —**in the light of** considering —**see the light (of day) 1** to come into existence **2** to come to public view **3** to understand

light² (līt) *adj.* [OE *leoht*] **1** having little weight; not heavy, esp. for its size **2** less than usual in weight, amount, force, etc. [a *light* blow] **3** not serious or profound [*light* verse] **4** easy to bear [a *light* tax] **5** easy to do [*light* work] **6** merry; happy **7** dizzy; giddy **8** containing fewer calories **9** moderate [a *light* meal] **10** moving with ease [*light* on one's feet] **11** producing small products

[*light* industry] —*adv.* LIGHTLY —*vi.* **light'ed** or **lit, light'ing 1** to come to rest after traveling through the air **2** to come or happen (*on* or *upon*) —**light into** [Inf.] to attack —**light out** [Inf.] to depart suddenly —**make light of** to treat as unimportant

light·en¹ *vt., vi.* **1** to make or become light or brighter **2** to shine; flash

light·en² *vt., vi.* **1** to make or become lighter in weight **2** to make or become more cheerful

light·er¹ *n.* a person or thing that starts something burning

light·er² *n.* [< MDu *licht*, LIGHT²] a large barge used to load or unload ships anchored in a harbor

light-fin·gered *adj.* **1** skillful at stealing **2** likely to steal

light-foot·ed *adj.* stepping lightly and gracefully

light·head·ed *adj.* **1** giddy; dizzy **2** flighty; frivolous

light·heart·ed *adj.* free from care; cheerful —**light'heart'ed·ly** *adv.* —**light'heart'ed·ness** *n.*

light heavyweight a boxer with a maximum weight of 175 lb.

light·house *n.* a tower with a very bright light to guide ships at night

light·ing *n.* the act or manner of giving light, or illuminating

light·ly *adv.* **1** with little weight or pressure; gently **2** to a small degree or amount **3** nimbly; deftly **4** cheerfully **5** without due care, consideration, etc.

light meter an instrument to measure intensity of light, used in photography

light-mind·ed *adj.* silly; frivolous

light·ness¹ *n.* **1** the amount of light; brightness **2** paleness in color

light·ness² *n.* **1** a being light, not heavy **2** mildness, nimbleness, etc.

light·ning (-niŋ) *n.* a flash of light in the sky caused by the discharge of atmospheric electricity

lightning bug FIREFLY

lightning rod a metal rod placed high on a building and grounded to divert lightning from the structure

light opera OPERETTA

light·weight *n.* a boxer with a maximum weight of 135 lb. —*adj.* light in weight

light-year *n.* a unit of distance equal to the distance light travels in one year, *c.* 6 trillion miles

lig·nite (lig'nīt) *n.* [< L *lignum*, wood] a soft coal, brownish-black in color and retaining the texture of the original plant material from which it was formed

lik·a·ble (līk'ə bəl) *adj.* pleasant, genial, etc.: also **like'a·ble** —**lik'a·ble·ness** *n.*, **lik'a·bil'i·ty**

like¹ (līk) *adj.* [OE *gelic*] having the same characteristics; similar; equal —*adv.* [Inf.] likely [*like* as not, he'll go] —*prep.* **1** similar to **2** similarly to [to sing *like* a bird] **3** characteristic of [not *like* her to cry] **4** in the mood for [to feel *like* sleeping] **5** indicative of [it looks *like* rain] **6** as for example [fruit, *like* pears and plums] —*conj.* [Inf.] **1** as [it's just *like* he said] **2** as if [it looks *like* he's late] —*n.* an equal or counterpart [I've never met her *like*] —**more like it** [Inf.] closer to being what is wanted —**nothing like** not at all like —**something like** almost like —**the like** others of the same kind —**the like (or likes) of** [Inf.] any person or thing like

like² (līk) *vi.* **liked, lik′ing** [OE *lician*] to be inclined [do as you *like*] —*vt.* **1** to be pleased with; enjoy **2** to wish [I'd *like* to go] —*n.* [*pl.*] preferences or tastes —**lik′er** *n.*

-like (līk) *suffix* like, characteristic of [*homelike*, bull-*like*]

like·li·hood (līk′lē hood′) *n.* a being likely to happen; probability

like·ly (līk′lē) *adj.* **-li·er, -li·est** [OE *gelīclic*] **1** credible [a *likely* cause] **2** reasonably to be expected [*likely* to rain] **3** suitable [a *likely* place to swim] —*adv.* probably [she'll *likely* go]

like-mind·ed *adj.* having the same ideas, plans, tastes, etc. —**like′-mind′ed·ness** *n.*

lik·en (līk′ən) *vt.* to compare

like·ness *n.* **1** a being like **2** (the same) form **3** a copy, portrait, etc.

like·wise *adv.* [< *in like wise*] **1** in the same manner **2** also; too

lik·ing (līk′iŋ) *n.* **1** fondness; affection **2** preference; taste; pleasure

li·lac (lī′lək, -läk′, -lak′) *n.* [ult. < Pers *līlak*, bluish] **1** a shrub with large clusters of tiny, fragrant flowers **2** pale purple —*adj.* pale-purple

Lil·li·pu·tian (lil′ə pyōō′shən) *adj.* [after *Lilliput*, place in J. Swift's *Gulliver's Travels*] **1** tiny **2** petty

lilt (lilt) *n.* [ME *lilten*, to sound] a light, swingy rhythm or tune —**lilt′ing** *adj.*

lil·y (lil′ē) *n., pl.* **lil′ies** [< L *lilium*] **1** a plant grown from a bulb and having typically trumpet-shaped flowers **2** its flower **3** any similar plant, as the waterlily —*adj.* like a lily, as in whiteness, purity, etc.

lil·y-liv·ered *adj.* cowardly; timid

lily of the valley *pl.* **lilies of the valley** a low plant with a spike of white, bell-shaped flowers

lily pad one of the large, flat, floating leaves of the waterlily

Li·ma (lē′mə) capital of Peru

li·ma bean (lī′mə) [after *Lima*, Peru] **1** a bean with broad pods **2** its broad, flat, edible seed

limb (lim) *n.* [OE *lim*] **1** an arm, leg, or wing **2** a large branch of a tree —**out on a limb** [Inf.] in a precarious position —**limb′less** *adj.*

lim·ber (lim′bər) *adj.* [< ? prec.] **1** easily bent; flexible **2** able to bend the body easily; supple —*vt., vi.* to make or become limber

lim·bo (lim′bō) *n., pl.* for **2** & **3** **-bos** [< L (*in*) *limbo*, (on) the border] **1** [*usually* **L-**] in some Christian theologies, the abode after death of unbaptized infants, etc. **2** an indefi-

nite state **3** a condition of neglect, oblivion, etc.

Lim·burg·er (cheese) (lim′burg′ər) a semisoft cheese with a strong odor, originally from Limburg, Belgium

lime¹ (līm) *n.* [OE *līm*] a white substance, calcium oxide, obtained from limestone, etc. and used in mortar and cement and to neutralize acid soil —*vt.* **limed, lim′ing** to treat with lime

lime² (līm) *n.* [< Ar *līmah*] a small, lemon-shaped, greenish-yellow citrus fruit with a juicy, sour pulp

lime·ade (-ād′) *n.* a drink made of lime juice, sugar, and water

lime·light *n.* **1** a brilliant light created by the incandescence of lime, formerly used in theaters **2** a prominent position before the public

lim·er·ick (lim′ər ik) *n.* [prob. after *Limerick*, Ir county] a rhymed nonsense poem of five lines

lime·stone *n.* rock consisting mainly of calcium carbonate

lim·i·nal (lim′i nəl) *adj.* at a boundary or transitional point between two conditions, stages, etc.

lim·it (lim′it) *n.* [< L *limes*] **1** the point, line, etc. where something ends; boundary **2** [*pl.*] bounds **3** the greatest amount allowed —*vt.* to set a limit to; restrict —**lim′i·ta′tion** *n.* —**lim′it·er** *n.* —**lim′it·less** *adj.*

lim·it·ed *adj.* **1** *a)* restricted *b)* narrow in scope *c)* brief **2** making a restricted number of stops: said of a train, bus, etc.

limn (lim) *vt.* **limned, limn·ing** (lim′iŋ, -nin) [< L *illuminare*, to illuminate] **1** to paint or draw **2** to describe

lim·nol·o·gy (lim näl′ə jē) *n.* [< Gr *limnē*, marsh + -LOGY] the science that deals with the properties and features of fresh waters, esp. lakes, etc.

lim·o (lim′ō) *n., pl.* **-os** [Inf.] LIMOUSINE

lim·ou·sine (lim′ə zēn′) *n.* [Fr, lit., cloak] a large, luxurious sedan, esp. one driven by a chauffeur

limp (limp) *vi.* [< OE *limpan*] to walk with or as with a lame leg —*n.* a lameness in walking —*adj.* lacking firmness; wilted, flexible, etc. —**limp′ly** *adv.* —**limp′ness** *n.*

lim·pet (lim′pit) *n.* [< ML *lempreda*] a mollusk that clings to rocks, etc.

lim·pid (lim′pid) *adj.* [< L *limpidus*] perfectly clear; transparent —**lim·pid′i·ty** *n.*

lim·y (līm′ē) *adj.* **-i·er, -i·est** of, like, or containing lime

lin·age (līn′ij) *n.* the number of written or printed lines, as on a page

linch·pin (linch′pin′) *n.* [OE *lynis*, linchpin] **1** a pin in an axle to keep the wheel from coming off **2** anything holding together the parts of a whole

Lin·coln¹ (liŋ′kən), **Abraham** 1809-65; 16th president of the U.S. (1861-65): assassinated

Lin·coln² (liŋ′kən) capital of Nebraska, in the SE part

lin·den (lin′dən) *n.* [OE] a tree with heart-shaped leaves

line[1] (līn) *n.* [< L *linea*, lit., linen thread] 1 a cord, rope, wire, etc. 2 any wire, pipe, etc., or system of these, conducting fluid, electricity, etc. 3 a thin, threadlike mark 4 a border or boundary 5 a limit 6 outline; contour 7 a row of persons or things, as of printed letters across a page 8 a succession of persons or things 9 lineage 10 a transportation system of buses, ships, etc. 11 the course a moving thing takes 12 a course of action, explanation, etc. 13 a person's trade or occupation 14 a stock of goods 15 a short letter, note, etc. 16 [*pl.*] all the speeches of a character in a play 17 the forward combat position in warfare 18 *Football* the players in the forward row 19 *Math.* the path of a moving point —*vt.* **lined, lin′ing** 1 to mark with lines 2 to form a line along —**bring (or come) into line** to bring (or come) into alignment or conformity —**down the line** completely; entirely —**draw the (or a) line** to set a limit —**hold the line** to stand firm —**in line for** being considered for —**line up** to form, or bring into, a line —**read between the lines** to discover a hidden meaning in something written, said, or done

line[2] (līn) *vt.* **lined, lin′ing** [< L *linum*, flax] to put, or serve as, a lining in

lin·e·age (lin′ē ij) *n.* [see LINE[1]] 1 direct descent from an ancestor 2 ancestry; family

lin·e·al (lin′ē əl) *adj.* 1 in the direct line of descent from an ancestor 2 hereditary 3 of lines; linear

lin·e·a·ment (lin′e ə mənt) *n.* [< L *linea*, line] a distinctive feature, esp. of the face: *usually used in pl.*

lin·e·ar (lin′ē ər) *adj.* 1 of, made of, or using a line or lines 2 logical and not complex 3 in relation to length only

line·back·er (līn′bak′ər) *n. Football* a defensive player directly behind the line

line drive a baseball hit in a nearly straight line parallel to the ground

line·man (-mən) *n., pl.* **-men** (-mən) 1 one who sets up and repairs telephone lines, electric power lines, etc. 2 *Football* a player in the line

lin·en (lin′ən) *n.* [< OE *lín*, flax: see LINE[2]] 1 thread or cloth made of flax 2 [*often pl.*] sheets, cloths, etc. of linen, or now more usually of cotton, etc.

lin·er (līn′ər) *n.* 1 a steamship, airplane, etc. in regular service for a specific line 2 LINE DRIVE 3 a cosmetic applied in a fine line, as along the eyelid

lines·man (līnz′mən) *n., pl.* **-men** (-mən) 1 *Football* an official who marks the yardage gained or lost 2 *Tennis* an official who decides whether the ball is inside or outside the lines

line·up *n.* an arrangement of persons or things in or as in a line

-ling (liŋ) [OE] *suffix* 1 small [*duckling*] 2 unimportant or contemptible [*hireling*]

lin·ger (liŋ′gər) *vi.* [OE *lengan*, to delay] 1 to continue to stay, esp. through reluctance to leave 2 to loiter —**lin′ger·er** *n.* —**lin′ger·ing** *adj.*

lin·ge·rie (län′zhə rā′) *n.* [Fr] women's underwear and nightclothes

lin·go (liŋ′gō) *n., pl.* **-goes** [< L *lingua*, tongue] [Inf.] a dialect, jargon, etc. that one is not familiar with

lin·gua fran·ca (liŋ′gwə fraŋ′kə) a hybrid language used for communication by speakers of different languages

lin·gual (liŋ′gwəl) *adj.* [see LANGUAGE] of, or pronounced with, the tongue

lin·gui·ne (liŋ gwē′nē) *n.* [< It *lingua*, tongue] pasta in thin, flat, narrow strips: also sp. **lin·gui′ni**

lin·guist (liŋ′gwist) *n.* [< L *lingua*, tongue] a specialist in linguistics

lin·guis·tics (-gwis′tiks) *n.* 1 the science of language 2 the study of the structure, development, etc. of a particular language —**lin·guis′tic** *adj.*

lin·i·ment (lin′ə mənt) *n.* [< L *linere*, to smear] a soothing medicated liquid for the skin

lin·ing (līn′iŋ) *n.* the material covering an inner surface

link (liŋk) *n.* [< Scand] 1 any of the loops making up a chain 2 *a)* a section of something like a chain [a *link* of sausage] *b)* an element in a series [a weak *link* in the evidence] 3 anything that connects [a *link* with the past] —*vt., vi.* to join; connect

link·age *n.* 1 a linking 2 a series or system of links

linking verb a verb that functions chiefly as a connection between a subject and a predicate (Ex.: *be, seem, become*)

links (liŋks) *pl.n.* [OE *hlinc*, a slope] GOLF COURSE

link·up *n.* a linking together

Lin·nae·us (li nē′əs, -nā′-), **Car·o·lus** (kar′ə ləs) 1707–78; Swed. botanist

lin·net (lin′it) *n.* [< L *linum*, flax: it feeds on flaxseed] a small finch of either an Old World or New World species

li·no·le·um (li nō′lē əm) *n.* [< L *linum*, flax + *oleum*, oil] 1 a smooth, washable floor covering, formerly much used, esp. in kitchens 2 any floor covering like linoleum

lin·seed (lin′sēd′) *n.* [OE *linsæd*] the seed of flax; flaxseed

linseed oil a yellowish oil extracted from flaxseed, used in oil paints, etc.

lint (lint) *n.* [< L *linum*, flax] bits of thread, fluff, etc. from cloth or yarn —**lint′y** *adj.*, **-i·er, -i·est**

lin·tel (lin′təl) *n.* [ult. < L *limen*, threshold] the horizontal crosspiece over a door, window, etc.

li·on (lī′ən) *n.* [< Gr *leōn*] 1 a large, powerful cat, found in Africa and SW Asia 2 a person of great courage or strength 3 a celebrity

li·on·ess (lī′ə nəs) *n.* a female lion

li·on·heart·ed *adj.* very brave

li·on·ize (lī′ə nīz′) *vt.* **-ized′, -iz′ing** to treat as a celebrity

lip (lip) *n.* [OE *lippa*] 1 either of the two fleshy folds forming the edges of the mouth 2 anything like a lip, as the rim of a pitcher 3

[Slang] insolent talk —**keep a stiff upper lip** [Inf.] to bear pain or distress bravely

lip·id (lip'id) *n.* [< Gr *lipos*, fat] any of a group of organic compounds consisting of the fats and other similar substances

lip·o·suc·tion (lip'ō suk'shən, li'pō–) *n.* [< prec. + SUCTION] surgical removal of fatty tissue under the skin by means of suction

lip·py (lip'ē) *adj.* -**pi·er**, -**pi·est** [Slang] impudent; insolent —**lip'pi·ness** *n.*

lip reading the act or skill of recognizing words by watching a speaker's lips: it is taught esp. to the deaf —**lip'-read'** *vt., vi.* —**lip reader**

lip service insincere words of support, etc.

lip·stick *n.* a small stick of cosmetic paste for coloring the lips

lip-sync or **lip-synch** (–siṇk') *vt., vi.* [< *lip sync(hronization)*] to move the lips silently so as to seem to be speaking or singing (something recorded)

liq·ue·fy (lik'wi fī') *vt., vi.* -**fied'**, -**fy'ing** [< L *liquere*, be liquid + *facere*, make] to change into a liquid —**liq'ue·fac'tion** (–fak'shən) *n.*

li·queur (li kur', –koor') *n.* [Fr] a sweet, syrupy, flavored alcoholic liquor

liq·uid (lik'wid) *adj.* [< L *liquidus*] 1 readily flowing; fluid 2 clear; limpid 3 flowing smoothly and musically, as verse 4 readily convertible into cash —*n.* a substance that, unlike a solid, flows readily but, unlike a gas, does not expand indefinitely —**liq·uid'i·ty** *n.*

liq·ui·date (lik'wi dāt') *vt.* -**dat'ed**, -**dat' ing** [see prec.] 1 to settle the accounts of (a business) by paying debts, apportioning assets, etc. 2 to pay (a debt) 3 to convert into cash 4 to get rid of, as by killing —**liq'ui·da' tion** *n.* —**liq'ui·da'tor** *n.*

liq·uid·ize (–wid iz') *vt.* -**ized'**, -**iz'ing** to cause to become liquid

liq·ui·fy (lik'wi fī') *vt., vi.* -**fied'**, -**fy'ing** *alt. sp. of* LIQUEFY

liq·uor (lik'ər) *n.* [L] 1 any liquid 2 an alcoholic drink, esp. a distilled drink, as whiskey or rum

li·ra (lir'ə) *n., pl.* **li're** (–ā) or **li'ras** [< L *libra*, a pound] the former monetary unit of Italy, superseded in 2002 by the EURO

Lis·bon (liz'bən) capital of Portugal

lisle (līl) *n.* [after Lisle (now Lille), city in France] 1 a fine, hard, extra-strong cotton thread 2 a fabric woven of lisle

lisp (lisp) *vi.* [< OE *wlisp*, a lisping] 1 to substitute the sounds (th) and (*th*) for the sounds of *s* and *z*, respectively 2 to speak imperfectly —*vt.* to utter with a lisp —*n.* the act or sound of lisping

lis·some or **lis·som** (lis'əm) *adj.* [< *lithesome*] lithe, supple, agile, etc.

list¹ (list) *n.* [< OE *liste*, border] a series of names, numbers, etc. set forth in order —*vt.* to enter in a list, directory, etc.

list² (list) *vi.* [prob. ult. < OE *lust*, desire] to tilt to one side: said of a ship, etc. —*n.* such a tilting

lis·ten (lis'ən) *vi.* [< OE *hlysnan*] 1 to make a conscious effort to hear 2 to give heed; take advice —**lis'ten·er** *n.*

list·ing *n.* 1 the making of a list 2 an entry in a list

list·less (–lis) *adj.* [< OE *lust*, desire + -LESS] indifferent because of illness, dejection, etc.; languid —**list'less·ly** *adv.* —**list'less·ness** *n.*

list price retail price as given in a list or catalog

lists (lists) *pl.n.* [< ME *liste*, border] a fenced area in which knights jousted

Liszt (list), **Franz** (fränts) 1811–86; Hung. composer & pianist

lit¹ (lit) *vt., vi. alt. pt. & pp. of* LIGHT¹

lit² *abbrev.* 1 liter(s) 2 literally 3 literary 4 literature

lit·a·ny (lit'n ē) *n., pl.* -**nies** [< Gr *litē*, a request] 1 a series of fixed invocations and responses, used as a prayer 2 a repetitive series, as of complaints, misfortunes, etc.

li·tchi (lē'chē') *n.* [< Chin] the raisinlike fruit of a Chinese evergreen tree, enclosed in a papery shell

lite (līt) *adj. informal sp. of* LIGHT² (*adj.* 8)

li·ter (lēt'ər) *n.* [< Gr *litra*, a pound] the basic metric unit of volume, equal to 1 cubic decimeter or 61.0237 cubic inches: Brit. sp. **li'tre**

lit·er·a·cy (lit'ər ə sē) *n.* the ability to read and write

lit·er·al (lit'ər əl) *adj.* [< L *littera*, a letter] 1 following exactly the wording of the original [a *literal* translation] 2 in a basic or strict sense [the *literal* meaning] 3 prosaic; matter-of-fact [a *literal* mind] 4 restricted to the facts [the *literal* truth] —**lit'er·al· ly** *adv.*

lit·er·ar·y (lit'ər er'ē) *adj.* 1 of or having to do with literature or books 2 familiar with or versed in literature

lit·er·ate (lit'ər it) *adj.* [< L *littera*, a letter] 1 able to read and write 2 well-educated —*n.* a literate person

lit·e·ra·ti (lit'ə rät'ē) *pl.n.* [It < L *litterati*: see prec.] writers, scholars, etc.

lit·er·a·ture (lit'ər ə chər') *n.* [< L *littera*, a letter] 1 *a)* all writings in prose or verse of an imaginative character *b)* all such writings having permanent value, excellence of form, etc. *c)* all the writings of a particular time, country, etc. *d)* all the writings on a particular subject 2 any printed matter

lithe (līth) *adj.* **lith'er**, **lith'est** [OE *lithe*, soft] bending easily; flexible; supple: also **lithe'some** (–səm)

lith·i·um (lith'ē əm) *n.* [< Gr *lithos*, stone] a soft, silver-white, chemical element: symbol, Li; at. no. 3

lithium carbonate a white, powdery salt, used in making glass, dyes, etc. and in treating bipolar disorders

lith·o·graph (lith'ə graf') *n.* a print made by lithography —*vi., vt.* to make (prints or copies) by this process —**li·thog·ra·pher** (li thäg' rə fər) *n.*

li·thog·ra·phy (li thäg'rə fē) *n.* [< Gr *lithos*, stone + -GRAPHY] printing from a flat stone or metal plate, parts of which have been treated to repel ink **—lith·o·graph·ic** (lith′ə graf′ik) *adj.*

lith·o·sphere (lith′ō sfir′) *n.* 〖< Gr *lithos*, stone + *sphaira*, sphere〗 the solid, rocky part of the earth; earth's crust

Lith·u·a·ni·a (lith′ōō ā′nē ə) country in N Europe **—Lith′u·a′ni·an** *adj., n.*

lit·i·gant (lit′ī gənt) *n.* 〖see fol.〗 a party to a lawsuit

lit·i·gate (-gāt′) *vt., vi.* **-gat′ed, -gat′ing** 〖< L *lis*, dispute + *agere*, do〗 to contest in a lawsuit **—lit′i·ga′tion** *n.* **—lit′i·ga′tor** *n.*

li·ti·gious (li tij′əs) *adj.* 〖see prec.〗 1 *a)* given to filing lawsuits *b)* quarrelsome 2 of lawsuits **—li·ti′gious·ness** *n.*

lit·mus (lit′məs) *n.* 〖< ON *litr*, color + *mosi*, moss〗 a purple coloring matter obtained from various lichens: paper treated with it (**litmus paper**) turns blue in bases and red in acids

litmus test a test in which a single factor determines the finding

LittD or **Litt.D.** *abbrev.* Doctor of Letters

lit·ter (lit′ər) *n.* 〖< L *lectus*, a couch〗 1 a framework enclosing a couch on which a person can be carried 2 a stretcher for carrying the sick or wounded 3 straw, hay, etc. used as bedding for animals 4 granular clay used in an indoor receptacle (**litter box**) to absorb cat waste 5 the young borne at one time by a dog, cat, etc. 6 things lying about in disorder, esp. bits of rubbish **—vt.** 1 to make untidy 2 to scatter about carelessly

lit·ter·bug (-bug′) *n.* [Inf.] one who litters public places with rubbish, etc.

lit·tle (lit′′l) *adj.* **lit′tler** or **less** or **less′er**, **lit′tlest** or **least** 〖OE *lytel*〗 1 small in size, amount, degree, etc. 2 short in duration; brief 3 small in importance or power [the rights of the *little* man] 4 narrow-minded [a *little* mind] **—adv. less, least** 1 slightly; not much 2 not in the least **—n.** a small amount, degree, etc. **—little by little** gradually **— make (or think) little of** to consider as not very important **—lit′tle·ness** *n.*

Little Dipper, the a dipper-shaped group of stars containing the North Star

Little Rock capital of Arkansas

lit·to·ral (lit′ər əl) *adj.* 〖< L *litus*, seashore〗 of or along the shore

lit·ur·gy (lit′ər jē) *n., pl.* **-gies** 〖ult. < Gr *leos, laos*, people + *ergon*, work〗 prescribed ritual for public worship **—li·tur′gi·cal** (lə tur′ji kəl) *adj.*

liv·a·ble (liv′ə bəl) *adj.* 1 fit or pleasant to live in [a *livable* house] 2 endurable: said as of a way of life Also sp. **live′a·ble**

live¹ (liv) *vi.* **lived, liv′ing** 〖OE *libban*〗 1 to have life 2 *a)* to remain alive *b)* to endure 3 to pass one's life in a specified manner 4 to enjoy life [to know how to *live*] 5 to feed [to *live* on fruit] 6 to reside **—vt.** 1 to carry out in one's life [to *live* one's faith] 2 to spend; pass [to *live* a useful life] **—live down** to live so as to wipe out the shame of (a misdeed, etc.) **—live up to** to live or act in accordance with (one's ideals, etc.)

live² (līv) *adj.* 〖< ALIVE〗 1 having life 2 of present interest [a *live* issue] 3 still burning [a *live* spark] 4 unexploded [a *live* shell] 5 carrying electrical current [a *live* wire] 6 *a)* in person *b)* broadcast, recorded, etc. during the actual performance 7 *Sports* in play [a *live* ball]

live·bear·er (līv′ber′ər) *n.* any of various small freshwater fishes of the American tropics, as the guppy and molly

-lived (līvd, livd) *combining form* having (a specified kind of) life [long-*lived*]

live-in *adj.* living in someone's residence as a domestic servant, lover, etc.

live·li·hood (līv′lē hood′) *n.* 〖< OE *lif*, life + *-lad*, course〗 means of living or of supporting life

live·long (liv′lôŋ′) *adj.* 〖ME *lefe longe*, lit., lief long: *lief* is merely intens.〗 long in passing; whole [the *livelong* day]

live·ly (līv′lē) *adj.* **-li·er, -li·est** 〖OE *liflic*〗 1 full of life; vigorous 2 full of spirit; exciting 3 animated, cheerful, etc. 4 vivid; keen 5 rebounding with great resilience [a *lively* ball] **—live′li·ness** *n.*

liv·en (līv′ən) *vt., vi.* to make or become lively; cheer: often with *up*

liv·er (liv′ər) *n.* 〖OE *lifer*〗 1 the largest glandular organ in vertebrate animals: it secretes bile and is important in metabolism 2 the liver of cattle, fowl, etc., used as food

liv·er·mo·ri·um (liv′ər môr′ē əm) *n.* 〖after the Lawrence Livermore National Laboratory in California〗 an artificially produced, radioactive, metallic chemical element: symbol, Lv; at. no. 116

Liv·er·pool (liv′ər pool′) seaport in NW England

liv·er·wurst (liv′ər wurst′) *n.* 〖< Ger *leber*, liver + *wurst*, sausage〗 a sausage containing ground liver

liv·er·y (liv′ər ē) *n., pl.* **-er·ies** 〖ME, gift of clothes to a servant〗 1 an identifying uniform as of a servant 2 *a)* the care and feeding of horses for a fee *b)* the keeping of horses or vehicles for hire *c)* a stable for this (usually **livery stable**) 3 a place where boats can be rented

lives (līvz) *n. pl. of* LIFE

live·stock (līv′stäk′) *n.* domestic animals raised for use and sale

liv·id (liv′id) *adj.* 〖< L *lividus*〗 1 discolored by a bruise; black-and-blue 2 grayish-blue: sometimes taken to mean pale or red [*livid* with rage] 3 very angry; enraged

liv·ing (liv′iŋ) *adj.* 1 alive; having life 2 in active operation or use [a *living* institution] 3 of persons alive [within *living* memory] 4 true; lifelike 5 of life [*living* conditions] **—n.** 1 a being alive 2 livelihood 3 manner of existence **—the living** those that are still alive

living room a room in a home, with sofas, chairs, etc., used for social activities, entertaining guests, etc.

living wage a wage sufficient to maintain a reasonable level of comfort

living will a document directing that the signer's life not be artificially supported during a terminal illness

liz·ard (liz′ərd) *n.* [< L *lacerta*] any of various slender, scaly reptiles with four legs and a tail, as the chameleon and iguana

ll *abbrev.* lines

LL *abbrev.* Late Latin

-'ll (əl) *suffix* will or shall: used in contractions [*she'll* sing]

lla·ma (lä′mə) *n.* [Sp < AmInd (Peru)] a South American beast of burden related to the camel but smaller and without a hump

lla·no (lä′nō) *n., pl.* **-nos** [Sp < L *planus*, plain] any of the level, grassy plains of Spanish America

LLB or **LL.B.** *abbrev.* Bachelor of Laws

LLD or **LL.D.** *abbrev.* Doctor of Laws

lo (lō) *interj.* [OE *la*] [Archaic] look! see!

load (lōd) *n.* [< OE *lad*, a course, journey] 1 an amount carried at one time 2 something borne with difficulty; burden 3 the amount of work assigned to a person, group, etc. 4 an amount put into a washing machine, dishwasher, etc. 5 [*often pl.*] [Inf.] a great amount or number 6 *Finance* an amount added to the price of mutual fund shares to cover costs, etc. —*vt.* 1 to put a (load) into or upon (a carrier) 2 to burden; oppress 3 to supply in large quantities 4 to put a charge of ammunition into (a firearm) 5 *Comput.* to transfer (a program or data) into main memory from a disk, etc. —**load′er** *n.* —**load′ing** *n.*

load·star (lōd′stär′) *n.* LODESTAR

load·stone (lōd′stōn′) *n.* LODESTONE

loaf¹ (lōf) *n., pl.* **loaves** (lōvz) [OE *hlaf*] 1 a portion of bread baked in one piece 2 any food baked in this shape

loaf² (lōf) *vi.* [prob. < fol.] to spend time idly; idle, dawdle, etc.

loaf·er¹ *n.* [prob. < Ger *landläufer*, a vagabond] one who loafs; idler

loaf·er² *n.* [orig. a trademark] a moccasinlike shoe for casual wear

loam (lōm) *n.* [OE *lam*] a rich soil, esp. a mixture of clay, sand, and organic matter —**loam′ y** *adj.* **-i·er**, **-i·est**

loan (lōn) *n.* [< ON *lān*] 1 the act of lending 2 something lent, esp. money at interest — *vt.*, *vi.* to lend

loan·er *n.* 1 one who loans something 2 an automobile, TV, etc. lent in place of one left for repair

loan shark [Inf.] one who lends money at illegal rates of interest

loan·word *n.* a word of one language taken into and used in another

loath (lōth) *adj.* [< OE *lath*, hostile] reluctant [to be *loath* to depart]

loathe (lōth) *vt.* **loathed**, **loath′ing** [< OE *lathian*, be hateful] to feel intense dislike or disgust for; abhor

loath·ing *n.* intense dislike, disgust, or hatred; abhorrence

loath·some *adj.* causing loathing; disgusting

loaves (lōvz) *n. pl. of* LOAF¹

lob (läb) *vt., vi.* **lobbed**, **lob′bing** [< ME *lobbe*, heavy] to toss or hit (a ball) in a high curve —**lob′ber** *n.*

lob·by (läb′ē) *n., pl.* **-bies** [LL *lobia*] 1 an entrance hall, as of a hotel or theater 2 a group of lobbyists representing the same interest —*vi.* **-bied**, **-by·ing** to act as a lobbyist

lob·by·ist *n.* a person, acting on behalf of a group, who tries to get legislators to support certain measures

lobe (lōb) *n.* [< Gr *lobos*] a rounded projecting part, as the lower part of the ear or any of the divisions of the lung

lo·bot·o·my (lō bät′ə mē) *n., pl.* **-mies** [< prec. + -TOMY] a surgical incision into a lobe of the brain: now rarely used as a treatment

lob·ster (läb′stər) *n.* [< OE *loppe*, spider + -*estre*, -ster] an edible sea crustacean usually with four pairs of legs and a pair of large pincers

lobster tail the tail of any of various crustaceans, prepared as food

lo·cal (lō′kəl) *adj.* [< L *locus*, a place] 1 of, characteristic of, or confined to a particular place 2 of or for a particular part of the body [*local* anesthesia] 3 making all stops along its run [a *local* bus] —*n.* 1 a local train, bus, etc. 2 a branch, as of a labor union 3 [Inf.] a resident of a particular place —**lo′cal·ly** *adv.*

lo·cale (lō kal′) *n.* [OFr *local*] a place or locality, esp. with reference to events, etc. associated with it

lo·cal·i·ty (lō kal′ə tē) *n., pl.* **-ties** a place; district; neighborhood

lo·cal·ize (lō′kəl īz′) *vt.* **-ized′**, **-iz′ing** to limit, confine, or trace to a particular place —**lo′cal·i·za′tion** *n.*

lo·cate (lō′kāt′, lō kāt′) *vt.* **-cat′ed**, **-cat′ing** [< L *locus*, a place] 1 to establish in a certain place [offices *located* downtown] 2 to discover the position of 3 to show the position of [to *locate* Guam on a map] —*vi.* [Inf.] to settle [she *located* in Ohio]

lo·ca·tion *n.* 1 a locating or being located 2 position; place —**on location** *Film* in an outdoor setting, away from the studio

loc. cit. *abbrev.* [L *loco citato*] in the place cited

loch (läk, läkh) *n.* [< Gael & Old Ir] [Scot.] 1 a lake 2 an arm of the sea

lock¹ (läk) *n.* [< OE *loc*, a bolt] 1 a mechanical device for fastening a door, strongbox, etc. as with a key or combination 2 an enclosed part of a canal, etc. equipped with gates for changing the water level to raise or lower boats 3 the mechanism of a firearm that explodes the charge 4 [Slang] a sure thing —*vt.* 1 to fasten with a lock 2 to shut (*up*, *in*, or *out*) by means of a lock 3 to link [to *lock* arms] 4 to jam together so as to make immovable 5 to make definite or unvarying [*locked* into a good interest rate] —*vi.* 1 to become locked 2 to interlock

lock² (läk) *n.* [OE *loc*] a curl of hair

lock·er *n.* 1 a chest, closet, etc. which can be locked 2 a large compartment for freezing and storing foods

lock·et (läk′it) *n.* ‖< OFr *loc*, a latch, lock‖ a small, hinged case of gold, etc. for holding a picture, lock of hair, etc.: usually worn on a necklace

lock·jaw *n.* a form of tetanus, in which the jaws become firmly closed

lock·out *n.* the shutdown of a plant to bring the workers to an agreement

lock·smith *n.* one whose work is making or repairing locks and making keys

lock·up *n.* a jail

lo·co (lō′kō) *adj.* ‖Sp, mad‖ [Slang] crazy; demented

loco disease a nervous disease of horses, cattle, etc. caused by locoweed poison

lo·co·mo·tion (lō′kə mō′shən) *n.* ‖< L *locus*, a place + MOTION‖ motion, or the power of moving, from one place to another

lo·co·mo·tive (-mōt′iv) *adj.* of or capable of locomotion —*n.* an electric, steam, or diesel engine on wheels, designed to push or pull a railroad train

lo·co·weed (lō′kō wēd′) *n.* a plant of W North America that causes the loco disease of cattle, horses, etc.

lo·cus (lō′kəs) *n., pl.* **lo′ci′** (-sī′) ‖L‖ 1 a place 2 *Math.* a line, plane, etc. every point of which satisfies a given condition

lo·cust (lō′kəst) *n.* ‖< L *locusta*‖ 1 a large grasshopper often traveling in swarms and destroying vegetation 2 SEVENTEEN-YEAR LOCUST 3 a tree of the E or Central U.S., with clusters of fragrant, white flowers

lo·cu·tion (lō kyōō′shən) *n.* ‖< L *loqui*, speak‖ a word, phrase, or expression

lode (lōd) *n.* ‖< OE *lad*, course‖ a vein, stratum, etc. of metallic ore

lode·star *n.* a star by which one directs one's course; esp., the North Star

lode·stone *n.* 1 a strongly magnetic variety of iron ore 2 something that attracts strongly

lodge (läj) *n.* ‖< OFr *loge*, arbor‖ 1 *a)* a small house for some special use [a hunting *lodge*] *b)* a resort hotel or motel 2 the local chapter or hall of a fraternal society —*vt.* **lodged, lodg′ing** 1 to house temporarily 2 to shoot, thrust, etc. firmly (*in*) 3 to bring (a complaint, etc.) before legal authorities 4 to confer (powers) upon: with *in* —*vi.* 1 to live (*with* or *in*) as a paying guest 2 to come to rest and stick firmly (*in*)

lodg·er *n.* one who lives in a rented room in another's home

lodg·ing *n.* 1 a place to live in, esp. temporarily 2 [*pl.*] a room or rooms rented in a private home

loft (lôft, läft) *n.* ‖< ON *lopt*, upper room, air‖ 1 the space just below the roof of a house, barn, etc. 2 an upper story of a warehouse or factory; specif., a dwelling space, artist's studio, etc. in such an upper story 3 a gallery [a choir *loft*] 4 height given to a ball hit or thrown —*vt.* to give (a ball) into a high curve

loft bed a bed on a platform or balcony allowing the use of the floor area below as part of a living room, etc.

loft·y *adj.* **-i·er, -i·est** 1 very high 2 elevated; noble 3 haughty; arrogant —**loft′i·ness** *n.*

log¹ (lôg, läg) *n.* ‖ME *logge*‖ 1 a section of the trunk or of a large branch of a felled tree 2 a device for measuring the speed of a ship 3 a record of progress, speed, etc., specif. one kept on a ship's voyage or aircraft's flight —*vt.* **logged, log′ging** 1 to saw (trees) into logs 2 to record in a log 3 to sail or fly (a specified distance) —*vi.* to cut down trees and remove the logs —**log on** (or **off**) to enter the necessary information to begin (or end) a session, as on a computer network

log² (lôg, läg) *n.* short for LOGARITHM

-log (lôg, läg) *combining form* -LOGUE

lo·gan·ber·ry (lō′gən ber′ē) *n., pl.* **-ries** [after J. H. *Logan*, who developed it (1881)] 1 a hybrid bramble developed from the blackberry and the red raspberry 2 its purplish-red fruit

log·a·rithm (lôg′ə rith əm, läg′–) *n.* ‖< Gr *logos*, ratio + *arithmos*, number] *Math.* the exponent expressing the power to which a fixed number must be raised to produce a given number —**log′a·rith′mic** *adj.*

loge (lōzh) *n.* ‖OFr: see LODGE‖ 1 a theater box or mezzanine section 2 a luxury suite in a stadium or arena

log·ger *n.* a person whose work is felling trees for use as lumber, etc.

log·ger·head *n.* ‖dial. *logger*, block of wood + HEAD‖ used chiefly in **at loggerheads,** in sharp disagreement

log·ic (läj′ik) *n.* ‖ult. < Gr *logos*, word] 1 correct reasoning, or the science of this 2 way of reasoning [bad *logic*] 3 what is expected by the working of cause and effect 4 *Comput.* the system of switching functions, circuits, or devices —**lo·gi·cian** (lō jish′ən) *n.*

log·i·cal (-i kəl) *adj.* ‖ML *logicalis*‖ 1 based on or using logic 2 expected because of what has gone before —**log′i·cal·ly** *adv.*

lo·gis·tics (lō jis′tiks) *n.* ‖< Fr *loger*, to quarter, lodge] 1 the military science of procuring, maintaining, and transporting materiel and personnel 2 the managing of the details of an undertaking —**lo·gis′tic** *adj.,* **lo·gis′ti·cal** —**lo·gis′ti·cal·ly** *adv.*

log·jam *n.* 1 an obstacle formed by logs jamming together in a stream 2 piled-up work, etc. that obstructs progress 3 a deadlock

lo·go (lō′gō) *n.* ‖< Gr *logos*, a word] a distinctive company signature, trademark, etc.: also **log·o·type** (lôg′ə tīp′, läg′–)

log·roll·ing *n.* 1 mutual exchange of favors, esp. among legislators 2 the sport of balancing oneself on a floating log while rotating it with one's feet

-logue (lôg, läg) ‖see LOGIC‖ *combining form* a (specified kind of) speaking or writing [*Decalogue*]

lo·gy (lō′gē) *adj.* **-gi·er, -gi·est** ‖< ? Du *log*, dull] [Inf.] dull or sluggish

-logy (lə jē) ‖see LOGIC‖ *combining form* 1 a (specified kind of) speaking [*eulogy*] 2 the science, doctrine, or theory of [*biology*]

loin (loin) *n.* ‖< L *lumbus*‖ 1 [*usually pl.*] the

lower part of the back between the hipbones and the ribs **2** the front part of the hindquarters of beef, lamb, etc. **3** [*pl.*] the hips and the lower abdomen regarded as the region of strength, etc.

loin·cloth *n.* a cloth worn about the loins, as by some peoples in warm climates

loi·ter (loit′ər) *vi.* [< MDu *loteren*] **1** to spend time idly; linger **2** to move slowly and idly —**loi′ter·er** *n.*

loll (läl) *vi.* [< MDu *lollen*, mumble, doze] **1** to lean or lounge about lazily **2** to hang loosely; droop (the camel's tongue *lolled* out) —*vt.* to let hang loosely

lol·li·pop or **lol·ly·pop** (läl′ē päp′) *n.* [prob. < dial. *lolly*, the tongue + *pop*] a piece of hard candy on the end of a stick

lol·ly·gag (läl′ē gag′) *vi.* **-gagged′**, **-gag′ ging** [var. of *lallygag* < ?] [Inf.] to waste time in trifling or aimless activity

Lon·don (lun′dən) capital of England & the United Kingdom

lone (lōn) *adj.* [< *alone*] **1** by oneself; solitary **2** isolated

lone·ly *adj.* **-li·er**, **-li·est 1** solitary or isolated **2** unhappy at being alone —**lone′li· ness** *n.*

lon·er (lōn′ər) *n.* [Inf.] one who prefers to be independent of others, as by living or working alone

lone·some *adj.* **1** having or causing a lonely feeling **2** unfrequented

long[1] (lôŋ) *adj.* [< OE] **1** measuring much in space or time **2** in length (six feet *long*) **3** of greater than usual length, quantity, etc. (a *long* list) **4** tedious; slow **5** far-reaching (a *long* view of the matter) **6** well-supplied (*long* on excuses) —*adv.* **1** for a long time **2** from start to finish (all day *long*) **3** at a remote time (*long* ago) —**as** (or **so**) **long as 1** during the time that **2** seeing that; since **3** provided that —**before long** soon

long[2] (lôŋ) *vi.* [< OE *langian*] to feel a strong yearning; wish earnestly

long[3] *abbrev.* longitude

Long Beach seaport in SW California, on the Pacific

long distance a telephone service for calls to and from distant places —**long′-dis′tance** *adj., adv.*

lon·gev·i·ty (län jev′ə tē, lôn-) *n.* [< L *longus*, long + *aevum*, age] long life

long-faced *adj.* glum

long·hair *adj.* [Inf.] of intellectuals or intellectual tastes

long·hand *n.* ordinary handwriting, as distinguished from shorthand or typed characters

long·ing *n.* strong desire; yearning —*adj.* feeling or showing a yearning

Long Island island in SE New York, in the Atlantic south of Connecticut

lon·gi·tude (län′jə tōōd′) *n.* [< L *longus*, long] distance east or west of the prime meridian, expressed in degrees or by the difference in time

lon·gi·tu·di·nal (-tōōd′′n əl) *adj.* **1** of or in

length **2** running or placed lengthwise **3** of longitude

long jump *Sports* a jump for distance made with a running start

long-lived (-līvd′, -livd′) *adj.* having or tending to have a long life span

long-range *adj.* **1** having a range of a great distance **2** taking the future into consideration

long·shore·man (lôŋ′shôr′mən) *n., pl.* **-men** (-mən) [< *alongshore* + MAN] a person who works on a waterfront loading and unloading ships; stevedore

long shot [Inf.] **1** in betting, a choice that is little favored and, hence, carries great odds **2** a venture with only a slight chance of success, but offering potentially great rewards

long-stand·ing *adj.* having continued for a long time

long-suf·fer·ing *adj.* bearing trouble, etc. patiently for a long time

long-term *adj.* for or extending over a long time

long ton TON (*n.* 2)

Lon·gueuil (lôn gāl′) city in S Quebec: suburb of Montreal

long-wind·ed (-win′did) *adj.* **1** speaking or writing at great length **2** tiresomely wordy

look (look) *vi.* [< OE *locian*] **1** to direct one's eyes in order to see **2** to search **3** to appear; seem **4** to be facing in a specified direction —*vt.* **1** to direct one's eyes on **2** to have an appearance befitting (to *look* the part) —*n.* **1** a looking; glance **2** appearance; aspect **3** [Inf.] *a*) [*usually pl.*] appearance *b*) [*pl.*] personal appearance —*interj.* **1** see! **2** pay attention! —**look after** to take care of —**look down on** (or **upon**) to regard with contempt —**look for** to expect —**look forward to** to anticipate —**look in** (**on**) to pay a brief visit (to) —**look into** to investigate —**look out** to be careful —**look over** to examine —**look to 1** to take care of **2** to rely on —**look up 1** to search for as in a reference book **2** [Inf.] to call on —**look up to** to admire —**look′er** *n.*

look·er-on *n., pl.* **look′ers-on′** an observer or spectator; onlooker

looking glass a (glass) mirror

look·out *n.* **1** a careful watching **2** a place for keeping watch **3** a person detailed to watch **4** [Inf.] concern

look-see *n.* [Inf.] a quick look

loom[1] (lōōm) *n.* [< OE (*ge*)*loma*, tool] a machine for weaving thread or yarn into cloth

loom[2] (lōōm) *vi.* [< ?] to come into sight indistinctly, esp. threateningly

loon[1] (lōōn) *n.* [< ON *lomr*] a fish-eating diving bird, noted for its wailing or laughlike calls

loon[2] (lōōn) *n.* [< ?] a stupid or crazy person

loon·ie *n.* [< LOON[1], depicted on the reverse] [Cdn.] the Canadian one-dollar coin

loon·y *adj.* **-i·er**, **-i·est** [< LUNATIC] [Slang] crazy; demented

loop (lōōp) *n.* [ME *loup*] **1** the figure made by a line, thread, etc. that curves back to cross itself **2** anything forming this figure **3** an intrauterine device **4** a segment of movie film or magnetic tape joined end to end so as to be played continuously —*vt.* **1** to make a loop in or of **2** to fasten with a loop —*vi.* to form a loop or loops

loop·hole *n.* [prob. < MDu *lupen*, to peer + HOLE] **1** a hole in a wall for looking or shooting through **2** a means of evading an obligation, etc.

loop·y *adj.* **-i·er, -i·est** [Slang] **1** slightly crazy **2** confused

loose (lōōs) *adj.* **loos'er, loos'est** [< ON *lauss*] **1** not confined or restrained; free **2** not firmly fastened **3** not tight or compact **4** not precise [a *loose* translation] **5** sexually immoral **6** [Inf.] relaxed —*adv.* loosely —*vt.* **loosed, loos'ing 1** to set free; unbind **2** to make less tight, compact, etc. **3** to relax **4** to release (an arrow, etc.) —**on the loose** not confined; free —**loose'ly** *adv.* —**loose'ness** *n.*

loose cannon an uncontrollable person whose unpredictable words or actions cause embarrassment or harm to others

loose ends unsettled details —**at loose ends** unsettled, idle, etc.

loose-leaf *adj.* having leaves, or sheets, that can be removed or replaced easily

loos·en (lōōs'ən) *vt., vi.* to make or become loose or looser

loose·strife (lōōs'strif') *n.* a plant with long spikes of purple flowers

loos·ey-goos·ey (lōō'sē gōō'sē) [Slang] *adj.* relaxed; easy *adv.* in a loose, relaxed way

loot (lōōt) *n.* [Hindi *lut*] **1** goods stolen or taken by force; plunder **2** [Slang] money, gifts, etc. —*vt., vi.* to plunder

lop¹ (läp) *vt.* **lopped, lop'ping** [< OE *loppian*] **1** to trim (a tree, etc.) by cutting off branches, etc. **2** to remove by or as by cutting off: usually with *off*

lop² (läp) *vi.* **lopped, lop'ping** [prob. akin to LOB] to hang down loosely

lope (lōp) *vi.* **loped, lop'ing** [< ON *hlaupa*, to leap] to move with a long, swinging stride —*n.* such a stride

lop·sid·ed (läp'sīd'id) *adj.* noticeably heavier, bigger, or lower on one side

lo·qua·cious (lō kwā'shəs) *adj.* [< L *loqui*, speak] very talkative —**lo·qua'cious·ness** *n.* —**lo·quac'i·ty** (-kwas'ə tē) *n.*

lord (lôrd) *n.* [< OE *hlaf*, loaf + *weard*, keeper] **1** a ruler; master **2** the head of a feudal estate **3** [L-] *a)* God *b)* Jesus Christ **4** in Great Britain, a titled nobleman —**lord it over** to be overbearing toward

lord·ly *adj.* **-li·er, -li·est 1** noble; grand **2** haughty —*adv.* in the manner of a lord —**lord'li·ness** *n.*

Lord's Day [*sometimes* L- d-] Sunday: with *the*

lord·ship *n.* **1** the rank or authority of a lord **2** rule; dominion **3** the territory of a lord **4** [*often* L-] a title used in speaking to or of a lord

Lord's Prayer the prayer beginning *Our Father*: Matt. 6:9–13

lore (lôr) *n.* [< OE *lar*] knowledge; learning, esp. when passed down over time

lor·gnette (lôr nyet') *n.* [Fr < OFr *lorgne*, squinting] eyeglasses, or opera glasses, attached to a handle

lo·ris (lô'ris, lōr'is) *n.* [ult. < Du *loer*, a clown] a small, slow-moving, large-eyed Asiatic lemur that lives in trees and is active at night

lor·ry (lôr'ē) *n., pl.* **-ries** [prob. < dial. *lurry*, to pull] [Brit.] a motor truck

Los Al·a·mos (lôs al'ə mōs') town in NC New Mexico: site of nuclear energy research facility where the atomic bomb was developed

Los An·ge·les (lôs an'jə ləs) city & seaport on the coast of S California

lose (lōōz) *vt.* **lost, los'ing** [OE *losian*] **1** to become unable to find [to *lose* one's keys] **2** to have taken from one by accident, death, removal, etc. **3** to fail to keep [to *lose* one's temper] **4** to fail to see, hear, or understand **5** to fail to have, get, etc. [to *lose* one's chance] **6** to fail to win **7** to cause the loss of **8** to wander from (one's way, etc.) **9** to squander **10** to go slower by [a watch that *loses* five minutes a day] —*vi.* to suffer (a) loss —**lose oneself** to become absorbed —**los'er** *n.*

loss (lôs, läs) *n.* [ME *los*] **1** a losing or being lost **2** the damage, trouble, etc. caused by losing **3** the person, thing, or amount lost —**at a loss to** uncertain how to

lost (lôst, läst) *vt., vi. pt. & pp.* of LOSE —*adj.* **1** ruined; destroyed **2** not to be found; missing **3** no longer held, seen, heard, etc. **4** not gained or won **5** having wandered astray **6** wasted

lot (lät) *n.* [< OE *hlot*] **1** the deciding of a matter by chance, as by drawing counters **2** the decision thus arrived at **3** one's share by lot **4** fortune [her unhappy *lot*] **5** a plot of ground **6** a group of persons or things **7** [*often pl.*] [Inf.] a great number or amount [a *lot* of cars, *lots* of fun] **8** [Inf.] sort [he's a bad *lot*] —**a (whole) lot** a great deal; very much: somewhat informal —**draw** (or **cast**) **lots** to decide by lot

Lo·thar·i·o (lō ther'ē ō') *n., pl.* **-i·os'** [after the rake in the play *The Fair Penitent* (1703)] [*often* l-] a seducer of women; rake

lo·tion (lō'shən) *n.* [< L *lavare*, to wash] a liquid preparation used, as on the skin, for cleansing, healing, etc.

lots *adv.* a great deal; very much: somewhat informal

lot·ter·y (lät'ər ē) *n., pl.* **-ies** [< MDu *lot*, lot] **1** a game of chance in which people buy numbered tickets on prizes, winners being chosen by lot **2** a drawing, event, etc. based on chance

lot·to (lät'ō) *n.* [It < MDu: see LOT] a game resembling bingo

lo·tus (lōt'əs) *n.* [< Gr *lōtos*] **1** Gr. Legend a plant whose fruit induced forgetfulness **2** any of several mostly tropical waterlilies

lotus position in yoga, an erect sitting position with the legs crossed, each foot resting on the opposite thigh

loud (loud) *adj.* [< OE *hlud*] **1** strongly audible: said of sound **2** making a loud sound **3** noisy **4** emphatic *[loud* denials] **5** [Inf.] flashy —*adv.* in a loud manner —**loud′ly** *adv.* —**loud′ness** *n.*

loud·mouthed (-mouthd′, -moutht′) *adj.* talking in a loud, irritating voice

loud·speak·er *n.* SPEAKER (*n. 2*)

Lou·is (lōō′ē; *Fr* lwē; *Eng* lōō′is) **1 Louis XIV** 1638–1715; king of France (1643–1715) **2 Louis XV** 1710–74; king of France (1715–74) **3 Louis XVI** 1754–93; king of France (1774–92): guillotined

Lou·i·si·an·a (loo ē′zē an′ə) state of the S U.S.; cap. Baton Rouge: abbrev. *LA* —**Lou·i′si·an′i·an** *adj., n.*, **Lou·i′si·an′an**

Lou·is·ville (lōō′ə vəl) city in N Kentucky

lounge (lounj) *vi.* **lounged, loung′ing** [Scot dial. < ? *lungis,* a laggard] **1** to move, sit, lie, etc. in a relaxed way **2** to spend time in idleness —*n.* **1** a room with comfortable furniture for lounging **2** a couch or sofa

lounge·wear *n.* loose-fitting clothing for casual wear, esp. at home

louse (lous) *n., pl.* **lice** [< OE *lus*] **1** a small, wingless insect parasitic on humans and other animals **2** any similar insect parasitic on plants **3** *pl.* **lous′es** [Slang] a mean, contemptible person —**louse up** [Slang] to spoil; ruin

lous·y (lou′zē) *adj.* **-i·er, -i·est 1** infested with lice **2** [Slang] *a)* disgusting *b)* poor; inferior **3** well supplied (*with*) —**lous′i·ness** *n.*

lout (lout) *n.* [prob. < or akin to ME *lutien,* to lurk] a clumsy, stupid fellow —**lout′ish** *adj.*

lou·ver (lōō′vər) *n.* [< MDu *love,* gallery] **1** an opening, window, etc. fitted with a series of sloping slats arranged so as to admit light and air but shed rain **2** any of these slats

love (luv) *n.* [< OE *lufu*] **1** strong affection or liking for someone or something **2** a passionate affection of one person for another **3** the object of such affection; a sweetheart or lover **4** *Tennis* a score of zero — *vt., vi.* to feel love (for) —**fall in love (with)** to begin to feel love (for), esp. romantic love —**in love** feeling love, esp. romantic love —**make love 1** to woo, embrace, etc. **2** to have sexual intercourse —**lov′a·ble** *adj.,* **love′a·ble** —**love′less** *adj.*

love affair a romantic relationship between two people who are not married to each other

love·bird *n.* any of various small Old World parrots often kept as cage birds

love handles [Slang] bulges of fat at the sides of the waist

love·lorn (-lôrn′) *adj.* [LOVE + obs. *lorn,* lost] sad because not loved in return

love·ly *adj.* **-li·er, -li·est 1** beautiful **2** [Inf.] highly enjoyable —**love′li·ness** *n.*

lov·er (luv′ər) *n.* **1** a person who greatly enjoys something **2** one who loves; specif., either partner in a sexual relationship **3** [*pl.*] a couple in a romantic or sexual relationship

love seat a small sofa for two people

lov·ing *adj.* feeling or expressing love —**lov′ing·ly** *adv.*

loving cup a large drinking cup with two handles, often given as a trophy

low[1] (lō) *adj.* [< ON *lagr*] **1** not high or tall **2** below the normal level *[low* ground] **3** shallow **4** less in size, degree, etc. than usual *[low* speed] **5** deep in pitch **6** depressed in spirits **7** not of high rank; humble **8** vulgar; coarse **9** poor; inferior **10** not loud —*adv.* in or to a low level, degree, etc. —*n.* **1** a low level, degree, etc. **2** an arrangement of gears giving the lowest speed and greatest power **3** *Meteorol.* an area of low barometric pressure —**lay low** to overcome or kill —**lie low** to keep oneself hidden —**low′ness** *n.*

low[2] (lō) *n., vi.* [< OE *hlowan*] MOO

low-born *adj.* of humble birth

low·boy *n.* a chest of drawers mounted on short legs

low·brow *n.* one considered to lack cultivated tastes —*adj.* of or for a lowbrow

Low Countries the Netherlands, Belgium, & Luxembourg

low·down (lō′doun′; *for adj.,* -doun′) *n.* [Slang] the true, pertinent facts: with *the* —*adj.* [Inf.] mean; contemptible

low-end *adj.* [Inf.] **1** inexpensive and low in quality **2** having only the basic features

low·er[1] (lō′ər) *adj.* (*compar.* of LOW[1]) **1** below in place, rank, etc. **2** less in amount, degree, etc. **3** farther south —*vt.* **1** to let or put down *[lower* the window] **2** to reduce in height, amount, etc. **3** to bring down in respect, etc. —*vi.* to become lower

low·er[2] (lou′ər) *vi.* [ME *louren*] **1** to scowl or frown **2** to appear dark and threatening: said as of the sky —**low′er·ing** *adj.* —**low′er·ing·ly** *adv.*

low·er·case (lō′ər kās′) *n.* small-letter type or writing, as distinguished from capital letters —*adj.* of or in lowercase

low·er·class·man (-klas′mən) *n., pl.* **-men** (-mən) a student in the freshman or sophomore class of a high school or college

low frequency any radio frequency between 30 and 300 kilohertz

Low German 1 the group of dialects of N Germany **2** the branch of Germanic languages including English, Dutch, Frisian, etc.

low-grade *adj.* of low quality, degree, etc.

low-key *adj.* of low intensity, tone, etc.; subdued: also **low′-keyed′**

low·land (-lənd, -land′) *n.* land below the level of the surrounding land —*adj.* of, in, or from such a region —**the Lowlands** lowland region of SC Scotland

low·life *n., pl.* **-lifes′** a vulgar or undignified person

low·ly *adj.* **-li·er, -li·est 1** of low position or rank **2** humble; meek —**low′li·ness** *n.*

low-mind·ed *adj.* having or showing a coarse, vulgar mind

low-spir·it·ed *adj.* sad; depressed

low tide 1 the lowest level reached by the ebbing tide **2** the time at which this occurs

lox[1] (läks) *n.* [< Yiddish < Ger *lachs,* salmon] a kind of smoked salmon

lox² (läks) *n.* ⟦*l(iquid) ox(ygen)*⟧ liquid oxygen, esp. when used in rockets: also **LOX**

loy·al (loi′əl) *adj.* ⟦see LEGAL⟧ **1** faithful to one's country, friends, ideals, etc. **2** showing such faithfulness —**loy′al·ly** *adv.* —**loy′al·ty** *n., pl.* **-ties**

loy·al·ist *n.* one who supports the government during a revolt

loz·enge (läz′ənj) *n.* ⟦< OFr *losenge*⟧ **1** RHOMBUS **2** a cough drop or piece of hard candy

LP *n.* ⟦*L(ong) P(laying)*⟧ a large-sized phonograph record, for playing at 33⅓ revolutions per minute

LPN *n., pl.* **LPNs** licensed practical nurse

Lr *Chem. symbol for* lawrencium

LSD *n.* ⟦*l(y)s(ergic acid) d(iethylamide)*⟧ a chemical compound used in the study of mental disorders and as a psychedelic drug

Lt *abbrev.* Lieutenant

Ltd or **ltd** *abbrev.* limited

lu·au (lōō′ou′) *n.* a traditional Hawaiian feast

lube (lōōb) *n.* **1** a lubricating oil for machinery: also **lube oil 2** [Inf.] a lubrication —*vt.* **lubed, lub′ing** [Inf.] to lubricate

lu·bri·cant (lōō′bri kənt) *adj.* reducing friction by providing a smooth film over parts coming into contact —*n.* a lubricant oil, etc.

lu·bri·cate (-kāt′) *vt.* **-cat′ed, -cat′ing** ⟦< L *lubricus*, smooth⟧ **1** to make slippery or smooth **2** to apply a lubricant to (machinery, etc.) —*vi.* to serve as a lubricant —**lu′bri·ca′tion** *n.* —**lu′bri·ca′tor** *n.*

lu·cid (lōō′sid) *adj.* ⟦< L *lucere*, to shine⟧ **1** [Old Poet.] shining **2** transparent **3** sane **4** clear; readily understood —**lu·cid′i·ty** *n.* —**lu′cid·ly** *adv.*

Lu·ci·fer (lōō′sə fər) *n.* Satan

Lu·cite (lōō′sīt′) ⟦< L *lux*, light⟧ *trademark for* an acrylic resin that is molded into transparent or translucent sheets, rods, etc.

luck (luk) *n.* ⟦prob. < MDu *gelucke*⟧ **1** the seemingly chance happening of events that affect someone; fortune; lot **2** good fortune —**luck out** [Inf.] to be lucky —**luck′less** *adj.*

luck·y *adj.* **-i·er, -i·est 1** having good luck **2** resulting fortunately **3** believed to bring good luck —**luck′i·ly** *adv.* —**luck′i·ness** *n.*

lu·cra·tive (lōō′krə tiv) *adj.* ⟦< L *lucrum*, riches⟧ producing wealth or profit; profitable

lu·cre (lōō′kər) *n.* ⟦< L *lucrum*, riches⟧ riches; money: chiefly humorously derogatory

lu·cu·brate (lōō′kə brāt′, -kyōō-) *vi.* **-brat′ed, -brat′ing** ⟦< L *lucubrare*, to work by candlelight⟧ to work, study, or write laboriously, esp. late at night —**lu′cu·bra′tion** *n.*

lu·di·crous (lōō′di krəs) *adj.* ⟦< L *ludus*, a game⟧ causing laughter because absurd or ridiculous —**lu′di·crous·ly** *adv.* —**lu′di·crous·ness** *n.*

luff (luf) *vi.* ⟦< ME *lof*⟧ **1** to turn the bow of a ship toward the wind **2** to flutter: used of a sail

lug (lug) *vt.* **lugged, lug′ging** ⟦prob. < Scand⟧ to carry or drag (something heavy) —*n.* **1** an earlike projection by which a thing is held or supported **2** a heavy bolt, used, with a nut (**lug nut**), to secure a wheel to an axle

lug·gage (lug′ij) *n.* ⟦< prec.⟧ suitcases, trunks, etc.; baggage

lu·gu·bri·ous (lə gōō′brē əs) *adj.* ⟦< L *lugere*, mourn⟧ very sad or mournful, esp. in an exaggerated way —**lu·gu′bri·ous·ly** *adv.* —**lu·gu′bri·ous·ness** *n.*

Luke (lōōk) *n. Bible* **1** an early Christian, the reputed author of the third Gospel **2** this Gospel

luke·warm (lōōk′wôrm′) *adj.* ⟦< ME *luke*, tepid + *warm*, warm⟧ **1** slightly warm **2** lacking enthusiasm —**luke′warm′ly** *adv.* —**luke′warm′ness** *n.*

lull (lul) *vt.* ⟦ME *lullen*⟧ **1** to calm by gentle sound or motion **2** to bring into a specified condition by soothing and reassuring —*vi.* to become calm —*n.* a short period of calm

lull·a·by (-ə bī′) *n., pl.* **-bies** ⟦< ME, echoic⟧ a song for lulling a baby to sleep

lum·ba·go (lum bā′gō) *n.* ⟦L < *lumbus*, loin⟧ pain in the lower back

lum·bar (lum′bär) *adj.* ⟦< L *lumbus*, loin⟧ of or near the loins

lum·ber¹ (lum′bər) *n.* ⟦< ? pawnbrokers of Lombardy, Italy; hence, stored articles⟧ timber sawed into boards, etc. —*vi.* to cut down timber and saw it into lumber —**lum′ber·er** *n.* —**lum′ber·ing** *n.*

lum·ber² (lum′bər) *vi.* ⟦< ? Scand⟧ to move heavily and noisily —**lum′ber·ing** *adj.*

lum·ber·jack (-jak′) *n.* LOGGER

lum·ber·man (-mən) *n., pl.* **-men** (-mən) one who deals in lumber

lu·mi·nar·y (lōō′mə ner′ē) *n., pl.* **-nar′ies** ⟦< L *lumen*, a light⟧ **1** a body that gives off light, such as the sun **2** a famous or notable person

lu·mi·nes·cence (lōō′mə nes′əns) *n.* ⟦< L *lumen*, a light + -ESCENCE⟧ the giving off of light without heat, as in fluorescence or phosphorescence —**lu′mi·nes′cent** *adj.*

lu·mi·nous (lōō′mə nəs) *adj.* ⟦< L *lumen*, a light⟧ **1** giving off light; bright **2** clear; readily understood —**lu′mi·nos′i·ty** (-näs′ə tē) *n.*

lum·mox (lum′əks) *n.* ⟦< ?⟧ [Inf.] a clumsy, stupid person

lump¹ (lump) *n.* ⟦ME *lompe*⟧ **1** an indefinitely shaped mass of something **2** a swelling **3** [pl.] [Inf.] hard blows, criticism, etc. —*adj.* in a lump or lumps —*vt.* **1** to put together in a lump or lumps **2** to treat or deal with in a mass —*vi.* to become lumpy —**lump′i·ness** *n.* —**lump′y** *adj.* **-i·er, -i·est**

lump² (lump) *vt.* ⟦< ?⟧ [Inf.] to have to put up with [like it or *lump* it]

lump sum a gross, or total, sum paid at one time

lu·na·cy (lōō′nə sē) *n.* ⟦< LUNATIC⟧ **1** insanity **2** great folly or a foolish act

lu·nar (lōō′nər) *adj.* ⟦< L *luna*, the moon⟧ of or like the moon

lu·na·tic (lōō′nə tik) *adj.* ⟦< L *luna*, the moon⟧ **1** insane or for insane persons **2** utterly foolish —*n.* an insane person

lunch (lunch) *n.* ⟦< ? Sp *lonja*, slice of ham⟧ a light meal; esp., the midday meal between breakfast and dinner —*vi.* to eat lunch

lunch·eon (lun′chən) *n.* a lunch; esp., a formal lunch

lunch·eon·ette (-et′) *n.* a place where light lunches are served

lunch·meat *n.* meat processed in the form of loaves, sausages, etc. and ready to eat: also **luncheon meat**

lung (luŋ) *n.* ⟦OE *lungen*⟧ either of the two spongelike organs in the thorax of air-breathing vertebrates

lunge (lunj) *n.* ⟦< Fr *allonger*, lengthen⟧ 1 a sudden thrust as with a sword 2 a sudden plunge forward — *vi., vt.* **lunged, lung′ing** to move, or cause to move, with a lunge

lung·fish (luŋ′fish′) *n., pl.* **-fish** or **-fish′es** any of various fishes having lungs as well as gills

lunk·head (luŋk′hed′) *n.* ⟦prob. echoic alteration of LUMP¹ + HEAD⟧ [Inf.] a stupid person: also **lunk**

lu·pine (lōō′pīn′; *for n.,* -pin) *adj.* ⟦< L *lupus*, wolf⟧ of or like a wolf —*n.* a plant with long spikes of white, rose, yellow, or blue flowers

lu·pus (lōō′pəs) *n.* ⟦< L, a wolf⟧ any of various diseases with skin lesions

lurch¹ (lurch) *vi.* ⟦< ?⟧ 1 to pitch or sway suddenly to one side 2 to stagger —*n.* a lurching movement

lurch² (lurch) *n.* ⟦prob. < OFr *lourche*, duped⟧ a difficult situation: only in **leave someone in the lurch**

lure (loor) *n.* ⟦< OFr *loirre*⟧ 1 anything that tempts or entices 2 a bait used in fishing —*vt.* **lured, lur′ing** to attract; tempt; entice

lu·rid (loor′id) *adj.* ⟦L *luridus*, ghastly⟧ 1 glowing through a haze: said as of flames hidden by smoke 2 shocking; sensational —**lu′rid·ly** *adv.* —**lu′rid·ness** *n.*

lurk (lurk) *vi.* ⟦ME *lurken*⟧ to stay hidden, ready to attack, spring out, etc.

lus·cious (lush′əs) *adj.* ⟦ME *lucius*⟧ 1 highly gratifying to taste or smell; delicious 2 delighting any of the senses —**lus′cious·ness** *n.*

lush¹ (lush) *adj.* ⟦< ? OFr *lasche*, lax⟧ 1 of or showing luxuriant growth 2 rich, abundant, extravagant, etc. —**lush′ness** *n.*

lush² (lush) *n.* [Slang] an alcoholic

lust (lust) *n.* ⟦OE, pleasure⟧ 1 bodily appetite; esp., excessive sexual desire 2 overwhelming desire *[a lust for power]* —*vi.* to feel an intense desire —**lust′ful** *adj.* —**lust′ful·ly** *adv.* —**lust′ful·ness** *n.*

lus·ter (lus′tər) *n.* ⟦< L *lustrare*, illumine⟧ 1 gloss; sheen 2 brightness; radiance 3 brilliant beauty or fame; glory Also [Chiefly Brit.] **lus′tre**

lus·trous (-trəs) *adj.* having luster; shining

lust·y (lus′tē) *adj.* **-i·er, -i·est** full of vigor; robust —**lust′i·ly** *adv.* —**lust′i·ness** *n.*

lute (lōōt) *n.* ⟦ult. < Ar *al'ūd*, the wood⟧ an old stringed instrument like the guitar, with a rounded body

lu·te·nist (lōōt′'n ist) *n.* a lute player: also **lu′ta·nist**

lu·te·ti·um (lōō tē′shē əm) *n.* ⟦< L *Lutetia*, ancient name of Paris, France⟧ a soft, silvery-white chemical element: symbol, Lu; at. no. 71

Lu·ther (lōō′thər), **Mar·tin** (märt′'n) 1483-1546; Ger. Reformation leader

Lu·ther·an *adj.* of the Protestant denomination founded by Luther —*n.* a member of a Lutheran Church —**Lu′ther·an·ism′** *n.*

lut·ist (lōōt′ist) *n.* LUTENIST

Lux·em·bourg (luk′səm burg′) grand duchy in W Europe, north of France

lux·u·ri·ant (lug zhoor′ē ənt) *adj.* ⟦see LUXURY⟧ 1 growing with vigor and in abundance 2 having rich ornamentation, etc. —**lux·u′ri·ance** *n.*

lux·u·ri·ate (-āt′) *vi.* **-at′ed, -at′ing** 1 to live in great luxury 2 to revel (*in*) —**lux·u′ri·a′tion** *n.*

lux·u·ri·ous (-əs) *adj.* 1 fond of or indulging in luxury 2 constituting luxury; rich, comfortable, etc. —**lux·u′ri·ous·ly** *adv.*

lux·u·ry (luk′shə rē, lug′zhə rē) *n., pl.* **-ries** ⟦< L *luxus*⟧ 1 the use and enjoyment of the best and most costly things 2 anything contributing to such enjoyment, usually something not necessary —*adj.* characterized by luxury

Lu·zon (lōō zän′) main island of the Philippines

-ly¹ (lē) ⟦< OE *-lic*⟧ *suffix* 1 like or characteristic of *[manly]* 2 happening (once) every (specified period of time) *[monthly, hourly]*

-ly² (lē) ⟦< OE *-lice*⟧ *suffix* 1 in a (specified) manner or direction, to a (specified) extent, in or at a (specified) time or place *[harshly, inwardly, hourly]* 2 in the (specified) order *[thirdly]*

ly·ce·um (lī sē′əm) *n.* ⟦< Gr *Lykeion*, grove at Athens where Aristotle taught⟧ 1 a lecture hall 2 an organization presenting lectures, etc.

ly·chee (lē′chē′) *n. alt. sp. of* LITCHI

Ly·cra (lī′krə) *trademark for* a spandex fabric used in athletic apparel, etc.

lye (lī) *n.* ⟦OE *leag*⟧ any strongly alkaline substance, used in cleaning, making soap, etc.

ly·ing¹ (lī′iŋ) *vi. prp. of* LIE¹

ly·ing² (lī′iŋ) *vt., vi. prp. of* LIE² —*adj.* false; not truthful —*n.* the telling of a lie or lies

ly·ing-in *n.* confinement in childbirth —*adj.* of or for childbirth

lymph (limf) *n.* ⟦L *lympha*, spring water⟧ a clear, yellowish body fluid, found in the spaces between cells and in the lymphatic vessels

lym·phat·ic (lim fat′ik) *adj.* containing lymph

lymph node any of the small, compact structures lying in groups along the course of the lymphatic vessels

lym·pho·cyte (lim′fō sīt′) *n.* a leukocyte formed in lymphatic tissue, important in the synthesis of antibodies

lymph·oid (lim′foid′) *adj.* of or like lymph or the tissue of the lymph nodes

lym·pho·ma (lim fō′mə) *n.* any of a group of diseases resulting from the proliferation of malignant lymphoid cells

lynch (linch) *vt.* ⟦after W. *Lynch*, vigilante in VA in 1780⟧ to murder (an accused person) by mob action and without lawful trial, as by hanging —**lynch′ing** *n.*

lynx (liŋks) *n.* [< Gr *lynx*] any of several wild-cats, esp. of N parts of Eurasia and North America, having a short tail and tufted ears

lynx-eyed (-īd′) *adj.* keen-sighted

Lyon (lyōn′) city in EC France

ly·on·naise (lī′ə nāz′) *adj.* [Fr] prepared with sliced onions

lyre (līr) *n.* [< Gr *lyra*] a small stringed instrument of the harp family, used by the ancient Greeks

lyr·ic (lir′ik) *adj.* [< Gr *lyrikos*] 1 suitable for singing; specif., designating or of poetry expressing the poet's personal emotion 2 of or having a high voice with a light, flexible quality [a *lyric* tenor] —*n.* 1 a lyric poem 2 [*usually pl.*] the words of a song

lyr·i·cal (-i kəl) *adj.* 1 LYRIC 2 expressing rapture or great enthusiasm

lyr·i·cism (-ə siz′əm) *n.* lyric quality or style

lyr·i·cist (-ə sist) *n.* a writer of lyrics, esp. lyrics for popular songs

ly·ser·gic acid (lī sur′jik) *see* LSD

-ly·sis (lə sis, li-) [< Gr *lysis*, a loosening] *combining form* a loosening, dissolving, destruction, etc. [*catalysis, electrolysis*]

-lyte (līt) [< Gr *lyein*, dissolve] *combining form* a substance undergoing decomposition [*electrolyte*]

M

m¹ or **M** (em) *n., pl.* **m's, M's** the 13th letter of the English alphabet

m² *abbrev.* 1 married 2 masculine 3 medium 4 meter(s) 5 mile(s) 6 minute(s)

M¹ (em) *n.* a Roman numeral for 1,000

M² *abbrev.* 1 male 2 married 3 medium 4 Monday 5 Monsieur

ma (mä) *n.* [Inf.] MOTHER (*n.* 1)

MA *abbrev.* 1 Massachusetts 2 [L *Magister Artium*] Master of Arts: also **M.A.**

ma'am (mam, mäm) *contr. n.* [Inf.] madam: used in direct address

ma·ca·bre (mə käb′rə, mə käb′) *adj.* [< OFr (*danse*) *Macabré*, (dance) of death] grim and horrible; gruesome

mac·ad·am (mə kad′əm) *n.* [after J. L. McAdam (1756-1836), Scot engineer] small broken stones used in making roads, esp. such stones mixed with tar or asphalt

Ma·cao (mə kou′) administrative zone of China, near Hong Kong: formerly under Portuguese administration

mac·a·ro·ni (mak′ə rō′nē) *n.* [It *maccaroni*, ult. < Gr *makar*, blessed] pasta in the form of tubes, etc.

mac·a·roon (mak′ə rōōn′) *n.* [see prec.] a small, chewy cookie made with crushed almonds or coconut

ma·caw (mə kô′) *n.* [prob. < AmInd (Brazil)] any of several large, bright-colored parrots of Central and South America

Mac·beth (mək beth′) *n.* a Scot. king, the title character of a tragedy by Shakespeare

Mac·ca·bees (mak′ə bēz′) *n.* a family of Jewish patriots who led a successful revolt against the Syrians (175-164 B.C.)

mace¹ (mās) *n.* [OFr *masse*] 1 a heavy, spiked war club, used in the Middle Ages 2 a staff used as a symbol of authority by certain officials

mace² (mās) *n.* [< ML *macis*] a spice made from the husk of the nutmeg

Mace (mās) [< MACE¹] *trademark for* a gas, sold in aerosol containers, that temporarily stuns its victims —*n.* [*often* m-] such a substance, or a container of it —*vt.* **Maced, Mac′ing** [*often* m-] to spray with Mace

Mac·e·do·ni·a (mas′ə dō′nē ə) 1 ancient kingdom in SE Europe 2 country in the Balkan Peninsula —**Mac′e·do′ni·an** *adj., n.*

mac·er·ate (mas′ər āt′) *vt.* **-at′ed, -at′ing** [< L *macerare*, soften] 1 to soften and separate into parts by soaking in liquid 2 to steep (fruit or vegetables), as in wine 3 loosely, to tear, chop, etc. into bits —**mac′er·a′tion** *n.*

ma·che·te (mə shet′ē, -chet′ē) *n.* [Sp < L *marcus*, hammer] a large knife used for cutting sugar cane, underbrush, etc., esp. in Central and South America

Mach·i·a·vel·li·an (mak′ē ə vel′ē ən, mäk′-) *adj.* [after N. *Machiavelli* (1469-1527), It statesman] crafty; deceitful

mach·i·na·tion (mak′ə nā′shən) *n.* [< L *machinari*, to plot] a plot or scheme, esp. one with evil intent: *usually used in pl.*

ma·chine (mə shēn′) *n.* [< Gr *mēchos*, contrivance] 1 *a*) a device with various moving parts, for doing some kind of work *b*) an electronic device, as a computer 2 an organization functioning like a machine 3 the controlling group in a political party 4 *Mech.* a device, as the lever, that transmits, or changes the application of, energy —*adj.* 1 of machines 2 done by machinery —*vt.* **-chined′, -chin′ing** to make, shape, etc. by machinery

machine gun an automatic gun, firing a rapid stream of bullets

machine language a language entirely in binary digits, used directly by a computer

ma·chin·er·y (mə shēn′ər ē, -shēn′rē) *n., pl.*

-ies 1 machines collectively **2** the working parts of a machine **3** the means for keeping something going

ma·chin·ist (mə chēz'mō) *n.* one who makes, repairs, or operates machinery

ma·chis·mo (mä chēz'mō) *n.* [Sp < *macho*, masculine + *-ismo*, -ISM] overly assertive or exaggerated masculinity

Mach number (mäk) [after E. *Mach* (1838-1916), Austrian physicist] [*also* **m- n-**] a number indicating the ratio of an object's speed to the speed of sound in the surrounding medium: written as **Mach 1, Mach 2,** etc.

ma·cho (mä'chō) *adj.* [Sp, masculine] exhibiting or characterized by assertive, exaggerated masculinity

mack·er·el (mak'ər əl) *n., pl.* **-el** or **-els** [< OFr *maquerel*] an edible fish of the North Atlantic

Mack·i·naw (coat) (mak'ə nô') [after *Mackinac* Island in N Lake Huron] [*also* **m-**] a short, heavy, double-breasted woolen coat, usually plaid

mack·in·tosh (mak'in täsh') *n.* [after C. *Macintosh* (1766-1843), Scot inventor] a raincoat, orig., one made of rubberized cloth

mac·ra·mé (mak'rə mā') *n.* [Fr, ult. < Ar *miqramah*, a veil] a coarse fringe or lace made as of cord knotted in designs

mac·ro (mak'rō) *n., pl.* **-ros** [< MACROIN-STRUCTION] a single computer instruction that represents a given sequence of instructions

macro- [< Gr *makros*, long] *combining form* long, large, enlarged

mac·ro·bi·ot·ics (-bī ät'iks) *pl.n.* [< prec. + Gr *bios*, life] [*with sing. v.*] the attempt to promote health and prolong life by the use of special diets, etc. —**mac'ro·bi·ot'ic** *adj.*

mac·ro·cosm (-käz'əm) *n.* [see MACRO- & COSMOS] **1** the universe **2** any large, complex entity

ma·cron (mä'krən) *n.* [< Gr *makros*, long] a mark (̄) placed over a vowel to indicate its pronunciation

mad (mad) *adj.* **mad'der, mad'dest** [< OE *(ge)mǣdan*, make mad] **1** insane **2** frantic [*mad* with fear] **3** foolish and rash **4** infatuated [he's *mad* about her] **5** wildly amusing **6** having rabies [a *mad* dog] **7** angry: often with *at* —**mad'ly** *adv.* —**mad'ness** *n.*

Mad·a·gas·car (mad'ə gas'kər) island country off the SE coast of Africa

mad·am (mad'əm) *n., pl.* **mad'ams; for 1,** usually **mes·dames** (mā däm', -dam') [Fr *madame*, orig. *ma dame*, my lady] **1** a woman; lady: a polite term of address **2** a woman in charge of a brothel

ma·dame (mə däm', -dam'; mad'əm; Fr mä däm') *n., pl.* **mes·dames** (mā däm', -dam'; Fr mä däm') [Fr: see prec.] **1** a married woman: French title equivalent to *Mrs.* **2** a distinguished woman: used in English as a title of respect

mad·cap (mad'kap') *n.* [MAD + CAP¹, figurative for head] a zany, uninhibited person —*adj.* zany and uninhibited

mad·den (mad'n) *vt., vi.* to make or become insane, angry, or wildly excited —**mad'den·ing** *adj.* —**mad'den·ing·ly** *adv.*

mad·der (mad'ər) *n.* [OE *mædere*] **1** any of various related plants, esp. a vine with yellow flowers and a red root **2** a red dye made from this root

made (mād) *vt., vi. pt. & pp. of* MAKE

ma·de·moi·selle (mad'ə mə zel'; Fr mäd mwä zel') *n., pl.* **-selles'; mes·de·moi·selles** (mäd mwä zel') [Fr < *ma*, my + *demoiselle*, young lady] an unmarried woman or girl: French title equivalent to *Miss*

made-to-or·der *adj.* made to conform to the customer's specifications

made-up *adj.* **1** put together **2** invented; false [a *made-up* story] **3** with cosmetics applied

mad·house *n.* **1** an insane asylum: a dated term, now somewhat offensive **2** any place of turmoil, noise, etc.

Mad·i·son¹ (mad'ə sən), **James** 1751-1836; 4th president of the U.S. (1809-17)

Mad·i·son² (mad'ə sən) capital of Wisconsin

mad·man (-man', -mən) *n., pl.* **-men'** (-men', -mən) a man who is or seems to be mentally ill: not in scientific use

Ma·don·na (mə dän'ə) *n.* [It < *ma*, my + *donna*, lady] **1** Mary, mother of Jesus **2** a picture or statue of Mary

ma·dras (ma'drəs, mə dras') *n.* [after fol.] a fine, firm cotton cloth, usually striped or plaid

Ma·dras (mə dras', -dräs') seaport on the SE coast of India: now officially *Chennai*

ma·dras·sa or **ma·dras·a** (mə dras'ə, -drä'sə) *n.* [Ar *madrasa* < *darasa*, to study] a school for the study of Islam, often affiliated with a mosque

Ma·drid (mə drid') capital of Spain, in the central part

mad·ri·gal (ma'dri gəl) *n.* [< It] a part song, without accompaniment, popular in the 1400s to the 1600s

mad·wom·an *n., pl.* **-wom'en** a woman who is or seems to be mentally ill

mael·strom (māl'strəm) *n.* [< Du *malen*, to grind + *stroom*, a stream] **1** a large or violent whirlpool **2** an agitated state of mind, affairs, etc.

mae·stro (mīs'trō) *n., pl.* **-tros** or **-tri** (-trē) [It < L *magister*, master] a master in any art; esp., a great composer or conductor of music

Ma·fi·a (mä'fē ə) *n.* [It *maffia*] **1** a secret society of Italian origin engaged in illegal activities **2** [**m-**] any group engaged in organized crime

Ma·fi·o·so (mä'fē ō'sō) *n., pl.* **-si** (-sē) [*also* **m-**] a member of the Mafia

mag·a·zine (mag'ə zēn') *n.* [< Ar *makhzan*, storehouse] **1** a military supply depot **2** a space in which explosives are stored, as in a fort **3** a supply chamber, as in a rifle or camera **4** a periodical publication containing stories, articles, etc.

Ma·gel·lan (mə jel'ən), **Fer·di·nand** (furd'n and') 1480?-1521; Port. navigator in the service of Spain

ma·gen·ta (mə jen′tə) *n.* [after *Magenta,* town in Italy] **1** a purplish-red dye **2** purplish red —*adj.* purplish-red

mag·got (mag′ət) *n.* [ME *magotte*] a wormlike insect larva, as of the housefly —**mag′got·y** *adj.*

Ma·gi (mā′jī′) *pl.n., sing.* **-gus** (-gəs) [< Old Pers *magus,* magician] the wise men who came bearing gifts to the infant Jesus

mag·ic (maj′ik) *n.* [< Gr *magikos,* of the Magi, ancient Persian priests] **1** the use of charms, spells, etc. in seeking or pretending to control events **2** any mysterious power [the *magic* of love] **3** the art of producing illusions by sleight of hand, etc. —*adj.* **1** of, produced by, or using magic **2** producing extraordinary results, as if by magic —**mag′i·cal** *adj.* —**mag′i·cal·ly** *adv.*

magic bullet an invention, discovery, etc. that solves a particular problem; esp., a medicine that can cure a disease

ma·gi·cian (mə jish′ən) *n.* [< OFr *magicien*] an expert in magic

mag·is·te·ri·al (maj′is tir′ē əl) *adj.* **1** of or suitable for a magistrate or master **2** authoritative —**mag′is·te′ri·al·ly** *adv.*

mag·is·trate (maj′is trāt′) *n.* [< L *magister,* master] **1** a civil officer empowered to administer the law **2** a minor official, as a justice of the peace

mag·ma (mag′mə) *n.* [< Gr *massein,* knead] molten rock in the earth, which solidifies to produce igneous rock

Mag·na Car·ta or **Mag·na Char·ta** (mag′nə kär′tə) [ML, great charter] the royal charter, granted in 1215, that guarantees certain civil and political liberties to the English people

mag·nan·i·mous (mag nan′ə məs) *adj.* [< L *magnus,* great + *animus,* soul] generous in overlooking injury or insult; rising above pettiness; noble —**mag′na·nim′i·ty** (-nə nim′ə tē) *n.* —**mag·nan′i·mous·ly** *adv.*

mag·nate (mag′nāt) *n.* [< L *magnus,* great] a very influential person, esp. in business

mag·ne·sia (mag nē′zhə, -shə) *n.* [ModL, ult. < Gr *Magnēsia,* ancient Gr city] magnesium oxide, a white powder, used as a mild laxative and antacid

mag·ne·si·um (-zē əm) *n.* [ModL: see prec.] a lightweight, metallic chemical element: symbol, Mg; at. no. 12

mag·net (mag′nit) *n.* [see MAGNESIA] **1** any piece of iron or certain other materials that has the property of attracting similar material **2** one that attracts

mag·net·ic (mag net′ik) *adj.* **1** having the properties of a magnet **2** of, producing, or caused by magnetism **3** of the earth's magnetism **4** that can be magnetized **5** powerfully attractive —**mag·net′i·cal·ly** *adv.*

magnetic field a physical field arising from a magnet or from an electric charge in motion, producing a force on other magnetic materials or on moving electric charges

magnetic tape a thin plastic ribbon having a magnetized coating, used for recording sounds, digital computer data, etc.

mag·net·ism (mag′nə tiz′əm) *n.* **1** the property, quality, or condition of being magnetic **2** the force to which this is due **3** personal charm

mag·net·ite (-tīt′) *n.* [< Ger] black iron oxide, an important iron ore

mag·net·ize (-tīz′) *vt.* **-ized′, -iz′ing 1** to give magnetic properties to (steel, iron, etc.) **2** to charm (a person) —**mag′net·i·za′tion** *n.*

mag·ne·to (mag nēt′ō) *n., pl.* **-tos** an electric generator, often a small one, in which one or more permanent magnets produce the magnetic field

mag·ne·tom·e·ter (mag′nə täm′ət ər) *n.* **1** an instrument for measuring magnetic forces **2** such an instrument used as to detect concealed metal weapons at airports, etc.

magnet school a public school offering new and special courses to attract students from a broad urban area so as to bring about desegregation

mag·nif·i·cent (mag nif′ə sənt) *adj.* [< L *magnus,* great + *facere,* do] **1** splendid, stately, or sumptuous, as in form **2** exalted: said of ideas, etc. **3** [Inf.] excellent —**mag·nif′i·cence** *n.* —**mag·nif′i·cent·ly** *adv.*

mag·ni·fy (mag′nə fī′) *vt.* **-fied′, -fy′ing** [see prec.] **1** to exaggerate **2** to increase the apparent size of, esp. with a lens **3** [Archaic] to praise —*vi.* to have the power of increasing the apparent size of an object —**mag′ni·fi·ca′tion** *n.* —**mag′ni·fi′er** *n.*

mag·ni·tude (-tōōd′) *n.* [< L *magnus,* great] **1** greatness of size, extent, etc. **2** *a)* size *b)* loudness (of sound) *c)* importance **3** the degree of brightness of a star, etc.

mag·no·li·a (mag nō′lē ə, -nōl′yə) *n.* [after P. *Magnol* (1638-1715), Fr botanist] a tree with large, fragrant flowers of white, pink, or purple

mag·num (mag′nəm) *n.* [< L *magnus,* great] **1** a wine bottle holding 1.5 liters **2** [*usually* M-] a firearm, esp. a revolver, that fires magnum cartridges —*adj.* of or pertaining to a cartridge having great explosive force for its size

mag·num o·pus (mag′nəm ō′pəs) [L] a great work; masterpiece

mag·pie (mag′pī′) *n.* [< *Mag,* dim. of *Margaret* + *pie,* magpie] **1** a noisy, black-and-white bird related to the jay **2** a person who talks much and foolishly

Mag·yar (mag′yär′) *n.* **1** a member of the main ethnic group of Hungary **2** the language of this people; Hungarian

ma·ha·ra·jah or **ma·ha·ra·ja** (mä′hə rä′jə) *n.* [< Sans *mahā,* great + *rājā,* king] [Historical] in India, a prince, specif. one ruling any of the chief states

ma·ha·ra·ni (-nē) *n., pl.* **-nee** the wife of a maharajah

ma·ha·ri·shi (mä′hə rish′ē) *n.* [Hindi < *mahā,* great + *ṛshi,* sage] a Hindu teacher of mysticism

ma·hat·ma (mə hat′mə, -hät′-) *n.* [< Sans *mahā*, great + *ātman*, soul] in India, any of a class of wise and holy persons held in special regard

mah-jongg or **mah·jong** (mä′jôṅ′, -zhôṅ′) *n.* [< Chin *ma-ch'iao*, sparrow, a figure on one of the tiles] a game of Chinese origin played with small pieces called *tiles*

Mah·ler (mä′lər), **Gus·tav** (goos′täf′) 1860-1911; Austrian composer & conductor

ma·hog·a·ny (mə häg′ə nē, -hôg′-) *n., pl.* **-nies** [< ?] **1** *a)* a tropical American tree *b)* the reddish-brown wood of this tree **2** reddish brown

Ma·hom·et (mə häm′it) *var. of* MUHAMMAD

ma·hout (mə hout′) *n.* [< Hindi] in India, an elephant driver or keeper

maid (mād) *n.* **1** [Now Chiefly Literary] a girl or young unmarried woman **2** a female servant

maid·en (mād′n) *n.* [OE *mægden*] [Now Chiefly Literary] a girl or young unmarried woman —*adj.* **1** of or for a maiden **2** unmarried or virgin **3** untried **4** first [a *maiden* voyage] —**maid′en·hood′** *n.* —**maid′en·ly** *adj.*

maid·en·hair (fern) a delicate fern

maid·en·head (-hed′) *n.* the hymen

maiden name the surname that a married woman had when not yet married

maid of honor an unmarried woman acting as chief attendant to a bride

maid·ser·vant *n.* a female servant

mail¹ (māl) *n.* [< OHG *malaha*, wallet] **1** letters, packages, etc. transported and delivered by the post office **2** a postal system **3** EMAIL —*adj.* of mail —*vt.* to send by mail —**mail′er** *n.*

mail² (māl) *n.* [< L *macula*, mesh of a net] flexible body armor made of small metal rings, scales, etc.

mail·box *n.* **1** a box into which mail is put when delivered **2** a box into which mail is put for collection **3** *Comput.* the location of incoming messages in an email system Also **mail box**

mail carrier a person who carries and delivers mail

mail·man (-man′, -mən) *n., pl.* **-men′** (-men′, -mən) a man who is a mail carrier

mail order an order for goods to be sent by mail —**mail′-or′der** *adj.*

maim (mām) *vt.* [OFr *mahaigner*] to disable; mutilate

main (mān) *n.* [OE *mægen*, strength] **1** a principal pipe in a distribution system for water, gas, etc. **2** [Old Poet.] the ocean —*adj.* chief in size, importance, etc.; principal —**by main force (or strength)** by sheer force (or strength) —**in the main** mostly; chiefly —**with might and main** with all one's strength

main clause *Gram.* INDEPENDENT CLAUSE

main drag [Slang] the principal street of a city or town

Maine (mān) New England state of the U.S.; cap. Augusta: abbrev. ME —**Main·er** (mā′nər) *n.*

main·frame (mān′frām′) *n.* **1** the central processing unit of a large computer **2** a very large computer, to which several terminals may be connected

main·land (-land′, -lənd) *n.* the principal landmass of a continent or large island, in relation to smaller islands nearby —**main′land′er** *n.*

main·line *n.* the principal road, course, etc. —*vt.* **-lined′, -lin′ing** [Slang] to inject (a narcotic drug) directly into a large vein

main·ly *adv.* chiefly; principally

main·mast (-mast′; *naut.,* -məst) *n.* the principal mast of a vessel

main·sail (-sāl′; *naut.,* -səl) *n.* the principal sail of a vessel, set from the mainmast

main·spring *n.* **1** the principal spring in a clock, watch, etc. **2** the chief motive or cause

main·stay *n.* **1** the supporting line extending forward from the mainmast **2** a chief support

main·stream *n.* a major trend or line of thought, action, etc. —*vt.* to cause to undergo mainstreaming

main·stream·ing *n.* the placement of disabled people into regular school classes, workplaces, etc.

main·tain (mān tān′) *vt.* [< L *manu tenere*, hold in the hand] **1** to keep or keep up; carry on **2** to keep in continuance or in a certain state, as of repair **3** to affirm or assert **4** to support by providing what is needed —**main·tain′a·ble** *adj.*

main·te·nance (mänt′n əns) *n.* a maintaining or being maintained

mai tai (mī′ tī′) [Tahitian, lit., good] [*often* M- T-] a cocktail of rum, fruit juices, etc.

mai·tre d' (māt′ər dē′) [< fol.] [Inf.] MAÎTRE D'HÔTEL

maî·tre d'hô·tel (me tr′ dô tel′) [Fr, master of the house] a supervisor of waiters and waitresses

maize (māz) *n.* [< WInd *mahiz*] **1** *chiefly Brit.* name for CORN¹ (*n.* 2) **2** yellow

Maj *abbrev.* Major

ma·jes·tic (mə jes′tik) *adj.* grand; stately —**ma·jes′ti·cal·ly** *adv.*

maj·es·ty (maj′is tē) *n., pl.* **-ties** [< L *magnus*, great] **1** [M-] a title used in speaking to or of a sovereign **2** grandeur

ma·jol·i·ca (mə jäl′i kə) *n.* [It] Italian glazed pottery

ma·jor (mā′jər) *adj.* [L, compar. of *magnus*, great] **1** great or greater in size, amount, importance, etc. **2** *Music* designating an interval greater than the corresponding minor by a half tone —*vi. Educ.* to specialize (*in* a field of study) —*n.* **1** *U.S. Mil.* an officer ranking just above a captain **2** a field of study in which a student specializes

ma·jor-do·mo (-dō′mō) *n., pl.* **-mos** [< L *major*, greater + *domus*, house] a man in charge of a great household

ma·jor·ette (-et′) *n.* a girl or woman with a baton, who leads or accompanies a marching band; drum majorette

major general *pl.* **major generals** *U.S. Mil.* an

officer ranking just above a brigadier general

ma·jor·i·ty (mə jôr′ə tē) *n., pl.* **-ties** [see MAJOR] **1** [*also with pl. v.*] the greater number; more than half of a total **2** the number by which the votes cast for the candidate who receives more than half the votes, exceed the remaining votes **3** full legal age **4** the military rank of a major

major scale a musical scale with semitones between the third and fourth and the seventh and eighth tones, and whole tones in all other positions

make (māk) *vt.* **made, mak′ing** [OE *macian*] **1** to bring into being; build, create, produce, etc. **2** to cause to be or become [*made* king, *made* sad] **3** to prepare for use [*make* the beds] **4** to amount to [two pints *make* a quart] **5** to have the qualities of [to *make* a fine leader] **6** to acquire; earn **7** to cause the success of [that venture *made* her] **8** to regard as the meaning (*of*) [what do you *make* of that?] **9** to execute, do, etc. [to *make* a speech] **10** to cause or force: with an infinitive without *to* [*make* him behave] **11** to arrive at; reach [the ship *made* port] **12** [Inf.] to get on or in [to *make* the team] —*vi.* **1** to behave as specified [*make* bold] **2** to cause something to be as specified [*make* ready] —*n.* **1** the way in which something is made; style **2** a type or brand —**make away with** to steal —**make believe** to pretend —**make someone's day** [Inf.] to give pleasure that will be the high point of someone's day —**make do** to manage with what is available —**make for 1** to go toward **2** to help effect —**make good** [Inf.] **1** to repay or replace **2** to fulfill **3** to succeed —**make it** [Inf.] to achieve a certain thing —**make off with** to steal —**make out 1** to see with difficulty **2** to understand **3** to fill out (a check, etc.) **4** to (try to) show or prove to be **5** to succeed; get along **6** [Slang] *a*) to kiss and caress as lovers *b*) to have sexual intercourse —**make over 1** to change; renovate **2** to transfer the ownership of —**make something of 1** to treat as of great importance **2** [Inf.] to make an issue of —**make up 1** to put together **2** to form; constitute **3** to invent **4** to complete by providing what is lacking **5** to compensate (*for*) **6** to become friendly again after a quarrel **7** to put on cosmetics, etc. —**make up one's mind** to come to a decision —**make up to** [Inf.] to try to win over, as by flattering —**make′a·ble** *adj.* **mak′a·ble** —**mak′er** *n.*

make-be·lieve *n.* pretense; feigning —*adj.* pretended; feigned

make·o·ver *n.* **1** a renovation **2** a change in someone's appearance made by altering makeup, hairstyle, etc.

make·shift *n.* a temporary substitute or expedient —*adj.* serving as a temporary substitute

make·up or **make-up** *n.* **1** the way something is put together; composition **2** nature; disposition **3** the cosmetics, etc. used by an actor **4** cosmetics generally

make-work *adj.* that serves no other purpose

than to give an idle or unemployed person something to do [a *make-work* project]

mal- [< L *malus*, bad] *prefix* bad or badly, wrong, ill

mal·ad·just·ed (mal′ə jus′tid) *adj.* poorly adjusted; specif., unable to adjust to the stresses of daily life —**mal′ad·just′ment** *n.*

mal·a·droit (mal′ə droit′) *adj.* [Fr: see MAL- & ADROIT] awkward; clumsy; bungling —**mal′a·droit′ly** *adv.*

mal·a·dy (mal′ə dē) *n., pl.* **-dies** [< VL *male habitus*, badly kept] a disease

ma·laise (ma lāz′) *n.* [Fr < *mal*, bad + *aise*, ease] **1** a vague feeling of illness **2** a pervasive sense of depression or trouble

mal·a·mute (mal′ə myōōt′) *n.* [< *Malemute*, an Eskimo people] a strong dog developed in North American arctic regions for pulling sleds

mal·a·prop·ism (mal′ə prăp′iz′əm) *n.* [after Mrs. *Malaprop* in Sheridan's play *The Rivals* (1775)] a ludicrous misuse of words that sound alike

ma·lar·i·a (mə ler′ē ə) *n.* [It < *mala aria*, bad air] an infectious disease transmitted by the anopheles mosquito, characterized by severe chills and fever —**ma·lar′i·al** *adj.*

ma·lar·key or **ma·lar·ky** (mə lär′kē) *n.* [< ?] [Slang] nonsensical talk

mal·a·thi·on (mal′ə thī′än′) *n.* [< chemical names] an organic insecticide

Ma·la·wi (mä′lä wē′) country in SE Africa

Ma·lay (mā′lā′, mə lā′) *n.* **1** any of a group of languages spoken by indigenous peoples of the Malay Peninsula and the Malay Archipelago, including the official languages of Malaysia and Indonesia **2** a member of any of these peoples —*adj.* of these peoples or their language or culture

Mal·a·ya·lam (mal′ə yä′ləm) *n.* a language of the SW coast of India

Malay Archipelago large group of islands between SE Asia & Australia

Malay Peninsula peninsula in SE Asia

Ma·lay·sia (mə lā′zhə) **1** MALAY ARCHIPELAGO **2** country in SE Asia, mostly on the Malay Peninsula —**Ma·lay′sian** *adj., n.*

mal·con·tent (mal′kən tent′) *adj.* [OFr: see MAL- & CONTENT¹] dissatisfied or rebellious —*n.* a malcontent person

Mal·dives (mal′dīvz) country on a group of islands (**Mal′dive Islands**) in the Indian Ocean

male (māl) *adj.* [< L *mas*, a male] designating of or the sex that fertilizes the ovum **2** of, like, or suitable for men or boys; masculine **3** having a part shaped to fit into a corresponding hollow part (called *female*): said of electric plugs, etc. —*n.* a male person, animal, or plant

mal·e·dic·tion (mal′ə dik′shən) *n.* [see MAL- & DICTION] a curse

mal·e·fac·tor (–fak′tər) *n.* [< L *male*, evil + *facere*, do] an evildoer or criminal —**mal′e·fac′tion** *n.*

ma·lef·i·cent (mə lef′ə sənt) *adj.* [< L: see prec.] harmful —**ma·lef′i·cence** *n.*

ma·lev·o·lent (mə lev′ə lənt) *adj.* [< L *male*, evil + *velle*, to wish] wishing evil or harm to others; malicious —**ma·lev′o·lence** *n.*

mal·fea·sance (mal fē′zəns) *n.* [< Fr *mal*, evil + *faire*, do] wrongdoing, esp. by a public official

mal·for·ma·tion (mal′fôr mā′shən) *n.* faulty or abnormal formation of a body or part —**mal·formed′** *adj.*

mal·func·tion (mal funk′shən) *vi.* to fail to function as it should —*n.* an instance of malfunctioning

Ma·li (mä′lē) country in W Africa

mal·ice (mal′is) *n.* [< L *malus*, bad] 1 active ill will; desire to harm another 2 *Law* evil intent

ma·li·cious (mə lish′əs) *adj.* having, showing, or caused by malice; spiteful —**ma·li′cious·ly** *adv.*

ma·lign (mə līn′) *vt.* [< L *male*, ill + *genus*, born] to speak evil of; slander —*adj.* 1 malicious 2 evil; baleful 3 very harmful

ma·lig·nan·cy (-nən sē) *n.* 1 malignant quality 2 *pl.* **-cies** a malignant tumor

ma·lig·nant (mə lig′nənt) *adj.* [see MALIGN] 1 having an evil influence 2 wishing evil 3 very harmful 4 causing or likely to cause death; specif., cancerous —**ma·lig′ni·ty** (-nə tē) *n., pl.* **-ties**

ma·lin·ger (mə lin′gər) *vi.* [< Fr *malingre*, sickly] to feign illness so as to escape duty —**ma·lin′ger·er** *n.*

mall (môl) *n.* [< *maul*, mallet: from use in a game on outdoor lanes] 1 a shaded walk or public promenade 2 *a)* a shop-lined street for pedestrians only *b)* an often enclosed shopping center

mal·lard (mal′ərd) *n.* [< OFr *malart*] the common wild duck

mal·le·a·ble (mal′ē ə bəl) *adj.* [< L *malleus*, a hammer] 1 that can be hammered, pounded, or pressed into various shapes without breaking 2 adaptable —**mal′le·a·bil′i·ty** *n.*

mal·let (mal′ət) *n.* [< L *malleus*, a hammer] 1 a short-handled hammer with a wooden head, for driving a chisel, etc. 2 any similar, long-handled hammer, as for use in croquet or polo 3 a small hammer for playing a xylophone, etc.

mal·low (mal′ō) *n.* [< L *malva*] any of a family of plants, including the hollyhock, cotton, and okra, with large, showy flowers

mal·nour·ished (mal nur′isht) *adj.* improperly nourished

mal·nu·tri·tion (mal′noo trish′ən) *n.* faulty or inadequate nutrition or nourishment

mal·oc·clu·sion (-ə kloo′zhən) *n.* improper meeting of the upper and lower teeth

mal·o·dor·ous (-ō′dər əs) *adj.* having a bad odor; stinking

mal·prac·tice (-prak′tis) *n.* professional misconduct or improper practice, esp. by a physician

malt (môlt) *n.* [OE *mealt*] barley or other grain soaked until it sprouts, then dried in a kiln: used in brewing and distilling —*adj.* made with malt

Mal·ta (môl′tə) country on a group of islands in the Mediterranean, south of Sicily

malt·ed (milk) a drink made by mixing a preparation of powdered malt and dried milk, with milk, ice cream, etc.

Mal·tese (môl tēz′) *n.* 1 the language of Malta, closely related to Arabic 2 *pl.* **Maltese′** a person born or living in Malta —*adj.* of Malta or its people, language, etc.

malt liquor beer, ale, or the like made of malt by fermentation

mal·treat (mal trēt′) *vt.* [see MAL- & TREAT] to treat roughly, unkindly, or brutally; abuse —**mal·treat′ment** *n.*

mal·ware (mal′wer′) *n.* [*mal(icious soft)ware*] any unauthorized program or set of instructions, as a virus, designed to disrupt the normal functioning of a computer

ma·ma or **mam·ma** (mä′mə, mə mä′) *n. child's term for* MOTHER (n. 1)

mam·mal (mam′əl) *n.* [< L *mamma*, breast] any of a large group of warmblooded vertebrates the females of which have milk-secreting glands (**mam′ma·ry glands**) for feeding their offspring —**mam·ma·li·an** (mə mā′lē ən) *adj., n.*

mam·mo·gram (mam′ə gram′) *n.* an X-ray obtained by mammography

mam·mog·ra·phy (mə mäg′rə fē) *n.* [< L *mamma*, breast + -GRAPHY] an X-ray technique for detecting breast tumors before they can be seen or felt

mam·mon (mam′ən) *n.* [< Aram] [*often* M-] riches regarded as an object of worship and greedy pursuit

mam·moth (mam′əth) *n.* [< Russ *mamont*] an extinct elephant with long tusks and hairy skin, adapted to cold climates —*adj.* huge; enormous

man (man) *n., pl.* **men** (men) [OE *mann*] 1 a human; person 2 the human race; humankind 3 an adult male person 4 an adult male servant, employee, etc. 5 a husband or male lover 6 any of the pieces used in chess, checkers, etc. —*vt.* **manned, man′ning** 1 to furnish with a labor force for work, defense, etc. 2 to take one's station in or at 3 to strengthen; brace [to *man* oneself for an ordeal] —**as a (or one) man** in unison; unanimously —**to a man** with no exception

Man (man), **Isle of** one of the British Isles, between Ireland & Great Britain: a British dependency

-man (mən, man) *combining form* man or person of a (specified) kind, in a (specified) activity, etc.: now often replaced by -PERSON or -WOMAN

man·a·cle (man′ə kəl) *n.* [< L *manus*, hand] a handcuff: *usually used in pl.* —*vt.* **-cled, -cling** 1 to put handcuffs on 2 to restrain

man·age (man′ij) *vt.* **-aged, -ag·ing** [< L *manus*, hand] 1 to control the movement or behavior of 2 to have charge of; direct [to *manage* a hotel] 3 to succeed in accomplishing —*vi.* 1 to carry on business 2 to contrive to get along —**man′age·a·ble** *adj.*

managed care a plan or system for providing medical services at reduced costs to patients who agree to use specified doctors and hospitals

man·age·ment *n.* **1** a managing or being managed **2** the persons managing a business, institution, etc.

man·ag·er *n.* one who manages; esp., one who manages a business, etc.

man·a·ge·ri·al (man′ə jir′ē əl) *adj.* of a manager or management

ma·ña·na (mä nyä′nä) *n., adv.* ⟦Sp⟧ tomorrow or (at) an indefinite future time

Ma·nas·sas (mə nas′əs) city in NE Virginia: site of two Civil War battles

man·a·tee (man′ə tē′) *n.* ⟦< WInd native name⟧ a large, herbivorous aquatic mammal of tropical waters

Man·ches·ter (man′ches′tər) city & port in NW England

Man·chu (man choo′, man′choo) *n.* **1** *pl.* **-chus′** or **-chu′** a member of a Mongolian people of Manchuria that ruled China from 1644 to 1912 **2** the language of this people —*adj.* of the Manchus, their language, etc.

Man·chu·ri·a (man choor′ē ə) region in NE China —**Man·chu′ri·an** *adj., n.*

man·da·rin (man′də rin) *n.* ⟦< Sans *mantrin*, counselor⟧ **1** a high official in the Chinese empire **2** [**M-**] the main dialect of Chinese **3** a small, sweet orange: in full **mandarin orange**

man·date (man′dāt′) *n.* ⟦< L *mandare*, to command⟧ **1** an order or command **2** [Historical] *a*) a League of Nations commission to a country to administer some region *b*) this region **3** the will of voters as expressed in an election —*vt.* **-dat′ed, -dat′ing** to require as by law

man·da·to·ry (man′də tôr′ē) *adj.* authoritatively commanded; obligatory

man·di·ble (man′də bəl) *n.* ⟦< L *mandere*, chew⟧ the jaw; specif., *a*) the lower jaw of a vertebrate *b*) either jaw of a beaked animal

man·do·lin (man′də lin′) *n.* ⟦< Gr *pandoura*, kind of lute⟧ a lute-like musical instrument with four to six pairs of strings

man·drake (man′drāk′) *n.* ⟦< Gr *mandragoras*⟧ a poisonous plant of the nightshade family

man·drill (man′dril) *n.* ⟦MAN + *drill*, kind of monkey⟧ a baboon of W Africa: the male has blue and scarlet patches on the face and rump

mane (mān) *n.* ⟦OE *manu*⟧ the long hair growing on the neck of the horse, lion, etc. —**maned** *adj.*

man-eat·er *n.* an animal that eats human flesh —**man′-eat′ing** *adj.*

ma·neu·ver (mə noo′vər) *n.* ⟦< L *manu operare*, to work by hand⟧ **1** a planned and controlled movement of troops, warships, etc. **2** a skillful change of direction **3** a skillful or shrewd move; stratagem —*vi., vt.* **1** to perform or cause to perform a maneuver or maneuvers **2** to manage or plan skillfully **3** to move, get, make, etc. by some scheme —**ma·neu′ver·a·ble** *adj.*

man·ful (man′fəl) *adj.* manly; brave, resolute, etc. —**man′ful·ly** *adv.*

man·ga (mäŋ′gə, maŋ′-) *n.* ⟦Jpn, random pictures⟧ a Japanese genre of comic books and graphic novels, having stylized art and often adult themes —*pl.n.* such comic books and graphic novels

man·ga·nese (maŋ′gə nēs′, -nēz′) *n.* ⟦ult. < ML *magnesia*: see MAGNESIA⟧ a grayish-white, metallic chemical element, used in alloys: symbol, Mn; at. no. 25

mange (mānj) *n.* ⟦< OFr *mangeue*, an itch⟧ a skin disease of mammals, causing itching, hair loss, etc.

man·ger (mān′jər) *n.* ⟦< L *mandere*, chew⟧ a box or trough to hold fodder for horses or cattle to eat

man·gle¹ (maŋ′gəl) *vt.* **-gled, -gling** ⟦prob. < OFr *mehaigner*, maim⟧ **1** to mutilate by roughly cutting, tearing, crushing, etc. **2** to spoil; botch; mar

man·gle² (maŋ′gəl) *n.* ⟦< Gr *manganon*, war machine⟧ a machine for pressing laundry between rollers

man·go (maŋ′gō) *n., pl.* **-goes** or **-gos** ⟦< Tamil *mān-kāy*⟧ **1** the yellow-red, somewhat acid fruit of a tropical tree **2** this tree

man·grove (maŋ′grōv) *n.* ⟦< WInd name⟧ a tropical tree of swampy areas, usually with roots that rise out of the water

man·gy (mān′jē) *adj.* **-gi·er, -gi·est 1** having mange **2** filthy, low, etc. —**man′gi·ness** *n.*

man·han·dle (man′han′dəl) *vt.* **-dled, -dling** to handle roughly

Man·hat·tan¹ (man hat′'n) *n.* ⟦after fol.⟧ [*often* **m-**] a cocktail made of whiskey and sweet vermouth

Man·hat·tan² (man hat′'n) island in SE New York: borough of New York City

man·hole *n.* a hole through which one can enter a sewer, conduit, etc.

man·hood *n.* **1** the state or time of being a man **2** manly qualities; manliness **3** men collectively

man-hour *n.* a time unit equal to one hour of work done by one person

man·hunt *n.* a hunt for a fugitive

ma·ni·a (mā′nē ə) *n.* ⟦Gr, madness⟧ **1** wild or violent mental disorder **2** an excessive enthusiasm

-ma·ni·a (mā′nē ə) ⟦see prec.⟧ *combining form* **1** a (specified) type of mental disorder **2** an intense enthusiasm for

ma·ni·ac (mā′nē ak′) *adj.* wildly insane —*n.* a violently insane person —**ma·ni·a·cal** (mə nī′ə kəl) *adj.*

man·ic (man′ik) *adj.* **1** having, characterized by, or like mania **2** [Inf.] very excited, elated, etc. —**man′ic·al·ly** *adv.*

man·ic-de·pres·sive (-dē pres′iv) *adj.* BIPOLAR (*adj.* 2)

man·i·cure (man′i kyoor′) *n.* ⟦< L *manus*, a hand + *cura*, care⟧ a trimming, polishing, etc. of the fingernails —*vt.* **-cured′, -cur′ing 1** to trim, polish, etc. (fingernails) **2** [Inf.] to trim, clip, etc. meticulously —**man′i·cur′ist** *n.*

man·i·fest (man'ə fest') *adj.* ⟦< L *manifestus*, lit., struck by the hand⟧ apparent to the senses or the mind; obvious —*vt.* to show plainly; reveal —*n.* an itemized list of a craft's cargo or passengers —**man'i·fest'ly** *adv.*

man·i·fes·ta·tion (-fes tā'shən) *n.* **1** a manifesting or being manifested **2** something that manifests or is manifested

man·i·fes·to (-fes'tō) *n., pl.* **-toes** or **-tos** ⟦It < *manifestare*, to manifest⟧ a public declaration of policies or principles, as by a political or artistic group

man·i·fold (man'ə fōld') *adj.* ⟦see MANY & -FOLD⟧ **1** having many forms, parts, etc. **2** of many sorts —*n.* a pipe with several outlets, as for conducting cylinder exhaust from an engine

man·i·kin (man'i kin) *n.* ⟦Du *manneken* < *man*, man + *-ken*, -KIN⟧ **1** a little man; dwarf **2** an anatomical model of the human body, used as in art classes **3** MANNEQUIN

Ma·nil·a (mə nil'ə) capital & seaport of the Philippines, in SW Luzon

Manila hemp ⟦after prec.⟧ [*often* **m- h-**] a strong fiber from the leafstalks of a Philippine plant, used for making rope, paper, etc.

Manila paper [*often* **m- p-**] a strong, buff-colored paper, orig. made of Manila hemp

man in the street the average person

ma·nip·u·late (mə nip'yoo lāt', -yə-) *vt.* **-lat'ed, -lat'ing** ⟦ult. < L *manus*, a hand + *plere*, to fill⟧ **1** to handle skillfully **2** to manage artfully or shrewdly, often in an unfair way **3** to falsify (figures, etc.) for one's own purposes —**ma·nip'u·la'tion** *n.* —**ma·nip'u·la'tor** *n.*

Man·i·to·ba (man'ə tō'bə) province of SC Canada; cap. Winnipeg: abbrev. **MB** —**Man'i·to'ban** *adj., n.*

man·kind (man'kīnd') *n.* **1** the human race; humankind **2** all human males

man·ly (man'lē) *adj.* **-li·er, -li·est** having the qualities regarded as suitable for a man; virile, brave, etc. —**man'li·ness** *n.*

man-made *adj.* artificial or synthetic

man·na (man'ə) *n.* ⟦< Heb *mān*⟧ **1** *Bible* food miraculously provided for the Israelites in the wilderness: Exodus 16:11-18 **2** anything badly needed that comes unexpectedly

man·ne·quin (man'ə kin) *n.* ⟦see MANIKIN⟧ **1** a model of the human body, used as for displaying clothes in shop windows **2** a woman who models clothes

man·ner (man'ər) *n.* ⟦< L *manus*, a hand⟧ **1** a way in which something is done or happens **2** a way, esp. a usual way, of acting **3** [*pl.*] *a*) ways of social behavior [bad *manners*] *b*) polite ways of social behavior [to learn *manners*] **4** kind; sort

man·nered (-ərd) *adj.* **1** having manners of a specified sort [ill-*mannered*] **2** artificial, stylized, etc.

man·ner·ism *n.* **1** excessive use of some distinctive manner or style in art, literature, etc. **2** a peculiarity of manner in behavior, speech, etc.

man·ner·ly *adj.* polite

man·ni·kin (man'ə kin) *n. alt. sp. of* MANIKIN

man·nish (man'ish) *adj.* like a man or man's: used in referring to a woman having characteristics generally attributed to men

ma·noeu·vre (mə nōō'vər) *n., vi., vt.* **-vred, -vring** *chiefly Brit. sp. of* MANEUVER

man of letters a writer, scholar, editor, etc., esp. in the field of literature

man of the world a man who is familiar with various sorts of people

man-of-war *n., pl.* **men'-of-war'** an armed naval vessel; warship

ma·nom·e·ter (mə näm'ət ər) *n.* ⟦Fr < Gr *manos*, rare (as in "thin, sparse") + Fr *-mètre*, -METER⟧ an instrument for measuring the pressure of gases or liquids

man on the street *var. of* MAN IN THE STREET

man·or (man'ər) *n.* ⟦< L *manere*, remain, dwell⟧ **1** in England, an estate **2** the main house on an estate —**ma·no·ri·al** (mə nôr'ē əl) *adj.*

man·pow·er *n.* **1** power furnished by human strength **2** the collective strength or availability for work of the people of an area, nation, etc.

man·qué (män kā') *adj.* ⟦Fr < *manquer*, be lacking⟧ unfulfilled; would-be [a poet *manqué*]

man·sard (roof) (man'särd) ⟦after F. *Mansard* (1598-1666), Fr architect⟧ a roof with two slopes on each of four sides, the lower steeper than the upper

manse (mans) *n.* ⟦see MANOR⟧ **1** the residence of a minister; parsonage **2** a large, imposing house

man·ser·vant *n., pl.* **men'ser'vants** a male servant: also **man servant**

-man·ship (mən ship') *combining form* talent or skill (esp. in gaining advantage) in connection with [grants*manship*]

man·sion (man'shən) *n.* ⟦< L *manere*, remain, dwell⟧ a large, imposing house

man-sized *adj.* [Inf.] of a size fit for a man; big: also **man'-size'**

man·slaugh·ter (-slôt'ər) *n.* the killing of a human by another, esp. when unlawful but without malice

man·ta (man'tə) *n.* ⟦Sp < LL *mantum*, a cloak⟧ a giant ray, with winglike pectoral fins: also **manta ray**

man·tel (man'təl) *n.* ⟦var. of MANTLE⟧ **1** the facing of stone, etc. about a fireplace, including a projecting shelf **2** this shelf: also **man'tel·piece'**

man·til·la (man til'ə, -tē'ə) *n.* ⟦Sp: see MANTA⟧ a woman's scarf, as of lace, worn over the hair and shoulders

man·tis (man'tis) *n., pl.* **-tis·es** or **-tes'** (-tēz') ⟦< Gr, prophet⟧ any of several predatory insects with forelegs often held up together as if praying

man·tis·sa (man tis'ə) *n.* ⟦L, (useless) addition⟧ the decimal part of a logarithm

man·tle (man'təl) *n.* ⟦< L *mantellum*⟧ **1** a loose, sleeveless cloak: sometimes used figuratively to connote authority **2** anything that envelops or conceals **3** a small hood which when placed over a flame gives off incandescent light —*vt.* **-tled, -tling** to cover as with a mantle —*vi.* to blush

man-to-man *adj.* frank; candid

man·tra (man′trə, män′-) *n.* ⟦Sans⟧ **1** a chant of a Vedic hymn, text, etc. **2** a syllable, word, etc. repeated during meditation **3** a word or slogan often repeated, as for inspiration

man·u·al (man′yōō əl) *adj.* ⟦< L *manus*, a hand⟧ **1** of the hands **2** made, done, or worked by hand **3** involving skill or hard work with the hands —*n.* **1** a book of facts, etc. for use as a reference **2** prescribed drill in the handling of a weapon —**man′u·al·ly** *adv.*

man·u·fac·ture (man′yōō fak′chər, -yə-) *n.* ⟦< L *manus*, a hand + *facere*, make⟧ **1** the making of goods, esp. by machinery and on a large scale **2** the making of something in any way, esp. when regarded as merely mechanical —*vt.* **-tured, -tur·ing 1** to make, esp. by machinery **2** to make up (excuses, etc.); fabricate —**man′u·fac′tur·er** *n.*

man·u·mit (man′yōō mit′) *vt.* **-mit′ted, -mit′ting** ⟦< L *manus*, hand + *mittere*, send⟧ to free from slavery —**man′u·mis′sion** *n.*

ma·nure (mə noor′) *vt.* **-nured′, -nur′ing** ⟦< OFr *manouvrer*, work with the hands⟧ to put manure on or into —*n.* animal excrement, etc. used to fertilize soil

man·u·script (man′yōō skript′, -yə-) *adj.* ⟦< L *manus*, hand + *scriptus*, written⟧ written by hand or typewritten —*n.* **1** a written or type written document, book, etc., esp. one submitted to a publisher **2** writing as opposed to print

Manx (maŋks) *n.* the Celtic language of the Isle of Man, now nearly extinct —*adj.* of the Isle of Man or its people, etc.

man·y (men′ē) *adj.* **more, most** ⟦OE *manig*⟧ numerous —*pl.n.* a large number (of persons or things) —*pron.* many persons or things

Ma·o·ri (mä′ō rē, mou′rē) *n.* **1** *pl.* **-ris** or **-ri** a member of a Polynesian people native to New Zealand **2** the language of this people —*adj.* of the Maoris or their language, etc.

Mao Tse-tung (mou′ dzu′doōŋ′) 1893-1976; Chinese Communist leader: Pinyin *Mao Zedong* —**Mao′ism′** *n.* —**Mao′ist** *adj., n.*

map (map) *n.* ⟦< L *mappa*, napkin, cloth⟧ **1** a representation of all or part of the earth's surface, showing countries, bodies of water, cities, etc. **2** a representation of the sky, showing the stars, etc. —*vt.* **mapped, map′ping 1** to make a map of **2** to plan

ma·ple (mā′pəl) *n.* ⟦OE *mapel*⟧ **1** any of a large group of trees with two-winged fruits, grown for wood, sap, or shade **2** the hard, light-colored wood **3** the flavor of the sugary syrup (**maple syrup**) made from the sap

mar (mär) *vt.* **marred, mar′ring** ⟦OE *mierran*, hinder⟧ to injure or damage so as to make imperfect, etc.; spoil

mar·a·bou (mar′ə boō′) *n.* ⟦Fr < Ar *murābit*, hermit⟧ a large-billed African stork

ma·ra·ca (mə rä′kə) *n.* ⟦Port *maracá* < native name in Brazil⟧ a percussion instrument that is a dried gourd or a gourd-shaped rattle with pebbles, etc. in it

mar·a·schi·no (mar′ə shē′nō, -skē′-) *n.* ⟦It < *marasca*, kind of cherry⟧ a liqueur made from a sour cherry

maraschino cherries cherries in a syrup flavored with maraschino or imitation maraschino

mar·a·thon (mar′ə thän′) *n.* ⟦after *Marathon*, plain in ancient Greece⟧ **1** a race on foot, 26 miles and 385 yards in length **2** any contest or endeavor testing endurance —**mar′a·thon′er** *n.*

ma·raud (mə rôd′) *vi., vt.* ⟦< Fr *maraud*, vagabond⟧ to raid and plunder —**ma·raud′er** *n.*

mar·ble (mär′bəl) *n.* ⟦< Gr *marmaros*, white stone⟧ **1** a metamorphosed limestone, white, colored, or mottled, which takes a high polish **2** a piece of this stone, used in sculpture, etc. **3** anything like marble in hardness, coldness, coloration, etc. **4** *a*) a little ball of stone, glass, etc. *b*) [*pl., with sing. v.*] a children's game played with such balls **5** [*pl.*] [Slang] mental soundness; wits —*adj.* of or like marble —*vt.* **-bled, -bling** to decorate (paper, etc.) with a mottled pattern resembling that of marble

mar·bled *adj.* **1** mottled or streaked **2** streaked with fat: said of meat

mar·ble·ize (-īz′) *vt.* **-ized′, -iz′ing** to make look like marble

mar·bling *n.* a streaked or mottled appearance like that of marble

march[1] (märch) *vi.* ⟦Fr *marcher*⟧ **1** to walk with regular steps, as in military formation **2** to advance steadily —*vt.* to cause to march —*n.* **1** a marching **2** a steady advance; progress **3** a regular, steady step **4** the distance covered in marching **5** a piece of music with a beat suitable for marching —**on the march** marching or advancing —**steal a march on** to get an advantage over secretly —**march′er** *n.*

march[2] (märch) *n.* ⟦< OFr⟧ a border or frontier

March (märch) *n.* ⟦< L *Mars*, the god Mars⟧ the third month of the year, having 31 days: abbrev. **Mar.**

March hare a hare in breeding time, proverbially an example of madness

marching orders 1 orders to march, go, or leave **2** notice of dismissal

mar·chion·ess (mär′shən is) *n.* **1** the wife or widow of a marquess **2** a lady of the rank of a marquess

Mar·co·ni (mär kō′nē), **Gu·gliel·mo** (goō lyel′mō) 1874-1937; It. physicist: developed wireless telegraphy

Mar·di Gras (mär′dē grä′) ⟦Fr, fat Tuesday⟧ **1** [*sometimes* **M- g-**] the last day before Lent; Shrove Tuesday: a day of carnival in New Orleans, etc. **2** the carnival period culminating with this day

mare[1] (mer) *n.* ⟦< OE *mere*⟧ a mature female horse, mule, donkey, etc.

ma·re² (mä′rā′) *n., pl.* **ma·ri·a** (mä′rē ə) ⟦L, sea⟧ a large, dark area on the moon

mare's-nest (merz′nest′) *n.* 1 a hoax 2 a jumble; mess

mar·ga·rine (mär′jə rin) *n.* ⟦Fr⟧ a spread or cooking fat of vegetable oils processed to give them the consistency of butter

mar·gin (mär′jən) *n.* ⟦< L *margo*⟧ 1 a border; edge 2 the blank border of a printed or written page 3 an amount beyond what is needed 4 provision for increase, error, etc. 5 the amount or degree by which things differ 6 the difference between the cost and the selling price of goods 7 collateral deposited with a broker, either to meet legal requirements or to insure against loss on contracts, as for buying stocks

mar·gin·al *adj.* 1 of, in, or near the margin 2 limited or minimal

mar·gi·na·li·a (mär′jə nä′lē ə) *pl.n.* notes written or printed in the margin

mar·gin·al·ize *vt.* **-ized′, -iz′ing** to exclude or ignore

ma·ri·a·chi (mär′ē ä′chē) *n., pl.* **-chis** ⟦MexSp < Fr *mariage*, marriage: from playing at wedding celebrations⟧ 1 a member of a strolling band of musicians in Mexico 2 such a band 3 its music

Mar·i·an (mer′ē ən, mar′-) *adj.* of the Virgin Mary

Ma·rie An·toi·nette (mə rē′ an′twə net′) 1755–93; wife of Louis XVI: queen of France (1774–92): guillotined

mar·i·gold (mar′ə gōld′) *n.* ⟦< *Marie* (prob. the Virgin Mary) + GOLD⟧ a plant of the composite family, with red, yellow, or orange flowers

mar·i·jua·na or **mar·i·hua·na** (mar′ə wä′nə) *n.* ⟦AmSp⟧ 1 HEMP (*n.* 1) 2 its dried leaves and flowers, smoked or ingested for euphoric effects

ma·rim·ba (mə rim′bə) *n.* ⟦< native name in Africa⟧ a kind of xylophone with a resonant tube beneath each bar

ma·ri·na (mə rē′nə) *n.* ⟦< L *mare*, sea⟧ a small harbor with docks, services, etc. for pleasure craft

mar·i·nade (mar′ə nād′) *n.* ⟦Fr < Sp *marinar*, to pickle⟧ a spiced pickling solution for steeping meat, fish, etc., often before cooking —*vt.* **-nad′ed, -nad′ing** MARINATE

mar·i·na·ra (mä′rə nä′rə, mär′ə ner′ə) *adj.* designating or of a tomato sauce seasoned with garlic, spices, etc.

mar·i·nate (mar′ə nāt′) *vt.* **-nat′ed, -nat′ing** ⟦< It *marinare*, to pickle⟧ to steep in a marinade

ma·rine (mə rēn′) *adj.* ⟦< L *mare*, sea⟧ 1 of or found in the sea 2 *a)* maritime; nautical *b)* naval —*n.* 1 a member of a military force trained for service at sea 2 [*often* M-] a member of the MARINE CORPS

Marine Corps a branch of the United States armed forces trained for land, sea, and aerial combat

mar·i·ner (mar′ə nər) *n.* a sailor

mar·i·o·nette (mar′ē ə net′, mer′-) *n.* ⟦Fr < *Marie*, Mary⟧ a jointed puppet moved by strings or wires

mar·i·tal (mar′ət'l) *adj.* ⟦< L *maritus*, a husband⟧ of marriage; matrimonial —**mar′i·tal·ly** *adv.*

mar·i·time (mar′ə tīm′) *adj.* ⟦< L *mare*, sea⟧ 1 on, near, or living near the sea 2 of sea navigation, shipping, etc.

mar·jo·ram (mär′jə rəm) *n.* ⟦prob. ult. < Gr *amarakos*⟧ a fragrant herb of the mint family, used in cooking

mark¹ (märk) *n.* ⟦OE *mearc*, boundary⟧ 1 a line, dot, spot, scratch, etc. on a surface 2 a printed or written symbol [punctuation *marks*] 3 a brand or label on an article showing the maker, etc. 4 an indication of some quality 5 a grade [a *mark* of B in Latin] 6 a standard of quality 7 impression; influence 8 an object of known position, serving as a guide 9 a line, dot, etc. indicating position, as on a graduated scale 10 an object aimed at; target 11 a goal; aim 12 *a)* an object to be attacked, criticized, etc. *b)* [Slang] an intended victim, as of a swindle —*vt.* 1 to put or make a mark or marks on 2 to identify as by a mark 3 to indicate by a mark 4 to show plainly [her smile *marked* her joy] 5 to set off; characterize 6 to listen to [*mark* my words] 7 to grade; rate —**make one's mark** to achieve fame —**mark down (or up)** to mark for sale at a reduced (or an increased) price —**mark time** to keep time while at a halt by lifting the feet as if marching 2 to suspend progress for a time

mark² (märk) *n.* ⟦< ON *mǫrk⟧* DEUTSCHE MARK

Mark (märk) *Bible* 1 one of the four Evangelists, the reputed author of the second Gospel 2 this Gospel

mark·down *n.* 1 a selling at a reduced price 2 the amount of reduction in price

marked (märkt) *adj.* 1 having a mark or marks 2 noticeable; obvious —**mark·ed·ly** (märk′id lē) *adv.*

mark·er (märk′ər) *n.* one that marks, specif., *a)* a felt-tipped pen for drawing thick lines *b)* a device for keeping score *c)* a milestone, etc.

mar·ket (mär′kit) *n.* ⟦ult. < L *merx*, merchandise⟧ 1 a gathering of people for buying and selling things 2 an open space or a building where goods are shown for sale: also **mar′ket·place′** 3 a shop for the sale of provisions [a meat *market*] 4 a region in which goods can be bought and sold [the European *market*] 5 trade; buying and selling 6 demand (for goods, etc.) [a good *market* for tea] —*vt.* 1 to offer for sale 2 to sell —*vi.* to buy provisions —**mar′ket·a·ble** *adj.* —**mar′ket·eer′** (-kə tir′) *n.* —**mar′ket·er** *n.*

mar·ket·ing *n.* 1 a buying or selling in a market 2 the total of activities involved in the moving of goods from the producer to the consumer, including selling, advertising, etc.

market share a company's percentage of the total sales of some commodity

mark·ing *n.* **1** a mark or marks **2** the characteristic arrangement of marks, as of an animal

marks·man (märks′mən) *n., pl.* **-men** (-mən) a person who shoots, esp. one who shoots well —**marks′man·ship′** *n.*

mark·up *n.* **1** a selling at an increased price **2** the amount of increase in price

mar·lin (mär′lin) *n.,* *pl.* **-lin** or **-lins** [< fol. : from the shape] a large, slender deep-sea fish

mar·line·spike (mär′lin spīk′) *n.* [< Du *marlijn*, small cord + SPIKE[1]] a pointed metal tool for separating the strands of a rope in splicing

mar·ma·lade (mär′mə lād′) *n.* [ult. < Gr *meli*, honey + *mēlon*, apple] a jamlike preserve made from the pulp and peel of oranges, etc.

mar·mo·set (mär′mə zet′, -set′) *n.* [< OFr *marmouset*, grotesque figure] a small monkey of South and Central America

mar·mot (mär′mət) *n.* [prob. < L *mus montanus*, mountain mouse] any of a group of thick-bodied rodents, as the woodchuck

ma·roon[1] (mə rōōn′) *n., adj.* [Fr *marron*, chestnut] dark brownish red

ma·roon[2] (mə rōōn′) *vt.* [< AmSp *cimarrón*, wild] **1** to put (a person) ashore in a lonely place and abandon that person **2** to leave abandoned, helpless, etc.

marque (märk) *n.* [Fr, a sign] a distinctive emblem on an automobile

mar·quee (mär kē′) *n.* [< Fr *marquise*, awning] a rooflike projection over an entrance, as to a theater

mar·quess (mär′kwis) *n.* [var. of MARQUIS] **1** a British nobleman ranking above an earl **2** MARQUIS

mar·que·try (mär′kə trē) *n.* [Fr, ult. < *marque*, a mark] decorative inlaid work, as in furniture

mar·quis (mär′kwis, mär kē′) *n.* [< ML *marchisus*, prefect] in some European countries, a nobleman ranking above an earl or count

mar·quise (mär kēz′) *n.* **1** the wife or widow of a marquis **2** a lady of the rank of a marquis

mar·qui·sette (mär′ki zet′, -kwi-) *n.* [see MARQUEE] a thin, meshlike fabric used for curtains, etc.

mar·riage (mar′ij) *n.* **1** the state of being married **2** the act of marrying; wedding **3** a close union —**mar′riage·a·ble** *adj.*

mar·ried (mar′ēd) *adj.* **1** living together as spouses; joined in wedlock **2** having a spouse **3** of marriage —*n.* a married person

mar·row (mar′ō) *n.* [OE *mearg*] the soft, fatty tissue that fills the cavities of most bones

mar·ry (mar′ē) *vt.* **-ried, -ry·ing** [< L *maritus*, husband] **1** to join as spouses **2** to take as a spouse **3** to unite —*vi.* to get married —**marry off** to give in marriage

Mars (märz) *n.* **1** the Roman god of war **2** a planet of the solar system: see PLANET

Mar·seille (mär sā′) seaport in SE France: Eng. sp. **Mar·seilles′**

marsh (märsh) *n.* [OE *merisc*] a wetland covered with grasses, reeds, etc. —**marsh′y** *adj.* **-i·er, -i·est**

mar·shal (mär′shəl) *n.* [< OHG *marah*, horse + *scalh*, servant] **1** in various foreign armies, a general officer of the highest rank **2** an official in charge of ceremonies, parades, etc. **3** in the U.S., *a)* a federal officer appointed to a judicial district with duties like those of a sheriff *b)* the head of some police or fire departments —*vt.* **-shaled** or **-shalled, -shal·ing** or **-shal·ling 1** to arrange (troops, ideas, etc.) in order **2** to guide

Mar·shall (mär′shəl), **John** 1755-1835; U.S. chief justice (1801-35)

Marshall Islands country on a group of islands in the W Pacific

marsh·mal·low (märsh′mel′ō) *n.* [orig. made of the root of a mallow found in marshes] a soft, spongy confection of sugar, gelatin, etc.

mar·su·pi·al (mär sōō′pē əl) *adj.* [< Gr *marsypos*, pouch] of a group of mammals that carry their incompletely developed young in an external abdominal pouch on the mother —*n.* such an animal, as a kangaroo or opossum

mart (märt) *n.* [MDu *markt*] a market

mar·ten (märt′'n) *n.* [< OFr *martre*] **1** a small mammal like a weasel, with soft, thick fur **2** the fur

mar·tial (mär′shəl) *adj.* [< L *martialis*, of Mars] **1** of or suitable for war **2** warlike; bold **3** military —**mar′tial·ly** *adv.*

martial arts systems of self-defense originating in E Asia, such as karate or kung fu, also engaged in for sport

martial law temporary rule by military authorities over civilians, as during a war or natural disaster

Mar·tian (mär′shən) *adj.* of Mars —*n.* a being from or living on Mars, as in science fiction

mar·tin (märt′'n) *n.* [Fr] any of several birds of the swallow family

mar·ti·net (märt′'n et′) *n.* [after J. *Martinet* (died 1762), Fr general] a very strict disciplinarian

mar·ti·ni (mär tē′nē) *n., pl.* **-nis** [< ?] a cocktail made of gin (or vodka) and dry vermouth

mar·tyr (märt′ər) *n.* [< Gr *martyr*, a witness] **1** one who chooses to suffer or die for one's faith or principles **2** one who suffers great pain or misery for a long time —*vt.* to kill or persecute for a belief —**mar′tyr·dom** *n.*

mar·vel (mär′vəl) *n.* [< L *mirari*, wonder at] a wonderful thing —*vi.* **-veled** or **-velled, -vel·ing** or **-vel·ling** to be filled with wonder —*vt.* to wonder at or about: followed by a clause

mar·vel·ous (-və ləs) *adj.* **1** causing wonder; extraordinary, etc. **2** fine; splendid Also [Chiefly Brit.] **mar′vel·lous** —**mar′vel·ous·ly** *adv.*

Marx (märks), **Karl** (kärl) 1818-83; Ger. founder of modern socialism

Marx·ism *n.* the system of thought developed by Karl Marx and Friedrich Engels (1820-95, Ger. socialist leader & writer), serving as a basis for socialism and communism —**Marx′ist** *adj., n.,* **Marx′i·an** (-ē ən)

Mar·y (mer′ē) *n. Bible* mother of Jesus

Mar·y·land (mer′ə lənd) state of the E U.S.;

cap. Annapolis: abbrev. **MD** —**Mar′y·land·er** (-lən dər, -lan′-) n.

Mary Mag·da·lene (mag′də lən) *Bible* a follower of Jesus and witness to his crucifixion and resurrection

mar·zi·pan (mär′zi pan′) n. ⟦Ger < It *marzapane*⟧ a confection that is a paste of ground almonds, sugar, and egg white, variously shaped

masc or **mas** *abbrev.* masculine

mas·car·a (mas kar′ə) n. ⟦< It *maschera*, mask⟧ a cosmetic for darkening the eyelashes —*vt.* -**car′aed, -car′a·ing** to put mascara on

mas·cot (mas′kät′) n. ⟦< Prov *masco*, sorcerer⟧ **1** any person, animal, or thing supposed to bring good luck **2** any person, animal, or thing adopted, as by a sports team, as a symbol

mas·cu·line (mas′kyə lin) adj. ⟦< L *mas*, male⟧ **1** male; of men or boys **2** suitable to or having qualities regarded as typical of men; strong, vigorous, manly, etc. **3** mannish: said of women **4** *Gram.* designating or of the gender of words referring to males as well as to various other words to which no sex is attributed —**mas′cu·lin′i·ty** n.

mash (mash) n. ⟦< OE *mascwyrt*⟧ **1** crushed malt or meal soaked in hot water for making wort **2** a mixture of watered bran, meal, etc. for feeding horses, etc. **3** any soft mass —*vt.* **1** to change into a soft mass by beating, crushing, etc. **2** to crush and injure

mash-up (-up′) n. **1** [Inf.] a mixture of incongruous elements, esp. when startling, inept, or inelegant **2** a recorded composition of digitally blended sections of other recordings

mask (mask) n. ⟦< Fr < It *maschera*⟧ **1** a covering to conceal or protect the face **2** anything that conceals or disguises **3** *a)* a molded likeness of the face *b)* a grotesque representation of a face, worn to amuse or frighten —*vt.* to conceal or cover with or as with a mask —**masked** adj.

mas·o·chism (mas′ə kiz′əm) n. ⟦after L. von Sacher-*Masoch* (1835-95), Austrian writer⟧ the getting of pleasure, often sexual pleasure, from being hurt or humiliated —**mas′o·chist** n. —**mas′o·chis′tic** adj. —**mas′o·chis′ti·cal·ly** adv.

ma·son (mā′sən) n. ⟦< ML *macio*⟧ **1** one whose work is building with stone, brick, etc. **2** [**M-**] FREEMASON

Ma·son-Dix·on line (mā′sən dik′sən) ⟦after C. *Mason* & J. *Dixon*, who surveyed it, 1763-67⟧ boundary line between Pennsylvania & Maryland, regarded as separating the North from the South

Ma·son·ic (mə sän′ik) adj. [*also* m-] of Freemasons or Freemasonry

ma·son·ry (mā′sən rē) n. **1** a mason's trade **2** pl. **-ries** something built, as by a mason, of stone, brick, etc. **3** [*usually* **M-**] FREEMASONRY

masque (mask) n. [see MASK] **1** MASQUERADE (n. 1) **2** a former kind of dramatic entertainment, often allegorical, with lavish costumes, music, etc. —**masqu′er** n.

mas·quer·ade (mas′kə rād′) n. [see MASK] **1** a ball or party at which masks and fancy costumes are worn **2** *a)* a disguise *b)* an acting under false pretenses —*vi.* -**ad′ed, -ad′ing 1** to take part in a masquerade **2** to act under false pretenses

mass (mas) n. ⟦< Gr *maza*, barley cake⟧ **1** a quantity of matter of indefinite shape and size; lump **2** a large quantity or number [a *mass* of bruises] **3** bulk; size **4** the main part **5** *Physics* the quantity of matter in a body as measured by its inertia —*adj.* of or for the masses or for a large number —*vt., vi.* to gather or form into a mass —**the masses** the common people

Mass (mas) n. ⟦< L *missa* in the words said by the priest: *ite, missa est* (*contio*), go, (the meeting) is dismissed⟧ [*also* **m-**] *R.C.Ch.* the service that includes the Eucharist

Mas·sa·chu·setts (mas′ə chōō′sits) New England state of the U.S.; cap. Boston: abbrev. **MA**

mas·sa·cre (mas′ə kər) n. ⟦< OFr *maçacre*, butchery⟧ the indiscriminate, merciless killing of many people or animals —*vt.* -**cred, -cring** (-kər iŋ, -kriŋ) to kill in large numbers

mas·sage (mə säzh′) n. ⟦Fr < Ar *massa*, to touch⟧ a rubbing, kneading, etc. of part of the body, as to stimulate circulation or relieve tension —*vt.* -**saged′, -sag′ing 1** to give a massage to **2** to alter or manipulate (information, etc.)

mas·seur (mə sur′, -sōōr′) n. ⟦Fr⟧ a man whose work is giving massages

mas·seuse (mə sōōz′, -sōōs′) n. a woman whose work is giving massages

mas·sive (mas′iv) adj. **1** forming or consisting of a large mass; big and solid **2** large and imposing —**mas′sive·ly** adv. —**mas′sive·ness** n.

mass-mar·ket (mas′mär′kit) adj. designating goods (such as paperback books) produced less expensively through large-scale manufacturing for a wide range of consumers —**mass′-mar′ket** vt.

mass media those means of communication that reach and influence large numbers of people, as newspapers, radio, and TV

mass noun a noun denoting an abstraction or something that cannot be counted (Ex.: *love, water, news*)

mass number the number of neutrons and protons in the nucleus of an atom

mass production quantity production of goods, esp. by machinery and division of labor —**mass′-pro·duce′** vt. -**duced′, -duc′ing**

mast (mast) n. ⟦OE *mæst*⟧ **1** a tall vertical spar used to support the sails, yards, etc. on a ship **2** a vertical pole

mas·tec·to·my (mas tek′tə mē) n., pl. **-mies** the surgical removal of all or part of a breast

mas·ter (mas′tər) n. ⟦< L *magister*⟧ **1** a man who rules others or has control over something; specif., *a)* one who is head of a household *b*) an employer *c*) one who owns a slave or an animal *d*) the captain of a merchant ship 2 *a*) a person very skilled and able in some work, profession, science, etc.; expert *b*) an artist regarded as great 3 [**M-**] a title applied to a boy too young to be addressed as *Mr.* —*adj.* 1 being a master 2 of a master —*vt.* 1 to become master of 2 to become an expert in (an art, science, etc.)

mas·ter·ful *adj.* 1 acting the part of a master; domineering 2 expert; skillful —**mas′ter·ful·ly** *adv.*

master key a key that will open every one of a set of locks

mas·ter·ly *adj.* expert; skillful

mas·ter·mind *n.* a very clever person, esp. one who plans or runs a project —*vt.* to be the mastermind of

Master of Arts (*or* **Science,** *etc.*) a degree given by a university for completion of a prescribed course at the first level of graduate study: also **master's (degree)**

master of ceremonies one who supervises or presides over a ceremony, program, etc.

mas·ter·piece *n.* [< Ger *meisterstück*] 1 a thing made or done with masterly skill 2 the greatest work of a person or group

master sergeant *U.S. Mil.* a noncommissioned officer of high rank

mas·ter·stroke *n.* a masterly action, move, or achievement

mas·ter·work *n.* MASTERPIECE

mas·ter·y *n., pl.* **-ies** 1 rule; control 2 ascendancy or victory 3 expert skill or knowledge

mast·head *n.* 1 the top part of a ship's mast 2 a box or section in a newspaper or magazine, listing the owner, editors, etc.

mas·ti·cate (mas′ti kāt′) *vt.* **-cat′ed, -cat′ing** [ult. < Gr *mastax*, mouth] to chew —**mas′ti·ca′tion** *n.*

mas·tiff (mas′tif) *n.* [< L *mansuetus*, tame] a large, powerful dog with a short, thick coat

mas·to·don (mas′tə dän′) *n.* [< Gr *mastos*, breast + *odous*, tooth: from the nipplelike processes on its molar] a large, extinct mammal resembling the elephant but larger

mas·toid (mas′toid′) *adj.* [< Gr *mastos*, breast + *-eidēs*, -OID] designating, of, or near a projection of the temporal bone behind the ear —*n.* the mastoid projection

mas·tur·bate (mas′tər bāt′) *vi.* **-bat′ed, -bat′ing** [< L *masturbari*] to manipulate the genitals for sexual gratification —**mas′tur·ba′tion** *n.*

mat¹ (mat) *n.* [< LL *matta*] 1 a flat piece of cloth, rubber, woven straw, etc. used for protection, as on a floor or under a vase 2 a thickly padded floor covering, esp. one used for wrestling, etc. 3 anything densely interwoven or growing in a thick tangle — *vt., vi.* **mat′ted, mat′ting** 1 to cover as with a mat 2 to form into a thick tangle —**go to the mat** [Inf.] to engage in a struggle or dispute

mat² (mat) *n.* [< OFr] 1 MATTE 2 a border, as of cardboard, put around a picture —*vt.* **mat′ted, mat′ting** to frame with a mat

mat·a·dor (mat′ə dôr′) *n.* [< Sp *matar*, to kill] a bullfighter whose specialty is killing the bull

match¹ (mach) *n.* [< OFr *mesche*] a slender piece of wood, cardboard, etc. tipped with a substance that catches fire by friction

match² (mach) *n.* [OE (ge)*mæcca*, mate] 1 any person or thing equal or similar to another 2 two persons or things that go well together 3 a contest or game 4 a marriage or mating —*vt.* 1 to put in opposition (*with*); pit (*against*) 2 to be equal or similar to 3 to make or get a counterpart or equivalent to 4 to fit (one thing) to another —*vi.* to be equal, similar, suitable, etc.

match·book *n.* a folder of book matches

match·less *adj.* having no equal

match·mak·ing *n.* the bringing together of unmarried persons in the hope they will become romantically involved —**match′mak′er** *n.*

match·stick *n.* a thin strip of wood, cardboard, etc., as or like that of a match

mate (māt) *n.* [< MDu] 1 a companion or fellow worker 2 one of a matched pair 3 *a*) a husband or wife *b*) the male or female of paired animals 4 an officer of a merchant ship, ranking below the captain — *vt., vi.* **mat′ed, mat′ing** 1 to join as a pair 2 to couple in marriage or sexual union

ma·te·ri·al (mə tir′ē əl) *adj.* [< L *materia*, matter] 1 of matter; physical [a *material* object] 2 of the body or bodily needs, comfort, etc.; not spiritual 3 important, pertinent, etc. —*n.* 1 what a thing is, or may be, made of; elements or parts 2 cloth; fabric 3 [*pl.*] tools, articles, etc. needed to make or do something

ma·te·ri·al·ism *n.* 1 the doctrine that everything in the world, including thought, can be explained in terms of matter alone 2 the tendency to be more concerned with material possessions, money, etc. than with spiritual or intellectual values —**ma·te′ri·al·ist** *n., adj.* —**ma·te′ri·al·is′tic** *adj.*

ma·te·ri·al·ize (-īz′) *vt.* **-ized′, -iz′ing** to give material form to —*vi.* 1 to become fact; be realized 2 to take on bodily form: said of spirits, etc. —**ma·te′ri·al·i·za′tion** *n.*

ma·te·ri·al·ly *adv.* 1 physically 2 to a great extent; substantially

ma·te·ri·el *or* **ma·té·ri·el** (mə tir′ē el′) *n.* [Fr] necessary materials and tools, esp. military weapons, equipment, etc.

ma·ter·nal (mə tur′nəl) *adj.* [< L *mater*, mother] 1 of, like, or from a mother 2 related through the mother's side of the family —**ma·ter′nal·ly** *adv.*

ma·ter·ni·ty (-nə tē) *n.* the state of being a mother; motherhood —*adj.* 1 for pregnant women 2 for the care of mothers and their newborn babies

math (math) *n.* [Inf.] mathematics

math·e·mat·i·cal (math′ə mat′i kəl) *adj.* [< Gr *manthanein*, learn] 1 of, like, or concerned with mathematics 2 very precise, accurate, etc. —**math′e·mat′i·cal·ly** *adv.*

math·e·mat·ics (math′ə mat′iks) *n.* [see prec. & -ICS] the science dealing with quantities, forms, etc. and their relationships, by the use of numbers and symbols —**math′e‧ma‧ti′cian** (-mə tish′ən) *n.*

mat‧i‧nee or **mat‧i‧née** (mat′'n ā′) *n.* ⟦< Fr *matin*, morning⟧ an afternoon performance of a play, etc.

mat‧ins (mat′'nz) *pl.n.* ⟦< L *matutinus*, of the morning⟧ [*often* **M-**] [*usually with sing. v.*] a church service of morning prayer

Ma‧tisse (må tēs′), **Hen‧ri** (än rē′) 1869-1954; Fr. painter

matri- ⟦< L *mater*⟧ *combining form* mother: also **matr-**

ma‧tri‧arch (mā′trē ärk′) *n.* ⟦prec. + -ARCH⟧ 1 a woman who rules a family, tribe, etc. 2 a highly respected elderly woman —**ma′tri‧ar′chal** (-är′kəl) *adj.* —**ma′tri‧arch′y** *n., pl.* **-ies**

mat‧ri‧cide (ma′trə sīd′) *n.* 1 the murdering of one's mother 2 a person who does this —**mat′ri‧ci′dal** *adj.*

ma‧tric‧u‧late (mə trik′yoo lāt′, -yə-) *vt., vi.* **-lat′ed, -lat′ing** ⟦< LL: see MATRIX⟧ to enroll, esp. as a student in a college —**ma‧tric′u‧la′tion** *n.*

mat‧ri‧mo‧ny (ma′trə mō′nē) *n., pl.* **-nies** ⟦< L *mater*, mother⟧ 1 the act or rite of marriage 2 married life —**mat′ri‧mo′ni‧al** *adj.*

ma‧trix (mā′triks) *n., pl.* **ma‧tri‧ces** (mā′trə sēz′, ma′trə-) or **ma′trix′es** ⟦< L *mater*, mother⟧ that within which something originates or develops

ma‧tron (mā′trən) *n.* ⟦< L *mater*, mother⟧ 1 a wife or widow, esp. one with a mature appearance and manner 2 a woman manager of the domestic arrangements of a hospital, school dormitory, etc. —**ma′tron‧ly** *adj.*

matron of honor a married woman acting as chief attendant to a bride

matte (mat) *n.* ⟦var. of MAT²⟧ a dull surface or finish —*adj.* not shiny Also **matt**

mat‧ted (mat′id) *adj.* closely tangled in a dense mass [*matted hair*]

mat‧ter (mat′ər) *n.* ⟦< L *materia*⟧ 1 what a thing is made of; material 2 whatever occupies space and is perceptible to the senses 3 any specified substance [*coloring matter*] 4 material of thought or expression 5 an amount or quantity [*a matter of a few days*] 6 *a)* a thing or affair *b)* cause or occasion [*no laughing matter*] 7 importance [*it's of no matter*] 8 trouble; difficulty: with *the* [*what's the matter?*] 9 mail —*vi.* to be of importance —**as a matter of fact** *see this phrase at* FACT —**no matter** 1 it is not important 2 regardless of

mat‧ter-of-fact *adj.* sticking to facts; literal, unimaginative, etc.

Mat‧thew (math′yoō′) *n. Bible* 1 a Christian apostle, reputed author of the first Gospel 2 this Gospel: abbrev. **Matt.**

mat‧ting (mat′iŋ) *n.* 1 a woven fabric of fiber, as straw, for mats, etc. 2 mats collectively

mat‧tock (mat′ək) *n.* ⟦OE *mattuc*⟧ a tool like a pickax, for loosening the soil, digging roots, etc.

mat‧tress (ma′trəs) *n.* ⟦< Ar *matraḥ*, cushion⟧ a casing of strong cloth filled with cotton, foam rubber, coiled springs, etc., used on a bed

ma‧ture (mə toor′, -choor′) *adj.* ⟦< L *maturus*, ripe⟧ 1 full-grown; ripe 2 fully developed 3 due: said of a note, bond, etc. — *vt., vi.* **-tured′, -tur′ing** to make or become mature —**mat‧u‧ra‧tion** (mach′ə rā′shən) *n.* —**ma‧ture′ly** *adv.* —**ma‧tu′ri‧ty** *n.*

mat‧zo (mät′sə, -sō) *n., pl.* **mat′zot, mat′zoth** (-sōt), or **mat′zos** ⟦Heb *matstsāh*, unleavened⟧ 1 thin, crisp unleavened bread eaten during the Passover 2 a piece of this

maud‧lin (môd′lin) *adj.* ⟦< ME *Maudeleyne*, (Mary) Magdalene (often represented as weeping)⟧ foolishly, often tearfully, sentimental

maul (môl) *n.* ⟦< L *malleus*, a hammer⟧ a heavy hammer for driving stakes, etc. —*vt.* 1 to bruise or lacerate 2 to handle roughly; manhandle

maun‧der (môn′dər) *vi.* ⟦< earlier *mander*, to grumble⟧ to talk or move in a confused way

Mau‧ri‧ta‧ni‧a (môr′ə tā′nē ə) country in NW Africa, on the Atlantic

Mau‧ri‧ti‧us (mô rish′ē əs, -rish′əs) island country in the Indian Ocean

mau‧so‧le‧um (mô′sə lē′əm, mä′-; -zə-) *n., pl.* **-le′ums** or **-le′a** (-ə) [after the tomb of King *Mausolus*, in ancient Asia Minor] 1 a large, imposing tomb 2 a building with spaces for entombing a number of bodies

mauve (mōv, môv) *n.* ⟦Fr, mallow⟧ any of several shades of pale purple —*adj.* of such a color

mav‧er‧ick (mav′ər ik) *n.* ⟦after S. *Maverick*, 19th-c. Texan whose cattle had no brand⟧ 1 an unbranded animal, esp. a lost calf 2 [Inf.] one who takes an independent stand, as in politics

maw (mô) *n.* ⟦OE *maga*⟧ 1 [Archaic] the stomach 2 the throat, jaws, or mouth of a voracious animal

mawk‧ish (mô′kish) *adj.* ⟦< ON *mathkr*, maggot⟧ sentimental in a weak, insipid way —**mawk′ish‧ly** *adv.*

max¹ (maks) [Slang] *n., adj.* maximum —**to the max** to the greatest possible degree

max² *abbrev.* maximum

maxi- ⟦< MAXI(MUM)⟧ *combining form* maximum, very large, very long

max‧il‧la (mak sil′ə) *n., pl.* **-lae** (-ē) [L] the upper jawbone —**max′il‧lar′y** (-sə ler′ē) *adj.*

max‧im (mak′sim) *n.* ⟦< LL *maxima* (*propositio*), the greatest (premise)⟧ a concise rule of conduct

max‧i‧mize (mak′sə mīz′) *vt.* **-mized′, -miz′ing** to increase to the maximum

max‧i‧mum (mak′sə məm) *n., pl.* **-mums** or **-ma** (-mə) ⟦< L superl. of *magnus*, great⟧ 1 the greatest possible or allowable quantity, number, etc. 2 the highest degree or point reached —*adj.* greatest possible, allowable, or reached —**max′i‧mal** (-məl) *adj.*

may (mā) *v.aux. pt.* **might** ⟦OE *mæg*⟧ used

to express *a*) possibility [it *may* rain] *b*) permission [you *may* go] (see also CAN[1]) *c*) contingency [they died that we *may* be free] *d*) a wish or hope [*may* he live]

May (mā) *n.* [< L *Maius*] the fifth month of the year, having 31 days

Ma·ya (mä′yə, mī′ə) *n.* [Sp < native name] 1 *pl.* **-ya** or **-yas** a member of an American Indian people of Central America whose highly developed civilization flourished esp. in the period from A.D. 300 to 900 2 the language of this people —**Ma′yan** *adj.*, *n.*

may·be (mā′bē) *adv.* [ME (for *it may be*)] perhaps

May Day May 1: a traditional spring festival, now also a labor holiday in many countries

may·flow·er *n.* 1 an early spring flower, as the trailing arbutus 2 [M-] the ship on which the Pilgrims came to America (1620)

may·fly *n.*, *pl.* **-flies′** [thought to be prevalent in May] a delicate insect with gauzy wings

may·hem (mā′hem, -əm) *n.* [see MAIM] 1 *Law* the offense of maiming a person 2 any deliberate destruction

may·o (mā′ō) *n.* short for [Inf.] MAYONNAISE

may·on·naise (mā′ə nāz′) *n.* [after *Mahón*, port on a Sp island] a creamy sauce of egg yolks, oil, vinegar, etc. beaten together

may·or (mā′ər) *n.* [< L *major*, greater] the chief administrative official of a city, town, etc. —**may·or·al** (mā′ər əl, mā ôr′əl) *adj.*

may·or·al·ty *n.*, *pl.* **-ties** the office or term of office of a mayor

may·pole (mā′pōl′) *n.* [*often* M-] a high pole with flowers, streamers, etc., for dancing around on May Day

Ma·za·tlán (mä′sät län′) seaport & resort on the Pacific coast of Mexico

maze (māz) *n.* [< OE *amasian*, to amaze] 1 a confusing, intricate network of pathways 2 a confused state

maz·el tov (mä′zəl tōv′, -tôf′) [Heb, good luck] used to express congratulations: also **maz′el·tov′** *interj.*

ma·zur·ka or **ma·zour·ka** (mə zur′kə) *n.* [Pol] a lively Polish folk dance in 3/4 or 3/8 time

MB *abbrev.* 1 Manitoba 2 megabyte(s): also **mb**

MBA or **M.B.A.** *abbrev.* Master of Business Administration

MC *abbrev.* 1 Master of Ceremonies 2 Member of Congress

Mc·Kin·ley[1] (mə kin′lē), **William** 1843-1901; 25th president of the U.S. (1897-1901): assassinated

Mc·Kin·ley[2] (mə kin′lē), **Mount** former name for DENALI

MD *abbrev.* 1 [L *Medicinae Doctor*] Doctor of Medicine: also **M.D.** 2 Maryland

mdse *abbrev.* merchandise

me (mē) *pron.* [OE] objective form of I[2]

ME *abbrev.* Maine

mead[1] (mēd) *n.* [OE *meodu*] an alcoholic beverage made of fermented honey and water

mead[2] (mēd) *n. var. of* [Old Poet.] MEADOW

mead·ow (med′ō) *n.* [< OE *mæd*] 1 a grass-land where the grass is grown for hay 2 low, level grassland

mea·ger (mē′gər) *adj.* [< L *macer*, lean] 1 thin; lean 2 poor; not full or rich; inadequate Brit. sp. **mea′gre** —**mea′ger·ly** *adv.* —**mea′ger·ness** *n.*

meal[1] (mēl) *n.* [OE *mæl*] 1 any of the times for eating, as lunch or dinner 2 the food eaten or served at such a time

meal[2] (mēl) *n.* [OE *melu*] 1 any edible grain, coarsely ground [*cornmeal*] 2 any substance similarly ground —**meal′y** *adj.* **-i·er, -i·est**

meal·y-mouthed (mēl′ē mouthd′) *adj.* not outspoken or blunt; euphemistic

mean[1] (mēn) *vt.* **meant** (ment), **mean′ing** [OE *mænan*] 1 to have in mind; intend [he *means* to go] 2 to intend to express [say what you *mean*] 3 to signify; denote [the German word "*ja*" means "yes"] —*vi.* to have a (specified) degree of importance, effect, etc. [honors *mean* little to him] —**mean well** to have good intentions

mean[2] (mēn) *adj.* [OE (*ge*)*mæne*] 1 low in quality or value; paltry 2 poor in appearance; shabby 3 petty 4 stingy 5 pettily bad-tempered, disagreeable, etc. 6 [Slang] *a*) hard to cope with *b*) skillful —**mean′ly** *adv.* —**mean′ness** *n.*

mean[3] (mēn) *adj.* [< L *medius*, middle] 1 halfway between extremes 2 average —*n.* 1 what is between extremes 2 *Math.* a number between the smallest and largest values of a set of quantities; esp., an average

me·an·der (mē an′dər) *vi.* [< Gr *Maiandros*, a winding river in Asia Minor] 1 to take a winding course: said of a stream 2 to wander idly —*n.* an aimless wandering

mean·ie or **mean·y** (mē′nē) *n.*, *pl.* **-ies** [Inf.] one who is mean, selfish, etc.

mean·ing *n.* what is meant; what is intended to be signified, understood, indicated, etc. [the *meaning* of a word] —**mean′ing·ful** *adj.* —**mean′ing·less** *adj.*

means (mēnz) *pl.n.* [< MEAN[3], *n.*] 1 [*with sing. or pl. v.*] that by which something is done or obtained; agency [a *means* of travel] 2 resources; wealth —**by all means** 1 without fail 2 certainly —**by means of** by using —**by no means** not at all

means test an investigation of a person's financial resources, to determine that person's eligibility for welfare payments, etc.

meant (ment) *vt.*, *vi. pt. & pp. of* MEAN[1]

mean·time *n.* the intervening time [in the *meantime*] —*adv.* mean′while′

mean·while *adv.* 1 in or during the intervening time 2 at the same time

mea·sles (mē′zəlz) *n.* [ME *maseles*] 1 an acute, infectious, communicable viral disease, usually of children, characterized by small, red spots on the skin, high fever, etc. 2 a similar but milder disease; esp., rubella (*German measles*)

mea·sly (mēz′lē) *adj.* **-sli·er, -sli·est** [Inf.] contemptibly slight or worthless

meas·ure (mezh′ər) *n.* [< L *metiri*, to measure⟧ **1** the extent, dimensions, capacity, etc. of anything **2** a determining of this; measurement **3** *a)* a unit of measurement *b)* any standard of valuation **4** a system of measurement **5** an instrument for measuring **6** a definite quantity measured out **7** a course of action [reform *measures*] **8** a statute; law **9** a rhythmical pattern or unit; specif., the notes and rests between two bars on a musical staff —*vt.* **-ured, -ur·ing 1** to find out or estimate the extent, dimensions, etc. of, esp. by a standard **2** to mark off by measuring: often with *off* or *out* **3** to be a measure of —*vi.* **1** to take measurements **2** to be of a specified dimension, etc. —**beyond measure** exceedingly —**for good measure** as a bonus or something extra —**measure up to** to reach (a standard, etc.) —**meas′ur·a·ble** *adj.* —**meas′ur·a·bly** *adv.* —**meas′ure·less** *adj.*

meas·ured *adj.* **1** determined or marked off by a standard **2** regular or steady [*measured* steps] **3** careful and guarded: said of speech, etc.

meas·ure·ment *n.* **1** a measuring or being measured **2** extent or quantity determined by measuring **3** a system of measuring or of measures

meat (mēt) *n.* ⟦OE *mete*⟧ **1** food: now archaic except in **meat and drink 2** the flesh of animals, esp. of mammals, used as food **3** the edible, inner part [the *meat* of a nut] **4** the substance or essence —**meat′y** *adj.* **-i·er, -i·est**

meat-and-po·ta·toes *adj.* [Inf.] **1** basic; fundamental **2** ordinary; everyday

meat·pack·ing *n.* the process or industry of slaughtering animals and preparing their meat for market

Mec·ca¹ (mek′ə) *n.* [after fol.] [*often* m-] any place many people feel drawn to [a tourist *mecca*]

Mec·ca² (mek′ə) city in W Saudi Arabia: birthplace of Muhammad & hence a holy city of Islam

me·chan·ic (mə kan′ik) *n.* ⟦< Gr *mēchanē*, machine⟧ a worker skilled in using tools, repairing machines, etc.

me·chan·i·cal *adj.* **1** having to do with machinery or tools **2** produced or operated by machinery or a mechanism **3** of the science of mechanics **4** machinelike; lacking warmth, spontaneity, etc. —**me·chan′i·cal·ly** *adv.*

me·chan·ics *n.* **1** the science of motion and of the action of forces on bodies **2** knowledge of machinery —*pl.n.* [*sometimes with sing. v.*] the technical part [the *mechanics* of writing]

mech·a·nism (mek′ə niz′əm) *n.* ⟦< Gr *mēchanē*, machine⟧ **1** the working parts of a machine **2** any system of interrelated parts **3** any physical or mental process by which a result is produced —**mech′a·nis′tic** *adj.*

mech·a·nize (-nīz′) *vt.* **-nized′, -niz′ing 1** to make mechanical **2** to equip (an industry) with machinery or (an army, etc.) with motor vehicles, tanks, etc. —**mech′a·ni·za′tion** *n.*

med *abbrev.* **1** medical **2** medicine **3** medium

med·al (med′'l) *n.* ⟦< LL *medialis*, medial⟧ **1** a small, flat piece of stamped or inscribed metal commemorating some event or awarded for some distinguished action, merit, etc. **2** a similar piece of metal bearing a religious figure or symbol

med·al·ist *n.* one awarded a medal

me·dal·lion (mə dal′yən) *n.* ⟦Fr *médaillon*⟧ **1** a large medal **2** a design, portrait, etc. resembling a medal

med·dle (med′'l) *vi.* **-dled, -dling** ⟦< L *miscere*, to mix⟧ to interfere in another's affairs —**med′dler** *n.* —**med′dle·some** (-səm) *adj.*

me·di·a (mē′dē ə) *n.* alt. pl. of MEDIUM: see MEDIUM (*n.* 3 & 6) —**the media** [*usually with sing. v.*] all the means of communication such as newspapers, radio, and TV

me·di·al (mē′dē əl) *adj.* ⟦< L *medius*⟧ **1** of or in the middle **2** average

me·di·an (mē′dē ən) *adj.* **1** middle; intermediate **2** designating the middle number in a series —*n.* **1** a median number, point, line, etc. **2** the strip of land separating the lanes of opposing traffic of a divided highway: in full **median strip**

me·di·ate (mē′dē āt′) *vi.* **-at′ed, -at′ing** ⟦< L *medius*, middle⟧ to be an intermediary —*vt.* to settle (differences) between persons, nations, etc. by friendly or diplomatic intervention —**me′di·a′tion** *n.* —**me′di·a′tor** *n.*

med·ic (med′ik) *n.* ⟦< L *medicus*⟧ **1** [Inf.] a physician or surgeon **2** a medical officer who gives first aid in combat

Med·ic·aid (-i kād′) *n.* [fol. + AID] [*also* m-] a state and federal health program for paying certain medical expenses of persons of low income

med·i·cal (-i kəl) *adj.* of or connected with the practice or study of medicine —**med′i·cal·ly** *adv.*

medical jurisprudence the application of medical knowledge to questions of law

Med·i·care (-i ker′) *n.* ⟦MEDI(CAL) + CARE⟧ [*also* m-] a federal health program for paying certain medical expenses of the aged and the needy

med·i·cate (-kāt′) *vt.* **-cat′ed, -cat′ing** ⟦< L *medicari*, heal⟧ to treat with medicine —**med′i·ca′tion** *n.*

me·dic·i·nal (mə dis′ən əl) *adj.* of, or having the properties of, medicine

med·i·cine (med′i sən) *n.* ⟦< L *medicus*, physician⟧ **1** the science and art of treating and preventing disease **2** any substance, as a drug, used in treating disease, relieving pain, etc.

medicine man among North American Indians, etc., a man supposed to have supernatural powers for healing the sick, etc.

me·di·e·val (mē′dē ē′vəl, mi dē′vəl) *adj.* ⟦< L *medius*, middle + *aevum*, age⟧ of or characteristic of the Middle Ages

me·di·o·cre (mē′dē ō′kər) *adj.* ⟦< L *medius*, middle + *ocris*, peak⟧ **1** ordinary; average **2** inferior —**me′di·oc′ri·ty** (-äk′rə tē) *n.*, *pl.* **-ties**

med·i·tate (med'ə tāt') *vt.* **-tat'ed, -tat'ing** [< L *meditari*] to plan —*vi.* to think deeply —**med'i·ta'tion** *n.* —**med'i·ta'tive** *adj.*

Med·i·ter·ra·ne·an (med'ə tə rā'nē ən) *adj.* 1 of the large sea (**Mediterranean Sea**) surrounded by Europe, Africa, & Asia 2 of the regions near this sea —*n.* a Mediterranean person

me·di·um (mē'dē əm) *n., pl.* **-di·ums** or **-di·a** (-ə) [L < *medius*, the middle] 1 an intermediate thing or state 2 an intervening thing through which a force acts 3 *pl. usually* **me·dia** any means, agency, etc.; specif., a means of communication that reaches the general public: a singular form **media** (*pl.* **medias**) is now often used 4 any surrounding substance or environment 5 *pl.* **mediums** one through whom messages are supposedly sent from the dead 6 *pl. usually* **media** any material or technique used for expression in art —*adj.* intermediate in size, quality, etc.

med·ley (med'lē) *n., pl.* **-leys** [< L *miscere*, to mix] 1 a mixture of dissimilar things 2 a musical piece made up of various tunes or passages

me·dul·la (mi dul'ə) *n., pl.* **-las** or **-lae** (-ē) [L, marrow] *Anat.* 1 a widening of the spinal cord forming the lowest part of the brain: in full **medulla ob·lon·ga·ta** (äb'läŋ gät'ə) 2 the inner substance of an organ, as of the kidney

meek (mēk) *adj.* [< ON *miukr*, gentle] 1 patient and mild 2 too submissive; spiritless —**meek'ly** *adv.* —**meek'ness** *n.*

meer·schaum (mir'shəm, -shôm') *n.* [Ger, sea foam] 1 a white, claylike, heat-resistant mineral used for tobacco pipes, etc. 2 a pipe made of this

meet[1] (mēt) *vt.* **met, meet'ing** [OE *metan*] 1 to come upon; encounter 2 to be present at the arrival of [to *meet* a bus] 3 to come into contact with 4 to be introduced to 5 to contend with; deal with 6 to experience [to *meet* disaster] 7 to be perceived by (the eye, etc.) 8 *a*) to satisfy (a demand, etc.) *b*) to pay (a bill, etc.) —*vi.* 1 to come together 2 to come into contact, etc. 3 to be introduced 4 to assemble —*n.* a meeting as for a sporting competition —**meet with** 1 to experience 2 to receive

meet[2] (mēt) *adj.* [OE *(ge)mæte*, fitting] [Now Rare] suitable; proper

meet·ing *n.* 1 a coming together 2 a gathering of people 3 a junction

mega- [Gr < *megas*, great] *combining form* 1 large, great, powerful 2 one million Also, **meg-**

meg·a·byte (meg'ə bīt') *n.* [prec. + BYTE] a unit of storage capacity in a computer system, equal to 2²⁰ bytes, or, loosely, one million bytes

meg·a·hertz (-hurts') *n., pl.* **-hertz'** [MEGA- + HERTZ] one million hertz

meg·a·lo·ma·ni·a (meg'ə lō mā'nē ə) *n.* [< Gr *megas*, large + -MANIA] a mental disorder characterized by delusions of grandeur, power, etc. —**meg'a·lo·ma'ni·ac** *adj., n.*

meg·a·lop·o·lis (meg'ə läp'ə lis) *n.* [Gr, great city] a vast, continuously urban area, including any number of cities

meg·a·phone (-fōn') *n.* [MEGA- + -PHONE] a cone-shaped device for increasing the volume of the voice

meg·a·ton (-tun') *n.* [MEGA- + TON] the explosive force of a million tons of TNT

meit·ner·i·um (mīt nir'ē əm) *n.* [after Lise *Meitner* (1878-1968), Swed physicist born in Austria] an artificially produced radioactive chemical element: symbol, Mt; at. no. 109

Me·kong (mā'käŋ', -kôŋ') river in SE Asia, flowing into the South China Sea

mel·a·mine (mel'ə mēn') *n.* [Ger *melamin*] a white, crystalline compound used in making synthetic resins

mel·an·cho·li·a (mel'ən kō'lē ə) *n.* 1 DEPRESSION (*n.* 4) 2 melancholy

mel·an·chol·y (-käl'ē) *n., pl.* **-ies** [< Gr *melas*, black + *cholē*, bile] sadness and depression of spirits —*adj.* 1 sad and depressed 2 causing sadness —**mel'an·chol'ic** *adj.*

Mel·a·ne·sia (mel'ə nē'zhə) group of islands in the S Pacific —**Mel'a·ne'sian** *adj., n.*

mé·lange (mā lônzh', -lônj') *n.* [Fr < *mêler*, to mix] a mixture; medley

mel·a·nin (mel'ə nin) *n.* [< Gr *melas*, black] a blackish pigment found in skin, hair, etc.

mel·a·no·ma (-nō'mə) *n., pl.* **-mas** or **-ma·ta** (-mə tə) [< Gr *melas*, black + -*ōma*, mass] a skin tumor derived from cells capable of melanin formation

Mel·ba toast (mel'bə) [after N. *Melba* (1861-1931), Australian soprano] [*also* **m- t-**] very crisp, thinly sliced toast

Mel·bourne (mel'bərn) seaport in SE Australia

meld (meld) *vt., vi.* [< MELT + WELD] to blend; merge

me·lee or **mê·lée** (mā'lā', mā lā') *n.* [Fr] a confused fight or hand-to-hand struggle

mel·io·rate (mēl'yə rāt') *vt., vi.* **-rat'ed, -rat'ing** [< L *melior*, better] to make or become better

mel·lif·lu·ous (mə lif'loo əs) *adj.* [< L *mel*, honey + *fluere*, to flow] sounding sweet and smooth —**mel·lif'lu·ence** *n.*

mel·low (mel'ō) *adj.* [ME *melwe*, ripe] 1 full-flavored: said of wine, etc. 2 full, rich, soft, etc.; not harsh: said of sound, light, etc. 3 made gentle, understanding, etc. by age 4 [Inf.] genial, as from drinking liquor — *vt., vi.* to make or become mellow

me·lo·di·ous (mə lō'dē əs) *adj.* 1 producing melody 2 pleasing to hear; tuneful —**me·lo'di·ous·ly** *adv.*

mel·o·dra·ma (mel'ō drä'mə, -dram'ə) *n.* [< Fr < Gr *melos*, song + LL *drama*, drama] 1 a drama with exaggerated conflicts and emotions, stereotyped characters, etc. 2 an excessively emotional situation, interaction, etc. —**mel'o·dra·mat'ic** (-drə mat'ik) *adj.*

mel·o·dra·mat·ics (-drə mat'iks) *pl.n.* melodramatic behavior

mel·o·dy (mel'ə dē) *n., pl.* **-dies** [< Gr *melos*,

song + *aeidein*, sing] **1** pleasing sounds in sequence **2** *Music a)* a tune, song, etc. *b)* the leading part in a harmonic composition —**me·lod·ic** (mə läd′ik) *adj.* —**me·lod′i·cal·ly** *adv.*

mel·on (mel′ən) *n.* [< Gr *mēlon*, apple] the large, juicy, thick-skinned, many-seeded fruit of certain trailing plants, as the watermelon or cantaloupe

melt (melt) *vt., vi.* [OE *m(i)eltan*] **1** to change from a solid to a liquid state, generally by heat **2** to dissolve **3** to disappear or cause to disappear gradually **4** to soften; become gentle, tender, etc.

melt·down *n.* a dangerous situation in which a nuclear reactor begins to melt its fuel rods

melting pot a country, etc. in which people of various nationalities and races are assimilated

Mel·ville (mel′vil), **Her·man** (hur′mən) 1819–91; U.S. novelist

mem·ber (mem′bər) *n.* [< L *membrum*] **1** a limb or other part of a person, animal, or plant **2** a distinct part of a whole **3** a person belonging to some group, society, etc.

mem·ber·ship *n.* **1** the state of being a member: with *in* **2** members collectively, as of a group **3** the number of members

mem·brane (mem′brān′) *n.* [< L *membrum*, member] a thin, soft layer, esp. of animal or plant tissue, that covers or lines an organ, part, etc. —**mem′bra·nous** (-brə nəs) *adj.*

me·men·to (mə men′tō) *n., pl.* -**tos** or -**toes** [< L *meminisse*, remember] a souvenir

mem·o (mem′ō) *n., pl.* -**os** *short for* MEMO·RANDUM

mem·oirs (mem′wärz′) *pl.n.* [< L *memoria*, memory] **1** an autobiography **2** a record of events based on the writer's personal knowledge

mem·o·ra·bil·i·a (mem′ə rə bil′ē ə, -bil′yə; -bēl′-) *pl.n.* [L] things kept for their sentimental or historical value

mem·o·ra·ble (mem′ə rə bəl) *adj.* worth remembering; notable; remarkable —**mem′o·ra·bly** *adv.*

mem·o·ran·dum (mem′ə ran′dəm) *n., pl.* -**dums** or -**da** (-də) [L] **1** a short note written to remind one of something **2** an informal written communication, as in an office **3** *Law* a short written statement of the terms of an agreement, etc.

me·mo·ri·al (mə môr′ē əl) *adj.* [< L *memoria*, memory] serving to help people remember —*n.* anything meant to help people remember a person or event, as a monument or holiday —**me·mo′ri·al·ize** (-īz′) *vt.* -**ized′**, -**iz′ing**

Memorial Day a legal holiday in the U.S. (the last Monday in May in most states) in memory of members of the armed forces killed in war

mem·o·rize (mem′ə rīz′) *vt.* -**rized′**, -**riz′ing** to commit to memory —**mem′o·ri·za′tion** *n.*

mem·o·ry (mem′ə rē, mem′rē) *n., pl.* -**ries** [< L *memor*, mindful] **1** the power or act of remembering **2** all that one remembers **3** something remembered **4** the period of remembering [within my *memory*] **5** commemoration **6** storage capacity, as of a computer or disk

Mem·phis (mem′fis) city in SW Tennessee

men (men) *n. pl. of* MAN

men·ace (men′əs) *n.* [< L *minari*, threaten] **1** a threat **2** [Inf.] one who is a nuisance —*vt., vi.* -**aced**, -**ac·ing** to threaten —**men′ac·ing·ly** *adv.*

mé·nage or **me·nage** (mā näzh′, mə-) *n.* [Fr < OFr *manoir*, stay, dwell] a household

mé·nage à trois (mā näzh ȧ trwä′) *pl.* **mé·nages à trois** (mā näzh ȧ trwä′) [Fr, household of three] [*often not in italics*] **1** an arrangement by which a married couple and the lover of one of them live together **2** any sexual relationship involving three people, esp. when they live together

me·nag·er·ie (mə naj′ər ē, -nazh′-) *n.* [see prec.] a collection of wild animals kept in cages, etc. for exhibition

mend (mend) *vt.* [< ME *amenden*, amend] **1** to repair **2** to make better; reform —*vi.* **1** to improve, esp. in health **2** to heal, as a fracture —*n.* **1** a mending **2** a mended place —**on the mend** improving, esp. in health —**mend′er** *n.*

men·da·cious (men dā′shəs) *adj.* [< L *mendax*] not truthful; lying —**men·dac′i·ty** (-das′ə tē) *n., pl.* -**ties**

Men·del (men′dəl), **Gre·gor** (grā′gôr) 1822–84; Austrian monk & geneticist

men·de·le·vi·um (men′də lē′vē əm) *n.* [after Dmitri *Mendeleev* (1834–1907), Russ chemist] an artificially produced radioactive, metallic chemical element: symbol, Md; at. no. 101

Men·dels·sohn (men′dəl sən, -sōn′), **Fe·lix** (fā′liks) 1809–47; Ger. composer

men·di·cant (men′di kənt) *adj.* [< L *mendicus*, needy] begging —*n.* **1** a beggar **2** a mendicant friar

men·folk (-fōk′) *pl.n.* [Inf. or Dial.] men: also **men′folks′**

men·ha·den (men hād′'n) *n., pl.* -**den** or -**dens** [< AmInd] a common fish of the W Atlantic, used for bait or for making oil and fertilizer

me·ni·al (mē′nē əl) *adj.* [< L *mansio*, house] **1** of or fit for servants **2** servile; low —*n.* **1** a domestic servant **2** a servile, low person —**me′ni·al·ly** *adv.*

me·nin·ges (mə nin′jēz′) *pl.n., sing.* **me·ninx** (mē′niŋks′) [< Gr *mēninx*, membrane] the three membranes that envelop the brain and the spinal cord —**me·nin′ge·al** (-jē əl) *adj.*

men·in·gi·tis (men′in jīt′is) *n.* [ModL: see prec. & -ITIS] inflammation of the meninges

me·nis·cus (mə nis′kəs) *n., pl.* -**cus·es** or -**ci′** (-ī′) [< Gr dim. of *mēnē*, the moon] **1** a crescent or crescent-shaped thing **2** fibrous cartilage in a joint, esp. the knee **3** the convex or concave upper surface of a column of liquid

Men·non·ite (men′ən it′) *n.* [after *Menno* Simons (1492–1559), Du reformer] a member of an evangelical Christian sect that opposes military service and favors plain living and dress

men·o·pause (men′ə pôz′) *n.* ⟦< Gr *mēn*, month + *pauein*, to end⟧ the permanent cessation of menstruation

me·no·rah (mə nô′rə, -nôr′ə) *n.* ⟦Heb *menora*, lamp stand⟧ a candelabrum with seven (or nine) branches: a symbol of Judaism

men·ses (men′sēz′) *pl.n.* ⟦L, pl. of *mensis*, month⟧ the periodic flow, usually monthly, of blood from the uterus

men·stru·ate (men′strōō āt′, -strāt′) *vi.* **-at′ed, -at′ing** ⟦< L *mensis*, month⟧ to have a discharge of the menses —**men′strual** (-strəl) *adj.* —**men′stru·a′tion** *n.*

men·su·ra·tion (men′sə rā′shən) *n.* ⟦< L *mensura*, measure⟧ a measuring

-ment (mənt, mint) ⟦< L *-mentum*⟧ *suffix* **1** a result **2** a means of **3** an act **4** a state [*enchantment*]

men·tal (ment′l) *adj.* ⟦< L *mens*, the mind⟧ **1** of, for, by, or in the mind **2** of, having, or related to mental illness **3** for the mentally ill [a *mental* hospital] —**men′tal·ly** *adv.*

men·tal·ist *n.* MIND READER

men·tal·i·ty (men tal′i tē) *n., pl.* **-ties 1** mental capacity or power **2** mental attitude or outlook

mental reservation a qualification (of a statement) that one makes to oneself but does not express

mental retardation a condition, usually congenital, characterized by subnormal intelligence

men·ta·tion (men tā′shən) *n.* ⟦< L *mens*, mind + -ATION⟧ the act or process of using the mind

men·thol (men′thôl′) *n.* ⟦Ger < L *mentha*, MINT²⟧ a white, crystalline alcohol obtained from oil of peppermint and used in medicine, cosmetics, etc. —**men′tho·lat′ed** (-thə lāt′id) *adj.*

men·tion (men′shən) *n.* ⟦< L *mens*, the mind⟧ **1** a brief reference **2** a citing for honor —*vt.* to refer to briefly or incidentally —**make mention of** to mention —**not to mention** with it being unnecessary to mention

men·tor (men′tər, -tôr′) *n.* ⟦after Mentor, friend and advisor of Odysseus⟧ **1** a wise advisor **2** a teacher or coach

men·u (men′yōō) *n., pl.* **-us** ⟦Fr, small, detailed⟧ **1** a detailed list of the foods served at a meal or those available at a restaurant **2** a list, as on a computer screen, of the various choices available to the user

me·ow or **me·ou** (mē ou′) *n.* ⟦echoic⟧ the characteristic vocal sound made by a cat —*vi.* to make such a sound

mer·can·tile (mur′kən til′, -til) *adj.* ⟦Fr⟧ of or characteristic of merchants or trade

mer·ce·nar·y (mur′sə ner′ē) *adj.* ⟦< L *merces*, wages⟧ working or done for payment only —*n., pl.* **-ies** a soldier hired to serve in a foreign army

mer·cer·ize (-īz′) *vt.* **-ized′, -iz′ing** ⟦after J. Mercer (1791-1866), Eng calico dealer⟧ to

treat (cotton thread or fabric) with a sodium hydroxide solution to strengthen it, give it a silky luster, etc.

mer·chan·dise (mur′chən dīz′; for *n.*, also, -dis′) *n.* ⟦see fol.⟧ things bought and sold; goods; commodities —*vt., vi.* **-dised′, -dis′ing 1** to buy and sell **2** to promote the sale of (a product) Also, for v., **mer′chan·dize′** (-dīz′) **-dized′, -diz′ing** —**mer′chan·dis′er** *n.*, **mer′chan·diz′er** *n.*

mer·chant (mur′chənt) *n.* ⟦ult. < L *merx*, wares⟧ **1** one whose business is buying and selling goods **2** a retail dealer; storekeeper —*adj.* mercantile; commercial

mer·chant·man (-mən) *n., pl.* **-men** (-mən) a ship used in commerce

merchant marine 1 all of a nation's commercial ships **2** their personnel

mer·ci (mer sē′) *interj.* ⟦Fr⟧ thank you

mer·ci·ful (mur′si fəl) *adj.* having or showing mercy; compassionate; lenient —**mer′ci·ful·ly** *adv.*

mer·ci·less *adj.* without mercy; pitiless —**mer′ci·less·ly** *adv.*

mer·cu·ri·al (mər kyoor′ē əl) *adj.* **1** of or containing mercury **2** quick, changeable, fickle, etc.

Mer·cu·ry (mur′kyoor ē) *n.* **1** Rom. Myth. the messenger of the gods **2** the smallest planet in the solar system: see PLANET **3** [m-] a heavy, silver-white metallic chemical element, liquid at ordinary temperatures, used in thermometers, etc.: symbol, Hg; at. no. 80 —**mer·cu′ric** (mər kyoor′ik) *adj.* —**mer·cu′rous** *adj.*

mer·cy (mur′sē) *n., pl.* **-cies** ⟦< L *merces*, payment⟧ **1** a refraining from harming offenders, enemies, etc. **2** a disposition to forgive or be kind **3** the power to forgive **4** kind or compassionate treatment **5** a lucky thing; blessing —**at the mercy of** completely in the power of

mercy killing EUTHANASIA

mere (mir) *adj. superl.* **mer′est** ⟦< L *merus*, pure⟧ nothing more or other than [a *mere* boy]

mere·ly *adv.* only; no more than

mer·e·tri·cious (mer′ə trish′əs) *adj.* ⟦< L *meretrix*, a prostitute⟧ **1** attractive in a flashy way **2** superficially plausible; specious

mer·gan·ser (mər gan′sər) *n.* ⟦< L *mergus*, diver (bird) + *anser*, goose⟧ a fish-eating, diving duck with a long bill

merge (murj) *vi., vt.* **merged, merg′ing** ⟦L *mergere*, to dip⟧ **1** to lose or cause to lose identity by being absorbed or combined **2** to unite; combine

merg·er (mur′jər) *n.* a merging; specif., a combining of two or more companies into one

me·rid·i·an (mə rid′ē ən) *n.* ⟦< L *meridies*, noon⟧ **1** the highest point of power, etc. **2** *a)* a circle on the earth's surface passing through the geographical poles and any given point *b)* any of the lines of longitude

me·ringue (mə raŋ′) *n.* ⟦Fr⟧ egg whites

beaten with sugar until stiff: used as a pie covering, etc.

me·ri·no (mə rē′nō) *n.*, *pl.* **-nos** ‖Sp‖ **1** any of a breed of hardy, white-faced sheep with long, fine wool **2** the wool **3** yarn or cloth made of it

mer·it (mer′it) *n.* ‖< L *merere,* deserve‖ **1** worth; value; excellence **2** something deserving reward, praise, etc. **3** [*pl.*] intrinsic rightness or wrongness —*vt.* to deserve

mer·i·to·ri·ous (mer′i tôr′ē əs) *adj.* having merit; deserving reward, praise, etc. —**mer′i·to′ri·ous·ly** *adv.*

Mer·lin (mur′lin) *n.* Arthurian Legend a magician and seer, mentor to King Arthur

mer·maid (mur′mād′) *n.* ‖< OE *mere,* sea + MAID‖ an imaginary sea creature with the head and upper body of a woman and the tail of a fish

mer·man (-man′) *n.*, *pl.* **-men′** (-men′) an imaginary sea creature like a mermaid, but with the upper body of a man

mer·ri·ment (mer′i mənt) *n.* merrymaking; gaiety and fun; mirth

mer·ry (mer′ē) *adj.* **-ri·er, -ri·est** ‖< OE *myrge,* pleasing‖ **1** full of fun; lively **2** festive —**make merry** to be festive and have fun —**mer′ri·ly** *adv.* —**mer′ri·ness** *n.*

mer·ry-go-round *n.* a circular, revolving platform with seats in the form of animals, used as an amusement at carnivals, etc.

mer·ry·mak·ing *n.* fun; conviviality; festivity —**mer′ry·mak′er** *n.*

me·sa (mā′sə) *n.* ‖Sp < L *mensa,* a table‖ a small, high plateau with steep sides

Me·sa (mā′sə) city in SC Arizona

mes·cal (mes kal′) *n.* ‖Sp < AmInd (Mex) *mexcalli*‖ a small cactus of N Mexico and the SW U.S.

mes·ca·line (mes′kə lin) *n.* a psychedelic drug obtained from the mescal

mes·clun (mes′klən) *n.* ‖Fr‖ a mixture of salad greens and herbs

mes·dames (mā däm′; Fr, –dàm′) *n. pl. of* MA-DAME, MADAM (n. 1), or MRS.

mes·de·moi·selles (mād mwà zel′) *n. pl. of* MADEMOISELLE

mesh (mesh) *n.* ‖prob. < MDu *mæsche*‖ **1** any of the open spaces of a net, screen, etc. **2** a net or network **3** a netlike material, as for stockings **4** the engagement of the teeth of gears — *vt., vi.* **1** to entangle or become entangled **2** to engage or become engaged: said of gears **3** to interlock

mes·mer·ize (mez′mər iz′) *vt.* **-ized′, -iz′ing** [after F. A. *Mesmer* (1734-1815), Ger physician] **1** [Archaic] to hypnotize **2** to spellbind —**mes′mer·ism′** *n.* —**mes′mer·ist** *n.*

Mes·o·a·mer·i·ca (mes′ō ə mer′i kə, mez′-) region including parts of modern Mexico and Central America, formerly inhabited by the Maya, the Aztecs, etc.

mes·on (mes′än′, mez′-) *n.* ‖< Gr *mesos,* middle + (ELECTR)ON‖ any of a group of unstable subatomic particles having a mass between those of an electron and a proton

Mes·o·po·ta·mi·a (mes′ə pə tā′mē ə) ancient country in SW Asia, between the upper Tigris & Euphrates rivers

Mes·o·zo·ic (mes′ə zō′ik, mez′-) *adj.* ‖< Gr *mesos,* middle + ZO(O)- + -IC‖ designating the geologic era (c. 251 to 65 million years ago) characterized by dinosaurs and by the appearance of flowering plants, mammals, birds, etc.

mes·quite or **mes·quit** (me skēt′) *n.* ‖< AmInd(Mex) *mizquitl*‖ a thorny tree or shrub of Mexico and the SW U.S.

mess (mes) *n.* ‖< L *missus,* course (at a meal)‖ **1** a portion of food for a meal **2** a group of people who regularly eat together, as in the army **3** the meal they eat **4** a jumble **5** a state of trouble, disorder, or confusion **6** [Inf.] a person in such a state **7** [Inf.] an untidy place —*vt.* **1** to make dirty or untidy **2** to muddle; botch Often with *up* —*vi.* **1** to eat as one of a mess **2** to make a mess **3** to putter or meddle (*in* or *with*) —**mess′y** *adj.* **-i·er, -i·est** —**mess′i·ly** *adv.* —**mess′i·ness** *n.*

mes·sage (mes′ij) *n.* ‖< L *mittere,* send‖ **1** a communication sent by speech, in writing, etc. **2** the chief idea that an artist, writer, etc. seeks to communicate in a work —**get the message** [Inf.] to understand a hint, etc. —**on (or off) message** [Inf.] following (or deviating from) an intended set of remarks or positions

mes·sen·ger (mes′ən jər) *n.* one who carries a message or goes on an errand

messenger RNA a single-stranded form of RNA, derived from DNA, that carries the genetic information needed to form proteins

mess hall a room or building where soldiers, etc. regularly have meals

Mes·si·ah (mə sī′ə) *n.* ‖< Heb *māshīaḥ,* anointed‖ **1** Judaism the expected deliverer of the Jews **2** Christianity Jesus **3** [**m-**] any expected savior or liberator —**Mes′si·an′ic** *adj.,* **mes·si·an·ic** (mes′ē an′ik) *adj.*

mes·sieurs (mes′ərz; Fr mā syö′) *n. pl. of* MONSIEUR

Messrs (mes′ərz) *abbrev.* messieurs: now used chiefly as the pl. of MR.

mes·ti·zo (me stē′zō) *n.*, *pl.* **-zos** or **-zoes** ‖Sp < L *miscere,* to mix‖ a person of mixed parentage, esp. Spanish and American Indian

met¹ (met) *vt., vi. pt. & pp. of* MEET¹

met² *abbrev.* metropolitan

meta- ‖< Gr *meta,* after‖ *prefix* **1** changed [*metathesis*] **2** after, beyond, higher [*metaphysics*]

me·tab·o·lism (mə tab′ə liz′əm) *n.* ‖< Gr *meta,* beyond + *ballein,* throw‖ the chemical processes continuously going on in living organisms and cells, including the changing of food into living tissue and the changing of living tissue into waste products and energy —**met·a·bol·ic** (met′ə bäl′ik) *adj.* —**me·tab′o·lize′** (-līz′) *vt., vi.* **-lized′, -liz′ing**

met·a·car·pus (met′ə kär′pəs) *n.*, *pl.* **-pi′** (-pī′) ‖< Gr *meta,* over + *karpos,* wrist‖ the part of the hand between the wrist and the fingers —**met′a·car′pal** *adj., n.*

met·al (met′l) *n.* ‖< Gr *metallon,* a mine‖ **1** *a)* any of a class of chemical elements, as iron or gold, that have luster, can conduct heat and electricity, etc. *b)* an alloy of such elements, as brass **2** anything consisting of metal —**me·tal·lic** (mə tal′ik) *adj.*

met·al·lur·gy (met′ə lur′jē) *n.* [< Gr *metallon*, metal + *ergon*, work] the science of separating metals from their ores and preparing them for use, by smelting, refining, etc. —**met′al·lur′gi·cal** *adj.* —**met′al·lur′gist** *n.*

met·a·mor·phose (met′ə môr′fōz′, -fōs′) *vt.,* *vi.* **-phosed′, -phos′ing** to change in form; transform

met·a·mor·pho·sis (-môr′fə sis) *n., pl.* **-ses′** (-sēz′) [< Gr *meta*, over + *morphē*, form] **1** a change of form, structure, substance, or function; specif., the physical change undergone by some animals during development, as of the tadpole to the frog **2** a marked change of character, appearance, condition, etc. —**met′a·mor′phic** *adj.*

met·a·phor (met′ə fôr′) *n.* [< Gr *meta*, over + *pherein*, to bear] a figure of speech in which one thing is spoken of as if it were another (Ex.: "all the world's a stage") —**met′a·phor′ic** *adj.,* **met′a·phor′i·cal**

met·a·phys·i·cal (met′ə fiz′i kəl) *adj.* **1** of or relating to metaphysics **2** very abstract or subtle **3** supernatural

met·a·phys·ics (-iks) *n.* [< Gr *meta* (*ta*) *physika*, after (the) *Physics* (of Aristotle)] **1** the branch of philosophy that seeks to explain the nature of being and reality **2** speculative philosophy in general

me·tas·ta·sis (mə tas′tə sis) *n., pl.* **-ses′** (-sēz′) [< Gr *meta*, after + *histanai*, to place] the spread of disease from one part of the body to another, esp. the spread of cancer cells by way of the bloodstream —**me·tas′ta·size′** (-sīz′) *vi.* **-sized′, -siz′ing**

met·a·tar·sus (met′ə tär′səs) *n., pl.* **-si′** (-sī′) [< Gr *meta*, over + *tarsos*, flat of the foot] the part of the human foot between the ankle and the toes —**met′a·tar′sal** *adj., n.*

me·tath·e·sis (mə tath′ə sis) *n., pl.* **-ses′** (-sēz′) [< Gr *meta*, over + *tithenai*, to place] transposition, specif. of sounds in a word

mete (mēt) *vt.* **met′ed, met′ing** [OE *metan*, to measure] to allot; distribute: usually with *out*

me·tem·psy·cho·sis (mi tem′sī kō′sis) *n., pl.* **-ses′** (-sēz′) [< Gr *meta*, over + *en,* in + *psychē*, soul] transmigration of souls

me·te·or (mēt′ē ər, -ôr′) *n.* [< Gr *meta*, beyond + *eōra*, a hovering] **1** the streak of light, etc. observed when a meteoroid enters the earth's atmosphere; shooting star **2** loosely, a meteoroid or meteorite

me·te·or·ic (-ôr′ik) *adj.* **1** of a meteor **2** like a meteor; momentarily brilliant, swift, etc.

me·te·or·ite (-ər īt′) *n.* that part of a meteoroid that survives passage through the atmosphere of a planet and falls to its surface

me·te·or·oid (-ər oid′) *n.* a small, solid body traveling through outer space, seen as a meteor when in the earth's atmosphere

me·te·or·ol·o·gy (-ə räl′ə jē) *n.* [see METEOR & -LOGY] the science of the atmosphere and its phenomena; study of weather —**me′te·or·o·log′i·cal** (-ə läj′i kəl) *adj.* —**me′te·or·ol′o·gist** *n.*

me·ter¹ (mēt′ər) *n.* [< Gr *metron*, a measure] **1** measured arrangement of syllables in verse according to stress or syllable length **2** the basic pattern of beats in a piece of music **3** [Fr *mètre*] the basic metric unit of length, equal to 39.3701 inches

me·ter² (mēt′ər) *n.* [METE + -ER] **1** an apparatus for measuring and recording the quantity of gas, water, etc. passing through it **2** PARKING METER

-me·ter (mēt′ər, mi tər) [< Gr *metron*, a measure] *combining form* a device for measuring [*barometer*]

meth·a·done (meth′ə dōn′) *n.* [< its chemical name] a synthetic narcotic drug used in medicine to treat heroin and morphine addicts

meth·ane (meth′ān′) *n.* [< METHYL] a colorless, odorless, flammable gas formed by the decomposition of vegetable matter, as in marshes

meth·a·nol (meth′ə nôl′) *n.* [< prec. + (ALCO-H)OL] a colorless, flammable, poisonous liquid used as a fuel, solvent, antifreeze, etc.

me·thinks (mē thiŋks′) *v.impersonal pt.* **-thought′** (-thôt′) [OE *me*, to me + *thyncth*, it seems] [Archaic] it seems to me

meth·od (meth′əd) *n.* [< Fr < Gr *meta*, after + *hodos*, a way] **1** a way of doing anything; procedure; process **2** orderliness in doing things or handling ideas

me·thod·i·cal (mə thäd′i kəl) *adj.* characterized by method; orderly; systematic —**me·thod′i·cal·ly** *adv.*

Meth·od·ist (meth′ə dist) *n.* a member of a Protestant Christian denomination that developed from the teachings of John Wesley —**Meth′od·ism′** *n.*

meth·od·ol·o·gy (meth′ə däl′ə jē) *n., pl.* **-gies** a system of methods, as in a science

Me·thu·se·lah (mə thōō′zə lə) *n. Bible* a patriarch who lived 969 years

meth·yl (meth′əl) *n.* [< Gr *methy*, wine + *hylē*, wood] a hydrocarbon radical found in methanol

methyl alcohol METHANOL

me·tic·u·lous (mə tik′yōō ləs, -yə-) *adj.* [< L *metus*, fear] extremely or excessively careful about details; scrupulous or finicky —**me·tic′u·lous·ly** *adv.*

mé·tier (mā tyā′) *n.* [Fr, a trade] work that one is particularly suited for

me·tre (mēt′ər) *n. Brit. sp. of* METER¹

met·ric (me′trik) *adj.* **1** METRICAL **2** *a)* of the METER¹ (*n.* 3) *b)* of the metric system

met·ri·cal (me′tri kəl) *adj.* **1** of or composed in meter or verse **2** of or used in measurement —**met′ri·cal·ly** *adv.*

met·ri·cate (me′tri kāt′) *vt.* **-cat′ed, -cat′ing** to change over to the metric system —**met′ri·ca′tion** *n.*

metric system a decimal system of weights

and measures in which the kilogram (2.2046 pounds), the meter (39.3701 inches), and the liter (1,000 cubic centimeters or 1.0567 quarts) are the basic units

met·ro¹ (me′trō) *adj.* short for METROPOLITAN

met·ro² (me′trō) *n., pl.* **-ros** ⟦ult. < *metro(politan)*⟧ ⟦*often* M-⟧ a subway

met·ro·nome (me′trə nōm′) *n.* ⟦< Gr *metron*, measure + *nomos*, law⟧ a device that beats time at a desired rate, as for piano practice

me·trop·o·lis (mə trǎp′ə lis) *n.* ⟦< Gr *mētēr*, mother + *polis*, city⟧ 1 the main city of a country, state, etc. 2 any large or important city —**met·ro·pol·i·tan** (me′trə pǎl′i tən) *adj.*

met·tle (met′'l) *n.* ⟦var. of METAL⟧ spirit; courage; ardor —**on one's mettle** prepared to do one's best

met·tle·some (-səm) *adj.* full of mettle; spirited; ardent, brave, etc.

mew (myōō) *n.* ⟦echoic⟧ the characteristic vocal sound made by a cat —*vi.* to make this sound

mewl (myōōl) *vi.* ⟦< prec.⟧ to cry weakly, like a baby; whimper

mews (myōōz) *pl.n.* ⟦< L *mutare*, to change⟧ ⟦*usually with sing. v.*⟧ 1 [Chiefly Brit.] stables or carriage houses in a court or alley 2 a former stable or carriage house converted into a dwelling

Mex (meks) 1 Mexican 2 Mexico

Mex·i·ca·li (mek′si kä′lē) city in NW Mexico, on the U.S. border

Mex·i·co (mek′si kō′) 1 country in North America, south of the U.S. 2 Gulf of arm of the Atlantic, east of Mexico —**Mex′i·can** *adj., n.*

Mexico City capital of Mexico

mez·za·nine (mez′zə nēn′, mez′ə nēn′) *n.* ⟦< It *mezzano*, middle⟧ 1 a low-ceilinged story between two main stories, usually in the form of a balcony over the main floor 2 the first few rows of the balcony in some theaters

mez·zo-so·pra·no (met′sō sə pran′ō) *n., pl.* **-nos** or **-ni** (-ē) ⟦It < *mezzo*, medium + SOPRANO⟧ 1 the range of a female voice between soprano and contralto 2 a voice or singer with such a range

MFA or **M.F.A.** *abbrev.* Master of Fine Arts

mfg *abbrev.* manufacturing

mfr *abbrev.* 1 manufacture 2 manufacturer

mg *abbrev.* milligram(s)

Mg *Chem. symbol for* magnesium

Mgr or **mgr** *abbrev.* manager

MHz *abbrev.* megahertz

mi¹ (mē) *n.* ⟦ML⟧ *Music* the third tone of the diatonic scale

mi² *abbrev.* 1 mile(s) 2 mill(s)

MI *abbrev.* 1 Michigan 2 middle initial

Mi·am·i (mī am′ē) city on the SE coast of Florida —**Mi·am′i·an** *n.*

mi·as·ma (mī az′mə, mē-) *n.* ⟦< Gr *miainein*, pollute⟧ 1 a vapor as from marshes, formerly supposed to poison the air 2 an unwholesome atmosphere or influence

mi·ca (mī′kə) *n.* ⟦L, a crumb⟧ a mineral that crystallizes in thin, flexible layers, resistant to heat and electricity

mice (mīs) *n. pl. of* MOUSE

Mi·chel·an·ge·lo (mī′kəl an′jə lō′, mik′əl-) 1475-1564; It. sculptor, painter, & architect

Mich·i·gan (mish′i gən) 1 Midwestern state of the U.S.; cap. Lansing: abbrev. **MI** 2 Lake one of the Great Lakes, between Michigan & Wisconsin —**Mich′i·gan′der** (-gan′dər) *n.* —**Mich′i·ga′ni·an** (-gä′nē ən) *adj., n.*, **Mich′i·gan·ite′**

Mick·ey Finn (mik′ē fin′) *n.* ⟦< ?⟧ ⟦*also* m- f-⟧ [Slang] a drink of liquor to which a narcotic, etc. has been added, given to an unsuspecting person: often shortened to **Mick′ey** or **mick′ey** *n., pl.* **-eys**

micro- ⟦< Gr *mikros*, small⟧ *combining form* 1 little, small ⟦*microcosm*⟧ 2 enlarging ⟦*microscope*⟧ 3 involving microscopes ⟦*microsurgery*⟧ 4 one millionth ⟦*microsecond*⟧ Also, **micr-**

mi·crobe (mī′krōb′) *n.* ⟦< Gr *mikros*, small + *bios*, life⟧ a microorganism, esp. one causing disease

mi·cro·bi·ol·o·gy (mī′krō bī äl′ə jē) *n.* the branch of biology dealing with microorganisms —**mi′cro·bi·ol′o·gist** *n.*

mi·cro·brew·er·y *n., pl.* **-er·ies** a small brewery producing high-quality beer, typically for local consumption

mi·cro·chip *n.* INTEGRATED CIRCUIT

mi·cro·com·put·er *n.* a small, inexpensive computer having a microprocessor and used in the home, etc.

mi·cro·cosm (-käz′əm) *n.* ⟦see MICRO- & COSMOS⟧ something regarded as a world in miniature

mi·cro·dot *n.* a copy, as of written or printed matter, photographically reduced to pinhead size, used in espionage, etc.

mi·cro·ec·o·nom·ics *n.* a branch of economics dealing with the behavior of individual consumers and businesses

mi·cro·fiche (-fēsh′) *n., pl.* **-fich′es** or **-fiche′** ⟦Fr < *micro-*, MICRO- + *fiche*, small card⟧ a small sheet of microfilm containing a group of microfilmed pages

mi·cro·film *n.* film on which documents, etc. are photographed in a reduced size for storage, etc. —*vt., vi.* to photograph on microfilm

mi·cro·man·age *vt.* **-aged**, **-ag·ing** to manage or control closely, often so closely as to be counterproductive

mi·crom·e·ter¹ (mī kräm′ət ər) *n.* ⟦< Fr: see MICRO- & -METER⟧ a tool for measuring very small distances, angles, etc.

mi·cro·me·ter² (mī′krō mē′tər) *n.* MICRON

mi·cron (mī′krän′) *n.* ⟦< Gr *mikros*, small⟧ one millionth of a meter

Mi·cro·ne·sia (mī′krə nē′zhə) country on a group of islands in the Pacific east of the Philippines —**Mi′cro·ne′sian** *adj., n.*

mi·cro·or·gan·ism (mī′krō ôr′gə niz′əm) *n.* a microscopic animal, plant, bacterium, virus, etc.

mi·cro·phone (mī′krə fōn′) *n.* ⟦MICRO- + -PHONE⟧ an instrument for converting sound waves into an electric signal

mi·cro·proc·es·sor (mī′krō prä′ses′ər) *n.* a chip that functions to control the operation of a microcomputer

mi·cro·scope (mī′krə skōp′) *n.* [[see MICRO- & -SCOPE]] **1** an instrument consisting of a combination of lenses, for making very small objects, as microorganisms, look larger **2** an electronic device, such as an electron microscope, used for the same purpose

mi·cro·scop·ic (-skäp′ik) *adj.* **1** so small as to be invisible or obscure except through a microscope; minute **2** of, with, or like a microscope —**mi′cro·scop′i·cal·ly** *adv.*

mi·cro·sur·ger·y (mī′krō sur′jər ē) *n.* surgery performed using a microscope and minute instruments or laser beams

mi·cro·wave *adj.* **1** designating equipment, etc. using microwaves for radar, communications, etc. **2** designating an oven that cooks quickly using microwaves —*vt.* **-waved′, -wav′ing** to cook in a microwave oven —*n.* **1** an electromagnetic wave with a frequency of about 300,000 megahertz to 300 megahertz **2** a microwave oven

mid¹ (mid) *adj.* [[OE *midd-*]] middle

mid² (mid) *prep.* [Old Poet.] amid: also **'mid**

mid- *combining form* middle, middle part of [*mid*-May]

mid·air *n.* any point in space not in contact with the ground or any other surface

Mi·das (mī′dəs) *Gr. Myth.* a king granted the power to turn everything he touches into gold

mid·course *adj.* happening in the middle of a journey or a course of action

mid·day *n., adj.* [[OE *middæg*]] noon

mid·dle (mid′'l) *adj.* [[OE *middel*]] **1** halfway between two given points, times, etc. **2** intermediate **3** [**M-**] designating a stage in language development intermediate between *Old* and *Modern* [*Middle* English] —*n.* **1** a middle point, part, time, etc. **2** something intermediate **3** the middle part of the body; waist

middle age the time between youth and old age —**mid′dle-aged′** *adj.*

Middle Ages the period of European history between ancient and modern times, A.D. 476–c. 1450

Middle America the American middle class, esp. when seen as being conventional or conservative

mid·dle·brow (-brou′) *n.* [Inf.] one regarded as having conventional, middle-class tastes or opinions —*adj.* of or for a middlebrow

middle class the social class between the aristocracy or very wealthy and the lower working class —**mid′dle-class′** *adj.*

middle ear the part of the ear including the eardrum and the adjacent cavity containing three small bones

Middle East area from Afghanistan to Libya, including Arabia, Cyprus, & Asiatic Turkey —**Middle Eastern**

Middle English the English language between c. 1100 and c. 1500

mid·dle·man (-man′) *n., pl.* **-men′** (-men′) **1** a trader who buys from a producer and sells at wholesale or retail **2** a go-between

mid·dle·most *adj.* MIDMOST

mid·dle-of-the-road *adj.* avoiding extremes, esp. political extremes

middle school a school with three or four grades, variously including grades 5 through grade 8

mid·dle·weight *n.* a boxer with a maximum weight of 160 pounds

Middle West MIDWEST —**Middle Western**

mid·dling (mid′liŋ) *adj.* of medium size, quality, etc. —*adv.* [Inf.] somewhat

mid·dy (mid′ē) *n., pl.* **-dies** [[< MIDSHIPMAN]] a loose blouse with a sailor collar, worn by women and children

Mid·east MIDDLE EAST —**Mid·east′ern** *adj.*

midge (mij) *n.* [[OE *mycg*]] a small, gnatlike insect

midg·et (mij′it) *n.* **1** a very small person: now often offensive **2** anything very small of its kind —*adj.* very small of its kind

mid·land (mid′lənd) *n.* the middle region of a country; interior —*adj.* in or of the midland

mid·most *adj.* exactly in the middle, or nearest the middle

mid·night *n.* twelve o'clock at night —*adj.* **1** of or at midnight **2** like midnight; very dark

mid·point *n.* a point at or close to the middle or center

mid·riff (mid′rif) *n.* [[< OE *midd-*, MID¹ + *hrif*, belly]] **1** DIAPHRAGM (*n.* 1) **2** the middle part of the torso, between the abdomen and the chest

mid·ship·man (mid′ship′mən) *n., pl.* **-men** (-mən) a student in training to be a naval officer

mid-size or **mid·size** (mid′sīz′) (mid′sīz′) *adj.* of a size intermediate between large and small [a *mid-size* car]

mldst (midst) *n.* the middle; central part —*prep.* [Old Poet.] in the midst of; amid —**in our** (or **your** or **their**) **midst** among us (or you or them) —**in the midst of 1** in the middle of **2** during

mid·stream *n.* the middle of a stream

mid·sum·mer *n.* **1** the middle of summer **2** the time of the summer solstice, about June 21

mid·term *adj.* in the middle of the term —*n.* [Inf.] a midterm examination, as at a college

mid·town *adj.* of or in the central part of a city, esp. a large city —*n.* a midtown area

mid·way *n.* that part of a fair where sideshows, rides, concessions, etc. are located —*adj., adv.* in the middle of the way or distance; halfway

Mid·west region of the NC U.S. between the Rocky Mountains & the E border of Ohio & the S borders of Kansas & Missouri —**Midwest′ern** *adj.* —**Mid·west′ern·er** *n.*

mid·wife (-wīf′) *n., pl.* **-wives′** [[< ME *mid*, with + *wif*, woman]] a person who helps women in childbirth —**mid′wife′ry** (-wīf′rē) *n.*

mid·win·ter *n.* **1** the middle of winter **2** the time of the winter solstice, about Dec. 22

mid·year *adj.* in the middle of the year —*n.* [Inf.] a midyear examination, as at a college

mien (mēn) *n.* ⟦short for DEMEAN²⟧ one's appearance, bearing, or manner

miff (mif) *vt.* ⟦prob. orig. cry of disgust⟧ [Inf.] to offend

MIG (mig) *n.* ⟦after Mi(koyan) & G(urevich), Soviet aircraft designers⟧ any of a series of Soviet or Russian jet fighter planes: also **MiG**

might¹ (mīt) *v.aux.* ⟦OE mihte⟧ **1** pt. of MAY **2** used as an auxiliary generally equivalent to MAY [it might rain]

might² (mīt) *n.* ⟦OE miht⟧ strength, power, or vigor

might·y *adj.* **-i·er, -i·est 1** powerful; strong **2** remarkably large, etc.; great —*adv.* [Inf.] very —**might'i·ly** *adv.* —**might'i·ness** *n.*

mi·gnon·ette (min'yə net') *n.* ⟦< Fr mignon, small⟧ a plant with spikes of small greenish, whitish, or reddish flowers

mi·graine (mī'grān') *n.* ⟦< Gr hēmi-, half + kranion, skull⟧ an intense, periodic headache, usually limited to one side of the head

mi·grant (mī'grənt) *adj.* migrating —*n.* **1** one that migrates **2** a farm laborer who moves from place to place to harvest seasonal crops

mi·grate (mī'grāt') *vi.* **-grat'ed, -grat'ing** ⟦< L migrare⟧ **1** to settle in another country or region **2** to move to another region with the change in seasons, as many birds do —**mi·gra·to·ry** (mī'grə tôr'ē) *adj.*

mi·gra·tion (mī grā'shən) *n.* **1** a migrating **2** a group of people, birds, etc., migrating together

mi·ka·do (mi kä'dō) *n.,* pl. **-dos** ⟦< Jpn mi, an honorific title + kado, gate⟧ [often **M-**] the emperor of Japan: title no longer used

mike (mīk) [Inf.] *n.* a microphone —*vt.* **miked, mik'ing** to record, amplify, etc. with a microphone

mil¹ (mil) *n.* ⟦L mille, thousand⟧ a unit of linear measure, equal to ¹/₁₀₀₀ inch

mil² (mil) *n.* [Slang] short for million

Mi·lan (mi lan', -län') city in NW Italy

milch (milch) *adj.* ⟦ME milche⟧ kept for milking [milch cows]

mild (mīld) *adj.* ⟦OE milde⟧ **1** gentle or kind; not severe **2** having a soft, pleasant flavor [a mild cheese] —**mild'ly** *adv.* —**mild'ness** *n.*

mil·dew (mil'dōō') *n.* ⟦OE meledeaw, honeydew⟧ a fungus that attacks some plants or appears on damp cloth, etc. as a whitish coating —*vt., vi.* to affect or be affected with mildew

mile (mīl) *n.* ⟦< L milia (passuum), thousand (paces)⟧ a unit of linear measure equal to 5,280 feet

mile·age *n.* **1** an allowance per mile for traveling expenses **2** total miles traveled **3** the average number of miles that can be traveled, as per gallon of fuel

mile·post *n.* a signpost showing the distance in miles to or from a place

mil·er *n.* one who competes in mile races

mile·stone *n.* **1** a stone set up to show the distance in miles to or from a place **2** a significant event in history, in a career, etc.

mi·lieu (mēl yœ', -yoo', -yōo'; mil-) *n.,* pl. **-lieus'** ⟦Fr < L medius, middle + locus, a place⟧ environment; esp., social setting

mil·i·tant (mil'i tənt) *adj.* ⟦< L miles, soldier⟧ **1** fighting **2** ready to fight, esp. for some cause —*n.* a militant person —**mil'i·tan·cy** *n.* —**mil'i·tant·ly** *adv.*

mil·i·ta·rism (mil'ə tə riz'əm) *n.* **1** military spirit **2** a policy of aggressive military preparedness —**mil'i·ta·rist** *n.* —**mil'i·ta·ris'tic** *adj.*

mil·i·ta·rize (-rīz') *vt.* **-rized', -riz'ing** to equip and prepare for war

mil·i·tar·y (mil'ə ter'ē) *adj.* ⟦< L miles, soldier⟧ **1** of, for, or done by soldiers **2** of, for, or fit for war **3** of the army —**the military** the armed forces

military police soldiers assigned to police duties in the army

military time a system for measuring time of day expressed as a four-digit numeral, the hour followed by minutes and starting with midnight at 0000 (midnight may also be expressed as 2400) (Ex.: 1:30 A.M. = 0130, 1:30 P.M. = 1330)

mil·i·tate (mil'ə tāt') *vi.* **-tat'ed, -tat'ing** ⟦< L militare, be a soldier⟧ to operate or work (against)

mi·li·tia (mə lish'ə) *n.* ⟦< L miles, soldier⟧ **1** an army composed of citizens rather than professional soldiers, called up in time of emergency **2** a group of disaffected citizens organized like an army and opposing federal authority —**mi·li'tia·man** (-mən) *n.,* pl. **-men** (-mən)

milk (milk) *n.* ⟦OE meolc⟧ **1** a white fluid secreted by the mammary glands of female mammals as nourishment for their young **2** cow's milk, etc., drunk by humans as a food or used to make butter, cheese, etc. **3** any liquid like this, as the liquid in coconuts —*vt.* **1** to squeeze milk from (a cow, goat, etc.) **2** to extract money, ideas, etc. from as if by milking —**milk'er** *n.*

milk glass a nearly opaque whitish glass

milk·maid *n.* a girl or woman who milks cows or works in a dairy

milk·man (-man') *n.,* pl. **-men** (-mən') a man who sells or delivers milk for a dairy

milk of magnesia a milky-white suspension of magnesium hydroxide in water, used as a laxative and antacid

milk·shake *n.* a drink made of milk, flavoring, and ice cream, mixed or shaken until frothy

milk·sop (-säp') *n.* a man thought of as timid, ineffectual, etc.

milk tooth any of the temporary, first teeth of a child or young animal

milk·weed *n.* any of a group of plants with a milky juice

milk·y *adj.* **-i·er, -i·est 1** like milk; esp., white as milk **2** of or containing milk —**milk'i·ness** *n.*

Milky Way the galaxy containing our sun: seen as a broad, faintly luminous band of very distant stars and interstellar gas arching across the night sky

mill¹ (mil) *n.* ⟦< L *mola*, millstone⟧ **1** a building with machinery for grinding grain into flour or meal **2** any of various machines for grinding, crushing, cutting, etc. **3** a factory, esp. one that processes raw materials [a textile *mill*] **4** a place where something is produced in great numbers, esp. unethically: [diploma *mill*, puppy *mill*] —*vt.* **1** to grind, form, etc. by or in a mill **2** to raise and ridge the edge of (a coin) —*vi.* to move (*around* or *about*) confusedly —**in the mill** in preparation —**through the mill** [Inf.] through a hard, painful, instructive experience

mill² (mil) *n.* ⟦< L *mille*, thousand⟧ ¹⁄₁₀ of a cent: unit used in calculating

mill·age *n.* taxation in mills per dollar of valuation

mil·len·ni·um (mi len′ē əm) *n., pl.* **-ni·ums** or **-ni·a** (-ə) ⟦< L *mille*, thousand + *annus*, year⟧ **1** a thousand years **2** *Christian Theol.* the period of a thousand years during which Christ will reign on earth: with *the* **3** any period of great happiness, peace, etc.

mill·er *n.* one who owns or operates a mill, esp. a flour mill

mil·let (mil′it) *n.* ⟦< L *milium*⟧ **1** a cereal grass whose grain is used for food in Europe and Asia **2** any of several similar grasses

milli- ⟦< L *mille*, thousand⟧ *combining form* one thousandth part of [*millimeter*]

mil·li·gram (mil′i gram′) *n.* one thousandth of a gram

mil·li·li·ter (-lēt′ər) *n.* one thousandth of a liter: Brit. sp. **mil′li·li′tre**

mil·li·me·ter (-mēt′ər) *n.* one thousandth of a meter

mil·li·ner (mil′i nər) *n.* ⟦< *Milaner*, vendor of dress wares from Milan⟧ one who makes or sells women's hats

mil·li·ner·y (mil′i ner′ē) *n.* **1** women's hats, headdresses, etc. **2** the work or business of a milliner

mil·lion (mil′yən) *n.* ⟦< L *mille*, thousand⟧ a thousand thousands; 1,000,000

mil·lion·aire (-yə ner′) *n.* a person whose wealth comes to at least a million dollars, pounds, francs, etc.

mil·li·pede (mil′i pēd′) *n.* ⟦< L *mille*, thousand + *pes*, foot⟧ a many-legged arthropod with an elongated body

mill·race *n.* the channel in which water runs to turn the wheel driving the machinery in a mill

mill·stone *n.* **1** either of a pair of round, flat stones used for grinding grain, etc. **2** a heavy burden

mill·stream *n.* the water flowing in a millrace

mill·wright *n.* a worker who builds or repairs the machinery in a mill

milt (milt) *n.* ⟦prob. < Scand⟧ the sex glands or sperm of male fishes

Mil·ton (milt′n), **John** 1608-74; Eng. poet

Mil·wau·kee (mil wô′kē) city & port in SE Wisconsin, on Lake Michigan

mime (mīm) *n.* ⟦< Gr *mimos*, imitator⟧ **1** the representation of an action, mood, etc. by gestures, not words **2** a mimic or pantomimist —*vt.* **mimed, mim′ing** to mimic or pantomime

mi·met·ic (mi met′ik, mī-) *adj.* ⟦< Gr *mimeisthai*, to imitate⟧ **1** imitative **2** characterized by mimicry

mim·ic (mim′ik) *adj.* ⟦< Gr *mimos*, actor⟧ imitative —*n.* an imitator; esp., an actor skilled in mimicry —*vt.* **-icked, -ick·ing** to imitate, often so as to ridicule **2** to copy or resemble closely

mim·ic·ry (mim′ik rē) *n., pl.* **-ries** the practice or art of mimicking

mi·mo·sa (mi mō′sə) *n.* [see MIME] a tree, shrub, or herb growing in warm regions and usually having spikes of white, yellow, or pink flowers

min *abbrev.* **1** minimum **2** minute(s)

min·a·ret (min′ə ret′) *n.* ⟦< Ar *manāra(t)*, lighthouse⟧ a high, slender tower attached to a mosque

min·a·to·ry (min′ə tôr′ē) *adj.* ⟦< L *minari*, threaten⟧ menacing

mince (mins) *vt.* **minced, minc′ing** ⟦< L *minutus*, small⟧ **1** to cut up (meat, etc.) into small pieces **2** to lessen the force of [to *mince* no words] —*vi.* to speak, act, or walk with an affected daintiness —**minc′ing** *adj.*

mince·meat *n.* a mixture of chopped apples, spices, suet, raisins, etc., and sometimes meat, used as a pie filling

mind (mīnd) *n.* ⟦< OE *(ge)mynd*⟧ **1** memory [to bring to *mind* a story] **2** opinion [speak your *mind*] **3** the seat of consciousness, in which thinking, feeling, etc. takes place **4** intellect **5** PSYCHE (*n.* 2) **6** reason; sanity —*vt.* **1** to pay attention to; heed **2** to obey **3** to take care of [*mind* the baby] **4** to be careful about [*mind* the stairs] **5** to care about; object to [they don't *mind* the noise] —*vi.* **1** to pay attention **2** to be obedient **3** to be careful **4** to care; object —**bear** (or **keep**) **in mind** to remember —**change one's mind** to change one's opinion, purpose, etc. —**have in mind** to intend —**never mind** don't be concerned —**on someone's mind 1** filling someone's thoughts **2** worrying someone —**out of one's mind 1** insane **2** frantic (*with* worry, etc.)

mind-blow·ing *adj.* [Slang] **1** causing shock, etc.; overwhelming **2** hard to comprehend

mind-bog·gling *adj.* [Slang] **1** hard to comprehend **2** surprising, overwhelming, etc.

mind·ed *adj.* having a (specified kind of) mind: used in compounds [high-*minded*]

mind·ful (-fəl) *adj.* having in mind; aware or careful (*of*) —**mind′ful·ly** *adv.* —**mind′ful·ness** *n.*

mind·less (-lis) *adj.* stupid or foolish

mind reader one who seems or professes to be able to perceive another's thoughts

mind's eye the imagination

mine¹ (mīn) *pron.* ⟦OE *min*⟧ that or those belonging to me: poss. form of I² [this is *mine*; *mine* are better]

mine² (mīn) *n.* ⟦< Fr⟧ **1** a large excavation made in the earth, from which to extract ores, coal, etc. **2** a deposit of ore, coal, etc. **3** any great source of supply [a *mine* of a information] **4** *Mil.* *a)* a tunnel dug under an enemy's fort, etc., in which an explosive is placed *b)* an explosive charge hidden underground or in the sea, for destroying enemy vehicles, ships, etc. — *vt., vi.* **mined, min'ing 1** to dig (ores, etc.) from (the earth) **2** to dig or lay military mines in or under **3** to undermine

min·er *n.* one whose work is digging coal, ore, etc. in a mine

min·er·al (min'ər əl) *n.* [< ML *minera*, ore] **1** an inorganic substance found naturally in the earth, as metallic ore **2** any substance that is neither vegetable nor animal —*adj.* of or containing a mineral

mineral jelly PETROLATUM

min·er·al·o·gy (min'ər äl'ə jē) *n.* the scientific study of minerals —**min'er·al'o·gist** *n.*

mineral oil a colorless, tasteless oil derived from petroleum, used as a laxative

mineral water water impregnated with mineral salts or gases

Mi·ner·va (mi nur'və) *n. Rom. Myth.* the goddess of wisdom

mi·ne·stro·ne (min'ə strō'nē) *n.* [It.: ult. < L *ministrare*, serve] a thick vegetable soup in a meat broth

min·gle (miŋ'gəl) *vt.* **-gled, -gling** [< OE *mengan*, to mix] to mix together; blend —*vi.* **1** to become mixed or blended **2** to join or unite with others

mini- [< fol.] *combining form* miniature, very small, very short [*miniskirt*]

min·i·a·ture (min'ē ə chər, min'i chər) *n.* [< L *miniare*, to paint red] **1** a small painting, esp. a portrait **2** a copy or model on a very small scale —*adj.* done on a very small scale

min·i·a·tur·ize (-īz') *vt.* **-ized', -iz'ing** to make in a small and compact form —**min'i·a·tur'i·za'tion** *n.*

min·i·bike (min'ē bīk') *n.* a compact motorcycle, usually used as an off-road vehicle

min·i·mal (min'i məl) *adj.* **1** smallest or least possible **2** of minimalism —**min'i·mal·ly** *adv.*

min·i·mal·ism *n.* a movement in art, music, etc. in which only the simplest design, forms, etc. are used, often repetitiously —**min'i·mal·ist** *adj., n.*

min·i·mal·ize (-īz') *vt.* **-ized', -iz'ing** to reduce to basic components

min·i·mize (min'i mīz') *vt.* **-mized', -miz'ing** to reduce to or estimate at a minimum

min·i·mum (-məm) *n., pl.* **-mums** or **-ma** (-mə) [L, least] **1** the smallest possible or allowable quantity, number, etc. **2** the lowest degree or point reached —*adj.* smallest possible, permissible, or reached

min·ion (min'yən) *n.* [Fr *mignon*, darling] **1** a favorite, esp. one who is a servile follower: term of contempt **2** a subordinate official

min·is·cule (min'i skyōōl') *adj. disputed var. of* MINUSCULE

min·i·se·ries (min'ē sir'ēz) *n., pl.* **-ries** a TV drama broadcast serially in a limited number of episodes

min·i·skirt (min'ē skurt') *n.* a very short skirt ending well above the knee

min·is·ter (min'is tər) *n.* [L, a servant] **1** a person appointed to head a governmental department **2** a diplomat representing his or her government in a foreign nation **3** one authorized to conduct religious services in a church, esp. a Protestant church —*vi.* **1** to serve as a minister in a church **2** to give help (*to*) —**min'is·te'ri·al** (-tir'ē əl) *adj.* —**min'is·trant** (-trənt) *adj., n.*

min·is·tra·tion (-trā'shən) *n.* the act of giving help or care; service

min·is·try (-is trē) *n., pl.* **-tries 1** the act of ministering, or serving **2** *a)* the office or function of a religious minister *b)* ministers of religion collectively; clergy **3** *a)* the department under a minister of government *b)* the minister's term of office *c)* the ministers of a government as a group

min·i·van (min'ē van') *n.* a passenger vehicle like a van but smaller, usually with windows all around and removable rear seats

mink (miŋk) *n.* [< Scand] **1** a slim carnivore living in water part of the time **2** its valuable, white to brown fur

Min·ne·ap·o·lis (min'ē ap'ə lis) city in E Minnesota

Min·ne·so·ta (min'ə sōt'ə) Midwestern state of the U.S.; cap. St. Paul: abbrev. *MN* —**Min'ne·so'tan** *adj., n.*

min·now (min'ō) *n.* [< OE *myne*] any of various, usually small, freshwater fishes used commonly as bait

Mi·no·an (mi nō'ən) *adj.* [after *Minos*, mythical king of Crete] of an advanced prehistoric culture in Crete from *c.* 3000 to *c.* 1100 B.C.

mi·nor (mī'nər) *adj.* [< L] **1** lesser in size, amount, importance, etc. **2** *Music a)* of or being a minor scale *b)* lower than the corresponding major by a half tone —*vi. Educ.* to have a secondary field of study (*in*) —*n.* **1** a person under full legal age **2** *Educ.* a secondary field of study

mi·nor·i·ty (mī nôr'ə tē, mi-) *n., pl.* **-ties 1** the lesser part or smaller number **2** a racial, religious, or political group that differs from the larger, controlling group **3** the period or state of being under full legal age

minor scale an eight-tone musical scale with a semitone between the second and third tones

Min·o·taur (min'ə tôr') *n. Gr. Myth.* a monster with the body of a man and the head of a bull

min·ox·i·dil (min äk'sə dil) *n.* a drug that dilates blood vessels, used in treating high blood pressure and baldness

min·strel (min'strəl) *n.* [see MINISTER] **1** a medieval traveling singer **2** [Historical] a member of a comic variety show (**minstrel show**) in which the performers blacken their faces —**min'strel·sy** (-sē) *n., pl.* **-sies**

mint¹ (mint) *n.* [< L < *Moneta*, epithet for Juno, whose temple was the Roman mint] **1** a place where a government coins money **2** a large amount —*adj.* new, as if freshly minted —*vt.* to coin (money) —**mint'age** (-ij) *n.*

mint² (mint) *n.* [< Gr *mintha*] **1** an aromatic plant whose leaves are used for flavoring **2 a** candy flavored with mint

mint julep an iced drink of bourbon, sugar, and mint leaves

min·u·end (min′yōō end′) *n.* [< L *minuere*, lessen] the number from which another is to be subtracted

min·u·et (min′yōō et′) *n.* [< Fr < OFr *menu*, small: from the small steps taken] **1** a slow, stately dance **2** the music for this

mi·nus (mī′nəs) *prep.* [< L *minor*, less] **1** reduced by subtraction of; less [four *minus* two] **2** [Inf.] without [*minus* a toe] —*adj.* **1** involving subtraction [a *minus* sign] **2** negative **3** less than [a grade of A *minus*] —*n.* a sign (−), indicating subtraction or negative quantity: in full **minus sign**

mi·nus·cule (min′i skyōōl′, mi nus′kyōōl′) *adj.* [L *minusculus*] very small

min·ute¹ (min′it) *n.* [see fol.] **1** the sixtieth part of an hour, or of a degree of an arc **2** a moment **3** a specific point in time **4** [*pl.*] an official record of a meeting, etc. —**the minute (that)** just as soon as

mi·nute² (mī nōōt′, -nyōōt′) *adj.* [< L *minor*, less] **1** very small **2** of little importance **3** of or attentive to tiny details; precise —**mi·nute′ly** *adv.*

minute hand (min′it) the longer hand of a clock, indicating the minutes

min·ute·man (min′it man′) *n., pl.* **-men′** (-men′) [*also* **M-**] a member of a local militia group in New England at the time of the American Revolution

minute steak (min′it) a small, thin steak that can be cooked quickly

mi·nu·ti·ae (mi nōō′shə, -nyōō′-) *pl.n., sing.* **-ti·a** (-shə) [see MINUTE²] small or unimportant details

minx (miŋks) *n.* [< ?] a pert, saucy girl

mir·a·cle (mir′ə kəl) *n.* [< L *mirus*, wonderful] **1** an event or action that apparently contradicts known scientific laws **2** a remarkable thing

mi·rac·u·lous (mi rak′yōō ləs, -yə-) *adj.* **1** having the nature of, or like, a miracle **2** able to work miracles —**mi·rac′u·lous·ly** *adv.* —**mi·rac′u·lous·ness** *n.*

mi·rage (mi räzh′) *n.* [< VL *mirare*, look at] an optical illusion, caused by the refraction of light by layers of hot and cold air, in which a distant object appears to be nearby, inverted, etc.

mire (mīr) *n.* [< ON *myrr*] **1** an area of wet, soggy ground **2** deep mud —*vt.* **mired, mir′ing 1** to cause to get stuck as in mire **2** to soil with mud, etc. —*vi.* to sink in mud —**mir′y** *adj.* **-i·er, -i·est**

mir·ror (mir′ər) *n.* [< L *mirare*, look at] **1** a smooth, reflecting surface; esp., a glass coated as with silver on the back **2** anything giving a true representation —*vt.* to reflect, as in a mirror

mirth (murth) *n.* [< OE *myrig*, pleasant] joyfulness or gaiety, esp. when shown by laughter —**mirth′ful** *adj.* —**mirth′less** *adj.*

MIRV (murv) *n., pl.* **MIRV's** [*m(ultiple) i(ndependently) targeted) r(eentry) v(ehicle)*] an intercontinental ballistic missile whose several warheads can be launched individually

mis- [< OE *mis-* or OFr *mes-*] *prefix* **1** wrong(ly), bad(ly) **2** no, not

mis·ad·ven·ture (mis′əd ven′chər) *n.* a mishap; an instance of bad luck

mis·an·thrope (mis′ən thrōp′) *n.* [Gr *misein*, to hate + *anthrōpos*, man] a person who hates or distrusts all people: also **mis·an·thro·pist** (mi san′thrə pist) —**mis′an·throp′ic** (-thräp′ik) *adj.* —**mis·an′thro·py** *n.*

mis·ap·ply *vt.* **-plied′, -ply′ing** to use badly, improperly, or wastefully

mis·ap·pre·hend (-ap rē hend′) *vt.* to misunderstand —**mis′ap·pre·hen′sion** *n.*

mis·ap·pro·pri·ate *vt.* **-at′ed, -at′ing** to appropriate to a wrong or dishonest use —**mis′ap·pro′pri·a′tion** *n.*

mis·be·got·ten *adj.* **1** wrongly or unlawfully begotten; illegitimate **2** badly conceived

mis·be·have *vt., vi.* **-haved′, -hav′ing** to behave (oneself) wrongly —**mis′be·hav′ior** *n.*

misc *abbrev.* **1** miscellaneous **2** miscellany

mis·cal·cu·late *vt., vi.* **-lat′ed, -lat′ing** to calculate incorrectly; miscount or misjudge —**mis′cal·cu·la′tion** *n.*

mis·call *vt.* to call by a wrong name

mis·car·ry (mis kar′ē, mis′kar′ē) *vi.* **-ried, -ry·ing 1** to go wrong; fail: said of a plan, etc. **2** to fail to arrive: said of mail, freight, etc. **3** to give birth to a fetus before it has developed enough to live —**mis·car′riage** *n.*

mis·cast *vt.* **-cast′, -cast′ing** to cast (an actor, a play, etc.) unsuitably

mis·ce·ge·na·tion (mi sej′ə nā′shən) *n.* [< L *miscere*, to mix + *genus*, race] marriage or sexual relations between a man and woman of different races: term used in the context of racial segregation

mis·cel·la·ne·ous (mis′ə lā′nē əs) *adj.* [< L *miscere*, to mix] consisting of various kinds or qualities

mis·cel·la·ny (mis′ə lā′nē) *n., pl.* **-nies** a miscellaneous collection, esp. of literary works

mis·chance *n.* bad luck

mis·chief (mis′chif) *n.* [< OFr *mes-*, MIS- + *chief*, end] **1** harm or damage **2** a cause of harm or annoyance **3** a prank

mis·chie·vous (mis′chə vəs) *adj.* **1** causing mischief; specif., *a)* harmful *b)* prankish **2** inclined to annoy with playful tricks —**mis′chie·vous·ly** *adv.* —**mis′chie·vous·ness** *n.*

mis·ci·ble (mis′ə bəl) *adj.* [< L *miscere*, to mix] that can be mixed

mis·com·mu·ni·ca·tion *n.* failure to fully or clearly communicate

mis·con·ceive (mis′kən sēv′) *vt., vi.* **-ceived′, -ceiv′ing** to misunderstand —**mis′con·cep′tion** (-sep′shən) *n.*

mis·con·duct *n.* **1** bad or dishonest management **2** willfully improper behavior

mis·con·strue (mis′kən strōō′) *vt.* **-strued′, -stru′ing** to misinterpret —**mis′con·struc′tion** (-struk′shən) *n.*

mis·count (mis kount′; *for n.* mis′kount′) *vt., vi.* to count incorrectly —*n.* an incorrect count

mis·cre·ant (mis′krē ənt) *adj.* [< OFr *mes-*, MIS- + *croire*, believe] villainous —*n.* a criminal; villain

mis·deal (mis dēl′; *for n.* mis′dēl′) *vt., vi.* -dealt′, -deal′ing to deal (playing cards) incorrectly —*n.* an incorrect deal

mis·deed *n.* a wrong or wicked act; crime, sin, etc.

mis·de·mean·or (mis′də mēn′ər) *n. Law* any minor offense bringing a lesser punishment than a felony

mis·di·rect *vt.* to direct wrongly or badly —**mis′di·rec′tion** *n.*

mis·do·ing *n.* wrongdoing

mi·ser (mī′zər) *n.* [< L, wretched] a greedy, stingy person who hoards money for its own sake —**mi′ser·ly** *adj.* —**mi′ser·li·ness** *n.*

mis·er·a·ble (miz′ər ə bəl, miz′rə bəl) *adj.* 1 in misery 2 causing misery, discomfort, etc. 3 bad; inadequate 4 pitiable —**mis′er·a·bly** *adv.*

mis·er·y (miz′ər ē) *n., pl.* -ies [see MISER] 1 a condition of great suffering; distress 2 a cause of such suffering; pain, poverty, etc.

mis·file *vt.* -filed′, -fil′ing to file (papers, etc.) in the wrong place

mis·fire *vi.* -fired′, -fir′ing 1 to fail to go off or ignite properly: said of a firearm or engine 2 to fail to achieve a desired effect —*n.* a misfiring

mis·fit (mis fit′; *for n.* mis′fit′) *vt., vi.* -fit′ted, -fit′ting to fit badly —*n.* 1 an improper fit 2 a maladjusted person

mis·for·tune *n.* 1 ill fortune; trouble 2 a mishap, calamity, etc.

mis·giv·ing *n.* a disturbed feeling of fear, doubt, etc.: *usually used in pl.*

mis·gov·ern *vt.* to govern badly —**mis′gov′ern·ment** *n.*

mis·guide (-gīd′) *vt.* -guid′ed, -guid′ing to lead into error or misconduct —**mis·guid′ance** *n.* —**mis′guid′ed·ly** *adv.*

mis·han·dle *vt.* -dled, -dling to handle badly or roughly; abuse or mismanage

mis·hap (mis′hap′) *n.* an unlucky or unfortunate accident

mis·hear *vt., vi.* -heard′, -hear′ing to hear wrongly

mish·mash (mish′mash′) *n.* a jumble

mis·in·form *vt.* to supply with false or misleading information —**mis′in·for·ma′tion** *n.*

mis·in·ter·pret *vt.* to interpret wrongly —**mis′in·ter′pre·ta′tion** *n.*

mis·judge *vt., vi.* -judged′, -judg′ing to judge wrongly or unfairly —**mis·judg′ment** *n.*

mis·la·bel *vt.* -beled or -belled, -bel·ing or -bel·ling to label incorrectly or improperly

mis·lay (-lā′) *vt.* -laid′, -lay′ing to put in a place that is then forgotten

mis·lead *vt.* -led′, -lead′ing 1 to lead in a wrong direction 2 to deceive 3 to lead into wrongdoing

mis·man·age *vt., vi.* -aged, -ag·ing to manage badly or dishonestly —**mis·man′age·ment** *n.*

mis·match (mis mach′; *for n.* mis′mach′) *vt.* to match badly or unsuitably —*n.* a bad match

mis·name *vt.* -named′, -nam′ing to give an inappropriate name to

mis·no·mer (mis nō′mər) *n.* [< OFr < *mes-*, MIS- + *nommer*, to name] a wrong name

mi·sog·y·ny (mi säj′ə nē) *n.* [< Gr *misein*, to hate + *gynē*, woman] hatred of women —**mi·sog′y·nist** *n.*

mis·place (mis plās′) *vt.* -placed′, -plac′ing 1 to put in a wrong place 2 to bestow (one's trust, etc.) unwisely 3 MISLAY

mis·play (mis plā′; *for n.* mis′plā′) *vt., vi.* to play wrongly or badly, as in games or sports —*n.* a wrong or bad play

mis·print (mis print′; *for n.* mis′print′) *vt.* to print incorrectly —*n.* a printing error

mis·pri·sion (-prizh′ən) *n.* [< OFr *mesprendre*, take wrongly] 1 misconduct or neglect of duty by a public official 2 misunderstanding or misinterpretation, as of a text

mis·pro·nounce *vt., vi.* -nounced′, -nounc′ing to pronounce differently from the accepted pronunciations —**mis′pro·nun′ci·a′tion** *n.*

mis·quote *vt., vi.* -quot′ed, -quot′ing to quote incorrectly —**mis′quo·ta′tion** *n.*

mis·read (-rēd′) *vt., vi.* -read′ (-red′), -read′ing (-rēd′iŋ) to read wrongly, esp. so as to misunderstand

mis·rep·re·sent *vt.* to represent falsely; give an untrue idea of —**mis′rep·re·sen·ta′tion** *n.*

mis·rule (mis rool′) *vt.* -ruled′, -rul′ing to rule badly; misgovern —*n.* misgovernment

miss¹ (mis) *vt.* [OE *missan*] 1 to fail to hit, meet, do, attend, see, hear, etc. 2 to let (a chance, etc.) go by 3 to avoid [he just *missed* being hit] 4 to notice or feel the absence or loss of 5 to lack [this book is *missing* a page] —*vi.* 1 to fail to hit something 2 to fail to be successful 3 to misfire: said of an engine —*n.* a failure to hit, meet, etc.

miss² (mis) *n., pl.* **miss′es** [< MISTRESS] 1 [M-] a title used before the name of an unmarried woman or a girl 2 a young unmarried woman or a girl

mis·sal (mis′əl) *n.* [< LL *missa*, Mass] [*often* M-] a book of prayers, readings, etc. authorized by the Roman Catholic Church for the celebration of Mass

mis·shape *vt.* -shaped′, -shap′ing to shape badly; deform —**mis·shap′en** *adj.*

mis·sile (mis′əl) *n.* [< L *mittere*, send] an object, as a spear, bullet, or rocket, designed to be thrown, fired, or launched toward a target

mis·sile·ry (-rē) *n.* 1 the science of building and launching guided missiles 2 such missiles

miss·ing (mis′iŋ) *adj.* absent; lost

mis·sion (mish′ən) *n.* [< L *mittere*, send] 1 a sending out or being sent out to perform a special service 2 *a)* a group of persons sent by a religious body to spread its religion, esp. in a foreign land *b)* its headquarters 3 a diplomatic delegation 4 a group of technicians, specialists, etc. sent to a foreign country **5** the special duty for which one is sent **6** a special task to which one devotes one's life; calling

mis·sion·ar·y (-er′ē) *adj.* of religious missions or missionaries —*n., pl.* **-ies** a person sent on a religious mission

Mis·sis·sip·pi (mis′ə sip′ē) **1** river in the central U.S., flowing from NC Minnesota to the Gulf of Mexico **2** Southern state of the U.S.; cap. Jackson: abbrev. *MS* —**Mis′sis·sip′pi·an** *adj., n.*

mis·sive (mis′iv) *n.* ⟦< L *mittere*, send⟧ a letter or written message

Mis·sou·ri (mi zoor′ē, -ə) **1** river in the central U.S., flowing from SW Montana into the Mississippi **2** Midwestern state of the U.S.; cap. Jefferson City: abbrev. *MO* —**Mis·sou′ri·an** *adj., n.*

mis·spell *vt., vi.* **-spelled′** or **-spelt′, -spell′ ing** to spell incorrectly

mis·spend *vt.* **-spent′, -spend′ing** to spend improperly or wastefully

mis·state *vt.* **-stat′ed, -stat′ing** to state incorrectly or falsely —**mis·state′ment** *n.*

mis·step *n.* **1** a wrong or awkward step **2** a mistake in conduct

mist (mist) *n.* ⟦OE⟧ **1** a large mass of water vapor, less dense than a fog **2** a mass of tiny droplets suspended in air **3** anything that dims or obscures — *vt., vi.* to make or become misty

mis·take (mi stāk′) *vt.* **-took′, -tak′en, -tak′ ing** ⟦< ON *mistaka*, take wrongly⟧ to understand or perceive wrongly —*n.* an idea, answer, act, etc. that is wrong; error or blunder —**mis·tak′a·ble** *adj.*

mis·tak·en *adj.* **1** wrong; having an incorrect understanding **2** incorrect: said of ideas, etc. —**mis·tak′en·ly** *adv.*

mis·ter¹ (mis′tər) *n.* ⟦< MASTER⟧ [M-] a title used before the name of a man or his office and usually written Mr.

mist·er² *n.* a bottle for directing a fine spray of water onto a houseplant, etc.

mis·time (mis tīm′) *vt.* **-timed′, -tim′ing** to do or say at the wrong time

mis·tle·toe (mis′əl tō′) *n.* ⟦< OE *mistel*, mistletoe + *tan*, a twig⟧ a parasitic evergreen plant with yellowish flowers and poisonous, white berries

mis·took (mis took′) *vt., vi. pt. of* MISTAKE

mis·treat *vt.* to treat wrongly or badly —**mis· treat′ment** *n.*

mis·tress (mis′tris) *n.* ⟦< OFr, fem. of *maistre*, master⟧ **1** a woman who is head of a household or institution **2** a woman, nation, etc. that has control, power, etc. **3** a woman in a sexual relationship with another person's spouse **4** [M-] [Obs.] a title used before the name of a woman: now replaced by Mrs., Miss, or Ms.

mis·tri·al *n. Law* a trial made void, as by an error in the proceedings or by the inability of the jury to reach a verdict

mis·trust *n.* lack of trust or confidence — *vt.,*

vi. to have no trust in; doubt —**mis·trust′ful** *adj.*

mist·y *adj.* **-i·er, -i·est** **1** of, like, or covered with mist **2** blurred, as by mist; vague —**mist′i·ly** *adv.* —**mist′i·ness** *n.*

mis·un·der·stand *vt.* **-stood′, -stand′ing** to fail to understand correctly; misinterpret

mis·un·der·stand·ing *n.* **1** a failure to understand **2** a quarrel

mis·use (mis yoōz′; *for n.,* -yoōs′) *vt.* **-used′, -us′ing** **1** to use improperly **2** to treat badly or harshly —*n.* incorrect or improper use

mite (mīt) *n.* ⟦OE⟧ **1** a tiny arachnid, often parasitic upon animals or plants **2** a very small sum of money **3** a very small creature or object

mi·ter (mīt′ər) *n.* ⟦< Gr *mitra*, headband⟧ **1** a tall, ornamented cap worn by bishops and abbots **2** *Carpentry* a joint formed by fitting together two pieces beveled to form a corner: now usually **miter joint**

mit·i·gate (mit′ə gāt′) *vt., vi.* **-gat′ed, -gat′ ing** ⟦< L *mitis*, soft⟧ **1** to make or become less severe, less painful, etc. **2** [< confusion with MILITATE] to operate or work (*against*): a loose usage —**mit′i·ga′tion** *n.*

mi·to·sis (mī tō′sis) *n.* ⟦< Gr *mitos*, thread⟧ the process by which a cell divides into two with the nucleus of each new cell having the full number of chromosomes —**mi·tot′ic** (-tät′ik) *adj.*

mitt (mit) *n.* ⟦< fol.⟧ **1** [Slang] a hand **2** *a*) *Baseball* a padded glove, worn for protection *b*) a boxing glove **3** a mitten

mit·ten (mit′'n) *n.* ⟦< OFr *mitaine*⟧ a glove with a thumb but no separately divided fingers

mix (miks) *vt.* ⟦< L *miscere*⟧ **1** to blend together in a single mass **2** to make by blending ingredients [to *mix* a drink] **3** to combine [to *mix* work and play] **4** to blend electronically (recorded sounds, etc.) —*vi.* **1** to be mixed or blended **2** to get along together —*n.* **1** a mixture **2** a commercial mixture of ingredients [a cake *mix*] **3** MIXER (*n.* 4) **4** the blend of sounds in a recording, etc. —**mix up 1** to mix thoroughly **2** to confuse **3** to involve or implicate (*in*): usually used in the passive —**mix′a·ble** *adj.*

mixed (mikst) *adj.* **1** blended **2** made up of different parts, classes, races, etc., or of both sexes **3** confused; muddled

mixed number a number consisting of a whole number and a fraction, as 3 ⅔

mixed-up *adj.* confused, troubled, etc.

mix·er *n.* **1** a person with reference to the ability to get along with others **2** a machine for mixing ingredients together **3** a social dance for helping people meet one another **4** a beverage for mixing with alcoholic beverages

mix·ture (miks′chər) *n.* **1** a mixing or being mixed **2** something made by mixing

mix-up *n.* a confusion; tangle

miz·zen·mast (miz′ən mast′; *naut.,* -məst) *n.* ⟦< L *medius*, middle⟧ the mast aft of the mainmast on a sailing vessel

mkt *abbrev.* market

ml *abbrev.* milliliter(s)

MLB *abbrev. service mark* Major League Baseball

Mlle *abbrev.* Mademoiselle

mm *abbrev.* millimeter(s)

MM *abbrev.* Messieurs

Mme *abbrev.* Madame

Mmes *abbrev.* mesdames

MMR *abbrev.* measles, mumps, and rubella (vaccine or vaccination)

Mn *Chem. symbol for* manganese

MN *abbrev.* Minnesota

mne·mon·ic (nē män′ik) *adj.* [< Gr *mnēmōn*, mindful] of or helping the memory

mo *abbrev.* month

Mo *Chem. symbol for* molybdenum

MO *abbrev.* 1 Missouri 2 [L *modus operandi*] mode of operation

moan (mōn) *n.* [prob. < OE *mænan*, complain] a low, mournful sound, as of sorrow or pain —*vi., vt.* 1 to utter or say with a moan 2 to complain (about)

moat (mōt) *n.* [< OFr *mote*, a mound] a deep, broad ditch, often filled with water, around a fortress or castle

mob (mäb) *n.* [< L *mobile (vulgus)*, movable (crowd)] 1 a disorderly, lawless crowd 2 any crowd 3 the masses: contemptuous term 4 [Inf.] a gang of criminals —*vt.* **mobbed, mob′bing** 1 to crowd around and attack, annoy, etc. 2 to throng; crowd into

mo·bile (mō′bəl, -bil′; *for n.,* -bēl′) *adj.* [< L *movere*, to move] 1 moving or movable 2 movable by means of a motor vehicle [a *mobile* X-ray unit] 3 that can change rapidly or easily; adaptable 4 characterized by ease in change of social status —*n.* a piece of abstract sculpture consisting of an arrangement of thin forms, rings, etc. suspended and set in motion by air currents —**mo·bil′i·ty** (-bil′ə tē) *n.*

-mo·bile (mō bēl′) [< (AUTO)MOBILE] *combining form* motorized vehicle [*bookmobile*]

mo·bile home (mō′bəl) a movable dwelling set more or less permanently at a location: cf. MOTOR HOME

mo·bi·lize (-bə līz′) *vt., vi.* **-lized′, -liz′ing** to make or become prepared or active, as for war —**mo′bi·li·za′tion** *n.*

mob·ster (mäb′stər) *n.* [Slang] a gangster

moc·ca·sin (mäk′ə sən) *n.* [< AmInd] 1 a heelless slipper of soft, flexible leather 2 any similar heeled slipper

mo·cha (mō′kə) *n.* a choice grade of coffee grown esp. in Arabia —*adj.* flavored with coffee or coffee and chocolate

mock (mäk) *vt.* [< OFr *mocquer*] 1 to ridicule 2 to mimic, as in fun or derision —*vi.* to express scorn, ridicule, etc. —*adj.* sham; imitation; pretended —*adv.* falsely or insincerely

mock·er·y (-ər ē) *n., pl.* **-ies** 1 a mocking 2 a person or thing receiving or deserving ridicule 3 a derisive imitation

mock·ing·bird *n.* a bird of the U.S. that imitates the calls of other birds

mock-up *n.* [< Fr *maquette*] a model built to scale, often full-sized, for teaching, testing, etc.

mod (mäd) *adj.* [< MOD(ERN)] up-to-date, fashionable, stylish, etc.

mode (mōd) *n.* [< L *modus*] 1 a manner or way of acting, doing, or being 2 customary usage or current fashion 3 *Gram.* MOOD²

mod·el (mäd′'l) *n.* [< L *modus*, a measure] 1 a small representation of a planned or existing object 2 a hypothetical description, often based on an analogy, used in analyzing something 3 a person or thing regarded as a standard of excellence to be imitated 4 a style or design 5 *a)* one who poses for an artist or photographer *b)* one employed to display clothes by wearing them —*adj.* 1 serving as a model 2 representative of others of the same style, etc. [a *model* home] —*vt.* **-eled** or **-elled, -el·ing** or **-el·ling** 1 *a)* to make a model of *b)* to plan or form after a model 2 to display (clothes) by wearing —*vi.* to serve as a MODEL (*n.* 5)

mo·dem (mō′dəm) *n.* [MO(DULATOR) + DEM(ODULATION)] a device that converts data for transmission, as by telephone, between computers

mod·er·ate (mäd′ər it; *for v.,* -āt′) *adj.* [< L *moderare*, restrain] 1 within reasonable limits; avoiding extremes 2 mild; calm 3 of medium quality, amount, etc. —*n.* one holding moderate opinions —*vt., vi.* **-at′ed, -at′ing** 1 to make or become moderate 2 to preside over (a meeting, etc.) —**mod′er·ate·ly** *adv.*

mod·er·a·tion *n.* 1 a moderating 2 avoidance of extremes 3 calmness

mod·er·a·tor *n.* one who presides at an assembly, debate, etc.

mod·ern (mäd′ərn) *adj.* [< L *modo*, just now] 1 of the present or recent times; specif., up-to-date 2 [*often* M-] designating the most recent form of a language 3 breaking with tradition, as by employing radically innovative styles, etc. —*n.* a person living in modern times, having modern ideas, etc. —**mo·der·ni·ty** (mä dur′nə tē) *n.*

Modern English the English language since about the mid-1400s

mod·ern·ism *n.* 1 (a) modern usage, practice, thought, etc. 2 [*often* M-] a movement of the early 1900s in the arts, breaking with established traditions and styles —**mod′ern·ist** *n., adj.* —**mod′ern·is′tic** *adj.*

mod·ern·ize *vt., vi.* **-ized′, -iz′ing** to make or become modern —**mod′ern·i·za′tion** *n.*

mod·est (mäd′ist) *adj.* [< L *modus*, a measure] 1 not vain or boastful 2 shy or reserved 3 decorous; decent 4 unpretentious —**mod′est·ly** *adv.* —**mod′es·ty** *n.*

mod·i·cum (mäd′i kəm) *n.* [< L, moderate] a small amount; bit

mod·i·fy (mäd′ə fī′) *vt.* **-fied′, -fy′ing** [< L *modificare*, to limit] 1 to change partially in character, form, etc. 2 to limit slightly 3 *Gram.* to limit in meaning —**mod′i·fi·ca′tion** *n.* —**mod′i·fi′er** *n.*

mod·ish (mōd′ish) *adj.* fashionable; stylish —**mo′dish·ly** *adv.* —**mod′ish·ness** *n.*

mod·u·lar (mäj′ə lər) *adj.* of modules

mod·u·late (-lāt′) *vt.* **-lat′ed, -lat′ing** [< L *modus*, a measure] **1** to regulate or adjust **2** to vary the pitch, intensity, etc. of (the voice) **3** *Radio* to vary the frequency of (radio waves, etc.) —**mod′u·la′tion** *n.* —**mod′u·la′tor** *n.*

mod·ule (mäj′ool) *n.* [Fr < L *modus*, a measure] **1** a standard or unit of measurement, as of building materials **2** any of a set of units to be variously fitted together **3** a detachable unit with a specific function, as in a spacecraft

mo·gul (mō′gul′) *n.* [Pers *Mughul*, Mongol] a powerful or important person

mo·hair (mō′her′) *n.* [< Ar *mukhayyar*, fine cloth] **1** the hair of the Angora goat **2** yarn or fabric made of this

Mo·ham·med (mō ham′id) *var. of* MUHAMMAD

Mo·ham·med·an *adj.* of Muhammad or Islam —*n.* MUSLIM A somewhat archaic term once widely used by non-Muslims

moi·e·ty (moi′ə tē) *n., pl.* **-ties** [< L *medius*, middle] **1** a half **2** an indefinite part

moire (mwär, môr) *n.* [Fr] a fabric, esp. silk, etc., having a wavy pattern: also **moi·ré** (mwä rä′, mô-)

moist (moist) *adj.* [< L *mucus*, mucus] slightly wet; damp —**moist′ly** *adv.* —**moist′ness** *n.*

mois·ten (mois′ən) *vt., vi.* to make or become moist

mois·ture (-chər) *n.* water or other liquid causing a slight wetness

mois·tur·ize (-īz′) *vt., vi.* **-ized′, -iz′ing** to make (the skin, air, etc.) moist —**mois′tur·iz′er** *n.*

Mo·ja·ve Desert (mō hä′vē) desert in SE California: also sp. **Mo·ha′ve Desert**

mo·lar (mō′lər) *adj.* [< L *mola*, millstone] designating a tooth or teeth adapted for grinding —*n.* a molar tooth

mo·las·ses (mə las′iz) *n.* [< L *mel*, honey] a thick, dark-brown syrup produced as a by-product of refining sugar

mold¹ (mōld) *n.* [< L *modus*, a measure] **1** a hollow form for giving a certain shape to something plastic or molten **2** a frame on which something is modeled **3** a pattern; model **4** something that is formed in or on a mold **5** distinctive character —*vt.* **1** to make in or on a mold **2** to form; shape

mold² (mōld) *n.* [ME *moul*] **1** a fungus producing a furry growth on the surface of organic matter **2** this growth —*vi.* to become moldy

mold³ (mōld) *n.* [OE *molde*] loose, soft soil rich in decayed organic matter

mold·er (mōl′dər) *vi.* [< OE *molde*, dust] to crumble into dust

mold·ing (mōl′diŋ) *n.* **1** the act of one that molds **2** something molded **3** a shaped strip of wood, etc., as around the upper walls of a room

Mol·do·va (mōl dō′və) country in E Europe

mold·y *adj.* **-i·er, -i·est 1** covered or over-

grown with mold **2** musty or stale —**mold′i·ness** *n.*

mole¹ (mōl) *n.* [OE *mal*] a small, congenital spot on the human skin, usually dark-colored and raised

mole² (mōl) *n.* [ME *molle*] **1** a small, burrowing mammal with soft fur **2** a spy who infiltrates an enemy's intelligence agency, etc. long before engaging in spying

mole³ (mōl) *n.* [< L *moles*, a dam] a breakwater

mol·e·cule (mäl′i kyool′) *n.* [< ModL dim. of L *moles*, a mass] **1** the smallest particle of an element or compound that can exist in the free state and still retain the characteristics of the substance **2** a small particle —**mo·lec·u·lar** (mō lek′yoo lər) *adj.*

mole·hill *n.* a small ridge of earth, formed by a burrowing mole

mole·skin *n.* a napped cotton fabric

mo·lest (mə lest′) *vt.* [< L *moles*, a burden] **1** to annoy or to meddle with so as to trouble or harm **2** to make improper sexual advances to **3** to assault or attack (esp. a child) sexually —**mo·les·ta·tion** (mō′les tā′shən) *n.* —**mo·lest′er** *n.*

Mo·lière (mōl yer′) 1622–73; Fr. dramatist

mol·li·fy (mäl′ə fī′) *vt.* **-fied′, -fy′ing** [< L *mollis*, soft + *facere*, make] **1** to soothe; appease **2** to make less severe or violent

mol·lusk (mäl′əsk) *n.* [< L *mollis*, soft] any of a group of invertebrates, as an oyster or snail, having a soft body, often in a shell

mol·ly (mäl′ē) *n., pl.* **-lies** [after F. N. *Mollien* (1758–1850), Fr statesman] any of various brightly colored fishes often kept in aquariums: also **mol′lie**

mol·ly·cod·dle (mäl′ē käd′'l) *vt.* **-dled, -dling** [< *Molly*, dim. of *Mary* + CODDLE] to pamper; coddle

Mo·lo·tov cocktail (mäl′ə tôf′) [after V. Molotov, Soviet statesman] a crude grenade, typically a bottle containing gasoline and a fuse

molt (mōlt) *vi.* [< L *mutare*, to change] to shed fur, skin, feathers, etc. prior to replacement by a new growth

mol·ten (mōlt′'n) *vt., vi.* [ME] *archaic pp. of* MELT —*adj.* melted by heat

mo·lyb·de·num (mə lib′də nəm) *n.* [ult. < Gr *molybdos*, lead] a silvery metallic chemical element, used in alloys: symbol, Mo; at. no. 42

mom (mäm) *n.* [Inf.] MOTHER (*n.* 1)

mo·ment (mō′mənt) *n.* [< L *momentum*, movement] **1** an indefinitely brief period of time; instant **2** a definite point in time **3** a brief time of importance **4** importance

mo·men·tar·i·ly (mō′mən ter′ə lē) *adv.* **1** for a short time **2** in an instant **3** at any moment

mo·men·tar·y (mō′mən ter′ē) *adj.* lasting for only a moment; passing

mo·men·tous (mō men′təs) *adj.* very important —**mo·men′tous·ness** *n.*

mo·men·tum (mō men′təm) *n., pl.* **-tums** or **-ta** (-tə) [L: see MOMENT] the impetus of a moving object, equal to the product of its mass and its velocity

mom·my (mäm′ē) *n., pl.* **-mies** *child's term for* MOTHER (*n.* 1)

Mon *abbrev.* Monday

Mon·a·co (män′ə kō) independent principality on the Mediterranean: an enclave in SE France

mon·arch (män′ərk, -ärk′) *n.* [< Gr *monos*, alone + *archein*, to rule] **1** a hereditary ruler; king, queen, etc. **2** a large butterfly of North America, having black-edged orange wings —**mo·nar·chi·cal** (mə när′ki kəl) *adj.*

mon·ar·chist (-ər kist) *n.* one who favors monarchical government

mon·ar·chy (-kē) *n., pl.* **-chies** a government or state headed by a monarch

mon·as·ter·y (män′ə ster′ē) *n., pl.* **-ies** [< Gr *monos*, alone] the residence of a group of monks, etc. living in seclusion for religious reasons

mo·nas·tic (mə nas′tik) *adj.* of or like that of a monastery, monk, nun, etc.: also **mo·nas′ti·cal** —**mo·nas′ti·cism′** (-tə siz′əm) *n.*

mon·au·ral (män ôr′əl) *adj.* of sound reproduction in which only one source of sound is used

Mon·day (mun′dā) *n.* [OE *monandæg*, moon's day] the second day of the week: abbrev. *Mon*

mon·e·tar·y (män′ə ter′ē) *adj.* [< L *moneta*, a MINT¹] **1** of the coinage or currency of a country **2** of money —**mon′e·tar′i·ly** *adv.*

mon·ey (mun′ē) *n., pl.* **-eys** or **-ies** [< L *moneta*, a MINT¹] **1** stamped pieces of metal, or any paper notes, authorized by a government as a medium of exchange **2** property; wealth —**for my money** [Inf.] in my opinion —**in the money** [Slang] **1** among the winners in a race, etc. **2** wealthy —**make money** to gain profits; become wealthy —**on the money** [Slang] exact; correct —**put money into** to invest money in

mon·ey·bag *n.* **1** a bag for money **2** [*pl., with sing. v.*] [Inf.] a rich person

mon·eyed (mun′ēd) *adj.* rich; wealthy

mon·ey·mak·er *n.* **1** one successful at acquiring money **2** something profitable —**mon′ey·mak′ing** *adj., n.*

money market the short-term system for lending and borrowing funds, esp. by governments and large corporations

money market fund a mutual fund that puts funds into short-term investments, as government treasury bills

money order an order for payment of a specified sum of money, issued for a fee at one post office, bank, etc. and payable at another

mon·ger (muŋ′gər) *n.* [< OE *mangere*] [Chiefly Brit.] a dealer or trader: usually in compounds

Mon·gol (män′gəl) *n.* a person born or living in Mongolia —*adj.* MONGOLIAN

Mon·go·li·a (mäŋ gō′lē ə) **1** region in EC Asia, consisting of the country of Mongolia and a region of China (*Inner Mongolia*) **2** country in EC Asia

Mon·go·li·an (mäŋ gō′lē ən) *n.* **1** MONGOL **2** a family of languages spoken in Mongolia

—*adj.* **1** of Mongolia or its peoples, languages, etc. **2** [Obs.] affected with Down syndrome

Mon·gol·oid (mäŋ′gəl oid′) *adj.* **1** *var. of* MONGOLIAN **2** designating or of a human racial group including most of the peoples native to SE and E Asia and the Americas: no longer in scientific use **3** [*often* **m-**] affected with Down syndrome: now offensive —*n.* **1** a member of the Mongoloid population of humans: no longer in scientific use **2** [*often* **m-**] one affected with Down syndrome: now offensive

mon·goose (mäŋ′gōos′) *n., pl.* **-goos′es** [< native name in India] a civetlike Old World carnivore that kills snakes, rodents, etc.

mon·grel (mäŋ′grəl) *n.* [< OE *mengan*, to mix] an animal or plant, esp. a dog, of mixed breed —*adj.* of mixed breed, origin, character, etc.

mon·ied (mun′ēd) *adj.* MONEYED

mon·i·ker (män′i kər) *n.* [< ?] [Slang] a person's name: also **mon′ick·er**

mo·ni·tion (mō nish′ən) *n.* [< L *monere*, warn] admonition; warning

mon·i·tor (män′i tər) *n.* [< L *monere*, warn] **1** a student chosen to help the teacher **2** any device for regulating the performance of a machine, an aircraft, etc. **3** a device allowing someone to view or hear activities in another room, etc. **4** *Comput.* a video screen for displaying data, images, etc. **5** *Radio, TV* a receiver for checking the quality of transmission — *vt., vi.* to watch or check on (a person or thing)

monk (muŋk) *n.* [< Gr *monos*, alone] a man who is a member of an ascetic religious order

mon·key (muŋ′kē) *n., pl.* **-keys** [< ? Fr or Sp *mona*, ape + LowG *-ke*, -KIN] **1** a primate having a flat, hairless face and a long tail **2** loosely, another, similar primate, as a chimpanzee —*vi.* [Inf.] to play, trifle, or meddle (*around* or *with*)

monkey business [Inf.] foolishness, mischief, or deceit

mon·key·shines (-shīnz′) *pl.n.* [Inf.] playful tricks or pranks

monkey wrench a wrench with an adjustable jaw —**throw a monkey wrench into** [Inf.] to disrupt the orderly functioning of

monk's cloth a heavy cloth with a basket weave, used for drapes, etc.

mon·o (män′ō) *adj. short for* MONOPHONIC —*n.* [Inf.] *short for* MONONUCLEOSIS

mono- [< Gr *monos*, single] *prefix* one, alone, single

mon·o·chrome (män′ə krōm′) *adj.* [< prec. + -CHROME] in one color or shades of one color

mon·o·cle (män′ə kəl) *n.* [ult. < Gr *monos*, single + L *oculus*, eye] an eyeglass for one eye only

mon·o·clon·al (män′ō klōn′əl) *adj.* of cells derived or cloned from one single cell

mon·o·cot·y·le·don (män′ō kät′ə lēd′'n) *n. Bot.* a plant having an embryo with only one cotyledon, or seed leaf: also **mon′o·cot′**

mo·nog·a·my (mə näg′ə mē) *n.* [ult. < Gr

monos, single + *gamos*, marriage] the practice or state of being married to only one person at a time —**mo·nog′a·mous** *adj.*

mon·o·gram (män′ə gram′) *n.* [< Gr *monos*, single + *gramma*, letter] the initials of a name, combined in a single design —*vt.* **-grammed′, -gram′ming** to put a monogram on

mon·o·graph (-graf′) *n.* [MONO- + -GRAPH] a book or long article, esp. a scholarly one, on a single, usually fairly narrow topic

mon·o·lin·gual (män′ō liŋ′gwəl) *adj.* using or knowing only one language

mon·o·lith (män′ə lith′) *n.* [< Gr *monos*, single + *lithos*, stone] 1 a single large block of stone, as one made into an obelisk 2 any massive, unyielding structure —**mon′o·lith′ic** *adj.*

mon·o·logue or **mon·o·log** (män′ə lôg′) *n.* [< Gr *monos*, single + *legein*, speak] 1 a long speech 2 a soliloquy 3 a skit, etc. for one actor only

mon·o·ma·ni·a (män′ō mā′nē ə) *n.* an excessive interest in or enthusiasm for some one thing; craze —**mon′o·ma′ni·ac′** (-mā′nē ak′) *n.* —**mon′o·ma·ni′a·cal** (-mə ni′ə kəl) *adj.*

mon·o·nu·cle·o·sis (män′ō nōō′klē ō′sis) *n.* [MONO- + NUCLE(US) + -OSIS] an acute disease, with fever, swollen lymph nodes, etc.

mon·o·phon·ic (-fän′ik) *adj.* of sound reproduction using a single channel to carry sounds

mo·nop·o·list (mə näp′ə list) *n.* one who has a monopoly or favors monopoly —**mo·nop′o·lis′tic** *adj.*

mo·nop·o·lize (-līz′) *vt.* **-lized′, -liz′ing** 1 to get, have, or exploit a monopoly of 2 to get full control of [he *monopolized* the conversation]

mo·nop·o·ly (-lē) *n., pl.* **-lies** [< Gr *monos*, single + *pōlein*, sell] 1 exclusive control of a commodity or service in a given market 2 such control granted by a government 3 something held as a monopoly 4 a company that has a monopoly

mon·o·rail (män′ə rāl′) *n.* 1 a single rail that is a track for cars suspended from it or balanced on it 2 a railway with such a track

mon·o·so·di·um glu·ta·mate (män′ō sō′dē əm glōō′tə māt′) a white powder made from vegetable protein, used to intensify flavor in foods

mon·o·syl·la·ble (män′ō sil′ə bəl) *n.* a word of one syllable —**mon′o·syl·lab′ic** (-si lab′ik) *adj.*

mon·o·the·ism (-thē iz′əm) *n.* [MONO- + THEISM] the belief that there is only one God —**mon′o·the·ist′** *n.* —**mon′o·the·is′tic** *adj.*

mon·o·tone (män′ə tōn′) *n.* [see MONO- & TONE] 1 utterance of successive words without change of pitch or key 2 tiresome sameness of style, color, etc. 3 a single, unchanging tone

mo·not·o·nous (mə nät′'n əs) *adj.* 1 going on in the same tone 2 having no variety 3 tiresome because unvarying —**mo·not′o·ny** *n.*

Mon·roe (mən rō′), **James** 1758-1831; 5th president of the U.S. (1817-25)

mon·sieur (mə syur′; *Fr* mə syö′) *n., pl.*

mes·sieurs (mes′ərz; *Fr* mä syö′) [Fr, lit., my lord] 1 a gentleman 2 [M-] French title, equivalent to *Mr.* or *Sir*

Mon·si·gnor (män sēn′yər) *n., pl.* **-gnors** [It, lit., my lord] *R.C.Ch.* a title of certain Roman Catholic prelates

mon·soon (män sōōn′) *n.* [< Ar *mausim*, a season] 1 a seasonal wind of the Indian Ocean and S Asia 2 the rainy season during which this wind blows from the southwest 3 a similar wind, as in the SW United States 4 a heavy rainstorm, esp. with high winds

mon·ster (män′stər) *n.* [< L *monere*, warn] 1 any grotesque imaginary creature 2 a very wicked person 3 any huge animal or thing —*adj.* huge

mon·strance (män′strəns) *n.* [ult. < L *monstrare*, to show] *R.C.Ch.* a receptacle for displaying the consecrated Host

mon·strous (män′strəs) *adj.* 1 huge; enormous 2 greatly malformed 3 horrible; hideous 4 evil —**mon·stros′i·ty** (-sträs′ə tē) *n., pl.* **-ties**

mon·tage (män täzh′) *n.* [Fr < *monter*, to mount] 1 a composite picture 2 a rapid sequence of film scenes, often superimposed

Mon·taigne (män tān′), **Mi·chel de** (mē shel′ də) 1533-92; Fr. essayist

Mon·tan·a (män tan′ə) Mountain State of the NW U.S.; cap. Helena: abbrev. *MT* —**Mon·tan′an** *adj., n.*

Mon·te Car·lo (mänt′ə kär′lō) district in Monaco: gambling resort

Mon·te·ne·gro (mänt′ə nē′grō, neg′rō) country in SE Europe

Mon·tes·so·ri method (mänt′ə sôr′ē) [after M. *Montessori* (1870-1952), It educator] a method of teaching young children, emphasizing sensory training

Mon·te·vi·de·o (mänt′ə və dā′ō) capital & seaport of Uruguay

Mont·gom·er·y (munt gum′ər ē, -gum′rē) capital of Alabama

month (munth) *n.* [OE *monath*] 1 any of the twelve divisions of the calendar year 2 a period of four weeks or 30 days 3 one twelfth of the solar year

month·ly *adj.* done, happening, payable, etc. every month —*n., pl.* **-lies** a periodical published once a month —*adv.* once a month; every month

Mon·ti·cel·lo (män′tə sel′ō, -chel′ō) home & burial place of Thomas Jefferson, in central Virginia

Mont·pel·ier (mänt pēl′yər) capital of Vermont

Mon·tre·al (män′trē ôl′) city & seaport in SW Quebec, Canada, on an island in the St. Lawrence River

mon·u·ment (män′yōō mənt) *n.* [< L *monere*, remind] 1 something set up to keep alive the memory of a person or event, as a tablet or statue 2 a work of enduring significance

mon·u·men·tal (-ment′'l) *adj.* 1 of or serving as a monument 2 like a monument; massive 3 very great; colossal

moo (mōō) *n., pl.* **moos** ⟦echoic⟧ a cow's vocal sound —*vi.* **mooed, moo′ing** to make this sound

mooch (mōōch) *vi., vt.* ⟦ult. < OFr *muchier,* to hide⟧ [Slang] to get (food, money, etc.) by begging, imposition, etc. —**mooch′er** *n.*

mood[1] (mōōd) *n.* ⟦< OE *mod,* mind⟧ **1** a particular state of mind or feeling **2** a predominant or pervading feeling or spirit

mood[2] (mōōd) *n.* ⟦< MODE⟧ a characteristic of verbs that indicates whether the action expressed is regarded as a fact, supposition, or command

mood·y *adj.* **-i·er, -i·est 1** changing in mood **2** gloomy —**mood′i·ly** *adv.* —**mood′i·ness** *n.*

moon (mōōn) *n.* ⟦OE *mona*⟧ [*often* M-] **1** the celestial body that revolves around the earth once about every 29 ½ days **2** anything shaped like the moon (i.e., an orb or crescent) **3** any natural satellite of a planet —*vi.* to behave in an idle or abstracted way

moon·beam *n.* a ray of moonlight

moon·light *n.* the light of the moon —*vi.* to engage in moonlighting

moon·light·ing *n.* the holding of a second job along with one's main job

moon·lit *adj.* lighted by the moon

moon·scape (-skāp′) *n.* ⟦MOON + (LAND)-SCAPE⟧ the surface of the moon or a representation of it

moon·shine *n.* **1** MOONLIGHT **2** foolish talk, plans, etc. **3** [Inf.] whiskey unlawfully distilled —**moon′shin′er** *n.*

moon·shot *n.* the launching of a spacecraft to the moon

moon·stone *n.* a feldspar with a pearly luster, used as a gem

moon·struck *adj.* **1** crazed; lunatic **2** romantically dreamy

moon·walk *n.* a walking about by an astronaut on the surface of the moon

moor[1] (moor) *n.* ⟦OE *mor*⟧ [Brit.] open wasteland covered with heather or other low-growing plants

moor[2] (moor) *vt.* ⟦< ? MDu *maren,* to tie⟧ **1** to hold (a ship, etc.) in place by cables attached to a pier **2** to secure —*vi.* to moor a ship, etc.

Moor (moor) *n.* a member of a Muslim people of NW Africa —**Moor′ish** *adj.*

moor·ing *n.* **1** [*often pl.*] the cables, etc. by which a ship is moored **2** [*pl.*] a place where a ship is moored

moose (mōōs) *n., pl.* **moose** ⟦< AmInd⟧ a large deer of N regions, the male of which has broad, flat antlers

moot (mōōt) *adj.* ⟦OE *mot,* a meeting⟧ **1** debatable **2** resolved and thus not worthy of discussion

mop (mäp) *n.* ⟦earlier *mappe*⟧ **1** a bundle of rags or yarns, a sponge, etc. fastened to the end of a stick, as for washing floors **2** anything suggesting this, as a thick head of hair —*vt.* **mopped, mop′ping** to wash or wipe with a mop —**mop up** [Inf.] **1** to finish **2** to clear remnants of beaten enemy forces from

mope (mōp) *vi.* **moped, mop′ing** ⟦akin to MDu *mopen*⟧ to be gloomy and apathetic —**mop′ey, mop′y,** or **mop′ish** *adj.*

mop·pet (mäp′it) *n.* ⟦< ME *moppe,* rag doll⟧ [Inf.] a little child

MOR *abbrev.* middle-of-the-road: used in radio broadcasting to designate styles of popular music that are not extreme

mo·raine (mə rān′) *n.* ⟦Fr⟧ a mass of rocks, sand, etc. left by a glacier

mor·al (môr′əl, mär′-) *adj.* ⟦< L *mos,* pl. *mores,* morals⟧ **1** dealing with, or capable of distinguishing between, right and wrong **2** of, teaching, or in accordance with the principles of right and wrong **3** good in conduct or character; specif., sexually virtuous **4** involving sympathy without action [*moral* support] **5** virtually such because of effects on thoughts or attitudes [a *moral* victory] **6** based on probability [a *moral* certainty] —*n.* **1** a moral lesson taught by a fable, event, etc. **2** [*pl.*] principles or standards with respect to right or wrong in conduct —**mor′al·ly** *adv.*

mo·rale (mə ral′) *n.* mental condition related to courage, confidence, enthusiasm, etc.

mor·al·ist (môr′əl ist) *n.* **1** a teacher of or writer on morals **2** one who seeks to impose his or her own morals on others —**mor′al·is′tic** *adj.*

mo·ral·i·ty (mō ral′i tē, mə-) *n., pl.* **-ties 1** rightness or wrongness, as of an action **2** right or moral conduct **3** moral principles

mor·al·ize (môr′əl īz′) *vi.* **-ized′, -iz′ing** to think, write, etc. about moral questions, often in a self-righteous or tedious way

mo·rass (mə ras′) *n.* ⟦< OFr *maresc*⟧ a bog, marsh, or swamp: often used figuratively of a difficult or troublesome situation

mor·a·to·ri·um (môr′ə tôr′ē əm) *n., pl.* **-ri·ums** or **-ri·a** (-ə) ⟦< L *mora,* a delay⟧ **1** a legal authorization to delay payment of money due **2** any authorized delay of a specified activity

mo·ray (eel) (môr′ā) *n.* ⟦< Gr *myraina*⟧ a voracious, brilliantly colored eel

mor·bid (môr′bid) *adj.* ⟦< L *morbus,* disease⟧ **1** of or caused by disease; diseased **2** resulting as from a diseased state of mind **3** tending to dwell on gruesome or gloomy matters **4** gruesome [*morbid* details] —**mor·bid′i·ty** *n.* —**mor′bid·ly** *adv.*

mor·dant (môr′dənt) *adj.* ⟦< L *mordere,* to bite⟧ caustic; sarcastic —*n.* a substance that fixes colors in dyeing —**mor′dan·cy** *n.* —**mor′dant·ly** *adv.*

more (môr) *adj.* ⟦OE *mara*⟧ **1** greater in amount, degree, or number: comparative of MUCH or MANY **2** additional [take *more* tea] —*n.* **1** a greater amount or degree **2** [*with pl. v.*] a greater number (*of*) **3** something additional —*adv.* **1** in or to a greater degree or extent **2** in addition

more·o·ver *adv.* in addition to what has been said; besides

mo·res (môr′āz′) *pl.n.* ⟦L, customs⟧ ways of

thinking and behaving shared by a society or group

more·so (môr′sō′) *adv. disputed sp. of* more so

morgue (môrg) *n.* [Fr] 1 a place where the bodies of unknown dead persons or those dead of unknown causes are temporarily kept 2 the file of back numbers, photographs, etc. kept as in a newspaper's office

mor·i·bund (môr′i bund′) *adj.* [< L *mori*, to die] dying

Mor·mon (môr′mən) *n.* a member of the Church of Jesus Christ of Latter-day Saints, founded (1830) in the U.S. —**Mor′mon·ism′** *n.*

morn (môrn) *n.* [Old Poet.] morning

morn·ing (môr′niŋ) *n.* [OE *morgen*] the first or early part of the day, from midnight, or esp. dawn, to noon

morning glory a twining vine with trumpet-shaped flowers

morning sickness nausea, vomiting, etc. affecting many women early in pregnancy, occurring usually in the morning

mo·roc·co (mə rä′kō) *n.* [< fol.] a fine, soft leather

Mo·roc·co (mə rä′kō) kingdom on the NW coast of Africa —**Mo·roc′can** *adj., n.*

mo·ron (môr′än′) *n.* [< Gr *mōros*, foolish] a very foolish or stupid person —**mo·ron′ic** *adj.*

mo·rose (mə rōs′) *adj.* [< L *mos*, manner] ill-tempered; gloomy, sullen, etc. —**mo·rose′ly** *adv.*

morph (môrf) *vt., vi.* to transform or be transformed as by morphing

mor·pheme (môr′fēm′) *n.* [< Gr *morphē*, a form] the smallest meaningful unit in a language, as an affix or base

mor·phine (môr′fēn′) *n.* [after *Morpheus*, Gr god of dreams] an alkaloid derived from opium and used in medicine to relieve pain

morph·ing *n.* [< (META)MORPH(OSIS) + -*ing*] a film or video process in which persons or objects seem to change form through a continuous series of images created by a computer

mor·phol·o·gy (môr fäl′ə jē) *n.* [Ger < Gr *morphē*, form + Ger -*logie*, -LOGY] the study of form and structure, as in biology or linguistics

mor·row (mär′ō, môr′-) *n.* [< OE *morgen*, morning] [Archaic] 1 morning 2 the next day

Morse (môrs) *adj.* [after S. Morse (1791-1872), U.S. inventor] [*often* m-] designating or of a code of dots and dashes used in telegraphy

mor·sel (môr′səl) *n.* [< L *morsum*, a bite] a small piece or amount, as of food

mor·tal (môr′t'l) *adj.* [< L *mors*, death] 1 that must eventually die 2 of a human seen as a being who must eventually die 3 of death 4 causing physical or spiritual death; deadly [a *mortal* wound; a *mortal* sin] 5 very intense [*mortal* terror] —*n.* a human —**mor′tal·ly** *adv.*

mor·tal·i·ty (môr tal′ə tē) *n.* 1 the mortal nature of humans 2 death on a large scale, as from war 3 the ratio of deaths to population

mor·tar (môr′tər) *n.* [< L *mortarium*] 1 a bowl in which substances are pulverized with a pestle 2 a short-barreled cannon which hurls shells in a high trajectory 3 a mixture of cement or lime with sand and water, used to bind bricks or stones

mor·tar·board *n.* 1 a square board for holding mortar 2 an academic cap with a square, flat top

mort·gage (môr′gij) *n.* [< OFr *mort*, dead + *gage*, pledge] 1 the pledging of property to a creditor as security for the payment of a debt 2 the deed by which this is done —*vt.* -gaged, -gag·ing 1 to pledge (property) by a mortgage 2 to put an advance claim on [to *mortgage* one's future] —**mort′ga·gor** *n.,* **mort′gag·er** (-gi jər)

mort·ga·gee (-gə jē′) *n.* a person to whom property is mortgaged

mor·ti·cian (môr tish′ən) *n.* [< L *mors*, death] FUNERAL DIRECTOR

mor·ti·fy (môr′tə fi′) *vt.* -fied′, -fy′ing [< L *mors*, death + *facere*, make] 1 to subdue (physical desires) by self-denial, fasting, etc. 2 to humiliate —**mor′ti·fi·ca′tion** *n.*

mor·tise (môr′tis) *n.* [< Ar *murtazza*, joined] a hole or recess cut, as in a piece of wood, to receive a projecting part (*tenon*) shaped to fit into it

mor·tu·ar·y (môr′chōō er′ē) *n., pl.* -ies a place where dead bodies are kept before burial or cremation; morgue or funeral home

mo·sa·ic (mō zā′ik) *n.* [< L *musivus*, artistic] 1 the making of pictures or designs by inlaying small bits of colored stone, etc. in mortar 2 a picture or design so made

Mo·sa·ic (mō zā′ik) *adj.* of Moses or the laws, etc. attributed to him

Mos·cow (mäs′kō, -kou′) capital of Russia, in the W part

Mo·ses (mō′zəz, -zəs) *n. Bible* the leader and lawgiver who brought the Israelites out of slavery in Egypt

mo·sey (mō′zē) *vi.* [prob. < VAMOOSE] [Slang] to stroll or amble along

Mos·lem (mäz′ləm) *n., adj.* MUSLIM

mosque (mäsk) *n.* [< Ar *masjid*, temple] a Muslim place of worship

mos·qui·to (mə skēt′ō) *n., pl.* -toes or -tos [Sp & Port < L *musca*, a fly] a two-winged insect, the female of which sucks blood from animals, including humans

moss (môs, mäs) *n.* [OE *mos*, a swamp] a very small, green plant that grows in velvety clusters on rocks, trees, etc. —**moss′y** *adj.* -i·er, -i·est

moss·back *n.* [Inf.] an old-fashioned or very conservative person

most (mōst) *adj.* [OE *mæst*] 1 greatest in amount, degree, or number: superlative of MUCH or MANY 2 in the greatest number of instances [*most* fame is fleeting] —*n.* 1 the greatest amount, quantity, or degree 2 [*with pl. v.*] the greatest number (*of*) —*adv.* in or to the greatest degree or extent

most·ly *adv.* **1** for the most part **2** chiefly; principally **3** usually

mote (mōt) *n.* ⟦OE *mot*⟧ a speck, as of dust

mo·tel (mō tel′) *n.* ⟦< MO(TOR) + (HO)TEL⟧ a hotel for motorists, usually with easy access between the rooms and a parking lot

moth (môth) *n.*, *pl.* **moths** (môthz, môths) ⟦OE *moththe*⟧ a four-winged, chiefly night-flying insect, similar to the butterfly: the larvae of one kind feed on wool, etc.

moth·ball *n.* a small ball, as of naphthalene, the fumes of which repel moths from woolens, etc. —**in mothballs** put into storage or reserve

moth·er (muth′ər) *n.* ⟦OE *modor*⟧ **1** a female parent **2** the origin or source of something **3** [*often* **M-**] a woman who is the head (**mother superior**) of a religious establishment —*adj.* **1** of or like a mother **2** native [*mother tongue*] —*vt.* **1** to be the mother of **2** to care for as a mother does —**moth′er·hood′** *n.* —**moth′er·less** *adj.*

Mother Goose the imaginary creator of a collection of nursery rhymes

moth·er-in-law *n.*, *pl.* **moth′ers-in-law′** the mother of one's husband or wife

moth·er·land *n.* one's native land

moth·er·ly *adj.* of or like a mother; protective, nurturing, etc. —**moth′er·li·ness** *n.*

moth·er-of-pearl *n.* the hard, iridescent internal layer of the shell of the pearl oyster, etc., used to make buttons, etc.

mother tongue one's native language

mo·tif (mō tēf′) *n.* ⟦Fr: see MOTIVE⟧ **1** *Art, Literature, Music* a main theme for development **2** a repeated figure in a design

mo·tile (mōt′'l) *adj.* ⟦< L *movere*, to move⟧ *Biol.* capable of or exhibiting spontaneous motion —**mo·til′i·ty** *n.*

mo·tion (mō′shən) *n.* ⟦< L *movere*, to move⟧ **1** a moving from one place to another; movement **2** a moving of a part of the body; specif., a gesture **3** a proposal formally made in an assembly —*vi.* to make a meaningful movement of the hand, etc.; gesture —*vt.* to direct by a meaningful gesture —**go through the motions** to do something as from habit, without enthusiasm —**in motion** moving —**mo′tion·less** *adj.*

motion picture FILM (*n.* 4)

motion sickness nausea, vomiting, etc. caused by the motion of a car, boat, etc.

mo·ti·vate (mōt′ə vāt′) *vt.* **-vat′ed, -vat′ing** to provide with, or affect as, a motive; incite

mo·ti·va·tion (mōt′ə vā′shən) *n.* **1** the act or an instance of motivating **2** anything that motivates **3** desire or enthusiasm to accomplish or achieve something [a talented athlete who lacks *motivation*] —**mo′ti·va′tion·al** *adj.*

mo·tive (mōt′iv) *n.* ⟦< L *movere*, to move⟧ **1** an emotion, impulse, etc. that causes one to act **2** MOTIF (*n.* 1)

-mo·tive (mōt′iv) *combining form* moving, of motion [*automotive*]

mot·ley (mät′lē) *adj.* ⟦< ?⟧ **1** of many colors **2** of many different or clashing elements

mo·to·cross (mō′tō krôs′) *n.* ⟦Fr⟧ a cross-country race for lightweight motorcycles

mo·tor (mōt′ər) *n.* ⟦L < *movere*, to move⟧ **1** anything that produces motion **2** an engine; esp., an internal-combustion engine **3** a machine for converting electric energy into mechanical energy —*adj.* **1** producing motion **2** of or powered by a motor **3** of, by, or for motor vehicles **4** of or involving muscular movements [*motor* skills] —*vi.* to travel by automobile

mo·tor·bike *n.* [Inf.] **1** a motor-driven bicycle **2** a light motorcycle — **1** a motor-driven bicycle **2** a light motorcycle

mo·tor·boat *n.* a small motor-driven boat

mo·tor·cade (-kād′) *n.* ⟦MOTOR + -CADE⟧ a procession of motor vehicles

mo·tor·car *n.* [Now Chiefly Brit.] an automobile — an automobile

mo·tor·cy·cle (-sī′kəl) *n.* a two-wheeled vehicle propelled by an internal-combustion engine

motor home a motor vehicle with a truck chassis, outfitted as a traveling home

mo·tor·ist (mōt′ər ist) *n.* one who drives an automobile or travels by automobile

mo·tor·ize (-īz′) *vt.* **-ized′, -iz′ing** to equip with a motor or with motor-driven vehicles

motor vehicle an automotive vehicle, esp. an automobile, truck, or bus

mot·tle (mät′'l) *vt.* **-tled, -tling** ⟦< MOTLEY⟧ to mark with blotches, etc. of different colors

mot·to (mät′ō) *n.*, *pl.* **-toes** or **-tos** ⟦It, a word⟧ a word or saying that expresses the goals, ideals, etc. of an individual or group

mould (mōld) *n.*, *vt.*, *vi.* chiefly Brit. sp. of MOLD[1], MOLD[2], MOLD[3]

mould·ing *n.* chiefly Brit. sp. of MOLDING

mould·y *adj.* chiefly Brit. sp. of MOLDY

moult (mōlt) *vi.* chiefly Brit. sp. of MOLT

mound (mound) *n.* ⟦< ? MDu *mond*, protection⟧ a heap or bank of earth, sand, etc. —*vt.* to heap up

mount[1] (mount) *n.* ⟦< L *mons*⟧ a mountain

mount[2] (mount) *vi.* ⟦< L *mons*, mountain⟧ **1** to climb; ascend **2** to climb up on something, as onto a horse **3** to increase in amount —*vt.* **1** to go up; ascend [to *mount* stairs] **2** to get up on (a horse, platform, etc.) **3** to provide with horses [*mounted* police] **4** to place or fix (a jewel, picture, etc.) on or in the proper support, backing, etc. **5** to arrange (a dead animal, etc.) for exhibition **6** to place (a gun) into proper position for use **7** to prepare for and undertake (an expedition, etc.) —*n.* **1** the act of mounting **2** a horse, etc. for riding **3** the support, setting, etc. on or in which a thing is mounted

moun·tain (mount′'n) *n.* ⟦ult. < L *mons*⟧ **1** a natural raised part of the earth, larger and usually more rugged than a hill **2** a large pile, amount, etc. —*adj.* of or in the mountains

mountain bike a heavy-duty bicycle with wide tires for use on and off regular road surfaces

moun·tain·eer (-ir′) *n.* **1** one who lives in a mountainous region **2** a mountain climber

moun·tain·eer·ing *n.* the climbing of mountains, esp. using special equipment and techniques on rock, ice, or snow

mountain goat a long-haired, goatlike mammal of the Rocky Mountains

mountain lion COUGAR

moun·tain·ous *adj.* 1 full of mountains 2 huge

mountain sickness weakness, nausea, etc. caused by thin air at high altitudes

Mountain State any of the six states of the W U.S. through which the Rocky Mountains pass; Montana, Idaho, Wyoming, Utah, Colorado, or New Mexico

moun·te·bank (mount′ə baŋk′) *n.* ⟦It *montambanco*, lit., mounted on a bench: orig. a person on a bench selling quack medicines⟧ a charlatan or quack

mount·ed *adj.* 1 on horseback, a bicycle, etc. 2 on or in a mounting

mount·ing *n.* something serving as a backing, support, setting, etc.

mourn (môrn) *vi., vt.* ⟦OE *murnan*⟧ 1 to feel or express sorrow for (something regrettable) 2 to grieve for (someone who has died) —**mourn′er** *n.*

mourn·ful *adj.* 1 feeling or expressing grief or sorrow 2 causing sorrow

mourn·ing *n.* 1 the expression of grief, esp. at someone's death 2 black clothes, etc., worn as such an expression 3 the period during which one mourns

mouse (mous; *for v.*, *also* mouz) *n.*, *pl.* **mice**; *for 3, also* **mous′es** ⟦OE *mus*⟧ 1 any of many small rodents, esp. a species that commonly infests buildings 2 a timid person 3 a handheld device for controlling the video display of a computer —*vi.* **moused, mous′ing** to hunt mice

mous·sa·ka (moō sä′kə, moō′sä kä′) *n.* ⟦ModGr⟧ a Greek dish of sliced eggplant and ground meat arranged in layers, baked with a top layer of white sauce and cheese

mousse (moōs) *n.* ⟦Fr, foam⟧ 1 a light, chilled dessert made with egg white, whipped cream, etc. 2 an aerosol foam used to keep hair in place, etc. —*vt.* **moussed, mouss′ing** to style (hair) using mousse

mous·tache (mus′tash′, məs tash′) *n. alt. sp. of* MUSTACHE

mous·y (mous′ē, mouz′-) *adj.* **-i·er, -i·est** of or like a mouse; specif., timid, drab, etc.: *also* **mous′ey** —**mous′i·ness** *n.*

mouth (mouth; *for v.* mouth) *n., pl.* **mouths** (mouthz) ⟦OE *muth*⟧ 1 the opening in the head through which food is taken in and sounds are made 2 any opening regarded as like this [the *mouth* of a jar, river, etc.] —*vt.* 1 to say, esp. insincerely 2 to form (a word) with the mouth silently —**down in** (or **at**) **the mouth** [Inf.] unhappy —**mouth off** [Slang] to talk loudly, impudently, etc.

mouth·ful *n., pl.* **-fuls′** 1 as much as the mouth can hold 2 as much as is usually taken into the mouth 3 [Slang] a pertinent remark: chiefly in **say a mouthful**

mouth organ HARMONICA

mouth·piece *n.* 1 a part, as of a musical instrument, held in or to the mouth 2 a person, periodical, etc. which expresses the views as of a group

mouth·wash *n.* a flavored, often antiseptic liquid for rinsing the mouth

mouth·wa·ter·ing *adj.* appetizing; tasty

mouth·y *adj.* **-i·er, -i·est** talkative, esp. in a bombastic or rude way —**mouth′i·ness** *n.*

mou·ton (moō′tän′) *n.* ⟦Fr, sheep⟧ lambskin or sheepskin made to resemble beaver, seal, etc.

mov·a·ble (moō′və bəl) *adj.* that can be moved from one place to another —*n.* 1 something movable 2 *Law* personal property, esp. furniture: *usually used in pl.* Also **move′a·ble**

move (moōv) *vt.* **moved, mov′ing** ⟦< L *movere*⟧ 1 to change the place or position of 2 to set or keep in motion 3 to cause (*to do, say,* etc.) 4 to arouse the emotions, etc. of 5 to propose formally, as in a meeting —*vi.* 1 to change place or position 2 to change one's residence 3 to be active 4 to make progress 5 to take action 6 to be, or be set, in motion 7 to make a formal application (*for*) 8 to evacuate: said of the bowels 9 to be sold: said of goods —*n.* 1 act of moving 2 an action toward some goal 3 a change of residence 4 *Chess, Checkers, etc.* the act of moving a piece, or one's turn to move —**move up** to promote or be promoted —**on the move** [Inf.] moving about from place to place

move·ment *n.* 1 a moving or manner of moving 2 an evacuation (of the bowels) 3 a change in the location of troops, etc. 4 organized action by people working toward a goal 5 the moving parts of a mechanism, as of a clock 6 *Music a)* a principal division of a symphony, etc. *b)* rhythm

mov·er (moō′vər) *n.* one that moves; specif., one whose work is moving furniture, etc. for those changing residence

mov·ie (-vē) *n.* ⟦< *moving picture*⟧ FILM (*n.* 4) —**the movies** 1 the film industry 2 a showing of a film

moving van a large van for transporting belongings, as of a person moving to a new residence

mow¹ (mō) *vt., vi.* **mowed, mowed** or **mown** (mōn), **mow′ing** ⟦OE *mawan*⟧ to cut down (grass, etc.) from (a lawn, etc.) —**mow down** 1 to cause to fall like cut grass 2 to overwhelm (an opponent) —**mow′er** *n.*

mow² (mou) *n.* ⟦OE *muga*⟧ a heap of hay, etc., esp. in a barn

Mo·zam·bique (mō′zəm bēk′) country in SE Africa

Mo·zart (mō′tsärt′), **Wolf·gang A·ma·de·us** (vôlf′gäŋk′ ä′mä dā′ oos) 1756–91; Austrian composer

MP *abbrev.* 1 Member of Parliament 2 Military Police

mpg *abbrev.* miles per gallon

mph *abbrev.* miles per hour

MP3 (em′pē′thrē′) *n.* ⟦*MP(EG)*, abbrev. of *Motion Picture Experts Group* + (*audio layer*)⟧

3, a coding format] **1** a format for processing digital audio files that removes unneeded data, producing a smaller file for transmission and use **2** an audio file so produced

Mr. or **Mr** (mis′tər) *abbrev.* mister: used before a man's name or title: pl. **Messrs**

MRI *n.* [[*m*(agnetic) *r*(esonance) *i*(maging)]] imaging making use of the properties of atomic nuclei in a strong magnetic field, used in medical diagnosis

Mrs. or **Mrs** (mis′iz) *abbrev.* mistress: now used before a married woman's name: pl. **Mmes**

MS *abbrev.* **1** manuscript: also **ms 2** Master of Science: also **M.S., MSc,** or **M.Sc. 3** Mississippi **4** multiple sclerosis

Ms. or **Ms** (miz) *abbrev.* a title, free of reference to marital status, used in place of *Miss* or *Mrs.*

MSG *abbrev.* monosodium glutamate

Msgr *abbrev.* Monsignor

MSRP *abbrev.* Manufacturer's Suggested Retail Price

MST *abbrev.* Mountain Standard Time

MSW or **M.S.W.** *abbrev.* Master of Social Work

Mt *abbrev.* **1** Mount **2** Mountain

MT *abbrev.* **1** Montana **2** megaton **3** Mountain Time

mtg *abbrev.* **1** meeting **2** mortgage: also **mtge**

MTV *trademark for* Music Television

mu (mo͞o, myo͞o) *n.* the 12th letter of the Greek alphabet (M, μ)

much (much) *adj.* **more, most** [[< OE *mycel*]] great in quantity, degree, etc. —*adv.* **more, most 1** to a great degree or extent **2** nearly [*much* the same] —*n.* **1** a great amount **2** something great or outstanding [not *much* to look at]

mu·ci·lage (myo͞o′si lij′) *n.* [[< L *mucere,* be moldy]] **1** a thick, sticky substance in certain plants **2** any watery solution of gum, glue, etc. used as an adhesive

muck (muk) *n.* [[ME *muk*]] **1** moist manure **2** black earth with decaying matter, used as fertilizer **3** mud; dirt; filth —**muck′y** *adj.* **-i·er, -i·est**

muck·rake *vi.* **-raked′, -rak′ing** [see prec. & RAKE[1]] to search for and publicize real or alleged corruption in politics, etc. —**muck′rak′er** *n.*

mu·cous (myo͞o′kəs) *adj.* **1** of, containing, or secreting mucus **2** slimy

mucous membrane a mucus-secreting lining of certain body cavities

mu·cus (myo͞o′kəs) *n.* [[L]] the thick, slimy fluid secreted by mucous membranes for moistening and protection

mud (mud) *n.* [[ME]] **1** wet, soft, sticky earth **2** defamatory remarks

mud·dle (mud′l) *vt.* **-dled, -dling** [< prec.] **1** to mix up; bungle **2** to confuse mentally; befuddle —*vi.* to act or think confusedly —*n.* **1** a mess, jumble, etc. **2** mental confusion —**mud′dler** *n.*

mud·dle-head·ed *adj.* confused

mud·dy *adj.* **-di·er, -di·est 1** full of or spattered with mud **2** not clear; cloudy [muddy

coffee] **3** confused, obscure, etc. [muddy thinking] —*vt., vi.* **-died, -dy·ing** to make or become muddy —**mud′di·ness** *n.*

mud flat an expanse of low, muddy land that is underwater at high tide

mud·sling·ing *n.* the making of unscrupulous, malicious attacks, as against a political opponent —**mud′sling′er** *n.*

mu·ez·zin (myo͞o ez′in) *n.* [< Ar *adhana,* proclaim] a Muslim crier who calls the people to prayer

muff (muf) *n.* [< Fr *moufle,* mitten] **1** a cylindrical covering, as of fur, to warm the hands **2** any bungled action —*vt.* to bungle; specif., to miss (a catch, etc.)

muf·fin (muf′ən) *n.* [< ?] a quick bread baked in a cup-shaped mold

muf·fle (muf′əl) *vt.* **-fled, -fling** [prob. < OFr *moufle,* mitten] **1** to wrap or cover so as to keep warm, deaden sound, etc. **2** to deaden (a sound)

muf·fler (-lər) *n.* **1** a scarf worn around the neck, as for warmth **2** a device for deadening noise, esp. of a car's exhaust

muf·ti (muf′tē) *n., pl.* **-tis** [< Ar] **1** an interpreter of Islamic law **2** ordinary clothes, esp. when worn by one usually wearing a uniform

mug (mug) *n.* [prob. < Scand] **1** a sturdy drinking cup with a handle **2** as much as a mug will hold **3** [Slang] the face —*vt.* **mugged, mug′ging** to assault, usually with intent to rob —*vi.* [Slang] to grimace, esp. in overacting —**mug′ger** *n.*

mug·gy (mug′ē) *adj.* **-gi·er, -gi·est** [< dial. *mug,* mist] hot, damp, and close —**mug′gi·ness** *n.*

mug shot a police photograph of the face of a criminal or suspect

Mu·ham·mad (mo͞o ham′əd) A.D. 570?-632; Arab prophet: founder of Islam

mu·ja·hi·deen (mo͞o′jä hə dēn′) *pl.n., sing.* **mu′ja·hid′** (-hid′) [Ar, persons who fight in a jihad] (the members of) a Muslim guerrilla force that claims divine authority for its activities: often sp. **mu′ja·hi·din′**

muk·luk (muk′luk′) *n.* [Esk *muklok,* a seal] an Eskimo boot of sealskin or caribou skin

mu·lat·to (mə lät′ō, -lat′ō) *n., pl.* **-toes** or **-tos** [Sp & Port *mulato*] a person who has one black parent and one white parent: term now often regarded as disparaging or insulting

mul·ber·ry (mul′ber′ē, -bər ē) *n., pl.* **-ries** [< OE *morberie*] **1** a tree with usually purplish-red, edible, berrylike fruit **2** the fruit

mulch (mulch) *n.* [ME *molsh,* soft] leaves, straw, etc., spread around plants to prevent freezing of roots, etc. —*vt.* to apply mulch to

mulct (mulkt) *vt.* [< L *mul(c)ta,* a fine] **1** to fine **2** to take (money, etc.) from (someone) by fraud —*n.* a fine

mule[1] (myo͞ol) *n.* [< L *mulus*] **1** the offspring of a jackass and a female horse **2** [Inf.] a stubborn person **3** [Slang] a drug smuggler

mule[2] (myo͞ol) *n.* [< L *mulleus,* red shoe] a lounging slipper that does not cover the heel

mu·le·teer (myo͞o′lə tir′) *n.* [OFr *muletier*]

a driver of mules: also [Inf.] **mule skin·ner** (skin′ər)

mul·ish *adj.* stubborn; obstinate

mull¹ (mul) *vt., vi.* ⟦ME *mullen*, to grind⟧ to ponder (*over*)

mull² (mul) *vt.* ⟦< ?⟧ to heat, sweeten, and spice (wine, cider, etc.)

mul·lah or **mul·la** (mul′ə, mōōl′ə) *n.* ⟦ult. < Ar *maulā*, a master⟧ a Muslim teacher or interpreter of religious laws

mul·let (mul′it) *n.* ⟦< L *mullus*⟧ an edible, spiny-finned fish of fresh and salt waters

mul·li·gan stew (mul′i gən) a stew made of bits of meat and vegetables, esp. as by hobos

mul·li·ga·taw·ny (mul′i gə tô′nē) *n.* ⟦Tamil *miḷagutaṇṇir*, lit., pepper water⟧ an East Indian soup of meat, etc., flavored with curry

mul·lion (mul′yən) *n.* ⟦prob. < OFr *moien*, median⟧ a vertical dividing bar, as between windowpanes

multi- ⟦L < *multus*, many⟧ *combining form* **1** having many **2** more than two **3** many times more than

mul·ti·cul·tur·al·ism (mul′tē kul′chər əl iz′ əm) *n.* the practice of publicly recognizing the needs and contributions of all cultural groups, esp. traditionally underrepresented minority groups, in a society —**mul′ti·cul′ tur·al** *adj.*

mul·ti·fac·et·ed (-fas′ət id) *adj.* having a variety of features, parts, etc. [a *multifaceted* career]

mul·ti·far·i·ous (mul′tə far′ē əs) *adj.* ⟦< L⟧ having many kinds of parts or elements; diverse

mul·ti·lat·er·al (mul′ti lat′ər əl) *adj.* involving more than two parties, nations, etc.

mul·ti·lin·gual (mul′ti liŋ′gwəl) *adj.* of, in, or capable of using several languages

mul·ti·me·di·a (-mē′dē ə) *adj.* combining or using several media, as film and live performance or TV, radio, and printed matter

mul·ti·mil·lion·aire *n.* one whose wealth amounts to many millions of dollars, pounds, etc.

mul·ti·na·tion·al *adj.* **1** of many nations **2** having offices, etc. in many nations —*n.* a multinational corporation

mul·ti·ple (mul′tə pəl) *adj.* ⟦< L *multiplex*⟧ **1** having many parts, elements, etc. **2** shared by or involving many —*n.* a number which is a product of some specified number and another number

mul·ti·ple-choice *adj.* listing several answers from which the correct one is to be chosen

multiple sclerosis a disease of the central nervous system, with loss of muscular coordination, etc.

mul·ti·plex (mul′tə pleks′) *adj.* ⟦L, multiple⟧ designating a system for sending two or more signals simultaneously over a common circuit, etc. —*n.* a film-theater complex with three or more screens —**mul′ti·plex′er** *n.*, **mul′ti·plex′or**

mul·ti·pli·cand (-pli kand′) *n.* a number to be multiplied by another

mul·ti·pli·ca·tion (-pli kā′shən) *n.* a multiplying or being multiplied; specif., the process of finding the quantity obtained by repeated additions of a specified quantity a specified number of times

mul·ti·plic·i·ty (-plis′ə tē) *n.* a great number or variety (*of*)

mul·ti·pli·er (-plī′ər) *n.* the number by which another is to be multiplied

mul·ti·ply (-plī′) *vt., vi.* -**plied′**, -**ply′ing** ⟦see MULTIPLE⟧ **1** to increase in number, degree, etc. **2** to find the product (of) by multiplication

mul·ti·proc·es·sor (mul′ti prä′ses′ər) *n.* a computer system capable of processing many programs at once

mul·ti·stage *adj.* having more than one stage, as a missile, process, etc.

mul·ti·task·ing (-task′iŋ) *n.* the act or an instance of performing various tasks more or less simultaneously —**mul′ti·task′er** *n.*

mul·ti·tude (mul′tə tōōd′) *n.* ⟦< L *multus*, many⟧ a large number; host

mul·ti·tu·di·nous (-tōōd′'n əs) *adj.* very numerous; many

mum¹ (mum) *n.* [Inf.] a chrysanthemum

mum² (mum) *adj.* ⟦ME *momme*⟧ silent; not speaking

Mum·bai (moom′bī′) seaport in W India

mum·ble (mum′bəl) *vt., vi.* -**bled**, -**bling** ⟦ME *momelen*⟧ to speak or say indistinctly; mutter —*n.* a mumbled utterance —**mum′bler** *n.*

mum·bo jum·bo (mum′bō jum′bō) ⟦of Afr orig.⟧ meaningless ritual, talk, etc.

mum·mer (mum′ər) *n.* ⟦< OFr *momo*, grimace⟧ an actor, esp. one who wears a mask or costume —**mum′mer·y** *n.*

mum·mi·fy (mum′ə fī′) *vt., vi.* -**fied′**, -**fy′ing** to make into or become (like) a mummy

mum·my (mum′ē) *n., pl.* -**mies** ⟦ult. < Pers *mum*, wax⟧ a dead body preserved by embalming, as by the ancient Egyptians

mumps (mumps) *n.* ⟦< obs. *mump*, a grimace⟧ an acute communicable disease characterized by swelling of the salivary glands

mun *abbrev.* municipal

munch (munch) *vt., vi.* ⟦ME *monchen*⟧ to chew steadily, often with a crunching sound

mun·dane (mun′dān′, mun dān′) *adj.* ⟦< L *mundus*, world⟧ **1** of the world; worldly **2** commonplace, ordinary, etc. —**mun′dane′ ly** *adv.*

Mu·nich (myōō′nik) city in SE Germany

mu·nic·i·pal (myōō nis′ə pəl) *adj.* ⟦< L *municeps*, inhabitant of a free town⟧ of or having to do with a city, town, etc. or its local government

mu·nic·i·pal·i·ty (-pal′ə tē) *n., pl.* -**ties** a city, town, etc. having its own incorporated government

mu·nif·i·cent (myōō nif′ə sənt) *adj.* ⟦< L *munus*, a gift + *facere*, make⟧ very generous; lavish —**mu·nif′i·cence** *n.*

mu·ni·tions (myōō nish′ənz) *pl.n.* ⟦< L *munire*, fortify⟧ weapons and ammunition for war

mu·ral (myoor′əl) *adj.* ⟦< L *murus*, wall⟧ of,

on, or for a wall —*n*. a picture, esp. a large one, painted directly on a wall —**mu′ral·ist** *n*.

mur·der (mur′dər) *n*. [OE *morthor*] 1 the unlawful and malicious or premeditated killing of a person 2 [Inf.] something very hard, unsafe, etc. to do or deal with —*vt*. 1 to kill (a person) unlawfully and with malice 2 to spoil, mar, etc., as in performance [to *murder* a song] —**mur′der·er** *n*.

mur·der·ous *adj*. 1 of or characteristic of murder; brutal 2 capable or guilty of, or intending, murder —**mur′der·ous·ly** *adv*.

murk (murk) *n*. [< ON *myrkr*, dark] darkness; gloom

murk·y *adj*. **-i·er, -i·est** dark or gloomy —**murk′i·ness** *n*.

mur·mur (mur′mər) *n*. [< L] 1 a low, steady sound 2 a mumbled complaint 3 *Med*. an abnormal sound in the body, esp. in the heart —*vi*. to make a murmur —*vt*. to say in a murmur

mus·cat (mus′kət) *n*. [< LL *muscus*, musk] a sweet European grape

mus·ca·tel (-kə tel′) *n*. a sweet wine made from the muscat

mus·cle (mus′əl) *n*. [< L *musculus*, lit., little mouse] 1 any body organ consisting of fibrous tissue that can be contracted and expanded to produce bodily movements 2 this tissue 3 muscular strength —*vi*. **-cled, -cling** [Inf.] to force one's way (*in*)

mus·cle-bound *adj*. having some of the muscles enlarged and less elastic, as from too much exercise

mus·cu·lar (mus′kyoo lər, -kyə-) *adj*. 1 of, consisting of, or done by muscles 2 having well-developed muscles; strong —**mus′cu·lar′i·ty** (-lar′ə tē) *n*.

muscular dys·tro·phy (dis′trə fē) a chronic disease characterized by a progressive wasting of the muscles

mus·cu·la·ture (mus′kyoo lə chər, -kyə-) *n*. [Fr] the muscular system of a body, limb, etc.

muse (myooz) *vi*. **mused, mus′ing** [< OFr *muser*, ponder] to think deeply; meditate

Muse (myooz) *n*. [< Gr *mousa*] 1 *Gr. Myth*. any of the nine goddesses of literature and of the arts and sciences 2 [**m-**] a person regarded as the object of love and as a source of inspiration

mu·sette (bag) (myoo zet′) [< OFr, bagpipe] a bag with a shoulder strap, carried as by soldiers

mu·se·um (myoo zē′əm) *n*. [< Gr *mousa*, Muse] a place for preserving and exhibiting artistic or historical objects

mush¹ (mush) *n*. [prob. var. of MASH] 1 a thick porridge of boiled meal 2 any thick, soft mass 3 [Inf.] maudlin sentimentality —**mush′y** *adj*. **-i·er, -i·est**

mush² (mush) *interj*. [prob. < Fr *marchons*, let's go] a shout to urge on sled dogs —*vi*. to travel on foot over snow with a dog sled

mush·room *n*. [< LL *mussirio*] any of various fleshy fungi, typically with a stalk capped by an umbrellalike top —*adj*. of or like a

mushroom —*vi*. to grow or spread rapidly

mu·sic (myoo′zik) *n*. [< Gr *mousikē* (*technē*), art of the Muses] 1 the art of combining tones to form expressive compositions 2 such compositions 3 any rhythmic sequence of pleasing sounds —**face the music** [Inf.] to accept the consequences

mu·si·cal (-zi kəl) *adj*. 1 of or for music 2 melodious or harmonious 3 fond of or skilled in music 4 set to music —*n*. a play or film with a musical score featuring songs and dances —**mu′si·cal·ly** *adv*.

mu·si·cale (myoo′zi kal′) *n*. [Fr] a social affair featuring a musical program

mu·si·cian (myoo zish′ən) *n*. one skilled in music; esp., a performer

mu·si·col·o·gy (-zi käl′ə jē) *n*. the study of the history, forms, etc. of music —**mu′si·col′o·gist** *n*.

musk (musk) *n*. [< Sans *muṣka*, testicle] a strong-smelling animal secretion, used in perfumes —**musk′y** *adj*. **-i·er, -i·est**

mus·kel·lunge (mus′kə lunj′) *n*. [< AmInd] a very large, edible pike of North America: also **mus′kie** (-kē)

mus·ket (mus′kət) *n*. [< L *musca*, a fly] a former kind of firearm with a long barrel and smooth bore

mus·ket·eer (mus′kə tir′) *n*. a soldier armed with a musket

musk·mel·on *n*. any of various sweet, juicy melons, as the cantaloupe

musk ox a hardy oxlike mammal of arctic North America with a long, coarse coat and a musklike odor

musk·rat *n*. 1 an American water rodent with webbed hind feet and a musklike odor 2 its fur

Mus·lim (muz′ləm, mooz′-, moos′-) *n*. [Ar, true believer < *aslama*, to resign oneself (to God)] an adherent of Islam —*adj*. of Islam or the Muslims

mus·lin (muz′lin) *n*. [after *Mosul*, city in Iraq] a strong, plain-woven cotton cloth

muss (mus) *n*. [prob. var. of MESS] [Inf.] a mess; disorder —*vt*. to make messy or disordered: often with *up* —**muss′y** *adj*. **-i·er, -i·est**

mus·sel (mus′əl) *n*. [< OE *muscle*] any of various bivalve mollusks; specif., an edible variety

must (must) *v.aux. pt*. **must** [< OE *moste*] used to express: 1 necessity [I *must* go] 2 probability [it *must* be Joe] 3 certainty [all men *must* die] —*n*. [Inf.] something that must be done, had, etc.

mus·tache (mus′tash′, məs tash′) *n*. [ult. < Gr *mystax*] hair growing on the upper lip; esp., the hair that a man has let grow

mus·tang (mus′taŋ′) *n*. [< L *mixtus*, a mingling] a small wild horse of the SW plains

mus·tard (mus′tərd) *n*. [< OFr] 1 an herb with yellow flowers and round seeds in slender pods 2 a pungent seasoning made from the ground seeds

mustard gas [< its mustardlike odor] an oily liquid used in warfare for its blistering and disabling effects

mus·ter (mus'tər) *vt.* ⟦< L *monstrare*, to show⟧ 1 to assemble (troops, etc.) 2 to collect; summon: often with *up* —*vi.* to assemble, as troops —*n.* 1 a gathering or assembling, as of troops for inspection 2 the persons or things assembled —**muster in** (or **out**) to enlist in (or discharge from) military service —**pass muster** to meet the required standards

mus·ty (mus'tē) *adj.* **-ti·er, -ti·est** ⟦< ? MOIST⟧ 1 having a stale, moldy smell or taste 2 stale or trite; antiquated —**mus'ti·ly** *adv.* —**mus'ti·ness** *n.*

mu·ta·ble (myo͞ot'ə bəl) *adj.* ⟦< L *mutare*, to change⟧ 1 that can be changed 2 inconstant; fickle —**mu'ta·bil'i·ty** *n.* —**mu'ta·bly** *adv.*

mu·tant (myo͞ot'nt) *adj.* of mutation —*n.* an organism with inheritable characteristics that differ from those of the parents; sport

mu·ta·tion (myo͞o tā'shən) *n.* 1 a change, as in form, nature, etc. 2 a sudden variation in some inheritable characteristic of an organism —**mu'tate'** *vi., vt.* **-tat'ed, -tat'ing**

mute (myo͞ot) *adj.* ⟦< L *mutus*⟧ 1 not speaking; silent 2 unable to speak —*n.* 1 a deaf-mute 2 a device that softens the sound of a musical instrument —*vt.* **mut'ed, mut'ing** to soften the sound of

mu·ti·late (myo͞ot''l āt') *vt.* **-lat'ed, -lat'ing** ⟦< L *mutilus*, maimed⟧ to cut off, damage, or mar an important part of —**mu'ti·la'tion** *n.* —**mu'ti·la'tor** *n.*

mu·ti·ny (myo͞ot''n ē) *n., pl.* **-nies** ⟦< L *movere*, to move⟧ revolt against authority; esp., rebellion of soldiers or sailors against their officers —*vi.* **-nied, -ny·ing** to take part in a mutiny —**mu'ti·neer'** *n.* —**mu'ti·nous** *adj.*

mutt (mut) *n.* ⟦Slang⟧ a mongrel dog

mut·ter (mut'ər) *vi., vt.* ⟦ME *moteren*⟧ 1 to speak or say in low, indistinct tones 2 to grumble —*n.* 1 a muttering 2 something muttered

mut·ton (mut''n) *n.* ⟦< OFr, a ram⟧ the flesh of a sheep, esp. a grown sheep, used as food

mu·tu·al (myo͞o'cho͞o əl) *adj.* ⟦< L *mutare*, to exchange⟧ 1 *a)* done, felt, etc. by each of two or more for or toward the other or others *b)* of each other 2 in common ⟦our *mutual* friend⟧ —**mu'tu·al·ly** *adv.*

mutual fund a fund of securities owned jointly by investors who have purchased shares of it 2 a corporation which manages such a fund or funds

muu·muu (mo͞o'mo͞o') *n.* ⟦< Haw⟧ a long, loose dress of Hawaiian style

Mu·zak (myo͞o'zak') *trademark for* a system of transmitting recorded background music to stores, etc. —*n.* this music, variously regarded as unobtrusive, bland, etc.

muz·zle (muz'əl) *n.* ⟦< ML *musum*⟧ 1 the mouth, nose, and jaws of a dog, horse, etc. 2 a device put over the mouth of an animal to prevent its biting or eating 3 the front end of the barrel of a firearm —*vt.* **-zled, -zling** 1 to put a muzzle on (an animal) 2 to prevent from talking

my (mī) *poss. pronominal adj.* ⟦< OE *min*⟧ of, belonging to, or done by me —*interj.* used to express surprise, dismay, etc. ⟦oh, *my!*⟧

Myan·mar (myän'mär') country in SE Asia

my·col·o·gy (mī käl'ə jē) *n.* the study of fungi —**my·col'o·gist** *n.*

my·e·li·tis (mī'ə līt'is) *n.* ⟦< Gr *myelos*, marrow + -ITIS⟧ inflammation of the spinal cord or the bone marrow

My·lar (mī'lär') *trademark for* a strong, thin polyester used for helium balloons, food packaging, fabrics, etc. —*n.* ⟦*occas.* **m-**⟧ this substance

my·na or **my·nah** (mī'nə) *n.* ⟦Hindi *mainā*⟧ any of various tropical birds of Southeast Asia: some can mimic speech

my·o·pi·a (mī ō'pē ə) *n.* ⟦< Gr *myein*, to close + *ōps*, eye⟧ nearsightedness —**my·op'ic** (-äp'ik) *adj.*

myr·i·ad (mir'ē əd) *n.* ⟦< Gr *myrios*, countless⟧ a great number —*adj.* countless; innumerable

myr·mi·don (mur'mə dän', -dən) *n.* ⟦after name of a Gr tribe led by Achilles⟧ an unquestioning follower

myrrh (mur) *n.* ⟦< Ar *murr*⟧ a fragrant gum resin of Arabia and E Africa, used in incense, etc.

myr·tle (murt''l) *n.* ⟦< Gr *myrtos*⟧ 1 an evergreen shrub with white or pink flowers and dark berries 2 any of various other plants, as the periwinkle

my·self (mī self') *pron.* a form of I, used as an intensive ⟦I went *myself*⟧, as a reflexive ⟦I hurt *myself*⟧, or with the meaning "my true self" ⟦I am not *myself* today⟧

mys·te·ri·ous (mis tir'ē əs) *adj.* of, containing, implying, or characterized by mystery —**mys·te'ri·ous·ly** *adv.* —**mys·te'ri·ous·ness** *n.*

mys·ter·y (mis'tə rē) *n., pl.* **-ies** ⟦< Gr *mystērion*, secret rite⟧ 1 something unexplained or secret 2 a story involving unknown persons, facts, etc. ⟦a murder *mystery*⟧ 3 secrecy

mys·tic (mis'tik) *adj.* 1 of esoteric rites or doctrines 2 MYSTICAL 3 mysterious —*n.* a believer in mysticism

mys·ti·cal (-ti kəl) *adj.* 1 spiritually significant or symbolic 2 of mystics or mysticism 3 occult —**mys'ti·cal·ly** *adv.*

mys·ti·cism (mis'tə siz'əm) *n.* 1 belief in the possibility of attaining direct communion with God or knowledge of spiritual truths, as by meditation 2 obscure thinking or belief

mys·ti·fy (-fī') *vt.* **-fied', -fy'ing** to puzzle or perplex —**mys'ti·fi·ca'tion** *n.*

mys·tique (mis tēk') *n.* ⟦Fr, mystic⟧ a mysterious and fascinating quality

myth (mith) *n.* ⟦< Gr *mythos*⟧ 1 a traditional story serving to explain some phenomenon, custom, etc. 2 mythology 3 any fictitious story, person, or thing —**myth'ic** *adj.* —**myth'i·cal** *adj.*

my·thol·o·gy (mi thäl'ə jē) *n., pl.* **-gies** 1 the study of myths 2 myths collectively, as of a specific people —**myth·o·log·i·cal** (mith'ə läj'i kəl) *adj.*

N

n¹ or **N** (en) *n., pl.* **n's, N's** the 14th letter of the English alphabet

n² *abbrev.* 1 name 2 neuter 3 new 4 nominative 5 noun 6 number

N¹ *abbrev.* 1 Navy 2 no 3 north 4 northern 5 November

N² *Chem. symbol for* nitrogen

Na [L *natrium*] *Chem. symbol for* sodium

NA *abbrev.* North America

NAACP *abbrev.* National Association for the Advancement of Colored People

nab (nab) *vt.* **nabbed, nab'bing** [prob. < dial. *nap*, to snatch] [Inf.] 1 to snatch or seize 2 to arrest or catch (a felon or wrongdoer)

na·bob (nā'bäb') *n.* [< Ar *nā'ib*, deputy] a very rich or important man

na·cre (nā'kər) *n.* [Fr < Ar *naqqārah*, small kettledrum] MOTHER-OF-PEARL

na·dir (nā'dər, -dir') *n.* [< Ar *nazīr*, opposite] 1 the point opposite the zenith and directly below the observer 2 the lowest point

nae (nā) [Scot.] *adv.* no; not —*adj.* no

nag¹ (nag) *vt., vi.* **nagged, nag'ging** [< ON *gnaga*] 1 to annoy by continual scolding, urging, etc. 2 to keep troubling [nagged by doubts] —*n.* one who nags: also **nag'ger**

nag² (nag) *n.* [ME *nagge*] an old or inferior horse

Na·ga·sa·ki (nä'gə sä'kē) seaport in SW Japan: U.S. atomic-bomb target (1945)

Na·go·ya (nä'gō yä') seaport in S Honshu, Japan

nai·ad (nā'ad', nī'-) *n.* [< Gr *naein*, to flow] [*also* N-] *Gr. & Rom. Myth.* a nymph living in a spring, river, etc.

nail (nāl) *n.* [< OE *nægl*] 1 the thin, horny growth at the ends of fingers and toes 2 a tapered, pointed piece of metal driven with a hammer, as to join pieces of wood —*vt.* 1 to fasten, secure, etc. with or as with nails 2 [Inf.] to catch, capture, etc. 3 [Inf.] to hit hard

nail-bit·er (-bit'ər) *n.* [Inf.] a suspenseful drama, sports event, etc.

Nai·ro·bi (nī rō'bē) capital of Kenya

na·ive or **na·ïve** (nä ēv') *adj.* [Fr < L *nativus*, natural] 1 unaffectedly simple 2 credulous —**na·ive'ly** *adv.*, **na·ïve'ly** —**na·ive·té'** *n.*, **na·ïve·té'** (-tā')

na·ked (nā'kid) *adj.* [OE *nacod*] 1 completely unclothed; nude 2 without covering 3 without additions, disguises, etc.; plain [the naked truth] —**na'ked·ly** *adv.* —**na'ked·ness** *n.*

nam·by-pam·by (nam'bē pam'bē) *adj.* [after *Namby-Pamby*, a satire on the poetry of *Ambrose* Philips by H. Carey (1687?-1743)] weak, insipid, indecisive, etc. —*n., pl.* **-bies** a namby-pamby person

name (nām) *n.* [OE *nama*] 1 a word or phrase by which a person, thing, or class is known; title 2 a word or words considered descriptive; epithet, often an abusive one 3 reputation —*adj.* well-known —*vt.* **named, nam'ing** 1 to give a name to 2 to mention by name 3 to identify by the right name [name the oceans] 4 to appoint to an office, etc. 5 to specify (a date, price, etc.) —**in name only** called such but not actually such —**in the name of** by the authority of

name·less *adj.* 1 not having a name 2 left unnamed 3 indescribable

name·ly *adv.* that is to say; to wit

name·sake *n.* a person with the same name as another, esp. if named after the other

Na·mib·i·a (nə mib'ē ə) country in S Africa —**Na·mib'i·an** *adj., n.*

Nan·jing (nän'jiŋ') city in E China, on the Chang

Nan·king (nan'kiŋ', nän'-) *a former transliteration of* NANJING

nan·ny (nan'ē) *n., pl.* **-nies** [< the name *Nan*] a person whose work is caring for a young child in the child's home

nanny goat a female goat

nano- [< Gr *nanos*, dwarf] *combining form* 1 one billionth [nanosecond] 2 of or having to do with nanotechnology [nanochip]

na·nom·e·ter (nan'ō mēt'ər) *n.* one billionth of a meter

na·no·scale (nan'ə skāl') *adj.* of or measured in nanometers

na·no·sec·ond (-sek'ənd) *n.* one billionth of a second

na·no·tech·nol·o·gy (nan'ō tek näl'ə jē) *n.* a branch of technology dealing with the manipulation of atoms and molecules, as in the production of high-tech materials or microscopic devices —**na'no·tech·nol'o·gist** *n.*

nap¹ (nap) *vi.* **napped, nap'ping** [OE *hnappian*] to sleep lightly for a short time —*n.* a brief, light sleep

nap² (nap) *n.* [ME *noppe*] the downy or hairy surface of cloth or suede formed by short hairs or fibers —**nap'less** *adj.*

na·palm (nā'päm') *n.* [na(phthene) + palm(i-tate)] a jellylike substance used in flame throwers and fire bombs —*vt.* to attack or burn with napalm

nape (nāp) *n.* [ME] the back of the neck

naph·tha (naf'thə, nap'-) *n.* [< Pers *neft*, pitch] a flammable liquid distilled from petroleum, used as a fuel, solvent, etc.

naph·tha·lene (-lēn') *n.* [< prec.] a white crystalline hydrocarbon distilled from coal tar, used in moth repellents, dyes, etc.

nap·kin (nap'kin) *n.* [< L *mappa*] 1 a small piece of cloth or paper used while eating to protect the clothes and wipe the lips **2** any small cloth, towel, etc.

Na·ples (nā′pəlz) seaport in S Italy

Na·po·le·on (nə pō′lē ən) *see* BONAPARTE, Napoleon, Napoleon

narc (närk) *n.* ⟦< NARC(OTIC)⟧ [Slang] **1** a police agent who enforces laws dealing with illegal drugs, esp. an undercover agent **2** an informer

nar·cis·sism (när′sə siz′əm) *n.* ⟦< fol.⟧ self-love; specif., excessive interest in one's own appearance, comfort, etc. —**nar′cis·sist** *n.*, *adj.* —**nar′cis·sis′tic** *adj.*

Nar·cis·sus (när sis′əs) *n.* **1** *Gr. Myth.* a youth who falls in love with his reflection in a pool and changes into the narcissus **2** *pl.* **-cis′sus, -cis′sus·es,** or **-cis′si** (-ī) [**n**—] any of various bulb plants, such as the daffodil, whose flowers have six parts and a cuplike or tube-like center

nar·co·sis (när kō′sis) *n.*, *pl.* **-ses′** (-sēz′) unconsciousness caused by a narcotic

nar·cot·ic (när kät′ik) *n.* ⟦< Gr *narkē*, numbness⟧ a drug, as morphine, used to relieve pain and induce sleep: narcotics are often addictive —*adj.* of or having to do with narcotics

nar·co·tize (när′kə tīz′) *vt.* **-tized′, -tiz′ing** to subject to a narcotic —**nar′co·ti·za′tion** *n.*

nark (närk) *n.* alt. sp. of [Slang] NARC

nar·rate (nar′āt′, na rāt′) *vt.*, *vi.* **-rat′ed, -rat′ing** ⟦< L *narrare*, tell⟧ to tell (a story), relate (events), etc.

nar·ra·tion (na rā′shən) *n.* **1** a narrating **2** a narrative

nar·ra·tive (nar′ə tiv) *adj.* in story form —*n.* **1** a story; account **2** the art or practice of narrating

nar·row (nar′ō) *adj.* [OE *nearu*] **1** small in width; not wide **2** limited in meaning **3** limited in outlook; not liberal **4** with limited margin [*a narrow escape*] —*vi.*, *vt.* to decrease or limit in width, extent, etc. —*n.* [*usually pl.*] a narrow passage; strait

nar·row·cast (-kast′) *vt.*, *vi.* **-cast′, -cast′ing** to transmit by cable TV to a selected audience —*n.* a narrowcasting

nar·row-mind·ed *adj.* limited in outlook; bigoted; prejudiced —**nar′row-mind′ed·ness** *n.*

nar·whal (nar′wəl) *n.* ⟦< ON *nahvalr*, lit., corpse whale⟧ a small arctic whale: the male has a long, straight, spiral-grooved tusk

nar·y (ner′ē) *adj.* ⟦< *ne'er a*, never a⟧ [Dial.] not any; no: with *a* or *an* [*nary a doubt*]

NASA (nas′ə) *abbrev.* National Aeronautics and Space Administration

na·sal (nā′zəl) *adj.* ⟦< L *nasus*, nose⟧ **1** of the nose **2** uttered so that the breath passes through the nose

na·sal·ize (-īz′) *vt.*, *vi.* **-ized′, -iz′ing** to pronounce or speak with a nasal sound —**na′sal·i·za′tion** *n.*

NASCAR (nas′kär′) *trademark for* National Association for Stock Car Auto Racing

nas·cent (nas′ənt, nā′sənt) *adj.* ⟦< L *nasci*, be born⟧ **1** coming into being **2** beginning to form or develop: said of ideas, etc.

NASDAQ (naz′dak′) *service mark* National Association of Securities Dealers Automated Quotations: often written **Nasdaq**

Nash·ville (nash′vil) capital of Tennessee

nas·tur·tium (nə stur′shəm) *n.* ⟦< L *nasus*, nose + *torquere*, to twist: from its pungent odor⟧ **1** a plant with trumpet-shaped, red, yellow, or orange flowers **2** its flower

nas·ty (nas′tē) *adj.* **-ti·er, -ti·est** ⟦< ?⟧ **1** filthy **2** morally offensive **3** very unpleasant **4** mean; malicious —**nas′ti·ly** *adv.* —**nas′ti·ness** *n.*

na·tal (nāt′'l) *adj.* ⟦< L *nasci*, be born⟧ of or relating to one's birth

na·tion (nā′shən) *n.* ⟦< L *natus*, born⟧ **1** a stable community of people with a territory, culture, and language in common **2** the people united under a single government; country

na·tion·al (nash′ə nəl) *adj.* of or affecting a nation as a whole —*n.* a citizen —**na′tion·al·ly** *adv.*

National Guard the organized militia forces of the individual U.S. states, part of the U.S. Army when called into active federal service

na·tion·al·ism *n.* **1** devotion to one's nation; patriotism **2** the advocacy of national independence —**na′tion·al·ist** *n.*, *adj.* —**na′tion·al·is′tic** *adj.*

na·tion·al·i·ty (-nal′ə tē) *n.*, *pl.* **-ties 1** the status of belonging to a nation by birth or naturalization **2** a national group, esp. of immigrants

na·tion·al·ize (-nə līz′) *vt.* **-ized′, -iz′ing 1** to make national **2** to transfer ownership or control of (land, industries, etc.) to the government —**na′tion·al·i·za′tion** *n.*

na·tion·wide *adj.* by or throughout the whole nation; national

na·tive (nāt′iv) *adj.* ⟦< L *natus*, born⟧ **1** inborn **2** belonging to a place by birth; production, or growth **3** being, or connected with, the place of one's birth [one's *native* land or language] **4** as found in nature; natural **5** of or characteristic of the original inhabitants of a place —*n.* **1** a person born in the place indicated **2** an original inhabitant **3** an indigenous plant or animal

Native American AMERICAN INDIAN

na·tive-born *adj.* of a specified place by birth

na·tiv·i·ty (nə tiv′ə tē) *n.*, *pl.* **-ties** ⟦see NATIVE⟧ birth —**the Nativity** the birth of Jesus

natl *abbrev.* national

NATO (nā′tō) *n.* North Atlantic Treaty Organization

nat·ty (nat′ē) *adj.* **-ti·er, -ti·est** ⟦< ? NEAT⟧ trim and stylish —**nat′ti·ly** *adv.*

nat·u·ral (nach′ər əl) *adj.* ⟦< L *naturalis*, by birth⟧ **1** of or dealing with nature **2** produced or existing in nature; not artificial **3** innate; not acquired **4** true to nature; lifelike **5** normal [a *natural* result] **6** free from affectation; at ease **7** *Music* neither sharped nor flatted —*n.* [Inf.] a person or thing sure to be successful

natural childbirth childbirth without anesthesia but with prior training

natural gas a mixture of gaseous hydrocarbons, chiefly methane, occurring naturally in the earth and used as fuel

natural history the study of the animal, vegetable, and mineral world

nat·u·ral·ism *n.* 1 action or thought based on natural desires 2 *Literature, Art, etc.* the realistic portrayal of persons or things 3 *Philos.* the belief that the natural world is all that exists

nat·u·ral·ist *n.* 1 one who studies animals and plants 2 a proponent of naturalism

nat·u·ral·ize (-īz′) *vt.* **-ized′, -iz′ing** to confer citizenship upon (an alien) —**nat′u·ral·i·za′tion** *n.*

nat·u·ral·ly *adv.* 1 in a natural manner 2 by nature; innately 3 of course

natural number any positive integer, as 1, 2, or 3

natural resource something of value supplied by nature, as coal, oil, or water power

natural science the systematized knowledge of nature, including biology, chemistry, physics, etc.

natural selection the evolutionary process by which the organisms best adapted to their environment are most likely to survive and reproduce

na·ture (nā′chər) *n.* [< L *natus*, born] 1 the essential quality of a thing; essence 2 inherent tendencies of a person 3 kind; type 4 *a)* the physical universe *b)* [*sometimes* **N-**] the power, force etc. that seems to regulate this 5 the primitive state of humans 6 natural scenery —**by nature** naturally; inherently

Naug·a·hyde (nôg′ə hīd′) [arbitrary coinage] *trademark for* an imitation leather, used for upholstery, luggage, etc. —*n.* [**n-**] this material

naught (nôt) *n.* [OE *nawiht*] 1 nothing 2 *Arith.* the figure zero (0)

naugh·ty (nôt′ē) *adj.* **-ti·er, -ti·est** [ME *naugti*] 1 mischievous or disobedient 2 indelicate; improper —**naugh′ti·ly** *adv.* —**naugh′ti·ness** *n.*

Na·u·ru (nä ōō′rōō) country on an island in the W Pacific, south of the equator

nau·sea (nô′shə, -zhə; -sē ə, -zē ə) *n.* [< Gr *nausia*, seasickness] 1 a sick feeling in the stomach, with an impulse to vomit 2 disgust; loathing

nau·se·ate (-shē āt′, -zhē-, -sē-, -zē-) *vt.* **-at′ed, -at′ing** to cause to feel nausea

nau·seous (nô′shəs, -zē əs, -sē-) *adj.* 1 causing nausea 2 feeling nausea; nauseated: usage objected to by some

nau·ti·cal (nôt′i kəl) *adj.* [< Gr *naus*, ship] of sailors, ships, or navigation —**nau′ti·cal·ly** *adv.*

nautical mile a unit of linear measure used in navigation, equal to 1.1508 miles or 1,852 meters

nau·ti·lus (nôt′'l əs) *n., pl.* **-lus·es** or **-li′** (-ī′) [< Gr *naus*, ship] a tropical mollusk with a spiral shell divided into many chambers —[**N-**] *trademark for* a type of mechanical weight-lifting equipment

Nav·a·jo (nav′ə hō′) *n. pl.* **-jos′** or **-jo′** a member of a North American Indian people of the SW U.S.: also sp. **Nav′a·ho′, -ho′** or **-ho′**

na·val (nā′vəl) *adj.* [< L *navis*, a ship] 1 of or relating to a navy 2 having a navy [*a naval power*]

nave (nāv) *n.* [< L *navis*, a ship] the main part of a church, from the chancel to the principal entrance

na·vel (nā′vəl) *n.* [OE *nafela*] the small scar in the abdomen marking the place where the umbilical cord was attached to the fetus

navel orange a seedless orange with a navel-like hollow at its apex

nav·i·ga·ble (nav′i gə bəl) *adj.* 1 wide or deep enough for ships to pass 2 that can be steered —**nav′i·ga·bil′i·ty** *n.*

nav·i·gate (nav′ə gāt′) *vt., vi.* **-gat′ed, -gat′ing** [< L *navis*, a ship + *agere*, to lead] 1 to steer or direct (a ship or aircraft) 2 to travel through or over (water, air, etc.) in a ship or aircraft 3 to walk or make one's way (on or through)

nav·i·ga·tion (-gā′shən) *n.* 1 the science of locating the position and plotting the course of ships and aircraft 2 traffic by ship

nav·i·ga·tor *n.* one skilled or employed in the navigation of a ship or aircraft

na·vy (nā′vē) *n., pl.* **-vies** [< L *navis*, a ship] 1 all the warships of a nation 2 [*often* **N-**] a nation's entire military sea force, including ships, personnel, stores, etc. 3 NAVY BLUE

navy bean [from use in U.S. *Navy*] a small white variety of kidney bean

navy blue very dark, purplish blue

nay (nā) *adv.* [< ON *ne*, not + *ei*, ever] 1 no: now used only in voice votes 2 not that only, but also [*I permit, nay encourage it*] —*n.* 1 a denial 2 a negative vote or a person voting negatively

nay·say·er (nā′sā′ər) *n.* one who opposes, refuses, etc., esp. habitually

Na·zi (nät′sē) *adj.* [Ger contr. of the party name] designating or of the German fascist political party which ruled Germany under Hitler (1933-45) —*n.* a member of this party

NB *abbrev.* New Brunswick

n.b. *abbrev.* [L *nota bene*] note well

NC *abbrev.* North Carolina

NCO *abbrev.* noncommissioned officer

NC-17 *trademark for* a film rating indicating that no one under 17 may be admitted

ND *abbrev.* North Dakota

Ne *Chem. symbol for* neon

NE *abbrev.* 1 Nebraska 2 northeast 3 northeastern

Ne·an·der·thal (nē an′dər thôl′, -täl′) *adj.* [after a Ger valley] 1 designating or of a widespread form of early human of the Pleistocene Epoch 2 primitive or regressive —*n.* 1 a Neanderthal human 2 one who is crude, primitive, etc.

neap (nēp) *adj.* [OE *nep-* in *nepflod*, neap tide] designating either of the two lowest high tides in the month —*n.* neap tide

Ne·a·pol·i·tan (nē′ə päl′ə tən) *adj.* of Naples

—*n.* a person born or living in Naples

Neapolitan ice cream brick ice cream in layers of different flavors and colors

near (nir) *adv.* [OE compar. of *neah*, nigh] 1 at a short distance in space or time 2 closely; intimately —*adj.* 1 close in distance or time 2 close in relationship; akin 3 close in friendship 4 close in degree [a *near* escape] 5 short or direct [the *near* way] —*prep.* close to — *vt., vi.* to draw near (to); approach —**near′ness** *n.*

near·by *adj., adv.* near; close at hand

Near East countries near the E end of the Mediterranean, including those of SW Asia, the Arabian Peninsula, & NE Africa

near·ly *adv.* almost; not quite

near miss 1 a result that is nearly but not quite successful 2 a near escape

near·sight·ed *adj.* having better vision for near objects than for objects that are distant; myopic —**near′sight′ed·ness** *n.*

neat (nēt) *adj.* [< L *nitere*, to shine] 1 unmixed; undiluted [whiskey *neat*] 2 clean and tidy 3 skillful and precise 4 well-proportioned 5 cleverly said or done 6 [Slang] nice, pleasing, etc. —**neat′ly** *adv.* —**neat′ness** *n.*

neat·en *vt.* to make clean, tidy, orderly, etc.: often with *up*

'neath or **neath** (nēth) *prep.* [Old Poet.] *short for* BENEATH

neb·bish (neb′ish) *n.* [< Yiddish *nebekh*, pity] [Slang] one who is pitifully inept, dull, etc.

Ne·bras·ka (nə bras′kə) Midwestern state of the U.S.; cap. Lincoln: abbrev. NE —**Ne·bras′kan** *adj., n.*

neb·u·la (neb′yə lə) *n., pl.* **-lae′** (-lē′) or **-las** [L, mist] 1 a cloud of interstellar gas or dust 2 formerly, any hazy, distant celestial object, as a star cluster —**neb′u·lar** *adj.*

neb·u·lous (-ləs) *adj.* unclear; vague

nec·es·sar·i·ly (nes′ə ser′ə lē) *adv.* 1 because of necessity 2 as a necessary result

nec·es·sar·y (-ser′ē) *adj.* [< L *ne-*, not + *cedere*, give way] 1 essential; indispensable 2 inevitable 3 required —*n., pl.* **-sar′ies** something necessary

ne·ces·si·tate (nə ses′ə tāt′) *vt.* **-tat′ed, -tat′ing** to make necessary or unavoidable

ne·ces·si·ty (-tē) *n., pl.* **-ties** [see NECESSARY] 1 natural causation; fate 2 great need 3 something that cannot be done without —**of necessity** necessarily

neck (nek) *n.* [OE *hnecca*] 1 that part of a human or animal joining the head to the body 2 the part of a garment near the neck 3 a necklike part; specif., *a)* a narrow strip of land *b)* the narrowest part of a bottle, etc. *c)* a strait —*vt., vi.* [Slang] to hug, kiss, and caress passionately —**neck and neck** very close, as in a race —**neck of the woods** [Inf.] a locality —**stick one's neck out** [Inf.] to expose oneself to possible failure, ridicule, etc.

neck·er·chief (nek′ər chif, -chēf′) *n.* [see prec. & KERCHIEF] a handkerchief or scarf worn around the neck

neck·lace (-lis) *n.* [NECK + LACE] an ornamental string of beads, chain of gold, etc., worn around the neck

neck·tie *n.* a band worn around the neck under a collar and tied in front

neck·wear *n.* articles worn about the neck, as neckties or scarves

ne·crol·o·gy (ne kräl′ə jē) *n., pl.* **-gies** [ult. < Gr *nekros*, corpse + -LOGY] a list of people who have died

nec·ro·man·cy (nek′rə man′sē) *n.* [< Gr *nekros*, corpse + *manteia*, divination] 1 divination by alleged communication with the dead 2 black magic; sorcery —**nec′ro·man′cer** *n.*

ne·cro·sis (ne krō′sis) *n., pl.* **-ses′** (-sēz′) [< Gr *nekros*, corpse] the death or decay of tissue in a part of the body

nec·tar (nek′tər) *n.* [< Gr *nektar*] 1 *Gr. & Rom. Myth.* the drink of the gods 2 any very delicious beverage 3 the sweetish liquid in many flowers, used by bees to make honey

nec·tar·ine (nek′tə rēn′, nek′tə rēn′) *n.* [< prec.] a kind of smooth-skinned peach

nee or **née** (nā; *now often* nē) *adj.* [Fr] born: used to preface a maiden name [Mrs. Helen Jones, *nee* Smith]

need (nēd) *n.* [OE *nied*] 1 necessity 2 a lack of something useful, required, or desired [to have *need* of a rest] 3 something required or desired that is lacking [your daily *needs*] 4 *a)* a condition in which help is required [a friend in *need*] *b)* poverty —*vt.* 1 to have need of; require 2 to be obliged; must [she needs to be careful] —*vi.* to be in need —**have need to** to be required to —**if need be** if it is required

need·ful *adj.* necessary; required

nee·dle (nēd′'l) *n.* [OE *nædl*] 1 a small, slender, pointed piece of steel with a hole for thread, used for sewing 2 a slender rod of steel, bone, etc. used for crocheting or knitting 3 STYLUS (2b) 4 the pointer of a compass, gauge, etc. 5 the thin, short, pointed leaf of a pine, spruce, etc. 6 the sharp, slender metal tube at the end of a hypodermic syringe —*vt.* **-dled, -dling** [Inf.] 1 to goad; prod 2 to tease —**nee′dler** *n.*

nee·dle·point *n.* 1 embroidery of woolen threads upon canvas 2 lace made on a paper pattern, with a needle

need·less *adj.* not needed; unnecessary [*needless* cruelty] —**need′less·ly** *adv.*

nee·dle·work *n.* work done with a needle; embroidery, crocheting, sewing, etc.

need·n't (nēd′'nt) *contr.* need not

needs (nēdz) *adv.* [OE *nedes*] of necessity: with *must* [he must *needs* obey]

need·y *adj.* **-i·er, -i·est** very poor —**need′i·ness** *n.*

ne'er (ner) *adv.* [Old Poet.] never

ne'er-do-well *n.* a shiftless, irresponsible person

ne·far·i·ous (nə fer′ē əs) *adj.* [< L *ne-*, not + *fas*, lawful] very wicked; villainous —**ne·far′i·ous·ly** *adv.* —**ne·far′i·ous·ness** *n.*

ne·gate (ni gāt′) *vt.* **-gat′ed, -gat′ing** [< L *negare*, deny] 1 to deny 2 to make ineffective

ne·ga·tion (ni gā'shən) *n.* **1** the act or an instance of denying **2** the lack or opposite of something positive

neg·a·tive (neg'ə tiv) *adj.* **1** expressing denial or refusal; saying "no" **2** opposite to or lacking in that which is positive [a *negative* force] **3** *Math.* designating a quantity less than zero, or one to be subtracted **4** *Med.* not showing the presence of a condition, infection, etc. **5** *Photog.* reversing the relation of light and shade of the subject **6** *Elec. a)* of, generating, or charged with negative electricity *b)* having an excess of electrons —*n.* **1** a negative word, reply, etc. **2** the point of view that opposes the positive **3** the plate in a battery having an excess of electrons flowing out toward the positive **4** an exposed and developed photographic film or plate on which light and shadow are reversed —**in the negative** with a negative answer —**neg'a·tive·ly** *adv.* —**neg'a·tiv·i·ty** *n.*

ne·glect (ni glekt') *vt.* [< L *neg-*, not + *legere*, gather] **1** to ignore or disregard **2** to fail to attend to properly **3** to leave undone —*n.* **1** a neglecting **2** lack of proper care **3** the state of being neglected —**ne·glect'ful** *adj.*

neg·li·gee (neg'lə zhā') *n.* [< Fr *négliger*, to neglect] a woman's loosely fitting dressing gown

neg·li·gent (neg'lə jənt) *adj.* **1** habitually failing to do the required thing; neglectful **2** careless, inattentive, etc. —**neg'li·gence** *n.*

neg·li·gi·ble (-jə bəl) *adj.* that can be neglected or disregarded; trifling

ne·go·ti·ate (ni gō'shē āt') *vi.* **-at'ed, -at'ing** [< L *negotium*, business] to discuss a matter with a view to reaching agreement —*vt.* **1** to settle (a business transaction, treaty, etc.) **2** to transfer or sell (bonds, stocks, etc.) **3** to succeed in crossing, passing, etc. [safely *negotiated* the rapids] —**ne·go'ti·a·ble** (-shē ə bəl, -shə bəl) *adj.* —**ne·go'ti·a'tion** *n.* —**ne·go'ti·a'tor** *n.*

neg·ri·tude (neg'rə tōōd', nē'grə-) *n.* [Fr *négritude*] [*also* **N-**] an awareness and affirmation by black people of their distinctive cultural heritage

Ne·gro (nē'grō) *n., pl.* **-groes** [Sp & Port *negro*, black] **1** a member of any of the indigenous dark-skinned peoples of Africa **2** a person having some African ancestors; a black person —*adj.* of or for Negroes: In all senses now somewhat offensive

Ne·groid (-groid') *adj.* designating or of a human racial group including most of the peoples native to Africa: no longer in scientific use

Neh·ru (nā'rōō), **Ja·wa·har·lal** (jə wä'hər läl') 1889-1964; prime minister of India (1947-64)

neigh (nā) *vi.* [OE *hnǽgan*] to utter the characteristic cry of a horse —*n.* this cry; a whinny

neigh·bor (nā'bər) *n.* [OE *neah*, nigh + *gebur*, freeholder] **1** one who lives or is situated near another **2** a fellow human — *vt., vi.* to live or be situated near (someone or something) Brit. sp. **neigh'bour** —**neigh'bor·ing** *adj.*

neigh·bor·hood *n.* **1** a particular community, district, or area **2** the people living near one another —**in the neighborhood of** [Inf.] **1** near **2** about; approximately

neigh·bor·ly *adj.* like or appropriate to neighbors; friendly, helpful, etc. —**neigh'bor·li·ness** *n.*

nei·ther (nē'thər, nī'-) *adj., pron.* [OE *nahwæther*, lit., not whether] not one or the other (of two); not either [*neither* boy went; *neither* of them was invited] —*conj.* not either [I could *neither* laugh nor cry]

nem·a·tode (nem'ə tōd') *n.* [ult. < Gr *nēma*, thread] a long, cylindrical, unsegmented worm; roundworm

nem·e·sis (nem'ə sis) *n., pl.* **-ses'** (-sēz') [< Gr *nemein*, deal out] **1** *a)* just punishment *b)* one who imposes this **2** anyone or anything that seems inevitably to defeat or frustrate someone

neo- [< Gr *neos*] *combining form* [*often* **N-**] **1** new, recent **2** in a new way

ne·o·clas·sic (nē'ō klas'ik) *adj.* designating or of a revival of classic style and form in art, literature, etc.: also **ne'o·clas'si·cal** —**ne'o·clas'si·cism'** *n.*

ne·o·co·lo·ni·al·ism *n.* exploitation by a foreign power of a region that has ostensibly achieved independence

ne·o·dym·i·um (nē'ō dim'ē əm, nē'ə-) *n.* [ModL] a silver-colored chemical element, used esp. for coloring glass: symbol, Nd; at. no. 60

ne·ol·o·gism (nē äl'ə jiz'əm) *n.* [see NEO-, -LOGY, & -ISM] a new word or a new meaning for an established word

ne·on (nē'än') *n.* [ult. < Gr *neos*, new] a nonreactive, gaseous chemical element found in small amounts in the earth's atmosphere: symbol, Ne; at. no. 10 —*adj.* **1** containing neon [a *neon* light] **2** lighted by a neon light **3** very intense [*neon* blue]

ne·o·nate (nē'ō nāt') *n.* [ModL < neo-, NEO- + L *natus*, born] a newborn infant —**ne'o·na'tal** *adj.*

ne·o·phyte (nē'ō fīt') *n.* [< Gr *neos*, new + *phyein*, to produce] **1** a new convert **2** a beginner; novice

ne·o·plasm (nē'ō plaz'əm) *n.* [< NEO- + Gr *plassein*, to form] an abnormal growth of tissue, as a tumor

ne·o·prene (-prēn') *n.* a synthetic rubber resistant to oil, heat, etc.

Ne·pal (nə pôl', -päl') country in the Himalayas —**Nep·a·lese** (nep'ə lēz') *adj., n.*

neph·ew (nef'yōō) *n.* [< L *nepos*] the son of one's brother or sister, or of one's brother-in-law or sister-in-law

ne·phri·tis (nə frīt'əs) *n.* [< Gr *nephros*, kidney + -ITIS] a disease of the kidneys, characterized by inflammation

ne·phro·sis (nə frō'sis) *n.* [< Gr *nephros*, kidney + -OSIS] a degenerative disease of the kidneys, characterized by edema

ne plus ul·tra (nā plus ul′trə) ⟦L, no more beyond⟧ the ultimate

nep·o·tism (nep′ə tiz′əm) *n.* ⟦< L *nepos*, nephew⟧ favoritism shown to relatives, esp. in providing jobs —**nep′o·tis′tic** *adj.*

Nep·tune (nep′tōōn′) *n.* **1** the Roman god of the sea **2** the planet eighth in distance from the sun: see PLANET

nep·tu·ni·um (nep tōō′nē əm) *n.* ⟦after prec.⟧ a radioactive chemical element produced by irradiating uranium atoms: symbol, Np; at. no. 93

nerd (nurd) *n.* ⟦Slang⟧ a person regarded as dull, socially awkward, excessively studious, etc. —**nerd′y** *adj.*

Ne·ro (nir′ō) A.D. 37-68; emperor of Rome (54-68)

nerve (nurv) *n.* ⟦< L *nervus*⟧ **1** any of the cord-like fibers carrying impulses between body organs and the central nervous system **2** coolness in danger; courage **3** [*pl.*] nervousness **4** [Inf.] impudent boldness —*vt.* **nerved, nerv′ing** to give strength or courage to —**get on someone's nerves** [Inf.] to make someone irritable or exasperated

nerve center a control center; headquarters

nerve gas a poisonous gas causing paralysis of the respiratory and nervous systems

nerve·less *adj.* **1** without strength, vigor, etc.; weak **2** not nervous; cool; controlled —**nerve′less·ly** *adv.*

nerve-rack·ing or **nerve-wrack·ing** (-rak′iŋ) *adj.* very trying to one's patience or equanimity

nerv·ous (nur′vəs) *adj.* **1** animated **2** of or made up of nerves **3** emotionally tense, restless, etc. **4** fearful —**nerv′ous·ly** *adv.* —**nerv′ous·ness** *n.*

nervous system all the nerve cells and nervous tissues in an organism, including, in the vertebrates, the brain, spinal cord, nerves, etc.

nerv·y *adj.* **-i·er, -i·est 1** bold **2** [Inf.] impudent

-ness (nis, nəs) ⟦OE *-nes(s)*⟧ *suffix* state, quality, or instance of being [*togetherness, sadness*]

nest (nest) *n.* ⟦OE⟧ **1** the structure or place where a bird lays its eggs and shelters its young **2** the place used by insects, fish, etc. for spawning or breeding **3** a cozy place; retreat **4** *a)* a haunt or den *b)* the people who frequent such a place [*a nest of thieves*] **5** a set of things, each fitting within the one next larger — *vi., vt.* **1** to build or settle in (a nest) **2** to fit (an object) closely within another

nest egg money, etc. put aside as a reserve or to establish a fund

nes·tle (nes′əl) *vi.* **-tled, -tling** ⟦OE *nestlian*⟧ **1** to settle down comfortably **2** to press close for comfort or in affection **3** to lie sheltered —*vt.* to cause to rest snugly

nest·ling (nest′liŋ) *n.* a young bird not yet ready to leave the nest

net[1] (net) *n.* ⟦OE *nett*⟧ **1** a loose fabric of woven or knotted string, etc., used to snare birds, fish, etc. **2** a trap; snare **3** a loose fabric of woven or knotted threads, etc., esp. one used to hold, protect, or cover. [*a hairnet*] **4** [*usually* **N-**] [Inf.] *Comput. short for* INTERNET: with *the* —*vt.* **net′ted, net′ting** to snare or enclose, as with a net

net[2] (net) *adj.* ⟦Fr, clear⟧ remaining after deductions or allowances have been made —*n.* a net amount, profit, weight, price, etc. —*vt.* **net′ted, net′ting** to clear as profit, etc.

net·book (net′book′) *n.* ⟦< *netBook*, former trademark < (INTER)NET + (NOTE)BOOK⟧ a small notebook computer with limited processing power and storage, used chiefly for transmitting email, browsing the internet, and using applications via Wi-Fi

neth·er (neth′ər) *adj.* ⟦OE *neothera*⟧ lower or under [*the nether world*]

Neth·er·lands (neth′ər ləndz) country in W Europe; : usually used with *the* —**Neth′er·land′er** (-land′ər, -lən dər) *n.*

neth·er·most *adj.* lowest

net·ting *n.* NET[1] (*n.* 1 & 3)

net·tle (net′'l) *n.* ⟦OE *netele*⟧ a weed with stinging hairs —*vt.* **-tled, -tling** to irritate; annoy; vex

net·tle·some (-səm) *adj.* that nettles, or irritates

net·work *n.* **1** an arrangement of parallel wires, etc. crossed at intervals by others so as to leave open spaces **2** anything like this, as a system of interconnected roads, individuals, or computers **3** *Radio, TV* a chain of transmitting stations —*adj.* broadcast over a radio or TV

net·work·ing *n.* **1** the developing of contacts or exchanging of information, as to further a career **2** the interconnection of computer systems

neu·ral (noor′əl) *adj.* ⟦NEUR(O)- + -AL⟧ of a nerve, nerves, or the nervous system

neu·ral·gi·a (noo ral′jə) *n.* ⟦see NEURO- & -ALGIA⟧ severe pain along a nerve —**neu·ral′gic** (-jik) *adj.*

neu·ras·the·ni·a (noor′əs thē′nē ə) *n.* ⟦< NEURO- + Gr *asthenia*, weakness⟧ a former category of mental disorder, characterized by fatigue, anxiety, etc. —**neu′ras·then′ic** (-then′ik) *adj., n.*

neu·ri·tis (noo rīt′əs) *n.* ⟦fol. + -ITIS⟧ inflammation of a nerve or nerves —**neu·rit′ic** (-rit′ik) *adj.*

neuro- ⟦< Gr *neuron*, nerve⟧ *combining form* of a nerve or the nervous system: also **neur-**

neu·rol·o·gy (noo räl′ə jē) *n.* ⟦prec. + -LOGY⟧ the branch of medicine dealing with the nervous system and its diseases —**neu·ro·log·i·cal** (noor′ə läj′i kəl) *adj.* —**neu·rol′o·gist** *n.*

neu·ro·mus·cu·lar (noor′ō mus′kyōō lər) *adj.* of or involving both nerves and muscles

neu·ron (noor′än′) *n.* the nerve cell body and all its processes

neu·ro·sis (noo rō′sis) *n., pl.* **-ses′** (-sēz′) ⟦NEUR(O)- + -OSIS⟧ any of various mental disorders characterized by anxiety, compulsions, phobias, etc.

neu·ro·sur·ger·y (noor'ō sur'jər ē) *n.* the branch of surgery involving the brain, spinal cord, or smaller nerves —**neu'ro·sur'geon** *n.*

neu·rot·ic (noo rät'ik) *adj.* of, characteristic of, or having a neurosis —*n.* a neurotic person —**neu·rot'i·cal·ly** *adv.*

neu·ro·trans·mit·ter (noor'ō trans'mit'ər) *n.* a biochemical substance that transmits or inhibits nerve impulses at a synapse

neu·ter (noot'ər) *adj.* [< L *ne*-, not + *uter*, either] 1 *Biol.* *a)* having no sexual organ *b)* having undeveloped sexual organs in the adult 2 *Gram.* designating or of the gender of words that are neither masculine nor feminine —*vt.* to castrate or spay (an animal)

neu·tral (noo'trəl) *adj.* [see prec.] 1 supporting neither side in a quarrel or war 2 of neither option or extreme in type, kind, etc.; indefinite 3 having little or no decided color; not vivid 4 having no net effect [a carbon-*neutral* energy policy] —*n.* 1 a neutral person or nation 2 a neutral color 3 *Mech.* a disengaged position of gears —**neu'tral·ly** *adv.*

neu·tral·ism (-iz'əm) *n.* a policy of remaining neutral, esp. in international conflicts —**neu'tral·ist** *adj., n.*

neu·tral·i·ty (-tral'ə tē) *n.* 1 a being neutral 2 the status or policy of a neutral nation

neu·tral·ize (noo'trə līz') *vt.* **-ized'**, **-iz'ing** to destroy or counteract the effectiveness, force, etc. of —**neu'tral·i·za'tion** *n.* —**neu'tral·iz'er** *n.*

neutral spirits ethyl alcohol of 190 proof or over, used in blended whiskeys, liqueurs, etc.

neu·tri·no (noo trē'nō) *n., pl.* **-nos** [It, little neutron] any of three leptons having almost no mass

neu·tron (noo'trän') *n.* [< NEUTRAL] an elementary particle in the nucleus of an atom, carrying no electrical charge

neutron bomb a small thermonuclear bomb designed to emit large numbers of neutrons to kill enemy soldiers without destroying buildings, etc.

neutron star a collapsed star of extremely high density composed almost entirely of neutrons

Ne·vad·a (nə vad'ə, -väd'ə) Mountain State of the W U.S.; cap. Carson City: abbrev. NV —**Ne·vad'an** *adj., n.*

nev·er (nev'ər) *adv.* [< OE *ne*, not + *æfre*, ever] 1 not ever; at no time 2 not at all; in no case

nev·er·more *adv.* never again

nev·er-nev·er land [after a place in *Peter Pan* (1904), play by Brit. author J. M. Barrie] an unreal or unrealistic place or situation

nev·er·the·less (-thə les') *adv.* in spite of that; however

Ne·vis (nē'vis, nev'is) island of the West Indies: see ST. KITTS AND NEVIS

ne·vus (nē'vəs) *n., pl.* **ne'vi'** (-vī') [< L *naevus*] a birthmark or mole

new (noo) *adj.* [OE *niwe*] 1 appearing, thought of, developed, made, etc. for the first time 2 different from (the) one in the past [a *new*

hairdo] 3 strange; unfamiliar 4 *a)* recently grown; fresh *b)* harvested early [*new* potatoes] 5 unused 6 modern; recent 7 more; additional 8 starting as a repetition of a cycle, series, etc. [the *new* moon] 9 having just reached a position, rank, etc. [a *new* arrival] —*adv.* 1 again 2 recently —**new'ness** *n.*

New Age [*often* n- a-] of or pertaining to a cultural movement variously combining belief in reincarnation, astrology, meditation, etc.

new blood new people as a potential source of new ideas, vigor, etc.

new·born *adj.* 1 recently born 2 reborn —*n.* a newborn infant

New Bruns·wick (brunz'wik) province of SE Canada; cap. Fredericton: abbrev. NB

new·com·er (-kum'ər) *n.* a recent arrival

New Deal the principles and policies adopted by President Franklin D. Roosevelt in the 1930s to advance economic recovery and social welfare

New Delhi capital of India, adjacent to the old city of Delhi

new·el (noo'əl) *n.* [ult. < L *nux*, nut] 1 the pillar around which the steps of a winding staircase turn 2 the post that supports the handrail of a flight of stairs: also **newel post**

New England the six NE states of the U.S.: Maine, Vermont, New Hampshire, Massachusetts, Rhode Island, and Connecticut —**New Eng'land·er**

new·fan·gled (-faŋ'gəld) *adj.* [ME *newe*, new + -*fangel* < OE *fon*, to take] new; novel: a humorously derogatory term

new·found (-found') *adj.* newly acquired

New·found·land and Labrador (noo'fənd lənd, -land') province of Canada, including Labrador and an island (**Newfoundland**) off the E coast; cap. St. John's: abbrev. NL

New Guinea large island in the East Indies, north of Australia

New Hamp·shire (hamp'shir) New England state of the U.S.; cap. Concord: abbrev. NH —**New Hamp'shir·ite'**

New Jer·sey (jur'zē) state of the E U.S.; cap. Trenton: abbrev. NJ —**New Jer'sey·ite'**

new·ly *adv.* recently; lately

new·ly·wed *n.* a recently married person

New Mexico Mountain State of the SW U.S.; cap. Santa Fe: abbrev. NM —**New Mexican**

new moon 1 the moon in its first thin crescent phase 2 the moon when it is between the earth and the sun, with its dark side toward the earth

New Or·le·ans (ôr'lē ənz, -lənz; ôr lēnz') city & port in SE Louisiana

news (nooz) *n.* 1 new information; information previously unknown 2 *a)* recent happenings *b)* reports of these 3 *short for* NEWSCAST —**make news** to do something apt to be reported as news

news·cast *n.* a radio or television news broadcast —**news'cast'er** *n.*

news·deal·er *n.* a retailer of newspapers, magazines, etc.

news·let·ter *n.* a bulletin issued regularly to subscribers, employees, club members, etc., containing news of upcoming events, etc.

news·man (-man', -mən) *n., pl.* **-men'** (-men', -mən) a man who is a newscaster or reporter

news·pa·per *n.* a regular publication, usually daily or weekly, containing news, opinions, advertising, etc.

news·print *n.* a cheap, low-grade paper used chiefly for newspapers

news·stand *n.* a stand at which newspapers, magazines, etc. are sold

news·wom·an *n., pl.* **-wom'en** a woman who is a newscaster or reporter

news·wor·thy (-wur'thē) *adj.* timely and important or interesting

news·y *adj.* **-i·er, -i·est** [Inf.] containing much news

newt (nōōt) *n.* ⟦by merging of ME *(a)n eute,* a newt⟧ any of various small, largely aquatic salamanders

New Testament the part of the Bible that contains the life and teachings of Jesus and his followers

new·ton (nōōt'ʼn) *n.* ⟦after fol.⟧ a unit of force

New·ton (nōōt'ʼn), Sir **Isaac** 1642-1727; Eng. mathematician & natural philosopher

New World the Western Hemisphere

New Year's (Day) Jan. 1

New Year's Eve 1 the evening before New Year's Day **2** the day of December 31

New York (yôrk) **1** state of the NE U.S.; cap. Albany: abbrev. **NY 2** city & port in SE New York: often **New York City** —**New York'er**

New Zea·land (zē'lənd) country made up of two large islands in the S Pacific, southeast of Australia —**New Zea'land·er**

next (nekst) *adj.* ⟦OE *neahst,* superl. of *neah, nigh*⟧ nearest; immediately preceding or following —*adv.* **1** in the nearest time, place, rank, etc. **2** on the first subsequent occasion

next-door *adj.* in or at the next house, building, etc.

nex·us (nek'səs) *n., pl.* **nex'us·es** or **nex'us** ⟦L⟧ a connection, tie, or link

Nfld & Lab *abbrev.* Newfoundland and Labrador

NH New Hampshire

Ni *Chem. symbol for* nickel

ni·a·cin (nī'ə sin) *n.* ⟦NI(COTINIC) AC(ID) + *in*⟧ a white, crystalline substance, a member of the vitamin B complex

Ni·ag·a·ra Falls (nī ag'rə) large waterfall on a river (**Niagara River**) flowing from Lake Erie into Lake Ontario

nib (nib) *n.* ⟦< ME *nebb,* a bird's beak⟧ a point, esp. a pen point

nib·ble (nib'əl) *vt., vi.* **-bled, -bling** ⟦ME *nebyllen*⟧ **1** to eat (food) with quick, small bites **2** to bite (*at*) lightly and intermittently —*n.* a small bite —**nib'bler** *n.*

nibs (nibz) *n.* ⟦< ?⟧ [Inf.] a self-important person: preceded by *his* or *her*

Nic·a·ra·gua (nik'ə rä'gwə) country in Central America —**Nic'a·ra'guan** *adj., n.*

nice (nīs) *adj.* **nic'er, nic'est** ⟦< L *nescius,* ignorant⟧ **1** fastidious; refined **2** delicate; precise; subtle [a *nice* distinction] **3** calling for care, tact, etc. **4** pleasant, attractive, kind, good, etc.: a generalized term of approval —**nice'ly** *adv.* —**nice'ness** *n.*

ni·ce·ty (nī'sə tē) *n., pl.* **-ties 1** precision; accuracy **2** fastidiousness; refinement **3** a subtle or minute detail, distinction, etc.

niche (nich, nēsh) *n.* ⟦Fr < L *nidus,* a nest⟧ **1** a recess in a wall, for a statue, vase, etc. **2** an especially suitable place or position **3** a specialized business market

nick (nik) *n.* ⟦ME *nyke*⟧ a small cut, chip, etc. made on a surface —*vt.* **1** to make a nick or nicks in **2** to wound superficially —**in the nick of time** exactly when needed

nick·el (nik'əl) *n.* ⟦< Ger *kupfernickel,* copper devil: the copperlike ore contains no copper⟧ **1** a hard, silver-white, metallic chemical element, much used in alloys: symbol, Ni; at. no. 28 **2** a U.S. or Canadian coin of nickel and copper, equal to five cents

nick·el·o·de·on (nik'əl ō'dē ən) *n.* ⟦prec. + (*mel*)*odeon,* a small keyboard organ⟧ **1** a movie theater of the early 1900s **2** a coin-operated player piano or early type of jukebox

nick·er (nik'ər) *vi., n.* NEIGH

nick·name (nik'nām') *n.* ⟦by merging of ME *(a)n ekename,* a surname⟧ **1** a substitute, often descriptive, name given in fun, etc., as "Shorty" **2** a familiar form of a proper name, as "Dick" for "Richard" —*vt.* **-named', -nam'ing** to give a nickname to

nic·o·tine (nik'ə tēn') *n.* ⟦Fr, after J. *Nicot* (1530?-1600), Fr diplomat who introduced tobacco into France⟧ a toxic alkaloid found in tobacco leaves

nic·o·tin·ic acid (-tin'ik) NIACIN

niece (nēs) *n.* ⟦< L *neptis*⟧ the daughter of one's brother or sister or of one's brother-in-law or sister-in-law

Nie·tzsche (nē'chə), **Fried·rich** (frē'driH) 1844-1900; Ger. philosopher

nif·ty (nif'tē) *adj.* **-ti·er, -ti·est** ⟦prob. < *magnificent*⟧ [Slang] attractive, smart, stylish, etc.

Ni·ger (nī'jər) country in WC Africa, north of Nigeria

Ni·ger·i·a (nī jir'ē ə) country on the W coast of Africa —**Ni·ger'i·an** *adj., n.*

nig·gard (nig'ərd) *n.* ⟦prob. < Scand⟧ a stingy person; miser —**nig'gard·ly** *adj., adv.* —**nig'gard·li·ness** *n.*

nig·gle (nig'əl) *vi.* **-gled, -gling** ⟦prob. akin to Norw *nigla*⟧ to be finicky —**nig'gler** *n.* —**nig'gling** *adj., n.*

nigh (nī) *adv., adj., prep.* ⟦OE *neah*⟧ [Now Chiefly Dial.] NEAR

night (nīt) *n.* ⟦OE *niht*⟧ **1** the period of darkness from sunset to sunrise **2** any period or condition of darkness or gloom

night blindness imperfect vision in the dark or in dim light

night·cap *n.* **1** a cap worn to bed, esp. formerly **2** [Inf.] an alcoholic drink taken just before going to bed

night·clothes *n.* clothes to be worn in bed, as pajamas

night·club *n.* a place of entertainment for eating, drinking, dancing, etc. at night

night crawl·er a large earthworm that comes to the surface at night

night·fall *n.* the time in the evening when daylight is last visible; dusk

night·gown *n.* a loose gown worn in bed by women or girls

night·hawk *n.* 1 any of various usually nocturnal birds that feed on insects 2 NIGHT OWL

night·ie (-ē) *n.* [Inf.] NIGHTGOWN

night·in·gale (nīt′'n gāl′) *n.* [< OE *niht*, night + *galan*, sing] a small European songbird: the male sings melodiously, esp. at night

Night·in·gale (nīt′'n gāl′), **Florence** 1820-1910; Eng. nurse: regarded as the founder of modern nursing

night·jar *n.* [NIGHT + JAR¹: from the whirring noise made by the male] any of various nocturnal, insect-eating birds with long wings

night life pleasure-seeking activity at night, as in nightclubs

night·ly *adj.* done or occurring every night —*adv.* night after night; every night

night·mare (-mer′) *n.* [ME < *niht*, night + *mare*, demon] 1 a dream that is frightening 2 any frightening experience —**night′mar′ish** *adj.*

night owl a person who works at night or otherwise stays up late

night·shade *n.* 1 a chiefly tropical plant with five-lobed leaves and flowers of various colors 2 BELLADONNA

night·shirt *n.* a loose garment like a long shirt, worn in bed

night·spot *n.* NIGHTCLUB

night stand a small bedside table

night·stick *n.* a policeman's club; billy

night·time *n.* the time between dusk and dawn

night·wear *n.* NIGHTCLOTHES

NIH *abbrev.* National Institutes of Health

ni·hil·ism (nī′ə liz′əm, nē′-) *n.* [< L *nihil*, nothing] the general rejection of customary beliefs in morality, religion, etc. —**ni′hil·ist** *n.* —**ni′hil·is′tic** *adj.*

Ni·hon (nē′hôn) *Jpn. name for* JAPAN

nil (nil) *n.* [L, contr. of *nihil*] nothing

Nile (nīl) river in NE Africa, flowing through Egypt into the Mediterranean

nim·ble (nim′bəl) *adj.* **-bler, -blest** [< OE *niman*, to take] 1 quick-witted; alert 2 moving quickly and lightly —**nim′bly** *adv.*

nim·bus (nim′bəs) *n., pl.* **-bi** (-bī′) or **-bus·es** [L] 1 any rain-producing cloud 2 a halo that is around the head of a saint, etc., as in a painting

Nim·rod (nim′räd′) *n.* *Bible* a mighty hunter

nin·com·poop (nin′kəm pōōp′) *n.* [< ?] a stupid, silly person; fool

nine (nīn) *adj., n.* [OE *nigon*] one more than eight; 9; IX —**ninth** (nīnth) *adj., n.*

9/11 (nīn′i lev′ən) September 11, 2001, the day on which four airliners were hijacked by terrorists for use in an attack on the U.S.

9-1-1 or **911** (nīn′wun wun′) [the specific digits in the number] a three-digit telephone number for emergencies

nine·pins *n.* a British version of the game of tenpins, played with nine pins

nine·teen *adj., n.* nine more than ten; 19; XIX —**nine′teenth′** (-tēnth′) *adj., n.*

nine·ty (nīn′tē) *adj., n., pl.* **-ties** nine times ten; 90; XC (or LXXXX) —**the nineties** the numbers or years, as of a century, from 90 through 99 —**nine′ti·eth** (-ith) *adj., n.*

nin·ja (nin′jə) *n.* [Jpn] any of a class of feudal Japanese warriors employed as spies and assassins

nin·ny (nin′ē) *n., pl.* **-nies** [< (a)n inn(ocent)] a fool; dolt

ni·o·bi·um (nī ō′bē əm) *n.* [after *Niobe*, in Gr. myth] a soft, ductile, metallic chemical element, used in alloy steels, superconducting alloys, etc.: symbol, Nb; at. no. 41

nip¹ (nip) *vt.* **nipped, nip′ping** [prob. < earlier LowG *nippen*] 1 to pinch or bite 2 to sever (shoots, etc.) by clipping 3 to check the growth of 4 to have a painful or injurious effect on because of cold —*n.* 1 a nipping; pinch; bite 2 a stinging, as in cold air 3 stinging cold; frost —**nip and tuck** so close as to leave the outcome in doubt

nip² (nip) *n.* [prob. < Du *nippen*, to sip] a small drink of liquor —*vt., vi.* **nipped, nip′ping** to drink in nips

nip·per (nip′ər) *n.* 1 anything that nips 2 [*pl.*] pliers, pincers, etc. 3 the claw of a crab or lobster

nip·ple (nip′əl) *n.* [prob. < earlier *neb*, a beak] 1 the small protuberance on a breast or udder through which, in the female, the milk passes; teat 2 the teatlike part in the cap of a baby's bottle

Nip·pon (nip′än′, ni pän′) *var. of* NIHON

nip·py (nip′ē) *adj.* **-pi·er, -pi·est** bitingly cold

nir·va·na (nir vä′nə) *n.* [< Sans] [*also* N-] 1 *Buddhism* the state of perfect blessedness attained by the extinction of the individual self or of desires, passions, etc. 2 a place or condition of great bliss

ni·sei (nē′sā′) *n., pl.* **-sei** or **-seis′** [Jpn, second generation] [*also* N-] a native U.S. or Canadian citizen born of immigrant Japanese parents

nit (nit) *n.* [OE *hnitu*] 1 the egg of a louse or similar insect 2 a young louse, etc.

nite (nīt) *n. inf. sp. of* NIGHT

ni·ter (nīt′ər) *n.* [< Gr *nitron*] potassium nitrate or sodium nitrate, used in making explosives, fertilizers, etc.; saltpeter: also [Chiefly Brit.] **ni′tre**

nit-pick·ing (nit′pik′iŋ) *adj., n.* stressing petty details; niggling —**nit′-pick′er** *n.*

ni·trate (nī′trāt′) *n.* a salt of nitric acid, as sodium nitrate —*vt.* **-trat′ed, -trat′ing** to combine with nitric acid or, esp., to make into a nitrate

ni·tric acid (nī′trik) a colorless, corrosive acid containing nitrogen

ni·tro·cel·lu·lose (nī′trō sel′yŏo lōs′) *n.* a substance obtained by treating cellulose with nitric acid, used in making explosives, lacquers, etc.

ni·tro·gen (nī′trə jən) *n.* [< Fr: see NITER & -GEN] a colorless, odorless, gaseous chemical element forming nearly four fifths of the atmosphere: symbol, N; at. no. 7 —**ni·trog′e·nous** (-träj′ə nəs) *adj.*

ni·tro·glyc·er·in or **ni·tro·glyc·er·ine** (nī′trō glis′ər in) *n.* a thick, explosive oil prepared by treating glycerin with nitric and sulfuric acids: used in making dynamite

ni·trous oxide (nī′trəs) a colorless gas containing nitrogen, used as an anesthetic and in aerosols

nit·ty-grit·ty (nit′ē grit′ē) *n.* [Slang] the actual, basic facts, issues, etc.

nit·wit *n.* [? NIT + WIT¹] a stupid or silly person

nix (niks) [Slang] *adv.* [Ger *nichts*] 1 no 2 not at all —*interj.* 1 stop! 2 I forbid, disagree, etc. —*vt.* to disapprove of or put a stop to

Nix·on (nik′sən), **Richard M(ilhous)** 1913–94; 37th president of the U.S. (1969–74): resigned

Nizh·ny Nov·go·rod (nēzh′nē nôv′gə rət) city in central European Russia

NJ *abbrev.* New Jersey

NL Newfoundland and Labrador

NM *abbrev.* New Mexico

no¹ (nō) *adv.* [< OE *ne a*, not ever] 1 not at all [*no* worse] 2 nay; not so: used to deny, refuse, or disagree —*adj.* not any; not one [*no* errors] —*n., pl.* **noes** or **nos** 1 a refusal or denial 2 a negative vote or voter

no² *abbrev.* [L *numero*] number

Noah (nō′ə) *n. Bible* the patriarch commanded by God to build the ARK (*n.* 3)

no·bel·i·um (nō bel′ē əm) *n.* [after A. B. *Nobel*: see fol.] a radioactive, metallic chemical element artificially produced in trace amounts: symbol, No; at. no. 102

No·bel prizes (nō bel′) [after A. B. *Nobel* (1833–96), Swed inventor who established them] annual international prizes given for distinction in physics, chemistry, economics, medicine, and literature, and for promoting peace

no·bil·i·ty (nō bil′ə tē) *n., pl.* **-ties** 1 a being noble 2 high rank in society 3 the class of people of noble rank

no·ble (nō′bəl) *adj.* **-bler, -blest** [< L *nobilis*, well-known] 1 having high moral qualities 2 excellent 3 grand; stately 4 of high hereditary rank —*n.* one having hereditary rank or title —**no′ble·ness** *n.* —**no·bly** (nō′blē) *adv.*

no·ble·man (-mən) *n., pl.* **-men** (-mən) a man of noble rank

no·blesse o·blige (nō bles′ ō blēzh′) [Fr, nobility obliges] the inferred obligation of people of high rank to behave honorably or kindly, esp. toward those of lower rank

no·ble·wom·an *n., pl.* **-wom′en** a woman of noble rank

no·bod·y (nō′bäd′ē, -bud′ē, -bə dē) *pron.* not anybody; no one —*n., pl.* **-ies** a person of no importance

no-brain·er (nō′brān′ər) *n.* [Inf.] something so obvious, simple, etc. as to require little thought

noc·tur·nal (näk tur′nəl) *adj.* [< L *nox, night*] 1 of the night 2 functioning, done, or active during the night —**noc·tur′nal·ly** *adv.*

noc·turne (näk′turn′) *n.* [Fr, nocturnal] a romantic or dreamy musical composition

nod (näd) *vi.* **nod′ded, nod′ding** [ME *nodden*] 1 to bend the head forward quickly, as in agreement, greeting, etc. 2 to let the head fall forward because of drowsiness —*vt.* 1 to bend (the head) forward quickly 2 to signify (assent, etc.) by doing this —*n.* a nodding

node (nōd) *n.* [L *nodus*] 1 a knot; knob; swelling 2 a point where lines, etc. meet or intersect 3 that part of a stem from which a leaf starts to grow —**nod·al** (nōd′′l) *adj.*

nod·ule (näj′ōol′) *n.* [L *nodulus*] a small knot or rounded lump

No·el or **No·ël** (nō el′) *n.* [Fr < L *natalis*, natal] CHRISTMAS

no-fault *adj.* 1 designating a form of automobile insurance in which those injured collect damages without blame being fixed 2 designating a form of divorce granted without blame being charged

nog·gin (näg′in) *n.* [prob. < Brit dial. *nog*, strong ale] 1 a small cup or mug 2 [Inf.] the head

no-good *adj.* [Slang] contemptible

noir (nwär) *n.* [Fr, black] a film, novel, etc. pessimistic or cynical in mood and often dealing with urban crime —**noir′ish** *adj.*

noise (noiz) *n.* [< OFr] 1 din of voices; clamor 2 any sound; specif., a loud, disagreeable sound —*vt.* **noised, nois′ing** to spread (a report, rumor, etc.) *about, around*, etc.

noise·less *adj.* with little or no noise; very quiet —**noise′less·ly** *adv.*

noi·some (noi′səm) *adj.* [see ANNOY & -SOME¹] 1 injurious to health; harmful 2 foul-smelling

nois·y (noiz′ē) *adj.* **-i·er, -i·est** 1 making noise 2 full of noise —**nois′i·ly** *adv.* —**nois′i·ness** *n.*

no-load (nō′lōd′) *adj.* designating mutual funds charging no commissions on sales

no·mad (nō′mad′) *n.* [< Gr *nemein*, to pasture] 1 any of a people having no permanent home, but moving about constantly, as in search of pasture 2 a wanderer —**no·mad′ic** *adj.*

no man's land the unoccupied region separating opposing armies

nom de plume (näm′ də ploom′) [Fr] a pen name

no·men·cla·ture (nō′mən klā′chər) *n.* [< L *nomen*, a name + *calare*, to call] the system of names used in a science, etc. or for the parts of a device

-nom·ics (näm′iks) *combining form* economics: also **-om′ics**

nom·i·nal (näm′ə nəl) *adj.* [< L *nomen*, a name] 1 in name only, not in fact [a *nominal* leader] 2 relatively very small —**nom′i·nal·ly** adv.

nom·i·nate (-nāt′) vt. -**nat′ed, -nat′ing** [< L nomen, a name] 1 to appoint to an office or position 2 to name as a candidate for election —**nom′i·na′tion** n.

nom·i·na·tive (-nə tiv) n. Gram. the case of the subject of a verb

nom·i·nee (-ə nē′) n. a person who is nominated

non- [< L non, not] prefix not: less emphatic than IN-[2] and UN-, which often give a word a strong opposite or reverse meaning: the terms in the following list will be understood if "not" is used before the meaning of the base word:

nonabrasive	nondestructive
nonabsorbent	nondetachable
nonactive	nondisciplinary
nonaddictive	nondramatic
nonadministrative	nondrinker
nonaggression	nondrying
nonaggressive	noneducational
nonalcoholic	noneffective
nonallergenic	nonenforceable
nonallergic	nonessential
nonassignable	nonexclusive
nonathletic	nonexempt
nonattendance	nonexistence
nonautomotive	nonexistent
nonavailability	nonexplosive
nonbasic	nonfactual
nonbeliever	nonfading
nonbelligerent	nonfat
nonbreakable	nonfatal
nonburnable	nonfiction
nonchargeable	nonfictional
nonclerical	nonflammable
nonclinical	nonflowering
noncollectable	nonfluctuating
noncombustible	nonflying
noncommercial	nonfreezing
noncommunicable	nonfunctional
noncompeting	nongranular
noncompetitive	nonhazardous
noncompliance	nonhereditary
noncomplying	nonhuman
nonconducting	nonidentical
nonconforming	noninclusive
nonconsecutive	nonindependent
nonconsensual	nonindustrial
nonconstructive	noninfected
noncontagious	noninflationary
noncontributory	nonintellectual
noncontroversial	noninterference
nonconvertible	nonintoxicating
noncorroding	nonirritating
noncorrosive	nonjudicial
noncriminal	nonlegal
noncritical	nonliterary
noncrystalline	nonmagnetic
noncumulative	nonmalignant
nondeductible	nonmember
nondelivery	nonmigratory
nondepartmental	nonmilitant
nondepreciating	nonmilitary

nonnarcotic	nonscientific
nonnegotiable	nonscoring
nonnumerical	nonseasonal
nonobjective	nonsecular
nonobligatory	nonsensitive
nonobservance	nonsmoker
nonobservant	nonsocial
nonoccurrence	nonspeaking
nonofficial	nonspecializing
nonoperational	nonspiritual
nonoperative	nonstaining
nonpaying	nonstandard
nonpayment	nonsticking
nonperishable	nonstrategic
nonphysical	nonstriking
nonpoisonous	nonstructural
nonpolitical	nonsuccessive
nonporous	nonsupporting
nonprejudicial	nonsustaining
nonprescriptive	nontaxable
nonproductive	nontechnical
nonprofitable	nontheatrical
nonpunishable	nonthinking
nonracial	nontoxic
nonreactive	nontransparent
nonreciprocal	nontropical
nonrecoverable	nonuniform
nonrecurring	nonuser
nonredeemable	nonvenomous
nonrefillable	nonverbal
nonreligious	nonviable
nonrenewable	nonvirulent
nonresidential	nonvocal
nonresidual	nonvoice
nonresistant	nonvoter
nonreturnable	nonvoting
nonrhythmic	nonvolatile
nonrigid	nonwhite
nonsalaried	nonyielding

non·age (nän′ij, nō′nij) n. [see prec. & AGE] the state of being under full legal age

non·a·ge·nar·i·an (nän′ə jə ner′ē ən) n. [< L nonaginta, ninety] a person between the ages of 90 and 100

non·a·ligned (-ə līnd′) adj. not aligned with either side in a conflict —**non′a·lign′ment** n.

no-name adj. not famous or distinguished

non·bind·ing (-bīn′diŋ) adj. not holding one to an obligation, promise, etc.

non·book (nän′book′) n. a book produced cheaply and quickly, often in response to a current fad, etc.

nonce (näns) n. [by merging of ME (for then) ones, lit., (for the) once] the present use, occasion, or time: chiefly in **for the nonce**

nonce word a word coined and used for a single occasion

non·cha·lant (nän′shə länt′) adj. [Fr, ult. < L non, not + calere, be warm] casually indifferent —**non′cha·lance′** (-läns′) n.

non·com (nän′käm′) n. [Inf.] short for NONCOMMISSIONED OFFICER

non·com·bat·ant (nän′kəm bat′′nt) n. 1 a member of the armed forces not engaged in actual combat 2 any civilian in wartime

non·com·mis·sioned officer (nän′kə mish′

ənd) an enlisted person of any of various grades in the armed forces: in the U.S. Army, from corporal to sergeant major inclusive

non·com·mit·tal (-kə mit'l) *adj.* not committing one to a definite point of view or course of action

non com·pos men·tis (nän' käm'pəs men'tis) ⟦L⟧ *Law* not of sound mind

non·con·duc·tor (-kən duk'tər) *n.* a substance that does not readily transmit sound, heat, or, esp., electricity

non·con·form·ist (-kən fôr'mist) *n.* 1 one who does not conform to prevailing beliefs and practices 2 [N-] an English or Welsh Protestant who is not Anglican —**non'con·form'i·ty** *n.*

non·cus·to·di·al (-kəs tō'dē əl) *adj.* without custody, as of one's children after divorce

non·dair·y (nän'der'ē) *adj.* containing no milk or milk products

non·de·script (nän'di skript') *adj.* ⟦< L *non*, not + *describere*, describe⟧ 1 belonging to no definite class or type; hard to classify or describe 2 not interesting; colorless

none (nun) *pron.* ⟦< OE *ne*, not + *an*, one⟧ 1 no one; not anyone 2 [*with pl. v.*] not any [there are *none* on the table] —*n.* not any (of); no part [I want *none* of it] —*adv.* not at all [*none* the worse for wear]

non·en·ti·ty (nän'en'tə tē) *n., pl.* -**ties** a person or thing of little importance

none·the·less (nun'thə les') *adv.* nevertheless: also **none the less**

non·e·vent (nän'ē vent') *n.* [Inf.] an event that is boring or that is deliberately staged for publicity

non·fer·rous (-fer'əs) *adj.* 1 not containing iron 2 designating or of metals other than iron

non·in·ter·ven·tion (-in'tər ven'shən) *n.* refusal to interfere; esp., a refusal by one nation to interfere in another's affairs

non·in·va·sive (-in vā'siv) *adj. Med.* not entering the skin or a body cavity

non·judg·men·tal (-juj ment'l) *adj.* objective; tolerant

non·met·al (-met'l) *n.* any chemical element, as oxygen, carbon, nitrogen, fluorine, etc., lacking the characteristics of a metal —**non'me·tal'lic** *adj.*

no-no *n., pl.* -**nos'** [Slang] something forbidden or considered unwise to do, say, etc.

no-non·sense *adj.* practical and serious

non·pa·reil (nän'pə rel') *adj.* ⟦Fr < *non*, not + *pareil*, equal⟧ unequaled; unrivaled; peerless —*n.* 1 one that has no equal 2 a small candy used esp. in decorating cakes, etc.

non·par·ti·san (-pärt'ə zən) *adj.* not partisan; esp., not connected with any single political party

non·per·son (-pur'sən) *n.* a person officially ignored by the government

non·plus (nän plus') *vt.* -**plused'** or -**plussed'**, -**plus'ing** or -**plus'sing** ⟦L *non*, not + *plus*, more⟧ to greatly perplex or bewilder

non·prof·it (-präf'it) *adj.* not established or done to earn a profit: said as of a charity

non·res·i·dent (-rez'ə dənt) *adj.* not residing in the locality where one works, attends school, etc. —*n.* a nonresident person

non·re·stric·tive (nän'ri strik'tiv) *adj. Gram.* designating a clause, phrase, or word felt as not essential to the sense, usually set off by commas (Ex.: John, *who is tall*, is Bill's brother)

non·sched·uled (nän'skej'oold) *adj.* licensed for commercial air flights as demand warrants rather than on a schedule

non·sec·tar·i·an (-sek ter'ē ən) *adj.* not confined to any specific religion

non·sense (nän'sens') *n.* words, actions, etc. that are absurd or meaningless —*interj.* how absurd!: an exclamation —**non·sen'si·cal** (-sen'si kəl) *adj.*

non se·qui·tur (nän' sek'wi tər) ⟦L, it does not follow⟧ 1 *Logic* a conclusion which does not follow from the premises 2 a remark having no bearing on what has just been said

non·skid (-skid') *adj.* having a surface made so as to reduce slipping or skidding

non·start·er (-stärt'ər) *n.* [Inf.] a proposal, etc. regarded as having no chance of success or acceptance

non·stop (-stäp') *adj., adv.* without a stop

non·sup·port (-sə pôrt') *n.* failure to provide for a legal dependent

non·un·ion (-yoon'yən) *adj.* 1 not belonging to a labor union 2 not made or serviced by union workers

non·vi·o·lence (-vī'ə ləns) *n.* an abstaining from violence or the use of force, as in efforts to obtain civil rights —**non'vi'o·lent** *adj.*

noo·dle¹ (nood'l) *n.* [< ?] [Slang] the head

noo·dle² (nood'l) *n.* ⟦Ger *nudel*⟧ a flat, narrow strip of dry dough, usually made with egg and served in soup, etc.

nook (nook) *n.* ⟦ME *nok*⟧ 1 a corner or separate part of a room 2 a small, secluded spot

noon (noon) *n.* [< L *nona* (*hora*), ninth (hour)] twelve o'clock in the daytime; midday —*adj.* of or at noon Also **noon'time'** or **noon'day'**

no one not anyone; nobody

noose (noos) *n.* [< L *nodus*, knot] a loop in a rope, etc. formed by a slipknot so that the loop tightens as the rope is pulled

nor (nôr) *conj.* ⟦ME < *ne-*, not, + *or*, other⟧ and not; and not either [I can neither go *nor* stay]

Nor·dic (nôr'dik) *adj.* ⟦OE *north*, north⟧ 1 of or relating to Scandinavia 2 of or relating to cross-country skiing

norm (nôrm) *n.* ⟦L *norma*, rule⟧ a standard or model for a group

nor·mal (nôr'məl) *adj.* 1 conforming with an accepted standard or norm; natural; usual 2 average in intelligence, etc. —*n.* 1 anything normal 2 the usual state, amount, etc. —**nor'mal·cy** (-sē) *n.*, **nor·mal'i·ty** (-mal'ə tē) —**nor'mal·ize'** *vt., vi.* -**ized'**, -**iz'ing** —**nor'mal·i·za'tion** *n.*

nor·mal·ly *adv.* 1 in a normal manner 2 under normal circumstances

Nor·man (nôr′mən) *n.* [< OFr] **1** a member of the people of Normandy that conquered England in 1066 **2** a person born or living in Normandy —*adj.* of Normandy or its people, etc.

Nor·man·dy (nôr′mən dē) historical region in NW France, on the English Channel

norm·a·tive (nôr′mə tiv) *adj.* of or establishing a norm

Norse (nôrs) *adj., n.* [prob. < Du *noord*, north] **1** SCANDINAVIAN **2** (of) the Scandinavian group of languages

Norse·man (-mən) *n., pl.* **-men** (-mən) a member of any of the medieval Scandinavian peoples

north (nôrth) *n.* [OE] **1** the direction to the right of one facing the sunset (0° or 360° on the compass) **2** a region in or toward this direction —*adj.* **1** in, of, toward, or facing the north **2** from the north [*a north* wind] —*adv.* in or toward the north —**the North** that part of the U.S. north of Maryland, the Ohio River, and Missouri

North America N continent in the Western Hemisphere —**North American**

North Car·o·li·na (kar′ə li′nə) state of the SE U.S.; cap. Raleigh: abbrev. *NC* —**North Car′o·lin′i·an** (-lin′ē ən)

North Da·ko·ta (də kōt′ə) Midwestern state of the U.S.; cap. Bismarck: abbrev. *ND* —**North Da·ko′tan**

north·east *n.* **1** the direction halfway between north and east **2** a region in or toward this direction —*adj.* **1** in, of, or toward the northeast **2** from the northeast [*a northeast* wind] —*adv.* in or toward the northeast —**north′east′er·ly** *adj., adv.* —**north′east′ern** *adj.* —**north′east′ward** *adj., adv.* —**north′east′wards** *adv.*

north·er·ly (nôrth′ər lē) *adj., adv.* **1** toward the north **2** from the north

north·ern (nôr′thərn) *adj.* **1** in, of, or toward the north **2** from the north **3** [N-] of the North

north·ern·er *n.* a person born or living in the north

Northern Hemisphere the half of the earth north of the equator

Northern Ireland division of the United Kingdom, in the NE part of the island of Ireland

northern lights [*also* N- L-] the aurora borealis

Northern Ma·ri·an·a Islands (mer′ē an′ə) group of islands in the W Pacific: a commonwealth associated with the U.S.: also **Northern Marianas**

North Pole the northern end of the earth's axis

North Sea arm of the Atlantic, between Great Britain and the N European mainland

North Star POLARIS

north·ward *adv., adj.* toward the north: also **north′wards** *adv.*

north·west *n.* **1** the direction halfway between north and west **2** a region in or toward this direction —*adj.* **1** in, of, or toward the northwest **2** from the northwest [*a northwest* wind] —*adv.* in or toward the north-

west —**north′west′er·ly** *adj., adv.* —**north′west′ern** *adj.* —**north′west′ward** *adj., adv.* —**north′west′wards** *adv.*

Northwest Territories division of N Canada; cap. Yellowknife: abbrev. *NT*

Norw *abbrev.* **1** Norway **2** Norwegian

Nor·way (nôr′wā′) country in N Europe

Nor·we·gian (nôr wē′jən) *n.* **1** the language of Norway **2** a person born or living in Norway —*adj.* of Norway or its people, language, etc.

nose (nōz) *n.* [OE *nosu*] **1** the part of the face above the mouth, having two openings for breathing and smelling; in animals, the snout, muzzle, etc. **2** the sense of smell **3** anything like a nose in shape or position —*vt.* **nosed, nos′ing 1** to nuzzle **2** to push (a way, etc.) with the front forward —*vi.* **1** to pry inquisitively **2** to move forward —**by a nose** [< horse racing] by a very small margin —**nose out 1** to defeat by a very small margin **2** to discover, as by smelling —**on the nose** [Slang] precisely

nose·bleed *n.* a bleeding from the nose —*adj.* in or of the highest section of seats in a stadium, etc.

nose cone the cone-shaped foremost part of a rocket or missile

nose dive 1 a swift, steep downward plunge of an airplane, nose first **2** any sudden, sharp drop, as in profits —**nose′-dive′** *vi.* **-dived′, -div′ing**

nose drops medication administered through the nose with a dropper

nose·gay (nōz′gā′) *n.* [NOSE + GAY (obs. sense "bright object")] a small bouquet

nose guard *Football* the defensive lineman directly opposite the offensive center: also **nose tackle**

nosh (näsh) *vt., vi.* [< Yiddish < Ger *nashchen*, to nibble] [Slang] to eat (a snack) —*n.* [Slang] a snack —**nosh′er** *n.*

no-show *n.* one who fails to claim or cancel a reservation

nos·tal·gi·a (nä stal′jə) *n.* [< Gr *nostos*, a return + -ALGIA] a longing for something far away or long ago —**nos·tal′gic** (-jik) *adj.*

nos·tril (näs′trəl) *n.* [< OE *nosu*, nose + *thyrel*, hole] either of the external openings of the nose

nos·trum (näs′trəm) *n.* [L, ours] **1** a quack medicine **2** a panacea

nos·y or **nos·ey** (nō′zē) *adj.* **-i·er, -i·est** [Inf.] prying; inquisitive

not (nät) *adv.* [< ME *nought*] in no manner, to no degree, etc.

no·ta·ble (nōt′ə bəl) *adj.* [< L *notare*, to note] worthy of notice; remarkable; outstanding —*n.* a person of distinction —**no′ta·bly** *adv.*

no·ta·rize (nōt′ə rīz′) *vt.* **-rized′, -riz′ing** to certify or attest (a document) as a notary public

no·ta·ry (-rē) *n., pl.* **-ries** [< L *notare*, to note] an official authorized to certify or attest documents, take affidavits, etc.: in full **notary public**

no·ta·tion (nō tā′shən) *n.* **1** the use of signs

or symbols to represent words, quantities, etc. **2** any such system of signs or symbols, as in mathematics or music **3** a brief note or noting

notch (näch) *n.* ⟦prob. < ME *(a)n oche*, a notch⟧ **1** a V-shaped cut in an edge or surface **2** a narrow pass with steep sides **3** [Inf.] a step; degree —*vt.* to cut a notch or notches in

note (nōt) *n.* ⟦< L *nota*, a mark⟧ **1** a distinguishing feature [*a note* of sadness] **2** importance, distinction, etc. [a person of *note*] **3** a brief writing to aid the memory; memorandum **4** a comment or explanation; annotation **5** notice; heed [worthy of *note*] **6** a short, informal letter **7** a written acknowledgment of a debt **8** *Music a)* a tone of definite pitch *b)* a symbol for a tone, indicating its duration and pitch —*vt.* **not′ed, not′ing 1** to heed; observe **2** to set down in writing **3** to mention particularly —**compare notes** to exchange views

note·book *n.* **1** a book in which notes, or memorandums, are kept **2** a small laptop computer

not·ed (nōt′id) *adj.* renowned; famous

note·wor·thy *adj.* worthy of note; outstanding; remarkable —**note′wor′thi·ness** *n.*

noth·ing (nuth′iŋ) *pron.* ⟦OE *na thing*⟧ **1** no thing; not anything **2** a person or thing considered of little or no importance —*n.* **1** nothingness **2** a thing that does not exist **3** a person or thing considered of little or no importance **4** a zero; cipher —*adv.* not at all; in no way —**for nothing 1** free **2** in vain **3** without reason —**nothing doing** [Slang] **1** no: used as a refusal **2** no result, accomplishment, etc.

noth·ing·ness *n.* **1** the condition of not existing **2** insignificance **3** unconsciousness or death

no·tice (nōt′is) *n.* ⟦see NOTE⟧ **1** announcement or warning **2** a brief article about a book, play, etc. **3** a sign giving some public information, warning, etc. **4** attention; heed **5** a formal warning of intention to end an agreement or contract at a certain time —*vt.* **-ticed, -tic·ing** to observe; pay attention to —**take notice** to pay attention

no·tice·a·ble *adj.* readily noticed; conspicuous —**no′tice·a·bly** *adv.*

no·ti·fy (nōt′ə fī′) *vt.* **-fied′, -fy′ing** ⟦< L *notus*, known + *facere*, make⟧ to give notice to; inform —**no′ti·fi·ca′tion** (-fi kā′shən) *n.*

no·tion (nō′shən) *n.* ⟦see NOTE⟧ **1** a general idea **2** a belief; opinion **3** an inclination; whim **4** [*pl.*] small, useful articles, as needles and thread, sold in a store —**no′tion·al** *adj.*

no·to·ri·e·ty (nōt′ə rī′ə tē) *n.* a being notorious

no·to·ri·ous (nō tôr′ē əs) *adj.* ⟦see NOTE⟧ widely known, esp. unfavorably —**no·to′ri·ous·ly** *adv.*

not·with·stand·ing (nät′with stan′diŋ, nät′with-) *prep.* in spite of —*adv.* nevertheless —*conj.* although

nou·gat (nōō′gət) *n.* ⟦< Prov *noga*, nut⟧ a confection of sugar paste with nuts

nought (nôt) *n.* ⟦< OE *ne*, not + *awiht*, aught⟧ alt. sp. of NAUGHT

noun (noun) *n.* ⟦< L *nomen*, a name⟧ *Gram.* a word that names or denotes a person, thing, place, action, quality, etc.

nour·ish (nur′ish) *vt.* ⟦< L *nutrire*⟧ **1** to provide with substances necessary to life and growth **2** to foster; promote —**nour′ish·ing** *adj.*

nour·ish·ment (-mənt) *n.* **1** a nourishing or being nourished **2** food

nou·veau riche (nōō′vō rēsh′) *pl.* **nou·veaux riches** (nōō′vō rēsh′) ⟦Fr⟧ a newly rich person, esp. one lacking culture, taste, or gentility

no·va (nō′və) *n., pl.* **-vas** or **-vae** (-vē) ⟦< L, new⟧ a star that brightens intensely and then gradually dims

No·va Sco·tia (nō′və skō′shə) province of SE Canada; cap. Halifax: abbrev. *NS* —**No′va Sco′tian**

nov·el (näv′əl) *adj.* ⟦< L dim. of *novus*, new⟧ new and unusual —*n.* a relatively long fictional prose narrative

nov·el·ette (-et′) *n.* a short novel

nov·el·ist *n.* one who writes novels

nov·el·ize (-īz′) *vt.* **-ized′, -iz′ing** to make into or like a novel; specif., to use (a film script) as the basis of a novel

nov·el·ty *n., pl.* **-ties 1** the quality of being novel; newness **2** something new, fresh, or unusual **3** a small, often cheap, cleverly made article: *usually used in pl.*

No·vem·ber (nō vem′bər) *n.* ⟦< L *novem*, nine: ninth month in Roman year⟧ the 11th month of the year, having 30 days: abbrev. **Nov.**

no·ve·na (nō vē′nə) *n.* ⟦< L *novem*, nine⟧ *R.C.Ch.* the offering of special prayers and devotions for nine days

nov·ice (näv′is) *n.* ⟦< L *novus*, new⟧ **1** a person on probation in a religious order before taking final vows **2** a person new to something; beginner

no·vi·ti·ate (nō vish′it) *n.* the period or state of being a religious novice

No·vo·cain (nō′və kān′) ⟦L *nov(us)*, new + (C)OCAIN(E)⟧ *trademark for* PROCAINE

now (nou) *adv.* ⟦OE *nu*⟧ **1** *a)* at the present time *b)* at once **2** at that time; then **3** with things as they are [*now* we'll never know] —*conj.* since; seeing that —*n.* the present time [that's all for *now*] —*adj.* of the present time —**just now** recently —**now and then** (or **again**) occasionally

now·a·days (-ə dāz′) *adv.* at the present time

no·way (nō′wā′) *adv.* by no means; not at all: now often **no way**, used with the force of an interjection

no·where *adv.* not in, at, or to any place —**nowhere near** not by a wide margin

no-win (nō′win′) *adj.* designating or of a situation, policy, etc. that cannot lead to success no matter what measures are taken

no·wise (-wīz′) *adv.* in no manner; noway

nox·ious (näk′shəs) *adj.* ⟦< L *nocere*, to hurt⟧ harmful to health or morals —**nox′ious·ness** *n.*

noz·zle (näz′əl) *n.* ⟦dim. of *nose*⟧ the spout at the end of a hose, pipe, etc.

Np *Chem. symbol for* neptunium

NR *abbrev.* not rated: said of films

NS *abbrev.* Nova Scotia

NT *abbrev.* 1 New Testament 2 Northwest Territories

-n't *suffix* not: used with certain verbs in contractions [*aren't*]

nth (enth) *adj.* of the indefinitely large or small quantity represented by *n*

nt wt *abbrev.* net weight

nu (nōō, nyōō) *n.* the 13th letter of the Greek alphabet (N, v)

NU *abbrev.* Nunavut

nu·ance (nōō′äns′) *n.* ⟦Fr < *nuer*, to shade⟧ a slight variation in tone, color, meaning, etc. —**nu′anced′** *adj.*

nub (nub) *n.* ⟦var. of *knub*, knob⟧ 1 a lump or small piece 2 [Inf.] the main point; gist

nub·bin (nub′in) *n.* ⟦dim. of prec.⟧ a small thing

nub·by (nub′ē) *adj.* **-bi·er**, **-bi·est** having a rough, knotted surface [a *nubby* fabric]

nu·bile (nōō′bəl, -bīl′) *adj.* ⟦< L *nubere*, marry⟧ 1 marriageable 2 sexually attractive Said of a young woman

nu·cle·ar (nōō′klē ər) *adj.* 1 of, like, or forming a nucleus 2 of or relating to atomic nuclei [*nuclear* energy] 3 of or operated by the use of nuclear energy [*nuclear* weapons] 4 of or involving nuclear weapons [*nuclear* warfare]

nuclear energy the energy released from atoms in nuclear reactions, esp. in nuclear fission or nuclear fusion

nuclear family a basic social unit consisting of parents and their children living in one household

nuclear fission the splitting of the nuclei of atoms, accompanied by conversion of part of their mass into energy, as in the atomic bomb

nuclear fusion the fusion of lightweight atomic nuclei into a nucleus of heavier mass with a resultant loss in the combined mass, which is converted into energy, as in the hydrogen bomb

nuclear physics the branch of physics dealing with the structure of atomic nuclei, nuclear forces, etc.

nuclear reactor a device for creating a controlled nuclear chain reaction using atomic fuel, as for the production of energy

nuclear winter a hypothetical condition following nuclear war in which sunlight is cut off by clouds of smoke and dust, resulting in very low temperatures, destruction of life forms, etc.

nu·cle·ate (nōō′klē it; *for v.,* -āt′) *adj.* having a nucleus —*vt., vi.* **-at′ed**, **-at′ing** to form into a nucleus —**nu′cle·a′tion** *n.*

nu·cle·ic acid (nōō klē′ik, -klā′-) any of a group of essential complex organic acids found in all living cells: the two types are DNA and RNA

nucleo- *combining form* 1 nucleus 2 nuclear 3 nucleic acid Also, **nucle-**

nu·cle·o·lus (nōō klē′ə ləs) *n., pl.* **-li′** (nyōō-) ⟦< LL, dim. of L *nucleus*⟧ a conspicuous, usually spherical, dense body in the nucleus of most cells, consisting of protein and RNA

nu·cle·us (nōō′klē əs) *n., pl.* **-cle·i′** (-ī′) or **-cle·us·es** ⟦< L, kernel⟧ 1 a central thing or part around which others are grouped; core 2 any center of growth or development 3 the positively charged central part of an atom, made up of protons and neutrons 4 the central mass of protoplasm in a cell

nude (nōōd) *adj.* ⟦L *nudus*⟧ naked; bare —*n.* 1 a nude human figure, esp. in a work of art 2 the state of being nude [in the *nude*] —**nu′di·ty** *n.*

nudge (nuj) *vt.* **nudged**, **nudg′ing** ⟦< ?⟧ to push gently, esp. with the elbow, in order to get the attention of, hint slyly, etc. —*n.* a gentle push

nud·ism (nōō′diz′əm) *n.* the practice of going nude, esp. as a group lifestyle —**nud′ist** *n., adj.*

nu·ga·to·ry (nōō′gə tôr′ē) *adj.* ⟦< L *nugari*, to trifle⟧ 1 trifling; worthless 2 not operative; invalid

nug·get (nug′ət) *n.* ⟦prob. < dial. *nug*, a lump⟧ 1 a lump; esp., a lump of native gold 2 a small portion of something valuable [a *nugget* of wisdom]

nui·sance (nōō′səns) *n.* ⟦< L *nocere*, annoy⟧ an act, thing, or person causing trouble, annoyance, etc.

nuke (nōōk) [Slang] *n.* ⟦< NUCLEAR⟧ a nuclear weapon —*vt.* **nuked**, **nuk′ing** 1 to attack with nuclear weapons 2 [Inf.] to microwave (food)

null (nul) *adj.* ⟦< L *nullus*, none⟧ 1 without legal force; invalid: usually in the phrase **null and void** 2 amounting to naught 3 of no value, effect, etc.

nul·li·fy (nul′ə fī′) *vt.* **-fied′**, **-fy′ing** ⟦< L *nullus*, none + *facere*, to make⟧ 1 to make legally null or valueless 2 to cancel out —**nul′li·fi·ca′tion** *n.*

numb (num) *adj.* ⟦< ME *nimen*, to take⟧ deadened; insensible —*vt.* to make numb —**numb′ly** *adv.* —**numb′ness** *n.*

num·ber (num′bər) *n.* ⟦< L *numerus*⟧ 1 a symbol or word showing how many or which one in a series (Ex.: 2, 35, four, ninth) 2 [*pl.*] ARITHMETIC 3 the sum of persons or things; total 4 *a*) [*often pl.*] many *b*) [*pl.*] numerical superiority 5 quantity 6 *a*) a single issue of a periodical *b*) a single song, dance, etc. in a program of entertainment 7 [Inf.] a person or thing singled out 8 *Gram.* the form of a word as indicating either singular or plural —*vt.* 1 to count; enumerate 2 to give a number to 3 to include as one of a group 4 to limit the number of 5 to have or comprise; total —*vi.* to be included —**a number of** several or many; some —**beyond** (or **without**) **number** too numerous to be counted —**the numbers** an illegal lottery based on certain numbers published in newspapers: also **numbers game** (or **racket**)

num·ber·less *adj.* countless

Num·bers (num′bərz) *n.* the fourth book of the Pentateuch in the Bible: abbrev. **Num.**

nu·mer·al (nōō′mər əl) *adj.* ⟦< L *numerus*, number⟧ of or denoting a number or numbers —*n.* a figure, a letter, or a group of figures or letters, expressing a number

nu·mer·ate (-it) *adj.* able to understand basic mathematical concepts, etc.

nu·mer·a·tor (-āt′ər) *n.* the part of a fraction above the line

nu·mer·i·cal (nōō mer′i kəl) *adj.* 1 of, or having the nature of, number 2 in or by numbers 3 expressed by numbers, not letters —**nu·mer′i·cal·ly** *adv.*

nu·mer·ol·o·gy (nōō′mər äl′ə jē) *n.* divination by numbers, as with birth dates

nu·mer·ous (nōō′mər əs) *adj.* 1 consisting of many persons or things 2 very many

nu·mi·nous (nōō′mə nəs) *adj.* ⟦< L *numen*, deity⟧ having a deeply spiritual or mystical effect

nu·mis·mat·ics (nōō′miz mat′iks, -mis-) *n.* ⟦< L *numisma*, a coin⟧ the study or collection of coins, paper money, etc. —**nu·mis′ma·tist** (-mə tist) *n.*

num·skull (num′skul′) *n.* ⟦NUM(B) + SKULL⟧ a dunce

nun (nun) *n.* ⟦< LL *nonna*⟧ a woman devoted to a religious life, esp. one living in a convent under vows

Nu·na·vut (nōō′nə vōōt′) territory of N Canada; cap. Iqaluit: abbrev. *NU*

nun·ci·o (nun′shō′, -sē ō′) *n.,* *pl.* **-ci·os′** ⟦< It < L *nuntius*, messenger⟧ a papal ambassador to a foreign state

nun·ner·y (nun′ər ē) *n.,* *pl.* **-ies** *former term for* CONVENT

nup·tial (nup′shəl, -chəl) *adj.* ⟦< L *nubere*, marry⟧ of marriage or a wedding —*n.* [*pl.*] a wedding

nurse (nʉrs) *n.* ⟦< L *nutrire*, nourish⟧ 1 a woman hired to care for another's children 2 a person trained to care for the sick, assist surgeons, etc. —*vt.* **nursed, nurs′ing** 1 to suckle (an infant) 2 to take care of (a child, invalid, etc.) 3 to nourish, foster, etc. 4 to try to cure [to *nurse* a cold] 5 to use or handle so as to protect or conserve —*vi.* 1 to feed at the breast; suckle 2 to serve as a nurse

nurse·maid *n.* a woman hired to care for a child or children

nurs·er·y (nʉrs′ə rē) *n.,* *pl.* **-ies** 1 a room set aside for children 2 a place where parents may temporarily leave children to be cared for 3 a place where young trees or other plants are raised for transplanting, etc.

nurs·er·y·man (-mən) *n.,* *pl.* **-men** (-mən) one who owns or works in a tree nursery

nursery rhyme a poem for children

nursery school PRESCHOOL

nursing home a residence providing care for the infirm, chronically ill, disabled, etc.

nur·ture (nʉr′chər) *n.* ⟦< L *nutrire*, nourish⟧ training; rearing —*vt.* **-tured, -tur·ing** 1 to nourish 2 to train, educate, rear, etc. —**nur′tur·er** *n.*

nut (nut) *n.* ⟦OE *hnutu*⟧ 1 a dry, one-seeded fruit, consisting of a kernel, often edible, in a woody shell, as the walnut 2 the kernel itself 3 loosely, any hard-shelled, relatively nonperishable fruit, as the peanut 4 a small metal block with a threaded hole for screwing onto a bolt, etc. 5 [Slang] *a)* a crazy or eccentric person *b)* a devotee; fan

nut case [Slang] one who is eccentric or crazy: also **nut′case′** *n.*

nut·crack·er *n.* 1 an instrument for cracking nutshells 2 a crowlike bird that feeds on nuts

nut·hatch *n.* a small nut-eating bird with a sharp beak

nut·meat *n.* the kernel of a nut

nut·meg (-meg′) *n.* ⟦< L *nux*, nut + LL *muscus*, musk⟧ the aromatic seed of an East Indian tree, grated and used as a spice

nu·tri·a (nōō′trē ə) *n.* ⟦Sp < L *lutra*, otter⟧ 1 a large, aquatic rodent of South America 2 its soft, brown fur

nu·tri·ent (nōō′trē ənt) *adj.* ⟦< L *nutrire*, nourish⟧ nourishing —*n.* anything nutritious

nu·tri·ment (-trə mənt) *n.* anything that nourishes; food

nu·tri·tion (nōō trish′ən) *n.* ⟦see NUTRIENT⟧ 1 the process by which an organism takes in and assimilates food 2 anything that nourishes; food 3 the study of diet and health —**nu·tri′tion·al** *adj.* —**nu·tri′tion·al·ly** *adv.* —**nu′tri·tive** (-trə tiv) *adj.*

nu·tri·tious (-trish′əs) *adj.* nourishing

nuts (nuts) [Slang] *adj.* crazy; foolish —*interj.* used to express disgust, scorn, refusal, etc. —**be nuts about** 1 to be greatly in love with 2 to be very enthusiastic about

nuts and bolts [Inf.] the basic elements or practical aspects of something —**nuts′-and-bolts′** *adj.*

nut·shell *n.* the shell enclosing the kernel of a nut —**in a nutshell** in concise form; in a few words

nut·ty *adj.* **-ti·er, -ti·est** 1 containing nuts 2 having a nutlike flavor 3 [Slang] *a)* very enthusiastic *b)* foolish, crazy, etc. —**nut′ti·ness** *n.*

nuz·zle (nuz′əl) *vt., vi.* **-zled, -zling** ⟦< ME *nose,* NOSE⟧ 1 to push (against) or rub with the nose, snout, etc. 2 to nestle; snuggle —**nuz′zler** *n.*

NV *abbrev.* Nevada

NW *abbrev.* 1 northwest 2 northwestern

NY *abbrev.* New York

NYC or **N.Y.C.** *abbrev.* New York City

ny·lon (nī′län′) *n.* ⟦arbitrary coinage⟧ 1 an elastic, very strong synthetic material that is made into fiber, yarn, bristles, etc. 2 [*pl.*] stockings made of this

nymph (nimf) *n.* ⟦< Gr *nymphē*⟧ 1 *Gr. & Rom. Myth.* any of a group of minor nature goddesses, living in rivers, trees, etc. 2 the young of an insect with incomplete metamorphosis

nym·pho·ma·ni·a (nim′fō mā′nē ə) *n.* uncontrollable desire by a woman for sexual intercourse —**nym′pho·ma′ni·ac′** *adj., n.*

O

o or **O** (ō) *n.*, *pl.* **o's**, **O's** the 15th letter of the English alphabet

O¹ (ō) *n.*, *pl.* **O's** **1** the numeral zero **2** a blood type

O² (ō) *interj.* **1** used in direct address [*O Lord!*] **2** OH

O³ *abbrev.* **1** Ocean **2** *Physics* ohm **3** Old **4** *Baseball* out(s)

O⁴ *Chem. symbol for* oxygen

-o (ō) *suffix* forming slangy words, as slang nouns from adjectives [*weirdo, sicko*]

oaf (ōf) *n.* [< ON *alfr*, elf] a stupid, clumsy fellow; lout —**oaf′ish** *adj.*

O·a·hu (ō ä′hōō) most populous island of Hawaii

oak (ōk) *n.* [OE *ac*] **1** a large hardwood tree with nuts called *acorns* **2** its wood —*adj.* of oak —**oak′en** *adj.*

Oak·land (ōk′lənd) seaport in W California

oa·kum (ō′kəm) *n.* [< OE *a-*, out + *camb*, a comb] stringy hemp fiber gotten by taking apart old ropes, used as a caulking material esp. for wooden ships

oar (ôr) *n.* [OE *ar*] a long pole with a broad blade at one end, used in rowing —**oars·man** (ôrz′mən) *n.*, *pl.* **-men** (-mən)

oar·lock *n.* a device, often U-shaped, for holding an oar in place in rowing

OAS *abbrev.* Organization of American States

o·a·sis (ō ā′sis) *n.*, *pl.* **-ses′** (-sēz′) [< Gr, fertile spot] **1** a fertile place in a desert, resulting from the presence of water **2** any place offering welcome relief, refreshment, etc.

oat (ōt) *n.* [OE *ate*] [*usually pl.*] **1** a hardy cereal grass **2** its edible grain —**oat′en** *adj.*

oat·cake *n.* a thin, flat cake made of oatmeal

oath (ōth) *n.*, *pl.* **oaths** (ōthz, ōths) [OE *ath*] **1** a declaration based on an appeal to God that one will speak the truth, keep a promise, etc. **2** a swearword; curse

oat·meal *n.* **1** oats ground or rolled into meal or flakes **2** a porridge of this

OB *abbrev.* **1** obstetrician **2** obstetrics

ob. *abbrev.* [L *obiit*] he (or she) died

ob- [< L *ob*] *prefix* **1** to, toward, before [*obtrude*] **2** against [*obstinate*] **3** upon, over [*obscure*] **4** completely [*obdurate*]

O·bam·a (ō bä′mə), **Ba·rack Hus·sein Jr.** (bə räk′ hōō sän′) (born *Barack Hussein Obama II* 1961-   ; 44th president of the U.S. (2009-   )

ob·bli·ga·to (äb′li gät′ō) *n.*, *pl.* **-tos** or **-ti** (-ē) [See OBLIGE] a musical accompaniment, usually by a solo instrument

ob·du·rate (äb′door it) *adj.* [< L *obduratus* < *ob-*, intens. + *durus*, hard] **1** hardhearted **2** stubborn; obstinate —**ob′du·ra·cy** (-ə sē) *n.*

o·be·di·ent (ō bē′dē ənt) *adj.* obeying or willing to obey —**o·be′di·ence** *n.* —**o·be′di·ent·ly** *adv.*

o·bei·sance (ō bā′səns, -bē′-) *n.* [< OFr *obeir*, obey] **1** a gesture of respect, as a bow **2** homage; deference —**o·bei′sant** *adj.*

ob·e·lisk (äb′ə lisk, ō′bə-) *n.* [< Gr *obelos*, needle] a tall, four-sided stone pillar tapering to a pyramidal top

o·bese (ō bēs′) *adj.* [< L *obesus* < *ob-* (see OB-) + *edere*, to eat] very fat; stout —**o·be′si·ty** (-ə tē) *n.*

o·bey (ō bā′) *vt.* [< L *obedire* < *ob-* (see OB-) + *audire*, hear] **1** to carry out the orders of **2** to carry out (an order, etc.) **3** to be guided by [*obey* one's conscience] —*vi.* to be obedient

ob·fus·cate (äb′fəs kāt′, äb fus′kāt′) *vt.* **-cat′ed**, **-cat′ing** [< L *obfuscatus* < *ob-* (see OB-) + *fuscus*, dark] to obscure; confuse —**ob′fus·ca′tion** *n.*

ob·i·ter dic·tum (äb′i tər dik′təm, ō bi-) *pl.* **ob′i·ter dic′ta** (-tə) an incidental remark

o·bit·u·ar·y (ō bich′ōō er′ē) *n.*, *pl.* **-ar′ies** [< L *obire*, to die] a notice of someone's death, usually with a brief biography: also **o·bit** (ō′bit)

obj *abbrev.* **1** object **2** objective

ob·ject (äb′jikt; *for v.* äb jekt′) *n.* [< ML *objectum*, thing thrown in the way < L *objectus* < *ob-* (see OB-) + *jacere*, to throw] **1** a thing that can be seen or touched **2** a person or thing to which action, feeling, etc. is directed **3** purpose; goal **4** *Gram.* a noun, pronoun, etc. receiving the action of a verb or governed by a preposition —*vt.* to state by way of objection —*vi.* to feel or express disapproval or opposition —**ob·jec′tor** *n.*

ob·jec·ti·fy (əb jek′tə fī′) *vt.* **-fied′**, **-fy′ing** **1** to regard or treat (someone) superficially or as an object **2** to make objective or concrete —**ob·jec′ti·fi·ca′tion** *n.*

ob·jec·tion (əb jek′shən) *n.* **1** a feeling or expression of opposition or disapproval **2** a reason for objecting

ob·jec·tion·a·ble *adj.* **1** open to objection **2** disagreeable; offensive

ob·jec·tive (əb jek′tiv) *adj.* **1** existing as an object or fact, independent of the mind; real **2** determined by the realities of the thing dealt with rather than the thoughts of the writer or speaker **3** without bias or prejudice **4** *Gram.* designating or of the case of an object of a preposition or verb —*n.* **1** something aimed at **2** the lens or lenses nearest the object being viewed, as in a microscope —**ob·jec′tive·ly** *adv.* —**ob·jec·tiv·i·ty** (äb′jek tiv′ə tē) *n.*, **ob·jec′tive·ness** *n.*

object lesson an actual or practical demonstration or exemplification of some principle

ob·jet d'art (äb′zhä där′) *pl.* **ob′jets d'art** (-zhä-) [Fr] a small object of artistic value, as a figurine

ob·jur·gate (äb′jər gāt′) *vt.* **-gat′ed, -gat′ing** [< L *objurgatus* < *ob-* (see OB-) + *jurgare,* chide] to upbraid sharply; rebuke

ob·late (äb′lāt′) *adj.* [ModL *oblatus,* thrust forward] *Geom.* flattened at the poles

ob·la·tion (äb lā′shən) *n.* [< L *oblatus,* offered] an offering or sacrifice to God or a god

ob·li·gate (äb′li gāt′) *vt.* **-gat′ed, -gat′ing** [see OBLIGE] to bind by a promise, sense of duty, etc.

ob·li·ga·tion (-gā′shən) *n.* **1** an obligating or being obligated **2** a binding contract, promise, responsibility, etc. **3** the binding power of a contract, etc. **4** a being indebted for a favor, etc.

ob·lig·a·to·ry (ə blig′ə tôr′ē, äb′lə gə-) *adj.* legally or morally binding

o·blige (ə blīj′) *vt.* **o·bliged′, o·blig′ing** [< L *obligare* < *ob-* (see OB-) + *ligare,* to bind] **1** to compel by moral, legal, or physical force **2** to make indebted for a favor; do a favor for

o·blig·ing *adj.* helpful; accommodating —**o·blig′ing·ly** *adv.*

ob·lique (ō blēk′) *adj.* [< L *obliquus* < *ob-* (see OB-) + *liquis,* awry] **1** slanting **2** indirect or evasive —**ob·lique′ly** *adv.* —**ob·liq·ui·ty** (ə blik′wə tē) *n.,* **ob·lique′ness** *n.*

ob·lit·er·ate (ə blit′ər āt′) *vt.* **-at′ed, -at′ing** [< L *obliteratus* < *ob-* (see OB-) + *littera,* a letter] **1** to blot out; efface **2** to destroy —**ob·lit′er·a′tion** *n.*

ob·liv·i·on (ə bliv′ē ən) *n.* [< L *oblivisci,* forget] **1** forgetfulness **2** the condition of being forgotten

ob·liv·i·ous (-əs) *adj.* forgetful or indifferent: usually with *to* or *of*

ob·long (äb′lôŋ′) *adj.* [< L *oblongus,* rather long < *ob-* (see OB-) + *longus,* long] longer in one direction than in another —*n.* an oblong figure

ob·lo·quy (äb′lə kwē) *n.,* pl. **-quies** [< L *obloqui* < *ob-* (see OB-) + *loqui,* speak] **1** widespread censure or abuse **2** disgrace resulting from this

ob·nox·ious (əb näk′shəs, äb-) *adj.* [< L *obnoxiosus* < *ob-* (see OB-) + *noxa,* harm] very unpleasant; offensive; repugnant —**ob·nox′ious·ly** *adv.* —**ob·nox′ious·ness** *n.*

o·boe (ō′bō) *n.* [< Fr *haut,* high (pitch) + *bois,* wood] a double-reed woodwind instrument having a high, penetrating tone —**o′bo·ist** *n.*

obs *abbrev.* obsolete

ob·scene (äb sēn′) *adj.* [< L *obscenus,* filthy] **1** offensive to modesty or decency; lewd **2** repulsive —**ob·scen′i·ty** (-sen′ə tē) *n.,* pl. **-ties**

ob·scure (əb skyoor′) *adj.* [< L *obscurus,* covered over] **1** dim; dark **2** not easily seen; faint **3** vague; ambiguous [an *obscure* answer] **4** inconspicuous or hidden [an *obscure* actor] —*vt.* **-scured′, -scur′ing** to make obscure —**ob·scure′ly** *adv.* —**ob·scu′ri·ty** *n.*

ob·se·quies (äb′si kwēz′) *pl.n.* [< L *obsequium,* compliance, substituted for L *exsequiae,* funeral] funeral rites

ob·se·qui·ous (əb sē′kwē əs) *adj.* [< L *obsequi,* to comply with] servile or fawning

ob·serv·ance (əb zurv′əns) *n.* **1** the observing of a law, custom, etc. **2** a customary act, rite, etc.

ob·serv·ant (-ənt) *adj.* **1** strict in observing a law, custom, etc. **2** paying careful attention **3** perceptive or alert

ob·ser·va·tion (äb′zər vā′shən) *n.* **1** *a)* the act or power of noticing *b)* something noticed **2** a being seen **3** a noting and recording of facts, as for research **4** a comment or remark

ob·serv·a·to·ry (əb zurv′ə tôr′ē) *n.,* pl. **-ries** a building equipped for scientific observation, esp. one with a large telescope for astronomical research

ob·serve (-zurv′) *vt.* **-served′, -serv′ing** [< L *observare* < *ob-* (see OB-) + *servare,* to keep] **1** to adhere to (a law, custom, etc.) **2** to celebrate (a holiday, etc.) **3** *a)* to notice (something) *b)* to pay special attention to **4** to say; remark **5** to examine scientifically —**ob·serv′a·ble** *adj.* —**ob·serv′er** *n.*

ob·sess (əb ses′) *vt.* [< L *obsessus* < *ob-* (see OB-) + *sedere,* sit] to haunt or trouble in mind; preoccupy —*vi.* to be obsessed or preoccupied: usually with *about, over,* or *on* —**ob·ses′sive** *adj.* —**ob·ses′sive·ly** *adv.*

ob·ses·sion (-sesh′ən) *n.* **1** a being obsessed **2** an idea, desire, etc. that obsesses one

ob·sid·i·an (əb sid′ē ən) *n.* [ModL *obsidianus,* ult. after *Obsius,* finder of a similar stone in ancient times] a hard, dark, volcanic glass

ob·so·les·cent (äb′sə les′ənt) *adj.* becoming obsolete —**ob′so·les′cence** *n.*

ob·so·lete (äb′sə lēt′) *adj.* [< L *obsoletus* < *ob-* (see OB-) + *exolescere,* to grow out of use] **1** no longer used **2** outdated

ob·sta·cle (äb′stə kəl) *n.* [< L *obstaculum* < *ob-* (see OB-) + *stare,* to stand] anything that stands in the way; obstruction

ob·stet·rics (əb stet′riks) *n.* [< L *obstetrix,* midwife] the branch of medicine concerned with the care and treatment of women during pregnancy and childbirth —**ob·stet′ric** *adj.,* **ob·stet′ri·cal** *adj.* —**ob·ste·tri·cian** (äb′stə trish′ən) *n.*

ob·sti·nate (äb′stə nət) *adj.* [< L *obstinare,* resolve on] **1** determined to have one's own way; stubborn **2** hard to treat or cure [an *obstinate* fever] —**ob′sti·na·cy** (-nə sē) *n.* —**ob′sti·nate·ly** *adv.*

ob·strep·er·ous (əb strep′ər əs) *adj.* [< L *obstreperus* < *ob-* (see OB-) + *strepere,* to roar] noisy or unruly, esp. in resisting —**ob·strep′er·ous·ly** *adv.* —**ob·strep′er·ous·ness** *n.*

ob·struct (əb strukt′) *vt.* [< L *obstructus* < *ob-* (see OB-) + *struere,* to pile up] **1** to block or stop up (a passage) **2** to hinder (progress, etc.) **3** to cut off from view —**ob·struc′tive** *adj.* —**ob·struc′tive·ly** *adv.* —**ob·struc′tive·ness** *n.*

ob·struc·tion (-struk′shən) *n.* **1** an obstructing **2** anything that obstructs; hindrance

ob·struc·tion·ist *n.* one who obstructs progress —*adj.* that obstructs progress

ob·tain (əb tān′) *vt.* [< L *obtinere* < *ob-* (see OB-) + *tenere*, to hold] to get possession of by trying; procure —*vi.* to prevail or be in effect —**ob·tain′a·ble** *adj.* —**ob·tain′ment** *n.*

ob·trude (əb trōōd′, äb-) *vt.* **-trud′ed, -trud′ing** [< L *obtrudere* < *ob-* (see OB-) + *trudere*, to thrust] to force (oneself, one's opinions, etc.) upon others unasked or unwanted —*vi.* to obtrude oneself (*on* or *upon*) —**ob·tru′sion** *n.* —**ob·tru′sive** *adj.* —**ob·tru′sive·ly** *adv.* —**ob·tru′sive·ness** *n.*

ob·tuse (äb tōōs′, əb-) *adj.* [< L *obtundere*, to strike upon, blunt] **1** blunt **2** greater than 90° and less than 180° [an *obtuse* angle] **3** slow to understand —**ob·tuse′ly** *adv.* —**ob·tuse′ness** *n.*

ob·verse (äb vurs′; *also, and for n. always,* äb′vurs′) *adj.* [< L *obversus* < *ob-* (see OB-) + *vertere*, to turn] **1** turned toward the observer **2** forming a counterpart —*n.* **1** the side, as of a coin or medal, bearing the main design **2** a counterpart

ob·vi·ate (äb′vē āt′) *vt.* **-at′ed, -at′ing** [see fol.] to do away with or prevent by effective measures; make unnecessary —**ob′vi·a′tion** *n.*

ob·vi·ous (äb′vē əs) *adj.* [L *obvius*, in the way] easy to see or understand; evident —**ob′vi·ous·ly** *adv.* —**ob′vi·ous·ness** *n.*

oc- *prefix* OB-: used before *c* [*occur*]

oc·a·ri·na (äk′ə rē′nə) *n.* [It < LL *auca*, goose: from its shape] a small, ovoid wind instrument with finger holes and a mouthpiece

occas *abbrev.* occasional(ly)

oc·ca·sion (ə kā′zhən, ō-) *n.* [< L *occasio* < *ob-* (see OB-) + *cadere*, to fall] **1** a favorable time; opportunity **2** an event, etc. that makes something else possible **3** *a)* a happening *b)* a particular time **4** a special time or event **5** need arising from circumstances —*vt.* to cause —**on occasion** sometimes

oc·ca·sion·al *adj.* **1** of or for special occasions **2** happening now and then; infrequent —**oc·ca′sion·al·ly** *adv.*

oc·ci·dent (äk′sə dənt, -dent′) *n.* [< L *occidere*, to fall: with reference to the setting sun] [Old Poet.] the west —**the Occident** Europe and the Americas —**oc′ci·den′tal** *adj., n.,* **Oc′ci·den′tal**

oc·clude (ə klōōd′) *vt.* **-clud′ed, -clud′ing** [< L *occludere* < *ob-* (see OB-) + *claudere*, to shut] **1** to close or block (a passage) **2** to shut in or out —*vi.* Dentistry to meet with the cusps fitting closely —**oc·clu′sion** (-klōō′zhən) *n.* —**oc·clu′sive** (ə klōō′siv) *adj.*

oc·cult (ə kult′) *adj.* [< L *occulere*, to conceal] **1** hidden **2** secret **3** mysterious **4** of mystic arts, such as magic, astrology, etc.

oc·cu·pan·cy (äk′yōō pən sē) *n., pl.* **-cies 1** an occupying; a taking or keeping in possession **2** the condition of being occupied, esp. by a given number of people [a single-*occupancy* room]

oc·cu·pant (-pənt) *n.* one who occupies

oc·cu·pa·tion (äk′yōō pā′shən) *n.* **1** an occupying or being occupied **2** that which occupies one's time; work; profession —**oc′cu·pa′tion·al** *adj.*

oc·cu·py (äk′yōō pī′) *vt.* **-pied′, -py′ing** [< L *occupare* < *ob-* (see OB-) + *capere*, seize] **1** to take possession of by settlement or seizure **2** to hold possession of; specif., *a)* to dwell in *b)* to hold (a position or office) **3** to take up (space, time, etc.) **4** to employ (oneself, one's mind, etc.)

oc·cur (ə kur′) *vi.* **-curred′, -cur′ring** [< L *occurrere* < *ob-* (see OB-) + *currere*, to run] **1** to be found; exist **2** to come to mind [an idea *occurred* to me] **3** to take place; happen

oc·cur·rence (-əns) *n.* **1** the act or fact of occurring **2** an event; incident

o·cean (ō′shən) *n.* [< Gr *Ōkeanos*] **1** the body of salt water covering about 71% of the earth's surface **2** any of its four principal divisions: the Atlantic, Pacific, Indian, or Arctic Ocean **3** a great quantity —**o·ce·an·ic** (ō′shē an′ik) *adj.*

o·cean·go·ing (-gō′iŋ) *adj.* of, or made for, travel on the ocean

O·ce·an·i·a (ō′shē an′ē ə) islands in the S, W, and central Pacific, including Melanesia, Micronesia, & Polynesia —**O′ce·an′i·an** *adj., n.*

o·cean·og·ra·phy (ō′shə näg′rə fē) *n.* the study of the environment in the ocean, its plants and animals, etc. —**o′cean·o·graph′ic** (-nō′graf′ik) *adj.* —**o′cean·og′ra·pher** *n.*

o·cean·ol·o·gy (-näl′ə jē) *n.* **1** the study of the sea in all its aspects, including oceanography, undersea exploration, etc. **2** OCEANOGRAPHY

o·ce·lot (äs′ə lət, -lät′) *n.* [Fr < AmInd] a spotted wildcat of North and South America

o·cher or **o·chre** (ō′kər) *n.* [< Gr *ōchros*, paleyellow] **1** a yellow or reddish-brown clay containing iron oxides, used as a pigment **2** its color

o′clock (ə kläk′, ō-) *adv.* of or according to the clock [nine *o'clock* at night]

octa- [< Gr *oktō*, eight] *combining form* eight [*octagon*]

oc·ta·gon (äk′tə gän′) *n.* [< Gr: see prec. & -GON] a plane figure with eight angles and eight sides —**oc·tag′o·nal** (-tag′ə nəl) *adj.*

octane number (*or* **rating**) (äk′tān′) a number representing the antiknock properties of a gasoline, etc.

oc·tave (äk′tiv, -tāv′) *n.* [< L *octavus*, eighth] **1** any group of eight **2** *Music a)* the eighth tone of a diatonic scale, or a tone seven degrees above or below a given tone *b)* the interval of seven degrees between a tone and either of its octaves *c)* the series of tones within this interval, or the keys of an instrument producing such a series

oc·ta·vo (äk tā′vō, -tä′-) *n., pl.* **-vos** [< L *(in) octavo*, (in) eight] **1** the page size (usually 6 by 9 in.) of a book made up of printer's sheets folded into eight leaves **2** a book of such pages

oc·tet or **oc·tette** (äk tet′) *n.* [OCT(A)- + (DU)-

ET] **1** a composition for eight voices or instruments **2** the eight performers of this

Oc·to·ber (äk tō′bər) *n.* ⟦< L *octo*, eight: eighth month in Roman calendar⟧ the tenth month of the year, having 31 days: abbrev. **Oct.**

oc·to·ge·nar·i·an (äk′tə ji ner′ē ən) *n.* ⟦< L *octoginta*, eighty⟧ a person between the ages of 80 and 90

oc·to·pus (äk′tə pəs) *n., pl.* **-pus·es, -pi′** (-pī′) ⟦< Gr *oktō*, eight + *pous*, foot⟧ a mollusk with a soft body and eight arms covered with suckers

oc·u·lar (äk′yoō lər) *adj.* ⟦< L *oculus*, eye⟧ **1** of, for, or like the eye **2** by eyesight

oc·u·list (-list) *n. former term for* OPHTHALMOLOGIST

OD¹ (ō′dē′) [Slang] *n., pl.* **ODs** or **OD's** an overdose, esp. of a narcotic —*vi.* **OD'd** or **ODed, OD′ing** or **ODing** to take an overdose, esp. a fatal overdose of a narcotic

OD² *abbrev.* ⟦L⟧ Doctor of Optometry

o·da·lisque or **o·da·lisk** (ō′də lisk′) *n.* ⟦Fr < Turk *ōdalīk*, chambermaid⟧ a female slave or concubine in a harem

odd (äd) *adj.* ⟦< ON *oddi*⟧ **1** remaining or separated from a pair, set, etc. **2** having a remainder of one when divided by two **3** with a few more: usually in hyphenated compounds [*sixty-odd* years ago] **4** occasional [*odd* jobs] **5** peculiar or eccentric —**odd′ly** *adv.* —**odd′ness** *n.*

odd·ball *adj., n.* [Slang] strange or eccentric (person)

odd·i·ty (-ə tē) *n.* **1** strangeness **2** *pl.* **-ties** an odd person or thing

odds (ädz) *pl.n.* **1** difference in favor of one side over the other; advantage **2** an equalizing advantage in betting, based on a bettor's assumed chance of winning and expressed as a ratio [*odds* of 3 to 1] —**at odds** quarreling

odds and ends scraps; remnants

odds·mak·er *n.* an expert who estimates the odds in betting, etc.

odds-on *adj.* having a good chance of winning [an *odds-on* favorite]

ode (ōd) *n.* ⟦< Gr *ōidē*, song⟧ a lyric poem characterized by lofty feeling, elaborate form, and dignified style

-ode (ōd) ⟦< Gr *hodos*⟧ *suffix* way, path [*electrode*]

O·des·sa (ō des′ə) seaport in S Ukraine, on the Black Sea

O·din (ō′din) *n. Norse Myth.* the chief deity, god of art, war, and the dead

o·di·ous (ō′dē əs) *adj.* ⟦< L *odium*, hatred⟧ disgusting; offensive —**o′di·ous·ly** *adv.* —**o′di·ous·ness** *n.*

o·di·um (ō′dē əm) *n.* ⟦< L *odi*, I hate⟧ **1** hatred **2** the disgrace brought on by hateful action

o·dom·e·ter (ō däm′ət ər) *n.* ⟦< Gr *hodometros* < *hodos*, way + *metron*, a measure⟧ an instrument for measuring the distance traveled by a vehicle

o·dor (ō′dər) *n.* ⟦L⟧ a smell; scent; aroma Brit. sp. **o′dour** —**o′dor·less** *adj.* —**o′dor·ous** *adj.*

o·dor·if·er·ous (ō′dər if′ər əs) *adj.* ⟦< L *odor*, odor + *ferre*, to bear⟧ giving off an odor, now often, specif., a strong or offensive one

O·dys·se·us (ō dis′ē əs, ō dis′yoōs′) *n.* ⟦Gr⟧ the hero of the *Odyssey*, one of the Greek leaders in the Trojan War

Od·ys·sey (äd′i sē) *n.* **1** an ancient Greek epic poem, ascribed to Homer, about the wanderings of Odysseus after the fall of Troy **2** *pl.* **-seys** [o-] any extended journey

OE *abbrev.* Old English

Oed·i·pal (ed′i pəl) *adj.* [*also* o-] of or relating to the Oedipus complex

Oed·i·pus (ed′i pəs, ē′di-) *n. Gr. Myth.* a king who unwittingly kills his father and marries his mother

Oedipus complex *Psychoanalysis* the unconscious tendency of a child, esp. a male child, to be attached to the parent of the opposite sex

oe·nol·o·gy (ē näl′ə jē) *n.* ⟦< Gr *oinos*, wine + -LOGY⟧ the science or study of wines and winemaking —**oe·nol′o·gist** *n.*

oe·no·phile (ē′nə fīl′) *n.* a connoisseur of wine

o′er (ō′ər, ôr) *prep., adv.* [Old Poet.] OVER

oeu·vre (ë′vr′) *n., pl.* **-vres** (-vr′) ⟦Fr⟧ all the works of a writer, artist, or composer

of (uv) *prep.* ⟦OE⟧ **1** from; specif., *a)* coming from [men *of* Ohio] *b)* resulting from [to die *of* fever] *c)* at a distance from [east *of* the city] *d)* by [the poems *of* Poe] *e)* separated from [robbed *of* his money] *f)* from the whole constituting [one *of* her hats] *g)* made from [a sheet *of* paper] **2** belonging to [the pages *of* a book] **3** *a)* possessing [a man *of* wealth] *b)* containing [a bag *of* nuts] **4** specified as [a height *of* six feet] **5** characterized by [a man *of* honor] **6** concerning; about [think *of* me] **7** during [*of* recent years]

of- *prefix* OB-: used before *f* [*offer*]

off (ôf) *adv.* [ME var. of *of*] **1** so as to be away, at a distance, etc. **2** so as to be no longer on, attached, etc. [take *off* your hat] **3** (a specified distance) away in space or time [20 yards *off*] **4** so as to be no longer in operation, etc. [turn the motor *off*] **5** so as to be less, etc. [5% *off* for cash] **6** away from one's work [take a week *off*] —*prep.* **1** (so as to be) no longer (or not) on, attached, etc. [*off* the road] **2** from the substance of [live *off* the land] **3** away from [a mile *off* shore] **4** branching out from [an alley *off* Main Street] **5** relieved from [*off* duty] **6** not up to the usual standard, etc. of [*off* one's game] —*adj.* **1** not on or attached **2** not in operation **3** on the way [*off* to bed] **4** away from work [we are *off* today] **5** not up to the usual standard, etc. **6** more remote [on the *off* chance] **7** in (specified) circumstances [to be well *off*] **8** wrong [his figures are *off*] —*vt.* [Slang] to kill; murder —*interj.* go away! —**off and on** now and then

-off (ôf, äf) *combining form* a contest of skill in a (specified) activity or field [a chili cook-*off*]

of·fal (ôf′əl) *n.* ⟦ME *ofall*, lit., off-fall⟧ **1** [with *sing. or pl. v.*] the entrails, etc. of a butchered animal **2** refuse; garbage

off·beat *n. Music* a beat having a weak accent —*adj.* [Inf.] unconventional, unusual, strange, etc.

off-col·or *adj.* **1** varying from the standard color **2** improper; risqué

of·fend (ə fend′) *vi.* [< L *offendere*, to strike against < *ob*– (see OB–) + *fendere*, to hit] **1** to commit a sin or crime **2** to create resentment, anger, etc. —*vt.* **1** to hurt the feelings of; insult **2** to be displeasing to (the taste, sense, etc.) —**of·fend′er** *n.*

of·fense (ə fens′; *also, esp. for 5 & 6,* ô′fens′) *n.* **1** a sin or crime **2** a creating of resentment, displeasure, etc. **3** a feeling hurt, angry, etc. **4** something that causes anger, etc. **5** the act of attacking **6** the side that is attacking or seeking to score in any contest Brit. sp. **of·fence′** —**take offense** to become offended

of·fen·sive *adj.* **1** attacking or for attack **2** unpleasant; disgusting **3** insulting —*n.* **1** attitude or position of attack: often with *the* **2** an attack, esp. as part of a larger campaign —**of·fen′sive·ly** *adv.* —**of·fen′sive·ness** *n.*

of·fer (ôf′ər, äf′–) *vt.* [< L *offerre* < *ob*– (see OB–) + *ferre*, to bear] **1** to present in worship [to *offer* prayers] **2** to present for acceptance [to *offer* help] **3** to suggest; propose **4** to show or give signs of [to *offer* resistance] **5** to bid (a price, etc.) —*n.* the act of offering or thing offered

of·fer·ing *n.* **1** the act of making an offer **2** something offered; specif., *a*) a gift *b*) presentation in worship

of·fer·to·ry (–tôr′ē) *n., pl.* **-ries** [often O–] **1** *a*) the part of a Eucharistic service in which the bread and wine are offered to God *b*) the prayers said, or music used, then **2** *a*) the part of a church service during which money offerings are collected *b*) the collection itself

off·hand *adv.* without preparation; extemporaneously —*adj.* **1** said or done offhand **2** casual, curt, etc. Also **off′hand′ed**

off-hour *adj.* not for or during rush hour or other busy periods

of·fice (ôf′is, äf′–) *n.* [< L *officium*] **1** a service done for another **2** a duty, esp. as a part of one's work **3** a position of authority or trust, as in government **4** *a*) the place where the affairs of a business, etc. are carried on *b*) the people working there **5** [often O–] a religious service or set of prayers

of·fice·hold·er *n.* a government official

of·fi·cer (ôf′i sər, äf′–) *n.* **1** anyone holding an office, or position of authority, in a government, business, club, etc. **2** a police officer **3** one holding a position of authority, esp. by commission, in the armed forces

of·fi·cial (ə fish′əl) *adj.* **1** of or holding an office, or position of authority **2** authorized or authoritative **3** formal —*n.* a person holding office —**of·fi′cial·dom** (–dəm) *n.* —**of·fi′cial·ly** *adv.*

of·fi·ci·ate (ə fish′ē āt′) *vi.* **-at′ed, -at′ing** **1**

to perform the duties of an office **2** to perform the functions of a priest, minister, rabbi, etc. at a religious ceremony

of·fi·cious (ə fish′əs) *adj.* [see OFFICE] offering unwanted advice or services; meddlesome, esp. overbearingly so —**of·fi′cious·ly** *adv.* —**of·fi′cious·ness** *n.*

off·ing (ôf′iŋ) *n.* [< OFF] used chiefly in **in the offing**, at some indefinite future time

off-key *adj.* **1** *Music* flat or sharp **2** not harmonious

off-lim·its *adj.* declared to be a place that cannot be entered, etc. by a specified group

off-line or **off·line** *adj.* **1** designating or of equipment not directly connected to and controlled by the central processing unit of a computer **2** not connected to a computer network

off·load *vt., vi.* UNLOAD (1*a*, 2*b*, 4)

off-put·ting *adj.* distracting, annoying, etc.

off-road *adj.* designating or of a vehicle for use off regular highways, streets, etc.

off-sea·son *n.* a time of the year when the usual activity is reduced or not carried on

off·set (ôf set′; *for n.* ôf′set′) *vt.* **-set′, -set′ting** to balance, compensate for, etc. —*n.* **1** a thing that offsets another **2** OFFSET PRINTING

offset printing a printing process in which the inked impression is first made on a rubber-covered roller, then transferred to paper

off·shoot *n.* anything that derives from a main source; specif., a shoot growing from the main stem of a plant

off·shore *adj.* **1** moving away from the shore **2** at some distance from the shore **3** engaged in outside the U.S. as by U.S. banks or manufacturers [*offshore* investments] —*adv.* **1** away from the shore **2** outside the U.S. [to borrow *offshore*]

off·side *adj. Sports* not in the proper position for play: also **off′sides′**

off·spring *n., pl.* **-spring′** or **-springs′** a child or children; progeny; young

off·stage *n.* the part of the stage not seen by the audience —*adj.* in or from this —*adv.* to the offstage

off-the-wall *adj.* [Slang] very unusual, unconventional, eccentric, etc.

off-track *adj.* designating or of legalized betting on horse races, carried on away from the racetrack

off-white *adj.* grayish-white or yellowish-white

off year **1** a year in which a major election does not take place **2** a year of little production

oft (ôft) *adv.* [OE] *literary var. of* OFTEN

of·ten (ôf′ən, –tən) *adv.* [ME var. of prec.] many times; frequently: also **of′ten·times′**

o·gle (ō′gəl) *vi., vt.* **o′gled, o′gling** [prob. < LowG *oog,* an eye] to gaze (at) lustfully —*n.* an ogling look —**o′gler** *n.*

o·gre (ō′gər) *n.* [Fr] **1** in fairy tales and folklore, a man-eating giant **2** a hideous, cruel man

oh (ō) *interj., n., pl.* **oh's** or **ohs** an exclamation of surprise, fear, pain, etc.

O·hi·o (ō hī′ō) **1** river flowing from W Pennsylvania into the Mississippi **2** Midwestern state of the U.S.; cap. Columbus: abbrev. **OH** —**O·hi′o·an** *adj., n.*

ohm (ōm) *n.* ⟦after G. S. Ohm (1789-1854), Ger physicist⟧ unit of electrical resistance

ohm·me·ter *n.* an instrument for measuring electrical resistance in ohms

o·ho (ō hō′) *interj.* used to express surprise or triumph

-o·hol·ic (ə häl′ik) *combining form* –AHOLIC

-oid (oid) ⟦< Gr *eidos*, a form⟧ *suffix* like or resembling [*crystalloid*]

oil (oil) *n.* ⟦< L *oleum*⟧ **1** any of various greasy, combustible, liquid substances obtained from animal, vegetable, or mineral matter **2** PETROLEUM **3** *a)* OIL PAINT *b)* OIL PAINTING —*vt.* to lubricate or supply with oil —*adj.* of, from, or like oil

oil·cloth *n.* cloth made waterproof by being treated with oil or paint

oil·man (-mən) *n.*, *pl.* **-men** (-mən) an entrepreneur or executive in the petroleum industry

oil paint paint made by grinding a pigment in oil: also **oil color**

oil painting 1 a picture painted in oil paints **2** the art of painting in oil paints

oil shale shale from which oil can be extracted by distillation

oil·skin *n.* **1** cloth made waterproof by treatment with oil **2** [*often pl.*] a garment or outfit made of this

oil well a well that supplies petroleum

oil·y (oi′lē) *adj.* **-i·er**, **-i·est 1** of, like, or containing oil **2** greasy **3** too suave or smooth; unctuous —**oil′i·ness** *n.*

oink (oiŋk) *n.* [echoic] the grunt of a pig —*vi.* to make this sound

oint·ment (oint′mənt) *n.* ⟦< L *unguentum*, a salve⟧ a fatty substance used on the skin for healing or cosmetic purposes; salve

OJ or **oj** (ō′jā) *n.* [Slang] orange juice

OK or **O.K.** (ō kā′) [Inf.] *adj., adv., interj.* ⟦< "oll korrect," facetious misspelling of *all correct*⟧ all right; correct —*n.*, *pl.* **OK's** or **O.K.'s** approval —*vt.* **OK'd** or **O.K.'d**, **OK'ing** or **O.K.'ing** to approve or endorse Also **o′kay′**

O·kla·ho·ma (ō′klə hō′mə) state of the SC U.S.; cap. Oklahoma City: abbrev. **OK** **O′kla·ho′man** *adj., n.*

Oklahoma City capital of Oklahoma

o·kra (ō′krə) *n.* ⟦< WAfr name⟧ **1** a plant with sticky green pods **2** the pods, used in soups, stews, etc.

Ok·to·ber·fest (äk tō′bər fest′) *n.* ⟦Ger⟧ a beer-drinking festival held in Germany and elsewhere in the fall

old (ōld) *adj.* **old′er** or **eld′er**, **old′est** or **eld′est** ⟦OE *ald*⟧ **1** having lived or existed for a long time **2** of aged people **3** of a specified age [*two years old*] **4** not new **5** worn out by age or use **6** former **7** experienced [*an old hand*] **8** ancient **9** [*often* **O-**] designating the earliest form of a language [*Old English*] **10** designating the earlier or earliest of two or more [*the Old World*] —*n.* **1** time long past [*days of old*] **2** something old: with *the* —**old′ness** *n.*

Old Church Sla·von·ic (slə vän′ik) the South Slavic language now used only as a liturgical language by Orthodox Slavs: also called **Old Church Slavic** or **Old Bulgarian**

old country the country, esp. in Europe, from which an immigrant came

old·en (ōl′dən) *adj.* [Old Poet.] (of) old

Old English the Germanic language of the Anglo-Saxons, spoken in England from *c.* A.D. 400 to *c.* 1100

old-fash·ioned *adj.* suited to or favoring the styles, ideas, etc. of past times —*n.* [*also* **Old-Fashioned**] a cocktail made with whiskey, bitters, sugar, and fruit

old fogy or **old fogey** *see* FOGY

Old French the French language from *c.* A.D. 800 to *c.* 1550

Old Glory *name for* the flag of the United States

old-growth *adj.* designating or of a forest having very large, very old trees

old guard ⟦transl. < Fr⟧ [*sometimes* **O- G-**] the conservative element of a group, party, etc.

old hat [Slang] old-fashioned or stale

Old High German the High German language before the 1100s

old·ie (ōl′dē) *n.*, *pl.* **-ies** [Inf.] an old song, joke, saying, movie, etc.

old lady [Slang] **1** one's mother **2** one's wife

old-line *adj.* long-established, traditional, conservative, etc.

Old Low German the Low German language before the 1100s

old maid 1 a woman, esp. an older woman, who has never married: now somewhat offensive **2** a prim, prudish, fussy person

old man [Slang] **1** one's father **2** one's husband **3** [*usually* **O- M-**] any man in authority: with *the*

old master 1 any of the great European painters before the 1700s **2** a painting by any of these

Old Norse the Germanic language of the Scandinavians before the 1300s

Old Saxon the Low German dialect of the Saxons before the 900s

old school a group of people who cling to traditional or conservative ideas, methods, etc. —**old′-school′** *adj.*

old·ster (-stər) *n.* [Inf.] an old or elderly person

Old Testament *Christian designation for* the Holy Scriptures of Judaism, the first of the two general divisions of the Christian Bible

old-time *adj.* **1** of past times **2** of long standing

old-tim·er *n.* [Inf.] a long-time resident, employee, member, etc.

old-tim·ey (-tīm′ē) *adj.* [Inf.] reminiscent of the past, usually in a positive way

old-world *adj.* **1** of or from the Eastern Hemisphere, esp. Europe **2** reminiscent of European customs, manners, etc.

o·lé (ō lā′) *interj., n.* ⟦Sp⟧ used to express approval, triumph, joy, etc.

o·le·ag·i·nous (ō′lē aj′i nəs) *adj.* [< L *olea*, olive tree] oily; unctuous

o·le·an·der (ō′lē an′dər) *n.* [ML] a poisonous evergreen shrub with fragrant white, pink, or red flowers and narrow, leathery leaves

o·le·o·mar·ga·rine (ō′lē ō mär′jə rin) *n.* [< L *oleum*, oil + MARGARINE] *former term for* MARGARINE

ol·fac·to·ry (äl fak′tə rē, ôl–) *adj.* [< L *olere*, have a smell + *facere*, make] of the sense of smell

ol·i·gar·chy (äl′i gär′kē) *n., pl.* **-chies** [< Gr *oligos*, few + -ARCHY] 1 government in which ruling power belongs to a few persons 2 a state governed in this way 3 the persons ruling such a state —**ol′i·gar′chic** *adj.*

ol·ive (äl′iv) *n.* [< L *oliva*] 1 *a)* an evergreen tree of S Europe and the Near East *b)* its small, oval fruit, eaten green or ripe as a relish or pressed, when ripe, to extract its oil (**olive oil**) 2 the yellowish-green color of the unripe fruit

olive branch the branch of the olive tree, a symbol of peace

O·lym·pi·a (ō lim′pē ə) capital of Washington

O·lym·pic games (ō lim′pik) *n.* [< *Olympia*, plain in Greece, site of ancient games] an international athletic competition now held every two years, alternating between summer games and winter games: also **O·lym′pics**

O·lym·pus (ō lim′pəs), **Mount** mountain in N Greece: in Greek mythology, the home of the gods —**O·lym′pi·an** (-pē ən) *adj., n.*

om (ōm) *n.* [Sans] Hinduism a word intoned as during meditation

O·ma·ha (ō′mə hô) city in E Nebraska

O·man (ō män′) country on the SE coast of Arabia —**O·man′i** (-ē) *adj., n.*

om·buds·man (äm′bədz mən) *n., pl.* **-men** (-mən) [Swed < *ombud*, a deputy] a public official appointed to investigate citizens' complaints

o·me·ga (ō mä′gə) *n.* [Gr *ō* + *mega*, great, i.e., long o: see OMICRON] the 24th & final letter of the Greek alphabet (Ω, ω)

om·e·let or **om·e·lette** (äm′lət) *n.* [< L *lamella*, small plate] eggs beaten and cooked in a pan, often with cheese, meat, vegetables, etc.

o·men (ō′mən) *n.* [L] a thing or happening supposed to foretell a future event, either good or evil

om·i·cron (äm′i krän′, ō′mi–) *n.* [Gr *o mikron*, small o: see OMEGA] the 15th letter of the Greek alphabet (O, o)

om·i·nous (äm′ə nəs) *adj.* of or serving as an evil omen; threatening —**om′i·nous·ly** *adv.*

o·mis·sion (ō mish′ən) *n.* 1 an omitting 2 something omitted

o·mit (ō mit′) *vt.* **o·mit′ted**, **o·mit′ting** [< L *omittere* < *ob-* (see OB-) + *mittere*, send] 1 to fail to include; leave out 2 to fail to do; neglect

omni- [L < *omnis*, all] *combining form* all, everywhere

om·ni·bus (äm′ni bəs) *n., pl.* **-bus·es** [< L, for all] 1 BUS 2 a collection of stories, articles, etc., as on one theme —*adj.* including many things

om·nip·o·tent (äm nip′ə tənt) *adj.* [< L *omnis*, all + *potens*, able] having unlimited ability or authority; all-powerful —**the Omnipotent**, God —**om·nip′o·tence** *n.*

om·ni·pres·ent (äm′ni prez′ənt) *adj.* present in all places at the same time —**om′ni·pres′ence** *n.*

om·nis·cient (äm nish′ənt) *adj.* [< L *omnis*, all + *sciens*, knowing] knowing all things —**the Omniscient** God —**om·nis′cience** *n.*

om·niv·o·rous (äm niv′ə rəs) *adj.* [< L *omnis*, all + *vorare*, devour] 1 eating any sort of food, esp. both animal and vegetable food 2 taking in everything indiscriminately —**om·niv′o·rous·ly** *adv.* —**om·niv′o·rous·ness** *n.*

on (än, ôn) *prep.* [OE] 1 in contact with, supported by, or covering 2 in the surface of [scars on it] 3 *a)* near to [on my left] *b)* having as its location [a house on Main Street] 4 at the time of [on Monday] 5 connected with [on the team] 6 engaged in [on a trip] 7 in a state of [on parole] 8 as a result of [a profit on the sale] 9 in the direction of [light shone on us] 10 through the use of [lived on bread] 11 concerning [an essay on war] 12 onto 13 at the expense of [a drink on the house] 14 [Inf.] using; under the influence of [on drugs] —*adv.* 1 in a situation of contacting, being supported by, or covering 2 in a direction toward [he looked on] 3 forward [move on] 4 without stopping [she sang on] 5 into action or operation [turn on the light] —*adj.* 1 in action or operation [the TV is on] 2 [Slang] performing very well [she is really on today] —**and so on** and more like the preceding —**on and off** intermittently —**on and on** for a long time; continuously —**on to** [Slang] aware of the real nature or meaning of

ON *abbrev.* Ontario

once (wuns) *adv.* [ME *ones*] 1 one time only 2 at any time; ever 3 formerly [a once famous woman] 4 by one degree [a cousin once removed] —*conj.* as soon as [once he is tired, he will quit] —*n.* one time [go this once] —**at once** 1 immediately 2 at the same time —**once (and) for all** conclusively —**once in a while** now and then

once-o·ver *n.* [Inf.] a quick look

on·co·gene (äŋ′kə jēn′) *n.* [< Gr *onkos*, a mass + GENE] a gene that, when activated as by a virus, may cause a normal cell to become cancerous

on·col·o·gy (än käl′ə jē, äŋ–) *n.* [< Gr *onkos*, a mass + -LOGY] the branch of medicine dealing with tumors —**on·col′o·gist** *n.*

on·com·ing (än′kum′iŋ) *adj.* coming nearer in position or time

on·co·vi·rus (äŋ′kə vī′rəs) *n.* a virus that causes cancer

one (wun) *adj.* [OE *an*] 1 being a single thing or unit 2 united [with one accord] 3 a certain but unnamed [take one path or the other, one day last week] 4 the same 5 unique; only [the *one* solution] —*n.* **1** the first and lowest cardinal number; 1; I **2** a single person or thing —*pron.* **1** a certain person or thing **2** any person or thing —**at one** in accord —**one another** each one the other or others; each other —**one by one** individually in succession

one-di·men·sion·al *adj.* **1** *Math.* existing in a single dimension **2** having one dominant aspect, quality, etc. and hence narrow, limited, etc.

O'Neill (ō nēl′), **Eu·gene** (yōō jēn′) 1888-1953; U.S. playwright

one·ness *n.* **1** singleness; unity **2** unity of mind, feeling, etc.

one-on-one *adj., adv.* in direct personal confrontation

on·er·ous (än′ər əs) *adj.* [< L *onus*, a load] burdensome; oppressive

one·self *pron.* a person's own self: also **one's self** —**be oneself 1** to function normally **2** to be natural —**by oneself** alone

one-sid·ed *adj.* **1** on, having, or involving only one side **2** unfair **3** uneven or unequal [a *one-sided* race]

one-stop *adj.* designating of a store, bank, etc. that offers a complete range of goods or services

one·time *adj.* former: also **one′-time′**

one-track *adj.* [Inf.] limited in scope

one-up [Inf.] *adj.* having an advantage (over another) —*vt.* **-upped′, -up′ing** to gain an advantage over

one-up·man·ship (-up′mən ship′) *n.* [Inf.] skill in seizing an advantage over others

one-way *adj.* moving, or allowing movement, in one direction only

on·go·ing *adj.* going on; progressing

on·ion (un′yən) *n.* [< L *unus*, one] **1** a plant of the lily family with an edible bulb **2** this bulb, having a strong, sharp smell and taste

on·ion·skin *n.* a tough, thin, translucent paper

on·line or **on-line** *adj.* **1** designating or of equipment directly connected to and controlled by the central processing unit of a computer **2** connected to a computer network

on·look·er *n.* a spectator

on·ly (ōn′lē) *adj.* [< OE *an*, one + *-lic*, -ly] **1** alone of its or their kind; sole **2** alone in superiority; best —*adv.* **1** and no other; and no more; solely **2** (but) in the end [to meet one crisis, *only* to face another] **3** as recently as —*conj.* [Inf.] except that; but —**only too** very; exceedingly

on·o·mat·o·poe·ia (än′ō mat′ō pē′ə, -mät′-) *n.* [< Gr *onoma*, a name + *poiein*, make] the formation of words by imitating sounds (Ex.: *buzz, thump*)

on·rush *n.* a headlong dash forward

on·set *n.* **1** an attack **2** a start

on·slaught (än′slôt′) *n.* [< Du *slagen*, to strike] a violent attack

On·tar·i·o (än ter′ē ō) **1** province of SC Canada; cap. Toronto: abbrev. **ON 2** Lake smallest of the Great Lakes, between New York & Ontario, Canada —**On·tar′i·an** *adj., n.*

on·to (än′tōō) *prep.* **1** to a position on **2** [Slang] aware of the real meaning or nature of

on·tog·e·ny (än täj′ə nē) *n.* [ult. < Gr *einai*, to be + *-genēs*, born] the development of a single organism from embryo to adult

o·nus (ō′nəs) *n.* [L] **1** a burden, unpleasant duty, etc. **2** blame

on·ward *adv.* toward or at a position ahead; forward: also **on′wards** —*adj.* advancing

on·yx (än′iks) *n.* [< Gr, fingernail] a type of agate with alternate colored layers

oo·dles (ōōd′lz) *pl.n.* [< ?] [Inf.] a great amount; very many

ooze[1] (ōōz) *n.* [OE *wos*, sap] **1** an oozing **2** something that oozes —*vi.* **oozed, ooz′ing** to flow or leak out slowly —*vt.* to give forth (a fluid)

ooze[2] (ōōz) *n.* [OE *wase*] soft mud or slime, as at the bottom of a lake

op- *prefix* OB-: used before *p* [*oppress*]

o·pal (ō′pəl) *n.* [< Sans *úpalaḥ*, (precious) stone] an iridescent mineral of various colors, used esp. as a gemstone —**o·pal·es·cent** (ō′pəl es′ənt) *adj.*

o·paque (ō pāk′) *adj.* [< L *opacus*, shady] **1** not transparent **2** dull or dark **3** hard to understand —**o·pac·i·ty** (ō pas′ə tē) *n.*, **o·paque′ness** *n.* —**o·paque′ly** *adv.*

op art (äp) a style of abstract painting creating optical effects, as the illusion of movement

op. cit. *abbrev.* [L *opere citato*] in the work cited

OPEC (ō′pek′) *n.* Organization of Petroleum Exporting Countries

Op-Ed (äp′ed′) *adj.* [*Op(posite) Ed(itorial page)*] designating or on a page in a newspaper featuring a wide variety of columns, letters, etc.

o·pen (ō′pən) *adj.* [OE] **1** not closed, covered, clogged, or shut **2** not enclosed [*open* fields] **3** spread out; unfolded [an *open* book] **4** having gaps, holes, etc. **5** free to be entered, used, etc. [an *open* meeting] **6** not decided [an *open* question] **7** not closed to new ideas, etc. [an *open* mind] **8** generous **9** free from legal or discriminatory restrictions [*open* season, *open* housing] **10** not sexually or romantically exclusive [*open* marriage] **11** not already taken [the job is *open*] **12** not secret; public **13** frank; candid [an *open* manner] —*vt., vi.* **1** to cause to be, or to become, open **2** to spread out; expand; unfold **3** to begin; start **4** to start operating —**open to 1** willing to receive, discuss, etc. **2** liable to **3** available to —**the open 1** the outdoors **2** public knowledge —**o′pen·er** *n.* —**o′pen·ly** *adv.* —**o′pen·ness** *n.*

open air the outdoors —**o′pen-air′** *adj.*

o·pen-and-shut *adj.* easily decided

o·pen-end·ed (-en′ded) *adj.* unlimited

o·pen-eyed (-īd′) *adj.* with the eyes wide open, as in awe or watchfulness

o·pen-faced *adj.* **1** having a frank, honest face **2** designating a sandwich without a top slice of bread Also **o′pen-face′**

o·pen-hand·ed *adj.* generous

o·pen-heart·ed *adj.* **1** not reserved; frank **2** kindly; generous

o·pen-hearth *adj.* **1** designating or using a furnace with a wide hearth and low roof, for making steel **2** of or relating to the use of an open fireplace, esp. for cooking

o·pen-heart surgery surgery on the heart during which the blood is diverted, circulated, and oxygenated by mechanical means

open house 1 an informal reception at one's home **2** a time when an institution is open to visitors

o·pen·ing *n.* **1** an open place; hole; gap **2** a clearing **3** a beginning **4** start of operations **5** a favorable chance **6** an unfilled job

o·pen-mind·ed *adj.* having a mind open to new ideas; unprejudiced

o·pen·work *n.* ornamental work, as in cloth, with openings in it

op·er·a¹ (äp′ə rə, äp′rə) *n.* ⟦< L, a work⟧ a play having its text set to music and sung to orchestral accompaniment —**op′er·at′ic** (-ə rat′ik) *adj.*

o·pe·ra² (ō′pə rə, äp′ə rə) *n. pl. of* OPUS

op·er·a·ble (äp′ər ə bəl) *adj.* ⟦see OPERATE & -ABLE⟧ **1** able to function **2** that can be treated by surgery

opera glasses a small binocular telescope used in theaters, etc.

op·er·ate (äp′ə rāt′) *vi.* **-at·ed, -at·ing** ⟦< L *operari*, to work⟧ **1** to be in action; act; work **2** to have an effect **3** to perform a surgical operation —*vt.* **1** to put or keep in action **2** to direct; manage

op·er·a·tion (-rā′shən) *n.* ⟦< L *operatio*⟧ **1** the act or method of operating **2** a being in action or at work **3** a process or action that is part of a series in some work **4** any surgical procedure to remedy a physical ailment

op·er·a·tion·al *adj.* **1** of or having to do with the operation of a device, system, process, etc. **2** *a)* that can be used or operated *b)* in use; operating

op·er·a·tive (-rə tiv′, -rāt′iv) *adj.* **1** in operation **2** effective **3** connected with physical work or mechanical action

op·er·a·tor (-rāt′ər) *n.* **1** one who operates a machine [a telephone *operator*] **2** one engaged in commercial or industrial operations **3** [Slang] a clever, persuasive person

op·er·et·ta (äp′ə ret′ə) *n.* ⟦It, dim. of *opera*, OPERA¹⟧ an amusing opera with spoken dialogue between musical numbers

oph·thal·mic (äf thal′mik, äp′-) *adj.* ⟦< Gr *ophthalmos*, the eye⟧ of or involving the eye

oph·thal·mol·o·gy (äf′thal mäl′ə jē, äp′thə-) *n.* ⟦< Gr *ophthalmos*, the eye + -LOGY⟧ the branch of medicine dealing with the eye and its diseases —**oph′thal·mol′o·gist** *n.*

o·pi·ate (ō′pē it) *n.* ⟦ML *opiatum*⟧ **1** a drug containing, or derived from, opium **2** anything that quiets, soothes, or deadens

o·pine (ō pīn′) *vt., vi.* **o·pined′, o·pin′ing** ⟦< L *opinari*, think⟧ to express (an opinion)

o·pin·ion (ə pin′yən) *n.* ⟦< L *opinari*, think⟧ **1** a belief based not on certainty but on what seems true or probable **2** an evaluation, estimation, etc. **3** formal expert judgment

o·pin·ion·at·ed (-āt′id) *adj.* holding obstinately to one's opinions

o·pi·oid (ō′pē oid′) *adj.* designating or of a group of natural or synthetic chemicals that relieve pain in the same way that opiates do —*n.* any such chemical

o·pi·um (ō′pē əm) *n.* ⟦< Gr *opos*, vegetable juice⟧ a narcotic drug prepared from the seed of a certain poppy

o·pos·sum (ə päs′əm) *n.* ⟦< AmInd, white beast⟧ a small, nocturnal, tree-dwelling American marsupial that plays dead when threatened

op·po·nent (ə pō′nənt) *n.* ⟦< L *ob-* (see OB-) + *ponere*, to place⟧ one who opposes, as in a game; adversary

op·por·tune (äp′ər tōōn′) *adj.* ⟦< L *ob-* (see OB-) + *portus*, PORT¹⟧ **1** suitable: said of time **2** well-timed

op·por·tun·ism *n.* the adapting of one's actions, thoughts, etc. to circumstances, as in politics, without regard for principles —**op′por·tun′ist** *n., adj.* —**op′por·tun·is′tic** (-tōō nis′tik) *adj.*

op·por·tu·ni·ty (äp′ər tōō′nə tē) *n., pl.* **-ties 1** a combination of circumstances favorable for the purpose **2** a good chance, as to advance oneself

op·pose (ə pōz′) *vt.* **-posed′, -pos′ing** ⟦< L *ob-* (see OB-) + *ponere*, to place⟧ **1** to place opposite **2** to contend with; resist —**op·pos′a·ble** *adj.*

op·po·site (äp′ə zit) *adj.* ⟦< L *ob-* (see OB-) + *ponere*, to place⟧ **1** set against; in a contrary direction: often with *to* **2** entirely different; exactly contrary —*n.* anything opposed —*prep.* across from —**op′po·site·ly** *adv.*

opposite number one whose position, rank, etc. parallels another's in a different place or organization

op·po·si·tion (-zish′ən) *n.* **1** an opposing **2** resistance, contrast, hostility, etc. **3** *a)* one that opposes *b)* [*often* O-] a political party opposing the party in power

op·press (ə pres′) *vt.* ⟦< L *ob-* (see OB-) + *premere*, to press⟧ **1** to weigh heavily on the mind of; worry **2** to keep down by the cruel or unjust use of authority —**op·pres′sor** *n.*

op·pres·sion (ə presh′ən) *n.* **1** an oppressing or being oppressed **2** a thing that oppresses **3** physical or mental distress

op·pres·sive (ə pres′iv) *adj.* **1** causing discomfort **2** tyrannical **3** distressing —**op·pres′sive·ly** *adv.*

op·pro·bri·ous (ə prō′brē əs) *adj.* expressing opprobrium; abusive

op·pro·bri·um (-əm) *n.* ⟦< L *ob-* (see OB-) + *probrum*, a disgrace⟧ **1** the disgrace attached to shameful conduct **2** contempt for something regarded as inferior

opt (äpt) *vi.* 〚< L *optare*, to wish〛 to make a choice: often with *for* —**opt out (of)** to choose not to be or continue in (some activity, organization, etc.)

op·tic (äp′tik) *adj.* 〚< Gr *ōps*, an eye〛 of the eye or sense of sight

op·ti·cal (äp′ti kəl) *adj.* **1** of the sense of sight; visual **2** of optics **3** for aiding vision —**op′ti·cal·ly** *adv.*

optical disc (*or* **disk**) any disk on which data, as computer files or music, is stored in the form of microscopic pits to be read by a laser

op·ti·cian (äp tish′ən) *n.* one who makes or sells eyeglasses, etc.

op·tics (äp′tiks) *n.* **1** the branch of physics dealing with light and vision **2** [Slang] the way a situation, actions, etc., appears to the public

op·ti·mism (äp′tə miz′əm) *n.* 〚< L *optimus*, best〛 **1** the doctrine or belief that good ultimately prevails over evil **2** the tendency to take the most hopeful view of matters —**op′ti·mist** *n.* —**op′ti·mis′tic** *adj.* —**op′ti·mis′ti·cal·ly** *adv.*

op·ti·mum (-məm) *n.,* pl. **-mums** *or* **-ma** (-mə) 〚see prec.〛 the best or most favorable degree, condition, etc. —*adj.* most favorable; best: also **op′ti·mal** (-məl)

op·tion (äp′shən) *n.* 〚< L *optare*, to wish〛 **1** a choosing; choice **2** the right of choosing **3** something that is or can be chosen **4** the right to buy, sell, or lease at a fixed price within a specified time —**op′tion·al** *adj.*

op·tom·e·try (äp räm′ə trē) *n.* 〚< Gr *optikos*, optic + *metron*, a measure〛 the profession of testing and examining the eyes and prescribing glasses to correct vision problems —**op·tom′e·trist** *n.*

op·u·lent (äp′yōō lənt, -yə-) *adj.* 〚< L *ops*, riches〛 **1** very wealthy **2** abundant —**op′u·lence** *n.*

o·pus (ō′pəs) *n.,* pl. **o·pe·ra** (ō′pə rə, äp′ə rə) *or* **o′pus·es** 〚L, a work〛 **1** a creative work, as of composition **2** any of the numbered musical works of a composer

or (ôr) *conj.* 〚OE *oththe*〛 a coordinating conjunction introducing: *a*) an alternative [red *or* blue] or the last in a series of choices *b*) a synonymous word or phrase [oral, *or* spoken]

OR *abbrev.* Oregon

-or (ər, ôr) 〚< L〛 *suffix* a person or thing that (does a specified thing) [*inventor*]

or·a·cle (ôr′ə kəl) *n.* 〚< L *orare*, pray〛 **1** among the ancient Greeks and Romans, *a*) the place where, or medium by which, deities were consulted *b*) the revelation of a medium or priest **2** *a*) a person of great knowledge *b*) statements of such a person —**o·rac·u·lar** (ō rak′yōō lər) *adj.*

o·ral (ôr′əl) *adj.* 〚< L *os*, the mouth〛 **1** uttered; spoken **2** of or near the mouth —**o′ral·ly** *adv.*

oral history 1 the gathering of personal recollections, esp. in recorded interviews **2** a historical account based on this

or·ange (ôr′inj, är′-) *n.* 〚< Sans *naranga*〛 **1** a round, edible, reddish-yellow citrus fruit, with a sweet, juicy pulp **2** the evergreen tree it grows on **3** reddish yellow

or·ange·ade *n.* a drink made of orange juice, water, and sugar

o·rang·u·tan (ō raŋ′ōō tan′,-taŋ′) *n.* 〚< Malay *oraṅ*, man + *utan*, forest〛 an ape of Borneo and Sumatra with shaggy, reddish-brown hair and very long arms

o·rate (ō rāt′, ôr′āt′) *vi.* **-rat′ed, -rat′ing** to make an oration; speak in a pompous or bombastic way

o·ra·tion (ō rā′shən, ô-) *n.* 〚< L *orare*, speak〛 a formal speech, esp. one given at a ceremony

or·a·tor (ôr′ət ər, är′-) *n.* an eloquent public speaker

or·a·to·ri·o (ôr′ə tôr′ē ō′) *n.,* pl. **-os′** 〚It, small chapel〛 a long, dramatic musical work, usually on a religious theme, sung but not acted out

or·a·to·ry (ôr′ə tôr′ē, är′-) *n.,* pl. **-ries** 〚< L *oratoria*〛 skill in public speaking —**or′a·tor′i·cal** *adj.*

orb (ôrb) *n.* 〚L *orbis*, a circle〛 **1** a sphere, esp. a celestial body, as the sun or moon **2** a sphere topped with a cross: a symbol of royal power

or·bit (ôr′bit) *n.* 〚< L *orbis*, a circle〛 **1** the path of a celestial body during its revolution around another **2** the path of an artificial satellite or spacecraft around a celestial body **3** the sphere of influence, as of a nation —*vi.,* *vt.* to move in, or put into, an orbit —**or′bit·al** *adj.*

or·ca (ôr′kə) *n.* 〚L〛 KILLER WHALE

or·chard (ôr′chərd) *n.* 〚OE *ortgeard*〛 **1** land for growing fruit trees **2** the trees

or·ches·tra (ôr′kis trə, -kes′-) *n.* 〚< Gr *orcheisthai*, to dance〛 **1** the space in front of a theater stage, where the musicians sit: in full **orchestra pit 2** the seats on the main floor of a theater **3** *a*) a group of musicians playing together *b*) their instruments —**or·ches′tral** (-kes′trəl) *adj.*

or·ches·trate (-trāt′) *vt., vi.* **-trat′ed, -trat′ing 1** to arrange (music) for an orchestra **2** to coordinate or arrange (something) —**or′ches·tra′tion** *n.*

or·chid (ôr′kid) *n.* 〚< Gr *orchis*, testicle: from the shape of the roots〛 **1** a perennial plant having flowers with three petals, one of which is lip-shaped **2** this flower **3** pale purple

or·dain (ôr dān′) *vt.* 〚< L *ordo*, an order〛 **1** to decree; establish; enact **2** to invest with the office of minister, priest, or rabbi —**or·dain′ment** *n.*

or·deal (ôr dēl′) *n.* 〚OE *ordal*〛 any difficult or painful experience

or·der (ôr′dər) *n.* 〚< L *ordo*, straight row〛 **1** social position **2** a state of peace; orderly conduct **3** arrangement of things or events; series **4** a definite plan; system **5** a military, monastic, or social brotherhood **6** a condition in which everything is in its place and working properly **7** condition in general [in working *order]* 8 an authoritative command, instruction, etc. 9 a class; kind 10 an established method, as of conduct in meetings, etc. 11 *a)* a request to supply something [an *order* for books] *b)* the goods supplied 12 [*usually pl.*] the position of ordained minister, priest, etc. [to take holy *orders*] —*vt., vi.* 1 to put or keep (things) in order; arrange 2 to command 3 to request (something to be supplied) —**in (or out of) order 1** in (or not in) proper position **2** in (or not in) good condition **3** in (or not in) accordance with the rules —**in order that** so that —**in order to** for the purpose of —**in short order** quickly —**on the order of** similar to —**to order** in accordance with the buyer's specifications

or·der·ly *adj.* **1** neat or tidy **2** well-behaved —*n., pl.* **-lies 1** an enlisted person assigned to perform personal services for an officer **2** a hospital attendant —**or′der·li·ness** *n.*

or·di·nal (ôrd′'n əl) *adj.* [< L *ordo,* order] expressing order in a series —*n.* any number showing order in a series (e.g., first, tenth): in full **ordinal number**

or·di·nance (ôrd′'n əns) *n.* [< L *ordo,* an order] a statute or regulation, esp. a municipal one

or·di·nar·i·ly (ôrd′'n er′ə lē) *adv.* usually; as a rule

or·di·nar·y (ôrd′'n er′ē) *adj.* [< L *ordo,* an order] **1** customary; usual **2** familiar; unexceptional; common —**out of the ordinary** unusual

or·di·nate (ôrd′'n it, -āt′) *n.* [< L (*linea*) *ordinate (applicata),* line applied in ordered manner] *Math.* the vertical distance of a point from a horizontal axis

or·di·na·tion (ôrd′'n ā′shən) *n.* an ordaining or being ordained to the clergy

ord·nance (ôrd′nəns) *n.* [< ORDINANCE] **1** artillery **2** all military weapons, ammunition, etc.

or·dure (ôr′jər) *n.* [< L *horridus,* horrid] dung

ore (ôr) *n.* [OE *ar,* brass] a natural combination of minerals, esp. one from which a metal or metals can be profitably extracted

o·reg·a·no (ô reg′ə nō, ə-) *n.* [< Sp < Gr *origanon*] an herb of the mint family, with fragrant leaves used for seasoning

Or·e·gon (ôr′i gən, -gän′) NW coastal state of the U.S.; cap. Salem: abbrev. OR —**Or′e·go′ni·an** (-gō′nē ən) *adj., n.*

or·gan (ôr′gən) *n.* [< Gr *organon,* an implement] **1** *a)* a keyboard musical instrument with sets of graduated pipes through which compressed air is passed, causing sound by vibration *b)* any keyboard musical instrument producing similar sounds **2** in animals and plants, a part adapted to perform a specific function **3** a means for performing some action **4** a means of communicating ideas, as a periodical

or·gan·dy or **or·gan·die** (ôr′gən dē) *n., pl.* **-dies** [Fr *organdi*] a very sheer, crisp cotton fabric

or·gan·elle (ôr′gə nel′) *n.* [< L *organum,* tool

+ dim. of *-ellus*] a discrete structure within a cell, as a chloroplast, having specialized functions, a distinctive chemical composition, etc.

or·gan·ic (ôr gan′ik) *adj.* **1** of or having to do with a bodily organ **2** inherent; inborn **3** systematically arranged **4** designating or of any chemical compound containing carbon **5** of, like, or derived from living organisms **6** grown without synthetic fertilizers, pesticides, etc. —**or·gan′i·cal·ly** *adv.*

or·gan·ism (ôr′gə niz′əm) *n.* any living thing

or·gan·ist *n.* an organ player

or·gan·i·za·tion (ôr′gə ni zā′shən) *n.* **1** an organizing or being organized **2** any organized group, as a club —**or′gan·i·za′tion·al** *adj.*

or·gan·ize (ôr′gə nīz′) *vt.* **-ized′, -iz′ing 1** to provide with an orderly structure or arrangement **2** to arrange for **3** to institute; establish **4** to persuade to join a cause, group, etc. —*vi.* to become organized —**or′gan·iz′er** *n.*

or·gan·za (ôr gan′zə) *n.* a thin, stiff fabric of rayon, silk, etc.

or·gasm (ôr′gaz′əm) *n.* [< Gr *organ,* to swell] the climax of a sexual act —**or·gas′mic** *adj.*

or·gy (ôr′jē) *n., pl.* **-gies** [< Gr *orgia,* secret rites] **1** a wild party, esp. with sexual activity **2** unrestrained indulgence in any activity

o·ri·el (ôr′ē əl, ôr′-) *n.* [< ML *oriolum,* porch] a bay window resting on a bracket or a corbel

o·ri·ent (ôr′ē ənt; *for v.,* -ent′, -ənt) *n.* [< L *oriri,* arise: used of the rising sun] [Old Poet.] the east —*vt.* to adjust (oneself) to a particular situation, with regard to direction or position, etc. —**the Orient** the East, or Asia; esp. the Far East

O·ri·en·tal (-ent′'l) *adj.* of the Far East or its people, etc.: now often regarded as a term of disparagement

o·ri·en·ta·tion (ôr′ē en tā′shən) *n.* **1** an orienting or being oriented **2** position, esp. relative to the points of the compass **3** familiarization with and adjustment to a new situation **4** SEXUAL ORIENTATION

or·i·fice (ôr′ə fis, är′-) *n.* [< L *os,* a mouth + *facere,* make] a mouth of a tube, cavity, etc.; opening

orig *abbrev.* **1** origin **2** original **3** originally

o·ri·ga·mi (ôr′ə gä′mē) *n.* [Jpn] the Japanese art of folding paper to form flowers, animals, etc.

or·i·gin (ôr′ə jin, är′-) *n.* [< L *oriri,* to rise] **1** a coming into existence or use; beginning **2** parentage; birth **3** source; root; cause

o·rig·i·nal (ə rij′i nəl) *adj.* **1** first; earliest **2** never having been before; new; novel **3** capable of creating something new **4** that from which copies are made —*n.* **1** a primary type that has given rise to varieties **2** an original work, as of art or literature —**o·rig′i·nal′i·ty** (-nal′ə tē) *n.* —**o·rig′i·nal·ly** *adv.*

o·rig·i·nate (-nāt′) *vt.* **-nat′ed, -nat′ing** to bring into being; esp., to invent —*vi.* to begin; start —**o·rig′i·na′tion** *n.* —**o·rig′i·na′tor** *n.*

O-ring (ô′riŋ′) *n.* a ring-shaped seal of rubber, plastic, etc., used to prevent leaks

o·ri·ole (ôr′ē ōl′) *n.* ‖< L *aurum,* gold‖ a bright-orange and black American bird that builds a hanging nest

O·ri·on (ō rī′ən) *n.* a very bright equatorial constellation

Or·lon (ôr′län′) *trademark for* a synthetic acrylic fiber similar to nylon, or a fabric made from this fiber

or·mo·lu (ôr′mə loō′) *n.* ‖Fr *or moulu,* ground gold‖ a copper and tin alloy used to imitate gold

or·na·ment (ôr′nə mənt; *for v.,* -ment′) *n.* ‖< L *ornare,* adorn‖ 1 anything that adorns; decoration 2 one who is a source of pride, honor, etc., as to a group —*vt.* to decorate —**or′na·men′tal** *adj.* —**or′na·men·ta′tion** *n.*

or·nate (ôr nāt′) *adj.* ‖< L *ornare,* adorn‖ heavily ornamented; showy —**or·nate′ly** *adv.* —**or·nate′ness** *n.*

or·ner·y (ôr′nər ē) *adj.* ‖< ORDINARY‖ [Inf.] 1 mean; nasty 2 obstinate —**or′ner·i·ness** *n.*

or·ni·thol·o·gy (ôr′nə thäl′ə jē) *n.* ‖< Gr *ornis,* bird + -LOGY‖ the branch of zoology dealing with birds —**or′ni·thol′o·gist** *n.*

o·ro·tund (ôr′ə tund′) *adj.* ‖< L *os,* mouth + *rotundas,* round‖ 1 resonant: said of the voice 2 bombastic or pompous

or·phan (ôr′fən) *n.* ‖< Gr *orphanos* ‖ a child whose parents are dead —*adj.* 1 being an orphan 2 of or for orphans —*vt.* to cause to become an orphan

or·phan·age (-ij) *n.* an institution that is a home for orphans

Or·phe·us (ôr′fē əs) *n.* Gr. Myth. a poet-musician with magic musical powers

or·ris (ôr′is, är′-) *n.* ‖< Gr *iris, iris* ‖ a European iris, esp. one with a root (**or′ris·root′**) pulverized for perfumery, etc.

ortho- ‖< Gr *orthos,* straight‖ *combining form* 1 straight [*orthodontics*] 2 proper; correct [*orthodox*] Also **orth-**

or·tho·don·tics (ôr′thə dän′tiks) *n.* ‖< prec. + Gr *odōn,* tooth + -ICS‖ the branch of dentistry concerned with correcting tooth irregularities: also **or′tho·don′tia** (-dän′shə, -shē ə) —**or′tho·don′tist** *n.*

or·tho·dox (ôr′thə däks′) *adj.* ‖< Gr *orthos,* straight + *doxa,* opinion‖ conforming to the usual beliefs or established doctrines; approved or conventional —**or′tho·dox′y** *n., pl.* **-ies**

or·thog·ra·phy (ôr thäg′rə fē) *n., pl.* **-phies** ‖< Gr: see ORTHO- & -GRAPHY‖ 1 correct spelling 2 spelling as a subject for study —**or·tho·graph·ic** (ôr′thə graf′ik) *adj.*

or·tho·pe·dics or **or·tho·pae·dics** (ôr′thə pē′diks) *n.* ‖< Gr *orthos,* straight + *paideia,* training of children‖ the branch of medicine dealing with deformities, diseases, and injuries of the bones, joints, muscles, etc. —**or′tho·pe′dic** *adj.,* **or′tho·pae′dic** —**or′tho·pe′dist** *n.,* **or′tho·pae′dist**

or·thot·ic (ôr thät′ik) *adj.* ‖< ORTH(O)- + -OTIC‖ of or having to do with orthotics [an *orthotic* shoe] —*n.* any brace, support, insert, or other device used in orthotics

or·thot·ics (ôr thät′iks) *n.* the science of developing and fitting orthopedic devices

-o·ry (ôr′ē, ər ē) ‖< L *-orius* ‖ *suffix* 1 of, having the nature of [*sensory*] 2 a place or thing for [*crematory*]

OS *abbrev.* Old Saxon

O·sa·ka (ō sä′kə) seaport in S Honshu, Japan

os·cil·late (äs′ə lāt′) *vi.* -**lat′ed,** -**lat′ing** ‖< L *oscillum,* a swing‖ 1 to swing to and fro 2 to vacillate 3 *Physics* to vary regularly between high and low values: said as of an electric current —**os′cil·la′tion** *n.* —**os′cil·la′tor** *n.*

os·cil·lo·scope (ə sil′ə skōp′) *n.* ‖< L *oscillare,* to swing + -SCOPE‖ an instrument that visually displays an electrical wave on a fluorescent screen

os·cu·late (äs′kyoō lāt′, -kyə-) *vt., vi.* -**lat′ed,** -**lat′ing** ‖< L *osculum,* little mouth‖ to kiss: a facetious usage —**os′cu·la′tion** *n.*

-ose¹ (ōs) ‖Fr < (*gluc)ose*‖ *suffix* 1 a carbohydrate [*sucrose*] 2 the product of a protein hydrolysis

-ose² (ōs) ‖L *-osus*‖ *suffix* full of, like

o·sier (ō′zhər) *n.* ‖< ML *auseria,* willow‖ a willow with branches used for baskets and furniture

-o·sis (ō′sis) ‖< Gr‖ *suffix* 1 condition, action [*hypnosis*] 2 an abnormal or diseased condition [*psychosis*]

Os·lo (äz′lō, äs′-) seaport & capital of Norway

os·mi·um (äz′mē əm) *n.* ‖< Gr *osmē,* odor‖ a very hard, metallic chemical element, used in making pen points and other wear resistant items: symbol, Os; at. no. 76

os·mo·sis (äs mō′sis, äz–) *n.* ‖< Gr *ōsmos,* impulse‖ 1 the tendency of fluids to pass through a membrane so as to equalize concentrations on both sides 2 the movement of fluids through a membrane 3 an apparently effortless absorption of ideas, feelings, etc. —**os·mot′ic** (-mät′ik) *adj.*

os·prey (äs′prē, -prā) *n., pl.* -**preys** ‖< L *os,* a bone + *frangere,* to break‖ a bird of prey that feeds mainly on fish

os·si·fy (äs′ə fī′) *vt., vi.* -**fied′,** -**fy′ing** ‖< L *os,* a bone + -FY‖ 1 to change into bone 2 to fix rigidly in a custom, practice, etc. —**os′si·fi·ca′tion** *n.*

os·ten·si·ble (ä sten′sə bəl) *adj.* ‖< L *ostendere,* to show‖ apparent; seeming —**os·ten′si·bly** *adv.*

os·ten·ta·tion (äs′tən tā′shən) *n.* ‖< L *ostendere,* to show‖ showy display; pretentiousness —**os′ten·ta′tious** *adj.*

osteo- ‖< Gr *osteon,* a bone‖ *combining form* bone or bones

os·te·o·ar·thri·tis (äs′tē ō′är thrīt′is) *n.* ‖prec. + ARTHRITIS‖ a common form of arthritis marked by cartilage degeneration and bone enlargement

os·te·op·a·thy (äs′tē äp′ə thē) *n.* ‖ModL: see OSTEO- & -PATHY‖ a school of medicine and surgery that emphasizes the interrelationship of muscles and bones to other body systems —**os·te·o·path** (äs′tē ə path′) *n.* —**os′te·o·path′ic** *adj.*

os·te·o·po·ro·sis (äs′tē ō′pə rō′sis) *n.* ⟦OSTEO- + L *porus,* a pore + -OSIS⟧ a bone disorder marked by porous, brittle bones

os·to·my (äs′tə mē) *n., pl.* **-mies** any surgery connecting a hollow organ to the outside of the body or to another hollow organ

os·tra·cize (äs′trə sīz′) *vt.* **-cized′, -ciz′ing** ⟦< Gr *ostrakon,* a shell or potsherd (cast as a ballot)⟧ 1 to banish from a group, society, etc. 2 to exclude socially —**os′tra·cism′** (-siz′əm) *n.*

os·trich (äs′trich, ôs′-) *n.* ⟦< L *avis,* bird + *struthio,* ostrich⟧ a large, swift-running, flightless bird of Africa and SW Asia

OT *abbrev.* 1 Old Testament 2 overtime

O·thel·lo (ō thel′ō) *n.* a noble Moor, the title character of a tragedy by Shakespeare

oth·er (uth′ər) *adj.* ⟦OE⟧ 1 being the remaining one or ones [Bill and the *other* boys] 2 different or distinct from that or those referred to or implied [use your *other* foot] 3 additional [he has no *other* coat] —*pron.* 1 the other one 2 some other one [do as *others* do] —*adv.* otherwise [he can't do *other* than go] —**the other day** (or **night,** etc.) on a recent day (or night, etc.)

oth·er·wise *adv.* 1 in another manner; differently [she believes *otherwise*] 2 in all other respects [he is *otherwise* intelligent] 3 in other circumstances [do it now; *otherwise,* you'll forget it] —*adj.* different

oth·er·world·ly *adj.* being apart from earthly interests; spiritual

o·ti·ose (ō′shē ōs′) *adj.* ⟦< L *otium,* leisure⟧ 1 futile 2 useless

Ot·ta·wa (ät′ə wə, -wä′) capital of Canada, in SE Ontario

ot·ter (ät′ər) *n.* ⟦OE *oter*⟧ 1 a furry, carnivorous mammal with a long body and webbed feet 2 its fur

ot·to·man (ät′ə mən) *n.* ⟦Fr *ottomane*⟧ a low, cushioned seat or footstool

ouch (ouch) *interj.* used to express sudden pain

ought (ôt) *v.aux.* used with infinitives and meaning: 1 to be compelled by obligation, duty, or desirability [you *ought* to eat more] 2 to be expected [it *ought* to be over soon]

oui (wē) *adv., interj.* [Fr] yes

Oui·ja (wē′jə, -jē) ⟦< prec. + Ger *ja,* yes⟧ *trademark for* a board with the alphabet and various symbols on it and a sliding pointer: believed by some to convey messages from spirits

ounce (ouns) *n.* ⟦< L *uncia,* a twelfth⟧ 1 a unit of weight, $\frac{1}{16}$ pound avoirdupois or $\frac{1}{12}$ pound troy 2 fluid ounce, $\frac{1}{16}$ pint

our (our) *poss. pronominal adj.* ⟦OE *ure*⟧ of, belonging to, or done by us

ours (ourz) *pron.* that or those belonging to us: poss. form of WE [that book is *ours; ours* are better]

our·selves (our selvz′) *pron.* a form of WE, used as an intensive [we went *ourselves*], as a reflexive [we saw *ourselves* in the mirror], or with the meaning "our true selves" [we are not *ourselves* when we are sick]

-ous (əs) ⟦< L *-osus*⟧ *suffix* having, full of, characterized by [*beauteous*]

oust (oust) *vt.* ⟦< L *ostare,* obstruct⟧ to force out; expel; dispossess

oust·er *n.* an ousting or being ousted

out (out) *adv.* ⟦OE *ut*⟧ 1 away or removed from a place, position, etc. 2 into the open air 3 into existence or activity [disease broke *out*] 4 *a)* to a conclusion [argue it *out*] *b)* completely [tired *out*] 5 into sight or notice [the moon came *out*] 6 from existence or activity [fade *out*] 7 aloud [sing *out*] 8 beyond a regular surface, condition, etc. [stand *out*] 9 into disuse [long skirts went *out*] 10 from a group or stock [pick *out*] 11 [Slang] into unconsciousness 12 *Baseball* in a manner that results in an out [to fly *out*] —*adj.* 1 external: usually in combination [*outpost*] 2 beyond regular limits 3 away from work, etc. 4 in error [*out* in one's estimates] 5 not in use, operation, etc. 6 [Inf.] having suffered a financial loss [*out* twenty dollars] 7 [Inf.] outmoded 8 *Baseball* having failed to get on base —*prep.* 1 out of 2 along, and away from a central location —*n.* 1 something that is out 2 [Slang] a way out; excuse 3 *Baseball* the failure of a player to reach base safely —*vi.* to become known [the truth will *out*] —*vt.* [Inf.] 1 to expose (a person) as being gay, lesbian, or bisexual 2 to publicly reveal an aspect of the identity of (a person) —**on the outs** [Inf.] on unfriendly terms —**out for** trying to get or do —**out of** 1 from inside of 2 beyond 3 from (material, etc.) [made *out of* stone] 4 because of [*out of* spite] 5 having no [*out of* gas] 6 so as to deprive —**out of it** [Slang] 1 mentally dulled 2 not stylish or sophisticated —**out to** trying or determined to

out- *combining form* 1 at or from a point away, outside, etc. [*outpatient*] 2 going away or forth, outward [*outbound*] 3 better or more than [*outdo*]

out·age (out′ij) *n.* an interruption of operation, as of electric power

out-and-out *adj.* thorough

out·back *n.* any remote, sparsely settled region, esp. in Australia

out·bid *vt.* **-bid′, -bid′ding** to bid or offer more than (someone else)

out·board *adj.* outside the hull of a ship or boat [an *outboard* motor]

out·bound *adj.* outward bound

out·break *n.* a breaking out; sudden occurrence, as of disease or rioting

out·build·ing *n.* a structure, as a shed, separate from the main building

out·burst *n.* a sudden release, as of feeling or energy

out·cast *adj.* driven out; rejected —*n.* a person rejected, as by society

out·class *vt.* to surpass

out·come *n.* result; consequence

out·crop *n.* 1 the emergence of a mineral at the earth's surface 2 any rock formation exposed at the surface

out·cry *n.*, *pl.* **-cries'** 1 a crying out 2 a strong objection

out·dat·ed *adj.* no longer current

out·dis·tance *vt.* **-tanced, -tanc·ing** to get ahead of, as in a race

out·do *vt.* **-did', -done', -do'ing** to exceed or surpass —**outdo oneself** to do better than one expected to do

out·door *adj.* 1 being or taking place outdoors 2 of or fond of the outdoors

out·doors *adv.* in or into the open; outside —*n.* any area outside of a building

out·er *adj.* farther out or away

out·er·most *adj.* farthest out

outer space space beyond the earth's atmosphere or beyond the solar system

out·er·wear *n.* garments, as overcoats, worn over the usual clothing

out·field *n. Baseball* 1 the playing area beyond the infield 2 the players (**out'field'ers**) positioned there

out·fit *n.* 1 the equipment used in an activity 2 clothing worn together; ensemble 3 a group associated in an activity —*vt.* **-fit'ted, -fit'ting** to furnish as with an outfit —**out'fit'ter** *n.*

out·flank *vt.* to go around and beyond the flank of (enemy troops)

out·fox *vt.* to outsmart

out·go *n.*, *pl.* **-goes'** that which is paid out; expenditure

out·go·ing *adj.* 1 *a*) leaving *b*) retiring from office 2 sociable, friendly, etc.

out·grow *vt.* **-grew', -grown', -grow'ing** 1 to grow faster or larger than 2 to lose in becoming mature 3 to grow too large for

out·growth *n.* 1 a growing out or that which grows out 2 a result or development

out·guess *vt.* to outwit in anticipating

out·house *n.* a small outdoor structure used as a toilet, having a seat with a hole over a deep pit

out·ing *n.* 1 a pleasure trip 2 an outdoor walk, ride, etc.

out·land·ish (-lan'dish) *adj.* very odd or strange; fantastic; bizarre

out·last *vt.* to endure longer than

out·law *n.* a habitual or notorious criminal —*vt.* to declare illegal

out·lay *n.* 1 a spending (*of* money, etc.) 2 money, etc. spent

out·let *n.* 1 a passage for letting something out 2 a means of expression [an *outlet* for anger] 3 a retail store selling surplus goods, esp. of a single manufacturer, at a discount: in full **outlet store** 4 a point in an electric circuit where a plug can be inserted to connect with a power supply

out·line *n.* 1 a line bounding the limits of an object 2 a sketch showing only contours 3 [*also pl.*] a general plan 4 a systematic summary —*vt.* **-lined', -lin'ing** 1 to draw in outline 2 to give or write the main points of

out·live *vt.* **-lived', -liv'ing** to live or endure longer than; outlast

out·look *n.* 1 the view from a place 2 viewpoint 3 expectation or prospect

out·ly·ing *adj.* relatively far out from a certain point; remote

out·ma·neu·ver or **out·ma·noeu·vre** *vt.* **-vered** or **-vred, -ver·ing** or **-vring** to outwit by maneuvering

out·match *vt.* to be superior to; outdo

out·mod·ed *adj.* no longer in fashion or accepted; obsolete

out·num·ber *vt.* to exceed in number

out-of-date *adj.* no longer in style or use; old-fashioned

out-of-doors *adj.* OUTDOOR — *adv.*, *n.* OUT-DOORS

out-of-the-way *adj.* 1 secluded 2 not common; unusual

out-of-town·er *n.* a visitor from another town or city

out·pa·tient *n.* a patient treated at a hospital, etc. without staying overnight

out·place·ment *n.* assistance in finding a new job, provided to an employee by the employer

out·play *vt.* to play better than

out·post *n.* 1 *Mil. a*) a small group stationed at a distance from the main force *b*) the station occupied by such a group *c*) a foreign base 2 a frontier settlement

out·pour·ing *n.* 1 the action of pouring out 2 that which pours out 3 a release or display of strong feeling

out·put *n.* 1 the work done or amount produced, esp. over a given period 2 information delivered by a computer 3 *Elec.* the useful voltage, current, or power delivered

out·rage *n.* [ult. < L *ultra*, beyond] 1 an extremely vicious or violent act 2 a deep insult or offense 3 great anger, etc. aroused by this —*vt.* **-raged', -rag'ing** 1 to commit an outrage upon or against 2 to cause outrage in

out·ra·geous (-rā'jəs) *adj.* 1 involving or doing great injury or wrong 2 very offensive or shocking —**out'ra'geous·ly** *adv.* —**out'ra'geous·ness** *n.*

out·rank *vt.* to exceed in rank

ou·tré (ōō trā') *adj.* [Fr] 1 exaggerated 2 eccentric; bizarre

out·reach (out'rēch'; for *v.*, also out'rēch') *vt.*, *vi.* to reach farther (than) —*n.* a reaching out —*adj.* designating or of a program extending assistance, services, etc. to people in the community

out·rid·er *n.* 1 a rider on horseback who accompanies a stagecoach, etc. 2 a cowboy riding a range, as to keep cattle from straying 3 a forerunner

out·rig·ger (-rig'ər) *n.* 1 a float rigged out from the side of certain canoes to prevent tipping 2 a canoe of this type

out·right (out'rīt', out'rīt') *adj.* 1 without reservation 2 complete —*adv.* 1 entirely 2 openly 3 at once

out·run *vt.* **-ran', -run', -run'ning** 1 to run faster than 2 to exceed

out·sell *vt.* **-sold', -sell'ing** to sell in greater amounts than

out·set *n.* a setting out; beginning

out·shine *vt.* **-shone′** or **-shined′**, **-shin′ing** 1 to shine brighter or longer than (another) 2 to surpass; excel

out·side (out′sīd′, out′sīd′) *n.* 1 the outer side or part; exterior 2 outward appearance 3 any area not inside —*adj.* 1 of or on the outside; outer 2 extreme [an *outside* estimate] 3 slight [an *outside* chance] —*adv.* 1 on or to the outside 2 outdoors —*prep.* 1 on or to the outer side of 2 beyond the limits of —**outside of 1** outside 2 [Inf.] other than

out·sid·er (out′sīd′ər, out′sīd′ər) *n.* one who is not included in a given group

out·size *n.* an unusually large size —*adj.* unusually large

out·skirts *pl.n.* districts remote from the center, as of a city

out·smart *vt.* to overcome by cunning or cleverness; outwit —**outsmart oneself** to harm oneself by one's own efforts at cunning or cleverness

out·source *vt.* **-sourced′**, **-sourc′ing** to transfer (manufacturing tasks, etc.) to outside contractors, esp. in order to reduce operating costs

out·spo·ken *adj.* 1 unrestrained in speech 2 spoken boldly or candidly

out·spread *adj.* spread out; extended

out·stand·ing *adj.* 1 prominent; distinguished 2 unpaid; uncollected 3 issued and sold: said of stocks and bonds 4 unusually fine, enjoyable, etc.

out·sta·tion *n.* a post or station in a remote or unsettled area

out·stretch *vt.* to stretch out; extend

out·strip *vt.* **-stripped′**, **-strip′ping** 1 to go at a faster pace than 2 to excel; surpass

out·take *n.* a filmed scene, defective recording, etc. not used as or in the final version

out·vote *vt.* **-vot′ed**, **-vot′ing** to defeat in a vote

out·ward *adj.* 1 having to do with the outside; outer 2 clearly apparent 3 away from the interior —*adv.* toward the outside: also **out′wards** —**out′ward·ly** *adv.*

out·wear *vt.* **-wore′**, **-worn′**, **-wear′ing** to outlast

out·weigh *vt.* 1 to weigh more than 2 to be more important than

out·wit *vt.* **-wit′ted**, **-wit′ting** to get the better of by cleverness

o·va (ō′və) *n. pl. of* OVUM

o·val (ō′vəl) *adj.* [< L *ovum*, egg] egg-shaped; elliptical —*n.* anything oval

o·va·ry (ō′və rē) *n.*, *pl.* **-ries** [< L *ovum*, egg] 1 a female reproductive gland producing eggs 2 *Bot.* the enlarged, hollow part of the pistil, containing ovules —**o·var·i·an** (ō ver′ ē ən) *adj.*

o·vate (ō′vāt′) *adj.* egg-shaped; oval

o·va·tion (ō vā′shən) *n.* [< L *ovare*, celebrate a triumph] enthusiastic applause or an enthusiastic public welcome

ov·en (uv′ən) *n.* [OE *ofen*] a heated compartment or receptacle for baking, roasting, etc.

ov·en·proof *adj.* able to withstand the high temperatures of an oven without being damaged

o·ver (ō′vər) *prep.* [OE *ofer*] 1 *a*) in, at, or to a position above *b*) across and down from [fell *over* a cliff] 2 so as to cover [shutters *over* the windows] 3 upon [to cast a spell *over* someone] 4 above in authority, power, etc. 5 on or to the other side of [fly *over* the lake] 6 throughout [*over* the whole city] 7 during [*over* the years] 8 more than [*over* ten cents] 9 in preference to 10 concerning —*adv.* 1 *a*) above or across *b*) across the edge 2 more [three hours or *over*] 3 from start to finish [think it *over*] 4 *a*) from an upright position [to fall *over*] *b*) upside down [turn the cup *over*] 5 again [do it *over*] 6 at, to, or in a specified place [*over* in Spain] 7 from one belief, etc. to another [win him *over*] —*adj.* 1 upper, outer, superior, excessive, etc. [*overseer*] 2 finished; past 3 having reached the other side 4 [Inf.] as a surplus; extra

over- *combining form* 1 above in position, rank, etc. [*overlord*] 2 passing across or beyond [*overrun*] 3 excessively [*oversell*] The list below includes some common compounds formed with *over-* that can be understood if "too much" or "excessively" is added to the meaning of the base word:

overabundance	overgenerous
overactive	overheat
overambitious	overindulge
overanxious	overindulgence
overbid	overload
overburden	overpay
overcautious	overpopulate
overconfident	overproduce
overcook	overproduction
overcritical	overrefined
overcrowd	overripe
overdevelop	oversell
overeager	oversensitive
overeat	overspecialize
overemphasize	overspend
overenthusiastic	overstimulate
overexercise	overstock
overexert	overstrict
overexpose	oversupply
overextend	overtire

o·ver·a·chieve *vi.* **-chieved′**, **-chiev′ing** 1 to do better, as in school, than expected 2 to drive oneself to reach unreasonable goals —**o′ver·a·chieve′ment** *n.* —**o′ver·a·chiev′er** *n.*

o·ver·act *vt.*, *vi.* to act (a dramatic role) with exaggeration

o·ver·age¹ (ō′vər āj′) *adj.* over the age fixed as a standard

o·ver·age² (ō′vər ij) *n.* [OVER + -AGE] a surplus or excess

o·ver·all (ō′vər ôl′, ō′vər ôl′) *adj.* 1 from end to end 2 including everything; total —*adv.* 1 from end to end 2 in general

o·ver·alls (-ôlz′) *pl.n.* loose trousers extending up over the chest, worn, usually over other clothing, to protect against dirt

o·ver·arch·ing *adj.* including or linking all that is within its scope [an *overarching* theory]

o·ver·awe *vt.* **-awed′, -aw′ing** to overcome or subdue by inspiring awe

o·ver·bal·ance *vt.* **-anced, -anc·ing** OUT-WEIGH

o·ver·bear·ing *adj.* arrogant; domineering

o·ver·bite *n.* a dental condition in which the upper incisors and canines project over the lower ones to an abnormal extent

o·ver·blown (-blōn′) *adj.* **1** overdone; excessive **2** pompous or bombastic

o·ver·board *adv.* from a ship into the water —**go overboard** [Inf.] to go to extremes

o·ver·book *vt., vi.* to issue more reservations for (a flight, hotel, etc.) than can be accommodated

o·ver·cast *adj.* cloudy; dark: said of the sky

o·ver·charge (ō′vər chärj′; *also, and for n. always,* ō′vər chärj′) *vt., vi.* **-charged′, -charg′ing 1** to charge too high a price (to) **2** to overload —*n.* **1** an excessive charge **2** too full a load

o·ver·cloud *vt., vi.* to make or become cloudy, gloomy, etc.

o·ver·coat *n.* a heavy coat worn over the usual clothing for warmth

o·ver·come *vt.* **-came′, -come′, -com′ing 1** to get the better of in competition, etc. **2** to master, prevail over, or surmount —*vi.* to win

o·ver·de·ter·mine *vt.* **-mined, -min·ing** to bring about through many causes or factors

o·ver·do *vt.* **-did′, -done′, -do′ing 1** to do too much **2** to exaggerate **3** to overcook —*vi.* to exhaust oneself by doing too much

o·ver·dose (ō′vər dōs′; *for v. also* ō′vər dōs′) *n.* too large a dose —*vi.* **dosed′, dos′ing** to take too large an amount of a narcotic, etc.

o·ver·draw *vt.* **-drew′, -drawn′, -draw′ing** to draw on in excess of the amount available —**o′ver·draft′** *n.*

o·ver·dress *vt., vi.* **1** to dress too warmly **2** to dress too showily or formally

o·ver·dub *n.* a recording of sounds, music, etc. superimposed on another recording — *vt., vi.* **-dubbed′, -dub′bing** to add (sounds, music, etc.) to (a recording)

o·ver·due *adj.* past the time for payment, arrival, etc.

o·ver·es·ti·mate *vt.* **-mat′ed, -mat′ing** to set too high an estimate on or for

o·ver·flight *n.* the flight of an aircraft over a foreign territory, as in reconnaissance

o·ver·flow (ō′vər flō′; *also, and for n. always,* ō′vər flō′) *vt.* **1** to flow across; flood **2** to flow over the brim of —*vi.* **1** to run over **2** to be superabundant —*n.* **1** an overflowing **2** the amount that overflows **3** an outlet for overflowing liquids

o·ver·grow *vt.* **-grew′, -grown′, -grow′ing** to overspread with foliage so as to cover —*vi.* to grow too fast or beyond normal size —**o′ver·grown′** *adj.* —**o′ver·growth′** *n.*

o·ver·hand *adj., adv.* with the hand raised above the elbow or the arm above the shoulder

o·ver·hang (ō′vər haŋ′; *also, and for n. always,* ō′vər haŋ′) *vt., vi.* **-hung′, -hang′ing** to hang over or project beyond (something) —*n.* the projection of one thing over or beyond another

o·ver·haul (ō′vər hôl′; *also, and for n. always,* ō′vər hôl′) *vt.* **1** *a)* to check thoroughly for needed repairs *b)* to restore (a motor, etc.) to good working order **2** to catch up with —*n.* an overhauling

o·ver·head (ō′vər hed′; *for adv.* ō′vər hed′) *adj.* **1** above the head **2** in the sky **3** on a higher level, with reference to related objects —*n.* the general, continuing costs of a business, as of rent, maintenance, etc. —*adv.* above the head; aloft

o·ver·hear *vt.* **-heard′, -hear′ing** to hear (something spoken or a speaker) without the speaker's knowledge or intention

o·ver·joyed *adj.* feeling great joy

o·ver·kill *n.* much more of something than is necessary, appropriate, etc.

o·ver·land (-land′, -lənd) *adv., adj.* by, on, or across land

o·ver·lap (ō′vər lap′; *also, and for n. always,* ō′vər lap′) *vt., vi.* **-lapped′, -lap′ping** to extend over a part of (something) so as to coincide with this part —*n.* an overlapping part or amount

o·ver·lay *vt.* **-laid′, -lay′ing 1** to lay or spread over **2** to cover, as with a decorative layer

o·ver·lie *vt.* **-lay′, -lain′, -ly′ing** to lie on or over

o·ver·look (ō′vər look′; *for n.* ō′vər look′) *vt.* **1** to look at from above **2** to give a view of from above **3** *a)* to fail to notice *b)* to ignore; neglect **4** to excuse —*n.* a height from which to view surroundings

o·ver·lord *n.* person having great authority over others

o·ver·ly *adv.* too or too much

o·ver·mas·ter *vt.* to overcome; subdue

o·ver·much *adj., adv., n.* too much

o·ver·night (ō′vər nīt′, ō′vər nīt′) *adv.* **1** during the night **2** suddenly —*adj.* **1** done or going on during the night **2** staying through the night [an *overnight* guest] **3** of or for a brief trip [an *overnight* bag]

o·ver·pass *n.* a bridge, etc. over a road, railway, etc.

o·ver·play *vt.* to overact, overdo, or overemphasize

o·ver·pow·er *vt.* to get the better of; subdue or overwhelm —**o′ver·pow′er·ing** *adj.*

o·ver·price *vt.* **-priced′, -pric′ing** to offer for sale at too high a price

o·ver·pro·tect *vt.* to protect more than necessary, as by exercising control over (one's child, etc.) in trying to shield from hurt, disappointment, etc.

o·ver·qual·i·fied *adj.* having more knowledge, education, etc. than needed for a particular job

o·ver·rate *vt.* **-rat′ed, -rat′ing** to rate or estimate too highly

o·ver·reach *vt.* to reach beyond or above —*vi.*

to attempt too much —**overreach oneself** to fail because of trying to do too much

o·ver·re·act *vi.* to react in an overly emotional way

o·ver·ride *vt.* **-rode′, -rid′den, -rid′ing 1** to prevail over **2** to disregard or nullify

o·ver·rule *vt.* **-ruled′, -rul′ing 1** to set aside or decide against by virtue of higher authority; annul; reverse **2** to prevail over

o·ver·run *vt.* **-ran′, -run′, -run′ning 1** to spread out over so as to cover **2** to swarm over, as vermin do **3** to extend beyond (certain limits)

o·ver·seas *adv.* over or beyond the sea —*adj.* **1** foreign **2** over or across the sea

o·ver·see *vt.* **-saw′, -seen′, -see′ing** to supervise; superintend —**o′ver·se′er** (-sē′ ər) *n.*

o·ver·sexed (-sekst′) *adj.* having excessive sexual drive or interest in sex

o·ver·shad·ow *vt.* **1** *a)* to cast a shadow over *b)* to darken **2** to be more important than by comparison

o·ver·shoe *n.* a boot of rubber, etc. worn over the regular shoe to protect against water, mud, cold, etc.

o·ver·shoot *vt.* **-shot′, -shoot′ing 1** to shoot or pass beyond (a target, mark, etc.) **2** to exceed

o·ver·sight *n.* **1** supervision **2** a careless mistake or omission

o·ver·sim·pli·fy *vt., vi.* **-fied′, -fy′ing** to simplify to the point of distortion —**o′ver·sim′pli·fi·ca′tion** *n.*

o·ver·size *adj.* **1** too large **2** larger than the usual Also **o′ver·sized′**

o·ver·sleep *vi.* **-slept′, -sleep′ing** to sleep longer than intended

o·ver·spread *vt.* **-spread′, -spread′ing** to spread or cover over

o·ver·state *vt.* **-stat′ed, -stat′ing** to exaggerate —**o′ver·state′ment** *n.*

o·ver·stay *vt.* to stay beyond the time or limit of

o·ver·step *vt.* **-stepped′, -step′ping** to go beyond the limits of

o·ver·strung *adj.* high-strung; tense

o·ver·stuff *vt.* **1** to stuff with too much of something **2** to upholster with deep stuffing

o·vert (ō vurt′, ō′vurt′) *adj.* [< L *aperire,* to open] not hidden; apparent; open —**o·vert′ly** *adv.*

o·ver·take *vt.* **-took′, -tak′en, -tak′ing 1** to catch up with **2** to come upon suddenly

o·ver·tax *vt.* **1** to tax too heavily **2** to make excessive demands on

o·ver-the-count·er *adj.* **1** designating or of securities sold directly to buyers **2** sold legally without prescription: said of some drugs

o·ver-the-top *adj.* outrageously or ridiculously excessive

o·ver·throw (ō′vər thrō′; *also & for n.* ō′ vər thrō′) *vt.* **-threw′, -thrown′, -throw′ ing 1** to overcome; conquer **2** to throw beyond —*n.* **1** an overthrowing or being overthrown **2** destruction; end

o·ver·time *n.* **1** time beyond the established limit, as of working hours **2** pay for work done in such time —*adj., adv.* of, for, or during overtime

o·ver·tone *n.* **1** a faint, higher tone accompanying a fundamental tone produced by a musical instrument **2** an implication; nuance: *usually used in pl.*

o·ver·ture (ō′vər chər) *n.* [< L *apertura,* opening] **1** an introductory proposal or offer **2** *a)* a musical introduction to an opera, etc. *b)* an independent composition resembling this

o·ver·turn *vt.* **1** to turn over **2** to conquer —*vi.* to tip over; capsize

o·ver·ween·ing (-wēn′iŋ) *adj.* [< OE *ofer,* over + *wenan,* to think] **1** arrogant **2** excessive

o·ver·weight (ō′vər wāt′, ō′vər wāt′) *adj.* above the normal or allowed weight

o·ver·whelm *vt.* **1** to pour down upon and bury beneath **2** to crush; overpower —**o′ver·whelm′ing** *adj.*

o·ver·work (ō′vər wurk′, ō′vər wurk′) *vt.* to work or use to excess —*vi.* to work too hard or too long —*n.* severe or burdensome work

o·ver·wrought (ō′vər rôt′) *adj.* **1** very nervous or excited **2** too elaborate

Ov·id (äv′id) 43 B.C.–A.D. 17?; Rom. poet

o·vi·duct (ō′vi dukt′, äv′i-) *n.* [< L *ovum,* egg + DUCT] a tube through which the ova pass from an ovary to the uterus or to the outside of the body

o·vip·a·rous (ō vip′ə rəs) *adj.* [< L *ovum,* egg + *parere,* to bear] producing eggs which hatch after leaving the female's body

o·void (ō′void′) *adj.* [< L *ovum,* egg + -OID] egg-shaped —*n.* anything ovoid

ov·u·late (äv′yə lāt′) *vi.* **-lat′ed, -lat′ing** [< L *ovum,* egg] to produce and discharge ova from the ovary —**ov′u·la′tion** *n.*

ov·ule (äv′yōōl′, ō′vyōōl′) *n.* [< L *ovum,* egg] a small egg or seed, esp. one in an early stage of development —**ov′u·lar** *adj.*

o·vum (ō′vəm) *n., pl.* **o·va** (ō′və) [L, egg] a mature female germ cell

ow (ou) *interj.* a cry of pain

owe (ō) *vt.* **owed, ow′ing** [OE *agan,* to own] **1** to be indebted to the amount of **2** to have the need to do, give, etc., as because of gratitude **3** to be indebted *to* someone for the existence of

ow·ing (ō′iŋ) *adj.* [ME *owynge*] due; unpaid —**owing to** because of

owl (oul) *n.* [OE *ule*] **1** a predatory night bird having a large, flat face, large eyes, and a short, hooked beak **2** a person of nocturnal habits, solemn appearance, etc. —**owl′ish** *adj.*

owl·et (-it) *n.* a young or small owl

own (ōn) *adj.* [OE *agan,* possess] belonging or relating to oneself or itself [his *own* book] —*n.* that which belongs to oneself [that is her *own*] —*vt.* **1** to possess; have **2** to admit; acknowledge —*vi.* to confess (*to*) —**on one's own** [Inf.] by one's own efforts —**own′er** *n.* —**own′er·ship′** *n.*

ox (äks) *n., pl.* **ox'en** [OE *oxa*] any of certain cud-chewing, cattlelike mammals, esp. a castrated, domesticated bull used as a draft animal

ox·blood *n.* a deep-red color

ox·bow (-bō´) *n.* **1** the U-shaped part of an ox yoke which passes under and around the animal's neck **2** *a*) a bend in a meandering river *b*) the land within such a bend

ox·ford (äks´fərd) *n.* [after *Oxford*, England] [*sometimes* **O-**] **1** a low shoe laced over the instep: also **oxford shoe 2** a cotton or rayon fabric with a basketlike weave: also **oxford cloth**

Ox·ford (äks´fərd) city in SC England; site of Oxford University

ox·i·dant (äk´si dənt) *n.* an oxidizing agent

ox·i·da·tion (äk´si dā´shən) *n.* an oxidizing or being oxidized

ox·ide (äk´sīd´) *n.* [Fr] a compound of oxygen with another element or a radical

ox·i·dize (äk´si dīz´) *vt.* **-dized´, -diz´ing** to unite with oxygen, as in burning or rusting —*vi.* to become oxidized —**ox´i·diz´er** *n.*

ox·y·a·cet·y·lene (äk´sē ə set´'l ēn´) *adj.* of or using a mixture of oxygen and acetylene, as for producing a hot flame used in welding

ox·y·gen (äk´si jən) *n.* [Fr *oxygène*] a colorless, odorless, gaseous chemical element: it is essential to life processes and to combustion: symbol, 0; at. no. 8

ox·y·gen·ate (-jə nāt´) *vt.* **-at´ed, -at´ing** to treat or combine with oxygen —**ox´y·gen·a´tion** *n.*

oxygen tent a transparent enclosure filled with oxygen, fitted around a bed patient to aid breathing

ox·y·mo·ron (äk´si môr´än´) *n., pl.* **-mo´ra** (-rə) [< Gr *oxys*, sharp + *mōros*, foolish] a figure of speech in which contradictory ideas or terms are combined (Ex.: thunderous silence)

oys·ter (ois´tər) *n.* [< Gr *ostreon*] an edible bivalve mollusk with an irregular shell

oz *symbol* ounce(s)

o·zone (ō´zōn´) *n.* [Fr < Gr *ozein*, to smell] **1** an unstable, pale-blue form of oxygen with a strong odor, formed by an electrical discharge in air and used as a bleaching agent, water purifier, etc. **2** [Slang] pure, fresh air

ozone layer the layer of ozone within the stratosphere that absorbs much ultraviolet radiation

P

p¹ or **P** (pē) *n., pl.* **p's, P's** the 16th letter of the English alphabet

p² *abbrev.* **1** page **2** participle **3** past **4** per **5** pint

P¹ *abbrev.* petite

P² *Chem. symbol for* phosphorus

pa (pä) *n.* [Inf.] FATHER

PA *abbrev.* **1** Pennsylvania **2** public address (system)

pab·lum (pab´ləm) *n.* [< *Pablum*, trademark for a soft, bland baby food] simplistic or bland writing, ideas, etc.

PAC *n.* political action committee

pace (pās) *n.* [< L *passus*, a step] **1** a step in walking, etc. **2** the length of a step or stride **3** the rate of speed in walking, etc. **4** rate of progress, etc. **5** a gait **6** the gait of a horse in which both legs on the same side are raised together —*vt.* **paced, pac´ing 1** to walk back and forth across **2** to measure by paces **3** to set the pace for (a runner, etc.) —*vi.* **1** to walk with regular steps **2** to move at a pace: said of a horse —**put through one's paces** to test one's ability, skills, etc. —**pac´er** *n.*

pace·mak·er *n.* **1** one that leads the way: also **pace´set´ter** (-set´ər) **2** an electronic device placed in the body to regulate the heartbeat

pach·y·derm (pak´ə durm´) *n.* [< Gr *pachys*,

thick + *derma*, skin] a large, thick-skinned, hoofed animal, as the elephant or rhinoceros

pach·y·san·dra (pak´ə san´drə) *n.* [< ModL name of genus] a low, hardy evergreen plant often used for a ground cover in the shade

pa·cif·ic (pə sif´ik) *adj.* [see PACIFY] **1** making peace **2** of a peaceful nature; tranquil; calm

Pa·cif·ic Ocean (pə sif´ik) largest of the earth's oceans, between Asia and the American continents

pac·i·fi·er (pas´ə fī´ər) *n.* **1** one that pacifies **2** a nipple or teething ring for babies

pac·i·fism (-fiz´əm) *n.* opposition to the use of force under any circumstances; specif., refusal to participate in war —**pac´i·fist** *n., adj.*

pac·i·fy (pas´ə fī´) *vt.* **-fied´, -fy´ing** [< L *pax*, peace + *facere*, make] to make peaceful, calm, nonhostile, etc. —**pac´i·fi·ca´tion** *n.*

pack¹ (pak) *n.* [< MDu *pak*] **1** a bundle of things tied up for carrying **2** a number of similar persons or things; specif., *a*) a group [a *pack* of lies] *b*) a package of a standard number [a *pack* of cigarettes] *c*) a number of wild animals living together —*vt.* **1** to make a pack of **2** *a*) to put together in a box, trunk, etc. *b*) to fill (a box, etc.) **3** to crowd; cram [the hall was *packed*] **4** to fill in tightly, as for prevention of leaks **5** to carry in a pack **6** to send (*off*) [to *pack* him off to school] **7** [Slang] to carry (a gun, etc.) **8** [Slang] to be able to deliver (a punch, etc.) with force —*vi.* **1** to make up packs **2** to put one's clothes, etc. into luggage for a trip **3** to crowd together **4** to settle into a compact mass —*adj.* used for carrying packs, loads, etc. [a *pack* animal] —**send packing** to dismiss abruptly

pack² (pak) *vt.* to choose (a jury, etc.) so as to get desired results

pack·age (pak′ij) *n.* **1** a wrapped or boxed thing or group of things; parcel **2** a number of items, plans, etc. offered as a unit —*vt.* **-aged, -ag·ing 1** to make a package of **2** to offer or present in an enticing way —**pack′ag·er** *n.*

package store a store where alcoholic beverages are sold by the bottle

pack·et (-it) *n.* **1** a small package **2** a boat that travels a regular route carrying passengers, freight, and mail: in full **packet boat**

pack·ing *n.* **1** the act or process of a person or thing that packs **2** any material used to pack

pack·ing·house *n.* a plant where meats, etc. are processed and packed for sale

pack rat 1 a North American rat that often hides small articles in its nest **2** [Inf.] one who hoards miscellaneous items

pack·sad·dle *n.* a saddle with fastenings to secure the load carried by a pack animal

pact (pakt) *n.* [< L *paciscere*, agree] an agreement; compact

pad¹ (pad) *n.* [echoic] the dull sound of a footstep —*vi.* **pad′ded, pad′ding** to walk, esp. with a soft step

pad² (pad) *n.* [? var. of POD] **1** anything soft to protect against friction, pressure, etc.; cushion **2** the cushionlike sole of an animal's paw **3** the floating leaf of a water plant, as the waterlily **4** a number of sheets of paper glued along one edge; tablet **5** a keypad or other device for entering information **6** [Slang] the place where one lives —*vt.* **pad′ded, pad′ding 1** to stuff or cover with soft material **2** to lengthen (a speech, etc.) with unnecessary material **3** to fill (an expense account, etc.) with invented or inflated entries

pad·ding *n.* anything used to pad

pad·dle¹ (pad′'l) *n.* [ME *padell*, small spade] **1** a short pole with a wide blade at one or both ends, used to propel a canoe, kayak, etc. **2** an implement shaped like this, used to hit a ball, beat something, etc. —*vt., vi.* **-dled, -dling 1** to propel (a canoe, etc.) with a paddle **2** to beat as with a paddle; spank —**pad′dler** *n.*

pad·dle² (pad′'l) *vi.* **-dled, -dling** [prob. < PAD¹] to move the hands or feet about in the water, as in playing —**pad′dler** *n.*

paddle ball a game like handball played with a short-handled paddle

paddle wheel a wheel with boards around it for propelling a steamboat

pad·dock (pad′ək) *n.* [OE *pearruc*, enclosure] **1** a small enclosure near a stable, in which horses are exercised **2** an enclosure at a racetrack, where horses are saddled

pad·dy (pad′ē) *n., pl.* **-dies** [Malay *padi*, rice in the husk] a rice field

pad·lock (pad′läk′) *n.* a removable lock with a hinged link to be passed through a staple, chain, or eye —*vt.* to fasten or close up as with a padlock

pa·dre (pä′drā′) *n.* [< L *pater*] **1** father: the title of a priest in Italy, Spain, etc. **2** [Inf.] a priest or chaplain

pae·an (pē′ən) *n.* [< Gr *paian*, hymn] a song of joy, triumph, etc.

pa·gan (pā′gən) *n.* [< L *paganus*, peasant] **1** [Historical] one following a religion other than Judaism, Christianity, or Islam **2** one who has no religion: often derogatory **3** one who worships nature or the earth —*adj.* of pagans —**pa′gan·ism′** *n.*

page¹ (pāj) *n.* [< L *pangere*, fasten] **1** *a*) one side of a leaf of a book, etc. *b*) an entire leaf in a book, etc. **2** [*often pl.*] a record of events **3** WEB PAGE —*vi.* **paged, pag′ing** to look (*through*) by turning the pages

page² (pāj) *n.* [OFr] **1** a boy attendant **2** a young person who runs errands —*vt.* **paged, pag′ing 1** to try to find by calling out the name of **2** to contact with a pager

pag·eant (paj′ənt) *n.* [ME *pagent*, stage scene] **1** a spectacular exhibition, parade, etc. **2** an elaborate outdoor drama celebrating a historical event **3** a beauty contest

pag·eant·ry (-ən trē) *n., pl.* **-ries 1** grand spectacle; gorgeous display **2** empty show or display

pag·er (pā′jər) *n.* a portable electronic device used to contact people for messages

pag·i·na·tion (paj′ə nā′shən) *n.* **1** the numbering of pages **2** the arrangement and number of pages

pa·go·da (pə gō′də) *n.* [prob. < Pers *but*, idol + *kadah*, house] in Asia, a temple in the form of a pyramidal tower of several stories

paid (pād) *vt., vi. pt. & pp.* of PAY —*adj.* **1** settled by payment **2** with pay [a *paid* vacation]

pail (pāl) *n.* [< OE *pægel*, wine vessel] **1** a container, usually with a handle, for holding liquids, etc.; bucket **2** the amount held by a pail: also **pail′ful′**, *pl.* **-fuls′**

pain (pān) *n.* [< Gr *poinē*, penalty] **1** physical or mental suffering caused by injury, disease, grief, anxiety, etc. **2** [*pl.*] great care [take *pains* with one's work] —*vt.* to cause pain to; hurt —**on** (or **under**) **pain of** at the risk of a penalty —**pain′ful** *adj.* —**pain′ful·ly** *adv.* —**pain′less** *adj.*

Paine (pān), **Thom·as** (täm′əs) 1737-1809; Am. Revolutionary patriot & writer

pain·kill·er *n.* a medicine that relieves pain

pains·tak·ing (pānz′tā′kiŋ) *adj.* requiring or showing great care; very careful

paint (pānt) *vt.* [< L *pingere*] **1** *a*) to make (a picture, etc.) in colors applied to a surface *b*) to depict with paints **2** to describe vividly **3** to cover or decorate with paint —*vi.* to paint pictures —*n.* **1** a mixture of a pigment with oil, water, etc., used as a covering or coloring **2** a dried coat of paint

paint·ball *n.* a game where players, using air guns, shoot pellets filled with colored gel at each other

paint·er *n.* **1** an artist who paints pictures **2** one whose work is covering walls, etc. with paint

paint·ing *n.* a painted picture

pair (per) *n., pl.* **pairs** or **pair** [< L *par*, equal] **1** two corresponding things associated or used together [a *pair* of shoes] **2** a single unit of two corresponding parts [a *pair* of pants] **3** any two persons or animals regarded as a unit — *vi., vt.* **1** to form a pair (of) **2** to mate

pais·ley (pāz′lē) *adj.* [after *Paisley*, Scotland] [*also* **P-**] having an intricate, multicolored pattern of swirls, etc.

pa·ja·mas (pə jä′məz, –jam′əz) *pl.n.* [< Pers *pāi*, a leg + *jāma*, garment] a loosely fitting sleeping or lounging suit consisting of jacket (or blouse) and trousers

Pa·ki·stan (pak′i stan′, pä′ki stän′) country in S Asia, west of India —**Pak′i·stan′i** (-ē) *adj., n.*

pal (pal) *n.* [Romany, brother, ult. < Sans] [Inf.] a close friend

pal·ace (pal′əs) *n.* [< L *Palatium*, one of the Seven Hills of Rome] **1** the official residence of a king, etc. **2** any large, magnificent building

pal·at·a·ble (pal′it ə bəl) *adj.* pleasant or acceptable to the taste or mind

pal·ate (pal′it) *n.* [< L *palatum*] **1** the roof of the mouth **2** sense of taste **pal′a·tal** (-it′l) *adj.*

pa·la·tial (pə lā′shəl) *adj.* [see PALACE] **1** suitable for, or like a palace **2** magnificent; stately

pal·a·tine (pal′ə tīn′, -tin) *adj.* [see PALACE] designating or of a count or earl who ruled in his own territory

Pa·lau (pä lou′) country on a group of islands in the W Pacific

pa·lav·er (pə lav′ər) *n.* [Port *palavra*, a word] talk, esp. idle talk —*vi.* to talk idly

pale¹ (pāl) *adj.* **pal′er, pal′est** [< L *pallidus*] **1** of a whitish or colorless complexion **2** faint; dim **3** feeble; weak —*vi.* **paled, pal′ing** to become pale —**pale′ly** *adv.* —**pale′ness** *n.*

pale² (pāl) *n.* [< L *palus*, a stake] **1** a pointed stake used in fences **2** a boundary; restriction: now chiefly figurative

pale·face *n.* a white person: a term allegedly first used by North American Indians

pa·le·on·tol·o·gy (pā′lē on täl′ə jē) *n.* [< Fr] the branch of geology studying prehistoric life by means of fossils —**pa′le·on·tol′o·gist** *n.*

Pa·le·o·zo·ic (-ə zō′ik) *adj.* [< Gr *palaios*, ancient + ZO(O)- + -IC] designating the geologic era (*c.* 542-251 million years ago) characterized by the first fishes, reptiles, and land plants

Pal·es·tine (pal′əs tīn′) historical region in SW Asia at the E end of the Mediterranean, including modern Israel & Jordan as well as other nearby areas

Pal·es·tin·i·an (-tin′ē ən) *n.* a person, esp. an Arab, born or living in Palestine —*adj.* of Palestine or the Palestinians

pal·ette (pal′it) *n.* [Fr < L *pala*, a shovel] **1** a thin board on which an artist arranges and mixes paints **2** the colors used for a painting

pal·frey (pôl′frē) *n., pl.* **-freys** [ult. < Gr *para*, beside + L *veredus*, post horse] [Archaic] a saddle horse, esp. a gentle one for a woman

pal·i·mo·ny (pal′ə mō′nē) *n.* [PAL + (ALI)MONY] an allowance or a property settlement claimed by or granted to one member of an unmarried couple who separate after having lived together

pal·imp·sest (pal′imp sest′) *n.* [< Gr *palimpsēstos*, lit., rubbed again] a parchment previously written upon that bears traces of the erased texts

pal·in·drome (pal′in drōm′) *n.* [< Gr *palindromos*, running back] a word, phrase, or sentence that reads the same backward or forward (Ex.: madam)

pal·ing (pāl′iŋ) *n.* a fence made of pales

pal·i·sade (pal′ə sād′) *n.* [< Fr < L *palus*, a stake] **1** a row of large, pointed stakes forming a fence as for fortification **2** [*pl.*] a line of steep cliffs

pall¹ (pôl) *vi.* **palled, pall′ing** [ME *pallen*, appall] **1** to become cloying, insipid, boring, etc. **2** to become satiated

pall² (pôl) *n.* [< L *pallium*, a cover] **1** a cloth covering for a coffin **2** a dark or gloomy covering

pal·la·di·um (pə lā′dē əm) *n.* [after the asteroid *Pallas*] a rare, ductile, metallic chemical element alloyed for use in electric contacts, surgical instruments, etc.: symbol, Pd; at. no. 46

pall·bear·er (pôl′ber′ər) *n.* [PALL² + BEARER] one of the persons who attend or carry the coffin at a funeral

pal·let¹ (pal′it) *n.* [see PALETTE] a low, portable platform used for stacking materials, as in a warehouse

pal·let² (pal′it) *n.* [< L *palea*, chaff] a small bed or a pad filled as with straw and used on the floor

pal·li·ate (pal′ē āt′) *vt.* **-at′ed, -at′ing** [< L *pallium*, a cloak] **1** to lessen the severity of without curing; alleviate **2** to make (an offense) appear less serious; excuse —**pal′li·a′tion** *n.* —**pal′li·a′tive** (-āt′iv, -ə tiv) *adj., n.*

pal·lid (pal′id) *adj.* [L *pallidus*, pale] faint in color; pale —**pal′lid·ly** *adv.*

pal·lor (pal′ər) *n.* [< L *pallere*, be pale] unnatural paleness

palm¹ (päm, pälm, pôlm) *n.* [< L *palma*: from its handlike leaf] **1** any of a large group of tropical or subtropical trees or shrubs with a branchless trunk and a bunch of large leaves at the top **2** a leaf of such a tree carried as a symbol of victory, etc.

palm² (päm, pälm, pôlm) *n.* [< L *palma*] the inner surface of the hand between the fingers and wrist —*vt.* to hide (something) in the palm, as in a sleight-of-hand trick —**palm off** [Inf.] to pass off by fraud

pal·met·to (pal met′ō) *n., pl.* **-tos** or **-toes** any of certain palms with fan-shaped leaves

palm·is·try (päm′is trē, pälm′-, pôlm′-) *n.* [prob. < ME *paume*, PALM² + *maistrie*, mastery] fortunetelling by interpreting the lines, etc. on the palm of a person's hand —**palm′ist** *n.*

Palm Springs resort city in SW California

Palm Sunday the Sunday before Easter, commemorating Jesus' entry into Jerusalem, when palm branches were strewn before him

palm·y (päm′ē) *adj.* **-i·er**, **-i·est** 1 of, like, or full of palm trees 2 prosperous [*palmy* days]

pal·o·mi·no (pal′ə mē′nō) *n., pl.* **-nos** [AmSp < Sp, dove-colored] a golden or cream-colored horse with a white tail

pal·pa·ble (pal′pə bəl) *adj.* [< L *palpare*, to touch] 1 that can be touched, felt, etc. 2 easily perceived by the senses; perceptible 3 obvious; plain —**pal′pa·bly** *adv.*

pal·pi·tate (pal′pə tāt′) *vi.* **-tat′ed**, **-tat′ing** [< L *palpare*, to feel] 1 to beat rapidly, as the heart 2 to throb —**pal′pi·ta′tion** *n.*

pal·sy (pôl′zē) *n., pl.* **-sies** [ult. < L *paralysis*, paralysis] paralysis of a muscle, sometimes with involuntary tremors —*vt.* **-sied**, **-sy·ing** to affect with or as with palsy

pal·try (pôl′trē) *adj.* **-tri·er**, **-tri·est** [prob. < LowG *palte*, rag] almost worthless; trifling —**pal′tri·ness** *n.*

Pam·pas (pam′pəz, päm′-), **the** [AmSp < AmInd *pampa*, plain, field] an extensive, treeless plain of S South America

pam·per (pam′pər) *vt.* [ME *pampren*, to feed too much < LowG] to be overindulgent with; coddle

pam·phlet (pam′flit) *n.* [< OFr *Pamphilet*, shortened name of a ML poem] a thin, unbound booklet, often on some topic of current interest —**pam′phlet·eer′** (-flə tir′) *n.*

pan¹ (pan) *n.* [OE *panne*] 1 any broad, shallow container used in cooking, etc. 2 a pan-shaped part or object —*vt.* **panned**, **pan′ning** 1 [Inf.] to criticize unfavorably 2 *Mining* to wash (gravel) in a pan, as to separate (gold) —*vi. Mining* to wash gravel in a pan, searching for gold —**pan out** [Inf.] to turn out; esp., to succeed

pan² (pan) *Film, TV, etc. vt., vi.* **panned**, **pan′ning** [< PAN(ORAMA)] to move (a camera) so as to get a panoramic effect —*n.* the act of panning

Pan (pan) *n. Gr. Myth.* a god of fields, forests, flocks, and shepherds, represented as having the legs of a goat

pan- [< Gr *pan*, all, every] *combining form* 1 all [*pantheism*] 2 [**P-**] of, comprising, or uniting every [*Pan-American*]

pan·a·ce·a (pan′ə sē′ə) *n.* [< Gr *pan*, all + *akos*, healing, medicine] a supposed remedy for all ills

pa·nache (pə nash′, -näsh′) *n.* [Fr, ult. < L *pinna*, feather] dashing elegance of manner or style

Pan·a·ma (pan′ə mä′, -mô′) country in Central America, a strip of land connecting Central & South America —**Pan′a·ma′ni·an** (-mā′nē ən) *adj., n.*

Panama Canal ship canal across Panama, connecting the Atlantic & Pacific

Panama (hat) [*also* **p-**] a hand-woven hat made with strawlike strips of the leaves of a tropical plant

Pan-A·mer·i·can *adj.* of North, South, and Central America, collectively

pan·cake (pan′kāk′) *n.* a flat cake of batter fried on a griddle or in a pan

pan·chro·mat·ic (pan′krō mat′ik) *adj.* sensitive to light of all colors [*panchromatic* film]

pan·cre·as (pan′krē əs, pan′-) *n.* [< Gr *pan*, all + *kreas*, flesh] a large gland that secretes a digestive juice into the small intestine and produces insulin —**pan′cre·at′ic** (-at′ik) *adj.*

pan·da (pan′də) *n.* [< native name in Nepal] 1 a black-and-white, herbivorous bear of China: in full **giant panda** 2 a reddish, raccoonlike mammal of the Himalayas: in full **lesser panda**

pan·dem·ic (pan dem′ik) *adj.* [< Gr *pan*, all + *dēmos*, the people] epidemic over a large region

pan·de·mo·ni·um (pan′də mō′nē əm) *n.* [< name of demons' abode in Milton's *Paradise Lost* < Gr *pan*, all + *daimōn*, evil spirit] wild disorder or noise

pan·der (pan′dər) *n.* [< L *Pandarus*, lovers' go-between in Chaucer, etc.] 1 a procurer; pimp 2 one who helps others to satisfy their vices, etc. Also **pan′der·er** —*vi.* to act as a pander (*to*)

P & H *abbrev.* postage and handling

Pan·do·ra (pan dôr′ə) *n.* [< Gr *pan*, all + *dōron*, gift] *Gr. Myth.* the first mortal woman: she opens a box, letting all human ills into the world

pane (pān) *n.* [< L *pannus*, piece of cloth] a sheet of glass in a frame of a window, etc.

pan·e·gyr·ic (pan′ə jir′ik) *n.* [< Gr *panēgyris*, public meeting] 1 a formal speech or piece of writing praising a person or event 2 high praise

pan·el (pan′əl) *n.* [see PANE] 1 *a*) a section or division, usually rectangular, forming a part of a wall, door, etc. *b*) a board for instruments or controls 2 a lengthwise strip in a skirt, etc. 3 a list of persons summoned for jury duty 4 a group of persons selected for judging, discussing, etc. —*vt.* **-eled** or **-elled**, **-el·ing** or **-el·ling** to provide with panels

pan·el·ing or **pan·el·ling** *n.* 1 panels collectively 2 sheets of plastic, wood, etc. from which to cut panels

pan·el·ist *n.* a member of a PANEL (*n.* 4)

panel truck an enclosed pickup truck

pang (paŋ) *n.* [< ?] a sudden, sharp pain, physical or emotional

pan·han·dle¹ (pan′han′dəl) *n.* a strip of land projecting like the handle of a pan

pan·han·dle² (pan′han′dəl) *vi.* **-dled**, **-dling** [Inf.] to beg on the streets —**pan′han′dler** *n.*

pan·ic (pan′ik) *n.* [< Gr *panikos*, of Pan, as inspirer of sudden fear] a sudden, unreasoning fear, often spreading quickly —*vt.* **-icked**, **-ick·ing** to affect with panic —*vi.* to show panic —**pan′ick·y** *adj.*

pan·ic-strick·en *adj.* badly frightened: also **pan′ic-struck′**

pan·nier or **pan·ier** (pan′yər, -ē ər) *n.* [< L *panis*, bread] **1** a large basket for carrying loads on the back **2** a pack used on a horse, bicycle, etc.

pan·o·ply (pan′ə plē) *n., pl.* **-plies** [< Gr *pan*, all + *hopla*, arms] **1** a complete suit of armor **2** any complete or magnificent covering or array

pan·o·ram·a (pan′ə ram′ə) *n.* [< PAN- + Gr *horáma*, a view] **1** a wide view in all directions **2** a constantly changing scene —**pan′o·ram′ic** *adj.*

pan·sy (pan′zē) *n., pl.* **-sies** [< Fr *penser*, think] a small plant of the violet family, with velvety petals

pant (pant) *vi.* [ult. < L *phantasia*, nightmare] **1** to breathe rapidly and heavily, as from running fast **2** to yearn eagerly: with *for* or *after* —*vt.* to gasp out —*n.* any of a series of rapid, heavy breaths; gasp

pan·ta·loons (pan′tə lōōnz′) *pl.n.* [< It: ult. after St. *Pantalone*] [Historical] trousers

pan·the·ism (pan′thē iz′əm) *n.* [< Gr *pan*, all + *theos*, a god + -ISM] **1** the doctrine that all forces, manifestations, etc. of the universe are God **2** the worship of all gods —**pan′the·ist** *n.*

pan·the·on (pan′thē än′) *n.* [< Gr *pan*, all + *theos*, a god] **1** all the gods of a people **2** [*often* P-] a building in which famous dead persons of a nation are entombed or commemorated

pan·ther (pan′thər) *n.* [< Gr *panthēr*] **1** a leopard, specif. one that is black **2** COUGAR

pant·ies (pan′tēz) *pl.n.* women's or children's short underpants: also **pant′ie**

pan·to·mime (pan′tə mīm′) *n.* [ult. < Gr *pan*, all + *mimos*, a mimic] **1** a drama played without words, using only action and gestures **2** action or gestures without words — *vt., vi.* **-mimed′**, **-mim′ing** to express or act in pantomime —**pan′to·mim′ist** (-mīm′ist) *n.*

pan·to·then·ic acid (pan′tō then′ik) [< Gr *pantothen*, from every side] a viscous oil, part of the vitamin B complex, occurring widely in animal and plant tissues and thought essential for cell growth

pan·try (pan′trē) *n., pl.* **-tries** [< L *panis*, bread] a small room off the kitchen, where cooking ingredients and utensils, china, etc. are kept

pants (pants) *pl.n.* [< PANTALOONS] **1** a two-legged outer garment that covers the body from the waist down **2** drawers or panties

pant·suit *n.* matched pants and jacket for women: also **pants suit**

pant·y·hose (pan′tē hōz′) *n.* a stretchable one-piece undergarment consisting of hose attached to a top that resembles underpants

pant·y·waist *n.* [Slang] a sissy

pap (pap) *n.* [ME] **1** any soft food for babies or invalids **2** any oversimplified or tasteless writing, ideas, etc.

pa·pa (pä′pə, pə pä′) *n.* [< baby talk] *child's term for* FATHER

pa·pa·cy (pā′pə sē) *n., pl.* **-cies** [LL *papa*, pope] **1** the rank of pope **2** the term of office of a pope **3** the governing of the Roman Catholic Church by the pope, its head

pa·pal (pā′pəl) *adj.* of or relating to a pope or the papacy

pa·pa·raz·zi (pä′pä rät′tsē) *pl.n.* photographers who take candid shots of celebrities

pa·paw (pə pô′, pô′pô′) *n.* [< fol.] **1** PAPAYA **2** *a)* a tree of central s and S U.S. with an oblong, yellowish, edible fruit *b)* its fruit

pa·pa·ya (pə pî′ə) *n.* [Sp < WInd name] **1** a tropical American tree with a large, oblong, yellowish-orange fruit **2** its fruit

pa·per (pā′pər) *n.* [ult. < Gr *papyros*, papyrus] **1** a thin, flexible material in sheets, made from rags, wood, etc. and used for writing or printing on, for packaging, etc. **2** a single sheet of this **3** an official document **4** an essay, dissertation, etc. **5** a newspaper **6** wallpaper **7** [*pl.*] credentials —*adj.* **1** of, or made of, paper **2** like paper; thin —*vt.* to cover with wallpaper —**pa′per·y** *adj.*

pa·per·back *n.* a book bound in paper covers

pa·per·boy *n.* a boy who sells or delivers newspapers

paper clip a flexible clasp for holding loose sheets of paper together

pa·per·girl *n.* a girl who sells or delivers newspapers

pa·per·hang·er *n.* a person whose work is covering walls with wallpaper

pa·per-ma·ché (pā′pər mə shā′) *n. var. of* PAPIER-MÂCHÉ

paper tiger a person, nation, etc. that seems to pose a threat but is really powerless

paper trail written records that serve as evidence of a person's actions

pa·per·weight *n.* any small, heavy object set on papers to keep them from being scattered

pa·per·work *n.* the keeping of records, etc. incidental to some task

pa·pier-mâ·ché (pā′pər mə shā′) *n.* [Fr < *papier*, paper + *mâcher*, to chew] a material made of paper pulp mixed with size, glue, etc., and molded into various objects when moist

pa·pil·la (pə pil′ə) *n., pl.* **-lae** (-ē) [L < *papula*, pimple] any small nipplelike projection of tissue, as on the surface of the tongue —**pap·il·lar·y** (pap′ə ler′ē) *adj.*

pa·poose (pə pōōs′, pa-) *n.* [< AmInd] [Historical] a North American Indian baby

pa·pri·ka (pə prē′kə) *n.* [Hung., ult. < Gr *peperi*, pepper] a mild or hot, red, powdered condiment ground from the fruit of certain pepper plants

Pap test (pap) [after G. *Papanicolaou* (1883-1962), U.S. pathologist] a test for uterine cancer

Pap·u·a New Guinea (pap′yōō ə) country

occupying the E half of the island of New Guinea & nearby islands

pa·py·rus (pə pī′rəs) *n., pl.* **-ri′** (-rī′) or **-rus·es** [< Gr *papyros*] 1 a tall water plant of Egypt 2 a writing material made from the pith of this plant by the ancients

par (pär) *n.* [L, an equal] 1 the established value of a currency in terms of the money of another country 2 an equal status, level, etc.: usually in **on a par (with)** 3 the average state, condition, etc. [work that is above *par*] 4 the face value of stocks, etc. 5 *Golf* the number of strokes established as a skillful score for a hole or course —*adj.* 1 of or at par 2 average

par *abbrev.* 1 paragraph 2 parish

para- *prefix* 1 beside, beyond [*parapsychology*] 2 helping, accessory [*paramedical*]

par·a·ble (par′ə bəl) *n.* [< Gr *parabolē*, analogy < *para-*, beside + *ballein*, to throw] a short, simple story teaching a moral lesson

pa·rab·o·la (pə rab′ə lə) *n.* [see prec.] *Geom.* a curve formed by the intersection of a cone with a plane parallel to its side —**par·a·bol·ic** (par′ə bäl′ik) *adj.*

par·a·chute (par′ə shōōt′) *n.* [Fr < *para-*, protecting + *chute*, a fall] a cloth contrivance usually shaped like an umbrella when expanded, and used to retard the speed of one dropping from an airplane, etc. — *vt., vi.* **-chut′ed, -chut′ing** to drop by parachute —**par′a·chut′ist** *n.*

pa·rade (pə rād′) *n.* [< L *parare*, prepare] 1 ostentatious display 2 a review of marching troops 3 any organized procession or march, as for display —*vt.* **-rad′ed, -rad′ing** 1 to march or walk through, as for display 2 to show off [to *parade* one's knowledge] —*vi.* 1 to march in a parade 2 to walk about ostentatiously

par·a·digm (par′ə dīm′) *n.* [< Gr *para-*, beside + *deigma*, example] 1 an example or model 2 a generally accepted concept that explains a complex idea, set of data, etc. 3 *Gram.* an example of a declension or conjugation, giving all the inflections of a word

Par·a·dise (par′ə dīs′) *n.* [< Gr *paradeisos*, garden] 1 the garden of Eden 2 heaven 3 [*p-*] any place or state of great happiness

par·a·dox (par′ə däks′) *n.* [< Gr *para-*, beyond + *doxa*, opinion] 1 a statement that seems contradictory, or absurd but may be true in fact 2 a statement that is self-contradictory and, hence, false 3 any person or thing having contradictory qualities —**par′a·dox′i·cal** *adj.* —**par′a·dox′i·cal·ly** *adv.*

par·af·fin (par′ə fin) *n.* [Ger < L *parum*, too little + *affinis*, akin: from its inertness] a white, waxy substance obtained from petroleum and used for making candles, etc.

par·a·gon (par′ə gän′) *n.* [< It *paragone*, touchstone] a model of perfection or excellence

par·a·graph (par′ə graf′) *n.* [< Gr *para-*, beside + *graphein*, write] a distinct section of a piece of writing, begun on a new line and often indented —*vt.* to arrange in paragraphs

Par·a·guay (par′ə gwä′, -gwī′) inland country in SC South America —**Par′a·guay′an** *adj., n.*

par·a·keet (par′ə kēt′) *n.* [prob. < MFr *perrot, parrot*] a small, slender parrot with a long tail

par·a·le·gal (par′ə lē′gəl) *adj.* designating or of persons trained to aid lawyers but not licensed to practice law —*n.* such a person

par·al·lax (par′ə laks′) *n.* [< Gr *para-*, beyond + *allassein*, to change] the apparent change in the position of an object resulting from a change in the viewer's position

par·al·lel (par′ə lel′) *adj.* [< Gr *para-*, side by side + *allēlos*, one another] 1 extending in the same direction and at the same distance apart, so as never to meet 2 similar or corresponding —*n.* 1 a parallel line, surface, etc. 2 any person or thing similar to another; counterpart 3 any comparison showing likeness 4 any of the imaginary lines parallel to the equator and representing degrees of latitude: in full **parallel of latitude** —*vt.* **-leled′** or **-lelled′, -lel′ing** or **-lel′ling** 1 to be parallel with 2 to match; equal —**par′al·lel·ism′** *n.*

par·al·lel·o·gram (-ə gram′) *n.* a four-sided plane figure having the opposite sides parallel and equal

parallel parking the parking of vehicles close to and parallel to the curb

pa·ral·y·sis (pə ral′ə sis) *n., pl.* **-ses′** (-sēz′) [< Gr *paralyein*, to loosen or weaken at the side] 1 partial or complete loss of voluntary motion or of sensation in part or all of the body 2 any condition of helpless inactivity —**par·a·lyt·ic** (par′ə lit′ik) *adj., n.*

par·a·lyze (par′ə līz′) *vt.* **-lyzed′, -lyz′ing** 1 to cause paralysis in 2 to make ineffective or powerless

par·a·me·ci·um (par′ə mē′sē əm, -shē əm) *n., pl.* **-ci·a** (-ə) [< Gr *paramēkēs*, oval] an elongated protozoan that moves by means of cilia

par·a·med·ic (par′ə med′ik) *n.* a person in paramedical work, specif. one working from an ambulance

par·a·med·i·cal (-med′i kəl) *adj.* [PARA- + MEDICAL] of auxiliary medical personnel

pa·ram·e·ter (pə ram′ət ər) *n.* [< Gr *para-*, beside + *metron*, a measure] 1 any of a set of interdependent variables 2 *a)* a boundary or limit *b)* a characteristic (*usually used in pl.*)

par·a·mil·i·tar·y (par′ə mil′ə ter′ē) *adj.* [PARA- + MILITARY] of forces working along with, or in place of, a regular military organization —*n., pl.* **-tar′ies** a member of such a force

par·a·mount (par′ə mount′) *adj.* [< OFr *par*, by + *amont*, uphill] ranking higher than any other; chief

par·a·mour (par′ə moor′) *n.* [< OFr *par amour*, with love] a lover or mistress; esp., the illicit sexual partner of a married man or woman

par·a·noi·a (par′ə noi′ə) *n.* [< Gr *para-*, beside + *nous*, the mind] a mental disorder characterized by delusions, as of grandeur or, esp., persecution —**par′a·noid′** *adj., n.*

par·a·nor·mal *adj.* of psychic, occult, or supernatural phenomena

par·a·pet (par′ə pet′, -pət) *n.* ⟦< It *parare*, to guard + *petto*, breast⟧ **1** a wall or bank for screening troops from enemy fire **2** a low wall or railing

par·a·pher·na·li·a (par′ə fər nāl′yə, -nā′lē ə) *pl.n.* ⟦< Gr *para-*, beyond + *phernē*, dowry⟧ [*often with sing. v.*] **1** personal belongings **2** equipment

par·a·phrase (par′ə frāz′) *n.* ⟦< Gr *para-*, beside + *phrazein*, say⟧ a rewording of the meaning of something spoken or written — *vt., vi.* **-phrased′, -phras′ing** to express (something) in a paraphrase

par·a·ple·gi·a (par′ə plē′jē ə, -jə) *n.* ⟦< Gr *para-*, beside + *plēgē*, a stroke⟧ paralysis of the lower half of the body —**par′a·ple′gic** (-plē′jik) *adj., n.*

par·a·pro·fes·sion·al *n.* [see PARA-] a trained assistant to licensed professionals, as in medicine

par·a·psy·chol·o·gy *n.* [see PARA-] psychology that investigates psychic phenomena, such as telepathy

par·a·sail *n.* [< PARACHUTE] a kind of parachute worn by a person who is pulled by a boat, car, etc. fast enough to glide in the air —**par′a·sail′ing** *n.*

par·a·site (par′ə sīt′) *n.* ⟦< Gr *para-*, beside + *sitos*, food⟧ **1** one who lives at others' expense without making any useful return **2** a plant or animal that lives on or in another organism, usually with harmful effects —**par′a·sit′ic** (-sit′ik) *adj.*

par·a·sol (par′ə sôl′) *n.* ⟦< It *parare*, ward off + *sole*, sun⟧ a lightweight umbrella used for protection from the sun's rays

par·a·sym·pa·thet·ic (par′ə sim′pə thet′ik) *adj.* ⟦PARA- + SYMPATHETIC⟧ *Physiology* designating the part of the autonomic nervous system whose functions include constricting the pupils of the eyes, slowing the heartbeat, and stimulating some digestive glands

par·a·thi·on (par′ə thī′än′) *n.* ⟦PARA- + Gr *theion*, sulfur⟧ a highly poisonous insecticide

par·a·thy·roid (-thī′roid′) *adj.* ⟦PARA- + THYROID⟧ designating or of the small glands near the thyroid that regulate calcium and phosphorus metabolism

par·a·troops (par′ə trōōps′) *pl.n.* ⟦< PARA(CHUTE) + TROOP⟧ troops trained and equipped to parachute into a combat area —**par′a·troop′er** *n.*

par·boil (pär′boil′) *vt.* ⟦< L *per*, through + *bullire*, to boil: infl. by *part*⟧ to boil until partly cooked

par·cel (pär′səl) *n.* ⟦ult. < L *pars*, part⟧ **1** a small, wrapped bundle; package **2** a group or collection [*a parcel of fools*] **3** a piece (of land) —*vt.* **-celed** or **-celled**, **-cel·ing** or **-cel·ling** to separate into parts and distribute: with *out*

parcel post a mail service for parcels not over a specified weight and size

parch (pärch) *vt.* ⟦< ?⟧ **1** to make hot and dry **2** to make very thirsty —*vi.* to become very dry, hot, thirsty, etc.

parch·ment (pärch′mənt) *n.* ⟦< L (*charta*) *Pergamena*, (paper) of Pergamum, city in Asia Minor⟧ **1** the skin of a sheep, goat, etc. prepared as a surface for writing **2** paper like parchment **3** a manuscript on parchment

par·don (pärd′'n) *vt.* ⟦< L *per-*, through + *donare*, give⟧ **1** to release from further punishment **2** to forgive (an offense) **3** to excuse (a person) for a fault, etc. —*n.* **1** forgiveness **2** an official document granting a pardon —**par′don·a·ble** *adj.*

pare (per) *vt.* **pared**, **par′ing** ⟦< L *parare*, prepare⟧ **1** to cut or trim away (the rind, skin, etc.) of; peel **2** to reduce gradually: often with *down*

par·e·gor·ic (par′ə gôr′ik) *n.* ⟦< Gr *parēgoros*, soothing⟧ a tincture of opium, used to relieve diarrhea

par·ent (per′ənt) *n.* ⟦< L *parere*, beget⟧ **1** a person in relation to his or her offspring; a mother or father **2** any organism in relation to its offspring **3** a source; origin —*adj.* of a corporation in relation to a subsidiary that it owns —**pa·ren·tal** (pə rent′'l) *adj.* —**par′ent·hood′** *n.*

par·ent·age *n.* descent from parents or ancestors; lineage

pa·ren·the·sis (pə ren′thə sis) *n., pl.* **-ses′** (-sēz′) ⟦< Gr *para-*, beside + *entithenai*, to insert⟧ **1** a word, clause, etc. added as an explanation or comment within a sentence **2** either or both of the curved lines, ( ), used to set this off —**par·en·thet·i·cal** (par′ən thet′i kəl) *adj.*, **par′en·thet′ic**

par·ent·ing *n.* the work or skill of a parent in raising a child or children

pa·re·sis (pə rē′sis) *n., pl.* **-ses′** (-sēz′) ⟦Gr < *parienai*, relax⟧ **1** partial paralysis **2** a brain disease caused by syphilis of the central nervous system

par ex·cel·lence (pär′ ek′sə läns′) ⟦< Fr⟧ in the greatest degree of excellence

par·fait (pär fā′) *n.* ⟦Fr, lit., perfect⟧ a frozen dessert of cream, eggs, etc., or of layers of ice cream, crushed fruit, etc. in a tall glass

pa·ri·ah (pə rī′ə) *n.* ⟦< Tamil *paraiyan*, drummer⟧ **1** a member of one of the lowest social castes in India **2** any outcast

par·i·mu·tu·el (par′ə myōō′chōō əl) *n.* ⟦Fr, lit., a mutual bet⟧ a system of betting on races in which the winning bettors share the net of each pool in proportion to their wagers

par·ing (per′in) *n.* a piece pared off

Par·is[1] (par′is) *n. Gr. Legend* a prince of Troy: see HELEN OF TROY

Par·is[2] (par′is; *Fr* pä′rē′) capital of France —**Pa·ri·sian** (pə rē′zhən) *adj., n.*

par·ish (par′ish) *n.* ⟦< Gr *paroikia*, diocese⟧ **1** a part of a diocese, under the charge of a priest or minister **2** the congregation of a church **3** a civil division in Louisiana, corresponding to a county

pa·rish·ion·er (pə rish′ə nər) *n.* a member of a parish

par·i·ty (par′ə tē) *n.* ⟦< L *par*, equal⟧ **1** equality in power, value, etc. **2** equality of value at a given ratio between different kinds of money, etc. **3** *Math.* the condition of being even or odd

park (pärk) *n.* [< ML *parricus*] **1** wooded land held as part of an estate or preserve **2** an area of public land, with walks, playgrounds, etc., for recreation **3** the system in an automatic transmission that locks the drive wheels of a motor vehicle — *vt., vi.* **1** to leave (a vehicle) in a place temporarily **2** to maneuver (a vehicle) into a space where it can be left temporarily

par·ka (pär′kə) *n.* [< Russ, fur coat] a heavy jacket with a hood

parking meter a timing device installed near a parking space: drivers pay to park there for a certain length of time as by inserting coins in it

Par·kin·son's disease (pär′kin sənz) [after J. *Parkinson* (1755-1824), Eng physician] a degenerative disease of later life, causing a rhythmic tremor and muscular rigidity

park·way *n.* a broad roadway landscaped with trees, bushes, etc.

par·lance (pär′ləns) *n.* [< OFr *parler*, speak] language or idiom

par·lay (pär′lā) *vt., vi.* [< It *paro*, a pair] **1** to bet (an original wager plus its winnings) on another race, etc. **2** to exploit (an asset) successfully —*n.* a parlayed bet

par·ley (pär′lē) *vi.* [< Fr *parler*, speak] to confer, esp. with an enemy —*n., pl.* **-leys** a conference, as to settle a dispute or discuss terms

par·lia·ment (pär′lə mənt) *n.* [< OFr *parler*, speak] **1** an official legislative council **2** [P-] the national legislative body of certain countries, esp. Great Britain

par·lia·men·tar·i·an (-men ter′ē ən) *n.* one skilled in parliamentary rules or debate

par·lia·men·ta·ry (-ment′ə rē, -men′trē) *adj.* **1** of or by a parliament **2** conforming to the rules of a parliament

par·lor (pär′lər) *n.* [< OFr *parler*, speak] **1** [Old-fashioned] any living room **2** any of certain kinds of business establishment [a beauty *parlor*]

Parmesan (cheese) (pär′mə zän′, -zhän′) [after *Parma*, It city] a very hard, dry cheese orig. of Italy

par·mi·gia·na (pär′mə zhä′nə, pär′mə zhän′) *adj.* prepared with Parmesan cheese

pa·ro·chi·al (pə rō′kē əl) *adj.* [see PARISH] **1** of or in a parish or parishes **2** narrow in scope; provincial

parochial school a school supported and run by a church

par·o·dy (par′ə dē) *n., pl.* **-dies** [< Gr *para-*, beside + *ōidē*, song] a humorous imitation of a literary or musical work or style —*vt.* **-died, -dy·ing** to make a parody of

pa·role (pə rōl′) *n.* [< LL *parabola*, a speech] the release of a prisoner whose sentence has not expired, on condition of future good behavior —*vt.* **-roled′, -rol′ing** to release on parole

par·ox·ysm (par′ək siz′əm) *n.* [< Gr *para-*,

beyond + *oxynein*, sharpen] **1** a sudden attack of a disease **2** a sudden outburst as of laughter

par·quet (pär kā′) *n.* [Fr, < MFr *parchet*, dim. of *parc*, park] **1** the main floor of a theater: usually called *orchestra* **2** a flooring of parquetry —*vt.* **-queted′** (-kād′), **-quet′ing** (-kā′iŋ) to make of parquetry

parquet circle the part of a theater beneath the balcony on the main floor

par·quet·ry (pär′kə trē) *n.* inlaid wooden flooring in geometric forms

par·ri·cide (par′ə sīd′) *n.* [< L *paricida*: see -CIDE] **1** the act of murdering one's parent, close relative, etc. **2** one who does this

par·rot (par′ət) *n.* [Fr dial. *perrot*] **1** a tropical bird with a hooked bill and brightly colored feathers: some parrots can learn to imitate human speech **2** one who simply repeats what others say —*vt.* to repeat without understanding

par·ry (par′ē) *vt.* **-ried, -ry·ing** [prob. ult. < L *parare*, prepare] **1** to ward off (a blow, etc.) **2** to evade (a question, etc.) —*n., pl.* **-ries** a parrying

parse (pärs) *vt., vi.* **parsed, pars′ing** [< L *pars (orationis)*, part (of speech)] **1** to separate (a sentence) into its parts, giving the form and function of each part **2** to use analytical skills to comprehend

par·si·mo·ny (pär′sə mō′nē) *n.* [< L *parcere*, to spare] stinginess; extreme frugality —*par′si·mo′ni·ous adj.*

pars·ley (pärs′lē) *n.* [< Gr *petros*, stone + *selinon*, celery] a plant with aromatic, often curled leaves used to flavor or garnish some foods

pars·nip (pärs′nip′) *n.* [< L *pastinare*, dig up] **1** a plant with a long white root used as a vegetable **2** its root

par·son (pär′sən) *n.* [see PERSON] **1** an Anglican minister having a parish **2** [Inf.] any minister

par·son·age *n.* the dwelling provided by a church for its minister

part (pärt) *n.* [< L *pars*] **1** a portion, division, etc. of a whole [a *part* of a book] **2** an essential, separable element [automobile *parts*] **3** a portion or share; specif., *a*) a share of work [to do one's *part*] *b*) [usually *pl.*] talent; ability [a man of *parts*] *c*) a role in a play *d*) any of the voices or instruments in a musical ensemble, or the score for this **4** [usually *pl.*] a portion of a country **5** a dividing line formed in combing the hair —*vt.* **1** to break or divide into parts **2** to comb (the hair) so as to leave a part **3** to break or hold apart —*vi.* **1** to break or divide into parts **2** to separate and go different ways **3** to cease associating **4** to go away; leave: with *from* —*adj.* partial —**for one's part** as far as one is concerned —**for the most part** mostly —**in part** partly —**part with** to relinquish —**take part** to participate —**take someone's part** to side with someone

par·take (pär tāk′) *vi.* **-took′, -tak′en, -tak′ing** [< *part taker*] **1** to participate (*in* an activity) **2** to eat or drink something, esp. with others: usually with *of* —**par·tak′er** *n.*

part·ed (pärt′id) *adj.* separated; divided

par·terre (pär ter′) *n.* ⟦Fr < *par*, on + *terre*, earth⟧ **1** a garden with patterned flower beds **2** PARQUET CIRCLE

par·the·no·gen·e·sis (pär′thə nō jen′ə sis) *n.* ⟦see fol. & GENESIS⟧ reproduction from an unfertilized ovum, seed, or spore

Par·the·non (-nän′) *n.* ⟦< Gr *parthenos*, a virgin (i.e., Athena)⟧ the Doric temple of Athena on the Acropolis

par·tial (pär′shəl) *adj.* ⟦< L *pars*, a part⟧ **1** favoring one person, faction, etc. more than another; biased **2** not complete —**partial to** fond of —**par′ti·al′i·ty** (-shē al′ə tē) *n.* —**par′tial·ly** *adv.*

par·tic·i·pate (pär tis′ə pāt′) *vi.* -**pat′ed**, -**pat′ing** ⟦< L *pars*, a part + *capere*, to take⟧ to have or take a share with others (*in* some activity) —**par·tic′i·pant** *adj., n.* —**par·tic′i·pa′tion** *n.* —**par·tic′i·pa′tor** *n.* —**par·tic′i·pa·to′ry** (-pə tôr′ē) *adj.*

par·ti·ci·ple (pärt′i sip′əl) *n.* ⟦see prec.⟧ a verbal form having characteristics of both verb and adjective —**par′ti·cip′i·al** (-sip′ē əl) *adj.*

par·ti·cle (pärt′i kəl) *n.* ⟦< L *pars*, a part⟧ **1** a tiny fragment or trace **2** a short, usually invariable word, as an article or preposition **3** *Physics* a subatomic particle that cannot be divided

par·ti·col·ored (pär′ti kul′ərd) *adj.* ⟦< Fr *parti*, divided + COLORED⟧ having different colors in different parts

par·tic·u·lar (pür tik′yə lər) *adj.* ⟦< L *particula*, particle⟧ **1** of or belonging to a single person, group, or thing **2** regarded separately; specific **3** unusual **4** exacting; fastidious —*n.* a distinct fact, item, detail, etc. —**in particular** especially —**par·tic′u·lar′i·ty** (-lar′ə tē) *n.*, *pl.* -**ties**

par·tic·u·lar·ize (-lər īz′) *vt., vi.* -**ized′**, -**iz′ing** to give particulars or details (of) —**par·tic′u·lar·i·za′tion** *n.*

par·tic·u·lar·ly *adv.* **1** in detail **2** especially **3** specifically

par·tic·u·late (-lit, -lāt′) *adj.* of or formed of separate tiny particles

part·ing *adj.* **1** dividing; separating **2** departing **3** given, spoken, etc. at parting —*n.* **1** a breaking or separating **2** a departure

par·ti·san (pärt′ə zən) *n.* ⟦< L *pars*, a part⟧ **1** a strong supporter of a faction, party, etc. **2** a guerrilla fighter —*adj.* of or like a partisan Also sp. **par′ti·zan** —**par′ti·san·ship′** *n.*

par·ti·tion (pär tish′ən) *n.* ⟦< L *partitio*⟧ **1** division into parts **2** something that divides, as a wall separating rooms —*vt.* **1** to divide into parts; apportion **2** to divide by a partition

part·ly *adv.* not fully or completely

part·ner (pärt′nər) *n.* ⟦< ME⟧ **1** one who joins in an activity with another or others; specif., one of two or more persons jointly owning a business **2** a spouse **3** either of two persons not married to each other but in an intimate, spouse-like relationship **4** either of two per-

sons dancing together **5** either of two players on the same side or team —**part′ner·ship′** *n.*

part of speech any of the classes to which a word can be assigned as by form, function, or meaning; noun, verb, adverb, etc.

par·took (pär took′) *vi. pt. of* PARTAKE

par·tridge (pär′trij) *n.* ⟦< Gr *perdix*⟧ any of several short-tailed game birds, esp. one with an orange-brown head and grayish neck

part song a song for several voices, usually without accompaniment

part-time *adj.* designating, of, or engaged in work, study, etc. taking less time than a regular or full schedule

part-tim·er *n.* a part-time employee, student, etc.

par·tu·ri·tion (pär′too rish′ən) *n.* ⟦< L *parere*, bring forth⟧ childbirth

part·way *adv.* to some degree, but not fully

par·ty (pär′tē) *n., pl.* -**ties** ⟦< L *pars*, a part⟧ **1** a group of people working to promote a political platform or group of candidates, a cause, etc. **2** a group acting together to accomplish a task **3** a gathering for social entertainment **4** one concerned in an action, plan, lawsuit, etc. [*a party* to the action] **5** [Inf.] a person —*vi.* -**tied**, -**ty·ing** to attend or hold social parties, esp. with consumption of alcohol or drugs

par·ty·go·er (-gō′ər) *n.* a person who attends a party or many parties

party line 1 a single circuit connecting two or more telephone users with the exchange **2** the policies of a political party

par·ve·nu (pär′və nōō′) *n.* ⟦< L *pervenire*, arrive⟧ a newly rich person who is considered an upstart

pas·chal (pas′kəl) *adj.* ⟦< LL < Gr < Heb *pesach*, Passover⟧ **1** of Passover **2** of Easter

pa·sha (pä′shə, pə shä′) *n.* ⟦Turk⟧ [Historical] in Turkey, a title of rank or honor placed after the name

pass (pas) *vi.* ⟦< L *passus*, a step⟧ **1** to go or move forward, through, etc. **2** to go or be conveyed from one place, form, condition, etc. to another **3** *a)* to cease *b)* to depart **4** to die: usually with *away* or *on* **5** to go by **6** to elapse [an hour *passed*] **7** to make a way: with *through* or *by* **8** to be accepted without question **9** to be approved, as by a legislature **10** to go through a test, course, etc. successfully **11** to give a judgment, sentence, etc.: with *on* or *upon* **12** *Card Games* to decline a chance to bid —*vt.* **1** to go by, beyond, over, or through; specif., *a)* to leave behind *b)* to go through (a test, course, etc.) successfully **2** to cause or allow to go or proceed; specif., *a)* to ratify; enact *b)* to spend (time) *c)* to excrete **3** to cause to move from place to place; circulate **4** to give (an opinion or judgment) —*n.* **1** an act of passing; passage **2** a condition; situation [a strange *pass*] **3** *a)* a ticket, etc. giving permission to come or go freely or without charge *b) Mil.* a brief leave of absence **4** a motion of the hand, as in card tricks or hypnotism, or as if to strike **5** a tentative attempt **6** a narrow passage, etc., esp. between mountains **7** [Inf.] an implicit or explicit proposal of sexual intimacy **8** *Sports* a transfer of a ball, etc. to another player during play —**come (or bring) to pass** to (cause to) happen —**pass for** to be accepted as —**pass off** to cause to be accepted through deceit —**pass out 1** to distribute **2** to faint —**pass over** to disregard; ignore —**pass up** [Inf.] to refuse or let go by —**pass′er** *n.*

pass·a·ble *adj.* **1** that can be passed, traveled over, etc. **2** adequate; fair —**pass′a·bly** *adv.*

pas·sage (pas′ij) *n.* **1** a passing; specif., *a)* migration *b)* transition *c)* the enactment of a law **2** permission or right to pass **3** a voyage **4** a means of passing; road, passageway, etc. **5** an exchange, as of blows or words **6** a portion of a book, musical composition, etc.

pas·sage·way *n.* a narrow way for passage, as a hall or alley

pass·book *n.* BANKBOOK

pas·sé (pa sā′) *adj.* [Fr, past] out-of-date; old-fashioned

pas·sel (pas′əl) *n.* [< PARCEL] [Inf. or Dial.] a group, esp. a fairly large one

pas·sen·ger (pas′ən jər) *n.* [< OFr *passage*, passage] a person traveling in a train, boat, car, etc.

pass·er·by *n.,* *pl.* **pass′ers·by′** one who passes by: also **pass′er-by′,** *pl.* **pass′ers-by′**

pass-fail *adj. Educ.* designating a grading system recording "pass" or "fail" instead of a letter or number grade

pass·ing *adj.* **1** going by, beyond, etc. **2** fleeting **3** casual [a *passing* remark] **4** satisfying given requirements [a *passing* grade] —*n.* the act of one that passes; specif., death —**in passing** incidentally

pas·sion (pash′ən) *n.* [< L *pati*, endure] **1** any emotion, as hate, love, or fear **2** intense emotional excitement, as rage, enthusiasm, or lust **3** the object of any strong desire **4** [P-] the sufferings of Jesus, beginning after the Last Supper and continuing to his death on the Cross

pas·sion·ate (-ə nit) *adj.* **1** having or showing strong feelings **2** hot-tempered **3** ardent; intense **4** sensual —**pas′sion·ate·ly** *adv.*

pas·sive (pas′iv) *adj.* [see PASSION] **1** inactive, but acted upon **2** offering no resistance; submissive **3** *Gram.* denoting the voice of a verb whose subject is the recipient of the action —**pas′sive·ly** *adv.* —**pas·siv·i·ty** (pa siv′ə tē) *n.*

pas·sive-ag·gres·sive *adj. Psychol.* showing disguised aggression or resistance to others' expectations, as by procrastination or inefficiency

passive resistance opposition to a government, etc. by refusal to comply or by nonviolent acts such as fasting

pass·key *n.* **1** *a)* MASTER KEY *b)* SKELETON KEY **2** any private key

Pass·o·ver (pas′ō′vər) *n.* a Jewish holiday commemorating deliverance of the ancient Hebrews from slavery in Egypt

pass·port *n.* a government document carried by a citizen traveling abroad, certifying identity and citizenship

pass·word *n.* **1** a secret term used for identification, as in passing a guard **2** any means of gaining entrance

past (past) *vi., vt. rare pp.* of PASS —*adj.* **1** gone by; ended **2** of a former time **3** immediately preceding **4** *Gram.* indicating an action completed, or a condition in existence, at a former time [the *past* tense] —*n.* **1** time gone by **2** the history of a person, group, etc. **3** a personal background that is hidden or questionable —*prep.* beyond in time, space, etc. —*adv.* to and beyond some point

pas·ta (päs′tə) *n.* [It] **1** a flour paste or dough of which spaghetti, etc. is made **2** any food made of this

paste (pāst) *n.* [< Gr *pastē*, porridge] **1** dough for making pastry, etc. **2** any soft, moist, smooth preparation [*toothpaste*] **3** a mixture of flour, water, etc. used as an adhesive **4** the hard, brilliant glass of artificial gems —*vt.* **past′ed, past′ing 1** to make adhere with paste **2** [Slang] to hit

paste·board *n.* a stiff material made as of layers of paper pasted together

pas·tel (pas tel′) *n.* [< LL *pasta*, paste] **1** a crayon of ground coloring matter **2** a picture drawn with such crayons **3** a soft, pale shade of a color —*adj.* soft and pale: said of colors

pas·tern (pas′tərn) *n.* [< L *pastor*, shepherd] the part of the foot of a horse, dog, etc. just above the hoof or toes

Pas·teur (pas tur′), **Louis** 1822–95; Fr. chemist & bacteriologist

pas·teur·ize (pas′chər īz′, -tər-) *vt.* **-ized′, -iz′ing** [after prec.] to destroy bacteria in (milk, etc.) by heating to a prescribed temperature for a specified time —**pas′teur·i·za′tion** *n.*

pas·tiche (pas tēsh′) *n.* [Fr] **1** an artistic composition made up of bits from various sources **2** an artistic imitation of another's style

pas·time (pas′tīm′) *n.* a way of spending spare time; diversion

past master [for *passed master*] a person of long experience in an occupation, art, etc.; expert

pas·tor (pas′tər) *n.* [L, a shepherd] a priest or minister in charge of a congregation —**pas′tor·ate** (-it) *n.*

pas·to·ral (-tə rəl) *adj.* **1** of or relating to a pastor **2** of shepherds **3** of rustic life **4** peaceful; simple

past participle *Gram.* a participle used *a)* to express completed action (Ex.: *gone* in "he has gone") *b)* to form the passive voice (Ex.: *done* in "the deed was done") *c)* as an adjective (Ex.: *fried* in "fried fish")

pas·tra·mi (pə strä′mē) *n.* [E Yiddish, ult. < Turk *basdyrma*, dried meat] highly spiced smoked beef

pas·try (pās′trē) *n., pl.* **-tries** [see PASTE & -ERY] **1** pies, tarts, etc. with crusts baked from flour dough made with shortening **2** broadly, all fancy baked goods

pas·tur·age (pas′chər ij) *n.* PASTURE

pas·ture (pas′chər) *n.* ⟦< L *pascere*, to feed⟧ 1 grass, etc. used as food by grazing animals 2 ground suitable for grazing —*vt.* **-tured, -tur·ing** to put (cattle, etc.) out to graze in a pasture

past·y (pās′tē) *adj.* **-i·er, -i·est** of or like paste in color or texture

pat¹ (pat) *n.* ⟦prob. echoic⟧ 1 a gentle tap or stroke with the hand or a flat object 2 the sound made by this 3 a small lump, as of butter —*vt.* **pat′ted, pat′ting** 1 to tap or stroke gently, esp. with the hand 2 to shape or apply by patting —*adj.* 1 exactly suitable 2 so glibly plausible as to seem contrived —**pat on the back** 1 a compliment 2 to praise —**stand pat** [Inf.] to refuse to change an opinion, etc.

pat² *abbrev.* 1 patent 2 patented

patch (pach) *n.* ⟦ME *pacche*⟧ 1 a piece of material applied to mend a hole or strengthen a weak spot 2 a bandage 3 an area or spot [*patches* of blue sky] 4 a small plot of land 5 a scrap; bit 6 an adhesive pad containing a drug or hormone that is absorbed through the skin —*vt.* 1 to put a patch on 2 to produce crudely or hurriedly —**patch up** to settle (differences, a quarrel, etc.)

patch test *Med.* a test for allergy, made by attaching a sample of a substance to the skin and observing the reaction

patch·work *n.* 1 something made of irregular or miscellaneous parts 2 needlework, as a quilt, made of patches of cloth sewn together at their edges

patch·y *adj.* **-i·er, -i·est** 1 made up of patches 2 not consistent or uniform; irregular —**patch′i·ness** *n.*

pate (pāt) *n.* ⟦< ?⟧ the head, esp. the top of the head: a humorous term

pâ·té (pä tā′) *n.* ⟦Fr⟧ a meat paste or pie

pa·tel·la (pə tel′ə) *n., pl.* **-las** or **-lae** (-ē) ⟦< L *patina*, a pan⟧ a movable bone at the front of the human knee

pat·ent (pat′′nt; *also for adj.* 1, pāt′-) *adj.* ⟦< L *patere*, be open⟧ 1 obvious; plain 2 of or having to do with patents —*n.* 1 a document granting the exclusive right to produce or sell an invention, etc. for a specified time 2 *a)* the right so granted *b)* the thing protected by such a right —*vt.* to secure a patent for

patent leather (pat′′nt) ⟦formerly patented⟧ leather with a hard, glossy finish

patent medicine (pat′′nt) a trademarked medical preparation

pa·ter·nal (pə tur′nəl) *adj.* ⟦< L *pater*, father⟧ 1 of, like, or from a father 2 related through the father's side of the family —**pa·ter′nal·ly** *adv.*

pa·ter·nal·ism *n.* the governing or controlling of a country, employees, etc. in a manner suggesting a father's relationship with his children —**pa·ter·nal·is′tic** *adj.*

pa·ter·ni·ty (-nə tē) *n.* 1 the state of being a father 2 male parentage

pa·ter·nos·ter (pät′ər näs′tər) *n.* ⟦L, our father⟧ the Lord's Prayer, esp. in Latin: often **Pater Noster**

path (path) *n.* ⟦OE *pæth*⟧ 1 a way worn by footsteps 2 a walk for the use of people on foot 3 a line of movement 4 a course of conduct, thought, etc. —**path′less** *adj.*

pa·thet·ic (pə thet′ik) *adj.* ⟦see PATHOS⟧ 1 arousing pity, sorrow, etc.; pitiful 2 contemptibly unsuccessful, ineffective, etc. —**pa·thet′i·cal·ly** *adv.*

pathetic fallacy in literature, the attribution of human feelings and characteristics to inanimate things (Ex.: the angry sea)

patho- ⟦< Gr: see PATHOS⟧ *combining form* suffering, disease, feeling: also **path-**

path·o·gen (path′ə jən) *n.* ⟦prec. + -GEN⟧ a microorganism, etc. capable of causing disease —**path′o·gen′ic** (-jen′ik) *adj.*

pa·thol·o·gy (pə thäl′ə jē) *n., pl.* **-gies** ⟦< Gr *pathologia*: see fol. & -LOGY⟧ 1 the branch of medicine that deals with the nature of disease, esp. with structural and functional effects 2 any abnormal variation from a sound condition —**path·o·log·i·cal** (path′ə läj′i kəl) *adj.* —**pa·thol′o·gist** *n.*

pa·thos (pā′thäs′) *n.* ⟦Gr, suffering, disease, feeling⟧ the quality in something which arouses pity, sorrow, sympathy, etc.

path·way *n.* PATH

-pathy (pə thē) ⟦< Gr: see PATHOS⟧ *combining form* 1 feeling [*telepathy*] 2 (treatment of) disease [*osteopathy*]

pa·tience (pā′shəns) *n.* a being patient; calm endurance

pa·tient (-shənt) *adj.* ⟦< L *pati*, endure⟧ 1 enduring pain, trouble, etc. without complaining 2 calmly tolerating delay, confusion, etc. 3 diligent; persevering —*n.* one receiving medical care —**pa′tient·ly** *adv.*

pat·i·na (pat′′n ə, pə tē′nə) *n.* ⟦Fr < It⟧ a fine greenish crust on bronze or copper, formed by oxidation

pa·ti·o (pat′ē ō′) *n., pl.* **-os′** ⟦Sp⟧ 1 a courtyard open to the sky 2 a paved area adjoining a house, for outdoor lounging, dining, etc.

pa·tois (pa′twä′) *n., pl.* **-tois′** (-twäz′) ⟦Fr⟧ a provincial or local dialect

pat pend *abbrev.* patent pending

patri- ⟦< Gr *patēr*⟧ *combining form* father: also **patr-**

pa·tri·arch (pā′trē ärk′) *n.* ⟦< Gr *patēr*, father + *archein*, to rule⟧ 1 the father and head of a family or tribe, as Abraham, Isaac, or Jacob in the Bible 2 a man of great age and dignity 3 [*often* P-] a high-ranking bishop, as in the Eastern Orthodox Church

pa·tri·ar·chal (pā′trē är′kəl) *adj.* of a patriarch or patriarchy

pa·tri·arch·y (-är′kē) *n., pl.* **-ies** 1 a form of social organization in which the father is head of the family, descent being traced through the male line 2 rule or domination by men

pa·tri·cian (pə trish′ən) *n.* ⟦< L *pater*, father⟧ an aristocrat

pat·ri·cide (pa′trə sīd′) *n.* 1 the murdering of one's father 2 a person who does this

pat·ri·mo·ny (-mō′nē) *n., pl.* **-nies** ⟦< L *pater*, father⟧ property or traditions inherited from one's father or ancestors —**pat′ri·mo′ni·al** *adj.*

pa·tri·ot (pā′trē ət) *n.* ⟦< Gr *patris*, fatherland⟧ one who loves and zealously supports one's own country —**pa′tri·ot′ic** (-ät′ik) *adj.* —**pa′tri·ot′i·cal·ly** *adv.* —**pa′tri·ot·ism′** *n.*

pa·trol (pə tröl′) *vt., vi.* **-trolled′, -trol′ling** ⟦Fr *patrouiller*⟧ to make a regular, repeated circuit (of) in guarding —*n.* **1** a patrolling **2** a person or group patrolling

patrol car a police car used to patrol an area

pa·trol·man (-mən) *n., pl.* **-men** (-mən) a policeman who patrols a certain area

patrol wagon an enclosed truck used by police to carry prisoners

pa·trol·wom·an *n., pl.* **-wom′en** a policewoman who patrols a certain area

pa·tron (pā′trən) *n.* ⟦< L *pater*, father⟧ one who supports, sponsors, or protects some person, activity, etc. **2** a regular customer

pa·tron·age (pā′trə nij, pa′-) *n.* **1** support, encouragement, etc. given by a patron **2** *a)* clientele *b)* business; trade **3** *a)* the power to grant political favors *b)* such favors

pa·tron·ess (pā′trə nis) *n.* a woman who supports, sponsors, or protects some person, activity, etc.

pa·tron·ize (pā′trə nīz′, pa′-) *vt.* **-ized′, -iz′ing 1** to sponsor; support **2** to be kind or helpful to, but in a haughty or snobbish way **3** to be a regular customer of

patron saint a saint looked upon as a special guardian

pat·ro·nym·ic (pa′trə nim′ik) *n.* ⟦< Gr *patēr*, father + *onyma*, name⟧ a name showing descent from a given person (Ex.: *Johnson*, son of John)

pat·sy (pat′sē) *n., pl.* **-sies** [Slang] a person easily imposed upon or victimized

pat·ter′ (pat′ər) *vi.* ⟦< PAT¹⟧ to make, or move so as to make, a patter —*n.* a series of quick, light taps [*the patter* of rain]

pat·ter² (pat′ər) *vi.* ⟦< PATERNOSTER⟧ to speak rapidly or glibly —*n.* **1** glib, rapid speech, as of salespeople or comedians **2** idle chatter

pat·tern (pat′ərn) *n.* ⟦< OFr *patrun*, patron⟧ **1** a model or plan used in making things **2** a design **3** a regular way of acting or doing **4** a predictable or repeating arrangement, sequence, etc. —*vt.* to make or do in imitation of a pattern

pat·ty (pat′ē) *n., pl.* **-ties** ⟦Fr *pâté*, pie⟧ **1** a small pie **2** a small, flat cake of ground meat, fish, etc.

pau·ci·ty (pô′sə tē) *n.* ⟦< L *paucus*, few⟧ **1** smallness of number or amount **2** scarcity

Paul (pôl) (original name *Saul*) (died A.D. 67?); the Apostle of Christianity to the Gentiles; author of several Epistles in the New Testament: also **Saint Paul**

paunch (pônch) *n.* ⟦< L *pantex*, belly⟧ a potbelly —**paunch′y** *adj.*

pau·per (pô′pər) *n.* ⟦L⟧ an extremely poor person, esp. one who lives on charity —**pau′per·ize′** *vt.* **-ized′, -iz′ing**

pause (pôz) *n.* ⟦< Gr *pauein*, to bring to an end⟧ a temporary stop or rest —*vi.* **paused, paus′ing** to make a pause; stop

pave (pāv) *vt.* **paved, pav′ing** ⟦< L *pavire*, to beat⟧ to cover the surface of (a road, etc.), as with concrete —**pave the way (for)** to prepare the way (for)

pave·ment *n.* a paved surface, as of concrete; specif., a paved road, etc.

pa·vil·ion (pə vil′yən) *n.* ⟦< L *papilio*, tent⟧ **1** a large tent **2** a building, often partly open, for exhibits, etc., as at a fair or park **3** any of a group of related buildings, as of a hospital

Pav·lov (pav′lôv′), **I·van** (i vän′) 1849-1936; Russ. physiologist

paw (pô) *n.* ⟦< OFr *poue*⟧ **1** the foot of a four-footed animal having claws **2** [Inf.] a hand —*vt., vi.* **1** to touch, dig, hit, etc. with paws or feet **2** to handle clumsily or roughly

pawl (pôl) *n.* ⟦<?⟧ a device, as a hinged tongue which engages cogs in a wheel, allowing rotation in only one direction

pawn¹ (pôn) *n.* ⟦< L *pannus*, cloth⟧ **1** anything given as security, as for a debt **2** the state of being pledged [a ring in *pawn*] —*vt.* **1** to give as security **2** to wager or risk

pawn² (pôn) *n.* ⟦< ML *pedo*, foot soldier⟧ **1** a chess piece of the lowest value **2** a person used to advance another's purposes

pawn·bro·ker *n.* a person licensed to lend money at interest on personal property left as security

pawn·shop *n.* a pawnbroker's shop

paw-paw (pô′pô′) *n. var. of* PAPAW

pay (pā) *vt.* **paid** or [Obs.] (except in **pay out**) **payed, pay′ing** ⟦< L *pacare*, pacify⟧ **1** to give to (a person) what is due, as for goods or services **2** to give (what is due) in return, as for goods or services **3** to settle (a debt, etc.) **4** *a)* to give (a compliment, etc.) *b)* to make (a visit, etc.) **5** to be profitable to —*vi.* **1** to give due compensation **2** to be profitable —*n.* money paid; esp., wages or salary —*adj.* **1** operated by the insertion of coins [a *pay* phone] **2** designating a service, etc. paid for by fees [*pay* TV] —**in the pay of** employed and paid by —**pay back 1** to repay **2** to retaliate upon —**pay down** to pay (part of the price) at purchase as an installment —**pay for** to suffer or atone for (a wrong) —**pay off 1** to pay all that is owed on or for **2** to yield full recompense **3** [Inf.] to succeed —**pay out** to let out (a rope, cable, etc.) —**pay up** to pay in full or on time —**pay′er** *n.*

pay·a·ble *adj.* **1** that can be paid **2** due to be paid (on a specified date)

pay·check *n.* a check in payment of wages or salary —*adj.* designating or of a short-term loan to be paid back from the borrower's next paycheck

pay·day *n.* the day on which salary or wages are paid

pay dirt soil, ore, etc. rich in valuable minerals —**hit (or strike) pay dirt** [Inf.] to discover a source of wealth, success, etc.

pay·ee (pā ē′) *n.* one to whom a payment is made or owed

pay·load *n.* **1** a cargo **2** a load, as a warhead or satellite, carried by an aircraft, rocket, etc. but not essential to its flight operations

pay·mas·ter *n.* the official in charge of paying employees

pay·ment *n.* **1** a paying or being paid **2** something that is paid

pay·off *n.* **1** a settlement, reckoning, or payment **2** [Inf.] a bribe **3** [Inf.] a climax or culmination

pay·o·la (pā ō′lə) *n.* [Slang] **1** a bribe **2** bribery

pay·out *n.* **1** a paying out; disbursement **2** an amount paid out; dividend

pay-per-view *adj.* TV of a system for paying for single showings of films or programs, as by cable or satellite —*n.* such a system

pay phone a public telephone, usually coin-operated or accepting credit cards

pay·roll *n.* **1** a list of employees to be paid, with the amount due to each **2** the total amount needed for this

pay·wall *n.* a system designed to prevent the viewing of a website if a subscription fee has not been paid

Pb [L *plumbum*] *abbrev. Chem. symbol for* lead

PB&J *abbrev.* peanut butter and jelly (sandwitch)

PBX *n.* [p(*rivate*) b(*ranch*) (e)x(*change*)] a telephone system within an organization, having outside lines

PC¹ *n., pl.* **PCs** or **PC's** PERSONAL COMPUTER

PC² *abbrev.* politically correct or political correctness

pct *abbrev.* percent

PCV valve [p(*ositive*) c(*rankcase*) v(*entilation*)] a valve regulating the pollution control system of a motor vehicle

pd *abbrev.* paid

Pd *Chem. symbol for* palladium

PE *abbrev.* **1** physical education **2** Prince Edward Island

pea (pē) *n., pl.* **peas** [< ME *pese*, a pea, taken as pl.; ult. < Gr *pison*] **1** a climbing plant with green pods **2** its small round seed, used as a vegetable

peace (pēs) *n.* [< L *pax*] **1** freedom from war **2** an agreement to end war **3** law and order **4** harmony; concord **5** serenity or quiet —**hold (or keep) one's peace** to be silent —**peace′a·ble** *adj.*

peace·ful *adj.* **1** not quarrelsome **2** free from disturbance; calm **3** of or in a time of peace —**peace′ful·ly** *adv.*

peace·mak·er *n.* a person who makes peace, as by settling quarrels —**peace′mak′ing** *n., adj.*

peace officer an officer entrusted with maintaining law and order, as a sheriff

peace pipe CALUMET

peace·time *n.* a time of freedom from war —*adj.* of such a time

peach (pēch) *n.* [< L *Persicum* (*malum*), Persian (apple)] **1** a tree with round, juicy, orange-yellow fruit having a fuzzy skin and a rough pit **2** its fruit **3** the color of this fruit **4** [Slang] a well-liked person or thing

pea·cock (pē′käk′) *n.* [< L *pavo*, peacock] a male peafowl, having a long, showy tail that can be spread out like a fan

pea·fowl (pē′foul′) *n.* any of various pheasantlike birds of S and SE Asia or central Africa

pea·hen (pē′hen′) *n.* a female peafowl

pea jacket (pē) [< Du *pijjekker*] a hip-length, double-breasted coat of heavy woolen cloth, worn orig. by seamen

peak (pēk) *n.* [var. of Brit dial. *pike*, prob. < ON *pic*] **1** a pointed end or top, as of a cap or roof **2** *a)* the summit of a hill or mountain ending in a point *b)* a mountain with such a summit **3** the highest or utmost point of anything —*adj.* maximum —*vi.* to come to a peak

peak·ed (pē′kid) *adj.* [< ?] thin and drawn, or weak and pale, as from illness

peal (pēl) *n.* [ME *apele*, appeal] **1** the loud ringing of a bell or bells **2** a set of tuned bells **3** a loud, prolonged sound, as of thunder or laughter —*vi., vt.* to sound in a peal; ring

pea·nut *n.* **1** a vine related to the pea, with underground pods containing edible seeds **2** the pod or any of its seeds **3** [*pl.*] [Slang] a trifling sum of money

peanut butter a food paste or spread made by grinding roasted peanuts

pear (per) *n.* [< L *pirum*] **1** a tree with greenish-yellow, brown, or reddish fruit **2** the juicy fruit, round at the base and narrowing toward the stem

pearl (purl) *n.* [< L *perna*, sea mussel] **1** a smooth, hard, usually white or bluish-gray object, a roundish growth formed within the shell of some oysters and other mollusks: used as a gem **2** MOTHER-OF-PEARL **3** any person or thing like a pearl in beauty, value, etc. **4** bluish-gray —**pearl′y** *adj.* **-i·er, -iest**

Pearl Harbor inlet on the S coast of Oahu, Hawaii: site of a U.S. naval base bombed by Japan on Dec. 7, 1941

peas·ant (pez′ənt) *n.* [< LL *pagus*, district] **1** one who owns or works on a small farm, esp. in a traditional society **2** a person regarded as boorish, ignorant, etc. —**peas′ant·ry** *n.*

peat (pēt) *n.* [< ML *peta*, piece of turf] partly decayed plant matter from ancient swamps, used for fuel

peat moss peat composed of residues of mosses, used as mulch

peb·ble (peb′əl) *n.* [< OE *papol-*(*stan*), pebble (stone), prob. echoic] a small stone worn smooth and round, as by running water —**peb′bly** *adj.* **-bli·er, -bli·est**

pe·can (pē kän′, -kan′; pi-; pē′kän′, -kan′) *n.* [< AmInd] **1** an edible nut with a thin, smooth shell **2** the tree it grows on

pec·ca·dil·lo (pek′ə dil′ō) *n., pl.* **-loes** or **-los** [< Sp < L *peccare*, to sin] a small fault or offense

pec·ca·ry (pek′ə rē) *n., pl.* **-ries** [< native name] a piglike animal of North and South America, with sharp tusks

peck¹ (pek) *vt.* [ME *picken*, to pick] **1** to strike, as with a beak **2** to make by doing this [to *peck* a hole] **3** to pick up with the beak —*vi.* to make strokes as with a pointed object —*n.* **1** a stroke so made **2** [Inf.] a quick, casual kiss —**peck at** [Inf.] **1** to eat very little of **2** to criticize constantly

peck² (pek) *n.* [< OFr *pek*] a unit of dry measure, ¼ bushel or eight quarts

pecking order a hierarchy of members of a group, based on status, relative power, etc.

pecs (peks) *pl.n.* [Slang] pectoral muscles

pec·tin (pek′tin) *n.* [< Gr *pēktos*, congealed] a carbohydrate, obtained from certain fruits, which forms a gel that is the basis of jellies and jams

pec·to·ral (pek′tə rəl) *adj.* [< L *pectus*, breast] of or located in or on the chest or breast

pec·u·la·tion (pek′yoo lā′shən) *n.* [ult. < L *culium*, private property] embezzlement

pe·cu·liar (pi kyoōl′yər) *adj.* [< L *peculium*: see prec.] **1** of only one person, thing, etc.; exclusive **2** special **3** odd; strange —**pe·cu′liar·ly** *adv.*

pe·cu·li·ar·i·ty (pi kyoō′lē er′ə tē) *n.* **1** a being peculiar **2** *pl.* **-ties** something that is peculiar, as a trait

pe·cu·ni·ar·y (pi kyoō′nē er′ē) *adj.* [< L *pecunia*, money] of or involving money

ped·a·gogue or **ped·a·gog** (ped′ə gäg′) *n.* [< Gr *paidagōgos* < *pais*, child + *agein*, to lead] a teacher, esp. a pedantic one

ped·a·gog·y (-gäj′ē, -gō′jē) *n.* **1** the act of teaching **2** the art or science of teaching —**ped′a·gog′ic** *adj.*, **ped′a·gog′i·cal**

ped·al (ped′'l) *adj.* [< L *pes*, FOOT] of the foot or feet —*n.* a lever operated by the foot, as on a bicycle or organ —*vt.*, *vi.* **-aled** or **-alled**, **-al·ing** or **-al·ling** to operate by pedals; use the pedals of

ped·ant (ped′nt) *n.* [ult. < Gr *paidagōgos*: see PEDAGOGUE] **1** one who emphasizes trivial points of learning **2** a narrow-minded teacher who insists on exact adherence to rules —**pe·dan′tic** *adj.* —**ped′ant·ry** *n.*

ped·dle (ped′'l) *vt.*, *vi.* **-dled**, **-dling** [< ? *ped*, basket] to go from place to place selling (small articles) —**ped′dler** *n.*

-pede (pēd) [< L *pes*] *combining form* foot or feet [*centipede*]

ped·er·as·ty (ped′ər as′tē) *n.* [< Gr *paiderastēs*, lover of boys] sodomy between a man and a boy —**ped′er·ast′** *n.*

ped·es·tal (ped′əs təl) *n.* [< It *piè*, foot + *di*, of + *stal*, a rest] a bottom support of a pillar, statue, etc.

pe·des·tri·an (pi des′trē ən) *adj.* [< L *pes*, foot] **1** going or done on foot **2** of or for pedestrians **3** ordinary and dull; prosaic —*n.* one who goes on foot; walker

pe·di·at·rics (pē′dē a′triks) *n.* [< Gr *pais*, child + *iatros*, physician] the branch of medicine dealing with the care of infants and children —**pe′di·a·tri′cian** (-ə trish′ən) *n.* —**pe′di·at′ric** *adj.*

ped·i·cab (ped′i kab′) *n.* [< L *pes*, foot + CAB] a three-wheeled carriage pedaled like a bicycle by the driver

ped·i·cure (ped′i kyoor′) *n.* [< L *pes*, FOOT + *cura*, care] a trimming, polishing, etc. of the toenails

ped·i·gree (ped′i grē′) *n.* [< MFr *pié de grue*, lit., crane's foot: from lines in genealogical tree] **1** a list of ancestors **2** descent; lineage **3** a known line of descent, esp. of a purebred animal —**ped′i·greed′** *adj.*

ped·i·ment (ped′i mənt) *n.* [< earlier *periment*, prob. < PYRAMID] an ornamental gable or triangular piece on the front of a building, over a doorway, etc.

pe·dom·e·ter (pē däm′ət ər, pi-) *n.* [< L *pes*, foot + Gr *metron*, a measure] an instrument carried to measure the distance walked

ped·o·phil·i·a (ped′ə fil′ē ə, pēd′ə-) *n.* [< Gr *pais*, child + *philos*, loving] an abnormal condition in which an adult has a sexual attraction to children —**pe′do·phile′** *n.*

pe·dun·cle (pē dun′kəl, pēd′un′-) *n.* [< L *pes*, foot] a stalklike part in some plants, animals, etc.

pee (pē) [Inf.] *vi.*, *vt.* **peed, pee′ing** to urinate —*n.* **1** urine **2** an act of urination

peek (pēk) *vi.* [ME *piken*] to look quickly and furtively —*n.* such a look

peel (pēl) *vt.* [< L *pilare*, make bald] to cut away (the rind, skin, etc.) of —*vi.* **1** to shed skin, etc. **2** to come off in layers or flakes —*n.* the rind or skin of a fruit —**peel′er** *n.*

peel·ing *n.* a peeled-off strip

peen (pēn) *n.* [prob. < Scand] the end of a hammerhead opposite the flat striking surface, usually ball-shaped or wedge-shaped

peep¹ (pēp) *vi.* [echoic] to make the short, high-pitched cry of a young bird —*n.* a peeping sound

peep² (pēp) *vi.* [ME *pepen*] **1** to look through a small opening or from a place of hiding **2** to appear gradually or partially —*n.* a brief look; furtive glimpse —**peep′er** *n.*

peep·hole *n.* a hole to peep through

peeping Tom [after legendary tailor who peeped at Lady GODIVA] one who gets sexual pleasure from furtively watching others

peer¹ (pir) *n.* [< L *par*, an equal] **1** a person or thing of the same rank, ability, etc.; an equal **2** a British noble —**peer′age** (-ij) *n.*

peer² (pir) *vi.* [< ? APPEAR] to look closely, as in trying to see more clearly

peer·ess (pir′is) *n.* a British noblewoman

peer·less *adj.* without equal

peeve (pēv) [Inf.] *vt.* **peeved, peev′ing** to make peevish; annoy —*n.* an annoyance

pee·vish (pē′vish) *adj.* [ME *pevische*] irritable; fretful; cross —**pee′vish·ly** *adv.* —**pee′vish·ness** *n.*

pee·wee (pē′wē′) *n.* [< ?] [Inf.] an unusually small person or thing

peg (peg) *n.* [ME *pegge*] **1** a short piece of wood, metal, etc. used to hold parts together, hang things on, etc. **2** a step or degree **3** [Inf.] a throw —*vt.* **pegged, peg′ging** to fasten, fix, secure, mark, etc. with pegs

Peg·a·sus (peg′ə səs) *n.* Gr. Myth. a winged horse

peg·board *n.* a piece of boardlike material with rows of holes for hooks or pegs to hold displays, tools, etc.

peign·oir (pān wär′, pen-) *n.* ⟦Fr⟧ a woman's full, loose dressing gown

Pei·ping (bā′piŋ′) *a former transliteration of* BEIJING

pe·jo·ra·tive (pi jôr′ə tiv) *adj.* ⟦< L *pejor*, worse⟧ disparaging or derogatory —**pe·jo′ra·tive·ly** *adv.*

Pe·king (pē′kiŋ′) *a former transliteration of* BEIJING

Pe·king·ese (pē′kə nēz′) *n., pl.* **-ese′** a small dog with a long, straight coat, short legs, and a short, wrinkled muzzle: also **Pe′kin·ese′** (-kə nēz′)

pe·koe (pē′kō) *n.* ⟦< Chin dial. *pek-ho*, white down (on the leaves used)⟧ a black tea of Sri Lanka and India

pe·lag·ic (pi laj′ik) *adj.* ⟦< Gr *pelagos*, sea⟧ of the open sea or ocean

pelf (pelf) *n.* ⟦< ? MFr *pelfre*, booty⟧ money or wealth regarded with contempt

pel·i·can (pel′i kən) *n.* ⟦< Gr *pelekan*⟧ a large, web-footed water bird with an expandable pouch in the lower bill for scooping up fish

pel·la·gra (pə lā′grə, -lag′rə) *n.* ⟦It ult. < L *pellis*, skin + Gr *agra*, seizure⟧ a chronic disease caused by a lack of niacin in the diet, characterized by skin eruptions and mental disorders

pel·let (pel′it) *n.* ⟦< L *pila*, a ball⟧ 1 a little ball, as of clay or medicine 2 a bullet, piece of lead shot, etc.

pell-mell (pel′mel′) *adv., adj.* ⟦< OFr *mesler*, to mix⟧ 1 in a jumble 2 in wild, disorderly haste Also **pell′mell′**

pel·lu·cid (pə lōō′sid) *adj.* ⟦< L *per*, through + *lucere*, to shine⟧ 1 transparent; clear 2 easy to understand

pelt[1] (pelt) *vt.* ⟦ME *pelten*⟧ 1 to throw things at 2 to beat repeatedly —*vi.* to strike heavily or steadily: said as of hard rain

pelt[2] (pelt) *n.* ⟦prob. < OFr *pel*, a skin⟧ the skin of a fur-bearing animal, esp. when stripped from the carcass

pel·vis (pel′vis) *n., pl.* **-vis·es** or **-ves′** (-vēz′) ⟦L, basin⟧ 1 the basinlike cavity in the posterior part of the trunk in many vertebrates: in humans, it supports the spinal column and rests on the legs 2 the bones forming this cavity —**pel′vic** *adj.*

pem·mi·can (pem′i kən) *n.* ⟦< AmInd⟧ a concentrated food made of dried beef, suet, dried fruit, etc.

pen[1] (pen) *n.* ⟦OE *penn*⟧ 1 a small enclosure for domestic animals 2 any small enclosure —*vt.* **penned** or **pent**, **pen′ning** to enclose as in a pen

pen[2] (pen) *n.* ⟦< L *penna*, a feather⟧ a device used in writing, etc., having a pointed end supplied with ink either from an internal reservoir or from an inkwell —*vt.* **penned**, **pen′ning** to write with or as with a pen

pen[3] (pen) *n.* ⟦Slang⟧ a penitentiary

Pen or **pen** *abbrev.* peninsula

pe·nal (pē′nəl) *adj.* ⟦< Gr *poinē*, penalty⟧ of, for, constituting, or making a person liable to punishment

pe·nal·ize (pē′nə līz′, pen′ə-) *vt.* **-ized′, -iz′ing** to impose a penalty on; punish —**pe′nal·i·za′tion** *n.*

pen·al·ty (pen′əl tē) *n., pl.* **-ties** 1 a punishment 2 the handicap, etc. imposed on an offender, as a fine

pen·ance (pen′əns) *n.* ⟦see PENITENT⟧ voluntary self-punishment to show repentance for wrongdoing, sins, etc.

pence (pens) *n. pl. of* ⟦Brit.⟧ PENNY

pen·chant (pen′chənt) *n.* ⟦Fr < *pencher*, to incline⟧ a strong liking

pen·cil (pen′səl) *n.* ⟦< L *penis*, a tail⟧ a rod-shaped instrument with a core of graphite, crayon, etc. that is sharpened to a point for writing, drawing, etc. —*vt.* **-ciled** or **-cilled**, **-cil·ing** or **-cil·ling** to write, etc. with a pencil

pend (pend) *vi.* ⟦< L *pendere*, hang⟧ to await judgment or decision

pend·ant (pen′dənt) *n.* ⟦see prec.⟧ a hanging ornamental object, as one on a necklace or earring

pend·ent (pen′dənt) *adj.* ⟦see PEND⟧ 1 suspended 2 overhanging 3 undecided; pending

pend·ing *adj.* ⟦prp. of PEND, infl. by Fr *pendant*, L *pendens*⟧ 1 not decided 2 impending —*prep.* until

pen·du·lous (pen′dyoo ləs, -joo-) *adj.* ⟦see PEND⟧ hanging freely; drooping

pen·du·lum (pen′dyoo ləm, -joo-) *n.* ⟦see PEND⟧ a weight hung so as to swing freely to and fro: used to regulate clock movements

pen·e·trate (pen′i trat′) *vt., vi.* **-trat·ed, -trat′ing** ⟦< L *penitus*, inward⟧ 1 to enter by or as by piercing 2 to have an effect throughout 3 to affect deeply 4 to understand —**pen′e·tra·ble** (-trə bəl) *adj.* —**pen′e·tra′tion** *n.*

pen·e·trat·ing (pen′i trāt′iŋ) *adj.* 1 that penetrates 2 sharp; piercing 3 acute; discerning Also **pen′e·tra′tive** (-trāt′iv)

pen·guin (peŋ′gwin, pen′-) *n.* ⟦prob. < Welsh⟧ a flightless bird of the Southern Hemisphere with webbed feet and flippers for swimming

pen·i·cil·lin (pen′i sil′in) *n.* ⟦< L *penicillus*, brush⟧ an antibiotic obtained from certain molds or produced synthetically

pen·in·su·la (pə nin′sə lə) *n.* ⟦< L *paene*, almost + *insula*, isle⟧ a land area almost surrounded by water —**pen·in′su·lar** *adj.*

pe·nis (pē′nis) *n., pl.* **-nis·es** or **-nes′** (-nēz′) ⟦L⟧ the male organ of sexual intercourse —**pe′nile** (-nīl′) *adj.*

pen·i·tent (pen′i tənt) *adj.* ⟦< L *paenitere*, repent⟧ sorry for having done wrong and willing to atone —*n.* a penitent person —**pen′i·tence** *n.* —**pen′i·ten′tial** (-ten′shəl) *adj.* —**pen′i·tent·ly** *adv.*

pen·i·ten·tia·ry (pen′i ten′shə rē) *n., pl.* **-ries** a state or federal prison for persons convicted of serious crimes

pen·knife *n., pl.* **-knives′** (-nīvz′) a small pocketknife

pen·light or **pen·lite** *n.* a flashlight about the size of a fountain pen

pen·man·ship *n.* handwriting as an art or skill

Penn (pen), **William** 1644-1718; Eng. Quaker: founder of Pennsylvania

pen name a pseudonym

pen·nant (pen′ənt) *n.* [< PENNON] 1 any long, narrow flag 2 such a flag symbolizing a championship, esp. in baseball

pen·ne (pen′ā′) *n.* pasta in the form of tubes, cut diagonally on the ends

pen·ni·less (pen′ə lis) *adj.* without even a penny; extremely poor

pen·non (pen′ən) *n.* [< L *penna*, a feather] a flag or pennant

Penn·syl·va·ni·a (pen′səl vān′yə) state of the NE U.S.; cap. Harrisburg: abbrev. *PA* —**Penn′syl·va′ni·an** *adj., n.*

pen·ny (pen′ē) *n., pl.* **-nies** or **pence** (pens) [< OE *penig*] 1 in the United Kingdom, 1/100 of a pound 2 a U.S. or Canadian cent

pen·ny-an·te *adj.* [Inf.] having a contemptibly small value

penny arcade a building, as at an amusement park, with coin-operated games, etc.

penny pincher a miserly person —**pen′ny-pinch′ing** *n., adj.*

pen·ny·weight *n.* a unit of weight, equal to 1/20 ounce troy weight

pen·ny-wise *adj.* thrifty in small matters —**penny-wise and pound-foolish** thrifty in small matters but wasteful in major ones

pe·nol·o·gy (pē näl′ə jē) *n.* [< Gr *poinē*, punishment + -LOGY] the study of prison management

pen pal a person, esp. a stranger in another country, with whom one exchanges letters

pen·sion (pen′shən) *n.* [< L *pensio*, a paying] a regular payment, not wages, as to one who is retired or disabled —*vt.* to grant a pension to

pen·sion·er *n.* one who receives a pension

pen·sive (pen′siv) *adj.* [< L *pensare*, consider] thoughtful or reflective, often in a melancholy way —**pen′sive·ly** *adv.* —**pen′sive·ness** *n.*

pent (pent) *vt. alt. pt. & pp. of* PEN[1] —*adj.* held or kept in; penned: often with *up*

penta- [< Gr *pente*, FIVE] *combining form* five

pen·ta·gon (pen′tə gän′) *n.* [< Gr *penta-*, five + *gōnia*, an angle] a plane figure with five angles and five sides —**the Pentagon** the pentagonal office building of the Defense Department, located near Washington, DC —**pen·tag′o·nal** (-tag′ə nəl) *adj.*

pen·tam·e·ter (pen tam′ət ər) *n.* [see PENTA- & METER[1]] a line of verse containing five metrical feet; esp., English iambic pentameter (Ex.: "Hĕ jésts| ăt scárs| whŏ név′| ĕr félt| ă woúnd")

Pen·ta·teuch (pen′tə tōōk′) *n.* [< Gr *penta-*, five + *teuchos*, book] the first five books of the Bible; the Torah

pen·tath·lon (pen tath′län′) *n.* [< Gr *penta-*, five + *athlon*, a contest] an athletic contest in which each contestant takes part in five events —**pen·tath′lete** (-lēt′) *n.*

Pen·te·cost (pen′tə kôst′) *n.* [< Gr *pentēkostē* (*hēmera*), the fiftieth (day)] a Christian festival on the seventh Sunday after Easter

Pen·te·cos·tal (pen′tə kôs′təl) *adj.* designating or of any of various Protestant fundamentalist sects often stressing direct inspiration by the Holy Spirit —**Pen′te·cos′tal·ism′** *n.*

pent·house (pent′hous′) *n.* [ult. < L *appendere*, append] an apartment on the roof or on the top floor of a building

pent-up (pent′up′) *adj.* held in check; curbed [*pent-up* emotion]

pe·nu·che or **pe·nu·chi** (pə nōō′chē) *n.* [var. of PANOCHA] a candy similar to fudge

pe·nul·ti·mate (pē nul′tə mət) *adj.* [< L *paene*, almost + ULTIMATE] next to the last

pe·nu·ri·ous (pe nyoor′ē əs, -noor′-) *adj.* [see fol.] 1 miserly; stingy 2 impoverished —**pe·nu′ri·ous·ly** *adv.*

pen·u·ry (pen′yōō rē, -yə-) *n.* [< L *penuria*, want] extreme poverty

pe·on (pē′än′) *n.* [< ML *pedo*, foot soldier] 1 in Spanish America, a member of the laboring class 2 [Historical] in the SW U.S., a person forced into servitude to work off a debt —**pe′on·age** (-ə nij) *n.*

pe·o·ny (pē′ə nē) *n., pl.* **-nies** [< Gr *Paiōn*, Apollo as god of medicine: from its former medicinal use] 1 a plant with large, showy, pink, white, red, or yellow flowers 2 the flower

peo·ple (pē′pəl) *n., pl.* **-ples** [< L *populus*, nation, crowd] all the persons of a racial or ethnic group; nation, race, etc. —*pl.n.* 1 *pl. of* PERSON (*n.* 1) 2 the persons of a certain place, group, or class 3 one's family; relatives 4 the populace 5 persons considered indefinitely [what will *people* say?] 6 humans —*vt.* **-pled, -pling** to populate

pep (pep) [Inf.] *n.* [< fol.] energy; vigor —*vt.* **pepped, pep′ping** to fill with pep; invigorate: with *up* —**pep′py** *adj.* **-pi·er, -pi·est**

pep·per (pep′ər) *n.* [< Gr *peperi*] 1 *a*) a pungent condiment ground from the dried fruits of an East Indian vine *b*) this vine 2 a plant with red or green, sweet or hot pods —*vt.* 1 to season with ground pepper 2 to pelt with small objects

pep·per·corn *n.* the dried berry of the pepper

pepper mill a hand mill used to grind peppercorns

pep·per·mint *n.* 1 a plant of the mint family that yields a pungent oil used for flavoring 2 the oil 3 a candy flavored with this oil

pep·per·o·ni (pep′ər ō′nē) *n., pl.* **-nis** or **-ni** [< It *peperoni*] a hard, highly spiced Italian sausage

pepper shaker a container for ground pepper, with a perforated top

pep·per·y *adj.* 1 of, like, or highly seasoned with pepper 2 sharp or fiery, as words 3 hot-tempered

pep·sin (pep′sin) *n.* [< Gr *peptein*, to digest] a stomach enzyme, aiding in the digestion of proteins

pep talk a talk, as to an athletic team by its coach, to instill enthusiasm, determination, etc.

pep·tic (pep′tik) *adj.* ⟦see PEPSIN⟧ **1** of or aiding digestion **2** caused by digestive secretions [a *peptic* ulcer]

per (pur) *prep.* ⟦L⟧ **1** through; by; by means of **2** for each [fifty cents *per* yard] **3** [Inf.] according to

per- [< prec.] *prefix* **1** through, throughout **2** thoroughly

per·ad·ven·ture (pur′əd ven′chər) *adv.* ⟦< OFr *par*, by + *aventure*, chance⟧ [Archaic] possibly

per·am·bu·late (pər am′byŏŏ lāt′) *vt., vi.* -**lat**′**ed**, -**lat**′**ing** ⟦< L *per*, through + *ambulare*, to walk⟧ to walk (through, over, etc.)

per·am·bu·la·tor (-lāt′ər) *n.* [Chiefly Brit.] a baby carriage

per an·num (pər an′əm) ⟦L⟧ yearly

per·cale (pər kāl′) *n.* ⟦Fr < Pers *pargāla*, scrap⟧ fine, closely woven cotton cloth, used for sheets, etc.

per cap·i·ta (pər kap′i tə) ⟦ML, lit., by heads⟧ for each person

per·ceive (pər sēv′) *vt., vi.* -**ceived**′, -**ceiv**′**ing** ⟦< L *per*, through + *capere*, take⟧ **1** to understand **2** to become aware (of) through the senses

per·cent (pər sent′) *adv., adj.* ⟦< L *per centum*] in, to, or for every hundred: symbol, %: also **per cent** —*n.* [Inf.] percentage

per·cent·age *n.* **1** a given part in every hundred **2** part; portion **3** [Inf.] advantage; profit

per·cen·tile (pər sen′til′, -sent′′l) *n.* *Statistics* any of 100 divisions of a series, each of equal frequency

per·cep·ti·ble (pər sep′tə bəl) *adj.* that can be perceived —**per·cep′ti·bly** *adv.*

per·cep·tion (-shən) *n.* ⟦< L *percipere*, perceive⟧ **1** the mental grasp of objects, etc. through the knowledge, etc. **2** insight or intuition **3** the knowledge, etc. gotten by perceiving —**per·cep′tion·al** *adj.*

per·cep·tive (-tiv) *adj.* **1** of perception **2** able to perceive quickly —**per·cep′tive·ly** *adv.* —**per·cep′tive·ness** *n.*

per·cep·tu·al (-chōō əl) *adj.* of or involving perception

perch[1] (purch) *n., pl.* -**es** ⟦< Gr *perkē*⟧ **1** a small, spiny-finned, freshwater food fish **2** any of various other spiny-finned fishes

perch[2] (purch) *n.* ⟦< L *pertica*, pole⟧ **1** a horizontal pole, etc. serving as a roost for birds **2** any high resting place — *vi., vt.* to rest or place on or as on a perch

per·chance (pər chans′) *adv.* ⟦< OFr *par*, by + *chance*, chance⟧ [Archaic] **1** by chance **2** perhaps

per·co·late (pur′kə lāt′) *vt.* -**lat**′**ed**, -**lat**′**ing** ⟦< L *per*, through + *colare*, to strain⟧ to filter (a liquid) through a porous substance —*vi.* to ooze through a porous substance

per·co·la·tor (-lāt′ər) *n.* a coffeepot in which the boiling water bubbles up through a tube and filters back down through the ground coffee

per·cus·sion (pər kush′ən) *n.* ⟦< L *per-*, thor-

oughly + *quatere*, shake⟧ **1** the hitting of one body against another **2** the shock, vibration, etc. from this —*adj.* of a musical instrument producing a tone when struck, as a drum, cymbal, etc.

per·cus·sion·ist *n.* a musician who plays percussion instruments

per di·em (pər dē′əm) ⟦L⟧ daily

per·di·tion (pər dish′ən) *n.* ⟦< L *perdere*, to lose⟧ *Theol.* **1** the loss of the soul **2** HELL

per·dure (pər door′) *vi.* -**dured**′, -**dur**′**ing** ⟦< L *perdurare*, to endure⟧ to remain in existence; last

per·e·gri·nate (per′ə gri nāt′) *vt., vi.* -**nat**′**ed**, -**nat**′**ing** ⟦see PILGRIM⟧ to travel (along, over, or through) —**per′e·gri·na′tion** *n.*

per·e·grine (falcon) (per′ə grin) a swift falcon much used in falconry

per·emp·to·ry (pər emp′tə rē) *adj.* ⟦< L *perimere*, destroy⟧ **1** *Law* barring further action; final **2** that cannot be denied, delayed, etc., as a command **3** dogmatic; imperious

per·en·ni·al (pə ren′ē əl) *adj.* ⟦< L *per-*, through + *annus*, year⟧ **1** continuing for a long time **2** becoming active again and again **3** living more than two years: said of plants —*n.* a perennial plant

per·fect (pur′fikt; *for v.* pər fekt′) *adj.* ⟦< L *per-*, through + *facere*, do⟧ **1** complete in all respects; flawless **2** excellent, as in skill or quality **3** completely accurate **4** utter; absolute [a *perfect* fool] **5** *Gram.* expressing a state or action completed at the time being spoken about —*vt.* **1** to complete **2** to make perfect or nearly perfect —**per′fect·ly** *adv.*

per·fec·ta (pər fek′tə) *n.* ⟦Sp, perfect⟧ a bet in which one wins if one correctly picks the first and second place finishers in a race

per·fect·i·ble (pər fek′tə bəl) *adj.* that can become, or be made, perfect

per·fec·tion (pər fek′shən) *n.* **1** the act of perfecting **2** a being perfect **3** a person or thing that is the perfect embodiment of some quality

per·fec·tion·ism *n.* obsessive striving for perfection —**per·fec′tion·ist** *n., adj.*

perfect storm a situation marked by an extraordinary convergence of conditions conducive to a given outcome

per·fi·dy (pur′fə dē) *n., pl.* -**dies** ⟦< L *per*, through + *fides*, faith⟧ betrayal of trust; treachery —**per·fid·i·ous** (pər fid′ē əs) *adj.*

per·fo·rate (pur′fə rāt′) *vt., vi.* -**rat**′**ed**, -**rat**′**ing** ⟦< L *per*, through + *forare*, to bore⟧ **1** to make a hole or holes through (something), as by boring **2** to pierce with holes in a row —**per′fo·ra′tion** *n.*

per·force (pər fôrs′) *adv.* ⟦< OFr: see PER & FORCE⟧ necessarily

per·form (pər fôrm′) *vt.* ⟦< OFr *parfournir*⟧ **1** to do (a task, etc.) **2** to fulfill (a promise, etc.) **3** to render or enact (a piece of music, dramatic role, etc.) —*vi.* to execute an action or process, esp. as in a play or other performance —**per·form′er** *n.*

per·form·ance *n.* **1** the act of performing **2**

functional effectiveness **3** deed or feat **4** *a)* a formal exhibition or presentation, as a play *b)* one's part in this

performance art an art form combining elements as of dance, theater, etc., often presenting startling or provocative actions or events

performing arts arts, such as drama, for performance before an audience

per·fume (pər fyōōm'; *for n. usually* pur' fyōōm') *vt.* **-fumed', -fum'ing** ⟦< L *per-*, intens. + *fumare*, to smoke⟧ **1** to scent **2** to put perfume on —*n.* a pleasing odor, or a substance producing this, as a volatile oil extracted from flowers

per·fum·er·y (-fyōō'mə rē) *n., pl.* **-ies** perfumes collectively

per·func·to·ry (pər funk'tə rē) *adj.* ⟦< L *per-*, intens. + *fungi*, perform⟧ **1** done without care or interest; superficial **2** indifferent; unconcerned —**per·func'to·ri·ly** *adv.*

per·go·la (pur'gə lə) *n.* ⟦< L *pergula*⟧ an arbor with a latticework roof

per·haps (pər haps') *adv.* ⟦PER + pl. of *hap*, chance⟧ possibly; maybe

peri- ⟦Gr⟧ *prefix* **1** around; about **2** near

per·i·car·di·um (per'ə kär'dē əm) *n., pl.* **-di·a** (-ə) ⟦< Gr *peri-*, around + *kardia*, heart⟧ in vertebrates, the thin, closed sac surrounding the heart —**per'i·car'di·al** *adj.*

Per·i·cles (per'ə klēz') 495?–429 B.C.; Athenian statesman & general

per·i·gee (per'ə jē') *n.* ⟦< Gr *peri-*, near + *gē*, earth⟧ the point nearest to the earth in the orbit of the moon or of a man-made satellite

per·i·he·li·on (per'ə hē'lē ən) *n., pl.* **-li·ons** or **-li·a** (-ə) ⟦< Gr *peri-*, around + *hēlios*, sun⟧ the point nearest the sun in the orbit of a planet, comet, spacecraft, etc.

per·il (per'əl) *n.* ⟦< L *periculum*, danger⟧ **1** exposure to potential harm or injury **2** something that may cause harm

per·il·ous (-ə ləs) *adj.* involving peril or risk; dangerous —**per'il·ous·ly** *adv.*

pe·rim·e·ter (pə rim'ə tər) *n.* ⟦< Gr *peri-*, around + *metron*, measure⟧ **1** the outer boundary of a figure or area **2** the total length of this

per·i·ne·um (per'ə nē'əm) *n., pl.* **-ne'a** (-ə) ⟦< Gr *perineon*⟧ the small area between the anus and the genitals

pe·ri·od (pir'ē əd) *n.* ⟦< Gr *periodos*, a cycle⟧ **1** the interval between successive occurrences of an event **2** a portion of time characterized by certain processes, etc. [a *period* of change] **3** any of the portions of time into which a game, school day, etc. is divided **4** the menses **5** an end, conclusion **6** *a)* the pause in speaking or a mark of punctuation (.) used at the end of a sentence *b)* the dot (.) following many abbreviations —*interj.* an exclamation used for emphasis

pe·ri·od·ic (pir'ē äd'ik) *adj.* **1** appearing or recurring at regular intervals **2** intermittent

pe·ri·od·i·cal *adj.* **1** PERIODIC **2** published at regular intervals, as weekly, etc. **3** of a peri-

odical —*n.* a periodical publication —**pe'ri·od'i·cal·ly** *adv.*

periodic table an arrangement of the chemical elements according to their atomic numbers

pe·ri·od·i·za·tion (pir'ē ə də zā'shən) *n.* the dividing, as of history, into chronological periods

per·i·o·don·tal (per'ē ə dänt'l) *adj.* ⟦< PERI- + Gr *odōn*, tooth⟧ occurring around a tooth or affecting the gums

per·i·pa·tet·ic (per'i pə tet'ik) *adj.* ⟦< Gr *peri-*, around + *patein*, walk⟧ walking or moving about; itinerant

pe·riph·er·al (pə rif'ər əl) *adj.* **1** of or forming a periphery **2** outer; external —*n.* a piece of equipment used with a computer to increase its range or efficiency, as a disk, etc.

pe·riph·er·y (pə rif'ər ē) *n., pl.* **-ies** ⟦< Gr *peri-*, around + *pherein*, to bear⟧ **1** an outer boundary, esp. of a rounded object **2** surrounding space

pe·riph·ra·sis (pə rif'rə sis) *n., pl.* **-ses'** (-sēz') ⟦< Gr *peri-*, around + *phrazein*, to speak⟧ the use of many words where a few would do —**per·i·phras·tic** (per'ə fras'tik) *adj.*

per·i·scope (per'ə skōp') *n.* ⟦PERI- + -SCOPE⟧ an optical instrument which allows one to see around or over an obstacle: used on submarines, etc.

per·ish (per'ish) *vi.* ⟦< L *per-*, through + *ire*, go⟧ **1** to be destroyed or ruined **2** to die, esp. violently

per·ish·a·ble (per'ish ə bəl) *adj.* that may perish; esp., liable to spoil, as some foods —*n.* something, esp. a food, liable to spoil

per·i·stal·sis (per'ə stal'sis, -stôl'-) *n., pl.* **-ses'** (-sēz') ⟦< Gr *peri-*, around + *stellein*, to place⟧ the contractions and dilations of the alimentary canal, moving the contents onward —**per'i·stal'tic** *adj.*

per·i·to·ne·um (per'ə tə nē'əm) *n., pl.* **-ne'a** (-ə) or **-ne'ums** ⟦< Gr *peri-*, around + *tein-ein*, to stretch⟧ the serous membrane lining the abdominal cavity

per·i·to·ni·tis (-nīt'is) *n.* inflammation of the peritoneum

per·i·wig (per'ə wig') *n.* ⟦altered < Fr *perruque*⟧ a wig of a type worn by men esp. in the late 1600s and 1700s

per·i·win·kle¹ (per'ə wiŋ'kəl) *n.* ⟦< L *pervin-cire*, entwine⟧ a creeping plant with blue, white, or pink flowers

per·i·win·kle² (per'ə wiŋ'kəl) *n.* ⟦OE *pine-wincle*⟧ a small saltwater snail with a nearly spherical shell

per·jure (pur'jər) *vt.* **-jured, -jur·ing** ⟦< L *per*, through + *jurare*, swear⟧ to make (oneself) guilty of perjury —**per'jur·er** *n.*

per·ju·ry (pur'jə rē) *n., pl.* **-ries** ⟦< L *perjurus*, false⟧ the willful telling of a lie while under oath

perk¹ (purk) *vt.* ⟦ME *perken*⟧ **1** to raise (the head, ears, etc.) **2** briskly **3** to give a smart, fresh, or vivacious look to Often with *up* —*vi.* to become lively: with *up* —**perk'y** *adj.* **-i·er, -i·est**

perk² (purk) *vt., vi.* [Inf.] *short for* PERCOLATE

perk³ (purk) *n.* [Inf.] *short for* PERQUISITE

perm (purm) [Inf.] *n. short for* PERMANENT —*vt.* to give a permanent to

per·ma·frost (pur'mə frôst') *n.* permanently frozen subsoil

per·ma·nent (pur'mə nənt) *adj.* [< L *per*, through + *manere*, remain] lasting or intended to last indefinitely or for a long time —*n.* a long-lasting hair wave produced by use of chemicals or heat

per·me·a·ble (pur'mē ə bəl) *adj.* that can be permeated, as by fluids —**per'me·a·bil'i·ty** *n.*

per·me·ate (-āt') *vt., vi.* -at'ed, -at'ing [< L *per*, through + *meare*, to glide] to spread or diffuse; penetrate (*through* or *among*)

per·mis·si·ble (pər mis'ə bəl) *adj.* that can be permitted; allowable

per·mis·sion (pər mish'ən) *n.* the act of permitting; esp., formal consent

per·mis·sive (-mis'iv) *adj.* 1 that permits 2 allowing freedom; lenient —**per·mis'sive·ly** *adv.* —**per·mis'sive·ness** *n.*

per·mit (pər mit'; *for n.* pur'mit', pər mit') *vt.* -mit'ted, -mit'ting [< L *per*, through + *mit tere*, send] 1 to allow; consent to 2 to authorize —*vi.* to give opportunity [*if time permits*] —*n.* a license

per·mu·ta·tion (pur'myoo tā'shən) *n.* [< L *per*-, intens. + *mutare*, change] 1 any radical alteration 2 any of the total number of groupings possible within a group

per·ni·cious (pər nish'əs) *adj.* [< L < *per*, thoroughly + *necare*, kill] very harmful or destructive —**per·ni'cious·ly** *adv.*

per·o·ra·tion (per'ə rā'shən) *n.* [< L *per*, through + *orare*, speak] the concluding part of a speech

per·ox·ide (pər äk'sīd') *n.* [< L *per*, through + OXIDE] any oxide containing the oxygen group linked by a single bond; specif., hydrogen peroxide —*vt.* -id'ed, -id'ing to bleach (hair, etc.) with hydrogen peroxide

per·pen·dic·u·lar (pur'pən dik'yoo lər, -yə-) *adj.* [< L *perpendiculum*, plumb line] 1 at right angles to a given plane or line 2 exactly upright; vertical —*n.* a line or plane at right angles to another line or plane

per·pe·trate (pur'pə trāt') *vt.* -trat'ed, -trat'ing [< L *per*, thoroughly + *patrare*, to effect] 1 to do (something evil, criminal, etc.) 2 to commit (a blunder, etc.) —**per'pe·tra'tion** *n.* —**per'pe·tra'tor** *n.*

per·pet·u·al (pər pech'oo əl) *adj.* [< L *perpetuus*, constant] 1 lasting forever or for a long time 2 continuing without interruption; constant —**per·pet'u·al·ly** *adv.*

per·pet·u·ate (-āt') *vt.* -at'ed, -at'ing to make perpetual; cause to continue or be remembered —**per·pet'u·a'tion** *n.*

per·pe·tu·i·ty (pur'pə too'ə tē) *n., pl.* -ties unlimited time; eternity —**in perpetuity** forever

per·plex (pər pleks') *vt.* [< L *per*, through + *plectere*, twist] to make (a person) uncertain, doubtful, etc.; confuse —**per·plex'ing** *adj.* —**per·plex'i·ty** *n., pl.* -ties

per·qui·site (pur'kwi zit) *n.* [< L *per*-, intens. + *quaerere*, seek] something in addition to regular pay for one's work, as a tip

per se (pur' sā', -sē') [L] by (or in) itself; intrinsically

per·se·cute (pur'si kyoot') *vt.* -cut'ed, -cut'ing [< L *per*, through + *sequi*, follow] to afflict constantly so as to injure or distress, as for reasons of religion, race, etc. —**per'se·cu'tion** *n.* —**per'se·cu'tor** *n.*

per·se·vere (pur'sə vir') *vi.* -vered', -ver'ing [< L *per*-, intens. + *severus*, severe] to continue a course of action, etc. in spite of difficulty, opposition, etc. —**per'se·ver'ance** *n.*

Per·sia (pur'zhə) *former name for* IRAN

Per·sian (pur'zhən) *adj.* of Persia or its people, language, etc. —*n.* 1 person born or living in Persia 2 the language of Iran 3 a variety of domestic cat with a long, thick, glossy coat

Persian Gulf arm of the Indian Ocean, between Iran & Arabia

Persian lamb the pelt of karakul lambs

per·si·flage (pur'sə fläzh') *n.* [Fr < L *per*, through + *sifilare*, to hiss] frivolous talk or writing

per·sim·mon (pər sim'ən) *n.* [< AmInd] 1 a hardwood tree with plumlike fruit 2 the fruit

per·sist (pər sist') *vi.* [< L *per*, through + *sistere*, cause to stand] 1 to refuse to give up, esp. when faced with opposition 2 to continue insistently 3 to endure; remain

per·sist·ent *adj.* 1 continuing, esp. in the face of opposition, etc. 2 continuing to exist or endure 3 constantly repeated —**per·sist'ence** *n.*

per·snick·e·ty (pər snik'ə tē) *adj.* [< Scot dial.] [Inf.] too particular or precise; fussy

per·son (pur'sən) *n.* [< L *persona*] 1 a human: now usually pluralized as *people* 2 the human body 3 personality; self 4 *Gram.* any of the three sets of pronouns and corresponding verb forms: see FIRST PERSON, SECOND PERSON, THIRD PERSON 5 *Law* any individual or incorporated group having certain legal rights and responsibilities —**in person** actually present

-per·son (pur'sən) *combining form* person in a (specified) activity: used to avoid the masculine implication of *-man [chairperson]*

per·son·a·ble *adj.* [ME *personabilis*] having a pleasing appearance and personality

per·son·age *n.* a person; esp., an important person; notable

per·son·al (-nəl) *adj.* 1 private; individual 2 done in person 3 involving humans [*personal* relationships] 4 of the body or physical appearance 5 *a)* having to do with the character, conduct, etc. of a person [*a personal* remark] *b)* tending to make personal, esp. derogatory, remarks 6 *Gram.* indicating PERSON (n. 4) 7 *Law* of property (**personal property**) that is movable

personal computer MICROCOMPUTER

personal effects personal belongings, esp. those worn or carried

per·son·al·i·ty (pur'sə nal'ə tē) *n., pl.* **-ties** 1 distinctive individual qualities of a person, considered collectively 2 such qualities seen as being attractive to others 3 a notable person

per·son·al·ize (pur'sə nə līz') *vt.* **-ized', -iz' ing** 1 to apply to a particular person, esp. to oneself 2 to have marked with one's name, etc.

per·son·al·ly *adv.* 1 in person 2 as a person [I dislike him *personally*] 3 in one's own opinion 4 as though directed at oneself

per·so·na non gra·ta (pər sän'ə nän grät'ə) [L] an unwelcome person

per·son·i·fy (pər sän'ə fī') *vt.* **-fied', -fy'ing** 1 to think of or represent (a thing) as a person 2 to typify; embody —**per·son'i·fi·ca'tion** *n.*

per·son·nel (pur'sə nel') *n.* [Fr] 1 persons employed in any work, enterprise, service, etc. 2 a personnel department or office —*adj.* of or relating to the division within a business, etc. responsible for hiring and training employees, etc.

per·spec·tive (pər spek'tiv) *n.* [< L *per*, through + *specere*, look] 1 the art of picturing objects so as to show relative distance or depth 2 the appearance of objects as determined by their relative distance and positions 3 sense of proportion 4 *a)* a specific point of view in understanding things or events *b)* the ability to see things in a true relationship

per·spi·ca·cious (pur'spi kā'shəs) *adj.* [see prec.] having keen judgment; discerning —**per'spi·ca'cious·ly** *adv.* —**per'spi·cac'i·ty** (-kas'ə tē) *n.*

per·spic·u·ous (pər spik'yōō əs) *adj.* [see PERSPECTIVE] easily understood; lucid —**per·spi·cu·i·ty** (pur'spi kyōō'ə tē) *n.*

per·spi·ra·tion (pur'spə rā'shən) *n.* 1 the action of perspiring 2 sweat

per·spire (pər spīr') *vt., vi.* **-spired', -spir' ing** [< L *per*-, through + *spirare*, breathe] to sweat

per·suade (pər swād') *vt.* **-suad'ed, -suad' ing** [< L *per*-, intens. + *suadere*, to urge] to cause to do or believe something by reasoning, urging, etc.; induce or convince —**per·suad'er** *n.*

per·sua·sion (pər swā'zhən) *n.* 1 a persuading or being persuaded 2 power of persuading 3 a strong belief 4 a particular religious belief

per·sua·sive *adj.* having the power, or tending, to persuade —**per·sua'sive·ly** *adv.*

pert (purt) *adj.* [< L *apertus*, open] 1 impudent; saucy 2 chic and jaunty —**pert'ly** *adv.*

per·tain (pər tān') *vi.* [< L *per*-, intens. + *tenere*, hold] 1 to belong; be connected or associated 2 to be appropriate 3 to have reference

per·ti·na·cious (purt''n ā'shəs) *adj.* [< L *per*-, intens. + *tenax*, holding fast] 1 holding firmly to some purpose, belief, etc. 2 hard to get rid of —**per'ti·nac'i·ty** (-as'ə tē) *n.*

per·ti·nent (purt''n ənt) *adj.* [see PERTAIN] having some connection with the matter at hand —**per'ti·nence** *n.*

per·turb (pər turb') *vt.* [< L *per*-, intens. + *turbare*, disturb] to cause to be alarmed, agitated, or upset —**per·tur·ba'tion** (pur'tər bā' shən) *n.*

per·tus·sis (pər tus'is) *n.* WHOOPING COUGH

Pe·ru (pə rōō') country in W South America, on the Pacific —**Pe·ru'vi·an** (-vē ən) *adj., n.*

pe·ruke (pə rōōk') *n.* [Fr *perruque*] PERIWIG

pe·ruse (pə rōōz') *vt.* **-rused', -rus'ing** [prob. < L *per*-, intens. + ME *usen*, to use] 1 to read carefully; study 2 to read in a leisurely way —**pe·rus'al** *n.*

per·vade (pər vād') *vt.* **-vad'ed, -vad'ing** [< L *per*, through + *vadere*, go] to spread or be prevalent throughout —**per·va'sive** (-vā' siv) *adj.*

per·verse (pər vurs') *adj.* [see PERVERT] 1 deviating from what is considered right or good 2 stubbornly contrary 3 obstinately disobedient —**per·verse'ly** *adv.* —**per· verse'ness** *n.*, **per·ver'si·ty** *n.*

per·ver·sion (pər vur'zhən) *n.* 1 a perverting or being perverted 2 something perverted 3 any sexual act or practice considered abnormal

per·vert (pər vurt'; *for n.* pur'vurt') *vt.* [< L *per*-, intens. + *vertere*, turn] 1 to lead astray; corrupt 2 to misuse 3 to distort —*n.* one inclined to sexual acts considered abnormal —**per·vert'ed** *adj.*

pe·se·ta (pə sāt'ə) *n.* [Sp, dim. of *peso*, peso] the former monetary unit of Spain

pes·ky (pes'kē) *adj.* **-ki·er, -ki·est** [prob. var. of *pesty*] [Inf.] annoying; troublesome —**pes'ki·ness** *n.*

pe·so (pā'sō) *n., pl.* **-sos** [Sp < L *pensum*, something weighed] the monetary unit of various countries, including Mexico, Colombia, Chile, etc.

pes·si·mism (pes'ə miz'əm) *n.* [< L *pessimus*, worst] 1 the belief that the evil in life outweighs the good 2 the tendency to expect the worst —**pes'si·mist** *n.* —**pes'si·mis'tic** *adj.* —**pes'si·mis'ti·cal·ly** *adv.*

pest (pest) *n.* [< L *pestis*, plague] a person or thing that is troublesome, destructive, etc.; specif., a rat, fly, weed, etc.

pes·ter (pes'tər) *vt.* [< OFr *empestrer*, entangle] to annoy; vex

pes·ti·cide (pes'tə sīd') *n.* any chemical for killing insects, weeds, etc.

pes·tif·er·ous (pes tif'ər əs) *adj.* [< L *pestis*, plague + *ferre*, to bear] 1 noxious 2 [Inf.] annoying

pes·ti·lence (pes'tə ləns) *n.* 1 a deadly epidemic disease; plague 2 anything regarded as harmful

pes·ti·lent (pes'tə lənt) *adj.* [< L *pestis*, plague] 1 likely to cause death 2 dangerous to society [the *pestilent* threat of war] 3 annoying

pes·tle (pes'əl) *n.* [< L *pinsere*, to pound] a tool used to pound or grind substances, esp. in a mortar

pes·to (pes′tō) *n.* 〚see prec.〛 a sauce for pasta, of ground basil, garlic, nuts, etc. mixed with olive oil

pet¹ (pet) *n.* 〚orig. Scot dial.〛 **1** an animal that is domesticated and kept as a companion **2** a person treated with particular indulgence —*adj.* **1** kept or treated as a pet **2** especially liked **3** particular [a *pet* peeve] **4** showing fondness [a *pet* name] —*vt.* **pet′ted, pet′ting** to stroke or pat gently; caress —*vi.* [Inf.] to kiss, embrace, etc. as lovers do

pet² (pet) *n.* 〚< ?〛 a sulky mood

pet·al (pet′'l) *n.* 〚< Gr *petalos*, outspread〛 any of the leaflike parts of a blossom

pe·tard (pi tärd′) *n.* 〚< Fr〛 [Historical] a kind of explosive device: now used chiefly in **hoist with (or by) one's own petard**, destroyed by the very thing with which one meant to destroy others

pet·cock (pet′käk′) *n.* 〚< L *pedere*, break wind + *cock*, valve〛 a small valve for draining pipes, etc.

pe·ter (pēt′ər) *vi.* 〚< ?〛 [Inf.] to become gradually smaller, weaker, etc. and then disappear: with *out*

Pe·ter (pēt′ər) *n. Bible* (original name *Simon*) (died A.D. 64?); one of the twelve Apostles, a fisherman: reputed author of two Epistles: also **Saint Peter**

Peter I 1672-1725; czar of Russia (1682-1725): called *Peter the Great*

pet·i·ole (pet′ē ōl′) *n.* 〚< L *pes*, FOOT〛 LEAF-STALK

pe·tite (pə tēt′) *adj.* 〚Fr〛 small and trim in figure: said of a woman

pe·tit four (pet′ē fôr′) *pl.* **pe·tits fours** or **pe·tit fours** (pet′ē fôrz′) 〚Fr, lit., small oven〛 a tiny, frosted cake

pe·ti·tion (pə tish′ən) *n.* 〚< L *petere*, seek〛 **1** a solemn, earnest request; entreaty **2** a formal document embodying such a request, often signed by many people **3** *Law* a written formal request asking for a specific court action —*vt.* to address a petition to —*vi.* to make a petition —**pe·ti′tion·er** *n.*

petit jury (pet′ē) a group of citizens picked to decide the issues of a trial in court

pet·rel (pe′trəl) *n.* 〚< ?〛 a small sea bird with long wings

pet·ri·fy (pe′tri fī′) *vt.* **-fied′, -fy′ing** 〚< L *petra*, rock + *facere*, make〛 **1** to turn into stone **2** to harden or deaden **3** to paralyze, as with fear

petro- 〚< Gr *petra*, rock〛 *combining form* **1** rock or stone **2** petroleum **3** of or relating to the petroleum business

pet·ro·chem·i·cal (pe′trō kem′i kəl) *n.* a chemical made from petroleum

pet·ro·dol·lars *pl.n.* revenue from the sale of petroleum

pet·rol (pe′trəl) *n.* 〚see PETROLEUM〛 *Brit. term for* GASOLINE

pet·ro·la·tum (pe′trə lāt′əm) *n.* 〚< fol.〛 a greasy, jellylike substance derived from petroleum and used in ointments, etc.: also **petroleum jelly**

pe·tro·le·um (pə trō′lē əm) *n.* 〚< L *petra*, rock + *oleum*, oil〛 an oily, liquid solution of hydrocarbons, occurring naturally in certain rock strata: it yields kerosene, gasoline, etc.

PET (scan) (pet) 〚*p*(*ositron*) *e*(*mission*) *t*(*omography*)〛 an X-ray technique〛 a type of X-raying that shows metabolic activity, used to detect abnormalities, esp. of the brain

pet·ti·coat (pet′ē kōt′, pet′i-) *n.* 〚< PETTY + COAT〛 a woman's underskirt

pet·ti·fog·ger (pet′i fäg′ər, -fôg′-; pet′ē-) *n.* 〚< PETTY + *fogger* < ?〛 **1** a lawyer who handles petty cases, esp. unethically **2** one who quibbles —**pet′ti·fog′** *vi.* **-fogged′, -fog′ging**

pet·tish (pet′ish) *adj.* 〚< PET²〛 peevish; petulant —**pet′tish·ly** *adv.*

pet·ty (pet′ē) *adj.* **-ti·er, -ti·est** 〚< OFr *petit*〛 **1** relatively unimportant **2** smallminded; mean **3** relatively low in rank —**pet′ti·ness** *n.*.

petty cash a cash fund for incidentals

petty officer *U.S. Navy* a naval enlisted person who is a noncommissioned officer

pet·u·lant (pech′ə lənt) *adj.* 〚< L *petere*, to rush at〛 impatient or irritable, esp. over a petty annoyance —**pet′u·lance** *n.* —**pet′u·lant·ly** *adv.*

pe·tu·ni·a (pə tōōn′yə) *n.* 〚ult. < AmInd (Brazil)〛 a plant with showy, funnel-shaped flowers

pew (pyōō) *n.* 〚ult. < Gr *pous*, foot〛 any of the benches with a back that are fixed in rows in a church

pe·wee (pē′wē′) *n.* 〚echoic of its call〛 a small flycatcher

pew·ter (pyōōt′ər) *n.* 〚OFr *peautre*〛 **1** an alloy of tin with antimony, copper, lead, etc. **2** articles made of this

pe·yo·te (pā ōt′ē) *n.* 〚AmSp < AmInd (Mexico) *peyotl*, caterpillar〛 MESCAL: see also MESCALINE

pf or **pfd** *abbrev.* preferred

PFC or **Pfc** *abbrev.* Private First Class

pg *abbrev.* page

PG *trademark for* a film rating indicating parents may find some content unsuitable for children

PG-13 *trademark for* a film rating indicating parents may find some content especially unsuitable for children under 13

pH (pē′āch′) *n.* 〚< Fr *p*(*ouvoir*) *h*(*ydrogène*), lit., hydrogen power〛 the degree of acidity or alkalinity of a solution

pha·e·ton or **pha·ë·ton** (fā′ə tən) *n.* 〚after *Phaëton*, son of Helios, Gr sun god〛 **1** a light, four-wheeled carriage **2** an early type of open automobile

phag·o·cyte (fag′ə sīt′) *n.* 〚< Gr *phagein*, to eat + *kytos*, hollow〛 any cell, esp. a leukocyte, that destroys foreign matter in the blood and tissues

pha·lan·ger (fə lan′jər) *n.* 〚< Gr *phalanx*, bone between fingers or toes〛 a small, tree-dwelling Australian marsupial

pha·lanx (fā′laŋks′) *n., pl.* **pha′lanx′es**; also, and for 3 always, **pha·lan·ges** (fə lan′jēz′)

〖Gr, line of battle〗 **1** an ancient close-ranked infantry formation **2** any massed group **3** any of the bones forming the fingers or toes

phal·lo·cen·tric (fal′ō sen′trik) *adj.* dominated by attitudes regarded as typically masculine

phal·lus (fal′əs) *n., pl.* **-li′** (-ī′) or **-lus·es** 〖Gr *phallos*〗 **1** an image of the penis **2** the penis —**phal′lic** *adj.*

phan·tasm (fan′taz′əm) *n.* 〖< Gr *phantazein*, to show〗 **1** a figment of the mind **2** a deceptive likeness

phan·tas·ma·go·ri·a (fan taz′mə gôr′ē ə) *n.* 〖< Gr *phantasma*, phantasm + *ageirein*, assemble〗 a rapid sequence of images, as in a dream

phan·tom (fan′təm) *n.* 〖see PHANTASM〗 **1** an apparition; specter **2** an illusion —*adj.* of or like a phantom; illusory

Phar·aoh (far′ō, fā′rō′) *n.* [*sometimes* **p-**] the title of the kings of ancient Egypt

Phar·i·see (far′ə sē′) *n.* **1** a member of an ancient Jewish group that observed both the written and the oral law **2** 〖< characterization in NT〗 [**p-**] a self-righteous, hypocritical person —**phar′i·sa′ic** (-sā′ik) *adj.*

phar·ma·ceu·ti·cal (fär′mə sōōt′i kəl) *adj.* 〖< Gr *pharmakon*, a drug〗 of pharmacy or drugs: also **phar′ma·ceu′tic** —*n.* a drug or medicine

phar·ma·cist (fär′mə sist) *n.* one licensed to practice pharmacy; druggist

phar·ma·col·o·gy (-käl′ə jē) *n.* 〖< Gr *pharmakon*, a drug〗 the science dealing with the effect of drugs on living organisms

phar·ma·co·pe·ia or **phar·ma·co·poe·ia** (-kō pē′ə) *n.* 〖< Gr *pharmakon*, a drug + *poiein*, to make〗 an official listing of drugs and medicines

phar·ma·cy (fär′mə sē) *n., pl.* **-cies** 〖< Gr *pharmakon*, a drug〗 **1** the art or profession of preparing drugs and medicines **2** a drugstore

phar·yn·gi·tis (far′in jīt′is) *n.* inflammation of the pharynx; sore throat

phar·ynx (far′iŋks) *n., pl.* **pha·ryn·ges** (fə rin′jēz′) or **phar′ynx·es** 〖Gr *pharynx*, throat〗 the cavity leading from the mouth and nasal passages to the larynx and esophagus —**pha·ryn·ge·al** (fə rin′jē əl) *adj.*

phase (fāz) *n.* 〖< Gr *phainesthai*, appear〗 **1** any stage in a series or cycle of changes, as in the moon's illumination **2** an aspect or side, as of a problem —*vt.* **phased, phas′ing** to introduce or carry out in stages: often with *in* or *into* —**in** (or **out of**) **phase** in (or not in) synchronization —**phase out** to bring or come to an end by stages

phase-out *n.* a phasing out; gradual termination or withdrawal

PhD or **Ph.D.** *abbrev.* 〖L *Philosophiae Doctor*〗 Doctor of Philosophy

pheas·ant (fez′ənt) *n.* 〖< Gr *phasianos*, (bird) of *Phasis*, river in Asia〗 a large game bird with a long, sweeping tail and brilliant feathers

phe·nac·e·tin (fē nas′ə tin) *n.* a white, crystalline powder used to reduce fever, relieve headaches, etc.

phe·no·bar·bi·tal (fē′nə bär′bi tôl′) *n.* an odorless, white, crystalline powder used as a sedative

phe·nol (fē′nōl′, -nôl′, -näl′) *n.* a white, crystalline compound, corrosive and poisonous, used to make synthetic resins, etc. and, in dilute solution (*carbolic acid*) as an antiseptic

phe·nol·phthal·ein (fē′nōl thal′ēn′, -ē in) *n.* a white to pale-yellow, crystalline powder used as an acid-base indicator in chemical analysis, etc.

phe·nom (fē′näm) *n.* 〖< fol.〗 [Slang] one who is very talented or skilled; specif., a young, very gifted athlete

phe·nom·e·non (fə näm′ə nən, -nän′) *n., pl.* **-na** (-nə); also, esp. for 2 and usually for 3, **-nons′** 〖< Gr *phainesthai*, appear〗 **1** any observable fact or event that can be scientifically described **2** anything very unusual **3** [Inf.] an extraordinary person; prodigy —**phe·nom′e·nal** *adj.*

pher·o·mone (fer′ə mōn′) *n.* 〖< Gr *pherein*, carry + (HOR)MONE〗 a chemical substance secreted by certain animals, as ants, that conveys information to others of the same species

phi (fī, fē) *n.* the 21st letter of the Greek alphabet (Φ, φ)

phi·al (fī′əl) *n.* 〖< Gr *phialē*, shallow bowl〗 a small glass bottle; vial

Phil·a·del·phi·a (fil′ə del′fē ə) city & port in SE Pennsylvania

Philadelphia lawyer [Inf.] a shrewd or tricky lawyer

phi·lan·der (fi lan′dər, fə-) *vi.* 〖ult. < Gr *philos*, loving + *anēr*, a man〗 to engage lightly in love affairs, esp. unfaithfully: said of a man —**phi·lan′der·er** *n.*

phi·lan·thro·py (fə lan′thrə pē) *n.* 〖< Gr *philein*, to love + *anthrōpos*, human〗 **1** a desire to help humankind, esp. as shown by gifts to institutions, etc. **2** *pl.* **-pies** a philanthropic gift, institution, etc. —**phil·an·throp·ic** (fil′ən thräp′ik) *adj.* —**phi·lan′thro·pist** *n.*

phi·lat·e·ly (fə lat′′l ē) *n.* 〖< Fr < Gr *philos*, loving + *ateleia*, exemption from (further) tax (meaning "postage prepaid")〗 the collection and study of postage stamps, postmarks, etc. —**phi·lat′e·list** *n.*

-phile (fīl, fil) 〖< Gr *philos*, loving〗 *combining form* one that loves or is attracted to

Phil·har·mon·ic (fil′här män′ik) *adj.* 〖ult. < Gr *philos*, loving + *harmonia*, harmony〗 designating a group formed to sponsor a symphony orchestra —*n.* an orchestra so sponsored

phi·lip·pic (fi lip′ik) *n.* 〖< Gr *Philippos*, Philip, Macedonian king denounced by Demosthenes〗 a bitter verbal attack

Phil·ip·pines (fil′ə pēnz′) country consisting of *c.* 7,100 islands (**Philippine Islands**) in the SW Pacific off the SE coast of Asia —**Phil′ip·pine′** (-pēn′) *adj.*

Phil·is·tine (fil′ə stēn′) *n.* **1** a member of a non-Semitic people of SW Palestine in biblical times **2** 〖< a Ger slang word〗 [*often* **p-**] a person regarded as smugly conventional, lacking culture, etc.

Phil·lips (fil′ips) [after H. F. *Phillips* (?-1958), its U.S. developer] *trademark for* a screwdriver (**Phillips screwdriver**) with a cross-shaped, pointed tip

philo- [< Gr *philos*, loving] *combining form* loving, liking

phil·o·den·dron (fil′ə den′drən) *n.* [< Gr *philos*, loving + *dendron*, tree] a tropical American vine used as a houseplant

phi·lol·o·gy (fi läl′ə jē) *n.* [< Gr *philein*, to love + *logos*, word] *former term for* LINGUISTICS —**phil·o·log·i·cal** (fil′ə läj′i kəl) *adj.* —**phi·lol′o·gist** *n.*

phi·los·o·pher (fə läs′ə fər) *n.* [< Gr *philos*, loving + *sophos*, wise] 1 one who is an expert in philosophy 2 one who expounds a system of philosophy 3 one who meets difficulties calmly

phil·o·soph·ic (fil′ə säf′ik) *adj.* 1 of philosophy or philosophers 2 sensibly composed or calm Also **phil′o·soph′i·cal**

phi·los·o·phize (fə läs′ə fīz′) *vi.* **-phized′, -phiz′ing** 1 to think or reason like a philosopher 2 to moralize, express truisms, etc.

phi·los·o·phy (fə läs′ə fē) *n.* [see PHILOSOPHER] 1 the study of the principles underlying conduct, thought, and the nature of the universe 2 the general principles of a field of knowledge 3 *pl.* **-phies** a particular system of principles for the conduct of life

phil·ter (fil′tər) *n.* [< Gr *philein*, to love] a magic potion, esp. one thought to arouse sexual love: also [Chiefly Brit.] **phil′tre** (-tər)

phle·bi·tis (flə bīt′is) *n.* [< Gr *phleps*, vein + -ITIS] inflammation of a vein

phle·bot·o·my (fli bät′ə mē) *n.* [< Gr *pheps*, vein + *temnein*, to cut] the practice of taking blood from the body for therapeutic purposes

phlegm (flem) *n.* [< Gr *phlegma*, inflammation] 1 thick mucus discharged from the throat, as during a cold 2 sluggishness or apathy

phleg·mat·ic (fleg mat′ik) *adj.* [see prec.] sluggish or unexcited —**phleg·mat′i·cal·ly** *adv.*

phlo·em (flō′em′) *n.* [< Gr *phloos*, bark] the vascular tissue through which food is distributed in a plant

phlox (fläks) *n.* [Gr, lit., a flame] a North American plant with clusters of white, pink, or bluish flowers

-phobe (fōb) [< Gr *phobos*, fear] *combining form* one who fears or hates

pho·bi·a (fō′bē ə) *n.* [see prec.] an irrational, excessive, and persistent fear of some thing or situation —**pho′bic** *adj.*

-pho·bi·a (fō′bē ə) [Gr *-phobia* < *phobos*, fear] *combining form* fear, dread, hatred

phoe·be (fē′bē) *n.* [echoic, with sp. after *Phoebe*, Gr goddess of the moon] an American bird with a grayish or brown back, that catches insects in flight

Phoe·ni·cia (fə nish′ə, -nē′shə) ancient region at the E end of the Mediterranean —**Phoe·ni′cian** *adj., n.*

phoe·nix (fē′niks) [< Gr *phoinix*] Egypt. Myth. a bird that lives for 500 years and then sets itself on fire, rising renewed from the ashes

Phoe·nix (fē′niks) capital of Arizona

phone (fōn) *n., vt., vi.* **phoned, phon′ing** *short for* TELEPHONE

-phone (fōn) [< Gr *phōnē*, a sound] *combining form* 1 a device producing or transmitting sound 2 a telephone

phone card a prepaid card or credit card for long-distance telephone calls

pho·neme (fō′nēm′) *n.* [< Fr < Gr *phōnē*, voice] *Linguistics* a set of related speech sounds with slight variations, that are heard as the same sound by native speakers —**pho·ne·mic** (fō nē′mik, fə-) *adj.*

pho·net·ics (fō net′iks, fə-) *n.* [< Gr *phōnē*, a sound] the study of the production of speech sounds and their representation in written symbols —**pho·net′ic** *adj.* —**pho·ne·ti·cian** (fō′nə tish′ən) *n.*

phon·ics (fän′iks) *n.* [< Gr *phōnē*, a sound] a phonetic method of teaching reading —**phon′ic** *adj.*

phono- [< Gr *phōnē*, a sound] *combining form* sound, tone, speech [*phonology*]

pho·no·graph (fō′nə graf′) *n.* [prec. + -GRAPH] a device for reproducing sound recorded in a spiral groove on a revolving disk —**pho′no·graph′ic** *adj.*

pho·nol·o·gy (fō näl′ə jē, fə-) *n.* [PHONO- + -LOGY] 1 the study of speech sounds 2 a description of the sounds of a given language —**pho′no·log′i·cal** (-nō läj′i kəl, -nə-) *adj.* —**pho·nol′o·gist** *n.*

pho·ny (fō′nē) [Inf.] *adj.* **-ni·er, -ni·est** [< Brit thieves' argot *fawney*, gilt ring] not genuine; false —*n., pl.* **-nies** something or someone not genuine; fraud; fake Also sp. **pho′ney** —**pho′ni·ness** *n.*

phooey (fōō′ē) *interj.* [echoic] used to express scorn, disgust, etc

phos·phate (fäs′fāt′) *n.* [Fr] 1 a salt or ester of phosphoric acid 2 a fertilizer containing phosphates

phos·phor (fäs′fər, -fôr′) *n.* [see PHOSPHORUS] a phosphorescent or fluorescent substance

phos·pho·res·cence (fäs′fə res′əns) *n.* 1 the property of giving off a lingering emission of light after exposure to radiant energy such as light 2 a continuing luminescence without noticeable heat —**phos′pho·res′cent** *adj.*

phos·phor·ic acid (fäs fôr′ik) any of several oxygen acids of phosphorus

phos·pho·rus (fäs′fə rəs) *n.* [< Gr *phōs*, a light + *pherein*, to bear] a nonmetallic chemical element, a waxy solid that ignites spontaneously at room temperature: symbol, P; at. no. 15

pho·to (fōt′ō) *n., pl.* **-tos** *short for* PHOTOGRAPH

photo- *combining form* 1 [< Gr *phōs*, a light] of or produced by light 2 [< PHOTOGRAPH] photograph, photography

pho·to·cop·y (fōt′ō käp′ē) *n., pl.* **-ies** a photographic reproduction, as of a book page, made by a special device (**pho′to·cop′i·er**)

pho·to·e·lec·tric cell any device in which light controls an electric circuit that operates a mechanical device, as for opening doors

pho·to·en·grav·ing *n.* 1 a process by which photographs are reproduced on relief printing plates 2 such a plate, or a print made from it —**pho′to·en·grave′** *vt.* -**graved′**, -**grav′ing** —**pho′to·en·grav′er** *n.*

photo essay a group of photographs arranged, often with text, to tell a story, evoke a mood, etc.

photo finish a race finish so close that the winner can be determined only from a photograph of the finish

pho·to·fin·ish·ing *n.* the process of developing photographic film, making prints, etc.

pho·to·gen·ic (fōt′ə jen′ik) *adj.* ⟦PHOTO- + -genic, suitable for⟧ likely to look attractive in photographs

pho·to·graph (fōt′ə graf′) *n.* a picture made by photography —*vt.* to take a photograph of —*vi.* to appear (as specified) in photographs —**pho·tog·ra·pher** (fə tägʹrə fər) *n.*

pho·tog·ra·phy (fə tägʹrə fē) *n.* ⟦PHOTO- + -GRAPHY⟧ the art or process of capturing images, as on light-sensitive film or in digital form —**pho·to·graph·ic** (fōt′ə grafʹik) *adj.*

pho·ton (fōʹtän′) *n.* ⟦PHOT(O)- + (ELECTR)ON⟧ a subatomic particle that is a quantum of electromagnetic energy, including light

pho·to·off·set *n.* offset printing in which the text or pictures are photographically transferred to a metal plate from which inked impressions are made on the roller

pho·to·syn·the·sis (fōt′ō sinʹthə sis) *n.* the production of organic substances, esp. sugars, from carbon dioxide and water by the action of light on the chlorophyll in green plant cells

pho·to·syn·the·size (-sīz′) *vi.*, *vt.* -**sized′**, -**siz′ing** to carry on, or produce by, photosynthesis

phrase (frāz) *n.* ⟦< Gr *phrazein*, speak⟧ 1 a short, colorful expression 2 a group of words, not a full sentence or clause, conveying a single thought 3 a short, distinct musical passage —*vt.*, *vi.* **phrased**, **phras′ing** to express in words —**phras·al** (frāʹzəl) *adj.*

phra·se·ol·o·gy (frā′zē älʹə jē) *n.*, *pl.* -**gies** choice and pattern of words

phre·net·ic (fri netʹik) *adj.* ⟦< Gr *phrenētikos*, mad⟧ *archaic sp. of* FRENETIC

phre·nol·o·gy (fri nälʹə jē, frə-) *n.* ⟦< Gr *phrēn*, mind + -LOGY⟧ a system, popular esp. in the 1800s, based on the assumption that character can be analyzed based on the shape of the skull

phy·lac·ter·y (fi lakʹtər ē) *n.*, *pl.* -**ies** ⟦< Gr *phylaktērion*, safeguard⟧ TEFILLIN

phyl·lo (fēʹlō, fiʹ-) *n.* ⟦< Gr *phyllon*, leaf⟧ dough in very thin sheets that becomes very flaky when baked

phy·log·e·ny (fī läjʹə nē) *n.*, *pl.* -**nies** ⟦< Gr *phylon*, tribe + -*geneia*, origin⟧ the origin and evolution of a group or race of animals or plants

phy·lum (fīʹləm) *n.*, *pl.* -**la** (-lə) ⟦< Gr *phylon*, tribe⟧ a major category in the classification of organisms, esp. animals

phys *abbrev.* 1 physical 2 physician 3 physics

phys·ic (fizʹik) *n.* ⟦< Gr *physis*, nature⟧ a medicine, esp. a laxative

phys·i·cal (fizʹi kəl) *adj.* 1 of nature and all matter; material 2 of or according to the laws of nature 3 of, or produced by the forces of, physics 4 of the body as opposed to the mind —*n.* a general medical examination —**phys′i·cal·ly** *adv.*

physical anthropology a major division of anthropology that deals with the physical characteristics and evolution of humans

physical education instruction in physical exercise and in the care of the body, including sports, calisthenics, and hygiene

physical science any science dealing with nonliving matter or energy, as physics, chemistry, geology, or astronomy

physical therapy the treatment of disease, injury, etc. by physical means, as by exercise or massage

phy·si·cian (fi zishʹən) *n.* ⟦see PHYSIC⟧ a doctor of medicine

phys·ics (fizʹiks) *n.* ⟦see PHYSIC⟧ the science dealing with the properties, changes, interactions, etc. of matter and energy —**phys′i·cist** (-ə sist) *n.*

phys·i·og·no·my (fiz′ē ägʹnə mē) *n.* ⟦< Gr *physis*, nature + *gnōmōn*, one who knows⟧ facial features and expression

phys·i·ol·o·gy (-älʹə jē) *n.* ⟦< Gr *physis*, nature + -LOGY⟧ the science dealing with the functions and vital processes of living organisms —**phys′i·o·log′i·cal** (-ə läjʹi kəl) *adj.* —**phys′i·ol′o·gist** *n.*

phys·i·o·ther·a·py (fiz′ē ō′therʹə pē) *n.* PHYSICAL THERAPY —**phys′i·o·ther′a·pist** *n.*

phy·sique (fi zēkʹ) *n.* ⟦Fr⟧ the structure or form of the body; build

pi (pī) *n.* 1 the 16th letter of the Greek alphabet (Π, π) 2 the symbol (π) designating the ratio of the circumference of a circle to its diameter, about 3.1416

pi·a·nis·si·mo (pē′ə nisʹi mō′) *adj.*, *adv.* ⟦It⟧ *Music* very soft(ly)

pi·an·ist (pēʹə nist, pē anʹist) *n.* one who plays the piano

pi·a·no¹ (pē äʹnō) *adj.*, *adv.* ⟦It⟧ *Music* soft(ly)

pi·an·o² (pē anʹō) *n.*, *pl.* -**os** ⟦< fol.⟧ a large, stringed keyboard instrument: each key operates a felt-covered hammer that strikes a corresponding wire or wires

pi·an·o·for·te (pē an′ō fôrt′, pē an′ō fôrʹtā) *n.* ⟦It < *piano*, soft + *forte*, loud⟧ PIANO²

pi·as·ter (pē asʹtər) *n.* ⟦ult. < L *emplastrum*, plaster⟧ a 100th part of a pound in Egypt, Lebanon, and Syria

pi·az·za (pē ätʹsə; *for 2* pē azʹə) *n.* 1 in Italy, a public square 2 [Dial.] a large, covered porch; a veranda

pi·broch (pēʹbräk′) *n.* ⟦< Gael *piob*, bagpipe⟧ music for the bagpipe, usually of a martial or dirgelike kind

pi·ca (pī′kə) *n.* ⟦< ? ML, a directory⟧ a size of printing type, 12 point

pi·can·te (pē kän′tā) *adj.* ⟦Sp⟧ designating, prepared with, or served with a hot, spicy sauce

pic·a·resque (pik′ə resk′) *adj.* ⟦< Sp *pícaro*, rascal⟧ dealing with sharp-witted vagabonds or rogues and their adventures ⟦a *picaresque* novel⟧

Pi·cas·so (pi kä′sō), **Pa·blo** (pä′blō) 1881-1973; Sp. painter & sculptor in France

pic·a·yune (pik′ə yōōn′, pik′ə yōōn′) *adj.* ⟦< Fr *picaillon*, small coin⟧ trivial or petty

pic·ca·lil·li (pik′ə lil′ē) *n.* ⟦prob. < PICKLE⟧ a relish of chopped vegetables, mustard, vinegar, and hot spices

pic·co·lo (pik′ə lō′) *n., pl.* **-los′** ⟦< It, small⟧ a small flute, pitched an octave above the ordinary flute

pick¹ (pik) *n.* ⟦OE pic, PIKE²⟧ 1 any of several pointed tools or instruments for picking, esp. a heavy one used in breaking up soil, rock, etc. 2 PLECTRUM

pick² (pik) *vt.* ⟦ME picken⟧ 1 to probe, scratch at, etc. so as to remove or clear something from 2 to gather (flowers, berries, etc.) 3 to prepare (a fowl) by removing the feathers 4 to choose; select 5 to provoke (a quarrel or fight) 6 to pluck (the strings) of (a guitar, etc.) 7 to open (a lock) with a wire, etc. instead of a key 8 to steal from (another's pocket, etc.) —*vi.* 1 to use a pick 2 to select, esp. in a fussy way —*n.* 1 the act of choosing or the choice made 2 the best —**pick at** to eat small amounts of, esp. fussily —**pick off** 1 to remove by picking 2 to hit with a carefully aimed shot —**pick on** [Inf.] to single out for criticism or abuse; annoy; tease —**pick out** to choose —**pick up** 1 to grasp and lift 2 to get, find, or learn, esp. by chance 3 to stop for and take along 4 to gain (speed) 5 to improve 6 [Inf.] to become acquainted with casually, esp. for sexual activity —**pick′er** *n.*

pick·ax or **pick·axe** (pik′aks′) *n.* ⟦< OFr *picquois*⟧ a pick with a point at one end of the head and a chisel-like edge at the other

pick·er·el (pik′ər əl) *n., pl.* **-el** or **-els** ⟦ME < *pik,* PIKE³⟧ any of various small North American freshwater fishes

pick·et (pik′it) *n.* ⟦< Fr *pic,* PIKE²⟧ 1 a pointed stake used in a fence, as a hitching post, etc. 2 a soldier or soldiers stationed to guard against surprise attack 3 a person, as a member of a striking labor union, stationed outside a factory, store, etc. to demonstrate opposition, keep workers out, etc. —*vt.* 1 to hitch (an animal) to a picket 2 to post as a military picket 3 to place pickets, or serve as a picket, at (a factory, etc.)

picket line a line or cordon of people serving as pickets

pick·ings *pl.n.* [occas. *sing.*] something picked; specif., *a)* scraps; remains *b)* something gotten by effort, often dishonestly

pick·le (pik′əl) *n.* ⟦< MDu *pekel*⟧ 1 any brine, vinegar, etc. used to preserve or marinate food 2 a vegetable, specif. a cucumber, preserved in this 3 [Inf.] an awkward situation —*vt.* **-led, -ling** to treat or preserve in a pickle solution

pick·pock·et *n.* a thief who steals from pockets, as in a crowd

pick·up *n.* 1 a picking up 2 the process or power of increasing in speed 3 a small, open delivery truck 4 [Inf.] a casual acquaintance, esp. one formed for sexual purposes 5 [Inf.] improvement 6 a device for producing electric currents from vibrations —*adj.* [Inf.] assembled informally for a single occasion

pick·y *adj.* **-i·er, -i·est** [Inf.] overly fastidious; fussy

pic·nic (pik′nik) *n.* ⟦< Fr⟧ a pleasure outing at which a meal is eaten outdoors —*vi.* **-nicked, -nick·ing** to have a picnic —**pic′nick·er** *n.*

pi·cot (pē′kō) *n., pl.* **-cots** ⟦< Fr *pic,* a point⟧ any of the small loops forming a fancy edge, as on lace

pic·to·graph (pik′tə graf′) *n.* 1 a picture or picturelike symbol used in a system of writing 2 a graph using pictures to convey data

pic·to·ri·al (pik tôr′ē əl) *adj.* 1 of, containing, or expressed in pictures 2 suggesting a mental image; vivid —**pic·to′ri·al·ly** *adv.*

pic·ture (pik′chər) *n.* ⟦< L *pingere,* to paint⟧ 1 a likeness of a person, scene, etc. produced by drawing, painting, photography, etc. 2 a perfect likeness or image [the *picture* of health] 3 anything suggestive of a beautiful painting, drawing, etc. 4 a vivid description 5 FILM (*n.* 4) 6 the image on a TV screen —*vt.* **-tured, -tur·ing** 1 to make a picture of 2 to show visibly 3 to describe 4 to imagine —**in (or out of) the picture** considered (or not considered) as being involved in a situation

pic·ture-per·fect *adj.* perfect or flawless

pic·tur·esque (-chər esk′) *adj.* like or suggesting a picture; beautiful, vivid, quaint, etc.

picture window a large window that seems to frame the outside view

pid·dle (pid′'l) *vi., vt.* **-dled, -dling** ⟦< ?⟧ to dawdle; trifle

pid·dling (pid′liŋ) *adj.* insignificant; trifling

pid·dly (pid′lē) *adj.* PIDDLING

pidg·in (pij′in) *n.* ⟦supposed Chin pronunciation of *business*⟧ a mixed language for trade purposes, using words from one language and simplified grammar from another

pie (pī) *n.* ⟦ME⟧ a baked dish of fruit or of meat, with an under crust or upper crust, or both —**(as) easy as pie** [Inf.] extremely easy

pie·bald (pī′bôld′) *adj.* ⟦< *pie,* magpie + BALD⟧ covered with patches of two colors —*n.* a piebald horse, etc.

piece (pēs) *n.* ⟦OFr *pece*⟧ 1 a part broken or separated from the whole 2 a section of a whole regarded as complete in itself 3 any single thing, specimen, example, etc. [a *piece* of music] 4 a quantity, as of cloth, manufactured as a unit —*vt.* **pieced, piec′ing** 1 to add pieces to, as in repairing 2 to join (together) the pieces of —**go to pieces** 1 to fall apart 2 to lose self-control

pièce de ré·sis·tance (pyes də rä zēs täns′) [Fr, piece of resistance] 1 the principal dish of a meal 2 the main item in a series

piece goods YARD GOODS

piece·meal *adv.* [< ME *pece*, a piece + -*mele*, part] piece by piece —*adj.* made or done piecemeal

piece·work *n.* work paid for at a fixed rate (**piece rate**) per piece of work done

pie chart a graph in the form of a circle divided into sectors in which relative quantities are indicated by the sizes of the sectors

pied (pīd) *adj.* [< *pie*, magpie] spotted with various colors

pied-à-terre (pyä dà ter′) *n., pl.* **pieds-à-terre** (pyä dà ter′) [Fr, foot on the ground] a residence, esp. one used only part of the time or temporarily

pie-eyed *adj.* [Slang] intoxicated

pier (pir) *n.* [< ML *pera*] 1 a structure supporting the spans of a bridge 2 a structure built out over the water and supported by pillars: used as a landing place, pavilion, etc. 3 *Archit.* a heavy column used to support weight

pierce (pirs) *vt.* **pierced, pierc′ing** [< OFr *percer*] 1 to pass into or through as a pointed instrument does; stab 2 to make a hole in 3 to force a way into; break through 4 to sound sharply through 5 to penetrate with the sight or mind —*vi.* to penetrate

Pierce (pirs), **Franklin** 1804–69; 14th president of the U.S. (1853-57)

pierc·ing (pir′siŋ) *n.* 1 a hole pierced in an earlobe, nostril, or other body part for inserting a ring, stud, or other ornament 2 an ornament so worn —*adj.* that can pierce; specif., *a*) penetrating or sharp to the senses [a *piercing* wind] *b*) caustic; cutting; sarcastic [*piercing* criticism] *c*) having or showing keen intelligence, perception, or judgment [a *piercing* wit]

Pierre (pir) capital of South Dakota

pi·e·ty (pī′ə tē) *n., pl.* -ties [< L *pius*, pious] 1 devotion to religious duties, etc. 2 devotion to parents, family, etc. 3 a pious act

pif·fle (pif′əl) *n.* [Inf.] anything that is regarded as insignificant or nonsensical —**pif′fling** (pif′liŋ) *adj.*

pig (pig) *n.* [ME *pigge*] 1 any swine, esp. the young of the thick-bodied domesticated species 2 a greedy or filthy person

pi·geon (pij′ən) *n.* [< L *pipire*, to chirp] any of various related birds with a small head, a plump body, and short legs

pi·geon·hole *n.* a small, open compartment, as in a desk, for filing papers —*vt.* -**holed′, -hol′ing** 1 to put in the pigeonhole of a desk, etc. 2 to put aside indefinitely 3 to classify, esp. in an overly reductive way

pi·geon-toed (-tōd′) *adj.* having the toes or feet turned in

pig·gish (pig′ish) *adj.* like a pig; gluttonous or filthy —**pig′gish·ness** *n.*

pig·gy (pig′ē) *n., pl.* -**gies** a little pig: also sp. **pig′gie** —*adj.* -**gi·er, -gi·est** PIGGISH

pig·gy·back *adv., adj.* 1 on the shoulders or back 2 by or of a transportation system in which truck trailers are carried on flatcars 3 carried by or connected with something else as an adjunct —*vt.* 1 to carry piggyback 2 to place on something in piggyback fashion 3 to include with something else

pig·head·ed *adj.* stubborn

pig iron crude iron, as it comes from the blast furnace

pig·ment (pig′mənt) *n.* [< L *pingere*, to paint] 1 coloring matter used to make paints 2 any coloring matter in the tissues of plants or animals

pig·men·ta·tion (pig′mən tā′shən) *n.* coloration in plants or animals due to pigment in the tissue

Pig·my (pig′mē) *adj., n., pl.* -**mies** *alt. sp. of* PYGMY

pig·pen *n.* a pen where pigs are kept: also **pig′sty** (-stī′), **-sties**

pig·skin *n.* 1 leather made from the skin of a pig 2 [Inf.] a football

pig·tail *n.* a ponytail of hair hanging at the back or side of the head, esp. as one of a pair

pike¹ (pīk) *n.* a highway: now chiefly in [Inf.] **come down the pike,** to happen or appear

pike² (pīk) *n.* [Fr *pique*] a weapon, formerly for foot soldiers, consisting of a metal spearhead on a long wooden shaft (**pike′staff′**)

pike³ (pīk) *n., pl.* **pike** *or* **pikes** [ME *pīk*] a slender, freshwater bony fish with a narrow, pointed head

pik·er (pīk′ər) *n.* [< ? *Pike* County, Missouri] [Slang] a person who does things in a petty or stingy way

pi·laf *or* **pi·laff** (pē′läf′) *n.* [Pers *pilāv*] a dish made of rice boiled in a seasoned liquid

pi·las·ter (pi las′tər) *n.* [< L *pila*, a pile] a supporting column projecting partially from a wall

Pi·late (pī′lət), **Pon·tius** (pun′chəs, pä′-) 1st c. A.D.; Rom. procurator of Judea (26?-36?) who condemned Jesus to be crucified

pil·chard (pil′chərd) *n.* [< ?] 1 a small, oily marine fish, the commercial sardine of W Europe 2 any of several related fishes

pile¹ (pīl) *n.* [< L *pila*, pillar] 1 a mass of things heaped together 2 a heap of wood, etc. on which a corpse or sacrifice is burned 3 a large building 4 [Inf.] a large amount —*vt.* **piled, pil′ing** 1 to heap up 2 to load 3 to accumulate Often with *up* —*vi.* 1 to form a pile 2 to move in a mass: with *in, into, out, on,* etc.

pile² (pīl) *n.* [< L *pilus,* hair] a soft, velvety, raised surface of yarn loops, often sheared, as on a rug

pile³ (pīl) *n.* [OE *pīl*] a long, heavy beam driven into the ground to support a bridge, dock, etc.

pile driver (or engine) a machine for driving piles by raising and dropping a heavy weight on them

piles (pīlz) *pl.n.* [< L *pila,* a ball] hemorrhoids

pile·up *n.* 1 an accumulation of tasks, etc. 2 [Inf.] a collision involving several vehicles

pil·fer (pil'fər) *vt.*, *vi.* [< MFr *pelfre*, booty] to steal (esp. small sums, etc.) —**pil'fer·age** (-ij) *n.* —**pil'fer·er** *n.*

pil·grim (pil'grəm) *n.* [< L *peregrinus*, foreigner] 1 a wanderer 2 one who travels to a shrine or holy place as a religious act 3 [P-] any of the band of English Calvinists who founded Plymouth Colony in 1620

pil·grim·age *n.* 1 a journey made by a pilgrim, esp. to a shrine or holy place 2 any long journey

pill (pil) *n.* [< L *pila*, a ball] a small ball, tablet, etc. of medicine to be swallowed whole —**the pill** (or **Pill**) [Inf.] any contraceptive drug for women, in the form of a pill

pil·lage (pil'ij) *n.* [< MFr *piller*, to rob] 1 a plundering 2 goods stolen or taken by force —*vt.*, *vi.* **-laged**, **-lag·ing** to plunder

pil·lar (pil'ər) *n.* [< L *pila*, column] 1 a slender, vertical structure used as a support or monument; column 2 a main support of something

pill·box *n.* 1 a small box for holding pills 2 an enclosed gun emplacement of concrete and steel

pil·lion (pil'yən) *n.* [< L *pellis*, a skin] an extra seat behind the saddle on a horse or motorcycle

pil·lo·ry (pil'ə rē) *n.*, *pl.* **-ries** [< OFr *pilori*] a device consisting of a board with holes for the head and hands, in which petty offenders were formerly locked and exposed to public scorn —*vt.* **-ried**, **-ry·ing** 1 to punish by placing in a pillory 2 to subject to public scorn or ridicule

pil·low (pil'ō) *n.* [OE *pyle*] a cloth case filled with down, foam rubber, etc., used as a support, as for the head in sleeping —*vt.* to rest as on a pillow

pil·low·case *n.* a removable covering for a pillow: also **pil'low·slip'**

pi·lot (pi'lət) *n.* [< Gr *pēdon*, oar] 1 *a*) [Archaic] HELMSMAN *b*) a person licensed to direct ships into or out of a harbor or through difficult waters 2 a qualified operator of aircraft or spacecraft 3 a guide; leader 4 pilot light 5 an episode produced as the opening of a projected series of TV shows —*vt.* 1 to act as a pilot of, on, etc. 2 to guide —*adj.* serving as a trial unit in testing

pi·lot·house *n.* an enclosure for the helmsman on the upper deck of a ship

pilot light a small gas burner that is kept burning for use in lighting a main burner

Pil·sen·er or **Pil·sner** (pilz'nər) *n.* [*often* p-] a light lager beer

pi·men·to (pi men'tō) *n.*, *pl.* **-tos** [< Sp < L *pigmentum*, pigment] a variety of sweet red pepper: also **pi·mien'to** (-myen'-, -men'-)

pimp (pimp) *n.* [< ?] a prostitute's agent —*vi.* to act as a pimp

pim·ple (pim'pəl) *n.* [< OE *piplian*, to break out in pimples] a small, usually inflamed swelling of the skin —**pim'ply** *adj.* **-pli·er**, **-pli·est**

pin (pin) *n.* [OE *pinn*] 1 a peg, as of wood,

or a pointed piece of stiff wire, for fastening things together, etc. 2 anything like a pin 3 an ornament or badge with a pin or clasp for fastening to clothing 4 *Bowling* one of the bottle-shaped wooden objects at which the ball is rolled —*vt.* **pinned**, **pin'ning** 1 to fasten as with a pin 2 to hold firmly in one position —**pin down** 1 to get (someone) to make a commitment, etc. 2 to determine (a fact, etc.) —**pin something on someone** [Inf.] to lay the blame for something on someone

PIN (pin) *n.* [**p**(*ersonal*) **i**(*dentification*) **n**(*umber*)] an identification number, as for use at an ATM

pin·a·fore (pin'ə fôr') *n.* [PIN + archaic *afore*, before] a sleeveless garment worn over a dress

pi·ña·ta (pē nyä'tä) *n.* [Sp, ult. < L *pinus*, pine tree] in Mexico, a papier-mâché container hung from the ceiling in a game in which blindfolded children take turns trying to break it open and release the toys, candy, etc. inside

pin·ball machine a game machine consisting of an inclined board and a rolling ball that hits objects, etc. on it to score points

pince-nez (pans'nā') *n.* [Fr, nose-pincher] *pl.* **pince'-nez'** (-nāz', -nā') eyeglasses kept in place by a spring gripping the bridge of the nose

pin·cer (pin'sər) *n.* [< OFr *pincier*, to pinch] 1 [*usually pl.*] a tool formed of two pivoted parts, used in gripping things 2 a grasping claw, as of a crab

pinch (pinch) *vt.* [ME *pinchen* < OFr *pincier*] 1 to squeeze between a finger and the thumb or between two edges, surfaces, etc. 2 to press painfully upon (some part of the body) 3 to make cramped, thin, etc., as by hunger or cold 4 [Slang] *a*) to steal *b*) to arrest —*vi.* 1 to squeeze painfully 2 to be stingy or frugal —*n.* 1 a squeeze or nip 2 *a*) an amount squeezed between finger and thumb *b*) a small amount 3 distress or difficulty 4 an emergency: usually in **in a pinch** —*adj. Baseball* substitute

pinch-hit *vi.* **-hit'**, **-hit'ting** 1 *Baseball* to bat in place of the batter whose turn it is 2 to substitute in an emergency (*for*) —**pinch hitter**

pin curl a strand of hair kept curled with a bobby pin while it sets

pin·cush·ion *n.* a small cushion to stick pins in to keep them handy

pine[1] (pīn) *n.* [< L *pinus*] 1 an evergreen tree with cones and needle-shaped leaves 2 its wood

pine[2] (pīn) *vi.* **pined**, **pin'ing** [< L *poena*, a pain] 1 to waste (*away*) through grief, etc. 2 to yearn

pin·e·al gland (pin'ē əl) [< L *pinea*, pine cone] a small, cone-shaped body in the brain that produces a hormone

pine·ap·ple (pīn'ap'əl) *n.* [ME *pinappel*, pine cone] 1 a juicy, edible tropical fruit somewhat resembling a pine cone 2 the plant it grows on

pine tar a thick, dark liquid obtained from pine wood, used in disinfectants, paints, etc.

pin·feath·er *n.* an undeveloped, emerging feather

ping (piŋ) *n.* ⟦echoic⟧ the sound made as by a bullet striking something sharply — *vi., vt.* to make or cause to make this sound

Ping-Pong (piŋ′pôŋ′) ⟦echoic⟧ *trademark for* table-tennis equipment —*n.* [*often* ping-pong] TABLE TENNIS

pin·head *n.* 1 the head of a pin 2 a person regarded as stupid or silly

pin·hole *n.* 1 a tiny hole as from a pin 2 a hole to stick a pin into

pin·ion (pin′yən) *n.* ⟦< L *pinna*, feather⟧ 1 a small cogwheel that meshes with a larger gear or with a RACK[1] (*n.* 2) 2 a wing; specif., the outer part of a bird's wing —*vt.* 1 to bind the wings or arms of 2 to shackle

pink[1] (piŋk) *n.* ⟦< ?⟧ 1 any of certain plants with white, pink, or red flowers 2 the flower 3 pale red 4 the highest degree, finest example, etc. —*adj.* 1 pale-red 2 [Inf.] somewhat leftist: a derogatory term —**in the pink** [Inf.] healthy; fit

pink[2] (piŋk) *vt.* ⟦ME *pynken*⟧ 1 to cut a saw-toothed edge on (cloth, etc.) 2 to prick or stab

pink·eye *n.* a contagious eye infection in which the eyeball and the lining of the eyelid are red and inflamed

pink·ie or **pink·y** (piŋ′kē) *n., pl.* **-ies** the smallest finger

pink·ing shears (piŋ′kiŋ) shears with notched blades, for pinking edges of cloth

pink slip [Inf.] notice to an employee that he or she is fired

pin money a small sum of money, as for incidental minor expenses

pin·na·cle (pin′ə kəl) *n.* ⟦< L *pinna*, feather⟧ 1 a small turret or spire 2 a slender, pointed formation, as a mountain peak 3 the highest point

pin·nate (pin′āt′, -it) *adj.* ⟦< L *pinna*, feather⟧ *Bot.* with leaflets on each side of a common stem

pi·noch·le or **pi·noc·le** (pē′nuk′əl) *n.* ⟦< Fr *binocle*, pince-nez⟧ a card game played with a 48-card deck (two of every card above the eight)

pi·not noir (pē′nō nwär′, pē nô′-) [*also* P-N-] 1 the main red-wine grape of the Burgundy region 2 a dry red wine made from this grape

pin·point *vt.* to locate precisely —*adj.* precise

pin·prick *n.* 1 a tiny puncture as by a pin 2 a minor annoyance

pins and needles a tingling feeling as in a numb limb —**on pins and needles** in anxious suspense

pin·set·ter *n.* a person or automatic device that sets up bowling pins on the alley: also **pin′spot′ter**

pin·stripe *n.* a pattern of very narrow stripes in suit fabrics, etc.

pint (pīnt) *n.* ⟦< ML⟧ a unit of measure equal to ½ quart

pin·to (pin′tō) *adj.* ⟦< obs. Sp, spotted⟧ having patches of white and some other color —*n., pl.* **-tos** a pinto horse

pinto bean a kind of mottled kidney bean grown in the SW U.S.

pin-up *n.* 1 a poster or large picture of a sexually attractive person 2 a person depicted in such a poster or picture

pin·wheel *n.* a small wheel with vanes of paper, etc., pinned to a stick so as to revolve in the wind

Pin·yin (pin′yin′) *n.* ⟦Chin *pinyin*, lit., phonetic sound⟧ [*also* p-] system for transcribing Chinese words in the Latin alphabet

pi·o·neer (pī′ə nir′) *n.* ⟦< OFr *peonier*, foot soldier⟧ one who goes before, preparing the way for others, as an early settler —*vi.* to be a pioneer —*vt.* to be a pioneer in or of

pi·ous (pī′əs) *adj.* ⟦< L *pius*⟧ 1 having or showing religious devotion 2 only seemingly virtuous 3 sacred —**pi′ous·ly** *adv.*

pip[1] (pip) *n.* ⟦< PIPPIN⟧ a small seed, as of an apple

pip[2] (pip) *n.* ⟦< ?⟧ any of the figures or spots on playing cards, dice, or dominoes

pip[3] (pip) *n.* ⟦< L *pituita*, phlegm⟧ a contagious disease of fowl

pipe (pīp) *n.* ⟦< L *pipare*, chirp⟧ 1 a tube of wood, metal, etc. for making musical sounds 2 [*pl.*] the bagpipe 3 a long tube for conveying water, gas, etc. 4 a tube with a small bowl at one end in which tobacco is smoked 5 any tubular part, organ of the body, etc. —*vi.* piped, pip′ing 1 to play on a pipe 2 to utter shrill sounds —*vt.* 1 to play (a tune) on a pipe 2 to utter in a shrill voice 3 to bring, call, etc. by piping 4 to convey (water, gas, etc.) by pipes —**pipe down** [Slang] to stop shouting, talking, etc. —**pip′er** *n.*

pipe dream [Inf.] a fantastic idea, vain hope or plan, etc.

pipe fitter a mechanic who installs and maintains plumbing pipes, etc.

pipe·line *n.* 1 a line of pipes for conveying water, gas, oil, etc. 2 any means whereby something is passed on

pipe organ ORGAN (*n.* 1a)

pi·pette or **pi·pet** (pi pet′, pī-) *n.* a slender tube for taking up and measuring small amounts of a liquid

pip·ing (pīp′iŋ) *n.* 1 music made by pipes 2 a shrill sound 3 a pipelike fold of material for trimming seams, etc. —**piping hot** very hot

pip·it (pip′it) *n.* ⟦echoic⟧ a small bird with a slender bill, streaked breast, and the habit of walking rather than hopping

pip·pin (pip′in) *n.* ⟦< OFr *pepin*, seed⟧ any of several varieties of apple

pip·squeak (pip′skwēk′) *n.* [Inf.] anyone or anything regarded as small or insignificant

pi·quant (pē′kənt) *adj.* ⟦Fr < *piquer*, to prick⟧ 1 agreeably pungent to the taste 2 exciting interest; stimulating —**pi′quan·cy** (-kən sē) *n.*

pique (pēk) *n.* ⟦see prec.⟧ resentment at

being slighted —*vt.* **piqued**, **piqu′ing** 1 to arouse such resentment in 2 to stir up; excite

pi·qué or **pi·que** (pē kā′) *n.* ⟦see PIQUANT⟧ a cotton fabric with ribbed or corded wales

pi·ra·cy (pī′rə sē) *n., pl.* **-cies** 1 robbery of ships on the high seas 2 the unauthorized use of copyrighted or patented work

pi·ra·nha (pi rä′nə) *n.* ⟦< Brazilian Port < AmInd (Brazil) *pirá*, fish + *sainha*, tooth⟧ any of various small, freshwater South American fishes: they hunt in schools, attacking any animals

pi·rate (pī′rət) *n.* ⟦< Gr *peirān*, to attack⟧ one who practices piracy —*vt., vi.* **-rat·ed**, **-rat·ing** 1 to take (something) by piracy 2 to publish, reproduce, etc. (a book, recording, etc.) in violation of a copyright —**pi·rat′i·cal** (-rat′i kəl) *adj.*

pi·ro·gi (pi rō′gē) *n., pl.* **-gi** or **-gies** ⟦Russ⟧ a small pastry turnover filled with meat, cheese, etc.

pir·ou·ette (pir′ōō et′) *n.* ⟦Fr, spinning top⟧ a whirling on one foot or the point of the toe —*vi.* **-et′ted**, **-et′ting** to do a pirouette

pis·ca·to·ri·al (pis′kə tôr′ē əl) *adj.* ⟦< L *piscator*, fisherman⟧ of fishes or fishing

Pis·ces (pī′sēz′) *n.* ⟦L, pl. of *piscis*, fish⟧ the 12th sign of the zodiac

pis·mire (pis′mīr′, piz′-) *n.* ⟦< ME *pisse*, urine + *mire*, ant⟧ ⟦Archaic⟧ an ant

piss·ant (pis′ant′) *adj., n.* ⟦Slang⟧ insignificant and contemptible (person)

pis·tach·i·o (pi stash′ē ō′) *n., pl.* **-o′** ⟦< OPers *pistah*⟧ 1 a small tree of the cashew family 2 its edible, greenish seed (**pistachio nut**)

pis·til (pis′təl) *n.* ⟦< L *pistillum*, pestle⟧ the seed-bearing organ of a flower —**pis′til·late′** *adj.*

pis·tol (pis′təl) *n.* ⟦< Czech *píšťal*⟧ a small firearm operated with one hand

pis·tol-whip *vt.* **-whipped′**, **-whip′ping** to beat with a pistol, esp. about the head

pis·ton (pis′tən) *n.* ⟦ult. < L *pinsere*, to pound⟧ the snug-fitting engine part that is forced back and forth within a cylinder by the pressure of combustion, steam, etc. and a reciprocating connecting rod (**piston rod**)

piston ring a split ring fitted into a groove around a piston to seal the cylinder, transfer heat, etc.

pit¹ (pit) *n.* ⟦< MDu *pitte*⟧ the hard stone, as of the plum, peach, or cherry, containing the seed —*vt.* **pit′ted**, **pit′ting** to remove the pit from

pit² (pit) *n.* ⟦< L *puteus*, a well⟧ 1 a hole in the ground 2 an abyss 3 hell: used with *the* 4 a pitfall 5 an enclosed area in which animals are kept or made to fight 6 a small hollow in a surface, as a scar left by smallpox 7 the section for the orchestra in front of the stage 8 a work area for mechanics beside an auto-racing track —*vt.* **pit′ted**, **pit′ting** 1 to make pits or scars in 2 to set in competition (*against*)

pi·ta (pēt′ə) *n.* ⟦< Heb < Modern Greek⟧ a round, flat bread of the Middle East: also **pita bread**

pit·a·pat (pit′ə pat′) *adv.* with rapid beating —*n.* a rapid series of beats or taps

pit bull a short, heavy dog with powerful jaws

pitch¹ (pich) *n.* ⟦< L *pix*⟧ a black, sticky substance formed from coal tar, etc. and used for roofing, etc.

pitch² (pich) *vt.* ⟦ME *picchen*⟧ 1 to set up [*pitch* a tent] 2 *a*) to throw or toss *b*) to throw away 3 to fix at a certain point, degree, key, etc. 4 *Baseball a*) to throw (the ball) to the batter *b*) to act as pitcher for (a game, etc.) —*vi.* 1 to pitch a ball, etc. 2 to plunge forward or dip downward 3 to rise and fall, as a ship in rough water —*n.* 1 a throw or toss 2 anything pitched 3 a point or degree 4 the degree of slope 5 [Inf.] a line of talk for persuading 6 *Music, etc.* the highness or lowness of a sound due to vibrations of sound waves —**pitch in** [Inf.] 1 to begin working hard 2 to make a contribution —**pitch into** [Inf.] to attack

pitch-black *adj.* very black

pitch·blende (-blend′) *n.* ⟦< Ger *pech*, PITCH¹ + *blenden*, to blind⟧ a dark mineral, a major source of uranium

pitch-dark *adj.* very dark

pitched battle 1 a battle in which troop placement is relatively fixed beforehand 2 a hard-fought battle

pitch·er¹ *n.* ⟦< OFr *pichier*⟧ a container, usually with a handle and lip, for holding and pouring liquids

pitch·er² *n.* ⟦PITCH² + -ER⟧ the baseball player who pitches the ball to the batters

pitcher plant a plant with pitcherlike leaves that trap and digest insects

pitch·fork *n.* a large, long-handled fork for lifting and tossing hay, etc.

pitch·man (-mən) *n., pl.* **-men** (-mən) 1 a hawker of novelties, as at a carnival 2 [Inf.] any high-pressure salesman

pitch pipe a small pipe that produces a fixed tone used as a standard in tuning instruments, etc.

pit·e·ous (pit′ē əs) *adj.* arousing or deserving pity —**pit′e·ous·ly** *adv.*

pit·fall (-fôl′) *n.* ⟦< PIT² + OE *fealle*, a trap⟧ 1 a lightly covered pit for trapping animals 2 an unsuspected danger, etc.

pith (pith) *n.* ⟦OE *pitha*⟧ 1 the soft, spongy tissue in the center of certain plant stems 2 the essential part; gist

pith·y *adj.* **-i·er**, **-i·est** 1 of, like, or full of pith 2 terse and full of meaning —**pith′i·ly** *adv.*

pit·i·ful (pit′i fəl) *adj.* 1 arousing or deserving pity 2 contemptible Also **pit·i·a·ble** (pit′ē ə bəl) —**pit′i·ful·ly** *adv.*

pit·i·less (-lis) *adj.* without pity

pi·ton (pē′tän′) *n.* ⟦Fr < MFr, a spike⟧ a metal spike with an eye for a rope, driven into rock or ice for support in mountain climbing

pit stop 1 a temporary stop in the PIT² (*n.* 8) by a racing car 2 [Slang] *a*) a pause for food, etc. during a journey *b*) a visit to a restroom

pit·tance (pit′′ns) *n.* ⟦< OFr *pitance*, food

allowed a monk‖ **1** a meager allowance of money **2** any small amount or share

pit·ter-pat·ter (pit′ər pat′ər) *n.* ⟦echoic⟧ a rapid succession of light tapping sounds

Pitts·burgh (pits′burg′) city in SW Pennsylvania

pi·tu·i·tar·y (pi tōō′ə ter′ē) *adj.* ⟦< L *pituita*, phlegm⟧ of a small, oval endocrine gland (**pituitary gland**) attached to the brain: it secretes hormones affecting growth, etc.

pit viper any of several poisonous vipers with a heat-sensitive pit on each side of the head

pit·y (pit′ē) *n., pl.* **-ies** ⟦< L *pietas*, piety⟧ **1** sorrow for another's suffering or misfortune **2** a cause for sorrow or regret —*vt., vi.* **-ied, -y·ing** to feel pity (for)

piv·ot (piv′ət) *n.* ⟦Fr⟧ **1** a point, shaft, etc. on which something turns **2** a person or thing on which something depends, etc. **3** a pivoting movement —*vt.* to provide with a pivot —*vi.* to turn as on a pivot —**piv′ot·al** *adj.*

pix·el (pik′səl) *n.* ⟦< *pic(ture)s* + *el(ement)*⟧ any of the dots that make up an image on a video screen

pix·ie or **pix·y** (pik′sē) *n., pl.* **-ies** ⟦< Brit dial.⟧ a fairy, elf, etc.

pi·zazz or **piz·zazz** (pi zaz′) *n.* [Inf.] **1** vigor **2** style, flair, etc.

piz·za (pēt′sə) *n.* ⟦It⟧ an Italian dish made by baking thin dough covered with tomatoes, cheese, etc.

piz·ze·ri·a (pēt′sə rē′ə) *n.* ⟦It⟧ a place where pizzas are made and sold

piz·zi·ca·to (pit′si kät′ō) *adj.* ⟦It⟧ *Music* plucked: a note to pluck the strings with the finger instead of bowing: also written *piz′zi·ca′to*

pj's (pē′jāz′) *pl.n. inf. var. of* PAJAMAS

pk *abbrev.* **1** pack **2** park **3** peck

pkg *abbrev.* package(s)

Pkwy or **Pky** *abbrev.* Parkway

pl *abbrev.* **1** place: also **Pl 2** plural

plac·ard (plak′ärd; -ərd) *n.* ⟦< MDu *placke*, a piece⟧ a notice for display in a public place —*vt.* to place placards on or in

pla·cate (plā′kāt′) *vt.* **-cat′ed, -cat′ing** ⟦< L *placare*⟧ to appease; pacify —**pla·ca′tion** *n.*

place (plās) *n.* ⟦< Gr *plateia*, a street⟧ **1** a court or short street in a city **2** space; room **3** a region **4** *a)* the part of space occupied by a person or thing *b)* situation **5** a city, town, etc. **6** a residence **7** a building or space devoted to a special purpose [a *place* of amusement] **8** a particular point, part, position, etc. [a sore *place* on the leg, a *place* in history] **9** a step or point in a sequence **10** the proper position, time, etc. **11** a space, seat, etc. reserved or occupied by a person **12** a job or position **13** the duties of any position **14** the second position at the finish of a race —*vt.* **placed, plac′ing 1** *a)* to put in a particular place, condition, or relation *b)* to recognize or identify **2** to find employment for **3** to repose (trust) *in* a person or thing **4** to finish in (a specified position) in a race —*vi.* to finish second or among

the first three in a race —**take place** to occur

pla·ce·bo (plə sē′bō) *n., pl.* **-bos** or **-boes** ⟦< L, I shall please⟧ a harmless, unmedicated preparation given as a medicine, as to humor a patient or as a control in a research study

place mat a small mat serving as an individual table cover for a person at a meal

place·ment *n.* **1** a placing or being placed **2** location or arrangement

pla·cen·ta (plə sen′tə) *n., pl.* **-tas** or **-tae** (-tē) ⟦ult. < Gr *plax*, a flat object⟧ the structure in the uterus through which the fetus is nourished: cf. AFTERBIRTH —**pla·cen′tal** *adj.*

plac·er (plas′ər) *n.* ⟦< Sp *placel*⟧ a deposit of gravel or sand containing particles of gold, etc. that can be washed out

place setting the dishes, utensils, etc. used for setting one place at a table for a meal

plac·id (plas′id) *adj.* ⟦L *placidus*⟧ calm; quiet —**pla·cid·i·ty** (plə sid′ə tē) *n.* —**plac′id·ly** *adv.*

plack·et (plak′it) *n.* ⟦< ?⟧ a slit at the waist of a skirt or collar of a shirt, to make it easy to put on and take off

pla·gi·a·rize (plā′jə rīz′) *vt., vi.* **-rized′, -riz′ing** ⟦< L *plagiarius*, kidnapper⟧ to take (ideas, writings, etc.) from (another) and pass them off as one's own —**pla′gi·a·rism′** (-riz′əm) *n.* —**pla′gi·a·rist** *n.*

plague (plāg) *n.* ⟦< Gr *plēgē*, a misfortune⟧ **1** any affliction or calamity **2** any deadly epidemic disease **3** bubonic plague —*vt.* **plagued, plagu′ing 1** to afflict with a plague **2** to vex; torment

plaice (plās) *n., pl.* **plaice** or **plaic′es** any of various American and European flounders

plaid (plad) *n.* ⟦Gael *plaide*, a blanket⟧ **1** cloth with a crossbarred pattern **2** any pattern of this kind —*adj.* having such a pattern

plain (plān) *adj.* ⟦< L *planus*, flat⟧ **1** open; clear [in *plain* view] **2** clearly understood; obvious **3** outspoken; straightforward **4** not luxurious or ornate **5** not complicated; simple **6** homely **7** pure; unmixed **8** common; ordinary [a *plain* man] —*n.* an extent of level country —*adv.* clearly —**plain′ly** *adv.* —**plain′ness** *n.*

plain·clothes *adj.* wears civilian clothes while on duty to avoid being identified as police or security

plain·song *n.* a very old, plain kind of church music chanted in unison

plaint (plānt) *n.* ⟦< L *plangere*, to lament⟧ a complaint or lament

plain·tiff (plān′tif) *n.* [see prec.] one who brings a suit into a court of law

plain·tive (-tiv) *adj.* [see PLAINT] expressing sorrow or melancholy; mournful; sad

plait (plāt) *n.* ⟦< L *plicare*, to fold⟧ a braid of hair, etc. —*vt.* to braid

plan (plan) *n.* ⟦Fr, plan, foundation⟧ **1** a diagram showing the arrangement of a structure, piece of ground, etc. **2** a scheme for making, doing, or arranging something **3** any outline or sketch —*vt.* **planned, plan′ning 1** to make a plan of (a structure, etc.) **2** to devise a scheme for doing, etc. **3** to have in mind as a project or purpose —*vi.* to make plans —**plan′ner** *n.*

plane¹ (plān) *adj.* ⟦L *planus*⟧ **1** flat; level **2** of or having to do with flat surfaces or points, lines, etc. on them [*plane* geometry] —*n.* **1** a flat, level surface **2** a level of achievement, etc. **3** *short for* AIRPLANE

plane² (plān) *n.* ⟦< L *planus*, level⟧ a carpenter's tool for shaving a wood surface to make it smooth or level —*vt.* **planed**, **plan′ing** to smooth or level with a plane

plan·et (plan′it) *n.* ⟦< Gr *planan*, wander⟧ any celestial body that revolves about a star; esp., one of the sun's eight major planets: Mercury, Venus, Earth, Mars, Jupiter, Saturn, Uranus, and Neptune —**plan′e·tar′y** (-ə ter′ē) *adj.*

plan·e·tar·i·um (plan′ə ter′ē əm) *n., pl.* **-i·ums** or **-i·a** (-ə) **1** a revolving projector used to simulate the past, present, or future motions or positions of the sun, planets, etc. on the inside of a large dome **2** the room or building containing this

plane tree any of various trees with ball-shaped fruits and bark that sheds in large patches; sycamore

plan·gent (plan′jənt) *adj.* ⟦< L *plangere*, to beat⟧ loud or resonant, and, often, mournful-sounding

plank (plaŋk) *n.* ⟦< LL *planca*⟧ **1** a long, broad, thick board **2** an item in the platform of a political party —*vt.* **1** to cover with planks **2** to broil and serve [steak, fish, etc.] on a board

plank·ing *n.* **1** planks in quantity **2** the planks of a structure

plank·ton (plaŋk′tən) *n.* ⟦< Gr *planktos*, wander⟧ the microscopic animal and plant life found floating in bodies of water

plant (plant) *n.* ⟦< L *planta*, a sprout⟧ **1** any of a group of living organisms, excluding animals, bacteria, and certain other simple organisms, typically having leaves, stems, and roots and the ability to carry on photosynthesis **2** an herb, as distinguished from a tree or shrub **3** the machinery, buildings, etc. of a factory, etc. —*vt.* **1** to put into the ground to grow **2** to set firmly in position **3** to settle; establish **4** [Slang] to place (a person or thing) in such a way as to trick, trap, etc.

plan·tain¹ (plan′tin) *n.* ⟦< L *plantago*⟧ a plant with basal leaves and spikes of tiny, greenish flowers

plan·tain² (plan′tin, plan tān′) *n.* ⟦< Sp *plátano*, banana tree⟧ a hybrid banana plant yielding a starchy fruit that is usually cooked while green

plan·tar (plant′ər) *adj.* ⟦< L *planta*, sole⟧ of or on the sole of the foot

plan·ta·tion (plan tā′shən) *n.* ⟦< L *plantare*, to plant⟧ **1** an estate, esp. in a warm climate, cultivated by workers living on it **2** a large, cultivated planting of trees

plant·er (plant′ər) *n.* **1** the owner of a plantation **2** one that plants **3** a decorative container for plants

plant·ing *n.* **1** the act of putting seeds or young plants into soil **2** something that is planted

plant louse APHID

plaque (plak) *n.* ⟦Fr < MDu *placke*, disk⟧ **1** a flat, inscribed piece of wood or metal, used to commemorate an event, etc. **2** a thin film of matter on uncleaned teeth

plash (plash) *vt., vi., n.* ⟦echoic⟧ SPLASH

plas·ma (plaz′mə) *n.* ⟦Ger < Gr, something molded⟧ **1** the fluid part of blood, lymph, or milk **2** a high-temperature, ionized gas that is electrically neutral

plasma membrane a very thin living membrane surrounding a plant or animal cell

plas·ter (plas′tər) *n.* ⟦< Gr *emplassein*, to daub over⟧ **1** a pasty mixture, as of lime, sand, and water, that hardens when it dries, for coating walls, etc. **2** PLASTER OF PARIS **3** a pasty, medicinal preparation spread on cloth and applied to the body —*vt.* **1** to cover as with plaster **2** to apply like a plaster [to *plaster* posters on walls] **3** to make lie smooth and flat —**plas′ter·er** *n.*

plas·ter·board *n.* thin board consisting of plaster of Paris covered with heavy paper, used in wide sheets for walls, etc.

plaster of Paris ⟦from use of gypsum from *Paris*, France⟧ a thick paste of gypsum and water that sets quickly: used for casts, statuary, etc.

plas·tic (plas′tik) *adj.* ⟦< L *plassein*, to form⟧ **1** molding or shaping matter; formative **2** that can be molded or shaped **3** made of plastic —*n.* **1** any of various nonmetallic compounds, synthetically produced, which can be molded and hardened for commercial use **2** [Inf.] a credit card or credit cards, or credit based on their use —**plas·tic′i·ty** (-tis′ə tē) *n.*

plas·ti·cize (-tə sīz′) *vt., vi.* **-cized′**, **-ciz′ing** to make or become plastic

plastic surgery surgery dealing with the repair, restoration, or modification of parts of the body —**plastic surgeon**

plat (plat) *n.* ⟦var. of PLOT⟧ **1** a small piece of ground **2** a map or plan, as of a subdivision —*vt.* **plat′ted**, **plat′ting** to make a map or plan of

plate (plāt) *n.* ⟦< Gr *platys*, broad⟧ **1** a smooth, flat, thin piece of metal, etc., specif. one on which an engraving is cut **2** an impression taken from an engraved surface **3** dishes, utensils, etc. of, or plated with, silver or gold **4** a shallow dish **5** the food in a dish; a course **6** a denture, specif. that part of it which fits to the mouth **7** *Baseball short for* HOME PLATE **8** *Photog.* a sheet of glass, metal, etc. coated with a film sensitive to light **9** *Printing* a cast to be printed from —*vt.* **plat′ed**, **plat′ing 1** to coat with gold, silver, etc. **2** to cover with metal plates

pla·teau (pla tō′) *n.* ⟦Fr: see prec.⟧ **1** an elevated tract of level land **2** a period of relative stability or little change

plate glass polished, clear glass in thick sheets, for windows, mirrors, etc.

plate·let (plāt′lit) *n.* a small blood cell involved in clotting

plat·en (plat′'n) *n.* ⟦< OFr *plat*, flat⟧ 1 in a printing press, a flat metal plate which presses the paper against the type 2 a typewriter roller on which the keys strike

plate tec·ton·ics (tek tän′iks) [*with sing. v.*] *Geol.* the theory that the earth's surface consists of plates whose constant motion explains continental drift, etc.

plat·form (plat′fôrm′) *n.* ⟦Fr *plate-forme*, lit., flat form⟧ 1 a raised horizontal surface, as a stage for speakers, etc. 2 a statement of policy, esp. of a political party 3 *Comput.* a hardware design for use with an operating system, etc. 4 an opportunity to express one's views

plat·i·num (plat′'n əm) *n.* ⟦< Sp *plata*, silver⟧ a silvery, metallic chemical element, resistant to corrosion: used for jewelry, etc.: symbol, Pt; at. no. 78

plat·i·tude (plat′ə tōōd′) *n.* ⟦Fr < *plat*, flat, after *latitude*, etc.⟧ a commonplace or trite remark

Pla·to (plāt′ō) 427?-347? B.C.; Gr. philosopher

Pla·ton·ic (plə tän′ik) *adj.* 1 of Plato or his philosophy 2 [*usually* p-] not sexual but purely spiritual: said of a relationship, etc.

pla·toon (plə tōōn′) *n.* ⟦Fr *peloton*, a ball, group⟧ 1 a military unit composed of two or more squads 2 *Sports* any of the specialized squads making up a team

plat·ter (plat′ər) *n.* ⟦< OFr *plat*, flat⟧ a large, shallow dish, usually oval, for serving food

plat·y·pus (plat′ə pəs) *n., pl.* **-pus·es** or **-pi′** (-pī′) ⟦< Gr *platys*, flat + *pous*, foot⟧ a small, egg-laying water mammal of Australia, with webbed feet and a ducklike bill; duckbill

plau·dit (plô′dit) *n.* ⟦< L *plaudere*, applaud⟧ [*usually pl.*] applause or praise

plau·si·ble (plô′zə bəl) *adj.* ⟦< L *plaudere*, applaud⟧ seemingly true, trustworthy, honest, etc. —**plau′si·bil′i·ty** *n.*

play (plā) *vi.* ⟦OE *plegan*⟧ 1 to move lightly, rapidly, etc. [*sunlight played* on the water] 2 to engage in recreation 3 to take part in a game or sport 4 to trifle (*with* a thing or person) 5 to perform on a musical instrument 6 to give out sounds 7 to act in a specified way [to *play* dumb] 8 to act in a drama 9 to impose unscrupulously (*on* another's feelings) —*vt.* 1 to take part in (a game or sport) 2 to oppose (a person, team, etc.) in a game 3 to do, as in fun [to *play* tricks] 4 to bet on 5 to cause to move, etc.; wield 6 to cause [to *play* havoc] 7 to perform (music, a drama, etc.) 8 to perform on (an instrument) 9 to act the part of [to *play* Hamlet] —*n.* 1 motion or activity, esp. when free or rapid 2 freedom for motion or action 3 recreation; sport 4 fun; joking 5 the playing of a game 6 a move or act in a game 7 a dramatic composition or performance; drama —**in** (or **out of**) **play** *Sports* (in or not in) the condition for continuing play: said of a ball, etc. —**play down** to attach little importance to —**played out** exhausted —**play up** [Inf.] to give promi-

nence to —**play up to** [Inf.] to try to please by flattery

play·act *vi.* 1 to pretend 2 to behave in an affected or dramatic manner —**play′act′ing** *n.*

play·back *n.* 1 reproduction of sounds, images, etc. from a recorded disc, digital file, etc. 2 the control or device for such reproduction

play·bill *n.* 1 a poster advertising a play 2 a program of a play, listing the cast, etc.

play·boy *n.* a man of means who is given to pleasure-seeking

play·er *n.* 1 one who plays a specified game, instrument, etc. 2 an actor

play·ful *adj.* 1 fond of play or fun 2 jocular —**play′ful·ly** *adv.* —**play′ful·ness** *n.*

play·ground *n.* a place, often near a school, that has equipment for children's outdoor recreation

play·house *n.* 1 a theater for live dramatic productions 2 a small house for children to play in

playing cards cards used in playing various games, arranged in four suits

play·mate *n.* a companion in games and recreation

play·off *n.* a contest to break a tie or to decide a championship

play on words a pun or punning

play·pen *n.* a portable enclosure for an infant to play or crawl in safely

play·thing *n.* a toy

play·wright (-rīt′) *n.* one who writes plays

pla·za (plä′zə, plaz′ə) *n.* ⟦Sp < L *platea*, street⟧ 1 a public square in a city or town 2 a shopping center 3 a service area along a superhighway

plea (plē) *n.* ⟦< L *placere*, to please⟧ 1 a statement in defense; excuse 2 a request; appeal 3 *Law* the response of a defendant to criminal charges

plea-bar·gain *vi.* to engage in plea bargaining

plea bargaining pretrial negotiations in which the defendant agrees to plead guilty to a lesser charge if more serious charges are dropped

plead (plēd) *vi.* **plead′ed** or **pled** or **plead** (pled), **plead′ing** [see PLEA] 1 to present a plea in a law court 2 to make an appeal; beg —*vt.* 1 to argue (a law case) 2 to answer (guilty or not guilty) to a charge 3 to offer as an excuse —**plead′er** *n.*

pleas·ant (plez′ənt) *adj.* ⟦< Fr *plaisir*, to please⟧ 1 agreeable to the mind or senses; pleasing 2 having an agreeable manner, look, etc.; amiable —**pleas′ant·ly** *adv.* —**pleas′ant·ness** *n.*

pleas·ant·ry (-ən trē) *n., pl.* **-ries** 1 a humorous remark 2 a polite social remark [to exchange *pleasantries*]

please (plēz) *vt.* **pleased, pleas′ing** ⟦< L *placere*⟧ 1 to be agreeable to; satisfy 2 to be the wish of [it *pleased* him to go] —*vi.* 1 to be agreeable; satisfy 2 to have the wish; like [to do as one *pleases*] *Please* is also used in polite requests [*please* sit down]

pleas·ing *adj.* giving pleasure —**pleas′ing·ly** *adv.*

pleas·ure (plezh′ər) *n.* **1** a pleased feeling; delight **2** one's wish, will, or choice **3** a thing that gives delight or satisfaction —*vt.* **-ured, -ur·ing** to give sexual pleasure to —**pleas′ur·a·ble** (-ə bəl)

pleat (plēt) *n.* ⟦ME *pleten*⟧ a flat double fold in cloth, etc. pressed or stitched in place —*vt.* to lay and press (cloth) in a pleat or pleats

ple·be·ian (pli bē′ən) *n.* ⟦< L *plebs*, the common people⟧ **1** one of the common people **2** a vulgar person —*adj.* vulgar or common

pleb·i·scite (pleb′ə sīt′) *n.* ⟦< L *plebs*, the common people + *scitum*, a decree⟧ a direct vote of the people on a political issue, such as independent nationhood or annexation

plec·trum (plek′trəm) *n., pl.* **-trums** or **-tra** (-trə) ⟦L < Gr *plēssein*, to strike⟧ a thin piece of metal, plastic, etc., for plucking the strings of a guitar, etc.; pick

pled (pled) *vt., vi. pt. & pp. of* PLEAD

pledge (plej) *n.* ⟦prob < OS *plegan*, to warrant⟧ **1** the condition of being given or held as security for a contract, payment, etc. **2** a person or thing given or held thus as security **3** a promise or agreement **4** something promised —*vt.* **pledged, pledg′ing 1** to give as security **2** to bind by a promise **3** to promise to give

Pleis·to·cene (plīs′tə sēn′) *adj.* ⟦< Gr *pleistos*, most + *kainos*, recent⟧ designating an epoch in the Cenozoic Era, characterized by the appearance of modern humans

ple·na·ry (plē′nə rē, plen′ə-) *adj.* ⟦< L *plenus*, full⟧ **1** full; complete **2** for attendance by all members *[a plenary session]*

plen·i·po·ten·ti·ar·y (plen′i pō ten′she er′ē) *adj.* ⟦< L *plenus*, full + *potens*, powerful⟧ having or conferring full authority —*n., pl.* **-ar′ies** a diplomat given full authority

plen·i·tude (plen′i tōōd′) *n.* ⟦< L *plenus*, full⟧ **1** fullness; completeness **2** abundance

plen·te·ous (plen′tē əs) *adj.* plentiful

plen·ti·ful (plen′ti fəl) *adj.* **1** having or yielding plenty **2** abundant —**plen′ti·ful·ly** *adv.*

plen·ty (plen′tē) *n.* ⟦< L *plenus*, full⟧ **1** prosperity; opulence **2** a sufficient supply; enough or more than enough **3** a large number —*adv.* [Inf.] fully; quite

pleth·o·ra (pleth′ə rə) *n.* ⟦< Gr *plēthein*, to be full⟧ an overabundance

pleu·ra (ploor′ə) *n., pl.* **-rae** (-ē) ⟦< Gr, rib, side⟧ the thin membrane that covers a lung and lines the chest cavity in mammals

pleu·ri·sy (ploor′ə sē) *n.* ⟦< Gr *pleura*, rib, side⟧ inflammation of the pleura, characterized by painful breathing

Plex·i·glas (plek′si glas′) *trademark for* a lightweight, transparent thermoplastic substance

plex·i·glass (plek′si glas′) *n.* a material like Plexiglas

plex·us (plek′səs) *n., pl.* **-us·es** or **-us** ⟦< L *plectere*, to twine⟧ a network of blood vessels, nerves, etc.

pli·a·ble (plī′ə bəl) *adj.* ⟦< L *plicare*, to fold⟧ **1** easily bent; flexible **2** easily influenced or persuaded **3** adaptable —**pli′a·bil′i·ty** *n.*

pli·ant (plī′ənt) *adj.* **1** easily bent; pliable **2** compliant —**pli′an·cy** *n.*

pli·ers (plī′ərz) *pl.n.* ⟦< PLY¹⟧ small pincers for gripping small objects, bending wire, etc.

plight¹ (plīt) *n.* ⟦< OFr *pleit*, a fold⟧ a distressing situation

plight² (plīt) *vt.* ⟦< OE *pliht*, a pledge, danger⟧ to pledge, or bind by a pledge

plinth (plinth) *n.* ⟦< Gr *plinthos*, a brick⟧ the block at the base of a column, pedestal, etc.

plod (pläd) *vi.* **plod′ded, plod′ding** ⟦of echoic orig.⟧ **1** to move heavily and laboriously; trudge **2** to work steadily —**plod′der** *n.*

plop (pläp) *vt., vi.* **plopped, plop′ping** to drop with a sound like that of something flat falling into water —*n.* such a sound

plot (plät) *n.* ⟦OE⟧ **1** a small area of ground **2** a secret, usually evil, scheme **3** the plan of action of a play, novel, etc.: also **plot′line′** —*vt.* **plot′ted, plot′ting 1** to mark or trace on a chart or map **2** to make secret plans for —*vi.* to scheme —**plot′ter** *n.*

plov·er (pluv′ər, plō′vər) *n.* ⟦< L *pluvia*, rain⟧ a bird living near the shore, having a short tail and long, pointed wings

plow (plou) *n.* ⟦OE *plōh*⟧ **1** a farm implement used to cut and turn up the soil **2** any implement like this, as a snowplow —*vt.* **1** to cut and turn up (soil) with a plow **2** to clear with a snowplow **3** to make (one's way) through by or as if by plowing —*vi.* **1** to use a plow **2** to move (*through, into*, etc.) with force **3** to plod **4** to begin work vigorously: with *into* Also [Chiefly Brit.] **plough** (plou) —**plow′man** (-mən) *n., pl.* **-men** (-mən)

plow·share *n.* the cutting blade of a plow

ploy (ploi) *n.* ⟦? < (EM)PLOY⟧ an action intended to outwit someone

pluck (pluk) *vt.* ⟦OE *pluccian*⟧ **1** to pull off or out; pick **2** to snatch **3** to pull feathers or hair from **4** to pull at (a guitar string, etc.) and release quickly —*vi.* to pull: often with *at* —*n.* **1** a pulling; tug **2** courage

pluck·y *adj.* **-i·er, -i·est** brave; spirited —**pluck′i·ness** *n.*

plug (plug) *n.* ⟦MDu *plugge*⟧ **1** an object used to stop up a hole, etc. **2** a cake of pressed tobacco **3** an electrical device, as with prongs, for making contact or closing a circuit **4** a kind of fishing lure **5** [Inf.] a free boost, advertisement, etc. —*vt.* **plugged, plug′ging 1** to fill (a hole, etc.) with a plug **2** to insert a plug of **3** [Inf.] to advertise with a plug **4** [Slang] to shoot a bullet into —*vi.* [Inf.] to work doggedly —**plug in** to connect (an electrical device) by inserting a plug into a jack, socket, etc.

plug-in (plug′in′) *n.* a piece of software designed to enhance another, larger program

plum (plum) *n.* ⟦OE *plume*⟧ **1** *a*) a tree bearing a smooth-skinned fruit with a flattened stone *b*) the fruit **2** a raisin *[plum pudding]* **3** the purplish-red color of some plums **4** something desirable

plum·age (plōō′mij) *n.* ⟦Fr < *plume*, a feather⟧ a bird's feathers

plumb (plum) *n.* ⟦< L *plumbum*, LEAD²⟧ a

lead weight (**plumb bob**) hung at the end of a line (**plumb line**), used to determine how deep water is or whether a wall, etc. is vertical —*adj.* perfectly vertical —*adv.* **1** straight down **2** [Inf.] entirely —*vt.* **1** to test or sound with a plumb **2** to probe or fathom —**out of** (or **off**) **plumb** not vertical

plumb·er (plum′ər) *n.* ⟦see prec.⟧ a skilled worker who installs and repairs pipes, fixtures, etc., as of water systems

plumb·ing (plum′iŋ) *n.* **1** the work of a plumber **2** the pipes and fixtures with which a plumber works

plume (ploõm) *n.* ⟦< L *pluma*⟧ **1** a feather, esp. a large, showy one **2** a group of these —*vt.* **plumed, plum′ing 1** to adorn with plumes **2** to preen **3** to think favorably of (oneself)

plum·met (plum′it) *n.* ⟦see PLUMB⟧ **1** a plumb **2** a thing that weighs heavily —*vi.* **1** to fall straight downward **2** to decrease rapidly

plump¹ (plump) *adj.* ⟦< MDu *plomp*, bulky⟧ full and rounded in form; chubby

plump² (plump) *vi.*, *vt.* ⟦echoic⟧ to drop or bump suddenly or heavily —*n.* **1** a falling, bumping, etc. **2** the sound of this —*adv.* **1** suddenly; heavily **2** straight down

plun·der (plun′dər) *vt.*, *vi.* ⟦< Ger *plunder*, baggage⟧ **1** to rob or pillage **2** to take (property) by force or fraud —*n.* **1** a plundering **2** things taken by force or fraud

plunge (plunj) *vt.* **plunged, plung′ing** to thrust or throw suddenly (*into* a liquid, condition, etc.) —*vi.* **1** to dive or rush **2** to move violently and rapidly downward or forward —*n.* **1** a dive or fall **2** [Inf.] a gamble

plung·er *n.* **1** one who plunges **2** a large rubber suction cup used to free clogged drains **3** any cylindrical device that operates with a plunging motion, as a piston

plunk (pluŋk) *vt.* ⟦echoic⟧ **1** to strum (a banjo, etc.) **2** to throw or put down heavily —*vi.* **1** to give out a twanging sound **2** to fall heavily —*n.* the sound made by plunking —**plunk down** [Inf.] to give in payment

plu·ral (ploõr′əl) *adj.* ⟦< L *plus*, more⟧ more than one —*n.* Gram. the form of a word designating more than one (Ex.: *hands*, *men*)

plu·ral·ism *n.* **1** a state of society in which various ethnic, religious, etc. groups coexist peacefully **2** a policy embracing this —**plu′ral·ist** *n.*, *adj.* —**plu′ral·is′tic** *adj.*

plu·ral·i·ty (ploō ral′ə tē) *n.*, *pl.* **-ties 1** a being plural or numerous **2** *a)* the excess of votes in an election that the leading candidate has over the nearest rival *b)* the largest number, as of votes won

plu·ral·ize (ploõr′ə līz′) *vt.*, *vi.* **-ized′, -iz′ing** to make plural

plus (plus) *prep.* ⟦L, more⟧ **1** added to [2 *plus* 2] **2** in addition to —*adj.* **1** indicating addition **2** positive [a *plus* quantity] **3** somewhat higher than [a grade of B *plus*] **4** [Inf.] and more [*personality plus*] —*n.*, *pl.* **plus′es** or **plus′ses 1** a sign (+) indicating addition or positive quantity: in full **plus sign 2** something added **3** an advantage; benefit

plush (plush) *n.* ⟦< L *pilus*, hair⟧ a fabric with a soft, thick pile —*adj.* [Inf.] luxurious: also **plush′y, -i·er, -i·est**

Plu·tarch (ploõ′tärk′) A.D. 46?–120?; Gr. biographer & historian

Plu·to (ploõt′ō) *n.* **1** Rom. Myth. the god of the lower world **2** dwarf planet beyond Neptune

plu·toc·ra·cy (ploō täk′rə sē) *n.*, *pl.* **-cies** ⟦< Gr *ploutos*, wealth + *kratein*, to rule⟧ **1** government by the wealthy **2** a group of wealthy people who control a government

plu·to·crat (ploõt′ə krat′) *n.* **1** a member of a plutocracy **2** one whose wealth is the source of control or influence —**plu′to·crat′ic** *adj.*

plu·to·ni·um (ploō tō′nē əm) *n.* ⟦after PLUTO (dwarf planet)⟧ a radioactive metallic chemical element: symbol, Pu; at. no. 94

plu·vi·al (ploõ′vē əl) *adj.* ⟦< L *pluvia*, rain⟧ of, or having much, rain

ply¹ (plī) *vt.* **plied, ply′ing** ⟦< L *plicare*, to fold⟧ [Now Rare] to twist, fold, etc. —*n.*, *pl.* **plies 1** a thickness or layer, as of cloth or plywood **2** one of the twisted strands in rope, yarn, etc.

ply² (plī) *vt.* **plied, ply′ing** ⟦contr. < APPLY⟧ **1** to use (a tool, faculty, etc.), esp. with energy **2** to work at (a trade) **3** to keep supplying, assailing, etc. (*with*) **4** to sail back and forth across —*vi.* **1** to keep busy (*at*) **2** to travel regularly (*between* places)

Ply·mouth (plim′əth) town in SE Massachusetts: settled by the Pilgrims (1620)

ply·wood *n.* ⟦PLY¹ + WOOD⟧ a construction material made of thin layers of wood glued together

Pm *abbrev.* Chem. symbol for promethium

PM *abbrev.* **1** ⟦L *post meridiem*⟧ after noon: used for the time from noon to midnight : also **P.M.** or **p.m.** or **pm 2** Postmaster **3** Prime Minister

PMS *abbrev.* ⟦p(re)m(enstrual) s(yndrome)⟧ the physical and emotional symptoms that may precede menstruation

pneu·mat·ic (noō mat′ik) *adj.* ⟦< Gr *pneuma*, breath⟧ **1** of or containing wind, air, or gases **2** filled with or worked by compressed air

pneu·mo·ni·a (noō mōn′yə) *n.* ⟦< Gr *pneumōn*, lung < *pnein*, breathe⟧ inflammation of the lungs caused by bacteria or viruses

Po (pō) river in N Italy, flowing from the Alps into the Adriatic

PO *abbrev.* **1** Post Office **2** post office box

poach¹ (pōch) *vt.* ⟦< MFr *poche*, pocket: the yolk is "pocketed" in the white⟧ to cook (fish, an egg without its shell, etc.) in or over boiling water

poach² (pōch) *vt.*, *vi.* ⟦< MHG *puchen*, to plunder⟧ **1** to trespass on (private property), esp. to hunt or fish **2** to hunt or catch (game or fish) illegally —**poach′er** *n.*

pock (päk) *n.* ⟦OE *pocc*⟧ **1** a pustule caused by smallpox, etc. **2** POCKMARK —**pocked** *adj.*

pock·et (päk′it) *n.* ⟦< Fr *poque*, a pouch⟧ **1** a little bag or pouch, esp. one sewn into clothing, for carrying small articles **2** a pouchlike cavity or hollow **3** a small area or group [a *pocket* of poverty] **—adj. 1** that can be carried in a pocket **2** small **—vt. 1** to put into a pocket **2** to envelop; enclose **3** to take (money, etc.) dishonestly **4** to suppress [to *pocket* one's pride] **—out of pocket** to be paid from one's own financial resources **—pock′et·ful′** *n.*, *pl.* **-fuls′**

pock·et·book *n.* **1** a woman's purse or handbag **2** monetary resources

pock·et·knife *n.*, *pl.* **-knives′** a knife with a blade or blades that fold into the handle

pock·mark *n.* a scar left by a pustule, as of smallpox

pod (päd) *n.* [< ?] a dry fruit or seed vessel, as of peas or beans

-pod (päd) [< Gr *pous*, foot] *combining form* **1** foot **2** (one) having (a specified number or kind of) feet Also **-pode** (pōd)

pod·cast *n.* [< *iPod*, trademark for a portable electronic device + (BROAD)CAST] a recorded program of talk, music, etc. made available over the internet as a downloadable file **—vt.**, **vi.** to make (a program) available as a podcast

po·di·a·try (pō dī′ə trē) *n.* [< Gr *pous*, foot + -IATRY] the profession dealing with the care and treatment of the feet **—po·di′a·trist** *n.*

po·di·um (pō′dē əm) *n.* [L < Gr *pous*, foot] **1** a small platform, as for an orchestra conductor **2** LECTERN

Poe (pō), **Ed·gar Al·lan** (ed′gər al′ən) 1809-49; U.S. poet & short-story writer

po·em (pō′əm) *n.* [< Gr *poiein*, to make] an arrangement of words, esp. a rhythmical composition, sometimes rhymed, in a style more imaginative than ordinary speech or prose

po·e·sy (pō′ə sē′) *n. old-fashioned var. of* PO-ETRY

po·et (pō′ət) *n.* **1** one who writes poems or verses **2** one who displays imaginative power and beauty of thought, language, etc.

po·et·as·ter (pō′ə tas′tər) *n.* [< prec. + L -*aster*, dim. suffix] a writer of mediocre verse

po·et·ess (pō′ə tis) *n.* a woman who writes poems or verses: a dated and now often dismissive term

po·et·ic (pō et′ik) *adj.* **1** of or for poets or poetry **2** displaying the beauty, imaginative qualities, etc. found in good poetry Also **po·et′i·cal** *adj.* **—po·et′i·cal·ly** *adv.*

poetic justice justice, as in stories, applied in an especially fitting way

poetic license deviation from strict fact or rules, for artistic effect

poet laureate the official poet of a nation, appointed to write poems celebrating national events, etc.

po·et·ry (pō′ə trē) *n.* **1** the art, theory, or structure of poems **2** poems **3** poetic qualities

po·grom (pō′grəm, -gräm′) *n.* [< Russ, earlier, riot, storm] an organized massacre, as of Jews in czarist Russia

poi (poi) *n.* [Haw] a Hawaiian food that is a paste of taro root

poign·ant (poin′yənt) *adj.* [< L *pungere*, to prick] **1** pungent **2** *a)* sharply painful to the feelings *b)* emotionally moving **3** sharp, biting, pointed, etc. **—poign′an·cy** *n.*

poin·ci·an·a (poin′sē an′ə) *n.* [after M. de *Poinci*, early governor of the Fr West Indies] a small tropical tree or shrub with showy red, orange, or yellow flowers

poin·set·ti·a (poin set′ə, -set′ē ə) *n.* [after J. R. *Poinsett* (1779-1851), U.S. ambassador to Mexico] a tropical shrub with yellow flowers and petal-like red leaves

point (point) *n.* [< L *pungere*, to prick] **1** a dot in writing, etc. [a decimal *point*] **2** a position or location **3** the exact moment **4** a condition reached [boiling *point*] **5** a detail; item [*point* by *point*] **6** a distinguishing feature **7** a unit, as of value or game scores **8** a sharp end **9** a projecting piece of land; cape **10** the essential fact or idea [the *point* of a joke] **11** a purpose; object **12** a convincing idea or fact **13** a helpful hint **14** a mark showing direction on a compass **15** *Finance a)* a $1 change in the price of a stock *b)* a unit or amount equal to one percent **16** *Printing* a measuring unit for type, about 1/72 of an inch **—vt. 1** to sharpen to a point **2** to give (a story, etc.) emphasis: usually with *up* **3** to show: usually with *out* [*point* out the way] **4** to aim **—vi. 1** to direct one's finger (*at* or *to*) **2** to call attention (*to*) **3** to be directed (*to* or *toward*) **—at the point of** very close to **—beside the point** irrelevant **—to the point** pertinent; apt

point-blank *adj.*, *adv.* [prec. + *blank* (white center of a target)] **1** (aimed) straight at a mark **2** direct(ly); blunt(ly)

point·ed *adj.* **1** having a sharp end **2** sharp; incisive **3** aimed at someone: said as of a remark **4** very evident **—point′ed·ly** *adv.*

poin·telle (poin tel′) *n.* a lacy, loosely formed fabric, often of acrylic, used for blouses, sweaters, etc.

point·er *n.* **1** a long, tapered rod for pointing to things **2** an indicator on a meter, etc. **3** a large, muscular hunting dog with a smooth coat **4** [Inf.] a helpful hint or suggestion

poin·til·lism (pwan′tə liz′əm, poin′-) *n.* [Fr] a style of painting using dots of color that blend together when seen from a distance **—poin′til·list** *n.*, *adj.*

point·less *adj.* **1** without a point **2** without meaning or force; senseless

point man 1 the soldier in the front position in a patrol **2** anyone in the forefront of a movement attacking or supporting a political program, etc.

point of view 1 the way in which something is viewed **2** a mental attitude or opinion

point spread SPREAD (*n.* 7)

point·y *adj.* **-i·er**, **-i·est 1** coming to a sharp point **2** many-pointed

poise (poiz) *n.* [< L *pendere*, weigh] **1** balance; stability **2** ease and dignity of manner **3** carriage, as of the body **—vt.**, **vi.** poised, pois′ing to balance or be balanced

poised *adj.* **1** calm; self-assured **2** readied

poi·son (poi′zən) *n.* [< L *potio*, potion] a substance that can cause illness or death when ingested even in small quantities —*vt.* 1 to harm or kill with poison 2 to put poison into 3 to influence wrongly —*adj.* poison-ous

poison ivy a plant having leaves of three leaflets and ivory-colored berries: it can cause a severe rash if touched

poi·son·ous *adj.* that can injure or kill by or as by poison; toxic —**poi′son·ous·ly** *adv.*

poison pill any defensive measure that makes the takeover of a corporation prohibitively expensive

poke[1] (pōk) *vt.* **poked, pok′ing** [< MDu *poken*] 1 *a)* to prod, as with a stick *b)* [Slang] to hit 2 to make (a hole, etc.) by poking —*vi.* 1 to jab (*at*) 2 to pry or search (*about* or *around*) 3 to move slowly (*along*) —*n.* 1 a jab; thrust 2 [Slang] a blow with the fist —**poke fun at** to ridicule

poke[2] (pōk) *n.* [OFr.] [Dial.] a sack

pok·er[1] (pōk′ər) *n.* [< ? Ger *pochspiel*, lit., game of defiance] a card game in which the players bet on the value of their hands

pok·er[2] (pō′kər) *n.* a rod, usually of iron, for stirring a fire

poker face an expressionless face, as of a poker player trying to conceal the nature of his or her hand

pok·y (pō′kē) *adj.* **-i·er, -i·est** [POKE[1] + -Y[2]] 1 slow, dull, etc. 2 small and uncomfortable [a *poky* room] Also **pok′ey**

pol (päl) *n.* [Slang] a politician

Pol *abbrev.* 1 Poland 2 Polish

Po·land (pō′lənd) country in EC Europe, on the Baltic Sea

po·lar (pō′lər) *adj.* 1 of or near the North or South pole 2 of a pole or poles

polar bear a large white bear of coastal arctic regions

Po·la·ris (pō lar′is) *n.* the bright star almost directly above the North Pole

po·lar·i·ty (pō lar′ə tē) *n., pl.* **-ties** 1 the tendency of bodies having opposite magnetic poles to have their ends point to the earth's magnetic poles 2 the tendency to turn, grow, think, etc. in contrary directions, as if because of magnetic repulsion 3 the condition of being electrically positive or negative

po·lar·i·za·tion (pō′lə ri zā′shən) *n.* 1 a polarizing or being polarized 2 *Optics* the condition of electromagnetic waves in which the motion of the wave is confined to one plane or one direction

po·lar·ize (pō′lə rīz′) *vt.* **-ized′, -iz′ing** to give polarity to —*vi.* to acquire polarity; specif., to separate into opposed or antagonistic groups, viewpoints, etc.

Po·lar·oid (pō′lə roid′) *trademark for:* 1 a transparent material capable of polarizing light 2 a camera and film that produce instant photographs

pole[1] (pōl) *n.* [< L *palus*, a stake] a long, slender piece of wood, metal, etc. —*vt.* **poled, pol′ing** to push along with a pole

pole[2] (pōl) *n.* [< Gr *polos*] 1 either end of any axis, as of the earth's axis 2 either of two op-

posed forces, parts, etc., as the ends of a magnet or the terminals of a battery

Pole (pōl) *n.* a person born or living in Poland

pole·cat (pōl′kat′) *n.* [prob. < OFr *poule*, hen + CAT] 1 a small Old World weasel 2 SKUNK

po·lem·ic (pō lem′ik) *adj.* [< Gr *polemos*, war] of or involving dispute: also **po·lem′i·cal** —*n.* a verbal attack or disputation

po·lem·ics *n.* [*sometimes with pl. v.*] the art or practice of disputation —**po·lem′i·cist** (-i sist) *n.*

pole·star *n.* 1 Polaris, the North Star: usually **Pole Star** 2 a guiding principle

pole vault a leap for height by jumping over a bar with the aid of a long pole —**pole′-vault′** *vi.* —**pole′-vault′er** *n.*

po·lice (pə lēs′) *n.* [Fr: ult. < Gr *polis*, city] 1 the governmental department (of a city, state, etc.) for keeping order, detecting crime, etc. 2 [*with pl. v.*] the members of such a department: also **police force** —*vt.* **-liced′, -lic′ing** 1 to control, protect, etc. with police or a similar force 2 to keep (a military camp, etc.) clean and orderly

po·lice·man (-mən) *n., pl.* **-men** (-mən) a man who is a member of a police force

police officer a member of a police force

police state a government that seeks to suppress political opposition by means of police

po·lice·wom·an *n., pl.* **-wom′en** a woman who is a member of a police force

pol·i·cy[1] (päl′ə sē) *n., pl.* **-cies** [see POLICE] 1 wise management 2 a principle, plan, etc., as of a government

pol·i·cy[2] (päl′ə sē) *n., pl.* **-cies** [< Gr *apodeixis*, proof] a written insurance contract: in full **insurance policy**

pol·i·cy·hold·er *n.* a person to whom an insurance policy is issued

po·li·o·my·e·li·tis (pō′lē ō mī′ə līt′is) *n.* [< Gr *polios*, gray + MYELITIS] an acute infectious disease caused by viral inflammation of the gray matter of the spinal cord, often resulting in muscular paralysis: also **po′li·o′**

pol·ish (päl′ish) *vt.* [< L *polire*] 1 to smooth and brighten, as by rubbing 2 to refine (manners, style, etc.) —*vi.* to take a polish —*n.* 1 a surface gloss 2 elegance, refinement, etc. 3 a substance used to polish —**polish off** [Inf.] to finish (a meal, job, etc.) completely

Pol·ish (pōl′ish) *adj.* of Poland or its people, language, etc. —*n.* the Slavic language of Poland

po·lite (pə līt′) *adj.* [< L *polire*, to polish] 1 cultured; refined 2 courteous; mannerly —**po·lite′ly** *adv.* —**po·lite′ness** *n.*

pol·i·tesse (päl′i tes′) *n.* [Fr] politeness

pol·i·tic (päl′ə tik′) *adj.* [see POLICE] 1 having practical wisdom; prudent 2 expedient: said of a plan —*vi.* **-ticked′, -tick′ing** to campaign in politics

po·lit·i·cal (pə lit′i kəl) *adj.* 1 of, concerned with, or engaged in government, politics, etc. 2 of or characteristic of political parties or politicians —**po·lit′i·cal·ly** *adv.*

politically correct holding orthodox liberal

political views: usually used disparagingly to connote dogmatism, etc. —**political correctness**

political science the science of the principles, organization, and methods of government —**political scientist**

pol·i·ti·cian (päl′ə tish′ən) *n.* one actively engaged in politics: often used with implications of seeking personal or partisan gain, scheming, etc.

po·lit·i·cize (pə lit′ə sīz′) *vt.* -**cized**′, -**ciz**′**ing** to make political in tone, character, etc.

po·lit·i·co (pə lit′ə kō′) *n., pl.* -**cos**′ ⟦< Sp or It⟧ POLITICIAN

pol·i·tics (päl′ə tiks) *pl.n.* [*with sing. or pl. v.*] **1** the science and art of government **2** political affairs **3** political methods, tactics, etc. **4** political opinions, etc. **5** factional scheming for power

pol·i·ty (-ə tē) *n., pl.* -**ties** ⟦see POLICE⟧ **1** governmental organization **2** a society with a government; state

Polk (pōk), **James K.** 1795-1849; 11th president of the U.S. (1845-49)

pol·ka (pōl′kə) *n.* ⟦Czech, Polish dance⟧ **1** a fast dance for couples **2** music for this

pol·ka dot (pō′kə, pōl′kə) any of a regular pattern of small, round dots on cloth

poll (pōl) *n.* ⟦ME *pol*⟧ **1** the head **2** a counting, listing, etc. of persons, esp. of voters **3** the number of votes recorded **4** [*pl.*] a place where votes are cast **5** a canvassing of people's opinions on some question —*vt.* **1** to register the votes of **2** to require each member of (a jury, etc.) to declare individual votes **3** to receive (a specified number of votes) **4** to canvass in a POLL (5)

pol·lack (päl′ək) *n.* alt. sp. of POLLOCK

pol·len (päl′ən) *n.* ⟦L, dust⟧ the fine, dustlike mass in the anthers of seed plants, containing male sexual cells

pollen count the number of grains of pollen, esp. of ragweed, in a given volume of air at a specified time and place

pol·li·nate (päl′ə nāt′) *vt.* -**nat**′**ed**, -**nat**′**ing** to transfer pollen to the pistil of (a flower) —**pol′li·na′tion** *n.* —**pol′li·na′tor** *n.*

pol·li·wog (päl′ē wäg′, -wôg′) *n.* ⟦< ME: see POLL + WIGGLE⟧ TADPOLE: also **pol′ly·wog**′

pol·lock (päl′ək) *n., pl.* -**lock** or -**locks** any of several food fishes of the N Atlantic and Pacific, related to the cod

poll·ster (pōl′stər) *n.* one whose work is taking public-opinion polls

pol·lute (pə lōōt′) *vt.* -**lut**′**ed**, -**lut**′**ing** ⟦< L *polluere*⟧ to make unclean or impure —**pol·lu**′**tant** *n.* —**pol·lu**′**tion** *n.*

Pol·ly·an·na (päl′ē an′ə) *n.* ⟦after the young heroine of a novel (1913) by E. H. Porter⟧ an excessively optimistic person

po·lo (pō′lō) *n.* ⟦ult. < Tibetan *pulu*, ball⟧ a game played on horseback by two teams, using a wooden ball and long-handled mallets

Po·lo (pō′lō), **Mar·co** (mär′kō) 1254-1324; Venetian traveler in E Asia

po·lo·naise (päl′ə nāz′) *n.* ⟦Fr, Polish⟧ a stately Polish dance

po·lo·ni·um (pə lō′nē əm) *n.* ⟦< ML *Polonia*, Poland⟧ a radioactive, nonmetallic chemical element that occurs naturally by the disintegration of radium or artificially: symbol, Po; at. no. 84

pol·ter·geist (pōl′tər gīst′) *n.* ⟦Ger < *poltern*, to rumble + *geist*, ghost⟧ a ghost supposed to be responsible for mysterious noisy disturbances

pol·troon (päl trōōn′) *n.* ⟦< It *poltrone*⟧ a thorough coward

poly- ⟦< Gr⟧ *combining form* much, many

pol·y·es·ter (päl′ē es′tər) *n.* ⟦POLY(MER) + ESTER⟧ a polymeric resin used in making plastics, fibers, etc.

pol·y·eth·yl·ene (päl′ē eth′ə lēn′) *n.* ⟦POLY(MER) + ETHYLENE⟧ a thermoplastic resin used in making plastics, films, etc.

po·lyg·a·my (pə lig′ə mē) *n.* ⟦< Gr *poly-*, many + *gamos*, marriage⟧ the practice of having two or more spouses at the same time —**po·lyg′a·mist** *n.* —**po·lyg′a·mous** *adj.*

pol·y·glot (päl′i glät′) *adj.* ⟦< Gr *poly-*, many + *glōtta*, tongue⟧ **1** knowing several languages **2** written in several languages —*n.* a polyglot person

pol·y·gon (-gän′) *n.* ⟦< Gr: see POLY- & -GON⟧ a closed plane figure consisting of straight lines —**po·lyg·o·nal** (pə lig′ə nəl) *adj.*

pol·y·graph (-graf′) *n.* ⟦see POLY- & -GRAPH⟧ a device measuring changes in respiration, pulse rate, etc.: see LIE DETECTOR

pol·y·he·dron (-hē′drən) *n.* ⟦< Gr: see POLY- & -HEDRON⟧ a solid figure having an outer surface composed of polygons

pol·y·math (-ə math′) *n.* ⟦< Gr *poly-*, much + *manthanein*, learn⟧ a person of great and varied learning

pol·y·mer (-mər) *n.* ⟦Ger < Gr *poly-*, many + *meros*, part⟧ a substance consisting of giant molecules formed from polymerization —**pol′y·mer′ic** (-mer′ik) *adj.*

po·lym·er·i·za·tion (pō lim′ər ə zā′shən) *n.* a chaining together of many simple molecules to form a more complex molecule with different properties —**po·lym′er·ize** (-īz′) *vt., vi.* -**ized**′, -**iz**′**ing**

Pol·y·ne·sia (päl′i nē′zhə) group of Pacific islands, east of Micronesia, including Hawaii, Samoa, Tahiti, etc. —**Pol′y·ne′sian** *adj., n.*

pol·y·no·mi·al (päl′i nō′mē əl) *n.* ⟦POLY- + (BI)NOMIAL⟧ a mathematical expression containing three or more terms (Ex: $x^3 + 3x + 2$)

pol·yp (päl′ip) *n.* ⟦< Gr *poly-*, many + *pous*, foot⟧ **1** a cnidarian with many small tentacles at the top of a tubelike body **2** a growth of mucous membrane in the bladder, rectum, etc.

po·lyph·o·ny (pə lif′ə nē) *n.* ⟦< Gr *poly-*, many + *phōnē*, a sound⟧ *Music* a combining of independent, harmonizing melodies, as in a fugue; counterpoint —**pol·y·phon·ic** (päl′i fän′ik) *adj.* —**pol′y·phon′i·cal·ly** *adv.*

pol·y·rhythm (päl′i rith′əm) *n. Music* **1** the

pol·y·sty·rene (-stī'rēn') *n.* ⟦POLY(MER) + *styrene*, an organic compound⟧ a clear polymer used to make containers, etc.

pol·y·syl·lab·ic (päl'i si lab'ik) *adj.* 1 having four or more syllables 2 characterized by polysyllabic words —**pol'y·syl'la·ble** (-sil'ə bəl) *n.*

pol·y·tech·nic (-tek'nik) *n., adj.* ⟦< Gr *poly-*, many + *technē*, art⟧ (school) providing instruction in many scientific and technical subjects

pol·y·the·ism (-thē iz'əm) *n.* ⟦< Gr *poly*, many + *theos*, god⟧ belief in more than one god —**pol'y·the·ist** *adj., n.* —**pol'y·the·is'tic** *adj.*

pol·y·un·sat·u·rat·ed (päl'ē un sach'ə rāt' id) *adj.* designating any of certain vegetable and animal fats and oils that may help reduce blood cholesterol levels

pol·y·u·re·thane (-yoor'ə thān') *n.* ⟦POLY- + URETHANE⟧ any of various synthetic polymers used in cushions, coatings, etc.

pol·y·vi·nyl (päl'i vī'nəl) *adj.* designating or of any of a group of polymerized vinyl compounds

po·made (päm äd', pō mād') *n.* ⟦< It *pomo*, apple (orig. an ingredient)⟧ a perfumed ointment, as for the hair

pome·gran·ate (päm'ə gran'it) *n.* ⟦ult. < L *pomum*, fruit + *granum*, seed⟧ 1 a round, red fruit with a hard rind and many seeds 2 the bush or tree it grows on

pom·mel (päm'əl; *for v.* pum'əl) *n.* ⟦< L *pomum*, fruit⟧ 1 the knob on the end of the hilt of some swords and daggers 2 the rounded, upward-projecting part at the front of a saddle —*vt.* **-meled** or **-melled, -mel·ing** or **-mel·ling** PUMMEL

pomp (pämp) *n.* ⟦< Gr *pompē*, solemn procession⟧ 1 stately display 2 ostentatious show or display

pom·pa·dour (päm'pə dôr') *n.* ⟦after Mme. *Pompadour*, mistress of Louis XV⟧ a hairdo in which the hair is brushed up high from the forehead

pom·pa·no (päm'pə nō') *n., pl.* **-no'** or **-nos'** ⟦< Sp⟧ a food fish of North America and the West Indies

pom·pom (päm'päm') *n.* ⟦see POMP⟧ an ornamental tuft of silk, etc., used on clothing, etc. or waved as by a cheerleader: also **pom'pon'** (-pän')

pom·pous (päm'pəs) *adj.* pretentious; self-important —**pom·pos'i·ty** (-päs'ə tē) *n.*

pon·cho (pän'chō) *n., pl.* **-chos** ⟦AmSp < AmInd, woolen cloth⟧ a cloak like a blanket with a hole in the middle for the head, esp. a waterproof one worn as a raincoat

pond (pänd) *n.* ⟦< ME *pounde*, enclosure⟧ a body of water smaller than a lake

pon·der (pän'dər) *vt., vi.* ⟦< L *ponderare*, weigh⟧ to think deeply (about); consider carefully

pon·der·o·sa (pine) (pän'dər ō'sə) ⟦< L *ponderosus*, very heavy⟧ a yellow pine of W North America

pon·der·ous *adj.* 1 very heavy 2 unwieldy 3 labored and dull

pone (pōn) *n.* ⟦< AmInd⟧ [Chiefly South] corn bread in the form of small ovals

pon·gee (pän jē', pun-) *n.* ⟦< Mandarin Chin dial. *pen-chi*, one's own loom⟧ a soft, thin silk cloth, usually left in its natural light-brown color

pon·iard (pän'yərd) *n.* ⟦ult. < L *pugnus*, fist⟧ a dagger

pon·tiff (pänt'if) *n.* ⟦< L *pontifex*, high priest⟧ 1 a bishop 2 [P-] the pope

pon·tif·i·cal (pän tif'i kəl) *adj.* ⟦see prec.⟧ 1 having to do with a bishop, the pope, etc. 2 pompous, dogmatic, etc.

pon·tif·i·cate (-i kit; *for v.,* -kāt') *n.* the office or term of a pontiff —*vi.* **-cat'ed, -cat'ing** 1 to officiate as a pontiff 2 to be pompous or dogmatic

pon·toon (pän tōōn') *n.* ⟦< L *pons*, a bridge⟧ 1 a flat-bottomed boat 2 any of a row of boats or floating objects used to support a temporary bridge 3 a float, as on an aircraft's landing gear

po·ny (pō'nē) *n., pl.* **-nies** ⟦prob. < L *pullus*, foal⟧ 1 a horse of any small breed 2 a small liqueur glass 3 [Inf.] a literal translation of a foreign work, used in doing schoolwork

po·ny·tail *n.* a hair style in which the hair is tied tightly at the back and hangs down

pooch (pōōch) *n.* ⟦< ?⟧ [Inf.] a dog

poo·dle (pōōd'l) *n.* ⟦Ger *pudel*⟧ a dog with a thick, wiry coat of tight curls in a solid color

pooh (pōō) *interj.* used to express disdain, disbelief, or impatience

pooh-pooh (pōō'pōō') *vt.* to treat disdainfully; make light of

pool[1] (pōōl) *n.* ⟦OE *pol*⟧ 1 a small pond 2 a small collection of liquid, as a puddle 3 a tank for swimming

pool[2] (pōōl) *n.* ⟦< LL *pulla*, hen⟧ 1 a game related to billiards, played on a table with six pockets 2 a combination of resources, funds, supplies, etc. for some common purpose 3 the parties forming such a combination —*vt., vi.* to contribute to a common fund

poop[1] (pōōp) *n.* ⟦< L *puppis*, stern of a ship⟧ a raised deck at the stern of a sailing ship: also **poop deck**

poop[2] (pōōp) *vt.* [Slang] to tire

poop[3] (pōōp) *n.* 1 [Inf.] excrement 2 [Slang] current inside information —*vi.* [Inf.] to defecate

poor (poor) *adj.* ⟦< L *pauper*, poor⟧ 1 having little or no means to support oneself; needy 2 lacking in some quality; specif., *a)* inadequate *b)* inferior or worthless *c)* contemptible 3 worthy of pity; unfortunate —**the poor** poor, or needy, people —**poor'ly** *adv.*

poor·house *n.* [Historical] a publicly supported institution for paupers

pop[1] (päp) *n.* ⟦echoic⟧ 1 a sudden, light explosive sound 2 any carbonated, nonalcoholic beverage 3 *Baseball* POP-UP[1] (*n.* 1) —*vi.* **popped, pop'ping** 1 to make, or burst with, a pop **2** to move, go, etc. suddenly **3** to open wide or bulge: said of the eyes **4** *Baseball* to hit the ball high into the infield —*vt.* **1** to cause to pop, as corn by heating it **2** to put suddenly [to pop one's head in] **3** [Slang] to swallow (a pill, etc.) —**pop′per** *n.*

pop² (päp) *n.* [< PAPA] [Inf.] FATHER

pop³ (päp) *adj.* **1** of music popular with the general public **2** intended for the popular taste, esp. as exploited commercially [*pop* culture] **3** of a realistic art style using techniques and subjects adapted from commercial art, comic strips, posters, etc. —*n.* pop music, etc.

pop⁴ *abbrev.* **1** popular **2** popularly **3** population

pop·corn *n.* **1** a variety of corn with hard grains that pop open into a white, puffy mass when heated **2** the popped grains

pope (pōp) *n.* [< Gr *pappas,* father] [*often* P-] R.C.Ch. the bishop of Rome and head of the Church

Pope (pōp), **Alexander** 1688-1744; Eng. poet

pop·gun *n.* a toy gun that shoots a piece of cork, etc. by air compression, with a pop

pop·in·jay (päp′in jā′) *n.* [< Ar *babghā',* a parrot] a conceited person

pop·lar (päp′lər) *n.* [< L *populus*] **1** a tree of the willow family having soft wood **2** its wood

pop·lin (päp′lin) *n.* [prob. after *Poperinge,* city in Flanders] a sturdy ribbed fabric of cotton, silk, etc.

pop·o·ver *n.* a very light, puffy, hollow muffin

pop·py (päp′ē) *n., pl.* **-pies** [< L *papaver*] **1** a plant with a milky juice and variously colored flowers **2** its flower

pop·py·cock (-käk′) *n.* [Inf.] foolish talk; nonsense

poppy seed the small, dark seed of the poppy, used in baking, etc.

pops (päps) *adj.* of a symphony orchestra that plays light classical music or arrangements of popular music —*n.* a pops orchestra, concert, etc.

Pop·si·cle (päp′si kəl) [blend of POP¹ + I(CICLE)] *trademark for* a flavored ice frozen around a stick —*n.* [*also* p-] such a confection

pop-top (päp′täp′) *n.* a container with a tab or ring pulled or pushed to make an opening in the top

pop·u·lace (päp′yə lis) *n.* [< L *populus*] **1** the common people; the masses **2** POPULATION (1*a*)

pop·u·lar (päp′yə lər) *adj.* [< L *populus,* the people] **1** of, carried on by, or intended for people generally **2** not expensive [*popular* prices] **3** commonly accepted; prevalent **4** liked by many people —**pop′u·lar′i·ty** (-lar′ə tē) *n.* —**pop′u·lar·ly** *adv.*

pop·u·lar·ize (päp′yə lə rīz′) *vt.* **-ized′, -iz′ing** to make popular —**pop′u·lar·i·za′tion** *n.*

pop·u·late (-lāt′) *vt.* **-lat′ed, -lat′ing** [< L *populus,* the people] **1** to inhabit **2** to supply with inhabitants **3** Comput. to fill in (a field, as in a spreadsheet) with data

pop·u·la·tion *n.* **1** *a)* all the people in a country, region, etc. *b)* the number of these **2** a populating or being populated

population explosion a great and rapid increase in human population

pop·u·list (päp′yə list) *n.* a politician, etc. who claims to represent the common people: often used to suggest demagogy —*adj.* of a populist —**pop′u·lism′** *n.*

pop·u·lous (-ləs) *adj.* full of people; thickly populated

pop-up *n.* **1** *Baseball* a ball hit high in the air, usually not beyond the infield **2** *Comput.* a window, typically an advertisement, that appears superimposed over the window in use —*adj.* of or designating a book with cut-out portions of an illustration that lift out when opened to its page, producing a three-dimensional effect

por·ce·lain (pôr′sə lin) *n.* [< It *porcellana*] a hard, white, translucent variety of ceramic ware

porch (pôrch) *n.* [< L *porta,* gate] **1** a covered entrance to a building **2** an open or enclosed gallery or room on the outside of a building

por·cine (pôr′sīn′, -sin) *adj.* [< L *porcus,* hog] of or like pigs or hogs

por·cu·pine (pôr′kyə pīn′) *n.* [< L *porcus,* pig + *spina,* spine] a rodent having coarse hair mixed with long, stiff, sharp spines

pore¹ (pôr) *vi.* **pored, por′ing** [ME *poren*] **1** to study carefully: with *over* **2** to ponder: with *over*

pore² (pôr) *n.* [< Gr *poros,* passage] a tiny opening, as in skin or plant leaves, for absorbing or discharging fluids

pork (pôrk) *n.* [< L *porcus,* pig] the flesh of a pig, used as food

pork barrel [Inf.] government appropriations for political patronage

pork·y *adj.* **-i·er, -i·est** **1** of or like pork **2** fat

porn (pôrn) *n., adj.* [Slang] *short for* PORNOGRAPHY, PORNOGRAPHIC: also **por·no** (pôr′nō)

por·nog·ra·phy (pôr näg′rə fē) *n.* [< Gr *pornē,* a prostitute + *graphein,* write] writings, pictures, etc. intended to arouse sexual desire —**por·nog′ra·pher** *n.* —**por′no·graph′ic** (-nə graf′ik) *adj.*

po·rous (pôr′əs) *adj.* full of pores, through which fluids, air, or light may pass —**po·ros·i·ty** (pō rӓs′ə tē) *n.*

por·phy·ry (pôr′fə rē) *n., pl.* **-ries** [< Gr *porphyros,* purple] any igneous rock with large, distinct crystals

por·poise (pôr′pəs) *n.* [< L *porcus,* pig + *piscis,* a fish] **1** a small whale with a blunt snout **2** a dolphin

por·ridge (pôr′ij) *n.* [< POTTAGE by confusion with VL *porrata,* leek broth] [Chiefly Brit.] a soft food of cereal or meal boiled in water or milk

por·rin·ger (-in jər) *n.* [< Fr *potager,* soup dish: infl. by prec.] a small, shallow bowl

port¹ (pôrt) *n.* [< L *portus,* haven] **1** a har-

bor 2 a city with a harbor where ships load and unload cargo

port² (pôrt) *n.* ⟦after *Oporto*, city in Portugal⟧ a sweet, dark-red wine

port³ (pôrt) *vt.* ⟦< L *portare*, carry⟧ to hold (a rifle, etc.) diagonally in front of one, as for inspection

port⁴ (pôrt) *n.* ⟦< PORT¹⟧ the left side of a ship, etc. as one faces forward —*adj.* of or on this side

port⁵ (pôrt) *n.* ⟦< L *porta*, door⟧ **1** PORT-HOLE **2** an opening, as in a valve face, for the passage of steam, etc. **3** *Comput.* the circuit, outlet, etc. which connects a computer to another device

Port *abbrev.* **1** Portugal **2** Portuguese

port·a·ble (pôr′tə bəl) *adj.* ⟦< L *portare*, carry⟧ **1** that can be carried **2** easily carried —*n.* something portable —**port′a·bil′i·ty** *n.*

por·tage (pôr′tij, pôr täzh′) *n.* ⟦< L *portare*, carry⟧ **1** a carrying of boats and supplies over-land between navigable lakes, rivers, etc. **2** any route over which this is done — *vt., vi.,* **-taged, -tag·ing** to carry (boats, etc.) over a portage

por·tal (pôrt′'l) *n.* ⟦< L *porta*, door⟧ **1** a door-way, gate, or entrance **2** *Comput.* a website offering access to various other sites or services

port·cul·lis (pôrt kul′is) *n.* ⟦< MFr *porte*, gate + *coleïce*, sliding⟧ a heavy grating lowered to bar the gateway of a castle or fortified town

por·tend (pôr tend′) *vt.* ⟦< L *por-*, forth + *tendere*, to stretch⟧ **1** to be an omen of; presage **2** to signify

por·tent (pôr′tent′) *n.* **1** something that portends an event **2** significance

por·ten·tous (pôr ten′təs) *adj.* **1** portending evil; ominous **2** amazing **3** pompous; self-important —**por·ten′tous·ly** *adv.*

por·ter¹ (pôr′tər) *n.* ⟦< L *porta*, gate⟧ a door-man or gatekeeper

por·ter² (pôr′tər) *n.* ⟦< L *portare*, carry⟧ **1** one who carries luggage, etc. for hire **2** an employee who sweeps, cleans, etc. in a bank, store, etc. **3** a railroad attendant for passengers as on a sleeper **4** a dark-brown beer

por·ter·house *n.* ⟦orig. a tavern: see prec.⟧ a choice cut of beef next to the sirloin: in full **porterhouse steak**

port·fo·li·o (pôrt fō′lē ō′) *n., pl.* **-li·os′** ⟦< L *portare*, carry + *folium*, leaf⟧ **1** a flat, portable case, for loose papers; briefcase **2** the office of a minister of state **3** a list of an investor's securities **4** a selection from an artist's, etc. work

port·hole (pôrt′hōl′) *n.* an opening in a ship's side to admit light and air

por·ti·co (pôr′ti kō′) *n., pl.* **-coes′** or **-cos′** ⟦< L *porticus*, porch⟧ a porch or covered walk, consisting of a roof supported by columns

por·tiere or **por·tière** (pôr tyer′) *n.* ⟦Fr < *porte*, door⟧ a curtain hung in a doorway

por·tion (-shən) *n.* ⟦< L *portio*⟧ **1** a part, esp. that allotted to a person; share **2** one's fate **3** a helping of food —*vt.* to give out in portions

Port·land (pôrt′lənd) city & port in NW Oregon

port·ly (pôrt′lē) *adj.* **-li·er, -li·est 1** large and stately **2** stout; corpulent —**port′li·ness** *n.*

port·man·teau (pôrt man′tō) *n., pl.* **-teaus** or **-teaux** (-tōz) ⟦< Fr *porter*, carry + *manteau*, cloak⟧ a stiff suitcase that opens into two compartments

portmanteau word a word that is a combination of two other words (Ex.: *smog*, from *smoke* and *fog*)

por·to·bel·lo mushroom (pôr′tə bel′ō) a dark, flavorful mushroom with a broad cap: also **portobello** *n., pl.* **-los**

port of entry a place where customs officials check people and goods entering a country

por·trait (pôr′trit, -trāt′) *n.* ⟦see PORTRAY⟧ a painting, photograph, etc. of a person, esp. of the face **2** a description, portrayal, etc.

por·trai·ture (-tri chər) *n.* the practice or art of making portraits

por·tray (pôr trā′) *vt.* ⟦< L *pro-*, forth + *tra-here*, draw⟧ **1** to make a portrait of **2** to describe graphically **3** to play the part of as in a play or movie —**por·tray′al** *n.*

Por·tu·gal (pôr′chə gəl) country in SW Europe, on the Atlantic

Por·tu·guese (pôr′chə gēz′, -gēs′) *adj.* of Portugal or its people, language, etc. —*n.* **1** *pl.* **-guese′** a person born or living in Portugal **2** a Romance language of Portugal and Brazil

por·tu·lac·a (pôr′chə lak′ə) *n.* ⟦< L *portula*, small door: from the opening in its seed capsule⟧ a fleshy plant with yellow, pink, or purple flowers

POS *abbrev.* point-of-sale

pose (pōz) *vt.* **posed, pos′ing** ⟦< L *pausare*, to stop⟧ **1** to propose (a question, etc.) **2** to put (a model, etc.) in a certain attitude —*vi.* **1** to assume a certain attitude, as in modeling for an artist **2** to strike attitudes for effect **3** set oneself up *(as)* [to *pose* as an officer] —*n.* **1** a bodily attitude, esp. one held for an artist, etc. **2** a way of behaving assumed for effect

Po·sei·don (pō sī′dən) *n.* the Greek god of the sea

pos·er (pō′zər) *n.* one who poses; esp., a poseur

po·seur (pō zur′) *n.* ⟦Fr⟧ one who assumes attitudes or manners merely for effect

posh (päsh) *adj.* ⟦< ?⟧ **1** [Inf.] luxurious and fashionable **2** [Chiefly Brit.] upper-class

pos·it (päz′it) *vt.* ⟦see foll.⟧ to suppose to be a fact; postulate

po·si·tion (pə zish′ən) *n.* ⟦< L *ponere*, to place⟧ **1** the way in which a person or thing is placed or arranged **2** one's attitude or opinion **3** the place where one is; location **4** the usual or proper place **5** rank, esp. high rank **6** a post of employment; job —*vt.* to put into a certain position

pos·i·tive (päz′ə tiv) *adj.* ⟦see prec.⟧ **1** definitely set; explicit [*positive* instructions] **2** *a)* having the mind set; confident *b)* overconfident or dogmatic **3** showing agreement; affirmative **4** constructive [*positive* criticism] **5** regarded as having real existence [a *positive* good] **6** based on facts [*positive proof*] **7** *Elec.* of the kind of electricity predominating in objects that have a deficiency of electrons **8** *Gram.* of an adjective or adverb in its uncompared degree **9** *Math.* greater than zero **10** *Med.* showing the presence of a condition, infection, etc. **11** *Photog.* with the light and shade corresponding to those of the subject —*n.* **1** something positive, as a degree, quality, quantity, photographic print, etc. **2** the terminal in a battery that takes in electrons passing through the circuit —**pos′i·tive·ly** *adv.*

pos·i·tron (-trän′) *n.* ⟦prec. + (ELEC)TRON⟧ the positive antiparticle of an electron, having the same mass and magnitude of charge

poss *abbrev.* **1** possessive **2** possibly

pos·se (päs′ē) *n.* ⟦< L, be able⟧ **1** ⟦Historical⟧ a band of men, usually armed, summoned to assist the sheriff in keeping the peace, etc. **2** [Slang] an entourage

pos·sess (pə zes′) *vt.* ⟦< L *possidere*⟧ **1** to have as belonging to one; own **2** to have as an attribute, quality, etc. **3** to gain control over [*possessed* by an idea] —**pos·ses′sor** *n.*

pos·sessed *adj.* **1** owned **2** controlled, as if by a demon; crazed

pos·ses·sion (-zesh′ən) *n.* **1** a possessing or being possessed **2** anything possessed **3** [*pl.*] property **4** territory ruled by an outside country

pos·ses·sive (-zes′iv) *adj.* **1** of possession **2** showing or desiring possession, domination, control, influence, etc. **3** *Gram.* designating or of a case, form, or construction expressing possession (Ex: *my, Bill's*) —*n. Gram.* **1** the possessive case **2** a word or phrase in this case —**pos·ses′sive·ness** *n.*

pos·si·ble (päs′ə bəl) *adj.* ⟦< L *posse*, be able⟧ **1** that can be or exist **2** that may or may not happen **3** that can be done, selected, etc. **4** permissible —**pos′si·bil′i·ty** (-bil′ə tē) *n.*, *pl.* **-ties**

pos·si·bly (-blē) *adv.* **1** by any possible means **2** perhaps; maybe

pos·sum (päs′əm) [Inf.] *n.* OPOSSUM —**play possum** to pretend to be asleep, dead, ill, etc.

post¹ (pōst) *n.* ⟦< L *postis*⟧ **1** a piece of wood, metal, etc. set upright to support a building, sign, etc. **2** the starting point of a horse race **3** a message added as to a blog —*vt.* **1** to put up (a poster, etc.) on (a wall, etc.) **2** to announce by posting notices [to *post* a reward] **3** to warn against trespassing on by posted notices **4** to put (a name) on a posted or published list **5** to make available for viewing as on a blog

post² (pōst) *n.* ⟦< Fr < It *posto*⟧ **1** the place where a soldier, guard, etc. is stationed **2** a place where troops are garrisoned **3** the place assigned to one **4** a job or duty —*vt.* **1** to assign to a post **2** to put up (a bond, etc.)

post³ (pōst) *n.* ⟦< Fr < It *posta*⟧ [Chiefly Brit.] (the) mail —*vi.* to travel fast; hasten —*vt.* **1** [Chiefly Brit.] to mail **2** to inform [keep me *posted*]

post- ⟦L < *post*, after⟧ *prefix* **1** after in time, later (than) [*postnatal*] **2** behind

post·age (pōs′tij) *n.* the amount charged for mailing a letter, etc.

post·al (pōs′təl) *adj.* ⟦Fr⟧ of mail or post offices

post-bel·lum (pōst bel′əm) *adj.* ⟦L⟧ after the war; specif., after the American Civil War

post·card *n.* a card, usually with a picture on one side, for sending short messages by mail

post·date *vt.* **-dat′ed, -dat′ing 1** to assign a later date to than the actual date **2** to be subsequent to

post·er (pōs′tər) *n.* a large advertisement or notice posted publicly

pos·te·ri·or (päs tir′ē ər) *adj.* ⟦L < *post*, after⟧ **1** later; following **2** at the rear; behind —*n.* the buttocks

pos·ter·i·ty (päs ter′ə tē) *n.* [see prec.] **1** all of a person's descendants **2** all succeeding generations

post·grad·u·ate *adj.* of or taking a course of study after graduation, esp. after receipt of the bachelor's degree

post·hole *n.* a hole dug to hold the end of an upright post

post·hu·mous (päs′choo məs, -tyoo-) *adj.* ⟦< L *postumus*, last⟧ **1** published after the author's death **2** arising or continuing after one's death —**post′hu·mous·ly** *adv.*

post·hyp·not·ic *adj.* in the time after a hypnotic trance [*posthypnotic* suggestion]

pos·til·ion or **pos·til·lion** (pōs til′yən, päs-) *n.* ⟦Fr < It *posta*, a post⟧ one who rides the leading left-hand horse of a team drawing a carriage

post·in·dus·tri·al *adj.* of a society in which the economy has shifted from heavy industry to service industries, technology, etc.

Post-it *trademark for* small sheets of adhesive-backed paper for attaching notes —*n.* a sheet of this

post·lude (pōst′lood′) *n.* ⟦POST- + (PREL)UDE⟧ a concluding musical piece

post·man (-mən) *n. pl.* **-men** (-mən) MAILMAN

post·mark *n.* a post-office mark stamped on mail, canceling the postage stamp and recording the date and place —*vt.* to stamp with a postmark

post·mas·ter *n.* the manager of a post office

postmaster general *pl.* **postmasters general** the head of a government's postal system

post me·ri·di·em (mə rid′ē əm) ⟦L⟧ after noon: abbrev. *P.M., p.m., PM,* or *pm*

post·mod·ern·ism *n.* **1** an eclectic artistic trend of the late 1900s **2** modern critical and social theories questioning objective truth, intrinsic meaning, etc. —**post′mod′ern** *adj.* —**post′mod′ern·ist** *adj., n.*

post-mor·tem (pōst′môr′təm) *adj.* ⟦L⟧ **1** after death **2** of a post-mortem —*n.* **1** AUTOPSY **2** an evaluation of some event just ended

post·na·sal drip (pōst′nā′zəl) a discharge of mucus from behind the nose onto the pharynx, due to a cold, allergy, etc.

post·na·tal (-nāt′'l) *adj.* after birth

post office 1 the governmental department in charge of the mail **2** a place where mail is sorted, postage stamps are sold, etc.

post·op·er·a·tive (-äp′ər ə tiv) *adj.* occurring after a surgical operation: also **post′op′**

post·paid *adj.* with postage prepaid

post·par·tum (-pär′təm) *adj.* ⟦L < *post*-, after + *parere*, to bear⟧ of the time after childbirth

post·pone (pōst pōn′) *vt.* **-poned′, -pon′ing** ⟦< L *post*-, after + *ponere*, put⟧ to put off until later; delay —**post·pone′ment** *n.*

post·script *n.* ⟦< L *post*-, after + *scribere*, write⟧ a note added below the signature in a letter

post·sea·son (pōst′sē′zən) *Sports n.* the period just after the regular season, during which playoffs are held —*adj.* of the postseason

post time the scheduled starting time of a horse race

post-trau·mat·ic stress disorder a disorder characterized by recurring flashbacks, anxiety, depression, etc., occurring after a traumatic event, as combat or rape

pos·tu·late (päs′chə lāt′; *for n.,* -lit) *vt.* **-lat′ed, -lat′ing** ⟦< L *postulare*, to demand⟧ to assume to be true, real, etc., esp. as a basis for argument —*n.* something postulated

pos·ture (päs′chər) *n.* ⟦MFr < L *ponere*, to place⟧ **1** the position or carriage of the body **2** a position assumed as in posing **3** an official stand or position [*our national posture*] —*vi.* to pose or assume an attitude merely for effect

post·war *adj.* after the (or a) war

po·sy (pō′zē) *n.,* pl. **-sies** ⟦< POESY⟧ [Old-fashioned] a flower or bouquet

pot¹ (pät) *n.* ⟦OE *pott*⟧ **1** a round vessel for holding liquids, for cooking, etc. **2** a pot with its contents **3** [Inf.] all the money bet at a single time —*vt.* **pot′ted, pot′ting** to put into a pot —**go to pot** [Inf.] to go to ruin —**pot′ful′** *n.,* pl. **-fuls′**

pot² (pät) *n.* ⟦< AmSp *potiguaya*⟧ [Slang] MARIJUANA

po·ta·ble (pōt′ə bəl) *adj.* ⟦< L *potare*, to drink⟧ drinkable —*n.* a beverage —**po′ta·bil′i·ty** *n.*

pot·ash *n.* ⟦< Du *pot*, POT¹ + *asch*, ASH³⟧ any of various potassium compounds used in fertilizers, soaps, etc.

po·tas·si·um (pə tas′ē əm) *n.* ⟦see prec.⟧ a soft, silver-white, metallic chemical element: symbol, K; at. no. 19

po·ta·to (pə tāt′ō) *n.,* pl. **-toes** ⟦< WInd⟧ **1** the starchy tuber of a widely cultivated plant, eaten as a cooked vegetable **2** this plant

potato chip a very thin slice of potato fried crisp and then salted

pot·bel·lied *adj.* **1** having a potbelly **2** having bulging sides [a *potbellied* stove]

pot·bel·ly *n.,* pl. **-lies** a protruding belly

pot·boil·er *n.* a piece of writing, etc., done quickly and for money only

pot-bound *adj.* having outgrown its container: said of a potted plant

po·tent (pōt′'nt) *adj.* ⟦< L *posse*, be able⟧ **1** having authority or power **2** convincing; cogent **3** effective, as a drug **4** able to have sexual intercourse: said of a male —**po′ten·cy** *n.*

po·ten·tate (pōt′'n tāt′) *n.* a person having great power; ruler; monarch

po·ten·tial (pō ten′shəl) *adj.* ⟦see POTENT⟧ that can come into being; possible; latent —*n.* **1** something potential **2** the difference in voltage between two points in an electric circuit or field —**po·ten′ti·al′i·ty** (-shē al′ə tē) *n.,* pl. **-ties** —**po·ten′tial·ly** *adv.*

pot·herb *n.* any herb whose leaves and stems are boiled and eaten or used as a flavoring

pot·hold·er *n.* a small pad, or piece of thick cloth, for handling hot pots, etc.

pot·hole *n.* **1** a deep hole or pit **2** a rough hole in pavement

pot·hook *n.* an S-shaped hook for hanging a pot over a fire

po·tion (pō′shən) *n.* ⟦< L *potare*, to drink⟧ a drink as of medicine, poison, or a supposedly magic substance

pot·luck *n.* **1** whatever the family meal happens to be [to take *potluck*] **2** a dinner to which everyone brings a dish to share: in full **potluck dinner**

Po·to·mac (pə tō′mək) river in the E U.S., flowing into Chesapeake Bay

pot·pie *n.* a meat pie made in a deep dish

pot·pour·ri (pō′pŏŏ rē′) *n.* ⟦Fr < *pot*, a pot + *pourrir*, to rot⟧ **1** a mixture of dried flowers, spices, etc., kept for its fragrance **2** a medley or miscellany; mixture

pot roast a large cut of beef cooked in one piece by braising

pot·sherd (pät′shurd′) *n.* ⟦see POT¹ & SHARD⟧ a piece of broken pottery

pot·shot *n.* **1** an easy or random shot **2** a haphazard try **3** a random attack

pot·tage (pät′ij) *n.* ⟦< earlier Fr *pot*, a pot⟧ a kind of thick soup or stew

pot·ter *n.* one who makes earthenware pots, dishes, etc.

potter's field a burial ground for paupers or unknown persons

potter's wheel a rotating disk upon which clay is molded into bowls, etc.

pot·ter·y *n.,* pl. **-ies 1** a potter's workshop **2** the art of a potter; ceramics **3** pots, dishes, etc. made of clay hardened by heat

pot·ty (pät′ē) *n.,* pl. **-ties 1** a child's chair incorporating a chamberpot for toilet training: in full **potty chair 2** a toilet: a child's word

pouch (pouch) *n.* ⟦< earlier Fr *poche*⟧ **1** a small bag or sack [a tobacco *pouch*] **2** a mailbag **3** a saclike structure, as that on the abdomen of the kangaroo, etc. for carrying young —*vi.* to form a pouch

poul·tice (pōl′tis) *n.* ⟦< ML *pultes*, pap⟧ a hot, soft, moist mass applied to a sore part of the body —*vt.* **-ticed, -tic·ing** to apply a poultice to

poul·try (pōl′trē) *n.* ⟦< L *pullus*, chicken⟧ domestic fowls; chickens, ducks, etc.

pounce (pouns) *n.* ⟦ME *pownce*, talon⟧ a

pouncing —*vi.* **pounced, pounc'ing** to swoop down or leap (*on, upon,* or *at*) in, or as in, seizing

pound¹ (pound) *n., pl.* **pounds;** sometimes, after a number, **pound** [< L *pondus,* weight] **1** a unit of weight equal to 16 oz. avoirdupois or 12 oz. troy: abbrev. **lb. 2** the monetary unit of the United Kingdom: symbol, £ **3** the monetary unit of various other countries, as Egypt and Syria

pound² (pound) *vt.* [OE *punian*] **1** to beat to a pulp, powder, etc. **2** to hit hard —*vi.* **1** to deliver repeated, heavy blows (*at* or *on*) **2** to move with heavy steps **3** to throb

pound³ (pound) *n.* [< OE *pund-*] **1** a municipal enclosure for stray animals [a dog *pound*] **2** a place where impounded vehicles are held

pound·cake *n.* a rich cake made (orig. with a pound each) of flour, butter, sugar, etc.

pound sign a symbol (#) on a button on a keyboard or keypad

pour (pôr) *vt.* [ME *pouren*] **1** to cause to flow in a continuous stream **2** to emit, utter, etc. profusely or steadily —*vi.* **1** to flow freely, continuously, etc. **2** to rain heavily

pout (pout) *vi.* [ME *pouten*] **1** to thrust out the lips, as in sullenness **2** to sulk —*n.* the act of pouting —**pout'er** *n.*

POV *abbrev.* point of view

pov·er·ty (päv'ər tē) *n.* [< L *pauper,* poor] **1** the condition or quality of being poor; need **2** deficiency; inadequacy **3** scarcity

pov·er·ty-strick·en *adj.* very poor

POW *n., pl.* **POW's** prisoner of war

pow·der (pou'dər) *n.* [< L *pulvis,* dust] **1** any dry substance in the form of fine, dustlike particles, produced by crushing, grinding, etc. **2** a specific kind of powder [bath *powder*] —*vt.* **1** to sprinkle, etc. with powder **2** to make into powder —**pow'der·y** *adj.*

powder keg 1 a keg for gunpowder **2** a potential source of violence, war, etc.

powder room a lavatory for women

pow·er (pou'ər) *n.* [ult. < L *posse,* be able] **1** ability to do or act **2** vigor; force; strength **3** *a*) authority; influence *b*) legal authority **4** *a*) physical force or energy [electric *power*] *b*) the rate at which physical work is done **5** a person or thing having great influence, force, or authority **6** a nation with influence over other nations **7** the product of the multiplication of a quantity by itself **8** the degree of magnification of a lens —*vt.* to supply with a source of power —*adj.* **1** operated by electricity, a fuel engine, etc. [*power* tools] **2** served by an auxiliary system that reduces effort [*power* steering] **3** carrying electricity

pow·er·ful *adj.* strong, mighty, influential, etc. —**pow'er·ful·ly** *adv.*

pow·er·house *n.* **1** a building where electric power is generated **2** [Inf.] a powerful person, team, etc.

pow·er·less (pou'ər lis) *adj.* without power; weak, unable, etc. —**pow'er·less·ly** *adv.*

power of attorney written legal authority for one person to act for another

power strip an electrical device consisting of a block of sockets by which a single outlet can power multiple appliances

pow·er·train *n.* DRIVETRAIN

pow·wow (pou'wou') *n.* [< AmInd] **1** a conference of or with North American Indians **2** [Inf.] any conference

pox (päks) *n.* [for *pocks:* see POCK] **1** a disease characterized by skin eruptions, as smallpox **2** syphilis: with *the*

pp *abbrev.* **1** pages **2** past participle **3** postpaid **4** prepaid Also, for 3 & 4, **ppd**

PPO *n., pl.* **PPO's** [p(referred) p(rovider) o(rganization)] a healthcare system having certain hospitals, doctors, etc. under contract at a reduced cost

P.P.S. or **p.p.s.** or **PPS** or **pps** *abbrev.* [L *post postscriptum*] an additional postscript

PPV *abbrev.* pay-per-view

pr *abbrev.* **1** pair(s) **2** price

Pr *abbrev.* Provençal

PR or **P.R.** *abbrev.* **1** public relations **2** Puerto Rico

prac·ti·ca·ble (prak'ti kə bəl) *adj.* **1** that can be put into practice; feasible **2** that can be used; useful —**prac'ti·ca·bil'i·ty** *n.* —**prac'ti·ca·bly** *adv.*

prac·ti·cal (prak'ti kəl) *adj.* **1** of or obtained through practice or action **2** useful **3** concerned with the application of knowledge to useful ends [*practical* science] **4** dealing realistically and sensibly with everyday matters **5** that is so in practice, if not in theory, law, etc. —**prac'ti·cal'i·ty** (-kal'ə tē) *n., pl.* **-ties**

practical joke a trick played on someone in fun —**practical joker**

prac·ti·cal·ly (prak'tik lē, -tik ə lē) *adv.* **1** in a practical manner **2** from a practical viewpoint **3** in effect; virtually **4** [Inf.] nearly

practical nurse a nurse with less training than a registered nurse, often one licensed by a U.S. state (**licensed practical nurse**) for specified duties

prac·tice (prak'tis) *vt.* **-ticed, -tic·ing** [< Gr *prassein,* do] **1** to do or engage in frequently; make a habit of **2** to do repeatedly so as to become proficient **3** to work at, esp. as a profession —*vi.* to do something repeatedly so as to become proficient; drill Chiefly Brit. sp. **prac'tise** —*n.* **1** a practicing; habit, custom, etc. **2** *a*) repeated action to acquire proficiency *b*) proficiency so acquired **3** the actual doing of something **4** *a*) the exercise of a profession *b*) a business based on this

prac·ticed *adj.* experienced; skilled

prac·ti·cum (prak'ti kəm) *n.* [see PRACTICE] a course involving activities emphasizing the practical application of theory, as on-the-job experience in a field of study

prac·ti·tion·er (prak tish'ə nər) *n.* one who practices a profession

Prae·to·ri·an (prē tôr'ē ən) *adj.* [< L *praetor,* magistrate] of or belonging to the bodyguard (**Praetorian Guard**) of a Roman emperor

prag·mat·ic (prag mat′ik) *adj.* [< Gr *pragma*, thing done] 1 practical 2 testing the validity of all concepts by their practical results —**prag′mat′i·cal·ly** *adv.* —**prag′ma·tism′** (-mə tiz′əm) *n.* —**prag′ma·tist** *n.*

Prague (präg) capital of the Czech Republic

prai·rie (prer′ē) *n.* [Fr < L *pratum*, meadow] a large area of level or rolling, grassy land

prairie dog a small, burrowing rodent of North America

prairie schooner a box-shaped covered wagon

praise (präz) *vt.* **praised, prais′ing** [< L *pretium*, worth, price] 1 to express approval or admiration of 2 to glorify (God, etc.), as in song —*n.* a praising or being praised; commendation

praise·wor·thy *adj.* worthy of praise —**praise′wor′thi·ly** *adv.* —**praise′wor′thi·ness** *n.*

pra·line (prä′lēn′, prā′-) *n.* [Fr] any of various soft or crisp candies made of nuts, sugar, etc.

prance (prans) *vi.* **pranced, pranc′ing** [< ?] 1 to rise up, or move along, on the hind legs, as a horse does 2 to caper or strut —*n.* a prancing —**pranc′er** *n.* —**pranc′ing·ly** *adv.*

prank (praŋk) *n.* [< ?] a mischievous trick —**prank′ster** *n.*

pra·se·o·dym·i·um (prā′zē ō dim′ē əm, -sē-) *n.* [ModL] a silvery, malleable chemical element used to color glasses and enamels: symbol, Pr; at. no. 59

prate (prāt) *vi., vt.* **prat′ed, prat′ing** [< MDu *praten*] to talk much and foolishly; chatter

prat·tle (prat′'l) *vi., vt.* **-tled, -tling** [LowG *pratelen*] to prate or babble —*n.* chatter or babble

prawn (prôn) *n.* [< ?] a large shrimp or other similar crustacean

pray (prā) *vt.* [< L *prex*, prayer] 1 to implore [(I) *pray* (you) tell me] 2 to ask for by prayer —*vi.* to say prayers, as to God

prayer¹ (prer) *n.* 1 the act of praying 2 an entreaty; supplication 3 *a)* a humble request, as to God *b)* any set formula for this 4 [*often pl.*] a devotional service chiefly of prayers 5 something prayed for 6 [Inf.] a chance to succeed —**prayer′ful** *adj.* —**prayer′ful·ly** *adv.*

pray·er² (prā′ər) *n.* one who prays

praying mantis MANTIS

pre- [< L *prae*, before] *prefix* before in time, place, rank, etc.

preach (prēch) *vi.* [< L *prae-*, before + *dicare*, proclaim] 1 to give a religious sermon 2 to give moral advice, esp. in a tiresome manner —*vt.* 1 to urge as by preaching 2 to deliver (a sermon) —**preach′ment** *n.*

preach·er *n.* one who preaches; esp., a member of the Protestant clergy

preach·y *adj.* **-i·er, -i·est** [Inf.] given to or marked by preaching, or moralizing

pre·am·ble (prē′am′bəl) *n.* [< L *prae-*, before + *ambulare*, go] an introduction, esp. one to a constitution, statute, etc., stating its purpose

pre·ap·prove (-ə prōōv′) *vt.* **-proved′, -prov′ing** to authorize before an application is submitted

pre·ar·range (-ə ränj′) *vt.* **-ranged′, -rang′ing** to arrange beforehand

pre·can·cer·ous (prē kan′sər əs) *adj.* likely to become cancerous

pre·car·i·ous (prē ker′ē əs) *adj.* [see PRAY] dependent upon circumstances or chance; uncertain; risky —**pre·car′i·ous·ly** *adv.*

pre·cau·tion (pri kô′shən) *n.* [< L *prae-*, before + *cavere*, take care] care taken beforehand, as against danger or failure —**pre·cau′tion·ar′y** *adj.*

pre·cede (prē sēd′) *vt., vi.* **-ced′ed, -ced′ing** [< L *prae-*, before + *cedere*, to go] to be, come, or go before in time, place, rank, etc.

prec·e·dence (pres′ə dəns, pri sēd′'ns) *n.* the act, right, or fact of preceding in time, order, rank, etc.

prec·e·dent (pres′ə dənt) *n.* an act, statement, etc. that may serve as an example or justification for a later one

pre·ced·ing *adj.* that precedes

pre·cept (prē′sept′) *n.* [< L *prae-*, before + *capere*, take] a rule of moral conduct; maxim

pre·cep·tor (prē sep′tər) *n.* a teacher

pre·cinct (prē′siŋkt′) *n.* [< L *prae-*, before + *cingere*, surround] 1 [*usually pl.*] an enclosure between buildings, walls, etc. 2 [*pl.*] environs 3 *a)* police district *b)* a subdivision of a voting ward 4 a limited area

pre·ci·os·i·ty (presh′ē äs′ə tē, pres′ē-) *n., pl.* **-ties** [see fol.] affectation, esp. in language

pre·cious (presh′əs) *adj.* [< L *pretium*, a price] 1 of great price or value; costly 2 beloved; dear 3 very fastidious, affected, etc. —**pre′cious·ly** *adv.*

precious stone a rare and costly gem: applied to the diamond, emerald, ruby, and sapphire

prec·i·pice (pres′i pis) *n.* [< L *prae-*, before + *caput*, a head] a vertical or overhanging rock face

pre·cip·i·tant (prē sip′i tənt) *adj.* [see prec.] PRECIPITATE

pre·cip·i·tate (prē sip′ə tāt′; *for adj. &* *n.,* -tit, -tāt′) *vt.* **-tat′ed, -tat′ing** [see PRECIPICE] 1 to hurl downward 2 to cause to happen before expected, needed, etc. 3 *Chem.* to separate (a soluble substance) out of a solution —*vi.* 1 *Chem.* to be precipitated 2 *Meteorol.* to condense and fall as rain, snow, etc. —*adj.* 1 acting or done hastily or rashly 2 very sudden or abrupt —*n.* a substance precipitated out of a solution

pre·cip·i·ta·tion (-tā′shən) *n.* 1 a headlong fall or rush 2 rash haste; impetuosity 3 a bringing on suddenly 4 *Chem.* a precipitating or being precipitated from a solution 5 *Meteorol.* rain, snow, etc.

pre·cip·i·tous (-təs) *adj.* 1 steep like a precipice 2 rash; impetuous

pré·cis (prā sē′) *n., pl.* **-cis′** (-sēz′) [Fr: see fol.] a concise summary

pre·cise (prē sīs′) *adj.* [< L *prae-*, before + *caedere*, to cut] 1 accurately stated; definite 2 minutely exact 3 strict; scrupulous; fastidious —**pre·cise′ly** *adv.* —**pre·cise′ness** *n.*

pre·ci·sion (prē sizh′ən) *n.* the quality of being precise; exactness —*adj.* requiring exactness [*precision* work]

pre·clude (prē klōōd′) *vt.* **-clud′ed, -clud′ing** [< L *prae-*, before + *claudere*, to close] to make impossible, esp. in advance; prevent —**pre·clu′sion** (-klōō′zhən) *n.*

pre·co·cious (prē kō′shəs) *adj.* [< L *prae-*, before + *coquere*, to cook] matured earlier than usual [a *precocious* child] —**pre·coc′i·ty** (-käs′ə tē) *n.*

pre·cog·ni·tion (prē′käg nish′ən) *n.* [see PRE- & COGNITION] *Parapsychology* the perception of an event, etc. before it occurs, esp. by extrasensory means —**pre·cog′ni·tive** (-nə tiv) *adj.*

pre-Co·lum·bi·an (prē′kə lum′bē ən) *adj.* of any period in the Americas before Columbus's voyages

pre·con·ceive (prē′kən sēv′) *vt.* **-ceived′, -ceiv′ing** to form (an opinion) in advance —**pre′con·cep′tion** (-sep′shən) *n.*

pre·con·di·tion (-dish′ən) *vt.* to prepare (someone) to behave, react, etc. in a certain way under certain conditions —*n.* a condition required beforehand if something else is to occur

pre·cur·sor (prē kur′sər, prē′kur′-) *n.* [< L *praecurrere*, run ahead] 1 a forerunner 2 a predecessor —**pre·cur′so·ry** *adj.*

pred·a·to·ry (pred′ə tôr′ē) *adj.* [< L *praeda*, a prey] 1 of or living by plundering, robbing, or exploiting 2 preying on other animals —**pred′a·tor** (-tər) *n.*

pre·de·cease (prē′dē sēs′) *vt.* **-ceased′, -ceas′ing** to die before (someone else)

pred·e·ces·sor (pred′ə ses′ər) *n.* [< L *prae-*, before + *decedere*, go away] a person preceding another, as in office

pre·des·ti·na·tion (prē des′tə nā′shən) *n.* 1 *Theol.* the doctrine that *a*) God foreordained everything that would happen *b*) God predestines souls to salvation or to damnation 2 one's destiny

pre·des·tine (-des′tin) *vt.* **-tined, -tin·ing** to destine beforehand; foreordain

pre·de·ter·mine (-dē tur′min) *vt.* **-mined, -min·ing** to determine beforehand

pre·dic·a·ment (prē dik′ə mənt) *n.* [see PREACH] an unpleasant or embarrassing situation

pred·i·cate (pred′i kāt′; *for n. & adj.,* -kit) *vt.* **-cat′ed, -cat′ing** [see PREACH] 1 to affirm as a quality or attribute 2 to base (something) *on* or *upon* facts, conditions, etc. —*n. Gram.* the word or words that make a statement about the subject —*adj. Gram.* of a predicate —**pred′i·ca′tion** *n.*

pre·dict (prē dikt′) *vt., vi.* [< L *prae-*, before + *dicere*, tell] to say in advance (what one believes will happen); foretell —**pre·dict′a·ble** *adj.* —**pre·dic′tion** *n.* —**pre·dic′tor** *n.*

pre·di·gest (prē′di jest′, -dī-) *vt.* to treat (food) as with enzymes for easier digestion when eaten

pred·i·lec·tion (pred′ə lek′shən, prē′də-) *n.*

[< L *prae-*, before + *diligere*, prefer] a partiality or preference (*for*)

pre·dis·pose (prē′di spōz′) *vt.* **-posed′, -pos′ing** to make receptive or susceptible (*to*); incline —**pre′dis·po·si′tion** (-dis pə zish′ən) *n.*

pre·dom·i·nant (prē däm′ə nənt) *adj.* 1 having authority or influence over others; superior 2 most frequent; prevailing —**pre·dom′i·nance** *n.* —**pre·dom′i·nant·ly** *adv.*

pre·dom·i·nate (prē däm′ə nāt′) *vi.* **-nat′ed, -nat′ing** 1 to have authority or influence (*over* others) 2 to be dominant in amount, number, etc.; prevail

pre·em·i·nent (prē em′ə nənt) *adj.* eminent above others; surpassing —**pre·em′i·nence** *n.* —**pre·em′i·nent·ly** *adv.*

pre·empt or **pre-empt** (prē empt′) *vt.* [ult. < L *prae-*, before + *emere*, buy] 1 to gain the right to buy (public land) by settling on it 2 to seize before anyone else can 3 to act in advance of 4 *Radio, TV* to replace (a scheduled program) with a special broadcast

pre·emp·tion (-emp′shən) *n.* 1 a preempting 2 action taken to check other action beforehand —**pre·emp′tive** *adj.*

preen (prēn) *vt.* [< ME *proinen*, to dress up] 1 to clean and trim (the feathers) with the beak 2 to dress up or adorn (oneself)

pre·ex·ist (prē′eg zist′) *vt., vi.* to exist previously or before (another person or thing) —**pre′ex·ist′ence** *n.*

pref *abbrev.* 1 preface 2 preferred 3 prefix

pre·fab (prē′fab′) *n.* [Inf.] a prefabricated building

pre·fab·ri·cate (prē fab′ri kāt′) *vt.* **-cat′ed, -cat′ing** to build (a house, etc.) in standardized sections for shipment and quick assembly

pref·ace (pref′is) *n.* [< L *prae-*, before + *fari*, speak] an introduction to a book, speech, etc. —*vt.* **-aced, -ac·ing** 1 to furnish with a preface 2 to introduce —**pref′a·to·ry** (-ə tôr′ē) *adj.*

pre·fect (prē′fekt′) *n.* [< L *praeficere*, to set over] any of various administrators —**pre′fec′ture** (-fek′chər) *n.*

pre·fer (prē fur′, pri-) *vt.* **-ferred′, -fer′ring** [< L *prae-*, before + *ferre*, to bear] 1 to put before a court, etc. for consideration 2 to like better

pref·er·a·ble (pref′ər ə bəl) *adj.* more desirable —**pref′er·a·bly** *adv.*

pref·er·ence (-əns) *n.* 1 a preferring or being preferred 2 something preferred 3 advantage given to one person, country, etc. over others —**pref′er·en′tial** (-ər en′shəl) *adj.*

pre·fer·ment (prē fur′mənt) *n.* an advancement in rank, etc.; promotion

pre·fig·ure (prē fig′yər) *vt.* **-ured, -ur·ing** to suggest beforehand; foreshadow

pre·fix (prē′fiks′; *for v., also* prē fiks′) *vt.* [< L *prae-*, before + *figere*, fix] to fix to the beginning of a word, etc.; esp., to add as a prefix —*n.* a syllable, group of syllables, or word joined to the beginning of another word or a base to alter its meaning

preg·nant (preg′nənt) *adj.* [< L *pregnans*] **1** having (an) offspring developing in the uterus; with child **2** mentally fertile; inventive **3** full of meaning, etc. [a *pregnant* silence] —**preg′nan·cy** *n.*, *pl.* -**cies**

pre·hen·sile (prē hen′səl) *adj.* [< L *prehendere*, take] adapted for seizing or grasping, esp. by wrapping around something: said as of a monkey's tail

pre·his·tor·ic (prē′his tôr′ik) *adj.* of the period before recorded history

pre·ig·ni·tion (prē′ig nish′ən) *n.* in an internal-combustion engine, ignition occurring before the intake valve is closed or before the spark plug fires

pre·judge (prē juj′) *vt.* -**judged′**, -**judg′ing** to judge beforehand or without all the evidence —**pre·judg′ment** *n.*

prej·u·dice (prej′ə dis) *n.* [< L *prae-*, before + *judicium*, judgment] **1** a preconceived, usually unfavorable idea **2** an opinion held in disregard of facts that contradict it; bias **3** intolerance or hatred of other races, etc. **4** injury or harm as from some judgment —*vt.* -**diced**, -**dic·ing 1** to injure or harm, as by some judgment **2** to cause to have prejudice; bias —**prej′u·di′cial** (-dish′əl) *adj.*

prel·ate (prel′it) *n.* [< L *praelatus*, placed before] a high-ranking member of the clergy, as a bishop —**prel′a·cy** *n.*, *pl.* -**cies**

pre·lim·i·nar·y (prē lim′ə ner′ē, pri-) *adj.* [< L *prae-*, before + *limen*, threshold] leading up to the main action, discussion, etc.; introductory —*n.*, *pl.* -**ies** [*often pl.*] a preliminary step, procedure, etc.

pre·lit·er·ate (prē lit′ər it) *adj.* of a society not having a written language

prel·ude (prā′lood, prel′yood) *n.* [< Fr < L *prae-*, before + *ludere*, to play] **1** a preliminary part **2** *Music a)* an introductory instrumental composition, as the overture to an opera *b)* a short, romantic composition

pre·mar·i·tal (prē mar′ət'l) *adj.* occurring before marriage

pre·ma·ture (prē′mə toor′, -choor′) *adj.* [< L *prae-*, before + *maturus*, ripe] happening, done, arriving, etc. before the proper or usual time; too early —**pre′ma·ture′ly** *adv.*

pre·med·i·tate (-med′ə tāt′) *vt.*, *vi.* -**tat′ed**, -**tat′ing** to think (out) or plan beforehand —**pre·med′i·ta′tion** *n.*

pre·men·stru·al (prē men′strəl) *adj.* occurring before a menstrual period

pre·mier (pri mir′, -myir′) *adj.* [Fr < L *primus*, first] first in importance; foremost —*n.* a chief official; specif., a prime minister —**pre·mier′ship** *n.*

pre·mière or **pre·miere** (pri mir′, -myer′) *n.* [Fr: see prec.] a first performance of a play, movie, etc.

prem·ise (prem′is) *n.* [< L *prae-*, before + *mittere*, send] **1** a previous statement serving as a basis for an argument **2** [*pl.*] a piece of real estate —*vt.* -**ised**, -**is·ing** to state as a premise

pre·mi·um (prē′mē əm) *n.*, *pl.* -**ums** [< L *prae-*, before + *emere*, get, buy] **1** a reward or prize, esp. as an inducement to buy **2** an additional amount paid or charged **3** a payment, as for an insurance policy **4** very high value [to put a *premium* on wit] —**at a premium** very valuable because of scarcity

pre·mo·ni·tion (prem′ə nish′ən, prē′mə-) *n.* [< L *prae-*, before + *monere*, warn] **1** a forewarning **2** a foreboding —**pre·mon·i·to·ry** (prē män′i tôr′ē) *adj.*

pre·na·tal (prē nāt′'l) *adj.* before birth

pre·nup·tial (prē nup′shəl) *adj.* before a marriage or wedding

pre·oc·cu·pied *adj.* completely absorbed in one's thoughts; engrossed

pre·oc·cu·py (prē äk′yoo pī′) *vt.* -**pied′**, -**py′ing** [< L *prae-*, before + *occupare*, seize] to wholly occupy the thoughts of; engross —**pre·oc′cu·pa′tion** (-pā′shən) *n.*

pre·op·er·a·tive (prē äp′ər ə tiv, -ər āt′iv) *adj.* occurring before a surgical operation

pre·or·dain (prē′ôr dān′) *vt.* to ordain or decree beforehand

pre·owned *adj.* previously owned; used

prep[1] (prep) *adj. short for* PREPARATORY [a *prep* school] —*vt.* **prepped**, **prep′ping** to prepare (a patient) for surgery, etc.

prep[2] *abbrev.* **1** preparatory **2** preposition

pre·pack·age (prē pak′ij) *vt.* -**aged**, -**ag·ing** to package (foods, etc.) in standard units before selling

pre·paid (prē pād′) *vt.* *pt.* & *pp. of* PREPAY

prep·a·ra·tion (prep′ə rā′shən) *n.* **1** a preparing or being prepared **2** a preparatory measure **3** something prepared, as a medicine or cosmetic

pre·par·a·to·ry (prē par′ə tôr′ē, prep′ə rə-) *adj.* serving to prepare; introductory

preparatory school a private secondary school that prepares students for college

pre·pare (prē par′, pri-) *vt.* -**pared′**, -**par′ing** [< L *prae-*, before + *parare*, get ready] **1** to make ready **2** to equip or furnish **3** to put together [to *prepare* dinner] —*vi.* **1** to make things ready **2** to make oneself ready

pre·par·ed·ness (-par′id nəs) *n.* the state of being prepared, as for waging war

pre·pay *vt.* -**paid′**, -**pay′ing** to pay or pay for in advance —**pre·pay′ment** *n.*

pre·pon·der·ate (prē pän′dər āt′, pri-) *vi.* -**at′ed**, -**at′ing** [< L *prae-*, before + *ponderare*, weigh] to be superior in amount, power, etc. —**pre·pon′der·ance** *n.* —**pre·pon′der·ant** *adj.*

prep·o·si·tion (prep′ə zish′ən) *n.* [< L *prae-*, before + *ponere*, to place] a word, as *in, by, or to,* that connects a noun or pronoun to another element of a sentence —**prep′o·si′tion·al** *adj.*

pre·pos·sess (prē′pə zes′) *vt.* to bias, esp. favorably

pre·pos·sess·ing *adj.* that impresses favorably

pre·pos·ter·ous (prē päs′tər əs, pri-) *adj.* [< L *prae-*, before + *posterus*, following] absurd; ridiculous; laughable

prep·py or **prep·pie** (prep'ē) [Inf.] *n., pl.* **-pies** a student at or graduate of a preparatory school —*adj.* **-pi·er**, **-pi·est** of or like such students, their clothes, manners, etc.

pre·puce (prē'pyoos') *n.* [< L *praeputium*] FORESKIN

pre·re·cord (prē'ri kôrd') *vt. Film, Radio, TV* to record (music, a program, etc.) for later use

pre·re·cord·ed *adj.* recorded ahead of time for later playback or broadcast

pre·req·ui·site (prē rek'wə zit, pri-) *adj.* required beforehand as a necessary condition —*n.* something prerequisite

pre·rog·a·tive (prē răg'ə tiv, pri-) *n.* [< L *prae-*, before + *rogare*, ask] an exclusive right or privilege

pres *abbrev.* present

Pres *abbrev.* President

pres·age (pres'ij; *for v., usually* prē sāj', pri-) *n.* [< L *prae-*, before + *sagire*, perceive] 1 an omen; portent 2 a foreboding —*vt.* **-aged'**, **-ag'ing** to give warning of

pres·by·ter (prez'bi tər) *n.* [see PRIEST] 1 in the Presbyterian Church, an elder 2 in the Episcopal Church, a priest

Pres·by·te·ri·an (-tir'ē ən) *adj.* designating or of a church of a traditionally Calvinistic Protestant denomination governed by presbyters —*n.* a member of a Presbyterian church

pre·school *adj.* of or for a child between infancy and school age —*n.* a school for very young children, usually those three to five years of age —**pre'school'er** *n.*

pre·science (prē'shəns, -shē əns) *n.* [< L *prae-*, before + *scire*, know] foreknowledge; foresight —**pres'cient** *adj.*

pre·scribe (prē skrīb', pri-) *vt.* **-scribed'**, **-scrib'ing** [< L *prae-*, before + *scribere*, write] 1 to order; direct 2 to order as a medicine or treatment: said as of physicians

pre·script (prē'skript') *n.* a prescribed rule —**pre·scrip'tive** *adj.*

pre·scrip·tion (prē skrip'shən, pri-) *n.* 1 something prescribed 2 *a)* a written direction for the preparation and use of medicine *b)* such a medicine

pre·sea·son (prē'sē'zən) *Sports n.* the period just prior to the regular season, when teams practice and play exhibition games —*adj.* of the preseason

pres·ence (prez'əns) *n.* 1 the fact or state of being present 2 immediate surroundings [in his *presence*] 3 *a)* a person's bearing or appearance *b)* impressive bearing, personality, etc.

presence of mind ability to think and act quickly in an emergency

pres·ent (prez'ənt; *for v.* prē zent', pri-) *adj.* [< L *prae-*, before + *esse*, be] 1 being at the specified place 2 existing or happening now 3 *Gram.* indicating action or state occurring now or action that is always the same [*present* tense] —*n.* 1 the present time 2 the present tense 3 a gift —*vt.* **pre·sent'** 1 to introduce (a person) 2 to exhibit; show 3 to

offer for consideration 4 to give (a gift, etc.) to a person, etc. —**present arms** to hold a rifle vertically in front of the body

pre·sent·a·ble (prē zent'ə bəl, pri-) *adj.* 1 suitable for presentation 2 suitably groomed for meeting people

pres·en·ta·tion (prez'ən tā'shən, prē'zən-) *n.* 1 a presenting or being presented 2 something presented

pres·ent-day *adj.* of the present time

pre·sen·ti·ment (prē zent'ə mənt, pri-) *n.* [see PRE- & SENTIMENT] a feeling that something, esp. of an unfortunate nature, is about to take place

pres·ent·ly *adv.* 1 soon; shortly 2 at present; now: a usage objected to by some

pre·sent·ment (prē zent'mənt, pri-) *n.* presentation

present participle a participle used *a)* to express present or continuing action or existence (Ex.: he is *growing*) *b)* as an adjective (Ex.: a *growing* boy)

pres·er·va·tion·ist (prez'ər vā'shən ist) *n.* one who advocates positive measures to preserve historic buildings, wilderness lands, etc.

pre·serv·a·tive (prē zurv'ə tiv, pri-) *adj.* preserving —*n.* anything that preserves [a *preservative* added to foods]

pre·serve (prē zurv', pri-) *vt.* **-served'**, **-serv'ing** [< L *prae-*, before + *servare*, to keep] 1 to protect from harm, damage, etc. 2 to keep from spoiling 3 to prepare (food), as by canning, for future use 4 to carry on; maintain —*n.* 1 [*usually pl.*] fruit preserved by cooking with sugar 2 a place where game, fish, etc. are maintained —**pres·er·va·tion** (prez'ər vā'shən) *n.* —**pre·serv'er** *n.*

pre·set (prē set') *vt.* **-set'**, **-set'ting** to set (automatic controls) beforehand

pre·shrink (prē shriŋk') *vt.* **-shrank'** or **-shrunk'**, **-shrunk'** or **-shrunk'en**, **-shrink'ing** to shrink by a special process in manufacture, to minimize further shrinkage in laundering —**pre'shrunk'** *adj.*

pre·side (prē zīd', pri-) *vi.* **-sid'ed**, **-sid'ing** [< L *prae-*, before + *sedere*, sit] 1 to serve as chairman 2 to have control or authority (*over*)

pres·i·dent (prez'ə dənt) *n.* [see prec,] 1 the highest executive officer of a company, club, etc. 2 [*often* P-] the chief executive (as in the U.S.), or the nominal head (as in Italy), of a republic —**pres'i·den·cy** *n., pl.* **-cies** —**pres'i·den'tial** (-den'shəl) *adj.*

press' (pres) *vt.* [< L *premere*] 1 *a)* to act on with steady force or weight; push against, squeeze, compress, etc. *b)* to push against (a button, key, etc.) as in using an elevator, keyboard, etc. 2 to squeeze (juice, etc.) from 3 to iron (clothes, etc.) 4 to embrace closely 5 to urge persistently; entreat 6 to try to force 7 to emphasize 8 to distress or trouble [I'm *pressed* for time] 9 to urge on —*vi.* 1 to exert pressure; apply weight 2 to go forward with determination 3 to crowd —*n.* 1 pressure, urgency, etc. 2 a crowd 3 a machine for crushing, stamping, etc. **4** *a)* *short for* PRINTING PRESS *b)* a printing establishment *c)* newspapers, magazines, etc., or the persons who write for them *d)* publicity, etc. in newspapers, etc. **5** a closet for storing clothes, etc. —**press′er** *n.*

press² (pres) *vt.* [< L *praes*, surety + *stare*, to stand] to force into service, esp. military or naval service

press agent one whose work is to get publicity for a client

press box a place for reporters at sports events, etc.

press conference a group interview granted to media personnel as by a celebrity

press·ing *adj.* calling for immediate attention; urgent

press secretary one whose job is to deal with the news media on behalf of a prominent person

pres·sure (presh′ər) *n.* **1** a pressing or being pressed **2** a state of distress **3** a compelling influence [social *pressure*] **4** urgent demands; urgency **5** *Physics* force per unit of area exerted upon a surface, etc. —*vt.* **-sured, -sur·ing** to exert pressure on

pressure cooker a container for quick cooking by steam under pressure

pressure group a group trying to influence government through lobbying, propaganda, etc.

pres·sur·ize (-īz′) *vt.* **-ized′, -iz′ing** to keep nearly normal atmospheric pressure inside (an airplane, etc.), as at high altitudes —**pres′sur·i·za′tion** *n.*

pres·ti·dig·i·ta·tion (pres′tə dij′i tā′shən) *n.* [Fr < *preste*, quick + L *digitus*, finger] sleight of hand

pres·tige (pres tēzh′, -tēj′) *n.* [< L *praestrigiae*, deceptions] **1** the power to impress or influence **2** reputation based on high achievement, character, etc.

pres·ti·gious (-tij′əs, -tē′jəs) *adj.* having or imparting prestige or distinction

pres·to (pres′tō) *adv., adj.* [It, quick] **1** fast or at once **2** *Music* in fast tempo Also written **pres′to**

pre·stressed concrete (prē′strest′) concrete containing tensed steel cables for strength

pre·sume (prē zōōm′, pri-) *v.* **-sumed′, -sum′ing** [< L *prae-*, before + *sumere*, take] **1** to dare (to say or do something); venture **2** to take for granted; suppose —*vi.* to act presumptuously; take liberties —**pre·sum′a·ble** *adj.* —**pre·sum′a·bly** *adv.*

pre·sump·tion (prē zump′shən, pri-) *n.* **1** a presuming; specif., *a)* an overstepping of proper bounds *b)* a taking of something for granted **2** the thing presumed **3** a reason for presuming —**pre·sump′tive** *adj.*

pre·sump·tu·ous (-chōō əs) *adj.* too bold or forward

pre·sup·pose (prē′sə pōz′) *vt.* **-posed′, -pos′ing 1** to suppose or assume beforehand **2** to require or imply as a preceding condition —**pre′sup·po·si′tion** (-sup ə zish′ən) *n.*

pre·teen (prē′tēn′) *n.* a child nearly a teenager

pre·tend (prē tend′, pri-) *vt.* [< L *prae-*, before + *tendere*, to stretch] **1** to profess [to *pretend* ignorance] **2** to feign; simulate [to *pretend* anger] **3** to make believe [to *pretend* to be astronauts] —*vi.* to lay claim (*to*) —**pre·tend′er** *n.*

pre·tense (prē tens′, pri-; prē′tens′) *n.* **1** a claim; pretension **2** a false claim **3** a false show of something **4** a pretending, as at play Brit. sp. **pre·tence′**

pre·ten·sion (prē ten′shən, pri-) *n.* **1** a pretext **2** a claim **3** pretentiousness

pre·ten·tious (-shəs) *adj.* **1** making claims to some distinction, importance, etc. **2** affectedly grand; ostentatious —**pre·ten′tious·ly** *adv.* —**pre·ten′tious·ness** *n.*

pret·er·it or **pret·er·ite** (pret′ər it) *adj.* [< L *praeter-*, beyond + *ire*, go] *Gram.* expressing past action or state —*n.* the past tense

pre·term (prē′turm′) *adj.* of premature birth

pre·ter·nat·u·ral (prēt′ər nach′ər əl) *adj.* [ML *praeternaturalis*] **1** differing from or beyond what is natural; abnormal **2** SUPERNATURAL

pre·test (prē test′) *vt., vi.* to test in advance

pre·text (prē′tekst′) *n.* [< L *prae-*, before + *texere*, weave] a false reason put forth to hide the real one

Pre·to·ri·a (prē tôr′ē ə) administrative capital of South Africa

pret·ti·fy (prit′i fī′) *vt.* **-fied′, -fy′ing** to make pretty

pret·ty (prit′ē) *adj.* **-ti·er, -ti·est** [OE *prættig*, crafty] attractive in a dainty, graceful way —*adv.* fairly; somewhat —*vt.* **-tied, -ty·ing** to make pretty: usually with *up* —**pret′ti·ly** *adv.* —**pret′ti·ness** *n.*

pret·zel (pret′səl) *n.* [< L *brachium*, an arm] a hard, salted biscuit, often formed in a loose knot

pre·vail (prē vāl′, pri-) *vi.* [< L *prae-*, before + *valere*, be strong] **1** to be victorious; triumph: often with *over* or *against* **2** to succeed **3** to be or become more widespread **4** to be prevalent —**prevail on** (or **upon** or **with**) to persuade

pre·vail·ing *adj.* **1** superior in strength or influence **2** prevalent

prev·a·lent (prev′ə lənt) *adj.* [see PREVAIL] widely existing; generally accepted, used, etc. —**prev′a·lence** *n.*

pre·var·i·cate (pri var′i kāt′) *vi.* **-cat′ed, -cat′ing** [< L *prae-*, before + *varicare*, straddle] **1** to evade the truth **2** to lie —**pre·var′i·ca′tion** *n.* —**pre·var′i·ca′tor** *n.*

pre·vent (prē vent′, pri-) *vt.* [< L *prae-*, before + *venire*, come] to stop or keep from doing or happening; hinder —**pre·vent′a·ble** *adj.,* **pre·vent′i·ble** —**pre·ven′tion** *n.*

pre·ven·tive (-vent′iv) *adj.* preventing or serving to prevent —*n.* anything that prevents Also **pre·vent′a·tive** (-vent′ə tiv)

pre·view (prē′vyōō′) *n.* **1** an advance, restricted showing, as of a movie **2** a showing of scenes from a movie, etc. to advertise it

pre·vi·ous (prē′vē əs) *adj.* [< L *prae-*, before + *via*, a way] occurring before; prior —**previous to** before —**pre′vi·ous·ly** *adv.*

pre·war (prē′wôr′) *adj.* before a (or the) war

prex·y (prek′sē) *n., pl.* **-ies** [Slang] the president, esp. of a college, etc.

prey (prā) *n.* [< L *prehendere*, seize] 1 an animal hunted for food by another animal 2 a victim 3 the mode of living by preying on other animals [a bird of *prey*] —*vi.* 1 to plunder 2 to hunt other animals for food 3 to weigh as an obsession Generally used with *on* or *upon*

pri·ap·ic (prī ap′ik) *adj.* [after *Priapos*, Gr god of procreation] 1 of a phallus 2 of exaggerated masculine sexuality

price (prīs) *n.* [< L *pretium*] 1 the amount of money, etc. asked or paid for something; cost 2 value or worth 3 the cost, as in life, labor, etc., of obtaining some benefit —*vt.* **priced, pric′ing** 1 to fix the price of 2 [Inf.] to find out the price of

price·less *adj.* of inestimable value; invaluable

pric·y *adj.* **pric′i·er, pric′i·est** [Inf.] expensive: also sp. **pric′ey**

prick (prik) *n.* [OE *prica*, a point] 1 a tiny puncture made by a sharp point 2 a sharp pain caused as by being pricked —*vt.* 1 to make (a hole) in (something) with a sharp point 2 to pain sharply —**prick up one's ears** 1 to raise the ears erect 2 to listen closely

prick·le (prik′əl) *n.* [OE *prica*, a point] 1 a small, sharply pointed growth, as a thorn: also **prick′er** 2 a tingling sensation *vt., vi.* **-led, -ling** to tingle

prick·ly (prik′lē) *adj.* **-li·er, -li·est** 1 full of prickles 2 stinging; smarting; tingling 3 irritable or argumentative —**prick′li·ness** *n.*

prickly heat a skin eruption caused by inflammation of the sweat glands

pride (prīd) *n.* [< OE *prut*, proud] 1 *a)* an unduly high opinion of oneself *b)* haughtiness; arrogance 2 dignity and self-respect 3 satisfaction in something done, owned, etc. 4 a person or thing in which pride is taken 5 a group or family: said of lions —**pride oneself on** to be proud of —**pride′ful** *adj.*

pri·er (prī′ər) *n.* one who pries

priest (prēst) *n.* [< Gr *presbys*, old] 1 a person of special rank who performs religious rites in a temple of God or a god 2 *R.C.Ch.* a clergyman ranking next below a bishop —**priest′-hood′** *n.* —**priest′ly** *adj.* **-li·er, -li·est**

priest·ess (prēs′tis) *n.* a pagan female priest

prig (prig) *n.* [?] one who smugly affects great propriety or morality —**prig′gish** *adj.*

prim (prim) *adj.* **prim′mer, prim′mest** [< ?] stiffly formal, precise, or moral —**prim′ly** *adv.*

pri·ma·cy (prī′mə sē) *n., pl.* **-cies** [< L *primus*, first] 1 a being first in time, rank, etc.; supremacy 2 the rank or office of a primate

pri·ma don·na (prē′mə dän′ə, prim′ə) pl. **pri′-ma don′nas** [It, lit., first lady] 1 the principal woman singer in an opera 2 [Inf.] a vain, temperamental person

pri·ma fa·ci·e (prī′mə fā′shə) [L, lit., at first sight] 1 self-evident 2 *Law* designating evidence that establishes a fact unless refuted

pri·mal (prī′məl) *adj.* [< L *primus*, first] 1 first in time; original 2 first in importance; chief 3 fundamental; basic [*primal* instincts]

pri·mar·i·ly (prī mer′ə lē) *adv.* 1 at first; originally 2 mainly; principally

pri·mar·y (prī′mer′ē) *adj.* [< L *primus*, first] 1 first in time or order; original 2 from which others are derived; fundamental [*primary* colors] 3 first in importance; chief —*n., pl.* **-ries** 1 something first in order, importance, etc. 2 a preliminary election at which candidates are chosen for the final election

primary school 1 ELEMENTARY SCHOOL 2 a school including the first three elementary grades and, sometimes, kindergarten

primary stress (or accent) the heaviest stress (′) in pronouncing a word

pri·mate (prī′mit; *for* 2, -māt′) *n.* [< L *primus*, first] 1 an archbishop, or the highest-ranking bishop in a province, etc. 2 any of the order of mammals that includes humans, the apes, monkeys, etc.

prime (prīm) *adj.* [< L *primus*, first] 1 first in time; original 2 first in rank or importance; chief; principal 3 first in quality 4 fundamental 5 *Math.* that can be evenly divided by no other whole number than itself and 1 —*n.* 1 the first or earliest part 2 the best or most vigorous period 3 the best part —*vt.* **primed, prim′ing** 1 to make ready; prepare 2 to get (a pump) into operation by pouring water into it 3 to apply an undercoat, as of size, before painting 4 to provide with facts, answers, etc. beforehand

prime meridian the meridian at Greenwich, England, from which longitude is measured east and west

prime minister in some countries, the chief executive of the government

prim·er¹ (prim′ər) *n.* [< L *primus*, first] 1 a simple book for teaching reading 2 any elementary textbook

prim·er² (prī′mər) *n.* a thing that primes; specif., *a)* an explosive cap, etc. used to set off a main charge *b)* a preliminary coat of paint, etc.

prime rate the most favorable interest rate charged on bank loans to large corporations: also **prime interest rate** or **prime lending rate**

prime time *Radio*, TV the hours when the largest audience is available

pri·me·val (prī mē′vəl) *adj.* [< L *primus*, first + *aevum*, an age] of the earliest times or ages; primordial

prim·i·tive (prim′i tiv) *adj.* [< L *primus*, first] 1 of the earliest times; original 2 crude; simple 3 primary; basic —*n.* a primitive person or thing

pri·mo·gen·i·ture (prī′mə jen′i chər) *n.* [< L *primus*, first + *genitura*, a begetting] the exclusive right of inheritance of the eldest son

pri·mor·di·al (prī môr′dē əl) *adj.* [< L *primus*, first + *ordiri*, begin] primitive; fundamental

primp (primp) *vt., vi.* ⟦prob. < PRIM⟧ to groom or dress up in a fussy way

prim·rose (prim′rōz′) *n.* ⟦altered (after *rose*) < ML *primula*⟧ a plant with tubelike, often yellow flowers

primrose path 1 the path of pleasure, self-indulgence, etc. **2** a course of action that seems easy but that can lead to disaster

prince (prins) *n.* ⟦< L *princeps*, chief⟧ **1** a ruler ranking below a king; head of a principality **2** a son of a sovereign **3** any preeminent person

prince consort the husband of a reigning queen

Prince Edward Island island province of SE Canada; cap. Charlottetown: abbrev. *PE*

prince·ly *adj.* **-li·er, -li·est** of a prince **2** magnificent; generous —**prince′li·ness** *n.*

prin·cess (prin′sis, -ses′) *n.* **1** a daughter of a sovereign **2** the wife of a prince

prin·ci·pal (prin′sə pəl) *adj.* ⟦see PRINCE⟧ first in rank, importance, etc. —*n.* **1** a principal person or thing **2** the head of a school **3** the amount of a loan, on which interest is computed —**prin′ci·pal·ly** *adv.*

prin·ci·pal·i·ty (-pal′ə tē) *n., pl.* **-ties** the territory ruled by a prince

principal parts the principal inflected forms of a verb: in English, the infinitive, past tense, and past participle (Ex: *drink, drank, drunk*)

prin·ci·ple (prin′sə pəl) *n.* ⟦see PRINCE⟧ **1** a fundamental truth, law, etc. upon which others are based **2** *a*) a rule of conduct *b*) adherence to such rules; integrity **3** *a*) the scientific law explaining a natural action *b*) the method of a thing's operation

prin·ci·pled *adj.* having principles, as of conduct

print (print) *n.* ⟦< L *premere*, to press⟧ **1** a mark made on a surface by pressing or stamping **2** cloth printed with a design **3** the impression of letters, designs, etc. made by inked type or from a plate, block, etc. **4** a photograph, esp. one made from a negative — *vt., vi.* **1** to stamp (a mark, letter, etc.) on a surface **2** to produce on (paper, etc.) the impression of inked type, etc. **3** to produce (a book, etc.) **4** to write in letters resembling printed ones **5** to make (a photographic print) —**in** (or **out of**) **print** still (or no longer) being sold by the publisher: said of books, etc. —**print′a·ble** *adj.* —**print′er** *n.*

printed circuit an electrical circuit of conductive material, as in fine lines, applied to an insulating sheet

print·ing *n.* **1** the act of one that prints **2** something printed **3** all the copies printed at one time

printing press a machine for printing from inked type, plates, or rolls

print-out *n.* a paper copy of computer output, made by a printer

pri·or (prī′ər) *adj.* ⟦L⟧ **1** earlier; previous **2** preceding in order or importance —*n.* the head of a priory —**prior to** before in time

pri·or·ess (-is) *n.* a woman who heads a priory of nuns

pri·or·i·tize (prī ôr′ə tīz′) *vt.* **-tized′, -tiz′ing** to arrange (items) in order of importance

pri·or·i·ty (prī ôr′ə tē) *n., pl.* **-ties 1** a being prior; precedence **2** a prior right to get, buy, or do something **3** something more urgent or important

pri·o·ry (prī′ə rē) *n., pl.* **-ries** a monastery governed by a prior, or a convent governed by a prioress

prism (priz′əm) *n.* ⟦< Gr *prizein*, to saw⟧ **1** *Geom.* a solid figure whose ends are parallel and equal in size and shape, and whose sides are parallelograms **2** a transparent, triangular prism used to disperse light into the spectrum —**pris·mat·ic** (priz mat′ik) *adj.*

pris·on (priz′ən) *n.* ⟦< L *prehendere*, take⟧ a place of confinement for convicted criminals or persons who are awaiting trial

prison camp 1 a camp with minimum security for holding reliable prisoners **2** a camp for confining prisoners of war

pris·on·er *n.* one held captive or confined, esp. in prison

pris·sy (pris′ē) *adj.* **-si·er, -si·est** ⟦prob. PR(IM) + (S)ISSY⟧ [Inf.] very prim or prudish —**pris′si·ness** *n.*

pris·tine (pris′tēn′, pris tēn′) *adj.* ⟦L *pristinus*, former⟧ **1** characteristic of the earliest period **2** unspoiled

prith·ee (prith′ē) *interj.* ⟦< *pray thee*⟧ [Archaic] I pray thee; please

pri·va·cy (prī′və sē) *n., pl.* **-cies 1** a being private; seclusion **2** secrecy **3** one's private life

pri·vate (prī′vət) *adj.* ⟦< L *privus*, separate⟧ **1** of or concerning a particular person or group **2** not open to or controlled by the public [a *private* school] **3** for an individual person [a *private* room] **4** not holding public office [a *private* citizen] **5** secret [a *private* matter] —*n.* **1** [*pl.*] the genitals: also **private parts 2** an enlisted person of the lowest rank in either the U.S. Army or Marine Corps —**go private** to restore private corporate ownership by buying back publicly held stock —**in private** not publicly —**pri′vate·ly** *adv.*

pri·va·teer (prī′və tir′) *n.* **1** a privately owned ship commissioned in war to capture enemy ships **2** a commander or crew member of a privateer

private eye [Slang] a private detective

pri·va·tion (prī vā′shən) *n.* the lack of ordinary necessities or comforts

pri·va·tize (prī′və tīz′) *vt.* **-tized′, -tiz′ing** to turn over (a public property, etc.) to private interests —**pri′va·ti·za′tion** *n.*

priv·et (priv′it) *n.* ⟦< ?⟧ an evergreen shrub used for hedges

priv·i·lege (priv′ə lij, priv′lij) *n.* ⟦< L *privus*, separate + *lex*, law⟧ a special right, favor, etc. granted to some person or group —*vt.* **-leged, -leg·ing** to grant a privilege to

priv·y (priv′ē) *adj.* private: now only in such phrases as **privy council**, a body of confidential advisers named by a ruler —*n., pl.* **priv′ies** an outhouse —**privy to** privately informed about

prize¹ (prīz) *vt.* **prized, priz′ing** [see PRICE] to value highly; esteem —*n.* **1** something given to the winner of a contest, etc. **2** anything worth striving for —*adj.* **1** that has won or is worthy of a prize **2** given as a prize

prize² (prīz) *n.* [< L *prehendere*, to take] something taken by force, esp. a captured ship —*vt.* **prized, priz′ing** to pry, as with a lever

prize·fight *n.* a professional boxing match —**prize′fight′er** *n.*

pro¹ (prō) *adv.* [L, for] favorably —*adj.* favorable —*n., pl.* **pros** **1** a person or vote on the affirmative side **2** an argument in favor of something

pro² (prō) *adj., n., pl.* **pros** *short for* PROFESSIONAL

pro-¹ [Gr < *pro*, before] *prefix* before in place or time

pro-² [L < *pro*, forward] *prefix* **1** moving forward or ahead of [*proclivity*] **2** forth [*produce*] **3** substituting for [*pronoun*] **4** defending, supporting [*prolabor*]

pro-am (prō′am′) *n.* a sports competition for both amateurs and professionals

prob *abbrev.* **1** probably **2** problem

prob·a·bil·i·ty (präb′ə bil′ə tē) *n., pl.* **-ties** **1** a being probable; likelihood **2** something probable **3** *Math.* degree of likelihood

prob·a·ble (präb′ə bəl) *adj.* [< L *probare*, prove] **1** likely to occur or be **2** reasonably so, but not proved —**prob′a·bly** *adv.*

pro·bate (prō′bāt′) *n.* [see PROBE] the act or process of probating —*adj.* having to do with probating [*probate* court] —*vt.* **-bat′ed, -bat′ing** to establish officially that (a document, esp. a will) is genuine

pro·ba·tion (prō bā′shən) *n.* [see PROBE] **1** a testing, as of one's character, ability, etc. **2** the conditional suspension of a convicted person's sentence **3** the status of being allowed to prove one's worthiness, etc. —**pro·ba′tion·ar′y** *adj.*

pro·ba·tion·er *n.* a person on probation

probation officer an officer who watches over persons on probation

probe (prōb) *n.* [< L *probare*, to test] **1** a surgical instrument for exploring a wound, etc. **2** a searching examination **3** a device, as a spacecraft with instruments, used to get information about an environment —*vt.* **probed, prob′ing** **1** to explore (a wound, etc.) with a probe **2** to investigate thoroughly —*vi.* to search

pro·bi·ty (prō′bə tē, präb′ə-) *n.* [< L *probus,* good] honesty; integrity

prob·lem (präb′ləm) *n.* [< Gr *problēma*] **1** a question proposed for solution **2** a perplexing or difficult matter, person, etc.

prob·lem·at·ic (präb′lə mat′ik) *adj.* **1** hard to solve **2** uncertain

pro·bos·cis (prō bäs′is) *n., pl.* **-cis·es** [< Gr *pro-*, before + *boskein*, to feed] an elephant's trunk, or any similar long, flexible snout

pro·caine (prō′kān′) *n.* [PRO-² + (CO)CAINE] a synthetic compound used as a local anesthetic

pro·ce·dure (prō sē′jər, prə-) *n.* the act or method of proceeding in an action —**pro·ce′dur·al** *adj.*

pro·ceed (prō sēd′, prə-) *vi.* [< L *pro-*, forward + *cedere*, go] **1** to go on, esp. after stopping **2** to carry on some action **3** to take legal action (*against*) **4** to come forth or issue (*from*)

pro·ceed·ing *n.* **1** a going on with what one has been doing **2** a course of action **3** [*pl.*] a record of the business carried on, as by a learned society **4** [*pl.*] legal action

pro·ceeds (prō′sēdz′) *pl.n.* the sum derived from a sale, business venture, etc.

proc·ess (prä′ses′) *n.* [see PROCEED] **1** the course of being done: chiefly in **in process 2** course (*of* time, etc.) **3** a continuing development involving many changes [the *process* of digestion] **4** a method of doing something, with all the steps involved **5** *Biol.* a projecting part **6** *Law* a court summons —*vt.* to prepare by or subject to a special process —**pro′cess·or** *n.*

pro·ces·sion (prō sesh′ən, prə-) *n.* [see PROCEED] a number of persons or things moving forward, as in a parade

pro·ces·sion·al *n.* a hymn sung at the beginning of a church service during the entrance of the clergy

pro-choice *adj.* advocating the legal right to obtain an abortion —**pro′-choic′er** *n.*

pro·claim (prō klām′) *vt.* [< L *pro-*, before + *clamare*, cry out] to announce officially; announce to be

proc·la·ma·tion (präk′lə mā′shən) *n.* **1** a proclaiming **2** something that is proclaimed

pro·cliv·i·ty (prō kliv′ə tē) *n., pl.* **-ties** [< L *pro-*, before + *clivus*, a slope] a tendency or inclination

pro·cras·ti·nate (prō kras′tə nāt′) *vi., vt.* **-nat′ed, -nat′ing** [< L *pro-*, forward + *cras,* tomorrow] to put off doing (something) until later; delay —**pro·cras′ti·na′tion** *n.* —**pro·cras′ti·na′tor** *n.*

pro·cre·ate (prō′krē āt′) *vt., vi.* **-at′ed, -at′ing** [< L *pro-*, before + *creare*, create] to produce (young); beget (offspring) —**pro′cre·a′tion** *n.*

proc·tor (präk′tər) *n.* [see PROCURE] one who supervises students, as at an examination —*vt.* to supervise (an academic examination)

proc·u·ra·tor (präk′yōō rāt′ər) *n.* [see fol.] in the Roman Empire, the governor of a lesser province

pro·cure (prō kyoor′) *vt.* **-cured′, -cur′ing** [< L *pro-*, before + *curare*, attend to] to obtain; get —**pro·cur′a·ble** *adj.* —**pro·cure′ment** *n.*

pro·cur·er *n.* a pimp

prod (präd) *vt.* **prod′ded, prod′ding** [< ?] **1** to jab as with a pointed stick **2** to goad into action —*n.* **1** a jab or thrust **2** something that prods

prod·i·gal (präd′i gəl) *adj.* [< L *pro-*, forth + *agere*, to drive] **1** exceedingly or recklessly wasteful 2 extremely abundant —*n.* a spend-thrift —**prod'i·gal'i·ty** (-gal'ə tē) *n., pl.* **-ties**

pro·di·gious (prō dij'əs, prə-) *adj.* [see fol.] 1 wonderful; amazing 2 enormous; huge —**pro·di'gious·ly** *adv.*

prod·i·gy (präd'ə jē) *n., pl.* **-gies** [< L *prodigium,* omen] 1 a child having extraordinary talent 2 an extraordinary person, thing, or act

pro·duce (prə doos'; *for n.* prō'doos') *vt.* **-duced', -duc'ing** [< L *pro-,* forward + *ducere,* to lead] 1 to bring to view; show [to *produce* an ID card] 2 to bring forth; bear 3 to make or manufacture 4 to cause 5 to get (a play, etc.) ready for presentation —*vi.* to yield something —*n.* something produced; esp., fruit and vegetables —**pro·duc'er** *n.*

prod·uct (präd'əkt) *n.* 1 something produced by nature, industry, or art 2 result; outgrowth 3 *Math.* the quantity obtained by multiplying two or more quantities together

pro·duc·tion (prə duk'shən) *n.* a producing or something produced

pro·duc·tive *adj.* 1 fertile 2 marked by abundant production 3 bringing as a result (with *of*) [war is *productive* of misery] —**pro·duc'tive·ly** *adv.* —**pro·duc·tiv·i·ty** (prō'dək tiv'ə tē) *n.,* pro·duc'tive·ness

prof (präf) *n.* [Inf.] *short for* PROFESSOR

Prof *abbrev.* Professor

pro·fane (prō fān') *adj.* [< L *pro-,* before + *fanum,* temple] 1 not connected with religion; secular 2 showing disrespect or contempt for sacred things —*vt.* **-faned', -fan'ing** 1 to treat (sacred things) with irreverence or contempt 2 to debase; defile —**prof·a·na·tion** (präf'ə nā'shən) *n.* —**pro·fane'ly** *adv.* —**pro·fane'ness** *n.*

pro·fan·i·ty (-fan'ə tē) *n.* 1 a being profane 2 *pl.* **-ties** profane language; swearing

pro·fess (prō fes', prə-) *vt.* [< L *pro-,* before + *fateri,* avow] 1 to declare openly; affirm 2 to claim to have (some feeling, etc.): often insincerely 3 to declare one's belief in —**pro·fessed'** *adj.*

pro·fes·sion (prō fesh'ən, prə-) *n.* 1 a professing, or declaring; avowal 2 an occupation requiring advanced academic training, as medicine, law, etc. 3 all the persons in such an occupation

pro·fes·sion·al *adj.* 1 of or engaged in a profession 2 engaged in some sport or in a specified occupation for pay —*n.* a person who is professional —**pro·fes'sion·al·ly** *adv.*

pro·fes·sor (prō fes'ər, prə-) *n.* a college or university teacher, esp. one of the highest rank —**pro·fes·so·ri·al** (prō'fə sôr'ē əl, prä'-) *adj.* —**pro·fes'sor·ship'** *n.*

prof·fer (präf'ər) *vt.* [< OFr: see PRO-² & OFFER] to offer (usually something intangible) [to *proffer* friendship] —*n.* an offer

pro·fi·cient (prō fish'ənt, prə-) *adj.* [< L *pro-,* forward + *facere,* make] highly competent; skilled —**pro·fi'cien·cy** *n.* —**pro·fi'cient·ly** *adv.*

pro·file (prō'fīl') *n.* [< It *profilare,* to out-line] 1 a side view of the face 2 a drawing of this 3 an outline 4 a short, vivid biography 5 a degree of public exposure [keeping a low *profile*] —*vt.* 1 to draw or write a profile 2 to identify or single out by profiling

pro·fil·ing *n.* the use of a set of characteristics to identify those thought likely to belong to a certain group, as in detaining suspected criminals

prof·it (präf'it) *n.* [see PROFICIENT] 1 advantage; gain 2 [*often pl.*] financial gain; esp. the sum remaining after deducting costs —*vt., vi.* 1 to be of advantage (to) 2 to benefit —**prof'it·a·bil'i·ty** *n.* —**prof'it·a·ble** *adj.* —**prof'it·a·bly** *adv.* —**prof'it·less** *adj.*

prof·it·eer (präf'i tir') *n.* one who makes excessive profits by charging exorbitant prices —*vi.* to be a profiteer

pro·fi·te·role (prə fit'ə rōl') *n.* a small cream puff

prof·li·gate (präf'li git) *adj.* [< L *pro-,* forward + *fligere,* to drive] 1 dissolute 2 recklessly wasteful —**prof'li·ga·cy** (-gə sē) *n.*

pro for·ma (prō fôr'mə) [L] for (the sake of) form; as a matter of form

pro·found (prō found', prə-) *adj.* [< L *pro-,* forward + *fundus,* bottom] 1 marked by intellectual depth 2 deeply felt [*profound* grief] 3 thoroughgoing [*profound* changes] —**pro·found'ly** *adv.* —**pro·fun·di·ty** (-fun'də tē) *n., pl.* **-ties**

pro·fuse (prō fyoos', prə-) *adj.* [< L *pro-,* forth + *fundere,* pour] giving or given freely and abundantly —**pro·fuse'ly** *adv.* —**pro·fu'sion** (-fyoo'zhən) *n.*

pro·gen·i·tor (prō jen'ə tər) *n.* [< L *pro-,* forth + *gignere,* beget] 1 an ancestor in direct line 2 a precursor

prog·e·ny (präj'ə nē) *n., pl.* **-nies** [see prec.] children; offspring

pro·ges·ter·one (prō jes'tər ōn') *n.* a female hormone secreted by the ovary or made synthetically

prog·na·thous (präg'nə thəs) *adj.* [PRO-¹ + Gr *gnathos,* jaw] having the jaws projecting beyond the upper face

prog·no·sis (präg nō'sis) *n., pl.* **-no'ses'** (-sēz') [< Gr *pro-,* before + *gignōskein,* know] a prediction, esp. of the course of a disease

prog·nos·tic (-näs'tik) *adj.* [see prec.] 1 foretelling 2 of a medical prognosis

prog·nos·ti·cate (-näs'ti kāt') *vt.* **-cat'ed, -cat'ing** [see PROGNOSIS] to foretell —**prog·nos'ti·ca'tion** *n.* —**prog·nos'ti·ca'tor** *n.*

pro·gram (prō'gram', -grəm) *n.* [< Gr *pro-,* before + *graphein,* write] 1 a list of the acts, speeches, musical pieces, etc. as of an entertainment 2 a plan or procedure 3 a scheduled radio or TV broadcast 4 a logical sequence of coded instructions specifying operations to be performed as by a computer —*vt.* **-grammed'** or **-gramed', -gram'ming** or **-gram'ing** 1 to schedule in a program 2 to prepare (a textbook, etc.) for use in programmed instruction **3** to write a computer program for **4** to furnish (a computer) with a program Also [Chiefly Brit.] **pro′gramme′** —**pro·gram·ma·ble** (prō′gram′ə bəl, prō gram′-) *adj.*, *n.* —**pro′gram′mer** *n.*, **pro′ gram′er**

pro·gram·mat·ic (prō′grə mat′ik) *adj.* of or like a program; often, specif., predictable, mechanical, uninspired, etc.

prog·ress (präg′res; *for v.* prō gres′, prə-) *n.* ⟦< L *pro-*, before + *gradi*, to step⟧ **1** a moving forward or onward **2** development **3** improvement —*vi.* **1** to move forward or onward **2** to move forward toward completion **3** to improve

pro·gres·sion (prō gresh′ən, prə-) *n.* **1** a moving forward **2** a succession, as of events **3** *Math.* a series of numbers, each of which is obtained from its predecessor by the same rule

pro·gres·sive (-gres′iv, prə-) *adj.* **1** moving forward **2** continuing by successive steps **3** of or favoring progress, reform, etc. **4** *Gram.* indicating continuing action or state, as certain verb forms —*n.* one who is politically progressive —**pro·gres′sive·ly** *adv.*

pro·hib·it (prō hib′it, prə-) *vt.* ⟦< L *pro-*, before + *habere*, have⟧ **1** to forbid by law or an order **2** to prevent; hinder —**pro·hib′i·tive** *adj.*

pro·hi·bi·tion (prō′i bish′ən) *n.* **1** a prohibiting **2** the forbidding by law of the manufacture or sale of alcoholic beverages —**pro′hi·bi′tion·ist** *n.*

proj·ect (prä′jekt′; *for v.* prō jekt′, prə-) *n.* ⟦< L *pro-*, before + *jacere*, to throw⟧ **1** a proposal; scheme **2** an organized undertaking —*vt.* **pro·ject′ 1** to propose (a plan) **2** to throw forward **3** to cause to jut out **4** to cause (a shadow, image, etc.) to fall upon a surface —*vi.* to jut out —**pro·jec′tion** *n.*

pro·jec·tile (prō jek′təl, prə-; -til′) *n.* **1** an object designed to be shot forward, as a bullet **2** anything thrown or hurled forward —*adj.* thrown or shot

projection booth a small chamber, as in a theater, from which images on film, slides, etc. are projected

pro·jec·tion·ist *n.* the operator of a projector ·

pro·jec·tor *n.* a machine for projecting images onto a screen

pro·lapse (prō laps′, prō′laps′) *n.* ⟦L *pro-*, forward + *labi*, to fall⟧ *Med.* the slipping out of place of an internal organ: said as of the uterus

pro·le·tar·i·at (prō′lə ter′ē ət) *n.* ⟦< L *proletarius*, a citizen of the lowest class⟧ the working class; esp., the industrial working class —**pro′ le·tar′i·an** *adj.*, *n.*

pro-life *adj.* opposing the legal right to abortion —**pro′-lif′er** *n.*

pro·lif·er·ate (prō lif′ər āt′, prə-) *vi.* **-at′ ed, -at′ing** ⟦ult. < L *proles*, offspring + *ferre*, to bear⟧ to increase rapidly —**pro·lif′er·a′ tion** *n.*

pro·lif·ic (prō lif′ik, prə-) *adj.* ⟦< L *proles*,

offspring + *facere*, make⟧ **1** producing many young or much fruit **2** turning out many products of the mind —**pro·lif′i·cal·ly** *adv.*

pro·lix (prō liks′, prō′liks′) *adj.* ⟦< L *prolixus*, extended⟧ wordy or long-winded —**pro·lix′i· ty** *n.*

pro·logue (prō′lôg′) *n.* ⟦< Gr *pro-*, before + *logos*, discourse⟧ **1** an introduction to a poem, play, etc. **2** any preliminary act, event, etc.

pro·long (prō lôŋ′, prə-) *vt.* ⟦< L *pro-*, forth + *longus*, long⟧ to lengthen in time or space —**pro·lon·ga·tion** (prō′lôŋ gā′shən) *n.*

prom (präm) *n.* ⟦< fol.⟧ a dance, as of a particular class in a school

prom·e·nade (präm′ə nād′, -näd′) *n.* ⟦Fr < L *pro-*, forth + *minare*, to herd⟧ **1** a leisurely walk taken for pleasure, display, etc. **2** a public place for walking —*vi.*, *vt.* **-nad′ed, -nad′ ing** to take a promenade (along or through)

Pro·me·the·us (prō mē′thē əs) *n. Gr. Myth.* a Titan who steals fire from heaven for the benefit of humans

pro·me·thi·um (prō mē′thē əm) *n.* ⟦see prec.⟧ a radioactive chemical element, one isotope of which is used as a source of beta rays: symbol, Pm; at. no. 61

prom·i·nent (präm′ə nənt) *adj.* ⟦< L *prominere*, to project⟧ **1** sticking out; projecting **2** noticeable; conspicuous **3** widely and favorably known —**prom′i·nence** *n.* —**prom′i· nent·ly** *adv.*

pro·mis·cu·ous (prō mis′kyoō əs, prə-) *adj.* ⟦< L *pro-*, forth + *miscere*, to mix⟧ **1** consisting of different elements indiscriminately mingled **2** characterized by a lack of discrimination, esp. in sexual liaisons —**prom·is·cu·i· ty** (präm′is kyoō′ə tē) *n.*, *pl.* **-ties** —**pro· mis′cu·ous·ly** *adv.*

prom·ise (präm′is) *n.* ⟦< L *pro-*, forth + *mittere*, send⟧ **1** an agreement to do or not to do something **2** indication, as of a successful future **3** something promised — *vi.*, *vt.* **-ised, -is·ing 1** to make a promise of (something) **2** to give a basis for expecting (something)

Promised Land *Bible* Canaan, promised by God to Abraham and his descendants: Genesis 17:8

prom·is·so·ry (präm′i sôr′ē) *adj.* containing a promise

pro·mo (prō′mō) [Inf.] *adj.* of or engaged in the promotion or advertising of a product, etc. —*n.*, *pl.* **-mos** a recorded announcement, radio or TV commercial, etc. used in advertising, etc.

prom·on·to·ry (präm′ən tôr′ē) *n.*, *pl.* **-ries** ⟦prob. < L *prominere*, to project⟧ a peak of high land that juts out into a body of water; headland

pro·mote (prə ōt′) *vt.* **-mot′ed, -mot′ing** ⟦< L *pro-*, forward + *movere*, to move⟧ **1** to raise to a higher position or rank **2** to further the growth, establishment, sales, etc. of —**pro· mo′tion** *n.* —**pro·mo′tion·al** *adj.*

pro·mot·er *n.* one who begins, organizes, and furthers an undertaking

prompt (prämpt) *adj.* ⟦< L *pro-*, forth + *emere*, take⟧ 1 ready, punctual, etc. 2 done, spoken, etc. without delay —*vt.* 1 to urge into action 2 to remind (a person) of something he or she has forgotten; specif., to help (an actor, etc.) with a cue 3 to inspire —**prompt'er** *n.* —**prompt'ly** *adv.* —**prompt'ness** *n.,* **promp'ti·tude'** *n.*

prom·ul·gate (präm'əl gāt', prō mul'gāt') *vt.* **-gat'ed, -gat'ing** ⟦< L *promulgare*, publish⟧ 1 to make known officially 2 to make widespread —**prom'ul·ga'tion** *n.*

pron *abbrev.* 1 pronoun 2 pronunciation

prone (prōn) *adj.* ⟦< L *pronus*⟧ 1 lying face downward or prostrate 2 disposed or inclined (*to*) [*prone to* error]

prong (prôŋ) *n.* ⟦ME *pronge*⟧ 1 any of the pointed ends of a fork; tine 2 any projecting part —**pronged** *adj.*

prong·horn *n.* an animal of the W U.S. having curved horns and resembling both the deer and the antelope

pro·noun (prō'noun') *n.* ⟦< L *pro*, for + *nomen*, noun⟧ *Gram.* a word used in place of a noun (Ex.: *I, he, them, ours, which, yourself, anyone*) —**pro·nom'i·nal** (-näm'i nəl) *adj.*

pro·nounce (prə nouns', prō-) *vt.* **-nounced', -nounc'ing** ⟦< L *pro-*, before + *nuntiare*, announce⟧ 1 to declare officially, solemnly, etc. 2 to utter or articulate (a sound or word) —**pro·nounce'a·ble** *adj.*

pro·nounced *adj.* clearly marked; decided [a *pronounced* change]

pro·nounce·ment *n.* a formal statement, as of an opinion

pron·to (prän'tō) *adv.* ⟦Sp: see PROMPT⟧ [Slang] at once; quickly

pro·nun·ci·a·tion (prə nun'sē ā'shən, prō-) *n.* 1 the act or manner of pronouncing words 2 an accepted way of pronouncing a word; also, a rendering of this in symbols

proof (prōōf) *n.* ⟦see PROBE⟧ 1 a proving or testing of something 2 evidence that establishes the truth of something 3 the relative strength of an alcoholic liquor 4 *Photog.* a trial print of a negative 5 a sheet printed from set type, for checking errors, etc. —*adj.* of tested strength in resisting: with *against*

-proof (prōōf) ⟦< prec.⟧ *combining form* 1 impervious to [*waterproof*] 2 protected from or resistant to [*fireproof*]

proof·read (-rēd') *vt., vi.* to read and mark corrections on (printers' proofs, etc.) —**proof'read'er** *n.*

prop¹ (präp) *n.* ⟦< MDu *proppe*⟧ a support, as a pole, placed under or against something: often used figuratively —*vt.* **propped, prop'ping** 1 to support with or as with a prop: often with *up* 2 to lean (something) *against* a support

prop² (präp) *n.* short for PROPERTY (*n.* 4)

prop³ (präp) *n.* short for PROPELLER

prop⁴ *abbrev.* 1 proper(ly) 2 property 3 proposition 4 proprietor

prop·a·gan·da (präp'ə gan'də) *n.* ⟦ModL: see fol.⟧ 1 any widespread promotion of particular ideas, doctrines, etc. 2 ideas, etc. so spread —**prop'a·gan'dist** *n., adj.* —**prop'a·gan'dize'** (-dīz') *vt., vi.* **-dized', -diz'ing**

prop·a·gate (präp'ə gāt') *vt.* **-gat'ed, -gat'ing** ⟦< L *propago*, slip (of a plant)⟧ 1 to cause (a plant or animal) to reproduce itself 2 to reproduce (itself): said of a plant or animal 3 to spread (ideas, customs, etc.) —*vi.* to reproduce: said of plants or animals —**prop'a·ga'tion** *n.*

pro·pane (prō'pān') *n.* a gaseous hydrocarbon obtained from petroleum, used as a fuel

pro·pel (prə pel', prō-) *vt.* **-pelled', -pel'ling** ⟦< L *pro-*, forward + *pellere*, to drive⟧ to drive onward or forward

pro·pel·lant or **pro·pel·lent** *n.* one that propels; specif., the fuel for a rocket

pro·pel·ler *n.* a device having two or more blades in a revolving hub, for propelling a ship or aircraft

pro·pen·si·ty (prə pen'sə tē) *n., pl.* **-ties** ⟦< L *propendere*, hang forward⟧ a natural inclination or tendency

prop·er (präp'ər) *adj.* ⟦< L *proprius*, one's own⟧ 1 specially suitable; appropriate; fitting 2 naturally belonging (*to*) 3 conforming to a standard; correct 4 decent; decorous 5 in the most restricted sense [*Chicago proper* (i.e., apart from its suburbs)] 6 designating a noun that names a specific individual, place, etc. (Ex.: *Bill, Paris*) —**prop'er·ly** *adv.*

prop·er·ty (präp'ər tē) *n., pl.* **-ties** ⟦see prec.⟧ 1 ownership 2 something owned, esp. real estate 3 a characteristic or attribute 4 any of the movable articles used in a play, movie, etc. —**prop'er·tied** (-tēd) *adj.*

proph·e·cy (präf'ə sē) *n., pl.* **-cies** ⟦see PROPHET⟧ 1 prediction of the future, as by divine guidance 2 something predicted

proph·e·sy (-sī') *vt., vi.* **-sied', -sy'ing** 1 to predict as by divine guidance 2 to predict in any way

proph·et (präf'it) *n.* ⟦< Gr *pro-*, before + *phanai*, speak⟧ 1 a religious leader regarded as, or claiming to be, divinely inspired 2 one who predicts the future 3 [**P-**] *Islam* Muhammad

proph·et·ess (präf'i tis) *n.* a woman who is a prophet: a dated term

pro·phet·ic (prə fet'ik, prō-) *adj.* 1 of or like a prophet 2 like or containing a prophecy —**pro·phet'i·cal·ly** *adv.*

pro·phy·lac·tic (prō'fə lak'tik) *adj.* ⟦< Gr *pro-*, before + *phylassein*, to guard⟧ preventive or protective; esp., preventing disease —*n.* 1 a prophylactic medicine, device, etc. 2 a condom

pro·phy·lax·is (-lak'sis) *n., pl.* **-lax·es'** (-sēz') 1 prophylactic treatment 2 *Dentistry* a cleaning of the teeth to remove plaque and tartar

pro·pin·qui·ty (prō piŋ'kwə tē) *n.* ⟦< L *propinquus*, near⟧ nearness

pro·pi·ti·ate (prō pish'ē āt', prə-) *vt.* **-at'ed, -at'ing** ⟦see fol.⟧ to win the good will of; appease —**pro·pi'ti·a'tion** *n.* —**pro·pi'ti·a·to'ry** (-ē ə tôr'ē) *adj.*

pro·pi·tious (prō pish′əs, prə-) *adj.* [< L *pro-*, before + *petere*, seek] 1 favorably inclined 2 favorable; auspicious

prop·jet *n.* TURBOPROP

pro·po·nent (prə pō′nənt, prō-) *n.* [see PROPOSE] one who espouses or supports a cause, etc.

pro·por·tion (prə pôr′shən, prō-) *n.* [< L *pro,* for + *portio,* a part] 1 the comparative relation in size, amount, etc. between things; ratio 2 a part, share, etc. in its relation to the whole 3 balance or symmetry 4 [*pl.*] dimensions —*vt.* 1 to put in proper relation with something else 2 to arrange the parts of (a whole) so as to be harmonious —**pro·por′tion·al** *adj.* —*n.,* **pro·por′tion·ate** (-shə nit) *adj.*

pro·pos·al (prə pōz′əl) *n.* 1 a proposing 2 a proposed plan, etc. 3 an offer of marriage

pro·pose (prə pōz′) *vt.* -**posed′,** -**pos′ing** [< L *pro-,* forth + *ponere,* to place] 1 to put forth for consideration, approval, etc. 2 to plan or intend —*vi.* to offer marriage

prop·o·si·tion (präp′ə zish′ən) *n.* 1 something proposed; plan 2 a proposed deal, as in business 3 an undertaking, etc. to be dealt with 4 a subject to be discussed 5 *Math.* a problem to be solved —*vt.* to propose sexual relations with

pro·pound (prə pound′, prō-) *vt.* [see PROPOSE] to put forward for consideration

pro·pri·e·tar·y (prə prī′ə tər ē, prō-) *adj.* [see PROPERTY] belonging to a proprietor, as under a patent, trademark, or copyright

pro·pri·e·tor *n.* an owner, as of a business —**pro·pri′e·tor·ship′** *n.*

pro·pri·e·ty (-tē) *n., pl.* -**ties** [see PROPER] 1 the quality of being proper, fitting, etc. 2 conformity with accepted standards of behavior

pro·pul·sion (prə pul′shən) *n.* [see PROPEL] 1 a propelling or being propelled 2 something that propels —**pro·pul′sive** *adj.*

pro·rate (prō rāt′, prō′rāt′) *vt., vi.* -**rat′ed,** -**rat′ing** [< L *pro rata,* in proportion] to divide or assess proportionally

pro·sa·ic (prō zā′ik) *adj.* [< L *prosa,* prose] commonplace; dull

pro·sce·ni·um (prō sē′nē əm) *n., pl.* -**ni·ums** or -**ni·a** (-ə) [< Gr *pro-,* before + *skēnē,* tent] in a theater, the portion of the stage in front of the arch (**proscenium arch**) within which the curtain is hung

pro·scribe (prō skrīb′) *vt.* -**scribed′,** -**scrib′ing** [< L < *pro-,* before + *scribere,* write] 1 to outlaw 2 to banish; exile 3 to denounce or forbid the use, etc. of —**pro·scrip′tion** (-skrip′shən) *n.*

prose (prōz) *n.* [< L *prorsus,* straight on] ordinary language; writing that is not poetry

pros·e·cute (präs′ə kyōōt′) *vt.* -**cut′ed,** -**cut′ing** [< L *pro-,* before + *sequi,* follow] 1 to carry on 2 to conduct legal action against —**pros′e·cu′tion** *n.* —**pros′e·cu′tor** *n.* —**pros′e·cu·to′ri·al** *adj.*

pros·e·lyte (präs′ə līt′) *n.* [< Gr *prosēlytos,* a stranger] one who has been converted from one religion, sect, etc. to another

pros·e·lyt·ize (präs′ə li tīz′) *vi., vt.* -**ized′,** -**iz′ing** 1 to try to convert (a person), esp. to one's religion 2 to persuade to do or join something —**pros′e·lyt·ism′** (-li tiz′əm) *n.* —**pros′e·lyt·iz′er** *n.*

pro·sim·i·an (prō sim′ē ən) *n.* any of various small, arboreal primates

pros·o·dy (präs′ə dē) *n.* [< Gr *prosōidia,* accent] versification; study of meter, rhyme, etc.

pros·pect (präs′pekt′) *n.* [< L *pro-,* forward + *specere,* to look] 1 a broad view; scene 2 a viewpoint; outlook 3 anticipation 4 *a)* something expected *b)* [*usually pl.*] apparent chance for success 5 a likely customer, candidate, etc. —*vi.* to explore or search (*for*) —**pros′pec′tor** *n.*

pro·spec·tive (prə spek′tiv, prä-, prō-) *adj.* expected; likely

pro·spec·tus (-spek′təs) *n.* [L: see PROSPECT] a statement of the features of a new work, enterprise, etc.

pros·per (präs′pər) *vi.* [< L *prospere,* fortunately] to succeed; thrive

pros·per·i·ty (präs per′ə tē) *n., pl.* -**ties** prosperous condition; wealth

pros·per·ous (präs′pər əs) *adj.* 1 prospering; successful 2 wealthy —**pros′per·ous·ly** *adv.*

pros·tate (präs′tāt′) *adj.* [< Gr *prostatēs,* one standing before] of or designating a gland surrounding the male urethra at the base of the bladder —*n.* this gland: in full **prostate gland**

pros·the·sis (präs thē′sis) *n., pl.* -**ses** (-sēz′) *Med.* 1 the replacement of a missing part of the body, as a limb, by an artificial substitute 2 such a substitute —**pros·thet′ic** (-thet′ik) *adj.* —**pros·thet′ics** *n.*

pros·ti·tute (präs′tə tōōt′) *n.* [< L *pro-,* before + *statuere,* cause to stand] one who engages in promiscuous sexual activity for pay —*vt.* -**tut′ed,** -**tut′ing** 1 to offer (oneself) as a prostitute 2 to sell (oneself, one's talents, etc.) for base purposes —**pros′ti·tu′tion** *n.*

pros·trate (präs′trāt′) *adj.* [< L *pro-,* before + *sternere,* stretch out] 1 lying face downward 2 lying prone or supine 3 laid low; overcome —*vt.* -**trat′ed,** -**trat′ing** 1 to lay flat on the ground 2 to lay low; subjugate —**pros·tra′tion** *n.*

pros·y (prō′zē) *adj.* -**i·er,** -**i·est** prosaic; commonplace, dull, etc.

pro·tac·tin·i·um (prō′tak tin′ē əm) *n.* [PRO-T(O)- + ACTINIUM] a rare, toxic, radioactive, metallic chemical element: symbol, Pa; at. no. 91

pro·tag·o·nist (prō tag′ə nist) *n.* [< Gr *prōtos,* first + *agōnistēs,* actor] the main character in a drama, novel, etc.

pro·te·an (prōt′ē ən, prō tē′ən) *adj.* [after *Proteus,* Gr god who changes his form] readily taking on different forms

pro·tect (prə tekt′, prō-) *vt.* [< L *pro-,* before + *tegere,* to cover] to shield from injury, danger, etc.; defend —**pro·tec′tor** *n.*

pro·tec·tion *n.* 1 a protecting or being protected **2** a person or thing that protects **3** a device, such as a condom, to prevent conception or sexually transmitted diseases **4** [Inf.] money extorted by a racketeer

pro·tec·tive *adj.* **1** protecting **2** *Economics* intended to protect domestic industry from foreign competition [a *protective* tariff] —**pro·tec'tive·ly** *adv.* —**pro·tec'tive·ness** *n.*

pro·tec·tor·ate (-tər it) *n.* a weak state under the control of a strong state

pro·té·gé (prōt′ə zhā′) *n.* [Fr: see PROTECT] a person guided and helped in his or her career by another person

pro·tein (prō'tēn′, prō'tē in) *n.* [< Gr *prōtos,* first] any of numerous nitrogenous substances occurring in all living matter and essential to diet

pro tem·po·re (prō tem'pə rē′) [L] for the time being: shortened to **pro tem**

pro·test (prō test′; *also, and for n. always* prō'test′) *vt.* [< L *pro-,* forth + *testari,* affirm] **1** to state positively **2** to speak strongly against —*vi.* to express disapproval; object —*n.* **1** an objection **2** a formal statement of objection —**prot·es·ta·tion** (prät′es tā'shən) *n.* —**pro'test'er** *n.*

Prot·es·tant (prät'əs tənt) *n.* [see prec.] a member of one of the Christian churches descended from those that split from the Roman Catholic Church in the 1500s —**Prot'es·tant·ism'** *n.*

proto- [< Gr *prōtos,* first] *combining form* **1** first in time, original **2** first in importance, chief

pro·to·col (prōt'ə kôl′) *n.* [< Gr *prōtokollon,* contents page] **1** an original draft of a document, etc. **2** a code of ceremonial forms prescribed for official dealings, as between heads of state **3** a standard procedure for regulating the transmission of data between computers

pro·ton (prō'tän′) *n.* [< Gr *prōtos,* first] an elementary particle in the nucleus of all atoms, carrying a unit positive charge of electricity

pro·to·plasm (prōt'ə plaz'əm) *n.* [see PROTO- & PLASMA] a semifluid, viscous colloid, the essential living matter of all animal and plant cells —**pro'to·plas'mic** (-plaz'mik) *adj.*

pro·to·type (prōt'ə tīp′) *n.* the first thing or being of its kind; model

pro·to·zo·an (prōt'ə zō'ən) *n., pl.* **-zo'a** (-ə) [< Gr *prōtos,* first + *zōion,* an animal] any of various microscopic, single-celled animals: also **pro'to·zo'on'** (-än′), *pl.* **-zo'a** (-ə)

pro·tract (prō trakt′, prə-) *vt.* [< L *pro-,* forward + *trahere,* draw] to draw out; prolong —**pro·trac'tion** *n.*

pro·trac·tor (prō'trak′tər) *n.* a device for plotting and measuring angles

pro·trude (prō trōōd′, prə-) *vt., vi.* **-trud'ed, -trud'ing** [< L *pro-,* forth + *trudere,* to thrust] to jut out; project —**pro·tru'sion** (-trōō'zhən) *n.*

pro·tu·ber·ance (prō tōō'bər əns, prə-) *n.* a part or thing that protrudes; bulge —**pro·tu'ber·ant** *adj.*

proud (proud) *adj.* [< LL *prode,* beneficial] **1** having a proper pride in oneself **2** arrogant; haughty **3** feeling or causing great pride or joy **4** caused by pride **5** stately; splendid [a *proud* fleet] —**proud of** highly pleased with —**proud'ly** *adv.*

proud flesh [from the notion of swelling up] an abnormal growth of flesh around a healing wound

Proust (prōōst), **Mar·cel** (mär sel′) 1871–1922; Fr. novelist

prove (prōōv) *vt.* **proved, proved** or **prov'en, prov'ing** [< L *probare,* to test] **1** to test by experiment, a standard, etc. **2** to establish as true —*vi.* to be found by experience or trial —**prov'a·bil'i·ty** *n.* —**prov'a·ble** *adj.*

prov·e·nance (präv'ə nəns) *n.* [< L *provenire,* come forth] origin; source

Pro·ven·çal (prō'vən säl′) *n.* **1** the vernacular of S France, a Romance language **2** the medieval literary language of S France

prov·en·der (präv'ən dər) *n.* [< L *praebere,* give] **1** dry food for livestock **2** [Inf.] food

prov·erb (präv'ərb) *n.* [< L *pro-,* PRO-[2] + *verbum,* word] a short, traditional saying expressing an obvious truth —**pro·ver·bi·al** (prō vur'bē əl) *adj.*

Prov·erbs *n.* a book of the Bible containing maxims

pro·vide (prə vīd′, prō-) *vt.* **-vid'ed, -vid'ing** [< L *pro-,* PRO-[2] + *videre,* see] **1** to make available; supply **2** to furnish (someone) *with* something **3** to stipulate —*vi.* **1** to prepare (*for* or *against* a possible situation, etc.) **2** to furnish support (*for*) —**pro·vid'er** *n.*

pro·vid·ed or **pro·vid·ing** *conj.* on the condition or understanding (*that*)

prov·i·dence (präv'ə dəns) *n.* **1** provident management **2** the benevolent guidance of God or nature **3** [P-] God

Prov·i·dence (präv'ə dəns) capital of Rhode Island

prov·i·dent (-dənt) *adj.* [see PROVIDE] **1** providing for the future **2** prudent or economical —**prov'i·dent·ly** *adv.*

prov·i·den·tial (-den'shəl) *adj.* of, by, or as if decreed by divine providence

prov·ince (präv'ins) *n.* [< L *provincia*] **1** an administrative division of a country; specif., of Canada **2** *a)* a district; territory *b)* [pl.] the parts of a country removed from the major cities **3** range of duties or work; sphere

pro·vin·cial (prə vin'shəl, prō-) *adj.* **1** of a province **2** having the ways, speech, etc. of a certain province **3** countrylike; rustic **4** narrow; limited —**pro·vin'cial·ism'** *n.*

proving ground a place for testing new equipment, new theories, etc.

pro·vi·sion (prə vizh'ən, prō-) *n.* **1** a providing or preparing **2** something provided for the future **3** [pl.] a stock of food **4** a stipulation; proviso —*vt.* to supply with provisions

pro·vi·sion·al *adj.* temporary —**pro·vi'sion·al·ly** *adv.*

pro·vi·so (prə vī'zō, prō-) *n., pl.* **-sos'** or **-soes'** [see PROVIDE] a condition or stipulation, or a clause making one

prov·o·ca·tion (präv'ə kā'shən) *n.* 1 a provoking 2 something that provokes; incitement

pro·voc·a·tive (prə väk'ə tiv, prō–) *adj.* provoking or tending to provoke, as to action, thought, or feeling —**pro·voc'a·tive·ly** *adv.*

pro·voke (prə vōk', prō–) *vt.* **-voked', -vok'ing** [< L *pro-*, forth + *vocare*, to call] 1 to excite to some action or feeling 2 to anger or irritate 3 to stir up (action or feeling) 4 to evoke —**pro·vok'er** *n.* —**pro·vok'ing** *adj.*

pro·vost (prō'vōst') *n.* [< L *praepositus*, chief] a high executive official, as in some colleges

prow (prou) *n.* [< Gr *prōira*] the forward part of a ship, etc.

prow·ess (prou'is) *n.* [< OFr *prouesse*] 1 bravery; valor 2 superior ability, skill, etc.

prowl (proul) *vi., vt.* [< ?] to roam about furtively (in), as in search of prey or loot —*n.* a prowling —**prowl'er** *n.*

prowl car PATROL CAR

prox·im·i·ty (präk sim'ə tē) *n.* [< L *prope*, near] nearness

prox·y (präk'sē) *n., pl.* **-ies** [< ME *procuracie*, function of a procurator] 1 the authority to act for another, as in voting 2 one given such authority

Pro·zac (prō'zak') *trademark for* a drug used in treating depression, eating disorders, etc.

prude (prood) *n.* [Fr < *prudefemme*, excellent woman] one who is overly modest or proper in behavior, dress, etc. —**prud'er·y** *n.* —**prud'ish** *adj.* —**prud'ish·ness** *n.*

pru·dent (prood'ənt) *adj.* [< L *providens*, provident] 1 exercising sound judgment in practical matters 2 cautious in conduct; not rash 3 managing carefully —**pru'dence** *n.* —**pru·den'tial** (proo den'shəl) *adj.*

prune¹ (proon) *n.* [< Gr *proumnon*, plum] a dried plum

prune² (proon) *vt.* **pruned, prun'ing** [< OFr *prooignier*] 1 to trim dead or living parts from (a plant) 2 to cut out (unnecessary parts)

pru·ri·ent (proor'ē ənt) *adj.* [< L *prurire*, to itch] tending to excite lust; lewd —**pru'ri·ence** *n.*

Prus·sia (prush'ə) former kingdom in N Europe & later the dominant state of the German Empire (1871-1919) —**Prus'sian** *adj., n.*

pry¹ (prī) *n., pl.* **pries** [< PRIZE²] a lever or crowbar —*vt.* **pried, pry'ing** 1 to raise or move with a pry 2 to obtain with difficulty

pry² (prī) *vi.* **pried, pry'ing** [< ?] to look closely and inquisitively; snoop

pry·er *n.* PRIER

PS *abbrev.* Public School

P.S., p.s., or **PS** *abbrev.* postscript

psalm (säm; sälm, sôlm) *n.* [<ᵗGr *psallein*, to pluck (a harp)] 1 a sacred song or poem 2 [*usually* P-] any of the songs in praise of God constituting the Book of Psalms —**psalm'ist** *n.*

Psalms (sämz; sälmz, sôlmz) *n.* a book of the Bible consisting of 150 psalms

Psal·ter (sôl'tər) *n.* [< Gr *psaltērion*, a harp] 1 PSALMS 2 [*also* p–] a version of the Book of Psalms for use in religious services

pseu·do (soo'dō) *adj.* [ME: see fol.] sham; false; spurious

pseudo- [< Gr *pseudein*, deceive] *combining form* sham, counterfeit

pseu·do·nym (soo'də nim') *n.* [< Gr *pseudēs*, false + *onyma*, a name] a fictitious name, esp. one assumed by an author; pen name

pshaw (shô) *n., interj.* (an exclamation) used to express impatience, disgust, etc.

psi¹ (sī, psē) *n.* the 23d letter of the Greek alphabet (Ψ, ψ)

psi² (sī) *adj.* psychic or paranormal

psi³ *abbrev.* pounds per square inch

psit·ta·co·sis (sit'ə kō'sis) *n.* [< Gr *psittakos*, parrot + -OSIS] a disease of birds, esp. parrots, often transmitted to humans

pso·ri·a·sis (sə rī'ə sis) *n.* [ult. < Gr *psōra*, an itch] a chronic skin disease characterized by scaly, reddish patches

psst (pst) *interj.* [Inf.] used to attract someone's attention quietly

PST *abbrev.* Pacific Standard Time

psych¹ (sīk) *vt.* **psyched, psych'ing** [< PSYCHOANALYZE] [Slang] 1 to outwit, overcome, etc. by psychological means: often with *out* 2 to prepare (oneself) psychologically: often with *up*

psych² *abbrev.* psychology

psych- *combining form* PSYCHO-

psy·che (sī'kē) *n.* [Gr *psychē*] 1 the soul 2 the mind regarded as an entity with its own complex processes 3 [P-] *Rom. Folklore* the wife of Cupid

psy·che·del·ic (sī'kə del'ik) *adj.* [< prec. + Gr *dēloun*, make manifest] 1 of or causing extreme changes in the conscious mind, as hallucinations 2 of psychedelic drugs

psy·chi·a·try (sī kī'ə trē) *n.* [see PSYCHO- & -IATRY] the branch of medicine dealing with disorders of the mind, including psychoses and neuroses —**psy·chi·at·ric** (sī'kē a'trik) *adj.* —**psy'chi'a·trist** *n.*

psy·chic (sī'kik) *adj.* [see PSYCHE] 1 of the psyche, or mind 2 beyond known physical processes 3 apparently sensitive to forces beyond the physical world Also **psy'chi·cal** —*n.* 1 a person apparently sensitive to nonphysical forces 2 MEDIUM (*n.*5) —**psy'chi·cal·ly** *adv.*

psy·cho (sī'kō) *adj., n.* [Inf.] *short for* PSYCHOTIC, PSYCHOPATHIC, *and* PSYCHOPATH

psycho- [see PSYCHE] *combining form* mind or mental processes

psy·cho·a·nal·y·sis (sī'kō ə nal'ə sis) *n.* a method of treating some mental disorders by analyzing repressed feelings, emotional conflicts, etc. through the use of free association, dream analysis, etc. —**psy'cho·an'a·lyst** (-an'ə list) *n.* —**psy'cho·an'a·lyze'** (-līz') *vt.* **-lyzed', -lyz'ing**

psy·cho·bab·ble *n.* [Inf.] talk or writing that uses psychological terms and concepts in a trite or superficial way

psy·cho·gen·ic (-jen'ik) *adj.* [see PSYCHO- & GENESIS] originating in the mind or caused by mental conflicts

psy·chol·o·gy (sī kälʹə jē) *n., pl.* **-gies** ⟦see PSYCHO- & -LOGY⟧ **1** the science dealing with the mind and with mental and emotional processes **2** the science of human and animal behavior —**psyʹcho·logʹi·cal** (-kə läjʹi kəl) *adj.* —**psy·cholʹo·gist** *n.*

psy·cho·neu·ro·sis (sīʹkō nōō rōʹsis) *n., pl.* **-ses'** (-sēz') NEUROSIS

psy·cho·path (-path') *n.* ⟦see PSYCHO- & -PATHY⟧ one who has a severe mental disorder and whose behavior is asocial —**psyʹcho·pathʹic** *adj.*

psy·cho·sis (sī kōʹsis) *n., pl.* **-ses'** (-sēz') ⟦see PSYCHO- & -OSIS⟧ a mental disorder in which the personality is seriously disorganized and contact with reality is usually impaired —**psy·chotʹic** (-kätʹik) *adj.*

psy·cho·so·mat·ic (-sō matʹik) *adj.* ⟦PSYCHO- + SOMATIC⟧ designating or of a physical disorder brought on, or made worse, by one's emotional state

psy·cho·ther·a·py (-therʹə pē) *n.* ⟦PSYCHO- + THERAPY⟧ treatment of mental disorders by counseling, psychoanalysis, etc. —**psyʹcho·therʹa·pist** *n.*

pt *abbrev.* **1** part **2** pint(s) **3** point

Pt¹ *abbrev.* **1** Point **2** Port

Pt² *Chem. symbol for* platinum

PT *abbrev.* Pacific Time

PTA *abbrev.* Parent–Teacher Association

ptar·mi·gan (tärʹmi gən) *n.* ⟦< Scot *tarmachan*⟧ a grouse of northern regions

ptero- ⟦< Gr *pteron*, wing⟧ *combining form* feather, wing

pter·o·dac·tyl (terʹə dakʹtəl) *n.* ⟦see prec. & DACTYL⟧ an extinct flying reptile with wings of skin stretched from the hind limbs to the long digits of each forelimb

Ptol·e·my (tälʹə mē) 2d c. A.D.; Greco-Egyptian astronomer & mathematician

pto·maine (tōʹmān') *n.* ⟦< Gr *ptōma*, corpse⟧ an alkaloid substance, often poisonous, formed in decaying matter

PTSD *abbrev.* post-traumatic stress disorder

Pu *Chem. symbol for* plutonium

pub (pub) *n.* ⟦< *pub(lic house)*⟧ a bar or tavern

pu·ber·ty (pyōōʹbər tē) *n.* ⟦< L *puber*⟧ the stage of physical development when sexual reproduction first becomes possible —**puʹber·tal** *adj.*

pu·bes·cent (pyōō besʹənt) *adj.* ⟦see prec.⟧ reaching or having reached puberty —**pu·besʹcence** *n.*

pu·bic (-bik) *adj.* of or in the region of the genitals

pub·lic (pubʹlik) *adj.* ⟦ult. < L *populus*, the people⟧ **1** of the people as a whole **2** for the use or benefit of all [a *public* park] **3** acting officially for the people [a *public* prosecutor] **4** known by, open to, or available to most or all people [to make *public*, a *public* company] —*n.* **1** the people as a whole **2** a specific part of the people [the reading *public*] —**in public** openly —**pubʹlic·ly** *adv.*

pub·li·can (pubʹli kən) *n.* **1** in ancient Rome, a tax collector **2** [Brit.] a proprietor of a pub

pub·li·ca·tion (pubʹli kāʹshən) *n.* ⟦see PUBLISH⟧ **1** public notification **2** the printing and distribution of books, magazines, etc. **3** something published, as a periodical or book

public defender an attorney employed at public expense to defend indigent people who are accused of crimes

public domain the condition of being free from copyright or patent

pub·li·cist (pubʹlə sist) *n.* a person whose business is publicity

pub·lic·i·ty (pub lisʹə tē) *n.* **1** *a)* any information or action that brings a person, cause, etc. to public notice *b)* work concerned with such promotional matters **2** notice by the public

pub·li·cize (pubʹlə sīz') *vt.* **-cized'**, **-ciz'ing** to give publicity to

public relations relations of an organization, etc. with the general public as through publicity

public school 1 in the U.S., an elementary or secondary school maintained by public taxes, free to students, and supervised locally **2** in England, a private boarding school

public servant a government official or a civil-service employee

pub·lic-spir·it·ed *adj.* having or showing zeal for the public welfare

public utility an organization supplying water, electricity, etc. to the public

pub·lish (pubʹlish) *vt.* ⟦< L *publicare*⟧ **1** to make publicly known; announce **2** to issue (a printed work) for sale —*vi.* **1** to issue books, newspapers, etc. to the public **2** to write books, etc. that are published —**pubʹlish·er** *n.*

Puc·ci·ni (pōō chēʹnē), **Gia·co·mo** (jäʹkō mō') 1858–1924; It. operatic composer

puck (puk) *n.* ⟦< dial. *puck*, to strike⟧ the hard rubber disk used in ice hockey

puck·er (pukʹər) *vt., vi.* ⟦< POKE²⟧ to gather into wrinkles or small folds —*n.* a wrinkle or small fold made by puckering

puck·ish (pukʹish) *adj.* ⟦after Puck, elf in a Shakespeare play⟧ mischievous

pud·ding (pōōdʹiŋ) *n.* ⟦ME *puddyng*, a sausage⟧ a soft, sweet food made of eggs, milk, fruit, etc.

pud·dle (pudʹl) *n.* ⟦dim. < OE *pudd*, a ditch⟧ a small pool of water, esp. stagnant, spilled, or muddy water

pud·dling (-liŋ) *n.* the making of wrought iron from pig iron melted and stirred in an oxidizing atmosphere

pudg·y (pujʹē) *adj.* **-i·er**, **-i·est** ⟦< Scot *pud*, belly⟧ short and fat

pueb·lo (pwebʹlō) *n., pl.* **-los** (-lōz) ⟦Sp < L *populus*, people⟧ an Amerindian communal village, as in the SW U.S., of terraced adobe dwellings

pu·er·ile (pyōōʹər əl, pyoorʹil') *adj.* ⟦< L *puer*, boy⟧ childish; silly —**puʹer·ilʹi·ty** *n.*

Puer·to Ri·co (pwerʹtə rēʹkō, pôrʹ-) island in the West Indies: a commonwealth associated with the U.S.; cap. San Juan —**Puerʹto Riʹcan** (-kən)

puff (puf) *n.* 〖OE *pyff*〗 1 a short, sudden gust or expulsion of air, breath, smoke, etc. 2 a draw at a cigarette, etc. 3 a light pastry filled with whipped cream, etc. 4 a soft pad [a powder *puff*] —*vi.* 1 to blow in puffs 2 to breathe rapidly 3 to fill or swell (*out* or *up*) 4 to take puffs at a cigarette, etc. —*vt.* 1 to blow, smoke, etc. in or with puffs 2 to swell; inflate 3 to praise unduly —**puff′y** *adj.* **-i·er**, **-i·est** —**puff′i·ness** *n.*

puff·ball *n.* a fungus that bursts at the touch and discharges a cloud of spores

puff·er *n.* a small saltwater fish that can expand its body by swallowing water or air

puf·fin (puf′in) *n.* 〖ME *poffin*〗 a northern sea bird with a brightly colored, triangular beak

puff pastry rich, flaky pastry made of many thin layers of dough

pug (pug) *n.* 〖< ? *Puck*: see PUCK〗 any of a breed of small, short-haired, snub-nosed dog

pug·gle (pug′əl) *n.* 〖< PUG + BEAGLE〗 a dog crossbred from a pug and a beagle

pu·gil·ism (pyōō′jə liz′əm) *n.* 〖L. *pugil*, boxer〗 the sport of boxing —**pu′gil·ist** *n.* —**pu′gil·is′tic** *adj.*

pug·na·cious (pug nā′shəs) *adj.* 〖< L *pugnare*, to fight〗 eager and ready to fight; quarrelsome —**pug·na′cious·ly** *adv.* —**pug·nac′i·ty** (-nas′ə tē) *n.*

pug nose a short, thick, turned-up nose —**pug′-nosed′** *adj.*

puke (pyōōk) *n., vt., vi.* **puked, puk′ing** 〖< ?〗 [Inf.] VOMIT

puk·ka (puk′ə) *adj.* 〖Hindi *pakka*, ripe〗 [Brit.] genuine; real

pul·chri·tude (pul′krə tōōd′) *n.* 〖< L *pulcher*, beautiful〗 physical beauty

pule (pyōōl) *vi.* **puled, pul′ing** 〖echoic〗 to whimper or whine, as a sick or fretful child does

pull (pool) *vt.* 〖< OE *pullian*, to pluck〗 1 to exert force on so as to move toward the source of the force 2 to pluck out [to *pull* a tooth] 3 to rip; tear 4 to strain (a muscle) 5 [Inf.] to carry out; perform [to *pull* a raid] 6 [Inf.] to restrain [to *pull* one's punches] 7 [Inf.] to draw out (a gun, etc.) —*vi.* 1 to exert force in dragging, tugging, or attracting something 2 to be capable of being pulled 3 to move (*away, ahead,* etc.) —*n.* 1 the act, force, or result of pulling; a tugging, attracting, etc. 2 a difficult, continuous effort 3 something to be pulled, as a handle 4 [Inf.] *a)* influence *b)* drawing power —**pull for** [Inf.] to cheer on —**pull off** [Inf.] to accomplish —**pull oneself together** to regain one's poise, etc. —**pull out** to depart or withdraw —**pull through** [Inf.] to get over (an illness, etc.) —**pull up** 1 to bring or come to a stop 2 to move ahead —**pull′er** *n.*

pull·back *n.* a pulling back; esp., a planned military withdrawal

pul·let (pool′it) *n.* 〖ult. < L *pullus*, chicken〗 a young hen

pul·ley (pool′ē) *n., pl.* **-leys** 〖< medieval Gr *polos*, pivot〗 a small wheel with a grooved rim in which a rope, belt, etc. runs, as to raise weights or transmit power

Pull·man (pool′mən) *n.* 〖after G. M. *Pullman* (1831–97), U.S. inventor〗 a railroad car with convertible berths for sleeping: also **Pullman car**

pull·out *n.* 1 a pulling out; esp. removal, withdrawal, etc. 2 something to be pulled out, as a magazine insert

pull·o·ver *adj.* that is put on by being pulled over the head —*n.* a pullover sweater, shirt, etc.

pull-up or **pull·up** *n.* the act of chinning oneself

pul·mo·nar·y (pul′mə ner′ē) *adj.* 〖< L *pulmo*, lung〗 of the lungs

pulp (pulp) *n.* 〖< L *pulpa*, flesh〗 1 a soft, moist, sticky mass 2 the soft, juicy part of a fruit or the pith inside a plant stem 3 the soft, sensitive tissue in the center of a tooth 4 ground-up, moistened fibers of wood, rags, etc., used to make paper —**pulp′y** *adj.* **-i·er**, **-i·est**

pul·pit (pool′pit) *n.* 〖< L *pulpitum*, a stage〗 1 a raised platform from which a member of the clergy preaches in a church 2 preachers collectively

pul·sar (pul′sär′) *n.* 〖< PULSE〗 any of several celestial objects that emit radio waves at short, regular intervals

pul·sate (pul′sāt′) *vi.* **-sat′ed, -sat′ing** 〖< L *pulsare*, to beat〗 1 to beat or throb rhythmically 2 to vibrate; quiver —**pul·sa′tion** *n.*

pulse (puls) *n.* 〖< L *pulsus*, a beating〗 1 the regular beating in the arteries, caused by the contractions of the heart 2 any regular beat 3 a brief, abnormal burst or surge, as of electric current —*vi.* **pulsed, puls′ing** to pulsate; throb

pul·ver·ize (pul′vər īz′) *vt., vi.* **-ized′, -iz′ing** 〖< L *pulvis*, powder〗 to grind or be ground into powder

pu·ma (pōō′mə, pyōō′-) *n.* 〖AmSp〗 COUGAR

pum·ice (pum′is) *n.* 〖< L *pumex*〗 a light, porous volcanic rock used for scouring, polishing, etc.

pum·mel (pum′əl) *vt.* **-meled** or **-melled**, **-mel·ing** or **-mel·ling** 〖< POMMEL〗 to hit with repeated blows, esp. with the fist

pump¹ (pump) *n.* 〖< Sp *bomba*〗 a machine that forces a liquid or gas into, or draws it out of, something —*vt.* 1 to move (fluids) with a pump 2 to remove water, etc. from 3 to drive air into with a pump 4 to draw out, move up and down, pour forth, etc. as a pump does 5 [Inf.] to question persistently, or to elicit (information) by this —**pump′er** *n.*

pump² (pump) *n.* 〖prob. < Fr *pompe*, boot〗 a low-cut shoe without straps or ties

pumped *adj.* [Slang] full of confidence, enthusiasm, etc.

pum·per·nick·el (pum′pər nik′əl) *n.* 〖Ger〗 a coarse, dark rye bread

pump·kin (pump′kin) *n.* 〖< Gr *pepōn*, ripe〗 a large, round, orange-yellow, edible fruit that grows on a vine

pun (pun) *n.* ⟦< ? It *puntiglio*, fine point⟧ the humorous use of a word, or of different words sounded alike, so as to play on the various meanings —*vi.* **punned, pun′ning** to make puns

punch¹ (punch) *n.* ⟦ult. < L *pungere*, to prick⟧ a tool driven against a surface that is to be stamped, pierced, etc. —*vt.* **1** to pierce, stamp, etc. with a punch **2** to make (a hole) with or as with a punch

punch² (punch) *vt.* ⟦ME *punchen*⟧ **1** to prod with a stick **2** to herd (cattle) as by prodding **3** to strike with the fist —*n.* **1** a thrusting blow with the fist **2** [Inf.] effective force —**punch in** (or **out**) to record with a time clock one's arrival (or departure)

punch³ (punch) *n.* ⟦Hindi *pañca*, five⟧ a sweet drink made with fruit juices, sherbet, etc., often mixed with wine or liquor

punch card a machine-readable card in which a pattern of punched holes encodes information for interpretation by a data-processing machine

punch-drunk *adj.* [Inf.] confused, unsteady, etc., as from many blows to the head in boxing

punch line the surprise line carrying the point of a joke

punch·y *adj.* **-i·er, -i·est** [Inf.] **1** forceful; vigorous **2** PUNCH-DRUNK

punc·til·i·ous (puŋk til′ē əs) *adj.* ⟦see fol.⟧ **1** very careful about fine points of behavior **2** very exact; scrupulous

punc·tu·al (puŋk′chōō əl) *adj.* ⟦< L *punctus*, a point⟧ on time; prompt —**punc′tu·al′i·ty** (-al′ə tē) *n.* —**punc′tu·al·ly** *adv.*

punc·tu·ate (-āt′) *vt.* **-at′ed, -at′ing** ⟦see prec.⟧ **1** to use standardized marks (**punctuation marks**), as the period and comma, in (written matter) to clarify meaning **2** to interrupt [a speech *punctuated* with applause] **3** to emphasize —**punc′tu·a′tion** *n.*

punc·ture (puŋk′chər) *n.* ⟦< L *pungere*, pierce⟧ **1** a piercing **2** a hole made by a sharp point — *vt., vi.* **-tured, -tur·ing** to pierce or be pierced with or as with a sharp point

pun·dit (pun′dit) *n.* ⟦< Sans *paṇḍita*⟧ someone who has or professes to have great expertise

pun·gent (pun′jənt) *adj.* ⟦< L *pungere*, pierce⟧ **1** producing a sharp sensation of taste and smell **2** sharp, biting, or stimulating [*pungent* wit] —**pun′gen·cy** *n.* —**pun′gent·ly** *adv.*

pun·ish (pun′ish) *vt.* ⟦< L *punire*⟧ **1** to cause to undergo pain, loss, etc., as for a crime **2** to impose a penalty for (an offense) —**pun′ish·a·ble** *adj.*

pun·ish·ment *n.* **1** a punishing or being punished **2** the penalty imposed **3** harsh treatment

pu·ni·tive (pyōō′ni tiv) *adj.* inflicting, or concerned with, punishment —**pu′ni·tive·ly** *adv.*

punk¹ (puŋk) *n.* ⟦prob. < SPUNK⟧ **1** decayed wood used as tinder **2** a substance that smolders when ignited, used to light fireworks, etc.

punk² (puŋk) *n.* ⟦< ?⟧ **1** [Slang] *a)* a young hoodlum *b)* a young person regarded as inexperienced, insignificant, etc. **2** PUNK ROCK —*adj.* **1** [Slang] poor; inferior **2** of punk rock or its fans

punk rock a loud, fast, and deliberately offensive style of rock music

pun·ster (pun′stər) *n.* one who is fond of making puns

punt¹ (punt) *n.* ⟦< ? dial. *bunt*, to kick⟧ *Football* a kick in which the ball is dropped and kicked before it hits the ground — *vt., vi.* to kick (a football) in this way

punt² (punt) *n.* ⟦< L *ponto*⟧ a flat-bottomed boat with square ends — *vt., vi.* to propel (a punt) with a long pole

pu·ny (pyōō′nē) *adj.* **-ni·er, -ni·est** ⟦< OFr *puis*, after + *né*, born⟧ of inferior size, strength, or importance —**pu′ni·ness** *n.*

pup (pup) *n.* **1** a young dog; puppy **2** a young fox, seal, etc.

pu·pa (pyōō′pə) *n., pl.* **-pae** (-pē) or **-pas** ⟦< L, a doll⟧ an insect in the stage between the last larval form and the adult form

pu·pil¹ (pyōō′pəl) *n.* ⟦< L *pupillus*, a ward⟧ a person taught under the supervision of a teacher or tutor

pu·pil² (pyōō′pəl) *n.* ⟦< L *pupilla*, figure reflected in the eye⟧ the contractile circular opening, apparently black, in the center of the iris of the eye

pup·pet (pup′ət) *n.* ⟦< L *pupa*, a doll⟧ **1** a small figure, as of a person, moved by strings or the hands, as in a performance (**puppet show**) **2** one whose actions, ideas, etc. are controlled by another —**pup′pet·ry** *n.*

pup·pet·eer (-ə tir′) *n.* one who operates, designs, etc. puppets

pup·py (pup′ē) *n., pl.* **-pies** ⟦< medieval Fr *popee*, a doll⟧ a young dog

pup tent a small, portable tent

pur·blind (pur′blīnd′) *adj.* ⟦ME *pur blind*, quite blind⟧ **1** partly blind **2** slow in understanding

pur·chase (pur′chəs) *vt.* **-chased, -chas·ing** ⟦< OFr *pour*, for + *chacier*, to chase⟧ to buy —*n.* **1** anything bought **2** the act of buying **3** a firm hold applied to move something heavy or to keep from slipping —**pur′chas·a·ble** *adj.* —**pur′chas·er** *n.*

pure (pyoor) *adj.* **pur′er, pur′est** ⟦< L *purus*⟧ **1** free from anything that adulterates, taints, etc.; unmixed **2** simple; mere **3** utter; absolute **4** faultless **5** blameless **6** virgin or chaste **7** abstract or theoretical [*pure* physics] —**pure′ly** *adv.* —**pure′ness** *n.*

pure·bred *adj.* belonging to a recognized breed with genetic attributes maintained through generations of unmixed descent —*n.* a purebred animal or plant

pu·rée or **pu·ree** (pyoo rā′) *n.* ⟦Fr: see PURE⟧ **1** cooked food pressed through a sieve or whipped in a blender to a soft, smooth consistency **2** a thick soup made with this —*vt.* **-réed′** or **-reed′, -rée′ing** or **-ree′ing** to make a purée of

pur·ga·tive (pur′gə tiv) *adj.* purging —*n.* a purging substance; cathartic

pur·ga·to·ry (pur′gə tôr′ē) *n.*, *pl.* **-ries** [see fol.] [*often* P-] *Theol.* a state or place after death, in some Christian doctrine, for expiating sins by suffering —**pur′ga·to′ri·al** *adj.*

purge (purj) *vt.* **purged, purg′ing** [< L *purus*, clean + *agere*, do] 1 to cleanse of impurities, etc. 2 to cleanse of sin 3 to rid (a nation, party, etc.) of (individuals held to be disloyal) 4 to empty (the bowels) —*vi.* to vomit, esp. intentionally —*n.* a purging —**purg′er** *n.*

pu·ri·fy (pyoor′ə fī′) *vt.* **-fied′, -fy′ing** [see PURE & -FY] 1 to rid of impurities, etc. 2 to free from guilt, sin, etc. —*vi.* to become purified —**pu′ri·fi·ca′tion** *n.*

Pu·rim (poor′im) *n.* [Heb] a Jewish holiday commemorating Esther's deliverance of the Jews from a massacre

pu·rine (pyoor′ēn, -in) *n.* [Ger *purin*] 1 a colorless, crystalline organic compound, from which is derived a group of compounds including uric acid and caffeine 2 a purine derivative, as adenine

pur·ism (pyoor′iz′əm) *n.* strict or excessive observance of precise usage or formal rules in language, style, etc. —**pur′ist** *n.*

Pu·ri·tan (pyoor′i tən) *n.* [see fol.] 1 a member of a group in the 1500s and 1600s in England and America that wanted to make the Church of England simpler in its forms and stricter about morality 2 [p-] a person regarded as excessively strict in morals and religion —**pu′ri·tan′i·cal** (-tan′i kəl) *adj.* —**Pu′ri·tan·ism′** *n.*, **pu′ri·tan·ism′**

pu·ri·ty (-tē) *n.* [< LL *puritas*] a being pure; specif., *a*) freedom from adulterating matter *b*) cleanness *c*) chastity

purl¹ (purl) *vi.* [< ? Scand] to move in ripples or with a murmur —*n.* the sound of purling water

purl² (purl) *vt.*, *vi.* [earlier *pirl*, prob. ult. < It] to invert (stitches) in knitting

pur·lieu (purl′yōō) *n.* [< OFr *pur-*, through + *aler*, go] 1 [*pl.*] environs 2 an outlying part

pur·loin (pər loin′, pur′loin′) *vt.*, *vi.* [< OFr *pur-*, for + *loin*, far] to steal

pur·ple (pur′pəl) *n.* [ult. < Gr *porphyra*, shellfish yielding a dye] 1 a dark bluish red 2 crimson cloth or clothing, esp. as an emblem of royalty —*adj.* 1 bluish-red 2 imperial 3 ornate [*purple* prose]

pur·port (pər pôrt′; *for n.* pur′pôrt′) *vt.* [< OFr *por-*, forth + *porter*, to bear] 1 to profess or claim as its meaning 2 to give the appearance, often falsely, of being, intending, etc. —*n.* 1 meaning; sense 2 intention —**pur·port′ed** *adj.* —**pur·port′ed·ly** *adv.*

pur·pose (pur′pəs) *vt.*, *vi.* **-posed, -pos·ing** [see PROPOSE] to intend or plan —*n.* 1 something one intends to get or do; aim 2 determination 3 the object for which something exists or is done —**on purpose** by design; intentionally —**pur′pose·ful** *adj.* —**pur′pose·less** *adj.*

pur·pose·ly *adv.* with a definite purpose; intentionally; deliberately

pur·pos·ive (pur′pəs iv, pər pō′siv) *adj.* serving or having a purpose

purr (pur) *n.* [echoic] a low, vibratory sound made by a cat at ease —*vi.*, *vt.* to make, or express by, such a sound

purse (purs) *n.* [< Gr *byrsa*, a hide] 1 a small bag for carrying money 2 finances; money 3 a sum of money for a present or prize 4 a woman's handbag —*vt.* **pursed, purs′ing** to draw (the lips) tightly, as in disapproval

purs·er (pur′sər) *n.* [ME, purse-bearer] a ship's officer in charge of accounts, tickets, etc.

pur·su·ance (pər sōō′əns) *n.* a pursuing of a project, plan, etc.

pur·su·ant *adj.* [Now Rare] pursuing —**pursuant to** in accordance with

pur·sue (pər sōō′) *vt.* **-sued′, -su′ing** [< L *pro-*, forth + *sequi*, follow] 1 to follow in order to overtake or capture; chase 2 to follow (a specified course, action, etc.) 3 to strive for —**pur·su′er** *n.*

pur·suit (-sōōt′) *n.* 1 a pursuing 2 an occupation, interest, etc.

pu·ru·lent (pyoor′ə lənt) *adj.* [< L *pus*, pus] of, like, or discharging pus —**pu′ru·lence** *n.*

pur·vey (pər vā′) *vt.* [see PROVIDE] to supply (esp. food) —**pur·vey′or** *n.*

pur·view (pur′vyōō) *n.* [< OFr *pourveii*, provided] scope or extent, as of control

pus (pus) *n.* [L] the yellowish-white liquid matter produced by an infection

push (poosh) *vt.* [< L *pulsare*, to beat] 1 to press against so as to move 2 to press or urge on 3 to urge the use, sale, etc. of —*n.* 1 a pushing 2 a vigorous effort 3 an advance against opposition 4 [Inf.] aggressiveness; drive

push button a small knob pushed to operate something, as with electricity

push·er *n.* 1 one that pushes 2 [Slang] one who sells drugs, esp. narcotics, illegally

push·o·ver *n.* [Inf.] 1 anything very easy to do 2 one easily persuaded, defeated, etc.

push-up or **push·up** *n.* an exercise in which a prone person, with hands under shoulders, raises the body by pushing down on the palms

push·y *adj.* **-i·er, -i·est** [Inf.] annoyingly aggressive and persistent —**push′i·ness** *n.*

pu·sil·lan·i·mous (pyōō′si lan′ə məs) *adj.* [< L *pusillus*, tiny + *animus*, the mind] timid; cowardly —**pu′sil·la·nim′i·ty** (-si lə nim′ə tē) *n.*

puss (poos) *n.* [< ?] a cat: also **puss′y·cat′** or **puss′y,** *pl.* **-ies**

puss·y·foot *vi.* [Inf.] 1 to move with stealth or caution, like a cat 2 to avoid committing oneself

pussy willow a willow bearing silvery, velvet-like catkins

pus·tule (pus′chōōl′) *n.* [L *pustula*] a pus-filled blister or pimple

put (poot) *vt.* **put, put′ting** [< or akin to OE *potian*, to push] 1 *a*) to thrust; drive *b*) to propel with an overhand thrust [to *put* the shot] 2 to cause to be in a certain place, condition, relation, etc.; place; set **3** to impose (a tax, etc.) **4** to attribute; ascribe **5** to express *[put* it plainly] **6** to present for decision *[put* the question] **7** to bet (money) *on* —*n. Finance* an option to sell a stock, etc. —*adj.* [Inf.] fixed *[stay put]* —**put across** [Inf.] to cause to be understood or accepted —**put aside** (or **by**) to reserve for later use —**put down 1** to crush; repress **2** to write down **3** [Slang] to belittle or humiliate —**put in for** to apply for —**put it** (or **something**) **over on** [Inf.] to deceive; trick —**put off 1** to postpone; delay **2** to evade; divert —**put on 1** to clothe oneself with **2** to stage (a play) **3** [Slang] to fool; hoax —**put out 1** to expel; dismiss **2** to extinguish (a fire or light) **3** to inconvenience **4** *Baseball* to retire (a batter or runner) —**put through 1** to carry out **2** to cause to do or undergo —**put up 1** to offer **2** to preserve (fruits, etc.) **3** to build **4** to provide lodgings for **5** to provide (money) **6** to arrange (the hair) with curlers, etc. **7** [Inf.] to incite *to* some action —**put up with** to tolerate

pu·ta·tive (pyōot′ə tiv) *adj.* [< L *putare,* suppose] generally considered or deemed such; reputed

put-down *n.* [Inf.] a belittling remark or crushing retort

put-on *n.* [Slang] a hoax

put·out *n. Baseball* a play in which a runner or the batter is retired

pu·tre·fy (pyōo′trə fī′) *vt., vi.* -**fied**′, -**fy**′**ing** [see PUTRID & -FY] to make or become putrid; rot —**pu′tre·fac′tion** (-fak′shən) *n.*

pu·tres·cent (pyōo tres′ənt) *adj.* putrefying; rotting —**pu·tres′cence** *n.*

pu·trid (pyōo′trid) *adj.* [< L *putrere,* to rot] rotten and foul-smelling

putt (put) *n.* [< PUT, v.] *Golf* a shot which attempts to roll the ball into the hole —*vt., vi.* to hit (the ball) in making a putt

putt·er¹ (put′ər) *n. Golf* a short, straight-faced club used in putting

putt·er² (put′ər) *vi.* [< OE *potian,* to push] to busy oneself in an ineffective or aimless way (with *along, around,* etc.) —*vt.* to fritter (*away*)

put·ty (put′ē) *n.* [Fr *potée,* lit., potful] a soft, plastic mixture used to fill small cracks, etc. —*vt.* -**tied**, -**ty·ing** to cement or fill with putty

put-up *adj.* [Inf.] planned secretly beforehand

putz (puts) *n.* [Yiddish < Ger] [Slang] a stupid or foolish person

puz·zle (puz′əl) *vt.* -**zled**, -**zling** [< ?] to perplex; bewilder —*vi.* **1** to be perplexed **2** to exercise one's mind, as over a problem —*n.* **1** something that puzzles **2** a toy or problem for testing skill or ingenuity —**puzzle out** to solve by deep study —**puz′zle·ment** *n.* —**puz′zler** *n.*

PVC *n.* [*p(oly)v(inyl) c(hloride)*] a type of

polymer used in packaging materials, plumbing, etc.

Pvt *abbrev. Mil.* Private

PX *service mark for* a general store at an army base

Pyg·my (pig′mē) *n., pl.* -**mies** [< Gr *pygmaios,* of a forearm's length] **1** a member of any of several groups of African or Asian peoples of small stature **2** [p-] a dwarf —*adj.* **1** of the Pygmies **2** [p-] very small

py·ja·mas (pə jä′məz, -jam′əz) *pl.n. Brit. sp. of* PAJAMAS

py·lon (pī′län′) *n.* [Gr *pylōn,* gateway] **1** a gateway, as of an Egyptian temple **2** a tower-like structure supporting electric lines, marking a flight course, etc.

py·lo·rus (pī lôr′əs) *n., pl.* -**ri** (-rī) [< Gr *pylōros,* gatekeeper] the opening from the stomach into the duodenum —**py·lor′ic** *adj.*

py·or·rhe·a (pī′ə rē′ə) *n.* [< Gr *pyon,* pus + *rheein,* to flow] a periodontal infection with formation of pus and loosening of teeth —**py′or·rhe′al** *adj.*

pyr·a·mid (pir′ə mid) *n.* [< Gr *pyramis*] **1** a huge structure with a square base and four triangular sides meeting at the top, as a royal tomb of ancient Egypt **2** *Geom.* a solid figure with a polygonal base, the sides of which form the bases of triangular surfaces meeting at a common vertex —**py·ram·i·dal** (pi ram′i dəl) *adj.*

pyre (pīr) *n.* [< Gr *pyr,* fire] a pile of wood on which a dead body is burned in funeral rites

Pyr·e·nees (pir′ə nēz′) mountain range between France & Spain

py·ret·ic (pī ret′ik) *adj.* [< Gr *pyretos,* fever] of, causing, or characterized by fever

Py·rex (pī′reks′) [arbitrary coinage < *pie*] *trademark for* a heat-resistant glassware used for cooking, lab work, etc.

py·rite (pī′rīt′) *n., pl.* **py·ri·tes** (pi rīt′ēz′, pī′rīts′) [< Gr *pyritēs,* flint] iron sulfide, a lustrous yellow mineral used as a source of sulfur

pyro- [< Gr *pyr,* fire] *combining form* fire, heat

py·ro·ma·ni·a (pī′rə mā′nē ə) *n.* [ModL: see prec. & -MANIA] a compulsion to start destructive fires —**py′ro·ma′ni·ac′** *n., adj.*

py·ro·tech·nic (pī′rə tek′nik) *adj.* [< Gr *pyr,* fire + *technē,* art] **1** of fireworks **2** brilliant; dazzling

py·ro·tech·nics *pl.n.* **1** a display of fireworks **2** a dazzling display, as of wit

Pyr·rhic victory (pir′ik) [after *Pyrrhus,* Gr king who won such victories over the Romans, 280 and 279 B.C.] a too costly victory

Py·thag·o·ras (pi thag′ə rəs) 6th c. B.C.; Gr. philosopher & mathematician —**Py·thag′o·re′an** (-ə rē′ən) *adj., n.*

py·thon (pī′thän′, -thən) *n.* [< Gr *Pythōn,* a serpent slain by Apollo] a large, nonpoisonous snake of Asia, Africa, and Australia, that squeezes its prey to death

Q

q¹ or **Q** (kyōō) *n., pl.* **q's, Q's** the 17th letter of the English alphabet

q² *abbrev.* **1** quart **2** question

Qa·tar (kä tär′, kut′ər) country on a peninsula of E Arabia, on the Persian Gulf

QB *abbrev.* Football quarterback

QC *abbrev.* Quebec

Q.E.D. or **q.e.d.** *abbrev.* ⟦L *quod erat demonstrandum*⟧ which was to be demonstrated or proved

qt *abbrev.* quart(s)

q.t. *n.* ⟦< *q(uie)t*⟧ [Inf.] quiet: chiefly in **on the q.t.,** secretly: also **Q.T.**

qua (kwā, kwä) *prep.* ⟦L < *qui,* who⟧ in the function or character of; as ⟦the President *qua* Commander in Chief⟧

quack¹ (kwak) *vi.* ⟦echoic⟧ to utter the sound or cry of a duck —*n.* this sound

quack² (kwak) *n.* ⟦ult. < MDu *quacken,* to brag⟧ **1** a person who practices medicine fraudulently **2** one who falsely pretends to have knowledge or a skill —*adj.* fraudulent —**quack′er·y** *n.*

quad¹ (kwäd) *n.* short for: **1** QUADRANGLE **2** QUADRICEPS **3** QUADRUPLET

quad² *abbrev.* **1** quadrangle **2** quadrant **3** quadruplicate

quad·ran·gle (kwä′draŋ′gəl) *n.* ⟦see QUADRI- & ANGLE¹⟧ **1** *Geom.* a plane figure with four angles and four sides **2** an area surrounded on its four sides by buildings —**quad·ran′gu·lar** *adj.*

quad·rant (kwä′drənt) *n.* ⟦< L *quadrans,* fourth part⟧ **1** an arc of 90° **2** a quarter section of a circle **3** an instrument formerly used in measuring angular elevation of celestial objects in navigation, etc.

quad·rat·ic (kwä drat′ik) *adj. Algebra* involving a quantity or quantities that are squared but none that are raised to a higher power

quad·ren·ni·al (kwä dren′ē əl) *adj.* ⟦< L *quadri-* (see foll.) + *annus,* year⟧ **1** happening every four years **2** lasting four years

quadri- ⟦L < *quattuor,* four⟧ *combining form* four, four times

quad·ri·ceps (kwä′dri seps′) *n.* ⟦< prec. + L *caput,* the head⟧ a muscle with four points of origin; esp., the large muscle at the front of the thigh

quad·ri·lat·er·al (kwä′dri lat′ər əl) *adj.* ⟦see QUADRI- & LATERAL⟧ four-sided —*n. Geom.* a plane figure having four sides and four angles

qua·drille (kwə dril′, kwä–) *n.* ⟦Fr: ult. < L *quadra,* a square⟧ a square dance performed by four couples

quad·ri·ple·gi·a (kwä′dri plē′jē ə, -jə) *n.* ⟦ModL < QUADRI- + Gr *plēgē,* a stroke⟧ total paralysis of the body from the neck down —**quad′ri·ple′gic** (-plē′jik) *adj., n.*

quad·ru·ped (kwä′droo ped′) *n.* ⟦< L *quadru-,* four + *pes,* foot⟧ an animal, esp. a mammal, with four feet —**quad′ru·ped′al** *adj.*

quad·ru·ple (kwä droo′pəl) *adj.* ⟦< L *quadru-,* four + *-plus,* -fold⟧ **1** consisting of four **2** four times as much or as many —*n.* an amount four times as much or as many —*vt., vi.* **-pled, -pling** to make or become four times as much or as many

quad·ru·plet (kwä droo′plit, -drup′lit) *n.* any of four offspring from the same pregnancy

quad·ru·pli·cate (kwä droo′pli kät′; *for adj. & n.,* -kit, -kät′) *vt.* **-cat′ed, -cat′ing** to make four identical copies of —*adj.* **1** fourfold **2** being the last of four identical copies —*n.* any one of such copies —**in quadruplicate** in four such copies —**quad·ru′pli·ca′tion** *n.*

quaff (kwäf, kwaf) *vt., vi.* ⟦prob. < LowG *quassen,* overindulge⟧ to drink deeply and heartily —*n.* a quaffing

quag·mire (kwag′mīr′) *n.* ⟦*quag,* a bog + MIRE⟧ **1** wet, boggy ground **2** a situation from which one cannot extricate oneself

qua·hog or **qua·haug** (kō′hâg′) *n.* ⟦AmInd⟧ an edible clam of the E coast of North America

quail¹ (kwāl) *vi.* ⟦prob. < L *coagulare,* coagulate⟧ to recoil in fear

quail² (kwāl) *n.* ⟦< OFr *quaille*⟧ a small, short-tailed bird resembling a partridge

quaint (kwānt) *adj.* ⟦< OFr *cointe* < L *cognitus,* known⟧ **1** pleasingly odd or old-fashioned **2** unusual; curious **3** fanciful; whimsical —**quaint′ly** *adv.* —**quaint′ness** *n.*

quake (kwāk) *vi.* **quaked, quak′ing** ⟦< OE *cwacian*⟧ **1** to tremble or shake **2** to shiver, as from fear or cold —*n.* **1** a shaking or tremor **2** an earthquake —**quak′y** *adj.* **-i·er, -i·est**

Quak·er (kwā′kər) *n.* ⟦< founder's admonition to "quake" at the word of the Lord⟧ *name for* a member of the SOCIETY OF FRIENDS

qual·i·fi·ca·tion (kwôl′ə fi kā′shən) *n.* **1** a qualifying or being qualified **2** a restriction; limiting condition **3** any skill, etc. that fits one for a job, etc.

qual·i·fied (kwôl′ə fīd′) *adj.* **1** fit; competent **2** limited; modified

qual·i·fi·er (-fī′ər) *n.* **1** one that qualifies **2** an adjective or adverb

qual·i·fy (-fī′) *vt.* **-fied′, -fy′ing** ⟦< L *qualis,* of what kind + *facere,* make⟧ **1** to make fit for a job, etc. **2** to make legally capable **3** to modify; restrict **4** to moderate; soften —*vi.* to be or become qualified

qual·i·ta·tive (-tāt′iv) *adj.* having to do with quality or qualities —**qual′i·ta′tive·ly** *adv.*

qual·i·ty (-tē) *n., pl.* **-ties** ⟦< L *qualis,* of what kind⟧ **1** a characteristic element or attribute **2** basic nature; kind **3** the degree of excellence of a thing 4 excellence —*adj.* of high quality

qualm (kwäm) *n.* ⟦OE *cwealm*, disaster⟧ 1 a sudden, brief feeling of sickness, faintness, etc. 2 a doubt; misgiving 3 a twinge of conscience

quan·da·ry (kwän′də rē, -drē) *n., pl.* **-ries** ⟦prob. < L⟧ a state of uncertainty; dilemma

quan·ti·fy (kwänt′ə fī′) *vt.* **-fied′, -fy′ing** ⟦< L *quantus*, how much + *facere*, make⟧ 1 to determine or express the quantity of 2 to express as a quantity or number —**quan′ti·fi′er** *n.*

quan·ti·ta·tive (-tāt′iv) *adj.* having to do with quantity

quan·ti·ty (-tē) *n., pl.* **-ties** ⟦< L *quantus*, how great⟧ 1 an amount; portion 2 any indeterminate bulk or number 3 [*also pl.*] a great amount 4 that property by which a thing can be measured 5 a number or symbol expressing this property

quan·tum (kwän′təm) *n., pl.* **-ta** (-tə) ⟦L, how much⟧ *Physics* a fixed, elemental unit, esp. of energy: the **quantum theory** states that energy is radiated discontinuously in quanta

quantum jump (*or* **leap**) a sudden, extensive change

quar·an·tine (kwôr′ən tēn) *n.* ⟦< L *quadraginta*, forty⟧ 1 the period, orig. 40 days, during which a vessel suspected of carrying contagious disease is detained in port 2 any isolation imposed to keep contagious diseases, etc. from spreading —*vt.* **-tined′, -tin′ing** to place under quarantine

quark (kwôrk) *n.* ⟦arbitrary coinage⟧ any of a set of elementary particles that bind together to form protons, neutrons, mesons, etc.

quar·rel (kwôr′əl) *n.* ⟦< L *queri*, complain⟧ 1 a cause for dispute 2 a dispute, esp. an angry one —*vi.* **-reled** *or* **-relled, -rel·ing** *or* **-rel·ling** 1 to find fault 2 to dispute heatedly 3 to have a breach in friendship —**quar′rel·er** *n.*, **quar′rel·ler** — **quar′rel·some** *adj.*

quar·ry¹ (kwôr′ē) *n., pl.* **-ries** ⟦< OFr *cuiree*, parts of prey fed to dogs⟧ an animal, etc. being hunted

quar·ry² (kwôr′ē) *n., pl.* **-ries** ⟦< L *quadrare*, to square⟧ a place where stone is excavated —*vt.* **-ried, -ry·ing** to excavate from a quarry

quart (kwôrt) *n.* ⟦< L *quartus*, fourth⟧ 1¼ gallon in liquid measure 2⅛ peck in dry measure

quar·ter (-ər) *n.* ⟦< L *quartus*, fourth⟧ 1 a fourth of something 2 *a)* one fourth of a year *b)* any of the three terms of about eleven weeks each in an academic year 3 one fourth of an hour 4 one fourth of a dollar; 25 cents, or a coin of this value 5 any leg of a four-legged animal, with the adjoining parts 6 a particular district or section 7 [*pl.*] lodgings 8 mercy granted to a surrendering foe 9 a particular source [*news from high quarters*] —*vt.* 1 to divide into four equal parts 2 to provide lodgings for —*adj.* constituting a quarter —**at close quarters** close together

quar·ter·back *n. Football* the offensive back who calls the play, passes the ball, etc.

quar·ter·deck *n.* the after part of the upper deck of a ship, usually for officers

quar·ter·fi·nal *adj.* coming just before the semifinals —*n.* a quarterfinal match, etc.

quarter horse ⟦< its speed in a *quarter*-mile sprint⟧ any of a breed of muscular, solid-colored horse

quar·ter·ly *adj.* occurring regularly four times a year —*adv.* once every quarter of the year —*n., pl.* **-lies** a publication issued every three months

quar·ter·mas·ter *n.* 1 *Mil.* an officer who provides troops with quarters, clothing, equipment, etc. 2 *Naut.* a petty officer or mate involved in steering and navigating a ship

quarter note *Music* a note having one fourth the duration of a whole note

quar·tet (kwôr tet′) *n.* ⟦ult. < L *quartus*, fourth⟧ 1 a group of four 2 *Music a)* a composition for four voices or instruments *b)* the four performers of this

quar·to (kwôrt′ō) *n., pl.* **-tos** ⟦< L (*in*) *quarto*, (in) a fourth⟧ 1 the page size (about 9 by 12 in.) of a book made up of sheets each of which is folded twice to form four leaves, or eight pages 2 a book with pages of this size

quartz (kwôrts) *n.* ⟦Ger *quarz*⟧ a hard crystalline mineral, a form of silica, often white or colorless

quartz crystal *Electronics* a piece of quartz cut and ground so as to vibrate at a particular frequency

qua·sar (kwā′zär′) *n.* ⟦< *quas*(*i-stell*)*ar* (*radio source*)⟧ a distant celestial object that emits immense quantities of light and radio waves

quash¹ (kwäsh) *vt.* ⟦< L *cassus*, empty⟧ *Law* to set aside (an indictment)

quash² (kwäsh) *vt.* ⟦< L *quatere*, to break⟧ to quell (an uprising)

qua·si (kwā′zī′, kwä′zē′) *adv.* ⟦L⟧ as if; seemingly; in part —*adj.* seeming Often hyphenated as a prefix [*quasi*-legal]

quat·rain (kwä′trān′) *n.* ⟦< L *quattuor*, four⟧ a stanza of four lines

qua·ver (kwā′vər) *vi.* ⟦ME *cwafien*⟧ 1 to shake or tremble 2 to be tremulous: said of the voice —*n.* a tremulous quality in a voice or tone

quay (kē) *n.* ⟦ult. < Celt⟧ a wharf, usually of concrete or stone

quea·sy (kwē′zē) *adj.* **-si·er, -si·est** ⟦ME *qwesye* < Gmc⟧ 1 affected with nausea 2 squeamish; easily nauseated

Que·bec (kwi bek′) 1 province of E Canada: abbrev. QC 2 its capital, on the St. Lawrence River

queen (kwēn) *n.* ⟦< OE *cwen*⟧ 1 the wife of a king 2 a female monarch in her own right 3 a woman noted for her beauty or accomplishments 4 the fully developed, reproductive female in a colony of bees, ants, etc. 5 a playing card with a picture of a queen on it 6 *Chess* the most powerful piece —**queen′ly** *adj.* **-li·er, -li·est**

Queens (kwĕnz) borough of New York City, on W Long Island

queen-size *adj.* larger than usual, but smaller than king-size *[a queen-size bed is 60 by 80 in.]*

queer (kwir) *adj.* [< ? Ger *quer*, crosswise] 1 different from the usual; strange 2 [Inf.] eccentric —*vt.* [Slang] to spoil the success of

quell (kwel) *vt.* [OE *cwellan*, kill] 1 to subdue 2 to quiet; allay

quench (kwench) *vt.* [OE *cwencan*] 1 to extinguish *[to quench* a fire with water*]* 2 to satisfy *[to quench* one's thirst*]* 3 to cool (hot steel, etc.) suddenly by plunging into water, etc. —**quench′less** *adj.*

quer·u·lous (kwer′yo͞o ləs, -ə-) *adj.* [< L *queri*, complain] 1 inclined to find fault 2 full of complaint; peevish —**quer′u·lous·ly** *adv.*

que·ry (kwir′ē) *n., pl.* **-ries** [< L *quaerere*, ask] a question; inquiry —*vt., vi.* **-ried, -ry·ing** to question

quest (kwest) *n.* [see prec.] 1 a seeking 2 a journey in pursuit of a lofty goal —*vi.* to go in pursuit

ques·tion (kwes′chən) *n.* [see QUERY] 1 an asking; inquiry 2 something asked 3 doubt; uncertainty 4 a matter open to discussion 5 a difficult matter *[it's not a question* of money*]* 6 a point being debated before an assembly —*vt.* 1 to ask questions of 2 to express doubt about 3 to dispute; challenge —*vi.* to ask questions —**out of the question** impossible

ques·tion·a·ble *adj.* 1 that can be questioned or doubted 2 suspected of being immoral, dishonest, etc. 3 uncertain

question mark a mark of punctuation (?) put after a sentence, word, etc. to indicate a direct question or to express doubt, etc.

ques·tion·naire (-chə ner′) *n.* a written or printed set of questions used in gathering information from people

queue (kyo͞o) *n.* [< L *cauda*, tail] 1 a pigtail 2 [Chiefly Brit.] a line, as of persons waiting to be served 3 stored computer data or programs waiting to be processed —*vi.* **queued, queu′ing** [Chiefly Brit.] to line up in a queue: often with *up*

quib·ble (kwib′əl) *n.* [< L *qui*, who] a petty evasion or criticism —*vi.* **-bled, -bling** to evade the truth of a point under discussion by caviling

quiche (kēsh) *n.* a dish consisting of unsweetened custard baked in a pastry shell with ingredients such as bacon, cheese, or spinach

quick (kwik) *adj.* [< OE *cwicu*, living] 1 *a)* rapid; swift *[a quick* walk*] b)* prompt *[a quick* reply*]* 2 prompt to understand or learn *[a quick* mind*]* 3 easily stirred *[a quick* temper*]* —*adv.* quickly; rapidly —*n.* 1 the living: esp. in **the quick and the dead** 2 the sensitive flesh under the nails 3 the deepest feelings *[hurt to the quick]* —**quick′ly** *adv.* —**quick′ness** *n.*

quick bread any bread leavened with baking powder, soda, etc. and baked as soon as the batter is mixed

quick·en *vt.* 1 to animate; enliven; revive 2 to cause to move more rapidly —*vi.* 1 to become enlivened; revive 2 to begin to show signs of life, as a fetus 3 to become more rapid

quick-freeze *vt.* **-froze′, -fro′zen, -freez′ing** to subject (food) to sudden freezing for long storage

quick·ie *n.* [Inf.] anything done or made quickly and, often, cheaply

quick·lime *n.* unslaked lime

quick·sand *n.* [< ME: see QUICK & SAND] a loose, deep sand deposit, engulfing heavy objects easily

quick·sil·ver *n.* mercury

quick-tem·pered *adj.* easily angered

quick-wit·ted *adj.* mentally nimble

quid (kwid) *n.* [var. of CUD] a piece, as of tobacco, to be chewed

quid pro quo (kwid′ prō kwō′) [L] one thing in return for another

qui·es·cent (kwī es′ənt) *adj.* [< L *quiescere*, become quiet] still; inactive —**qui·es′cence** *n.*

qui·et (kwī′ət) *adj.* [< L *quies*, rest] 1 still; motionless 2 *a)* not noisy; hushed *b)* not speaking; silent 3 not easily excited 4 not showy 5 not forward; unobtrusive 6 peaceful and relaxing —*n.* 1 calmness, stillness, etc. 2 a quiet or peaceful quality —*vt.* to make quiet —*vi.* to become quiet: usually with *down* —**qui′et·ly** *adv.*

qui·e·tude (kwī′ə to͞od′) *n.* a state of being quiet; calmness

qui·e·tus (kwī ēt′əs) *n.* [< ML *quietus (est)*, (he is) released from an obligation] 1 discharge from debt, etc. 2 death

quill (kwil) *n.* [prob. < LowG or MDu] 1 a large, stiff feather 2 *a)* the hollow stem of a feather *b)* anything made from this, as a pen 3 a spine of a porcupine or hedgehog

quilt (kwilt) *n.* [< L *culcita*, bed] a bedcover filled with down, cotton, etc. and stitched together in lines or patterns —*vt.* to stitch like a quilt —*vi.* to make a quilt —**quilt′er** *n.*

quince (kwins) *n.* [< Gr *kydōnion*] 1 a yellowish, apple-shaped fruit, used in preserves 2 the tree it grows on

qui·nine (kwī′nīn′) *n.* [< *quina*, cinchona bark] a bitter, crystalline alkaloid extracted from cinchona bark, used for treating malaria

quin·tes·sence (kwin tes′əns) *n.* [< ML *quinta essentia*] the pure essence or perfect type

quin·tet or **quin·tette** (kwin tet′) *n.* [ult. < L *quintus*, a fifth] 1 a group of five 2 Music *a)* a composition for five voices or instruments *b)* the five performers of this

quin·tu·ple (kwin to͞o′pəl) *adj.* [< L *quintus*, a fifth + *-plex*, *-fold*] 1 consisting of five 2 five times as much or as many —*vt., vi.* **-pled, -pling** to make or become five times as much or as many

quin·tu·plet (kwin tup′lit, -to͞o′plit) *n.* any of five offspring from the same pregnancy

quip (kwip) *n.* [< L *quippe*, indeed] a witty or sarcastic remark or reply —*vi.* **quipped, quip′ping** to utter quips —**quip′ster** *n.*

quire (kwīr) *n.* [< L *quaterni*, four each] a set

of 24 or 25 sheets of paper of the same size and stock

quirk (kwʉrk) *n.* ⟦< ?⟧ **1** a sudden twist or turn **2** a peculiarity —**quirk′i·ness** *n.* —**quirk′y** *adj.* **-i·er, -i·est**

quirt (kwʉrt) *n.* ⟦AmSp *cuarta*⟧ a riding whip with a braided leather lash and a short handle

quis·ling (kwiz′liŋ) *n.* ⟦after V. *Quisling*, Norw collaborator with the Nazis⟧ a traitor

quit (kwit) *vt.* **quit, quit′ting** ⟦< ML *quittus*, free⟧ **1** to free (oneself) *of* **2** to stop having, using, or doing **3** to depart from **4** to resign from —*vi.* **1** to stop doing something **2** to give up one's job

quit·claim *n.* a deed relinquishing a claim, as to property

quite (kwit) *adv.* ⟦see QUIT⟧ **1** completely **2** really; positively **3** very or fairly [*quite* warm] —**quite a few** (or **bit,** etc.) [Inf.] more than a few (or bit, etc.)

Qui·to (kē′tō) capital of Ecuador

quits (kwits) *adj.* ⟦< ML *quittus*, free⟧ on even terms, as by discharge of a debt, retaliation, etc. —**call it quits** [Inf.] **1** to stop working, etc. **2** to end an association

quit·tance (kwit′ns) *n.* ⟦see QUIT⟧ **1** discharge from a debt **2** recompense

quit·ter *n.* [Inf.] one who quits or gives up easily, without trying hard

quiv·er¹ (kwiv′ər) *vi.* ⟦< OE *curifer-*, eager⟧ to shake tremulously; tremble —*n.* a quivering; tremor

quiv·er² (kwiv′ər) *n.* ⟦< OFr *coivre*⟧ a case for holding arrows

quoth (kwōth) *vt.* ⟦< OE *cwethan*, speak⟧ [Archaic] said

quix·ot·ic (kwik sät′ik) *adj.* ⟦after DON QUIXOTE⟧ extravagantly chivalrous or foolishly idealistic

quiz (kwiz) *n., pl.* **quiz′zes** ⟦prob. < L *quis*, what⟧ a questioning; esp., a short examination to test knowledge —*vt.* **quizzed, quiz′zing** to ask questions, or test the knowledge, of —**quiz′zer** *n.*

quiz·zi·cal (-i kəl) *adj.* **1** teasing **2** perplexed —**quiz′zi·cal·ly** *adv.*

quoin (koin, kwoin) *n.* ⟦var. of COIN⟧ **1** the external corner of a building; esp., any of the large stones at such a corner **2** a wedge–shaped block

quoit (kwoit) *n.* ⟦prob. < OFr *coite*, a cushion⟧ **1** a ring of rope or metal **2** [*pl.*, *with sing. v.*] a game somewhat like horseshoes, in which such rings are thrown at a peg

quon·dam (kwän′dəm) *adj.* ⟦L⟧ former

Quon·set hut (kwän′sit) ⟦< *Quonset*, a trademark⟧ a prefabricated, metal shelter like a half cylinder on its flat side

quo·rum (kwôr′əm) *n.* ⟦< L *qui*, who⟧ the minimum number of members required to be present before an assembly can transact business

quot *abbrev.* quotation

quo·ta (kwōt′ə) *n.* ⟦< L *quota pars*, how large a part⟧ **1** a share or proportion assigned to each of a number **2** a maximum or minimum number allowed

quotation mark either of a pair of punctuation marks (" " or ' ') used to enclose a direct quotation

quote (kwōt) *vt.* **quot′ed, quot′ing** ⟦< L *quotus*, of what number⟧ **1** to repeat a passage from or statement of **2** to repeat (a passage, statement, etc.) **3** to state the price of (something) —*n.* [Inf.] **1** something quoted **2** QUOTATION MARK —**quot′a·ble** *adj.* —**quo·ta·tion** (kwō tā′shən) *n.*

quo·tid·i·an (kwō tid′ē ən) *adj.* ⟦< L *quotidie*⟧ **1** daily **2** ordinary

quo·tient (kwō′shənt) *n.* ⟦< L *quot*, how many⟧ *Math.* the result obtained when one number is divided by another

Qu·ran or **Qu·r'an** (koo rän′) *n.* var. of KORAN: now often the preferred form

q.v. *abbrev.* ⟦L *quod vide*⟧ which see

R

r¹ or **R** (är) *n., pl.* **r's, R's** the 18th letter of the English alphabet

r² *abbrev.* radius

R¹ *trademark for* a film rating indicating that no one under 17 may be admitted unless accompanied by a parent or guardian

R² *abbrev.* **1** [L *Rex*] king **2** [L *Regina*] queen **3** Republican **4** right **5** River **6** Road **7** route **8** *Baseball* run(s): also **r**

Ra¹ (rä) *n. Egypt. Myth.* the sun god and chief deity

Ra² *Chem. symbol for* radium

rab·bet (rab′it) *n.* ⟦< OFr *rabattre*, beat down⟧ a cut made in a board so that another may be fitted into it — *vt., vi.* to cut, or be joined by, a rabbet

rab·bi (rab′i) *n., pl.* **-bis** ⟦< Heb *rabi*, my master⟧ an ordained teacher of the Jewish law

rab·bin·ate (rab′i nit, -nāt′) *n.* **1** the position of a rabbi **2** rabbis collectively —**rab·bi·ni·cal** (rə bin′i kəl) *adj.*

rab·bit (rab′it) *n.* ⟦ME *rabette*⟧ a swift, burrowing mammal with soft fur and long ears

rabbit punch *Boxing* a short, sharp blow to the back of the neck

rab·ble (rab′əl) *n.* ⟦< ?⟧ a mob

rab·ble-rous·er (-rou'zər) *n.* one who tries to arouse people to violent action by appeals to emotions, prejudices, etc.

Ra·be·lais (rab'ə lā'), **Fran·çois** (frän swä') 1494?-1553; Fr. satirist & humorist

Ra·be·lai·si·an (rab'ə lā'zhən, -zē ən) *adj.* [after prec.] broadly and coarsely humorous or satirical

rab·id (rab'id) *adj.* [< L *rabere*, to rage] 1 violent; raging 2 fanatic 3 of or having rabies

ra·bies (rā'bēz) *n.* [L, madness] an infectious disease characterized by convulsions, etc., transmitted to people by the bite of an infected animal

rac·coon (ra kōōn') *n.* [< AmInd *aroughcun*] 1 a small, tree-climbing, American mammal, with yellowish-gray fur and a black-ringed tail 2 its fur

race[1] (rās) *n.* [< ON *rās*, a running] 1 a competition of speed in running, etc. 2 any similar contest [the *race* for mayor] 3 a swift current of water, or its channel —*vi.* **raced, rac'ing** 1 to take part in a race 2 to go or move swiftly —*vt.* 1 to compete with in a race 2 to enter or run (a horse, etc.) in a race 3 to cause to go swiftly —**rac'er** *n.*

race[2] (rās) *n.* [Fr < It *razza*] 1 any of the different varieties of humans distinguished by physical traits, blood types, etc. 2 loosely, any geographical population sharing the same habits, ideas, etc. 3 any distinct group of people

race·horse *n.* a horse bred and trained for racing

ra·ceme (rā sēm', rə-) *n.* [L *racemus*, cluster of grapes] a flower cluster having a central stem along which individual flowers grow on small stalks

race·track *n.* a course prepared for racing, esp. an oval track for horse races

race·way *n.* 1 a narrow channel for water 2 a racetrack for harness racing, drag racing, etc.

ra·cial (rā'shəl) *adj.* 1 of or characteristic of a RACE[2] 2 between races —**ra'cial·ly** *adv.*

rac·i·ness (rā'sē nis) *n.* racy quality

racing form a chart, etc. of information about an upcoming program of horse races

rac·ism (rā'siz'əm) *n.* the practice of racial discrimination, segregation, etc. —**rac'ist** *n., adj.*

rack[1] (rak) *n.* [< LowG *rack*] 1 a framework, etc. for holding or displaying various things [dish *rack*] 2 a toothed bar into which a pinion, etc. meshes 3 a pair of antlers 4 an instrument of torture which stretches the victim's limbs —*vt.* 1 to arrange in or on a rack 2 to torture on a rack 3 to torment —**rack one's brains** to try hard to think of something —**rack up** [Slang] to score or achieve

rack[2] (rak) *n.* [var. of WRACK] used only in **go to rack and ruin**, to become ruined

rack[3] (rak) *n.* [< ? RACK[1]] the rib section of mutton: the full **rack of lamb**

rack·et[1] (rak'it) *n.* [prob. echoic] 1 a noisy confusion 2 *a)* a method or scheme for obtaining money illegally *b)* [Inf.] any dishonest practice *c)* [Inf.] an easy way of making money

rack·et[2] (rak'it) *n.* [< Ar *rāḥa(t)*, palm of the hand] a light bat for tennis, etc., with a network, as of catgut or nylon, in an oval frame attached to a handle: also sp. **rac'quet**

rack·et·eer (rak'ə tir') *n.* one who obtains money illegally, as by fraud, extortion, etc. —**rack'et·eer'ing** *n.*

rac·on·teur (rak'än tur') *n.* [Fr < *raconter*, to recount] one skilled at telling stories or anecdotes

rac·quet·ball (rack'it bôl') *n.* a game like handball, but played with a short racket

rac·y (rā'sē) *adj.* **-i·er, -i·est** [RACE[2] + -Y[2]] 1 having the characteristic taste or quality of the genuine type [*racy* fruit] 2 lively; spirited 3 pungent 4 risqué

rad (rad) *n.* [< RAD(IATION)] a dosage of absorbed radiation

ra·dar (rā'där') *n.* [*ra*(*dio*) *d*(*etecting*) *a*(*nd*) *r*(*anging*)] an apparatus that transmits radio waves to a reflecting object, as an aircraft, to determine its location, speed, etc. by the reflected waves

ra·di·al (rā'dē əl) *adj.* [< L *radius*, ray] 1 of or like a ray or rays; branching out from a center 2 of a radius —*n.* a radial tire

radial (ply) tire an automobile tire with plies of rubberized cords at right angles to the center line of the tread

ra·di·ant (rā'dē ənt) *adj.* [< L *radius*, ray] 1 shining brightly 2 showing pleasure, etc.; beaming 3 issuing (from a source) in or as in rays —**ra'di·ance** *n.* —**ra'di·ant·ly** *adv.*

ra·di·ate (rā'dē āt') *vi.* **-at'ed, -at'ing** [< L *radius*, ray] 1 to send out rays of heat, light, etc. 2 to branch out in lines from a center —*vt.* 1 to send out (heat, light, etc.) in rays 2 to give forth or spread (happiness, love, etc.)

ra·di·a·tion *n.* 1 a radiating 2 the rays sent out 3 energy emitted as nuclear particles, etc.

radiation sickness sickness produced by overexposure to X-rays, radioactive matter, etc.

ra·di·a·tor *n.* 1 an apparatus for radiating heat, as into a room 2 a device for circulating coolant, etc., as for a car engine

rad·i·cal (rad'i kəl) *adj.* [< L *radix*, root] 1 fundamental; basic 2 favoring basic change, as in the social or economic structure —*n.* 1 a person holding radical views 2 *Chem.* a group of two or more atoms acting as a single atom 3 *Math.* the sign (√) used with a quantity to show that its root is to be extracted —**rad'i·cal·ism'** *n.* —**rad'i·cal·ly** *adv.*

ra·dic·chio (rə dē'kyō) *n., pl.* **-chios** [It] a variety of chicory used in salads

ra·di·i (rā'dē ī') *n.* alt. *pl.* of RADIUS

ra·di·o (rā'dē ō') *n.* [< *radio*(*telegraphy*)] 1 the transmission of sounds or signals by electromagnetic waves directly through space to a receiving set 2 *pl.* **-os'** such a set 3 broadcasting by radio as an industry, entertainment, etc. —*adj.* 1 of, using, used in, or sent by radio 2 of electromagnetic wave frequencies between *c.* 10 kilohertz and *c.* 300,000 megahertz —*vt., vi.* **-oed′, -o′ing** to transmit, or communicate with, by radio

radio- 〖< L *radius,* ray〗 *combining form* **1** ray, raylike **2** by radio **3** using radiant energy **4** radioactive [*radiotherapy*]

ra·di·o·ac·tive *adj.* giving off radiant energy in the form of particles or rays by the disintegration of atomic nuclei —**ra′di·o·ac·tiv′i·ty** *n.*

radio astronomy astronomy in which radio waves from space are observed in order to obtain information about the universe

ra·di·o·gram *n.* a message sent by radio

ra·di·o·i·so·tope *n.* a radioactive isotope of a chemical element

ra·di·ol·o·gy (rā′dē äl′ə jē) *n.* the use of radiant energy, as X-rays, in medical diagnosis and therapy —**ra′di·ol′o·gist** *n.*

ra·di·o·paque (-ō pāk′) *adj.* 〖RADIO- + (O)PAQUE〗 not allowing the passage of X-rays, etc.

radio telescope a radio antenna for receiving and measuring radio waves from stars, spacecraft, etc.

ra·di·o·ther·a·py *n.* the treatment of disease by the use of X-rays or rays from a radioactive substance

rad·ish (rad′ish) *n.* 〖< L *radix,* root〗 **1** an annual plant with an edible root **2** the pungent root, eaten raw

ra·di·um (rā′dē əm) *n.* 〖< L *radius,* ray〗 a radioactive, metallic chemical element found in some uranium, which undergoes spontaneous atomic disintegration: symbol, Ra; at. no. 88

ra·di·us (rā′dē əs) *n., pl.* **-di·i′** (-ī′) or **-us·es** 〖L, ray〗 **1** any straight line from the center to the periphery of a circle or sphere **2** the circular area limited by the sweep of such a line [*within a radius of two miles*] **3** the shorter, thicker bone of the forearm

ra·don (rā′dän′) *n.* 〖< RADIUM〗 a radioactive chemical element, a nonreactive gas, formed in the atomic disintegration of radium: symbol, Rn; at. no. 86

RAF *abbrev.* Royal Air Force

raf·fi·a (raf′ē ə) *n.* 〖< native name〗 **1** a palm tree of Madagascar, with large leaves **2** fiber from its leaves, used as string or for weaving

raff·ish (raf′ish) *adj.* 〖(RIFF)RAFF + -ISH〗 **1** carelessly unconventional **2** vulgar; low

raf·fle (raf′əl) *n.* 〖ME *rafle*〗 a lottery in which each participant buys a chance or chances to win a prize —*vt.* **-fled, -fling** to offer as a prize in a raffle: often with *off*

raft¹ (raft) *n.* 〖< ON *raptr,* a log〗 **1** a flat, buoyant structure of logs, etc. fastened together **2** a flat-bottomed, inflatable boat —*vi.* to travel on a raft

raft² (raft) *n.* 〖< Brit dial. *raff,* rubbish〗 [Inf.] a large quantity

raf·ter (raf′tər) *n.* 〖OE *ræfter*〗 any of the beams that slope from the ridge of a roof to the eaves

rag¹ (rag) *n.* 〖< ON *rögg,* tuft of hair〗 **1** a waste piece of cloth, esp. one old or torn **2** a small piece of cloth for dusting, etc. **3** [*pl.*] old, worn clothes

rag² (rag) *vt.* **ragged, rag′ging** 〖< ?〗 [Slang] to tease or scold: often with *on*

rag³ (rag) *n.* a tune in ragtime

ra·ga (rä′gə) *n.* 〖Sans *rāga,* color〗 any of various traditional melody patterns improvised on by Hindu musicians

rag·a·muf·fin (rag′ə muf′in) *n.* 〖ME *Ragamoffyn,* name of a demon〗 a poor, ragged child

rag·bag *n.* **1** a bag for rags **2** a collection of odds and ends

rage (rāj) *n.* 〖< LL *rabia,* madness〗 **1** a furious, uncontrolled anger **2** a great force, violence, etc. —*vi.* **raged, rag′ing 1** to show violent anger in action or speech **2** to be forceful, violent, etc. **3** to spread unchecked, as a disease —**(all) the rage** a fad

ragg (rag) *adj.* designating or made of sturdy yarn having a speckled pattern

rag·ged (rag′id) *adj.* **1** shabby or torn from wear **2** wearing shabby or torn clothes **3** uneven; imperfect **4** shaggy [*ragged* hair] —**run ragged** to tire out; exhaust —**rag′ged·ness** *n.*

rag·ged·y *adj.* tattered

rag·lan (rag′lən) *n.* 〖after Lord *Raglan* (1788-1855), Brit general〗 a loose coat with sleeves that continue in one piece to the collar —*adj.* designating or having such a sleeve

ra·gout (ra gōō′) *n.* 〖< Fr *ragoûter,* revive the appetite of〗 a highly seasoned stew of meat and vegetables

rag·time *n.* 〖prob. < *ragged time*〗 **1** a type of American music (*c.* 1890-1920), with a strongly syncopated melody and a steady beat in the accompaniment **2** its rhythm

rag·weed *n.* 〖< its ragged-looking leaves〗 a weed whose pollen is a common cause of hay fever

rah (rä) *interj.* hurrah: used as by cheerleaders

raid (rād) *n.* 〖dial. var. of ROAD〗 **1** a sudden, hostile attack, esp. by troops or bandits **2** a sudden invasion of a place by police, for discovering violations of the law — *vt., vi.* to make a raid (on) —**raid′er** *n.*

rail¹ (rāl) *n.* 〖< L *regula,* a rule〗 **1** a bar of wood, metal, etc. placed between posts as a barrier or support **2** any of the parallel metal bars forming a track for a railroad, etc. **3** railroad or railway —*vt.* to supply with rails or a railing —*adj.* of a railway or railroad

rail² (rāl) *vi.* 〖< LL *ragere,* to bellow〗 to speak bitterly; complain violently

rail³ (rāl) *n.* 〖< Fr *raaler,* to screech〗 a marsh bird with a harsh cry

rail·ing *n.* **1** materials for rails **2** a fence, etc. made of rails and posts

rail·ler·y (rāl′ər ē) *n., pl.* **-ies** 〖see RAIL²〗 light, good-natured ridicule

rail·road *n.* **1** a track of parallel steel rails for a train **2** a complete system of such tracks, trains, etc. —*vt.* **1** to transport by railroad **2** [Inf.] to rush through quickly, so as to prevent careful consideration —*vi.* to work on a railroad —**rail′road′er** *n.* —**rail′road′ing** *n.*

rail·way n. 1 any track with rails for guiding wheels 2 RAILROAD

rai·ment (rā′mənt) n. ⟦see ARRAY & -MENT⟧ [Archaic] clothing; attire

rain (rān) n. ⟦OE regn⟧ 1 water falling in drops condensed from the atmosphere 2 the falling of such drops 3 a rapid falling of many small objects —vi. 1 to fall: said of rain 2 to fall like rain —vt. 1 to pour down 2 to give in large quantities —**rain out** to cause (an event) to be postponed because of rain —rain′y adj. -i·er, -i·est

rain·bow (-bō′) n. ⟦OE regnboga⟧ an arc containing the colors of the spectrum, formed in the sky by the refraction, reflection, and dispersion of light in rain or fog

rain check 1 a ticket stub to a ballgame, etc. allowing future admission if the event is rained out 2 a promise to renew an unaccepted offer at some future time

rain·coat n. a water-repellent coat

rain·drop n. a single drop of rain

rain·fall n. 1 a falling of rain 2 the amount of rain over a given area during a given time

rain forest a dense, evergreen forest in a rainy, usually tropical region

rain·storm n. a storm with heavy rain

rain·wa·ter n. water that is falling or has fallen as rain

raise (rāz) vt. raised, rais′ing ⟦< ON reisa⟧ 1 to cause to rise; lift 2 to construct; build 3 to increase in size, intensity, amount, degree, etc. [to raise prices, raise one's voice] 4 to provoke; inspire 5 to present for consideration [raise a question] 6 to collect (an army, money, etc.) 7 to end [raise a siege] 8 a) to cause to grow b) to rear (children) —n. 1 a raising 2 an increase in salary or in a bet —**raise Cain** (or **hell,** etc.) [Slang] to create a disturbance

rai·sin (rā′zən) n. ⟦< L racemus, cluster of grapes⟧ a dried sweet grape

rai·son d'être (rā′zōn det′, -det′rə) [Fr] reason for being; justification for existence

raj (räj) n. ⟦Hindi: see fol.⟧ in India, rule; government —**the Raj** [Historical] the British government in, or its dominion over, India

ra·jah or **ra·ja** (rä′jə) n. ⟦< Sans rāj, to rule⟧ a prince in India

rake[1] (rāk) n. ⟦OE raca⟧ a long-handled tool with teeth at one end, for gathering loose hay, leaves, etc. or for smoothing a bed of soil, sand, etc. —vt. raked, rak′ing 1 to gather or smooth with a rake 2 to search through minutely 3 to direct gunfire along (a line of troops, etc.) —**rake in** to gather a great amount of rapidly —**rake up** to uncover facts or gossip about (the past, etc.)

rake[2] (rāk) n. [contr. of rakehell] a dissolute, debauched man

rake[3] (rāk) vi., vt. raked, rak′ing ⟦< ?⟧ to slant —n. a slanting

rake-off n. [Inf.] a commission or rebate, esp. when illegitimate

rak·ish (rāk′ish) adj. ⟦< RAKE[3] + -ISH⟧ 1 having a trim appearance suggesting speed: said

of a ship 2 dashing; jaunty —rak′ish·ly adv.

Ra·legh or **Ra·leigh** (rô′lē, rä′lē), Sir **Wal·ter** (wôl′tər) 1552?-1618; Eng. explorer & poet

Ra·leigh (rô′lē, rä′lē) capital of North Carolina

ral·ly[1] (ral′ē) vt., vi. -lied, -ly·ing ⟦< OFr re-, again + alier, join⟧ 1 to bring back together in, or come back to, a state of order: said of troops 2 to bring or come together for a common purpose 3 to recover; revive —n., pl. -lies 1 a rallying or being rallied; esp., a gathering of people for some purpose 2 an organized automobile run designed to test driving skills

ral·ly[2] (ral′ē) vt., vi. -lied, -ly·ing ⟦see RAIL[2]⟧ to tease or ridicule

ram (ram) n. ⟦OE ramm⟧ 1 a male sheep 2 BATTERING RAM —vt. rammed, ram′ming 1 to strike against with great force 2 to force into place; press down

RAM (ram) n. random-access memory

ram·ble (ram′bəl) vi. -bled, -bling ⟦< ME romen⟧ 1 to roam about; esp., to stroll about idly 2 to talk or write aimlessly 3 to spread in all directions, as a vine does —n. a stroll

ram·bler (-blər) n. a person or thing that rambles; esp., a climbing rose

ram·bunc·tious (ram buŋk′shəs) adj. ⟦altered, (after RAM) < earlier robustious⟧ disorderly, boisterous, unruly, etc. —ram·bunc′tious·ness n.

ram·e·kin or **ram·e·quin** (ram′ə kin) n. ⟦< Fr < MDu⟧ a small individual baking dish

ra·men (rä′mən) pl.n. [sometimes with sing. v.] Japanese wheat noodles

ram·i·fy (ram′ə fī′) vt., vi. -fied′, -fy′ing ⟦< L ramus, a branch + facere, make⟧ to divide or spread out into branches or branchlike divisions —ram′i·fi·ca′tion n.

ramp (ramp) n. ⟦< OFr ramper, to climb⟧ 1 a sloping surface, walk, etc. joining different levels 2 a means for boarding a plane, as a movable staircase 3 a sloping runway, as for launching boats —**ramp up** [Inf.] to increase

ram·page (ram′pāj′) vi. -paged′, -pag′ing to rush about wildly; rage —n. an outbreak of violent, raging behavior: chiefly in **on the** (or **a**) **rampage**

ramp·ant (ram′pənt) adj. ⟦< OFr ramper, to climb⟧ growing unchecked; widespread

ram·part (ram′pärt′, -pərt) n. ⟦< Fr re-, again + emparer, fortify⟧ an embankment of earth surmounted by a parapet for defending a fort, etc.

ram·rod n. a rod for ramming down the charge in a muzzle-loading gun —vt. -rod′ded, -rod′ding to manage or direct in an unyielding way

ram·shack·le (ram′shak′əl) adj. ⟦< RANSACK⟧ loose and rickety; likely to fall to pieces

ran (ran) vi., vt. pt. of RUN

ranch (ranch) n. ⟦< Sp rancho, small farm⟧ 1 a large farm, esp. in the W U.S., for raising cattle, horses, or sheep 2 a style of house with all the rooms on one floor: in full **ranch house** 3 creamy buttermilk salad dressing: in full **ranch dressing** —vi. to work on or manage a ranch —ranch′er n.

ran·cid (ran′sid) *adj.* [< L *rancere*, to be rank] smelling or tasting of stale fats or oils; spoiled

ran·cor (raŋ′kər) *n.* [< L *rancere*, to be rank] a continuing and bitter hate or ill will: Brit. sp. **ran′cour** —**ran′cor·ous** *adj.* —**ran′cor·ous·ly** *adv.*

rand (rand) *n., pl.* **rand** the monetary unit of South Africa

R & B or **r & b** *abbrev.* rhythm and blues

R & D *abbrev.* research and development

ran·dom (ran′dəm) *adj.* [< OFr *randir*, run violently] purposeless; haphazard —**at random** haphazardly —**ran′dom·ly** *adv.*

ran·dom-ac·cess *adj. Comput.* of a kind of memory that allows data to be directly accessible

ran·dom·ize (-īz′) *vt.* **-ized′, -iz′ing** to select or choose (items of a group) in a random order

ran·dy (ran′dē) *adj.* **-di·er, -di·est** amorous; lustful

rang (raŋ) *vi., vt. pt. of* RING¹

range (rānj) *vt.* **ranged, rang′ing** [< OFr *renc*, a ring] 1 to arrange in order; set in a row or rows 2 to place (esp. oneself) with others in a cause, etc. 3 to roam through —*vi.* 1 to extend in a given direction 2 to roam 3 to vary between stated limits —*n.* 1 a row, line, or series 2 a series of connected mountains 3 the distance that a weapon can fire its projectile 4 *a)* a place for shooting practice *b)* a place for testing rockets in flight 5 extent; scope 6 a large, open area for grazing livestock 7 the limits of possible variations of amount, degree, pitch, etc. [a wide *range* of prices] 8 a cooking stove

rang·er (rān′jər) *n.* 1 *a)* a mounted trooper who patrols a region *b)* [*often* R-] a soldier trained for raiding and close combat 2 a warden who patrols parks and forests

Ran·goon (ran gōōn′) *former name for* YANGON

rang·y (rān′jē) *adj.* **-i·er, -i·est** long-limbed and slender —**rang′i·ness** *n.*

rank¹ (raŋk) *n.* [< OFr *renc*] 1 a row, line, or series 2 a social class 3 a high position in society 4 an official grade [the *rank* of major] 5 a relative position in a scale [a poet of the first *rank*] 6 *a)* a row of soldiers, etc. placed side by side *b)* [*pl.*] the army; esp., enlisted soldiers —*vt.* 1 to place in a rank 2 to assign a position to 3 to outrank —*vi.* to hold a certain position —**rank and file** 1 enlisted soldiers 2 the common people, as distinguished from leaders

rank² (raŋk) *adj.* [OE *ranc*, strong] 1 growing vigorously and coarsely [*rank* grass] 2 strong and offensive in smell or taste 3 in bad taste 4 complete; utter [*rank* deceit]

rank·ing *adj.* 1 of the highest rank 2 prominent or outstanding

ran·kle (raŋ′kəl) *vi., vt.* **-kled, -kling** [ult. < L dim. of *draco*, dragon] 1 [Obs.] to fester 2 to cause, or cause to have, long-lasting anger, rancor, etc.

ran·sack (ran′sak′) *vt.* [< ON *rann*, house + *sœkja*, seek] 1 to search thoroughly 2 to plunder

ran·som (ran′səm) *n.* [see REDEEM] 1 the redeeming of a captive by paying money or complying with demands 2 the price thus paid or demanded —*vt.* to obtain the release of (a captive, etc.) by paying the demanded price

rant (rant) *vi., vt.* [< obs. Du *ranten*] to speak or write in a loud, wild, extravagant way —*n.* a wild, extravagant speech or piece of writing

rap (rap) *vt.* **rapped, rap′ping** [prob. echoic] 1 to strike quickly and sharply; tap 2 [Slang] to criticize sharply —*vi.* 1 to knock sharply 2 [Slang] to talk —*n.* 1 a quick, sharp knock 2 [Slang] blame or punishment 3 a kind of popular music in which rhymed verses are chanted over repetitive rhythms

ra·pa·cious (rə pā′shəs) *adj.* [< L *rapere*, seize] 1 greedy; voracious 2 predatory —**ra·pa′cious·ly** *adv.* —**ra·pac′i·ty** (-pas′ə tē) *n.*

rape¹ (rāp) *n.* [prob. < L *rapere*, seize] 1 the crime of having sexual intercourse with a person forcibly and without consent 2 the plundering (*of* a city, etc.), as in warfare —*vt.* **raped, rap′ing** 1 to commit rape on; violate 2 to plunder or destroy —*vi.* to commit rape —**rap′ist** *n.*

rape² (rāp) *n.* [< L *rapa*, turnip] an annual plant whose leaves are used for fodder and as a source of oil

Raph·a·el (rä′fā el′, -fī-) 1483-1520; It. painter & architect

rap·id (rap′id) *adj.* [< L *rapere*, to rush] moving or occurring with speed; swift; quick —*n.* [*usually pl.*] a part of a river where the current is swift —**ra·pid·i·ty** (rə pid′ə tē) *n.* —**rap′id·ly** *adv.*

rapid transit a system of public transportation in an urban area, using electric trains along an unimpeded right of way

ra·pi·er (rā′pē ər) *n.* [Fr *rapière*] a light, sharp-pointed sword used only for thrusting

rap·ine (rap′in) *n.* [< L *rapere*, seize] plunder; pillage

rap·pel (ra pel′) *n.* [Fr, lit., a recall] a descent by a mountain climber, usu. by sliding down a doubled rope, using friction to control the speed of descent —*vi.* **-pelled′, -pel′ling** to make such a descent

rap·per *n.* a performer of rap music

rap·port (ra pôr′) *n.* [Fr] close relationship; harmony

rap·proche·ment (ra′prōsh män′) *n.* [Fr] an establishing of friendly relations

rap·scal·lion (rap skal′yən) *n.* [< RASCAL] a rascal

rap sheet [Slang] one's police record of arrests and convictions

rapt (rapt) *adj.* [< L *rapere*, seize] 1 carried away with joy, love, etc. 2 completely engrossed (*in* meditation, study, etc.)

rap·tor (rap′tər, -tôr′) *n.* [< L *rapere*, to snatch] a bird, as a hawk, that preys on other animals

rap·ture (rap′chər) *n.* the state of being carried

away with joy, love, etc.; ecstasy —**the Rapture** *Christian Theol.* the bodily ascent into heaven of those who are saved, just before Armageddon —**rap′tur·ous** *adj.* —**rap′tur·ous·ly** *adv.*

ra·ra a·vis (rer′ə ā′vis) *pl.* **ra·rae a·ves** (rer′ē ā′vēz) ⟦L, lit., strange bird⟧ an extraordinary person or thing

rare¹ (rer) *adj.* **rar′er, rar′est** ⟦< L *rarus*⟧ 1 not frequently encountered; scarce; unusual 2 unusually good; excellent 3 not dense [*rare* atmosphere] —**rare′ness** *n.*

rare² (rer) *adj.* **rar′er, rar′est** ⟦OE *hrere*⟧ not completely cooked; partly raw: said esp. of meat —**rare′ness** *n.*

rare³ (rer) *vi.* **rared, rar′ing** [Inf.] to be eager: used in prp. [*raring* to go]

rare·bit (rer′bit) *n.* WELSH RABBIT

rar·e·fy (rer′ə fī′) *vt., vi.* **-fied, -fy′ing** ⟦< L *rarus*, RARE¹ + *facere*, make⟧ to make or become less dense —**rar′e·fac′tion** (-fak′shən) *n.*

rare·ly (rer′lē) *adv.* 1 infrequently; seldom 2 uncommonly

rar·i·ty (rer′ə tē) *n.* 1 a being rare; specif., *a*) scarcity *b*) lack of density 2 *pl.* **-ties** something remarkable or valuable because rare

ras·cal (ras′kəl) *n.* ⟦< OFr *rascaille*, rabble⟧ 1 a rogue 2 a mischievous child —**ras·cal′i·ty** (-kal′ə tē) *n.* —**ras′cal·ly** *adj., adv.*

rash¹ (rash) *adj.* ⟦ME *rasch*⟧ too hasty in acting or speaking; reckless —**rash′ly** *adv.* —**rash′ness** *n.*

rash² (rash) *n.* ⟦< OFr *rascaille*, rabble⟧ 1 an eruption of spots on the skin 2 a sudden appearance of a large number of instances

rash·er *n.* ⟦< L *radere*, to scrape⟧ a thin slice of bacon, etc., or a serving of several such slices

rasp (rasp) *vt.* ⟦< OHG *raspon*, to scrape together⟧ 1 to scrape as with a file 2 to grate upon; irritate —*vi.* 1 to grate 2 to make a rough, grating sound —*n.* 1 a type of rough file 2 a rough, grating sound —**rasp′y** *adj.* **-i·er, -i·est**

rasp·ber·ry (raz′ber′ē, -bər-) *n., pl.* **-ries** ⟦< earlier *raspis*⟧ 1 a small, juicy, edible, usu. reddish fruit of a plant related to the rose 2 this plant 3 [Slang] a sound of derision

rat (rat) *n.* ⟦OE *ræt*⟧ 1 a long-tailed rodent, resembling, but larger than, the mouse 2 [Slang] a sneaky, contemptible person; esp., an informer —*vi.* **rat′ted, rat′ting** [Slang] to inform (*on*) —**smell a rat** to suspect a trick, plot, etc.

ratch·et (rach′it) *n.* ⟦< It *rocca*, distaff⟧ 1 a toothed wheel (in full **ratchet wheel**) or bar whose sloping teeth catch a pawl, preventing backward motion 2 such a pawl

rate¹ (rāt) *n.* ⟦< L *reri*, reckon⟧ 1 the amount, degree, etc. of anything in relation to units of something else [*rate* of pay] 2 price, esp. per unit —*vt.* **rat′ed, rat′ing** 1 to appraise 2 to consider 3 [Inf.] to deserve —*vi.* to have value, status, etc. —**at any rate** 1 in any event 2 anyway

rate² (rāt) *vt., vi.* **rat′ed, rat′ing** ⟦< L *reputare*, to count⟧ to scold; chide

rath·er (rath′ər) *adv.* ⟦OE *hræthe*, quickly⟧ 1 more willingly; preferably 2 with more justice, reason, etc. [I, *rather* than you, should pay] 3 more accurately [my son, or *rather*, stepson] 4 on the contrary 5 somewhat [*rather* hungry] —**rather than** instead of

raths·kel·ler (rath′skel′ər) *n.* ⟦Ger < *rat*, council, town hall + *keller*, cellar⟧ a restaurant, usually below the street level, where beer is served

rat·i·fy (rat′ə fī′) *vt.* **-fied′, -fy′ing** ⟦< L *ratus*, reckoned + *facere*, make⟧ to approve; esp., to give official sanction to —**rat′i·fi·ca′tion** *n.*

rat·ing (rāt′iŋ) *n.* 1 a rank or grade, as of military personnel 2 a placement in a certain rank or class 3 an evaluation; appraisal 4 *Film* a classification, based on content, restricting the age of those who may attend 5 *Radio, TV* the relative popularity of a program according to sample polls

ra·tio (rā′shō, -shē ō′) *n., pl.* **-tios** ⟦L, a reckoning⟧ a fixed relation in degree, number, etc. between two similar things; proportion

ra·ti·oc·i·nate (rash′ē äs′ə nāt′) *vi.* **-nat′ed, -nat′ing** [see prec.] to think or argue logically; reason —**ra′ti·oc′i·na′tion** *n.*

ra·tion (rash′ən, rā′shən) *n.* [see RATIO] 1 a fixed portion; share 2 a fixed allowance of food, as a daily allowance for a soldier 3 [*pl.*] food supply —*vt.* to distribute (food, clothing, etc.) in rations, as in times of scarcity

ra·tion·al (rash′ən əl) *adj.* [see RATIO] 1 of or based on reasoning 2 able to reason; reasoning 3 sensible or sane —**ra′tion·al′i·ty** (-ə nal′ə tē) *n.* —**ra′tion·al·ly** *adv.*

ra·tion·ale (rash′ə nal′) *n.* ⟦< L *rationalis*, rational⟧ 1 the reasons or rational basis for something 2 an explanation of principles

ra·tion·al·ism *n.* the practice of accepting reason as the only authority in determining one's opinions or course of action —**ra′tion·al·ist** *n., adj.* —**ra′tion·al·is′tic** *adj.*

ra·tion·al·ize *vt., vi.* **-ized′, -iz′ing** 1 to make or be rational or reasonable 2 to devise plausible explanations for (one's acts, beliefs, etc.), usually in self-deception —**ra′tion·al·i·za′tion** *n.*

rat·line (rat′lin) *n.* ⟦< ?⟧ any of the horizontal ropes which join the shrouds of a ship and serve as a ladder: also sp. **rat′lin**

rat race [Inf.] a mad scramble or intense struggle, as in the business world

rat·tan (ra tan′) *n.* ⟦Malay *rotan*⟧ 1 a tall palm tree with long, slender, tough stems 2 its stem, used in making furniture, etc.

rat·tle (rat′l) *vi.* **-tled, -tling** ⟦prob. echoic⟧ 1 to make a series of sharp, short sounds 2 to chatter: often with *on* —*vt.* 1 to cause to rattle 2 to confuse or upset —*n.* 1 a series of sharp, short sounds 2 a series of horny rings at the end of a rattlesnake's tail 3 a baby's toy, a percussion instrument, etc. made to rattle when shaken

rat·tler *n.* a rattlesnake

rat·tle·snake *n.* a poisonous American snake with horny rings at the end of the tail that rattle when shaken

rat·tle·trap *n.* a rickety old car

rat·tling (-liŋ) *adj.* 1 that rattles 2 [Inf.] very fast, good, etc. —*adv.* [Inf.] very [a *rattling* good time]

rat·trap *n.* 1 a trap for rats 2 [Inf.] a dirty, run-down building

rat·ty (rat′ē) *adj.* **-ti·er, -ti·est** [Slang] shabby or run-down

rau·cous (rô′kəs) *adj.* [L *raucus*] 1 hoarse 2 loud and rowdy —**rau′cous·ly** *adv.* —**rau′ cous·ness** *n.*

raun·chy (rôn′chē) *adj.* **-chi·er, -chi·est** [< ?] [Slang] 1 dirty, sloppy, etc. 2 risqué, lustful, etc.

rav·age (rav′ij) *n.* [see RAVISH] destruction; ruin —*vt.* **-aged, -ag·ing** to destroy violently; ruin

rave (rāv) *vi.* **raved, rav′ing** [< OFr *raver*, roam] 1 to talk incoherently or wildly 2 to talk with great enthusiasm (*about*) —*n.* [Inf.] a very enthusiastic commendation

rav·el (rav′əl) *vt., vi.* **-eled** or **-elled, -el·ing** or **-el·ling** [< MDu *ravelen*] to separate into its parts, esp. threads; fray —*n.* a raveled part in a fabric

ra·ven (rā′vən) *n.* [OE *hræfn*] the largest crow, with a straight, sharp beak —*adj.* black and lustrous [*raven* hair]

rav·en·ing (rav′ə niŋ) *adj.* [ult. < L *rapere*, seize] greedily searching for prey [*ravening* wolves]

rav·e·nous (rav′ə nəs) *adj.* [< L *rapere*, seize] 1 greedily hungry 2 rapacious —**rav′ e·nous·ly** *adv.*

ra·vine (rə vēn′) *n.* [Fr, flood] a long, deep hollow in the earth, esp. one worn by a stream; gorge

rav·ing *adj.* 1 that raves; frenzied 2 [Inf.] exciting enthusiastic admiration [a *raving* beauty] —*adv.* so as to cause raving [*raving* mad]

ra·vi·o·li (rav′ē ō′lē) *n., pl.* **-li** or **-lis** [It] small casings of dough filled with meat, cheese, etc.

rav·ish (rav′ish) *vt.* [< L *rapere*, seize] 1 to seize and carry away forcibly 2 to rape (a woman) 3 to transport with joy or delight —**rav′ish·ment** *n.*

rav·ish·ing *adj.* causing great joy

raw (rô) *adj.* [OE *hreaw*] 1 not cooked 2 in its natural condition; not processed [*raw* silk] 3 inexperienced [a *raw* recruit] 4 abraded and sore 5 uncomfortably cold and damp [a *raw* wind] 6 brutal, coarse, indecent, etc. 7 [Inf.] harsh or unfair [a *raw* deal] —**in the raw** 1 in the natural state 2 naked —**raw′ness** *n.*

raw bar a place serving uncooked shellfish

raw·boned (-bōnd′) *adj.* lean; gaunt

raw·hide *n.* 1 untanned cattle hide 2 a whip made of this

ray¹ (rā) *n.* [< L *radius*] 1 any of the thin lines, or beams, of light that appear to come from a bright source 2 any of several lines radiating from a center 3 a tiny amount [a *ray* of hope] 4 a beam of radiant energy, radioactive particles, etc.

ray² (rā) *n.* [< L *raia*] a cartilaginous fish with a broad, flat body, widely expanded fins on both sides, and a whiplike tail

ray·on (rā′än) *n.* [< RAY¹] 1 a textile fiber made from a cellulose solution 2 a fabric of such fibers

raze (rāz) *vt.* **razed, raz′ing** [< L *radere*, to scrape] to tear down completely; demolish

ra·zor (rā′zər) *n.* [see prec.] an instrument with a blade or blades, for shaving, trimming hair, etc.

razor wire sharp-edged wire, as for fences

razz (raz) *vt.* [< RASPBERRY] [Slang] to tease, ridicule, etc.

raz·zle-daz·zle (raz′əl daz′əl) *n.* [Slang] a flashy, deceptive display

razz·ma·tazz (raz′mə taz′) *n.* [prob. < prec.] [Slang] 1 lively spirit 2 flashy display

RB *abbrev. Football* running back

RBI *n., pl.* **RBIs** or **RBI** *Baseball* run batted in

RC *abbrev.* Roman Catholic

rd *abbrev.* 1 rod 2 round

Rd *abbrev.* Road

RDA *abbrev.* Recommended Daily (or Dietary) Allowance: the amount of protein, vitamins, etc. suggested for various age groups

re¹ (rā) *n.* [It] *Music* the second tone of the diatonic scale

re² (rē, rā) *prep.* [L < *res*, thing] in the matter of; as regards

re- [< Fr or L] *prefix* 1 back 2 again; anew It is sometimes hyphenated, as before a word beginning with *e* or to distinguish between such forms as *re-cover* (to cover again) and RECOVER The words in the following list can be understood if "again" or "anew" is added to the meaning of the base word:

reacquaint	redesign
reacquire	redirect
readjust	rediscover
readmit	redistribute
reaffirm	redivide
realign	redraw
reappear	reedit
reapply	reeducate
reappoint	reelect
reappraise	reembark
rearm	reemerge
reassemble	reemphasize
reassert	reenact
reassess	reenlist
reassign	reenter
reawaken	reestablish
reborn	reevaluate
rebroadcast	reexamine
rebuild	reexplain
recharge	refashion
recheck	refasten
reclassify	rethink
recommence	retrain
reconquer	retrial
reconvene	reunite
reconvert	reupholster
recopy	refinance
redecorate	reformulate
rededicate	refuel

refurnish

rehear

reheat

rehire

reinfect

reinsert

reinspect

reinvest

reissue

rekindle

relearn

reload

remake

remarry

rematch

remix

rename

renegotiate

renominate

renumber

reoccupy

reoccur

reopen

reorder

repack

repackage

repaint

rephrase

replay

re-press

reprint

republish

reread

rerelease

reroute

reschedule

resell

reset

resettle

reshuffle

respell

restate

restring

restudy

restyle

resupply

retell

retest

reuse

revitalize

rewash

reweigh

rework

rezone

reach (rēch) *vt.* ⟦OE *ræcan*⟧ **1** to thrust out (the hand, etc.) **2** to extend to by thrusting out, etc. **3** to obtain and hand over [*reach* me the salt] **4** to go as far as; attain **5** to influence; affect **6** to get in touch with, as by telephone —*vi.* **1** to thrust out the hand, etc. **2** to extend in influence, space, amount, etc. **3** to carry: said of sight, sound, etc. **4** to try to get something —*n.* **1** a stretching or thrusting out **2** the power of, or the extent covered in, stretching, obtaining, etc. **3** a continuous extent, esp. of water

re·act (rē akt′) *vi.* **1** to act in return or reciprocally **2** to act in opposition **3** to act in a reverse way; go back to a former condition, stage, etc. **4** to respond to a stimulus **5** *Chem.* to act with another substance in a chemical change

re·act·ant (rē ak′tənt) *n.* any substance involved in a chemical reaction

re·ac·tion (rē ak′shən) *n.* **1** a return or opposing action, force, etc. **2** a response, as to a stimulus or influence **3** a movement back to a former or less advanced condition; extreme conservatism **4** a chemical change **5** a change in an atomic nucleus **6** *Med.* a response to a substance, as in an allergy

re·ac·tion·ar·y (-shə ner′ē) *adj.* of, characterized by, or advocating reaction, esp. in politics —*n., pl.* -ies an advocate of reaction, esp. in politics

re·ac·ti·vate (rē ak′tə vāt′) *vt., vi.* -vat′ed, -vat′ing to make or be made active again; specif., to return (a military unit, ship, etc.) to active status —re·ac′ti·va′tion *n.*

re·ac·tive (-tiv) *adj.* **1** tending to react **2** of, from, or showing reaction —re·ac·tiv′i·ty *n.*

re·ac·tor (-tər) *n.* NUCLEAR REACTOR

read¹ (rēd) *vt.* read (red), read·ing (rēd′iŋ) ⟦< OE *rǣdan*, to counsel⟧ **1** to get the meaning of (writing) by interpreting the characters **2** to utter aloud (written matter) **3** to understand or interpret **4** to foretell (the future) **5** [Brit.] to study [to *read* law] **6** to register: said as of a gauge **7** [Slang] to hear and understand [I *read* you] **8** *Comput.* to access (data) from (a disk, flash drive, etc.) —*vi.* **1** to read something written **2** to learn by reading: with *about* or *of* **3** to contain certain words —**read into** to attribute (a particular meaning) to —**read out of** to expel from (a group) —read′a·bil′i·ty *n.* —read′a·ble *adj.* —read′er *n.*

read² (red) *vt., vi. pt. & pp. of* READ¹ —*adj.* informed by reading [well-*read*]

read·er·ship (rēd′ər ship′) *n.* the people who read a certain publication, author, etc.

read·i·ly (red′ə lē) *adv.* **1** willingly **2** easily

read·ing (rēd′iŋ) *n.* **1** the act of one who reads **2** material to be read **3** the amount measured by a barometer, thermometer, etc. **4** a particular interpretation or performance

read·out (rēd′out′) *n.* **1** the retrieving of information from a computer **2** information from a computer, thermostat, etc. displayed visually or recorded, as on tape

read·y (red′ē) *adj.* -i·er, -i·est ⟦OE *rǣde*⟧ **1** prepared to act or be used immediately **2** willing **3** likely or liable; apt [*ready* to cry] **4** dexterous **5** prompt [a *ready* reply] **6** available at once [*ready* cash] —*vt.* -ied, -y·ing to prepare —**at the ready** prepared for immediate use —read′i·ness *n.*

read·y-made *adj.* made so as to be ready for use or sale at once: also, as applied to clothing, read′y-to-wear′

Rea·gan (rā′gən), **Ron·ald (Wilson)** (rän′əld) 1911-2004; 40th president of the U.S. (1981-89)

re·a·gent (rē ā′jənt) *n. Chem.* a substance used to detect, measure, or react with another substance

re·al (rē′əl, rēl) *adj.* ⟦< L *res*, thing⟧ **1** existing as or in fact; actual; true **2** authentic; genuine **3** *Law* of or relating to permanent, immovable things [*real* property] —*adv.* [Inf.] very —**for real** [Slang] real or really

real estate 1 land, including the buildings, etc. on it **2** the buying and selling of this

re·al·ism (rē′ə liz′əm) *n.* **1** a tendency to face facts and be practical **2** the picturing in art and literature of people and things as they really appear to be —re′al·ist *n.* —re′al·is′tic *adj.* —re′al·is′ti·cal·ly *adv.*

re·al·i·ty (rē al′ə tē) *n., pl.* -ties **1** the quality or fact of being real **2** a person or thing that is real; fact —*adj.* of or being TV programming featuring nonactors in unscripted but contrived situations —**in reality** in fact; actually

re·al·ize (rē′ə līz′) *vt.* -ized′, -iz′ing **1** to make real; achieve **2** to understand fully **3** to convert (assets, rights, etc.) into money **4** to gain; obtain [to *realize* a profit] **5** to be sold for (a specified sum) —re′al·i·za′tion *n.*

re·al-life *adj.* actual; not imaginary

re·al·ly *adv.* 1 in reality 2 truly —*interj.* indeed: used to express surprise, doubt, etc.

realm (relm) *n.* 〚see REGAL〛 1 a kingdom 2 a region; sphere

real-time *adj.* of or pertaining to a mode of computer operation in which the computer collects data, computes with it, and uses the results to control a process as it happens

Re·al·tor (rē′əl tər, -tôr′) *trademark for* a real estate broker or appraiser who is a member of the National Association of Realtors —*n.* [r-] a real estate agent

re·al·ty (rē′əl tē) *n.* REAL ESTATE

ream¹ (rēm) *n.* 〚< Ar *rizma*, a bale〛 1 a quantity of paper varying from 480 to 516 sheets 2 [*pl.*] [Inf.] a great amount

ream² (rēm) *vt.* 〚OE *reman*〛 to enlarge (a hole) as with a reamer

ream·er *n.* 1 a sharp-edged tool for enlarging or tapering holes 2 a juicer

re·an·i·mate (rē an′ə māt′) *vt.* -**mat′ed**, -**mat′ing** to give new life, power, or vigor to —**re·an′i·ma′tion** *n.*

reap (rēp) *vt., vi.* 〚OE *ripan*〛 1 to cut (grain) with a scythe, reaper, etc. 2 to gather (a harvest) 3 to obtain as the reward of action, etc.

reap·er *n.* 1 one who reaps 2 a machine for reaping grain

re·ap·por·tion (rē′ə pôr′shən) *vt.* to apportion again; specif., to change the distribution of (a legislature) so that members represent constituents equally —**re′ap·por′tion·ment** *n.*

rear¹ (rir) *n.* 〚see ARREARS〛 1 the back part 2 the position behind or at the back 3 the part of an army, etc. farthest from the enemy 4 [Slang] the buttocks —*adj.* of, at, or in the rear —**bring up the rear** to come at the end

rear² (rir) *vt.* 〚OE *ræran*〛 1 to put upright; elevate 2 to build; erect 3 to grow or breed 4 to educate, train, etc. [to *rear* a child] —*vi.* 1 to rise on the hind legs, as a horse does 2 to rise (*up*), in anger, etc. 3 to rise high

rear admiral a naval officer ranking above a captain

rear-end *vt.* to crash into, or cause one's vehicle to crash into, the back end of (another vehicle)

rear·most *adj.* farthest in the rear

re·ar·range (rē′ə rānj′) *vt.* -**ranged′**, -**rang′ing** to arrange again or in a different way

rear·ward *adj.* at, in, or toward the rear —*adv.* toward the rear: also **rear′wards**

rea·son (rē′zən) *n.* 〚< L *ratio*, a reckoning〛 1 an explanation of an act, idea, etc. 2 a cause or motive 3 the ability to think, draw conclusions, etc. 4 good sense 5 sanity —*vi., vt.* 1 to think logically (about); analyze 2 to argue or infer —**stand to reason** to be logical —**rea′son·ing** *n.*

rea·son·a·ble *adj.* 1 able to reason 2 fair; just 3 sensible 4 not excessive —**rea′son·a·bly** *adv.*

re·as·sure (rē′ə shoor′) *vt.* -**sured′**, -**sur′ing** to restore to confidence —**re′as·sur′ance** *n.*

re·bate (rē′bāt′) *vt.* -**bat′ed**, -**bat′ing** 〚< OFr *re-*, RE- + *abattre*, beat down〛 to give back (part of a payment) —*n.* a return of part of a payment

Re·bek·ah (ri bek′ə) *n. Bible* the wife of Isaac: also sp. **Re·bec′ca**

reb·el (reb′əl; *for v.* ri bel′) *n.* 〚< L *re-*, again + *bellare*, wage war〛 one who resists authority —*adj.* 1 rebellious 2 of rebels —*vi.* **re·bel′**, -**belled′**, -**bel′ling** 1 to resist authority 2 to feel or show strong aversion

re·bel·lion (ri bel′yən) *n.* 1 armed resistance to one's government 2 a defiance of any authority

re·bel·lious (-yəs) *adj.* 1 resisting authority 2 opposing control; defiant

re·birth (rē burth′) *n.* 1 a new or second birth 2 a reawakening; revival

re·boot (rē boot′; *for n.* rē′boot′) *vi., vt.* 1 *Comput.* to boot again, as to restore normal operation 2 [Inf.] to restart or remake —*n.* [Inf.] the act or an instance of rebooting

re·bound (ri bound′; *for n.* rē′bound′) *vi.* to spring back, as upon impact —*n.* a rebounding, or a ball, etc. that rebounds —**on the rebound** 1 after it bounces back 2 just after being jilted

re·buff (ri buf′) *n.* 〚< It *rabbuffare*, disarrange〛 1 an abrupt refusal of offered advice, help, etc. 2 any repulse —*vt.* 1 to snub 2 to check or repulse

re·buke (ri byook′) *vt.* -**buked′**, -**buk′ing** 〚< OFr *re-*, back + *buchier*, to beat〛 to scold in a sharp way; reprimand —*n.* a reprimand

re·bus (rē′bəs) *n.* 〚L, lit., by things〛 a puzzle consisting of pictures, etc. combined to suggest words or phrases

re·but (ri but′) *vt.* -**but′ted**, -**but′ting** 〚< OFr *re-*, back + *buter*, to thrust〛 to contradict or oppose, esp. in a formal manner by argument, proof, etc. —**re·but′tal** (-′l) *n.*

rec (rek) *n.* short for RECREATION: used in compounds, as **rec center** or **rec room**

re·cal·ci·trant (ri kal′si trənt) *adj.* 〚< L *re-*, back + *calcitrare*, to kick〛 1 refusing to obey authority, etc. 2 hard to handle —**re·cal′ci·trance** *n.*

re·call (ri kôl′; *for n.* rē′kôl′) *vt.* 1 to call back; specif., to ask purchasers to return (a potentially defective product) 2 to remember 3 to take back; revoke —*n.* 1 a recalling 2 memory 3 the removal of, or right to remove, an official from office by popular vote

re·cant (ri kant′) *vt., vi.* 〚< L *re-*, back + *canere*, sing〛 to renounce formally (one's beliefs, remarks, etc.) —**re·can·ta·tion** (rē′kan tā′shən) *n.*

re·cap¹ (rē kap′; *also, and for n. always,* rē′kap′) *vt.* -**capped′**, -**cap′ping** to put a new tread on (a worn tire) —*n.* such a tire

re·cap² (rē′kap′) *n.* a recapitulation, or summary —*vt., vi.* -**capped′**, -**cap′ping** to recapitulate

re·ca·pit·u·late (rē′kə pich′ə lāt′) *vi., vt.* -**lat′ed**, -**lat′ing** 〚see RE- & CAPITULATE〛 to repeat briefly; summarize —**re′ca·pit′u·la′tion** *n.*

re·cap·ture (rē kap/chər) *vt.* **-tured, -turing 1** to capture again; retake **2** to remember —*n.* a recapturing

recd or *contr.* **rec'd** *abbrev.* received

re·cede (ri sēd/) *vi.* **-ced/ed, -ced/ing** [see RE- & CEDE] **1** to go, move, or slope backward **2** to diminish

re·ceipt (ri sēt/) *n.* [see RECEIVE] **1** old-fashioned var. of RECIPE **2** a receiving or being received **3** a written acknowledgment that something has been received **4** [*pl.*] the amount, as of money, received —*vt.* to write a receipt for (goods, etc.)

re·ceiv·a·ble (ri sēv/ə bəl) *adj.* **1** that can be received **2** due —*n.* [*pl.*] outstanding bills, loans, etc.

re·ceive (ri sēv/) *vt.* **-ceived/, -ceiv/ing** [< L *re-*, back + *capere*, take] **1** to take or get (something given, thrown, sent, etc.) **2** to experience; undergo [to *receive* acclaim] **3** to bear or hold **4** to react to in a specified way **5** to learn [to *receive* news] **6** to let enter **7** to greet (visitors, etc.)

re·ceived *adj.* accepted; considered as standard

re·ceiv·er *n.* one that receives; specif., *a*) a device that converts electrical waves or signals into audible or visual signals *b*) a football player designated to receive a forward pass *c*) one appointed by a court to administer or hold in trust property in bankruptcy or in a lawsuit —**re·ceiv/er·ship/** *n.*

re·cen·sion (ri sen/shən) *n.* [< L *recensere*, revise] a revision of a text based on a critical study of sources

re·cent (rē/sənt) *adj.* [< L. *recens*] **1** done, made, etc. just before the present; new **2** of a time just before the present —**re/cent·ly** *adv.*

re·cep·ta·cle (ri sep/tə kəl) *n.* [see RECEIVE] a container

re·cep·tion (ri sep/shən) *n.* **1** *a*) a receiving or being received *b*) the manner of this **2** a social function for the receiving of guests **3** *Radio, TV* the receiving of signals, with reference to the quality of reproduction

re·cep·tion·ist *n.* an office employee who receives callers, etc.

re·cep·tive *adj.* able or ready to accept new ideas, suggestions, etc.

re·cep·tor *n.* a nerve ending or group of nerve endings specialized for receiving stimuli

re·cess (rē/ses; *also, & for v. usually, ri ses*/) *n.* [< L. *recedere*, recede] **1** a hollow place, as in a wall **2** a hidden or inner place **3** a temporary halting as of work, a session, etc. —*vt.* **1** to place in a recess **2** to halt temporarily —*vi.* to take a recess

re·ces·sion (ri sesh/ən) *n.* **1** a going back; withdrawal **2** a temporary falling off of business activity

re·ces·sion·al *n.* a piece of music at the end of a church service played when the clergy, etc. march out

re·ces·sive (ri ses/iv) *adj.* **1** tending to recede **2** *Genetics* designating or of that one of any pair of hereditary factors which remains latent —*n.* *Genetics* a recessive character or characters

re·cher·ché (rə sher/shā/) *adj.* [Fr] **1** rare; choice **2** refined; esp., too refined

re·cid·i·vism (ri sid/ə viz/əm) *n.* [< L *re-*, back + *cadere*, to fall] habitual or chronic relapse, esp. into crime

rec·i·pe (res/ə pē/) *n.* [L < *recipere*, receive] **1** a list of materials and directions for preparing a dish or drink **2** a way to achieve something

re·cip·i·ent (ri sip/ē ənt) *n.* [see RECEIVE] one that receives

re·cip·ro·cal (ri sip/rə kəl) *adj.* [< L *reciprocus*, returning] **1** done, given, etc. in return **2** mutual [*reciprocal* love.] **3** corresponding but reversed **4** corresponding or complementary —*n.* **1** a complement, counterpart, etc. **2** *Math.* the quantity resulting from the division of 1 by the given quantity [the *reciprocal* of 7 is ⅟₇]

re·cip·ro·cate (-kāt/) *vt., vi.* **-cat/ed, -cat/ing 1** to give and get reciprocally **2** to do, feel, etc. in return **3** to move alternately back and forth —**re·cip/ro·ca/tion** *n.*

rec·i·proc·i·ty (res/ə präs/ə tē) *n., pl.* **-ties 1** reciprocal state **2** mutual exchange as of special privileges between two countries, clubs, etc.

re·cit·al (ri sīt/'l) *n.* **1** a reciting **2** the account, story, etc. told **3** a musical or dance program

rec·i·ta·tion (res/ə tā/shən) *n.* **1** a reciting, as of facts, events, etc. **2** *a*) a saying aloud in public of something memorized *b*) a piece so presented **3** a reciting by pupils of answers to questions on a prepared lesson

rec·i·ta·tive (-tə tēv/) *n.* [< It: see fol.] a type of declamation, as for operatic dialogue, with the rhythms of speech, but in musical tones

re·cite (ri sīt/) *vt., vi.* **-cit/ed, -cit/ing** [see RE- & CITE] **1** to say aloud from memory, as a poem, lesson, etc. **2** to tell in detail; relate

reck·less (rek/lis) *adj.* [OE *recceleas*] careless; heedless —**reck/less·ly** *adv.* —**reck/less·ness** *n.*

reck·on (rek/ən) *vt.* [OE *-recenian*] **1** to count; compute **2** to estimate **3** [Inf. or Dial.] to suppose —*vi.* **1** to count up **2** [Inf.] to rely (*on*) —**reckon with** to take into consideration

reck·on·ing *n.* **1** count or computation **2** the settlement of an account

re·claim (ri klām/) *vt.* [see RE- & CLAIM] **1** to bring back (a person) from error, vice, etc. **2** to make (wasteland, etc.) usable **3** to recover (useful materials) from waste products —**rec·la·ma·tion** (rek/lə mā/shən) *n.*

re·cline (ri klīn/) *vt., vi.* **-clined/, -clin/ing** [< L *re-*, back + *clinare*, lean] to lie or cause to lie down

re·clin·er *n.* an upholstered armchair with an adjustable back and seat for reclining: also **reclining chair**

rec·luse (rek/lōōs, ri klōōs/) *n.* [< L *re-*, back + *claudere*, shut] one who lives a secluded, solitary life —**re·clu/sive** *adj.*

rec·og·ni·tion (rek/əg nish/ən) *n.* **1** acknowledgment, approval, or gratitude as for services rendered **2** identification of a person or thing as having been known before **3** formal acknowledgment of sovereignty

re·cog·ni·zance (ri käg′ni zəns, -kän′i-) *n.* ‖< L *re-*, again + *cognoscere*, know‖ *Law* a bond binding one to some act, as to appear in court

rec·og·nize (rek′əg nīz′) *vt.* **-nized′, -niz′ ing** ‖see prec.‖ **1** to be aware of as someone or something known before **2** to know by some detail, as of appearance **3** to perceive **4** to accept as a fact [to *recognize* defeat] **5** to acknowledge as worthy of approval **6** to acknowledge the status of (a government, etc.) **7** to grant the right to speak in a meeting —**rec′og·niz′a·ble** *adj.*

re·coil (ri koil′; *also for n.* rē′koil′) *vi.* ‖< L *re-*, back + *culus*, buttocks‖ **1** to draw back, as in fear, etc. **2** to spring or kick back, as a gun when fired —*n.* a springing or kicking back

rec·ol·lect (rek′ə lekt′) *vt., vi.* ‖see RE- & COLLECT‖ to remember, esp. with some effort —**rec′ol·lec′tion** *n.*

re·com·bi·nant DNA (rē käm′bə nənt) DNA formed in the laboratory by splicing together pieces of DNA from different species, as to create new life forms

rec·om·mend (rek′ə mend′) *vt.* ‖see RE- & COMMEND‖ **1** to entrust **2** to suggest favorably as suited for some position, etc. **3** to make acceptable **4** to advise; counsel —**rec′om·men·da′tion** *n.*

re·com·mit (rē′kə mit′) *vt.* **-mit′ted, -mit′ ting 1** to commit again **2** to refer (a question, bill, etc.) back to a committee

rec·om·pense (rek′əm pens′) *vt.* **-pensed′, -pens′ing** ‖see RE- & COMPENSATE‖ **1** to repay or reward **2** to compensate (a loss, etc.) —*n.* **1** requital; reward **2** compensation

rec·on·cile (rek′ən sīl′) *vt.* **-ciled′, -cil′ing** ‖see RE- & CONCILIATE‖ **1** to make friendly again **2** to settle (a quarrel, etc.) **3** to make (ideas, accounts, etc.) consistent **4** to make acquiescent (*to*) —**rec′on·cil′a·ble** *adj.* —**rec′on·cil′i·a′tion** (-sil′ē ā′shən) *n.*

rec·on·dite (rek′ən dīt′) *adj.* ‖< L *re-*, back + *condere*, to hide‖ beyond ordinary understanding; abstruse

re·con·di·tion (rē′kən dish′ən) *vt.* to put back in good condition, as by repairing

re·con·nais·sance (ri kän′ə səns) *n.* ‖Fr: see RECOGNIZANCE‖ a survey of a region, as in seeking out information about enemy positions

rec·on·noi·ter (rek′ə noit′ər, rē′kə-) *vt., vi.* to make a reconnaissance (of): also [Chiefly Brit.] **rec′on·noi′tre, -tred, -tring**

re·con·sid·er (rē′kən sid′ər) *vt., vi.* to think over again, esp. with a view to changing a decision

re·con·sti·tute (rē kän′stə tōōt′) *vt.* **-tut′ ed, -tut′ing** to constitute again; specif., to restore (a dried or condensed substance) to its full liquid form by adding water

re·con·struct (rē′kən strukt′) *vt.* **1** to construct again; rebuild **2** to build up, as from remains, an image of the original

re·con·struc·tion *n.* **1** a reconstructing **2** [R-] the process or period, after the Civil War, of reestablishing the Southern states in the Union

re·cord (ri kôrd′; *for n. & adj.* rek′ərd) *vt.* ‖< L *recordari*, remember‖ **1** to write down for future use **2** to register, as on a graph **3** to register (sound or visual images) on a disc, tape, etc. for later reproduction —*n.* **rec′ ord 1** the condition of being recorded **2** anything written down and preserved; account of events **3** *a)* the known facts about anyone or anything *b)* the recorded crimes of a person **4** *a)* a grooved disc for playing on a phonograph *b)* a musical recording in any medium **5** the best official performance achieved —*adj.* **rec′ord** being the best, largest, etc. —**on** (or **off the**) **record** publicly (or confidentially) declared

re·cord·er *n.* **1** an official who keeps records **2** a machine or device that records; esp., a TAPE RECORDER **3** an early wind instrument

re·cord·ing *n.* **1** that which is recorded, as on a disc or tape **2** a record, disc, etc.

re·count¹ (ri kount′) *vt.* ‖see RE- & COUNT¹‖ to tell in detail; narrate

re·count² (rē′kount′; *for n.* rē′kount′) *vt.* to count again —*n.* a recounting, as of votes

re·coup (ri kōōp′) *vt.* ‖< Fr *re-*, again + *couper*, to cut‖ to make up for or regain [to *recoup* a loss]

re·course (rē′kôrs′, ri kôrs′) *n.* ‖see RE- & COURSE‖ **1** a turning for aid, safety, etc. **2** that to which one turns seeking aid, safety, etc.

re·cov·er (ri kuv′ər) *vt.* ‖< L *recuperare*‖ **1** to get back (something lost, etc.) **2** to regain (health, etc.) **3** to make up for [to *recover* losses] **4** to save (oneself) from a fall, etc. **5** to reclaim (land from the sea, etc.) **6** *Sports* to get control of (a fumbled ball, etc.) —*vi.* **1** to regain health, balance, or control **2** *Sports* to regain control of a fumbled ball, etc.

re·cov·er·y *n., pl.* **-ies** a recovering; specif., *a)* a regaining of something lost *b)* a return to health *c)* a retrieval of a capsule, etc. after a spaceflight

recovery room a hospital room where postoperative patients are kept for close observation and care

rec·re·ant (rek′rē ənt) [Archaic] *adj.* ‖< OFr *recreire*, surrender allegiance‖ **1** cowardly **2** disloyal —*n.* **1** a coward **2** a traitor

rec·re·a·tion (rek′rē ā′shən) *n.* ‖< L *recreare*, refresh‖ any form of play, amusement, etc. used to relax or refresh the body or mind —**rec′re·ate′** *vt., vi.* **-at′ed, -at′ing** —**rec′ re·a′tion·al** *adj.*

re·crim·i·nate (ri krim′ə nāt′) *vi.* **-nat′ed, -nat′ing** ‖< L *re-*, back + *crimen*, offense‖ to answer an accuser by accusing that person in return —**re·crim′i·na′tion** *n.*

re·cru·desce (rē′krōō des′) *vi.* **-desced′, -desc′ing** ‖< L *re-*, again + *crudus*, raw‖ to break out again after being inactive —**re′cru· des′cence** *n.* —**re′cru·des′cent** *adj.*

re·cruit (ri krōōt′) *vt., vi.* [< L *re-*, again + *crescere*, grow] **1** to enlist (personnel) into an army or navy **2** to enlist (new members) for an organization —*n.* **1** a newly enlisted or drafted soldier, etc. **2** a new member of any group —**re·cruit′er** *n.*

rec·tal (rek′təl) *adj.* of, for, or near the rectum

rec·tan·gle (rek′taŋ′gəl) *n.* [< L *rectus*, straight + *angulus*, a corner] a plane figure with four sides and four right angles —**rec·tan′gu·lar** (-gyə lər) *adj.*

rec·ti·fy (rek′tə fī′) *vt.* **-fied′, -fy′ing** [< L *rectus*, straight + *facere*, make] **1** to put right; correct **2** *Elec.* to convert (alternating current) to direct current —**rec′ti·fi·ca′tion** *n.* —**rec′ti·fi′er** *n.*

rec·ti·lin·e·ar (rek′tə lin′ē ər) *adj.* bounded or formed by straight lines

rec·ti·tude (rek′tə tōōd′) *n.* [< L *rectus*, right] strict honesty; uprightness of character

rec·tor (rek′tər) *n.* [< L *regere*, to rule] **1** in some churches, a clergyman in charge of a parish **2** the head of certain schools, colleges, etc.

rec·to·ry (rek′tər ē) *n., pl.* **-ries** the house of a minister or priest

rec·tum (rek′təm) *n., pl.* **-tums** or **-ta** (-tə) [< L *rectum (intestinum)*, straight (intestine)] the lowest, or last, segment of the large intestine

re·cum·bent (ri kum′bənt) *adj.* [< L *re-*, back + *-cumbere*, lie down] lying down; reclining

re·cu·per·ate (ri kōō′pə rāt′) *vt., vi.* **-at′ed, -at′ing** [< L *recuperare*, recover] **1** to get well again **2** to recover (losses, etc.) —**re·cu′per·a′tion** *n.* —**re·cu′per·a′tive** (-pə rāt′iv, -pə rə tiv) *adj.*

re·cur (ri kur′) *vi.* **-curred′, -cur′ring** [< L *re-*, back + *currere*, run] **1** to return in thought, talk, etc. **2** to occur again or at intervals —**re·cur′rence** *n.* —**re·cur′rent** *adj.*

re·cy·cle (rē si′kəl) *vt.* **-cled, -cling** **1** to pass through a cycle again **2** to use again and again, as the same water **3** *a)* to process in order to use again [*to recycle paper*] *b)* to gather up and turn in (newspapers, etc.) for such processing

red (red) *n.* [OE *read*] **1** the color of blood **2** any red pigment **3** [*often* R-] [Inf.] a communist —*adj.* **red′der, red′dest 1** of the color red **2** [*often* R-] communist —**in the red** losing money —**see red** [Inf.] to become angry —**red′dish** *adj.* —**red′ness** *n.*

re·dact (ri dakt′) *vt.* [< L *redigere*, get in order] **1** to prepare for publication; edit **2** to delete (sensitive information) from a document —**re·dac′tion** *n.* —**re·dac′tor** *n.*

red blood cell or **red corpuscle** ERYTHROCYTE

red-blood·ed *adj.* high-spirited and strongwilled; vigorous

red·cap *n.* a baggage porter, as in a railroad station

red carpet a very grand or impressive welcome and entertainment: with *the* —**red′-car′pet** *adj.*

red·coat *n.* a British soldier in a uniform with a red coat, as during the American Revolution

Red Cross an international society for the relief of suffering in time of war or disaster

redd (red) *vt., vi.* **redd** or **redd′ed, redd′ing** [< OE *hreddan*, take away] [Inf. or Dial.] to put in order; tidy: usually with *up*

red deer a deer of Europe and Asia

red·den (red′n) *vt.* to make red —*vi.* to become red; esp., to blush

re·deem (ri dēm′) *vt.* [< L *re(d)-*, back + *emere*, get] **1** to buy or get back; recover **2** to pay off (a mortgage, etc.) **3** to turn in (a coupon, etc.) for a discount, premium, etc. **4** to ransom **5** to deliver from sin **6** to fulfill (a promise) **7** *a)* to make amends or atone for *b)* to restore (oneself) to favor —**re·deem′a·ble** *adj.* —**re·deem′er** *n.* —**re·demp·tion** (ri demp′shən) *n.*

re·de·ploy (rē′di ploi′) *vt., vi.* to move (troops, etc.) from one front or area to another —**re′de·ploy′ment** *n.*

re·de·vel·op (rē′di vel′əp) *vt.* **1** to develop again **2** to rebuild or restore —**re′de·vel′op·ment** *n.*

red-flag *vt.* **-flagged′, -flag′ging** to mark or otherwise indicate as being risky, etc.

red-hand·ed *adv.* in the very commission of crime or wrongdoing

red·head *n.* a person with red hair

red herring [< herring drawn across the trace in hunting to divert the hounds] something used to divert attention from the basic issue

red-hot *adj.* **1** hot enough to glow **2** very excited, angry, etc. **3** very new

re·dis·trict *vt.* to divide anew into districts

red-let·ter *adj.* designating a memorable or joyous day or event

red·lin·ing (-līn′iŋ) *n.* [from outlining such areas in red on a map] the refusal by some banks or companies to issue loans or insurance on property in certain neighborhoods

re·do (rē dōō′) *vt.* **-did′, -done′, -do′ing 1** to do again **2** to redecorate

red·o·lent (red′′l ənt) *adj.* [< L *re(d)-*, intens. + *olere*, to smell] **1** sweet-smelling **2** smelling (*of*) **3** suggestive (*of*) —**red′o·lence** *n.*

re·dou·ble (rē dub′əl) *vt., vi.* **-bled, -bling** to make or become twice as much or twice as great

re·doubt (ri dout′) *n.* [see REDUCE] **1** a breastwork **2** any stronghold

re·doubt·a·ble *adj.* [< L *re-*, intens. + *dubitare*, to doubt] formidable —**re·doubt′a·bly** *adv.*

re·dound (ri dound′) *vi.* [< L *re(d)-*, intens. + *undare*, to surge] **1** to have a result (*to* the credit or discredit of) **2** to come back; react (*upon*)

re·dress (ri dres′; *for n., usually* rē′dres′) *vt.* [see RE- & DRESS] to compensate for (a wrong, etc.) —*n.* **1** compensation **2** a redressing

Red Sea sea between NE Africa & W Arabia

red snapper a reddish, edible, deep-water fish

red state [< the media's use of red on maps to designate "Republican"] a U.S. state whose voters chose predominantly the Republican candidate in the most recent presidential election

red tape [< tape for tying official papers] rules and details that waste time and effort

red tide sea water discolored by red algae poisonous to marine life

re·duce (ri dōōs′) *vt.* **-duced′, -duc′ing** [< L *re-*, back + *ducere*, to lead] 1 to lessen, as in size, price, etc. 2 to put into a different form 3 to lower, as in rank or condition —*vi.* to lose weight, as by dieting

re·duc·tion (ri duk′shən) *n.* 1 a reducing or being reduced 2 anything made by reducing 3 the amount by which anything is reduced

re·dun·dant (ri dun′dənt) *adj.* [see REDOUND] 1 excess; superfluous 2 wordy 3 unnecessary to the meaning: said of words and affixes —**re·dun′dan·cy** *n.*

red·wood *n.* 1 a giant evergreen of the Pacific coast 2 its reddish wood

reed (rēd) *n.* [OE *hreod*] 1 a tall, slender grass 2 a rustic musical instrument made from a hollow stem 3 *Music* a thin strip of wood, plastic, etc. placed against the mouthpiece, as of a clarinet, and vibrated by the breath to produce a tone —**reed′y** *adj.* **-i·er, -i·est**

reef[1] (rēf) *n.* [prob. < ON *rif*, a rib] a ridge of rock, coral, or sand at or near the surface of the water

reef[2] *n.* [ME *riff*] a part of a sail which can be folded or rolled up and made fast to reduce the area exposed to the wind — *vt., vi.* to reduce the size of (a sail) by taking in part of it

reef·er *n.* [Slang] a marijuana cigarette

reek (rēk) *n.* [OE *rec*] a strong, unpleasant smell —*vi.* to have a strong, offensive smell

reel[1] (rēl) *n.* [OE *hreol*] 1 a spool on which wire, film, fishing line, etc. is wound 2 the quantity of wire, film, etc. usually wound on one reel —*vt.* to wind on a reel —*vi.* 1 to sway, stagger, etc. as from drunkenness or dizziness 2 to spin; whirl —**reel in** 1 to wind on a reel 2 to pull in (a fish) by using a reel —**reel off** to tell, write, etc. easily and quickly —**reel out** to unwind from a reel

reel[2] (rēl) *n.* [prob. < prec.] a lively dance

re-en·try or **re-en·try** (rē en′trē) *n., pl.* **-tries** 1 a coming back, as of a space vehicle, into the earth's atmosphere 2 a repeated or second entry

ref[1] (ref) *n., vt., vi.* [Inf.] *short for* REFEREE

ref[2] *abbrev.* 1 referee 2 reference 3 reformed 4 refund

re·face (rē fās′) *vt.* **-faced′, -fac′ing** to put a new facing or covering on

re·fec·tion (ri fek′shən) *n.* [< L *re-*, again + *facere*, make] a light meal; lunch

re·fec·to·ry (ri fek′tə rē) *n., pl.* **-ries** a dining hall, as in a monastery

re·fer (ri fur′) *vt.* **-ferred′, -fer′ring** [< L *re-*, back + *ferre*, to bear] 1 to submit (a quarrel, etc.) for settlement 2 to direct *to* someone or something for aid, information, etc. —*vi.* 1

to relate or apply (*to*) 2 to direct attention (*to*) 3 to turn (*to*) for information, aid, etc. —**re·fer′rer** *n.*

ref·er·ee (ref′ə rē′) *n.* 1 one to whom something is referred for decision 2 an official who enforces the rules in certain sports contests — *vt., vi.* **-eed′, -ee′ing** to act as referee (in)

ref·er·ence (ref′ər əns, ref′rəns) *n.* 1 a referring or being referred 2 relation [in *reference* to his letter] 3 *a*) the directing of attention to a person or thing *b*) a mention 4 *a*) an indication, as in a book, of some other source of information *b*) such a source 5 *a*) one who can offer information or recommendation *b*) a statement of character, ability, etc. by such a person —*adj.* used for research [*reference* books]

ref·er·en·dum (ref′ə ren′dəm) *n., pl.* **-dums** or **-da** (-də) [L: see REFER] 1 the submission of a law to a direct vote of the people 2 the vote itself

ref·er·ent (ref′ər ənt) *n.* the thing referred to, esp. by a word or expression

re·fer·ral (ri fur′əl) *n.* 1 a referring or being referred 2 a person who is referred to another

re·fill (rē fil′; *for n.* rē′fil′) *vt., vi.* to fill again —*n.* 1 a unit to refill a special container 2 a refilling of a medical prescription —**re·fill′a·ble** *adj.*

re·fine (ri fīn′) *vt.* **-fined′, -fin′ing** [RE- + *fine*, make fine] 1 to free from impurities, etc. 2 to make more polished or elegant

re·fined *adj.* 1 made free from impurities; purified 2 cultivated, elegant, etc. 3 subtle, precise, etc.

re·fine·ment *n.* 1 *a*) a refining or being refined *b*) the result of this 2 delicacy or elegance of manners, etc. 3 an improvement 4 a fine distinction; subtlety

re·fin·er·y *n., pl.* **-er·ies** a plant for purifying materials, as oil, sugar, etc.

re·fin·ish (rē fin′ish) *vt.* to change or restore the finish of (furniture, etc.) —**re·fin′ish·er** *n.*

re·fit (rē fit′) *vt., vi.* **-fit′ted, -fit′ting** to make or be made fit for use again by repairing, reequipping, etc.

re·flect (ri flekt′) *vt.* [< L *re-*, back + *flectere*, to bend] 1 to throw back (light, heat, or sound) 2 to give back an image of 3 to bring as a result [to *reflect* honor on the city] —*vi.* 1 to throw back light, heat, etc. 2 to give back an image 3 to think seriously (*on* or *upon*) 4 to cast blame or discredit (*on* or *upon*) —**re·flec′tive** *adj.*

re·flec·tion *n.* 1 a reflecting or being reflected 2 anything reflected 3 contemplation 4 a thoughtful idea or remark 5 blame; discredit

re·flec·tor *n.* a surface, object, etc. that reflects light, sound, heat, etc.

re·flex (rē′fleks′) *adj.* [see REFLECT] designating or of an involuntary action, as a sneeze, resulting from the direct transmission of a stimulus to a muscle or gland —*n.* a reflex action

re·flex·ive (ri flek′siv) *adj.* **1** designating a grammatical relation in which a verb's subject and object refer to the same person or thing (Ex.: I wash myself) **2** designating a verb, pronoun, etc. in such a relation —**re·flex′ive·ly** *adv.*

re·for·est (rē fôr′ist) *vt., vi.* to plant new trees on (land once forested) —**re′for·est·a′tion** *n.*

re·form (ri fôrm′) *vt.* [see RE- & FORM] **1** to make better as by stopping abuses **2** to cause (a person) to behave better —*vi.* to become better in behavior —*n.* a reforming

re·form (rē fôrm′) *vt., vi.* to form again

ref·or·ma·tion (ref′ər mā′shən) *n.* a reforming or being reformed —**the Reformation** the religious movement of the 1500s that resulted in establishing the Protestant churches

re·form·a·to·ry (ri fôr′mə tôr′ē) *n., pl.* -ries an institution to which young offenders are sent to be reformed

re·form·er *n.* one who seeks to bring about political or social reform

re·fract (ri frakt′) *vt.* [< L *refractus*, turned aside <*re*–, back + *frangere*, to break] to cause (a ray of light, etc.) to undergo refraction

re·frac·tion *n.* the bending of a ray or wave, as of light or sound, as it passes from one medium to another

re·frac·to·ry (ri frak′tər ē) *adj.* [see REFRACT] hard to manage; stubborn

re·frain¹ (ri frān′) *vi.* [< L *re*–, back + *frenare*, to curb] to hold back; keep oneself (*from doing something)

re·frain² (ri frān′) *n.* [see REFRACT] a phrase or verse repeated at intervals in a song or poem

re·fresh (ri fresh′) *vt.* **1** to make fresh by cooling, wetting, etc. **2** to make (a person) feel cooler, stronger, etc., as by food, sleep, etc. **3** to replenish **4** to stimulate (the memory, etc.) **5** *Comput.* to load (a webpage, etc.) again

re·fresh·ing *adj.* **1** that refreshes **2** pleasingly new or different

re·fresh·ment *n.* **1** a refreshing or being refreshed **2** something that refreshes **3** [*pl.*] food or drink or both

re·frig·er·ant (rē frij′ə rənt) *n.* a substance used in refrigeration

re·frig·er·ate (ri frij′ə rāt′) *vt.* -at′ed, -at′ing [< L *re*–, intens. + *frigus*, cold] to make or keep cool or cold, as for preserving —**re·frig′er·a′tion** *n.*

re·frig·er·a·tor *n.* a box or room in which food, drink, etc. are kept cool

ref·uge (ref′yōōj) *n.* [< L *re*–, back + *fugere*, flee] (a) shelter or protection from danger, difficulty, etc.

ref·u·gee (ref′yoo jē′, ref′yoo jē′) *n.* one who flees from home or country to seek refuge elsewhere

re·ful·gent (ri ful′jənt) *adj.* [< L *re*–, back + *fulgere*, shine] shining; radiant; glowing —**re·ful′gence** *n.*

re·fund (ri fund′; *for n.* rē′fund′) *vt., vi.*

[< L *re*–, back + *fundere*, pour] to give back (money, etc.); repay —*n.* a refunding or the amount refunded

re·fur·bish (ri fur′bish) *vt.* [RE- + FURBISH] to renovate —**re·fur′bish·ment** *n.*

re·fuse¹ (ri fyōōz′) *vt., vi.* -fused′, -fus′ing [< L *re*–, back + *fundere*, pour] **1** to decline to accept **2** to decline (to do something), to grant the request of (someone), etc. —**re·fus′al** *n.*

ref·use² (ref′yōōs, -yōōz) *n.* [see prec.] waste; trash; rubbish

re·fute (ri fyōōt′) *vt.* -fut′ed, -fut′ing [L *refutare*, repel] to prove to be false or wrong —**re·fut′a·ble** *adj.* —**ref·u·ta·tion** (ref′yə tā′shən)

reg *abbrev.* **1** registered **2** regular **3** regulation

re·gain (ri gān′) *vt.* **1** to get back; recover **2** to get back to

re·gal (rē′gəl) *adj.* [< L *rex*, king] of, like, or fit for a monarch

re·gale (ri gāl′) *vt.* -galed′, -gal′ing [< Fr *ré*- (see RE-) + OFr *gale*, joy] to amuse or delight as with a story

re·ga·li·a (ri gāl′yə) *pl.n.* [see REGAL] **1** royal insignia **2** the insignia as of a rank or society **3** finery

re·gard (ri gärd′) *n.* [see RE- & GUARD] **1** a steady look; gaze **2** consideration; concern **3** respect and affection **4** reference; relation [in *regard* to your plan] **5** [*pl.*] good wishes —*vi.* **1** to look at attentively **2** to consider **3** to hold in affection and respect **4** to concern or involve —**as regards** concerning

re·gard·ing *prep.* concerning; about

re·gard·less *adv.* [Inf.] without regard for objections, etc.; anyway —**regardless of** in spite of

re·gat·ta (ri gät′ə) *n.* [< It] **1** a boat race **2** a series of boat races

re·gen·er·ate (ri jen′ə rit; *for v.,* -rāt′) *adj.* [see RE- & GENERATE] **1** spiritually reborn **2** renewed or restored —*vt.* -at′ed, -at′ing **1** to cause to be spiritually reborn **2** to cause to be completely reformed **3** to bring into existence again —*vi.* to form again, or be made anew —**re·gen′er·a′tion** *n.* —**re·gen′er·a′tive** (-rāt′iv, -rə tiv) *adj.*

re·gent (rē′jənt) *n.* [< L *regere*, to rule] **1** a person appointed to rule when a monarch is absent, too young, etc. **2** a member of a governing board, as of a university —**re′gen·cy** *n.*

reg·gae (reg′ā) *n.* [< ?] a form of popular Jamaican music with a strongly accented offbeat

reg·i·cide (rej′ə sīd′) *n.* [< L *regis*, of a king + -*cida* (see -CIDE)] **1** one who kills a monarch **2** the killing of a monarch

re·gime or **ré·gime** (rə zhēm′, rā-) *n.* [see fol.] **1** a political system **2** an administration

reg·i·men (rej′ə mən) *n.* [< L *regere*, to rule] a system of diet, exercise, etc. to improve health

reg·i·ment (rej′ə mənt; *for v.,* -ment′) *n.* [< L *regere*, to rule] a military unit, smaller than a division —*vt.* 1 to organize systematically 2 to subject to strict discipline and control —**reg′i•men′tal** *adj.* —**reg′i•men•ta′tion** *n.*

Re•gi•na (ri jī′nə) capital of Saskatchewan, Canada

re•gion (rē′jən) *n.* [< L *regere*, to rule] 1 a large, indefinite part of the earth's surface 2 a division or part, as of an organism —**re′gion•al** *adj.*

re•gion•al•ism *n.* 1 regional quality or character in life or literature 2 a word, etc. peculiar to some region

reg•is•ter (rej′is tər) *n.* [< L *regerere*, to record] 1 *a)* a list of names, items, etc. *b)* a book in which this is kept 2 a device for recording [a cash *register*] 3 an opening into a room by which the amount of warm or cold air passing through can be controlled 4 *Music* a part of the range of a voice or instrument —*vt.* 1 to enter in a list 2 to indicate on or as on a scale 3 to show, as by facial expression [to *register* surprise] 4 to protect (mail) by paying a fee to have it handled by with special care and security —*vi.* 1 to enter one's name in a list, as of voters 2 to enroll in a school 3 to make an impression —**reg′is•trant** (-trənt) *n.*

registered nurse a trained nurse who has passed a state examination

reg•is•trar (rej′i strär′) *n.* one who keeps records, as in a college

reg•is•tra•tion (rej′i strā′shən) *n.* 1 a registering or being registered 2 an entry in a register 3 the number of persons registered 4 a document certifying that a car, etc. has been registered

reg•is•try (-is trē) *n., pl.* **-tries** 1 a registering 2 an office where registers are kept 3 an official record or list

reg•nant (reg′nənt) *adj.* 1 ruling 2 predominant 3 prevalent

re•gress (rē′gres; *for v.* ri gres′) *n.* [< L *re-*, back + *gradi*, go] backward movement —*vi.* to go back —**re•gres′sion** *n.* —**re•gres′sive** *adj.*

re•gret (ri gret′) *vt.* **-gret′ted**, **-gret′ting** [< OFr *regreter*, mourn] to feel sorry about (an event, one's acts, etc.) —*n.* remorse, esp. over one's acts or omissions —**(one's) regrets** a polite declining of an invitation —**re•gret′ful** *adj.* —**re•gret′ta•ble** *adj.*

re•group *vt., vi.* 1 to reassemble or reorganize 2 to collect oneself, as after a setback

reg•u•lar (reg′yə lər) *adj.* [< L *regula*, a rule] 1 conforming to a rule, type, etc.; orderly; symmetrical 2 conforming to a fixed principle or procedure 3 customary or established 4 consistent [a *regular* customer] 5 functioning in a normal way [a *regular* pulse] 6 properly qualified [a *regular* doctor] 7 designating or of the standing army of a country 8 [Inf.] thorough; complete [a *regular* nuisance] —*n.* 1 a regular soldier or a player who is not a substitute 2 [Inf.] one who is regular in attendance 3 *Politics* a loyal party member —**reg′u•lar′i•ty** (-lar′ə tē) *n., pl.* **-ties** —**reg′u•lar•ize′** *vt.* -ized′, -iz′ing —**reg′u•lar•ly** *adv.*

reg•u•late (reg′yə lāt′) *vt.* **-lat′ed**, **-lat′ing** [< L *regula*, a rule] 1 to control or direct according to a rule, principle, etc. 2 to adjust to a standard, rate, etc. 3 to adjust for accurate operation —**reg′u•la′tor** *n.* —**reg′u•la•to′ry** (-lə tôr′ē) *adj.*

reg•u•la•tion *n.* 1 a regulating or being regulated 2 a rule or law regulating conduct —*adj.* usual; regular

re•gur•gi•tate (ri gur′jə tāt′) *vi., vt.* **-tat′ed**, **-tat′ing** [< ML *re-*, back + LL *gurgitare*, to flood] to bring (partly digested food) back up to the mouth —**re•gur′gi•ta′tion** *n.*

re•hab (rē′hab′) *n. short for* REHABILITATION —*vt.* **-habbed′**, **-hab′bing** *short for* REHABILITATE

re•ha•bil•i•tate (rē′hə bil′ə tāt′) *vt.* **-tat′ed**, **-tat′ing** [< L *re-*, back + *habere*, have] 1 to restore to rank, reputation, etc. which one has lost 2 to put back in good condition 3 to bring or restore to a state of health, constructive activity, etc. —**re′ha•bil′i•ta′tion** *n.* —**re′ha•bil′i•ta′tive** *adj.*

re•hash (rē′hash′; *for v., also* rē hash′) *vt.* [RE- + HASH] to work up again or go over again —*n.* a rehashing

re•hearse (ri hurs′) *vt., vi.* **-hearsed′**, **-hears′ing** [< OFr *re-*, again + *hercer*, to harrow] to practice (a play, etc.) for public performance —**re•hears′al** *n.*

reign (rān) *n.* [< L *regere*, to rule] 1 royal power 2 dominance or sway 3 the period of rule, dominance, etc. —*vi.* 1 to rule as a sovereign 2 to prevail [peace *reigns*]

re•im•burse (rē′im burs′) *vt.* **-bursed′**, **-burs′ing** [RE- + archaic *imburse*, to pay] to pay back —**re′im•burse′ment** *n.*

rein (rān) *n.* [see RETAIN] 1 a narrow strap of leather attached in pairs to a horse's bit and manipulated to control the animal: *usually used in pl.* 2 [pl.] a means of controlling, etc. —**give (free) rein to** to allow to act without restraint

re•in•car•na•tion (rē′in kär nā′shən) *n.* [see RE- & INCARNATE] rebirth of the soul in another body —**re′in•car′nate** *vt.* -nat′ed, -nat′ing

rein•deer (rān′dir′) *n., pl.* **-deer** [< ON *hreinn*, reindeer + *dȳr*, animal] a large deer found in northern regions and domesticated there as a beast of burden

re•in•force (rē′in fôrs′) *vt.* **-forced′**, **-forc′ing** [RE- + var. of ENFORCE] 1 to strengthen (a military force) with more troops, ships, etc. 2 to strengthen, as by patching, propping, or adding new material —**re′in•force′ment** *n.*

re•in•state (rē′in stāt′) *vt.* **-stat′ed**, **-stat′ing** to restore to a former state, position, etc. —**re′in•state′ment** *n.*

re•it•er•ate (rē it′ə rāt′) *vt.* -at′ed, -at′ing [< L *re-*, back + *iterare*, repeat] to say or do again or repeatedly —**re•it′er•a′tion** *n.* —**re•it′er•a′tive** (-ə rāt′iv, -ər ə tiv) *adj.*

re•ject (ri jekt′; *for n.* rē′jekt) *vt.* [< L *re-*, back + *jacere*, to throw] 1 to refuse to take, agree to, use, believe, etc. 2 to discard —n. a rejected thing or person —re·jec'tion n.

re·jig·ger (rē jig'ər) vt. to adjust or alter the structure, terms, etc. of

re·joice (ri jois') vi., vt. -joiced', -joic'ing [< OFr re-, again + joïr, be glad] to be glad or happy

re·join (rē join') vt., vi. 1 to join again; reunite 2 to answer

re·join·der (ri join'dər) n. [see RE- & JOIN] an answer, esp. to a reply

re·ju·ve·nate (ri jōō'və nāt') vt. -nat'ed, -nat'ing [< RE- + L juvenis, young] to cause to feel or seem young again —re·ju've·na'tion n.

rel abbrev. 1 relative(ly) 2 religion

re·lapse (ri laps'; for n., usually rē'laps) vi. -lapsed', -laps'ing [see RE- & LAPSE] to slip back into a former state, esp. into illness after apparent recovery —n. a relapsing

re·late (ri lāt') vt. -lat'ed, -lat'ing [< L relatus, brought back] 1 to tell the story of; narrate 2 to connect, as in thought or meaning —vi. 1 to have some connection or relation (to) 2 to feel sympathetic understanding

re·lat·ed adj. connected by kinship, origin, marriage, etc.

re·la·tion n. 1 a narrating 2 a narrative; account 3 connection, as in thought or meaning 4 connection by blood or marriage 5 a relative 6 [pl.] the connections between or among persons, nations, etc. —in (or with) relation to concerning; regarding —re·la'tion·ship' n.

rel·a·tive (rel'ə tiv) adj. 1 related each to the other 2 pertinent; relevant 3 comparative [living in relative comfort] 4 meaningful only in relationship ["cold" is a relative term] 5 Gram. that refers to an antecedent [a relative pronoun] —n. one related by blood or marriage —rel'a·tive·ly adv.

relative humidity the ratio of the amount of moisture in the air to the maximum amount possible at the given temperature

rel·a·tiv·i·ty (rel'ə tiv'ə tē) n. 1 a being relative 2 Physics the theory of the relative, rather than absolute, character of motion, velocity, mass, etc., and the interdependence of matter, time, and space

re·lax (ri laks') vt., vi. [< L re-, back + laxare, loosen] 1 to make or become less firm, tense, severe, etc. 2 to rest, as from work —re·lax'er n.

re·lax·ant adj. causing relaxation, esp. of muscles —n. a relaxant drug

re·lax·a·tion (rē'lak sā'shən) n. 1 a relaxing or being relaxed 2 a) rest from work or effort b) recreation

re·lay (rē'lā'; for v., also ri lā') n. [< Fr re-, back + laier, to leave] 1 a fresh supply of horses, etc., as for a stage of a journey 2 a race (in full relay race) between teams, each member of which goes a part of the distance —vt. -layed', -lay'ing to get and pass on

re·lease (ri lēs') vt. -leased', -leas'ing [see RELAX] 1 to set free from confinement, work,

pain, etc. 2 to let go [to release an arrow] 3 to permit to be issued, published, etc. —n. 1 a releasing, as from prison 2 a film, news story, etc. released to the public 3 a written surrender of a claim, etc.

rel·e·gate (rel'ə gāt') vt. -gat'ed, -gat'ing [< L re-, away + legare, send] 1 to exile or banish (to) 2 to consign or assign, esp. to an inferior position 3 to refer or hand over for decision —rel'e·ga'tion n.

re·lent (ri lent') vi. [< L re-, again + lentus, pliant] to become less severe, stern, or stubborn; soften

re·lent·less adj. 1 harsh; pitiless 2 not letting up; persistent —re·lent'less·ly adv. —re·lent'less·ness n.

rel·e·vant (rel'ə vənt) adj. [see RELIEVE] relating to the matter under consideration; pertinent —rel'e·vance n., rel'e·van·cy

re·li·a·ble (ri lī'ə bəl) adj. that can be relied on; dependable —re·li'a·bil'i·ty n. —re·li'a·bly adv.

re·li·ance (-əns) n. 1 a relying 2 trust, dependence, or confidence 3 a thing relied on —re·li'ant adj.

rel·ic (rel'ik) n. [see RELINQUISH] 1 an object, custom, etc. surviving from the past 2 a souvenir 3 [pl.] ruins 4 the venerated remains, etc. of a saint

re·lief (ri lēf') n. 1 a relieving of pain, anxiety, a burden, etc. 2 anything that lessens tension, or offers a pleasing change 3 aid, esp. by a public agency to the needy 4 release from work or duty, or those bringing it 5 the projection of sculptured forms from a flat surface 6 the differences in height, collectively, of land forms shown as by lines on a map (relief map) —adj. Baseball designating a pitcher who replaces another during a game —in relief carved so as to project from a surface

re·lieve (ri lēv') vt. -lieved', -liev'ing [< L re-, again + levare, to raise] 1 to ease (pain, anxiety, etc.) 2 to free from pain, anxiety, a burden, etc. 3 to give or bring aid to 4 to set free from duty or work by replacing 5 to make less tedious, etc. by providing a pleasing change —relieve oneself to urinate or defecate

re·li·gion (ri lij'ən) n. [< L religio, holiness] 1 belief in and worship of God or gods 2 a specific system of belief, worship, etc., often involving a code of ethics

re·li·gios·i·ty (-ē äs'ə tē) n. a being religious, esp. excessively or sentimentally religious

re·li·gious (-əs) adj. 1 devout; pious 2 of or concerned with religion 3 conscientiously exact; scrupulous —n., pl. -gious a monk or nun —re·li'gious·ly adv.

re·lin·quish (ri liŋ'kwish) vt. [< L re-, from + linquere, to leave] 1 to give up (a plan, etc.) or let go (one's grasp, etc.) 2 to renounce or surrender (property, a right, etc.) —re·lin'quish·ment n.

rel·ish (rel'ish) n. [< OFr relais, something remaining] 1 an appetizing flavor 2 enjoyment; zest [to listen with relish] 3 a food, as pickles or raw vegetables, served with a meal to add flavor **4** a condiment of chopped pickles, spices, etc. for use as on hot dogs —*vt.* to enjoy; like

re·live (rē liv′) *vt.* **-lived′, -liv′ing** to experience again (a past event) as in the imagination

re·lo·cate (rē lō′kāt′) *vt., vi.* **-cat′ed, -cat′ing** to move to a new location —**re′lo·ca′tion** *n.*

re·luc·tant (ri luk′tənt) *adj.* [< L *re-*, against + *luctari*, to struggle] **1** unwilling; disinclined **2** marked by unwillingness [a *reluctant* answer] —**re·luc′tance** *n.* —**re·luc′tant·ly** *adv.*

re·ly (ri lī′) *vi.* **-lied′, -ly′ing** [< L *re-*, back + *ligare*, bind] to trust or depend: used with *on* or *upon*

rem (rem) *n., pl.* **rem** [r(oentgen) e(quivalent), m(an)] a dose of ionizing radiation with a biological effect equal to one roentgen of X-rays

REM (rem) *n.* [r(apid) e(ye) m(ovement)] the rapid, jerky movement of the eyeballs during stages of sleep associated with dreaming

re·main (ri mān′) *vi.* [< L *re-*, back + *manere*, to stay] **1** to be left over when the rest has been taken away, etc. **2** to stay **3** to continue [to *remain* a cynic] **4** to be left to be done, said, etc.

re·main·der *n.* **1** those remaining **2** what is left when a part is taken away **3** what is left when a smaller number is subtracted from a larger **4** what is left undivided when a number is divided by another that is not one of its factors

re·mains *pl.n.* **1** what is left after use, destruction, etc. **2** a dead body

re·mand (ri mand′) *vt.* [< L *re-*, back + *mandare*, to order] to send back (a prisoner, etc.) into custody

re·mark (ri märk′) *vt.* [< Fr *re-*, again + *marquer*, to mark] **1** to notice or observe **2** to say or write as a comment —*vi.* to make a comment: with *on* or *upon* —*n.* a brief comment

re·mark·a·ble *adj.* worthy of notice; extraordinary —**re·mark′a·bly** *adv.*

Rem·brandt (rem′brant′) 1606-69; Du. painter & etcher

re·me·di·al (ri mē′dē əl) *adj.* **1** providing a remedy **2** for correcting deficiencies: said as of some courses of study

re·me·di·ate (-āt′) *vt.* **-at′ed, -at′ing** to provide a remedy for

rem·e·dy (rem′ə dē) *n., pl.* **-dies** [< L *re-*, again + *mederi*, heal] **1** any medicine or treatment for a disease **2** something to correct a wrong —*vt.* **-died, -dy·ing** to cure, correct, etc.

re·mem·ber (ri mem′bər) *vt.* [< L *re-*, again + *memorare*, bring to mind] **1** to think of again **2** to bring back to mind by an effort; recall **3** to be careful not to forget **4** to mention (a person) to another as sending greetings —*vi.* to bear something in mind or call something back to mind

re·mem·brance (-brəns) *n.* **1** a remembering or being remembered **2** the power to remember **3** a souvenir

re·mind (ri mīnd′) *vt., vi.* to put (a person) in mind (*of* something); make remember —**re·mind′er** *n.*

rem·i·nisce (rem′ə nis′) *vi.* **-nisced′, -nisc′ing** [< fol.] to think, talk, or write, esp. pleasurably, about remembered events

rem·i·nis·cence (-əns) *n.* [Fr < L *re-*, again + *memini*, remember] **1** a remembering **2** a memory **3** [*pl.*] an account of remembered experiences —**rem′i·nis′cent** *adj.*

re·miss (ri mis′) *adj.* [see REMIT] careless; negligent —**re·miss′ness** *n.*

re·mis·sion (ri mish′ən) *n.* [see fol.] **1** forgiveness; pardon **2** release from a debt, tax, etc. **3** a lessening of pain, etc. **4** a diminishment or disappearance of a disease

re·mit (ri mit′) *vt.* **-mit′ted, -mit′ting** [< L *re-*, back + *mittere*, send] **1** to forgive or pardon **2** to refrain from exacting (a payment), inflicting (punishment), etc. **3** to slacken; decrease **4** to send (money) in payment —**re·mit′tance** *n.*

rem·nant (rem′nənt) *n.* [see REMAIN] what is left over, as a piece of cloth at the end of a bolt

re·mod·el (rē mäd′'l) *vt.* **-eled or -elled, -el·ing or -el·ling** to make over; rebuild

re·mon·strate (ri män′strāt′) *vt.* **-strat′ed, -strat′ing** [< L *re-*, again + *monstrare*, to show] to say in protest, objection, etc. —*vi.* to protest; object —**re·mon′strance** (-strəns) *n.*

re·morse (ri môrs′) *n.* [< L *re-*, again + *mordere*, to bite] a torturing sense of guilt for one's actions —**re·morse′ful** *adj.* —**re·morse′less** *adj.*

re·mote (ri mōt′) *adj.* **-mot′er, -mot′est** [< L *remotus*, removed] **1** distant in space or time **2** distant in connection, relation, etc. **3** distantly related **4** aloof **5** slight [a *remote* chance] —*n.* a remote control —**re·mote′ly** *adv.*

remote control 1 control of aircraft, etc. from a distance, as by radio waves **2** a device to control a TV set, recorder, etc. from a distance

re·move (ri mōōv′) *vt.* **-moved′, -mov′ing** [see RE- & MOVE] **1** to move (something) from where it is; take away or off **2** to dismiss, as from office **3** to get rid of —*vi.* to move away, as to another residence —*n.* a step or degree away —**re·mov′a·ble** *adj.* —**re·mov′al** *n.* —**re·mov′er** *n.*

re·mu·ner·ate (ri myōō′nə rāt′) *vt.* **-at′ed, -at′ing** [< L *re-*, again + *munus*, gift] to pay (a person) for (work, a loss, etc.) —**re·mu′ner·a′tion** *n.* —**re·mu′ner·a′tive** *adj.*

ren·ais·sance (ren′ə säns′) *n.* [Fr] a rebirth; renascence —**the Renaissance** the great revival of art and learning in Europe in the 1300s, 1400s, and 1500s

Renaissance man a man skilled and knowledgeable in many fields

Renaissance woman a woman skilled and knowledgeable in many fields

re·nal (rē′nəl) *adj.* ⟦< L *renes*, kidneys⟧ of or near the kidneys

re·nas·cence (ri nas′əns, -nās′-) *n.* ⟦< L *renasci*, be born again⟧ [*also* R-] RENAISSANCE

rend (rend) *vt.* **rent, rend′ing** ⟦OE *rendan*⟧ to tear or split with violence —*vi.* to tear; split apart

ren·der (ren′dər) *vt.* ⟦ult. < L *re*(*d*)-, back + *dare*, give⟧ **1** to submit, as for approval or payment **2** to give in return or pay as due [*render* thanks] **3** to cause to be **4** to give (aid) or do (a service) **5** to depict, as by drawing **6** to play (music), act (a role), etc. **7** to translate **8** to melt down (fat) **9** to pronounce (a verdict)

ren·dez·vous (rän′dā vōō′) *n., pl.* **-vous** (-vōōz′) ⟦< Fr *rendez-vous*, present yourself⟧ **1** a meeting place **2** an agreement to meet **3** the meeting itself — *vi., vt.* **-voused'** (-vōōd′), **-vous'ing** (-vōō′iŋ) to meet or assemble at a certain time or place

ren·di·tion (ren dish′ən) *n.* **1** a rendering; performance, translation, etc. **2** the handing over of a fugitive to the state having jurisdiction

ren·e·gade (ren′ə gād′) *n.* ⟦< L *re*-, again + *negare*, deny⟧ one who abandons a party, movement, etc. to join the opposition; turncoat

re·nege (ri nig′) *vi.* **-neged′, -neg′ing** ⟦see prec.⟧ to go back on a promise

re·new (ri nōō′) *vt.* **1** to make new or fresh again **2** to reestablish; revive **3** to resume **4** to put in a fresh supply of **5** to give or get an extension of [*renew* a lease] —**re·new′a·ble** *adj.* —**re·new′al** *n.*

ren·net (ren′it) *n.* ⟦< ME *rennen*, coagulate⟧ an extract from the stomach of calves, etc. used to curdle milk

Re·noir (rən wär′, ren′wär′), **Pierre Au·guste** (pyer ô güst′) 1841-1919; Fr. painter

re·nounce (ri nouns′) *vt.* **-nounced′, -nounc′ing** ⟦< L *re*-, back + *nuntiare*, tell⟧ **1** to give up formally (a claim, etc.) **2** to give up (a habit, etc.) **3** to disown —**re·nounce′ment** *n.*

ren·o·vate (ren′ə vāt′) *vt.* **-vat′ed, -vat′ing** ⟦< L *re*-, again + *novus*, new⟧ to make as good as new; restore —**ren′o·va′tion** *n.* —**ren′o·va′tor** *n.*

re·nown (ri noun′) *n.* ⟦< OFr *re*-, again + *nom*(*m*)*er*, to name < L *nominare*⟧ great fame or reputation —**re·nowned′** *adj.*

rent¹ (rent) *n.* ⟦< L *reddita*, paid⟧ a stated payment at fixed intervals for the use of a house, land, etc. —*vt.* to get or give use of in return for rent —*vi.* to be let for rent —**for rent** available to be rented —**rent′er** *n.*

rent² (rent) *vt., vi. pt. & pp. of* REND —*n.* a hole or gap made by tearing

rent·al (rent′′l) *n.* **1** an amount paid or received as rent **2** a house, car, etc. offered for rent **3** a renting —*adj.* of a rental

re·nun·ci·a·tion (ri nun′sē ā′shən) *n.* a renouncing, as of a right

re·or·gan·ize (rē ôr′gə nīz′) *vt., vi.* **-ized′, -iz′ing** to organize (a business, etc.) anew —**re·or′gan·i·za′tion** *n.*

rep¹ (rep) *n.* [Inf.] *short for:* **1** REPRESENTATIVE **2** REPUTATION **3** REPETITION

rep² *abbrev.* **1** repeat **2** report(ed) **3** reporter

Rep *abbrev.* **1** Representative **2** Republican

re·paid (ri pād′) *vt., vi. pt. & pp. of* REPAY

re·pair¹ (ri per′) *vt.* ⟦< L *re*-, again + *parare*, prepare⟧ **1** to put back in good condition; fix; renew **2** to make amends for —*n.* **1** a repairing **2** [*usually pl.*] work done in repairing **3** the state of being repaired [kept in *repair*] —**re·pair′a·ble** *adj.* —**re·pair′man** (-mən) *n., pl.* **-men** (-mən)

re·pair² (ri per′) *vi.* ⟦< L *re*-, back + *patria*, native land⟧ to go (*to* a place)

rep·a·ra·tion (rep′ə rā′shən) *n.* ⟦see REPAIR¹⟧ **1** a making of amends **2** [*usually pl.*] compensation, as for war damage

rep·ar·tee (rep′är tē′, -tā′) *n.* ⟦< Fr *repartir*, to return a blow quickly⟧ a series of quick, witty retorts; banter

re·past (ri past′) *n.* ⟦< OFr *re*-, RE- + *past*, food⟧ food and drink; a meal

re·pa·tri·ate (rē pā′trē āt′) *vt., vi.* **-at′ed, -at′ing** ⟦see REPAIR²⟧ to return to the country of birth, citizenship, etc. —**re·pa′tri·a′tion** *n.*

re·pay (ri pā′) *vt.* **-paid′, -pay′ing 1** to pay back **2** to make return to for (a favor, etc.) —**re·pay′ment** *n.*

re·peal (ri pēl′) *vt.* ⟦see RE- & APPEAL⟧ to revoke; cancel; annul —*n.* revocation; abrogation

re·peat (ri pēt′) *vt.* ⟦< L *re*-, again + *petere*, to demand⟧ **1** to say again **2** to recite (a poem, etc.) **3** to say (something) as said by someone else **4** to tell to someone else [to *repeat* a secret] **5** to do or make again —*vi.* to say or do again —*n.* **1** a repeating **2** anything said or done again, as a rebroadcast of a television program **3** *Music a*) a passage to be repeated *b*) a symbol for this —**re·peat′er** *n.*

re·peat·ed *adj.* said, made, or done again, or often —**re·peat′ed·ly** *adv.*

re·pel (ri pel′) *vt.* **-pelled′, -pel′ling** ⟦< L *re*-, back + *pellere*, to drive⟧ **1** to drive or force back **2** to reject **3** to cause dislike in; disgust **4** to be resistant to (water, dirt, etc.) —**re·pel′lent** *adj., n.*

re·pent (ri pent′) *vi., vt.* ⟦< L *re*-, again + *poenitere*, repent⟧ **1** to feel sorry for (an error, sin, etc.) **2** to feel such regret over (an action, intention, etc.) as to change one's mind (about) —**re·pent′ance** *n.* —**re·pent′ant** *adj.*

re·per·cus·sion (rē′pər kush′ən) *n.* ⟦see RE- & PERCUSSION⟧ **1** reverberation **2** a far-reaching, often indirect reaction to some event

rep·er·toire (rep′ər twär′) *n.* ⟦< Fr < L *reperire*, discover⟧ the stock of plays, songs, etc. that a company, singer, etc. is prepared to perform

rep·er·to·ry (rep′ər tôr′ē) *n., pl.* **-ries 1** REPERTOIRE **2** the system of alternating several plays throughout a season with a permanent group of actors

rep·e·ti·tion (rep′ə tish′ən) *n.* 〖< L *repetitio*〗 1 a repeating 2 something repeated —**rep′e·ti′tious** *adj.* —**re·pet·i·tive** (ri pet′ə tiv) *adj.*

re·pine (ri pīn′) *vi.* -**pined′**, -**pin′ing** 〖RE- + PINE²〗 to feel or express unhappiness or discontent

re·place (ri plās′) *vt.* -**placed′**, -**plac′ing** 1 to put back in a former or the proper place 2 to take the place of 3 to provide an equivalent for —**re·place′a·ble** *adj.* —**re·place′ment** *n.*

re·plen·ish (ri plen′ish) *vt.* 〖< L *re-*, again + *plenus*, full〗 1 to make full or complete again 2 to supply again —**re·plen′ish·ment** *n.*

re·plete (ri plēt′) *adj.* 〖< L *re-*, again + *plere*, to fill〗 1 plentifully supplied 2 stuffed; gorged —**re·ple′tion** *n.*

rep·li·ca (rep′li kə) *n.* [see REPLY] a reproduction or close copy, as of a work of art

rep·li·cate (rep′li kāt′) *vt.* -**cat′ed**, -**cat′ing** 〖see REPLY〗 to repeat or duplicate

rep·li·ca·tion *n.* 1 a replicating 2 a copy; reproduction

re·ply (ri plī′) *vi.* -**plied′**, -**ply′ing** 〖< L *re-*, back + *plicare*, to fold〗 to answer or respond —*n., pl.* -**plies′** an answer or response

re·port (ri pôrt′) *vt.* 〖< L *re-*, back + *portare*, carry〗 1 to give an account of, as for publication 2 to carry and repeat (a message, etc.) 3 to announce formally 4 to make a charge about (something) or against (someone) to one in authority —*vi.* 1 to make a report 2 to present oneself, as for work 3 to be subordinate (to) —*n.* 1 rumor 2 a statement or account 3 a formal presentation of facts 4 the noise of an explosion —**re·port′ed·ly** *adv.*

re·port·age (ri pôrt′ij, rep′ər täzh′) *n.* 1 the reporting of the news 2 journalistic writings

report card a periodic written report on a student's progress: often used figuratively

re·port·er *n.* one who reports; specif., one who gathers and reports news for a newspaper, etc. —**rep·or·to·ri·al** (rep′ər tôr′ē əl) *adj.*

re·pose¹ (ri pōz′) *vt.* -**posed′**, -**pos′ing** 〖< L *re-*, again + *pausare*, to rest〗 to lay or place for rest —*vi.* 1 to lie at rest 2 to rest from work, etc. 3 to lie dead —*n.* 1 a) rest b) sleep 2 composure 3 calm; peace —**re·pose′ful** *adj.*

re·pose² (ri pōz′) *vt.* -**posed′**, -**pos′ing** 〖see fol.〗 1 to place (trust, etc.) *in* someone 2 to place (power, etc.) *in* the control of some person or group

re·pos·i·to·ry (ri päz′ə tôr′ē) *n., pl.* -**ries** 〖< L *re-*, back + *ponere*, to place〗 a box, room, etc. in which things may be placed for safekeeping

re·pos·sess (rē′pə zes′) *vt.* to take back, as from a buyer who has missed payments —**re′pos·ses′sion** *n.*

rep·re·hend (rep′ri hend′) *vt.* 〖< L *re-*, back + *prehendere*, take〗 to rebuke, blame, or censure

rep·re·hen·si·ble (-hen′sə bəl) *adj.* deserving to be reprehended —**rep′re·hen′si·bly** *adv.*

rep·re·sent (rep′ri zent′) *vt.* 〖< L *re-*, again + *praesentare*, to present〗 1 to present to the mind 2 to present a likeness of 3 to describe 4 to stand for; symbolize 5 to be the equivalent of 6 to act (a role) 7 to act in place of, esp. by conferred authority 8 to serve as an example of

rep·re·sen·ta·tion *n.* 1 a representing or being represented, as in a legislative assembly 2 legislative representatives, collectively 3 a likeness, image, picture, etc. 4 [*often pl.*] a statement of facts, arguments, etc. meant to influence action, make protest, etc. —**rep′re·sen·ta′tion·al** *adj.*

rep·re·sent·a·tive *adj.* 1 representing 2 of or based on representation of the people by elected delegates 3 typical —*n.* 1 an example or type 2 one authorized to act for others; delegate, agent, salesman, etc. 3 [**R-**] a member of the lower house of Congress or of a state legislature

re·press (ri pres′) *vt.* 〖see RE- & PRESS¹〗 1 to hold back; restrain 2 to put down; subdue 3 *Psychiatry* to force (painful ideas, etc.) into the unconscious —**re·pres′sion** *n.* —**re·pres′sive** *adj.*

re·prieve (ri prēv′) *vt.* -**prieved′**, -**priev′ing** 〖< Fr *reprendre*, take back〗 1 to postpone the punishment of, esp. the execution of 2 to give temporary relief to —*n.* a reprieving or being reprieved

rep·ri·mand (rep′rə mand′) *n.* 〖< L *reprimere*, repress〗 a severe or formal rebuke —*vt.* to rebuke severely or formally

re·pris·al (ri prī′zəl) *n.* [see REPREHEND] injury done in return for injury received

re·proach (ri prōch′) *vt.* 〖< L *re-*, back + *prope*, near〗 to accuse of a fault; rebuke —*n.* 1 shame, disgrace, etc. or a cause of this 2 rebuke or censure —**re·proach′ful** *adj.*

re·pro·bate (rep′rə bāt′) *adj.* 〖LL *reprobare*, reprove〗 unprincipled or depraved —*n.* a reprobate person

re·proc·ess (rē prä′ses) *vt.* to process again so as to reuse; esp., to recover plutonium, etc. from

re·pro·duce (rē′prə dōōs′) *vt.* -**duced′**, -**duc′ing** to produce again; specif., *a*) to produce by propagation *b*) to make a copy of —*vi.* to produce offspring —**re′pro·duc′i·ble** *adj.*

re·pro·duc·tion (-duk′shən) *n.* 1 a reproducing 2 a copy, imitation, etc. 3 any of the processes by which living things produce new individuals —**re′pro·duc′tive** *adj.*

re·proof (ri prōōf′) *n.* a reproving; rebuke: also **re·prov′al** (-prōō′vəl)

re·prove (ri prōōv′) *vt.* -**proved′**, -**prov′ing** 〖see RE- & PROVE〗 1 to rebuke 2 to express disapproval of (something done or said)

rep·tile (rep′tīl′) *n.* 〖< L *repere*, to creep〗 a usu. coldblooded vertebrate covered with scales or horny plates, as a snake, lizard, turtle, or dinosaur —**rep·til·i·an** (rep til′ē ən) *adj.*

re·pub·lic (ri pub′lik) *n.* 〖< L *res*, thing + *publica*, public (adj.)〗 a state or government, specif. one headed by a president, in which the power is exercised by officials elected by the voters

re·pub·li·can (-li kən) *adj.* 1 of or like a republic 2 [**R-**] of or belonging to the Republican

Party —*n.* **1** one who favors a republican form of government **2** [R-] a member of the Republican Party

Republican Party one of the two major political parties in the U.S.

re·pu·di·ate (ri pyōō'dē āt') *vt.* **-at'ed, -at'ing** [< L *repudium*, separation] **1** to refuse to have anything to do with **2** to refuse to accept or support (a belief, treaty, etc.) —**re·pu'di·a'tion** *n.*

re·pug·nant (ri pug'nənt) *adj.* [< L *re-*, back + *pugnare*, fight] **1** contradictory **2** distasteful; offensive —**re·pug'nance** *n.*

re·pulse (ri puls') *vt.* **-pulsed', -puls'ing** [see REPEL] **1** to drive back (an attack, etc.) **2** to refuse or reject with discourtesy, etc.; rebuff —*n.* a repelling or being repelled

re·pul·sion (ri pul'shən) *n.* **1** a repelling or being repelled **2** strong dislike **3** *Physics* the mutual action by which bodies tend to repel each other

re·pul·sive (-siv) *adj.* causing strong dislike or aversion; disgusting —**re·pul'sive·ly** *adv.* —**re·pul'sive·ness** *n.*

re·pur·pose (rē pur'pəs) *vt., vi.* **-posed, -posing** to use or reuse (something that already exists) for another purpose or in another form

rep·u·ta·ble (rep'yə tə bəl) *adj.* having a good reputation —**rep'u·ta·bil'i·ty** *n.* —**rep'u·ta·bly** *adv.*

rep·u·ta·tion (rep'yōō tā'shən) *n.* [see fol.] **1** a commonly held opinion about a person or thing **2** favorable public opinion

re·pute (ri pyōōt') *vt.* **-put'ed, -put'ing** [< L *re-*, again + *putare*, think] to consider or regard [*reputed* to be rich] —*n.* REPUTATION (*n.* 1)

re·put·ed *adj.* generally supposed to be such [the *reputed* owner] —**re·put'ed·ly** *adv.*

re·quest (ri kwest') *n.* [see REQUIRE] **1** an asking for something **2** something asked for **3** the state of being asked for; demand —*vt.* **1** to ask for **2** to ask (a person) to do something

Re·qui·em (rek'wē əm, rā'kwē-) *n.* [< L, rest] [*also* r-] **1** R.C.Ch. a Mass for a dead person or persons **2** a musical setting for this

re·quire (ri kwīr') *vt.* **-quired', -quir'ing** [< L *re-*, again + *quaerere*, ask] **1** to insist upon; demand **2** to order **3** to need —**re·quire'ment** *n.*

req·ui·site (rek'wə zit) *adj.* [see prec.] required; necessary; indispensable —*n.* something that is necessary

req·ui·si·tion (rek'wə zish'ən) *n.* **1** a requiring; formal demand **2** a formal written order, as for equipment —*vt.* **1** to demand or take, as by authority **2** to submit a written request for

re·quite (ri kwīt') *vt.* **-quit'ed, -quit'ing** [RE- + *quite*, obs. var. of QUIT] to repay (someone) for (a benefit, service, etc. or an injury, wrong, etc.) —**re·quit'al** *n.*

re·run (rē'run') *n.* the showing of a film or TV program after the first run or showing

re·sale *n.* a selling of something bought to a third party

re·scind (ri sind') *vt.* [< L *re-*, back + *scindere*, to cut] to revoke or cancel (a law, etc.) —**re·scis'sion** (-sizh'ən) *n.*

res·cue (res'kyōō) *vt.* **-cued, -cu·ing** [ult. < L *re-*, again + *ex-*, off + *quatere*, to shake] to free or save from danger, imprisonment, evil, etc. —*n.* a rescuing; deliverance —**res'cu·er** *n.*

re·search (rē'surch', ri surch') *n.* [see RE- & SEARCH] careful, systematic study and investigation in some field of knowledge — *vi., vt.* to do research (on or in) —**re'search'er** *n.*

re·sec·tion (ri sek'shən) *n.* [< L *re-*, back + *secare*, to cut] *Surgery* the removal of part of an organ, bone, etc.

re·sem·blance (ri zem'bləns) *n.* a similarity of appearance; likeness

re·sem·ble (-bəl) *vt.* **-bled, -bling** [ult. < L *re-*, again + *simulare*, feign] to be like or similar to

re·sent (ri zent') *vt.* [ult. < L *re-*, again + *sentire*, to feel] to feel or show displeasure and hurt or indignation over or toward —**re·sent'ful** *adj.* —**re·sent'ful·ly** *adv.* —**re·sent'ment** *n.*

re·ser·pine (ri sur'pin, -pēn) *n.* [Ger] a crystalline alkaloid used in treating hypertension, mental illness, etc.

res·er·va·tion (rez'ər vā'shən) *n.* **1** a reserving or that which is reserved; specif., *a*) a withholding *b*) public land set aside for a special use, as for American Indians *c*) holding of a hotel room, etc. until called for **2** a limiting condition **3** a doubt or misgiving

re·serve (ri zurv') *vt.* **-served', -serv'ing** [< L *re-*, back + *servare*, to keep] **1** to keep back or set apart for later or special use **2** to keep back for oneself —*n.* **1** something kept back or stored up, as for later use **2** the keeping of one's thoughts, feelings, etc. to oneself **3** reticence; silence **4** [*pl.*] troops, players, etc. kept out of action for use as replacements **5** land set apart for a special purpose **6** cash, etc. held back to meet future demands —**in reserve** reserved for later use —**without reserve** subject to no limitation

re·served *adj.* **1** kept in reserve; set apart **2** self-restrained; reticent

re·serv·ist *n.* a member of a country's military reserves

res·er·voir (rez'ər vwär', -vwôr') *n.* [< Fr: see RESERVE] **1** a place where water is collected and stored for use **2** a receptacle for holding a fluid **3** a large supply

re·side (ri zīd') *vi.* **-sid'ed, -sid'ing** [< L *re-*, back + *sedere*, sit] **1** to dwell for a long time; live (*in* or *at*) **2** to be present or inherent (*in*): said of qualities, etc.

res·i·dence (rez'i dəns) *n.* **1** a residing **2** the place where one resides —**res'i·den'tial** (-den'shəl) *adj.*

res·i·den·cy (-dən sē) *n., pl.* **-cies 1** RESIDENCE (*n.* 1) **2** a period of advanced, specialized medical or surgical training at a hospital

res·i·dent (-dənt) *adj.* **1** residing; esp., living in a place while working, etc. **2** filling a given role, as in an organization —*n.* **1** one who lives in a place, not just a visitor **2** a doctor who is serving a residency

re·sid·u·al (ri zij′ōō əl) *adj.* of or being a residue; remaining —*n.* **1** something remaining **2** [*often pl.*] the fee paid for reruns on television, etc.

res·i·due (rez′ə dōō′) *n.* ⟦< L *residuus*, remaining⟧ that which is left after part is taken away; remainder

re·sid·u·um (ri zij′ōō əm) *n., pl.* **-u·a** (-ə) RESIDUE

re·sign (ri zīn′) *vt., vi.* ⟦< L *re–*, back + *signare*, to sign⟧ to give up (a claim, position, etc.) —**resign oneself (to)** to become reconciled (to)

res·ig·na·tion (rez′ig nā′shən) *n.* **1** *a*) the act of resigning *b*) formal notice of this **2** patient submission

re·signed (ri zīnd′) *adj.* feeling or showing resignation; submissive —**re·sign′ed·ly** (-zīn′id lē) *adv.*

re·sil·ient (ri zil′yənt) *adj.* ⟦< L *re–*, back + *salire*, to jump⟧ **1** springing back into shape, etc. **2** recovering strength, spirits, etc. quickly —**re·sil′ience** n., **re·sil′ien·cy**

res·in (rez′ən) *n.* ⟦< L *resina*⟧ **1** a substance exuded from various plants and trees and used in varnishes, plastics, etc. **2** a synthetic substance similar to this **3** ROSIN —**res′in·ous** *adj.*

re·sist (ri zist′) *vt.* ⟦< L *re–*, back + *sistere*, to set⟧ **1** to withstand; fend off **2** to oppose actively; fight against —*vi.* to oppose or withstand something —**re·sist′er** n. —**re·sist′i·ble** *adj.*

re·sist·ance n. **1** a resisting **2** power to resist, as to ward off disease **3** opposition of some force, thing, etc. to another, as to the flow of an electric current —**re·sist′ant** *adj.*

re·sist·less *adj.* **1** irresistible **2** unable to resist

re·sis·tor n. a device used in an electrical circuit to provide resistance

re·sole (rē sōl′) *vt.* **-soled′, -sol′ing** to put a new sole on (a shoe, etc.)

res·o·lute (rez′ə lōōt′) *adj.* ⟦see RE- & SOLVE⟧ fixed and firm in purpose; determined —**res′o·lute′ly** *adv.*

res·o·lu·tion n. **1** the act or result of resolving something **2** a thing determined upon; decision as to future action **3** a resolute quality of mind **4** a formal statement of opinion or determination by an assembly, etc.

re·solve (ri zälv′, -zôlv′) *vt.* **-solved′, -solv′ing** ⟦see RE- & SOLVE⟧ **1** to break up into separate parts **2** to change: used reflexively **3** to reach a decision; determine [*to resolve to go*] **4** to solve (a problem) **5** to decide by vote —*n.* **1** firm determination **2** a formal resolution —**re·solv′a·ble** *adj.*

re·solved *adj.* determined; resolute

res·o·nant (rez′ə nənt) *adj.* ⟦< L *resonare*, resound⟧ **1** resounding **2** intensifying sound [*resonant* walls] **3** sonorous; vibrant [*a resonant* voice] —**res′o·nance** n. —**res′o·nate′** (-nāt′) *vi., vt.* **-nat′ed, -nat′ing**

res·o·na·tor n. a device that produces, or increases sound by, resonance

re·sort (ri zôrt′) *vi.* ⟦< OFr *re–*, again + *sortir*, go out⟧ to have recourse; turn (*to*) for help, etc. [*to resort to* lies] —*n.* **1** a place to which people go often or generally, as on vacation **2** a source of help, support, etc.; recourse —**as a last resort** as the last available means

re·sound (ri zound′) *vi.* ⟦< L *resonare*⟧ **1** to reverberate **2** to make a loud, echoing sound —**re·sound′ing** *adj.* —**re·sound′ing·ly** *adv.*

re·source (rē′sôrs′, ri sôrs′) *n.* ⟦< OFr *re–*, again + *sourdre*, spring up⟧ **1** something that lies ready for use or can be drawn upon for aid **2** [*pl.*] wealth; assets **3** resourcefulness

re·source·ful *adj.* able to deal effectively with problems, etc. —**re·source′ful·ness** n.

re·spect (ri spekt′) *vt.* ⟦< L *re–*, back + *specere*, look at⟧ **1** to feel or show honor or esteem for **2** to show consideration for —*n.* **1** honor or esteem **2** consideration or regard **3** [*pl.*] expressions of regard **4** a particular detail **5** reference; relation [*with respect* to the problem] —**re·spect′ful** *adj.* —**re·spect′ful·ly** *adv.*

re·spect·a·ble *adj.* **1** worthy of respect or esteem **2** proper; correct **3** fairly good in quality or size **4** presentable —**re·spect′a·bil′i·ty** n. —**re·spect′a·bly** *adv.*

re·spect·ing *prep.* concerning; about

re·spec·tive *adj.* as relates individually to each one

re·spec·tive·ly *adv.* in regard to each, in the order named

res·pi·ra·tion (res′pə rā′shən) *n.* ⟦< L *re–*, back + *spirare*, breathe⟧ act or process of breathing —**res·pi·ra·to·ry** (res′pər ə tôr′ē, ri spī′rə–) *adj.*

res·pi·ra·tor n. **1** a mask, as of gauze, to prevent the inhaling of harmful substances **2** an apparatus to maintain breathing by artificial means

res·pite (res′pit) *n.* ⟦see RESPECT⟧ **1** a delay or postponement **2** temporary relief, as from pain or work; lull

re·splend·ent (ri splen′dənt) *adj.* ⟦< L *re–*, again + *splendere*, to shine⟧ shining brightly; dazzling —**re·splend′ence** n. —**re·splend′ent·ly** *adv.*

re·spond (ri spänd′) *vi.* ⟦< L *re–*, back + *spondere*, to pledge⟧ **1** to answer; reply **2** to react **3** to have a favorable reaction —**re·spond′er** n.

re·spond·ent *adj.* responding —*n.* *Law* a defendant, as in divorce proceedings

re·sponse (ri späns′) *n.* ⟦see RESPOND⟧ **1** something said or done in answer; reply **2** words sung or spoken by the congregation or choir replying to the clergyman **3** any reaction to a stimulus

re·spon·si·bil·i·ty (ri spän′sə bil′ə tē) *n., pl.* **-ties** **1** a being responsible; obligation **2** a thing or person that one is responsible for

re·spon·si·ble (-bəl) *adj.* **1** expected or obliged to account (*for*); answerable (*to*) **2** involving obligation or duties **3** that is the cause of something **4** able to distinguish between right and wrong **5** dependable; reliable —**re·spon′si·bly** *adv.*

re·spon·sive *adj.* reacting readily, as to suggestion or appeal —**re·spon′sive·ness** *n.*

rest¹ (rest) *n.* ⟦OE⟧ **1** sleep or repose **2** ease or inactivity after exertion **3** relief from anything distressing, tiring, etc. **4** absence of motion **5** a resting place **6** a supporting device **7** *Music* a measured interval of silence between tones, or a symbol for this —*vi.* **1** to get ease and refreshment by sleeping or by ceasing from work **2** to be at ease **3** to be or become still **4** to lie, sit, or lean **5** to be placed or based (*in, on,* etc.) **6** to be found [the fault *rests* with him] **7** to rely; depend —*vt.* **1** to give rest to **2** to put for ease, support, etc. [*rest* your head here] **3** *Law* to finish introducing evidence in (a case) —**lay to rest** to bury

rest² (rest) *n.* ⟦< L *restare,* remain⟧ **1** what is left **2** [*with pl. v.*] the others —*vi.* to go on being [*rest* assured]

res·tau·rant (res′tə ränt′, res′tränt′) *n.* ⟦Fr: see RESTORE⟧ a place where meals can be bought and eaten

res·tau·ra·teur (res′tə rə tur′, -toor′) *n.* ⟦Fr⟧ one who owns or operates a restaurant: also **res·tau·ran·teur** (res′tə rän′tur′, -toor′)

rest·ful (rest′fəl) *adj.* **1** full of or giving rest **2** quiet; peaceful

rest home a residence that provides care for aged persons or convalescents

res·ti·tu·tion (res′tə too′shən) *n.* ⟦< L *re-,* again + *statuere,* set up⟧ **1** a giving back of something that has been lost or taken away; restoration **2** reimbursement, as for loss

res·tive (res′tiv) *adj.* ⟦< OFr *rester,* remain⟧ **1** unruly or balky **2** nervous under restraint; restless —**res′tive·ly** *adv.* —**res′tive·ness** *n.*

rest·less *adj.* **1** unable to relax; uneasy **2** giving no rest, disturbed [*restless* sleep] **3** rarely quiet or still; active **4** discontented —**rest′less·ly** *adv.* —**rest′less·ness** *n.*

res·to·ra·tion (res′tə rā′shən) *n.* **1** a restoring or being restored **2** something restored, as by rebuilding

re·stor·a·tive (ri stôr′ə tiv) *adj.* able to restore health, consciousness, etc. —*n.* something that is restorative

re·store (ri stôr′) *vt.* **-stored′, -stor′ing** ⟦< L *re-,* again + *-staurare,* to erect⟧ **1** to give back (something taken, lost, etc.) **2** to return to a former or normal state, or to a position, rank, use, etc. **3** to bring back to health, strength, etc.

re·strain (ri strān′) *vt.* ⟦< L *re-,* back + *stringere,* draw tight⟧ **1** to hold back from action; check; suppress **2** to limit; restrict

re·straint (ri strānt′) *n.* **1** a restraining or being restrained **2** a means or instrument of restraining **3** confinement **4** control of emotions, impulses, etc.; reserve

re·strict (ri strikt′) *vt.* ⟦see RESTRAIN⟧ to keep within limits; confine —**re·strict′ed** *adj.* —**re·stric′tion** *n.*

re·stric·tive *adj.* **1** restricting **2** *Gram.* designating a modifier, as a subordinate clause or phrase, that limits the reference of the word it modifies and is customarily not set off by punctuation

rest·room *n.* a room in a public building, equipped with toilets, washbowls, etc.: also **rest room**

re·struc·ture (rē struk′chər) *vt.* **-tured, -tur·ing 1** to plan or provide a new structure or organization for **2** to change the terms of (a loan, etc.)

re·sult (ri zult′) *vi.* ⟦< L *resultare,* to rebound⟧ **1** to happen as an effect **2** to end as a consequence (*in* something) —*n.* **1** *a)* anything that comes about as an effect *b)* [*pl.*] the desired effect **2** the number, etc. obtained by mathematical calculation —**re·sult′ant** *adj., n.*

re·sume (ri zoom′) *vt.* **-sumed′, -sum′ing** ⟦< L *re-,* again + *sumere,* take⟧ **1** to take or occupy again **2** to continue after interruption —*vi.* to proceed after interruption —**re·sump′tion** (-zump′shən) *n.*

ré·su·mé (rez′ə mā′) *n.* ⟦Fr: see prec.⟧ a summary, esp. of education and employment experience: also written **resume** or **resumé**

re·sur·face (rē sur′fis) *vt.* **-faced, -fac·ing** to put a new surface on —*vi.* to come to the surface again

re·sur·gent (ri sur′jənt) *adj.* ⟦see foll.⟧ rising or tending to rise again —**re·sur′gence** *n.*

res·ur·rec·tion (rez′ə rek′shən) *n.* ⟦< L *resurgere,* rise again⟧ **1** a rising from the dead **2** a coming back into notice, use, etc.; revival —**the Resurrection** *Theol.* **1** the rising of Jesus from the dead **2** the raising of the dead before the Last Judgment —**res·ur·rect′** *vt.*

re·sus·ci·tate (ri sus′ə tāt′) *vt., vi.* **-tat′ed, -tat′ing** ⟦< L *re-,* again + *suscitare,* revive⟧ to revive when apparently dead or in a faint, etc. —**re·sus′ci·ta′tion** *n.* —**re·sus′ci·ta′tor** *n.*

ret *abbrev.* **1** retired **2** return(ed)

re·tail (rē′tāl′) *n.* ⟦< OFr *re-,* again + *tailler,* to cut⟧ the sale of goods in small quantities directly to the consumer —*adj.* of or engaged in such sale —*adv.* at a retail price —*vt., vi.* to sell or be sold directly to the consumer —**re′tail′er** *n.*

re·tain (ri tān′) *vt.* ⟦< L *re-,* back + *tenere,* hold⟧ **1** to keep in possession, use, etc. **2** to hold in **3** to keep in mind **4** to hire by paying a retainer

re·tain·er *n.* **1** something that retains **2** a servant, attendant, etc. **3** a fee paid in advance to engage the services of a lawyer, etc.

retaining wall a wall for keeping earth from sliding or water from flooding

re·take (rē tāk′; *for n.* rē′tāk′) *vt.* **-took′, -tak′en, -tak′ing 1** to take again; recapture **2** to photograph again —*n.* a scene, etc. rephotographed

re·tal·i·ate (ri tal′ē āt′) *vi.* **-at′ed, -at′ing** ⟦< L *re-,* back + *talio,* punishment in kind⟧ to return like for like, esp. injury for injury —**re·tal′i·a′tion** *n.* —**re·tal′i·a·to′ry** *adj.*

re·tard (ri tärd′) *vt.* [< L *re-*, back + *tardare*, make slow] to hinder, delay, or slow the progress of —**re·tar·da·tion** (rē′tär dā′shən) *n.*

re·tard·ant *n.* something that retards; esp., a substance that delays a chemical reaction —*adj.* that retards

re·tard·ed *adj.* slowed or delayed in development, esp. mentally: term now often considered offensive

retch (rech) *vi.* [OE *hræcan,* clear the throat] to strain to vomit, esp. without bringing anything up

re·ten·tion (ri ten′shən) *n.* 1 a retaining or being retained 2 capacity for retaining 3 a remembering; memory —**re·ten′tive** *adj.*

ret·i·cent (ret′ə sənt) *adj.* [< L *re-*, again + *tacere,* be silent] disinclined to speak; taciturn —**ret′i·cence** *n.*

ret·i·na (ret′′n ə) *n., pl.* **-nas** or **-nae′** (-ē′) [prob. < L *rete,* a net] the innermost coat lining the eyeball, containing light-sensitive cells that are directly connected to the brain

ret·i·nue (ret′′n ōō′) *n.* [< OFr, ult. < L: see RETAIN] a group of persons attending a person of rank or importance

re·tire (ri tīr′) *vi.* **-tired′, -tir′ing** [< Fr *re-*, back + *tirer,* draw] 1 to withdraw to a secluded place 2 to go to bed 3 to retreat, as in battle 4 to give up one's work, business, etc., esp. because of age —*vt.* 1 to pay off (bonds, etc.) 2 to cause to retire from a position, office, etc. 3 to withdraw from use 4 *Baseball* to put out (a batter, side, etc.) —**re·tir′ee′** *n.* —**re·tire′ment** *n.*

re·tired *adj.* 1 secluded 2 no longer working, etc. as because of age

re·tir·ing *adj.* reserved; modest; shy

re·tool (rē tōōl′) *vt., vi.* 1 to adapt (factory machinery) for a different product 2 to reorganize to meet new or different needs or conditions

re·tort[1] (ri tôrt′) *vt.* [< L *re-*, back + *torquere,* to twist] to say in reply —*vi.* to make a sharp, witty reply —*n.* a sharp, witty reply

re·tort[2] (ri tôrt′) *n.* [< ML *retorta:* see prec.] a glass container with a long tube, in which substances are distilled

re·touch (rē tuch′) *vt.* to touch up details in (a photograph, essay, etc.) so as to improve or change it

re·trace (rē trās′) *vt.* **-traced′, -trac′ing** [see RE- & TRACE[1]] to go back over again [to *retrace* one's steps]

re·tract (ri trakt′) *vt., vi.* [< L *re-*, back + *trahere,* draw] 1 to draw back or in 2 to withdraw (a statement, charge, etc.) —**re·tract′a·ble** *adj.,* **re·trac′tile** (-trak′təl, -til′) —**re·trac′tion** *n.*

re·tread (rē tred′; *for n.* rē′tred′) *vt., n.* RE-CAP[1]

re·treat (ri trēt′) *n.* [< L *retrahere:* see RETRACT] 1 a withdrawal, as from danger 2 a safe, quiet place 3 a period of seclusion, esp. for spiritual renewal 4 *a*) the forced withdrawal of troops under attack *b*) a signal for this *c*) a signal, as by bugle, or a ceremony at sunset for lowering the national flag —*vi.* to withdraw; go back

re·trench (rē trench′) *vi.* [< Fr: see RE- & TRENCH] 1 to cut down expenses; economize 2 to reorganize for renewed effort —**re·trench′ment** *n.*

ret·ri·bu·tion (re′trə byōō′shən) *n.* [< L *re-*, back + *tribuere,* to pay] punishment for evil done —**re·trib·u·tive** (ri trib′yoo tiv) *adj.*

re·trieve (ri trēv′) *vt.* **-trieved′, -triev′ing** [< OFr *re-*, again + *trouver,* find] 1 to get back; recover 2 to restore 3 to make good (a loss, error, etc.) 4 to access (data) stored in a computer 5 to find and bring back (killed or wounded game) —*vi.* to retrieve game —**re·triev′al** *n.*

re·triev·er *n.* a dog trained or bred to retrieve game

ret·ro (re′trō) *adj.* of a revival of an earlier style: said of clothing, hairstyles, etc.

retro- [< L] *combining form* backward, back, behind

ret·ro·ac·tive (re′trō ak′tiv) *adj.* having an effect on things that are already past —**ret′ro·ac′tive·ly** *adv.*

ret·ro·fire (re′trə fīr′) *vt.* **-fired′, -fir′ing** to ignite (a retrorocket)

ret·ro·fit (-fit′) *n.* a change in design or equipment, as of an aircraft already in operation, so as to incorporate later improvements — *vt., vi.* **-fit′ted, -fit′ting** to modify with a retrofit

ret·ro·grade (-grād′) *adj.* [< L: see RETRO- & GRADE] 1 moving backward 2 going back to a worse condition

ret·ro·gress (-gres′) *vi.* [< L: see prec.] to move backward, esp. into a worse condition; degenerate —**ret′ro·gres′sion** *n.* —**ret′ro·gres′sive** *adj.*

ret·ro·rock·et (re′trō räk′it) *n.* a small rocket, as on a spacecraft, producing thrust opposite to the direction of flight to reduce speed, as for maneuvering

ret·ro·spect (re′trə spekt′) *n.* [< L *retro-*, back + *specere,* to look] contemplation of the past —**ret′ro·spec′tion** *n.*

ret·ro·spec·tive *adj.* looking back on the past —*n.* a representative show of an artist's lifetime work

ret·si·na (ret sē′nə) *n.* [ModGr, prob. < It *resina,* resin] a Greek wine flavored with pine resin

re·turn (ri turn′) *vi.* [< OFr: see RE- & TURN] 1 to go or come back 2 to answer; reply —*vt.* 1 to bring, send, or put back 2 to do in reciprocation [*return* a visit] 3 to yield (a profit, etc.) 4 to report officially 5 to elect or reelect —*n.* 1 a coming or going back 2 a bringing, sending, or putting back 3 something returned 4 a recurrence 5 repayment; requital 6 [*often pl.*] yield or profit, as from investments 7 an answer; reply 8 *a*) an official report [election *returns*] *b*) a filled-out form for computing income tax —*adj.* 1 of or for a return [*return* postage] 2 given, done, etc. in return —**in return** as a return; as an equivalent, response, etc. —**re·turn′a·ble** *adj.*

re·turn·ee *n.* one who returns, as home from military service

Reu·ben (sandwich) (rōō′bən) a sandwich of rye bread, corned beef, sauerkraut, Swiss cheese, etc., served hot

re·u·ni·fy (rē yōōn′nə fī′) *vt., vi.* **-fied′, -fy′ing** to unify again after being divided —**re·u′ni·fi·ca′tion** *n.*

re·un·ion (rē yōōn′yən) *n.* a coming together again, as after separation

re-up (rē up′) *vi.* **-upped′, -up′ping** ⟦RE- + (sign) up⟧ [Inf.] to enlist or enroll again

rev¹ (rev) *vt.* **revved, rev′ving** ⟦< REV(OLUTION)⟧ [Inf.] **1** to increase the speed of (an engine) **2** to accelerate, intensify, etc. Usually with *up*

rev² *abbrev.* **1** revenue **2** revise(d) **3** revolution

Rev *abbrev.* **1** *Bible* Revelation **2** Reverend

re·vamp (rē vamp′) *vt.* to renovate; redo

re·veal (ri vēl′) *vt.* ⟦< L *re-*, back + *velum*, veil⟧ **1** to make known (something hidden or secret) **2** to show; exhibit; display

rev·eil·le (rev′ə lē) *n.* ⟦< Fr < L *re-*, again + *vigilare*, to watch⟧ a signal on a bugle, drum, etc. in the morning to waken soldiers, etc.

rev·el (rev′əl) *vi.* **-eled** or **-elled, -el·ing** or **-el·ling** ⟦< MFr < L *rebellare*, to rebel: see REBEL⟧ **1** to be festive; make merry **2** to take much pleasure (*in*) —*n.* merrymaking —**rev′el·er** *n.*, **rev′el·ler** —**rev′el·ry** *n.,* pl. **-ries**

rev·e·la·tion (rev′ə lā′shən) *n.* **1** a revealing **2** a striking disclosure **3** *Theol.* God's disclosure to humanity of divine truth, etc. —[R-] the last book of the New Testament

re·venge (ri venj′) *vt.* **-venged′, -veng′ing** ⟦< OFr: see RE- & VENGEANCE⟧ to inflict harm in return for (an injury, etc.) —*n.* **1** the act or result of revenging **2** desire to take vengeance —**re·venge′ful** *adj.*

rev·e·nue (rev′ə nōō′) *n.* ⟦< MFr, returned⟧ **1** return, as from investment; income **2** the income from taxes, licenses, etc., as of a city or nation

re·ver·ber·ate (ri vur′bə rāt′) *vi., vt.* **-at′ed, -at′ing** ⟦< L *re-*, again + *verberare*, to beat⟧ to reecho or cause to reecho —**re·ver′ber·a′tion** *n.*

re·vere (ri vir′) *vt.* **-vered′, -ver′ing** ⟦< L *re-*, again + *vereri*, to fear⟧ to regard with deep respect, love, etc.

Re·vere (ri vir′), **Paul** 1735-1818; Am. silversmith & patriot

rev·er·ence (rev′ə rəns) *n.* a feeling of deep respect, love, and awe —*vt.* **-enced, -enc·ing** to treat or regard with reverence; venerate —**rev′er·ent** *adj.*, **rev′er·en′tial** (-ə ren′shəl) —**rev′er·ent·ly** *adv.*

rev·er·end (rev′ə rənd) *adj.* worthy of reverence: used with *the* as a title of respect for a member of the clergy [the *Reverend* A. B. Smith]

rev·er·ie (rev′ə rē) *n.* ⟦< Fr⟧ daydreaming or a daydream

re·verse (ri vurs′) *adj.* [see fol.] **1** turned backward; opposite or contrary **2** causing

movement in the opposite direction —*n.* **1** the opposite or contrary **2** the back of a coin, medal, etc. **3** a change from good fortune to bad **4** a mechanism for reversing, as a gear on a machine —*vt.* **-versed′, -vers′ing 1** to turn backward, in an opposite position or direction, upside down, or inside out **2** to change to the opposite **3** *Law* to revoke or annul (a decision, etc.) —*vi.* to go or turn in the opposite direction —**re·ver′sal** (-vur′səl) *n.* —**re·vers′i·ble** *adj.* —**re·vers′i·bly** *adv.*

re·vert (ri vurt′) *vi.* ⟦< L *re-*, back + *vertere*, to turn⟧ **1** to go back, as to a former practice, state, subject, etc. **2** *Biol.* to return to a former or primitive type **3** *Law* to go back to a former owner or his or her heirs —**re·ver′sion** (-vur′zhən) *n.* —**re·vert′i·ble** *adj.*

re·vet·ment (ri vet′mənt) *n.* ⟦< Fr⟧ **1** a facing of stone, cement, etc., as to protect an embankment **2** RETAINING WALL

re·view (ri vyōō′) *n.* ⟦< L *re-*, again + *videre*, see⟧ **1** a looking at or looking over again **2** a general survey or report **3** a looking back on (past events, etc.) **4** reexamination, as of the decision of a lower court **5** a critical evaluation of a book, play, etc. **6** a formal inspection, as of troops on parade —*vt.* **1** to look back on **2** to survey in thought, speech, etc. **3** to inspect (troops, etc.) formally **4** to give a critical evaluation of (a book, etc.) **5** to study again —**re·view′er** *n.*

re·vile (ri vīl′) *vt.* **-viled′, -vil′ing** ⟦< OFr: see RE- & VILE⟧ to use abusive language to or about —**re·vile′ment** *n.* —**re·vil′er** *n.*

re·vise (ri vīz′) *vt.* **-vised′, -vis′ing** ⟦< L *re-*, back + *visere*, to survey⟧ **1** to read over carefully and correct, improve, or update **2** to change or amend —**re·vi′sion** (-vizh′ən) *n.*

re·vi·sion·ist *n.* a person who revises, or favors the revision of, some accepted theory, doctrine, etc. —*adj.* of revisionists or their policy or practice —**re·vi′sion·ism′** *n.*

re·vis·it (rē viz′it) *vt.* **1** to visit again **2** to reconsider or reevaluate

re·viv·al (ri vī′vəl) *n.* **1** a reviving or being revived **2** a bringing or coming back into use, being, etc. **3** a new presentation of an earlier play, etc. **4** restoration to vigor or activity **5** a meeting led by an evangelist to stir up religious feeling —**re·viv′al·ist** *n.*

re·vive (ri vīv′) *vi., vt.* **-vived′, -viv′ing** ⟦< L *re-*, again + *vivere*, to live⟧ **1** to return to life or consciousness **2** to return to health or vigor **3** to come or bring back into use, attention, popularity, etc.

re·viv·i·fy (ri viv′ə fī′) *vt.* **-fied′, -fy′ing** to put new life or vigor into —*vi.* to revive —**re·viv′i·fi·ca′tion** *n.*

re·voke (ri vōk′) *vt.* **-voked′, -vok′ing** ⟦< L *re-*, back + *vocare*, to call⟧ to withdraw, repeal, or cancel (a law, etc.) —**rev·o·ca·ble** (rev′ə kə bəl, ri vōk′ə-) *adj.* —**rev′o·ca′tion** (-kā′shən) *n.*

re·volt (ri vōlt′) *n.* ⟦< Fr: see REVOLVE⟧ a rebelling against the government or any authority —*vi.* to rebel against authority —*vt.* to disgust —**re·volt′ing** *adj.* —**re·volt′ing·ly** *adv.*

rev·o·lu·tion (rev′ə lōō′shən) *n.* [see REVOLVE] **1** the movement of a body in an orbit **2** a turning around an axis; rotation **3** a complete cycle of events **4** a complete change **5** overthrow of a government, social system, etc. —**rev′o·lu′tion·ar′y** *adj., n., pl.* **-ies** —**rev′o·lu′tion·ist** *n.*

Revolutionary War *see* AMERICAN REVOLUTION

rev·o·lu·tion·ize (-shə nīz′) *vt.* **-ized′, -iz′ing** to make a fundamental change in

re·volve (ri välv′, -vôlv′) *vt.* **-volved′, -volv′ing** [< L *re-*, back + *volvere*, to roll] to turn over in the mind —*vi.* **1** to move in a circle or orbit **2** to rotate —**re·volv′a·ble** *adj.*

re·volv·er *n.* a handgun with a revolving cylinder containing cartridges

re·vue (ri vyōō′) *n.* [Fr, review] a musical show with skits, dances, etc., often parodying recent events

re·vul·sion (ri vul′shən) *n.* [< L *re-*, back + *vellere*, to pull] extreme disgust; loathing

re·ward (ri wôrd′) *n.* [< OFr *regarde*: see REGARD] **1** something given in return for something done **2** money offered, as for capturing a criminal —*vt.* to give a reward to (someone) for (service, etc.)

re·ward·ing *adj.* giving a sense of reward or worthwhile return

re·wind (rē wīnd′) *vt.* **-wound′, -wind′ing** to wind again; specif., to wind (film or tape) back on the original reel

re·word *vt.* to change the wording of

re·write *vt., vi.* **-wrote′, -writ′ten, -writ′ing** **1** to write again **2** to revise (something written)

Rey·kja·vík (rā′kyə vēk′, -vik′) seaport & capital of Iceland

RFD *abbrev.* Rural Free Delivery

rhap·so·dize (rap′sə dīz′) *vi., vt.* **-dized′, -diz′ing** to speak or write in an ecstatic or enthusiastic manner

rhap·so·dy (-sə dē) *n., pl.* **-dies** [< Gr *rhaptein*, stitch together + *ōidē*, song] **1** any ecstatic or enthusiastic speech or writing **2** a musical composition of free, irregular form, suggesting improvisation —**rhap·sod′ic** (-säd′ik) *adj.*, **rhap·sod′i·cal**

rhe·a (rē′ə) *n.* [< Gr] a large, flightless South American bird, like an ostrich but smaller

rhe·ni·um (rē′nē əm) *n.* [< L *Rhenus*, Rhine] a rare metallic chemical element with a high melting point, used for electrical contacts: symbol, Re; at. no. 75

rhe·o·stat (rē′ə stat′) *n.* [< Gr *rheos*, current + -STAT] a device for varying the resistance of an electric circuit, used as for dimming or brightening electric lights

rhesus (monkey) (rē′səs) [< Gr proper name] a brownish-yellow monkey native to India: used in medical research

rhet·o·ric (ret′ə rik) *n.* [< Gr *rhētōr*, orator] **1** the art of using words effectively; esp., the art of prose composition **2** showy, elaborate language that is empty or insincere —**rhe-**

tor·i·cal (ri tôr′i kəl) *adj.* —**rhet′o·ri′cian** (-ə rish′ən) *n.*

rhetorical question a question asked only for rhetorical effect, no answer being expected

rheum (rōōm) *n.* [< Gr *rheuma*, a flow] watery discharge from the eyes, nose, etc., as in a cold

rheumatic fever an acute or chronic disease, usually of children, with fever, swelling of the joints, inflammation of the heart, etc.

rheu·ma·tism (rōō′mə tiz′əm) *n.* [see RHEUM] *nontechnical term for* a painful condition of the joints and muscles —**rheu·mat′ic** (-mat′ik) *adj., n.* —**rheu′ma·toid′** (-mə toid′) *adj.*

rheumatoid arthritis a chronic disease with painful swelling of joints, often leading to deformity

Rh factor (är′āch′) [first discovered in RH(ESUS) monkeys] a group of antigens, usually present in human blood: people who have this factor are **Rh positive**; those who do not are **Rh negative**

Rhine (rīn) river in W Europe, flowing from E Switzerland through Germany & the Netherlands into the North Sea

rhine·stone (rīn′stōn′) *n.* a bright, colorless artificial gem of hard glass, often cut to resemble a diamond

Rhine wine a light white wine, esp. one produced in the valley of the Rhine

rhi·ni·tis (rī nīt′is) *n.* [< Gr *rhis*, nose + -ITIS] inflammation of the nasal mucous membrane

rhi·no (rī′nō) *n., pl.* **-nos** or **-no** *short for* RHINOCEROS

rhi·noc·er·os (rī näs′ər əs) *n.* [< Gr *rhis*, nose + *keras*, horn] a large, thick-skinned, plant-eating mammal of Africa and Asia, with one or two upright horns on the snout

rhi·zome (rī′zōm′) *n.* [< Gr *rhiza*, a root] a horizontal stem on or under soil, bearing leaves near its tips and roots from its undersurface

rho (rō) *n.* the 17th letter of the Greek alphabet (P, ρ)

Rhode Island (rōd) New England state of the U.S.; cap. Providence: abbrev. *RI* —**Rhode Islander**

Rhodes (rōdz) large Greek island in the Aegean

rho·di·um (rō′dē əm) *n.* [< Gr *rhodon*, rose] a hard, metallic chemical element used to form high-temperature alloys with platinum: symbol, Rh; at. no. 45

rho·do·den·dron (rō′də den′drən) *n.* [< Gr *rhodon*, rose + *dendron*, tree] any of various trees or shrubs, mainly evergreen, with showy flowers

rhom·boid (räm′boid′) *n.* [< Fr: see fol. & -OID] a parallelogram with oblique angles and only the opposite sides equal

rhom·bus (räm′bəs) *n., pl.* **-bus·es** or **-bi′** (-bī′) [L < Gr *rhombos*, turnable object] an equilateral parallelogram, esp. one with oblique angles

Rhone or **Rhône** (rōn) river flowing through

SW Switzerland & France into the Mediterranean

rhu·barb (rōo′bärb′) *n.* ⟦< Gr *rhēon*, rhubarb + *barbaron*, foreign⟧ a plant with long, thick stalks that are cooked into a sauce, etc.

rhyme (rīm) *n.* ⟦< OFr⟧ 1 a poem or verse with like recurring sounds, esp. at ends of lines 2 such verse, poetry, or likeness of sounds 3 a word like another in end sound —*vi.* **rhymed, rhym′ing** 1 to make (rhyming) verse 2 to form a rhyme ["more" *rhymes* with "door"] —*vt.* 1 to put into rhyme 2 to use as a rhyme —**rhyme or reason** order or sense

rhym·er *n.* a maker of rhymes, esp. a rhymester

rhyme·ster *n.* a maker of trivial rhyme

rhythm (rith′əm) *n.* ⟦< Gr *rhythmos*, measure⟧ 1 movement, flow, etc. characterized by regular recurrence of beat, accent, etc. 2 the pattern of this in music, verse, etc. —**rhyth′mic** (-mik) *adj.*, **rhyth′mi·cal** —**rhyth′mi·cal·ly** *adv.*

rhythm and blues the form of American popular music from which rock-and-roll derives

rhythm method a method of attempting to prevent pregnancy by abstaining from intercourse during ovulation

rhythm section those supporting instruments in a band that supply rhythm

RI *abbrev.* Rhode Island

rib (rib) *n.* ⟦OE⟧ 1 any of the arched bones attached to the spine and enclosing the chest cavity 2 anything like a rib in appearance or function —*vt.* **ribbed, rib′bing** 1 to strengthen or form with ribs 2 [Slang] to make fun of; kid

rib·ald (rib′əld) *adj.* ⟦< OHG *riban*, to rub⟧ coarse or vulgar in joking, speaking, etc. —**rib′ald·ry** *n.*

rib·bon (rib′ən) *n.* ⟦< MFr *ruban*⟧ 1 a narrow strip of silk, rayon, etc. used for decoration, tying, etc. 2 [*pl.*] torn shreds 3 an inked strip for printing, as in a typewriter, etc.

rib·bon-cut·ting *n.* a ceremony to officially open a new building, construction site, etc.

rib-eye (steak) boneless beefsteak from the rib section

ri·bo·fla·vin (rī′bə flā′vin) *n.* ⟦< *ribose*, a sugar + L *flavus*, yellow⟧ a B vitamin found in milk, eggs, fruits, etc.: see VITAMIN B (COMPLEX)

rice (rīs) *n.* ⟦< Gr *oryza*⟧ 1 an aquatic cereal grass grown widely in warm climates, esp. in East Asia 2 the starchy grains of this grass, used as food —*vt.* **riced, ric′ing** to make rice-like granules from (cooked potatoes, etc.) using a utensil (**ric′er**) with small holes

rich (rich) *adj.* ⟦< OFr⟧ 1 owning much money or property; wealthy 2 well-supplied (*with*); abounding (*in*) 3 valuable or costly 4 full of choice ingredients, as butter, sugar, etc. [*rich* pastries] 5 *a*) full and mellow (said of sounds) *b*) deep; vivid (said of colors) *c*) very fragrant 6 abundant 7 yielding in abundance, as soil 8 [Inf.] very amusing —**the rich** wealthy people collectively —**rich′ly** *adv.* —**rich′ness** *n.*

Rich·ard I (rich′ərd) 1157-99; king of England (1189-99): called **Richard Coeur de Li·on** (kur′ də lē′ən) or **Richard the Li′on-Heart′ed**

rich·es (rich′iz) *pl.n.* ⟦< OFr *richesse*⟧ wealth

Rich·mond (rich′mənd) capital of Virginia

Rich·ter scale (rik′tər) ⟦devised by C. **Richter** (1900-85), U.S. geologist⟧ a scale for measuring the magnitude of earthquakes

rick (rik) *n.* ⟦OE *hreac*⟧ a stack of hay, straw, etc.

rick·ets (rik′its) *n.* ⟦< ? Gr *rhachis*, spine⟧ a disease, chiefly of children, characterized by a softening and, often, bending of the bones

rick·et·y (rik′it ē) *adj.* 1 feeble; weak 2 likely to fall down or apart

rick·shaw or **rick·sha** (rik′shô′) *n.* JINRIKISHA

ric·o·chet (rik′ə shā′) *n.* ⟦Fr⟧ the oblique rebound of a bullet, etc. after striking a surface at an angle —*vi.* **-cheted** (-shād′), **-chet′ing** (-shā′iŋ) to make a ricochet

ri·cot·ta (ri kät′ə) *n.* ⟦It < L *recocta*, recooked⟧ a soft cheese made from whey, whole milk, or both

rid (rid) *vt.* **rid** or **rid′ded, rid′ding** ⟦< ON *rythja*, to clear (land)⟧ to free or relieve, as of something undesirable —**get rid of** to give or throw away or to destroy

rid·dance (rid′ns) *n.* a ridding or being rid —**good riddance** an expression of satisfaction at being rid of something

rid·den (rid′n) *vi., vt. pp. of* RIDE —*adj.* dominated: used in compounds [fear-*ridden*]

rid·dle¹ (rid′l) *n.* ⟦OE *rædels*⟧ 1 a puzzling question, etc. requiring some ingenuity to answer 2 any puzzling person or thing

rid·dle² (rid′l) *vt.* **-dled, -dling** ⟦< OE *hriddel*, a sieve⟧ 1 to make many holes in 2 to affect every part of [*riddled* with errors]

ride (rīd) *vi.* **rode, rid′den, rid′ing** ⟦OE *ridan*⟧ 1 to be carried along by a horse, in a vehicle, etc. 2 to be supported in motion (*on* or *upon*) [tanks *ride* on treads] 3 to admit of being ridden [the car *rides* smoothly] 4 to move or float on water 5 [Inf.] to continue undisturbed [let the matter *ride*] —*vt.* 1 to sit on or in and control so as to move along 2 to move over, along, or through (a road, area, etc.) by horse, car, etc. 3 to control, dominate, etc. [*ridden* by doubts] 4 [Inf.] to tease with ridicule, etc. —*n.* 1 a riding 2 a means of riding 3 a thing to ride at an amusement park

rid·er *n.* 1 one who rides 2 an addition or amendment to a document

rid·er·ship *n.* the passengers of a particular transportation system

ridge (rij) *n.* ⟦< OE *hrycg*, animal's spine⟧ 1 the long, narrow crest of something 2 a long, narrow elevation of land 3 any raised narrow strip 4 the horizontal line formed by the meeting of two sloping surfaces —*vt., vi.* **ridged, ridg′ing** to mark or be marked with, or form into, ridges

ridge·pole *n.* the horizontal beam at the ridge of a roof, to which the rafters are attached

rid·i·cule (rid′i kyool′) *n.* ⟦< L *ridere*, to laugh⟧ 1 the act of making someone the object of scornful laughter **2** words or actions intended to produce such laughter —*vt.* **-culed', -cul'ing** to make fun of; deride; mock

ri·dic·u·lous (ri dik'yə ləs) *adj.* deserving ridicule —**ri·dic'u·lous·ly** *adv.* —**ri·dic'u·lous·ness** *n.*

rife (rīf) *adj.* 〖OE *ryfe*〗 **1** widespread **2** abounding [*rife* with error]

riff (rif) *n.* 〖prob. altered < REFRAIN²〗 **1** in jazz and pop music, a constantly repeated musical phrase **2** [Inf.] one of several improvised variations, as in dialogue —*vi.* to perform a riff

rif·fle (rif'əl) *n.* 〖< ?〗 **1** a ripple in a stream, produced by a submerged rock, etc. **2** a certain way of shuffling cards —*vt., vi.* **-fled, -fling** to shuffle (playing cards) by letting a divided deck fall together as the corners are slipped through one's thumbs

riff·raff (rif'raf') *n.* 〖< OFr〗 those people regarded as worthless, disreputable, etc.

ri·fle' (rī'fəl) *vt.* **-fled, -fling** 〖Fr *rifler,* to scrape〗 to cut spiral grooves within (a gun barrel, etc.) —*n.* a gun, fired from the shoulder, with a rifled barrel to spin the bullet for greater accuracy

ri·fle² (rī'fəl) *vt.* **-fled, -fling** 〖< OFr *rifler*〗 to ransack and rob —**ri'fler** *n.*

ri·fling (rī'fliŋ) *n.* spiral grooves cut within a gun barrel to make the projectile spin

rift (rift) *n.* 〖< Dan, fissure〗 an opening caused by splitting; cleft — *vt., vi.* to burst open; split

rig (rig) *vt.* **rigged, rig'ging** 〖< Scand〗 **1** to fit (a ship, mast, etc.) with (sails, shrouds, etc.) **2** to assemble **3** to equip **4** to arrange dishonestly **5** [Inf.] to dress: with *out* —*n.* **1** the way sails, etc. are rigged **2** equipment; gear **3** oil-drilling equipment **4** a tractor-trailer

rig·a·ma·role (rig'ə mə rōl') *n. var. of* RIGMAROLE

rig·ging *n.* the ropes, chains, etc. for a vessel's masts, sails, etc.

right (rīt) *adj.* 〖< OE *riht,* straight〗 **1** with a straight line or plane perpendicular to a base [a *right* angle] **2** upright; virtuous **3** correct **4** fitting; suitable **5** designating the side or surface meant to be seen **6** mentally or physically sound **7** *a)* designating or of that side of the body toward the east when one faces north *b)* designating or of the corresponding side of anything *c)* closer to the right side of one who is facing the thing mentioned —*n.* **1** what is right, just, etc. **2** power, privilege, etc. belonging to one by law, nature, etc. **3** the right side **4** the right hand **5** [*often* R-] *Politics* a conservative or reactionary position, party, etc.: often with *the* —*adv.* **1** straight; directly [*go right* home] **2** properly; fittingly **3** completely **4** exactly [*right* here] **5** according to law, justice, etc. **6** correctly **7** on or toward the right side **8** very: in certain titles [the *right* reverend] —*interj.* agreed! OK! —*vt.* **1** to put upright **2** to cor-

rect **3** to put in order —**right away** (or **off**) at once —**right on!** [Slang] that's right! —**right'ly** *adv.* —**right'ness** *n.*

right angle an angle of 90 degrees

right·eous (rī'chəs) *adj.* **1** acting in a just, upright manner; virtuous **2** morally right or justifiable —**right'eous·ly** *adv.* —**right'eous·ness** *n.*

right·ful *adj.* **1** fair and just; right **2** having a lawful claim —**right'ful·ly** *adv.* —**right'ful·ness** *n.*

right-hand *adj.* **1** on or toward the right **2** of, for, or with the right hand **3** most helpful or reliable [a *right-hand* man]

right-hand·ed *adj.* **1** using the right hand more skillfully than the left **2** done with or made for use with the right hand —*adv.* **1** with the right hand **2** in such a way that the bat, club, etc. swings leftward —**right'-hand'ed·ness** *n.*

right·ist *n., adj.* conservative or reactionary

right-mind·ed *adj.* having sound principles

right of way *n.* **1** the right to move first at intersections **2** land over which a road, power line, etc. passes **3** right of passage, as over another's property Also **right'-of-way'**

right-to-life *adj.* designating any movement, party, etc. opposed to abortion —**right'-to-lif'er** *n.*

right triangle a triangle with a right angle

right wing the more conservative or reactionary section of a political party or group —**right'-wing'** *adj.* —**right'-wing'er** *n.*

rig·id (rij'id) *adj.* 〖< L *rigere,* be stiff〗 **1** not bending or flexible; stiff **2** not moving; fixed **3** severe; strict —**ri·gid·i·ty** (ri jid'ə tē) *n.,* **rig'id·ness** —**rig'id·ly** *adv.*

rig·ma·role (rig'mə rōl') *n.* 〖< ME *rageman rolle,* long list〗 **1** nonsense **2** a foolishly complicated procedure

rig·or (rig'ər) *n.* 〖< L *rigere:* see RIGID〗 **1** severity; strictness **2** hardship Brit. sp. **rig'our** —**rig'or·ous** *adj.* —**rig'or·ous·ly** *adv.*

rigor mor·tis (môr'tis) 〖L, stiffness of death〗 the stiffening of the muscles after death

rile (rīl) *vt.* **riled, ril'ing** [var. of ROIL] [Inf. or Dial.] to anger; irritate

rill (ril) *n.* 〖< Du *ril*〗 a rivulet

rim (rim) *n.* 〖OE *rima*〗 **1** an edge, border, or margin, esp. of something circular **2** the outer part of a wheel —*vt.* **rimmed, rim'ming** to put a rim or rims on or around —**rim'less** *adj.*

rime' (rīm) *n., vi., vt.* **rimed, rim'ing** RHYME

rime² (rīm) *n.* 〖OE *hrim*〗 frost formed by the freezing of water droplets in fog, etc.

rind (rīnd) *n.* 〖OE〗 a hard outer layer or covering

ring' (riŋ) *vi.* **rang** or [Now Chiefly Dial.] **rung, rung, ring'ing** 〖OE *hringan*〗 **1** to give forth a resonant sound, as a bell **2** to seem [to *ring* true] **3** to sound a bell, esp. as a summons **4** to resound [to *ring* with laughter] **5** to have a ringing sensation, as the ears —*vt.* **1** to cause (a bell, etc.) to ring **2** to signal, announce, etc., as by ringing **3** to call by telephone —n. 1 the sound of a bell 2 a characteristic quality [the *ring* of truth] 3 the act of ringing a bell 4 a telephone call —**ring a bell** to evoke a vague memory

ring² (riŋ) n. ⟦OE *hring*⟧ 1 an ornamental circular band worn on a finger 2 any similar band [a key *ring*] 3 a circular line, mark, figure, or course 4 a group of people or things in a circle 5 a group working to advance its own interests, esp. by dishonest means 6 an enclosed area for contests, exhibitions, etc. [a circus *ring*] 7 prizefighting: with *the* —vt. **ringed, ring′ing** 1 to encircle 2 to form into a ring

ring·er¹ n. a horseshoe, etc. thrown so that it encircles the peg

ring·er² n. 1 one that rings a bell, etc. 2 [Slang] *a)* a person or thing closely resembling another *b)* one entered unfairly in a competition

ring·lead·er n. one who leads others, esp. in unlawful acts, etc.

ring·let (-lit) n. a long curl of hair

ring·mas·ter n. a person who directs and introduces the performances in a circus ring

ring·side n. 1 the place just outside a boxing or circus ring 2 any place providing a close view

ring·tone n. a digital recording of music or other sound that plays when a call is received on a cellular phone

ring·worm n. a contagious skin disease caused by a fungus

rink (riŋk) n. ⟦< OFr *renc*, a rank⟧ 1 an expanse of ice for skating 2 a smooth floor for roller-skating

rinse (rins) vt. **rinsed, rins′ing** ⟦ult. < L *recens*, fresh⟧ 1 to wash or flush lightly 2 to remove soap, etc. from with clear water —n. 1 a rinsing or the liquid used 2 a solution used to rinse or tint hair

Ri·o de Ja·nei·ro (rē′ō dā′ zhə ner′ō) city & seaport in SE Brazil

Ri·o Gran·de (rē′ō grand′, -gran′dē) river flowing from S Colorado into the Gulf of Mexico: the S border of Texas

ri·ot (rī′ət) n. ⟦< OFr *riote*, dispute⟧ 1 wild or violent disorder, confusion, etc.; esp., a violent public disturbance 2 a brilliant display 3 [Inf.] something very funny —vi. to take part in a riot —**read someone the riot act** [Inf.] to upbraid or forcefully warn someone —**run riot** 1 to act wildly 2 to grow wild in abundance —**ri′ot·er** n. —**ri′ot·ous** adj.

rip (rip) vt. **ripped, rip′ping** ⟦ME *rippen*⟧ 1 *a)* to cut or tear apart roughly *b)* to remove in this way (with *off, out*, etc.) *c)* to sever the threads of (a seam) 2 to saw (wood) along the grain —vi. 1 to become ripped 2 [Inf.] to rush; speed —n. a ripped place —**rip into** [Inf.] to attack, esp. verbally —**rip off** [Slang] 1 to steal 2 to cheat or exploit —**rip′per** n.

R.I.P. or **RIP** abbrev. may he (she) rest in peace

rip cord a cord, etc. pulled to open a parachute during descent

ripe (rīp) adj. ⟦OE⟧ 1 ready to be harvested, as grain or fruit 2 of sufficient age, etc. to be used [*ripe* cheese] 3 fully developed; mature 4 fully prepared; ready [*ripe* for action] 5 having a strong, unpleasant smell —**ripe′ly** adv. —**ripe′ness** n.

rip·en (rī′pən) vi., vt. to become or make ripe; mature, age, etc.

rip-off n. [Slang] the act or an instance of stealing, cheating, etc.

ri·poste or **ri·post** (ri pōst′) n. ⟦Fr < L *respondere*, to answer⟧ a sharp, swift response; retort

rip·ple (rip′əl) vi., vt. **-pled, -pling** ⟦prob. < RIP⟧ to have or form little waves on the surface (of) —n. 1 a small wave 2 a rippling 3 [R-] any cheap wine

ripple effect the spreading effects caused by a single event

rip-roar·ing (-rôr′iŋ) adj. [Slang] boisterous; uproarious

rip·saw n. a saw with coarse teeth, for cutting wood along the grain

rip·tide n. a current opposing other currents, esp. a narrow band of current flowing seaward from a shore: also **rip tide**

rise (rīz) vi. **rose, ris·en** (riz′ən), **ris′ing** ⟦< OE *risan*⟧ 1 to stand or sit up after sitting, kneeling, or lying 2 to rebel; revolt 3 to go up; ascend 4 to appear above the horizon, as the sun 5 to attain a higher level, rank, etc. 6 to extend, slant, or move upward 7 to increase in amount, degree, etc. 8 to expand and swell, as dough with yeast 9 to originate; begin 10 *Theol.* to return to life —n. 1 upward movement; ascent 2 an advance in status, rank, etc. 3 a slope upward 4 an increase in degree, amount, etc. 5 beginning; origin —**give rise to** to bring about

ris·er n. 1 one that rises 2 a vertical piece between the steps in a stairway 3 an elevated platform as for singers on a stage

ris·i·ble (riz′ə bəl) adj. ⟦< L *ridere*, to laugh⟧ causing laughter; funny —**ris′i·bil′i·ty** n.

ris·ing n. an uprising; revolt

risk (risk) n. ⟦< Fr < It *risco*⟧ the chance of injury, damage, or loss —vt. 1 to expose to risk [to *risk* one's life] 2 to incur the risk of [to *risk* a war] —**risk′y** adj. **-i·er, -i·est**

ris·qué (ris kā′) adj. ⟦Fr < *risquer*, to risk⟧ very close to being improper or indecent; suggestive

Rit·a·lin (rit′′l in) trademark for a stimulant drug used to treat depression, hyperactivity, etc.

rite (rīt) n. ⟦L *ritus*⟧ a ceremonial, solemn act, as in religious use

rite of passage a significant event, ceremony, etc. in a person's life

rit·u·al (rich′oo əl) adj. of, like, or done as a rite —n. a set form or system of rites, religious or otherwise —**rit′u·al·ism′** n. —**rit′u·al·ly** adv.

ri·val (rī′vəl) n. ⟦< L *rivalis*⟧ one who tries to equal or surpass another; competitor —adj. acting as a rival; competing —vt. **-valed** or **-valled, -val·ing** or **-val·ling** 1 to try to equal or surpass 2 to equal in some way —**ri′val·rous** *adj.* —**ri′val·ry** *n.*, *pl.* **-ries**

riv·en (riv′ən) *adj.* torn apart or split

riv·er (riv′ər) *n.* [< L *ripa*, a bank] a natural stream of water flowing into an ocean, a lake, etc.

river basin the area drained by a river and its tributaries

riv·er·bed *n.* the channel in which a river flows or has flowed

riv·er·side *n.* the bank of a river

riv·et (riv′it) *n.* [Fr < *river*, to clinch] a metal bolt with a head and a plain end that is flattened after the bolt is passed through parts to be held together —*vt.* 1 to fasten with rivets 2 to hold (someone's attention or interest) firmly —**riv′et·er** *n.*

Riv·i·er·a (riv′ē er′ə) strip of the Mediterranean coast of SE France & NW Italy: a resort area

riv·u·let (riv′yo͞o lit) *n.* [< L *rivus*, brook] a little stream

rm *abbrev.* 1 ream 2 room

Rn *Chem. symbol for* radon

RN *abbrev.* Registered Nurse

RNA *n.* [r(ibo)n(ucleic) a(cid)] an essential component of all living matter: one form carries genetic information

roach[1] (rōch) *n. short for* COCKROACH

roach[2] (rōch) *n.*, *pl.* **roach** or **roach′es** [< OFr *roche*] a freshwater fish of the carp family

road (rōd) *n.* [OE *rad*, a ride] 1 a way made for traveling; highway 2 a way; course [the *road* to fortune] 3 [*often pl.*] a place near shore where ships can ride at anchor —**on the road** traveling, as by a salesman or a touring troupe of actors

road·bed *n.* the foundation laid for railroad tracks, a highway, etc.

road·block *n.* 1 a blockade set up in a road as to prevent movement 2 any hindrance

road·kill *n.* [Slang] the body of an animal killed by a passing vehicle

road rage angry or violent behavior by motorists, as caused by stress in traffic

road·run·ner *n.* a long-tailed, swift-running desert bird of the SW U.S. and N Mexico: also **road runner**

road·show *n.* a touring theatrical show

road·side *n.* the side of a road —*adj.* on or at the side of a road

road·way *n.* a road; specif., the part of a road used by vehicles

road·work *n.* work done in repairing or building roads

roam (rōm) *vi.*, *vt.* [ME *romen*] to wander aimlessly (over or through) —**roam′er** *n.*

roan (rōn) *adj.* [< OSp *roano*] bay, black, etc. thickly sprinkled with white —*n.* a roan horse

roar (rôr) *vi.* [OE *rarian*] 1 to make a loud, deep, rumbling sound 2 to laugh boisterously —*vt.* to say loudly —*n.* a loud, deep, rumbling sound

roast (rōst) *vt.* [< OFr *rostir*] 1 to cook (meat, etc.) with little or no moisture, as in an oven or over an open fire 2 to process (coffee, etc.) by exposure to heat 3 to expose to great heat 4 [Inf.] to criticize severely 5 [Inf.] to mock affectionately as at a banquet —*vi.* 1 to undergo roasting 2 to be or become very hot —*n.* 1 roasted meat 2 a cut of meat for roasting 3 a picnic at which food is roasted 4 [Inf.] a banquet at which the guest of honor is affectionately mocked —*adj.* roasted [*roast* pork] —**roast′er** *n.*

rob (räb) *vt.* **robbed, rob′bing** [< OFr *rober*] 1 to take money, etc. from unlawfully by force; steal from 2 to deprive of something unjustly or injuriously —*vi.* to be one who robs —**rob′ber** *n.* —**rob′ber·y** *n.*, *pl.* **-ies**

robe (rōb) *n.* [< OFr] 1 a long, loose outer garment 2 such a garment worn to show rank or office, as by a judge 3 a bathrobe or dressing gown 4 a covering or wrap [a lap *robe*] —*vt.*, *vi.* **robed, rob′ing** to dress in a robe

rob·in (räb′ən) *n.* [< OFr dim. of *Robert*] a North American thrush with a dull-red breast in the male

Robin Hood *Eng. Legend* 12th-c. outlaw who robbed the rich to help the poor

ro·bot (rō′bät′) *n.* [< Czech < OSlav *rabu*, servant] 1 a mechanical device to automatically perform complex or repetitive tasks 2 a person who acts or works in a machinelike manner —**ro·bot′ic** *adj.*

ro·bot·ics *n.* the science or technology of robots, their design, use, etc.

ro·bust (rō bust′, rō′bust′) *adj.* [< L *robur*, oak] strong and healthy —**ro·bust′ly** *adv.* —**ro·bust′ness** *n.*

rock[1] (räk) *n.* [< ML *rocca*] 1 a large mass of stone 2 broken pieces of stone 3 mineral matter formed in masses in the earth's crust 4 anything like a rock; esp., a firm support —**on the rocks** [Inf.] 1 in trouble or near ruin 2 served over ice cubes: said of liquor, etc.

rock[2] (räk) *vt.*, *vi.* [OE *roccian*] 1 to move back and forth or from side to side 2 to sway strongly; shake —*n.* 1 a rocking motion 2 ROCK-AND-ROLL

rock·a·bil·ly (-ə bil′ē) *n.* [fol. + -a- + (HILL)-BILLY] an early form of rock-and-roll with a strong country music influence

rock-and-roll *n.* a form of popular music that evolved from rhythm and blues, characterized by a strong rhythm with an accent on the offbeat

rock bottom the lowest level

rock·bound *adj.* surrounded or covered by rocks

rock candy large, hard, clear crystals of sugar formed on a string

rock·er *n.* 1 either of the curved pieces on which a cradle, etc. rocks 2 a chair mounted on such pieces: also **rocking chair**

rocker panel any panel section below the doors of an automotive vehicle

rock·et (räk′it) *n.* [It *rocchetta*, spool] any device driven forward by gases escaping through a rear vent, as a firework, a projectile weapon, or the propulsion mechanism of a spacecraft —*vi.* to move in or like a rocket; soar

rock·et·ry (-ə trē) *n.* the science of building and launching rockets

rock garden a garden of flowers, etc. in ground studded with rocks

rocking horse a toy horse on rockers or springs, for a child to ride

rock lobster SPINY LOBSTER

rock-ribbed *adj.* 1 having rocky ridges 2 firm; unyielding

rock salt common salt in rocklike masses

rock wool a fibrous material made from molten rock, used for insulation

rock·y (räk′ē) *adj.* **-i·er, -i·est** 1 full of rocks 2 consisting of rock 3 like a rock; firm, hard, etc. 4 full of obstacles or difficulties —**rock′i·ness** *n.*

Rocky Mountains mountain system in W North America, extending from New Mexico to N British Columbia: also **Rock′ies**

Rocky Mountain sheep BIGHORN

ro·co·co (rə kō′kō) *n.* ⟦Fr < *rocaille*, shell work⟧ [*occas.* **R-**] a style of architecture, art, music, etc. marked by profuse and delicate ornamentation, etc. —*adj.* 1 of or in rococo 2 too elaborate

rod (räd) *n.* ⟦< OE *rodd*, straight shoot or stem⟧ 1 a straight stick or bar 2 a stick for beating as punishment 3 a staff carried as a symbol of office; scepter 4 a pole for fishing 5 a measure of length equal to 5½ yards 6 [Slang] a pistol

rode (rōd) *vi., vt. pt. & archaic pp. of* RIDE

ro·dent (rōd′ʼnt) *n.* ⟦< L *rodere*, gnaw⟧ any of an order of gnawing mammals, as rats or mice

ro·de·o (rō′dē ō′) *n., pl.* **-os′** ⟦Sp < L *rotare*, to turn⟧ a public exhibition of the skills of cowboys, with contests in bull riding, lassoing, etc.

Ro·din (rō dan′), **(François) Au·guste (René)** (ō güst′) 1840-1917; Fr. sculptor

roe[1] (rō) *n.* ⟦ME *rowe*⟧ fish eggs

roe[2] (rō) *n., pl.* **roe** or **roes** ⟦< OE *rā*⟧ a small, agile deer of Europe and Asia

roe·buck *n.* the male roe deer

roent·gen (rent′gən) *n.* ⟦after W. K. Roentgen (1845-1923), Ger physicist⟧ the unit for measuring the radiation of X-rays or gamma rays

roent·gen·i·um (rent gen′ē əm) *n.* ⟦after W. K. Roentgen (1845-1923), Ger physicist⟧ an artificially produced, radioactive chemical element: symbol, Rg; at. no. 111

Rog·er (rä′jər) *interj.* ⟦< name of signal flag for R⟧ [*also* **r-**] 1 received 2 [Inf.] right! OK!

rogue (rōg) *n.* ⟦< ?⟧ 1 a scoundrel 2 a mischievous person —**ro·guer·y** (rō′gər ē) *n., pl.* **-ies** —**ro·guish** (rō′gish) *adj.*

rogues gallery a police collection of photographs of criminals

roil (roil) *vt.* ⟦< L *robigo*, rust⟧ 1 to make (a liquid) cloudy, muddy, etc. by stirring up sediment 2 to vex

roist·er (rois′tər) *vi.* ⟦see RUSTIC⟧ to revel noisily —**roist′er·er** *n.*

role (rōl) *n.* ⟦Fr⟧ 1 the part played by an actor 2 a function assumed by someone [an advisory *role*] Often **rôle**

role model a person so effective or inspiring as to be a model for others

role-play·ing *n. Psychol.* a technique in which participants act out roles as to practice appropriate behavior, etc.

roll (rōl) *vi.* ⟦< L *rota*, a wheel⟧ 1 to move by turning around or over and over 2 to move on wheels 3 to pass [the years *roll* by] 4 to extend in gentle swells 5 to make a loud rising and falling sound [thunder *rolls*] 6 to rock from side to side —*vt.* 1 to make move by turning around or over and over 2 to make move on wheels 3 to utter with full, flowing sound 4 to pronounce with a trill [to *roll* one's r's] 5 to give a swaying motion to 6 to move around or from side to side [to *roll* one's eyes] 7 to make into a ball or cylinder [*roll* up the rug] 8 to flatten or spread with a roller, etc. —*n.* 1 a rolling 2 a scroll 3 a list of names 4 something rolled into a cylinder 5 a very small loaf of bread, etc. 6 a swaying motion 7 a loud, reverberating sound, as of thunder 8 a slight swell on a surface —**be on a roll** [Inf.] to have a series of successes —**roll back** to reduce (prices) to a previous level —**roll over** to refinance or reinvest by means of a ROLLOVER

roll·back *n.* a rolling back, esp. of prices to a previous level

roll call the reading aloud of a roll to find out who is absent

roll·er (rōl′ər) *n.* 1 one that rolls 2 a cylinder of metal, wood, etc. on which something is rolled, or one used to crush, smooth, or spread something

roller bearing a bearing in which the shaft turns with rollers in a circular track

Roll·er·blade *trademark for* a kind of IN-LINE SKATE —*n.* [**r-**] any IN-LINE SKATE —**roll′er·blad′ing** *n.*

roller coaster an amusement ride in which small open cars move on tracks that dip and curve sharply

roller skate SKATE[1] (*n.* 2) —**roll′er-skate′** *vi.* **-skat′ed, -skat′ing** —**roll′er skater**

rol·lick·ing (räl′ik iŋ) *adj.* ⟦< ? FROLIC⟧ playfully lively

rolling pin a smooth, heavy cylinder of wood, etc. used to roll out dough

roll·o·ver *n.* 1 the refinancing of a maturing note, etc. 2 the reinvesting of funds to defer the payment of taxes 3 a traffic accident in which a vehicle rolls over

roll-top *adj.* having a sliding, flexible top of parallel slats [a *roll-top* desk]

roll-up *n.* a cylindrical food, typically a tortilla rolled around meat, vegetables, or other fillings: also written **roll′up′**

Ro·lo·dex (rō′lə deks′) *trademark for* a desktop file holding cards with names and addresses for ready reference

ro·ly-po·ly (rō′lē pō′lē) *adj.* ⟦< ROLL⟧ short and plump; pudgy

Rom *abbrev.* Roman

ROM (räm) *n.* ⟦r(ead-)o(nly) m(emory)⟧ 1 computer memory whose contents can be read but not altered **2** a memory chip like this

Ro·ma (rō′mə) *pl.n., sing.* **Rom** (räm) [see ROMANI] a traditionally itinerant people, believed to be orig. from India —*adj.* of or relating to this people

ro·maine (rō mān′) *n.* [Fr., ult. < L *Romanus*, Roman] a type of lettuce with long leaves forming a slender head

Ro·man (rō′mən) *adj.* **1** of or characteristic of ancient or modern Rome or its people, etc. **2** of the Roman Catholic Church **3** [*usually* r-] designating or of the usual upright style of printing types; not italic —*n.* **1** a person born or living in ancient or modern Rome **2** [*usually* r-] roman type or characters

Roman candle a firework consisting of a tube that sends out balls of fire, etc.

Roman Catholic 1 of the Christian church (**Roman Catholic Church**) headed by the pope **2** a member of this church

ro·mance (rō mans′, rō′mans′) *adj.* [ult. < L *Romanicus*, Roman] [R-] designating or of any of the languages derived from Vulgar Latin, as Italian, Spanish, or French —*n.* **1** a long poem or tale about the adventures of knights **2** a novel of love, adventure, etc. **3** excitement, love, etc. of the kind found in such literature **4** a love affair —*vt.* **-manced′, -manc′ing** to make love to; woo

Roman Empire empire of the ancient Romans (27 B.C.–A.D. 395), including W & S Europe, N Africa, & SW Asia

Rom·a·ni (räm′ə nē, rō′mə-) *n.* [Romani < *rom*, a man; ult. < Sans] the language of the Roma; also sp. **Rom′a·ny**

Ro·ma·ni·a (rō mā′nē ə) country in SE Europe —**Ro·ma′ni·an** *adj., n.*

Roman numerals Roman letters used as numerals: I = 1, V = 5, X = 10, L = 50, C = 100, D = 500, and M = 1,000

ro·man·tic (rō man′tik) *adj.* **1** of, like, or characterized by romance **2** fanciful or fictitious **3** not practical; visionary **4** full of thoughts, feelings, etc. of romance **5** suited for romance **6** [*often* R-] of a cultural movement of the 1800s characterized by freedom of form and spirit, emphasis on feeling and originality, etc. —*n.* a romantic person —**ro·man′ti·cal·ly** *adv.*—**ro·man′ti·cism′** (-tə siz′əm) *n.*

ro·man·ti·cize (-tə sīz′) *vt.* **-cized′, -ciz′ing** to treat or regard romantically —*vi.* to have romantic ideas, etc.

Rome (rōm) capital of Italy &, formerly, of the Roman Empire

Ro·me·o (rō′mē ō′) *n.* the hero of Shakespeare's *Romeo and Juliet* (c. 1595)

romp (rämp) *n.* [prob. < OFr *ramper*, to climb] boisterous, lively play —*vi.* to play in a boisterous, lively way

romp·er *n.* **1** one who romps **2** [*pl.*] a loose, one-piece outer garment for a small child

Rom·u·lus (räm′yoo ləs) *n. Rom. Myth.* founder and first king of Rome: he and his twin brother Remus are suckled by a female wolf

rood (rood) *n.* [OE *rod*] **1** a crucifix **2** [Brit.] an old unit of area equal to ¼ acre

roof (roof, roof) *n., pl.* **roofs** [OE *hrof*] **1** the outside top covering of a building **2** anything like this in position or use [the *roof* of the mouth] —*vt.* to cover with or as with a roof —**roof′less** *adj.*

roof·er *n.* a roof maker or repairer

roof·ing *n.* material for roofs

roof·top *n.* the roof of a building

rook[1] (rook) *n.* [OE *hroc*] a European crow —*vt., vi.* to swindle; cheat

rook[2] (rook) *n.* [< Pers *rukh*] a chess piece that can move horizontally or vertically

rook·er·y *n., pl.* **-ies** a breeding place of rooks, or of seals, penguins, etc.

rook·ie (rook′ē) *n.* [Slang] **1** an inexperienced army recruit **2** [Inf.] any beginner

room (room, room) *n.* [OE *rum*] **1** space to contain something **2** suitable scope [*room* for doubt] **3** an interior space enclosed or set apart by walls **4** [*pl.*] living quarters [the people in a room] —*vi., vt.* to have or provide with lodgings —**room′ful′** *n.* —**room′y** *adj.* **-i·er, -i·est** —**room′i·ness** *n.*

room and board lodging and meals

room·er *n.* one who rents a room or rooms to live in; lodger

rooming house a house with furnished rooms for rent

room·mate *n.* a person with whom one shares a room or rooms

Roo·se·velt (rō′zə velt′) **1 Franklin De·la·no** (del′ə nō′) 1882–1945; 32d president of the U.S. (1933–45) **2 Theodore** 1858–1919; 26th president of the U.S. (1901–09)

roost (roost) *n.* [OE *hrost*] **1** a perch on which birds, esp. domestic fowls, can rest **2** a place with perches for birds **3** a place for resting, sleeping, etc. —*vi.* **1** to perch on a roost **2** to stay or settle down, as for the night

roost·er *n.* a male chicken

root[1] (root, root) *n.* [< ON *rot*] **1** the part of a plant, usually underground, that anchors the plant, draws water from the soil, etc. **2** the embedded part of a tooth, a hair, etc. **3** a source or cause **4** a supporting or essential part **5** a quantity that, multiplied by itself a specified number of times, produces a given quantity **6** the basic element of a word or form, without affixes or phonetic changes —*vi.* to take root —*vt.* **1** to fix the roots of in the ground **2** to establish; settle —**root up** (or **out**) to pull up by the roots; destroy completely —**take root 1** to begin growing by putting out roots **2** to become fixed, settled, etc.

root[2] (root, root) *vt.* [< OE *wrot*, snout] to dig (*up* or *out*) with or as with the snout —*vi.* **1** to search about; rummage **2** to cheer for or favor a team, etc.: usually with *for*

root beer a carbonated drink made or flavored with certain plant root extracts

root canal 1 a tubular channel in a tooth's root **2** a treatment involving opening, cleaning, filling, etc. such a channel

root·let (-lit) *n.* a little root

rope (rōp) *n.* [OE *rap*] 1 a thick, strong cord made of strands of fiber, etc. twisted together 2 a ropelike string, as of pearls —*vt.* **roped, rop′ing** 1 to fasten or tie with a rope 2 to mark off or enclose with a rope 3 to catch with a lasso —**know the ropes** [Inf.] to be well acquainted with a procedure, etc. —**rope in** [Slang] to entice or trick into doing something

rope tow a kind of ski lift for pulling skiers up a slope on their skis

Roque·fort (rōk′fərt) [after *Roquefort*, France, where made] *trademark for* a strong French cheese with a bluish mold

Ror·schach test (rôr′shäk′) [after H. *Rorschach* (1884-1922), Swiss psychiatrist] *Psychol.* a personality test in which the subject's interpretations of standard inkblot designs are analyzed

ro·sa·ry (rō′zər ē) *n., pl.* **-ries** [ML *rosarium*] *R.C.Ch.* a string of groups of beads, used to keep count in saying repeated prayers

rose[1] (rōz) *n.* [< L *rosa* < Gr *rhodon*] 1 a shrub with prickly stems and with flowers of red, pink, white, yellow, etc. 2 its flower 3 pinkish red or purplish red —*adj.* of this color

rose[2] (rōz) *vi. pt. of* RISE

ro·sé (rō zā′) *n.* [Fr, pink] a pink wine, tinted by the grape skins early in fermentation

ro·se·ate (rō′zē it) *adj.* rose-colored

rose·bud *n.* the bud of a rose

rose·bush *n.* a shrub that bears roses

rose-col·ored *adj.* 1 pinkish-red or purplish-red 2 optimistic —**through rose-colored glasses** with optimism, esp. undue optimism

rose·mar·y (rōz′mer′ē) *n.* [< L *ros marinus*, sea dew] an evergreen herb of the mint family, with fragrant leaves used in perfumes, in cooking, etc.

ro·sette (rō zet′) *n.* an ornament or arrangement, as of ribbons, resembling a rose

rose water a preparation of water and attar of roses, used as a perfume

rose window a circular window with a roselike pattern of tracery

rose·wood *n.* [< its odor] 1 a hard, reddish wood, used in furniture, etc. 2 a tropical tree yielding this wood

Rosh Ha·sha·na (rōsh′ hə shô′nə, -shä′-) the Jewish New Year

ros·in (räz′ən) *n.* [see RESIN] the hard resin left after the distillation of turpentine: it is rubbed on violin bows, used in making varnish, etc.

ros·ter (räs′tər) *n.* [< Du *rooster*] a list or roll, as of military personnel

ros·trum (räs′trəm) *n., pl.* **-trums** or **-tra** (-trə) [L, beak] a platform for public speaking

ros·y (rō′zē) *adj.* **-i·er, -i·est** [ME] 1 rose in color 2 bright, promising, etc. [a *rosy* future] —**ros′i·ly** *adv.* —**ros′i·ness** *n.*

rot (rät) *vi., vt.* **rot′ted, rot′ting** [OE *rotian*] to decompose; decay —*n.* 1 a rotting or something rotten 2 a disease characterized by decay 3 [Slang] nonsense

ro·ta·ry (rōt′ər ē) *adj.* [< L *rota*, wheel] 1 turning around a central axis, as a wheel does 2 having rotating parts [a *rotary* press] —*n., pl.* **-ries** 1 a rotary machine 2 TRAFFIC CIRCLE

ro·tate (rō′tāt′) *vi., vt.* **-tat′ed, -tat′ing** [< L *rota*, wheel] 1 to turn around an axis 2 to change or cause to change in regular succession —**ro·ta′tion** *n.* —**ro·ta′tor** *n.*

ROTC *abbrev.* Reserve Officers' Training Corps

rote (rōt) *n.* [ME] a fixed, mechanical way of doing something —**by rote** by memory alone, without thought

rot·gut (rät′gut′) *n.* [Slang] raw, low-grade whiskey or other liquor

ro·tis·ser·ie (rō tis′ər ē) *n.* [Fr < earlier Fr *rostir*, to roast] a grill with an electrically turned spit

ro·to·gra·vure (rōt′ə grə vyoor′) *n.* [< L *rota*, wheel + Fr *gravure*, engraving] a printing process using a rotary press with cylinders etched from photographic plates

ro·tor (rōt′ər) *n.* 1 the rotating part of a motor, etc. 2 a system of rotating airfoils, as on a helicopter

ro·to·till·er (rōt′ə til′ər) *n.* a motorized machine with rotary blades, for loosening the earth around growing plants —**ro′to·till′** *vt.*

rot·ten (rät′'n) *adj.* [< ON *rotinn*] 1 decayed; spoiled 2 foul-smelling 3 morally corrupt 4 unsound, as if decayed within 5 [Slang] very bad, unpleasant, etc. —**rot′ten·ness** *n.*

Rot·ter·dam (rät′ər dam′) seaport in SW Netherlands

ro·tund (rō tund′) *adj.* [L *rotundus*] plump or stout —**ro·tun′di·ty** *n.,* **ro·tun′dness**

ro·tun·da (rō tun′də) *n.* [see prec.] a round building, hall, or room, esp. one with a dome

rou·é (rōō ā′) *n.* [Fr < L *rota*, wheel] a dissipated man; rake

rouge (rōōzh) *n.* [Fr, red] a reddish cosmetic powder or paste for adding color to the cheeks —*vt.* **rouged, roug′ing** to use cosmetic rouge on

rough (ruf) *adj.* [OE *ruh*] 1 not smooth or level; uneven 2 shaggy [a *rough* coat] 3 stormy [*rough* weather] 4 disorderly [*rough* play] 5 harsh or coarse 6 lacking comforts and conveniences 7 not polished or finished; crude 8 approximate [a *rough* guess] 9 [Inf.] difficult [a *rough* time] —*n.* 1 rough ground, material, condition, etc. 2 *Golf* any part of the course with grass, etc. left uncut —*adv.* in a rough way —*vt.* 1 to roughen: often with *up* 2 to treat roughly: usually with *up* 3 to sketch, shape, etc. roughly: usually with *in* or *out* —**rough it** to live without customary comforts, etc. —**rough′ly** *adv.* —**rough′ness** *n.*

rough·age *n.* rough or coarse food containing bran, peel, or other sources of cellulose

rough·en *vt., vi.* to make or become rough

rough-hew *vt.* **-hewed′, -hewed′** or **-hewn′, -hew′ing** 1 to hew (timber, stone, etc.) roughly, or without smoothing 2 to form roughly Also sp. **rough′hew′**

rough·house *vt., vi.* **-housed′, -hous′ing** [Inf.] to treat or act roughly or boisterously

rough·neck *n.* 1 [Inf.] a rowdy 2 a worker on an oil rig —*vi.* to work as a roughneck

rough·shod *adj.* shod with horseshoes having metal points —**ride roughshod over** to treat harshly and arrogantly

rou·lette (rōō let′) *n.* [Fr < L *rota*, wheel] a gambling game played by tossing a small ball into a whirling shallow bowl (**roulette wheel**) with numbered, red or black compartments

round (round) *adj.* [< L *rotundus*, rotund] 1 shaped like a ball, circle, or cylinder 2 plump 3 full; complete [a *round* dozen] 4 expressed by a whole number or in tens, hundreds, etc. —*n.* 1 something round, as the rung of a ladder 2 the part of a beef animal between the rump and the leg 3 a series or succession [a *round* of parties] 4 [*often pl.*] a regular, customary circuit, as by a watchman 5 a single serving of one drink apiece 6 a single shot from a gun, or from several guns together; also, the ammunition for this 7 a single outburst, as of applause 8 a single period of action, as in boxing 9 a short song which one group begins singing when another reaches the second phrase, etc. —*vt.* 1 to make round 2 to express as a round number: with *off* 3 to finish: with *out* or *off* 4 to go around —*vi.* 1 to turn; reverse direction 2 to become plump: often with *out* —*adv.* 1 AROUND 2 through a recurring period of time [to work the year *round*] 3 for each of several 4 in a roundabout way —*prep.* AROUND —**in the round** 1 in an arena theater 2 in full, rounded form: said of sculpture 3 in full detail —**round about** in or to the opposite direction —**round up** to collect in a herd, group, etc. —**round′ness** *n.*

round·a·bout *adj.* indirect; circuitous

roun·de·lay (roun′də lā′) *n.* [< OFr *rondel*, a short lyrical poem] a simple song in which some phrase, line, etc. is continually repeated

round·house *n.* a circular building for storing and repairing locomotives

round·ly *adv.* 1 in a round form 2 vigorously 3 fully; completely and thoroughly

round-shoul·dered *adj.* having the shoulders bent forward

round steak a steak cut from a round of beef

round·ta·ble *n.* [< fol.] a group gathered together for an informal discussion or conference

Round Table in legend, the circular table around which King Arthur and his knights sit

round-the-clock *adj., adv.* throughout the day and night; continuous(ly)

round trip a trip to a place and back again —**round′-trip′** *adj.*

round·up *n.* 1 a driving together of cattle, etc. on the range, as for branding 2 any similar collecting 3 a summary, as of news

round·worm *n.* NEMATODE

rouse (rouz) *vt., vi.* **roused, rous′ing** [prob. < earlier Fr] 1 to excite or become excited 2 to wake

Rous·seau (rōō sō′), **Jean Jacques** (zhän zhȧk′) 1712–78; Fr. philosopher & writer, born in Switzerland

roust·a·bout (rous′tə bout′) *n.* [< ROUSE + ABOUT] an unskilled or transient laborer, as on a wharf or in an oil field

rout¹ (rout) *n.* [< L *rupta*, broken] 1 a disorderly flight 2 an overwhelming defeat —*vt.* 1 to put to flight 2 to defeat overwhelmingly

rout² (rout) *vt.* [< ROOT²] to force out —**rout out** 1 to gouge out 2 to make (a person) get out

route (rōōt, rout) *n.* [< L *rupta* (*via*), (path) broken through] a road or course for traveling; often, a regular course, as in delivering mail —*vt.* **rout′ed, rout′ing** 1 to send by a certain route 2 to arrange the route for

rout·er¹ (rout′ər) *n.* [see ROUT²] 1 a tool for gouging out recesses and smoothing grooves 2 a machine for routing out areas on wood or metal surfaces

rout·er² (rout′ər) *n.* [< ROUTE] 1 one that routes 2 a device that coordinates the transmission of data packets within and between computer networks

rou·tine (rōō tēn′) *n.* [see prec.] a regular procedure, customary or prescribed —*adj.* like or using routine —**rou·tine′ly** *adv.*

rou·tin·ize (-tē′nīz) *vt.* **-ized, -iz·ing** to make routine; reduce to a routine —**rou′tin·i·za′tion** *n.*

rove (rōv) *vi., vt.* **roved, rov′ing** [ME *roven*] to roam —**rov′er** *n.*

row¹ (rō) *n.* [OE *ræw*] 1 a number of people or things in a line 2 a line of seats in a theater, etc. —**in a row** in succession; consecutively

row² (rō) *vt., vi.* [OE *rowan*] 1 to propel (a boat) with oars 2 to carry in a rowboat —*n.* a trip by rowboat

row³ (rou) *n., vi.* [< ? ROUSE] quarrel or brawl

row·boat (rō′bōt′) *n.* a small boat made for rowing

row·dy (rou′dē) *n., pl.* **-dies** [< ? ROW³] a rough, quarrelsome, and disorderly person —*adj.* **-di·er, -di·est** rough, quarrelsome, disorderly, etc. —**row′di·ness** *n.* —**row′dy·ism′** *n.*

row·el (rou′əl) *n.* [ult. < L *rota*, wheel] a small wheel with sharp points, at the end of a spur

row house (rō) any of a line of identical houses joined by common walls

roy·al (roi′əl) *adj.* [< L *regalis*] 1 of a king or queen 2 like, or fit for, a king or queen; magnificent, majestic, etc. 3 of a kingdom, its government, etc. —**roy′al·ly** *adv.*

roy·al·ist *n.* one who supports a monarch or a monarchy

roy·al·ty *n., pl.* **-ties** 1 the rank or power of a king or queen 2 a royal person or persons 3 royal quality 4 a share of the proceeds from a patent, book, etc. paid to the owner, author, etc.

RPG (är′pē′jē′) *n., pl.* **RPGs** [prob. < *r*(*ocket-*) *p*(*ropelled*) *g*(*renade*) (*launcher*)] 1 a type of grenade equipped with a simple rocket-propulsion system 2 a grenade launcher that shoots this type of grenade

rpm *abbrev.* revolutions per minute

rps *abbrev.* revolutions per second

RR *abbrev.* 1 railroad 2 Rural Route: also **R.R.**

RSV *abbrev.* Revised Standard Version (of the Bible)

RSVP (är′es vē pē′) *n.* [< Fr *répondez s'il vous plaît*, please reply] a reply to an invitation —*vi.* to reply to an invitation

rte *abbrev.* route

rub (rub) *vt.* **rubbed, rub′bing** [ME *rubben*] 1 to move (one's hand, a cloth, etc.) over (something) with pressure and friction 2 to apply (polish, etc.) in this way 3 to move (things) over each other with pressure and friction 4 to make sore by rubbing 5 to remove by rubbing (*out, off*, etc.) —*vi.* 1 to move with pressure and friction (*on*, etc.) 2 to rub something —*n.* 1 a rubbing 2 an obstacle, difficulty, or source of irritation —**rub down** 1 to massage 2 to smooth, polish, etc. by rubbing —**rub elbows with** to associate or mingle with: also **rub shoulders with** —**rub it in** [Slang] to keep reminding someone of his or her mistake —**rub the wrong way** to annoy

ru·ba·to (rōō bät′ō) *adj., adv.* [It, stolen] *Music* intentionally and temporarily not in strict tempo

rub·ber (rub′ər) *n.* 1 one that rubs 2 [< orig. use as an eraser] an elastic substance made from the milky sap of various tropical plants or made synthetically 3 something made of this substance; specif., a) a low-cut overshoe b) [Slang] a condom c) *Baseball* a rubber slab set into the pitcher's mound —*adj.* made of rubber —**rub′ber·y** *adj.*

rubber band a small loop of rubber for holding small objects together

rubber cement an adhesive of unvulcanized rubber in a solvent that quickly evaporates

rubber check [from the notion that it "bounces": see BOUNCE (*vi.* 3)] [Slang] a check that is worthless because of insufficient funds in the writer's account

rubber game (rub′ər) [< ?] the deciding game in a series

rub·ber·ize (-īz′) *vt.* **-ized′, -iz′ing** to coat or impregnate with rubber

rub·ber·neck [Inf.] *vi.* to look at things or gaze about in curiosity by stretching the neck or turning the head, as a sightseer might do —**rub′ber·neck′er** *n.*

rubber plant 1 any plant yielding latex 2 a house plant with large, glossy leaves

rub·ber-stamp *vt.* to give routine or automatic approval to

rub·bish (rub′ish) *n.* [ME *robous*] 1 any material thrown away as worthless; trash 2 nonsense

rub·ble (rub′əl) *n.* [ME *robel*] rough, broken pieces of stone, brick, etc.

rub·down *n.* a brisk rubbing of the body, as in massage

rube (rōōb) *n.* [< name *Reuben*] [Slang] an unsophisticated rustic

ru·bel·la (rōō bel′ə) *n.* [< L *ruber*, red] an infectious disease causing small red spots on the skin; German measles

Ru·bens (rōō′bənz), **Peter Paul** 1577-1640; Fl. painter

ru·bi·cund (rōō′bə kund′) *adj.* [< L *ruber*, red] reddish; ruddy

ru·bid·i·um (rōō bid′ē əm) *n.* [< L *rubidus*, red] a soft, alkali, metallic chemical element that ignites spontaneously in air and reacts violently with water: symbol, Rb; at. no. 37

ru·ble (rōō′bəl) *n.* [Russ *rubl'*] the monetary unit of Russia, Belarus, & Tajikistan

ru·bric (rōō′brik) *n.* [< L *ruber*, red] 1 in early books, a section-heading, letter, etc., often printed in red 2 any rule, explanatory comment, etc.

ru·by (rōō′bē) *n., pl.* **-bies** [ult. < L *rubeus*, reddish] 1 a clear, deep-red precious stone: a variety of corundum 2 deep red —*adj.* deep-red

ruck·sack (ruk′sak′, rook′-) *n.* [Ger, back sack] a kind of knapsack

ruck·us (ruk′əs) *n.* [prob. merging of RUMPUS & *ruction*, uproar] [Inf.] noisy confusion or disturbance

rud·der (rud′ər) *n.* [OE *rother*] a broad, flat, movable piece hinged to the rear of a ship or aircraft, used for steering —**rud′der·less** *adj.*

rud·dy (rud′ē) *adj.* **-di·er, -di·est** [OE *rudig*] 1 having a healthy red color 2 reddish —**rud′di·ness** *n.*

rude (rōōd) *adj.* **rud′er, rud′est** [< L *rudis*] 1 crude; rough 2 uncouth 3 discourteous 4 unskillful —**rude′ly** *adv.* —**rude′ness** *n.*

ru·di·ment (rōō′də mənt) *n.* [see prec.] [*usually pl.*] 1 a first principle as of a subject to be learned 2 a first slight beginning of something —**ru′di·men′ta·ry** (-men′tər ē) *adj.*

rue[1] (rōō) *vt., vi.* **rued, ru′ing** [OE *hreowan*] 1 to feel remorse for (a sin, fault, etc.) 2 to regret (an act, etc.) —*n.* [Archaic] sorrow —**rue′ful** *adj.* —**rue′ful·ly** *adv.*

rue[2] (rōō) *n.* [< Gr *rhytē*] a strong-scented shrub with bitter leaves

ruff (ruf) *n.* [< RUFFLE] 1 a high, frilled starched collar of the 1500s and 1600s 2 a band of colored or protruding feathers or fur about an animal's neck

ruf·fi·an (ruf′ē ən) *n.* [< It *ruffiano*, a pimp] a rowdy or hoodlum

ruf·fle (ruf′əl) *vt.* **-fled, -fling** [< ON or LowG] 1 to disturb the smoothness of 2 to make (feathers, etc.) stand up 3 to disturb or annoy —*vi.* to become uneven —*n.* a strip of cloth, lace, etc. gathered along one edge, used as a trimming

rug (rug) *n.* [< Scand] a piece of thick fabric used as a floor covering

rug·by (rug′bē) *n.* [first played at *Rugby* School in England] a game from which American football developed

rug·ged (rug′id) *adj.* [ME] 1 uneven; rough 2 severe; harsh 3 not refined 4 strong; robust —**rug′ged·ly** *adv.* —**rug′ged·ness** *n.*

Ruhr (rōōr) 1 river in WC Germany, flowing into the Rhine 2 major coal-mining & industrial region along this river: also called **Ruhr Basin**

ru·in (rōō′ən) *n.* [< L *ruere*, to fall] **1** [*pl.*] the remains of something destroyed, decayed, etc. **2** anything destroyed, etc. **3** downfall, destruction, etc. **4** anything causing this —*vt.* to bring to ruin; destroy, spoil, bankrupt, etc. —ru′in·a′tion *n.* —ru′in·ous *adj.*

rule (rōōl) *n.* [< L *regere*, to rule] **1** an established regulation or guide for conduct, procedure, usage, etc. **2** custom **3** the customary course **4** government; reign **5** RULER (*n.* 2) —*vt., vi.* **ruled, rul′ing 1** to have an influence (over); guide **2** to govern **3** to determine officially **4** to mark lines (on) as with a ruler —**as a rule** usually —**rule out** to exclude

rule of thumb a practical, though imprecise or unscientific, method

rul·er *n.* **1** one who governs **2** a strip of wood, etc. with a straight edge, used in drawing lines, measuring length, etc.

rul·ing *adj.* that rules —*n.* an official decision, as of a court

rum (rum) *n.* [< ?] an alcoholic liquor distilled from fermented sugar cane

Ru·ma·ni·a (rōō mā′nē ə) *var. of* ROMANIA —**Ru·ma′ni·an** *adj., n.*

rum·ba (room′bə, rum′-) *n.* [AmSp] a dance of Cuban origin, or music for it —*vi.* to dance the rumba

rum·ble (rum′bəl) *vi., vt.* **-bled, -bling** [ME *romblen*] **1** to make or cause to make a continuous deep, rolling sound **2** to move with such a sound —*n.* **1** a rumbling sound **2** [Slang] a fight between teenage gangs

ru·mi·nant (rōō′mə nənt) *adj.* [see fol.] of or belonging to the group of cud-chewing animals —*n.* any of a group of cud-chewing mammals, as cattle, deer, or camels, having a stomach with three or four chambers

ru·mi·nate (-nāt′) *vi.* **-nat′ed, -nat′ing** [< L *ruminare*] **1** to chew a cud **2** to turn something over in the mind —*vt.* **ru′mi·na′tion** *n.*

rum·mage (rum′ij) *vt., vi.* **-maged, -mag·ing** [< Fr *rum*, ship's hold] to search through (a place, etc.) thoroughly

rummage sale a sale of contributed miscellaneous articles, as for charity

rum·my (rum′ē) *n.* [< ?] a card game in which the object is to match cards into sets and sequences

ru·mor (rōō′mər) *n.* [L, noise] **1** general talk not based on definite knowledge **2** an unconfirmed report, story, etc. in general circulation —*vt.* to tell or spread by rumor Brit. sp. **ru′mour**

rump (rump) *n.* [< ON *rumpr*] **1** the hind part of an animal, where the legs and back join **2** the buttocks

rum·ple (rum′pəl) *n.* [< MDu *rompe*] an uneven crease; wrinkle —*vt., vi.* **-pled, -pling** to wrinkle; muss

rum·pus (rum′pəs) *n.* [< ?] [Inf.] an uproar or commotion

run (run) *vi.* **ran, run, run′ning** [< ON & OE] **1** to go by moving the legs faster than in walking **2** to go, move, etc. easily and freely **3** to flee **4** to make a quick trip (*up to, down to,* etc.) **5** to compete in a race, election, etc. **6** to ply between two points: said as of a train **7** to ravel: said as of a stocking **8** to operate: said of a machine, computer program, etc. **9** to flow **10** to spread over cloth, etc. when moistened, as colors do **11** to discharge pus, etc. **12** to extend in time or space; continue **13** to pass into a specified condition, etc. [*to run into trouble*] **14** to be written, etc. in a specified way **15** to be at a specified size, price, etc. [*eggs run high*] —*vt.* **1** to follow (a specified course) **2** to perform as by running [*run a race*] **3** to incur (a risk) **4** to get past [*run a blockade*] **5** to cause to run, move, compete, etc. **6** to drive into a specified condition, place, etc. **7** to drive (an object) into or against something **8** to make flow in a specified way, place, etc. **9** to manage (a business, etc.) **10** to undergo (a fever, etc.) **11** to publish (a story, etc.) in a newspaper —*n.* **1** an act or period of running **2** the distance covered in running **3** a trip; journey **4** a route [*a delivery run*] **5** *a)* movement onward, progression, or trend [*the run of events*] *b)* a continuous period [*a run of good luck*] **6** a continuous course of performances, etc., as of a play **7** a continued series of demands, as on a bank **8** a brook **9** a kind or class; esp., the average kind **10** the output during a period of operation **11** an enclosed area for domestic animals **12** freedom to move about at will [*the run of the house*] **13** a large number of fish migrating together **14** a ravel, as in a stocking **15** *Baseball* a scoring point, made by a successful circuit of the bases —**in the long run** in the final outcome —**on the run** running or running away —**run across** to encounter by chance: also **run into** —**run along** to leave or depart —**run down 1** to stop operating **2** to run against so as to knock down **3** to pursue and capture or kill **4** to speak of disparagingly —**run out** to come to an end; expire —**run out of** to use up —**run over 1** to ride over **2** to overflow **3** to examine, rehearse, etc. rapidly —**run through 1** to use up quickly or recklessly **2** to pierce —**run up 1** to raise, rise, or accumulate rapidly **2** to sew rapidly

run·a·round *n.* [Inf.] a series of evasions

run·a·way *n.* **1** a fugitive **2** a horse, etc. that runs away —*adj.* **1** escaping, fleeing, etc. **2** easily won: said as of a race **3** rising rapidly: said as of prices

run-down *n.* a concise summary

run-down *adj.* **1** not wound and therefore not running, as a watch **2** in poor physical condition, as from overwork **3** fallen into disrepair

rune (rōōn) *n.* [OE *run*] **1** any of the characters of an ancient Germanic alphabet **2** [*often pl.*] writing in these characters —**ru′nic** *adj.*

rung[1] (run) *n.* [OE *hrung*, staff] a rod or bar forming a step of a ladder, a crosspiece on a chair, etc.

rung[2] (run) *vi., vt. pp. of* RING[1]

run-in *n.* [Inf.] a quarrel, fight, etc.

run·nel (run′əl) *n.* [OE *rynel*] a small stream

run·ner *n.* **1** *a)* one that runs, as a racer *b)* a messenger, etc. *c)* a smuggler **2** a long, narrow cloth or rug **3** a ravel, as in hosiery **4** a long, trailing stem, as of a strawberry **5** either of the long, narrow pieces on which a sled, etc. slides

run·ner-up *n., pl.* **-ners-up'** a person or team that finishes second, etc. in a contest

run·ning *n.* the act of one that runs; racing, managing, etc. —*adj.* **1** that runs (in various senses) **2** measured in a straight line **3** continuous [*a running* commentary] **4** current or concurrent —*adv.* in succession [for five days *running*] —**in** (or **out of) the running** having a (or no) chance to win

running back *Football* an offensive back, responsible primarily for rushing the ball

running lights the lights that a ship or aircraft must display at night

running mate 1 the candidate for the lesser of two closely associated offices, as for the vice-presidency **2** either of two candidates running for office together

run·ny *adj.* **-ni·er, -ni·est 1** flowing, esp. too freely **2** discharging mucus [a *runny* nose]

run·off *n.* **1** something that runs off, as rain that is not absorbed into the ground **2** a deciding, final contest

run-of-the-mill *adj.* ordinary; average

runt (runt) *n.* [< ?] **1** a stunted animal, plant, or (contemptuously) person **2** the smallest animal of a litter —**runt'y** *adj.* **-i·er, -i·est**

run-through *n.* a complete rehearsal, from beginning to end

run·way *n.* a channel, track, etc. in, on, or along which something moves; esp., *a)* a strip of leveled ground for use by airplanes in taking off and landing *b)* a narrow platform extending from a stage into the audience, as at a fashion show

ru·pee (rōō'pē, rōō pē') *n.* [< Sans *rūpyah*, wrought silver] the monetary unit of India, Nepal, Pakistan, Sri Lanka, etc.

rup·ture (rup'chər) *n.* [< L *rumpere*, to break] **1** a breaking apart or being broken apart; breach **2** a hernia —*vt., vi.* **-tured, -tur·ing** to cause or suffer a rupture

ru·ral (roor'əl) *adj.* [< L *rus*, the country] of, like, or living in the country; rustic —**ru'ral·ism'** *n.*

ruse (rōōz) *n.* [< OFr *reuser*, deceive] a stratagem, trick, or artifice

rush¹ (rush) *vi., vt.* [< Fr *ruser*, repel] **1** to move, push, drive, etc. swiftly or impetuously **2** to make a sudden attack (*on*) **3** to pass, go, send, act, do, etc. with unusual haste; hurry **4** *Football* to run with (the ball) on a running play —*n.* **1** a rushing **2** an eager movement of many people to get to a place **3** busyness; haste [the *rush* of modern life] **4** a press, as of business, necessitating unusual haste **5** [Slang] a sudden thrill, etc.

rush² (rush) *n.* [OE *risc*] a grasslike marsh plant with round stems used in making mats, etc.

rush hour a time of the day when business, traffic, etc. typically is heavy

rusk (rusk) *n.* [Sp *rosca*, twisted bread roll] **1** sweet, raised bread or cake toasted until browned and crisp **2** a piece of this

Russ *abbrev.* **1** Russia **2** Russian

rus·set (rus'it) *n.* [< L *russus*, reddish] **1** yellowish brown or reddish brown **2** a winter apple with a mottled skin

Rus·sia (rush'ə) **1** former empire (1547–1917) in E Europe & N Asia: in full **Russian Empire 2** loosely, the UNION OF SOVIET SOCIALIST REPUBLICS **3** country in E Europe and N Asia, stretching from the Baltic Sea to the Pacific: formerly a republic of the U.S.S.R.

Rus·sian (rush'ən) *adj.* of Russia or its people, language, etc. —*n.* **1** a person born or living in Russia **2** the East Slavic language of the Russians

rust (rust) *n.* [OE] **1** the reddish-brown coating on iron or steel caused by oxidation during exposure to air and moisture **2** any stain resembling this **3** a reddish brown **4** a plant disease causing spotted stems and leaves —*vi., vt.* **1** to form rust (on) **2** to deteriorate, as through disuse

rus·tic (rus'tik) *adj.* [< L *rus*, the country] **1** rural **2** simple or artless **3** rough or uncouth —*n.* a country person —**rus'ti·cal·ly** *adv.*

rus·ti·cate (rus'tə kāt') *vi., vt.* **-cat'ed, -cat'ing 1** to go or send to live in the country **2** to become or make rustic —**rus'ti·ca'tion** *n.*

rus·tle¹ (rus'əl) *vi., vt.* **-tled, -tling** [ult. echoic] to make or cause to make soft sounds, as of moving leaves, etc. —*n.* a series of such sounds

rus·tle² (rus'əl) [Inf.] *vi., vt.* **-tled, -tling** [< ?] to steal (cattle, etc.) —**rustle up** to gather together —**rus'tler** *n.*

rust·proof *vt., adj.* (make) resistant to rust

rust·y (rus'tē) *adj.* **-i·er, -i·est 1** coated with rust, as a metal **2** *a)* impaired by disuse, neglect, etc. *b)* having lost facility through lack of practice **3** rust-colored; reddish-brown —**rust'i·ly** *adv.* —**rust'i·ness** *n.*

rut¹ (rut) *n.* [< ? Fr *route*, route] **1** a groove, track, etc., as made by wheels **2** a fixed, routine course of action, thought, etc. —*vt.* **rut'ted, rut'ting** to make ruts in —**rut'ty** *adj.* **-ti·er, -ti·est**

rut² (rut) *n.* [< L *rugire*, to roar] the periodic sexual excitement of certain male mammals —*vi.* **rut'ted, rut'ting** to be in rut —**rut' tish** *adj.*

ru·ta·ba·ga (rōōt'ə bā'gə) *n.* [Swed dial. *rotabagge*] **1** a turniplike plant with a large, yellow root **2** this root

Ruth¹ (rōōth) *n. Bible* a woman devoted to her mother-in-law, for whom she left her own people

Ruth² (rōōth), **Babe** (bāb) (born *George Herman Ruth*) 1895-1948; U.S. baseball player

ru·the·ni·um (rōō thē'nē əm) *n.* [< ML *Ruthenia*, Russia] a rare hard chemical element used to harden platinum and palladium: symbol, Ru; at. no. 44

ruth·er·for·di·um (ruth'ər fôr'dē əm) *n.* [after Ernest *Rutherford* (1871-1937), N.Z.

physicist] an artificially produced, radioactive chemical element: symbol, Rf; at. no. 104

ruth·less (-lis) *adj.* [OE *hreowan*, to rue] without pity or compassion —**ruth′less·ly** *adv.* —**ruth′less·ness** *n.*

RV *n.*, *pl.* **RVs** [*R*(*ecreational*) *V*(*ehicle*)] a camper, trailer, motor home, etc. outfitted for living in

Rwan·da (rōō än′də) country in EC Africa, east of Democratic Republic of the Congo

Rx *symbol* PRESCRIPTION (*n. 2a*)

-ry (rē) *suffix* -ERY [*foundry*]

rye (rī) *n.* [OE *ryge*] 1 a hardy cereal grass 2 its grain or seeds, used for making flour, etc. 3 whiskey distilled from this grain

S

s¹ or **S** (es) *n.*, *pl.* **s′s, S′s** the 19th letter of the English alphabet —*adj.* shaped like S

s² *abbrev.* 1 second(s) 2 shilling(s)

S¹ *abbrev.* 1 Saturday 2 small 3 south 4 southern 5 Sunday

S² *Chem. symbol for* sulfur

-s [alt. of -ES] *suffix* 1 forming the plural of most nouns [*hips*] 2 forming the 3d pers. sing., pres. indic., of most verbs [*shouts*]

-'s¹ [OE] *suffix* forming the possessive of singular nouns and some pronouns, and of plural nouns not ending in s [*boy's, men's*]

-'s² *suffix* 1 is [*he's a sailor*] 2 has [*she's asked them both*] 3 [Inf.] does [*what's it matter?*] 4 us [*let's go*]

SA South America

Saar (sär, zär) rich coal-mining region in a river valley of SW Germany: also called **Saar Basin**

Sab·bath (sab′əth) *n.* [< Heb *shabat*, to rest] 1 the seventh day of the week (Saturday), set aside in Jewish scripture for rest and worship 2 Sunday as the usual Christian day of rest and worship

Sab·bat·i·cal (sə bat′i kəl) *adj.* 1 of the Sabbath 2 [s-] bringing a period of rest —*n.* [s-] SABBATICAL LEAVE

sabbatical leave [orig. given every seven years] a period of absence with pay, for study, travel, etc., given as to professors: also **sabbatical year**

sa·ber (sā′bər) *n.* [< Hung *szablya*] a heavy cavalry sword with a slightly curved blade: also **sa′bre**

Sa·bin vaccine (sā′bin) [after Dr. A. B. *Sabin* (1906-93), its U.S. developer] a polio vaccine taken orally

sa·ble (sā′bəl) *n.* [< Russ *sobol′*] 1 any marten 2 its costly fur pelt —*adj.* black or dark brown

sa·bot (sa bō′, sab′ō) *n.* [Fr, ult. < Ar *sabbāṭ*, sandal] a shoe shaped from a single piece of wood

sab·o·tage (sab′ə täzh′) *n.* [Fr < *sabot*, wooden shoe + -AGE: from damage done to machinery by sabots] deliberate destruction or obstruction, as of railroads, bridges, etc.

by enemy agents — *vt.*, *vi.* **-taged′, -tag′ing** to commit sabotage (on) —**sab′o·teur′** (-tur′) *n.*

sa·bra (sä′brə) *n.* [Heb *sabra*, a native cactus fruit] [*sometimes* **S-**] a native-born Israeli Jew

sabre saw a portable electric saw with a narrow, oscillating blade

sac (sak) *n.* [see SACK¹] a pouchlike part in a living thing

sac·cha·rin (sak′ə rin′) *n.* [< Gr *sakcharon*] a white, crystalline coal-tar compound used as a sugar substitute

sac·cha·rine (-rin′) *adj.* 1 of or like sugar 2 too sweet [*a saccharine voice*]

sac·er·do·tal (sas′ər dōt′'l; *occas.* sak′-) *adj.* [< L *sacerdos*, priest] of priests or the office of priest

sa·chem (sā′chəm) *n.* [AmInd] among some North American Indian tribes, the chief

sa·chet (sa shā′) *n.* [Fr] a small perfumed packet used to scent clothes

sack¹ (sak) *n.* [ult. < Heb *saq*] 1 a bag, esp. a large one of coarse cloth 2 [Slang] dismissal from a job: with *the* 3 *Football* a sacking of a quarterback —*vt.* 1 to put into sacks 2 [Slang] to fire (a person) 3 *Football* to tackle (a quarterback) behind the line of scrimmage —**hit the sack** [Slang] to go to bed: also **sack out**

sack² (sak) *n.* [see prec.] the plundering of a city, etc. —*vt.* to plunder

sack³ (sak) *n.* [< Fr (*vin*) *sec*, dry (wine) < L] a dry, white Spanish wine popular in England during the 1500s and 1600s

sack·cloth *n.* 1 SACKING 2 [Historical] coarse cloth worn as a symbol of mourning

sack·ing *n.* a cheap, coarse cloth used for sacks

sac·ra·ment (sak′rə mant) *n.* [< L *sacer*, holy] any of certain Christian rites, as baptism, the Eucharist, etc. —**sac′ra·men′tal** (-ment′l) *adj.*

Sac·ra·men·to (sak′rə men′tō) capital of California

sa·cred (sā′krid) *adj.* [< L *sacer*, holy] 1 consecrated to a god or God; holy 2 having to do with religion 3 venerated; hallowed 4 inviolate —**sa′cred·ly** adv. —**sa′cred·ness** n.

sac·ri·fice (sak′rə fīs′) n. ⟦< L sacrificium < sacer, sacred + facere, make⟧ 1 an offering, as of a life or object, to a deity 2 a giving up of one thing for the sake of another — vt., vi. **-ficed′**, **-fic′ing** 1 to offer as a sacrifice to a deity 2 to give up one thing for the sake of another 3 to sell at less than the supposed value —**sac′ri·fi′cial** (-fish′əl) adj.

sac·ri·lege (sak′rə lij) n. ⟦< L sacer, sacred + legere, take away⟧ desecration of what is sacred —**sac′ri·le′gious** (-lij′əs, -lē′jəs) adj.

sac·ris·tan (sak′ris tən) n. a person in charge of a sacristy

sac·ris·ty (-tē) n., pl. **-ties** ⟦ult. < L sacer, sacred⟧ a room in a church for sacred vessels, etc.

sac·ro·il·i·ac (sak′rō il′ē ak′, sā′krō-) n. ⟦ModL, ult. < L sacrum, bone at bottom of spine + ileum, flank, groin⟧ the joint between the top part of the hipbone and the fused bottom vertebrae

sac·ro·sanct (sak′rō saŋkt′) adj. ⟦< L sacer, sacred + sanctus, holy⟧ very sacred, holy, or inviolable

sad (sad) adj. **sad′der**, **sad′dest** ⟦OE sæd, sated⟧ 1 having or expressing low spirits; unhappy; sorrowful 2 causing dejection, sorrow, etc. 3 [Inf.] very bad; deplorable —**sad′ly** adv. —**sad′ness** n.

sad·den vt., vi. to make or become sad

sad·dle (sad′l) n. ⟦OE sadol⟧ 1 a seat for a rider on a horse, bicycle, etc. 2 a cut of lamb, etc., including part of the backbone and the two loins —vt. **-dled**, **-dling** 1 to put a saddle upon 2 to encumber or burden —**in the saddle** in control

sad·dle·bag n. 1 a bag hung behind the saddle of a horse, etc. 2 a bag carried on a bicycle, etc.

saddle horse a horse for riding

saddle shoes white oxford shoes with a contrasting band across the instep

Sad·du·cee (saj′oo sē′) n. a member of an ancient Jewish sect that accepted only the written law

sad·ism (sā′diz′əm, sad′iz′əm) n. ⟦after Marquis de Sade (1740-1814), Fr writer⟧ the getting of pleasure, esp. sexual pleasure, from mistreating others —**sad′ist** n. —**sa·dis′tic** adj. —**sa·dis′ti·cal·ly** adv.

sad·o·mas·o·chism (sā′dō mas′ə kiz′əm, sad′ō-) n. the getting of sexual pleasure from sadism or masochism, or both —**sad′o·mas′o·chist** n. —**sad′o·mas′o·chis′tic** adj.

sa·fa·ri (sə fär′ē) n., pl. **-ris** ⟦< Ar safar, to journey⟧ a trip for hunting or observing animals, esp. in E or S Africa

safe (sāf) adj. **saf′er**, **saf′est** ⟦< L salvus⟧ 1 a) free from damage, danger, etc.; secure b) having escaped injury; unharmed 2 a) giving protection b) trustworthy —n. a locking metal container for valuables —**safe′ly** adv. —**safe′ness** n.

safe-con·duct n. permission to travel safely through enemy regions

safe-de·pos·it adj. designating or of a box or vault, as in a bank, for storing valuables: also **safe′ty-de·pos′it**

safe·guard n. a protection; precaution —vt. to protect or guard

safe house a house, etc. used as a refuge or hiding place, as by an underground organization

safe·keep·ing n. protection or custody

safe sex sexual activity incorporating practices, as condom use, that reduce the risk of spreading sexually transmitted diseases

safe·ty (sāf′tē) n., pl. **-ties** 1 a being safe; security 2 any device for preventing an accident 3 Football a) a grounding of the ball by the offense behind its own goal line, that scores two points for the defense b) a defensive back responsible for covering pass receivers in the middle of the field —adj. giving safety

safety glass shatterproof glass

safety match a match that lights only when struck on a prepared surface

safety net 1 a net suspended as beneath aerialists 2 any protection against failure or loss

safety pin a pin bent back on itself and having the point held in a guard

safety razor a razor with a detachable blade held between guards

safety valve 1 an automatic valve that releases steam if the pressure in a boiler, etc. becomes excessive 2 any outlet for the release of strong emotion, etc.

saf·flow·er (saf′lou′ər) n. ⟦ult. < Ar aṣfar, yellow⟧ a thistlelike, annual plant with large, orange flowers and seeds yielding an edible oil

saf·fron (saf′rən) n. ⟦< Ar za′farān⟧ 1 a plant having orange stigmas 2 the dried stigmas, used as a dye and flavoring 3 orange yellow

sag (sag) vi. **sagged**, **sag′ging** ⟦prob. < Scand⟧ 1 to sink, esp. in the middle, from weight or pressure 2 to hang down unevenly 3 to weaken through weariness, age, etc. —n. 1 a sagging 2 a sagging place —**sag′gy** adj. **-gi·er**, **-gi·est**

sa·ga (sä′gə) n. ⟦ON, a tale⟧ 1 a medieval Scandinavian story relating the legendary history of a family 2 any long story of heroic deeds

sa·ga·cious (sə gā′shəs) adj. ⟦< L sagax, wise⟧ very wise; shrewd —**sa·gac′i·ty** (-gas′ə tē) n.

sage[1] (sāj) adj. **sag′er**, **sag′est** ⟦ult. < L sapere, know⟧ 1 wise, discerning, etc. 2 showing wisdom —n. a very wise man

sage[2] (sāj) n. ⟦< L salvus, safe: from its reputed healing powers⟧ 1 a plant of the mint family with leaves used for seasoning meats, etc. 2 SAGEBRUSH

sage·brush n. a plant with aromatic leaves, in the dry areas of the W U.S.

Sag·it·tar·i·us (saj′ə ter′ē əs) n. ⟦L, archer⟧ the ninth sign of the zodiac

sa·go (sā′gō) n., pl. **-gos** an edible starch from a Malayan palm tree, etc.

sa·gua·ro (sə gwär′ō) n., pl. **-ros** ⟦< native

name] a giant cactus of the SW U.S. and N Mexico

Sa·ha·ra (sə harʹə) vast desert region extending across N Africa

sa·hib (säʹib) *n.* ⟦Hindi < Ar⟧ sir; master: title used esp. in colonial India when speaking to or of a European

said (sed) *vt., vi. pt. & pp. of* SAY —*adj.* aforesaid

Sai·gon (sī gänʹ) *former name for* HO CHI MINH CITY

sail (sāl) *n.* ⟦OE *segl*⟧ **1** a sheet, as of canvas, spread to catch the wind, so as to drive a vessel forward **2** sails collectively **3** a trip in a ship or boat **4** anything like a sail —*vi.* **1** to be moved forward by means of sails **2** to travel on water **3** to begin a trip by water **4** to manage a sailboat **5** to glide or move smoothly **6** [Inf.] to move quickly —*vt.* **1** to move upon (a body of water) in a vessel **2** to manage or navigate (a vessel) —**set** (or **make**) **sail** to begin a trip by water —**under sail** sailing

sail·board *n.* a board used in windsurfing

sail·boat *n.* a boat propelled by a sail or sails

sail·cloth *n.* canvas or other cloth for making sails, tents, etc.

sail·fish *n., pl.* **-fish** or **-fish·es** a large marine fish with a sail-like dorsal fin

sail·or *n.* **1** a person whose work is sailing **2** an enlisted person in the navy

sail·plane *n.* a light glider

saint (sānt) *n.* ⟦< L *sanctus*, holy⟧ **1** a holy person **2** a person who is exceptionally charitable, patient, etc. **3** in certain Christian churches, a person officially recognized for having attained heaven after an exceptionally holy life —**saintʹli·ness** *n.* —**saintʹly** *adj.* **-li·er, -li·est**

Saint Ber·nard (bər närdʹ) a large dog of a breed once used to rescue travelers lost in the snow

Saint Nich·o·las (nikʹə ləs) SANTA CLAUS: also **Saint Nick**

Saint Pat·rick's Day (paʹtriks) March 17, observed by the Irish in honor of the patron saint of Ireland

Saint Valentine's Day February 14, observed in honor of a martyr of the 3d c. and as a day for sending valentines

saith (seth) *vt., vi.* [Archaic] says

sake[1] (sāk) *n.* ⟦OE *sacu*, suit at law⟧ **1** motive; cause [for the *sake* of money] **2** behalf [for my *sake*]

sa·ke[2] (säʹkē) *n.* ⟦Jpn⟧ a Japanese alcoholic beverage made from rice: also sp. **saʹki**

sa·laam (sə lämʹ) *n.* ⟦Ar *salām*, peace⟧ a greeting in the Near East, etc. made by bowing low in respect or obeisance

sal·a·ble (sālʹə bəl) *adj.* that can be sold; marketable: also sp. **saleʹa·ble**

sa·la·cious (sə lāʹshəs) *adj.* ⟦< L *salire*, to leap⟧ **1** lustful **2** obscene —**sa·laʹcious·ly** *adv.* —**sa·laʹcious·ness** *n.*

sal·ad (salʹəd) *n.* ⟦< L *sal*, salt⟧ a dish, usually cold, of vegetables (esp. lettuce), meat, eggs, etc. usually mixed with salad dressing

salad bar a buffet in a restaurant, at which diners make their own salads

salad dressing oil, vinegar, spices, etc. put on a salad

sa·lade niçoise (salʹəd nē swäzʹ) a salad of tuna, tomatoes, etc. with a garlic vinaigrette

sal·a·man·der (salʹə manʹdər) *n.* ⟦< Gr *salamandra*⟧ **1** a mythological reptile said to live in fire **2** an amphibian with a tail and soft, moist skin

sa·la·mi (sə läʹmē) *n.* ⟦It < L *sal*, salt⟧ a spiced, salted sausage

sal·a·ry (salʹə rē) *n., pl.* **-ries** ⟦< L *salarium*, orig. part of a soldier's pay for buying salt < *sal*, salt⟧ a fixed payment at regular intervals for work —**salʹa·ried** (-rēd) *adj.*

sale (sāl) *n.* ⟦< ON *sala*⟧ **1** a selling **2** opportunity to sell; market **3** an auction **4** a special offering of goods at reduced prices **5** [*pl.*] receipts in business **6** [*pl.*] the work of, or a department involved in, selling [a job in *sales*] —**for sale** to be sold —**on sale** for sale, esp. at a reduced price

Sa·lem (sāʹləm) **1** capital of Oregon, in the NW part **2** city in NE Massachusetts: site of witch trials (1692)

sales·clerk (sālzʹklurk′) *n.* a person employed to sell goods in a store

sales·man (-mən) *n., pl.* **-men** (-mən) a man who is a salesperson

sales·man·ship *n.* the skill of selling

sales·per·son *n., pl.* **-peoʹple** a person employed to sell goods or services

sales representative a salesperson, esp. one employed as an agent for a manufacturer, etc.

sales slip a receipt or bill of sale

sales tax a tax on sales

sales·wom·an *n., pl.* **-wom′en** a woman who is a salesperson

sal·i·cyl·ic acid (salʹə silʹik) ⟦< L *salix*, willow⟧ a crystalline compound used to make aspirin, etc.

sa·lient (sālʹyənt) *adj.* ⟦< L *salire*, to leap⟧ **1** pointing outward; jutting **2** conspicuous; prominent —*n.* a salient angle, part, etc. —**saʹlience** *n.*

sa·line (sāʹlēn′, -lin′) *adj.* ⟦< L *sal*, salt⟧ of, like, or containing salt —*n.* a saline solution used in medicine, etc. —**sa·lin·i·ty** (sə linʹ ə tē) *n.*

sa·li·va (sə līʹvə) *n.* ⟦L⟧ the watery fluid secreted by glands in the mouth: it aids in digestion —**sal·i·var·y** (salʹə verʹē) *adj.*

sal·i·vate (salʹə vāt′) *vi.* **-vat′ed, -vat′ing** ⟦< L *salivare*⟧ to secrete saliva —**sal′i·va′tion** *n.*

sal·low (salʹō) *adj.* ⟦ME *salou*⟧ of a sickly, pale-yellowish complexion

sal·ly (salʹē) *n., pl.* **-lies** ⟦< L *salire*, to leap⟧ **1** a sudden rushing forth, as to attack **2** a witty remark; quip **3** an excursion —*vi.* **-lied, -ly·ing** to rush or set (*forth* or *out*) on a sally

salm·on (samʹən) *n., pl.* **-on** or **-ons** ⟦< L *salmo*⟧ **1** a game and food fish with orangish-pink flesh, that lives usually in salt water and spawns in fresh water **2** orangish pink

sal·mo·nel·la (salʹmə nelʹə) *n., pl.* **-nelʹlae**

(-ē), **-nel′la**, or **-nel′las** [after D. E. Salmon (1850–1914), U.S. doctor] any of a genus of bacilli that cause typhoid fever, food poisoning, etc.

sa·lon (sə län′) *n.* [Fr: see fol.] **1** a large reception hall or drawing room **2** a regular gathering of distinguished guests for informal conversation **3** a shop furnished to provide some personal service [beauty *salon*]

sa·loon (sə lōōn′) *n.* [< Fr < L *sala*] **1** any large room or hall for receptions, etc. **2** [Old-fashioned] a place where alcoholic drinks are sold; bar

sal·sa (säl′sə) *n.* [AmSp, sauce < L, salted food] **1** a kind of Latin American dance music usually played at fast tempos **2** a hot sauce made with chilies, tomatoes, etc.

salt (sôlt) *n.* [OE *sealt*] **1** a white, crystalline substance, sodium chloride, found in natural beds, in sea water, etc., and used for seasoning food, etc. **2** a chemical compound derived from an acid by replacing hydrogen with a metal **3** piquancy; esp., pungent wit **4** [pl.] mineral salts used as a cathartic or restorative **5** [Inf.] a sailor —*adj.* containing, preserved with, or tasting of salt —*vt.* to sprinkle, season, or preserve with salt —**salt away** [Inf.] to store or save (money, etc.) —**salt of the earth** any person or persons regarded as simple, authentic, etc. —**with a grain of salt** with allowance for exaggeration, etc.; skeptically —**salt′ed** *adj.*

salt·cel·lar (-sel′ər) *n.* [< prec. + Fr *salière*, saltcellar] **1** a small dish for holding salt **2** a saltshaker

salt·ine (sôl tēn′) *n.* [SALT + -INE³] a flat, crisp, salted cracker

Salt Lake City capital of Utah

salt lick a natural deposit or a block of rock salt which animals lick

salt·pe·ter (-pēt′ər) *n.* [< L *sal*, salt + *petra*, rock] NITER

salt pork pork cured in salt

salt·shak·er *n.* a container for salt, with a perforated top

salt·wa·ter *adj.* of salt water or the sea

salt·y *adj.* **-i·er**, **-i·est 1** of or having salt **2** suggesting the sea **3** *a)* sharp; witty *b)* coarse *c)* cross or caustic

sa·lu·bri·ous (sə lōō′brē əs) *adj.* [< L *salus*, health] healthful; wholesome

sal·u·tar·y (sal′yōō ter′ē) *adj.* [see prec.] **1** healthful **2** beneficial

sal·u·ta·tion (sal′yōō tā′shən) *n.* [see fol.] **1** the act of greeting, addressing, etc. **2** a form of greeting, as the "Dear Sir" of a letter

sa·lute (sə lōōt′) *vt., vi.* **-lut′ed**, **-lut′ing** [< L *salus*, health] **1** to greet with friendly words or ceremonial gesture **2** to honor by performing a prescribed act, such as raising the right hand to the head, in military and naval practice **3** to praise; commend —*n.* an act or remark made in saluting

sal·vage (sal′vij) *n.* [see SAVE¹] **1** *a)* the rescue of a ship and cargo from shipwreck, etc. *b)* compensation paid for such res-

cue **2** *a)* the rescue of any property from destruction or waste *b)* the property saved —*vt.* **-vaged**, **-vag·ing** to save or rescue from shipwreck, fire, etc.

sal·va·tion (sal vā′shən) *n.* [< L *salvare*, save] **1** a saving or being saved **2** a person or thing that saves **3** *Theol.* deliverance from sin and from the penalties of sin; redemption

salve (sav) *n.* [OE *sealf*] **1** any soothing or healing ointment for wounds, burns, etc. **2** anything that soothes —*vt.* **salved**, **salv′ing** to soothe

sal·ver (sal′vər) *n.* [ult. < L *salvare*, save] a tray

sal·vo (sal′vō) *n., pl.* **-vos** or **-voes** [< It < L *salve*, hail!] a discharge of a number of guns, in salute or at a target

SAM (sam) *n.* surface-to-air missile

sa·mar·i·um (sə mer′ē əm, -mar′-) *n.* [ult. after V. E. *Samarsky*-Bykhovets (1803–70), Russ mining official] a silvery or pale-gray chemical element: symbol, Sm; at. no. 62

sam·ba (sam′bə, säm′-) *n.* [Port] a Brazilian dance of African origin, or music for it

same (sām) *adj.* [< ON *samr*] **1** being the very one; identical **2** alike in kind, quality, amount, etc. **3** unchanged [to keep the *same* look] **4** before-mentioned: in all senses usually used with *the* —*pron.* the same person or thing —*adv.* in like manner: usually with *the* —**same′ness** *n.*

Sa·mi (sä′mē) *n., pl.* **-mi** or **-mis** [Lapp] LAPP: for those in this ethnic group, now the preferred term

sam·iz·dat (säm′iz dät′) *n.* [Russ, self-published] in the U.S.S.R., a system by which writings officially disapproved of were circulated secretly

Sa·mo·a (sə mō′ə) country in the SW Pacific, consisting of two large islands & several small ones —**Sa·mo′an** *adj., n.*

sam·o·var (sam′ə vär′) *n.* a Russian metal urn with a spigot, for heating water in making tea

sam·pan (sam′pan′) *n.* [< Chin dial.] a small boat used in China and Japan, rowed with a scull from the stern

sam·ple (sam′pəl) *n.* [see EXAMPLE] **1** a part or item taken as representative of a whole thing, group, etc.; specimen **2** an example **3** a short excerpt from one recording used in another —*vt.* **-pled**, **-pling 1** to take (and test) a sample of **2** to include a short excerpt from (one recording) in another

sam·pler (-plər) *n.* **1** one who samples **2** a collection of representative selections **3** a cloth embroidered with designs, mottoes, etc. in different stitches

Sam·son (sam′sən) *n. Bible* an Israelite noted for his great strength

Sam·u·el (sam′yōō əl) *n. Bible* a Hebrew leader and prophet

sam·u·rai (sam′ə rī′) *n., pl.* **-rai′** [Jpn] a member of a military class in feudal Japan

San An·to·ni·o (san′ an tō′nē ō′) city in SC Texas: site of the Alamo

san·a·to·ri·um (san′ə tôr′ē əm) *n., pl.* **-ri·ums**

or **-ri·a** (-ə) *chiefly Brit. var. of* SANITARIUM

sanc·ti·fy (saŋk′tə fī′) *vt.* **-fied′, -fy′ing** ⟦see SAINT & -FY⟧ **1** to set apart as holy; consecrate **2** to make free from sin **—sanc′ti·fi·ca′tion** *n.*

sanc·ti·mo·ni·ous (saŋk′tə mō′nē əs) *adj.* pretending to be pious **—sanc′ti·mo′ni·ous·ly** *adv.*

sanc·ti·mo·ny *n.* ⟦< L *sanctus*, holy⟧ pretended piety

sanc·tion (saŋk′shən) *n.* ⟦see SAINT⟧ **1** authorization **2** support; approval **3** a coercive measure, as an official trade boycott against a nation defying international law: *often used in pl.* **—vt. 1** to confirm; ratify **2** to authorize; permit **3** to penalize, as by instituting trade sanctions

sanc·ti·ty (saŋk′tə tē) *n., pl.* **-ties** ⟦< L *sanctus*, holy⟧ **1** holiness **2** sacredness

sanc·tu·ar·y (saŋk′chōō er′ē) *n., pl.* **-ies** ⟦< L *sanctus*, sacred⟧ **1** a holy place; specif., *a)* a church, temple, etc. *b)* a particularly holy place within a church or temple **2** a place of refuge or protection

sanc·tum (saŋk′təm) *n.* ⟦L⟧ **1** a sacred place **2** a private room where one is not to be disturbed

sand (sand) *n.* ⟦OE⟧ **1** loose, gritty grains of eroded rock, as on beaches, in deserts, etc. **2** [*usually pl.*] a tract of sand **—vt. 1** to sprinkle with sand **2** to smooth or polish, as with sandpaper **—sand′er** *n.*

san·dal (san′dəl) *n.* ⟦< Gr *sandalon*⟧ a shoe made of a sole fastened to the foot by straps

san·dal·wood *n.* ⟦ult. < Sans⟧ **1** the hard, sweet-smelling wood at the core of certain Asiatic trees **2** such a tree

sand·bag *n.* a bag filled with sand, used for ballast, protecting levees, etc. **—vt. -bagged′, -bag′ging 1** to put sandbags in or around **2** [Inf.] to force into doing something

sand·bar *n.* a ridge of sand, as one formed in a river or along a shore: also **sand bar** or **sand′bank′**

sand·blast *vt.* to clean with a current of air or steam carrying sand at a high velocity,

sand·box *n.* a box containing sand for children to play in

sand dollar any of various flat, round, disklike echinoderms that live on sandy ocean beds

S & H *abbrev.* shipping and handling

sand·hog *n.* a laborer in underground or underwater construction

San Di·e·go (san′ dē ā′gō) seaport in S California

S & L *abbrev.* savings and loan (association)

sand·lot *adj.* of or having to do with baseball played by amateurs, orig. on a sandy lot

sand·man *n. Folklore* a person supposed to make children sleepy by dusting sand in their eyes

sand·pa·per *n.* paper coated on one side with sand, used for smoothing and polishing **—vt.** to smooth or polish with sandpaper

sand·pip·er (-pī′pər) *n.* a small shorebird with a long, soft-tipped bill

sand·stone *n.* a sedimentary rock composed of sand grains cemented together, as by silica

sand·storm *n.* a windstorm in which large quantities of sand are blown about in the air

sand trap a hollow filled with sand, serving as a hazard on a golf course

sand·wich (sand′wich′) *n.* ⟦after 4th Earl of *Sandwich* (1718–92)⟧ slices of bread with meat, cheese, etc. between them **—vt.** to place or squeeze between other persons, things, etc.

sand·y (san′dē) *adj.* **-i·er, -i·est 1** of or like sand **2** pale reddish-yellow

sane (sān) *adj.* ⟦L *sanus*, healthy⟧ **1** mentally healthy; rational **2** sound; sensible **—sane′ly** *adv.*

San Fran·cis·co (san′ frən sis′kō) seaport on the coast of central California

San Francisco Bay an inlet of the Pacific in WC California: the harbor of San Francisco

sang (saŋ) *vi., vt. alt. pt. of* SING[1]

sang-froid (sän frwä′) *n.* ⟦Fr, lit., cold blood⟧ cool self-possession or composure

san·gri·a (san grē′ə, saŋ-) *n.* ⟦Sp < *sangre*, blood⟧ an iced punch made with red wine, fruit juice, pieces of fruit, etc.

san·gui·nar·y (saŋ′gwi ner′ē) *adj.* ⟦see fol.⟧ **1** accompanied by much bloodshed **2** bloodthirsty

san·guine (saŋ′gwin) *adj.* ⟦< L *sanguis*, blood⟧ **1** of the color of blood; ruddy **2** cheerful; confident

san·i·tar·i·um (san′ə ter′ē əm) *n., pl.* **-i·ums** or **-i·a** (-ə) ⟦ModL < L *sanitas*, health⟧ **1** a resort where people go to regain health **2** an institution for the care of invalids or convalescents

san·i·tar·y (san′ə ter′ē) *adj.* ⟦< L *sanitas*, health⟧ **1** of or bringing about health and healthful conditions **2** in a clean, healthy condition

sanitary napkin an absorbent pad worn by women during menstruation

san·i·ta·tion (san′ə tā′shən) *n.* **1** the science and practice of effecting hygienic conditions **2** drainage and disposal of sewage

san·i·tize (san′ə tīz′) *vt.* **-tized′, -tiz′ing 1** to make sanitary **2** to free from anything considered undesirable, damaging, etc.

san·i·ty (san′ə tē) *n.* **1** the state of being sane **2** soundness of judgment

San Jo·se (san′ hō zā′) city in WC California

San Juan (san′ hwän′) seaport & capital of Puerto Rico

sank (saŋk) *vi., vt. alt. pt. of* SINK

San Ma·ri·no (san′ mə rē′nō) independent country within E Italy

sans (sanz; Fr sän) *prep.* ⟦Fr < L *sine*⟧ without

San·skrit (san′skrit′) *n.* the classical literary language of ancient India

San·ta An·a (san′tə an′ə) hot desert wind from the east or northeast in S California

San·ta Claus (san′tə klôz′) ⟦< Du *Sant Nikolaas*, St. Nicholas⟧ *Folklore* a fat, white-bearded, jolly old man in a red suit, who distributes gifts at Christmas

San·ta Fe (san′tə fā′) capital of New Mexico

San·ti·a·go (sän′tē ä′gō, san′-) capital of Chile

São Pau·lo (soun pou′loo) city in SE Brazil

São To·mé and Prín·ci·pe (tō mĕ′ and prin′sə pē′) country off the W coast of Africa, comprising two islands (**São Tomé** and **Príncipe**)

sap¹ (sap) *n.* ⟦OE *sæp*⟧ **1** the juice that circulates through a plant, bearing water, food, etc. **2** vigor; energy **3** [Slang] a fool —**sap′less** *adj.*

sap² (sap) *vt.* **sapped, sap′ping** ⟦< Fr *sappe*, a hoe⟧ **1** to dig beneath; undermine **2** to weaken

sa·pi·ent (sā′pē ənt) *adj.* ⟦< L *sapere*, to taste, know⟧ wise —**sa′pi·ence** *n.*

sap·ling (sap′liŋ) *n.* a young tree

sap·phire (saf′īr) *n.* ⟦< Sans *śanipriya*⟧ a precious stone of a clear, deep-blue corundum

sap·py (sap′ē) *adj.* **-pi·er, -pi·est 1** full of sap; juicy **2** [Slang] foolish or silly, esp. in a sentimental way —**sap′pi·ness** *n.*

sap·ro·phyte (sap′rə fīt′) *n.* ⟦< Gr *sapros*, rotten + *phyton*, a plant⟧ any plant that lives on dead or decaying organic matter, as some fungi —**sap′ro·phyt′ic** (-fit′ik) *adj.*

sap·suck·er *n.* an American woodpecker that often drills holes in trees for the sap

Sar·a·cen (sar′ə sən) *n.* any Arab or any Muslim at the time of the Crusades

Sar·ah (ser′ə) *n. Bible* the wife of Abraham and mother of Isaac

Sa·ra·je·vo (sar′ə yä′vō) capital of Bosnia and Herzegovina

sa·ran (sə ran′) *n.* ⟦arbitrary coinage⟧ a thermoplastic substance used in various fabrics, wrapping material, etc.

sar·casm (sär′kaz′əm) *n.* ⟦< Gr *sarkazein*, to tear flesh⟧ **1** a taunting or caustic remark, generally ironic **2** the making of such remarks

sar·cas·tic (sär kas′tik) *adj.* **1** of, like, or full of sarcasm **2** using sarcasm —**sar·cas′ti·cal·ly** *adv.*

sar·co·ma (sär kō′mə) *n., pl.* **-mas** or **-ma·ta** (-mə tə) ⟦< Gr *sarx*, flesh⟧ a malignant tumor in connective tissue

sar·coph·a·gus (sär käf′ə gəs) *n., pl.* **-gi′** (-jī′) or **-gus·es** ⟦< Gr *sarx*, flesh + *phagein*, to eat⟧ a stone coffin, esp. one exposed to view, as in a tomb

sar·dine (sär dēn′) *n.* ⟦< L *sarda*, a fish⟧ any of various small ocean fishes preserved in tightly packed cans for eating

sar·don·ic (sär dän′ik) *adj.* ⟦< Gr *sardonios*⟧ scornfully or bitterly sarcastic —**sar·don′i·cal·ly** *adv.*

sa·ri (sä′rē) *n.* ⟦< Sans⟧ the outer garment of a woman of India, Pakistan, etc., consisting of a long cloth wrapped around the body

sa·rong (sə rôŋ′, -räŋ′) *n.* ⟦Malay *sarung*⟧ a garment of men and women in the East Indies, etc., consisting of a cloth worn like a skirt

sar·sa·pa·ril·la (sas′pə ril′ə) *n.* ⟦< Sp *zarza*, bramble + *parra*, vine⟧ **1** a tropical American vine with fragrant roots **2** a carbonated drink flavored with or as with the dried roots

sar·to·ri·al (sär tôr′ē əl) *adj.* ⟦< LL *sartor*, tailor⟧ **1** of tailors or their work **2** of men's dress

SASE *abbrev.* self-addressed, stamped envelope

sash¹ (sash) *n.* ⟦Ar *shāsh*, muslin⟧ an ornamental band, ribbon, etc. worn over the shoulder or around the waist

sash² (sash) *n.* ⟦< Fr *châssis*, a frame⟧ a frame for holding the glass pane of a window or door, esp. a sliding frame

sa·shay (sa shā′) *vi.* ⟦< Fr *chassé*, a dance step⟧ [Inf.] **1** to walk or go, esp. casually **2** to move, walk, etc. so as to attract attention

Sas·katch·e·wan (sas kach′ə wän′) province of SC Canada; cap. Regina: abbrev. *SK*

sass (sas) [Inf.] *n.* ⟦var. of SAUCE⟧ impudent talk —*vt.* to talk impudently to

sas·sa·fras (sas′ə fras′) *n.* ⟦Sp *sasafras*⟧ **1** a small tree having small, bluish fruits **2** its dried root bark, used for flavoring

sass·y (sas′ē) *adj.* **-i·er, -i·est** ⟦var. of SAUCY⟧ [Inf.] impudent; saucy

sat (sat) *vi., vt. pt. & pp. of* SIT

Sat *abbrev.* Saturday

SAT *trademark for* Scholastic Assessment Tests

Sa·tan (sāt′n) *n.* ⟦< Heb *satan*, adversary⟧ the Devil

sa·tan·ic (sā tan′ik, sə-) *adj.* like Satan; wicked —**sa·tan′i·cal·ly** *adv.*

Sa·tan·ism (sāt′n iz′əm) *n.* ⟦< Fr *satanisme*⟧ [*also* **S-**] worship of Satan or celebration of principles associated with Satan —**Sa′tan·ist** *n.*

satch·el (sach′əl) *n.* ⟦< L *saccus*, a bag⟧ a small bag for carrying clothes, books, etc.

sate (sāt) *vt.* **sat′ed, sat′ing** ⟦prob. < L *satiare*, fill full⟧ **1** to satisfy (an appetite, etc.) completely **2** to satiate

sa·teen (sa tēn′) *n.* ⟦< SATIN⟧ a cotton cloth made to imitate satin

sat·el·lite (sat′′l īt′) *n.* ⟦< L *satelles*, an attendant⟧ **1** *a)* a celestial body revolving around a larger celestial body *b)* a man-made object rocketed into orbit around the earth, moon, etc. **2** a small state dependent on a larger one

sa·ti·ate (sā′shē āt′) *vt.* **-at′ed, -at′ing** ⟦< L *satis*, enough⟧ to provide with more than enough, so as to weary or disgust; glut

sa·ti·e·ty (sə tī′ə tē) *n.* a being satiated

sat·in (sat′′n) *n.* ⟦< Ar *zaitūnī*, of *Zaitūn*, former name of a Chinese seaport⟧ a fabric of silk, nylon, rayon, etc. with a smooth, glossy finish on one side —**sat′in·y** *adj.*

sat·in·wood *n.* **1** a smooth wood used in fine furniture **2** any of the trees yielding such a wood

sat·ire (sa′tīr′) *n.* ⟦< L *satira*⟧ **1** a literary or artistic work in which vices, follies, etc. are held up to ridicule and contempt **2** the use of ridicule, sarcasm, etc. to attack vices, follies, etc. —**sa·tir·i·cal** (sə tir′i kəl) *adj.* —**sat·i·rist** (sat′ə rist) *n.*

sat·i·rize (sat′ə rīz′) *vt.* **-rized′, -riz′ing** to attack with satire

sat·is·fac·tion (sat′is fak′shən) *n.* **1** a satisfying or being satisfied **2** something that satisfies; specif., *a)* anything that brings pleasure or contentment *b)* settlement of debt

sat·is·fac·to·ry (-tə rē) *adj.* good enough to fulfill a need, wish, etc.; satisfying or adequate —**sat′is·fac′to·ri·ly** *adv.*

sat·is·fy (sat′is fī′) *vt.* **-fied′, -fy′ing** [< L *satis*, enough + *facere*, make] **1** to fulfill the needs or desires of; content **2** to fulfill the requirements of **3** to free from doubt; convince **4** *a)* to give what is due to *b)* to discharge (a debt, etc.)

sa·to·ri (sä tôr′ē) *n.* [Jpn] in Zen, spiritual enlightenment

sa·trap (sā′trap′, sa′-) *n.* [< Pers] a petty tyrant, esp. one subordinate to another ruler

sat·u·rate (sach′ə rāt′) *vt.* **-rat′ed, -rat′ing** [< L *satur*, full] **1** to make thoroughly soaked **2** to cause to be filled, charged, etc. with the most it can absorb —**sat′u·ra′tion** *n.*

Sat·ur·day (sat′ər dā′) *n.* [< OE *Sæterdæg*, Saturn's day] the seventh and last day of the week

Saturday night special [from their use in weekend crimes] [Slang] any small, cheap handgun

Sat·urn (sat′ərn) *n.* **1** the Roman god of agriculture **2** the second largest planet of the solar system, with thin, icy rings of particles orbiting above its equator: see PLANET

sat·ur·nine (sat′ər nīn′) *adj.* [< supposed influence of planet Saturn] sluggish, gloomy, grave, etc.

sat·yr (sät′ər, sat′-) *n.* [< Gr *satyros*] **1** *Gr. Myth.* a lecherous woodland deity represented as a man with a goat's legs, pointed ears, and short horns **2** a lecherous man

sat·y·ri·a·sis (sät′ə rī′ə sis, sat′-) *n.* [< Gr: see prec.] uncontrollable desire by a man for sexual intercourse

sauce (sôs) *n.* [< L *sal*, salt] **1** a liquid or soft mixture served with food to add flavor **2** stewed or preserved fruit **3** [Inf.] impudence **4** [Slang] alcoholic liquor: with *the*

sauce·pan *n.* a small pot with a projecting handle, used for cooking

sau·cer (sô′sər) *n.* [see SAUCE] **1** a small, round, shallow dish, esp. one designed to hold a cup **2** anything shaped like a saucer

sau·cy (sô′sē) *adj.* **-ci·er, -ci·est** [SAUC(E) + -y²] **1** rude; impudent **2** pert; sprightly —**sau′ci·ly** *adv.* —**sau′ci·ness** *n.*

Sa·u·di Arabia (sou′dē, sô′-) kingdom occupying most of Arabia

sau·er·bra·ten (sou′ər brät′'n, zou′ər-) *n.* [Ger *sauer*, sour + *braten*, roast] beef marinated in vinegar with onions, spices, etc. before cooking

sau·er·kraut (sou′ər krout′) *n.* [Ger *sauer*, sour + *kraut*, cabbage] chopped cabbage fermented in brine

Saul (sôl) *n. Bible* first king of Israel

sau·na (sô′nə, sä′-) *n.* [Finnish] a bath involving exposure to hot, dry air

saun·ter (sôn′tər) *vi.* [ME *santren*, to muse] to walk about idly; stroll —*n.* a leisurely walk; stroll

sau·ri·an (sôr′ē ən) *adj.* [< Gr *sauros*, lizard] of or like lizards

sau·ro·pod (sôr′ə päd′) *n.* [< Gr *sauros*, lizard + -POD] a gigantic dinosaur with a long neck and tail and a small head, as an apatosaurus

sau·sage (sô′sij) *n.* [see SAUCE] pork or other meat, chopped fine, seasoned, and often stuffed into a casing

sau·té (sô tā′, sō-) *vt.* **-téed′, -té′ing** [Fr < *sauter*, to leap] to fry quickly with a little fat

Sau·ternes (sō turn′) *n.* [after *Sauternes*, town in France] [*often* **s-**] any of various white wines, of varying sweetness: also sp. **Sau·terne′**

sav·age (sav′ij) *adj.* [< L *silva*, a wood] **1** fierce; untamed [a *savage* tiger] **2** primitive; barbarous **3** cruel; pitiless —*n.* **1** a member of a preliterate, often tribal, culture: now often offensive **2** a brutal or crude person —**sav′age·ly** *adv.* —**sav′age·ry** *n.*

sa·van·na or **sa·van·nah** (sə van′ə) *n.* [Sp *sabana*] a treeless plain or a grassland with scattered trees

Sa·van·nah (sə van′ə) seaport in SE Georgia

sa·vant (sə vänt′, -vant′; sav′ənt) *n.* [Fr < *savoir*, know] a learned person

save¹ (sāv) *vt.* **saved, sav′ing** [< L *salvus*, safe] **1** to rescue or preserve from harm or danger **2** to preserve for future use **3** to prevent loss or waste of [to *save* time] **4** to prevent or lessen [to *save* expense] **5** *Theol.* to deliver from sin —*vi.* **1** to avoid expense, waste, etc. **2** to store (*up*) money or goods —*n. Sports* an action that keeps an opponent from scoring or winning —**sav′er** *n.*

save² (sāv) *prep., conj.* [< OFr *sauf*, safe] except; but

sav·ing (sā′viŋ) *adj.* that saves; specif., *a)* economizing or economical *b)* redeeming —*n.* **1** [*often pl., with sing. v.*] any reduction in expense, time, etc. **2** [*pl.*] sums of money saved

saving grace a compensating or redeeming quality or feature

sav·ior or **sav·iour** (sāv′yər) *n.* [< L *salvare*, to save] **1** one who saves **2** [S-] Jesus

sa·voir-faire (sav′wär fer′) *n.* [Fr, to know (how) to do] ready knowledge of what to do or say in any situation

sa·vor (sā′vər) *n.* [< L *sapor*] **1** a particular taste or smell **2** distinctive quality —*vi.* to have the distinctive taste, smell, or quality (*of*) —*vt.* to taste with delight Brit. sp. **sa′vour**

sa·vor·y *adj.* **-i·er, -i·est 1** pleasing to the taste or smell **2** pleasant, agreeable, etc. **3** salty or piquant; not sweet Brit. sp. **sa′vour·y**

sav·vy (sav′ē) [Slang] *n.* [< Port *saber*, to know] shrewdness or understanding —*adj.* shrewd or discerning

saw¹ (sô) *n.* [OE *sagu*] a cutting tool consisting of a thin metal blade or disk with sharp teeth —*vt.* to cut or shape with a saw —*vi.* **1**

to cut with or as with a saw **2** to be cut with a saw

saw² (sô) *n.* [OE *sagu*] a maxim; proverb

saw³ (sô) *vt., vi. pt. of* SEE¹

saw·dust *n.* fine particles of wood formed in sawing wood

sawed-off *adj.* short or shortened

saw·horse *n.* a rack on which wood is placed while being sawed

saw·mill *n.* a factory where logs are sawed into boards

saw-toothed *adj.* having notches along the edge like the teeth of a saw: also **saw'tooth'**

saw·yer (sô'yər) *n.* one whose work is sawing wood

sax (saks) *n.* [Inf.] *short for* SAXOPHONE

Sax·on (sak'sən) *n.* **1** a member of an ancient Germanic people, some of whom settled in England **2** an Anglo-Saxon **3** any dialect of the Saxons

sax·o·phone (sak'sə fōn') *n.* [Fr, after A. J. *Sax* (1814–94), Belgian inventor + -PHONE] a single-reed, keyed woodwind instrument with a metal body —**sax'o·phon'ist** (-fōn'ist) *n.*

say (sā) *vt.* **said, say'ing** [OE *secgan*] **1** to utter or speak **2** to express in words; state **3** to state positively or as an opinion **4** to indicate or show [the clock *says* one] **5** to recite [to *say* one's prayers] **6** to estimate; assume [he is, I'd *say*, forty] —*n.* **1** a chance to speak [I had my *say*] **2** authority, as to make a final decision: often with *the* —**that is to say** in other words

say·ing *n.* an adage, proverb, or maxim

say-so *n.* [Inf.] **1** one's word, assurance, etc. **2** right of decision

Sb [L *stibium*] *Chem. symbol for* antimony

sc *abbrev.* Printing small capitals

SC *abbrev.* South Carolina

scab (skab) *n.* [< ON *skabb*] **1** a crust forming over a sore during healing **2** a worker who replaces a striking worker —*vi.* **scabbed, scab'bing** to become covered with a scab —**scab'by** *adj.* -bi·er, -bi·est —**scab'bi·ness** *n.*

scab·bard (skab'ərd) *n.* [< ? OHG *scar*, sword] a sheath for the blade of a sword, dagger, etc.

sca·bies (skā'bēz) *n.* [L, the itch] a contagious, itching skin disease caused by a mite

scab·rous (skab'rəs, skā'brəs) *adj.* [< L *scabere*, to scratch] **1** scaly or scabby **2** indecent, shocking, etc.

scads (skadz) *pl.n.* [< ?] [Inf.] a very large number or amount

scaf·fold (skaf'əld) *n.* [< OFr *escafalt*] **1** a temporary framework for supporting workers during the repairing, painting, etc. of a building, etc. **2** a raised platform on which criminals are executed

scaf·fold·ing *n.* **1** the materials forming a scaffold **2** a scaffold

scal·a·wag (skal'ə wag') *n.* [< ?] [Inf.] a scamp; rascal

scald (skôld) *vt.* [< L *ex-*, intens. + *calidus*, hot] **1** to burn with hot liquid or steam **2** to heat almost to the boiling point **3** to use boiling liquid on —*n.* a burn caused by scalding

scale¹ (skāl) *n.* [< L *scala*, ladder] **1** *a)* a series of marks along a line used in measuring [the *scale* of a thermometer] *b)* any instrument so marked **2** the proportion that a map, etc. bears to the thing it represents [a *scale* of one inch to a mile] **3** *a)* a series of degrees classified by size, amount, etc. [a wage *scale*] *b)* any degree in such a series **4** *Music* a series of tones, rising or falling in pitch, according to a system of intervals —*vt.* **scaled, scal'ing 1** to climb up or over **2** to make according to a scale —**scale back (or down)** to reduce according to a fixed ratio —**scale up** to increase according to a fixed ratio

scale² (skāl) *n.* [< OFr *escaille*, shell] **1** any of the thin, flat horny plates covering many fishes, reptiles, etc. **2** any thin, platelike layer or piece —*vt.* **scaled, scal'ing** to scrape scales from —*vi.* to flake or peel off in scales —**scal'y** *adj.* -i·er, -i·est

scale³ (skāl) *n.* [< ON *skāl*, bowl] **1** either pan of a balance **2** [*often pl.*] *a)* DALANCE (*n.* 1) *b)* any weighing machine —*vt.* **scaled, scal'ing** to weigh —**turn the scales** to decide or settle

scale insect any of various small insects destructive to plants: the females secrete a waxy scale

sca·lene (skā'lēn', skā lēn') *adj.* [< Gr *skalēnos*, uneven] having unequal sides [a *scalene* triangle]

scal·lion (skal'yən) *n.* [< L (*caepa*) *Ascalonia*, (onion of) Ascalon (Philistine city)] any of various onions or onionlike plants, as the shallot, green onion, or leek

scal·lop (skäl'əp, skal'-) *n.* [< OFr *escalope*] **1** *a)* any of various edible mollusks with two curved, hinged shells *b)* one of the shells **2** any of a series of curves, etc. forming an ornamental edge —*vt.* **1** to cut the edge of in scallops **2** to bake until brown, usually with a creamy sauce and bread crumbs

scalp (skalp) *n.* [< Scand] the skin on the top and back of the head, usually covered with hair —*vt.* **1** to cut or tear the scalp from **2** [Inf.] to buy (theater tickets, etc.) and resell them at higher prices —**scalp'er** *n.*

scal·pel (skal'pəl) *n.* [< L *scalprum*, a knife] a small, sharp, straight knife used in surgery, etc.

scam (skam) [Inf.] *n.* [prob. < obs. *scamp*, to roam] a swindle or fraud, esp. a CONFIDENCE GAME —*vt.* **scammed, scam'ming** to cheat or swindle, as in a confidence game

scamp (skamp) *n.* [< It *scampare*, to flee] a mischievous fellow; rascal

scam·per (skam'pər) *vi.* [see prec.] to run or go quickly —*n.* a scampering

scam·pi (skam'pē) *n., pl.* -pi or -pies [It] shrimp or prawns, esp. prepared with butter, garlic, and white wine

scan (skan) *vt.* **scanned, scan'ning** [< L *scandere*, to climb] **1** to analyze (verse) by marking the metrical feet **2** to look at closely **3** to glance at quickly **4** to examine the structure or condition of (an internal body organ) with ultrasound, etc. **5** to pass radar beams over (an area) —*vi.* to conform to metrical principles: said of poetry —*n.* the act or an instance of scanning

Scan or **Scand** *abbrev.* Scandinavia(n)

scan·dal (skan′dəl) *n.* ⟦< Gr *skandalon*, a snare⟧ **1** anything that offends moral feelings and leads to disgrace **2** shame, outrage, etc. caused by this **3** disgrace **4** malicious gossip

scan·dal·ize (-də liz′) *vt.* **-ized′, -iz′ing** to outrage the moral feelings of by improper conduct

scan·dal·mon·ger (-dəl muŋ′gər, -dəl mäŋ′-) *n.* one who spreads scandal or gossip

scan·dal·ous (-də ləs) *adj.* **1** causing scandal; shameful **2** spreading slander —**scan′dal·ous·ly** *adv.*

Scan·di·na·vi·a (skan′də nā′vē ə) region in N Europe, including Norway, Sweden, & Denmark and, sometimes, Iceland and Finland

Scan·di·na·vi·an (skan′də nā′vē ən) *adj.* of Scandinavia or its peoples, languages, etc. —*n.* **1** a person born or living in Scandinavia **2** the subbranch of the Germanic languages spoken by most Scandinavians

scan·di·um (skan′dē əm) *n.* ⟦< L *Scandia*, Scandinavia⟧ a soft, rare, metallic chemical element: symbol, Sc; at. no. 21

scan·sion (skan′shən) *n.* ⟦Fr < L *scansio*⟧ the act of scanning, or analyzing, poetry

scant (skant) *adj.* ⟦< ON *skammr*, short⟧ **1** inadequate; meager **2** not quite up to full measure

scant·y *adj.* **-i·er, -i·est 1** barely sufficient **2** insufficient; not enough —**scant′i·ly** *adv.* —**scant′i·ness** *n.*

scape·goat (skāp′gōt′) *n.* ⟦< ESCAPE + GOAT; see Lev. 16:7-26⟧ one who bears the blame for the mistakes of others —*vt.* to make a scapegoat of

scape·grace (skāp′grās′) *n.* ⟦< ESCAPE + GRACE⟧ a rogue; scamp

scap·u·la (skap′yə lə) *n., pl.* **-lae′** (-lē′) or **-las** ⟦< L⟧ either of the two flat bones in the upper back; shoulder blade

scar (skär) *n.* ⟦< Gr *eschara*, orig., fireplace⟧ **1** a mark left after a wound, burn, etc. has healed **2** the lasting mental or emotional effects of suffering —*vt.* **scarred, scar′ring** to mark as with a scar —*vi.* to form a scar in healing

scar·ab (skar′əb) *n.* ⟦< L *scarabaeus*⟧ **1** a large, black beetle **2** a carved image of such a beetle

scarce (skers) *adj.* ⟦ult. < L *excerpere*, pick out⟧ **1** not common; rarely seen **2** not plentiful; hard to get —*adv.* scarcely —**make oneself scarce** [Inf.] to go or stay away —**scarce′ness** *n.*

scarce·ly *adv.* **1** hardly; only just **2** probably not or certainly not

scar·ci·ty (sker′sə tē) *n., pl.* **-ties 1** an inadequate supply; dearth **2** rarity; uncommonness

scare (sker) *vt.* **scared, scar′ing** ⟦< ON *skjarr*, timid⟧ to fill with sudden fear —*vi.* to become frightened —*n.* a sudden fear —**scare away** (or **off**) to drive away by frightening —**scare up** [Inf.] to produce or gather quickly

scare·crow (sker′krō′) *n.* a human figure made with sticks, old clothes, etc., put in a field to scare birds away from crops

scarf (skärf) *n., pl.* **scarves** (skärvz) or sometimes **scarfs** ⟦< OFr *escharpe*, purse hung from the neck⟧ **1** a piece of cloth worn about the neck, head, etc. **2** a long, narrow covering for a table, etc.

scar·i·fy (skar′ə fi′) *vt.* **-fied′, -fy′ing** ⟦< L *scarifare*⟧ to make small cuts in (the skin, etc.) —**scar′i·fi·ca′tion** *n.*

scar·let (skär′lit) *n.* ⟦< ML *scarlatum*⟧ very bright red —*adj.* **1** of this color **2** sinful; specif., whorish

scarlet fever an acute contagious disease characterized by sore throat, fever, and a scarlet rash

scar·y (sker′ē) *adj.* **-i·er, -i·est** [Inf.] frightening —**scar′i·ness** *n.*

scat¹ (skat) *vi.* **scat′ted, scat′ting** ⟦? short for SCATTER⟧ [Inf.] to go away: usually in the imperative

scat² (skat) *adj.* ⟦< ?⟧ Jazz using improvised, meaningless syllables in singing —*n.* such singing —*vi.* **scat′ted, scat′ting** to sing scat

scath·ing (skā′thiŋ) *adj.* ⟦< ON *skathi*, harm⟧ harsh or caustic [*scathing* remarks] —**scath′ing·ly** *adv.*

sca·tol·o·gy (skə täl′ə jē) *n.* ⟦< Gr *skōr*, excrement⟧ obsession with excrement or excretion in literature —**scat·o·log·i·cal** (skat′ə läj′i kəl) *adj.*

scat·ter (skat′ər) *vt.* ⟦ME *skateren*⟧ **1** to throw here and there **2** to separate and drive in many directions; disperse —*vi.* to separate and go off in several directions

scat·ter·brain *n.* one who is forgetful or easily distracted

scatter rug a small rug

scav·eng·er (skav′in jər) *n.* ⟦< NormFr *es·cauwer*, to inspect⟧ **1** one who gathers things discarded by others **2** any animal that eats refuse and decaying matter —**scav′enge** (-inj) *vt., vi.* **-enged, -eng·ing**

scavenger hunt a contest in which participants are given a list of miscellaneous objects which they must find and acquire without buying them

sce·nar·i·o (sə ner′ē ō′, -när′-) *n., pl.* **-os′** [see fol.] **1** *a*) an outline of a play, etc. *b*) the script of a film **2** an outline for any series of events, real or imagined —**sce·nar′ist** *n.*

scene (sēn) *n.* ⟦< Gr *skēnē*, stage⟧ **1** the place where an event occurs **2** the setting of a play, story, etc. **3** a division of a play, usually part of an act **4** a unit of action in a play, film, etc. **5** SCENERY (*n.* 1) **6** a display of strong feeling [to make a *scene*] **7** [Inf.] the locale for a specified activity

sce·ner·y (sēn′ə rē) *n., pl.* **-ies 1** painted

screens, backdrops, etc., used on the stage to represent places, as in a play, etc. **2** the features of a landscape

sce·nic (sē'nik) *adj.* **1** of stage scenery **2** *a)* of natural scenery *b)* having beautiful scenery

scent (sent) *vt.* ⟦ult. < L *sentire*, to feel⟧ **1** to smell **2** to get a hint of **3** to fill with an odor; perfume —*n.* **1** an odor **2** the sense of smell **3** a perfume **4** an odor left by an animal, by which it is tracked —**scent′ed** *adj.*

scep·ter (sep'tər) *n.* ⟦< Gr *skēptron*, staff⟧ a staff held by a ruler as a symbol of sovereignty: chiefly Brit. sp. **scep′tre**

scep·tic (skep'tik) *n., adj. chiefly Brit. sp. of* SKEPTIC —**scep′ti·cal** *adj.* —**scep′ti·cism′** *n.*

sched·ule (ske'jool; *Brit & often Cdn* shej'ool) *n.* ⟦< L *scheda*, a strip of papyrus⟧ **1** a list of details **2** a list of times of recurring events, projected operations, etc.; timetable **3** a timed plan for a project —*vt.* **-uled, -ul·ing 1** to place in a schedule **2** to plan for a certain time

sche·mat·ic (skē mat'ik) *adj.* of or like a scheme, diagram, etc.

scheme (skēm) *n.* ⟦< Gr *schēma*, a form⟧ **1** *a)* a systematic program for attaining some end *b)* a secret plan; plot **2** an orderly combination of things on a definite plan **3** a diagram — *vt., vi.* **schemed, schem′ing** to devise or plot —**schem′er** *n.*

scher·zo (sker'tsō) *n., pl.* **-zos** or **-zi** (-tsē) ⟦It, a jest⟧ *Music* a lively composition, usually in 3/4 time, as the third movement of a symphony, etc.

schism (siz'əm, skiz'-) *n.* ⟦< Gr *schizein*, to cleave⟧ a split, as in a church, because of difference of opinion, doctrine, etc. —**schis·mat′ic** (-mat'ik) *adj.*

schist (shist) *n.* ⟦< Gr *schistos*, easily cleft⟧ a rock usually containing mica and easily split into layers

schiz·o·phre·ni·a (skit'sə frē'nē ə) *n.* ⟦< Gr *schizein*, cleave + *phrēn*, the mind⟧ a mental disorder characterized by separation between thought and emotions, by delusions, bizarre behavior, etc. —**schiz′oid** (-soid) *adj., n.,* **schiz′o·phren′ic** (-ə fren'ik)

schle·miel (shlə mēl′) *n.* ⟦Yiddish⟧ [Slang] a bungling person who habitually fails or is easily victimized

schlep or **schlepp** (shlep) [Slang] *vt.* **schlepped, schlep′ping** ⟦via Yiddish < LowG *slepen*, to drag⟧ to carry, haul, etc. —*vi.* to go or move with effort

schlock (shläk) [Slang] *n.* ⟦< ? Ger *schlacke*, dregs⟧ anything cheap or inferior; trash —*adj.* cheap; inferior: also **schlock′y -i·er, -i·est**

schmaltz (shmälts, shmôlts) *n.* ⟦? via Yiddish < Ger *schmaltz*, rendered fat⟧ [Slang] highly sentimental music, literature, etc.

schnapps (shnäps) *n., pl.* **schnapps** ⟦Ger, a nip < Du *snaps*, a gulp⟧ a strong alcoholic liquor: also sp. **schnaps**

schnau·zer (shnou'zər) *n.* ⟦Ger < *schnauzen*, to snarl⟧ a sturdily built dog with a wiry coat and bushy eyebrows

schol·ar (skäl'ər) *n.* ⟦< L *schola*, a school⟧ **1** a learned person **2** a student or pupil —**schol′ar·ly** *adj.*

schol·ar·ship *n.* **1** the quality of knowledge a student shows **2** the systematized knowledge of a scholar **3** a gift of money, etc. as by a foundation, to help pay student's expenses

scho·las·tic (skə las'tik) *adj.* ⟦see fol.⟧ of schools, colleges, students, etc.; educational; academic

school¹ (skool) *n.* ⟦< Gr *scholē*, leisure⟧ **1** a place or institution, with its buildings, etc., for teaching and learning **2** all of its students and teachers **3** a regular session of teaching **4** formal education; schooling **5** a particular division of a university **6** a group following the same beliefs, methods, etc. —*vt.* **1** to train; teach **2** to discipline or control —*adj.* of a school or schools

school² (skool) *n.* ⟦Du, a crowd⟧ a group of fish, etc. swimming together

school board an elected or appointed group of people in charge of public or private schools

school·book *n.* a textbook

school·boy *n.* a boy attending school

school·girl *n.* a girl attending school

school·house *n.* a building used as a school

school·ing *n.* training or education; esp., formal instruction at school

school·marm (-märm', -mäm') *n.* **1** [Old-fashioned] a woman schoolteacher **2** [Inf.] any person who tends to be prudish, pedantic, etc.

school·mas·ter *n.* [Old-fashioned] a man who teaches in a school

school·mate *n.* a companion or acquaintance at school

school·mis·tress *n.* [Old-fashioned] a woman who teaches in a school

school·room *n.* a room in which pupils are taught, as in a school

school·teach·er *n.* one who teaches in a school

school·work *n.* lessons worked on in classes or done as homework

school·yard *n.* the ground around a school, used as a playground, etc.

school year the part of a year when school is in session, usually September to June

schoon·er (skoon'ər) *n.* ⟦< ?⟧ **1** a ship with two or more masts, rigged fore and aft, with the foremast usually shorter **2** a large beer glass

Schu·bert (shoo'bərt), **Franz** (fränts) 1797-1828; Austrian composer

schuss (shoos) *n.* ⟦Ger, lit., shot⟧ a straight run down a hill in skiing —*vi.* to do a schuss

schwa (shwä) *n.* ⟦Ger < Heb *sheva*⟧ **1** the neutral vowel sound of most unstressed syllables in English, as of *e* in *agent* **2** the symbol (ə) for this

sci·at·ic (sī at'ik) *adj.* ⟦see fol.⟧ of or in the hip or its nerves

sci·at·i·ca (sī at'i kə) *n.* ⟦< Gr *ischion*, the hip⟧ any painful condition in the hip or thigh; esp., neuritis of the long nerve (**sciatic nerve**) passing down the back of the thigh

sci·ence (sī′əns) *n.* ‖< L *scire*, know‖ **1** systematized knowledge derived from observation, study, etc. **2** a branch of knowledge, esp. one that systematizes facts, principles, and methods, as NATURAL SCIENCE **3** skill or technique

science fiction highly imaginative fiction typically involving some actual or projected scientific phenomenon or technology

sci·en·tif·ic (sī′ən tif′ik) *adj.* **1** of or dealing with science **2** based on, or using, the principles and methods of science; systematic and exact —**sci′en·tif′i·cal·ly** *adv.*

sci·en·tist *n.* a specialist in science, as in biology, chemistry, or physics

sci-fi (sī′fī′) *n.* [Inf.] *short for* SCIENCE FICTION

scim·i·tar (sim′ə tər) *n.* ‖It *scimitarra*‖ a short, curved sword historically used by Turks and Arabs

scin·til·la (sin til′ə) *n.* [L] **1** a spark **2** a particle; the least trace: figurative only

scin·til·late (sint′'l āt′) *vi.* -**lat′ed**, -**lat′ing** ‖< L *scintilla*, a spark‖ **1** to sparkle or twinkle **2** to be brilliant and witty —**scin′til·la′tion** *n.*

sci·on (sī′ən) *n.* ‖< OFr *cion*‖ **1** a shoot or bud of a plant, esp. one for grafting **2** a descendant; heir

scis·sor (siz′ər) *vt.* ‖< fol.‖ to cut, cut off, or cut out with scissors —*n.* SCISSORS, esp. in adjectival use

scis·sors (siz′ərz) *n.* ‖< LL *cisorium*, cutting tool‖ [*also with pl. v.*] a cutting instrument with two opposing blades pivoted together so that they can work against each other as the instrument is closed on paper, etc.: also called **pair of scissors**

scle·ra (sklir′ə) *n.*, *pl.* -**ras** or -**rae** (-ē) ‖< Gr *sklēros*, hard‖ the tough, white membrane covering all of the eyeball except the area covered by the cornea

scle·ro·sis (skli rō′sis) *n.*, *pl.* -**ses** (-sēz′) ‖< Gr *sklēros*, hard‖ an abnormal hardening of body tissues —**scle·rot′ic** (-rät′ik) *adj.*

scoff (skäf, skôf) *n.* an expression of scorn or derision — *vt.*, *vi.* to mock or jeer (at) —**scoff′er** *n.*

scoff·law *n.* [Inf.] one who flouts traffic laws, liquor laws, etc.

scold (skōld) *n.* ‖< ON *skald*, poet (prob. of satirical verses)‖ a person, esp. a woman, who habitually uses abusive language — *vt.*, *vi.* to find fault (with) angrily; to rebuke —**scold′ing** *adj.*, *n.*

sco·li·o·sis (skō′lē ō′sis) *n.* ‖< Gr *skolios*, crooked‖ lateral curvature of the spine

sconce (skäns) *n.* ‖ult. < L *abscondere*, to hide‖ a wall bracket for a candle, electric light, etc.

scone (skōn, skän) *n.* ‖Scot‖ a light cake resembling a biscuit and often quadrant-shaped

scooch (skōōch) *vi.* [Inf.] **1** to scrunch (*down*, *through*, etc.) **2** to slide jerkily

scoop (skōōp) *n.* ‖< MDu *schope*, bailing vessel, *schoppe*, a shovel‖ **1** any of various small, shovel-like utensils, as for taking up flour or ice cream **2** the deep shovel of a dredge, etc. **3** the act or motion of scooping **4** the amount scooped up at one time **5** [Inf.] *a)* the publication or broadcast of a news item before a competitor *b)* such a news item —*vt.* **1** to take up or out with or as with a scoop **2** to hollow (*out*) **3** [Inf.] to publish news before (a competitor)

scoot (skōōt) *vi.*, *vt.* ‖prob. < ON *skjōta*, to shoot‖ [Inf.] to go or move quickly; hurry (off)

scootch (skōōch) *vi.* [Inf.] *alt. sp. of* SCOOCH

scoot·er *n.* ‖< SCOOT‖ **1** a usually two-wheeled vehicle moved by pushing one foot against the ground **2** a similar, motor-driven vehicle with a seat: in full **motor scooter**

scope (skōp) *n.* ‖< Gr *skopos*, watcher‖ **1** the extent of the mind's grasp **2** the range or extent of action, inclusion, inquiry, etc. **3** room or opportunity for freedom of action or thought

-scope (skōp) ‖< Gr *skopein*, see‖ *combining form* an instrument, etc. for seeing or observing [*telescope*, *kaleidoscope*]

scorch (skôrch) *vt.* ‖< ? Scand‖ **1** to burn slightly or superficially **2** to parch by intense heat —*vi.* to become scorched —*n.* a superficial burn

score (skôr) *n.* ‖< ON *skor*‖ **1** a scratch, mark, notch, incised line, etc. **2** an account or debt **3** a grievance one seeks to settle **4** a reason or motive **5** the number of points made, as in a game **6** a grade, as on a test **7** *a)* twenty people or things *b)* [*pl.*] very many **8** a copy of a musical composition showing all parts for the instruments or voices **9** [Inf.] the basic facts [to know the *score*] **10** [Slang] the act of acquiring or stealing —*vt.* **scored**, **scor′ing 1** to mark with notches, cuts, lines, etc. **2** *a)* to make (runs, points, etc.) in a game *b)* to record the score of **3** to achieve [*score* a success] **4** to evaluate, as in testing **5** *Music* to arrange in a score **6** [Slang] to acquire or steal —*vi.* **1** to make points, as in a game **2** to keep the score of a game **3** to gain an advantage, a success, etc. —**scor′er** *n.*

score·board *n.* a large board for posting scores, etc., as in a stadium

score·less *adj.* with no points scored

scorn (skôrn) *n.* ‖< OFr *escharnir*, to scorn‖ extreme, often indignant, contempt —*vt.* **1** to regard with scorn **2** to refuse or reject with scorn —**scorn′ful** *adj.* —**scorn′ful·ly** *adv.*

Scor·pi·o (skôr′pē ō′) *n.* ‖L, scorpion‖ the eighth sign of the zodiac

scor·pi·on (-ən) *n.* ‖< Gr *skorpios*‖ an arachnid with a long tail ending in a poisonous sting

Scot[1] (skät) *n.* a person born or living in Scotland

Scot[2] *abbrev.* **1** Scotland **2** Scottish

scotch (skäch) *vt.* ‖prob. < OFr *coche*, a nick‖ **1** to maim **2** to put an end to; stifle [to *scotch* a rumor]

Scotch (skäch) *adj.* of Scotland: cf. SCOTTISH —*n.* **1** SCOTTISH **2** [*often* **s-**] whiskey distilled in Scotland from malted barley: in full **Scotch whisky**

Scotch tape [< *Scotch,* a trademark] a thin, transparent adhesive tape

scot-free (skät′frē′) *adv., adj.* [< earlier *scot,* a tax] without being punished or hurt

Scot·land (skät′lənd) division of the United Kingdom: the N half of Great Britain —**Scots′man** (-mən) *n., pl.* **-men** (-mən) —**Scots′wom′an** (-,woom′ən) *n.* **-wom′en**

Scotland Yard the London police headquarters, esp. its detective bureau

Scots (skäts) *n.* the variety of English spoken in Scotland —*adj.* Scottish

Scot·tie or **Scot·ty** (skät′ē) *n., pl.* **-ties** SCOTTISH TERRIER

Scot·tish (skät′ish) *adj.* of Scotland or its people, variety of English, etc.: *Scottish* is formal usage, but with some words, *Scotch* is used (e.g., tweed, whisky), with others, *Scots* (e.g., law) —*n.* **Scots** —**the Scottish** the Scottish people

Scottish terrier a short-legged terrier with a wiry coat

scoun·drel (skoun′drəl) *n.* [prob. ult. < L *ab*(-)-, from + *condere,* to hide] a mean, immoral, or wicked person

scour[1] (skour) *vt., vi.* [< ? L *ex*-, intens. + *cura,* care] **1** to clean by rubbing hard, as with abrasives **2** to clean or clear out as by a flow of water

scour[2] (skour) *vt.* [< L *ex*-, out + *currere,* to run] to pass over quickly, or range over, as in searching [to *scour* a library for a book]

scourge (skurj) *n.* [< L *ex,* off + *corrigia,* a whip] **1** a whip **2** any cause of serious affliction —*vt.* **scourged, scourg′ing 1** to whip or flog **2** to punish or afflict severely

scout (skout) *n.* [< L *auscultare,* to listen] **1** a soldier, plane, etc. sent to spy out the enemy's strength, actions, etc. **2** a person sent out to survey a competitor, find new talent, etc. **3** [S-] a Boy Scout or Girl Scout —*vt., vi.* **1** to reconnoiter **2** to go in search of (something)

scout·ing *n.* **1** the act of one who scouts **2** [*often* **S-**] the activities of the Boy Scouts or Girl Scouts

scout·mas·ter *n.* the adult leader of a troop of Boy Scouts

scow (skou) *n.* [Du *schouw*] a large, flat-bottomed boat used for carrying loads, often towed by a tugboat

scowl (skoul) *vi.* [prob. < Scand] to look angry, sullen, etc., as by contracting the eyebrows —*n.* a scowling look —**scowl′er** *n.*

scrab·ble (skrab′əl) *vi.* **-bled, -bling** [< Du *schrabben,* to scrape] **1** to scratch, scrape, etc. as though looking for something **2** to struggle

scrag·gly (skrag′lē) *adj.* **-gli·er, -gli·est** [prob. < ON] uneven, ragged, etc. in growth or form

scram (skram) *vi.* **scrammed, scram′ming** [< fol.] [Slang] to get out, esp. in a hurry

scram·ble (skram′bəl) *vi.* **-bled, -bling** [< ?] **1** to climb, crawl, etc. hurriedly **2** to scuffle or struggle for something —*vt.* **1** to mix haphazardly **2** to stir and cook (slightly beaten eggs) **3** to make (transmitted signals) unintelligible without special receiving equipment —*n.* **1** a hard climb or advance **2** a disorderly struggle, as for something prized

scrap[1] (skrap) *n.* [ult. < ON *skrapa,* to scrape] **1** a small piece; fragment **2** discarded material **3** [*pl.*] bits of food —*adj.* **1** in the form of pieces, leftovers, etc. **2** used and discarded —*vt.* **scrapped, scrap′ping 1** to make into scrap **2** to discard; junk —**scrap′per** *n.*

scrap[2] (skrap) *n., vi.* **scrapped, scrap′ping** [< ? SCRAPE] [Inf.] fight or quarrel —**scrap′per** *n.* —**scrap′py** *adv.* **-pi·er, -pi·est**

scrap·book *n.* a book in which to mount clippings, pictures, etc.

scrape (skrāp) *vt.* **scraped, scrap′ing** [< ON *skrapa*] **1** to make smooth or clean by rubbing with a tool or abrasive **2** to remove in this way: with *off, out,* etc. **3** to scratch or abrade **4** to gather slowly and with difficulty [*scrape* up some cash] —*vi.* **1** to rub against something harshly; grate **2** to manage to get by: with *through, along, by* —*n.* **1** a scraping **2** a scraped place **3** a grating sound **4** a predicament —**scrap′er** *n.*

scrap·heap (-hēp′) *n.* a pile of discarded material, as of scrap iron —**throw** (or **toss, cast,** etc.) **on the scrapheap** to get rid of as useless or obsolete

scratch (skrach) *vt.* [ME *scracchen*] **1** to mark, break, or cut the surface of slightly **2** to tear or dig with the nails or claws **3** to scrape lightly to relieve itching **4** to scrape with a grating noise **5** to write hurriedly or carelessly **6** to strike out (writing, etc.) **7** *Sports* to withdraw (a contestant, etc.) —*vi.* **1** to use nails or claws in digging, wounding, etc. **2** to scrape —*n.* **1** a scratching **2** a mark, tear, etc. made by scratching **3** a grating or scraping sound —*adj.* used for hasty notes, figuring etc. [*scratch* paper] —**from scratch 1** from the beginning **2** without using preassembled ingredients or components —**up to scratch** [Inf.] up to standard —**scratch′y** *adj.* **-i·er, -i·est** —**scratch′i·ly** *adv.* —**scratch′i·ness** *n.*

scratch·pad *n.* a pad of paper for jotting notes

scrawl (skrôl) *vt., vi.* [< ?] to write or draw hastily, carelessly, etc. —*n.* sprawling, often illegible handwriting

scraw·ny (skrô′nē) *adj.* **-ni·er, -ni·est** [prob. < Scand] very thin; skinny —**scraw′ni·ness** *n.*

scream (skrēm) *vi.* [ME *screamen*] **1** to utter a shrill, piercing cry in fright, pain, etc. **2** to shout, laugh, etc. wildly —*vt.* to utter with or as with a scream —*n.* **1** a sharp, piercing cry or sound **2** [Inf.] a very funny person or thing

screech (skrēch) *vi., vt.* [< ON *skraekja*] to utter (with) a shrill, high-pitched sound —*n.* such a sound —**screech′y** *adj.* **-i·er, -i·est**

screen (skrēn) *n.* [< OFr *escren*] **1** a partition, curtain, etc. used to separate, conceal, etc. **2** anything that shields, conceals, etc. **3** a coarse mesh of wire, etc., used as a sieve **4** a frame covered with a mesh [a window *screen*] **5** *a*) a surface on which films, slides, etc. are projected *b*) the film industry *c*) the surface of a TV set, computer, etc. on which images are formed —*vt.* **1** to conceal or protect, as with a screen **2** to sift through a screen **3** to separate according to skills, etc. **4** to check or test, as for disease **5** to show (a film, etc.) to critics, the public, etc.

screen·play *n.* the script from which a film is produced

screen saver *Comput.* a software program that displays constantly shifting or changing images when the screen is inactive

screen·writ·er *n.* the writer of a script for a film —**screen′writ′ing** *n.*

screw (skr‾oo) *n.* [< Fr *escroue*, hole in which the screw turns] **1** a cylindrical or conical piece of metal threaded in an advancing spiral, for fastening things: it penetrates when turned **2** any spiral thing like this **3** anything operating or threaded like a screw —*vt.* **1** to twist; turn **2** to fasten, tighten, etc. as with a screw **3** to contort —*vi.* **1** to go together or come apart by being turned like a screw [the lid *screws* on] **2** to twist or turn —**put the screws on** (or **to**) [Inf.] to subject to great pressure; coerce —**screw up** [Inf.] to bungle

screw·ball *n.* [Slang] an erratic, irrational or unconventional person

screw·driv·er *n.* a tool used for turning screws

screw·worm *n.* the larva of an American blowfly that infests wounds, and the nostrils, navel, etc. of animals

screw·y (skr‾oo′ē) *adj.* -i·er, -i·est [Slang] **1** crazy **2** peculiar, eccentric

scrib·ble (skrib′əl) *vt., vi.* -bled, -bling [< L *scribere*, write] **1** to write carelessly, hastily, etc. **2** to make meaningless or illegible marks (on) —*n.* scribbled writing —**scrib′bler** *n.*

scribe (skrīb) *n.* [< L *scribere*, write] **1** a person who copied manuscripts before the invention of printing **2** a writer

scrim (skrim) *n.* [< ?] **1** a light, sheer, loosely woven cotton or linen cloth **2** such a cloth used as a stage backdrop or semitransparent curtain

scrim·mage (skrim′ij) *n.* [< SKIRMISH] *Football* play that follows the snap from center **2** a practice game —*vi.* -maged, -mag·ing to take part in a scrimmage

scrimp (skrimp) *vt., vi.* [< ? Scand] to be sparing or frugal (with)

scrim·shaw (-shô′) *n.* intricate engraving on bone, ivory, etc. done esp. by sailors

scrip (skrip) *n.* [< fol.] a certificate of a right to receive something, as money or goods

script (skript) *n.* [< L *scribere*, to write] **1** handwriting **2** a copy of the text of a play, film etc.

scrip·ture (skrip′chər) *n.* [see prec.] **1** any sacred writing **2** [S—] [*often pl.*] the Jewish Bible **3** [S—] [*often pl.*] the Christian Bible —**scrip′tur·al** *adj.*

script·writ·er *n.* one who writes scripts for films, TV, etc.

scrod (skräd) *n.* [prob. < MDu *schrode*, piece cut off] a young codfish or haddock, esp. one prepared for cooking

scrof·u·la (skräf′yə lə) *n.* [< L *scrofa*, a sow] tuberculosis of the lymphatic glands, esp. of the neck —**scrof′u·lous** *adj.*

scroll (skrōl) *n.* [< ME *scrowle*] **1** a roll of parchment, paper, etc., usually with writing on it **2** an ornamental design in coiled or spiral form —*vi.* to move lines of text, etc. vertically on a video screen

scro·tum (skrōt′əm) *n., pl.* -ta (-ə) or -tums [L] the pouch of skin holding the testicles

scrounge (skrounj) *vt.* scrounged, scroung′ing [< ?] [Inf.] **1** to get by begging or sponging; mooch **2** to pilfer —*vi.* [Inf.] to seek (*around*) for something —**scroung′er** *n.*

scrub[1] (skrub) *n.* [ME, var. of *shrubbe*, shrub] **1** a thick growth of stunted trees or bushes **2** any person or thing smaller than the usual, or inferior **3** *Sports* a substitute player —*adj.* small, stunted, inferior, etc. —**scrub′by** *adj.* -bi·er, -bi·est

scrub[2] (skrub) *vt., vi.* scrubbed, scrub′bing [prob. < Scand] **1** to clean or wash by rubbing hard **2** to rub hard —*n.* a scrubbing —**scrub′ber** *n.*

scruff (skruf) *n.* [< ON *skrufr*, a tuft of hair] the nape of the neck

scruff·y (skruf′ē) *adj.* -i·er, -i·est [< SCURF + -Y²] shabby; unkempt —**scruff′i·ness** *n.*

scrum (skrum) *n.* *Rugby* a play in which the forwards, lined up facing each other, try to kick the ball back to a teammate

scrump·tious (skrump′shəs) *adj.* [< SUMPTUOUS] [Inf.] very pleasing, esp. to the taste

scrunch (skrunch) *vt., vi.* [< CRUNCH] **1** to crunch, crush, etc. **2** to huddle, squeeze, etc. —*n.* a crunching or crumpling sound

scru·ple (skr‾oo′pəl) *n.* [< L *scrupulus*, small stone] **1** a very small quantity **2** doubt arising from difficulty in deciding what is right —*vt., vi.* -pled, -pling to hesitate (at) from doubt

scru·pu·lous (-pyə ləs) *adj.* **1** having or showing scruples; conscientiously honest **2** careful of details; precise —**scru′pu·los′i·ty** (-läs′ət ē) *n., pl.* -ties —**scru′pu·lous·ly** *adv.*

scru·ti·nize (skr‾oot′'n īz′) *vt.* -nized′, -niz′ing to examine closely

scru·ti·ny (skr‾oot′'n ē) *n., pl.* -nies [< L *scrutari*, examine] **1** a close examination or watch **2** a lengthy, searching look

scu·ba (sk‾oo′bə) *n.* [s(elf-)c(ontained) u(nderwater) b(reathing) a(pparatus)] a diver's equipment with compressed-air tanks for breathing underwater

scud (skud) *vi.* scud′ded, scud′ding [prob. < ON] to move swiftly —*n.* a scudding

scuff (skuf) *vt., vi.* [prob. < ON *skufa*, to shove] **1** to wear or get a rough place on the surface (of) **2** to drag (the feet) —*n.* **1** a worn or rough spot **2** a flat-heeled house slipper with no back upper part

scuf·fle (skuf'əl) *vi.* **-fled, -fling** [< prec.] **1** to struggle or fight in rough confusion **2** to drag the feet —*n.* **1** a confused fight **2** a shuffling of feet

scull (skul) *n.* [ME *skulle*] **1** an oar worked from side to side over the stern of a boat **2** a light rowboat for racing — *vt., vi.* to propel with a scull

scul·ler·y (skul'ər ē) *n., pl.* **-ies** [< L *scutella*, tray] [Now Rare] a room near the kitchen, where pots, pans, etc. are cleaned and stored

scul·lion (skul'yən) *n.* [ult. < L *scopa*, a broom] [Archaic] a servant doing menial tasks in a kitchen or scullery

sculpt (skulpt) *vt., vi.* SCULPTURE

sculp·tor (skulp'tər) *n.* an artist who creates works of sculpture

sculp·ture (skulp'chər) *n.* [< L *sculpere*, to carve] **1** the art of shaping stone, clay, wood, metal, etc. into statues, figures, etc. **2** a work or works of sculpture — *vt., vi.* **-tured, -turing** **1** to cut, carve, chisel, etc. (statues, figures, etc.) **2** to make or form like sculpture —**sculp'tur·al** *adj.*

scum (skum) *n.* [< MDu *schum*] **1** a thin layer of impurities on the top of a liquid **2** refuse **3** [Inf.] a despicable person or persons —*vi.* to become covered with scum —**scum'my** *adj.* **-mi·er, -mi·est**

scup·per (skup'ər) *n.* [< OFr *escopir*, to spit] an opening in a ship's side to allow water to run off the deck

scurf (skurf) *n.* [< ON] **1** little, dry scales shed by the skin, as dandruff **2** any scaly coating —**scurf'y** *adj.* **-i·er, -i·est**

scur·ril·ous (skur'ə ləs) *adj.* [< L *scurra*, buffoon] vulgarly abusive —**scur·ril·i·ty** (skə ril'ə tē) *n., pl.* **-ties** —**scur'ri·lous·ly** *adv.*

scur·ry (skur'ē) *vi.* **-ried, -ry·ing** [< ?] to run hastily; scamper —*n.* a scurrying

scur·vy (skur'vē) *adj.* **-vi·er, -vi·est** [< SCURF] low; mean —*n.* a disease resulting from a deficiency of vitamin C, characterized by weakness, anemia, spongy gums, etc. —**scur'vi·ly** *adv.*

scut·tle¹ (skut'l) *n.* [< L *scutella*, tray] a bucket for carrying coal

scut·tle² (skut'l) *vi.* **-tled, -tling** [ME *scutlen*] to scamper —*n.* a scamper

scut·tle³ (skut'l) *n.* [< Sp *escotilla*, an indentation] an opening fitted with a cover, as in the hull or deck of a ship —*vt.* **-tled, -tling** to cut holes through the lower hull of (a ship, etc.) to sink it

scut·tle·butt (skut'l but') *n.* [< *scuttled butt*, lidded cask] [Inf.] rumor or gossip

scuz·zy (skuz'ē) *adj.* **-zi·er, -zi·est** [< ?] [Slang] dirty, shabby, etc.

scythe (sīth) *n.* [OE *sithe*] a tool with a long, single-edged blade on a long, curved handle, for cutting grass, grain, etc.

SD *abbrev.* South Dakota

Se *Chem. symbol for* selenium

SE *abbrev.* **1** southeast **2** southeastern

sea (sē) *n.* [OE *sæ*] **1** the ocean **2** any of various smaller bodies of salt water [the Red

Sea] **3** a large body of fresh water [*Sea of Galilee*] **4** the condition of the surface of the ocean [a calm *sea*] **5** a heavy wave **6** a very great amount [a *sea* of debt] —**at sea 1** on the open sea **2** uncertain; bewildered

sea anemone a sea polyp with a gelatinous body and petal-like tentacles

sea bass (bas) a saltwater food fish

sea·bed *n.* the mineral-rich ocean floor

sea·board *n.* [SEA + BOARD] land bordering on the sea —*adj.* bordering on the sea

sea·bor·gi·um (sē bôr'gē əm) *n.* [after Glenn *Seaborg* (1912-99), U.S. chemist] an artificially produced, radioactive chemical element: symbol, Sg; at. no. 106

sea change [used by SHAKESPEARE in *The Tempest*, I, ii (1610)] an essential or notable transformation

sea·coast *n.* land bordering on the sea

sea cow a large sea mammal with a cigar-shaped body and a blunt snout, as the manatee

sea·far·er (-fer'ər) *n.* a sea traveler; esp., a sailor —**sea'far·ing** *adj., n.*

sea·floor *n.* the ground along the ocean bottom

sea·food *n.* food prepared from or consisting of saltwater fish or shellfish

sea·go·ing *adj.* **1** made for use on the open sea **2** SEAFARING

sea gull GULL¹

sea horse a small semitropical fish with a head somewhat like that of a horse

seal¹ (sēl) *n.* [< L *sigillum*] **1** *a)* a design or initial impressed, often into wax, on a letter or document as a mark of authenticity *b)* a stamp or ring for making such an impression **2** a piece of paper, etc. bearing an impressed design recognized as official **3** something that seals or closes tightly **4** anything that guarantees; pledge **5** an ornamental paper stamp —*vt.* **1** to mark with a seal, as to authenticate or certify **2** to close or shut tight as with a seal **3** to confirm the genuineness of (a promise, etc.) **4** to decide finally

seal² (sēl) *n.* [OE *seolh*] **1** a sea mammal with a torpedo-shaped body and flippers **2** the fur of some seals —*vi.* to hunt seals —**seal'er** *n.*

seal·ant (sēl'ənt) *n.* a substance, as a wax or plastic, used for sealing

sea legs the ability to walk without loss of balance on board a ship at sea

sea level the mean level of the sea's surface: used in measuring heights

sea lion a seal of the N Pacific

seal·skin *n.* **1** the skin of the seal **2** a garment made of this

seam (sēm) *n.* [OE] **1** a line formed where two pieces of material are sewn together **2** a line that marks adjoining edges **3** a mark like this, as a scar or wrinkle **4** a layer of ore, coal, etc. —*vt.* **1** to join together so as to form a seam **2** to mark with a seamlike line, etc. —**seam'less** *adj.*

sea·man (sē'mən) *n., pl.* **-men** (-mən) **1** a

sailor **2** *U.S. Navy* an enlisted person ranking below a petty officer —**sea′man·ship′** *n.*

seam·stress (sēm′stris) *n.* a woman whose occupation is sewing

seam·y *adj.* **-i·er, -i·est** unpleasant or sordid [the *seamy* side of life]

sé·ance (sā′äns) *n.* ⟦Fr < L *sedere,* to sit⟧ a meeting at which a medium seeks to communicate with the spirits of the dead

sea·plane *n.* an airplane designed to land on and take off from water

sea·port *n.* a port or harbor used by ocean ships

sear (sir) *vt.* ⟦< OE *sear,* dry (adj.)⟧ **1** to burn the surface of **2** to brand

search (surch) *vt.* ⟦< LL *circare,* go about⟧ **1** to look through in order to find something **2** to examine (a person) for something concealed **3** to examine carefully; probe —*vi.* to make a search —*n.* a searching —**in search of** making a search for —**search′er** *n.*

search engine 1 software for locating documents, websites, etc. on a specified topic, etc. **2** a website designed to search the internet in this manner

search·ing *adj.* **1** examining thoroughly **2** piercing; penetrating

search·light *n.* **1** an apparatus on a swivel that projects a strong beam of light **2** such a beam

search warrant a legal document authorizing a police search

sea·scape (-skāp′) *n.* ⟦SEA + (LAND)SCAPE⟧ **1** a view of the sea **2** a drawing, painting, etc. of such a scene

sea·shell *n.* a saltwater mollusk shell

sea·shore *n.* land along the sea

sea·sick·ness *n.* nausea, dizziness, etc. caused by the rolling and pitching of a ship or boat —**sea′sick′** *adj.*

sea·side *n.* SEASHORE

sea·son (sē′zən) *n.* ⟦< VL *satio,* season for sowing⟧ **1** any of the four divisions of the year; spring, summer, fall, or winter **2** the time when something takes place, is popular, is permitted, etc. **3** the suitable time —*vt.* **1** to make (food) more tasty by adding salt, spices, etc. **2** to add zest to **3** to make more usable, as by aging **4** to make used to; accustom —*vi.* to become seasoned

sea·son·a·ble *adj.* **1** suitable to the season **2** opportune; timely

sea·son·al *adj.* of or depending on the season —**sea′son·al·ly** *adv.*

sea·son·ing *n.* anything that adds zest; esp., salt, spices, etc. added to food

season ticket a ticket or set of tickets for an entire season's program of events, such as concerts or baseball games

seat (sēt) *n.* ⟦ON *sæti*⟧ **1** *a)* a place to sit *b)* a thing to sit on; chair, etc. **2** *a)* the buttocks *b)* the part of a chair, garment, etc. that one sits on **3** the right to sit as a member [a *seat* on the council] **4** the center or the chief location [the *seat* of government] —*vt.* **1** to set in or on a seat **2** to have seats for [the car *seats* six] **3** to put or fix in a place, position,

etc. —**be seated** to sit down: also **take a seat**

seat belt straps across the hips and often the chest, to protect a seated rider in a vehicle: also **seat′belt′** *n.*

Se·at·tle (sē at′l) seaport in WC Washington

sea urchin a small sea animal with a round body in a shell covered with sharp spines

sea·ward *adj., adv.* toward the sea: also **sea′wards** *adv.*

sea·way *n.* an inland waterway to the sea for ocean ships

sea·weed *n.* a sea plant, esp. an alga

sea·wor·thy (-wur′thē) *adj.* fit to travel on the sea: said of a ship

se·ba·ceous (sə bā′shəs) *adj.* ⟦< L *sebum,* tallow⟧ of, like, or secreting fat or a fatty substance [*sebaceous* glands]

seb·or·rhe·a or **seb·or·rhoe·a** (seb′ə rē′ə) *n.* ⟦ult. < L *sebum,* tallow + Gr *rheein,* flow⟧ an excessive discharge from the sebaceous glands, causing abnormally oily skin

sec *abbrev.* **1** second(s) **2** secondary **3** secretary **4** section(s)

SEC *abbrev.* Securities and Exchange Commission

se·cede (si sēd′) *vi.* **-ced′ed, -ced′ing** ⟦< L *se-,* apart + *cedere,* to go⟧ to withdraw formally from a group, organization, etc.

se·ces·sion (si sesh′ən) *n.* **1** a seceding **2** [*often* S-] the withdrawal of the Southern states from the United States of America at the start of the Civil War —**se·ces′sion·ist** *n.*

se·clude (si klōōd′) *vt.* **-clud′ed, -clud′ing** ⟦< L *se-,* apart + *claudere,* to close⟧ to shut off from others; isolate

se·clu·sion (si klōō′zhən) *n.* a secluding or being secluded; retirement; isolation

sec·ond (sek′ənd) *adj.* ⟦< L *sequi,* follow⟧ **1** coming next after the first; 2d or 2nd **2** another of the same kind; other [a *second* chance] **3** next below the first in rank, value, etc. —*n.* **1** one that is second **2** an article of merchandise not of first quality **3** an aide or assistant, as to a duelist or boxer **4** the gear next after first gear **5** [*pl.*] a second helping of food —*vt.* **1** to assist **2** to indicate formal support of (a motion) before discussion or a vote —*adv.* in the second place, group, etc.

sec·ond² (sek′ənd) *n.* ⟦< ML (*pars minuta*) *secunda,* second (small part): from being a further division⟧ **1** the sixtieth part of a minute of time or of angular measure **2** a moment

sec·ond·ar·y (sek′ən der′ē) *adj.* **1** second in order, rank, importance, place, etc.; subordinate; minor **2** derived, not primary; derivative —*n., pl.* **-ar′ies 1** a secondary person or thing **2** *Football* the defensive backfield —**sec′ond·ar′i·ly** *adv.*

secondary school a school, esp. a high school, coming after elementary school

secondary stress (or **accent**) a weaker stress (′) than the primary stress of a word

sec·ond-class *adj.* **1** of the class, rank, etc. next below the highest, best, etc. **2** of a cheaper mail class, as for periodicals **3** inferior, inadequate, etc. or treated as such —*adv.*

by second-class mail or travel accommodations

sec·ond-guess vt., vi. [Inf.] to criticize or contradict, esp. in retrospect

sec·ond·hand adj. 1 not from the original source 2 used before; not new 3 of or dealing in used merchandise

second lieutenant Mil. a commissioned officer of the lowest rank

sec·ond·ly adv. in the second place

second nature an acquired habit, etc. deeply fixed in one's nature

second person the form of a pronoun or verb that refers to the person or persons spoken to

sec·ond-rate adj. 1 second in quality, rank, etc. 2 inferior

sec·ond-string adj. Sports [Inf.] that is a substitute player at a specified position —**sec′ond-string′er** n.

second thought a change in thought after reconsidering —**on second thought** after reconsideration

second wind 1 the return of easy breathing after initial exhaustion, as while running 2 any fresh ability to continue

se·cre·cy (sē′krə sē) n., pl. **-cies** 1 a being secret 2 a tendency to keep things secret

se·cret (sē′krit) adj. [< L se-, apart + cernere, sift] 1 kept from the knowledge of others 2 beyond general understanding; mysterious 3 concealed from sight; hidden —n. a secret fact, cause, process, etc. —**in secret** secretly —**se′cret·ly** adv.

sec·re·tar·i·at (sek′rə ter′ē ət) n. a staff headed by a secretary; specif., an administrative staff, as in a government

sec·re·tar·y (sek′rə ter′ē) n., pl. **-tar′ies** [< ML secretarius, one entrusted with secrets] 1 one who keeps records, handles correspondence, etc. for an organization or person [often S-] the head of a government department 3 a writing desk —**sec′re·tar′i·al** adj.

se·crete (si krēt′) vt. **-cret′ed, -cret′ing** [see SECRET] 1 to hide; conceal 2 to form and release (a substance) as a gland, etc. does

se·cre·tion (si krē′shən) n. 1 a secreting 2 a substance secreted as by a gland

se·cre·tive (sē′krə tiv) adj. concealing one's thoughts, etc.; not frank or open —**se′cre·tive·ly** adv. —**se′cre·tive·ness** n.

se·cre·to·ry (si krēt′ər ē) adj. having the function of secreting, as a gland

Secret Service a division of the U.S. Treasury Department for uncovering counterfeiters, guarding the President, etc.

sect¹ (sekt) n. [< L sequi, follow] 1 a religious denomination 2 any group of people having a common philosophy, set of beliefs, etc.

sect² abbrev. section

sec·tar·i·an (sek ter′ē ən) adj. 1 of or devoted to some sect 2 narrow-minded —n. a sectarian person —**sec·tar′i·an·ism′** n.

sec·tion (sek′shən) n. [< L secare, to cut] 1 a cutting or cutting apart 2 a part cut off; portion 3 any distinct part, group, district, etc. 4 a drawing, etc. of a thing as it would appear if cut straight through —vt. to divide into sections

sec·tion·al adj. 1 of or characteristic of a given section or district 2 made up of sections —**sec′tion·al·ism′** n.

sec·tor (sek′tər) n. [< L secare, to cut] 1 part of a circle bounded by any two radii and the included arc 2 any of the districts into which an area is divided for military operations 3 a distinct part of society or of an economy, group, etc.

sec·u·lar (sek′yə lər) adj. [< LL saecularis, worldly] not religious; not connected with a church —**sec′u·lar·ism′** n.

sec·u·lar·ize (-lə rīz′) vt. **-ized′, -iz′ing** to change from religious to civil use, control, influence, etc. —**sec′u·lar·i·za′tion** n.

se·cure (si kyoor′) adj. [< L se-, free from + cura, care] 1 free from fear, care, etc. 2 free from danger, risk, etc.; safe 3 firm, stable, etc. [make the knot secure] —vt. **-cured′, -cur′ing** 1 to make secure; protect 2 to make certain, as with a pledge 3 to make firm, fast, etc. 4 to obtain or bring about —**se·cure′ly** adv.

se·cu·ri·ty (si kyoor′ə tē) n., pl. **-ties** 1 a feeling secure; freedom from fear, doubt, etc. 2 protection; safeguard 3 something given as a pledge of repayment, etc. 4 [pl.] bonds, stocks, etc. 5 a private police force

secy or **sec′y** abbrev. secretary

se·dan (si dan′) n. [< ? L sedere, to sit] an automobile usually having four doors, a permanent rigid top, and a full-sized rear seat

se·date¹ (si dāt′) adj. [< L sedare, to settle] calm or composed; esp., serious and unemotional —**se·date′ly** adv.

se·date² (si dāt′) vt. **-dat′ed, -dat′ing** to dose with a sedative —**se·da′tion** n.

sed·a·tive (sed′ə tiv) adj. [see SEDATE¹] tending to soothe or quiet; lessening excitement, irritation, nervousness, etc. —n. a sedative medicine

sed·en·tar·y (sed′′n ter′ē) adj. [< L sedere, to sit] marked by much sitting

Se·der (sā′dər) n., pl. **Se·ders** or **Se·dar·im** (sə där′im) [Heb lit., arrangement] [also s-] Judaism the feast of Passover as observed in the home on the eve of the first (by some also of the second) day of the holiday

sedge (sej) n. [OE secg] a coarse, grasslike plant growing in wet ground

sed·i·ment (sed′ə mənt) n. [< L sedere, sit] 1 matter that settles to the bottom of a liquid 2 Geol. matter deposited by water or wind

sed·i·men·ta·ry (-men′tər ē) adj. 1 of or containing sediment 2 formed by the deposit of sediment, as certain rocks

sed·i·men·ta·tion (-men tā′shən, -mən-) n. the depositing of sediment

se·di·tion (si dish′ən) n. [< L sed-, apart + itio, a going] a stirring up of rebellion against the government —**se·di′tion·ist** n. —**se·di′tious** adj.

se·duce (si doos′) vt. **-duced′, -duc′ing** [< L se-, apart + ducere, to lead] 1 to tempt to wrongdoing 2 to entice into having sexual intercourse —se·duc'er n. —se·duc'tion (-duk'shən) n. —se·duc'tive adj. —se·duc'tress (-tris) n.

sed·u·lous (sej'oo ləs) adj. [L sedulus] diligent

se·dum (sē'dəm) n. [< L] any of various succulent plants having white, yellow, or pink flowers

see¹ (sē) vt. saw, seen, see'ing [OE seon] 1 to get knowledge of through the eyes; look at 2 to understand 3 to learn; find out 4 to experience 5 to make sure [see that he goes] 6 to escort [see her to her door] 7 to encounter 8 to call on; consult 9 to receive [too ill to see anyone] —vi. 1 to have the power of sight 2 to understand 3 to think [let me see, who's next?] —see off to accompany (someone) to the place from which that person is to depart, as on a journey —see through 1 to perceive the true nature of 2 to finish 3 to help through difficulty —see to to attend to

see² (sē) n. [< L sedes, a seat] the official seat or jurisdiction of a bishop

seed (sēd) n., pl. seeds or seed [OE sæd] 1 a) the part of a plant, containing the embryo, from which a new plant can grow b) such seeds collectively 2 the source of anything 3 [Archaic] descendants; posterity 4 sperm or semen 5 a seeded contestant —vt. 1 to plant with seeds 2 to remove the seeds from 3 to distribute (contestants in a tournament) so that the best teams or players are not matched in early rounds —vi. to produce seeds —go (or run) to seed 1 to shed seeds after flowering 2 to deteriorate, weaken, etc. —seed'less adj.

seed·ling (-liŋ) n. 1 a plant grown from a seed 2 a young tree

seed money money to begin a long-term project

seed·y adj. -i·er, -i·est 1 full of seed 2 gone to seed 3 shabby, rundown, etc. —seed'i·ness n.

seek (sēk) vt. sought, seek'ing [OE secan] 1 to try to find; search for 2 to try to get 3 to aim at 4 to try; attempt [to seek to please] —seek'er n.

seem (sēm) vi. [prob. < ON sœma, conform to] 1 to appear to be [to seem happy] 2 to give the impression: usually with an infinitive [she seems to know]

seem·ing adj. that seems real, true, etc. without necessarily being so; apparent —seem'ing·ly adv.

seem·ly adj. -li·er, -li·est suitable, proper, etc. —seem'li·ness n.

seen (sēn) vt., vi. pp. of SEE¹

seep (sēp) vi. [OE sipian, to soak] to leak through small openings; ooze —seep'age n.

seer (sir, sē'ər) n. one who supposedly foretells the future

seer·suck·er (sir'suk'ər) n. [< Pers shir u shakar, lit., milk and sugar] a crinkled fabric of linen, cotton, etc.

see·saw (sē'sô') n. [< SAW¹] 1 a plank or

beam balanced at the middle on which children at play, riding the ends, rise and fall alternately 2 any up-and-down or back-and-forth motion or change — vt., vi. to move up and down or back and forth

seethe (sēth) vi. seethed, seeth'ing 1 to boil, surge, or bubble 2 to be violently agitated

seg·ment (seg'mənt; for v., -ment) n. [< L secare, to cut] any of the parts into which something is or can be separated; section — vt., vi. to divide into segments —seg'men·ta'tion n.

seg·re·gate (seg'rə gāt') vt. -gat'ed, -gat'ing [< L se-, apart + grex, a flock] to set apart from others; specif., to impose racial segregation on

seg·re·ga·tion n. the policy of compelling different, esp. racial, groups to live apart, use separate schools, facilities, etc. —seg're·ga'tion·ist n.

se·gue (seg'wā, sā'gwä) vi. -gued, -gue·ing [It, (it follows) < L sequi, to follow] to continue without break (to or into the next part) —n. an immediate transition to the next part

sei·gnior (sān'yər, sān yôr') n. [< OFr seignor < L senior] a feudal lord

seine (sān) n. [< Gr sagēnē] a large fishing net weighted along the bottom — vt., vi. seined, sein'ing to fish with a seine —sein'er n.

Seine (sān; Fr sen) river in N France, flowing through Paris

seis·mic (sīz'mik) adj. [< Gr seismos, earthquake] of or caused by an earthquake —seis'mi·cal·ly adv.

seis·mo·graph (-mə graf') n. [see prec. & -GRAPH] an instrument that records the intensity and duration of earthquakes

seis·mol·o·gy (sīz mäl'ə jē) n. [see SEISMIC & -LOGY] the science dealing with earthquakes —seis·mo·log·i·cal (-mə läj'ik əl) adj. —seis·mol'o·gist n.

seize (sēz) vt. seized, seiz'ing [< ML sacire] 1 a) to take legal possession of b) to capture; arrest 2 to take forcibly and quickly 3 to grasp suddenly 4 to attack or afflict suddenly [seized with pain] —vi. to stick or jam: said of a machine: often with up

sei·zure (sē'zhər) n. 1 a seizing or being seized 2 a sudden attack, as of epilepsy

sel·dom (sel'dəm) adv. [OE seldan, strange] rarely; infrequently

se·lect (sə lekt') adj. [< L se-, apart + legere, to choose] 1 chosen in preference to others 2 choice; excellent 3 exclusive — vt., vi. to choose or pick out —se·lec'tor n.

se·lec·tion (-lek'shən) n. 1 a selecting or being selected 2 that or those selected

se·lec·tive adj. 1 of selection 2 careful in choosing; discriminating —se·lec'tiv'i·ty n.

selective service compulsory military service set by age, fitness, etc.

se·lect·man (-mən) n., pl. -men (-mən) one of a board of governing officers in most New England towns

se·lect·wom·an n., pl. -wom'en a woman who is one of a board of governing officers in most New England towns

se·le·ni·um (sə lēʹnē əm) *n.* ⟦ModL < Gr *selēnē*, the moon⟧ a nonmetallic chemical element, used in photoelectric devices: symbol, Se; at. no. 34

self (self) *n., pl.* **selves** ⟦OE⟧ **1** the identity, character, or essential qualities of any person or thing **2** one's own person as distinct from all others **3** one's own welfare or interest —*adj.* of the same kind, color, material, etc. [drapes with a *self* lining]

self- *prefix* of, by, in, to, or with oneself or itself The following list includes some common compounds formed with *self-* that do not have special meanings:

self-abasement	self-imposed
self-advancement	self-induced
self-appointed	self-indulgence
self-awareness	self-indulgent
self-complacent	self-inflicted
self-deception	self-love
self-defeating	self-pity
self-delusion	self-proclaimed
self-deprecating	self-protection
self-destructive	self-reproach
self-discipline	self-sealing
self-employed	self-supporting
self-examination	self-sustaining

self-ad·dressed *adj.* addressed to oneself [a *self-addressed* envelope]

self-ad·he·sive *adj.* made to stick without moistening

self-as·ser·tion *n.* a demanding to be acknowledged or an insisting upon one's rights, etc.

self-as·sur·ance *n.* confidence in oneself —**self'-as·sured'** *adj.*

self-cen·tered *adj.* **1** egocentric **2** selfish

self-con·fi·dence *n.* confidence in one's own abilities, etc. —**self'-con'fi·dent** *adj.*

self-con·scious *adj.* unduly conscious of oneself as an object of notice; specif., ill at ease —**self'-con'scious·ly** *adv.* —**self'-con'scious·ness** *n.*

self-con·tained *adj.* **1** keeping one's affairs to oneself **2** showing self-control **3** complete within itself

self-con·trol *n.* control of one's own emotions, desires, actions, etc. —**self'-con·trolled'** *adj.*

self-de·fense *n.* defense of oneself or of one's rights, beliefs, actions, etc.

self-de·ni·al *n.* denial or sacrifice of one's own desires or pleasures

self-de·scribed *adj.* described so by the person himself or herself [a *self-described* expert]

self-de·struct *vi.* **1** to destroy itself automatically **2** to greatly harm oneself as the result of inherent flaws

self-de·ter·mi·na·tion *n.* **1** a making up one's own mind **2** the right of a people to choose its own form of government —**self'-de·ter'mined** *adj.*

self-dis·cov·er·y *n.* a becoming aware of one's true potential, character, motives, etc.

self-ed·u·cat·ed *adj.* educated by oneself, with little formal schooling

self-ef·fac·ing *adj.* modest; retiring —**self'-ef·face'ment** *n.*

self-es·teem *n.* **1** self-respect **2** undue pride in oneself; conceit

self-ev·i·dent *adj.* evident without need of proof

self-ex·plan·a·to·ry *adj.* explaining itself; obvious

self-ex·pres·sion *n.* expression of one's own personality or emotions, esp. in the arts

self-ful·fill·ing *adj.* **1** bringing about one's personal goals **2** brought about chiefly as an effect of having been expected or predicted

self-gov·ern·ment *n.* government of a group by its own members —**self'-gov'ern·ing** *adj.*

self-help *n.* care for or improvement of oneself by one's own efforts

self·ie (selʹfē) *n.* ⟦SELF + -IE⟧ [Slang] a photograph that one takes of oneself, esp. with a cell phone

self-im·age *n.* one's conception of oneself and of one's own abilities, worth, etc.

self-im·por·tant *adj.* having an exaggerated opinion of one's own importance —**self'-im·por'tance** *n.*

self-in·ter·est *n.* **1** one's own interest or advantage **2** an exaggerated regard for this

self·ish *adj.* having or showing too much concern for one's own interests, etc., with little concern for others —**self'ish·ly** *adv.* —**self'ish·ness** *n.*

self·less *adj.* having or showing devotion to others' welfare; unselfish —**self'less·ly** *adv.* —**self'less·ness** *n.*

self-made *adj.* **1** made by oneself or itself **2** successful through one's own efforts

self-por·trait *n.* a portrait of oneself, done by oneself

self-pos·ses·sion *n.* full control of one's feelings, actions, etc. —**self'-pos·sessed'** *adj.*

self-pro·pelled *adj.* propelled by its own motor or power

self-re·crim·i·na·tion *n.* a blaming of oneself

self-reg·u·lat·ing *adj.* regulating oneself or itself, so as to function automatically or without outside control

self-re·li·ance *n.* reliance on one's own judgment, abilities, etc. —**self'-re·li'ant** *adj.*

self-re·spect *n.* proper respect for oneself —**self'-re·spect'ing** *adj.*

self-re·straint *n.* restraint imposed on oneself by oneself; self-control

self-right·eous *adj.* regarding oneself as being morally superior to others; smugly virtuous —**self'-right'eous·ly** *adv.* —**self'-right'eous·ness** *n.*

self-sac·ri·fice *n.* sacrifice of oneself or one's own interests for the benefit of others —**self'-sac'ri·fic'ing** *adj.*

self·same *adj.* identical

self-sat·is·fied *adj.* feeling or showing an often smug satisfaction with oneself —**self'-sat'is·fac'tion** *n.*

self-seek·er *n.* one who seeks mainly to further his or her own interests —**self'-seek'ing** *n., adj.*

self-serve *adj.* short for SELF-SERVICE

self-serv·ice *adj.* of or being a store, cafeteria, etc. set up so that customers serve themselves

self-serv·ing *adj.* serving one's own selfish interests

self-styled *adj.* so called only or primarily by oneself

self-suf·fi·cient *adj.* able to get along without help; independent —**self'-suf·fi'cien·cy** *n.*

self-taught *adj.* having taught oneself through one's own efforts

self-willed *adj.* stubborn; obstinate

self-wind·ing (-wīn'diŋ) *adj.* wound automatically, as some wristwatches

sell (sel) *vt.* **sold**, **sell'ing** 〚OE *sellan*, to give〛 **1** to exchange (goods, services, etc.) for money, etc. **2** to offer for sale **3** to promote the sale of —*vi.* **1** to engage in selling **2** to be sold (*for* or *at*) **3** to attract buyers —**sell out 1** to get rid of completely by selling **2** [*Inf.*] *a*) to betray *b*) to compromise one's principles for profit —**sell'er** *n.*

sell·out *n.* [*Inf.*] **1** a selling out; betrayal **2** a show, game, etc. for which all seats have been sold

selt·zer (selt'sər) *n.* 〚< *Niederselters*, Germany〛 **1** [*often* **S-**] natural, effervescent mineral water **2** any carbonated water, often flavored

sel·vage or **sel·vedge** (sel'vij) *n.* 〚< SELF + EDGE〛 a specially woven edge that prevents cloth from raveling

selves (selvz) *n. pl. of* SELF

se·man·tics (sə man'tiks) *pl.n.* 〚< Gr *sēmainein*, to show〛 the study of the meanings of words —**se·man'tic** *adj.*

sem·a·phore (sem'ə fôr') *n.* 〚< Gr *sēma*, sign + *pherein*, to bear〛 any apparatus or system for signaling, as by lights, flags, etc.

sem·blance (sem'bləns) *n.* 〚< L *similis*, like〛 **1** outward appearance **2** a likeness or copy

se·men (sē'mən) *n.* 〚L, seed〛 the fluid secreted by the male reproductive organs, containing sperm cells

se·mes·ter (sə mes'tər) *n.* 〚< L *sex*, six + *mensis*, month〛 either of the two terms usually making up a school year

sem·i (sem'ī') *n.* [*Inf.*] a semitrailer and its attached TRACTOR (*n.* 2)

semi- 〚L〛 *prefix* **1** half **2** partly, not fully **3** twice in a (specified period)

sem·i·an·nu·al (sem'ē an'yŏō əl) *adj.* happening, coming, etc. every half year

sem·i·au·to·mat·ic *adj.* designating an automatic weapon requiring a trigger pull for each round fired —*n.* a semiautomatic firearm

sem·i·cir·cle (sem'i sur'kəl) *n.* a half circle —**sem'i·cir'cu·lar** (-kyə lər) *adj.*

sem·i·co·lon *n.* a mark of punctuation (;) indicating a degree of separation greater than that marked by the comma

sem·i·con·duc·tor *n.* a substance, as germanium, used as in transistors

sem·i·con·scious *adj.* not fully conscious or awake

sem·i·fi·nal (sem'i fīn'əl; *for n.,* sem'ī fīn'əl) *adj.* coming just before the final match, as of a tournament —*n.* a semifinal match, etc.

sem·i·month·ly (sem'i munth'lē) *adj.* done, happening, etc. twice a month —*adv.* twice monthly

sem·i·nal (sem'ə nəl) *adj.* 〚see SEMEN〛 **1** of seed or semen **2** being a source **3** of essential importance; specif., *a*) basic; central *b*) crucial

sem·i·nar (sem'ə när') *n.* 〚see fol.〛 **1** a group of supervised students doing research **2** a course for such a group

sem·i·nar·y (sem'ə ner'ē) *n., pl.* **-nar'ies** 〚< L *seminarium*, nursery for plants〛 a school where ministers, priests, or rabbis are trained —**sem'i·nar'i·an** *n.*

Sem·i·nole (sem'ə nōl') *n., pl.* **-noles'** or **-nole'** a member of a North American Indian people of S Florida & Oklahoma

se·mi·ot·ics (sē'mē ät'iks) *n.* 〚< Gr *sēmeion*, sign〛 *Philos.* a general theory of signs and symbols; esp., the analysis of signs in language

sem·i·pre·cious (sem'i presh'əs) *adj.* designating gems, as the garnet, turquoise, etc., of lower value than precious stones

sem·i·pri·vate *adj.* of a hospital room with two, three, or sometimes four beds

sem·i·pro·fes·sion·al *n.* a person who engages in a sport for pay but not as a regular occupation: also **sem'i·pro'**

sem·i·skilled *adj.* of or doing manual work requiring only limited training

Sem·ite (sem'īt') *n.* 〚< Heb *Shem*, son of Noah〛 a member of any of the peoples speaking a Semitic language

Se·mit·ic (sə mit'ik) *n.* a major group of African and Asian languages, including Hebrew, Arabic, etc. —*adj.* designating or of the Semites or their languages, etc.

sem·i·tone (sem'i tōn') *n. Music* the difference in pitch between any two immediately adjacent keys on the piano

sem·i·trail·er *n.* a detachable trailer designed to be attached to a coupling at the rear of a TRACTOR (*n.* 2)

sem·i·trop·i·cal *adj.* almost tropical; subtropical

sem·i·week·ly *adj.* done, happening, etc. twice a week —*adv.* twice weekly

sem·o·li·na (sem'ə lē'nə) *n.* 〚It〛 coarse flour from hard wheat

Sen *abbrev.* **1** Senate **2** Senator **3** [*also* **s-**] senior

sen·ate (sen'it) *n.* 〚< L *senex*, old〛 **1** a legislative assembly **2** [**S-**] the upper house of the U.S. Congress or of most of the U.S. state legislatures

sen·a·tor (sen'ət ər) *n.* a member of a senate —**sen·a·to·ri·al** (sen'ə tôr'ē əl) *adj.*

send (send) *vt.* **sent**, **send'ing** 〚OE *sendan*〛 **1** to cause to go or be transmitted; dispatch; transmit **2** to cause (a person) to go **3** to impel; drive **4** to cause to happen, come, etc. —**send for 1** to summon **2** to place an order for —**send'er** *n.*

send-off *n.* [Inf.] **1** a farewell demonstration for someone starting out on a trip, career, etc. **2** a start given to someone or something

Sen·e·gal (sen′i gôl′) country on the W coast of Africa

se·nile (sē′nīl′) *adj.* [< L *senex*, old] **1** of or resulting from old age **2** showing the deterioration accompanying old age, esp. confusion, memory loss, etc. —**se·nil·i·ty** (si nil′ə tē) *n.*

sen·ior (sēn′yər) *adj.* [< L *senex*, old] **1** older: written *Sr.* after a father's name if his son's name is the same **2** of higher rank or longer service **3** of or for seniors —*n.* **1** one who is older, of higher rank, etc. **2** a student in the last year of high school or college **3** *short for* SENIOR CITIZEN

senior citizen an elderly person, esp. one who is retired

senior high school high school, usually grades 10, 11, and 12

sen·ior·i·ty (sēn yôr′ə tē) *n., pl.* **-ties 1** a being senior **2** status, priority, etc. achieved by length of service in a given job

sen·na (sen′ə) *n.* [< Ar *sanā*, cassia plant] the dried leaflets of a tropical cassia plant used, esp. formerly, as a laxative

se·ñor (se nyôr′) *n., pl.* **se·ño·res** (-nyô′res) [Sp] a man; gentleman: as a title, equivalent to *Mr.* or *Sir*

se·ño·ra (se nyô′rä) *n.* [Sp] a married woman: as a title, equivalent to *Mrs.* or *Madam*

se·ño·ri·ta (se′nyô rē′tä) *n.* [Sp] an unmarried woman or girl: as a title, equivalent to *Miss*

sen·sa·tion (sen sā′shən) *n.* [< L *sensus*, sense] **1** the receiving of sense impressions through hearing, seeing, etc. **2** a conscious sense impression **3** a generalized feeling [a *sensation* of joy] **4** *a*) a feeling of general excitement *b*) the cause of such a feeling

sen·sa·tion·al *adj.* **1** arousing intense interest **2** intended to shock, thrill, etc. —**sen·sa′tion·al·ism′** *n.*

sense (sens) *n.* [< L *sentire*, to feel] **1** any faculty of receiving impressions through body organs; sight, touch, taste, smell, or hearing **2** *a*) feeling, perception, etc. through the senses *b*) a generalized feeling or awareness **3** an ability to appreciate some quality [a *sense* of humor] **4** sound judgment **5** [*pl.*] normal ability to reason [to come to one's *senses*] **6** meaning, as of a word —*vt.* **sensed, sens′ing 1** to perceive **2** to detect as by sensors —**in a sense** to a limited degree —**make sense** to be intelligible or logical

sense·less *adj.* **1** unconscious **2** stupid; foolish **3** meaningless

sen·si·bil·i·ty (sen′sə bil′ə tē) *n., pl.* **-ties 1** the ability to respond to stimuli **2** [*often pl.*] (sensitive) awareness or responsiveness

sen·si·ble (-bəl) *adj.* **1** that can cause physical sensation **2** easily perceived **3** aware **4** having or showing good sense; wise —**sen′si·bly** *adv.*

sen·si·tive (-tiv) *adj.* **1** keenly susceptible to stimuli **2** tender; raw **3** highly perceptive or responsive **4** easily offended; touchy **5** detecting or reacting to slight changes [*sensitive* instruments] **6** of delicate or secret matters —**sen′si·tiv′i·ty** *n.*

sen·si·tize (-tīz′) *vt.* **-tized′, -tiz′ing** to make sensitive

sen·sor (sen′sər) *n.* a device to detect, measure, or record physical phenomena, as radiation, heat, etc.

sen·so·ry (sen′sər ē) *adj.* of the senses or sensation

sen·su·al (sen′shōō əl) *adj.* [< L *sensus*, sense] **1** of the body and the senses as distinguished from the intellect or spirit **2** connected or preoccupied with sexual pleasure —**sen′su·al′i·ty** (-al′ə tē) *n.* —**sen′su·al·ly** *adv.*

sen·su·ous (sen′shōō əs) *adj.* **1** of, derived from, or perceived by the senses **2** enjoying sensation

sent (sent) *vt., vi. pt. & pp. of* SEND

sen·tence (sen′təns) *n.* [< L *sententia*, opinion] **1** *a*) a decision as of a court; esp., the determination by a court of a punishment *b*) the punishment **2** a word or group of words, usually containing a subject and predicate, that states, asks, etc. —*vt.* **-tenced, -tenc·ing** to pronounce punishment upon (a convicted person)

sen·ten·tious (sen ten′shəs) *adj.* characterized by pompous moralizing

sen·tient (sen′shənt) *adj.* [see SENSE] of or capable of perception; conscious

sen·ti·ment (sen′tə mənt) *n.* [see SENSE] **1** a complex combination of feelings and opinions **2** an opinion, etc., often, one colored by emotion: *often used in pl.* **3** tender feelings **4** appeal to the emotions in literature, etc. **5** maudlin emotion

sen·ti·men·tal (sen′tə ment′'l) *adj.* **1** having or showing tender or delicate feelings **2** maudlin; mawkish **3** of or resulting from sentiment —**sen′ti·men′tal·ism′** *n.* —**sen′ti·men′tal·ist** *n.* —**sen′ti·men·tal′i·ty** (-tal′ə tē) *n.* —**sen′ti·men′tal·ly** *adv.*

sen·ti·men·tal·ize (-īz′) *vi., vt.* **-ized′, -iz′ing** to be sentimental or treat in a sentimental way

sen·ti·nel (sent′'n əl) *n.* [< L *sentire*, to sense] a guard or sentry

sen·try (sen′trē) *n., pl.* **-tries** [< ? obs. *centrinell*, var. of prec.] a sentinel; esp., a soldier posted to guard against danger

Seoul (sōl) capital of South Korea

se·pal (sē′pəl) *n.* [< Gr *skepē*, a covering + *petalon*, petal] any of the leaflike parts of the calyx of a flower

sep·a·ra·ble (sep′ə rə bəl) *adj.* that can be separated —**sep′a·ra·bly** *adv.*

sep·a·rate (sep′ə rāt′; *for adj.* sep′ə rit, sep′rit) *vt.* **-rat′ed, -rat′ing** [< L *se-*, apart + *parare*, arrange] **1** to set apart into sections, groups, etc.; divide **2** to keep apart by being between —*vi.* **1** to withdraw **2** to part, become disconnected, etc. **3** to go in different directions **4** to stop living together without a divorce —*adj.* 1 not joined, united, etc.; severéd 2 distinct; individual 3 not shared —**sep′a·rate·ly** *adv.* —**sep′a·ra′tor** *n.*

sep·a·ra·tion (sep′ə rā′shən) *n.* 1 a separating or being separated 2 the place this occurs; break; division 3 something that separates

sep·a·ra·tism (-rə tiz′əm) *n.* advocacy of political, religious, or racial separation —**sep′a·ra·tist** *n.*

se·pi·a (sē′pē ə) *n., adj.* [< Gr *sēpia*, cuttlefish secreting inky fluid] (of) a dark reddish-brown color

sep·sis (sep′sis) *n.* [see SEPTIC] a poisoning caused by the absorption of pathogenic microorganisms into the blood

Sep·tem·ber (sep tem′bər) *n.* [< L *septem*, seven: seventh month in Roman calendar] the ninth month of the year, having 30 days: abbrev. **Sept.**

sep·tet (sep tet′) *n.* [< L *septem*, seven] *Music* 1 a composition for seven voices or instruments 2 the seven performers of this

sep·tic (sep′tik) *adj.* [< Gr *sēpein*, to make putrid] causing, or resulting from, sepsis or putrefaction

sep·ti·ce·mi·a (sep′tə sē′mē ə) *n.* [see prec.] a disease caused by infectious microorganisms in the blood

septic tank an underground tank in which waste matter is putrefied and decomposed by bacteria

sep·tu·a·ge·nar·i·an (sep′tōō ə jə ner′ē ən) *n.* [< L *septuaginta*, seventy] a person between the ages of 70 and 80

Sep·tu·a·gint (sep′tōō ə jint′) *n.* [< L *septuaginta*, seventy: in tradition, done in 70 days] a translation into Greek of the Hebrew Scriptures

sep·tum (sep′təm) *n., pl.* **-tums** or **-ta** (-tə) [< L *saepire*, enclose, fence] *Biol.* a wall or part that separates, as in the nose or in a fruit

sep·ul·cher (sep′əl kər) *n.* [< L *sepelire*, bury] a vault for burial; tomb

se·pul·chral (sə pul′krəl) *adj.* 1 of sepulchers, burial, etc. 2 suggestive of the grave or burial; gloomy 3 deep and melancholy: said of sound

seq. *abbrev.* [L *sequentes*] the following

se·quel (sē′kwəl) *n.* [< L *sequi*, follow] 1 something that follows; continuation 2 a result; consequence 3 any literary work, film, etc. continuing a story begun in an earlier one

se·quence (sē′kwəns) *n.* [< L *sequi*, follow] 1 *a)* the coming of one thing after another; succession *b)* the order in which this occurs 2 a series 3 a resulting event 4 *Film* a succession of scenes forming a single episode

se·quen·tial (si kwen′shəl) *adj.* of or occurring in a sequence —**se·quen′tial·ly** *adv.*

se·ques·ter (si kwes′tər) *vt.* [< L *sequester*, trustee] 1 to set off or apart 2 to withdraw; isolate —**se·ques·tra·tion** (sē′kwə strā′shən) *n.*

se·quin (sē′kwin) *n.* [Fr; ult. < Ar *sikka*, a stamp, die] a spangle, esp. one of many sewn on fabric for decoration —**se′quined** *adj.*, **se′quinned**

se·quoi·a (si kwoi′ə) *n.* [after *Sequoyah* (1760?-1843), Cherokee scholar and metalsmith] 1 a very large coniferous tree of E Central California 2 REDWOOD (*n.* 1)

se·ra (sir′ə) *n.* alt. *pl.* of SERUM

se·ra·glio (si ral′yō) *n., pl.* **-glios** [< L *sera*, a lock] HAREM (*n.* 1)

se·ra·pe (sə rä′pē) *n.* [MexSp] a bright-colored wool blanket used as a garment by men in Mexico, etc.

ser·aph (ser′əf) *n., pl.* **-aphs** or **-a·phim′** (-ə fim′) [< Heb *serafim*, pl.] *Theol.* a heavenly being, or any of the highest order of angels —**se·raph·ic** (sə raf′ik) *adj.* —**se·raph′i·cal·ly** *adv.*

Serb (surb) *n.* 1 a person born or living in Serbia 2 a member of a Slavic people of Serbia and adjacent areas —*adj.* SERBIAN

Ser·bi·a (sur′bē ə) country in SE Europe —**Ser′bi·an** *adj., n.*

Ser·bo-Cro·a·tian (sur′bō krō ā′shən) *n.* the major Slavic language of Serbia, Montenegro, Bosnia and Herzegovina, and Croatia

ser·e·nade (ser′ə nād′) *n.* [ult. < L *serenus*, clear] 1 music played or sung at night, esp. by a lover 2 a piece of music like this —*vt., vi.* **-nad′ed**, **-nad′ing** to play or sing a serenade (to)

ser·en·dip·i·ty (ser′ən dip′ə tē) *n.* [after Pers tale *The Three Princes of Serendip*] 1 a seeming gift for finding good things accidentally 2 a fortunate, unexpected discovery —**ser′en·dip′i·tous** *adj.*

se·rene (sə rēn′) *adj.* [L *serenus*] 1 clear; unclouded 2 undisturbed; calm —**se·rene′ly** *adv.* —**se·ren′i·ty** (-ren′ə tē) *n.*, **se·rene′ness**

serf (surf) *n.* [< L *servus*, a slave] a person in feudal servitude, bound to a master's land and transferred with it to a new owner —**serf′dom** *n.*

serge (surj) *n.* [< L *sericus*, silken] a strong twilled fabric

ser·geant (sär′jənt) *n.* [< L *servire*, serve] 1 a noncommissioned officer ranking above a corporal 2 a police officer ranking next below a captain or a lieutenant

ser·geant-at-arms *n., pl.* **ser′geants-at-arms′** an officer appointed to keep order, as in a court or legislature

sergeant major *pl.* **sergeants major** the highest ranking noncommissioned officer

se·ri·al (sir′ē əl) *adj.* [< L *series*, a row, order] 1 appearing in a series of continuous parts at regular intervals 2 committing a given act repeatedly [a *serial* killer] —*n.* a story, etc. presented in serial form —**se′ri·al·i·za′tion** *n.* —**se′ri·al·ize′** *vt.* **-ized′**, **-iz′ing**

serial number one of a series of numbers given for identification

se·ries (sir′ēz) *n., pl.* **-ries** [L < *serere*, join together] a number of similar things or persons arranged in a row or coming one after another

se·ri·ous (sir′ē əs) *adj.* [< L *serius*] 1 earnest, grave, sober, etc. 2 not joking; sincere 3 requiring careful consideration 4 weighty 5 dangerous —**se'ri·ous·ly** *adv.* —**se'ri·ous·ness** *n.*

ser·mon (sur'mən) *n.* 〖< L *sermo*, a discourse〗 1 a speech on religion or morals, esp. by a member of the clergy 2 any serious talk on behavior, duty, etc., esp. a tedious one —**ser'mon·ize'** *vi.* **-ized', -iz'ing**

se·rous (sir'əs) *adj.* 1 of or containing serum 2 thin and watery

ser·pent (sur'pənt) *n.* 〖< L *serpere*, to creep〗 a snake

ser·pen·tine (-pən tēn', -tīn') *adj.* of or like a serpent; esp., *a*) cunning; treacherous *b*) coiled; winding —*n.* a mottled, greenish variety of rock

ser·rate (ser'āt') *adj.* 〖< L *serra*, a saw〗 having sawlike notches along the edge: said of some leaves : also **ser'rat'ed** —**ser·ra'tion** *n.*

ser·ried (ser'ēd) *adj.* 〖< LL *serare*, to lock〗 placed close together

se·rum (sir'əm) *n., pl.* **-rums** or **-ra** (-ə) 〖L, whey〗 1 a clear, watery animal fluid, as the yellowish fluid (**blood serum**) separating from a blood clot after coagulation 2 blood serum used esp. as an antitoxin, taken from an animal inoculated with a specific antigen

serv·ant (sur'vənt) *n.* 〖ult. < L *servire*, serve〗 1 a person employed by another, esp. to do household duties 2 a person devoted to another or to a cause, creed, etc.

serve (surv) *vt.* **served, serv'ing** 〖< L *servus*, slave〗 1 to work for as a servant 2 to do services for; aid; help 3 to do military or naval service for 4 to spend (a term of imprisonment, etc.) [to *serve* ten years] 5 to provide (customers, etc.) with goods or services 6 to set food, etc. before (a person) 7 to meet the needs of 8 to be used by [this hospital *serves* the whole city] 9 to function for [if memory *serves* me well] 10 to deliver (a summons, etc.) to (someone) 11 to hit (a tennis ball, etc.) in order to start play —*vi.* 1 to work as a servant 2 to do service [to *serve* in the navy] 3 to carry out the duties of an office 4 to be of service 5 to meet needs 6 to provide guests with food or drink 7 to be favorable: said of weather, etc. —*n.* a serving of the ball in tennis, etc. —**serve someone right** to be what someone deserves, for doing wrong

serv·er *n.* 1 one who serves 2 a thing for serving, as a tray 3 *Comput.* the central computer in a network, on which shared files, etc. are stored

serv·ice (sur'vis) *n.* 〖< L *servus*, slave〗 1 the occupation of a servant 2 *a*) public employment [diplomatic *service*] *b*) a branch of this; specif., the armed forces 3 work done for others [repair *service*] 4 any religious ceremony 5 *a*) benefit; advantage *b*) [*pl.*] friendly help; also, professional aid 6 the act or manner of serving food 7 a set of articles used in serving [a tea *service*] 8 a system of providing people with some utility, as water or gas 9 the act or manner of serving the ball in tennis, etc. —*vt.* **-iced, -ic·ing** 1 to furnish with a service 2 to make fit for service, as by repairing —**at someone's service** 1 ready to serve someone 2 ready for someone's use —**in service** functioning; operational —**of service** helpful

serv·ice·a·ble *adj.* 1 that can be of service; useful 2 that will give good service; durable

serv·ice·man (-man', -mən) *n., pl.* **-men'** (-men', -mən) 1 a member of the armed forces 2 a person whose work is repairing something [a TV *serviceman*]: also **service man**

service mark a word, etc. used like a trademark by a supplier of a service

service station a place selling gasoline, oil, etc., for motor vehicles

serv·ice·wom·an *n., pl.* **-wom'en** a woman who is a member of the armed forces

ser·vile (sur'vəl, -vīl') *adj.* 〖< L *servus*, slave〗 1 of slaves 2 like that of slaves or servants 3 humbly submissive —**ser·vil·i·ty** (sər vil'ə tē) *n.*

serv·ing *n.* a single portion of food; helping

ser·vi·tude (sur'və tōōd') *n.* 〖see SERF〗 1 slavery or bondage 2 work imposed to punish a crime

ser·vo (sur'vō) *n., pl.* **-vos** *short for:* 1 SERVOMECHANISM 2 SERVOMOTOR

ser·vo·mech·a·nism *n.* a system using one or more sensors and usually an electric motor to provide fine mechanical control

ser·vo·mo·tor *n.* an electric motor used in a servomechanism

ses·a·me (ses'ə mē') *n.* 〖of Semitic origin〗 1 a plant whose edible seeds yield an oil 2 its seeds

ses·qui·cen·ten·ni·al (ses'kwi sen ten'ē əl) *adj.* 〖< L *sesqui-*, more by a half + CENTENNIAL〗 of a period of 150 years —*n.* a 150th anniversary

ses·sion (sesh'ən) *n.* 〖< L *sedere*, sit〗 1 *a*) the meeting of a court, legislature, etc. *b*) a series of such meetings *c*) the period of these 2 a school term 3 a period of activity of any kind

set (set) *vt.* **set, set'ting** 〖OE *settan*〗 1 to cause to sit; seat 2 to put in a specified place, condition, etc. [to *set* books on a shelf, *set* slaves free] 3 to put in a proper condition; fix (a trap for animals), adjust (a clock or dial), arrange (a table for a meal), fix (hair) in a desired style, etc., put (a broken bone, etc.) into normal position, etc. 4 to make settled, rigid, or fixed [pectin *sets* jelly] 5 to mount (gems) 6 to direct; point 7 to appoint; establish; fix (boundaries, the time for an event, a rule, a quota, etc.) 8 to furnish (an example) for others 9 to fit (words *to* music or music *to* words) 10 to arrange (type) for printing —*vi.* 1 to sit on eggs: said of a fowl 2 to become firm, hard, or fixed [this cement *sets* quickly] 3 to begin to move (*out, forth, off*, etc.) 4 to sink below the horizon [the sun *sets*] —*adj.* 1 fixed; established [a *set* time] 2 intentional 3 fixed; rigid; firm 4 obstinate 5 ready [get *set*] —*n.* 1 a setting or being set **2** the way or position in which a thing is set [the *set* of his jaw] **3** direction; tendency **4** the scenery for a play, etc. **5** a group of persons or things classed or belonging together **6** assembled equipment for radio or TV reception, etc. **7** *Tennis* a group of six or more games won by a margin of at least two —**set about** (or **in** or **to**) to begin —**set down** 1 to put in writing 2 to establish (rules, etc.) —**set forth** 1 to publish 2 to state —**set off** 1 to make prominent or enhance by contrast 2 to make explode —**set on** (or **upon**) to attack —**set up** 1 to erect 2 to establish; found

set·back *n.* 1 a reversal in progress 2 a required minimum distance, as of a building from a road

set·screw *n.* a screw used in regulating the tension of a spring, etc.

set·tee (se tē′) *n.* 1 a seat or bench with a back 2 a small sofa

set·ter *n.* a long-haired dog trained to hunt

set·ting *n.* 1 the act of one that sets 2 the position of a dial, etc. that has been set 3 a mounting, as of a gem 4 the time, place, etc., as of a story 5 actual physical surroundings

set·tle (set′′l) *vt.* **-tled, -tling** [< OE *setl*, a seat] 1 to put in order; arrange [to *settle* one's affairs] 2 to set in place firmly or comfortably 3 to colonize 4 to cause to sink and become more compact 5 to free (the nerves, etc.) from disturbance 6 to decide (doubt) 7 to end (a dispute) 8 to pay (a debt, etc.) —*vi.* 1 to stop moving and stay in one place 2 to descend, as fog does over a landscape, or gloom over a person 3 to become localized: said as of pain 4 to take up permanent residence 5 to sink [the house *settled*] 6 to become more dense by sinking, as sediment does 7 to become more stable 8 to reach an agreement or decision (*with* or *on*) 9 to accept less than one would ideally like —**set′tler** *n.*

set·tle·ment *n.* 1 a settling or being settled 2 a new colony 3 a village 4 an agreement

set-to *n.*, *pl.* **-tos′** [Inf.] 1 a fight 2 an argument

set·up *n.* 1 *a*) the plan, makeup, or arrangement of equipment, an organization, etc. *b*) the details of a situation, plan, etc. 2 [Inf.] a situation that has been unfairly prearranged for a desired result

sev·en (sev′ən) *adj.*, *n.* [OE *seofon*] one more than six; 7; VII —**sev′enth** *adj.*, *n.*

sev·en·teen (-tēn′) *adj.*, *n.* seven more than ten; 17; XVII —**sev′en·teenth′** (-tēnth′) *adj.*, *n.*

seventeen-year locust a cicada which lives underground for 13-17 years before emerging as an adult

seventh heaven perfect happiness

sev·en·ty (sev′ən tē) *adj.*, *n.*, *pl.* **-ties** seven times ten; 70; LXX —**the seventies** the years, from 70 through 79, as of a century —**sev′en·ti·eth** (-ith) *adj.*, *n.*

sev·er (sev′ər) *vt.*, *vi.* [ult. < L *separare*] to separate, divide, or divide off —**sev′er·ance** *n.*

sev·er·al (sev′ər əl) *adj.* [ult. < L *separ*] 1 separate; distinct 2 different; respective 3 more than two but not many; few —*pl.n.* a small number (*of*) —*pron.* [with *pl. v.*] a few —**sev′er·al·ly** *adv.*

se·vere (sə vir′) *adj.* **-ver′er, -ver′est** [< L *severus*] 1 harsh or strict, as in treatment 2 serious or grave, as in expression 3 rigidly accurate or demanding 4 extremely plain [a dress with *severe* lines] 5 intense [*severe* pain] 6 rigorous; trying —**se·vere′ly** *adv.* —**se·vere′ness** *n.*, **se·ver′i·ty** (-ver′ə tē)

Se·ville (sə vil′) city in SW Spain

Sè·vres (sev′rə; *Fr* se′vr′) *n.* [after *Sèvres*, SW suburb of Paris, where made] a type of fine French porcelain

sew (sō) *vt.*, *vi.* **sewed, sewn** (sōn) or **sewed, sew′ing** [OE *siwian*] 1 to fasten with stitches made with needle and thread 2 to make, mend, etc. by sewing —**sew up** [Inf.] to get full control of 2 to make sure of success in —**sew′er** *n.*

sew·age (sōō′ij) *n.* the waste matter carried off by sewers or drains

sew·er (sōō′ər) *n.* [ult. < L *ex*, out + *aqua*, water] a pipe or drain, usually underground, used to carry off water and waste matter

sew·er·age *n.* 1 a system of sewers 2 SEWAGE

sew·ing *n.* 1 the act of one who sews 2 something to be sewn

sewing machine a machine with a mechanically driven needle used for sewing

sex (seks) *n.* [< L *sexus*] 1 either of two divisions, male or female, into which persons, animals, or plants are divided 2 the character of being male or female 3 the attraction between the sexes 4 sexual intercourse —*adj.* SEXUAL

sex- [< L *sex*, six] *combining form* six

sex·a·ge·nar·i·an (sek′sə ji ner′ē ən) *n.* [< L] a person between the ages of 60 and 70

sex appeal the physical charm that makes someone sexually attractive

sex chromosome a sex-determining chromosome in the germ cells: eggs carry an X chromosome and spermatozoa either an X or a Y chromosome, with a female resulting from an XX pairing and a male from an XY

sex·ism *n.* discrimination against people, esp. women, on the basis of sex —**sex′ist** *adj.*, *n.*

sex·tant (seks′tənt) *n.* [< L *sextans*, a sixth part (of a circle)] an instrument for measuring the angular distance of the sun, a star, etc. from the horizon, as to determine position at sea

sex·tet (seks tet′) *n.* [ult. < L *sex*, six] 1 a group of six 2 *Music* a composition for six voices or instruments, or its six performers

sex·ton (seks′tən) *n.* [ult. < L *sacer*, sacred] a church official who maintains church property

sex·u·al (sek′shōō əl) *adj.* of or involving sex, the sexes, the sex organs, etc. —**sex′u·al·ly** *adv.* —**sex·u·al′i·ty** (-al′ə tē) *n.*

sexual harassment inappropriate, unwelcome behavior, esp. by an employer or colleague, that is sexual in nature

sexual intercourse a joining of the sexual organs of a male and a female human

sexual orientation the direction of one's sexual interest toward members of the same, opposite, or both sexes

sex·y *adj.* **-i·er, -i·est 1** [Inf.] exciting or intended to excite sexual desire **2** [Slang] exciting, glamorous, etc. —**sex′i·ly** *adv.* —**sex′i·ness** *n.*

Sey·chelles (sā shelz′, –shelz′) country on a group of islands in the Indian Ocean, northeast of Madagascar

sf or **SF** *abbrev.* science fiction

Sgt *abbrev.* Sergeant

sh (sh) *interj.* used to ask for silence

shab·by (shab′ē) *adj.* **-bi·er, -bi·est** ⟦OE *sceabb*, scab⟧ **1** rundown; dilapidated **2** *a*) ragged; worn *b*) wearing worn clothing **3** mean; shameful [*shabby* treatment] —**shab′bi·ly** *adv.* —**shab′bi·ness** *n.*

shack (shak) *n.* ⟦< ?⟧ a small, crudely built house or cabin; shanty

shack·le (shak′əl) *n.* ⟦OE *sceacel*⟧ **1** a metal fastening, usually in pairs, for the wrist or ankle of a prisoner; fetter **2** anything that restrains freedom, as of expression **3** a device for fastening or coupling —*vt.* **-led, -ling 1** to put shackles on **2** to restrain in freedom of expression or action

shad (shad) *n., pl.* **shad** or **shads** ⟦OE *sceadd*⟧ an American coastal food fish

shade (shād) *n.* ⟦OE *sceadu*⟧ **1** comparative darkness caused by an object cutting off rays of light **2** an area with less light than its surroundings **3** degree of darkness of a color [*shades* of blue] **4** *a*) a small difference [*shades* of opinion] *b*) a slight amount or degree **5** [Chiefly Literary] a ghost **6** a device used to screen from light [a window *shade*] **7** [*pl.*] [Slang] sunglasses —*vt.* **shad′ed, shad′ing 1** to screen from light **2** to darken; dim **3** to represent shade in (a painting, etc.) —*vi.* to change slightly or by degrees —**shades of** *exclamation used to refer to a reminder of the past* —**the shades** Gr. & Rom. Myth. the spirits of the dead in Hades

shad·ing *n.* **1** a shielding against light **2** shade in a picture **3** a small variation

shad·ow (shad′ō) *n.* ⟦< OE *sceadu*, shade⟧ **1** (a) shade cast by a body intercepting light rays **2** gloom or that which causes gloom **3** a shaded area in a picture **4** a ghost **5** a remnant; trace —*vt.* **1** to throw a shadow upon **2** to follow closely, esp. in secret —**shad′ow·y** *adj.*

shad·ow·box *vi.* Boxing to spar with an imaginary opponent in training

shad·y (shā′dē) *adj.* **-i·er, -i·est 1** giving shade **2** shaded; full of shade **3** [Inf.] of questionable character —**shad′i·ness** *n.*

shaft (shaft) *n.* ⟦OE *sceaft*⟧ **1** an arrow or spear, or its stem **2** anything hurled like a missile [*shafts* of wit] **3** a long, slender part

or object, as a pillar, a bar transmitting motion to a mechanical part, or either of the poles between which an animal is harnessed to a vehicle **4** a long, narrow passage sunk into the earth **5** a vertical opening passing through a building, as for an elevator —*vt.* [Slang] to cheat, trick, exploit, etc.

shag[1] (shag) *n.* ⟦< OE *sceacga*, rough hair⟧ a rough, heavy nap, as on some cloth

shag[2] (shag) *vt.* **shagged, shag′ging** to chase after and retrieve (baseballs hit in batting practice)

shag·gy *adj.* **-gi·er, -gi·est 1** covered with long, coarse hair or wool **2** unkempt, straggly, etc. **3** having a rough nap [a *shaggy* carpet]

shah (shä) *n.* ⟦Pers *šāh*⟧ the title of any of the former rulers of Iran

shake (shāk) *vt., vi.* **shook, shak′en, shak′ing** ⟦OE *sceacan*⟧ **1** to move quickly up and down, back and forth, etc. **2** to bring, force, mix, etc. by brisk movements **3** to tremble or cause to tremble **4** *a*) to become or cause to become unsteady *b*) to unnerve or become unnerved **5** to clasp (another's hand), as in greeting **6** [Inf.] to get away from or rid of: often with *off* —*n.* **1** an act of shaking **2** a wood shingle **3** *short for* MILKSHAKE **4** [*pl.*] [Inf.] a convulsive trembling: usually with *the* —**no great shakes** [Inf.] not outstanding —**shake down 1** to cause to fall by shaking **2** [Slang] to extort money from

shake·down *n.* **1** [Slang] an extortion of money, as by blackmail **2** a thorough search —*adj.* for testing new equipment, etc. [a *shakedown* cruise]

shake·out *n.* a drop in economic activity that eliminates unprofitable businesses, etc.

shak·er *n.* **1** one that shakes **2** a device used in shaking **3** [S–] a member of a religious sect that founded celibate communities in the U.S. in the 1700s and 1800s

Shake·speare (shāk′spir), **William** 1564–1616; Eng. poet & dramatist —**Shake·spear′e·an** *adj., n.*, **Shake·spear′i·an**

shake·up *n.* a shaking up; specif., an extensive reorganization

shak·y *adj.* **-i·er, -i·est 1** not firm; weak or unsteady **2** *a*) trembling *b*) nervous **3** not reliable; questionable —**shak′i·ness** *n.*

shale (shāl) *n.* ⟦< OE *scealu*, shell⟧ a rock formed of hard clay: it splits easily into thin layers

shale oil oil distilled from a hard shale containing a greasy organic solid

shall (shal) *v.aux. pt.* **should** ⟦OE *sceal*⟧ **1** used in the first person to indicate simple future time **2** used in the second or third person, esp. in formal speech or writing, to express determination, compulsion, obligation, or necessity See usage note at WILL[2]

shal·lot (shə lät′, shal′ət) *n.* ⟦< OFr *eschaloigne*, scallion⟧ **1** a small onion whose clustered bulbs are used for flavoring **2** GREEN ONION

shal·low (shal′ō) *adj.* ⟦ME *shalowe*⟧ **1** not deep **2** lacking depth of character, intellect, etc. —*n*. [*usually pl., often with sing. v.*] SHOAL² (*n*. 1)

shalt (shalt) *v.aux. archaic* 2d pers. sing., pres. indic., of SHALL: used with *thou*

sham (sham) *n*. ⟦< ? shame⟧ something false or fake; person or thing that is a fraud —*adj*. false or fake —*vt., vi.* **shammed, sham′ming** to pretend; feign

sham·ble (sham′bəl) *vi.* -**bled, -bling** ⟦< obs. use in *shamble legs*, bench legs⟧ to walk clumsily; shuffle —*n*. a shambling walk

sham·bles *n*. ⟦ME *schamel*, butcher's bench; ult. < L⟧ 1 a slaughterhouse 2 a scene of great slaughter, destruction, or disorder

shame (shām) *n*. ⟦OE *scamu*⟧ 1 a painful feeling caused by awareness of one's improper behavior, etc. 2 dishonor or disgrace 3 something regrettable or outrageous —*vt*. **shamed, sham′ing** 1 to cause to feel shame 2 to dishonor or disgrace 3 to force by a sense of shame —**put to shame** 1 to cause to feel shame 2 to surpass; outdo —**shame′ful** *adj*. —**shame′ful·ly** *adv*. —**shame′ful·ness** *n*.

shame·faced *adj*. showing shame; ashamed

shame·less *adj*. having or showing no shame, modesty, or decency; brazen —**shame′less·ly** *adv*. —**shame′less·ness** *n*.

sham·poo (sham poo̅′) *vt.* **-pooed′, -poo′ing** ⟦Hindi *chāmpnā*, to press⟧ 1 to wash (the hair) 2 to wash (a rug, sofa, etc.) —*n*. 1 a shampooing 2 a liquid soap, etc. used for this

sham·rock (sham′räk′) *n*. ⟦Ir *seamar*, clover⟧ a plant, esp. a clover, with leaflets in groups of three: the emblem of Ireland

shang·hai (shaŋ′hī′) *vt.* ⟦< such kidnapping for crews on route to China⟧ to kidnap, usually by drugging, for service aboard ship

Shang·hai (shaŋ′hī′) seaport in E China

shank (shaŋk) *n*. ⟦OE *scanca*⟧ 1 the part of the leg between the knee and ankle in humans, or a corresponding part in animals 2 the whole leg 3 the part between the handle and the working part of a tool, etc. 4 [Slang] a homemade or contraband knife —**shank of the evening** early evening

shan't (shant) *contr*. shall not

shan·ty (shan′tē) *n., pl.* **-ties** ⟦< CdnFr *chantier*, workshop⟧ a small, shabby dwelling; shack; hut

shape (shāp) *n*. ⟦< OE (*ge*)*sceap*, a form⟧ 1 that quality of a thing which depends on the relative position of all the points on its surface; physical form 2 the contour of the body 3 definite or regular form [to begin to take *shape*] 4 good physical condition —*vt*. **shaped, shap′ing** 1 to give definite shape to 2 to arrange, express, etc. (a plan, etc.) in definite form 3 to adapt [*shaped* to our needs] —**shape up** [Inf.] 1 to develop to a definite form, satisfactorily, etc. 2 to behave as required —**take shape** to begin to have definite form —**shape′less** *adj*. —**shape′less·ness** *n*.

shape·ly *adj.* **-li·er, -li·est** having a pleasing figure: used esp. of a woman

shard (shärd) *n*. ⟦OE *sceard*⟧ a broken piece, esp. of pottery

share¹ (sher) *n*. ⟦OE *scearu*⟧ 1 a portion that belongs to an individual 2 any of the equal parts of capital stock of a corporation —*vt*. **shared, shar′ing** 1 to distribute in shares 2 to receive, use, etc. in common with others —*vi*. to have a share (*in*)

share² (sher) *n*. ⟦OE *scear*⟧ a plowshare

share·crop *vi., vt.* **-cropped′, -crop′ping** to work (land) for a share of the crop, esp. as a tenant farmer —**share′crop′per** *n*.

share·hold·er *n*. a person who owns shares of stock in a corporation

shark¹ (shärk) *n*. ⟦prob. < Ger *schurke*, scoundrel⟧ 1 a swindler 2 [Slang] an expert in an activity

shark² (shärk) *n*. ⟦< ?⟧ a large, predatory sea fish with a tough, usually grayish skin

shark·skin *n*. a smooth, silky cloth of cotton, wool, rayon, etc.

sharp (shärp) *adj*. ⟦OE *scearp*⟧ 1 having a fine edge or point for cutting or piercing 2 having a point or edge; not rounded 3 not gradual; abrupt 4 clearly defined; distinct [a *sharp* contrast] 5 quick in perception; clever 6 attentive; vigilant 7 crafty; underhanded 8 harsh; severe [a *sharp* temper] 9 violent [a *sharp* attack] 10 brisk; active 11 intense [a *sharp* pain] 12 pungent 13 nippy [a *sharp* wind] 14 [Slang] stylishly dressed 15 *Music* above the true pitch —*adv*. 1 in a sharp manner; specif., *a*) abruptly or briskly *b*) attentively or alertly *c*) *Music* above the true pitch 2 precisely [one o'clock *sharp*] —*n*. 1 [Inf.] an expert or adept 2 *Music a*) a tone one half step above another *b*) the symbol (♯) for such a note —*vt., vi. Music* to make, sing, or play sharp —**sharp′ly** *adv*. —**sharp′ness** *n*.

sharp·en *vt., vi.* to make or become sharp or sharper —**sharp′en·er** *n*.

sharp·er *n*. a swindler or cheat

sharp-eyed *adj*. having keen sight or perception: also **sharp′-sight′ed** *adj*.

sharp·shoot·er *n*. a good marksman

sharp-tongued *adj*. using sharp or harshly critical language

sharp-wit·ted (-wit′id) *adj*. thinking quickly and effectively

shat·ter (shat′ər) *vt., vi.* ⟦ME *schateren*, scatter⟧ 1 to break or burst into pieces suddenly, as with a blow 2 to damage or be damaged severely

shat·ter·proof *adj*. that will resist shattering

shave (shāv) *vt.* **shaved, shaved** or **shav′en, shav′ing** ⟦OE *sceafan*⟧ 1 to cut away thin slices or sections from 2 *a*) to cut off (hair) at the surface of the skin *b*) to cut the hair to the surface of (the face, etc.) *c*) to cut the beard of (a person) 3 to barely touch in passing; graze —*vi*. to cut off a beard with a razor, etc. —*n*. the act or an instance of shaving

shav·er *n*. 1 a person who shaves 2 an instrument used in shaving, esp. one with electrically operated cutters 3 [Inf.] a boy; lad

shav·ing *n*. 1 the act of one who shaves 2 a thin piece of wood, metal, etc. shaved off

Shaw (shô), **George Ber·nard** (bər närd′,

bur'nərd) 1856-1950; Brit. dramatist & critic, born in Ireland —**Sha·vi·an** (shā'vē ən) *adj., n.*

shawl (shôl) *n.* ⟦prob. < Pers *shāl*⟧ a cloth worn as a covering for the head or shoulders

shay (shā) *n.* ⟦< CHAISE, assumed as pl.⟧ [Dial.] a light carriage; chaise

she (shē) *pron., pl.* see THEY ⟦< OE *seo*⟧ the woman, girl, or female animal previously mentioned —*n., pl.* **shes** a female

sheaf (shēf) *n., pl.* **sheaves** ⟦OE *sceaf*⟧ 1 a bundle of cut stalks of grain, etc. 2 a collection, as of papers, bound in a bundle

shear (shir) *vt.* **sheared**, **sheared** or **shorn**, **shear'ing** ⟦OE *scieran*⟧ 1 to cut with or as with shears 2 to clip (hair) from (the head), (wool) from (sheep), etc. 3 to divest (someone) *of* a power, etc. —*n.* a shearing —**shear' er** *n.*

shears *pl.n.* 1 a large pair of scissors 2 a large cutting tool or machine with opposed blades

sheath (shēth) *n., pl.* **sheaths** (shēthz, shēths) ⟦OE *sceath*⟧ 1 a case for the blade of a knife, sword, etc. 2 a covering resembling this, as the membrane around a muscle 3 a woman's closefitting dress

sheathe (shēth) *vt.* **sheathed**, **sheath'ing** 1 to put into a sheath 2 to enclose in a case or covering

sheath·ing (shē'thiŋ) *n.* something that sheathes, as boards, etc. forming the base for roofing or siding

she·bang (shə baŋ') *n.* ⟦prob. < Ir⟧ [Inf.] an affair, business, contrivance, etc.: chiefly in **the whole shebang**

shed' (shed) *n.* ⟦OE *scead*⟧ a small structure for shelter or storage

shed² (shed) *vt.* **shed**, **shed'ding** ⟦< OE *sceadan*, to separate⟧ 1 to pour out; emit 2 to cause to flow [to *shed* tears] 3 to cause to flow off [*oilskin sheds* water] 4 to cast off or lose (a natural growth, as hair, etc.) 5 to get rid of (something unwanted) [to *shed* a few pounds] —*vi.* to shed hair, etc. —**shed blood** to kill violently

sheen (shēn) *n.* ⟦< OE *sciene*, beautiful⟧ brightness; luster

sheep (shēp) *n., pl.* **sheep** ⟦< OE *sceap*⟧ 1 a cud-chewing mammal with heavy wool and edible flesh called *mutton*, closely related to goats, antelope, etc. 2 one who is timid, submissive, etc.

sheep·dog *n.* a dog trained to herd sheep

sheep·fold *n.* a pen or enclosure for sheep: also, chiefly Brit., **sheep'cote'** (-kōt') *n.*

sheep·herd·er *n.* a person who herds a flock of sheep; shepherd

sheep·ish *adj.* 1 embarrassed or chagrined 2 shy or bashful —**sheep'ish·ly** *adv.* —**sheep' ish·ness** *n.*

sheep·skin *n.* 1 the skin of a sheep 2 parchment or leather made from it 3 [Inf.] a diploma

sheer' (shir) *vi., vt.* ⟦var. of SHEAR⟧ to turn aside or cause to turn aside from a course; swerve

sheer² (shir) *adj.* ⟦< ON *skœrr*, bright⟧ 1 very thin; transparent: said of textiles 2 absolute; utter [*sheer* folly] 3 extremely steep 4 not mixed with anything; pure [*sheer* ice] —*adv.* very steeply

sheet' (shēt) *n.* ⟦OE *sceat*⟧ 1 a large piece of cotton, linen, etc., used on a bed 2 *a)* a single piece of paper *b)* [Inf.] a newspaper 3 a broad, continuous surface or expanse, as of flame or ice 4 a broad, thin piece of any material, as glass, plywood, or metal

sheet² (shēt) *n.* ⟦short for OE *sceatline*⟧ a rope for controlling the set of a sail

sheet·ing *n.* 1 cotton or linen material used for making sheets 2 material used to cover or line a surface [copper *sheeting*]

sheet lightning a sheetlike flash of light in the sky, caused by lightning reflected by thunderclouds

sheet metal metal rolled thin in the form of a sheet

sheet music music printed on unbound sheets of paper

sheik or **sheikh** (shēk, shāk) *n.* ⟦Ar *shaikh*, lit., old man⟧ the chief of an Arab family, tribe, or village

shek·el (shek'əl) *n.* ⟦Heb < *shakal*, weigh⟧ 1 a gold or silver coin of the ancient Hebrews 2 the monetary unit of Israel 3 [*pl.*] [Slang] money

shelf (shelf) *n., pl.* **shelves** ⟦prob. < MLowG *schelf*⟧ 1 a thin, flat board fixed horizontally to a wall, used for holding things 2 something like a shelf; specif., *a)* a ledge *b)* a sandy reef —**on the shelf** out of use, activity, etc.

shelf life the length of time a packaged food, etc. can be stored without deteriorating

shell (shel) *n.* ⟦OE *sciel*⟧ 1 a hard outer covering, as of a turtle, egg, nut, etc. 2 something like a shell in being hollow, empty, a covering, etc. 3 a light, narrow racing boat rowed by a team 4 an explosive artillery projectile 5 a small-arms cartridge —*vt.* 1 to remove the shell or covering from [to *shell* peas] 2 to bombard with shells from a large gun —**shell out** [Inf.] to pay out (money)

shel·lac or **shel·lack** (shə lak') *n.* ⟦< prec. & LAC⟧ a thin varnish containing lac and alcohol —*vt.* **-lacked'**, **-lack'ing** 1 to apply shellac to 2 [Slang] to defeat decisively

-shelled (sheld) *combining form* having a (specified kind of) shell

Shel·ley (shel'ē) 1 **Mary Woll·stone·craft** (wool'stən kraft') 1797-1851; Eng. novelist: second wife of Percy 2 **Per·cy Bysshe** (pur' sē bish) 1792-1822; Eng. poet

shell·fire *n.* the firing of artillery shells

shell·fish *n., pl.* **-fish'** or **-fish'es** any aquatic animal with a shell, esp. an edible one, as the clam or lobster

shel·ter (shel'tər) *n.* ⟦< ? OE *scield*, shield + *truma*, a troop⟧ 1 something that protects, as from the elements, danger, etc. 2 a being covered, protected, etc.; protection 3 a place that provides food and lodging on a temporary basis —*vt.* to provide shelter for; protect —*vi.* to find shelter

shelve (shelv) *vt.* **shelved**, **shelv'ing** 1 to

equip with shelves **2** to put on a shelf **3** to put aside; defer

shelves (shelvz) *n. pl. of* SHELF

shelv·ing (shel′viŋ) *n.* **1** material for shelves **2** shelves collectively

she·nan·i·gan (shi nan′i gən) *n.* ⟦altered < ? Ir *sionnachuighim*, I play the fox⟧ [Inf.] a deceitful or mischievous trick: *usually used in pl.*

shep·herd (shep′ərd) *n.* ⟦see SHEEP & HERD⟧ **1** one who herds or tends sheep **2** a religious leader **3** GERMAN SHEPHERD —*vt.* to herd, lead, etc. as a shepherd

shep·herd·ess (shep′ər·dis) *n.* a woman or girl who herds or tends sheep

sher·bet (shur′bət) *n.* ⟦< Ar *sharba(t)*, a drink⟧ a frozen dessert like an ice but with gelatin and, often, milk added: also, erroneously, **sher′bert** (-bərt)

sher·iff (sher′if) *n.* ⟦< OE *scir*, shire + *gerefa*, chief officer⟧ the chief law-enforcement officer of a county

Sher·lock Holmes (shur′läk′ hōmz, hōlmz) fictitious detective with great powers of deduction, in stories by Brit. writer Arthur Conan Doyle

Sher·pa (shur′pə, sher′-) *n. pl.* **-pas** or **-pa** a member of a Tibetan people of Nepal, famous as porters and guides in Himalayan mountaineering

sher·ry (sher′ē) *n., pl.* **-ries** ⟦after *Jerez*, Spain⟧ **1** a yellow or brown Spanish fortified wine **2** any similar wine

shh (sh: *often a prolonged sound*) *interj.* used to ask for silence

Shi·a (shē′ə) *n., pl.* **Shi′as** or **Shi′a** ⟦Ar *shī′a*, followers, faction, sect⟧ *var. of* SHIITE

shib·bo·leth (shib′ə leth′, -ləth) *n.* ⟦< Heb *shibolet*, a stream⟧ **1** *Bible* the test word used to distinguish the enemy: Judg. 12:4-6 **2** any phrase, custom, etc. peculiar to a certain party, class, etc.

shied (shīd) *vi., vt. pt. & pp. of* SHY¹, SHY²

shield (shēld) *n.* ⟦OE *scield*⟧ **1** a flat piece of metal, etc. worn on the forearm to ward off blows, etc. **2** one that guards, protects, etc. **3** anything shaped like a triangular shield with two curved sides — *vt., vi.* to defend; protect

shift (shift) *vt.* ⟦OE *sciftan*, to divide⟧ **1** to move from one person or place to another **2** to replace by another or others **3** to change the arrangement of (gears) —*vi.* **1** to change position, direction, etc. **2** to get along; manage [to *shift* for oneself] —*n.* **1** a shifting; transfer **2** a plan of conduct, esp. for an emergency **3** an evasion; trick **4** a gearshift **5** *a)* a group of people working earlier or later hours than another group at the same location *b)* their regular work period

shift·less *adj.* incapable, inefficient, lazy, etc. —**shift′less·ness** *n.*

shift·y *adj.* **-i·er**, **-i·est** of a tricky or deceitful nature; evasive —**shift′i·ly** *adv.* —**shift′i·ness** *n.*

Shih Tzu (shēd′zoō′, shēt′soō′) *pl.* **Shih Tzus** or **Shih Tzu** ⟦Mandarin *shihtzu*, lion⟧ a small dog with long, silky hair and short legs

shii·ta·ke (shē tä′kē) *n.* ⟦Jpn⟧ an edible Japanese mushroom

Shi·ite (shē′īt′) *n.* ⟦< SHIA⟧ an adherent of the second most widely practiced branch of Islam, revering a succession of 12 Imams as the rightful successors of Muhammad

shill (shil) [Slang] *n.* **1** a confederate of a gambler, auctioneer, etc. who pretends to bet, bid, etc. so as to lure others **2** one who promotes another's cause, esp. shamelessly —*vi.* to act as a shill

shil·le·lagh (shi lā′lē, -lə) *n.* ⟦after *Shillelagh*, Ir village⟧ a club or cudgel: used chiefly of or by the Irish

shil·ling (shil′iŋ) *n.* ⟦OE *scylling*⟧ **1** a former British monetary unit and coin, equal to ¹⁄₂₀ of a pound **2** the basic monetary unit of various countries

shil·ly-shal·ly (shil′ē shal′ē) *vi.* **-lied**, **-ly·ing** ⟦< *shall* I?⟧ to vacillate, esp. over trifles

shim (shim) *n.* ⟦< ?⟧ a thin wedge of wood, metal, etc. used as for filling space

shim·mer (shim′ər) *vi.* ⟦OE *scymrian*⟧ to shine with an unsteady light; glimmer —*n.* a shimmering light

shim·my (shim′ē) *n.* ⟦< a jazz dance < CHEMISE⟧ a marked vibration or wobble, as in a car's front wheels —*vi.* **-mied**, **-my·ing 1** to vibrate or wobble **2** to move by wiggling the torso [*shimmied* up a tree]

shin (shin) *n.* ⟦OE *scinu*⟧ the front part of the leg between the knee and the ankle —*vi.* **shinned**, **shin′ning** to climb a pole, etc. by gripping with hands and legs: with *up* or *down*: also **shin′ny**, **-nied**, **ny·ing**

shin·bone *n.* TIBIA

shin·dig (shin′dig′) *n.* ⟦< old informal *shindy*, commotion⟧ [Inf.] a dance, party, or other informal gathering

shine (shin) *vi.* **shone**, **shined**, **shin′ing** ⟦OE *scinan*⟧ **1** to emit or reflect light **2** to stand out; excel **3** to exhibit itself clearly [love *shining* from her face] —*vt.* **1** to direct the light of **2** to make shiny by polishing [to *shine* shoes] —*n.* **1** brightness **2** luster; gloss **3** *short for* SHOESHINE

shin·er (shi′nər) *n.* [Slang] BLACK EYE

shin·gle (shiŋ′gəl) *n.* ⟦OE *scindel*⟧ **1** a thin, wedge-shaped piece of wood, slate, etc. laid with others in overlapping rows, as in covering roofs **2** a small signboard, as that of a doctor —*vt.* **-gled**, **-gling** to cover (a roof, etc.) with shingles

shin·gles (shiŋ′gəlz) *n.* ⟦< L *cingere*, to gird⟧ *nontechnical name for* HERPES ZOSTER

shin-guard (shin′gärd′) *n.* a padded guard worn to protect the shins in some sports

shin·splints *pl.n.* ⟦< SHIN & *splint*, growth on bone of a horse's leg⟧ [*with sing. or pl. v.*] painful strain of muscles of the lower leg

Shin·to (shin′tō) *n.* ⟦Jpn < Chin *shen*, god + *tō*, *dō*, way⟧ a religion of Japan, emphasizing ancestor worship —**Shin′to·ism′** *n.*

shin·y (shi′nē) *adj.* **-i·er**, **-i·est 1** bright; shining **2** highly polished —**shin′i·ness** *n.*

ship (ship) *n.* ⟦OE *scip*⟧ **1** any large vessel for

traveling on deep water **2** an aircraft —*vt.*
shipped, ship′ping 1 to put or take on board
a ship **2** to send or transport by any carrier
[to *ship* coal by rail] **3** to take in (water)
over the side, as in a stormy sea **4** to put (an
object) in place on a vessel **5** [Inf.] to send
(*away, out,* etc.); get rid of —*vi.* to go aboard,
or travel by, ship —**ship′per** *n.*

-ship (ship) ⟦OE *-scipe*⟧ *suffix* **1** the quality
or state of being [*friendship*] **2** *a*) the rank
or office of [*professorship*] *b*) one having the
rank of [*lordship*] **3** skill as [*leadership*] **4** all
persons (of a specified group) collectively
[*readership*]

ship·board *n.* used chiefly in **on shipboard,**
aboard a ship

ship·build·er *n.* one whose business is building
ships —**ship′build′ing** *n.*

ship·mate *n.* a fellow sailor on the same ship

ship·ment *n.* **1** the shipping of goods **2** goods
shipped

ship of the line [Historical] a warship of the
largest class

ship·ping *n.* **1** the act or business of transporting goods **2** ships collectively, as of a nation
or port

shipping clerk an employee who prepares
goods for shipment, and keeps records of
shipments made

ship·shape *adj.* having everything neatly in
place; trim

ship·wreck *n.* **1** the remains of a wrecked
ship **2** the loss of a ship through storm, etc. **3**
ruin; failure —*vt.* to cause to undergo shipwreck

ship·yard *n.* a place where ships are built and
repaired

shire (shīr) *n.* ⟦OE *scir,* office⟧ in England, a
county

shirk (shurk) *vt., vi.* ⟦< ?⟧ to neglect or evade
(a duty, etc.) —**shirk′er** *n.*

shirr (shur) *vt.* ⟦< ?⟧ **1** to make shirring in
(cloth) **2** to bake (eggs) in buttered dishes

shirr·ing *n.* a gathering made in cloth by drawing the material up on parallel rows of short
stitches

shirt (shurt) *n.* ⟦OE *scyrte*⟧ **1** a garment worn
on the upper part of the body, usually with a
collar and a buttoned front **2** an undershirt
—**keep one's shirt on** [Slang] to remain patient or calm

shirt·tail *n.* the part of a shirt extending below
the waist

shirt·waist *n.* [Archaic] a woman's blouse tai-
lored like a shirt

shish ke·bab (shish′ kə bäb′) ⟦< Ar *shīsh,*
skewer + *kabāb,* kebab⟧ a dish of kebabs, esp.
lamb, stuck on a skewer, often with vegetables, and broiled

shiv (shiv) *n.* ⟦prob. < Romany *chiv,* blade⟧
[Slang] a knife

Shi·va (shē′və) *n.* Hindu god of destruction
and reproduction

shiv·er¹ (shiv′ər) *n.* ⟦ME *schievere*⟧ a fragment
—*vt., vi.* to break into fragments; shatter

shiv·er² (shiv′ər) *vi.* ⟦< ? OE *ceafl,* jaw⟧ to

shake or tremble, as from fear or cold —*n.* a
shaking, trembling, etc. —**shiv′er·y** *adj.*

shlep or **shlepp** (shlep) *n., vt., vi.* **shlepped,
shlep′ping** [Slang] *alt. sp. of* SCHLEP

shmaltz (shmôlts, shmälts) *n.* [Slang] *alt. sp.
of* SCHMALTZ

shoal¹ (shōl) *n.* ⟦OE *scolu*⟧ a school of fish

shoal² (shōl) *n.* ⟦< OE *sceald,* shallow⟧ **1** a
shallow place in a river, sea, etc. **2** a sandbar
forming a shallow place

shoat (shōt) *n.* ⟦ME *schote*⟧ a young, weaned
pig

shock¹ (shäk) *n.* ⟦< MFr *choquer,* to collide⟧ **1**
a sudden, powerful blow, shake, etc. **2** *a*) a
sudden emotional disturbance *b*) the cause
of this **3** an extreme stimulation of the nerves
by the passage of electric current through the
body **4** [Inf.] *short for* SHOCK ABSORBER **5** a
disorder of the blood circulation produced by
hemorrhage, disturbance of heart function,
etc. —*vt.* **1** to astonish, horrify, etc. **2** to produce electrical shock in —**shock′er** *n.*

shock² (shäk) *n.* ⟦ME *schokke*⟧ a number of
grain sheaves stacked together

shock³ (shäk) *n.* ⟦< ? prec.⟧ a thick, bushy
mass of hair

shock absorber a device, as on a motor vehicle, that absorbs the force of bumps and
jarring

shock·ing *adj.* **1** causing great surprise and
distress **2** disgusting —**shock′ing·ly** *adv.*

shock·proof *adj.* able to absorb shock without
being damaged

shock therapy the treatment of certain mental disorders by using electricity or drugs to
produce convulsions or coma

shock troops troops trained to lead an attack

shod (shäd) *vt. alt. pt. & pp. of* SHOE

shod·dy (shäd′ē) *n., pl.* **-dies** ⟦< ?⟧ an inferior
woolen cloth made from used fabrics —*adj.*
-di·er, -di·est 1 made of inferior material **2**
poorly done or made **3** contemptible; low
—**shod′di·ly** *adv.* —**shod′di·ness** *n.*

shoe (sho͞o) *n.* ⟦OE *sceoh*⟧ **1** an outer covering for the foot **2** *short for* HORSESHOE **3** the
part of a brake that presses against a wheel
—*vt.* **shod** or **shoed, shoe′ing** to furnish with
shoes —**fill someone's shoes** to take someone's place

shoe·horn *n.* an implement used to help slip
the heel of a foot into a shoe —*vt.* to force or
squeeze into a narrow space

shoe·lace *n.* a length of cord, etc. used for lac-
ing and fastening a shoe

shoe·mak·er *n.* one whose business is making
or repairing shoes

shoe·shine *n.* the cleaning and polishing of a
pair of shoes

shoe·string *n.* **1** a shoelace **2** a small amount
of capital [a business started on a *shoestring*]
—*adj.* **1** like a shoestring; long and narrow **2**
of or characterized by a small amount of
money

shoe tree a form made of wood, etc. inserted
in a shoe to stretch it or preserve its shape

sho·gun (shō′gun′) *n.* ⟦< Chin *chiang-chun*⟧

any of the hereditary governors of Japan who, until 1867, were de facto absolute rulers —**sho′gun·ate** (-gə nit) *n.*

shone (shōn) *vi., vt. alt. pt. & pp. of* SHINE

shoo (sho͞o) *interj.* go away! get out! —*vt.* **shooed, shoo′ing** to drive away, as by crying "shoo"

shoo-in *n.* [Inf.] one expected to win easily in a race, etc.

shook (sho͝ok) *vt., vi. pt. and dial. pp. of* SHAKE —**shook up** [Inf.] upset; agitated

shoot (sho͞ot) *vt.* **shot, shoot′ing** [OE *sceotan*] 1 to move swiftly over, by, etc. [to *shoot* the rapids] 2 to streak or vary (*with* another color, etc.) 3 to thrust or put forth 4 to discharge or fire (a bullet, arrow, etc.) 5 to send forth swiftly or with force 6 to hit, wound, etc. with a bullet, arrow, etc. 7 to photograph or film 8 *Sports a)* to throw or drive (a ball, etc.) toward the objective *b)* to score (a goal, points, etc.) —*vi.* 1 to move swiftly 2 to be felt suddenly, as pain 3 to grow rapidly 4 to jut out 5 to send forth a missile; discharge bullets, etc. 6 to use guns, etc. as in hunting —*n.* 1 a shooting trip, contest, etc. 2 a new growth; sprout 3 a session for photographing or filming —**shoot at** (or **for**) [Inf.] to strive for —**shoot′er** *n.*

shooting star METEOR (*n.* 1)

shoot-out or **shoot·out** *n.* 1 a battle with handguns, etc., as between police and criminals 2 *Sports* a procedure used to break a tie at the end of a game, esp. in soccer

shop (shäp) *n.* [OE *sceoppa*, booth] 1 a place where certain things are offered for sale; esp., a small store 2 a place where a particular kind of work is done —*vi.* **shopped, shop′ping** to visit shops to examine or buy goods —*vt.* [Inf.] to offer for sale to various prospective buyers: often with *around* —**talk shop** to discuss one's work

shop·keep·er *n.* one who owns or operates a shop, or small store

shop·lift *vt., vi.* to steal (articles) from a store during shopping hours —**shop′lift′er** *n.*

shop·per *n.* 1 one who shops 2 one hired to shop for others 3 one hired by a store to check competitors' prices, etc.

shopping center a complex of stores, restaurants, etc. with a common parking area

shop talk *n.* 1 the specialized words and idioms of those in the same work 2 talk about work, esp. after hours

shop·worn *adj.* soiled, faded, etc., as from having been displayed in a shop

shore¹ (shôr) *n.* [ME *schore*] land at the edge of a body of water

shore² (shôr) *n.* [ME *schore*] a prop, beam, etc. used for support, etc. —*vt.* **shored, shor′ing** to support as with shores; prop (*up*)

shore·bird *n.* a bird that lives or feeds near the shore

shore·line *n.* the edge of a body of water

shore patrol a detail of the U.S. Navy, Coast Guard, or Marine Corps acting as military police on shore

shorn (shôrn) *vt., vi. alt. pp. of* SHEAR

short (shôrt) *adj.* [OE *scort*] 1 not measuring much from end to end in space or time 2 not great in range or scope 3 not tall 4 brief; concise 5 not retentive [a *short* memory] 6 curt; abrupt 7 less than a sufficient or correct amount 8 crisp or flaky, as pastry rich in shortening 9 designating a sale of securities, etc. which the seller does not yet own but expects to buy later at a lower price —*n.* 1 something short 2 [*pl.*] *a)* short trousers *b)* a man's undergarment like these 3 *short for: a)* SHORTSTOP *b)* SHORT CIRCUIT —*adv.* 1 abruptly; suddenly 2 briefly; concisely 3 so as to be short in length 4 by surprise [caught *short*] —*vt., vi.* 1 to give less than what is needed or usual 2 *short for: a)* SHORTCHANGE *b)* SHORT-CIRCUIT —**in short** briefly —**run short** to have less than enough —**short of** 1 less than or lacking 2 without actually resorting to —**short′ness** *n.*

short·age *n.* a deficiency in the amount needed or expected; deficit

short·bread *n.* a rich, crumbly cake or cookie made with much shortening

short·cake *n.* a light biscuit or a sweet cake served with fruit, etc.

short·change *vt., vi.* **-changed′, -chang′ing** [Inf.] 1 to give less money than is due in change 2 to cheat by depriving of something due

short circuit 1 a usually accidental connection between two points in an electric circuit, resulting in excessive current flow that causes damage 2 popularly, a disrupted electric circuit caused by this —**short′-cir′cuit** *vt., vi.*

short·com·ing *n.* a defect or deficiency

short·cut *n.* 1 a shorter route 2 any way of saving time, effort, etc.

short·en *vt., vi.* to make or become short or shorter

short·en·ing (shôrt′'n iŋ, shôrt′niŋ) *n.* edible fat used to make pastry, etc. crisp or flaky

short·fall *n.* a falling short, or the amount of the shortage

short·hand *n.* any system of speed writing using symbols for words

short-hand·ed *adj.* short of workers

short-lived (-līvd′, -livd′) *adj.* having a short life span or existence

short·ly *adv.* 1 briefly 2 soon 3 abruptly and rudely; curtly

short order any food that can be cooked or served quickly when ordered

short-range *adj.* reaching over a short distance or period of time

short ribs the rib ends from the front half of a side of beef

short shrift very little care or attention —**make short shrift of** to dispose of quickly and impatiently

short·sight·ed *adj.* 1 NEARSIGHTED 2 lacking in foresight —**short′sight′ed·ly** *adv.* —**short′sight′ed·ness** *n.*

short-spo·ken *adj.* using few words, esp. to the point of rudeness; curt

short·stop *n. Baseball* the infielder usually positioned to the left of second base

short story a piece of prose fiction shorter than a short novel

short subject a short film, as that shown with a film feature

short-tem·pered *adj.* easily or quickly angered

short-term *adj.* for or extending over a short time

short ton 2,000 pounds: see TON

short-waist·ed (-wās'tid) *adj.* unusually short between shoulders and waistline

short·wave *n.* 1 a radio wave 200 meters or less in length: shorter than the waves used in commercial broadcasting 2 a radio or radio band for broadcasting or receiving short-waves: in full **shortwave radio**

short-wind·ed (-win'did) *adj.* easily put out of breath by exertion

shot¹ (shät) *n.* ⟦OE *sceot*⟧ 1 the act of shooting 2 range; scope 3 an attempt or try 4 a pointed, critical remark 5 the path of an object thrown, etc. 6 *a)* a projectile for a gun *b)* projectiles collectively 7 small pellets of lead or steel for a shotgun 8 the heavy metal ball used in the shot put 9 a marksman 10 a photograph or a film sequence 11 a hypodermic injection 12 a drink of liquor —**call the shots** [Inf.] to direct or control what is done

shot² (shät) *vt., vi. pt. & pp.* of SHOOT —*adj.* [Inf.] ruined or worn out

shot·gun *n.* 1 a gun for firing a charge of shot at short range 2 *Football* a formation in which the quarterback stands several yards behind the line of scrimmage to receive the ball —**ride shotgun** [Slang] to ride next to the driver of a vehicle

shot put a contest in which a heavy metal ball is propelled with an overhand thrust from the shoulder —**shot'-put'ter** *n.* —**shot'-put'ting** *n.*

should (shood) *v.aux.* ⟦OE *sceolde*⟧ 1 *pt.* of SHALL 2 used to express: *a)* obligation, duty, etc. [you *should* help] *b)* expectation or probability [he *should* be here soon] *c)* a future condition [if I *should* die tomorrow]

shoul·der (shōl'dər) *n.* ⟦OE *sculdor*⟧ 1 *a)* the joint connecting the arm or forelimb with the body *b)* the part of the body including this joint 2 [pl.] the two shoulders and the part of the back between them 3 a shoulderlike projection 4 the land along the edge of a paved road —*vt.* 1 to push along or through, as with the shoulder 2 to carry upon the shoulder 3 to assume the burden of — **turn (or give) a cold shoulder to** to snub or shun

shoulder blade SCAPULA

shoulder harness an anchored strap passing across the chest, used with a seat belt, as in a car: also called **shoulder belt**

shout (shout) *n.* ⟦ME *schoute*⟧ a loud cry or call — *vt., vi.* to utter or cry out in a shout —**shout'er** *n.*

shout-out *n.* [Slang] a public acknowledg-ment of recognition, gratitude, respect, etc.

shove (shuv) *vt., vi.* **shoved, shov'ing** ⟦OE *scufan*⟧ 1 to push, as along a surface 2 to push roughly —*n.* a push —**shove off** 1 to push (a boat) away from shore 2 [Inf.] to leave

shov·el (shuv'əl) *n.* ⟦OE *scofl*⟧ a tool with a broad scoop or blade and a long handle, for lifting and moving loose material —*vt.* **-eled** or **-elled, -el·ing** or **-el·ling** 1 to move with a shovel 2 to dig out with a shovel

shov·el·ful *n., pl.* **-fuls'** as much as a shovel will hold

show (shō) *vt.* **showed, shown** or **showed, show'ing** ⟦< OE *sceawian*⟧ 1 to bring or put in sight 2 to guide; conduct 3 to point out 4 to reveal, as by behavior 5 to prove; demonstrate 6 to bestow (favor, mercy, etc.) —*vi.* 1 to be or become seen; appear 2 to be noticeable 3 to finish third or better in a horse race —*n.* 1 a showing or demonstration 2 pompous display 3 pretense [sorrow that was mere *show*] 4 a public display or exhibition 5 a presentation of entertainment —**show off** 1 to make a display of 2 to attract attention to oneself intentionally —**show up** 1 to expose 2 to be seen 3 to arrive 4 to outperform

show·biz (-biz') *n.* [Inf.] SHOW BUSINESS

show·boat *n.* 1 a boat with a theater and actors who play river towns 2 [Slang] a showoff —*vi.* [Slang] to show off

show business the theater, films, TV, etc. as a business or industry

show·case *n.* a glass-enclosed case for displaying things, as in a store —*vt.* **-cased', -cas'ing** to display to good advantage

show·down *n.* [Inf.] a decisive confrontation or contest

show·er (shou'ər) *n.* ⟦OE *scur*⟧ 1 a brief fall of rain, etc. 2 a sudden, abundant fall or flow, as of sparks 3 a party at which gifts are presented to the guest of honor 4 a bath in which the body is sprayed from overhead with fine streams of water —*vt.* 1 to spray with water, etc. 2 to pour forth as in a shower —*vi.* 1 to fall or come as a shower 2 to bathe under a shower —**show'er·y** *adj.*

show·ing (shō'iŋ) *n.* 1 a bringing to view or notice; exhibition 2 a performance, appearance, etc. [a good *showing* in the contest]

show·man (shō'mən) *n., pl.* **-men** (-mən) 1 one whose business is producing shows 2 a person skilled at presenting anything in a striking manner —**show'man·ship'** *n.*

shown (shōn) *vt., vi. alt. pp.* of SHOW

show·off *n.* one who shows off

show of hands a raising of hands, as in voting or volunteering

show·piece *n.* 1 something displayed or exhibited 2 something that is a fine example of its kind

show·place *n.* 1 a place displayed to the public for its beauty, etc. 2 any beautiful place

show·room *n.* a room where merchandise is displayed for advertising or sale

show·time *n.* the time when a show begins

show·y *adj.* **-i·er, -i·est** 1 of striking appearance 2 attracting attention in a gaudy way —**show′i·ness** *n.*

shpt *abbrev.* shipment

shrank (shraŋk) *vt., vi. alt. pt. of* SHRINK

shrap·nel (shrap′nəl) *n.* [after Gen. H. *Shrapnel* (1761-1842), its Brit inventor] 1 an artillery shell filled with an explosive charge and small metal balls 2 these balls 3 any fragments scattered by an exploding shell, bomb, etc.

shred (shred) *n.* [OE *screade*] 1 a narrow strip cut, torn off, etc. 2 a fragment —*vt.* **shred′ded** or **shred, shred′ding** to cut or tear into shreds —**shred′da·ble** *adj.*

shred·der *n.* 1 one that shreds 2 a device that shreds paper, esp. as in destroying confidential documents

shrew (shrōō) *n.* [< OE *screawa*] 1 a small, mouselike insectivorous mammal with a long snout 2 a nagging, bad-tempered woman —**shrew′ish** *adj.*

shrewd (shrōōd) *adj.* [see prec.] clever or sharp in practical affairs; astute —**shrewd′ly** *adv.* —**shrewd′ness** *n.*

shriek (shrēk) *vi., vt.* [ME *schriken*] to make or utter with a loud, piercing cry —*n.* such a cry

shrift (shrift) *n.* [ult. < L *scribere*, write] [Archaic] confession to and absolution by a priest: see also SHORT SHRIFT

shrike (shrīk) *n.* [OE *scric*] a shrill-voiced, predatory songbird with a hooked beak

shrill (shril) *adj.* [echoic] producing a high, thin, piercing sound — *vi., vt.* to utter (with) a shrill sound —**shril′ly** *adv.* —**shrill′ness** *n.*

shrimp (shrimp) *n., pl.* **shrimps** or **shrimp** [OE *scrimman*, to shrink] 1 a small, long-tailed crustacean, valued as food 2 [Inf.] a small or insignificant person —**shrimp′y** *adj.*

shrine (shrīn) *n.* [< L *scrinium*, box] 1 a container holding sacred relics 2 a saint's tomb 3 a place of worship 4 any hallowed place

shrink (shriŋk) *vi.* **shrank** or **shrunk, shrunk** or **shrunk′en, shrink′ing** [OE *scrincan*] 1 to contract, as from heat, cold, desiccation, etc. 2 to lessen, as in amount 3 to draw back; flinch —*vt.* to make shrink —**shrink′a·ble** *adj.*

shrink·age *n.* 1 a shrinking 2 the amount of shrinking

shrinking violet a very shy person

shrink-wrap (-rap′) *vt.* **-wrapped′, -wrap′ping** to wrap in a plastic material that is then shrunk by heating to fit tightly —*n.* a wrapping of such material

shrive (shrīv) *vt.* **shrived** or **shrove, shriv·en** (shriv′ən) or **shrived, shriv′ing** [OE *scrifan*] [Archaic] to hear the confession of and absolve

shriv·el (shriv′əl) *vt., vi.* **-eled** or **-elled, -el·ing** or **-el·ling** [prob. < Scand] to shrink and wrinkle or wither

shroud (shroud) *n.* [OE *scrud*] 1 a cloth used to wrap a corpse for burial 2 something that

covers, veils, etc. 3 any of the ropes from a ship's side to a masthead —*vt.* to hide; cover

Shrove Tuesday [see SHRIVE] the last day before Lent

shrub (shrub) *n.* [OE *scrybb*, brushwood] a low, woody plant with several stems; bush —**shrub′by** *adj.*

shrub·ber·y (-ər ē) *n.* shrubs collectively

shrug (shrug) *vt., vi.* **shrugged, shrug′ging** [ME *schruggen*] to draw up (the shoulders), as in indifference, doubt, etc. —*n.* the gesture so made —**shrug off** to dismiss or disregard in a carefree way

shrunk (shruŋk) *vi., vt. alt. pt. & pp. of* SHRINK

shrunk·en *vi., vt. alt. pp. of* SHRINK —*adj.* contracted in size; shriveled

shtick (shtik) *n.* [Yiddish] [Slang] 1 a comic scene or gimmick 2 an attention-getting device

shuck (shuk) *n.* [< ?] a shell, pod, or husk —*vt.* to remove shucks from

shucks (shuks) *interj.* used to express mild disappointment, embarrassment, etc.

shud·der (shud′ər) *vi.* [ME *schoderen*] to shake or tremble, as in horror —*n.* a shuddering

shuf·fle (shuf′əl) *vt., vi.* **-fled, -fling** [prob. < LowG *schuffeln*] 1 to move (the feet) with a dragging gait 2 to mix (playing cards) 3 to mix together in a jumble —*n.* a shuffling —**shuf′fler** *n.*

shuf·fle·board *n.* [< earlier *shovel board*] a game in which disks are pushed with a cue toward numbered spaces on a diagram

shun (shun) *vt.* **shunned, shun′ning** [OE *scunian*] to keep away from; avoid scrupulously

shunt (shunt) *vt., vi.* [ME *schunten*] 1 to move or turn to one side 2 to switch from one track to another: said as of a train —*n.* 1 a shunting 2 a railroad switch 3 a surgically created channel allowing flow from one organ, etc. to another

shush (shush, shoosh) *interj.* [echoic] hush! be quiet! —*vt.* to say "shush" to

shut (shut) *vt.* **shut, shut′ting** [OE *scyttan*] 1 to move (a door, lid, etc.) so as to close (an opening, container, etc.) 2 *a*) to prevent entrance to or exit from *b*) to confine *in* a room, etc. 3 to bring together the parts of (a book, the eyes, etc.) —*vi.* to be or become shut —*adj.* closed, fastened, etc. —**shut down** to cease operating —**shut off** to prevent passage of or through —**shut out** 1 to deny entrance to 2 to prevent from scoring —**shut up** 1 to confine 2 [Inf.] to stop or cause to stop talking

shut·down *n.* a stoppage of work or activity, as in a factory

shut-eye *n.* [Slang] sleep

shut-in *adj.* confined indoors by illness —*n.* an invalid who is shut-in

shut·out *n.* a game in which a team is kept from scoring

shut·ter (shut′ər) *n.* 1 a person or thing that shuts 2 a movable cover for a window 3 a device for opening and closing the aperture of

a camera lens —*vt.* to close or furnish with
a shutter

shut·tle (shut′'l) *n.* [< OE *scytel*, missile] **1** a
device that carries thread back and forth, as in
weaving **2** *a)* a traveling back and forth over
a short route *b)* an airplane, bus, etc. used in
a shuttle *c) short for* SPACE SHUTTLE —*vt., vi.*
-tled, -tling to move back and forth rapidly

shut·tle·cock (-käk′) *n.* in badminton, a
rounded piece of cork having a flat end stuck
with feathers, or a similar plastic device

shy¹ (shī) *adj.* **shy′er** or **shi′er, shy′est**
or **shi′est** [OE *sceoh*] **1** easily frightened;
timid **2** not at ease with others; bashful **3**
distrustful; wary **4** [Slang] lacking —*vi.*
shied, shy′ing 1 to move suddenly as when
startled **2** to be or become cautious, etc.
—**shy′ly** *adv.* —**shy′ness** *n.*

shy² (shī) *vt., vi.* **shied, shy′ing** [< ?] to fling,
esp. sideways

shy·ster (shī′stər) *n.* [prob. < Ger *scheisser*,
one who defecates] [Slang] a lawyer who
uses unethical or tricky methods

Si *Chem. symbol for* silicon

Si·am (sī am′) *former name for* THAILAND

Si·a·mese (sī′ə mēz′) *n., pl.* **-mese′ 1** *former
name for* THAI **2** a domestic cat with blue eyes
and a light-colored coat —*adj. former term
for* THAI

Siamese twins [after such a pair born in
Siam] any pair of twins born with bodies
joined together

Si·ber·i·a (sī bir′ē ə) region in N Asia, between
the Urals & the Pacific; Asian section of Russia **Si·ber′i·an** *adj., n.*

sib·i·lant (sib′ə lant) *adj.* [< L *sibilare*, to hiss]
having or making a hissing sound —*n.* a sibi-
lant consonant, as (s) or (z)

sib·ling (sib′liŋ) *n.* [< OE *sib*, kinsman +
-LING] a brother or sister

sib·yl (sib′əl) *n.* [< Gr *sibylla*] ancient Greek
or Roman prophetess —**sib′yl·line** (-īn′,
-ēn′) *adj.*

sic (sik) *vt.* **sicced** or **sicked, sic′cing** or
sick′ing [< SEEK] to incite (a dog) to attack

sic (sik, sēk) *adv.* [L] thus; so: used within
brackets [*sic*], to show that a quoted passage,
esp. one containing an error, is reproduced
accurately

Sic·i·ly (sis′ə lē) island of Italy, off its S tip
—**Si·cil·i·an** (si sil′yən) *adj., n.*

sick¹ (sik) *adj.* [OE *seoc*] **1** suffering from
disease; ill **2** having nausea **3** of or for sick
people [*sick* leave] **4** deeply disturbed, as
by grief **5** disgusted by an excess [*sick* of ex-
cuses] **6** [Inf.] sadistic, morbid, etc. [a *sick*
joke] —**the sick** sick people —**sick′ish** *adj.*

sick² (sik) *vt. alt. sp. of* SIC (incite)

sick bay a hospital and dispensary on a ship

sick·bed *n.* the bed of a sick person

sick·en *vt., vi.* to make or become ill, disgusted, etc. —**sick′en·ing** *adj.*

sick·le (sik′əl) *n.* [ult. < L *secare*, to cut] a tool
having a crescent-shaped blade on a short
handle, for cutting tall grasses and weeds

sickle cell anemia an inherited chronic ane-

mia found chiefly among black people, in
which defective hemoglobin causes sickle-
shaped red blood cells

sick·ly *adj.* **-li·er, -li·est 1** in poor health **2**
produced by sickness [a *sickly* pallor] **3**
faint **4** weak

sick·ness *n.* **1** a being sick or diseased **2** a
malady **3** nausea

sick·o (-ō) *n.* [Slang] a sick person, esp. one
who is emotionally disturbed, sadistic, etc.

sick·room *n.* the room of a sick person

side (sīd) *n.* [OE] **1** the right or left half, as of
the body **2** a position beside one **3** *a)* any of
the lines or surfaces that bound something *b)*
either of the two bounding surfaces of an object
that are not the front, back, top, or bottom **4**
either of the two surfaces of paper, cloth, etc. **5**
an aspect [his cruel *side*] **6** any location, etc.
with reference to a central point **7** the position
or attitude of one person or faction opposing
another **8** one of the parties in a contest, conflict, etc. **9** a line of descent —*adj.* **1** of, at, or
on a side **2** to or from one side [a *side* glance] **3**
secondary [a *side* issue] —*vi.* to align oneself
(with a faction, etc.) —**side by side** together
—**take sides** to support a faction

side·arm *adj., adv.* with a forward arm motion
at or below shoulder level

side arm a weapon worn at the side or waist, as
a sword or pistol

side·bar *n.* a short article about a sidelight of
a major news story and printed alongside it

side·board *n.* a piece of furniture for holding
linen, china, silverware, etc.

side·burns *pl.n.* [< *burnsides*, side whiskers
worn by A. E. *Burnside*, Civil War general] the
hair growing on the sides of a man's face, just
in front of the ears

side·car *n.* a small car attached to the side of
a motorcycle

side dish any food served along with the main
course, usually in a separate dish

side effect an incidental effect, as an unrelated symptom produced by a drug

side·kick *n.* [Inf.] **1** a close friend **2** a partner;
confederate

side·light *n.* a bit of incidental knowledge or
information

side·line *n.* **1** either of two lines marking the
side limits of a playing area, as in football **2**
a secondary line of merchandise, work, etc.

side·long *adv.* toward the side —*adj.* directed
to the side: said as of a glance

side·man (-man′) *n., pl.* **-men′** (-men′) a
band member other than the leader or soloist

side·piece *n.* a piece on the side of something

si·de·re·al (sī dir′ē əl) *adj.* [< L *sidus*, star]
with reference to the stars

side·sad·dle *n.* a saddle designed for a rider
sitting with both legs on the same side of the
animal —*adv.* on or as if on a sidesaddle

side·show *n.* a small show in connection with
the main show, as of a circus

side·slip *vi.* **-slipped′, -slip′ping** to slip or
skid sideways —*vt.* to cause to sideslip —*n.* a
slip or skid to the side

side·split·ting *adj.* **1** very hearty: said of laughter **2** very funny

side-step *vt., vi.* **-stepped′, -step′ping** to dodge as by stepping aside

side·swipe *vt.* **-swiped′, -swip′ing** to hit along the side in passing —*n.* such a glancing blow

side·track *vt., vi.* **1** to switch (a train) to a siding **2** to turn away from the main issue

side·walk *n.* a path for pedestrians, usually paved, along the side of a street

side·wall *n.* the side of a tire between the tread and the wheel rim

side·ways (-wāz′) *adv., adj.* **1** toward or from one side **2** with one side forward

sid·ing (sīd′iŋ) *n.* **1** a covering, as of overlapping boards, for the outside of a frame building **2** a short railroad track connected with a main track by a switch and used for unloading, etc.

si·dle (sīd′'l) *vi.* **-dled, -dling** [< *sideling,* sideways] to move sideways, esp. shyly or stealthily

SIDS (sīdz) *abbrev.* SUDDEN INFANT DEATH SYNDROME

siege (sēj) *n.* [ult. < L *sedere,* sit] **1** the encirclement of a fortified place by an enemy intending to take it **2** any persistent attempt to gain control, etc. —**lay siege to** to subject to a siege

si·en·na (sē en′ə) *n.* [It] yellowish brown or reddish brown

si·er·ra (sē er′ə) *n.* [Sp < L *serra,* a saw] a range of hills or mountains with a sawtoothed appearance

Si·er·ra Le·one (sē er′ə lē ōn′) country in W Africa, on the Atlantic

si·es·ta (sē es′tə) *n.* [Sp < L *sexta* (*hora*), sixth (hour), noon] a brief nap or rest after the noon meal

sieve (siv) *n.* [OE *sife*] a utensil with many small holes for straining liquids, etc.; strainer

sift (sift) *vt.* [OE *siftan*] **1** to pass (flour, etc.) through a sieve **2** to examine (evidence, etc.) with care **3** to separate [to *sift* fact from fable] —*vi.* to pass as through a sieve —**sift′er** *n.*

sigh (sī) *vi.* [< OE *sican*] **1** to take in and let out a long, deep, audible breath, as in sorrow, relief, or longing **2** to feel longing or grief (*for*) —*n.* the act or sound of sighing

sight (sīt) *n.* [< OE *seon,* to see] **1** something seen or worth seeing **2** the act of seeing **3** a device to aid the eyes in aiming a gun, etc. **4** aim or an observation taken, as on a sextant **5** the power or range of seeing; eyesight **6** [Inf.] anything that looks unpleasant, odd, etc. —*vt.* **1** to glimpse; see **2** to aim at **3** to adjust the sights of —*vi.* to look carefully [*sight* along the line] —**at (or on) sight** as soon as seen —**by sight** by appearance —**not by a long sight 1** not nearly **2** not at all —**out of sight 1** not in sight **2** far off **3** [Inf.] beyond reach **4** [Slang] excellent; wonderful

sight·ed *adj.* **1** having sight; not blind **2** having (a specified kind of) sight [*farsighted*]

sight·ing *n.* an observation, as of something rare

sight·less *adj.* blind

sight·ly *adj.* **-li·er, -li·est** pleasant to the sight —**sight′li·ness** *n.*

sight reading the skill of performing written music on first sight —**sight′-read′** *vt., vi.*

sight·see·ing *n.* the visiting of places of interest —**sight′se′er** (-sē′ər) *n.*

sig·ma (sig′mə) *n.* the eighteenth letter of the Greek alphabet (Σ, σ, ς)

sign (sīn) *n.* [< L *signum*] **1** something that indicates a fact, quality, etc.; token **2** a gesture that conveys information, etc. **3** a mark or symbol having a specific meaning [a dollar *sign* ($)] **4** a placard, etc. bearing information, advertising, etc. **5** any trace or indication —*vt.* **1** to write (one's name) on (a letter, check, contract, etc.) **2** to engage by written contract —*vi.* to write one's signature —**sign in** (or **out**) to sign a register on arrival (or departure) —**sign off** to stop broadcasting, as for the day —**sign off on** to approve

sign·age *n.* public signs collectively, often, specif., when graphically coordinated

sig·nal (sig′nəl) *n.* [< L *signum,* a sign] **1** a sign or event that initiates action [a bugle *signal* to attack] **2** a gesture, device, etc. that conveys command, warning, etc. **3** in radio, etc., the electrical impulses transmitted or received —*adj.* **1** remarkable; notable **2** used as a signal —*vt., vi.* **-naled** or **-nalled, -nal·ing** or **-nal·ling 1** to make a signal or signals (to) **2** to communicate by signals

sig·nal·ize (-nə līz′) *vt.* **-ized′, -iz′ing** to make known or draw attention to

sig·nal·ly *adv.* in a signal way; notably

sig·na·to·ry (sig′nə tôr′ē) *adj.* having joined in signing something —*n., pl.* **-ries** a signatory person, nation, etc.

sig·na·ture (sig′nə chər) *n.* [< L *signare,* to sign] **1** a person's name written by that person **2** *Music* a staff sign showing key or time

sign·board (sīn′bôrd′) *n.* a board bearing a sign or advertisement

sig·net (sig′nit) *n.* [< Fr *signe,* a sign] a seal, as on a ring, used in marking documents as official, etc.

sig·nif·i·cance (sig nif′ə kəns) *n.* **1** that which is signified; meaning **2** the quality of being significant; expressiveness **3** importance

sig·nif·i·cant (-kənt) *adj.* [< L *significare,* signify] **1** having or expressing a meaning, esp. a special or hidden one **2** full of meaning **3** important —**sig·nif′i·cant·ly** *adv.*

significant other a person with whom one has an intimate, often long-term and usually sexual, relationship

sig·ni·fy (sig′nə fī′) *vt.* **-fied′, -fy′ing** [< L *signum,* a sign + *facere,* make] **1** to be an indication of; mean **2** to make known by a sign, words, etc. —*vi.* to be important —**sig′ni·fi·ca′tion** *n.*

sign language hand signals and gestures used, as by the deaf, as a language

sign of the cross an outline of a CROSS (*n.* 2)

made ritually by moving the hand or fingers

sign of the zodiac any of the twelve divisions of the zodiac, each represented by a symbol

si·gnor (sē nyôr′) *n., pl.* **-gno′ri** (-nyô′rē) ⟦It⟧ **1** [S-] Mr.: Italian title **2** a man; gentleman

si·gno·ra (sē nyô′rä) *n., pl.* **-gno′re** (-re) ⟦It⟧ **1** [S-] Mrs.; Madam: Italian title **2** a married woman

si·gno·ri·na (sē′nyô rē′nä) *n., pl.* **-ri′ne** (-ne) ⟦It⟧ **1** [S-] Miss: Italian title **2** an unmarried woman or a girl

sign·post *n.* **1** a post bearing a sign **2** an obvious clue, symptom, etc.

Sikh (sēk, sik) *n.* ⟦Hindi, disciple⟧ a member of a monotheistic religion founded in N India in the 1500s

si·lage (sī′lij) *n.* green fodder preserved in a silo

si·lence (sī′ləns) *n.* **1** a keeping silent **2** absence of sound **3** an omission of mention —*vt.* **-lenced, -lenc·ing 1** to make silent **2** to put down; repress —*interj.* be silent!

si·lenc·er *n.* **1** one that silences **2** a device to muffle the sound of a gun

si·lent (sī′lənt) *adj.* ⟦< L *silere*, be silent⟧ **1** making no vocal sound; mute **2** not talkative **3** still; noiseless **4** not expressed; tacit **5** not active [a *silent* partner] —**si′lent·ly** *adv.*

sil·hou·ette (sil′ə wet′) *n.* ⟦Fr, after E. de *Silhouette* (1709-67), Fr statesman⟧ **1** a solid, usually black, outline drawing, esp. a profile **2** any dark shape seen against a light background —*vt.* **-et′ted, -et′ting** to show in silhouette

sil·i·ca (sil′i kə) *n.* ⟦< L *silex*, flint⟧ a hard, glassy mineral found in a variety of forms, as in quartz, opal, or flint —**si·li·ceous** (sə lish′əs) *adj.*

sil·i·cate (-kit, -kāt′) *n.* a salt or ester derived from silica

sil·i·con (-kän′, -kən) *n.* ⟦ult. < L *silex*, flint⟧ a nonmetallic chemical element found always in combination: symbol, Si; at. no. 14

sil·i·cone (-kōn′) *n.* an organic silicon compound highly resistant to heat, water, etc.

Silicon Valley ⟦after the material used for electronic chips⟧ *name for* an area near San Francisco: a center of high-technology industries

sil·i·co·sis (-kō′sis) *n.* ⟦see SILICON & -OSIS⟧ a chronic lung disease from inhaling silica dust

silk (silk) *n.* ⟦ult. < ? L *sericus*, (fabric) of the *Seres*, prob. the Chinese⟧ **1** *a)* the fine, soft fiber produced by silkworms *b)* thread or fabric made from this **2** any silklike filament or substance —**silk′en** *adj.* —**silk·y** (sil′kē) *adj.* **-i·er, -i·est** —**silk′i·ness** *n.*

silk-screen 1 a stencil method of printing a color design through a piece of silk or other fine cloth on which parts of the design not to be printed have been blocked out **2** a print made this way —**silk′-screen′** *vt.*

silk·worm *n.* any of certain moth caterpillars that produce cocoons of silk fiber

sill (sil) *n.* **1** a heavy horizontal timber or line of masonry supporting a house wall, etc. **2** a horizontal piece forming the bottom frame of a window or door opening

sil·ly (sil′ē) *adj.* **-li·er, -li·est** ⟦< OE *sælig*, happy⟧ having or showing little sense, judgment, or sobriety; foolish, absurd, etc. —**sil′li·ness** *n.*

si·lo (sī′lō) *n., pl.* **-los** ⟦< Gr *siros*⟧ **1** an airtight pit or tower in which green fodder is preserved **2** an underground facility for a long-range ballistic missile

silt (silt) *n.* ⟦prob. < Scand⟧ a fine-grained, sandy sediment carried or deposited by water —*vt., vi.* to fill or choke up with silt

sil·ver (sil′vər) *n.* ⟦< OE *seolfer*⟧ **1** a white metallic chemical element that is very ductile and malleable: a precious metal: symbol, Ag; at. no. 47 **2** *a)* silver coin *b)* money; riches **3** silverware **4** a lustrous, grayish white —*adj.* **1** of, containing, or plated with silver **2** silvery **3** marking a 25th anniversary —*vt.* to cover with or as with silver

sil·ver·fish *n., pl.* **-fish′** a wingless insect with silvery scales and long feelers, found in damp places

silver lining some basis for hope or comfort in the midst of disappointment

silver nitrate a colorless crystalline salt, used in photography, as an antiseptic, etc.

sil·ver·smith *n.* an artisan who makes and repairs silver articles

sil·ver·tongued (-tuŋd′) *adj.* eloquent

sil·ver·ware *n.* **1** articles, esp. tableware, made of or plated with silver **2** any metal tableware

sil·ver·y *adj.* **1** of, like, or containing silver **2** soft and clear in tone

sim·i·an (sim′ē ən) *adj., n.* ⟦< L *simia*, an ape⟧ (of or like) an ape or monkey

sim·i·lar (sim′ə lər) *adj.* ⟦< L *similis*⟧ **1** nearly but not exactly the same or alike **2** *Geom.* having the same shape but not necessarily the same size —**sim′i·lar′i·ty** (-ler′ə tē) *n., pl.* **-ties** —**sim′i·lar·ly** *adv.*

sim·i·le (sim′ə lē′) *n.* ⟦< L, a likeness⟧ a figure of speech likening one thing to another by the use of *like, as,* etc. (Ex.: tears flowed like wine)

si·mil·i·tude (sə mil′ə tōōd′) *n.* ⟦< L *similitudo*⟧ likeness; resemblance

sim·mer (sim′ər) *vi.* ⟦echoic⟧ **1** to remain at or just below the boiling point **2** to be about to break out, as in anger or revolt —*vt.* to keep at or just below the boiling point —*n.* a simmering

si·mon-pure (sī′mən pyoor′) *adj.* ⟦after *Simon Pure*, a character in a play by S. Centlivre (1669-1723)⟧ genuine; authentic

si·mo·ny (sī′mə nē, sim′ə-) *n.* ⟦after *Simon Magus*: Acts 8:9-24⟧ the buying or selling of holy orders, benefices, etc.

sim·pa·ti·co (sim pät′i kō, -pat′-) *adj.* ⟦< It or Sp⟧ compatible or congenial

sim·per (sim′pər) *vi.* ⟦early Modern Eng⟧ to smile in a silly or affected way —*n.* such a smile

sim·ple (sim′pəl) *adj.* **-pler, -plest** [< L *simplus*] **1** having only one or a few parts; uncomplicated **2** easy to do or understand **3** without additions [the *simple* facts] **4** not ornate or luxurious; plain **5** without guile or deceit **6** without ostentation; natural **7** of low rank or position **8** stupid or foolish —**sim′ple·ness** *n.*

simple interest interest computed on principal alone, and not on principal plus interest already accrued

sim·ple-mind·ed *adj.* **1** artless; unsophisticated **2** foolish **3** intellectually disabled

sim·ple·ton (-tən) *n.* a fool

sim·plic·i·ty (sim plis′ə tē) *n., pl.* **-ties 1** a simple state or quality; freedom from complexity **2** absence of elegance, luxury, etc.; plainness

sim·pli·fy (sim′plə fī′) *vt.* **-fied′, -fy′ing** to make simpler or less complex —**sim′pli·fi·ca′tion** *n.*

sim·plis·tic (sim plis′tik) *adj.* making complex problems unrealistically simple —**sim·plis′ti·cal·ly** *adv.*

sim·ply (sim′plē) *adv.* **1** in a simple way **2** merely [*simply* trying] **3** completely [*simply* furious]

sim·u·late (sim′yōō lāt′) *vt.* **-lat′ed, -lat′ing** [< L *simulare*] **1** to give a false appearance of; feign **2** to look or act like —**sim′u·la′tion** *n.* —**sim′u·la′tor** *n.*

si·mul·cast (sī′məl kast′) *vt.* **-cast′** or **-cast′ed, -cast′ing** to broadcast (a program) simultaneously by radio and television —*n.* a program so broadcast

si·mul·ta·ne·ous (sī′məl tā′nē əs, sim′əl-) *adj.* [< L *simul*, together] occurring, done, etc. at the same time —**si′mul·ta·ne′i·ty** (-tə nē′ə tē, -nā′-) *n.* —**si′mul·ta′ne·ous·ly** *adv.*

sin (sin) *n.* [OE *synne*] **1** the willful breaking of religious or moral law **2** any offense or fault —*vi.* **sinned, sin′ning** to commit a sin

Si·nai (sī′nī′), **Mount** *Bible* the mountain where Moses received the law from God: Exodus 19

since (sins) *adv.* [ult. < OE *sith*, after + *thæt*, that] **1** from then until now [I've been here ever *since*] **2** at some time between then and now [he has *since* recovered] **3** before now; ago [long *since* gone] —*prep.* **1** continuously from (then) until now [*since* noon] **2** during the period between (then) and now [twice *since* May] —*conj.* **1** after the time that [two years *since* they met] **2** continuously from the time when [lonely ever *since* she left] **3** because [*since* you're done, let's go]

sin·cere (sin sir′) *adj.* **-cer′er, -cer′est** [< L *sincerus*, pure] **1** truthful; honest **2** genuine [*sincere* grief] —**sin·cere′ly** *adv.* —**sin·cer′i·ty** (-ser′ə tē) *n.*

si·ne·cure (sī′nə kyoor′, sin′ə-) *n.* [< L *sine*, without + *cura*, care] a position providing an income but requiring little or no work

si·ne di·e (sī′nē dī′ē) [LL, without a day] for an indefinite period

si·ne qua non (sī′nē kwä nän′, sin′ā kwä nōn′) [L, without which not] an indispensable condition or thing

sin·ew (sin′yōō) *n.* [OE *seonwe*] **1** a tendon **2** muscular power; strength —**sin′ew·y** *adj.*

sin·ful *adj.* wicked; immoral —**sin′ful·ly** *adv.*

sing[1] (sin) *vi.* **sang, sung, sing′ing** [OE *singan*] **1** to produce musical sounds with the voice **2** to use song or verse in praise, etc. [of thee I *sing*] **3** to make musical sounds, as a songbird does **4** to hum, buzz, etc., as a bee does **5** [Slang] to confess to or implicate another in a crime —*vt.* **1** to render (a song, etc.) by singing **2** to extol, etc. in song **3** to bring or put by singing [to *sing* a baby to sleep] —*n.* [Inf.] group singing —**sing′er** *n.*

sing[2] *abbrev.* singular

sing·a·long *n.* an informal gathering of people to sing songs

Sin·ga·pore (sin′ə pôr′) **1** island country off the S tip of the Malay Peninsula **2** its capital, a seaport on the S coast

singe (sinj) *vt.* **singed, singe′ing** [OE *sengan*] **1** to burn superficially **2** to expose (an animal carcass) to flame in removing feathers, etc. —*n.* **1** a singeing **2** a superficial burn

sin·gle (sin′gəl) *adj.* [< L *singulus*] **1** *a)* one only *b)* separate and distinct [every *single* time] **2** solitary **3** of or for one person or family **4** between two persons only [*single* combat] **5** unmarried **6** having only one part; not multiple, etc. **7** whole; unbroken [a *single* front] —*vt.* **-gled, -gling** to select from others: usually with *out* —*vi. Baseball* to hit a single —*n.* **1** a single person or thing **2** a one-dollar bill **3** *Baseball* a hit on which the batter reaches first base **4** [*pl.*] *Racket Sports* a match with only one player on each side —**sin′gle·ness** *n.*

sin·gle-breast·ed (-bres′tid) *adj.* overlapping in front enough to fasten [a *single-breasted* coat]

single file 1 a single line of people or things, one behind another **2** in such a line

sin·gle-hand·ed *adj., adv.* **1** using only one hand **2** without help —**sin′gle-hand′ed·ly** *adv.*

sin·gle-mind·ed *adj.* with only one aim or purpose —**sin′gle-mind′ed·ly** *adv.*

sin·gle·ton (-tən) *n.* **1** a playing card that is the only one of its suit held by a player **2** a single person or thing

sin·gle-track *adj.* ONE-TRACK

sin·gle·tree (-trē′) *n.* [< ME *swingle*, rod + *tre*, tree] the crossbar on the hitch of a wagon, etc. to which the traces of a horse's harness are hooked

sin·gly (sin′glē) *adv.* **1** alone **2** one by one **3** unaided

sing·song *n.* a monotonous rise and fall of tone, as in speaking

sin·gu·lar (sin′gyə lər) *adj.* [< L *singulus*, single] **1** unique **2** extraordinary; remarkable **3** peculiar; odd **4** *Gram.* designating only one —*n. Gram.* the singular form of a word —**sin′gu·lar′i·ty** (-ler′ə tē) *n.* —**sin′gu·lar·ly** *adv.*

Sin·ha·lese (sin′hə lēz′, -lēs′) *adj.* of Sri Lanka (island country of S Asia) or its principal people, language, etc. —*n.* 1 *pl.* **-lese′** a member of the Sinhalese people 2 the language of this people

sin·is·ter (sin′is tər) *adj.* [< L *sinister*, left-hand (side)] 1 [Archaic] on or to the left-hand side 2 threatening harm, evil, etc. 3 wicked; evil

sink (siŋk) *vi.* **sank** or **sunk, sunk, sink′ing** [OE *sincan*] 1 to go beneath the surface of water, etc. 2 to go down slowly 3 to appear to descend, as the sun does 4 to become lower, as in level, value, or rank 5 to subside: said as of wind or sound 6 to become hollow: said as of the cheeks 7 to pass gradually (*into* sleep, etc.) 8 to approach death —*vt.* 1 to cause to sink 2 to make (a mine, engraving, etc.) by digging, cutting, etc. 3 to invest 4 to defeat; undo —*n.* 1 a cesspool or sewer 2 a basin, as in a kitchen, with a drainpipe 3 an area of sunken land —**sink in** [Inf.] to be understood in full —**sink′a·ble** *adj.*

sink·er *n.* 1 one that sinks 2 a lead weight used in fishing

sink·hole *n.* a surface depression resulting when ground collapses

sinking fund a fund built up over time to pay off a future debt, as of a company

sin·ner *n.* a person who sins

Sino- [< Gr *Sinai*] *combining form* Chinese and

sin tax a tax on something seen as sinful or harmful, as on liquor or gambling

sin·u·ous (sin′yoo əs) *adj.* [< L *sinus*, a bend] bending or winding in and out; wavy —**sin′u·os′i·ty** (-äs′ə tē) *n.* —**sin′u·ous·ly** *adv.*

si·nus (sī′nəs) *n.* [L, a bend] a cavity, hollow, etc.; specif., any of the air cavities in the skull opening into the nasal cavities

si·nus·i·tis (-īt′is) *n.* inflammation of the sinuses, esp. those of the skull

Sioux (sōō) *n., pl.* **Sioux** (sōō, sōōz) a member of a group of Indian tribes of the N U.S. and S Canada —*adj.* of these tribes

sip (sip) *vt., vi.* **sipped, sip′ping** [ME *sippen*] to drink a little at a time —*n.* 1 the act of sipping 2 a quantity sipped —**sip′per** *n.*

si·phon (sī′fən) *n.* [< Gr *siphōn*, tube] a bent tube for carrying liquid out over the edge of a container to a lower level —*vt.* to draw off through or as through a siphon

sir (sur) *n.* [ME < *sire*, fol.] 1 [*sometimes* S-] a respectful term of address used to a man: not followed by the name 2 [S-] the title used before the name of a knight or baronet

sire (sīr) *n.* [< OFr < L *senior*, compar. of *senex*, old] 1 [S-] a title of respect used in addressing a king 2 [Old Poet.] a father or forefather 3 the male parent of a four-legged mammal —*vt.* **sired, sir′ing** to beget: said esp. of animals

si·ren (sī′rən) *n.* [< Gr *Seirēn*] 1 Gr. & Rom. Myth. any of several sea nymphs whose singing lures sailors to their death on rocky coasts 2 a woman considered seductive 3 a warning device producing a loud, wailing sound

sir·loin (sur′loin′) *n.* [< OFr *sur*, over + *loigne*, loin] a choice cut of beef from the loin end in front of the rump

si·roc·co (sə räk′ō) *n., pl.* **-cos** [It < Ar *sharq*, the east] a hot, oppressive wind blowing from the deserts of N Africa into S Europe

sir·ree or **sir·ee** (sə rē′) *interj.* [< SIR] used to provide emphasis after *yes* or *no*

sir·up (sur′əp, sir′-) *n. alt. sp. of* SYRUP

sis (sis) *n.* [Inf.] *short for* SISTER (*n.* 1, 2, & 3)

si·sal (sī′səl, sis′əl) *n.* [after *Sisal*, in SE Mexico] a strong fiber obtained from the leaves of an agave

sis·sy (sis′ē) *n., pl.* **-sies** [dim. of SIS] [Inf.] 1 an effeminate boy or man: a derogatory term 2 a timid person —**sis′si·fied′** (-ə fīd′) *adj.*

sis·ter (sis′tər) *n.* [< ON *systir*] 1 a woman or girl as she is related to the other children of her parents 2 a half sister or stepsister 3 a female friend who is like a sister 4 a female fellow member of the same race, organization, etc. 5 [*often* S-] a nun 6 something of the same kind, model, etc. —**sis′ter·hood′** *n.* —**sis′ter·ly** *adj.*

sis·ter-in-law *n., pl.* **sis′ters-in-law′** 1 the sister of one's spouse 2 the wife of one's brother 3 the wife of the brother of one's spouse

Sis·y·phus (sis′ə fəs) Gr. Myth. a greedy king doomed in Hades to roll uphill a stone which always rolls down again

sit (sit) *vi.* **sat, sit′ting** [OE *sittan*] 1 *a*) to rest oneself upon the buttocks, as on a chair *b*) to rest on the haunches with the forelegs braced (said of a dog, etc.) *c*) to perch (said of a bird) 2 to cover and warm eggs for hatching; brood 3 *a*) to occupy a seat as a judge, legislator, etc. *b*) to be in session (said as of court) 4 to pose, as for a portrait 5 to be located 6 to rest or lie as specified [cares *sit* lightly on him] 7 BABY-SIT —*vt.* 1 to cause to sit; seat 2 to keep one's seat on (a horse, etc.) —**sit down** to take a seat —**sit in** to attend: often with *on* —**sit out** to take no part in (a dance, etc.) —**sit up** 1 to sit erect 2 to postpone going to bed 3 [Inf.] to become suddenly alert —**sit′ter** *n.*

si·tar (si tär′, si′tär′) *n.* [Hindi *sttār*] a lute-like instrument of India with a long, fretted neck

sit·com (sit′käm′) *n.* [Inf.] *short for* SITUATION COMEDY

sit-down (strike) a strike in which the strikers refuse to leave the premises

site (sīt) *n.* [< L *situs*, position] a location or scene

sit-in *n.* a method of protest in which demonstrators sit in, and refuse to leave, a public place

sit·ting *n.* 1 the act or position of one that sits 2 a session, as of a court 3 a period of being seated

sitting duck [Inf.] a person or thing especially vulnerable to attack; easy target

sit·u·ate (sich′ <del>oo</del> āt′) *vt.* **-at′ed, -at′ing** [see SITE] to put in a certain place or position; place; locate

sit·u·a′tion *n.* **1** location; position **2** condition with regard to circumstances **3** state of affairs **4** a position of employment

situation comedy a comic TV series made up of episodes involving the same group of characters

sit-up *n.* an exercise in which a person lying supine rises to a sitting position without using the hands

sitz bath (sits, zits) [< Ger] a therapeutic bath in which only the hips and buttocks are immersed

six (siks) *adj., n.* [OE *sex*] one more than five; 6; VI —**sixth** *adj., n.*

six-pack *n.* a package of six units, as one with six cans of beer

six-shoot·er *n.* [Inf.] a revolver having a cylinder that holds six cartridges: also **six′-gun′**

six·teen (siks tēn′) *adj.* [OE *syxtene*] six more than ten; 16; XVI —**six′teenth′** *adj., n.*

sixth sense intuitive power

six·ty (siks′tē) *adj., n., pl.* **-ties** [OE *sixtig*] six times ten; 60; LX —**the sixties** the numbers or years, as of a century, from 60 through 69 —**six′ti·eth** (-ith) *adj., n.*

siz·able (sī′zə bəl) *adj.* quite large or bulky: also sp. **size′able**

size¹ (sīz) *n.* [ult. < L *sedere*, sit] **1** that quality of a thing which determines how much space it occupies; dimensions or magnitude **2** any of a series of graded classifications of measure into which merchandise is divided —*vt.* **sized, siz′ing** to make or grade according to size —**size up** [Inf.] **1** to make an estimate or judgment of **2** to meet requirements

size² (sīz) *n.* [ME *syse*] a pasty substance used as a glaze or filler on plaster, paper, cloth, etc. —*vt.* **sized, siz′ing** to fill, stiffen, or glaze with size

-sized (sīzd) *combining form* having a (specified) size [medium-*sized*]: also **-size**

siz·ing *n.* **1** SIZE² **2** the act of applying SIZE²

siz·zle (siz′əl) *vi.* **-zled, -zling** [echoic] **1** to make a hissing sound when in contact with heat **2** to be extremely hot —*n.* a sizzling sound

S.J. *abbrev.* Society of Jesus

SK Saskatchewan

skank (skaŋk) *n.* [Slang] one who is considered to be sleazy, sexually promiscuous, etc.: an insulting term used esp. of a woman —**skank′y** *adj.* **-i·er, -i·est**

skate¹ (skāt) *n.* [< OFr *eschace*, stilt] **1** a metal runner in a frame, fastened to a shoe for gliding on ice **2** a similar frame or shoe with wheels, for gliding on a floor, sidewalk, etc. —*vi.* **skat′ed, skat′ing** to glide or roll on or as on skates —**skat′er** *n.*

skate² (skāt) *n.* [< ON *skata*] any of various species of rays

skate·board *n.* a short, oblong board with two wheels at each end, ridden standing up, as down an incline —*vi.* to ride on a skateboard

ske·dad·dle (ski dad′'l) *vi.* **-dled, -dling** [< ?] [Inf.] to run away

skeet (skēt) *n.* [< ON *skeyti*, projectile] trapshooting in which the shooter fires from different angles

skein (skān) *n.* [< MFr *escaigne*] a quantity of thread or yarn in a coil

skel·e·ton (skel′ə tən) *n.* [< Gr *skeletos*, dried up] **1** the hard framework of bones of an animal body **2** a supporting framework **3** an outline, as of a book —*adj.* greatly reduced [a *skeleton* crew] —**skel′e·tal** *adj.*

skeleton key a key that can open many simple locks

skep·tic (skep′tik) *n.* [L < Gr *skeptikos*, inquiring] **1** an adherent of skepticism **2** one who habitually questions matters generally accepted **3** one who doubts religious doctrines

skep·ti·cal (-ti kəl) *adj.* doubting; questioning —**skep′ti·cal·ly** *adv.*

skep·ti·cism (-tə siz′əm) *n.* **1** the doctrine that the truth of all knowledge must always be in question **2** skeptical attitude **3** doubt about religious doctrines

sketch (skech) *n.* [ult. < Gr *schedios*, extempore] **1** a rough drawing or design, done rapidly **2** a brief outline **3** a short, light story, play, etc. —*vt., vi.* make a sketch or sketches (of)

sketch·y *adj.* **-i·er, -i·est 1** of or resembling a sketch **2** [Inf.] potentially unsafe or unreliable

skew (skyōō) *vi., vt.* [< OFr *eschiver*, shun < OHG] **1** to slant or set at a slant **2** to distort —*adj.* slanting —*n.* a slant or twist

skew·er (skyōō′ər) *n.* [< ON *skifa*, a slice] a long pin used to hold meat, etc. together while cooking —*vt.* to fasten or pierce with or as with skewers

ski (skē) *n., pl.* **skis** [Norw < ON *skith*, snowshoe] either of a pair of long runners with upturned tips, fastened to shoes for gliding over snow —*vi.* **skied, ski′ing** to glide on skis —**ski′er** *n.*

skid (skid) *n.* [prob. < ON *skith*, snowshoe] **1** a plank, log, etc., often used as a track upon which to slide a heavy object **2** a low, wooden platform for holding loads **3** a runner on aircraft landing gear **4** a sliding wedge used to brake a wheel **5** the act of skidding — *vt., vi.* **skid′ded, skid′ding** to slide or slip, as a vehicle on ice —**be on** (or **hit**) **the skids** [Slang] to be on the decline, or to fail

skid row [altered < *skid road*, trail to skid logs along] a section of a city frequented by vagrants, derelicts, etc.

skiff (skif) *n.* [< It *schifo*] any light, open boat propelled by oars, motor, or sail

ski lift an endless cable with seats, enclosed pods, etc. for carrying skiers up a slope

skill (skil) *n.* [< ON *skil*, distinction] **1** great ability or proficiency **2** *a)* an art, craft, etc., esp. one involving the hands or body *b)* ability in such an art, etc. —**skilled** *adj.* —**skill′ful** *adj.*, **skil′ful**

skil·let (skil′it) *n.* ⟦< ? L *scutra*, dish⟧ a pan for frying

skim (skim) *vt., vi.* **skimmed, skim′ming** ⟦ME *skimen*⟧ 1 to remove (floating matter) from (a liquid) 2 to glance through (a book, etc.) without reading word for word 3 to glide lightly (over)

skim milk milk with the cream removed: also **skimmed milk**

skimp (skimp) *vi., vt.* SCRIMP

skimp·y *adj.* **-i·er, -i·est** [Inf.] barely enough; scanty

skin (skin) *n.* ⟦< ON *skinn*⟧ 1 the outer covering of the animal body 2 a pelt 3 something like skin, as fruit rind, etc. —*vt.* **skinned, skin′ning** 1 to remove skin from 2 to injure by scraping (one's knee, etc.) 3 [Inf.] to swindle

skin diving underwater swimming with such gear as a face mask, flippers, snorkel, etc. —**skin′-dive′** *vi.* **-dived′, -div′ing** —**skin diver**

skin flick *n.* [Slang] a film emphasizing nudity or explicit sexual activity

skin·flint *n.* [lit., one who would skin a flint for economy] a miser

-skinned *combining form* having (a specified kind of) skin [dark-*skinned*]

skin·ny *adj.* **-ni·er, -ni·est** without much flesh; very thin —*n.* [Slang] inside information —**skin′ni·ness** *n.*

skin·ny-dip [Inf.] *vi.* **-dipped′, -dip′ping** to swim nude —*n.* a swim in the nude

skin·tight *adj.* tightfitting [skintight jeans]

skip (skip) *vi., vt.* **skipped, skip′ping** ⟦ME *skippen*⟧ 1 to move along by hopping on first one foot and then the other 2 to ricochet or bounce 3 to pass from one point to another, omitting or ignoring (what lies between) 4 [Inf.] to leave (town, etc.) hurriedly —*n.* a skipping —**skip it!** [Inf.] it doesn't matter

skip·per (skip′ər) *n.* ⟦< MDu *schip*, a ship⟧ the captain of a ship

skir·mish (skur′mish) *n.* ⟦< It *schermire* < Gmc⟧ 1 a brief fight between small groups, as in a battle 2 any slight, unimportant conflict —*vi.* to take part in a skirmish

skirt (skurt) *n.* ⟦< ON *skyrt*, shirt⟧ 1 that part of a dress, coat, etc. that hangs below the waist 2 a woman's garment that hangs from the waist 3 something like a skirt —*vt., vi.* to be on, or move along, the edge (of)

ski run a slope or course for skiing

skit (skit) *n.* ⟦prob. ult. < ON *skjota*, to shoot⟧ a short, humorous sketch, as in the theater

skit·ter (skit′ər) *vi.* ⟦< Scand⟧ to move along quickly and lightly

skit·tish (skit′ish) *adj.* ⟦see SKIT & -ISH⟧ 1 lively; playful 2 easily frightened; jumpy 3 fickle

skiv·vy (skiv′ē) *n., pl.* **-vies** ⟦< ?⟧ [Slang] 1 a man's, esp. a sailor's, short-sleeved undershirt: usually **skivvy shirt** 2 [pl.] men's underwear

skoal (skōl) *interj.* ⟦< ON *skāl*, a bowl⟧ to your health!: used as a toast

skul·dug·ger·y or **skull·dug·ger·y** (skul dug′ər ē) *n.* ⟦< obs. Scot⟧ [Inf.] sneaky, dishonest behavior; trickery

skulk (skulk) *vi.* ⟦ME *sculken*⟧ to move in a stealthy manner; slink

skull (skul) *n.* ⟦< Scand⟧ 1 the bony framework of the head, enclosing the brain 2 the head; mind

skull·cap *n.* a light, closefitting, brimless cap, usually worn indoors

skunk (skuŋk) *n.* ⟦< AmInd⟧ 1 a small, bushytailed mammal having black fur with white stripes down the back: it ejects a foul-smelling liquid when disturbed or frightened 2 its fur 3 [Inf.] a despicable person

sky (skī) *n., pl.* **skies** ⟦< ON, a cloud⟧ 1 [often pl.] the upper atmosphere [blue *skies*, a cloudy *sky*] 2 the firmament 3 heaven

sky·box *n.* a private section of seats, often luxurious and usually elevated, in a stadium, etc.

sky·cap *n.* a porter at an airport terminal

sky diving parachute jumping involving freefall maneuvers

sky-high *adj.* very high —*adv.* 1 very high 2 in or to pieces

sky·jack *vt.* to hijack (an aircraft) —**sky′jack′er** *n.*

sky·lark *n.* a Eurasian lark famous for the song it utters as it soars —*vi.* to romp or frolic

sky·light *n.* a window in a roof or ceiling

sky·line *n.* 1 the visible horizon 2 the outline, as of a city, seen against the sky

sky·rock·et *n.* a fireworks rocket that explodes aloft —*vi., vt.* to rise or cause to rise rapidly

sky·scrap·er *n.* a very tall building

sky·ward *adv., adj.* toward the sky: also **sky′wards** *adv.*

sky·way *n.* 1 AIR LANE 2 an elevated highway or walkway

sky·writ·ing *n.* the tracing of words, etc. in the sky by trailing smoke from an airplane —**sky′writ′er** *n.*

slab (slab) *n.* ⟦ME *sclabbe*⟧ a flat, broad, and fairly thick piece

slack¹ (slak) *adj.* ⟦< OE *slæc*⟧ 1 slow; sluggish 2 not busy; dull [a *slack* period] 3 loose; not tight 4 careless [a *slack* worker] —*vt.* to make slack —*vi.* 1 to become slack 2 to avoid work —*n.* 1 a part that hangs loose 2 a lack of tension 3 a dull period; lull —**cut someone some slack** [Slang] to demand less of someone —**slack off** to slacken —**slack′ness** *n.*

slack² (slak) *n.* ⟦ME *sleck*⟧ a mixture of small pieces of coal, coal dust, etc. left from screening coal

slack·en (slak′ən) *vt., vi.* 1 to make or become less active, brisk, etc. 2 to loosen or relax, as rope

slack·er *n.* one who is unambitious or avoids work

slacks (slaks) *pl.n.* trousers for men or women

slag (slag) *n.* ⟦< earlier LowG *slagge*⟧ the fused refuse separated from metal in smelting

slain (slān) *vt. pp. of* SLAY

slake (slāk) *vt.* **slaked, slak′ing** [< OE *slæc,* SLACK¹] **1** to satisfy (thirst, etc.) **2** to produce a chemical change in (lime) by mixing with water

sla·lom (slä′ləm) *n.* [Norw] a race, as on skis, over a zigzag course —*vi.* to take part in a slalom

slam (slam) *vt.* **slammed, slam′ming** [prob. < Scand] **1** to shut, hit, throw, or put with force and noise **2** [Inf.] to criticize severely —*n.* **1** a slamming **2** [Inf.] a severe criticism

slam-bang [Inf.] *adv.* **1** swiftly or abruptly and recklessly **2** noisily —*adj.* lively, noisy, etc.

slam-dunk *n. Basketball* a forceful shot from directly above the basket

slam·mer (slam′ər) *n.* [Slang] a prison or jail

slan·der (slan′dər) *n.* [see SCANDAL] **1** the utterance of a falsehood that damages another's reputation **2** such a spoken statement —*vt.* to utter a slander about —**slan′der·er** *n.* —**slan′der·ous** *adj.*

slang (slaŋ) *n.* [< ?] highly informal, nonstandard speech consisting of coined words and phrases or of new meanings given to established terms —**slang′y** *adj.* **-i·er, -i·est**

slant (slant) *vt., vi.* [< Scand] **1** to incline; slope **2** to tell so as to express a particular bias —*n.* **1** an oblique surface, line, etc. **2** a point of view or attitude —*adj.* sloping

slap (slap) *n.* [echoic] **1** a blow with something flat, as the palm of the hand **2** an insult or rebuff —*vt.* **slapped, slap′ping 1** to strike with something flat **2** to put, hit, etc. with force

slap·dash *adj., adv.* hurried(ly), careless(ly), haphazard(ly), etc.

slap-hap·py *adj.* [Slang] **1** dazed, as by blows **2** silly or giddy

slap·stick *n.* crude comedy full of horseplay —*adj.* characterized by such comedy

slash (slash) *vt.* [< ? OFr *eschlachier,* to break] **1** to cut with sweeping strokes, as of a knife **2** to cut slits in **3** to reduce drastically [*slash* prices] —*vi.* to make a sweeping stroke as with a knife —*n.* **1** a slashing **2** a cut made by slashing **3** a virgule —**slash′er** *n.*

slash-and-burn *adj.* **1** of a method of clearing fields by cutting down and burning vegetation **2** indiscriminately destructive

slat (slat) *n.* [< OFr *esclat,* fragment] a narrow strip of wood, metal, etc.

slate (slāt) *n.* [see prec.] **1** a hard, fine-grained rock that cleaves into thin, smooth layers **2** a thin piece of slate or slatelike material, as a roofing tile or writing tablet **3** the bluish-gray color of much slate: also **slate blue** —*vt.* **slat′ed, slat′ing 1** to cover with slate **2** to designate, as for candidacy —**a clean slate** a record showing no marks of discredit, dishonor, etc.

slath·er (slath′ər) *vt.* [< ?] [Inf. or Dial.] to cover or spread on thickly

slat·tern (slat′ərn) *n.* [< dial. *slatter,* to slop] a slovenly or sluttish woman —**slat′tern·ly** *adj.*

slaugh·ter (slôt′ər) *n.* [< ON *slátr,* lit., slain flesh] **1** the killing of animals for food; butchering **2** the brutal killing of a person **3** the killing of many people, as in battle —*vt.* **1** to kill (animals) for food; butcher **2** to kill (people) brutally or in large numbers —**slaugh′ter·er** *n.*

slaugh·ter·house *n.* a place where animals are butchered for food

Slav (släv, slav) *n.* a member of a group of peoples of E and SE Europe, including Russians, Serbs, Czechs, Poles, etc. —*adj. var. of* SLAVIC

slave (slāv) *n.* [< Gr *Sklabos,* ult. < OSlav *Slověne,* first used of captive Slavs] **1** a human who is owned as property by another **2** one dominated by some influence, etc. **3** one who slaves —*vi.* **slaved, slav′ing** to work like a slave; drudge

slave driver 1 one who oversees slaves **2** any merciless taskmaster

slav·er (slav′ər) *vi.* [< Scand] to drool

slav·er·y (slā′vər ē) *n.* **1** the owning of slaves as a practice **2** the condition of a slave; bondage **3** drudgery; toil

Slav·ic (släv′ik, slav′-) *adj.* of the Slavs, their languages, etc. —*n.* a family of languages, including Russian, Polish, Czech, Bulgarian, etc.

slav·ish (slā′vish) *adj.* **1** of or like slaves; servile **2** blindly dependent or imitative —**slav′ish·ly** *adv.*

slaw (slô) *n.* [Du *sla* < Fr *salade,* salad] *short for* COLESLAW

slay (slā) *vt.* **slew, slain, slay′ing** [OE *slean*] to kill in a violent way —**slay′er** *n.*

sleaze (slēz) *n.* [< SLEAZY] [Slang] **1** sleaziness **2** someone or something sleazy

slea·zy (slē′zē) *adj.* **-zi·er, -zi·est** [< *silesia,* orig. cloth made in central Europe] [Inf.] shabby, immoral, etc. —**slea′zi·ly** *adv.* —**slea′zi·ness** *n.*

sled (sled) *n.* [ME *sledde*] a vehicle on runners for moving over snow, ice, etc. —*vt., vi.* **sled′ded, sled′ding** to carry or ride on a sled —**sled′der** *n.*

sledge¹ (slej) *n.* [OE *slecge*] SLEDGEHAMMER

sledge² (slej) *n.* [MDu *sleedse*] a sled or sleigh

sledge·ham·mer *n.* [see SLEDGE¹] a long, heavy hammer, usually held with both hands

sleek (slēk) *adj.* [var. of SLICK] **1** smooth and shiny; glossy **2** of well-fed or well-groomed appearance **3** suave, elegant, etc. —*vt.* to make sleek —**sleek′ly** *adv.* —**sleek′ness** *n.*

sleep (slēp) *n.* [OE *slæp*] **1** the natural, regularly recurring rest for the body, during which there is little or no conscious thought **2** any state like this —*vi.* **slept, sleep′ing** to be in a state of or like sleep —**sleep off** to rid oneself of by sleeping —**sleep′less** *adj.* —**sleep′less·ness** *n.*

sleep·er *n.* **1** one who sleeps **2** a railroad car with berths for sleeping: also **sleeping car 3** a beam laid flat to support something **4** something that achieves an unexpected success

sleeping bag a warmly lined, zippered bag for sleeping in, as when camping

sleeping sickness an infectious disease, esp. of Africa, transmitted by the tsetse fly and characterized by lethargy, prolonged coma, etc.

sleep·o·ver *n.* a spending the night at another's home, as by a group of young people for fun

sleep·walk·ing *n.* the act of walking while asleep —**sleep′walk′er** *n.*

sleep·wear *n.* NIGHTCLOTHES

sleep·y *adj.* **-i·er, -i·est** 1 ready or inclined to sleep; drowsy 2 dull; idle [a *sleepy* town] —**sleep′i·ly** *adv.* —**sleep′i·ness** *n.*

sleet (slēt) *n.* ⟦ME *slete*⟧ 1 partly frozen rain 2 the icy coating formed when rain freezes on trees, etc. —*vi.* to fall as sleet —**sleet′y** *adj.*

sleeve (slēv) *n.* ⟦OE *sliefe*⟧ 1 that part of a garment that covers the arm 2 a tubelike part fitting over or around another part —**roll up one's sleeves** prepare for a difficult task —**up one's sleeve** hidden but ready at hand —**sleeve′less** *adj.*

sleigh (slā) *n.* ⟦Du *slee*⟧ a vehicle on runners, usually horse-drawn, for moving over snow, ice, etc.

sleight of hand (slīt) ⟦< ON *slœgr*, crafty⟧ 1 skill with the hands, esp. in deceiving onlookers, as in magic 2 a trick thus performed

slen·der (slen′dər) *adj.* ⟦ME *s(c)lendre* < ?⟧ 1 long and thin 2 slim of figure 3 small in amount, size, force, etc. —**slen′der·ness** *n.*

slen·der·ize *vt., vi.* **-ized′, -iz′ing** to make or become slender

slept (slept) *vi., vt. pt. & pp. of* SLEEP

sleuth (slooth) *n.* ⟦< ON *slóth*, a trail⟧ a detective

slew¹ (sloo) *n.* ⟦Ir *sluagh*, a host⟧ [Inf.] a large number or amount

slew² (sloo) *vt. pt. of* SLAY

slew³ (sloo) *vt., vi.* **slewed, slew′ing** ⟦< ?⟧ to turn or swing around, as on a pivot

slice (slīs) *n.* ⟦< OFr *esclicier*⟧ 1 a relatively thin, broad piece cut from something 2 a part or share —*vt.* **sliced, slic′ing** 1 to cut into slices 2 to cut off as in a slice or slices: often with *off, from, away,* etc. 3 to hit (a ball) so that it curves to the right if right-handed or the left if left-handed —**slic′er** *n.*

slick (slik) *vt.* ⟦OE *slician*⟧ 1 to make smooth 2 [Inf.] to make smart, neat, etc.: usually with *up* —*adj.* 1 sleek; smooth 2 slippery 3 adept; clever 4 [Inf.] smooth but superficial, tricky, etc. —*n.* 1 a smooth area on the water, as from a layer of oil 2 a slippery, oily area on the surface of a road —**slick′ly** *adv.* —**slick′ness** *n.*

slick·er *n.* 1 a loose, waterproof coat 2 [Inf.] a tricky or sophisticated person

slide (slīd) *vi.* **slid** (slid), **slid′ing** ⟦OE *slidan*⟧ 1 to move along in constant contact with a smooth surface, as on ice 2 to glide 3 to slip [it *slid* from his hand] —*vt.* 1 to cause to slide 2 to place quietly or deftly (*in* or *into*) —*n.* 1 a sliding 2 a smooth, often inclined surface for sliding down 3 something that works by sliding 4 a photographic

transparency for use with a viewer or projector 5 a small glass plate on which objects are mounted for microscopic study 6 the fall of a mass of rock, snow, etc. down a slope 7 a digital image used as in a presentation —**let slide** to fail to attend to properly

slid·er *n.* 1 one that slides 2 *Baseball* a fast pitch that curves

sliding scale a schedule, as of fees, wages, etc., that varies with given conditions, as cost of living, etc.

slight (slīt) *adj.* ⟦OE *sliht*⟧ 1 *a)* light in build; slender *b)* frail; fragile 2 lacking strength, importance, etc. 3 small in amount or extent —*vt.* 1 to neglect 2 to treat with disrespect 3 to treat as unimportant —*n.* a slighting or being slighted —**slight′ly** *adv.* —**slight′ness** *n.*

slim (slim) *adj.* **slim′mer, slim′mest** ⟦< Du, bad⟧ 1 small in girth; slender 2 small in amount, degree, etc. —*vt., vi.* **slimmed, slim′ming** to make or become slim —**slim′ness** *n.*

slime (slīm) *n.* ⟦OE *slim*⟧ any soft, moist, slippery, often sticky matter —**slim′y** *adj.* **-i·er, -i·est**

sling (sliŋ) *n.* ⟦prob. < ON *slyngua*, to throw⟧ 1 a primitive instrument whirled by hand for throwing stones 2 a cast; throw; fling 3 *a)* a supporting band, etc. as for raising a heavy object *b)* a cloth looped from the neck under an injured arm for support —*vt.* **slung, sling′ing** 1 to throw as with a sling 2 to suspend

sling·back *n.* an open-heeled shoe held in place with a strap around the back of the ankle

sling·shot *n.* a Y-shaped piece of wood, etc. with an elastic band attached to it for shooting stones, etc.

slink (sliŋk) *vi.* **slunk, slink′ing** ⟦OE *slincan*, to creep⟧ to move in a furtive or sneaking way

slink·y *adj.* **-i·er, -i·est** 1 furtive; sneaking 2 [Inf.] sinuous in movement or line

slip¹ (slip) *vi.* **slipped, slip′ping** ⟦ME *slippen*, ult. < Ger⟧ 1 to go quietly or secretly [to *slip* out of a room] 2 to pass smoothly or easily 3 to escape from one's memory, grasp, etc. 4 to slide, lose footing, etc. 5 to make a mistake; err 6 to become worse —*vt.* 1 to cause to slip 2 to put, pass, etc. deftly or stealthily 3 to escape from (the memory) —*n.* 1 a space between piers for docking ships 2 a woman's undergarment the length of a skirt 3 a pillowcase 4 a slipping or falling down 5 an error or mistake —**let slip** to say without intending to —**slip up** to make a mistake

slip² (slip) *n.* ⟦< MDu *slippen*, to cut⟧ 1 a stem, root, etc. of a plant, used for planting or grafting 2 a young, slim person 3 a small piece of paper

slip·case *n.* a boxlike container for a book or books, open at one end

slip·cov·er *n.* a removable, fitted cloth cover for a chair, sofa, etc.

slip·knot *n.* a knot that will slip along the rope around which it is tied

slip·page (slip′ij) *n.* a slipping, as of one gear past another

slipped disk a ruptured cartilaginous disk between vertebrae

slip·per (slip′ər) *n.* a light, low shoe easily slipped on the foot, esp. one for indoor wear —**slip′pered** *adj.*

slip·per·y (slip′ər ē, slip′rē) *adj.* **-i·er, -i·est 1** liable to cause slipping, as a wet surface **2** tending to slip away, as from a grasp **3** unreliable; deceitful

slip·shod (-shäd′) *adj.* ⟦< obs. *slip-shoe*, a slipper⟧ careless, as in workmanship

slip·stream *n.* the current of air thrust backward by a spinning aircraft propeller

slip-up *n.* [Inf.] an error: also **slip′up′**

slit (slit) *vt.* **slit, slit′ting** ⟦ME *slitten*⟧ **1** to cut or split open, esp. lengthwise **2** to cut into strips —*n.* a straight, narrow cut, opening, etc.

slith·er (slith′ər) *vi.* ⟦< OE *slidan*, to slide⟧ to slip, slide, or glide along —**slith′er·y** *adj.*

sliv·er (sliv′ər) *n.* ⟦< OE *slifan*, to split⟧ a thin, sharp piece cut or split off; splinter — *vt., vi.* to cut or break into slivers

slob (släb) *n.* ⟦Ir *slab*, mud⟧ [Inf.] a sloppy or coarse person

slob·ber (släb′ər) *vi.* ⟦prob. < LowG *slubberen*, to swig⟧ to drool

sloe (slō) *n.* ⟦OE *sla*⟧ **1** the blackthorn **2** its small, plumlike fruit

sloe-eyed *adj.* **1** having large, dark eyes **2** having almond-shaped eyes

sloe gin a liqueur of gin flavored with sloes

slog (släg) *vt., vi.* **slogged, slog′ging** ⟦ME *sluggen*, go slowly⟧ **1** to make (one's way) with great effort; plod **2** to toil (at) —*n.* an arduous trip, task, etc. —**slog′ger** *n.*

slo·gan (slō′gən) *n.* ⟦< Gael *sluagh*, a host + *gairm*, a call: orig., a battle cry⟧ **1** a motto associated with a political party, etc. **2** a catchy phrase used in advertising —**slo′gan·eer′** *n.*

sloop (slōōp) *n.* ⟦< LowG *slupen*, to glide⟧ a sailing vessel having a single mast with a mainsail and a jib

slop (släp) *n.* ⟦OE *sloppe*⟧ **1** watery snow or mud; slush **2** a puddle of spilled liquid **3** unappetizing, watery food **4** [*often pl.*] liquid waste — *vi., vt.* **slopped, slop′ping** to spill or splash

slope (slōp) *n.* ⟦< OE *slupan*, to glide⟧ **1** rising or falling ground **2** any inclined line, surface, etc.; slant **3** the amount or degree of deviation from the horizontal or vertical —*vi.* sloped, slop′ing to have an upward or downward inclination; incline; slant —*vt.* to cause to slope

slop·py (släp′ē) *adj.* **-pi·er, -pi·est 1** splashy; slushy **2** *a)* slovenly *b)* slipshod **3** [Inf.] gushingly sentimental —**slop′pi·ness** *n.*

sloppy Joe (jō) ground meat cooked with tomato sauce, spices, etc. and served on a bun

slosh (släsh) *vi.* ⟦var. of SLUSH⟧ **1** to splash through water, mud, etc. **2** to splash about: said of a liquid —*n.* the sound of sloshing liquid —**slosh′y** *adj.*

slot (slät) *n.* ⟦< OFr *esclot*, hollow between the breasts⟧ **1** a narrow opening, as for a coin in a vending machine **2** a position in a group, etc. —*vt.* **slot′ted, slot′ting 1** to make a slot in **2** to place in a series or sequence

sloth (slôth, släth; *also* slōth) *n.* ⟦< OE *slaw*, slow⟧ **1** laziness; idleness **2** a slow-moving, tree-dwelling mammal of tropical America that hangs, back down, from branches —**sloth′ful** *adj.* —**sloth′ful·ness** *n.*

slot machine a gambling device activated by the insertion of a coin, ticket, etc. in a slot

slouch (slouch) *n.* ⟦< ON *slōka*, to droop⟧ **1** a lazy or incompetent person **2** a drooping or slovenly posture —*vi.* to sit, stand, walk, etc. in a slouch —**slouch′y** *adj.* **-i·er, -i·est**

slough¹ (sluf) *n.* ⟦ME *slouh*, a skin⟧ a castoff layer or covering, as the skin of a snake —*vt.* to throw off; discard

slough² (slou) *n.* ⟦OE *sloh*⟧ **1** a place full of soft, deep mud **2** deep, hopeless dejection

Slo·vak (slō′väk′, -vak′) *n.* **1** a member of a Slavic people living chiefly in Slovakia **2** the language of this people —*adj.* of the Slovaks

Slo·va·ki·a (slō vä′kē ə) country in central Europe: formerly the E republic of Czechoslovakia

slov·en (sluv′ən) *n.* ⟦prob. < MDu *slof*, lax⟧ a careless, untidy person —**slov′en·ly** *adj.* **-li·er, -li·est** —*adv.*

Slo·ve·ni·a (slō vē′nē ə) country in SE Europe —**Slo·ve′ni·an** *adj., n.,* **Slo·ve′ne′**

slow (slō) *adj.* ⟦OE *slaw*⟧ **1** not quick in understanding **2** taking a longer time than is usual **3** marked by low speed, etc.; not fast **4** behind the correct time, as a clock **5** passing tediously; dull — *vt., vi.* to make or become slow or slower: often with *up* or *down* —*adv.* in a slow manner —**slow′ly** *adv.* —**slow′ness** *n.*

slow-mo·tion *adj.* **1** moving slowly **2** designating a film or taped TV sequence showing the action slowed down

slow·poke (-pōk′) *n.* [Slang] a person who acts or moves slowly

slow-wit·ted *adj.* mentally slow; dull

SLR *n.* ⟦*s(ingle) l(ens) r(eflex)*⟧ a camera allowing the photographer to see the subject through the same lens that will be used in taking the picture

slub (slub) *n.* ⟦< ?⟧ a soft, thick lump or irregularity in yarn or fabric

sludge (sluj) *n.* ⟦var. of *slutch*, mud⟧ any heavy, slimy deposit, sediment, etc.

slug¹ (slug) *n.* ⟦ME *slugge*, clumsy one⟧ a small mollusk like a shell-less snail

slug² (slug) *n.* ⟦prob. < prec.⟧ a small piece of metal; specif., a bullet or counterfeit coin

slug³ (slug) *n.* ⟦prob. < Dan *sluge*, to gulp⟧ [Slang] a drink of liquor

slug⁴ (slug) [Inf.] *vt.* **slugged, slug′ging** ⟦< ON *slag*⟧ to hit hard, esp. with the fist or a bat —*n.* a hard blow or hit —**slug′ger** *n.*

slug·gard (slug′ərd) *n.* ⟦< ME *sluggen*, be lazy⟧ a lazy person

slug·gish (-ish) *adj.* ⟦< SLUG¹⟧ **1** lacking energy or alertness **2** slow or slow-moving **3** not functioning with normal vigor —**slug′gish·ness** *n.*

sluice (slo͞os) *n.* ⟦< L *excludere*, to shut out⟧ **1** an artificial channel for water, with a gate to regulate the flow **2** such a gate: also **sluice gate 3** any channel for excess water **4** a sloping trough, as for washing gold ore —*vt.* **sluiced, sluic′ing 1** to draw off through a sluice **2** to wash with water from a sluice

slum (slum) *n.* ⟦< ?⟧ a populous area characterized by poverty, poor housing, etc. —*vi.* **slummed, slum′ming** to visit a slum, etc. as out of condescension or for amusement —**slum′my** *adj.* **-mi·er, -mi·est**

slum·ber (slum′bər) *vi.* ⟦OE *sluma*⟧ **1** to sleep **2** to be inactive —*n.* **1** sleep **2** an inactive state

slum·lord *n.* [Slang] an absentee landlord who exploits slum property

slump (slump) *vi.* ⟦prob. < Ger⟧ **1** to fall or sink suddenly **2** to slouch —*n.* a decline in activity, prices, performance, etc.

slung (sluŋ) *vt. pt. & pp. of* SLING

slunk (sluŋk) *vi. pt. & pp. of* SLINK

slur (slur) *vt.* **slurred, slur′ring** ⟦prob. < MDu *sleuren*, to drag⟧ **1** to pass over lightly: often with *over* **2** to pronounce indistinctly **3** to disparage **4** *Music* to produce (successive notes) by gliding without a break —*n.* **1** a slurring **2** an aspersion **3** *Music* a curved line connecting notes to be slurred

slurp (slurp) [Slang] *vt., vi.* ⟦Du *slurpen*, to sip⟧ to drink or eat noisily —*n.* a loud sipping or sucking sound

slur·ry (slur′ē) *n., pl.* **-ries** ⟦< MDu *slore*, thin mud⟧ a thin, watery mixture of clay, cement, etc.

slush (slush) *n.* ⟦prob. < Scand⟧ **1** partly melted snow or ice **2** soft mud **3** sentimentality; drivel —**slush′y** *adj.* **-i·er, -i·est**

slush fund 1 money used for bribery, political pressure, etc. **2** funds set aside for indefinite future use

slut (slut) *n.* ⟦ME *slutte*⟧ **1** a dirty, slovenly woman **2** a sexually promiscuous woman: a derogatory term —**slut′tish** *adj.*

sly (slī) *adj.* **sli′er** or **sly′er, sli′est** or **sly′est** ⟦< ON *slœgr*⟧ **1** skillful at trickery; crafty **2** cunningly underhanded **3** playfully mischievous —**on the sly** secretly —**sly′ly** *adv.*, **sli′ly** —**sly′ness** *n.*

smack¹ (smak) *n.* ⟦OE *smæc*⟧ **1** a slight taste or flavor **2** a small amount; trace —*vi.* to have a smack (*of*)

smack² (smak) *n.* ⟦< ?⟧ **1** a sharp noise made by parting the lips suddenly **2** a loud kiss **3** a slap —*vt.* **1** to part (the lips) with a smack **2** to slap loudly —*adv.* **1** with a smack **2** directly

smack³ (smak) *n.* ⟦prob. < Du *smak*⟧ a fishing boat with a well for keeping fish alive

smack⁴ (smak) *n.* ⟦< ?⟧ [Slang] heroin

smack·er *n.* [Old Slang] a dollar

small (smôl) *adj.* ⟦OE *smæl*⟧ **1** comparatively little in size; not big **2** little in quantity, extent, duration, etc. **3** of little importance; trivial **4** young [*small* children] **5** mean; petty **6** lowercase —*n.* the small part [the *small* of the back]

small arms firearms of small caliber, as pistols, rifles, etc.

small fry ⟦see FRY²⟧ **1** children **2** persons considered insignificant

small intestine the narrow section of the intestines, extending from the stomach to the large intestine

small-mind·ed *adj.* mean, narrow-minded, or selfish

small·pox *n.* an acute, contagious viral disease, now eradicated, characterized by fever and pustules

small talk light conversation about common, everyday things; chitchat

small-time *adj.* [Inf.] minor or petty

smarm·y (smär′mē) *adj.* **-i·er, -i·est** ⟦< *smarm*, to smear⟧ [Inf., Chiefly Brit.] flattering in an insincere way

smart (smärt) *vi.* ⟦OE *smeortan*⟧ **1** *a)* to cause sharp, stinging pain, as a slap does *b)* to feel such pain **2** to feel mental distress or irritation —*n.* **1** a stinging sensation **2** [*pl.*] [Slang] intelligence —*adj.* **1** causing sharp pain **2** sharp, as pain **3** brisk; lively [a *smart* pace] **4** intelligent **5** neat; trim **6** stylish **7** [Inf.] insolent **8** *Comput. a)* working by means of a computer or microchip *b)* programmed in advance —**smart′ly** *adv.* —**smart′ness** *n.*

smart al·eck or **smart al·ec** (al′ik) ⟦prec. + *Aleck*, dim. of *Alexander*⟧ [Inf.] one who makes an impudent display of wit or cleverness

smart bomb [Inf.] a bomb directed to its target by electronic means

smart·en *vt., vi.* to make or become smart or smarter: usually with *up*

smart·phone *n.* a cellular phone that allows text messaging, information storage, internet access, etc.

smash (smash) *vt., vi.* ⟦prob. < MASH⟧ **1** to break into pieces with noise or violence **2** to hit, collide, or move with force **3** to destroy or be destroyed —*n.* **1** a hard, heavy hit **2** a violent, noisy breaking **3** a violent collision **4** a popular success

smash·ing *adj.* [Inf.] extraordinary

smash-up *n.* **1** a violent wreck or collision **2** total failure; ruin

smat·ter·ing (smat′ər iŋ) *n.* ⟦ME *smateren*, to chatter⟧ **1** a slight knowledge **2** a small number or limited amount

smear (smir) *vt.* ⟦< OE *smerian*, to anoint⟧ **1** to cover or soil with something greasy, sticky, etc. **2** to apply (something greasy, etc.) **3** to streak by rubbing **4** to slander —*vi.* to be or become smeared —*n.* **1** a mark made by smearing **2** slander —**smear′y** *adj.* **-i·er, -i·est**

smell (smel) *vt.* **smelled** or [Chiefly Brit.] **smelt, smell′ing** ⟦ME *smellen*⟧ **1** to be aware of through the nose; detect the odor of [to *smell* trouble] **2** to sense the presence of —*vi.* **1** to use the sense of smell; sniff **2** to have an odor **3** to stink —*n.* **1** the sense by which odors are perceived **2** odor; scent **3** a smelling

smelling salts an ammonia compound sniffed to relieve faintness

smell·y *adj.* **-i·er, -i·est** having an unpleasant smell

smelt¹ (smelt) *n.* ⟦OE⟧ a small, silvery food fish found esp. in northern seas

smelt² (smelt) *vt.* ⟦< MDu *smelten*⟧ 1 to melt (ore, etc.) so as to extract the pure metal 2 to refine (metal) in this way

smelt³ (smelt) *vt., vi.* chiefly Brit. *pt. & pp. of* SMELL

smelt·er *n.* 1 one whose work is smelting 2 a place for smelting

smidg·en (smij′ən) *n.* ⟦prob. < dial. *smidge*, particle⟧ [Inf.] a small amount; bit: also **smidge**

smile (smīl) *vi.* **smiled, smil′ing** ⟦ME *smilen*⟧ to show pleasure, amusement, affection, etc. by an upward curving of the mouth —*vt.* to express with a smile —*n.* the act or expression of smiling —**smil′ing·ly** *adv.*

smirch (smurch) *vt.* ⟦prob. < OFr *esmorcher*, to hurt⟧ 1 to soil or stain 2 to dishonor —*n.* 1 a smudge; smear 2 a stain on reputation, etc.

smirk (smurk) *vi.* ⟦< OE *smearcian*, to smile⟧ to smile in a conceited or complacent way —*n.* such a smile

smite (smīt) *vt.* **smote, smit′ten** or **smote, smit′ing** ⟦OE *smitan*⟧ 1 to strike with powerful effect 2 to affect or impress strongly

smith (smith) *n.* 1 one who makes or repairs metal objects 2 *short for* BLACKSMITH

Smith (smith), Captain **John** 1580?-1631; Eng. explorer and colonist in America

smith·er·eens (smith′ər ēnz′) *pl.n.* ⟦Ir *smidirín*⟧ [Inf.] fragments; bits

smith·y (smith′ē) *n., pl.* **-ies** the workshop of a smith, esp. a blacksmith

smock (smäk) *n.* ⟦OE *smoc*⟧ a loose, shirtlike outer garment worn to protect the clothes

smock·ing *n.* decorative stitching used to gather cloth and make it hang in folds

smog (smäg, smôg) *n.* ⟦fol. + (F)OG⟧ a low-lying, perceptible layer of polluted air —**smog′gy** *adj.* **-gi·er, -gi·est**

smoke (smōk) *n.* ⟦OE *smoca*⟧ 1 the vaporous matter arising from something burning 2 any vapor, etc. like this 3 an act of smoking tobacco, etc. 4 a cigarette, cigar, etc. —*vi.* **smoked, smok′ing** 1 to give off smoke 2 *a*) to draw in and exhale the smoke of tobacco, etc. *b*) to be a habitual user of cigarettes, etc. —*vt.* 1 to cure (meat, etc.) with smoke 2 to use (a pipe, cigarette, etc.) in smoking 3 to drive out as with smoke —**smoke out** to force out of hiding —**smoke′less** *adj.* —**smok′er** *n.*

smoke detector a warning device that sets off a loud signal when excessive smoke or heat is detected

smoke·house *n.* a building where meats, fish, etc. are cured with smoke

smoke-screen *n.* 1 a cloud of smoke for hiding troop movements, etc. 2 anything said or done to conceal or mislead

smoke·stack *n.* a pipe for discharging smoke from a factory, etc.

smok·y (smō′kē) *adj.* **-i·er, -i·est** 1 giving off smoke 2 of or like smoke 3 filled with smoke —**smok′i·ness** *n.*

smol·der (smōl′dər) *vi.* ⟦ME *smoldren*⟧ 1 to burn and smoke without flame 2 to exist in a suppressed state —*n.* a smoldering

smooch (smōōch) *n., vt., vi.* [Slang] kiss

smoosh (smōōsh) *vt. alt. sp. of* [Inf.] SMUSH

smooth (smōōth) *adj.* ⟦OE *smoth*⟧ 1 having an even surface, with no roughness 2 without lumps 3 even or gentle in movement [a *smooth* voyage] 4 free from interruptions, obstacles, etc. 5 pleasing to the taste; not harsh or bitter 6 having an easy, flowing rhythm or sound 7 polished or ingratiating, esp. in an insincere way —*vt.* 1 to make level or even 2 to remove lumps or wrinkles from 3 to free from difficulties, etc.; make easy 4 to make calm; soothe 5 to polish or refine —*adv.* in a smooth manner —**smooth′ly** *adv.* —**smooth′ness** *n.*

smooth·ie (smōō′thē) *n.* a drink of fruits, juices, vegetables, crushed ice, and usually milk or yogurt, whipped in a blender until smooth

smooth muscle involuntary muscle tissue found in the uterus, stomach, blood vessels, etc.

smooth-spo·ken *adj.* speaking in a pleasing, persuasive, or polished manner

smor·gas·bord or **smör·gås·bord** (smôr′gəs bôrd′, smur′-) *n.* ⟦Swed⟧ 1 a wide variety of appetizers, cheeses, meats, etc., served buffet style 2 a varied assortment of options

smote (smōt) *vt., vi. pt. & alt. pp. of* SMITE

smoth·er (smuth′ər) *vt.* ⟦< ME *smorther*, dense smoke⟧ 1 to keep from getting air; suffocate 2 to cover over thickly 3 to stifle [to *smother* a yawn] —*vi.* to be suffocated

smoul·der (smōl′dər) *vi., n.* Brit. sp. of SMOLDER

smudge (smuj) *vt., vi.* **smudged, smudg′ing** ⟦ME *smogen*⟧ to make or become dirty; smear —*n.* 1 a dirty spot 2 a fire made to produce dense smoke —**smudg′y** *adj.* **-i·er, -i·est**

smug (smug) *adj.* **smug′ger, smug′gest** ⟦prob. < LowG *smuk*, trim, neat⟧ annoyingly self-satisfied; complacent —**smug′ly** *adv.* —**smug′ness** *n.*

smug·gle (smug′əl) *vt.* **-gled, -gling** ⟦< LowG *smuggeln*⟧ 1 to bring into or take out of a country secretly or illegally 2 to bring, take, etc. secretly —*vi.* to practice smuggling —**smug′gler** *n.*

smush (smōōsh) *vt.* [Inf.] to smash, squeeze, etc.

smut (smut) *n.* ⟦< LowG *smutt*⟧ 1 a particle of soot 2 a fungal disease of plants 3 indecent talk, writing, etc. —**smut′ty** *adj.* **-ti·er, -ti·est**

Sn ⟦L *stannum*⟧ *Chem. symbol for* tin

snack (snak) *n.* ⟦< ME *snaken*, to bite⟧ a light meal between regular meals —*vi.* to eat a snack

snack bar a counter for serving snacks

snag (snag) *n.* ⟦< Scand⟧ 1 a sharp point or

projection 2 an underwater tree stump or branch 3 a tear, as in cloth, made by a snag, etc. 4 an unexpected or hidden difficulty, etc. —*vt.* **snagged, snag′ging 1** to catch, tear, etc. on a snag **2** to impede with a snag **3** to grab or get quickly

snail (snāl) *n.* 〖OE *snægl*〗 a slow-moving mollusk having a wormlike body and a spiral protective shell

snake (snāk) *n.* 〖OE *snaca*〗 **1** a long, scaly, limbless reptile with a tapering tail **2** a treacherous or deceitful person **3** a plumber's tool for clearing pipes —*vi.* **snaked, snak′ing** to move, twist, etc. like a snake —**snake′like′** *adj.*

snak·y (snā′kē) *adj.* **-i·er, -i·est 1** of or like a snake or snakes **2** winding; twisting **3** cunningly treacherous or evil

snap (snap) *vi., vt.* **snapped, snap′ping** 〖< MDu *snappen*〗 **1** to bite or grasp suddenly: with *at* **2** to speak or utter sharply: often with *at* **3** to break suddenly **4** to make or cause to make a sudden, cracking sound **5** to close, fasten, etc. with this sound **6** to move or cause to move suddenly and smartly [to snap to attention] **7** to take a snapshot (of) —*n.* **1** a sudden bite, grasp, etc. **2** a sharp cracking sound [the *snap* of a whip] **3** a brief period of cold weather **4** a fastening that closes with a click **5** a hard, thin cookie **6** *short for* SNAPSHOT **7** [Slang] an easy job, problem, etc. —*adj.* **1** made or done quickly [a *snap* decision] **2** that fastens with a snap **3** [Slang] easy —**snap back** to recover quickly —**snap out of it** to improve or recover quickly —**snap′per** *n.*

snap bean a green bean or wax bean

snap·drag·on *n.* 〖SNAP + DRAGON: from the mouth-shaped flowers〗 a plant with saclike, two-lipped flowers

snap·pish *adj.* **1** likely to bite **2** irritable

snap·py *adj.* **-pi·er, -pi·est 1** cross; irritable **2** that snaps **3** [Inf.] brisk or lively **4** [Inf.] stylish

snap·shot *n.* an informal photograph taken with a hand camera

snare (sner) *n.* 〖< ON *snara*〗 **1** a trap for small animals **2** anything dangerous, etc. that tempts or attracts **3** a length usually of coiled wire across the bottom of a drum to give a sharper sound —*vt.* **snared, snar′ing** to catch as in a snare; trap

snarl¹ (snärl) *vi.* 〖< earlier *snar*, to growl〗 **1** to growl, baring the teeth, as a dog does **2** to speak sharply, as in anger —*vt.* to utter with a snarl —*n.* a fierce growl —**snarl′ing·ly** *adv.*

snarl² (snärl) *n., vt., vi.* 〖< SNARE〗 tangle —**snarl′y** *adj.* **-i·er, -i·est**

snatch (snach) *vt.* 〖ME *snacchen*〗 to take suddenly, specif. without right or warning —*vi.* **1** to try to seize; grab (*at*) **2** to take advantage of a chance, etc. eagerly: with *at* —*n.* **1** a snatching **2** a brief period **3** a fragment; bit

sneak (snēk) *vt., vi.* **sneaked** or **snuck, sneak′ing** 〖prob. < OE *snican*, to crawl〗 to move, act, give, put, take, etc. secretly or

stealthily —*n.* **1** one who sneaks **2** a sneaking —*adj.* without warning [a *sneak* attack] —**sneak′y** *adj.* **-i·er, -i·est**

sneak·er *n.* a shoe for athletics or informal wear, having a soft rubber sole

sneak preview 1 an advance showing of a film, as for evaluating audience reaction **2** [Inf.] an early chance to look at something

sneer (snir) *vi.* 〖ME *sneren*〗 **1** to show scorn as by curling the upper lip **2** to express derision, etc. in speech or writing —*n.* a sneering

sneeze (snēz) *vi.* **sneezed, sneez′ing** 〖ME *snesen*〗 to exhale breath from the nose and mouth in an involuntary, explosive action —*n.* a sneezing

snick·er (snik′ər) *vi.* 〖echoic〗 to laugh in a sly, partly stifled way —*n.* a snickering

snide (snīd) *adj.* 〖prob. < Du dial.〗 slyly malicious or derisive

sniff (snif) *vi., vt.* 〖ME *sniffen*〗 **1** to draw in (air) forcibly through the nose **2** to express (disdain, etc.) by sniffing **3** to smell by sniffing —*n.* **1** an act or sound of sniffing **2** something sniffed

snif·fle (snif′əl) *vi.* **-fled, -fling** to sniff repeatedly, as in checking mucus running from the nose —*n.* an act or sound of sniffling —**the sniffles** [Inf.] a head cold

snif·ter (snif′tər) *n.* 〖< *snift*, var. of SNIFF〗 a goblet tapering to a small opening to concentrate the aroma, as of brandy

snig·ger (snig′ər) *vi., n.* 〖echoic〗 SNICKER

snip (snip) *vt., vi.* **snipped, snip′ping** 〖Du *snippen*〗 to cut or cut off in a short, quick stroke, as with scissors —*n.* **1** a small piece cut off **2** [Inf.] a young or insignificant person

snipe (snip) *n.* 〖< ON *snipa*〗 a long-billed wading bird —*vi.* **sniped, snip′ing** to shoot from a hidden position, as at individuals —**snip′er** *n.*

snip·pet (snip′it) *n.* 〖dim. of SNIP〗 a small piece or scrap, specif. of information

snip·py *adj.* **-pi·er, -pi·est** [Inf.] brusquely finding fault or taking offense

snit (snit) *n.* 〖< ? prec. + (F)IT〗 a fit of anger, resentment, etc.: usually in (or **into**) **a snit**

snitch (snich) [Slang] *vt.* to steal; pilfer —*vi.* to tattle (*on*) —*n.* an informer

sniv·el (sniv′əl) *vi.* **-eled** or **-elled, -el·ing** or **-el·ling** 〖ME *snivelen*〗 **1** to cry and sniffle **2** to complain and whine **3** to make a tearful, often false display of grief, etc. —**sniv′el·er** *n.*

snob (snäb) *n.* 〖< ?〗 one who disdains supposed inferiors —**snob′bish** *adj.* —**snob′bish·ness** *n.,* **snob′ber·y**

snood (snōod) *n.* 〖OE *snod*〗 a baglike net worn at the back of a woman's head to hold the hair

snook·er (snook′ər) *n.* a variety of the game of pool —*vt.* [Slang] to deceive

snoop (snōop) [Inf.] *vi.* 〖Du *snoepen*, eat on the sly〗 to pry about in a sneaking way —*n.* one who snoops: also **snoop′er** —**snoop′y** *adj.* **-i·er, -i·est**

snoot (snōot) *n.* 〖see SNOUT〗 [Inf.] the nose

snoot·y *adj.* **-i·er, -i·est** [Inf.] haughty; snobbish —**snoot′i·ness** *n.*

snooze (snōōz) *n., vi.* [< LowG *snusen*, to snore] **snoozed, snooz′ing** [Inf.] nap; doze —**snooz′er** *n.*

snore (snôr) *vi.* **snored, snor′ing** [see SNARL¹] to breathe, while asleep, with harsh sounds —*n.* the act or sound of snoring —**snor′er** *n.*

snor·kel (snôr′kəl) *n.* [Ger *schnorchel*, inlet] a breathing tube extending above the water, used in swimming just below the surface —*vi.* **-keled, -kel·ing** to swim underwater using a snorkel —**snor′kel·er** *n.*

snort (snôrt) *vi.* **1** to force breath audibly through the nostrils **2** to express contempt, etc. by a snort —*vt.* **1** to express with a snort **2** [Slang] to inhale (a drug) through the nose —*n.* **1** a snorting **2** [Slang] a quick drink of liquor

snot (snät) *n.* [OE *(ge)snot*, mucus] [Inf.] **1** nasal mucus: considered mildly vulgar **2** an impudent young person —**snot′ty** *adj.* **-ti·er, -ti·est**

snout (snout) *n.* [prob. < MDu *snute*] the projecting nose and jaws of an animal

snow (snō) *n.* [OE *snaw*] **1** frozen particles of water vapor that fall to earth as soft, white flakes **2** a falling of snow —*vi.* to fall as or like snow —*vt.* **1** to cover or obstruct with snow: with *in, up, under*, etc. **2** [Slang] to deceive or mislead —**snow under 1** to overwhelm with work, etc. **2** to defeat decisively —**snow′y** *adj.* **-i·er, -i·est**

snow·ball *n.* a mass of snow packed into a ball —*vi.* to grow rapidly like a ball of snow rolling downhill

snow·bank *n.* a large mass of snow

Snow·belt the N and NE U.S., characterized by cold, snowy winters: also **Snow Belt**

snow·board *n.* a board for sliding down snowy hills, having bindings for the rider's boots —*vi.* to use a snowboard —**snow′board′er** *n.*

snow·bound *adj.* shut in or blocked off by snow

snow·cone *n.* crushed ice mixed with a flavored syrup, served in a paper cone

snow·drift *n.* a heap of snow piled up by the wind

snow·drop *n.* a small plant with small, bell-shaped, white flowers that appear in late winter or early spring

snow·fall *n.* a fall of snow or the amount of this in a given area or time

snow fence a light fence of lath and wire to control the drifting of snow

snow·flake *n.* a single snow crystal

snow·man (-man′) *n., pl.* **-men′** (-men′) a figure made of large spheres of packed snow, vaguely suggestive of the human form

snow·mo·bile *n.* a motor vehicle with steerable runners at the front and tractor treads at the rear, used on snow —*vi.* **-biled′, -bil′ing** to travel by snowmobile

snow·plow *n.* a plowlike machine used to clear snow off a road, etc.

snow·shoe *n.* one of a pair of oblong rounded frames crisscrossed with straps, etc., worn on the feet to prevent sinking in deep snow

snow·storm *n.* a storm with a heavy snowfall

snow·suit *n.* a child's heavily lined, hooded garment for cold weather

snow tire a tire with a deep tread for added traction on snow or ice

snub (snub) *vt.* **snubbed, snub′bing** [< ON *snubba*, chide] **1** to treat with scorn, disdain, etc. **2** to check suddenly the movement of (a rope, etc.) —*n.* scornful treatment —*adj.* short and turned up: said of a nose

snub-nosed *adj.* **1** having a snub nose **2** having a short barrel: said of a handgun

snuck (snuk) *vi., vt. alt. pt. & pp. of* SNEAK

snuff¹ (snuf) *vt.* [ME] **1** to trim off the charred end of (a wick) **2** to put out (a candle) —**snuff out 1** to extinguish **2** to destroy —**snuff′er** *n.*

snuff² (snuf) *vt., vi.* [< MDu *snuffen*] to sniff or smell —*n.* **1** a sniff **2** powdered tobacco taken up into the nose or put on the gums —**up to snuff** [Inf.] up to the usual standard

snuff·box *n.* a small box for snuff

snuf·fle (snuf′əl) *n., vi.* **-fled, -fling** [< SNUFF²] SNIFFLE

snug (snug) *adj.* **snug′ger, snug′gest** [prob. < Scand] **1** warm and cozy **2** neat; trim [a *snug* cottage] **3** tight in fit —**snug′ly** *adv.*

snug·gle (-əl) *vi., vt.* **-gled, -gling** [< prec.] to nestle; cuddle

so (sō) *adv.* [OE *swa*] **1** as shown or described [hold the bat just *so*] **2** *a)* to such an extent [why are you *so* late?] *b)* very [they are *so* happy] *c)* [Inf.] very much [she *so* wants to go] **3** therefore [they were tired, and *so* left] **4** more or less [fifty dollars or *so*] **5** also; likewise [I am going, and *so* are you] **6** then [and *so* to bed] —*conj.* **1** in order (*that*) **2** with the result that —*pron.* that which has been specified or named [he is a friend and will remain *so*] —*interj.* used to express surprise, triumph, etc. —*adj.* true [that's *so*] —**and so on** (or **forth**) and the rest; et cetera —**so as** with the purpose or result —**so what?** [Inf.] even if so, what then?

SO *abbrev.* strikeout(s)

soak (sōk) *vt.* [OE *socian*] **1** to make thoroughly wet **2** to take in; absorb: usually with *up* **3** [Inf.] to overcharge —*vi.* **1** to stay in a liquid for wetting, softening, etc. **2** to penetrate —*n.* a soaking or being soaked

so-and-so *n., pl.* **so′-and-sos′** [Inf.] an unspecified person or thing: often used euphemistically

soap (sōp) *n.* [OE *sape*] **1** a substance, usually a salt derived from fatty acids, used with water to produce suds for washing **2** [Slang] SOAP OPERA —*vt.* to lather, etc. with soap —**soap′y** *adj.* **-i·er, -i·est**

soap·box *n.* any improvised platform used in speaking to a street audience

soap opera [Inf.] a radio or television serial melodrama

soap·stone *n.* a soft rock containing talc, used as an insulator, etc.

soap·suds *pl.n.* foamy, soapy water

soar (sôr) *vi.* [ult. < L *ex-*, out + *aura*, air] **1** to rise or fly high into the air **2** to glide along high in the air **3** to rise above the usual level

So·a·ve (sə wä′vä, swä′vä) *n.* [It] an Italian dry white wine

sob (säb) *vi.* **sobbed**, **sob′bing** [ME *sobben*] to weep aloud with short, gasping breaths —*vt.* to utter with sobs —*n.* the act or sound of sobbing

so·ber (sō′bər) *adj.* [< L *sobrius*] **1** temperate, esp. in the use of liquor **2** not drunk **3** serious, reasonable, sedate, etc. **4** not flashy; plain — *vt., vi.* to make or become sober: often with *up* —**so′ber·ly** *adv.* —**so′ber·ness** *n.*

so·bri·e·ty (sə brī′ə tē) *n.* a being sober; specif., *a*) temperance, esp. in the use of liquor *b*) seriousness

so·bri·quet (sō′brə kā′, -ket′) *n.* [Fr] **1** a nickname **2** an assumed name

soc *abbrev.* **1** social **2** socialist **3** society

so-called *adj.* **1** known by this term **2** inaccurately or questionably designated as such [a *so-called* liberal]

soc·cer (säk′ər) *n.* [alt. < (as)soc(iation football)] a team game played by kicking a round ball

so·cia·ble (sō′shə bəl) *adj.* [see fol.] **1** friendly; gregarious **2** characterized by informal conversation and companionship —**so′cia·bil′i·ty** *n.* —**so′cia·bly** *adv.*

so·cial (sō′shəl) *adj.* [< L *soctus*, companion] **1** of or having to do with humans, etc. in their living together **2** living with others; gregarious [man as a *social* being] **3** of or having to do with society, esp. fashionable society **4** sociable **5** of or for companionship **6** of or doing welfare work —*n.* an informal gathering —**so′cial·ly** *adv.*

social disease [Old-fashioned] a sexually transmitted disease

so·cial·ism *n.* **1** a theory or system of ownership of the means of production and distribution by society rather than by individuals **2** [often **S-**] a political movement for establishing such a system —**so′cial·ist** *n., adj.* —**so′cial·is′tic** *adj.*

so·cial·ite (sō′shə līt′) *n.* a person prominent in fashionable society

so·cial·ize (-shə līz′) *vt.* **-ized′, -iz′ing** **1** to make fit for living in a group **2** to subject to governmental ownership or control —*vi.* to take part in social activity —**so′cial·i·za′tion** *n.*

socialized medicine a system supplying complete medical and hospital care to all through public funds

social media SOCIAL NETWORKING applications regarded collectively as a type of communications media

social networking open, Web-based networking in which users can share messages, videos, photographs, etc.

social science a field of study, as economics or anthropology, dealing with the structure, etc. of society —**social scientist**

Social Security [*sometimes* **s- s-**] a federal system of old-age, unemployment, or disability insurance

social studies a course of study including history, geography, etc.

social work any service or activity promoting the welfare of the community and the individual, as through counseling services, etc. —**social worker**

so·ci·e·ty (sə sī′ə tē) *n., pl.* **-ties** [< L *socius*, companion] **1** a group of persons, etc. forming a single community **2** the system of living together in such a group **3** all people, collectively **4** companionship **5** an organized group with some interest in common **6** the wealthy, dominant class —**so·ci′e·tal** (-təl) *adj.*

Society of Friends a Christian denomination that believes in plain worship, pacifism, etc.: see also QUAKER

so·ci·o·e·co·nom·ic (sō′sē ō ē′kə näm′ik, -shē-; -ek′ə-) *adj.* of or involving both social and economic factors

so·ci·ol·o·gy (sō′sē äl′ə jē, -shē-) *n.* [see SOCIAL & -LOGY] the science of social relations, organization, and problems —**so′ci·o·log′i·cal** (-ə lä′ji kəl) *adj.* —**so′ci·ol′o·gist** *n.*

so·ci·o·path (sō′sē ə path′, -shē-) *n.* an aggressively antisocial psychopath

sock¹ (säk) *n., pl.* **socks** *or* **sox** [< L *soccus*, type of light shoe] a knitted covering for the foot, usually worn under a shoe —**sock away** [Inf.] to set aside (money) as savings

sock² (säk) [Slang] *vt.* to hit with force —*n.* a blow

sock·et (säk′it) *n.* [< OFr *soc*, plowshare] a hollow part into which something fits [an eye *socket*]

sock·eye salmon (säk′ī′) a red-fleshed salmon of the N Pacific

Soc·ra·tes (säk′rə tēz′) 470?-399 B.C.; Athenian philosopher & teacher —**So·crat·ic** (sə krat′ik) *adj., n.*

sod (säd) *n.* [prob. < MDu *sode*] **1** a surface layer of earth containing grass with its roots; turf **2** a piece of this —*vt.* **sod′ded, sod′ding** to cover with sod

so·da (sō′də) *n.* [ML] **1** *a*) SODIUM BICARBONATE *b*) SODA WATER *c*) SODA POP **2** a confection of soda water, syrup, and ice cream

soda cracker a light, crisp cracker made from flour, water, and leavening, orig. baking soda

soda fountain a counter for making and serving soft drinks, sodas, etc.

soda pop a flavored, carbonated soft drink

soda water water charged under pressure with carbon dioxide gas

sod·den (säd′'n) *adj.* **1** soaked through **2** soggy from improper cooking **3** dull or stupefied, as from liquor —**sod′den·ly** *adv.*

so·di·um (sō′dē əm) *n.* [< *soda*] an alkaline, metallic chemical element: symbol, Na; at. no. 11

sodium bicarbonate a white powder, used in baking powder, as an antacid, etc.

sodium chloride common salt

sodium hydroxide a caustic base used in oil refining, etc.

sodium nitrate a clear, crystalline salt used in explosives, fertilizers, etc.

sodium pen·to·thal (pen′tə thôl′) a yellowish powder injected in solution as a general anesthetic

Sod·om and Go·mor·rah (säd′əm and gə môr′ ə) *Bible* two sinful cities destroyed by fire

sod·om·y (säd′ə mē) *n.* 〖after *Sodom*〗 any sexual intercourse held to be abnormal —**sod′ om·ite′** (-mīt′) *n.*

so·fa (sō′fə) *n.* 〖< Ar *ṣuffa*, a platform〗 an upholstered couch with fixed back and arms

sofa bed a sofa that can be opened into a bed

So·fi·a (sō′fē ə, sō fē′ə) capital of Bulgaria

soft (sôft) *adj.* 〖OE *softe*, gentle〗 **1** giving way easily under pressure **2** easily cut, marked, shaped, etc. [a *soft* metal] **3** not as hard as is normal, desirable, etc. [*soft* butter] **4** smooth to the touch **5** easy to digest: said of a diet **6** nonalcoholic: said of drinks **7** having few of the mineral salts that keep soap from lathering **8** mild, as a breeze **9** weak; not vigorous **10** easy [a *soft* job] **11** kind or gentle **12** not bright: said of color or light **13** gentle; low: said of sound —*adv.* gently; quietly —**soft′ly** *adv.* —**soft′ness** *n.*

soft·ball *n.* **1** a kind of baseball played with a larger ball **2** this ball

soft-boiled *adj.* boiled a short time to keep the yolk soft: said of an egg

soft coal BITUMINOUS COAL

soft drink a nonalcoholic drink, esp. one that is carbonated

soft·en (sôf′ən) *vt., vi.* to make or become soft or softer —**soft′en·er** *n.*

soft·heart·ed *adj.* **1** full of compassion **2** not strict or severe; lenient

soft landing a landing of a spacecraft without damage to the craft or its contents

soft money money donated to a political party but not for a particular candidate

soft palate the soft, fleshy part at the rear of the roof of the mouth; velum

soft-ped·al *vt.* **-aled** or **-alled, -al·ing** or **-al·ling** 〖from pedal to soften an instrument's tone〗 [Inf.] to make less emphatic; tone down; play down

soft sell selling that relies on subtle inducement or suggestion

soft soap [Inf.] flattery or smooth talk —**soft′-soap′** *vt.*

soft·ware *n.* the programs, routines, etc. for a computer

soft·wood *n.* **1** any light, easily cut wood **2** *a)* the wood of any tree bearing cones, as the pine *b)* such a tree

soft·y *n., pl.* **soft′ies** [Inf.] one who is too sentimental or trusting

sog·gy (säg′ē, sôg′ē) *adj.* **-gi·er, -gi·est** 〖prob. < ON *sea*, a sucking〗 soaked; moist and heavy —**sog′gi·ness** *n.*

soil¹ (soil) *n.* 〖< L *solum*〗 **1** the surface layer of earth, supporting plant life **2** land; country [native *soil*] **3** ground or earth [barren *soil*]

soil² (soil) *vt.* 〖ult. < L *sus*, pig〗 **1** to make dirty; stain **2** to disgrace —*vi.* to become soiled or dirty —*n.* a soiled spot; stain

soi·ree or **soi·rée** (swä rā′) *n.* 〖< Fr *soir*, evening〗 an evening party

so·journ (sō′jurn; *also, for v.*, sō jurn′) *vi.* 〖< L *sub-*, under + *diurnus*, of a day〗 to live somewhere temporarily —*n.* a brief stay; visit

sol (sōl) *n.* 〖< ML〗 *Music* the fifth tone of the diatonic scale

Sol (säl) *n.* 〖L〗 **1** *Rom. Myth.* the sun god **2** the sun personified

sol·ace (säl′is) *n.* 〖< L *solacium*〗 **1** an easing of grief, loneliness, etc. **2** a comfort or consolation —*vt.* **-aced, -ac·ing** to comfort; console

so·lar (sō′lər) *adj.* 〖< L *sol*, the sun〗 **1** of or having to do with the sun **2** produced by or coming from the sun

so·lar·i·um (sō ler′ē əm) *n., pl.* **-i·a** (-ē ə) 〖< L *sol*, sun〗 a glassed-in porch, etc. to sun oneself

solar panel an assembly of cells (**solar cells**) used to convert solar energy into electric power

solar plexus a network of nerves in the abdomen behind the stomach

solar system 1 the sun and all the planets, asteroids, etc. orbiting it **2** any similar system consisting of a star, its planets, etc.

sold (sōld) *vt., vi.* pt. & pp. of SELL

sol·der (säd′ər) *n.* 〖ult. < L *solidus*, solid〗 a metal alloy heated and used to join or patch metal parts, etc. — *vt., vi.* to join with solder

sol·dier (sōl′jər) *n.* 〖< LL *solidus*, a coin〗 **1** a member of an army **2** an enlisted person, as distinguished from an officer **3** one who works for a specified cause —*vi.* **1** to serve as a soldier **2** to proceed stubbornly (*on*) —**sol′ dier·ly** *adj.*

soldier of fortune a mercenary or any adventurer

sole¹ (sōl) *n.* 〖< L *solum*, a base〗 **1** the bottom surface of the foot **2** the part of a shoe, etc. corresponding to this —*vt.* **soled, sol′ing** to furnish (a shoe, etc.) with a sole

sole² (sōl) *adj.* 〖< L *solus*〗 without another; single; one and only

sole³ (sōl) *n., pl.* **sole** or **soles** 〖< L *solea*, SOLE¹: from its shape〗 a sea flatfish valued as food

sol·e·cism (säl′ə siz′əm) *n.* 〖< Gr *soloikos*, speaking incorrectly〗 a violation of conventional grammar, usage, etc.

sole·ly (sōl′lē) *adv.* **1** alone **2** only, exclusively, or merely

sol·emn (säl′əm) *adj.* 〖< L *sollemnis*, annual, hence religious: said of festivals〗 **1** sacred **2** formal **3** serious; grave; earnest —**sol′emn· ly** *adv.*

so·lem·ni·ty (sə lem′nə tē) *n., pl.* **-ties 1** solemn ceremony, ritual, etc. **2** seriousness; gravity

sol·em·nize (säl′əm nīz′) *vt.* **-nized′, -niz′ing 1** to celebrate formally or according to ritual **2** to perform the ceremony of (marriage, etc.)

so·le·noid (sō′lə noid′, säl′-) *n.* [< Gr *sōlēn*, channel + *eidos*, a form] a coil of wire with a movable iron core, used as an electromagnetic switch

so·lic·it (sə lis′it) *vt., vi.* [see SOLICITOUS] **1** to appeal to (persons) for (aid, donations, etc.) **2** to entice or lure **—so·lic′i·ta′tion** *n.*

so·lic·i·tor *n.* **1** one who solicits trade, contributions, etc. **2** in England, a lawyer other than a barrister **3** the chief lawyer for a city, etc.

so·lic·i·tous (sə lis′ə təs) *adj.* [< L *sollus*, whole + *ciere*, set in motion] **1** showing care or concern [*solicitous* for her welfare] **2** desirous; eager

so·lic·i·tude (-tōōd′) *n.* a being solicitous; care, concern, etc.

sol·id (säl′id) *adj.* [< L *solidus*] **1** relatively firm or compact; neither liquid nor gaseous **2** not hollow **3** having three dimensions **4** firm; strong; substantial **5** having made bases or divisions **6** of one color, material, etc. **7** showing unity; unanimous **8** reliable or dependable *—n.* **1** a solid substance, not a liquid or gas **2** an object having length, breadth, and thickness **—sol′id·ly** *adv.* **—sol′id·ness** *n.*

sol·i·dar·i·ty (säl′ə dar′ə tē) *n.* complete unity, as of opinion or feeling

so·lid·i·fy (sə lid′ə fī′) *vt., vi.* **-fied′, -fy′ing** to make or become solid, hard, etc. **—so·lid′i·fi·ca′tion** *n.*

so·lid·i·ty (-tē) *n.* a being solid

sol·id-state *adj.* **1** of the branch of physics dealing with the structure, properties, etc. of solids **2** equipped with transistors, etc.

so·lil·o·quy (sə lil′ə kwē) *n., pl.* **-quies** [< L *solus*, alone + *loqui*, speak] **1** a talking to oneself **2** lines in a drama spoken by a character as if to himself or herself **—so·lil′o·quize** (sə lil′ə kwīz′) *vi., vt.* **-quized′, -quiz′ing**

sol·i·taire (säl′ə ter′) *n.* [Fr: see fol.] **1** a diamond or other gem set by itself **2** a card game for one player

sol·i·tar·y (-ter′ē) *adj.* [< L *solus*, alone] **1** living or being alone **2** single; only [a *solitary* example] **3** lonely; remote **4** done in solitude

sol·i·tude (-tōōd′) *n.* [see prec.] **1** a being solitary, or alone; seclusion **2** a secluded place

so·lo (sō′lō) *n., pl.* **-los** or **-li** (-lē) [It < L *solus*, alone] **1** a musical piece or passage to be performed by one person **2** any performance by one person alone *—adj.* for or by a single person *—adv.* alone *—vi.* **-loed, -lo·ing** to perform a solo **—so′lo·ist** *n.*

Sol·o·mon (säl′ə mən) *n. Bible* king of Israel noted for his wisdom

Solomon Islands country on a group of islands in the SW Pacific, east of New Guinea

So·lon (sō′lən, -län′) 640?-559? B.C.; Athenian statesman & lawgiver

so long [Inf.] GOODBYE

sol·stice (sōl′stis, säl′-) *n.* [< L *sol*, sun + *sistere*, to stand] the time of the year when the sun reaches the point farthest north (about June 21) or farthest south (about Dec. 21) of the equator: in the Northern Hemisphere, the **summer solstice** and **winter solstice**, respectively

sol·u·ble (säl′yə bəl) *adj.* [see SOLVE] **1** that can be dissolved **2** capable of being solved

sol·ute (säl′yōōt′) *n.* the substance dissolved in a solution

so·lu·tion (sə lōō′shən) *n.* [see fol.] **1** the solving of a problem **2** an answer, explanation, etc. **3** the dispersion of one substance in another, usually a liquid, so as to form a homogeneous mixture **4** the mixture so produced

solve (sälv, sôlv) *vt.* **solved, solv′ing** [< L *se-*, apart + *luere*, let go] to find the answer to (a problem, etc.) **—solv′a·ble** *adj.* **—solv′er** *n.*

sol·vent (säl′vənt, sôl′-) *adj.* [see prec.] **1** able to pay all one's debts **2** able to dissolve another substance *—n.* a substance that can dissolve another substance **—sol′ven·cy** *n.*

So·ma·li·a (sō mä′lē ə) country of E Africa, on the Indian Ocean

so·mat·ic (sō mat′ik) *adj.* [< Gr *sōma*, body] of the body; physical

somatic cell any of the cells that form the tissues and organs of the body: opposed to GERM CELL

som·ber (säm′bər) *adj.* [< L *sub*, under + *umbra*, shade] **1** dark and gloomy **2** melancholy **3** solemn Also [Chiefly Brit.] **som′bre** **—som′ber·ly** *adv.*

som·bre·ro (säm brer′ō) *n., pl.* **-ros** [Sp < *sombra*, shade: see prec.] a broad-brimmed, tall-crowned hat worn in Mexico, the Southwest, etc.

some (sum) *adj.* [OE *sum*] **1** certain but not specified or known [open *some* evenings] **2** of an unspecified quantity, degree, etc. [have *some* candy] **3** about [*some* ten of them] **4** [Inf.] remarkable, striking, etc. [it was *some* fight] *—pron.* an unspecified number, quantity, etc. [*some* of them agree] *—adv.* **1** approximately [*some* ten men] **2** [Inf.] to some extent; somewhat [slept *some*] **3** [Inf.] to a great extent or at a great rate [must run *some* to catch up] **—and then some** [Inf.] and more than that

-some¹ (səm) [OE *-sum*] *suffix* tending to (be) [tiresome]

-some² (sōm) [< Gr *sōma*, body] *combining form* body [chromosome]

some·bod·y (sum′bäd′ē, -bud′ē) *pron.* a person unknown or not named; someone *—n., pl.* **-bod′ies** an important person

some·day *adv.* at some future day or time

some·how *adv.* in a way or by a method not known or stated: often in **somehow or other**

some·one *pron.* SOMEBODY

som·er·sault (sum′ər sôlt′) *n.* [< L *supra*, over + *saltus*, a leap] an acrobatic stunt performed by turning the body one full revolution, heels over head *—vi.* to perform a somersault

some·thing *pron.* **1** a thing not definitely known, understood, etc. [*something* went wrong] **2** a definite but unspecified thing [have *something* to eat] **3** a bit; a little —*adv.* **1** somewhat [looks *something* like me] **2** [Inf.] really; quite [sounds *something* awful] —**something else** [Slang] one that is quite remarkable

some·time *adv.* at some unspecified or future time —*adj.* **1** former **2** occasional

some·times *adv.* occasionally

some·way *adv.* in some way: also **some′ways′**

some·what *pron.* some degree, part, amount, etc. —*adv.* to some extent or degree; a bit

some·where *adv.* **1** in, to, or at some place not known or specified **2** at some time, degree, age, etc. (with *about, around, near, in, between,* etc.)

som·nam·bu·lism (säm nam′byōō liz′əm) *n.* [< L *somnus,* sleep + *ambulare,* to walk] sleepwalking —**som·nam′bu·list** *n.*

som·no·lent (säm′nə lənt) *adj.* [< L *somnus,* sleep] **1** sleepy **2** inducing drowsiness —**som′no·lence** *n.*

son (sun) *n.* [OE *sunu*] **1** a boy or man as he is related to his parents **2** a male descendant —**the Son** *Christian Theol.* Jesus

so·nar (sō′när′) *n.* [*so*(*und*) *n*(*avigation*) *a*(*nd*) *r*(*anging*)] an apparatus that transmits sound waves in water, used to find depths, etc.

so·na·ta (sə nät′ə) *n.* [It < L *sonare,* to sound] a musical composition for one or two instruments, usually consisting of several movements

song (sôŋ) *n.* [OE *sang*] **1** the act or art of singing **2** a piece of music for singing **3** *a)* [Old Poet.] poetry *b)* a lyric set to music **4** a sound like singing —**for a song** [Inf.] for a small sum; cheap

song·bird *n.* a bird that makes vocal sounds that are like music

song·fest *n.* [SONG + -FEST] an informal gathering of people for singing, esp. folk songs

song·ster (-stər) *n.* **1** a singer **2** a songwriter

song·writ·er *n.* one who writes the words or music for songs

son·ic (sän′ik) *adj.* [< L *sonus,* a sound] of or having to do with sound or the speed of sound

sonic boom the explosive sound of a supersonic jet passing overhead

son-in-law *n., pl.* **sons′-in-law′** the husband of one's child

son·net (sän′it) *n.* [ult. < L *sonus,* a sound] a poem normally of fourteen lines in any of several rhyme schemes

son·ny (sun′ē) *n., pl.* **-nies** little son: used as a familiar term of address to a young boy

So·no·ra (sə nō′rä) state of NW Mexico

so·no·rous (sə nôr′əs, sän′ər əs) *adj.* [< L *sonor,* a sound] **1** producing sound; resonant **2** full, deep, or rich in sound —**so·nor′i·ty** (-ə tē) *n., pl.* **-ties**

soon (sōōn) *adv.* [OE *sona,* at once] **1** in a short time [will *soon* be there] **2** promptly; quickly [as *soon* as possible] **3** ahead of time; early [we left too *soon*] **4** readily; willingly [as *soon* go as stay] —**sooner or later** inevitably; eventually

soot (soot) *n.* [OE *sot*] a black substance consisting chiefly of carbon particles, in the smoke of burning matter —**soot′y** *adj.* **-i·er, -i·est**

sooth (sōōth) *n.* [OE *soth*] [Archaic] truth

soothe (sōōth) *vt.* **soothed, sooth′ing** [OE *sothian,* prove true] **1** to make calm or composed, as by gentleness or flattery **2** to relieve (pain, etc.) —**sooth′er** *n.* —**sooth′ing** *adj.*

sooth·say·er (sōōth′sā′ər) *n.* [ME *sothseyere,* one who speaks the truth] [Historical] a person who professes to predict the future —**sooth′say′ing** *n.*

sop (säp) *n.* [OE *sopp*] **1** a piece of food, as bread, soaked in milk, etc. **2** *a)* something given to appease *b)* a bribe —*vt., vi.* **sopped, sop′ping 1** to soak, steep, etc. **2** to take up (liquid) by absorption: usually with *up*

SOP *abbrev.* standard operating procedure

soph·ism (säf′iz′əm) *n.* [< Gr *sophos,* clever] a clever and plausible but fallacious argument

soph·ist *n.* one who uses clever, specious reasoning —**so·phis·ti·cal** (sə fis′ti kəl) *adj.*

so·phis·ti·cate (sə fis′tə kāt′; *for n., usually,* -kit) *vt.* **-cat′ed, -cat′ing** [ult. < Gr *sophistēs,* wise man] to change from a natural or simple state; make worldly-wise —*n.* a sophisticated person

so·phis·ti·cat·ed *adj.* **1** not simple, naive, etc.; worldly-wise **2** for sophisticated people **3** highly complex or developed —**so·phis′ti·ca′tion** *n.*

soph·ist·ry (säf′is trē) *n.* misleading but clever reasoning

Soph·o·cles (säf′ə klēz′) 496?–406 B.C.; Gr. writer of tragic dramas

soph·o·more (säf′môr′, säf′ə môr′) *n.* [< obs. *sophumer,* sophism] a student in the second year of college or the tenth grade in high school —*adj.* of or for sophomores

soph·o·mor·ic *adj.* of or like sophomores; seen as opinionated, immature, etc.

-so·phy (sə fē) [< Gr *sophia,* wisdom] *combining form* knowledge

sop·o·rif·ic (säp′ə rif′ik, sō′pə-) *adj.* [< L *sopor,* sleep + -FIC] causing sleep —*n.* a soporific drug, etc.

sop·py (säp′ē) *adj.* **-pi·er, -pi·est 1** very wet: also **sop′ping 2** [Inf.] sentimental

so·pra·no (sə pran′ō, -prä′nō) *n., pl.* **-nos** or **-ni** (-nē) [It < *sopra,* above] **1** the range of the highest voice of women or boys **2** a voice, singer, or instrument with such a range **3** a part for a soprano —*adj.* of or for a soprano

sor·bet (sôr bā′, sôr′bət) *n.* [Fr < Ar *sharba*(*t*), a drink] a tart ice, as of fruit juice

sor·cer·y (sôr′sər ē) *n., pl.* **-ies** [< L *sors,* lot, chance] **1** the supposed use of an evil supernatural power over people **2** charm, influence, etc. —**sor′cer·er** *n.* —**sor′cer·ess** *n.*

sor·did (sôr′did) *adj.* [< L *sordes,* filth] **1** dirty; filthy **2** squalid; wretched **3** base; ignoble; mean —**sor′did·ly** *adv.* —**sor′did·ness** *n.*

sore (sôr) *adj.* **sor′er, sor′est** 〖OE *sar*〗 1 giving or feeling pain; painful 2 filled with grief 3 causing irritation [a *sore* point] 4 [Inf.] angry; offended —*n.* a sore, usually infected spot on the body —*adv.* [Archaic] greatly —**sore′ness** *n.*

sore·head *n.* [Inf.] a person easily angered, made resentful, etc.

sore·ly *adv.* 1 grievously; painfully 2 urgently [*sorely* needed]

sor·ghum (sôr′gəm) *n.* 〖< It *sorgo*〗 1 a cereal grass grown for grain, syrup, fodder, etc. 2 syrup made from its juices

so·ror·i·ty (sə rôr′ə tē) *n., pl.* **-ties** 〖< L *soror*, sister〗 a group of women or girls joined together for fellowship, etc., as at some colleges

sor·rel¹ (sôr′əl, sär′-) *n.* 〖< OFr *surele*〗 any of various plants with edible sour leaves

sor·rel² (sôr′əl, sär′-) *n.* 〖< OFr *sor*, light brown〗 1 light reddish brown 2 a horse, etc. of this color

sor·row (sär′ō, sôr′ō) *n.* 〖OE *sorg*〗 1 mental suffering caused by loss, disappointment, etc.; grief 2 that which causes such suffering —*vi.* to grieve —**sor′row·ful** *adj.* —**sor′row·ful·ly** *adv.*

sor·ry (sär′ē, sôr′ē) *adj.* **-ri·er, -ri·est** 〖< OE *sar*, sore〗 1 full of sorrow, pity, or regret 2 inferior; poor 3 wretched —**sor′ri·ly** *adv.* —**sor′ri·ness** *n.*

sort (sôrt) *n.* 〖< L *sors*, lot, chance〗 1 any group of related things; kind; class 2 quality or type —*vt.* to arrange according to class or kind —**of sorts** of an inferior or approximate kind: also **of a sort** —**out of sorts** [Inf.] not in good humor or health —**sort of** [Inf.] somewhat

sor·tie (sôrt′ē) *n.* 〖Fr < *sortir*, go out〗 1 a quick raid by forces from a besieged place 2 one mission by a single military plane

SOS (es′ō′es′) *n.* a signal of distress, as in wireless telegraphy

so-so *adj., adv.* just passable or passably; fair

sot (sät) *n.* 〖< ML *sottus*, a fool〗 a drunkard —**sot′tish** *adj.*

sot·to vo·ce (sät′ō vō′chē) 〖It, under the voice〗 in a low voice, so as not to be overheard

souf·flé (sōō flā′) *n.* 〖Fr < L *sufflare*, puff out〗 a baked food made light and puffy by beaten egg whites added before baking

sough (sou, suf) *n.* 〖OE *swogan*, to sound〗 a soft sighing or rustling sound —*vi.* to make a sough

sought (sôt) *vt., vi. pt. & pp. of* SEEK

soul (sōl) *n.* 〖OE *sawol*〗 1 an entity without material reality, regarded as the spiritual part of a person 2 the moral or emotional nature of a person 3 spiritual or emotional warmth, force, etc. 4 vital or essential part, quality, etc. 5 a person [I didn't see a *soul*] 6 the deep spiritual and emotional quality deemed characteristic of black American culture; also, the expression of this, as in music

soul food [Inf.] food items, as chitterlings, popular orig. in the South, esp. among blacks

soul·ful *adj.* full of deep feeling —**soul′ful·ly** *adv.* —**soul′ful·ness** *n.*

soul mate [Inf.] a person, esp. a romantic partner, with whom one is deeply compatible

sound¹ (sound) *n.* 〖< L *sonus*〗 1 that which is heard, resulting from stimulation of auditory nerves by vibrations (**sound waves**) in the air; also the vibrations 2 the distance within which a sound may be heard; earshot 3 the mental impression produced [the *sound* of his report] —*vi.* 1 to make a sound 2 to seem upon being heard [to *sound* troubled] —*vt.* 1 to cause to sound 2 to signal, express, etc. 3 to utter distinctly [to *sound* one's r's] —**sound′less** *adj.*

sound² (sound) *adj.* 〖OE (*ge*)*sund*〗 1 free from defect, damage, or decay 2 healthy [a *sound* body] 3 safe; stable [a *sound* bank] 4 based on valid reasoning; sensible 5 thorough; forceful [a *sound* defeat] 6 deep and undisturbed: said of sleep 7 honest, loyal, etc. —*adv.* deeply [*sound* asleep] —**sound′ly** *adv.* —**sound′ness** *n.*

sound³ (sound) *n.* 〖< OE & ON *sund*〗 1 a wide channel linking two large bodies of water or separating an island from the mainland 2 a long inlet or arm of the sea

sound⁴ (sound) *vt.* 〖< L *sub*, under + *unda*, a wave〗 1 to measure the depth of (water), esp. with a weighted line 2 to try to find out the opinions of (a person), usually subtly: often with *out* —*vi.* 1 to measure the depth of water 2 to dive: used as of a whale —**sound′ing** *n.*

sound barrier the large increase in air resistance encountered by aircraft flying near the speed of sound

sound bite a brief, quotable remark, as by a politician, suitable for use in radio or TV news

sounding board 1 something to increase resonance or reflect sound: often **sound′board′** 2 a person on whom one tests one's ideas, etc.

sound·proof *adj.* that keeps sound from coming through —*vt.* to make soundproof

sound·stage *n.* an enclosed soundproof area for producing films or TV shows

sound·track *n.* 1 the sound portion of a film 2 a recording of the music used in a film

soup (sōōp) *n.* 〖Fr *soupe*〗 a liquid food made by cooking meat, vegetables, etc. in water, milk, etc. —**soup up** [Slang] to increase the capacity for speed of (an engine, etc.)

soup·çon (sōōp sôn′) *n.* 〖Fr < L *suspicio*, suspicion〗 1 a slight trace, as of a flavor 2 a tiny bit

soup·y (sōō′pē) *adj.* **-i·er, -i·est** 1 watery like soup 2 [Inf.] foggy

sour (sour) *adj.* 〖OE *sur*〗 1 having the sharp, acid taste of vinegar, etc. 2 made acid or rank by fermentation 3 cross; bad-tempered 4 distasteful or unpleasant —*vt., vi.* to make or become sour —**sour′ly** *adv.* —**sour′ness** *n.*

source (sôrs) *n.* 〖< L *surgere*, to rise〗 1 a spring, etc. from which a stream arises 2 a place or thing from which something originates or develops **3** a person, book, etc. that provides information

sour cream cream that has been thickened and soured by bacterial fermentation

sour·dough (sour′dō′) *n.* **1** bread made from fermented dough **2** a lone prospector for gold, etc., as in the W U.S.

sour grapes a scorning of something only because it cannot be had or done

sour·puss (-poos′) *n.* [Slang] a gloomy or disagreeable person

souse (sous) *n.* [< OHG *sulza*, brine] **1** a pickled food, as pigs' feet **2** liquid for pickling; brine **3** a plunging into a liquid **4** [Slang] a drunkard — *vt., vi.* **soused, sous′ing 1** to pickle **2** to plunge into a liquid **3** to make or become soaking wet

soused *adj.* [Slang] drunk

south (south) *n.* [OE *suth*] **1** the direction to the left of one facing the sunset (180° on the compass) **2** a region in or toward this direction —*adj.* **1** in, of, or toward the south **2** from the south —*adv.* in or toward the south —**go south** [Inf.] to decline, deteriorate, fail, etc. —**the South** that part of the U.S. south of Pennsylvania and the Ohio River, and generally east of the Mississippi; specif., the states that formed the Confederacy

South Africa country in southernmost Africa

South America S continent in the Western Hemisphere —**South American**

South Car·o·li·na (kar′ə lī′nə) state of the SE U.S.; cap. Columbia: abbrev. *SC* —**South Car′o·lin′i·an** (-lin′ē ən)

South China Sea arm of the W Pacific, between SE Asia & the Philippines

South Da·ko·ta (də kōt′ə) Midwestern state of the U.S.; cap. Pierre: abbrev. *SD* —**South Da·ko′tan**

south·east *n.* **1** the direction halfway between south and east **2** a region in or toward this direction —*adj.* **1** in, of, or toward the southeast **2** from the southeast —*adv.* in or toward the southeast —**south′east′er·ly** *adj., adv.* —**south′east′ern** *adj.* —**south′east′ward** *adv., adj.* —**south′east′wards** *adv.*

south·er·ly (suth′ər lē) *adj., adv.* **1** toward the south **2** from the south

south·ern (suth′ərn) *adj.* **1** in, of, or toward the south **2** from the south **3** of the south

south·ern·er *n.* a person born or living in the south

Southern Hemisphere that half of the earth south of the equator

southern lights [*also* **S- L-**] aurora australis

south·paw (south′pô′) *n.* [Inf.] a left-handed person; esp., a left-handed baseball pitcher

South Pole the southern end of the earth's axis

South Sea Islands the islands in the S Pacific

South Sudan country in NE Africa

south·ward *adv., adj.* toward the south: also **south′wards** *adv.*

south·west *n.* **1** the direction halfway between south and west **2** a region in or toward this direction —*adj.* **1** in, of, or toward the southwest **2** from the southwest [*a southwest* wind] —*adv.* toward or in the southwest —**south′west′er·ly** *adj., adv.* —**south′west′ern** *adj.* —**south′west′ward** *adv., adj.* —**south′west′wards** *adv.*

sou·ve·nir (soo′və nir′) *n.* [< Fr < L *subvenire*, come to mind] something kept as a reminder of a place, person, etc.

sov·er·eign (säv′rən, -ər in) *adj.* [< L *super*, above] **1** above all others; chief; supreme **2** supreme in power, rank, etc. **3** independent of all others [*a sovereign* state] —*n.* **1** a monarch or ruler **2** a British gold coin worth one pound: no longer minted

sov·er·eign·ty *n.* **1** the status, rule, etc. of a sovereign **2** supreme and independent political authority

so·vi·et (sō′vē et′) *n.* [Russ *sovyet*, council] **1** in Russia, Uzbekistan, and, formerly, the Soviet Union, any of the various elected governing councils, local, intermediate, and national **2** any similar council in a socialist governing system —*adj.* [**S-**] of or connected with the Soviet Union

Soviet Union UNION OF SOVIET SOCIALIST REPUBLICS

sow¹ (sou) *n.* [OE *sugu*] an adult female pig

sow² (sō) *vt.* **sowed, sown** (sōn) *or* **sowed, sow′ing** [OE *sawan*] **1** to scatter (seed) for growing **2** to plant seed in (a field, etc.) **3** to spread or scatter —*vi.* to sow seed —**sow′er** *n.*

sox (säks) *n. alt. pl. of* SOCK¹

soy (soi) *n.* [Jpn] **1** a dark, salty sauce made from fermented soybeans: in full **soy sauce 2** the soybean plant or its seeds Also [*Chiefly* Brit.] **soy·a** (soi′ə)

soy·bean *n.* **1** a plant widely grown for its seeds, which contain much protein and oil **2** its seed

sp *abbrev.* **1** special **2** spelling

Sp *abbrev.* **1** Spain **2** Spanish

spa (spä) *n.* [*after* Spa, resort in Belgium] **1** a health resort having a mineral spring **2** a commercial establishment with exercise rooms, saunas, etc.

space (spās) *n.* [< L *spatium*] **1** *a*) the continuous, three-dimensional expanse in which all things are contained *b*) OUTER SPACE **2** *a*) the distance, area, etc. between or within things *b*) room for something [a parking *space*] **3** an interval of time —*vt.* **spaced, spac′ing** to arrange with space or spaces between

space·craft *n., pl.* **-craft′** any vehicle or satellite for orbiting the earth, travel through the solar system, etc.

spaced-out *adj.* [Slang] under or as if under the influence of a drug

space·flight *n.* flight in a spacecraft

space heater a small heating unit for a room or other confined area

space·port *n.* a center for assembling, testing, and launching spacecraft

space·ship *n.* a spacecraft, esp. if manned

space shuttle an airplanelike spacecraft designed to carry personnel and equipment between earth and a space station

space station a spacecraft in long-term orbit serving as a launch pad, research center, etc.

space·suit *n.* a garment pressurized for use by astronauts

space·walk *n.* the act of an astronaut in moving about in space outside a spacecraft

spac·y or **spac·y** (spā′sē) *adj.* **-i·er, -i·est** [Slang] **1** SPACED-OUT **2** *a)* eccentric or unconventional *b)* flighty, irresponsible, forgetful, etc. —**spac′i·ness** *n.*

spa·cious (spā′shəs) *adj.* having more than enough space; vast —**spa′cious·ly** *adv.* —**spa′cious·ness** *n.*

Spack·le (spak′əl) [prob. < Ger *spachtel*, spatula] *trademark for* a powder mixed with water to form a paste that dries hard, used to fill holes, cracks, etc. in wallboard, wood, etc. —*n.* [s-] this substance —*vt.* **-led, -ling** [s-] to fill or cover with spackle

spade[1] (spād) *n.* [OE *spadu*] a flat-bladed, long-handled digging tool, like a shovel —*vt.*, *vi.* **spad′ed, spad′ing** to dig with or as with a spade —**spade′ful** *n.*

spade[2] (spād) *n.* [ult. < Gr *spathē*, flat blade] **1** any of a suit of playing cards marked with black figures like this ♠ **2** [*pl.*] this suit

spade·work *n.* preparatory work for some main project, esp. when tiresome

spa·dix (spā′diks) *n., pl.* **-dix·es** or **-di·ces′** (-də sēz′) [ult. < Gr] a spike of tiny flowers, usually enclosed in a spathe

spaet·zle (shpet′slə, -səl) *n.* [< Ger dial. *spätzle*, lit., little sparrows] a dish of egg noodles or dumplings made by pressing dough through a coarse sieve into boiling water

spa·ghet·ti (spə get′ē) *n.* [It < *spago*, small cord] pasta in long, thin strings, boiled or steamed

Spain (spān) country in SW Europe

spake (spāk) *vi., vt. archaic pt. of* SPEAK

spam (spam) *Comput. n.* unsolicited email, often advertisements, sent to many addresses over a computer network, usually indiscriminately — *vt., vi.* **spammed, spam′ming** to send such email to (a user or users) —**spam′mer** *n.*

span (span) *n.* [OE *sponn*] **1** the distance (about 9 in.) between the tips of the thumb and little finger when fully extended **2** *a)* the full extent between any two limits *b)* the distance between ends or supports [the *span* of an arch] *c)* the full duration (*of*) [a *span* of attention] **3** a part between two supports —*vt.* **spanned, span′ning 1** to measure, esp. by the span of the hand **2** to extend over

Span *abbrev.* Spanish

span·dex (span′deks′) *n.* [< EXPAND] an elastic synthetic fiber used in girdles, etc.

span·gle (span′gəl) *n.* [< OE *spang*, a clasp] a small piece of bright metal sewn on fabric for decoration —*vt.* **-gled, -gling** to decorate as with spangles

Span·iard (span′yərd) *n.* a person born or living in Spain

span·iel (span′yəl) *n.* [< MFr *espagnol*, lit.,

Spanish] any of several breeds of dog with large, drooping ears and a dense, wavy coat

Span·ish (span′ish) *adj.* of Spain or its people, language, etc. —*n.* the language of Spain and Spanish America —**the Spanish** the people of Spain

Spanish America those countries south of the U.S. in which Spanish is the chief language —**Span′ish-A·mer′i·can** *adj., n.*

Spanish moss a rootless plant that grows in long, graceful grayish strands from tree branches in the SE U.S.

spank (spaŋk) *vt.* [echoic] to strike with the open hand, etc., esp. on the buttocks, as in punishment —*n.* a smack given in spanking

spank·ing *adj.* **1** swiftly moving **2** brisk: said of a breeze —*adv.* [Inf.] completely [*spanking* new]

spar[1] (spär) *n.* [< ON *sparri* or MDu *sparre*] any pole, as a mast or yard, supporting a sail of a ship

spar[2] (spär) *vi.* **sparred, spar′ring** [prob. < It *parare*, to parry] **1** to box with feinting movements, landing few heavy blows **2** to wrangle

spare (sper) *vt.* **spared, spar′ing** [OE *sparian*] **1** to refrain from killing, hurting, etc. **2** to save or free (a person) from something **3** to avoid using or use frugally **4** to part with or give up conveniently [can you *spare* a dime?] —*adj.* **1** not in regular use; extra **2** free [*spare* time] **3** meager; scanty **4** lean; thin —*n.* **1** a spare, or extra, thing **2** *Bowling* a knocking down of all the pins with two rolls of the ball —**spare′ly** *adv.*

spare·ribs *pl.n.* a cut of meat, esp. pork, consisting of the thin end of the ribs

spar·ing *adj.* careful; frugal —**spar′ing·ly** *adv.*

spark (spärk) *n.* [OE *spearca*] **1** a glowing bit of matter, esp. one thrown off by a fire **2** any flash or sparkle **3** a particle or trace **4** a brief flash of light accompanying an electric discharge as through air —*vi.* to make sparks —*vt.* to stir up; activate

spar·kle (spär′kəl) *vi.* **-kled, -kling 1** to throw off sparks **2** to glitter **3** to effervesce or bubble **4** to be brilliant and lively —*n.* **1** a sparkling **2** brilliance; liveliness —**spar′kler** (-klər) *n.*

spark plug an electrical device fitted into a cylinder of an engine to ignite the fuel mixture by making sparks

spar·row (spar′ō) *n.* [OE *spearwa*] any of numerous small, perching songbirds

sparse (spärs) *adj.* [< L *spargere*, scatter] thinly spread; not dense —**sparse′ly** *adv.* —**sparse′ness** *n.*, **spar′si·ty** (-sə tē)

Spar·ta (spärt′ə) ancient city in S Greece: a military power

Spar·tan (spärt′'n) *adj.* **1** of ancient Sparta or its people or culture **2** like the Spartans; warlike, hardy, disciplined, etc. *n.* a Spartan person

spasm (spaz′əm) *n.* [< Gr *spasmos*] **1** a sudden, involuntary muscular contraction **2** any sudden, violent, temporary activity, feeling, etc. —*vi.* to undergo a spasm

spas·mod·ic (spaz mäd′ik) *adj.* ⟦see prec. & -OID⟧ of or like spasms; fitful —**spas·mod′i·cal·ly** *adv.*

spas·tic (spas′tik) *adj.* of or characterized by muscular spasms —*n.* one having spastic paralysis

spat¹ (spat) [Inf.] *n.* ⟦prob. echoic⟧ a brief, petty quarrel —*vi.* **spat′ted, spat′ting** to engage in a spat

spat² (spat) *n.* ⟦< *spatterdash*, a legging⟧ a gaiterlike covering for the instep and ankle

spat³ (spat) *vt., vi. alt. pt. & pp. of* SPIT²

spate (spāt) *n.* ⟦< ?⟧ an unusually large flow, as of words

spathe (spāth) *n.* ⟦< L *spatha*, a flat blade⟧ a large, leaflike part enclosing a flower cluster

spa·tial (spā′shəl) *adj.* ⟦< L *spatium*, space⟧ of, or existing in, space

spat·ter (spat′ər) *vt., vi.* ⟦< ?⟧ 1 to scatter or spurt out in drops 2 to splash —*n.* 1 a spattering 2 a mark caused by spattering

spat·u·la (spach′ə lə) *n.* ⟦L < Gr *spathē*, flat blade⟧ an implement with a broad, flat, flexible blade for spreading or blending foods, paints, etc.

spat·u·late (-lāt′) *adj.* shaped like a spatula

spav·in (spav′in) *n.* ⟦< MFr *esparvain*⟧ a disease that lames horses in the hock joint —**spav′ined** *adj.*

spawn (spôn) *vt., vi.* ⟦< L *expandere*: see EXPAND⟧ 1 to produce or deposit (eggs, sperm, or young) 2 to bring forth or produce prolifically —*n.* 1 the mass of eggs or young produced by fish, mollusks, etc. 2 something produced, esp. in great quantity, as offspring

spay (spā) *vt.* ⟦< Gr *spathē*, flat blade⟧ to sterilize (a female animal) by removing the ovaries

speak (spēk) *vi.* **spoke, spo′ken, speak′ing** ⟦OE *sp(r)ecan*⟧ 1 to utter words; talk 2 to communicate as by talking 3 to make a request (*for*) 4 to make a speech —*vt.* 1 to make known as by speaking 2 to use (a given language) in speaking 3 to utter (words) —**so to speak** that is to say —**speak out (or up)** to speak clearly or freely —**speak to** to respond to, deal with, etc. —**speak well for** to say or indicate something favorable about

speak-eas·y (-ē′zē) *n., pl.* **-ies** [Old Slang] a place where alcoholic drinks are sold illegally

speak·er *n.* 1 one who speaks; esp., *a*) an orator *b*) the presiding officer of various lawmaking bodies *c*) [**S-**] the presiding officer of the U.S. House of Representatives 2 a device for converting electrical signals to audible sound waves

spear (spir) *n.* ⟦OE *spere*⟧ 1 a weapon with a long shaft and a sharp point, for thrusting or throwing 2 ⟦var. of SPIRE⟧ a long blade or shoot, as of grass —*vt.* to pierce or stab with or as with a spear

spear·fish *n., pl.* **-fish′** or **-fish′es** any of a group of large food and game fishes of the open seas —*vi.* to fish with a spear, etc.

spear·head *n.* 1 the pointed head of a spear 2 the leading person or group, as in an attack —*vt.* to take the lead in (an attack, etc.)

spear·mint *n.* ⟦prob. from the shape of its flower heads⟧ a fragrant plant of the mint family, used for flavoring

spec¹ (spek) [Inf.] *n. short for:* 1 SPECIFICATION (*n.* 1) 2 SPECULATION —**on spec** 1 according to specification(s) 2 as a speculation or gamble; without a prior commission or contract

spec² *abbrev.* 1 special 2 specifically

spe·cial (spesh′əl) *adj.* ⟦< L *species*, kind⟧ 1 distinctive or unique 2 exceptional; unusual 3 highly valued 4 of or for a particular purpose, etc. 5 not general; specific —*n.* a special thing, as, specif., a sale item —**spe′cial·ly** *adv.*

special delivery mail delivery by a special messenger, for a special fee

spe·cial·ist *n.* one who specializes in a particular field of study, work, etc.

spe·cial·ize *vi.* **-ized′, -iz′ing** to concentrate on a particular branch of study, work, etc. —**spe′cial·i·za′tion** *n.*

spe·cial·ty *n., pl.* **-ties** 1 a special quality, feature, etc. 2 a special interest, study, etc. 3 a special product, service, etc.

spe·cie (spē′shē, -sē) *n.* ⟦< L *species*, kind⟧ coin, rather than paper money

spe·cies (spē′shēz, -sēz) *n., pl.* **-cies** ⟦L, appearance, kind⟧ 1 a distinct kind; sort 2 any of the groups of related plants or animals that usually breed only among themselves: similar species form a genus

specif *abbrev.* specifically

spe·cif·ic (spə sif′ik) *adj.* ⟦< L *species*, kind + *-ficus*, -FIC⟧ 1 definite; explicit 2 peculiar to or characteristic of something 3 of a particular kind 4 specially indicated as a cure for some disease —*n.* 1 a specific cure 2 a distinct item or detail; particular —**spe·cif′i·cal·ly** *adv.*

-spe·cif·ic *combining form* limited or specific to

spec·i·fi·ca·tion (spes′ə fi kā′shən) *n.* 1 [*usually pl.*] a statement or enumeration of particulars, as to size, quality, or terms 2 something specified

specific gravity the ratio of the mass of a given volume of a substance to that of an equal volume of water or another substance used as a standard

spec·i·fy (spes′ə fī′) *vt.* **-fied′, -fy′ing** ⟦< LL *specificus*, specific⟧ 1 to state definitely 2 to include in a set of specifications

spec·i·men (spes′ə mən) *n.* ⟦L < *specere*, see⟧ 1 a part or individual used as a sample of a whole or group 2 *Med.* a sample, as of urine, for analysis

spe·cious (spē′shəs) *adj.* ⟦< L *species*, appearance⟧ seeming to be good, sound, correct, etc. without really being so —**spe′cious·ly** *adv.*

speck (spek) *n.* ⟦OE *specca*⟧ 1 a small spot, mark, etc. 2 a very small bit —*vt.* to mark with specks

speck·le (spek′əl) *n.* a small speck —*vt.* **-led, -ling** to mark with speckles

specs (speks) *pl.n.* [Inf.] 1 spectacles; eyeglasses 2 specifications

spec·ta·cle (spek′tə kəl) *n.* [< L *specere*, see] 1 a remarkable thing or sight 2 a large public show 3 [*pl.*] [Old-fashioned] a pair of eyeglasses

spec·tac·u·lar (spek tak′yə lər) *adj.* unusual to a striking degree —*n.* an elaborate show or display —**spec·tac′u·lar·ly** *adv.*

spec·ta·tor (spek′tāt′ər) *n.* [L < *spectare*, behold] one who watches without taking an active part

spec·ter (spek′tər) *n.* [< L *spectare*, behold] a ghost; apparition: Brit. sp. **spec′tre**

spec·tral (-trəl) *adj.* 1 of or like a specter 2 of a spectrum

spec·tro·scope (spek′trə skōp′) *n.* [< Ger., ult. < L *spectare*, behold] an optical instrument used for forming spectra for study —**spec·tro·scop·ic** (-skäp′ik) *adj.* —**spec·tros′co·py** (-träs′kə pē) *n.*

spec·trum (spek′trəm) *n.*, *pl.* **-tra** (-trə) or **-trums** [< L: see SPECTER] 1 the series of colored bands separated and arranged in order of their respective wavelengths by the passage of white light through a prism, etc. 2 a continuous range or entire extent

spec·u·late (spek′yə lāt′) *vi.* **-lat′ed, -lat′ing** [< L *specere*, see] 1 to ponder; esp., to conjecture 2 to take part in any risky venture (as buying or selling certain stocks, etc.) on the chance of making huge profits —**spec′u·la′tion** *n.* —**spec′u·la′tive** (-lāt′iv, -lə tiv) *adj.* —**spec′u·la′tor** *n.*

speech (spēch) *n.* [< OE *sprecan*, speak] 1 the act of speaking 2 the power to speak 3 that which is spoken; utterance, remark, etc. 4 a talk given to an audience 5 the language of a certain people

speech·less *adj.* 1 incapable of speech 2 silent, as from shock

speed (spēd) *n.* [OE *spœd*, success] 1 swiftness; quick motion 2 rate of movement; velocity 3 an arrangement of gears, as for the drive of an engine 4 [Inf.] one's kind of taste, capability, etc. 5 [Slang] any of various amphetamine compounds —*vi.* **sped** (sped) or **speed′ed, speed′ing** to move rapidly, esp. too rapidly —*vt.* 1 to help to succeed; aid 2 to cause to speed —**speed up** to increase in speed —**up to speed** 1 working, etc. at full speed 2 [Inf.] fully informed —**speed′er** *n.*

speed·boat *n.* a fast motorboat

speed·om·e·ter (spi däm′ət ər) *n.* a device attached to a motor vehicle, etc. to indicate speed

speed·ster (spēd′stər) *n.* a very fast car, driver, etc.

speed·way *n.* a track for racing automobiles or motorcycles

speed·y *adj.* **-i·er, -i·est** 1 rapid; fast; swift 2 without delay; prompt —**speed′i·ly** *adv.*

spe·le·ol·o·gy (spē′lē äl′ə jē) *n.* [< Gr *spēlaion*, a cave] the scientific study of caves —**spe′le·ol′o·gist** *n.*

spell¹ (spel) *n.* [OE, a saying] 1 a word or

formula thought to have some magic power 2 irresistible influence; charm; fascination

spell² (spel) *vt.* **spelled** or **spelt, spell′ing** [< OFr *espeller*, explain] 1 to name, write, etc. in order the letters of (a word) 2 to form (a word, etc.): said of specified letters 3 to mean [red *spells* danger] —*vi.* to spell words —**spell out** to explain in detail

spell³ (spel) *vt.* **spelled, spell′ing** [OE *spelian*] [Inf.] to work in place of (another) for an interval; relieve —*n.* 1 a period of work, duty, etc. 2 a period of anything [a *spell* of brooding] 3 [Inf.] a fit of illness

spell·bind *vt.* **-bound′, -bind′ing** to cause to be spellbound; fascinate —**spell′bind′er** *n.*

spell·bound *adj.* held by or as if by a spell; fascinated

spell-check·er *n.* a word-processing program used to check the spelling of words in a document

spell·er *n.* 1 one who spells words 2 a textbook for teaching spelling

spell·ing *n.* 1 the act of one who spells words 2 the way a word is spelled; orthography

spelling bee a spelling contest, esp. one in which a contestant is eliminated after misspelling a word

spe·lunk·er (spi lun′kər) *n.* [< Gr *spēlynx*, a cave] a cave explorer —**spe·lunk′ing** *n.*

spend (spend) *vt.* **spent, spend′ing** [< L *expendere*: see EXPEND] 1 to use up, exhaust, etc. [his fury was *spent*] 2 to pay out (money) 3 to devote (time, labor, etc.) to something 4 to pass (time) —*vi.* to pay out or use up money, etc. —**spend′a·ble** *adj.* —**spend′er** *n.*

spend·thrift *n.* one who wastes money —*adj.* wasteful

spent (spent) *vt.*, *vi. pt. & pp. of* SPEND —*adj.* 1 tired out; exhausted 2 used up; worn out

sperm (spurm) *n.* [< Gr *sperma*, seed] 1 SEMEN 2 *pl.* **sperm** or **sperms** a male germ cell, esp. a spermatozoon

sper·ma·to·zo·on (spur′mə tə zō′än′, -ən) *n.*, *pl.* **-zo′a** (-zō′ə) [< Gr *sperma*, seed + *zōion*, animal] the male germ cell, found in semen, which penetrates the egg of the female to fertilize it

sperm·i·cide (spur′mə sīd′) *n.* [SPERM + -i- + -CIDE] an agent that kills spermatozoa —**sperm′i·cid′al** *adj.*

sperm whale the largest species of toothed whale, formerly widely hunted for the oil (**sperm oil**) found in its head

spew (spyōō) *vt.*, *vi.* [OE *spiwan*] 1 to throw up (something) from or as from the stomach; vomit 2 to flow or cause to flow or gush forth —*n.* something spewed

sp gr *abbrev.* specific gravity

sphere (sfir) *n.* [< L *sphaira*] 1 any round body having the surface equally distant from the center at all points; globe; ball 2 the place, range, or extent of action, existence, knowledge, experience, etc. —**spher·i·cal** (sfer′i kəl, sfir′-) *adj.*

sphe·roid (sfir′oid) *n.* a body that is almost but not quite a sphere —**sphe·roi′dal** *adj.*

sphinc·ter (sfiŋk′tər) *n.* 〚< Gr *sphingein*, to draw close〛 a ring-shaped muscle at a body orifice

sphinx (sfiŋks) *n.* 〚< Gr, strangler〛 1 *Gr. Myth.* a winged monster with a lion's body and a woman's head 2 [**S-**] a statue with a lion's body and a man's head, near Cairo, Egypt 3 one who is difficult to know or understand

spice (spīs) *n.* 〚< L *species*, kind〛 1 an aromatic vegetable substance, as nutmeg or pepper, used to season food 2 that which adds zest or interest —*vt.* **spiced, spic′ing** 1 to season with spice 2 to add zest to —**spic′y** *adj.* **-i·er, -i·est**

spick-and-span (spik′′n span′) *adj.* 〚< *spike*, nail + ON *spānn*, a chip〛 1 new or fresh 2 neat and clean

spic·ule (spik′yōōl) *n.* 〚< L *spica*, a point〛 a hard, needlelike part

spi·der (spī′dər) *n.* 〚< OE *spinnan*, to spin〛 any of various arachnids that spin webs

spi·der·y *adj.* like a spider

spiel (spēl, shpēl) *n.* 〚Ger, play〛 [Inf.] a talk or harangue, as in selling

spiff·y (spif′ē) *adj.* **-i·er, -i·est** 〚< dial. *spiff*, well-dressed person〛 [Slang] spruce, smart, or dapper

spig·ot (spig′ət, spik′-) *n.* 〚ME *spigote*〛 a faucet

spike[1] (spīk) *n.* 〚< ON *spīkr* or MDu *spīker*〛 1 a long, heavy nail 2 a sharp-pointed projection, as on the sole of a shoe to prevent slipping —*vt.* **spiked, spik′ing** 1 to fasten or fit as with spikes 2 to pierce with, or impale on, a spike 3 to thwart (a scheme, etc.) 4 [Inf.] to add alcoholic liquor to (a drink) 5 *Sports* to hit or throw a ball forcefully toward the ground —*vi.* to rise suddenly and rapidly

spike[2] (spīk) *n.* 〚L *spica*〛 1 an ear of grain 2 a long flower cluster

spill (spil) *vt.* **spilled** or [Chiefly Brit.] **spilt** (spilt), **spill′ing** 〚OE *spillan*, destroy〛 1 to allow or cause, esp. unintentionally, to run, scatter, or flow over from a container 2 to shed (blood) 3 to throw off (a rider, etc.) 4 [Inf.] to let (a secret) become known —*vi.* to be spilled; overflow —*n.* 1 a spilling 2 a fall or tumble —**spill′age** *n.*

spill·way *n.* a channel to carry off excess water, as around a dam

spin (spin) *vt.* **spun, spin′ning** 〚OE *spinnan*〛 1 *a)* to draw out and twist fibers of (wool, cotton, etc.) into thread *b)* to make (thread, etc.) thus 2 to make (a web, cocoon, etc.), as a spider does 3 to draw *out* (a story) to a great length 4 to rotate swiftly —*vi.* 1 to spin thread or yarn 2 to form a web, cocoon, etc. 3 to whirl 4 to seem to be spinning from dizziness 5 to move along swiftly and smoothly —*n.* 1 a spinning or rotating movement 2 a ride in a motor vehicle 3 a descent of an airplane, nose first along a spiral path 4 a particular emphasis or slant given to news, etc. —**spin off** to produce as

an outgrowth or secondary development, etc. —**spin′ner** *n.*

spi·na bi·fi·da (spī′nə bif′i də) a congenital defect in which part of the spinal column is exposed, causing paralysis, etc.

spin·ach (spin′ich) *n.* 〚ult. < Pers *aspanākh*〛 1 a plant with dark-green, juicy, edible leaves 2 these leaves

spi·nal (spī′nəl) *adj.* of or having to do with the spine or spinal cord —*n.* a spinal anesthetic

spinal column the series of joined vertebrae forming the axial support for the skeleton; spine; backbone

spinal cord the thick cord of nerve tissue in the spinal column

spin·dle (spin′dəl) *n.* 〚< OE *spinnan*, to spin〛 1 a slender rod used in spinning for twisting, winding, or holding thread 2 a spindlelike thing 3 any rod or pin that revolves or serves as an axis for a revolving part

spin·dly (spind′lē) *adj.* **-dli·er, -dli·est** long or tall and very thin

spin doctor [Slang] a person employed as by a politician to use spin in presenting information in a favorable light

spine (spīn) *n.* 〚< L *spina*, thorn〛 1 *a)* a sharp, stiff projection, as on a cactus *b)* anything like this 2 *a)* SPINAL COLUMN *b)* anything like this, as the part of a book covering the seam where the pages are bound together —**spin′y** *adj.* **-i·er, -i·est**

spine·less *adj.* 1 having no spine or spines 2 lacking courage or willpower

spin·et (spin′it) *n.* 〚< It *spinetta*〛 a small upright piano

spine-tin·gling *adj.* very thrilling, terrifying, etc.

spin·ner·et (spin′ə ret′) *n.* the organ in spiders, caterpillars, etc., that spins thread for webs or cocoons

spinning wheel a simple machine for spinning thread with a spindle driven by a large wheel spun as by a treadle

spin-off (spin′ôf′) *n.* a secondary benefit, product, development, etc.

spin·ster (spin′stər) *n.* 〚ME < *spinnen*, to spin〛 [Old-fashioned] an unmarried woman, esp. an elderly one —**spin′ster·hood′** *n.*

spiny lobster a type of lobster with a spiny shell and no pincers

spi·ra·cle (spir′ə kəl) *n.* 〚< L < *spirare*, breathe〛 an opening for breathing, as on the sides of an insect's body or on the top of a whale's head

spi·ral (spī′rəl) *adj.* 〚< Gr *speira*, a coil〛 circling around a point in constantly increasing (or decreasing) curves, or in constantly changing planes —*n.* 1 a spiral curve, coil, path, etc. 2 a continuous, widening decrease or increase [an inflationary *spiral*] — *vi.*, *vt.* **-raled** or **-ralled, -ral·ing** or **-ral·ling** to move in or form a spiral

spire (spīr) *n.* 〚OE *spir*〛 1 the top part of a pointed, tapering object 2 anything tapering to a point, as a steeple

spi·re·a (spī rē′ə) *n.* [< Gr *speira*, a coil] a plant of the rose family, with dense clusters of small, pink or white flowers: also sp. **spi·rae′a**

spir·it (spir′it) *n.* [< L *spirare*, breathe] 1 *a)* the life principle, esp. in humans *b)* SOUL (*n.* 1) 2 [*also* S-] life, will, thought, etc., regarded as separate from matter 3 a supernatural being, as a ghost or angel 4 an individual [a brave *spirit*] 5 [*usually pl.*] disposition; mood [high *spirits*] 6 vivacity, courage, etc. 7 enthusiastic loyalty [school *spirit*] 8 real meaning [the *spirit* of the law] 9 a pervading animating principle or characteristic quality [the *spirit* of the times] 10 [*usually pl.*] distilled alcoholic liquor —*vt.* to carry (*away, off,* etc.) secretly and swiftly —**spir′it·less** *adj.*

spir·it·ed *adj.* lively; animated

spir·it·u·al (spir′i chōō əl) *adj.* 1 relating to the spirit or the soul 2 consisting of spirit; not corporeal 3 of religion; sacred —*n.* a folk hymn, specif. one originating among S U.S. blacks —**spir′it·u·al′i·ty** (-al′ə tē) *n.* —**spir′it·u·al·ly** *adv.*

spir·it·u·al·ism *n.* the belief that the dead survive as spirits that can communicate with the living —**spir′it·u·al·ist** *n.* —**spir′it·u·al·is′tic** *adj.*

spir·it·u·ous (spir′i chōō əs) *adj.* of or containing distilled alcohol

spi·ro·chete (spī′rō kēt′) *n.* [< Gr *speira,* a coil + *chaitē,* hair] any of various spiral-shaped bacteria

spit[1] (spit) *n.* [OE *spitu*] 1 a thin, pointed rod on which meat is roasted over a fire, etc. 2 a narrow point of land extending into the water —*vt.* **spit′ted, spit′ting** to fix as on a spit

spit[2] (spit) *vt.* **spit** or **spat, spit′ting** [OE *spittan*] 1 to eject from the mouth 2 to eject explosively —*vi.* 1 to eject saliva from the mouth 2 to rain or snow lightly or briefly —*n.* 1 a spitting 2 saliva

spit·ball *n.* 1 paper chewed up into a wad for throwing 2 *Baseball* a pitch, now illegal, made to curve by wetting one side of the ball as with spit

spite (spīt) *n.* [see DESPITE] ill will; malice —*vt.* **spit′ed, spit′ing** to vent one's spite upon by hurting, frustrating, etc. —**in spite of** regardless of —**spite′ful** *adj.*

spit·fire *n.* a woman or girl easily aroused to violent anger

spitting image [Inf.] a near-perfect likeness

spit·tle (spit′'l) *n.* saliva; spit

spit·toon (spi tōōn′) *n.* a container to spit into

splash (splash) *vt.* [echoic] 1 to cause (a liquid) to fly in drops or blobs 2 to dash a liquid, mud, etc. on, so as to wet or soil —*vi.* to move, strike, etc. with a splash —*n.* 1 a splashing 2 a spot made by splashing —**make a splash** [Inf.] to attract great attention

splash·down *n.* a spacecraft's soft landing on the sea

splash·y *adj.* **-i·er, -i·est** 1 splashing or apt to splash; wet, muddy, etc. 2 [Inf.] spectacular —**splash′i·ly** *adv.* —**splash′i·ness** *n.*

splat[1] (splat) *n.* [< SPLIT] a thin slat of wood, as in a chair back

splat[2] (splat) *n., interj.* [echoic] (used to suggest) a splattering or wet, slapping sound —*vi.* 1 to make such a sound 2 to flatten on impact

splat·ter (splat′ər) *n., vt., vi.* spatter or splash

splay (splā) *vt., vi.* [ME *splaien*] to spread out or apart: often with *out* —*adj.* spreading outward

splay·foot *n., pl.* **-feet′** a foot that is flat and turned outward —**splay′foot′ed** *adj.*

spleen (splēn) *n.* [< Gr *splēn*] 1 a large lymphatic organ in the upper left part of the abdomen: it modifies the blood structure 2 malice; spite

splen·did (splen′did) *adj.* [< L *splendere,* to shine] 1 shining; brilliant 2 magnificent; gorgeous 3 grand; illustrious 4 [Inf.] very good; fine —**splen′did·ly** *adv.*

splen·dor (splen′dər) *n.* [see prec.] 1 great luster; brilliance 2 pomp; grandeur Brit. sp. **splen′dour**

sple·net·ic (spli net′ik) *adj.* 1 of the spleen 2 bad-tempered; irritable

splice (splīs) *vt.* **spliced, splic′ing** [MDu *splissen*] 1 to join (ropes) by weaving together their strands 2 to join the ends of (timbers) by overlapping 3 to fasten the ends of (wire, film, etc.) together, as by soldering or twisting —*n.* a joint made by splicing —**splic′er** *n.*

splint (splint) *n.* [prob. < MDu *splinte*] 1 a thin strip of wood, etc. woven with others to make baskets, etc. 2 a thin, rigid strip of wood, etc. used to hold a broken bone in place

splin·ter (splin′tər) *vt., vi.* [see prec.] to break or split into thin, sharp pieces —*n.* a thin, sharp piece, as of wood, made by splitting, etc.; sliver

split (split) *vt., vi.* **split, split′ting** [MDu *splitten*] 1 to separate lengthwise into two or more parts 2 to break or tear apart 3 to divide into shares 4 to disunite 5 *a)* to break (a molecule) into atoms *b)* to produce nuclear fission in (an atom) 6 *Finance* to divide (stock) by converting each share into two or more shares with the same overall value —*n.* 1 a splitting 2 a break; crack 3 a division in a group, etc. 4 [*often pl.*] the feat of spreading the legs apart on the floor until they lie flat —*adj.* divided; separated

split-lev·el *adj.* having floor levels staggered about a half story apart

split pea a green or yellow pea shelled, dried, and split: used esp. for soup

split·ting *adj.* severe, as a headache

splotch (splä ch) *n.* [prob. < SPOT + BLOTCH] an irregular spot, splash, or stain —*vt., vi.* to mark or be marked with splotches —**splotch′y** *adj.* **-i·er, -i·est**

splurge (splurj) [Inf.] *n.* [echoic] an instance or spree of extravagant spending —*vi.* **splurged, splurg′ing** to spend money freely

splut·ter (splut′ər) *vi.* [var. of SPUTTER] 1 to

make hissing or spitting sounds **2** to speak hurriedly and confusedly —*n.* a spluttering sound or utterance

spoil (spoil) *vt.* **spoiled** or [Brit.] **spoilt**, **spoil′ing** [< L *spolium*, plunder] **1** to damage so as to make useless, etc. **2** to impair the enjoyment, etc. of **3** to cause to expect too much by overindulgence —*vi.* to become spoiled; decay, etc., as food does —*n.* [*usually pl.*] plunder; booty —**spoil′age** *n.*

spoil·er *n.* **1** one that spoils **2** one that has no chance of winning but spoils another's chances for success **3** a projecting device that breaks up airflow around a body, as on an airplane wing or the rear of a car **4** an instance of revealing, as in a review, a key part of the plot of a book or movie

spoil·sport *n.* one whose actions ruin the pleasure of others

spoils system the practice of rewarding supporters of a victorious political candidate with public offices

Spo·kane (spō kan′) city in E Washington

spoke[1] (spōk) *n.* [OE *spaca*] any of the braces or bars extending from the hub to the rim of a wheel

spoke[2] (spōk) *vi., vt. pt. & archaic pp.* of SPEAK

spo·ken (spō′kən) *vi., vt. pp.* of SPEAK —*adj.* **1** uttered; oral **2** having a (specified) kind of voice [soft-*spoken*]

spokes·man (spōks′mən) *n., pl.* **-men** (-mən) a man who is a spokesperson

spokes·per·son *n.* a person who speaks for another or for a group

spokes·wom·an *n., pl.* **-wom′en** a woman who is a spokesperson

spo·li·a·tion (spō′lē ā′shən) *n.* [< L *spoliatio*] robbery; plundering

sponge (spunj) *n.* [< Gr *spongia*] **1** a stationary aquatic animal with a porous structure **2** the highly absorbent skeleton of such animals, used for washing surfaces, etc. **3** any substance like this, as a piece of light, porous cellulose, rubber, etc. —*vt.* **sponged**, **spong′ing 1** to dampen, wipe, absorb, etc. as with a sponge **2** [Inf.] to get as by begging, imposition, etc. —*vi.* [Inf.] to live as a parasite upon other people —**spong′er** *n.* —**spon′gy** *adj.* **-gi·er, -gi·est**

sponge bath a bath taken by using a wet sponge or cloth without getting into water

sponge·cake *n.* a light, spongy cake without shortening: also **sponge cake**

spon·sor (spän′sər) *n.* [L < *spondere*, promise solemnly] **1** one who assumes responsibility for something; proponent, underwriter, endorser, etc. **2** a godparent **3** a business firm, etc. that pays for a radio or TV program advertising its product —*vt.* to act as sponsor for —**spon′sor·ship′** *n.*

spon·ta·ne·i·ty (spän′tə nē′ə tē, -nā′-) *n.* **1** a being spontaneous **2** *pl.* **-ties** spontaneous behavior, action, etc.

spon·ta·ne·ous (spän tā′nē əs) *adj.* [< L *sponte*, of free will] **1** acting or resulting from a natural feeling or impulse, without

constraint, effort, etc. **2** occurring through internal causes

spontaneous combustion the process of catching fire through heat generated by internal chemical action

spoof (spōōf) *n.* **1** a hoax or joke **2** a light satire — *vt., vi.* **1** to fool; deceive **2** to satirize playfully

spook (spōōk) [Inf.] *n.* [Du] a ghost — *vt., vi.* to frighten or become frightened

spook·y *adj.* **-i·er, -i·est** [Inf.] **1** weird; eerie **2** easily frightened; nervous, jumpy, etc.

spool (spōōl) *n.* [< MDu *spoele*] **1** a cylinder on which thread, wire, etc. is wound **2** the material wound on a spool

spoon (spōōn) *n.* [< OE *spon*, a chip] **1** a utensil consisting of a small, shallow bowl and a handle, used for eating, stirring, etc. **2** something shaped like a spoon, as a shiny, curved fishing lure —*vt.* to take up with a spoon —**spoon′ful′** *n., pl.* **-fuls′**

spoon·bill *n.* a wading bird whose flat bill is spoon-shaped at the tip

spoon·er·ism (spōōn′ər iz′əm) *n.* [after Rev. W. A. *Spooner* (1844-1930), of England, who made such slips] an unintentional interchange of the initial sounds of words (Ex.: "a well-boiled icicle" for "a well-oiled bicycle")

spoon-feed *vt.* **-fed′, -feed′ing 1** to feed with a spoon **2** to pamper; coddle

spoor (spoor) *n.* [Afrik] the track or trail of a wild animal

spo·rad·ic (spə rad′ik) *adj.* [< Gr *sporas*, scattered] happening or appearing in isolated instances [*sporadic* storms] —**spo·rad′i·cal·ly** *adv.*

spore (spôr) *n.* [< Gr *spora*, a seed] a small reproductive body produced by algae, ferns, etc. and capable of giving rise to a new individual asexually

sport (spôrt) *n.* [< DISPORT] **1** any recreational activity; specif., a game, competition, etc. requiring bodily exertion **2** fun or play **3** [Inf.] a sportsmanlike person **4** [Inf.] a showy, flashy fellow **5** *Biol.* a plant or animal markedly different from the normal type —*vt.* [Inf.] to display [to *sport* a loud tie] —*vi.* to play —*adj.* **1** of or for sports **2** suitable for casual wear [a *sport* coat] Also, for adj., **sports** —in (or for) sport in jest —**make sport of** to mock or ridicule

sport·ing *adj.* **1** of or interested in sports **2** sportsmanlike; fair **3** of games, races, etc. involving gambling or betting

spor·tive (spôrt′iv) *adj.* **1** full of sport or fun **2** done in fun —**spor′tive·ly** *adv.*

sports car a small car characterized by above-average speed and handling

sports·cast *n.* a broadcast of sports news on radio or TV —**sports′cast′er** *n.*

sports·man (-mən) *n., pl.* **-men** (-mən) **1** a man who is active in sports **2** one who exhibits sportsmanship

sports·man·ship (-mən ship) *n.* qualities and behaviors befitting a SPORTSMAN (*n.* 2)

sports·wom·an *n., pl.* **-wom′en** a woman who is active in sports

sport utility vehicle a vehicle like a station wagon, but with a small-truck chassis and, usually, four-wheel drive

sport·y *adj.* **-i·er, -i·est** [Inf.] **1** sporting or sportsmanlike **2** showy —**sport′i·ness** *n.*

spot (spät) *n.* [prob. < MDu *spotte*] **1** *a*) a small area differing in color, etc. from the surrounding area *b*) a stain, speck, etc. **2** a flaw or defect **3** a locality; place —*vt.* **spot′ted, spot′ting 1** to mark with spots **2** to stain; blemish **3** to place; locate **4** to see; recognize **5** [Inf.] to allow as a handicap [to *spot* an opponent points] **6** [Slang] to lend **7** *Sports* to assist (a gymnast, weight-lifter, etc.) by standing nearby to prevent injury —*vi.* **1** to become marked with spots **2** to make a stain —*adj.* **1** ready [*spot* cash] **2** made at random [a *spot* survey] —**hit the spot** [Inf.] to satisfy a craving or need —**in a (bad) spot** [Inf.] in trouble —**on the spot** [Inf.] in a bad or demanding situation —**spot′less** *adj.* —**spot′less·ly** *adv.* —**spot′ted** *adj.* —**spot′ter** *n.*

spot-check *vt.* to check or examine at random or by sampling —*n.* such a checking

spot·light *n.* **1** *a*) a strong beam of light focused on a particular person, thing, etc. *b*) a lamp used to project such a beam **2** public notice or prominence —*vt.* to light or draw attention to, by or as by a spotlight

spot·ty *adj.* **-ti·er, -ti·est 1** having, occurring in, or marked with spots **2** not uniform or consistent —**spot′ti·ly** *adv.*

spouse (spous) *n.* [< L *sponsus*, betrothed] (one's) husband or wife —**spous·al** (spou′zəl) *adj.*

spout (spout) *n.* [< ME *spouten*, to spout] **1** a lip, orifice, or projecting tube by which a liquid is poured or discharged **2** a stream, etc. as of liquid from a spout —*vt., vi.* **1** to shoot out (liquid, etc.) as from a spout **2** to speak or utter (words, etc.) in a loud, pompous manner

sprain (sprān) *vt.* [< ? L *ex-*, out + *premere*, to press] to wrench a ligament or muscle of (a joint) without dislocating the bones —*n.* an injury resulting from this

sprang (spraŋ) *vi., vt. alt. pt. of* SPRING

sprat (sprat) *n.* [OE *sprott*] a small European herring

sprawl (sprôl) *vi.* [< OE *spreawlian*, move convulsively] **1** to sit or lie with the limbs in a relaxed or awkward position **2** to spread out awkwardly or unevenly —*n.* **1** a sprawling movement or position **2** the uncontrolled spread of real-estate development into areas around a city

spray¹ (sprā) *n.* [prob. < MDu *spraeien*] **1** a mist of fine liquid particles **2** *a*) a jet of such particles, as from a spray gun *b*) a device for spraying **3** something likened to a spray —*vt., vi.* **1** to direct a spray (on) **2** to shoot out in a spray —**spray′er** *n.*

spray² (sprā) *n.* [ME] a small branch of a tree or plant, with leaves, flowers, etc.

spray can a can from which gas under pressure sprays out the contents

spray gun a device that shoots out a spray of liquid, as paint or insecticide

spread (spred) *vt., vi.* **spread, spread′ing** [OE *sprēdan*] **1** to open or stretch out; unfold **2** to move (the fingers, wings, etc.) apart **3** to distribute or be distributed over an area or surface **4** to extend in time **5** to make or be made widely known, felt, etc. **6** to set (a table) for a meal **7** to push or be pushed apart —*n.* **1** the act or extent of spreading **2** an expanse **3** a cloth cover for a table, bed, etc. **4** jam, butter, etc. used on bread **5** a meal with many different foods **6** a ranch or other large estate **7** in betting, the expected point differential between two teams —**spread′er** *n.*

spread-ea·gle *adj.* having the figure of an eagle with wings and legs spread —*vt.* **-gled, -gling** to stretch out in this form, as for a flogging

spread·sheet *n.* a computer program that organizes numerical data into rows and columns on a video screen

spree (sprē) *n.* [< earlier *spray*] **1** a noisy frolic **2** a period of drunkenness **3** a period of uninhibited activity [a shopping *spree*]

sprig (sprig) *n.* [ME *sprigge*] a little twig or spray

spright·ly (sprīt′lē) *adj.* **-li·er, -li·est** [< *spright*, var. of SPRITE] full of energy and spirit; lively —*adv.* in a sprightly manner —**spright′li·ness** *n.*

spring (spriŋ) *vi.* **sprang** or **sprung, sprung, spring′ing** [OE *springan*] **1** to leap; bound **2** to come, appear, etc. suddenly **3** to bounce **4** to arise as from some source; grow or develop **5** to become warped, split, etc. Often followed by *up* —*vt.* **1** to cause (a trap, etc.) to snap shut **2** to cause to warp, split, etc. **3** to make known suddenly **4** [Slang] to get (someone) released from jail —*n.* **1** a leap, or the distance so covered **2** elasticity; resilience **3** a device, as a coil of wire, that returns to its original form after being forced out of shape **4** a flow of water from the ground **5** a source or origin **6** *a*) the season of the year following winter, when plants begin to grow *b*) any period of beginning —*adj.* **1** of, for, appearing in, or planted in the spring **2** having or supported on springs [a *spring* mattress] **3** coming from a spring [*spring* water] —**spring a leak** to begin unexpectedly to leak —**spring for** [Inf.] to bear the cost of for someone else

spring·board *n.* a springy board used as a take-off in leaping or diving

spring fever the laziness or restlessness that many people feel in the early days of spring

Spring·field (spriŋ′fēld′) **1** city in SW Missouri **2** capital of Illinois

spring·time *n.* the season of spring

spring·y *adj.* **-i·er, -i·est** having spring; elastic, resilient, etc. —**spring′i·ness** *n.*

sprin·kle (spriŋ′kəl) *vt., vi.* **-kled, -kling** [ME *sprinklen*] **1** to scatter or fall in drops or particles **2** to scatter drops or particles (upon) **3** to rain lightly —*n.* **1** a sprinkling **2** a light rain —**sprin′kler** *n.*

sprin·kling (-kliŋ) *n.* a small number or amount, esp. when scattered thinly

sprint (sprint) *vi., n.* ⟦ME *sprenten*⟧ run or race at full speed for a short distance —**sprint′er** *n.*

sprite (sprīt) *n.* ⟦< L *spiritus*, spirit⟧ *Folklore* an imaginary being, as an elf

spritz (sprits, shprits) *vt., vi., n.* ⟦< Ger *spritzen* & Yiddish *shprits*⟧ [Inf.] squirt or spray

spritz·er *n.* a drink consisting of white wine and soda water

sprock·et (spräk′it) *n.* ⟦< ?⟧ 1 any of the teeth, as on the rim of a wheel, arranged to fit the links of a chain 2 a wheel fitted with such teeth: in full **sprocket wheel**

sprout (sprout) *vi.* ⟦OE *sprutan*⟧ to begin to grow; give off shoots —*vt.* to cause to sprout or grow —*n.* 1 a young growth on a plant; shoot 2 a new growth from a bud, etc. 3 a new growth from a seed of alfalfa, etc., used as in salads

spruce[1] (sproos) *n.* ⟦ME *Spruce*, Prussia⟧ 1 an evergreen tree with slender needles 2 its wood

spruce[2] (sproos) *adj.* **spruc′er, spruc′est** ⟦< *Spruce leather* (see prec.)⟧ neat and trim in a smart way —*vt., vi.* **spruced, spruc′ing** to make (oneself) spruce: usually with *up*

sprung (spruŋ) *vt., vi. pp.* & *alt. pt. of* SPRING

spry (sprī) *adj.* **spri′er** or **spry′er, spri′est** or **spry′est** ⟦< Scand⟧ full of life; active, esp. though elderly —**spry′ly** *adv.* —**spry′ness** *n.*

spud (spud) *n.* [Inf.] a potato

spume (spyoom) *n.* ⟦< L *spuma*⟧ foam, froth, or scum —*vi.* **spumed, spum′ing** to foam; froth

spu·mo·ni (spə mō′nē) *n.* ⟦It < L *spuma*, foam⟧ Italian ice cream in variously flavored and colored layers

spun (spun) *vt., vi. pt.* & *pp. of* SPIN

spunk (spuŋk) *n.* ⟦Ir *sponc*, tinder⟧ [Inf.] courage; spirit —**spunk′y** *adj.* **-i·er, -i·est**

spur (spur) *n.* ⟦OE *spura*⟧ 1 a pointed device worn on the heel by a rider, used to urge a horse forward 2 anything that urges; stimulus 3 any spurlike projection 4 a short railroad track connected with the main track —*vt.* **spurred, spur′ring** 1 to prick with spurs 2 to urge or incite —**on the spur of the moment** abruptly and impulsively

spurge (spurj) *n.* ⟦< earlier Fr *espurger*, to purge⟧ any of a group of plants with milky juice and tiny flowers

spu·ri·ous (spyoor′ē əs, spur′-) *adj.* ⟦L *spurius*, illegitimate⟧ not genuine; false —**spu′ri·ous·ly** *adv.* —**spu′ri·ous·ness** *n.*

spurn (spurn) *vt.* ⟦OE *spurnan*⟧ to reject with contempt; scorn

spurt (spurt) *vt.* ⟦prob. < OE *sprutan*, to sprout⟧ to expel in a stream or jet —*vi.* 1 to gush forth in a stream or jet 2 to show a sudden, brief burst of energy, etc. —*n.* 1 a sudden shooting forth; jet 2 a sudden, brief burst of energy, etc.

sput·nik (spoot′nik, sput′-) *n.* ⟦Russ, lit., co-traveler⟧ any of a series of man-made satellites launched by the U.S.S.R. starting in 1957

sput·ter (sput′ər) *vi., vt.* ⟦< MDu *spotten*, to spit⟧ 1 to spit out (bits, drops, etc.) explosively, as when talking excitedly 2 to speak or utter in a confused, explosive way 3 to make sharp, sizzling sounds, as frying fat does —*n.* a sputtering

spu·tum (spyoot′əm) *n., pl.* **-ta** (-ə) ⟦< L *spuere*, to spit⟧ saliva, usually mixed with mucus, ejected from the mouth

spy (spī) *vt.* **spied, spy′ing** ⟦< OHG *spehōn*, examine⟧ 1 to watch closely and secretly: often with *out* 2 to catch sight of; see —*vi.* to watch closely and secretly; act as a spy —*n., pl.* **spies** 1 one who keeps close and secret watch on others 2 one employed by a government to get secret information about another government

spy·glass *n.* a small telescope

sq *abbrev.* 1 sequence 2 squadron 3 square

sqq *abbrev.* ⟦L *sequentes; sequentia*⟧ the following ones; what follows

squab (skwäb) *n.* ⟦prob. < Scand⟧ a nestling pigeon

squab·ble (skwäb′əl) *vi.* **-bled, -bling** ⟦< Scand⟧ to quarrel noisily over a small matter; wrangle —*n.* a noisy, petty quarrel —**squab′bler** *n.*

squad (skwäd) *n.* ⟦< Sp *escuadra* or It *squadra*, a square⟧ 1 a small group of soldiers, often a subdivision of a platoon 2 any small group of people working together

squad car PATROL CAR

squad·ron (-rən) *n.* ⟦< It *squadra*, a square⟧ a unit of warships, military aircraft, etc.

squal·id (skwäl′id, skwôl′id) *adj.* ⟦< L *squalere*, be foul⟧ 1 foul or unclean 2 wretched

squall[1] (skwôl) *n.* ⟦< Scand⟧ a brief, violent windstorm, usually with rain or snow —**squall′y** *adj.* **-i·er, -i·est**

squall[2] (skwôl) *vi., vt.* ⟦< ON *skvala*⟧ to cry or scream loudly and harshly —*n.* a harsh cry or loud scream

squal·or (skwäl′ər, skwôl′ər) *n.* a being squalid; filth and wretchedness

squa·mous (skwā′məs) *adj.* ⟦< L *squama*, a scale⟧ like, formed of, or covered with scales

squan·der (skwän′dər) *vt.* ⟦prob. < dial. *squander*, to scatter⟧ to spend or use wastefully or extravagantly

square (skwer) *n.* ⟦< L *ex*, out + *quadrare*, to square⟧ 1 *a)* a plane figure having four equal sides and four right angles *b)* anything of or approximating this shape 2 an open area bounded by several streets, used as a park, etc. 3 an instrument for drawing or testing right angles 4 the product of a number multiplied by itself 5 [Inf.] a person who is SQUARE (*adj.* 10) —*vt.* **squared, squar′ing** 1 to make square 2 to make straight, even, right-angled, etc. 3 to settle; adjust [to *square* accounts] 4 to make conform [to *square* a statement with the facts] 5 to multiply (a quantity) by itself —*vi.* to fit; agree; accord (*with*) —*adj.* **squar′er, squar′est** 1 having four equal sides and four right angles **2** forming a right angle **3** straight, level, even, etc. **4** leaving no balance; even **5** just; fair **6** direct; straightforward **7** designating a unit of surface measure in the form of a square [a *square* foot] **8** sturdy and somewhat rectangular [a *square* jaw] **9** [Inf.] substantial [a *square* meal] **10** [Inf.] old-fashioned, unsophisticated, etc. —*adv.* in a square manner —**square off** to assume a posture of attack or self-defense —**square'ly** *adv.* —**square'ness** *n.* —**squar'ish** *adj.*

square dance a dance with various steps, in which four couples are grouped in a square —**square'-dance'** *vi.* **-danced', -danc'ing**

square-rigged *adj.* rigged with square sails as the principal sails

square root the number or quantity which when squared will produce a given number or quantity [3 is the *square root of* 9]

squash¹ (skwôsh, skwäsh) *vt.* [< L *ex-*, intens. + *quatere*, to shake] **1** to crush into a soft or flat mass; press **2** to suppress; quash —*vi.* **1** to be squashed **2** to make a sound of squashing —*n.* **1** the act or sound of squashing **2** a game played in a walled court with rackets and a rubber ball —**squash'y** *adj.* **-i·er, -i·est**

squash² (skwôsh, skwäsh) *n.* [< AmInd] the fleshy fruit of various plants of the gourd family, eaten as a vegetable

squat (skwät) *vi.* **squat'ted, squat'ting** [ult. < L *ex-*, intens. + *cogere*, to force] **1** to crouch so as to sit on the heels with knees bent and weight resting on the balls of the feet **2** to crouch close to the ground **3** to settle on land without right or title **4** to settle on public land in order to get title to it —*adj.* **-ter, -test** short and heavy or thick; also **squat'ty, -ti·er, -ti·est** —*n.* **1** the act or position of squatting **2** [Slang] nothing —**squat'ness** *n.* —**squat'ter** *n.*

squaw (skwô) *n.* [< AmInd] [Now Rare] a North American Indian woman or wife: term now considered offensive

squawk (skwôk) *vi.* [echoic] **1** to utter a loud, harsh cry **2** [Inf.] to complain loudly —*n.* **1** a loud, harsh cry **2** [Inf.] a loud complaint

squeak (skwēk) *vi.* [ME *squeken*] to make or utter a sharp, high-pitched sound or cry —*vt.* to say in a squeak —*n.* a thin, sharp sound or cry —**narrow** (or **close**) **squeak** [Inf.] a narrow escape —**squeak through** (or **by,** etc.) [Inf.] to succeed, survive, etc. with difficulty —**squeak'y** *adj.* **-i·er, -i·est**

squeak·er *n.* [Inf.] a narrow escape, victory, etc.

squeal (skwēl) *vi.* [ME *squelen*] **1** to utter or make a long, shrill cry or sound **2** [Slang] to act as an informer —*vt.* to utter in a squeal —*n.* a squealing —**squeal'er** *n.*

squeam·ish (skwē'mish) *adj.* [ME *squaimous*] **1** easily nauseated **2** easily shocked —**squeam'ish·ly** *adv.* —**squeam' ish·ness** *n.*

squee·gee (skwē'jē) *n.* [prob. < fol.] a rubber-edged tool for scraping water from a flat surface

squeeze (skwēz) *vt.* **squeezed, squeez'ing** [< OE *cwysan*] **1** to press hard, esp. from two or more sides **2** to extract (juice, etc.) from (fruit, etc.) **3** to force (*into, out,* etc.) by pressing **4** to embrace closely; hug —*vi.* **1** to yield to pressure **2** to exert pressure **3** to force one's way by pushing (*in, out,* etc.) —*n.* **1** a squeezing or being squeezed **2** a close embrace; hug **3** the state of being closely pressed or packed; crush **4** a period of scarcity, hardship, etc.

squeeze bottle a plastic bottle that is squeezed to eject its contents

squelch (skwelch) *n.* [prob. echoic] [Inf.] a crushing retort, rebuke, etc. —*vt.* to suppress or silence completely

squib (skwib) *n.* [prob. echoic] **1** a firecracker that burns with a hissing noise before exploding **2** a short, witty attack in words; lampoon **3** a short news item

squid (skwid) *n.* [prob. < *squit,* dial. for SQUIRT] a long, slender sea mollusk with eight arms and two long tentacles

squig·gle (skwig'əl) *n.* [SQU(IRM) + (W)IGGLE] a short, wavy line or illegible scrawl —*vt., vi.* **-gled, -gling** to write as, or make, a squiggle or squiggles

squint (skwint) *vi.* [< (a)*squint,* with a squint < ME *on skwyn,* sideways] **1** to peer with the eyes partly closed **2** to be cross-eyed —*n.* **1** a squinting **2** a being cross-eyed **3** [Inf.] a quick look

squire (skwīr) *n.* [see ESQUIRE] **1** in England, the owner of a large, rural estate **2** [Old-fashioned] a man escorting a woman —*vt.* **squired, squir'ing** to escort

squirm (skwurm) *vi.* [prob. echoic, infl. by WORM] **1** to twist and turn the body; wriggle **2** to show or feel shame or embarrassment —*n.* a squirming —**squirm'y** *adj.* **-i· er, -i·est**

squir·rel (skwur'əl, skwurl) *n.* [< Gr *skia,* shadow + *oura,* tail] **1** a small, tree-dwelling rodent with heavy fur and a long, bushy tail **2** its fur

squirt (skwurt) *vt.* [prob. < LowG *swirtjen*] **1** to shoot out (a liquid) in a jet; spurt **2** to wet with liquid so shot out —*n.* **1** a jet of liquid **2** [Inf.] a small or young person, esp. an impudent one

squish (skwish) *vi.* [echoic var. of SQUASH¹] to make a soft, splashing sound when squeezed, etc. —*vt.* [Inf.] to squash —*n.* **1** a squishing sound **2** [Inf.] a squashing —**squish'y** *adj.* **-i·er, -i·est**

Sr¹ *abbrev.* **1** Senior **2** Sister

Sr² *abbrev. Chem.* symbol for strontium

Sri Lan·ka (srē län'ka) island country off the SE tip of India —**Sri Lan'kan**

SRO *abbrev.* **1** single room occupancy **2** standing room only

SS *abbrev.* **1** Social Security **2** steamship

SSN *abbrev.* Social Security number

SST *abbrev.* supersonic transport

St *abbrev.* **1** Saint **2** Strait **3** Street

stab (stab) *n.* [prob. < ME *stubbe,* stub] **1** a

wound made by stabbing **2** a thrust, as with a knife **3** a sudden, sharp pain — *vt.*, *vi.* **stabbed, stab′bing 1** to pierce or wound as with a knife **2** to thrust (a knife, etc.) into something **3** to pain sharply —**make (or take) a stab at** [Inf.] to make an attempt at

sta·bil·i·ty (stə bil′ə tē) *n.* **1** a being stable; steadiness **2** firmness of character, purpose, etc. **3** permanence

sta·bi·lize (stā′bə līz′) *vt.* **-lized′, -liz′ing 1** to make stable **2** to keep from changing **3** to give stability to (a plane or ship) —*vi.* to become stabilized —**sta′bi·li·za′tion** *n.* —**sta′bi·liz′er** *n.*

sta·ble¹ (stā′bəl) *adj.* **-bler, -blest** [< L *stare*, to stand] **1** not likely to give way; firm; fixed **2** firm in character, purpose, etc.; steadfast **3** not likely to change; lasting

sta·ble² (stā′bəl) *n.* [see prec.] **1** a building in which horses or cattle are sheltered and fed **2** all the racehorses belonging to one owner **3** [Inf.] all the athletes, performers, etc. under one management — *vt.*, *vi.* **-bled, -bling** to lodge, keep, or be kept in or as in a stable

stac·ca·to (stə kät′ō) *adj.*, *adv.* [It < *distac-care*, detach] *Music* with distinct breaks between successive tones

stack (stak) *n.* [< ON *stakkr*] **1** a large, neatly arranged pile of straw, hay, etc. **2** any orderly pile **3** SMOKESTACK **4** [*pl.*] a series of bookshelves, as in a library —*vt.* **1** to arrange in a stack **2** to rig so as to predetermine the outcome —**stack up** to stand in comparison (*with* or *against*)

sta·di·um (stā′dē əm) *n.* [< Gr *stadion*, ancient unit of length, *c.* 607 feet] a large structure as for sports events, with tiers of seats for spectators

staff (staf) *n.*, *pl.* **staffs**; also, for 1 & 4, **staves** [OE *stæf*] **1** a stick or rod used as a support, a symbol of authority, etc. **2** a group of people assisting a leader **3** a specific group of workers [a teaching *staff*] **4** *Music* the horizontal lines on and between which notes are written —*vt.* to provide with a staff, as of workers

staff·er *n.* a member of a staff, as of a newspaper

stag (stag) *n.* [OE *stagga*] a full-grown male deer —*adj.* for men only [a *stag* dinner]

stage (stāj) *n.* [< L *stare*, to stand] **1** a platform **2** *a)* an area or platform on which plays, etc. are presented *b)* the theater, or acting as a profession (with *the*) **3** the scene of an event **4** a stopping place, or the distance between stops, on a journey **5** *short for* STAGECOACH **6** a period or level in a process of development [the larval *stage*] **7** any of the propulsion units used in sequence to launch a missile, spacecraft, etc. —*vt.* **staged, stag′ing 1** to present as on a stage **2** to plan and carry out [to *stage* an attack]

stage·coach *n.* a horse-drawn public coach that, formerly, traveled a regular route

stage fright nervousness felt when appearing as a speaker or performer before an audience

stage·hand *n.* one who sets up scenery, furniture, lights, etc. for a stage play

stage-struck *adj.* having an intense desire to become an actor or actress

stag·ger (stag′ər) *vi.* [< ON *stakra*, totter] to totter, reel, etc. as from a blow or fatigue —*vt.* **1** to cause to stagger, as with a blow **2** to affect strongly with astonishment, grief, etc. **3** to set or arrange alternately, as on either side of a line; make zigzag **4** to arrange so as to come at different times [to *stagger* employees' vacations] —*n.* **1** a staggering **2** [*pl.*, *with sing. or pl. v.*] a nervous disease of horses, etc. causing this

stag·nant (stag′nənt) *adj.* [see fol.] **1** not flowing or moving **2** foul from lack of movement: said of water **3** dull; sluggish

stag·nate (-nāt′) *vi.*, *vt.* **-nat′ed, -nat′ing** [< L *stagnare*] to become or make stagnant —**stag·na′tion** *n.*

staid (stād) *vi.*, *vt.* archaic *pt.* & *pp.* of STAY³ —*adj.* sober; sedate —**staid′ly** *adv.*

stain (stān) *vt.* [ult. < L *dis-*, from + *tingere*, to tinge] **1** to spoil by discoloring or spotting **2** to disgrace; dishonor **3** to color (wood, etc.) with a dye —*n.* **1** a color or spot resulting from staining **2** a moral blemish **3** a dye for staining wood, etc.

stain·less steel steel alloyed with chromium, etc., which renders it virtually immune to rust and corrosion

stair (ster) *n.* [OE *stæger*] **1** [*usually pl.*] a stairway **2** a single step, as of a stairway

stair·case *n.* a stairway in a building, usually with a handrail

stair·way *n.* a means of access, as from one level of a building to another, consisting of a series of stairs

stair·well *n.* a vertical shaft (in a building) containing a staircase

stake (stāk) *n.* [OE *staca*] **1** a pointed length of wood or metal for driving into the ground **2** the post to which a person was tied for execution by burning **3** [*often pl.*] money risked, as in a wager or business venture **4** [*often pl.*] the winner's prize in a race, etc. —*vt.* **staked, stak′ing 1** to mark the boundaries of [to *stake* out a claim] **2** to fasten to a stake or stakes **3** to gamble **4** [Inf.] to furnish with money or resources —**at stake** being risked —**pull up stakes** [Inf.] to change one's residence, etc. —**stake out** to put under police surveillance

stake·out *n.* **1** the putting of a suspect or a place under police surveillance **2** an area under such surveillance

sta·lac·tite (stə lak′tīt) *n.* [< Gr *stalaktos*, trickling] an icicle-shaped mineral deposit hanging from a cave roof

Sta·lag (shtä′läk; *E* stä′läg) *n.* [Ger] a German prisoner-of-war camp, esp. in WWII

sta·lag·mite (stə lag′mīt′) *n.* [< Gr *stalagmos*, a dropping] a cone-shaped mineral deposit built up on a cave floor by dripping water

stale (stāl) *adj.* **stal′er, stal′est** [prob. < OFr *estale*, quiet] **1** no longer fresh; flat, dry, etc. **2** trite [a *stale* joke] **3** out of condition, bored, etc.

stale·mate *n.* [< OFr *estal*, fixed location] **1** *Chess* any situation in which a player cannot move: it results in a draw **2** any deadlock —*vt.* **-mat'ed, -mat'ing** to bring into a stalemate

Sta·lin (stä'lin), **Joseph** 1878-1953; Soviet premier (1941-53) —**Sta'lin·ist** *adj., n.*

stalk[1] (stôk) *vi., vt.* [OE *stealcian*] **1** to walk (through) in a stiff, haughty manner **2** to advance grimly **3** *a)* to pursue (game, etc.) stealthily *b)* to pursue (a person) in a persistent, harassing, obsessive way —*n.* **1** a slow, stiff, haughty stride **2** a stalking —**stalk'er** *n.*

stalk[2] (stôk) *n.* [ME *stalke*] **1** any stem or stemlike part **2** the main stem of a plant

stall[1] (stôl) *n.* [OE *steall*] **1** a partitioned-off area for one animal in a stable **2** *a)* a booth, etc. as at a market *b)* a pew in a church **3** the state of being in a stop or standstill, as a result of some malfunction —*vt., vi.* **1** to keep or be kept in a stall **2** to bring or be brought to a standstill, esp. unintentionally

stall[2] (stôl) *vi., vt.* [< *stall*, a decoy] to act evasively so as to deceive or delay —*n.* any action used in stalling

stal·lion (stal'yən) *n.* [< OFr *estalon*] an uncastrated male horse

stal·wart (stôl'wərt) *adj.* [< OE *stathol*, foundation + *wyrthe*, worth] **1** strong; sturdy **2** brave; valiant **3** resolute; firm —*n.* a stalwart person

sta·men (stä'mən) *n.* [< L, thread] the pollen-bearing organ in a flower

stam·i·na (stam'ə nə) *n.* [L, pl. of STAMEN] resistance to fatigue, illness, hardship, etc.; endurance

stam·mer (stam'ər) *vt., vi.* [OE *stamerian*] to speak or say with involuntary pauses and rapid repetitions of some sounds —*n.* a stammering —**stam'mer·er** *n.*

stamp (stamp) *vt.* [ME *stampen*] **1** to bring (the foot) down forcibly **2** to crush or pound with the foot **3** to imprint or cut out (a design, etc.) **4** to cut (*out*) by pressing with a die **5** to put a stamp on —*vi.* **1** to bring the foot down forcibly **2** to walk with loud, heavy steps, as in anger —*n.* **1** a stamping **2** *a)* a machine, tool, or die for stamping *b)* a mark or form made by stamping **3** any of various seals, gummed pieces of paper, etc. used to show that a fee, as for postage, has been paid **4** any similar stamp **5** class; kind —**stamp out 1** to crush by treading on forcibly **2** to suppress or put down —**stamp'er** *n.*

stam·pede (stam pēd') *n.* [< Sp *estampar*, to stamp] a sudden, headlong rush or flight, as of a herd of cattle —*vi.* **-ped'ed, -ped'ing** to move, or take part, in a stampede

stamping ground [Inf.] STOMPING GROUND: *also used in pl.*

stance (stans) *n.* [< L *stare*, to stand] **1** the way one stands, esp. the placement of the feet **2** the attitude taken in a given situation

stanch *vt., vi., adj. see* STAUNCH

stan·chion (stan'chən) *n.* [see STANCE] **1** an upright post or support **2** a device for confining a cow, fitted loosely around the neck

stand (stand) *vi.* **stood, stand'ing** [OE *standan*] **1** to be in, or assume, an upright position on the feet **2** to be supported on a base, pedestal, etc. **3** to take or be in a (specified) position, attitude, etc. **4** to have a (specified) height when standing **5** to be placed or situated **6** to gather and remain: said as of water **7** to remain unchanged **8** to make resistance **9** *a)* to halt *b)* to be stationary —*vt.* **1** to place upright **2** to endure **3** to withstand **4** to undergo [to *stand* trial] —*n.* **1** a standing; esp., a halt or stop **2** an act of stopping as to fight back **3** a position; station **4** a view, opinion, etc. **5** a structure to stand or sit on **6** a place of business, esp. a stall, etc. where goods are sold **7** a rack, small table, etc. for holding things **8** a growth of trees, etc. —**make a stand** to make an act of resistance or self-defense —**stand a chance** to have a chance (*of* winning, surviving, etc.) —**stand by 1** to be ready if needed **2** to aid —**stand down** to reduce, or order a reduction in, military activity —**stand for 1** to represent; mean **2** [Inf.] to tolerate —**stand in for** to substitute for —**stand on 1** to be founded on **2** to insist upon —**stand out 1** to project **2** to be distinct, prominent, etc. —**stand up 1** to rise to a standing position **2** to prove valid, durable, etc. **3** [Inf.] to fail to keep a date with —**take the stand** to testify in court

stand·ard (stan'dərd) *n.* [< OFr *estendard*] **1** a flag or banner used as an emblem of a military unit, etc. **2** something established for use as a rule or basis of comparison in measuring **3** an upright support —*adj.* **1** used as, or conforming to, a standard, rule, model, etc. **2** generally accepted as reliable or authoritative **3** typical; ordinary

stand·ard-bear·er *n.* **1** one who carries the flag **2** the leader of a movement, political party, etc.

stand·ard·ize *vt.* **-ized', -iz'ing** to make standard or uniform —**stand'ard·i·za'tion** *n.*

standard time *n.* the time in any of the time zones, usually an hour apart, into which the earth is divided based on their approximate longitude

stand·by *n., pl.* **-bys'** a person or thing that is dependable or is a possible substitute

stand·ee (stan dē') *n.* one who stands, as in a theater or bus

stand-in *n.* a temporary substitute, as for an actor at rehearsals

stand·ing *n.* **1** status or reputation [in good *standing*] **2** duration [a rule of long *standing*] —*adj.* **1** upright or erect **2** from a standing position [a *standing* jump] **3** stagnant: said as of water **4** lasting; permanent [a *standing* order]

stand·off *n.* a tie in a game or contest

stand·off·ish *adj.* reserved; aloof

stand·out *n.* [Inf.] a person or thing outstanding in performance or quality

stand·pipe n. a high vertical pipe or cylindrical tank, as in a town's water-supply system, for storing water at a desired pressure

stand·point n. point of view

stand·still n. a stop or halt

stand-up adj. 1 in a standing position 2 designating a comedian who tells jokes, etc., as in a nightclub 3 [Slang] loyal and courageous

stank (staŋk) vi. alt. pt. of STINK

stan·za (stan′zə) n. [It: ult. < L stare, to stand] a group of lines of verse forming a division of a poem or song

staph (staf) n. short for STAPHYLOCOCCUS

staph·y·lo·coc·cus (staf′ə lō kä′kəs) n., pl. **-coc′ci** (-käk′sī′) [< Gr staphylē, bunch of grapes + kokkos, kernel] any of certain spherical bacteria, a common source of infection

sta·ple¹ (stā′pəl) n. [< MDu stapel, mart] 1 a chief commodity made or grown in a particular place 2 a chief part or element in anything 3 a regularly stocked item of trade, as flour, salt, etc. 4 the fiber of cotton, wool, etc. —adj. 1 regularly stocked, produced, or used 2 most important; principal

sta·ple² (stā′pəl) n. [OE stapol, a post] a U-shaped piece of metal with sharp ends, driven into wood, etc. as to fasten something, or through papers as a binding —vt. **-pled**, **-pling** to fasten or bind with a staple or staples —**sta′pler** n.

star (stär) n. [OE steorra] 1 any of the luminous celestial objects seen as points of light in the sky; esp., any far-off, self-luminous one 2 such an object regarded as influencing one's fate: often used in pl. 3 a conventionalized figure with five or six points, or anything like this 4 ASTERISK 5 one who excels, as in a sport 6 a leading actor or actress —vt. **starred**, **star′ring** 1 to mark with stars as a decoration, etc. 2 to feature (an actor or actress) in a leading role —vi. 1 to perform brilliantly 2 to perform as a star, as in films —adj. 1 having great skill; outstanding 2 of a star

star·board (stär′bərd, -bôrd′) n. [< OE steoran, to steer (rudder formerly on right side) + bord, side (of ship)] the right-hand side of a ship, etc. as one faces forward —adj. of or on this side

starch (stärch) n. [< OE stearc, stiff] 1 a white, tasteless, odorless food substance found in potatoes, cereals, etc. 2 a powdered form of this, used in laundering for stiffening cloth, etc. —vt. to stiffen as with starch —**starch′y** adj. **-i·er**, **-i·est**

star-crossed adj. [see STAR, n. 2] ill-fated

star·dom (stär′dəm) n. the status of a star, as of films

stare (ster) vi. **stared**, **star′ing** [OE starian] to gaze steadily and intently —n. a steady, intent look —**stare down** to stare at (another) boldly until he or she looks away —**star′er** n.

star·fish n., pl. **-fish′** or **-fish′es** a small, star-shaped sea animal

star·gaze vi. **-gazed′**, **-gaz′ing** 1 to gaze at the stars 2 to indulge in dreamy thought —**star′gaz′er** n.

stark (stärk) adj. [OE stearc] 1 rigorous; severe 2 sharply outlined 3 bleak; desolate 4 sheer; downright —adv. utterly; wholly

star·less adj. with no stars visible

star·let (stär′lit) n. a young actress being promoted as a future star

star·light n. light given by the stars —**star′lit′** adj.

star·ling (stär′liŋ) n. [OE stær] any of an Old World family of birds; esp., the **common starling** with iridescent plumage, introduced into the U.S.

Star of David a six-pointed star: symbol of Judaism and now of the state of Israel

star·ry adj. **-ri·er**, **-ri·est** full of stars

star·ry-eyed adj. 1 with sparkling eyes 2 overly optimistic

Stars and Stripes name for the U.S. flag

star·ship n. a spaceship for interstellar travel

star-span·gled adj. studded with stars

Star-Spangled Banner [with reference to the U.S. flag] the U.S. national anthem

star-struck or **star·struck** adj. fascinated by celebrities, esp. by stars of movies, etc.

start (stärt) vi. [OE styrtan] 1 to make a sudden or involuntary move 2 to go into action or motion; begin; commence 3 to spring into being, activity, etc. —vt. 1 to flush (game) 2 to displace, loosen, etc. [to start a seam] 3 a) to begin to play, do, etc. b) to set into motion, action, etc. 4 to cause to be an entrant in a race, etc. 5 to play in (a game) at the beginning —n. 1 a sudden, startled reaction or movement 2 a starting, or beginning 3 a) a place or time of beginning b) a lead or other advantage 4 an opportunity of beginning a career —**start out (or off)** to start a journey, project, etc. —**start′er** n.

star·tle (stärt′'l) vt. **-tled**, **-tling** [< ME sterten, to start] to surprise or frighten suddenly; esp., to cause to start —vi. to be startled

start-up adj., n. (of) a new business venture

starve (stärv) vi. **starved**, **starv′ing** [< OE steorfan, to die] 1 to die from lack of food 2 to suffer from hunger 3 to suffer great need: with for —vt. 1 to cause to starve 2 to force by starvation —**star·va·tion** (stär vā′shən) n.

starve·ling (-liŋ) n. a person or animal that is weak from lack of food

stash (stash) [Inf.] vt. [< ?] to put or hide away (money, etc.) —n. 1 a place for hiding things 2 something hidden away

stat (stat) n. [Inf.] short for STATISTIC

-stat (stat) combining form a device or agent that keeps something (specified) stable [thermostat]

state (stāt) n. [< L stare, to stand] 1 a set of circumstances, etc. characterizing a person or thing; condition 2 condition as regards structure, form, etc. 3 rich display; pomp 4 [sometimes S-] a body of people politically organized under one government; nation 5 [often S-] any of the political units forming a federal government, as in the U.S. 6 civil government [church and state] —adj. 1 formal; ceremonial 2 [sometimes S-] of the government or of a state —*vt.* **stat′ed, stat′ing** 1 to establish by specifying 2 to set forth in words —**lie in state** to be displayed formally before burial —**the States** the United States

state·hood *n.* the condition of being a state

state·house *n.* [*often* S-] the official legislative meeting place of each U.S. state

state·less *adj.* having no state or nationality

state·ly *adj.* -li·er, -li·est 1 imposing; majestic 2 slow, dignified, etc. —**state′li·ness** *n.*

state·ment *n.* 1 *a)* a stating *b)* a declaration, assertion, etc. 2 *a)* a financial account *b)* a bill; invoice

Stat·en Island (stat′n) island borough of New York City

state-of-the-art *adj.* of the current level of sophistication, as of technology

state·room *n.* a private room on a ship or train

state·side [Inf.] *adj.* of or in the U.S. (as viewed from abroad) —*adv.* in or to the U.S.

states·man (stāts′mən) *n., pl.* -men (-mən) one who is wise or experienced in the business of government or diplomacy —**states′man·ship′** *n.*

states·wom·an *n., pl.* -wom′en a woman who is wise or experienced in the business of government

stat·ic (stat′ik) *adj.* [< Gr *statikos*, causing to stand] 1 of masses, forces, etc. at rest or in equilibrium 2 at rest; inactive 3 of or producing stationary electrical charges, as from friction 4 of or having to do with static —*n.* 1 noise in radio or TV reception, caused by atmospheric electrical discharges 2 [Slang] adverse criticism —**stat′i·cal·ly** *adv.*

sta·tion (stā′shən) *n.* [< L *stare*, to stand] 1 the place where a person or thing stands or is located; esp., an assigned post 2 a building, etc. at which a service, etc. is provided [police *station*] 3 a regular stopping place, as on a railroad 4 social standing 5 *a)* a place equipped for radio or TV transmission *b)* its assigned frequency or channel —*vt.* to assign to a station

sta·tion·ar·y (stā′shə ner′ē) *adj.* 1 not moving; fixed 2 unchanging

station break a pause in radio or TV programs for station identification

sta·tion·er (stā′shə nər) *n.* [< ML *stationarius*, shopkeeper] a dealer in office supplies, etc.

sta·tion·er·y (-ner′ē) *n.* writing materials; specif., paper and envelopes

station wagon a sedan with a tailgate and extra room for seating or cargo

sta·tis·tics (stə tis′tiks) *pl.n.* [< L *status*, standing] numerical data assembled and classified so as to present significant information —*n.* the science of compiling such data —**sta·tis′tic** *n.* **sta·tis′ti·cal** *adj.* —**stat·is·ti·cian** (stat′is tish′ən) *n.*

stats (stats) *pl.n.* [Inf.] short for STATISTICS

stat·u·ar·y (stach′oo er′ē) *n.* statues collectively

stat·ue (stach′oo) *n.* [< L *statuere*, to set] a figure, as of a person, or an abstract form carved in stone, cast in bronze, etc.

stat·u·esque (-esk′) *adj.* tall and stately

stat·u·ette (-et′) *n.* a small statue

stat·ure (stach′ər) *n.* [< L *statura*] 1 standing height, esp. of a person 2 level of attainment [moral *stature*]

sta·tus (stat′əs, stāt′-) *n., pl.* -tus·es [L, standing] 1 legal condition [the *status* of a minor] 2 *a)* position; rank *b)* prestige 3 state, as of affairs

status quo (kwō′) [L, the state in which] the existing state of affairs

status symbol a possession regarded as a mark of high social status

stat·ute (stach′oot) *n.* [see STATUE] 1 an established rule 2 a law passed by a legislative body

statute of limitations a statute limiting the time for legal action

stat·u·to·ry (stach′oo tôr′ē) *adj.* 1 fixed or authorized by statute 2 punishable by statute

satutory rape the crime of having sexual intercourse with someone who is legally underage

St. Au·gus·tine (ô′gəs tēn′) seaport in NE Florida: oldest city (founded 1565) in the U.S.

staunch (stônch, stänch) *vt.* [< L *stare*, to stand] to check the flow of (blood, etc.) from (a cut, etc.) —*vi.* to stop flowing —*adj.* 1 steadfast; loyal 2 strong; solid Also, esp. for v., **stanch** (stänch, stonch) —**staunch′ly** *adv.*

stave (stāv) *n.* [< *staves*, pl. of STAFF] 1 any of the shaped strips of wood forming the wall of a barrel, bucket, etc. 2 a stick or staff 3 a stanza —*vt.* **staved** or **stove, stav′ing** to smash or break (*in*) —**stave off** to hold off or put off

staves (stāvz) *n.* 1 *alt. pl.* of STAFF 2 *pl.* of STAVE

stay¹ (stā) *n.* [OE *stæg*] a heavy rope or cable, used as a brace or support

stay² (stā) *n.* [Fr *estaie*] 1 a support or prop 2 a strip of stiffening material used in a corset, shirt collar, etc. —*vt.* to support, or prop up

stay³ (stā) *vi.* **stayed, stay′ing** [< L *stare*, to stand] 1 to continue in the place or condition specified; remain 2 to live; dwell 3 to stop; halt 4 to pause; delay 5 [Inf.] to continue; last —*vt.* 1 to stop or check 2 to hinder or detain 3 to postpone (legal action) 4 to satisfy (thirst, etc.) for a time 5 *a)* to remain to the end of *b)* to be able to last through —*n.* 1 *a)* a stopping or being stopped *b)* a halt or pause 2 a postponement in legal action 3 the action of remaining, or the time spent, in a place —**stay put** [Inf.] to remain in place or unchanged

staying power endurance

St. Chris·to·pher (kris′tə fər) St. Kitts: see ST. KITTS AND NEVIS

STD *abbrev.* sexually transmitted disease

Ste [Fr *Sainte*] *abbrev.* 1 Saint (female) 2 Suite

stead (sted) *n.* [OE *stede*] the place of a person or thing as filled by a substitute —**stand**

someone in good stead to give someone good service

stead·fast *adj.* ⟦OE *stedefeeste*⟧ **1** firm; fixed **2** constant —**stead'fast'ly** *adv.*

stead·y *adj.* **-i·er, -i·est** ⟦STEAD + -Y²⟧ **1** firm; stable; not shaky **2** constant, regular, or uniform [*a steady gaze*] **3** constant in behavior, loyalty, etc. **4** habitual or regular; by habit [*a steady customer*] **5** calm and controlled [*steady nerves*] **6** sober; reliable — *vt., vi.* **-ied, -y·ing** to make or become steady —*n.* [Inf.] a person one dates exclusively —*adv.* in a steady manner —**go steady** [Inf.] to date someone (or each other) exclusively —**stead'i·ly** *adv.* —**stead'i·ness** *n.*

steak (stāk) *n.* ⟦< ON *steikja*, to roast on a spit⟧ a slice of beef, fish, etc. for broiling or frying

steal (stēl) *vt.* **stole, stol'en, steal'ing** ⟦OE *stelan*⟧ **1** to take (another's property, etc.) dishonestly or unlawfully, esp. in a secret manner **2** to take (a look, etc.) slyly **3** to gain insidiously or artfully [*he stole her heart*] **4** to move, put, etc. stealthily (*in, from,* etc.) **5** *Baseball* to gain (a base), as by running to it from another base while the pitch is being delivered —*vi.* **1** to be a thief **2** to move, etc. stealthily —*n.* [Inf.] an extraordinary bargain

stealth (stelth) *n.* ⟦< ME *stelen,* to steal⟧ secret or furtive action —*adj.* **1** of or using technology that prevents detection by enemy radar **2** achieving some aim by going undetected —**stealth'i·ly** *adv.* —**stealth'i·ly** *adj.*

steam (stēm) *n.* ⟦OE⟧ **1** water as converted into a vapor by being heated to the boiling point **2** the power of steam under pressure **3** condensed water vapor **4** [Inf.] vigor; energy —*adj.* using, conveying, or operated by, steam —*vi.* **1** to give off steam **2** to become covered or coated with condensed steam: usually with *up* **3** to move by steam power —*vt.* to cook, remove, etc. with steam —**steam'y** *adj.* **-i·er, -i·est**

steam·boat *n.* a small steamship

steam engine an engine using steam under pressure to supply mechanical energy

steam·er *n.* **1** something operated by steam, as a steamship **2** a container for cooking, cleaning, etc. with steam

steam·fit·ter *n.* one whose work is installing boilers, pipes, etc. in steam-pressure systems

steam·roll·er *n.* a construction machine or vehicle with a heavy roller — *vt., vi.* to move, crush, override, etc. as (with) a steamroller: also **steam'roll'**

steam·ship *n.* a ship driven by steam power

steam shovel a large, mechanically operated digger

steed (stēd) *n.* ⟦OE *steda*⟧ a horse for riding

steel (stēl) *n.* ⟦OE *stiele*⟧ **1** a hard, tough alloy of iron with carbon **2** a thing of steel **3** great strength or hardness —*adj.* of or like steel —*vt.* to make hard, tough, etc. —**steel'y** *adj.* **-i·er, -i·est**

steel wool long, thin shavings of steel in a pad, used for scouring, polishing, etc.

steel·yard *n.* ⟦STEEL + obs. *yard,* rod⟧ a scale consisting of a metal arm suspended from above with a sliding weight on one end and a hook for the object to be weighed on the other

steep¹ (stēp) *adj.* ⟦OE *steap,* lofty⟧ **1** having a sharp rise or slope; precipitous **2** [Inf.] excessive; extreme —**steep'ly** *adv.* —**steep'ness** *n.*

steep² (stēp) *vt.* ⟦ME *stepen*⟧ to soak, saturate, imbue, etc.

stee·ple (stē'pəl) *n.* ⟦OE *stepel*⟧ **1** a tower rising above the main structure, as of a church **2** a spire

stee·ple·chase *n.* a horse race run over a course obstructed with ditches, hedges, etc.

stee·ple·jack *n.* one who builds or repairs steeples, smokestacks, etc.

steer¹ (stir) *vt., vi.* ⟦OE *stieran*⟧ **1** to guide (a ship, etc.) with a rudder **2** to direct the course of (an automobile, etc.) **3** to follow (a course) —**steer clear of** to avoid —**steer'a·ble** *adj.*

steer² (stir) *n.* ⟦OE *steor*⟧ a castrated male ox, esp. one raised for beef

steer·age (stir'ij) *n.* **1** a steering **2** [Historical] a section in a ship for the passengers paying the lowest fare

steg·o·sau·rus (steg'ə sôr'əs) *n., pl.* **-ri** (-ī) ⟦< Gr *stegos,* roof + *sauros,* lizard⟧ a large dinosaur with pointed, bony plates along the backbone: also **steg'o·saur'**

stein (stīn) *n.* ⟦Ger⟧ a beer mug

stein·bok (-bäk') *n.* ⟦Ger *steinbock*⟧ an African antelope

stel·lar (stel'ər) *adj.* ⟦< L *stella,* a star⟧ **1** of a star **2** excellent **3** leading; chief [*a stellar role*]

stem¹ (stem) *n.* ⟦OE *stemm*⟧ **1** the main stalk of a plant **2** any stalk or part supporting leaves, flowers, or fruit **3** a stemlike part, as of a pipe, goblet, etc. **4** the prow of a ship; bow **5** the part of a word to which inflectional endings are added —*vt.* **stemmed, stem'ming** to make headway against [*to stem the tide*] —*vi.* to derive

stem² (stem) *vt.* **stemmed, stem'ming** ⟦< ON *stemma*⟧ to stop or check by or as if by damming up

stem cell *Biol.* an unspecialized cell that has the potential to develop into one or more different types of specialized cells

stem·ware *n.* goblets, wineglasses, etc. having stems

stench (stench) *n.* ⟦< OE *stincan,* to stink⟧ an offensive smell; stink

sten·cil (sten'səl) *vt.* **-ciled** or **-cilled, -cil·ing** or **-cil·ling** ⟦ult. < L *scintilla,* a spark⟧ to make or mark with a stencil —*n.* **1** a thin sheet, as of paper, cut through so that when ink, etc. is applied, designs, letters, etc. form on the surface beneath **2** a design, etc. so made

ste·nog·ra·phy (stə näg'rə fē) *n.* shorthand writing, as of dictation, testimony, etc., for later transcription —**ste·nog'ra·pher** *n.* —**sten·o·graph·ic** (sten'ə graf'ik) *adj.*

stent (stent) *n.* ⟦after C.R. *Stent*, Brit dentist⟧ a surgical device used to hold tissue in place, as inside a blood vessel to keep it open

sten·to·ri·an (sten tôr'ē ən) *adj.* ⟦after *Stentor*, Gr herald in the *Iliad*⟧ very loud vocally

step (step) *n.* ⟦OE *stepe*⟧ **1** a single movement of the foot, as in walking **2** the distance covered by such a movement **3** a short distance **4** a manner of stepping **5** the sound of stepping **6** a rest for the foot in climbing, as a stair **7** a degree; level; stage **8** any of a series of acts, processes, etc. —*vi.* **stepped, step'ping** **1** to move by executing a step **2** to walk a short distance **3** to move briskly (*along*) **4** to enter (*into* a situation, etc.) **5** to press the foot down (*on*) —**in** (or **out of**) **step** conforming (or not conforming) to a rhythm, a regular procedure, etc. —**step by step 1** gradually **2** by noting each stage in a process —**step down** to resign —**step in** to intervene —**step on it** [Inf.] to go faster —**step up 1** to advance **2** to increase, as in rate —**take steps** to do the things needed —**step'per** *n.*

step-broth·er *n.* one's stepparent's son by a former union

step·child *n.*, *pl.* **-chil'dren** ⟦< OE *steop-*, orphaned + *cild*, child⟧ one's spouse's child (**step'daugh'ter** or **step'son'**) by a former union

step-down *n.* a decrease, as in amount, intensity, etc.

step·lad·der *n.* a four-legged ladder with broad, flat steps

step·par·ent *n.* the person (**step'fa'ther** or **step'moth'er**) who has married one's parent, as after the death of or divorce from one's other parent

steppe (step) *n.* ⟦Russ *styep'*⟧ any of the great plains of SE Europe and Asia, having few trees

step·ping·stone *n.* **1** a stone to step on, as in crossing a stream **2** a means of bettering oneself

step-sis·ter *n.* one's stepparent's daughter by a former union

step-up *n.* an increase, as in amount, intensity, etc.

-ster (stər) ⟦OE *-estre*⟧ *suffix* one who is, does, creates, or is associated with (something specified) [*trickster, gangster*]

ster·e·o (ster'ē ō') *n.*, *pl.* **-os'** a stereophonic device, system, effect, etc. —*adj. short for* STEREOPHONIC

stereo- ⟦< Gr *stereos*, solid⟧ *combining form* solid, firm, three-dimensional [*stereoscope*]

ster·e·o·phon·ic (ster'ē ə fän'ik) *adj.* designating or of sound reproduction using two or more channels to carry sounds from separate sources through separate speakers

ster·e·o·scop·ic (-skäp'ik) *adj.* appearing three-dimensional

ster·e·o·type (-tīp') *n.* ⟦see STEREO- & -TYPE⟧ **1** a printing plate cast from a mold, as a page of set type **2** a fixed or conventional notion or conception —*vt.* **-typed', -typ'ing** to make a stereotype of —**ster'e·o·typed'** *adj.*

ster·e·o·typ·i·cal (-tip'i kəl) *adj.* **1** stereotyped **2** hackneyed

ster·ile (ster'əl) *adj.* ⟦L *sterilis*⟧ **1** incapable of producing offspring, fruit, etc.; barren **2** lacking in interest or stimulation [*sterile decor*] **3** free from living microorganisms —**ste·ril·i·ty** (stə ril'ə tē) *n.*

ster·i·lize (-ə līz') *vt.* **-lized', -liz'ing** to make sterile; specif., *a*) to make incapable of reproduction *b*) to make free of germs, etc. —**ster'i·li·za'tion** *n.* —**ster'i·liz'er** *n.*

ster·ling (stur'liŋ) *n.* ⟦ME *sterling*, Norman coin⟧ **1** sterling silver **2** British money —*adj.* **1** of silver that is at least 92.5 percent pure **2** of British money **3** made of sterling silver **4** excellent [*a sterling reputation*]

stern' (sturn) *adj.* ⟦OE *styrne*⟧ **1** severe; strict [*stern measures*] **2** grim [*a stern face*] **3** relentless or firm —**stern'ly** *adv.* —**stern'ness** *n.*

stern² (sturn) *n.* ⟦< ON *styra*, to steer⟧ the rear end of a ship, etc.

ster·num (stur'nəm) *n.*, *pl.* **-nums** or **-na** (-nə) ⟦< Gr *sternon*⟧ the flat, bony structure to which most of the ribs are joined, in front of the chest; breastbone

ster·oid (stir'oid', ster'oid') *n.* ⟦< (CHOLE)S-TER(OL) + -OID⟧ **1** any of a group of compounds including the bile acids, sex hormones, etc. **2** a compound of this group that promotes muscle growth —**ste·roi'dal** *adj.*

stet (stet) *v. imper.* ⟦L⟧ let it stand: printer's term indicating that matter marked for deletion or change is to remain —*vt.* **stet'ted, stet'ting** to mark with "stet"

steth·o·scope (steth'ə skōp') *n.* ⟦< Gr *stēthos*, chest + -SCOPE⟧ *Med.* an instrument used to examine the heart, lungs, etc. by listening to the sounds they make

ste·ve·dore (stē'və dôr') *n.* ⟦ult. < L *stipare*, cram⟧ LONGSHOREMAN

Ste·ven·son (stē'vən sən), **Rob·ert Lou·is** (rä'bərt loo'is) 1850–94; Scot. writer

stew (stoo) *vt., vi.* ⟦ult. < L *ex-*, out + Gr *typhos*, steam⟧ **1** to cook by simmering or boiling slowly **2** to worry —*n.* **1** a dish, esp. of meat and vegetables, cooked by stewing **2** a state of worry

stew·ard (stoo'ərd) *n.* ⟦< OE *stig*, hall + *weard*, keeper⟧ **1** a person put in charge of a large estate **2** an administrator, as of finances and property **3** one responsible for the food and drink, etc. in a club, etc. **4** an attendant, as on a ship or airplane **5** a union representative —**stew'ard·ship'** *n.*

stew·ard·ess (-ər dis) *n.* a woman flight attendant

stick (stik) *n.* ⟦OE *sticca*⟧ **1** a twig or small branch broken or cut off **2** a long, slender piece of wood, as a club, cane, etc. **3** any sticklike piece [*a stick of gum*] —*vt.* **stuck, stick'ing 1** to pierce, as with a pointed instrument **2** to pierce with (a knife, pin, etc.) **3** to thrust (*in, into, out*, etc.) **4** to attach by gluing, pinning, etc. **5** to obstruct, detain, etc. [*the wheels were stuck*] **6** [Inf.]

to place; put; set **7** [Inf.] to puzzle; baffle **8** [Slang] *a)* to impose a burden, etc. upon *b)* to defraud —*vi.* **1** to be fixed by a pointed end, as a nail **2** to adhere; cling; remain **3** to persevere [to *stick at a job*] **4** to remain firm and resolute [he *stuck* with us] **5** to become embedded, jammed, etc. **6** to become stopped or delayed **7** to hesitate; scruple [he'll *stick* at nothing] **8** to protrude or project (*out*, *up*, etc.) —**stick by** to remain loyal to —**stick up for** [Inf.] to uphold; defend —**the sticks** [Inf.] the rural districts

stick·er *n.* a person or thing that sticks; specif., a gummed label

stick-in-the-mud *n.* [Inf.] one who resists change, new ideas, etc.

stick·le·back (stik′əl bak′) *n.* a small, bony-plated fish with sharp dorsal spines

stick·ler (stik′lər) *n.* ⟦prob. < ME *stightlen*, to order⟧ **1** one who insists on a certain way of doing things [a *stickler* for discipline] **2** [Inf.] something difficult to solve

stick·pin *n.* an ornamental pin worn in a necktie, on a lapel, etc.

stick shift a gearshift, as on a car, operated manually

stick·um (-əm) *n.* ⟦STICK + 'em, short for THEM⟧ [Inf.] any adhesive substance

stick·up *n.* slang term for HOLDUP (*n.* 2)

stick·y *adj.* **-i·er, -i·est 1** that sticks; adhesive **2** [Inf.] hot and humid **3** [Inf.] troublesome —**stick′i·ness** *n.*

stiff (stif) *adj.* ⟦OE *stif*⟧ **1** hard to bend or move; rigid; firm **2** sore or limited in movement: said of joints and muscles **3** not fluid; thick **4** strong; powerful [a *stiff* wind] **5** harsh [*stiff* punishment] **6** difficult [a *stiff* climb] **7** very formal or awkward **8** [Inf.] excessive [a *stiff* price] —*vt.* **stiffed, stiff′ing** [Slang] to cheat —**stiff′ly** *adv.* —**stiff′ness** *n.*

stiff-arm *vt.* to push (someone) away with one's arm out straight

stiff·en *vt., vi.* to make or become stiff or stiffer —**stiff′en·er** *n.*

stiff-necked (-nekt′) *adj.* stubborn

sti·fle (stī′fəl) *vt.* **-fled, -fling** ⟦< Fr *estouffer*⟧ **1** to suffocate; smother **2** to suppress; hold back; stop [to *stifle* a sob] —*vi.* to die or suffer from lack of air —**sti′fling·ly** *adv.*

stig·ma (stig′mə) *n., pl.* **-mas;** usually for 2 & 3, **stig·ma·ta** (-mät′ə) ⟦< Gr, lit., a puncture made with a sharp instrument⟧ **1** a mark of disgrace or reproach **2** a spot on the skin, esp. one that bleeds **3** the upper tip of the pistil of a flower, on which pollen falls and develops —**stig·mat′ic** (-mat′ik) *adj.*

stig·ma·tize (-tīz′) *vt.* **-tized′, -tiz′ing** to mark or characterize as disgraceful

stile (stīl) *n.* ⟦< OE *stigan*, to climb⟧ a set of steps for climbing over a fence or wall

sti·let·to (sti let′ō) *n., pl.* **-tos** or **-toes** ⟦It < L *stilus*, pointed tool⟧ a small dagger with a slender blade

still¹ (stil) *adj.* ⟦OE *stille*⟧ **1** noiseless; silent **2** stationary **3** tranquil; calm **4** designating or of a single photograph taken from a film —*n.* **1** silence; quiet **2** a still photograph —*adv.* **1** at or up to the time indicated **2** even; yet [*still* colder] **3** nevertheless; yet [*rich* but *still* unhappy] —*conj.* nevertheless; yet —*vt., vi.* to make or become still —**still′ness** *n.*

still² (stil) *n.* ⟦< obs. *still*, to distill⟧ an apparatus used for distilling liquids, esp. alcoholic liquors

still·birth *n.* **1** the birth of a stillborn fetus **2** such a fetus

still·born *adj.* **1** dead when delivered from the uterus **2** unsuccessful from the start

still life *pl.* **still lifes** a picture of inanimate objects, as fruit, flowers, etc.

stilt (stilt) *n.* ⟦ME *stilte*⟧ **1** either of a pair of poles, each with a footrest, used for walking high off the ground **2** any of a number of long posts used to hold a building, etc. above ground or out of water **3** a bird with a long, slender bill and long legs

stilt·ed (stil′tid) *adj.* pompous, affected, etc.

stim·u·lant (stim′yə lant) *n.* anything, as a drug, that stimulates

stim·u·late (-lāt′) *vt.* **-lat′ed, -lat′ing** ⟦see fol.⟧ to rouse or excite to activity or increased activity —**stim′u·la′tion** *n.*

stim·u·lus (-ləs) *n., pl.* **-li′** (-lī′) ⟦L, a goad⟧ **1** an incentive **2** any action or agent that causes an activity in an organism, organ, etc.

sting (stiŋ) *vt.* **stung, sting′ing** ⟦OE *stingan*⟧ **1** to prick or wound with a sting **2** to cause sudden, pricking pain to **3** to make unhappy **4** [Slang] to cheat —*vi.* to cause or feel sharp, smarting pain —*n.* **1** a stinging **2** a pain or wound resulting from stinging **3** a sharp-pointed organ, as in insects and plants, that pricks, wounds, etc. **4** [Inf.] *a)* a swindling, as in a confidence game *b)* a scheme by police, etc. for entrapping lawbreakers

sting·er *n.* one that stings; specif., a STING (*n.* 3)

sting·ray *n.* a large ray with one or more venomous spines that can inflict painful wounds

stin·gy (stin′jē) *adj.* **-gi·er, -gi·est** ⟦< dial. form of STING⟧ **1** giving or spending grudgingly; miserly **2** less than needed; scanty —**stin′gi·ly** *adv.* —**stin′gi·ness** *n.*

stink (stiŋk) *vi.* **stank** or **stunk, stunk, stink′ing** ⟦OE *stincan*⟧ **1** to give off a strong, unpleasant smell **2** to be very offensive or abhorrent **3** [Inf.] to be of low standard or quality —*n.* a strong, unpleasant smell; stench —**stink′er** *n.* —**stink′y** *adj.* **-i·er, -i·est**

stint (stint) *vt.* ⟦< OE *styntan*, to blunt⟧ to restrict to a certain quantity, often small —*vi.* to be sparing in giving or using —*n.* **1** restriction; limit **2** an assigned task or period of work —**stint′er** *n.*

sti·pend (stī′pənd) *n.* ⟦< L *stips*, coin + *pendere*, to pay⟧ a regular or fixed payment, as a salary

stip·ple (stip′əl) *vt.* **-pled, -pling** [< Du *stippel*, a speckle] to paint, draw, or engrave in small dots

stip·u·late (stip′yə lāt′) *vt.* **-lat′ed, -lat′ing** [< L *stipulari*, to bargain] 1 to specify or require, esp. as a condition of agreement 2 to concede for the purposes of argument —**stip′u·la′tion** *n.*

stir¹ (stur) *vt., vi.* **stirred, stir′ring** [OE *styrian*] 1 to move, esp. slightly 2 to make or be active 3 to mix (a liquid, etc.) as by agitating with a spoon 4 to excite the feelings (of) 5 to incite: often with *up* —*n.* 1 a stirring 2 movement; activity 3 excitement; tumult —**stir′rer** *n.*

stir² (stur) *n.* [< Romani *stariben*] [Slang] a prison

stir-cra·zy *adj.* [Slang] anxious, tense, etc. from long, close confinement, specif. in prison

stir-fry *vt.* **-fried′, -fry′ing** to fry (diced or sliced vegetables, meat, etc.) quickly in a wok while stirring constantly

stir·ring *adj.* 1 active; busy 2 rousing; exciting

stir·rup (stur′əp) *n.* [OE *stigrap*] 1 a flat-bottomed ring hung from a saddle and used as a footrest 2 one of the three small bones in the middle ear

stitch (stich) *n.* [OE *stice*, a puncture] 1 *a)* a single complete in-and-out movement of a needle in sewing, etc. *b)* a suture 2 a loop, knot, etc. made by stitching 3 a particular kind of stitch or style of stitching 4 a sudden, sharp pain 5 a bit or piece — *vi., vt.* to make stitches (in); sew —**in stitches** in a state of uproarious laughter

stitch·er·y (-ər ē) *n.* ornamental needlework

St. John's seaport & capital of Newfoundland and Labrador

St. Kitts and Nevis (kits) country in the Leeward Islands, consisting of two islands, St. Kitts & Nevis

St. Lawrence river flowing from Lake Ontario into the Atlantic: the main section of an inland waterway (**St. Lawrence Seaway**) connecting the Great Lakes with the Atlantic

St. Lou·is (lōō′is, lōō′ē) city & port in E Missouri, on the Mississippi

St. Lu·ci·a (lōō′shē ə, lōō sē′ə) island country of the West Indies

stoat (stōt) *n.* [ME *stote*] a large European ermine, esp. in its brown summer coat

stock (stäk) *n.* [OE *stocc*] 1 the trunk of a tree 2 *a)* descent; lineage *b)* a strain, race, etc. of animals or plants 3 a supporting or main part of an implement, etc., as the wooden handle to which the barrel of a rifle is attached 4 [*pl.*] a wooden frame with holes for confining the ankles or wrists, formerly used for punishment 5 raw material 6 water in which meat, fish, etc. has been boiled, used in soups 7 livestock 8 a supply of goods on hand in a store, etc. 9 (a certificate for) a share or shares of corporate ownership 10 a stock company or its repertoire —*vt.* 1 to furnish (a farm, shop, etc.) with stock 2 to keep a supply of, as for sale or for future use —*vi.* to put in a stock, or supply: with *up* —*adj.* 1 kept in stock [*stock* sizes] 2 common or trite [a *stock* excuse] 3 that deals with stock 4 relating to a stock company —**in** (or **out of**) **stock** (not) available for sale or use —**take stock** 1 to inventory the stock on hand 2 to make an appraisal — **take** (or **put**) **stock in** to have faith in

stock·ade (stä kād′) *n.* [< Prov *estaca*, a stake] 1 a barrier of stakes driven into the ground side by side, for defense 2 an enclosure, as a fort, made with such stakes 3 an enclosure for military prisoners

stock·bro·ker *n.* one who acts as an agent in buying and selling stocks, bonds, etc.

stock car a standard automobile, modified for racing

stock company a theatrical company presenting a repertoire of plays

stock exchange 1 a place where stocks and bonds are bought and sold 2 an association of stockbrokers Also **stock market**

stock·hold·er *n.* one owning stock in a given company

Stock·holm (stäk′hōm′, -hōlm′) seaport & capital of Sweden

stock·ing *n.* [< obs. sense of *stock*] a closefitting covering, usually knitted, for the foot and leg

stocking cap a long, tapered knitted cap, often with a tassel at the end

stock·pile *n.* a reserve supply of goods, raw material, etc. — *vt., vi.* **-piled′, -pil′ing** to accumulate a stockpile (of)

stock-still *adj.* motionless

stock·y *adj.* **-i·er, -i·est** heavily built; short and thickset —**stock′i·ness** *n.*

stock·yard *n.* an enclosure where cattle, hogs, etc. are kept before slaughtering

stodg·y (stä′jē) *adj.* **-i·er, -i·est** [< *stodge*, heavy food] 1 dull; uninteresting 2 old-fashioned; conventional —**stodg′i·ness** *n.*

sto·gie or **sto·gy** (stō′gē) *n., pl.* **-gies** [after *Conestoga* Valley, PA] a cigar, esp. one that is inexpensive

Sto·ic (stō′ik) *n.* [< Gr *stoa*, a colonnade: where first Stoics met] 1 a member of an ancient Greek school of philosophy 2 [s-] a stoical person —*adj.* [s-] STOICAL —**sto′i·cism′** (-i siz′əm) *n.*

sto·i·cal (-i kəl) *adj.* showing indifference to joy, grief, pleasure, or pain; impassive —**sto′i·cal·ly** *adv.*

stoke (stōk) *vt., vi.* **stoked, stok′ing** [< Du *stoken*, to poke] 1 to stir up and feed fuel to (a fire) 2 to tend (a furnace, boiler, etc.) —**stok′er** *n.*

STOL *abbrev.* short takeoff and landing

stole¹ (stōl) *n.* [< Gr *stolē*, garment] 1 a long strip of cloth worn about the neck by members of the clergy at various rites 2 a woman's long scarf of cloth or fur worn around the shoulders

stole² (stōl) *vt., vi. pt. of* STEAL

stol·en (stō′lən) *vt., vi. pp. of* STEAL

stol·id (stäl′id) *adj.* ⟦L *stolidus,* slow⟧ having or showing little or no emotion; unexcitable —**sto·lid·i·ty** (stə lid′ə tē) *n.* —**stol′id·ly** *adv.*

sto·lon (stō′län′) *n.* ⟦< L *stolo,* a shoot⟧ a creeping stem lying above the soil surface and bearing leaves, as in the strawberry

stom·ach (stum′ək) *n.* ⟦ult. < Gr *stoma,* mouth⟧ **1** the saclike digestive organ into which food passes from the esophagus **2** the abdomen, or belly **3** appetite for food **4** desire or inclination —*vt.* **1** to be able to eat or digest **2** to tolerate; bear

stom·ach·ache *n.* pain in the stomach or abdomen

stom·ach·er *n.* an ornamented piece of cloth formerly worn over the chest and abdomen, esp. by women

stomp (stämp) *vt., vi. var. of* STAMP (*vt.* 1 & 2; *vi.* 1 & 2)

stomping ground [Inf.] a favorite gathering place: *also used in pl.*

stone (stōn) *n.* ⟦OE *stan*⟧ **1** the hard, solid, nonmetallic mineral matter of which rock is composed **2** a piece of rock **3** the seed of certain fruits **4** *short for* PRECIOUS STONE **5** *pl.* **stone** [Brit.] 14 pounds avoirdupois **6** an abnormal stony mass formed in the kidney, gall bladder, etc. —*vt.* **stoned, ston′ing 1** to pelt or kill with stones **2** to remove the stone from (a peach, etc.) —*adv.* completely

stone- ⟦< prec.⟧ *combining form* completely [*stone*-blind]

Stone Age the period in human culture when stone tools were used

stoned *adj.* [Slang] drunk or under the influence of a drug

ston·er *n.* ⟦< STONED⟧ [Slang] a habitual user of marijuana

stone's throw a short distance

stone·wall *vi.* [Inf.] to behave in an obstructive manner, as by withholding information, etc.

stone·ware *n.* a dense, opaque, glazed or unglazed pottery

ston·y *adj.* **-i·er, -i·est 1** full of stones **2** of or like stone; specif., unfeeling; pitiless —**ston′i·ness** *n.*

stood (stood) *vi., vt. pt. & pp. of* STAND

stooge (stooj) *n.* ⟦< ?⟧ [Inf.] **1** an actor who serves as the victim of a comedian's jokes, pranks, etc. **2** anyone who acts as a foil or underling

stool (stool) *n.* ⟦OE *stol*⟧ **1** a single seat having no back or arms **2** feces

stool pigeon [Inf.] a spy or informer, esp. for the police

stoop¹ (stoop) *vi.* ⟦OE *stupian*⟧ **1** to bend the body forward **2** to carry the head and shoulders habitually bent forward **3** to degrade oneself —*n.* the act or position of stooping

stoop² (stoop) *n.* ⟦Du *stoep*⟧ a small porch at the door of a house

stop (stäp) *vt.* **stopped, stop′ping** ⟦< L *stuppa,* a kind of stuffing material⟧ **1** to close by filling, shutting off, etc. **2** to cause to cease motion, activity, etc. **3** to block; intercept; prevent **4** to cease; desist from [*stop* talking] —*vi.* **1** to cease moving, etc.; halt **2** to leave off doing something **3** to cease operating **4** to become clogged **5** to tarry or stay —*n.* **1** a stopping or being stopped **2** a finish; end **3** a stay or sojourn **4** a place stopped at, as on a bus route **5** an obstruction, plug, etc. **6** a finger hole in a wind instrument, closed to produce a desired tone **7** a pull, lever, etc. for controlling a set of organ pipes —**pull out all the stops** [Inf.] to use every means —**stop off** to stop for a while en route to a place —**stop over** to visit for a while: also **stop in** (or **by**)

stop·cock *n.* a cock or valve to stop or regulate the flow of a fluid

stop·gap *n.* a person or thing serving as a temporary substitute

stop·light *n.* a traffic light, esp. when red to signal vehicles to stop

stop·o·ver *n.* a brief stop or stay at a place in the course of a journey

stop·page (-ij) *n.* **1** a stopping or being stopped **2** an obstructed condition; block

stop·per *n.* something inserted to close an opening; plug

stop·watch *n.* a watch that can be started and stopped instantly, as for timing races

stor·age (stôr′ij) *n.* **1** a storing or being stored **2** a place for, or the cost of, storing goods **3** computer memory

storage battery a battery for producing electric current, with cells that can be recharged

store (stôr) *vt.* **stored, stor′ing** ⟦< L *instaurare,* restore⟧ **1** to put aside for use when needed **2** to furnish with a supply **3** to put, as in a warehouse, for safekeeping —*n.* **1** a supply (*of* something) for use when needed; stock **2** [*pl.*] supplies, esp. of food, clothing, etc. **3** a retail establishment where goods are offered for sale —**in store** set aside for the future; in reserve —**set** (or **put** or **lay**) **store by** to value

store·front *n.* a front room on the ground floor of a building, designed for use as a retail store and usually having one or more large windows

store·house *n.* a place where things are stored; esp., a warehouse

store·keep·er *n.* **1** a person in charge of military or naval stores **2** a retail merchant

store·room *n.* a room where things are stored

sto·rey *n., pl.* **-reys** *Brit. sp. of* STORY²

sto·ried (stôr′ēd) *adj.* famous in story or history

stork (stôrk) *n.* ⟦OE *storc*⟧ a large, long-legged wading bird with a long neck and bill

storm (stôrm) *n.* ⟦OE⟧ **1** a strong wind, with rain, snow, thunder, etc. **2** any heavy fall of snow, rain, etc. **3** a strong emotional outburst **4** any strong disturbance **5** a sudden, strong attack on a fortified place —*vi.* **1** to blow rain, snow, etc. violently **2** to rage; rant **3** to rush violently [to *storm* into a room] —*vt.* to attack vigorously

storm door (or **window**) a door (or window) placed outside the regular one to make the opening more weathertight

storm·y *adj.* **-i·er, -i·est** 1 of or characterized by storms 2 violent, raging, etc. —**storm'i·ly** *adv.* —**storm'i·ness** *n.*

sto·ry[1] (stôr'ē) *n., pl.* **-ries** [< Gr *historia*, narrative] 1 the telling of an event or events; account; narration 2 a fictional prose narrative shorter than a novel 3 the plot of a novel, play, etc. 4 [Inf.] a falsehood 5 a news report

sto·ry[2] (stôr'ē) *n., pl.* **-ries** [< prec.] a horizontal division of a building, from a floor to the ceiling above it

sto·ry·board *n.* a large board on which sketches, etc. for shots or scenes of a film, etc. are arranged in sequence —*vt.* to make a storyboard of (a shot or scene) for (a film, etc.)

sto·ry·book *n.* a book of stories, esp. one for children

sto·ry·tell·er *n.* one who narrates stories —**sto'ry·tell'ing** *n.*

stoup (stoop) *n.* [< ON *staup*, cup] a font for holy water

stout (stout) *adj.* [< OFr *estout*, bold] 1 courageous 2 strong; sturdy; firm 3 powerful; forceful 4 fat; thickset —*n.* a very dark-brown beer —**stout'ly** *adv.* —**stout'ness** *n.*

stout·heart·ed *adj.* courageous; brave

stove[1] (stōv) *n.* [< MDu, heated room] an apparatus for heating, cooking, etc.

stove[2] (stōv) *vt., vi. alt. pt. & pp. of* STAVE

stove·pipe *n.* a metal pipe used to carry off smoke from a stove

stow (stō) *vt.* [< OE *stowe*, a place] to pack in an orderly way —**stow away** 1 to put or hide away 2 to be a stowaway —**stow'age** *n.*

stow·a·way (-ə wā') *n.* one who hides aboard a ship, airplane, etc. as to get free passage

St. Paul capital of Minnesota

St. Pe·ters·burg (pēt'ərz burg') seaport in NW Russia

strad·dle (strad'l) *vt.* **-dled, -dling** [< STRIDE] 1 to stand or sit astride of 2 to take or appear to take both sides of (an issue) —*n.* a straddling —**strad'dler** *n.*

strafe (strāf) *vt.* **strafed, straf'ing** [< Ger *Gott strafe England* (God punish England)] to attack with machine-gun fire from low-flying aircraft

strag·gle (strag'əl) *vi.* **-gled, -gling** [prob. < ME *straken*, roam] 1 to wander from the main group 2 to be scattered over a wide area; ramble 3 to hang in an unkempt way, as hair —**strag'gler** *n.* —**strag'gly** *adj.*

straight (strāt) *adj.* [< ME *strecchen*, to stretch] 1 having the same direction throughout its length; not crooked, bent, etc. 2 direct; undeviating; etc. 3 in order; properly arranged, etc. 4 honest; sincere 5 undiluted 6 [Slang] normal or conventional 7 [Slang] heterosexual —*adv.* 1 in a straight line 2 upright; erectly 3 without detour, delay, etc. —*n. Poker* a hand of five cards in sequence —**straight away** (or **off**) without delay —**straight'ness** *n.*

straight arrow [Inf.] one who is proper, conscientious, etc. and often regarded as stodgy or dull —**straight'-ar'row** *adj.*

straight·a·way (strāt'ə wā'; *for adv.,* strāt'ə wā') *n.* a straight section of a racetrack, highway, etc. —*adv.* without delay

straight·edge *n.* a strip of wood, etc. having a perfectly straight edge, used in drawing straight lines

straight·en *vt., vi.* to make or become straight —**straighten out** 1 to make or become less confused, easier to deal with, etc. 2 to reform —**straight'en·er** *n.*

straight face a facial expression showing no amusement or other emotion —**straight'-faced'** *adj.*

straight·for·ward *adj.* 1 moving or leading straight ahead; direct 2 honest; frank —*adv.* in a straightforward manner: also **straight'for'wards**

straight man an actor whose remarks have a comedian answers with a quip

straight shooter [Inf.] a person who is honest, sincere, etc.

straight ticket a ballot cast for candidates of only one party

straight·way *adv.* [Now Chiefly Literary] at once

strain[1] (strān) *vt.* [< L *stringere*] 1 to stretch tight 2 to exert to the utmost 3 to injure by overexertion [to *strain* a muscle] 4 to stretch beyond normal limits 5 to pass through a screen, sieve, etc.; filter —*vi.* to strive hard —*n.* 1 a straining or being strained 2 great effort, exertion, etc. 3 a bodily injury from overexertion 4 stress or force 5 a great demand on one's emotions, resources, etc.

strain[2] (strān) *n.* [< OE *strynan,* to produce] 1 ancestry; lineage 2 race; stock; line 3 a line of individuals differentiated from its species or race 4 an inherited tendency 5 a musical tune

strained *adj.* not natural or relaxed

strain·er *n.* a device for straining, sifting, or filtering; sieve, filter, etc.

strait (strāt) *adj.* [< L *stringere,* draw tight] [Archaic] narrow or strict —*n.* 1 [*often pl.*] a narrow waterway connecting two large bodies of water 2 [*usually pl.*] difficulty; distress

strait·en *vt.* to bring into difficulties: usually in **in straitened circumstances,** lacking enough money

strait·jack·et *n.* a coatlike device for restraining violent persons

strait·laced *adj.* narrowly strict in behavior or moral views

strand[1] (strand) *n.* [OE] shore, esp. ocean shore —*vt., vi.* 1 to run or drive aground, as a ship 2 to put or be put into an isolated and helpless position [*stranded* abroad with no money]

strand[2] (strand) *n.* [ME *stronde*] 1 any one of the threads, wires, etc. that are twisted together to form a string, cable, etc. 2 a ropelike length of anything [a *strand* of pearls]

strange (strānj) *adj.* **strang'er, strang'est** [< L *extraneus,* foreign] 1 not previously known, seen, etc.; unfamiliar 2 unusual; extraordinary 3 peculiar; odd —**strange'ly** *adv.* —**strange'ness** *n.*

stran·ger (strān′jər) *n.* **1** a newcomer **2** a person not known to one

stran·gle (straŋ′gəl) *vt., vi.* **-gled, -gling** [< Gr *strangos*, twisted] **1** to choke to death **2** to suppress, stifle, or repress —**stran′gler** *n.*

stran·gle·hold *n.* **1** an illegal wrestling hold that chokes an opponent **2** a force or action that suppresses freedom

stran·gu·late (straŋ′gyə lāt′) *vt.* **-lat′ed, -lat′ing 1** STRANGLE **2** *Med.* to block (a tube, etc.) by constricting —**stran′gu·la′tion** *n.*

strap (strap) *n.* [dial. form of STROP] a narrow strip of leather, etc., as for securing things —*vt.* **strapped, strap′ping** to fasten with a strap

strap·less *adj.* having no shoulder straps

strapped *adj.* [Inf.] in great need of money

strap·ping *adj.* [Inf.] tall and well-built; robust

stra·ta (strāt′ə, strat′ə) *n. alt. pl. of* STRATUM

strat·a·gem (strat′ə jəm) *n.* [< Gr *stratos*, army + *agein*, to lead] **1** a trick, plan, etc. for deceiving an enemy in war **2** any tricky scheme

strat·e·gy (strat′ə jē) *n., pl.* **-gies 1** the science of planning and directing military operations **2** skill in managing or planning **3** a stratagem, plan, etc. —**stra·te·gic** (strə tē′jik) *adj.* —**stra·te′gi·cal·ly** *adv.* —**strat′e·gist** *n.* —**strat′e·gize′** *vi.* **-gized′, -giz′ing**

strat·i·fy (strat′ə fī′) *vt., vi.* **-fied′, -fy′ing** [< L *stratum*, layer + *facere*, make] to form in layers or strata —**strat′i·fi·ca′tion** *n.*

strat·o·sphere (-ə sfir′) *n.* [< ModL *stratum*, stratum + Fr *sphère*, sphere] **1** the atmospheric zone at an altitude of *c.* 20 to 50 km **2** an extremely high point, level, etc. —**strat′o·spher′ic** (-sfer′ik, -sfir′-) *adj.*

stra·tum (strāt′əm, strat′-) *n., pl.* **-ta** (-ə) or **-tums** [ModL < L *stratus*, a spreading] **1** a horizontal layer of matter, as of sedimentary rock **2** any of the socioeconomic groups of a society

stra·tus (-əs) *n., pl.* **-ti** (-ī) [see prec.] a uniform, low, gray cloud layer

Strauss (strous), **Jo·hann** (yō′hän′) 1825-99; Austrian composer, esp. of waltzes

Stra·vin·sky (strə vin′skē), **I·gor** (ē′gôr) 1882-1971; Russ. composer & conductor, in the U.S. after 1940

straw (strô) *n.* [OE *streaw*] **1** hollow stalks of grain after threshing **2** a single one of these **3** a tube used for sucking beverages **4** a trifle —*adj.* **1** straw-colored; yellowish **2** made of straw

straw·ber·ry (-ber′ē, -bər ē) *n., pl.* **-ries** [prob. from the strawlike seeds on the fruit] **1** the small, red, fleshy fruit of a vinelike plant of the rose family **2** this plant

straw boss [Inf.] one having subordinate authority

straw vote (*or* **poll**) an unofficial vote taken to determine general group opinion

stray (strā) *vi.* [< LL *strata*, street] **1** to wander from a given place, course, etc. **2** to deviate (*from* what is right) —*n.* one that strays;

esp., a lost domestic animal —*adj.* **1** having strayed; lost **2** isolated or incidental [a few *stray* words]

streak (strēk) *n.* [< OE *strica*] **1** a long, thin mark or stripe **2** a layer, as of fat in meat **3** a tendency in behavior, etc. [a nervous *streak*] **4** a period, as of luck —*vt.* to make streaks on or in —*vi.* **1** to become streaked **2** to go fast **3** to dash naked in public as a prank —**streak′er** *n.* —**streak′y** *adj.* **-i·er, -i·est**

stream (strēm) *n.* [OE] **1** a current of water; specif., a small river **2** a steady flow, as of air, light, etc. **3** a continuous series [a *stream* of cars] **4** a continuous flow of data, as over the internet —*vi.* **1** to flow as in a stream **2** to move swiftly —*vt.* to transmit or receive by STREAMING

stream·er *n.* **1** a long, narrow flag **2** any long, narrow strip hanging loose at one end

stream·ing *n.* a method of transmitting audio or video content, as over the internet, the content being played continuously as it is received

stream·line *vt.* **-lined′, -lin′ing** to make streamlined —*adj.* STREAMLINED

stream·lined *adj.* **1** having a contour designed to offer the least resistance in moving through air, water, etc. **2** efficient, trim, simplified, etc.

street (strēt) *n.* [< L *strata* (*via*), paved (road)] **1** a public road in a town or city, esp. a paved one **2** such a road with its sidewalks, buildings, etc. **3** the people living, working, etc. along a given street

street·car *n.* a car on rails for public transportation along certain streets

street·light *n.* a lamp on a post for lighting a street: also **street′lamp′**

street-smart *adj.* [Inf.] STREETWISE

street smarts [Inf.] the skills required to get by in an urban environment having much poverty, crime, etc.

street·walk·er *n.* a prostitute who solicits customers along the streets —**street′walk′ing** *n.*

street·wise *adj.* [Inf.] experienced in dealing with people in urban areas where poverty, crime, etc. are common

strength (streŋkth) *n.* [OE *strengthu*] **1** the state or quality of being strong; force; power **2** toughness; durability **3** the power to resist attack **4** potency or concentration, as of drugs, etc. **5** intensity, as of sound, etc. **6** force of an army, etc., as measured in numbers —**on the strength of** based or relying on

strength·en *vt., vi.* to make or become stronger —**strength′en·er** *n.*

stren·u·ous (stren′yōō əs) *adj.* [L *strenuus*] requiring or characterized by great effort or energy —**stren′u·ous·ly** *adv.* —**stren′u·ous·ness** *n.*

strep (strep) *n. short for:* **1** STREPTOCOCCUS **2** STREP THROAT

strep throat [Inf.] a sore throat caused by a streptococcus, with inflammation and fever

strep·to·coc·cus (strep′tə käk′əs) *n., pl.* **-coc′ci** (-käk′sī′) [< Gr *streptos*, twisted

+ **coccus**] any of various spherical bacteria that occur in chains: some cause diseases

strep·to·my·cin (-mī′sin) *n.* [< Gr *streptos*, bent + *mykēs*, fungus] an antibiotic drug used in treating various diseases

stress (stres) *n.* [< L *strictus*, strict] 1 strain; specif., force that strains or deforms 2 emphasis; importance 3 *a*) mental or physical tension *b*) urgency, pressure, etc. causing this 4 the relative force of utterance given a syllable or word; accent —*vt.* 1 to put stress or pressure on 2 to accent 3 to emphasize —*vi.* [Inf.] to feel stress: often with *out*

stressed-out *adj.* [Inf.] tired, nervous, etc. as from overwork, mental pressure, etc.

stress fracture a leg fracture caused by repetitive stress, as in marathon running

stretch (strech) *vt.* [OE *streccan*] 1 to reach out; extend 2 to draw out to full extent or to greater size 3 to cause to extend too far; strain 4 to strain in interpretation, scope, etc. —*vi.* 1 *a*) to spread out to full extent or beyond normal limits *b*) to extend over a given distance or time 2 *a*) to extend the body or limbs to full length *b*) to lie down (usually with *out*) 3 to become stretched —*n.* 1 a stretching or being stretched 2 an unbroken period [a ten-day *stretch*] 3 an unbroken length, tract, etc. 4 *short for* HOMESTRETCH 5 an action that exceeds someone's normal powers —*adj.* 1 made of elasticized fabric so as to stretch easily 2 designating a vehicle built extra long to enlarge seating capacity [a *stretch* limousine] —**stretch′a·ble** *adj.* —**stretch′y** *adj.* **-i·er, -i·est**

stretch·er *n.* 1 one that stretches 2 a frame for carrying the sick or injured

strew (strōō) *vt.* **strewed, strewed** or **strewn, strew′ing** [OE *streawian*] 1 to spread here and there; scatter 2 to cover as by scattering

stri·at·ed (strī′āt′id) *adj.* [< L *striare*, to groove] marked with parallel lines, bands, furrows, etc.

strick·en (strik′ən) *vt., vi. alt. pp. of* STRIKE —*adj.* 1 struck or wounded 2 afflicted, as by something painful

strict (strikt) *adj.* [< L *stringere*, draw tight] 1 exact or precise 2 *a*) enforcing rules carefully *b*) closely enforced —**strict′ly** *adv.* —**strict′ness** *n.*

stric·ture (strik′chər) *n.* [see prec.] 1 adverse criticism 2 a limiting; restriction 3 an abnormal narrowing of a passage in the body

stride (strīd) *vi.* **strode, strid′den, strid′ing** [OE *stridan*] 1 to walk with long steps 2 to take a single, long step (esp. *over* something) —*n.* 1 a long step 2 the distance covered by such a step 3 [*usually pl.*] progress [to make *strides*]

stri·dent (strīd′nt) *adj.* [< L *stridere*, to rasp] harsh-sounding; shrill; grating —**stri′dent·ly** *adv.*

strife (strīf) *n.* [< OFr *estrif*] 1 contention or fighting or quarreling; struggle

strike (strīk) *vt.* **struck, struck,** or, esp. for *vt.*

7 & 10 **strick′en, strik′ing** [OE *strican*, to go, advance] 1 to hit with the hand, a tool, etc. 2 to make by stamping, etc. [to *strike* coins] 3 to announce (time), as with a bell: said of clocks, etc. 4 to ignite (a match) or produce (a light, etc.) by friction 5 to collide with or cause to collide [he *struck* his head on a beam] 6 to attack 7 to afflict, as with disease, pain, etc. 8 to come upon; notice, find, etc. 9 to affect as if by contact, etc.; occur to [an idea *struck* me] 10 to remove (from a list, record, etc.) 11 to make (a bargain, truce, etc.) 12 to lower (a sail, flag, etc.) 13 to assume (an attitude, pose, etc.) —*vi.* 1 to hit (*at*) 2 to attack 3 to make sounds as by being struck: said of a bell, clock, etc. 4 to collide; hit (*against, on,* or *upon*) 5 to seize bait: said of a fish 6 to come suddenly (*on* or *upon*) 7 to refuse to continue to work until certain demands are met 8 to proceed, esp. in a new direction —*n.* 1 the act of striking; specif., a military attack 2 a refusal by employees to go on working, in an attempt to gain better working conditions, etc. 3 the discovery of a rich deposit of oil, etc. 4 *Baseball* a pitched ball missed, or fouled off, by the batter or called a good pitch by the umpire 5 *Bowling* a knocking down of all the pins on the first roll —**strike out** 1 to erase 2 to start out 3 *Baseball* to put out, or be put out, on three strikes —**strike up** to begin —**strik′er** *n.*

strike·out *n. Baseball* an out made by a batter charged with three strikes

strik·ing *adj.* very impressive, attractive, etc.

string (striŋ) *n.* [OE *streng*] 1 a thin line of fiber, leather, etc. used for tying, pulling, etc. 2 a group of like things on a string [a *string* of pearls] 3 a row, series, etc. of like things [a *string* of houses] 4 *a*) a slender cord of wire, gut, etc. bowed, plucked, or struck to make a musical sound *b*) [*pl.*] all the stringed instruments of an orchestra 5 [Inf.] a condition attached to a plan, offer, etc.: *usually used in pl.* 6 *Physics* a hypothetical tiny, vibrating stringlike particle thought to be the basic unit of matter —*vt.* **strung, string′ing** 1 to provide with strings 2 to thread on a string 3 to tie, hang, etc. with a string 4 to remove the fibers from (beans, etc.) 5 to arrange in a row 6 to extend [*string* a cable] —**pull strings** to get someone to use influence in one's behalf, often secretly —**string along** [Inf.] 1 to go along with another 2 to dupe with false premises —**string up** [Slang] to kill by hanging —**string′y** *adj.* **-i·er, -i·est**

string bean SNAP BEAN

stringed instrument (striŋd) a musical instrument with vibrating strings, as a violin or guitar

strin·gent (strin′jənt) *adj.* [see STRICT] strict; severe —**strin′gen·cy** *n.*

string·er *n.* 1 a long horizontal piece in a structure 2 a part-time, local correspondent for a newspaper, magazine, etc.

strip¹ (strip) *vt.* **stripped, strip′ping** [OE *stripan*] 1 to remove (the clothing, etc.) from (a person) **2** to dispossess of (honors, titles, etc.) **3** to plunder; rob **4** to take off (a covering, etc.) from (a person or thing) **5** to make bare by taking away removable parts, etc. **6** to break the thread of (a nut, bolt, etc.) or the teeth of (a gear) —*vi.* to take off all clothing —**strip′per** *n.*

strip² (strip) *n.* [< STRIP] **1** a long, narrow piece, as of land, tape, etc. **2** *short for* AIR-STRIP

stripe (strīp) *n.* [< MDu *strip*] **1** a long, narrow band differing from the surrounding area **2** a strip of cloth on a uniform to show rank, years served, etc. **3** kind; sort [a man of his *stripe*] —*vt.* **striped**, **strip′ing** to mark with stripes

strip mall a shopping center of connected storefronts with a parking area in front

strip mining mining, as for coal, by laying bare a mineral deposit near the surface of the earth

stripped-down *adj.* reduced to essentials

strip-search *vt.* to search (a person) by requiring removal of the clothes —*n.* such a search Also **strip search**

strip-tease *n.* an entertainment in which the performer undresses slowly, usually to musical accompaniment

strive (strīv) *vi.* **strove** or **strived**, **striv·en** (striv′ən) or **strived**, **striv′ing** [< OFr *estrif*, effort] **1** to make great efforts; try very hard **2** to struggle

strobe (light) (strōb) [< Gr *strobus*, a twisting around] an electronic tube emitting rapid, brief, and brilliant flashes of light

strode (strōd) *vi.*, *vt. pt. of* STRIDE

stroke (strōk) *n.* [ME] **1** a blow of an ax, whip, etc. **2** a sudden action or event [a *stroke* of luck] **3** an interruption of normal blood flow to the brain, as from a hemorrhage, blood clot, etc., causing paralysis, etc. **4** a single strong effort **5** the sound of striking, as of a clock **6** *a)* a single movement, as with a tool, racket, etc. *b)* any of a series of repeated motions made in rowing, swimming, etc. **7** a mark made by a pen, etc. —*vt.* **stroked**, **strok′ing** to draw one's hand, a tool, etc. gently over the surface of

stroll (strōl) *vi.* [prob. < Ger *strolch*, vagabond] **1** to walk about leisurely; saunter **2** to wander —*vt.* to stroll along or through —*n.* a leisurely walk

stroll·er *n.* **1** one who strolls **2** a light, chair-like baby carriage

strom·bo·li (sträm bō′lē) *n.* [< ?] an Italian-American dish consisting of meat, cheese, etc. rolled into flattened bread dough and baked

strong (strôŋ) *adj.* [OE *strang*] **1** *a)* physically powerful *b)* healthy; hearty **2** morally or intellectually powerful [a *strong* will] **3** firm; durable **4** powerful in wealth, numbers, etc. **5** of a specified number [troops 6,000 *strong*] **6** having a powerful effect **7** intense in degree or quality **8** forceful; vigorous, etc. —*adv.* strong′ly

strong-arm [Inf.] *adj.* using physical force —*vt.* to use force or the threat of force upon

strong·box *n.* a heavily made box or safe for storing valuables

strong·hold *n.* a fortress

strong-mind·ed *adj.* unyielding; determined: also **strong′-willed′**

stron·ti·um (strän′shəm, stränt′ē əm) *n.* [ult. after *Strontian*, Scotland] a metallic chemical element resembling calcium in its properties: symbol, Sr; at. no. 38

strop (sträp) *n.* [OE] a leather band for sharpening razors —*vt.* **stropped**, **strop′ping** to sharpen on a strop

stro·phe (strō′fē) *n.* [Gr *strophē*, a turning] a stanza of a poem

strove (strōv) *vi. alt. pt. of* STRIVE

struck (struk) *vt.*, *vi. pt. & pp. of* STRIKE

struc·ture (struk′chər) *n.* [< L *struere*, arrange] **1** something built or constructed, as a building or dam **2** the arrangement of all the parts of a whole **3** something composed of related parts —*vt.* **-tured**, **-tur·ing** to put together systematically —**struc′tur·al** *adj.*

stru·del (strōōd′'l) *n.* [Ger] a pastry made of a thin sheet of dough filled with apples, etc., rolled up, and baked

strug·gle (strug′əl) *vi.* **-gled**, **-gling** [ME *strogelen*] **1** to fight violently with an opponent **2** to make great efforts; strive; labor —*n.* **1** great effort **2** conflict; strife

strum (strum) *vt.*, *vi.* **strummed**, **strum′ming** [echoic] to play (a guitar, etc.) with long strokes across the strings, often casually

strum·pet (strum′pit) *n.* [ME] [Old-fashioned] a female prostitute

strung (struŋ) *vt.*, *vi. pt. & alt. pp. of* STRING

strut (strut) *vi.* **strut′ted**, **strut′ting** [OE *strutian*, stand rigid] to walk in a swaggering manner —*n.* **1** a swaggering walk **2** a brace fitted into a framework to stabilize the structure **3** a shock absorber and its mounting plates in a single assembly

strych·nine (strik′nīn, -nēn′, -nīn′) *n.* [< Gr *strychnos*, nightshade] a colorless, highly poisonous, crystalline alkaloid

stub (stub) *n.* [OE *stybb*] **1** a tree or plant stump **2** a short piece left over [a pencil *stub*] **3** any short or blunt projection **4** the part of a ticket, bank check, etc. kept as a record —*vt.* **stubbed**, **stub′bing** **1** to strike (one's toe, etc.) against something **2** to put out (a cigarette, etc.) by pressing the end against a surface: often with *out*

stub·ble (stub′əl) *n.* [< L *stipula*, a stalk] **1** short stumps of grain, corn, etc., left after harvesting **2** any short, bristly growth, as of a beard

stub·born (stub′ərn) *adj.* [ME *stoburn*] **1** refusing to yield or comply; obstinate **2** done in an obstinate or persistent way **3** hard to handle or deal with —**stub′born·ly** *adv.* —**stub′born·ness** *n.*

stub·by (stub′ē) *adj.* **-bi·er**, **-bi·est 1** covered with stubs or stubble **2** short and thickset

stuc·co (stuk′ō) *n.*, *pl.* **-coes** or **-cos** [It] plaster or cement for surfacing walls, etc. —*vt.* **-coed**, **-co·ing** to cover with stucco

stuck (stuk) *vt.*, *vi.* *pt.* & *pp. of* STICK

stuck-up *adj.* [Inf.] snobbish; conceited

stud[1] (stud) *n.* [OE *studu*, a post] 1 any of a series of small knobs, etc. used to ornament a surface 2 a small, buttonlike device for fastening a shirt front, etc. 3 an upright piece in the wall of a building, to which panels, laths, etc. are nailed —*vt.* **stud'ded, stud'ding** 1 to set or decorate with studs, etc. 2 to be set thickly on [*rocks stud* the hill]

stud[2] (stud) *n.* [OE] 1 a male animal, esp. a horse (**stud'horse'**), kept for breeding 2 [Slang] a virile or sexually promiscuous man

stud-book *n.* a register of purebred animals, esp. racehorses: also **stud book**

stud-ding *n.* studs, esp. for walls

stu-dent (stōōd''nt) *n.* [< L *studere*, to study] 1 one who studies, or investigates 2 one who is enrolled for study at a school, college, etc.

stud-ied (stud'ēd) *adj.* 1 prepared by careful study 2 deliberate

stu-di-o (stōō'dē ō') *n.*, *pl.* **-os'** [It] 1 a place where an artist, etc. works or where music or dancing lessons, etc. are given 2 a place where films, radio or TV programs, etc. are produced

studio apartment a one-room apartment with a kitchen area and a bathroom

stu-di-ous (stōō'dē əs) *adj.* [< L *studiosus*] 1 devoted to study 2 zealous or attentive

stud-y (stud'ē) *n.*, *pl.* **-ies** [< L *studere*, to study] 1 the acquiring of knowledge, as by reading or investigating 2 careful examination of a subject, event, etc. 3 a branch of learning 4 [*pl.*] formal education; schooling 5 an essay, thesis, etc. containing the results of an investigation 6 a room for study, etc. —*vt.* **-ied, -y·ing** 1 to try to learn or understand by reading, thinking, etc. 2 to investigate carefully 3 to read (a book, etc.) intently 4 to take a course in, as at a school —*vi.* 1 to study something 2 to be a student 3 to meditate

stuff (stuf) *n.* [< OFr *estoffe*] 1 the material out of which anything is made 2 essence; character 3 matter of an unspecified kind 4 cloth, esp. woolen cloth 5 objects; things 6 worthless objects; junk 7 [Inf.] ability, skill, etc. —*vt.* 1 to fill or pack; specif., *a*) to fill the skin of (a dead animal) in taxidermy *b*) to fill (a turkey, etc.) with seasoning, bread crumbs, etc. before roasting 2 to fill too full; cram 3 to plug; block —*vi.* to eat too much

stuffed shirt [Slang] a pompous, pretentious person

stuff-ing *n.* something used to stuff, as padding in cushions or a seasoned mixture for stuffing fowl

stuff-y (stuf'ē) *adj.* **-i·er, -i·est** 1 poorly ventilated; close 2 having the nasal passages stopped up, as from a cold 3 [Inf.] dull, conventional, or pompous —**stuff'i·ness** *n.*

stul-ti-fy (stul'tə fī') *vt.* **-fied', -fy'ing** [< L *stultus*, foolish + *facere*, make] 1 to make seem

foolish, stupid, etc. 2 to make worthless, etc. 3 to cause to be dull, torpid, etc.

stum-ble (stum'bəl) *vi.* **-bled, -bling** [ME *stumblen*] 1 to trip in walking, running, etc. 2 to walk unsteadily 3 to speak, act, etc. in a blundering way 4 to do wrong 5 to come by chance —*n.* a stumbling —**stum'bler** *n.*

stumbling block a difficulty or obstacle

stump (stump) *n.* [ME *stumpe*] 1 the end of a tree or plant left in the ground after the upper part has been cut off 2 the part of a limb, tooth, etc. left after the rest has been removed 3 the place where a political speech is made —*vt.* 1 to travel over (a district), making political speeches 2 [Inf.] to puzzle or perplex —*vi.* 1 to walk with a heavy step 2 to travel about, making political speeches —**stump'y** *adj.* **-i·er, -i·est**

stun (stun) *vt.* **stunned, stun'ning** [ult. < L *ex-*, intens. + *tonare*, to thunder] 1 to make unconscious, as by a blow 2 to daze; shock

stung (stuŋ) *vt.*, *vi. pt.* & *pp. of* STING

stunk (stuŋk) *vi. pp.* & *alt. pt. of* STINK

stun-ning (stun'iŋ) *adj.* [Inf.] remarkably attractive, excellent, etc.

stunt[1] (stunt) *vt.* [< OE, stupid] 1 to check the growth or development of 2 to hinder (growth, etc.)

stunt[2] (stunt) *n.* [< ?] something done to show one's skill or daring, get attention, etc. —*vi.* to do a stunt

stu-pe-fy (stōō'pə fī') *vt.* [< L *stupere*, be stunned + *facere*, make] 1 to produce stupor in; stun 2 to astound; bewilder —**stu'pe-fac'tion** (-fak'shən) *n.*

stu-pen-dous (stōō pen'dəs) *adj.* [< L *stupere*, be stunned] 1 astonishing 2 astonishingly great

stu-pid (stōō'pid) *adj.* [see prec.] 1 lacking normal intelligence 2 foolish; silly [a *stupid* idea] 3 dull and boring —**stu-pid'i·ty** *n.*, *pl.* **-ties**

stu-por (stōō'pər) *n.* [see STUPENDOUS] a state in which the mind and senses are dulled; loss of awareness

stur-dy (stur'dē) *adj.* **-di·er, -di·est** [< OFr *estourdi*, hard to control] 1 firm; resolute 2 strong; vigorous 3 strongly constructed —**stur'di·ly** *adv.* —**stur'di·ness** *n.*

stur-geon (stur'jən) *n.* [< OFr *esturjon*] a large food fish valuable as a source of caviar

stut-ter (stut'ər) *vt.*, *vi.*, *n.* [< ME *stutten*] STAMMER

Stutt-gart (stoot'gärt'; *Ger* shtoot'gärt') city in SW Germany

St. Vin-cent and the Gren-a-dines (sānt vin' sənt and *thə* gren'ə dēnz') country consisting of the island of St. Vincent and the N Grenadines, in the West Indies

sty[1] (stī) *n.*, *pl.* **sties** [< OE *sti*, hall, enclosure] 1 a pen for pigs 2 any foul place

sty[2] or **stye** (stī) *n.*, *pl.* **sties** or **styes** [ult. < OE *stigan*, to rise] a small, inflamed swelling on the rim of an eyelid

Styg-i-an (stij'ē ən, stij'ən) *adj.* 1 of the Styx 2 [*also* **s-**] *a*) infernal *b*) dark or gloomy

style (stīl) *n.* [< L *stilus*, pointed writing tool] 1 a stylus 2 *a)* manner of expression in language *b)* characteristic manner of expression, design, etc. in any art, period, etc. *c)* excellence of artistic expression 3 *a)* fashion *b)* something stylish —*vt.* **styled, styl′ing** 1 to name; call 2 to design the style of 3 to arrange (hair) by cutting, etc.

styl·ish (stī′lish) *adj.* conforming to current style, as in dress; fashionable

styl·ist (-list) *n.* 1 a writer, etc. whose work has style and distinction 2 a person who styles hair —**sty·lis′tic** *adj.* —**sty·lis′ti·cal·ly** *adv.*

styl·ize (-līz′) *vt.* **-ized′, -iz′ing** to design or represent according to a style rather than nature

sty·lus (stī′ləs) *n., pl.* **-lus·es** or **-li** (-lī) [L, for *stilus*, pointed instrument] 1 a sharp, pointed marking device 2 the short, pointed piece that moves in the grooves of a phonograph record and that transmits vibrations

sty·mie (stī′mē) *n.* [prob. < Scot, person partially blind] *Golf* a situation in which a ball to be putted has another ball between it and the hole —*vt.* **-mied, -mie·ing** to block; impede

sty·my *n., pl.* **-mies** *vt.* **-mied, -my·ing** *alt. sp.* of STYMIE

styp·tic pencil (stip′tik) a piece of astringent, used to stop minor bleeding

Sty·ro·foam (stī′rə fōm′) *trademark for* a rigid, lightweight polystyrene foam —*n.* [*also* **s-**] this substance

Styx (stiks) *n. Gr. Myth.* the river crossed by dead souls entering Hades

sua·sion (swā′zhən) *n.* [< L *suadere*, to persuade] PERSUASION: now chiefly in **moral suasion**, a persuading by appealing to one's sense of morality

suave (swäv) *adj.* [< L *suavis*, sweet] smoothly gracious or polite; polished —**suave′ly** *adv.* —**suav′i·ty** *n.*

sub (sub) *n. short for:* 1 SUBMARINE 2 SUBSTITUTE 3 SUBMARINE SANDWICH —*vi.* **subbed, sub′bing** [Inf.] to be a substitute (for someone)

sub- [< L *sub*, under] *prefix* 1 under [*submarine*] 2 lower than; inferior to [*subhead*] 3 to a lesser degree than [*subhuman*]

sub·a·tom·ic (sub′ə täm′ik) *adj.* of or being a particle smaller than an atom

sub·branch *n.* a division of a branch

sub·com·mit·tee *n.* a small committee chosen from a main committee

sub·com·pact *n.* an automobile model smaller than a compact

sub·con·scious *adj.* occurring with little or no conscious perception on the part of the individual: said of mental processes and reactions —**the subconscious** subconscious mental activity —**sub·con′scious·ly** *adv.*

sub·con·ti·nent *n.* 1 a large land mass smaller than a continent 2 a large, geographically distinct part of a continent

sub·con·tract *n.* a secondary contract undertaking some or all obligations of another con-

tract —*vt., vi.* to make a subcontract (for) —**sub′con′trac′tor** *n.*

sub·cul·ture *n.* 1 a distinctive social group within a larger social group 2 its cultural patterns

sub·cu·ta·ne·ous *adj.* beneath the skin

sub·dea·con *n.* a cleric ranking below a deacon

sub·dis·trict *n.* a subdivision of a district

sub·di·vide *vt., vi.* **-vid′ed, -vid′ing** 1 to divide further 2 to divide (land) into small parcels —**sub′di·vi′sion** *n.*

sub·due (səb dōō′) *vt.* **-dued′, -du′ing** [< L *subducere*, take away] 1 to conquer 2 to overcome; control 3 to make less intense; diminish

sub·fam·i·ly *n., pl.* **-lies** a main subdivision of a family, as of plants or of languages

sub·head *n.* a subordinate heading or title, as of a magazine article

subj *abbrev.* 1 subject 2 subjunctive

sub·ject (sub′jikt, -jekt′; *for v.* səb jekt′) *adj.* [< L *sub-*, under + *jacere*, to throw] 1 under the authority or control of another 2 having a tendency [*subject* to anger] 3 exposed [*subject* to censure] 4 contingent upon: with *to* [*subject* to approval] —*n.* 1 one under the authority or control of another, esp. a monarch or empire 2 one made to undergo a treatment, experiment, etc. 3 something dealt with in discussion, study, etc.; theme 4 a course of study in a school or college 5 *Gram.* the noun, etc. in a sentence about which something is said —*vt.* 1 to bring under the authority or control of 2 to cause to undergo something [to *subject* someone to questioning] —**sub·jec′tion** *n.*

sub·jec·tive (səb jek′tiv) *adj.* of or resulting from the feelings of the person thinking; not objective; personal —**sub·jec·tiv·i·ty** (sub′jek tiv′ə tē) *n.*

sub·join (səb join′) *vt.* [see SUB- & JOIN] to append

sub·ju·gate (sub′jə gāt′) *vt.* **-gat′ed, -gat′ing** [< L *sub-*, under + *jugum*, a yoke] to bring under control; conquer —**sub′ju·ga′tion** *n.*

sub·junc·tive (səb juŋk′tiv) *adj.* [< L *subjungere*, subjoin] designating or of the mood of a verb that is used to express supposition, desire, possibility, etc., rather than to state an actual fact

sub·lease (sub′lēs′; *for v.* sub lēs′) *n.* a lease granted by a lessee —*vt.* **-leased′, -leas′ing** to grant or hold a sublease of

sub·let (sub let′) *vt.* **-let′, -let′ting** 1 to rent to another (property which one is renting) 2 to rent (property) from someone who is the lessee rather than the owner 3 to let out (work) to a subcontractor

sub·li·mate (sub′lə māt′) *vt.* **-mat′ed, -mat′ing** 1 to cause (a solid) to change to a gas, or (a gas) to change to a solid, without becoming a liquid 2 to express (unacceptable impulses) in acceptable forms, often unconsciously —*vi.* to change from solid to gas or from gas to solid without becoming a liquid —**sub′li·ma′tion** *n.*

sub·lime (sə blīm′) *adj.* [< L *sub-*, up to + *limen*, lintel] **1** noble; exalted **2** inspiring awe or admiration —*vt.* -limed′, -lim′ing SUBLIMATE (*vt.* 1) —*vi.* SUBLIMATE —**sub·lim·i·ty** (sə blim′ə tē) *n.*

sub·lim·i·nal (sub lim′ə nəl) *adj.* [< SUB- + L *limen*, threshold + -AL] below the threshold of consciousness

sub·ma·chine gun a portable automatic fire-arm

sub·mar·gin·al (sub mär′jə nəl) *adj.* below minimum requirements or standards

sub·ma·rine (sub′mə rēn′, sub′mə rēn′) *adj.* being, living, etc. underwater —*n.* a ship, esp. a warship, that can operate under water

submarine sandwich HERO SANDWICH

sub·merge (səb murj′) *vt., vi.* -merged′, -merg′ing [< L *sub-*, under + *mergere*, to plunge] to place or sink beneath the surface, as of water —**sub·mer′gence** (-mur′jəns) *n.*

sub·merse (-murs′) *vt.* -mersed′, -mers′ing SUBMERGE —**sub·mers′i·ble** *adj.* —**sub·mer′sion** *n.*

sub·mis·sion (səb mish′ən) *n.* **1** a submitting or surrendering **2** obedience; resignation **3** *a)* the submitting of something to another *b)* the thing submitted, as a manuscript —**sub·mis′sive** *adj.*

sub·mit (-mit′) *vt.* -mit′ted, -mit′ting [< L *sub-*, down + *mittere*, send] **1** to present to others for consideration, etc. **2** to yield to the control or power of another **3** to offer as an opinion —*vi.* to yield; give in

sub·nor·mal (sub nôr′məl) *adj.* below normal, esp. in intelligence

sub·or·bit·al (-ôr′bit′l) *adj.* designating a flight in which a rocket, spacecraft, etc. follows a trajectory of less than one orbit

sub·or·di·nate (sə bôrd′′n it; *for v.,* -bôr′də nāt′) *adj.* [< L *sub-*, under + *ordinare*, to order] **1** below another in rank, importance, etc. **2** under the authority of another **3** *Gram.* having the function of a noun, adjective, or adverb within a sentence [a *subordinate clause*] —*n.* one that is subordinate —*vt.* -nat′ed, -nat′ing to place in a subordinate position —**sub·or′di·na′tion** *n.*

subordinate clause *Gram.* DEPENDENT CLAUSE

sub·orn (sə bôrn′) *vt.* [< L *sub-*, under + *ornare*, furnish] to induce (another) to commit perjury —**sub·or·na·tion** (sub′ôr nā′shən) *n.*

sub·plot *n.* a secondary plot in a play, novel, etc.

sub·poe·na (sə pē′nə) *n.* [< L *sub poena*, under penalty] a written legal order directing a person to appear in court to testify, etc. —*vt.* -naed, -na·ing to summon with such an order Also **sub·pe′na**

sub·prime (sub′prīm′) *adj.* designating of of mortgage loans made to higher-risk borrowers

sub ro·sa (sub rō′zə) [L, under the rose, ancient symbol of secrecy] secretly; privately

sub·scribe (səb skrīb′) *vt., vi.* -scribed′, -scrib′ing [< L *sub-*, under + *scribere*, write] **1** to sign (one's name) at the end of a document, etc. **2** to give support or consent (to) **3** to promise to contribute (money) **4** to agree to receive and pay for a periodical, service, etc. (with *to*) —**sub·scrib′er** *n.*

sub·script (sub′skript′) *n.* [see prec.] a figure, letter, or symbol written below and to the side of another

sub·scrip·tion (səb skrip′shən) *n.* **1** a subscribing **2** money subscribed **3** a formal agreement to receive and pay for a periodical, cable TV service, etc.

sub·se·quent (sub′si kwənt) *adj.* [< L *sub-*, after + *sequi*, follow] coming after; following —**subsequent to** after —**sub′se·quent·ly** *adv.*

sub·ser·vi·ent (səb sur′vē ənt) *adj.* [< L *sub-*, under + *servire*, to serve] **1** that is of service, esp. in a subordinate capacity **2** submissive —**sub·ser′vi·ence** *n.*

sub·set (sub′set′) *n.* a mathematical set containing some or all of the elements of a given set

sub·side (səb sīd′) *vi.* -sid′ed, -sid′ing [< L *sub-*, under + *sidere*, to settle] **1** to sink to the bottom or to a lower level **2** to become less active, intense, etc. —**sub·sid′ence** *n.*

sub·sid·i·ar·y (səb sid′ē er′ē) *adj.* [see SUBSIDY] **1** giving aid, service, etc.; auxiliary **2** being in a subordinate relationship —*n., pl.* -ies one that is subsidiary; specif., a company controlled by another company

sub·si·dize (sub′sə dīz′) *vt.* -dized′, -diz′ing to support with a subsidy —**sub′si·di·za′tion** *n.*

sub·si·dy (sub′sə dē) *n., pl.* -dies [< L *subsidium*, auxiliary forces] a grant of money, as from a government to a private enterprise

sub·sist (səb sist′) *vi.* [< L *sub-*, under + *sistere*, to stand] **1** to continue to be or exist **2** to continue to live; remain alive (*on* or *by*)

sub·sist·ence *n.* **1** existence **2** the act of providing sustenance **3** means of support or livelihood, esp. the barest means

sub·soil (sub′soil′) *n.* the layer of soil beneath the topsoil

sub·son·ic (sub sän′ik) *adj.* designating, of, or moving at a speed less than that of sound

sub·stance (sub′stəns) *n.* [< L *substare*, be present] **1** the real or essential part of anything; essence **2** *a)* the physical matter of which a thing consists *b)* matter of a particular kind or composition **3** *a)* solid or substantial quality *b)* consistency; body **4** the real meaning; gist **5** wealth **6** a drug: see CONTROLLED SUBSTANCE

sub·stand·ard *adj.* below standard

sub·stan·tial (səb stan′shəl) *adj.* **1** having substance **2** real; true **3** strong; solid **4** ample; large **5** important **6** wealthy **7** with regard to essential elements —**sub·stan′tial·ly** *adv.*

sub·stan·ti·ate (-shē āt′, *vt.* -at′ed, -at′ing [see SUBSTANCE] to show to be true or real by giving evidence —**sub·stan′ti·a′tion** *n.*

sub·stan·tive (sub′stən tiv) *adj.* [see

SUBSTANCE] of or dealing with essentials —*n. Gram.* a noun or any other word or group of words used as a noun

sub·sta·tion *n.* a lesser station, as in an electric power grid

sub·sti·tute (sub′stə tōōt′) *n.* [< L *sub-*, under + *statuere*, put] a person or thing serving or used in place of another — *vt., vi.* **-tut′ed, -tut′ing** to put, use, or serve in place of (another) —**sub′sti·tu′tion** *n.*

sub·stra·tum (sub′strāt′əm, -strat′-) *n., pl.* **-ta** (-ə) or **-tums** a part, substance, etc. which lies beneath and supports another

sub·struc·ture *n.* a part or structure that is a support, base, etc.

sub·sume (sub sōōm′) *vt.* **-sumed′, -sum′ing** [< L *sub-*, under + *sumere*, take] to include within a larger class

sub·ten·ant *n.* a person who rents from a tenant —**sub·ten′an·cy** *n.*

sub·ter·fuge (sub′tər fyōōj′) *n.* [< L *subter*, secretly + *fugere*, flee] any plan or action used to hide or evade something

sub·ter·ra·ne·an (sub′tə rā′nē ən) *adj.* [< L *sub-*, under + *terra*, earth] **1** underground **2** secret; hidden

sub·text (sub′tekst′) *n.* an underlying meaning, theme, etc.

sub·ti·tle *n.* **1** a secondary or explanatory title **2** one or more lines of translated dialogue, etc. at the bottom of a film or video image —*vt.* **-ti·tled, -ti·tling** to add a subtitle or subtitles to

sub·tle (sut′'l) *adj.* **-tler** (-lər, -'l ər), **-tlest** [< L *subtilis*, fine, thin] **1** thin; not dense **2** mentally keen **3** delicately skillful **4** crafty **5** not obvious —**sub′tle·ty** *n., pl.* **-ties** —**sub′tly** *adv.*

sub·to·tal *n.* a total that is part of a complete total — *vt., vi.* **-taled** or **-talled, -tal·ing** or **-tal·ling** to add up so as to form a subtotal

sub·tract (səb trakt′) *vt., vi.* [< L *sub-*, under + *trahere*, to draw] to take away or deduct (one quantity from another) —**sub·trac′tion** *n.*

sub·tra·hend (sub′trə hend′) *n.* a quantity to be subtracted from another (the *minuend*)

sub·trop·i·cal (sub trä′pi kəl) *adj.* of or like regions bordering on the tropics

sub·urb (sub′ərb) *n.* [< L *sub-*, near + *urbs*, town] a district, town, etc. on the outskirts of a city —**sub·ur·ban** (sə bur′bən) *adj.*

sub·ur·ban·ite (sə bur′bən īt′) *n.* a person living in a suburb

sub·ur·bi·a (-bē ə) *n.* the suburbs or suburbanites collectively

sub·ven·tion (səb ven′shən) *n.* [< LL *subventio*, aid] a subsidy

sub·ver·sive (səb vur′siv) *adj.* tending to subvert —*n.* a person seen as being subversive

sub·vert (səb vurt′) *vt.* [< L *sub-*, under + *vertere*, to turn] **1** to overthrow or destroy (something established) **2** to corrupt, as in morals —**sub·ver′sion** (-vur′zhən) *n.*

sub·way *n.* an underground, electric metropolitan railway

suc- *prefix* SUB-: used before *c* [*succumb*]

suc·ceed (sək sēd′) *vi.* [< L *sub-*, under + *cedere*, go] **1** to follow, as into office **2** to be successful —*vt.* to come after; follow

suc·cess (sək ses′) *n.* **1** a favorable result **2** the gaining of wealth, fame, etc. **3** a successful person or thing

suc·cess·ful *adj.* **1** turning out as was hoped for **2** having gained wealth, fame, etc. —**suc·cess′ful·ly** *adv.*

suc·ces·sion (sək sesh′ən) *n.* **1** *a)* the act of succeeding another, as to an office *b)* the right to do this **2** a number of persons or things coming one after another

suc·ces·sive (-ses′iv) *adj.* coming one after another —**suc·ces′sive·ly** *adv.*

suc·ces·sor *n.* one that succeeds another, as to an office

suc·cinct (sək siŋkt′) *adj.* [< L *sub-*, under + *cingere*, gird] clear and brief; terse —**suc·cinct′ly** *adv.* —**suc·cinct′ness** *n.*

suc·cor (suk′ər) *vt.* [< L *sub-*, under + *currere*, to run] to help in time of need or distress —*n.* aid; relief

suc·co·tash (suk′ə tash′) *n.* [< AmInd] a dish of lima beans and corn kernels cooked together

suc·cu·bus (suk′yōō bəs) *n., pl.* **-bi′** (-bī′) [ML] a demon who haunts sleeping men

suc·cu·lent (suk′yōō lənt) *adj.* [< L *sucus*, juice] full of juice —**suc′cu·lence** *n.,* **suc′cu·len·cy**

suc·cumb (sə kum′) *vi.* [< L *sub-*, under + *cumbere*, to lie] **1** to give way (to) **2** to die

such (such) *adj.* [OE *swilc*] **1** *a)* of the kind mentioned *b)* of the same or a similar kind **2** whatever [at *such* time as you go] **3** so extreme, so much, etc. [*such* an honor] —*adv.* to so great a degree [*such* good news] —*pron.* **1** such a person or thing **2** the person or thing mentioned [*such* was her nature] —**as such 1** as being what is indicated **2** in itself —**such as** for example

such and such (being) something particular but not named or specified [*such and such* a place]

such·like *adj.* of such a kind —*pron.* persons or things of such a kind

suck (suk) *vt.* [< OE *sucan*] **1** to draw (liquid) into the mouth **2** to take in by or as by sucking **3** to suck liquid from (fruit, etc.) **4** to hold (ice, etc.) in the mouth and lick so as to dissolve **5** to place (the thumb, etc.) in the mouth and draw on —*vi.* **1** to suck something **2** [Slang] to be contemptible or of low quality —*n.* the act of sucking

suck·er *n.* **1** one that sucks **2** a freshwater bony fish with a mouth adapted for sucking **3** a part used for sucking or for holding fast by suction **4** LOLLIPOP **5** [Slang] one easily duped **6** *Bot.* a subordinate shoot on the root or stem of a plant

suck·le (suk′əl) *vt.* **-led, -ling** [ME *sokelen*] **1** to cause to suck at the breast or udder; nurse **2** to bring up; rear —*vi.* to suck at the breast or udder

suck·ling *n.* an unweaned young animal

su·crose (sōō′krōs′) *n.* [< Fr *sucre*, sugar + -OSE¹] a sugar extracted from sugar cane or sugar beets

suc·tion (suk′shən) *n.* [< L *sugere*, to suck] 1 a sucking 2 the production of a vacuum in a cavity or over a surface so that external atmospheric pressure forces fluid in or causes something to adhere to the surface

Su·dan (sōō dan′) country in NE Africa: often preceded by *the* —**Su·da·nese** (sōō′də nēz′) *adj., n., pl.* -**nese′**

sud·den (sud′'n) *adj.* [< L *sub-*, under + *ire*, go] 1 *a)* happening or coming unexpectedly *b)* sharp or abrupt 2 quick or hasty —**all of a sudden** unexpectedly —**sud′den·ly** *adv.* —**sud′den·ness** *n.*

sudden death *Sports* an extra period added to a tied game: the game ends when one side scores

sudden infant death syndrome the sudden death of an apparently healthy infant, possibly caused by a breathing problem

su·do·ku (sōō dō′kōō) *n.* [Jpn] [*often* S-] a puzzle in which a player must fill in empty squares in a grid with numerals, with no numeral repeated in any row, column, or region of the grid

suds (sudz) *pl.n.* [prob. < MDu *sudse*, marsh water] 1 soapy, frothy water 2 foam —**suds′y** *adj.* -**i·er**, -**i·est**

sue (sōō) *vt., vi.* **sued**, **su′ing** [< L *sequi*, follow] 1 to appeal (to); petition 2 to prosecute (any process) in a court seeking justice, etc.

suede or **suède** (swād) *n.* [< Fr *gants de Suède*, Swedish gloves] 1 tanned leather with the flesh side buffed into a nap 2 a kind of cloth resembling this

su·et (sōō′it) *n.* [ult. < L *sebum*, tallow] the hard fat of cattle and sheep: used in cooking, etc.

Su·ez Canal (sōō ez′) ship canal joining the Mediterranean & Red seas

suf or **suff** *abbrev.* suffix

suf- *prefix* SUB-: used before *f*

suf·fer (suf′ər) *vt., vi.* [< L *sub-*, under + *ferre*, to bear] 1 to undergo (pain, injury, grief, etc.) 2 to experience (any process) 3 to permit; tolerate —**suf′fer·er** *n.*

suf·fer·ance (suf′ər əns, suf′rəns) *n.* 1 the capacity to endure pain, etc. 2 consent, permission, etc. implied by failure to prohibit

suf·fer·ing (-ər iŋ, -riŋ) *n.* 1 the bearing of pain, distress, etc. 2 something suffered

suf·fice (sə fīs′) *vi.* -**ficed′**, -**fic′ing** [< L *sub-*, under + *facere*, make] to be enough or adequate

suf·fi·cient (sə fish′ənt) *adj.* as much as is needed; enough —**suf·fi′cien·cy** *n.* —**suf·fi′cient·ly** *adv.*

suf·fix (suf′iks) *n.* [< L *sub-*, under + *figere*, fix] a syllable or syllables joined to the end of a word to alter its meaning, etc. (Ex.: -*ness* in *darkness*)

suf·fo·cate (suf′ə kāt′) *vt.* -**cat′ed**, -**cat′ing** [< L *sub-*, under + *fauces*, throat] 1 to kill by cutting off the supply of air for breathing 2

to smother, suppress, etc. —*vi.* 1 to die by being suffocated 2 to choke; stifle —**suf′fo·ca′tion** *n.*

suf·frage (suf′rij) *n.* [< L *suffragium*, a ballot] 1 a vote or voting 2 the right to vote; franchise

suf·fra·gette (suf′rə jet′) *n.* [< prec. + -ETTE] [Old-fashioned] a woman advocating female suffrage: term now considered patronizing

suf·fra·gist *n.* one who believes in extending the right to vote, esp. to women

suf·fuse (sə fyōōz′) *vt.* -**fused′**, -**fus′ing** [< L *sub-*, under + *fundere*, pour] to overspread so as to fill with a glow, etc. —**suf·fu′sion** *n.*

sug- *prefix* SUB-: used before *g*

sug·ar (shoog′ər) *n.* [< Sans *sárkarâ*] any of a class of sweet, soluble carbohydrates, as sucrose or glucose; specif., sucrose used as a food and sweetening agent —*vt.* to sweeten, etc. with sugar —*vi.* to form sugar —**sug′ar·less** *adj.* —**sug′ar·y** *adj.*

sugar beet a beet having a white root with a high sugar content

sugar cane a very tall tropical grass cultivated as the main source of sugar

sug·ar·coat *vt.* 1 to coat with sugar 2 to make (something disagreeable) seem more pleasant

sug·ar·plum *n.* a round piece of sugary candy

sug·gest (səg jest′) *vt.* [< L *sub-*, under + *gerere*, carry] 1 to bring to the mind for consideration 2 to call to mind by association of ideas 3 to propose as a possibility 4 to show indirectly; imply

sug·gest·i·ble *adj.* readily influenced by suggestion —**sug·gest′i·bil′i·ty** *n.*

sug·ges·tion (-jes′chən) *n.* 1 a suggesting or being suggested 2 something suggested 3 a hint or trace

sug·ges·tive *adj.* 1 tending to suggest ideas 2 tending to suggest something considered improper or indecent —**sug·ges′tive·ly** *adv.*

su·i·cide (sōō′ə sīd′) *n.* [L *sui*, of oneself + -CIDE] 1 the act of killing oneself intentionally 2 one who commits suicide —**su′i·ci′dal** *adj.*

su·i ge·ne·ris (sōō′ē jen′ər is) [L, of his (or her or its) own kind] being the only one of the kind; unique

suit (sōōt) *n.* [< L *sequi*, follow] 1 a set of clothes; esp., a coat and trousers (or skirt) 2 any of the four sets of playing cards 3 action to secure justice in a court of law 4 an act of suing, pleading, etc. 5 courtship —*vt.* 1 to be appropriate to 2 to make right or appropriate; fit 3 to please; satisfy [nothing *suits* him] —**follow suit** to follow the example set —**suit oneself** to act according to one's own wishes —**suit up** to put on an athletic uniform, spacesuit, etc. in preparation for a particular activity

suit·a·ble *adj.* that suits a given purpose, etc.; appropriate —**suit′a·bil′i·ty** *n.* —**suit′a·bly** *adv.*

suit·case *n.* a travel case for clothes, etc.

suite (swēt; *for 3, also* sōōt) *n.* [Fr: see SUIT] 1

a group of attendants; staff **2** a set of connected rooms, as an apartment **3** a set of matched furniture for a given room **4** a musical composition with several movements

suit·ing *n.* cloth for making suits

suit·or *n.* **1** a man courting a woman **2** a corporation seeking to take over another

su·ki·ya·ki (sōō'kē yä'kē) *n.* ⟦Jpn⟧ a Japanese dish of thinly sliced meat and vegetables, cooked quickly with soy sauce, sake, etc.

Suk·kot or **Suk·koth** (sook'ŏt, sook'ŏs) *n.* ⟦Heb, lit., tabernacles⟧ a Jewish fall festival commemorating the wandering of the Hebrews during the Exodus

sul·fa (sul'fə) *adj.* of a family of drugs used in combating certain bacterial infections

sul·fate (sul'fāt') *n.* a salt or ester of sulfuric acid

sul·fide (-fīd') *n.* a compound of sulfur with another element or a radical

sul·fur (sul'fər) *n.* ⟦< L *sulphur*⟧ a paleyellow, nonmetallic chemical element: it burns with a blue flame and a stifling odor: symbol, S; at. no. 16

sul·fu·ric (sul fyoor'ik) *adj.* of or containing sulfur

sulfuric acid an oily, colorless, corrosive liquid used in making dyes, explosives, fertilizers, etc.

sul·fu·rous (sul'fər əs, sul fyoor'əs) *adj.* **1** of or containing sulfur **2** like burning sulfur in odor, color, etc.

sulk (sulk) *vi.* ⟦< fol.⟧ to be sulky —*n.* a sulky mood

sulk·y (sul'kē) *adj.* -i·er, -i·est ⟦prob. < OE *-seolcan*, become slack⟧ quietly resentful or ill-humored —*n.*, *pl.* -ies a light, twowheeled carriage for one person —**sulk'i·ly** *adv.* —**sulk'i·ness** *n.*

sul·len (sul'ən) *adj.* ⟦< L *solus*, alone⟧ **1** showing resentment and ill humor by morose, unsociable withdrawal **2** gloomy; sad —**sul'len·ly** *adv.* —**sul'len·ness** *n.*

sul·ly (sul'ē) *vt.* -lied, -ly·ing ⟦prob. < OFr *soillier*⟧ to soil, tarnish, etc., esp. by disgracing

sul·phur (sul'fər) *n.* chiefly Brit. sp. of SULFUR

sul·tan (sult'n) *n.* ⟦Fr < Ar *sultān*⟧ a Muslim ruler

sul·tan·a (sul tan'ə) *n.* **1** a sultan's wife, mother, sister, or daughter **2** a small, white, seedless grape used for raisins

sul·tan·ate (sult'n it, -āt') *n.* a sultan's authority, office, or domain

sul·try (sul'trē) *adj.* -tri·er, -tri·est ⟦< SWELTER⟧ **1** oppressively hot and moist **2** suggesting or showing passion, lust, etc.

sum (sum) *n.* ⟦< L *summus*, highest⟧ **1** an amount of money **2** gist; summary **3** the result obtained by adding quantities; total —**sum up** to summarize

su·mac or **su·mach** (sōō'mak', shōō'-) *n.* ⟦< Ar *summāq*⟧ any of numerous poisonous and nonpoisonous trees and shrubs of the cashew family

Su·ma·tra (sōō mä'trə) large island of Indonesia

sum·ma·rize (sum'ə rīz') *vt.* -rized', -riz'ing to make or be a summary of

sum·ma·ry (-rē) *adj.* ⟦< L *summa*, a sum⟧ **1** summarizing; concise **2** prompt and without formality **3** hasty and arbitrary —*n.*, *pl.* -ries a brief statement covering the main points; digest —**sum·mar·i·ly** (sə mer'ə lē) *adv.*

sum·ma·tion (sə mā'shən) *n.* a final summary of arguments, as in a trial

sum·mer (sum'ər) *n.* ⟦< OE *sumor*⟧ the warmest season of the year, following spring —*adj.* of or typical of summer —*vi.* to pass the summer —**sum'mer·y** *adj.*

sum·mer·house *n.* a small, open structure in a garden, park, etc.

sum·mer·sault *n.*, *vi.* alt. sp. of SOMERSAULT

summer sausage a type of hard, dried or smoked sausage

sum·mer·time *n.* the summer season

sum·mit (sum'it) *n.* ⟦< L *summus*, highest⟧ **1** the highest or utmost point; top; apex **2** a conference between high-ranking leaders, as of several nations

sum·mit·ry (sum'i trē) *n.*, *pl.* -ries the use of conferences between heads of state to resolve problems of diplomacy

sum·mon (sum'ən) *vt.* ⟦< L *sub-*, under + *monere*, warn⟧ **1** to call together; order to meet **2** to call or send for with authority **3** to rouse [*summon* up one's strength] —**sum'mon·er** *n.*

sum·mons (-ənz) *n.*, *pl.* -mons·es ⟦see prec.⟧ **1** an order or command to come, attend, etc. **2** Law an official order to appear in court

su·mo (wrestling) (sōō'mō) ⟦Jpn *sumo*, compete⟧ [*sometimes* S- w-] Japanese wrestling by large, extremely heavy men

sump (sump) *n.* ⟦ME *sompe*, swamp⟧ a pit, cistern, cesspool, etc. for draining, collecting, or storing liquids

sump·tu·ous (sump'chōō əs) *adj.* ⟦< L *sumptus*, expense⟧ **1** costly; lavish **2** magnificent

sun (sun) *n.* ⟦OE *sunne*⟧ **1** the gaseous, selfluminous central star of the solar system **2** the heat or light of the sun **3** any star that is the center of a planetary system —*vt.*, *vi.* sunned, sun'ning to expose (oneself) to direct sunlight

Sun abbrev. Sunday

sun·bathe *vi.* -bathed', -bath'ing to expose the body to direct sunlight —**sun'bath'er** *n.*

sun·beam *n.* a beam of sunlight

Sun·belt in the U.S., the S and SW states having a sunny climate: also **Sun Belt**

sun·block *n.* SUNSCREEN

sun·bon·net *n.* a bonnet for shading the face and neck from the sun

sun·burn *n.* an inflammation of the skin from exposure to the sun's rays or to a sunlamp —*vi.*, *vt.* -burned' or -burnt', -burn'ing to get or cause to get a sunburn

sun·burst *n.* **1** sudden sunlight **2** a decorative pattern representing the sun with spreading rays

sun·dae (sun'dā, -dē) *n.* ⟦prob. < fol.⟧ a serving of ice cream covered with a syrup, fruit, nuts, etc.

Sun·day (sun′dā) *n.* 〖OE *sunnandæg,* sun day〗 the first day of the week: it is the Sabbath for most Christians: abbrev. **Sun**

sun·der (sun′dər) *vt., vi.* 〖< OE *sundor,* asunder〗 to break apart; split

sun·di·al *n.* an instrument that shows time by the shadow of a pointer cast by the sun onto a dial

sun·down *n.* SUNSET

sun·dries (-drēz) *pl.n.* sundry items

sun·dry (-drē) *adj.* 〖< OE *sundor,* apart〗 miscellaneous

sun·fish *n., pl.* **-fish′** or **-fish′es** 1 any of a family of North American freshwater fishes 2 a large, sluggish ocean fish

sun·flow·er *n.* a tall plant having large, yellow, daisylike flowers

sung (suŋ) *vi., vt. pp. & rare pt. of* SING[1]

sun·glass·es *pl.n.* eyeglasses with tinted lenses to shade the eyes

sunk (suŋk) *vi., vt. pp. & alt. pt. of* SINK

sunk·en (-ən) *adj.* 1 submerged 2 below the general level [a *sunken* patio] 3 deeply set; hollow [*sunken* cheeks]

sun·lamp *n.* an ultraviolet-ray lamp, used for tanning the body, etc.

sun·light *n.* the light of the sun

sun·lit *adj.* lighted by the sun

Sun·ni (soon′ē) 〖< Ar *sunna,* tradition〗 *n., pl.* **Sun′ni** an adherent of the most widely practiced branch of Islam, accepting the first four caliphs as successors to Muhammad —*adj.* of the Sunni or their branch of Islam

sun·ny (-ē) *adj.* **-ni·er, -ni·est** 1 full of sunshine 2 bright; cheerful —**sun′ni·ness** *n.*

sunny side 1 the sunlit side 2 the brighter aspect —**sunny side up** fried on one side only and with unbroken yolk: said of an egg

sun·rise *n.* 1 the daily appearance of the sun above the E horizon 2 the varying time of this

sun·roof *n.* a panel in a car roof, that opens to let in light and air: also **sun roof**

sun·room *n.* a room with large windows to let in sunlight

sun·screen *n.* a lotion, cream, etc. to block certain ultraviolet rays of the sun and reduce the danger of sunburn

sun·set *n.* 1 the daily disappearance of the sun below the W horizon 2 the varying time of this

sun·shine *n.* 1 the shining of the sun 2 the light and heat from the sun 3 a sunny place 4 cheerfulness, happiness, etc. —**sun′shin′y** *adj.*

sun·spot *n.* any of the temporarily cooler regions appearing cyclically as dark spots on the sun

sun·stroke *n.* a form of heatstroke caused by excessive exposure to the sun

sun·tan *n.* a darkened condition of the skin resulting from exposure to the sun

sun·up *n.* SUNRISE

sup (sup) *vi.* **supped, sup′ping** 〖< OFr *soupe,* soup〗 to have supper

sup- *prefix* SUB-: used before *p*

su·per (soo′pər) *n.* 〖< fol.〗 short for SUPERINTENDENT (*n.* 2) —*adj.* 1 〖Inf.〗 outstanding; exceptionally fine 2 great, extreme, or excessive

super- 〖L < *super,* above〗 *prefix* 1 over, above [*superstructure*] 2 *a*) surpassing [*superabundant*] *b*) greater or better than others of its kind [*supermarket*] 3 additional [*supertax*]

su·per·a·bun·dant *adj.* being more than enough —**su′per·a·bun′dance** *n.*

su·per·an·nu·at·ed (soo′pər an′yoo āt′id) *adj.* 〖< L *super,* above + *annus,* year〗 1 too old for service 2 retired, esp. with a pension, because of old age 3 obsolete; old-fashioned

su·perb (sə purb′, soo-) *adj.* 〖see SUPER-〗 1 noble or majestic 2 rich or magnificent 3 extremely fine; excellent —**su·perb′ly** *adv.*

su·per·car·go *n., pl.* **-goes** or **-gos** an officer on a merchant ship in charge of the cargo

su·per·charge *vt.* **-charged′, -charg′ing** to increase the power of (an engine), as with a device (**su′per·charg′er**) that forces extra air and fuel into the cylinders

su·per·cil·i·ous (soo′pər sil′ē əs) *adj.* 〖< L *super-,* above + *cilium,* eyelid, hence (in allusion to raised eyebrows) haughtiness〗 disdainful or contemptuous; haughty

su·per·con·duc·tiv·i·ty *n. Physics* the lack of resistance to electrical current in certain metals, etc. when cooled to very low temperatures

su·per·con·duc·tor *n.* any material that exhibits superconductivity

su·per·e·go (-ē′gō) *n., pl.* **-gos** *Psychoanalysis* that part of the psyche that enforces moral standards

su·per·e·ro·ga·tion (-er′ə gā′shən) *n.* 〖< L *super-,* above + *erogare,* pay out〗 a doing more than is needed or expected —**su′per·e·rog′a·to′ry** (-i rãg′ə tôr′ē) *adj.*

su·per·fi·cial (-fish′əl) *adj.* 〖< L *super-,* above + *facies,* face〗 1 of or being on the surface 2 concerned with and understanding only the obvious; shallow 3 quick and cursory 4 seeming such only at first glance —**su′per·fi′ci·al′i·ty** (-fish′ē al′ə tē) *n., pl.* **-ties** —**su′per·fi′cial·ly** *adv.*

su·per·flu·ous (sə pur′floo əs, soo-) *adj.* 〖< L *super-,* above + *fluere,* to flow〗 excessive or unnecessary —**su·per·flu′i·ty** (soo′pər floo′ə tē) *n., pl.* **-ties**

su·per·he·ro *n., pl.* **-roes** a nearly invincible hero, as in comic books, often having extraordinary powers

su·per·high·way *n.* EXPRESSWAY

su·per·hu·man *adj.* 1 having a nature above that of humans; divine 2 greater than that of a normal human

su·per·im·pose *vt.* **-posed′, -pos′ing** to put, lay, or stack on top of something else

su·per·in·tend (soo′pər in tend′) *vt.* to act as superintendent of; supervise; manage —**su′per·in·tend′ence** *n.,* **su′per·in·tend′en·cy** *n.*

su·per·in·tend·ent (-ten′dənt) *n.* 〖< LL *superintendere,* superintend〗 1 a person in charge of a department, institution, etc.; director 2 a person responsible for the maintenance of a building

su·pe·ri·or (sə pir′ē ər) *adj.* ⟦see SUPER-⟧ **1** higher in space, order, rank, etc. **2** greater in quality or value than: with *to* **3** above average in quality; excellent **4** refusing to give in to or be affected by: with *to* **5** showing a feeling of being better than others; haughty —*n.* **1** a superior person or thing **2** the head of a religious community —**su·pe′ri·or′i·ty** (-ôr′ə tē) *n.*

Su·pe·ri·or (sə pir′ē ər), **Lake** largest of the Great Lakes, between N Michigan & W Ontario, Canada

superl *abbrev.* superlative

su·per·la·tive (sə pur′lə tiv, soo-) *adj.* ⟦< L *super-*, above + *latus*, pp. of *ferre*, to bear, carry⟧ **1** superior to all others; supreme **2** *Gram.* designating the extreme degree of comparison of adjectives and adverbs —*n.* **1** the highest degree; peak **2** *Gram.* the superlative degree ["finest" is the *superlative* of "fine"] —**su·per′la·tive·ly** *adv.*

su·per·ma·jor·i·ty *n.* the quantity of votes, above a mere majority, required to pass certain bills, etc.

su·per·man (-man′) *n., pl.* **-men** (-men′) an apparently superhuman man

su·per·mar·ket *n.* a large retail food store or market

su·per·nal (soo purn′əl) *adj.* ⟦< L *supernus*, upper⟧ celestial or divine

su·per·nat·u·ral *adj.* not explainable by the known forces or laws of nature; specif., of or involving gods, ghosts, spirits, etc.

su·per·no·va *n., pl.* **-vas** or **-vae** (-vē) a rare, extremely bright nova

su·per·nu·mer·a·ry (soo′pər noo′mə rer′ ē) *n., pl.* **-ies** ⟦< L *super*, above + *numerus*, number⟧ **1** an extra person or thing **2** *Theater* a person with a small, nonspeaking part

su·per·pose (-pōzed′, -pos′ing ⟦see SUPER- & POSE⟧ to place on or above something else —**su′per·pos′a·ble** *adj.* —**su′per·po·si′ tion** *n.*

su·per·pow·er *n.* an extremely powerful, influential nation

su·per·sat·u·rate *vt.* **-rat′ed, -rat′ing** to make more concentrated than in normal saturation —**su′per·sat′u·ra′tion** *n.*

su·per·script *n.* ⟦see SUPER- & SCRIPT⟧ a figure, letter, or symbol written above and to the side of another

su·per·sede (soo′pər sēd′) *vt.* **-sed′ed, -sed′ing** ⟦< L *supersedere*, sit over⟧ to replace or succeed

su·per·son·ic *adj.* ⟦SUPER- + SONIC⟧ designating, of, or moving at a speed greater than that of sound

su·per·star *n.* a star performer, as in sports or entertainment

su·per·sti·tion (soo′pər stish′ən) *n.* ⟦< L *superstitio*, lit., a standing (in awe) over⟧ **1** any belief that is inconsistent with known facts or rational thought, esp. such a belief in omens, the supernatural, etc. **2** any action or practice

based on such a belief —**su′per·sti′tious** *adj.*

su·per·store *n.* a very large retail store with a wide variety of goods

su·per·struc·ture *n.* **1** a structure built on top of another **2** that part of a building above the foundation **3** that part of a ship above the main deck

su·per·tank·er *n.* an extremely large tanker ship, of 300,000 tons or more

su·per·vene (soo′pər vēn′) *vi.* **-vened′, -ven′ing** ⟦< L *super-*, over + *venire*, come⟧ to come or happen as something extraneous or unexpected

su·per·vise (soo′pər vīz′) *vt., vi.* **-vised′, -vis′ing** ⟦< L *super-*, over + *videre*, see⟧ to oversee or direct (work, workers, etc.) —**su′ per·vi′sion** (-vizh′ən) *n.* —**su′per·vi′sor** *n.* —**su′per·vi′so·ry** *adj.*

su·pine (soo pīn′) *adj.* ⟦L *supinus*⟧ **1** lying on the back, face upward **2** inactive; sluggish; listless

supp or **suppl** *abbrev.* **1** supplement **2** supplementary

sup·per (sup′ər) *n.* ⟦see SUP⟧ an evening meal

supper club a nightclub offering restaurant service, live music, and often dancing

sup·plant (sə plant′) *vt.* ⟦< L *sub-*, under + *planta*, sole of the foot⟧ **1** to take the place of, esp. by force or plotting **2** to remove in order to replace with something else

sup·ple (sup′əl) *adj.* **-pler, -plest** ⟦< L *supplex*, submissive⟧ **1** easily bent; flexible **2** lithe; limber **3** adaptable

sup·ple·ment (sup′lə mənt; *for v.*, -ment′) *n.* ⟦see SUPPLY⟧ **1** something added, esp. to make up for a lack **2** a section of additional material in a book, newspaper, etc. —*vt.* to provide a supplement to —**sup′ple·men′tal** *adj.*, **sup′ple·men′ta·ry**

sup·pli·ant (sup′lē ənt) *n.* one who supplicates —*adj.* supplicating

sup·pli·cant (-lə kənt) *adj., n.* SUPPLIANT

sup·pli·cate (sup′lə kāt′) *vt., vi.* **-cat′ed, -cat′ing** ⟦< L *sub-*, under + *plicare*, to fold⟧ **1** to ask for (something) humbly **2** to make a humble request (of) —**sup′pli·ca′tion** *n.*

sup·ply (sə plī′) *vt.* **-plied′, -ply′ing** ⟦< L *sub-*, under + *plere*, fill⟧ **1** to furnish or provide (what is needed) to (someone) **2** to compensate for (a deficiency, etc.); make good —*n., pl.* **-plies′ 1** the amount available for use or sale; stock **2** [*pl.*] needed materials, provisions; etc. —**sup·pli′er** *n.*

sup·ply-side *adj.* designating or of an economic theory that increasing money available for private investment, as by lowering taxes, will stimulate economic growth

sup·port (sə pôrt′) *vt.* ⟦< L *sub-*, under + *portare*, carry⟧ **1** to carry the weight of; hold up **2** to encourage; help **3** to advocate; uphold **4** to maintain (a person, institution, etc.) with money or subsistence **5** to help prove, vindicate, etc. **6** to bear; endure **7** to keep up; maintain **8** to have a role subordinate to (a star) in a play —*n.* **1** a supporting or being supported **2** a person or thing that supports **3** a means of maintaining a livelihood —**sup·port'a·ble** *adj.* —**sup·port'er** *n.*

sup·port·ive *adj.* giving support or help

sup·pose (sə pōz') *vt.* **-posed', -pos'ing** ⟦< L *sub-*, under + *ponere*, put⟧ **1** to assume to be true, as for argument's sake **2** to believe, think, etc. **3** to consider as a possibility [*suppose I go*] **4** to expect [I'm *supposed* to sing] —*vi.* to conjecture —**sup·posed'** *adj.* —**sup·pos'ed·ly** *adv.*

sup·po·si·tion (sup'ə zish'ən) *n.* **1** a supposing **2** something supposed

sup·pos·i·to·ry (sə päz'ə tôr'ē) *n.,* pl. **-ries** ⟦see SUPPOSE⟧ a small piece of medicated substance placed in the rectum or vagina, where it melts

sup·press (sə pres') *vt.* ⟦< L *sub-*, under + *premere*, to press⟧ **1** to put down by force; quell **2** to keep from being known, published, etc. **3** to keep back; restrain —**sup·pres'sion** (-presh'ən) *n.*

sup·pres·sant (-ənt) *n.* a drug, etc. that tends to suppress an action, condition, etc.

sup·pu·rate (sup'yōō rāt') *vi.* **-rat'ed, -rat' ing** ⟦< L *sub-*, under + *pus*, pus⟧ to form or discharge pus

supra- ⟦< L *supra*, above⟧ *prefix* above, over, beyond

su·pra·na·tion·al (sōō'prə nash'ə nəl) *adj.* of, for, or above all or a number of nations

su·prem·a·cist (sə prem'ə sist, sōō-) *n.* one who believes in the supremacy of a particular group

su·prem·a·cy (-sē) *n.,* pl. **-cies** supreme condition or power

su·preme (-prēm') *adj.* ⟦< L *superus*, that is above⟧ **1** highest in rank, power, etc. **2** highest in quality, achievement, etc. **3** highest in degree **4** final; ultimate —**su·preme'ly** *adv.*

Supreme Being God

Supreme Court 1 the highest U.S. federal court **2** the highest court in most U.S. states

Supreme Soviet 1 a part of the legislature of Russia **2** formerly, the parliament of the U.S.S.R.

Supt *abbrev.* Superintendent

sur- ⟦< L *super*, over⟧ *prefix* over, upon, above, beyond

sur·cease (sur'sēs') *n.* ⟦< L *supersedere*, refrain from⟧ an end, or cessation

sur·charge (sur'chärj') *vt.* **-charged', -charg'ing** ⟦see SUR- & CHARGE⟧ **1** to overcharge **2** to mark (a postage stamp) with a surcharge —*n.* **1** an additional charge **2** a new valuation printed over the original valuation on a postage stamp

sur·cin·gle (sur'siŋ'gəl) *n.* ⟦< OFr *sur-*, over + L *cingulum*, a belt⟧ a strap passed around a horse's body to bind on a saddle, pack, etc.

sure (shoor) *adj.* **sur'er, sur'est** ⟦< L *securus*⟧ **1** that will not fail [a *sure* method] **2** that cannot be doubted or questioned **3** having no doubt; confident [*sure* of the facts] **4** that can be counted on to be or happen [a *sure* defeat] **5** certain (to do, be, etc.) [*sure* to lose] —*adv.*

[Inf.] certainly; indeed —**for sure** certain(ly) —**sure enough** [Inf.] **1** without doubt **2** as expected or feared —**sure'ness** *n.*

sure·fire or **sure-fire** (-fīr') *adj.* [Inf.] sure to be successful or as expected

sure·foot·ed *adj.* not likely to stumble, slip, fall, or err —**sure'-foot'ed·ness** *n.*

sure·ly *adv.* **1** with confidence **2** without a doubt; certainly

sure·ty (shoor'ə tē, shoor'tē) *n.,* pl. **-ties 1** something that gives assurance, as against loss, etc. **2** one who takes responsibility for another

surf (surf) *n.* ⟦prob. var. of SOUGH⟧ the waves of the sea breaking on the shore or a reef —*vi.* to engage in surfing —*vt.* [Inf.] to browse a succession of (TV channels, websites, etc.) on (a TV, computer network, etc.) —**surf' er** *n.*

sur·face (sur'fis) *n.* ⟦< Fr *sur-*, over + *face*, a face⟧ **1** *a*) the exterior of an object *b*) any of the faces of a solid **2** superficial features or outward appearance —*adj.* **1** of, on, or at the surface **2** external; superficial —*vt.* **-faced, -fac·ing** to give a surface to, as in paving —*vi.* **1** to rise to the surface of the water **2** to become known

surf·board *n.* a long, narrow board used in the sport of surfing

surf·cast *vi.* **-cast', -cast'ing** to fish by casting into the surf from or near the shore

sur·feit (sur'fit) *n.* ⟦< OFr *sorfaire*, overdo⟧ **1** too great an amount **2** overindulgence, esp. in food or drink **3** disgust, nausea, etc. resulting from excess —*vt.* to feed or supply to excess

surf·ing (sur'fiŋ) *n.* the sport of riding in toward shore on the front slope of a wave, esp. on a surfboard

surge (surj) *n.* ⟦< L *surgere*, to rise⟧ **1** a large wave of water **2** a sudden, powerful forward motion **3** a sudden, strong increase, as of power —*vi.* **surged, surg'ing 1** to move in or as in a surge **2** to increase suddenly

sur·geon (sur'jən) *n.* a doctor who specializes in surgery

sur·ger·y (sur'jər ē) *n.,* pl. **-ger·ies** ⟦< Gr *cheir*, the hand + *ergein*, to work⟧ **1** the treatment of disease, injury, etc. by manual or instrumental operations **2** a room used for this

sur·gi·cal (-ji kəl) *adj.* **1** of surgeons or surgery **2** very accurate, precisely targeted, etc. —**sur'gi·cal·ly** *adv.*

Su·ri·name (soor'i näm') country in NE South America: formerly **Su'ri·nam'**

sur·ly (sur'lē) *adj.* **-li·er, -li·est** ⟦earlier *sirly*, imperious < *sir*, sir⟧ bad-tempered; sullenly rude

sur·mise (sər mīz') *n.* ⟦OFr *sur-*, upon + *mettre*, put⟧ a conjecture —*vt., vi.* **-mised', -mis'ing** to guess

sur·mount (sər mount') *vt.* ⟦SUR- & MOUNT²⟧ **1** to overcome (a difficulty) **2** to be at the top of; rise above **3** to climb up and across (a height, etc.) —**sur·mount'a· ble** *adj.*

sur·name (sur′nām′) *n.* ⟦< OFr *sur–* (see SUR–) + *nom*, name⟧ the family name, or last name

sur·pass (sər pas′) *vt.* ⟦< Fr *sur–* (see SUR–) + *passer*, to pass⟧ 1 to excel or be superior to 2 to go beyond the limit, capacity, etc. of

sur·plice (sur′plis) *n.* ⟦< L *super–*, above + *pelliceum*, fur robe⟧ a loose, white ecclesiastical vestment, usually worn over a cassock

sur·plus (sur′plus′) *n.* ⟦< OFr *sur–*, above (see SUR–) + L *plus*, more⟧ a quantity over and above what is needed or used *—adj.* excess; extra

sur·prise (sər prīz′) *vt.* **–prised′, –pris′ing** ⟦< OFr *sur–* (see SUR–) + *prendre*, to take⟧ 1 to come upon suddenly or unexpectedly; take unawares 2 to amaze; astonish *—n.* 1 a being surprised 2 something that surprises

sur·re·al (sə rē′əl) *adj.* 1 of or like surrealism 2 bizarre; fantastic

sur·re·al·ism *n.* ⟦see SUR– & REAL⟧ a modern movement in the arts in which the workings of the unconscious are depicted *—sur·re′al·is′tic adj. —sur·re′al·ist adj., n.*

sur·ren·der (sə ren′dər) *vt.* ⟦< Fr *sur–*, up + *rendre*, render⟧ 1 to give up possession of; yield to another on compulsion 2 to give up or abandon *—vi.* to give oneself up, esp. as a prisoner *—n.* the act of surrendering

sur·rep·ti·tious (sur′əp tish′əs) *adj.* ⟦< L *sub–*, under + *rapere*, seize⟧ done, gotten, acting, etc. in a stealthy way

sur·rey (sur′ē) *n., pl.* **–reys** ⟦after Surrey, county in England⟧ a light, four-wheeled carriage with two seats and a flat top

sur·ro·gate (sur′ə git, –gāt′) *n.* ⟦< L *sub–*, in place of + *rogare*, ask⟧ 1 a deputy or substitute 2 in some U.S. states, a probate court judge 3 a woman who bears a child for another woman, who will raise it *—sur′ro·ga·cy n., pl.* **–cies**

sur·round (sə round′) *vt.* ⟦< L *super–*, over + *undare*, to rise⟧ to encircle on all or nearly all sides

sur·round·ings *pl.n.* the things, conditions, etc. around a person or thing

sur·tax (sur′taks′) *n.* an extra tax on top of the regular tax

sur·veil·lance (sər vā′ləns) *n.* ⟦Fr < *sur–* (see SUR–) + *veiller*, to watch⟧ close watch kept over someone, esp. a suspect

sur·vey (sər vā′; *for n.* sur′vā′) *vt.* ⟦< OFr *sur–* (see SUR–) + *veoir*, see⟧ 1 to examine or consider in detail or comprehensively 2 to determine the location, form, or boundaries of (a tract of land) 3 to gather information from (multiple people) as by means of a questionnaire *—n., pl.* **–veys** a detailed study, as by gathering information from multiple people and analyzing it 2 a general study or course of study, as of a topic 3 *a)* the process of surveying a tract of land *b)* a written description of this *—sur·vey′or n.*

sur·vey·ing *n.* the science or work of making land surveys

sur·viv·al·ist (sər vī′vəl ist) *n.* one who takes

measures, as storing food and weapons, to ensure survival after an economic collapse, nuclear war, etc.

sur·vive (sər vīv′) *vt.* **–vived′, –viv′ing** ⟦< L *super–*, above + *vivere*, to live⟧ to remain alive or in existence after *—vi.* to continue living or existing *—sur·viv′al n.*

sur·vi·vor (–ər) *n.* 1 one that survives 2 one who is capable of surviving changing conditions, misfortune, etc.

sus·cep·ti·ble (sə sep′tə bəl) *adj.* ⟦< L *sus–*, under + *capere*, take⟧ easily affected emotionally *—susceptible of* admitting; allowing [*testimony susceptible of* error] *—susceptible to* easily influenced or affected by *—sus·cep′ti·bil′i·ty n.*

su·shi (sōō′shē) *n.* ⟦Jpn⟧ a dish consisting of small cakes of cold rice garnished with raw or cooked fish, vegetables, etc.

sus·pect (sə spekt′; *for adj. & n.* sus′pekt′) *vt.* ⟦< L *sus–*, under + *spicere*, to look⟧ 1 to believe to be guilty on little or no evidence 2 to believe to be bad, wrong, etc.; distrust 3 to guess; surmise *—adj.* suspected *—n.* one suspected of a crime, etc.

sus·pend (sə spend′) *vt.* ⟦< L *sus–*, under + *pendere*, hang⟧ 1 to exclude as a penalty from an office, school, etc., for a time 2 to stop temporarily 3 to hold back (judgment, etc.) 4 to hang by a support from above 5 to hold in place as though hanging [dust particles *suspended* in the air]

suspended animation a temporary cessation of the vital functions, resembling death

sus·pend·ers *pl.n.* a pair of straps passed over the shoulders to hold up trousers

sus·pense (sə spens′) *n.* ⟦< L *suspendere*, suspend⟧ 1 a state of uncertainty 2 the growing excitement felt while awaiting a climax of a novel, play, etc. *—sus·pense′ful adj.*

sus·pen·sion (sə spen′shən) *n.* 1 a suspending or being suspended 2 the system of springs, etc. supporting a vehicle upon its undercarriage or axles 3 a mixture in which particles are dispersed through a fluid but not dissolved in it

suspension bridge a bridge suspended from cables anchored at either end and supported by towers at intervals

sus·pi·cion (sə spish′ən) *n.* ⟦< L *suspicere*, suspect⟧ 1 a suspecting 2 the feeling or state of mind of one who suspects 3 a very small amount; trace *—vt.* [Inf. or Dial.] to suspect

sus·pi·cious *adj.* 1 arousing suspicion 2 showing or feeling suspicion *—sus·pi′cious·ly adv.*

sus·tain (sə stān′) *vt.* ⟦< L *sus–*, under + *tenere*, to hold⟧ 1 to keep in existence; maintain or prolong 2 to provide sustenance for 3 to carry the weight of; support 4 to endure; withstand 5 to comfort or encourage 6 to suffer (an injury, loss, etc.) 7 to uphold the validity of 8 to confirm; corroborate

sus·te·nance (sus′tə nəns) *n.* 1 a sustaining 2 means of livelihood 3 nourishment; food

sut·ler (sut′lər) *n.* ⟦< Obs. Du *soeteler*⟧ [Historical] a person following an army to sell things to its soldiers

su·ture (sōō′chər) *n.* [< L *suere*, sew] **1** the line of junction of two parts, esp. of bones of the skull **2** *a)* the stitching together of the two edges of a wound or incision *b)* the thread, etc. used or any of the stitches so made

SUV *abbrev.* SPORT UTILITY VEHICLE

su·ze·rain (sōō′zə rin′, -rān′) *n.* [Fr < L *sursum*, above] **1** a feudal lord **2** a state in relation to another over which it has some political control

svelte (svelt) *adj.* [Fr] slender; lithe

Sw *abbrev.* **1** Sweden **2** Swedish

SW *abbrev.* **1** southwest **2** southwestern

swab (swäb) *n.* [< Du *zwabben*, do dirty work] **1** a yarn mop **2** a small piece of cotton, etc. used to medicate or cleanse a bodily orifice or a wound **3** [Slang] a sailor —*vt.* **swabbed, swab′bing** to use a swab on

swad·dle (swäd′'l) *vt.* **-dled, -dling** [prob. < OE *swathian*, swathe] to wrap (a newborn baby) in a blanket or, formerly, in long, narrow bands of cloth **(swaddling clothes)**

swag (swag) *vt.* **swagged, swag′ging** [see SWAGGER] to hang in a swag —*n.* **1** a valance, garland, etc. hanging decoratively in a curve **2** [Slang] loot

swage (swāj) *n.* a tool for bending or shaping metal

swag·ger (swag′ər) *vi.* [prob. < Norw *svagga*, sway] **1** to walk with a bold, arrogant stride **2** to boast or brag loudly —*n.* swaggering walk or manner

Swa·hi·li (swä hē′lē) *n.* [< Ar *sawāhil*, the coasts] a Bantu language used as a lingua franca in E Africa

swain (swān) *n.* [< ON *sveinn*, boy] [Archaic] **1** a country youth **2** a lover

swal·low¹ (swäl′ō) *n.* [OE *swealwe*] a small, swift-flying bird with long, pointed wings and a forked tail

swal·low² (swäl′ō) *vt.* [OE *swelgan*] **1** to pass (food, etc.) from the mouth into the stomach **2** to take in; absorb: often with *up* **3** to retract (words said) **4** to put up with [to *swallow* insults] **5** to suppress [to *swallow* one's pride] **6** [Inf.] to accept as true without question —*vi.* to perform the actions of swallowing something, esp. as a result of emotion —*n.* **1** a swallowing **2** the amount swallowed at one time

swam (swam) *vi., vt. pt. of* SWIM¹ & SWIM²

swa·mi (swä′mē) *n., pl.* **-mis** [< Sans *svāmin*, lord] lord; master: title of respect for a Hindu religious teacher

swamp (swämp, swômp) *n.* [prob. < LowG] a piece of wet, spongy land, esp. one with trees or shrubs —*vt.* **1** to plunge or sink in a swamp, water, etc. **2** to flood as with water **3** to overwhelm [*swamped* by debts] **4** to sink (a boat) by filling with water —**swamp′y** *adj.* **-i·er, -i·est**

swan (swän, swôn) *n.* [OE] a large waterfowl, usually white, with a long, graceful neck

swank (swaŋk) [Inf.] *n.* [akin to OE *swancor*, pliant] ostentatious display —*adj.* ostentatiously stylish

swank·y *adj.* **-i·er, -i·est** [Inf.] ostentatiously stylish

swan's-down *n.* **1** the soft down of the swan, used for trimming clothes, etc. **2** a soft, thick flannel Also sp. **swans′down′**

swan song [after the song sung, in ancient fable, by a dying swan] the last act, final creative work, etc. of a person

swap (swäp, swôp) *vt., vi.* **swapped, swap′ping** [ME *swappen*, to strike] to trade; barter

sward (swôrd) *n.* [< OE *sweard*, a skin] grass-covered soil; turf

swarm (swôrm) *n.* [OE *swearm*] **1** a large number of bees, led by a queen, leaving a hive to start a new colony **2** a colony of bees in a hive **3** a moving mass, crowd, or throng —*vi.* **1** to fly off in a swarm: said of bees **2** to move, be present, etc. in large numbers **3** to be crowded

swarth·y (swôr′thē, -thē) *adj.* **-i·er, -i·est** [< OE *sweart*] having a dark complexion

swash·buck·ler (-buk′lər) *n.* [< *swash*, to swagger + *buckler*, a shield] **1** a blustering, swaggering fighting man **2** [Inf.] a romantic historical novel or movie featuring daring adventures —**swash′buck′ling** *n., adj.*

swas·ti·ka (swäs′ti kə) *n.* [< Sans *svasti*, well-being] **1** an ancient design and mystic symbol in the form of a cross with four equal arms, each bent in a right angle **2** this design with the arms bent clockwise, used as an emblem of Nazism and anti-Semitism

swat (swät) *vt.* **swat′ted, swat′ting** [echoic] to hit with a quick, sharp blow —*n.* a quick, sharp blow —**swat′ter** *n.*

SWAT (swät) *n.* [S(pecial) W(eapons) a(nd) T(actics)] a special police unit trained to deal with violence, riots, terrorism, etc.: in full **SWAT team**

swatch (swäch) *n.* [orig., a cloth tag or label] a sample piece of cloth, etc.

swath (swäth, swôth) *n.* [OE *swathu*, a track] **1** the width covered with one cut of a scythe or other mowing device **2** a strip, row, etc. that has been mowed **3** a strip, streak, or zone

swathe (swäth, swāth) *vt.* **swathed, swath′ing** [OE *swathian*] **1** to wrap up in a long strip of cloth **2** to envelop; enclose

sway (swā) *vi.* [< ON *sveigja*, to turn, bend] **1** to swing or move from side to side or to and fro **2** to lean or go to one side —*vt.* **1** to cause to sway **2** to influence —*n.* **1** a swaying or being swayed **2** influence [the *sway* of passion] —**hold sway** to reign or prevail

sway-backed (-bakt′) *adj.* having a sagging spine: said as of some horses

Swa·zi·land (swä′zē land′) country in SE Africa

swear (swer) *vi.* **swore, sworn, swear′ing** [OE *swerian*] **1** to make a solemn declaration with an appeal to God to confirm it **2** to make a solemn promise; vow **3** to use profane language; curse —*vt.* to declare, pledge, or vow on oath —**swear in** to administer an oath to (a person taking office, a witness, etc.) —**swear off** to renounce —**swear out** to obtain (a warrant for arrest) by making a charge under oath —**swear′er** *n.*

swear·word *n.* a profane word or phrase

sweat (swet) *vi., vt.* **sweat** or **sweat′ed, sweat′ing** ⟦< OE *swat,* sweat⟧ 1 to give forth or cause to give forth a salty moisture through the pores of the skin; perspire 2 to give forth or condense (moisture) on its surface 3 to work hard enough to cause sweating 4 [Inf.] to experience anxiety or distress (over) —*n.* 1 the salty liquid given forth in perspiration 2 moisture collected in droplets on a surface 3 a sweating or being sweated 4 a condition of eagerness, anxiety, etc. 5 [*pl.*] clothes worn for exercising, etc.; specif., a sweat suit —**sweat out** [Inf.] 1 to get rid of by sweating [to *sweat out* a cold] 2 to wait anxiously for or through —**sweat′y** *adj.* **-i·er, -i·est**

sweat·er *n.* a knitted or crocheted outer garment for the upper body

sweat·shirt a heavy, long-sleeved pullover or zippered jacket, usually of cotton jersey, sometimes with matching loose trousers (**sweat pants**) in an ensemble (**sweat suit**)

sweat·shop *n.* a shop where employees work long hours at low wages under poor conditions

Swed *abbrev.* 1 Sweden 2 Swedish

Swede (swēd) *n.* a person born or living in Sweden

Swe·den (swēd′'n) country in N Europe

Swed·ish (swē′dish) *adj.* of Sweden or its people, language, etc. —*n.* the Germanic language of Sweden

sweep (swēp) *vt.* **swept, sweep′ing** ⟦OE *swapan*⟧ 1 to clean (a floor, etc.) as by brushing with a broom 2 to remove (dirt, etc.) as with a broom 3 to strip, carry away, or destroy with a forceful movement 4 to touch in moving across [hands *sweeping* the keyboard] 5 to pass swiftly over or across 6 *a)* to win all the games of (a series, etc.) *b)* to win overwhelmingly —*vi.* 1 to clean a floor, etc. as with a broom 2 to move steadily with speed or grace 3 to extend in a long curve or line [a road *sweeping* up the hill] —*n.* 1 the act of sweeping 2 a steady sweeping movement 3 range or scope 4 extent, as of land; stretch 5 a line, curve, etc. that seems to flow or move 6 one whose work is sweeping [a chimney *sweep*] —**sweep′er** *n.* —**sweep′ing** *adj.* —**sweep′ing·ly** *adv.*

sweep·ings *pl.n.* things swept up, as litter from a floor

sweep·stakes *n., pl.* **-stakes′** 1 a lottery in which the winner or winners are determined by the result of a horse race or other contest 2 any of various other lotteries, often used for promotional purposes

sweet (swēt) *adj.* ⟦OE *swete*⟧ 1 having a taste of, or like that of, sugar 2 *a)* having an

agreeable taste, smell, sound, etc. *b)* gratifying *c)* friendly, kind, etc. 3 *a)* not rancid or sour *b)* not salty or salted —*n.* [*pl.*] sweet foods —**sweet′ish** *adj.* —**sweet′ly** *adv.* —**sweet′ness** *n.*

sweet·bread (-bred′) *n.* the thymus or pancreas of a calf, lamb, etc., when used as food: *usually used in pl.*

sweet·bri·er or **sweet·bri·ar** (-brī′ər) *n.* EG-LANTINE

sweet corn a variety of corn eaten fresh as a table vegetable

sweet·en *vt.* 1 to make sweet 2 to make pleasant or agreeable 3 [Inf.] to increase the value of (collateral, an offer, etc.)

sweet·en·er *n.* a sweetening agent, esp. a synthetic one, as saccharin

sweet·heart *n.* a loved one; lover

sweetheart contract a contract arranged by collusion between union officials and an employer with terms disadvantageous to union members

sweet·meat *n.* a candy

sweet pea a climbing plant with usually pink to purple flowers

sweet pepper 1 a red pepper plant producing a large, mild fruit 2 the fruit

sweet potato 1 a tropical plant with a fleshy, brownish root used as a vegetable 2 its root

sweet-talk *vt., vi.* [Inf.] to talk in a flattering way (to)

sweet tooth [Inf.] a fondness or craving for sweets

swell (swel) *vi., vt.* **swelled, swelled** or **swol′len, swell′ing** ⟦OE *swellan*⟧ 1 to expand as a result of pressure from within 2 to curve out; bulge 3 to fill (*with* pride, etc.) 4 to increase in size, force, intensity, loudness, etc. —*n.* 1 a part that swells; specif., a large, rolling wave 2 an increase in size, amount, degree, etc. 3 [Inf.] a person of high social standing a crescendo —*adj.* [Slang] excellent

swell·head *n.* [Inf.] a conceited person —**swell′head′ed** *adj.*

swell·ing *n.* 1 an increase in size, volume, etc. 2 a swollen part

swel·ter (swel′tər) *vi.* ⟦< OE *sweltan,* to die, faint⟧ to feel uncomfortably hot; sweat, feel weak, etc. from great heat

swel·ter·ing *adj.* very hot; sultry

swept (swept) *vt., vi. pt. & pp. of* SWEEP

swept·back *adj.* having a backward slant: said of the wings of an aircraft

swerve (swurv) *vi., vt.* **swerved, swerv′ing** ⟦< OE *sweorfan,* to scour⟧ to turn aside from a straight line, course, etc. —*n.* a swerving

swift (swift) *adj.* ⟦OE⟧ 1 moving with great speed; fast 2 coming, acting, etc. quickly —*n.* a swift-flying, swallowlike bird —**swift′ly** *adv.* —**swift′ness** *n.*

Swift (swift), **Jon·a·than** (jän′ə thən) 1667-1745; Eng. satirist, born in Ireland

swig (swig) [Inf.] *vt., vi.* **swigged, swig′ging** ⟦< ?⟧ to drink in gulps —*n.* a big gulp, as of liquor

swill (swil) *vt., vi.* ⟦OE *swilian*⟧ 1 to drink

greedily **2** to feed swill to (pigs, etc.) —*n.* **1** liquid garbage fed to pigs **2** garbage

swim¹ (swim) *vi.* **swam**, **swum**, **swim′ming** ⟦OE *swimman*⟧ **1** to move through water by moving arms, legs, fins, etc. **2** to move along smoothly **3** to float on or in a liquid **4** to overflow [eyes *swimming* with tears] —*vt.* to swim in or across —*n.* the act of swimming —*adj.* [Inf.] of or for swimming [*swim trunks*] —**in the swim** active in what is popular at the moment —**swim′mer** *n.*

swim² (swim) *vi.* **swam**, **swum**, **swim′ming** ⟦OE *swima*⟧ **1** to be dizzy **2** to seem to whirl [the room *swam* before me]

swimming hole a deep place in a river, creek, etc. used for swimming

swim·ming·ly *adv.* easily and with success

swim·suit *n.* a garment worn for swimming

swin·dle (swin′dəl) *vt., vi.* **-dled**, **-dling** [< Ger *schwindeln*] to defraud (another) of money or property; cheat —*n.* an act of swindling; trick; fraud —**swin′dler** *n.*

swine (swīn) *n., pl.* **swine** ⟦OE *swīn*⟧ **1** a pig or hog: usually used collectively **2** a vicious, contemptible person

swing (swiŋ) *vi.* **swung**, **swing′ing** ⟦OE *swingan*⟧ **1** to sway or move backward and forward **2** to walk, trot, etc. with relaxed movements **3** to strike (*at*) **4** to turn, as on a hinge **5** to move in a curve **6** to hang; be suspended **7** [Slang] to engage in casual sexual relations —*vt.* **1** to move, lift, etc. with a sweeping motion **2** to cause to move backward and forward **3** to cause to turn, as on a hinge **4** to cause to move in a curve [*swing* the car around] **5** [Inf.] to cause to come about successfully [to *swing* an election] —*n.* **1** a swinging **2** the arc through which something swings **3** the manner of swinging a golf club, etc. **4** a relaxed motion, as in walking **5** a sweeping blow **6** the course of some activity, etc. **7** rhythm, as of music **8** a seat hanging from ropes, etc. on which one can swing **9** a trip or tour **10** jazz (c. 1935-45) characterized by large bands and written arrangements —*adj.* having decisive power, as in determining an election [the *swing* vote]

swing·er *n.* [Slang] a sophisticated, uninhibited, pleasure-seeking person

swing shift [Inf.] the evening work shift in a factory, etc., commonly from 4:00 P.M. to midnight

swipe (swīp) *n.* [prob. var. of SWEEP] [Inf.] **1** a hard, sweeping blow **2** a sweeping motion —*vt.* **swiped**, **swip′ing 1** to hit with a swipe **2** to pass across or through with a sweeping motion **3** [Slang] to steal

swirl (swurl) *vi., vt.* ⟦ME (Scot) *swyrl*⟧ to move or cause to move with a whirling motion —*n.* **1** a whirl; eddy **2** a twist; curl —**swirl′y** *adj.*

swish (swish) *vi.* [echoic] **1** to move with a sharp, hissing sound: said as of a cane swung through the air **2** to move with a light, brushing sound: said as of skirts in walking —*vt.* **1** to cause to swish **2** to move (liquid), esp. in

the mouth, with a hissing or gurgling sound —*n.* a swishing sound or movement

Swiss (swis) *adj.* of Switzerland or its people, etc. —*n., pl.* **Swiss** a person born or living in Switzerland

Swiss chard CHARD

Swiss (cheese) a hard, pale-yellow cheese with many large holes

Swiss steak a thick cut of round steak pounded with flour and braised with vegetables

switch (swich) *n.* ⟦Early Modern Eng *swits*⟧ **1** a thin, flexible stick used for whipping **2** a separate tress of hair, used as part of a coiffure **3** a device used to open, close, or divert an electric circuit **4** a device used to transfer a train from one track to another **5** a shift; change —*vt.* **1** to whip as with a switch **2** to jerk sharply [the cow *switched* its tail] **3** to shift; change **4** to turn (an electric light, etc.) *on* or *off* **5** to transfer (a train, etc.) to another track **6** to change or exchange —*vi.* to shift —**switch′er** *n.*

switch·back *n.* **1** a road, railroad, etc. following a zigzag course up a steep grade **2** a segment or bend of such a road, railroad, etc.

switch·blade (knife) a large jackknife that snaps open when a release button is pressed

switch·board *n.* a panel for controlling a system of electric circuits, as in a telephone exchange

switch-hit·ter *n.* a baseball player who can bat right-handed and left-handed

Swit·zer·land (swit′sər lənd) country in WC Europe

swiv·el (swiv′əl) *n.* [< OE *swifan*, to revolve] a coupling device that allows free turning of the parts attached to it —*vi., vt.* **-eled** or **-elled**, **-el·ing** or **-el·ling** to turn or cause to turn on or as on a swivel or pivot

swiz·zle stick (swiz′əl) [< ?] a small rod for stirring mixed drinks

swol·len (swōl′ən) *vi., vt. alt. pp.* of SWELL —*adj.* blown up; distended; bulging

swoon (swōōn) *vi., n.* [< OE *geswogen*, unconscious] FAINT

swoop (swōōp) *vi.* [< OE *swapan*, sweep along] to pounce or sweep (*down* or *upon*), as a bird does in hunting —*n.* the act of swooping

swop (swäp) [Inf., Chiefly Brit.] *alt. sp.* of SWAP

sword (sôrd) *n.* ⟦OE *sweord*⟧ a hand weapon with a long, sharp-pointed blade set in a hilt —**at swords′ points** ready to quarrel or fight

sword·fish *n., pl.* **-fish′** a large marine food fish with an upper jawbone extending in a swordlike point

sword·play *n.* the act or skill of using a sword, as in fencing

swords·man (sôrdz′mən) *n., pl.* **-men** one skilled in using a sword

swore (swôr) *vi., vt. pt.* of SWEAR

sworn (swôrn) *vi., vt. pp.* of SWEAR —*adj.* bound, pledged, etc. by or as by an oath

swum (swum) *vi., vt. pp.* of SWIM¹ & SWIM²

swung (swuŋ) *vi.*, *vt. pp. & pt. of* SWING

syb·a·rite (sib′ə rīt′) *n.* [after *Sybaris*, ancient Gr city in Italy] anyone very fond of luxury and pleasure —**syb′a·rit′ic** (-rit′ik) *adj.*

syc·a·more (sik′ə môr′) *n.* [< Gr *sykomoros*, a fig tree mentioned in the Bible] 1 a maple tree of Europe and Asia 2 an American tree with bark that sheds in patches

syc·o·phant (sik′ə fənt) *n.* [< Gr *sykophantēs*, informer] one who seeks favor by flattering people of wealth or influence —**syc′o·phan·cy** *n.*

Syd·ney (sid′nē) seaport in SE Australia

syl·lab·i·cate (si lab′i kāt′) *vt.* -cat′ed, -cat′ing SYLLABIFY —**syl·lab′i·ca′tion** *n.*

syl·lab·i·fy (si lab′ə fī′) *vt.* -fied′, -fy′ing [ult. < L *syllaba*, syllable + *facere*, make] to form or divide into syllables —**syl·lab′i·fi·ca′tion** *n.*

syl·la·ble (sil′ə bəl) *n.* [< Gr *syn*-, together + *lambanein*, to hold] 1 a word or part of a word pronounced with a single, uninterrupted sounding of the voice 2 one or more letters used to represent a spoken syllable —**syl·lab′ic** (si lab′ik) *adj.*

syl·la·bus (sil′ə bəs) *n.*, *pl.* -bus·es or -bi′ (-bī′) [ult. < Gr *sittybos*, strip of leather] a summary or outline, esp. of a course of study

syl·lo·gism (sil′ə jiz′əm) *n.* [< Gr *syn*-, together + *logizesthai*, to reason] a form of reasoning in which two premises are made and a conclusion is drawn from them

sylph (silf) *n.* [Mod L *sylphus*, a spirit] 1 an imaginary being supposed to inhabit the air 2 a slender, graceful woman or girl —**sylph′like′** *adj.*

syl·van (sil′vən) *adj.* [< L *silva*, forest] 1 of, characteristic of, or living in the woods or forest 2 covered with trees; wooded

sym·bi·o·sis (sim′bī ō′sis, -bē-) *n.* [< Gr *symbioun*, to live together] the living together of two kinds of organisms to their mutual advantage —**sym′bi·ot′ic** (-ät′ik) *adj.*

sym·bol (sim′bəl) *n.* [< Gr *syn*-, together + *ballein*, to throw] 1 an object used to represent something abstract [the dove is a peace *symbol*] 2 a mark, letter, etc. standing for an object, quality, quantity, process, etc., as in music or chemistry —**sym·bol′ic** (-bäl′ik) *adj.* —**sym·bol′i·cal·ly** *adv.*

sym·bol·ism *n.* 1 representation by symbols 2 a system of symbols 3 symbolic meaning

sym·bol·ize *vt.* -ized′, -iz′ing 1 to be a symbol of; stand for 2 to represent by a symbol or symbols

sym·me·try (sim′ə trē) *n.*, *pl.* -tries [< Gr *syn*-, together + *metron*, a measure] 1 correspondence of opposite parts in size, shape, and position 2 balance or beauty of form resulting from this —**sym·met·ri·cal** (si me′tri kəl) *adj.* —**sym·met′ri·cal·ly** *adv.*

sym·pa·thet·ic (sim′pə thet′ik) *adj.* 1 of, feeling, or showing sympathy 2 in agreement with one's tastes, mood, etc. 3 *Physiology* designating the part of the autonomic nervous system involved esp. in communicating the involuntary response to alarm, as by speeding the heart rate —**sym′pa·thet′i·cal·ly** *adv.*

sym·pa·thize (-thīz′) *vi.* -thized′, -thiz′ing 1 to share the feelings or ideas of another 2 to feel or express sympathy —**sym′pa·thiz′er** *n.*

sym·pa·thy (-thē) *n.*, *pl.* -thies [< Gr *syn*-, together + *pathos*, feeling] 1 sameness of feeling 2 mutual liking or understanding 3 *a)* ability to share another's ideas, emotions, etc. *b)* pity or compassion for another's trouble or suffering

sym·pho·ny (sim′fə nē) *n.*, *pl.* -nies [< Gr *syn*-, together + *phōnē*, a sound] 1 harmony of sounds, color, etc. 2 an extended musical composition in several movements, for full orchestra 3 SYMPHONY ORCHESTRA —**sym·phon′ic** (-fän′ik) *adj.*

symphony orchestra a large orchestra for playing symphonic works

sym·po·si·um (sim pō′zē əm) *n.*, *pl.* -si·ums or -si·a (-ə) [< Gr *syn*-, together + *posis*, a drinking] 1 a conference to discuss a topic 2 a published group of opinions on a topic

symp·tom (simp′təm) *n.* [< Gr *syn*-, together + *piptein*, to fall] any circumstance or condition that indicates the existence of something, as a particular disease —**symp′to·mat′ic** (-tə mat′ik) *adj.*

syn *abbrev.* synonym

syn- [Gr] *prefix* with, together, at the same time

syn·a·gogue (sin′ə gäg′, -gôg′) *n.* [< Gr *syn*-, together + *agein*, do] 1 an assembly of Jews for worship and religious study 2 a building or place for such assembly —**syn′a·gog′al** *adj.*

syn·apse (sin′aps′) *n.* [< Gr *syn*-, together + *apsis*, a joining] the space between nerve cells where nerve impulses are transmitted

sync or **synch** (siŋk) *vi.*, *vt.* **synced** or **synched**, **sync′ing** or **synch′ing** *short for* SYNCHRONIZE —*n. short for* SYNCHRONIZATION —**in** (or **out of**) **sync** in (or out of) synchronization or harmony (*with*)

syn·chro·nize (siŋ′krə nīz′) *vi.* -nized′, -niz′ing [< Gr *syn*-, together + *chronos*, time] to move or occur at the same time or rate —*vt.* to cause to agree in time or rate of speed —**syn′chro·ni·za′tion** *n.*

syn·chro·nous *adj.* happening at the same time or at the same rate

syn·co·pate (siŋ′kə pāt′) *vt.* -pat′ed, -pat′ing [< Gr *syn*-, together + *koptein*, to cut] *Music* to shift (the accent), as by beginning a tone on an unaccented beat and continuing it through the next accented beat —**syn′co·pa′tion** *n.*

syn·di·cate (sin′də kit; *for v.*, -kāt′) *n.* [< Gr *syn*-, together + *dikē*, justice] 1 an association of individuals or corporations formed to carry out a project requiring much capital 2 any group, as of criminals, organized for some undertaking 3 an organization selling articles or features to many newspapers, etc. —*vt.* -cat′ed, -cat′ing 1 to manage as or form into a syndicate **2** *a)* to sell (an article, etc.) through a syndicate *b)* to sell (a program, etc.) to a number of radio or TV stations —*vi.* to form a syndicate —**syn'di·ca'tion** *n.*

syn·drome (sin'drōm') *n.* ⟦< Gr *syn-*, with + *dramein*, to run⟧ a set of symptoms characterizing a disease or condition

syn·er·gism (sin'ər jiz'əm) *n.* ⟦< Gr *syn-*, together + *ergon*, work⟧ an interaction of several things that results in a greater effect than the sum of the things' individual effects: said esp. of drugs —**syn'er·gis'tic** *adj.* —**syn'er·gy** *n.*

syn·fu·el (sin'fyōō'əl) *n.* ⟦SYN(THETIC) + FUEL⟧ a fuel, as oil or gas made from coal, used as a substitute for petroleum or natural gas

syn·od (sin'əd) *n.* ⟦< Gr *syn-*, together + *hodos*, way⟧ **1** an ecclesiastical council **2** a high governing body in certain Christian churches

syn·o·nym (sin'ə nim) *n.* ⟦< Gr *syn-*, together + *onyma*, a name⟧ a word having the same or nearly the same meaning as another in the same language —**syn·on·y·mous** (si nän'ə məs) *adj.*

syn·op·sis (si näp'sis) *n., pl.* **-ses'** (-sēz') ⟦< Gr *syn-*, together + *opsis*, a seeing⟧ a brief, general review or condensation; summary

syn·tax (sin'taks') *n.* ⟦< Gr *syn-*, together + *tassein*, arrange⟧ the arrangement of and relationships among words, phrases, and clauses forming sentences —**syn·tac'tic** (-tak'tik) *adj.,* **syn·tac'ti·cal**

syn·the·sis (sin'thə sis) *n., pl.* **-ses'** (-sēz') ⟦< Gr *syn-*, together + *tithenai*, to place⟧ the combining of parts or elements so as to form a whole, a compound, etc. —**syn'the·size'** (-sīz') *vt.* **-sized'**, **-siz'ing**

syn·the·siz·er *n.* an electronic device producing sounds unobtainable from ordinary musical instruments or imitating instruments and voices

syn·thet·ic (-thet'ik) *adj.* **1** of or involving synthesis **2** produced by chemical synthesis, rather than of natural origin **3** not real; artificial —*n.* something synthetic —**syn·thet'i·cal·ly** *adv.*

syph·i·lis (sif'ə lis) *n.* ⟦after *Syphilus*, hero of a L poem (1530)⟧ a sexually transmitted disease caused by a spirochete —**syph'i·lit'ic** *adj., n.*

Syr·i·a (sir'ē ə) country in SW Asia, at the E end of the Mediterranean —**Syr'i·an** *adj., n.*

sy·ringe (sə rinj', sir'inj) *n.* ⟦< Gr *syrinx*, a pipe⟧ **1** a device consisting of a tube with a rubber bulb or piston at one end, for drawing in a liquid and then ejecting it in a stream: used to inject fluids into body cavities, etc. **2** HYPODERMIC SYRINGE —*vt.* **-ringed'**, **-ring'ing** to cleanse, inject, etc. by using a syringe

syr·up (sur'əp, sir'-) *n.* ⟦< OFr *sirop* < ML *sirupus* < Ar *sharāb*, a drink⟧ any thick, sweet liquid; specif., a solution of sugar and water boiled together

syr·up·y *adj.* **1** like syrup **2** overly sentimental

sys·tem (sis'təm) *n.* ⟦< Gr *syn-*, together + *histanai*, to set⟧ **1** a set or arrangement of things related so as to form a whole [a solar *system*, a school *system*] **2** a set of facts, rules, etc. arranged to show a logical plan linking them **3** a method or plan **4** an established, orderly way of doing something **5** the body, or a number of bodily organs, functioning as a unit

sys·tem·at·ic (-tə mat'ik) *adj.* **1** constituting or based on a system **2** according to a system; orderly —**sys'tem·at'i·cal·ly** *adv.*

sys·tem·a·tize (-tə mə tīz') *vt.* **-tized'**, **-tiz'ing** to arrange according to a system; make systematic —**sys'tem·a·ti·za'tion** *n.*

sys·tem·ic (sis tem'ik) *adj.* of or affecting the body as a whole

sys·to·le (sis'tə lē') *n.* ⟦< Gr *syn-*, together + *stellein*, to set up⟧ the usual rhythmic contraction of the heart —**sys·tol'ic** (-täl'ik) *adj.*

T

t¹ or **T** (tē) *n., pl.* **t's**, **T's** the 20th letter of the English alphabet —**to a T** to perfection; exactly

t² *abbrev.* **1** teaspoon(s) **2** temperature **3** tense **4** ton(s) **5** transitive

T *abbrev.* **1** tablespoon(s) **2** temperature **3** Thursday **4** Tuesday

't- *prefix* it: used chiefly in poetry [*'twas*]

TA (tē'ā') *n., pl.* **TA's** [Inf.] TEACHING ASSISTANT

tab¹ (tab) *n.* ⟦< ?⟧ **1** a small, flat loop or strap fastened to something **2** a projecting piece as of a file folder, used in filing

tab² (tab) *n.* ⟦prob. < TABULATION⟧ [Inf.] **1** a bill, as for expenses **2** total cost —**keep tabs (or a tab) on** [Inf.] to check up on regularly

Ta·bas·co (tə bas'kō) *trademark for* a very hot sauce made from a tropical American hot red pepper

tab·bou·leh (tə bōō'lē, -le) *n.* [Ar] a salad of coarsely ground wheat with chopped parsley, tomatoes, scallions, etc.

tab·by (tab'ē) *n., pl.* **-bies** [ult. < Ar] **1** a light-colored cat with darker stripes **2** a domestic cat, esp. a female

tab·er·nac·le (tab'ər nak'əl) *n.* ⟦< L *taberna*,

hut] **1** a large place of worship **2** [T—] the portable sanctuary carried by the Jews during the Exodus

tab·la (täb′lä) *n.* [< Ar *ṭabla*, a drum] a set of two small drums whose pitch can be varied, used esp. in India and played with the hands

ta·ble (tā′bəl) *n.* [< L *tabula*, a board] **1** [Obs.] a thin slab of metal, stone, etc. **2** *a)* a piece of furniture having a flat top set on legs *b)* such a table set with food *c)* food served *d)* the people seated at a table **3** *a)* a systematic list of details, contents, etc. *b)* an orderly arrangement of facts, figures, etc. **4** any flat, horizontal surface, piece, etc. —*vt.* **-bled, -bling** to postpone indefinitely the consideration of (a legislative bill, etc.) —**at table** at a meal —**on the table 1** postponed **2** subject to discussion or negotiation —**turn the tables** to reverse a situation

tab·leau (tab′lō′, ta blō′) *n., pl.* **-leaux′** (-lōz′) or **-leaus** [Fr < OFr, dim. of *table*] a striking, dramatic scene or picture

ta·ble·cloth *n.* a cloth for covering a table, esp. at meals

ta·ble d'hôte (tä′bəl dōt′) [Fr, table of the host] a complete meal served at a restaurant for a set price

ta·ble-hop *vi.* **-hopped′, -hop′ping** to leave one's table, as at a restaurant, and visit at other tables

ta·ble·land *n.* a plateau

ta·ble·spoon *n.* **1** a large spoon for serving or for eating soup **2** a measuring spoon holding ½ fluid ounce —**ta′ble·spoon′ful** *n., pl.* **-fuls**

tab·let (tab′lit) *n.* [see TABLE] **1** a thin, flat piece of stone, metal, etc. with an inscription **2** a writing pad of paper sheets glued together at one edge **3** a small, flat piece of compressed material, as of medicine **4** a lightweight computer with a touchscreen

table tennis a game somewhat like tennis, played on a table with a small, hollow celluloid ball

ta·ble·ware (-wer′) *n.* dishes, glassware, silverware, etc. for use at a meal

tab·loid (tab′loid′) *n.* [TABL(ET)+-OID] a newspaper, usually half size, with many pictures and short, often sensational, news stories

ta·boo (tə bōō′, ta-) *n.* [< a Polynesian language] **1** among some Polynesian peoples, a sacred prohibition making certain people or things untouchable, etc. **2** any conventional social restriction —*adj.* prohibited by taboo —*vt.* **-booed′, -boo′ing 1** to put under taboo **2** to prohibit or forbid Also **ta·bu′**

ta·bou·li (tə bōō′lē) *n. var. of* TABBOULEH

tab·u·lar (tab′yə lər) *adj.* [see TABLE] **1** flat **2** of, arranged in, or computed from a table or list

tab·u·late (-lāt′) *vt.* **-lat′ed, -lat′ing** to put (facts, statistics, etc.) in a table —**tab′u·la′tion** *n.* —**tab′u·la′tor** *n.*

ta·chom·e·ter (ta käm′ət ər) *n.* [< Gr *tachos*, speed + -METER] a device that measures the rate of rotation of a revolving shaft, as of an engine

tach·y·car·di·a (tak′i kär′dē ə) *n.* [< Gr *tachys*, swift + *kardia*, heart] an abnormally fast heartbeat

tac·it (tas′it) *adj.* [< L *tacere*, be silent] **1** unspoken **2** not expressed openly, but implied or understood —**tac′it·ly** *adv.* —**tac′it·ness** *n.*

tac·i·turn (tas′ə turn′) *adj.* [see prec.] almost always silent; not liking to talk —**tac′i·tur′ni·ty** *n.*

tack (tak) *n.* [< MDu *tacke*, twig, point] **1** a short nail or pin with a sharp point and a large, flat head **2** a temporary stitch **3** a course of action **4** *a)* the direction a ship goes in relation to the position of the sails *b)* a change of a ship's direction —*vt.* **1** to fasten with tacks **2** to attach or add **3** to change the course of (a ship) —*vi.* to change course suddenly

tack·le (tak′əl) *n.* [< MDu *takel*] **1** equipment; gear **2** a system of ropes and pulleys for moving weights **3** a tackling, as in football **4** *Football* a lineman next to the end —*vt.* **tack′led, tack′ling 1** to take hold of; seize **2** to try to do; undertake **3** *Football* to throw (the ball carrier) to the ground —**tack′ler** *n.*

tack·y (tak′ē) *adj.* **-i·er, -i·est 1** sticky: said as of drying varnish **2** dowdy or shabby **3** in poor taste —**tack′i·ness** *n.*

ta·co (tä′kō) *n., pl.* **-cos** [Sp, light lunch] a fried or soft tortilla folded around chopped meat, shredded lettuce, grated cheese, etc.

tact (takt) *n.* [< L *tangere*, to touch] delicate perception of the right thing to say or do without offending —**tact′ful** *adj.* —**tact′ful·ly** *adv.* —**tact′less** *adj.*

tac·tics (tak′tiks) *pl.n.* [< Gr *tassein*, arrange] **1** [*with sing. v.*] the science of maneuvering military and naval forces **2** any skillful methods to gain an end —**tac′ti·cal** *adj.* —**tac·ti′cian** (-tish′ən) *n.*

tac·tile (tak′təl) *adj.* [< L *tangere*, to touch] of, having, or perceived by the sense of touch

tad (tad) *n.* [prob. < fol.] a small amount or degree: often used adverbially [a *tad* tired after the hike]

tad·pole (tad′pōl′) *n.* [ME *tadde*, toad + *poll*, head] the larva of a frog or toad, having gills and a tail and living in water

taf·fe·ta (taf′i tə) *n.* [< Pers *tāftan*, to weave] a fine, stiff fabric of silk, nylon, etc., with a sheen

taff·rail (taf′rāl′) *n.* [< Du] the rail around the stern of a ship

taf·fy (taf′ē) *n.* [< ?] a chewy candy made of sugar or molasses

Taft (taft), **William How·ard** (hou′ərd) 1857-1930; 27th president of the U.S. (1909-13): chief justice of the U.S. (1921-30)

tag (tag) *n.* [prob. < Scand] **1** a hanging end or part **2** a hard-tipped end on a cord or lace **3** a card, etc. attached as a label **4** an epithet **5** ending for a story, etc. **6** TAG LINE **7** a children's game in which one player chases the others with the object of touching one of them **8** *Comput.* a sequence of characters providing extra information about a document —*vt.* **tagged, tag′ging 1** to provide with a tag; label **2** to choose or select **3** to touch in playing tag **4** [Inf.] to strike or hit hard —*vi.* [Inf.] to follow closely: with *along, after*, etc. —**tag′ger** *n.*

Ta·ga·log (tä gä′lôg) *n.* **1** *pl.* **-logs′** or **-log′** a member of the ethnic group native to the Manila region in the Philippines **2** the language of this group, an official language of the Republic of the Philippines

tag line the last line or lines of a speech, etc.

tag-team *adj.* ⟦orig. a wrestling term⟧ [Inf.] of any activity in which participants work together by taking turns

Ta·hi·ti (tə hēt′ē) French island in the S Pacific —**Ta·hi′ti·an** (-hēsh′ən) *adj., n.*

Tai (tī) *n.* **1** a group of languages spoken esp. in SE Asia **2** a member of a group of peoples of SE Asia that speak these languages —*adj.* of these languages or peoples

tai chi (tī′ jē′, tī chē′) ⟦Mandarin⟧ a Chinese exercise system consisting of a series of slow, relaxed movements: in full **t′ai chi ch′uan** (chwän)

tai·ga (tī′gə) *n.* ⟦Russ⟧ a type of plant community in the far north, having mostly coniferous trees

tail (tāl) *n.* ⟦OE *tægel*⟧ **1** the rear end of an animal's body, esp. when a distinct appendage **2** anything like an animal's tail in form or position **3** the hind, bottom, last, or inferior part of anything **4** [*often pl.*] the reverse side of a coin **5** [*pl.*] full-dress attire for men **6** [Inf.] one that follows another, esp. in surveillance —*adj.* **1** at the rear or end **2** from the rear [a *tail* wind] —*vt.* [Slang] to follow stealthily —*vi.* [Inf.] to follow close behind —**turn tail** to run from danger or difficulty

tail·back *n.* *Football* the offensive back farthest from the line

tail·bone *n.* COCCYX

tail end 1 the rear of anything **2** the concluding part

tail fin a fin that forms the tail of a fish, etc. **2** a finlike projection at the rear of a rocket, car, etc.

tail·gate *n.* the hinged or removable gate at the back of a wagon, truck, etc. —*vi.* **-gat′ed, -gat′ing 1** to drive too closely behind another vehicle **2** to party or picnic beside a parked vehicle —*vt.* to drive too closely behind (another vehicle) —**tail′gat′er** *n.*

tail·ings *pl.n.* waste or refuse left after milling, mining, etc.

tail·light *n.* a light, usually red, at the rear of a vehicle to warn vehicles coming from behind

tai·lor (tā′lər) *n.* ⟦< VL *taliare*, to cut⟧ one who makes, repairs, or alters clothes —*vt.* **1** to make by tailor's work **2** to form, alter, etc. for a certain purpose

tail·pipe *n.* the exhaust pipe coming from the muffler of a motor vehicle

tail·spin *n.* SPIN (*n.* 3)

taint (tānt) *vt.* ⟦< ?⟧ **1** to affect with something injurious, unpleasant, etc.; infect, spoil, etc. **2** to make morally corrupt —*n.* a trace of contamination, corruption, etc.

Tai·pei (tī′pā′) capital of Taiwan

Tai·wan (tī′wän′) island province of China, off the SE coast: together with nearby islands it forms the *Republic of China*

Ta·jik·i·stan (tä jik′i stan′) country in WC Asia

take (tāk) *vt.* **took, tak′en, tak′ing** ⟦< ON *taka*⟧ **1** to get possession of; capture, seize, etc. **2** to get hold of **3** to capture the fancy of; charm **4** to obtain, acquire, assume, etc. **5** to use, consume, etc. **6** to buy, rent, subscribe to, etc. **7** to join with (one side in a disagreement, etc.) **8** to choose; select **9** to travel by [to *take* a bus] **10** to deal with; consider **11** to occupy [*take* a chair] **12** to require; demand [it *takes* money] **13** to derive (a name, quality, etc.) from **14** to study **15** to write down [*take* notes] **16** to make by photographing **17** to win (a prize, etc.) **18** to undergo [*take* punishment] **19** to occupy oneself in; enjoy [*take* a nap] **20** to accept (an offer, bet, etc.) **21** to react to [*take* a joke in earnest] **22** to understand **23** to suppose; presume **24** to feel [*take* pity] **25** to lead, escort, etc. **26** to carry **27** to remove, as by stealing **28** to subtract **29** [Slang] to cheat; trick **30** *Gram.* to be used with [the verb "hit" *takes* an object] —*vi.* **1** to take root: said of a plant **2** to catch [the fire *took*] **3** to gain favor, success, etc. **4** to be effective [the vaccination *took*] **5** [Inf. or Dial.] to become (sick) —*n.* **1** a taking **2** *a)* the amount taken *b)* [Slang] receipts or profit —**on the take** [Slang] taking bribes, etc. —**take after** to be, act, or look like —**take back** to retract (something said, etc.) —**take down** to put in writing; record —**take for 1** to regard as **2** to mistake for —**take in 1** to admit; receive **2** to make smaller **3** to understand **4** to cheat; trick —**take off 1** to leave the ground, etc. in flight **2** [Inf.] to start **3** [Inf.] to imitate in a burlesque manner: with *on* —**take on 1** to acquire; assume **2** to employ **3** to undertake (a task, etc.) —**take over** to assume control or possession (of) —**take to 1** to become fond of **2** to go to or withdraw to [to *take* to the hills] —**take up 1** to make tighter or shorter **2** to become interested in (an occupation, study, etc.) —**tak′er** *n.*

take·off *n.* **1** the act or place of leaving the ground, as in jumping or flight **2** [Inf.] a mocking imitation; caricature

take·out *n.* prepared food bought to be taken away —*adj.* designating of or such food

take·o·ver *n.* **1** the usurpation of power in a nation, organization, etc. **2** the assumption of management in acquiring a corporation

tak·ing (tāk′iŋ) *adj.* attractive; winning —*n.* **1** the act of one that takes **2** [*pl.*] earnings; profits

talc (talk) *n.* ⟦< Ar *ṭalq*⟧ **1** a soft mineral used to make talcum powder, etc. **2** *short for* TALCUM (POWDER)

tal·cum (powder) (tal′kəm) a powder for the body made of purified talc

tale (tāl) *n.* 〖OE *talu*〗 1 a story; narrative 2 idle or malicious gossip 3 a fiction; lie

tale-bear-er (-ber′ər) *n.* a gossip

tal-ent (tal′ənt) *n.* 〖< Gr *talanton*, a weight〗 1 an ancient unit of weight or money 2 any natural ability or power 3 a superior ability in an art, etc. 4 people, or a person, with talent —**tal′ent-ed** *adj.*

tal-is-man (tal′is mən, -iz-) *n.*, *pl.* **-mans** 〖< 5th-c. medieval Gr *telesma*, religious rite〗 1 a ring, stone, etc. bearing engraved figures thought to bring good luck, avert evil, etc. 2 a charm

talk (tôk) *vi.* 〖prob. < OE *talian*, reckon〗 1 to put ideas into words; speak 2 to express ideas by speech substitutes [*talk* by signs] 3 to chatter; gossip 4 to confer; consult 5 to confess or inform on someone —*vt.* 1 to use in speaking [to *talk* French] 2 to discuss 3 to put into a specified condition, etc. by talking —*n.* 1 the act of talking 2 conversation 3 a speech 4 a conference 5 gossip 6 the subject of conversation, gossip, etc. 7 speech; dialect —**talk back** to answer impertinently —**talk down to** to talk patronizingly to, as by simple speech —**talk over** to discuss —**talk up** to promote in discussion —**talk′er** *n.*

talk-a-tive (-ə tiv) *adj.* talking a great deal; loquacious

talk-ing-to (tôk′iŋ tōō′) *n.* [Inf.] a scolding

talk show *Radio, TV* a program in which a host talks with guest celebrities, experts, members of the audience, etc.

talk therapy PSYCHOTHERAPY

talk-y *adj.* **-i-er, -i-est** 1 talkative 2 containing too much talk, or dialogue

tall (tôl) *adj.* 〖< OE *(ge)tæl*, swift〗 1 higher in stature than the average 2 having a specified height 3 [Inf.] exaggerated [a *tall* tale] 4 [Inf.] large [a *tall* drink] —*adv.* in an upright, dignified manner [to stand *tall*] —**tall′ness** *n.*

Tal-la-has-see (tal′ə has′ē) capital of Florida

tal-low (tal′ō) *n.* 〖prob. < LowG *talg*〗 the solid fat of cattle, sheep, etc., used in candles, soaps, etc.

tal-ly (tal′ē) *n.*, *pl.* **-lies** 〖< L *talea*, a stick (notched to keep accounts)〗 1 anything used as a record for an account or score 2 an account, score, etc. 3 a tag or label —*vt.* **-lied, -ly-ing** 1 to put on or as on a tally 2 to add (*up*) —*vi.* 1 to score a point 2 to agree; correspond

Tal-mud (täl′mood, tal′məd) *n.* 〖Heb, learning〗 the body of early Jewish civil and religious law

tal-on (tal′ən) *n.* 〖< L *talus*, an ankle〗 the claw of a bird of prey

tam (tam) *n.* short for TAM-O′-SHANTER

ta-ma-le (tə mäl′lē) *n.* 〖< MexSp〗 a serving usually of minced meat wrapped in a dough of corn meal and steamed or boiled

tam-a-rack (tam′ə rak′) *n.* 〖< AmInd〗 1 an American larch tree usually found in swamps 2 its wood

tam-a-rind (tam′ə rind′) *n.* 〖< Ar *tamr hindī*, date of India〗 1 a tropical tree with yellow flowers and brown pods 2 its sharp-tasting, edible fruit

tam-bou-rine (tam′bə rēn′) *n.* 〖prob. < Ar *ṭanbūr*, stringed instrument〗 a shallow, single-headed hand drum with jingling metal disks in the rim: played by shaking, hitting, etc.

tame (tām) *adj.* **tam′er, tam′est** 〖OE *tam*〗 1 changed from a wild state and trained for human use 2 gentle; docile 3 without spirit or force; dull —*vt.* **tamed, tam′ing** 1 to make tame 2 to make gentle; subdue —**tam′a-ble** *adj.*, **tame′a-ble** —**tame′ly** *adv.* —**tame′ness** *n.* —**tam′er** *n.*

Tam-il (tam′əl) *n.* the language of the Tamils, a people of S India and N Sri Lanka

tam-o′-shan-ter (tam′ə shan′tər) *n.* 〖< title character of Robert Burns′s poem〗 a Scottish cap with a round, flat top, often having a pompom

tamp (tamp) *vt.* 〖< ? Fr *tampon*, a plug〗 to pack firmly or pound (*down*) by a series of blows or taps

tam-per (tam′pər) *vi.* 〖< TEMPER〗 1 to make secret, illegal arrangements (*with*) 2 to interfere (*with*) or meddle (*with*)

tam-pon (tam′pän′) *n.* 〖Fr〗 a plug of cotton, etc. put into a body cavity, etc., as to absorb blood during menstruation

tan (tan) *n.* 〖< ML *tanum*, a bark used to tan hides〗 1 a yellowish-brown color 2 a darkening of the skin as by exposure to the sun, etc. —*adj.* **tan′ner, tan′nest** yellowish-brown —*vt.* **tanned, tan′ning** 1 to change (hide) into leather by soaking in tannin 2 to produce a suntan in 3 [Inf.] to whip severely —*vi.* to become tanned

tan-a-ger (tan′ə jər) *n.* 〖< AmInd (Brazil) *tangara*〗 any of various small American songbirds: the males usually are brightly colored

tan-bark (tan′bärk′) *n.* any bark containing tannin, used to tan hides, etc.

tan-dem (tan′dəm) *adv.* 〖< punning use of L *tandem*, at length〗 one behind another; in single file —*n.* 1 teamwork between two persons, etc. [to work in *tandem*]

tang (taŋ) *n.* 〖< ON *tangi*, a sting〗 1 a prong on a file, etc., that fits into the handle 2 a strong, penetrating taste or odor —**tang′y** *adj.* **-i-er, -i-est**

tan-ge-lo (tan′jə lō′) *n.*, *pl.* **-los′** 〖TANG(ERINE) + (*pom*)*elo*, grapefruit〗 a fruit produced by crossing a tangerine with a grapefruit

tan-gent (tan′jənt) *adj.* 〖< L *tangere*, to touch〗 1 touching 2 *Geom.* touching a curved surface at one point but not intersecting it —*n.* a tangent line, curve, or surface —**go off at (or on) a tangent** to digress suddenly to another topic, etc. —**tan-gen′tial** (-jen′shəl) *adj.*

tan-ge-rine (tan′jə rēn′) *n.* 〖after *Tangier*, city in N Africa〗 a small, loose-skinned, reddish-yellow orange with easily separated segments

tan-gi-ble (tan′jə bəl) *adj.* 〖< L *tangere*, to touch〗 1 that can be touched or felt 2 definite; objective —*n.* [*pl.*] assets having real substance and able to be appraised for value —**tan′gi·bil′i·ty** *n.*

tan·gle (taŋ′gəl) *vt.* **-gled, -gling** [< ? Swed] 1 to catch as in a snare; trap 2 to make a snarl of; intertwine —*vi.* 1 to become tangled 2 [Inf.] to argue —*n.* 1 an intertwined, confused mass 2 a confused condition

tan·go (taŋ′gō) *n.*, *pl.* **-gos** [AmSp] 1 a South American dance for couples with long gliding steps and dips 2 music for this dance in 2/4 or 4/4 time —*vi.* to dance the tango

tank (taŋk) *n.* [in sense 1 < Sans] 1 any large container for liquid or gas 2 an armored combat vehicle with tractor treads —*vi.* [Slang] to fail

tank·ard (taŋ′kərd) *n.* [< OFr *tanquart*] a large drinking cup with a handle

tank·er (taŋ′kər) *n.* 1 a ship equipped to transport oil or other liquids 2 a plane designed to carry liquids, as for refueling another plane in flight 3 a truck, etc. equipped to transport liquids or dry commodities in bulk

tank top [orig. worn in swimming pools] a sleeveless casual shirt with shoulder straps

tank truck a motor truck built to transport gasoline, oil, etc.

tan·ner (tan′ər) *n.* a person whose work is making leather by tanning hides

tan·ner·y *n.*, *pl.* **-ner·ies** a place where leather is made by tanning hides

tan·nic acid (tan′ik) a yellowish, astringent substance used in tanning hides, dyeing, etc.

tan·nin (-in) *n.* [< *tan*, TAN + -*in*, -INE³] any of a group of compounds, as tannic acid, that are found in plants and convert hide into leather

tan·sy (tan′zē) *n.*, *pl.* **-sies** [< LL *tanacetum*] a plant with a strong smell and small, yellow flowers

tan·ta·lize (tan′tə liz′) *vt.* **-lized′, -liz′ing** [after *Tantalus*, in Gr myth, a king doomed in Hades to stand in water that always recedes when he wishes to drink and whose fruit he cannot reach] to promise or show something desirable and then withhold it; tease

tan·ta·lum (tan′tə ləm) *n.* [after *Tantalus*, in Gr myth] a hard, ductile, corrosion-resistant, metallic chemical element used in making nuclear reactors, electronic components, etc.: symbol, Ta; at. no. 73

tan·ta·mount (tant′ə mount′) *adj.* [< OFr *tant*, so much + *amont*, upward] equal (*to*) in value, effect, etc.

tan·tra (tun′trə, tän′-) *n.* [Sans] [*often* T-] a form of yoga teaching attainment of ecstasy —**tan′tric** *adj.*

tan·trum (tan′trəm) *n.* [< ?] a violent, willful outburst of rage, etc.

Tan·za·ni·a (tan′zə nē′ə) country in E Africa —**Tan′za·ni′an** *adj.*, *n.*

Tao·ism (dou′iz′əm-, tou′-) *n.* [Chin *tao*, the way] a Chinese religion and philosophy advocating simplicity, selflessness, etc. —**Tao′ist** *n.*, *adj.*

tap¹ (tap) *vt.*, *vi.* **tapped, tap′ping** [echoic] 1 to strike lightly 2 to make or do by tapping

[to *tap* a message] 3 to choose, as for membership in a club —*n.* a light, rapid blow

tap² (tap) *n.* [OE *tæppa*] 1 a faucet or spigot 2 a plug, cork, etc. for stopping a hole in a cask, etc. 3 a tool used to cut threads inside a nut, pipe, etc. 4 the act or an instance of wiretapping 5 *Elec.* a place in a circuit where a connection can be made —*vt.* **tapped, tap′ping** 1 to put a tap or spigot on 2 to make a hole in, or pull the plug from, for drawing off liquid 3 to draw off (liquid) 4 to make use of [to *tap* new resources] 5 to make a connection with (a pipe, circuit, etc.); specif., to wiretap —**on tap** 1 ready to be drawn from a cask: said as of beer 2 [Inf.] planned, available, or expected

tap dance a dance done with sharp, loud taps of the foot, toe, or heel at each step —**tap′-dance′** *vi.* **-danced′, -danc′ing** —**tap′-danc′er** *n.*

tape (tāp) *n.* [OE *tæppe*, a fillet] 1 a strong, narrow strip of cloth, paper, etc. used for binding, tying, etc. 2 *short for* MAGNETIC TAPE 3 *short for* TAPE MEASURE 4 paper, plastic, etc. in a long strip with adhesive on one side —*vt.* **taped, tap′ing** 1 to bind, tie, etc. with tape 2 to record on magnetic tape

tape deck a component of an audio system, that records and plays back magnetic tapes

tape measure a tape with marks in inches, feet, etc. for measuring

ta·per (tā′pər) *n.* [OE *tapur*] 1 a slender candle 2 a gradual decrease in width or thickness —*vt.*, *vi.* 1 to decrease gradually in width or thickness 2 to lessen; diminish Often with *off*

tape recorder a device for recording on magnetic tape and for playing back what has been recorded

tap·es·try (tap′əs trē) *n.*, *pl.* **-tries** [< Gr *tapes*, a carpet] a heavy woven cloth with decorative designs and pictures, used as a wall hanging, etc.

tape·worm *n.* a long, tapelike flatworm that lives as a parasite in the intestines

tap·i·o·ca (tap′ē ō′kə) *n.* [< AmInd (Brazil)] a starchy substance from cassava roots, used for puddings, etc.

ta·pir (tā′pər) *n.* [< AmInd (Brazil)] a large, hoglike mammal of tropical America and the Malay Peninsula

tapped out [Slang] 1 having no money; broke 2 exhausted or depleted

tap·room *n.* BARROOM

tap·root *n.* [TAP² + ROOT¹] a main root, growing downward, from which small branch roots spread out

taps (taps) *n.* [< TAP¹, because orig. a drum signal] [*with sing. or pl. v.*] a bugle call to put out lights in retiring for the night

tar¹ (tär) *n.* [OE *teru*] a thick, sticky, black liquid formed when coal, wood, etc. is broken down by heat in the absence of air —*vt.* **tarred, tar′ring** to cover or smear with tar —**tar′ry** *adj.* **-ri·er, -ri·est**

tar² (tär) *n.* [< TAR(PAULIN)] [Old Inf.] a sailor

ta·ran·tu·la (tə ran′choo lə) *n.* ⟦after *Taranto*, city in S Italy⟧ any of several large, hairy, somewhat poisonous spiders of S Europe and tropical America

tar·dy (tär′dē) *adj.* **-di·er, -di·est** ⟦< L *tardus*, slow⟧ **1** slow in moving, acting, etc. **2** late, delayed, etc. **—tar′di·ly** *adv.* **—tar′di·ness** *n.*

tare[1] (ter) *n.* ⟦ME⟧ **1** any of various vetches **2** *Bible* an undesirable weed

tare[2] (ter) *n.* ⟦< Ar *ṭaraḥa*, to reject⟧ the weight of a container, etc. deducted from the total weight to determine the net weight of the contents or load

tar·get (tär′git) *n.* ⟦< medieval Fr *targe*, a shield⟧ **1** a board, etc. marked as with concentric circles, aimed at in archery, rifle practice, etc. **2** any object that is shot at **3** an objective; goal **4** an object of attack, criticism, etc. **—vt.** to establish as a target, goal, etc.

tar·iff (tar′if) *n.* ⟦< Ar *ta‘rīf*, information⟧ **1** a list or system of taxes upon exports or, esp., imports **2** such a tax, or its rate **3** a list or scale of prices, charges, etc.

tar·mac (tär′mak′) *n.* ⟦ult. < TAR[1] + MAC(ADAM)⟧ [Chiefly Brit.] an airport runway or apron

tar·nish (tär′nish) *vt.* ⟦< Fr *ternir*, make dim⟧ **1** to dull the luster of **2** to sully or mar **—vi.** **1** to lose luster **2** to become sullied **—n.** **1** dullness **2** a stain **—tar′nish·a·ble** *adj.*

ta·ro (ter′ō, tär′ō) *n., pl.* **-ros** ⟦< a Polynesian language⟧ a tropical Asiatic plant with a starchy, edible root

tar·ot (tar′ō, -ət; ta rō′) *n.* ⟦Fr < Ar *ṭaraḥa*, to reject⟧ [*often* T-] any of a set of 22 cards with pictures, used in fortunetelling

tarp (tärp) *n. short for* TARPAULIN

tar·pau·lin (tär pô′lin, tär′pə-) *n.* ⟦< TAR[1] + PALL[2], a covering⟧ **1** canvas coated with a waterproofing compound **2** a sheet of this or some other waterproof material

tar·pon (tär′pən) *n.* ⟦<?⟧ a large, silvery game fish of the W Atlantic

tar·ra·gon (tar′ə gän′) *n.* ⟦< Sp < Ar < Gr *drakōn*, a dragon⟧ an Old World plant with fragrant leaves used for seasoning

tar·ry (tar′ē) *vi.* **-ried, -ry·ing** ⟦< OE *tergan*, to vex & prob. OFr *targer*, to delay⟧ **1** to delay; linger **2** to stay for a time **3** to wait

tart[1] (tärt) *adj.* ⟦OE *teart*⟧ **1** sharp in taste; sour; acid **2** sharp in meaning; cutting [a *tart* answer] **—tart′ly** *adv.* **—tart′ness** *n.*

tart[2] (tärt) *n.* ⟦< OFr *tarte*⟧ a small pastry shell filled with jam, jelly, etc.

tart[3] (tärt) *n.* ⟦< prec.⟧ [Old Inf.] a prostitute

tar·tan (tärt′'n) *n.* ⟦prob. < medieval Fr *tiretaine*, a cloth of mixed fibers⟧ a woolen cloth in any of various woven plaid patterns, worn as part of traditional Scottish attire

tar·tar (tärt′ər) *n.* ⟦< medieval Gr *tartaron*⟧ **1** cream of tartar, esp. the crude form present in grape juice and forming a crustlike deposit in wine casks **2** a hard deposit on the teeth

Tar·tar (tärt′ər) *n.* TATAR

tar·tar sauce (tärt′ər) ⟦Fr⟧ a seafood sauce consisting of mayonnaise with chopped pickles, olives, capers, etc.: also sp. **tar′tare sauce**

Tas·er (tā′zər) *trademark for* a weapon for delivering an incapacitating electric shock **—vt.** to stun with a Taser: also [Slang] **tase** (tāz)

task (task) *n.* ⟦ult. < L *taxare*, to rate⟧ **1** a piece of work to be done **2** any difficult undertaking **—vt.** to burden; strain **—take to task** to scold

task·mas·ter *n.* one who assigns tasks to others, esp. when severe

Tas·ma·ni·a (taz mā′nē ə) island of Australia, off its SE coast **—Tas·ma′ni·an** *adj., n.*

tas·sel (tas′əl) *n.* ⟦OFr, knob⟧ **1** an ornamental tuft of threads, etc. hanging loosely from a knob **2** something resembling this, as a tuft of corn silk

taste (tāst) *vt.* **tast′ed, tast′ing** ⟦< OFr *taster*⟧ **1** to test the flavor of by putting a little in one's mouth **2** to detect the flavor of by the sense of taste **3** to eat or drink a small amount of **4** to experience [to *taste* success] **—vi.** to have a specific flavor **—n.** **1** the sense by which flavor is perceived through the taste buds on the tongue **2** the quality so perceived; flavor **3** a small amount tasted as a sample **4** a slight experience of something **5** the ability to appreciate what is beautiful, appropriate, etc. **6** a specific preference **7** a liking; inclination **—in bad (or good) taste** in a style showing a bad (or good) sense of beauty, fitness, etc. **—taste′less** *adj.* **—tast′er** *n.*

taste bud any of the cells, esp. in the tongue, that are the organs of taste

taste·ful *adj.* having or showing good TASTE (*n.* 5) **—taste′ful·ly** *adv.*

tast·y (tās′tē) *adj.* **-i·er, -i·est** that tastes good; flavorful **—tast′i·ness** *n.*

tat[1] (tat) *vt.* **tat′ted, tat′ting** to make by tatting **—vi.** to do tatting

tat[2] (tat) *n.* [Inf.] short for TATTOO[1] (*n.*)

ta·ta·mi (tə tä′mē) *n., pl.* **-mi** or **-mis** ⟦Jpn⟧ a floor mat of rice straw, used traditionally in Japanese homes for sitting on

Ta·tar (tät′ər) *n.* **1** a member of any of the E Asian peoples that invaded W Asia and E Europe in the Middle Ages **2** a Turkic language

tat·ter (tat′ər) *n.* ⟦< ON *tǫturr*, rags⟧ **1** a torn and hanging piece, as of a garment **2** [*pl.*] torn, ragged clothes **— vt., vi.** to make or become ragged **—tat′tered** *adj.*

tat·ting (tat′iŋ) *n.* ⟦prob. < Brit dial. *tat*, to tangle⟧ **1** a fine lace made by looping and knotting thread **2** the act or process of making this

tat·tle (tat′'l) *vi.* **-tled, -tling** ⟦prob. < MDu *tatelen*⟧ **1** to talk idly **2** to reveal others' secrets **3** to inform against someone **—tat′tler** *n.*

tat·tle·tale *n.* an informer; a gossip

tat·too[1] (ta tōō′) *vt.* **-tooed′, -too′ing** ⟦< a Polynesian language⟧ to make (permanent designs) on (the skin) by puncturing and inserting indelible color **—n., pl.** **-toos′** a tattooed design

tat·too² (ta tōō′) *n., pl.* **-toos′** [< Du *tap toe*, tap to (shut): a signal for closing barrooms] **1** a signal on a drum or bugle, summoning military personnel to their quarters at night **2** a drumming, rapping, etc.

tau (tou, tô) *n.* the 19th letter of the Greek alphabet (Τ, τ)

taught (tôt) *vt., vi. pt. & pp. of* TEACH

taunt (tônt, tänt) *vt.* [< ? Fr *tant pour tant*, tit for tat] to reproach scornfully or sarcastically; mock —*n.* a scornful or jeering remark

taupe (tōp) *n.* [Fr < L *talpa*, mole] a dark, brownish gray

Tau·rus (tô′rəs) *n.* [L, a bull] the second sign of the zodiac

taut (tôt) *adj.* [ME *toght*, tight] **1** tightly stretched, as a rope **2** tense [a *taut* smile] **3** trim, tidy, etc. —**taut′ly** *adv.* —**taut′ness** *n.*

tau·tol·o·gy (tô tält′ə jē) *n., pl.* **-gies** [< Gr < *auto*, the same + -LOGY] needless repetition of an idea in a different word, phrase, etc.; redundancy —**tau′to·log′i·cal** *adj.*

tav·ern (tav′ərn) *n.* [< L *taberna*] **1** a saloon; bar **2** an inn

taw·dry (tô′drē) *adj.* **-dri·er, -dri·est** [after St. *Audrey laces*, sold at St. Audrey's fair in Norwich, England] **1** cheap and showy; gaudy **2** shameful

taw·ny (tô′nē) *adj.* **-ni·er, -ni·est** [< OFr *tanner*, to tan] brownish-yellow; tan —**taw′ni·ness** *n.*

tax (taks) *vt.* [< L *taxare*, appraise] **1** to require to pay a tax **2** to assess a tax on (income, purchases, etc.) **3** to put a strain on **4** to accuse; charge —*n.* **1** a compulsory payment of a percentage of income, property value, etc. for the support of a government **2** a heavy demand; burden —**tax′a·ble** *adj.* —**tax·a′tion** *n.*

tax·i (tak′sē) *n., pl.* **-is** *short for* TAXICAB —*vi.* **-ied, -i·ing** *or* **-y·ing** **1** to go in a taxicab **2** to move along the ground or on the water as before takeoff or after landing: said of an airplane

tax·i·cab *n.* [< *taxi(meter) cab*] an automobile in which passengers are carried for a fare

tax·i·der·my (tak′si dur′mē) *n.* [< Gr *taxis*, arrangement + *derma*, skin] the art of preparing, stuffing, etc. the skins of animals to make them appear lifelike —**tax′i·der′mist** *n.*

tax·i·me·ter (tak′sē mēt′ər) *n.* [< Fr, ult. < ML *taxa*, tax + *-meter*, -METER] an automatic device in taxicabs that registers the fare due

tax·on·o·my (tak sän′ə mē) *n., pl.* **-mies** [< Gr *taxis*, arrangement + *nomos*, law] classification, esp. of animals and plants —**tax·on′o·mist** *n.*

tax·pay·er *n.* one who pays a tax

tax shelter an investment made to reduce one's income tax

tax·us (tak′səs) *n.* [ModL] YEW (*n.* 1)

Tay·lor (tā′lər), **Zach·a·ry** (zak′ə rē) 1784–1850; U.S. general: 12th president of the U.S. (1849–50)

TB (tē′bē′) *n.* tuberculosis

TBA or **tba** *abbrev.* to be announced

T-ball (tē′bôl′) *n.* a baseball game for young children in which the ball is placed on and struck from a tall tee

TBD *abbrev.* to be determined

T-bone steak (tē′bōn′) a beefsteak with a T-shaped bone, containing some tenderloin

tbs or **tbsp** *abbrev.* **1** tablespoon(s) **2** tablespoonful(s)

T cell any of the lymphocytes affected by the thymus, that regulate immunity, reject foreign tissue, etc.: cf. B CELL

Tchai·kov·sky (chī kôf′skē), **Peter** 1840–93; Russ. composer

TD *abbrev.* touchdown: sometimes **td**

TDD *abbrev.* telecommunications device for the deaf

tea (tē) *n.* [< Chin dial. *t'e*] **1** an evergreen plant grown in Asia **2** its dried leaves, used to make a beverage **3** the beverage made by soaking such leaves in boiling water **4** a tealike beverage made from other plants or from a meat extract **5** [Chiefly Brit.] a light meal in the late afternoon, usually eaten with tea **6** an afternoon party at which tea, etc. is served **7** [Slang] marijuana

tea·ber·ry (tē′ber′ē) *n., pl.* **-ries 1** WINTERGREEN (*n.* 1) **2** the berry of the wintergreen

teach (tēch) *vt.* **taught, teach′ing** [OE *tæcan*] **1** to show or help (a person) to learn (*how*) to do something **2** to give lessons to (a student, etc.) **3** to give lessons in (a subject) **4** to provide with knowledge, insight, etc. —*vi.* to give lessons or instruction —**teach′a·ble** *adj.*

teach·er *n.* one who teaches, esp. as a profession

teach·ing *n.* **1** the profession of a teacher **2** something taught; precept, doctrine, etc.: *usually used in pl.*

tea·cup *n.* a cup for drinking tea, etc. —**tea′cup·ful′** *n., pl.* **-fuls′**

teak (tēk) *n.* [< Malayalam *tēkka*] **1** a tall tree of SE Asia, with hard, yellowish-brown wood **2** its wood: also **teak′wood′**

tea·ket·tle *n.* a kettle with a spout, for boiling water to make tea, etc.

teal (tēl) *n.* [ME *tele*] **1** a small, short-necked, freshwater wild duck **2** a dark grayish or greenish blue: also **teal blue**

team (tēm) *n.* [OE, offspring] **1** two or more horses, oxen, etc. harnessed to the same plow, etc. **2** a group of people working or playing together —*vi.* to join in cooperative activity: often with *up* —*adj.* of or done by a team

team·mate *n.* one on the same team

team·ster (-stər) *n.* one whose work is hauling loads, as with a horse-drawn wagon or a truck

team·work *n.* joint action by a group of people

tea·pot *n.* a pot with a spout and handle, for brewing and pouring tea

tear¹ (ter) *vt.* **tore, torn, tear′ing** [OE *teran*, rend] **1** to pull apart into pieces by force; rip **2** to make by tearing [to *tear* a hole] **3** to lacerate **4** to disrupt; split [ranks *torn* by dissensions] **5** to divide with doubt, etc. **6** to pull with force —*vi.* 1 to be torn 2 to move with force or speed —*n.* 1 a tearing 2 a torn place; rent —**on a tear** in a state of extreme activity —**tear down** 1 to wreck 2 to dismantle

tear² (tir) *n.* ⟦OE *tēar*⟧ a drop of the salty fluid which flows from the eye, as in weeping —**in tears** crying; weeping —**tear′ful** *adj.* —**tear′ful·ly** *adv.* —**tear′y** *adj.* **-i·er, -i·est**

tear·drop (tir′dräp′) *n.* a tear

tear gas (tir) a liquid or gas that causes irritation of the eyes, used as by the police to disperse rioters —**tear′-gas′** *vt.* **-gassed′, -gas′sing**

tear·jerk·er (tir′jur′kər) *n.* [Slang] a sad, overly sentimental film, play, etc.

tea·room *n.* a restaurant that serves tea, coffee, light lunches, etc.

tease (tēz) *vt.* **teased, teas′ing** ⟦OE *tǣsan*⟧ 1 *a*) to card or comb (flax, wool, etc.) *b*) to fluff (the hair) by combing toward the scalp 2 to annoy by mocking, poking fun, etc. 3 to beg; importune 4 to tantalize —*vi.* to indulge in teasing —*n.* one who teases

tea·sel (tē′zəl) *n.* ⟦see prec.⟧ a bristly plant with prickly flowers

teas·er (tē′zər) *n.* 1 a person or thing that teases 2 a puzzling problem

tea·spoon *n.* 1 a spoon for stirring tea, etc. 2 a spoon for measuring ⅓ tablespoon —**tea′spoon·ful′** *n., pl.* **-fuls′**

teat (tēt) *n.* ⟦< OFr *tete*⟧ a nipple, as on a breast or udder

tech *abbrev.* 1 technical 2 technician 3 technology

tech·ie (tek′ē) *n.* [Inf.] an expert in computer technology

tech·ne·ti·um (tek nē′shē əm, -shəm) *n.* ⟦< Gr *technētos,* artificial⟧ a radioactive, metallic chemical element: the first artificially produced element: symbol, Tc; at. no. 43

tech·ni·cal (tek′ni kəl) *adj.* ⟦< Gr *technē,* an art⟧ 1 dealing with the industrial or mechanical arts or the applied sciences 2 of a specific science, art, craft, etc. 3 of, in or showing technique 4 concerned with minute details —*n. Sports* a foul called usually for breaking a rule not involving active play: in full **technical foul** —**tech′ni·cal·ly** *adv.*

tech·ni·cal·i·ty (-kal′ə tē) *n., pl.* **-ties** 1 the state or quality of being technical 2 a technical point, detail, etc. 3 a minute point, detail, etc. brought to bear upon a main issue

tech·ni·cian (tek nish′ən) *n.* one skilled in the technique of some art, craft, or science

Tech·ni·col·or (tek′ni kul′ər) *trademark for* a process of making bright, intense color movies —*n.* [**t-**] this process

tech·nique (tek nēk′) *n.* ⟦Fr⟧ 1 the method of procedure in artistic work, scientific activity, etc. 2 the degree of expertness in following this

tech·noc·ra·cy (tek näk′rə sē) *n.* ⟦< Gr *technē,* an art + -CRACY⟧ government by scientists and engineers —**tech′no·crat′** (-nə krat′) *n.*

tech·nol·o·gy (tek näl′ə jē) *n.* ⟦Gr *technologia,*

systematic treatment⟧ 1 the science of the practical or industrial arts 2 applied science —**tech′no·log′i·cal** (-nə läj′i kəl) *adj.*

tech·no·phile (tek′nə fil′) *n.* one who is enthusiastic about advanced technology

tech·no·pho·bi·a *n.* dislike or fear of advanced technology —**tech′no·phobe′** *n.*

ted·dy bear (ted′ē) [after *Teddy* (Theodore) Roosevelt] a child's stuffed toy made to look like a bear cub

te·di·ous (tē′dē əs) *adj.* full of tedium; long and dull —**te′di·ous·ly** *adv.*

te·di·um (-əm) *n.* ⟦< L *taedet,* it offends⟧ the condition or quality of being tiresome, boring, etc.

tee (tē) *n.* ⟦prob. < Scot dial. *teaz*⟧ 1 *Golf a*) a small peg from which the ball is driven *b*) the place from which a player makes the first stroke on each hole 2 *Football* a small holder on which the ball is placed for kickoffs 3 a tall holder on which a ball is placed for hitting in T-ball —*vt., vi.* **teed, tee′ing** to place (a ball) on a tee —**tee off** 1 to play a golf ball from a tee 2 [Slang] to make angry

teem (tēm) *vi.* ⟦< OE *tēam,* progeny⟧ to be prolific; abound; swarm

teen (tēn) *n.* ⟦OE *tien,* ten⟧ 1 [*pl.*] the years from 13 through 19, as of a person's age 2 TEENAGER

teen·age (tēn′āj′) *adj.* 1 in one's teens 2 of or for people in their teens —**teen′ag′er** *n.*

tee·ny (tē′nē) *adj.* **-ni·er, -ni·est** *inf. var. of* TINY: also **teen·sy** (tēn′zē, -sē), **-si·er, -si·est**

tee·ny-wee·ny (tē′nē wē′nē) *adj.* [Inf.] tiny: also **teen·sy-ween·sy** (tēn′zē wēn′zē, tēn′sē wēn′sē)

tee·pee (tē′pē) *n. alt. sp. of* TEPEE

tee shirt *var. of* T-SHIRT

tee·ter (tēt′ər) *vi.* ⟦< ON *titra,* to tremble⟧ to totter, wobble, etc.

tee·ter-tot·ter (-tōt′ər, -tät′-) *n., vi.* SEE-SAW

teeth (tēth) *n. pl. of* TOOTH —**in the teeth of** 1 directly against 2 defying

teethe (tēth) *vi.* **teethed, teeth′ing** to grow teeth; cut one's teeth

tee·to·tal·er or **tee·to·tal·ler** (tē tōt′ˈlər) *n.* ⟦< doubling of initial *t* in *total*⟧ one who abstains from all alcoholic drinks

te·fil·lin (tə fil′in) *n.* either of two small, leather cases holding Scripture texts, worn in prayer on the forehead and arm by orthodox Jewish men

Tef·lon (tef′län′) *trademark for* a tough polymer, used as for nonsticking coatings on cookware —*n.* [**t-**] this substance

Teh·ran (te rän′) capital of Iran: also **Te·he·ran′**

tek·tite (tek′tīt′) *n.* ⟦< Gr *tēktos,* molten⟧ a small, dark, glassy body thought to have originated as a meteorite

tel *abbrev.* 1 telegram 2 telephone

Tel A·viv (tel′ ə vēv′) seaport in W Israel

tele- *combining form* 1 ⟦< Gr *tēle,* far off⟧ at, over, etc. a distance [*telegraph*] 2 ⟦<

TELE(VISION)] of, in, or by television [*telecast*]

tel·e·cast (tel′ə kast′) *vt., vi.* -**cast′** or -**cast′ed,** -**cast′ing** to broadcast by television —*n.* a television broadcast —**tel′e·cast′er** *n.*

tel·e·com·mu·ni·ca·tion *n.* [*also pl., with sing. or pl. v.*] communication by electronic or electrical means, as through radio, TV, computers, etc.: also **tel′e·com′** (-käm′)

tel·e·com·mute *vi.* to do office work at home using a computer —**tel′e·com·mut′er** *n.*

tel·e·con·fer·ence *n.* a conference of persons in different locations, as by telephone, TV, etc.

tel·e·gram *n.* a message transmitted by telegraph

tel·e·graph *n.* [see TELE- & -GRAPH] an apparatus or system that sends text via electrical impulses sent by wire or radio —*vt., vi.* to send (a message) to (a person) by telegraph —**tel′e·graph′ic** *adj.*

te·leg·ra·phy (tə leg′rə fē) *n.* the operation of telegraphs —**te·leg′ra·pher** *n.*

tel·e·ki·ne·sis (tel′ə ki nē′sis) *n.* [see TELE- & KINETIC] *Parapsychology* the causing of an object to move by psychic, rather than physical, force

tel·e·mar·ket·ing *n.* the use of the telephone in selling, market research, promotion, etc. —**tel′e·mar′ket·er** *n.*

tel·e·me·ter (tel′ə mēt′ər, tə lem′ət ər) *n.* a device for measuring and transmitting data about radiation, temperature, etc. from far away —**te·lem′e·try** *n.*

te·le·no·ve·la (tel′ə nō vel′ə, -vä′lä) *n.* [AmSp < *tele(visión)*, television + *novela*, novel] a Spanish-language TV soap opera

te·lep·a·thy (tə lep′ə thē) *n.* [TELE- & -PATHY] *Parapsychology* extrasensory communication between minds —**tel·e·path·ic** (tel′ə path′ik) *adj.*

tel·e·phone (tel′ə fōn′) *n.* [TELE- + -PHONE] an instrument or system for conveying speech or computerized information over distances, usually by converting sound into electrical impulses sent through a wire —*vt., vi.* -**phoned′, -phon′ing** to convey (a message) to (a person) by telephone —**tel′e·phon′ic** (-fän′ik) *adj.*

te·leph·o·ny (tə lef′ə nē) *n.* the making or operation of telephones

tel·e·pho·to (tel′ə fōt′ō) *adj.* designating or of a camera lens that produces a large image of a distant object

tel·e·promp·ter (-prämp′tər) *n.* [< *Tele-PrompTer*, a former trademark] an electronic device that unrolls a speech, script, etc. line by line, as an aid to a speaker, etc. on TV

tel·e·scope (tel′ə skōp′) *n.* [see TELE- & -SCOPE] an optical instrument for making distant objects appear nearer and larger —*vi., vt.* -**scoped′, -scop′ing** to slide one into another like the tubes of a collapsible telescope —**tel′e·scop′ic** (-skäp′ik) *adj.*

tel·e·thon (-thän′) *n.* [TELE(VISION) + (MARA)THON] a campaign, as on a lengthy telecast, seeking donations

Tel·e·type (tel′ə tīp′) *n. trademark* for a former kind of telegraphic apparatus for transmitting typed messages

tel·e·vise (tel′ə vīz′) *vt., vi.* -**vised′, -vis′ing** to transmit by television

tel·e·vi·sion (-vizh′ən) *n.* **1** the process of transmitting images by converting light rays into electrical signals: the receiver reconverts the signals to reproduce the images on a screen **2** television broadcasting **3** a television receiving set **4** a television program or programs

tel·ex (tel′eks′) *n.* **1** a device which sends typed messages over telephone lines **2** a message sent in this way —*vt.* to send by telex

tell (tel) *vt.* ` told, tell′ing [OE *tellan*, calculate] **1** to count; reckon [to *tell* time] **2** to narrate; relate [to *tell* a story] **3** to express in words; say [to *tell* the truth] **4** to reveal; disclose **5** to recognize; distinguish [to *tell* twins apart] **6** to inform [*tell* me later] **7** to order [*tell* him to go] —*vi.* **1** to give an account or evidence (*of* something) **2** to be effective [each blow *told*] —*n.* an unconscious signal, as of the strength of a cardplayer's hand —**tell off** [Inf.] to rebuke severely —**tell on 1** to have an adverse effect on **2** [Inf.] to inform against

tell·er *n.* **1** one who tells (a story, etc.) **2** a bank clerk who pays out or receives money

tell·ing *adj.* **1** forceful; striking **2** that reveals much —**tell′ing·ly** *adv.*

tell·tale *adj.* revealing what is meant to be kept secret or hidden

tel·lu·ri·um (te loor′ē əm) *n.* [< L *tellus*, earth] a rare, brittle chemical element used in compact discs, semiconductors, and ceramics: symbol, Te; at. no. 52

tel·ly (tel′ē) *n., pl.* -**lies** *Brit. inf.* term for TELEVISION

tem·blor (tem′blôr′, -blər) *n.* [Sp < *temblar*, to tremble] EARTHQUAKE

te·mer·i·ty (tə mer′ə tē) *n.* [< L *temere*, rashly] foolish or rash boldness

temp¹ (temp) *n.* [Inf.] one who works at a place on a temporary basis

temp² *abbrev.* **1** temperature **2** temporary

tem·per (tem′pər) *vt.* [< L *temperare*, regulate] **1** to moderate, as by mingling with something else [to *temper* blame with praise] **2** to bring to the proper condition by some treatment [to *temper* steel] **3** to toughen —*n.* **1** the degree of hardness and resiliency of a metal **2** frame of mind; disposition **3** calmness of mind: in **lose (or keep) one's temper 4** a tendency to become angry **5** anger; rage

tem·per·a (tem′pər ə) *n.* [It: see prec.] a process of painting with pigments mixed with size, casein, or egg

tem·per·a·ment (tem′pər ə mənt, -prə mənt) *n.* [see TEMPER] **1** one's natural disposition; nature **2** a nature that is excitable, moody, etc. —**tem′per·a·men′tal** *adj.*

tem·per·ance (tem′pər əns, -prəns) *n.* **1** self-restraint in conduct, indulgence of the appetites, etc.; moderation **2** moderation in drinking alcoholic liquors or total abstinence from them

tem·per·ate (tem′pər it, -prit) *adj.* ⟦see TEMPER⟧ **1** moderate, as in one's appetites, behavior, etc. **2** neither very hot nor very cold: said of climate, etc.

Temperate Zone either of the two zones of the earth (**North Temperate Zone** and **South Temperate Zone**) between the tropics and the polar circles

tem·per·a·ture (tem′pər ə chər, -prə chər) *n.* ⟦< L *temperatus,* temperate⟧ **1** the degree of hotness or coldness of anything **2** an excess of body heat over the normal; fever

tem·pered (tem′pərd) *adj.* **1** having been given the desired TEMPER (*n.* 1) **2** having a (specified) TEMPER (*n.* 2)

tem·pest (tem′pist) *n.* ⟦< L *tempus,* time⟧ a violent storm with high winds, esp. one accompanied by rain, hail, etc.

tem·pes·tu·ous (tem pes′choo əs) *adj.* of or like a tempest; violent

tem·plate (tem′plit) *n.* ⟦< L *templum,* small timber⟧ a pattern, as a thin metal plate, for making an exact copy

tem·ple¹ (tem′pəl) *n.* ⟦< L *templum*⟧ **1** a building for the worship of a god or gods **2** a large building for some special purpose [a *temple* of art]

tem·ple² (tem′pəl) *n.* ⟦< L *tempus*⟧ **1** the flat surface alongside the forehead, in front of each ear **2** either of the sidepieces of a pair of glasses

tem·po (tem′pō) *n., pl.* **-pos** or **-pi** (-pē) ⟦It < L *tempus,* time⟧ **1** the speed at which a musical composition is performed **2** rate of activity

tem·po·ral¹ (tem′pə rəl) *adj.* ⟦< L *tempus,* time⟧ **1** worldly; not spiritual **2** secular **3** of or limited by time

tem·po·ral² (tem′pə rəl) *adj.* of or near the temples (of the head)

tem·po·rar·y (-rer′ē) *adj.* ⟦< L *tempus,* time⟧ lasting only a while; not permanent —**tem′po·rar′i·ly** *adv.*

tem·po·rize (-rīz′) *vi.* **-rized′, -riz′ing 1** to act based on current conditions rather than on fixed principle **2** to evade decision, comply temporarily, etc., so as to gain time or avoid argument

tempt (tempt) *vt.* ⟦< L *temptare,* to test⟧ **1** to induce or entice, as to something immoral **2** to be inviting to; attract **3** to provoke or risk provoking (fate, etc.) **4** to incline strongly [to be *tempted* to accept] —**temp·ta·tion** (temp tā′shən) *n.*

tempt·ress (temp′tris) *n.* a woman who tempts, esp. sexually

tem·pu·ra (tem′poo rä′, tem poor′ə) *n.* ⟦Jpn⟧ a Japanese dish of deep-fried breaded shrimp, fish, vegetables, etc.

ten (ten) *adj., n.* ⟦OE⟧ one more than nine; 10; X

ten·a·ble (ten′ə bəl) *adj.* ⟦< L *tenere,* to hold⟧ that can be defended or believed —**ten′a·bil′i·ty** *n.*

te·na·cious (tə nā′shəs) *adj.* ⟦< L *tenere,* to hold⟧ **1** holding firmly [a *tenacious* grip] **2** retentive [a *tenacious* memory] **3** strongly cohesive or adhesive **4** persistent; stubborn [*tenacious* courage] —**te·na′cious·ly** *adv.* —**te·nac·i·ty** (tə nas′ə tē) *n.*

ten·ant (ten′ənt) *n.* ⟦see prec.⟧ **1** one who pays rent to occupy land, a building, etc. **2** an occupant —**ten′an·cy** *n., pl.* **-cies**

tenant farmer one who farms land owned by another and pays rent

Ten Commandments *Bible* the ten laws of moral and religious conduct given to Moses by God: Exodus 20:2-17

tend¹ (tend) *vt.* ⟦see ATTEND⟧ **1** to take care of **2** to manage or operate

tend² (tend) *vi.* ⟦< L *tendere,* to stretch⟧ **1** to be inclined, disposed, etc. (*to*) **2** to be directed (*to* or *toward*)

tend·en·cy (ten′dən sē) *n., pl.* **-cies** ⟦see prec.⟧ **1** an inclination to move or act in a particular direction or way **2** a course toward some object

ten·den·tious (ten den′shəs) *adj.* ⟦< Ger *tendenz,* prec.⟧ advancing a definite point of view [*tendentious* writings] —**ten·den′tious·ly** *adv.*

ten·der¹ (ten′dər) *adj.* ⟦< L *tener,* soft⟧ **1** soft and easily chewed, broken, cut, etc. **2** physically weak **3** immature **4** that requires careful handling **5** gentle or light **6** acutely sensitive, as to pain **7** sensitive to emotions, others' feelings, etc. —**ten′der·ly** *adv.* —**ten′der·ness** *n.*

ten·der² (ten′dər) *vt.* ⟦see TEND²⟧ to offer formally —*n.* **1** a formal offer **2** money, etc. offered in payment

tend·er³ (ten′dər) *n.* **1** one who tends something **2** a small ship for supplying a larger one **3** a railroad car attached behind, and carrying fuel and water for, a steam locomotive

ten·der⁴ (ten′dər) *n.* ⟦< TENDER(LOIN)⟧ a small strip of meat, esp of chicken breast, often served breaded and fried or baked

ten·der·foot *n., pl.* **-foots′** or **-feet′ 1** a newcomer to ranching in the West, unused to hardships **2** any novice

ten·der·heart·ed *adj.* quick to feel pity or compassion

ten·der·ize (ten′dər īz′) *vt.* **-ized′, -iz′ing** to make (meat) tender

ten·der·loin *n.* the tenderest part of a loin of beef, pork, etc.

ten·di·ni·tis (ten′də nīt′is) *n.* inflammation of a tendon

ten·don (ten′dən) *n.* ⟦< Gr *teinein,* to stretch⟧ any of the inelastic cords of tough connective tissue by which muscles are attached to bones, etc.

ten·dril (ten′drəl) *n.* ⟦prob. ult. < L *tener,* delicate⟧ a threadlike, clinging part of a climbing plant

ten·e·ment (ten′ə mənt) *n.* ⟦< L *tenere,* to hold⟧ a building divided into apartments; now specif., one that is run-down, overcrowded, etc.: in full **tenement house**

ten·et (ten′it) *n.* 〖L, he holds〗 a principle, doctrine, or belief held as a truth, as by some group

Ten·nes·see (ten′ə sē′) state of the EC U.S.; cap. Nashville: abbrev. *TN* —**Ten′nes·se′an** *adj., n.*

ten·nis (ten′is) *n.* 〖prob. < OFr *tenez*, hold (imperative)〗 a game in which players in a marked area (**tennis court**) hit a ball back and forth with rackets over a net

tennis elbow inflammation of the elbow tendons, caused by strain

tennis shoe a sneaker

Ten·ny·son (ten′i sən), **Al·fred** (al′frəd) 1809–92; Eng. poet: called *Alfred, Lord Tennyson*

ten·on (ten′ən) *n.* 〖ult. < L *tenere*, to hold〗 a projecting part cut on the end of a piece of wood for insertion into a mortise to make a joint

ten·or (ten′ər) *n.* 〖< L *tenere*, to hold〗 **1** general tendency **2** general meaning; drift **3** *a)* the range of the highest regular adult male voice *b)* a voice, singer, or instrument with such a range *c)* a part for a tenor —*adj.* of or for a tenor

ten·pins *n.* the game of bowling in which ten pins are used

tense[1] (tens) *adj.* **tens′er, tens′est** 〖< L *tendere*, to stretch〗 **1** stretched tight; taut **2** feeling or showing tension —*vt., vi.* **tensed, tens′ing** to make or become tense

tense[2] (tens) *n.* 〖< L *tempus*, time〗 any of the forms of a verb that show the time of its action or existence

ten·sile (ten′səl) *adj.* **1** of, undergoing, or exerting tension **2** capable of being stretched

ten·sion (ten′shən) *n.* **1** a tensing or being tensed **2** mental or nervous strain **3** a state of strained relations due to mutual hostility **4** VOLTAGE **5** stress on a material produced by the pull of forces causing extension

tent (tent) *n.* 〖< L *tendere*, to stretch〗 a portable shelter made of canvas, etc. stretched over poles — *vi., vt.* to lodge in a tent or tents

ten·ta·cle (ten′tə kəl) *n.* 〖< L *tentare*, to touch〗 a long, slender, flexible growth on the head of some invertebrates, used to grasp, feel, etc.

ten·ta·tive (ten′tə tiv) *adj.* 〖< L *tentare*, to try〗 **1** made, done, etc. provisionally; not final **2** indicating timidity or uncertainty —**ten′ta·tive·ly** *adv.*

ten·ter·hook (ten′tər hook′) *n.* 〖< L *tendere*, to stretch + HOOK〗 a kind of hooked nail —**on tenterhooks** in anxious suspense

tenth (tenth) *adj.* 〖OE *teogotha*〗 preceded by nine others in a series; 10th —*n.* **1** the one following the ninth **2** any of the ten equal parts of something; ¹⁄₁₀

ten·u·ous (ten′yo͞o əs) *adj.* 〖< L *tenuis*, thin〗 **1** slender or fine, as a fiber **2** rare, as air at high altitudes **3** flimsy [*tenuous* evidence]

ten·ure (ten′yər) *n.* 〖< medieval Fr < *tenir*, to hold〗 **1** the act or right of holding property, an office, etc. **2** the length of time, or the conditions under which, something is held **3** the status of holding one's position on a permanent basis, granted as to a professor

te·pee (tē′pē) *n.* 〖< AmInd *tʰípi*, dwelling〗 a cone-shaped tent used by some North American Indians

tep·id (tep′id) *adj.* 〖< L *tepidus*〗 **1** lukewarm **2** lacking enthusiasm

te·qui·la (tə kē′lə) *n.* 〖< AmInd (Mexico) *Tuiquila*, region in Mexico〗 an alcoholic liquor of Mexico, distilled from an agave mash

tera- 〖< Gr *teras*, monster〗 *combining form* one trillion [*terahertz*]

ter·a·byte (ter′ə bīt′) *n.* 〖prec. + BYTE〗 **1** a unit of storage capacity in a computer system, equal to 1,099,511,627,776 (2⁴⁰) bytes **2** loosely, one trillion bytes Abbrev. *TB*

ter·bi·um (tur′bē əm) *n.* 〖after *Ytterby*, Sweden〗 a soft, ductile chemical element, used in X-ray machines and lasers: symbol, Tb; at. no. 65

ter·cen·te·nar·y (tur′sen ten′ər ē, tər sen′tə ner′ē) *adj., n., pl.* **-ies** 〖L *ter*, three times + CENTENARY〗 TRICENTENNIAL

term (turm) *n.* 〖< L *terminus*, a limit〗 **1** a set date, as for payment, etc. **2** a set period of time [school *term*, *term* of office] **3** [*pl.*] conditions of a contract, etc. **4** [*pl.*] mutual relationship between persons [on speaking *terms*] **5** a word or phrase **6** *Math. a)* either quantity of a fraction or a ratio *b)* each quantity in a series or algebraic expression —*vt.* to call by a term; name —**bring (or come) to terms** to force into (or arrive at) an agreement

ter·mi·na·ble (tur′mi nə bəl) *adj.* that can be, or is, terminated

ter·mi·nal (tur′mə nəl) *adj.* 〖L *terminalis*〗 **1** of, at, or forming the end or extremity **2** concluding; final **3** close to causing death [*terminal* cancer] **4** of or at the end of a transportation line —*n.* **1** an end; extremity **2** a connective point on an electric circuit **3** either end of a transportation line, or a main station on it **4** a device, usually with a keyboard and video display, for putting data in, or getting it from, a computer

ter·mi·nate (tur′mə nāt′) *vt.* **-nat′ed, -nat′ing** 〖< L *terminus*, a limit〗 **1** to form the end of **2** to put an end to; stop **3** to dismiss from employment; fire —*vi.* **1** to come to an end **2** to have its end (*in* something) —**ter′mi·na′tion** *n.*

ter·mi·nol·o·gy (tur′mə näl′ə jē) *n., pl.* **-gies** the terms used in a specific science, art, etc.

term insurance life insurance that expires after a specified period

ter·mi·nus (tur′mə nəs) *n., pl.* **-ni′** (-nī′) or **-nus·es** 〖L, a limit〗 **1** a limit **2** an end; extremity or goal **3** either end of a transportation line

ter·mite (tur′mīt′) *n.* 〖< L *tarmes*, wood-boring worm〗 a social insect that feeds on dead plant material and is often very destructive to wooden structures

tern (turn) *n.* 〖< ON *therna*〗 a gull-like seabird with webbed feet and a straight bill

ter·race (ter'əs) *n.* [< L *terra*, earth] 1 a raised, flat mound of earth with sloping sides, esp. one in a series on a hillside 2 an unroofed, paved area, between a house and lawn 3 a row of houses on ground above street level 4 a small, usually roofed balcony, as outside an apartment —*vt.* -raced, -rac·ing to form into a terrace or terraces

ter·ra cot·ta (ter'ə kät'ə) [It, lit., baked earth] a hard, brown-red earthenware, or its color

ter·ra fir·ma (ter'ə fur'mə) [L] solid ground

ter·rain (tə rān') *n.* [< L *terra*, earth] a tract of ground, as with regard to its features

ter·ra·pin (ter'ə pin) *n.* [< Algonquian] 1 any of various terrestrial, freshwater or tidewater turtles 2 its edible flesh

ter·rar·i·um (tə rer'ē əm) *n., pl.* -i·ums or -i·a (-ə) [< L *terra*, earth + -*arium*, as in *aquarium*] a usually closed container, as of glass, in which small plants are grown or small land animals are kept

ter·raz·zo (tə raz'ō, tə rät'sō) *n.* [It] flooring of small chips of marble set in cement and polished

ter·res·tri·al (tə res'trē əl) *adj.* [< L *terra*, earth] 1 worldly; mundane 2 of the earth 3 consisting of land, not water 4 living on land

ter·ri·ble (ter'ə bəl) *adj.* [< L *terrere*, frighten] 1 causing terror 2 extreme; intense 3 [Inf.] very unpleasant, etc. —**ter'ri·bly** *adv.*

ter·ri·er (ter'ē ər) *n.* [< medieval Fr (*chien*) *terrier*, hunting (dog)] any of several breeds of small dog originally used for hunting rats, etc.

ter·rif·ic (tə rif'ik) *adj.* [< L *terrere*, frighten] 1 causing great fear 2 [Inf.] *a*) very great, intense, etc. *b*) unusually fine, admirable, etc.

ter·ri·fy (ter'ə fī') *vt.* -fied', -fy'ing to fill with terror; frighten greatly

ter·ri·to·ry (ter'ə tôr'ē) *n., pl.* -ries [< L *terra*, earth] 1 an area under the jurisdiction of a nation, ruler, etc. 2 a part of a country or empire that does not have full status 3 any large tract of land 4 an assigned area 5 a sphere of action, thought, etc. —**ter'ri·to'ri·al** *adj.*

ter·ror (ter'ər) *n.* [< L *terrere*, frighten] 1 intense fear 2 *a*) one that causes intense fear *b*) the quality of causing such fear 3 [Inf.] one who is very annoying or unmanageable, esp. a child

ter·ror·ism *n.* the use of violence or threats to intimidate, force, etc., esp. as a political policy —**ter'ror·ist** *n., adj.*

ter·ror·ize (-īz') *vt.* -ized', -iz'ing 1 to terrify 2 to coerce, make submit, etc. by filling with terror

ter·ry (ter'ē) *n.* [prob. < Fr *tirer*, to draw] cloth having a pile of uncut loops, esp. cotton cloth used for toweling: also **terry cloth**

terse (turs) *adj.* ters'er, ters'est [L *tersus*, wiped off] free of superfluous words; concise; succinct —**terse'ly** *adv.* —**terse'ness** *n.*

ter·ti·ar·y (tur'shē er'ē) *adj.* [< L *tertius*, third] third in order

tes·sel·late (tes'ə lāt') *vt.* -lat'ed, -lat'ing [< L *tessella*, little square stone] to lay out in a mosaic pattern of small, square blocks

test (test) *n.* [< OFr, assaying cup] 1 *a*) an examination or trial, as of something's value *b*) the method or a criterion used in this 2 an event, etc. that tries one's qualities 3 a set of questions, etc. for determining one's knowledge, etc. 4 *Chem.* a trial or reaction for identifying a substance —*vt.* to subject to a test; try —*vi.* to be rated by a test

tes·ta·ment (tes'tə mənt) *n.* [< L *testis*, a witness] 1 [T-] either of the two parts of the Christian Bible, the *Old Testament* and the *New Testament* 2 *a*) a testimonial *b*) an affirmation of beliefs 3 *Law* a will —**tes'ta·men'ta·ry** (-men'tə rē) *adj.*

tes·tate (tes'tāt') *adj.* [< L *testari*, make a will] having left a legally valid will

tes·ta·tor (tes'tāt'ər, tes tāt'-) *n.* one who has made a will

tes·ti·cle (tes'ti kəl) *n.* [< L *testis*] either of two male sex glands

tes·ti·fy (tes'tə fī') *vi.* -fied', -fy'ing [< L *testis*, a witness + *facere*, to make] 1 to give evidence, esp. under oath in court 2 to serve as evidence —*vt.* to affirm; declare, esp. under oath in court

tes·ti·mo·ni·al (tes'tə mō'nē əl) *n.* 1 a statement recommending a person or thing 2 something given or done to show gratitude or appreciation

tes·ti·mo·ny (tes'tə mō'nē) *n., pl.* -nies [< L *testis*, a witness] 1 a statement made under oath to establish a fact 2 any declaration 3 any form of evidence; proof

tes·tis (tes'tis) *n., pl.* -tes' (-tēz') [L] TES·TICLE

tes·tos·ter·one (tes täs'tər ōn') *n.* [see TESTICLE] a male sex hormone

test tube a tube of thin, transparent glass closed at one end, used in chemical experiments, etc.

test-tube *adj.* produced by in vitro fertilization [a *test-tube* baby]

tes·ty (tes'tē) *adj.* -ti·er, -ti·est [< L *testa*, the head] irritable; touchy

tet·a·nus (tet'ʼn əs, tet'nəs) *n.* [< Gr *tetanos*, spasm] an acute infectious disease, often fatal, caused by a toxin and characterized by spasmodic contractions and rigidity of muscles

tête-à-tête (tāt'ə tāt', tet'ə tet') *n.* [Fr, lit., head-to-head] a private conversation between two people

teth·er (teth'ər) *n.* [< ON *tjothr*] 1 a rope or chain that is fastened to an animal to keep it from roaming 2 the limit of one's abilities, resources, etc. —*vt.* to fasten with a tether

tet·ra (te'trə) *n.* [< ModL] a brightly colored, tropical American fish

tetra- [Gr < *tettares*, four] *combining form* four

tet·ra·cy·cline (te'trə sī'klin) *n.* a yellow crystalline compound used as an antibiotic

tet·ra·he·dron (te'trə hē'drən) *n., pl.* -drons

or **-dra** (-drə) [[see TETRA- & -HEDRON]] a solid figure with four triangular faces

te·tram·e·ter (te tram'ət ər) *n.* [[see TETRA- & METER[1]]] **1** a line of verse containing four metrical feet **2** verse consisting of such lines

Teu·ton·ic (tōō tän'ik) *adj.* designating of or a group of N European peoples, esp. the Germans —**Teu·ton** (tōōt'n) *n.*

Tex·as (tek'səs) state of the SW U.S.; cap. Austin: abbrev. TX —**Tex'an** *adj., n.*

Texas hold 'em a poker game in which players each receive two cards and share five cards

text (tekst) *n.* [< L *texere*, to weave]] **1** the actual words of an author, as distinguished from notes, etc. **2** any form in which a written work exists **3** the principal matter on a printed page, as distinguished from notes, headings, etc. **4** *a)* a Biblical passage used as the topic of a sermon, etc. *b)* any topic or subject **5** *short for* TEXTBOOK **6** letters, numbers, or symbols forming words, phrases, etc., used chiefly in a text message **7** *short for* TEXT MESSAGE —*vt.*, *vi.* to send a text message (to) —**tex·tu·al** (teks'chōō əl) *adj.*

text·book *n.* a book giving instructions in a subject of study —*adj.* so typical as to be a classic example or model of its kind

tex·tile (teks'tīl', -təl) *adj.* [[see TEXT]] **1** having to do with weaving **2** that has been or can be woven —*n.* **1** a woven or knitted fabric; cloth **2** raw material suitable for this

text·ing *n.* the act or practice of sending or receiving an electronic text message

text message a short communication in the form of TEXT (*n.* 6) sent or received by a portable electronic device, esp. a cell phone —**text messaging**

tex·ture (teks'chər) *n.* [< L *texere*, to weave]] **1** the character of a fabric, determined by the arrangement, size, etc. of its threads **2** the way something feels to the touch **3** the quality of the whole based on its constituent parts —**tex'tur·al** *adj.*

tex·tured *adj.* having an uneven surface; not smooth [*textured* wallpaper]

Th *abbrev. Chem. symbol for* thorium

-th[1] [[OE]] *suffix* **1** the act of ___ing [*growth*] **2** the state or quality of being or having [*wealth*]
-th[2] [< OE]] *suffix* forming ordinal numerals [*fourth, ninth*]

Thai (tī) *n.* **1** *pl.* **Thais** or **Thai** a person born or living in Thailand **2** the language of Thailand **3** *alt. sp. of* TAI —*adj.* of Thailand or its people, culture, etc.

Thai·land (tī'land') country in SE Asia

thal·a·mus (thal'ə məs) *n., pl.* **-mi'** (-mī') [< Gr *thalamos*, inner chamber]] a mass of gray matter at the base of the brain, involved in the transmission of certain sensations

thal·li·um (thal'ē əm) *n.* [< Gr *thallos*, young, green shoot (< its green spectral line)]] a soft, toxic, metallic chemical element, used in making photoelectric cells: symbol, Tl; at. no. 81

thal·lo·phyte (thal'ə fīt') *n.* [< Gr *thallos*, young shoot + *phyton*, a plant]] any of a large

group of plantlike organisms lacking true roots, leaves, or stems, as the fungi, the lichens, and most algae

Thames (temz) river in S England, flowing through London into the North Sea

than (than) *conj.* [[OE *thenne*]] introducing the second element in a comparison [A is taller *than* B]

thank (thaŋk) *vt.* [[OE *thancian*]] **1** to express gratitude to, as by saying "thank you" **2** to blame: an ironic use —**thank you** *short for* I thank you

thank·ful *adj.* feeling or expressing thanks —**thank'ful·ly** *adv.*

thank·less *adj.* **1** not feeling or expressing thanks; ungrateful **2** unappreciated

thanks (thaŋks) *pl.n.* an expression of gratitude —*interj.* I thank you —**thanks to** **1** let thanks be given to **2** on account of; because of

thanks·giv·ing *n.* **1** a formal public expression of thanks to God **2** [**T-**] an annual U.S. holiday observed on the fourth Thursday of November

that (that) *pron., pl.* **those** [[OE *thæt*]] **1** the person or thing mentioned [*that* is John] **2** the farther one or the other one [this is better than *that*] **3** who, whom, or which [the road *that* we took] **4** where [the place *that* I saw her] **5** when [the year *that* I was born] —*adj., pl.* **those 1** designating the one mentioned [*that* man is John] **2** designating the farther one or the other one [this house is larger than *that* one] —*conj.* subordinating conjunction used to introduce: *a)* a noun clause [*that* she's gone is obvious] *b)* an adverbial clause expressing purpose [they died *that* we might live], result [I ran so fast *that* I won], or cause [I'm glad *that* I won] *c)* an elliptical sentence expressing surprise, desire, etc. [oh, *that* she were here!] —*adv.* **1** to that extent [I can't see *that* far] **2** [Inf] to a great extent; very —**at that 1** at that point: also **with that 2** even so —**that is 1** to be specific **2** in other words

thatch (thach) *n.* [[OE *thæc*]] **1** a roof of straw, rushes, etc. **2** material for such a roof: also **thatch'ing 3** a layer of tangled, partly decayed leaves, stems, etc. lying on top of the soil —*vt.* to cover as with thatch

thaw (thô) *vi.* [[OE *thawian*]] **1** *a)* to melt (said of ice, snow, etc.) *b)* to pass to an unfrozen state (said of frozen foods) **2** to become warmer so that snow, etc. melts **3** to lose one's coldness of manner —*vt.* to cause to thaw —*n.* **1** a thawing **2** a spell of weather warm enough to allow thawing

THC *n.* [*t*(etra)*h*(ydro)*c*(annabinol)]] the principal mind-altering chemical in marijuana

ThD or **Th.D.** *abbrev.* [L *Theologiae Doctor*]] Doctor of Theology

the (thə; *before vowels* thē, thi) *definite article* [< OE *se* with *th-* from other forms]] *the* (as opposed to *a, an*) refers to: **1** a particular person, thing, or group [*the* story ended; *the* President] **2** a person or thing considered generically [*the* cow is a domestic animal; *the poor*] —*adv.* 1 that much [*the* better to see you with] 2 by how much . . . by that much [*the* sooner *the* better]

the·a·ter or **the·a·tre** (thē′ə tər) *n.* [< Gr *theasthai*, to view] 1 a place, esp. a building, where plays, operas, films, etc. are presented 2 any similar place with banked rows of seats 3 any place where events occur 4 *a*) the dramatic art *b*) the theatrical world 5 speech or actions that are only for show

the·at·ri·cal (thē a′tri kəl) *adj.* 1 having to do with the theater 2 dramatic; esp. (in disparagement), melodramatic —**the·at′ri·cal·ly** *adv.*

thee (thē) *pron.* [OE *the*] [Archaic] *objective form of* THOU

theft (theft) *n.* [OE *thiefth*] the act or an instance of stealing; larceny

their (ther) *poss. pronominal adj.* [< ON *theirra*] of, belonging to, or done by them

theirs (therz) *pron.* that or those belonging to them: poss. form of THEY [that book is *theirs*; *theirs* are better]

the·ism (thē′iz′əm) *n.* [< Gr *theos*, god] 1 belief in a god or gods 2 MONOTHEISM —**the′ist** *n., adj.* —**the·is′tic** *adj.*

them (them) *pron.* [< ON *theim*] *objective form of* THEY

theme (thēm) *n.* [< Gr *thema*, what is laid down] 1 a topic, as of an essay 2 a short essay 3 a short melody used as the subject of a musical composition 4 a recurring or identifying song in a film, musical, TV series, etc.: in full **theme song** —**the·mat·ic** (thē mat′ ik) *adj.*

them·selves (them selvz′) *pron.* a form of THEY, used as an intensive [they went *themselves*], as a reflexive [they hurt *themselves*], or with the meaning "their true selves" [they are not *themselves* when they are sick]

then (then) *adv.* [see THAN] 1 at that time [he was young *then*] 2 next [he took his hat and *then* left] 3 in that case [if she read it, *then* she knows] 4 furthermore [he likes to walk, and *then* it's good exercise] 5 at another time [now it's warm, *then* freezing] —*adj.* being such at that time [the *then* director] —*n.* that time [by *then*, they were gone]

thence (thens) *adv.* [OE *thanan*] 1 from that place 2 from that time; thenceforth

thence·forth *adv.* from that time onward; thereafter: also **thence·for′ward**

the·oc·ra·cy (thē äk′rə sē) *n., pl.* **-cies** [< Gr *theos*, god + *kratos*, rule, power] 1 government by a person or persons claiming divine authority 2 a country with this form of government

the·o·lo·gi·an (thē′ə lō′jən) *n.* a student of or specialist in theology

the·ol·o·gy (thē äl′ə jē) *n.* [< Gr *theos*, god + *logos*, word] the study of God, religious doctrines, etc. —**the′o·log′i·cal** (-ə läj′i kəl) *adj.*

the·o·rem (thē′ə rəm, thir′əm) *n.* [< Gr *theōrein*, to view] a proposition that can be proved from accepted premises; law or prin-

ciple 2 *Math., Physics* a proposition embodying something to be proved

the·o·ret·i·cal (thē′ə ret′i kəl) *adj.* 1 limited to or based on theory; hypothetical 2 tending to theorize; speculative Also **the′o·ret′ic** —**the′o·ret′i·cal·ly** *adv.*

the·o·rize (thē′ə rīz′) *vi.* **-rized′, -riz′ing** to form a theory or theories; speculate —**the′o·re·ti′cian** (-rə tish′ən) *n.,* **the′o·rist** (-rist) *n.*

the·o·ry (thē′ə rē, thir′ē) *n., pl.* **-ries** [< Gr *theōrein*, to view] 1 a speculative plan 2 a formulation of underlying principles of certain observed phenomena that has been verified to some degree 3 the principles of an art or science, rather than its practice 4 a conjecture or guess

the·os·o·phy (thē äs′ə fē) *n.* [< Gr *theos*, god + *sophia*, wisdom] [*also* T-] an eclectic set of occult beliefs, held to be based on mystical insight —**the′o·soph′ic** (-ə säf′ik) *adj.,* **the′o·soph′i·cal** *adj.* —**the·os′o·phist** *n.*

ther·a·peu·tic (ther′ə pyōōt′ik) *adj.* [< Gr *therapeuein*, to nurse] serving to cure or heal or to preserve health

ther·a·peu·tics *n.* the branch of medicine that deals with the treatment of diseases; therapy

ther·a·py (ther′ə pē) *n., pl.* **-pies** [see THERAPEUTIC] 1 the treatment of any physical or mental disorder by medical or physical means, usually excluding surgery 2 short for PSYCHOTHERAPY —**ther′a·pist** *n.*

there (ther) *adv.* [OE *ther*] 1 at, in, or to that place 2 at that point; then [*there* I paused] 3 in that respect [*there* you are wrong] *There* is also used in impersonal constructions in which the real subject follows the verb [*there* is little time] —*n.* that place —*interj.* used to express defiance, satisfaction, sympathy, etc. —**(not) all there** [Inf.] (not) mentally sound

there·a·bouts (-ə bouts′) *adv.* 1 near that place 2 near that time, number, degree, etc. Also **there′a·bout′**

there·af·ter *adv.* from then on

there·at *adv.* 1 at that place; there 2 at that time 3 for that reason

there·by *adv.* 1 by that means 2 connected with that

there·for *adv.* for this; for that; for it

there·fore (-fôr′) *adv.* for this or that reason; hence

there·in *adv.* 1 in or into that place 2 in that matter, detail, etc.

there·of *adv.* 1 of that 2 from that as a cause, reason, etc.

there·on *adv.* 1 on that or it 2 THEREUPON

there·to *adv.* to that place, thing, etc.: also **there·un·to** (ther un′tōō, ther′un tōō′)

there·to·fore *adv.* until that time

there·up·on *adv.* 1 immediately following that 2 as a consequence of that 3 on that subject, etc.

there·with *adv.* 1 along with that 2 immediately thereafter

ther·mal (thur′məl) *adj.* [< Gr *thermē*, heat] 1 having to do with heat 2 designating a loosely knitted material with air spaces for insulation —*n.* *Meteorol.* a rising column of warm air

thermal pollution the harmful discharge of heated liquid or air into the environment

thermo- ⟦< Gr *thermē*, heat⟧ *combining form* heat

ther·mo·dy·nam·ics (thur′mō dī nam′iks) *n.* the branch of physics dealing with the transformation of heat to and from other forms of energy —**ther′mo·dy·nam′ic** *adj.*

ther·mom·e·ter (thər mäm′ət ər) *n.* ⟦see THERMO- & -METER⟧ an instrument for measuring temperatures, as a graduated glass tube in which mercury, etc. rises or falls as it expands or contracts with changes in temperature

ther·mo·nu·cle·ar (thur′mō nōō′klē ər) *adj.* *Physics* 1 designating a reaction in which isotopes of a light element fuse, at extremely high heat, into heavier nuclei 2 of or using the heat energy released in nuclear fusion

ther·mo·plas·tic (thur′mə plas′tik) *adj.* soft and moldable when subjected to heat: said of certain plastics —*n.* a thermoplastic substance

Ther·mos (thur′məs) ⟦< Gr *thermos*, hot⟧ *trademark for* a vacuum-insulated container for keeping liquids hot or cold —*n.* [*usually* t-] such a container

ther·mo·stat (thur′mə stat′) *n.* ⟦THERMO- + -STAT⟧ an apparatus for regulating temperature, esp. one that automatically controls a heating or cooling unit

the·sau·rus (thi sô′rəs) *n., pl.* -**ri′** (-rī′) or -**rus·es** ⟦< Gr *thēsauros*, a treasure⟧ a book of synonyms and antonyms

these (thēz) *adj., pl. of* THIS

The·seus (thē′sōōs′, thē′sē əs) *n.* Gr. Legend a hero who kills the Minotaur and later becomes king of Athens

the·sis (thē′sis) *n., pl.* -**ses′** (-sēz′) ⟦< Gr *ti-thenai*, to put⟧ 1 a proposition to be defended in argument 2 a long research paper, esp. one written by a candidate for a master's degree

Thes·pi·an (thes′pē ən) *adj.* ⟦after *Thespis*, ancient Gr poet⟧ [*often* t-] having to do with the drama; dramatic —*n.* [*often* t-] an actor or actress

the·ta (thāt′ə, thēt′-) *n.* the eighth letter of the Greek alphabet (Θ, ϑ, θ)

thews (thyōōz) *pl.n., sing.* **thew** ⟦< OE *theaw*, habit⟧ muscles or sinews

they (thā) *pron., sing.* **he, she, it** ⟦< ON *their*⟧ 1 the persons, animals, or things previously mentioned 2 people generally [*they* say it's so]

thi·a·mine (thī′ə min, -mēn′) *n.* ⟦ult. < Gr *theion*, brimstone + (VIT)AMIN⟧ a white, crystalline B vitamin, found in cereals, egg yolk, liver, etc.; vitamin B_1: also **thi′a·min** (-min)

thick (thik) *adj.* ⟦OE *thicce*⟧ 1 of relatively great extent from side to side 2 as measured between opposite surfaces [one inch *thick*] 3 close and abundant [*thick* hair] 4 viscous 5 dense [*thick* smoke] 6 husky; blurred [*thick* speech] 7 [Inf.] stupid 8 [Inf.] close in

friendship —*n.* the thickest part —**thick′ly** *adv.* —**thick′ness** *n.*

thick·en *vt., vi.* 1 to make or become thick or thicker 2 to make or become more complex —**thick′en·ing** *n.*

thick·et (thik′it) *n.* ⟦see THICK⟧ a thick growth of shrubs or small trees

thick-set *adj.* 1 planted thickly or closely 2 thick in body; stocky

thick-skinned *adj.* insensitive, as to insult

thief (thēf) *n., pl.* **thieves** (thēvz) ⟦OE *theof*⟧ one who steals

thieve (thēv) *vt., vi.* **thieved, thiev′ing** to steal —**thiev′ish** *adj.*

thiev·er·y (-ər ē) *n., pl.* -**ies** the act or an instance of stealing; theft

thigh (thī) *n.* ⟦OE *theoh*⟧ that part of the leg between the knee and the hip

thigh-bone *n.* FEMUR

thim·ble (thim′bəl) *n.* ⟦< OE *thuma*, a thumb⟧ a small protective cap worn over the end of the finger that pushes the needle in sewing —**thim′ble·ful′** *n., pl.* -**fuls′**

thin (thin) *adj.* **thin′ner, thin′nest** ⟦OE *thynne*⟧ 1 of relatively little extent from side to side 2 lean; slender 3 not dense or compact [*thin* hair] 4 very fluid or watery [*thin* soup] 5 high-pitched and weak [a *thin* voice] 6 sheer: said as of fabric 7 flimsy or unconvincing [a *thin* excuse] 8 lacking substance, depth, etc.; weak — *vt., vi.* **thinned, thin′ning** to make or become thin or thinner —**thin′ly** *adv.* —**thin′ness** *n.*

thine (thīn) [Archaic] *pron.* ⟦OE *thin*⟧ that or those belonging to thee: poss. form of THOU —*poss. pronominal adj.* thy: used esp. before a vowel

thing (thiŋ) *n.* ⟦OE, council⟧ 1 any matter, affair, or concern 2 a happening, act, incident, event, etc. 3 *a*) a tangible object *b*) an inanimate object 4 an item, detail, etc. 5 *a*) [*pl.*] personal belongings *b*) a garment 6 [Inf.] a person [poor *thing*] 7 [Inf.] a point of contention; issue 8 [Inf.] an irrational liking, fear, etc. 9 [Inf.] what one wants to do or is adept at [to do one's own *thing*] —**see things** [Inf.] to have hallucinations

think (thiŋk) *vt.* **thought, think′ing** ⟦OE *thencan*⟧ 1 to form or have in the mind [*thinking* good thoughts] 2 to judge; consider [many *think* her charming] 3 to believe [I *think* I can come] —*vi.* 1 to use the mind; reason 2 to have an opinion, etc.: with *of* or *about* 3 to remember or consider: with *of* or *about* 4 to conceive (*of*) —**think up** to invent, plan, etc. by thinking —**think′er** *n.*

think tank a group or center organized to do intensive research and problem-solving

thin·ner (thin′ər) *n.* a substance added to paint, shellac, etc. to thin it

thin-skinned *adj.* sensitive, as to insult

third (thurd) *adj.* ⟦OE *thridda*⟧ preceded by two others in a series; 3d or 3rd —*adv.* in the third place, etc.: also **third′ly** —*n.* 1 the one following the second 2 any of the three equal parts of something; ⅓ 3 the third forward gear of a transmission, providing more speed but less power than second

third-class *adj.* 1 of the class, rank, etc. next below the second 2 of a low-cost mail class, as for advertisements —*adv.* by third-class mail or travel accommodations

third degree [Inf.] harsh interrogation intended to extract a confession: with *the*

third dimension 1 depth 2 solidity

third person the form of a pronoun or verb that refers to a person or thing other than the speaker or the one spoken to

third-rate *adj.* 1 third in quality or other rating 2 inferior; very poor

Third World [*also* t- w-] the economically underdeveloped countries of the world

thirst (thurst) *n.* [OE *thurst*] 1 the discomfort caused by a need for water 2 a strong desire; craving —*vi.* 1 to feel thirst 2 to have a strong desire or craving —**thirst′y** *adj.* -i-er, -i-est —**thirst′i-ly** *adv.*

thir-teen (thur′tēn′) *adj., n.* [OE *threotyne*] three more than ten; 13; XIII —**thir′teenth′** *adj., n.*

thir-ty (thurt′ē) *adj., n., pl.* -ties [OE *thritig*] three times ten; 30; XXX —**the thirties** the numbers or years, as of a century, from 30 through 39 —**thir′ti-eth** (-ith) *adj., n.*

this (this) *pron., pl.* **these** [OE *thes*] 1 the person or thing mentioned [*this* is John] 2 the nearer one or another one [*this* is older than that] 3 something about to be presented [listen to *this*] —*adj., pl.* **these** 1 designating the person or thing mentioned [*this* man is John] 2 designating the nearer one or another one [*this* desk is older than that one] 3 designating something about to be presented [hear *this* news] —*adv.* to this extent [it was *this* big]

this-tle (this′əl) *n.* [OE *thistel*] a plant with prickly leaves and white, purple, etc. flowers

this-tle-down *n.* the down growing from the seeds of a thistle

thith-er (thith′ər, thith′-) *adv.* [OE *thider*] to or toward that place; there

tho or **tho'** (thō) *conj., adv. phonetic sp. of* THOUGH

thole (thōl) *n.* [OE *thol*] one of a pair of pins set as an oarlock into the gunwale of a boat: also **thole′pin′**

-thon (thän) *suffix* -ATHON: used after a vowel [*radiothon*]

thong (thôŋ) *n.* [OE *thwang*] 1 a narrow strip of leather, etc. used as a lace, strap, etc. 2 an extremely brief bikini bottom or undergarment like this

Thor (thôr) *n. Norse Myth.* the god of thunder, war, and strength

tho-rax (thôr′aks′) *n., pl.* -rax′es *or* -ra·ces′ (-ə sēz′) [< Gr] 1 the part of the body between the neck and the abdomen; chest 2 the middle segment of an insect's body —**tho·rac·ic** (thō ras′ik, thô-) *adj.*

Tho-reau (thôr′ō, thə rō′), **Henry David** 1817-62; U.S. writer

tho-ri-um (thôr′ē əm) *n.* [< THOR] a rare, grayish, radioactive, metallic chemical element, used as a nuclear fuel: symbol, Th; at. no. 90

thorn (thôrn) *n.* [OE] 1 *a)* a very short, hard, leafless stem with a sharp point *b)* any small tree or shrub bearing thorns 2 a source of constant trouble or irritation —**thorn′y** *adj.* -i-er, -i-est

thor-ough (thur′ō) *adj.* [var. of THROUGH] 1 omitting nothing; complete 2 absolute [a *thorough* rascal] 3 very exact, accurate, or painstaking —**thor′ough-ly** *adv.* —**thor′ough-ness** *n.*

thor-ough-bred (thur′ō bred′, thur′ə-) *adj.* of pure stock —*n.* [T-] any of a breed of light horse developed primarily for racing

thor-ough-fare (-fer′) *n.* a public street open at both ends, esp. a main highway

thor-ough-go-ing *adj.* very thorough

those (thōz) *pron., adj. pl. of* THAT

thou (thou) *pron., pl.* **you** or **ye** [OE *thu*] [Archaic] you: in poetic or religious use

though (thō) *conj.* [OE *theah*] 1 in spite of the fact that [*though* it rained, he went] 2 and yet [they can win, *though* no one thinks so] 3 even if [*though* he may fail, he will have tried] —*adv.* however; nevertheless [she sings well, *though*]

thought¹ (thôt) *n.* [OE *thoht*] 1 the act or process of thinking 2 the power of reasoning 3 an idea, concept, etc. 4 attention; consideration 5 mental concentration [deep in *thought*]

thought² (thôt) *vt., vi. pt. & pp. of* THINK

thought-ful *adj.* 1 full of thought 2 considerate of others —**thought′ful-ly** *adv.* —**thought′ful-ness** *n.*

thought-less *adj.* 1 not stopping to think; careless 2 ill-considered; rash 3 inconsiderate —**thought′less-ly** *adv.* —**thought′less-ness** *n.*

thou-sand (thou′zənd) *n., adj.* [OE *thusend*] ten hundred; 1,000; M —**thou′sandth** (-zəndth) *adj., n.*

thrall (thrôl) *n.* [< ON *thræll*] 1 [Now Chiefly Literary] a slave 2 the condition of being dominated or enslaved, esp. psychologically: now used chiefly in **hold in thrall** —**thrall′dom** *n.,* **thral′dom** (-dəm)

thrash (thrash) *vt., vi.* [OE *therscan*] 1 THRESH 2 to beat; flog 3 to toss about violently 4 to defeat overwhelmingly —**thrash out** to settle by detailed discussion

thrash-er *n.* [E dial. *thresher*] a thrushlike American songbird

thread (thred) *n.* [OE *thræd*] 1 a fine, string-like length of spun cotton, silk, nylon, etc. used in sewing 2 any thin line, vein, etc. 3 something like a thread in its length, sequence, etc. [the *thread* of a story] 4 the spiral ridge of a screw, nut, etc. —*vt.* 1 to put a thread through (a needle, etc.) 2 to make (one's way) by twisting, weaving, etc. 3 to fashion a THREAD (*n.* 4) on or in (a screw, pipe, etc.)

thread-bare *adj.* 1 worn down so that the

threads show [a *threadbare* rug] **2** wearing worn clothes; shabby **3** stale; trite

threat (thret) *n.* [OE *threat*, pressure] **1** an expression of intention to hurt, destroy, punish, etc., esp. when intended to coerce **2** an indication of, or a source of, imminent danger, harm, etc.

threat·en *vt., vi.* **1** to make threats, as of injury (against) **2** to indicate the likely occurrence of (something dangerous, unpleasant, etc.) **3** to be a source of danger (to)

three (thrē) *adj., n.* [OE *threo*] one more than two; 3; III

three-deck·er (-dek′ər) *n.* anything having three levels, layers, etc.

three-di·men·sion·al *adj.* having or seeming to have depth or thickness

three·fold *adj.* **1** having three parts **2** having three times as much or as many —*adv.* three times as much or as many

three R's reading, writing, and arithmetic, regarded as the fundamentals of an education: with *the*

three·score (thrē′skôr′) *adj., n.* sixty

thren·o·dy (thren′ə dē) *n., pl.* **-dies** [< Gr *thrēnos*, lamentation + *ōidē*, song] a song of lamentation; dirge

thresh (thresh) *vt., vi.* [ME *threschen*: see THRASH] **1** to beat out (grain) from (husks), as with a flail **2** THRASH —**thresh′er** *n.*

thresh·old (thresh′ōld′, -hōld′) *n.* [OE *therscwold*] **1** a length of wood, stone, etc. along the bottom of a doorway **2** the beginning point **3** a limit beyond which something occurs [a high *threshold* for pain]

threw (thrōō) *vt., vi.* pt. of THROW

thrice (thrīs) *adv.* [OE *thriwa*] **1** three times **2** threefold

thrift (thrift) *n.* [< ON *thrifa*, to grasp] economy; frugality —**thrift′less** *adj.* —**thrift′y** *adj.* **-i·er, -i·est** —**thrift′i·ly** *adv.* —**thrift′i·ness** *n.*

thrift shop a store where castoff clothes, etc. are sold to raise money for charity

thrill (thril) *vi., vt.* [< OE *thurh*, through] **1** to feel or cause to feel emotional excitement **2** to quiver or cause to quiver —*n.* a thrilling or being thrilled —**thrill′er** *n.*

thrive (thrīv) *vi.* **thrived** or **throve, thrived** or **thriv·en** (thriv′ən), **thriv′ing** [< ON *thrifa*, to grasp] **1** to prosper or flourish; be successful **2** to grow vigorously or luxuriantly

throat (thrōt) *n.* [OE *throte*] **1** the front part of the neck **2** the upper part of the passage from the mouth and nose to the stomach and lungs **3** any narrow passage

throat·y *adj.* **-i·er, -i·est** **1** produced in the throat: said of some sounds **2** husky; hoarse

throb (thräb) *vi.* **throbbed, throb′bing** [ME *throbben*] **1** to beat, pulsate, vibrate, etc., esp. strongly or fast **2** to feel excitement —*n.* **1** a throbbing **2** a strong beat or pulsation

throe (thrō) *n.* [prob. < OE *thrawu*, pain] a spasm or pang of pain: *usually used in pl.* [the throes *of* childbirth, death *throes*] —**in the throes of** in the act of struggling with (a problem, task, etc.)

throm·bo·sis (thräm bō′sis) *n.* [< Gr *thrombos*, a clot] coagulation of the blood in the heart or a blood vessel, forming a clot

throm·bus (thräm′bəs) *n.* **-bi′** (-bī′) [see prec.] the clot attached at the site of thrombosis

throne (thrōn) *n.* [< Gr *thronos*, a seat] **1** the chair on which a king, bishop, etc. sits on formal occasions **2** the power or rank of a king, etc.

throng (thrôŋ) *n.* [OE *thringan*, to crowd] **1** a crowd **2** any great number of things considered together —*vi.* to gather together in a throng —*vt.* to crowd into

throt·tle (thrät′'l) *n.* [prob. dim. of THROAT] the valve, or its control lever or pedal, that regulates the amount of fuel entering an engine —*vt.* **-tled, -tling 1** to strangle **2** to censor or suppress **3** to slow by means of a throttle

through (thrōō) *prep.* [OE *thurh*] **1** in one side and out the other side of **2** in the midst of; among **3** by way of **4** around [touring *through* France] **5** *a)* from the beginning to the end of *b)* up to and including **6** by means of **7** as a result of [done *through* error] —*adv.* **1** in one side and out the other **2** from the beginning to the end **3** completely to the end [to see something *through*] **4** completely [soaked *through*]: also **through and through** —*adj.* **1** extending from one place to another [a *through* street] **2** traveling to the destination without stops [a *through* train] **3** finished [*through* with the job]

through·out *prep.* all the way through —*adv.* in every part; everywhere

through·way *n.* alt. sp. of THRUWAY: see EXPRESSWAY

throve (thrōv) *vi.* alt. pt. of THRIVE

throw (thrō) *vt.* **threw, thrown, throw′ing** [OE *thrawan*, to twist] **1** to send through the air by a rapid motion of the arm, etc. **2** to cause to fall; upset **3** to send rapidly [to *throw* troops into battle] **4** to put suddenly into a specified state, etc. [*throw* into confusion] **5** to move (a switch, etc.) so as to connect, disconnect, etc. **6** to direct, cast, etc. [*throw* a glance] **7** [Inf.] to lose (a game, etc.) deliberately **8** [Inf.] to give (a party, etc.) **9** [Inf.] to confuse or disconcert [the question *threw* him] **10** [Inf.] to have (a tantrum, etc.) —*n.* **1** the act of one who throws **2** the distance something is or can be thrown [a stone's *throw*] **3** a spread for a bed, etc. —**throw away 1** to discard **2** to waste —**throw in** to add on free or add to others —**throw off 1** to rid oneself of **2** to mislead or confuse **3** to expel, emit, etc. —**throw oneself at** to try very hard to win the love of —**throw out 1** to discard **2** to reject or remove —**throw over 1** to give up; abandon **2** to jilt —**throw together** to assemble hurriedly —**throw up** to vomit —**throw′er** *n.*

throw·a·way *n.* a leaflet, handbill, etc. given out on the streets, etc. —*adj.* for discarding after use

throw·back *n.* (a) reversion to an earlier or more primitive type

throw rug SCATTER RUG

thru (thrōō) *prep., adv., adj. informal sp. of* THROUGH

thrush (thrush) *n.* 〚OE *thrysce*〛 any of a family of songbirds, including the robin

thrust (thrust) *vt., vi.* **thrust, thrust′ing** 〚< ON *thrysta*〛 **1** to push with sudden force **2** to stab **3** to force or impose —*n.* **1** a sudden, forceful push **2** a stab **3** continuous pressure, as of a rafter against a wall **4** the forward force produced by a propeller, a jet or rocket engine, etc. **5** forward movement **6** the basic meaning; point

thru·way (thrōō′wā′) *n.* EXPRESSWAY

Thu·cyd·i·des (thōō sid′i dēz′) 460?–400? B.C.; Athenian historian

thud (thud) *vi.* **thud′ded, thud′ding** 〚prob. < OE *thyddan*, to strike〛 to hit or fall with a dull sound —*n.* a dull sound, as of an object dropping on a soft surface

thug (thug) *n.* 〚Hindi *thag*, swindler〛 a brutal hoodlum, gangster, etc. —**thug′gish** *adj.*

thu·li·um (thōō′lē əm) *n.* 〚< *Thule*, the northernmost part of the ancient world〛 a bright, silvery chemical element used in portable X-ray units: symbol, Tm; at. no. 69

thumb (thum) *n.* 〚OE *thuma*〛 the short, thick digit of the hand —*vt.* **1** to handle, soil, etc. as with the thumb **2** [Inf.] to solicit or get (a ride) in hitchhiking by signaling with the thumb —**all thumbs** clumsy —**under someone's thumb** under someone's influence

thumb·nail *n.* the nail of the thumb —*adj.* very small, brief, or concise

thumb·screw *n.* **1** a screw designed to be turned by the thumb and forefinger **2** a former instrument of torture for squeezing the thumbs

thumb·tack *n.* a tack with a wide, flat head that can be pressed into a board, etc. with the thumb

thump (thump) *n.* 〚echoic〛 **1** a blow with something heavy and blunt **2** the dull sound made by such a blow —*vt.* to strike with a thump —*vi.* **1** to hit or fall with a thump **2** to make a dull, heavy sound

thump·ing *adj.* **1** that thumps **2** [Inf.] very large; whopping

thun·der (thun′dər) *n.* 〚OE *thunor*〛 **1** the sound following a flash of lightning **2** any similar sound, as of cannons or surf —*vi.* to produce thunder or a sound like this —*vt.* to say very loudly —**thun′der·ous** *adj.*

thun·der·bolt *n.* **1** a flash of lightning and the accompanying thunder **2** something sudden and shocking, as bad news

thun·der·clap *n.* a clap, or loud crash, of thunder

thun·der·cloud *n.* a storm cloud charged with electricity and producing lightning and thunder

thun·der·head *n.* a high, round mass of cumulus clouds appearing before a thunderstorm

thun·der·show·er *n.* a shower accompanied by thunder and lightning

thun·der·storm *n.* a storm accompanied by thunder and lightning

thun·der·struck *adj.* struck with amazement, terror, etc.: also **thun′der·strick′en** (-strik′ ən)

Thurs·day (thurz′dā) *n.* 〚< ON *Thorsdagr*, Thor's day〛 the fifth day of the week: abbrev. **Thur** or **Thurs**

thus (*thus*) *adv.* 〚OE〛 **1** in this or that manner **2** to this or that degree or extent **3** therefore **4** for example

thwack (thwak) *vt., n.* 〚prob. echoic〛 WHACK

thwart (thwôrt) *n.* 〚< ON *thvert*, transverse〛 a seat or brace extending across a boat —*vt.* to obstruct, frustrate, or defeat (a person, plans, etc.)

thy (*thī*) *poss. pronominal adj.* 〚< ME *thin*〛 *archaic or poet. var, of* YOUR

thyme (tīm) *n.* 〚< Gr *thymon*〛 an herb of the mint family, with small leaves used for seasoning

thy·mo·sin (thī′mə sin) *n.* 〚< Gr *thymos*, thymus〛 a hormone secreted by the thymus that stimulates the immune system

thy·mus (thī′məs) *n.* 〚Gr *thymos*〛 an endocrine gland situated near the throat: also **thymus gland**

thy·roid (thī′roid′) *adj.* 〚< Gr *thyreos*, large shield〛 designating or of a large endocrine gland near the trachea, secreting a hormone that regulates growth —*n.* **1** the thyroid gland **2** an animal extract of this gland, used in treating goiter

thy·self (*thī* self′) *pron.* [Archaic] *reflexive or intensive form of* THOU

ti (tē) *n. Music* the seventh tone of the diatonic scale

Ti *Chem. symbol for* titanium

Tian·jin (tyen′jin′) seaport in NE China

ti·a·ra (tē er′ə, -ar′-, -är′-) *n.* 〚< Gr〛 **1** the pope's triple crown **2** a woman's crownlike ornament for the head

Ti·ber (tī′bər) river in central Italy, flowing through Rome

Ti·bet (ti bet′) plateau region of SW China, north of the Himalayas —**Ti·bet′an** *adj., n.*

tib·i·a (tib′ē ə) *n., pl.* **-i·ae′** (-ē ē′) or **-i·as** 〚L〛 the inner and thicker of the bones of the lower leg

tic (tik) *n.* 〚Fr < ?〛 any involuntary, regularly repeated, spasmodic contraction of a muscle

tick¹ (tik) *n.* 〚prob. echoic〛 **1** a light clicking sound, as of a clock **2** a mark made to check off items —*vi.* to make a tick or ticks —*vt.* to record, mark, or check by ticks —**tick off** [Slang] to make angry

tick² (tik) *n.* 〚OE *ticia*〛 a wingless mite that sucks the blood of humans, cattle, etc.

tick³ (tik) *n.* 〚< ? L *theca*, a cover〛 the cloth case of a mattress or pillow

ticked (tikt) *adj.* 〚< TICK OFF〛 [Slang] angry, annoyed, irritated, etc.

tick·er *n.* **1** one that ticks **2** a telegraphic device for recording stock market quotations, etc. on a paper tape (**ticker tape**) **3** [Slang] the heart

tick·et (tik′it) *n.* [< obs. Fr *etiquet*, etiquette] 1 a printed card, etc. that gives one a right, as to attend a theater 2 a license or certificate 3 a label on merchandise giving size, price, etc. 4 the list of candidates nominated by a political party 5 a summons to court for a traffic violation —*vt.* 1 to label with a ticket 2 to give a ticket to

tick·ing *n.* strong cloth, often striped, used for casings of pillows, etc.

tick·le (tik′əl) *vt.* **-led, -ling** [ME *tikelen*] 1 to please, gratify, delight, etc. 2 to stroke lightly so as to cause involuntary twitching, laughter, etc. —*vi.* to have or cause an itching or tingling sensation —*n.* a sensation of being tickled

tick·ler (tik′lər) *n.* a pad, file, etc. for noting matters to be remembered

tick·lish (-lish) *adj.* 1 sensitive to tickling 2 needing careful handling; precarious; delicate

tic-tac-toe or **tick-tack-toe** (tik′tak tō′) *n.* a game for two, each marking X (or O) in turn in a nine-square grid so as to complete any one row before the other can

tick·tock (tik′täk′) *n.* the sound made by a clock or watch

tid·al (tīd′l) *adj.* of, having, or caused by a tide or tides

tidal wave 1 *nontechnical term for* a tsunami or a similar huge wave caused by strong winds 2 any widespread movement, feeling, etc.

tid·bit (tid′bit′) *n.* [dial. *tid*, small object] a choice bit of food, gossip, etc.

tid·dly·winks (tid′lē wiŋks′) *n.* [< ?] a game in which little disks are snapped into a cup by pressing their edges with a larger disk

tide (tīd) *n.* [OE *tid*, time] 1 a period of time: now only in combination [*Eastertide*] 2 the alternate rise and fall, about twice a day, of the surface of oceans, seas, etc., caused by the attraction of the moon and sun 3 something that rises and falls like the tide 4 a stream, trend, etc. —*vi.* **tid′ed, tid′ing** to help along temporarily: with *over*

tide·land *n.* land uncovered at low tide

tide·wa·ter *n.* 1 water that is affected by the tide 2 land that is affected by the tide —*adj.* of or along a tidewater

ti·dings (tī′diŋz) *pl.n.* [OE *tidung*] news; information

ti·dy (tī′dē) *adj.* **-di·er, -di·est** [<OE *tid*, time] 1 neat in appearance, arrangement, etc.; orderly 2 [Inf.] rather large [a *tidy* sum] —*vt., vi.* **-died, -dy·ing** to make tidy: often with *up* —ti′di·ness *n.*

tie (tī) *vt.* **tied, ty′ing** or **tie′ing** [< OE *teag*, a rope] 1 to bind, as with string, rope, etc. 2 to knot the laces, etc. of 3 to make (a knot) in 4 to bind in any way 5 to equal the score of, as in a contest —*vi.* to make an equal score, as in a contest —*n.* 1 a string, cord, etc. used to tie things 2 something that connects, binds, etc. 3 a necktie 4 a beam, rod, etc. that holds parts together 5 any of the crossbeams to which the rails of a railroad are fastened 6 *a)* an equality of scores, etc. *b)* a contest in which this occurs —*adj.* that has been made equal [a *tie* score] —**tie down** to confine; restrict —**tie up** 1 to wrap up and tie 2 to moor to a dock 3 to obstruct; hinder 4 to cause to be already in use, committed, etc.

tie·back *n.* a band or ribbon used to tie curtains, etc. to one side

tie·break·er *n.* an additional game, period of play, etc. used to establish a winner from among those tied at the end of a contest

tie clasp a decorative clasp for fastening a necktie to the shirt: also **tie clip**

tie-dye *n.* a method of dyeing designs on cloth by tying bunches of it so that the dye affects only exposed parts —*vt.* **-dyed′, -dye′ing** to dye in this way

tie-in *n.* 1 a sale or campaign in which one item is offered along with another 2 a connection or relationship

Tien·tsin (tyen′tsin′) *a former transliteration of* TIANJIN

tier (tir) *n.* [< OFr *tire*, order] any of a series of rows arranged one above or behind another

tie rod a rod connecting certain parts in the steering linkage of a motor vehicle

tie tack a decorative pin fitted into a snap to fasten a necktie to a shirt

tie-up (tī′up′) *n.* 1 a temporary stoppage of production, traffic, etc. 2 a connection

tiff (tif) *n.* [< ?] a slight quarrel; spat

Tif·fa·ny (tif′ə nē) *adj.* [after L. C. *Tiffany* (1848–1933), U.S. designer] of a style of stained glass, often translucent or mottled and employing subtly varied colors

ti·ger (tī′gər) *n.* [< Gr *tigris*] 1 a large, fierce Asian cat, having a tawny coat striped with black 2 one who is dynamic, fierce, etc.

tight (tīt) *adj.* [< OE -*thight*, strong] 1 so compact in structure that water, air, etc. cannot pass through 2 drawn, packed, etc. closely together 3 fixed securely; firm 4 fully stretched; taut 5 fitting so closely as to be uncomfortable 6 difficult: esp. in **a tight corner** (or **squeeze**, etc.), a difficult situation 7 showing tension, etc. [a *tight* smile] 8 almost tied [a *tight* race] 9 sharp; abrupt [a *tight* turn in the road] 10 difficult to get; scarce 11 [Inf.] stingy 12 [Slang] drunk 13 [Slang] very familiar —*adv.* 1 securely 2 [Inf.] soundly [sleep *tight*] —**sit tight** [Inf.] to keep one's opinion or position and wait —**tight′ly** *adv.* —**tight′ness** *n.*

tight·en *vt., vi.* to make or become tight or tighter —**tight′en·er** *n.*

tight end *Football* an offensive end positioned close to the tackle, usu. for blocking purposes

tight·fist·ed *adj.* stingy

tight·fit·ting *adj.* fitting very tight

tight-lipped *adj.* secretive

tight·rope *n.* a tightly stretched rope on which acrobats perform

tights *pl.n.* a tightly fitting garment for the lower half of the body, as worn by acrobats or dancers

tight ship [Inf.] an efficient, orderly, well-disciplined organization

tight·wad *n.* ⟦TIGHT + *wad*, roll of money⟧ [Slang] a stingy person

ti·gress (tī′gris) *n.* a female tiger

Ti·gris (tī′gris) river flowing from EC Turkey to a juncture with the Euphrates in SE Iraq

Ti·jua·na (tē′ə wä′nə) city in Baja California, NW Mexico, on the U.S. border

til·de (til′də) *n.* ⟦Sp < L *titulus*, a sign⟧ a diacritical mark (~)

tile (tīl) *n.* ⟦< L *tegula*⟧ 1 a thin piece of stone, fired clay, etc. used for roofing, flooring, etc. 2 a similar piece of plastic, etc. 3 a drain of earthenware pipe —*vt.* **tiled, til′ing** to cover with tiles

til·ing *n.* tiles collectively

till[1] (til) *prep., conj.* ⟦OE *til*⟧ UNTIL

till[2] (til) *vt., vi.* ⟦< OE *tilian*, lit., strive for⟧ to prepare (land) for raising crops, as by plowing

till[3] (til) *n.* ⟦< ? ME *tillen*, to draw⟧ a drawer for keeping money, as at a store

till·age *n.* 1 the tilling of land 2 land that is tilled

till·er[1] (til′ər) *n.* ⟦< ML *telarium*, a weaver's beam⟧ a bar or handle for turning a boat's rudder

till·er[2] (til′ər) *n.* a person or machine that tills the soil

tilt (tilt) *vt.* ⟦ME *tilten*, totter⟧ to cause to slant; tip —*vi.* 1 to slope; incline 2 to charge (*at an opponent*) 3 to take part in a tilt —*n.* 1 a medieval contest in which two horsemen fight with lances 2 any spirited contest 3 a slope —**(at) full tilt** at full speed

tilt-top *adj.* of a table with a hinged top that can be tipped vertically

tim·bale (tim′bəl) *n.* ⟦Fr⟧ 1 chicken, lobster, etc. in a cream sauce, baked in a drum-shaped mold 2 a pastry shell, filled with a cooked food

tim·ber (tim′bər) *n.* ⟦OE⟧ 1 wood for building houses, ships, etc. 2 a wooden beam used in building 3 trees collectively 4 personal quality or character —**tim′bered** *adj.*

tim·ber·line *n.* the line above or beyond which trees do not grow, as on mountains

tim·bre (tam′bər, tim′-) *n.* ⟦< OFr, kind of drum⟧ the quality of sound that distinguishes one voice or musical instrument from another

time (tīm) *n.* ⟦OE *tima*⟧ 1 every moment there has ever been or ever will be 2 a system of measuring duration [standard *time*] 3 the period during which something exists, happens, etc. 4 [*often pl.*] a period of history; age, era, etc. 5 [*usually pl.*] prevailing conditions [*times* are good] 6 a set period or term, as of work, confinement, etc. 7 standard rate of pay 8 rate of speed in marching, driving, etc. 9 a precise or designated instant, moment, day, etc. 10 an occasion or repeated occasion [the fifth *time* it's been on TV] 11 *Music a)* rhythm as determined by the grouping of beats into measures *b)* tempo 12 *Sports* TIMEOUT —*vt.* **timed, tim′ing** 1 to arrange the time of so as to be suit-

able, opportune, etc. 2 to adjust, set, etc. so as to coincide in time [*time* our watches] 3 to calculate the pace, speed, etc. of —*adj.* 1 having to do with time 2 set to explode, open, etc. at a given time [a *time* bomb] 3 having to do with paying in installments —**ahead of time** early —**at the same time** however —**at times** occasionally —**do time** [Inf.] to serve a prison term —**for the time being** temporarily —**from time to time** now and then —**in time** 1 eventually 2 before it is too late 3 keeping the set tempo, pace, etc. —**make time** to travel, work, etc. rapidly —**on time** 1 at the appointed time 2 for or by payment by installments —**time after time** again and again: also **time and again** —**time out** *Comput.* to cancel or disconnect automatically after a time —**time was** there was a time

time clock a clock with a mechanism for recording the time an employee begins and ends a work period

time frame a given period of time

time-hon·ored *adj.* honored because of long existence or usage

time·keep·er *n.* one who keeps account of hours worked by employees or of the elapsed time in races, games, etc.

time-lapse *adj.* of photographing a slow process by shooting images at long intervals: the images are then projected or displayed in quick succession, showing the process greatly speeded up

time·less *adj.* 1 eternal 2 always valid or true

time·line *n.* a chronological chart or list of events, dates, plans, etc.

time·ly *adj.* **-li·er, -li·est** well-timed; opportune —**time′li·ness** *n.*

time machine in science fiction, a device for conveying a person into the past or the future

time·out *n.* 1 *Sports* any temporary suspension of play 2 a disciplinary measure in which a child is sent to be alone for a while

time·piece *n.* any device for measuring and recording time, as a clock or watch

tim·er (tīm′ər) *n.* a device for controlling the timing of some mechanism

time-re·lease *adj.* releasing active ingredients gradually

times (tīmz) *prep.* multiplied by

time sharing 1 a system for simultaneous computer use at many remote sites 2 a system for sharing ownership of a vacation home, etc., with each joint purchaser occupying the unit at a specific time each year: also **time share**

time sheet a sheet on which are recorded the hours an employee works

time·ta·ble *n.* a schedule of events, such as the times of arrival and departure of airplanes, trains, buses, etc.

time-test·ed *adj.* having value proved by long use or experience

time warp displacement from one point in time to another, as in science fiction

time·worn *adj.* 1 worn out by long use 2 hackneyed; trite

time zone *see* STANDARD TIME

tim·id (tim′id) *adj.* ⟦< L *timere*, to fear⟧ lacking self-confidence; shy; fearful; hesitant —**ti·mid·i·ty** (tə mid′ə tē) *n.* —**tim′id·ly** *adv.*

tim·ing (tīm′iŋ) *n.* the regulation of pace or speed as it affects performance

tim·or·ous (tim′ər əs) *adj.* ⟦< L *timor*, fear⟧ full of fear; timid; afraid

tim·o·thy (tim′ə thē) *n.* ⟦after a *Timothy* Hanson, *c.* 1720⟧ a perennial grass with dense spikes, grown for hay

tim·pa·ni (tim′pə nē) *pl.n., sing.* **-no′** (-nō′) ⟦It: see TYMPANUM⟧ ⟦*often with sing. v.*⟧ kettledrums; esp., a set of them played by one performer —**tim′pa·nist** *n.*

tin (tin) *n.* ⟦OE⟧ **1** a soft, silver-white, metallic chemical element: symbol, Sn; at. no. 50 **2** TIN PLATE **3** *a)* a pan, box, etc. made of tin plate *b)* [Chiefly Brit.] CAN² (*n.* 2 & 3) Variously used to connote cheapness, etc. of something —*vt.* **tinned, tin′ning 1** to plate with tin **2** [Chiefly Brit.] CAN² (*vt.* 1)

tin can CAN² (*n.* 2)

tinc·ture (tiŋk′chər) *n.* ⟦< L *tingere*, to dye⟧ **1** a light color; tinge **2** a slight trace **3** a dilute solution of a medicinal substance in alcohol —*vt.* **-tured, -tur·ing** to tinge

tin·der (tin′dər) *n.* ⟦OE *tynder*⟧ any dry, easily flammable material

tin·der·box *n.* **1** [Obs.] a box to hold tinder **2** a highly flammable building, etc. **3** a potential source of war, rebellion, etc.

tine (tīn) *n.* ⟦OE *tind*⟧ a slender, projecting point; prong ⟦fork *tines*⟧

tin·foil *n.* **1** tin in thin sheets **2** aluminum in thin sheets, used for wrapping food, etc.

tinge (tinj) *n.* ⟦see TINT⟧ **1** a slight coloring; tint **2** a slight trace, flavor, etc. —*vt.* **tinged, tinge′ing** or **ting′ing** to give a tinge to

tin·gle (tiŋ′gəl) *vi.* **-gled, -gling** ⟦var. of TINKLE⟧ to have a prickling or stinging feeling, as from cold, excitement, etc. —*n.* this feeling —**tin′gly** *adj.*

tin·ker (tiŋk′ər) *n.* ⟦ME *tinkere*⟧ one who mends pots, pans, etc. —*vi.* to make unskillful or experimental adjustments or modifications to something

tin·kle (tiŋk′əl) *vi.* **-kled, -kling** ⟦echoic⟧ to make a series of light sounds as of a tiny bell —*vt.* to cause to tinkle —*n.* a tinkling sound

tin·ny (tin′ē) *adj.* **-ni·er, -ni·est 1** of or like tin **2** high-pitched and lacking resonance ⟦*tinny* music⟧ —**tin′ni·ness** *n.*

tin plate thin sheets of iron or steel plated with tin

tin·sel (tin′səl) *n.* ⟦< L *scintilla*, a spark⟧ **1** thin strips of tin, metal foil, etc., as for decoration **2** something of little worth that glitters

tin·smith *n.* one who works in tin or tin plate

tint (tint) *n.* ⟦< L *tingere*, to dye⟧ **1** a pale color **2** a gradation of a color; shade **3** a hair dye —*vt.* to give a tint to

tin·tin·nab·u·la·tion (tin′ti nab′yoo lā′shən) *n.* ⟦< L *tintinnabulum*, little bell⟧ the ringing sound of bells

tin·type (tin′tīp′) *n.* an early type of photograph taken directly as a positive print on a treated iron plate

ti·ny (tī′nē) *adj.* **-ni·er, -ni·est** ⟦< ME *tine*, *n.*, a little⟧ very small

-tion (shən) ⟦< Fr < L⟧ *suffix* **1** the act of ___ing **2** the state of being ___ed **3** the thing that is ___ed

-tious (shəs) *suffix* of, having, or characterized by

tip¹ (tip) *n.* ⟦ME *tippe*⟧ **1** the point or end of something **2** something attached to the end, as a cap, etc. —*vt.* **tipped, tip′ping 1** to form a tip on **2** to cover the tip of

tip² (tip) *vt.* **tipped, tip′ping** ⟦< ?⟧ **1** to strike lightly and sharply **2** to give a gratuity to (a waiter, etc.) **3** [Inf.] to give secret information to: often with *off* —*vi.* to give a tip or tips —*n.* **1** a light, sharp blow **2** a piece of confidential information **3** a hint, warning, etc. **4** a gratuity —**tip one's hand** [Inf.] to reveal a secret, one's plans, etc., often without meaning to —**tip′per** *n.*

tip³ (tip) *vt., vi.* **tipped, tip′ping** ⟦ME *tipen*⟧ **1** to overturn or upset: often with *over* **2** to tilt or slant —*n.* a tilt; slant

tip-off *n.* a tip; confidential disclosure, hint, or warning

tipping point the minimum level or degree required for something, as a trend, to begin or prevail

tip·ple (tip′əl) *vi., vt.* **-pled, -pling** ⟦< ?⟧ to drink (alcoholic liquor) habitually —**tip′pler** *n.*

tip·ster (tip′stər) *n.* [Inf.] one who sells tips, as on horse races or the stock market

tip·sy (tip′sē) *adj.* **-si·er, -si·est 1** that tips easily; not steady **2** somewhat drunk —**tip′si·ly** *adv.*

tip·toe *vi.* **-toed′, -toe′ing** to walk carefully, with the heels raised —**on tiptoe 1** standing with the heels raised **2** excited, alert, etc. **3** silently and stealthily

tip-top *n.* ⟦TIP¹ + TOP¹⟧ the highest point —*adj., adv.* **1** at the highest point **2** [Inf.] at the highest point of excellence, health, etc.

ti·rade (tī′rād′) *n.* ⟦< It *tirare*, to fire⟧ a long, vehement speech or denunciation; harangue

tire¹ (tīr) *vt., vi.* **tired, tir′ing** ⟦OE *tiorian*⟧ to make or become weary, exhausted, bored, etc.

tire² (tīr) *n.* ⟦ME *tyre*⟧ **1** a hoop of iron or rubber around the wheel of a vehicle **2** an inflatable, vulcanized rubber or synthetic casing sealed to a wheel rim by air pressure

tired (tīrd) *adj.* **1** weary **2** hackneyed —**tired′ly** *adv.* —**tired′ness** *n.*

tire iron a crowbar with a built-in wrench, for changing automobile tires

tire·less *adj.* persistent, unwavering, etc. —**tire′less·ly** *adv.* —**tire′less·ness** *n.*

tire·some (-səm) *adj.* **1** tiring; boring **2** annoying —**tire′some·ly** *adv.* —**tire′some·ness** *n.*

Ti·rol (ti rōl′, -räl′) E Alpine region in W Austria & N Italy —**Ti·ro·le·an** (ti rō′lē ən, tī-) *adj., n.*

'tis (tiz) *contr.* [Old Poet.] it is

tis·sue (tish′o͞o) *n.* [< L *texere*, to weave] 1 light, thin cloth 2 an interwoven mass; mesh; web 3 a piece of soft, absorbent paper, used as a disposable handkerchief, etc. 4 TISSUE PAPER 5 the substance of an organic body, consisting of cells and intercellular material

tissue paper very thin wrapping paper

tit[1] (tit) *n.* a titmouse

tit[2] (tit) *n.* [OE] 1 NIPPLE (*n.* 1) 2 a woman's breast: in this sense somewhat vulgar

ti·tan (tīt′'n) *n.* [< Gr *Titan*, a giant deity] any person or thing of great size or power

ti·tan·ic (tī tan′ik) *adj.* of great size, strength, or power

ti·ta·ni·um (tī tā′nē əm) *n.* [see TITAN] a silvery or dark-gray, metallic chemical element used in manufacturing: symbol, Ti; at. no. 22

tit for tat [var. of earlier *tip for tap*] this for that: phrase indicating retribution

tithe (tīth) *n.* [OE *teothe*, a tenth] a tenth of one's income paid to a church —*vi.* **tithed**, **tith′ing** to pay a tithe

tit·il·late (tit′'l āt′) *vt.* -**lat′ed**, -**lat′ing** [< L *titillare*, tickle] to excite pleasurably —**tit′il·la′tion** *n.*

ti·tle (tīt′'l) *n.* [< L *titulus*] 1 the name of a book, poem, picture, etc. 2 an epithet 3 an appellation indicating one's rank, profession, etc. 4 a claim 5 *Film, TV* a subtitle, credit, etc. 6 *Law a)* a right to ownership, esp. of real estate *b)* a deed 7 *Sports, etc.* a championship —*vt.* -**tled**, -**tling** to give a title to

ti·tled *adj.* having a title, esp. of nobility

ti·tle·hold·er *n.* the holder of a title; specif., the champion in some sport

title role (*or* **character**) the character in a play, film, etc. whose name is used as or in its title

ti·tlist (tīt′'l ist) *n.* a champion in some sport

tit·mouse (tit′mous′) *n., pl.* -**mice** (-mīs′) [ME *titemose*] a small bird with ashy-gray feathers

tit·ter (tit′ər) *vi.* [echoic] to laugh in a half-suppressed way; giggle —*n.* a tittering

tit·tle (tit′'l) *n.* [ME *title*] a very small particle; jot

tit·u·lar (tich′ə lər, tit′yə-) *adj.* [see TITLE] 1 of a title 2 having a title 3 in name only [a *titular* sovereign]

tiz·zy (tiz′ē) *n., pl.* -**zies** [< ?] [Inf.] a state of frenzied excitement

tko *or* **TKO** *n. Boxing* a technical knockout

TLC *abbrev.* tender, loving care

TM *abbrev.* trademark

tn *abbrev.* ton(s)

TN *abbrev.* Tennessee

TNT *n.* [*t*(*ri*)*n*(*itro*)*t*(*oluene*)] a high explosive used for blasting, etc.

to (to͞o, too, tə) *prep.* [OE] 1 toward [turn to the left] 2 so as to reach [she went to Boston] 3 as far as [wet to the skin] 4 into a condition of [a rise to fame] 5 *a)* on, onto, against, at, etc. [tied to a post] *b)* in front of [face to face] 6 *a)* until [from noon to night] *b)* before [the time is ten to six] 7 for the purpose of [come to dinner] 8 as regards [open to attack] 9 with the result of producing [torn to bits] 10 along with [add this to the rest] 11 belonging with [a key to the house] 12 as compared with [a score of 10 to 0] 13 in agreement with [not to my taste] 14 constituting [four quarts to a gallon] 15 with (a specified person or thing) as the recipient of the action [give it to me] 16 in honor of [a toast to you] 17 by [known to me] *To* is also a sign of the infinitive (Ex.: I want to stay) —*adv.* 1 forward [wrong side to] 2 shut; closed [pull the door to] 3 into a state of consciousness [the boxer came to] —**to and fro** first in one direction and then in the opposite

toad (tōd) *n.* [OE *tadde*] a froglike amphibian that lives on moist land

toad·stool (-sto͞ol′) *n.* a mushroom; esp., any poisonous mushroom

toad·y (tō′dē) *n., pl.* -**ies** [short for *toadeater*, quack doctor's assistant] a servile flatterer —*vt., vi.* -**ied**, -**y·ing** to be a toady (to)

toast[1] (tōst) *vt.* [< L *torrere*, parch] 1 to brown the surface of (bread, cheese, etc.) by heating 2 to warm thoroughly —*vi.* to become toasted —*n.* sliced bread made brown and crisp by heat —**toast′er** *n.*

toast[2] (tōst) *n.* [from the use of toasted spiced bread to flavor the wine] 1 a drink, or a proposal to drink, in honor of some person, etc. 2 someone greatly admired or acclaimed [the *toast* of Broadway] —*vt., vi.* to propose or drink a toast (to)

toast·mas·ter *n.* the person at a banquet who proposes toasts, introduces after-dinner speakers, etc.

toast·y *adj.* -**i·er**, -**i·est** warm and comfortable or cozy

to·bac·co (tə bak′ō) *n., pl.* -**cos** [Sp *tabaco* < ?] 1 a plant with large leaves that contain nicotine and are used for smoking, chewing, etc. 2 cigars, cigarettes, etc.

to·bac·co·nist (tə bak′ə nist) *n.* a dealer in tobacco

to·bog·gan (tə bäg′ən) *n.* [< AmInd] a long, flat sled without runners, for coasting down-hill —*vi.* 1 to coast on a toboggan 2 to decline rapidly

toc·ca·ta (tə kät′ə) *n.* a musical work in free style for the organ, piano, etc., often a prelude to a fugue

toc·sin (täk′sin) *n.* [Fr < Prov *toc*, a stroke + *senh*, a bell] an alarm bell or its sound

to·day (tə dā′) *adv.* [OE < *dæg*] 1 on or during the present day 2 in the present time —*n.* 1 the present day 2 the present time

tod·dle (täd′'l) *vi.* -**dled**, -**dling** [? < *totter*] to walk with short, uncertain steps

tod·dler *n.* a very young child, esp. one just learning to walk

tod·dy (täd′ē) *n., pl.* -**dies** [< Hindi] a drink of whiskey, etc. mixed with hot water, sugar, etc.: also **hot toddy**

to-do (tə do͞o′) *n., pl.* -**dos′** [Inf.] a commotion; fuss

toe (tō) *n.* [OE *ta*] 1 *a)* any of the digits of the foot *b)* the forepart of the foot 2 any-

thing like a toe in location, shape, or use —*vt.*
toed, toe′ing to touch, kick, etc. with the toes —*vi.* to stand, walk, etc. with the toes in a specified position [he *toes* in] —**on one's toes** [Inf.] alert —**toe the line (or mark)** to follow orders, rules, etc. strictly

toed (tōd) *adj.* having (a specified kind or number of) toes: usually in compounds [two-*toed*]

toe dance a dance performed on the tips of the toes, as in ballet —**toe′-dance′** *vi.* **-danced′, -danc′ing** —**toe′-danc′er** *n.*

toe·hold *n.* 1 a small space to support the toe in climbing, etc. 2 a slight footing or advantage

toe·less *adj.* having the toe open or uncovered [a *toeless* shoe]

toe·nail *n.* the nail of a toe

toe-to-toe *adv.* in direct competition

tof·fee (tôf′ē, täf′ē) *n.* [< TAFFY] a hard, chewy candy, a kind of taffy

to·fu (tō′fōō) *n.* [Jpn] a food consisting of pressed soybean curds

to·ga (tō′gə) *n., pl.* **-gas** *or* **-gae** (-jē, -gē) [L < *tegere*, to cover] in ancient Rome, a loose outer garment worn in public by male citizens

to·geth·er (tə geth′ər) *adv.* [< OE *to*, to + *gædre*, together] 1 in or into one group, place, etc. [we ate *together*] 2 in or into contact, union, etc. [the cars skidded *together*] 3 considered collectively [he lost more than all of us *together*] 4 at the same time [gunshots fired *together*] 5 in succession [sulking for three days *together*] 6 in or into agreement, cooperation, etc. [to get *together* on a deal] —*adj.* 1 with one another; not apart 2 [Slang] having a harmoniously organized personality

to·geth·er·ness *n.* the sense of unity fostered, as in a family, by spending time together

tog·gle switch (täg′əl) a switch consisting of a lever moved back and forth to open or close an electric circuit

To·go (tō′gō) country on the W coast of Africa

togs (tägz, tôgz) *pl.n.* [ult. < L *toga*, toga] [Inf.] clothes

toil (toil) *vi.* [< L *tudiculare*, to stir about] 1 to work hard and continuously 2 to proceed laboriously —*n.* hard, tiring work —**toil′er** *n.*

toi·let (toi′lit) *n.* [< OFr *toile*, cloth < L *tela*, a web] 1 TOILETTE 2 (a room with) a bowl-shaped fixture for defecation or urination

toilet paper (*or* **tissue**) soft paper for cleaning oneself after defecation or urination

toi·let·ry (-lə trē) *n., pl.* **-ries** soap, lotion, etc. used in grooming oneself

toi·lette (twä let′, toi-) *n.* [Fr] 1 the process of grooming oneself 2 dress; attire

toilet water a lightly scented liquid containing alcohol, applied to the skin after bathing, etc.

toils (toilz) *pl.n.* [< L *tela*, web] any snare suggestive of a net

toil·some (toil′səm) *adj.* laborious

toke (tōk) [Slang] *n.* [? < fol.] a puff on a cigarette, esp. one of marijuana or hashish —*vi.* **toked, tok′ing** to take such a puff

to·ken (tō′kən) *n.* [OE *tacn*] 1 a sign, indication, symbol, etc. [a *token* of one's affection] 2 a keepsake 3 a metal disk to be used in place of currency, as for transportation fares 4 one included in a group to avoid the appearance of discrimination —*adj.* 1 symbolic 2 merely simulated; slight [*token* resistance] —**by the same token** for the same reason

to·ken·ism *n.* the making of small, often merely formal concessions to a demand, etc.; specif., token integration of blacks, as in jobs

To·ky·o (tō′kē ō′) capital of Japan, on S Honshu

told (tōld) *vt., vi. pt. & pp. of* TELL —**all told** all things considered

tole (tōl) *n.* [Fr *tôle*, sheet iron] a type of lacquered or enameled metalware used for lamps, trays, etc.

tol·er·a·ble (täl′ər ə bəl) *adj.* 1 endurable 2 fairly good; passable —**tol′er·a·bly** *adv.*

tol·er·ance (-əns) *n.* 1 a being tolerant of others' views, beliefs, practices, etc. 2 the amount of variation allowed from a standard 3 *Med.* the (developed) resistance to the effects of a drug, etc.

tol·er·ant (-ənt) *adj.* having or showing tolerance of others' beliefs, etc.

tol·er·ate (-āt′) *vt.* **-at′ed, -at′ing** [< L *tolerare*, to bear] 1 to allow 2 to respect (others' beliefs, practices, etc.) without sharing them 3 to bear (someone or something disliked); put up with 4 *Med.* to have tolerance for —**tol′er·a′tion** *n.*

toll[1] (tōl) *n.* [ult. < Gr *telos*, tax] 1 a tax or charge for a privilege, as for the use of a turnpike 2 a charge for service, as for a long-distance telephone call 3 the number lost, etc. [the tornado took a heavy *toll* of lives]

toll[2] (tōl) *vt.* [ME *tollen*, to pull] 1 to ring (a church bell, etc.) with slow, regular strokes 2 to announce, summon, etc. by this —*vi.* to ring slowly: said of a bell —*n.* the sound of a bell tolling

toll·booth *n.* a booth at which a toll is collected, as before entering a toll road

toll·gate *n.* a gate for stopping travel to collect a toll

toll road *n.* a road on which a toll must be paid: also **toll′way′** *n.*

Tol·stoy *or* **Tol·stoi** (tōl′stoi′), Count **Le·o** (lē′ō) 1828–1910; Russ. novelist

tol·u·ene (täl′yōō ēn′) *n.* [Sp *tolu*, after *Tolú*, seaport in Colombia + (BENZ)ENE] a colorless, poisonous liquid obtained from coal tar or petroleum and used in making dyes, explosives, etc.

tom (täm) *adj.* [after the name *Tom*] male [a *tomcat*, a tom turkey]

tom·a·hawk (täm′ə hôk′) *n.* [< AmInd] a light ax used by North American Indians as a tool and a weapon

to·ma·to (tə māt′ō, -mät′ō) *n., pl.* **-toes** [< AmInd (Mexico)] 1 a red or yellowish edible fruit with a juicy and somewhat sweet pulp 2 the plant it grows on

tomb (tōōm) *n.* [< Gr *tymbos*] a vault or grave for the dead

tom·boy (täm′boi′) *n.* a girl who behaves in ways considered typical of active boys

tomb·stone (tōōm′stōn′) *n.* a stone or monument marking a tomb or grave

tom·cat (täm′kat′) *n.* a male cat

tome (tōm) *n.* [< Gr *tomos*, piece cut off] a book, esp. a large one

tom·fool·er·y (täm′fōōl′ər ē) *n.*, *pl.* **-ies** foolish behavior; silliness

tom·my gun (täm′ē) [*sometimes* T- g-] [Inf.] a submachine gun

to·mog·ra·phy (tə mäg′rə fē) *n.* [< Gr *temnein*, to cut + -GRAPHY] an X-ray process for producing an image of a single plane of an object, used in medical diagnosis

to·mor·row (tə mär′ō, -môr′-) *adv.* [OE *to morgen*] on the day after today —*n.* the day after today

tom·tit (täm tit′, täm′tit′) *n.* [Chiefly Brit.] a titmouse or other small bird

tom-tom (täm′täm′) *n.* [Hindi *ṭamṭam*] a simple kind of drum, usually beaten with the hands

-to·my (tə mē) [< Gr < *tomē*, a cutting] combining form a surgical operation

ton (tun) *n.* [var. of TUN] 1 a unit of weight equal to 2,000 pounds 2 in Great Britain, a unit of weight equal to 2,240 pounds 3 in the metric system, a unit of weight equal to 1,000 kilograms

ton·al (tōn′nəl) *adj.* of a tone —**ton′al·ly** *adv.*

to·nal·i·ty (tō nal′ə tē) *n.*, *pl.* **-ties** Music 1 KEY¹ (*n.* 6) 2 tonal character, as determined by the relationship of the tones to the keynote

tone (tōn) *n.* [< Gr *teinein*, to stretch] 1 a vocal or musical sound, or its quality as to pitch, intensity, etc. 2 a manner of expression showing a certain attitude [a friendly *tone*] 3 style, character, spirit, etc. 4 elegance 5 a quality of color; shade 6 normal, healthy condition of a muscle, organ, etc. 7 Music *a*) a sound of distinct pitch *b*) any of the full intervals of a diatonic scale —*vt.* **toned, ton′ing** to give a tone to —**tone down** (or **up**) to give a less (or more) intense tone to —**tone′less** *adj.*

tone·arm *n.* the pivoted arm beside a phonograph turntable, holding the stylus

tone-deaf *adj.* 1 unable to distinguish differences in musical pitch 2 [Inf.] insensitive to how one's statements may cause offense, be misinterpreted, etc.

ton·er (tō′nər) *n.* 1 the black or colored powder used to form images in xerography 2 a facial cleanser

tone row (*or* **series**) see TWELVE-TONE

tong (tôŋ, täŋ) *n.* [Mandarin *t'ang*, meeting place] a Chinese association, society, etc.

Ton·ga (täŋ′gə) kingdom on a group of islands (**Tonga Islands**) in the SW Pacific, east of Fiji —**Ton′gan** *n.*

tongs (tôŋz, täŋz) *pl.n.* [OE *tange*] [*sometimes with sing. v.*] a device for seizing or lifting objects, having two long arms pivoted or hinged together

tongue (tuŋ) *n.* [OE *tunge*] 1 the movable, muscular structure in the mouth, used in eating, tasting, and (in humans) speaking 2 talk; speech 3 the act, power, or manner of speaking 4 a language or dialect 5 something like a tongue in shape, position, use, etc., as the flap under the laces of a shoe —**hold one's tongue** to refrain from speaking —**speak in tongues** to utter unintelligible sounds, as while in a religious trance —**(with) tongue in cheek** in a humorously ironic or insincere way —**tongue′less** *adj.*

tongue-and-groove joint a joint in which a projection on one board fits into a groove in another

tongue-lash·ing *n.* [Inf.] a harsh scolding or reproving; reprimand

tongue-tied *adj.* speechless from amazement, embarrassment, etc.

tongue twister a phrase or sentence hard to say fast (Ex.: six sick sheiks)

ton·ic (tän′ik) *adj.* [see TONE] 1 of or producing good muscular tone 2 Music designating or based on a keynote —*n.* 1 anything that invigorates, as a drug or medicine 2 a quinine-flavored beverage served with gin, vodka, etc.: also **tonic water** 3 Music a keynote

to·night (tə nit′) *adv.* [OE to *niht*] on or during the present or coming night —*n.* the present or coming night

ton·nage (tun′ij) *n.* 1 the total amount of shipping of a country or port, calculated in tons 2 the carrying capacity of a ship, calculated in tons

ton·sil (tän′səl) *n.* [L *tonsillae*, pl.] either of a pair of oval masses of tissue at the back of the mouth

ton·sil·lec·to·my (tän′sə lek′tə mē) *n.*, *pl.* **-mies** [prec. + -ECTOMY] the surgical removal of the tonsils

ton·sil·li·tis (-līt′is) *n.* [ModL < L *tonsillae*, tonsils + -ITIS] inflammation of the tonsils

ton·so·ri·al (tän sôr′ē əl) *adj.* [see fol.] of a barber or barbering: often humorous [a *tonsorial* artist]

ton·sure (tän′shər) *n.* [< L *tondere*, to clip] 1 a shaving off of part of the hair of the head, done as a sign of entrance into the clerical or monastic state 2 the head area so shaved

ton·y (tō′nē) *adj.* **-i·er, -i·est** [Slang] very elegant and high-class

too (tōō) *adv.* [stressed form of TO] 1 in addition; also 2 more than enough [the hat is *too* big] 3 extremely; very [it was just *too* delicious!]

took (took) *vt.*, *vi. pt. of* TAKE

tool (tōōl) *n.* [OE *tol*] 1 any hand implement, instrument, etc. used for some work 2 any similar instrument that is the working part of a machine, as a drill 3 anything that serves as a means 4 a stooge —*vt.* to impress designs on (leather, etc.) with a tool —*vi.* to install the tools, equipment, etc. needed: often with *up*

toot (tōōt) *vi.*, *vt.* [echoic] to sound (a horn,

whistle, etc.) in short blasts —*n.* a short blast of a horn, whistle, etc.

tooth (tōōth) *n., pl.* **teeth** (tēth) [OE *toth*] **1** any of the hard, bonelike structures in the jaws, used for biting, chewing, etc. **2** a tooth-like part, as on a saw, comb, gearwheel, etc.; tine, prong, cog, etc. **3** [*pl.*] effective means of enforcement [a law with *teeth*] —**tooth and nail** with all one's strength —**toothed** *adj.* —**tooth′less** *adj.*

tooth·ache *n.* pain in a tooth

tooth·brush *n.* a small brush for cleaning the teeth

tooth·paste *n.* a paste used for brushing the teeth

tooth·pick *n.* a very small, pointed stick for removing bits of food from between the teeth

tooth powder a powder used like toothpaste

tooth·some (-səm) *adj.* tasty; savory

tooth·y *adj.* **-i·er, -i·est** having or exposing teeth that show prominently —**tooth′i·ly** *adv.*

top¹ (täp) *n.* [OE] **1** the head or crown **2** the highest point or surface of anything **3** the part of a plant above ground **4** the uppermost part or covering, as a lid, cap, etc. **5** the highest degree [at the *top* of his voice] **6** the highest rank [the *top* of the class] **7** a garment for the upper body —*adj.* of, at, or being the top; highest or foremost —*vt.* **topped, top′ping 1** to take off the top of (a plant, etc.) **2** to provide with a top **3** to be a top for **4** to reach the top of **5** to exceed in amount, etc. **6** to surpass; outdo —**blow one's top** [Slang] to lose one's temper —**on top** successful —**on top of 1** resting upon **2** besides **3** controlling successfully —**top off** to complete by adding a finishing touch —**top′per** *n.*

top² (täp) *n.* [OE] a toy with a wide body and a narrow base, tapering to a point upon which it is spun

to·paz (tō′paz′) *n.* [< *L* *topazos*] any of various yellow gems, esp. a variety of aluminum silicate

top brass [Slang] important officials

top·coat *n.* a lightweight overcoat

top-drawer (-drôr′) *adj.* of first importance

top-dress·ing *n.* material applied to a surface, as fertilizer on land

To·pe·ka (tə pē′kə) capital of Kansas

top·er (tō′pər) *n.* [< archaic *tope*, to drink (much liquor)] a drunkard

top-flight *adj.* [Inf.] first-rate

top hat a man's tall, black, cylindrical silk hat, worn in formal dress

top-heav·y *adj.* too heavy at the top, so as to be unstable

top·ic (täp′ik) *n.* [ult. < Gr *topos*, place] the subject of an essay, speech, discussion, etc.

top·i·cal *adj.* dealing with topics of the day; of current or local interest

top·knot *n.* a tuft of hair or feathers on the top of the head

top·less *adj.* without a top: said as of a costume exposing the breasts

top-lev·el *adj.* of or by persons of the highest office or rank

top·mast *n.* the second mast above the deck of a sailing ship, supported by the lower mast

top·most *adj.* at the very top

top-notch *adj.* [Inf.] first-rate; excellent

to·pog·ra·phy (tə päg′rə fē) *n., pl.* **-phies** [see TOPIC & -GRAPHY] **1** the science of representing surface features of a region on maps and charts **2** these surface features —**top·o·graph·ic** (täp′ə graf′ik) *adj.*, **top′o·graph′i·cal**

top·ping (täp′iŋ) *n.* something put on top of something else, as a condiment on food

top·ple (täp′əl) *vi.* **-pled, -pling** [< TOP¹] to fall top forward; fall (*over*) because top-heavy, etc. —*vt.* **1** to cause to topple; overturn **2** to depose [*topple* a dictator]

top·sail (täp′sāl′; *naut.*, -səl) *n.* in a square-rigged vessel, the square sail next above the lowest sail on a mast

top-se·cret *adj.* designating or of the most secret information

top·side *adv.* on or to an upper deck or the main deck of a ship

top·soil *n.* the upper layer of soil, usually richer than the subsoil

top·sy-tur·vy (täp′sē tur′vē) *adv., adj.* [prob. < *top*, highest part + ME *terven*, to roll] **1** upside down; in a reversed condition **2** in disorder

toque (tōk) *n.* [Fr] a woman's small, round, usually brimless hat

To·rah (tō′rə, tô′rə) [*occas.* t-] *n.* [< Heb, law] **1** the body of Jewish religious literature **2** the Pentateuch

torch (tôrch) *n.* [see TORQUE] **1** a portable flaming light **2** a device for producing a very hot flame, as in welding **3** [Brit.] a flashlight —*vt.* [Slang] to set fire to, as in arson

torch·bear·er *n.* **1** one who carries a torch **2** *a)* one who brings enlightenment, truth, etc. *b)* an inspirational leader, as in some movement

torch·light *n.* the light of a torch or torches —*adj.* done by torchlight

torch song a sentimental song of unrequited love —**torch singer**

tore (tôr) *vt., vi. pt. of* TEAR¹

tor·e·a·dor (tôr′ē ə dôr′) *n.* [Sp < L *taurus*, a bull] a bullfighter

tor·ment (tôr′ment′; *for v.* tôr ment′) *n.* [OFr < L; see TORQUE] **1** great pain or anguish **2** a source of pain, anxiety, etc. —*vt.* **1** to cause great physical pain or mental anguish in **2** to annoy; harass —**tor·ment′ing·ly** *adv.* —**tor·men′tor** *n.*, **tor·ment′er**

torn (tôrn) *vt., vi. pp. of* TEAR¹

tor·na·do (tôr nā′dō) *n., pl.* **-does** or **-dos** [< Sp < L *tonare*, to thunder] a violently whirling column of air seen as a funnel-shaped cloud that usually destroys everything in its narrow path

To·ron·to (tə ränt′ō) capital of Ontario, Canada

tor·pe·do (tôr pē′dō) *n., pl.* **-does** [< L: see fol.] **1** a large, cigar-shaped, self-propelled underwater projectile containing explosives **2** any of various explosive devices —*vt.* **-doed, -do·ing** to attack, destroy, etc. as with a torpedo

tor·pid (tôr′pid) *adj.* [< L *torpere*, be numb] **1** dormant or inactive **2** dull; sluggish

tor·por (-pər) *n.* [L] **1** a torpid state; sluggishness; stupor **2** dullness; apathy

torque (tôrk) *n.* [< L *torquere*, to twist] **1** *Physics* a measure of the tendency of a force to cause rotation **2** a forceful twist —*vt.* **torqued, torqu′ing** to twist forcefully

tor·rent (tôr′ənt, tär′-) *n.* [< L *torrens*, rushing] **1** a swift, violent stream, esp. of water **2** a flood or rush of words, mail, etc. —**tor·ren·tial** (tô ren′shəl) *adj.*

tor·rid (tôr′id, tär′-) *adj.* [< L *torrere*, to dry] **1** subjected to intense heat, esp. of the sun; parched **2** very hot; scorching **3** passionate; ardent

Torrid Zone the tropics

tor·sion (tôr′shən) *n.* [see TORQUE] **1** a twisting or being twisted **2** the stress produced in a rod, wire, etc. by twisting along a longitudinal axis

tor·so (tôr′sō) *n., pl.* **-sos** or **-si** (-sē) [< Gr *thyrsos*, a stem] the trunk of the human body

tort (tôrt) *n.* [< L *torquere*, to twist] *Law* a wrongful act or damage (not involving a breach of contract), for which a civil action can be brought

torte (tôrt; *Ger* tôr′tə) *n., pl.* **tortes** or Ger. **tor·ten** (tôr′tən) [Ger < It < LL *torta*, a twisted bread] a rich cake, as one made of eggs, finely chopped nuts, crumbs, etc.

tor·tel·li·ni (tôrt′ə lē′nē) *n.* [It] pasta in tiny ring-shaped pieces filled with meat, etc.

tor·til·la (tôr tē′ə) *n.* [Sp, dim. of *torta*, a cake] a flat cake of unleavened cornmeal or flour

tor·toise (tôrt′əs) *n.* [< ? c. 4th-c. Gr *tartarouchos*, evil demon] a turtle, esp. one that lives on land

tor·toise-shell *n.* **1** the hard, mottled, yellow-and-brown shell of some turtles **2** a synthetic substance resembling this

tor·to·ni (tôr tō′nē) *n.* [prob. alt. < It *tortone*, lit., big pastry tart] an ice cream made with heavy cream, maraschino cherries, almonds, etc.

tor·tu·ous (tôr′chōō əs) *adj.* [see TORQUE] **1** full of twists, turns, etc.; crooked **2** deceitful or tricky

tor·ture (tôr′chər) *n.* [see TORQUE] **1** the inflicting of severe pain, as to elicit information or force a confession **2** any severe physical or mental pain; agony —*vt.* **-tured, -tur·ing 1** to subject to torture **2** to twist or distort (meaning, etc.) —**tor′tur·er** *n.*

To·ry (tôr′ē) *n., pl.* **-ries** [Ir *tóruidhe*, robber] **1** after 1689, a member of the major conservative party of England **2** in the American Revolution, one loyal to Great Britain **3** [*often* t-] any extreme conservative

toss (tôs, täs) *vt.* [prob. < Scand] **1** to throw about [*waves tossed* the boat] **2** to throw lightly from the hand **3** to jerk upward [to *toss* one's head] —*vi.* **1** to be thrown about **2** to fling oneself about in sleep, etc. —*n.* a tossing or being tossed

toss·up *n.* [Inf.] **1** the flipping of a coin to decide something **2** an even chance

tot¹ (tät) *n.* [prob. < ON] **1** a young child **2** [Chiefly Brit.] a small drink of alcoholic liquor

tot² (tät) *vt., vi.* **tot′ted, tot′ting** [Inf., Chiefly Brit.] to total: with *up*

to·tal (tōt′'l) *adj.* [< L *totus*, all] **1** constituting a whole **2** complete; utter [a total loss] —*n.* the whole amount; sum —*vt.* **-taled** or **-talled, -tal·ing** or **-tal·ling 1** to find the total of **2** to add up to **3** [Slang] to demolish —**to′tal·ly** *adv.*

to·tal·i·tar·i·an (tō tal′ə ter′ē ən) *adj.* [prec. + (AUTHOR)ITARIAN] designating or of a government in which one political group maintains complete control, esp. under a dictator —*n.* one who favors such a government —**to·tal′i·tar′i·an·ism′** *n.*

to·tal·i·ty (tō tal′ə tē) *n., pl.* **-ties** the total amount or sum

tote (tōt) *vt.* **tot′ed, tot′ing** [< ?] [Inf.] to carry or haul —*n.* **1** a small piece of luggage **2** a large, open handbag: in full **tote bag**

to·tem (tōt′əm) *n.* [< Algonquian] **1** among some peoples, an animal or natural object taken as the symbol of a family or clan **2** an image of this

totem pole a pole carved and painted with totems by Indian tribes of NW North America

tot·ter (tät′ər) *vi.* [prob. < Scand] **1** to rock as if about to fall **2** to be unsteady on one's feet; stagger

tou·can (tōō′kan′) *n.* [< AmInd (Brazil)] a brightly colored bird of tropical America, with a very large beak

touch (tuch) *vt.* [< OFr *tochier*] **1** to put the hand, etc. on, so as to feel **2** to bring (something), or come, into contact with (something else) **3** to border on **4** to strike lightly **5** to give a light tint, aspect, etc. to [*touched* with pink] **6** to handle; use **7** to come up to; reach **8** to compare with; equal **9** to affect; concern **10** to arouse sympathy, gratitude, etc. in **11** [Slang] to seek a loan or gift of money from —*vi.* **1** to touch a person or thing **2** to be or come in contact **3** to verge (*on* or *upon*) **4** to pertain; bear (*on* or *upon*) **5** to treat in passing: with *on* or *upon* —*n.* **1** a touching or being touched; specif., a light tap **2** the sense by which physical objects are felt **3** a special quality or skill **4** a subtle change or addition in a painting, story, etc. **5** a trace, tinge, etc. **6** a slight attack [a *touch* of the flu] **7** contact or communication [keep in *touch*] **8** [Slang] *a*) the act of seeking or getting a loan or gift of money *b*) one from whom money is sought [a soft *touch*] **9** *Music* the manner of striking the keys of a piano, etc. —**touch down** to land: said of an aircraft or spacecraft —**touch up** to improve by minor changes

touch-and-go *adj.* uncertain, risky, etc.

touch·down *n.* **1** the moment at which an aircraft or spacecraft lands **2** *Football* a play, scoring six points, in which a player carries, catches, or recovers the ball past the opponent's goal line

tou·ché (tōō shā′) *interj.* [Fr] touched: said when one's opponent in fencing scores a point, or as to acknowledge a clever retort

touched (tucht) *adj.* **1** emotionally affected; moved **2** slightly demented

touch·ing *adj.* arousing tender emotions; moving

touch·less (-lis) *adj.* not requiring physical contact for activation [*touchless* faucets]

touch-screen (-skrēn′) *n. Comput.* a computer screen that allows an icon, menu item, etc. to be selected by touching that portion of the screen displaying it: also **touch′-screen′**

touch·stone *n.* **1** a stone formerly used to test the purity of gold or silver **2** any test of genuineness

touch-type *vi.* **-typed′, -typ′ing** to type without looking at the keyboard by regularly touching a given key with a specific finger

touch·y *adj.* **-i·er, -i·est** **1** easily offended; oversensitive; irritable **2** very risky or precarious

touch·y-feel·y (-fē′lē) *adj.* [Inf.] having or showing too much affection, compassion, etc.

tough (tuf) *adj.* [OE *toh*] **1** that will bend, etc. without tearing or breaking **2** not easily cut or chewed [*tough* steak] **3** strong; hardy **4** stubborn **5** brutal or rough **6** very difficult; laborious [*tough* job] —*n.* a tough person; thug

tough·en *vt., vi.* to make or become tough or tougher   **tough′en·er** *n.*

tou·pee (tōō pā′) *n.* [< Fr < OFr *toup,* tuft of hair] a man's small wig, used to cover a bald spot

tour (toor) *n.* [< OFr *tourner,* to turn] **1** a turn, period, etc., as of military duty **2** a long trip, as for sightseeing **3** any trip, as for inspection, for giving performances, etc. —*vt., vi.* to go on a tour (through)

tour de force (toor′ da fôrs′) *pl.* **tours de force** (toor′) [Fr] an unusually skillful or ingenious creation or performance, sometimes a merely clever one

Tou·rette's syndrome (tōō rets′) [after G. de la *Tourette* (1857-1904), Fr doctor] a nervous disorder characterized by involuntary movements, obscene utterances, etc.: also **Tourette syndrome**

tour·ism *n.* tourist travel

tour·ist *n.* one who tours, esp. for pleasure —*adj.* of or for tourists

tour·ma·line (toor′mə lin, -lēn′) *n.* [Fr] a crystalline mineral used as a gemstone, etc.

tour·na·ment (toor′mə mənt, tur′-) *n.* [< OFr *tourner,* to turn] **1** in the Middle Ages, a contest between knights on horseback who tried to unseat one another with lances **2** a series of contests in competition for a championship **3** tour′ney (-nē) *n., pl.* **-neys**

tour·ni·quet (toor′ni kit, tur′-) *n.* [Fr < L *tunica,* tunic] a device for compressing a blood vessel to stop bleeding, as a bandage twisted about a limb and released at intervals

tou·sle (tou′zəl) *vt.* **-sled, -sling** [< ME *tusen,* to pull] to disorder, dishevel, muss, etc.

tout (tout) [Inf.] *vi., vt.* [OE *totian,* to peep] **1** to praise highly **2** to sell betting tips on (racehorses) —*n.* one who touts

tow (tō) *vt.* [OE *togian*] to pull, as by a rope or chain —*n.* **1** a towing or being towed **2** something towed **3** TOWLINE —**in tow 1** being towed **2** in one's company or charge

toward (tôrd, twôrd) *prep.* [see TO & -WARD] **1** in the direction of **2** facing **3** along a likely course to [steps *toward* peace] **4** just before [*toward* noon] **5** for [save *toward* a car] Also **towards**

tow·el (tou′əl) *n.* [< OFr *toaille*] a piece of cloth or paper for wiping or drying things —*vt.* **-eled** or **-elled, -el·ing** or **-el·ling** to wipe or dry with a towel —**throw** (or **toss,** etc.) **in the towel** [Inf.] to admit defeat

tow·el·ing or **tow·el·ling** *n.* material for making towels

tow·er (tou′ər) *n.* [< L *turris*] **1** a high structure, often part of a building **2** such a structure used as a fortress, etc. —*vi.* to rise high like a tower —**tow′er·ing** *adj.*

tow·head (tō′hed′) *n.* [< *tow,* fibers of flax, etc.] a person with pale-yellow hair —**tow′head′ed** *adj.*

tow·hee (tō′hē, -ē) *n.* [echoic] any of various small North American sparrows

tow·line (tō′līn′) *n.* a rope, etc. used for towing

town (toun) *n.* [OE *tun*] **1** a concentration of houses, etc. somewhat larger than a village **2** a city **3** a township **4** the people of a town —**on the town** [Inf.] out for a good time

town crier one who, formerly, cried public announcements through the streets of a village or town

town hall a building in a town, housing the offices of officials, etc.

town·house a two-story or three-story dwelling, esp. one attached to others of similar design

town meeting a meeting of the voters of a town or township, as in New England

town·ship *n.* a division of a county, constituting a unit of local government

towns·peo·ple *pl.n.* the people of a town: also **towns′folk′**

tow·path (tō′path′) *n.* a path along a canal, that is used by men or animals towing freight-carrying boats

tow·rope *n.* a rope used in towing

tox·e·mi·a (täk sē′mē ə) *n.* [see fol. & -EMIA] a condition in which the blood contains poisonous substances, esp. toxins produced by pathogenic bacteria —**tox·e′mic** *adj.*

tox·ic (täk′sik) *adj.* [< Gr *toxicon,* a poison] **1** of, affected by, or caused by a toxin **2** poisonous

tox·i·col·o·gy (täk′si käl′ə jē) *n.* [see prec. & -LOGY] the science of poisons and their effects, antidotes, etc. —**tox′i·col′o·gist** *n.*

tox·in (täk′sin) *n.* [< TOXIC] 1 any of various poisons produced by microorganisms and causing certain diseases 2 any poison secreted by plants or animals

toy (toi) *n.* [< ? MDu *toi*, finery] 1 a trifle 2 a plaything for children —*adj.* 1 like a plaything in size, use, etc. 2 made as a toy —*vi.* to trifle (*with* a thing, an idea, etc.)

tr *abbrev.* 1 translated 2 translation 3 translator 4 transpose

trace¹ (trās) *n.* [< L *trahere*, to draw] 1 a mark, track, sign, etc. left by a person, animal, or thing 2 a barely perceptible amount —*vt.* **traced, trac′ing** 1 to follow the trail of; track 2 *a)* to follow the development or history of *b)* to determine (a source, etc.) by this procedure 3 to draw, outline, etc. 4 to copy (a drawing, etc.) by following its lines on a superimposed transparent sheet —**trace′a·ble** *adj.* —**trac′er** *n.*

trace² (trās) *n.* [see TRAIT] either of two straps, etc. connecting a draft animal's harness to the vehicle drawn

trace element a chemical element, as copper, zinc, etc., essential in nutrition, but only in minute amounts

trac·er·y (trās′ər ē) *n.,* pl. **-ies** [< TRACE¹ + -ERY] ornamental work of interlacing or branching lines

tra·che·a (trā′kē ə) *n.,* pl. **-che·ae′** (-ē′) or **-che·as** [< Gr *tracheia (arteria)*, rough (windpipe)] the passage that conveys air from the larynx to the bronchi; windpipe —**tra′che·al** *adj.*

tra·che·ot·o·my (trā′kē ät′ə mē) *n.,* pl. **-mies** [see prec. & -TOMY] an incision of the trachea to aid breathing in an emergency

trac·ing (trās′iŋ) *n.* something traced; specif., *a)* a copy of a drawing, etc. *b)* a traced line made by a recording instrument

track (trak) *n.* [< Fr *trac*] 1 a mark left in passing, as a footprint, wheel rut, etc. 2 a path or trail 3 a sequence of ideas, events, etc. 4 a path or circuit laid out for racing, etc. 5 a pair of parallel metal rails on which trains, etc. run 6 *a)* sports performed on a track, as running, hurdling, etc. *b)* these sports along with other contests in jumping, throwing, etc. (in full **track and field**) 7 *a)* any of the separate recording divisions on a phonographic record, compact disc, magnetic tape, etc. *b)* the contents of one of these divisions —*vt.* 1 to follow the track of 2 to trace by means of evidence, etc. 3 to plot the path of, as with radar 4 to leave tracks of (mud, etc.) on: often with *up* —**in one's tracks** where one is at the moment —**keep (or lose) track of** to stay (or fail to stay) informed about —**track′less** *adj.*

track lighting a method of lighting a room with movable spotlights inserted along a narrow, electrified track

track record [Inf.] the record of the performance of a person, etc. as in some activity

tract¹ (trakt) *n.* [< L *trahere*, to draw] 1 a continuous expanse of land 2 a system of organs having some special function [the digestive *tract*]

tract² (trakt) *n.* [< LL *tractatus*, treatise] a propagandizing pamphlet

trac·ta·ble (trak′tə bəl) *adj.* [< L *trahere*, to draw] easily managed; docile; compliant

tract house a house built to a design that is used many times throughout a housing development

trac·tion (trak′shən) *n.* [< L *trahere*, to draw] 1 *a)* a pulling or drawing *b)* a being pulled or drawn *c)* the kind of power used for pulling [electric *traction*] 2 the power, as of tires on pavement, to hold to a surface without slipping

trac·tor (trak′tər) *n.* [see prec.] 1 a powerful, motor-driven vehicle for pulling farm machinery, etc. 2 a truck with a driver's cab and no body, for hauling large trailers

trac·tor-trail·er *n.* a TRACTOR (*n.* 2) combined with a trailer or semitrailer, used for transporting goods

trade (trād) *n.* [< LowG, a track] 1 occupation; esp., skilled work 2 all the persons in a particular business 3 buying and selling; commerce 4 customers 5 an exchange; swap —*vi.* **trad′ed, trad′ing** 1 to carry on a business 2 to have business dealings (*with*) 3 to make an exchange (*with*) 4 [Inf.] to be a customer (*at* a certain store) —*vt.* to exchange; barter —**trade on (or upon)** to take advantage of

trade-in *n.* a thing given or taken as part payment for something else

trade journal (or magazine) a magazine devoted to a specific trade or industry

trade·mark *n.* 1 a symbol, word, etc. that is used by a manufacturer or dealer to distinguish a product: usually protected by law 2 [Inf.] a distinctive, identifying feature or characteristic

trade name 1 the name by which a commodity is commonly known by those who deal in it 2 a name used as a trademark 3 the business name of a company

trade-off *n.* an exchange in which one benefit is given up for another considered more desirable: also **trade′off′**

trad·er *n.* 1 one who trades; merchant 2 a ship used in trade

trades·man (trādz′mən) *n.,* pl. **-men** (-mən) 1 one engaged in skilled work, such as an electrician or plumber 2 [Chiefly Brit.] a storekeeper

trade union LABOR UNION

trade wind a consistent northeasterly or southeasterly wind that blows toward the equator in the tropics

trading post a store in an outpost, settlement, etc., where trading is done

tra·di·tion (trə dish′ən) *n.* [< L *tradere*, deliver] 1 the handing down orally of beliefs, customs, etc. from generation to generation 2 a story, belief, custom, etc. handed down in this way

tra·di·tion·al *adj.* of, handed down by, or conforming to tradition

tra·di·tion·al·ism *n.* adherence to tradition —**tra·di'tion·al·ist** *n.*

tra·duce (trə dōos', -dyōos') *vt.* -**duced'**, -**duc'ing** [< L *trans*, across + *ducere*, to lead] to slander

traf·fic (traf'ik) *n.* [< It *traffico* < L *trans*, across + It *ficcare*, bring] 1 buying and selling; trade 2 dealings (*with* someone) 3 the movement or number of automobiles, pedestrians, etc. along a street, etc. 4 the business done by a transportation company —*adj.* of or having to do with traffic —*vi.* -**ficked**, -**fick·ing** 1 to carry on traffic (*in* a commodity) 2 to have dealings (*with* someone) —**traf'fick·er** *n.*

traffic circle a circular road at the intersection of several streets: vehicles move on it in one direction only

traffic light (*or* **signal**) a set of signal lights at a street intersection for regulating traffic

tra·ge·di·an (trə jē'dē ən) *n.* 1 a writer of tragedy 2 an actor in tragedies

trag·e·dy (traj'ə dē) *n., pl.* -**dies** [< Gr *tragos*, goat + *ōidē*, song] 1 a serious play with an unhappy ending 2 a very sad or tragic event; disaster

trag·ic (traj'ik) *adj.* 1 of or like a tragedy 2 disastrous, fatal, etc. —**trag'i·cal·ly** *adv.*

trail (trāl) *vt.* [< L *trahere*, to draw] 1 to drag or let drag behind one 2 to follow the tracks of; track 3 to hunt by tracking 4 to follow behind —*vi.* 1 to drag along on the ground, etc. 2 to grow along the ground, etc., as some plants do 3 to flow behind: said as of smoke 4 to follow or lag behind; straggle 5 to grow weaker, dimmer, etc.: with *off* or *away* —*n.* 1 something that trails behind 2 a mark, scent, etc. left by a person, animal, or thing that has passed 3 a beaten path

trail·blaz·er *n.* 1 one who blazes a trail 2 a pioneer in any field

trail·er *n.* 1 one that trails 2 *a*) a wagon, van, etc. designed to be pulled by an automobile, truck, etc. *b*) such a vehicle designed to be lived in

trailer park an area, usually with piped water, electricity, etc., for trailers, esp. mobile homes

trail mix a mixture of raisins, nuts, etc. eaten as by hikers for quick energy

train (trān) *n.* [< L *trahere*, to pull] 1 something that drags along behind, as a trailing skirt 2 a group of followers; retinue 3 a procession; caravan 4 any connected order; sequence [a *train* of thought] 5 a line of connected railroad cars pulled by a locomotive —*vt.* 1 to guide the growth of (a plant) 2 to guide the mental, moral, etc. development of; rear 3 to instruct so as to make proficient 4 to make fit for an athletic contest, etc. 5 to aim (a gun, etc.) —*vi.* to undergo training —**train·ee** (trān ē') *n.* —**train'er** *n.*

training wheels a pair of small wheels attached to a bicycle's rear wheel to provide stability for someone learning to ride

traipse (trāps) *vi., vt.* **traipsed**, **traips'ing** [< ?] to walk, wander, or tramp

trait (trāt) *n.* [< L *trahere*, to draw] a distinguishing quality or characteristic

trai·tor (trāt'ər) *n.* [< L *tradere*, betray] one who betrays one's country, cause, friends, etc. —**trai'tor·ous** *adj.*

tra·jec·to·ry (trə jek'tə rē) *n., pl.* -**ries** [ult. < L *trans*, across + *jacere*, to throw] the curved path of something hurtling through space

tram (tram) *n.* [prob. < LowG *traam*, a beam] 1 an aerial cable car 2 [Brit.] a streetcar

tram·mel (tram'əl) *n.* [< L *tres*, three + *macula*, a mesh] [*usually pl.*] something that confines or restrains —*vt.* -**meled** or -**melled**, -**mel·ing** or -**mel·ling** to confine, restrain, etc.

tramp (tramp) *vi.* [ME *trampen*] 1 to walk or step heavily 2 to travel about on foot —*vt.* 1 to step on heavily 2 to walk through —*n.* 1 a vagrant; hobo 2 the sound of heavy steps 3 a journey on foot; hike 4 a freight ship with no schedule, that picks up cargo, etc. as it goes along 5 [Slang] a sexually promiscuous woman: in this sense, a term of contempt

tram·ple (tram'pəl) *vi.* -**pled**, -**pling** [see prec.] to tread heavily —*vt.* to crush, destroy, etc. by or as by treading heavily on

tram·po·line (tram'pə lēn', -lin) *n.* [< It] a sheet of strong canvas stretched tightly on a frame with springs, used in acrobatic tumbling and jumping

trance (trans) *n.* [< L *transire*, go across, die] 1 a state of altered consciousness, resembling sleep, as in hypnosis 2 a daze; stupor 3 a state of great mental abstraction

tran·quil (traŋ'kwol) *adj.* -**quil·er** or -**quil·ler**, -**quil·est** or -**quil·lest** [L *tranquillus*] calm, serene, placid, etc. —**tran·quil'li·ty** *n.*, **tran·quil'i·ty** (-kwil'ə tē) —**tran'quil·ly** *adv.*

tran·quil·ize or **tran·quil·lize** (-kwə liz') *vt., vi.* -**ized'** or -**lized'**, -**iz'ing** or -**liz'ing** to make or become tranquil

tran·quil·iz·er or **tran·quil·liz·er** *n.* a drug used as a calming agent in treating various emotional disturbances, etc.

trans *abbrev.* 1 translated 2 translation 3 translator 4 transportation

trans- [L < *trans*, across] *prefix* over, across, beyond, through

trans·act (tran zakt', -sakt') *vt.* [< L *trans-*, over + *agere*, to drive] to carry on or complete (business, etc.)

trans·ac·ti·nide series (trans ak'tə nīd', tranz-) *n.* a group of radioactive chemical elements with an atomic number 104 or higher

trans·ac·tion *n.* 1 a transacting 2 something transacted; specif., *a*) a business deal *b*) [*pl.*] a record of the proceedings of a society, etc.

trans·at·lan·tic (trans'at lan'tik, tranz'-) *adj.* 1 crossing the Atlantic 2 on the other side of the Atlantic

trans·ceiv·er (tran sē'vər) *n.* a radio transmitter and receiver in a single housing

tran·scend (tran send') *vt.* [< L *trans-*, over

+ *scandere*, climb] **1** to go beyond the limits of; exceed **2** to surpass; excel —**tran·scend′ent** *adj.*

tran·scen·den·tal (tran′sen dent′′l) *adj.* **1** supernatural **2** abstract —**tran′scen·den′tal·ly** *adv.*

tran·scen·den·tal·ism *n.* [*often* T–] a philosophy based on a search for reality through spiritual intuition

trans·con·ti·nen·tal (trans′kän tə nent′′l, tranz′–) *adj.* **1** that crosses a continent **2** on the other side of a continent

tran·scribe (tran skrīb′) *vt.* -**scribed′**, -**scrib′ing** **1** to write out or type out in full (shorthand notes, etc.) **2** to represent (speech sounds) in symbols

tran·script (tran′skript′) *n.* **1** a written, typewritten, or printed copy **2** a copy, esp. an official copy, as of a student's record

tran·scrip·tion (–skrip′shən) *n.* **1** a transcribing **2** a transcript; copy **3** an arrangement of a piece of music for an instrument or voice other than that for which it was written

trans·duc·er (trans dōōs′ər, tranz–) *n.* [< L *trans*-, over + *ducere*, to lead] a device that transmits energy from one system to another, sometimes converting the energy to a different form

tran·sept (tran′sept′) *n.* [< L *trans*-, across + *septum*, enclosure] the part of a cross-shaped church at right angles to the nave, or either of its arms

tran·sex·u·al (tran sek′shōō əl) *adj., n. var. of* TRANSSEXUAL

trans fat (trans, tranz) a partially hydrogenated, unsaturated fatty acid, used in foods to increase shelf life and maintain flavor: also **trans fatty acid**

trans·fer (trans′fər) *vt.* -**ferred**, -**fer·ring** [< L *trans*-, across + *ferre*, to bear] **1** to carry, send, etc. to another person or place **2** to make over (property, etc.) to another **3** to convey (a picture, etc.) from one surface to another —*vi.* **1** to transfer oneself or be transferred **2** to change as to another school or another bus —*n.* **1** a transferring or being transferred **2** one that is transferred **3** a ticket entitling the bearer to change to another bus, etc. —**trans·fer′ral** (–fur′–) *n.*

trans·fer·ence (trans′fər əns, trans fur′–) *n.* a transferring or being transferred

trans·fig·ure (trans fig′yər) *vt.* -**ured**, -**ur·ing** [< L *trans*-, across + *figura*, figure] **1** to change the form or appearance of **2** to transform so as to glorify —**trans·fig′u·ra′tion** *n.*

trans·fix (trans fiks′) *vt.* [< L *trans*-, through + *figere*, to fix] **1** to pierce through; impale **2** to make motionless, as if impaled

trans·form (trans fôrm′) *vt.* [< L *trans*-, over + *forma*, a form] **1** to change the form or appearance of **2** to change the condition, nature, or function of —**trans′for·ma′tion** *n.*

trans·form·er *n.* a device for changing alternating current to a different voltage

trans·fuse (–fyōōz′) *vt.* -**fused′**, -**fus′ing** [< L *trans*-, across + *fundere*, pour] **1** to instill;

imbue **2** to transfer (blood, etc.) into a blood vessel —**trans·fu′sion** *n.*

trans·gen·der *adj.* identifying as or having undergone medical treatment to become a member of the opposite sex

trans·gress (trans gres′, tranz–) *vt., vi.* [< L *trans*-, over + *gradi*, to step] **1** to break (a law, command, etc.); sin (against) **2** to go beyond (a limit, etc.) —**trans·gres′sion** (–gresh′ən) *n.* —**trans·gres′sor** *n.*

tran·sient (tran′shənt, –zē ənt) *adj.* [< L *trans*-, over + *ire*, to go] **1** passing away with time; temporary **2** passing quickly; fleeting **3** staying only a short time —*n.* a transient person —**tran′sience** *n.*, **tran′sien·cy**

tran·sis·tor (tran zis′tər, –sis′–) *n.* [TRAN(S-FER) + (RE)SISTOR] a compact electronic device, composed of semiconductor material, that controls current flow —**tran·sis′tor·ize′** *vt.* -**ized′**, -**iz′ing**

trans·it (tran′sit, –zit) *n.* [< L *trans*-, over + *ire*, to go] **1** passage through or across **2** *a)* a carrying through or across; conveyance *b)* a system of urban public transportation **3** a surveying instrument for measuring horizontal angles

tran·si·tion (tran zish′ən) *n.* a passing from one condition, place, etc. to another —*vi.* to make or undergo a transition —**tran·si′tion·al** *adj.*

tran·si·tive (tran′sə tiv, –zə–) *adj.* designating a verb that takes a direct object

tran·si·to·ry (tran′sə tôr′ē, –zə–) *adj.* not enduring; temporary; fleeting

transl *abbrev.* **1** translated **2** translation

trans·late (trans lāt′, tranz–) *vt.* -**lat′ed**, -**lat′ing** [< L *translatus*, transferred] **1** to move from one place or condition to another **2** to put into the words of a different language **3** to put into different words —**trans·la′tor** *n.*

trans·la·tion *n.* **1** a translating **2** writing or speech translated into another language

trans·lit·er·ate (trans lit′ər āt′, tranz–) *vt.* -**at′ed**, -**at′ing** [< TRANS- + L *litera*, letter] to write (words, etc.) in the characters of another alphabet —**trans·lit′er·a′tion** *n.*

trans·lu·cent (–lōō′sənt) *adj.* [< L *trans*-, through + *lucere*, to shine] letting light pass through, but not transparent

trans·mi·grate (–mī′grāt′) *vi.* -**grat′ed**, -**grat′ing** [see TRANS- & MIGRATE] to pass into another body at death: said of the soul, as in Hindu religious belief —**trans′mi·gra′tion** *n.*

trans·mis·sion (–mish′ən) *n.* **1** a transmitting **2** something transmitted **3** the part of a motor vehicle that adjusts the relative speed of the engine and wheels

trans·mit (–mit′) *vt.* -**mit′ted**, -**mit′ting** [< L *trans*-, over + *mittere*, send] **1** to cause to go to another person or place; transfer **2** to hand down by heredity, inheritance, etc. **3** *a)* to pass (light, heat, etc.) through some medium *b)* to conduct [water *transmits* sound] **4** to convey (force, movement, etc.)

to **5** to send out (radio or television broadcasts) —**trans·mis′si·ble** (-mis′ə bəl) *adj.* —**trans·mit′ta·ble** *adj.* —**trans·mit′tal** *n.*

trans·mit·ter *n.* the apparatus that transmits signals in telephony, radio, etc.

trans·mute (-myo̅o̅t′) *vt., vi.* -**mut′ed**, -**mut′ing** [< L *trans-*, over + *mutare*, to change] to change from one form, nature, substance, etc. into another; transform —**trans′mu·ta′tion** *n.*

trans·na·tion·al (-nash′ə nəl) *adj.* transcending the limits, interests, etc. of a single nation

trans·o·ce·an·ic (-ō′shē an′ik) *adj.* crossing the ocean

tran·som (tran′səm) *n.* [prob. < L *transtrum*, crossbeam] **1** a horizontal crossbar, as across the top of a door or window **2** a small window just above a door or window **3** the squared-off stern of a ship or boat

trans·pa·cif·ic (trans′pə sif′ik) *adj.* **1** crossing the Pacific **2** on the other side of the Pacific

trans·par·en·cy (trans per′ən sē) *n., pl.* -**cies** a transparent film or slide having an image that can be projected on a screen

trans·par·ent *adj.* [< L *trans-*, through + *parere*, appear] **1** transmitting light rays so that objects on the other side can be seen clearly **2** so fine in texture as to be seen through **3** easily understood or detected; clear; obvious —**trans·par′ent·ly** *adv.*

tran·spire (tran spīr′) *vi.* -**spired′**, -**spir′ing** [< L *trans-*, through + *spirare*, breathe] **1** to give off vapor, moisture, etc., as through pores **2** to become known **3** to happen

trans·plant (trans plant′; *also, and for n. always,* trans′plant′) *vt.* **1** to remove from one place and plant, resettle, etc. in another **2** *Surgery* to transfer (tissue or an organ) from one to another; graft —*n.* **1** a transplanting **2** something or someone transplanted —**trans′plan·ta′tion** (-plan tā′shən) *n.*

tran·spon·der (tran spän′dər) *n.* [< TRAN(SMITTER) & RESPOND] a transceiver that automatically transmits signals

trans·port (trans pôrt′; *for n.* trans′pôrt′) *vt.* [< L *trans-*, over + *portare*, carry] **1** to carry from one place to another **2** to carry away with emotion —*n.* **1** a transporting; transportation **2** strong emotion, esp. joy **3** a vehicle for transporting

trans·por·ta·tion (-pər tā′shən) *n.* **1** a transporting or being transported **2** a means of conveyance **3** fare or a ticket for being transported

trans·pose (trans pōz′) *vt., vi.* -**posed′**, -**pos′ing** [see TRANS- & POSE] **1** to change the usual order or position of; interchange **2** to rewrite or play (a musical composition) in a different key —**trans′po·si′tion** (-pə zish′ən) *n.*

trans·sex·u·al (trans sek′sho̅o̅ əl) *adj.* identifying as, or having undergone medical treatment to become, a member of the opposite sex —*n.* a person who is transsexual

trans·ship (trans ship′) *vt., vi.* -**shipped′**, -**ship′ping** to transfer from one ship, train,

etc. to another for further shipment —**trans·ship′ment** *n.*

trans·verse (trans vurs′, tranz-; *also, and for n. usually,* trans′vurs′, tranz′-) *adj.* [< L *trans-*, across + *vertere*, to turn] situated across; crosswise —*n.* a transverse part, etc.

trans·ves·tite (trans ves′tit′, tranz-) *n.* [< TRANS- + L *vestire*, to dress] one who adopts the clothing and deportment regarded as typical of the opposite sex

trap (trap) *n.* [< OE *træppe*] **1** a device for catching animals, as one that snaps shut tightly when stepped on **2** any stratagem designed to catch or trick **3** a device, as in a drainpipe, for preventing the escape of gas, etc. —*vt.* trapped, trap′ping to catch in or as in a trap —*vi.* to trap animals, esp. for their furs —**trap′per** *n.*

trap·door *n.* a hinged or sliding door in a roof, ceiling, or floor

tra·peze (tra pēz′) *n.* [see fol.] a short horizontal bar, hung high by two ropes, on which gymnasts, etc. swing

tra·pe·zi·um (trə pē′zē əm) *n., pl.* -**zi·ums** or -**zi·a** (-ə) [< Gr *trapeza*, table] a plane figure with four sides, no two of which are parallel

trap·e·zoid (trap′i zoid′) *n.* [see prec.] a plane figure with four sides, only two of which are parallel —**trap′e·zoi′dal** *adj.*

trap·pings *pl.n.* [< OFr *drap*, cloth] **1** an ornamental covering for a horse **2** adornments

trap·shoot·ing *n.* the sport of shooting at clay disks sprung into the air from throwing devices

trash (trash) *n.* [prob. < Scand] **1** broken, discarded, or worthless things; rubbish **2** a person or people regarded as disreputable, etc. —*vt.* [Slang] **1** to destroy (property) as by vandalism **2** to criticize or insult (a person, etc.) sharply or maliciously —**trash′y** *adj.* -**i·er**, -**i·est**

trau·ma (trô′mə, trä′-) *n., pl.* -**mas** or -**ma·ta** (-mə tə) [Gr] **1** a bodily injury or shock **2** an emotional shock, often having a lasting psychic effect —**trau·mat′ic** (trô mat′ik) *adj.*

trau·ma·tize (-tīz′) *vt.* -**tized′**, -**tiz′ing** to subject to a physical or mental trauma

trav·ail (trə vāl′, trav′āl′) *n.* [< L *tri-*, three + *palus*, stake: referring to a torture device] **1** very hard work **2** intense pain; agony

trav·el (trav′əl) *vi.* -**eled** or -**elled**, -**el·ing** or -**el·ling** [var. of prec.] **1** to go from one place to another **2** to move, pass, or be transmitted —*vt.* to make a journey over or through —*n.* **1** a traveling **2** [pl.] trips, journeys, etc. —**trav′el·er** *n.*, -**trav′el·ler**

traveler's check a check in a fixed denomination, sold to a traveler who signs it at issuance and again when cashing it

trav·e·logue or **trav·e·log** (trav′ə lôg′) *n.* **1** an illustrated lecture on travels **2** a short film about a place, esp. one that is foreign, unusual, etc.

tra·verse (trə vurs′; *for n. & adj.* trav′ərs) *vt.* -**versed′**, -**vers′ing** [< L *trans-*, across + *vertere*, to turn] to pass over, across, or through —*n.* **trav′erse** **1** something that traverses or crosses, as a crossbar **2** a traversing —*adj.* **trav′erse** **1** extending across **2** designating or of draperies drawn by pulling a cord at the side

trav·es·ty (trav′is tē) *n., pl.* **-ties** [< L *trans-*, over + *vestire*, to dress] **1** a farcical imitation in ridicule **2** a ridiculous representation [a *travesty* of justice] —*vt.* **-tied, -ty·ing** to make a travesty of

trawl (trôl) *n.* [< ? MDu *traghel*, dragnet] **1** a large dragnet for fishing **2** a long line supported by buoys, from which fishing lines are hung —*vi., vt.* to fish or catch with a trawl

trawl·er *n.* a boat used in trawling

tray (trā) *n.* [< OE *treg*, wooden board] a flat receptacle with raised edges, for holding or carrying things

treach·er·ous (trech′ər əs) *adj.* **1** characterized by treachery; disloyal **2** untrustworthy or insecure —**treach′er·ous·ly** *adv.*

treach·er·y (trech′ər ē) *n., pl.* **-ies** [< OFr *trichier*, to cheat] **1** betrayal of trust; disloyalty **2** treason

trea·cle (trē′kəl) *n.* [< Gr (*antidotos*) *thēriakē*, (remedy) for venom] [Brit.] **1** molasses **2** anything very sweet or cloying —**trea′cly** (-klē) *adj.*

tread (tred) *vt.* **trod, trod′den** or **trod, tread′ing** [OE *tredan*] **1** to walk on, in, along, etc. **2** to do or follow by walking, dancing, etc. **3** to press or beat with the feet —*vi.* **1** to walk **2** to set one's foot (*on, across,* etc.) **3** to trample (*on* or *upon*) —*n.* **1** the manner or sound of treading **2** something for treading or moving on, as a shoe sole or surface of a stair **3** the thick outer layer of an automotive tire —**tread water** *pt. & pp. usually* **treaded** **1** to stay upright in swimming by moving the legs and arms back and forth **2** to expend effort simply remaining in one's current position

trea·dle (tred′'l) *n.* [< OE *tredan,* to tread] a lever moved by the foot as to turn a wheel

tread·mill *n.* **1** a mill wheel turned by an animal treading an endless belt **2** any monotonous work in which one seems to make no progress **3** an exercise machine with an endless belt on which one walks or runs

treas *abbrev.* **1** treasurer **2** treasury

trea·son (trē′zən) *n.* [< L *trans-,* over + *dare,* give] betrayal of one's country to an enemy —**trea′son·a·ble** *adj.,* **trea′son·ous**

treas·ure (trezh′ər) *n.* [< Gr *thēsauros*] **1** accumulated wealth, as money or jewels **2** any person or thing considered valuable —*vt.* **-ured, -ur·ing** **1** to save up for future use **2** to value greatly

treas·ur·er (trezh′ər ər) *n.* one in charge of a treasury, as of a government or club

treas·ure-trove (-trōv′) *n.* [*trove* < OFr *trover,* find] **1** treasure found hidden, the original owner of which is unknown **2** a valuable source or collection

treas·ur·y (trezh′ər ē) *n., pl.* **-ies** **1** a place where treasure or funds are kept **2** the funds or revenues of a state, corporation, etc. **3** [T-] the department of government in charge of revenue, taxation, and public finances

treat (trēt) *vi.* [ult. < L *trahere,* to draw] **1** to discuss terms (*with*) **2** to speak or write (*of*) —*vt.* **1** to deal with (a subject) in writing, music, etc. in a specified manner **2** to act toward (someone or something) in a specified manner **3** to pay for the food, etc. of (another) **4** to subject to some process, chemical, etc. **5** to give medical care to —*n.* **1** a meal, drink, etc. paid for by another **2** anything that gives great pleasure

trea·tise (trēt′is) *n.* [see prec.] a formal article or book on some subject

treat·ment (trēt′mənt) *n.* **1** act, manner, method, etc. of treating **2** medical or surgical care **3** an outline or summary of a screenplay

trea·ty (trēt′ē) *n., pl.* **-ties** [< L *trahere,* to draw] a formal agreement between two or more nations

tre·ble (treb′əl) *adj.* [< L *triplus,* triple] **1** threefold; triple **2** of, for, or performing the treble —*n.* **1** the highest part in musical harmony; soprano **2** a high-pitched voice or sound —*vt., vi.* **-bled, -bling** to make or become threefold

tree (trē) *n.* [OE *trēow*] **1** a large, woody perennial plant with one main trunk and many branches *a)* anything resembling a tree *b)* FAMILY TREE —*vt.* treed, tree/ing to chase up a tree —**tree′less** *adj.* —**tree′like** *adj.*

tre·foil (trē′foil′) *n.* [< L *tri-,* three + *folium,* leaf] **1** a plant with leaves divided into three leaflets, as the clover **2** a design, etc. shaped like such a leaf

trek (trek) *vi.* **trekked, trek′king** [Afrik < Du *trekken,* to pull] **1** to travel slowly or laboriously **2** [Inf.] to go on foot —*n.* **1** a journey **2** a migration

trel·lis (trel′is) *n.* [< L *trilix,* triple-twilled] a lattice on which vines are trained

trem·a·tode (trem′ə tōd′, trē′mə-) *n.* [< Gr *trēmatōdēs,* perforated] a parasitic flatworm with muscular suckers; fluke

trem·ble (trem′bəl) *vi.* **-bled, -bling** [< L *tremere*] **1** to shake or shiver from cold, fear, etc. **2** to feel great anxiety **3** to quiver, vibrate, etc. —*n.* **1** a trembling **2** [*sometimes pl.*] a fit of trembling

tre·men·dous (tri men′dəs) *adj.* [< L *tremere,* to tremble] **1** very large; great **2** [Inf.] wonderful, amazing, etc. —**tre·men′dous·ly** *adv.*

trem·o·lo (trem′ə lō′) *n., pl.* **-los′** [It] *Music* a tremulous effect produced by rapid reiteration of the same tone

trem·or (trem′ər) *n.* [< L *tremere,* to tremble] **1** a trembling, shaking, etc. **2** a trembling sensation

trem·u·lous (trem′yōō ləs) *adj.* [< L *tremere,* to tremble] **1** trembling; quivering **2** fearful; timid

trench (trench) *vt.* [< OFr *trenchier,* to cut] **1** to dig a ditch or ditches in —*n.* **1** a deep furrow **2** a long, narrow ditch dug by soldiers as a makeshift fortification

trench·ant (tren'chənt) *adj.* [see prec.] **1** sharp; incisive [*trenchant* words] **2** forceful; effective [a *trenchant* argument] —**trench'ant·ly** *adv.*

trench coat a belted raincoat in a military style

trench·er *n.* [see TRENCH] [Archaic] a wooden platter for meat

trench foot a diseased condition of the feet from prolonged exposure to wet and cold

trench mouth an infectious disease of the mucous membranes of the mouth and throat

trend (trend) *vi.* [OE *trendan*] **1** to have a general direction or tendency **2** to be increasingly prominent or popular —*n.* **1** a general tendency or course; drift **2** a current style

trend·y (tren'dē) *adj.* **-i·er, -i·est** [Inf.] of or in the latest style, or trend

Tren·ton (trent'’n) capital of New Jersey

trep·i·da·tion (trep'ə dā'shən) *n.* [< L *trepidus*, disturbed] fearful uncertainty; anxiety

tres·pass (tres'pas, -pas') *vi.* [< L *trans-*, across + *passus*, a step] **1** to go beyond the limits of what is considered right; do wrong; transgress **2** to enter another's property without permission or right —*n.* a trespassing; specif., a moral offense —**tres'pass·er** *n.*

tress (tres) *n.* [< OFr *tresse*, braid of hair] **1** a lock of human hair **2** [*pl.*] a woman's or girl's hair, esp. when long

tres·tle (tres'əl) *n.* [< L *transtrum*, a beam] **1** a horizontal beam fastened to two pairs of spreading legs, used as a support **2** a framework of uprights and crosspieces, supporting a bridge, etc.

trey (trā) *n.* [< L *tres*, three] a playing card with three spots

tri- [< Fr, L, or Gr] *prefix* **1** having or involving three **2** three times, into three **3** every third

tri·ad (trī'ad') *n.* [< Gr *treis*, three] a group of three

tri·age (trē äzh', trē'äzh') *n.* [< Fr *trier*, sift] a system of establishing the order in which acts are to be carried out in an emergency, esp. acts of medical assistance —*vt.* **-aged', -ag'ing** to prioritize (patients, problems, etc.)

tri·al (trī'əl) *n.* [see TRY] **1** the act or process of trying, testing, etc.; test; probation **2** a hardship, suffering, etc. **3** a source of annoyance **4** a hearing and deciding of a case in a court of law **5** an attempt; effort —*adj.* **1** of a trial **2** for the purpose of trying, testing, etc. —**on trial** in the process of being tried

trial and error the process of making repeated trials, tests, and adjustments until the desired result is attained

trial balloon something said or done to test public opinion on an issue

tri·an·gle (trī'aŋ'gəl) *n.* [see TRI- & ANGLE!] **1** a plane figure having three angles and three sides **2** anything with three sides or three corners **3** a situation involving three persons [a love *triangle*] —**tri·an'gu·lar** (-gyōō lər) *adj.*

tri·an·gu·late (-gyə lāt') *vt.* **-lat'ed, -lat'ing** to divide (an area) into triangles in order to

determine distance or relative positions —**tri·an'gu·la'tion** *n.*

tri·ath·lon (trī ath'län', -lən) *n.* [TRI- + Gr *athlon*, a contest] an endurance race combining events in swimming, bicycling, and running

tribe (trīb) *n.* [< L *tribus*] **1** a group of persons or clans descended from a common ancestor and living under a leader or chief **2** a natural group of related plants or animals —**trib'al** *adj.* —**trib'al·ly** *adv.* —**tribes'man** (-mən) *n., pl.* **-men** (-mən)

trib·u·la·tion (trib'yə lā'shən) *n.* [< L *tribulare*, to press] **1** great misery or distress, or the cause of it **2** something that presents great inconvenience or difficulty

tri·bu·nal (trī byōō'nəl, tri-) *n.* [see fol.] **1** a seat for a judge in a court **2** a court of justice

trib·une (trib'yōōn'; *for 2, often* tri byōōn') *n.* [< L *tribus*, tribe] **1** in ancient Rome, a magistrate appointed to protect the rights of plebeians **2** a champion of the people: often used in newspaper names

trib·u·tar·y (trib'yōō ter'ē) *adj.* **1** paying tribute **2** subject [a *tributary* nation] **3** flowing into a larger one [a *tributary* stream] —*n., pl.* **-ies 1** a tributary nation **2** a tributary river

trib·ute (trib'yōōt) *n.* [< L *tribuere*, allot] **1** money paid regularly by one nation to another as acknowledgment of subjugation, for protection, etc. **2** any forced payment **3** something given, done, or said to show gratitude, honor, or praise

trice (trīs) *n.* [< MDu *trisen*, to pull] an instant; moment: now only in **in a trice**

tri·cen·ten·ni·al (trī'sen ten'ē əl) *adj.* happening once every 300 years —*n.* a 300th anniversary

tri·ceps (trī'seps') *n., pl.* **-ceps'** or **-ceps'es** [L < *tri-*, three + *caput*, head] a muscle with three points of origin, esp. the muscle on the back of the upper arm

tri·cer·a·tops (trī ser'ə täps') *n.* [< TRI- + Gr *keras*, horn + *ōps*, eye] a plant-eating dinosaur having a bony crest over the neck and three horns

tri·chi·na (tri kī'nə) *n., pl.* **-nae** (-nē) [< Gr *trichinos*, hairy] a very small worm that causes trichinosis

trich·i·no·sis (trik'i nō'sis) *n.* [< Gr *trichinos*, hairy] a disease caused by intestinal worms, and acquired by eating insufficiently cooked pork from an infested hog

trick (trik) *n.* [< OFr *trichier*, to cheat] **1** something designed to deceive, cheat, etc. **2** a practical joke; prank **3** a clever act intended to amuse **4** any feat requiring skill **5** a personal mannerism **6** a round of duty; shift **7** *Card Games* the cards won in a single round —*vt.* to deceive or swindle —*adj.* **1** having to do with a trick or tricks **2** apt to malfunction [a *trick* knee] —**do (or turn) the trick** [Inf.] to produce the desired result —**not miss a trick** [Inf.] to be very alert —**trick'er·y** *n., pl.* **-ies**

trick·le (trik'əl) *vi.* **-led, -ling** [ME *triklen* <

?**]** 1 to flow slowly in a thin stream or fall in drops 2 to move slowly [the crowd *trickled* away] —*n.* a slow, small flow

trick·le·down *adj.* of an economic theory holding that government aid to the largest businesses will ultimately benefit the poor

trick-or-treat·er *n.* a person in costume who goes from door to door on Halloween asking for candy

trick·ster (-stər) *n.* a person who tricks; cheat

trick·y *adj.* -i·er, -i·est 1 given to or characterized by trickery 2 like a trick in deceptiveness or intricacy 3 requiring great skill or care

tri·col·or (trī′kul′ər) *n.* a flag having three colors in large areas; esp., the flag of France

tri·cy·cle (trī′sə kəl) *n.* [Fr: see TRI- & CYCLE] a child's three-wheeled vehicle operated by pedals

tri·dent (trīd′′nt) *n.* [< L *tri-*, three + *dens*, tooth] a three-pronged spear

tried (trīd) *vt., vi. pt. & pp.* of TRY —*adj.* 1 tested; proved 2 trustworthy

tri·en·ni·al (trī en′ē əl) *adj.* [< L *tri-*, three + *annus*, year] 1 happening every three years 2 lasting three years —**tri·en′ni·al·ly** *adv.*

Tri·este (trē est′) seaport in NE Italy

tri·fle (trī′fəl) *n.* [< OFr *truffe*, deception] 1 something of little value or importance 2 a small amount of money —*vi.* -fled, -fling 1 to talk or act jokingly [to toy (with) —*vt.* to waste [to *trifle* the hours away] —**tri′fler** *n.*

tri·fling (-fliŋ) *adj.* 1 frivolous; shallow 2 of little importance; trivial

tri·fo·cals (trī′fō′kəlz) *pl.n.* eyeglasses like bifocals, but with a third area in the lens ground for viewing objects at an intermediate distance

trig (trig) *n. short for* TRIGONOMETRY

trig·ger (trig′ər) *n.* [< Du *trekken*, to pull] a lever pulled to release a catch, etc., esp. one pressed to activate the firing mechanism on a firearm —*vt.* to initiate (an action)

trig·ger-hap·py *adj.* 1 tending to resort to force rashly or irresponsibly 2 ready to start a war for the slightest cause

tri·glyc·er·ide (trī glis′ər īd′) *n.* [TRI- + Gr *glykeros*, sweet] an ester derived from glycerol: the chief component of fats and oils

trig·o·nom·e·try (trig′ə näm′ə trē) *n.* [< Gr *trigōnon*, triangle + *-metria*, measurement] the branch of mathematics concerning the relations between the sides and angles of triangles —**trig′o·no·met′ric** (-nə me′trik) *adj.*

trill (tril) *n.* [ult. echoic] 1 a rapid alternation of a musical tone with a slightly higher tone 2 a warble 3 a rapid vibration of the tongue or uvula —*vt., vi.* to sound, speak, or play with a trill

tril·lion (tril′yən) *n.* 1 1 followed by 12 zeros 2 [Brit.] 1 followed by 18 zeros —**tril′lionth** *adj., n.*

tril·li·um (tril′ē əm) *n.* [ModL < L *tri-*, three] a woodland plant having a single flower with three petals and three sepals

tril·o·gy (tril′ə jē) *n., pl.* -gies [see TRI- & -LOGY] a set of three related plays, novels, etc.

trim (trim) *vt.* trimmed, trim′ming [< OE *trymman*, make firm] 1 to put in proper order; make neat or tidy [to *trim* hair] 2 to clip, lop, cut, etc. 3 to decorate, as by adding ornaments, etc. 4 *a)* to balance (a ship) by ballasting, etc. *b)* to put (sails) in order for sailing 5 to balance (a flying aircraft) 6 [Inf.] to beat, punish, defeat, cheat, etc. —*vi.* to adjust one's opinions or position according to expediency —*n.* 1 order; arrangement 2 good condition 3 a trimming, as by clipping 4 decorative parts or borders —*adj.* trim′mer, trim′mest 1 orderly; neat 2 well-proportioned 3 in good condition —**trim′ly** *adv.* —**trim′mer** *n.* —**trim′ness** *n.*

tri·ma·ran (trī′mə ran′) *n.* a boat like a catamaran, but with three parallel hulls

tri·mes·ter (trī mes′tər, trī′mes′-) *n.* [< L *tri-*, three + *mensis*, month] 1 a three-month period, as of pregnancy 2 in some colleges, any of the three periods of the academic year

trim·ming (trim′iŋ) *n.* 1 decoration; ornament 2 [*pl.*] *a)* the side dishes of a meal *b)* parts trimmed off 3 [Inf.] a beating, defeat, cheating, etc.

Trin·i·dad and To·ba·go (trin′i dad′ and tə bā′gō) island country in the West Indies

trin·i·ty (trin′i tē) *n., pl.* -ties [< L *trinitas*] a set of three —**the Trinity** *Christian Theol.* the union of Father, Son, and Holy Spirit in one Godhead

trin·ket (triŋ′kit) *n.* [ME *trenket*] 1 a small, cheap ornament, piece of jewelry, etc. 2 a trifle or toy

tri·o (trē′ō) *n., pl.* -os [< L *tres*, three] 1 a group of three 2 *Music a)* a composition for three voices or three instruments *b)* the three performers of such a composition

trip (trip) *vi., vt.* tripped, trip′ping [< OFr *treper*] 1 to move or perform with light, rapid steps; skip 2 to stumble or cause to stumble 3 to make or cause to make a mistake 4 to release (a spring, wheel, etc.) 5 to cause (a mechanism, etc.) to start operating —*n.* 1 a light, quick tread 2 a journey, jaunt, etc. 3 a stumble or a causing to stumble 4 [Slang] *a)* an experience induced by a psychedelic drug, esp. LSD *b)* an experience that is pleasing, exciting, etc. —**trip up** to catch in a lie, error, etc. —**trip′per** *n.*

tri·par·tite (trī pär′tīt′) *adj.* [< L *tri-*, three + *partire*, to part] 1 having three parts 2 made between three parties, as an agreement

tripe (trīp) *n.* [prob. ult. < Ar *tharb*, layer of fat lining the intestines] 1 part of the stomach of an ox, etc., used as food 2 [Slang] anything worthless, etc.; nonsense

trip-ham·mer *n.* a heavy, power-driven hammer, alternately raised and allowed to fall by a tripping device: also **trip hammer**

tri·ple (trip′əl) *adj.* [< L *triplus*] 1 consisting of three; threefold 2 three times as much or as many —*n.* 1 an amount three times as much or as many 2 *Baseball* a hit on which the batter reaches third base —*vt., vi.* tri′pled, tri′pling 1 to make or become three times as much or as many **2** *Baseball* to hit a triple —**tri′ply** *adv.*

tri·plet (trip′lit) *n.* **1** a group of three, as three successive lines of poetry **2** any of three offspring from the same pregnancy

trip·li·cate (trip′li kit; *for v.,* -kāt′) *adj.* [< L *triplex*] **1** threefold **2** being the last of three identical copies —*n.* any one of such copies —*vt.* -**cat′ed, -cat′ing** to make three identical copies of —**in triplicate** in three identical copies

tri·pod (trī′päd′) *n.* [< Gr *tri-*, three + *pous*, foot] a three-legged support

trip·tych (trip′tik) *n.* [< Gr *tri-*, three + *ptychē*, a fold] a set of three hinged panels with pictures, etc., commonly placed above and behind an altar

tri·sect (trī sekt′, trī′sekt′) *vt.* [< TRI- + L *secare*, to cut] to cut or divide into three equal parts

tri·state (trī′stāt′) *adj.* of an area consisting of all or parts of three contiguous states

trite (trīt) *adj.* **trit′er, trit′est** [< L *terere*, wear out] worn out by constant use; stale —**trite′ness** *n.*

trit·i·um (trit′ē əm) *n.* a radioactive isotope of hydrogen having an atomic weight of 3

Tri·ton (trīt′'n) *n.* Gr. Myth. a sea god having the tail of a fish and the head and upper body of a man

tri·umph (trī′əmf) *n.* [< L *triumphus*] **1** a victory; success **2** exultation or joy over a victory, etc. —*vi.* **1** to gain victory or success **2** to rejoice over victory, etc. —**tri·um′phal** (-um′fəl) *adj.*

tri·um·phal·ism *n.* an arrogant confidence in a set of beliefs —**tri·um′phal·ist** *adj., n.*

tri·um·phant (-fant) *adj.* **1** successful; victorious **2** rejoicing over victory —**tri·um′phant·ly** *adv.*

tri·um·vir (trī um′vir′) *n., pl.* -**virs′** or -**vi·ri′** (-vi rī′) [L: see fol.] in ancient Rome, any of three administrators sharing authority

tri·um·vi·rate (trī um′və rit) *n.* [< L *trium virum,* of three men] government by three persons or parties

tri·va·lent (trī vā′lənt) *adj. Chem.* having three valences or a valence of three

triv·et (triv′it) *n.* [< L *tripes,* tripod] **1** a three-legged stand for holding pots, etc. near a fire **2** a short-legged stand for hot dishes to rest on

triv·i·a (triv′ē ə) *pl.n.* [*usually with sing. v.*] unimportant matters

triv·i·al (triv′ē əl) *adj.* [< L *trivialis,* commonplace] unimportant; insignificant —**triv′i·al′i·ty** (-al′ə tē) *n.*

triv·i·al·ize (-īz′) *vt.* -**ized′, -iz′ing** to regard or treat as trivial; make seem unimportant

-trix (triks) [L] *suffix* forming feminine nouns of agency

tro·chee (trō′kē) *n.* [< Gr *trechein,* to run] a metrical foot of one accented syllable followed by one unaccented syllable —**tro·cha′ic** (- kā′ik) *adj.*

trod (träd) *vt., vi. pt. & alt. pp. of* TREAD

trod·den (träd′'n) *vt., vi. alt. pp. of* TREAD

trog·lo·dyte (träg′lə dīt′) *n.* [< Gr *trōglē,* hole + *dyein,* enter] **1** any of the prehistoric people who lived in caves **2** someone considered culturally undeveloped

troi·ka (troi′kə) *n.* [Russ] **1** a vehicle drawn by three horses abreast **2** an association of three in authority

Tro·jan (trō′jən) *adj.* of ancient Troy or its people or culture —*n.* a person born or living in ancient Troy

Trojan horse 1 *Gr. Legend* a huge, hollow wooden horse with Greek soldiers inside: it is brought into Troy, the soldiers creep out and open the gates, and the Greek army destroys the city **2** one that subverts a nation, etc. from within **3** a computer program that contains hidden instructions for an unauthorized, disruptive operation

troll¹ (trōl) *vt., vi.* [ME *trollen,* to roll] **1** to sing in a full voice **2** to fish (in) with a baited line trailed behind a slowly moving boat **3** to visit (one or more areas) in search of something **4** [infl. by TROLL²] to post inflammatory or malicious content on (an electronic forum) —*n.* [infl. by TROLL²] one who posts maliciously on electronic forums, etc. —**troll′er** *n.*

troll² (trōl) *n.* [ON] *Scand. Folklore* a supernatural being, as a giant or dwarf, living in a cave

trol·ley (trä′lē) *n., pl.* -**leys** [< TROLL¹] **1** a wheeled basket, etc. that runs suspended from an overhead track **2** a grooved wheel at the end of a pole, for transmitting electric current from an overhead wire to a streetcar, etc. **3** a trolley car

trolley car an electric streetcar that gets its power from a trolley

trol·lop (trä′ləp) *n.* [prob. < Ger *trolle,* wench] [Old-fashioned] a prostitute

trom·bone (träm bōn′) *n.* [It < *tromba,* a trumpet] a large brass instrument, usually with a slide, or movable section —**trom·bon′ist** *n.*

troop (trōōp) *n.* [< ML *troppus,* flock] **1** a group of persons or animals **2** [*pl.*] soldiers **3** a subdivision of a cavalry regiment **4** a unit of Boy Scouts or Girl Scouts —*vi.* **1** to gather or go together in a group **2** to walk or go

troop·er *n.* [prec. + -ER] **1** a soldier in the mounted cavalry **2** a mounted police officer **3** in the U.S., a state police officer **4** [Inf.] one who is steady, dependable, etc. during trying times

trope (trōp) *n.* [< Gr *tropos,* a turning] **1** a word used in a figurative sense **2** a conventional theme, motif, etc.

tro·phy (trō′fē) *n., pl.* -**phies** [< Gr *tropaion*] a memorial of victory in war, sports competition, etc.; prize

trop·ic (träp′ik) *n.* [< Gr *tropikos,* of a turn (of the sun at the solstices)] **1** either of two parallels of latitude, one, the **Tropic of Cancer,** *c.* 23° 27′ north, and the other, the **Tropic of**

Capricorn, c. 23° 27' south **2** [also **T-**] [pl.] the region between these latitudes —adj. of the tropics; tropical

trop·i·cal (-i kəl) adj. **1** of, in, characteristic of, or suitable for the tropics **2** very hot; sultry; torrid

tropical storm a tropical cyclone having winds that move slower than a hurricane (73 mph) but faster than a breeze (31 mph)

tro·pism (trō′piz′əm) n. [< Gr tropē, a turn] the tendency of a plant or animal to grow or turn toward, or away from, a stimulus, as light

tro·po·sphere (trō′pə sfir′, träp′ə-) n. [Fr < Gr tropos, a turning + Fr sphère, sphere] the lowest layer of the atmosphere, characterized by water vapor, weather, and decreasing temperatures with increasing altitude

trot (trät) vt., vi. **trot′ted, trot′ting** [< OHG trottōn, to tread] **1** to move, ride, go, etc. at a trot **2** to hurry; run —n. **1** a gait, as of a horse, in which a front leg and the opposite hind leg are lifted at the same time **2** a jogging gait of a person —**trot′ter** n.

troth (trōth, trôth) n. [ME trouthe] [Archaic] **1** faithfulness; loyalty **2** truth **3** a promise, esp. to marry

trou·ba·dour (trōō′bə dôr′) n. [Fr < Prov trobar, compose] **1** any of a class of lyric poets and poet-musicians in S France, N Spain, and Italy in the 1000s to the 1200s **2** a minstrel or singer

trou·ble (trub′əl) vt. **-bled, -bling** [< L turba, crowd] **1** to disturb or agitate **2** to worry; harass **3** to cause inconvenience to [don't trouble yourself] —vi. to take pains; bother —n. **1** a state of mental distress; worry **2** a misfortune; calamity **3** a person, event, etc. causing annoyance, distress, etc. **4** public disturbance **5** effort; bother [take the trouble to listen]

trou·ble·mak·er n. one who incites others to quarrel, rebel, etc. —**trou′ble·mak′ing** n., adj.

trou·ble·shoot·er n. one whose work is to locate and fix breakdowns, eliminate the source of trouble in work flow, etc. —**trou′ble·shoot′ing** n.

trou·ble·some (-səm) adj. characterized by or causing trouble

trough (trôf, träf) n. [OE trog] **1** a long, narrow, open container, esp. one to hold water or food for animals **2** a channel or gutter for carrying off rainwater **3** a long, narrow hollow, as between waves **4** a low in an economic cycle **5** a long, narrow area of low barometric pressure

trounce (trouns) vt. **trounced, trounc′ing** [< ?] **1** to beat; flog **2** [Inf.] to defeat —**trounc′er** n.

troupe (trōōp) n. [Fr] a group of actors, singers, etc. —vi. **trouped, troup′ing** to travel as a member of a troupe

troup·er n. a member of a troupe

trou·sers (trou′zərz) pl.n. [< Gael triubhas] pants, esp. for men and boys, extending usually to the ankles

trous·seau (trōō sō′, trōō′sō) n., pl. **-seaux′** (-sōz′) or **-seaus′** [Fr < OFr trousse, a bundle] a bride's clothes, linens, etc.

trout (trout) n., pl. **trout** or **trouts** [< Gr trōgein, gnaw] a food and game fish, related to the salmon, found chiefly in fresh water

trow (trō, trou) vi., vt. [< OE treow, faith] [Archaic] to believe

trow·el (trou′əl) n. [< L trua, ladle] **1** a flat hand tool for smoothing plaster or applying mortar **2** a scooplike tool for loosening soil, etc. —vt. **-eled** or **-elled, -el·ing** or **-el·ling** to spread, smooth, dig, etc. with a trowel

troy (troi) adj. [after Troyes, city in France, where first used] of or by a system of weights (**troy weight**) for gold, silver, gems, etc.

Troy (troi) ancient city in NW Asia Minor

tru·ant (trōō′ənt) n. [< OFr, beggar] **1** a pupil who stays away from school without permission **2** one who neglects duties —adj. **1** that is a truant **2** errant; straying —**tru′an·cy** n., pl. **-cies**

truce (trōōs) n. [< OE treow, faith] **1** a temporary cessation of warfare by agreement between the belligerents **2** respite from conflict, trouble, etc.

truck[1] (truk) n. [< Gr trochos, wheel] **1** a low, two-wheeled frame for carrying heavy articles **2** an automotive vehicle for hauling loads **3** a swiveling, wheeled frame under each end of a railroad car, etc. —vt. to carry on a truck —vi. to drive a truck —**truck′er** n.

truck[2] (truk) vt., vi. [< Fr troquer] to exchange; barter —n. **1** small articles of little value **2** vegetables raised for market **3** [Inf.] dealings **4** [Inf.] trash; rubbish

truck farm a farm where vegetables are grown to be marketed

truck·le (truk′əl) n. [< Gr trochos, wheel] TRUNDLE BED: in full **truckle bed** —vi. **-led, -ling** to be servile; submit (to)

truc·u·lent (truk′yōō lənt, -yə-) adj. [< L trux] **1** fierce; cruel; savage **2** pugnacious —**truc′u·lence** n. —**truc′u·lent·ly** adv.

trudge (truj) vi. **trudged, trudg′ing** [< ?] to walk, esp. wearily or laboriously —n. a wearying walk

true (trōō) adj. **tru′er, tru′est** [OE treowe] **1** faithful; loyal **2** in accordance with fact; not false **3** conforming to standard, etc.; correct **4** rightful; lawful **5** accurately fitted, shaped, etc. **6** real; genuine —adv. **1** truly **2** Biol. without variation from type —vt. **trued, tru′ing** or **true′ing** to fit, place, or shape accurately: often with up —n. that which is true: with the

true believer a dedicated follower, esp. one who follows unquestioningly

true bill a bill of indictment endorsed by a grand jury

true-blue adj. very loyal; staunch

truf·fle (truf′əl) n. [ult. < L tuber, knob] a fleshy, edible underground fungus

tru·ism (trōō′iz′əm) n. a statement the truth of which is obvious

tru·ly adv. **1** in a true manner; accurately, genuinely, etc. **2** really; indeed **3** sincerely

Tru·man (trōō′mən), **Har·ry S.** (har′ē) 1884–1972; 33d president of the U.S. (1945-53)

trump (trump) *n.* ⟦< TRUMPH⟧ **1** any playing card of a suit ranked higher than any other suit for a given hand **2** such a suit **3** any advantage held in reserve —*vt.* **1** to play a trump on (a trick, etc.) **2** to surpass or outrank —**trump up** to devise fraudulently

trump·er·y (trump′ər ē) *n., pl.* **-ies** ⟦< Fr *tromper*, deceive⟧ **1** something showy but worthless **2** nonsense

trum·pet (trum′pit) *n.* ⟦< OFr *trompe*⟧ **1** a brass instrument consisting of a looped tube with a flared bell and three valves **2** a trumpetlike device for channeling sound, as an early kind of hearing aid **3** a sound like that of a trumpet —*vt.* to make the sound of a trumpet —*vt.* to proclaim loudly —**trum′pet·er** *n.*

trun·cate (truŋ′kāt′) *vt.* **-cat′ed, -cat′ing** ⟦< L *truncus*, stem⟧ to cut off a part of —**trun·ca′tion** *n.*

trun·cheon (trun′chən) *n.* ⟦< L *truncus*, stem⟧ [Chiefly Brit.] a policeman's stick or billy

trun·dle (trun′dəl) *vt., vi.* **-dled, -dling** ⟦< OE *trendan*, to roll⟧ to roll along —**trun′dler** *n.*

trundle bed a low bed on small wheels, that can be rolled under another bed when not in use

trunk (truŋk) *n.* ⟦< L *truncus*⟧ **1** the main stem of a tree **2** a human or animal body, not including the head and limbs **3** a long snout, as of an elephant **4** a large, reinforced box to hold clothes, etc. in travel **5** [*pl.*] shorts worn by men esp. for swimming **6** a compartment in a car, usually in the rear, for luggage, etc.

trunk line a main line of a railroad, telephone system, etc.

truss (trus) *vt.* ⟦< OFr *trousser*⟧ **1** to tie, bind, or bundle: often with *up* **2** to support with a truss —*n.* **1** a bundle or pack **2** a framework for supporting a roof, bridge, etc. **3** a padded device for giving support in cases of rupture or hernia

trust (trust) *n.* ⟦< ON *traust*⟧ **1** firm belief in the honesty, reliability, etc. of another; faith **2** confident expectation, hope, etc. **3** responsibility resulting from confidence placed in one **4** care; custody **5** something entrusted to one **6** faith in a buyer's ability to pay; credit **7** a combination of corporations to establish a monopoly **8** *Law a)* the fact of having nominal ownership of property to keep, use, or administer for another *b)* such property —*vi.* to be confident —*vt.* **1** to have confidence in **2** to commit (something) to a person's care **3** to allow to do something without misgivings **4** to believe **5** to hope; expect —*adj.* **1** relating to a trust **2** acting as trustee —**in trust** entrusted to another's care

trust·ee (trus tē′) *n.* **1** one to whom another's property or its management is entrusted **2** a member of a board managing the affairs of a college, hospital, etc. —**trust·ee′ship** *n.*

trust·ful *adj.* full of trust; ready to confide; trusting —**trust′ful·ly** *adv.* —**trust′ful·ness** *n.*

trust fund money, securities, etc. held in trust

trust·ing *adj.* that trusts; trustful —**trust′ing′ly** *adv.*

trust territory a territory placed under the administrative authority of a country by the United Nations

trust·wor·thy *adj.* **-thi·er, -thi·est** worthy of trust; reliable —**trust′wor′thi·ness** *n.*

trust·y *adj.* **-i·er, -i·est** dependable; trustworthy —*n., pl.* **-ies** a convict granted special privileges as a trustworthy person

truth (trōōth) *n., pl.* **truths** (trōōthz, trōōths) ⟦OE *treowth*⟧ **1** a being true; specif., *a)* sincerity; honesty *b)* conformity with fact *c)* reality; actual existence *d)* correctness; accuracy **2** that which is true **3** an established fact —**in truth** truly

truth·ful *adj.* **1** telling the truth; honest **2** corresponding with fact or reality —**truth′ful·ly** *adv.* —**truth′ful·ness** *n.*

try (trī) *vt.* **tried, try′ing** ⟦< OFr *trier*⟧ **1** to melt out or render (fat, etc.) **2** to conduct the trial of in a law court **3** to put to the proof; test **4** to subject to trials, etc.; afflict **5** to experiment with [to *try* a recipe] **6** to attempt; endeavor —*vi.* to make an effort, attempt, etc. —*n., pl.* **tries** an attempt; effort; trial —**try on** to test the fit of (something to wear) by putting it on —**try out 1** to test by putting into use **2** to test one's fitness, as for a place on a team

try·ing *adj.* that tries one's patience; annoying; irksome —**try′ing·ly** *adv.*

try·out *n.* a test to determine fitness, etc.

tryst (trist) *n.* ⟦< OFr *triste*, hunting station⟧ **1** an appointment to meet, esp. one made by lovers **2** an appointed meeting or meeting place

tsar (tsär, zär) *n. alt. sp. of* CZAR (n. 1)

tset·se fly (tset′sē, tsēt′-) ⟦< Bantu name⟧ a small fly of central and S Africa: one kind carries sleeping sickness

T-shirt *n.* a collarless pullover knit shirt usu ally having short sleeves

tsp *abbrev.* teaspoon(s) or teaspoonful(s)

T square a T-shaped ruler for drawing parallel lines

tsu·na·mi (tsōō nä′mē) *n., pl.* **-mis** or **-mi** ⟦Jpn < *tsu*, a harbor + *nami*, a wave⟧ a huge sea wave caused by an undersea earthquake, volcanic eruption, etc.

tub (tub) *n.* ⟦< MDu *tubbe*⟧ **1** a round, wooden container, usually with staves and hoops **2** any large, open container, as of metal **3** a bathtub

tu·ba (tōō′bə) *n.* ⟦L, trumpet⟧ a large, low-pitched brass musical instrument

tub·al (tōō′bəl) *adj.* of or in a tube, esp. a fallopian tube [a *tubal* pregnancy]

tub·by (tub′ē) *adj.* **-bi·er, -bi·est 1** shaped like a tub **2** fat and short

tube (tōōb) *n.* ⟦< L *tubus*, pipe⟧ **1** a slender pipe of metal, glass, etc. for conveying fluids **2** a tubelike part, organ, etc. **3** a pliable cylinder with a screw cap, for holding paste, etc. **4** *short for: a)* ELECTRON TUBE *b)*

VACUUM TUBE 5 [Brit.] a subway —**the tube** [Inf.] television —**tube′less** *adj.*

tu·ber (tōō′bər) *n.* ⟦L., lit., a swelling⟧ a short, thick part of an underground stem, as a potato —**tu′ber·ous** *adj.*

tu·ber·cle (-kəl) *n.* ⟦see prec.⟧ 1 a small, rounded projection, as on a bone or a plant root 2 any abnormal hard nodule or swelling; specif., the typical lesion of tuberculosis

tu·ber·cu·lin (tōō bur′kyə lin) *n.* a solution injected into the skin as a test for tuberculosis

tu·ber·cu·lo·sis (-lō′sis) *n.* ⟦see TUBERCLE & -OSIS⟧ an infectious disease characterized by the formation of tubercles in body tissue; specif., tuberculosis of the lungs —**tu·ber′cu·lar** *adj.*, **tu·ber′cu·lous**

tube sock a stretchable sock in the form of a long tube with no shaped heel

tube top a tight-fitting, one-piece, sleeveless and strapless women's garment for the upper body

tub·ing (tōō′biŋ) *n.* 1 a system of tubes 2 material in the form of a tube

tu·bu·lar (tōō′byə lər) *adj.* ⟦< L *tubus*, pipe⟧ 1 of or like a tube 2 made with a tube or tubes

tu·bule (-byōōl′) *n.* a small tube

tuck (tuk) *vt.* ⟦< MDu *tucken*⟧ 1 to pull or gather (*up*) in folds or folds 2 to sew a fold or folds in (a garment) 3 to fold the edges of (a sheet, etc.) under or in, to make secure 4 to press snugly into a small space —*n.* 1 a sewed fold in a garment 2 [Inf.] cosmetic plastic surgery to remove fat

tuck·er (tuk′ər) *vt.* ⟦prob. < prec., in obs. sense "to punish, rebuke"⟧ [Inf.] to tire (*out*); weary

Tuc·son (tōō′sän′) city in S Arizona

-tude (tōōd, tyōōd) ⟦< L *-tudo*⟧ *suffix* state, quality, or instance of being

Tues·day (tōōz′dā) *n.* ⟦OE *Tiwes dæg*, day of the god of war *Tiu*⟧ the third day of the week: abbrev. **Tue, Tues**

tuft (tuft) *n.* ⟦< OFr *tufe*⟧ 1 a bunch of hairs, feathers, grass, etc. growing closely together 2 any soft cluster, as the fluffy ball at the end of a cluster of threads drawn through a mattress —*vt.* to provide with tufts —**tuft′ed** *adj.*

tug (tug) *vi., vt.* **tugged, tug′ging** ⟦prob. < ON *toga*, to pull⟧ 1 to pull hard; drag; haul 2 to tow with a tugboat —*n.* 1 a hard pull 2 a tugboat

tug·boat (tug′bōt′) *n.* a sturdy, powerful boat for towing or pushing ships, barges, etc.

tug of war 1 a contest in which two teams pull at opposite ends of a rope 2 a power struggle

tu·i·tion (tōō ish′ən) *n.* ⟦< L *tueri*, protect⟧ the charge for instruction, as at a college

tu·la·re·mi·a (tōō′lə rē′mē ə) *n.* ⟦after Tulare County, CA⟧ an infectious disease of rodents, esp. rabbits, transmissible to humans

tu·lip (tōō′lip) *n.* ⟦< Turk *tülbend*, turban: from its shape⟧ 1 a bulb plant with a large, cup-shaped flower 2 the flower

tulle (tōōl) *n.* ⟦after *Tulle*, city in France⟧ a fine netting of silk, rayon, nylon, etc., used as for veils and scarves

Tul·sa (tul′sə) city in NE Oklahoma

tum·ble (tum′bəl) *vi.* **-bled, -bling** ⟦< OE *tumbian*, to jump⟧ 1 to do somersaults or similar acrobatic feats 2 to fall suddenly or helplessly 3 to toss or roll about 4 to move in a hasty, disorderly manner —*vt.* 1 to cause to tumble 2 to put into disorder; disarrange —*n.* 1 a fall 2 disorder

tum·ble·down *adj.* dilapidated

tum·bler (-blər) *n.* 1 an acrobat who does somersaults, etc. 2 a drinking glass with no handle or stem 3 a part of a lock that must be rotated by a key to release the bolt

tum·ble·weed *n.* a plant that breaks off near the ground in autumn and is blown about by the wind

tum·brel or **tum·bril** (tum′brəl) *n.* ⟦< Fr *tomber*, to fall⟧ a cart that can be tilted for emptying

tu·mes·cence (tōō mes′əns) *n.* ⟦see fol.⟧ 1 a swelling; distention 2 a swollen or distended part —**tu·mes′cent** *adj.*

tu·mid (tōō′mid) *adj.* ⟦< L *tumere*, to swell⟧ 1 swollen; bulging 2 inflated or pompous —**tu·mid′i·ty** *n.*

tum·my (tum′ē) *n., pl.* **-mies** [Inf.] the stomach or abdomen

tu·mor (tōō′mər) *n.* ⟦L., a swelling⟧ an abnormal growth of new tissue, independent of its surrounding structures; neoplasm: Brit. sp. **tu′mour**

tu·mult (tōō′mult′) *n.* ⟦< L *tumere*, to swell⟧ 1 noisy commotion 2 confusion; disturbance

tu·mul·tu·ous (tōō mul′chōō əs) *adj.* full of tumult, uproar, etc.

tun (tun) *n.* ⟦OE *tunne*⟧ a large cask

tu·na (tōō′nə) *n., pl.* **-na** or **-nas** ⟦AmSp⟧ 1 a large, edible ocean fish, as the albacore 2 the flesh of the tuna, canned for food: also **tuna fish**

tun·dra (tun′drə) *n.* ⟦Russ⟧ a vast, treeless arctic plain

tune (tōōn) *n.* ⟦ME, var. of *tone*, tone⟧ 1 a rhythmic succession of musical tones; melody 2 *a)* correct musical pitch *b)* agreement; concord: now used chiefly in the phrases **in tune** and **out of tune** —*vt.* **tuned, tun′ing** 1 to adjust (a musical instrument) to some standard of pitch 2 to adapt to some condition, mood, etc. 3 to adjust (a motor, circuit, etc.) for proper performance —**to the tune of** [Inf.] to the sum, price, or extent of —**tune in** to adjust a radio or TV receiver so as to receive (a station, etc.) —**tune out** [Inf.] to ignore (a distraction, etc.) —**tun′er** *n.*

tune·ful *adj.* full of music; melodious

tune·less *adj.* 1 not melodious 2 not producing music —**tune′less·ly** *adv.* —**tune′less·ness** *n.*

tune-up or **tune·up** *n.* an adjusting, as of an engine, to the proper condition

tung·sten (tuŋ′stən) *n.* ⟦Swed < *tung*, heavy + *sten*, stone⟧ a hard, heavy metallic chemical element, used in steel, etc.: symbol, W; at. no. 74

tu·nic (tōō′nik, tyōō′-) *n.* [L *tunica*] **1** a loose, gownlike garment worn by men and women in ancient Greece and Rome **2** a blouselike garment extending to the hips, often belted

tuning fork a two-pronged steel instrument which when struck sounds a certain fixed tone in perfect pitch

Tu·nis (tōō′nis) seaport & capital of Tunisia

Tu·ni·si·a (tōō nē′zhə) country in N Africa, on the Mediterranean —**Tu·ni′si·an** *adj., n.*

tun·nel (tun′əl) *n.* [< Fr *tonnelle*, a vault] **1** an underground passageway, as for autos, etc. **2** any tunnel-like passage, as in a mine — *vt., vi.* -**neled** or -**nelled,** -**nel·ing** or -**nel·ling** to make a tunnel (through or under) —**tun′nel·er** *n.,* **tun′nel·ler**

tunnel vision a narrow outlook, as on a particular problem

tun·ny (tun′ē) *n., pl.* -**nies** TUNA (*n.* 1)

tur·ban (tur′bən) *n.* [< Pers *dulbānd*] **1** a headdress worn by men in parts of Asia, consisting of cloth wound in folds about the head **2** any similar headdress

tur·bid (tur′bid) *adj.* [< L *turba,* a crowd] **1** muddy or cloudy from stirring sediment **2** thick, dense, or dark, as clouds **3** confused

tur·bine (tur′bin, -bīn′) *n.* [< L *turbo,* a whirl] an engine driven as by the pressure of steam, water, or air against the curved vanes of a wheel

tur·bo·charge (tur′bō chärj′) *vt.* -**charged′,** -**charg′ing** to increase the power of (an engine) by using a type of compressor (**tur′bo·charg′er**) driven by a turbine powered by exhaust gases

tur·bo·fan (-fan′) *n.* a turbojet engine developing extra thrust from air that bypasses the combustion chamber and is accelerated by a fan: in full **turbofan engine**

tur·bo·jet (-jet′) *n.* **1** a jet engine in which the energy of the jet spins a turbine which drives the air compressor: in full **turbojet engine 2** an aircraft with such an engine

tur·bo·prop (-präp′) *n.* **1** a turbojet engine whose turbine shaft drives a propeller: in full **turboprop engine 2** an aircraft with such an engine

tur·bot (tur′bət) *n., pl.* -**bot** or -**bots** [< OFr *tourbout*] any of various flounders highly regarded as food

tur·bu·lent (tur′byə lənt) *adj.* [< L *turba,* a crowd] **1** wild or disorderly **2** full of violent motion —**tur′bu·lence** *n.* —**tur′bu·lent·ly** *adv.*

tu·reen (too rēn′) *n.* [< Fr *terrine,* earthen vessel] a large, deep dish with a lid, for soups, etc.

turf (turf) *n.* [OE] **1** *a)* a top layer of earth containing grass with its roots; sod *b)* [Chiefly Brit.] a piece of this **2** a track for horse racing; also, horse racing: usually with *the* **3** [Inf.] *a)* an area seen by a street gang as its territory to be defended *b)* one's own territory —*vt.* to cover with turf —**turf′y** *adj.*

tur·gid (tur′jid) *adj.* [< L *turgere,* to swell] **1** swollen; distended **2** bombastic; pompous —**tur·gid′i·ty** *n.,* **tur′gid·ness** —**tur′gid·ly** *adv.*

Tu·rin (toor′in) city in NW Italy

Turk¹ (turk) *n.* a person born or living in Turkey

Turk² *abbrev.* **1** Turkey **2** Turkish

tur·key (tur′kē) *n.* [< similarity to a fowl formerly imported through *Turkey*] **1** a large North American bird with a spreading tail **2** its flesh, used as food

Tur·key (tur′kē) country occupying Asia Minor & a SE part of the Balkan Peninsula

turkey vulture a dark-colored vulture of temperate and tropical America: also **turkey buzzard**

Turk·ic (tur′kik) *adj.* designating or of a family of languages including Turkish, Tatar, etc.

Turk·ish (tur′kish) *adj.* of Turkey or its people, language, etc. —*n.* the language of Turkey

Turkish bath a bathhouse with steam rooms, showers, massage, etc.

Turk·men·i·stan (tәrk men′i stan′) country in central Asia

tur·mer·ic (tur′mər ik) *n.* [< ML *terra merita,* deserved earth] an East Indian plant whose powdered root is used as a yellow dye and as a seasoning

tur·moil (tur′moil′) *n.* [< ?] tumult; commotion

turn (turn) *vt.* [ult. < Gr *tornos,* a lathe] **1** to rotate (a wheel, etc.) **2** to move around or partly around [*turn* the key] **3** to give form to, as in a lathe **4** to change the position or direction of **5** to reverse the position or sides of **6** to wrench [*turn* one's ankle] **7** to upset (the stomach) **8** to deflect; divert **9** to cause to change actions, beliefs, aims, etc. **10** to go around (a corner, etc.) **11** to reach or pass (a certain age, amount, etc.) **12** to drive, set, let go, etc. [*turn* the dog loose] **13** to direct, point, aim, etc. **14** to change [to *turn* cream into butter] **15** to make sour **16** to affect in some way —*vi.* **1** to rotate or revolve; pivot **2** to move around or partly around **3** to reel; whirl **4** to become upset: said of the stomach **5** to change or reverse course, direction, etc., or one's feelings, allegiance, etc. **6** to refer (*to*) **7** to apply (*to*) for help **8** to shift one's attention [he *turned* to music] **9** to make a sudden attack (*on*) **10** to be contingent or depend (*on* or *upon*) **11** to become [to *turn* cold] **12** to change to another form [the rain *turned* to snow] **13** to become rancid, sour, etc. —*n.* **1** a turning around; rotation; revolution **2** a single twist, winding, etc. **3** a change or reversal of course or direction **4** a short walk, ride, etc. **5** a bend; curve [a *turn* in the road] **6** a change in trend, events, etc. **7** a sudden shock or fright **8** an action or deed [a good *turn*] **9** the right, duty, or chance to do something in regular order [my *turn* to go] **10** a distinctive form, detail, etc. [an odd *turn* of speech] **11** natural inclination [a curious *turn* of mind] —**in** (or **out of**) **turn** (not) in proper sequence —**take turns** to act or speak, one person at a time in order —**turn**

down to reject (a request, etc.) —**turn in 1** to deliver; hand in **2** [Inf.] to go to bed —**turn off 1** to stop the flow of (water, gas, etc.) **2** to make (an electrical device) stop functioning **3** [Inf.] to cause to be uninterested, displeased, etc. —**turn on 1** to start the flow of **2** to make (an electrical device) start functioning **3** [Inf.] to make or become interested, enthusiastic, etc. —**turn out 1** to put out (a light, etc.) **2** to dismiss **3** to come out or assemble **4** to produce **5** to result **6** to prove to be **7** [Inf.] to get out of bed —**turn over 1** to ponder **2** to hand over; transfer —**turn up** to happen, appear, arrive, etc. —**turn′er** n.

turn·a·bout n. a shift or reversal of position, allegiance, opinion, etc.

turn·a·round n. **1** TURNABOUT **2** a wide area, as in a driveway, for turning a vehicle around **3** the time taken to complete a task

turn·buck·le n. an adjustable coupling for two rods, etc., consisting of a metal sleeve with opposite internal threads at each end

turn·coat n. a renegade; traitor

turn·ing n. **1** the action of one that turns **2** a place where a road, etc. turns

turning point a point in time when a decisive change occurs

tur·nip (turr′nip) n. [prob. < Fr tour, round + ME nepe, turnip] a plant related to cabbage and broccoli, with a light-colored, roundish, edible root **2** the root

turn·key n., pl. **-keys′** [Archaic] a jailer

turn·off n. **1** a turning off **2** a place to turn off, as a road ramp **3** [Slang] someone or something regarded as being boring, distasteful, etc.

turn-on n. [Slang] someone or something regarded as being interesting, exciting, etc.

turn·out n. **1** a gathering of people, as for a meeting **2** a wider part of a narrow road, enabling vehicles to pass each other

turn·o·ver n. **1** a small pie with half the crust folded back over the other half **2** a) the number of times a stock of goods is sold and replaced in a given period b) the amount of business done during a given period **3** the rate of replacement as of workers

turn·pike n. [ME turnpyke, a spiked road barrier] a toll road, esp. one that is an expressway

turn·stile (-stīl′) n. a device, as a post with revolving horizontal bars, placed in an entrance to allow the passage of persons one at a time

turn·ta·ble n. a circular rotating platform, as for supporting a phonograph record being played

turn·ta·blist (-tā′bəl ist) n. a disc jockey who manipulates records on a turntable to create distinctive sounds

tur·pen·tine (turr′pən tīn′) n. [< Gr terebinthos, tree yielding this substance] a colorless, volatile oil distilled from a substance extracted from various coniferous trees: used in paints, etc.

tur·pi·tude (turr′pi tōōd′) n. [< L turpis, vile] baseness; vileness

tur·quoise (turr′koiz′, -kwoiz′) n. [< OFr turqueis, Turkish] **1** a greenish-blue semiprecious stone **2** its color

tur·ret (turr′it) n. [see TOWER] **1** a small tower projecting from a building, usually at a corner **2** a dome or revolving structure for guns, as on a warship, tank, or airplane **3** a rotating attachment for a lathe, etc. holding cutting tools

tur·tle (turt′'l) n. [< Fr tortue, tortoise] any of various land or water reptiles having a soft body encased in a tough shell

tur·tle·dove n. [< L echoic turtur] a wild dove with a plaintive call

tur·tle·neck n. **1** a high, snug, turned-down collar completely encircling the neck, as on a pullover sweater **2** a sweater, etc. with such a collar

tusk (tusk) n. [OE tucs] a very long, large, pointed tooth projecting outside the mouth

tus·sle (tus′əl) vi. **-sled, -sling** [< ME tusen, to pull] struggle; scuffle

tus·sock (tus′ək) n. [< ?] a thick tuft or clump of grass, sedge, etc.

tu·te·lage (tōōt′'l ij) n. [< L tutela, protection] **1** guardianship; care, protection, etc. **2** instruction —**tu′te·lar′y** (-er′ē) adj.

tu·tor (tōōt′ər) n. [< L tueri, to guard] a private teacher — vt., vi. to act as a tutor (to); teach —**tu·to·ri·al** (tōō tôr′ē əl, tyōō-) adj., n.

tut·ti-frut·ti (tōōt′ē frōōt′ē) n. [It, all fruits] **1** made with mixed fruits **2** combining a number of fruit flavors

tu·tu (tōō′tōō′) n. [Fr] a very short, full, projecting skirt worn by ballerinas

Tu·va·lu (tōō′va lōō′) country on a group of islands in the WC Pacific, north of Fiji

tux (tuks) n., pl. **tux′es** [Inf.] short for TUXEDO

tux·e·do (tuk sē′dō) n., pl. **-dos** [after a country club near Tuxedo Lake, NY] a man's semiformal suit with a tailless jacket

TV n. **1** television **2** pl. **TVs** or **TV′s** a television receiving set

TVA abbrev. Tennessee Valley Authority

TV dinner a frozen, precooked dinner packaged in a divided tray

twad·dle (twäd′'l) n. [prob. var. of TATTLE] foolish, empty talk or writing; nonsense

twain (twān) adj., n. [OE twegen, two] archaic var. of TWO

Twain (twān), Mark pseud. for Samuel Langhorne CLEMENS

twang (twaŋ) n. [echoic] **1** a sharp, vibrating sound, as of a plucked string **2** a sharply nasal way of speaking — vi., vt. to make or cause to make a twang —**twang′y** adj. **-i·er, -i·est**

'twas (twuz, wäz) contr. [Old Poet.] it was

tweak (twēk) vt. [OE twiccan, to twitch] **1** to give a twisting pinch to (someone's nose, ear, etc.) **2** to make a slight adjustment to —n. such a pinch or adjustment

tweed (twēd) n. [< misreading of tweel, Scot form of TWILL] **1** a rough wool fabric in a weave of two or more colors **2** [pl.] clothes of tweed

tweed·y *adj.* **-i·er, -i·est** **1** of, like, or wearing tweeds **2** having an informal style, a fondness for the outdoors, etc.

'tween (twēn) *contr. prep.* ⟦ME *twene*⟧ [Old Poet.] between

tweet (twēt) *interj., n.* ⟦echoic⟧ (used to signify or imitate) the thin, chirping sound of a small bird —*vi.* to make this sound

tweet·er *n.* a small, high-fidelity speaker for reproducing high-frequency sounds

tweeze (twēz) *vt.* **tweezed, tweez′ing** to pluck with tweezers

tweez·ers (twē′zərz) *pl.n.* ⟦< obs. *tweeze*, surgical set⟧ [*also with sing. v.*] a small tool having two arms joined at one end, for plucking out hairs, etc.

twelfth (twelfth) *adj.* ⟦OE *twelfta*⟧ preceded by eleven others; 12th —*n.* **1** the one following the eleventh **2** any of the twelve equal parts of something; ¹⁄₁₂

Twelfth Day Epiphany, the twelfth day after Christmas: **Twelfth Night** is the evening before, or of, Epiphany

twelve (twelv) *adj., n.* ⟦OE *twelf*⟧ two more than ten; 12; XII

12-step or **twelve-step** *adj.* designating or of any rehabilitation program modeled on that of AA

twelve-tone *adj. Music* of composition in which the twelve tones of the chromatic scale are fixed in some arbitrary succession (*tone row*)

twen·ty (twent′ē) *adj., n., pl.* **-ties** ⟦OE *twegentig*⟧ two times ten; 20; XX —**the twenties** the numbers or years, as of a century, from 20 through 29 —**twen′ti·eth** (-ith) *adj., n.*

twen·ty-one *n.* BLACKJACK (*n.* 2)

twen′ty-twen′ty (*or* 20/20) **vision** normal visual ability, i.e., seeing clearly at 20 feet what the normal eye sees at 20 feet

twerp (twərp) *n.* ⟦ult. < ? Dan *tver*, perverse⟧ [Slang] a person regarded as insignificant, contemptible, etc.

twice (twīs) *adv.* ⟦OE *twiga*⟧ **1** two times **2** two times as much or as many

twid·dle (twid′'l) *vt., vi.* **-dled, -dling** ⟦prob. < TW(IST) + (d)iddle, move back and forth rapidly⟧ to twirl or play with (something) lightly or idly —**twiddle one's thumbs** to be idle

twig (twig) *n.* ⟦OE *twigge*⟧ a small branch of a tree or shrub

twi·light (twī′līt′) *n.* ⟦ME⟧ **1** the subdued light just after sunset **2** the period from sunset to dark **3** a gradual decline —*adj.* of twilight

twi·lit (twī′lit) *adj.* in the subdued light of twilight

twill (twil) *n.* ⟦OE *twilic*, woven of double thread⟧ a kind of cloth having parallel diagonal ribs —**twilled** *adj.*

twin (twin) *adj.* ⟦OE *twinn*, double⟧ **1** consisting of, or being one of a pair of, two similar things **2** being a twin or twins —*n.* **1** either of two offspring from the same pregnancy **2**

either of two persons or things that are very much alike

twin bed either of a pair of single beds

twine (twīn) *n.* ⟦OE *twin*⟧ strong thread, string, etc. of strands twisted together —*vt., vi.* **twined, twin′ing** **1** to twist together **2** to wind (around)

twinge (twinj) *vt., vi.* **twinged, twing′ing** ⟦OE *twengan*, to squeeze⟧ to (cause to) have a sudden, sharp pain, qualm, etc. —*n.* such a pain, etc.

twi-night or **twi·night** (twī′nīt′) *adj.* ⟦TWI(LIGHT) + NIGHT⟧ *Baseball* designating a double-header starting in late afternoon and going into evening

twin·kle (twiŋ′kəl) *vi.* **-kled, -kling** ⟦OE *twinclian*⟧ **1** to shine with quick, intermittent gleams **2** to light up, as with amusement: said of the eyes **3** to move to and fro quickly: said as of a dancer's feet —*n.* **1** a glint in the eye **2** a gleam; sparkle

twin·kling *n.* an instant

twin-size *adj.* of or being the standard size of a twin bed: also **twin′-sized′**

twirl (twərl) *vt., vi.* ⟦prob. < Scand⟧ **1** to rotate rapidly; spin **2** to whirl in a circle —*n.* **1** a twirling **2** a twist, coil, etc. —**twirl′er** *n.*

twist (twist) *vt.* ⟦< OE *-twist*, a rope⟧ **1** to wind (strands, etc.) around one another **2** to wind (rope, etc.) around something **3** to give spiral shape to **4** *a)* to subject to torsion *b)* to wrench; sprain **5** to contort or distort **6** to confuse **7** to pervert the meaning of **8** to cause to rotate **9** to break (*off*) by turning the end —*vi.* **1** to undergo twisting **2** to spiral, twine, (*around or about*) **3** to revolve or rotate **4** to wind, as a path does **5** to squirm; writhe —*n.* **1** something twisted **2** a twisting or being twisted **3** stress produced by twisting **4** a contortion **5** a wrench or sprain **6** a turn; bend **7** distortion, as of meaning **8** an unexpected or different direction, method, slant, etc.

twist·er *n.* **1** a person or thing that twists **2** [Inf.] a tornado or cyclone

twist-tie *n.* a short wire covered with paper or plastic, twisted to tie closed a plastic bag, etc.

twit¹ (twit) *vt.* **twit′ted, twit′ting** ⟦< OE *æt*, at + *witan*, accuse⟧ to reproach, taunt, etc.

twit² (twit) *n.* ⟦< ?⟧ [Inf.] a foolish, contemptible person

twitch (twich) *vt., vi.* ⟦< OE *twiccian*, to pluck⟧ to pull (at) or move with a quick, slight jerk —*n.* **1** a twitching **2** a sudden, quick motion, esp. a spasmodic one

twitch·y *adj.* **-i·er, -i·est** [Inf.] nervous; jittery

twit·ter (twit′ər) *vi.* ⟦ME *twiteren*⟧ **1** to chirp rapidly **2** *a)* to chatter *b)* to giggle **3** to tremble with excitement —*n.* **1** a twittering **2** a condition of trembling excitement

'twixt (twikst) *prep.* [Old Poet.] betwixt; between

two (tōō) *adj., n.* ⟦OE *twa*⟧ one more than one; 2; II —**in two** in two parts

two-bit *adj.* [Slang] cheap, inferior, etc.

two bits [Old Inf.] twenty-five cents

two-by-four *n.* a piece of lumber two inches thick and four inches wide when untrimmed (1½ by 3½ inches trimmed)

two cents a person's opinion

two-edged *adj.* 1 having two cutting edges 2 that can be taken two ways [a *two-edged* remark]

two-faced *adj.* 1 having two faces, surfaces, etc. 2 deceitful; hypocritical

two·fer (tōō′fər) *n.* [altered < *two for*] [Inf.] a pair, as of theater tickets, sold for the price of one

two-fist·ed *adj.* [Inf.] 1 able to use both fists 2 vigorous; virile

two·fold *adj.* 1 having two parts 2 having twice as much or as many —*adv.* twice as much or as many

two-hand·ed *adj.* 1 requiring the use of both hands 2 operated, played, etc. by two persons

two·pence (tup′əns) *n.* two pence

two-ply *adj.* having two layers, strands, etc.

two·some (-səm) *n.* two people; a couple

two-time *vt.* -timed′, -tim′ing [Slang] to be unfaithful to —**two′-tim′er** *n.*

two-tone *adj.* of or having two colors

two-way *adj.* 1 allowing passage in either direction 2 involving two or used in two ways

Twp *abbrev.* township

TX *abbrev.* Texas

-ty (tē, ti) [< L *-tas*] *suffix* quality of, condition of

ty·coon (tī kōōn′) *n.* [< Jpn < Chin *tai*, great + *kuan*, official] a wealthy, powerful industrialist, financier, etc.

ty·ing (tī′iŋ) *vt., vi. prp. of* TIE

tyke (tīk) *n.* [< ON *tik*, a female dog] [Inf.] a small child

Ty·ler (tī′lər), **John** 1790–1862; 10th president of the U.S. (1841–45)

tym·pa·ni (tim′pə nē) *pl.n., sing.* **-no′** (-nō′) *alt. sp. of* TIMPANI —**tym′pa·nist** *n.*

tym·pan·ic membrane (tim pan′ik) a thin membrane inside the ear that vibrates when struck by sound waves

tym·pa·num (tim′pə nəm) *n., pl.* **-nums** or **-na** (-nə) [L, a drum] 1 MIDDLE EAR 2 TYMPANIC MEMBRANE

type (tīp) *n.* [< Gr *typos*, a mark] 1 the characteristic form, plan, style, etc. of a class or group 2 a class, group, etc. with characteristics in common 3 a person, animal, or thing representative of a class 4 a perfect example; model 5 *a)* a piece of metal or wood with a raised letter, etc. in reverse on its top, used in printing *b)* such pieces collectively *c)* a printed or photographically reproduced character or characters —*vt.* **typed, typ′ing** 1 to classify 2 to write using the keyboard of a typewriter or computer —*vi.* to use the keyboard of a typewriter or computer

-type (tīp) *combining form* 1 type, representative form, example [*stereotype*] 2 print, printing type

type·cast *vt.* -cast′, -cast′ing to cast (an actor) repeatedly in the same type of part

type·script *n.* typewritten matter

type·set *vt.* -set′, -set′ting to set in type; compose

type·set·ter *n.* 1 a person who sets type 2 a machine for setting type

type·write *vt., vi.* -wrote′, -writ′ten, -writ′ing to write with a typewriter: now usually *type*

type·writ·er *n.* a writing machine with a keyboard, for printing text on a sheet of paper

ty·phoid (tī′foid′) *n.* [TYPH(US) + -OID] an acute infectious disease caused by a bacillus and acquired by ingesting contaminated food or water: characterized by fever, intestinal disorders, etc.: in full **typhoid fever**

ty·phoon (tī fōōn′) *n.* [< Chin *tai-fung*, great wind] a violent tropical cyclone originating in the W Pacific

ty·phus (tī′fəs) *n.* [< Gr *typhos*, fever] an acute infectious disease caused by certain bacteria, transmitted by fleas, lice, etc., and characterized by fever, skin rash, etc.: in full **typhus fever**

typ·i·cal (tip′i kəl) *adj.* 1 serving as a type 2 having the distinguishing characteristics of a class, group, etc.; representative —**typ′i·cal·ly** *adv.*

typ·i·fy (tip′i fī′) *vt.* -fied′, -fy′ing to have the characteristics of; be typical of; exemplify —**typ′i·fi·ca′tion** *n.*

typ·ist (tīp′ist) *n.* a person skilled at or employed to do typing

ty·po (tī′pō) *n., pl.* **-pos** [Inf.] an error made in setting type or in typing

ty·pog·ra·phy (tī päg′rə fē) *n.* [see TYPE & -GRAPHY] 1 setting, and printing with, type 2 the arrangement, style, etc. of matter printed from type —**ty·pog′ra·pher** *n.* —**ty′po·graph′i·cal** (-pə graf′i kəl) *adj.* —**ty′po·graph′i·cal·ly** *adv.*

ty·ran·ni·cal (tə ran′i kəl, tī-) *adj.* 1 of or suited to a tyrant 2 harsh, cruel, unjust, etc. Also **ty·ran′nic** —**ty·ran′ni·cal·ly** *adv.*

tyr·an·nize (tir′ə nīz′) *vi.* -nized′, -niz′ing 1 to govern as a tyrant 2 to govern or use authority harshly or cruelly —*vt.* to treat tyrannically; oppress

ty·ran·no·saur (tə ran′ə sôr′) *n.* [< Gr *tyrannos*, tyrant + *sauros*, lizard] a huge, two-footed, flesh-eating dinosaur: also **ty·ran′no·saur′us** (-əs)

tyr·an·ny (tir′ə nē) *n., pl.* **-nies** 1 the authority, government, etc. of a tyrant 2 cruel and unjust use of power 3 a tyrannical act —**tyr′an·nous** *adj.*

ty·rant (tī′rənt) *n.* [< Gr *tyrannos*] 1 an absolute ruler 2 a cruel, oppressive ruler, master, etc.

ty·ro (tī′rō) *n., pl.* **-ros** [< L *tiro*, young soldier] a beginner in learning something; novice

Ty·rol (ti rōl′, -räl′) *alt. sp. of* TIROL

tzar (tsär, zär) *n. var. of* CZAR (*n.* 1)

U

u¹ or **U** (yōō) *n., pl.* **u's, U's** the 21st letter of the English alphabet

u² *abbrev.* unit(s)

U¹ *abbrev.* **1** Union **2** United **3** University

U² *Chem. symbol for* uranium

UAW *abbrev.* United Automobile Workers (of America)

u·biq·ui·tous (yōō bik′wə təs) *adj.* [< L *ubique*, everywhere] (seemingly) present everywhere at the same time —**u·biq′ui·ty** *n.*

U-boat *n.* [< Ger *Unterseeboot*, undersea boat] a German submarine

U bolt a U-shaped bolt with threads and a nut at each end

ud·der (ud′ər) *n.* [OE *udr*] a baglike, milk-secreting organ with two or more teats, as in cows

UFO *n., pl.* **UFOs** or **UFO's** an unidentified flying object, esp. when regarded as a spacecraft from another planet

u·fol·o·gy (yōō fäl′ə jē) *n.* the study of UFOs —**u·fol′o·gist** *n.*

U·gan·da (yōō gan′də, -gän′–) country in EC Africa —**U·gan′dan** *adj., n.*

ugh (ōōkh, ōō, ug, *etc.*) *interj.* used to express disgust, horror, etc.

ug·ly (ug′lē) *adj.* **-li·er, -li·est** [< ON *uggr*, fear] **1** unpleasing to look at **2** bad, disgusting, etc. [an *ugly* lie] **3** ominous [*ugly* storm clouds] **4** [Inf.] cross; quarrelsome [an *ugly* mood] —**ug′li·ness** *n.*

uh (u, un) *interj.* **1** HUH **2** used when hesitating in speaking

UHF or **uhf** *abbrev.* ultrahigh frequency

UK *abbrev.* United Kingdom

u·kase (yōō′kās′, -kāz′) *n.* [Russ *ukaz*, edict] an official decree

U·kraine (yōō krān′) country in SE Europe —**U·krain′i·an** *n., adj.*

u·ku·le·le (yōō′kə lā′lē) *n.* [Haw, leaping flea] a small, four-stringed, guitarlike musical instrument

UL *trademark for* Underwriters Laboratories

ul·cer (ul′sər) *n.* [L *ulcus*] **1** an open sore, often one discharging pus, on the skin or some mucous membrane **2** any corrupt condition —**ul′cer·ous** *adj.*

ul·cer·ate (-āt′) *vt., vi.* **-at·ed, -at·ing** to make or become ulcerous —**ul′cer·a′tion** *n.*

ul·na (ul′nə) *n., pl.* **-nae** (-nē) or **-nas** [L, the elbow] the larger of the two bones of the forearm —**ul′nar** *adj.*

ul·ster (ul′stər) *n.* [after Ulster, in N Ireland] a long, loose, heavy overcoat

ult *abbrev.* ultimate(ly)

ul·te·ri·or (ul tir′ē ər) *adj.* [L: see ULTRA-] **1** lying beyond or on the farther side **2** beyond what is expressed or implied; undisclosed

ul·ti·mate (ul′tə mit) *adj.* [< L *ultimus*, last] **1** beyond which it is impossible to go **2** final; conclusive **3** basic **4** greatest possible —*n.* a final point or result —**ul′ti·mate·ly** *adv.*

ul·ti·ma·tum (ul′tə mät′əm) *n., pl.* **-tums** or **-ta** (-ə) [see prec.] a final offer or demand, as in negotiations

ul·tra (ul′trə) *adj.* [< fol.] going beyond the usual limit; extreme

ultra- [L < *ultra*, beyond] *prefix* **1** beyond [*ultrasonic*] **2** extremely [*ultraconservative*]

ul·tra·con·serv·a·tive (ul′trə kən sur′və tiv) *adj.* extremely conservative

ul·tra·high frequency (ul′trə hī′) any radio frequency between 300 and 3,000 megahertz

ul·tra·ma·rine (-mə rēn′) *adj.* deep-blue —*n.* deep blue

ul·tra·son·ic (-sän′ik) *adj.* above the range of sound audible to the human ear

ul·tra·sound (-sound′) *n.* ultrasonic waves, used in medical diagnosis and therapy, etc.

ul·tra·vi·o·let (-vī′ə lit) *adj.* of or designating those rays that are just beyond the violet end of the visible spectrum

u·lu·late (yōōl′yōō lāt′, ul′-) *vi.* **-lat·ed, -lat′ing** [< L *ululare*, to howl] to howl, hoot, or wail loudly —**ul′u·la′tion** *n.*

U·lys·ses (yōō lis′ēz′) *n. Latin name for* ODYSSEUS

um·bel (um′bəl) *n.* [L *umbella*, parasol: see UMBRELLA] a cluster of flowers with stalks of similar length springing from the same point

um·ber (um′bər) *n.* [< It (*terra d'*)*ombra*, (earth of) shade] **1** a kind of earth used as a yellowish-brown or reddish-brown pigment **2** a yellowish-brown or reddish-brown color

um·bil·i·cal (um bil′i kəl) *adj.* [< L *umbilicus*, navel] of a cordlike structure (**umbilical cord**) connecting a fetus's navel to the placenta, for conveying nourishment to, and removing waste from, the fetus

um·bil·i·cus (um bil′i kəs) *n., pl.* **-ci′** (-sī′) [L] NAVEL

um·bra (um′brə) *n., pl.* **-brae** (-brē) or **-bras** [L, a shade] **1** shade or a shadow **2** the dark cone of complete shadow from a planet or satellite on the side opposite the sun

um·brage (um′brij) *n.* [< L *umbra*, a shade] **1** [Obs.] shade **2** offense or resentment

um·brel·la (um brel′ə) *n.* [< L *umbra*, a shade] **1** a screen, usually of cloth on a folding frame, carried for protection against rain or sun **2** any comprehensive, protective alliance, strategy, device, etc.

u·mi·ak (ōō′mē ak′) *n.* [Esk] a large, open boat made of skins on a wooden frame, used by the Yupik and Inuit

um·laut (ōōm′lout) *n.* [Ger < *um*, about + *laut*, a sound] *Linguistics* **1** a vowel changed in sound by its assimilation to another vowel **2** the mark (¨) placed over such a vowel, as in German

ump (ump) *n., vt., vi.* [Inf.] *short for* UMPIRE

um·pire (um′pīr′) *n.* [< Fr *nomper*, uneven, hence a third person] **1** a person chosen to judge a dispute **2** an official who administers the rules in certain sports — *vt., vi.* **-pired′, -pir′ing** to act as umpire (in or of)

ump·teen (ump′tēn′) *adj.* [Slang] very many —**ump′teenth′** *adj.*

UN *abbrev.* United Nations

un- *prefix* **1** [OE] not, lack of, the opposite of [*unconcern*] **2** [OE *un-*, *on-*] back: indicating a reversal of action [*unfold*] The following list includes some common compounds formed with *un-* (either sense) that do not have special meanings:

unabashed	unconfirmed	unfocused	unpardonable
unable	unconnected	unforeseen	unpaved
unabridged	uncontaminated	unforgivable	unpin
unaccented	uncontrollable	unforgotten	unplanned
unacceptable	uncontrolled	unfulfilled	unpolished
unaccompanied	uncontroversial	unfurnished	unpolluted
unacquainted	unconventional	ungrammatical	unpredictable
unadorned	unconvinced	ungrateful	unprejudiced
unadulterated	uncooked	unhampered	unpremeditated
unafraid	uncooperative	unharmed	unprepared
unaided	uncoordinated	unhealthful	unpretentious
unaltered	uncultivated	unheeded	unprofitable
unambiguous	undamaged	unhesitating	unpromising
unannounced	undefeated	unhitch	unprotected
unanswered	undemocratic	unhook	unproven
unashamed	undependable	unhurried	unprovoked
unasked	undeserved	unhurt	unpunished
unassailable	undesirable	unidentified	unquenchable
unassisted	undeveloped	unimaginable	unquestioned
unattainable	undigested	unimaginative	unquestioning
unattractive	undiminished	unimpaired	unreadable
unauthorized	undisciplined	unimportant	unrealistic
unavailable	undisclosed	unimproved	unrealized
unavoidable	undiscovered	unincorporated	unrecognized
unbearable	undisguised	uninformed	unrecorded
unbeaten	undisputed	uninhabited	unrefined
unbiased	undisturbed	uninjured	unregulated
unbleached	undivided	uninspired	unrelated
unblemished	undomesticated	uninsured	unreliable
unbound	uneducated	unintelligent	unrelieved
unbreakable	unemotional	unintelligible	unrepentant
unbroken	unending	unintentional	unresponsive
unbuckle	unenlightened	uninteresting	unrestricted
unbutton	unenviable	uninterrupted	unsafe
uncap	unethical	uninvited	unsanitary
unceasing	uneventful	uninviting	unsatisfactory
uncensored	unexpired	unjustifiable	unsatisfied
unchallenged	unexplained	unjustified	unscientific
unchanged	unexplored	unknowing	unscripted
unchanging	unexpressed	unknown	unseasoned
unchecked	unexpurgated	unlace	unseeing
uncivilized	unfair	unlatch	unseen
unclassified	unfashionable	unleavened	unsegmented
unclean	unfasten	unlicensed	unselfish
unclear	unfathomable	unlined	unshackle
uncomplaining	unfavorable	unlisted	unshakable
uncompleted	unfit	unloved	unshaken
unconcealed	unflattering	unmanageable	unshaven
		unmannerly	unsociable
		unmarked	unsold
		unmarried	unsolicited
		unmatched	unsought
		unmerited	unspoiled
		unmoved	unspoken
		unnamed	unsuccessful
		unnoticed	unsuitable
		unobserved	unsullied
		unobstructed	unsupervised
		unobtainable	unsure
		unobtrusive	unsurpassed
		unoccupied	unsuspecting
		unofficial	unsweetened
		unopened	unsympathetic
		unopposed	untainted
		unorthodox	untamed
		unpaid	untarnished
		unpalatable	

untenable
untested
untiring
untouched
untrained
untried
untroubled
untrue
untrustworthy

unvarying
unverified
unwanted
unwarranted
unwavering
unwed
unworkable
unyielding
unzip

un·ac·count·a·ble (un′ə kount′ə bəl) *adj.* **1** that cannot be explained; strange **2** not responsible

un·ac·cus·tomed *adj.* **1** not accustomed (*to*) **2** not usual; strange

un·ad·vised *adj.* **1** without counsel or advice **2** indiscreet; rash

un·af·fect·ed *adj.* **1** not affected or influenced **2** without affectation; simple; sincere

un-A·mer·i·can *adj.* regarded as contrary to the principles, traditions, etc. of the U.S.

u·nan·i·mous (yōō nan′ə məs) *adj.* ⟦< L *unus*, one + *animus*, the mind⟧ agreeing completely; without dissent —**u·nan·im·i·ty** (yōō′nə nim′ə tē) *n.* —**u·nan′i·mous·ly** *adv.*

un·ap·proach·a·ble *adj.* **1** not to be approached; inaccessible; aloof **2** having no equal; unmatched

un·armed *adj.* having no weapons

un·as·sum·ing *adj.* not forward; modest

un·at·tached *adj.* **1** not attached **2** not engaged or married

un·at·tend·ed *adj.* **1** not waited on **2** not accompanied (*by*) **3** neglected

un·a·vail·ing (-ə vāl′iŋ) *adj.* futile; useless

un·a·ware *adj.* not aware or conscious —*adv.* UNAWARES

un·a·wares *adv.* **1** unintentionally **2** unexpectedly

un·bal·anced *adj.* **1** not in balance **2** *a*) mentally deranged *b*) erratic or unstable

un·bar *vt.* **-barred′, -bar′ring** to remove the bar or bars from; open

un·be·com·ing *adj.* not appropriate or suited to one's appearance, character, etc.; unattractive, indecorous, etc.

un·be·known (un′bē nōn′) *adj.* without one's knowledge; unknown: usually with *to*: also **un′be·knownst′** (-nōnst′)

un·be·lief *n.* lack of belief, esp. in religion

un·be·liev·a·ble *adj.* beyond belief; astounding; incredible

un·be·liev·er *n.* **1** one who does not believe **2** one who does not accept any, or some particular, religious belief

un·bend *vt., vi.* **-bent′** or **-bend′ed, -bend′ing 1** to relax, as from formality **2** to straighten

un·bend·ing *adj.* **1** rigid; stiff **2** firm; resolute **3** aloof; austere

un·bid·den *adj.* **1** not commanded **2** not invited

un·blush·ing *adj.* **1** not blushing **2** shameless —**un·blush′ing·ly** *adv.*

un·bolt *vt., vi.* to withdraw the bolt or bolts of (a door, etc.); open

un·born *adj.* **1** not born **2** still in the mother's uterus **3** yet to be

un·bos·om (-booz′əm) *vt., vi.* to tell or reveal (feelings, secrets, etc.) —**unbosom oneself** to reveal one's feelings, secrets, etc.

un·bound·ed *adj.* **1** without bounds or limits **2** not restrained

un·bowed (-boud′) *adj.* not yielding or giving in

un·bri·dled *adj.* **1** having no bridle on: said of a horse, etc. **2** uncontrolled

un·bur·den *vt.* **1** to free from a burden **2** to relieve (oneself, one's mind, etc.) by disclosing (guilt, etc.)

un·but·toned *adj.* **1** with buttons unfastened **2** free and easy; casual

un·called-for *adj.* **1** not needed **2** inappropriately rude or hurtful

un·can·ny (un kan′ē) *adj.* **1** mysterious and eerie; weird **2** so good, acute, etc. as to seem preternatural —**un·can′ni·ly** *adv.*

un·cared-for *adj.* not cared for or looked after; neglected

un·cer·e·mo·ni·ous *adj.* **1** not ceremonious; informal **2** curt; abrupt

un·cer·tain *adj.* **1** *a*) not surely or certainly known *b*) not sure or certain in knowledge; doubtful **2** vague **3** not dependable or reliable **4** varying —**un·cer′tain·ty** *n., pl.* **-ties**

un·char·i·ta·ble *adj.* harsh or severe, as in opinion —**un·char′i·ta·bly** *adv.*

un·chart·ed *adj.* not marked on a chart or map; unexplored or unknown

un·chris·tian *adj.* **1** not Christian **2** lacking the qualities, esp. charity, considered appropriate for a Christian

un·ci·al (un′shē əl, -shəl) *adj.* ⟦L *uncialis*, inch-high⟧ designating or of the large, rounded letters of Greek and Latin manuscripts between A.D. 300 and 900 —*n.* uncial script or an uncial letter

un·cir·cum·cised *adj.* **1** not circumcised **2** not Jewish; gentile

un·civ·il *adj.* not civil; impolite

un·clad *adj.* alt. *pt. & pp. of* UNCLOTHE

un·clasp *vt.* **1** to unfasten the clasp of **2** to release from a clasp or grasp

un·cle (uŋ′kəl) *n.* ⟦< L *avunculus*⟧ the brother or brother-in-law of one's father or mother

Uncle Sam ⟦< abbrev. *U.S.*⟧ [Inf.] the U.S. (government or people), personified as a tall man with a goatee, dressed in red, white, and blue

Uncle Tom ⟦after main character in novel *Uncle Tom's Cabin* (1852)⟧ [Inf.] a black person regarded as servile toward whites: a term of contempt

un·cloak *vt.* to reveal; expose

un·clothe *vt.* **-clothed′** or **-clad′, -cloth′ing** to undress, uncover, etc.

un·coil *vt., vi.* to unwind

un·com·fort·a·ble *adj.* **1** feeling discomfort **2** causing discomfort **3** ill at ease —**un·com′fort·a·bly** *adv.*

un·com·mit·ted *adj.* **1** not committed or pledged **2** not taking a stand

un·com·mon *adj.* **1** rare; not common or usual **2** strange; remarkable

un·com·mu·ni·ca·tive *adj.* not communicative; reserved; taciturn

un·com·pro·mis·ing *adj.* not yielding; firm; inflexible

un·con·cern *n.* 1 apathy; indifference 2 lack of concern or worry

un·con·cerned *adj.* 1 indifferent 2 not solicitous or anxious —**un'con·cern'ed·ly** *adv.*

un·con·di·tion·al *adj.* without conditions or reservations; absolute

un·con·scion·a·ble (un kän'shən ə bəl) *adj.* 1 not guided or restrained by conscience 2 unreasonable or excessive 3 not fair or just —**un·con'scion·a·bly** *adv.*

un·con·scious *adj.* 1 deprived of consciousness 2 not aware (*of*) 3 not doing or done on purpose [an *unconscious* habit] —**the unconscious** *Psychoanalysis* the sum of all thoughts, impulses, etc. of which the individual is not conscious but which influence the emotions and behavior —**un·con'scious·ly** *adv.*

un·con·sti·tu·tion·al *adj.* not in accordance with a constitution, specif. the U.S. constitution

un·cool *adj.* [Slang] 1 unsophisticated 2 unfashionable, unacceptable, etc.

un·cork *vt.* to pull the cork out of

un·count·ed *adj.* 1 not counted 2 inconceivably numerous

un·cou·ple *vt.* **-pled, -pling** to unfasten (things coupled together)

un·couth (un kōōth') *adj.* [OE < *un-*, not + *cunnan*, know] 1 awkward; ungainly 2 not cultured; crude

un·cov·er *vt.* 1 to disclose 2 to remove the cover from 3 to remove the hat, etc. from (the head) —*vi.* to bare the head, as in respect

unc·tion (uŋk'shən) *n.* [< L *ungere*, anoint] 1 *a*) the act of anointing, as for medical or religious purposes *b*) the oil, ointment, etc. used for this 2 anything that soothes or comforts

unc·tu·ous (uŋk'chōō əs) *adj.* [see prec.] 1 oily or greasy 2 characterized by a smooth but insincere show of deep or earnest feeling

un·cut *adj.* not cut; specif., *a*) not ground to shape (said of a gem) *b*) not abridged or shortened

un·daunt·ed *adj.* not hesitating because of fear or discouragement

un·de·ceive *vt.* **-ceived', -ceiv'ing** to cause to be no longer deceived or misled

un·de·cid·ed *adj.* 1 not decided 2 not having come to a decision

un·de·mon·stra·tive *adj.* not demonstrative; not showing feelings openly; reserved

un·de·ni·a·ble *adj.* that cannot be denied; indisputable —**un'de·ni'a·bly** *adv.*

un·der (un'dər) *prep.* [OE] 1 in, at, or to a position down from; below 2 beneath the surface of 3 below and to the other side of [drive *under* the bridge] 4 covered by [a vest *under* his coat] 5 *a*) lower in rank, position, amount, etc. than *b*) lower than the required degree of [*under* age] 6 subject to the control, limitations, etc. of [*under* oath] 7 undergoing [*under* repair] 8 with the disguise of [*under* an alias] 9 in (the designated category) 10 during the rule of [*under* Elizabeth I] 11 being the subject of [*under* discussion] 12 because of [*under* the circumstances] 13 authorized by —*adv.* 1 in or to a lower position or state 2 so as to be covered, concealed, etc. —*adj.* lower in position, amount, etc.

under- *prefix* 1 in, on, to, or from a lower place; beneath [*undertow*] 2 in a subordinate position [*undersecretary*] 3 too little; insufficiently [*underdeveloped*]

un·der·a·chieve (un'dər ə chēv') *vi.* **un'der·a·chieved', un'der·a·chiev'ing** to fail to do as well as might be expected based on one's abilities —**un'der·a·chiev'er** *n.*

un·der·act *vt., vi.* to act (a theatrical role) with insufficient emphasis or too great restraint

un·der·age *adj.* below the age required by law

un·der·arm *adj.* 1 of, for, in, or used on the area under the arm, or the armpit 2 UNDERHAND (*adj.* 1) —*adv.* UNDERHAND

un·der·bel·ly *n.* 1 the lower, posterior part of an animal's belly 2 any vulnerable area, point, etc.

un·der·bid *vt., vi.* **-bid', -bid'ding** 1 to bid lower than (another person) 2 to bid less than the worth of (a thing, as one's hand in bridge)

un·der·brush *n.* small trees, shrubs, etc. growing in woods or forests

un·der·car·riage *n.* a supporting frame, as of an automobile

un·der·charge *vt., vi.* **-charged', -charg'ing** 1 to charge too low a price (to) 2 to provide with too small or low a charge

un·der·class *n.* the socioeconomic class with incomes below subsistence level

un·der·class·man (-mən) *n., pl.* **-men** (-mən) a freshman or sophomore in high school or college

un·der·clothes *pl.n.* UNDERWEAR: also **un'der·cloth'ing** *sing.n.*

un·der·coat *n.* 1 a tarlike coating applied to the underside of a motor vehicle to retard rust, etc. 2 a coat of paint, etc. applied before the final coat Also **un'der·coat'ing** —*vt.* to apply an undercoat to

un·der·cov·er *adj.* acting or carried out in secret

un·der·cur·rent *n.* 1 a current flowing beneath the surface 2 an underlying tendency, opinion, etc.

un·der·cut *vt.* **-cut', -cut'ting** 1 to make a cut below or under 2 to undersell or work for lower wages than 3 to weaken or undermine

un·der·de·vel·oped *adj.* inadequately developed, esp. economically and industrially

un·der·dog *n.* 1 a person or team that is losing or expected to lose 2 a person at a disadvantage because of injustice, prejudice, etc.

un·der·done *adj.* not cooked enough

un·der·em·ployed *adj.* 1 working less than

full time 2 working at low-skilled, poorly paid jobs when capable of doing more highly skilled work

un·der·es·ti·mate *vt.* **-mat'ed, -mat'ing** to set too low an estimate on or for —**un'der·es'ti·ma'tion** *n.*

un·der·ex·pose *vt.* **-posed', -pos'ing** to expose (photographic film, etc.) to inadequate light or for too short a time

un·der·foot *adv., adj.* 1 under the foot or feet 2 in the way

un·der·gar·ment *n.* a piece of underwear

un·der·go *vt.* **-went', -gone', -go'ing** to experience; go through

un·der·grad·u·ate *n.* a college student who has not yet earned a degree

un·der·ground *adj.* 1 under the earth's surface 2 secret; hidden 3 of newspapers, movies, etc. that are unconventional, radical, etc. —*adv.* 1 under the earth's surface 2 in or into secrecy —*n.* 1 the region under the earth's surface 2 a secret movement in a country to oppose the government or enemy occupation forces 3 [Brit.] a subway

un·der·growth *n.* UNDERBRUSH

un·der·hand *adj.* 1 done with the hand below the level of the elbow or shoulder 2 UNDERHANDED —*adv.* with an underhand motion

un·der·hand·ed *adj.* deceitful, treacherous, etc. —**un'der·hand'ed·ly** *adv.*

un·der·lie *vt.* **-lay', -lain', -ly'ing** 1 to lie beneath 2 to be the basis for; form the foundation of

un·der·line *vt.* **-lined', -lin'ing** 1 to draw a line beneath 2 to stress

un·der·ling (un'dər lin) *n.* ‖OE: see UNDER- & -LING‖ a person in a subordinate position; inferior: usually a contemptuous term

un·der·ly·ing *adj.* 1 lying under 2 fundamental; basic

un·der·mine *vt.* **-mined', -min'ing** 1 to dig beneath, so as to form a tunnel or mine 2 to wear away and weaken the supports of 3 to injure or weaken, esp. by subtle or insidious means

un·der·most *adj., adv.* lowest in place, position, rank, etc.

un·der·neath (un'dər nēth') *adv., prep.* ‖< OE *under*, UNDER + *neothan*, below‖ under; below

un·der·nour·ished *adj.* not getting the food needed for health and growth

un·der·pants *pl.n.* pants, usually short, for use as an undergarment

un·der·pass *n.* a passage under something; esp., a road or passageway passing under a highway or railway

un·der·per·form *vi.* to be less successful than expected or needed —*vt.* to produce a smaller return than: said of stocks, etc.

un·der·pin·ning (-pin'in) *n.* a support or prop

un·der·play *vt., vi.* 1 UNDERACT 2 to make seem less important

un·der·priv·i·leged *adj.* deprived of a decent standard of living and economic security through poverty, discrimination, etc.

un·der·pro·duce *vt., vi.* **-duced', -duc'ing** to produce less than is needed or wanted

un·der·rate *vt.* **-rat'ed, -rat'ing** to rate or estimate too low

un·der·score *vt.* **-scored', -scor'ing** UNDERLINE

un·der·sea *adj., adv.* beneath the surface of the sea: also **un'der·seas'** *adv.*

un·der·sec·re·tar·y *n., pl.* **-ies** an assistant secretary

un·der·sell *vt.* **-sold', -sell'ing** 1 to sell at a lower price than 2 to publicize or promote in a restrained or inadequate manner

un·der·shirt *n.* a collarless shirt for use as an undergarment

un·der·shot *adj.* 1 with the lower part extending past the upper [an *undershot* jaw] 2 driven by water flowing along the lower part [an *undershot* water wheel]

un·der·side *n.* the side or surface that is underneath

un·der·signed *adj.* whose name is signed at the end —**the undersigned** the person or persons having signed at the end

un·der·skirt *n.* a skirt worn under another

un·der·staffed *adj.* having fewer workers on the staff than are needed

un·der·stand *vt.* **-stood', -stand'ing** ‖< OE *understandan*, lit., to stand among‖ 1 to perceive the meaning of 2 to assume from what is heard, etc.; infer 3 to take as meant; interpret 4 to take as a fact 5 to know the nature, character, etc. of 6 to have a sympathetic rapport with —*vi.* 1 to have understanding, comprehension, etc. 2 to be informed; believe —**un'der·stand'a·ble** *adj.* —**un'der·stand'a·bly** *adv.*

un·der·stand·ing *n.* 1 comprehension 2 the power to think and learn; intelligence 3 a specific interpretation 4 mutual agreement, esp. one that settles differences —*adj.* that understands; sympathetic

un·der·state *vt.* **-stat'ed, -stat'ing** 1 to state too weakly 2 to state in a restrained style —**un'der·state'ment** *n.*

un·der·stud·y *n., pl.* **-ies** an actor prepared to substitute for another —*vt., vi.* **-ied, -y·ing** to learn (a part) as an understudy (to)

un·der·take *vt.* **-took', -tak'en, -tak'ing** 1 to take upon oneself (a task, etc.) 2 to promise; guarantee

un·der·tak·er *n.* FUNERAL DIRECTOR

un·der·tak·ing *n.* 1 something undertaken; task; enterprise 2 a promise; guarantee

un·der-the-coun·ter *adj.* [Inf.] done secretly in an unlawful way: also **un'der-the-ta'ble**

un·der·things *pl.n.* women's or girls' underwear

un·der·tone *n.* 1 a low tone of voice 2 a subdued color 3 an underlying quality, factor, etc.

un·der·tow *n.* a current of water moving beneath the surface water and in a different direction

un·der·wa·ter *adj.* 1 being, done, etc. beneath the surface of the water 2 relating to an asset that is worth less than the amount owed or paid for it

un·der·way *adj.* 1 moving; making progress 2 *Naut.* not anchored or moored or aground

un·der·wear *n.* clothing worn under one's outer clothes, usually next to the skin, as undershirts

un·der·weight (un'dər wāt', un'dər wāt') *adj.* below the normal, desirable, or allowed weight

un·der·world *n.* 1 the mythical world of the dead; Hades 2 criminals regarded as a group

un·der·write *vt.* -wrote', -writ'ten, -writ'ing 1 to agree to market (an issue of securities), guaranteeing to buy any part remaining unsubscribed 2 to agree to pay the cost of or cover the losses of (an undertaking, etc.) 3 to sign one's name to (an insurance policy), thus assuming liability —un'der·writ'er *n.*

un·dies (un'dēz') *pl.n.* [Inf.] underwear, esp. underpants

un·do *vt.* -did', -done', -do'ing 1 to untie, open, etc. 2 to do away with; cancel 3 to bring to ruin

un·doc·u·ment·ed *adj.* resident in a country without the proper visa [an *undocumented* alien]

un·do·ing *n.* 1 an annulling 2 a bringing to ruin 3 the cause of ruin

un·done *adj.* 1 not done; not performed, accomplished, etc. 2 ruined 3 emotionally upset

un·doubt·ed *adj.* not doubted or disputed; certain —un·doubt'ed·ly *adv.*

un·dreamed *adj.* not even dreamed (*of*) or imagined: also **un·dreamt'** (-dremt')

un·dress *vt.* to take off the clothing of —*vi.* to take off one's clothes

un·due *adj.* 1 not appropriate; improper 2 excessive; immoderate

un·du·lant (un'jə lənt, -dyə-) *adj.* undulating

un·du·late (-lāt') *vi., vt.* [< L *unda*, a wave] 1 to move or cause to move in waves 2 to have or cause to have a wavy form or surface —un'du·la'tion *n.*

un·du·ly *adv.* 1 improperly 2 excessively

un·dy·ing *adj.* immortal or eternal

un·earned *adj.* not earned by work or service; specif., obtained as a return on an investment [*unearned* income]

un·earth *vt.* 1 to dig up from the earth 2 to bring to light; disclose

un·earth·ly *adj.* 1 supernatural 2 weird; mysterious 3 [Inf.] fantastic, outlandish, etc.

un·eas·y *adj.* -i·er, -i·est 1 having, showing, or allowing no ease of body or mind; uncomfortable 2 awkward; constrained 3 anxious; apprehensive —un·eas'i·ly *adv.* —un·eas'i·ness *n.*

un·em·ploy·a·ble *adj.* not employable, as because of severe physical or mental disability, outmoded skills, etc.

un·em·ployed *adj.* 1 not employed; without work 2 not being used —un'em·ploy'ment *n.*

un·e·qual *adj.* 1 not equal, as in size, strength, ability, or value 2 not balanced, even, regular, etc. 3 not adequate (*to*)

un·e·qualed or **un·e·qualled** *adj.* not equaled; unmatched; unrivaled

un·e·quiv·o·cal *adj.* not equivocal; plain; clear

un·err·ing (un ur'iŋ, -er'-) *adj.* 1 free from error 2 not missing or failing; sure; exact

UNESCO (yoō nes'kō) *n.* United Nations Educational, Scientific, and Cultural Organization

un·e·ven *adj.* 1 not even, level, smooth, regular, etc. 2 unequal 3 *Math.* odd —un·e'ven·ly *adv.* —un·e'ven·ness *n.*

un·ex·am·pled *adj.* having no parallel or precedent; unprecedented

un·ex·cep·tion·a·ble *adj.* without fault; beyond criticism

un·ex·cep·tion·al *adj.* ordinary

un·ex·pect·ed *adj.* not expected; unforeseen —un'ex·pect'ed·ly *adv.*

un·fail·ing *adj.* 1 not failing 2 never ceasing or falling short; inexhaustible 3 always reliable

un·faith·ful *adj.* 1 lacking or breaking faith or loyalty 2 not true, accurate, etc. 3 adulterous —un·faith'ful·ness *n.*

un·fa·mil·iar *adj.* 1 not well-known; strange 2 not acquainted (*with*) —un'fa·mil'i·ar'i·ty *n.*

un·feel·ing *adj.* 1 incapable of feeling; insensible 2 hardhearted; cruel —un·feel'ing·ly *adv.*

un·feigned (un fānd') *adj.* genuine

un·fin·ished *adj.* 1 not finished; incomplete 2 not painted, varnished, etc.

un·flap·pa·ble (-flap'ə bəl) *adj.* [< UN- + FLAP (*n.* 3) + -ABLE] [Inf.] not easily excited; imperturbable

un·flinch·ing *adj.* steadfast; firm

un·fold *vt.* 1 to open and spread out (something folded) 2 to lay open to view; reveal, explain, etc. —*vi.* 1 to become unfolded 2 to develop fully

un·for·get·ta·ble *adj.* so beautiful, shocking, etc. as never to be forgotten

un·for·giv·ing *adj.* 1 not willing or not able to forgive 2 exacting, inflexible, harsh, etc.

un·for·tu·nate *adj.* 1 having or bringing bad luck; unlucky 2 not suitable or successful —*n.* an unfortunate person —un·for'tu·nate·ly *adv.*

un·found·ed *adj.* not founded on fact or truth

un·friend·ly *adj.* -li·er, -li·est 1 not friendly or kind 2 not favorable —un·friend'li·ness *n.*

un·frock *vt.* to deprive of the rank of priest or minister

un·furl *vt., vi.* to open or spread out from a furled state

un·gain·ly (un gān'lē) *adj.* [< ME *un-*, not + ON *gegn*, ready] awkward; clumsy

un·god·ly *adj.* 1 not godly or religious 2 [Inf.] outrageous —un·god'li·ness *n.*

un·gov·ern·a·ble *adj.* that cannot be governed or controlled; unruly

un·gra·cious *adj.* 1 not gracious; rude 2 unpleasant; unattractive

un·guard·ed *adj.* 1 unprotected 2 without guile or cunning 3 careless; imprudent

un·guent (uŋ'gwənt) *n.* [< L *unguere*, anoint] a salve or ointment

un·gu·late (uŋ′gyŏō lit, -lāt′) *adj.* ‖< L *unguis*, a nail‖ having hoofs —*n.* a mammal having hoofs

un·hand *vt.* to release from the hand or hands; let go of

un·hap·py *adj.* **-pi·er, -pi·est 1** unfortunate **2** sad; wretched **3** not suitable —**un·hap′pi·ly** *adv.* —**un·hap′pi·ness** *n.*

un·health·y *adj.* **-i·er, -i·est 1** sickly; not well **2** harmful to health **3** harmful to morals **4** dangerous or risky —**un·health′i·ness** *n.*

un·heard *adj.* **1** not perceived by the ear **2** not given a hearing

un·heard-of *adj.* **1** not heard of before; unprecedented or unknown **2** unacceptable or outrageous

un·hinge *vt.* **-hinged′, -hing′ing 1** to remove from the hinges **2** to unbalance (the mind) of (someone)

un·ho·ly *adj.* **-li·er, -li·est 1** not sacred, hallowed, etc. **2** wicked; profane **3** [Inf.] outrageous

un·horse *vt.* **-horsed′, -hors′ing** to throw (a rider) from a horse

uni- ‖< *unus*, one‖ *prefix* one; having only one

u·ni·cam·er·al (-kam′ər əl) *adj.* ‖< UNI- + L *camera*, chamber‖ of or having a single legislative chamber

UNICEF (yŏō′nə sef′) *n.* United Nations Children's Fund: formerly, *United Nations International Children's Emergency Fund*

u·ni·corn (yŏō′nə kôrn′) *n.* ‖< L *unus*, one + *cornu*, horn‖ a mythical horselike animal with a single horn growing from its forehead

u·ni·cy·cle (yŏō′nə sī′kəl) *n.* ‖UNI- + (BI)CYCLE‖ a one-wheeled vehicle straddled by the rider who pushes its pedals —**u′ni·cy′clist** *n.*

u·ni·form (yŏō′nə fôrm′) *adj.* ‖< L *unus*, one + *-formis*, -FORM‖ **1** not varying in form, rate, degree, etc. **2** like others of the same class —*n.* the distinctive clothes identifying members of a particular group, as of soldiers —*vt.* to supply with a uniform —**u′ni·form′i·ty** *n.* —**u′ni·form′ly** *adv.*

u·ni·fy (yŏō′nə fī′) *vt., vi.* **-fied′, -fy′ing** ‖see UNI- & -FY‖ to become or make united —**u′ni·fi·ca′tion** *n.*

u·ni·lat·er·al (yŏō′nə lat′ər əl) *adj.* **1** of, occurring on, or affecting one side only **2** involving only one of several parties; not reciprocal

un·im·peach·a·ble (un′im pēch′ə bəl) *adj.* that cannot be doubted or discredited; irreproachable

un·in·hib·it·ed *adj.* without inhibition; esp., free of the usual social or psychological restraints on one's behavior

un·in·ter·est·ed *adj.* not interested; indifferent

un·ion (yŏōn′yən) *n.* ‖< L *unus*, one‖ **1** a uniting or being united; combination **2** a grouping together of nations, etc. for some specific purpose **3** marriage **4** something united **5** *short for* LABOR UNION **6** a design symbolizing political union, used as in a flag **7** a device for joining parts, as of a machine —**the Union 1** the United States **2** the North in the Civil War

un·ion·ize (-īz′) *vt., vi.* **-ized′, -iz′ing** to organize into a labor union —**un′ion·i·za′tion** *n.*

Union Jack the flag of the United Kingdom

Union of Soviet Socialist Republics former country in E Europe & N Asia: formed as a union of 15 constituent republics, it was disbanded in 1991

u·nique (yŏō nēk′) *adj.* ‖< L *unus*, one‖ **1** one and only; sole **2** without like or equal **3** very unusual: a usage still objected to by some

u·ni·sex (yŏō′nə seks′) *adj.* **1** of or involving a fashion, as in haircuts, that is not differentiated for the sexes **2** intended for both sexes

u·ni·son (yŏō′nə sən, -zən) *n.* ‖< L *unus*, one + *sonus*, a sound‖ **1** a musical interval consisting of two identical pitches **2** agreement —**in unison 1** with all the voices or instruments performing the same part **2** speaking the same words at the same time

u·nit (yŏō′nit) *n.* ‖< UNITY‖ **1** the smallest whole number; one **2** a standard basic quantity, measure, etc. **3** a single person or group, esp. as a part of a whole **4** a distinct part or object with a specific purpose

U·ni·tar·i·an (yŏō′nə ter′ē ən) *n.* a member of a religious denomination of Christian origin that rejects the doctrine of the Trinity, holding that God is a single being

u·ni·tar·y (yŏō′nə ter′ē) *adj.* **1** of a unit or units **2** of or based on unity

u·nite (yŏō nīt′) *vt., vi.* **-nit′ed, -nit′ing** ‖< L *unus*, one‖ **1** to put or join together so as to make one; combine **2** to bring or come together in common cause, action, etc.

United Arab E·mir·ates (em′ər əts) country in E Arabia, on the Persian Gulf

United Arab Republic *former name for* Egypt (1961-71)

United Kingdom country in W Europe, consisting of Great Britain & Northern Ireland

United Nations an international organization of nations for world peace and security: formed in 1945

United States of America country including 49 states in North America, and Hawaii; cap. Washington, D.C.: also called **United States**

u·nit·ize (yŏō′nə tīz′) *vt.* **-ized′, -iz′ing** to make into a single unit

unit pricing a system of showing prices, as of foods, in terms of standard units

u·ni·ty (yŏō′nə tē) *n., pl.* **-ties** ‖< L *unus*, one‖ **1** a being united; oneness **2** a single, separate thing **3** harmony; agreement **4** a complex that is a union of related parts **5** a harmonious, unified arrangement of parts in an artistic work **6** continuity of purpose, action, etc. **7** *Math.* any quantity, etc. identified as a unit, or 1

univ *abbrev.* university

u·ni·va·lent (yŏō′nə vā′lənt) *adj. Chem.* **1** having one valence **2** having a valence of one

u·ni·valve (yōo'nə valv') *n.* a mollusk with a one-piece shell, as a snail

u·ni·ver·sal (yōo'nə vur'səl) *adj.* 1 of the universe; present everywhere 2 of, for, or including all or the whole 3 used, or intended to be used, for all kinds, sizes, etc. or by all people —**u'ni·ver·sal'i·ty** (-vər sal'ə tē) *n.*

u·ni·ver·sal·ize *vt.* **-ized', -iz'ing** to make universal

universal joint (*or* **coupling**) a joint or coupling that permits a swing of limited angle in any direction, esp. one for transmitting rotary motion from one shaft to another not in line with it

u·ni·ver·sal·ly *adv.* 1 in every instance 2 in every part or place

Universal Product Code a patterned series of vertical bars printed on consumer products: it can be read by computerized scanners for pricing, etc.

u·ni·verse (yōo'nə vurs') *n.* [< L *unus*, one + *vertere*, to turn] 1 the totality of all things that exist in a system of space and time 2 the world

u·ni·ver·si·ty (yōo'nə vur'sə tē) *n., pl.* **-ties** [see prec.] 1 an educational institution offering bachelor's and advanced degrees 2 the grounds, buildings, etc. of a university

un·just (un just') *adj.* not just or right; unfair —**un·just'ly** *adv.*

un·kempt (-kempt') *adj.* [UN- + *kempt* < dial. *kemben*, to comb] 1 tangled, disheveled, etc. 2 not tidy; slovenly

un·kind *adj.* not kind; specif., *a)* not considerate of others *b)* harsh, severe, cruel, etc. —**un·kind'ness** *n.*

un·kind·ly *adj.* UNKIND —*adv.* in an unkind way

un·known *adj.* not known; specif., *a)* unfamiliar (*to*) *b)* not identified, etc. —*n.* an unknown person or thing

un·law·ful *adj.* 1 against the law; illegal 2 immoral —**un·law'ful·ly** *adv.* —**un·law'ful·ness** *n.*

un·lead·ed *adj.* not containing lead compounds: said of gasoline

un·learn *vt., vi.* to forget or try to forget (something learned)

un·learn·ed (-lur'nid; *for* 2, -lurnd') *adj.* 1 not having much learning; uneducated 2 not learned or memorized [*unlearned* lessons]

un·leash *vt.* to release from or as from a leash

un·less (un les') *conj.* [< ME *on lesse that*, at less than] except if; except that

un·let·tered *adj.* 1 ignorant; uneducated 2 illiterate

un·like *adj.* not alike; different —*prep.* 1 not like; different from 2 not characteristic of

un·like·ly *adj.* 1 not likely; improbable 2 not likely to succeed —**un·like'li·hood** *n.*

un·lim·ber *vt., vi.* to get ready for use or action

un·lim·it·ed *adj.* 1 without limits or restrictions 2 vast; immeasurable

un·load *vt., vi.* 1 *a)* to remove (a load) *b)* to take a load from 2 *a)* to tell (one's troubles, etc.) without restraint *b)* to relieve of something that troubles 3 to remove the charge from (a gun) 4 to get rid of

un·lock *vt.* 1 *a)* to open (a lock) *b)* to open the lock of (a door, etc.) 2 to let loose; release 3 to reveal

un·looked-for *adj.* not expected

un·loose *vt.* **-loosed', -loos'ing** to set loose; loosen, release, etc.

un·luck·y *adj.* **-i·er, -i·est** having or bringing bad luck; unfortunate

un·make *vt.* **-made', -mak'ing** 1 to cause to be as before; undo 2 to ruin; destroy 3 to depose from a position or rank

un·man·ly *adj.* **-li·er, -li·est** not manly; specif., *a)* cowardly, weak, etc. *b)* effeminate; womanish

un·manned *adj.* without people aboard and operating by remote control

un·mask *vi., vt.* 1 to remove a mask or disguise (from) 2 to disclose the true nature or character (of)

un·mean·ing *adj.* lacking in meaning or sense

un·men·tion·a·ble *adj.* not fit to be mentioned

un·mer·ci·ful *adj.* having or showing no mercy; cruel; pitiless

un·mis·tak·a·ble *adj.* that cannot be mistaken or misinterpreted; clear —**un'mis·tak'a·bly** *adv.*

un·mit·i·gat·ed *adj.* 1 not lessened or eased 2 out-and-out; absolute

un·mor·al *adj.* AMORAL

un·nat·u·ral *adj.* 1 contrary to nature; abnormal 2 artificial 3 very cruel —**un·nat'u·ral·ly** *adv.*

un·nec·es·sar·y *adj.* not necessary; needless —**un·nec'es·sar'i·ly** *adv.*

un·nerve *vt.* **-nerved', -nerv'ing** to cause to lose one's self-confidence, courage, etc.

un·num·bered *adj.* 1 not counted 2 innumerable 3 having no identifying number

un·or·gan·ized *adj.* not organized; specif., not belonging to a labor union

un·pack *vt., vi.* 1 to remove (the contents of a trunk, suitcase, etc.) 2 to take things out of (a trunk, etc.)

un·par·al·leled *adj.* that has no parallel, equal, or counterpart

un·pleas·ant *adj.* offensive; disagreeable —**un·pleas'ant·ly** *adv.* —**un·pleas'ant·ness** *n.*

un·plumbed *adj.* 1 of unknown depth 2 not fully understood

un·pop·u·lar *adj.* not liked by the public or by the majority —**un'pop·u·lar'i·ty** (-lar'ə tē) *n.*

un·prac·ticed *adj.* 1 not habitually or repeatedly done, etc. 2 not skilled or experienced

un·prec·e·dent·ed *adj.* having no precedent or parallel; unheard-of

un·prin·ci·pled *adj.* lacking moral principles; unscrupulous

un·print·a·ble *adj.* not fit to be printed, as because of obscenity

un·pro·fes·sion·al *adj.* not professional; esp., violating the ethical code of a given profession

un·qual·i·fied *adj.* 1 lacking the necessary qualifications 2 not limited; absolute

un·ques·tion·a·ble *adj.* not to be questioned,

doubted, or disputed; certain —**un·ques'tion·a·bly** adv.

un·quote interj. I end the quotation

un·rav·el vt. **-eled** or **-elled, -el·ing** or **-el·ling 1** to separate the threads of (something woven, tangled, etc.) **2** to make clear; solve —vi. to become unraveled

un·read (-red') adj. **1** not read, as a book **2** having read little or nothing

un·re·al adj. not real or actual; imaginary, fanciful, false, etc.

un·rea·son·a·ble adj. **1** not reasonable or rational **2** excessive; immoderate —**un·rea'son·a·bly** adv.

un·rea·son·ing adj. not reasoning or reasoned; irrational

un·re·con·struct·ed adj. holding to an earlier, outmoded practice or point of view

un·re·gen·er·ate adj. stubbornly defiant

un·re·lent·ing adj. **1** inflexible; relentless **2** without mercy; cruel **3** not relaxing in effort, speed, etc.

un·re·mit·ting adj. not stopping, relaxing, etc.; incessant; persistent

un·re·quit·ed adj. not reciprocated

un·re·served adj. not reserved; specif., a) frank or open in speech b) without limitations —**un're·serv'ed·ly** adv.

un·rest n. restlessness; specif., angry discontent verging on revolt

un·ripe adj. not ripe or mature; green

un·ri·valed or **un·ri·valled** adj. having no rival, equal, or competitor

un·roll vt. **1** to open (something rolled up) **2** to display —vi. to become unrolled

un·ruf·fled adj. not ruffled or disturbed; calm; smooth; serene

un·rul·y (un rōō'lē) adj. **-i·er, -i·est** hard to control, restrain, or keep in order —**un·rul'i·ness** n.

un·sad·dle vt. **-dled, -dling** to take the saddle off (a horse, etc.)

un·said adj. not expressed

un·sat·u·rat·ed (-sach'ə rāt'id) adj. **1** not saturated **2** designating or of a fat composed chiefly of fatty acids having one or more double bonds in the carbon chain **3** capable of dissolving more of a solute

un·sa·vor·y adj. **1** unpleasant to taste or smell **2** morally offensive

un·scathed (-skāthd') adj. [< un- + ON skathi, harm] unharmed

un·schooled adj. not educated or trained, esp. by formal schooling

un·scram·ble vt. **-bled, -bling** to cause to be no longer scrambled, mixed up, or unintelligible

un·screw vt. to detach or loosen by removing screws, or by turning

un·script·ed adj. without or not in a prepared script

un·scru·pu·lous adj. not restrained by ideas of right and wrong; unprincipled

un·seal vt. **1** to break the seal of **2** to open

un·sea·son·a·ble adj. **1** not usual for the season **2** at the wrong time

un·seat vt. **1** to dislodge from a seat **2** to remove from office

un·seem·ly adj. not seemly; not decent or proper; unbecoming

un·set·tle vt., vi. **-tled, -tling** to make or become unstable; disturb or displace

un·set·tled adj. **1** not settled; not fixed, orderly, stable, calm, decided, etc. **2** not paid **3** having no settlers

un·sheathe (un shēth') vt. **-sheathed', -sheath'ing** to remove (a sword, etc.) from a sheath

un·sight·ly adj. not sightly or pleasant to look at; ugly —**un·sight'li·ness** n.

un·skilled adj. having or requiring no special skill or training

un·skill·ful adj. having little or no skill; awkward

un·snap vt. **-snapped', -snap'ping** to undo the snaps of, so as to loosen or detach

un·snarl vt. to untangle

un·so·phis·ti·cat·ed adj. not sophisticated; simple, ingenuous, etc.

un·sound adj. not sound; specif., a) not healthy, safe, firm, etc. b) not reliable, sensible, etc.

un·spar·ing adj. **1** not sparing; lavish **2** not merciful; severe

un·speak·a·ble adj. **1** that cannot be spoken **2** so bad, foul, evil, etc. as to defy description or be unfit for discussion [unspeakable depravity] —**un·speak'a·bly** adv.

un·sta·ble adj. not stable; specif., a) easily upset b) changeable c) unreliable d) emotionally or psychologically unsettled e) Chem. tending to decompose

un·stead·y adj. not steady; specif., a) not firm; shaky b) changeable; inconstant c) erratic in habits, purpose, etc.

un·stop vt. **-stopped', -stop'ping 1** to remove the stopper from **2** to clear (a pipe, etc.) of an obstruction

un·struc·tured adj. not formally organized; loose, free, open, etc.

un·strung adj. **1** nervous or upset **2** with the strings loosened or detached, as a bow or racket

un·stuck adj. loosened or freed from being stuck

un·stud·ied adj. not gotten by study or conscious effort; spontaneous; natural

un·sub·stan·tial adj. **1** having no material substance **2** not solid; flimsy **3** unreal; visionary

un·sung adj. not honored or celebrated, as in song or poetry

un·tan·gle vt. **-gled, -gling 1** to free from a snarl or tangle **2** to free from confusion; put in order

un·taught adj. **1** not taught; uneducated **2** acquired without being taught

un·think·a·ble adj. **1** that cannot be imagined; inconceivable **2** so foul, etc. as to be unfit to be considered [unthinkable war crimes]

un·think·ing adj. thoughtless; heedless

un·ti·dy adj. **-di·er, -di·est** not neat; messy

un·tie vt. **-tied', -ty'ing** or **-tie'ing 1** to unfasten (a thing tied or knotted) **2** to free, as from restraint

un·til (un til′) *prep.* ⟦ME *untill*⟧ **1** up to the time of [*until* death] **2** before [not *until* tomorrow] —*conj.* **1** up to the time when or that [*until* you leave] **2** to the point, degree, etc. that [cook *until* it is done] **3** before [not *until* I die]

un·time·ly *adj., adv.* **1** before the proper time; premature(ly) **2** at the wrong time —**un·time′li·ness** *n.*

un·to (un′tōō, -tōō) *prep.* ⟦ME⟧ *old poet. var. of:* **1** TO **2** UNTIL

un·told *adj.* **1** not told or revealed **2** too many to be counted **3** indescribably great [*untold* misery]

un·touch·a·ble *adj.* that cannot or should not be touched —*n.* DALIT: in this sense, *untouchable* is no longer the preferred term

un·to·ward (un tô′ərd, -tôrd′) *adj.* **1** improper, unseemly, etc. **2** not favorable; adverse

un·trav·eled or **un·trav·elled** *adj.* **1** not used or frequented by travelers **2** not having done much traveling

un·truth *n.* **1** falsity **2** a falsehood; lie —**un·truth′ful** *adj.*

un·tu·tored *adj.* uneducated

un·twist *vt., vi.* to loosen or separate, as something twisted together; unwind

un·used *adj.* **1** not in use **2** never used before **3** unaccustomed (*to*)

un·u·su·al *adj.* not usual or common; rare —**un·u′su·al·ly** *adv.*

un·ut·ter·a·ble *adj.* inexpressible

un·var·nished *adj.* **1** not varnished **2** plain; simple; unadorned

un·veil *vt.* to reveal as by removing a veil from —*vi.* to take off one's veil

un·voiced *adj.* **1** not expressed; not spoken **2** Phonet. pronounced without vibrating the vocal cords

un·war·y *adj.* not wary or cautious

un·wea·ried (-wir′ēd) *adj.* ⟦ME *unweried* (see UN- & WEARY)⟧ never wearying; tireless; indefatigable

un·well *adj.* not well; sick

un·whole·some *adj.* **1** harmful to body or mind **2** of unsound health or unhealthy appearance **3** morally harmful —**un·whole′some·ness** *n.*

un·wield·y *adj.* hard to wield, manage, etc., as because of large size

un·will·ing *adj.* **1** not willing; reluctant **2** done, said, etc. reluctantly —**un·will′ing·ly** *adv.*

un·wind (-wīnd′) *vt.* **-wound′, -wind′ing 1** to wind off or undo (something wound) **2** to untangle (something involved) —*vi.* **1** to become unwound **2** to become relaxed

un·wise *adj.* having or showing a lack of wisdom or sound judgment

un·wit·ting *adj.* **1** not knowing; unaware **2** unintentional

un·wont·ed *adj.* not common, usual, or habitual

un·wor·thy *adj.* **-thi·er, -thi·est 1** lacking

merit or value; worthless **2** not deserving (*of*) **3** not fit or becoming: usually with *of* —**un·wor′thi·ness** *n.*

un·wrap *vt.* **-wrapped′, -wrap′ping** to take off the wrapping of

un·writ·ten *adj.* **1** not in writing **2** operating only through custom or tradition [an *unwritten* rule]

up¹ (up) *adv.* ⟦OE⟧ **1** to, in, or on a higher place or level **2** to a later period **3** to or into a higher condition, amount, etc. **4** *a*) in or into a standing or upright position *b*) out of bed **5** in or into action, view, consideration, etc. **6** aside; away [lay *up* wealth] **7** so as to be even with in time, degree, etc. **8** completely; thoroughly [eat *up* the cake] **9** Baseball to one's turn at batting **10** used with verbs: *a*) to form idioms with meanings different from the simple verb [look *up* this word] *b*) as an intensive [dress *up*] —*prep.* up to, toward, along, through, into, or upon —*adj.* **1** directed toward a higher position **2** in a higher place or position **3** advanced in amount, degree, etc. [rents are *up*] **4** in a standing or upright position **5** in an active or excited state **6** at an end; over [time's *up*] **7** [Inf.] going on [what's *up*] **8** Baseball at bat —*n.* **1** an upward slope **2** an upward movement, etc. —*vi.* **upped, up′ping** [Inf.] to get up; rise —*vt.* [Inf.] **1** to put up, lift up, etc. **2** to cause to rise [to *up* prices] —**on the up and up** [Slang] honest —**up against** [Inf.] confronted with —**up on** (or **in**) [Inf.] well-informed concerning —**ups and downs** good periods and bad periods —**up to 1** doing or scheming **2** capable of (doing, etc.) **3** as many as **4** as far as **5** dependent upon —**up with!** give or restore power, favor, etc. to!

up² (up) *adv.* ⟦phonetic respelling of *ap(iece)*⟧ apiece [a score of ten *up*]

up- *combining form* up

up-and-com·ing *adj.* **1** enterprising, promising, etc. **2** gaining in prominence

up·beat *n.* Music a beat that is ordinarily unaccented —*adj.* [Inf.] cheerful; optimistic

up·braid (up brād′) *vt.* ⟦< OE *up-*, up + *bregdan*, to pull⟧ to rebuke severely; censure; scold

up·bring·ing *n.* the training and education received while growing up

UPC *abbrev.* Universal Product Code

up·chuck *vi., vt., n.* [Slang] VOMIT

up·com·ing *adj.* coming soon

up·coun·try *adj., adv.* in or toward the interior of a country

up·date (up dāt′; *also, and for n. always,* up′ dāt′) *vt.* **-dat′ed, -dat′ing** to make up-to-date; make conform to the most recent facts, methods, etc. —*n.* **1** an updating **2** an updated report, etc.

up·end *vt., vi.* **1** to set, turn, or stand on end **2** to topple

up·front [Inf.] *adj.* **1** forthright **2** in advance [*upfront* money] —*adv.* in advance Also **up′-front′**

up·grade (up′grād′; *also, and for v. usually,* up

grād′) *n.* 1 an upward slope 2 an improvement —*adj., adv.* uphill; upward —*vt., vi.* **-grad′ed, -grad′ing** to raise or improve in value, rank, etc.

up·heav·al (up hē′vəl) *n.* 1 a heaving up 2 a sudden, violent change

up·hill *adv.* 1 toward the top of a hill; upward 2 with difficulty —*adj.* 1 going or sloping up 2 laborious; tiring

up·hold *vt.* **-held′, -hold′ing** 1 to hold up 2 to keep from falling; support 3 to confirm; sustain

up·hol·ster (up hōl′stər) *vt.* [ult. < ME *upholder*, tradesman] to fit out (furniture, etc.) with coverings, padding, springs, etc. —**up·hol′ster·er** *n.*

up·hol·ster·y *n., pl.* **-ies** 1 the material used in upholstering 2 the work of an upholsterer

up·keep *n.* 1 maintenance 2 state of repair 3 the cost of maintenance

up·land (-lənd, -land′) *n.* land elevated above other land —*adj.* of or situated in upland

up·lift (up lift′; *also, and for n. always,* up′lift′) *vt.* 1 to lift up 2 to raise to a higher moral, social, or cultural level —*n.* 1 a lifting up 2 a movement for moral, social, or cultural betterment

up·load *vt., vi.* to transfer (information) as from a personal computer to a main computer —*n.* a file transferred this way

up·mark·et *adj.* UPSCALE

up·on (ə pän′, ə pôn′) *prep.* on, or up and on: used interchangeably with *on* —*adv.* on

up·per (up′ər) *adj.* 1 higher in place 2 higher in rank, etc. 3 farther north —*n.* 1 the part of a shoe above the sole 2 [Slang] any drug that is a stimulant

up·per·case (up′ər kas′) *n.* capital letters, as distinguished from small letters —*adj.* of or in uppercase

upper class the social class having the most wealth, prestige, or power —**up′per·class′** *adj.*

up·per·class·man (-mən) *n., pl.* **-men** (-mən) a junior or senior in high school or college

up·per·cut *n.* Boxing a short, swinging blow directed upward

upper hand the position of advantage or control

up·per·most *adj.* highest in place, authority, etc. —*adv.* in the highest place, rank, etc.

Upper Vol·ta (väl′tə) *former name for* BURKINA FASO

up·pi·ty (up′ə tē) *adj.* [Inf.] haughty, arrogant, snobbish, etc.

up·raise *vt.* **-raised′, -rais′ing** to raise up; lift

up·rear *vt.* to lift up —*vi.* to rise up

up·right (up′rīt′; *for adj. and adv., also* up rīt′) *adj.* 1 standing, pointing, etc. straight up; erect 2 honest and just —*adv.* in an upright position or direction —*n.* something in an upright position

upright piano a piano with a vertical, rectangular body

up·ris·ing *n.* a revolt

up·riv·er *adv., adj.* in the direction against the current of a river

up·roar (up′rôr′) *n.* [Du *oproer*, a stirring up] 1 violent disturbance; tumult 2 loud, confused noise

up·roar·i·ous (up rôr′ē əs) *adj.* 1 making an uproar 2 boisterous 3 causing loud laughter

up·root *vt.* 1 to tear up by the roots 2 to destroy or remove utterly

up·scale *adj.* of or for people who are affluent, stylish, etc.

up·set (up set′; *for n.,* up′set′) *vt.* **-set′, -set′ting** 1 *a*) to tip over; overturn *b*) to defeat unexpectedly 2 *a*) to disturb the functioning of [to *upset* a schedule] *b*) to disturb emotionally or physically —*vi.* to become overturned or upset —*n.* 1 an upsetting 2 an unexpected victory or defeat 3 a disturbance —*adj.* 1 tipped over 2 overthrown or defeated 3 disturbed or disordered

up·shot *n.* [orig., final shot in an archery match] the conclusion; result

up·side¹ *prep.* [Chiefly Dial.] on or against the side of [struck *upside* the head]

up·side² *n.* 1 the upper side or part 2 appreciation or gain, as on an investment 3 a favorable aspect of something

upside down 1 with the top side or part underneath or turned over; inverted 2 in disorder —**up′side′-down′** *adj.*

up·si·lon (ōōp′sə län′, up′-) *n.* the twentieth letter of the Greek alphabet (Υ, υ)

up·stage (up′stāj′; *for v.,* up stāj′) *adv., adj.* toward or at the rear of a stage —*vt.* **-staged′, -stag′ing** 1 to move upstage relative to (another actor) 2 to draw attention away from

up·stairs *adv.* 1 up the stairs 2 on or to an upper floor or higher level 3 [Inf.] in the mind —*adj.* on an upper floor —*n.* an upper floor

up·stand·ing *adj.* 1 erect 2 upright in character; honorable

up·start *n.* one who has recently come into wealth, power, etc., esp. one who is presumptuous, aggressive, etc. —*adj.* of or like an upstart

up·state *adj., adv.* in, to, or from the northerly part of a U.S. state

up·stream *adv., adj.* in the direction against the current of a stream

up·surge *n.* a surge upward

up·swing *n.* a swing, trend, or movement upward

up·take *n.* a taking up —**quick** (or **slow**) **on the uptake** [Inf.] quick (or slow) to comprehend

up·tight *adj.* [Slang] 1 very tense, nervous, etc. 2 overly strict or conventional

up-to-date *adj.* 1 extending to the present time 2 keeping up with what is most recent

up·town *adj., adv.* in or toward the residential part of a city —*n.* the uptown section of a city

up·turn (-turn′; *for n.,* up′turn′) *vt., vi.* to turn up or over —*n.* an upward turn or trend —**up′turned′** *adj.*

up·ward *adv., adj.* toward a higher place, posi-

tion, etc.: also up'wards _adv._ —**upwards** (or **upward) of** more than —**up'ward·ly** _adv._

upward mobility movement to a higher social and economic status

up·wind _adv., adj._ in the direction from which the wind is blowing or usually blows

Ur (oor, ur) ancient city on the Euphrates River

u·ra·cil (yoor'ə sil') _n._ a colorless, crystalline base that is a constituent of RNA

U·ral Mountains (yoor'əl) mountain system in Russia, regarded as the boundary between Europe & Asia: also **Urals**

u·ra·ni·um (yoo rā'nē əm) _n._ ⟦after fol.⟧ a very hard, heavy, silver-colored, radioactive, metallic chemical element: used as a fuel in nuclear reactors and in nuclear weapons: symbol, U; at. no. 92

U·ra·nus (yoor'ə nəs, yoo rā'nəs) _n._ ⟦< Gr _Ouranos_, heaven⟧ the planet seventh in distance from the sun: see PLANET

ur·ban (ur'bən) _adj._ ⟦< L _urbs_, city⟧ 1 of, in, or constituting a city 2 characteristic of cities

ur·bane (ur bān') _adj._ ⟦see prec.⟧ polite in a smooth, polished way; refined —**ur·ban'i·ty** (-ban'ə tē) _n._

ur·ban·ize (ur'bə nīz') _vt._ **-ized', -iz'ing** to change from rural to urban —**ur'ban·i·za'tion** _n._

urban legend (_or_ **myth**) a widely circulating secondhand anecdote describing a purportedly true incident

urban renewal rehabilitation of deteriorated urban areas, as by slum clearance and housing construction

urban sprawl the spread of urban congestion into surrounding areas

ur·chin (ur'chin) _n._ ⟦< L _ericius_, hedgehog⟧ a small child; esp., a mischievous boy

-ure (ər) ⟦Fr < L _-ura_⟧ _suffix_ 1 act, process, or result [_exposure_] 2 agent of 3 state of being __ed [_composure_] 4 office, rank, or collective body [_legislature_]

u·re·a (yoo rē'ə) _n._ ⟦< Gr _ouron_, urine⟧ a soluble, crystalline solid found in urine or made synthetically, esp. for use in fertilizers

u·re·mi·a (yoo rē'mē ə) _n._ ⟦< Gr _ouron_, urine + _haima_, blood⟧ a toxic condition caused by the presence in the blood of waste products normally eliminated in the urine —**u·re'mic** _adj._

u·re·ter (yoo rēt'ər) _n._ ⟦< Gr _ourein_, urinate⟧ a tube carrying urine from a kidney to the bladder

u·re·thane (yoor'ə thān') _n._ ⟦< Fr⟧ a white, crystalline compound used as a hypnotic and sedative, a solvent, etc.

u·re·thra (yoo rē'thrə) _n., pl._ **-thrae** (-thrē') or **-thras** ⟦< Gr _ouron_, urine⟧ the duct through which urine is discharged from the bladder: in males, also the duct for semen

urge (urj) _vt._ **urged, urg'ing** ⟦L _urgere_, press hard⟧ 1 _a)_ to press upon the attention; advocate _b)_ to plead with; ask earnestly 2 to incite; provoke 3 to drive or force onward —_n._ 1 an urging 2 an impulse

ur·gent (ur'jənt) _adj._ ⟦see prec.⟧ 1 calling for haste, immediate action, etc. 2 insistent —**ur'gen·cy** _n., pl._ **-cies** —**ur'gent·ly** _adv._

-ur·gy (ur'jē) ⟦< Gr _ergon_, work⟧ _combining form_ a working with or by means of (something specified) [_chemurgy_]

u·ric (yoor'ik) _adj._ of, in, or from urine

u·ri·nal (yoor'ə nəl) _n._ 1 a receptacle or fixture for urinating 2 a place for urinating

u·ri·nal·y·sis (yoor'ə nal'ə sis) _n., pl._ **-ses'** (-sēz') chemical or microscopic analysis of urine

u·ri·nar·y (yoor'ə ner'ē) _adj._ 1 of urine 2 of the organs that secrete and discharge urine

u·ri·nate (yoor'ə nāt') _vi._ **-nat'ed, -nat'ing** to discharge urine from the body —**u'ri·na'tion** _n._

u·rine (yoor'in) _n._ ⟦< L _urina_⟧ the yellowish liquid, containing waste products, secreted by the kidneys and discharged through the urethra

URL _n._ ⟦_u(niform) r(esource) l(ocator)_⟧ an address on the World Wide Web

urn (urn) _n._ ⟦< L _urna_⟧ 1 _a)_ a vase with a pedestal _b)_ such a vase used to hold ashes after cremation 2 a metal container with a faucet, for making or serving hot coffee, tea, etc.

u·ro·gen·i·tal (yoor'ō jen'i təl) _adj._ of the urinary and genital organs

u·rol·o·gy (yoo räl'ə jē) _n._ ⟦< Gr _ouron_, urine + -LOGY⟧ the branch of medicine dealing with the urinary and genital organs and their diseases —**u·rol'o·gist** _n._

Ur·sa Major (ur'sə) ⟦L, lit., Great Bear⟧ a prominent N constellation

Ursa Minor ⟦L, lit., Little Bear⟧ a N constellation, containing Polaris

ur·sine (ur'sīn', -sin) _adj._ ⟦< L _ursus_, a bear⟧ of or like a bear

ur·ti·car·i·a (urt'i ker'ē ə) _n._ ⟦< L _urtica_, a nettle⟧ HIVES

U·ru·guay (yoor'ə gwā', oor'-; -gwī') country in SE South America —**Ur'u·guay'an** _adj., n._

us (us) _pron._ _objective form of_ WE

US or **U.S.** _abbrev._ United States

USA _abbrev._ 1 United States of America: also **U.S.A.** 2 United States Army

us·a·ble or **use·a·ble** (yoo'zə bəl) _adj._ that can be used; fit for use —**us'a·bil'i·ty** (-bil'ə tē) _n._, **use'a·bil'i·ty**

USAF _abbrev._ United States Air Force

us·age (yoo'sij) _n._ 1 the act, way, or extent of using; treatment 2 established practice; custom; habit 3 the way in which a word, phrase, etc. is used to express a particular idea

USB _abbrev._ Universal Serial Bus: used to designate a kind of standard interface for connecting peripherals to a computer

USCG _abbrev._ United States Coast Guard

USDA _abbrev._ United States Department of Agriculture

use (yooz; _for n.,_ yoos) _vt._ **used, us'ing** ⟦< L _uti_⟧ 1 to put into action or service 2 to exercise [_use_ your judgment] 3 to deal with; treat [to _use_ a friend badly] 4 to consume, expend: often with _up_ 5 to consume habitually [to _use_ drugs] 6 to exploit (someone) —_vi._ [Slang] to take drugs, esp. habitually —_n._ 1 a using or being used 2 the ability to use 3 the right to use **4** the need or opportunity to use **5** a way of using **6** usefulness **7** the purpose for which something is used **8** function —**used to** (yōōs′tə, -tōō) **1** did at one time [I *used to* live here] **2** accustomed to

used (yōōzd) *vt. pt. & pp.* of USE —*adj.* not new; secondhand

use·ful (yōōs′fəl) *adj.* that can be used; serviceable; helpful —**use′ful·ly** *adv.* —**use′ful·ness** *n.*

use·less (-lis) *adj.* **1** having no use **2** to no purpose —**use′less·ly** *adv.* —**use′less·ness** *n.*

us·er (yōō′zər) *n.* one that uses something; specif., one who uses drugs habitually, a computer, etc.

us·er-friend·ly *adj.* easy to use or understand: said esp. of computer hardware, programs, etc.

ush·er (ush′ər) *n.* [< L *ostiarius*, doorkeeper] **1** one who shows people to their seats in a theater, church, etc. **2** a bridegroom's attendant —*vt.* **1** to escort (others) to seats, etc. **2** to be a forerunner of: often with *in*

USMC *abbrev.* United States Marine Corps

USN *abbrev.* United States Navy

USO *abbrev.* United Service Organizations

USP *abbrev.* United States Pharmacopoeia

USPS *abbrev.* United States Postal Service

USS *abbrev.* United States Ship

USSR or **U.S.S.R.** *abbrev.* Union of Soviet Socialist Republics

u·su·al (yōō′zhə wəl) *adj.* [see USE] such as is most often seen, used, etc.; common; customary —**u′su·al·ly** *adv.*

u·surp (yōō surp′, -zurp′) *vt., vi.* [< L *usus*, a use ɪ *rapere*, to seize] to take (power, a position, etc.) by force —**u·sur·pa·tion** (yōō′zər pā′shən, -sər-) *n.* —**u·surp′er** *n.*

u·su·ry (yōō′zhə rē) *n., pl.* **-ries** [see USE] **1** the lending of money at an excessive rate of interest **2** an excessive interest rate —**u′su·rer** *n.* —**u·su·ri·ous** (yōō zhoor′ē əs) *adj.*

U·tah (yōō′tô′, -tä′) state of the W U.S.; cap. Salt Lake City: abbrev. UT —**U′tah′an** *adj., n.*, (local usage) **U·tahn** (yōō′tôn′, -tän′)

u·ten·sil (yōō ten′səl) *n.* [< L *uti*, to use] an implement or container, esp. one for use in a kitchen

u·ter·us (yōōt′ə rəs) *n., pl.* **-ter·i′** (-ī′) or **-us·es** [L] a hollow organ of female mammals in which the embryo and fetus are developed; womb —**u′ter·ine** (-rin, -rīn′) *adj.*

u·til·i·tar·i·an (yōō til′ə ter′ē ən) *adj.* **1** of or having to do with utility **2** stressing usefulness over beauty or other considerations

u·til·i·tar·i·an·ism *n.* **1** the doctrine that worth or value is determined solely by utility **2** the doctrine that the purpose of all action should be to bring about the greatest happiness of the greatest number

u·til·i·ty (yōō til′ə tē) *n., pl.* **-ties** [< L *uti*, to use] **1** usefulness **2** something useful **3** a company providing gas, water, etc. to the public **4** *Comput.* a program to perform a basic task

utility room a room containing laundry appliances, heating equipment, etc.

u·ti·lize (yōōt′'l īz′) *vt.* **-lized′, -liz′ing** to put to profitable use; make use of —**u′ti·li·za′tion** *n.*

ut·most (ut′mōst′) *adj.* [< OE superl. of *ut*, out] **1** farthest of the greatest degree, amount, etc. —*n.* the most that is possible

U·to·pi·a (yōō tō′pē ə) *n.* [< Gr *ou*, not + *topos*, a place] **1** an imaginary island with a perfect political and social system, described in *Utopia* (1516) by Sir Thomas More, Eng. statesman **2** [*often* **u-**] *a*) any idealized place of perfection *b*) any visionary scheme for a perfect society —**U·to′pi·an** *adj., n.*, **u·to′pi·an**

ut·ter¹ (ut′ər) *adj.* [< OE compar. of *ut*, out] **1** complete; total **2** unqualified; absolute; unconditional —**ut′ter·ly** *adv.*

ut·ter² (ut′ər) *vt.* [< ME *utter*, outward] to speak or express audibly (sounds, words, etc.)

ut·ter·ance *n.* **1** an uttering **2** the power or style of speaking **3** that which is uttered

ut·ter·most *adj., n.* UTMOST

U-turn *n.* **1** a turn by a car made so as to head in the opposite direction **2** a reversal of opinion, strategy, etc.

UV or **uv** *abbrev.* ultraviolet

u·vu·la (yōō′vyə lə) *n., pl.* **-las** or **-lae′** (-lē′) [< L *uva*, grape] the small, fleshy part hanging down from the soft palate above the back of the tongue —**u′vu·lar** *adj.*

ux·o·ri·ous (uk sôr′ē əs, -zôr′-) *adj.* [< L < *uxor*, wife] dotingly fond of or submissive to one's wife

Uz·bek·i·stan (ooz bek′i stan′) country in central Asia

U·zi (ōō′zē) *trademark for* a small submachine gun

V

v¹ or **V** (vē) *n., pl.* **v's, V's** the 22d letter of the English alphabet

v² *abbrev.* **1** [L *vide*] see **2** velocity **3** verb **4** versus **5** volt(s) **6** volume

V¹ (vē) *n.* a Roman numeral for 5

V² *abbrev.* **1** velocity **2** volt(s) **3** volume

V³ *Chem. symbol for* vanadium

VA *abbrev.* **1** Veterans Administration **2** Virginia

va·can·cy (vā′kən sē) *n., pl.* **-cies 1** a being vacant **2** empty or vacant space **3** an unoccupied position, office, quarters, etc.

va·cant (vā′kənt) *adj.* ⟦< L *vacare*, be empty⟧ **1** having nothing in it **2** not held, occupied, etc., as a seat or house **3** free from work; leisure [*vacant* time] **4** without thought, interest, etc.

va·cate (–kāt′) *vt.* **-cat′ed, -cat′ing 1** to cause (an office, house, etc.) to be vacant **2** *Law* to make void; annul

va·ca·tion (vā kā′shən, və–) *n.* ⟦< L *vacatio*⟧ a period of rest from work, study, etc. —*vi.* to take one's vacation —**va·ca′tion·er** *n.,* **va·ca′tion·ist**

vac·ci·nate (vak′sə nāt′) *vt., vi.* **-nat′ed, -nat′ing** to inoculate with a vaccine to prevent disease —**vac′ci·na′tion** *n.*

vac·cine (vak sēn′) *n.* ⟦< L *vacca*, cow: from use of cowpox virus in smallpox vaccine⟧ any preparation introduced into the body to produce immunity to a specific disease

vac·il·late (vas′ə lāt′) *vi.* **-lat′ed, -lat′ing** ⟦< L *vacillare*⟧ **1** to sway to and fro; waver **2** to fluctuate **3** to show indecision —**vac′il·la′tion** *n.*

va·cu·i·ty (va kyōō′ə tē) *n., pl.* **-ties** ⟦< L *vacuus*, empty⟧ **1** emptiness **2** an empty space **3** emptiness of mind **4** something senseless or silly

vac·u·ous (vak′yōō əs) *adj.* ⟦L *vacuus*⟧ **1** empty **2** stupid; senseless —**vac′u·ous·ly** *adv.*

vac·uum (vak′yōōm) *n., pl.* **-ums** or **-u·a** (–yōō ə) ⟦L⟧ **1** space with nothing at all in it **2** a space from which most of the air or gas has been taken **3** any void **4** *short for* vacuum cleaner —*adj.* **1** of or used to make a vacuum **2** having or working by a vacuum —*vt., vi.* to clean with a vacuum cleaner

vacuum cleaner a machine for cleaning carpets, floors, etc. by suction

vac·uum-packed *adj.* packed in a sealed container from which air has been removed to maintain freshness

vacuum tube an electron tube from which most of the air has been evacuated, containing one or more grids, used as an amplifier, etc.

vag·a·bond (vag′ə bänd′) *adj.* ⟦< L *vagari*, wander⟧ **1** wandering **2** living a drifting or irresponsible life; shiftless —*n.* **1** one who wanders from place to place **2** a wandering beggar **3** an idle or shiftless person —**vag′a·bond′age** *n.*

va·gar·y (vā′gə rē, və ger′ē) *n., pl.* **-ies** [see prec.] **1** an odd or eccentric action **2** a whimsical or freakish notion; caprice —**va·gar′i·ous** *adj.*

va·gi·na (və jī′nə) *n., pl.* **-nas** or **-nae** (–nē) ⟦L, sheath⟧ in female mammals, the canal from the vulva to the uterus —**vag′i·nal** (vaj′ə nəl) *adj.*

va·grant (vā′grənt) *n.* ⟦prob. < OFr *walcrer*, wander⟧ one who wanders from place to place supporting oneself by begging, etc. —*adj.* **1** nomadic **2** of or like a vagrant **3** wayward, erratic, etc. —**va′gran·cy** *n., pl.* **-cies**

vague (vāg) *adj.* **va′guer, va′guest** ⟦< L *vagus*, wandering⟧ **1** indefinite in shape or form **2** not sharp, certain, or precise in thought or expression —**vague′ly** *adv.* —**vague′ness** *n.*

vain (vān) *adj.* ⟦< L *vanus*, empty⟧ **1** having no real value; worthless [*vain* pomp] **2** without effect; futile [a *vain* endeavor] **3** having an excessively high regard for one's self, looks, etc.; conceited —**in vain 1** fruitlessly **2** profanely

vain·glo·ry (–glôr′ē) *n.* ⟦< L *vana gloria*, empty boasting⟧ excessive vanity —**vain′glo′ri·ous** *adj.*

val *abbrev.* **1** valuation **2** value

val·ance (val′əns, vā′ləns) *n.* ⟦ME < ?⟧ a short curtain forming a border, esp. across the top of a window

vale (vāl) *n.* [Old Poet.] VALLEY

val·e·dic·to·ri·an (val′ə dik tôr′ē ən) *n.* the student, usually the one with the highest grades, who delivers the valedictory at graduation

val·e·dic·to·ry (–tər ē) *n., pl.* **-ries** ⟦< L *vale*, farewell + *dicere*, to say⟧ a farewell speech, esp. at graduation

va·lence (vā′ləns) *n.* ⟦< L *valere*, be strong⟧ *Chem.* the combining capacity of an element or radical as measured by the number of hydrogen or chlorine atoms which one radical or atom of the element will combine with or replace: also **va′len·cy,** *pl.* **-cies**

Va·len·ci·a (və len′shē ə, –shə) seaport in E Spain

val·en·tine (val′ən tīn′) *n.* **1** a sweetheart chosen or greeted on Saint Valentine's Day **2** a greeting card or gift sent on this day

val·et (va lā′, *Brit.* val′it) *n.* ⟦Fr, a groom⟧ **1** a personal manservant who takes care of a man's clothes, helps him dress, etc. **2** an employee, as of a hotel, who cleans or presses clothes, parks cars, etc.

val·e·tu·di·nar·i·an (val′ə tōō′də ner′ē ən) *n.* ⟦< L *valetudo*, state of health, sickness⟧ **1** a person in poor health **2** one who worries about one's health

Val·hal·la (val hal′ə, väl häl′ə) *n.* Norse Myth. the great hall where Odin feasts the souls of heroes slain in battle

val·iant (val′yənt) *adj.* ⟦< L *valere*, be strong⟧ brave; courageous —**val′iance** *n.* —**val′iant·ly** *adv.*

val·id (val′id) *adj.* ⟦< L *valere*, be strong⟧ **1** having legal force **2** based on evidence or sound reasoning —**val′id·ly** *adv.* —**val′id·ness** *n.*

val·i·date (val′ə dāt′) *vt.* **-dat′ed, -dat′ing 1** to make legally valid **2** to prove to be valid

va·lid·i·ty (və lid′ə tē) *n., pl.* **-ties** the quality or fact of being valid

va·lise (və lēs′) *n.* ⟦Fr < L *valesium* < ?⟧ [Old-fashioned] a piece of hand luggage

Val·i·um (val′ē əm) *trademark for* a tranquilizing drug

Val·kyr·ie (val kir′ē, val′ki rē) *n. Norse Myth.* any of the maidens of Odin who conduct the souls of heroes slain in battle to Valhalla

val·ley (val′ē) *n., pl.* **-leys** [< L *vallis*] **1** low land lying between hills or mountains **2** the land drained by a river system **3** any valley-like dip

Valley Forge village in SE Pennsylvania: scene of Washington's winter encampment (1777-78)

val·or (val′ər) *n.* [< L *valere*, be strong] courage or bravery: Brit. sp. **val′our** —**val′or·ous** *adj.*

Val·pa·rai·so (val′pə rā′zō, -rī′sō) seaport in central Chile

val·u·a·ble (val′yə bəl, -yōō ə bəl) *adj.* **1** having value, esp. great monetary value **2** highly important, esteemed, etc. —*n.* an article of value: *usually used in pl.*

val·u·a·tion (val′yōō ā′shən) *n.* **1** the determining of the value of anything **2** determined or estimated value

val·ue (val′yōō) *n.* [< L *valere* be worth] **1** the worth of a thing in money or goods **2** estimated worth **3** purchasing power **4** that quality of a thing which makes it more or less desirable, useful, etc. **5** a thing or quality having intrinsic worth **6** [*pl.*] beliefs or standards **7** relative duration, intensity, etc. —*vt.* **val′ued, val′u·ing 1** to estimate the value of; appraise **2** to place a certain estimate of worth on [*to value* health above wealth] **3** to think highly of —**val′ue·less** *adj.*

val·ue-add·ed tax a tax based and paid on products, etc. at each stage of production or distribution, and included in the cost to the consumer

val·ued *adj.* highly thought of

value judgment an estimate made of the worth, goodness, etc. of a person, action, etc., esp. when such a judgment is not called for or desired

valve (valv) *n.* [< L *valva*, leaf of a folding door] **1** *Anat.* a membranous structure which permits body fluids to flow in one direction only, or opens and closes a tube, etc. **2** any device in a pipe, etc. that regulates the flow by means of a flap, lid, etc. **3** *Music* a device, as in the trumpet, that changes the tube length so as to change the pitch **4** *Zoology* one of the parts making up the shell of a mollusk, clam, etc.

va·moose (va mōōs′) *vi.* **-moosed′, -moos′ing** [< Sp *vamos*, let us go] [Old Slang] to leave quickly

vamp (vamp) *n.* [< OFr *avant*, before + *pié*, foot] **1** the part of a boot or shoe covering the instep **2** *Music* a simple, indefinitely repeated passage, often with improvisation —*vi. Music* to play a vamp

vam·pire (vam′pīr′) *n.* [< Slavic] **1** in folklore, a reanimated corpse that sucks the blood of living persons **2** one who preys ruthlessly on others

vampire bat a tropical American bat that lives on the blood of animals

van¹ (van) *n. short for* VANGUARD

van² (van) *n.* [< CARAVAN] a large, closed truck used as for moving, or a small one used for deliveries, fitted out as an RV, etc.

va·na·di·um (və nā′dē əm) *n.* [< ON *Vanadis*, goddess of love] a ductile, metallic chemical element used in steel alloys, etc.: symbol, V; at. no. 23

Van Al·len belt (van al′ən) [after J. *Van Allen* (1914-2006), U.S. physicist] a broad belt of radiation encircling the earth at varying levels

Van Bu·ren (van byoor′ən), **Mar·tin** (märt′'n) 1782-1862; 8th president of the U.S. (1837-41)

Van·cou·ver (van kōō′vər) seaport in SW British Columbia, Canada

Van·dal (van′dəl) *n.* **1** a member of a Germanic people that sacked Rome (A.D. 455) **2** [v-] one who maliciously destroys property

van·dal·ize (van′də līz′) *vt.* **-ized′, -iz′ing** to destroy or damage (property) maliciously —**van′dal·ism′** *n.*

Van·dyke (beard) (van dīk′) a closely trimmed, pointed beard

vane (vān) *n.* [< OE *fana*, a flag] **1** a free-swinging piece of metal, etc. that shows which way the wind is blowing; weather vane **2** any of the flat pieces set around an axle and rotated about it by moving air, water, etc. or rotated to move the air or water

van Gogh (van gō′, -gôkh′), **Vin·cent** (vin′sənt) 1853-90; Du. painter

van·guard (van′gärd′) *n.* [< OFr *avant*, before + *garde*, guard] **1** the part of an army which goes ahead of the main body **2** the leading position or persons in a movement

va·nil·la (və nil′ə) *n.* [< Sp *vaina*, pod] **1** a climbing orchid with podlike capsules (**vanilla beans**) **2** a flavoring made from these capsules —*adj.* **1** of or flavored with vanilla **2** [in allusion to the commonness of *vanilla* ice cream] [Inf.] bland, plain, or basic

van·ish (van′ish) *vi.* [see EVANESCENT] **1** to pass suddenly from sight; disappear **2** to cease to exist

van·i·ty (van′ə tē) *n., pl.* **-ties** [< L *vanus*, vain] **1** anything that is vain or futile **2** worthlessness or futility **3** a being vain, or too proud of oneself **4** a small table with a mirror for use while putting on cosmetics, etc. **5** a bathroom cabinet containing a washbowl

vanity case a woman's small traveling case for carrying cosmetics, toilet articles, etc.

van·quish (vaŋ′kwish, van′-) *vt.* [< L *vincere*] to conquer or defeat

van·tage (van′tij) *n.* [see ADVANTAGE] **1** a favorable position **2** a position allowing a clear view, understanding, etc.: also **vantage point**

Va·nua·tu (van′wä tōō′) country on a group of islands in the SW Pacific, west of Fiji

vap·id (vap′id) *adj.* [L *vapidus*] tasteless; dull —**va·pid·i·ty** (va pid′ə tē) *n.,* **vap′id·ness** *n.*

va·por (vā′pər) *n.* [L] **1** *a)* visible particles of moisture floating in the air, as fog or steam *b)* smoke, fumes, etc. **2** the gaseous form of any substance normally a liquid or solid Brit. sp. **va′pour**

va·por·ize (-pə rīz′) *vt., vi.* **-ized′, -iz′ing** to change into vapor —**va′por·i·za′tion** *n.* —**va′por·iz′er** *n.*

va·por·ous (vā′pər əs) *adj.* **1** forming or full of vapor; foggy; misty **2** like vapor

vapor trail CONTRAIL

va·que·ro (vä ker′ō) *n., pl.* **-ros** ⟦Sp < *vaca*, cow⟧ [Southwest] a man who herds cattle; cowboy

var *abbrev.* **1** variant(s) **2** various

var·i·a·ble (ver′ē ə bəl, var′-) *adj.* **1** apt to change or vary; changeable, inconstant, etc. **2** that can be changed or varied —*n.* anything changeable; a thing that varies —**var′i·a·bil′i·ty** *n.*

var·i·ance (-əns) *n.* **1** a varying or being variant **2** degree of change or difference; discrepancy **3** official permission to bypass regulations —**at variance** not in agreement or accord

var·i·ant (-ənt) *adj.* varying; different in some way from others of the same kind —*n.* anything variant, as a different spelling of the same word

var·i·a·tion (-ā′shən) *n.* **1** a varying; change in form, extent, etc. **2** the degree of such change **3** a thing somewhat different from another of the same kind **4** *Music* the repetition of a theme with changes in rhythm, key, etc.

var·i·col·ored (ver′i kul′ərd, var′-) *adj.* of several or many colors

var·i·cose (var′ə kōs′) *adj.* ⟦< L *varix*, enlarged vein⟧ abnormally and irregularly swollen [*varicose* veins].

var·ied (ver′ēd, var′-) *adj.* **1** of different kinds; various **2** changed; altered

var·i·e·gat·ed (ver′ē ə gāt′id, var′-) *adj.* ⟦< L *varius*, various⟧ **1** marked with different colors in spots, streaks, etc. **2** having variety; varied

va·ri·e·tal (və rī′ə təl) *adj.* **1** of or being a variety **2** designating a wine named after the kind of grape from which it is made —*n.* a varietal wine

va·ri·e·ty (-tē) *n., pl.* **-ties 1** the state of being various or varied **2** a different form of some thing, condition, etc.; kind **3** a collection of different things

variety store a retail store selling many small, inexpensive items

var·i·ous (ver′ē əs, var′-) *adj.* ⟦L *varius*, diverse⟧ **1** differing one from another; of several kinds **2** several or many —**var′i·ous·ly** *adv.*

var·let (vär′lit) *n.* ⟦OFr, a page⟧ [Archaic] a scoundrel; knave

var·mint (vär′mənt) *n.* ⟦var. of VERMIN⟧ [Inf. or Dial.] a person or animal regarded as objectionable

var·nish (vär′nish) *n.* ⟦< ML *veronix*, resin⟧ **1** a preparation of resinous substances dissolved in oil, alcohol, etc., used to give a hard, glossy surface to wood, metal, etc. **2** this surface **3** a surface smoothness, as of manner —*vt.* **1** to cover with varnish **2** to make superficially attractive

var·si·ty (vär′sə tē) *n., pl.* **-ties** ⟦< UNIVERSITY⟧ the main team representing a university, school, etc., as in a sport

var·y (ver′ē, var′ē) *vt.* **var′ied, var′y·ing** ⟦< L *varius*, various⟧ **1** to change; alter **2** to make different from one another **3** to give variety to [to *vary* one's reading] —*vi.* **1** to undergo change **2** to be different **3** to deviate or depart (*from*)

vas·cu·lar (vas′kyə lər) *adj.* ⟦< L *vas*, vessel⟧ of or having vessels or ducts for conveying blood, sap, etc.

vase (vās, vāz) *n.* ⟦< L *vas*, vessel⟧ an open container used for decoration, displaying flowers, etc.

vas·ec·to·my (va sek′tə mē) *n., pl.* **-mies** ⟦< L *vas*, vessel + -ECTOMY⟧ the surgical removal or tying of the duct carrying sperm from the testicle

Vas·e·line (vas′ə lēn′) ⟦< Ger *was(ser)*, water + Gr *el(aion)*, oil⟧ *trademark for* petrolatum —*n.* [v-] petrolatum

vas·o·mo·tor (vas′ō mōt′ər, vä′zō-) *adj.* ⟦< L *vas*, vessel + MOTOR⟧ regulating the diameter of blood vessels: said of a nerve, drug, etc.

vas·sal (vas′əl) *n.* ⟦< ML *vassus*, servant⟧ **1** under feudalism, one who held land, owing fealty to an overlord **2** a subordinate, servant, slave, etc. —**vas′sal·age** (-ij) *n.*

vast (vast) *adj.* ⟦L *vastus*⟧ very great in size, degree, etc. —**vast′ly** *adv.* —**vast′ness** *n.*

vat (vat) *n.* ⟦< OE *fæt*, cask⟧ a large container for holding liquids

VAT (vē′ā′tē′, vat) *abbrev.* value-added tax

Vat·i·can (vat′i kən) *n.* **1** the papal palace in Vatican City **2** the papal government

Vatican City independent papal state, an enclave in Rome (Italy), including the Vatican

vaude·ville (vôd′vil) *n.* ⟦Fr, after *Vau-de-Vire*, a valley in Normandy, famous for convivial songs⟧ a staged entertainment, popular in the early 1900s, presenting acts such as slapstick comedy, song, dance, etc.

vault¹ (vôlt) *n.* ⟦< L *volvere*, to roll⟧ **1** an arched roof or ceiling **2** an arched chamber or space **3** a cellar room used for storage **4** a burial chamber **5** a room for the safekeeping of valuables, as in a bank —*vt.* to cover with, or build as, a vault —*vi.* to curve like a vault

vault² (vôlt) *vi., vt.* ⟦< earlier It *voltare*⟧ to jump over (a barrier), esp. with the hands supported on the barrier or holding a long pole —*n.* a vaulting —**vault′er** *n.*

vault·ing *adj.* **1** leaping **2** unduly confident [*vaulting* ambition] **3** used in vaulting —*n.* the structure or material of a vaulted ceiling

vaunt (vônt) *vi., n.* ⟦< L *vanus*, vain⟧ boast —**vaunt′ed** *adj.*

VCR *n.* VIDEOCASSETTE RECORDER

VD *abbrev.* venereal disease

VDT *n.* a video display terminal

-'ve (v, əv) *suffix* have: used in contractions [*we've* seen it]

veal (vēl) *n.* [< L *vitulus*, calf] the flesh of a young calf, used as food

vec·tor (vek′tər) *n.* [< L *vehere*, to carry] 1 an animal that transmits a disease-producing organism 2 *Math. a)* a quantity, such as velocity, that has both magnitude and direction *b)* a line segment representing such a quantity 3 the compass heading of an aircraft, etc.

Ve·da (vā′də, vē′-) *n.* [Sans *veda*, knowledge] any of four ancient sacred books of Hinduism —**Ve′dic** *adj.*

Veep (vēp) *n.* [*sometimes* v-] [Inf.] a vice-president

veer (vir) *vi., vt.* [< Fr *virer*, turn around] to change in direction; shift; turn —*n.* a change of direction

veg (vej) *n., pl.* **veg** [Inf., Chiefly Brit.] a vegetable

ve·gan (vē′gən) *n.* [< VEG(ETABLE) + -AN] a vegetarian who eats no animal products

veg·e·ta·ble (vej′tə bəl, vej′ə tə-) *adj.* [see VEGETATE] 1 of plants in general 2 of, from, or like edible vegetables —*n.* 1 any plant, as distinguished from animal or inorganic matter 2 a plant eaten whole or in part, raw or cooked 3 [Inf.] a person thought of as like a vegetable, as a person in a coma

veg·e·tar·i·an (vej′ə ter′ē ən) *n.* one who eats no meat —*adj.* 1 of vegetarians 2 consisting only of vegetables

veg·e·tate (vej′ə tāt′) *vi.* **-tat′ed, -tat′ing** [< L *vegere*, quicken] 1 to grow as plants 2 to lead a dull, inactive life —**veg′e·ta′tive** *adj.*

veg·e·ta·tion (-tā′shən) *n.* 1 a vegetating 2 plant life in general

veg·gie (vej′ē) *n.* 1 [Inf.] a vegetable 2 [Slang] a vegetarian —*adj.* [Inf.] vegetarian

ve·he·ment (vē′ə mənt) *adj.* [< L *vehere*, carry] 1 violent; impetuous 2 full of intense or strong passion —**ve′he·mence** *n.,* **ve′he·men·cy** —**ve′he·ment·ly** *adv.*

ve·hi·cle (vē′ə kəl) *n.* [< L *vehere*, to carry] 1 any device for carrying or conveying persons or objects 2 a means of expressing thoughts, etc. —**ve·hic′u·lar** (-hik′yōō lər) *adj.*

veil (vāl) *n.* [< L *velum*, cloth] 1 a piece of light fabric, as of net, worn, esp. by women, over the face or head 2 anything used to conceal, cover, separate, etc. [a *veil* of silence] 3 a part of a nun's headdress —*vt.* 1 to cover with a veil 2 to hide or disguise —**take the veil** to become a nun

veiled (vāld) *adj.* 1 wearing a veil 2 concealed, hidden, etc. 3 not openly expressed

vein (vān) *n.* [< L *vena*] 1 any blood vessel carrying blood to the heart 2 any of the ribs of an insect's wing or of a leaf blade 3 a body of minerals occupying a fissure in rock 4 a lode 5 a streak of a different color, etc., as in marble 6 a distinctive quality in one's character, speech, etc. 7 a mood —*vt.* to mark as with veins

Vel·cro (vel′krō) *trademark for* a nylon material for fastenings, made up of matching strips with tiny hooks and adhesive pile, that can be easily pressed together or pulled apart —*n.* [*occas.* v-] this material

veld or **veldt** (velt) *n.* [Afrik < MDu *veld*, field] in S & E Africa, open, grassy country, with few bushes or trees

vel·lum (vel′əm) *n.* [< L *vitulus*, calf] 1 a fine parchment prepared from calfskin, lambskin, etc. used for writing on or for binding books 2 a strong paper made to resemble this

ve·loc·i·ty (və läs′ə tē) *n., pl.* **-ties** [< L *velox*, swift] 1 quickness of motion; speed 2 *Physics* speed and direction of motion

ve·lour or **ve·lours** (və loor′) *n., pl.* **-lours′** (-loorz′, -loor′) [Fr < L *villus*, shaggy hair] a fabric with a soft nap like velvet

ve·lum (vē′ləm) *n., pl.* **-la** (-lə) [L, a veil] SOFT PALATE

vel·vet (vel′vət) *n.* [< L *villus*, shaggy hair] 1 a rich fabric of silk, rayon, etc. with a soft, thick pile 2 anything like velvet in texture —*adj.* 1 made of velvet 2 like velvet —**vel′vet·y** *adj.*

vel·vet·een (-və tēn′) *n.* a cotton cloth with a short, thick pile like velvet

ve·nal (vē′nəl) *adj.* [L *venalis*, for sale] open to, or characterized by, bribery or corruption —**ve·nal·i·ty** (vi nal′ə tē) *n.*

vend (vend) *vt., vi.* [< L *venum dare*, offer for sale] to sell (goods) —**ven′dor** *n.,* **vend′er**

ven·det·ta (ven det′ə) *n.* [It < L *vindicta*, vengeance] a bitter feud, as between families

vending machine an automated machine for selling small articles, refreshments, etc.

ve·neer (və nir′) *vt.* [< Fr *fournir*, furnish] to cover with a thin layer of more costly material; esp., to cover (wood) with wood of finer quality —*n.* 1 a thin surface layer, as of fine wood, laid over a base of common material 2 superficial appearance [a *veneer* of culture]

ven·er·a·ble (ven′ər ə bəl) *adj.* worthy of respect because of age, dignity, etc. —**ven′er·a·bil′i·ty** *n.*

ven·er·ate (ven′ər āt′) *vt.* **-at′ed, -at′ing** [< L *venerari*, to worship] to look upon with feelings of deep respect; revere —**ven′er·a′tion** *n.*

ve·ne·re·al (və nir′ē əl) *adj.* [< L *venus*, love] 1 of sexual intercourse 2 transmitted by sexual intercourse [*venereal* disease]

Ve·ne·tian (və nē′shən) *adj.* of Venice or its people or culture —*n.* a person born or living in Venice

Venetian blind [*also* v- b-] a window blind of thin, horizontal slats that can be set at any angle

Ven·e·zue·la (ven′ə zwā′lə) country in N South America —**Ven′e·zue′lan** *adj., n.*

venge·ance (venj′əns) *n.* [< L *vindicare*, avenge] the return of an injury for an injury, as in retribution; revenge —**with a vengeance 1** with great force or fury **2** excessively

venge·ful (venj′fəl) *adj.* seeking vengeance; vindictive —**venge′ful·ly** *adv.*

ve·ni·al (vēn′yəl, vē′nē əl) *adj.* [< L *venia*, a grace] that may be forgiven; pardonable [a *venial* sin]

Ven·ice (ven′is) seaport in N Italy built on more than 100 small islands

ve·ni·re·man (və nī′rē mən) *n., pl.* **-men** (-mən) [< ML *venire facias*, cause to come] one of a group of people from among whom a jury will be selected

ven·i·son (ven′i sən, -zən) *n.* [< L *venari*, to hunt] the flesh of a deer, used as food

ven·om (ven′əm) *n.* [< L *venenum*, a poison] 1 the poison secreted by some snakes, spiders, etc. 2 malice

ven·om·ous *adj.* 1 full of venom; poisonous 2 spiteful; malicious

ve·nous (vē′nəs) *adj.* [L *venosus*] 1 of veins 2 designating blood carried in veins

vent¹ (vent) *n.* [< L *ventus*, wind] 1 expression; release [giving *vent* to emotion] 2 a small opening to permit passage or escape, as of a gas —*vt.* 1 to make a vent in or for 2 to express; let out

vent² (vent) *n.* [< L *findere*, to split] a vertical slit in a garment

ven·ti·late (vent′'l āt′) *vt.* **-lat′ed, -lat′ing** [< L *ventus*, wind] 1 to circulate fresh air in (a room, etc.) 2 to provide with an opening for the escape of air, gas, etc. —**ven′ti·la′tion** *n.*

ven·ti·la·tor *n.* 1 an opening or a device used to bring in fresh air and drive out foul air 2 a device providing artificial respiration

ven·tral (ven′trəl) *adj.* [< L *venter*, belly] of, near, or on the belly

ven·tri·cle (ven′tri kəl) *n.* [see prec.] either of the two lower chambers of the heart —**ven·tric′u·lar** (-trik′yə lər) *adj.*

ven·tril·o·quism (ven′tril′ə kwiz′əm) *n.* [< L *venter*, belly + *loqui*, speak] the art of speaking so that the voice seems to come from a source other than the speaker —**ven·tril′o·quist** *n.*

ven·ture (ven′chər) *n.* [see ADVENTURE] 1 a risky undertaking, as in business 2 something on which a risk is taken —*vt.* **-tured, -tur·ing** 1 to expose to danger or chance of loss 2 to express at the risk of criticism [to *venture* an opinion] —*vi.* to do or go at some risk

ven·ture·some (-səm) *adj.* 1 inclined to venture; daring 2 risky; hazardous Also **ven′tur·ous** (-əs)

ven·ue (ven′yo͞o′) *n.* [< L *venire*, come] 1 *Law a)* the locality in which a cause of action or a crime occurs *b)* the locality in which a jury is drawn and a case is tried 2 the scene of a large gathering for some event

Ve·nus (vē′nəs) *n.* 1 the Roman goddess of love and beauty 2 the planet second in distance from the sun: see PLANET

Venus' fly·trap (flī′trap′) a swamp plant with hinged leaves that snap shut, trapping insects

Ve·nu·si·an (vi no͞o′shən) *adj.* of the planet Venus —*n.* a being from or living on Venus, as in science fiction

ve·ra·cious (və rā′shəs) *adj.* [< L *verus*, true] 1 habitually truthful; honest 2 true; accurate

ve·rac·i·ty (və ras′ə tē) *n.* 1 honesty 2 accuracy 3 truth

Ver·a·cruz (ver′ə kro͞oz′) state of Mexico, on the E coast

ve·ran·da or **ve·ran·dah** (və ran′də) *n.* [< Port

varanda, balcony] an open porch or portico, usually roofed, along the outside of a building

verb (vurb) *n.* [L *verbum*, a word] a word expressing action, existence, or occurrence

ver·bal (vur′bəl) *adj.* 1 of, in, or by means of words 2 in speech; oral 3 of, like, or derived from a verb —**ver′bal·ly** *adv.*

ver·bal·ize *vi.* **-ized′, -iz′ing** to use words for communication —*vt.* to express in words —**ver′ba·li·za′tion** *n.*

verbal noun *Gram.* a noun derived from a verb (Ex.: *swimming* is fun)

ver·ba·tim (vər bāt′əm) *adv., adj.* [< L *verbum*, a word] word for word

ver·be·na (vər bē′nə) *n.* [L, foliage] an ornamental plant with spikes or clusters of showy red, white, or purplish flowers

ver·bi·age (vur′bē ij′) *n.* [Fr < L *verbum*, a word] an excess of words; wordiness

ver·bose (vər bōs′) *adj.* [< L *verbum*, a word] using too many words; wordy —**ver·bos′i·ty** (-bäs′ə tē) *n.*

ver·dant (vur′dənt) *adj.* [prob. VERD(URE) + -ANT] 1 green 2 covered with green vegetation

Ver·di (ver′dē), **Giu·sep·pe** (jo͞o zep′pe) 1813-1901; It. operatic composer

ver·dict (vur′dikt) *n.* [< L *vere*, truly + *dictum*, a thing said] 1 the formal finding of a judge or jury 2 any decision or judgment

ver·di·gris (vur′di grēs′, -gris) *n.* [< OFr *vert de Grece*, lit., green of Greece] a greenish coating that forms on brass, bronze, etc.

ver·dure (vur′jər) *n.* [< OFr *verd*, green] 1 the fresh-green color of growing things 2 green vegetation

verge¹ (vurj) *n.* [< L *virga*, rod] the edge, brink, or margin (*of* something) —*vi.* **verged, verg′ing** to be on the verge: usually with *on* or *upon*

verge² (vurj) *vi.* **verged, verg′ing** [L *vergere*, to bend, turn] 1 to tend or incline (*to* or *toward*) 2 to change or pass gradually (*into*)

verg·er (vur′jər) *n.* [ME, ult. < L *virga*, rod] a church caretaker or usher

Ver·gil (vur′jəl) *alt. sp. of* VIRGIL

ver·i·fy (ver′ə fī′) *vt.* **-fied′, -fy′ing** [< L *verus*, true + *-ficare*, -FY] 1 to prove to be true by demonstration, evidence, etc.; confirm 2 to test the accuracy of —**ver′i·fi′a·ble** *adj.* —**ver′i·fi·ca′tion** *n.*

ver·i·ly (ver′ə lē) *adv.* [Archaic] truly

ver·i·si·mil·i·tude (ver′ə si mil′ə to͞od′) *n.* [< L *verus*, true + *similis*, like] the appearance of being true or real

ver·i·ta·ble (ver′i tə bəl) *adj.* [see fol.] true; actual

ver·i·ty (ver′ə tē) *n.* [< L *verus*, true] 1 truth; reality 2 *pl.* **-ties** a principle, belief, etc. taken to be fundamentally true; a truth

ver·mi·cel·li (vur′mə sel′ē, -chel′ē) *n.* [It < L *vermis*, a worm] pasta like thin spaghetti

ver·mic·u·lite (vər mik′yə lit′) *n.* [< L *vermis*, a worm] a hydrous silicate mineral that expands when heated, used as in insulation

ver·mi·form (vur′mə fôrm′) *adj.* [< L *vermis*, a worm + -FORM] shaped like a worm

vermiform appendix the appendix extending from the cecum of the large intestine

ver·mil·ion (vər mil′yən) *n.* [< L *vermis*, a worm] 1 a bright-red pigment 2 a bright red or scarlet

ver·min (vur′mən) *n., pl.* **-min** [< L *vermis*, a worm] 1 [*pl.*] various destructive insects or small animals regarded as pests, as rats 2 a vile person

Ver·mont (vər mänt′) New England state of the U.S.; cap. Montpelier: abbrev. *VT* —**Ver·mont′er** *n.*

ver·mouth (vər mōōth′) *n.* [< Ger *wermut*, wormwood] a white fortified wine flavored with herbs, used in cocktails and as an aperitif

ver·nac·u·lar (vər nak′yə lər) *adj.* [< L *vernaculus*, indigenous] 1 of, in, or using the native language of a place 2 native to a country —*n.* 1 the native language or dialect of a country or place 2 the common, everyday language of a people 3 the jargon of a profession or trade

ver·nal (vur′nəl) *adj.* [< L *ver*, spring] 1 of or in the spring 2 springlike 3 youthful

ver·ni·er scale (vur′nē ər) [after P. *Vernier* (1580?–1637), Fr mathematician] a graduated scale with increments fractionally smaller than those on the scale it slides along, allowing precise measurement

Ver·sailles (vər sī′) city in NC France, near Paris: site of a palace built by Louis XIV

ver·sa·tile (vur′sə təl) *adj.* [< L *vertere*, to turn] competent in many things —**ver′sa·til′i·ty** (-til′ə tē) *n.*

verse (vurs) *n.* [< L *vertere*, to turn] 1 a single line of poetry 2 poetry 3 a particular form of poetry 4 a poem 5 a stanza 6 *Bible* any of the short divisions of a chapter

versed (vurst) *adj.* [< L *versari*, be busy] skilled or learned (*in* a subject)

ver·si·fy (vur′sə fī′) *vi.* **-fied′, -fy′ing** [< L *versus*, a verse + *facere*, make] to compose verses —*vt.* 1 to tell about in verse 2 to put into verse form —**ver′si·fi·ca′tion** *n.* —**ver′si·fi′er** *n.*

ver·sion (vur′zhən) *n.* [see VERSE] 1 a translation, esp. of the Bible 2 an account showing one point of view 3 a particular form of something

ver·sus (vur′səs) *prep.* [ML < L, toward] 1 against 2 in contrast with

ver·te·bra (vur′tə brə) *n., pl.* **-brae′** (-brē′, -brā′) or **-bras** [L < *vertere*, to turn] any of the single bones of the spinal column —**ver′te·bral** *adj.*

ver·te·brate (-brit, -brāt′) *adj.* 1 having a backbone, or spinal column 2 of the vertebrates —*n.* any of a large division of animals having a spinal column, as mammals, birds, etc.

ver·tex (vur′teks′) *n., pl.* **-tex′es** or **-ti·ces′** (-tə sēz′) [L] 1 the highest point; top 2 *Geom.* the point of intersection of the two sides of an angle or of three or more faces of a polyhedron

ver·ti·cal (vur′ti kəl) *adj.* 1 of or at the ver-

tex 2 upright, straight up or down, etc. —*n.* a vertical line, plane, etc. —**ver′ti·cal·ly** *adv.*

ver·tig·i·nous (vər tij′ə nəs) *adj.* of, having, or causing vertigo

ver·ti·go (vur′ti gō′) *n.* [L < *vertere*, to turn] a sensation of dizziness

verve (vurv) *n.* [Fr < OFr, manner of speech] vigor; energy; enthusiasm

ver·y (ver′ē) *adj.* [< L *verus*, true] 1 complete; absolute [the *very* opposite] 2 same [the *very* hat I lost] 3 being just what is needed 4 actual [caught in the *very* act]: often an intensive [the *very* rafters shook] —*adv.* 1 extremely 2 truly; really [the *very* same man]

very high frequency any radio frequency between 30 and 300 megahertz

very low frequency any radio frequency between 10 and 30 kilohertz

ves·i·cant (ves′i kənt) *adj.* [< L *vesica*, a blister] causing blisters —*n.* a vesicant agent, as mustard gas used in warfare to blister skin and lungs

ves·i·cle (-kəl) *n.* [< L *vesica*, bladder] a small, membranous cavity, sac, or cyst —**ve·sic·u·lar** (və sik′yə lər) *adj.*, **ve·sic′u·late** (-lit)

ves·pers (ves′pərz) *n.* [ult. < L *vespera*, evening] [*often* V-] [*sometimes with pl. v.*] an evening prayer or service

Ves·puc·ci (ves pōōt′chē), **A·me·ri·go** (ä′me rē′gō) (L. name *Americus Vespucius*) 1454–1512; It. navigator & explorer

ves·sel (ves′əl) *n.* [< L *vas*] 1 a utensil for holding something, as a bowl, kettle, etc. 2 a boat or ship 3 a tube or duct of the body, containing a fluid

vest (vest) *n.* [< L *vestis*, garment] a short, sleeveless garment, esp. one worn under a suit coat by men —*vt.* 1 to dress, as in clerical robes 2 to place (authority, etc.) in someone 3 to put (a person) in control of, as power, etc. —*vi.* to pass to a person; become vested (*in* a person), as property

ves·tal (ves′təl) *adj.* [< L *Vesta*, goddess of the hearth] chaste; pure —*n.* a virgin priestess of the Roman goddess Vesta: in full **vestal virgin**

vest·ed (ves′tid) *adj.* [pp. of VEST] *Law* fixed; settled; absolute [a *vested* right]

vested interest 1 an established right, as to some future benefit 2 [*pl.*] groups pursuing selfish goals and exerting controlling influence

ves·ti·bule (ves′tə byōōl′) *n.* [L *vestibulum*] a small entrance hall, as to a building

ves·tige (ves′tij) *n.* [< L *vestigium*, footprint] 1 a trace, mark, or sign, esp. of something that has passed away 2 *Biol.* a degenerate part, more fully developed in an earlier stage —**ves·tig′i·al** (-tij′ē əl, -tij′əl) *adj.*

vest·ing *n.* the partial or complete retention of pension rights as by a former employee

vest·ment (vest′mənt) *n.* [< L *vestire*, clothe] a garment or robe, esp. one worn by a clergy

vest-pock·et *adj.* very small, or unusually small

ves·try (ves′trē) *n., pl.* **-tries** [< L *vestis*,

garment] **1** a room in a church where vestments, etc. are kept **2** a room in a church, used as a chapel **3** a group of church members managing the temporal affairs of the church

Ve·su·vi·us (və sōō′vē əs) active volcano in S Italy, near Naples

vet[1] (vet) *vt.* to evaluate thoroughly or expertly

vet[2] *abbrev.* **1** veteran **2** veterinarian **3** veterinary

vetch (vech) *n.* [< L *vicia*] a leafy, climbing or trailing plant of the pea family, grown for fodder

vet·er·an (vet′ər ən, ve′trən) *adj.* [< L *vetus*, old] **1** old and experienced **2** of veterans —*n.* **1** one who has served in the armed forces **2** one who has served long in some position

Veterans Day a legal holiday in the U.S. honoring all veterans of the armed forces: observed on ARMISTICE DAY

vet·er·i·nar·i·an (vet′ər ə ner′ē ən) *n.* one who practices veterinary medicine or surgery

vet·er·i·nar·y (-ē) *adj.* [< L *veterina*, beasts of burden] designating or of the branch of medicine dealing with nonhuman animals —*n.*, *pl.* **-ies** VETERINARIAN

ve·to (vē′tō) *n.*, *pl.* **-toes** [L, I forbid] **1** *a*) an order prohibiting some act *b*) the power to prohibit action **2** *a*) the power of one branch of government to reject bills passed by another *b*) the exercise of this power —*vt.* **-toed, -to·ing 1** to prevent (a bill) from becoming law by a veto **2** to forbid

vex (veks) *vt.* [< L *vexare*, agitate] **1** to disturb; annoy, esp. in a petty way **2** to distress; afflict

vex·a·tion (vek sā′shən) *n.* **1** a vexing or being vexed **2** something that vexes —**vex·a′tious** *adj.*

VHF or **vhf** *abbrev.* very high frequency

VHS [*v*(*ideo*) *h*(*ome*) *s*(*ystem*)] *trademark for* a format for videocassettes

vi *abbrev.* intransitive verb

VI *abbrev.* Virgin Islands: also **V.I.**

vi·a (vī′ə, vē′ə) *prep.* [L, way] by way of

vi·a·ble (vī′ə bəl) *adj.* [< L *vita*, life] **1** sufficiently developed to be able to live outside the uterus **2** able to survive and grow [*viable seeds*] **3** workable [*viable ideas*] —**vi′a·bil′i·ty** *n.*

vi·a·duct (vī′ə dukt′) *n.* [< VIA + (AQUE)DUCT] a bridge consisting of a series of short spans, supported on piers or towers

Vi·a·gra (vī ag′rə) *trademark for* a compound used to treat erectile dysfunction of the penis

vi·al (vī′əl) *n.* [< OFr *fiole*] a small vessel or bottle for liquids

vi·and (vī′ənd) *n.* [< L *vivere*, to live] an article of food

vibe (vīb) *n.* [Inf.] a distinctive mood surrounding a person, thing, or place, as sensed by another person

vibes (vībz) *pl.n.* **1** VIBRAPHONE **2** [Slang] qualities thought of as being like vibrations which produce an emotional reaction in others

vi·brant (vī′brənt) *adj.* **1** quivering or vibrating **2** produced by vibration **3** vigorous, vivacious, etc. —**vi′bran·cy** *n.* —**vi′brant·ly** *adv.*

vi·bra·phone (vī′brə fōn′) *n.* a musical instrument like the marimba, with electrically operated resonators —**vi′bra·phon′ist** *n.*

vi·brate (vī′brāt′) *vt.* **-brat′ed, -brat′ing** [< L *vibrare*] to set in to-and-fro motion —*vi.* **1** to swing back and forth; oscillate **2** to move rapidly back and forth; quiver **3** to resound **4** to be emotionally stirred —**vi·bra′tion** *n.* —**vi′bra·tor** *n.*

vi·bra·to (vi brät′ō) *n.*, *pl.* **-tos** [It] a pulsating effect produced by rapid but slight oscillation in the pitch of a musical tone

vi·bra·to·ry (vī′brə tôr′ē) *adj.* **1** of, like, or causing vibration **2** vibrating or capable of vibrating

vi·bur·num (vī bur′nəm) *n.* [L, wayfaring tree] a shrub or small tree with white flowers

vic·ar (vik′ər) *n.* [< L *vicis*, a change] **1** *Anglican Ch.* a parish priest receiving a stipend **2** *R.C.Ch.* a church officer acting as a deputy of a bishop

vic·ar·age *n.* **1** the residence of a vicar **2** the position or duties of a vicar

vi·car·i·ous (vī ker′ē əs) *adj.* [< L *vicarius*, substituted] **1** endured or performed by one person in place of another **2** shared in by imagined participation in another's experience [a *vicarious* thrill] —**vi·car′i·ous·ly** *adv.*

vice (vīs) *n.* [< L *vitium*] **1** *a*) an evil action or habit *b*) evil conduct *c*) prostitution **2** a trivial fault or failing

vice- [L < *vicis*, a change] *prefix* a subordinate; deputy [*vice*-president]

vice·ge·rent (vīs′jir′ənt) *n.* [< prec. + L *gerere*, to direct] a deputy

vice-pres·i·dent *n.* an officer next in rank below a president, acting during the president's absence or incapacity: for the U.S. official, usually **Vice President** —**vice′-pres′i·den·cy** *n.*

vice·roy (vīs′roi′) *n.* [MFr < *vice*- (see VICE-) + *roy*, king] a person ruling a region as the deputy of a sovereign

vi·ce ver·sa (vī′sə vur′sə, vīs′ vur′sə) [L] the relation being reversed

vi·chys·soise (vē′shē swäz′, vish′ē-) *n.* a thick, cold soup of potatoes, leeks, and cream

vi·cin·i·ty (və sin′ə tē) *n.*, *pl.* **-ties** [< L *vicus*, village] **1** nearness; proximity **2** the surrounding area

vi·cious (vish′əs) *adj.* [< L *vitium*, vice] **1** characterized by vice; evil or depraved **2** faulty; flawed **3** unruly [a *vicious* horse] **4** malicious; spiteful [a *vicious* rumor] **5** very intense, forceful, etc. [a *vicious* blow] —**vi′cious·ly** *adv.* —**vi′cious·ness** *n.*

vicious circle a situation in which the solution of one problem gives rise to another, eventually bringing back the first problem: also **vicious cycle**

vi·cis·si·tudes (vi sis′ə tōōdz′) *pl.n.* [< L *vi-*

cis, a turn] unpredictable changes in life; ups and downs

Vicks·burg (viks′burg′) city in W Mississippi: besieged & captured by Grant in the Civil War (1863)

vic·tim (vik′təm) *n.* [L *victima*] 1 someone or something killed, destroyed, sacrificed, etc. 2 one who suffers some loss, esp. by being swindled

vic·tim·ize (-īz′) *vt.* **-ized′, -iz′ing** to make a victim of

vic·tor (vik′tər) *n.* [< L *vincere*, conquer] the winner in a battle, struggle, etc.

Vic·to·ri·a¹ (vik tôr′ē ə) 1819-1901; queen of Great Britain & Ireland (1837-1901)

Vic·to·ri·a² (vik tôr′ē ə) capital of British Columbia, Canada

Vic·to·ri·an *adj.* 1 of or characteristic of the period of the reign of Queen Victoria 2 showing the respectability, prudery, etc. attributed to the Victorians —*n.* a person of that time —**Vic·to′ri·an·ism′** *n.*

vic·to·ri·ous (vik tôr′ē əs) *adj.* 1 having won a victory; triumphant 2 of or bringing about victory

vic·to·ry (vik′tər ē, -trē) *n., pl.* **-ries** [< L *vincere*, conquer] the winning of a battle, war, or any struggle

vict·uals (vit′lz) *pl.n.* [< L *victus*, food] [Inf. or Dial.] articles of food

vi·cu·ña (vi kōō′nya) *n.* [Sp] 1 a small llama of South America 2 its soft, shaggy wool

vi·de (vī′dē) *v.* [L] see; refer to (a certain page, etc.)

vid·e·o (vid′ē ō′) *adj.* [L, I see] 1 of television 2 of the picture portion of a telecast, recording, etc. 3 of data display on a computer —*n., pl.* **-os′** 1 TELEVISION 2 *short for* VIDEOCASSETTE, VIDEOTAPE, etc.

vid·e·o·cas·sette *n.* a cassette of videotape

videocassette recorder a device for recording on and playing back videocassettes: also **vid′e·o·re·cord′er** *n.*

vid·e·o·con·fer·enc·ing *n.* the holding of a conference at several locations using video equipment

vid·e·o·disc *n.* a disc on which images and sounds can be recorded for later playback: also **vid′e·o·disk′**

video game any of various games involving images, controlled by players, on a TV screen, computer monitor, etc.

vid·e·o·tape *n.* a magnetic tape on which images and sounds can be recorded for later playback —*vt.* **-taped′, -tap′ing** to record on videotape

vie (vī) *vi.* **vied, vy′ing** [< L *invitare*, invite] to struggle for superiority (*with* someone); compete

Vi·en·na (vē en′ə) capital of Austria —**Vi·en·nese** (vē′ə nēz′) *adj., n., pl.* **-nese′**

Vi·et·nam (vē′et näm′, -nam′) country on the E coast of Indochina: partitioned into two republics (**North Vietnam** & **South Vietnam**) in 1954, and reunified in 1976 —**Vi′et·nam·ese′** (-nə mēz′) *adj., n., pl.* **-ese′**

view (vyōō) *n.* [< L *videre*, to see] 1 a seeing or looking, as in inspection 2 range of vision 3 mental survey [a correct *view* of a situation] 4 a scene or prospect [a room with a *view*] 5 manner of regarding something; opinion —*vt.* 1 to inspect; scrutinize 2 to see; behold 3 to survey mentally; consider —**in view** 1 in sight 2 under consideration 3 as a goal or hope —**in view of** because of —**on view** displayed publicly —**with a view to** with the purpose or hope of

view·er *n.* 1 one who views something 2 an optical device for individual viewing of slides

view·find·er *n.* a camera device for viewing what will appear in the photograph

view·point *n.* the mental position from which things are viewed and judged; point of view

vig·il (vij′əl) *n.* [< L, awake] 1 *a)* a watchful staying awake *b)* a watch kept 2 the eve of a church festival 3 a peaceful assembly in support of a cause

vig·i·lant (vij′ə lənt) *adj.* [< L *vigil*, awake] staying watchful and alert to danger or trouble —**vig′i·lance** *n.*

vig·i·lan·te (vij′ə lan′tē) *n.* [Sp, watchman] one who acts outside the law to punish or avenge a crime —**vig′i·lan′tism′** *n.* —**vig′i·lan′tist** *adj.*

vi·gnette (vin yet′) *n.* [Fr < *vigne*, vine] 1 an ornamental design used on a page of a book, etc. 2 a picture shading off gradually at the edges 3 a short literary sketch, scene in a film, etc.

vig·or (vig′ər) *n.* [< L *vigere*, be strong] active force or strength; vitality; energy: Brit. sp. **vig′our** —**vig′or·ous** *adj.* —**vig′or·ous·ly** *adv.*

vik·ing (vī′kiŋ) *n.* [ON *vikingr*] [*also* V-] any of the Scandinavian pirates of the 8th to the 10th c.

vile (vīl) *adj.* [< L *vilis*, cheap, base] 1 morally evil; wicked 2 disgusting 3 degrading; mean 4 very bad [*vile* weather] —**vile′ness** *n.*

vil·i·fy (vil′ə fī′) *vt.* **-fied′, -fy′ing** [see prec. & -FY] to use abusive language about or of; defame —**vil′i·fi·ca′tion** *n.*

vil·la (vil′ə) *n.* [It < L, a farm] a country house or estate, esp. a large one

vil·lage (vil′ij) *n.* [see prec.] 1 a community smaller than a town 2 the populace of such a community —**vil′lag·er** *n.*

vil·lain (vil′ən) *n.* [< VL *villanus*, a farm servant] a wicked or evil person, or such a character in a play, etc. —**vil′lain·ous** *adj.*

vil·lain·y *n., pl.* **-ies** 1 wickedness; evil 2 a villainous act

vil·lein (vil′ən) *n.* [see VILLAIN] a feudal serf who had become a freeman, except to his lord

vim (vim) *n.* [prob. echoic] vigor

vin (van; *E* vin) *n.* [Fr] wine

vin·ai·grette (vin′ə gret′) *n.* [Fr < *vinaigre*, vinegar] a salad dressing of vinegar, oil, etc.

Vinci, Leonardo da *see* DA VINCI, Leonardo

vin·di·cate (vin′də kāt′) *vt.* **-cat′ed, -cat′ing** [< L *vis*, force + *dicere*, say] 1 to clear from criticism, blame, etc. 2 to defend against opposition **3** to justify —**vin′di·ca′tion** *n.* —**vin′di·ca′tor** *n.*

vin·dic·tive (vin dik′tiv) *adj.* [see prec.] **1** revengeful in spirit **2** said or done in revenge —**vin·dic′tive·ly** *adv.* —**vin·dic′tive·ness** *n.*

vine (vīn) *n.* [< L *vinum*, wine] **1** a grapevine **2** *a)* a plant with a long, thin stem that grows along the ground or climbs a support *b)* the stem of such a plant

vin·e·gar (vin′ə gər) *n.* [< medieval Fr *vin*, wine + *aigre*, sour] a sour liquid made by fermenting cider, wine, etc. and used as a condiment and preservative —**vin′e·gar·y** *adj.*

vine·yard (vin′yərd) *n.* land devoted to cultivating grapevines

vi·no (vē′nō), *n.* [It & Sp] wine

vin ro·sé (rō zā′; E rō zā′) [Fr] ROSÉ

vin·tage (vin′tij) *n.* [< L *vinum*, wine + *demere*, remove] **1** the grape crop of a single season **2** the wine of a particular region and year **3** the model of a particular period [a car of prewar *vintage*] —*adj.* **1** of a particular vintage: said of wine **2** representative of the best [*vintage* Hemingway] **3** of a past period [*vintage* clothes]

vint·ner (vint′nər) *n.* [< ME < L *vinum*, wine] one who sells or makes wine

vi·nyl (vī′nəl) *n.* [< L *vinum*, wine] **1** any of various compounds polymerized to form resins and plastics (**vinyl plastics**) **2** phonograph records, considered collectively

vi·ol (vī′əl) *n.* [< VL *vitula*, a fiddle] any of an early family of stringed instruments, usually having six strings, frets, and a flat back

vi·o·la (vē ō′lə, vī–) *n.* [It] a stringed instrument of the violin family, slightly larger than a violin

vi·o·la·ble (vī′ə lə bəl) *adj.* that can be, or is likely to be, violated

vi·o·late (vī′ə lāt′) *vt.* -**lat′ed**, -**lat′ing** [< L *violare*, use violence] **1** to fail to obey or keep (a law, etc.) **2** to rape **3** to desecrate (something sacred) **4** to break in upon; disturb —**vi′o·la′tor** *n.*

vi·o·la·tion (-lā′shən) *n.* a violating or being violated; specif., *a)* infringement, as of a law *b)* rape *c)* desecration of something sacred *d)* disturbance

vi·o·lence (-ləns) *n.* [< L *violentus*, violent] **1** physical force used so as to injure **2** powerful force, as of a hurricane **3** harm done by violating rights, etc. **4** a violent act or deed

vi·o·lent *adj.* **1** acting with or having great physical force **2** caused by violence **3** furious [*violent* language] **4** extreme; intense [a *violent* storm] —**vi′o·lent·ly** *adv.*

vi·o·let (vī′ə lit) *n.* [< L *viola*] **1** a plant with white, blue, purple, or yellow flowers **2** a bluish–purple color —*adj.* bluish-purple

vi·o·lin (vī′ə lin′) *n.* [< VIOLA] any of the modern family of four-stringed musical instruments played with a bow; specif., the smallest and highest-pitched one of this family —**vi′o·lin′ist** *n.*

vi·ol·ist (vī′əl ist; *for 2* vē ō′list) *n.* **1** a viol player **2** a viola player

vi·o·lon·cel·lo (vē′ə län chel′ō, vī′ə lən-) *n., pl.* -**los** CELLO

VIP (vē′ī′pē′) *n.* [*v(ery) i(mportant) p(erson)*] a high-ranking official or important guest

vi·per (vī′pər) *n.* [OFr < L *vipera*] **1** a venomous snake **2** a malicious or treacherous person —**vi′per·ous** *adj.*

vi·ral (vī′rəl) *adj.* **1** of or caused by a virus **2** circulated widely and rapidly, as by social media —**go viral** [Inf.] to be circulated broadly and rapidly by social media

vir·e·o (vir′ē ō′) *n., pl.* -**os′** [L, a type of finch] a small American songbird, with olive-green or gray feathers

Vir·gil (vur′jəl) 70-19 B.C.; Rom. poet: author of the *Aeneid*

vir·gin (vur′jən) *n.* [< L *virgo*, a maiden] one, esp. a young woman, who has never had sexual intercourse —*adj.* **1** being a virgin **2** chaste; modest **3** untouched, unused, pure, etc. [*virgin* land] —**the Virgin** Mary, the mother of Jesus

vir·gin·al *adj.* VIRGIN

Vir·gin·ia (vər jin′yə) state of the S U.S.; cap. Richmond: abbrev. **VA** —**Vir·gin′i·an** *adj., n.*

Virginia Beach city in SE Virginia, on the Atlantic

Virginia creeper WOODBINE (*n.* 2)

Virginia reel an American variety of reel danced by couples in two parallel rows

Virgin Islands group of islands in the West Indies, divided between those forming a British territory & those constituting a U.S. territory (**Virgin Islands of the United States**)

vir·gin·i·ty (vər jin′ə tē) *n.* the state of being a virgin

Virgin Mary Mary, the mother of Jesus

Vir·go (vur′gō′) *n.* [L, virgin] the sixth sign of the zodiac

vir·gule (vur′gyōōl′) *n.* [< L *virgula*, small rod] a diagonal line (/) used in dates or fractions (3/8) and also standing for "or," "per," etc.

vir·ile (vir′əl) *adj.* [< L *vir*, a man] **1** of or characteristic of a man; masculine **2** having manly strength or vigor **3** sexually potent —**vi·ril·i·ty** (və ril′ə tē) *n.*

vi·rol·o·gy (vi räl′ə jē) *n.* [< VIR(US) + -o- + -LOGY] the study of viruses and virus diseases —**vi·rol′o·gist** *n.*

vir·tu·al (vur′chŏŏ əl) *adj.* being so in effect, although not in actual fact or name —**vir′tu·al·ly** *adv.*

virtual reality computer simulation of three-dimensional images, with which one may seemingly interact using special electronic devices

vir·tue (vur′chōō) *n.* [< L *virtus*, worth] **1** general moral excellence **2** a specific moral quality regarded as good **3** chastity **4** *a)* excellence in general *b)* a good quality **5** efficacy, as of a medicine —**by (or in) virtue of** because of

vir·tu·o·so (vur′chōō ō′sō) *n., pl.* -**sos** or -**si** (-sē) [It, skilled] one with great skill in a fine art —**vir′tu·os′i·ty** (-äs′ə tē) *n.*

vir·tu·ous (vur'chōō əs) *adj.* **1** having, or characterized by, moral virtue **2** chaste: said of a woman —**vir'tu·ous·ly** *adv.*

vir·u·lent (vir'yoo lənt, -oo-) *adj.* [see fol.] **1** *a)* extremely poisonous *b)* full of hate **2** *Med. a)* violent and rapid in its course *b)* highly infectious —**vir'u·lence** *n.*

vi·rus (vī'rəs) *n.* [L, a poison] **1** a microscopic infectious agent causing various diseases **2** any harmful influence **3** an unauthorized, disruptive, spreadable set of computer program instructions

vi·sa (vē'zə, -sə) *n.* [< L *videre*, see] an endorsement on a passport, granting entry into a country

vis·age (viz'ij) *n.* [see prec.] **1** the face; countenance **2** aspect; look

vis-à-vis (vē'zə vē') *adj., adv.* [Fr] face to face; opposite —*prep.* **1** opposite to **2** in relation to

vis·cer·a (vis'ər ə) *pl.n.* [L] the internal organs of the body, as the heart, lungs, intestines, etc.

vis·cer·al *adj.* **1** of the viscera **2** intuitive, emotional, etc. rather than intellectual

vis·cid (vis'id) *adj.* [< LL *viscidus*, sticky] thick, syrupy, and sticky

vis·cose (vis'kōs') *n.* [see prec.] a syruplike solution of cellulose, used in making rayon and cellophane

vis·cos·i·ty (vis käs'ə tē) *n., pl.* **-ties 1** a viscous quality **2** *Physics* the resistance of a fluid to flowing freely

vis·count (vī'kount') *n.* [see VICE- & COUNT²] a nobleman next below an earl or count and above a baron

vis·count·ess (vī'koun'tis) *n.* **1** the wife or widow of a viscount **2** a noblewoman holding the rank of viscount in her own right

vis·cous (vis'kəs) *adj.* [see VISCID] **1** syrupy; viscid **2** *Physics* having viscosity

vise (vīs) *n.* [< L *vitis*, vine, lit., that which winds] a device having two jaws closed by a screw, used for holding firmly an object being worked on

Vish·nu (vish'nōō) *n.* a Hindu god worshiped as protector and preserver

vis·i·bil·i·ty (viz'ə bil'ə tē) *n., pl.* **-ties 1** a being visible **2** *a)* the relative possibility of being seen under the prevailing conditions of distance, light, etc. [red has good *visibility*] *b)* range of vision

vis·i·ble (viz'ə bəl) *adj.* [< L *videre*, to see] **1** that can be seen **2** apparent —**vis'i·bly** *adv.*

vi·sion (vizh'ən) *n.* [see prec.] **1** the power of seeing **2** something seen in a dream, trance, etc., or supernaturally revealed **3** a mental image **4** the ability to perceive or foresee something, as through mental acuteness **5** something or someone of great beauty

vi·sion·ar·y (-er'ē) *adj.* **1** seen in a vision **2** not realistic; impractical [a *visionary* scheme] —*n., pl.* **-ies 1** one who sees visions **2** one whose ideas, etc. are impractical

vis·it (viz'it) *vt.* [< L *videre*, to see] **1** to go or come to see **2** to stay with as a guest **3** to af-

flict or trouble —*vi.* **1** to make a social call **2** [Inf.] to chat —*n.* **1** a social call **2** a stay as a guest

vis·it·ant *n.* a visitor

vis·i·ta·tion (viz'ə tā'shən) *n.* **1** an official visit, as to inspect **2** a reward or punishment, as sent by God **3** the legal right to visit one's children, as after divorce **4** the visiting of a family in mourning

vis·i·tor *n.* a person making a visit

vi·sor (vī'zər) *n.* [< OFr *vis*, a face] **1** a part of a helmet that protects the face, often one that can be raised and lowered **2** a projecting brim, as of a cap, for shading the eyes

vis·ta (vis'tə) *n.* [< L *videre*, to see] **1** a view, esp. of distant objects seen through an opening **2** a mental view of events

vis·u·al (vizh'ōō əl) *adj.* [< L *videre*, to see] **1** of or used in seeing **2** based on the use of sight **3** that can be seen; visible

vis·u·al·ize *vt., vi.* **-ized', -iz'ing** to form a mental image of (something not actually seen) —**vis'u·al·i·za'tion** *n.*

vi·ta (vīt'ə, vēt'ə) *n.* [< *curriculum vitae* < L, course of life] a summary of one's personal history and professional qualifications, as that submitted by a job applicant; résumé

vi·tal (vīt'l) *adj.* [< L *vita*, life] **1** of or concerned with life **2** essential to life [*vital* organs] **3** fatal [a *vital* wound] **4** *a)* essential; indispensable *b)* very important **5** full of life; energetic —*n.* [*pl.*] **1** the vital organs, as the heart, brain, etc. **2** any essential parts —**vi'tal·ly** *adv.*

vi·tal·i·ty (vī tal'ə tē) *n., pl.* **-ties 1** power to live **2** power to endure **3** mental or physical vigor

vi·tal·ize (vīt'l īz') *vt.* **-ized', -iz'ing** to make vital; give life or vigor to

vital signs the pulse, respiration, and body temperature

vital statistics data on births, deaths, marriages, etc.

vi·ta·min (vīt'ə min) *n.* [< L *vita*, life] any of certain complex substances found variously in foods and essential to good health

vitamin A a fat-soluble alcohol found in fish-liver oil, egg yolk, carrots, etc.: a deficiency of this results in impaired vision in the dark

vitamin B (complex) a group of unrelated water-soluble substances including *a)* **vitamin B₁** (see THIAMINE) *b)* **vitamin B₂** (see RIBOFLAVIN) *c)* NIACIN *d)* **vitamin B₁₂**, a vitamin containing cobalt, used in treating anemia

vitamin C a compound occurring in citrus fruits, tomatoes, etc.: a deficiency of this results in scurvy

vitamin D any of several fat-soluble vitamins found in fish-liver oils, milk, etc.: a deficiency of this results in rickets

vitamin E a vitamin occurring in wheat germ, etc., vital to the reproductive processes in some animals

vitamin K a vitamin occurring in green vegetables, fish meal, etc., that clots blood

vi·ti·ate (vish'ē āt') *vt.* **-at'ed, -at'ing** [< L

vitium, a vice‖ **1** to spoil; corrupt; pervert **2** to invalidate (a contract, etc.) —**vi'ti·a'tion** *n.*

vit·re·ous (vi'trē əs) *adj.* ‖< L *vitrum*, glass‖ **1** of or like glass **2** derived from or made of glass

vitreous humor (*or* **body**) the transparent, jellylike substance filling the eyeball between the retina and the lens

vit·ri·fy (vi'trə fī') *vt., vi.* **-fied', -fy'ing** ‖< L *vitrum*, glass + Fr *-fier*, -ꜰʏ‖ to change into glass or a glasslike substance by heat

vit·rine (vi trēn', vi'trēn') *n.* ‖see VITREOUS‖ a glass-paneled cabinet or display case

vit·ri·ol (vi'trē ôl') *n.* ‖< L *vitreus*, glassy‖ **1** *a*) any of several sulfates of metals, as of copper (*blue vitriol*) or iron (*green vitriol*) *b*) SULFURIC ACID **2** caustic remarks —**vit'ri·ol'ic** (-äl'ik) *adj.*

vi·tu·per·ate (vī tōō'pər āt', vi-) *vt.* **-at'ed, -at'ing** ‖< L *vitium*, a fault, + *parare*, prepare‖ to speak abusively to or about —**vi·tu'per·a'tion** *n.* —**vi·tu'per·a'tive** *adj.*

vi·va (vē'vä) *interj.* ‖It & Sp‖ long live (some-one specified)!

vi·va·ce (vē vä'chä) *adj., adv.* ‖It‖ *Music* in a lively, spirited manner: also written **vivace**

vi·va·cious (vī vā'shəs, vi-) *adj.* ‖< L *vivere*, to live‖ full of animation; lively —**vi·va'cious·ly** *adv.* —**vi·vac'i·ty** (-vas'ə tē) *n.*, **vi·va'ci·ous·ness**

vive (vēv) *interj.* ‖Fr‖ long live (someone specified)!

viv·id (viv'id) *adj.* ‖< L *vivere*, to live‖ **1** full of life **2** intensely bright: said as of colors **3** of or presenting lifelike images [a *vivid* imagination] —**viv'id·ly** *adv.* —**viv'id·ness** *n.*

viv·i·fy (viv'ə fī') *vt.* **-fied', -fy'ing** ‖< L *vivus*, alive + *facere*, make‖ to give life to

vi·vip·a·rous (vī vip'ər əs) *adj.* ‖< L *vivus*, alive + *parere*, produce‖ bearing living young, instead of laying eggs

viv·i·sec·tion (viv'ə sek'shən) *n.* ‖< L *vivus*, alive + SECTION‖ surgery performed on a living animal in medical research —**viv'i·sec'tion·ist** *n.*

vix·en (vik'sən) *n.* ‖OE *fyxe*, female fox‖ **1** a female fox **2** a sexually alluring woman

viz. or **viz** *abbrev.* ‖< L *videlicet*‖ that is; namely

vi·zier (vi zir', viz'yər) *n.* ‖< Ar *wazara*, bear a burden‖ a high government official in the Turkish empire (*c.* 1300–1918): also sp. **vi·zir'**

viz·or (vī'zər) *n. alt. sp. of* VISOR

VLF or **vlf** *abbrev.* very low frequency

vo·cab·u·lar·y (vō kab'yə ler'ē) *n., pl.* **-ies** ‖ult. < L *vocare*, to call‖ **1** a list of words, etc. as in a dictionary or glossary **2** all the words used in a language or by a person, group, etc.

vo·cal (vō'kəl) *adj.* ‖< L *vox*, voice‖ **1** of or produced by the voice **2** sung **3** capable of making oral sounds **4** speaking freely —**vo'cal·ly** *adv.*

vocal cords membranous folds in the larynx that vibrate to produce voice sounds

vo·cal·ic (vō kal'ik) *adj.* of, like, or involving a vowel or vowels

vo·cal·ist (vō'kəl ist) *n.* a singer

vo·cal·ize *vt., vi.* **-ized', -iz'ing** to speak or sing

vo·ca·tion (vō kā'shən) *n.* ‖< L *vocare*, to call‖ **1** the career to which one feels one is called **2** any trade or occupation

vo·ca·tion·al *adj.* **1** of a vocation **2** designating or of training, etc. for an occupation or trade

voc·a·tive (väk'ə tiv) *n.* ‖see VOCATION‖ *Gram.* a case indicating the person or thing addressed

vo·cif·er·ate (vō sif'ər āt') *vt., vi.* **-at'ed, -at'ing** ‖< L *vox*, voice + *ferre*, to bear‖ to shout loudly; clamor —**vo·cif'er·a'tion** *n.*

vo·cif·er·ous (vō sif'ər əs) *adj.* noisy; clamorous

vod·ka (väd'kə) *n.* ‖Russ < *voda*, water‖ a colorless alcoholic liquor distilled from rye, wheat, etc.

vogue (vōg) *n.* ‖Fr‖ **1** the current fashion **2** popularity —*adj.* in vogue: also **vogu·ish** (vō'gish)

voice (vois) *n.* ‖< L *vox*‖ **1** sound made through the mouth, esp. by humans **2** the ability to make such sounds **3** anything regarded as like vocal utterance **4** an expressed wish, opinion, etc. **5** the right to express one's wish, etc.; vote **6** utterance or expression **7** a verb form showing the relation of the subject to the action: see ACTIVE (*adj.* 4), PASSIVE (*adj.* 3) **8** singing ability —*vt.* **voiced, voic'ing** to give utterance or expression to —**with one voice** unanimously —**voice'less** *adj.*

voice box LARYNX

voice-mail *n.* **1** an electronic system whereby voice messages can be recorded, stored, and then delivered **2** such messages

voice-o·ver *n.* the voice of an unseen announcer or narrator, as on TV

void (void) *adj.* ‖< L *vacare*, be empty‖ **1** containing nothing **2** devoid (*of*) [*void* of common sense] **3** ineffective; useless **4** of no legal force —*n.* **1** an empty space **2** a feeling of emptiness —*vt.* **1** to empty **2** to make void; annul —**void'a·ble** *adj.*

voi·là (vwä lä') *interj.* ‖Fr‖ behold; there it is

voile (voil) *n.* ‖Fr, a veil‖ a thin fabric, as of cotton

vol *abbrev.* volume

vol·a·tile (väl'ə təl) *adj.* ‖< L *volare*, to fly‖ **1** evaporating quickly **2** *a*) unstable; explosive [a *volatile* temper] *b*) fickle —**vol'a·til'i·ty** (-til'ə tē) *n.* —**vol'a·til·ize'** (-iz') *vt., vi.* **-ized', -iz'ing**

vol·can·ic (väl kan'ik, vôl-) *adj.* **1** of or caused by a volcano **2** like a volcano; violently explosive

vol·ca·no (väl kā'nō, vôl-) *n., pl.* **-noes** or **-nos** ‖< L *Volcanus*, Vulcan‖ **1** a vent in the earth's crust through which molten rock, ashes, etc. are ejected **2** a cone-shaped mountain of ejected material built up around such a vent

vole (vōl) *n.* ‖< earlier *vole mouse* < Scand, as in ON *vollr*, meadow‖ any of various small rodents with a stout body and short tail

Vol·ga (väl′gə, vōl′-) river in European Russia, flowing into the Caspian Sea

vo·li·tion (vō lish′ən) n. [ult. < L velle, be willing] the act or power of using the will —**vo·li′tion·al** adj.

vol·ley (väl′ē) n., pl. **-leys** [< L volare, to fly] **1** a) the simultaneous discharge of a number of weapons b) the bullets, etc., so discharged **2** a burst of words or acts **3** Sports a) a returning of a ball, etc. before it touches the ground b) an extended exchange of shots, as in tennis —vt., vi. **-leyed, -ley·ing 1** to discharge or be discharged as in a volley **2** Sports to return (the ball, etc.) as a volley

vol·ley·ball n. **1** a team game played by hitting a large, light, inflated ball back and forth over a net with the hands **2** this ball

volt (vōlt) n. [after A. Volta (1745-1827), It physicist] the basic unit of electromotive force

volt·age (vōl′tij) n. electromotive force expressed in volts

vol·ta·ic (väl tā′ik) adj. of or by electricity produced by chemical action

Vol·taire (vōl ter′) 1694-1778; Fr. writer & philosopher

volt·me·ter n. an instrument for measuring voltage

vol·u·ble (väl′yə bəl) adj. [< L volvere, to roll] characterized by a great flow of words; talkative —**vol′u·bil′i·ty** n. —**vol′u·bly** adv.

vol·ume (väl′yōōm) n. [< L volumen, a scroll] **1** a) a book b) one of a set of books **2** the amount of space occupied in three dimensions **3** a) a quantity, bulk, or amount b) a large quantity **4** the loudness of sound

vo·lu·mi·nous (və lōōm′ə nəs) adj. **1** producing or consisting of enough to fill volumes **2** large; bulky; full —**vo·lu′mi·nous·ly** adv.

vol·un·ta·rism (väl′ən tər iz′em) n. (system of) voluntary participation in a course of action

vol·un·tar·y (-ter′ē) adj. [< L voluntas, free will] **1** brought about by one's own free choice **2** acting on one's own accord **3** intentional **4** controlled by one's mind or will —**vol′un·tar′i·ly** adv.

vol·un·teer (väl′ən tir′) n. **1** one who chooses freely to do something, as entering military service **2** one who willingly works without pay —adj. **1** serving as a volunteer **2** of a volunteer or volunteers —vt. to offer or give of one's own free will —vi. to offer to enter into any service of one's own free will, esp. without pay —**vol′un·teer′ism** n.

vo·lup·tu·ar·y (və lup′chōō er′ē) n., pl. **-ar′ies** [< L voluptas, pleasure] one devoted to sensual pleasures

vo·lup·tu·ous (-chōō əs) adj. full of, producing, or fond of sensual pleasures —**vo·lup′tu·ous·ness** n.

vo·lute (və lōōt′) n. [< L volvere, to roll] a spiral or whorl

vom·it (väm′it) n. [< L vomere, to vomit] matter ejected from the stomach through the mouth —vt., vi. **1** to eject (the contents of the stomach) through the mouth; throw up **2** to discharge or be discharged with force —**vom′i·tous** (-ə təs) adj.

voo·doo (vōō′dōō) n., pl. **-doos** [of WAfr orig.] a religion of the West Indies, based on a belief in magic, charms, etc. —adj. of or resembling voodoo

vo·ra·cious (vô rā′shəs) adj. [< L vorare, devour] **1** greedy in eating; ravenous **2** very eager [a voracious reader] —**vo·rac′i·ty** (-ras′ə tē) n.

vor·tex (vôr′teks) n., pl. **-tex′es** or **-ti·ces′** (-tə sēz′) [< L vertere, to turn] **1** a whirlpool **2** a whirlwind **3** anything like a whirlwind, etc. in effect

vo·ta·ry (vōt′ə rē) n., pl. **-ries** [< L vovere, to vow] **1** one bound by a vow, esp. by religious vows, as a monk or nun **2** one devoted to a cause, study, etc.

vote (vōt) n. [< L votum, a vow] **1** a decision on a proposal, etc., or a choice between candidates for office **2** a) the expression of such a decision or choice b) the ballot, etc. by which it is expressed **3** the right to vote **4** votes collectively —vi. vot′ed, vot′ing to give or cast a vote —vt. to decide or enact by vote —**vot′er** n.

vo·tive (vōt′iv) adj. [see prec.] designed to fulfill a promise, express devotion, etc.

vouch (vouch) vi. [< L vocare, to call] to give, or serve as, assurance, a guarantee, etc. (for) [to vouch for someone's honesty]

vouch·er n. **1** one who vouches **2** a paper serving as evidence or proof; specif., a receipt

vouch·safe (vouch sāf′) vt. **-safed′, -saf′ing** [< ME vouchen safe, vouch as safe] to be kind enough to give or grant

vow (vou) n. [< L votum] **1** a solemn promise, esp. one made to God **2** a promise of love and fidelity [marriage vows] —vt. to promise or declare solemnly —vi. to make a vow —**take vows** to enter a religious order

vow·el (vou′əl) n. [< L vocalis, vocal] **1** a speech sound in which the air passes in a continuous stream through the open mouth **2** a letter representing such a sound, as a, e, i, o, or u

voy·age (voi′ij) n. [< L via, way] a relatively long journey by ship or spacecraft —vi. **-aged, -ag·ing** to make a voyage —**voy′ag·er** n.

voy·eur (voi ur′, vwä yur′) n. [< L videre, see] **1** one who derives pleasure from viewing sexual activity or nudity **2** one who obsessively or secretly observes the private lives of others —**voy′eur·ism′** n. —**voy′eur·is′tic** adj.

VP abbrev. Vice-President

vs. or **vs** abbrev. versus

vt abbrev. transitive verb

VT abbrev. Vermont

Vul·can (vul′kən) n. the Roman god of fire and of metalworking

vul·can·ize (vul′kən iz′) vt. **-ized′, -iz′ing** to treat (crude rubber) with sulfur under heat to make it stronger and more elastic —**vul′can·i·za′tion** n.

Vulg *abbrev.* Vulgate

vul·gar (vul′gər) *adj.* ⟦< L *vulgus*, common people⟧ 1 of people in general; popular 2 vernacular 3 lacking culture, taste, etc.; crude; boorish 4 indecent or obscene —**vul′gar·ly** *adv.*

vul·gar·i·an (-ger′ē ən) *n.* a vulgar person, esp. a rich person with coarse, showy tastes

vul·gar·ism (-gər iz′əm) *n.* 1 a word, phrase, etc. used widely but regarded as nonstandard or unrefined 2 vulgarity

vul·gar·i·ty (-ger′ə tē) *n.* 1 a being vulgar 2 *pl.* **-ties** a vulgar act, habit, usage in speech, etc.

vul·gar·ize (-gər iz′) *vt.* **-ized′, -iz′ing** 1 to popularize 2 to make vulgar, coarse, obscene, etc. —**vul′gar·i·za′tion** *n.*

Vulgar Latin the everyday Latin spoken by ancient Romans as distinguished from standard written Latin

Vul·gate (vul′gāt′) *n.* ⟦ML *vulgata (editio)*, popular (edition)⟧ a Latin version of the Bible, used in the Roman Catholic Church

vul·ner·a·ble (vul′nər ə bəl) *adj.* ⟦< L *vulnus*, a wound⟧ 1 that can be wounded or injured 2 open to, or easily hurt by, criticism or attack 3 affected by a specified influence, temptation, etc. —**vul′ner·a·bil′i·ty** *n.* —**vul′ner·a·bly** *adv.*

vul·pine (vul′pīn) *adj.* ⟦< L *vulpes*, a fox⟧ of or like a fox; cunning

vul·ture (vul′chər) *n.* ⟦< L, akin to *vellere*, to tear⟧ 1 a large bird that lives chiefly on carrion 2 a greedy, ruthless person

vul·va (vul′və) *n., pl.* **-vae** (-vē) or **-vas** ⟦L, womb⟧ the external genital organs of the female

vy·ing (vī′iŋ) *adj.* that vies; competing

w¹ or **W** (dub′əl yōō′) *n., pl.* **w's, W's** the 23d letter of the English alphabet

w² *abbrev.* 1 waist 2 watt(s) 3 week(s) 4 weight 5 *a*) west *b*) western 6 wide 7 width 8 with 9 win(s)

W¹ *abbrev.* 1 watt(s) 2 Wednesday 3 *a*) west *b*) western 4 win(s)

W² *abbrev.* ⟦*w(olfram)*, alt. name of tungsten⟧ *Chem.* symbol for tungsten

WA *abbrev.* Washington (state)

Wac (wak) *n.* a member of the Women's Army Corps (**WAC**)

wack·o (wak′ō) [Slang] *adj. var. of* WACKY —*n., pl.* **-os** one who is wacko

wack·y (wak′ē) *adj.* **-i·er, -i·est** ⟦< ?⟧ [Slang] erratic, eccentric, or irrational —**wack′i·ness** *n.*

wad (wäd) *n.* ⟦ML *wadda*, wadding⟧ 1 a small, soft mass, as of cotton or paper 2 a lump or small, firm mass —*vt.* **wad′ded, wad′ding** 1 to compress, or roll up, into a wad 2 to plug or stuff with a wad or wadding

wad·ding *n.* any soft material for use in padding, packing, etc.

wad·dle (wäd′əl) *vi.* **-dled, -dling** ⟦< fol.⟧ to walk with short steps, swaying from side to side, as a duck does —*n.* a waddling gait

wade (wäd) *vi.* **wad′ed, wad′ing** ⟦OE *waden*, go⟧ 1 to walk through any resisting substance, as water, mud, etc. 2 to proceed with difficulty [to *wade* through a dull book] 3 [Inf.] to attack with vigor: with *in* or *into* —*vt.* to cross by wading

wad·er *n.* 1 one that wades 2 [*pl.*] *a*) high waterproof boots *b*) waterproof overalls with bootlike parts for the feet

wa·di (wä′dē) *n., pl.* **-dis** or **-dies** ⟦Ar *wādī*⟧ in Arabia, N Africa, etc., a ravine or watercourse that is usually dry

wading bird any long-legged bird that wades in shallow water in search of food

wa·fer (wā′fər) *n.* ⟦< MDu *wafel*⟧ 1 a thin, flat, crisp cracker or cookie 2 any disklike thing resembling this

waf·fle¹ (wä′fəl) *n.* [see prec.] a crisp batter cake baked in a waffle iron

waf·fle² (wä′fəl) *vi.* **-fled, -fling** ⟦< echoic *waff*, to yelp⟧ to speak or write in a wordy or vague way

waffle iron a utensil with two flat, studded plates pressed together to bake a waffle

waft (wäft, waft) *vt., vi.* ⟦< Du *wachter*, watcher⟧ to carry (sounds, odors, etc.) lightly through the air or over water or to move in this way —*n.* 1 an odor, sound, etc. carried through the air 2 a gust of wind 3 a wafting movement

wag¹ (wag) *vt., vi.* **wagged, wag′ging** ⟦ME *waggen*⟧ to move rapidly back and forth, up and down, etc. —*n.* a wagging

wag² (wag) *n.* ⟦prob. < obs. *waghalter*, joker⟧ a comical person; wit —**wag′ger·y** *n., pl.* **-ies**

wage (wāj) *vt.* **waged, wag′ing** ⟦< OFr *gage*, a pledge⟧ to engage in or carry on (a war, etc.) —*n.* 1 [*often pl.*] money paid for work done 2 [*usually pl.*] what is given in return

wa·ger (wā′jər) *n.* [see prec.] a bet — *vt., vi.* to bet

wag·gish (wag′ish) *adj.* 1 of or like a wag; roguishly merry 2 playful; jesting

wag·gle (wag′əl) *vt., vi.* **-gled, -gling** ⟦< WAG¹⟧ to wag, esp. with short, quick movements —*n.* a waggling —**wag′gly** *adj.*

Wag·ner (väg′nər), **Rich·ard** (riH′ärt) 1813–83; Ger. composer

wag·on (wag′ən) *n.* ⟦Du *wagen*⟧ **1** a four-wheeled vehicle, esp. one for hauling heavy loads **2** *short for* STATION WAGON —**on** (or **off**) **the wagon** [Slang] no longer (or once again) drinking alcohol, taking drugs, etc.

waif (wāf) *n.* [< NormFr] a homeless person, esp. a child

wail (wāl) *vi.* [< ON *wæ*, woe] to make a long, loud, sad cry, as in grief or pain —*n.* such a cry

wain (wān) *n.* ⟦OE *wægn*⟧ [Old Poet.] a wagon

wain·scot (wān′skät′, -skət) *n.* [< MDu *wagenschot*] a wood paneling on the walls of a room, sometimes on the lower part only —*vt.* **-scot·ed** or **-scot′ted**, **-scot′ing** or **-scot′ting** to line (a wall) with wood, etc.

wain·scot·ing or **wain·scot·ting** *n.* **1** WAINSCOT **2** material used to wainscot

wain·wright (wān′rīt′) *n.* [WAIN + WRIGHT] one who builds or repairs wagons

waist (wāst) *n.* [< OE *weaxan*, grow] **1** the part of the body between the ribs and the hips **2** the part of a garment that covers the body from the shoulders to the waistline **3** the narrow part of any object that is wider at the ends

waist·band *n.* a band encircling the waist, as on slacks or a skirt

waist·coat (wes′kət, wāst′kōt′) *n.* [Brit.] a man's vest

waist·line *n.* (the circumference of) the narrowest part of the waist

wait (wāt) *vi.* [< NormFr *waittier*] **1** to remain (until something expected happens) **2** to be ready **3** to remain undone [it can *wait*] **4** to serve food at a meal: with *at* or *on* —*vt.* **1** to await **2** [Inf.] to delay serving (a meal) —*n.* an act or period of waiting —**lie in wait (for)** to wait so as to catch after planning a trap [*for*] —**wait on** (or **upon**) **1** to act as a servant to **2** to serve (a customer) —**wait table** to serve food to people at a table —**wait up** to delay going to bed until someone arrives, etc.

wait·er *n.* one who waits; esp., a man who waits on tables, as in a restaurant

wait·ing *adj.* **1** that waits **2** of or for a wait —*n.* the act of one that waits —**in waiting** in attendance, as on a king

waiting game a scheme by which one wins out over another by delaying action until one has an advantage

waiting list a list of applicants, in the order of their application

waiting room a room in which people wait, as in a bus station or doctor's office

wait·per·son *n.* a waiter or waitress

wait·ress (wā′tris) *n.* a woman who waits on tables, as in a restaurant

waive (wāv) *vt.* **waived**, **waiv′ing** [< ON *veifa*, fluctuate] **1** to give up or forgo (a right, etc.) **2** to postpone; defer

waiv·er (wā′vər) *n. Law* a waiving of a right, claim, etc.

wake¹ (wāk) *vi.* **woke** or **waked**, **waked** or **wok′en**, **wak′ing** [< OE *wacian*, be awake & *wacan*, arise] **1** to come out of sleep; awake: often with *up* **2** to stay awake **3** to become active: often with *up* **4** to become alert (*to* a realization, etc.) —*vt.* **1** to cause to wake: often with *up* **2** to arouse (passions, etc.) —*n.* a time set aside for viewing a corpse before burial

wake² (wāk) *n.* [< ON *vök*, hole] **1** the track left in water by a moving ship **2** the track or course of anything —**in the wake of** following closely

wake·ful *adj.* **1** alert; watchful **2** unable to sleep —**wake′ful·ness** *n.*

wak·en (wā′kən) *vi., vt.* to awake

Wal·dorf salad (wôl′dôrf′) [after the old *Waldorf*-Astoria Hotel in New York City] a salad made of diced raw apples, celery, and walnuts, with mayonnaise

wale (wāl) *n.* ⟦OE *walu*, weal⟧ **1** a welt raised by a whip, etc. **2** a ridge on the surface of cloth, as corduroy

Wales (wālz) constituent country of the United Kingdom: a peninsula of WC Great Britain

walk (wôk) *vi.* ⟦OE *wealcan*, to roll⟧ **1** to go on foot at a moderate pace **2** to follow a certain course [*walk* in the ways of peace] **3** *Baseball* to go to first base after the pitching of four balls —*vt.* **1** to go over, along, etc. on foot **2** to cause (a dog, etc.) to walk, as for exercise **3** to accompany on a walk or stroll [to *walk* a friend home] **4** *Baseball* to advance (a batter) to first base by pitching four balls —*n.* **1** the act of walking **2** a stroll or hike **3** a distance walked [an hour's *walk*] **4** a sphere of activity, occupation, etc. [people from all *walks* of life] **5** a path for walking **6** *Baseball* the walking of a batter —**walk (all) over** [Inf.] to domineer over —**walk away** (or **off**) **with** **1** to steal **2** to win easily —**walk out** to go on strike —**walk out on** [Inf.] to desert; abandon

walk·a·way *n.* an easily won victory

walk·er *n.* **1** one that walks **2** a frame with wheels used as a support in walking, as by the lame or by babies learning to walk

walk·ie-talk·ie (wôk′ē tôk′ē) *n.* a compact, portable radio transmitter and receiver

walking stick a stick for carrying when walking; cane

walk-on *n.* a minor role in which the actor has few or no lines

walk·out *n.* a labor strike

walk-up *n.* **1** an upstairs apartment or office in a building without an elevator **2** the building

walk·way *n.* a path, passage, etc. for pedestrians, esp. one that is sheltered

wall (wôl) *n.* [< L *vallus*, palisade] **1** an upright structure of wood, stone, etc., serving to enclose, divide, or protect **2** something like a wall in appearance or function —*vt.* **1** to enclose, divide, etc. with or as with a wall **2** to close up (an opening) with a wall: usually with *up* —**drive up the wall** [Inf.] to cause to be extremely frustrated or angry —**hit the (or a) wall** [Inf.] to lose strength or effectiveness suddenly —**off the wall** [Slang] **1** insane; crazy **2** very eccentric

wal·la·by (wä′lə bē) *n., pl.* **-bies** [< Australian native name *wolabā*] a marsupial of Australia, etc., like a small kangaroo

wall·board (wôl′bôrd′) *n.* fibrous material in thin slabs for making or covering walls and ceilings

wal·let (wä′lit) *n.* [ME *walet*] a flat case or folder, as of leather, for carrying money, cards, etc.

wall-eye *n.* [< ON *vagl*, a beam + *eygr*, eye] **1** an eye that turns outward, showing much white **2** a fish with large, glossy eyes, esp. a North American freshwater perch

wall-flow·er *n.* [Inf.] a person who merely looks on at a dance, etc. as from shyness

Wal·loon (wä lōōn′) *n.* ·[< OHG *walh*, foreigner] **1** a member of a chiefly Celtic people in S Belgium **2** the French dialect of this people

wal·lop (wä′ləp) [Inf.] *vt.* [< OFr *galoper*, to gallop] **1** to beat or defeat soundly **2** to strike hard —*n.* **1** a hard blow **2** a thrill

wal·low (wä′lō) *vi.* [OE *wealwian*, to roll around] **1** to roll about, as in mud **2** to indulge oneself fully (*in* a specified thing) —*n.* **1** a wallowing **2** a muddy or dusty place

wall·pa·per *n.* decorative paper, fabric, etc. for covering the walls of a room —*vt.* to hang wallpaper on or in

Wall Street 1 street in New York City; financial center of the U.S. **2** U.S. financiers and their power, policies, etc. **3** the U.S. securities market

wall-to-wall *adj.* **1** covering a floor completely **2** [Inf.] *a)* pervasive *b)* comprehensive

wal·nut (wôl′nut′) *n.* [< OE *wealh*, foreign + *hnutu*, nut] **1** a shade tree valued for its nuts and wood **2** its edible nut **3** its wood

wal·rus (wôl′rəs) *n.* [< Dan *hvalros*] a massive arctic sea mammal somewhat like a seal, having two tusks projecting from the upper jaw

waltz (wôlts) *n.* [< Ger *walzen*, dance about] **1** a ballroom dance for couples, in 3/4 time **2** music for this —*vi.* **1** to dance a waltz **2** to move lightly

wam·pum (wäm′pəm) *n.* [< AmInd] small beads made of shells and used by North American Indians as money, for ornament, etc.

wan (wän) *adj.* **wan′ner, wan′nest** [OE *wann*, dark] **1** sickly pale **2** feeble or weak [a *wan* smile]

wand (wänd) *n.* [< ON *vondr*] **1** a staff symbolizing authority **2** a rod regarded as having magical powers **3** any of various rod-shaped devices, as for scanning for metal objects at security checkpoints

wan·der (wän′dər) *vi.* [OE *wandrian*] **1** to roam aimlessly; ramble **2** to stray (*from* a path, etc.) **3** to go astray in mind or purpose **4** to meander, as a river —*vt.* to roam in or over —**wan′der·er** *n.*

wan·der·lust *n.* [Ger] an urge to wander or travel

wane (wān) *vi.* **waned, wan′ing** [OE *wanian*, to decrease] **1** to grow gradually less in extent: said of the visible face of the moon **2** to grow dim **3** to decline in power, etc. **4** to approach the end —*n.* a waning

wan·gle (waŋ′gəl) [Inf.] *vt., vi.* **-gled, -gling** [< ? WAGGLE] to get or cause (something) by persuasion, tricks, etc.

wan·na·be (wä′nə bē′) *n.* [Slang] one who wants to be like someone else or attain some status: also **wan′na-be′**

want (wänt, wônt) *vt.* [< ON *vanta*] **1** to lack **2** to wish for; desire **3** to wish to see or apprehend [*wanted* by the police] **4** [Chiefly Brit.] to require —*vi.* to have a need or lack: usually with *for* — *n.* **1** a shortage; lack **2** poverty **3** a craving **4** something needed

want ad [Inf.] an advertisement for something wanted, as a job

want·ing *adj.* **1** lacking **2** not up to standard —*prep.* without or minus —**wanting in** deficient in

wan·ton (wänt′'n) *adj.* [< OE *wan*, lacking + *teon*, educate] **1** sexually unrestrained **2** [Old Poet.] playful **3** unprovoked or malicious **4** recklessly ignoring justice, decency, etc. —*n.* a wanton person; esp., a sexually unrestrained woman

wap·i·ti (wä′pə tē) *n.* [< AmInd] a large North American deer with widely branching antlers; elk

war (wôr) *n.* [< NormFr *werre*] **1** open armed conflict as between nations **2** any active hostility or struggle **3** military operations as a science —*adj.* of, in, or from war —*vi.* **warred, war′ring 1** to carry on war **2** to contend; strive —**at war** in a state of active armed conflict

war·ble (wôr′bəl) *vt., vi.* **-bled, -bling** [< NormFr *werbler*] to sing (a song, etc.) melodiously, with trills, quavers, etc., as a bird does —*n.* a warbling

war·bler (wôr′blər) *n.* **1** one that warbles **2** a small, often brightly colored songbird

war crime a violation of laws or norms of humane behavior, committed during war

ward (wôrd) *vt.* [OE *weardian*, to guard] to turn aside; fend (*off*) —*n.* **1** a being under guard **2** one under the care of a guardian or court **3** a division of a jail, hospital, etc. **4** a division of a city or town, for purposes of voting, etc.

-ward (wərd) [OE *-weard*] *suffix* in a (specified) direction [*inward*]: also **-wards** (wərdz)

war·den (wôrd′'n) *n.* [< NormFr *wardein*] **1** one who guards, or has charge of, something [game *warden*] **2** the chief official of a prison

ward·er *n.* a watchman

ward heeler a follower of a politician, who solicits votes, etc.: often used with mild contempt

ward·robe (wôr′drōb′) *n.* **1** a closet, cabinet, etc. for holding clothes **2** one's supply of clothes

ward·room *n.* in a warship, a room used for

eating, socializing, etc. by commissioned officers

ware (wer) *n.* ⟦OE *waru*⟧ 1 anything for sale: *usually used in pl.* 2 pottery

-ware (wer) *combining form* computer software [*courseware, shareware*]

ware·house *n.* a building where goods are stored —*vt.* **-housed′, -hous′ing** to store in a warehouse

war·fare (wôr′fer′) *n.* (armed) conflict

war·head *n.* the front part of a torpedo, missile, etc., containing the explosive

war·horse *n.* [Inf.] 1 one who has been through many struggles; veteran 2 a symphony, play, etc. that has been performed many times

war·i·ly (wer′ə lē) *adv.* cautiously —**war′i·ness** (-ē nis) *n.*

war·like *adj.* 1 fond of or ready for war 2 of war 3 threatening war

war·lock (wôr′läk′) *n.* ⟦OE *wœrloga*, liar⟧ a man who practices black magic

war·lord *n.* 1 a high military officer in a warlike nation 2 a local ruler or bandit leader

warm (wôrm) *adj.* ⟦OE *wearm*⟧ 1 *a)* having or giving off a moderate degree of heat *b)* hot [*a warm night*] 2 that keeps body heat in [*a warm hat*] 3 ardent; enthusiastic 4 lively, vigorous, etc. 5 quick to anger 6 *a)* genial; cordial [*a warm welcome*] *b)* sympathetic or loving 7 newly made; fresh, as a trail 8 [Inf.] close to discovering something — *vt., vi.* to make or become warm —**warm up** to practice or exercise, as before going into a game, contest, etc. —**warm′er** *n.* —**warm′ish** *adj.* —**warm′ly** *adv.*

warm·blood·ed *adj.* having a body temperature that is relatively constant and usually higher than that of the surroundings

warmed-o·ver *adj.* 1 reheated 2 presented again without significant change, as ideas

warm front the forward edge of a warm air mass advancing into a colder mass

warm·heart·ed *adj.* kind, sympathetic, friendly, loving, etc.

war·mon·ger (-muŋ′gər, -mäŋ′-) *n.* one who tries to cause war —**war′mon′ger·ing** *adj., n.*

warmth (wôrmth) *n.* 1 *a)* the state of having heat *b)* mild heat 2 *a)* enthusiasm, ardor, etc. *b)* affectionate feelings

warm-up *n.* the act of warming up

warn (wôrn) *vt., vi.* ⟦OE *wearnian*⟧ 1 to tell of a danger, coming evil, etc. 2 to caution about certain acts 3 to notify in advance; inform

warn·ing *n.* 1 the act of one that warns 2 something that serves to warn —*adj.* that warns

warp (wôrp) *n.* ⟦OE *weorpan*, to throw⟧ 1 *a)* a distortion, as a twist or bend, in wood *b)* any similar distortion 2 a mental quirk, bias, etc. 3 *Weaving* the threads running lengthwise in the loom —*vt.* 1 to bend or twist out of shape 2 to distort, pervert, etc.: said of the mind, character, etc. —*vi.* to become bent or twisted

war·path *n.* the path taken by American Indians on a warlike expedition —**on the warpath 1** ready for war **2** actively angry; ready to fight

warp speed ⟦< (TIME) WARP + SPEED⟧ [Slang] in science fiction, a very high rate of speed

war·rant (wôr′ənt, wär′-) *n.* ⟦< NormFr *warant*⟧ 1 *a)* authorization, as by law *b)* justification for some act, belief, etc. 2 something serving as a guarantee of some event or result 3 *Law* a writ authorizing an arrest, search, etc. —*vt.* 1 to authorize 2 to serve as justification for (an act, belief, etc.) 3 to guarantee

warrant officer a military officer ranking above a noncommissioned officer but below a commissioned officer

war·ran·ty (wôr′ən tē, wär′-) *n., pl.* **-ties** an assurance by a seller that goods will be repaired or replaced if not as represented; guarantee

war·ren (wôr′ən, wär′-) *n.* ⟦< NormFr *warir*, to preserve⟧ 1 an area in which rabbits breed or are numerous 2 any crowded building or cluster of buildings

war·rior (wôr′yər, -ē ər) *n.* ⟦see WAR⟧ a person experienced in conflict, esp. war; soldier

War·saw (wôr′sô′) capital of Poland

war·ship *n.* any combat ship, as a battleship

wart (wôrt) *n.* ⟦OE *wearte*⟧ 1 a small, usually hard, tumorous growth on the skin, caused by a virus 2 a small protuberance, as on a plant —**wart′y** *adj.* **-i·er, -i·est**

wart hog a wild African hog with large tusks, and wartlike lumps below the eyes

war·y (wer′ē) *adj.* **-i·er, -i·est** ⟦OE *wœr*, aware⟧ on one's guard; cautious —**wary of** careful of

was (wuz, wäz) *vi.* ⟦OE *wœs*⟧ 1st & 3d pers. sing., pt., of BE

wash (wôsh, wäsh) *vt.* ⟦OE *wœscan*⟧ 1 to clean with water or other liquid 2 to purify 3 to wet or moisten 4 to flow over, past, or against: said of a sea, waves, etc. 5 to soak (*out*), flush (*off*), or carry (*away*) with water 6 to erode; wear (*out* or *away*) by flowing over [the flood *washed* out the road] —*vi.* 1 to wash oneself 2 to wash clothes 3 to undergo washing 4 to be removed by washing: usually with *out* or *away* 5 to be worn or carried (*out* or *away*) by the action of water [the bridge had *washed* out] 6 [Inf.] to withstand examination [that excuse won't *wash*] —*n.* 1 a washing 2 a quantity of clothes, etc. washed, or to be washed 3 the rush or surge of water 4 the eddy of water or air caused by a propeller, etc. 5 silt, mud, etc. carried and dropped by running water 6 a liquid for cosmetic or medicinal use [*mouthwash*] 7 in the W U.S., the dry bed of a stream 8 [Inf.] a situation in which gains and losses offset each other —*adj.* that can be washed without damage; washable —**wash down** to follow (food, etc.) with a drink —**wash′a·ble** *adj., n.*

wash-and-wear *adj.* of fabrics that need little or no ironing after washing

wash·board *n.* a ridged board for scrubbing dirt out of clothes

wash·bowl *n.* a bowl, esp. a bathroom fixture, for use in washing one's hands, etc.: also **wash'ba'sin**

wash·cloth *n.* a small cloth used in washing the body: also **wash'rag'**

washed-out *adj.* 1 faded 2 [Inf.] tired; spiritless; pale and wan

washed-up *adj.* 1 [Inf.] tired; exhausted 2 [Slang] finished; done for; having failed

wash·er *n.* 1 one who washes 2 a flat ring of metal, rubber, etc., used with a nut, faucet valve, bolt, etc. 3 a machine for washing; specif., washing machine

wash·ing *n.* clothes, etc. to be washed

washing machine a machine for washing clothes, linens, etc.

Wash·ing·ton' (wôsh'iŋ tən, wäsh'-), **George** 1732–99; 1st president of the U.S. (1789–97)

Wash·ing·ton² 1 NW coastal state of the U.S.; cap. Olympia: abbrev. **WA** 2 capital of the U.S., coextensive with the District of Columbia: also called **Washington, D.C.** —**Wash'ing·to'ni·an** (-tō'nē ən) *adj., n.*

wash·out *n.* 1 the washing away of soil, etc. by water 2 [Slang] a failure

wash·room *n.* 1 a room for washing 2 REST-ROOM

wash·stand *n.* a table or plumbing fixture with a washbowl, etc.

wash·tub *n.* a tub, often with faucets and a drain, for washing clothes, etc.

wasp (wäsp, wôsp) *n.* [OE *wæsp*] a winged insect with a slender body and, in the females and workers, a painful sting

WASP or **Wasp** (wäsp, wôsp) *n.* a white Anglo-Saxon Protestant

wasp·ish *adj.* bad-tempered; snappish

was·sail (wäs'əl, -āl') *n.* [< ON *ves heill*, be hearty] 1 a toast formerly used to drink to the health of a person 2 the spiced ale, etc. with which such toasts were drunk 3 a drinking party — *vi., vt.* to drink a wassail (to)

wast·age (wās'tij) *n.* 1 loss by use, decay, etc. 2 anything wasted

waste (wāst) *vt.* **wast'ed, wast'ing** [< L *vastare*] 1 to devastate; ruin 2 to wear away 3 to make weak or emaciated [*wasted* by age] 4 to use up needlessly; squander 5 to fail to take advantage of 6 [Slang] to kill —*vi.* 1 to lose strength, etc., as by disease 2 to be used up or worn down gradually —*adj.* 1 uncultivated or uninhabited; desolate 2 left over or superfluous 3 excreted from the body 4 used for waste —*n.* 1 uncultivated or uninhabited land 2 a devastated area 3 a wasting or being wasted 4 discarded material, as ashes 5 excretions from the body, as urine —**go to waste** to be wasted —**lay waste (to)** to destroy —**wast'er** *n.*

waste·bas·ket *n.* a container for wastepaper, etc.: also **wastepaper basket**

wast·ed (wās'təd) *adj.* [Slang] 1 intoxicated by a drug 2 drunk

waste·ful *adj.* using more than is necessary —**waste'ful·ly** *adv.* —**waste'ful·ness** *n.*

waste·land *n.* 1 barren land 2 any unproductive place, activity, etc. 3 a place that lacks cultural or intellectual activity

waste·pa·per *n.* paper thrown away after use: also **waste paper**

waste·wa·ter *n.* water discharged as sewage

wast·rel (wās'trəl) *n.* one who wastes; esp., a spendthrift

watch (wäch, wôch) *n.* [OE *wœcce*] 1 a keeping awake, esp. in order to guard 2 close observation for a time 3 a guard, or the period of duty of a guard 4 a small timepiece carried in the pocket or worn on the wrist 5 *a)* any of the periods of duty (usually four hours) on shipboard *b)* the crew on duty during such a period —*vi.* 1 to stay awake, esp. at night; keep vigil 2 to be on the alert 3 to look or observe 4 to be looking or watching attentively: with *for* —*vt.* 1 to guard or tend 2 to observe carefully 3 to wait and look for —**watch oneself** to be careful —**watch out** to be alert or careful —**watch over** to protect from harm —**watch'er** *n.*

watch·band *n.* a band of leather, metal, etc. to hold a watch on the wrist

watch·dog *n.* 1 a dog kept to guard property 2 one that keeps watch in order to prevent waste, unethical practices, etc.

watch·ful *adj.* watching closely; vigilant; alert —**watch'ful·ly** *adv.* —**watch'ful·ness** *n.*

watch·man (-mən) *n., pl.* **-men** (-mən) a man hired to stand guard or keep watch

watch·tow·er *n.* a high tower from which watch is kept, as for forest fires

watch·word *n.* 1 a password 2 a slogan or cry

wa·ter (wôt'ər, wät'-) *n.* [OE *wæter*] 1 *a)* the colorless liquid found in rivers, lakes, etc. and in the bodies of living things *b)* the compound, H_2O, forming this liquid, ice, snow, etc., occurring also as a gas in the atmosphere 2 water with reference to its depth, surface, or level [above *water*] 3 a body secretion, as urine 4 a wavy, lustrous finish given to linen, silk, metal, etc. —*vt.* 1 to give (animals) water to drink 2 to supply (crops, etc.) with water 3 to moisten, soak, or dilute with water 4 to give a wavy luster to (silk, etc.) —*vi.* 1 to fill with tears: said of the eyes 2 to secrete saliva [his mouth *watered*] 3 to take on a supply of water 4 to drink water —*adj.* of, for, in, on, near, from, or by water —**hold water** to remain sound, logical, etc. —**water down** to weaken the intensity or effectiveness of

water bed *n.* a heavy vinyl bag filled with water and used as a bed or mattress: also **wa'ter·bed'** *n.*

water buffalo a slow, powerful buffalo of S Asia used as a draft animal

water chestnut 1 a Chinese sedge with a nut-like tuber 2 this tuber

water closet TOILET (*n.* 2)

wa·ter·col·or *n.* 1 a pigment mixed with water for use as a paint 2 a painting done with such paints 3 the art of painting with watercolors

wa·ter–cooled *adj.* cooled by water circulated around or through it

wa·ter·course *n.* 1 a stream, river, etc. 2 a channel for water, as a canal

wa·ter·craft *n.*, *pl.* **-craft**′ a boat, ship, or other water vehicle

wa·ter·cress *n.* a white-flowered water plant: its leaves are used in salads, etc.

wa·ter·fall *n.* a steep fall of water, as of a stream, from a height

wa·ter·fowl *n.* a water bird, esp. one that swims

wa·ter·front *n.* land or docks at the edge of a stream, harbor, etc.

watering hole 1 a small pond from which animals drink 2 [Inf.] a place, such as a bar, where people gather to drink and socialize

wa·ter·lil·y *n.*, *pl.* **-lil′ies** 1 a water plant with large, flat, floating leaves and showy flowers 2 the flower

wa·ter·line *n.* the line to which the surface of the water comes on the side of a ship or boat

wa·ter·logged (-lôgd′) *adj.* soaked or filled with water so as to be heavy and sluggish

Wa·ter·loo¹ (wôt′ər loo′, wät′-) *n.* [after fol.] any disastrous or decisive defeat

Wa·ter·loo² town in central Belgium: scene of Napoleon's final defeat (1815)

water main a main pipe in a system of water pipes

wa·ter·mark *n.* 1 a mark showing the limit to which water has risen 2 a mark in paper, produced by pressure of a design, as in the mold 3 information coded into a digital file, as to indicate its creator —*vt.* to mark (paper or a digital file) with a watermark

wa·ter·mel·on *n.* a large, green melon with sweet, juicy, red pulp

water moccasin a large, poisonous water snake of the SE U.S.

water park an amusement park featuring swimming pools and rides that involve water

water pipe 1 a pipe for water 2 a smoking pipe using water, as a hookah

water polo a water game played with a ball by two teams of swimmers

water power *n.* the power of running or falling water, used to drive machinery, etc.: also **wa′ter·pow′er** *n.*

wa·ter·proof *adj.* that keeps out water, as by being treated with rubber, etc. —*vt.* to make waterproof

water rat any of various rodents living on the banks of streams and ponds

wa·ter·re·pel·lent *adj.* that repels water but is not fully waterproof

wa·ter·shed *n.* 1 a ridge dividing the areas drained by different river systems 2 the area drained by a river system 3 a critical turning point

wa·ter·side *n.* land at the edge of a body of water —*adj.* of, at, or on the waterside

wa·ter·ski *vi.* **-skied′**, **-ski′ing** to be towed on skilike boards (**water skis**) by a line attached to a speedboat —**wa′ter-ski′er** *n.*

wa·ter·spout *n.* 1 a pipe for spouting water 2 a whirling funnel-shaped column of air full of spray occurring over a body of water

water table the level below which the ground is saturated with water

wa·ter·tight *adj.* 1 so snugly put together that no water can get in or through 2 that cannot be misconstrued, nullified, etc.; flawless

water tower an elevated tank for water storage

wa·ter·way *n.* 1 a channel through which water runs 2 any body of water suitable for boats, ships, etc., as a canal or river

water wheel a wheel turned by running water, as for power

water wings an inflated device to keep one afloat, as while learning to swim

wa·ter·works *pl.n.* [*often with sing. v.*] a system of reservoirs, pumps, etc. supplying water to a city

wa·ter·y *adj.* 1 of or like water 2 full of water 3 thin; diluted 4 tearful 5 weak —**wa′ter·i·ness** *n.*

watt (wät) *n.* [after James *Watt* (1736-1819), Scot inventor of steam engine] a unit of electrical power, equal to the power developed in a circuit by a current of one ampere flowing through a potential difference of one volt

watt·age *n.* amount of electrical power, expressed in watts

wat·tle (wät′'l) *n.* [OE *watul*] 1 a woven work of sticks intertwined with twigs or branches 2 a fleshy flap of skin hanging from the throat as of certain birds or lizards —*vt.* **-tled**, **-tling** 1 to intertwine (sticks, twigs, etc.) 2 to build of or with wattle

wave (wāv) *vi.* **waved**, **wav′ing** [OE *wafian*] 1 to move or sway to and fro 2 to signal by moving a hand, arm, etc. to and fro 3 to have the form of a series of curves —*vt.* 1 to cause to wave 2 to brandish (a weapon) 3 *a)* to move or swing (something) as a signal *b)* to signal (something) to (someone) by doing this 4 to give an undulating form to (hair, etc.) —*n.* 1 a ridge or swell moving along the surface of the ocean, etc. 2 an undulation or curve, as in the hair 3 a motion to and fro, as with the hand in signaling 4 a thing like a wave in action or effect; specif., an upsurge [a crime *wave*] 5 *Physics* a periodic motion or disturbance, as in the propagation of sound or light

Wave (wāv) *n.* [< W(*omen*) A(*ccepted for*) V(*oluntary*) E(*mergency*) S(*ervice*)] a member of the women's branch of the U.S. Navy (**WAVES**)

wave·length *n.* 1 *Physics* the distance measured along a wave from any given point to the next similar point 2 [Inf.] chiefly in the phrase **on the same wavelength**, in accord

wave·let (-lit) *n.* a little wave

wa·ver (wā′vər) *vi.* [< ME *waven*, to wave] 1 to sway to and fro 2 to show indecision; vacillate 3 to falter, flicker, tremble, etc. —*n.* a wavering

wav·y (wā′vē) *adj.* **-i·er**, **-i·est** 1 having or like waves 2 moving in a wavelike motion —**wav′i·ness** *n.*

wax[1] (waks) *n.* ⟦OE *weax*⟧ 1 a plastic, dull-yellow substance secreted by bees; beeswax 2 any plastic substance like this; specif., *a*) paraffin *b*) a substance exuded by the ears —*vt.* to rub, polish, cover, or treat with wax

wax[2] (waks) *vi.* **waxed, wax′ing** ⟦OE *weaxan*, grow⟧ 1 to increase in strength, size, etc. 2 to become gradually full: said of the moon 3 [Literary] to become; grow [to *wax* angry]

wax bean a variety of the common garden bean with long, edible, yellow pods

wax·en (wak′sən) *adj.* 1 made of wax 2 pale

wax museum an exhibition of wax figures, as of famous persons

wax myrtle an evergreen shrub with grayish-white, wax-coated berries

wax paper a paper made moisture-proof by a wax coating: also **waxed paper**

wax·wing *n.* a fruit-eating bird with brown or gray silky plumage, a pointed crest, and scarlet tips on the wings

wax·works *n.* an exhibition of wax figures

wax·y *adj.* **-i·er, -i·est** of, full of, or like wax —**wax′i·ness** *n.*

way (wā) *n.* ⟦ME < OE *weg*⟧ 1 a road, street, path, etc. 2 space for passing 3 a route or course 4 course of life or conduct [avoid evil *ways*] 5 a method of doing something 6 a manner of living, acting, etc. [the *way* of the world] 7 distance [a long *way* off] 8 direction of movement or action 9 movement forward 10 respect; specific point [right in some *ways*] 11 wish; will [get one's own *way*] 12 [Inf.] *a*) a condition [he's in a bad *way*] *b*) a locality [out our *way*] 13 [*pl.*] a timber framework on which a ship is built —*adv.* [Inf.] away; far [*way* behind] —**by the way** incidentally —**by way of** 1 passing through 2 as a method, etc. of —**give way** 1 to yield 2 to break down —**lead the way** to be a guide or example —**make way** 1 to clear a passage 2 to make progress —**under way** moving; advancing

way·far·er (-fer′ər) *n.* a traveler, esp. on foot —**way′far′ing** *adj., n.*

way·lay (wā′lā′) *vt.* **-laid′, -lay′ing** 1 to lie in wait for and attack 2 to wait for and accost (a person) on the way

way-out *adj.* [Inf.] very unusual or unconventional

-ways (wāz) ⟦ME < *way* (see WAY)⟧ *suffix* in a (specified) direction, position, or manner [sideways]

ways and means methods of raising money; specif., such methods, including legislation, in government

way·side *n.* the edge of a road

way·ward *adj.* ⟦see AWAY & -WARD⟧ 1 headstrong, willful, disobedient, etc. 2 unpredictable; erratic —**way′ward·ly** *adv.* —**way′ward·ness** *n.*

we (wē) *pron., sing.* **I** ⟦OE⟧ 1 the persons speaking or writing 2 I: used by a monarch, editor, etc. when speaking with formal authority

weak (wēk) *adj.* ⟦< ON *veikr*⟧ 1 lacking physical strength; feeble 2 lacking moral strength or willpower 3 lacking mental power 4 lacking power, authority, force, etc. 5 easily torn, broken, etc. [a *weak* railing] 6 lacking intensity, etc. [a *weak* voice] 7 diluted [*weak* tea] 8 unconvincing [a *weak* argument]

weak·en *vt., vi.* to make or become weak or weaker

weak-kneed (-nēd′) *adj.* lacking in courage, determination, resistance, etc.

weak·ling *n.* one that is low in physical or moral strength

weak·ly *adj.* **-li·er, -li·est** sickly; feeble —*adv.* in a weak manner

weak·ness *n.* 1 state of being weak 2 a weak point 3 an immoderate fondness (*for* something)

weal[1] (wēl) *n.* ⟦< WALE⟧ a mark raised on the skin, as by a blow; welt

weal[2] (wēl) *n.* ⟦< OE *wela*, wealth, well-being⟧ well-being; welfare [the public *weal*]

wealth (welth) *n.* ⟦< prec.⟧ 1 much money or property; riches 2 a large amount [a *wealth* of ideas] 3 valuable products, contents, etc. 4 everything having monetary value

wealth·y (wel′thē) *adj.* **-i·er, -i·est** having wealth; rich —**wealth′i·ness** *n.*

wean (wēn) *vt.* ⟦OE *wenian*, to accustom, train⟧ 1 to accustom (a child or young animal) to take food other than by suckling 2 to withdraw (a person) by degrees (*from* a habit, etc.)

weap·on (wep′ən) *n.* ⟦OE *wæpen*⟧ 1 any instrument used to injure or kill 2 any means of attack or defense —**weap′on·less** *adj.*

weap·on·ize (wep′ən īz′) *vt.* **-ized′, -iz′ing** to develop for use as a lethal agent in warfare [to *weaponize* the smallpox virus] —**weap′on·i·za′tion** *n.*

weap·on·ry *n.* weapons collectively

wear (wer) *vt.* **wore, worn, wear′ing** ⟦OE *werian*⟧ 1 to have (clothing, etc.) on the body 2 to show in one's appearance [to *wear* a smile] 3 to impair or diminish by use, friction, etc.: often with *away* 4 to make by rubbing, flowing, etc. [to *wear* a hole in the rug] 5 to tire or exhaust —*vi.* 1 to become impaired or diminished, as by use 2 to hold up in use [that suit *wears* well] 3 to have an irritating effect (*on*) —*n.* 1 a wearing or being worn 2 things worn; clothes [women's *wear*] 3 impairment or loss, as from use, friction, etc. —**wear off** to diminish by degrees —**wear′a·ble** *adj.* —**wear′er** *n.*

wear and tear loss and damage resulting from use

wea·ri·some (wir′i səm) *adj.* causing weariness; tiresome or tedious —**wea′ri·some·ly** *adv.*

wea·ry (wir′ē) *adj.* **-ri·er, -ri·est** ⟦OE *werig*⟧ 1 tired; worn out 2 without further patience, zeal, etc. 3 tiring —*vt., vi.* **-ried, -ry·ing** to make or become weary —**wea′ri·ly** *adv.* —**wea′ri·ness** *n.*

wea·sel (wē′zəl) *n.* ⟦OE *wesle*⟧ 1 an agile flesh-eating mammal with a long, slender body and short legs **2** a sly, cunning person —*vi.* [Inf.] to avoid a commitment: with *out*

weath·er (weth′ər) *n.* ⟦OE *weder*⟧ **1** the condition of the atmosphere with regard to temperature, moisture, etc. **2** storm, rain, etc. —*vt.* **1** to expose to the action of weather **2** to pass through safely [to *weather* a storm] **3** *Naut.* to pass to the windward of —*vi.* **1** to become worn, etc. by exposure to the weather —**under the weather** [Inf.] ill

weath·er-beat·en *adj.* showing the effect of exposure to sun, rain, etc.

weath·er·cock *n.* a weather vane in the shape of a rooster

weath·er·ing *n.* the effects of the forces of weather on rock surfaces

weath·er·ize *vt.* **-ized′, -iz′ing** to weatherstrip, insulate, etc. (a building) —**weath′er·i·za′tion** *n.*

weath·er·man (-man′) *n., pl.* **-men′** (-men′) a man who forecasts and reports the weather

weath·er·proof *adj.* that can be exposed to wind, snow, etc. without damage —*vt.* to make weatherproof

weath·er·strip *n.* a thin strip of metal, felt, etc. covering the joint between a door or window and the casing, to keep out drafts, etc.: also **weath′er·strip′ping** —*vt.* **-stripped′, weath′er·strip′ping** to provide with weatherstrips

weather vane a vane for showing which way the wind is blowing

weave (wēv) *vt.* **wove** or chiefly for *vt.* **5** & *vi.* **2 weaved, wo′ven** or **wove,** or chiefly for *vt.* **5** & *vi.* **2 weaved, weav′ing** ⟦OE *wefan*⟧ **1** to make (a fabric, basket, etc.) by interlacing (threads, straw, etc.), as on a loom **2** to construct in the mind **3** to twist (something) into or through **4** to spin (a web), as spiders do **5** to make (one's way) by moving from side to side or in and out —*vi.* **1** to do weaving **2** to move from side to side or in and out —*n.* a method or pattern of weaving —**weav′er** *n.*

web (web) *n.* ⟦OE *webb*⟧ **1** any woven fabric **2** the network of silky strands spun by a spider, etc. **3** a carefully woven trap **4** a network **5** a membrane joining the digits of various water birds, etc. **6** [*usually* **W-**] *Comput.* WORLD WIDE WEB: also with *the* —*vt.* **webbed, web′bing** to join by, or cover as with, a web

web·bing *n.* a strong fabric woven in strips and used for belts, etc.

web·cam *n.* a camera designed for use with a computer, as to transmit images, esp. live video images, over a website

web·cast *n.* a performance, newscast, or other public event, transmitted over the World Wide Web

web·foot *n., pl.* **-feet′** a foot with the toes webbed —**web′-foot′ed** *adj.*

web·i·nar (web′ə när′) *n.* a seminar, workshop, lecture, etc. conducted over the internet, often with participant interaction

Web page a single file on the World Wide Web, providing text, pictures, etc.: also **web′page′**

web·site *n.* a location on the World Wide Web, consisting of one Web page or several such pages connected with hyperlinks: also **Web site**

Web·ster (web′stər), **No·ah** (nō′ə) 1758-1843; U.S. lexicographer

wed (wed) *vt., vi.* **wed′ded, wed′ded** or **wed, wed′ding** ⟦OE *weddian*⟧ **1** to marry **2** to unite or join

Wed *abbrev.* Wednesday

wed·ded (wed′id) *adj.* **1** married **2** of marriage **3** devoted [*wedded* to one's work] **4** joined

wed·ding *n.* **1** the marriage ceremony **2** a joining together

wedge (wej) *n.* ⟦OE *wecg*⟧ **1** a piece of wood, metal, etc. tapering to a thin edge: used to split wood, lift a weight, etc. **2** anything shaped like a wedge **3** any act serving to open the way for change, etc. —*vt.* **wedged, wedg′ing 1** to force apart, or fix in place, with a wedge **2** to crowd together or pack (*in*) —*vi.* to push or be forced as or like a wedge

wedg·ie (-ē) *n.* a shoe having a wedge-shaped piece under the heel, which forms a solid, flat sole

wed·lock *n.* ⟦OE *wedlac*⟧ the state of being married

Wednes·day (wenz′dā) *n.* ⟦< *Woden,* Germanic god⟧ the fourth day of the week

wee (wē) *adj.* **we′er, we′est** ⟦OE *wege*⟧ **1** very small; tiny **2** very early [*wee* hours of the morning]

weed (wēd) *n.* ⟦OE *weod*⟧ any undesired, uncultivated plant, esp. one that crowds out desired plants —*vt., vi.* **1** to remove weeds from (a garden, etc.) **2** to remove as useless, harmful, etc.: often with *out* —**weed′er** *n.* —**weed′less** *adj.*

weeds (wēdz) *pl.n.* ⟦< OE *wæde,* garment⟧ black mourning clothes, esp. those worn by a widow

weed·y *adj.* **-i·er, -i·est** **1** full of weeds **2** of or like a weed

week (wēk) *n.* ⟦OE *wicu*⟧ **1** a period of seven days, esp. one from Sunday through Saturday **2** the hours or days of work in this period

week·day *n.* any of the days of the week from Monday through Friday

week·end or **week-end** *n.* the period from Friday night or Saturday to Monday morning: also **week end** —*vi.* to spend the weekend

week·ly *adj.* **1** done, happening, etc. once every week **2** of a week, etc. —*adv.* once a week; every week —*n., pl.* **-lies** a periodical published once a week

ween (wēn) *vi., vt.* ⟦OE *wenan*⟧ [Archaic] to think

weep (wēp) *vi., vt.* **wept, weep′ing** ⟦OE *wepan*⟧ **1** to shed (tears) **2** to mourn (*for*) **3** to drip or exude (water, etc.) —**weep′er** *n.*

weep·ing *n.* the act of one who weeps —*adj.* **1** that weeps **2** having graceful, drooping branches

weeping willow an ornamental willow tree with drooping branches

weep·y *adj.* **-i·er, -i·est** (inclined to) weeping

wee·vil (wē′vəl) *n.* ⟦OE *wifel*⟧ a beetle whose larvae feed on grain, cotton, etc.

weft (weft) *n.* ⟦< OE *wefan*, to weave⟧ *Weaving* the yarns carried back and forth across the warp

weigh (wā) *vt.* ⟦OE *wegan*, carry⟧ **1** to determine the weight of **2** to have (a specified) weight **3** to consider and choose carefully [*weigh* one's words] —*vi.* **1** to have significance, importance, etc. **2** to be a burden —**weigh anchor** to hoist a ship's anchor —**weigh down** to burden or bear down on

weight (wāt) *n.* ⟦OE *wiht*⟧ **1** a quantity weighing a definite amount **2** *a)* heaviness *b) Physics* the force of gravity acting on a body **3** amount of heaviness **4** *a)* any unit of heaviness *b)* any system of such units *c)* a piece having a specific amount of heaviness, placed on a balance or scale in weighing **5** any mass of material used for its heaviness [a *paperweight*] **6** a burden, as of sorrow **7** importance or consequence **8** influence; power —*vt.* **1** to add weight to **2** to burden **3** to assign a specified degree of importance to, as in statistics

weight·less *adj.* having little or no apparent weight: said of an astronaut floating freely in an orbiting space vehicle —**weight′less·ness** *n.*

weight lifting the athletic exercise or sport of lifting barbells —**weight lift′er**

weight·y *adj.* **-i·er, -i·est 1** very heavy **2** burdensome **3** significant; important —**weight′i·ness** *n.*

weir (wir) *n.* ⟦OE *wer*⟧ **1** a low dam built to back up water, as for a mill **2** a fence, as of brushwood, in a stream, etc., for catching fish

weird (wird) *adj.* ⟦< OE *wyrd*, fate⟧ **1** of or about ghosts, etc.; mysterious, eerie, etc. **2** strange; bizarre —**weird′ly** *adv.* —**weird′ness** *n.*

weird·o (wir′dō) *n., pl.* **-os** [Slang] one that is weird, bizarre, etc.

wel·come (wel′kəm) *adj.* ⟦OE *wilcuma*, welcome guest⟧ **1** gladly received [a *welcome* guest] **2** freely permitted [he is *welcome* to use my car] —*n.* a welcoming —*vt.* **-comed, -com·ing** to greet or receive with pleasure, etc. —**you're welcome** the conventional response to "thank you"

weld (weld) *vt.* ⟦< obs. *well*⟧ **1** to unite (pieces of metal, etc.) by heating until fused or until soft enough to hammer together **2** to unite closely —*vi.* to be welded —*n.* **1** a welding **2** a joint formed by welding —**weld′a·ble** *adj.* —**weld′er** *n.*

wel·fare (wel′fer′) *n.* ⟦ME: see WELL[2] & FARE⟧ **1** a condition of health, happiness, prosperity, etc.; well-being **2** *a)* the organized efforts of government agencies granting aid to the poor, the unemployed, etc. *b)* such aid —**on welfare** receiving government aid because of poverty, etc.

wel·kin (wel′kin) *n.* ⟦< OE *wolcen*, a cloud⟧ [Archaic] the vault of the sky

well¹ (wel) *n.* ⟦OE *wella*⟧ **1** a natural spring and pool **2** a hole sunk into the earth to get water, oil, etc. **3** a source of abundant supply **4** a shaft, etc. resembling a well **5** a container for a liquid, as an inkwell — *vi., vt.* to flow or gush from or as from a well

well² (wel) *adv.* **bet′ter, best** ⟦OE *wel*⟧ **1** in a satisfactory, proper, or excellent manner [treat her *well*; you sing *well*] **2** prosperously [to live *well*] **3** with good reason [one may *well* ask] **4** to a considerable degree [*well* advanced] **5** thoroughly [stir it *well*] **6** with certainty; definitely **7** familiarly [I know her *well*] —*adj.* **1** suitable, proper, etc. **2** in good health **3** favorable; comfortable —*interj.* used variously to express surprise, agreement, etc. —**as well 1** in addition **2** equally —**as well as** in addition to

well-ad·vised (wel′əd vizd′) *adj.* showing or resulting from careful consideration or sound advice; prudent

well-ap·point·ed *adj.* excellently furnished

well-bal·anced *adj.* **1** precisely adjusted or regulated **2** sane, sensible, etc.

well-be·haved *adj.* displaying good manners

well-be·ing *n.* the state of being well, happy, or prosperous; welfare

well-born *adj.* born into a family of high social position

well-bred *adj.* showing good breeding; courteous and considerate

well-dis·posed *adj.* friendly (*toward* a person) or receptive (*to* an idea, etc.)

well-done *adj.* **1** performed with skill **2** thoroughly cooked: said esp. of meat

well-fed *adj.* plump or fat

well-fixed *adj.* [Inf.] wealthy

well-found·ed *adj.* based on facts, good evidence, or sound judgment

well-groomed *adj.* clean and neat

well-ground·ed *adj.* having a thorough basic knowledge of a subject

well·head *n.* **1** a source; fountainhead **2** the top of a well, as an oil or gas well

well-in·formed *adj.* having considerable knowledge of a subject or of many subjects

Wel·ling·ton (wel′iŋ tən) capital of New Zealand

well-in·ten·tioned *adj.* having or showing good or kindly intentions

well-knit *adj.* **1** well constructed; firm and strong **2** having a sturdy, muscular physique

well-known *adj.* **1** widely known; famous **2** thoroughly known

well-made *adj.* skillfully and soundly put together

well-man·nered *adj.* polite; courteous

well-mean·ing *adj.* **1** having good intentions **2** said or done with good intentions: also **well′-meant′**

well·ness *n.* the condition of being healthy

well-nigh *adv.* very nearly; almost

well-off *adj.* **1** in a fortunate condition **2** prosperous

well-pre·served *adj.* in good condition or looking good, in spite of age

well-read (-red′) *adj.* having read much

well-round·ed *adj.* **1** well-planned for proper balance **2** showing diverse talents **3** shapely

well-spo·ken *adj.* **1** speaking easily, graciously, etc. **2** properly or aptly spoken

well·spring *n.* **1** the source of a stream, etc. **2** a source of abundant supply

well-tak·en *adj.* apt and sound or cogent

well-thought-of *adj.* having a good reputation

well-timed *adj.* timely; opportune

well-to-do *adj.* prosperous; wealthy

well-turned *adj.* **1** gracefully shaped **2** expressed or worded well [a *well-turned* phrase]

well-wish·er *n.* one who wishes well to another or to a cause, etc.

well-worn *adj.* much worn or used

welsh (welsh) *vi.* [Slang] to fail to pay a debt, fulfill an obligation, etc.: often with *on* —**welsh′er** *n.*

Welsh (welsh) *adj.* [OE *Wealh*, foreigner] the Celtic language of Wales —*adj.* of Wales or its people, language, etc. —**the Welsh** the people of Wales —**Welsh′man** (-mən) *n.*, *pl.* **-men**

Welsh cor·gi (kôr′gē) a dog with short legs, a foxlike head, and erect ears

Welsh rabbit a dish of melted cheese served on toast or crackers: also **Welsh rarebit**

welt (welt) *n.* [OE *welte*] **1** a strip of leather in the seam between the sole and upper of a shoe **2** a ridge raised on the skin as by a blow

wel·ter (wel′tər) *vi.* [< MDu *welteren*] to roll about or wallow —*n.* a confusion; turmoil

wel·ter·weight (wel′tər wāt′) *n.* [prob. < *welt*, to beat] a boxer with a maximum weight of 147 pounds

wen (wen) *n.* [OE *wenn*] a benign skin tumor

wench (wench) *n.* [OE *wencel*, child] a young woman: derogatory or jocular term

wend (wend) *vt.* **wend′ed**, **wend′ing** [OE *wendan*, to turn] to go on (one's way)

went (went) *vi.*, *vt. pt. of* GO

wept (wept) *vi.*, *vt. pt. & pp. of* WEEP

were (wur) *vi.* [OE *wæron*] *pl. & 2d pers. sing.*, *past indic.*, *and the past subjunctive*, *of* BE

we're (wir) *contr.* we are

were·wolf (wer′woolf′, wir′-) *n.*, *pl.* **-wolves′** [OE *wer*, man + *wulf*, wolf] *Folklore* a person who changes or has changed into a wolf

Wes·ley (wes′lē, wez′-), **John** 1703-91; Eng. clergyman; founder of Methodism —**Wes′ley·an** *adj.*, *n.*

west (west) *n.* [OE] **1** the direction in which sunset occurs at the equinoxes (270° on the compass) **2** a region in or toward this direction —*adj.* **1** in, of, toward, or facing the west **2** from the west [a *west* wind] —*adv.* in or toward the west —**the Old West** the W frontier of the U.S. in the second half of the 1800s —**the West 1** the western part of the U.S. **2** Europe and the Western Hemisphere

west·er·ly *adj.*, *adv.* **1** toward the west **2** from the west

west·ern *adj.* [OE *westerne*] **1** in, of, or toward the west **2** from the west **3** [W-] of the West —*n.* a movie, book, etc. about life in the western U.S., esp. during the frontier period

west·ern·er *n.* a person born or living in the west

Western Hemisphere that half of the earth which includes North & South America

west·ern·ize *vt.* **-ized′**, **-iz′ing** to make Western in habits, ideas, etc.

Western Samoa *former name for* SAMOA

West In·dies (in′dēz′) large group of islands in the Atlantic between North America & South America —**West Indian**

West Point military reservation in SE New York: site of the U.S. Military Academy

West Virginia state of the E U.S.; cap. Charleston: abbrev. WV —**West Virginian**

west·ward *adv.*, *adj.* toward the west: also **west′wards** *adv.*

wet (wet) *adj.* **wet′ter**, **wet′test** [OE *wæt*] **1** covered or saturated with water or other liquid **2** rainy; misty **3** not yet dry [*wet* paint] —*n.* **1** water or other liquid; moisture **2** rain or rainy weather — *vt.*, *vi.* **wet** or **wet′ted**, **wet′ting** to make or become wet —**all wet** [Slang] mistaken or misinformed

wet blanket a person or thing whose presence or influence lessens the enthusiasm of others

wet·land *n.* [*usually pl.*] **1** swamps or marshes **2** an area of swampy or marshy land

wet nurse a woman hired to suckle another's child —**wet′-nurse′** *vt.* **-nursed′**, **-nurs′ing**

wet suit a closefitting suit of rubber worn by skin divers for warmth: also **wet′suit′** *n.*

whack (hwak) *vt.*, *vi.* [echoic] to strike with a sharp, resounding blow —*n.* **1** a sharp, resounding blow **2** the sound of this —**have** (or **take**) **a whack at** [Inf.] **1** to aim a blow at **2** to make an attempt at —**out of whack** [Inf.] not in proper working condition —**whack′-er** *n.*

whale[1] (hwāl) *n.* [OE *hwæl*] a large, warmblooded sea mammal that breathes air —*vi.* **whaled**, **whal′ing** to hunt whales —**a whale of a** [Inf.] an exceptionally large, fine, etc. example of a (class or group)

whale[2] (hwāl) *vt.* **whaled**, **whal′ing** [prob. < WALE] [Inf.] to beat, whip, etc.

whale·bone *n.* BALEEN

whal·er *n.* **1** a whaling ship **2** one whose work is whaling

wham (hwam) *interj.* used to suggest the sound of a heavy blow, explosion, etc. —*n.* a heavy blow, etc. — *vt.*, *vi.* **whammed**, **wham′ming** to strike, explode, etc. loudly

wham·my *n.*, *pl.* **-mies** [Slang] a jinx

wharf (hwôrf) *n.*, *pl.* **wharves** or **wharfs** [OE *hwerf*, a dam] a structure on a shore, at which ships are loaded or unloaded; dock

what (hwut, hwät) *pron.* [OE *hwæt*, neuter of *wha*, who] **1** which thing, event, etc. [*what* is that object?] **2** that or those which [to know *what* one wants] —*adj.* **1** which or which kind of: used interrogatively or relatively **2** as much, or as many, as [take *what* men you need] **3** how great, surprising, etc. [*what* nonsense!] —*adv.* **1** in what way? how? [*what* does it matter?] **2** how greatly, etc. [*what* tragic news!] —*interj.* used to express surprise, anger, etc. —**what about** what do you think, feel, etc. concerning? —**what for 1** why? **2** [Slang] a severe reprimand or punishment —**what is with** [Inf.] **1** what's the reason for **2** what's wrong with —**what with** because of [*what with* the bad weather, we'll be late]

what·ev·er *pron.* what: an emphatic variant; specif., *a)* which thing, event, etc.? *b)* anything that [say *whatever* you like] *c)* no matter what [*whatever* you do, don't hurry] —*adj.* **1** of any kind [I have no plans *whatever*] **2** being who it may be [*whatever* man said that, it is not true]

what·not *n.* a set of open shelves, as for bric-a-brac

what's (hwuts) *contr.* **1** what is **2** what has **3** [Inf.] what does [*what's* he want?] —**what's what** the true state of affairs

what·so·ev·er (hwut'sō ev'ər) *pron., adj.* whatever: an emphatic form

wheal[1] (hwēl) *n.* [ME *whele*] a small, itching elevation of the skin, as from an insect bite

wheal[2] (hwēl) *n.* WEAL[1]

wheat (hwēt) *n.* [OE *hwæte*] a cereal grass having spikes containing grains used in making flour, cereals, etc.

wheat germ the highly nutritious embryo of the wheat kernel, milled out as a flake

whee·dle (hwēd'l) *vt., vi.* **-dled, -dling** [< ?] to influence or persuade (a person), or get (something), by flattery, coaxing, etc.

wheel (hwēl) *n.* [OE *hweol*] **1** a circular disk or frame turning on a central axis **2** anything like a wheel in shape, movement, etc. **3** the steering wheel of a motor vehicle **4** [*pl.*] [Slang] an automobile **5** [*usually pl.*] the moving forces [the *wheels* of progress] **6** a turning movement — *vt., vi.* **1** to move on or in (a wheeled vehicle) **2** to turn, revolve, etc. **3** to turn so as to change direction —*at (or behind) the wheel* steering a motor vehicle, ship, etc. —**wheel and deal** [Slang] to negotiate or make bargains

wheel·bar·row *n.* a kind of cart for carrying small loads, having a wheel in front and two shafts with handles in back for raising the vehicle off its two back legs and moving it

wheel·base *n.* the length of a motor vehicle between the centers of the front and rear wheels

wheel·chair *n.* a chair mounted on large wheels, for persons unable to walk

wheeled (hwēld) *adj.* having wheels

wheel·house *n.* PILOTHOUSE

wheel·wright *n.* one who makes and repairs wheels and wheeled vehicles

wheeze (hwēz) *vi.* **wheezed, wheez'ing** [< ON *hvæsa*, to hiss] to breathe hard with a whistling, breathy sound, as in asthma —*n.* a wheezing —**wheez'y** *adj.* **-i·er, -i·est**

whelk (hwelk) *n.* [OE *wioluc*] a kind of large marine snail

whelm (hwelm) *vt.* [ME *welmen*] **1** to submerge **2** to overpower or crush

whelp (hwelp) *n.* [OE *hwelp*] a young dog,

etc. — *vt., vi.* to give birth to (young): said of some animals

when (hwen) *adv.* [OE *hwænne*] **1** at what time? [*when* did they leave?] **2** on what occasion? —*conj.* **1** at what time [tell me *when* to go] **2** at the time that [*when* we were young] **3** at which [a time *when* people must work] **4** as soon as [we will eat *when* he comes] **5** although **6** if —*pron.* what or which time —*n.* the time (*of* an event)

whence (hwens) *adv.* [ME *whennes*] from what place, cause, etc.? [*whence* do you come?]

when·ev·er *adv.* [Inf.] when: an emphatic form —*conj.* at whatever time [go *whenever* you can]

where (hwer) *adv.* [OE *hwær*] **1** in or at what place? [*where* is it?] **2** to or toward what place? [*where* did he go?] **3** in what respect? [*where* is he to blame?] **4** from what place or source? [*where* did he learn it?] —*conj.* **1** at what place [I see *where* it is] **2** at which place [I went home, *where* I ate dinner] **3** wherever **4** to the place to which [we go *where* you go] —*pron.* **1** the place at which [it's a mile to *where* I live] **2** what place [*where* are you from?] —*n.* the place (*of* an event)

where·a·bouts (-ə bouts') *adv.* near or at what place? —*n.* [*usually with pl. v.*] the place where one is

where·as *conj.* **1** in view of the fact that **2** while on the contrary [I'm slim, *whereas* he is fat]

where·at *conj.* [Archaic] at which point

where·by *conj.* by which

where·fore (-fôr') *adv.* [Archaic] for what reason? why? —*conj.* [Archaic] **1** for which **2** because of which —*n.* the reason; cause

where·in *conj.* in which

where·of *adv., conj.* of what, which, or whom [the things *whereof* he spoke]

where·on *conj.* on which

where·up·on *conj.* at which

wher·ev·er (-ev'ər) *adv.* [Inf.] where: an emphatic form —*conj.* in, at, or to whatever place or situation [go *wherever* you like]

where·with *conj.* [Archaic] with which

where·with·al (-with ôl') *n.* the necessary means, esp. money: usually with *the*

wher·ry (hwer'ē) *n., pl.* **-ries** [ME *whery*] a light rowboat

whet (hwet) *vt.* **whet'ted, whet'ting** [< OE *hwæt*, keen] **1** to sharpen by rubbing or grinding (the edge of a knife or tool) **2** to stimulate

wheth·er (hweth'ər) *conj.* [OE *hwæther*] **1** if it be the case that [ask *whether* she sings] **2** equally or similarly in two or more specified cases [*whether* it rains or snows]

whet·stone (hwet'stōn') *n.* an abrasive stone for sharpening knives, etc.

whew (hyōō) *interj.* [echoic] used to express relief, surprise, dismay, etc.

whey (hwā) *n.* [OE *hwæg*] the watery part of milk, that separates from the curds

which (hwich) *pron.* [OE *hwylc*] **1** what one

(or ones) of several? [*which* do you want?] **2** the one (or ones) that [he knows *which* he wants] **3** that [the boat *which* sank] —*adj.* what one or ones [*which* man (or men) left?]

which·ev·er pron., adj. **1** any one [take *whichever* (desk) you like] **2** no matter which [*whichever* (desk) he chooses, they won't be pleased]

whiff (hwif) *n.* ⟦echoic⟧ **1** a light puff or gust of air, etc. **2** a slight odor **3** a hint or trace —*vi.* [Inf.] to miss when swinging at something

whif·fle·tree (hwif′əl trē′) *n. var. of* WHIPPLETREE

Whig (hwig) *n.* ⟦< *whiggamore* (derisive term for Scottish Presbyterians)⟧ **1** a member of a former English political party that championed reform **2** a supporter of the American Revolution **3** a member of a U.S. political party (c. 1834-56)

while (hwīl) *n.* ⟦OE *hwīl*⟧ a period of time [a short *while*] —*conj.* **1** during the time that [I read *while* I eat] **2** although; whereas [*while* not poor, she's not rich] —*vt.* **whiled**, **whil′ing** to spend (time) in a pleasant way: often with *away*

whi·lom (hwī′ləm) *adj.* ⟦< OE⟧ former

whilst (hwīlst) *conj.* [Chiefly Brit.] WHILE

whim (hwim) *n.* a sudden, passing idea or desire

whim·per (hwim′pər) *vi., vt.* ⟦? akin to WHINE⟧ to cry or utter with low, whining, broken sounds —*n.* a whimpering sound or cry

whim·si·cal (hwim′zi kəl) *adj.* **1** full of whims or whimsy **2** oddly out of the ordinary —**whim′si·cal′i·ty** (-kal′ə tē) *n.* —**whim′si·cal·ly** *adv.*

whim·sy (hwim′zē) *n., pl.* **-sies** ⟦< ?⟧ **1** a sudden, odd notion **2** quaint or fanciful humor Also sp. **whim′sey**, *pl.* **-seys**

whine (hwīn) *vi.* **whined**, **whin′ing** ⟦OE *hwīnan*⟧ **1** *a)* to utter a high-pitched, nasal sound, as in complaint *b)* to make a prolonged sound like this **2** to complain in a childish way —*n.* **1** a whining **2** a complaint uttered in a whining tone —**whin′y** *adj.* **-i·er**, **-i·est**

whin·ny (hwin′ē) *vi.* **-nied**, **-ny·ing** [prob. echoic] to neigh in a low, gentle way: said of a horse —*n., pl.* **-nies** a whinnying

whip (hwip) *vt.* **whipped**, **whip′ping** ⟦< MDu *wippen*, to swing⟧ **1** to move, pull, throw, etc. suddenly [to *whip* out a knife] **2** to strike, as with a strap; lash **3** to wind (cord, etc.) around (a rope, etc.) so as to prevent fraying **4** to beat into a froth [to *whip* cream] **5** [Inf.] to defeat —*vi.* **1** to move quickly and suddenly **2** to flap about —*n.* **1** a flexible instrument for striking or flogging **2** a blow, etc. as with a whip **3** an officer of a political party in a legislature who maintains discipline, etc. **4** a whipping motion —**whip up 1** to rouse (interest, etc.) **2** [Inf.] to prepare quickly

whip·cord *n.* **1** a hard, twisted or braided cord **2** a strong, diagonally ribbed worsted cloth

whip hand control or advantage

whip·lash *n.* **1** the lash of a whip **2** a sudden, severe jolting of the neck, as in an automobile accident

whip·per·snap·per *n.* an insignificant person, esp. a young person who appears presumptuous

whip·pet (hwip′it) *n.* ⟦< WHIP⟧ a swift dog resembling a small greyhound, used in racing

whip·ple·tree (hwip′əl trē) *n.* ⟦< WHIP + TREE⟧ SINGLETREE

whip·poor·will (hwip′ər wil′) *n.* ⟦echoic⟧ a dark-colored bird of E North America, active at night

whir or **whirr** (hwur) *vi., vt.* **whirred**, **whir′ring** ⟦ME *quirren*⟧ to fly, revolve, vibrate, etc. with a whizzing or buzzing sound —*n.* such a sound

whirl (hwurl) *vi.* ⟦< ON *hvirfla*⟧ **1** to move rapidly in a circle or orbit **2** to rotate or spin fast **3** to seem to spin [my head is *whirling*] —*vt.* to cause to rotate, revolve, or spin rapidly —*n.* **1** a whirling motion **2** a confused or giddy condition —**give it a whirl** [Inf.] to make an attempt

whirl·i·gig (hwur′li gig′) *n.* a child's toy that whirls or spins, as a pinwheel

whirl·pool *n.* **1** water in violent, whirling motion, tending to draw floating objects into its center **2** a bath in which an agitating device propels a current of warm water with a swirling motion: in full **whirlpool bath**

whirl·wind *n.* **1** a forward-moving current of air whirling violently in a vertical spiral **2** anything like a whirlwind —*adj.* impetuous; speedy

whisk (hwisk) *n.* ⟦< ON *visk*, a brush⟧ **1** a brushing with a quick, light, sweeping motion **2** such a motion **3** a kitchen utensil of wire loops in a handle, for whipping cream, etc. —*vt.* to move, carry, brush (*away, off, out, etc.*) with a quick, sweeping motion —*vi.* to move quickly or nimbly

whisk broom a small, short-handled broom for brushing clothes, etc.

whisk·er (hwis′kər) *n.* **1** [*pl.*] the hair growing on a man's face, esp. on the cheeks **2** any of the long, bristly hairs on the upper lip of a cat, rat, etc. **3** a very small amount or margin

whis·key (hwis′kē) *n., pl.* **-keys** or **-kies** ⟦< Ir *uisce*, water + *beathadh*, life⟧ a strong alcoholic liquor distilled from the fermented mash of grain: also sp. **whis′ky**, *pl.* **-kies**: in general, U.S. and Irish usage favors *whiskey*, and Brit. and Cdn. usage favors *whisky*

whis·per (hwis′pər) *vi., vt.* ⟦< OE *hwisprian*⟧ **1** to speak or say very softly, esp. without vibrating the vocal cords **2** to talk or tell furtively, as in gossiping **3** to make a rustling sound —*n.* **1** a whispering **2** something whispered **3** a soft, rustling sound

whist (hwist) *n.* ⟦< earlier *whisk*⟧ a card game that is the forerunner of bridge

whis·tle (hwis′əl) *vi.* **-tled**, **-tling** ⟦OE *hwistlian*⟧ **1** to make a clear, shrill sound as by blowing through puckered lips **2** to move with a shrill sound, as the wind does **3** *a*) to blow a whistle *b*) to have its whistle blown [the train *whistled*] —*vt.* **1** to produce (a tune, etc.) by whistling **2** to signal, etc. by whistling —*n.* **1** a device for making whistling sounds **2** a whistling —**whis′tler** *n.* —**blow the whistle (on)** [Inf.] to report or inform (on or about)

whis·tle·blow·er *n.* one who reports wrongdoing, as by his or her employer

whis·tle-stop *n.* **1** a small town **2** a brief stop in a small town on a tour

whit (hwit) *n.* [< OE *wiht*, wight] the least bit; jot

white (hwīt) *adj.* **whit′er, whit′est** [OE *hwīt*] **1** having the color of pure snow or milk; opposite to black **2** of a light or pale color **3** pale; wan **4** lacking color **5** pure; innocent **6** [*sometimes* **W-**] having light-colored skin; Caucasoid —*n.* **1** *a*) white color *b*) a white pigment **2** a white or light-colored part, as the albumen of an egg or the white part of the eyeball **3** [*sometimes* **W-**] a person with light-colored skin —**white′ness** *n.*

white blood cell (*or* **corpuscle**) LEUKOCYTE

white·board *n.* a smooth, glossy white surface on which to write using erasable markers

white-bread *adj.* [Inf.] **1** of or like the white middle class, its values, etc. **2** bland, conventional, etc.

white·cap *n.* a wave with its crest broken into white foam

white-col·lar *adj.* designating or of office or professional workers

white-collar crime fraud, embezzlement, etc., committed by a person in business, government, or a profession

white elephant 1 an albino elephant **2** something of little use, but expensive to maintain **3** any object no longer wanted by its owner, but possibly useful to another

white·fish *n.*, *pl.* **-fish′** *or* **-fish′es** a white or silvery, edible fish, found in cool lakes of the Northern Hemisphere

white flag a white banner or cloth hoisted as a signal of truce or surrender

white gold a gold alloy that looks like platinum

white goods 1 household linens, as sheets and towels **2** large household appliances, as refrigerators and stoves

white heat 1 a temperature at which material glows white **2** a state of intense emotion, excitement, etc. —**white′-hot′** *adj.*

White·horse capital of the Yukon Territory, Canada

White House, the 1 official residence of the President of the U.S. in Washington, DC **2** the executive branch of the U.S. government

white lead a poisonous, white powder, lead carbonate, used in paint

white lie a lie about a trivial matter, often told to spare someone's feelings

white metal any of various light-colored alloys, esp. one containing much lead or tin, as pewter

whit·en (hwīt′'n) *vt.*, *vi.* to make or become white or whiter —**whit′en·er** *n.* —**whit′en·ing** *n.*

white·out *n.* a weather condition in which heavy windblown or falling snow greatly reduces visibility

white-out *n.* [< *Wite-Out*, a trademark] a quick-drying, white fluid that is brushed on to cover printed errors and allow for corrections

white paper 1 an official government report **2** any in-depth, authoritative report

white sale a sale of household linens

white·wall *adj.* designating or of a tire with a circular white band on the side —*n.* such a tire

white·wash *n.* **1** a mixture of lime, chalk, water, etc., as for whitening walls, etc. **2** a concealing of faults in order to exonerate —*vt.* **1** to cover with whitewash **2** to conceal the faults of **3** *Sports* [Inf.] to defeat (an opponent) soundly

white·wa·ter *adj.* of or having to do with recreational kayaking, rafting, etc. on rivers with rapids —*n.* the turbulent, foamy water in such rivers

whith·er (hwith′ər) [Now Rare] *adv.* [OE *hwider*] to what place, condition, result, etc.? —*conj.* **1** to which place, result, etc. **2** wherever

whit·ing[1] (hwīt′iŋ) *n.* [< MDu *wit*, white] any of various unrelated food fishes of North America, Europe, etc.

whit·ing[2] (hwīt′iŋ) *n.* [ME *hwiting*] powdered chalk used in paints, etc.

whit·ish *adj.* somewhat white

Whit·man (hwit′mən), **Walt(er)** 1819–92; U.S. poet

Whit·ney (hwit′nē), **Mount** mountain in EC California: 14,495 ft.

Whit·sun·day (hwit′sun′dā) *n.* [OE *Hwita Sunnandæg*, lit., white Sunday] PENTECOST

whit·tle (hwit′'l) *vt.* **-tled, -tling** [< OE *thwitan*, to cut] **1** *a*) to cut thin shavings from (wood) with a knife *b*) to carve (an object) thus **2** to reduce gradually —*vi.* to whittle wood —**whit′tler** *n.*

whiz *or* **whizz** (hwiz) *vi.* **whizzed, whiz′zing** [echoic] **1** to move swiftly with a buzzing or hissing sound **2** to make this sound —*n.* **1** this sound **2** [Slang] an expert [a *whiz* at football]

who (hōō) *pron.* [OE *hwa*] **1** what or which person or persons [*who* is he? I asked *who* he was] **2** the person or persons that, or a person that [a man *who* knows]

WHO *abbrev.* World Health Organization

whoa (hwō) *interj.* **1** stop!: used esp. in directing a horse to stand still **2** used to express awe, amazement, etc.

who·dun·it (hōō dun′it) *n.* [< WHO + DONE + IT] [Inf.] a mystery novel, play, etc.

who·ev·er *pron.* **1** any person that **2** no matter who [*whoever* said it, it's not so] **3** who?: an emphatic usage [*whoever* told you that?]

whole (hōl) *adj.* [OE *hal*] **1** healthy; not diseased or injured **2** not broken, damaged, etc.; intact **3** containing all the parts; complete **4** not divided up; in a single unit **5** not a fraction —*n.* **1** the entire amount **2** a thing complete in itself —**on the whole** in general —**whole′ness** *n.*

whole-heart·ed *adj.* with all one's energy, enthusiasm, etc.; sincere

whole-hog *adj., adv.* [Slang] without reservation; complete(ly)

whole milk milk from which no butterfat, etc. has been removed

whole note *Music* a note having four times the duration of a quarter note

whole·sale *n.* the selling of goods in large quantities and at lower prices, esp. to retailers —*adj.* **1** of or having to do with such selling **2** extensive or indiscriminate [*wholesale* criticism] —*adv.* **1** at wholesale prices **2** extensively or indiscriminately —*vt., vi.* **-saled′, -sal′ing** to sell wholesale —**whole′sal′er** *n.*

whole·some *adj.* 〖ME *holsom*〗 **1** promoting good health or well-being; healthful **2** improving the mind or character **3** healthy; sound — **whole′some·ness** *n.*

whole tone *Music* an interval consisting of two adjacent semitones: also **whole step**

whole-wheat *adj.* ground from whole kernels of wheat or made of flour so ground

whol·ly (hōl′lē) *adv.* to the whole amount or extent; totally; entirely

whom (hōōm) *pron. objective case of* WHO

whom·ev·er (-ev′ər) *pron. objective case of* WHOEVER

whoop (hwōōp, wōōp, hōōp) *n.* 〖< ? OFr *houper*, cry out〗 **1** a loud shout, cry, etc., as of joy **2** the convulsive intake of air following a fit of coughing in whooping cough —*vt., vi.* to utter (with) a whoop or whoops

whoop·ing cough (hōō′piŋ, hwōō′-) an acute infectious disease, esp. of children, with coughing fits that end in a whoop

whop·per (hwäp′ər, wäp′ər) *n.* [Inf.] **1** anything extraordinarily large **2** a great lie

whop·ping *adj.* [Inf.] extraordinarily large

whore (hôr) *n.* 〖OE *hore*〗 a prostitute

who're (hōō′ər) *contr.* who are

whorl (hwôrl, hwurl) *n.* 〖ME *whorwyl*〗 anything with a coiled or spiral appearance, as any of the circular ridges that form the patterns of a fingerprint —**whorled** *adj.*

who's (hōōz) *contr.* **1** who is **2** who has

whose (hōōz) *pron.* 〖OE *hwæs*〗 that or those belonging to whom —*poss. pronominal adj.* of, belonging to, or done by whom or which

who·so·ev·er (hōō′sō ev′ər) *pron.* whoever

why (hwī, wī) *adv.* 〖OE *hwæt*, what〗 for what reason, cause, or purpose? [*why* eat?] —*conj.* **1** because of which [no reason *why* you shouldn't go] **2** the reason for which [that is *why* he went] —*n., pl.* **whys** the reason; cause —*interj.* an exclamation of surprise, impatience, etc.

WI *abbrev.* Wisconsin

Wic·ca (wik′ə) *n.* a nature-based religion typically centering on a mother goddess or goddess-god pair

wick (wik) *n.* 〖OE *weoca*〗 a piece of cord, etc., as in a candle or oil lamp, that draws fuel up to the flame

wick·ed (wik′id) *adj.* 〖ME < *wikke*, evil〗 **1** morally bad; evil **2** generally bad, unpleasant, etc. [a *wicked* storm] **3** mischievous [a *wicked* sense of humor] **4** [Slang] showing great skill —**wick′ed·ly** *adv.* —**wick′ed·ness** *n.*

wick·er (wik′ər) *n.* 〖< Scand〗 **1** a thin, flexible twig **2** *a)* such twigs or long, woody strips woven together, as in making baskets *b)* WICKERWORK (*n.* 1) —*adj.* made of wicker

wick·er·work *n.* **1** things made of wicker **2** WICKER (*n.* 2a)

wick·et (wik′it) *n.* 〖ME *wiket*〗 **1** a small door or gate, esp. one in or near a larger one **2** a small window, as in a box office **3** *Croquet* any of the small wire arches through which balls are hit

wide (wīd) *adj.* **wid′er, wid′est** 〖OE *wid*〗 **1** extending over a large area, esp. from side to side **2** of a specified extent from side to side **3** of great extent [a *wide* variety] **4** open fully [eyes *wide* with fear] **5** far from the point, etc. aimed at: usually with *of* [*wide* of the target] —*adv.* **1** over a relatively large area **2** to a large or full extent [*wide* open] **3** so as to miss the point, etc. aimed at; astray —**wide′ly** *adv.* —**wide′ness** *n.*

-wide (wīd) *combining form* existing or extending throughout [*statewide*]

wide-an·gle *adj.* designating or of a camera lens having a wider than ordinary angle of view

wide-a·wake *adj.* **1** completely awake **2** alert

wide-eyed *adj.* **1** with the eyes opened widely, as in surprise or fear **2** naive or unsophisticated

wid·en (wīd′'n) *vt., vi.* to make or become wider

wide-o·pen *adj.* **1** opened wide **2** having no or few legal restrictions against prostitution, gambling, etc. [a *wide-open* city]

wide·spread *adj.* occurring over a wide area

widg·eon (wij′ən) *n.* alt. *sp. of* WIGEON

wid·ow (wid′ō) *n.* 〖OE *widewe*〗 a woman whose spouse has died and who has not remarried —*vt.* to cause to become a widow or widower —**wid′ow·hood′** *n.*

wid·ow·er *n.* a man whose spouse has died and who has not remarried

width (width) *n.* **1** distance from side to side **2** a piece of a certain width [two *widths* of cloth]

wield (wēld) *vt.* 〖OE *wealdan*〗 **1** to handle (a tool, etc.), esp. with skill **2** to exercise (power, influence, etc.)

wie·ner (wē′nər) *n.* 〖< Ger *Wiener wurst*, Vienna sausage〗 a smoked link sausage; frankfurter: also [Inf.] **wie′nie** (-nē)

wife (wīf) *n., pl.* **wives** 〖OE *wif*, woman〗 a married woman —**wife′less** *adj.* —**wife′ly** *adj.*

Wi-Fi (wī′fī′) 〖< *wi(reless) fi(delity)*, after HI-FI〗 *service mark for* a wireless local area network that uses radio waves to connect computers and other devices to the internet

wig (wig) *n.* 〖< PERIWIG〗 a covering of real or

synthetic hair worn as to hide baldness —*vt.*

wigged, wig′ging 1 to furnish with a wig **2** [Slang] to make excited, crazy, etc.: often with *out* —*vi.* [Slang] to be or become upset, excited, etc.: often with *out*

wi·geon (wij′ən) *n.* [prob. < L *vipio*, small crane] any of certain wild, freshwater ducks

wig·gle (wig′əl) *vt., vi.* **-gled, -gling** [ME *wigelen*] to move or cause to move with short, jerky motions from side to side —*n.* a wiggling —**wig′gler** *n.* —**wig′gly** *adj.* **-gli·er, -gli·est**

wiggle room [Inf.] space, room, or opportunity to make adjustments or to deviate from a standard or requirement

wight (wīt) *n.* [OE *wiht*] [Archaic] a human

wig·wag (wig′wag′) *vt., vi.* **-wagged′, -wag′ging** [< obs. *wig*, to move + WAG¹] **1** to move back and forth; wag **2** to send (a message) by a visible code —*n.* the sending of messages in this way

wig·wam (wig′wäm′) *n.* [< Algonquian] a North American dwelling consisting of a dome-shaped framework of poles covered with mats or bark

wik·i (wik′ē) *n.* [Haw, lit., fast] **1** a Web application that allows anyone to edit that website's content **2** such a website

wild (wīld) *adj.* [OE *wilde*] **1** living or growing in its original, natural state **2** not lived in or cultivated; waste **3** not civilized; savage **4** not easily controlled [a *wild* child] **5** lacking social or moral restraint; dissolute [a *wild* time] **6** turbulent; stormy **7** enthusiastic [*wild* about golf] **8** fantastically impractical; reckless **9** missing the target [a *wild* shot] **10** *Card Games* having any desired value: said of a card —*adv.* in a wild manner —*n.* [*usually pl.*] a wilderness or wasteland —**the wild** a natural or undomesticated state —**wild′ly** *adv.* —**wild′ness** *n.*

wild·cat *n.* **1** any fierce, medium-sized, undomesticated cat, as the bobcat, ocelot, etc. **2** an oil well in a previously unproductive area —*adj.* **1** unsound or risky **2** illegal or unauthorized [a *wildcat* strike] —*vi.* **-cat′ted, -cat′ting** to drill for oil in a previously unproductive area

wil·de·beest (wil′də bēst′, vil′-) *n.* [Afrik] GNU

wil·der·ness (wil′dər nis) *n.* [< OE *wilde*, wild + *deor*, animal] an uncultivated region

wild-eyed *adj.* **1** staring in a wild or demented way **2** very foolish or impractical

wild·fire *n.* a fire that spreads widely and rapidly

wild·flow·er *n.* **1** any flowering plant growing wild in fields, etc. **2** its flower Also **wild flower**

wild·fowl *n., pl.* **-fowls′** or **-fowl′** a wild bird, esp. a game bird: also **wild fowl**

wild-goose chase a protracted or pointless search or pursuit

wild·life *n.* wild animals and birds

wild oats a wild grass common in the W U.S. —**sow one's wild oats** to be promiscuous or dissolute in one's youth

wild rice 1 an aquatic grass of the U.S. and Canada **2** its edible grain

Wild West [*also* **w- W-**] the western U.S. in its early frontier period of lawlessness

wile (wīl) *n.* [< OE *wigle*, magic] **1** a sly trick; stratagem **2** a beguiling trick: *usually used in pl.* —*vt.* **wiled, wil′ing** to beguile; lure —**wile away** to while away (time, etc.)

wil·ful (wil′fəl) *adj. alt. sp. of* WILLFUL

will¹ (wil) *n.* [OE *willa*] **1** the power of making a reasoned choice or of controlling one's own actions **2** determination **3** attitude toward others [a man of good *will*] **4** *a*) a particular desire, choice, etc. of someone *b*) mandate [the *will* of the people] **5** a legal document directing the disposal of one's property after death —*vt.* **1** to desire; want [to *will* to live] **2** to control by the power of the will **3** to bequeath by a will —*vi.* to wish, desire, or choose —**at will** when one wishes

will² (wil) *v.aux. pt.* **would** [OE *willan*, to desire] **1** used to indicate simple future time [when *will* she arrive?] **2** used to express determination, obligation, etc. [you *will* listen to me] **3** used in polite questions [*will* you have some wine?] **4** used to express habit, custom, etc. [they *will* talk for hours] **5** used to express expectation or surmise

USAGE—the distinction between WILL² and SHALL in expressing simple future time or determination, etc. is today virtually nonexistent in North American English; WILL² and SHALL and their respective past tenses WOULD and SHOULD are usually interchangeable, with WILL² (and WOULD) being the preferred form in all persons

will·ful (-fəl) *adj.* **1** said or done deliberately **2** doing as one pleases —**will′ful·ly** *adv.* —**will′ful·ness** *n.*

Wil·liam I (wil′yəm) 1027?-87; duke of Normandy who invaded England: king of England (1066-87): called *William the Conqueror*

wil·lies (wil′ēz) *pl.n.* [< ?] [Slang] a nervous feeling; jitters: with *the*

will·ing *adj.* **1** favorably disposed; consenting [*willing* to play] **2** acting, giving, etc. or done, given, etc. readily and cheerfully —**will′ing·ly** *adv.* —**will′ing·ness** *n.*

wil·li·waw (wil′i wô′) *n.* **1** a violent, cold wind blowing from mountain passes toward the coast **2** confusion; turmoil

will-o'-the-wisp (wil′ə thə wisp′) *n.* **1** a naturally occurring light sometimes seen at night hovering over swampy or marshy ground **2** a delusive hope or goal

wil·low (wil′ō) *n.* [OE *welig*] **1** a tree with narrow leaves, and flexible twigs used in weaving baskets, etc. **2** its wood

wil·low·y *adj.* like a willow; slender, lithe, etc.

will·pow·er *n.* strength of will, mind, or determination; self-control

wil·ly-nil·ly (wil′ē nil′ē) *adv., adj.* [contr. < *will I, nill I: nill* < OE *nyllan*, be unwilling] **1** (happening) whether one wishes it or not **2** in a disordered way; helter-skelter

Wil·son (wil′sən), **(Thomas) Wood·row**

(wood′rō) 1856-1924; 28th president of the U.S. (1913-21)

wilt (wilt) *vi.* 〚< obs. *welk*, to wither〛 **1** to become limp, as from heat or lack of water; droop: said of plants **2** to become weak or faint; lose strength or courage —*vt.* to cause to wilt

wil·y (wī′lē) *adj.* **-i·er, -i·est** full of wiles; crafty; sly —**wil′i·ness** *n.*

wimp (wimp) *n.* 〚< ?〛 [Inf.] a weak, ineffectual, or insipid person —**wimp′ish** *adj.* —**wimp′y** *adj.* **-i·er, -i·est**

wim·ple (wim′pəl) *n.* 〚OE *wimpel*〛 a nun's head covering that leaves only the face exposed

win (win) *vi.* **won, win′ning** 〚< OE *winnan*, to fight〛 **1** *a)* to gain a victory *b)* to finish first in a race, etc. **2** to succeed in reaching a specified condition or place; get [to *win* back to health] —*vt.* **1** to get by labor, struggle, etc. **2** to be victorious in (a contest, etc.) **3** to get to with effort [they *won* the camp by noon] **4** to prevail upon; persuade: often with *over* **5** to gain (the sympathy, favor, etc.) of (someone) **6** to persuade to marry one —*n.* a victory

wince (wins) *vi.* **winced, winc′ing** 〚< OFr *guenchir*〛 to shrink or draw back slightly, usually with a grimace, as in pain —*n.* a wincing

winch (winch) *n.* 〚OE *wince*〛 **1** a crank with a handle for transmitting motion **2** a machine for hoisting, etc. using a cylinder upon which is wound the rope, etc. attached to an object

Win·ches·ter (win′ches′tər) 〚after O. F. *Winchester* (1810-80), the manufacturer〛 *trademark for* a type of repeating rifle

wind¹ (wīnd) *vt.* **wound** (wound) *or* 〚Rare〛 **wind′ed, wind′ing** 〚OE *windan*〛 **1** to turn [to *wind* a crank] **2** to coil into a ball or around something else; twine **3** to cover by entwining **4** *a)* to make (one's way) in a twisting course *b)* to cause to move in a twisting course **5** to tighten the spring of (a clock, etc.) as by turning a stem: often with *up* —*vi.* **1** to move or go in a curving or sinuous manner **2** to take a devious course **3** to coil (*about* or *around* something) —*n.* a turn; twist —**wind down 1** to bring or come to an end **2** to become relaxed; unwind —**wind up 1** to wind into a ball, etc. **2** to bring to an end; settle **3** to make very tense, excited, etc. **4** *Baseball* to perform a WINDUP (*n.* 2) —**wind′er** *n.*

wind² (wind) *n.* 〚OE〛 **1** air in motion **2** a strong current of air; gale **3** air bearing a scent, as in hunting **4** air regarded as bearing information, etc. [a rumor in the *wind*] **5** breath or the power of breathing **6** empty talk **7** [*pl.*] the wind instruments of an orchestra —*vt.* **1** to get the scent of **2** to put out of breath —**break wind** to expel gas from the bowels —**get wind of** to hear of —**in the wind** happening or about to happen

wind·bag (wind′bag′) *n.* [Inf.] one who talks much but says little of importance

wind·break *n.* a hedge, fence, etc. serving as a protection from wind

wind·break·er *n.* a jacket made of lightweight, wind-resistant material

wind·burn *n.* a reddened, sore skin condition, caused by overexposure to the wind

wind-chill factor an estimated measure of the cooling effect of wind and wind speed on exposed skin

wind chimes (*or* **bells**) a cluster of small chimes or pendants hung so that they strike one another and tinkle when blown by the wind

wind·ed (win′did) *adj.* out of breath

wind·fall (wind′fôl′) *n.* an unexpected gain, stroke of good luck, etc.

wind farm an array of modern, high-speed windmills for generating electricity

wind·ing sheet (wīn′diŋ) a shroud

wind instrument (wind) a musical instrument sounded by blowing air through it, as a flute or trumpet

wind·jam·mer (wind′jam′ər) *n.* **1** a sail-powered cargo ship **2** a schooner or other large sailing vessel that offers cruises

wind·lass (wind′ləs) *n.* 〚< ON *vinda*, to WIND¹ + *ass*, a beam〛 a winch, esp. one worked by a crank

wind·mill *n.* **1** a mill operated by the wind's rotation of large vanes radiating from a shaft **2** a device like this, as one to harness wind power

win·dow (win′dō) *n.* 〚< ON *vindr*, WIND² + *auga*, an eye〛 **1** an opening in a building, vehicle, etc. for letting in light, air, etc. usually having a pane of glass in a movable frame **2** a windowpane **3** an opening resembling a window **4** the interval during which something can be done **5** *Comput.* a separate data display on a screen

window box a long, narrow box on or outside a window ledge, for growing plants

window dressing 1 the display of goods in a store window **2** that which is meant to make something seem better than it really is —**win′dow-dress′** *vt.* —**window dresser**

win·dow·pane *n.* a pane of glass in a window

win·dow-shop *vi.* **-shopped′, -shop′ping** to look at goods in store windows without entering to buy

win·dow·sill *n.* the sill of a window

wind·pipe (wind′pīp′) *n.* TRACHEA

wind·row (-rō′) *n.* **1** a row of hay, etc. raked together to dry **2** a long pile of some material

wind shear a sudden change in wind direction, esp., dangerous vertical wind shifts

wind·shield *n.* in automobiles, etc., a glass screen, in front, to protect from wind, etc.

wind·sock *n.* a long, cloth cone flown at an airfield to show wind direction: also **wind sleeve**

Wind·sor knot (win′zər) a double slipknot in a four-in-hand necktie

wind·storm *n.* a storm with a strong wind but little or no rain, hail, etc.

wind·surf *vi.* to ride for sport on a kind of surfboard with a pivoting sail —**wind′surf′ing** *n.*

wind tunnel a tunnel-like chamber through which air is forced, for testing the effects of wind pressure on aircraft, motor vehicles, etc.

wind-up (wīnd′up′) *n.* **1** a conclusion; end **2** *Baseball* the motion of the pitcher leading up to throwing the ball

wind-ward (wīnd′wǝrd) *n.* the direction from which the wind blows —*adv.* toward the wind —*adj.* **1** moving windward **2** on the side from which the wind blows

Windward Islands S group of islands in the West Indies, south of the Leeward Islands

wind-y (wīn′dē) *adj.* -i·er, -i·est **1** with much wind [a *windy* city] **2** stormy, blustery, etc. **3** long-winded, pompous, etc. —**wind′i·ness** *n.*

wine (wīn) *n.* [< L *vinum*] fermented juice, esp. of grapes, used as an alcoholic beverage —*vt., vi.* wined, win′ing usually in the phrase **wine and dine**, to entertain lavishly

wine-col·ored *adj.* dark purplish-red

win·er·y (wīn′ǝr ē) *n., pl.* -ies an establishment where wine is made

wing (wiŋ) *n.* [ON *vaengr*] **1** either of the paired organs of flight of a bird, bat, insect, etc. **2** something like a wing in use, position, etc., esp., *a*) a (or the) main lateral supporting surface of an airplane *b*) a subordinate, projecting part of a building *c*) either side of the stage out of sight of the audience **3** the section of an army, fleet, etc. to the right (or left) of the center **4** a section, as of a political party, with reference to its radicalism or conservatism **5** a unit in an air force —*vt.* **1** to provide with wings **2** *a*) to send swiftly as on wings *b*) to make (one's way) by flying *c*) to pass through or over, as by flying **3** to wound in the wing, arm, etc. —*vi.* to fly —**on the wing** (while) flying —**take wing** to fly away —**under one's wing** under one's protection, etc. —**wing it** [Inf.] to improvise in acting, etc. —**winged** (wiŋd; *poet.* wiŋ′id) *adj.* —**wing′less** *adj.*

wing-ding (-diŋ′) *n.* [< ?] [Slang] an event, party, etc. that is very festive, lively, etc.

wing-span *n.* **1** the distance between the tips of an airplane's wings **2** WINGSPREAD (*n.* 1)

wing-spread *n.* **1** the distance between the tips of fully spread wings **2** WINGSPAN (*n.* 1)

wink (wiŋk) *vi.* [OE *wincian*] **1** to close the eyelids and open them again quickly **2** to close and open one eyelid quickly, as a signal, etc. **3** to twinkle —*vt.* to make (an eye) wink —*n.* **1** a winking **2** an instant **3** a signal given by winking **4** a twinkle —**wink at** to pretend not to see

win·ner (win′ǝr) *n.* one that wins

win·ning (win′iŋ) *adj.* **1** victorious **2** attractive; charming —*n.* **1** a victory **2** [*pl.*] money won

Win·ni·peg (win′ǝ peg′) capital of Manitoba, Canada

win·now (win′ō) *vt., vi.* [< OE *wind*, WIND²] **1** to blow (chaff) from (grain) **2** to scatter **3** to sift out

win·o (wī′nō) *n., pl.* -os [Slang] an alcoholic who drinks cheap wine

win·some (win′sǝm) *adj.* [OE *wynsum*, pleasant] sweetly attractive; charming —**win′some·ly** *adv.*

win·ter (win′tǝr) *n.* [OE] **1** the coldest season of the year, following autumn **2** a period of decline, distress, etc. —*adj.* of, during, or for winter —*vi.* to pass the winter —*vt.* to keep, feed, etc. during winter

win·ter·green *n.* **1** an evergreen plant with white flowers and red berries **2** an aromatic oil (**oil of wintergreen**) distilled from its leaves or from birch twigs or synthesized and used as a flavoring **3** the flavor

win·ter·ize *vt.* -ized′, -iz′ing to put into condition for winter

win·ter·kill *vt., vi.* to kill or die by exposure to winter cold or excessive snow and ice —*n.* the process or an instance of winterkilling

win·ter·time *n.* the winter season

win·try (win′trē) *adj.* -tri·er, -tri·est of or like winter; cold, bleak, etc. [a *wintry* day]

win-win *adj.* **1** designating or of an interaction that benefits both parties involved **2** designating or of a situation from which all possible outcomes are satisfactory

win·y (wī′nē) *adj.* -i·er, -i·est like wine in taste, smell, color, etc.

wipe (wīp) *vt.* wiped, wip′ing [OE *wipian*] **1** to clean or dry by rubbing with a cloth, etc. **2** to rub (a cloth, etc.) over something **3** to apply or remove by wiping —*n.* a wiping —**wipe out 1** to remove; erase **2** to kill off **3** to destroy —**wip′er** *n.*

wiped-out *adj.* [Inf.] exhausted

wire (wīr) *n.* [OE *wīr*] **1** metal drawn into a long thread **2** a length of this **3** a telegram **4** the finish line of a horse race —*adj.* made of wire —*vt.* wired, wir′ing **1** to furnish, connect, etc. with wire **2** to telegraph —*vi.* to telegraph

wired (wīrd) *adj.* **1** [Inf.] provided with concealed electronic listening or recording equipment **2** [Slang] extremely excited, nervous, etc.

wire·hair *n.* a fox terrier with a wiry coat: also called **wire′-haired′ terrier**

wire·less (-lis) *adj.* operating by electromagnetic waves, not with conducting wire —*n.* **1** wireless telegraphy or telephony **2** [Chiefly Brit.] *old-fashioned term for* RADIO

wire service an agency sending news electronically to subscribing newspapers, etc.

wire·tap *vi., vt.* -tapped′, -tap′ping to tap (a telephone line, etc.) to get information secretly —*n.* a wiretapping

wir·ing *n.* a system of wires, as to provide a house with electricity

wir·y (wīr′ē) *adj.* -i·er, -i·est **1** of wire **2** like wire; stiff **3** lean and strong —**wir′i·ness** *n.*

Wis·con·sin (wis kän′sǝn) Midwestern state of the U.S.; cap. Madison: abbrev. WI —**Wis·con′sin·ite′** *n.*

wis·dom (wiz′dǝm) *n.* [OE: see WISE¹ & -DOM] **1** the quality of being wise; good judgment **2** learning; knowledge

wisdom tooth the back tooth on each side of each jaw

wise¹ (wīz) *adj.* wis′er, wis′est [OE *wīs*] **1** having or showing good judgment **2** informed [none the *wiser*] **3** learned **4** shrewd; cunning **5** [Slang] conceited, impudent, fresh, etc. —**wise′ly** *adv.*

wise² (wīz) *n.* [OE] way; manner

-wise (wīz) [< prec.] *suffix* **1** in a (specified) direction, position, or manner [*lengthwise*] **2** in a manner characteristic of [*clockwise*] **3** with regard to [*budgetwise*]

wise·a·cre (wīz′ā′kər) *n.* [ult. < OHG *wizzago*, prophet] one who makes impudent displays of knowledge

wise·crack [Slang] *n.* a flippant or facetious remark —*vi.* to make wisecracks

wise guy [Slang] **1** one who is offensively brash **2** a member of the Mafia

wish (wish) *vt.* [OE *wyscan*] **1** to have a longing for; want **2** to express a desire concerning [I *wish* you well] **3** to request [I *wish* you to go] —*vi.* **1** to long; yearn **2** to make a wish —*n.* **1** a wishing **2** something wished for **3** a polite request, almost an order **4** [*pl.*] expressed desire for a person's health, etc. [best *wishes*] —**wish′er** *n.*

wish·bone *n.* the forked bone in front of a bird's breastbone

wish·ful (-fəl) *adj.* having or showing a wish; desirous —**wish′ful·ly** *adv.*

wish·y-wash·y (wish′ē wôsh′ē) *adj.* [Inf.] **1** weak; feeble **2** vacillating; indecisive

wisp (wisp) *n.* [prob. < Scand] **1** a small bundle, as of straw **2** a thin or filmy piece, strand, etc. [a *wisp* of smoke] **3** something delicate, frail, etc. —**wisp′y** *adj.* **-i·er, -i·est**

wis·te·ri·a (wis tir′ē ə) *n.* [after C. *Wistar* (1761-1818), U.S. anatomist] a twining vine with showy clusters of flowers: also **wis·tar′i·a** (-ter′-)

wist·ful (wist′fəl) *adj.* [< earlier *wistly*, attentive] showing or expressing vague yearnings —**wist′ful·ly** *adv.* —**wist′ful·ness** *n.*

wit¹ (wit) *n.* [OE] **1** [*pl.*] powers of thinking; mental faculties **2** good sense **3** *a*) the ability to make clever remarks in a sharp, amusing way *b*) one characterized by wit —**at one's wits' end** having exhausted one's mental or emotional resources

wit² (wit) *vt., vi.* **wist** (wist), **wit′ting** [OE *witan*] [Archaic] to know —**to wit** namely

witch (wich) *n.* [OE *wicce*] **1** a woman thought to have supernatural power as by a compact with evil spirits **2** a spiteful, ill-tempered woman **3** [Inf.] a follower of Wicca

witch·craft *n.* the power or practices of witches

witch doctor in certain primitive societies, one thought able to cure sickness, ward off evil, etc. by using magic or incantations

witch·er·y (-ər ē) *n., pl.* **-ies 1** witchcraft; sorcery **2** bewitching charm

witch hazel [< OE *wice*] **1** a shrub bearing yellow flowers in the fall or winter **2** a lotion made from its leaves and bark, used on inflammations, etc.

witch hunt [in allusion to former persecutions of alleged witches] a highly publicized investigation carried out ostensibly to uncover disloyalty, etc., relying upon little evidence

with (with, with) *prep.* [OE] **1** in opposition to [to argue *with* a friend] **2** *a*) alongside of; near to *b*) in the company of *c*) into; among [mix blue *with* yellow] **3** as a member of [to play *with* a string quartet] **4** concerning [happy *with* his lot] **5** compared to **6** as well as [she rides *with* the best] **7** in the opinion of [it's OK *with* me] **8** as a result of [faint *with* hunger] **9** by means of [to part *with* one's gains] —**with that** after, or as a consequence of, that

with- *combining form* **1** away, back [*withdraw*] **2** against, from [*withhold*]

with·al (with ôl′, with-) *adv.* **1** besides **2** despite that

with·draw *vt.* **-drew′, -drawn′, -draw′ing 1** to take back; remove **2** to retract or recall (a statement, etc.) —*vi.* **1** to move back; go away; retreat **2** to remove oneself (*from* an organization, activity, etc.) **3** to become socially or emotionally detached

with·draw·al *n.* **1** the act of withdrawing **2** the process of giving up an addictive drug, typically accompanied by distressing physical and mental effects (**withdrawal symptoms**)

with·drawn *vt., vi. pp. of* WITHDRAW —*adj.* shy, reserved, etc.

withe (with, with) *n.* [< OE *withthe*] a tough, flexible twig of willow, osier, etc., used for binding

with·er (with′ər) *vi.* [< ME *wederen*, to weather] **1** to dry up; wilt, as plants **2** to become wasted or decayed **3** to weaken; languish —*vt.* **1** to cause to wither **2** to cause to feel abashed

with·ers (with′ərz) *pl.n.* [< OE, *wither*, against] the part of a horse's back between the shoulder blades

with·hold (with hōld′, with-) *vt.* **-held′, -hold′ing 1** *a*) to hold back; restrain *b*) to deduct (taxes, etc.) from wages **2** to refrain from granting

withholding tax the amount of income tax withheld, as payment in advance, from an employee's pay

with·in (with in′, with-) *adv.* [OE *withinnan*] **1** on or into the inside **2** indoors **3** inside the body, mind, etc. —*prep.* **1** in the inner part of **2** not beyond **3** inside the limits of —*n.* the inside

with·it (-it) *adj.* [Slang] **1** sophisticated, up-to-date, etc. **2** fashionable; stylish **3** mentally alert or competent

with·out *adv.* [OE *withutan*] **1** on the outside **2** out-of-doors —*prep.* **1** [Now Rare] at, on, or to the outside of **2** lacking **3** free from **4** with avoidance of [to pass by *without* speaking]

with·stand (-stand′) *vt., vi.* **-stood′, -stand′ing** to oppose, resist, or endure, esp. successfully

wit·less (wit′lis) *adj.* lacking wit; foolish —**wit′less·ly** *adv.*

wit·ness (wit′nis) *n.* [< OE *witan,* know] 1 evidence; testimony 2 one who saw, or can give a firsthand account of, something 3 one who testifies in court 4 one who observes, and attests to, a signing, etc. —*vt.* 1 to testify to 2 to serve as evidence of 3 to act as witness of 4 to be present at —**bear witness** to testify

wit·ti·cism (wit′ə siz′əm) *n.* [< WITTY] a witty remark

wit·ting (wit′iŋ) *adj.* [ME *wytting*] intentional

wit·ty (wit′ē) *adj.* **-ti·er, -ti·est** [OE *wittig*] having or showing wit; cleverly amusing —**wit′ti·ly** *adv.* —**wit′ti·ness** *n.*

wive (wīv) *vi., vt.* **wived, wiv′ing** [OE *wīfian*] [Archaic] to marry (a woman)

wives (wīvz) *n. pl. of* WIFE

wiz·ard (wiz′ərd) *n.* [ME *wisard*] 1 a magician; sorcerer 2 [Inf.] one very skilled at a specified activity

wiz·ard·ry *n.* magic; sorcery

wiz·ened (wiz′ənd) *adj.* [< OE *wisnian,* wither] dried up; withered

wk *abbrev.* 1 week 2 work

wkly. *abbrev.* weekly

WMD *abbrev.* weapon(s) of mass destruction

w/o *abbrev.* without

wob·ble (wäb′əl) *vi.* **-bled, -bling** [prob. < LowG *wabbeln*] 1 to move unsteadily from side to side 2 to shake 3 to vacillate —*vt.* to cause to wobble —*n.* wobbling motion —**wob′bly** *adj.* **-bli·er, -bli·est** —**wob′bli·ness** *n.*

woe (wō) *n.* [OE *wā*] 1 great sorrow; grief 2 trouble —*interj.* alas!

woe·be·gone (-bē gôn′, -bi-) *adj.* of woeful appearance; looking sad or wretched

woe·ful (-fəl) *adj.* 1 full of woe; sad 2 causing woe 3 pitiful; wretched —**woe′ful·ly** *adv.*

wok (wäk, wôk) *n.* [Chin] a bowl-shaped cooking pan used for frying, steaming, etc.

woke (wōk) *vi., vt. alt. pt. of* WAKE[1]

wok·en (wō′kən) *vi., vt. alt. pp. of* WAKE[1]

wolf (woolf) *n., pl.* **wolves** (woolvz) [OE *wulf*] 1 a wild, flesh-eating, doglike mammal of the Northern Hemisphere 2 *a)* a cruel or greedy person *b)* [Slang] a man who flirts aggressively with many women —*vt.* to eat greedily: often with *down* —**cry wolf** to give a false alarm —**wolf′ish** *adj.*

wolf·hound *n.* a breed of large dog, once used for hunting wolves

wol·ver·ine (wool′vər ēn′) *n.* [< WOLF] a stocky, flesh-eating mammal of N North America and N Eurasia

wolves (woolvz) *n. pl. of* WOLF

wom·an (woom′ən) *n., pl.* **wom·en** (wim′ən) [< OE *wīf,* a female + *mann,* human] 1 *a)* an adult female human *b)* women collectively 2 an adult female servant

-wom·an (woom′ən) *combining form* woman

of a (specified) kind, in a (specified) activity, etc.: sometimes used to avoid the masculine implications of -MAN

wom·an·hood *n.* 1 the state of being a woman 2 womanly qualities 3 women collectively

wom·an·ish *adj.* like or characteristic of a woman

wom·an·ize *vt.* **-ized′, -iz′ing** to make effeminate —*vi.* to be sexually promiscuous with women —**wom′an·iz′er** *n.*

wom·an·kind *n.* women in general

wom·an·ly *adj.* 1 womanish 2 characteristic of or fit for a woman —**wom′an·li·ness** *n.*

womb (woom) *n.* [OE *wamb*] UTERUS

wom·bat (wäm′bat′) *n.* [< native name] a burrowing marsupial resembling a small bear, found in Australia, etc.

wom·en (wim′in) *n. pl. of* WOMAN

wom·en·folk *pl.n.* [Inf. or Dial.] women or womankind: also **wom′en·folks′**

won (wun) *vi., vt. pt. & pp. of* WIN

won·der (wun′dər) *n.* [OE *wundor*] 1 a person, thing, or event causing astonishment and admiration; marvel 2 the feeling aroused by something strange, unexpected, etc. —*vi.* 1 to be filled with wonder; marvel 2 to have curiosity, sometimes mingled with doubt —*vt.* to have curiosity or doubt about [he *wondered* what happened]

won·der·ful *adj.* 1 that causes wonder; marvelous 2 excellent, fine, etc. —**won′der·ful·ly** *adv.*

won·der·land *n.* any place, real or imaginary, full of wonders

won·der·ment *n.* amazement

won·drous (wun′drəs) *adj.* wonderful: now chiefly literary —*adv.* [Archaic] surprisingly

wont (wônt, wōnt) *adj.* [< OE *wunian,* dwell] accustomed [she was *wont* to rise early] —*n.* usual practice; habit

won't (wōnt) *contr.* will not

wont·ed (wôn′tid, wōn′-) *adj.* customary

won ton (wän′ tän′) [Cantonese] Chinese dumplings of noodle dough filled with chopped meat, etc., often served in a soup (**won′-ton′** soup)

woo (woo) *vt.* [OE *wogian*] 1 to seek the love of, usually in order to propose marriage 2 to seek [to woo fame] —*vi.* to woo a person —**woo′er** *n.*

wood (wood) *n.* [OE *wudu*] 1 [usually *pl.,* with *sing.* or *pl. v.*] a thick growth of trees; forest 2 the hard, fibrous substance beneath the bark of trees and shrubs 3 lumber or timber 4 *Golf* any of certain clubs, originally with wooden heads —*adj.* 1 made of wood; wooden 2 growing or living in woods —**out of the woods** [Inf.] out of difficulty, danger, etc.

wood alcohol METHANOL

wood·bine (-bīn′) *n.* [< OE *wudu,* wood + *binde,* to bind] 1 a climbing honeysuckle 2 a climbing vine with dark-blue berries

wood·carv·ing *n.* 1 the art of carving wood by hand 2 an object so made —**wood′carv′er** *n.*

wood·chuck *n.* [< AmInd name] a burrowing and hibernating marmot of North America

wood·cock *n.* a small game bird with short legs and a long bill

wood·craft *n.* **1** skills relevant to traveling or living in the woods, as camping, hunting, etc. **2** WOODWORKING

wood·cut *n.* **1** a wooden block engraved with a design, etc. **2** a print from this

wood·cut·ter *n.* one who fells trees, cuts wood, etc. —**wood′cut′ting** *n.*

wood·ed *adj.* covered with trees

wood·en *adj.* **1** made of wood **2** stiff, lifeless, etc. **3** dull; insensitive —**wood′en·ly** *adv.*

wood·land (-lənd, -land′) *n.* land covered with woods —*adj.* of the woods

wood·lot *n.* a piece of land where trees are allowed to grow, as for firewood, lumber, etc.

wood·peck·er (-pek′ər) *n.* a climbing bird with a strong, pointed bill used to peck holes in trees to get insects

wood·pile *n.* a pile of wood, esp. of firewood

wood screw a screw with a sharp point, for use in wood

wood·shed *n.* a shed for storing firewood

woods·man (woodz′mən) *n., pl.* **-men** (-mən) **1** one who lives or works in the woods **2** one skilled in woodcraft

wood·sy (-zē) *adj.* **-si·er, -si·est** of or like the woods —**wood′si·ness** *n.*

wood·wind (wood′wind′) *n.* any of a family of wind instruments that produce sound through the vibration of a reed or by directing air across an opening

wood·work *n.* **1** work done in wood **2** the wooden moldings, doors, etc. of a house

wood·work·ing *n.* the art or work of making things of wood

wood·y *adj.* **-i·er, -i·est 1** covered with trees **2** consisting of or forming wood **3** like wood —**wood′i·ness** *n.*

woof¹ (woof) *n.* [ult. < OE *wefan*, to weave] WEFT

woof² (woof) *n.* [echoic] the gruff barking sound of a dog —*vi.* to make this sound

woof·er (woof′ər) *n.* a large, high-fidelity speaker for reproducing low-frequency sounds

wool (wool) *n.* [OE *wull*] **1** the soft, curly hair of sheep or of some other animals, as the goat **2** woolen yarn, cloth, clothing, etc. **3** anything that looks or feels like wool

wool·en *adj.* **1** made of wool **2** relating to wool or woolen cloth —*n.* [*pl.*] woolen goods Also [Chiefly Brit.] **wool′len**

Woolf (woolf), **Virginia** 1882-1941; Eng. novelist & critic

wool·gath·er·ing (-gath′ər iŋ) *n.* aimless daydreaming or speculation

wool·ly (wool′ē) *adj.* **-li·er, -li·est 1** of or like wool **2** bearing or covered with wool **3** rough and uncivilized: used chiefly in **wild and woolly 4** confused [*woolly* ideas] Also sp. **wool′y**

wooz·y (woo′zē, wooz′ē) *adj.* **-i·er, -i·est** [Inf.] dizzy or befuddled, as from drink or a blow —**wooz′i·ness** *n.*

Worces·ter·shire sauce (woos′tər shir′) a spicy sauce for meats, poultry, etc., containing soy, vinegar, and other ingredients: orig. made in Worcester, England

word (wurd) *n.* [OE] **1** *a*) a speech sound, or series of such sounds, having meaning as a unit of language *b*) the written or printed representation of this **2** a brief remark [a *word* of advice] **3** a promise or assurance [he gave his *word*] **4** news; information **5** *a*) a password *b*) a command, order, etc. **6** [*usually pl.*] *a*) speech *b*) lyrics **7** [*pl.*] a quarrel —*vt.* to put into words; phrase —**in a word** briefly —**in so many words** exactly and plainly —**the Word** the Bible, or, specif., the Gospels —**word for word** in precisely the same words

word·age *n.* **1** words **2** wordiness

word·ing *n.* choice of words; diction

word of honor solemn promise

word of mouth speech, as opposed to writing

word·play *n.* **1** repartee **2** punning

word processor a device or program for digitally composing and editing texts —**word processing**

Words·worth (wurdz′wərth), **William** 1770-1850; Eng. poet

word·y (wur′dē) *adj.* **-i·er, -i·est** containing or using too many words; verbose —**word′i·ness** *n.*

wore (wôr) *vt., vi. pt. of* WEAR

work (wurk) *n.* [OE *weorc*] **1** effort exerted to do or make something; labor; toil **2** employment; occupation **3** something one is making or doing; task **4** something made or done; specif., *a*) an act; deed (*usually used in pl.*) [*good works*] *b*) [*pl.*] collected writings *c*) [*pl.*] engineering structures, as bridges, dams, etc. **5** [*pl., with sing. v.*] a place where work is done, as a factory **6** workmanship **7** *Physics* force exerted multiplied by the distance over which it is exerted —*adj.* of, for, or used in work —*vi.* **worked** or **wrought**, **work′ing 1** to do work; labor; toil **2** to be employed **3** to function or operate, esp. effectively **4** to ferment **5** to move, proceed, etc. slowly and with difficulty **6** to come or become, as by repeated movement [the door *worked* loose] —*vt.* **1** to cause; bring about [his idea *worked* wonders] **2** to mold; shape **3** to solve (a mathematical problem, etc.) **4** to manipulate; knead **5** to bring into a specified condition, as by moving back and forth [to *work* a nail loose] **6** to cultivate (soil) **7** to operate; use **8** to cause to work [to *work* a crew hard] **9** to make (one's way, etc.) by effort **10** to provoke; rouse [to *work* oneself into a rage] **11** [Slang] to proceed ingratiatingly through (a crowd, etc.) —**at work** working —**in the works** in the process of being planned or done —**out of work** unemployed —**the works 1** the working parts (*of* a watch, etc.) **2** [Inf.] everything: also **the whole works** —**work off** to get rid of —**work on 1** to influence **2** to try to persuade —**work out 1** to solve **2** to result **3** to develop **4** to have a workout —**work up 1** to advance **2** to develop **3** to excite

work·a·ble (wurʹkə bəl) *adj.* **1** that can be worked **2** practicable; feasible

work·a·day (-dā′) *adj.* **1** of workdays; everyday **2** ordinary

work·a·hol·ic (-hôlʹik) *n.* ⟦WORK + -AHOLIC⟧ a person having an irrational need to work

work·bench *n.* a table at which work is done, as by a carpenter

work·book *n.* a book of questions, exercises, etc. for use by students

work·day *n.* **1** a day on which work is ordinarily done **2** the part of a day during which work is done

work·er *n.* **1** one who works for a living **2** one who works for a cause, etc. **3** a sterile female ant, bee, etc. that does work for the colony

work·fare *n.* ⟦WORK + (WEL)FARE⟧ a government program requiring employable recipients of welfare to register for work, training, etc.

work·flow *n.* the steps or operations into which a particular task is organized

work·force *n.* the total number of available workers

work·horse *n.* **1** a horse used for working **2** a reliable worker with a heavy workload

work·house *n.* **1** [Historical] a poorhouse having a program of compulsory labor **2** a prison where petty offenders are confined and made to work

work·ing *adj.* **1** that works **2** of, for, or used in work **3** sufficient to get work done **4** on which further work may be based [a *working* hypothesis] —*n.* the act of one that works

working class the social class consisting of industrial and manual workers

work·load *n.* the amount of work assigned for completion within a given time period

work·man (-mən) *n., pl.* **-men** (-mən) **1** a man who performs work for pay **2** a craftsman

work·man·like *adj.* capable; competent

work·man·ship *n.* skill of a workman or the quality of the work done

work·out *n.* a session of physical exercises or any strenuous work

work·place *n.* the office, factory, etc. where one works

work·sheet *n.* a paper sheet with working notes, etc., or with problems, etc. to be worked on by students

work·shop *n.* **1** a room or building where work is done **2** a seminar for specified intensive study, work, etc.

work·sta·tion *n.* **1** a person's work area, including furniture, etc. and, often, a computer **2** a terminal or personal computer connected to a network

work·ta·ble *n.* a table at which work is done

work·up *n.* a complete medical study of a patient, including tests

work·week *n.* the total number of hours or days worked in a week

world (wurld) *n.* ⟦OE *werold*⟧ **1** *a)* the earth *b)* the universe **2** *a)* humankind *b)* people generally; the public **3** *a)* [also **W-**] some part of the earth [the Old *World*] *b)* any sphere or domain [the animal *world*] **4** individual experience, outlook, etc. [her *world* is narrow] **5** secular life and interests, or people concerned with these **6** [*often pl.*] a large amount [a *world* of good] —**bring into the world 1** to give birth to **2** to assist in the delivery of (a baby) —**for all the world** exactly

world-class *adj.* of the highest class, as in international competition

world·ly *adj.* **-li·er, -li·est 1** of this world; secular **2** devoted to the affairs, pleasures, etc. of this world **3** worldly-wise —**world′li·ness** *n.*

world·ly-wise *adj.* wise in the ways or affairs of the world; sophisticated

world-shak·ing *adj.* of great significance, effect, or influence; momentous

world·view *n.* a comprehensive, esp. personal, philosophy of the world and of human life

World War I the war (1914-18) involving Great Britain, France, Russia, the U.S., etc. on one side and Germany, Austria-Hungary, etc. on the other

World War II the war (1939-45) involving Great Britain, France, the Soviet Union, the U.S., etc. on one side and Germany, Italy, Japan, etc. on the other

world-wea·ry *adj.* bored with living

world-wide *adj., adv.* (extending) throughout the world

World Wide Web a group of internet sources giving access to text, images, sound, etc.

worm (wurm) *n.* ⟦< OE *wyrm*, serpent⟧ **1** a long, slender, soft-bodied animal **2** an abject or contemptible person **3** something spiral in shape, etc., as the thread of a screw **4** [*pl.*] any disease caused by parasitic worms in the intestines, etc. **5** a computer virus that depletes memory by replicating itself —*vi.* to proceed like a worm, in a winding or devious manner —*vt.* **1** to bring about, get, make, etc. in a winding or devious manner **2** to purge of intestinal worms —**worm′y** *adj.* **-i·er, -i·est**

worm gear a gear consisting of a rotating screw meshed with a toothed wheel

worm·wood (-wood′) *n.* ⟦< OE *wermod*⟧ a strong-smelling plant that yields a bitter-tasting oil used in making absinthe

worn (wôrn) *vt., vi. pp. of* WEAR —*adj.* **1** damaged by use or wear **2** showing the effects of worry or anxiety

worn-out *adj.* **1** used until no longer effective, usable, etc. **2** exhausted; tired out

wor·ri·ment (wurʹē mənt) *n.* (a) worry

wor·ri·some (-səm) *adj.* causing worry

wor·ry (wurʹē) *vt.* **-ried, -ry·ing** ⟦< OE *wyrgan*, to strangle⟧ **1** to treat roughly, as with continual biting [a dog *worrying* a bone] **2** to annoy, bother, etc. **3** to make troubled or uneasy —*vi.* **1** to bite or tear (at an object) **2** to be anxious, troubled, etc. —*n., pl.* **-ries 1** a troubled state of mind; anxiety **2** a cause of this —**wor′ri·er** *n.*

wor·ry·wart (-wôrt´) *n.* 〖prec. + WART〗 [Inf.] one who tends to worry, esp. over trivial matters

worse (wurs) *adj.* 〖OE *wiersa*〗 **1** *compar. of* BAD[1] & ILL **2** *a)* bad, evil, harmful, etc. in a greater degree *b)* of inferior quality **3** in poorer health; more ill **4** in a less satisfactory condition —*adv.* **1** *compar. of* BADLY & ILL **2** in a worse manner **3** to a worse extent —*n.* that which is worse —**worse off** in worse circumstances

wor·sen (wur´sən) *vt., vi.* to make or become worse

wor·ship (wur´ship) *n.* 〖< OE *weorthscipe*〗 **1** a service or rite showing reverence for a deity **2** intense love or admiration **3** [W-] [Chiefly Brit.] a title of honor: used in addressing magistrates, etc. —*vt.* **-shiped** or **-shipped**, **-ship·ing** or **-ship·ping 1** to show religious reverence for **2** to have intense love or admiration for —*vi.* to engage in worship —**wor´-ship·er** *n.*, **wor´ship·per** *n.*

wor·ship·ful (-fəl) *adj.* feeling or offering great devotion or respect

worst (wurst) *adj.* 〖OE *wyrsta*〗 **1** *superl. of* BAD[1] & ILL **2** *a)* bad, evil, harmful, etc. in the highest degree *b)* of the lowest quality **3** in the least satisfactory condition —*adv.* **1** *superl. of* BADLY & ILL **2** in the worst manner **3** to the worst extent —*n.* that which is worst —*vt.* to defeat —**at worst** even under the worst circumstances —**if (the) worst comes to (the) worst** if the worst possible thing happens —**(in) the worst way** [Inf.] very much; greatly

wor·sted (woos´tid, wur´stid) *n.* 〖after Worstead, England〗 **1** a smooth, firmly twisted wool thread or yarn **2** fabric made from this

wort (wurt) *n.* 〖OE *wyrt*〗 a liquid, produced from malt, that can be fermented to make beer, etc.

worth (wurth) *n.* 〖OE *weorth*〗 **1** material value, esp. as expressed in terms of money **2** importance, value, merit, etc. **3** the quantity to be had for a given sum [a dollar's *worth*] —*prep.* **1** deserving or worthy of **2** equal in value to **3** having wealth amounting to

worth·less *adj.* without worth or merit; useless —**worth´less·ness** *n.*

worth·while *adj.* worth the time or effort spent

wor·thy (wur´thē) *adj.* **-thi·er, -thi·est 1** having worth, value, or merit **2** meriting —*n., pl.* **-thies** a person of outstanding worth, etc. —**wor´thi·ly** *adv.* —**wor´thi·ness** *n.*

would (wood) *v.aux.* 〖OE *wolde*〗 **1** *pt. of* WILL[2] **2** used to express a supposition or condition [he *would* write if he knew you *would* answer] **3** used to make a polite request [*would* you please open the window?] —*vt.* [Old Poet.] I wish: often used without an explicit grammatical subject [*would* that she were here] See usage note at WILL[2]

would-be *adj.* **1** wishing or pretending to be **2** intended to be

wound[1] (woond) *n.* 〖OE *wund*〗 **1** an injury in which tissue is cut, torn, etc. **2** any hurt to the feelings, honor, etc. —*vt., vi.* to inflict a wound (on or upon); injure

wound[2] (wound) *vt., vi. pt. & pp. of* WIND[1]

wove (wōv) *vt., vi. pt. & alt. pp. of* WEAVE

wo·ven (wō´vən) *vt., vi. alt. pp. of* WEAVE

wow (wou) *interj.* used to express surprise, pleasure, etc. —*vt.* [Slang] to arouse enthusiasm in

wpm *abbrev.* words per minute

wrack (rak) *n.* 〖< MDu *wrak*, a wreck〗 *alt. sp. of* RACK[2]

wraith (rāth) *n.* 〖Scot〗 a ghost

wran·gle[1] (raŋ´gəl) *vi.* **-gled, -gling** 〖< OE *wringan*, to press〗 to argue; quarrel, esp. noisily —*n.* a noisy dispute —**wran´gler** *n.*

wran·gle[2] (raŋ´gəl) *vt.* **-gled, -gling** 〖back-form. < WRANGLER[2]〗 to herd (livestock, esp. saddle horses)

wran·gler (-glər) *n.* 〖< AmSp *caballerango*, a groom〗 **1** a cowboy who herds livestock, esp. saddle horses **2** one who manages animals, as on a movie set —**wran´gle** *vt.* **-gled, -gling**

wrap (rap) *vt.* **wrapped, wrap´ping** 〖ME *wrappen*〗 **1** to wind or fold (a covering) around something **2** to enclose and fasten in paper, etc. —*vi.* to twine, coil, etc.: usually with *over, around*, etc. —*n.* **1** an outer covering or garment **2** [*pl.*] secrecy; censorship [to keep plans under *wraps*] **3** a sandwich made with folded flatbread **4** *Film* the completion of the filming of a scene, etc. —**wrapped up in** engrossed in or involved in —**wrap up** [Inf.] to conclude; settle

wrap·per *n.* **1** one that wraps **2** that in which something is wrapped **3** a woman's dressing gown

wrap·ping *n.* [*often pl.*] the material in which something is wrapped

wrap-up *n.* [Inf.] a concluding, summarizing statement, report, etc.

wrath (rath) *n.* 〖OE, angry〗 intense anger; rage; fury —**wrath´ful** *adj.*

wreak (rēk) *vt.* 〖OE *wrecan*, to revenge〗 **1** to give vent to (one's anger, etc.) **2** to inflict (vengeance, etc.)

wreath (rēth) *n., pl.* **wreaths** (rēthz, rēths) 〖OE *writha*〗 **1** a twisted ring of leaves, flowers, etc. **2** something like this in shape [*wreaths* of smoke]

wreathe (rēth) *vt.* **wreathed, wreath´ing 1** to form into a wreath **2** to coil or twist around; encircle **3** to decorate with wreaths

wreck (rek) *n.* 〖< ON *vrek*, driftwood〗 **1** a shipwreck **2** the remains of something destroyed **3** a run-down person **4** a wrecking or being wrecked —*vt.* **1** to destroy or damage badly **2** to tear down (a building, etc.) **3** to overthrow or thwart

wreck·age *n.* **1** a wrecking or being wrecked **2** the remains of something wrecked

wreck·er *n.* **1** one who wrecks **2** one that salvages or removes wrecks, esp. a tow truck used in salvaging vehicles

wren (ren) *n.* 〖OE *wrenna*〗 a small songbird with a stubby, erect tail

wrench (rench) *n.* 〖OE *wrenc*, a trick〗 **1** a sudden, sharp twist or pull **2** an injury caused by a twist, as to the back **3** a sudden feeling of grief, etc. **4** a tool for turning nuts, bolts, pipes, etc. —*vt.* **1** to twist or jerk violently **2** to injure with a twist **3** to distort (a meaning, etc.)

wrest (rest) *vt.* ⟦OE *wrǣstan*⟧ **1** to pull or force away violently with a twisting motion **2** to take by force

wres·tle (res**ʹ**əl; *often* ras**ʹ**-) *vi., vt.* **-tled, -tling** ⟦see prec.⟧ **1** to struggle hand to hand with (an opponent) in an attempt to throw or immobilize him or her **2** to contend (*with*) —*n.* a wrestling —**wres·tler** *n.*

wres·tling *n.* a sport in which the opponents wrestle, or struggle hand to hand

wretch (rech) *n.* ⟦OE *wrecca*, an outcast⟧ **1** a miserable or unhappy person **2** a despised person

wretch·ed *adj.* **1** very unhappy; miserable **2** distressing; dismal **3** poor in quality **4** contemptible —**wretch′ed·ly** *adv.* —**wretch′ed·ness** *n.*

wrig·gle (rig**ʹ**əl) *vi.* **-gled, -gling** ⟦medieval Low G *wriggeln*⟧ **1** to twist and turn; squirm **2** to move along with a twisting motion **3** to make one's way by shifty means —*n.* a wriggling —**wrig′gler** *n.* —**wrig′gly** *adj.* **-gli·er, -gli·est**

wright (rīt) *n.* ⟦< OE *wyrcan*, to work⟧ one who makes or constructs: chiefly in compounds [*shipwright*]

wring (riŋ) *vt.* **wrung, wring′ing** ⟦OE *wringan*⟧ **1** *a)* to squeeze, press, or twist *b)* to force out (water, etc.) by this means (usually with *out*) **2** to clasp and twist (the hands) in distress **3** to clasp (another's hand) forcefully in greeting **4** to extract by force, threats, etc. —*n.* a wringing

wring·er *n.* a machine with rollers to squeeze water from wet clothes

wrin·kle¹ (riŋ**ʹ**kəl) *n.* ⟦ME *wrinkel*⟧ **1** a small furrow in a normally smooth surface **2** a crease in the skin — *vt., vi.* **-kled, -kling** to form wrinkles (in); pucker; crease —**wrin′kly** *adj.* **-kli·er, -kli·est**

wrin·kle² (riŋ**ʹ**kəl) *n.* ⟦< OE *wrenc*, a trick⟧ [Inf.] a clever innovation

wrist (rist) *n.* ⟦OE⟧ the joint between the hand and forearm —**a slap** (or **tap**) **on the wrist** a token punishment

wrist·band *n.* a band that goes around the wrist, as on a cuff

wrist·watch *n.* a watch worn on a strap or band around the wrist

writ¹ (rit) *n.* ⟦OE < *writan*, write⟧ **1** a formal legal document ordering or prohibiting some action **2** scriptures

writ² (rit) *vt., vi. archaic pt. & pp. of* WRITE: now mainly in the phrase **writ large**, expressed or done on a larger scale, more clearly, or more emphatically

write (rīt) *vt.* **wrote, writ′ten, writ′ing** ⟦OE *writan*⟧ **1** to form (words, letters, etc.) on a surface, as with a pen **2** to compose (literary or musical material) **3** to communicate (with) in writing [she *wrote* (me) that she

was ill] **4** to cover with writing [to *write* three pages] **5** to fill in (a bank check, etc.) **6** to show clearly [anger was *written* on his face] **7** *Comput.* to record (information) on a disk, etc. —*vi.* to produce writing —**write off 1** to remove from accounts (bad debts, etc.) **2** to drop from consideration **3** to amortize —**write out 1** to put into writing **2** to write in full —**write up** to write an account of

write-in *n.* **1** a candidate whose name is not on the ballot, but is written in by a voter **2** a vote of this kind

write-off *n.* a cancelled debt, amortized expense, etc.

writ·er *n.* one who writes, esp. as an occupation; author

write-up *n.* [Inf.] a written report

writhe (rīth) *vi.* **writhed, writh′ing** ⟦OE *writhan*, to twist⟧ **1** to twist or turn; squirm [to *writhe* in agony] **2** to suffer great emotional distress

writ·ing (rīt**ʹ**iŋ) *n.* **1** the act of one who writes **2** something written **3** written form **4** *short for* HANDWRITING

writ·ten (rit**ʹ**n) *vt., vi. pp. of* WRITE

wrong (rôŋ) *adj.* ⟦< ON *rangr*, twisted⟧ **1** not in accordance with justice, law, morality, etc. **2** not suitable or appropriate **3** *a)* contrary to fact, etc.; incorrect *b)* mistaken **4** not functioning properly **5** not meant to be seen [the *wrong* side of a fabric] —*adv.* in a wrong manner, direction, etc. —*n.* an unjust, immoral, or illegal act —*vt.* to treat badly or unjustly —**wrong′ly** *adv.* —**wrong′ness** *n.*

wrong·do·ing *n.* any wrong act or behavior —**wrong′do′er** *n.*

wrong·ful *adj.* **1** unjust or injurious **2** unlawful —**wrong′ful·ly** *adv.*

wrong·head·ed *adj.* stubborn or perverse —**wrong′head′ed·ly** *adv.* —**wrong′head′ed·ness** *n.*

wrote (rōt) *vt., vi. pt. of* WRITE

wroth (rôth) *adj.* ⟦OE *wrath*⟧ angry

wrought (rôt) *vi., vt. alt. pt. & pp. of* WORK —*adj.* **1** formed; made **2** shaped by hammering, etc.: said of metals

wrought iron tough, ductile iron containing very little carbon —**wrought′-i′ron** *adj.*

wrought-up *adj.* very disturbed

wrung (ruŋ) *vt. pt. & pp. of* WRING

wry (rī) *adj.* **wri′er** or **wry′er, wri′est** or **wry′est** ⟦< OE *wrigian*, to turn⟧ **1** distorted in a grimace [a *wry* face] **2** ironic, dry, etc. [*wry* humor] —**wry′ly** *adv.* —**wry′ness** *n.*

wt *abbrev.* weight

Wu·han (wōō′hän′) city in EC China

wuss (woos) *n.* [Slang] a person who is regarded as weak, ineffectual, etc.; wimp: also **wuss′y,** *pl.* **wuss′ies**

WV *abbrev.* West Virginia

WWI *abbrev.* World War I

WWII *abbrev.* World War II

WWW or **www** *abbrev.* World Wide Web

Wy·o·ming (wī ō′miŋ) Mountain State of the W U.S.; cap. Cheyenne: abbrev. **WY** —**Wy·o′ ming·ite′** *n.*

x¹ or **X** (eks) *n., pl.* **x's, X's** **1** the 24th letter of the English alphabet **2** *Math.* an unknown quantity

x² *abbrev.* extra: also **X**

X (eks) *n.* **1** the Roman numeral 10 **2** a film rating meaning that no one under seventeen is to be admitted

X chromosome *see* SEX CHROMOSOME

Xe *Chem. symbol for* xenon

xe·non (zē′nän′) *n.* a colorless, nonreactive, gaseous chemical element: symbol, Xe; at. no. 54

xen·o·pho·bi·a (zen′ə fō′bē ə, zēn′ə-) *n.* [< Gr *xenos,* foreign + -PHOBIA] fear or hatred of strangers or foreigners —**xen′o·phobe′** (-fōb′) *n.* —**xen′o·pho′bic** (-fō′bik) *adj.*

xe·rog·ra·phy (zir äg′rə fē) *n.* [< Gr *xēros,* dry + -GRAPHY] a process for copying printed material, etc. by the action of light on an electrically charged surface

Xe·rox (zir′äks′) *trademark for* a device for copying by xerography —*vt., vi. [usually* **x-**] to reproduce by xerography —*n. [usually* **x-**] a copy so made

Xer·xes I (zurk′sēz′) 519?-465 B.C.; king of Persia (486-465)

xi (zī, sī) *n.* the 14th letter of the Greek alphabet (Ξ, ξ)

XL *abbrev.* extra large

X·mas (eks′məs) *n. inf. var. of* CHRISTMAS

X-rat·ed (eks′rāt′əd) *adj.* designating or like a film with a rating of X; explicit, obscene, etc.

X-ray (eks′rā′) *n.* **1** a type of electromagnetic wave of very short wavelength, that can penetrate solid substances: used to study internal body structures and treat various disorders **2** a photograph made by means of X-rays —*adj.* of or by X-rays —*vt.* to examine, treat, or photograph with X-rays Also **X ray, x-ray,** or **x ray**

XS *abbrev.* extra small

xy·lem (zī′ləm) *n.* [< Gr *xylon,* wood] the woody vascular tissue of a plant

xy·lo·phone (zī′lə fōn′) *n.* [< Gr *xylon,* wood + -PHONE] a musical percussion instrument consisting of a series of graduated wooden bars that are struck with small, wooden mallets —**xy′lo·phon′ist** (-fō′nist, zī läf′ə nist) *n.*

y or **Y** (wī) *n., pl.* **y's, Y's** the 25th letter of the English alphabet

Y¹ *abbrev. Chem. symbol for* yttrium

Y² *abbrev.* **1** yen: now usually ¥ **2** yes

-y¹ (ē, i) [ME] *suffix* little one, dear [*kitty, daddy*]

-y² (ē, i) [OE -*ig*] *suffix* **1** full of, like [*dirty*] **2** somewhat [*yellowy*] **3** tending to [*sticky*]

-y³ (ē, i) [< L -*ia*] *suffix* **1** quality or condition [*jealousy*] **2** a (specified) kind of shop, goods, or group [*bakery*]

-y⁴ (ē, i) [< L -*ium*] *suffix* action of [*inquiry*]

yacht (yät) *n.* [Du *jacht*] a small vessel for pleasure cruises, racing, etc. —**yacht·ing** (-iŋ) *n.* the sport of sailing a yacht —**yachts′man** (-mən) *n., pl.* **-men** (-mən)

ya·hoo (yä′hōō′) *n.* [after a race of people in Swift's novel *Gulliver's Travels*] a person regarded as vulgar, uneducated, etc. —*interj.* used to express triumph or great delight

Yah·weh (yä′we, -wä) *n.* [< Heb] God

yak¹ (yak) *n.* [< Tibet *g-yag*] a long-haired wild or domesticated ox of central Asia

yak² (yak) [echoic] *vi.* **yakked, yak′king** [echoic] to talk much or idly —*n.* a yakking

yam (yam) *n.* [< WAfr native name] **1** the edible, starchy, tuberous root of a tropical climbing plant **2** an orange-colored variety of sweet potato

yam·mer (yam′ər) *vi.* [< OE *geomerian,* to lament] **1** to shout, yell, etc. **2** to talk loudly or continuously —**yam′mer·er** *n.*

yang (yäŋ, yaŋ) *n.* [Chin] in Chinese philosophy, the masculine force or principle in the universe: cf. YIN

Yan·gon (yan gōn′) capital of Myanmar

Yang·tze (yaŋk′sē) *a former transliteration of* CHANG

yank (yaŋk) *n., vt., vi.* [< ?] [Inf.] jerk

Yank (yaŋk) *n.* [Slang] a Yankee

Yan·kee (yaŋ′kē) *n.* [< Du *Jan Kees,* a disparaging nickname] **1** a New Englander, esp. one of colonial English ancestry **2** a person born or living in the northern U.S. **3** a citizen of the U.S. —*adj.* of or like Yankees

yap (yap) *vi.* **yapped, yap′ping** [echoic] **1** to make a sharp, shrill bark **2** [Slang] to talk noisily and stupidly —*n.* **1** a sharp, shrill bark **2** [Slang] *a)* jabber *b)* the mouth

yard' (yärd) *n.* [OE *gierd*, rod] **1** a measure of length, 3 feet or 36 inches **2** *Naut.* a slender rod or spar fastened across a mast to support a sail

yard² (yärd) *n.* [OE *geard*, enclosure] **1** the ground around or next to a building **2** an enclosed place for a particular purpose [*ship-yard*]

yard·age *n.* **1** measurement in yards **2** the extent so measured

yard·arm *n.* *Naut.* either half of a yard supporting a square sail, etc.

yard goods textiles made in standard widths, usually sold by the yard

yard·man (yärd′man′, -mən) *n., pl.* **-men′** (-men′, -mən) a person who works in a yard, esp. a railroad yard

yard·sale *n.* GARAGE SALE

yard·stick *n.* **1** a graduated measuring stick one yard long **2** any standard used in judging, etc.

yard·work *n.* the work of caring for the lawn, trees, etc. of a yard adjacent to a house

yar·mul·ke (yär′məl kə, yä′-) *n.* [Yiddish < Pol] a skullcap traditionally worn by Jewish men, as at prayer: also sp. **yar′mel·ke**

yarn (yärn) *n.* [OE *gearn*] **1** fibers of wool, cotton, etc. spun into strands for weaving, knitting, etc. **2** [Inf.] a tale or story

yaw (yô) *vi.* [ON *jaga*, to sway] **1** to swing back and forth across its course, as a ship does when pushed by high waves **2** to rotate or oscillate about the vertical axis: said of a spacecraft, etc. —*n.* a yawing

yawl (yôl) *n.* [< Du *jol*] a fore-and-aft-rigged sailboat with a small second mast near the stern

yawn (yôn) *vi.* [ME *yanen*] **1** to open the mouth involuntarily and inhale, as when one is sleepy or bored **2** to open wide —*n.* a yawning

yaws (yôz) *n.* [of WInd origin] an infectious skin disease of the tropics

yay (yā) [Inf.] *adv.* this; so: often with a gesture indicating size —*interj.* YEA

Y chromosome *see* SEX CHROMOSOME

yd *abbrev.* yard(s): also, for the plural, **yds**

ye' (thə, thi, thē; now often erroneously or facetiously yē) *adj., definite article* archaic var. of THE

ye² (yē) *pron.* [OE *ge*] [Archaic] YOU

yea (yā) *adv.* [OE *gea*] **1** yes **2** indeed; truly —*n.* **1** an affirmative vote **2** a person voting in the affirmative —*interj.* [Inf.] hurray: a shout used in cheering for a team

yeah (ya, ye) *adv.* [Inf.] yes

year (yir) *n.* [OE *gear*] **1** a period of 365 days (366 days in leap year), divided into 12 months beginning Jan. 1 **2** the period (365 days, 5 hours, 48 minutes, and 46 seconds) of one revolution of the earth around the sun: also **solar year 3** a period of 12 calendar months reckoned from any date **4** an annual period of less than 365 days [a

school *year*] **5** [*pl.*] *a)* age [old for his *years*] *b)* a long time [*years* ago] —**year after year** every year

year·book *n.* an annual book; specif., *a)* a book giving data of the preceding year *b)* a publication of the graduating class of a school or college

year·ling *n.* an animal in its second year

year·ly *adj.* **1** done, happening, appearing, etc. once a year, or every year [a *yearly* event] **2** of a year, or of each year —*adv.* every year

yearn (yurn) *vi.* [< OE *georn*, eager] to be filled with longing or desire —**yearn′ing** *n.*

year·round *adj.* open, in use, operating, etc. throughout the year

yea·say·er *n.* one having a positive attitude toward life

yeast (yēst) *n.* [OE *gist*] **1** a moist, yellowish mass of certain fungi that cause fermentation: used in making beer, etc., and as leavening in baking **2** yeast dried in flakes or granules or compressed into cakes **3** ferment; agitation

yeast·y *adj.* **-i·er, -i·est 1** of, like, or containing yeast **2** in a ferment; restless

yell (yel) *vi., vt.* [OE *giellan*] to cry out loudly; scream —*n.* **1** a loud outcry **2** a rhythmic cheer in unison —**yell′er** *n.*

yel·low (yel′ō) *adj.* [OE *geolu*] **1** of the color of ripe lemons **2** having a somewhat yellow skin **3** [Inf.] cowardly **4** sensational: said of a newspaper —*n.* **1** a yellow color **2** an egg yolk —*vi.* to become yellow —**yel′low·ish** *adj.*

yel·low·cake *n.* a uranium concentrate extracted from ores

yellow fever an infectious tropical disease caused by a virus transmitted by the bite of a certain mosquito

yellow jacket a wasp or hornet having bright-yellow markings

Yel·low·knife capital of Northwest Territories, Canada

Yellow River HUANG

Yellow Sea arm of the East China Sea, between China & Korea

yelp (yelp) *vi.* [OE *gielpan*, to boast] to utter a short, sharp cry or bark, as a dog does —*n.* a short, sharp cry or bark

Yem·en (yem′ən) country in S Arabia —**Yem′en·ite′** *adj., n.*

yen' (yen) *n., pl.* **yen** [Jpn] the monetary unit of Japan

yen² (yen) *n.* [prob. < Chin *yan*, opium] [Inf.] a strong longing or desire

yeo·man (yō′mən) *n., pl.* **-men** (-mən) [ME *yeman*] **1** [Brit. Historical] a freeholder of a class below the gentry **2** *U.S. Navy* a petty officer assigned to clerical duty

yeo·man·ry *n.* yeomen collectively

yes (yes) *adv.* [OE *gese*] **1** aye; yea; it is so: expressing agreement, consent, etc. **2** not only that, but more [ready, *yes*, eager to help] —*n., pl.* **yes′es** an act of saying *yes*; an affirmative reply, vote, etc. — *vt., vi.* yessed, yes′sing to say *yes* (to)

ye·shi·va (yə shē′və; *Heb* ye shē vä′) *n., pl.*

-vas ⟦Heb., lit., act of sitting⟧ a Jewish school combining religious and secular studies

yes man [Inf.] one who uncritically agrees with what is said by a superior

yes·ter·day (yes′tər dā′) *n.* ⟦OE *geostran*, yesterday + *dæg*, day⟧ **1** the day before today **2** a recent day or time —*adv.* **1** on the day before today **2** recently

yes·ter·year (-yir′) *n., adv.* **1** last year **2** (in) past years

yet (yet) *adv.* ⟦OE *giet*⟧ **1** up to now; thus far [he hasn't gone *yet*] **2** at the present time; now [we can't go just *yet*] **3** still [there is *yet* a chance] **4** in addition; even [he was *yet* more kind] **5** nevertheless [she's kind, *yet* shy] —*conj.* but [she seems well, *yet* she is ill] —**as yet** up to now

yew (yōō) *n.* ⟦OE *iw*⟧ **1** an evergreen tree with flattened needles and bright red berrylike structures **2** its wood

Yid·dish (yid′ish) *n.* ⟦< Ger *jüdisch*, < L *Judaeus*, Jew⟧ a language derived from medieval High German, written in the Hebrew alphabet and spoken esp. by Eastern European Jews

yield (yēld) *vt.* ⟦OE *gieldan*, to pay⟧ **1** to produce as a crop, result, profit, etc. **2** to surrender **3** to concede —*vi.* **1** to produce **2** to surrender **3** to give way to physical force **4** to lose precedence, etc.: often with *to* —*n.* the amount yielded

yield·ing *adj.* **1** flexible **2** submissive

yin (yin) *n.* ⟦Chin⟧ in Chinese philosophy, the feminine force or principle in the universe: cf. YANG

yip (yip) *n.* ⟦echoic⟧ [Inf.] a yelp, or bark —*vi.* **yipped, yip′ping** [Inf.] to yelp, or bark

YMCA *abbrev.* Young Men's Christian Association

yo (yō) *interj.* [Inf.] used as to gain attention, greet someone, emphasize a remark, etc.

yo·del (yōd′'l) *vt., vi.* **-deled** or **-delled, -deling** or **-del·ling** ⟦Ger *jodeln*⟧ to sing with abrupt alternating changes in vocal register —*n.* a yodeling

yo·ga (yō′gə) *n.* ⟦Sans, union⟧ a mystical and ascetic Hindu discipline for achieving union with the supreme spirit through meditation, prescribed postures, controlled breathing, etc.

yo·gi (yō′gē) *n., pl.* **-gis** one who practices yoga: also **yo′gin** (-gin)

yo·gurt (yō′gərt) *n.* ⟦Turk *yogurt*⟧ a thick, somewhat solid food made from fermented milk: also sp. **yo′ghurt**

yoke (yōk) *n.* ⟦OE *geoc*⟧ **1** a wooden frame for harnessing together a pair of oxen, etc. **2** such a pair harnessed together **3** bondage; servitude **4** anything like a yoke, as something that binds or unites, or a part of a garment fitted to the shoulders or hips as a support for the gathered parts below —*vt.* **yoked, yok′ing 1** to harness (an animal) to (a plow, etc.) **2** to join together

yo·kel (yō′kəl) *n.* a person living in a rural area; bumpkin: a contemptuous term

Yo·ko·ha·ma (yō′kə hä′mə) seaport in S Honshu, Japan

yolk (yōk) *n.* ⟦OE *geolca*⟧ the yellow, principal substance of an egg

Yom Kip·pur (yäm′ ki poor′) the Day of Atonement: a major Jewish holiday and a day of fasting

yon (yän) *adj., adv.* ⟦OE *geon*⟧ [Now Chiefly Dial.] yonder: also **yond** (yänd)

yon·der (yän′dər) *adj., adv.* ⟦ME⟧ (being) at or in that (specified or relatively distant) place; over there

yoo-hoo (yōō′hōō′) *interj., n.* (a shout or call) used to attract someone's attention

yore (yôr) *adv.* ⟦OE *geara*⟧ [Obs.] long ago —**of yore** formerly

you (yōō) *pron., pl.* **you** ⟦OE *eow* < *ge*, YE²⟧ **1** the person or persons spoken to **2** a person or people generally; one [*you* can never tell!]

young (yuŋ) *adj.* **young′er** (-gər), **young′est** (-gəst) ⟦OE *geong*⟧ **1** being in an early period of life or growth **2** youthful; fresh; vigorous **3** in an early stage **4** inexperienced; immature —*n.* **1** young people: often with *the* **2** young offspring —**with young** pregnant —**young′ish** *adj.*

young adult an age group, from about 12 to about 18 years of age, used as a reader category as in libraries

young blood 1 young people; youth **2** youthful strength, vigor, etc.

young·ster *n.* a child or youth

your (yoor; *often* yôr) *poss. pronominal adj.* ⟦OE *eower*⟧ of, belonging to, or done by you: also used before some titles [*Your* Honor]

you're (yoor, yōōr) *contr.* you are

yours (yoorz; *often* yôrz) *pron.* that or those belonging to you: possessive form of YOU [that book is yours; yours are better]

your·self (yoor self′, yər-) *pron., pl.* **-selves** (-selvz′) a form of YOU, used as an intensive [you said so *yourself*], as a reflexive [you hurt *yourself*], or with the meaning "your customary self" [you are not *yourself* today]

yours truly 1 a phrase used in ending a letter **2** [Inf.] I or me

youth (yōōth) *n., pl.* **youths** (yōōthz, yōōths) ⟦OE *geoguthe*⟧ **1** the state or quality of being young **2** the period of adolescence **3** an early stage of growth or existence **4** young people collectively **5** a young person; esp., a young man

youth·ful *adj.* **1** young; not yet old or mature **2** of, like, or fit for youth **3** fresh; vigorous **4** new; early —**youth′ful·ly** *adv.* —**youth′ful·ness** *n.*

yowl (youl) *vi., n.* ⟦< ON *gaula*⟧ howl or wail

yo-yo (yō′yō′) *n., pl.* **yo′-yos′** ⟦< ?⟧ **1** a spool-like toy reeled up and let down by a string **2** [Slang] a person regarded as stupid, inept, etc. —*vi.* [Inf.] to move up and down; fluctuate

yr *abbrev.* **1** year(s) **2** your

yrs *abbrev.* **1** years **2** yours

YT *abbrev.* Yukon Territory

yt·ter·bi·um (i tʉr′bē əm) *n.* ⟦after *Ytterby*, Sweden⟧ a malleable chemical element used to increase the strength of certain alloys: symbol, Yb; at. no. 70

yt·tri·um (i′trē əm) *n.* ⟦after *Ytterby*, Sweden⟧ a silvery, malleable chemical element used to strengthen magnesium and aluminum alloys: symbol, Y; at. no. 39

Yu·ca·tán or **Yu·ca·tan** (yo͞o′kə tan′) a peninsula of SE Mexico separating the Gulf of Mexico from the Caribbean

yuc·ca (yuk′ə) *n.* ⟦< AmSp *yuca*⟧ 1 a desert plant with stiff leaves and white flowers 2 its flower

yuck¹ (yuk) *n., vi. alt. sp. of* YUK

yuck² (yuk) [Slang] *n.* something unpleasant, disgusting, etc. —*interj.* used to express distaste, disgust, etc. —**yuck′y** *adj.* **-i·er, -i·est**

Yu·go·slav·i·a (yo͞o′gō slä′vē ə, -gə-) former country in the NW Balkan Peninsula: beginning in 1991, broke up into Slovenia, Croatia, Bosnia and Herzegovina, Serbia, Montenegro, Kosovo, and Macedonia —**Yu′go·slav′** *adj., n.,* **Yu′go·sla′vi·an**

yuk (yuk) *n.* ⟦echoic⟧ [Slang] a loud laugh of amusement, or something causing such a laugh —*vi.* **yukked, yuk′king** [Slang] to laugh loudly

Yu·kon (yo͞o′kän′) territory of NW Canada, east of Alaska; cap. Whitehorse: abbrev. YT: usually used with *the:* in full **Yukon Territory**

yule (yo͞ol) *n.* ⟦OE *geol*⟧ [*often* Y-] Christmas or the Christmas season

yule·tide (-tīd′) *n.* [*often* Y-] the Christmas season

yum·my (yum′ē) *adj.* **-mi·er, -mi·est** [Inf.] very tasty; delectable

yup (yup) *adv.* [Slang] yes: an affirmative reply

Yu·pik (yo͞o′pik) *n.* **-pik, -piks** 1 a member of a group of peoples native to SW Alaska and extreme NE Russia 2 any of the languages of the Yupik —**Yu′pik** *adj.*

yup·pie (yup′ē) *n.* ⟦< *y(oung) u(rban) p(rofessional)*⟧ [Inf.] a young professional regarded as affluent, ambitious, materialistic, etc.

YWCA *abbrev.* Young Women's Christian Association

Z

z or **Z** (zē; *Brit* zed) *n., pl.* **z's, Z's** the 26th and last letter of the English alphabet

Za·ire or **Za·ïre** (zä ir′) 1 CONGO (River) 2 former name for Democratic Republic of the Congo: see CONGO

Zam·bi·a (zam′bē ə) country in S Africa

Zam·bo·ni (zam bō′nē) *trademark for* a machine like a tractor, used to smooth the ice in a rink

za·ny (zā′nē) *n., pl.* **-nies** ⟦< It dial. *zanni,* clown < *Giovanni,* John⟧ a silly or foolish person —*adj.* **-ni·er, -ni·est** amusingly eccentric or unpredictable —**za′ni·ness** *n.*

Zan·zi·bar (zan′zə bär′) island off the E coast of Africa: part of Tanzania

zap (zap) [Inf.] *vt.* **zapped, zap′ping** 1 ⟦echoic⟧ to move, strike, stun, kill, etc. suddenly and with great speed and force 2 to cook or heat in a microwave oven —*interj.* used to signify sudden, swift action or change —**zap′per** *n.*

zeal (zēl) *n.* ⟦< Gr *zēlos*⟧ strong interest or devotion; intense enthusiasm; fervor

zeal·ot (zel′ət) *n.* one who shows zeal, esp. fanatic zeal

zeal·ous (zel′əs) *adj.* of or showing zeal; fervent —**zeal′ous·ly** *adv.* —**zeal′ous·ness** *n.*

ze·bra (zē′brə) *n.* ⟦Port⟧ an African mammal related to the horse and having dark stripes on a white or tawny body

ze·bu (zē′byo͞o′) *n.* ⟦Fr *zébu* < ?⟧ a domesticated ox of Asia and Africa

zed (zed) *n.* ⟦< Gr *zēta*⟧ [Brit.] the letter Z, z

zeit·geist (tsīt′gīst′) *n.* ⟦Ger, time spirit⟧ the trend of thought and feeling at a particular moment in history

Zen (zen) *n.* ⟦Jpn ult. < Sans *dhyāna,* thinking⟧ a variety of Buddhism in which enlightenment is sought through introspection and intuition

ze·nith (zē′nith) *n.* ⟦ult. < L *semita,* path⟧ 1 the point in the sky directly overhead 2 the highest point

zeph·yr (zef′ər) *n.* ⟦< Gr *zephyros*⟧ a breeze

zep·pe·lin (zep′ə lin, zep′lin) *n.* ⟦after Count F. von *Zeppelin* (1838-1917), its Ger designer⟧ [*often* Z-] a type of rigid airship designed around 1900

ze·ro (zir′ō, zē′rō) *n., pl.* **-ros** or **-roes** ⟦< Ar *ṣifr,* cipher⟧ 1 the symbol 0, representing the absence of any quantity or magnitude; cipher; naught 2 the point, marked 0, from which quantities are reckoned on a graduated scale 3 nothing 4 the lowest point —*adj.* 1 of or at zero 2 not any: [soda with *zero* calories] —**zero in on** to concentrate attention on; focus on

zero hour 1 the time set for beginning an attack, etc. 2 any crucial moment

ze·ro-sum (-sum′) *adj.* of or being a situation

in which a gain for one must result in a loss for another or others

zero tolerance a policy so uncompromising that even slight infractions may be severely punished

zest (zest) *n.* [Fr *zeste*, orange peel] **1** a thin piece of orange or lemon peel used as flavoring **2** stimulating quality **3** keen enjoyment [a *zest* for life] —**zest′ful** *adj.*

ze·ta (zāt′ə) *n.* the sixth letter of the Greek alphabet (Z, ζ)

Zeus (zo͞os, zyo͞os) *n. Gr. Myth.* the king of the gods

Zhou En·lai (jō′en′lī′) 1898-1976; Chin. premier (1949-76)

zig·gu·rat (zig′o͞o rat′) *n.* [< Assyrian *ziqqurratu*] an ancient Assyrian or Babylonian temple tower in the form of a terraced pyramid

zig·zag (zig′zag′) *n.* [Fr] **1** a series of short, sharp angles in alternate directions **2** a design, path, etc. in this form —*adj.* having the form of a zigzag —*adv.* in a zigzag course —*vt., vi.* **-zagged′, -zag′ging** to form or move in a zigzag

zilch (zilch) *n.* [nonsense syllable] [Slang] nothing; zero

zil·lion (zil′yən) *n.* [< MILLION] [Inf.] a very large, indefinite number

Zim·ba·bwe (zim bäb′wä′) country in S Africa, north of South Africa

zinc (ziŋk) *n.* [Ger *zink*] a bluish-white, metallic chemical element, used in alloys, as a protective coating for iron, etc.: symbol, Zn; at. no. 30

zinc oxide a white powder used in making rubber articles, cosmetics, ointments, etc.

Zin·fan·del (zin′fən del′) *n.* [< ?] a dry red wine made chiefly in California

zing (ziŋ) *n.* [echoic] [Inf.] **1** a shrill, high-pitched sound, as of something moving fast **2** zest, vigor, etc.

zing·er *n.* [Inf.] **1** a clever, witty remark **2** a sharp, usually critical remark

zin·ni·a (zin′ē ə, zin′yə) *n.* [after J. G. *Zinn* (1727-59), Ger botanist] a plant having colorful composite flowers

Zi·on[1] (zī′ən) *n.* [< fol.] **1** the Jewish people **2** heaven

Zi·on[2] (zī′ən) **1** a hill in Jerusalem, site of Solomon's Temple **2** Jerusalem **3** Israel

Zi·on·ism *n.* a movement formerly for reestablishing, now for supporting, the state of Israel —**Zi′on·ist** *n., adj.*

zip (zip) *n.* [echoic] **1** a short, sharp hissing or whizzing sound **2** [Inf.] energy; vigor **3** [Slang] nothing —*vi.* **zipped, zip′ping 1** to make, or move with, a zip **2** [Inf.] to move with speed —*vt.* to fasten with a zipper

ZIP code or **zip code** (zip) [Z(one) I(mprovement) P(lan)] a code number assigned by the postal service, designating a delivery area

zip-line *n.* a pulley rigged to glide along a stretched cable for conveying a person or thing across an expanse

zip·per (zip′ər) *n.* a device used to fasten and unfasten two edges of material, as on clothing: it consists of two rows of interlocking teeth worked by a sliding part

zip·py *adj.* **-pi·er, -pi·est** [Inf.] full of energy; brisk

zir·con (zur′kän′) *n.* [ult. < Pers *zar*, gold] a crystalline silicate mineral, used as a gem

zir·co·ni·um (zər kō′nē əm) *n.* a ductile, metallic chemical element used in alloys, ceramics, etc.: symbol, Zr; at. no. 40

zit (zit) *n.* [Slang] a pimple, esp. one on the face

zith·er (zith′ər, zith′-) *n.* [< Gr *kithara*, lute] any of various musical instruments with strings stretched across a flat soundboard and plucked, bowed, struck with mallets, etc., as the dulcimer

Zn *Chem. symbol for* zinc

zo·di·ac (zō′dē ak′) *n.* [< Gr *zōdiakos (kyklos)*, (circle) of animals] **1** an imaginary belt across the sky extending on either side of the apparent path of the sun and divided into twelve equal parts, or signs, named for constellations **2** a diagram representing this —**zo·di′a·cal** (-dī′ə kəl) *adj.*

zom·bie (zäm′bē) *n.* [of Afr orig.] **1** in voodoo, a corpse animated by means of a spell **2** any animated corpse, as in horror films **3** [Inf.] one who is listless, etc.

zone (zōn) *n.* [Fr < Gr *zōnē*] **1** an encircling band, stripe, etc. **2** any of the five great latitudinal divisions of the earth's surface: see TORRID ZONE, TEMPERATE ZONE, and FRIGID ZONE **3** any area with reference to a specified use or restriction [a canal *zone*, war *zone*] —*vt.* **zoned, zon′ing** to mark off into zones —**in the (or a) zone** [Inf.] in a state producing high achievement, seemingly beyond explanation —**zon′al** *adj.*

zonked (zōŋkt, zäŋkt) *adj.* [Slang] **1** highly intoxicated or under the influence of a drug **2** exhausted

zoo (zo͞o) *n.* [< *zoo(logical garden)*] **1** a place where wild animals are kept for public showing **2** [Slang] a place of confusion, disorder, etc.

zoo- [< Gr *zōion*, animal] *combining form* animal(s) [*zoology*]

zo·ol·o·gy (zō äl′ə jē) *n.* [ModL *zoologia*: see prec. & -LOGY] the science that deals with animals and animal life —**zo′o·log′i·cal** (-ə läj′i kəl) *adj.* —**zo·ol′o·gist** *n.*

zoom (zo͞om) *vi.* [echoic] **1** to make a loud, low-pitched, buzzing sound **2** to climb in an airplane suddenly and sharply **3** to move speedily upward or forward **4** to focus as with a zoom lens —*vt.* to cause to zoom —*n.* a zooming

zoom lens a system of lenses, as in a film or TV camera, that can be rapidly adjusted for close-up or distant shots while keeping the image in focus

zo·o·phyte (zō′ə fīt′) *n.* [ult. < Gr *zōion*, an animal + *phyton*, a plant] any animal, as a coral or sponge, that looks and grows somewhat like a plant —**zo′o·phyt′ic** (-fit′ik) *adj.*

Zo·ro·as·ter (zō′rō as′tər) *c.* 6th or 7th c. B.C.; Pers. founder of Zoroastrianism

Zo·ro·as·tri·an·ism (zō′rō as′trē ən iz′əm) *n.* the religion of the ancient Persians before Islam

Zr *Chem. symbol for* zirconium

zuc·chi·ni (zōō kē′nē) *n., pl.* **-ni** or **-nis** ⟦It⟧ a summer squash that looks like a cucumber

Zu·lu (zōō′lōō) *n.* **1** *pl.* **-lus** or **-lu** a member of a people living in South Africa **2** the language of this people —*adj.* of the Zulus or their language, etc.

Zu·ni (zōō′nē) *n.* **1** *pl.* **-nis** or **-ni** a member of a pueblo-dwelling North American Indian people of W New Mexico **2** the language of this people Also, formerly, **Zu·ñi** (zōōn′yē)

Zur·ich (zoor′ik) city in N Switzerland

zwie·back (swē′bak′, swī′-) *n.* ⟦Ger < *zwie-*, twice + *backen*, to bake⟧ a kind of biscuit that is sliced and toasted after baking

zy·de·co (zī′də kō′) *n.* ⟦< ?⟧ a heavily syncopated dance music of S Louisiana, containing elements of blues, white Cajun music, etc.

zy·gote (zī′gōt′) *n.* ⟦< Gr *zygon*, a yoke⟧ a cell formed by the union of male and female gametes

zymo- ⟦< Gr *zymē*, a leaven⟧ *combining form* fermentation: also **zym-**

zy·mur·gy (zī′mər jē) *n.* ⟦*prec.* + -URGY⟧ the chemistry of fermentation, as applied in brewing, etc.

WEIGHTS AND MEASURES

Linear

12 inches	=	1 foot
3 feet	=	1 yard
5.5 yards	=	1 rod
40 rods	=	1 furlong
8 furlongs	=	1 mile

Liquid

16 ounces	=	1 pint
2 pints	=	1 quart
4 quarts	=	1 gallon
31.5 gallons	=	1 barrel
2 barrels	=	1 hogshead

Metric Equivalents

1 inch	=	2.54 centimeters
1 foot	=	0.3048 meter
1 yard	=	0.9144 meter
1 mile	=	1.6093 kilometers
1 centimeter	=	0.3937 inch
1 meter	=	39.3701 inches
1 kilometer	=	0.6214 mile
1 quart (dry)	=	1.1012 liters
1 quart (liquid)	=	0.9464 liter
1 gallon	=	3.7854 liters
1 liter	=	0.9081 dry quart
1 liter	=	1.0567 liquid quarts

Square

144 sq. inches	=	1 sq. foot
9 sq. feet	=	1 sq. yard
30.25 sq. yards	=	1 sq. rod
160 sq. rods	=	1 acre
640 acres	=	1 sq. mile

Circular

60 seconds	=	1 minute
60 minutes	=	1 degree
360 degrees	=	1 circle

Metric Equivalents

1 sq. inch	=	6.4516 sq. centimeters
1 sq. foot	=	929.0304 sq. centimeters
1 sq. mile	=	2.590 sq. kilometers
1 sq. centimeter	=	0.155 sq. inch
1 sq. meter	=	1.196 sq. yards
1 sq. kilometer	=	0.3861 sq. mile

Cubic Measure

1,728 cu. inches	=	1 cu. foot
27 cu. feet	=	1 cu. yard
128 cu. feet	=	1 cord (wood)

Dry

2 pints	=	1 quart
8 quarts	=	1 peck
4 pecks	=	1 bushel

Metric Equivalents

1 cu. inch	=	16.3871 cu. centimeters
1 cu. inch	=	16.3871 mililiters
1 cu. foot	=	0.0283 cu. meter
1 cu. foot	=	28.3169 liters
1 cu. meter	=	35.3147 cu. feet
1 ounce (avdp.)	=	28.3495 grams
1 pound	=	0.4536 kilogram
1 gram	=	0.0353 ounce
1 kilogram	=	2.2046 pounds
1 ton (2,000 pounds)	=	907.1847 kilograms

Temperature Conversion Formulas

$$°F = 32 + (1.8 \times °C)$$

$$°C = \frac{°F - 32}{1.8}$$

THE INTERNATIONAL SYSTEM OF UNITS (SI)

Any prefix can be combined with any unit; for example, milli- + ampere = milliampere (m + A = mA); kilo- + gram = kilogram (k + g = kg); mega + hertz = megahertz (M + H = MHz).

SI base units and prefixes

unit	symbol	quantity	prefix	symbol	multiplier*
ampere	A	electric current	yotta-	Y	$\times 10^{24}$
candela	cd	luminous	zetta-	Z	$\times 10^{21}$
		intensity	exa-	E	$\times 10^{18}$
kelvin	K	thermodynamic	peta-	P	$\times 10^{15}$
		temperature	tera-	T	$\times 10^{12}$
kilogram	kg	mass	giga-	G	$\times 10^{9}$
meter	m	length	mega-	M	$\times 10^{6}$
mole	mol	amount of	kilo-	k	$\times 10^{3}$
		substance	hecto-	h	$\times 10^{2}$
second	s	time	deka-; deca-	da	$\times 10$
			deci-	d	$\times 10^{-1}$
			centi-	c	$\times 10^{-2}$
			milli-	m	$\times 10^{-3}$
			micro-	μ	$\times 10^{-6}$
			nano-	n	$\times 10^{-9}$
			pico-	p	$\times 10^{-12}$
			femto-	f	$\times 10^{-15}$
			atto-	a	$\times 10^{-18}$
			zepto-	z	$\times 10^{-21}$
			yocto-	y	$\times 10^{-24}$

* $10^2 = 10 \times 10 = 100$; $10^3 = 10 \times 10 \times 10 = 1{,}000$; $10^{-1} = 1/10^1 = 0.1$; $10^{-2} = 1/10^2 = 0.01$
So, 2 km = 2×10^3 meters = 2,000 meters; 2 mm = 2×10^{-3} meter = 0.002 meter.

Common SI derived units with special names

name	symbol	quantity
coulomb	C	electric charge
°Celsius	°C	temperature (0°C = 273.16 K)
hertz	Hz	frequency
joule	J	energy; work
newton	N	force
ohm	Ω	electric resistance
pascal	Pa	pressure; stress
volt	V	electric potential; EMF
watt	W	power; radiant flux

Other common units used with the SI

name	symbol	quantity
hectare	ha	area
		= 10,000 m² or 2.471 acres
knot	kn; kt	speed (navigation)
		= 1 NM/hour or 1.1508 mph
liter	l; L	volume; capacity
		= 1,000 cm³ or 1.0567 qt
metric ton	t	mass
		= 1,000 kg or 2,204.623 lb
nautical mile	NM	distance (navigation) (U.S.)
		= 1.1508 statute miles
atmosphere	atm	atmospheric pressure
		= 101,325 Pa or 14.696 lb/in²

PRONUNCIATION KEY

Symbol	Vowel Sounds Key Words	IPA	Symbol	Consonant Sounds Key Words	IPA
a	at, cap, parrot	æ	b	bed, table, rob	b
ā	ape, play, sail	eɪ	d	dog, middle, sad	d
ä	cot, father, heart	ɑ	f	for, phone, cough	f
e	ten, wealth, merry	ɛ	g	get, wiggle, dog	g
ē	even, feet, money	i	h	hat, hope, ahead	h
i	is, stick, mirror	ɪ	hw	which, white	hw
ī	ice, high, sky	aɪ	j	joy, badge, agent	dʒ
ō	go, open, tone	oʊ	k	kill, cat, quiet	k
ô	all, law, horn	ɔ	l	let, yellow, ball	l
ʊʊ	could, look, pull	ʊ	'l	cattle, paddle	ļ
yʊʊ	cure, furious, globule, your	jʊ	m	meet, number, time	m
o͞o	boot, crew, tune	u	n	net, candle, ton	n
yo͞o	cute, few, use	ju	'n	sudden, sweeten	ņ
oi	boy, oil, royal	ɔɪ	p	put, sample, escape	p
ou	cow, out, sour	aʊ	r	red, wrong, born	ɹ
u	mud, ton, blood, trouble	ʌ	s	sit, castle, office	s
ʉr	her, sir, word	ɝ	t	top, letter, cat	t
ə	ago, agent, collect, focus	ə	v	voice, every, love	v
			w	wet, always, quart	w
			y	yes, canyon, onion	j
			z	zoo, misery, rise	z
			ch	chew, nature, punch	tʃ
			sh	shell, machine, bush	ʃ
			th	thin, nothing, truth	θ
			th	then, other, bathe	ð
			zh	beige, measure, seizure	ʒ
			ŋ	ring, anger, drink	ŋ

Symbols for foreign sounds are explained in the Guide to Pronunciation, p. vii.